CONSTITUTIONAL LAW OF CANADA

Fourth Edition

PETER W. HOGG

Professor of Law, Osgoode Hall Law School,
York University, Toronto

CARSWELL
Thomson Professional Publishing

The paper used in this publication meets the minimum requirements of the American National Standard for Information Sciences — Permanence of Paper for Printed Library Materials, ANSI Z39.48-1984.

Canadian Cataloguing in Publication Data

Hogg, Peter W.
Constitutional law of Canada

4th ed.
Includes bibliographical references and index.
ISBN 0-459-23855-8

1. Canada – Constitutional law. I. Title.

KE4219.H65 1997 342.71 C97-931927-7
KF4482.H65 1997

CARSWELL
Thomson Professional Publishing

One Corporate Plaza, 2075 Kennedy Road, Scarborough, Ontario M1T 3V4
Customer Service:
Toronto 1-416-609-3800
Elsewhere in Canada/U.S. 1-800-387-5164
Fax 1-416-298-5082

Preface to the Fourth Edition

This is the fourth edition of my *Constitutional Law of Canada*. The first edition was published in 1977, the second edition was published in 1985 and the third edition was published in 1992.

Since the third edition was published, the Supreme Court of Canada has decided nearly 200 constitutional cases, most of them under the Charter of Rights. On the political front, the set of amendments known as the Charlottetown Accord was defeated in a national referendum in 1992 (after the third edition had gone to press) and Quebec's proposal to become a sovereign state was defeated in a provincial referendum in 1995. There has been plenty to write about.

The third edition was published in a loose-leaf format as well as a bound format. I kept the loose-leaf version up to date by writing annual supplements that were sent out to subscribers for filing into the volumes. The fourth edition is a consolidation of all the supplementary material that has been included in the loose-leaf version up to September 1996. In addition, all textbook references have been brought up to date, the sections of each chapter and the footnotes have been renumbered, and some new writing has been introduced where I judged that pre-1996 developments had not been adequately treated in the annual supplements.

The fourth edition will be published in three formats. There will be a loose-leaf version (existing subscribers will receive the fourth edition automatically), a hardcover bound version and a softcover, abridged version for students (called 1997 student edition). Unfortunately, all three editions have to have different pagination (and of course the loose-leaf version will be annually revised). In cross-references and the index, I have avoided all references to pages and have referred only to the numbered sections of the text and to footnotes. This is probably the best practice for citation as well, but if page references are used, it is important to stipulate which version of the fourth edition is being cited.

The fourth edition, like its predecessor, is arranged in four parts. Part I, Basic Concepts, consists of 14 chapters, which cover the sources of constitutional law, the constitutional history of Canada, the status and amendment of the constitution, the theory of federalism and judicial review, and basic information about the structures of Canadian government. Part II, Distribution of Powers, consists of

16 chapters, which cover the federal distribution of powers, including the techniques of judicial review on federal grounds and paramountcy. Part III, Civil Liberties, consists of 24 chapters, which cover the protection of civil liberties, especially under the Charter of Rights. Part IV, Practice, consists of three chapters, which cover the effect of an unconstitutional law and the practice and procedure of constitutional litigation.

The book is about the law of Canada and makes no claim to be a comparative study. However, there are many references to the constitutional law of the United Kingdom, New Zealand, Australia and the United States. The American Bill of Rights is included as an appendix. The International Covenant on Civil and Political Rights is also included as an appendix, and some reference is made to that instrument and other international human rights instruments and their jurisprudential exegesis.

I have generally been sparing in citation, concentrating on the leading cases and commentaries. Decisions below the level of the Supreme Court of Canada and the secondary literature are cited only if they are especially interesting or important. I have also borne in mind the admonition of Dixon C.J. in the High Court of Australia that ''not everything that appears in the law reports'' is the law (*White* v. *The Queen* (1962) 107 C.L.R. 174, 175). There is accordingly much criticism of judicial reasoning, but always with a view to the recognition and application of sound principle. Others will not always agree with my ''sound principle'', but I have tried to be frank in identifying my own opinions so that they can be appropriately discounted by the reader. I appeared as counsel in some of the cases discussed in the text. In each case, that fact is disclosed in a footnote to the discussion, just in case my objectivity has been impaired.

In preparing the fourth edition, I am grateful to the able student research assistants who helped me prepare the annual supplements to the third edition. They are Randy Graham, LL.B. 1995, Eliza Erskine, LL.B. 1996, and Allison Bushell, LL.B. 1998. Allison Bushell also played an indispensable role in converting the loose-leaf text into a coherent fourth edition, updating the references, and in helping me with the new writing. Jill Whelan, LL.B. 1998, proof-read the entire manuscript and saved me from numerous errors. The path to publication was a smooth one, thanks to the efficiency of Karol Roseman, Lyn Northey and their colleagues at Carswell. Last but not least I thank my wife, Frances Hogg, who is unfailingly tolerant of my obsessive work habits, as well as being a joy to live with.

Toronto,
July 17, 1997

Peter W. Hogg

Contents

PART II
DISTRIBUTION OF POWERS

PART III
CIVIL LIBERTIES

PART IV
PRACTICE

APPENDICES

Table of Cases

References are to sections, not pages

TABLE OF CASES

References are to sections, not pages

TABLE OF CASES

References are to sections, not pages

TABLE OF CASES

References are to sections, not pages

TABLE OF CASES

References are to sections, not pages

TABLE OF CASES

References are to sections, not pages

TABLE OF CASES

References are to sections, not pages

TABLE OF CASES

References are to sections, not pages

TABLE OF CASES

References are to sections, not pages

TABLE OF CASES

References are to sections, not pages

TABLE OF CASES

References are to sections, not pages

TABLE OF CASES

References are to sections, not pages

TABLE OF CASES

References are to sections, not pages

References are to sections, not pages

TABLE OF CASES

References are to sections, not pages

TABLE OF CASES

References are to sections, not pages

TABLE OF CASES

References are to sections, not pages

TABLE OF CASES

References are to sections, not pages

TABLE OF CASES

References are to sections, not pages

TABLE OF CASES

References are to sections, not pages

TABLE OF CASES

References are to sections, not pages

TABLE OF CASES

References are to sections, not pages

TABLE OF CASES

References are to sections, not pages

TABLE OF CASES

References are to sections, not pages

TABLE OF CASES

References are to sections, not pages

TABLE OF CASES

References are to sections, not pages

TABLE OF CASES

References are to sections, not pages

TABLE OF CASES

References are to sections, not pages

TABLE OF CASES

References are to sections, not pages

TABLE OF CASES

References are to sections, not pages

I

BASIC CONCEPTS

1

Sources

1.1 Constitutional law

Constitutional law is the law prescribing the exercise of power by the organs of a State. It explains which organs can exercise legislative power (making new laws), executive power (implementing the laws) and judicial power (adjudicating disputes), and what the limitations on those powers are. In a federal state, the allocation of governmental powers (legislative, executive and judicial) among central and regional (state or provincial) authorities is a basic concern. The rules of federalism are especially significant in Canada because they protect the cultural, linguistic and regional diversity of the nation. Civil liberties are also part of constitutional law, because civil liberties may be created by the rules that limit the exercise of governmental power over individuals. A constitution has been described as "a mirror reflecting the national soul":[1] it must recognize and protect the values of a nation.

---

1 Cheffins and Tucker, *The Constitutional Process in Canada* (2nd ed., 1976), 4.

1.2 Constitution Act, 1867

In most countries, the bulk of the constitutional law is contained in a single constitutional document, which can be and usually is described as "the Constitution". In most cases, this document came into being after the gaining of independence, or after a revolution, or after a war, and was intended to symbolize and legitimize a new regime of law. In the United States, for example, the constitutional document of 1787 (and its amendments) is the Constitution.[2] It was adopted after the American colonists had won their independence from Britain by war. Naturally, the brilliant men who framed that document borrowed from their British traditions, as well as from other sources. But they wanted a document that would be complete in itself, for the previous constitutional rules had been irrevocably repudiated, and the new document was to be the foundation stone of the new nation. Accordingly, they set out the essentials of the entire scheme of government — legislative, executive and judicial — in one impressive document.

In Canada (as in the United Kingdom), there is no single document comparable to the Constitution of the United States, and the word "Constitution"[3] accordingly lacks a definite meaning.[4] The closest approximation to such a document is the British North America Act, 1867,[5] which was renamed the Constitution Act, 1867 in 1982.[6] The B.N.A. Act (as I shall continue to call it in historical contexts) created the new Dominion of Canada by uniting three of the colonies of British North America and by providing the framework for the admission of all the other British North American colonies and territories.[7] The B.N.A. Act established the rules of federalism, that is, the rules that allocate governmental power between the central institutions (especially the federal Parliament) and the provincial institutions (especially the provincial Legislatures). But the B.N.A. Act did not mark any break with the colonial past. Independence from the United Kingdom was not desired or even contemplated for the future. The new Dominion,

---

2 The document was adopted by a constitutional convention that met in Philadelphia in 1787. It was subject to ratification by the states, and was effective when the ninth state, New Hampshire, ratified it in 1788. The new government was organized in 1789.

3 For discussion of the meaning of "constitution", see Wheare, *Modern Constitutions* (2nd ed., 1966), 2-4.

4 There is a definition of "Constitution of Canada" in s. 52(2) of the Constitution Act, 1982. This definition applies when that term is used in the Constitution Act, 1982: see sec. 1.4, "Constitution of Canada", below.

5 The Constitution Act, 1867 (U.K.) is reproduced in R.S.C. 1985, Appendix II, No. 5. All the other instruments of the Constitution of Canada, as defined in s. 52(2) of the Constitution Act, 1982, are in the same Appendix II, along with some other instruments of constitutional interest. Department of Justice, Canada, *A Consolidation of the Constitution Acts, 1867 to 1982* (1989) is a convenient consolidation of the Constitution Acts. Part of this consolidation is printed with permission as an appendix to this book.

6 Constitution Act, 1982, s. 53(2).

7 The history of confederation is related in ch. 2, Reception, under heading, 2.4, "Confederation," below.

although enjoying a considerable degree of self-government, remained a British colony. In fact, of course, after 1867, there was an evolution to full independence, but it was a gradual process continuing well into the twentieth century.[8]

The B.N.A. Act did not follow the model of the Constitution of the United States in codifying all of the new nation's constitutional rules. On the contrary, the B.N.A. Act did no more than was necessary to accomplish confederation. The reason was stated in the preamble to the Act: the new nation was to have "a Constitution similar in principle to that of the United Kingdom". Apart from the changes needed to establish the new federation, the British North Americans wanted the old rules to continue in both form and substance exactly as before. After 1867, therefore, much of Canada's constitutional law continued to be found in a variety of sources outside the B.N.A. Act. Indeed, as will be elaborated later in this chapter, some of the most important rules were not matters of law at all, but were simply "conventions" which were unenforceable in the courts.

The best-known example of the colonists' reliance on the old regime is the absence of any general amending clause in the B.N.A. Act. We do not have definite information as to the reasons for this omission, because on this point (as on many others) there is no record of any discussion at the conferences in Charlottetown, Quebec and London which preceded the passage of the Act. But two facts may be assumed with confidence. First, the framers of the B.N.A. Act could not have overlooked such a vital matter: they were far too intelligent and pragmatic to imagine that they had drafted a document which would never require amendment, and they were very familiar with the United States' Constitution which of course contained an amending clause. Secondly, the framers must have known that the absence of an amending clause would mean that amendments would have to be enacted by the imperial Parliament. The conclusion is inescapable that the Canadian framers of the B.N.A. Act were content for the imperial Parliament to play a part in the process of amending the new Constitution.[9] Because of the absence of an amending clause in the B.N.A. Act, the imperial Parliament enacted amendments to the Act until 1982, when the Constitution Act, 1982 (itself an imperial statute) finally supplied amending procedures which could be operated entirely within Canada.[10]

Another gap in the B.N.A. Act concerns the office of Governor General. The Act, by s. 9, vests general executive authority for Canada in "the Queen", and confers several specific powers on a "Governor General". But the office of Governor General is nowhere created by the Act and no rules are provided for the appointment or tenure of that officer. The reason for this gap was the assump-

---

8 See ch. 3, Independence, under heading 3.1, "Bonds of Empire", below.

9 See also, Livingston, *Federalism and Constitutional Change* (1956), 19-21; Mallory, *The Structure of Canadian Government* (rev. ed., 1984), 420; Forsey, *Freedom and Order* (1974), 229.

10 The history of the search for a domestic amending formula is related in sec. 4.1(b) "The search for a domestic amending procedure", below.

tion that the office would be created and filled in the same way as colonial governorships had always been created and filled, that is, by the Queen acting on the advice of the British Colonial Secretary. The office of Governor General has never been formalized in an amendment to the B.N.A. Act. The office is still constituted by the royal prerogative,[11] and appointments are still made by the Queen, although, needless to say, she now acts on the advice of her Canadian ministers.[12]

The system of responsible (or cabinet) government, which had been achieved before confederation by the uniting colonies,[13] is another gap in the B.N.A. Act. It was intended in 1867 that this system would apply to the new federal government, but it never seems to have occurred to anyone to write the rules of the system into the B.N.A. Act, and so there is no mention of the Prime Minister, or of the cabinet, or of the dependence of the cabinet on the support of a majority in the House of Commons: the composition of the actual executive authority and its relationship to the legislative authority were left in the form of unwritten conventions — as in the United Kingdom. That is still their status today.[14]

Nor did the Canadians write into their B.N.A. Act a new supreme court on the model of the Supreme Court of the United States. The B.N.A. Act, by s. 101, gave authority for such a court to be established, but it did not actually establish it. The reason was simple. The framers were accustomed to look to the Judicial Committee of the Privy Council in England as the final appellate authority for British North America (and other colonies), and they were content to leave the appellate authority in those same safe British hands. This was regarded as so natural and obvious — like responsible government — that the Judicial Committee of the Privy Council is not mentioned anywhere in the B.N.A. Act. When the Supreme Court of Canada was established in 1875, it was established by an ordinary federal statute,[15] and the right of appeal to the Privy Council was retained; the abolition of Privy Council appeals did not occur finally until 1949.[16] It is still the case that the existence, composition and jurisdiction of the Supreme Court of Canada depend upon an ordinary federal statute.[17]

The Canadian framers of the B.N.A. Act even eschewed the alluring American precedent of a bill of rights, and instead left the civil liberties of Canadians to be protected by the moderation of their legislative bodies and the rules of the

---

11 Letters Patent constituting the office of Governor General of Canada, 1947, R.S.C. 1985, Appendix II, No. 31.

12 See ch. 9, Responsible Government, below.

13 The history of the development of responsible government is related in ch. 9, Responsible Government, below.

14 Responsible government is the subject of ch. 9, below.

15 The history of the Supreme Court of Canada is related in ch. 8, Supreme Court of Canada, below.

16 See ch. 8, Supreme Court of Canada, under heading 8.2, ''Abolition of Privy Council Appeals'', below.

17 Supreme Court Act, R.S.C. 1985, c. S-26.

common law — as in the United Kingdom.[18] When in 1960 Canada adopted the Canadian Bill of Rights,[19] it was enacted as a federal statute, not as an amendment to the B.N.A. Act, and it was made applicable only to federal laws. The Constitution Act, 1982 finally added to Canada's constitutional law a bill of rights — the Canadian Charter of Rights and Freedoms — which is entrenched (that is, alterable only by the process of constitutional amendment) and applicable to provincial as well as federal laws.

1.3 Constitution Act, 1982

As the foregoing account shows, the constitutional settlement of 1982 made some important repairs to Canada's constitutional law: a domestic amending formula was adopted; the authority over Canada of the United Kingdom (imperial) Parliament was terminated; and the Charter of Rights was adopted. But in terms of the accessibility and comprehensibility of Canada's constitutional law very little was accomplished. The leading instrument of the 1982 settlement was the Canada Act 1982,[20] a short statute of the United Kingdom Parliament, which terminated the authority over Canada of the United Kingdom Parliament. Schedule B of the Canada Act 1982 was the Constitution Act, 1982,[21] which contains the Charter of Rights, the amending formula and the other changes to Canada's constitutional law. Neither the Canada Act 1982 nor the Constitution Act, 1982 purports to be a codification or even consolidation of Canada's constitutional law. In fact, the two 1982 statutes are not even integrated into earlier constitutional instruments. The Canada Act 1982 consists of only four short sections,[22] none of which purports to be an amendment of the B.N.A. Act. The Constitution Act, 1982 is longer — 60 sections — and it makes a few amendments to the B.N.A. Act,[23] but for the most part it too is a self-sufficient instrument. In a sense, the two 1982 statutes worsen the formal state of Canada's constitutional law, because they add two more statutes to the variety of sources which existed before.

The Constitution Act, 1982 does do two things which are intended to effect some modernization and rationalization of Canada's constitutional law. First, the name of the B.N.A. Act is changed to the Constitution Act, 1867.[24] This change

---

18 The uniquely Canadian issues of language rights and denominational-school rights could not be evaded in 1867 and were dealt with in ss. 93 and 133 of the B.N.A. Act.

19 Canadian Bill of Rights, R.S.C. 1985, Appendix III. The Canadian Bill of Rights is set out in an appendix to this book. It is the subject of ch. 32, below.

20 U.K. Stats. 1982, c. 11. The Canada Act 1982 is set out in an appendix to this book.

21 The Constitution Act, 1982 is set out in an appendix to this book.

22 Section 1 incorporates the Constitution Act, 1982 as Schedule B to the Canada Act 1982. Section 2 terminates the authority over Canada of the United Kingdom Parliament. Section 3 incorporates a French version as Schedule A. Section 4 gives the short title.

23 Constitution Act, 1982, ss. 50, 51, 53 and schedule, item 1.

24 *Id.*, s. 53(2). The later B.N.A. Acts (amending the 1867 Act) are similarly changed to Constitution Acts.

seems to me to smack of re-writing history, and is likely to lead to confusion with the Constitution Act, 1982, which, as related above, is not technically an amendment to the B.N.A. Act (Constitution Act, 1867). Henceforth, to avoid ambiguity, the dates of the two instruments will always have to be used.

A second rationalization attempted by the Constitution Act, 1982 is the provision for the first time of a definition of the phrase ''Constitution of Canada''. That definition is discussed in the next section of this chapter.

1.4 Constitution of Canada

The phrase ''Constitution of Canada'' is defined in s. 52(2) of the Constitution Act, 1982, as follows:

> 52.(2) The Constitution of Canada includes
> (a) the Canada Act 1982, including this Act;
> (b) the Acts and orders referred to in the schedule; and
> (c) any amendment to any Act or order referred to in paragraph (a) or (b).

The definition of the Constitution of Canada includes three categories of instruments. The first category (paragraph (a)) is the Canada Act 1982, which includes the Constitution Act, 1982 (being Schedule B of the Canada Act 1982). The second category (paragraph (b)) is a list of 30 Acts and orders in the schedule to the Constitution Act, 1982. This list includes the Constitution Act, 1867 and its amendments, the orders in council and statutes admitting or creating new provinces or altering boundaries,[25] and the Statute of Westminster.[26] The third category (paragraph (c)) comprises the amendments which may in the future be made to any of the instruments in the first two categories.[27] At the time of writing (1997), there have been five such amendments.[28]

25 The admission or creation of new provinces after 1867 is described in ch. 2, Reception, under heading 2.5, ''Admission of new provinces and territories'', below.

26 The Statute of Westminster is described in ch. 3, Independence, under heading 3.3, ''Statute of Westminster, 1931'', below.

27 Section 52(2) does not contemplate a future addition to the Constitution that does not take the form of an amendment to the instruments already forming part of the Constitution of Canada. Suppose, for example, it was decided to entrench the letters patent constituting the office of Governor General, and the amending procedure of s. 41 of the Constitution Act, 1982 was operated to accomplish that result. This would be a free-standing addition to the Constitution that is not caught by the existing definition. It would be necessary to amend the definition by adding a reference to the new instrument. The Meech Lake Accord of 1987, now lapsed, proposed to remedy this defect in s. 52(2) by adding a new paragraph: ''(d) any other amendment to the Constitution of Canada''.

28 The five amendments are as follows:
(1) Constitution Amendment Proclamation, 1983, R.S.C. 1985, Appendix II, No. 46, amending s. 25(b), and adding ss. 35(3), 35(4), 35.1, 37.1 and 54.1 to the Constitution Act, 1982. This amendment was adopted by the Parliament and nine Legislatures (all except Quebec) under s. 38 of the Constitution Act, 1982.

The definition of the "Constitution of Canada" in s. 52(2) is introduced by the word "includes". In general, in Canadian statutes, the word "includes" indicates that the definition is not exhaustive. The word "means" is customary for an exhaustive definition. In *New Brunswick Broadcasting Co.* v. *Nova Scotia* (1993),[29] a majority of the Supreme Court of Canada held that the definition in s. 52(2) is not exhaustive. The Court held that the unwritten doctrine of parliamentary privilege should be included in the definition, although s. 52(2) makes no mention of parliamentary privilege. The inclusion of parliamentary privilege was said to be implied by the reference in the preamble of the Constitution Act, 1867 to "a constitution similar in principle to that of the United Kingdom". As Sopinka J. commented in a separate opinion,[30] this vague phrase is a frail foundation for the addition of new elements to the definition of the "Constitution of Canada" in s. 52(2). Moreover, the Court's decision means that the definition is capable of judicial expansion by virtue of implications from other parts of the Constitution. This raises the possibility of further additions, which destroys the certainty apparently afforded by the list of 30 instruments that is scheduled to s. 52(2).

The Court in *New Brunswick Broadcasting* did not add a new *document* to the scheduled list referred to in s. 52(2). What the Court added was the unwritten doctrine of parliamentary privilege. This was a surprising decision in that the definition in s. 52(2) is expressed solely in terms of written instruments, which seemed to presuppose that the Constitution of Canada was confined to written instruments. Could the Court now add additional written instruments to the sched-

---

(2) Constitution Act, 1985 (Representation), R.S.C. 1985, Appendix II, No. 47, repealing and replacing s. 51 of the Constitution Act, 1867. This was enacted by the Parliament of Canada alone, acting under s. 44 of the Constitution Act, 1982.

(3) Constitution Amendment, 1987 (Newfoundland Act), Can. Stat. Instruments, SI88-11, amending the Newfoundland Act with respect to denominational school rights. This amendment was adopted by the Parliament of Canada and Legislature of Newfoundland, acting under s. 43 of the Constitution Act, 1982.

(4) Constitution Amendment Proclamation, 1993 (New Brunswick Act), Can. Stat. Instruments, SI 93-54, amending the New Brunswick Act to give English and French linguistic communities "equality of status and equal rights and privileges." This amendment was adopted by the Parliament of Canada and the Legislature of New Brunswick, acting under s. 43 of the Constitution Act, 1982.

(5) Constitution Amendment Proclamation, 1993 (Prince Edward Island), Can. Stat. Instruments, SI 94-50, amending the Schedule to the P.E.I. Terms of Union to provide that a fixed crossing may substitute for a steam (ferry) service. This amendment was adopted by the Parliament of Canada and the Legislative Assembly of P.E.I., acting under s. 43 of the Constitution Act, 1982.

29 [1993] 1 S.C.R. 319. The majority opinion was written by McLachlin J., with whom La Forest, L'Heureux-Dubé, Gonthier and Iacobucci JJ. agreed. Lamer C.J. and Sopinka J., who each wrote a concurring opinion, and Cory J., who wrote a dissenting opinion, did not need to rule, and did not rule, on the question whether the definition of the Constitution of Canada was exhaustive, and, if not, whether it included parliamentary privilege.

30 *Id.*, 396.

uled list of Acts and orders? Obviously, this cannot be ruled out in view of the Court's holding that the definition in s. 52(2) is not exhaustive. But, considering the specificity of the scheduled list of Acts and orders, and the grave consequences (namely, supremacy and entrenchment, described in the next two paragraphs) of the inclusion of other instruments, a court would be very bold indeed to make additions[31] to the 30 instruments in the schedule.[32] On the whole, it seems best to confine the Court's ruling in *New Brunswick Broadcasting* to unwritten doctrine, and to treat the scheduled list of instruments as exhaustive.[33] It is important to note that the scheduled list omits many instruments of importance. For example, the definition omits the pre-1867 instruments which governed the territory now forming part of Ontario and Quebec: the Royal Proclamation of 1763, the Quebec Act of 1774, the Constitutional Act of 1791 and the Union Act of 1840.[34] Also excluded are the pre-1867 instruments which are still the constitutions of Nova Scotia (1749), Prince Edward Island (1769), New Brunswick (1784), Newfoundland (1832) and British Columbia (1866).[35] Nor does the definition include the Letters Patent of 1947,[36] which constitute the office of Governor General, or the Supreme Court Act,[37] which establishes the Supreme Court of Canada, or the Canadian Bill of Rights,[38] which remains in force notwithstanding the adoption of the Charter of Rights.

The definition of the "Constitution of Canada" in s. 52(2) is needed to give content to the supremacy clause and the entrenchment clause of the Constitution Act, 1982. The supremacy clause is s. 52(1), which provides as follows:

> 52.(1) The Constitution of Canada is the supreme law of Canada, and any law that is inconsistent with the provisions of the Constitution is, to the extent of the inconsistency, of no force or effect.

This gives priority to the "Constitution of Canada" where it is inconsistent with other laws.[39] This supremacy clause obviously calls for a definition of the Constitution of Canada to which supremacy is accorded.

The entrenchment clause is s. 52(3), which provides as follows:

---

31 A possible function for the word includes would be to catch future constitutional amendments that are missed by para. (c) of s. 52(2): see note 27, above. The argument for treating the definition as exhaustive is very powerful with respect to instruments that existed in 1982.

32 It has been suggested that the Supreme Court Act should be added: see ch. 4, Amendment, under heading 4.2(c), "Constitution of Canada", below.

33 So held in *Re Dixon* (1986) 31 D.L.R. (4th) 546, 556-557 (B.C.S.C.) (Constitution of B.C. not included); *MacLean* v. *A.G.N.S.* (1987) 35 D.L.R. (4th) 306 (N.S.S.C.) (Constitution of N.S. not included).

34 These instruments are described in ch. 2, Reception, below.

35 These instruments are also described in ch. 2, Reception, below.

36 R.S.C. 1985, Appendix II, No. 31.

37 R.S.C. 1985, c. S-26. But see note 32, above.

38 R.S.C. 1985, Appendix III.

39 The supremacy clause is discussed in ch. 5, Federalism, under heading 5.4, "Supremacy of the Constitution", below.

> 52.(3) Amendments to the Constitution of Canada shall be made only in accordance with the authority contained in the Constitution of Canada.

The effect of s. 52(3) is to entrench the "Constitution of Canada": it cannot be amended by ordinary legislative action, but only by the special amending procedures laid down by Part V of the Constitution Act, 1982.[40] This entrenchment clause obviously calls for a definition of the Constitution of Canada that is entrenched.

The definition of the Constitution of Canada in s. 52(2) is vital to the application of the supremacy clause and the entrenchment clause. But it will probably have little effect on the use of the term "constitution" in other contexts. That term will continue to take its colour from its context, sometimes meaning the definition in s. 52(2), sometimes including the whole of Canada's constitutional law, and sometimes meaning only the Constitution Act, 1867 or only the Constitution Act, 1982, or both the last two instruments. Canada's gradual evolution from colony to nation has denied it any single comprehensive constitutional document.

In the light of history it is perfectly understandable why Canada lacks a document which contains ringing declarations of national purpose and independence, and which is intended to state all of the most important constitutional rules. Some Canadians feel that the lack of such a document is a reproach to Canada's nationhood. But this kind of thinking, while clad in the garb of Canadian nationalism, is probably at bottom a desire to copy the United States; and the idea that a new constitution could somehow be manufactured which would be more Canadian, more legitimate and more inspiring is unhistorical and naive. The one real disadvantage of the absence of a comprehensive constitutional document is that the rules of the Constitution are not readily accessible to non-lawyers. The Constitution Act, 1867 and the Constitution Act, 1982 (especially the latter) are rather detailed lawyers' instruments, lacking in elegance and brevity and not always easy to understand. And, as emphasized above, they do not by any means include all of the rules of Canadian constitutional law. These rules have to be hunted down in a variety of places. In the following sections of this chapter, I shall briefly survey those various sources.

1.5 Imperial statutes

The Constitution Act, 1867 and the Constitution Act, 1982 are both imperial statutes, that is to say, statutes enacted for Canada by the United Kingdom Parliament in its role as imperial Parliament.[41] These two statutes are within the

40 The amending procedures of Part V are discussed in ch. 4, Amendment, below. Within Part V, two sections, namely, ss. 44 and 45, do authorize certain categories of amendments by ordinary legislative action, but all other categories require a special, more difficult procedure.

41 See ch. 2, Reception, under heading 2.6, "Imperial statutes", below.

definition of the "Constitution of Canada" in s. 52(2) of the Constitution Act, 1982, and they are the two most important elements of the Constitution of Canada. Also within the definition are 17 other imperial statutes, mostly amendments to the Constitution Act, 1867, and four orders in council made under the authority of s. 146 of the Constitution Act, 1867, admitting to Canada the federal territories and the provinces of British Columbia and Prince Edward Island.

1.6 Canadian statutes

The definition of the "Constitution of Canada" in s. 52(2) of the Constitution Act, 1982 includes eight Canadian statutes. Three of these created the provinces of Manitoba, Alberta and Saskatchewan. These statutes were enacted under the power to create provinces out of federal territories, which was granted to the federal Parliament by the Constitution Act, 1871.[42] The other five Canadian statutes were amendments to the Constitution Act, 1867. These statutes were enacted under limited powers of amendment granted to the federal Parliament by the Constitution Act, 1867 (including an amendment in 1949).[43]

The eight Canadian statutes forming part of the Constitution of Canada were of course enacted by the federal Parliament in the ordinary way. However, their inclusion in the definition of the "Constitution of Canada" means that they are now supreme over other federal statutes by virtue of s. 52(1) of the Constitution Act, 1982, and are entrenched (unalterable except by use of the amending procedures) by virtue of s. 52(3) of the Constitution Act, 1982.

There are other Canadian statutes, which, although not included in the definition of the "Constitution of Canada", are constitutional in the sense that they establish or regulate some of the important institutions of the country. The Canadian Bill of Rights of 1960,[44] which purports to limit the powers of the federal Parliament,[45] is the clearest example of such a statute. The statute that created the Supreme Court of Canada in 1875[46] is also in this category, and the statute that created the Federal Court of Canada in 1971[47] has a claim to be included as well. One might also include federal statutes upon such basic matters as the franchise and citizenship. In each province, too, there are statutes that establish the system of courts, that provide for elections to the Legislature and that regulate the proceedings of the Legislature; these statutes are clearly constitutional in character. As well, Saskatchewan, Alberta and Quebec have each enacted a Bill of Rights.[48]

42 See ch. 2, Reception, under heading 2.5(b), "Territories and prairie provinces", below.
43 See ch. 4, Amendment, under heading 4.6, "Federal Parliament alone (s. 44)", below.
44 R.S.C. 1985, Appendix III.
45 See ch. 32, Canadian Bill of Rights, below.
46 See ch. 8, Supreme Court of Canada, below.
47 See ch. 7, Courts, under heading 7.2(b), "Federal Court of Canada", below.
48 See ch. 31, Civil Liberties, under heading 31.3(b), "Statutory bills of rights", below.

1.7 Parliamentary Privilege

The federal Houses of Parliament and the provincial legislative assemblies possess a set of powers and privileges that are "necessary to their capacity to function as legislative bodies".[49] These powers and rights are known collectively as "parliamentary privilege". In *New Brunswick Broadcasting Co.* v. *Nova Scotia* (1993),[50] the Supreme Court of Canada held that the Nova Scotia legislative assembly could ban the televising of its proceedings, because the power to exclude "strangers" from the legislative chamber was part of the assembly's parliamentary privilege. Parliamentary privilege probably also includes freedom of speech in debate, including immunity from legal proceedings for things said in debate. It probably also includes exclusive control of the assembly's proceedings, as well as control of publication of debates and proceedings.[51]

Parliamentary privilege could be regarded as a branch of the common law in that it is not contained in any statute or other written instrument, and it is the courts who determine its existence and extent. In the *New Brunswick Broadcasting* case, for example, the Supreme Court of Canada asked itself whether the power to exclude strangers from the legislative chamber was necessary for the proper functioning of Nova Scotia's legislative assembly. Only after the Court had satisfied itself that the answer was yes did the Court uphold the existence of the power. In this respect, parliamentary privilege is like the royal prerogative, which is also circumscribed by the decisions of the courts.[52] However, in the *New Brunswick Broadcasting* case, the majority of the Supreme Court of Canada attributed two peculiar characteristics to parliamentary privilege that distinguish it from the royal prerogative and from other branches of the common law.

The first peculiar characteristic of parliamentary privilege, according to *New Brunswick Broadcasting*, is that parliamentary privilege is part of the "Constitution of Canada". This aspect of the decision has already been explained and criticized.[53] The second peculiar characteristic, according to *New Brunswick Broadcasting*, is that the powers authorized by parliamentary privilege are not subject to the Charter of Rights. In that case, for example, the majority of the Court, having determined that the legislative assembly had a parliamentary-privilege power to exclude strangers from the legislative chamber, did not need to consider, and did not consider, whether the assembly's denial of access to the

49 *New Brunswick Broadcasting Co.* v. *N.S.* [1993] 1 S.C.R. 319, 381 per McLachlin J. for the majority.

50 [1993] 1 S.C.R. 319. The majority opinion was written by McLachlin J., with the concurrence of La Forest, L'Heureux-Dubé, Gonthier and Iacobucci JJ. Separate concurring opinions were written by Lamer C.J. and Sopinka J. Cory J. dissented.

51 *Id.*, 385 per McLachlin J., pointing out that these powers and privileges are possessed by the Houses of Parliament in the United Kingdom, but noting that parliamentary privilege may be more extensive in the United Kingdom than in Canada.

52 See section 1.9, "Prerogative", below.

53 Section 1.4, "Constitution of Canada", at note 29, above.

television media was a breach of the freedom of the press guaranteed by s. 2(b) of the Charter. This immunity from the Charter distinguishes parliamentary privilege from the royal prerogative and other common law powers of government; all other common law powers must be exercised in conformity with the Charter of Rights.[54] The immunity from the Charter also distinguishes parliamentary privilege from other powers conferred by the Constitution of Canada on the federal Parliament and the provincial Legislatures; all the other powers of these legislative bodies must be exercised in conformity with the Charter of Rights.[55]

The powers and privileges of a provincial legislative assembly have been held to be alterable by a statute enacted by the provincial Legislature, on the basis that the powers and privileges are part of the "constitution of the province".[56] Since 1982, the power of each provincial Legislature over the constitution of the province is to be found in s. 45 of the Constitution Act, 1982. (The federal Parliament would possess a similar power over the powers and privileges of each of the two Houses of Parliament under s. 44 of the Constitution Act, 1982, which confers power over "the Senate and House of Commons".) It is not clear whether the decision in *New Brunswick Broadcasting*, by holding that the powers and privileges of provincial legislative assemblies are part of the Constitution of Canada, has deprived the provincial Legislatures of the power to amend the powers and privileges of their legislative assemblies. Sopinka J., in his separate opinion in *New Brunswick Broadcasting*,[57] expressed the opinion, obiter, that this was the result of the majority's decision, describing it as "a high price . . . to pay in order to escape the Charter". It is possible, however, that the powers and privileges of a provincial legislative assembly would remain part of the constitution of the province, and therefore amendable under s. 45, even if they are also part of the Constitution of Canada.[58]

1.8 Case law

The courts have the task of interpreting the Constitution Acts and the other constitutional statutes. Their decisions constitute precedents for later cases so that a body of judge-made or decisional law, usually called case law, develops in areas where there has been litigation. While the courts' role is simply one of interpretation, the cumulative effect of a series of precedents will constitute an important elaboration or even modification of the original text. In particular, the provisions

---

54 See ch. 34, Application of Charter, under heading 34.2(g), "Common law", below.

55 See ch. 34, Application of Charter, under heading 34.2(b), "Parliament or Legislature", below, where this part of the *New Brunswick Broadcasting* decision is criticized.

56 *Fielding* v. *Thomas* [1896] A.C. 600.

57 [1993] 1 S.C.R. 319, 396; Lamer C.J. (at p. 352) expresses a similar view.

58 The question whether s. 45 of the Constitution Act, 1982 extends to amendments of the Constitution of Canada is discussed in ch. 4, Amendment, under heading 4.7, "Provincial Legislature alone", below.

of the Constitution Act, 1867 that distribute legislative power between the central Parliament and the provincial Legislatures are now overlaid by such an accumulation of cases that it would be unthinkable to attempt to ascertain the relevant rules by recourse to the Act alone. The Charter of Rights (Part I of the Constitution Act, 1982) has also attracted a vast case law despite its much shorter life. Obviously, the case law that interprets the Constitution Acts and the other constitutional statutes is also constitutional law.

In addition, some of the common law, that is to say, case law which is independent of any statute or constitution, could be characterized as constitutional law. For example, the Crown (meaning the executive government) retains a few vestigial prerogative powers, which spring not from statute, but from the common law; the prerogative is discussed in the next section of this chapter. It is also the courts which have developed many of the rules concerning the liability of the Crown and its employees.[59] The courts have also made much of the law concerning civil liberties by establishing rules to limit the powers of government officials and administrative agencies, and procedures to enable private individuals to review administrative action.[60] In almost every field that initially developed purely as common law, there has been considerable statutory intervention, modifying the judge-made rules. That is true of the examples given, but much of the law is still case law.

1.9 Prerogative

The royal prerogative[61] consists of the powers and privileges accorded by the common law to the Crown. Dicey described it as "the residue of discretionary or arbitrary authority, which at any given time is left in the hands of the Crown".[62] The prerogative is a branch of the common law, because it is the decisions of the courts which have determined its existence and extent.[63]

The term prerogative should be confined to powers or privileges that are unique to the Crown. Powers or privileges enjoyed equally with private persons are not, strictly speaking, part of the prerogative. For example, the Crown has the power to acquire and dispose of property, and to enter into contracts, but these are not prerogative powers, because they are possessed by everyone. Sometimes,

---

59 See ch. 10, The Crown, below.

60 See ch. 31, Civil Liberties, under heading 31.2 "Common law", below.

61 See Mundell, "Legal Nature of Federal and Provincial Executive Governments" (1960) 2 Osgoode Hall L.J. 56; Cheffins and Tucker, *The Constitutional Process in Canada* (2nd ed., 1976), ch. 4; Munro, *Studies in Constitutional Law* (1987), ch. 8; Evatt, *The Royal Prerogative* (1987); MacDonald, *A Contemporary Analysis of the Prerogative* (LL.M. thesis, Osgoode Hall Law School, York University, 1988); de Smith and Brazier, *Constitutional and Administrative Law* (6th ed., 1989), ch. 6.

62 Dicey, *Law of the Constitution* (10th ed., 1965), 424; but see note 76, below.

63 *Case of Proclamations* (1611) 12 Co. Rep. 74, 77 E.R. 1352 (K.B.), holding that "the King hath no prerogative, but that which the law of the land allows him".

the term prerogative is used loosely, in a wider sense, as encompassing all the powers of the Crown that flow from the common law,[64] but this usage is historically inaccurate.[65]

In the next chapter, we shall see that the Crown possessed certain prerogative legislative powers over British colonies. The King, acting without the concurrence of Parliament, had the power to create the office of Governor, executive council, legislative assembly and courts for a colony. In the case of a conquered colony (as opposed to a settled colony), the King possessed a general power of legislation but only until such time as the colony was granted its own legislative assembly.[66] These powers are of mainly historical interest for Canada today; but the constitutions of Nova Scotia, New Brunswick and Prince Edward Island still consist of prerogative instruments,[67] and the office of Governor General still depends upon a prerogative instrument.[68]

Apart from the power over the colonies, the courts held that there was no prerogative power to legislate: only the Parliament could make new laws.[69] The Bill of Rights of 1688 denied the prerogative powers to "suspend" a law for a period of time, or to "dispense" with a law in a particular case.[70] The Bill of Rights of 1688 also affirmed that only Parliament could levy taxes.[71] And the courts established that only Parliament could authorize the expenditure of public funds.[72] The courts also held that there was no prerogative power to administer justice: only the courts could adjudicate disputes according to law.[73] These decisions confined the prerogative to executive governmental powers. And within this area the prerogative was further limited by the doctrine that most executive

---

64 Dicey, note 62, above, 455, said that "every act which the executive government can lawfully do without the authority of an Act of Parliament is done by virtue of the prerogative". For criticism of this usage, see Mundell, note 61, above, 58-59; Munro, note 61, above, 159-160.

65 Blackstone, *Commentaries* (1765), vol. 1, 239, says that: "It assumes in its etymology (from *prae* and *rogo*) something that is required or demanded before, or in preference to, all others".

66 See ch. 2, Reception, below.

67 *Id.*, under heading 2.2(c), "Amendment of received laws," below.

68 Letters Patent constituting the office of Governor General of Canada, 1947, R.S.C. 1985, Appendix II, No. 31.

69 *Case of Proclamations* (1611) 12 Co. Rep. 74, 77 E.R. 1352 (K.B.) (King by proclamation could not prohibit new buildings in London).

70 de Smith, note 61, above, 70-71; and see ch. 31, Civil Liberties, under heading 31.2, "Common law", below.

71 *Bowles* v. *Bank of England* [1913] 1 Ch. 57 (resolution of parliamentary committee, approved by House of Commons, cannot levy a tax).

72 *Auckland Harbour Bd.* v. *The King* [1924] A.C. 318 (P.C., N.Z.) (money spent by government without legislative appropriation is recoverable by government); Campbell, "Parliamentary Appropriations" (1971) 4 Adelaide L.R. 145.

73 *Prohibition del Roy* (1607) 12 Co. Rep. 63, 77 E.R. 1342 ("The King in his own person cannot adjudge any case, either criminal . . . or betwixt party and party").

action which infringed the liberty of the subject required the authority of a statute.[74] Moreover, the prerogative could be abolished or limited by statute, and, once a statute had occupied the ground formerly occupied by the prerogative, the Crown had to comply with the terms of the statute.[75] All of these rules, and especially the last (displacement by statute), have had the effect of shrinking the prerogative powers[76] of the Crown down to a very narrow compass. The conduct of foreign affairs, including the making of treaties and the declaring of war, continues to be a prerogative power in Canada. So is the appointment of the Prime Minister and other Ministers, the issue of passports, and the conferring of honours such as Queen's Counsel. But most governmental power in Canada[77] is exercised under statutory, not prerogative power.

It used to be asserted that the exercise of prerogative powers was not subject to judicial review.[78] The assertion is belied by the many cases in which the exercise or purported exercise of prerogative powers has been reviewed by the courts. The courts will determine whether a prerogative power that is asserted by the Crown does in fact exist,[79] and, if it does exist, what are its limits and whether any restrictions on the power have been complied with.[80] The courts will also determine whether a prerogative power has been displaced by statute.[81] The courts will also require, not only that prerogative powers be exercised in conformity with the

---

74 *Entick* v. *Carrington* (1765) 19 St. Tr. 1030, 95 E.R. 807 (K.B.), (no prerogative power of search and seizure). An exception was that property could be taken or destroyed in time of war, although the prerogative power was accompanied by an obligation to pay compensation: *Burmah Oil Co.* v. *Lord Advocate* [1965] A.C. 75 (H.L.) (Crown ordered to pay compensation for oil installations in Burma destroyed during second world war).

75 *A.G.* v. *De Keyser's Royal Hotel* [1920] A.C. 508 (H.L.) (Crown ordered to satisfy statutory requirement of compensation for building occupied in time of war). Cf. *Barton* v. *Cth. of Aust.* (1974) 131 C.L.R. 477 (extradition under prerogative upheld; not displaced by statute); *R.* v. *Home Secretary*; *Ex parte Northumbria Police Authority* [1989] Q.B. 26 (C.A.) (prerogative power to supply riot equipment to police not displaced by statute).

76 As well as prerogative powers, there are a number of prerogative privileges or immunities, which give to the Crown immunities from some kinds of legal proceedings, priority in the payment of debts, etc. This miscellaneous class of prerogatives, which is ignored in Dicey's definition accompanying note 62, above, has also been reduced by statute, but some of it lingers on. The part concerned with the liability of the Crown to legal proceedings is discussed in ch. 10, The Crown, below.

77 Canada being a federal state, the prerogative powers had to be distributed between the federal government (the Crown in right of Canada) and the provincial governments (the Crown in right of each province). The Constitution Act, 1867 was silent on the point. The courts held that the prerogative powers followed the comparable legislative powers: see ch. 9, Responsible Government, under heading 9.2, ''Law and Convention'', below.

78 de Smith, note 61, above, 129-130, rejecting the assertion.

79 The leading cases are cited in notes 69-74, above.

80 *Burmah Oil Co.* v. *Lord Advocate* [1965] A.C. 75 (H.L.) (prerogative power accompanied by a duty to pay compensation). Cf. judicial review of claims to withhold evidence by virtue of Crown privilege: ch. 10, The Crown, under heading 10.4, ''Crown privilege'', below.

81 Note 75, above.

Charter of Rights[82] and other constitutional norms,[83] but also that administrative-law norms such as the duty of fairness be observed.[84]

Before the development of responsible government, the prerogative powers of the Crown were exercised by the reigning monarch in accordance with his or her own discretion. Such powers could not survive the growth of democratic ideals, for the monarch was not (and still is not) an elected official. In most countries, the acceptance of democratic ideals led to the abolition of the monarchy: all executive and legislative powers were then conferred on elected officials. In the United Kingdom, the acceptance of democratic ideals led to the system of responsible government, under which the King (or Queen) continued as head of state, and retained many of his powers, but he exercised those powers only on the "advice" of (meaning at the direction of) his ministers. The ministers were the leaders of the party commanding a majority in the elected House of Commons. In this way, the requirements of democracy were satisfied without giving up the forms of monarchical government.

Responsible government had not been extended to the colonies by 1776. Indeed, it was not established in the United Kingdom itself until the nineteenth century. For the 13 American colonies that declared their independence in 1776, the democratic answer to rule by an absentee King and his appointed governors was independence under a republican form of government. For the loyal British North American colonies that remained in the Empire until after responsible government was established in the United Kingdom, the solution turned out to be the gradual extension of responsible government to each colony. At first just the colonial governor, but later the King or Queen as well, was to act on the advice of the ministers who enjoyed the confidence of the local representative assembly. At first various matters of imperial concern (for example, treaty-making) were excluded from responsible government and reserved for British decision, but eventually local responsible government extended to everything. The story of the extension of responsible government to British North America, and the working out of the full implications of that idea, is the story of Canada's achievement of independence.[85]

---

82 *Operation Dismantle* v. *The Queen* [1985] 1 S.C.R. 441 (weapon testing under prerogative upheld, but prerogative power in principle subject to Charter).

83 *Air Can.* v. *B.C.* [1986] 2 S.C.R. 539 (mandamus issued to overrule denial of royal fiat for proceedings against Crown to recover unconstitutional taxes).

84 *R.* v. *Criminal Injuries Comp. Bd.; Ex parte Lain* [1967] 2 Q.B. 864 (certiorari issued for error of law on face of record by board established under prerogative); *Council of Civil Service Unions* v. *Minr. for Civil Service* [1985] 1 A.C. 374 (H.L.) (remedy denied, but prerogative control of civil service held in principle to be subject to duty of fairness); *R.* v. *Foreign Secretary; Ex parte Everett* [1989] Q.B. 811 (C.A.) (remedy denied, but refusal of passport under prerogative held to be subject to duty of fairness). It seems likely, however, that there are still some prerogative powers that by their nature are not susceptible to judicial review: Evatt, note 61, above, C25 - C34 (by Zines); de Smith, note 61, above, 129-130.

85 The history of responsible government is related in ch. 9, Responsible Government, below.

An extraordinary feature of the system of responsible government is that its rules are not legal rules in the sense of being enforceable in the courts. They are conventions only. The exercise of the Crown's prerogative powers is thus regulated by conventions, not laws.[86] Conventions are the topic of the next section of this chapter.

1.10 Conventions

(a) Definition

Conventions are rules of the constitution that are not enforced by the law courts.[87] Because they are not enforced by the law courts, they are best regarded as non-legal rules, but because they do in fact regulate the working of the constitution, they are an important concern of the constitutional lawyer. What conventions do is to prescribe the way in which legal powers shall be exercised. Some conventions have the effect of transferring effective power from the legal holder to another official or institution. Other conventions limit an apparently broad legal power, or even prescribe that a legal power shall not be exercised at all.

Consider the following examples. (1) The Constitution Act, 1867, and many Canadian statutes, confer extensive powers on the Governor General or on the Governor General in Council, but a convention stipulates that the Governor General will exercise those powers only in accordance with the advice of the cabinet or in some cases the Prime Minister.[88] (2) The Constitution Act, 1867 makes the Queen, or the Governor General, an essential party to all federal legislation (s. 17), and it expressly confers upon the Queen and the Governor General the power to withhold the royal assent from a bill that has been enacted by the two Houses of Parliament (s. 55), but a convention stipulates that the royal assent shall never be withheld.[89]

Other developments, essentially elaborating the same idea, are related in ch. 3, Independence, below.

86 The Queen in the United Kingdom, and her representatives elsewhere in the Commonwealth, retain a few "personal prerogatives", namely, powers which are exercised at the personal discretion of the Queen (or Governor General or Lieutenant Governor). These powers are needed for the situation where there is no ministry that commands the confidence of the elected assembly. They are discussed in ch. 9, Responsible Government, under heading 9.6, "The Governor General's personal prerogatives", below.

87 The best-known of the abundant writings on conventions are Dicey, *The Law of the Constitution* (10th ed., 1965), chs. 14, 15; Jennings, *The Law and the Constitution* (5th ed., 1959), ch. 3; Wheare, *Modern Constitutions* (2nd ed., 1966), ch. 8; Marshall, *Constitutional Conventions* (1986); de Smith and Brazier, *Constitutional and Administrative Law* (6th ed., 1989), 28-47. A recent Canadian study is Heard, *Canadian Constitutional Conventions* (1991). Conventions are also discussed in Tremblay, *Droit Constitutionnel — Principles* (1993), 16-26.

88 See ch. 9, Responsible Government, below.

89 See ch. 9, Responsible Government, under heading 9.4, "The legislative branch", below.

Each of these two conventions is discussed later in this book, and many other examples will be encountered as well. The two that have been described are two of the most fundamental rules of the Canadian Constitution. Yet, like all conventions, they are not enforceable in the courts. If the Governor General exercised one of his powers without (or in violation of) ministerial advice, the courts would not deny validity to his act. If the Governor General withheld his assent to a bill enacted by both Houses of Parliament, the courts would deny the force of law to the bill, and they would not issue an injunction or other legal remedy to force the Governor General to give his assent. None of these things has ever happened, because conventions are in fact nearly always obeyed by the officials whose conduct they regulate.

If a convention is disobeyed by an official, then it is common, especially in the United Kingdom, to describe the official's act or omission as "unconstitutional". But this use of the term unconstitutional must be carefully distinguished from the case where a legal rule of the constitution has been disobeyed. Where unconstitutionality springs from a breach of law, the purported act is normally a nullity and there is a remedy available in the courts.[90] But where "unconstitutionality" springs merely from a breach of convention, no breach of the law has occurred and no legal remedy will be available.[91]

(b) Conventions in the courts

Although a convention will not be enforced by the courts, the existence of a convention has occasionally been recognized by the courts. For example, the courts have taken notice of the conventions of responsible government, which make a Minister accountable to Parliament, as a consideration in deciding to give a broad rather than a narrow interpretation to a statute conferring power on a Minister.[92] In these cases, and in other cases in which the existence of a convention has been recognized,[93] the existence of the convention was relevant to the dis-

---

90 In some cases of breach of a constitutional law, there is no remedy, for example, because the legal rule is held to be non-justiciable, or because the legal rule is held to be directory only and not mandatory, or because no individual is sufficiently affected by the breach of the legal rule to have "standing" to seek a judicial remedy, or because there is no appropriate remedy. But these are unusual cases.

91 In *Re Resolution to Amend the Constitution* [1981] 1 S.C.R. 753, 909, the Court distinguished between these two senses of the word unconstitutional, and held that breach of a convention did not cause invalidity or give rise to any remedy. Other cases where courts have explicitly refused to enforce a convention are *Re Disallowance and Reservation of Provincial Legislation* [1938] S.C.R. 71; *Currie* v. *MacDonald* (1949), 29 Nfld. & P.E.I.R. 294 (Nfld. C.A.); *Madzimbamuto* v. *Lardner-Burke* [1969] 1 A.C. 645 (P.C., So. Rhodesia).

92 E.g., *Liversidge* v. *Anderson* [1942] A.C. 206 (H.L.); *Carltona* v. *Commrs. of Works* [1943] 2 All E.R. 560 (C.A.); cf. *A.-G. Que.* v. *Blaikie* (No. 2) [1981] 1 S.C.R. 312, 320 (Acts include regulations in view of conventions linking government with Legislature).

93 Other cases are cited in *Re Resolution to Amend the Constitution* [1981] 1 S.C.R. 753, 775-784, 885. Add to these *OPSEU* v. *Ont.* [1987] 2 S.C.R. 2, 44-45 (convention of political neutrality of Crown servants recognized).

position of a legal issue, usually the interpretation of either a statute or a written constitution.

In the *Patriation Reference* (1981),[94] the Supreme Court of Canada was asked on a reference whether there was a convention requiring that the consent of the provinces be obtained before the federal government requested the United Kingdom Parliament to enact an amendment to the Constitution of Canada that would affect the powers of the provinces. The Court was also asked whether there was a legal requirement of provincial consent. The questions had been referred to the courts by three of the eight provinces that were opposed to Prime Minister Trudeau's proposals for a constitutional settlement to patriate the constitution and obtain an amending procedure and a charter of rights.[95] The Supreme Court of Canada obviously had to decide the legal question, and it did so by holding that there was no legal requirement of provincial consent to the constitutional proposals. But the Court went on to decide the convention question as well. A majority of the Court held that there was a convention, and that the convention required the federal government to obtain a ''substantial degree'' or ''substantial measure'' of provincial consent[96] before requesting the requisite legislation from the United Kingdom.[97]

The decision in the *Patriation Reference* did not, strictly speaking, enforce a convention. Indeed, as related above, the Court specifically held that there was no legal obligation upon the federal government to obtain the consent of the provinces. Nonetheless, as a matter of practical politics, the decision made it impossible for the federal government to proceed with its constitutional proposals without a ''substantial degree'' of provincial consent. After the decision, Prime Minister Trudeau and the Premiers met again to try and reach the agreement which had hitherto eluded them, and on November 5, 1981 they did in fact reach agreement on the constitutional settlement which became the Canada Act 1982 and the Constitution Act, 1982.

The Supreme Court of Canada in the *Patriation Reference* had said that the convention required a ''substantial degree'' of provincial consent to amendments as far-reaching as those proposed by Prime Minister Trudeau. After the agreement of November 5, 1981, doubt remained as to whether this rule had been satisfied. The agreement included nine of the ten provinces, but did not include Quebec, the only predominantly French-speaking province and one that included over 25 per cent of Canada's population. Was the consent of Quebec necessary as part of a ''substantial degree'' of provincial consent? Quebec referred this question to

---

94 *Re Resolution to Amend the Constitution* [1981] 1 S.C.R. 753.

95 The history of this constitutional settlement is related in ch. 4, Amendment, below.

96 [1981] 1 S.C.R. 753, 905.

97 Four opinions were written, none attributed to an individual judge. On the legal question, there was a majority opinion, signed by Laskin C.J., Dickson, Beetz, Estey, McIntyre, Chouinard and Lamer JJ., and a dissenting opinion, signed by Martland and Ritchie JJ. On the convention question, there was a majority opinion, signed by Martland, Ritchie, Dickson, Beetz, Chouinard and Lamer JJ., and a dissenting opinion signed by Laskin C.J., Estey and McIntyre JJ.

its Court of Appeal for answer. By the time the question reached the Supreme Court of Canada, the Canada Act 1982 had actually been enacted by the United Kingdom Parliament. Not only was the question solely about a convention, but the issue was moot even in a political sense. Nonetheless, in the *Quebec Veto Reference* (1982),[98] the Supreme Court of Canada answered the question, deciding that Quebec's consent was not necessary to make up the requisite ''substantial degree'' of provincial consent. By this decision the Court destroyed the spectre of an ''unconstitutional constitution''![99]

The convention questions in the *Patriation Reference* and *Quebec Veto Reference* raised no legal issues, and the answers could not lead to any legal consequences. Was the Supreme Court of Canada wrong to answer the questions? The Court pointed out that courts had in previous cases recognized the existence of conventions,[100] but, as mentioned earlier, in the previous cases the existence of the convention had been relevant to the disposition of a legal issue. That was not true in the *Patriation Reference*, where the answer to the convention question had no bearing on the answer to the legal question; nor was it true in the *Quebec Veto Reference*, where no legal question was asked. The Court also pointed out that the convention questions had been referred to the Court for answers,[101] but the Court has in the past often asserted (and exercised) a discretion not to answer questions referred to it that are unsuitable for judicial determination.[102] The issue really comes down to the question whether the convention questions were suitable for judicial determination. The only possible effect of answering the convention question in the *Patriation Reference* was to influence the outcome of the political negotiations over the 1981-82 constitutional settlement.[103] The answer to the convention question strengthened the hands of the provinces in that negotiation, and is probably the reason why the provinces were able to secure the insertion of the override clause in the Charter of Rights and the substitution of the opting-out amending formula — the two major concessions made by the federal government to achieve the agreement of November 5, 1981. In my view, the Court, which is not an elected body, and which is not politically accountable for its actions, should

---

98 *Re Objection by Que. to Resolution to Amend the Constitution* [1982] 2 S.C.R. 793.

99 Of course, if the decision had been otherwise, the Canada Act 1982 and the Constitution Act, 1982 would still have been valid; they would have been unconstitutional only in the conventional sense; see note 91, above.

100 [1981] 1 S.C.R. 753, 885.

101 [1981] 1 S.C.R. 753, 884.

102 The discretion not to answer questions posed on a reference is described in ch. 8, Supreme Court of Canada, under heading 8.6, ''Reference jurisdiction'', below.

103 In the *Que. Veto Reference*, note 98, above, even this effect was missing, since the amendments had been enacted. The Supreme Court of Canada (at pp. 805-806) gave two reasons for answering the question: (1) the Quebec Court of Appeal had answered it, and (2) ''it appears desirable that the constitutional question be answered in order to dispel any doubt over it''. It may be noted that the Court is rarely so deferential to the lower court, or so intolerant of doubt on questions that need not be decided.

have confined itself to answering the legal question, and should not have gone beyond the legal question to exert any further influence over the negotiations.[104]

(c) Convention and usage

Conventions are often distinguished from ''usages'': a convention is a rule which is regarded as obligatory by the officials to whom it applies; a usage is not a rule, but merely a governmental practice which is ordinarily followed, although it is not regarded as obligatory. An example of a usage is the practice of appointing to the position of Chief Justice of Canada the person who is the senior puisne judge of the Supreme Court of Canada at the time of the vacancy. This practice has been observed many times, but it is probable that the Prime Minister (who by convention makes the recommendation to the Governor General who by law makes the appointment) does not feel obliged to follow the practice, for it has been departed from in two recent appointments,[105] those of Chief Justice Laskin in 1973 and Chief Justice Dickson in 1984, neither of whom was the senior puisne judge at the time of his appointment. The practice was resumed with the appointment of Chief Justice Lamer in 1990.[106]

A usage may develop into a convention. If a practice is invariably followed over a long period of time, it may come to be generally regarded as obligatory and thereby cease to be merely a usage. The resulting convention may be called a custom. This process of evolution from usage to convention (or custom) is the way in which most conventions have been established. It should be noticed, however, that very little turns on the question whether a practice is a usage or a convention, because a convention is as unenforceable as a usage. The most that can be said is that there is a stronger moral obligation to follow a convention than a usage, and that departure from convention may be criticized more severely than departure from usage.

Before the *Patriation Reference* (1981),[107] it was generally assumed that there was no judicial procedure for adjudicating a dispute about whether a particular practice was a convention or a usage. Since no legal consequence could flow from the answer, the issue appeared to be non-justiciable. In the *Patriation Reference*, however, as we have seen, the Supreme Court of Canada undertook, for the first time in any common law jurisdiction, to adjudicate such a dispute. The issue was whether the past practice of securing provincial consents to con-

---

104 This position is argued, and other criticisms made of the *Patriation Reference*, in Hogg, Comment (1982) 60 Can. Bar Rev. 307.

105 Another departure occurred on the appointment of Anglin C.J. in 1924.

106 Another example of a usage is the practice of appointing three judges to the Supreme Court of Canada from Ontario. This practice was consistently followed until 1978 when Spence J. (from Ontario) retired and was replaced by McIntyre J. (from British Columbia). In 1982, when Martland J. (from Alberta) retired, he was replaced by Wilson J. (from Ontario), and Ontario's usual complement of three members was restored.

107 Note 94, above.

stitutional amendments affecting provincial powers was a usage (as the federal government and two provinces argued) or a convention (as eight provinces argued). In order to resolve the dispute, the Court looked at three questions: (1) what were the precedents? (2) what were the beliefs of the actors in the precedents? and (3) what was the reason for the practice?[108] With respect to the precedents, the Court surveyed the history of constitutional amendment in Canada and concluded that there had been an invariable practice of obtaining provincial consents to amendments that made a change in legislative powers. With respect to the beliefs of the actors, the Court concluded from statements in a federal white paper and by federal ministers that the actors on the federal side felt bound to obtain provincial consents to such amendments. With respect to the reason for the practice, the Court found it in a ''federal principle'' which condemned any modification of provincial powers ''by the unilateral action of the federal authorities''.[109] The Court accordingly concluded that there was a convention.

Having decided that there was a convention, the Court had to decide what the convention was. As noted earlier, the Court decided that the convention required a ''substantial degree'' or ''substantial measure'' of provincial consent, but that it was not necessary to decide exactly what the requisite degree was.[110] It was enough to decide that the constitutional proposals, which at that time enjoyed the support of only Ontario and New Brunswick, did not have ''a sufficient measure of provincial agreement''.[111] This part of the Court's decision was rather unsatisfactory, not only because it was an implausible reading of the history of constitutional amendment,[112] but also because it was so vague.

The vagueness of the ''substantial degree'' rule quickly led to further litigation. After the agreement of November 5, 1981, in which the federal government obtained the consents of nine out of ten provinces to a modified constitutional settlement, Quebec returned to the Supreme Court of Canada with a new reference, the *Quebec Veto Reference* (1982),[113] which asked whether the convention of a ''substantial degree'' of provincial consent required the consent of Quebec. With respect to the precedents, it was clear that Quebec's consent had always been required in the past. With respect to the reason for the practice, it could be found in a principle of ''duality'', which implied special protection of the powers of the only predominantly French-speaking province. But the Supreme Court of Canada concentrated its attention on the beliefs of the actors, finding that a Quebec veto

---

108 The three questions were taken from Jennings, *The Law and the Constitution* (5th ed., 1959), 136. The discussion of the questions is to be found in [1981] 1 S.C.R. 753, 888-909.

109 [1981] 1 S.C.R. 753, 905-906.

110 *Id.*, 905.

111 *Ibid.*

112 In my comment (1982) 60 Can. Bar Rev. 307, I argue that the history was consistent with either a convention of unanimity (contended for by seven provinces) or no convention at all (contended for by the federal government and two provinces), but not the substantial degree rule (contended for by only one province).

113 Note 98, above.

had never been articulated by any of the actors in the precedents (although it had never been denied either). In the Court's view, "a convention could not have remained wholly inarticulate, except perhaps at the inchoate stage when it has not yet been accepted as a binding rule".[114] The Court accordingly held that there was no requirement of Quebec's consent: the nine predominantly English-speaking provinces comprised a "substantial degree" of provincial consent, which satisfied the convention.

(d) Convention and agreement

As noticed above, most conventions have developed from a long history of past practice, which has eventually attracted a sense of obligation or normative character. But this process of evolution from usage to convention (or custom) is not the only way in which a convention may be established. If all the relevant officials agree to adopt a certain rule of constitutional conduct, then that rule may immediately come to be regarded as obligatory.[115] The resulting convention could hardly at the beginning be described as a custom. For example, in 1930 the Prime Ministers of the self-governing dominions of the Commonwealth agreed that thenceforth the King (or Queen) would appoint the Governor General of a dominion solely on the advice of the government of the dominion.[116] They also agreed that thenceforth the imperial Parliament would not enact a law for any of the dominions except at the request and with the consent of the dominion.[117] These agreements established conventions. It should be noticed too that conventions established by agreement will normally be written down by the officials concerned in precise and authoritative terms. Conventions are not necessarily unwritten rules,

114 [1982] 2 S.C.R. 793, 817. This point seems dubious. There is undoubtedly a convention that the Queen or Governor General or Lieutenant Governor will not withhold the royal assent from bills which have been passed by the appropriate legislative chambers, but I am not aware that any Queen or King or Governor General or Lieutenant Governor has ever explicitly acknowledged the obligation. The convention is well understood although tacit. For further criticism of the decision, see Petter, "The Quebec Veto Reference" (1984), 6 Supreme Court L.R. 387.

115 Latham, *The Law and the Commonwealth* (1949), 610, makes the point that "in domestic affairs agreement rarely, if ever, creates constitutional convention, because the usual parties namely, ministers, members of Parliament, the Houses of Parliament, and the King have no moral authority to bind their successors by mere agreement apart from precedent. But in Commonwealth relations it has long been recognized that the agreement of the executive government of a member binds its successors, because it would be derogatory to its autonomy if other members, in order to ascertain their rights and obligations in relation to it, were compelled to examine its internal affairs". It may perhaps be noticed that the problem of "moral authority to bind their successors" exists in Commonwealth relations too, but agreements to create conventions of Commonwealth relations have been made and observed.

116 See ch. 9, Responsible Government, under heading 9.2, "Law and Convention", below.

117 See ch. 3, Independence, under heading 3.3, "Statute of Westminster, 1931". This convention accorded with prior usage and may even have been established before the agreement in 1930, but the agreement settled its status as a convention.

although conventions established by custom are rarely written down in terms that are accepted as precise and authoritative.[118]

(e) Convention and law

A convention could be transformed into law by being enacted as a statute.[119] A convention would also be transformed into law if it were enforced by the courts. If a court gave a remedy for a breach of convention, for example, by ordering an unwilling Governor General to give his or her assent to a bill enacted by both Houses of Parliament, then we would have to change our language and say that the Governor General was under a legal obligation to assent, and not merely a conventional obligation. In that event, a convention would have been transformed into a rule of common law.

In the *Patriation Reference* (1981),[120] it was argued by the provinces that the convention requiring provincial consents to constitutional amendments had "crystallized" into law, so that there was a legal obligation to obtain provincial consents. But it was not clear how this process had occurred, and there seemed to be no precedents of crystallization. The Court rejected the argument in terms which suggested that a convention could never be transformed into a rule of common law. Their lordships pointed out that a convention develops through precedents established by political officials, while the common law develops through precedents established by the courts.[121] One of the opinions even disapproved my statement in an earlier edition of this book that a judicial decision could have the effect of transforming a convention into a legal rule.[122] But, with respect, the statement is true by definition. If a court did enforce a convention (and admittedly no court has ever done so), the convention would be transformed into a legal rule, because the rule would no longer be unenforceable in the courts, and that is the only characteristic which distinguishes a convention from a legal rule.

Since conventions are not legally enforceable, one may well ask: why are they obeyed? The primary reason is that breach of a convention would result in serious political repercussions, and eventually in changes in the law. An attempt by a Governor General to act without advice or to refuse assent to a bill would

118 The distinction between written and unwritten rules is hard to draw and is rarely useful. For example, even conventions established by custom are written down in textbooks on government or constitutional law, and such accounts are of persuasive authority in determining the existence or scope of a particular convention. Note also the *Quebec Veto Reference*, holding that no convention had been established, because the claimed rule had never been articulated: note 114 and accompanying text, above.

119 Legislation implementing a conventional rule, in this case the convention of public service neutrality, makes the rule subject to the Charter of Rights: *Osborne* v. *Can.* [1991] 2 S.C.R. 69 (restrictions on political activity by public servants held unconstitutional).

120 *Re Resolution to Amend the Constitution* [1981] 1 S.C.R. 753.

121 *Id.*, 774-775.

122 *Id.*, 856.

quickly be followed by his dismissal, and would lead to an irresistible demand to enact a statute embodying the terms of the convention. Similar kinds of grave political consequences would flow from breach of the other conventions, for example, the refusal of the Queen to appoint as Governor General the person recommended by the Canadian government, or the refusal by the Prime Minister to resign after losing his majority in the House of Commons.

Law and convention are "closely interlocked", as the examples given show; the conventions "do not exist in a legal vacuum".[123] They regulate the way in which legal powers shall be exercised, and they therefore presuppose the existence of the legal powers. Their purpose is "to ensure that the legal framework of the constitution will be operated in accordance with the prevailing constitutional values or principles of the period".[124] They bring outdated legal powers into conformity with current notions of government. Each convention takes a legal power that would be intolerable if it were actually exercised as written, and makes it tolerable. If the convention did not exist, the legal power would have to be changed. It would be intolerable to Canadians if the Queen or Governor General were actually to exercise significant governmental powers. Such powers would be inconsistent with representative democracy. But the legal powers can continue to exist, so long as they are invariably exercised in conformity with the conventions that assure democratic control of the powers. Thus, the conventions allow the law to adapt to changing political realities without the necessity for formal amendment.

Not only do conventions presuppose the existence of law, much law presupposes the existence of conventions. The Constitution Act, 1867 was drafted the way it was because the framers knew that the extensive powers vested in the Queen and Governor General would be exercised in accordance with the conventions of responsible government, that is to say, under the advice (meaning direction) of the cabinet or in some cases the Prime Minister. Modern statutes continue this strange practice of ignoring the Prime Minister (or provincial Premier) and his cabinet. They always grant powers to the Governor General in Council[125] (or the Lieutenant Governor in Council) when they intend to grant powers to the cabinet. The numerous statutes that do this are of course enacted in the certain knowledge that the conventions of responsible government will shift the effective power into the hands of the elected ministry where it belongs.

---

123 de Smith, note 87, above, 37-38.

124 *Re Resolution to Amend the Constitution* [1981] 1 S.C.R. 753, 880.

125 The actual phrase that is used in modern statutes is "the Governor in Council", which omits the word "General".

2

Reception

2.1 Rules of reception

How did Canada acquire its legal systems? The answer is that they were received from the former imperial power, the United Kingdom, and, to a much lesser extent, France, during the colonial period. This chapter explains how "reception"[1] occurred in British North America, and traces the process up to the present time.

Since British North America was eventually entirely colonized by the United Kingdom, we must look to the English common law of colonization for the basic

1 The process is usually described as "reception", although "adoption", "migration" and "introduction" are also occasionally used. For accounts of the process, see Anger and Honsberger, *Law of Real Property* (2nd ed., 1985), ch. 3; Jackett, "Foundations of Canadian Law in History and Theory" in Lang (ed.), *Contemporary Problems of Public Law in Canada* (1968), 3; Laskin, *The British Tradition in Canadian Law* (1969), 3-10; Lederman, *Continuing Canadian Constitutional Dilemmas* (1981), ch. 4; Brown, "British Statutes in the Emergent Nations of North America: 1606-1949" (1963) 7 Am. Jo. Legal History 95; Cote, "The Reception of English Law" (1977) 15 Alta. L. Rev. 29.

rules of reception. The common law distinguished between a colony acquired by the United Kingdom by settlement and a colony acquired by conquest. In the case of a colony acquired by settlement, the settlers brought with them English law, and this became the initial law of the colony. In the case of a colony acquired by conquest, the law of the conquered people continued in force, except to the extent necessary to establish and operate the governmental institutions of British colonial rule. A colony acquired by cession (that is, by transfer from another country) was treated as acquired by conquest.

In British North America, the two rules of reception were not as useful as they might appear. In the first place, they were often applied in disregard of the existence of the aboriginal peoples, who were in possession of much of British North America before the arrival of Europeans. Their presence, supported by their considerable military capability, may explain the survival of aboriginal customary law in parts of British North America.[2] It seems clear that all aboriginal customary law did not disappear at the time of European settlement, as the rule of reception for a settled British colony might imply. The account which follows will not pursue the complex issue of the survival of aboriginal customary law,[3] but will simply attempt to trace the reception of English and French law into British North America.

The reception of English and French law into British North America is by no means a straightforward story. In view of early French claims to large areas of British North America, it is not always clear whether a particular territory should be treated as having been acquired by the United Kingdom by settlement or by conquest (or cession). As we shall see, outside the territory now included in Ontario and Quebec (which was indisputably acquired by either conquest or cession), the tendency of the courts was to prefer the ''settled'' classification. The settled classification entailed the automatic reception of English, not French law, a result that was congenial to the English population. In the case of the three maritime provinces, which as a matter of historical fact were acquired by cession from France, the possibility of the survival of French law seems never to have been seriously considered. The reception of English law into these provinces has often been explained on the patently false basis that they were ''settled'' colonies.[4]

---

2 *Connolly* v. *Woolrich* (1867) 11 L.C. Jur. 197 (Que. S.C.); affd. (1869) 17 R.J.R.Q. 266 (Que. Q.B.).

3 The Eurocentric assumptions of international law and the domestic law of reception are questioned in Slattery, ''Aboriginal Sovereignty and Imperial Claims'' (1991) 29 Osgoode Hall L.J. 1. See also ch. 24, Aboriginal Peoples, below.

4 The leading case, *Uniacke* v. *Dickson* (1848) 2 N.S.R. 287 (S.C. N.S.), establishes that English law was received in Nova Scotia as of 1758, when the first legislative assembly was held. This decision proceeded from the premise that Nova Scotia was a settled colony. In fact, Nova Scotia (excepting Cape Breton Island) was ceded from France to Britain by the Treaty of Utrecht in 1713. (Some of New Brunswick may have been included — the boundaries are not clear.) Nova Scotia was therefore a conquered colony, but after a British colonial government was constituted by appointment of a governor in 1749, and especially after the expulsion of the French settlers

Settlement and conquest were not the only ways in which English and French laws were received in British North America. Adoption was a third way. The colonial Legislature could enact a statute adopting the laws of England as of a certain date. This would occur, either because the colony was not content with the body of law received by settlement or conquest, or because the date of reception was open to dispute. We shall see that reception of English laws in Ontario, the four western provinces and the two federal territories now depends upon adoption. A fourth mode of reception was imposition by the imperial power. We shall see that the King (exercising a prerogative power to legislate for a conquered colony) or the imperial Parliament could impose upon a colony the laws of England as of a certain date. We shall see that this occurred by royal proclamation in Quebec in 1763, although the pre-conquest French law was restored, this time by imperial statute, in 1774.

2.2 Settled colonies

(a) Date of reception

When an uninhabited territory was settled by British subjects, the rule of the common law was that the first settlers were deemed to have imported English law[5] with them. In the absence of any competing legal system, English law followed British subjects and filled the legal void in the new territory. The importation was deemed to have occurred on the date of the first settlement of the colony, but in practice settlement was a gradual process and the date of the

---

in the 1750's, the colony came to be treated as settled. Cape Breton Island, Prince Edward Island and New Brunswick (to the extent that it had not been ceded in 1713) were ceded from France to Britain by the Treaty of Paris in 1763, and were annexed to Nova Scotia in 1763. The effect of annexation would be to receive Nova Scotia's law which was English law as of 1758. This would continue to be the received law in Prince Edward Island after it was separated from Nova Scotia in 1769 and held its first legislative assembly in 1773. There does not seem to be a clear-cut decision in favour of 1758 for Prince Edward Island and commentators do not all agree on 1758: see note 1, above. The same date 1758 should also be the reception date of New Brunswick, which was separated from Nova Scotia in 1784 and held its first legislative assembly in 1786. However, the New Brunswick courts have held that 1660 is the reception date of New Brunswick, on the idiosyncratic basis that the Restoration of the Stuart Kings (Charles II) should be treated as the reception date for all North American colonies: *Scott* v. *Scott* (1970) 15 D.L.R. (3d) 374 (N.B.A.D.) (Abolition of Old Tenures Act, 1660 (Eng.), enacted after Restoration of Charles II, not in force in N.B.); and see Bell's two comments (1979) 28 U.N.B.L.J. 195; (1980) 29 U.N.B.L.J. 157. The constitutions of the maritime provinces are described, with references, in Read, ''The Early Provincial Constitutions'' (1948) 26 Can. Bar Rev. 621.

5 After the union of England and Scotland in 1707, when the United Kingdom of Great Britain was created, with two systems of private law, English and Scottish, equal in status, the law that automatically followed citizens of Great Britain to new colonies was English, not Scottish, law: Latham, *The Law and the Commonwealth* (1949), 517. See also note 69, below on the definition of the term ''United Kingdom''.

first settlement was unknown or disputable. The courts which later had to identify the rules of English law which had been received selected the date of ''the institution of a local legislature in the colony'' as the date of reception.[6] For example, Newfoundland, which had been settled (contrary to official British policy) for centuries, was deemed to have received English law in 1832 when the first legislative assembly was held.[7] The same principle probably yields dates of reception for Nova Scotia, New Brunswick and Prince Edward Island, on the dubious basis that they were settled (rather than conquered) colonies.[8] The dates of reception thus derived are quite artificial and are really cut-off dates, marking the end of a period of continuous reception, rather than a single event.

The law that was imported into a settled colony was the entire body of English law — statute law as well as common law — except to the extent that the law was unsuitable to the circumstances of the colony (an exception that will be discussed later). So far as statute law was concerned, the date of reception was important. If a statute was in force in England at the date of reception, then (unless it was unsuitable to the colony) it was imported to the colony. Its subsequent repeal in England would have no effect on its continued operation within the colony. By the same token, a statute enacted in England after the date of reception would not come into force in the colony. For example, Nova Scotia, with its reception date of 1758,[9] received the Statute of Uses, 1536 and the Statute of Frauds, 1677 (which established basic rules of property and contract law), but Nova Scotia did not receive the Divorce and Matrimonial Causes Act, 1857 (which introduced divorce). By contrast, Manitoba, Saskatchewan and Alberta, with an adopted reception date of 1870,[10] did receive the English law of divorce.

So far as common law[11] was concerned, the date of reception was not important. In colonial times, the common law was conceived of as a comprehensive body of doctrine, which was uniform throughout the British Empire, and which could provide a rule for any situation. The changes in the common law which in fact occurred as the courts fashioned new rules for new situations were regarded as merely the elaboration of pre-existing doctrine. This theory would have been hard to maintain if the common law had developed differently in different jurisdictions, but the Privy Council, as the final court of appeal for all

6 *Young* v. *Blaikie* (1822) 1 Nfld. L.R. 277, 283 (S.C. Nfld.), settling the date for Newfoundland.

7 *Ibid.*

8 See note 4 and accompanying text, above.

9 Note 4, above.

10 See sec. 2.5(b), ''Territories and prairie provinces'', below. The rules regarding the significance of the date of reception were the same regardless of whether the date was fixed by settlement or by legislative adoption.

11 By common law, I include all judge-made law, including the doctrines of equity. The problem of reception of equity in Upper Canada (now Ontario) (a conquered colony with a statutory reception of English law: see sec. 2.3(b), Ontario and Quebec'', below) stemmed, not from different rules of reception, but from the absence until 1837 of a court with equitable jurisdiction: see Cote (1977) 15 Alta. L. Rev. 29, 57-59.

British colonies, preserved the uniformity of the common law, not only throughout British North America but throughout the British Empire.[12] If different rules developed in different jurisdictions, one of those rules would eventually be declared to be the correct rule by either the Privy Council or the House of Lords and all common law jurisdictions would loyally accept the verdict of their lordships.[13]

In practice, the reception of common law was a continuous process, as the courts of each colonial jurisdiction absorbed without question developments in the common law of England as ''declared'' by the Privy Council and House of Lords. It was unusual for a colonial court to pay any attention to the date of reception of common law (as opposed to statute law).[14] Under the theory of a single, monolithic body of common law, it was only the fact of reception that mattered, not the date.[15]

(b) Unsuitable laws

The English laws which were received by a settled colony did not include those laws that were not suited to the circumstances of the colony. It was for a court of the colony, when adjudicating a dispute to which a rule of English law appeared relevant, to determine whether that rule was suited to the circumstances of the colony. If the court found it to be unsuitable, then the law was deemed never to have been received by the colony. In fact, colonial courts rarely found a

---

12 There was no mechanism to resolve differences between the House of Lords (with jurisdiction within the United Kingdom) and the Privy Council (with jurisdiction over overseas territories), because they were co-ordinate courts. But such differences (although not unknown) were rare because the same law lords sat on both courts. As well, the Privy Council acknowledged the position of the House of Lords as ''the supreme tribunal to settle English law'': *Robins* v. *National Trust Co.* [1927] A.C. 515, 519; in that case, the Privy Council said that colonial courts were bound to follow the House of Lords; the further implication was that the Privy Council itself would defer to the House of Lords.

13 The myth of the monolithic common law was not able to persist in the United States, where most issues of common law could not be appealed beyond the highest court of the state, so that permanent differences in the common law rules inevitably developed from state to state. Within the Commonwealth the same development is now occurring. Many jurisdictions have abolished appeals to the Privy Council and recognize their own highest court as able to depart from Privy Council or House of Lords precedents: see Bale, ''Casting off the Mooring Ropes of Binding Precedent'' (1980) 58 Can. Bar Rev. 255 (discussing rulings by the Supreme Court of Canada and High Court of Australia to that effect). Even in a jurisdiction which has retained the appeal to the Privy Council, the Privy Council has now accepted that the common law need not be the same as the common law of England: *Australian Consolidated Press* v. *Uren* [1969] 1 A.C. 590 (P.C., on appeal from Australia, refusing to follow *Rookes* v. *Barnard* [1964] A.C. 1129 (H.L.), allowing punitive damages for libel).

14 An exception is *Kungl* v. *Schiefer* [1962] S.C.R. 443, 448 (no action for alienation of affections recognized by English law at the date of reception for Ontario, namely, 1792); but compare *Fleming* v. *Atkinson* [1959] S.C.R. 513 (recognition of new common law duty to prevent domestic animals straying onto highway).

15 Lederman, *Continuing Canadian Constitutional Dilemmas* (1981), 68.

rule of common law to be unsuitable, although they frequently rejected a statutory rule on that ground.[16] This vague doctrine of unsuitability introduced even more uncertainty into the already hazardous tasks in each colony of determining the date of reception (which was not always free from doubt) and of determining exactly which English laws were in force on that date (which was often difficult to determine given the unsystematic English statute book).

(c) Amendment of received laws

The received laws of a settled colony could of course be altered by legislation. The legislation required to provide the institutions of government for the colony — a governor, a council, an assembly and courts — could be enacted by the King alone. Although the common law denied to the King (outside Parliament) any power to legislate for England,[17] it did accept a ''prerogative'' (common law) power to grant the institutions of government to a colony.[18] This explains why the constitutions of Nova Scotia, New Brunswick and Prince Edward Island consist, not of imperial statutes, but of prerogative instruments, namely, royal proclamations and commissions and instructions to colonial governors.[19] However, the King's prerogative power to legislate for a settled colony did not extend beyond the provision of the institutions of government. The English law which the settlers brought with them included the rule that the King had no general power of legislation. Any other changes in the received law of the colony could only be enacted by the imperial Parliament or (once it was established) the colonial legislative assembly.[20]

2.3 Conquered colonies

(a) General rules

When a colony was acquired by British conquest (or cession), as opposed to settlement, the rule of the common law was that the law of the conquered people

16 The case-law is discussed by Cote, note 1, above, 62-81.

17 *Case of Proclamations* (1611) 12 Co. Rep. 74, 77 E.R. 1352.

18 With respect to a conquered colony, this power existed as well, but went well beyond into a general power to legislate for the colony: see following text.

19 See Read, ''The Early Provincial Constitutions'' (1948) 26 Can. Bar Rev. 621, where the constitutions are described and full references given. See also note 4, above, for the principal historical dates. Newfoundland is exceptional in that its constitution has a statutory basis: Newfoundland Act, 1832 (U.K.), 2 & 3 Wm. IV, c. 78 (authorizing establishment of assembly), but this statute is very brief and the substance of the constitution is contained in four prerogative instruments of 1832: the Governor's Commission, the Governor's Instructions, a Despatch accompanying the Commission and Instructions, and the Proclamation for an election to the assembly. These instruments are reproduced in the Consolidated Stats. Nfld. (3rd series, 1916), vol. I, Appendix, pp. 3, 13, 33, 41.

20 The received law must be contrasted with the imperial statutes in force in a colony *ex proprio vigore*, which could not be altered by the colonial legislative assembly, although they could of course be altered by the imperial Parliament: see sec. 2.6, ''Imperial statutes'', below.

continued in force in the colony, except in matters involving the relationship between the conquered people and the new British sovereign. The effect of this rule was that the pre-existing private law (including criminal law) of the colony continued in force, while the public law of the colony (establishing British governmental institutions) was replaced by English law.

The received laws of a conquered colony could of course be altered by legislation. Obviously, legislation for the colony could be enacted by the imperial Parliament. In the case of a conquered colony, legislation could also be enacted by the King alone. This prerogative power extended beyond the provision of governmental institutions (which could be provided by the King alone even in settled colonies),[21] and was a general legislative power. However, the prerogative power of legislation terminated as soon as a conquered colony was granted its own legislative assembly. Thereafter, the law of the colony could not be altered by the King alone, but only by either the imperial Parliament or the colonial assembly. This temporal limitation on the prerogative was established by *Campbell* v. *Hall* (1774).[22] That case concerned the colony of Grenada, which had been acquired by conquest from France. The King issued a proclamation which granted an assembly to the colony. Then he issued another proclamation which purported to impose an export tax on the residents of the colony. The Court of Queen's Bench in England held that the tax was invalid. The prior grant of the assembly had terminated the King's prerogative power to legislate. Had the two proclamations been issued in the reverse order, so that the tax had been imposed before the assembly was granted, the tax would have been valid.

(b) Ontario and Quebec

The territory now comprising Ontario and Quebec was part of the French colony of New France. After the British victory on the Plains of Abraham in 1759, the whole of New France was ceded to Great Britain by France in the Treaty of Paris, 1763. New France was thus acquired by conquest. The Royal Proclamation of 1763,[23] an exercise of the King's prerogative power, provided for the government of "Quebec", which was a defined part of the valley of the St. Lawrence River — the area in fact settled by the French. This proclamation (at least by implication), reinforced by an ordinance of the first British governor, imposed English law on the colony,[24] thereby excluding the pre-existing French civil law, and changing the common law rule that the pre-conquest French civil law should continue as the private law of the conquered colony.

---

21 Text accompanying note 18, above.

22 (1774) 1 Cowp. 204, 98 E.R. 1045.

23 The Royal Proclamation, 1763 (U.K.), R.S.C. 1985, Appendix II, No. 1.

24 There was some doubt as to the efficacy of the imposition of English law: see Slattery, "The Land Rights of Indigenous Canadian Peoples as Affected by the Crown's Acquisition of Territories" (D. Phil. thesis, Oxford University, 1979), 206.

The Quebec Act, 1774,[25] by s. 8, restored the pre-conquest French civil law as the law of Quebec. Section 8 provided that "in all matters relative to property and civil rights, resort shall be had to the laws of Canada for the decision of the same". In this provision, the phrase "laws of Canada" meant the French-derived civil law which prevailed before the conquest. By s. 11 of the Act, English criminal law was continued in force, apparently because the French law at that time was particularly harsh.[26] The Quebec Act, 1774 was not a prerogative instrument like the Royal Proclamation of 1763. The prerogative authority of the King had terminated with the pledge of an assembly in the Royal Proclamation.[27] The Quebec Act, and the subsequent constitutional provisions for what is now Ontario and Quebec, had to take the form of an imperial statute.

The Quebec Act, 1774 differed from the Royal Proclamation of 1763 in two other respects that are relevant to the present account. First, the definition of the colony of Quebec was much wider in the Quebec Act, so that the colony encompassed much of what is now Ontario as well as Quebec. Secondly, the Quebec Act made no provision for an elected assembly. (The assembly authorized by the Royal Proclamation had never met.) The lack of an assembly became a source of grievance, especially after the immigration of English-speaking United Empire Loyalists following the American revolution. Many of the loyalists settled in the St. Lawrence valley, west of the French-speaking settlements, in what is now Ontario.

The Constitutional Act, 1791[28] separated the English and the French by dividing Quebec into two provinces, a predominantly English-speaking Upper Canada and a predominantly French-speaking Lower Canada, separated by the present boundary between Ontario and Quebec. The Act satisfied loyalist demands for an assembly by providing an elected assembly for each province. Section 33 of the Act provided that the laws of the former province of Quebec were to continue in force in both Upper and Lower Canada until altered by the assemblies of those provinces. This meant, of course, so far as private law was concerned, the French civil law. This was satisfactory to the province of Lower Canada, which made no general change in this received body of law. The continuance of French civil law did not, however, suit the Upper Canadians, and the first Act enacted by the Legislature of Upper Canada provided that "in all matters of controversy relative to property and civil rights, resort shall be had to the laws

---

25 Quebec Act, 1774 (U.K.), R.S.C. 1985, Appendix II, No. 2.

26 See Friedland, *A Century of Criminal Justice* (1984), 49; Edwards, "The Advent of English (Not French) Criminal Law and Procedure into Canada" (1984) 26 Crim. Law Q. 464.

27 *Campbell* v. *Hall* (1774) 1 Cowp. 204, 98 E.R. 1045, discussed in text accompanying note 22, above, was a decision based on the same Royal Proclamation of 1763, which made provision for the constitutions of Grenada, East Florida and West Florida, as well as Quebec.

28 The Constitutional Act, 1791 (U.K.), R.S.C. 1985, Appendix II, No. 3.

of England as the rule for the decision of the same''.[29] This was an adoption of English laws as of 1792, and it established 1792 as the date of reception of English law for what is now Ontario.

The elected assemblies constituted by the Constitutional Act, 1791 were in chronic conflict with the British governors and their appointed executive councils. In 1837, the inability of the popular assembly to control the executive led to armed rebellions in both provinces, and the appointment of Lord Durham to find a solution. The Durham Report (1839) recommended the institution of responsible government, a recommendation which was rejected at the time by the British government, but which was accepted within a decade when it became clear that it was the only viable solution to the conflict within the colonies.[30]

Lord Durham did not want to entrust a French majority with responsible government. In order to destroy French nationalism and to hasten what Lord Durham saw as the inevitable assimilation of the French-speaking Canadians into the English-speaking majority, Lord Durham recommended the union of the two Canadas. The Union Act, 1840[31] implemented this recommendation. The two provinces were fused into the united province of Canada with a single Legislature. The elected assembly included equal numbers of representatives from Upper Canada (now called Canada West) and Lower Canada (now called Canada East), despite the smaller population of Upper Canada. The motive was to ensure an English-speaking majority in the united assembly. Ironically, the population of Upper Canada quickly outgrew the population of Lower Canada, so that under-representation in the assembly became a grievance in Upper Canada. The achievement of representation by population became a major incentive for Upper Canadians to support a confederation scheme in which there would be representation by population in the lower house of the national Parliament.

The Union Act, 1840 did not change the two legal systems now so inappropriately united. Section 46 provided that all laws in force in Upper Canada and Lower Canada at the time of the union were to remain in force in the two parts of the united province of Canada. English law thus continued as the basis of the private law of Canada West, and French law continued as the basis of the private law of Canada East. The single Legislature of the united province had the power to change these bodies of law, of course, but it did not do so except in occasional and interstitial ways. Often, too, statutes enacted by the Legislature were applicable only to either Canada West or Canada East. Thus, the period of union, which lasted until confederation in 1867, did not disturb the essential differences between the English-derived laws of the predominantly English-speaking Canada

29 Stats. Upp. Can. 1792 (32 Geo. III), c. 1, s. 1. The phrase ''property and civil rights'' had also appeared, it will be recalled, in the Quebec Act, 1774 (U.K.), s. 8. The phrase was carried forward to s. 91(13) of the British North America Act, 1867: see ch. 21, Property and Civil Rights, under heading 21.2 ''History'' below.

30 The history of the development of responsible government is related in ch. 9, Responsible Government, under heading 9.1 ''History'', below.

31 The Union Act, 1840 (U.K.), R.S.C. 1985, Appendix II, No. 4.

West and the French-derived laws of the predominantly French-speaking Canada East.

2.4 Confederation

The confederation of the colonies of British North America received its major impetus from the political difficulties in the united province of Canada. For English-speaking Canada West, now more populous than Canada East, it offered representation by population in the new national Parliament, as well as a separate provincial Legislature. For French-speaking Canada East, it offered a separate provincial Legislature controlled by a French majority, with authority over education, culture, and most private law. More generally, confederation offered the prospect of greater military strength to resist the power of the United States, then engaged in civil war and on the union side hostile to English Canada. It also offered the economic advantages of a common market and the increased wealth to undertake large public projects, especially the building of a railway to link the Canadas with the ice-free ports of the maritimes, and the opening and settlement of the west.

The British North America Act, 1867[32] gave effect to the confederation scheme settled at conferences in Charlottetown (1864), Quebec City (1864) and London, England (1867).[33] It united the provinces of Canada, Nova Scotia and New Brunswick into a single ''Dominion'' under the name of Canada. It established a bi-cameral national Parliament with representation by population in the elected lower house — the House of Commons, and representation by region in the appointed upper house — the Senate. It established a common market, and allocated important economic powers to the new federal Parliament: over trade and commerce, transportation and communication, banking, currency, customs and excise and other forms of taxation; criminal law also became a federal responsibility, as did marriage and divorce. The provincial Legislatures were given other powers, notably, over ''property and civil rights'', municipal institutions, education and the administration of justice.[34] Nova Scotia and New Brunswick retained their existing Legislatures and other institutions of government. The province of Canada was divided into two new provinces, Ontario (the old Canada West, formerly Upper Canada) and Quebec (the old Canada East, formerly Lower Canada). The Act accordingly established a Legislature and other institutions of government for each of Ontario and Quebec.[35]

---

32 The British North America Act, 1867 (U.K.), R.S.C. 1985, Appendix II, No. 5; renamed the Constitution Act, 1867 by the Constitution Act, 1982, s. 53(2).

33 Browne, *Documents on the Confederation of British North America* (1969) is the best collection of source materials.

34 The list of federal powers is mainly in s. 91 of the Act; the provincial list is mainly in s. 92.

35 On the constitution of Quebec, see Morin, ''Pour une nouvelle Constitution du Québec'' (1985) 30 McGill L.J. 171.

At confederation, what happened to the legal systems, with their various reception dates and differing laws, in the uniting provinces? The answer is that they remained unchanged. Section 129 of the British North America Act continued in force the laws existing at the time of union in the united province of Canada and in Nova Scotia and New Brunswick. After confederation, these laws could be altered by either the new federal Parliament (acting within its limited powers) or a provincial Legislature (acting within its limited powers).[36]

The effect of s. 129 was to avoid a vacuum of law. With respect to matters within provincial legislative authority, each province retained its existing body of laws.[37] That body of laws had five sources: (1) the laws "received" from England or (in the case of Quebec) France by virtue of the rules discussed earlier in this chapter; (2) laws enacted for the province under the royal prerogative; (3) statute law enacted for the province by the imperial Parliament; (4) judicial developments in the common law (or civil law) since the date of reception; and (5) statute law enacted by the predecessor colonial Legislature. With respect to matters within federal legislative authority, there was no single body of law in 1867; such matters were regulated by a part of each of the five kinds of pre-confederation laws which were continued in force by s. 129. Gradually, of course, after 1867 the federal Parliament enacted statutes on the matters coming within its authority,[38] and thereby supplanted the diverse pre-confederation laws with a body of statute law which was usually uniform across the country.[39]

2.5 Admission of new provinces and territories

(a) Section 146

The British North America Act, by s. 146, contemplated the admission to Canada of the rest of British North America. In the case of the three remaining

---

36 The imperial Parliament (which had enacted the B.N.A. Act) also retained legislative power over Canada: see sec. 2.6, "Imperial statutes", below.

37 The boundaries of Quebec in 1898, and of Ontario, Quebec and Manitoba in 1912, were extended to include parts of the Northwest Territories, which of course had a different reception date than Ontario and Quebec and different laws than Ontario, Quebec or Manitoba. It has always been assumed that the effect of these annexations was to extend the laws of each province into the territory annexed to that province: Cote, note 1, above, 52. The statutes (which are silent on the reception point) are S.C. 1898, c. 3 (Quebec); S.C. 1912, c. 32 (Manitoba); S.C. 1912, c. 40 (Ontario); S.C. 1912, c. 45 (Quebec).

38 There is no constitutional requirement that the federal Parliament (or a provincial Legislature for that matter) actually exercise its authority. In the area of divorce (a federal responsibility under s. 91(26)), the federal Parliament was very tardy indeed, not enacting a Canada-wide statute until 1968. Before then the law differed from province to province, depending upon the state of the law initially received in that province. In some provinces, where reception yielded no divorce law, a territorially-limited federal statute was enacted to fill the vacuum: see, e.g., Divorce Act (Ontario), S.C. 1930, c. 14. See generally ch. 26, The Family, under heading, "Divorce", below.

39 There is no constitutional requirement that federal laws be uniform across the country, and there are many examples of territorially-limited federal statutes: see previous note.

colonies, namely, British Columbia, Prince Edward Island and Newfoundland, s. 146 provided that each could be admitted by imperial order in council at the request of the Legislature of the colony. In the case of the territories of Rupert's Land and the North-western Territory, s. 146 provided that each could be admitted by imperial order in council at the request of the Parliament of Canada.

(b) Territories and prairie provinces

From the Rocky Mountains eastward into what is now northern Ontario and northern Quebec[40] lay the huge territories of Rupert's Land and the North-western Territory. In 1870, the procedure established by s. 146 was employed to admit these territories to Canada.[41] On admission, they did not become provinces; they became federal territories, entirely subject to the authority of the federal Parliament.[42]

In 1870, immediately following the admission of the territories, the federal Parliament by statute created the province of Manitoba out of part of Rupert's Land.[43] What was left of Rupert's Land and the North-western Territory was renamed the Northwest Territories.[44] In 1898, in response to the influx of population caused by the gold rush, the Yukon Territory was carved out of the Northwest Territories and formed into a separate territory.[45] In 1905, the provinces of Alberta[46] and Saskatchewan[47] were created out of the Northwest Territories. As in the case of Manitoba, the provinces of Alberta and Saskatchewan were created by federal statute. The constitutions of Manitoba, Alberta and Saskatchewan thus take the curious form of a federal statute.

In the absence of legislation, the date of reception of English law into Rupert's Land and the North-western Territory and therefore into Manitoba, Alberta, Saskatchewan, the Northwest Territories and the Yukon Territory would be quite unclear. Happily, the reception date for these three provinces and two

---

40 In 1898 and 1912 the parts of the Northwest Territories lying north of Ontario, Quebec and Manitoba were annexed to those provinces: note 37, above.

41 Rupert's Land and North-Western Territory Order, 1870 (U.K.), R.S.C. 1985, Appendix II, No. 9. This did not cover all British territories in the north; the remaining (Arctic) territories were admitted by the Adjacent Territories Order, 1880 (U.K.), R.S.C. 1985, Appendix II, No. 14.

42 British North America Act, 1871 (U.K.) (now renamed the Constitution Act, 1871), R.S.C. 1985, Appendix II, No. 11, s. 4; and see next note.

43 Manitoba Act, 1870 (Can.), R.S.C. 1985, Appendix II, No. 8. The power of the federal Parliament to create provinces out of federal territories was not expressly conferred by the British North America Act, 1867. The power was granted retroactively (and the Manitoba Act confirmed) by ss. 2 and 5 of the British North America Act, 1871 (since renamed the Constitution Act, 1871). The same Act, by s. 4, conferred upon the federal Parliament full legislative authority over the federal territories.

44 Manitoba Act, 1870, s. 35.

45 Yukon Territory Act, 1898 (Can.), R.S.C. 1985, Appendix II, No. 19.

46 Alberta Act, 1905 (Can.), R.S.C. 1985, Appendix II, No. 20.

47 Saskatchewan Act, 1905 (Can.), R.S.C. 1985, Appendix II, No. 21.

territories has been fixed by statute as 1870.[48] When the Yukon Territory was created in 1898, and when Alberta and Saskatchewan were created in 1905, their constituent statutes preserved the reception date of 1870 by expressly continuing in force the laws in existence at the time of their creation.

(c) British Columbia

The province of British Columbia is the product of the fusion of two settled colonies, namely, Vancouver's Island and British Columbia (formerly New Caledonia).[49] Vancouver's Island was constituted by imperial statute in 1849,[50] and granted an assembly which first met in 1856. British Columbia, the mainland of present-day British Columbia, was constituted by imperial statute in 1858,[51] but no assembly was granted, the governor alone being authorized to make laws. The governor, by proclamation, stipulated 1858 as the date of reception of English laws. In 1866, the two colonies were amalgamated by imperial statute;[52] the new colony was called British Columbia. Legislative power over the enlarged colony was exercised by a Legislative Council composed of a majority of appointed members and a minority of elected members.[53] The Legislative Council, by ordinance, stipulated 1858 as the date of reception of English laws for the entire colony.[54]

British Columbia was admitted to Canada in 1871 by imperial order in council,[55] made at the request of its Legislative Council, which was the procedure provided by s. 146 of the British North America Act. The Terms of Union said nothing about the continuance in force of existing laws, but term 10 provided that the provisions of the British North America Act were to be applicable to British Columbia in the same way as they were applicable to the other provinces "as if the colony of British Columbia had been one of the provinces originally united by this Act". Term 10 made s. 129 of the B.N.A. Act applicable to British

48 After Manitoba was created, the provincial Legislature enacted the reception date of July 15, 1870: Queen's Bench Act, S.M. 1874, c. 12, s. 5. This law could only apply to matters within provincial jurisdiction, and so it was supplemented by a federal statute fixing the same date: Manitoba Supplementary Provision Act, S.C. 1888, c. 33, s. 4. The same date was provided for the Northwest Territories, including what later became the Yukon Territory, and the provinces of Alberta and Saskatchewan: North-West Territories Amendment Act, S.C. 1886, c. 25, s. 3.

49 See Read, note 4, above, 634-635; Lederman, note 1, above, 73-74; Cote, note 1, above, 91-92; Sharman, "The Strange Case of a Provincial Constitution: The British Columbia Constitution Act" (1984) 17 Can. J. Poli. Sci. 87.

50 Administration of Justice in Vancouver's Island Act, 1849 (U.K.), 12 & 13 Vict., c. 48.

51 Government of British Columbia Act, 1858 (U.K.), 21 & 22 Vict., c. 99.

52 British Columbia Act, 1866 (U.K.), 29 & 30 Vict., c. 67. All the constitutional documents (pre-confederation and post-confederation) relating to Vancouver Island and British Columbia are collected in R.S.B.C. 1979, vol. 7 (Appendices).

53 The people of Vancouver Island thereby lost their elected assembly.

54 The English Law Ordinance, 1867, S.B.C. 1867, c. 7.

55 British Columbia Terms of Union, 1871 (U.K.), R.S.C. 1985, Appendix II, No. 10.

Columbia, and thus continued in force the laws existing in British Columbia at the time of its admission. The reception date of 1858 was thus preserved.

British Columbia at the time of its admission in 1871 was unlike any of the other provinces in that its Legislature still consisted of a Legislative Council with a majority of appointed members, and it had not achieved responsible government. These disabilities were mentioned in term 14 of the Terms of Union, and their early elimination was contemplated. In 1871, British Columbia acquired a fully elected Legislature,[56] and, in 1872, the province achieved responsible government.[57]

(d) Prince Edward Island

Prince Edward Island was ceded from France to Britain by the Treaty of Paris in 1763, and was then annexed to Nova Scotia. It was separated from Nova Scotia and constituted as a separate colony in 1769.[58] It held its first legislative assembly in 1773. By virtue of the annexation to Nova Scotia in 1763, Prince Edward Island probably acquired the same reception date as Nova Scotia's, that is, 1758.[59]

Prince Edward Island, although a participant in the pre-confederation discussions in 1864 at Charlottetown (obviously) and Quebec City, did not become one of the original uniting provinces. The Island was not admitted to Canada until 1873. The instrument of admission was an imperial order in council,[60] made at the request of the Island's Legislature, which was the procedure provided by s. 146 of the B.N.A. Act. As in the case of British Columbia, the Terms of Union incorporated the provisions of the B.N.A. Act, including s. 129, and thus continued in force the laws existing in Prince Edward Island at the time of its admission.

(e) Newfoundland

We have already noted that Newfoundland was a settled colony, and that its date of reception had been judicially fixed at 1832 when its first assembly was held.[61] It achieved responsible government in 1855.[62]

---

56 The Legislative Council replaced itself with a fully elective Legislative Assembly: Constitution Act, 1871 (B.C.), 34 Vict., c. 147. The history of electoral representation in B.C. is related in *Re Dixon* (1986) 31 D.L.R. (4th) 546, 552-553 (B.C.S.C.).

57 After union, the Lieutenant Governor, on instructions from the federal government that appointed him, appointed a responsible ministry: Saywell, *The Office of Lieutenant-Governor* (1957), 79-87.

58 The Constitution consisted of two prerogative instruments of 1769, namely, the Commission and Instructions to the Governor: Read, note 4, above, 630 supplies references.

59 Note 4, above.

60 Prince Edward Island Terms of Union, 1873 (U.K.), R.S.C. 1985, Appendix II, No. 12.

61 Note 7, above.

62 Gunn, *The Political History of Newfoundland 1832-1864* (1966), ch. 9.

Newfoundland did not join confederation in 1867. It continued as a separate colony into the twentieth century, and indeed began to progress on the same path to independence that Canada, Australia and New Zealand followed. Like Canada, Australia and New Zealand, Newfoundland was described as a ''Dominion'' in the Balfour declaration of 1926 and in the Statute of Westminster of 1931.[63] But the depression so injured Newfoundland's economy that it was unable to pay its debts. In 1933, the Newfoundland Legislature formally requested the United Kingdom to suspend Newfoundland's constitution until Newfoundland became self-supporting again, and to replace the Legislature and other institutions of responsible government with a ''Commission of Government''. This request was implemented by an imperial statute,[64] and from 1934 Newfoundland was governed by a Commission of Government consisting of a Governor and a six-member Commission, all appointed by the United Kingdom Government. The Commission of Government exercised all legislative and executive power until 1949. In that year, Newfoundland was admitted to Canada.

Newfoundland's admission to Canada was effected by an imperial statute,[65] which followed two referenda in Newfoundland, the second of which had approved union with Canada by a narrow majority.[66] The procedure for the admission of new provinces in s. 146 of the B.N.A. Act, which had been used for the admission of British Columbia and Prince Edward Island, could not be used for Newfoundland, because s. 146 required that admission be requested by the Legislature of the province seeking admission, and in 1949 Newfoundland lacked a Legislature. The Terms of Union restored Newfoundland's Legislature and other

---

63 See ch. 3, Independence, under heading 3.3, ''Statute of Westminster, 1931'', below. Unlike the other dominions, however, Newfoundland had not signed the Treaty of Versailles separately from the United Kingdom; had never joined the League of Nations; and entrusted all of her external relations to the United Kingdom. Although the Statute of Westminster included Newfoundland in the definition of ''Dominion'', Newfoundland never adopted the operative provisions of the Statute. The Statute did not become operative within Newfoundland until union with Canada, by virtue of term 48 of the Terms of Union: note 65, below.

64 Newfoundland Act, 1933 (U.K.), 24 Geo. V, c. 2.

65 British North America Act, 1949 (U.K.) (since renamed the Newfoundland Act), R.S.C. 1985, Appendix II, No. 32. The Terms of Union are a schedule to the Act.

66 The 1949 statute (previous note) was, in my opinion, a breach of convention by the United Kingdom, because union with Canada had never been requested by the Newfoundland Legislature: see ch. 3, Independence, under heading 3.3, ''Statute of Westminster, 1931'', below. The Newfoundland Act, 1933 (U.K.), which instituted the Commission of Government, did not contemplate anything other than the restoration of responsible government to a separate Newfoundland. Fidelity to the original request for the Commission of Government required simply that the pre-1934 Legislature and responsible government be restored. The Legislature would then have been free to explore the question of confederation and, if desired, take the steps contemplated by s. 146 of the B.N.A. Act to achieve it. The validity of the 1949 statute was challenged on the basis of this breach of convention, but the Newfoundland courts held that the convention did not affect the legal authority of the United Kingdom Parliament to legislate as it pleased for Newfoundland: *Currie* v. *MacDonald* (1948) 29 Nfld. & P.E.I.R. 314 (Nfld. S.C.); affd. (1949) 29 Nfld. & P.E.I.R. 294 (Nfld. C.A.).

institutions of responsible government (which it needed to function as a province), by providing (in Term 7) that "the Constitution of Newfoundland as it existed prior to the sixteenth day of February, 1934 [when the Commission of Government had taken over], is revived at the date of Union".

As with the other provinces, Newfoundland's admission did not break the continuity of its laws. Term 18 of the Terms of Union continued in force the laws existing in Newfoundland at the time of admission. The reception date of 1832 was unaffected.

2.6 Imperial statutes

In the account so far, frequent reference has been made to imperial statutes. The instruments which mark the constitutional history of British North America include many imperial statutes: for example, the constitutions of several of the provinces, including the sequence of constitutions of what is now Ontario and Quebec, and, of course, the British North America Act, 1867 and most of its amendments.[67] As well as these constitutional instruments, many other imperial statutes were in force in colonial British North America, and a considerable number are in force in Canada today.[68]

From the earliest colonial times the Parliament at Westminster had the power not only to make laws for the United Kingdom,[69] but also to make laws for the overseas territories of the British Empire. In performing the latter function it was known as the imperial Parliament and its enactments were known as imperial statutes. An imperial statute applied in a colony, neither by virtue of the reception

67 Even the Canada Act 1982 and its schedule, the Constitution Act, 1982, is an imperial statute, that is, an enactment of the Parliament of the United Kingdom that is intended to regulate the affairs of a territory outside the United Kingdom, in this case, Canada.

68 There are perhaps one hundred currently in force in Canada: Ward, *Dawson's The Government of Canada* (6th ed., 1987), 296.

69 The United Kingdom now means the United Kingdom of Great Britain and Northern Ireland. It is in fact the union of four countries: England, Wales, Scotland and Northern Ireland. England annexed Wales in 1284 and Wales was fully integrated into English government and law in 1536, so much so that in most legal contexts the term England is taken to include Wales. In 1707 England (that is, England and Wales) united with Scotland and formed the United Kingdom of Great Britain (usually simply called Great Britain) under a single United Kingdom Parliament but retaining partially separate English and Scottish judicial and legal systems. In 1801 Great Britain (that is, England, Wales and Scotland) united with Ireland to form the United Kingdom of Great Britain and Ireland. There followed a succession of constitutional arrangements for Ireland which culminated in the creation in 1922 of a new "dominion", the Irish Free State (after 1937, Eire, and since 1949, the Republic of Ireland, no longer a member of the Commonwealth). Six northern counties remained in the United Kingdom, which thenceforth meant the United Kingdom of Great Britain and Northern Ireland. For a brief constitutional history of the United Kingdom, see Munro, *Studies in Constitutional Law* (1987), ch. 2; de Smith and Brazier, *Constitutional and Administrative Law* (6th ed., 1989), 48-57.

of English laws, nor by the adoption of the colonial legislature, but by the imperial statute's own force (ex proprio vigore).

In force in any colony there would be two classes of statute, both enacted by the Parliament of the United Kingdom. The first class consisted of those domestic statutes of the United Kingdom which were in force in England at the colony's reception date. These statutes had been enacted to regulate affairs within the United Kingdom, and had never been intended to apply outside the United Kingdom. Nevertheless, they became part of the law of a colony if they happened to be in force in England at the date upon which English laws were received into the colony.[70] This body of "received" statute law (like the common law) could be freely amended by the colonial legislature (within any limits imposed upon its authority). The only function of received law was to ensure that there was no vacuum of law in the colony. Received law was not a mechanism of imperial control over the colony and raised no question of independence from the imperial power.

The second class of statutes of the Parliament at Westminster that would be in force in a colony consisted of the imperial statutes in force ex proprio vigore. Those statutes had been passed to regulate the affairs of the colony or colonies to which they applied. They became law in the colony by their own terms, whether or not they were also in force in England (some were and some were not), and whether or not they were enacted before the date upon which the colony received English laws. Imperial statutes, unlike received statute law or common law, could not be amended by the colonial legislature.[71] Imperial statutes were a means by which the imperial power could impose its will on the colony. Once enacted, an imperial statute constituted a restriction on the power of the colonial legislature, a restriction which could be removed only by the imperial Parliament.[72] So long as a British territory included among its laws some that it was powerless to change, and so long as it remained vulnerable to future laws that it did not desire, that territory was a colony: its subservience to the imperial power was inconsistent with the independence that characterizes a sovereign state. The next chapter will relate how Canada gradually became free from the imperial power of the Parliament at Westminster, and thereby shed its colonial status.

---

70 The only exception was for those statutes judicially determined to be unsuitable to conditions in the colony: sec. 2.2(b), "Unsuitable laws", above.

71 An exception was the occasional imperial statute that expressly authorized its own amendment by the colonial Legislature. Parts of the British North America Act, 1867 could be amended within Canada for that reason.

72 The identification of the imperial statutes in force in a particular colony was exceedingly important. The Colonial Laws Validity Act, 1865 (U.K.), which is described in the next chapter, provided a rule of identification: an imperial statute was in force in a colony only if the statute, by its own terms, was applicable to the colony "by express words or necessary intendment". This rule is less than crystal clear, but it was a big improvement over the confusion that prevailed before 1865.

3

Indepedence

3.1 Bonds of Empire

The previous chapter, entitled Reception, has described the confederation of the colonies of British North America that took place in 1867.[1] But confederation must not be confused with independence. The British North America Act, while it created a new Dominion under the name of Canada, did not create an independent country. The federating provinces were all British colonies, although they had achieved responsible government and a large measure of self-government in local affairs. The new federation also became a British colony,[2] subordinate to the United Kingdom in international affairs, and subject to important imperial limitations in local affairs: the power of the imperial Parliament to enact

1 Ch. 2, Reception, under heading 2.4, "Confederation", above.

2 The term colony does not seem entirely appropriate for territories, such as Canada, Australia and New Zealand, which had achieved a considerable degree of self-government, and in the early 1900s the term "dominion" became usual to distinguish the more advanced colonies from the more dependent ones. However, even the dominions did not achieve full independence from the United Kingdom until well into the twentieth century: see note 10, below. For the dominions that remained in the Commonwealth, that is, Canada, Australia and New Zealand, and for other independent states within the Commonwealth, the term "Member of the Commonwealth" has become the preferred description. The history of the word "dominion" is related in ch. 5, Federalism, under heading 5.1(e), "Dominion and provinces", below.

statutes extending to Canada;[3] the powers of reservation and disallowance, which in effect allowed the British government to invalidate Canadian statutes;[4] the British appointment of Canada's Governor General;[5] the Canadian incapacity to enact any statute repugnant to an imperial statute extending to Canada;[6] the supposed incapacity to legislate with extra territorial effect;[7] the supposed incapacity to change the succession to the throne or the royal style and titles;[8] and the right to appeal from Canadian courts to the Privy Council.[9] As the footnotes have

---

3 See ch. 2, Reception, under heading 2.6, ''Imperial statutes'', above.

4 These powers are contained in ss. 55, 56 and 57 of the B.N.A. Act (Constitution Act, 1867). In the imperial conference of 1930 (note 18, and accompanying text, below) it was agreed that the power of disallowance would not be exercised by the United Kingdom government, and that the power of reservation would not be exercised under United Kingdom instructions by the Governor General of Canada. The powers have accordingly fallen into disuse; and even before 1930 this was arguably the case. Reservation had occurred 21 times between 1867 and 1878, but had never occurred after 1878 (when the royal instructions were changed); of the 21 bills reserved, six were denied the royal assent: Bourinot, *Parliamentary Procedure and Practice* (2nd ed., 1892), 648-650. Disallowance had occurred only once (in 1873): Mallory, *The Structure of Canadian Government* (rev. ed. 1984), 17, 23. Under s. 90 of the B.N.A. Act, provincial legislation is subject to powers of reservation and disallowance, but the power of disallowance is exercisable not by the United Kingdom government but by the Canadian federal government and so no issue of Canadian independence is thereby raised. Reservation and disallowance of provincial statutes is discussed in ch. 5, Federalism, under heading 5.3(e), ''Disallowance'', below.

5 The B.N.A. Act (Constitution Act, 1867) is silent on the appointment and tenure of the Governor General, and these matters were initially determined by the United Kingdom government, technically, the Queen, acting on the advice of her ministers in the United Kingdom. Since the imperial conference of 1930, however, it has been accepted that the appointment must always be made on the advice of the Canadian federal government, and it is the Canadian government that decides upon the term of office: see ch. 9, Responsible Government, under heading 9.2, ''Law and Convention''.

6 This incapacity and its removal is discussed later in this chapter.

7 See ch. 13, Extraterritorial Competence, below.

8 At the imperial conference of 1930 it was agreed that changes in the royal style and titles would be made by the United Kingdom Parliament only with the assent of the other Commonwealth countries. Since 1982, an Act of the United Kingdom Parliament, even if passed with Canada's assent, could not extend to Canada. Therefore, any change in the royal style and titles would require legislative action in Canada. Even before 1982, s. 91(1) of the Constitution Act, 1867 may have conferred the power on the federal Parliament alone after 1949 (when s. 91(1) was enacted); and s. 91(1) may be the constitutional basis for the Royal Style and Titles Act, R.S.C. 1985, c. R-12: see G. C. Eglinton, ''Authority to Change the Royal Style and Titles'' (1979) unpublished memorandum. In 1982, s. 91(1) was repealed and replaced by s. 44 of the Constitution Act, 1982. Section 44 is narrower than s. 91(1), and would not authorize laws in relation to the monarchy. Probably, the power must now be found in the federal Parliament's authority over the peace, order, and good government of Canada. A constitutional amendment under s. 41(a), which requires the unanimous consent of the provinces, would also be effective, but should not be necessary, because a change in the royal style and titles is not an amendment of the ''Constitution of Canada''.

9 This appeal and its abolition are discussed in ch. 8, Supreme Court of Canada, under heading 8.2, ''Abolition of Privy Council Appeals'', below.

indicated, these colonial limitations have now disappeared, by convention if not by law, as the British Empire has evolved into the Commonwealth, and the colonies have evolved into independent states within the Commonwealth. It is outside the scope of this book to describe all of the details of Canada's evolution to statehood.[10] However, the history of the status within Canada of imperial statutes is relevant to an understanding of the current foundation of much of Canada's constitutional law.

3.2 Colonial Laws Validity Act, 1865

In the previous chapter, entitled Reception, we noticed the dual capacity of the Parliament at Westminster, which functioned (1) as a Parliament for the United Kingdom, and (2) as a Parliament for the overseas territories of the British Empire.[11] In performing the latter function, it was known as the imperial Parliament, and its enactments were known as imperial statutes. The British North America Act was, as we have seen, an imperial statute. The significance of this fact can be understood only in the light of some history.

In the previous chapter, we also noticed the distinction between (1) "received" statutes (and common law), which applied in a colony by virtue of settlement, conquest or adoption, and (2) imperial statutes, which applied in a colony by virtue of their own force.[12] The distinction was important in colonial times, because received statutes and common law could be amended by the colonial legislature, but imperial statutes could not be. The Colonial Laws Validity Act, 1865[13] defined an imperial statute as an "Act of Parliament [i.e., of the

---

10 The important developments include: separate signature to the Treaty of Versailles, 1919; separate membership of the League of Nations, 1919; recognition of equal status in the Balfour declaration, 1926; acquisition of increased legal capacity by virtue of the Statute of Westminster, 1931; assumption of responsibility for external affairs, including treaty-making; separate declarations of war against Germany and Japan, 1939 and 1941; and membership of the United Nations, 1945. In *Re Offshore Mineral Rights of B.C.* [1967] S.C.R. 792, 816, the Supreme Court of Canada said that:

> There can be no doubt Canada has become a sovereign state. Its sovereignty was acquired in the period between its separate signature to the Treaty of Versailles in 1919 and the Statute of Westminster, 1931.

See generally, Kennedy, *The Constitution of Canada 1534-1937* (2nd ed., 1938), esp. chs. 21, 25, 28; Laskin, *Canadian Constitutional Law* (5th ed. 1986, by Finkelstein), 65-70; Stanley, *A Short History of the Canadian Constitution* (1969), ch. 7; Wheare, *The Constitutional Structure of the Commonwealth* (1960); Scott, "The End of Dominion Status" (1945) 23 Can. Bar Rev. 725; Rand, "Some Aspects of Canadian Constitutionalism" (1960) 38 Can. Bar Rev. 135.

11 Ch. 2, Reception, under heading 2.6, "Imperial statutes", above.

12 *Ibid*.

13 28 & 29 Vict., c. 63 (U.K.). For history, see Wheare, *The Statute of Westminster and Dominion Status* (5th ed., 1953), 74-79.

Parliament at Westminster] extending to the colony'', and provided that an Act of Parliament was deemed to extend to the colony only if it was made applicable to the colony ''by the express words or necessary intendment'' of the statute itself. The Colonial Laws Validity Act went on to provide that colonial laws were void if they were ''repugnant'' to an imperial statute (as defined), but were not void if they were repugnant to a received statute or rule of common law. The Colonial Laws Validity Act was intended to remove doubts as to the capacity of colonial legislatures to enact laws that were inconsistent with English law. By narrowly defining the class of imperial statutes, and thereby confining the doctrine of repugnancy, the Act was intended to extend rather than restrict the powers of the colonial legislatures. Nevertheless, the Act did leave the colonial legislatures powerless to alter any imperial statute which by its own terms applied to the colony. If the colony wished to alter or repeal such an imperial statute it had to persuade the imperial Parliament to enact the required law.

The B.N.A. Act was enacted in 1867, two years after the Colonial Laws Validity Act. Section 129 of the B.N.A. Act continued in force pre-confederation laws that were in force in the uniting provinces, and it gave to the federal Parliament or provincial Legislatures (depending upon which was competent) the power to repeal, abolish or alter such pre-confederation laws. However, s. 129 excluded from the power of repeal, abolition or alteration such laws ''as are enacted by or exist under Acts of the Parliament of Great Britain or of the Parliament of the United Kingdom of Great Britain and Ireland''. This exclusion made clear that the power conferred by s. 129 was subject to the restriction defined by the Colonial Laws Validity Act.[14]

3.3 Statute of Westminster, 1931

In 1926, two events made the Canadian government anxious to escape from the sovereignty of the imperial Parliament, and to secure equality of status as between the dominions and the United Kingdom. One event was the King-Byng dispute, which is related later in this book,[15] and which was treated by Prime Minister Mackenzie King as an issue of Canadian independence. The other event was the decision in *Nadan* v. *The King* (1926),[16] in which the Privy Council struck down a federal statute of 1888 (the statute purported to abolish appeals to the

14 Section 129's exclusion is in broad terms which would literally be apt to deny Canadian power to amend or repeal British statutes received by settlement, conquest or adoption, as well as those protected by the Colonial Laws Validity Act. However, it seems likely that s. 129 was intended to be no wider than the Colonial Laws Validity Act's definition of imperial statutes ''extending to the colony'': Laskin, *Canadian Constitutional Law* (5th ed., 1986, by Finkelstein), 66. The restriction on repealing or amending pre-confederation statutes was removed by the Statute of Westminster: see following text.

15 See ch. 9, Responsible Government, under heading 9.6(d), ''Dissolution of Parliament'', below.

16 [1926] A.C. 482.

Privy Council in criminal cases), on the ground that the statute exceeded Canadian legislative power by its extra territorial effect and its inconsistency with two imperial statutes.

The concerns of Canada and some of the other dominions[17] led to the "imperial conferences" (conferences of the Prime Ministers of the United Kingdom and the self-governing dominions) of 1926 and 1930, which grappled with the task of removing the remaining vestiges of colonial status from the dominions.[18] The conference of 1926 adopted the "Balfour Declaration" (named after the chairman of the drafting committee):[19]

> They [the United Kingdom and the dominions] are autonomous communities within the British Empire, equal in status, in no way subordinate one to another in any aspect of their domestic or external affairs, although united by a common allegiance to the Crown, and freely associated as members of the British Commonwealth of Nations.

The declaration was important, because it accepted the principle that the dominions were equal in status to the United Kingdom. However, the measures required to implement this principle were left to the conference of 1930.

The most difficult issue of equality concerned the power over the dominions of the imperial Parliament. How could that power be limited? The imperial conference of 1930 adopted a "convention"[20] that "no law hereafter made by the Parliament of the United Kingdom shall extend to any dominion otherwise than at the request and with the consent of that dominion"; the conference also recommended the enactment by the imperial Parliament of the Statute of Westminster.[21] The Statute of Westminster, 1931[22] was enacted by the imperial Parliament in pursuance of that recommendation: the Statute recited the convention in its preamble, and it provided, by s. 4, that hereafter no statute of the United Kingdom would extend to a dominion "unless it is expressly declared in that Act that the dominion has requested, and consented to, the enactment thereof". Notice how s. 4 of the Statute and the convention reinforce each other. Neither Statute nor convention purports to destroy the power of the imperial Parliament to enact

---

17 Another cause of concern was created by the Chanak crisis of 1922, when Britain almost went to war with Turkey, and made a last-minute appeal to the dominions for assistance. The crisis passed, but the dominions became concerned about Britain involving them in European wars, and wanted formal recognition of their autonomous status.

18 The dominions represented at the imperial conferences of 1926 and 1930 were Canada, Australia, New Zealand, Newfoundland, South Africa and the Irish Free State. (Newfoundland has since become a province of Canada. South Africa and the Irish Free State, which is now the Republic of Ireland, have since left the Commonwealth.) The records of the conferences are in Ollivier, *Colonial and Imperial Conferences* (1954), vol. 3, 137-344; there are also extracts in Dawson, *The Development of Dominion Status 1900-1936* (1955), 329-350, 394-411.

19 Ollivier, previous note, vol. 3, 146; Dawson, previous note, 331.

20 See ch. 1, Sources, under heading 1.10, "Conventions", above.

21 See Latham, *The Law of the Commonwealth* (1949); Marshall, *Parliamentary Sovereignty and the Commonwealth* (1957), ch. 6; Wheare, *The Statute of Westminster and Dominion Status* (5th ed., 1953); Wheare, *The Constitutional Structure of the Commonwealth* (1960).

22 R.S.C. 1985, Appendix II, No. 27.

statutes applying to the dominions; on the contrary, each expressly recognizes and preserves that power. But the convention defines the occasions when the power is to be exercised (only when the dominion concerned has requested and consented to its exercise), and the Statute defines how the power is to be exercised (only by including in the statute an express declaration that the dominion has requested and consented to the measure).[23]

The limitation of the power of the imperial Parliament, which was the object of the convention and s. 4, was not the only reform needed to eliminate the subjection of the dominions to imperial statutes. It was also necessary to increase the powers of the dominion legislatures so that the dominions could amend or repeal the imperial statutes which did apply to them. To that end, the Statute of Westminster, by s. 2(1), repealed the Colonial Laws Validity Act in its application to the dominions, and, by s. 2(2), granted to each dominion the power to repeal or amend imperial statutes which were part of the law of the dominion. Section 2(2) also stated that no dominion statute should be void for repugnancy to any existing or future imperial statute. Section 7(2) made clear that s. 2 applied to Canada's provincial Legislatures as well as to Canada's federal Parliament, but that each Legislature and the Parliament could only enact laws within their own competence under the B.N.A. Act. The power of amendment or repeal extended to future as well as existing imperial statutes.[24]

Section 7(1) of the Statute of Westminster provided that "nothing in this Act shall be deemed to apply to the repeal, amendment, or alteration of the British North America Acts, 1867 to 1930, or to any order, rule or regulation made thereunder". This provision was inserted because the Canadian delegates to the imperial conferences feared that without such a provision the Canadian Parliament and Legislatures would have gained the power to alter the B.N.A. Act by ordinary statute. In a unitary state, such as the United Kingdom, the power to alter the constitution by ordinary statute is not necessarily objectionable, but in a federal state it is essential that at least the distribution of powers between federal Parliament and provincial Legislatures be unalterable by either Parliament or a Legislature acting on its own. Before the Statute of Westminster, the supremacy of the B.N.A. Act was derived from the fact that it was an imperial statute protected from alteration by the Colonial Laws Validity Act. Therefore, when it was pro-

23 The efficacy of these attempts to limit imperial legislative power has been much debated in the books cited in note 21, above, and in the periodical literature. Fortunately, as the Privy Council once observed, disregard by the imperial Parliament of either the convention or s. 4 "is theory and has no relation to realities": *British Coal Corp.* v. *The King* [1935] A.C. 500, 520.

24 Section 129 of the B.N.A. Act, which continues in force the pre-confederation laws in the confederating provinces, and gives power to the competent Canadian legislative body to repeal or amend those laws, expressly excludes from the power of repeal or amendment those laws contained in imperial statutes. (One problem with this provision was referred to in note 14, above.) In *A Consolidation of the Constitution Acts, 1867-1982* (1996), the Department of Justice correctly asserts in a footnote to s. 129 that the restriction on repealing or amending pre-confederation imperial statutes "was removed by the Statute of Westminster".

posed to destroy the protected status of imperial statutes generally, Canada insisted on the exemption of its constituent statute.[25] That was the reason for s. 7 of the Statute of Westminster.[26]

3.4 Canada Act 1982

The final stage in the history of imperial statutes in Canada came with the passage of one last imperial statute, the Canada Act 1982 (which included, as Schedule B, the Constitution Act, 1982).

The Canada Act 1982 repealed s. 7(1) of the Statute of Westminster,[27] which was the provision that exempted the B.N.A. Act and its amendments from the liberating effect of the rest of the Statute of Westminster. However, this does not mean that the B.N.A. Act (Constitution Act, 1867) and its amendments are now vulnerable to ordinary legislative change just like other imperial statutes. The supremacy of the "Constitution of Canada", a defined phrase which includes the Constitution Act, 1867 and its amendments,[28] is maintained by s. 52(1) of the Constitution Act, 1982. Section 52(1) provides:

> The Constitution of Canada is the supreme law of Canada, and any law that is inconsistent with the provisions of the Constitution is, to the extent of the inconsistency, of no force or effect.

This provision serves exactly the same function as s. 7(1) of the Statute of Westminster formerly served. Section 7(1) preserved the doctrine of repugnancy expressed in the Colonial Laws Validity Act in its application to the B.N.A. Act and its amendments. Now s. 52(1) directly enacts a similar doctrine of repugnancy or inconsistency.[29] By virtue of s. 52(1), the Constitution of Canada is superior to all other laws in force in Canada, whatever their origin: federal statutes, provincial statutes, pre-confederation statutes, received statutes, imperial statutes and common law; all of these laws must yield to inconsistent provisions of the Constitution of Canada. Section 52(1) provides an explicit basis for judicial review of legislation in Canada, for, whenever a court finds that a law is inconsistent with the Constitution of Canada, the court must hold that law to be invalid ("of no force or effect").

---

25 See also ss. 8 and 9 exempting the constituent statutes of Australia and New Zealand; but note that New Zealand (a unitary state) acquired the power "to alter, suspend or repeal" its constituent statute in 1947: New Zealand Constitution (Amendment) Act, 1947 (U.K.), 11 Geo. VI, c. 4.

26 Wheare, *Constitutional Structure of the Commonwealth* (1960), 61. The question whether s. 7(1) was necessary in any event is considered in ch. 5, Federalism, under heading 5.5(a), "Development of judicial review", below.

27 Constitution Act, 1982, s. 53(1) and schedule, item 17.

28 See ch. 1, Sources, under heading 1.4, "Constitution of Canada", above.

29 *Re Manitoba Language Rights* [1985] 1 S.C.R. 721, 746 (recognizing that s. 52(1) has replaced the Colonial Laws Validity Act as the foundation of judicial review). The validity of s. 52(1) itself is analyzed in my article, "Supremacy of the Charter" (1983), 61 Can. Bar Rev. 69.

With respect to future imperial statutes, it will be recalled that s. 4 of the Statute of Westminster had expressly preserved the authority over the dominions of the United Kingdom Parliament. The Canada Act 1982 repealed s. 4 of the Statute of Westminster[30] and, by s. 2, formally terminated the authority over Canada of the United Kingdom Parliament.[31] The efficacy of this abdication of authority by the United Kingdom Parliament is discussed later in this chapter.[32] For the moment, it is sufficient to explain why such a provision could not have been enacted in the Statute of Westminster in 1931, but could be enacted in 1982.

There were two reasons why the Statute of Westminster did not terminate the authority of the United Kingdom Parliament over the dominions. The first reason was a theoretical one. In 1931, it was widely believed by constitutional lawyers that an attempt by the United Kingdom Parliament to terminate its authority over the dominions would be legally ineffective, on the basis that a sovereign Parliament could not abdicate any part of its sovereignty. Now, the more widely held belief is that an abdication of power over a former dominion or colony would be legally effective.[33]

In the case of Canada, there was in 1931 a second, more practical reason for the preservation of the legislative authority over the dominions of the United Kingdom Parliament, and that was the fact that the B.N.A. Act lacked any general procedure for its amendment within Canada. So long as that disability existed, the power over Canada of the Parliament of the United Kingdom had to be preserved, for that Parliament was the only body with legal authority to amend the B.N.A. Act. That disability was eliminated in 1982 by Part V of the Constitution Act, 1982, which provides procedures for the amendment of all parts of the Constitution of Canada without recourse to the United Kingdom. The adoption of these Canadian amending procedures rendered the continuing power of the United Kingdom Parliament unnecessary.[34]

Thus, in 1982, there was no longer any theoretical or practical justification for the continuing authority over Canada of the United Kingdom (imperial) Parliament. Indeed, the existence of the power was an affront to Canadian nationalism, and its abolition could be regarded as a "patriation" of the Canadian Constitution. It is to that idea that the final section of this chapter is addressed.

---

30 Constitution Act, 1982, s. 53(1) and schedule, item 17.

31 Australia and New Zealand subsequently adopted a similar provision: Australia Act 1986 (U.K.), 1986, c. 2, s. 1; Constitution Act 1986 (N.Z.), s. 15(2).

32 Section 3.5(d), "Termination of imperial authority", below.

33 *Ibid*.

34 Amendment of the Constitution of Canada is the topic of chapter 4, below.

3.5 Patriation of the Constitution

(a) Definition

The ''patriation'' of the Constitution means bringing it home to Canada.[35] The term ''patriation'' is a uniquely Canadian coinage, derived from the verb ''repatriate'' meaning ''to restore to one's own country''. As the B.N.A. Act has never been a Canadian Act, it cannot be *restored* to Canada; patriation conveys the idea of our Constitution *becoming* a Canadian instrument. There is no one accepted definition of what patriation involves. Several possible meanings are analyzed in the text that follows.

Patriation has not usually been regarded as entailing the abolition of the monarchy. Canada's link with the United Kingdom through recognition of the same Queen has of course been preserved. For practical purposes, however, the Queen's role for Canada is primarily as a ceremonial head of the Commonwealth, the Commonwealth being an informal association of countries that were formerly members of the old British Empire.[36]

(b) Canada Act 1982

The Canada Act 1982 and its Schedule B, the Constitution Act, 1982, were enacted by the United Kingdom Parliament on March 29, 1982, when they received the royal assent. The Canada Act 1982 came into force as Canadian law immediately. The Constitution Act, 1982, by virtue of s. 58, did not come into force until ''a day to be fixed by proclamation''. That proclamation was issued by the Queen, who came to Canada for that purpose, at a ceremony in Ottawa on April 17, 1982; and the proclamation fixed April 17, 1982 as the day upon which the Constitution Act, 1982 was to come into force. Did these events accomplish the ''patriation'' of Canada's Constitution?

At first blush, it does not seem plausible to regard the enactment of the Canada Act 1982 and the Constitution Act, 1982 as a patriation of the Canadian Constitution. Their enactment added two more imperial statutes to the series that existed before.[37] Since 1982, more, not less, of Canada's Constitution is to be found in the statute book of the United Kingdom.

---

35 This section of the book is adapted from my article, ''Patriation of the Canadian Constitution'' (1983), 8 Queen's L.J. 123. On the history of patriation, see Rémillard, ''Historique du rapatriement'' (1984) 25 Cahiers de Droit (Laval) 15; Rémillard, *Le Fédéralisme Canadien* , vol. 2 (1985). For analysis, see Oliver ''The 1982 Patriation of the Constitution . . .'' in Mélanges Jean Beetz (Les Éditions Thémis, 1995).

36 On the abolition of the monarchy, see ch. 9, Responsible Government, under heading 9.6(g), ''The Monarchy'', below.

37 The schedule to the Constitution Act, 1982 lists 22 United Kingdom statutes and orders in council as included in the ''Constitution of Canada''.

Nor have any formal steps been taken to give the Canada Act 1982 or the Constitution Act, 1982, or any of the other constitutional instruments enacted in the United Kingdom, some form of Canadian imprimatur. It is true that the two 1982 statutes were requested by a joint resolution of the two Houses of the Canadian Parliament;[38] but that has been true of every statute enacted for Canada by the United Kingdom Parliament since 1895,[39] and so it cannot be regarded as a new development, let alone as a patriation. It is also true that the terms of the joint resolution were agreed to by nine of the ten provincial Premiers at a meeting in Ottawa on November 5, 1981; but five previous statutes enacted for Canada by the United Kingdom Parliament were preceded by the unanimous agreement of the provincial Premiers, and so there is nothing of special note in that fact.[40] The enactment of the 1982 statutes has not been followed by ratification, either by Canadian legislative bodies or by popular referendum.

If the Constitution has been patriated — brought home to Canada — that event has obviously not occurred in the physical world. It must have occurred in a metaphysical world stocked with the ideas of constitutional lawyers. It is to that world that we must now turn our attention.

(c) Autochthony

One possible meaning of patriation could be the securing of constitutional autochthony. Autochthony[41] requires that a constitution be indigenous, deriving its authority solely from events within Canada. The Constitution of the United States is, of course, autochthonous, because its only claim to authority springs from within the United States: the American revolution had broken the chain of legal authority which in the colonial period had linked the American assemblies to the imperial Parliament. But in Canada no such revolution (or break in legal continuity) occurred — and certainly not in 1982. The legal force of the Canada Act 1982 and the Constitution Act, 1982, like other United Kingdom statutes extending to Canada, depends upon the power over Canada of the United Kingdom Parliament. These instruments have an external rather than a local root.[42]

38 The resolution was passed by the House of Commons on December 2, 1981 and by the Senate on December 8, 1981.

39 See ch. 4, Amendment, under heading 4.1, ''History of amendment'', below.

40 *Ibid*.

41 I am using the term in the sense employed by Wheare, *Constitutional Structure of the Commonwealth* (1960), ch. 4. The term is neither very clear nor very useful, as Marshall, *Constitutional Theory* (1971), 57-64, demonstrates. Indeed, the requirement of a break in legal continuity, which is assumed in my text, may be disputed. It may be said that every independent country has a local ''root'' to its legal system, since it is the fundamental rules of validity and change laid down by the local courts which at bottom determine which laws are to be accepted as valid: see Slattery, ''The Independence of Canada'' (1983), 5 Supreme Court L.R. 369.

42 The Committee on the Constitution of the Canadian Bar Association, *Towards a New Canada* (1978), 6 recommended that patriation be accomplished by action taken within Canada which constituted ''a break with the established legal order''. Other proposals for patriation have never gone that far.

If patriation means the securing of constitutional autochthony, I conclude that it has not been achieved.

(d) Termination of imperial authority

A second possible meaning of patriation could be the termination of the authority over Canada of the United Kingdom Parliament. Geoffrey Marshall has pointed out that the concern with autochthony (in the sense just described) involves a confusion between the continuity of new institutions with the old system, on the one hand, and the *subordination* of the new institutions to the old, on the other.[43] A break in continuity does not necessarily mean that British legislative authority no longer extends to the new institutions, and, if it still does so extend, then nothing important has been accomplished by the achievement of a "local root" to the new constitution. Marshall puts it this way:[44]

> The fundamental question raised by an assertion of "autochthony" is whether a legally effective abdication of British legislative authority has been made by the United Kingdom. If it has, further local operations, proclamations, and breaches of continuity are superfluous. If it has not, they are ineffective.

On this view, which seems sound, the question we should be asking is whether a legally effective termination[45] of British legislative authority has occurred.

The Canada Act 1982 contains an express abdication of British legislative authority over Canada. Section 2 provides as follows:

> No Act of the Parliament of the United Kingdom passed after the Constitution Act, 1982 comes into force shall extend to Canada as part of its law.

Has this provision accomplished the patriation of the Canadian constitution? On the argument accepted so far, the answer must be yes — if s. 2 is legally effective.

Under the traditional view of parliamentary sovereignty, s. 2 cannot be legally effective. The traditional view holds that a sovereign parliament cannot limit its own sovereignty.[46] In other words, s. 2 cannot be legally effective, because the United Kingdom Parliament could at any time in the future repeal s. 2 and re-assert its authority over Canada. This traditional view was generally accepted by

43 Marshall, note 41, above, 63.

44 *Id.* , 61. He is using the word "autochthony" in this passage in a broader sense than I have been using it in the text. He is really using it as equivalent to patriation.

45 Marshall uses the word "abdication", which is too narrow and perhaps even begs the question under consideration, since it implies the necessity of a voluntary surrender of authority by the United Kingdom Parliament. No such voluntary surrender occurred in respect of the thirteen American colonies, and yet after the revolutionary war the authority of the United Kingdom Parliament over the former colonies had obviously terminated. Even in the case of Canada (and other Commonwealth countries) it is arguable that the termination of British authority depends more on their accession to independence than on an "abdication" by the United Kingdom Parliament. This point is developed later in this section of the text.

46 de Smith and Brazier, *Constitutional and Administrative Law* (6th ed., 1989), ch. 4.

constitutional lawyers before the second world war, and their refusal to acknowledge the efficacy of an abdication of power is one reason why the Statute of Westminster, 1931 contained no such provision.[47] But the better view, which is now more widely accepted, is that, whatever view British courts would take,[48] the courts of the former colony would not accept a reversal of independence: "Freedom, once conferred, cannot be revoked".[49] If the United Kingdom Parliament did purport to repeal s. 2 of the Canada Act 1982, and enact a law purporting to extend to Canada, it is inconceivable that the Supreme Court of Canada would accept the resuscitated power and uphold the new law. Without doubt, the Canadian court would hold that the unwanted law had the same status in Canada as a law enacted for Canada by Portugal, and that is, no status at all: the law would be a nullity in Canada.[50]

If I am right that a law enacted for Canada after 1982 by the United Kingdom Parliament would be treated by Canadian courts as a nullity, does this establish that s. 2 of the Canada Act 1982 is a legally effective provision? The answer to this question is not necessarily yes. It can be plausibly argued that it is not s. 2 but the fact of Canadian independence which has terminated the United Kingdom's authority to enact laws for Canada. This is the view taken by S.A. de Smith in analyzing the situation of Mauritius, whose independence statute contained a provision similar to s. 2 of the Canada Act 1982. de Smith says that "the achievement of independence should in itself be understood as having liberated the legal order of Mauritius from its hierarchical subordination to that of the United Kingdom, so that the omnicompetence of the United Kingdom Parliament ceased to prevail in the local legal system".[51] If this view is correct, then the United Kingdom Parliament had lost much of its authority over Canada before 1982: what it retained was only what was necessary to fill the gaps in Canadian domestic legislative power.[52] Now that the new amending procedures contained in Part V

---

47 Wheare, *Constitutional Structure of the Commonwealth* (1960), 25.

48 A court in the United Kingdom would decline to hold invalid any statute duly enacted (in the correct "manner and form") by the United Kingdom Parliament: *Manuel* v. *A.-G.* [1982] 3 W.L.R. 821 (Eng. C.A.) (upholding validity of Canada Act 1982). But the question at issue is not the attitude of the courts in the United Kingdom, for they have no power to enforce their rulings in an independent country, but the attitude of the courts in the country to which the law purports to extend.

49 *Ndlwana* v. *Hofmeyr* [1937] A.D. 229, 237; and see de Smith, note 46, above, 76-78.

50 This would also have been the result before 1982 in respect of United Kingdom statutes enacted for Canada without any request or consent by Canada. Any other result would involve a denial of Canada's status as an independent country. See Hogg, Comment (1982) 60 Can. Bar Rev. 307, 330.

51 de Smith, note 46, above, 77-78.

52 It must be noted that this view is not easy to reconcile with obiter dicta in *Re Resolution to Amend the Constitution of Canada* [1981] 1 S.C.R. 753, 790, 794, 797, 799, 801, which suggested that there had been no diminution of the legal authority over Canada of the United Kingdom Parliament since colonial times. It is because of these dicta that this part of my text is expressed tentatively.

of the Constitution Act, 1982 leave no gaps in Canadian domestic legislative power, the authority over Canada of the United Kingdom Parliament has shrunk to nothing.

On this analysis, s. 2 of the Canada Act 1982 is not the reason for the termination of the authority over Canada of the United Kingdom Parliament. Canadian courts would now deny the existence of that authority, whether or not s. 2 of the Canada Act 1982 existed. That is the view of Brian Slattery, who says:[53]

> What residual power Westminster retained after independence stemmed from the absence of any corresponding local power. There is no longer any sphere in which Canada cannot act, and so Westminster's role automatically expires. What can be done in Canada cannot be done elsewhere if Canada is fully sovereign.

The inevitable conclusion from this line of reasoning is that s. 2 of the Canada Act 1982 is redundant.[54] It is not the reason for the termination of the authority over Canada of the United Kingdom Parliament, and therefore s. 2 does not accomplish the patriation of the Canadian Constitution.

(e) Autonomy

W.R. Lederman has suggested a third definition of patriation. He argued in 1967 that bringing the Constitution home meant "to make into law a set of amending procedures that can be carried out in Canada entirely by Canadian governments, legislative bodies, or electorates, acting severally or in combinations of some kind".[55] There is no doubt that the Constitution Act, 1982 has satisfied that definition of patriation. Section 52(2) defines the "Constitution of Canada", and s. 52(3) provides that amendments to the Constitution of Canada "shall be made only in accordance with the authority contained in the Constitution of Canada". The phrase "the authority contained in the Constitution of Canada" is a reference to the amending procedures established by Part V of the Constitution Act, 1982. These procedures fulfil Lederman's definition because they can be carried out entirely in Canada.[56]

Lederman's definition of patriation has been described as "autonomy", a condition that is achieved when "all processes for operating constitutional change

53 Slattery "The Independence of Canada" (1983), 5 Supreme Court L.R. 369, 403.

54 *Ibid.* Contra, Marshall, *Constitutional Conventions* (1984), 207-209.

55 Lederman, "The Process of Constitutional Amendment for Canada" (1967), 12 McGill L.J. 371, 377; reprinted in Lederman, *Continuing Canadian Constitutional Dilemmas* (1981), 85.

56 It is important to notice that the definition of the Constitution of Canada, which includes the list of instruments in the schedule to the Constitution Act, 1982, includes all of the British North America Acts (renamed Constitution Acts). By virtue of s. 7(1) of the Statute of Westminster, "the British North America Acts, 1867 to 1930" were before 1982 protected from amendment by legislative bodies in Canada. Since 1982 the position is that every law in force in Canada, whatever its source and whatever its name, can be amended by one of the three following Canadian procedures: (1) the Canadian Parliament, or (2) a provincial Legislature, or (3) one of the procedures stipulated by Part V of the Constitution Act, 1982.

are locally operated''.[57] But if the United Kingdom Parliament retains some authority over Canada, then Canada is still subject to the thrall, however theoretical, of the old imperial power. The achievement of an ''autonomy'' which could be overridden at any time by the United Kingdom hardly seems worth describing as a patriation. Once again we are driven back to Marshall's test: has there been a legally effective termination of British legislative power over Canada?

The principal consequence of Canada's achievement of autonomy, that is, the adoption of domestic amending procedures, is that Canada will never again request the United Kingdom to pass a law amending the Canadian Constitution (or making any other change in the law of Canada). In practice, this means of course that the United Kingdom Parliament will never again pass a law purporting to extend to Canada. But does the United Kingdom Parliament retain the legal power to enact a law extending to Canada? I think not. The achievement of autonomy, by eliminating the necessity for any continuing role for the United Kingdom Parliament in Canada's law-making process, has made Canada's legal system technically self-sufficient — perfectly independent of the United Kingdom.[58] If the United Kingdom Parliament were to do the unthinkable after 1982 and pass a law purporting to extend to Canada, and if such a law were challenged in the courts in Canada (as it obviously would be), the courts in Canada would ask whether such a law was authorized by the rules of the Canadian legal system. The only conceivable answer to that question would be no: Canada's legal system does not recognize the right of the United Kingdom (or Portugal or any other foreign country) to enact laws binding in Canada. Thus the achievement of autonomy has terminated the authority over Canada of the United Kingdom Parliament.[59] In that important sense, the patriation of the Canadian Constitution has been achieved.

57 Marshall, *Constitutional Theory* (1977), 58; see also Wheare, *Constitutional Structure of the Commonwealth* (1960), 58.

58 In a non-technical sense, Canada has been independent of the United Kingdom at least since 1931, because the conventions agreed to at the imperial conferences of 1926 and 1930 ensured that the residual powers over Canada of the United Kingdom Parliament and Government would be exercised only in accordance with the wishes of Canada.

59 Note 53 and accompanying text, above.

4

Amendment

4.1 History of amendment

(a) Imperial amendment

The British North America Act, 1867 (now the Constitution Act, 1867) differed from the constitutions of the United States and Australia (and other federal countries) in that it contained no general provision for its own amendment.[1] The reason for this omission[2] was that the framers were content for amendments to be made in the same way as the B.N.A. Act itself — by the imperial Parliament.[3] Until 1982, that was Canada's amending procedure: amendments to the B.N.A. Act had to be enacted by the United Kingdom (imperial) Parliament. In 1931, when the Statute of Westminster conferred upon Canada (and the other dominions) the power to repeal or amend imperial statutes applying to Canada, the B.N.A. Act and its amendments were excluded from the new power at Canada's insistence. This was done so that the B.N.A. Act could not be amended by an ordinary statute of either the federal Parliament or a provincial Legislature.[4] The idea was, and still is, that a constitution should be more difficult to amend than an Income Tax Act.

After the Statute of Westminster, while other imperial statutes had lost their protected status, the B.N.A. Act could still be amended only by the United Kingdom Parliament. This did not mean, however, that the amending process was outside the control of Canadians. At the imperial conference of 1930 (the same conference that recommended the enactment of the Statute of Westminster), it was agreed by the Prime Ministers of the United Kingdom and all the dominions that the United Kingdom Parliament would not enact any statute applying to a dominion except at the request and with the consent of that dominion.[5] This agreement, which reflected already longstanding practice, created a constitutional convention. The convention meant that the United Kingdom Parliament would not enact an amendment to the B.N.A. Act (or any other law applying to Canada) except at the request and with the consent of Canada.

The convention did not stipulate which governmental bodies in Canada should make the request for, and give the consent to, proposed amendments to the B.N.A. Act. However, long before 1930, the practice had developed of requesting amendments by a ''joint address'' of the Canadian House of Commons and the Canadian Senate. The joint address consisted of a resolution which requested the United Kingdom government to lay before the United Kingdom Parliament a bill to accomplish the desired amendment; the text of the bill was

---

1 For accounts of Canada's amending process before 1982, see Gérin-Lajoie, *Constitutional Amendment in Canada* (1950); Livingston, *Federalism and Constitutional Change* (1956), ch. 2; Favreau, *The Amendment of the Constitution of Canada* (1965); Lalonde and Basford, *The Canadian Constitution and Constitutional Amendment* (1978); Lederman, *Continuing Canadian Constitutional Dilemmas* (1981), chs. 5, 6.

2 There were some limited domestic powers of amendment, of which the most important were contained in s. 91(1) (power in the federal Parliament to amend a narrowly-defined ''Constitution of Canada'') and s. 92(1) (power in each provincial Legislature to amend the ''constitution of the province''). These provisions were both repealed by the Constitution Act, 1982. They have their counterparts within Part V of the Constitution Act, 1982, namely, ss. 44 and 45, discussed later in this chapter.

3 See ch. 1, Sources, under heading 1.2, ''Constitution Act, 1867'', above.

4 See ch. 3, Independence, under heading 3.3, ''Statute of Westminster, 1931'', above.

5 *Ibid.*

always included in the resolution. After the resolution was passed by the two Houses of Parliament, it was sent to the United Kingdom government for introduction in the United Kingdom Parliament, and enactment. This procedure became established in 1895 and was employed for every amendment to the B.N.A. Act which was enacted by the United Kingdom Parliament after that date.

What was the role of the provinces in the amending process which has just been described? Before the decision of the Supreme Court of Canada in the *Patriation Reference* (1981),[6] the position was unclear. There had been no consistent practice by the federal government of obtaining the consent of the provinces before requesting an amendment, although unanimous provincial consent had been obtained for all amendments directly affecting provincial powers.[7] When Prime Minister Trudeau proposed the amendments which ultimately (and after substantial change) became the Canada Act 1982 and the Constitution Act, 1982, he asserted that, if provincial consent could not be obtained, the federal government would proceed unilaterally to request the enactment of the amendments by the United Kingdom Parliament. The proposed amendments, including as they did a Charter of Rights and an amending formula, had a substantial direct effect on the powers of the provinces. Three provinces directed references to their Courts of Appeal, asking (1) whether there was a requirement of law that provincial consents be obtained, and (2) whether there was a requirement of convention that provincial consents be obtained. On appeal from a variety of answers in the three Courts of Appeal, the Supreme Court of Canada in the *Patriation Reference* (1981)[8] held that the consent of the provinces to the proposed amendments was not required "as a matter of law", but that a "substantial degree" of provincial consent was required "as a matter of convention".[9] After this decision, agreement was reached on November 5, 1981 between the Prime Minister and nine of the ten provincial Premiers[10] on an altered version of the amendments.[11] This agreed-

---

6 *Re Resolution to Amend the Constitution* [1981] 1 S.C.R. 753.

7 Favreau, *The Amendment of the Constitution of Canada* (1965), lists 22 amendments, and this list was reproduced by the Supreme Court of Canada in *Re Upper House* [1980] 1 S.C.R. 54, 60 and no less than three times in *Re Resolution to Amend the Constitution* [1981] 1 S.C.R. 753, 826, 859, 888. Of the 22 amendments, only five - in 1931, 1940, 1951, 1960 and 1964 - were preceded by the unanimous consent of the provinces. However, these five included the three amendments - in 1940, 1951 and 1964 - which had altered the distribution of legislative powers between the two levels of government; and they also included the Statute of Westminster, 1931, which was not literally an amendment to the B.N.A. Act, but which added to the powers of both levels of government. Of the other 17 amendments, none was preceded by unanimous provincial consent, and most were not preceded by provincial consultation.

8 *Re Resolution to Amend the Constitution* [1981] 1 S.C.R. 753. I have discussed this decision more fully in a comment in (1982) 60 Can. Bar Rev. 307.

9 As to the meaning of a "convention", see ch. 1, Sources, under heading 1.10, "Conventions", above.

10 The Premier of Quebec was the sole dissenter. This raised the question whether the conventional rule of a "substantial degree" of provincial consent had to include Quebec. On a reference of the question by Quebec, the Quebec Court of Appeal and, on appeal, the Supreme Court of

upon version was passed as a joint address by both Houses of the federal Parliament,[12] was sent to London, and was enacted by the United Kingdom Parliament as the Canada Act 1982,[13] which included, as Schedule B, the Constitution Act, 1982.[14]

The Constitution Act, 1982, by Part V, introduces into the Canadian Constitution a set of amending procedures which enable the B.N.A. Act (now renamed the Constitution Act, 1867) and its amendments to be amended within Canada without recourse to the United Kingdom Parliament. The role of the United Kingdom Parliament in Canada's amendment process is thus eliminated, and the Canada Act 1982 formally terminates the authority of the United Kingdom Parliament over Canada.[15] The roles of the federal and provincial governments in the amendment process are now defined in precise statutory language. The vague and unsatisfactory rules[16] laid down by the Supreme Court of Canada in the *Patriation Reference* have accordingly been supplanted and have no current relevance. The new procedures in Part V of the Constitution Act, 1982 constitute a complete code of legal (as opposed to conventional) rules which enable all parts of the "Constitution of Canada" to be amended. Those rules are described later in this chapter.

(b) The search for a domestic amending procedure

The Constitution Act, 1982 was the culmination of a search for a domestic amending procedure which started in 1927. The federal Minister of Justice had

---

Canada, in the *Que. Veto Reference*, answered no: *Re Objection by Que. to Resolution to Amend the Constitution* [1982] 2 S.C.R. 793.

11 The history of the 1982 amendments is analyzed by (among many others) McWhinney, *Canada and the Constitution 1979-1982* (1982); Banting and Simeon (eds.), *And No One Cheered* (1983); Romanow, Whyte, Leeson, *Canada ... Notwithstanding* (1984); Weiler and Elliot (eds.), *Litigating the Values of a Nation* (1986), Part I; Pelletier, *La modification constitutionnelle au Canada* (1996). The documentary sources are collected in Bayefsky, *Canada's Constitution Act, 1982 and Amendments: A Documentary History* (1989), 2 vols.

12 The resolution was passed by the House of Commons on December 2, 1981 and by the Senate on December 8, 1981.

13 Canada Act 1982 (U.K.), 1982, c. 11. The foregoing is the correct citation: see Banks, Comment (1983) 61 Can. Bar Rev. 499.

14 The reason for two Acts seems to have been to separate the provisions relating to the United Kingdom Parliament (in the Canada Act 1982) from the provisions relating to Canadian institutions (in the Constitution Act, 1982). The Canada Act 1982 came into force on March 29, 1982, when it received the royal assent. The Constitution Act, 1982, being a schedule to the Canada Act 1982, also became law at the same time; but under s. 58 its coming into force was postponed until "a day to be fixed by proclamation". The proclamation fixed April 17, 1982 as the in-force date: The Canada Gazette, Part III, p. 33 (21 September, 1982).

15 See ch. 3, Independence, under heading 3.5, "Patriation of the Constitution", above.

16 They were vague in their stipulation of a "substantial degree" of provincial consent. They were unsatisfactory in that this requirement was one of convention only; the provinces had no legal protection from changes to the Constitution initiated unilaterally by the federal Parliament, a situation inconsistent with principles of federalism.

placed the issue on the agenda of the dominion-provincial conference of 1927. He was influenced by the Balfour declaration of 1926, in which Canada had been recognized as the equal of the United Kingdom.[17] Equality plainly called for the elimination of the role of the United Kingdom Parliament in Canada's amendment process. But that could not be accomplished until a new domestic amending procedure had been enacted into Canada's Constitution. Until November 5, 1981, agreement on a domestic procedure had eluded Canada's political leaders. And even the 1981 agreement, as related above, did not include Quebec.

Agreement had nearly been reached on two earlier occasions. In 1964, the Fulton-Favreau formula was agreed to by all provinces except Quebec. It was almost an agreement not to agree, because it required the unanimous consent of the federal Parliament and all provincial Legislatures for most significant amendments. Even so, Quebec did not agree to it, and it was not proceeded with.[18] Then in 1970, the Victoria Charter formula was agreed to by the Prime Minister and all Premiers, but the agreement was subject to ratification by each provincial government, and Quebec decided not to ratify it.[19] For most amendments the Victoria Charter formula required the consent of the federal Parliament and a complex distribution of provinces: (1) any province that has had at any time 25 per cent of the population of Canada; (2) at least two of the Atlantic provinces; and (3) at least two of the Western provinces that have a combined population of at least 50 per cent of the population of all the Western provinces. Category (1) insured a permanent veto for Quebec (as well as Ontario). Even so, Quebec did not agree to it, and it was not proceeded with.[20]

It will be noticed that both the Fulton-Favreau formula and the Victoria Charter formula gave a veto to Quebec. Moreover, in 1964 and 1971, it was clear that all participants understood that Quebec had to be a party to whatever agreement was reached, because the sole dissent of Quebec was sufficient to abort both of these previous projects. When Prime Minister Trudeau tabled the constitutional proposals which evolved into the Constitution Act, 1982, the amending formula which he proposed was essentially the Victoria Charter formula. Eight provinces now opposed that formula,[21] and proposed an alternative ''Vancouver formula''. The Vancouver formula required for most amendments the agreement of the federal Parliament and two-thirds of the provincial Legislatures representing 50 per cent of the population of all the provinces. This formula did not give any province a veto; and it was formally proposed in a much-publicized eight-province accord which repeatedly affirmed the ''equality'' of the provinces.[22] Premier

17 See ch. 3, Independence, under heading 3.3, ''Statute of Westminster, 1931'', above.

18 Forsey, *Freedom and Order* (1974), 235-237.

19 All of the other provinces either did ratify it or would have done so if Quebec's refusal had not made the issue moot. Quebec was the only dissenter.

20 Forsey, note 18, above, 237-238.

21 Seven of these provinces had agreed to it as part of the Victoria Charter in 1971.

22 Constitutional Accord, April 16, 1981. The text of the Accord appeared in all newspapers of that evening or the next morning.

Levesque of Quebec was one of the eight signatories to that document: for the first time Quebec had formally abandoned its claim to a special status involving (at the minimum) a veto over constitutional amendments.[23]

The agreement of November 5, 1981 was achieved when the Prime Minister and his two provincial allies, the Premiers of Ontario and New Brunswick, gave up their support for the Victoria Charter formula and accepted instead a modified Vancouver formula.[24] Seven of the eight dissenting provincial Premiers, on their part, agreed to accept a modified Charter of Rights.[25] Premier Levesque did not agree with the compromise, and even found the new amending formula unacceptable, despite his earlier agreement to the very similar Vancouver formula.[26]

Once again, as in 1964 and 1971, there was an agreement on an amending formula which included all Premiers, except the Premier of Quebec. But this time the absence of Quebec from the agreement did not stop the process. The Prime Minister was determined to press on with the proposal despite the incomplete agreement, and the Supreme Court of Canada had ruled in the *Patriation Reference* that the consent of Quebec (or any other province) was not required by law, and was probably not required by convention either.[27] The federal-provincial agreement of November 5, 1981, supplemented by four changes agreed to later,[28] was accordingly embodied in a resolution for a joint address which passed both

---

23 The veto was replaced with an opting-out provision, which was available to any province. Opting out is discussed in sec. 4.3(d), "Opting out", below.

24 The only change was the elimination of a provision for payment of compensation to an opting-out province. However, after November 5, 1981, in an unsuccessful effort to secure Quebec's agreement, a right to compensation was restored for opting-out of amendments relating to "education or other cultural matters". This is now in s. 40 of the Constitution Act, 1982, and is discussed in sec. 4.3(c), "Compensation for opting out", below.

25 The major change in the Charter of Rights was the introduction of the override clause, now s. 33 of the Constitution Act, 1982, discussed in ch. 36, "Override of Rights", below.

26 Note 24, above.

27 Quebec had directed one of the three references to the Court on the amendment proposals, and it had not copied the questions submitted by Manitoba and Newfoundland (the other two provinces that had directed references). Instead, it drafted questions of its own, but none of its questions asked for a ruling on the question whether Quebec had a veto. The Supreme Court of Canada in the *Patriation Reference* (*Re Resolution to Amend the Constitution* [1981] 1 S.C.R. 753) accordingly did not address itself to that issue, simply providing the vague ruling that a "substantial degree" of provincial consent was required by convention. After the federal-provincial agreement of November 5, 1981, Quebec directed a second reference to the Court of Appeal asking whether Quebec's consent was necessary, by convention, as a pre-condition to the passage of the proposed amendments. Both the Quebec Court of Appeal and the Supreme Court of Canada answered no: note 10, above.

28 The four new elements were (1) an aboriginal rights clause (s. 35), (2) the removal of the sexual equality clause (s. 28) from the override power (s. 33), (3) compensation for opting out of amendments relating to education or culture (s. 40), and (4) limitation of minority language educational rights in Quebec (s. 59).

Houses of the federal Parliament in December 1981,[29] and was then transmitted to London. The Canada Act 1982 was enacted by the United Kingdom Parliament on March 29, 1982. When the Constitution Act, 1982 came into force on April 17, 1982,[30] Canada had at last acquired domestic amending procedures[31]. Those procedures are analyzed in a later section of this chapter.

(c) The failure to accommodate Quebec

The Constitution Act, 1982 was a major achievement, curing several long-standing defects in the Constitution of Canada. As well as the adoption of domestic amending procedures (ss. 38-49), a Charter of Rights was adopted (ss. 1-34), aboriginal rights were recognized (s. 35), equalization was guaranteed (s. 36), provincial powers over natural resources were extended (ss. 50-51), and the Constitution of Canada was defined and given supremacy over other laws (s. 52). But the Constitution Act, 1982 failed to accomplish one of the goals of constitutional reform, and that was the better accommodation of Quebec within the Canadian federation.

The Premier of Quebec had been the sole dissenter to the federal-provincial meeting of November 5, 1981; the Quebec National Assembly had passed a resolution condemning the constitutional settlement that had been agreed upon;[32] and Quebec had even sought relief in the courts, though without success.[33] Nor were Quebec's concerns without substance. The new amending procedures denied a veto to Quebec, something that in the past had always been recognized in practice. The new Charter of Rights restricted the powers of the provincial Legislatures, and in particular limited the capacity of the Quebec National Assembly to implement French-language policy.[34] Thus, the outcome of the constitutional changes of 1982 was a diminution of Quebec's powers and a profound sense of grievance in the province.

In assessing the gravity of Quebec's alienation from the constitutional changes of 1982, it is important to cast one's mind back to Quebec's referendum on sovereignty-association, which was held by the Parti Québécois government on May 20, 1980.[35] The referendum was defeated by a popular vote of 59.5 per

---

29 It is an interesting commentary on ''executive federalism'' that of the nine Premiers who signed the agreement of November 5, 1981 only one bothered to submit it to the Legislature for approval. It was approved by the Alberta Legislature on November 10, 1981, and it was disapproved by the Quebec National Assembly on December 1, 1981.

30 Note 14, above.

31 For references to the literature on the history of the 1982 settlement, see note 14, above.

32 Note 29, above.

33 Note 27, above.

34 This concern was shown to be justified by the later decisions of the Supreme Court of Canada in *A.G. Que.* v. *Que. Protestant School Bds.* [1984] 2 S.C.R. 66 (striking down Quebec's restrictions on admission to English-language schools) and *Ford* v. *Que.* [1988] 2 S.C.R. 712 (striking down Quebec's prohibition of English-language commercial signs).

35 See ch. 5, Federalism, under heading 5.7, ''Secession'', below.

cent to 40.5 per cent. In the referendum campaign, the federalist forces promised that a ''no'' to sovereignty-association was not a vote for the status quo, and the defeat of the referendum would be followed by constitutional change to better accommodate Quebec's aspirations. The defeat of the referendum was in fact immediately followed by a series of federal-provincial conferences in the summer and early fall of 1980, but these conferences failed to yield agreement on the specifics of constitutional change. On October 6, 1980, despite the absence of a federal-provincial agreement, Prime Minister Trudeau introduced in the House of Commons a resolution calling for the set of constitutional amendments that, after substantial alteration, became the Canada Act 1982 and the Constitution Act, 1982. For the reasons explained in the previous paragraph, these 1982 changes did not fulfil the promises made during the 1980 referendum campaign in Quebec.

Quebec was of course legally bound by the Constitution Act, 1982, because the Act had been adopted into law by the correct constitutional procedures. However, the government of Quebec thereafter refused to participate in constitutional changes that involved the new amending procedures. And the government ''opted out'' of the new Charter of Rights to the maximum extent possible under s. 33 by introducing a ''notwithstanding clause'' into each of its existing statutes, and into every newly-enacted statute.[36] In these ways, the point was made that the Constitution Act, 1982 lacked political legitimacy in the province of Quebec.

In 1984, Prime Minister Trudeau resigned, and, after an election later in the year, the Progressive Conservative government of Prime Minister Mulroney took office. One of the new government's policies was to achieve a reconciliation with Quebec. In 1985, an election was held in Quebec, and the Parti Québécois government was defeated. The new Liberal government of Premier Bourassa moved to seek a reconciliation with the rest of Canada. The government announced five conditions that were required for Quebec's acceptance of the Constitution Act, 1982. These were: (1) the recognition of Quebec as a distinct society; (2) a greater role in immigration; (3) a provincial role in appointments to the Supreme Court of Canada; (4) limitations on the federal spending power; and (5) a veto for Quebec on constitutional amendments.

The Prime Minister and the other provincial Premiers agreed to negotiate on Quebec's five conditions. The outcome of those negotiations was the Meech Lake Constitutional Accord of 1987[37] which was an agreement entered into by all

36 See ch. 36, Override of Rights, under heading 36.2, ''History of s. 33'', below.

37 The Meech Lake Constitutional Accord was made at Meech Lake, Quebec, on April 30, 1987. The actual constitutional text was settled at a second First Ministers' Conference in the Langevin Block, Ottawa, on June 3, 1987. The text, with explanatory commentary, is set out in Hogg, *Meech Lake Constitutional Accord Annotated* (1988). See also Schwartz, *Fathoming Meech Lake* (1987); Forest (ed.), *L'adhésion du Québec à l'Accord du Lac Meech* (1988); Swinton and Rogerson (eds.), *Competing Constitutional Visions: The Meech Lake Accord* (1988); Behiels (ed.), *The Meech Lake Primer* (1989); Monahan, *Meech Lake: The Inside Story* (1991). Many other books, articles and committee reports were also published on the Accord.

eleven first ministers on a set of amendments, essentially giving effect to Quebec's five conditions. This seemed at the time to be an immensely important development, reconciling the government of Quebec to the Constitution Act, 1982. However, in order to become law, the Accord had to be ratified by resolutions of the Senate and House of Commons and of the legislative assembly of every province.[38] It was ratified by the Senate and House of Commons[39] and by eight of the ten provinces, but it was not ratified by all ten provinces.[40] The Accord therefore lapsed.

In 1991, the process was resumed, but with an even more ambitious goal — to cure everybody's constitutional discontents as well as Quebec's. After a prolonged period of public consultation and discussion, in 1992 the eleven first ministers reached an agreement at Charlottetown, Prince Edward Island. The Charlottetown Accord[41] included all the elements of the Meech Lake Accord, and much else besides,[42] including provision for an elected Senate and for aboriginal self-government. In a radical break with past practice, the first ministers agreed

---

38 The unanimity procedure of s. 41 of the Constitution Act, 1982 was applicable, because the Accord included provisions relating to the composition of the Supreme Court of Canada (s. 41(d)) and a change in the amending procedures (s. 41(e)).

39 The Senate actually refused to ratify it, but was overridden by the House of Commons under s. 47 of the Constitution Act, 1982.

40 The government of New Brunswick changed in 1987 before ratification, and the Liberal government of Premier McKenna refused to ratify. The same thing happened in Manitoba in 1988 and the new Progressive Conservative government of Premier Filmon refused to ratify. The government of Newfoundland changed in 1989 after ratification, and the new Liberal government of Premier Wells acted under s. 46(2) of the Constitution Act, 1982 to revoke the previous ratification. In an attempt to bring the dissenters on board, a companion accord was agreed to by the First Ministers in Ottawa on June 6, 1990, which proposed some changes to the original Accord. This was followed by New Brunswick's ratification, but the legislative assemblies of Manitoba and Newfoundland adjourned without bringing the issue to a vote by June 23, 1990. Section 39(2) of the Constitution Act, 1982 caused the process to lapse on that date, which was three years from the date of the first legislative ratification, which had been by Quebec on June 23, 1987.

41 The Charlottetown Accord was made on August 28, 1992. It was an agreement of the eleven first ministers, the two territorial leaders and the leaders of the four national aboriginal organizations. The Accord was not in the form of a legal text, but a Draft Legal Text, prepared by officials, was issued on October 9, 1992. The text of the Accord and the Draft Legal Text is set out in the appendices to McRoberts and Monahan (eds.), *The Charlottetown Accord, the Referendum and the Future of Canada* (U. Toronto Press, 1993).

42 The provisions designed to appeal to Quebec included not only the five elements of the Meech Lake Accord, but also a perpetual guarantee for Quebec of 25 per cent of the seats in the House of Commons, a double-majority requirement for Senate passage of bills ''that materially affect French language or culture'', restrictions on the federal spending power and an explicit grant to the provinces of exclusive jurisdiction over culture in the province. The rest of the Accord was designed to appeal to western Canada (the Senate), aboriginal peoples (aboriginal self-government) and many other constituencies that sought constitutional recognition (an omnibus ''Canada clause'' and a ''social and economic charter'').

to submit the Accord to a national referendum[43] before proceeding to the legislative ratifications that were required by the Constitution's amending procedures.[44] The referendum was held on October 26, 1992, and decisively lost. The Accord was rejected by a national majority of 54.4 per cent to 44.6 per cent; the no side prevailed in six of the ten provinces, including Quebec.[45] The referendum result spelled the end of the Charlottetown Accord, which never even started on the process of legislative ratification. The referendum result, following as it did the failure of the Meech Lake Accord, also brought to an end the search for a constitutional accommodation with Quebec. Not only had all the political actors become weary of the long constitutional process, it had become clear that it was impossible to design a package of amendments that could command popular support in all regions of the country.[46]

The failure of the Meech Lake and Charlottetown Accords to accomplish any constitutional change led to a resurgence in the popular support for the separatist movement in Quebec. In the federal election of 1993, which was won by the Liberal Party under Prime Minister Chrétien, the separatist Bloc Québécois party took 52 of Quebec's 75 seats and actually became the official opposition in the federal Parliament. In Quebec's provincial election of 1994 the Liberals were defeated and the Parti Québécois, now under Premier Parizeau, once again formed the provincial government. The Parti Québécois had promised to hold a referendum on sovereignty if they were elected, and on October 30, 1995 they did so.[47] This time, the referendum did not propose merely a mandate to negotiate sovereignty-association (the 1980 question) but outright sovereignty, although the sovereignty was to be declared only after Quebec had ''made a formal offer to Canada for a new economic and political partnership''. Despite the stronger question, the referendum nearly passed. It was defeated by 50.6 per cent to 49.4 per cent. After the referendum vote, Premier Parizeau resigned, and was replaced

43 The referendum was a national one, held under the authority of federal law, everywhere except in Quebec, where the referendum was a provincial one, held under the authority of provincial law. Although, technically, there were two referendums, they were held at the same time on the same question and the results were amalgamated into national figures.

44 The unanimity procedure of s. 41 of the Constitution Act, 1982 was applicable, for the same reasons that made s. 41 applicable to the Meech Lake Accord: note 38, above.

45 The question to which the voters answered no was as follows:

> Do you agree that the Constitution of Canada should be renewed on the basis of the agreement reached on August 28, 1992?

It was understood that the referendum would have to pass in every province because no provincial Legislature would be willing to pass a resolution ratifying a proposal that had been rejected by that province's voters.

46 Although the vote in Quebec was similar to the vote in the rest of Canada, the reasons that caused the no vote were quite different. Outside Quebec, there was a widespread sentiment that Quebec had been given too much, while inside Quebec there was a widespread sentiment that Quebec had not been given enough!

47 See ch. 5, Federalism, under heading 5.7, ''Secession'', below.

by Premier Bouchard, who announced that, after the next Quebec election, if his government was re-elected, another referendum on sovereignty would be held.

The federal government of Prime Minister Chrétien reacted to the shock of the close vote in the referendum and to the prospect of another referendum with two measures. One was a resolution of the House of Commons that recognized Quebec as a ''distinct society'' and promised to be ''guided by that reality''.[48] The second was the regional veto statute,[49] which was enacted by the federal Parliament, and which purported to give a veto over future constitutional changes to Quebec (as well as to Ontario, British Columbia, a majority of Prairie provinces and a majority of Atlantic provinces). Neither of these measures was a constitutional amendment, and there was little general support for them. Both measures were criticized by the provincial premiers (who had not been consulted) and both were opposed by the Bloc Québécois, with the majority of seats in Quebec, and the Reform Party, with the majority of seats in the Western provinces. As measures to accommodate Quebec, they were modest—to say the least.

4.2 Part V of the Constitution Act, 1982

(a) Summary

Part V of the Constitution Act, 1982 is headed ''Procedure for Amending Constitution of Canada''. It provides five different amending procedures:[50]

(1) A general amending procedure (s. 38), for amendments not otherwise provided for (as well as for amendments listed in s. 42), requiring the assents of the federal Parliament and two-thirds of the provinces representing 50 per cent of the population;
(2) A unanimity procedure (s. 41), for five defined kinds of amendments, requiring the assents of the federal Parliament and all of the provinces;
(3) A some-but-not-all-provinces procedure (s. 43), for amendment of provisions not applying to all provinces, requiring the assents of the federal Parliament and only those provinces affected;

48 *House of Commons Debates* (29 November 1995) at 16971 (text of resolution); *House of Commons Debates* (11 December 1995) at 17536 (passage of resolution).

49 S.C. 1996, c. 1. The Act does not have an official short title; the long title is An Act respecting constitutional amendments. The Act is discussed in sec. 4.3(h), ''Regional veto statute'', below.

50 The amending procedures are analyzed by Cheffins, ''The Constitution Act, 1982 and the Amending Formula'' (1982) 4 Supreme Court L.R. 43; Scott, ''Pussycat, Pussycat or Patriation and the New Constitutional Amendment Processes'' (1982) 20 U. West. Ont. L. Rev. 247; Scott, ''The Canadian Constitutional Amendment Process'' (1982) 45 Law & Contemp. Problems 249; Meekison, ''The Amending Formula'' (1983) 8 Queen's L.J. 99; Lederman, ''Canadian Constitutional Amending Procedures, 1867-1982'' (1984) 32 Am. Jo. Comp. Law 339; Beaudoin, *La Constitution du Canada* (1990), ch. 6; Pelletier, *La modification constitutionnelle au Canada* (1996).

(4) The federal Parliament alone (s. 44) has power to amend provisions relating to the federal executive and Houses of Parliament; and
(5) Each provincial Legislature alone (s. 45) has power to amend ''the constitution of the province''.

Each of these procedures will be considered in turn in later sections of this chapter.

(b) Comparison with Australia and United States

Before turning to the detail and complexity of Canada's new amending procedures, it is interesting to contrast the simpler amending procedures of Australia and the United States. In the case of Australia, s. 128 of the Constitution requires approval by a simple majority in both Houses of the federal Parliament, followed by a popular referendum in which the amendment is approved by a ''double majority'' of votes: (1) a national majority, and (2) a state majority in a majority of states (that is, four of the six states).[51] In the case of the United States, Article V of the Constitution requires approval by a two-thirds majority in both Houses of the federal Congress followed by ratification by the Legislatures of three-quarters of the states (or, alternatively, at the discretion of the Congress, by constitutional conventions in three-quarters of the states — a method that has been used only once).[52]

51 The text of s. 128 of the Constitution of Australia is as follows:

> 128. This Constitution shall not be altered except in the following manner:
>
> The proposed law for the alteration thereof must be passed by an absolute majority of each House of the Parliament, and not less than two nor more than six months after its passage through both Houses the proposed law shall be submitted in each State and Territory to the electors qualified to vote for the election of members of the House of Representatives
>
> . . . .
>
> And if in a majority of the States a majority of the electors voting approve the proposed law, and if a majority of all the electors voting also approve the proposed law, it shall be presented to the Governor-General for the Queen's assent . . . .

On the Australian experience with s. 128, see Lumb, *The Constitution of the Commonwealth of Australia Annotated* (4th ed., 1986), ch. 8; Hanks, *Constitutional Law in Australia* (1991), 99-102. The latter work explains that, as of 1988, only eight of 42 proposals have carried.

52 The text of Article V of the Constitution of the United States is as follows:

> The Congress, whenever two thirds of both Houses shall deem it necessary, shall propose amendments to this Constitution, or, on the application of the legislatures of two thirds of the several States, shall call a convention for proposing amendments, which in either case, shall be valid to all intents and purposes, as part of this Constitution when ratified by the legislatures of three fourths of the several States, or by conventions in three fourths thereof, as the one or the other mode of ratification may be proposed by the Congress;
>
> . . .

On the American experience with Article V, see Nowak and Rotunda, *Constitutional Law* (4th ed., 1991), Appendix B.

(c) Constitution of Canada

The "Constitution of Canada" is defined in s. 52(2) of the Constitution Act, 1982.[53] The amending procedures of Part V of the Constitution Act, 1982 apply to amendments to the Constitution of Canada, as defined.[54] The amending procedures are not required for the amendment of statutes or instruments that are not part of the Constitution of Canada; anything that is not part of the Constitution of Canada can be amended by the ordinary action of the competent legislative body.

Section 41(a) of the Constitution Act, 1982 requires the unanimity procedure for amendments to the Constitution of Canada relating to "the office of the Queen, the Governor General and the Lieutenant Governor of the province". To the extent that these topics are provided for in the Constitution of Canada, they are specially entrenched by the severe rule of unanimity. But the Constitution of Canada does not include the Royal Style and Titles Act[55] or the Governor General's Act,[56] and although amendments to those Acts would be in relation to the office of the Queen or the Governor General, an ordinary statute would suffice.[57]

Nor is the Official Languages Act[58] part of the Constitution of Canada. It follows that the Act is freely amendable by the Parliament of Canada, employing the ordinary legislative process, even though "the use of the English or French language" is one of the topics listed in s. 41 as requiring the unanimity procedure.

The Supreme Court of Canada Act[59] is also not part of the Constitution of Canada. That is why, in 1987, the Parliament of Canada was able to enact extensive amendments to the Act[60] despite the fact that "the Supreme Court of Canada" is one of the topics listed in s. 42 as requiring the general (seven-fifty) amending procedure. The amending Act of 1987 did not change the number of judges on the Court or the requirement that three judges must be appointed from Quebec, but these are matters provided for in the Supreme Court Act, not the Constitution of Canada, and so they too are open to amendment by the ordinary legislative process, despite the fact that "the composition of the Supreme Court of Canada" is one of the topics listed in s. 41 as requiring the unanimity procedure.[61]

---

53 The definition is discussed in ch. 1, Sources, under heading 1.4, "Constitution of Canada", above.

54 An exception is the fifth procedure of s. 45 (provincial Legislature alone), which applies to amendments to "the constitution of the province".

55 R.S.C. 1985, c. R-12.

56 R.S.C. 1985, c. G-9.

57 The Governor General's Act was in fact amended in 1985 by the ordinary legislative process: S.C. 1985, c. 48. See also Banks, "If the Queen were to Abdicate: Procedure under Canada's Constitution" (1990) 28 Alta. L. Rev. 535.

58 R.S.C. 1985, c. O-3.

59 R.S.C. 1985, c. S-26.

60 S.C. 1987, c. 42.

61 The federal Parliament's power over the Supreme Court of Canada is granted by s. 101 of the Constitution Act, 1867. Section 101 itself would of course be protected by s. 42(d). However, the Constitution of Canada makes no other reference to the Supreme Court of Canada, and

(d) Charter of Rights

Must constitutional amendments conform to the Charter of Rights?

The Charter of Rights is itself part of the Constitution of Canada, and can be amended by the general (seven-fifty) amending procedure. It is therefore obvious that the general amending procedure (s. 38), or, a fortiori, the unanimity amending procedure (s. 41) cannot be constrained by the Charter of Rights. This conclusion is reinforced by s. 32 of the Charter of Rights, which makes the Charter applicable to the Parliament of Canada and the Legislatures of each province, but which makes no reference to the combinations of legislative resolutions that are required to operate three of the five amending procedures. It seems clear, therefore, that the Charter of Rights does not apply to the general amending procedure (s. 38), the unanimity procedure (s. 41), or the some-but-not-all-provinces procedure (s. 43).[62]

Under s. 44 of the Constitution Act, 1982, the Parliament of Canada alone has the power to enact amendments to the Constitution of Canada in relation to the federal executive and Houses of Parliament, and, under s. 45, each provincial Legislature alone has the power to enact amendments to ''the constitution of the province''. There is no reason why these two categories of legislation should be exempt from the Charter of Rights, and of course they are caught by the literal words of s. 32 of the Charter. Therefore, it has been held that provincial laws respecting electoral districts[63] and qualifications of candidates for election,[64] although constituting amendments to the constitution of the province, are subject to the Charter of Rights.

4.3 General amending procedure (s. 38)

(a) Section 38(1)

As related above, Part V of the Constitution Act, 1982 provides for five amending procedures. The general procedure, which applies when none of the

---

makes no provision for the composition of the Court. This has led some commentators to argue that the Supreme Court Act should be judicially added in whole or in part to the scheduled list of 30 pre-1982 instruments that is incorporated in the definition of s. 52(2): Cheffins, note 41, above, 53; Scott (Pussycat article), note 41, above, 273; Lederman, ''Constitutional Procedure and the Reform of the Supreme Court of Canada'' (1985) 26 Cahiers de droit (Laval) 195. In favour of this view is the use of the word ''includes'' (rather than ''means'') in s. 52(2). I prefer the view that the scheduled list is exhaustive: see ch. 1, Sources, under heading 1.4, ''Constitution of Canada'', above.

62 *Penikett* v. *Can.* (1987) 45 D.L.R. (4th) 108 (Y.T.C.A.); *Sibbeston* v. *Can.* (1988) 48 D.L.R. (4th) 691 (N.T.C.A.). Both cases held that the amendments comprising the (subsequently lapsed) Meech Lake Constitutional Accord, note 37, above, could not be challenged for breach of the Charter of Rights.

63 *Re Provincial Electoral Boundaries (Sask.)* [1991] 2 S.C.R. 158, 179.

64 *MacLean* v. *A.G.N.S.* (1987) 35 D.L.R. (4th) 306 (N.S.S.C.).

four more specific procedures (in ss. 41, 43, 44 and 45) is applicable, is stipulated by s. 38(1), which provides as follows:

> 38.(1) An amendment to the Constitution of Canada may be made by proclamation issued by the Governor General under the Great Seal of Canada where so authorized by
>
> (a) resolutions of the Senate and House of Commons; and
>
> (b) resolutions of the legislative assemblies of at least two-thirds of the provinces that have, in the aggregate, according to the then latest general census, at least fifty per cent of the population of all the provinces.

Section 38(1) requires that an amendment to the "Constitution of Canada"[65] be authorized by (a) resolutions of both Houses of the federal Parliament,[66] and (b) resolutions of the legislative assemblies[67] of at least two-thirds of the provinces, provided that they represent at least 50 per cent of the population of all the provinces. The two-thirds requirement means that at least seven of the ten provinces must agree to an amendment. Seven provinces would inevitably include at least one of the four western provinces and at least one of the four Atlantic provinces. The 50 per cent population requirement means that the agreeing provinces must include at least one of Ontario or Quebec, since the combined population of Ontario (9.1 million) and Quebec (6.5 million) is more than 50 per cent of the population of Canada (25 million). However, no single province has a constitutionally-entrenched veto over amendments.[68]

The general amending procedure is often called the seven-fifty formula, because of its requirements of seven provinces and 50 per cent of the population. Since 1982, it has been successfully operated once.[69]

(b) Proclamation

Once the authority for an amendment has been provided by the requisite number of resolutions of assent, s. 38(1) provides that the formal act of amendment

65 See sec. 4.2(b), "Constitution of Canada", above.

66 The Senate can be overridden by the House of Commons under s. 47. This was done in the case of the Meech Lake Constitutional Accord of 1987: note 39, above.

67 Section 38(1) does not stipulate any procedural requirements for the passage of a resolution of the House of Commons, the Senate or the legislative assembly of a province. It would therefore be the rules of the particular legislative chamber that would determine the quorum and other procedures. But s. 38(2) calls for a resolution "supported by a majority of the members" (as opposed to a majority of those present and voting) where the proposed amendment "derogates from the legislative powers, the proprietary rights or any other rights or privileges of the legislature or government of a province". (This is the same class of amendments in respect of which opting-out is available under s. 38(3).) Section 38(2) is a safeguard against a hasty decision by a poorly attended legislative chamber.

68 By virtue of the regional veto statute, S.C. 1996, c. 1, four provinces (Ontario, Quebec, British Columbia and Alberta) now have an indirect veto over constitutional amendments which come under s. 38(1): see sec. 4.3(h), "Regional veto statute", below.

69 Chapter 1, Sources, under heading 1.4, "Constitution of Canada".

is accomplished by a "proclamation issued by the Governor General under the Great Seal of Canada". Section 39 imposes time limits on the issue of this proclamation. Under s. 39(1), the proclamation is not to be issued until a full year has elapsed from the adoption of "the resolution initiating the amendment procedure",[70] unless before then all provinces have adopted resolutions of assent or dissent.[71] The purpose of this rule is to give each legislative assembly time to consider each proposal.[72] Under s. 39(2), the proclamation is not to be issued after three years have elapsed from the adoption of the resolution initiating the amendment procedure. The purpose of this rule is to prevent a proposed amendment from limping along for many years, gradually picking up assents, and eventually coming into force without ever having had widespread support.

(c) Initiation

The procedures for amendment "may be initiated either by the Senate or the House of Commons or by the legislative assembly of a province" (s. 46(1)). In other words, the amending procedure can start in any of the legislative chambers that have the power to authorize an amendment.

(d) Opting out

"Opting out" is permitted by s. 38(3) in respect of any amendment "that derogates from the legislative powers, the proprietary rights or any other rights or privileges of the legislature or government of a province".[73] Section 38(3) permits the legislative assembly of a province to pass a resolution of dissent to an amendment of the kind described, and then the amendment "shall not have effect in [that] province". Section 38(3) is not a unanimity requirement or a veto, because it does not permit a single province to block an amendment that is wanted by the federal government and seven provinces representing 50 per cent of the population. All that s. 38(3) does is to enable any province to opt out of an amendment that derogates from that province's powers, rights or privileges, and

---

70 This phrase is not defined, but it must mean the first of the authorizing resolutions to be passed under s. 38(1); see also the discussion of initiation in the following text.

71 Section 48 provides that the "Queen's Privy Council for Canada" (i.e., by convention, the cabinet) shall "advise" (i.e., direct) the Governor General to issue a proclamation "forthwith on the adoption of the resolutions required for an amendment ...". The word "forthwith" appears to contradict s. 39(1)'s requirement of a one-year delay. Section 48 must obviously be read as subject to the more specific requirement of s. 39(1).

72 This is particularly important with respect to proposals that would derogate from the powers, rights or privileges of the provinces. The one-year delay ensures that opting out under s. 38(3) (discussed in the following text), which is available only "prior to the issue of the proclamation", cannot be defeated by the speedy manoeuvering of those governments that desire an amendment.

73 Note also the procedural requirements for resolutions authorizing amendments of this kind: see note 67, above.

that is unacceptable to it. A maximum of three provinces could opt out of an amendment: if there were more than three dissenting provinces, the amendment would not have the support of two-thirds of the provinces and would therefore be defeated.

The operation of opting out may be illustrated by an example. Take the following hypothetical case:

> An amendment is proposed by the federal government to add to the list of exclusive federal powers "the regulation of product standards", a matter now within the exclusive provincial authority over property and civil rights in the province.[74] The proposed amendment is authorized by resolutions supported by a majority of the members of the Senate, the House of Commons and seven of the ten legislative assemblies, all except Quebec, Alberta and Newfoundland. The Quebec Legislature passes the resolution of dissent contemplated by s. 38(3). The Alberta and Newfoundland Legislatures do nothing. One year after the resolution initiating the amending procedure (see s. 39(1)) the Governor General issues the proclamation required by s. 38(1).

In this example, the amendment has been validly enacted, because the amendment has been authorized by resolutions of the Senate, the House of Commons and the legislative assemblies of two-thirds of the provinces (seven out of ten) having 50 per cent of the population of all the provinces. Therefore, the federal Parliament has acquired its new legislative power, and that power has effect not only in the provinces which agreed to the amendment, but also in Alberta and Newfoundland, which did not. In nine provinces, the provincial Legislatures would have lost their authority over the regulation of product standards. However, the amendment is one that derogates from the legislative powers of the provinces, and Quebec has passed a resolution of dissent under s. 38(3). Therefore the new federal power does not have effect in Quebec. In Quebec, the regulation of product standards remains within the authority of the Quebec Legislature. If the federal Parliament decides to exercise its new power of passing a law regulating product standards, the members of parliament and senators from Quebec will be allowed to vote on the bill (and may have to do so to preserve the government's majority),[75] but once the bill has been enacted into law the law will not apply in Quebec.

A resolution of dissent under s. 38(3) must be passed "prior to the issue of the proclamation to which the amendment relates" (s. 38(3)). In the example just discussed, neither Alberta nor Newfoundland could opt out of the amendment after the issue of the proclamation. However, if a resolution of dissent has been passed prior to the issue of the proclamation, it can be revoked "at any time before or after the issue of the proclamation" (s. 38(4)). In the example just discussed, Quebec can opt into the amendment at any time that its legislative

74 *Labatt Breweries* v. *A.-G. Can.* [1980] 1 S.C.R. 914.

75 This strange result has in the past been viewed as a grave defect in the idea of "special status" for one or more provinces: note 151, below.

assembly has a change of mind. A resolution of assent, on the other hand, may be revoked only before the issue of the proclamation (s. 46(2)). In the example just discussed, Ontario (or any of the other assenting provinces), having passed a resolution of assent prior to the issue of the proclamation, could not after the issue of the proclamation revoke its assent and thereby destroy the amendment.

(e) Compensation for opting out

Section 40 provides as follows:

> 40. Where an amendment is made under subsection 38(1) that transfers provincial legislative powers relating to education or other cultural matters from provincial legislatures to Parliament, Canada shall provide reasonable compensation to any province to which the amendment does not apply.

Section 40 imposes upon the federal government the obligation to provide ''reasonable compensation'' to any province that has opted out of an amendment that transfers ''provincial legislative powers relating to education or other cultural matters'' from the provincial Legislatures to the federal Parliament. The purpose of this obligation is to ensure that a province is not pressured by financial considerations into abandoning jurisdiction over educational or cultural matters. For example, if an amendment transferring legislative authority over universities from the provincial Legislatures to the federal Parliament could obtain the requisite two-thirds provincial support, in the absence of s. 40 there would be a powerful incentive on non-agreeing provinces not to opt out, because opting out would involve bearing a substantial expense (the cost of running the universities) from which other provincial governments would be freed by the amendment. With s. 40 in the Constitution Act, 1982, a province is freed from financial considerations in deciding whether or not to opt out of the amendment.

Amendments that do not relate to education or cultural matters do not carry any constitutional right to compensation for opting out. Take the example given earlier of an amendment transferring legislative authority over ''the regulation of product standards'' from the provincial Legislatures to the federal Parliament. If a province opted out of this amendment, it would have to continue to bear the cost of regulating product standards, a cost which in other provinces would now be borne by the federal government. It is in fact quite likely that the opting-out province would be successful in negotiating compensation (either in the form of extra tax room or a cash grant) for this extra burden,[76] but it could not invoke any constitutional right to compensation.

It will be recalled that the Vancouver formula, which was the first version of the present amending procedures, provided a right to compensation for opting out of all amendments. This part of the Vancouver formula was dropped in the federal-provincial agreement of November 5, 1981. Section 40 is a compromise

76 See ch. 6, Financial Arrangements, below.

between universal compensation and no compensation; it singles out education and culture because of their special significance to Quebec. Section 40 was agreed to by the Prime Minister and the nine Premiers of the English-speaking provinces after the agreement of November 5, 1981 in an attempt to make the amending formula more attractive to Quebec. However, the inclusion of s. 40 did not soften Quebec's opposition to the amending formula.[77]

(f) Revocation of assent or dissent

A resolution of assent may be revoked only before the issue of the proclamation authorized by the resolution (s. 46(2)). A revocation of assent after the issue of the proclamation cannot be permitted, because that would render every amendment permanently vulnerable to abrogation by the action of a single province or a few provinces.

A resolution of dissent (an opting-out resolution), on the other hand, may be revoked at any time, before or after the issue of the proclamation (s. 38(4)). A revocation of dissent after the issue of the proclamation is not objectionable, because it simply has the effect of extending to the opted-out province an amendment which is already applicable to the other provinces. Indeed, the checkerboard effect of opting out is so obviously undesirable that no obstacle should be raised to an opted-out province which, perhaps after a change of government, has now decided to opt in.

(g) Section 42

The point has already been made that the general amending procedure (the seven-fifty formula) is the correct one for the residual class of amendments which are not covered by the more specific procedures of ss. 41, 43, 44 and 45. In addition, s. 42 requires that the general amending procedure be used for six defined classes of amendments to the Constitution of Canada. Section 42 provides as follows:

> 42.(1) An amendment to the Constitution of Canada in relation to the following matters may be made only in accordance with subsection 38(1):
> (a) the principle of proportionate representation of the provinces in the House of Commons prescribed by the Constitution of Canada;
> (b) the powers of the Senate and the method of selecting Senators;
> (c) the number of members by which a province is entitled to be represented in the Senate and the residence qualifications of Senators;
> (d) subject to paragraph 41(d), the Supreme Court of Canada;
> (e) the extension of existing provinces into the territories; and

77 See note 24, above. Both the unsuccessful Meech Lake Accord of 1987, note 37, above, and the unsuccessful Charlottetown Accord of 1992, note 41, above, would have amended s. 40 so that the right to compensation would apply to all transfers of provincial legislative powers, not just those relating to education or other cultural matters.

(f) notwithstanding any other law or practice, the establishment of new provinces.

(2) Subsections 38(2) to (4) do not apply in respect of amendments in relation to matters referred to in subsection (1).

Section 42(1) lists six matters in respect of which an amendment to the Constitution of Canada may be made only in accordance with the general amending procedure of s. 38(1) (two-thirds provinces with 50 per cent population). Like ss. 38 and 41, s. 42 applies only to amendments to the "Constitution of Canada".[78]

Paragraph (a) of s. 42(1) refers to "the principle of proportionate representation of the provinces in the House of Commons". The principle of proportionate representation in the House of Commons was an essential element of the confederation scheme of 1867.[79] However, the principle has never been applied rigidly, and in 1915[80] the "Senate floor" of s. 51A was introduced into the Constitution Act, 1867, which guaranteed to each province a minimum number of Commons seats equal to the number of the province's Senate seats. The purpose was to limit the decline in representation of the maritime provinces that was caused by the relative decline in their populations. In 1985, the Representation Act, 1985, repealed and replaced s. 51 of the Constitution Act, 1867, which is the provision that provides for a readjustment of representation in the House of Commons every ten years, following a census, and provides the formula for that readjustment. The new s. 51 included a grandfather clause, which guaranteed that provinces with declining populations would not lose any seats on a readjustment. The effect of this clause was to further compromise the principle of representation by population. In *Campbell* v. *Canada* (1988),[81] it was held that a provision to protect the representation of declining provinces should not be regarded as offending "the principle" of proportionate representation, and did not require a seven-fifty amendment under s. 42(1)(a). The Act was to be characterized as a law in relation to the House of Commons; and it was a valid exercise of the federal Parliament's unilateral amending power under s. 44.

Paragraphs (b) and (c) of s. 42(1) refer to the powers of the Senate, the method of selecting senators and provincial representation in the Senate. These are all matters that (at least in theory) have significance to the provinces as well as to the central government. The effect of paras. (b) and (c) is to withdraw these matters from the federal Parliament's unilateral amending power under s. 44, and to require that any amendment be adopted by the seven-fifty formula of s. 38.

Paragraph (d) of s. 42(1) refers to the Supreme Court of Canada in all aspects other than its composition (which is specifically listed in s. 41(d) — the unanimity amendment procedure). The reference to the Supreme Court of Canada is puzzling, because, unlike the other matters listed in s. 42(1), the Supreme Court of

78 See sec. 4.2(c), "Constitution of Canada", above.

79 See ch. 2, Reception, under heading 2.4, "Confederation", above.

80 Constitution Act, 1915, R.S.C. 1985, Appendix II, No. 23.

81 (1988) 49 D.L.R. (4th) 321 (B.C.C.A.).

Canada is nowhere provided for in the Constitution of Canada. The Court is constituted by the Supreme Court Act, and the Supreme Court Act is a federal statute that is not one of the instruments forming part of the Constitution of Canada. Since s. 42 applies only to amendments to the "Constitution of Canada", it follows that the federal Parliament, acting under s. 101 of the Constitution Act, 1867, still has the power to amend the Supreme Court Act.[82] That power would cease, and s. 42(d) would become effective, if (as has often been advocated) steps were taken to adopt the Supreme Court of Canada into the Constitution of Canada.[83]

Paragraph (e) of s. 42(1) refers to the extension of existing provinces into the territories, and paragraph (f) to the establishment of new provinces. It is probably wrong to treat these paragraphs as requiring the seven-fifty formula for the extension of existing provinces or the establishment of new provinces. The Constitution Act, 1871, by s. 2, authorizes the federal Parliament to establish new provinces in federal territories, and, by s. 3, authorizes the federal Parliament, with the consent of a province, to extend the boundaries of a province. These provisions were not repealed or amended in 1982, and can still be operated without any change in the Constitution of Canada. The effect of paras. (e) and (f) of s. 42(1) is to protect ss. 2 and 3 of the Constitution Act, 1871 from repeal or amendment, except by the seven-fifty formula.[84]

Section 42(2) prohibits any province from opting out of amendments coming within s. 42. Thus, Quebec could not opt out of, let alone block, an amendment to the House of Commons or Supreme Court of Canada coming within s. 42(1), if the amendment was approved by the federal Parliament and seven provinces representing 50 per cent of the population. This illustrates the inferior protection provided to Quebec by the opting-out provision (even if accompanied by full compensation) in comparison with a veto over constitutional amendments.[85]

---

82 Note 61, above.

83 Texts were proposed in the unsuccessful Meech Lake Accord, note 37, above, and in the unsuccessful Charlottetown Accord, note 41, above.

84 In the 2nd edition of this book (1985), at p. 63, I took the position that ss. 2 and 3 of the Constitution Act, 1871 should be regarded as impliedly repealed by s. 42(1) (e) and (f). I now think that that position gives insufficient weight to the fact that s. 42(1) is directed only to amendments of the Constitution of Canada, and the extension of provinces and the establishment of new provinces requires no amendment of the Constitution of Canada. The position is not totally clear, however, especially having regard to the obscure notwithstanding clause in s. 42(1)(f). Other constitutional issues that would need to be resolved on the establishment of a new province are: representation in the Senate; representation in the House of Commons; and (perhaps) a modification of the amending formula.

85 Quebec would have obtained a veto under the Victoria Charter formula, which was abandoned in 1982 for the current formula: notes 21-26 and accompanying text, above. The unsuccessful Meech Lake Accord, note 37, above, would have moved the s. 42 list (of matters relating to the structure and central institutions of federalism) into s. 41, thereby requiring unanimity for their amendment and giving a veto to Quebec (and every other province).

(h) "Regional veto" statute

The general (seven-fifty) amending formula of s. 38 does not give any province a veto over constitutional amendments. It will be recalled that this was a conscious choice in 1982, when the Vancouver formula, which was based on the equality of the provinces, was preferred over the Victoria Charter formula, which was based on a system of regional vetoes (with Quebec as one of the required regions).[86] The fact that the seven-fifty formula does not give Quebec a veto has been occasionally advanced as a criticism of the Constitution Act, 1982. (However, it should be recalled that Premier Levesque of Quebec was one of the eight provincial premiers that had urged the adoption of the Vancouver formula, and persuaded Prime Minister Trudeau to shift his support away from the Victoria Charter formula.)[87] The Meech Lake and Charlottetown Accords had not proposed a reversion to the Victoria Charter formula: they had proposed a widening of the categories of amendments for which the unanimity procedure (a veto for all provinces) was required, and an extension of the right to compensation for opting out of amendments.[88]

After the narrow defeat of Quebec's 1995 referendum on sovereignty, the federal Parliament enacted a statute to ensure that Quebec would in future have a veto over most constitutional amendments. However, instead of revisiting the measures proposed in the Meech Lake and Charlottetown Accords, or conferring a veto on Quebec alone, the statute went back to the regional veto idea of the Victoria formula. The regional veto statute[89] provides as follows:

> No Minister of the Crown shall propose a motion for a resolution to authorize an amendment to the Constitution of Canada, other than an amendment in respect of which the legislative assembly of a province may exercise a veto under section 41 or 43 of the *Constitution Act, 1982* or may express its dissent under subsection 38(3) of that Act, unless the amendment has first been consented to by a majority of the provinces that includes
> (a) Ontario;
> (b) Quebec;
> (c) British Columbia;
> (d) two or more of the Atlantic provinces that have, according to the then latest general census, combined populations of at least fifty per cent of the population of all the Atlantic provinces; and
> (e) two or more of the Prairie provinces that have, according to the then latest census, combined populations of at least fifty per cent of the population of all the Prairie provinces.

---

86 See sec. 4.1(b), "The search for a domestic amending procedure", above.

87 The formula as enacted differed slightly from the Vancouver proposal, in particular, by limiting the entitlement to compensation for opting out: see sec. 4.3(e), "Compensation for opting out", above.

88 Note 100, below.

89 S.C. 1996, c. 1. The Act does not have an official short title. Its long title is "An Act respecting constitutional amendments".

The purpose of the statute is to import new conditions into the general (seven-fifty) formula for amending the Constitution of Canada. On top of the *constitutional* requirement of support by seven provinces representing 50 per cent of the population, the statute imposes the new *statutory* requirement that the seven agreeing provinces must include the five "regions" stipulated in the Act, namely, Ontario, Quebec, British Columbia, two Atlantic provinces and two Prairie provinces.[90]

The statute accomplishes its purpose indirectly. A direct alteration of the procedures for amending the Constitution could only be accomplished by constitutional amendment. As is explained in the next section of this chapter, an amendment of the amending procedures is one of the matters that requires the unanimous consent of Parliament and the provincial legislatures pursuant to s. 41(e) of the Constitution Act, 1982. So this Act purports to control only the action of Ministers of the Crown, who must refrain from proposing that Parliament adopt a resolution for a constitutional amendment unless the requirements of the statute have first been met.[91] Under the general (seven-fifty) procedure, resolutions of assent must be passed by both Houses of Parliament (unless the Senate has been by-passed under s. 47). The statute does not prohibit someone other than a Minister of the Crown from introducing a resolution for a constitutional amendment that lacks the regional support required by the statute, and it does not prohibit the Houses of Parliament from passing such a resolution.[92] But the political reality is that a resolution on a matter as important as amending the Constitution of Canada would be unlikely to pass if it had not been initiated by the government of the day, that is, by a Minister of the Crown. By binding Ministers of the Crown to its provisions, this statute effectively adds its own conditions to the general procedure for amending the Constitution. This means that all five of the "regions" defined by the statute must have given their consent to a proposed constitutional amendment before a Minister of the Crown is permitted to introduce a resolution of approval into either of the Houses of Parliament. The regions thereby obtain a veto by

---

90 The statutory regions differ from those in the Victoria Charter in two respects. First, British Columbia was not recognized as a separate region in the Victoria Charter, which required the assent of two of the "Western provinces" having a combined population of 50 per cent of all the Western provinces. By treating British Columbia as a separate region, the statute effectively grants Alberta a veto too, since its population exceeds that of the combined populations of Saskatchewan and Manitoba, the other Prairie provinces. Secondly, there was no requirement in the Victoria Charter that the two Atlantic provinces had to represent 50 per cent of the populations of all the Atlantic provinces. Under the Victoria Charter, any two Atlantic provinces would do.

91 The power of Parliament to enact such a statute probably comes from the peace, order, and good government power (see ch. 17, Peace, Order and Good Government, below), or possibly s. 44 of the Constitution Act, 1982 (see sec. 4.6, "Federal Parliament alone (s. 44)", below).

92 A statute that purported to restrict the discretion of the Houses of Parliament to pass future resolutions for constitutional amendments would be constitutionally suspect: see ch. 12, Parliamentary Sovereignty, under heading 12.3, "Self-imposed restraints on legislative power", below.

proxy. Of course, since the veto is statutory only, it could be repealed or amended by Parliament at any time in the future.

The regional veto statute only applies to amendments that are to follow the general (seven-fifty) amending procedure of s. 38, and that do not afford a dissenting province the constitutional right to ''opt out''. Amendments that require unanimity under s. 41, or that must be ratified by some-but-not-all provinces under s. 43, are expressly excluded. Amendments that come within the exclusive jurisdiction of the federal Parliament under s. 44 are excluded by implication, since s. 44 speaks of amendment by ''laws'' rather than by ''resolutions''. And amendments that are competent to the provinces alone under s. 45 are not affected by the statute, because they require no action by the Parliament of Canada.

The regional veto statute was hastily conceived and implemented after the Quebec sovereignty referendum of 1995. It was designed to achieve through federal legislation what the failed Meech and Charlottetown Accords had been unable to achieve through constitutional amendment, namely, a greater role for Quebec over future amendments of the Constitution. At the same time, a resolution recognizing Quebec as a ''distinct society'' was passed by the House of Commons—another matter that the Meech and Charlottetown Accords would have put into the Constitution. Even by the standard of accommodating the concerns of Quebec, the regional veto statute was probably an unwise initiative, because it makes the Constitution even more difficult to amend, and further reduces the faint hope of genuine constitutional change. For example, before the Act was enacted, the seven-fifty procedure[93] would have enabled a distinct society clause to be put into the Constitution without the assents of British Columbia or Alberta, where opposition to this element of the Meech Lake and Charlottetown Accords was most intense. The Act would now require the assents of both those provinces, since British Columbia is recognized as a region and Alberta has more than 50 per cent of the population of the Prairie provinces.

4.4 Unanimity procedure (s. 41)

Section 41 of the Constitution Act, 1982 provides as follows:

> 41. An amendment to the Constitution of Canada in relation to the following matters may be made by proclamation issued by the Governor General under the Great Seal of Canada only where authorized by resolutions of the Senate and House of Commons and of the legislative assembly of each province:
>
> (a) the office of the Queen, the Governor General and the Lieutenant Governor of a province;
>
> (b) the right of a province to a number of members in the House of Commons not less than the number of Senators by which the province is entitled to be represented at the time this Part comes into force;

93 It is possible that a distinct society clause could be put into the Constitution under s. 43, that is, with the consent of only Quebec and the federal Parliament, but the conventional wisdom is that the seven-fifty formula is required.

(c) subject to section 43, the use of the English or the French language;
(d) the composition of the Supreme Court of Canada; and
(e) an amendment to this Part.

Section 41 lists five matters in respect of which an amendment to the Constitution of Canada[94] requires the unanimous support of the provinces, as opposed to the two-thirds majority called for by the general amending procedure of s. 38(1). In respect of these matters, each province has a veto over amendments. The five listed topics are specially entrenched because they are deemed to be matters of national significance which should not be altered over the objection of even one province.

Paragraph (a) — "the office of the Queen, the Governor General and the Lieutenant Governor of a province" — has the effect of entrenching those provisions of the Constitution of Canada that deal with the monarchy and its representatives in Canada. If this topic were not listed in s. 41, it would be arguable that changes could be made for Canada by the federal Parliament alone under s. 44, and for a province by the provincial Legislature alone under s. 45.

Paragraph (b) of s. 41 entrenches the right of the least populous provinces to a minimum number of members in the House of Commons, thereby modifying the relentless application of representation by population. This provision, called the "Senate floor", was established, to limit the declining representation of the maritime provinces,[95] by the British North America Act, 1915,[96] which added a new s. 51A to the B.N.A. Act (now the Constitution Act, 1867). If s. 51A were not protected by s. 41, it would be arguable that it could be repealed or amended by the federal Parliament alone under s. 44.

Paragraph (c) of s. 41 entrenches those provisions of the Constitution of Canada that make provision for "the use of the English or French language".[97]

Paragraph (d) of s. 41 entrenches "the composition of the Supreme Court of Canada". The term "composition" is not entirely clear: the total number of judges, and the number of judges who must be drawn from a particular region,

94 See sec. 4.2(c), "Constitution of Canada", above.

95 Dawson, *The Government of Canada* (6th ed. by Ward, 1970), 89-90; *Campbell* v. *Can.* (1988) 49 D.L.R. (4th) 321, 324-327 (B.C.C.A.). At the present time, this provision benefits Prince Edward Island and New Brunswick.

96 Constitution Act, 1915, R.S.C. 1985, Appendix II, No. 23.

97 There are provisions of the Constitution of Canada in relation to the use of the English or French language in s. 133 of the Constitution Act, 1867, s. 23 of the Manitoba Act, 1870, and ss. 16 to 23 and 55 to 57 of the Constitution Act, 1982. However, not all of these provisions are caught by paragraph (c) of s. 41. Paragraph (c) is expressly subject to s. 43, which provides for the some-but-not-all-provinces procedure (discussed next). Section 43(b) covers those language provisions that apply to one or more but not all provinces and that relate to the use of the English or French language within a province. Many of the language provisions are in this category, and, once they are subtracted, the unanimity requirement of s. 41(c) applies only to s. 133 of the Constitution Act, 1867 in its application to federal institutions (but not Quebec institutions) and ss. 16(1), 16(3), 17(1), 18(1), 19(1), 20(1), 21, 22, 23 and 55 to 57 of the Constitution Act, 1982. See also note 105 below.

are probably aspects of composition; the mode of appointment is probably not.[98] However, since s. 41 applies only to amendments to the "Constitution of Canada", and since the rules regarding the composition of the Supreme Court of Canada are contained in the Supreme Court Act, which is not part of the "Constitution of Canada", paragraph (d) is probably ineffective. The composition of the Supreme Court of Canada can still be changed by the ordinary legislative process of the Parliament of Canada.[99]

Paragraph (e) provides that any amendment to the amending procedures themselves ("this Part" being Part V of the Constitution Act, 1982) can only be effected by the unanimity procedure of s. 41. Section 49 of the Constitution Act, 1982 also stipulates that the amending procedures must be reviewed at a constitutional conference to be held within 15 years of April 17, 1982 (when the Constitution Act, 1982 came into force). It is now apparent that s. 49 has expired without any alteration of the amending formula, a result which is not surprising in view of the unanimity requirement.[100]

An amendment made under the unanimity procedure of s. 41 is brought into force by a proclamation of the Governor General. However, the time-limits prescribed by s. 39 for the issue of the proclamation apply only to amendments made under the general (seven-fifty) procedure. It is easy to see why an amendment under the unanimity procedure should be able to be proclaimed in force without waiting for a minimum period of one year to elapse: since all legislative bodies have approved, there is no point in delay. It is not, however, easy to see why the maximum period of three years does not apply to amendments covered by the unanimity procedure; yet the three-year time limit of s. 39(2) is expressly applicable only to amendments under s. 38(1) — the general procedure. This means that the process of legislative ratification of an amendment covered by s. 41 — the unanimity procedure — is subject to no time limit. If it takes more than three years to secure all the required approvals, the amendment can still be proclaimed into law.

The Meech Lake Accord of 1987[101] raised an interesting point of interpretation regarding the three-year time-limit. The Accord was a package of related

98 Cheffins, note 50, above.

99 See sec. 4.2(c), "Constitution of Canada", above.

100 Proposals for changing the amending procedures were part of the unsuccessful Meech Lake Accord of 1987, note 37, above, and the unsuccessful Charlottetown Accord of 1992, note 41, above. Each would have effected two changes: (1) the expansion of the right to compensation for opting out in s. 40, so that it was no longer limited to education or other cultural matters; and (2) the expansion of the unanimity procedure of s. 41, so that it included the matters listed in s. 42 as well. Parliament effected an indirect *statutory* alteration of the general (seven-fifty) amending procedures by its passage of a 1996 Act; see sec. 4.3(h), "Regional veto statute", above. However, there was no *constitutional* change to the amending formulas before the April 1997 deadline. According to Prime Minister Chrétien, the obligation to reconsider the amending procedures was "discharged" after a brief discussion at a June 21, 1996 First Ministers' Conference: *The [Toronto] Globe and Mail* (22 June 1996).

101 Note 37, above.

amendments, some of which were subject to the seven-fifty procedure, and others of which (dealing with the Supreme Court of Canada and the amending procedures) were subject to the unanimity procedure. In order to bring the entire package into force, obviously the unanimity procedure had to be employed. Did this mean that no time-limit applied to the ratification of the Accord? Probably, the answer to that question was no: the existence within the package of seven-fifty amendments required that the time-limit be adhered to. Certainly, that was the view that was generally held, and the Accord was treated as having lapsed when two provincial legislative assemblies were still debating the Accord at the expiry of three years from the date of the initiating resolution.

4.5 Some-but-not-all-provinces procedure (s. 43)

Section 43 of the Constitution Act, 1982 provides as follows:

> 43. An amendment to the Constitution of Canada in relation to any provision that applies to one or more, but not all, provinces, including
> (a) any alteration to boundaries between provinces, and
> (b) any amendment to any provision that relates to the use of the English or the French language within a province,
>
> may be made by proclamation issued by the Governor General under the Great Seal of Canada only where so authorized by resolutions of the Senate and House of Commons and of the legislative assembly of each province to which the amendment applies.

There are provisions of the Constitution of Canada[102] which apply to one or more, but not all, provinces. For example, s. 93 of the Constitution Act, 1867 (education) applies to only six of the ten provinces; a similar but separate provision in each of the Manitoba Act, Alberta Act, Saskatchewan Act and Newfoundland Act (all included in the Constitution of Canada) applies to each of the other four provinces. Section 94 of the Constitution Act, 1867 (uniformity of laws) does not apply to Quebec. Section 97 of the Constitution Act, 1867 (qualifications of judges) does not apply to Quebec; s. 98 (on the same topic) applies only to Quebec. A number of language provisions apply only to Quebec or Manitoba or New Brunswick.[103] For the amendment of provisions of this kind, s. 43 requires authorizing resolutions of only those provinces to which the provision applies (as well as the Senate and House of Commons).[104] The obvious intent is to make such provisions somewhat easier to amend, but the ease of amendment will depend upon the number of provinces involved. In the case of s. 97 of the Constitution Act, 1867, which

---

102 See sec. 4.2(b), ''Constitution of Canada'', above.

103 Section 133 of the Constitution Act, 1867 applies only to Quebec (and the federal government), and s. 23 of the Manitoba Act applies only to Manitoba, and ss. 16(2), 17(2), 18(2), 19(2) and 20(2) of the Constitution Act, 1982 apply only to New Brunswick. See also note 97, above.

104 The procedure has been used three times since 1982: ch. 1, Sources, under heading 1.4, ''Constitution of Canada'', above.

is applicable to all provinces except Quebec, s. 43 would seem to require authorizing resolutions from all nine of the provinces to which it applies — a procedure that is more onerous than the seven-fifty requirement of s. 38.

Section 43 expressly applies to a provision of the Constitution of Canada which applies to only one province. The Constitution Act, 1867, which, it will be recalled, created Ontario and Quebec out of the old united province of Canada, contains a set of provisions (ss. 69 to 87) which are essentially the constitutions of those two provinces. Section 88 arguably incorporates by reference the pre-confederation constitutions of Nova Scotia and New Brunswick. The Constitution Act, 1867 is part of the Constitution of Canada, and therefore these provisions are part of the Constitution of Canada. As well, the instruments admitting or creating the remaining six provinces are part of the Constitution of Canada. Section 43, read by itself, seems to insist that any part of the constitution of a province that is to be found within the Constitution of Canada may be amended only by the procedure stipulated by s. 43; that procedure includes resolutions by the Senate and House of Commons. This is a strange result, because there is no good reason for any involvement by the federal Parliament in a province's decision to make some change in those provisions governing its Legislature, its executive or its courts, which happen to be within an instrument which is part of the Constitution of Canada.

Before the coming into force of the Constitution Act, 1982, a province was free to amend any part of the constitution of the province, including those parts provided for in the Constitution Act, 1867, without any federal involvement. Section 92(1) of the Constitution Act, 1867 authorized the Legislature of each province, by ordinary legislation, to amend the constitution of the province, "notwithstanding anything in this Act [the Constitution Act, 1867]". Section 92(1) has been repealed by the Constitution Act, 1982, and replaced by s. 45 of the Constitution Act, 1982, but s. 45 does not expressly authorize amendments to the Constitution of Canada. Section 43, on the other hand, does expressly authorize amendments to provisions of the Constitution of Canada that apply to only one province. One way of reconciling s. 43 with s. 45 would be to read s. 43 as applying to an amendment of a provision applying to a single province when that provision is contained in one of the instruments which comprise the Constitution of Canada, and to read s. 45 as applying to an amendment of the "constitution of the province" only when the provision to be amended is not to be found in any of the instruments comprising the Constitution of Canada. Nevertheless, I argue in the commentary to s. 45 (below) that s. 45 should be read as extending to the amendment of those provisions of the Constitution of Canada which can also be characterized as part of the constitution of the province. If this is correct, then s. 43 would be necessary to amend provisions of the Constitution of Canada which apply to only one province only if the provisions could not be characterized as part of the constitution of the province.[105]

4.6 Federal Parliament alone (s. 44)

Section 44 of the Constitution Act, 1982 provides as follows:

> 44. Subject to sections 41 and 42, Parliament may exclusively make laws amending the Constitution of Canada in relation to the executive government of Canada or the Senate and House of Commons.

Section 44 authorizes the federal Parliament, by ordinary legislation, to amend those parts of the Constitution of Canada[106] which relate to "the executive government of Canada or the Senate and House of Commons". Section 44 is subject to ss. 41 and 42 and those two sections entrench some aspects of the executive government of Canada, the Senate and House of Commons. The matters listed in s. 41 (which include the office of the Queen and the Governor General and the minimum provincial representation in the House of Commons) can be amended only with the unanimous consent of the provinces. The matters listed in s. 42 (which include some of the rules regarding the Senate and House of Commons) can be amended only by the general amending procedure of s. 38(1), which requires the consent of two-thirds of the provinces having at least 50 per cent of the population.[107]

Section 44 replaced s. 91(1) of the Constitution Act, 1867.[108] Section 91(1) was repealed by the Constitution Act, 1982. Section 91(1) conferred on the federal Parliament the power to amend the "Constitution of Canada". That phrase was

---

105 For example, even before 1982 it was held that language rights applicable to a single province are not part of the constitution of the province, because that would render them vulnerable to ordinary legislative change: *A.G. Que.* v. *Blaikie* [1979] 2 S.C.R. 1016; *A.G. Man.* v. *Forest* [1979] 2 S.C.R. 1032. Now, of course, s. 43(b) makes that explicit.

106 See sec. 4.2(b), "Constitution of Canada", above.

107 With respect to proportionate representation in the House of Commons, see *Campbell* v. *Can.*, note 81, above.

108 The text of s. 91(1) was as follows:

> The amendment from time to time of the Constitution of Canada, except as regards matters coming within the classes of subjects by this Act assigned exclusively to the Legislatures of the provinces, or as regards rights or privileges by this or any other Constitutional Act granted or secured to the Legislature or the Government of a province, or to any class of persons with respect to schools or as regards the use of the English or the French language or as regards the requirements that there shall be a session of the Parliament of Canada at least once each year, and that no House of Commons shall continue for more than five years from the day of the return of the Writs for choosing the House: provided, however, that a House of Commons may in time of real or apprehended war, invasion or insurrection be continued by the Parliament of Canada if such continuation is not opposed by the votes of more than one-third of the members of such House.

then undefined;[109] it was however given a very narrow meaning by the Supreme Court of Canada,[110] and it was subject to important exceptions which were expressed in s. 91(1) itself. The result is that the scope of s. 44 is similar to the scope of the old s. 91(1).[111]

4.7 Provincial Legislature alone (s. 45)

Section 45 of the Constitution Act, 1982 provides as follows:

> 45. Subject to section 41, the legislature of each province may exclusively make laws amending the constitution of the province.

Section 45 authorizes each provincial Legislature, by ordinary legislation, to amend the "constitution of the province". Section 45 is subject to s. 41, which by paragraph (a) requires that an amendment relating to the office of the Lieutenant Governor be made only with the unanimous consent of all the provinces. Section 45 differs from ss. 38, 41, 42, 43 and 44 in that s. 45 makes no reference to the "Constitution of Canada", a term which is defined in s. 52(2) of the Constitution Act, 1982. Instead, s. 45 refers to the "constitution of the province", which is not defined anywhere in the Constitution Act, 1982.

Section 45 replaced s. 92(1) of the Constitution Act, 1867.[112] Section 92(1) was repealed by the Constitution Act, 1982. Section 92(1) conferred on each provincial Legislature the power to amend the "constitution of the province". Subject to the doubt expressed in the next paragraph, the case-law under s. 92(1)[113] should continue to be relevant under s. 45.[114] Interpreting s. 92(1), the Supreme Court of Canada has said that a law is an amendment to the constitution of the province if "it bears on the operation of an organ of government of the province".[115] This definition embraces laws respecting the public service of the

---

109 It was defined for the first time in s. 52(2) of the Constitution Act, 1982.

110 *Re Upper House* [1980] 1 S.C.R. 54 (holding that s. 91(1) did not authorize the abolition or alteration of the Senate). For criticism of the decision, and analysis of the history and scope of s. 91(1) generally, see Hogg, Comment (1980) 58 Can. Bar Rev. 631.

111 In order to make the comparison, s. 44 must be read with s. 4 (restricting the extension of the House of Commons) and s. 41(c) (requiring unanimity for amendments relating to language).

112 The text of s. 92(1) was as follows:

> The amendment from time to time, notwithstanding anything in this Act, of the constitution of the province, except as regards the office of Lieutenant Governor.

113 See Forsey, *Freedom and Order* (1974), 205-207, 227; McConnell, *Commentary on the B.N.A. Act* (1977), 245-248; Banks, "Defining 'Constitution of the province'" (1986) 31 McGill L.J. 466.

114 *OPSEU* v. *Ont.* [1987] 2 S.C.R, 2, 33, per Beetz J. ("It may well be thought that the coming into force of the amending procedure has not altered the power of the province to amend its own constitution but I refrain from expressing any view on the matter").

115 *Id.*, 40.

province,[116] the powers and privileges of the legislative assembly,[117] and the term of the legislative assembly.[118] Some laws are expressly or impliedly withdrawn from the amending power of the province. The office of Lieutenant Governor was expressly exempted from 92(1),[119] and is also expressly exempted from s. 45.[120] The constitutional guarantees of language rights were held to be implicitly withdrawn from the provincial amending power in s. 92(1),[121] and are now explicitly withdrawn from s. 45.[122] It has been suggested as well that s. 92(1) would not authorize ''a profound constitutional upheaval by the introduction of political institutions foreign to and incompatible with the Canadian system''.[123]

The scope of s. 45 is somewhat obscured by s. 43 (the some-but-not-all-provinces procedure). As noted in the commentary to s. 43,[124] s. 43 explicitly authorizes an amendment to any provision of the Constitution of Canada which applies to a single province, and most of the important rules of each province's constitution are contained in instruments which form part of the Constitution of Canada.[125] But s. 43 requires the concurrence of the Senate and House of Commons for its amendments. The question is whether s. 45, which does not require the concurrence of the Senate and House of Commons, can be employed to amend those provisions of a province's constitution that are contained in instruments forming part of the Constitution of Canada. A negative answer to this question would mean that s. 45 was for no good reason much narrower than the old provincial amending power under s. 92(1), which extended to provisions of those instruments which are now called the ''Constitution of Canada''.[126] Indeed, a negative answer would leave s. 45 with very little work to do. The affirmative

116 *Ibid.*
117 *Fielding* v. *Thomas* [1896] A.C. 600; but see note 127, below.
118 *R. ex rel. Tolfree* v. *Clark* [1943] O.R. 501 (C.A.), but note that since 1982 there has been an express limitation to five years in s. 3 of the Charter of Rights.
119 This exception defeated the regime of direct democracy in *Re Initiative and Referendum Act* [1919] A.C. 935, although it was successfully circumvented in *R.* v. *Nat Bell Liquors* [1922] 2 A.C. 128. These cases are discussed in ch. 14, Delegation, ss. 14.2(d) and 14.2(e), below.
120 Section 45 is expressly subject to s. 41, which requires the unanimity procedure for amendments to the Constitution of Canada in relation to ''the office of ... the Lieutenant Governor of a province''.
121 Note 105, above.
122 Sections 41(c), 43(b).
123 *OPSEU* v. *Ont.* [1987] 2 S.C.R. 2, 47, citing *Re Initiative and Referendum Act* [1919] A.C. 935.
124 Section 4.5, ''Some-but-not-all-provinces procedure (s. 43)'', above.
125 The origins and sources of the constitutions of the provinces are described in ch. 2, Reception, above.
126 For example, Quebec has amended s. 71 of the Constitution Act, 1867 by abolishing its upper house: Legislative Council of Quebec Act, S.Q. 1968, c. 9; and Ontario and Quebec have amended s. 85 of the Constitution Act, 1867 by extending the term of each legislative assembly from four years to five: Legislative Assembly Act, R.S.O. 1980, c. 235, s. 3; Legislature Act, R.S.Q. 1977, c. L-1, s. 31. The Ontario extension of term was upheld in *R. ex rel. Tolfree* v. *Clark* [1943] O.R. 501 (C.A.).

answer seems the more plausible one, leaving s. 43 to apply to only those provisions of the Constitution of Canada which, although applicable to only one province, do not come within the phrase the ''constitution of the province''.[127]

4.8 Future amendments

(a) Forces of change

The movement for constitutional reform which led to the constitutional amendments of 1982, and which will lead to continuing efforts to adopt other amendments to the Constitution, is powered by a number of forces.[128]

First and foremost is French-Canadian nationalism.[129] French Canadians are a minority in the nation as a whole, but a majority in the province of Quebec. Their distinctive language and culture, nurtured by the memory of the conquest by the English and the constant danger of assimilation, has made them anxious to be masters in their own house. This inevitably leads to demands for greater power in the provincial Legislature in Quebec City — the Legislature that is controlled by a French-Canadian majority.

The extreme form of French-Canadian nationalism would be satisfied only by a separate nation in the territory of Quebec. On May 20, 1980, Quebecers voted in a referendum on a proposal to give to the government of Quebec a mandate to negotiate a sovereignty-association agreement with Canada. This proposal, which of course was far from a proposal of outright separation, was defeated by a majority of 59.5 per cent to 40.5 per cent.[130] However, the promises of constitutional change which were made by the ''no'' forces during the referendum campaign created a moral obligation to take steps to better accommodate Quebec's aspirations. Unfortunately, the constitutional amendments of 1982, which were the culmination of the process which followed the referendum, did not accomplish that goal; indeed, they reduced the powers of Quebec's National Assembly; and Quebec was the only province that did not agree to the amend-

---

127 Contra, *New Brunswick Broadcasting Co.* v. *Nova Scotia* [1993] 1 S.C.R. 319, 352 per Lamer C.J. obiter, 396 per Sopinka J. obiter, assuming that if parliamentary privilege were part of the ''Constitution of Canada'', as held by the majority, the provincial Legislature would have lost the power to amend it.

128 This section of the chapter draws to some extent on my article, ''The Theory and Practice of Constitutional Reform'' (1981) 3 Alta. L. Rev. 335; see also Lysyk, ''Reshaping Canadian Federalism'' (1979) 3 U.B.C. L. Rev. 1; Weiler, ''Confederation Discontents and Constitutional Reform'' (1979) 29 U. Toronto L.J. 253; The Task Force on Canadian Unity, *A Future Together* (1979).

129 For the recent history of Quebec within confederation, see McWhinney, *Quebec and the Constitution 1960-1978* (1979); McWhinney, *Canada and the Constitution 1979-1982* (1982); McRoberts, *Quebec: Social Change and Political Crisis* (3rd ed., 1988); Tremblay, *La Réforme de la Constitution au Canada* (1995).

130 See ch. 5, Federalism, under heading 5.7, ''Secession'', below.

ments. Even more unfortunately, the Meech Lake Accord of 1987, which was a set of amendments that would have reconciled Quebec to the Constitution of Canada, fell two provinces short of the unanimous ratification that was required for its passage.[131] The Charlottetown Accord of 1992 was another set of amendments with the same purpose; this Accord was agreed to by all first ministers, but was rejected in a national referendum, and never proceeded to legislative ratification.[132] The failure to accommodate the concerns of Quebecers in the Constitution of Canada led to a second Quebec referendum, on October 30, 1995.[133] That referendum proposed the negotiation of a "new economic and political partnership" between Canada and a sovereign Quebec, but it went beyond the 1980 referendum in authorizing the Quebec National Assembly to make a unilateral declaration of independence if negotiations should prove fruitless. The referendum was defeated again, but this time the vote was very close: 50.6 per cent for "no" and 49.4 per cent for "yes". After the close result, the Parti Québécois government announced that it would try again, with yet another referendum, although it would wait until after the next provincial election. Obviously, the need to better accommodate the concerns of Quebecers has taken on a truly urgent character, and has to take priority over any other constitutional change.

A second force of constitutional change is western regionalism. This is based, not on a distinctive language or culture, but on the distinctive economic base of the four western provinces. Their economies depend upon the primary production of grain, wood, metals, oil, gas and other minerals. Because the bulk of Canada's population is concentrated in Ontario and Quebec, federal policies have tended to favour the manufacturing industries and consumers of central Canada.[134] This tendency has been reflected in the tariffs that protect domestic manufacturing, in transportation policies, and for a time in federal control of the price of oil and gas. Two responses by western Canadians have inevitably been invoked. One is to seek to reduce the power of the federal government, which they cannot control, and to enhance the powers of the provincial governments, which they can control. The other response is to seek to make central institutions, that is, the institutions of the federal government, more responsive to regional interests. The latter idea is discussed later in this chapter. The 1982 amendments conferred some increase in provincial powers over natural resources,[135] but did nothing about central institutions.

---

131 See sec. 4.1(c), "The failure to accommodate Quebec", above.

132 *Ibid.*

133 The Quebec sovereignty referendum of October 30, 1995 is discussed in more detail in sec. 4.1(c), "The failure to accommodate Quebec", above, and in ch. 5, Federalism, under heading 5.7, "Secession", below.

134 There is a school of thought which holds that the west has been disadvantaged by free market forces rather than by federal policies: Smiley, *Canada in Question* (3rd. ed., 1980), 180 briefly summarizes the arguments. I am agnostic on this issue, but I believe that the text accurately reports widespread western perceptions, which are all that are relevant for present purposes.

135 Constitution Act, 1867, s. 92A, was added in 1982.

A third force of constitutional change is the demand by the aboriginal peoples of Canada — the Indian, Inuit and Métis peoples — for entrenchment of their traditional rights. The native peoples were successful in securing several provisions in the Constitution Act, 1982, including a guarantee of ''existing aboriginal and treaty rights'' (s. 35) and a commitment to further constitutional discussions (s. 37).[136] The settlement of their land claims is, of course, the overwhelming remaining problem, but they also seek entrenchment of an explicit right to self-government and a right to participate in the process of constitutional amendment, at least where aboriginal rights could be affected.[137] The Charlottetown Accord of 1992[138] would have recognized that aboriginal peoples have an inherent right of self-government within Canada, and would have required aboriginal consent to future amendments of constitutional provisions referring to aboriginal peoples. The defeat of the Accord in a national referendum blocked these proposals.

A fourth force of constitutional change has been Canadian nationalism, the constitutional dimension of which was addressed to the removal of the vestiges of the colonial relationship between Canada and the United Kingdom, the former imperial power. At the minimum, this required the ''patriation'' of the Constitution,[139] and (so that the constitution can be amended without recourse to the United Kingdom) the adoption of domestic amending procedures. The 1982 amendments accomplished these changes, although, as noted earlier, there will have to be an alteration in the amending procedures to meet Quebec's objections to them.[140] The patriation process did not touch the position of the Queen, who continues to be Canada's formal head of state, or Canada's membership of the Commonwealth of Nations (successor to the British Empire and later the British Commonwealth).

A fifth force of constitutional change is the civil libertarian impulse to entrench a Charter of Rights in the Constitution. This was accomplished by the 1982 amendments, although an override provision had to be inserted to secure the agreement of seven provincial governments. Quebec has never agreed to the Charter of Rights, although of course the Charter is legally binding on the province. In the Meech Lake Accord of 1987,[141] Quebec did not insist upon changes to the Charter, but only that the Constitution include a declaration that Quebec was a ''distinct society''. The legal effect of this declaration was not entirely clear, but it would probably have helped Quebec to sustain against Charter chal-

136 These provisions were amended again in 1983: Constitution Amendment Proclamation, 1983, R.S.C. 1985, Appendix II, No. 46.

137 For analysis of the constitutional provisions respecting aboriginal peoples, see ch. 24, Aboriginal Peoples, below.

138 Note 41, above.

139 See ch. 3, Independence, under heading 3.5, ''Patriation of the Constitution'', above.

140 The Meech Lake Accord of 1987, note 37, above, which has now lapsed, included an agreement to increase the number of matters that were subject to the unanimity procedure, and to extend the right to compensation for opting out of amendments.

141 Note 37, above.

lenge those laws that were designed to protect the French language and culture. The "distinct society" clause turned out to be the most controversial element of the Accord. The Accord did not receive the requisite level of provincial legislative approval and it lapsed in 1990. In the Charlottetown Accord of 1992,[142] the same issue was revived, and another "distinct society" clause was proposed for inclusion in the Constitution. The Charlottetown Accord was rejected in a national referendum held in 1992, which caused it to lapse.[143]

Sixthly, there will be a continuing need for amendments, not necessarily sponsored by interest-groups falling within any of the above five categories, but which are perceived as necessary to repair gaps in the existing constitutional provisions, to alter judicial interpretations that are unacceptable, or to give effect to values that were not recognized at the time of confederation. Examples from the past of this miscellaneous category are the amendments to confer powers over unemployment insurance[144] and old age pensions[145] on the federal Parliament, and the amendment imposing a retiring age on superior-court judges.[146]

(b) Division of powers

As noted earlier, the most obvious way to redress the grievances of French Canadians and western Canadians is to reduce the powers of the federal Parliament, which they do not control, and to increase the powers of the provincial Legislatures, which they do control.

The 1982 amendments made only one change in the division of powers between the two levels of government,[147] and that was an increase in the provincial power over natural resources.[148] This went some distance to meet western objections to two decisions of the Supreme Court of Canada which had narrowly defined

---

142 Note 41, above.

143 After the 1995 referendum on Quebec sovereignty was defeated by a very narrow margin, the House of Commons passed a resolution which declared that it recognized Quebec as a distinct society, and would be "guided by this reality": *House of Commons Debates* (29 November 1995) at 16971 (text of resolution); *House of Commons Debates* (11 December 1995) at 17536 (passage of resolution). This resolution did not meet Quebec's previous requests, which were for *constitutional* recognition of its distinctness. The 1995 referendum and the distinct society resolution are discussed in sec. 4.1(c), "The failure to accommodate Quebec", above.

144 Section 91(2A), conferring power over unemployment insurance, was added by the Constitution Act, 1940 (U.K.), R.S.C. 1985, Appendix II, No. 28. It abrogated the decision in *A.G. Can.* v. *A.G. Ont.* (Unemployment Insurance) [1937] A.C. 355.

145 Section 94A, conferring power over old age pensions, was added by the British North America Act, 1951 (U.K.), R.S.C. 1985, Appendix II, No. 35, and was expanded to include supplementary benefits by the Constitution Act, 1964 (U.K.), R.S.C. 1985, Appendix II, No. 38.

146 Section 99(2), imposing a retirement age for superior-court judges, was added by the Constitution Act, 1960 (U.K.), R.S.C. 1985, Appendix II, No. 37.

147 The Charter of Rights does not fall into this category, since it imposed limitations on the legislative powers of both levels of government and did not augment the powers of either level of government.

148 This is now Constitution Act, 1867, s. 92A.

the provincial powers to tax natural resources and to control the production and price of natural resources.[149]

Other changes in the division of powers which have been actively considered in recent years include: transferring to the provinces some aspects of control over communications, especially cable television; transferring marriage and divorce to the provinces; transferring fisheries and offshore resources to the provinces; transferring the residuary power to the provinces, and narrowly defining the federal power over the peace, order, and good government of Canada; limiting or abolishing the federal declaratory power; and limiting the federal spending power. On the federal side of the ledger, a case can be made for the enlargement of certain federal powers to facilitate effective national economic policies in areas where federal power is lacking or unclear or available only in an emergency, for example, foreign ownership, securities regulation and wage and price controls.[150] None of these changes was seriously proposed as part of the 1982 constitutional settlement.

The experience of federal-provincial negotiations shows that it is very difficult to secure agreement on changes in the division of powers. The overall thrust of most reform proposals has been in the direction of decentralization of powers. But the federal government naturally resists decentralization; and it is true that the Canadian provinces are already more powerful, in both legislative and fiscal terms, than are the American or Australian states in relation to their central governments. Moreover, the provinces differ so greatly in their size and wealth and aspirations that they do not agree on what new responsibilities they should assume and what they should give up.[151] The smaller provinces, in particular, cannot easily make common cause with the larger provinces: the smaller provinces are heavily dependent on federal funding to maintain the standard of living of their residents, are also dependent upon federal policies for protection from the unintended adverse effects of the policies of other provinces (for example, energy prices), and they lack the capacity to substantially increase their own responsibilities. It is only realistic to acknowledge that a substantial alteration in the division of powers between the federal and provincial governments is neither practicable nor desirable.

---

149 *Can. Industrial Gas and Oil* v. *Sask.* [1978] 2 S.C.R. 545; *Central Can. Potash Co.* v. *Sask.* [1979] 1 S.C.R. 42.

150 Arguments for reform in a wide range of areas are to be found in the studies collected in Beck and Bernier (eds.), *Canada and the New Constitution* (1983), vols. 1 and 2.

151 ''Special status'', under which one or more provinces could have different powers than the others, is a possible answer to the differing aspirations and capacities of the provinces. However, special status raises difficult questions about the role in the central institutions, especially the federal Parliament, of the representatives of the province or provinces with special status. It seems wrong that they should participate in decisions which in their province are a provincial responsibility. Yet their participation may be necessary to retain a government majority. Opting out, under the present amendment procedures, will lead to special status for the opted-out province (or provinces) and to the same difficulty regarding the role of its representatives in central institutions: see sec. 4.3(d), ''Opting out'', above.

(c) Central institutions

A different approach to constitutional change concentrates on reforming the institutions of the federal government so that regional attitudes and interests are more effectively represented within those institutions. The theory is that the more effectively these attitudes and interests are represented within the central institutions the wider is the range of powers that may be conferred on central institutions. If French Canadians and western Canadians could be confident that their interests would be fairly accommodated in the development of federal policies, then, so the argument goes, they would have less reason to demand that powers be transferred from federal institutions to provincial institutions. Thus, the reform of central institutions becomes an alternative to decentralization of powers as a means of redressing regional grievances. This approach to constitutional change has been dubbed ''intrastate federalism'' by political scientists in contrast to ''interstate federalism'', which involves the decentralization of powers.[152]

The most popular application of intrastate federalism by constitutional reformers has been to the Senate, the upper house of the federal Parliament. One idea, modelled on West Germany's upper house (the Bundesrat), is to convert the Senate into a ''House of the Provinces'' with members appointed by provincial governments. This would then become the means by which provincial governments could exercise a direct influence over federal policies. Another idea is to convert the Senate into an elected house, with equal representation from each province. The ''Triple-E'' Senate (equal, elected, effective) would operate, so it is claimed, to defend provincial interests in the formation of federal legislative policy. These ideas are discussed later in this book.[153]

The second most popular application of intrastate federalism has been to the Supreme Court of Canada, where attention has been directed to the introduction of a provincial role in the appointment of judges; to rules ensuring that the judges are drawn from all regions of the country; and to the restructuring of the Court to provide a special constitutional Court, or panel of the present Court, to decide constitutional cases. These ideas are discussed later in this book.[154]

Intrastate federalism does not stop with the Senate and Supreme Court of Canada. Smiley's study of the topic also addresses the House of Commons, the cabinet, the federal civil service, federal regulatory agencies and the political parties.[155] These institutions must also respond to the French, multicultural, aboriginal and regional interests. For the most part, however, changes in these institutions do not call for constitutional amendments.

---

152 Smiley, ''Central Institutions'' in Beck and Bernier (eds.), *Canada and the New Constitution* (1983), vol. 1, 19.

153 See ch. 9, Responsible Government, under heading 9.4(c), ''The Senate'', below.

154 Ch. 8, Supreme Court of Canada, under heading 8.8, ''Reform of Court'', below.

155 Note 152, above.

(d) Criticism of amending procedures

This chapter should not be permitted to end on a note that suggests flexibility and responsiveness on the part of the new amending procedures. It will be difficult to secure any amendment to the Constitution, because of the high level of agreement required by the general amending procedure.[156] Eight governments out of eleven is a group which is hard to assemble on anything, and, where opting out is available, there will be a strong impulse to proceed only when the assent of all governments is assured, since the "checkerboard constitution" which would develop through opting out would impose such severe strains on central institutions[157] that is likely to be unacceptable to the federal government and at least undesirable to most provincial governments.

The unanimity rule is even more difficult to operate. The Meech Lake Accord did achieve unanimous agreement at two First Ministers' Conferences held in 1987. However, over the next three years, provincial elections caused three changes of government before the process of ratification by all legislative assemblies was complete, and in each case the new government refused to respect the agreement of its predecessor. In the end, the Accord lapsed, because two of the newly-constituted legislative assemblies had not ratified it when the three-year time-limit for ratifications expired.[158] Unanimity was achieved a second time when the Charlottetown Accord was agreed to at a First Ministers' Conference in 1992. However, the first ministers agreed to put the Accord to a national referendum, with the understanding that it would need to be approved by eleven majorities, namely, a national majority and a majority in every one of the ten provinces. The referendum was held in 1992, and the voters rejected the Accord by a national majority, and by majorities in six provinces. The Accord, therefore, never started on the process of legislative ratification.[159]

The requirement of resolutions of assent by the Houses of Parliament and the legislative assemblies of the provinces dates only from 1982. Before 1982, an agreement by the first ministers was regarded as a sufficient manifestation of federal-provincial approval to enable an amendment to be transmitted to the United Kingdom for enactment.[160] Since 1982, any such executive agreement has to be ratified by the various legislative bodies. This adds a new hazard to the process, because it means that whatever agreement is achieved by first ministers must be maintained throughout the period of ratification. The three-year maximum period for ratification is far too long. In the case of the Meech Lake Accord, it allowed the process to drift on while elections were held and governments

156 There has been one amendment under the general amending procedure: Constitution Amendment Proclamation, 1983, R.S.C. 1985, Appendix II, No. 46, adding new provisions respecting aboriginal peoples. The details are described in ch. 24, Aboriginal Peoples, below.

157 See note 151, above.

158 The story is told in more detail in sec. 4.1(c), "The failure to accommodate Quebec", above.

159 *Ibid.*

160 Strayer, *The Patriation and Legitimacy of the Canadian Constitution* (1982), 3-13.

changed. A period of one year, or even six months, would surely be ample for legislative review of a constitutional proposal.

The requirement of legislative ratifications ensures that there is a public process to review any constitutional proposal. It was that public process that caused the destruction of the Meech Lake Accord. Ironically, it was a common complaint that the process was not public enough. What was lacking was a process of public scrutiny *before* the first ministers achieved their agreement. Whether this would have salvaged the Accord, or simply destroyed it earlier, cannot be known now.

In the case of the Charlottetown Accord, the agreement of the first ministers was preceded by an extraordinarily widespread public consultation. This started with a set of proposals for constitutional reform that was tabled in the federal Parliament by the federal government on September 24, 1991.[161] These proposals were referred to a Special Joint Committee of the House of Commons and the Senate, which received 3,000 submissions and listened to 700 individuals, and which produced a lengthy report on February 28, 1992.[162] During the same period all provinces and territories also established legislative committees to publicly examine the federal proposals. A series of five televised national conferences on the constitutional proposals was held between January and March of 1992. Starting in March, the federal and provincial governments, joined by the two territorial governments and the four aboriginal organizations, began multilateral discussions to reach an agreement. Those discussions culminated in a First Ministers' Conference at Charlottetown where the Charlottetown Accord was agreed to on August 28, 1992. Never in the history of Canada (and perhaps anywhere else) had there been such a thorough public consultation in preparation for a set of constitutional amendments. The first ministers decided to seek the definitive popular seal of approval for the Accord by putting it to a national referendum. A national referendum campaign followed in which the yes side (to approve the Accord) enjoyed the well-financed support of the federal government, all ten provincial governments, both territorial governments, most of the opposition leaders, all four aboriginal organizations, most business and labour organizations and most media editors and commentators. Despite this support (and all the earlier consultations), when the vote was held on October 26, 1992, it produced a decisive defeat for the yes side. The Accord was rejected by a majority of 54.4 per cent to 44.6 per cent. The process of legislative ratifications, which would have followed a yes vote, was never started.

The defeat of the Charlottetown Accord shows that no amount of public consultation guarantees the success of proposals to amend the Constitution. However, it is probably safe to assume that an absence of public consultation does guarantee failure. There is no escape from the conclusion that the Constitution's

161 Government of Canada, *Shaping Canada's Future Together: Proposals* (1991).

162 *Report of the Special Joint Committee on a Renewed Canada* (Beaudoin-Dobbie Report) (Government of Canada, 1992).

requirement of legislative ratifications of the text of any amendment must be supplemented by ample opportunities for public participation before the text has been settled. The Charlottetown process indicates some of the ways in which those opportunities can be structured. The hearings of the special joint committee and the five national conferences were particularly valuable vehicles for criticism of the proposals and for new ideas.

Whatever provision is made for public participation in the existing amending procedures, at some stage in the process of amendment there has to be an agreement of the first ministers. This is because they control their legislative bodies,[163] and it is highly unlikely that any significant number of legislative assents could be obtained for a constitutional proposal that had not first been agreed to by the first ministers. Unfortunately, obtaining an agreement from the first ministers inevitably turns into a process of bargaining, which excludes popular involvement at the crucial moment, and which leaves no assurance that any given position has been accepted or rejected on the merits. Moreover, the Prime Minister and Premiers are unlikely to agree to any significant restructuring of governmental institutions, since it is to the existing institutions that they owe their positions and powers.[164]

During the pre-1982 constitutional negotiations I argued[165] (without the slightest effect, needless to say) that one mode of constitutional amendment — not the only mode, but one mode — should be some form of ''initiative and referendum'',[166] under which a proposal for a constitutional amendment could be initiated by petition signed by a stipulated (fairly large) number of voters, and could be adopted by a referendum that obtained majorities in each region of the country.[167] The availability of an initiative and referendum procedure would place ultimate control over the amending power in the hands of the people, instead of the political elites. Note that governments would not be excluded from the initiative and referendum procedure. They could, and no doubt would, campaign for

163 See ch. 9, Responsible Government, below.

164 Accord, Cheffins, note 50, above.

165 Hogg, note 128, above, 348-351.

166 For discussion of initiative and referendum as a law-making process, as it was adopted in Alberta and Manitoba early this century, see ch. 14, Delegation, ss. 14.2(d) and 14.2(e), below. Australia and Switzerland use referenda as their amending procedures. In Australia, however, the referendum can only be initiated by the federal Parliament, while in Switzerland it can be initiated either by the federal Assembly or by popular initiative. Australia's amending procedure is set out in note 42, above. Switzerland's amending procedure is described in Government of Canada, *The Canadian Constitution and Constitutional Amendment* (1978), 4-5.

167 The requirement of regional majorities is necessary to avoid results like those of the national referendums on prohibition in 1898 and on conscription of 1942. In each case, the referendum was carried by an English-speaking majority despite French-speaking opposition. The only other national referendum that has ever been held was on the Charlottetown Accord in 1992; in that case, where the referendum was lost, Quebec was not isolated: the vote in Quebec was similar to that in the nation as a whole.

or against a particular proposal.[168] But the campaign would have to be addressed to the merits of the particular proposal. Support or opposition could no longer be simply a bargaining ploy, because that would not persuade the voters. Nor could radical proposals for change in the institutions of government be stifled or blocked by the existing institutions.

168 This is what happens in Australia, where state governments will often campaign against an amendment proposal that is supported by the federal government. Any fear that the resources of the federal government would enable it to win any referendum is not borne out by the Australian experience. In Australia, since federation in 1900, 42 proposed amendments have been put to referenda. In each instance the proposal was supported by the federal government (which must initiate the process). Only eight of the proposals have carried by the requisite "double majority" (a majority of all those voting and a majority of those voting in each of a majority of states): note 51, above.

5

Federalism

5.1 Distribution of governmental power

(a) Federalism

Canada is a federal state, or a federation. Other familiar examples of federal states are the United States of America and Australia. The United Kingdom and

New Zealand, by contrast, are unitary states. What is a federal state? How does it differ from a unitary state?

In a federal state, governmental power is distributed between a central (or national or federal) authority and several regional (or provincial or state) authorities, in such a way that every individual in the state is subject to the laws of two authorities, the central authority and a regional authority. For example, anyone in Ontario is subject to the laws of the Parliament of Canada (the central authority) and the Legislature of Ontario (the regional authority). The central authority and the regional authorities are ''coordinate'', that is to say, neither is subordinate to the other. The powers of the Legislature of Ontario are not granted by the Parliament of Canada, and they cannot be taken away, altered or controlled by the Parliament of Canada. And the Legislature of Ontario, even acting in concert with all the other provincial Legislatures, is likewise incompetent to take away, alter or control the powers of the Parliament of Canada.

In a unitary state, governmental power is vested in one national authority. There are, of course, local or municipal governments with law-making power over their local territories. But these local authorities differ from the provinces or states of a federation in that the local authorities are subordinate to the national authority. The powers of a city, borough or county are granted to it by the national legislature, and may be taken away, altered or controlled at any time by the national legislature; in fact, this happens quite often when local government is reorganized. This is also the position of local or municipal governments within a federal state. They are subordinate to a regional authority, for example, the city of Montreal to the province of Quebec.

In a federal state, it is common to speak of two ''levels'' of government. The metaphor is apt in that the power of the central authority extends throughout the country, and is in that sense ''higher'' than the power of each regional authority, which is confined to its region. Moreover, in every federation, in the event of inconsistency between a federal law and a provincial or state law, it is the federal or national law which prevails. But to speak of the central authority as a ''higher level'' of government must not carry the implication that the regional authorities are legally subordinate to the centre; on the contrary, they are coordinate or equal in status with the centre.

The notion of equality which is conveyed by the word ''coordinate'' does not necessarily imply equality of wealth, status or actual power. The tiny province of Prince Edward Island is not equal to the province of Ontario in that sense;[1] nor is any province equal to the federal government in that sense. Within every federation some regions are wealthier and more powerful than others, and the central authority is wealthier and more powerful than any of the regions. At different periods of a federal nation's history, the balance of power between the centre and the regions shifts. We shall see in the next chapter that during the

1 There are also some minor differences in the legal position of the provinces: see sec. 5.1(d), ''Special status'', below.

second world war, for example, the needs of national power led to enormous accretions in the wealth and power of the federal governments of Canada, Australia and the United States. Since then the balance of power has tended to shift back towards the regions, although this tendency has been less marked in Australia and the United States than it has been in Canada.

Depending upon the actual balance of power between the centre and the regions, federal states may be placed on a "spectrum" running from a point that is close to disintegration into separate countries to a point that is close to the centralized power of a unitary state or an empire.[2] With the growth of central power in the principal federations the question whether a state is still truly "federal" depends upon whether there is still "an area of guaranteed autonomy for each unit of the system".[3] It is this legal guarantee of autonomy to each of the regional authorities, however disparate in size and wealth they may be, which justifies the description of them as coordinate with the central authority. If in a once-federal country the area of guaranteed autonomy of the regions were attenuated to the point of triviality, then we would probably want to deny the term "federal" to the country. But it could not plausibly be argued that the growth of central power in Canada, or in Australia or the United States, has reached that point of substantial equivalence to a unitary state.

K.C. Wheare defined "the federal principle" as "the method of dividing powers so that the general and regional governments are each, within a sphere, co-ordinate and independent".[4] This definition has been criticized as unduly stressing the separate and distinct spheres of the central and regional authorities.[5] Other writers have contributed alternative definitions which emphasize the "interdependence" of central and regional authorities in a federal state,[6] or the "diversification" of the society within the federal state,[7] or the existence within the state of distinctive groups with common objectives,[8] or the constitutionally-entrenched incorporation of regional units in its decision-making procedures.[9] These writers have all contributed insights to the nature of federal states, but they have so eroded the concept of federalism that it has become too vague to be useful.

---

2 Livingston, *Federalism and Constitutional Change* (1956), 4; Riker, *Federalism, Origin, Operation, Significance* (1964), 5. Riker argues that the degree of centralization in any federal state may be measured by the degree of centralization in the organization of the political parties.

3 Sawer, *Modern Federalism* (1969), 27; Riker, note 2, above, 6.

4 Wheare, *Federal Government* (4th ed., 1963), 10; cf. Dicey, *The Law of the Constitution* (10th ed., 1960), 140, whose definition has obviously influenced Wheare's. For similar definitions, see Riker, note 2, above, 11; Sawer, *Australian Federalism in the Courts* (1967), 1; Smiley, *The Federal Condition in Canada* (1987), 2.

5 Birch, *Federalism, Finance and Social Legislation* (1955), 306.

6 Vile, *The Structure of American Federalism* (1961), 198-199.

7 Livingston, note 2, above, 4.

8 Friedrich, *Man and His Government* (1963), 594-595.

9 King, *Federalism and Federation* (1982), 77. Tremblay, *Droit Constitutionnel-Principles* (1993), 139.

In fact, however, there are very important differences in the constitutional law and governmental practices between ''federal'' states such as Canada, Australia and the United States on the one hand, and ''unitary'' states such as the United Kingdom and New Zealand on the other. There are a set of distinctive issues concerning the distribution of legislative power, the distribution of executive power and the administration of justice that have to be resolved in each of the federal states, and that are unimportant or non-existent in the unitary states; and these distinctive issues all relate to the fact that in a federal state the citizen is subject to two levels of government which are, to some degree at least, legally and politically independent of each other. It is true that in many spheres the central and regional powers overlap and that where they come into conflict the central power prevails. It is also true that financial arrangements between the central and regional governments have extended the powers of the financially dominant central authority deeply into spheres once reserved for the regions. And it is also true that the extent of modern governmental involvement in social and economic matters has produced policies which require constant interaction between each government, and in some cases the cooperative action of more than one government. So far as Canada is concerned these points will be amply demonstrated in succeeding chapters.

Perhaps Wheare did not sufficiently stress the elements of interdependence of central and regional authorities, but they are not inconsistent with his definition of federalism. If in a nation paramount central power completely overlapped regional power, then that nation would not be federal on his definition. The same conclusion would follow if the financial arrangements of a nation subjected the regions totally to central control.[10] It is only where overlapping of power is incomplete, or the scope of central control is limited, that we have a federal system. In that case there are two levels of government which are ''within a sphere'' coordinate and independent. That is true of Canada, Australia and the United States, and it is untrue of the United Kingdom and New Zealand.

(b) Confederation

Canada is often described as a ''confederation'', and the process of union which culminated in 1867 is often described as ''confederation''. Outside Canada the term confederation is usually used to mean a loose association of states in which the central government is subordinate to the states.[11] In a confederation in the technical sense the central government is the delegate of the states or provinces; its powers are delegated to it by the states or provinces, who retain the right to resume the delegated powers if they wish. It was a ''confederation'' that was established by the American colonies by the Articles of Confederation of 1777,

10 Wheare might prefer to say in this case that the ''constitution'' was still federal, but the ''government'' was unitary.

11 Wheare, note 4, above, 32.

because under that arrangement the central government was merely the delegate of the states. After the revolutionary war, the final constitution which was adopted by the United States in 1787 made the federal government independent of the states and coordinate with them.

In Canada, the union of the provinces, like the union of the United States, established a central government which was in no sense the delegate of the provinces. It was independent of the provinces and coordinate with them. Indeed, as we shall see later in this chapter, to the extent that the provinces and the central government are not coordinate, it is the provinces that are subordinate to the central government — the opposite of confederation. During the discussions of union in British North America before 1867, the terms union, federation and confederation were not used in any consistent or precise sense; and the term confederation has now become an accepted term for the Canadian union of provinces. There is no point in cavilling about this use of the word: for Canada, usage has made it correct.[12]

(c) Legislative union

The closest possible kind of union is a ''legislative union'', in which the united states or provinces form a new unitary state which incorporates the former units and subjects them to the authority of a single central legislature. The United Kingdom is a legislative union of England, Wales, Scotland and Northern Ireland. The Parliament at Westminster has full authority to legislate for all four regions.[13]

At the time of the union of the British North American colonies there was a good deal of sentiment in favour of a legislative union. John A. Macdonald wanted a legislative union, as did many people in Upper Canada (which became Ontario). But they had to settle for a federation because Lower Canada (which became Quebec) and the maritime provinces of New Brunswick, Nova Scotia and Prince Edward Island would not have agreed to a legislative union. Lower Canada feared that if it joined in a legislative union, its French language, culture and institutions and its Roman Catholic religion would be threatened by the English-speaking Protestant majority; the maritime provinces also feared for their local traditions

---

12 For extended discussion of the term confederation, see Kennedy, *The Constitution of Canada 1534-1937* (2nd ed., 1938), 401-404.

13 The history of the United Kingdom is related in ch. 2, Reception, under heading 2.6, ''Imperial statutes'', above. Northern Ireland has had a Parliament of its own since 1920, but the U.K. Parliament retains in reserve full power to legislate for Northern Ireland, and in 1972 the U.K. Parliament suspended the authority of the Northern Ireland Parliament and imposed direct rule on Northern Ireland. A new Northern Ireland Parliament was created in 1973, but after a short period direct rule was reimposed. This could not have occurred in a federal system. The organization of a country with regional authorities which are subordinate to the centre is often described as ''devolution''. Within Canada, the government of the two federal territories is based on devolution of power from the federal Parliament: the Territorial Councils have extensive legislative powers but they remain subordinate to the federal Parliament: Northwest Territories Act, R.S.C. 1985, c. N-27; Yukon Act, R.S.C. 1985, c. Y-2.

and institutions. On the other hand, union would provide the military strength needed for security, and the economic strength needed for prosperity. The compromise between these conflicting impulses was a federation, providing the unity necessary for military and economic strength, while allowing diversity of language, culture, religion and local institutions.[14] Even so, the maritime provinces were reluctant to join, and Prince Edward Island did not do so until 1873.[15]

(d) Special status

As noted earlier, the provinces are not equal in wealth, status or actual power. Nor is their constitutional situation exactly equal. A number of the provisions of the Constitution apply to only one or only some of the provinces.[16] And the terms upon which each province was admitted usually included unique terms[17] which operate as legally enforceable provisions applicable only to that province.[18]

While the provinces are not perfectly equal, the differences are not so marked as to justify the description ''special status'' for any province. ''Special status'' is the term which has been applied to proposals for constitutional change under which one province (most likely, Quebec) would possess larger powers than the other provinces.[19] This could arise under the new amending procedures if Quebec (or any other province) opted out of a constitutional amendment transferring a provincial power to the federal Parliament. As noted in the discussion of opting out,[20] special status for one or a few provinces would impose severe strains on central institutions, and especially the federal Parliament. If the Parliament had

---

14 Riker, note 2, above, (1964), ch. 2, argues that a similar set of conditions prevailed at the origin of every modern federal system.

15 Lower Canada had a special reason to support the federation. Since 1840 (as Canada East) it had been united with Upper Canada (Canada West) in the united province of Canada, and so federation offered more not less autonomy for French-speaking Canada. The maritime provinces had never been united and were reluctant to yield some of their autonomy: see generally Creighton, *The Road to Confederation* (1964).

16 For example, Constitution Act, 1867, ss. 93 (denominational schools), 94 (uniformity of laws), 133 (language); Constitution Act, 1982, ss. 6(4) (affirmative action), 16(2), 17(2), 18(2), 19(2), 20(2), 59 (language).

17 For example, the denominational schools guarantees in s. 20 of the Manitoba Act, 1870, s. 17 of the Alberta Act, s. 17 of the Saskatchewan Act and s. 17 of the Terms of Union of Newfoundland; the language guarantee in s. 23 of the Manitoba Act, 1870; and provisions regarding the natural resources of Manitoba, Alberta and Saskatchewan enacted by the Constitution Act, 1930.

18 *The Queen (Can.)* v. *The Queen (P.E.I.)* [1978] 1 F.C. 533 (C.A.) (enforcing terms of union promising ferry service); *Jack* v. *The Queen* [1980] 1 S.C.R. 294 (interpreting term of union regarding policy towards Indians); *Moosehunter* v. *The Queen* [1981] 1 S.C.R. 282 (enforcing term of natural resources agreement guaranteeing Indian hunting rights); *B.C.* v. *Can.* [1994] 2 S.C.R. 41 (interpreting term of union promising construction of railway).

19 ''Special status'', under which Quebec would remain within Canada, must be distinguished from ''sovereignty-association'', under which Quebec would secede from Canada and would retain only an economic association with (the rest of) Canada: see sec. 5.7, ''Secession'', below.

20 See ch. 4, Amendment, under heading 4.3(d), ''Opting out'', above.

authority to regulate a matter, say, product standards (to use my earlier example), everywhere except in Quebec, the members of parliament and senators from Quebec would presumably be permitted to vote on a bill regulating product standards, and they might have to do so in order to preserve a governmental majority, but the bill when enacted would not apply in Quebec. This problem has never been solved by political scientists, and it means that special status is a viable constitutional arrangement only up to a point. Of course, Quebec already enjoys a de facto special status, as the only province that has opted out of the Canada Pension Plan and the Hospital Insurance Plan (and some other national shared-cost programmes).[21] But these arrangements do not give to Quebec any special *constitutional* powers: the other nine provinces continue to possess the same powers as Quebec over pensions and hospital insurance, and they could if they chose follow an independent course like Quebec.

The Meech Lake Constitutional Accord of 1987[22] was a failed attempt to reconcile Quebec to the terms of the Constitution Act, 1982, by which the province was legally bound, but to which it had never given its assent. The Accord made provision for (1) the recognition of Quebec as a distinct society, (2) a provincial role in immigration, (3) a provincial role in appointments to the Supreme Court of Canada, (4) a limitation of the federal spending power and (5) a veto for Quebec over some kinds of constitutional amendments. Although these five points were sought by Quebec alone, the Accord was carefully drafted to avoid making special provision for Quebec, and the new provincial powers were conferred on all provinces, not just Quebec. This even included the veto over constitutional amendments, which took the form of a unanimity requirement, conferring a veto on all provinces.

The one point that would not yield to the ingenious avoidance of special provision for Quebec[23] was the recognition of Quebec as a "distinct society". In my opinion, even this provision could not plausibly be regarded as creating a special status for Quebec, in that it was an interpretative provision only. It did not directly confer any new powers on the province, and, if its interpretative role did lead to some expansion of Quebec's powers, that expansion was bound to be minor — well within the range of variation in provincial powers that is now to be found within the Constitution of Canada. Nevertheless, there was much public debate about the undesirability of special status for Quebec, and the distinct society clause was the major objection that led to the failure by two provinces to ratify the Accord, which caused the Accord to lapse.[24]

---

21 See ch. 6, Financial Arrangements, below.

22 See ch. 4, Amendment, under heading 4.1(c), "The failure to accommodate Quebec", above.

23 To be strictly accurate, the Accord also guaranteed that three of the judges of the Supreme Court of Canada would come from Quebec. This provision, although singling out Quebec for special treatment, was not controversial, because it constitutionalized a longstanding statutory requirement.

24 The "distinct society" clause was also part of the unsuccessful Charlottetown Accord of 1992 (see ch. 4, Amendment, under heading 4.1(c) "The failure to accommodate Quebec", above).

In 1995, the House of Commons, reacting to the close result in the sovereignty referendum that Quebec had held that year, passed a resolution declaring that the House recognized Quebec as a "distinct society", and would be "guided by this reality".[25] This is not a constitutional amendment (it is not even a statute), and so it does not confer any special constitutional status on Quebec. Even so, the resolution was opposed (because it went too far) by the Reform Party, with most of the seats in the western provinces, and (because it did not go far enough) by the Bloc Québécois, with most of the seats in Quebec.

(e) Dominion and provinces

In a federal state it is necessary to find suitable vocabulary to describe (1) the regional authorities, (2) the central authority, and (3) the nation as a whole. The first issue is rarely a problem. In Canada the regions are known as provinces, while in Australia and the United States they are known as states; and of course each province or state has a proper name of its own. It is, however, difficult to find a description for the central authority which is both accurate and dignified, and which at the same time distinguishes the central government apparatus from the nation as a whole. In Canada the terminological problem has not been satisfactorily resolved.

The British North America Act, 1867, by s. 3, created "one Dominion under the name of Canada". After 1867, the country was usually described officially as "the Dominion of Canada." When it was desired to distinguish the central government authority from the provinces, the central authority was called "the Dominion".

The term "dominion" gained currency outside Canada in the early 1900s to denote the self-governing countries of the British Empire. Canada, Australia, New Zealand and South Africa by then enjoyed a substantial measure of self-government, and it did not seem appropriate to describe them as colonies. In order to distinguish them from the more dependent territories of the Empire, they came to be called dominions. But terminology changed to meet changing facts and perceptions. The British Empire became the British Commonwealth and, later on, simply the Commonwealth. And after the second world war the term dominion became unfashionable. It was thought to carry a colonial connotation, and so, outside Canada, the term dominion has generally been superseded by the term

---

The Accord also repeated the guarantee that three judges of the Supreme Court of Canada would come from Quebec (see previous note). The Accord contained a new guarantee that Quebec's representation in the House of Commons would never fall below 25 per cent. This special provision for Quebec (along with the distinct society clause) seems to have been an important factor in the defeat of the Accord in the western provinces.

25 *House of Commons Debates* (29 November 1995) at 16971 (text of resolution); *House of Commons Debates* (11 December 1995) at 17536 (passage of resolution).

''member of the Commonwealth'' as a description of the self-governing countries of the Commonwealth.[26]

In Canada, the objections to the use of the word dominion were especially significant, since the word appeared as part of the official name of the country. In fact, however, s. 3 of the B.N.A. Act, although it used the word Dominion, did not actually name the country ''the Dominion of Canada'' but simply ''Canada''. In the 1930s, the federal government decided to switch the official name of the country from the Dominion of Canada to Canada. The substitution has been made in Acts of Parliament, for example, and efforts have been made to discontinue the use of the word Dominion wherever else it used to occur. Dominion-provincial conferences have since 1950 become federal-provincial conferences; the Dominion Bureau of Statistics has become Statistics Canada; and so on.

Most writers on constitutional law and government have continued to make discreet use of the term ''Dominion'', because it is convenient to have a name to distinguish the central authority from the provinces. It is of course possible to speak of the federal government or the national government, but these terms are not normally apt to include the legislative branch of government, and so clarity often requires that one use another term — the federal (or national) Parliament — when legislative power is in issue. The only proper noun which would replace Dominion is ''Canada'', but this causes ambiguity, since the central governmental authority is not the same as the nation as a whole. If one says that ''Canada has the power to regulate aeronautics'', it is not clear whether the statement means that the power to regulate aeronautics is one of the powers of the federal Parliament (which is a proposition about the distribution of legislative powers within the federal system), or whether the statement means that the power to regulate aeronautics exists somewhere in the country (which does not involve a proposition about the distribution of powers in the federal system).[27] The statement that ''the Dominion has the power to regulate aeronautics'' would in most contexts be an unambiguous statement about the distribution of legislative power within the federal system.

A related point of nomenclature concerns the names of the Canadian legislative bodies. These are all ''parliaments'' in the sense that each is modelled on the United Kingdom Parliament at Westminster. But the Canadian practice is to confine the term ''Parliament'' to the federal Parliament, and to use the term ''Legislature'' to describe each provincial parliament. This is the usage in the Constitution Acts, and it is almost invariable in Canadian constitutional writing.

---

26 Wheare, *The Constitutional Structure of the Commonwealth* (1960), 14-16.

27 The Constitution Act, 1867 is itself guilty of this ambiguity. While ''Canada'' usually means the nation as a whole, e.g., in ss. 3, 4, 5, 16, 22, in several places the word means the central governmental authority, e.g., in s. 101 (federal jurisdiction over ''laws of Canada'') and ss. 108, 111, 117, 119, 120, 125 (the public property provisions).

(f) Regions

The term "region" has no precise meaning in Canadian political discourse,[28] but the idea of region has been influential in several contexts.

Membership of the Senate of Canada[29] does not follow the American and Australian pattern of equal representation of each state. The numbers of the Canadian Senate are drawn equally from regions, which the Act describes as "divisions". Originally, three divisions were recognized, namely, Ontario, Quebec and the three maritime provinces, and each division was represented by 24 senators. In 1915, the four western provinces were recognized as a fourth division, also represented by 24 senators. In recent times, the regional logic has been compromised. On the admission of Newfoundland in 1949, the province was not included in the maritime division, but was allocated an additional six senators. And in 1975, the Yukon and Northwest Territories were given one senator each, also outside the existing divisions, but perhaps constituting a recognition of the North as a region.

Membership of the Supreme Court of Canada[30] has also been based on a regional idea. The Supreme Court Act requires that three of the nine judges be appointed from Quebec. This legal requirement has been supplemented by a practice of appointing three judges from Ontario, two judges from the four western provinces,[31] and one judge from the four Atlantic provinces.

The Victoria Charter amending formula, which was almost agreed to in 1970,[32] called for the agreement of provinces on a regional basis. An amendment would have required the consent of the federal Parliament and (1) any province that had at any time 25 per cent of the population of Canada (that is, Ontario and Quebec), (2) at least two of the four Atlantic provinces, and (3) at least two of the four western provinces having a combined population of at least 50 per cent of the population of all the western provinces. In 1981, a variant of the Victoria Charter formula was rejected by the first ministers in favour of the seven-fifty formula that is now embodied in s. 38 of the Constitution Act, 1982.[33]

The seven-fifty formula of s. 38 rejects the idea of regions in favour of the equality of the provinces. An amendment requires the consent of the federal Parliament and two-thirds of the provinces (that is, seven provinces) having a combined population of 50 per cent of the population of all the provinces. In fact, this formula does indirectly impose some regional requirements in that seven

28 See Smiley, note 4, above, 22-23.

29 The composition of the Senate is governed by s. 22 of the Constitution Act, 1867. The Senate is discussed in ch. 9, Responsible Government, under heading 9.4(c), "The Senate", below.

30 See ch. 8, Supreme Court of Canada, under heading 8.3, "Composition of Court", below.

31 Since 1978, one of the two western judges has been drawn from British Columbia, which may constitute a recognition that B.C. is a region separate from the prairies.

32 See ch. 4, Amendment, under heading 4.1(b), "The search for a domestic amending procedure", above.

33 See ch. 4, Amendment, under heading 4.3, "General amending procedure (s. 38)", above.

provinces will always include at least one western province and at least one Atlantic province, and 50 per cent of the population will always include either Ontario or Quebec, because the other eight provinces have less than 50 per cent of the population. What the seven-fifty formula avoids, however, is the explicit recognition of regions, which is particularly distasteful to the wealthy provinces of British Columbia (unless it is recognized as a region by itself) and Alberta (which dislikes being simply lumped in with the western provinces).

A "regional veto statute" passed by the federal Parliament in 1996, however, has the indirect effect of incorporating regions into the seven-fifty formula.[34] While the statute cannot properly be considered part of the constitutional amending formula, as it is an ordinary statute rather than a constitutional amendment, the statute does purport to prevent a Minister of the Crown from introducing any resolution authorizing an amendment into the House of Commons without prior consent by the Legislatures of:

(a) Ontario;
(b) Quebec;
(c) British Columbia;
(d) two or more of the Atlantic provinces representing at least fifty per cent of the population of the Atlantic provinces; and
(e) two or more of the Prairie provinces representing at least fifty per cent of the population of the Prairie provinces.

Practically speaking, since a resolution on a matter as significant as the amendment of the Constitution of Canada can only pass in the House of Commons with the support of the government of the day, this statute superimposes a requirement of regional consent on the seven-fifty formula.

The regions contemplated by the statute are similar to those which would have been created under the Victoria Charter formula. There are two differences, however. First, under the regional veto statute, British Columbia is a separate region which was not the case under the Victoria Charter. Secondly, under the regional veto statute, the two or more Atlantic provinces which support the amendment must represent at least fifty per cent of the population of the Atlantic provinces; under the Victoria charter, any two Atlantic provinces would suffice. By giving indirect vetos to the four most populous provinces,[35] the regional veto statute compromises the equality of the provinces envisioned in the seven-fifty formula. The idea behind the statute was, of course, to give Quebec a greater influence over future amendments of the Constitution.[36]

34 S.C. 1996, c. 1. For further discussion, see ch. 4, Amendment, under heading 4.3(h), "Regional veto statute", above.

35 The consent of the Legislatures of Ontario, Quebec and British Columbia are expressly required. The consent of the Alberta Legislature is also required because Alberta has more than fifty per cent of the population of the Prairie provinces.

36 See ch. 4, Amendment, under heading 4.1(c), "The failure to accommodate Quebec", above.

(g) Subsidiarity

Subsidiarity is a principle of social organization that prescribes that decisions affecting individuals should, as far as reasonably possible, be made by the level of government closest to the individuals affected.[37] The principle has been adopted in the European Community as a guideline for the division of responsibilities between the Community institutions in Brussels and the national institutions of the member states. In Canada, the principle has rarely been invoked in political discourse, but it does offer some useful ways of thinking about the Constitution of Canada.

One of the primary goals of confederation in 1867[38] was to preserve a considerable degree of autonomy for the four original provinces. It was critical to the acceptance of the plan by French Canadians that the Legislature of the new province of Quebec, in which French speakers would be in a majority, be invested with enough powers to safeguard the French language, culture and civil law tradition. New Brunswick and Nova Scotia had existing Legislatures and had enjoyed responsible government since 1848. They wanted their Legislatures to continue to regulate much of the daily life of the people as they had before confederation. The British North America Act, 1867 accordingly invested the provincial Legislatures with authority over such matters as property and civil rights, the courts and the police, municipal institutions, hospitals and education. This was consistent with the principle of subsidiarity.

Another of the primary goals of confederation was to provide the uniting provinces with the collective benefits of an economic union, greater financial strength and an increased capacity for defence. To these ends, the British North America Act, 1867 invested the federal Parliament with authority over such matters as customs and excise, interprovincial and international trade and commerce, banking and currency, all forms of taxation and national defence. This was consistent with the principle of subsidiarity. The catalogue of federal powers does include some that one might expect to find in the provincial list, for example, the criminal law, penitentiaries and marriage and divorce. These were powers that could have been exercised at the provincial level, but, for various reasons particular to the situation of the colonies in 1867, were entrusted to the federal level, contrary to the principle of subsidiarity.

Despite some departures, the division of powers in the British North America Act, 1867 did generally adhere to what we would now describe as the principle of subsidiarity. The principle was reinforced by the decisions of the courts in the early years of confederation, which established rules that continue to set the pattern of government in modern Canada. The provincial power over property

37 See my article ''Subsidiarity and the Division of Powers in Canada'' (1993) 3 N.J.C.L. 341; and see the other articles in the symposium on subsidiarity of which that article is one contribution: (1993) 3 N.J.C.L. 301-427.

38 See ch. 2, Reception, under heading 2.4, ''Confederation'', above.

and civil rights was given a broad interpretation, so that it now includes not only the private law of property, contract and torts, but also most of commercial law, consumer law, environmental law, labour law, health law and social-services law.[39] The result is that the laws that impact most directly on individuals are for the most part provincial. The early jurisprudence tended to interpret the principal federal powers narrowly, but since the second world war the Supreme Court of Canada has generally accepted the idea that, where matters take on a national dimension, they can be regulated by the federal Parliament under its powers over peace, order, and good government,[40] trade and commerce[41] and transportation and communication.[42] This is the corollary to subsidiarity, namely, that those matters that cannot be effectively regulated at the provincial level should be the responsibility of the more distant federal level of government.

5.2 Reasons for federalism

The genesis of the federal system in Canada was a political compromise between proponents of unity (who would have preferred a legislative union) and proponents of diversity (who were unwilling to submerge the separate identities of their provinces). Probably, a tension of this sort lies at the origin of all federal systems. But it should not be assumed that federalism is just a second-best alternative to a legislative union. The federal form of government has some distinctive advantages.[43]

In a country that covers a large area,[44] and includes diverse regions, there may be advantages of efficiency and accountability in dividing the powers of government so that a national government is responsible for matters of national importance and provincial or state governments are responsible for matters of local importance. There would inevitably be diseconomies of scale if all governmental decision-making was centralized in one unwieldy bureaucracy. And a more decentralized form of government can be expected to be able to identify and give effect to different preferences and interests in different parts of the country.

A related point is that a province or state, being more homogeneous than the nation as a whole, will occasionally adopt policies that are too innovative or

---

39 See ch. 21, Property and Civil Rights, below.

40 See ch. 17, Peace, Order, and Good Government, below.

41 See ch. 20, Trade and Commerce, below.

42 See ch. 22, Transportation and Communication, below.

43 A well-known account of the political merits of federalism is in Bryce, *The American Commonwealth* (1897), ch. 29. A modern Canadian discussion is in Smiley, *The Federal Condition in Canada* (1987), 15-22.

44 Federalism is also a convenient device for developing a new and large country, allowing the gradual expansion of settlement to be accompanied by local governments that are suitable to the needs of each new region. This is one of the "merits of the federal system" offered in Bryce, previous note, 248.

radical to be acceptable to the nation as a whole. In this way, a province or state may serve as a "social laboratory" in which new kinds of legislative programmes can be "tested".[45] If a new programme does not work out, the nation as a whole has not been placed at risk. If the programme works well, it will be copied by other provinces or states, and perhaps (if the Constitution permits) by the federal government. One can observe this kind of development in Canada with respect to social credit (which started in Alberta in 1935 and never took hold), medicare (which started in Saskatchewan in 1961 and became a national programme in 1968), family property regimes (which now exist in all provinces) and no-fault automobile insurance (which now exists in several provinces).

An entirely different argument in favour of federalism is that the division of governmental power inherent in a federal system operates to preclude an excessive concentration of power and thus as a check against tyranny.[46] The other side of that argument is that "federal government means weak government", because the dispersal of power makes it hard to enact and implement new public policies, especially radical policies.[47] In the right conditions, however, as we have noticed,[48] change can be initiated by a province or state, and later adopted more widely.

5.3 Federalism in Canada

(a) The terms of the Constitution

What is Canada's position on the "spectrum"[49] of federal states? There are many indications that the framers of the B.N.A. Act planned a strong central government. The Act gives the provinces only enumerated powers to make laws, giving the residue of power to the federal Parliament.[50] This was a departure from the American precedent[51] where residuary power had been left with the states.

---

45 *New State Ice Co.* v. *Liebmann* (1932) 285 U.S. 262, 311 per Brandeis J. ("It is one of the happy incidents of the federal system that a single courageous state may, if its citizens choose, serve as a laboratory; and try novel social and economic experiments without risk to the rest of the country.") See also Trudeau, *Federalism and the French Canadians* (1968), 124-150.

46 See Proudhon, *The Principle of Federation* (1863) (trans. by Vernon, U. Toronto Press, 1979), who extols federalism as the best possible compromise between liberty and authority; Hamilton, Madison and Jay, *The Federalist* papers (1787-1788), esp. Nos. 10, 51 by Madison, arguing that federalism is a protection for minorities (especially property-owning minorities) against the rule of the majority.

47 Dicey, note 4, above, 171; Smiley, note 43, above, 19-22.

48 Note 45, above.

49 Text accompanying note 2, above.

50 See ch. 17, Peace, Order and Good Government, under heading 17.1, "Residuary nature of power", below.

51 Lord Haldane seemed to think that this departure made Canada not truly federal: *A.-G. Aust.* v. *Colonial Sugar Refining Co.* [1914] A.C. 237, 252-254; criticized by Kennedy, *The Constitution of Canada 1534-1937* (2nd ed., 1938), 408-412; Wheare, *Federal Government* (4th ed., 1963), 12.

(When the Australian colonies united in 1900 they followed the American precedent.) And the list of specified heads of federal power included several topics left to the states in the United States (and, later, in Australia). Thus, the Canadian federal Parliament was given, by s. 91(2), the power to regulate ''trade and commerce'' without qualification, while the United States Congress had been given the more limited power to regulate ''commerce with foreign nations and among the several states and with the Indian tribes''.[52] Banking (s. 91(15)), marriage and divorce (s. 91(26)), the criminal law (s. 91(27)) and penitentiaries (s. 91(28)) were other topics allocated to the federal Parliament in Canada, but reserved to the states in the United States.[53] Even more significantly, the federal government was envisaged as fiscally dominant. The federal Parliament was given, by s. 91(3), the power to levy indirect as well as direct taxes while the provinces were confined, by s. 92(2), to direct taxes; in the 1860s, the indirect taxes of customs and excise accounted for 80 per cent of the uniting colonies' revenues, and so a system of federal grants to the provinces was established from the beginning in recognition that the provinces' tax-raising capacity would not be adequate for their needs.[54]

Not only did the B.N.A. Act's distribution of powers contemplate a more centralized system than that of the United States — the only useful federal precedent in existence in 1867,[55] in several respects, the provinces were actually made subordinate to the centre, in violation of the principle that in a federal state the regions should be coordinate with the centre. First, by s. 90 the federal government was given the power to disallow (i.e., invalidate) provincial statutes. Secondly, by s. 58, the federal government was given the power to appoint the Lieutenant Governor of each province (and, by s. 92(1), the provinces were denied the power to alter that part of their constitutions). Thirdly, by s. 96, the federal government was given the power to appoint the judges of the superior, district and county courts of each province. Fourthly, by s. 93, the federal government was given the power to determine appeals from provincial decisions affecting minority educational rights, and the federal Parliament was given the power to

52 United States Constitution, art. 1, s. 8(3). Ironically, the qualified language of the U.S. ''commerce clause'' has been given almost unlimited scope in the courts, while the unqualified language of the Canadian trade and commerce power has been severely restricted in the courts: see ch. 20, Trade and Commerce, below.

53 Australia's later federal list borrowed banking and marriage and divorce, but not the criminal law or penitentiaries.

54 Nowadays, of course, the ''direct'' taxation of personal and corporate income is the most lucrative source of governmental revenue; and the prohibition on ''indirect'' taxation has proved easy to circumvent. But these accretions in provincial fiscal capacity have still left the federal government fiscally dominant. This is related in detail in the next chapter, Chapter 6, Financial Arrangements.

55 The only other federal constitution in existence in 1867 was that of Switzerland, but its small geographic size, and different social and political environment made it a dubious precedent in comparison with the United States: see Birch, *Federalism, Finance and Social Legislation* (1955), xiv.

enforce a decision on appeal by the enactment of "remedial laws". Fifthly, by ss. 91(29) and 92(10)(c), the federal Parliament was given the power unilaterally to bring local works within exclusive federal legislative jurisdiction simply by declaring them to be "for the general advantage of Canada". None of these five matters is to be found among the federal powers in the earlier Constitution of the United States or in the later Constitution of Australia.

Wheare was so impressed by the elements of provincial subordination in the Constitution of Canada that he refused to describe it as federal; he preferred to say that "Canada has a quasi-federal constitution".[56] This judgment is fully justified by a literal reading of the terms of the Constitution. However, the subsequent development of case law, convention and practice has virtually eliminated the elements of provincial subordination in the Constitution.

(b) Early federal dominance

In the early years of confederation, the relationship between the new national government and the provinces was if anything understated by the term quasi-federal; it was more akin to a colonial relationship. The national government, with the bulk of the governmental revenues and most of the ablest politicians, exercised a control over the provinces not at all unlike that of an imperial government over its colonies.[57] Over the years, however, there has been a steady growth in the power and importance of the provinces.[58] If we re-examine the centralizing features of the Constitution of Canada in the light of the current body of case law, convention and practice, it is clear that Canada now has a federal Constitution on Wheare's definition, or any other reasonable definition, and indeed one that is less centralized than that of either the United States or Australia.

(c) Judicial interpretation of the distribution of powers

The Judicial Committee of the Privy Council was the final court of appeal for Canada in constitutional cases until appeals were abolished in 1949. Two figures dominated the course of decision in Canadian constitutional cases: Lord Watson, who was a law lord (and thus a member of the Privy Council) from 1880 to 1899,[59] and Lord Haldane, who was a law lord from 1911 to 1928.[60] They

---

56 Wheare, *Federal Government* (4th ed., 1963), 19, although he conceded (at p. 20) that the Constitution was "predominantly federal in practice".

57 See Mallory in Crépeau and Macpherson (eds.), *The Future of Canadian Federalism* (1965), 3.

58 See ch. 6, Financial Arrangements, below.

59 Lord Watson's influence is studied by Greenwood, "Lord Watson . . ." (1974) 9 U.B.C. L. Rev. 244 and Wexler, "The Urge to Idealize: Viscount Haldane . . ." (1984) 29 McGill L.J. 608; see also Haldane's eulogy of Watson (1899) 11 Juridical Review 278.

60 Lord Haldane's influence is studied by Robinson, "Lord Haldane and the B.N.A. Act" (1970) 20 U. Toronto L.J. 55; Wexler, previous note; see also Heuston, *Lives of the Lord Chancellors 1885-1940* (1964), 185-240.

believed strongly in provincial rights, and they established precedents that elevated the provinces to coordinate status with the Dominion,[61] and gave a narrow interpretation to the principal federal powers (the residuary power and the trade and commerce power) and a wide interpretation to the principal provincial power (over property and civil rights in the province).[62] The decisions of the Privy Council — the ''wicked stepfathers of confederation'', as Forsey calls them — were much criticized in English Canada[63] (although not in French Canada)[64] for their provincial bias.

In retrospect, the decisions of the Privy Council can be seen as consistent with other tendencies in Canada towards a less centralized federal system than that of the United States or Australia.[65] Recent appraisals of the work of the Privy Council have tended to recognize this, and have been much less critical.[66] Judicial interpretation since the abolition of appeals has permitted some growth of federal power, and this may well continue. However, it is unlikely that there will be any wholesale rejection of Privy Council decisions: the main lines of judicial inter-

---

61 *Hodge* v. *The Queen* (1883) 9 App. Cas. 117 (provincial legislative powers as plenary and ample as imperial Parliament); *Liquidators of the Maritime Bank* v. *Receiver General of N.B.* [1892] A.C. 437 (provincial executive powers match legislative powers).

62 For a full account see Scott, ''Centralization and Decentralization in Canadian Federalism'' (1951) 29 Can. Bar Rev. 1095; see also chs. 17, 20 and 21, below.

63 E.g., O'Connor Report (Senate of Canada, 1939); Laskin, ''Peace, Order and Good Government Re-Examined'' (1947) 25 Can. Bar Rev. 1054; Scott, previous note.

64 E.g., Tremblay Report (Quebec, 1956); Pigeon, ''The Meaning of Provincial Autonomy'' (1951) 29 Can. Bar Rev. 1126; Beetz in Crépeau and Macpherson, *The Future of Canadian Federalism* (1965), 113. Tremblay, *Les compétences législatives au Canada* (1967), although Tremblay concedes (at p. 47) that ''les intentions des péres de la fédration . . . étaient de créer un régime fortement centralisé''.

65 See ch. 6, Financial Arrangements, under heading 6.9, ''Conclusions'', below. McWhinney, *Judicial Review* (4th ed., 1969), 25-27, 70-71, argues that the Privy Council interpretations were consistent with the dominant political viewpoint in Canada at the time; he notes that from 1896 onwards, when the Privy Council rendered its pro-provincial decisions, Canada was mostly dominated by the Liberal Party, which depended upon the French Canadians for its parliamentary majority far more than the Conservative Party. Trudeau, *Federalism and the French Canadians* (1968), 198, says that ''if the law lords had not leaned in that [provincial] direction, Quebec separation might not be a threat today; it might be an accomplished fact.'' Gilbert, *Australian and Canadian Federalism 1867-1984* (1986) finds that Australian decisions tended to favour central power, while Canadian decisions tended to favour provincial power. Comparisons with the United States would produce the same, although more marked, divergence in trends of interpretation: on the commerce power, see Smith, *The Commerce Power in Canada and the United States* (1963).

66 The definitive study is Cairns, ''The Judicial Committee and its Critics'' (1971) 4 Can. J. Pol. Sci. 301. See also Browne, *The Judicial Committee and the British North America Act* (1967); Cheffins and Tucker, *The Constitutional Process in Canada* (2nd ed., 1976), 105-110; Lederman, ''Unity and Diversity in Canadian Federalism'' (1975) 53 Can. Bar Rev. 597; Vaughan, ''Critics of the Judicial Committee of the Privy Council'' (1986) 19 Can. Jo. Poli. Sci. 495.

pretation are probably irreversible.[67] For present purposes, the point is that the distribution of powers in the Constitution of Canada is much less favourable to the federal power than would be suggested merely by comparing the text with that of the American or Australian Constitutions.

(d) Federal-provincial financial arrangements

The fiscal dominance of the federal government which was established by the B.N.A. Act in 1867 has continued, but since the second world war there has been a substantial shift in power back to the provinces; and the present federal-provincial financial arrangements give the Canadian provinces more financial autonomy than is enjoyed by the states of the United States or Australia.[68] The financial arrangements are the subject of the next chapter.

(e) Disallowance

The federal power to disallow provincial statutes[69] was frequently exercised by the dominant federal government in the early years of confederation. Its use today would provoke intense resentment on the part of the provinces. If the federal objection to a provincial statute is that it is ultra vires or inconsistent with a federal law, the province may fairly insist that a court is the appropriate forum to determine the issue. If the federal objection to a provincial statute is that it is unwise, then the province may fairly reply that its voters should be left to determine the wisdom of the policies of the government which they have elected. In my view, the provincial case is unimpeachable: the modern development of ideas of judicial review and democratic responsibility has left no room for the exercise of the federal power of disallowance. This view has not been espoused in so many words by the federal government, but I think it may be safely assumed to be the prevailing official federal sentiment, since the power of disallowance has not been exercised since 1943.[70] The Charlottetown Accord of 1992[71] would have repealed the power

---

67 See the studies of the decisions of the Supreme Court of Canada since 1949 by Weiler, ''The Supreme Court and Canadian Federalism'' (1973) 23 U. Toronto L.J. 307; Hogg, ''Is the Supreme Court of Canada Biased in Constitutional Cases?'' (1979) 57 Can. Bar Rev. 721; Monahan, *Politics and the Constitution* (1987); Swinton, *The Supreme Court and Canadian Federalism* (1990).

68 See ch. 6, Financial Arrangements, under heading 6.9, ''Conclusions'', below.

69 Constitution Act, 1867, s. 90. This is not to be confused with the imperial power to disallow federal statutes: ch. 3, Independence, under heading 3.1, ''Bonds of Empire'', above.

70 For the history of federal disallowance of provincial legislation, see La Forest, *Disallowance and Reservation of Provincial Legislation* (1965); see also Saywell, *The Office of Lieutenant-Governor* (1957), ch. 8; Forsey, *Freedom and Order* (1974), 177-191; Wilson (1975) 39 Sask. L. Rev. 156; Vipond (1990) 39 U.N.B.L.J. 126. In *Re Powers of Disallowance and Reservation* [1938] S.C.R. 71, the Supreme Court of Canada held that the power of disallowance was ''still a subsisting power''. In *Re Resolution to Amend the Constitution* [1981] 1 S.C.R. 753, 802, the Court said, obiter, that ''reservation and disallowance of provincial legislation, although in law

of disallowance, but the defeat of that set of constitutional amendments has left the power in the Constitution.

(f) Appointment of Lieutenant Governors

The federal power to appoint Lieutenant Governors is another apparent breach of the federal principle. This power is regularly exercised by the federal government,[72] but once an appointment is made the Lieutenant Governor is in no sense the agent of the federal government:[73] he or she is obliged by the conventions of responsible government to act on the advice of the provincial cabinet.[74] The Lieutenant Governor does have power under s. 90 of the Constitution Act, 1867 to withhold his assent from a bill enacted by the provincial legislative assembly, and to "reserve" the bill for consideration by the federal government. But the power of reservation is as obsolete as the power of disallowance, and for the same reasons; the federal government would never today instruct a Lieutenant Governor to reserve a provincial bill. There have been occasional reservations in modern times, but they have been "almost wholly frivolous and acutely embarrassing to the federal government".[75]

(g) Appointment of judges

The federal power under s. 96 of the Constitution Act, 1867 to appoint the judges of the higher provincial courts is exercised by the federal cabinet whenever

---

still open, have, to all intents and purposes, fallen into disuse." In *The Queen* v. *Beauregard* [1986] 2 S.C.R. 56, 72, the Court said, obiter, that the disallowance power has fallen into "disuse". Some commentators would still support its occasional use, especially to protect civil liberties: e.g., Mallory, *The Structure of Canadian Government* (1984 rev. ed.), 369-370; Forsey, above, 167-171; while others argue that it is now (by convention) obsolete: e.g., Trudeau, note 65, above, 149; Cheffins and Tucker, note 66, above, 86, 123; Laskin, *The British Tradition in Canadian Law* (1969), 122 says that the power is "dormant, if not entirely dead." Dawson, *The Government of Canada* (6th ed., 1987 by Ward), 226, says that "some of the main reasons that might have been adduced to activate the disallowance power before 1982 seem to have been largely dissipated by the Charter . . .".

71 See ch. 4, Amendment, under heading 4.1(c), "The failure to accommodate Quebec", above.

72 See ch. 9, Responsible Government, under heading 9.2, "Law and convention", below.

73 *Ibid.*

74 The Lieutenant Governor also has certain "reserve powers" which are not exercised on the advice of the provincial cabinet. These powers are designed to bridge the situation where no government enjoys the confidence of the legislative assembly. The reserve powers would be exercised upon the Lieutenant Governor's personal discretion and not upon instructions from the federal government; if the federal government were asked for advice, it would undoubtedly refuse the request. The reserve powers are discussed in ch. 9, Responsible Government, under heading 9.6, "The Governor General's personal prerogatives", below.

75 Mallory, note 70, above, 371.

a superior, district or county court judgeship has to be filled.[76] Moreover, some federal governments have been wont to treat the power as one of patronage, and to give preference to supporters of the party in power in Ottawa (which is often not the party in power in the provincial capital). But the tradition of judicial independence is so strong that it has never been seriously claimed that the federally-appointed provincial judges would tend to favour the federal interest in disputes coming before them. In any event, cases involving important federal-provincial issues, for example, a challenge to the constitutionality of a statute, are usually appealed out of the provincial courts.

Before 1949, the final court of appeal was the Privy Council, whose members were appointed by the United Kingdom government. Since 1949, the final court of appeal has been the Supreme Court of Canada, which is a federal court created by a federal statute, whose judges are appointed and paid by the federal government. One of the contributions of French Canadian commentary in recent years has been to point out that the final court of appeal should not have its composition, and indeed its very existence, depend upon one government and Parliament. It is of course not seriously suggested that Ottawa would ever abolish the Court, take away the judges' tenure, attempt to influence its appointees, or "pack" the Court with centralists; but it is suggested that justice in federal-provincial controversies would be better seen to be done if the Court were entrenched in the constitution, and if the provinces had a role in appointing the judges. These ideas are pursued in the later chapter on the Supreme Court of Canada.[77]

(h) Educational appeals

The federal power under s. 93 of the Constitution Act, 1867 to enact remedial laws to correct provincial incursions on minority educational rights[78] has never been exercised, and has in practice become "obsolete".[79] It was almost exercised in 1896, when a Conservative government introduced in the federal Parliament a remedial bill to solve the Manitoba school question. But before the bill could be passed the government was defeated in an election fought on that issue. The new Liberal government of Prime Minister Laurier persuaded Manitoba itself to rectify the situation, which it did by statute in 1897.[80] Federal power under s. 93 has not been used (or seriously threatened) since 1896.

76 See ch. 7, Courts, below. Actually, as that chapter shows, the more important "unitary" feature of the administration of justice in Canada consists in the fact that provincial courts decide cases arising under federal as well as provincial laws, and their decisions are subject to appeal to the central general court of appeal, the Supreme Court of Canada.

77 Ch. 8, Supreme Court of Canada, under heading 8.8, "Reform of Court", below.

78 Cf. Constitution of the United States, thirteenth amendment, fourteenth amendment, fifteenth amendment, conferring upon the Congress the power to "enforce" those three amendments.

79 Dawson, *The Government of Canada* (6th ed., 1987 by Ward), 306.

80 See Schmeiser, *Civil Liberties in Canada* (1964), 158-166.

(i) Declaratory power

The federal Parliament's power under s. 92(10)(c) to bring a local work within federal jurisdiction by declaring it to be "for the general advantage of Canada" was frequently used in the past, mainly in respect of local railways. It has been used only sparingly in recent years.[81] The Charlottetown Accord of 1992[82] would have amended s. 92(10)(c) to make the declaratory power subject to the consent of the Legislature of the province in which the declared work was located. The defeat of the Accord has left the power in its original, unilateral condition.

(j) Conclusion

It is fair to conclude that the unitary elements of the Canadian Constitution are quite unimportant in relation to the federal elements, and that the Canadian Constitution is federal under any reasonable definition of that term.

5.4 Supremacy of the Constitution

The essential characteristic of a federal constitution, as we have seen, is the distribution of governmental power between coordinate central and regional authorities. This requires a constitution which defines the powers vested in the central and regional authorities. The constitution must be in writing, because such a vital matter could not be left to unwritten understandings.[83] The constitution must be "supreme", meaning that it must be binding on, and unalterable by, each of the central and regional authorities.[84] If either could unilaterally change the distribution of powers, then the authorities would not be coordinate: supreme power would lie with the authority having the power to change the constitution. The same idea is sometimes expressed by saying that a federal constitution must be "rigid". The term "rigid" does not imply that it cannot be amended — for all federal constitutions contain provision for amendment — but it does imply that the power-distributing parts of the constitution cannot be amended by ordinary legislative action: a special, and more difficult, process is required for amendment.

In most unitary states, the constitution is also rigid and in writing, but it does not have to be. In the United Kingdom or New Zealand, for example, the constitution is "flexible", meaning that any part of it can be altered by ordinary

81 See ch. 22, Transportation and Communication, under heading 22.8, "Works for the general advantage of Canada", below.

82 See ch. 4, Amendment, under heading 4.1(c), "The failure to accommodate Quebec", above.

83 Wheare, *Federal Government* (4th ed., 1963), 54; Dicey, *The Law of the Constitution* (10th ed., 1960), 146.

84 Wheare, previous note, 54; Dicey, previous note, 144.

legislative action. Much of the constitution of each country is not in writing; and those parts that are in writing are alterable by the ordinary legislative process.

In Canada, the powers of the Dominion and the provinces are defined in the Constitution Acts, 1867 to 1982, which are part of the "Constitution of Canada".[85] As explained in chapter 4, Amendment, neither the federal Parliament nor a provincial legislature has the powar to alter unilaterally the provisions of the Constitution of Canada: the amending procedures of Part V of the Constitution Act, 1982 must be used for that purpose.[86] For most amendments, Part V requires the assents of the two Houses of the federal Parliament and two-thirds of the provincial legislative assemblies representing 50 per cent of the population of all the provinces. This entrenchment of the Constitution of Canada makes it "rigid". As well, s. 52(1) of the Constitution Act, 1982 expressly affirms the supremacy over all other laws of the Constitution of Canada.[87]

5.5 Role of the courts

(a) Development of judicial review

We have seen that a distribution of legislative power among independent and coordinate authorities entails the supremacy of a written constitution. It has another consequence too. The provisions of a constitution distributing legislative power will be couched in general language which cannot possibly be free from doubt or ambiguity. And so there will be disputes as to whether or not a particular legislative body has the power to enact a particular statute. Any federal system therefore has to have a machinery for settling disputes about the distribution of legislative power. Neither the Constitution of the United States nor the Constitution of Canada expressly provides a machinery for settling disputes about the distribution of legislative power, and there is controversy as to what the framers of each constitution intended.[88]

In *Marbury* v. *Madison* (1803),[89] the Supreme Court of the United States, in an opinion delivered by Marshall C.J., took upon itself the power to settle disputes about the distribution of legislative power. The Court reached the momentous

---

85 The term is defined in s. 52(2) of the Constitution Act, 1982. The definition is discussed in ch. 1, Sources, under heading 1.4, "Constitution of Canada", above.

86 Within Part V, ss. 44 and 45 are exceptional in that they authorize limited kinds of amendment by the federal Parliament alone and the provincial Legislature alone, but ss. 44 and 45 do not extend to any of the power-distributing provisions of the Constitution of Canada.

87 Section 52(1) is discussed in ch. 3, Independence, under heading 3.4, "Canada Act 1982", above.

88 Strayer, *The Canadian Constitution and the Courts* (3rd ed., 1988), ch. 1; Smith, "The Origins of Judicial Review in Canada" (1983) 16 Can. Jo. Pol. Sci. 115. The later Australian constitution appears to envisage judicial review: Sawer, *Australian Federalism in the Courts* (1967), 76.

89 (1803) 5 U.S. (1 Cranch) 137.

decision that an Act of Congress was invalid as unconstitutional. The Act in question purported to give to the Supreme Court of the United States the jurisdiction to issue writs of mandamus against federal courts and officials. The Court held that this power was original jurisdiction and not appellate jurisdiction. But the Constitution stated that with certain specified exceptions the Supreme Court was to have only appellate jurisdiction. The Supreme Court's decision that the statute was invalid was based on very simple reasoning. (The question, the Court said, was "happily, not of an intricacy proportioned to its interest".) The Court said that its duty was to say what the law was. But here there were two inconsistent laws, the Constitution and the statute. It was therefore necessary to decide which one was in truth the law. The Court held that in a conflict between the Constitution and a statute, the Constitution should prevail, because it was superior to the statute. "The people", who had established the Constitution, had "supreme" authority; they could seldom act; and they intended the Constitution to be permanent. After *Marbury* v. *Madison*, it became accepted in the United States (though not immediately by the executive branch of the government) that the courts did have the role of settling disputes as to the distribution of powers under the Constitution, and therefore that the courts had the power to declare invalid the acts of a democratically elected legislature.

The Privy Council (as the ultimate court of appeal for Canada) and the provincial courts, in the years immediately after 1867, assumed the right to review the validity of legislation enacted by the Canadian legislative bodies. They used an argument similar to the one that had been accepted in *Marbury* v. *Madison*, although the Canadian rationale was "based more on imperialism than on constitutionalism".[90] If a statute was inconsistent with the B.N.A. Act, then the B.N.A. Act had to prevail, because it was an imperial statute. Imperial statutes extending to Canada had overriding force because the Colonial Laws Validity Act provided that colonial legislation repugnant to an imperial statute extending to the colony was invalid.[91] After the Supreme Court of Canada was established in 1875 it naturally assumed the same power.[92] Since 1982, of course, the doctrine of repugnancy defined by the Colonial Laws Validity Act has been replaced by the supremacy clause in s. 52(1) of the Constitution Act, 1982.[93] Section 52(1) stipulates that the "Constitution of Canada"[94] is "the supreme law of Canada", and that "any law that is inconsistent with the provisions of the Constitution is, to the extent of the inconsistency, of no force and effect". Section 52(1) is the current basis of judicial review in Canada.[95]

---

90 Russell, *The Judiciary in Canada* (1987), 93.

91 See ch. 3, Independence, under heading 3.2, "Colonial Laws Validity Act, 1865", above.

92 Strayer, note 88, above, ch. 1.

93 See ch. 3, Independence, under heading 3.3, "Canada Act 1982", above.

94 This term is defined in s. 52(2) of the Constitution Act, 1982.

95 This point is disputable. It could be argued that judicial review does not now depend on s. 52(1), and did not before 1982 depend on the Colonial Laws Validity Act. The argument is that judicial review depends, not on a doctrine of inconsistency or repugnancy, but on a doctrine of

The Constitution Act, 1982 also broadened the scope of judicial review by adding a Charter of Rights to the Constitution of Canada. A Charter of Rights is not essential to a federal system, of course, but when it exists it adds an additional set of provisions limiting the powers of legislative bodies. Those additional limits then give rise to judicial review in the same way as the limits created by the distribution-of-powers provisions. In the United States, judicial review under the Bill of Rights has become much more frequent than judicial review under the distribution-of-powers provisions of the Constitution. In Canada, the short experience with the Charter of Rights has established a similar trend here.

Within the existing institutional structure in Canada (and the United States and Australia) some degree of judicial review is inevitable.[96] It is true that the courts could have developed a quite different doctrine from that of *Marbury* v. *Madison* by holding that each legislative body is the interpreter of its own powers. But this would only have reduced judicial review.[97] It would not have eliminated it, because eventually the courts would have had to decide which of two inconsistent laws enacted by two different law-making bodies within the federation was valid. Even if this were the only task of the courts, it would be a very important and difficult one. There would be the problem (which arises now in fields of concurrent jurisdiction) of deciding when laws were inconsistent. Then there would be the problem of deciding which of two inconsistent laws should prevail. The latter task might involve interpreting the constitution in much the same way as occurs now. (If the courts simply accorded paramountcy to federal legislation, as they do now, then the Parliament would be legally able to take over the entire legislative field.) The fact is that disputes as to the distribution of legislative power

ultra vires. What is important about a constitution is, not that it is a supreme law, but that it limits the powers of legislative bodies. An attempt by a legislative body to act outside its powers is void because it is ultra vires. This argument is made in Wheare, *The Constitutional Structure of the Commonwealth* (1960), ch. 3. The argument suggests that s. 52(1) is not necessary to support judicial review. But the argument presupposes that it is possible to identify the provisions that limit the powers of legislative bodies. Even on the ultra vires rationale, s. 52(1) would serve the function of identifying all of the "Constitution of Canada" as constituting a set of limits on the powers of Canadian legislative bodies, since s. 52(1) declares that a law that is inconsistent with any provision of the Constitution of Canada is "of no force or effect". Thus, the difference between the inconsistency theory and the ultra vires theory now lacks practical importance for Canada, although, as Wheare shows, before 1982 in Canada and elsewhere in the Commonwealth the point was not wholly academic. It was treated in more length in the first edition of this book (1977) at pp. 43-45.

96 Accord, Kelsen, *General Theory of Law and State* (1946), 268.

97 It would, however, have eliminated judicial review under the bill of rights, and thereby rendered the bill of rights impotent, except to the extent that the bill of rights confers enforcement power on some body other than a court. Congressional enforcement is authorized by the thirteenth, fourteenth and fifteenth amendments of the Constitution of the United States, but judicial review has overwhelmingly dominated enforcement. Judicial review is the only means of enforcement of the Canadian Charter of Rights: legislative enforcement is expressly prohibited by s. 31.

are inevitable within a federation, and ultimately there is no body with power to decide them other than the courts.[98]

In a unitary state, the courts may also have the power to declare legislation invalid. This will be so in any unitary state that has adopted a rigid constitution. But in the United Kingdom and New Zealand the courts do not have this power. Setting aside the case where the Parliament has failed to follow the correct procedure (or manner and form) of legislation,[99] any law enacted by the United Kingdom or New Zealand Parliament will be held valid in the courts, even if it amends the constitution. This is just another way of saying that the constitutions of the United Kingdom and New Zealand are flexible.

(b) Limitations of judicial review

In a federal state such as Canada, where legislative powers are distributed between a central legislative body (the federal Parliament) and regional legislative bodies (the provincial Legislatures), one function of judicial review is to enforce the distribution-of-powers rules (the rules of federalism). The courts often have to determine whether a particular statute comes within the powers conferred by the Constitution on the legislative body that enacted the statute: if the statute is judicially determined to be outside the powers conferred upon the enacting body, then the statute is ultra vires and for that reason invalid. As well, a constitution, such as that of Canada, will contain some restrictions on legislative power which serve to protect civil libertarian values, or at any rate values other than the federal distribution of powers. Even before the adoption of the Charter of Rights in 1982, the Constitution of Canada contained various restrictions on legislative power,[100] and since 1982 the Charter of Rights has imposed a new set of restrictions on legislative power. A second function of judicial review is to enforce the Charter restrictions and the other non-federal restrictions. The courts often have to decide whether a statute violates a constitutional prohibition, for example, by unjustifiably abridging freedom of expression: if the statute is judicially determined to

---

98 Weiler, *In the Last Resort* (1974), ch. 6, argues that the courts should allow each legislative body to be the interpreter of its own powers, but he still concedes two functions to the courts: (1) resolving clashes between inconsistent laws (the point mentioned in the text), and (2) enforcing a prohibition on provincial laws discriminating against extra-provincial persons or products. He also leaves open the possibility of judicial review under a bill of rights. Weiler's argument is criticized in Swinton, *The Supreme Court and Canadian Federalism* (1990), ch. 2.

99 See ch. 12, Parliamentary Sovereignty, under heading 12.3(b), ''Manner and form of future laws'', below.

100 E.g., Constitution Act, 1867, s. 93 (denominational schools), ss. 96-100 (judiciary), s. 125 (intergovernmental taxation), s. 133 (language). There are many judicial decisions striking down laws for breach of each of these prohibitions.

violate the prohibition, then the statute is ultra vires[101] and for that reason invalid.

Whether judicial review takes place on distribution-of-powers (or federalism) grounds or on Charter grounds, it appears to be a normal judicial task, since it involves the interpretation of an authoritative text, the Constitution of Canada. This task is similar to the interpretation of a statute, a will or a contract, for example. Indeed, the Constitution, like a statute, a will or a contract, often provides a clear answer to the questions it addresses, which in the case of the Constitution are questions about the extent of governmental power. It is perfectly clear, for example, that the provincial Legislatures possess the power to regulate the disposition of property on death, and that the federal Parliament lacks this power.[102] It is equally clear that both the federal Parliament and the provincial Legislatures lack the power to prohibit criticism of the government.[103] No court has ever decided either of these points, and no court is likely to be called upon to do so: they are clear from the text of the Constitution. To these and many other constitutional questions, lawyers can and do give confident answers without recourse to the courts.[104]

The questions that come before the courts are those which are difficult or doubtful, and certainly there is no lack of these. The language of the Constitution is for the most part broad and vague. The rules that distribute the whole range of legislative power occupy only a few pages of text, as does the Charter of Rights. The scope of potential governmental activity that the rules address is so enormous that many problems will inevitably be overlooked by the framers of the text. Moreover, the passage of time produces social and economic change which throws up new problems which could not possibly have been foreseen by the framers of the text. For these reasons, the court probably has to apply a larger discretionary judgment to its constitutional decisions than it does to its decisions in other fields of the law. That is why Hughes C.J. of the United States Supreme Court made his celebrated remark that: ''We are under a Constitution, but the Constitution is what the judges say it is''.[105]

The judges upon whom the large task of judicial review rests are not well suited to the policy-making which is inevitably involved. Their mandate to make decisions differs from that of other public officials in that judges are not accountable to any electorate or to any government for their decisions; on the contrary,

---

101 Some constitutional lawyers would reserve the term ultra vires for breach of the distribution-of-powers rules, but I think it is better to regard the Charter and other prohibitions as additional restrictions on the powers of the legislative bodies.

102 The governing rule is the allocation to the provincial Legislatures of ''property and civil rights in the province'' by s. 92(13) of the Constitution Act, 1867.

103 The governing rule is the guarantee of ''freedom of . . . expression'' in s. 2(b) of the Charter of Rights.

104 Imagine how often lawyers have been asked by their clients, ''Is there any way I can challenge this statute?'', and have replied, ''No''.

105 Quoted, Corwin, *The Constitution and What it Means Today* (14th ed., 1978), xiii. Hughes was Governor of New York when he made the remark.

they occupy a uniquely protected place in the system of government, which is designed to guarantee their independence from political or other influences.[106] Their background is not broadly representative of the population: they are recruited exclusively from the small class of successful, middle-aged lawyers; they do not necessarily have much knowledge of or experience in public affairs, and after appointment they are expected to remain aloof from most public issues. The resources available to the judges are limited by the practice and procedure of an Anglo-Canadian court: they are obliged to decide cases on the basis of the limited information presented to them in court; they have no power to initiate inquiries or research, no staff of investigators or researchers, and of course no power to enact a law in substitution for one declared invalid.

These limitations of mandate, background, information and power led Sir Owen Dixon, the great Chief Justice of the High Court of Australia, to say that "there is no other safe guide to judicial decisions in great conflicts than a strict and complete legalism".[107] But a "strict and complete legalism" cannot be an answer to the exercise of political choice by judges. In those cases which find their way to the higher appellate courts, there are always competing plausible interpretations of the constitutional text and its case-law exegesis. The judges cannot escape making a choice, and the choice cannot be wholly explained by the pre-existing state of the law. It is undeniable that, as Oliver Wendell Holmes said long ago, a judicial decision may "depend on a judgment or intuition more subtle than any articulate major premise".[108]

Holmes' famous comment was made in dissent in *Lochner* v. *New York* (1905),[109] a case in which the Supreme Court of the United States struck down a state statute forbidding employment in a bakery for more than 60 hours per week or 10 hours per day. This law, the majority held, deprived the employer of his "liberty" of contract without "due process of law" in violation of the fourteenth amendment. Holmes J. pointed out in his dissenting opinion that this legal argument (substantive due process) masked an economic theory which had been rejected by the legislature. But the majority's ruling was applied in 159 later Supreme Court decisions, in which attempts by states to fix maximum working hours, minimum wages and maximum prices, and to prohibit anti-union activity, were held to be unconstitutional on similar grounds.[110] *Lochner* and the other substantive due process cases of that era were not overruled until 1937.[111]

The High Court of Australia — Dixon C.J.'s own court — is open to the charge that, under the cloak of "a strict and complete legalism", it was influenced by laissez faire economic theories. It blocked the major peace-time initiatives of

106 See ch. 7, Courts, under heading 7.1(c), "Tenure of provincial judges", below.

107 The statement was made on his appointment as Chief Justice: (1952) 85 C.L.R. xiv.

108 *Lochner* v. *New York* (1905) 198 U.S. 45, 76.

109 See previous note.

110 Lockhart, Kamisar, Choper, *Constitutional Law* (1980), 439.

111 *West Coast Hotel* v. *Parrish* (1937) 300 U.S. 379.

the federal Labour government that was in office from 1941 to 1949: federal legislation to provide medical security, to regulate state banking, and to nationalize the airlines and banks was held to be unconstitutional.[112] J.R. Mallory reaches a similar conclusion about the decisions of the Canadian courts in striking down legislation enacted by the Western provinces during the depression and drought of the 1930s to relieve their farmers of the burden of debt.[113] Another Canadian example is the line of seminal decisions of the Privy Council giving a provincial cast to the British North America Act's distribution-of-powers provisions. It is widely accepted that these decisions must be explained in part by conceptions of federalism held by Lords Watson and Haldane, the dominant members of the Privy Council between 1880 and 1928.[114]

There can be no doubt that judicial review permits, indeed requires, non-elected judges to make decisions of great political significance.[115] Yet Canada's adoption of the Charter of Rights in 1982 was a conscious decision to increase the scope of judicial review. It is hard to say whether public acceptance of judicial review flows from a belief in the myth of "a strict and complete legalism", or whether people really are content that some political choices be made by judges. It seems to me, however, that the judges' lack of democratic accountability, coupled with the limitations inherent in the adversarial judicial process, dictates that the appropriate posture for the courts in distribution of powers (or federalism) cases is one of restraint: the legislative decision should be overridden only where its invalidity is clear.[116] There should be, in other words, a presumption of con-

---

112 Galligan, *Politics of the High Court* (1987).

113 Mallory, *Social Credit and the Federal Power* (1954), esp. ch. 6.

114 See sec. 5.3(c), "Judicial interpretation of the distribution of powers", above.

115 I avoid the term "political decision", because I do not acknowledge that judges make political decisions similar to those made by politicians. To me, the element of political choice in a judicial decision is reduced to a very narrow compass by the substantive constraints of the language of the constitutional text and decided cases, and by the procedural constraints of the litigation process. A much wider choice of outcomes and reasoning is open to politicians. There is a vast American literature on the question whether and to what extent judicial decisions can be distinguished from political decisions. A seminal article is Wechsler, "Towards Neutral Principles of Constitutional Law" (1959) 73 Harv. L. Rev. 1, which probably exaggerates the neutrality of the process. The literature has reached avalanche proportions in recent years. Important books include Bickel, *The Least Dangerous Branch* (1962); Berger, *Government by Judiciary* (1977); Dworkin, *Taking Rights Seriously* (1977); Ely, *Democracy and Distrust* (1980); Choper, *Judicial Review and the National Political Process* (1980); Perry, *The Constitution, the Courts and Human Rights* (1982); Bobbitt, *Constitutional Fate* (1982). A Canadian contribution is Weiler, *In the Last Resort* (1974), esp. ch. 6.

116 This argument is pursued in the later chapter on Judicial Review on Federal Grounds: see ch. 15, under heading 15.5(g), "Criteria of choice", and (h), "Presumption of constitutionality", below. In Charter cases, however, where the constitutional contest is not between two levels of government, but between government and individual, and where the s. 33 override is available, the argument for judicial restraint is weaker; and in any event the language of s. 1 of the Charter is not consistent with judicial restraint. The scope of judicial review in Charter cases is examined in ch. 33, Charter of Rights, under heading 33.4, "Expansion of judicial review", and ch. 35, Limitation of Rights, under heading 35.5, "Presumption of constitutionality", below.

stitutionality. In this way a proper respect is paid to the legislators, and the danger of covert (albeit unconscious) imposition of judicial policy preferences is minimized.

(c) Alternatives to judicial review

It is inevitable that the role of "umpire" in a federal system will attract criticism, and criticism of the courts has sometimes led to suggestions that we take away from them the task of judicial review. The difficulty is that some other and better way of resolving federalism disputes has to be found. It is already true in Canada that federal-provincial conferences of various kinds now settle many of the problems of divided jurisdiction which would otherwise reach the courts. This tendency, which is discussed later in this chapter, and in more detail in the next chapter on federal-provincial financial arrangements, could be consummated by a constitutional amendment removing federalism disputes from the jurisdiction of the courts and remitting them for solution to direct negotiations between the interested governments.[117] But the danger of this proposal is that it might leave minority regional and cultural interests, and civil liberties, insufficiently protected from the acts of powerful majorities.

A quite different proposal for reform involves the establishment outside the ordinary courts of a specialized tribunal for constitutional disputes, which could include non-lawyers as well as lawyers, and which could be consciously composed so as to reflect different cultural and regional interests within Canada.[118] A less radical but similar proposal is to divide the Supreme Court of Canada into specialized divisions — a common law division, a civil law division and a constitutional law division; each division would be composed in such a way as to ensure maximum expertise in its own field of law, the constitutional division reflecting the different regional and cultural interests within the country.[119] But a specially-composed constitutional court or division would probably become an activist tribunal, assuming the role of giving positive direction to our constitutional law. In my view, the better posture of a court in federalism cases is one of restraint, endeavouring as far as possible to uphold the laws enacted by the elected legislative bodies.[120] Moreover, it is very difficult, and probably unwise, to isolate constitutional issues for determination by a special court or division, when they

---

117 This is Weiler's argument: note 98, above. As pointed out, however, this does not wholly eliminate the necessity for judicial review.

118 Morin, "A Constitutional Court for Canada" (1965) 43 Can. Bar Rev. 545; Morin, Le Québec et l'arbitrage constitutionnel" (1967) 45 Can. Bar Rev. 608.

119 McWhinney, in *The Confederation Challenge* (Ontario Advisory Committee on Confederation, 1967), 89; Abel, "The Role of the Supreme Court in Private Law Cases" (1965) 4 Alta. L.R. 39 argues for a similar result by removing from the Supreme Court's jurisdiction all private law cases in fields of provincial legislative authority; to like effect is Russell, "The Jurisdiction of the Supreme Court of Canada" (1968) 6 Osgoode Hall L.J. 1.

120 Note 116 and accompanying text, above.

usually arise in practice in a factual setting which also raises issues of statutory interpretation, common law and (in Quebec) civil law. Indeed, when constitutional issues have been decided in isolation from their factual setting, as they sometimes are now on constitutional references, most observers agree that the resulting opinions have often been too broad and abstract.[121] On the whole, there is much to be said in favour of the present system of judicial review by a court of general appellate jurisdiction.[122]

5.6 Amending power

Every nation requires the power to amend its constitution. In a unitary state with a flexible constitution, amendment is easy, requiring only an ordinary statute enacted by the state's single central legislative body. In a state with a rigid constitution, the process of amendment is by definition more difficult than the ordinary legislative process. We have already noticed that a federal state always has at least a partially rigid constitution, because it is essential that at least the power-distributing parts of the constitution be protected from change by the unilateral action of either the central or regional legislative bodies. It is therefore a feature of the federal constitutions of the United States, Australia and Canada that the amending process includes procedures designed to ensure that any amendment enjoys the support, not only of the federal legislative body (which is of course elected by all the people), but of some of the regional legislatures or governments or electorates as well.[123] Amendment is the topic of chapter 4 of this book.

5.7 Secession

(a) The power to secede

The question whether a province has the power to secede from the Canadian federation[124] became an issue after the election in Quebec in 1976 of the Parti Québécois. The Parti Québécois government held a referendum on May 20, 1980,

121 See ch. 8, Supreme Court of Canada, under heading 8.6, ''Reference jurisdiction'', below.

122 The case is well argued by Le Dain, ''Concerning the Proposed Constitutional and Civil Law Specialization at the Supreme Court Level'' (1967) 2 Revue Juridique Thémis 107.

123 Livingston, *Federalism and Constitutional Change* (1956) is a comparative study of the amending process in federal constitutions.

124 A comprehensive examination of the issue is in Brossard, *L'accessioné la souveraineté et le cas du Québec* (1976); see also Mayer, ''Legal Aspects of Secession'' (1968) 3 Man. L.J. 61; Matas, ''Can Quebec Separate?'' (1975) 21 McGill L.J. 387; Finkelstein and Vegh, ''The Separation of Quebec and the Constitution of Canada'' (Centre for Public Law and Public Policy, York University, Toronto, 1992); Williams, ''International Legal Effects of Secession by Quebec'' (Centre for Public Law and Public Policy, York University, Toronto, 1992).

asking the voters whether they would give to the government of Quebec a mandate to negotiate a ''sovereignty-association'' agreement with the government of Canada. Sovereignty-association was a compromise between outright separation and continuance as a province of Canada. Sovereignty-association did involve the secession of Quebec (hence ''sovereignty''), but it also involved an ''economic association'' between the new sovereign state of Quebec and (the rest of) Canada (hence ''association'').[125] This proposal was rejected by the Quebec voters by a majority of 59.5 per cent to 40.5 per cent.

The defeat of the 1980 referendum was followed by constitutional discussions, one purpose of which was to act on the grievances that contributed to nationalist sentiment in Quebec. Unfortunately, the Constitution Act, 1982, which emerged from this process, did not achieve the goal of an accommodation with Quebec, and Quebec was the only province that did not agree to the terms of the Constitution Act, 1982. After changes of government in Ottawa and Quebec City, Quebec did join an agreement that would have enabled it to give its approval to the Constitution Act, 1982. The Meech Lake Accord of 1987[126] seemed to provide an answer to the question, ''what does Quebec want?'', but unfortunately the Accord did not achieve the ratification by all provincial Legislatures that was necessary for it to come into force. The failure of the Accord led to another attempt to find an accommodation with Quebec, and this was achieved by first ministers in the Charlottetown Accord of 1992,[127] to which the Premier of Quebec was a party. Unfortunately, that Accord was also never implemented, because it was defeated in a national referendum held in 1992.

After the failures of the Meech Lake and Charlottetown Accords, the Parti Québécois won the Quebec election of 1994 with the mandate to hold another referendum on sovereignty. The referendum was held on October 30, 1995, and it asked the voters whether ''Quebec should become sovereign, after having made a formal offer to Canada for a new economic and political partnership . . .''.[128]

---

125 The full text in English of the question was as follows:

> The Government of Quebec has made public its proposal to negotiate a new agreement with the rest of Canada, based on the equality of nations; this agreement would enable Quebec to acquire the exclusive power to make its laws, administer its taxes and establish relations abroad in other words, sovereignty and at the same time, to maintain with Canada an economic association including a common currency; any change in political status resulting from these negotiations will be submitted to the people through a referendum; on these terms, do you agree to give the government of Quebec the mandate to negotiate the proposed agreement between Quebec and Canada? Yes/No.

126 See ch. 4, Amendment, under heading 4.1(c), ''The failure to accommodate Quebec'', above.

127 *Ibid.*

128 The full text in English of the question was:

> Do you agree that Quebec should become sovereign, after having made a formal offer to Canada for a new economic and political partnership, within the scope of the bill respecting the future of Quebec and of the agreement signed on June 12, 1995?

The ''bill respecting the future of Quebec'' was tabled in the Quebec National Assembly on September 7, 1995 as Bill 1, but was not to be enacted until after an affirmative vote in the

The referendum was defeated by the narrow margin of 50.6 per cent to 49.4 per cent. Although the question held out to voters the prospect of a continuing "economic and political partnership" with Canada, the question was stronger than the 1980 question for two reasons. First, whereas the 1980 referendum had merely sought a mandate to negotiate sovereignty-association with Canada, the terms of the 1995 referendum made clear that sovereignty was going to be declared regardless of whether Canada accepted the offer of partnership. The voters had to contemplate the possibility of sovereignty without association. Secondly, whereas the 1980 referendum question was explicit that a second referendum would be held to approve the outcome of the sovereignty-association negotiations, the terms of the 1995 referendum made clear that the Quebec National Assembly was empowered to proclaim Quebec as a sovereign state as soon as the partnership negotiations were completed or as soon as the partnership negotiations were judged to be fruitless.[129] In neither case was there to be a second referendum to enable the people to pass judgment on the actual arrangements for the separation of the province. The 1995 referendum also proceeded on the assumption that a unilateral declaration of independence would be legally effective to remove Quebec, with its present boundaries, from Canada without the need for any amendment of the Constitution of Canada and regardless of whether the terms of departure were agreed to by Canada. This assumption is false, as the next two sections of this chapter will explain. After the defeat of the referendum, Premier Parizeau resigned as the leader of the Parti Québécois and premier of the province, and was replaced by Premier Bouchard, who announced that another referendum on sovereignty would be held, although not until after the next Quebec election. Therefore, unless the Parti Québécois is defeated in the next election, it is very likely that another referendum will be held.[130]

---

referendum; it therefore was never enacted. This Bill purported to set out some of the arrangements for sovereignty, including assertions that Quebec's boundaries would remain the same (s. 10), that Quebec citizenship could be held concurrently with Canadian citizenship (s. 13), that Quebec's currency would remain the Canadian dollar (s. 14), and that Quebec would continue to be a party to the North American Free Trade Agreement (s. 15). The "agreement signed on June 12, 1995" was an agreement between the leaders of Quebec's three separatist parties: the Bloc Québécois, the Parti Québécois, and the Action démocratique du Québec. That agreement was scheduled to Bill 1 and it set out the terms of the "new economic and political partnership" that would be proposed to Canada following an affirmative vote. The terms included the creation of supra-national institutions in which Quebec would be equally represented with Canada and would have the power to veto Canadian policies in a wide range of economic and political matters.

129 Bill 1, previous note, s. 26.

130 There is wealth of recent commentary on the current Quebec situation and its legal implications, e.g., N. Finkelstein and G. Vegh, "The Separation of Quebec and the Constitution of Canada" (York University Centre for Public Law and Public Policy, 1992); Grand Council of the Crees, *Sovereign Injustice* (study by Paul Joffe, 1995); R.A. Young, *The Secession of Quebec and the Future of Canada* (1995); P.J. Monahan, M.J. Bryant and N.C. Coté, "Coming to Terms with Plan B: Ten Principles Governing Secession" (C.D. Howe Institute Commentary, June 1996).

There is no reason in principle why a federal constitution should not give a power of secession to its provinces or states.[131] In the United States, there was a long controversy as to the existence of such a power which was only settled by the civil war of 1861-1865. After the war was over, the Supreme Court of the United States declared that "the Constitution, in all its provisions, looks to an indestructible union, composed of indestructible states".[132] In Australia, the preamble to the Constitution describes the union as "indissoluble". In Canada, there is neither judicial decision nor explicit text to the same effect, but the absence of any provisions in the Constitution authorizing secession makes clear that no unilateral secession is possible.[133]

(b) Secession by amendment

Secession can, of course, be accomplished by amendment of the federal constitution — in the case of a Canadian province, by amendment of the Constitution of Canada. Such an amendment could not be enacted by the province desiring to secede, under s. 45 of the amending procedures (provincial Legislature alone),[134] because secession would not be simply an amendment of the "constitution of the province". It would involve a division of the national debt and of federal public property and, in the case of Quebec, arrangements for the shared use of the St. Lawrence Seaway and for land access between the Atlantic provinces and Ontario (and the west). Probably, secession could be accomplished under the general amending procedure of s. 38, that is, by the assents of both houses of the federal Parliament and of the legislative assemblies of two-thirds of the provinces representing 50 per cent of the population.[135]

The attitude of a federal government — any federal government — to a secession movement may be confidently predicted to be more or less hostile. The government may be expected to take the view that it did not assume office to preside over the dissolution of the federation. In the United States, the attempt by the southern states to secede in 1861 was opposed by the federal government and crushed by war. In Canada and Australia more cautious attempts to secede by

---

131 Wheare, *Federal Government* (4th ed., 1963), 85-87.

132 *Texas* v. *White* (1868) 74 U.S. (7 Wall.) 700, 725.

133 Wheare, note 131 above, 86; Brossard, note 124, above, 256; Matas, note 124, above, 388-389. The Monahan, Bryant and Coté study, note 130, above, reviews the constitutions of 89 states; of the 89, seven permit secession, 60 are silent on the issue, and 22 forbid secession. Of the seven that permit secession, none allow a unilateral declaration of independence, and none allow the seceding territory to set the question or conduct the referendum.

134 See sec. 4.7, "Provincial Legislature alone (s. 45)", above.

135 It is possible that the indirect impact of a secession on the matters enumerated in s. 41 makes the unanimity procedure applicable. This is in fact the majority view of academic commentators: see, e.g., N. Finkelstein and G. Vegh, "The Separation of Quebec and the Constitution of Canada" (York University Centre for Public Law and Public Policy, 1992), Part II; P.J. Monahan, "The Law and Politics of Quebec Secession" (1995) 33 Osgoode Hall L. J. 1. These two studies review the literature on the topic.

Nova Scotia in 1868 and by Western Australia in 1934 were successfully opposed by the federal government.[136] While the secession of the southern states in the United States was complicated by the slavery issue, there is no doubt that the secessionist movements in Nova Scotia and Western Australia enjoyed the support of a majority of the people in those regions;[137] yet this fact was not regarded as sufficient to justify federal cooperation or even acquiescence. Thus, even if a referendum showed that a majority of the people in a province wanted to secede, the referendum would have no constitutional significance of itself,[138] and there is no basis in history[139] or politics to suppose that the referendum would settle the policy of the federal government (or the other provincial governments). The federal government has to take a number of other considerations into account as well. It may well feel that it has no mandate to break up the country, or at least that the governments or people in other parts of the country should be consulted as to the appropriate federal attitude. The federal government will also be concerned that it has a responsibility towards the minority in the seceding province who desire to remain in Canada.[140] Finally, the federal government will want to consider whether the grievances which have provoked the secessionist movement are transitory, or could be met by means other than secession.

---

136 In 1868, Nova Scotia petitioned the imperial Parliament for an amendment allowing Nova Scotia to secede from Canada. Like all requests for amendments which did not come from the federal government, the petition was denied. In 1934, Western Australia requested an imperial amendment to the Australian Constitution allowing it to secede from the Commonwealth. A select committee of Lords and Commons decided that the request should not be considered because it had not come from the federal government (which was opposed): *Report to consider the petition of the State of Western Australia* (House of Commons, Parliamentary Papers, 1934-35, vol. 6). The precedents of Nova Scotia and Western Australia are examined by Brossard, note 124, above, 275-281; Matas, note 124, above, 392.

137 In Nova Scotia, nearly two-thirds of the voters had signed a petition in favour of secession; in Western Australia nearly two-thirds of the voters had voted for secession in a referendum: Matas, note 124, above, 402.

138 The referendum in Western Australia (previous note) illustrates this. Moreover, under existing Canadian constitutional law there are limits on the power of a province to give direct legal effect to a referendum: *Re Initiative and Referendum Act* [1919] A.C. 935; discussed in ch. 14, Delegation, under heading 14.2(d), ''Office of Lieutenant Governor or Governor General'', below.

139 A referendum was the basis for the admission of Newfoundland to confederation in 1949. The admission was accomplished by imperial amendment of the Constitution, but the request for the amendment was preceded by a referendum in Newfoundland in which a majority of votes cast favoured entry. However, the referendum was employed in that case only because Newfoundland had no Legislature in 1949 and the procedure for admission stipulated by s. 146 of the Constitution (addresses by the Parliament of Canada and Legislature of Newfoundland) had to be modified.

140 The special position of the Aboriginal people in Quebec, to whom the federal government owes a fiduciary duty, is the subject of a massive study, *Sovereign Injustice* (1995), which was prepared by Paul Joffe, and commissioned and published by the Grand Council of the Crees; it is a wide-ranging, scholarly examination of the domestic and international law on secession.

(c) Secession by unilateral act

It follows from what has just been said that there is a distinct possibility that if a majority of the people of Quebec voted in favour of secession, the assents of the two houses of the federal Parliament and of the legislative assemblies of two-thirds of the provinces representing 50 per cent of the population — the assents required by the general amending (seven-fifty) procedure — would not be forth-coming. In that event, could Quebec secede unilaterally?

A unilateral secession would, of course, be illegal because it would be unauthorized by the existing rules of constitutional law. But such a break in legal continuity may equally be regarded as a revolution, and it is a demonstrable fact that a successful revolution eventually becomes the foundation of a new and entirely legitimate legal order. The legal efficacy of a successful revolution is demonstrated by the fact that many countries whose regimes are universally recognized as lawful have had breaks in legal continuity at some time in their history. The United States springs most readily to mind: the declaration of independence in 1776, the adoption of state constitutions by each of the rebelling colonies after 1776, the adoption of the articles of confederation in 1777 and their replacement by the present federal constitution in 1787 were all unauthorized by any existing rules of constitutional law. Even the United Kingdom has had breaks in legal continuity: in 1649, when Charles I was executed and the Commonwealth was established under Cromwell; in 1660, when the Stuarts were restored to the throne; and in 1689, when William and Mary assumed the throne under the Bill of Rights.[141]

In assessing the legality of a regime established by revolution — meaning any break in legal continuity — the issue for the courts is simply whether or not the revolution has been successful. As de Smith says, "legal theorists have no option but to accommodate their concepts to the facts of political life".[142] In *Madzimbamuto* v. *Lardner-Burke* (1969),[143] the Privy Council had to decide whether validity should be accorded to the acts of the legislature and government of Southern Rhodesia after the "unilateral declaration of independence" (U.D.I.) from Britain in 1965. Their lordships held that the post-U.D.I. acts were not valid, because it could not be said "with certainty" that the break-away government was in effective control of the territory which it claimed the right to govern. Their lordships pointed out that Britain was still claiming to be the lawful government and was taking steps to regain control. In a later case, the Appellate Division of the High Court of Rhodesia decided that, having regard to developments since the decision of *Madzimbamuto*, it could "now predict with certainty that sanctions will not succeed in their objective of overthrowing the present government and

141 Jennings, *The Law and the Constitution* (5th ed., 1959), 159; de Smith and Brazier, *Constitutional and Administrative Law* (6th ed., 1989), 67.

142 de Smith, previous note, 68.

143 [1969] 1 A.C. 645.

of restoring the British government to the control of the government of Rhodesia''.[144] The Court accordingly held that the existing Rhodesian government was the legal government, and the post-U.D.I. constitution was the only valid constitution.[145]

Applying the same analysis to the hypothetical case of a unilateral declaration of independence by Quebec, the issue for the courts would be whether they could predict with certainty that the secession would be successful, that is to say, that federal authority would no longer be exercised in Quebec.[146] Obviously, the application of this criterion would depend a great deal on the attitude of the federal government. As long as it asserted its continuing authority over Quebec in areas of federal jurisdiction, it would be difficult for the courts to characterize the secession as successful. Notice that a mere likelihood of success would not justify the courts in ''changing sides'', for that would have the perverse effect of rendering illegal any efforts by the federal government to assert its authority, which would tend to implicate the courts in the political struggle.[147] The courts would have to uphold the pre-existing law of the federation until it was certain that it

144 *R.* v. *Ndhlovu* [1968] 4 S.A.L.R. 515, 532. The decision was never appealed to the Privy Council, probably because the Rhodesian government did not recognize the authority of the Privy Council (the government was not represented before the Privy Council in *Madzimbamuto*) and an appeal would have been futile.

145 Subsequent events suggested that this conclusion was premature. Guerilla war led the break-away government to seek a constitutional settlement with the United Kingdom (as well as with the blacks of Southern Rhodesia). A settlement was agreed upon at a conference in London in 1979, and independence and a new constitution (under which the white minority no longer held power) was granted to the state, now called Zimbabwe, by imperial statute: Zimbabwe Act 1979 (U.K.), c. 60; Zimbabwe Constitution Order 1979 (U.K.), S.I. 1979, No. 1600.

146 This would be the issue for the courts *inside* Quebec, and it must be remembered that the courts in Quebec are not federal courts, although the judges of the superior courts are federally appointed. Presumably, the Supreme Court of Canada, although a federal court, would decide issues arising on appeal from Quebec as if it were a Quebec court. The issue would be different for courts outside Quebec, whether Canadian or foreign; they would not exercise their own judgment as to the efficacy of the separatist regime, but would ascertain the attitude of their own government and act upon it as correct: *Carl Zeiss Stiftung* v. *Rayner and Keeler (No. 2)* [1967] 1 A.C. 853; contrast *R.* v. *Ndhlovu* (note 144, above) with *Adams* v. *Adams* [1971] P. 188 (P.D.A. Div.); if the separatist government were unrecognized, then its acts would be treated as invalid, although it is possible that effect could be given to some acts under the principle of necessity (note 148, below): [1967] 1 A.C. 853, 954; Hahlo, ''The Privy Council and the Gentle Revolution'' (1970) 16 McGill L.J. 92, 97-101; Hogg, ''Necessity in a Constitutional Crisis'' (1989) 15 Monash U.L. Rev. 253.

147 *Madzimbamuto* v. *Lardner-Burke* [1969] 1 A.C. 645, 725. The argument by Hahlo, previous note, 101-104, that the judges of the break-away country ''have no choice but to obey [the revolutionary government's] decrees'', apparently without regard for the question whether the revolution has been successful, seems objectionable in principle since it involves disregarding existing law in favour of the acts of a temporary usurper; it is also inconsistent with the decision in *Madzimbamuto*, in which, it must be remembered, the Privy Council was sitting as a Rhodesian court: [1969] 1 A.C. 645, 724.

had been effectively replaced.[148] Only after the federal government had expressly or impliedly abandoned its authority over Quebec (and there was no significant insurgency within Quebec), would the courts pronounce the separatist regime lawful.[149]

5.8 Cooperative federalism

The formal structure of the Constitution carries a suggestion of eleven legislative bodies each confined to its own jurisdiction, and each acting independently of the others. In some fields, that is exactly what happens.[150] However, in many fields, effective policies require the joint, or at least complementary, action of more than one legislative body. Particularly is this so where humanitarian and egalitarian sentiments have called for nation-wide minimum standards of health, education, income maintenance and other public services, most of which are within the territorially-limited jurisdiction of the provinces.

The formal structure of the Constitution also carries a suggestion of eleven separate fiscal systems, with each province levying taxes to raise the revenue it needs for its legislative policies, and the federal government doing the same. But if this were in fact the case the poorer provinces would be forced to provide much lower standards of public services, and much less economic opportunity, for their residents. In order to counter Canada's disparities in regional wealth, the richer regions have to help the poorer regions. To some extent they have always done so, but the current redistribution of governmental revenue through shared-cost programmes and equalization grants is on an unprecedented scale of size and complexity.

No federal nation could survive and flourish through war and peace, depression and inflation — to say nothing of shifting popular values — without the

---

148 It is possible that some acts of a usurping regime whose authority has not been successfully established could be recognized under a principle of "necessity": the necessity of preserving order and avoiding chaos. This principle was applied by the Supreme Court of the United States after the civil war to some of the internal acts performed by the confederate states during their unsuccessful secession: see, e.g., *Texas* v. *White* (1868) 7 Wall. (74 U.S.) 700, 733; *Horn* v. *Lockhart* (1873) 17 Wall. (84 U.S.) 570, 580; *Baldy* v. *Hunter* (1898) 64 Davis (171 U.S.) 388, 400, 491. It was applied by Lord Pearce in dissent in *Madzimbamuto* v. *Lardner-Burke*, note 143, above, but Lord Reid for the majority, without rejecting the principle, held it inapplicable to Southern Rhodesia on the ground that the United Kingdom had enacted a regime of law for the colony which left "no legal vacuum": *Id.*, 729. See also previous two notes.

149 See Brossard, note 124, above, 309; Matas, note 124, above, 393-395.

150 There is a school of thought that holds that competition between governments is more typical than cooperation, and more desirable, because competing governments are more likely to provide people with the policies they prefer: Royal Commission on the Economic Union and Development Prospects for Canada, *Report* (Macdonald Report) (1985) Supplementary Statement by Albert Breton, vol. 3, 486-526; Smiley, *The Federal Condition in Canada* (1987), 94-97. This model of "competitive federalism" is close to the idea of provinces as "social laboratories": note 45, above.

means of adapting its constitution to change. But the formal institutions lack the capacity to respond. Major change does not come through the courts: judicial interpretation accomplishes only incremental changes in the Constitution, and the changes do not necessarily reflect the needs of the day. Nor does change typically occur through the amending process. The amending procedures of the Constitution Act, 1982 require such broad consensus for most amendments that they cannot be a regular form of adaptation.

The related demands of interdependence of governmental policies, equalization of regional disparities, and constitutional adaptation have combined to produce what is generally described as "cooperative federalism".[151] The essence of cooperative federalism is a network of relationships between the executives of the central and regional governments. Through these relationships mechanisms are developed, especially fiscal mechanisms, which allow a continuous redistribution of powers and resources without recourse to the courts or the amending process. These relationships are also the means by which consultations occur on the many issues of interest to both federal and provincial governments. The area where cooperative federalism has been most dominant is in the federal-provincial financial arrangements. Changes in the financial arrangements have naturally altered the balance of powers within the federation. Yet the federal-provincial financial arrangements since the second world war have been worked out by the executives of the various governments, at first almost at the dictation of the federal government, latterly by intergovernmental negotiation leading to genuine agreements. The recent history of federal-provincial financial relations, and their enormous impact on the distribution of power within Canada, is the subject of the next chapter, Financial Arrangements. In that chapter, it will be explained how the taxing sources in Canada are shared between the federal and provincial governments, how federal intervention has secured nation-wide plans of health, education and welfare — matters within provincial jurisdiction, and how the richer regions of the country transfer wealth to the poorer regions. These arrangements are of course the fruits of cooperation between governments, and they in turn require that intergovernmental relations continue so that they can be maintained and adapted.

Most intergovernmental relationships depend upon informal arrangements which have no foundation in the Constitution, or in statutes, or in the conventions of parliamentary government. The most visible and important of these arrangements are the "first ministers' conferences",[152] which are federal-provincial con-

---

151 Lederman, *Continuing Canadian Constitutional Dilemmas* (1981), ch. 17; Smiley, previous note, ch. 4.

152 These conferences used to be called dominion-provincial conferences, until the term dominion fell out of favour, as related earlier in this chapter. The conferences were then called federal-provincial conferences, but there are now so many conferences between the federal and provincial governments at levels below that of first minister that the first ministers' conferences have had to have a distinctive name. Their history, functions and practices are described in

ferences of the provincial Premiers and the federal Prime Minister. It is at these conferences that the federal-provincial relationships are settled.[153] Their overweening importance stems primarily from the fact that a Premier or Prime Minister, with his supporting delegation of senior ministers and officials, is normally in a position to make commitments on behalf of his government, including commitments which require legislative action. In a system of responsible government, it is only in an unusual cabinet or parliamentary situation that there is any possibility of a Premier or Prime Minister having a commitment repudiated on his return home from a conference. Thus, the first ministers, when they meet, bring together the totality of executive power and (in practice) legislative power. As well, in Canada the relatively small number of provinces keeps the number of participants at a manageable level which facilitates direct relationships between the governments and ensures that each government has an influence on the result.

The picture of intergovernmental relations does not end at the level of the first ministers. There are several important standing federal-provincial committees of ministers, and nearly every cabinet minister meets with his counterparts in the other governments from time to time. It has been said only half in jest that there are usually more provincial cabinet ministers in Ottawa on any given day than there are federal cabinet ministers. Similarly, there are frequent meetings of permanent government officials from the provincial and federal governments. At any given time, there are over 150 organizations, conferences and committees involved in intergovernmental liaison, indicating the vast array of consultative organisms within the Canadian federation. In addition, of course, there are countless informal contacts among civil servants of all governments.[154]

The dominant role of the executive branch of government in working out intergovernmental relations has led Smiley to characterize the Canadian constitution today as ''executive federalism''.[155] It certainly must be frustrating for legislators to find that their role is confined to ratifying arrangements worked out elsewhere. But in any country, whether federal or unitary, which has adopted the system of responsible government, the legislative bodies have little real influence in policy-making in any case. The federal Parliament, despite its representation from all parts of the country, is too dominated by cabinet and the party system to be a suitable forum for federal-provincial adjustment; and it does not pretend to such a role.[156] It is the elected and permanent officials of the executive branches

---

MacKinnon, ''First Ministers' Conferences'' in Dwivedi (ed.), *Public Policy and Administrative Studies* (U. of Guelph, 1988), vol. 5, 38.

153 In practice, the amending procedures are normally initiated by a first ministers' conference, and this reality has been recognized by provision for first ministers' conferences in the Constitution Act, 1982, ss. 37, 37.1, 49.

154 Smiley, *Canada in Question* (3rd ed., 1980), 94.

155 Smiley, *The Federal Condition in Canada* (1987), 83.

156 In the United States' Congress the absence of strict party discipline has allowed regional interests to be somewhat better accommodated. This is one reason why there are fewer relations between governments in the United States than in Canada. For more comparisons in the financial area, see ch. 6, Financial Arrangements, under heading 6.9, ''Conclusions'', below.

of the federal and provincial governments who, through ''diplomacy'', search for cooperative means to accomplish limited social and economic objectives which require the action of more than one government.[157] The next chapter, Financial Arrangements, is almost a case-study of cooperative (or executive) federalism. It includes failures as well as successes, but the process which it describes is undeniably an important feature of Canada's constitutional law.

157 Simeon, *Federal-Provincial Diplomacy* (1972) is a study of three cases of federal-provincial negotiations.

6

Financial Arrangements

6.1 Confederation arrangements

At confederation,[1] the immediate and most urgent tasks facing Canada related to the economic development of the isolated pioneer communities which comprised British North America. The building of railways, roads, canals, harbours and bridges to link the provinces with each other and with the rest of the world was the prerequisite of economic development. This task, along with defence, was assigned to the new Dominion; the Dominion also assumed all the debts of the provinces. The functions assigned to the provinces were important too, for example, the administration of justice, municipal institutions, health, education, welfare and local matters; but in 1867, when laissez-faire was the prevailing philosophy of government, these functions were much less costly.

The initial financial arrangements reflected the allocation of functions. The most lucrative sources of revenue were the "indirect" taxes of customs and excise,

1 The sources of information on all the federal-provincial financial arrangements are diffuse and sometimes fugitive, and they become out-of-date very quickly. The Federal-Provincial Relations Office of the Government of Canada regularly issues *Federal-Provincial Programs and Activities: A Descriptive Inventory*. The Canadian Tax Foundation annually publishes *The National Finances*, and biennially publishes *Provincial and Municipal Finances*, and these are probably the easiest sources of up-to-date information; they also provide useful accounts of the history of the various arrangements.

which accounted for 80 per cent of the revenues of the uniting provinces just before confederation. By s. 122 of the B.N.A. Act "the customs and excise laws of each province" were transferred to the new Dominion, and by s. 91(3) — the power to raise money "by any mode or system of taxation" — the new Dominion received the power to impose any new taxes, direct or indirect, that it saw fit.

The less costly functions of the provinces were matched by the assignment to them of less extensive taxing powers. Section 92(2) conferred the power to impose only "direct" taxes, and s. 92(9) conferred the power to impose licence fees.[2] At the time of confederation, although some municipalities (not provinces) imposed property and income taxes, and all provinces received some revenue from their public property and imposed licence fees of various kinds, these sources of revenue amounted to less than 20 per cent of their revenue. Moreover, there are indications that it was not expected in 1867 that direct taxes on property or income would ever become particularly lucrative, because of their unpopularity. Accordingly, in order to enable the provinces to carry out their functions without the major sources of taxation, the B.N.A. Act provided for payment of annual subsidies by the Dominion to the provinces. These "statutory subsidies", as they are now called, were to comprise a major part of the expected revenues of the provinces. Although expressed by s. 118 of the B.N.A. Act to be "in full settlement of all future demands on Canada", they quickly proved inadequate for provincial needs; and they have been increased and varied in various ways for the original uniting provinces, and upon the entry of new provinces. The statutory subsidies continue to this day.

6.2 Development of direct taxation

The provinces were gradually driven to the levying of direct taxes. The first provincial personal income tax was levied by British Columbia in 1876, and the second by Prince Edward Island in 1894. They were the only provinces to levy such a tax in the half century after confederation. Between 1923 and 1939 five more provinces followed their example, and the remaining three waited until 1962. In some provinces, municipalities levied income taxes before any provincial tax was enacted. Corporation taxes and corporate income taxes were for most provinces an earlier source of revenue than the personal income tax. All provinces were taxing corporations on the basis of place of business, paid-up capital, and so on, by 1903, and corporate income taxes were general by the 1930s.

Inheritance taxes were another early source of provincial revenue. Ontario imposed a succession duty in 1892 which was quickly copied by all the other provinces.

---

2 The taxing powers in the Constitution, both federal and provincial, including the concepts of "direct" and "indirect" taxes, are discussed in ch. 30, Taxation, below.

Meanwhile, the customs and excise taxes did not continue to suffice for the federal government. Federal entry to the field of direct taxation occurred during the first world war with the enactment of the 1916 war profits tax, which was followed in 1917 by the introduction of personal and corporate income taxes. These were regarded as temporary measures only, because it was generally agreed then that the field of direct taxation should be left to the provinces; and indeed federal rates were substantially reduced in the period between the first and second world wars. The Dominion did not ''invade'' the inheritance tax field until the second world war, levying succession duties in 1941.

In 1937, after the depression and the rejection by the Privy Council of the Bennett New Deal, the Rowell-Sirois Commission was appointed to review the whole financial structure of Canadian government. The situation at that time was chaotic, with federal, provincial and municipal taxes of various kinds, at differing rates, on differing bases, producing a complex burden of taxation which varied greatly from municipality to municipality, and region to region. The Commission proposed that only the Dominion should levy the three standard taxes on personal income, corporate income and inheritances; and it proposed that the Dominion should pay ''national adjustment grants'' to the poorer provinces. The Rowell-Sirois Report[3] was rejected at the 1941 dominion-provincial conference because of the opposition of Alberta, British Columbia and Ontario, the three provinces which would have received nothing under the proposed system of adjustment grants.

6.3 Tax rental agreements: 1941-1962

Only months after the rejection of the Rowell-Sirois Report in January 1941, its recommendation that the provinces withdraw from the three standard tax fields was adopted, but as a temporary measure for the duration of the second world war. The federal government entered into agreements with the provinces under which the provinces abandoned their personal income taxes, corporate income taxes and inheritance taxes. In return, the provinces were to receive unconditional payments to compensate them for the lost revenue. The federal government, now alone in the three most lucrative tax fields, raised its rates of personal and corporate income taxes, and imposed succession duties for the first time. However, in the agreement with each province, the federal government undertook that at the end of the war it would reduce federal taxes so as to make ''room'' for the provinces to resume levying the three taxes.

At the end of the war, however, the federal government wished to continue to levy the major taxes in order to finance peacetime reconstruction and to use centralized fiscal policy as a tool of national economic management. In 1947, the federal government persuaded all provinces except Ontario and Quebec to enter

3 *Report of the Royal Commission on Dominion Provincial Relations* (1940).

into ''tax rental agreements'', under which the federal government ''rented'' from each agreeing province the right to levy personal income tax, corporate income tax and succession duty. The agreeing provinces did not levy these taxes, and received grants (''rent'') from the federal government to compensate for the foregone revenue. Ontario and Quebec, which did not sign rental agreements, in 1947 reimposed corporate income taxes and succession duties, but not personal income taxes. On the renewal of the agreements in 1952, Ontario joined the system, although it retained the right to levy succession duties. Quebec remained outside the system; and in 1954 it imposed a personal income tax, so that Quebec was then levying all three of the standard taxes.

In 1957, new tax rental agreements were entered into, but with several major changes in favour of the provinces. First, the rental payments were fixed as a percentage of the yield of each tax rented; the use of percentage points ensured that rental payments would rise at the same rate as federal tax collections, and it led the federal government to characterize the 1957 rental agreements as ''tax-sharing'' arrangements. Secondly, if a province preferred to levy its own tax, instead of renting the tax to the Dominion, then its residents would receive an ''abatement'' (or reduction) of federal tax of the same percentage as the rental payments; this was designed to leave room for a provincial tax. Eight provinces signed agreements to rent all three taxes. Ontario rented only personal income tax, and levied its own corporate income tax and succession duties. Quebec did not sign a rental agreement at all, and continued to levy all three standard taxes. The federal government accordingly allowed abatements of corporate income tax and succession duties to taxpayers in Ontario and abatements of these taxes and personal income tax to taxpayers in Quebec. Thirdly, the 1957 agreements provided that each province (whether or not it rented its taxes) would receive an ''equalization payment'' to bring its share of tax rental payments (or the value of its abatements) up to the same per capita figure as the average per capita yield in the two provinces whose yield was highest (at that time, Ontario and British Columbia).

6.4 Tax collection agreements: 1962-present

The tax rental agreements ended in 1962 and were replaced by the tax collection agreements. Under these agreements the provinces imposed their own income taxes at their own rates. Provided a province used the same tax base as the federal tax base,[4] the federal government would collect the provincial tax on

4 The use of the same tax base is ensured by stipulations in the agreements that provincial rates of personal income tax must be expressed as a percentage of the federal tax, and that provincial rates of corporate income tax must be expressed as a percentage of federally-defined taxable income. Without departing from these general rules, the federal government has agreed to administer some special provincial tax measures which produce some variation in the tax base from province to province.

behalf of the province free of charge. In this way taxpayers would only have to file a single return. To give the provinces room to levy their own taxes the federal government agreed to allow abatements (reductions) of corporate and personal income taxes to taxpayers in all provinces. All of the provinces except Quebec signed a collection agreement for personal income taxes, and all provinces except Ontario and Quebec signed a collection agreement for corporate income taxes.[5] Equalization payments continued.

The tax collection agreements continue to the present day. As of 1997, all provinces except Quebec have signed a collection agreement for personal income taxes; and all provinces except Quebec, Ontario and Alberta[6] have signed a collection agreement for corporate income taxes.[7] Quebec's personal income tax is collected by the province, as is the corporate income tax of Quebec, Ontario and Alberta. Equalization payments continue, although, as is related below, they have been substantially modified.

6.5 Tax abatements

An ''abatement'' is a reduction in a federal tax. It is not a ''grant'', because it does not involve the transfer of funds from the federal treasury to the provincial treasuries. But it is analogous to a grant in that it allows the provinces room to impose their own taxes. As noted, it is the vehicle by which the standard tax fields are shared. It is unconditional in the sense that the provinces are not obliged to levy their own taxes; if they do levy taxes, they are not obliged to do so at the same rate as the federal abatement, or to apply funds raised by their taxes for any particular purpose.

In 1972, the federal Income Tax Act was amended to conceal the abatement. Before 1972, a taxpayer would calculate his or her federal ''basic'' tax; and then he or she would deduct the abatement, which in 1971 was 28 per cent of the basic tax, in order to derive the actual federal tax liability. Then the taxpayer would

5 With respect to succession duty, in 1962 the provinces were given the choice, either of accepting 50 per cent of federal estate tax collections, or of levying their own succession duties in return for their deceaseds' estates receiving an abatement of 50 per cent of federal estate tax. In 1963 the provincial share was raised from 50 per cent to 75 per cent. Only Ontario and Quebec began the five-year period levying their own succession duties (which they had been doing, of course, since 1947), but they were joined by British Columbia in 1963. These arrangements continued until the end of 1971 when the federal Parliament repealed its estate tax. It agreed to collect provincial succession duties for a fee, so long as at least four provinces using the same tax base entered into three-year collection agreements. Six provinces enacted uniform succession duty statutes and entered into the collection agreement, leaving Alberta as a succession duty haven; British Columbia, Ontario and Quebec continued to collect their own succession duties. Subsequently, however, all provinces repealed their succession duty statutes.

6 Alberta began collecting its own corporate income tax in 1981.

7 The two territories levy personal and corporate income taxes, and have entered into collection agreements with the federal government for the taxes.

calculate the provincial tax, which like the abatement consisted of a percentage of the federal basic tax.[8] In 1972, the abatement was concealed from the taxpayer, by the federal government lowering its rates to produce a basic tax figure which was 28 per cent lower than in 1971, and by the provincial governments raising their rates so that their yield (which now had to be expressed as a percentage of the lower basic tax figure) was the same as before. In 1977, when further tax room (or tax ''points'')[9] was transferred to the provinces, the increased abatement was handled in the same way: federal rates were lowered and provincial rates were raised. It is questionable whether the word ''abatement'' is apt to describe a reduction in federal tax which takes the form of a lowering of rates. It is becoming increasingly common to describe these adjustments as ''tax point transfers'' or simply ''tax transfers''.[10]

Explicit abatements have not entirely disappeared. An explicit abatement is still allowed to corporate taxpayers to leave room for provincial corporate income taxes. And an explicit abatement of personal income tax is still allowed to Quebec taxpayers to compensate them for the foregone federal contributions to shared-cost programmes from which Quebec has opted out.[11]

There are two main sources of tax transfers (implicit and explicit abatements) to the provinces. First, and most important, is the reduction of federal tax which has been allowed to the provinces ever since 1962 in order to leave room for the provinces to impose their own personal and corporate income taxes.

Secondly, a reduction in federal tax is provided as part of the Canada Health and Social Transfer, a federal programme that provides funding for provincial health, post-secondary education and social programmes. The federal government has supported such programmes since shortly after the second world war, but its contributions once took the exclusive form of conditional cash grants to the universities (in the case of post-secondary education) and to the provinces (in the case of the other programmes). In 1967, when the grants for post-secondary education were made payable to the provinces rather than directly to the universities, a transfer of tax points replaced part of the grants for post-secondary education. In 1977, when post-secondary education and health were grouped together as ''established programmes'',[12] a transfer of additional tax points re-

---

8 See note 4, above.

9 Tax points are percentage points of federal tax on personal income (the income of individuals) and percentage points of the federally-defined taxable income of corporations: see note 4, above.

10 For example, the legislation enacting the Canada Health and Social Transfer (which inherits the tax points once allocated for the ''established programmes'') uses the term ''tax transfer'': Budget Implementation Act, 1995, S.C. 1995, c. 17.

11 See sec. 6.7, ''Conditional federal grants'', below.

12 They were described as established programmes in the Act which provided for their funding, namely, the Federal-Provincial Fiscal Arrangements and Federal Post-Secondary Education and Health Contributions Act, R.S.C. 1985, F-8, because they were regarded as having attained such a level of maturity that their continuance by the provinces was assured. Accordingly, in

placed part of the federal grants in aid of both purposes.[13] The federal contribution to provincial social programmes came through the Canada Assistance Plan and always took the form of cash grants. In 1996, the Canada Health and Social Transfer was implemented to replace both the Canada Assistance Plan and the established programmes funding. The Canada Health and Social Transfer involves no new tax points transfers, but ''inherits'' those that were allocated to fund the established programmes.

The transferred tax points do not provide the full federal contribution to the Canada Health and Social Transfer. The balance takes the form of a cash grant. This is vital to a continuing federal influence over health and social assistance, because it is the power to withhold all or part of the grant which is the sanction against non-compliance by a province with federal conditions.[14]

6.6 Equalization payments

The Rowell-Sirois Report had in 1940 recommended a system of equalization payments called ''national adjustment grants'', whereby the federal government would make special grants to the poorer provinces. This recommendation was rejected, but in 1957 equalization payments did become an explicit federal expenditure programme for the first time. There was in fact an equalizing element in the federal-provincial fiscal arrangements between 1941 and 1957, because grants were made to the provinces on a per capita basis, which naturally returned a larger share of revenue to the provinces with lower per capita tax yields. But under the 1957 tax rental (or tax-sharing) agreements, it will be recalled, each agreeing province received as ''rent'' a percentage share of the actual yield from its residents of the federal personal income tax, the federal corporate income tax and federal succession duties (later estate tax). Needless to say, rental payments varied greatly from the high per capita yields of Ontario and British Columbia down to the low per capita yields of Prince Edward Island and Newfoundland. The equalization payments were calculated to bring each province's rent up to the per capita average of the two highest-yielding provinces (at that time, Ontario and British Columbia). Even Quebec, which did not enter into a rental agreement, was included in the equalization system, and received payments calculated by

1977, federal control over the established programmes was considerably loosened. That loosening process continued with the Canada Health and Social Transfer, implemented by amendments to the same Act (now renamed the Federal-Provincial Fiscal Arrangements Act): see sec. 6.7, ''Conditional federal grants'', below.

13 For historical reasons (it had accepted a form of opting-out from some shared-cost programmes before 1977), Quebec received more tax points and less cash under the established programmes funding arrangements. The same is true for the Canada Health and Social Transfer. Except for this difference in apportionment, Quebec's entitlements were, and are, calculated in the same manner as those for the other provinces.

14 See sec. 6.7, ''Conditional federal grants'', below.

bringing her hypothetical yield from the provincial percentage of the three federal taxes up to the per capita average of the two highest-yielding provinces.

One defect in the original equalization formula was that it equalized only the yield from the three standard taxes, namely, those on personal income, corporate income and inheritances. However, the equalization base has gradually been broadened to comprise, not only the three standard taxes, but nearly all provincial revenue sources, including sales taxes, gasoline taxes, liquor taxes, movie admission taxes, race track taxes, motor vehicle registration fees, hospital and medical care insurance premiums, municipal property taxes, lottery profits, and revenues from oil, natural gas, water power and forestry. The result is that most provincial revenues are now equalized.

As the base of equalization has been expanded by the addition of further sources of provincial revenue, the cost of equalization has naturally increased. In 1967, in order to reduce the cost, the standard of equalization (the level to which provincial revenues were to be raised) was lowered from the average per capita yield of the two highest-yielding provinces down to the average per capita yield of all the provinces. Then, in 1973, and for some years thereafter, the price of oil rose so sharply that the revenues of the oil-producing provinces made even the lower national-average standard too expensive. At first, this problem was met by excluding from the equalization base a substantial part of provincial revenues from "non-renewable resources". In 1982, these revenues were restored in full to the base, but the standard of equalization was lowered again, this time to the average per capita yield of five "representative" provinces. The five provinces are British Columbia, Saskatchewan, Manitoba, Ontario and Quebec. The list thus excludes Alberta, which is far and away the largest recipient of revenue from non-renewable resources. The new "representative average" standard (which is still in force at the time of writing in 1997) is therefore not affected by Alberta's huge resource revenues.

The formula for calculating equalization payments[15] does not turn on the actual tax revenues of each province, because rates of tax and definitions of tax bases vary from province to province, depending on each province's discretionary tax policies. Instead, an attempt is made to measure the potential tax revenues of each province, that is, the tax-raising capacity or "fiscal capacity" of each province. This is done by estimating the revenue which each province would receive from a standard tax system with average provincial rates of tax. An estimate is made of the tax base in each province of each provincial source of revenue (amount of personal income, amount of corporate income, volume of retail sales, etc.). A single (national average) rate of tax for each base is then applied to each of the province's tax bases. The total of all these calculations yields the fiscal capacity of the province. The fiscal capacity of each province, divided by its population so as to give a per capita figure, is then compared with the average per capita

15 The equalization rules have of course always been contained in a federal statute. The current statute is the Federal-Provincial Fiscal Arrangements Act, note 12, above.

fiscal capacity of (under the current standard) the five representative provinces. If a province has a higher per capita fiscal capacity than the average of the five representative provinces (a fiscal capacity excess), that province is not entitled to equalization. If a province has a lower per capita fiscal capacity than the average of the five representative provinces (a fiscal capacity deficiency), that province is entitled to equalization; the amount of the equalization grant is the amount of the province's per capita deficiency multiplied by the province's population.

For the fiscal year 1996-97, the provinces that were entitled to equalization grants (the "have-not provinces") were Newfoundland, Prince Edward Island, Nova Scotia, New Brunswick, Quebec, Manitoba and Saskatchewan. There is a wide disparity between the fiscal capacity of the provinces,[16] and it is most marked at the top end of the scale. Alberta has nearly double the fiscal capacity of the second "have" province (British Columbia). This enables Alberta to enjoy the highest per capita revenues (and expenditures) with the lowest "tax effort" (low rates of income tax and no sales tax, for example). It must be emphasized, however, that the three "have" provinces of Alberta, British Columbia, and Ontario do not contribute to equalization grants. The grants come entirely from the federal government. That is why the rise in oil prices since 1973 has necessitated a lowering of the equalization standard. Increases in the resource revenues of the producing provinces swell the equalization entitlements of the have-not provinces, but the producing provinces do not contribute to the payments. This has led to suggestions that a portion of provincial resource revenues should be pooled and shared directly among all provinces.[17]

The total amount of equalization payments for 1996-97 was in excess of eight billion dollars. It is arguable that this vast sum would be better spent in the form of direct financial assistance to the poorest individuals (or families) in Canada, wherever they lived. Equalization payments swell the size of provincial governments, requiring the poor (and the rich for that matter)[18] in the have-not provinces to accept benefits in the form of enriched provincial public services.[19] However, the Constitution Act, 1982, by s. 36(2), explicitly recognizes "the principle of making equalization payments to ensure that provincial governments

---

16 For example, one percentage point of personal income tax yields $23.42 per capita in Ontario, and $18.63 in Alberta, but only $11.36 in Prince Edward Island; one percentage point of corporate income tax yields $28.41 in Alberta and $23.84 in Ontario, but only $9.39 in Prince Edward Island: 1988 taxation year, figures supplied by Department of Finance, Ottawa.

17 See e.g., Courchene, *Refinancing the Canadian Confederation* (1979), 39. See also note 20, below. The idea of direct sharing of provincial resource revenues is unlikely to be agreed to by the producing provinces.

18 Who benefits from equalization depends entirely on the design of the recipient province's public services. It is possible that equalization redistributes income from poor people in have provinces to rich people in have-not provinces.

19 If benefits were received directly by individuals or families, that would still leave inequality in the value of provincial public services (or burdens of taxation) as between residents of have provinces and residents of have-not provinces. The purpose of equalization is to reduce this inequality.

have sufficient revenues to provide reasonably comparable levels of public services at reasonably comparable levels of taxation''. This provision suggests that equalization payments will continue into the foreseeable future.

The constitutional obligation to make adequate equalization payments to the poorer provinces is probably too vague, and too political, to be justiciable. It is like the ''directive principles of state policy'' in the Constitution of India, which are statements of economic and social goals that ought to guide governments but which are not enforceable in court.[20] It should be noted, however, that there is room for doubt as to whether the federal government is in compliance with s. 36(2). The lowering of the equalization standard in 1982 to the average of the five representative provinces means that the low-income provinces are not even being brought up to the national average, and of course equalization does not bring the high-income provinces down. However, the size of the federal deficit and the federal government's lack of access to provincial resource revenues make it unrealistic to suppose that equalization could be significantly enriched in the foreseeable future.[21]

6.7 Conditional federal grants

A conditional grant is a transfer of funds which is made on condition that the grantee use the funds in accordance with the stipulations of the grantor. Within Canada, the federal government has used the device of the conditional grant to establish shared-cost programmes, under which the federal and provincial governments share the cost of a programme within a particular province. In broad terms, the shared-cost programmes were originally established in this way: the federal government decided upon the desirability of a particular programme, for example, the provision of insured hospital services; it worked out the details of the programme; and it proposed the programme as a joint venture to each province, on the basis that the federal government and the provincial government would each bear 50 per cent of the cost of the programme. The programme proposed may have been well down on the province's list of priorities, or a different kind of programme might have been preferable to the province; nevertheless, the federal offer was always very difficult to refuse, because refusal would deny to the province the federal grant. Indeed, refusal of a federal offer to share the costs

20 See Aikman, ''Fundamental Rights and Directive Principles of State Policy in India'' (1987) 17 Vict. U. Wgton. L. Rev. 373.

21 Cumming, ''Equitable Fiscal Federalism: The Problems in respect of Resources Revenue Sharing'' in Royal Commission on the Economic Union and Development Prospects for Canada (Macdonald Commission), *Report* (1985), vol. 65, 49-95, arguing that the disparity between have and have-not provinces is now so wide as to constitute a breach of s. 36(2); reporting and supporting the arguments by Courchene and other economists that provincial resource revenues should be shared by the producing provinces; and arguing that s. 36(2) should be amended to impose the obligation of equalization on the provinces as well as the federal government.

of a programme would have worn an aspect of taxation without benefit, since the residents of a non-participating province would still have had to pay the federal taxes which financed the federal share of the programme in the other provinces. The result was that the provinces usually felt sufficiently tempted by "50-cent dollars" to join the federally-initiated shared-cost programmes.

Since the second world war, at least 100 shared-cost programmes have been established on federal initiative. Some of the programmes were temporary and designed to fulfil a specific objective, such as building the Trans-Canada Highway. Of the continuing programmes, four were much more expensive and important than the others. The post-secondary education programme began in 1951 as a programme of federal grants to universities, and was reformed in 1967 into a programme of grants (and tax transfers) to the provinces to assist in the financing of their universities. The Canada Assistance Plan was created in 1966 to share the cost of various provincial social services and income-support programmes. The hospital insurance programme, under which hospital services were made universally available, began in 1958. The medical care programme, under which doctors' services were made universally available, began in 1968.

Except for university funding (where the federal grants did not match provincial costs), these major programmes began as traditional shared-cost programmes, with the federal government contributing a cash grant equal to half of the costs incurred by the provinces. A gradual transition has since occurred in the way in which they are funded and controlled. In 1977, federal support for post-secondary education and the two health services programmes was amalgamated into one annual transfer, termed "established programmes funding". The basis of the federal contribution (which took the form of a combination of tax points and cash grant) to the established programmes was changed to a formula that was independent of the actual costs of post-secondary education and health care services.[22] In 1996, Canada Assistance Plan transfers (which had continued to be based on actual costs) ended and these transfers, along with the established programmes, were replaced with the Canada Health and Social Transfer (CHST). The CHST is the federal contribution to provincial health and social programmes (embracing all four of the original shared-cost programmes) and, like the established programmes before it, the CHST transfers are based on a funding formula that is related to the gross national product and provincial populations, not to provincial spending levels. The cash component of the CHST transfers is still conditional in the sense that it is subject to provincial compliance with federal standards relating to health care programmes and entry to social assistance programmes.[23] However, the direct sharing of costs has been eliminated. This means

22 See sec. 6.5, "Tax abatements", above.

23 Current conditions require provinces to comply with the Canada Health Act (a statute which sets out the federal government's health care policy) and forbid them from setting minimum residency standards for social assistance; the federal government is also obliged not to impose any additional conditions without consulting first with the provinces: Budget Implementation Act, 1995, S.C. 1995, c. 17.

that provinces have a greater incentive to control their costs, and the federal government has no interest in controlling or auditing provincial expenditures.[24]

Shared-cost programmes have assured Canadians a high minimum level of some important social services. Without the federal initiative, and the federal sharing of the costs, it is certain that some at least of these services would have come later, at standards which varied from province to province, and not at all in some provinces. But the programmes have effected a substantial shift in the distribution of power within confederation. Since the provinces have traditionally borne half of the cost of most programmes, each province has been committed to substantial expenditures for purposes which have been selected, not by the province which raised the money, but by the federal government. This has locked a substantial portion of provincial budgets outside the normal provincial processes of priority setting and budgetary control. Thus shared-cost programmes have been pursued at the expense of provincial functions for which no federal assistance is available.

The federal government has over the past few decades shown increased sensitivity to the criticism that federal conditional grants amount in substance to federal dictation of provincial spending priorities. In a 1969 working paper it was proposed, not as a definite federal policy but as a suggestion for discussion, that for the future shared-cost programmes should be subject to two requirements. First, a shared-cost programme should be established only after a "broad national consensus in favour of the programme" had been demonstrated to exist, and this would be ascertained by prior submission of a federal proposal to provincial Legislatures. Secondly, "the decision of a provincial Legislature to exercise its constitutional right not to participate in any programme, even given a national consensus, should not result in a fiscal penalty being imposed on the people of the province."[25] These two points may probably be regarded as settled federal policy.[26] Certainly, since 1969, there have been no new programmes which have violated these precepts.

---

24 A source of conflict under the old shared-cost system was the unequal treatment of the provinces. As a cost-cutting measure in 1990, the CAP entitlements of the three "have" provinces of Alberta, British Columbia, and Ontario (but not of the seven other provinces) were restricted to a five per cent increase per year, and this quickly led to major reductions in the per capita grants to those provinces relative to the other seven. British Columbia unsuccessfully challenged the differential treatment in a reference: *Re Canada Assistance Plan* [1991] 2 S.C.R. 525. The Canada Health and Social Transfer, which replaced the CAP in 1996, does not restore an equal level of funding, but, according to the federal budget of March 6, 1996, the CHST is expected to reduce disparities in provincial per capita entitlements by half in its first five years.

25 Trudeau, *Federal-Provincial Grants and the Spending Power of Parliament* (1969), 36.

26 The Meech Lake Accord of 1987 and the Charlottetown Accord of 1992, both of which lapsed (see ch. 4, Amendment, under heading 4.1(c) "The failure to accommodate Quebec", above), would have added a new s. 106A to the Constitution Act, 1867, which would have obliged the federal government to provide for opting-out with reasonable compensation in any new shared-cost programme in an area of exclusive provincial jurisdiction. However, in order to qualify for the constitutional entitlement, the opting-out province would have had to itself carry out a

Substantial adjustments have also been made to existing programmes to increase provincial autonomy. In 1977, as has already been noted, funding for three of the four most significant shared-cost programmes was folded into "established programmes funding"; and in 1996, the established programmes funding and the Canada Assistance Plan (which was by then the last true shared-cost programme) were replaced by the Canada Health and Social Transfer, which combined all four of the original shared-cost programmes into one annual federal grant. The formulas for calculating the federal contribution to the post-1977 established programmes funding and the post-1996 Canada Health and Social Transfer were made independent of provincial expenditures. Because the federal government no longer shares the actual provincial costs of operating the programmes, the federal government has no interest in the actual level of each province's expenditures on the programmes and no incentive to control or monitor the province's expenditures. Under the established programmes formula, the federal contribution was not just cash, but a combination of cash and tax points, which gave the provinces additional "tax room" to generate their own funding for the programmes.[27] The same tax room was carried forward into the formula for the Canada Health and Social Transfer. To the extent that the federal contribution takes the form of tax points, there is a loss of federal influence over the provinces, because tax points cannot in practice be taken back by the federal government. It is the power to withhold the cash portion of the grant that is the only effective federal sanction against provincial non-compliance with federal standards.[28] Provincial concerns are given further recognition by Canada Health and Social Transfer provisions that give provincial governments a voice in setting future standards: the CHST legislation explicitly contemplates the participation of the provinces in developing "shared principles and objectives ... with respect to the operation of social programs".[29] This is a declaration that the federal government will in the future no longer set conditions on its funding by unilateral fiat, which is how the conditions were established for the original shared-cost programmes.

Before the terms of provincial participation in the shared-cost programmes were relaxed, provinces could still exercise a degree of autonomy by electing a form of opting-out. In 1959, the first opting-out arrangement was made whereby

---

programme which was "consistent with the national objectives". The new s. 106A would have been less tolerant of opting-out arrangements than the policy contemplated by the 1969 working paper. Yet s. 106A proved to be one of the more controversial elements of the Accords, on the basis that it weakened the federal government's ability to establish new shared-cost programmes.

27 See sec. 6.5, "Tax abatements", above.

28 The Budget Implementation Act, 1996, S.C. 1996, c. 18, recognizes the risk to federal influence of declining cash contributions by setting a floor of $11 billion per annum on the cash payments to the provinces under the Canada Health and Social Transfer; the payments cannot decline below the $11 billion figure.

29 Budget Implementation Act, 1995, S.C. 1995, c. 17.

Quebec was given an increased abatement of corporate income tax in return for assuming the entire financial responsibility for its universities. Similar opting-out provisions were later drafted for other shared-cost programmes. Only Quebec took advantage of those provisions, which carried with them additional tax abatements. When established programmes funding was implemented, those additional abatements became part of that programme and they were incorporated into the Canada Health and Social Transfer when it replaced the established programmes funding. While the original decision to opt out affects the split between tax points and cash transfers to Quebec, it has otherwise been reduced to an historical footnote.

Quebec also elected to opt out of the Canada Pension Plan. The establishment of this contributory scheme of retirement payments and supplementary benefits was preceded by a period of negotiation with Quebec. The original federal proposal was a "pay-as-you-go" or "non-funded" plan under which pensions and benefits would be paid out of current contributions. Quebec was determined to have a plan of its own which would be "funded", because this would result in the accumulation of a large investment fund which could be used as a source of capital by the province. The result of the negotiations between the federal and Quebec governments was that Quebec agreed to some modifications of the Quebec plan in order to facilitate the portability of pension rights for employees moving between Quebec and the other provinces, and Quebec added its consent to those of the other provinces to a constitutional amendment to give the federal government the power to include in the Canada plan benefits to survivors and to persons disabled before retirement age.[30] The federal government for its part agreed to put its plan on a partially funded basis, and to make the resulting investment fund available as a source of capital to the participating provinces. The federal government also agreed to permit opting out by a province with "a comparable plan". Only Quebec accepted this option. In 1965, two identical plans were enacted, the Canada Pension Plan[31] covering nine provinces, and the Quebec Régime de rentes[32] covering Quebec.

From a provincial perspective, a common flaw in all of these opting-out arrangements is that they have obliged the opting-out province to continue established programmes without significant change or, in the case of new programmes, to establish or continue comparable provincial programmes. Thus the "provincial autonomy" afforded by opting-out provisions has really amounted to nothing more than a transfer of administrative responsibility to the opting-out province.

30 Section 94A of the Constitution Act, 1867, which had been inserted by amendment in 1951, gave to the federal government the power "to make laws in relation to old age pensions in Canada". It was apparently believed by the federal government that this power would not authorize a pension plan which included "supplementary benefits, including survivors' and disability benefits irrespective of age", and so, after all provinces had agreed, in 1964 an amendment was obtained from the United Kingdom Parliament substituting a new s. 94A.

31 S.C. 1964-65, c. 51.

32 S.Q. 1964, c. 24.

It has not given that province the freedom to divert resources, which would otherwise be committed to a federally initiated programme, into other endeavours. Federal ''compensation'' to the opting-out province has been just as conditional as the federal contribution to participating provinces. The federal working paper of 1969 suggested (though it is not explicit) that the federal government may be willing to offer a real opting-out choice in future shared-cost proposals.[33] This would have to involve the offer of tax points or a grant of similar value to the federal share of the cost of the programme which would not be tied to the maintenance of the same or a similar programme, but would be available for use by the province in accordance with its own priorities. The trouble with this form of opting out is that it removes any incentive for a province to join the programme. This probably explains why the 1969 suggestion has never been implemented.

6.8 Spending power

(a) Federal power

When the federal government makes an unconditional grant to a province, the grant is of course used by the province for its own purposes. This means that funds raised by federal taxes end up being applied to objects which are outside federal legislative authority. When the federal government contributes to a shared-cost programme which lies within the legislative authority of the provinces, the same is true: federal funds are applied to provincial objects. If, in addition, those federal funds are granted on condition that the programme accord with federal stipulations, then those stipulations will effectively regulate the programme even though it lies outside federal legislative authority. In fact, many of the shared-cost programmes do lie outside federal legislative authority, and yet are administered in accordance with federally-imposed stipulations. We have already seen that the sum total of these programmes has amounted to a heavy federal presence in matters which are within provincial legislative responsibility.[34]

Take, for example, the programmes of hospital insurance and medicare, under which the provinces provide for the delivery of hospital and doctors' services to their residents. There is no doubt that these health care services come exclusively within the legislative competence of the provinces.[35] Yet both hospital

33 Trudeau, *Federal-Provincial Grants and the Spending Power of Parliament* (1969), 36. Cf. the constitutional proposals of 1987 and 1992, note 26, above.

34 See sec. 6.7, ''Conditional federal grants'', above.

35 Provincial authority over ''the establishment, maintenance, and management of hospitals'' is explicit in s. 92(7) of the Constitution Act, 1867. Provincial authority over the medical profession comes within ''property and civil rights in the province'' in s. 92(13) of the Constitution Act, 1867, below; as does provincial authority over a contributory insurance scheme: *A.G. Can.* v. *A.G. Ont.* (Unemployment Insurance) [1937] A.C. 355.

insurance and medicare were initiated by the federal government;[36] the federal government has legislated the most important terms of the programmes;[37] and the federal government makes a contribution of cash and tax points to each participating province to defray approximately one-half of each province's costs.

What is the constitutional basis for federal grants to the provinces, and for federal involvement in shared-cost programmes that are outside federal legislative competence? The only possible basis is the "spending power" of the federal Parliament, a power which is nowhere explicit in the Constitution Act, 1867, but which must be inferred from the powers to levy taxes (s. 91(3)), to legislate in relation to "public property" (s. 91(1A)), and to appropriate federal funds (s. 106). Plainly the Parliament must have the power to spend the money which its taxes yield, and to dispose of its own property. But of course the issue is whether this spending power authorizes payments for objects which are outside federal legislative competence.

Some constitutional lawyers, including Pierre Elliott Trudeau (before he assumed high federal office), have argued that the federal spending power is confined to objects within federal legislative competence.[38] The argument is that the general pattern of the distribution of powers in the Constitution Act, 1867 implicitly confines the taxing power of the federal Parliament in s. 91(3) to raising taxes for the legislative objects of the federal Parliament, and for no other objects; that provincial taxing power in s. 92(2) is also so limited; and that the spending powers of federal and provincial governments are also implicitly limited to their own legislative objects.

The political corollary to the narrow view of the spending power is the theory of "fiscal responsibility": each level of government should finance its own expenditures by its own taxation. On this theory, the federal government should levy no more taxes than are necessary to finance its own legislative responsibil-

---

36 The introduction of a national hospital insurance plan was proposed by the federal government in 1945 as part of its plan for postwar reconstruction. It was not, however, imposed upon the provinces by the federal government; there was a long period of intergovernmental discussion until general agreement was reached between the federal and provincial governments. The scheme started in 1958 with five provinces participating, and by 1961 all provinces were participating: see Carter, *Canadian Conditional Grants since World War II* (1971), 32-34. The introduction of many of the earlier postwar programmes, e.g., construction of the Trans-Canada highway, was not preceded by consultations with the provinces who would have to pay half the cost. Even so recent and so large a programme as Medicare became a federal commitment (it was an election promise) in 1963 without consultation of the provinces — although there was intergovernmental consultation as to the details before its introduction in 1968: Carter, 76.

37 See note 24, above.

38 Tremblay Report (*Report of the Royal Commission of Inquiry on Constitutional Problems*) (Quebec, 1956), vol. 2, 217-233; Trudeau, "Federal Grants to Universities" (1957) in *Federalism and the French Canadians* (1968), 79; Petter, "Federalism and the Myth of the Federal Spending Power" (1989) 68 Can. Bar Rev. 448 (although he suggests. at p. 468, that equalization is within federal legislative competence, even though equalization payments are applied to provincial objects).

ities, and each province should be given the taxing sources it needs to finance its legislative responsibilities without federal assistance. What this theory overlooks is the wide disparity of wealth and hence of tax-raising capacity among the provinces.[39] The fact is that unless federal grants are made to the poorer provinces their residents will have to accept either far higher levels of taxation or far lower levels of public services than the residents of the richer provinces. This is of course the reason for equalization payments; and for the ''implicit equalization'' in federal contributions to shared-cost programmes.[40] The theory, now embodied in s. 36 of the Constitution Act, 1982, is that Canadians in all provinces should receive ''reasonably comparable levels of public services at reasonably comparable levels of taxation''.

It is true that the framers of the Constitution could hardly have foreseen the rise of the welfare state with its enormous growth in provincial responsibilities. But to interpret the Constitution as impliedly forbidding the richer regions of the country from helping the poorer ones is to attribute a narrowness of vision to the framers which is thoroughly at odds with what we know of them. This is indeed the ''watertight compartments''[41] view of federalism carried to an extreme. And while the Constitution is generally silent on the spending power (which is what has led to this debate), let us not forget that it did from the beginning require federal grants to the provinces, including a special grant to the poorest of the original provinces, New Brunswick. We have already discussed the ''statutory subsidies'' provided for in the B.N.A. Act.[42] For present purposes, the point is that these subsidies (which still continue) would consist of money raised by federal taxation, which would be paid to the provinces and applied by them to provincial objects. Section 36 of the Constitution Act, 1982, expressing a commitment to redressing regional disparities and to making equalization payments, also seems to reinforce by implication a broad interpretation of the spending power.

It seems to me that the better view of the law is that the federal Parliament may spend or lend its funds to any government or institution or individual it chooses, for any purpose it chooses; and that it may attach to any grant or loan any conditions it chooses, including conditions it could not directly legislate. There is a distinction, in my view, between compulsory regulation, which can

---

39 The answer to Professor Trudeau (previous note) was given by Prime Minister Trudeau in a federal working paper: Trudeau, *Federal-Provincial Grants and the Spending Power of Parliament* (1969), 30. For examples of the disparities in tax-raising capacity, see note 16, above.

40 The per capita formula for federal financing of the three ''established'' programmes (post-secondary education, hospital insurance and medicare) has two consequences: (1) it redistributes tax revenue from the provinces with high per capita tax yields to the provinces with low per capita tax yields; and (2) it pays a higher proportion of the actual costs in provinces with low costs than in provinces with high costs. Both these effects work to the benefit of the have-not provinces with their lower tax yields and their less costly medical and post-secondary facilities.

41 The metaphor is Lord Atkin's: *A.G. Can.* v. *A.G. Ont* (Labour Conventions) [1937] A.C. 326, 354.

42 See sec. 6.1, ''Confederation arrangements'', above.

obviously be accomplished only by legislation enacted within the limits of legislative power, and spending or lending or contracting, which either imposes no obligations on the recipient (as in the case of family allowances) or obligations which are voluntarily[43] assumed by the recipient (as in the case of a conditional grant, a loan or a commercial contract). There is no compelling reason to confine spending or lending or contracting within the limits of legislative power, because in those functions the government is not purporting to exercise any peculiarly governmental authority over its subjects.

In *Re Canada Assistance Plan* (1991),[44] a constitutional challenge was brought by British Columbia to federal legislation amending the Canada Assistance Plan that would place a five per cent annual cap on the growth of federal contributions to the three ''have'' provinces of British Columbia, Alberta and Ontario. Under the Canada Assistance Plan (CAP), the federal government had entered into cost-sharing agreements with these three (and the other seven) provinces, under which the federal government undertook to pay 50 per cent of the costs incurred by the provinces in carrying out provincial welfare programmes that met the conditions stipulated in the CAP legislation. The practical effect of the amending legislation was to modify the federal government's obligations under the agreements. The amending legislation was challenged on a variety of grounds, all of which were rejected by the Supreme Court of Canada.

One of the grounds raised by the intervening province of Manitoba in the *CAP* case came dangerously close to a challenge to the power of the Parliament to make conditional grants to the provinces in a field of provincial jurisdiction. (The other participating provinces made no such challenge.) Sopinka J. for the unanimous Court said:[45]

> The written argument of the Attorney General of Manitoba was that the legislation ''amounts to'' regulation of a matter outside federal authority. I disagree. The Agreement under the Plan set up an open-ended cost-sharing scheme, which left it to British Columbia to decide which programmes it would establish and fund. The simple withholding of federal money which had previously been granted to fund a matter within provincial jurisdiction does not amount to the regulation of that matter.

This is a rather clear affirmation both of the Parliament's power to authorize grants to the provinces for use in fields of provincial jurisdiction and the power to impose conditions on the recipient provinces. Provided the Parliament's inter-

---

43 I appreciate that where there are discrepancies in bargaining power the recipient may not assume obligations ''voluntarily'' in the broadest sense of that term; but there is a legal distinction between the consensual assumption of an obligation and the compulsory imposition of an obligation. For example, in the realm of contract, a dominant contracting party may be able to secure the acceptance of a standard-form contract; that is still not legislating. Cf. *A.G.B.C.* v. *E. & N. Ry. Co.* [1950] A.C. 87, 110 (''Legislation and contract are entirely different methods of creating rights and liabilities and it is essential to keep them distinct'').

44 [1991] 2 S.C.R. 525. The opinion of the Court was written by Sopinka J. I disclose that I was one of the counsel for the Attorney General of Canada.

45 [1991] 2 S.C.R. 525, 567.

vention does not go beyond the granting or withholding of money, there is no unconstitutional trespass on provincial jurisdiction.

This broad interpretation of the federal spending power has been accepted by the federal government, of course, and probably by all provincial governments, despite occasional objections to federal intrusions on provincial autonomy.[46] It is, as noted, the basis of the federal-provincial financial arrangements of the last 30 years.[47] It is also the basis of the myriad of federal grants and loans to private firms or individuals,[48] of the tax expenditure provisions of the Income Tax Act,[49] and of the commercial activities of the federal government.[50] It is supported by the case-law[51] and by most commentators.[52]

---

46 The Meech Lake Accord of 1987, now lapsed (ch. 4, Amendment, under heading 4.1(c) ''The failure to accommodate Quebec'', above), proposed an amendment to the Constitution that would have confirmed the federal power to spend in areas of exclusive provincial jurisdiction, and the power to make its spending conditional (in order to establish a shared-cost programme), but would have required that any new national shared-cost programme in an area of exclusive provincial jurisdiction had to permit opting out with reasonable compensation for a province that itself established a programme that was ''compatible with the national objectives''. The Charlottetown Accord of 1992, also now lapsed (ch. 4, Amendment, under heading 4.1(c), ''The failure to accommodate Quebec'', above), repeated the same proposal, and also proposed an amendment that would have obligated the federal government, when requested by the government of a province, to negotiate an agreement to stop federal spending programmes in particular (listed) areas of provincial jurisdiction.

47 *Re Canada Assistance Plan* [1991] 2 S.C.R. 525; note 44, above; *Winterhaven Stables* v. *Can.* (1988) 53 D.L.R. (4th) 413 (Alta. C.A.) (upholding Canada Health Act, Canada Assistance Plan and the Federal-Provincial Fiscal Arrangements legislation). Cf. *Finlay* v. *Canada* [1986] 2 S.C.R. 607 (assuming validity of federal conditions on grants to provinces under Canada Assistance Plan). In the United States, conditional grants to the states have been upheld: *Oklahoma* v. *U.S. Civil Service Commn.* (1947) 330 U.S. 127 (upholding condition on federal highway grants that state officials not engage in political activities).

48 *Angers* v. *M.N.R.* [1957] Ex. C.R. 83 (upholding federal family allowances); *Central Mortgage and Housing Corp.* v. *Co-op College Residences* (1975) 13 O.R. (2d) 394 (C.A.) (upholding federal loans for student housing); *YMHA Jewish Community Centre* v. *Brown* [1989] 1 S.C.R. 1532 (upholding federal job creation programme, involving federal wages subsidy). Cf. *A.G. Can,* v. *A.G. Ont.* (Unemployment Insurance) [1937] A.C. 355 (refusing to uphold federal unemployment insurance as a spending measure, because it also established a contributory insurance scheme, involving the imposition of duties — to pay premiums — on employers and employees; dicta on extent of spending power at 366-367 per Lord Atkin are equivocal).

49 The Income Tax Act provides for many exemptions, deductions, credits and other preferences that pursue non-tax policies, e.g., to encourage manufacturing and processing, research and development, pollution control or charitable giving. It has become commonplace to describe these provisions as ''tax expenditures'', because their economic effect is equivalent to a direct expenditure equal to the tax foregone by the tax preference. The description reflects the interchangeability as policy instruments of direct expenditures and tax expenditures. Constitutional restrictions on the one would presumably apply to the other as well.

50 See ch. 28, Public Property, under heading 28.3, ''Executive power over public property'', below.

51 Notes 47-48, above.

52 Scott, ''The Constitutional Background of the Taxation Agreements'' (1955) 2 McGill L.J. 1, 6-7 (''Making a gift is not the same as making a law.''); Lederman, ''Some Forms and

(b) Provincial power

The understandable preoccupation of governments and commentators with the power to disburse from the federal purse has not been matched by an equivalent concern with the extent of the provincial spending power.[53] But the distinction between compulsory regulation, on the one hand, and spending or lending or contracting, on the other, is surely as valid for the provinces as it is for the Dominion. To be sure, the provincial taxing power is expressly limited to ''the raising of a revenue for provincial purposes'' (s. 92(2)), but Duff C.J. has said that the phrase ''for provincial purposes'' means only that the revenue raised is ''for the exclusive disposition of the legislature''.[54] In addition, there are cases which decide that a province may validly sell its property subject to conditions which would be outside its legislative competence.[55] In fact, the provinces have never recognized any limits on their spending power and have often spent money for purposes outside their legislative competence, for example, by running a commuter train service on interprovincial trackage,[56] by acquiring an airline,[57] or by giving international aid.[58]

6.9 Conclusions

The history of federal-provincial financial arrangements from 1867 to the present is a history of continuous constitutional adaptation to changing circumstances and values. The pendulum has swung several times between federal and provincial power as the balance has been altered by factors impinging on the

Limitations of Cooperative Federalism'' (1967) 45 Can. Bar Rev. 409, 433; Magnet, ''The Constitutional Distribution of Taxation Powers in Canada'' (1978) 10 Ottawa L. Rev. 473, 480; La Forest, *The Allocation of Taxing Power under the Canadian Constitution* (2nd ed., 1981), 51; Driedger, ''The Spending Power'' (1981) 7 Queen's L.J. 124, 133-134; Laskin, *Canadian Constitutional Law* (5th ed., 1986 by Finkelstein), 783-784.

53 See La Forest, previous note, 60-62; Driedger, previous note, 131-132; *Dunbar* v. *A.G. Sask.* (1984) 11 D.L.R. (4th) 374 (Sask. Q.B.) (upholding provincial appropriation for international aid).

54 *Unemployment Ins. Reference* [1936] S.C.R. 427, 434 per Duff C.J. dissenting. This makes the phrase ''for provincial purposes'' virtually meaningless, but the phrase ''with provincial objects'' in the incorporation power (s. 92(11)) has met a similar fate: see ch. 23, Companies, at note 16, below. The provincial appropriation power (the provincial equivalent to ss. 102 and 106) is s. 126, which uses the phrase ''for the public service of the province''. Driedger, note 52, above, 131-132, argues that this phrase (and its variants in ss. 102 and 106) does not import any restrictions on the purposes for which funds may be appropriated.

55 *Smylie* v. *The Queen* (1900) 27 O.A.R. 172; *Brooks-Bidlake and Whitall* v. *A.G. B.C.* [1923] A.C. 450; and see ch. 28, Public Property, under heading 28.2, ''Legislative power over public property'', below.

56 *The Queen (Ont.)* v. *Bd. of Transport Commrs.* (Go-Train) [1968] S.C.R. 118.

57 *The Queen (Alta.)* v. *Can. Transport Comm.* [1978] 1 S.C.R. 61.

58 *Dunbar* v. *A.-G. Sask.* (1984), 11 D.L.R. (4th) 374 (Sask. Q.B.).

economy or security of the nation.[59] The depression of the 1930s followed by the second world war led to a great increase in federal power. The depression, as well as nearly bankrupting some provinces, emphasized the importance of national monetary and banking systems as economic tools. The war effort required central direction of the economy, and enormous national resources. The resulting concentration of federal power continued well into the postwar period.

There were a number of reasons why the pendulum did not start to swing back until the mid-1950s. First of all, of course, the growth of federal power had altered the balance of bargaining power to a degree which would take years for the provinces to redress even if they strove single-mindedly to that end. Secondly, the problems of postwar reconstruction were comparable in magnitude to those of the war, and the federal government had in fact developed ambitious national policies for the transition to peace and an unprecedented level of prosperity. Thirdly, humanitarian and egalitarian ideals which emphasized governmental responsibility for the provision of minimum standards of income, health, education and welfare to all Canadians could only be fulfilled by action at the national level. Fourthly, the existence of only one taxing authority eliminated much complexity and duplication in collection machinery and in the obligations of taxpayers to file returns, and enabled one national fiscal policy to regulate the economy and stimulate employment. And fifthly, there were administrative and political advantages to the provinces in not having to administer a system of tax collection, and in not having to take responsibility for levying the most painful taxes. These factors all combined to produce a continuation of highly centralized fiscal arrangements well into the 1950s. (Some of the factors are, of course, enduring and will assure the federal government a major fiscal role into the foreseeable future.) In the tax rental agreements of 1947-1962, Ottawa remained the sole taxing authority, and it used the power of the purse to establish conditional grant and shared-cost programmes, which extended federal power deeply into the traditionally provincial domains of housing, highways, health and social welfare; these programmes, and the equalization payments, required Ottawa to raise taxes well in excess of its own legislative requirements.

But there were factors tugging in the opposite direction too, and especially autonomist sentiment in Quebec. Quebec had remained outside the rental system and had refused to join some of the shared-cost programmes, although it had joined some programmes and had accepted massive equalization payments. After the death of Premier Duplessis in 1959, and the election of a Liberal government under Premier Lesage in 1960, Quebec embarked on ambitious policies of social and economic reform, which inevitably brought it into conflict with Ottawa over money (for the policies were costly) and policy (for the policies often duplicated or clashed with federal policies). While the other provinces did not design their

59 See Advisory Commission on Intergovernmental Relations, *In Search of Balance — Canada's Intergovernmental Experience* (1971); Bastien, *Federalism and Decentralization: Where do we stand?* (1981).

policies in the service of cultural integrity, and did not make any such dramatic break with the past, they too by 1960 were becoming increasingly active in social and economic affairs. All of the provinces have grown stronger and more self-confident, and have recruited able public servants. Until recently, Ontario has been the wealthiest province, with the least to gain from centralized financial arrangements, and it is not surprising that it has never been a full participant in the tax rental or tax collection arrangements. Alberta, now far and away the wealthiest province (on a per capita basis), has withdrawn from the tax collection arrangements with respect to corporate income tax. Alberta is naturally suspicious of centralized financial arrangements, and especially of the proposals which surface periodically for the sharing of oil revenues.

What began to happen in the mid-1950s, and accelerated after 1960, was a swing of the pendulum back towards provincial power. After 1962, the provinces imposed their own taxes at their own rates, and these have steadily increased in relation to federal revenues. On the other hand, the federal government retains the dominant role in setting tax policy, because it is the federal Parliament which legislates the tax base, and all provinces within the collection system have to use the federal base. Equalization grants and other forms of provincial aid are accepted by the provinces, and these require the federal government to continue to raise much more revenue than it needs for strictly federal programmes. However, the federal government has modified many of its programmes to take account of provincial objections. The direct grants to provincial universities have been abandoned. Shared-cost programmes, once virtually dictated to the provinces by the federal government on a take-it-or-leave-it basis, have become a matter for prior consultation and discussion, and opting-out alternatives have been introduced. Even the cost-sharing aspect, implying federal control of provincial expenditures, has been abandoned with respect to all major programmes in favour of a formula which is independent of actual provincial expenditures, and which includes tax points as well as cash. All these developments have collectively enhanced the provinces' control over their universities, their social programmes and (to a lesser extent) their health care systems.[60]

If the fiscal arrangements in Canada still appear to be loaded in favour of the federal government, comparisons with Australia and the United States are instructive. In Australia,[61] as in Canada, the federal government assumed a monopoly of income taxation during the second world war. In Australia, however,

---

60 The Canada Health Act, R.S.C. 1985, c. C-6, which was enacted in 1984, is opposed to the general tendency, because it strengthened the federal conditions on grants to the provinces for insured health services (hospital insurance and medicare), and in particular required (on pain of financial penalty) provincial bans on extra-billing by doctors and user fees by hospitals. These conditions, which have made it very difficult for the provinces to control the cost of their provincial health care plans, have been carried forward to the Canadian Health and Social Transfer: note 23, above.

61 For comparisons, see Gilbert, *Australian and Canadian Federalism 1867-1984* (1986); Cullen, *Federalism in Action: the Australian and Canadian Offshore Disputes* (1990).

this has continued to the present. The states levy no income taxes, and if any did their residents would not receive any abatement of federal taxes.[62] The bulk of the states' revenue comes from grants from the federal government. The result is a high degree of uniformity in public services across the country, and a high degree of state dependence upon federal grants for revenue. These arrangements are much more centralized than in either Canada or the United States, reflecting the fact that Australia has only six states, and that they are relatively homogeneous. One could add the further speculation that Australia's relative isolation from European countries has fostered a sense of unity and acceptance of strong central government, especially in comparison with Canada.[63]

The fiscal arrangements of the United States[64] are highly uncoordinated, but the balance of power is nevertheless closer to the centre than it is in Canada. The federal government dominates the income tax field. The states can levy income taxes, and many do; but no federal abatements are available, and high federal rates allow room for only low rates of state tax, usually around five to seven per cent. Federal occupancy of most of the income tax field, coupled with wide acceptance of deficit financing at the federal level, has given overwhelming fiscal supremacy to the federal government. This has not been accompanied by Canadian-style tax-sharing arrangements with the states. The federal government does make conditional (or categorical) grants to states and municipalities, and these account for around 15 per cent of state and local revenue; but it makes few unconditional grants to states or municipalities. There are no equalization payments to allow the poorer states to bring their public services up to national average levels, and there is a wide disparity in state public services.[65] There is a continuing proliferation of different taxes on various bases, at various rates — like the situation in Canada before the second world war.

The relative lack of coordination between the two levels of government in the United States is the product of a number of distinctively American constitutional and cultural factors. For a start, there are practical difficulties in securing any general federal-state agreement on tax-sharing or anything else. There is no forum comparable to Canada's first ministers' conferences where an agreement could be struck between the federal and state governments. The state Governors, unlike provincial Premiers, are rarely in a position to make firm commitments on behalf of their states because, with the separation of executive and legislative branches and the absence of strict party discipline in the state Legislatures, a Governor is rarely in control of his state Legislature. The large number of states in comparison with provinces would in any case make general agreement difficult.

---

62 Abatements which varied from state to state would probably be unconstitutional in Australia, because the Constitution by s. 51(2) requires federal taxation to be uniform.

63 Gilbert, note 61, above, 156-157.

64 See *In Search of Balance — Canada's Intergovernmental Experience* (Advisory Commission on Intergovernmental Relations, Washington, D.C., 1971).

65 The disparity in welfare benefits is roughly four times the disparity between the rich provinces and poor provinces in Canada: *Id.*

(Of course some federal-state adjustment occurs within the federal Congress, which is not controlled by the executive and does not adhere to strict party discipline, and within the federal bureaucracy.) On top of the practical difficulties, Americans seem to be much less willing than Canadians or Australians to compromise the principle of "fiscal responsibility" — the principle that the spending authority should also be the taxing authority.

The uncoordinated situation is, as noted, one of unchallenged federal fiscal dominance. This is also reinforced by factors which are lacking in Canada. African-Americans in the United States are not concentrated in any one state, and their political influence has been unsympathetic to states' rights: they have tended to look to Washington for redress of grievances. In Canada, the concern of French Canadians to protect their language and cultural integrity has taken the form of a provincial rights movement, leading to Quebec's continual insistence that it be master in its own house. Moreover, Quebec, with 6.5 million people out of a total of 25 million, is much larger in relation to Canada as a whole than any one state is in relation to the United States as a whole, and Ontario is even larger. The Canadian provinces, or small groups of them, also come much closer to representing distinct economic regions of the country than do the American states, so that the provinces have become the natural advocates of regional interests.

Federalism in Canada, Australia and the United States, like other federal countries, is of necessity "cooperative", because of the high degree of interdependence between the parts of the system, but in the United States cooperation is much less evident than in Australia and Canada. In Canada, the centralized form of federalism which developed during and after the second world war has been replaced by a form of cooperative federalism in which the provinces have sufficient autonomy to influence the outcome of federal-provincial relationships. The ideal of cooperative federalism is that each government recognizes its interdependence with the other governments, and is concerned about the repercussions of its actions on the policies of the others. This requires much more than respect for the legislative authority of others; it involves consultation with others before exercising one's own undoubted legislative authority, in order to ensure that one's own actions are as far as possible compatible with the plans of others. In Canada, in the fiscal area, major federal developments have normally been preceded by a period of consultation leading to the agreement of all or most of the provinces. Indeed, fiscal cooperation is now institutionalized in the form of several intergovernmental committees which meet regularly, and do much of the work preparatory to the first ministers' conferences, which will of course continue to make the decisions. Cooperation has become the rule and unilateral initiative the exception.

7

Courts

7.1 Provincial courts

(a) Establishment of provincial courts

The Constitution Act, 1867, by s. 92(14), allocates to the provinces the power to make laws in relation to "the administration of justice in the province".[1] The power expressly includes "the constitution, maintenance, and organization of provincial courts, both of civil and criminal jurisdiction", and "procedure in civil matters in those courts". The power embraces courts of criminal as well as

1 See Russell, *The Judiciary in Canada* (1987); Beaudoin, *La Constitution du Canada* (1990), ch. 4.

civil jurisdiction, despite the fact that "the criminal law" is by s. 91(27) allocated to the federal Parliament; but the provincial power does not include criminal procedure, because "procedure in criminal matters" is by s. 91(27) allocated to the federal Parliament along with the substantive criminal law.[2]

At the time of confederation, each of the uniting provinces had its own system of courts modeled on the English courts. The system included a "superior" court or courts with jurisdiction throughout the province, unlimited by subject matter. Below the superior court in all provinces except Quebec were "county" or "district" courts with jurisdiction limited by territory to a local county or district as well as by subject matter. Below the county or district courts were "inferior" courts staffed by magistrates or justices of the peace with jurisdiction over small civil claims and minor criminal offences. All these courts were expressly continued after confederation by s. 129 of the Constitution Act, 1867, and their organization and jurisdiction remained the responsibility of the provinces by virtue of s. 92(14).[3]

The structure of the courts in each province, including those provinces admitted after confederation, did not until recently depart radically from the pre-confederation pattern. In each province, despite variations in nomenclature, organization and jurisdiction, it was still possible to identify the three tiers of the judicial system: (1) the "superior" court or courts, which in each province now includes a court of appeal as well as a trial division; (2) the "county" or "district" courts, which did not however exist in Quebec; and (3) the "inferior" courts, which in most provinces are now called "provincial courts".[4] In the 1970s, the idea of "amalgamating" the county and district courts into the superior court became popular among court reformers. What is involved in amalgamation is the abolition of the county and district courts and an increase in the size of the superior court. Amalgamation has now occurred in all nine provinces that originally had district or county courts. The intermediate tier of county or district courts no longer exists.

The administration of justice in Canada has important unitary as well as federal characteristics.[5] Of course, as one would expect in a federal country, there

---

2 The administration of justice in the province includes criminal justice, even though criminal law and procedure is a federal responsibility under s. 91(27). Criminal justice, including investigation of crime, policing, prosecution, punishment and public inquiries, is dealt with in ch. 18, Criminal Law, below.

3 The history is related in Laskin, *The British Tradition in Canadian Law* (1969), 10-21.

4 This change in nomenclature occasionally leads the ill-informed to assume that the superior, district and county courts in each province are "federal" courts. This is incorrect: these courts are also provincial, despite the national elements of the system, and despite federal appointment and payment of the judges, as described in the following text.

5 This idea is explored in more detail in Hogg, "Federalism and the Jurisdiction of Canadian Courts" (1981) 30 U.N.B.L.J. 9. The unitary elements of the system have been recognized in judicial dicta: *R.* v. *Thomas Fuller Construction* [1980] 1 S.C.R. 695, 706; *A.-G. Can.* v. *Law Society of B.C.* [1982] 2 S.C.R. 307, 327; *Ont.* v. *Pembina Exploration* [1989] 1 S.C.R. 206, 215, 217, 225, 226.

is a separate hierarchy of provincial courts in each province. But these courts, whether they were in existence at the time of confederation or were established later under s. 92(14), are not confined to deciding cases arising under provincial laws. The provincial power over the administration of justice in the province enables a province to invest its courts with jurisdiction over the full range of cases, whether the applicable law is federal or provincial or constitutional.[6] Then, there is an appeal from the provincial court of appeal, which stands at the top of each provincial hierarchy, to the Supreme Court of Canada. Although the Supreme Court of Canada is established by federal legislation, it is more of a national than a federal court, because it is a ''general court of appeal for Canada'', with power to hear appeals from the provincial courts (as well as from the federal courts, which are described later) in all kinds of cases, whether the applicable law is federal or provincial or constitutional.[7] The position of the Supreme Court of Canada, with its plenary jurisdiction, at the top of each provincial hierarchy, has the effect of melding the ten provincial hierarchies into a single national system. The national character of the system is reinforced by the judicature sections of the Constitution Act, 1867, which are described in the next section of this chapter, and which require that the judges of the superior, district and county courts of each province be appointed and paid by the federal government.

The general jurisdiction of the provincial courts means that there is no need for a separate system of federal courts to decide ''federal'' questions. Nor does the power to decide federal questions have to be specifically granted to the provincial courts by the federal Parliament. On the contrary, if federal law calls for the exercise of adjudication, but is silent as to the forum, the appropriate forum will be the provincial courts.[8] Thus, most disputes involving banking and commercial paper, although governed by federal law, are disposed of by provincial courts because the applicable federal law is silent on the question of adjudication.[9] The federal Parliament does have the power to stipulate the forum of adjudication over matters in relation to which it has legislative competence, and it may stipulate

---

6 *Valin* v. *Langlois* (1879) 3 S.C.R. 1, 19; *Ont.* v. *Pembina Exploration* [1989] 1 S.C.R. 206, 217.

7 The Supreme Court of Canada is the topic of the next chapter.

8 *Board* v. *Board* [1919] A.C. 956 (Supreme Court of Alberta has jurisdiction over divorce); *Ont.* v. *Pembina Exploration* [1989] 1 S.C.R. 206 (Small Claims Court of Ontario has jurisdiction over admiralty); *Knox Contracting* v. *Can.*, [1990] 2 S.C.R. 338, 360 (Court of Queen's Bench of New Brunswick has power to determine issue under Income Tax Act); Laskin, *The British Tradition in Canadian Law* (1969), 114. In *Kourtessis* v. *M.N.R.* [1993] 2 S.C.R. 53, the Court divided on the question whether the power to decide federal questions flowed from an assumed adoption by Parliament of the provincial forum (La Forest J. at 77) or from the plenary provincial power over the administration of justice (Sopinka J. at 105). The latter explanation is the orthodox one and, in my view, the correct one.

9 Judicial review of federal administrative tribunals was another example of provincial jurisdiction acquired by silence, but in 1971 that function was vested in the newly-established Federal Court: Federal Court Act, R.S.C. 1985, c. F-7, ss. 18, 28.

provincial courts or tribunals.[10] This has been done, for example, in the Criminal Code,[11] the Divorce Act[12] and the Young Offenders Act:[13] cases arising under those federal statutes are dealt with in the provincial courts under specific grants of jurisdiction contained in each statute.

While the Constitution Act, 1867 does not require a separate system of federal courts to decide federal questions, s. 101 does authorize the federal Parliament to establish federal courts ''for the better administration of the laws of Canada''. This power was exercised in 1875 by the establishment of the Exchequer Court of Canada. Then in 1971 the Exchequer Court was replaced by the Federal Court of Canada. These federal courts constitute an exception to the generally unitary character of the administration of justice in Canada; for since 1875 it has been necessary to bring certain kinds of ''federal'' cases in a federal court instead of a provincial court. The federal court system is discussed later in this chapter.[14]

(b) Appointment and payment of provincial judges

Section 92(4) of the Constitution Act, 1867 confers on each province the power to make laws in relation to ''the establishment and tenure of provincial offices and the appointment and payment of provincial officers''. Under this provision, the province appoints and pays the judges of the ''inferior'' courts. The province does not appoint and pay the judges of the ''superior'' courts, or the judges of the ''district'' or ''county'' courts (where they exist), because the judicature sections of the Constitution Act, 1867 (ss. 96 to 101) provide (among other things) for the appointment and payment of these judges by the federal government.

Section 96 of the Constitution Act, 1867 provides that ''the Governor General'', that is, the federal government, ''shall appoint the judges of the superior, district and county courts in each province''. On the face of it, this provision is an anomaly in a federal constitution.[15] Why should the federal government make

10 *Valin* v. *Langlois* (1879) 3 S.C.R. 1 (superior court); *Re Vancini* (1904) 34 S.C.R. 621 (police magistrate); *Coughlin* v. *Ont. Highway Transport Bd.* [1968] S.C.R. 569 (administrative tribunal); *Papp* v. *Papp* [1970] 1 O.R. 331 (Ont. C.A.) (superior court and master thereof); *R.* v. *Trimarchi* (1987) 63 O.R. (2d) 515 (C.A.) (provincial court); *Re Young Offenders Act* [1991] 1 S.C.R. 252 (youth court). The federal cause, if civil, will be regulated by the provincially-enacted procedure of the provincial court, although the federal Parliament may, if it chooses, stipulate the procedure to be followed: Laskin, *Canadian Constitutional Law* (5th ed., 1986 by Finkelstein), 184-188. It has done so in divorce, for example.

11 R.S.C. 1985, c. C-46, ss. 468, 798.

12 S.C. 1986, c. 4, s. 3.

13 R.S.C. 1985, c. Y-1, s. 2.

14 Section 7.2, ''Federal Courts'', below.

15 Section 96 has no counterpart in the Constitution of the United States and Australia, where the federal government plays no role in the selection of state judges.

appointments to the provinces' higher courts?[16] The answer that has become conventional is that s. 96 reinforces judicial independence by insulating the judges from local pressures. But this explanation, although enthusiastically endorsed by the Privy Council,[17] is not particularly convincing. There is no reason to suppose that judges appointed by the provinces would be less competent[18] or independent[19] than judges appointed by the federal government. I believe that the reason for s. 96 is to be found in the fact that the provincial courts are courts of general jurisdiction.[20] Since the provincial courts decide questions of federal law as well as provincial law, and questions of constitutional law as well as private law, some federal involvement in their establishment is appropriate.[21]

Associated with s. 96 are several other sections whose purpose is more obvious. Sections 97 and 98 require that the federally-appointed judges of the superior, district and county courts in each province be appointed from the bar of the province. This ensures that the judges be lawyers and that they be versed in the local law.

Section 100 provides that the salaries of the judges of the superior, district and county courts be "fixed and provided by the Parliament of Canada". This section makes clear that the federally-appointed judges are to be paid from the federal treasury, not the provincial treasury. In addition, however, by insisting that the salaries be fixed and provided by the Parliament, s. 100 protects the judiciary from executive power to impair judicial independence by reductions or

---

16 The legislative history is not clear: see Laskin, "Municipal Tax Assessment and Section 96" (1955) 33 Can. Bar Rev. 993, 998; Pepin, *Les tribunaux administratifs et la constitution* (1969), Part 1, ch. 1.

17 *Martineau & Sons* v. *Montreal* [1932] A.C. 113, 120; *Toronto* v. *York* [1938] A.C. 415, 426.

18 The provinces would undoubtedly appoint from the same group of senior lawyers as the federal government now appoints from. Considerations of provincial politics would sometimes operate in favour of different individuals, especially where the provincial government was controlled by a different political party than the federal government, but this would be unlikely to impair the relative quality of appointments.

19 The formal and informal guarantees of judicial independence, which are discussed in the next section of this chapter, would continue to apply if the s. 96 judges were appointed by the provinces.

20 This thesis is advanced in the article cited, note 5, above, and in Duplé's contribution to Beck and Bernier (eds.), *Canada and the New Constitution* (1983), vol. 1, 129.

21 This rationale is very powerful where there are no federal courts (the situation at confederation), or where the federal courts have very limited jurisdiction (the situation at the establishment of the Exchequer Court in 1875), but its force diminishes as more and more federal questions are removed from the jurisdiction of the provincial courts and vested in the federal courts (as has steadily occurred, especially at the establishment of the Federal Court of Canada in 1971). The establishment of these federal courts is described later in this chapter. However, the provincial courts still decide many issues under federal law, including the trial of all criminal offences, and they retain jurisdiction over constitutional cases — a jurisdiction that cannot be taken away from them: *A.G. Can.* v. *Law Society of B.C.* [1982] 2 S.C.R. 307; *Can. Labour Relations Bd.* v. *Paul L'Anglais* [1983] 1 S.C.R. 147.

raises of salary.[22] Of course, in a system of responsible government, the executive can usually rely upon the Parliament to do its bidding, but a government which had decided to tamper improperly with judicial salaries would have to expose its decision to parliamentary debate, and this would raise a storm of protest from the opposition and from the press. Indeed, during the depression of the 1930s, there was much controversy in Canada (and England) as to whether it was proper to reduce judicial salaries by ten per cent (20 per cent in England) by a statute which applied to the entire federal civil service as well. The argument that such a non-discriminatory reduction would threaten judicial independence seems fantastic, but it was seriously advanced by constitutional lawyers, judges, government ministers and members of parliament.[23]

The result of the judicature sections of the Constitution Act, 1867 is compulsory co-operative federalism. It is for the provinces under s. 92(14) to create all provincial courts, and to determine how many judges are to be appointed. But, with respect to the higher courts, the actual appointments must be made by the federal government (from the bar of the province), and the judges' salaries must be provided by the federal Parliament.[24] The federal appointments are made by the cabinet, with the federal Minister of Justice recommending the names of puisne judges, and the Prime Minister recommending the names of chief justices.[25] Salaries are fixed by the federal Judges Act.[26]

A reorganization of provincial courts sometimes gives rise to difficult questions as to the location of the required powers. There is a fine line between the reorganization of the provincial courts, which is competent to the province by virtue of s. 92(14), and the appointment of higher-court judges, which is incompetent to the province by virtue of s. 96. A provincial statute authorizing a county court judge to sit in a county other than that for which he was appointed has been

---

22 *Beauregard* v. *Can.* [1986] 2 S.C.R. 56, 75 (a condition of judicial independence is that a judge's right to salary or pension should "not be subject to arbitrary interference by the Executive").

23 The history is related by Lederman, "The Independence of the Judiciary" (1956) 34 Can. Bar Rev. 769, 789, 1139, 1164. There is an argument, based on the words "fixed and provided" in s. 100, that it would be unconstitutional to reduce judicial salaries even by a statute enacted by the federal Parliament; but the better view, it seems to me, is that this language does not prohibit a reduction in judicial salaries. In *Beauregard* v. *Can.* [1986] 2 S.C.R. 56, the Court held that an amendment to the federal Judges Act that required judges to contribute to the cost of their pensions (and which effectively reduced their salaries) was not prohibited by s. 100. Only a law respecting salaries that was "arbitrary" (p. 75), "colourable" or "discriminatory" (p. 77) would be vulnerable to attack under s. 100. Cf. *Re Public Sector Pay Reduction Act (P.E.I.)* (1994) 120 D.L.R. (4th) 449 (P.E.I. A.D.) (reduction of provincial judges' salaries in common with other public officials does not affect independence within s.11(d)).

24 Provincial requests for new judicial appointments are not always granted, and are sometimes granted on condition that reforms in provincial judicial management are carried out: Russell "Constitutional Reform of the Canadian Judiciary" (1967) 7 Alta. L. Rev. 103, 121.

25 Russell, note 1, above, 112.

26 R.S.C. 1985, c. J-1.

held to be valid.[27] But a provincial statute authorizing the Lieutenant Governor to assign superior court judges to a new appellate division of the court and to designate one of them as the Chief Justice has been struck down as a usurpation of the federal power of appointment.[28] It appears that, while the creation of new divisions of the superior court (or even of new superior courts) is competent to the provinces under s. 92(14), any such provincial reorganization must leave to the federal government the function of assigning or designating (appointing) judges to the new divisions or courts,[29] and the reorganization will be inoperative unless and until the federal government acts.[30]

The provisions of the Constitution Act, 1867 which have just been described (ss. 96, 97, 98 and 100) apply only to the higher courts, or, more precisely, to "the superior, district and county courts in each province". They do not apply to the courts below the level of the district and county courts. Some "inferior" courts existed at the time of confederation, and many more have been created since then under the provincial power over the administration of justice (s. 92(14)). For these courts, the Constitution is silent as to the qualifications of the presiding judges (or magistrates or justices of the peace): there is no constitutional requirement that the judges be members of the bar. Nor is there any constitutional requirement of federal appointment: the province makes the appointments and fixes and pays the salaries of the appointees.[31]

(c) Tenure of provincial judges: s. 99

Section 99 of the Constitution Act, 1867 guarantees the tenure of the judges of the superior courts. The section provides that "the judges of the superior courts shall hold office during good behaviour, but shall be removable by the Governor General on address of the Senate and House of Commons". Section 99, unlike the other judicature sections, applies only to superior courts, and does not extend to district or county courts. In its original form, s. 99 provided no retirement age. Successive federal governments took the view that s. 99 guaranteed tenure for life, and that the statutory imposition of a mandatory retirement age would be unconstitutional. In 1960, when it was decided to impose a mandatory retirement age, it was accomplished by amendment of the Constitution Act: a new subsection requiring retirement at age 75 was added to s. 99.[32]

---

27 *Re County Courts of B.C.* (1892) 21 S.C.R. 446.

28 *A.-G. Ont.* v. *A.-G. Can.* (Judges) [1925] A.C. 750.

29 *Scott* v. *A.-G. Can.* [1923] 3 W.W.R. 929 (P.C., unreported in A.C.).

30 See generally, Ontario Law Reform Commission, *Report on Administration of Ontario Courts: Part 1* (1973), 71-81.

31 The misleading practice of naming the inferior courts "Provincial Courts", as if the higher courts were not provincial courts, has been commented upon in note 4, above.

32 There has, however, been a statutory retirement age of 75 for judges of the Supreme Court of Canada since 1927: note 106, below.

The independence of the judiciary is a value which is now deeply rooted in Canada and elsewhere in the common law world. It is inherent in the concept of adjudication, at least as understood in the western world, that the judge must not be an ally or supporter of one of the contending parties.[33] Indeed, John Locke claimed that the adjudication of disputes by neutral judges was the most important benefit of civilization.[34] The independence of the judge from the other branches of government is especially significant, because it provides an assurance that the state will be subjected to the rule of law. If the state could count on the courts to ratify all legislative and executive actions, even if unauthorized by law, the individual would have no protection against tyranny. In England, the Stuart Kings badly impaired the independence of the judiciary by the practice of dismissing judges who rendered decisions unfavourable to them. Accordingly, as part of the revolution settlement on the accession of William and Mary, the English Parliament enacted the Act of Settlement, 1701, which guaranteed the tenure of the judges "during good behaviour", and which provided for their removal "upon the address of both Houses of Parliament". Section 99 of the Constitution Act, 1867 is closely modelled on the Act of Settlement.[35]

The independence of the judiciary has since become such a powerful tradition in the United Kingdom and Canada[36] that there may be little point in a fine analysis of the language of the provisions by which it is formally guaranteed. Nevertheless, the meaning of s. 99 of the Constitution Act, 1867 (and the similar language of the Act of Settlement) is not wholly free from doubt. The question is whether s. 99 provides for one mode of removal or two. It could be read as

---

33 Adjudication by courts is compulsory in that it does not depend upon the consent of the parties. Although the courts cannot themselves enforce their judgments, which has led to the description "the least dangerous branch", their judgments are enforceable, because they are backed by the coercive power of the state. (Arbitration, by contrast, depends upon the consent of the parties, and any relief will be enforceable only if the parties have previously so agreed. Mediation also depends upon the consent of the parties, although the mediator does not reach a decision but helps the parties to find their own solution. See Russell, note 1, above, 5.) Since parties that have taken a dispute to court cannot choose their judge, it is essential that they be confident that any judge will be a neutral third party.

34 Locke, *The Second Treatise on Government* (Peardon ed., Macmillan, N.Y., 1985), 9-10; quoted Russell, note 1, above, 20.

35 It is likely that s. 99 would preclude actions short of removal that would have the effect of impairing judicial independence. In *MacKeigan* v. *Hickman* [1989] 2 S.C.R. 796, the Court held that superior court judges could not be compelled to testify before a provincial commission of inquiry in order to elaborate on their written reasons for judgment; nor could the Chief Justice be compelled to testify as to his reasons for assigning a particular judge to a particular case. The decision was based on the interpretation of Nova Scotia's Public Inquiries Act, but the tenor of the judgments suggests that even an explicit statutory authority for the testimony would have been ineffective, because it would have been contrary to s. 99.

36 Judicial independence is examined in Shetreet, *Judges on Trial* (1976); Lederman, note 22, above; Deschênes, *Masters in their own House* (1981); Russell, note 1, above, chs. 4, 7; Friedland, *A Place Apart: Judicial Independence and Accountability in Canada* (Canadian Judicial Council, 1995).

meaning that a judge may be removed only by joint parliamentary address and then only for bad behaviour. But the section could also be read as meaning that a judge may be removed for bad behaviour by the government without the need for a joint parliamentary address, and may in addition be removed for any reason whatsoever (not necessarily involving bad behaviour) by a joint parliamentary address. On principle, the former interpretation is preferable, because it is more apt to secure the independence of the judiciary, which is the purpose of the provision.[37] In fact no Canadian government has ever attempted to by-pass the joint address procedure; and even the joint address procedure has never been carried to a conclusion, though it has been started on several occasions. It is a matter of record therefore that no superior court judge has ever been removed from office.[38]

Section 99 applies only to superior courts. There is no formal constitutional guarantee of tenure during good behaviour for the judges of county and district courts, even though they are also federally-appointed.[39] And, obviously, there is no formal constitutional guarantee of tenure for the judges of the inferior courts who are provincially-appointed. Of course, the powerful tradition of judicial independence would in practice protect them from arbitrary removal, and for most judges this tradition is reinforced by statutory guarantees of tenure. In the case of the federally-appointed county and district court judges, the federal Judges Act guarantees tenure "during good behaviour".[40] In the case of most provincially-

---

37 So held in *Gratton* v. *Can.* [1994] 2 F.C. 769 (T.D.), where the scholarly literature is reviewed by Strayer J. He went on to hold that a permanent infirmity (caused by a stroke in that case) would be a breach of good behaviour justifying dismissal under s. 99.

38 The federal Judges Act, R.S.C. 1985, c. J-1, Part II, establishes a Canadian Judicial Council, which is composed of the Chief Justice of Canada and the Chief Justices of all the superior courts, to inquire into complaints against judges of superior, district or county courts, as a precondition of removal.

39 Section 100 also plays a role in securing the independence of the judiciary by ensuring financial security and precluding "arbitrary interference" with the judges' financial security: *Beauregard* v. *Can.* [1986] 2 S.C.R. 56, 75. Section 100 applies to county and district court judges as well as superior court judges.

40 Judges Act, R.S.C. 1985, c. J-1, s. 67, provides for the removal by the Governor in Council of county and district court judges (but not superior court judges — no doubt, because of s. 99 of the Constitution Act, 1867). It is not entirely clear why the tenure of county and district court judges should be a matter within federal legislative competence. Nowhere in the Constitution Act, 1867 is it expressly assigned to the federal Parliament. However, perhaps Lederman, note 23, above, 1160, is right in asserting that "the cumulative effect of sections 96 to 100 inclusive is to assign by necessary implication to the federal parliament legislative power over the appointment, tenure and removal of provincial superior-court judges, subject to the limitations contained in those sections themselves" (he is using the term "superior-court judges" to include county and district court judges). Accord, *R.* v. *Moore; Ex parte Brooks* [1969] 2 O.R. 677 (Ont. H.C.) (upholding prohibition on judicial "moonlighting" in federal Judges Act); *Beauregard* v. *Can.* [1986] 2 S.C.R. 56 (upholding requirement in federal Judges Act that judges contribute to pension scheme); *Gratton* v. *Can.* [1994] 2 F.C. 769 (T.D.) (upholding provisions of federal Judges Act providing for investigation of complaints against judges).

appointed inferior court judges, similar guarantees are contained in provincial statutes.[41]

(d) Tenure of provincial judges: s. 11(d)

The Charter of Rights contains a guarantee of judicial independence in s. 11(d). Section 11(d) grants to ''any person charged with an offence'' the right:

> to be presumed innocent until proven guilty according to law in a fair and public hearing by an independent and impartial tribunal.

This right to ''an independent and impartial tribunal'' applies only to courts of criminal jurisdiction, because the right is possessed only by a person ''charged with an offence''. But the guarantee reaches deeply into the court system, because more than 90 per cent of criminal cases, including most of the cases involving serious indictable offences, are heard by inferior courts, that is, courts with provincially-appointed judges.[42]

(e) Inferior courts

In *Valente* v. *The Queen* (1985),[43] the question arose whether the provincially-appointed judges of Ontario's Provincial Court (Criminal Division) were disqualified from performing their functions by reason of s. 11(d). The argument was made that the degree of control over the judges that was possessed by the provincial Attorney General raised a reasonable apprehension that the judges would be biased in favour of the Crown. The argument could not be based on insecure tenure, because the judges had a statutory guarantee of tenure during good behaviour to age 65. But the argument enumerated a host of minor ways in which the judges remained subject to executive power: the judges were appointed by the Attorney General;[44] the Attorney General had discretions to designate a (higher-paid) ''senior judge'', to authorize leaves of absence, and to authorize

41 The position in the provinces is reviewed in Deschênes, note 36, above, 103-124; Russell, note 36, above, 178-190; Friedland, note 36, above, 105-113. In all provinces except Prince Edward Island, a guarantee of tenure during good behaviour is supplemented by the establishment of a judicial council — a committee of judges with power to inquire into complaints against judges and make recommendations as a precondition to disciplinary action. The size, composition and powers of provincial judicial councils vary from province to province, so that, for example, some provinces include federally-appointed judges on the council (e.g., Ontario), while others select only provincially-appointed judges (e.g., British Columbia). Unlike the federal Canadian Judicial Council, which is described in note 38, above, the provincial judicial councils are generally composed of both judges and lawyers, although the ratio varies across the country.

42 Russell, ''Constitutional Reform of the Judicial Branch'' (1984) 17 Can. Jo. Pol. Sci. 227.

43 [1985] 2 S.C.R. 673. The judgment of the Court was written by Le Dain J.

44 The powers of the Attorney General were in fact powers vested in the Lieutenant Governor in Council, i.e., by convention, the cabinet, but in practice in matters of this kind the advice of the Attorney General would be decisive.

paid extra-judicial work; the judges' salaries were fixed by regulation, not statute; and pensions were provided out of the general provincial civil service plan, not a special judges' plan.

The Supreme Court of Canada in *Valente* rejected the challenge to the Provincial Court (Criminal Division)'s jurisdiction. The Supreme Court held that "the essential conditions of judicial independence" were satisfied by the Provincial Court (Criminal Division). What were those conditions? First, the Supreme Court said, was "security of tenure". This did not need to be expressed to be "during good behaviour" (as in s. 99); nor was it necessary that a judge be removable only on an address of the Legislature (as in s. 99). What was required was that a judge be removable "only for cause related to the capacity to perform judicial functions".[45] Second, was "financial security". This did not require that salaries be fixed by the Legislature (as in s. 100), but it did require that the right to salary or pension be established by law, even if the law was (as Ontario's was) a regulation rather than a statute.[46] Third and last was "the institutional independence of the tribunal with respect to matters of administration bearing directly on the exercise of its judicial function".[47] This did not preclude involvement by the Attorney General in the administration of the courts, but it did require that the judges control the "assignment of judges, sittings of the court, and court lists".[48] The Court held that Ontario's Provincial Court (Criminal Division) did satisfy all three conditions of independence, and was accordingly capable of trying criminal cases without any breach of s. 11(d) of the Charter.

In *R.* v. *Lippé* (1990),[49] the question arose whether the municipal court judges of Quebec were disqualified from trying criminal cases by s. 11(d). The problem was that the municipal judges were part-time judges, who maintained private law practices when not serving on the bench. It was argued that the judges' continuing relationships with private clients gave them an appearance of bias and were therefore inconsistent with the independence and impartiality required by s. 11(d). The Supreme Court of Canada held that the test for bias under s. 11(d) was the same as in other legal contexts, namely, whether "an informed person, viewing

---

45 [1985] 2 S.C.R. 673, 697. The Court did find a breach of the security-of-tenure condition in the statutory provision for judges who were reappointed after retirement age to hold office during pleasure. However, the judge who declined jurisdiction in this case did not hold a post-retirement appointment, and in the meantime the statute had been amended to make the continuance in office after retirement dependant on the discretion, not of the Attorney General, but of the chief judge (for ages 65-70) and a judicial council (for ages 70-75). The new provisions created a post-retirement status that was "by no means ideal", but was sufficient for the purpose of s. 11(d).

46 See also *Re Public Sector Pay Reduction Act (P.E.I.)* (1994) 120 D.L.R. (4th) 449 (P.E.I. A.D.) (reduction of provincial judges' salaries by 7.5 per cent does not affect independence within s. 11(d)); *Lowther* v. *P.E.I.* (1995) 123 D.L.R. (4th) 648 (P.E.I. A.D.) (similar decision).

47 [1985] 2 S.C.R. 673, 708.

48 *Id.*, 709.

49 [1990] 2 S.C.R. 114. Lamer C.J. wrote a concurring opinion with the agreement of two others; Gonthier J. wrote a concurring opinion with the agreement of three others.

the matter realistically and practically'', would have a ''reasonable apprehension of bias''.[50] The Court determined that 11(d) was not offended, because the judges' oath of office, code of ethics, and the statutory rules of recusement (disqualification) to avoid conflicts of interest, were sufficient to allay any reasonable apprehension that the judges would be biased.[51]

(f) Court Martial

In *R.* v. *Généreux* (1992),[52] the question arose whether a Court Martial, constituted under the federal National Defence Act for the purpose of trying a member of the armed forces for a breach of the military Code of Service Discipline,[53] qualified as ''an independent and impartial tribunal'' for the purpose of s. 11(d). The Court Martial was presided over by a judge advocate, who was a legally trained officer of the armed forces serving in the legal branch of the forces. The judge advocate had the authority to determine questions of law or of mixed fact and law. The members of the Court Martial were between five and seven regular officers of the armed forces, and, under the direction of the judge advocate as to the applicable law, they had the authority to determine the guilt or innocence of the accused, and to determine the sentence in the event of a guilty verdict. The majority of the Supreme Court of Canada held that this tribunal did not satisfy the three conditions of judicial independence stipulated by the Court in *Valente*. With respect to ''security of tenure'', the Court noted that the judge advocate and the members of the Court Martial were appointed for a particular trial by their superior officers, and this would give rise to a reasonable apprehension that their careers in the armed forces might be affected by reaching a decision that was displeasing to their superiors. With respect to ''financial security'', there was a reasonable apprehension that future salary increases of the judge advocate and members might be determined by their superiors on the basis of their decision in the Court Martial. With respect to ''institutional independence'', there was no real independence from the superior officers who appointed the members and

---

50 The test was laid down in a pre-Charter case, *Committee for Justice and Liberty* v. *Nat. Energy Bd.* [1978] 1 S.C.R. 369, 394; and it has been applied in a variety of contexts, e.g., *R.* v. *Bain* [1992] 1 S.C.R. 91; *Nfld. Telephone Co.* v. *Nfld.* [1992] 1 S.C.R. 623; *Idziak* v. *Can.* [1992] 3 S.C.R. 631; *Ruffo* v. *Conseil de la Magistrature* [1995] 4 S.C.R. 267.

51 For Lamer C.J., there was no issue of independence, because ''independent'' in s. 11(d) meant only independent from government; the issue was one of impartiality. For Gonthier J. ''independent'' included independence from private parties, so that the words ''independent'' and ''impartial'' were overlapping requirements, both of which were in issue. Lamer C.J. and Gonthier J. agreed in the result, yielding a unanimous Court.

52 [1992] 1 S.C.R. 259. The judgment of the majority was written by Lamer C.J. with the agreement of four others. Stevenson J. wrote a concurring opinion with the agreement of two others. L'Heureux-Dubé J. dissented.

53 The breach was held to be an ''offence'' so as to make s. 11 applicable.

who also appointed the prosecutor. Therefore, the requirements of s. 11(d) were not met,[54] and the statutory provision for the Court Martial was unconstitutional.[55]

(g) Jury

Section 11(d) requires a fair hearing by an ''independent and impartial'' tribunal. It could not be doubted that a jury selected according to the rules of the Criminal Code would fully satisfy the three requirements stipulated in *Valente* for independence. But in *R.* v. *Bain* (1992),[56] the jury was successfully attacked as not meeting the requirement of impartiality.[57] The majority of the Supreme Court of Canada held that the Crown's ability to ''stand by'' up to 48 jurors gave to the prosecution an undue advantage in the composition of the jury. When the power of stand-by was exercised, the juror had to stand aside until the entire panel of jurors had been called. Although the juror was not dismissed, and could be called again if the jury was not filled by the time the jury list had been gone through once, in practice the power of stand-by operated in much the same way as a peremptory challenge, excluding the person from the jury without any showing of cause. Since the accused did not possess the power of stand-by, and only had a limited number of peremptory challenges,[58] the prosecution had a greater influence in the selection process than did the accused. For the minority of the Supreme Court of Canada, this was of no constitutional significance, because the Crown attorney was a public officer, who would be under a duty to use the power of stand-by in order to form an impartial jury, not in order to fashion a jury that would be predisposed to convict the accused. But, for the majority of the Court, the Crown attorney's greater role in the selection of the jury gave rise to a reasonable apprehension that the jury could be biased in favour of the Crown. This appearance of bias, whether or not reflected in fact, was a breach of the requirement of an ''impartial'' tribunal in s. 11(d).[59]

---

54 These breaches of independence were also held not to be necessary for the maintenance of discipline in the armed forces, and therefore to be unjustified under s. 1.

55 Accord, *R.* v. *Ingebrigston* (1990) 76 D.L.R. (4th) 481 (C.M.A.C.).

56 [1992] 1 S.C.R. 91. The majority opinion was written by Cory J. with the agreement of two others; Stevenson J. wrote a concurring opinion; Gonthier J. wrote a dissenting opinion with the agreement of two others.

57 The distinction between ''independent'' and ''impartial'' is also referred to in note 50, above.

58 The accused had four, twelve or twenty peremptory challenges, depending on the seriousness of the charge. The Crown had four peremptory challenges, regardless of the seriousness of the charge, as well as the power of stand-by. Both sides had unlimited challenges for cause.

59 The Court (at 165) permitted Parliament ''six months in which to provide new legislation, otherwise the Code provisions will be invalidated to the extent that they permit the impugned inequality''. Parliament acted on this instruction, amending the Criminal Code to repeal the Crown's power of stand-by, and to give the Crown the same number of peremptory challenges as the accused: S.C. 1992, c. 41, s. 1, amending s. 634 of the Criminal Code.

7.2 Federal courts

(a) Supreme Court of Canada

We have already noticed that the Constitution Act, 1867, by s. 92(14), confers on the provinces the power to establish and maintain provincial courts with jurisdiction encompassing matters arising under both provincial and federal laws. The Act, by s. 101, confers on the federal Parliament a less sweeping power to establish federal courts. Section 101 has two branches: it authorizes the establishment of (1) "a general court of appeal for Canada", and (2) "any additional courts for the better administration of the laws of Canada". Acting under the first branch of ss. 101, the Parliament of Canada in 1875 established the Supreme Court of Canada with civil and criminal appellate jurisdiction throughout Canada.[60] The Supreme Court of Canada is the topic of the next chapter of this book.

(b) Federal Court of Canada

The second branch of s. 101 of the Constitution Act, 1867, by conferring on the federal Parliament the power to establish "any additional courts for the better administration of the laws of Canada", authorizes the Parliament to establish a system of federal courts to determine cases arising under federal laws.[61] The federal Parliament has generally been content to leave the provincial courts with the jurisdiction to determine federal as well as provincial issues.[62] Until 1875, there were no federal courts at all. In 1875, the federal Parliament established the Exchequer Court of Canada, but gave it a very limited jurisdiction over cases involving the revenue and the Crown in right of Canada. This jurisdiction was gradually increased to cover copyright, trade marks, patents, admiralty, tax, citizenship and a few other matters regulated by federal laws.[63] In 1971, the Exchequer Court was replaced by the Federal Court of Canada.[64] The new Court inherited the jurisdiction of its predecessor, but was also given additional jurisdiction, including the power to review the decisions of federal agencies and officials and the power to entertain claims for relief in respect of aeronautics, interprovincial undertakings and certain kinds of commercial paper. The establishment of the

60 Supreme and Exchequer Courts Act, S.C. 1875, c. 11; see now Supreme Court Act, R.S.C. 1985, c. S-26.

61 The Parliament could probably even establish courts of criminal jurisdiction, despite their express allocation to the provinces in s. 92(14), because s. 101 is expressed to apply "notwithstanding anything in this Act". Doubt arises from the express exclusion from s. 91(27) of "the constitution of courts of criminal jurisdiction", and the existence of a notwithstanding clause in s. 91. See Laskin, *Canadian Constitutional Law* (5th ed., 1986 by Finkelstein), 179.

62 Notes 8 – 13, above.

63 Supreme and Exchequer Courts Act, S.C. 1875, c. 11; for jurisdiction in 1971, see Exchequer Court Act, R.S.C. 1970, c. E-11.

64 Federal Court Act, S.C. 1970-71-72, c. 1; now R.S.C. 1985, c. F-7.

Federal Court, with its broader jurisdiction and more elaborate structure (it has a trial division and an appeal division), is a step in the direction of the dual court system in the United States, a system which leads to multiple litigation and complex jurisdictional disputes.[65]

The power of the federal Parliament to establish federal courts is of course limited by the terms of s. 101 of the Constitution Act, 1867. Section 101 does not authorize the establishment of courts of general jurisdiction akin to the provincial courts. It only authorizes courts "for the better administration of the laws of Canada". This has two important consequences. First, it means that the Federal Court of Canada has no inherent jurisdiction; its jurisdiction is confined to those subject matters conferred upon it by the Federal Court Act or other statute. Secondly, it means that the Federal Court can be given jurisdiction over only subject matters governed by "the laws of Canada".

What are "the laws of Canada"? It is well settled that this phrase does not mean all laws in force in Canada whatever their source, but means federal laws.[66] The clearest example of a law of Canada is a federal statute, including, of course, a regulation or order made under a federal statute. Much of the subject matter of the jurisdiction of the Federal Court is governed by federal statute law, and this part of the Court's jurisdiction raises no constitutional issue. But some of the subject matter of the Court's jurisdiction is governed by provincial statute law or by the common law, and this part of the Court's jurisdiction does raise a constitutional issue.

Until 1976, there was substantial judicial support for the view that a federal court could be given jurisdiction over any matter in relation to which the federal Parliament had legislative competence, even if that matter was not in fact regulated by federal statute law. On this basis the "laws of Canada" could include a rule of provincial statute law or a rule of the common law if its subject matter was such that the law could have been enacted or adopted by the federal Parliament. However, in *Quebec North Shore Paper Co.* v. *Canadian Pacific* (1976),[67] the Supreme Court of Canada unexpectedly rejected the test of federal legislative competence. The Court held that the Federal Court had no jurisdiction over an action brought by Canadian Pacific against the Quebec North Shore Paper Co.

---

65 Russell, note 1, above, ch. 1, describes the history and functions of the Federal Court of Canada.

66 The Constitution Acts, 1867 to 1982 are not "laws of Canada", but the Federal Court does have jurisdiction to determine constitutional issues; like any other court or tribunal, the Federal Court, when called upon in the exercise of its jurisdiction to apply a law (in the case of the Federal Court, it will be a "law of Canada"), is under a duty to determine the constitutional validity of that law when the validity of the law is challenged: *Northern Telecom Can.* v. *Communications Workers of Can.* [1983] 1 S.C.R. 733. However, s. 101 does not authorize the federal Parliament to confer on the Federal Court exclusive jurisdiction to determine the constitutionality of federal laws: *A.-G. Can.* v. *Law Society of B.C.* [1982] 2 S.C.R. 307; or of federal administrative action: *Can. Labour Relations Bd.* v. *Paul L'Anglais* [1983] 1 S.C.R. 147.

67 [1977] 2 S.C.R. 1054.

for breach of a contract to build a marine terminal, which was part of a larger contract for the transportation of newsprint from a paper plant in Quebec to newspaper houses in the United States. The Federal Court Act included an express grant of jurisdiction over the case. The test of federal legislative competence was satisfied, because the Constitution Act, 1867, by ss. 91(29) and 92(10), confers on the federal Parliament legislative competence over the international transportation of goods. But the federal Parliament had not in fact enacted any law governing the contract, and the contract stipulated that it was to be interpreted in accordance with the civil law of Quebec. The Supreme Court of Canada held that the Federal Court could not constitutionally assume jurisdiction over the case because the case was not governed by ''applicable and existing federal law''.[68]

In *McNamara Construction* v. *The Queen* (1977),[69] the Supreme Court of Canada held that the Federal Court had no jurisdiction over an action brought by the Crown in right of Canada (the federal Crown) against a builder and an architect, alleging the breach of a contract to build a penitentiary in Alberta. Once again, the Federal Court Act included an express grant of jurisdiction over the case. Once again, the test of federal legislative competence was satisfied, because the Constitution Act, 1867 confers on the federal Parliament legislative competence over the federal Crown (s. 91(1A)) and over penitentiaries (s. 91(28)). But, because the applicable law was the common law, the Supreme Court of Canada held that its new requirement of ''applicable and existing federal law'' was not satisfied. Therefore, the Federal Court could not constitutionally assume jurisdiction over the case.

The decisions in *Quebec North Shore* and *McNamara Construction* are, in my view, open to serious criticism.[70] First, it seems to me that the test of federal legislative competence, which was well established before 1976,[71] is a perfectly defensible definition of ''laws of Canada'' in s. 101. Any laws within federal legislative competence could easily be converted into federal laws by the enactment of a federal statute incorporating them by reference (or adopting them) as

68 *Id.*, 1065-66. The adjectives ''applicable'' and ''existing'' seem to be redundant, especially the second of them, but that is the way Laskin C.J. phrased the requirement, and in this technical area it seems wise to repeat the precise language in which the rule has been judicially expressed.

69 [1977] 2 S.C.R. 655. The case was decided after *Quebec North Shore*, although reported earlier.

70 For more detailed criticism, see Hogg, Comment (1977) 55 Can. Bar Rev. 550; Hogg, ''Federalism and the Jurisdiction of Canadian Courts'' (1981) 30 U.N.B.L.J. 9; Laskin and Sharpe, ''Constricting Federal Court Jurisdiction'' (1980) 30 U. Toronto L.J. 283; Evans, Comment (1981) 59 Can. Bar Rev. 124; Scott, ''Canadian Federal Courts and the Constitutional Limits of their Jurisdiction'' (1982) 27 McGill L.J. 137; Evans and Slattery, Comment (1989) 68 Can. Bar Rev. 817; Crane, ''Constitutional Restraints on the Federal Court in relation to Crown litigation'' (1992) 2 N.J.C.L. 1.

71 It is accepted without question, for example, in the pre-1976 editions of Laskin, *Canadian Constitutional Law* see 3rd ed., 1969, at p. 817; 4th ed., 1975, at pp. 792-793.

federal statute law.[72] Since this can be so easily done, it seems to me that laws within federal legislative competence should be regarded as laws of Canada without requiring the referential incorporation.

Secondly, even if one accepts the requirement of "applicable and existing federal law", I can see no reason why the rules of the common law in a field of federal legislative competence should not qualify as "laws of Canada".[73] Indeed, it seems almost unarguable that "because the common law is potentially subject to overriding legislative power, there is federal common or decisional law and provincial common or decisional law according to the matters respectively distributed to each legislature by the B.N.A. Act".[74] But that is not what the Supreme Court of Canada has decided. According to the Court, the contracts in *Quebec North Shore* and *McNamara Construction*, although subject to overriding federal legislative power, were, as a matter of constitutional law, beyond the jurisdiction of the Federal Court. The same result has been reached with respect to a dispute over a contract to build a federal office building.[75] It is implicit in these decisions that there is no such thing as federal common law. And yet, the Supreme Court has from time to time made obscure reference to the existence of federal common law,[76] and has actually held that some parts of the common law do qualify as

---

72 Evans, note 70, above, 151 makes this suggestion. The Supreme Court of Canada has in fact protected the admiralty jurisdiction of the Federal Court by interpreting the Federal Court Act as not only conferring jurisdiction over admiralty cases, but as also incorporating by reference the applicable substantive law so as to convert it into a "law of Canada": *Tropwood A.G.* v. *Sivaco Wire and Nail Co.* [1979] 2 S.C.R. 157; *Antares Shipping Corp.* v. *The Ship "Capricorn"* [1980] 1 S.C.R. 553; *Aris Steamship Co.* v. *Associated Metals* [1980] 2 S.C.R. 322; *Wire Rope Industries* v. *B.C. Marine Shipbuilders* [1981] 1 S.C.R. 363; *Triglav* v. *Terrasses Jewellers* [1983] 1 S.C.R. 283; *ITO-International Terminal Operators* v. *Miida Electronics* [1986] 1 S.C.R. 752; *Ont.* v. *Pembina Exploration* [1989] 1 S.C.R. 206; *Monk Corp.* v. *Island Fertilizers* [1991] 1 S.C.R. 779.

73 In *McNamara Construction*, since the federal Parliament could have enacted a body of law regarding the construction of the penitentiary, there seems as much reason to describe the common law as federal law as there is to describe it as provincial law. It has a double aspect. Writing before *McNamara Construction*, Laskin, *Canadian Constitutional Law* (4th ed. rev., 1975), said (at pp. 792-793):

> "Laws of Canada" must also include common law which relates to the matters falling within classes of subjects assigned to the Parliament of Canada.

74 Laskin, previous note, 793. This approach could even be said to be imposed by s. 129 of the Constitution Act, 1867 for common law (as well as for pre-confederation colonial law and received English law): Scott, note 68, above, 159. Nor (as Scott comments) is it easy to devise another coherent or workable test.

75 *R.* v. *Thomas Fuller Construction* [1980] 1 S.C.R. 695. (The Federal Court did have jurisdiction over the liability of the federal Crown, but not other parties to the contracts.) Cf. *Southam* v. *Can.* [1990] 3 F.C. 465 (C.A.) (privileges, immunities and powers of the Senate are not laws of Canada).

76 *Que. North Shore Paper Co.* v. *CP* [1977] 2 S.C.R. 1054, 1063, 1065-1066; *McNamara Construction* v. *The Queen* [1977] 2 S.C.R. 655, 662-663; *Rhine* v. *The Queen* [1980] 2 S.C.R. 442, 447; *Northern Telecom Can.* v. *Communications Workers of Can.* [1983] 1 S.C.R. 733, 740.

federal law. One of these is the contractual liability of the federal Crown,[77] which has the curious consequence that a federal government contract is within Federal Court jurisdiction if the federal Crown is the defendant, but not if the federal Crown is the plaintiff.[78] Although the Court has never offered any criteria for the identification of these little enclaves of federal common law,[79] it may be that the Court has in mind those few common law doctrines that cannot be altered by the provincial Legislatures.[80]

A third criticism of the requirement of "applicable and existing federal law" is that it is exceedingly difficult to apply, often requiring litigation to determine the appropriate forum for cases in which the applicable laws come from a variety of sources.[81] Where a single cause of action is governed partly by federal law and partly by common law, the Supreme Court has in two cases been willing to concede federal jurisdiction.[82] In *Roberts* v. *Canada* (1989),[83] however, the Court disapproved of a dictum that it is sufficient "if the rights and obligations of the parties are to be determined to some material extent by federal law". In that case, the Court[84] also rejected the doctrine of "pendent jurisdiction", which has been developed by the federal courts of the United States to reduce the fragmentation of litigation between the federal and state court systems.[85] Under the doctrine of pendent jurisdiction, where a federal court has jurisdiction over a particular case, then the court has jurisdiction to determine all of the issues that are derived from the "common nucleus of operative fact," including "state" issues over which the federal court would have no independent jurisdiction. Why this sensible

---

77 *R.* v. *Thomas Fuller Construction* [1980] 1 S.C.R. 695.

78 *McNamara Construction* v. *The Queen* [1977] 2 S.C.R. 655. Another anomaly is that there is no Federal Court jurisdiction over a tort action against a Crown agent based on direct liability: *Can. Saltfish Corp.* v. *Rasmussen* [1986] 2 F.C. 500 (C.A.); but there is jurisdiction if the action is based on vicarious liability: *Briére* v. *Can. Mtge. & Housing Corp.* [1986] 2 F.C. 484.

79 Another area of federal common law is the law of aboriginal title: *Roberts* v. *Can.* [1989] 1 S.C.R. 322. Cf. *Bisaillon* v. *Keable* [1983] 2 S.C.R. 60 (police informer rule is a common law rule of criminal law that cannot be altered by the province).

80 The common law in fields of unexercised federal legislative competence is mainly subject to provincial alteration as well: note 73, above.

81 Without burdening this book with dozens of citations, I refer the reader to the index to each volume of the Federal Court Reports. That shows that many challenges to federal-court jurisdiction were made on constitutional grounds in the years following the decisions in *Quebec North Shore* and *McNamara Construction*. Thirteen of the cases ended up in the Supreme Court of Canada. Before 1976 such cases were rare.

82 *Rhine* v. *The Queen* [1980] 2 S.C.R. 442; *ITO-International Terminal Operators* v. *Miida Electronics* [1986] 1 S.C.R. 752.

83 [1989] 1 S.C.R. 322, 333.

84 *Id.*, 344; but compare the *ITO* case, note 82, above, 781-782, which seemed to accept the doctrine of pendent jurisdiction.

85 The Constitution of the United States, art. III, ss. 1, 2, confines the jurisdiction of the federal courts to cases or controversies coming within "the judicial power of the United States", a defined phrase of which a major element is cases arising under "the laws of the United States": see Wright, *Law of Federal Courts* (4th ed., 1983), chs. 1, 2.

doctrine would be unacceptable to the Supreme Court of Canada is a mystery. It means that there is no clear rule to deal with a cause of action governed by both federal and provincial law. And it means that where there are two causes of action against the same defendant, arising out of the same facts, only the cause of action based on federal law can be tried in the Federal Court; if the second cause of action is based on provincial law, a second proceeding must be brought in a provincial court.[86]

A fourth criticism of the requirement of ''applicable and existing federal law'' is that the Federal Court cannot dispose of the whole of a controversy when some issues are governed by federal law and some are not. We have noticed that proceedings against a single defendant may have to be split where there is more than one cause of action.[87] Where there is more than one defendant, or a third party, or a counterclaim, it is common to find that the liability of some parties is governed by federal law, and that of others is not. This situation is illustrated by *R.* v. *Thomas Fuller Construction* (1979).[88] In that case, an action was brought against the federal Crown by a contractor (Foundation) who was constructing a building for the federal government. This action was brought in the Federal Court, and it satisfied the requirements stipulated by the previous cases. The Federal Court Act granted jurisdiction over the cause of action. The Constitution Act, 1867, by s. 91(1A), conferred federal legislative competence over the liability of the federal Crown and over federal public property. And, in this case, the liability of the federal Crown was assumed to be governed by ''applicable and existing federal law''.[89] The principal action was therefore properly brought in the Federal Court and could in fact be brought in no other court, because federal-court jurisdiction over suits against the federal Crown was exclusive.[90] However, the federal Crown issued a third party notice against a contractor (Fuller) (also working on the same building), in which the Crown claimed indemnity against or contribution towards the Crown's liability to the plaintiff (Foundation). The problem was that the liability of the third party (Fuller) was not based on federal law, but on either (a) the contract between the federal Crown and the third party (Fuller), or (b) Ontario's Negligence Act providing for contribution between joint and concurrent tortfeasors. The Supreme Court of Canada, in a majority opinion written by Pigeon J., held, therefore, that the requirement of ''applicable and existing federal law'' was not satisfied, and the Federal Court was prohibited by the Constitution from taking jurisdiction over the third party proceeding. The

86 So held in *Que. Ready Mix* v. *Rocois Construction* [1989] 1 S.C.R. 695.

87 Previous note.

88 [1980] 1 S.C.R. 695.

89 Pigeon J. for the majority assumed without discussion that the principal action satisfied all three tests, although (at p. 707) he defined ''laws of Canada'' as ''laws enacted by Parliament'', i.e., as excluding the common law; and yet the only applicable law seemed to be the common law. Compare Martland J., dissenting, but not on this point, at pp. 703-704 (federal statute removing procedural bar of fiat was the ''law of Canada'').

90 This has since been changed: see text accompanying note 105, below.

decision in *Fuller Construction* meant that the federal Crown would have to bring a separate action in the Ontario courts in order to recover indemnity or contribution against the third party. A minimum of two lawsuits, and perhaps as many as four lawsuits, would be necessary to settle the rights and liabilities of the three parties.[91]

Fuller Construction is not an unusual case. Multi-party litigation in the Federal Court often has to be fragmented into federal and provincial components.[92] Recognizing this problem, Reed J. of the Federal Court, Trial Division, has held[93] that parties can be joined in the Federal Court when the two claims are ''so intertwined that findings of fact with respect to one defendant are intimately bound up with those that would have to be made with respect to the other''. This doctrine of intertwining has been rejected by the Federal Court of Appeal,[94] but given cautious approval in an obiter dictum of the Supreme Court of Canada.[95] The doctrine of intertwining, if it becomes established, would be a long step in the direction of the American doctrine of ''ancillary jurisdiction'', which permits a federal court in the United States, when it has jurisdiction over a particular proceeding, to take jurisdiction over an ''ancillary'' proceeding of which it could not take cognizance if it were independently presented.[96] Like the doctrine of pendent jurisdiction, mentioned above,[97] the doctrine of ancillary jurisdiction rests on the reasonable assumption that a federal court should have the power to resolve a case in its entirety.[98]

---

91 Note that Fuller had not been joined as a defendant by the plaintiff (Foundation), presumably because the suit against Fuller would have been outside the jurisdiction of the Federal Court. Foundation would probably want to sue Fuller directly in case the federal Crown was held not liable; that would require a third action in the courts of Ontario. But, if Fuller was sued in the courts of Ontario, he would not be able to claim contribution or indemnity from the federal Crown except by a fourth action in the Federal Court. Thus, four actions would be needed to fully determine the respective rights and liabilities of the three parties arising out of a single factual situation.

92 E.g., *Pacific Western Airlines* v. *The Queen* [1980] 1 F.C. 86 (C.A.); *Peel* v. *Can.* [1989] 2 F.C. 562 (C.A.).

93 *Marshall* v. *The Queen* [1986] 1 F.C. 437, 449. Reed J. is addressing the Court's statutory jurisdiction, but by implication she is also holding that the requirement of applicable and existing federal law is also satisfied.

94 *Varnam* v. *Can.* [1988] 2 F.C. 454 (C.A.).

95 *Roberts* v. *Can.* [1989] 1 S.C.R. 322, 333 (''*Marshall* seems to strike an appropriate balance by requiring the claim or claims against the private litigant to be inextricably linked with those against the Crown.'')

96 See generally Wright, *Law of Federal Courts* (4th ed., 1983), chs. 1, 2.

97 Note 85, above, and accompanying text.

98 It must be conceded that the *Canadian* authorities before *Marshall* provided little support for a doctrine of ancillary jurisdiction. The weight of authority held that the Federal Court could take jurisdiction over a third party notice, counterclaim or co-defendant only if the Court would have had jurisdiction if the issue had been presented independently in a separate proceeding. On third party notices, see *The King* v. *Hume*; *Consolidated Distilleries* v. *Consolidated Exporters Corp.* [1930] S.C.R. 531; *Bank of Montreal* v. *Royal Bank of Can.* [1933] S.C.R. 311; *McNamara Construction* v. *The Queen* [1977] 2 S.C.R. 654, 664; but compare *Schwella* v. *The Queen* [1957] Ex. C.R. 226, where ancillary jurisdiction over a third party notice seems

Fuller Construction illustrates the deficiencies of the Supreme Court of Canada's rigid approach to the requirement of "existing and applicable federal law". It also illustrates a deficiency in the Federal Court Act that has now, fortunately, been corrected. Until 1990, the Federal Court Act conferred on the Federal Court *exclusive* jurisdiction over proceedings against the federal Crown. This meant, obviously, that a plaintiff with a cause of action against the federal Crown had no choice but to sue in the Federal Court.[99] However, the Federal Court would normally have no jurisdiction over federal Crown servants,[100] or federal Crown agents,[101] who might also be involved in the dispute; and the Court would normally have no jurisdiction over other co-defendants,[102] third parties,[103] or counterclaims by the Crown.[104] In 1990, the Federal Court Act was amended to make the jurisdiction over proceedings against the Crown concurrent rather than exclusive.[105] Since this amendment, proceedings against the federal Crown can be brought in the appropriate provincial court, which is likely to have jurisdiction over all the other parties as well. If the plaintiff chooses the provincial forum, split proceedings can be avoided.[106]

The 1990 amendment to the Federal Court Act invites the question whether there is any reason to preserve even concurrent Federal Court jurisdiction over proceedings against the federal Crown. The same question could be posed with respect to other parts of the Federal Court's jurisdiction. As noted earlier in this chapter, Canada does not need a dual court system. The provincial courts have general jurisdiction over all causes of action; the judges of the higher courts are

---

to have been accepted. On counterclaims, see *Bow, McLachlan & Co.* v. *The Ship "Camosun"* [1909] A.C. 597; *A.-G. Can.* v. *Boeing Co.* (1983) 41 O.R. (2d) 777 (C.A.). On co-defendants, see *Pacific Western Airlines* v. *The Queen* [1980] 1 F.C. 86 (C.A.); but compare *The Ship "Sparrows Point"* v. *Greater Vancouver Water District* [1951] S.C.R. 396. However, most of these cases were decided before the decisions in *Quebec North Shore* and *McNamara Construction* made the problems more acute. I would argue that the Supreme Court of Canada should develop a doctrine of ancillary jurisdiction to mitigate the difficulties which it has created in those two decisions.

99 In *Rudolf Wolff & Co.* v. *Can.* [1990] 1 S.C.R. 695 and *Dywidag Systems* v. *Zutphen Bros.* [1990] 1 S.C.R. 705, it was held that the exclusive jurisdiction of the Federal Court, although admittedly a cause of hardship, delay and unnecessary expense, did not offend s. 15 of the Charter.

100 *Pacific Western Airlines* v. *The Queen* [1980] 1 F.C. 86 (C.A.).

101 *Can. Saltfish Corp.* v. *Rasmussen* [1986] 2 F.C. 500 (C.A.).

102 *Pacific Western Airlines* case, note 100, above.

103 *R.* v. *Thomas Fuller Construction* [1980] 1 S.C.R. 695.

104 Cf. *McNamara Construction* v. *The Queen* [1977] 2 S.C.R. 655 (proceedings by Crown outside federal jurisdiction).

105 S.C. 1990, c. 8, amending s. 17 of the Federal Court Act.

106 If the plaintiff chooses the federal forum, and the Crown wants to make a counterclaim or add a third party, the Attorney General is entitled to a stay of proceedings under s. 50.1 of the Federal Court Act (added in 1990). Although s. 50.1 refers only to the Attorney General, presumably it would also be possible for other parties to obtain a stay on the ground that the Federal Court is the less convenient forum.

federally appointed; and consistency of decisions is guaranteed by the appeal to the Supreme Court of Canada. The existence of a parallel hierarchy of federal courts cannot fail to give rise to wasteful jurisdictional disputes and multiple proceedings. I accordingly regret the expansion of the federal-court system which has occurred in Canada since 1875.[107] But it cannot be denied that the Constitution Act, 1867, by s. 101, authorizes the federal Parliament to create a federal-court system, and that the federal Parliament has deliberately chosen to do so. In these circumstances, it seems to me that the Supreme Court of Canada should develop rules which will enable the parallel jurisdictions to operate as smoothly as possible. It must be remembered that the burden of inadequate rules is borne not by governments but by individual litigants who have no means of escape from the uncertainties, expenses, delays, inconsistencies and injustices which are inherent in multiple lawsuits. The Supreme Court of Canada's rejection of the rule of legislative competence as the definition of ''laws of Canada'', and the Court's refusal to develop rules of ancillary and pendent jurisdiction, have exacerbated the problems of a dual court system.

(c) Tax Court of Canada

The Tax Court of Canada[108] was established in 1983, when it replaced an administrative tribunal, the Tax Review Board. The primary jurisdiction of the Tax Court is to hear income tax appeals.

(d) Territorial courts

For the sake of completeness it should also be mentioned that the federal Parliament has provided for a system of courts for each of the two federal territories, the Northwest Territories and the Yukon territory.[109] These courts are analogous to provincial courts, but of course they have to be established by the federal Parliament because it has plenary legislative powers over the two territories.[110]

(e) Appointment, payment and tenure of federal judges

Do the provisions of ss. 96 to 100 of the Constitution Act, 1867, dealing with appointment, payment and tenure of higher court judges, apply to the Supreme Court of Canada, the Federal Court of Canada and the higher territorial

107 The argument that, at least for Canada, federalism does not require the federalizing of the judiciary is made in Hogg (1981) 30 U.N.B.L.J. 9.

108 Tax Court of Canada Act, R.S.C. 1985, c. T-2.

109 Northwest Territories Act, R.S.C. 1985, c. N-27, Part II; Yukon Act, R.S.C. 1985, c. Y-2, Part II.

110 Constitution Act, 1871, s. 4.

courts?[111] There is no doubt that those courts are "superior courts". However, ss. 96 to 98, concerning appointment, are clearly confined to provincial courts, and s. 100, concerning salaries, should probably be read in the same sense. This reading of the sections is reinforced by the language of s. 101, which gives the federal Parliament power to create federal courts "notwithstanding anything in this Act".[112] In my opinion, therefore, ss. 96 to 100 of the Constitution Act, 1867 do not apply to the federal courts.[113] It follows that the federal Parliament could if it chose confer appointing power on some body other than the Governor General (despite s. 96), it could authorize the appointment of judges who were not members of the bar (despite ss. 97 and 98), and it could leave the judges' salaries to be determined administratively (despite s. 100).

The Parliament has done none of these things. The constituent statute of each of the federal courts (including the Tax Court) confers appointing power on the Governor in Council, and requires that an appointee either be a judge of a superior, district or county court in Canada, or be a member of at least ten years' standing of a provincial bar; the salaries of all federal judges are "fixed and provided" by the Judges Act,[114] the same statute that fixes and provides the salaries of the s. 96 judges. The conventions with respect to the mode of appointment of s. 96 judges are also observed in appointing federal judges, that is to say, puisne judges are appointed by the cabinet on the recommendation of the Minister of Justice, and the Chief Justices are appointed by the cabinet on the recommendation of the Prime Minister.[115] However, the point that sections 96, 97, 98 and 100 of the Constitution Act, 1867 do not apply is still important, because it means that the federal Parliament, unlike the provincial Legislatures, is not under any constitutional restraint in assigning jurisdiction to federal administrative tribunals or officials (or to federal inferior courts, if it chose to create some): such bodies may be invested with functions of a kind traditionally exercised by a superior, district or county court if the Parliament so enacts.[116]

111 The Tax Court of Canada is not expressed to be a superior court.

112 A possible response to this latter point is given in the text accompanying note 118, below.

113 *R.* v. *Can. Labour Relations Bd.*; *Ex parte Federal Elec. Corp.* (1964) 44 D.L.R. (2d) 440, 462-463 (Man. Q.B.) (federal administrative agency); *Papp* v. *Papp* [1970] 1 O.R. 331, 339 (C.A.) (Master); *A.-G. Can.* v. *Canard* [1976] 1 S.C.R. 170, 176 (federal minister), but compare the more guarded language at 202-203, 210; Laskin, *Canadian Constitutional Law* (5th ed., 1986 by Finkelstein), 112. Contra, *C.I.B.C.* v. *Rifou* [1986] 3 F.C. 486, 491, 493, but Stone J. dissented on this issue at 515 (C.A.); Lederman "The Independence of the Judiciary" (1956) 34 Can. Bar Rev. 1139, 1176; Elliot, Comment (1984) 18 U.B.C.L. Rev. 127. Note, however, that the federal Parliament may not be able to confer a s. 96 function on a *provincially-established* court or tribunal: *McEvoy* v. *A.-G.N.B.* [1983] 1 S.C.R. 704; discussed in ch. 19, Criminal Justice, under heading 19.2, "Courts of criminal jurisdiction", below.

114 R.S.C. 1985, c. J-1.

115 Note 25, above.

116 For the limits on provincial power to do these things, because of implications drawn judicially from s. 96, see sec. 7.3, "Implications of Constitution's judicature sections", below. With respect to the limits on federal power, see notes 112 to 114 and accompanying text, above.

What about s. 99, the section giving tenure ''during good behaviour''? Successive federal governments have taken the view that s. 99 does not apply to the federal courts. Thus, in 1927, when s. 99's guarantee of tenure was unqualified by the retirement provision which was inserted by amendment in 1960, it was provided by ordinary statute that the judges of the Supreme Court must retire at age 75.[117] And after s. 99 was amended to include a subsection providing for the retirement of superior court judges at age 75, the Federal Court Act initially provided that the judges of the Federal Court must retire at age 70.[118] (The retirement age has since been let out to 75, in line with all other federal judges.)[119] The arguments in favour of the federal government's position would be, no doubt, that (1) the term ''superior court'' in s. 99 takes its colour from the previous sections which are rather clearly limited to provincial ''superior, district or county courts'', and (2) the phrase in s. 101, ''notwithstanding anything in this Act'', exempts all federal courts from other provisions of the Constitution Act, 1867. These arguments are strong, but not conclusive. The term ''superior court'' in s. 99 could be read as applying to all superior courts in Canada; and the notwithstanding clause in s. 101 is primarily designed to override s. 92(14) (giving to the provinces the exclusive power to legislate for ''the administration of justice in the province'') and need not be read as overriding provisions such as s. 99 which are not directly inconsistent with s. 101.[120]

7.3 Implications of Constitution's judicature sections

(a) Separation of powers

There is no general ''separation of powers'' in the Constitution Act, 1867. The Act does not separate the legislative, executive and judicial functions and insist that each branch of government exercise only ''its own'' function. As between the legislative and executive branches, any separation of powers would make little sense in a system of responsible government;[121] and it is clearly established that the Act does not call for any such separation.[122] As between the judicial and the two political branches, there is likewise no general separation of powers. Either the Parliament or the Legislatures may by appropriate legislation

117 S.C. 1926-27, c. 38, s. 2.

118 S.C. 1970-71-72, c. 1, s. 8. This provision was held to be unconstitutional in *Addy* v. *The Queen* [1985] 2 F.C. 452 (T.D.), on the basis that s. 99 applied to federal as well as provincial superior courts. The federal government did not appeal, and s. 8 of the Federal Court Act was amended to raise the retirement age to 75: S.C. 1987, c. 21, s. 7.

119 Previous note.

120 Lederman, note 23 above, 1176, argues that s. 99 is applicable to the federal superior court judges. This position is supported by the *Addy* decision, note 118, above.

121 See ch. 9, Responsible Government, under heading 9.4(e), ''The Cabinet'', below.

122 See ch. 14, Delegation, under heading 14.2(a), ''Delegation of legislative power'', below.

confer non-judicial functions on the courts and (with one important exception, to be discussed) may confer judicial functions on bodies that are not courts.

Each Canadian jurisdiction has conferred non-judicial functions on its courts, by enacting a statute which enables the government to refer a question of law to the courts for an advisory opinion.[123] The rendering of advisory opinions to government is traditionally an "executive" function, performed by the law officers of the government. For that reason, the Supreme Court of the United States and the High Court of Australia have refused to render advisory opinions, reasoning that a separation of powers doctrine in their Constitutions confines the courts to the traditional judicial function of adjudicating upon genuine controversies. But in the *Reference Appeal* (1912),[124] the Privy Council refused to read any such limitation into Canada's Constitution. Their lordships upheld the federal reference statute, apparently as a law in relation to the Supreme Court of Canada (s. 101). The provincial reference statutes are also valid as laws in relation to the administration of justice in the province (s. 92(14)).

The conferral of judicial functions on bodies which are not courts is likewise subject to no general prohibition. However, here there is an important qualification to be made. The courts have held that the provincial Legislatures may not confer on a body other than a superior, district or county court judicial functions analogous to those performed by a superior, district or county court. This little separation of powers doctrine has been developed to preclude evasion of the stipulations of ss. 96 to 100 of the Constitution Act, 1867.

If ss. 96 to 100 of the Constitution Act, 1867 were read literally, they could easily be evaded by a province which wanted to assume control of its judicial appointments. The province could increase the jurisdiction of its inferior courts so that they assumed much of the jurisdiction of the higher courts; or the province could vest higher-court jurisdiction in a newly-established tribunal, and call that tribunal an inferior court or an administrative tribunal. It is therefore not surprising that the courts have added a gloss to s. 96 and the associated constitutional provisions. What they have said is this: if a province invests a tribunal with a jurisdiction of a kind that ought properly to belong to a superior, district or county court, then that tribunal, whatever its official name, is for constitutional purposes a superior, district or county court and must satisfy the requirements of s. 96 and the associated provisions of the Constitution Act, 1867. This means that such a tribunal will be invalidly constituted, unless its members (1) are appointed by the federal government in conformity with s. 96, (2) are drawn from the bar of the province in conformity with ss. 97 and 98, and (3) receive salaries that are fixed and provided by the federal Parliament in conformity with s. 100.

So far the law is clear, and the policy underlying it is comprehensible. But the difficulty lies in the definition of those functions that ought properly to belong

---

123 See ch. 8, Supreme Court of Canada, under heading 8.6, "Reference jurisdiction", below, where authority is provided for the statements in the text.

124 *A-G. Ont.* v. *A.-G. Can.* (Reference Appeal) [1912] A.C. 571.

to a superior, district or county court. The courts have attempted to fashion a judicially enforceable rule which would separate "s. 96 functions" from other adjudicatory functions. The attempt has not been successful, and it is difficult to predict with confidence how the courts will characterize particular adjudicatory functions. The uncertainty of the law, with its risk of nullification, could be a serious deterrent to the conferral of new adjudicatory functions on inferior courts or administrative tribunals, and a consequent impediment to much new regulatory or social policy. For the most part, the courts have exercised restraint in reviewing the provincial statutes which create new adjudicatory jurisdictions, so that the difficulty has not been as serious as it could have been. However, in the last two decades, there has been a regrettable resurgence of s. 96 litigation: six challenges to the powers of inferior courts or tribunals based on s. 96 have succeeded in the Supreme Court of Canada,[125] and these decisions have spawned many more challenges. These developments are described in the text that follows.

(b) Inferior courts

In the *Adoption Reference* (1938),[126] the Supreme Court of Canada had to pass on the validity of four Ontario statutes concerning adoption, neglected children, illegitimate children and deserted wives. This batch of social legislation gave rise to constitutional doubt because each statute conferred a new jurisdiction upon inferior courts presided over by justices of the peace or magistrates — officials who were appointed by the province. In a long and scholarly opinion written for the whole Court, Duff C.J. upheld the grants of new jurisdiction. He pointed out that s. 96 contemplated the existence of inferior courts whose judges could be appointed and paid by the province, and who need not be drawn from the ranks of the bar. The jurisdiction of these courts was not to be frozen at the limits in existence in 1867. Increases in their jurisdiction, or the establishment of new inferior courts, were within the legislative competence of the provinces. The only qualification to this power was that the new jurisdiction must "broadly conform to a type of jurisdiction generally exercisable by courts of summary conviction rather than the jurisdiction exercised by courts within the purview of s. 96".[127] In this case the provisions for making adoption orders, for enforcing obligations to maintain wives and children, for protecting neglected children and for trying juvenile offenders, were more closely

---

125 *A.-G. Que.* v. *Farrah* [1978] 2 S.C.R. 638; *Re Residential Tenancies Act* [1981] 1 S.C.R. 714; *Crevier* v. *A.-G. Que.* [1981] 2 S.C.R. 220; *Re B.C. Family Relations Act* [1982] 1 S.C.R. 62; *McEvoy* v. *A.-G.N.B.* [1983] 1 S.C.R. 704; *MacMillan Bloedel* v. *Simpson* [1995] 4 S.C.R. 725. Since the abolition of Privy Council appeals, two other challenges have also been successful, namely, *A.G. Ont.* v. *Victoria Medical Building* [1960] S.C.R. 32; *Seminary of Chicoutimi* v. *A.G. Que.* [1973] S.C.R. 681.

126 *Re Adoption Act* [1938] S.C.R. 398.

127 *Id.*, 421.

analogous to traditional inferior-court jurisdiction than to higher-court jurisdiction.

In *Re B.C. Family Relations Act* (1982),[128] the Supreme Court of Canada followed the *Adoption Reference* and upheld inferior-court jurisdiction over guardianship and custody, reasoning that, once adoption had been admitted to inferior-court jurisdiction, the lesser orders of guardianship and custody should not be treated differently. However, the Court struck down provisions purporting to confer on an inferior court the power to make orders with respect to the occupancy of (and access to) the family residence. This power was "more conformable to that exercised and exercisable by a s. 96 court", because it involved the adjudication of "proprietary rights" and the granting of relief "akin to injunctive relief".[129]

The test of "broad conformity" or "analogy", while providing a test for the allocation of new forms of jurisdiction, might be thought to prevent increases in traditional inferior-court jurisdiction which have the effect of transferring some higher-court jurisdiction to an inferior court.[130] This is the effect of an increase in the pecuniary limit of inferior-court jurisdiction, for example. But in *Re Quebec Magistrate's Court* (1965),[131] the Supreme Court upheld an increase in the jurisdiction of the Quebec Magistrate's Court from $200 to $500. This was a very modest increase, since the $200 limit dated from the establishment of the court in 1869. The Supreme Court had little trouble in determining that the increase in jurisdiction, "when considered in the light of the current value of the dollar", was constitutional; and the Court made clear that reasonable increases in inferior-court jurisdiction were within the *Adoption Reference* ruling.[132]

---

128 [1982] 1 S.C.R. 62. See also *Ont.* v. *Pembina Exploration* [1989] 1 S.C.R. 206 (admiralty jurisdiction was not exercised by superior, district or county courts at confederation); *Re Young Offenders Act* [1991] 1 S.C.R. 252 (youth court jurisdiction was exercised by inferior courts at confederation).

129 *Id.*, 87-91.

130 Note the more liberal way in which the test has been framed for administrative tribunals (as opposed to inferior courts) in *Re Residential Tenancies Act* [1981] 1 S.C.R. 714; discussed at note 149, below. In particular, the three-step test proposed in that case seems irrelevant to inferior courts, since their functions are nearly always judicial (step (2)), and an inferior court has no different expertise, resources or procedures than a s. 96 court has (step (3)). However, in *Re Young Offenders Act* [1991] 1 S.C.R. 252, a majority of the Court did apply the three-step test to an inferior court, although La Forest J. took the view that steps (2) and (3) were inapplicable.

131 [1965] S.C.R. 772 (opinion of Fauteux J. for the Court in French), (1965) 55 D.L.R. (2d) 701 (translation).

132 After the decision, Quebec rapidly further enlarged the jurisdiction of the Magistrate's Court, now called the Provincial Court, from the new limit of $500 to $1,000 (1965), and then to $3,000 (1969), and then to $6,000 (1979), and then to $10,000 (1982), and then to $15,000 (1984): see *Code of Civil Procedure*, R.S.Q. 1977, c. C-25, art. 34, as amended. Although Quebec had sought a ruling on the first step, from $200 to $500, it has not sought a ruling on the validity of the later, much greater increases. (Other provinces have also substantially increased the jurisdiction of their Provincial Courts.)

Quebec has had less success with another of its increases in inferior-court jurisdiction. In *Seminary of Chicoutimi* v. *A.-G. Que.* (1972),[133] the Supreme Court of Canada held that a transfer from the Quebec Superior Court to the Provincial Court of the power to quash municipal by-laws on grounds of illegality was unconstitutional. Fauteux C.J., who wrote the opinion for the Court, contented himself with the finding that the quashing of municipal by-laws had since before confederation been within the jurisdiction of s. 96 courts in Quebec. For this reason, without more, he held that the *Adoption Reference* test of ''broad conformity'' to inferior-court jurisdiction was not satisfied. The power to quash municipal by-laws could only be conferred upon a court which satisfied the stipulations of s. 96 of the Constitution Act, 1867. This reasoning is remarkably sparse. After all, in *Re Quebec Magistrate's Court*, it could have been said with equal truth that jurisdiction over pecuniary claims between $200 and $500 had always been exercised in Quebec by s. 96 courts. If the decline in the value of the dollar since confederation could justify an increase in the pecuniary limit, surely the vast increase in municipal functions and the consequent proliferation of by-laws since confederation might also justify the introduction of a speedier and cheaper means of testing the legality of by-laws. Perhaps in answer to this argument it could be said (although Fauteux C.J. did not say it) that the supervisory jurisdiction of the superior courts over inferior statutory bodies (such as municipalities) is too fundamental a guarantee of government according to law to be entrusted to a court constituted without the constitutional protections of ss. 96 to 100 of the Constitution Act, 1867.[134]

In *McEvoy* v. *A.-G. N.B.* (1983),[135] the Supreme Court of Canada held that the federal Parliament could not confer jurisdiction over all indictable offences on a provincial inferior court (a proposed ''unified criminal court''), because the trial of indictable offences was within superior-court jurisdiction in 1867. Unfortunately, the Court did not indicate any awareness of the fact that the present Criminal Code confers on provincial inferior courts jurisdiction over nearly all indictable offences. These jurisdictional provisions, although they have been upheld in earlier cases, are now vulnerable to attack on s. 96 grounds.[136]

In *MacMillan Bloedel* v. *Simpson* (1995),[137] the Supreme Court of Canada had to review a provision in the federal Young Offenders Act that purported to give the youth court of each province exclusive jurisdiction over ''every contempt

---

133 [1973] S.C.R. 681.

134 See the subsequent case of *Crevier* v. *A.-G. Que.* [1981] 2 S.C.R. 220, discussed at note 191, below.

135 [1983] 1 S.C.R. 704.

136 The prior cases had finessed the s. 96 issue by applying the rule that the federal Parliament was not bound by s. 96. *McEvoy*'s sudden rejection of that rule, and the implications for the present Criminal Code provisions, are discussed in sec. 19.2, ''Courts of criminal jurisdiction'', below.

137 [1995] 4 S.C.R. 725. The majority opinion of Lamer C.J. was concurred in by La Forest, Sopinka, Gonthier and Cory JJ.; the dissenting opinion of McLachlin J. was concurred in by L'Heureux-Dubé, Iacobucci and Major JJ.

of court committed by a young person'' except where the contempt was committed ''in the face'' of a court other than the youth court. The accused in *MacMillan Bloedel* was a 16-year-old boy who had disobeyed an injunction that had been issued by the Supreme Court of British Columbia (a superior court) and had therefore acted in contempt of that court. Since the contempt had not been committed ''in the face'' of the superior court, the Young Offenders Act purported to confer exclusive jurisdiction over the offence on the youth court. But the Supreme Court of Canada, by a majority, held that Parliament was barred from transferring to an inferior court (the youth court) exclusive jurisdiction over contempt committed against a superior court. The majority's reasoning to this result broke new ground. They held that there was a guaranteed core of superior-court jurisdiction which could not be removed from a superior court under any circumstances. The power of a superior court to punish contempts against itself, whether in the face of the court or outside the face of the court, was part of that guaranteed core. Therefore, it was contrary to s. 96 of the Constitution Act, 1867 to give *exclusive* jurisdiction to the youth court over a contempt committed against a superior court.

Before the *MacMillan Bloedel* case, the jurisprudence on the application of s. 96 to inferior courts had proceeded on a different track from the cases dealing with administrative tribunals. That is the reason why the present section of this chapter deals with inferior courts and a later section deals with administrative tribunals. As we shall see in that later section, the Supreme Court of Canada in *Re Residential Tenancies Act* (1981)[138] developed a rule (involving a three-step test) for the validity of a conferral of jurisdiction on administrative tribunals, but did not generally use that test in cases involving inferior courts. In the *MacMillan Bloedel* case, both the majority and the minority assumed that the *Residential Tenancies* rule was the appropriate one to test the validity of the jurisdiction of the youth court. All judges applied that rule, and all judges held that the youth court's jurisdiction did not offend s. 96 on the basis of that rule. For the minority, that resolved the issue in favour of the validity of the youth court's jurisdiction over contempt. However, the majority went on to add a new requirement to the rule in *Residential Tenancies,* namely, the requirement that there be no breach of the guaranteed core of superior-court jurisdiction. On the basis of this new requirement, the majority struck down the youth court's exclusive jurisdiction over contempt. Obviously, the rule establishing a guaranteed core of superior-court jurisdiction could be broken by a grant of exclusive jurisdiction to an administrative tribunal as well as to an inferior court. Therefore, a convergence of the inferior-court cases and the administrative-law cases has occurred. The validity of grants of jurisdiction to both inferior courts and administrative tribunals is now to be tested by the same rules: the *Residential Tenancies* rule supplemented by the rule that guarantees a core of superior-court jurisdiction. Both these rules are

138 Note 149 and accompanying text, below.

more fully described in the later section of this chapter headed ''Administrative tribunals''.[139]

(c) County or district courts

After confederation, the jurisdiction of county and district courts was steadily increased, to the point that in some provinces it became almost co-extensive with that of the superior courts. The cases so far discussed invite the question of whether the transfer of superior court powers to the district and county courts was constitutionally valid. County and district courts were s. 96 courts so that the federal appointment power would not have been violated by such transfers. But it will be recalled that s. 99 guarantees only the tenure of superior court judges. By analogy with the s. 96 reasoning, could it not be argued that s. 99 was offended when district or county court judges, whose tenure was not constitutionally guaranteed, decided cases which were traditionally decided by superior courts? The expansion of county and district court jurisdiction was never challenged,[140] however, and this question will not be answered as the county and district courts have now been eliminated in all of the provinces which once had them.[141]

(d) Superior courts

Section 96 and the other judicature provisions of the Constitution Act, 1867 do not impose any constraints on the jurisdiction that can be conferred on a *superior* court. A superior court is, of course, subject to the maximum constitutional protection. Therefore, there is no constitutional objection to the conferral on a superior court of a novel jurisdiction, or a jurisdiction traditionally exercised by inferior courts.[142] Note, however, that, according to the narrow majority in *MacMillan Bloedel* v. *Simpson* (1995),[143] there are constitutional restrictions on the jurisdiction that can be *withdrawn* from a superior court. No part of an ill-defined ''core'' of superior-court jurisdiction may be withdrawn from a superior court.[144] Apart from this exception, the nature and scope of superior-court juris-

---

139 Section 7.3(e), ''Administrative tribunals'', below.

140 In *Re Adoption Act* [1938] S.C.R. 398, 416-417, Duff, C.J. asserted, obiter, that increases in district or county court jurisdiction were not constitutionally vulnerable. Cf. *A.G. B.C.* v. *McKenzie* [1965] S.C.R. 490, 498-499 (upholding appointment of county court judges as local judges of the superior court, despite lack of independence guarantee for judges); *Re Judicature Amendment Act, 1970 (No. 4)* [1971] 2 O.R. 521 (C.A.) (same decision). These cases were discussed at more length in the 2nd edition of this book (1985), 154-155.

141 See sec. 7.1(a), ''Establishment of provincial courts'', above.

142 *Re Young Offenders Act* [1991] 1 S.C.R. 252, 274 (and answer to question 3(b)(ii) of the reference).

143 [1995] 4 S.C.R. 725; discussed in text accompanying note 137, above, and note 177, below.

144 *Id.*, para. 42. Lamer C.J. even said that a transfer of a core power to another superior court would be unconstitutional. Note, however, the contrary decisions cited in note 197, below.

diction are simply issues of policy to be resolved and enacted by the competent legislative body.[145]

(e) Administrative tribunals

The last 100 years have seen a great increase in the number of administrative tribunals in Canada (and elsewhere), to the point that administrative tribunals undoubtedly decide more cases and probably dispose of more dollars than do the ordinary courts. The cause of this development is the vast increase in social and economic regulation which has occurred in the last 100 years. The novel tasks of adjudication which are entailed by new schemes of regulation have commonly been entrusted to administrative tribunals rather than to the courts. Some of the reasons for this preference can be identified. First is the desire for a specialist body: specially qualified personnel can be appointed to a tribunal, and those who do not start off specially qualified can acquire experience and expertise in the field of regulation (whether it be labour relations, marketing of agricultural products, transportation, broadcasting, liquor licensing, or whatever). Second is the desire for innovation: a tribunal can be given broad discretion to develop the policies and remedies required to implement a new scheme of regulation (such as foreign investment review, control of pay television). Third is the desire for initiative: a tribunal (such as a human rights commission or a securities commission) can be given power to initiate proceedings, to undertake investigations, to do research, and to play an educative and policy-formulating role as well as an adjudicative one. Fourth is the problem of volume: if adjudication is required with great frequency (as in workers' compensation, unemployment insurance, immigration, income tax objections, for example), the tribunal can develop procedures to handle a case-load that would choke the ordinary court system. Fifth is economy: a tribunal can be structured and mandated to be less formal, speedier and less expensive than the ordinary courts (although in many fields the complexity of the issues and the sums at stake preclude this kind of advantage).[146]

When the advantages of administrative adjudication are reviewed, it is easy to see why legislative bodies have chosen to confer many adjudicative functions on administrative tribunals rather than the ordinary courts. But the ordinary courts, through their exegesis of s. 96 and the other judicature sections of the Constitution Act, 1867, have assumed the power to review legislation investing a provincially-established administrative tribunal[147] with adjudicative functions: if those functions ought properly to belong to a superior, district or county court, then the

145 Even non-judicial functions can be conferred: note 123 and accompanying text, above.

146 I have attempted to formulate a division of functions between administrative tribunals and courts in Hogg, "Judicial Review: How Much Do We Need?" (1974) 20 McGill L.J. 157.

147 Federally-established administrative tribunals are not vulnerable on this basis, although the federal investment of a provincially-established tribunal is: see note 135, above.

legislation will be unconstitutional.[148] By this means, the courts have erected constitutional barriers to legislative encroachments on their own traditional functions.

The leading case on the impact of s. 96 on the creation of provincial administrative tribunals is the decision of the Supreme Court of Canada in *Re Residential Tenancies Act* (1981).[149] In that case, Dickson J. for the Court suggested a three-step approach to the resolution of a s. 96 challenge to an administrative tribunal's powers.[150] The first step is an historical inquiry into whether the impugned power broadly conforms to a power exercised by a superior, district or county court at confederation. The second step, reached only if the answer to the historical inquiry is yes, is an inquiry into whether the impugned power is a ''judicial'' power. The third step, reached only if the answer to both the historical inquiry and the judicial inquiry is yes, is an inquiry into whether the power in its institutional setting has changed its character sufficiently to negate the broad conformity with superior, district or county court jurisdiction.

The first step — the historical inquiry — involves an investigation of whether the impugned power was one that was within the powers of a superior, district or county court at confederation. A negative answer to this inquiry will resolve the s. 96 issue in favour of the validity of the power without the necessity to proceed to steps (2) and (3).[151]

For a tribunal's power to be held to be a s. 96 power at confederation, it is clear that the impugned power must have been within the *exclusive* jurisdiction of s. 96 courts at confederation. If there was even concurrent jurisdiction in inferior courts or tribunals at confederation, then the tribunal will pass the historical inquiry.[152] This rule places great weight on the way in which the impugned power is characterized. For example, a tribunal's remedial powers may have been within the exclusive jurisdiction of s. 96 courts at confederation,[153] while its subject-

148 Unconstitutionality would be avoided, of course, if the tribunal's members (1) are appointed by the federal government in conformity with s. 96, (2) are drawn from the bar of the province in conformity with ss. 97 and 98, and (3) receive salaries which are fixed and provided by the federal Parliament in conformity with s. 100. So far as I am aware, no province has ever attempted to establish a tribunal on these terms, which would normally be inconsistent with the purposes of establishing a tribunal in the first place, and which would in any case have to be agreed to and implemented by the federal government.

149 [1981] 1 S.C.R. 714.

150 *Id.*, 734. The three-step test is summarized by Laskin C.J. in *Massey-Ferguson Industries* v. *Govt. of Sask.* [1981] 2 S.C.R. 413, 429.

151 E.g., *Jones* v. *Edmonton Catholic School Trustees* [1977] S.C.R. 872 (power of tribunal to resolve assessment disputes was exercised by similar tribunal at Alberta's entry to confederation).

152 *A.G. Que.* v. *Grondin* [1983] 2 S.C.R. 364; *Sobeys Stores* v. *Yeomans* [1989] 1 S.C.R. 238; *Re Young Offenders Act* [1991] 1 S.C.R. 252; *Re Residential Tenancies Act (N.S.)* [1996] 1 S.C.R. 186.

153 The character of the remedial powers was the critical issue in *Tomko* v. *Labour Rels. Bd. (N.S.)* [1977] 1 S.C.R. 112; *Re Residential Tenancies Act* [1981] 1 S.C.R. 714; but note *Sobey Stores*

matter jurisdiction was only concurrent. And with respect to subject-matter, jurisdiction can be expressed broadly (e.g., labour relations), which may give rise to concurrent jurisdiction, or narrowly (e.g., unjust dismissal), which may not. In *Sobeys Stores* v. *Yeomans* (1989),[154] which was a challenge to a reinstatement order made by a labour standards tribunal, Wilson J. for the majority of the Supreme Court of Canada recognized the existence of these choices. She suggested that the Court should lean in the direction of the choice that would fail (yield an affirmative answer to) the historical test, so as to protect the traditional jurisdiction of the s. 96 courts.[155] In that way, the historical inquiry would become a rather low threshold, easily crossed, and the issue of validity would be resolved in steps (2) and (3) of the s. 96 reasoning.

To which jurisdiction, and to which date, is the historical inquiry directed? The ten provinces entered confederation at different times, and the division of jurisdiction between s. 96 courts and inferior courts and tribunals at the time of entry differed from province to province. If the historical inquiry is addressed only to the situation of the province that established the impugned tribunal, then the outcome of the inquiry would not settle the same question for another province. In *Re Residential Tenancies Act* itself, the Court held that certain powers[156] of Ontario's rent tribunal to make orders evicting tenants and to make orders requiring landlords or tenants to comply with the rent control legislation failed all three tests and were accordingly unconstitutional for breach of s. 96. But in *A. G. Que.* v. *Grondin* (1983),[157] the Supreme Court of Canada upheld essentially similar powers in Quebec's rent tribunal, on the basis that the historical inquiry revealed that in Quebec, unlike Ontario, powers to resolve landlord-tenant disputes, including powers to order specific performance or rescission of the lease, were at the time of confederation possessed by inferior courts as well as superior courts.

The conflicting outcomes of the *Residential Tenancies* and *Grondin* cases made clear that litigation was required to settle the validity of the rent tribunal in each province that had established one.[158] Of course, the same was true for other kinds of tribunals. In *Sobeys Stores* v. *Yeomans* (1989),[159] a case concerning the power over unjust dismissal of a Nova Scotia labour standards tribunal, Wilson

---

v. *Yeomans* [1989] 1 S.C.R. 238, 255 ("It is, in my view, the type of dispute that must guide us and not the particular remedy sought.")

154 [1989] 1 S.C.R. 238.

155 *Id.*, 254. Accord, *Chrysler Can.* v. *Can.* [1992] 2 S.C.R. 394, 416 (power to punish for contempt for breach of tribunal's orders within exclusive jurisdiction of s. 96 courts at confederation).

156 The power to fix rents was not impugned, and could not be impugned: *A.-G. Que.* v. *Grondin* [1983] 2 S.C.R. 364, 376-377.

157 [1983] 2 S.C.R. 364.

158 E.g. *Re Proposed Legislation Concerning Leased Premises* (1978) 89 D.L.R. (3d) 460 (Alta. A.D.) (invalid in Alberta); *Re Pepita and Doukas* (1979) 101 D.L.R. (3d) 577 (B.C.C.A.) (valid in B.C.); *Re Fort Massey Realties* (1982) 132 D.L.R. (3d) 516 (N.S.A.D.) (valid in Nova Scotia).

159 [1989] 1 S.C.R. 238.

J. for the majority of the Court acknowledged the inconvenience of a single-province historical inquiry, and held that the inquiry ''should be expanded somewhat to include examination of the general historical conditions in all four original confederating provinces''.[160] Tribunals established in the other six provinces would be subjected to the same test, on the basis that provinces joining confederation after 1867 must be taken to have accepted the 1867 arrangements. In this way, there would be national uniformity in the answer to the historical inquiry, although of course different results could emerge from the answer to the second and third steps of the s. 96 inquiry. In *Sobeys Stores* itself, Wilson J. examined the state of the law at confederation in Ontario, Quebec and New Brunswick, as well as Nova Scotia, although it was Nova Scotia that had established the impugned tribunal. Wilson J.'s examination revealed an unexpected infirmity in the four-province test, because it produced a tie: two provinces passed the test, and two failed it! In order to break the tie, she said, it is necessary to look to the position in the United Kingdom in 1867. In the United Kingdom in 1867, she held, power over unjust dismissal was the exclusive preserve of the superior courts. Therefore, the historical test was failed. (The tribunal was saved by the institutional setting test.)

Whether the new four-province historical test has become established or not is unclear. In the first place, it means that either *Residential Tenancies* or *Grondin* is wrongly decided, because the only reason given in *Grondin* for the different outcome was that the law of Quebec in 1867 was different from the law of Ontario.[161] In the second place, Wilson J.'s opinion attracted only a bare majority of four of the seven-judge bench. La Forest J., writing for the other three (who concurred in the result), agreed that the inquiry should not be confined to the province that had established the impugned tribunal, but he did not agree that the inquiry should be confined to the four original provinces.[162]

The second step in the s. 96 reasoning — the ''judicial'' inquiry — involves the notoriously elusive task of characterizing the impugned power as ''judicial'' (in which case the s. 96 inquiry must proceed) or as ''administrative'' or ''legislative'' (in which case the s. 96 inquiry can stop). In *Re Residential Tenancies Act*,[163] Dickson J. suggested that a power was ''judicial'' if it involved (1) ''a private dispute between parties'', (2) that must be adjudicated ''through the

160 *Id.*, 265.

161 *Id.*, 266 (although not explicitly saying that one must be wrong).

162 *Id.*, 289. In *Re Young Offenders Act* [1991] 1 S.C.R. 252, Lamer C.J. (with two others) and Wilson J. (with one other) applied the four-province test. La Forest J. (with one other) said nothing about which provinces provided the historical comparison. In *Re Residential Tenancies Act (N.S.)* [1996] 1 S.C.R. 186, 225 (Lamer C.J. with two others), 235 (McLachlin J. with five others on this issue, including La Forest J.), all nine judges seem to accept the four-province test. The 1981 *Residential Tenancies* case was distinguished on the basis that it concerned only the two remedies of compliance orders and eviction orders.

163 [1981] 1 S.C.R. 714, 735; accord, *Massey-Ferguson Industries* v. *Govt. of Sask.* [1981] 2 S.C.R. 413, 429.

application of a recognized body of rules'', and (3) that must be adjudicated ''in a manner consistent with fairness and impartiality''. He concluded that these characteristics were all present in the powers of the rent tribunal in that case. Of course, in the case of an inferior court (as opposed to an administrative tribunal), the power in question is almost certain to be classified as judicial, and this step of the inquiry is not significant. Even in the case of an administrative tribunal, where the historical inquiry (the first step) has yielded the answer that the power in question was one that was exercised by a superior court at the time of confederation, in most cases the power will be classified as judicial. But in some cases a power, challenged for breach of s. 96, has been upheld as insufficiently judicial, either for absence of a private dispute between parties,[164] or for absence of a controlling body of rules,[165] or for both reasons.[166]

The third step in the s. 96 reasoning — the ''institutional setting'' inquiry — involves an examination of the power in its institutional setting to see whether it still broadly conforms to a s. 96 power. This step of the process had been emphasized before *Residential Tenancies* in *Tomko* v. *Labour Relations Board (Nova Scotia)* (1977),[167] where, in upholding a labour relations board's power to issue a cease and desist order, Laskin C.J. for the majority of the Supreme Court of Canada said that the superficially close analogy with superior-court injunctions was not decisive, because it was necessary to consider not the ''detached jurisdiction or power alone'', but rather ''its setting in the institutional arrangements in which it appears''. The Privy Council in the *John East* case (1949)[168] had also decided that the institutional setting of a labour relations regime transformed a power to enforce contracts into a non-s. 96 function. In both *Tomko* and *John East*, the court-like adjudicative function of the labour relations board was ancillary to a broader administrative and policy-making role as administrator of the labour relations legislation. A similar argument carried the day in *Sobeys Stores*,[169] where a labour standards tribunal's power to reinstate employees was upheld as ''a necessarily incidental aspect of the broader social policy goal of providing minimum standards of protection for non-unionized employees''. In settings other than labour relations, the institutional setting has sustained many other adjudicative functions vested in administrative tribunals.[170]

---

164 *Massey-Ferguson Industries* v. *Govt. of Sask.* [1981] 2 S.C.R. 413 (compensation board had self-initiated investigatory function).

165 *Ibid.* (compensation board not limited to legal considerations in fixing compensation); *Capital Regional District* v. *Concerned Citizens of B.C.* [1982] 2 S.C.R. 842 (provincial cabinet could affirm or reverse pollution tribunal on basis of policy).

166 *A.G. Que.* v. *Udeco* [1984] 2 S.C.R. 502 (Minister's power to suspend board of directors not judicial).

167 [1977] 1 S.C.R. 112, 120.

168 *Labour Rels. Bd. (Sask.)* v. *John East Ironworks* [1949] A.C. 134.

169 [1989] 1 S.C.R. 238, 282.

170 *Mississauga* v. *Peel* [1979] 2 S.C.R. 244 (Ontario Municipal Board's function ancillary to restructuring of municipalities under Board supervision); *Massey-Ferguson Industries* v. *Govt.*

The institutional setting will not save an adjudicative function which, having been held to be a s. 96 function at confederation (step (1)), and having been characterized as judicial (step (2)), is the "sole or central function" of the tribunal.[171] That was the case in *Re Residential Tenancies Act*,[172] where the Supreme Court of Canada held that, although the rent tribunal did perform other functions in the administration of Ontario's residential tenancy legislation, the other functions were ancillary to the central function of adjudicating disputes between landlords and tenants.

The institutional setting was also unavailing to save the impugned power in *A.-G. Que.* v. *Farrah* (1978),[173] where the sole function of the Quebec Transport Tribunal was to sit on appeal from a tribunal of first instance and decide "any question of law"; this was held to be an unconstitutional s. 96 function. That was also the holding in *Crevier* v. *A.-G. Que.* (1981),[174] where the sole function of the Quebec Professions Tribunal was to sit on appeal from several tribunals of first instance; the Professions Tribunal also had the power to decide questions of law. In both *Farrah* and *Crevier*, a privative clause purported to exclude superior-court review of the appellate tribunal's decisions; that aspect of the cases is discussed in the next section of this chapter. The three concurring opinions in *Farrah* emphasized the exclusion of superior-court review as if it was the unreviewable character of the authority of the Quebec Transport Tribunal that was important. But, in *Crevier* Laskin C.J. for the Court, as well as holding the privative clause unconstitutional, seemed to hold that the fact that the sole function of the Quebec Professions Tribunal was that of "a general tribunal of appeal" was a fatal flaw by itself.[175]

---

of Sask. [1981] 2 S.C.R. 413 (compensation board's function part of a public insurance plan); *Capital Regional District* v. *Concerned Citizens of B.C.* [1982] 2 S.C.R. 842 (provincial cabinet possessed administrative and regulatory authority as well as adjudicatory authority); *Chrysler Can.* v. *Can.* [1992] 2 S.C.R. 394 (Competition Tribunal required power to enforce its orders by punishment for contempt). Cases where the institutional setting has been ignored are *Toronto* v. *York* [1938] A.C. 415; *Quance* v. *Thomas A. Ivey & Sons* [1950] O.R. 397 (C.A.); *Toronto* v. *Olympia Edward Recreation Club* [1955] S.C.R. 454; these cases all concern the Ontario Municipal Board, holding that decisions regarding liability to assessment cannot be made by the Board (and the Act now remits these decisions to the Ontario Court of Appeal); in light of *John East* and the other authorities which rely on the institutional setting test, these cases are probably wrongly decided.

171 *Re Residential Tenancies Act* [1981] 1 S.C.R. 714, 736.

172 *Ibid.*

173 [1978] 2 S.C.R. 638.

174 [1981] 2 S.C.R. 220.

175 If this is correct, then the decision is not easy to understand. Laskin C.J. acknowledged in *Farrah* (at p. 642) that an administrative tribunal could be given authority to decide questions of law, and could be given appellate authority (extending to questions of law) over another tribunal. He could have added that superior-court jurisdiction over administrative tribunals has never (apart from statute) included appellate authority extending to all questions of law, but merely review authority over questions of jurisdiction and (on certiorari) errors of law on the face of the record. It would seem to follow that (apart from the privative clause issue, to be

The three-step approach now favoured by the Supreme Court of Canada is no doubt a sound synthesis of the prior case-law. But it is not satisfactory as constitutional-law doctrine. Each of the three steps is vague and disputable in many situations, and small differences between the provinces in their history or institutional arrangements can spell the difference between the validity and invalidity of apparently similar administrative tribunals. The Supreme Court of Canada's holdings of invalidity in the *Residential Tenancies*, *Farrah* and *Crevier* cases (as well as the *B.C. Family Relations Act*, *McEvoy* and *MacMillan Bloedel* cases, discussed in the earlier section of this chapter on inferior courts) have cast doubt on the constitutionality of many provincial administrative tribunals (and some inferior courts), have encouraged a spate of litigation on this issue, and have led to pressure from the provinces for an amendment to s. 96. I think an amendment is the only solution. The courts are unlikely to abandon doctrine which has been built up over a long time; nor are they likely to abandon their concern (which I regard as extravagant) to prevent the erosion of superior-court jurisdiction. To me, the allocation of jurisdiction between different levels of courts and administrative tribunals is primarily a political question, upon which the inevitably self-interested views of the courts should not be unduly influential. An amendment proposal which has been circulated for discussion by the federal Department of Justice would specifically grant to the provinces the power to confer on an administrative tribunal (but not an inferior court) any function within provincial legislative competence (including a s. 96 function), so long as the tribunal's decisions remained subject to superior-court review.[176] This proposal would remove a swamp of uncertainty from our constitutional law, and give to the provinces more security in assigning functions to administrative tribunals.

As was explained in the earlier section of this chapter on inferior courts, the Supreme Court of Canada in *MacMillan Bloedel* v. *Simpson* (1995)[177] decided that the *Residential Tenancies* three-step rule applies to the conferral of jurisdiction on inferior courts as well as administrative tribunals. The federal Young Offenders Act purported to invest a "youth court", which in British Columbia was an inferior court, with exclusive jurisdiction over the offence of contempt of court[178] when committed by a "young person". The accused, aged 16, was a

---

discussed in the next section of the chapter), the powers in *Farrah* and *Crevier* would fail the historical inquiry (step (1)), making it unnecessary to go on to steps (2) and (3). Yet in *Crevier*, Laskin C.J. (at p. 234) quoted with approval, and appeared to rely upon as an independent ground of decision, a dictum in *Re Residential Tenancies Act* that a scheme "is invalid when the adjudicative function is a sole or central function of the tribunal (*Farrah*) so that the tribunal can be said to be operating 'like a s. 96 court'."

176 *The Constitution of Canada: A Suggested Amendment Relating to Provincial Administrative Tribunals* (Department of Justice, Ottawa, 1983).

177 [1995] 4 S.C.R. 725; discussed at note 137, above.

178 The Act distinguished between contempt in the face of the court and contempt outside the face of the court. The youth court had exclusive jurisdiction over both categories where the contempt was committed against the youth court itself. The youth court had exclusive jurisdiction over

"young person" within the meaning of the Young Offenders Act, and he was arrested (along with many others) for disobeying an injunction issued by the Supreme Court of British Columbia that prohibited any obstruction of the logging operations of MacMillan Bloedel in an area of old growth forest in Clayoquot Sound on Vancouver Island. He was tried and convicted by the Supreme Court of British Columbia of the offence of contempt of court. He appealed the conviction, relying on the express language of the Young Offenders Act for the proposition that only the youth court possessed the jurisdiction over a contempt of court committed by a young person. The Supreme Court of Canada held that the power to punish for contempt of a superior court was within the exclusive jurisdiction of superior courts at Confederation (step (1)); and that the power was a judicial one (step (2)); but that in the institutional setting of a court with procedures and remedies tailored to the needs of young people (step (3)) the power lost its conformity with superior-court functions.

Because step (3) of the *Residential Tenancies* reasoning was answered in favour of the validity of the power, it followed that the youth court could be invested with jurisdiction over contempt of court. According to the prior case-law, it would make no difference whether the youth court's jurisdiction was exclusive or concurrent. This was the view of McLachlin J., who would have upheld the exclusive jurisdiction of the youth court, and would have held that the young person accused could not be tried by any court other than the youth court. But McLachlin J.'s opinion attracted the support of only three others, and was the dissenting opinion. Lamer C.J., writing with the support of four others (for a bare five-four majority), held that the *Residential Tenancies* tests exhausted the inquiry only when the challenged jurisdiction of the inferior court or tribunal was concurrent with the jurisdiction of the superior court. In his view, whenever *exclusive* jurisdiction was granted by statute to an inferior court or tribunal, it was necessary to ask a further question, which was whether the grant of exclusive jurisdiction took away any part of a superior court's "core" jurisdiction. Lamer C.J. held that the power of a superior court to punish breaches of its own orders through contempt outside the face of the court was part of the core of superior-court jurisdiction. Therefore, although a grant of concurrent jurisdiction could validly be made to the youth court (since the grant satisfied the *Residential Tenancies* third step), a grant of exclusive jurisdiction could not be. The majority of the Court concluded, therefore, that the Supreme Court of British Columbia had not lost its power to punish contempts against itself by young persons, which meant that the accused had been validly tried and convicted.

In my view, the theory that s. 96 guarantees a core of superior-court jurisdiction that cannot under any circumstances be taken away from a superior court is an unfortunate and needless supplement to what is already a complex body of law. First of all, it seems to me to be unwise to introduce even more restrictions

only the second category, namely, contempt outside the face of the court, where the contempt was committed against a court other than the youth court.

on the powers of Parliament and the Legislatures to constitute inferior courts and administrative tribunals. It is true that the doctrine of the core does not preclude the grant of concurrent powers, but concurrent powers lead to forum-shopping and the alternative of resorting to a superior court is likely to conflict with the legislative policy, as it obviously did in the case of the young person accused in *MacMillan Bloedel*, who was tried in an adult court without the protections and remedies of the youth court.[179] Secondly, the new restrictions are intolerably uncertain, because no one knows what is included in the guaranteed core. In *MacMillan Bloedel*, Lamer C.J. acknowledged that he was not able to specify the powers that comprised the core, but he said that it was "unnecessary in this case", because the power to punish for contempt was "obviously" within the core.[180] In other words, only a series of cases going all the way to the Supreme Court of Canada will chart the boundaries of the untouchable core. Thirdly, the policy reason supplied by Lamer C.J. seems exaggerated. He said that "destroying part of the core jurisdiction would be tantamount to abolishing the superior courts of general jurisdiction".[181] But it must be remembered that only those superior-court powers that satisfy the *Residential Tenancies* third step can be vested in an inferior court or tribunal, and any exercise of the powers by the inferior court or tribunal would be reviewable by a superior court: exclusivity does not exclude superior-court review on administrative-law grounds of jurisdictional error, unfairness, absence of evidence, bad faith, improper purpose, and the like. I find it hard to accept that the doctrine of the core is needed to maintain the institution of the superior court.[182]

(f) Privative clauses

The decisions of inferior courts and administrative tribunals have for centuries been subject to review by superior courts through the prerogative writs of certiorari, prohibition, mandamus, quo warranto and habeas corpus; and in more

179 The Supreme Court of British Columbia sentenced the accused to 45 days in prison and a fine of $1,000. In my opinion, no youth court would have imposed such a harsh penalty on a 16-year-old boy who was trying to protect the forest.

180 [1995] 4 S.C.R. 725, para. 38. As to the meaning of the core, Lamer C.J. used other descriptive phrases: "a core or inherent jurisdiction which is integral to their operations" (para. 15); "inherent jurisdiction" (para. 30); "powers which are 'hallmarks of superior courts' " (para. 35); "an essential attribute of superior courts" (para. 40). As to obviousness, it is by no means clear that a superior court must possess the power to punish contempt outside the face of the court. As McLachlin J. pointed out in dissent (paras. 84-88), there is no greater risk of non-compliance if a prosecution for contempt must be brought by the Attorney General in another court, in this case, the youth court.

181 *Id.*, para. 37.

182 The doctrine of the core was trenchantly criticized by McLachlin J. in dissent, who made the points in the text and some others as well, but unaccountably failed to attract the concurrence of more than three of her colleagues. On the other side of the argument, there has been academic support for a guaranteed core of superior-court jurisdiction: see note 194, below.

recent times by actions for a declaration or injunction; and even more recently in some jurisdictions by special statutory remedies such as an application for judicial review. Judicial review under these various procedures does not involve a full reconsideration of the merits of the decision under review, but it does enable the superior court to review certain aspects of the decision, and, in particular, whether the decision-maker had ''jurisdiction'' to render the decision. To the extent that superior-court review is available, the establishment of a new administrative tribunal does not involve a total exclusion of superior-court jurisdiction.

It is common for legislative bodies, when establishing a new administrative tribunal, to include in the constituent statute a ''privative clause'', which is a provision purporting to exclude judicial review of the tribunal's decision. Privative clauses come in a variety of fairly standard forms. There is the ''finality clause'', which declares that the decisions of the tribunal shall be ''final'' and not subject to review; the ''exclusive jurisdiction'' clause declares that the tribunal's jurisdiction to decide issues before it is exclusive and unreviewable; the ''no-certiorari clause'' declares that certiorari and other remedies which would otherwise be available for review purposes are not available to review the tribunal's decision; and one could also include ''notice clauses'' and ''limitation clauses'' which exclude review unless prior notice has been given or unless proceedings are brought within a short time. The superior courts have tended to give little effect to privative clauses. They have reasoned that any given privative clause could not have been intended to exclude judicial review in cases where the tribunal has (in the court's opinion) exceeded its jurisdiction, and they have accordingly ''interpreted'' the privative clause as not protecting a tribunal decision which is vitiated by a ''jurisdictional'' error. This result has traditionally been achieved by statutory interpretation, rather than by invocation of any constitutional doctrine. However, the Canadian courts have now developed a cluster of constitutional doctrines with respect to privative clauses, and the end result of that development seems to be a constitutional prohibition on privative clauses that purport to exclude judicial review for jurisdictional error.

There has always been at least one constitutional limit on the efficacy of privative clauses: they are ineffective to exclude a superior-court decision as to the constitutionality of a statute. This to so because the Constitution's distribution of powers has been assumed to require implicitly that the courts police the distribution to prevent usurpation by a legislative body of powers that do not belong to it.[183] For similar reasons, where an administrative tribunal is placed in the invidious position of having to decide a constitutional issue, its decision must be subject to review by a superior court notwithstanding any privative clause.[184] A

183 Laskin, *Canadian Constitutional Law* (5th ed., 1986 by Finkelstein), 68-69; Strayer, *The Canadian Constitution and the Courts* (3rd ed., 1988), ch. 3; *Amax Potash* v. *Govt. of Sask.* [1977] 2 S.C.R. 576 (Sask. cannot bar recovery by taxpayer of taxes found to be unconstitutional); *Air Canada* v. *B.C.* [1986] 2 S.C.R. 539 (B.C. cannot use fiat to bar recovery of unconstitutional taxes).

184 Chapter 37, Enforcement of Rights, under heading 37.3, ''Administrative tribunals,'' below.

common case is where a provincial labour relations board has to decide whether a particular industry is within federal or provincial jurisdiction. Since a provincial Legislature has no power to regulate labour relations in an industry within federal jurisdiction, it cannot authorize a provincial tribunal to determine conclusively whether or not a particular industry is within provincial or federal jurisdiction; otherwise, the tribunal by a wrong decision on the classification of the industry could extend provincial power into the forbidden federal area.[185]

In *A.-G. Can.* v. *Law Society of B.C.* (1982),[186] the Law Society of British Columbia brought an action in the superior court of British Columbia against the Attorney General of Canada, claiming a declaration that the Combines Investigation Act (now the Competition Act, Canada's anti-trust statute) was unconstitutional in its application to the legal profession. It was objected by the Attorney General that this was a matter within the exclusive jurisdiction of the Federal Court, so that the Law Society was suing in the wrong court. It was a difficult question of statutory interpretation as to whether the exclusive jurisdiction of the Federal Court covered an action for a declaration of invalidity. The Supreme Court of Canada, in an opinion written by Estey J., held that it was not necessary to decide the question of statutory interpretation, because the federal Parliament lacked the constitutional authority to invest the Federal Court with exclusive jurisdiction over a case that raised the constitutional validity of a federal statute. This was so because the federal Parliament's power in s. 101 of the Constitution Act, 1867, to create federal courts "for the better administration of the laws of Canada", did not authorize a provision which excluded the provincial superior courts from deciding constitutional questions. Therefore, even if the Federal Court Act purported to confer exclusive jurisdiction on the Federal Court, an action seeking a declaration of the invalidity of a federal statute could be brought in the superior court of any province.

The *Law Society of B.C.* case was taken a step further in *Canada Labour Relations Board* v. *Paul L'Anglais* (1983),[187] where the Supreme Court of Canada, in an opinion written by Chouinard J., held that the Federal Court could not be invested with exclusive jurisdiction to review the decisions of federal administrative tribunals in those cases where the application for judicial review was made on a constitutional ground. In that case, an employer had applied to the superior court of Quebec to review a decision of the federal labour relations board on the ground that the employment activities in issue (the sale of television commercial time and the production of commercials) fell outside the constitutional authority of the federal Parliament. The Supreme Court of Canada held that, since judicial review was applied for on this constitutional ground, the superior court of Quebec

185 For examples of these "constitutional jurisdictional facts", see *Can. Labour Relations Bd.* v. *Paul L'Anglais* [1983] 1 S.C.R. 147; *Northern Telecom Can.* v. *Communications Workers of Can.* [1983] 1 S.C.R. 733; and see Strayer, previous note, 95-96.

186 [1982] 2 S.C.R. 307.

187 [1983] 1 S.C.R. 147.

was properly seized of the case. A privative clause in the Canada Labour Relations Act, and an exclusive-jurisdiction clause in the Federal Court Act, both of which purported to exclude review of the board by provincial superior courts, were unconstitutional — but only to the extent that they purported to exclude based on the constitutional limits to the authority of the federal Parliament.

There can be no quarrel with the proposition that a legislative body should not be able to insulate its statutes or its administrative tribunals from judicial review on constitutional grounds. That does indeed seem to be entailed by the federal distribution of powers. But, in both the *Law Society of B.C.* case and the *Paul L'Anglais* case, judicial review had not been eliminated; it remained available, albeit in the Federal Court. It is not easy to see why the federal Parliament should be disabled from shifting the forum of judicial review from the superior courts of the provinces to the Federal Court. The Federal Court is a superior court staffed by judges with the same credentials as the judges of the superior courts of the provinces, and subject to an appeal to the Supreme Court of Canada.[188] Thus, the two decisions, although ostensibly resting on lofty principles of federalism, seem to fit more comfortably into that large category of cases that are really based on hostility to federal-court jurisdiction.[189]

None of these cases decided that superior-court review of administrative tribunals was constitutionally protected where no constitutional issue was involved.[190] That large step was taken in *Crevier* v. *A.-G. Que.* (1981),[191] where the Supreme Court of Canada struck down a privative clause in a Quebec statute that purported to exclude all judicial review of Quebec's Professions Tribunal. Laskin C.J.'s opinion for the Court acknowledged that a privative clause could constitutionally exclude review on questions of law not going to the limits of the tribunal's jurisdiction,[192] but, he held, a privative clause could not exclude all judicial review, including review on questions of the limits of the tribunal's jurisdiction.[193] Most of the language of Laskin C.J.'s opinion suggests that the

---

188 Cf. *Brink's Canada* v. *CLRB* [1985] 1 F.C. 898 (T.D.) (privative clause is effective to exclude judicial review by Federal Court, even on constitutional grounds).

189 Note 107 and accompanying text, above.

190 In Hogg, "Is Judicial Review of Administrative Action Guaranteed by the British North America Act?" (1976) 54 Can. Bar Rev. 716, I answered my question, no. The Supreme Court of Canada has now held that the answer is yes: see following text.

191 [1981] 2 S.C.R. 220.

192 *Id.*, 235. Subsequent cases have upheld privative clauses that did not exclude review for jurisdictional error: *Capital Regional District* v. *Concerned Citizens of B.C.* [1982] 2 S.C.R. 842; *A.-G. Que.* v. *Grondin* [1983] 2 S.C.R. 364.

193 The concept of jurisdictional error is one of the most elusive and susceptible to judicial manipulation in Anglo-Canadian law. Laskin C.J., [1981] 2 S.C.R. 220, at p. 236, invoking a gift of understatement, acknowledged that "there may be differences of opinion as to what are questions of jurisdiction", but he made no attempt to suggest a definition. It is alarming that this concept should now be enshrined in our constitutional law, immune from legislative change. This is a fundamental difficulty with the rule in *Crevier*: see Mullan, "The Uncertain Position of Canada's Administrative Appeal Tribunals" (1982) 14 Ottawa L. Rev. 239.

reason for the invalidity of the privative clause was that, by conferring unreviewable authority on the Professions Tribunal, the Quebec Legislature was attempting to constitute the tribunals as a s. 96 court.[194] In other words, it was the grant of unreviewable authority to the tribunal, rather than the taking away of the superior court's power of review,[195] that was unconstitutional. This is not a distinction without a difference, because, if it is the grant of unreviewable authority to the tribunal that is objectionable, then, since s. 96 does not apply to federal courts or tribunals,[196] the rule would not invalidate a privative clause protecting a federal administrative tribunal.[197] However, in *MacMillan Bloedel* v. *Simpson* (1995),[198] in which a majority of the Supreme Court of Canada committed themselves for the first time to the existence of a guaranteed core of superior-court jurisdiction, Lamer C.J. for the majority cited *Crevier* for the proposition that no part of the

---

194 There is one passage in the opinion, [1981] 2 S.C.R. 220, 236, in which Laskin C.J. describes "review of decisions on questions of jurisdiction" as standing "on the same footing" as review of decisions on questions of "constitutionality". The analogy seems strained to me, since the integrity of the federal system relies upon superior-court determinations of constitutionality, whereas no such issues are at stake when the question is simply the location of final decision-making power (court or tribunal) on issues entirely within provincial legislative competence. Nevertheless, the passage could be read as carrying the suggestion of a guaranteed core of superior-court jurisdiction. Elsewhere in the opinion, however, and indeed even in the passage referred to, Laskin C.J. is at pains always to frame his new rule as applicable to privative clauses protecting "provincial" administrative tribunals. The qualifying adjective would not be necessary if the decision was based on a guaranteed core of superior-court jurisdiction. See Mullan, previous note, 260; and see also next note.

195 Lederman, "The Independence of the Judiciary" (1956) 34 Can. Bar Rev. 769 and 1139, at p. 1174, has argued that a guaranteed core of superior-court jurisdiction should be derived from the judicature sections of the Constitution Act, 1867. For similar views, see Lyon (1971) 49 Can. Bar Rev. 365; Le Dain (1974) 12 Osgoode Hall L.J. 261, 334-336; Elliot (1982) 16 U.B.C.L. Rev. 313. The argument in essence is that judicature provisions in a constitution "are only meaningful as long as judges carry out meaningful tasks": Russell (1967) 7 Alta. L. Rev. 103, 108; compare the similar argument with respect to legislative bodies in ch. 14, Delegation, under heading 14.3(b) "Administrative inter-delegation". The implication of a guaranteed core of superior-court jurisdiction is that a privative clause is objectionable, not just because it confers unreviewable authority on an administrative tribunal, but because it takes away part of the superior court's guaranteed core of jurisdiction. On this basis, the federal Parliament would be as disabled as the provincial Legislatures from enacting a privative clause that excluded all provincial superior-court review. The theory of a guaranteed core of jurisdiction is attacked in my article, cited note 190, above, and is inconsistent with the cases in note 196, below. It is, of course, clear that there is no guaranteed core of *inferior*-court jurisdiction: *Re Young Offenders Act* [1991] 1 S.C.R. 252, 274.

196 See sec. 7.2(e), "Appointment, payment and tenure of federal judges", above.

197 In *Pringle* v. *Fraser* [1972] S.C.R. 821, the Supreme Court of Canada upheld a federal privative clause precluding review even on jurisdictional grounds of the decisions of the federal Immigration Appeal Board. The provisions of the Federal Court Act, conferring exclusive review power on the Federal Court, also have the effect of taking away the review power of the provincial superior courts, and their validity (except as to questions of constitutionality) has been recognized: *A.-G. Can.* v. *Canard* [1976] 1 S.C.R. 170, 202; *CLRB* v. *Paul L'Anglais* [1983] 1 S.C.R. 147, 154.

198 [1995] 4 S.C.R. 725; discussed at notes 137 and 177, above.

core jurisdiction could be taken away from superior courts.[199] This is rather a clear affirmation that a superior court's power of judicial review for jurisdictional error cannot be taken away in any circumstances by either the federal Parliament or a provincial Legislature. The position should probably not yet be regarded as settled, since the point was obiter in *MacMillan Bloedel*, was agreed to by only a bare majority, and is inconsistent with other cases.[200]

---

199 *Id.* , para. 35.
200 Note 197, above.

8

Supreme Court of Canada

8.1 Establishment of Court

The Supreme Court of Canada[1] was not established at confederation. It was not necessary, because the Judicial Committee of the Privy Council in the United Kingdom served as the final court of appeal from all British colonies, including those of British North America, and that right of appeal continued after confederation. (The abolition of Privy Council appeals is described in the next section of this chapter.) However, the Constitution Act, 1867 did make provision for the

---

1 For studies of the Supreme Court of Canada, see Brossard, *La cour suprême et la constitution* (1968); Russell, *The Supreme Court of Canada as a Bilingual and Bicultural Institution* (1969); Weiler, *In the Last Resort* (1974); Snell and Vaughan, *The Supreme Court of Canada: History of the Institution* (1985); Beaudoin (ed.), *The Supreme Court of Canada* (1986); Canadian Bar Association, Committee on the Supreme Court of Canada, *Report* (1987); Russell, *The Judiciary in Canada* (1987), ch. 14; Bushnell, *The Captive Court: A Study of the Supreme Court of Canada* (1992). The Supreme Court Law Review is an annual journal, established in 1980, which is devoted to the work of the Court.

later establishment of a Canadian court of appeal. Section 101 authorized the federal Parliament "to provide for the constitution, maintenance, and organization of a general court of appeal for Canada". Acting under this power, in 1875 the federal Parliament, by statute, established the Supreme Court of Canada.[2]

The Supreme Court of Canada's existence, and therefore the details of its composition and jurisdiction, depend upon an ordinary federal statute. As the following text will show, over the years there have been many changes in its composition and jurisdiction, and these have been accomplished by federal statutes. In theory, the Court could be abolished by the unilateral action of the federal Parliament.[3] In practice, of course, the Court has won a highly respected place in the scheme of Canadian government, and no federal government would ever contemplate the abolition or diminution of the Court.[4]

8.2 Abolition of Privy Council appeals

At confederation, the Judicial Committee of the Privy Council was the final court of appeal from all colonial courts, and to this day it continues to serve as a Commonwealth court for those members of the Commonwealth that have retained the appeal.[5]

The full Privy Council in the United Kingdom is a large body which now exercises only formal functions.[6] Its members are appointed by the Queen, acting on the advice of the Prime Minister, and they always include (among many others) the senior judges of the United Kingdom. The Judicial Committee is a committee of the Privy Council consisting of those Privy Councillors who are judges. The quorum of the Judicial Committee is three, but most appeals are heard by a bench of five, and these five are usually drawn from the law lords of the House of Lords.[7] Because the Judicial Committee is a committee rather than a court, it does not render a judgment, but merely "advises" the Queen as to the disposition of each

---

2 Supreme and Exchequer Courts Act, 1875, S.C. 1875, c. 11; see now Supreme Court Act, R.S.C. 1985, c. S-26.

3 It is possible that references to the Supreme Court of Canada in ss. 41(d) and 42(d) of the Constitution Act, 1982 have now placed the Court beyond the power of the federal Parliament. This issue is discussed in ch. 4, Amendment-secs. 4.3 and 4.4, above.

4 Proposals for reform of the Court are described later in this chapter, sec. 8.8, "Reform of Court", below.

5 The Privy Council in the United Kingdom and its Judicial Committee are described in de Smith and Brazier, *Constitutional and Administrative Law* (6th ed., 1989), ch. 8.

6 The Canadian equivalent, the Queen's Privy Council for Canada, is described in sec. 9.3(b), "The cabinet and the Privy Council", below.

7 The judicial members of the Privy Council and thus the members of the Judicial Committee include not only the Lords of Appeal in Ordinary (the law lords who sit in the House of Lords), but also the Master of the Rolls and the Lords Justices of Appeal (who sit in the Court of Appeal). As well, a few distinguished Commonwealth judges are appointed, and occasionally sit on appeals.

appeal. In practice, of course, the "advice" is treated as a binding judgment.[8] The Judicial Committee used to render its advice in the form of a single opinion. The theory was that advice to the Crown should not be divided. This meant that no dissenting opinion was ever written, and there was no disclosure of a dissenting view in the single opinion filed.[9] This practice was abandoned in 1966 (long after the abolition of Canadian appeals); dissenting opinions (but not separate concurring opinions) are now permitted.[10]

The jurisdiction of the Judicial Committee of the Privy Council (hereafter simply the Privy Council) comes partly from the royal prerogative and partly from a series of imperial statutes. The Privy Council's authority over the British North American colonies was continued for Canada by s. 129 of the Constitution Act, 1867. When the Supreme Court of Canada was established by federal statute in 1875, the right to appeal to the Privy Council was in no way impaired. Not only was there an appeal from the Supreme Court to the Privy Council,[11] but the pre-1875 appeals from the provincial courts directly to the Privy Council were preserved; these "per saltum" appeals enabled appellants to bypass the Supreme Court altogether.[12] Laskin C.J. aptly commented that the Supreme Court "was left in the ambiguous position where it could not command appeals to it nor effectively control appeals from it".[13]

The continuance of Privy Council appeals denied the Supreme Court a decisive voice in the development of Canadian law, including constitutional law. As the nation increased in maturity and shed other vestiges of colonial status, it became increasingly unacceptable that the rights of Canadian litigants, and the final say as to Canadian law, should be settled by a court in the United Kingdom. In 1887, the federal Parliament enacted an amendment to the Criminal Code which purported to abolish appeals to the Privy Council in criminal cases. Thirty-eight years later, in *Nadan* v. *The Queen* (1926),[14] the Privy Council held that the

---

8 The advisory character of its decisions may explain why the Judicial Committee never treated its prior decisions as strictly binding precedent, unlike the House of Lords before 1966: see sec. 8.7, "Precedent", below.

9 One of the law lords who sat in *A.-G. Can.* v. *A.-G. Ont.* (Labour Conventions) [1937] A.C. 326 disclosed in a published, extra-judicial speech that he had dissented in that case: see ch. 11, Treaties, under heading 11.5(c), "Evaluation of Labour Conventions case, below.

10 Judicial Committee (Dissenting Opinions) Order 1966 (U.K.) (S.I. 1966, No. 1100).

11 There was controversy about the retention of appeals between the Canadian government, which would have preferred to abolish them or seriously reduce them, and the British government, which wanted them retained; the British view prevailed: see Strayer, *The CanadianConstitution and the Courts* (3rd ed., 1988), 25.

12 "Per saltum" means by a leap or a bound. Per saltum appeals were not exceptional. Nearly half of the constitutional cases decided by the Privy Council were appealed directly from the provincial courts: Russell, *The Judiciary in Canada* (1987), 336.

13 "The Role and Function of Final Appellate Courts" (1975) 53 Can. Bar Rev. 459, 461.

14 [1926] A.C. 482.

statute was invalid, primarily because it conflicted with two imperial statutes.[15] We have already noticed that this unexpected decision was one factor leading to the imperial conference of 1926, which set afoot an inquiry into how the vestigial inequalities between the United Kingdom on the one hand and the dominions on the other could be removed.[16] After the Statute of Westminster had conferred on the dominions the capacity to repeal or amend imperial statutes, Canada re-enacted the 1888 statute, and as re-enacted it was held to be valid.[17]

In 1939, the federal government introduced a bill to abolish the remaining appeals to the Privy Council, and referred the bill to the Supreme Court of Canada for a decision as to its validity. There was little doubt that s. 101 of the Constitution Act, 1867 authorized the abolition of appeals from the Supreme Court of Canada to the Privy Council: that could fairly be characterized as a law in relation to ''a general court of appeal for Canada''. But this bill also purported to abolish the per saltum appeals, which lay from the provincial courts directly to the Privy Council. Was this not a matter solely within ''the administration of justice in the province'' and therefore outside federal competence? In the *Privy Council Appeals Reference* (1947),[18] the Privy Council, affirming the Supreme Court of Canada, held that the bill was within federal competence. The power to establish a general court of appeal for Canada included not only the power to make its jurisdiction ultimate, but also the power ''to deny appellate jurisdiction to any other court''.[19] After this decision, the bill was enacted,[20] and the new law came into force on December 23, 1949. Cases ''commenced'' before that date could still be carried to the Privy Council,[21] and the last Canadian appeal was not determined until 1959.[22] But for cases commenced since 1949 there is no longer any appeal to the Privy Council.[23]

---

15 A subsidiary ground of decision, which was almost certainly wrong, was that the statute purported to have extraterritorial effect: see ch. 13, Extraterritorial Competence, under heading 13.2, ''Federal Parliament'', below.

16 See ch. 3, Independence, under heading 3.3, ''Statute of Westminster, 1931'', above.

17 *British Coal Corp.* v. *The King* [1935] A.C. 500. The one point for decision was whether the Canadian Parliament could legislate upon the royal prerogative.

18 *A.-G. Ont.* v. *A.-G. Can.* (Privy Council Appeals) [1947] A.C. 127.

19 *Id.*, 153.

20 S.C. 1949 (2nd sess.), c. 37, s. 3.

21 *Id.*, s. 7.

22 *Ponoka-Calmar Oils.* v. *Wakefield* [1960] A.C. 18.

23 The Australian Constitution, adopted in 1900, also preserved appeals to the Privy Council, but under s. 74 (and supplementary legislation) questions as to the limits inter se of the constitutional powers of the Commonwealth and states (''inter se questions'') can be appealed to the Privy Council only with the leave of the High Court of Australia. Since inter se questions include most constitutional questions, and since the High Court of Australia has (with one exception) always denied leave to appeal inter se questions to the Privy Council, the High Court of Australia has in practice always been the final court of appeal on most constitutional questions. In 1968 appeals from the High Court of Australia to the Privy Council on all remaining questions of constitutional law (that is, questions other than inter se questions) were abolished. Appeals on federal law were also abolished in 1968; appeals on state law were abolished in 1975; and per

8.3 Composition of Court

The Supreme Court of Canada originally comprised six judges, and the Court's statute stipulated that at least two of them had to come from Quebec. In 1927 a seventh judge was added; and in 1949 two more judges were added, bringing the number to its present figure of nine, of whom three must come from Quebec. Since 1949 a pattern of regional representation has been maintained under which three judges come from Quebec (the statutory requirement), three from Ontario (on the basis that Ontario should have the same number of places as Quebec), two from the Western provinces and one from the Atlantic provinces.[24] The Chief Justiceship has usually alternated between French-speaking and English-speaking incumbents.[25]

Since the Court's beginning, five judges have constituted a quorum, and the quorum has not been increased as the membership has risen from six to nine.[26] For most of the Court's existence, including the period since 1949 when nine judges have been available, the majority of cases have been heard by a bare quorum of five judges. However, the more important cases have usually been heard by more than five judges and often by the full Court.[27] When the full Court does not sit, there is a tendency towards regional or provincial specialization by the inclusion in the panel for a particular case of the judges from the province or region in which the case arose. This is almost invariable in the case of appeals from Quebec. There are however no rules as to the composition of the bench for each case: it lies within the discretion of the Chief Justice.[28]

The Court has never accepted an obligation to announce its decisions in the form of a single opinion containing at least the lowest common denominator of

---

saltum appeals from state courts were abolished in 1986; no appeals remain. See generally, Hanks, *Constitutional Law in Australia* (1991), ch. 1.

24 This regional distribution has been disturbed only once, in 1978, when Spence J. from Ontario retired and was replaced by McIntyre J. from British Columbia. But in 1982, when Martland J. from Alberta retired, he was replaced by Wilson J. from Ontario, thus restoring the traditional regional distribution.

25 The practice of alternation, which had been followed since 1944, was departed from in 1984, when Dickson C.J. was appointed to succeed Laskin C.J. The practice was resumed when Lamer C.J. was appointed to succeed Dickson C.J.

26 There is provision in the Supreme Court Act (it is now s. 30) for the appointment of ad hoc judges "where at any time there is not a quorum" of permanent judges available to sit. Twenty-four ad hoc appointments have been made, but none since the increase in the number of judges to nine in 1949 made the quorum easy to achieve: Boult, "Ad Hoc Judges of the Supreme Court of Canada" (1978) 26 Chitty's L.J. 289.

27 Even numbers are avoided to eliminate the risk of an equal division, which causes the affirmation of the decision appealed from, as occurred in *Tiny Separate School Trustees* v. *The Queen* [1927] S.C.R. 637.

28 Apart from the power to preside over the hearings in which he participates, the selection of the bench of judges for each case appears to be the principal special power of the Chief Justice of Canada. He will also assign the writing of opinions where there are no volunteers. The functioning of the Court is described in Russell, *The Judiciary in Canada* (1987) 349-354.

agreement among the majority judges. In that respect it has not followed the practice of the Privy Council, or even of the Supreme Court of the United States, which, while not suppressing separate concurring opinions or dissenting opinions, does attempt to produce an official majority opinion. Sometimes, the Canadian Court will produce a proliferation of opinions, even though the opinion-writers agree on the result and, in substance, on the reasoning.[29] In recent years, however, it has become more common for only one or two or three judges to write opinions with each of the others simply expressing agreement with one of the written opinions.[30] Obviously, there is now some prior consultation and circulation of draft opinions among the judges, and some effort to avoid unnecessary extra opinions. However, an absence of coordination is still occasionally noticeable in that a dissenting opinion will not always directly refer to the language and ideas of the concurring opinion, and vice versa. Once again, the opinions in the Supreme Court of the United States, which are normally careful to address the opposing views of their colleagues, present a more disciplined collegiality.

8.4 Appointment of judges

The judges of the Court are appointed by the Governor in Council,[31] that is, by the federal cabinet. It is often said that the practices that are followed in the appointment of judges to the superior, district and county courts of the provinces are followed here too, that is, the Chief Justice is appointed on the recommendation of the Prime Minister, and the puisne judges are appointed on the recommendation of the federal Minister of Justice.[32] However, it seems more likely that the Prime Minister is usually involved in the selection of the puisne judges as well as the Chief Justice.

The only fetters imposed by the Supreme Court Act on the appointing power of the federal executive are rules regarding the qualifications of the appointees: each appointee must be either a judge of the superior court of a province, or a lawyer of at least ten years' standing at the bar of a province;[33] and at least three

29 E.g., *A.-G. N.S.* v. *A.-G. Can.* (Nova Scotia Inter-delegation) [1951] S.C.R. 31, where the seven-judge bench produced seven concurring opinions. This kind of proliferation was not unusual at that time.

30 Multi-author opinions are not unknown but are uncommon. In some constitutional cases, the Court has issued a single unanimous opinion which is described as that of ''The Court''.

31 Supreme Court Act, R.S.C. 1985, c. S-26, s. 4. For a thoughtful study, see Weinrub, ''Appointing Judges to the Supreme Court of Canada in the Charter Era: A Study in Institutional Function and Design'' in Ontario Law Reform Commission, *Appointing Judges: Philosophy, Politics and Practice* (1991).

32 See ch. 7, Courts, under heading 7.1(b), ''Appointment and payment of provincial judges'', above.

33 Section 5.

of the nine judges must come from Quebec.[34] There is no requirement that appointments be ratified by the Senate or the House of Commons or a legislative committee. In practice, there is confidential consultation with the organized bar, but no public scrutiny of appointments.

The provinces have no role in the selection of judges, and are not necessarily even consulted before an appointment is made. Since the Court has to decide constitutional disputes between the federal government and the provinces, it is arguable that the judges should not be appointed just by one side. Indeed, from time to time veiled accusations of a centralist bias are directed at the Court. Studies of the Court (including one commissioned by the Parti Québécois government of Quebec) have found no such bias.[35] Nevertheless, there is support in various reform proposals for incorporating some provincial role in the appointing process. The suggestions for reform of the Court are discussed later in this chapter.[36]

8.5 Appellate Jurisdiction

(a) Constitutional basis

The Supreme Court Act, by s. 35, provides that the Court ''shall have and exercise an appellate, civil and criminal jurisdiction within and throughout Canada''. The breadth of jurisdiction granted by this provision is fully justified by s. 101 of the Constitution Act, 1867, which authorizes the federal Parliament to establish ''a general court of appeal for Canada''.

The jurisdiction of the Supreme Court of Canada that is contemplated by s. 101 and is conferred by the Supreme Court Act is not a jurisdiction confined to cases arising under federal laws or otherwise coming within some limited area of federal jurisdiction. Now that Privy Council appeals have been abolished, the Supreme Court of Canada stands at the top of the hierarchy not only of federal courts but of provincial courts as well. It hears appeals not only from the Federal Court of Appeal but also from all the provincial courts of appeal, and those appeals may raise questions of constitutional law, federal law or provincial law. The Supreme Court of Canada is thus a powerful unitary element in the court system of Canada, uniting the ten provincial hierarchies of courts into what is

34 Section 6. This is supplemented by the conventions reported in the previous section of this chapter that three judges must come from Ontario, two from the Western provinces and one from the Atlantic provinces.

35 L'Ecuyer, *La Cour suprême du Canada et le partage des compétences 1949-1978* (Gouvernement du Québec, Ministère des affaires intergouvernementales, 1978); Hogg, ''Is the Supreme Court of Canada Biased in Constitutional Cases?'' (1979) 57 Can. Bar Rev. 721; Russell, ''The Supreme Court and Federal-Provincial Relations'' (1985) 11 Can. Public Policy 161.

36 Section 8.8, ''Reform of Court'', below.

essentially a single, national system.[37] Like the Privy Council before it, the Supreme Court of Canada is the final authority on the interpretation of the entire body of Canadian law, whatever its source. Unlike the Privy Council, which was an imperial or (latterly) a Commonwealth court, the Supreme Court of Canada is a federal court in the technical sense that it is established by federal law. But, from the standpoint of its plenary jurisdiction, it is as much a provincial court as a federal court. The fact that a case raises only a question of provincial law does not affect the right of appeal, and a large number of such cases are in fact appealed to and disposed of by the Court.

In the United States, there is no general court of appeal with jurisdiction over the entire body of the law. The jurisdiction of the Supreme Court of the United States is confined by article III, s. 1, of the Constitution to the ''judicial power of the United States''. The Constitution, by article III, s. 2, then defines the ''judicial power of the United States'' as follows:

> The judicial power shall extend to all cases, in law and equity, arising under this constitution, the laws of the United States, and treaties made, or which shall be made, under their authority; — to all cases affecting ambassadors, other public ministers and consuls; — to all cases of admiralty and maritime jurisdiction; — to controversies to which the United States shall be a party; to controversies between two or more states; — between a state and citizens of another state; between citizens of different states; between citizens of the same state claiming lands under the grants of different states, and between a state, or the citizens thereof, and foreign states, citizens or subjects.

The result is that the jurisdiction of the Supreme Court of the United States (and the lower federal courts)[38] cannot go beyond the ''cases'' and ''controversies'' coming within the judicial power of the United States. For the most part, these cases and controversies are matters governed by constitutional law or by federal law. When the Supreme Court of the United States (or a lower federal court) does have jurisdiction over a case which is not governed by constitutional law or by federal law, as occurs for example under its ''diversity jurisdiction'' (controversies between citizens of different states), the Court has decided in *Erie Railroad Co.* v. *Tompkins* (1938),[39] that it should defer to the law as laid down by the highest court of the state whose law is applicable. Thus, while most issues of state law cannot and do not go beyond the highest court of the state, even those that

---

37 The Supreme Court of Canada takes judicial notice of all laws in force in every province (and territory), not just those of the jurisdiction in which the appeal originated. In the Supreme Court of Canada, the laws of provinces other than the province in which the appeal originated are not ''foreign'' laws, and therefore need not be proved as facts, as they must be in the courts of a province. See ch. 13, Extraterritorial Competence, under heading 13.3(c), ''Impairment of extraprovincial rights'', below.

38 In addition to the Supreme Court, the federal courts of the United States consist of a District Court of original jurisdiction for each of 87 ''districts'' and a Court of Appeals of mainly appellate jurisdiction for each of ten ''circuits'' and for the District of Columbia. See generally Wright, *The Law of Federal Courts* (4th ed., 1983).

39 (1938) 304 U.S. 64.

do reach the Supreme Court of the United States are not decided in accordance with any nation-wide uniform rule. The inevitable consequence is that the common law, or at least that part of it within state jurisdiction, is not necessarily the same in each state, and on many topics divergent rules have in fact developed. For the same reason, a state statute which has been enacted in identical terms in several states could receive a different interpretation in the courts of one state than in the courts of another. The rule in *Erie Railroad Co.* v. *Tompkins* disables the Supreme Court from imposing uniformity on state law. This rule of restraint could be regarded as entailed by a federal system: the law of the several states is left to each state to develop judicially, just as it is legislatively.

When the Supreme Court of Canada has to determine a question of provincial law, it might perhaps be expected that it would defer to the decisions of the courts of that province (or at least decide the question as a court of that province would have done). This is not what has happened at all. *Erie Railroad Co.* v. *Tompkins* has no place in the law or practice of the Supreme Court of Canada. The Supreme Court of Canada always makes its own determination of any question before it, even if it is a question of provincial law, and it does not hesitate to reverse a decision rendered by a provincial court of appeal in a case raising only questions of provincial law. The Supreme Court of Canada does not tolerate divergences in the common law from province to province, or even divergences in the interpretation of similar provincial statutes. Such divergences do develop from time to time, of course, but they are eventually eliminated by the Supreme Court of Canada. The assumption of the Court, which is shared by the Canadian bar, is that, wherever variations can be avoided, Canadian law, whether federal or provincial, should be uniform. Needless to say, each province has a distinctive body of statute law, and Quebec also has a distinctive body of civil law (instead of common law); but the final interpretation of even these unique provincial laws lies with the Supreme Court of Canada.[40] But, apart from distinctive provincial statute law and Quebec's civil law, the law in Canada is generally uniform across the country, and does not differ from province to province.[41]

Albert Abel has argued that the Supreme Court of Canada should follow the lead of the Supreme Court of the United States and adopt a rule of restraint in provincial law cases like the rule in *Erie Railroad Co.* v. *Tompkins*. He argues that such a rule would make the law more responsive to the differing needs and

---

40 In the later section of this chapter on leave applications, I point out that the Court will often refuse leave to appeal a decision raising a question of law particular to a single province, but its power to grant the leave and hear the appeal is not in doubt. Appeals in civil law cases from Quebec are quite common, for example. With the great increase in constitutional law cases spawned by the Charter of Rights, the Court now has less time for cases raising issues of provincial law, and it therefore often denies leave to appeal such cases. In this way, Canada is creeping in the direction of *Erie Railroad Co.* v. *Tompkins*, as the provincial courts of appeal increasingly become the final arbiters of much provincial law.

41 Willis, ''Securing the Uniformity of Law in a Federal System — Canada'' (1944) 5 U. Toronto L.J. 352.

sentiments of the provinces.[42] This idea has a good deal of merit with respect to the civil law of Quebec with which only the three Quebec members of the Supreme Court of Canada are normally familiar, but with respect to the nine common law provinces it is easy to agree with Gibson that ''such a change would result in many more interprovincial legal discrepancies than could be attributed to cultural differences''.[43] It must be remembered that whenever a province does desire a different regime of law, it is free to enact a statute. In my opinion, the uniformity of the common law throughout Canada, while undoubtedly at variance with an ideal model of federalism, does not really impair provincial autonomy in any practical way. Moreover, the rule of uniformity makes Canada's laws much less complicated than those of the United States, and it allows the highest court (with presumably the best judges) to apply its talents to the development of all Canada's laws, both provincial and federal.

Quebec, with its distinctive civil law, is in a special situation. From the time of confederation to the present, Quebecers have found it hard to understand why a Court comprising a majority of common law judges should have the power to reverse a Quebec court of appeal in a case governed by the civil law; indeed, this concern was an important factor in delaying the establishment of the Supreme Court until 1875.[44] When the Court was established, the statutory provision for Quebec's representation was included to guarantee the membership of some civilian judges. Since 1949, when Quebec's representation was increased from two to three, it has been possible to assemble a quorum of five judges with a majority of civilians. This is now the usual composition of the bench when the Court hears a civil law appeal from Quebec. A bench so composed does not wholly meet the Quebec criticism, because, for example, two common law judges and one civilian could outvote two civilians and reverse a decision reached unanimously in Quebec; but it does offer some protection for the distinctiveness of Quebec's civil law.[45]

---

42 Abel, ''The role of the Supreme Court in Private Law Cases'' (1965) 4 Alta. L.R. 39; see also Russell, note 1, above, 218.

43 Gibson, Comment (1966) 44 Can. Bar Rev. 674, 679.

44 There was a substantial body of French Canadian opinion which regarded the Privy Council as better equipped to interpret Quebec's laws than any general Canadian court would be: Russell, *The Supreme Court of Canada as a Bilingual and Bicultural Institution* (1969), 7-9.

45 Russell, note 44, above, 60-63, and see Russell's ch. 4 for analysis of the influence of the common law judges in the outcome of appeals from Quebec. Russell's data covered the period from 1875 to 1964. Wheat, ''Disposition of Civil Law Appeals by the Supreme Court of Canada'' (1980) 1 Supreme Court L.R. 425, studying the period from 1965 to 1978, concluded (at pp. 451-452) that ''the common law members of the Court in fact have exercised very little influence over the outcome of civil law appeals''. Vaughan, ''Civil Code Influences on the Supreme Court of Canada, 1875-1980'' (1986) 20 Law Society of Upper Canada Gazette 48, reaches a similar conclusion. Of course, as Russell points out (at p. 173), opinions differ on the desirability of common law influences on the civil law. The ideological value of the ''purity'' of the civil law may be countered by the pragmatic value of critical re-examination of civil law doctrine in the light of ideas from the other system.

If a province would prefer that litigation in a field within provincial jurisdiction be finally disposed of at the level of the provincial court of appeal, it cannot constitutionally give effect to that preference. In *Crown Grain Co.* v. *Day* (1908),[46] the Privy Council struck down a Manitoba statute that provided that decisions of the Manitoba superior court in mechanics' liens actions were to be "final and binding", and that "no appeal shall lie therefrom". Their lordships held that this provision was inconsistent with the Supreme Court Act, which conferred a right of appeal to the Supreme Court of Canada from any "final judgment" of the highest court of final resort in a province.[47] Under the rule of federal paramountcy,[48] the Supreme Court Act's grant of a right of appeal prevailed over the Manitoba statute's purported denial of a right of appeal.[49] In *Re Sutherland* (1982),[50] the Manitoba Court of Appeal had to consider a Manitoba statute that purported to make "final" the decisions of the county court in cases relating to recovery of wages. The Manitoba Court of Appeal held that the provision was valid and effective to preclude appeals to the Manitoba Court of Appeal but that it could not be effective to preclude an appeal to the Supreme Court of Canada, and that it should be interpreted as not purporting to oust the jurisdiction of the Supreme Court of Canada. Therefore, the Supreme Court of Canada could still, if it chose, grant leave to appeal from a decision of the county court.

(b) Civil appeals

In civil matters, before 1975 there was an appeal as of right in cases where the amount in controversy exceeded $10,000. This loaded the Court's docket with cases that were unimportant except to the parties. In 1975 this appeal as of right was abolished.[51] Most civil appeals[52] now require leave.[53]

---

46 [1908] A.C. 504.

47 With some modifications that are irrelevant in this context, this provision is still in the current Supreme Court Act, R.S.C. 1985, c. S-26, s. 40.

48 Paramountcy is the subject of ch. 16, below.

49 Under the theory (note 3, above) that the Supreme Court Act has since 1982 become part of the Constitution of Canada, the provincial statute would today not merely be inoperative by virtue of paramountcy, but would be invalid by virtue of the supremacy clause in s. 52(1) of the Constitution Act, 1982. The possibility that the Charter provides constitutional appeal rights is discussed by Gibson, "The Crumbling Pyramid: Constitutional Appeal Rights in Canada" (1989) 38 U.N.B.L.J. 1.

50 (1982) 134 D.L.R. (3d) 177 (Man. C.A.).

51 S.C. 1974-75-76, c. 18, proclaimed in force January 27, 1975.

52 So far as I can work out, the only exceptions are (1) an appeal from the decision of a provincial court of appeal on a "reference" by the provincial government: Supreme Court Act, s. 36; and (2) an appeal from the decision of the Federal Court of Appeal in the case of a controversy between Canada and a province or between two or more provinces: Federal Court Act, s. 32.

In the case of appeals from provincial courts of appeal, leave can be granted by the provincial court of appeal itself "where, in the opinion of that court, the question involved in the appeal is one that ought to be submitted to the Supreme Court for decision".[54] The Federal Court of Appeal has an identically expressed power to grant leave to appeal from its own decisions.[55] The existence of these powers to grant leave is anomalous, because the main purpose of requiring leave for appeals is to enable the Supreme Court of Canada itself to control the size and nature of its caseload. This has been recognized by the courts of appeal, which have held that they should grant leave sparingly, doing so only in "obvious" or "special" cases.[56] In practice, the courts of appeal rarely grant leave.[57]

The important power to grant leave is the power possessed by the Supreme Court of Canada itself. It has this power:[58]

> where, with respect to the particular case sought to be appealed, the Supreme Court is of the opinion that any question involved therein is, by reason of its public importance or the importance of any issue of law or any issue of mixed law and fact involved in that question, one that ought to be decided by the Supreme Court or is, for any other reason, of such a nature or significance as to warrant decision by it, . . .

Because the Court does not give reasons for the grant or denial of leave to appeal, there is no case law on the kinds of considerations that the Court takes into account in determining applications for leave. Generally speaking, however, the broader the significance of the case, the more likely it is that leave will be granted. Appeals raising constitutional or civil liberties issues are likely to receive leave. Appeals arising out of an important federal statute, or of a provincial statute which has its counterparts in other provinces, or of an important point of common law, or of a will or contract which is a standard form, are more likely to receive leave than appeals arising out of a unique statute or contract or unusual problem or a fact-dominated case, which may lack the element of "public importance" even if a

---

In these two cases the appeal lies as of right. In criminal cases, there are still several categories of appeals as of right: see note 66, below.

53 See Crane, "Practice Note: Civil Appeals to the Supreme Court of Canada" (1977) 15 Osgoode Hall L.J. 389; Bushnell, "Leave to Appeal Applications to the Supreme Court of Canada" (1982) 2 Supreme Court L.R. 479. Sopinka, *The Conduct of an Appeal* (1993). Since 1986, each annual issue of the Supreme Court L.R. has included an analysis of leave to appeal applications for the previous year. An annual report on applications for leave is published by the law firm of Gowling, Strathy & Henderson, Ottawa.

54 Supreme Court Act, s. 37.

55 Federal Court Act, s. 31(1).

56 *MNR* v. *Creative Shoes* [1972] F.C. 1425, 1428 (C.A.); *Jodrey Estate* v. *Nova Scotia* (1978) 29 N.S.R. (2d) 369, 370 (N.S. A.D.); *CentralComputer Services* v. *Toronto Dominion Bank* (1980) 109 D.L.R. (3d) 660, 662-664 (Man. C.A.); *Campbell* v. *East-West Packers* (1982) 143 D.L.R. (3d) 136, 137 (Man. C.A.).

57 Crane, note 53, above, 390; Bushnell, note 53, above, 500.

58 Supreme Court Act, s. 40(1); Federal Court Act, s. 31(2); the quoted language is identical in each of the two provisions.

large sum of money is at stake.[59] A denial of leave to appeal does not imply that the leave-denying panel of the Supreme Court thought that the lower decision was rightly decided.[60]

On applications for leave to appeal, the practice of the Court used to be to sit in panels of three judges and hear brief oral argument by counsel for the parties. The Supreme Court Act required an oral hearing, and stipulated a quorum of three judges (instead of five).[61] In 1987, the Act was amended to allow applications for leave to appeal in ''clear'' cases to be determined on the basis of the written material, without an oral hearing.[62] The majority of applications are now disposed of in this way. For applications that are not ''clear'', the Court can order an oral hearing, in which case the pre-amendment practice is followed. The amendment did not change the quorum requirement, which remains at three, even if no hearing is held.[63] As noted earlier, decisions on applications for leave are rendered without reasons.

(c) Criminal appeals

Criminal law and procedure is a federal responsibility under s. 91(27) of the Constitution Act, 1867.[64] The federal Criminal Code[65] invests provincial courts with the jurisdiction to try criminal cases, and it makes provision for appeals from the provincial courts of appeal to the Supreme Court of Canada. In criminal cases there is still an extensive appeal as of right, that is, without leave. Generally speaking, this exists on any ''question of law'' on which a judge of the provincial court of appeal has dissented.[66] The appeal as of right thus depends upon the existence of a dissenting opinion in the provincial court of appeal. Where there is no such dissenting opinion, an appeal still lies, but only on a ''question of law'', and only with the leave of the Supreme Court of Canada.[67] Needless to say, there is a body of jurisprudence on what constitutes a ''question of law''.[68] These

---

59 The criteria for granting leave are discussed in Crane, note 53, above, 390-392 and Bushnell, note 53, above, 510-518.

60 *R.* v. *Côté* [1978] 1 S.C.R. 8, 16. Bushnell, note 53, above, 518, comments that ''in practice it would seem inevitable that the refusal to grant leave would have the effect of acting as some measure of approval in the eyes of the public and the legal profession''.

61 Supreme Court Act, s. 43; the general rule that five are a quorum is in s. 25.

62 S.C. 1987, c. 42, substituting a new s. 45 (43 in R.S.C. 1985).

63 Contrast the position in the United States where petitions for certiorari are considered by all Justices, although there is no oral hearing, and a petition is granted on the affirmative votes of four of the nine Justices.

64 Criminal law is the subject of ch. 18, below.

65 R.S.C. 1985, c. C-46.

66 *Id.*, ss. 691(1)(a), 692(3)(a), 693(1)(a). As well, an appeal as of right is provided for by s. 784(3) (denial of habeas corpus) and s. 691(2) (reversal of verdict of acquittal), even where there is no dissenting opinion in the court of appeal.

67 *Id.*, ss. 691(1)(b), 692(3)(b), 693(1)(b).

68 Greenspan, *Martin's Annual Criminal Code* (revised annually), commentary to ss. 691-693.

provisions (unlike the admittedly vague provisions regarding civil appeals) do not stipulate the grounds upon which leave should be granted or denied, and the Court does not give reasons for a grant or denial of leave, so that there is no case law on the point.[69]

8.6 Reference jurisdiction

(a) Federal references

The Supreme Court Act imposes on the Court the function of giving advisory opinions on questions referred to the Court by the federal government. Section 53 provides that ''the Governor in Council may refer to the court for hearing and consideration important questions of law or fact''; and, when such a reference is made, ''it is the duty of the Court to hear and consider it and to answer each question so referred''.

The reference procedure[70] has been used mainly for constitutional questions.[71] It has rarely been used to seek answers to non-constitutional questions, although it is available for that purpose as well. The questions referred are usually about the constitutionality of a federal law (or a proposed federal law), but the constitutionality of a provincial law can also be referred, and this has been done from time to time.[72]

The only body[73] that can direct a reference to the Court is the ''Governor in Council'', which means, by convention, the federal government (cabinet). The

---

69 The Supreme Court Act, s. 43, as amended by S.C. 1987, c. 42, permitting applications for leave to appeal in ''clear'' cases to be disposed of without an oral hearing, applies to criminal cases as well as to civil cases: *R.* v. *Chaulk* [1989] 1 S.C.R. 369.

70 See Strayer, *The Canadian Constitution and the Courts* (3rd ed., 1988), ch. 9; Huffman and Seathoff, ''Advisory Opinions and Canadian Constitutional Development'' (1990) 74 Minn. L. Rev. 1251.

71 Strayer, previous note, 334, reports that from 1867 to 1966, of the 197 constitutional cases reaching the highest available court (the Privy Council until 1949, the Supreme Court of Canada thereafter), 68 or about 35 per cent were references; in the period 1967 to 1986, of the 155 constitutional cases reaching the Supreme Court of Canada, 23 or about 15 per cent were references. He speculates that the relative decline in resort to the reference jurisdiction is explained by the greater ease of private access to the courts through acceptance of the action for a declaratory judgment as a means of constitutional challenge, liberal rules as to standing, legal aid, and more numerous special interest groups able to undertake or support litigation.

72 E.g., of federal references of provincial statutes, *A.-G.Alta.* v. *A.-G. Can.* (Bank Taxation) [1939] A.C. 117; *ReMinimum Wage Act* (Sask.) [1948] S.C.R. 248. The constitutionality of such references seems never to have been judicially doubted: Strayer, note 70, above, 322; for a doubt, see note 84, below.

73 A second kind of reference, authorized by the Supreme Court Act, s. 56, is the reference of a private bill by the Senate or House of Commons of the federal Parliament. There were some early references by the Senate, but, so far as I can tell, none by the House of Commons: Huffman, note 70, above, 1257, 1291.

reference procedure is therefore a privilege open only to government. A private person cannot direct a reference to the Court. However, the Court has compensated for this inequality by developing liberal rules of standing to allow a private person to bring a declaratory action to challenge the validity of a federal or a provincial law.[74] This procedure does not provide automatic access to the Supreme Court of Canada, but it does provide access to the superior court of the province, and normal rights of appeal are of course available.

(b) Provincial references

A provincial government has no power to direct a reference to the Supreme Court of Canada. However, each of the ten provinces has enacted legislation permitting the provincial government to direct a reference to the provincial court of appeal.[75] Each provincial law is broadly framed, allowing the constitutionality of federal laws as well as provincial laws to be referred,[76] as well as non-constitutional questions. Following the pattern of the federal legislation, each provincial law confines the power to direct a reference to the provincial government. A provincial reference will secure an advisory opinion from the provincial court of appeal. However, when the provincial court of appeal has rendered an opinion on a reference (as opposed to an actual case), there is an appeal as of right to the Supreme Court of Canada.[77] This right to appeal without leave means in effect that the provincial governments enjoy the same privilege as the federal government in being able to secure a ruling from the Supreme Court of Canada on a controverted point.

(c) Constitutional basis

The rendering of advisory opinions to government is not traditionally a judicial function for two reasons. First, it lacks the adversarial and concrete character of a genuine controversy; and, secondly, it is a function normally undertaken by the executive branch of government, specifically, the Attorney General. In Australia, the High Court of Australia has refused to render advisory

---

74 See ch. 56, Procedure, under heading 56.2, ''Standing'', below.

75 See Strayer, note 70, above, 315-318.

76 E.g., of provincial references of federal statutes, *A.-G.Ont.* v. *Can. Temperance Federation* [1946] A.C. 193; *ReAgricultural Products Marketing Act* [1978] 2 S.C.R. 1198; *Re Exported Natural Gas Tax* [1982] 1 S.C.R. 1004; *McEvoy* v. *A.-G. N.B.* [1983] 1 S.C.R. 704. In the last case (at pp. 708-709) ''the Court'' raised a doubt about the constitutionality of provincial references of federal legislation and said that ''we expressly refrain from comment on such issue''. Considering the broad jurisdiction of the provincial courts to decide federal as well as provincial questions, and the right of appeal to the Supreme Court of Canada, it is hard to see the basis for the Court's doubt. Strayer, note 70, above, 322, does not regard the point as doubtful.

77 Supreme Court Act, s. 36, requiring no leave to appeal.

opinions, on the ground that it is a non-judicial function.[78] And the Supreme Court of the United States has informally indicated a similar constitutional objection to the function.[79]

It would not have been surprising if the Canadian courts had held that the rendering of advisory opinions by the Supreme Court of Canada was precluded by the Constitution Act's description of the Court in s. 101 as ''a general court of appeal for Canada''. When the point was litigated up to the Privy Council in the *Reference Appeal* (1912),[80] the reference statute was upheld. Their lordships acknowledged that the function was not a judicial one, and emphasized that ''the answers are only advisory and will have no more effect than the opinions of the law officers'', but their lordships held nevertheless that the function could be conferred by statute on the Court. This decision is often taken as authority for the proposition that no separation-of-powers doctrine is to be read into the Constitution of Canada.[81] The provincial reference statutes seem never to have been squarely challenged, but have always been accepted as valid, apparently as laws in relation to the administration of justice in the province.[82]

A different kind of constitutional objection to federal (but not provincial) references would be based on the fact that they are an exercise of original rather than appellate jurisdiction by the Court. Section 101 of the Constitution Act, 1867 authorizes the establishment of ''a general court of appeal for Canada''. It will be recalled that in the United States it was the attempt to confer original jurisdiction on the Supreme Court of the United States that led to the celebrated case of *Marbury* v. *Madison* (1803), in which a federal statute was held unconstitutional for the very first time.[83] But this objection has never been taken to the reference jurisdiction of the Supreme Court of Canada, and the long acceptance of that jurisdiction must be regarded as an implicit rejection of the objection.[84]

---

78 *Re Judiciary and Navigation Act* (1921) 29 C.L.R. 257.

79 The refusal to render an advisory opinion is contained in correspondence in 1793 between the President and Secretary of State, on the one hand, and the judges of the Court, on the other. The refusal is undoubtedly consistent with the requirement of a ''case'' or ''controversy'' in the definition of the ''judicial power of the United States'', which limits the jurisdiction of the Supreme Court of the United States, as well as the lower federal courts. Several states authorize advisory opinions, however. See generally Note, ''Advisory Opinions on the Constitutionality of Statutes'' (1956) 69 Harv. L. Rev. 1302; Tribe, *American Constitutional Law* (2nd ed., 1988), 73-77.

80 *A.-G. Ont.* v. *A.-G. Can.* (Reference Appeal) [1912] A.C. 571.

81 See ch. 7, Courts, under heading 7.3(a), ''Separation of powers'', above.

82 Strayer, note 70, above, 139; see the rest of Strayer's ch. 5 on the constitutionality of references.

83 *Marbury* v. *Madison* (1803) 5 U.S. (1 Cranch) 137 is discussed in ch. 5, Federalism, under heading 5.5(a), ''Development of judicial review'', above. (The Supreme Court of the United States has some original jurisdiction, but only what is expressly authorized by the Constitution.)

84 In *Gulf Oil Corp.* v. *Gulf Canada* [1980] 2 S.C.R. 39, the Supreme Court of Canada, over objection, exercised an original jurisdiction to enforce letters rogatory conferred by the Canada Evidence Act. This relaxed attitude to its own jurisdiction, conferred by the first branch of s. 101, contrasts sharply with its narrow interpretations of the Federal Court's jurisdiction, conferred by the second branch of s. 101: see ch. 7, Courts, under heading 7.2(b), ''Federal Court

(d) Advisory character

In the *Reference Appeal* (1912),[85] as quoted above, the Privy Council held that the Court's answer to a question posed on a reference was ''advisory'' only and of ''no more effect than the opinions of the law officers''. It follows that the Court's answer is not binding even on the parties to the reference, and is not of the same precedential weight as an opinion in an actual case. This is certainly the black-letter law. But there do not seem to be any recorded instances where a reference opinion was disregarded by the parties, or where it was not followed by a subsequent court on the ground of its advisory character. In practice, reference opinions are treated in the same way as other judicial opinions.

The Supreme Court Act and the provincial reference statutes impose on the Court a duty to answer reference questions. However, the Court has often asserted and occasionally exercised a discretion not to answer a question posed on a reference.[86] It may exercise that discretion where the question is not yet ripe,[87] or has become moot,[88] or is not a legal question,[89] or is too vague to admit of a satisfactory answer.[90] However, as noted in the discussion of conventions in chapter 1,[91] in the reference litigation concerning the constitutional settlement of

---

of Canada'', above; see also Scott, ''Canadian Federal Courts and the Constitutional Limits of their Jurisdiction'' (1982) 27 McGill L.J. 137, 143. Where does the Supreme Court of Canada's capacity to exercise original jurisdiction come from? Perhaps, like the Federal Court's jurisdiction, it comes from the second branch of s. 101. In other words, when exercising original, as opposed to appellate, jurisdiction, the Supreme Court must come within the phrase ''any additional courts for the better administration of the laws of Canada''. If that is so, then it can exercise original jurisdiction only over the ''laws of Canada'', a phrase which excludes provincial laws. And yet, as pointed out, note 72, above, the Court has answered references by the federal government asking about the constitutionality of provincial statutes.

85 Note 80, above.

86 McEvoy, ''Separation of Powers and the Reference Power: Is there a Right to Refuse?'' (1988) 10 Supreme Court L.R. 429 argues that there is no discretion to refuse to answer a reference question, but he acknowledges the abundant authority to the contrary.

87 *A.-G. Ont.* v. *A.-G. Can.* (Local Prohibition) [1896] A.C. 348, 370 (refusing to answer questions that ''have not as yet given rise to any real and present controversy'' and are therefore ''academic rather than judicial'').

88 *Re Objection by Que. to Resolution to Amend the Constitution* [1982] 2 S.C.R. 793, 806 (asserting discretion not to answer a question ''where the issue has become moot'', while deciding to answer the question nonetheless).

89 *Re Can. Assistance Plan* [1991] 2 S.C.R. 525, 545 (asserting discretion to refuse to answer a ''purely political'' question, although the question in the case did have ''a sufficient legal component to warrant a decision by a court'').

90 In *McEvoy* v. *A.-G. N.B.* [1983] 1 S.C.R. 704, 707-715 where the Court in the end decided to answer a question which it described as suffering from ''excessive abstractness'', the Court cited four cases in which questions were not answered for lack of specificity. A fifth could be added: *A.-G. B.C.* v. *A.-G. Can.* (Fishing Rights) [1914] A.C. 153, 162. A sixth case is *Re GST* [1992] 2 S.C.R. 445, 485-486 (refusing to answer question on grounds that it was ''hypothetical'' and ''the answer given would not be precise or useful'').

91 Chpater 1, Sources, under heading 1.10, ''Conventions'', above.

1982, the Court was astonishingly liberal in the questions that it elected to answer. While acknowledging its power not to answer, the Court in the *Patriation Reference*[92] and the *Quebec Veto Reference*[93] answered questions about the existence and meaning of constitutional conventions — questions that raised no legal issue and had only political consequences.

Generally speaking, it is my opinion that the Court has not made sufficient use of its discretion not to answer a question posed on a reference. The reference procedure has often presented the Court with a relatively abstract question divorced from the factual setting which would be present in a concrete case. It has been a common and justified complaint that some of the opinions rendered in references have propounded doctrine that was too general and abstract to provide a satisfactory rule. A number of the most important Canadian cases are open to criticism on this ground.[94]

Even when the questions are specific and the factual setting is adequately presented, the lack of a concrete controversy can lead the Court to miss the point of an important question. *Re Agricultural Products Marketing Act* (1978)[95] is an example. The case concerned the validity of a complex scheme for regulating the market in eggs which had been enacted by complementary federal and provincial legislation. A series of specific questions was asked on a reference by the Ontario government. Large quantities of factual information were placed before the Court. Oral argument occupied four days. The Court took six months to write two concurring opinions. But when the opinions are analyzed, they are found to be unclear as to whether or not the levies imposed on egg producers by the federal egg marketing agency were wholly valid. Since this was one of the main points in dispute, which had led the Ontario government to direct the reference in the first place, the opinions were seriously deficient.[96] An action by the federal agency to collect unpaid levies, or a suit by a dissident producer to enjoin their collection, would have yielded a forthright outcome.

A balanced assessment of the reference procedure must acknowledge its utility as a means of securing an answer to a constitutional question. As noted earlier, the reference procedure has been used mainly in constitutional cases.[97] This is because it enables a government to obtain an early and (for practical

92 *Re Resolution to Amend the Constitution* [1981] 1 S.C.R. 753.

93 *Re Objection by Que. to Resolution to Amend the Constitution* [1982] 2 S.C.R. 793. In this case the only question posed was not only non-legal, it was also (as the Court acknowledged at pp. 805-806) ''moot'' even in a political sense.

94 Strayer, *The Canadian Constitution and the Courts* (3rd ed., 1988), 323-328.

95 [1978] 2 S.C.R. 1198.

96 I should disclose that I was one of the counsel in the case, and admit the possibility that counsel were at fault in not sufficiently emphasizing the significance of this issue. On the other hand, the majority opinion opened with the astonishing phrase (at p. 1289) ''Being pressed for time . . .''. Whoever was at fault, such an unsatisfactory outcome could only have been produced by the reference procedure.

97 Note 71, above.

purposes) authoritative ruling on the constitutionality of a legislative programme. Sometimes questions of law are referred in advance of the drafting of legislation; sometimes draft legislation is referred before it is enacted; sometimes a statute is referred shortly after its enactment; often a statute is referred after several private proceedings challenging its constitutionality promise a prolonged period of uncertainty as the litigation slowly works its way up the provincial or federal court system. The reference procedure enables an early resolution of the constitutional doubt.

(e) Proof of facts

Proof of facts in a reference is peculiarly difficult, because a reference originates in a court that is normally an appellate court: there is no trial, and no other procedure enabling evidence to be adduced. A statement of facts is sometimes included in the "order of reference", which is the document posing the questions that the government wishes the Court to answer. Sometimes, too, affidavits or Brandeis briefs or other material of a factual character are filed informally, or under the direction of the Court. The topic of evidence, including evidence in references, is taken up in chapter 57, Proof, below.[98]

8.7 Precedent

Canadian courts accept the doctrine of precedent (or stare decisis),[99] under which the decisions of a court are binding on courts lower in the judicial hierarchy.[100] Before the abolition of appeals to the Privy Council in 1949, the Supreme Court of Canada was lower in the judicial hierarchy and was accordingly bound by decisions[101] of the Privy Council.[102] During that period, the Supreme Court of Canada decided that it was also bound by its own prior decisions.[103] However, after its accession to final appellate status, the Court gradually came to accept that, while it should normally adhere to its prior decisions, it was not absolutely bound to do so; and the Court has explicitly refused to follow a prior decision in

---

98 Chapter 57, Proof, under heading 57.2, "Evidence", below.

99 Precedent or stare decisis is not to be confused with res judicata, under which the judgments of a court are permanently binding on the parties to the litigation.

100 See generally Murphy and Rueter, *Stare Decisis in Commonwealth Appellate Courts* (1981).

101 Decisions in reference cases, being advisory only, were not binding. However, as noted at note 85, above, in practice decisions in reference cases have been given the same weight as decisions in other cases.

102 The rule in *Robins* v. *National Trust Co.* [1927] A.C. 515, 519, that the House of Lords was "the supreme tribunal to settle English law", also made the decisions of the House of Lords binding on the Supreme Court of Canada.

103 *Stuart* v. *Bank of Montreal* (1909) 41 S.C.R. 516.

several cases.[104] Similarly, the Court gradually came to accept that the decisions of the Privy Council should have no more (and no less) binding force than its own decisions; and the Court has explicitly refused to follow a Privy Council precedent in two cases.[105]

The practice of other final appellate courts is similar.[106] The House of Lords was exceptional in holding itself to be bound by its own prior decisions,[107] but in 1966 it reversed this self-denying ordinance and assumed the power to refuse to follow its own prior decisions.[108] The Privy Council, however, never regarded itself as bound by its own prior decisions,[109] although in Canadian constitutional appeals there is no instance of an explicit refusal[110] to follow a prior decision.[111] The Supreme Court of the United States[112] and the High Court of Australia[113] are both free to refuse to follow their own prior decisions.

---

104 *Brant Dairy* v. *Milk Comm. of Ont.* [1973] S.C.R. 131, 152-153; *Paquette* v. *The Queen* [1977] 2 S.C.R. 189, 197; *McNamara Construction* v. *The Queen* [1977] 2 S.C.R. 655, 661; *Keizer* v. *Hanna* [1978] 2 S.C.R. 342, 347; *Vetrovec* v. *The Queen* [1982] 1 S.C.R. 811, 830; *Min. of Indian Affairs* v. *Ranville* [1982] 2 S.C.R. 518, 527; *Argentina* v. *Mellino* [1987] 1 S.C.R. 536, 547; *Re Bill 30 (Ont. Separate School Funding)* [1987] 1 S.C.R. 1148, 1195; *Clark* v. *CNR* [1988] 2 S.C.R. 680, 704; *Central Alta. Dairy Pool* v. *Alta.* [1990] 2 S.C.R. 489.

105 The first case is *Re Agricultural Products Marketing Act* [1978] 2 S.C.R. 1198, 1234, 1291. This is a strong example since (as Laskin C.J. acknowledged at p. 1256) the Privy Council case, *Lower Mainland Dairy Products* v. *Crystal Dairy* [1933] A.C. 168, had been followed by the Supreme Court of Canada in *Re Farm Products Marketing Act* [1957] S.C.R. 198, and the marketing levies successfully challenged in *Re Agricultural Products Marketing Act* had been enacted by the federal Parliament in reliance on the two decisions. Neither judicial re-affirmation nor legislative reliance sufficed to save the Privy Council decision. The second case is *Re Bill 30 (Ont. Separate School Funding)* [1987] 1 S.C.R. 1148, 1190-1196, overruling *Tiny Roman Catholic Separate School Trustees* v. *The King* [1928] A.C. 363.

106 Bale, ''Casting off the Mooring Ropes of Binding Precedent'' (1980) 58 Can. Bar Rev. 255.

107 *London Street Tramways Co.* v. *London County Council* [1898] A.C. 375 (H.L.).

108 Practice Statement (Judicial Precedent) [1966] 1 W.L.R. 1234.

109 *Tooth* v. *Power* [1891] A.C. 284, 292 (P.C., Aust.).

110 The Privy Council did occasionally depart from precedent, but never admitted that it was doing so. See for example, the tortuous history of the peace, order, and good government power, ch. 17, below, where there are several unacknowledged departures from prior precedent. Compare also the *Radio Reference* [1932] A.C. 304 with *A.-G. Can.* v. *A.-G. Ont.* (Labour Conventions) [1937] A.C. 326. The Privy Council did occasionally explicitly dissociate itself from dicta in earlier cases, e.g., *P.A.T.A.* v. *A.-G. Can.* [1931] A.C. 310, 326 per Lord Atkin, rejecting Lord Haldane's ''domain of criminal jurisprudence'' dictum; *A.-G. Ont.* v. *Can. Temperance Federation* [1946] A.C. 193, 206 per Viscount Simon, rejecting Lord Haldane's ''national binge'' explanation of *Russell*, note 111, below.

111 In *A.-G. Ont.* v. *Can. Temperance Federation* [1946] A.C. 193, in which the Privy Council reaffirmed the largely discredited decision in *Russell* v. *The Queen* (1882) 7 App. Cas. 829 primarily on the ground of its longevity, Viscount Simon said (at p. 206) that ''on constitutional questions it must be seldom indeed that the Board would depart from a previous decision which it may be assumed will have been acted on both by government and subjects''.

112 Note 116, below.

113 Note 117, below.

It is arguable that in constitutional cases the Court should be more willing to overrule prior decisions than in other kinds of cases.[114] In non-constitutional cases, there is always a legislative remedy if the doctrine developed by the courts proves to be undesirable: the unwanted doctrine can simply be changed by the competent legislative body. That is not true of constitutional doctrine, which after its establishment by the Court can be altered only by the difficult process of constitutional amendment. It follows that there is a greater need for judicial adaptation of constitutional law to keep the law abreast of new technology and new social and economic needs. There is sound policy in the dictum of Black J. of the Supreme Court of the United States that "the Court has a special responsibility where questions of constitutional law are involved to review its decisions from time to time and where compelling reasons present themselves to refuse to follow erroneous precedents; otherwise its mistakes in interpreting the Constitution are extremely difficult to alleviate and needlessly so".[115] The Supreme Court of the United States has often refused to follow constitutional precedents which it held to be "erroneous",[116] and the High Court of Australia has occasionally done the same.[117]

8.8 Reform of Court

Proposals to reform the Supreme Court of Canada[118] have focused on the idea of making the Court more acceptable to the provinces as an arbiter of federal-provincial constitutional conflict.[119]

114 It is even arguable that res judicata should be relaxed in constitutional litigation between entities in a federation; otherwise res judicata could lead "to just that rigidity in constitutional interpretation which the Court has otherwise successfully avoided in the application of the doctrine of precedent to its previous decisions": *Queensland* v. *Commonwealth* (1977) 139 C.L.R. 585, 605 (H.C. Aust.) per Stephen J.

115 *Green* v. *U.S.* (1958) 356 U.S. 165, 195. Accord, *Queensland* v. *Commonwealth* (1977) 139 C.L.R. 585, 593, 599, 604, 610; Laskin, *Canadian Constitutional Law* (5th ed., 1986, by Finkelstein), 311-313.

116 The best-known example is *Brown* v. *Bd. of Education* (1954) 347 U.S. 483, refusing to follow *Plessy* v. *Ferguson* (1896) 163 U.S. 537 which laid down the separate-but-equal doctrine which authorized racial segregation in public facilities. There are many other examples. Blaustein and Field (1958) 57 Mich. L.J. 151 report 90 overrulings between 1810 and 1956. Maltz [1980] Wisconsin L. Rev. 467 reports 47 overrulings between 1960 and 1979.

117 The best-known examples are *Amalgamated Society of Engineers* v. *Adelaide SS. Co.* (1920) 28 C.L.R. 129; *Victoria* v. *Commonwealth* (Second Uniform Tax Case) (1957) 99 C.L.R. 575; *Commonwealth* v. *Cigamatic* (1962) 108 C.L.R. 372; *Cole* v. *Whitfield* (1988) 165 C.L.R. 360. Other examples are given by Aickin J. in *Queensland* v. *Commonwealth* (1977) 139 C.L.R. 585, 620-631; Zines, *The High Court and the Constitution* (3rd ed., 1992), 348-9.

118 This section draws on part of my article "The Theory and Practice of Constitutional Reform" (1981) 19 Alta. L. Rev. 335. More comprehensive studies of proposals to reform the Supreme Court of Canada are Lederman, "Current Proposals for Reform of the Supreme Court of Canada" (1979) 57 Can. Bar Rev. 687; Beck and Bernier (eds.), *Canada and the New Consti-*

As noted earlier in this chapter,[120] the composition of the Court already reflects to some extent Canada's regional and linguistic differences. The Supreme Court Act stipulates that three of the nine judges must be appointed from Quebec; and, by convention, the remaining judges are appointed as follows: three from Ontario, two from the four Western provinces and one from the four Atlantic provinces. Of course, the nature of the judicial function, as understood in Canada and other countries in which the judiciary is independent, does not allow a judge to ''represent'' the region from which he or she was appointed in any direct sense, and certainly does not allow the judge to favour the arguments of persons or governments from that region. What regional representation does do, however, is to ensure that there are judges on the Court who are personally familiar with each major region of the country, and who can bring to the decision of a case from that region an understanding of the region's distinctive legal, social and economic character. When the Court does not sit as a full bench, one finds that the judges (or judge) from the region from which each appeal originated are nearly always assigned to that appeal; and that one of those judges will usually write the opinion of the majority.

The regional composition of the Court must enhance the sensitivity and acceptability of its opinions, but the structure of the Court has still attracted some strong criticisms which reveal considerable discontent, especially in Quebec and Western Canada.

The first point of criticism is that the Court's existence and jurisdiction are not guaranteed by the Constitution. The Court's existence and jurisdiction depend upon the Supreme Court Act, which is a federal statute enacted under s. 101 of the Constitution Act, 1867. As a matter of strict law, therefore, the Court could be abolished or radically altered by the federal Parliament.[121] Of course, this is not a practical possibility. Nevertheless, it is widely agreed that the existence and jurisdiction of the Court should be entrenched in the Constitution so that the Court is outside the reach of federal legislative power.[122] While this proposal is uncon-

---

tution (1983), vol. 1, 165 (by MacPherson); Russell, ''Constitutional Reform of the Judicial Branch'' (1984) 17 Can. J. Pol. Sci. 227; Lederman, ''Constitutional Procedure and the Reform of the Supreme Court of Canada'' (1985) 26 Cahiers de Droit (Laval) 195; Delpérée, ''Cour suprême, cour d'arbitrage ou cour constitutionnelle?'' (1985) 26 Cahiers de Droit (Laval) 205.

119 This is one aspect of the application of ''intrastate federalism'' to central institutions: see ch. 4, Amendment, under heading 4.8(c), ''Central institutions'', above.

120 Section 8.3, ''Composition'', above.

121 But note the argument that the Court has been protected from legislative change by ss. 41(d) and 42(d) of the Constitution Act, 1982: note 3, above.

122 This was agreed to as part of the Meech Lake Accord of 1987 (ch. 4, Amendment, at note 37, above). The text of new ss. 101A to 101E of the Constitution Act, 1867 was agreed to, which is set out with commentary in Hogg, *Meech Lake Constitutional Accord Annotated* (1988), ch. 7. The Accord was, however, never implemented by the process of amendment. The same text, with one additional provision (see next note), was agreed to as part of the Charlottetown Accord of 1992 (ch. 4, Amendment, under heading 4.1(c), ''The failure to accommodate Quebec'', above), but that Accord was also never implemented by the process of amendment.

troversial in principle, it should be noticed that it is not without difficulty. The difficulty lies in determining how much of the detail of the Court's organization and jurisdiction should be included in the constitutional text. It must be remembered that the matters dealt with in the constitutional text will become unchangeable except by constitutional amendment. That is the whole point of the exercise. But if too much detail is included, then the kinds of incremental change in the organization and jurisdiction of the Court that have occurred in the past will become exceedingly difficult in the future.

A second criticism of the structure of the Court is that the judges are appointed solely by the federal government. It has often been proposed that the provinces should play a role in the selection of judges to the Court. The principal argument for this proposal is that the Court serves as the "umpire of federalism", and it is inappropriate that the judges should be selected by only one of the contending levels of government. Since 1982, the Court has also been reviewing statutes under the Charter of Rights, and this power also has the potential to limit provincial (as well as federal) powers, which is an additional argument for some provincial influence on the composition of the Court. This could be accomplished by giving each provincial government a direct role in the selection of a judge from that province. For example, the federal government could be required to make its selection from names submitted by the provinces,[123] or selections could be made by a nominating commission comprised of representatives of both levels of government (as well as other interested groups).[124] If the initial selection continued to be made by the federal government alone, a provincial role could still be provided by a process of ratification by a reformed Senate or other legislative body or committee upon which the provinces are represented.[125]

A third point of criticism is that there are too few judges from Quebec on the Court. As noted earlier, the present position, mandated by the Supreme Court Act, is that three of the nine judges must come from Quebec. The argument that three are too few depends upon an evaluation of the Court's capacity to decide three classes of cases: (1) those in which the record and argument are in the French language, (2) those raising issues of civil law, and (3) those raising constitutional issues. The argument for increased representation from Quebec is quite strong

123 This was the mechanism agreed to in the Meech Lake Accord of 1987, previous note, and the Charlottetown Accord of 1992, previous note. Neither Accord established a procedure to resolve a deadlock, but the Charlottetown Accord provided for the appointment by the Chief Justice of an "interim judge" where a vacancy had not been filled after 90 days. The Victoria Charter of 1970 would have required agreement between the Attorney General of Canada and the Attorney General of the province, and in the case of a deadlock the choice would be made by a nominating council. None of these provisions was implemented.

124 Russell, note 1, above, 130-135.

125 The model here is article II, s. 2, of the Constitution of the United States, requiring ratification by the Senate of presidential appointments to the Supreme Court of the United States. For Canada, quite apart from provincial concerns, which have been the cause of proposals to reform the appointing procedure, the idea of a public scrutiny of the qualifications of proposed judges seems to me to be intrinsically sound.

with respect to the first two classes of case. The judges from Quebec would have a perfect fluency in French and a familiarity with the civil law which the judges from outside Quebec would often lack.

The argument that there should be more judges from Quebec to decide constitutional cases is not as strong. It depends upon the premise that Quebec has a special stake in the outcome of constitutional controversies. With respect to some issues, the premise is correct. Issues of culture, language and communications probably do have a deeper impact in Quebec than elsewhere. But with respect to other issues the premise is incorrect. Issues of resource ownership or control are of much greater interest to the Western provinces and (in the case of offshore resources) coastal provinces than they are to Quebec. Many other issues, for example, those relating to civil liberties, consumer protection or economic development, while they may be important to Quebec, have an equally significant impact in other provinces. It seems, therefore, that for many constitutional issues a larger complement of judges from Quebec would not lead to better informed decision-making, and might even lead to resentment in the under-represented parts of the country. I conclude that the case for larger Quebec representation on the Court should turn on the capacity of the Court to handle French language and civil law cases, rather than on the capacity of the Court to handle constitutional cases.

If it is agreed that there should be more judges from Quebec on the Court, the details of that change are still difficult to work out. Any increase in Quebec's numbers involves either a decrease in the numbers drawn from other regions or an increase in the size of the Court. The former alternative is hard to defend on principle and would obviously meet with resistance. The latter alternative — an increase in the size of the Court — carries risks to the quality of the oral argument before the Court and to the collegiality of the Court, which may lead to more fragmentation and more delay in the Court's decisions.[126]

Finally, in proposals to restructure the Supreme Court of Canada, it has occasionally been suggested that there should be a special constitutional court, or a special constitutional panel of the present Court, to decide constitutional cases. This suggestion has already been discussed in chapter 5, Federalism.[127] One version of this suggestion is premised on a dualist view of Canada, under which constitutional issues should be determined by a tribunal upon which French Canada has an equal voice with English Canada. As noted earlier, this is a dubious proposition having regard to the range and variety of constitutional issues which have as much or more impact on provinces other than Quebec. The dualist view of Canada also fails to reflect the actual composition of the Canadian population, which includes aboriginal people as well as those of neither English nor French

---

126 Note however that there are courts of last resort with more than nine judges, e.g., India, Japan, International Court of Justice. However, they tend to sit in panels rather than as a full court. See McWhinney, *Supreme Courts and Judicial Law-Making* (1986) 34-41.

127 Section 5.5(c), ''Alternatives to judicial review'', above.

heritage. To the extent that the proposal for a constitutional court is premised on the desire to assemble a broader range of talented individuals (not necessarily lawyers) to decide constitutional cases, it involves the risk of creating an active policy-making body which is not amenable to any of the processes of democratic accountability. And, as a technical matter, there is good reason not to try to decide constitutional issues in isolation from the other elements of a justiciable controversy, which supply the context and colour and are in my view indispensable to wise constitutional decision-making. My conclusion is that judicial review should continue to be the function of the same Supreme Court of Canada that serves as a general court of appeal for Canada.

9

Responsible Government

9.1 History

By 1832, the colonies of British North America had achieved representative government,[1] but they had not achieved responsible government. The government of each colony was ''representative'', because it included a legislative assembly

1 British Columbia was an exception. As related in ch. 2, Reception, British Columbia did not acquire a fully elective assembly until 1871. That chapter describes the establishment of assemblies in all the other colonies, the last being Newfoundland in 1832.

elected by the people of the colony. The assembly had the power to make laws, to raise taxes, and to grant supply (money) to the executive. But colonial government was not "responsible", because the executive was not responsible to the assembly. Executive power was possessed by the British-appointed governor, who was responsible to the Colonial Office of the United Kingdom government, which had appointed him, instructed him, and continued to supervise his work. The governor also received advice from a local executive council whom he appointed, but the members of the executive council in each province were drawn from a wealthy elite who not only lacked the confidence of the assembly but who often actively opposed the policies determined upon by the assembly. This meant that laws enacted by the assembly would often not be enforced; policies opposed by the assembly would often be implemented; civil servants regarded as unsuitable or incompetent by the assembly would often be appointed; and colonial revenues which did not come from taxes would often be spent for purposes of which the assembly disapproved.

In every colony, there was chronic conflict between the assembly and the governor (and his executive council). In Upper and Lower Canada, these frustrations led to armed rebellions in 1837. After the rebellions, Lord Durham was appointed governor of all the British North American colonies with instructions to report upon the causes of and remedies for the colonial discontent. Lord Durham reported in 1839.[2] He accurately identified the causes of conflict between assembly and executive, and he recommended the institution of responsible government: in Durham's view, the Colonial Office should instruct each governor to appoint to his executive council only persons who enjoyed the confidence of a majority of the assembly. This recommendation simply applied to the colonies the same system that had recently evolved in the United Kingdom to reconcile the powers of the representative Parliament and the hereditary King.[3] In the colonies, however, there was a further complication. How could the governor obey instructions from the Colonial Office in London as well as following the advice of his local executive council? Durham's solution was to distinguish between matters of imperial concern and matters of local concern. The only matters of imperial concern, he submitted, were constitutional arrangements, foreign affairs, external trade, and the disposal of public lands. On these matters, the governor would act

2 Lord Durham's Report (1839) has been published in an edited version by McClelland and Stewart: Craig (ed.), *Lord Durham's Report* (1963).

3 Lederman, *Continuing Canadian Constitutional Dilemmas* (1981), 50-51, notes that the thirteen American colonies, forming their new government in 1789 before responsible government had developed in the United Kingdom (the development was not complete until around the time of Lord Durham's report), created a President whose relationship to the Congress was similar to that of George III in relation to the British Parliament. Once a President has been elected, for his four-year term he possesses executive power independent of the Congress. Conflict between the legislative and executive branches is therefore a characteristic of the American Constitution to this day. The Americans thus froze this aspect of the constitutional arrangements of 1789, which in the United Kingdom continued to evolve into a new system of responsible government.

on the instructions of the Colonial Office. On all other matters, the governor would act on the advice of his local executive council.

At first, the government of the United Kingdom would not accept Lord Durham's wise recommendation (although it readily accepted his foolish plan for the union of Upper and Lower Canada).[4] But in 1846 a new Colonial Secretary, Earl Grey, did accept the recommendation and instructed the governors along the lines indicated by Lord Durham. In 1848 the new system was put to the test in Nova Scotia, when after a general election the assembly carried a vote of no confidence in the executive council. The council resigned and the governor appointed the leader of the majority party in the assembly to be premier with power to name the other members of the new council — all in accordance with the conventions of responsible government. Changes of government occurred in the same way in the united province of Canada and in New Brunswick also in 1848, in Prince Edward Island in 1851, and in Newfoundland in 1855. Responsible government was thus achieved in those provinces. British Columbia did not achieve responsible government until 1872, a year after its admission to Canada. Manitoba (created in 1870), Alberta (created in 1905) and Saskatchewan (also created in 1905) were each granted responsible government at the time of their creation.[5]

9.2 Law and convention

In a system of "responsible government" (or cabinet or parliamentary government, as it may also be called)[6] the formal head of state, whether King (or Queen), Governor General or Lieutenant Governor, must always act under the "advice" (meaning direction) of ministers who are members of the legislative branch and who enjoy the confidence of a majority in the elected house of the legislative branch. Responsible government is probably the most important non-federal characteristic of the Canadian Constitution. Yet the rules which govern it are almost entirely "conventional", that is to say, they are not to be found in the ordinary legal sources of statute or decided cases.[7]

As noted in the previous section of this chapter, responsible government had been achieved in each of the uniting colonies at the time of confederation in 1867.

4 See ch. 2, Reception, under heading 2.2(c), "Amendment of received laws", above.

5 See Dawson, *The Government of Canada* (5th ed., 1970), ch. 1 (not in 6th ed.). Some of the history of the provincial governments is also described in ch. 2, Reception, above.

6 See Dawson, *The Government of Canada* (6th ed., 1987 by Ward), chs. 9, 10; Mallory, *The Structure of Canadian Government* (rev. ed., 1984), chs. 1-3; de Smith and Brazier, *Constitutional and Administrative Law* (6th ed., 1989), Part 2; Forsey, *Freedom and Order* (1974), Parts 1, 2; Cheffins and Johnson, *The Revised Canadian Constitution* (1986), ch. 6; Beaudoin, *La Constitution du Canada* (1990), ch. 2.

7 Conventions and their role in the Constitution are discussed in sec. 1.10, "Conventions", above.

The intention to continue the same system after confederation was evidenced by the assertion in the preamble to the Constitution Act, 1867 that Canada was to have "a constitution similar in principle to that of the United Kingdom". Other than this vague reference, however, the Constitution Act is silent on responsible government; it confers powers on the Queen and the Governor General but makes no mention of the Prime Minister or the cabinet. Thus, s. 9 provides that the "executive government" of Canada is vested in "the Queen"; s. 10 contemplates that the Queen's powers may be exercised by a "Governor General"; and s. 11 establishes a "Queen's Privy Council for Canada" whose function is "to aid and advise in the government of Canada" and whose members are to be appointed and removed by the Governor General. The Governor General is also an essential part of the legislative branch in that a "bill" which has been enacted by both Houses of Parliament passes into law (and becomes a "statute") only after the Governor General (or the Queen) has given the royal assent to the bill (ss. 17, 55). In addition, the Governor General is given power to appoint the members of the appointed upper house, the Senate (s. 24), to summon into session the members of the elective lower house, the House of Commons (s. 38), to dissolve the House of Commons (s. 50), to withhold the royal assent from a bill passed by both Houses of Parliament or to "reserve" the bill "for the signification of the Queen's pleasure" (s. 55). The Queen herself has a discretion whether or not to assent to a bill reserved by the Governor General (s. 57), and she has the further power to "disallow" (annul) any statute enacted by the Canadian Parliament (s. 56).[8]

In each province, there is a "Lieutenant Governor" and an "Executive Council" with powers similar to those of the Governor General and Privy Council (ss. 58-68, 90). The Lieutenant Governors are appointed by the Governor General in Council (s. 58),[9] and it is the Governor General (rather than the Queen) to

8 Reservation and disallowance of federal statutes have been nullified by convention: see ch. 3, Independence, under heading 3.1, "Bonds of Empire", above.

9 The fact that the Lieutenant Governor is to be appointed by the Governor General (the federal government) led to early controversy as to whether he was a representative of the Crown or of the federal government. The issue was important because if the Lieutenant Governor were not the representative of the Crown then the provincial government would not be entitled to the executive powers and prerogatives of the Crown; all executive powers and prerogatives would rest with the central government, unless specifically delegated to the provinces. In *Liquidators of Maritime Bank* v. *Receiver General of N.B.* [1892] A.C. 437 the Privy Council, speaking through Lord Watson, emphatically rejected the view that the Lieutenant Governors (and their provincial governments) were subordinate to the Governor General (and his federal government): "a Lieutenant-Governor, when appointed, is as much the representative of Her Majesty for all purposes of provincial government as the Governor-General himself is for all purposes of Dominion government" (p. 443). It followed that the federal distribution of legislative power entailed a matching distribution of executive powers and prerogatives as well: see also *Bonanza Creek Gold Mining Co.* v. *The King* [1916] 1 A.C. 566. In the early years of confederation the Lieutenant Governors did also fulfil a secondary role as federal officers, but this has fallen into disuse: Hendry, *Memorandum on the Office of Lieutenant-Governor of a Province* (1955); Saywell, *The Office of Lieutenant-Governor* (1957), chs. 1, 7. For analysis of the significance

whom a Lieutenant Governor reserves a provincial bill; and it is the Governor General in Council (rather than the Queen in Council) in whom is vested the power of disallowance of a provincial statute (s. 90).[10] There are other provisions of the Constitution Act, 1867 which confer specific powers on the Governor General or the Lieutenant Governors. Furthermore, the statute books will reveal that the Canadian Parliament and provincial Legislatures to this day usually confer major powers of government upon the Governor General in Council or the Lieutenant Governor in Council.

The Constitution Act, 1867 also tells us that Canada is a monarchy, that is to say, the formal head of state is the Queen (s. 9). The Queen has in fact delegated all of her powers over Canada[11] to the Canadian Governor General, except of course for the power to appoint or dismiss the Governor General.[12] Moreover, most powers of government, whether conferred by the Constitution or by ordinary statute, are conferred upon the Governor General (or the Governor General in Council) directly. It is therefore simpler, and sufficiently accurate for most purposes, to speak of the Governor General being the formal head of state.[13] He or she is appointed by the Queen, and in colonial times of course the Queen acted

---

of these decisions, see Birks, ''The Survival of the Crown in the Canadian State'' (LL.M. thesis, Osgoode Hall Law School, York University, 1980).

10 Reservation and disallowance of provincial statutes have probably been nullified by convention: see ch. 5, Federalism, under heading 5.3(c), ''Judicial interpretation of the distribution of powers'', above.

11 An exception may be the power to appoint additional senators under s. 26 of the Constitution Act, 1867, which by referring to both the Governor General and the Queen perhaps implies a continuing non-delegable role for the Queen, to be exercised however only on the advice of Canadian ministers. When this power was exercised in 1990 (for the first time in Canadian history), a direction from the Queen was in fact obtained: see cases referred to in note 37, below.

12 Letters Patent constituting the office of Governor General of Canada (1947), R.S.C. 1985, Appendix II, No. 31, art. II; Mallory, *The Structure of Canadian Government* (rev. ed., 1984), 21, 37-39. As Mallory explains, a few powers are still in practice exercised by the Queen, but the delegation is complete so that they could be exercised by the Governor General. Needless to say, those powers which are conferred by the Constitution or by statute upon the Governor General directly do not require any delegation from the Queen for their exercise. Article VIII of the Letters Patent provides that the office devolves upon the Chief Justice of Canada ''in the event of the death, incapacity, removal, or absence of Our Governor General out of Canada''; and upon ''the senior judge for the time being of the Supreme Court of Canada'' in the event of ''the death, incapacity, removal or absence out of Canada of Our Chief Justice''; while the powers are vested in the Chief Justice or senior judge he is ''to be known as Our Administrator''.

13 Within each province the office of Lieutenant Governor is equivalent to that of Governor General of Canada (see note 9, above); to that extent the Letters Patent constituting the office of Governor General (1947) (see previous note) are misleading in their delegation of ''all powers and authorities'' to the Governor General. There is no provision in the Constitution Act, 1867 (or elsewhere) for an acting Lieutenant Governor in the event of the death or incapacity of the Lieutenant Governor; this means that government business requiring the imprimatur of the Lieutenant Governor, for example, new statutes and orders in council, has to await the appointment by the federal government of a replacement.

on the advice of her British ministers in making the appointment. However, the imperial conference of 1926 declared that the Governor General was not the "representative or agent" of the British government, and the imperial conference of 1930 resolved that thenceforth the Governor General would be appointed by the Queen acting on the advice of the ministers of the dominion concerned.[14] Since 1930, all Canadian Governors General have been selected by the Canadian Prime Minister with the Queen merely formalizing the appointment.[15] It is also the Canadian Prime Minister who determines the Governor General's term of office, and the Canadian Parliament that fixes the salary.[16]

The Governor General does not use any personal initiative or discretion in the exercise of the powers of government that belongs to the office, except for certain "reserve powers" or "personal prerogatives", which are exercisable only in exceptional circumstances, and which are discussed later in this chapter. The effect of responsible government is to transfer effective political power to elected officials.

9.3 The executive branch

(a) The ministry

What precisely are the conventions of responsible government? For convenience of exposition, I shall concentrate on Canada's federal government, but the rules are much the same in each of the provinces (and indeed in all those jurisdictions outside Canada whose governments are responsible in the technical

---

14 On the imperial conferences of 1926 and 1930, see ch. 3, Independence, above. No comparable convention has been established with respect to the appointment of Lieutenant Governors. Under s. 58 of the Constitution Act, 1867, such appointments are to be made by the Governor General in Council; this power is exercised on the advice of the federal Prime Minister (notes 15, 26, below) not the provincial Premier. This means that the appointee will often be a member of the political party in power in Ottawa, and the provincial Premier may not even be consulted, especially if he is not a member of that party: Saywell, *The Office of Lieutenant-Governor* (1957), ch. 1; MacKinnon, *The Government of Prince Edward Island* (1951), 144-149; Donnelly, *The Government of Manitoba* (1963), 115-116; Forsey, *Freedom and Order* (1974), 161-164. In Australia, the state governors are appointed on the advice of the state governments, not the federal government.

15 By convention the advice is tendered by the Prime Minister, and the decision is his alone, although no doubt he would usually consult his cabinet: Mallory, *The Structure of Canadian Government* (rev. ed., 1984), 93. Similarly, by convention it is the Prime Minister who tenders advice as to the appointment of Lieutenant Governors: Saywell, *The Office of Lieutenant-Governor* (1957), 24.

16 Constitution Act, 1867, s. 105, confers the power to fix the salary, but the Act is silent with respect to appointment and tenure.

sense).[17] Where there is any significant variation in provincial practice, that fact will be noted.

The narrative must start with an exercise by the Governor General of one of the exceptional reserve powers or personal prerogatives. In the formation of a government it is the Governor General's duty to select the Prime Minister. The Governor General must select a person who can form a government which will enjoy the confidence of the House of Commons. For reasons that will be explained later, the Governor General rarely has any real choice as to whom to appoint: he or she must appoint the parliamentary leader of the political party that has a majority of seats in the House of Commons. But it is still accurate to describe the Governor General's discretion as his or her own, because, unlike nearly all of his or her other decisions, it is not made upon ministerial advice.

When the Prime Minister has been appointed, he selects the other ministers, and advises the Governor General to appoint them. With respect to these appointments, the Governor General reverts to his or her normal non-discretionary role and is obliged by convention to make the appointments advised by the Prime Minister. If the Prime Minister later wishes to make changes in the ministry, as by moving a minister from one portfolio to another, or by appointing a new minister, or by removing a minister, then the Governor General will take whatever action is advised by the Prime Minister, including if necessary the dismissal of a minister who has refused the Prime Minister's request to resign.

It is basic to the system of responsible government that the Prime Minister and all the other ministers be members of Parliament.[18] Occasionally a person who is not a member of Parliament is appointed as a minister, but then the minister must quickly be elected to the House of Commons or appointed to the Senate. If the minister fails to win election, and is not appointed to the Senate, then he or she must resign (or be dismissed) from the ministry. The usual practice when a non-member of Parliament is appointed to the ministry is that a member of the Prime Minister's political party will be induced to resign from a ''safe seat'' in Parliament, which will precipitate a by-election in which the minister will be the candidate from the Prime Minister's party.

---

17 For the provinces, see MacKinnon, *The Government of Prince Edward Island* (1951); Beck, *The Government of Nova Scotia* (1957); Saywell, *The Office of Lieutenant-Governor* (1957); Donnelly, *The Government of Manitoba* (1963); Schindeler, *Responsible Government in Ontario* (1969); Bellamy, Pammett, Rowat (eds.), *The Provincial Political Systems* (1976), esp. ch. 20 (by Saywell).

18 The responsibility to Parliament of each minister is explained in sec. 9.3(d), ''Ministerial responsibility'', below. Note that the term ''deputy minister'' is used in Canada to describe the permanent head of a government department, who is of course a civil servant and not a member of Parliament. In Australia, New Zealand or the United Kingdom any title including the word ''minister'' would imply a parliamentary appointee.

(b) The cabinet and the Privy Council

When the ministers meet together as a group they constitute the cabinet.[19] The cabinet is not mentioned in the Constitution Act, 1867, although we have already noticed that a body called the Queen's Privy Council for Canada is established by s. 11.[20] The cabinet ministers are all appointed to the Queen's Privy Council for Canada. But the Privy Council includes many other people as well.[21] Appointments to the Privy Council are for life, so that its membership always includes not only the ministers of the government in office, but also all living persons who were ministers in past governments. Moreover, appointments to the Privy Council are often made to persons of distinction as an honour, so that its membership will include such persons as the Duke of Edinburgh, the Prince of Wales, a British Prime Minister, a Canadian High Commissioner, or a provincial Premier; and of course such honorific appointments will be for life. The whole Privy Council would be a body of some one hundred members of widely differing political persuasions. Such a body could not, and does not, conduct the business of government. The whole Privy Council meets very rarely, and then only for ceremonial occasions.[22]

The cabinet, which does meet regularly and frequently, is in most matters the supreme executive authority. (The "reserve powers" remain in the Governor General, and some powers are vested in the Prime Minister; these powers are discussed later.) The cabinet formulates and carries out all executive policies, and it is responsible for the administration of all the departments of government. It constitutes the only active part of the Privy Council, and it exercises the powers of that body. The Governor General does not preside over, or even attend, the meetings of the cabinet.[23] The Prime Minister presides. Where the Constitution or a statute requires that a decision be made by the "Governor General in Council" (and this requirement is very common indeed), there is still no meeting with the

19 The ministry and the cabinet are not necessarily identical. In the United Kingdom and Australia, for example, not all ministers are members of cabinet. Whether a particular minister is admitted to the cabinet lies in the discretion of the Prime Minister. The usual Canadian practice has been for the Prime Minister to admit all ministers to the cabinet: Dawson, *The Government of Canada* (6th ed., 1987 by Ward), 196; and this has been the general practice of the provincial Premiers as well.

20 Canada's Privy Council is of course modelled on the Privy Council in the United Kingdom, which is a body under the formal duty of advising the Queen as to the government of the United Kingdom. The United Kingdom's Privy Council used to have considerable significance for Canada in that its Judicial Committee was the final court of appeal for Canadian law-suits. The appeal to the Judicial Committee was abolished in 1949.

21 This is not true in the provinces, where the membership of the executive council and the cabinet is identical.

22 The last occasion was on April 17, 1982, when the Queen proclaimed into force the Constitution Act, 1982.

23 In the provinces, too, the Lieutenant Governor never presides over or attends meetings of the cabinet: Saywell, *The Office of Lieutenant-Governor* (1957), 35-36.

Governor General. The cabinet (or a cabinet committee to which routine Privy Council business has been delegated) will make the decision, and send an "order" or "minute" of the decision to the Governor General for signature (which by convention is automatically given).[24] Where a statute requires that a decision be made by a particular minister, then the cabinet will make the decision, and the relevant minister will formally authenticate the decision. Of course a cabinet will be content to delegate many matters to individual ministers, but each minister recognizes the supreme authority of the cabinet should the cabinet seek to exercise it.

(c) The Prime Minister

While in most matters the cabinet is the supreme executive authority, the Prime Minister (or provincial Premier)[25] has certain powers which he or she does not need to share with his or her colleagues.[26] Two of these are of great importance. First, there is the power to select the other ministers, and the power to promote, demote or dismiss them at pleasure. (Technically, of course, the Prime Minister only has power to recommend such measures to the Governor General, but the recommendations will invariably be acted upon.) Secondly, the Prime Minister is personally responsible for tendering advice to the Governor General as to when Parliament should be dissolved for an election, and when an elected Parliament should be summoned into session.[27]

Not only are these powers important in their own right, but the Prime Minister's possession of them also ensures that the Prime Minister's voice will be the most influential one within the cabinet. In addition, the Prime Minister enjoys the special authority which derives from having been selected by a political party as its leader, and from having led the party to victory in the previous election. Modern Canadian election campaigns have increasingly emphasized the qualities of the competing leaders, and this practice inevitably strengthens the position within the

---

24 Mallory, note 12, above, 74-75.

25 On the office of Prime Minister, see generally Hockin (ed.), *Apex of Power* (2nd ed., 1977).

26 Privy Council minute, P.C. 3374, October 25, 1935 provides:

> the following recommendations are the special prerogative of the prime minister: dissolution and convocation of Parliament: Appointment of — privy councillors; cabinet ministers; lieutenant governors (including leave of absence to same); provincial administrators, speaker of the Senate; Chief Justices of all courts, senators, sub-committees of council; Treasury Board; . . .

Not included in this list is the recommendation to the Queen for appointment of a Governor General, which is another power that, by convention, the Prime Minister may exercise independently of the other ministers.

27 These important powers are limited by the Constitution Act, 1982, s. 4 of which prescribes a maximum duration for the House of Commons or a provincial legislative assembly of five years, and s. 5 of which requires that there be a sitting of Parliament and of each Legislature at least once every twelve months. See also ss. 50 and 86 of the Constitution Act, 1867.

party of the leader of the victorious party. No doubt the extent of a Prime Minister's personal power varies from government to government, depending upon a number of factors. But in some governments a Prime Minister, who chooses to take on his own initiative, or on the advice of a few ministers, decisions which would traditionally be the preserve of the cabinet, is politically able to do so; and the extent to which the full cabinet plays a role in important decision-making may depend in large measure upon the discretion of the Prime Minister. In this connection it is important to notice that the Prime Minister calls the meetings of cabinet, settles the agenda, and presides over the meetings.[28]

(d) Ministerial responsibility

There is a minister at the head of each of the departments of government. Most of the cabinet ministers have charge of at least one department. (There are usually one or more ministers without portfolio who are members of the cabinet, but who do not have charge of a department.) Each minister who does have charge of a department has the administrative duties that go with such an office. In addition, the minister "represents" his or her department in Parliament: the minister pilots the departmental estimates of proposed expenditures through the House, explains and defends the policies and practices of the department, and introduces into Parliament any bills that relate to the work of the department.[29]

A government department is, of course, administered by civil servants, who, in contrast to the minister, are supposed to be politically neutral. The senior civil servant in each department, who in Canada is usually called a "deputy minister", is the link between the minister and the civil servants. The deputy minister acts both as an adviser to the minister and as the senior manager of the department. Of course, the minister is under no obligation to follow the advice of the deputy minister. The deputy minister is within the tradition of civil service neutrality: when the government changes, the deputy minister, like other career civil servants, will usually retain his or her position. However, the deputy minister is not appointed by normal civil service procedures: the appointment is made by order in

28 Criticism of the "imperial presidency" occasionally conveys the impression that the President of the United States is a more powerful figure within the American presidential system of government than is the Prime Minister (or provincial Premier) within a system of responsible government. This is incorrect. In a normal situation of majority government, the Prime Minister's leadership of the majority party in the House of Commons, reinforced by strict party discipline, and sanctioned by his power to dissolve the House, leads to a concentration of power in the hands of the Prime Minister that has no counterpart in the presidential (or gubernatorial) system.

29 In addition to one or more departments, a minister will often have a number of Crown corporations and regulatory agencies assigned to his or her ministry. These bodies are outside the departmental structure because they are intended to operate with more autonomy than a government department. However, because they are publicly funded, they have to be subjected to some degree of ministerial control; the mechanisms of that control differ greatly from one body to another.

council on the recommendation of the Prime Minister. The appointment is normally made from within the ranks of the career civil service, and is not treated as political patronage. Nevertheless, occasionally a particular deputy minister is perceived as too closely associated with the party in power, in which case he or she will be replaced when a new government takes office.

One aspect of the political neutrality of civil servants is the convention that they are anonymous in the sense that they should not be criticized personally or otherwise held accountable in Parliament. All the acts of the department are done in the name of the minister, and it is the minister who is responsible to Parliament for those acts. In this context, the word "responsible" is often said to entail two consequences. First, the minister is supposed to explain to Parliament, when asked, the actions of his or her department. This is a real responsibility, in that a minister will be frequently called upon by other members of Parliament to answer questions about the work of the department. Secondly, the minister is supposed to resign if a serious case of maladministration occurs within the department. This second aspect of ministerial responsibility is often asserted to exist, but is of much more doubtful strength. In a case of misconduct or serious maladministration by a minister personally, the principle would certainly apply and would require the resignation of the minister. In a case of misconduct or maladministration by a civil servant in the minister's department, a ministerial resignation is quite unlikely to follow in Canada. Accordingly, it may be more realistic (and therefore accurate) to define ministerial responsibility as not including an obligation to resign for merely departmental sins, although such resignations are often called for by the opposition and do occasionally occur.[30]

The notion of the responsibility of individual ministers is related to, but distinct from, the notion of the "collective responsibility" of the cabinet as a whole. All cabinet ministers collectively accept responsibility for cabinet decisions. This means that a cabinet minister is obliged to give public support to any decision reached by the cabinet, even if the minister personally opposed the decision within the cabinet and still disagrees with it. If the minister does decide to express dissent in public, then the minister should resign; and, if the minister does not resign, he or she can expect to be dismissed by the Prime Minister (although the Prime Minister might decide to tolerate the offence). Even after resignation or dismissal the obligation of unanimity is supposed to continue, but the Prime Minister will normally give permission to the minister to publish his or her reasons for resignation.

---

30 There is no personal *legal* responsibility on the part of a minister for torts or crimes committed by civil servants within a minister's department. In tort, vicarious liability for the acts of civil servants attaches to the Crown, which is the employer, not to individual ministers: *Bainbridge* v. *Postmaster-General* [1906] 1 K.B. 178 (C.A.) (minister not liable for torts committed by subordinates). In criminal law, there is no general doctrine of vicarious liability: *Bhatnager* v. *Can.* [1990] 2 S.C.R. 217 (ministers not liable for contempt of court order of which they were unaware).

Collective responsibility implies more than cabinet solidarity. Its most fundamental consequence is that if a cabinet decision is attacked in Parliament the issue is one of confidence in the government. As will be explained later in this chapter, if a government is defeated in the House of Commons[31] on an issue of confidence in the government, then the government must either resign or advise the Governor General to dissolve the House for an election. Consequently, the government will insist that its supporters in the House vote on party lines in favour of the government. Since the government is in office because it commands a majority of the members of the House, it is normally in a position to resist any opposition attack on its policies. The vigour of the doctrine of collective responsibility is what undermines the doctrine of individual responsibility. If a ministerial decision has been approved or ratified by the cabinet, then the individual minister will be protected by collective responsibility. More bluntly, one must acknowledge that if the government does not want a minister to resign, then no matter how clearly the facts would seem to warrant the minister's resignation, there is no way that the opposition can force it to happen.

9.4 The legislative branch

(a) The Parliament

The legislative power of the federal government is vested in the Parliament of Canada, which consists (in the language of s. 17 of the Constitution Act, 1867) "of the Queen, an upper house styled the Senate, and the House of Commons". There are thus three elements which must combine for passage of legislation and the cabinet is not one of them. Nevertheless the cabinet is able to control the legislative process. In order to see why this is so, let us examine separately each element of the process.

(b) The House of Commons

The House of Commons is a body which is elected on the basis of universal adult suffrage. As such it is representative of most shades of Canadian opinion.[32] But the Prime Minister and his cabinet (the government) are in office solely because they have the support of a majority of members in the House of Commons. In normal circumstances this support is unwavering and is available for every measure proposed by the government. Canada's political parties insist

31 The responsibility of the government and of individual ministers is to the elective lower house, and not to the Senate. A defeat in the Senate does not entail resignation or dissolution. For this reason only a few cabinet members are drawn from the Senate.

32 Note, however, the controversies about the merits of different electoral systems: Irvine, *Does Canada Need a New Electoral System?* (1979).

upon strict party discipline from their parliamentary members. Party discipline is effective to the point that each member of the government party can nearly always be relied upon to support all government measures. Very rarely does an issue arise which so divides the government party that any members will vote against the government. When that happens the combined votes of the opposition parties and the government defectors may defeat the government.

A more common situation in which the government may lose the support of a majority in the House of Commons is after a close election has given neither of the two major parties a majority in the House of Commons, and the control of the House depends upon one of the major parties being able to secure the cooperation of one of the minor parties. Here the cabinet's control is much more precarious, and the minor party can bring about the defeat of the government whenever it chooses. Sometimes this situation of "minority government" can be stabilized by the major party entering into coalition with the minor party and admitting its leaders to the cabinet. Coalition governments have not been uncommon in the provinces, and in countries outside Canada, but the Canadian federal government's only experience of this kind was the "union government" which was formed during the first world war. In recent years there have been frequent minority governments in which either the Progressive Conservative Party or the Liberal Party has had to depend upon the support of a third party,[33] but there does not seem to have been any serious consideration of coalition.[34] However, even a minority government is able to exercise very substantial control over the legislative process. The minor party is inhibited from voting against the government by the fact that, for reasons given later, a vote against the government is almost certain to force a new general election. An election is always expensive and exhausting and is not to be lightly precipitated, especially as a minor party which has overturned a government without a very good reason is almost certain to lose votes and seats.[35] On the whole then it is a fair generalization to say that all measures proposed by the cabinet are assured of passage through the House of Commons.

---

33 There have been six federal minority governments: (1) 1921-22, 1923-24 and 1925-26 (King); (2) 1926 (Meighen); (3) 1957-58 and 1962-63 (Diefenbaker); (4) 1963-68 (Pearson); (5) 1972-74 (Trudeau); (6) 1979-80 (Clark).

34 In Ontario in 1985, after an inconclusive election (Progressive Conservative Party (government) 52; Liberal Party 48; New Democratic Party 25), the two leaders of the opposition parties entered into a written, published agreement intended to give a minority Liberal government a secure term of two years: Globe and Mail newspaper, May 29, 1985. They then defeated the Progressive Conservative government in a confidence vote in the Legislature, and the Lieutenant Governor commissioned the Liberal leader, Mr. Peterson, to form the government. The agreement did not create a coalition, because the N.D.P. remained outside the cabinet. The Liberal minority government survived until 1987, when Premier Peterson advised dissolution, and in the ensuing election won a Liberal majority.

35 Federal governments have only been defeated by a withdrawal of the confidence of the House of Commons six times since Confederation, namely, 1873 (Macdonald), 1926 (King), 1926 (Meighen), 1963 (Diefenbaker), 1974 (Trudeau) and 1979 (Clark).

(c) The Senate

The second element in the legislative process is the Senate.[36] Its members are appointed by the Governor General, which of course means, by convention, the cabinet. The Constitution Act, 1867, by s. 21, provides for a fixed number of senators and, by s. 29, provides that once appointed a senator holds office until age 75. Since each government tends to appoint its own supporters to the Senate, a government which has been in office for a long time will have a majority and sometimes an overwhelming majority of its own party members in the Senate. After a long-standing government loses an election the new government will be faced with a Senate which is still controlled by the opposition party, and it may be a long time before deaths, retirements and resignations enable the new government to redress the unhappy balance.[37] Even in this situation, however, the Senate has rarely refused passage of measures proposed by the government.[38] Although the Constitution Act, 1867 gives to the Senate the same powers as the House of Commons (except that, by s. 53, money bills must originate in the House of Commons), it has to be (and usually is) accepted by opposition as well as

---

36 None of the provinces now has an upper house, although Manitoba, New Brunswick, Nova Scotia, Prince Edward Island and Quebec each used to have one (a Legislative Council) and subsequently abolished it: Forsey, *Freedom and Order* (1974), 227.

37 The Constitution Act, 1867, by s. 26, authorizes the appointment "at any time" of four or eight additional senators (drawn equally from the four divisions: note 40, below) as a remedy for the obstruction of government measures by the Senate. But the numbers four or eight are too small to redress the substantial imbalances that are common, and so the section has only been used once. That occasion, in 1990, was when a government (the Progressive Conservative government of Prime Minister Mulroney) was faced with an opposition majority that (after six years of Progressive Conservative government) had been reduced to less than eight. In that rare situation, s. 26 was an effective measure, enabling the government to secure Senate passage of the Goods and Services Tax Bill. The use of s. 26 was unsuccessfully challenged in the courts: *Re Appointment of Senators* (1991) 78 D.L.R. (4th) 245 (B.C.C.A.); *Singh* v. *Can.* (1991) 3 O.R. (3d) 429 (C.A.); *Weir* v. *Can.* (1991) 84 D.L.R. (4th) 39 (N.B.C.A.).

38 For figures as to amendments and rejections of bills by the Senate, see MacKay, *The Unreformed Senate of Canada* (rev. ed., 1963), 199 (Appendix A); Kunz, *The Modern Senate of Canada 1925-1963* (1965), 378 (Appendix 1). The pattern of restraint was broken by the Liberal majority in the Senate after the election in 1984 of the Progressive Conservative government of Prime Minister Mulroney. The Senate opposed some major government measures. The Senate refused to ratify the Meech Lake Constitutional Accord in 1987, and had to be overridden by the House of Commons under s. 47 of the Constitution Act, 1982. The Senate actually precipitated the election on Free Trade in 1988 by refusing to enact the government's bill to implement the Free Trade Agreement with the United States. The government won the election, and the Senate then passed the Bill. In the government's second term, the Senate refused to pass the Goods and Services Tax Bill, but by then the Liberal majority had been reduced to the point that the appointment under s. 26 (previous note) of eight additional senators tipped the balance and enabled the Bill to pass just before the GST's planned start-up date of January 1, 1991. In 1991, despite the government's slender majority, the Senate defeated with a tied vote the government's Abortion Bill, which had been passed by the House of Commons, but on a free vote. Throughout this period of activism, senators tended to vote on party lines, regardless of the region or province from which they were appointed.

government senators that the appointive nature of the Senate must necessarily make its role subordinate to the elective House.[39]

The Senate was intended to serve as a protector of regional interests, which is a traditional function of the upper house in federal systems. Its membership was drawn equally from the three original regions (or ''divisions'', as the Constitution calls them) of Canada, namely, Ontario, Quebec and the maritime provinces. The west later became a fourth region.[40] The plan was to offset representation by population in the House of Commons with equality of regions in the Senate. With hindsight, it is obvious that this plan was fatally flawed, because the senators were to be appointed rather than elected, and appointed by the federal government rather than by provincial governments. In any event, the Senate has never been an effective voice of regional or provincial interests.

Whether it is now feasible to reform the Senate[41] so as to restore the original plan is doubtful. The difficulty is that in a system of responsible government the cabinet is responsible to the House of Commons, not the Senate. If government policy is defeated in the House of Commons, then the government must resign and make way, either for a new government that can command the support of the House of Commons, or for an election that will provide a new House of Commons. An upper house has no obvious place in this scheme of things. That is why in so many jurisdictions with parliamentary systems the upper house has been abolished or reduced to impotence. And that is why the assertions of independence by the Australian Senate that led to the dismissal of Prime Minister Whitlam in 1975

---

39 The Senate of the United States is able to function as a strong upper house, partly because it is an elected body, and also because the President is elected separately from the legislative branch for a fixed term of office: he is not dependent upon a majority in the Congress for his continuance in office. In Australia, where the Senate is also elected but the system is one of responsible government, the Senate's occasional bursts of independence (as in the denials of supply to Prime Minister Whitlam in 1974 and 1975, the latter leading to the Prime Minister's dismissal) have created almost unbearable political tensions: see note 42, below. A strong upper house is not compatible with responsible government.

40 The Senate consists of 104 senators: Constitution Act, 1867, s. 22. There are 24 senators from each of four divisions, namely: (1) Ontario; (2) Quebec; (3) the three maritime provinces; and (4) the four western provinces. On Newfoundland's entry to confederation in 1949, six senators were added to represent that province, and in 1975 the Yukon and Northwest Territories were each given one senator. Under s. 26, the number can be increased by either four or eight senators, drawn equally from the four divisions. This power was exercised in 1990 (for the first time in Canadian history) by the appointment of eight additional senators: note 37, above. This increased the number of senators to 112, but, under s. 27, the increase is temporary only, because after such a s. 26 increase, the first two vacancies in each division cannot be filled.

41 A federal proposal for reform was held to be outside the competence of the federal Parliament in *Re Upper House* [1980] 1 S.C.R. 54. Since the adoption of the Constitution Act, 1982, by virtue of s. 42(1)(b), any change in ''the powers of the Senate and the method of selecting senators'' requires the general (seven-fifty) amending procedure; by virtue of s. 44, lesser changes can be made by the federal Parliament alone.

were so bitterly controversial in that country.[42] A powerful upper house could block major government bills (as the Australian Senate did), could refuse to vote supply to the government (as the Australian Senate did), and could eventually bring the government down (as the Australian Senate did). The Australian experience should also provide a warning that a powerful upper house would be more likely to vote on party lines (as the Australian Senate does) than to ignore party discipline in order to protect the interests of regions or provinces.

The Charlottetown Accord of 1992[43] proposed the creation of a new Senate. Its members were to be elected, and each province was to be represented by an equal number of six senators. The new Senate, although elected, was not to be a confidence chamber, so that the defeat of a government in the Senate would not entail the resignation of the government or the dissolution of Parliament. The new Senate was to have no power to block revenue and expenditure bills, merely a 30-day power of delay. In the case of most other bills,[44] defeat or amendment by the Senate would trigger a joint sitting of the Senate and House of Commons, where the fate of the bill would be determined by majority vote. Since the House of Commons would be five times more numerous than the Senate, the government's majority in the House of Commons would normally exceed the opposition's majority in the Senate, in which case the government's bill would be passed at the joint sitting. In these ways, the supremacy of the House of Commons was to be preserved. The defeat of the Charlottetown Accord in the referendum of 1992 spelled the end of this proposal for reform of the Senate, and the much-maligned existing Senate obtained a new lease on life.

In Canada, with few exceptions,[45] the Senate has not been a major obstruction to important government policy, even when its majority has been controlled by the opposition. This is so although the Canadian Senate's powers are, in law, as ample as those of the Australian Senate. The restraint by the Canadian Senate is caused by its recognition that, as an appointed body, it has no political mandate to obstruct the elected House of Commons. The Australian Senate, as an elected body, is not subject to the same inhibitions. If the Canadian Senate were reformed, either by making its membership elected or by making its membership appointed by provincial governments, it would naturally want to make more use of its

42 Of the vast literature on the Australian crisis, reference may be made to Sawer, *Federation under Strain* (1977); Evans (ed.), *Labour and the Constitution 1972-1975* (1977); Kerr, *Matters for Judgment* (1978) (the Governor General's version); Whitlam, *The Truth of the Matter* (1979) (the Prime Minister's version); Barwick, *Sir John Did His Duty* (1984) (the Chief Justice's version).

43 Chapter 4, Amendment, under heading 4.1(c), ''The failure to accommodate Quebec'', above.

44 Bills materially affecting French language or culture were a special category, requiring a ''double majority'' in the Senate, that is, passage by a majority of French-speaking Senators as well as by an overall majority; the defeat or amendment of such bills by the Senate could not be overcome by a joint sitting. Bills taxing natural resources were another special category, in which defeat or amendment by the Senate could not be overcome by a joint sitting.

45 I assume that the attitude of the Liberal majority in the Senate from 1984 to 1990 (note 38, above) was exceptional and anomalous.

powers. Serious obstruction of the House of Commons could be avoided if limitations were imposed on the powers of a reformed upper house. But, to the extent that the powers of a reformed upper house are limited, so also is its capacity to assert effectively regional and provincial interests.[46]

(d) The Governor General

The Governor General, who must complete the legislative process by conferring the royal assent, plays no discretionary role whatever. It is true, of course, that the Constitution Act, 1867, by s. 55, gives the Governor General the power to withhold the royal assent from a bill which has been enacted by both Houses of Parliament, and the power to reserve a bill for the signification of the Queen's pleasure; and by s. 56 gives to the Queen the power to disallow a Canadian statute. But the imperial conference of 1930 resolved that the powers of reservation and disallowance must never be exercised.[47] This conference and the full acceptance of responsible government have established a convention that the Governor General must always give the royal assent to a bill which has passed both Houses of Parliament. There is no circumstance which would justify a refusal of assent,[48] or a reservation, or a British disallowance.[49]

(e) The cabinet

It will now be obvious that in a system of responsible government there is no ''separation of powers'' between the executive and legislative branches of government. The head of the executive branch, the cabinet, draws its personnel and its power to govern from the legislative branch, the Parliament; and the cabinet controls the Parliament.[50] This contrasts with the presidential form of government

---

46 Reform of the Senate, like reform of the Supreme Court of Canada, is a central tenet of ''intrastate federalism'', designed to make central institutions more responsive to the various regions and cultures of the country. Intrastate federalism is discussed in ch. 4, Amendment, under heading 4.8(c), ''Central institutions'', above.

47 See ch. 3, Independence, under heading 3.1, ''Bonds of Empire'', above.

48 There has never been a refusal of assent (as opposed to a reservation) by the Governor General: Mallory, *The Structure of Canadian Government* (rev. ed., 1984), 241-2; although there have been refusals by the Lieutenant Governors: MacKinnon, *The Government of Prince Edward Island* (1951), 154-155; Beck, *The Government of Nova Scotia* (1957), 181-182. Refusals of assent are, however, as MacKinnon comments (p. 164), ''clearly incompatible with the principles of responsible government''.

49 By s. 90 provincial legislation is also made subject to reservation and disallowance, but the power of reservation is in the Lieutenant Governor (instead of the Governor General) and the power of disallowance is in the Governor General (instead of the Queen). It is less clear whether these powers have been effectively nullified by convention: see ch. 5, Federalism, under heading 5.3(e) ''Disallowance'', above.

50 There is a famous quotation from Walter Bagehot, *The English Constitution* (1872), 14: ''A cabinet is a combining committee — a hyphen which joins, a buckle which fastens, the legislative part of the state to the executive part of the state''.

in the United States, which was established at a time when the separation of the executive, legislative and judicial powers of government was regarded by influential political theorists as the ideal constitution for the preservation of individual liberty.[51] The President of the United States is not a member of the Congress, nor are the members of his cabinet; he is often not a member of the party with the majority of members in the Congress; and he is never able to exercise control over the Congress.

In Canada, the legislative programme for each session of Parliament is planned by the cabinet, and announced at the beginning of the session in the speech from the throne which is delivered by the Governor General. The speech is written by the Prime Minister. The cabinet determines the order of business in the Parliament, and generally exercises close control over the proceedings. Nearly all bills which are subsequently enacted are ''government bills'', that is to say, bills which have been approved by cabinet and introduced by one of the ministers. The Constitution Act, 1867, by s. 54, requires that a ''money bill'' must be introduced in the House of Commons only after it has been ''first recommended to that House by message of the Governor General''. Needless to say, it is the cabinet which prepares the message, and a minister who transmits the message to the House and introduces the bill. Other bills can be introduced in either House and by any member of Parliament, but the cabinet uses its majority in the House of Commons to ensure that the bulk of the Parliament's time is devoted to consideration of the government's own legislative programme, and, except for ''private bills'',[52] it is only the measures which have been approved by the cabinet and introduced by a minister (''government bills'') which stand any real chance of passage.

9.5 Defeat of the government

(a) Withdrawal of confidence

Since the major premise of responsible government is that the cabinet (or ''government'' or ''administration'') enjoys the confidence of a majority in the

51 See Jennings, *The Law and the Constitution* (5th ed., 1959), ch. 1 and Appendix 1; de Smith and Brazier, *Constitutional and Administrative Law* (6th ed., 1989), 18-22. The independence, if not formal separation, of the judicial branch from the executive and legislative branches is, however, still generally regarded as essential to the impartial administration of justice both in the United States and in countries such as Canada which have inherited their non-federal constitutional law from the United Kingdom.

52 ''Private bills'', which relate to a particular person or institution, or a particular locality, are enacted by a different and simpler procedure, which does not require government sponsorship, and they are often enacted after introduction by a private member. Private bills should not be confused with ''private members' bills'', which are bills introduced by private members. They may be either public or private bills, but when they are public bills they stand little chance of passage.

House of Commons, it follows that a cabinet which has lost that confidence cannot indefinitely continue in office. This is the primary meaning of the "collective responsibility" of the cabinet to the House of Commons.

If the House of Commons passed a motion of no confidence in the government, that would be the clearest possible evidence that the government had lost the confidence of the House of Commons; but the defeat of the government on any important vote is usually regarded as a withdrawal of confidence.[53] Where the defeat is on a matter of little importance, the defeat would not need to be treated as a withdrawal of confidence. A more difficult case is where the defeat occurs on a major measure, but is the result of a "snap vote" which catches the government party with some of its supporters inadvertently absent from the House at the time of the vote. A snap vote led to the defeat in the House of Commons of a government measure in 1968, and the Pearson government decided not to treat it as a withdrawal of confidence. The government reinforced its decision and acknowledged the primacy of the House by subsequently securing the passage of a resolution to the effect that the prior defeat was not to be interpreted as a withdrawal of confidence in the government.[54]

(b) Dissolution of Parliament

When a government measure is defeated in the House of Commons, then, subject to the comments made in the previous paragraph, the House of Commons is deemed to have withdrawn its confidence from the government. There are then only two alternatives: either the government must resign to make way for a new cabinet which will command the confidence of the House, or the House must be dissolved to make way for an election which will produce a new House of Commons.

It is the dissolution of the House of Commons which is the course normally favoured by a Prime Minister whose government has been defeated in the House,

---

53 The rule did not used to be so strict. Many British and Canadian governments were defeated in the House of Commons last century without either resigning or advising dissolution. The reason was the looser party discipline and the number of independent members. The strict rule is more appropriate today where party discipline is tight and there are very few or no independent members. But minority government restores some of the fluidity of former times, and it may be sensible and constitutional for a minority government to follow the earlier precedents and revert to a laxer rule as to what amounts to a withdrawal of confidence in the government. This position is cogently argued by Forsey, *Freedom and Order* (1974), 114-116; and there are precedents accumulating in its favour, e.g., the defeat of the British government on March 10, 1976: (1976) 53 The Parliamentarian 174; the defeat of the Ontario government on June 15, 1976: the Globe and Mail, June 16, 1976 and June 17, 1976. In neither case did the minority government resign.

54 Dawson, *The Government of Canada* (6th ed., 1987 by Ward), 145. In the United Kingdom since 1945 there have been several government defeats on "snap votes"; the government has in each case "mustered its full resources and procured a reversal of the vote": de Smith and Brazier, *Constitutional and Administrative Law* (6th ed., 1989), 186.

and that is the course which he will normally advise the Governor General to take. In the event of a dissolution the Prime Minister and his ministers remain in office, despite the fact that they have lost the confidence of the House of Commons. The period between the dissolution of one House of Commons and the election of another may be as long as several months, but the government must remain in office and exercise its functions: the country cannot be left without any government at all. The ensuing election may produce a new House of Commons which the government is able to control. If that happens the government will continue in office without a break. Thus, while the Constitution imposes a maximum duration for the House of Commons of five years,[55] there is no maximum duration for any particular government and most Canadian governments have lasted for longer than five years. It is the hope of continuance in office which makes dissolution a more attractive alternative than resignation for the government which has lost the confidence of the House of Commons.

As we shall see later in this chapter, it is probable that the Governor General has a reserve power to refuse to grant a dissolution to a Prime Minister whose government has lost the confidence of the House of Commons, but this has happened only once this century in Canada — in 1926. If a dissolution were refused, the Prime Minister whose government had lost the confidence of the House of Commons would have to resign, or be dismissed by the Governor General; and the resignation or dismissal of a Prime Minister involves the resignation or dismissal of the entire ministry.

(c) Resignation or dismissal

If a Prime Minister whose government has lost the support of the House of Commons does resign (whether voluntarily or because a dissolution has been refused by the Governor General), or is dismissed from office by the Governor General, then the Governor General would have to find a member of parliament who could become Prime Minister and form a government which would enjoy the confidence of the House. In selecting a new Prime Minister, as we have already noticed, the Governor General is entitled to exercise a personal discretion.[56]

9.6 The Governor General's personal prerogatives

(a) The principle

The Governor General has certain "personal prerogatives" or "reserve powers" which he or she may exercise upon his or her own personal discre-

---

55 Constitution Act, 1867, s. 50; Constitution Act, 1982, s. 4.

56 The narrow scope of the "discretion" is explained in the next section of this chapter.

tion.[57] Whereas in the exercise of governmental powers generally the Governor General must act in accordance with the advice of the Prime Minister or cabinet, there are some occasions on which he or she may act without advice, or even contrary to advice.

The definition of those occasions when the Governor General may exercise an independent discretion has caused much constitutional and political debate. But it is submitted that the basic premise of responsible government supplies the answer: so long as the cabinet enjoys the confidence of a majority in the House of Commons, the Governor General is always obliged to follow lawful and constitutional advice which is tendered by the cabinet. But there are occasions, as we have seen, when a government continues in office after it has lost the confidence of the House of Commons, or after the House of Commons has been dissolved. There are also occasions, for example, after a very close election, or after a schism in a political party, where for a period it is difficult to determine whether or not the government does enjoy the confidence of a majority in the House of Commons. In all these situations it is submitted that the Governor General has a discretion to refuse to follow advice which is tendered by the ministry in office.

When a government is in office without the support of the House of Commons, there are the makings of a constitutional crisis: not only can the government not secure the passage of any legislation, it cannot even secure parliamentary approval of supply to meet government expenditures. The crisis can be resolved or averted by a new election or by the resignation or dismissal of the ministry. But the ministry in office, which lacks the support of the House of Commons and which stands to lose most by the resolution of the crisis, is not the fittest group to determine the mode of resolution of the crisis. It is true of course that the Governor General has even less of a political base than the ministry in office, but it is for this very reason that the Governor General may reasonably be trusted to set aside partisan considerations and act impartially in the interests of the country as a whole. In this situation the role of Governor General is somewhat akin to that of a judge — another non-elected official to whom we readily entrust large powers in the expectation that they will be exercised impartially.

(b) Appointment of Prime Minister

Perhaps the clearest and least controversial of the Governor General's reserve powers or personal prerogatives is the power to select a Prime Minister.[58] This power has to be exercised whenever a Prime Minister resigns. The resignation of

57 There are two major studies of the reserve powers: Evatt, *The King and His Dominion Governors* (2nd ed., 1967) and Forsey, *The Royal Power of Dissolution of Parliament in the British Commonwealth* (1943, reprinted with new preface, 1968).

58 On the selection of provincial Premiers, see Saywell, *The Office of Lieutenant-Governor* (1957), ch. 4.

the Prime Minister (unless it is a personal retirement) automatically vacates all ministerial offices, and thus involves the resignation of the entire ministry or government. Resignation may occur, as we have seen, when the House of Commons withdraws its confidence from the government. The more usual case of resignation occurs after an election in which the government party has failed to obtain a majority of the seats in the House of Commons. The theory of responsible government indicates that the Prime Minister would be justified in remaining in office until the House of Commons assembles and votes against his government, but the modern practice (perhaps it is now a convention) is to resign as soon as the election results make clear that the opposition party has gained control of the House of Commons. However, if the election gave no party a clear majority, and it was not clear which major party would attract the support of minor parties or independent members, the Prime Minister would certainly be justified in awaiting a Commons vote.[59]

Once a government has resigned, for whatever reason, the appointment of a new Prime Minister has to be made by the Governor General. This decision is always a personal one in the sense that the Governor General does not act upon ministerial advice. But other conventions of responsible government have now severely limited the discretion which the Governor General really possesses. The Governor General must find the person who has the ability to form a government which will enjoy the support of the House of Commons. The only person with this qualification is the leader of the party which has a majority of seats in the House of Commons. Moreover, each Canadian party has procedures for selecting its own parliamentary leader. This means that in most cases the Governor General's ''choice'' is inevitable.

One situation which has occurred and could again is the death or retirement of a Prime Minister in office before his party has selected a successor. In that case, when the government still retains a majority in the House, the death or retirement is personal and the government as a whole does not vacate office. The country does not lack a government, but merely a Prime Minister. How is he to be replaced? Canadian political parties do not normally choose a deputy leader or second-in-command at the same time as they select a leader. The cabinet will

59 Prime Minister St. Laurent resigned after the election of 1957 as soon as the election results showed that his Liberal party had won fewer seats than the Progressive Conservative party, despite the fact that neither party had an absolute majority. He apparently did not want to appear to be clinging to office after an electoral ''defeat''. But since the election results did not answer the question of who could command the support of a majority in the House of Commons, it seems to me that the Prime Minister would have been fully justified in remaining in office until the parliamentary situation was clear, which might not have been until Parliament met. It turned out, however, that the Progressive Conservative party was able to form a government which lasted for a year so that Prime Minister St. Laurent's resignation could be interpreted as an accurate reading of the parliamentary situation. Prime Minister King had been faced with a similar situation after the election of 1925 in which his Liberal government won fewer seats than the Conservative party. He did not resign, and it turned out that he was able to continue in office for eight months with the support of Progressive, Labour and Independent members.

usually designate a minister to act as Prime Minister during the absence from Ottawa of the Prime Minister, but the Acting Prime Minister is not intended to be the successor to the Prime Minister in the event of the Prime Minister's death or retirement.[60] Before 1896, there were a number of occasions on which a Governor General had to use his own initiative to find a Prime Minister by reason of the death or retirement of the Prime Minister in office.[61] The situation has not recurred since 1896, because every Prime Minister since then has decently refrained from dying or retiring until his party has selected a successor. However, Dawson says that ''there is no reason whatever to assume that the power has vanished in the interval''.[62] But Dawson is probably wrong on this point. If a Prime Minister did die or retire in office without a successor, it is certain that the government party would want to choose the successor by its own procedures, and would not be content to accept the Governor General's choice. Given this political fact, the Governor General would be obliged to appoint the party's choice, for only the party's choice would be successful in forming a government. The utmost initiative which I can conceive of the Governor General exercising would be the appointment of a caretaker Prime Minister for the period when the party was making its choice; but even in this circumstance it is likely that the party, perhaps by vote of its parliamentary caucus, would also wish to designate the caretaker, and, in the absence of some gross impropriety in the mode of selection, a Governor General would be obliged to defer to the party's wish.[63]

(c) Dismissal of Prime Minister

The second reserve power of the Governor General is the power to dismiss the Prime Minister. The dismissal (or resignation) of a Prime Minister automatically involves the dismissal (or resignation) of the entire ministry. Thus what is formally a dismissal of a Prime Minister is in substance the dismissal of the ministry or government.

The power of dismissal has been exercised very rarely. In Canada no federal Prime Minister has ever been dismissed, and no provincial Premier has been dismissed since 1905.[64] In the United Kingdom no Prime Minister has been dismissed since 1783.[65]

---

60 Mallory, *The Structure of Canadian Government* (rev. ed. 1984), 98-99.

61 Mallory, previous note, 78-79; Dawson, *The Government of Canada* (6th ed., 1987 by Ward), 184.

62 Dawson, previous note, 184.

63 Three Quebec Premiers have recently died in office: Duplessis in 1959, Sauvé in 1960 and Johnson in 1968; in each case the parliamentary caucus of the governing Union Nationale party selected a successor, and presented a ''petition'' to the Lieutenant Governor asking him to commission the person chosen; the Lieutenant Governor complied. In the last case the Premier so chosen, Premier Bertrand, insisted upon his appointment also being ratified by a subsequent party leadership convention: see Mallory, note 60, above, 79-80.

64 Saywell, *The Office of Lieutenant-Governor* (1957), ch. 5.

65 de Smith and Brazier, *Constitutional and Administrative Law* (6th ed., 1989), 116.

When does the power of dismissal arise? It is obvious that a Governor General may not dismiss a ministry because he or she believes its policies to be unwise, or because he or she believes it to be incompetent. Those are judgments which in a democracy may be made only by the people or their elected representatives. Could the Governor General dismiss a ministry because he or she believed its policies to be illegal? There is a New South Wales precedent for such a dismissal, but it is soundly criticized by Evatt on the ground that the Governor of New South Wales (or any other head of state) has neither the competence nor the authority to assume to adjudicate a question of law and to provide a remedy for a finding of illegality; questions of illegality are properly justiciable and remediable in the courts.[66] There is also the recent Australian federal precedent of the dismissal in 1975 of Prime Minister Whitlam. The Whitlam Labour government had a secure majority in the lower house, but could not obtain supply from the upper house. This dismissal also seems improper since its effect was to install in office a government which the Governor General knew could not command a majority in the lower house. It is true that the Governor General stipulated that the new government should be a ''caretaker government'' only, which would ''make no appointments or dismissals or initiate new policies before a general election is held''; but to purport to bind a government to such conditions is itself an unprecedented and highly dubious exercise of vice-regal discretion.[67]

My opinion is that the only occasion upon which a Governor General would be justified in dismissing a ministry is when the ministry has lost the support of a majority of the House of Commons. When this happens, as we have already noticed, one of two changes must occur: either the House must be dissolved for an election which will produce a new House, or the ministry must resign to make way for a new ministry which will enjoy the confidence of the existing House. If a Prime Minister who had lost his parliamentary support refused to advise dissolution and refused to resign, then the Governor General would have no alternative but to dismiss the Prime Minister and call upon the leader of the opposition to form a government. If a Prime Minister who had lost his parliamentary support advised dissolution but had his advice rejected by the Governor General (the Governor General's power to refuse a dissolution is discussed in the next section of this chapter) and yet the Prime Minister refused to resign, then again the Governor General would have no alternative but to dismiss the Prime Minister. In Canada neither of these series of events is likely to occur, but if it did the Governor General's action of dismissal would be necessary to force an orderly transfer of power.

---

66 Evatt, *The King and His Dominion Governors* (2nd ed., 1967), chs. 19, 20.

67 The dismissal means that the Australian Senate can force a federal government out of office by denying supply, despite the fact that the government is not responsible to the Senate, and the action would not ordinarily involve the risk of the Senate's own dissolution. The Governor General's correct course, in my view, was to do nothing, and wait for a political resolution of the crisis. Commentary on the crisis is cited, note 42, above.

(d) Dissolution of Parliament

The Constitution Act, 1867, by s. 50, provides that a House of Commons "shall continue for five years" unless it is "sooner dissolved by the Governor General".[68] It is not the practice of Canadian federal Prime Ministers to allow the House of Commons to continue until the expiration of its five-year term. The usual practice is for the Prime Minister to select what he regards as a propitious time for an election and to advise the Governor General to dissolve the House in time for that election. In the normal situation the Prime Minister still has the confidence of the House of Commons, and he is simply seeking an earlier renewal of his government's mandate than would be provided by the eventual expiration of the House. No Canadian Governor General has ever refused a dissolution requested by a Prime Minister in command of a majority in the House, and it would probably be contrary to convention for a Governor General to do so.[69]

There is one famous Canadian precedent of a Governor General's refusal of a dissolution, but the request for a dissolution came from a Prime Minister who had lost the support of a majority in the House of Commons. In 1926, Prime Minister King's minority Liberal government lost the support of some of the Progressive, Labour and Independent members whose cooperation had provided the government with its majority.[70] Faced with an opposition motion of censure which was likely to carry (since the government had been defeated on motions to amend and to adjourn), Prime Minister King advised the Governor General, Lord Byng, to dissolve the House so as to lead to the calling of a general election. Lord Byng took the view that his personal discretion extended to the rejection of his Prime Minister's advice, and he refused the dissolution. Prime Minister King immediately resigned. Lord Byng then called upon the leader of the Conservative Party, Mr. Meighen, to form a new government. Mr. Meighen did so, but within a week his government was defeated, and so he advised Lord Byng to dissolve the House. Lord Byng accepted this advice, thereby granting to Mr. Meighen the dissolution which he had so recently refused Mr. King. In the ensuing election Mr. King's Liberal Party used the incident as an issue of Canadian independence from the Empire, and they won the election. It is clear that Lord Byng's failure to follow Prime Minister King's advice was unwise, since a dissolution in fact

---

68 To the same effect is the Constitution Act, 1982, s. 4.

69 Forsey, *The Royal Power of Dissolution in the British Commonwealth* (1943, reprinted, 1968), 146-162, takes the view that in some situations refusal of a dissolution would be appropriate, e.g., where a motion of censure is under debate in the House of Commons, or where the last election was very recent. For both these reasons he would support Lord Byng's refusal of a dissolution in 1926 (discussed in the text following) even if Mr. King still had the support of a majority in the House of Commons. For provincial precedents, see Saywell, *The Office of Lieutenant-Governor* (1957), ch. 6.

70 The exact standings of the parties in the House of Commons were: Liberals, 101; Conservatives, 116; Progressives, 24; and Labour and Independents, 4.

turned out to be necessary,[71] but there is no agreement among constitutional writers as to whether it was in violation of constitutional convention.[72]

There have been occasional suggestions in Canada that after an inconclusive election the Prime Minister would be justified in requesting a dissolution and therefore a second election without even waiting for the Parliament to meet. This view is almost certainly wrong. The House of Commons has been elected, and it should surely be allowed to meet and see if it can transact public business. If it turned out that the House could not even elect a speaker, or if it turned out that neither the Prime Minister nor the leader of any other party could command the support of a majority of members, then there would be no alternative to dissolution; but to dissolve the House before it had even met would be an abuse of the electoral system, and one which the Governor General would surely be entitled to refuse.[73]

(e) Appointments to Senate and bench

The Governor General's power to appoint senators (Constitution Act, 1867, s. 24) and judges (s. 96) is of course exercised on the advice of the cabinet.[74] In 1896, however, after Parliament had been dissolved and after a new election had decisively defeated the incumbent Conservative government of Prime Minister Tupper, the Tupper government advised the Governor General, Lord Aberdeen, to appoint a number of senators and judges. The Governor General refused to

71 The most thorough study of the King-Byng dispute is Forsey's *The Royal Power of Dissolution of Parliament in the British Commonwealth* (1943, reprinted, 1968), chs. 5, 6, and Forsey comes down strongly in support of Lord Byng's action: see note 69, above. My view that Lord Byng's refusal to dissolve Parliament was at least unwise is based on the fact that Lord Byng and Mr. Meighen must have known that Meighen would have great difficulty in forming a government because of the legal requirement of that time (it was repealed in 1931) that each minister with portfolio had to vacate his seat and seek re-election in a by-election. If Meighen had formed a ministry in the normal way he would have lost about 15 of his supporters in the House. Since he could not afford such a loss (see the voting figures: Forsey, 159), he formed a "temporary ministry" of ministers without portfolio who became "acting ministers" of the departments of government. This device evaded the necessity for ministerial by-elections, but led to a motion in the House of Commons condemning the device which passed by one vote: Forsey, 131-139. While the exact fashion of the Meighen government's downfall was obviously not foreseeable when Byng refused King's request for a dissolution, it was manifest at that time that the formation of a government by Meighen would present "unusual difficulties" (as Forsey, 135, admits). Marshall, *Constitutional Conventions* (1984), 39, suggests that convention authorizes the refusal of a dissolution only if the Governor General can rely on finding a Prime Minister who can form an alternative government; if this is correct, Lord Byng did not observe the convention.

72 The leading scholars are Forsey, who supports Lord Byng's refusal (notes 69 and 71, above) and Evatt, *The King and His Dominion Governors* (2nd ed., 1967), ch. 7, who argues that the refusal was contrary to convention.

73 Forsey, *Freedom and Order* (1974), 40.

74 To be precise, the appointment of Chief Justices and senators is made on the advice of the Prime Minister alone: note 26, above.

make the appointments. The Tupper government accordingly resigned (as it would have had to do anyway because of the election result). The Governor General then invited Mr. Laurier, the leader of the Liberal Party, which had won the election, to form a new government. Mr. Laurier did so, and his government filled the vacancies which the previous government had attempted to fill. The action of the Governor General in this case seems to me to be both wise and in accordance with convention. It was quite improper for the Tupper government to attempt to strengthen its support in the Senate and (less obviously) the bench after it had been defeated at the polls. True, the government was still in office, but the Governor General was entitled to recognize that it was not going to have a majority in the newly-elected House of Commons. In this circumstance the Governor General had a discretion to refuse to concur in an important and irrevocable decision which could await the early and inevitable formation of a new government which was bound to enjoy a majority in the House of Commons.[75]

(f) The justification for a formal head of state

A system of responsible government cannot work without a formal head of state who is possessed of certain reserve powers. While the occasions for the exercise of these powers arise very rarely, the powers are of supreme importance, for they insure against a hiatus in the government of the country or an illegitimate extension of power by a government which has lost its political support. The strength and the weakness of responsible government lie in the executive's dependence on support in the legislature. The strength lies in its provision of an executive which is in accord with the latest expression of the electorate's wishes and which is able to execute its policies. The weakness lies in the absence of clear legal rules as to when governmental power shall be assumed or relinquished and when elections shall be held. In situations where a discredited government is reluctant to relinquish its power, or where parliamentary support is fluid, the head of state is able to resolve the impasse impartially, either through formation of a government, or through an election.

This function of the head of state is unnecessary in a presidential (or gubernatorial) form of government, where the president (or governor) is directly elected for a fixed term and is not dependent upon the support of the legislative branch. The Americans have therefore been able to unite in the one office the formal head of state and the political executive of the nation (or state). The countries which have inherited the British system of responsible government have all had to establish a dual executive in which a formal head of state presides over a government which is actually administered by political officials. While the formal head of state rarely has to exercise the reserve powers, it should not be overlooked that he or she also performs many formal, ceremonial and social functions which are important in the life of the nation.

---

75 Accord, Mallory, *The Structure of Canadian Government* (rev. ed. 1984), 83.

(g) The monarchy

While responsible government requires a dual executive, it does not require that the formal head of state be the Queen. This is demonstrated by countries such as India, Ireland, Israel and South Africa, which possess responsible government, but no monarchy.[76] Canada could if it chose easily become a republic by the simple device of securing an amendment of the Constitution to make the Governor General the formal head of state in his or her own right.[77] Many constitutional and statutory powers are in any case conferred directly upon the Governor General or the Governor General in Council, and would need no alteration. Those powers that are expressly conferred on the Queen could easily be amended to substitute the Governor General for the Queen. The personal prerogatives which are nowhere authoritatively defined, but which are exercised by the Governor General under a delegation from the Queen, should probably be explicitly conferred on the Governor General directly, although it could be argued that they are implicit in the position of a head of state in a system of responsible government. Certainly, they would not need to be defined in detail, unless that exercise was regarded as worthwhile in itself.[78] A new mode of appointing the Governor General would have to be worked out, because at present the appointment is made by the Queen. But the Queen makes the appointment on the advice of the Canadian Prime Minister anyway, and so the real power of appointment has already been domesticated. In short, the shift from a monarchy to a republic could be accomplished with practically no disturbance of present constitutional practice. In considering the question whether Canada should make the change, the constitutional con-

76 Abolition of the monarchy would not entail leaving the Commonwealth. The Queen would no longer be Canada's head of state, and would play no role in the government of Canada, but she would still be recognized by Canada as the head of the Commonwealth and as the symbol of that association. This was the formula which was adopted in 1949 when India decided to become a republic within the Commonwealth; since then, of course, many of the members of the Commonwealth have become republics: Wheare, *The Constitutional Structure of the Commonwealth* (1960), ch. 7; de Smith and Brazier, *Constitutional and Administrative Law* (6th ed., 1989), 112.

77 The Constitution Act, 1982, by s. 41, requires the assents of the federal Parliament and all provinces (unanimity procedure) for an amendment in relation to ''the office of the Queen''.

78 Evatt in *The King and His Dominion Governors* (2nd ed., 1967) deplores the uncertainty in the scope of the personal prerogatives and argues that they should be reduced to writing and enacted as a statute. Significantly, however, he does not himself attempt to draft a model statute and that is the hard part. On the question of reducing conventions to writing, see also Keith (1967) 16 Int. Comp. L.Q. 542.

siderations may be dismissed as neutral or unimportant; obviously, such matters as tradition, sentiment and ceremony are the important considerations.[79]

79 For strong support of the monarchy, see MacKinnon, *The Crown in Canada* (1976). Forsey, *Freedom and Order* (1974), 21-32, in opposing the ''absurd'' suggestion that Canada might abolish the monarchy, exaggerates the constitutional problems which would be involved. The Canadian Bar Association's Committee on the Constitution has recommended the replacement of the monarchy with a Canadian Head of State chosen by the House of Commons: *Towards a New Canada* (1978), 34-35. The issue is discussed by Whyte, ''The Australian Republican Movement and its Implications for Canada'' (1993) 4 Constitutional Forum (U. of Alta.) 88.

siderations may be dismissed as immaterial or unimportant; obviously, such matters as tradition, sentiment and ceremony are the important considerations.[25]

25 For a strong support of the monarchy, see MacKinnon, *The Crown in Canada* (1976). Forsey, *Freedom and Order* (1974), 21-47, in opposing the "absurd" suggestion that Canada might abolish the monarchy, exaggerates the constitutional problems which would be involved. The Canadian Bar Association's Committee on the Constitution has recommended the replacement of the monarchy with a Canadian Head of State chosen by the House of Commons: *Towards a New Canada* (1978), 14-16. The issue is discussed by White, "The Australian Republican Movement and its Implications for Canada" (1993) 4 Constitutional Forum (U. of Alta.) 88.

10

The Crown

10.1 Definition

The juristic nature of the state (or the government) has given rise to controversy among legal theorists.[1] For our purposes it is probably sufficient to say that

---

1 Reference to the principal writings may be found in Hogg, *Liability of the Crown* (2nd ed., 1989), 9; see also Laskin, *The British Tradition in Canadian Law* (1969), 117-126; Mundell, "Legal Nature of Federal and Provincial Executive Governments" (1960) 2 Osgoode Hall L.J. 56; Lordon, *Crown Law* (1991), ch. 1.

the legal system of Canada recognizes the state as a legal person, capable of acquiring rights and liabilities under common law or statute law, capable of suing and being sued, and bound by the decisions of courts and other properly constituted tribunals. However, the state, although a legal person, is not subject to exactly the same laws as other legal persons, namely, corporations and private individuals. The state enjoys extensive powers that are not available to subjects: to collect taxes, to maintain an army, a police force and courts, and to exercise powers necessary to administer the myriad laws which regulate and provide state services in a modern society. In addition, the state enjoys certain privileges or exemptions from the general law of the land. Some of these are necessary to the effective exercise of state powers, for example, the privilege to withhold certain "classified" information from the courts. Others are the product of traditional notions of sovereignty, for example, the immunity of the state from certain kinds of legal proceedings.

In Canada, and in other Commonwealth countries which recognize the same Queen as the formal head of state, the state (or government) is commonly referred to as "the Crown". This usage dates from earlier times when all powers of government were vested in the monarch, and were exercised by delegation from the monarch. One could argue, with some support from the language of the Constitution, that this is still technically true of Canada today, but the theory bears no resemblance whatever to the actual lines of authority within Canadian governments.[2] Nevertheless, the "Crown" continues to be used as "a convenient symbol for the State", and we commonly speak of the Crown expropriating a house, of the Crown being sued for breach of contract, of the Crown being bound by a statute. In all of these propositions the state or the government could as well be used instead of the Crown.

There is only one individual at any time who is the Queen (or King). The Crown accordingly has a monolithic connotation, which has sometimes been articulated in dicta such as that the Crown is "one and indivisible". For nearly all purposes the idea of the Crown as one and indivisible is thoroughly misleading. Within the British Empire (or, later, the Commonwealth), once a territory acquired a degree of self-government, then, as to matters falling within the scope of self-government, the Queen was thereafter advised by her colonial ministers, not her British ministers; and the colonial government, with its power to raise taxes and create a separate treasury, would assume the responsibility for debts and other obligations pertaining to matters within the scope of self-government. When the colony achieved full independence, it became an entirely separate legal entity from the United Kingdom for all practical purposes, including the making of contracts, the holding of property and the capacity to sue and be sued. The divisibility of the Crown was explicitly recognized in the *Alberta Indians* case

2 See ch. 9, Responsible Government, above.

(1982),[3] when several associations of Canadian aboriginal peoples brought suit in the courts of the United Kingdom to enforce obligations to the aboriginal peoples undertaken by the Crown in treaties and other instruments in early colonial times. The English Court of Appeal held that these obligations had long since passed to Canada. They were enforceable only against the Crown in right of Canada and in the Canadian courts. The Crown was thus divisible: the Crown in right of Canada was a separate legal entity from the Crown in right of the United Kingdom.

Within Canada's federal system, legal recognition of the divisibility of the Crown may be dated from *Liquidators of the Maritime Bank* v. *Receiver General of New Brunswick* (1892),[4] which decided that a debt owing to a province was held by the Crown in right of the province, and the Crown in right of the province was entitled to the prerogative privilege of payment in priority to other creditors. This important case established that the Lieutenant Governor of each province, although appointed by the federal government, was not the representative of the federal government, but of the Queen. The executive government of each province therefore enjoyed the powers, privileges and immunities of the Crown. But each province was still a separate legal entity from each other province and from the federal government. The separate existence of each province and of the Dominion is, of course, manifested by a separate treasury, separate property, separate employees, separate courts, and a separate set of laws to administer.[5]

In order to reflect this strange notion of a single Queen recognized by many separate jurisdictions, it is usual to speak of the Crown "in right of" a particular jurisdiction. Thus, the government of the United Kingdom is described as the Crown in right of the United Kingdom; the federal government of Canada is the Crown in right of Canada (or the Dominion); and each of the provincial governments is the Crown in right of the province.

---

3 *R.* v. *Secretary of State for Foreign and Commonwealth Affairs; Ex parte Indian Assn. of Alta.* [1982] Q.B. 892 (C.A.).

4 [1892] A.C. 437.

5 The separate legal existence of the various governments is made abundantly clear by the governments suing each other, making conveyances to each other, and entering into agreements with each other, some of them judicially enforceable: e.g., *Can.* v. *Ont.* [1910] A.C. 637; *Re Troops in Cape Breton* [1930] S.C.R. 554; *Re Transfer of Natural Resources to Sask.* [1932] A.C. 28; *A.-G. Can.* v. *Higbie* [1945] S.C.R. 385; *Re Anti-Inflation Act* [1976] 2 S.C.R. 373; *The Queen (Can.)* v. *The Queen (P.E.I.)* [1978] 1 F.C. 533 (C.A.); *Man. Govt. Employees Assn.* v. *Govt. of Man.* [1978] 1 S.C.R. 1123; *B.C.* v. *Can.* [1994] 2 S.C.R. 41. As to court jurisdiction over intergovernmental suits, see Federal Court Act, R.S.C. 1985, c. F-7, s. 19; *Can. Javelin* v. *The Queen (Nfld.)* (1977) 77 D.L.R. (3d) 317 (Fed. C.A.); *Churchill Falls (Labrador) Corp.* v. *Commn. Hydro-Electrique de Qué.* [1982] 2 S.C.R. 79. For commentary, see Hogg, note 1, above, ch. 12.

10.2 Crown agency

(a) The issue

Do public corporations enjoy the same immunities and privileges as the Crown itself?[6] This issue has usually arisen when a public corporation claims immunity from a statute that does not bind the Crown, but the issue can arise in any situation where the Crown is entitled to a privilege or immunity that is not available to other persons or corporations. The issue is usually resolved by asking whether the corporation is an ''agent'' of the Crown. If the answer is yes, the corporation is entitled to share in the Crown's immunity. If the answer is no, the corporation is not entitled to the immunity.

In this context, the expression ''agent of the Crown'' is not a particularly happy one, because a public corporation will often perform legal acts, such as making contracts, holding property, suing and being sued, on its own behalf, rather than on behalf of the Crown.[7] Nevertheless, the corporation will be regarded as an agent of the Crown in this context if it satisfies the common law test of control (discussed next) or if it is expressly made an agent of the Crown (discussed later). The trouble is that none of the competing expressions captures the idea any better: the phrase ''servant of the Crown'', which is sometimes used, does not seem any more appropriate; and to describe a corporation as an ''instrumentality of the Crown'', ''emanation of the Crown'', or as ''within the shield of the Crown'', is positively misleading, since it conveys the impression that the public corporation is part of the Crown itself, whereas in fact it is a separate legal person.

(b) At common law

If there is no statutory provision expressly making a public corporation an agent of the Crown (such provisions are discussed in the next section of this chapter), the question whether a public corporation is an agent of the Crown depends upon ''the nature and degree of control which the Crown exercises over it''.[8] If the corporation is controlled by a minister (or a cabinet) in much the same way as a government department is controlled, then the corporation is an agent of the Crown. If, on the other hand, the corporation is largely free of ministerial

6 This issue is discussed in more detail in Hogg, note 1, above, ch. 11; Goldenberg in Law Society of Upper Canada, *New Developments in the Law of Torts*, Special Lectures 1973, 341, 365-389; Lordon, note 1, above, ch. 2.

7 A Crown agent was held to be liable to suit in contract in its own name in a court in which the Crown itself could not be sued in *Yeats* v. *Central Mortgage and Housing Corp.* [1950] S.C.R. 513 and *Northern Pipeline Agency* v. *Perehinec* [1983] 2 S.C.R. 513.

8 *Westeel-Rosco* v. *Bd. of Governors of South Sask. Hospital Centre* [1977] 2 S.C.R. 238, 249-250; *Fidelity Insurance Co.* v. *Cronkhite Supply* [1979] 2 S.C.R. 27, 29. *Northern Pipeline Agency* v. *Perehinec* [1983] 2 S.C.R. 513, 519.

control, then it is not an agent of the Crown.[9] Between the extremes of full control and no control lies a continuum in which the courts have ranged without clear rules, simply repeating that it is the ''nature and degree of control'' that has to be assessed.[10] As Dickson J. has said: ''the greater the control, the more likely it is that the person will be recognized as a Crown agent''.[11] However, the tendency of the decisions is to require a high degree of control; in other words, the tendency of the decisions is against the finding of Crown-agent status. The reason, without doubt, is a justified reluctance on the part of the courts to extend a special privilege of the Crown any further than necessary.

One rule that has become established, and that is useful, is that control means de jure control, not de facto control. It is the degree of control that the minister is legally entitled to exercise that is relevant, not the degree of control that is in fact exercised. The question is therefore resolved by an examination of the corporation's empowering statute, and does not involve an assessment of the actual relationship between the corporation and the government. The clearest example of de jure control is the case where a minister actually heads the corporation.[12] Another clear example is the case where there is a statutory requirement of the approval of a minister or of the cabinet for important transactions.[13] Such matters as the power to appoint directors[14] and to supply funding,[15] although they may provide opportunities for de facto control of the corporation's activities, are not sufficient by themselves to establish de jure control.

(c) By statute

If (as is common) a statute expressly provides that a public corporation is to be ''an agent of the Crown'', then the corporation will be an agent of the Crown.

---

9 An alternative to the control test is the ''functions'' test, under which one asks whether the functions performed by the public corporation are truly ''governmental'', as opposed to, say, ''commercial'': *Tamlin* v. *Hannaford* [1950] 1 K.B. 18, 25 (C.A.) seems to use a functions test. The functions test has never become established, because the only satisfactory criterion to determine whether a particular function is governmental or not is whether the government has chosen to assume control of it.

10 The leading cases establishing the control test are: *Fox* v. *Govt. of Nfld.* [1898] A.C. 667 (school board not entitled to Crown priority in payment of debts); *Metropolitan Meat Industry Bd.* v. *Sheedy* [1927] A.C. 899 (meat industry board not entitled to Crown priority in payment of debts); *Halifax* v. *Halifax Harbour Commrs.* [1935] S.C.R. 215 (harbour commission entitled to Crown immunity from business tax); *Westeel-Rosco* v. *Bd. of Governors of South Sask. Hospital Centre* [1977] 2 S.C.R. 238 (hospital board not entitled to Crown immunity from mechanics lien statute).

11 *R.* v. *Eldorado Nuclear* [1983] 2 S.C.R. 551, 573.

12 *Northern Pipeline Agency* v. *Perehinec* [1983] 2 S.C.R. 513.

13 *Halifax* v. *Halifax Harbour Commrs.* [1935] S.C.R. 215, 226; *R.* v. *Eldorado Nuclear* [1983] 2 S.C.R. 551, 571.

14 *Metropolitan Meat Industry Bd.* v. *Sheedy* [1927] A.C. 899, 905.

15 *Fox* v. *Govt. of Nfld.* [1898] A.C. 667, 671; *Westeel Rosco* v. *Bd. of Governors of South Sask. Hospital Centre* [1977] 2 S.C.R. 238, 252.

The Parliament or a Legislature, acting within its competence, is free to confer on a public corporation any privileges or immunities that it chooses. If it chooses to confer on the corporation the privileges and immunities of the Crown, that is a matter of legislative policy that is unreviewable by the courts. The express stipulation that a public corporation is to be an agent of the Crown is accordingly conclusive, even if the public corporation is not subject to the control of a minister of the Crown, and would for that reason not be treated as an agent of the Crown at common law.[16]

The Crown immunity that is possessed by a public corporation by virtue of an express designation as agent of the Crown is lost if the corporation acts outside its statutory purposes. In *Canadian Broadcasting Corporation* v. *The Queen* (1983),[17] the question arose whether the CBC was bound by the Criminal Code provision prohibiting the exhibition of obscene films. The Criminal Code provision did not bind the Crown. The federal statute that established the CBC provided that the corporation was "an agent of Her Majesty". Nevertheless, the Supreme Court of Canada held that the CBC was bound by the Criminal Code provision, and was liable to prosecution for exhibiting an obscene film. The CBC was subject to regulations which, among other things, expressly prohibited it from broadcasting obscene material. Therefore, the CBC, when broadcasting the obscene film, was acting outside its powers. This caused it to lose its Crown immunity.

It might be thought that compliance with the general law would always be a limitation on the powers of a public corporation. But the position is not so simple. In a 1959 case, also involving the CBC, *Canadian Broadcasting Corporation* v. *A.-G. Ont.* (1959),[18] the corporation was held to be entitled to Crown immunity from the provisions of the Lord's Day Act, so that the corporation was free to broadcast on Sundays. The Supreme Court of Canada held that it was sufficient to retain the Crown agency protection that the CBC's statutory mandate authorized the provision of a broadcasting service without any limitation as to time.

In *R.* v. *Eldorado Nuclear* (1983),[19] two public corporations engaged in the production of uranium, which had allegedly participated with other uranium producers in a price-fixing cartel, were held to be immune from the anti-trust provisions of the Combines Investigation Act (which did not bind the Crown). Each corporation was expressly designated an "agent of Her Majesty". Dickson J. for the majority of the Supreme Court of Canada held that this designation conferred immunity, because the purposes of each corporation were broad enough to authorize the "marketing arrangements" that were the subject of the anti-trust charge. The dissenting view of Wilson J. (and McIntyre J.) was that the general

16 *R.* v. *Eldorado Nuclear* [1983] 2 S.C.R. 551, 576 (Eldorado Nuclear entitled to Crown immunity by virtue of express statutory designation as agent, although not controlled by Crown).

17 [1983] 1 S.C.R. 339.

18 [1959] S.C.R. 188.

19 [1983] 2 S.C.R. 551.

purposes of a Crown agent should be interpreted as excluding illegal activity, unless the Crown agent could "show that he could not carry out his mandate without the commission of such [illegal] acts".[20]

10.3 Proceedings against the Crown

In England in the middle ages there was no formal procedure for suing the Crown (or government). In order to secure redress for an alleged wrong by government the subject would petition the King in much the same way as a subject would petition the King with any other kind of request. In due course the "petition of right", which asserted a legal right against the Crown, came to be treated differently from other kinds of petitions: it could be referred by the King to one of the ordinary courts to be tried.[21] However, the petition of right was subject to the fundamental limitation that it could only proceed to adjudication if the King in his discretion signified his consent by endorsing the petition "fiat justitiae" — let right be done. Of course, after the development of responsible government, the King's discretion to grant the "royal fiat" was in reality the discretion of the government of the day.

In 1947, the United Kingdom adopted a new Crown Proceedings Act. The new Act abolished the petition of right, replacing it with the remedies which would be available between subject and subject. The requirement of the fiat was also abolished, enabling the Crown to be sued without its consent. Many other special privileges which were enjoyed by the Crown as litigant were also swept away as Crown proceedings were assimilated to proceedings between subjects.

After the enactment of the Crown Proceedings Act 1947 in the United Kingdom, the Conference of Commissioners on Uniformity of Legislation in Canada prepared a model act for adoption by Canadian jurisdictions. The model act was based on the United Kingdom Act and incorporated its major provisions. Between 1951 and 1974, the model act was enacted in substance by all of the Canadian provinces, except Quebec. Quebec did not adopt the model act, but it did abolish the requirement of the fiat in 1965. The federal Parliament acted in stages, abolishing the requirement of the fiat in 1951, but retaining the petition of right as the procedure of suit until 1971 when it too was abolished.[22]

The present position in every province is that, in general, the Crown may be sued in the ordinary courts by the procedure which would be appropriate in suits between ordinary subjects. In the federal jurisdiction, suits against the Crown in right of Canada must be brought either in the Federal Court of Canada or in the

20 *Id.*, 585. A question which arises in all three of the cases discussed is whether a Crown agent can be guilty of a crime. This question is examined in Hogg, note 1, above, 232-235.

21 The history of proceedings against the Crown is related in Hogg, note 1, above, 3-9.

22 Detailed references are provided in Hogg, note 1, above, 3-9.

superior court of the province in which the claim arose.[23] However, the reforms in the law of Crown proceedings have not placed the Crown in exactly the same situation as a private litigant in all respects. In all Canadian jurisdictions, certain remedies are still unavailable against the Crown, for example, mandamus, injunction and execution of a judgment. In most jurisdictions, the Crown enjoys special advantages in the form of shorter limitation periods or notice requirements as a prelude to suits against the Crown. And, as we shall see in the next section of this chapter, in all jurisdictions, the Crown is entitled to claim ''Crown privilege'' and object to the admission of evidence which would be injurious to the public interest. These residual immunities and privileges vary from jurisdiction to jurisdiction depending upon the state of the statute law and case law in that jurisdiction.[24]

10.4 Crown privilege

(a) Definition

Crown privilege[25] (or public interest immunity, as it is now sometimes called) is a common law[26] rule of evidence[27] which provides that evidence that is relevant and otherwise admissible must be excluded if its admission would be injurious to the public interest.

A claim of Crown privilege may be made in any proceedings, civil or criminal, before any court or tribunal, and at any stage of the proceedings. Where the Crown is a party to civil proceedings, the claim is often made by the Crown

---

23 Federal Court Act, R.S.C. 1985, c. F-7, s. 17 (as amended by S.C. 1990, c. 8); Crown Liability and Proceedings Act, R.S.C. 1985, c. C-50, s. 21 (as amended by S.C. 1990, c. 8).

24 An account of the law of Canada is to be found in Hogg, note 1, above.

25 See Hogg, note 1, above, ch. 4; Sopinka, Lederman, Bryant, *The Law of Evidence in Canada* (1992), ch. 15; Schiff, *Evidence in the Litigation Process* (4th ed., 1993), 1115-1185.

26 In the federal jurisdiction, the law is codified in the Canada Evidence Act, R.S.C. 1985, c. C-5, ss. 37-39. In Quebec, the law is codified in article 308 of the Code of Civil Procedure: for discussion, see *Bisaillon* v. *Keable* [1983] 2 S.C.R. 60.

27 A rule which has traditionally been treated as a branch of Crown privilege is the rule prohibiting the disclosure of the identity of police informers (the police informer rule), which is necessary to enable the police to protect their sources of information. This rule is not absolute, giving way to the competing public interest where disclosure would tend to show the innocence of an accused: *Marks* v. *Beyfus* (1890) 25 Q.B.D. 494, 498. The accused's right to full answer and defence, which is protected by s. 7 of the Charter, also has implications for the police informer rule: *R.* v. *Khela* [1995] 4 S.C.R. 201; see also ch. 44, Fundamental Justice, under heading 44.16, ''Fair Trial'', below. Although this rule applies in civil as well as criminal proceedings (*Solicitor General Can.* v. *Royal Commission of Inquiry into Confidentiality of Health Records* [1981] 2 S.C.R. 494), in *Bisaillon* v. *Keable* [1983] 2 S.C.R. 60 Beetz J. for a unanimous Court held that the rule was best regarded as a rule of criminal law, which could be altered only by the federal Parliament and was therefore not affected by provincial codification of the law of Crown privilege. Accord, Mewett, ''State Secrets in Canada'' (1985) 63 Can. Bar Rev. 358.

in the process of discovery.[28] Where the Crown is not a party to proceedings, the Crown can still object to the production of evidence on the ground of Crown privilege, if necessary by intervening in the litigation to make the objection. A claim of Crown privilege need not, however, be made by the Crown: it can be made by a private party or private witness or even by the court of its own motion. A claim of Crown privilege, by whomever made, is customarily, though not necessarily, supported by the affidavit or certificate of a minister asserting that the public interest would be injured by disclosure of the evidence.

(b) Judicial review

In *Duncan* v. *Cammell Laird* (1942),[29] the House of Lords upheld a claim of Crown privilege in respect of the plans and specifications of a secret type of submarine. This decision, especially in its wartime context, was clearly correct, but Viscount Simon L.C. went beyond the necessity of the case to assert that a ministerial claim of privilege was conclusive and could not be reviewed by the courts. This position, which was inconsistent with a decision of the Privy Council,[30] has now been rejected by the House of Lords itself,[31] as well as by the High Court of Australia[32] and the Supreme Court of Canada.[33] It is now clear that no document or class of documents or other evidence enjoys absolute immunity from admission in litigation. It is for the court in which the claim is made to balance the injury to the public interest that is claimed to flow from the admission of the evidence against the injury to the administration of justice that would flow from the exclusion of the evidence. In making this assessment, the court is entitled to inspect the documents for which the privilege is claimed.[34]

(c) Class claims

A document whose particular contents are innocuous may be protected from disclosure by Crown privilege if it belongs to a class of documents that ought to be kept secret. An uncontroversial example might be a memorandum within the Department of External Affairs relating to the conduct of an international negotiation. In *Duncan* v. *Cammell Laird* (1942),[35] Viscount Simon L.C., again straying far beyond the necessity of the case, said that it was a sufficient ground for a

---

28 Crown immunity from discovery has been abolished in all Canadian jurisdictions: Hogg, note 1, above, 31.

29 [1942] A.C. 624.

30 *Robinson* v. *South Australia (No. 2)* [1931] A.C. 704.

31 *Conway* v. *Rimmer* [1968] A.C. 910; *Burmah Oil Co.* v. *Bank of England* [1980] A.C. 1090.

32 *Sankey* v. *Whitlam* (1978) 142 C.L.R. 1.

33 *R.* v. *Snider* [1954] S.C.R. 479; *Smallwood* v. *Sparling* [1982] 2 S.C.R. 686; *Carey* v. *Ont.* [1986] 2 S.C.R. 637.

34 *Carey* v. *Ont.*, previous note.

35 [1942] A.C. 624.

class-based claim of Crown privilege that disclosure of a particular document might prejudice the ''candour and completeness'' of communications within a government department[36] or might ''impair the proper functioning of the public service''.[37] When these generous definitions of class privilege were combined with the absence of judicial review, the power of a minister to successfully resist disclosure of government documents was broad indeed. It is now clear, however, that any claim of Crown privilege is reviewable by the courts, and that vague appeals to ''candour'' within the public service or the ''proper functioning'' of the public service are unlikely to outweigh the competing value of having all relevant material available in litigation. Even in respect of cabinet documents, which were at one time thought to enjoy an absolute immunity from production, a claim of Crown privilege will be reviewed by the courts, and disclosure has sometimes been ordered.[38]

(d) Oral testimony

Most claims of Crown privilege have concerned documents, but the rule applies to oral testimony as well: oral testimony is inadmissible if its reception would be contrary to the public interest.[39] But Crown privilege affords no general immunity for the oral testimony of a minister of the Crown (or a public servant): the minister is as competent and compellable as any other individual if called upon to testify in proceedings in which his or her testimony is relevant.[40] Any

36 *Id.*, 635.

37 *Id.*, 642.

38 *Sankey* v. *Whitlam* (1978) 142 C.L.R. 1 (H.C. Aust.) (production of cabinet minutes ordered); *Burmah Oil Co.* v. *Bank of England* [1980] A.C. 1090 (H.L.) (production of cabinet minutes denied, but only after judicial inspection); *Gloucester Properties* v. *The Queen (B.C.)* (1981) 129 D.L.R. (3d) 275 (B.C.C.A.) (production of cabinet minutes ordered); *Smallwood* v. *Sparling* [1982] 2 S.C.R. 686 (oral testimony of cabinet discussions ordered, subject to Crown privilege in respect of particular disclosures which could be proved to injure public interest); *Air Can.* v. *Secretary of State for Trade* [1983] 1 A.C. 394 (H.L.) (production of cabinet documents denied without judicial inspection); *Carey* v. *Ont.* [1986] 2 S.C.R. 637 (claim in respect of cabinet documents remitted to trial court for inspection and decision whether to order production). Note, however, that s. 39 of the Canada Evidence Act makes unreviewable a claim of Crown privilege in respect of ''a confidence of the Queen's Privy Council for Canada''.

39 *Smallwood* v. *Sparling*, previous note.

40 This is the common law rule in a court of law: *Can. Deposit Insurance Corp.* v. *Code* (1988) 49 D.L.R. (4th) 57 (Alta. C.A.). Outside a court of law, for example, in an administrative tribunal or commission of inquiry, the compellability of witnesses has to be created by statute. Any statute purporting to make witnesses compellable would have to be competent to the enacting Parliament or Legislature. In *A.-G. Que. and Keable* v. *A.-G. Can.* [1979] 1 S.C.R. 218, it was held that a provincial Legislature could not authorize an inquiry into the ''administration and management'' of the federal police force, the Royal Canadian Mounted Police; and, even for the purpose of an inquiry that was within provincial competence, could not compel federal ministers of the Crown to testify. In *Smallwood* v. *Sparling* [1982] 2 S.C.R. 686, it was held that no similar disability stopped the federal Parliament from authorizing a commission

claim of Crown privilege would have to be made in respect of answers to specific questions. Thus, in *Smallwood* v. *Sparling* (1982),[41] the Supreme Court of Canada held that Joseph R. Smallwood, the former Premier of Newfoundland, was obliged to comply with a subpoena requiring his testimony at a federal inquiry into the affairs of a corporation which had had dealings with the Newfoundland government while Mr. Smallwood was Premier. Mr. Smallwood sought an injunction to prevent the compelling of his testimony on the ground that his testimony would relate exclusively to his duties as Premier and would involve the disclosure of cabinet confidences. The Supreme Court of Canada held that there was no general immunity applicable to the testimony of ministers (or former ministers) of the Crown; and that even with respect to specific kinds of oral testimony (or specific documents) Crown immunity was not absolute but relative, involving an issue-by-issue determination by the courts in which the claimed injury to the public interest caused by disclosure would have to be balanced against the injury to the administration of justice caused by non-disclosure. The injunction was therefore denied as being too sweeping in its scope and premature in its timing.

10.5 Liability in contract

The petition of right was always available for the recovery of property from the Crown. The wide conception of property in the middle ages, and the imperfect recognition of other legal conceptions, brought within the ambit of the petition of right some claims which would now be thought of as contractual. After contract emerged as a distinct legal cause of action, the courts decided that the petition of right was available against the Crown as a general remedy for breach of contract. The Crown proceedings statutes of all Canadian jurisdictions preserve the Crown's liability in contract[42] while simplifying the procedure for suit.

10.6 Crown servants

The rule of the common law is that Crown servants are dismissible at pleasure.[43] This curious rule developed originally with respect to members of the armed

---

of inquiry into the affairs of a federally-incorporated company to compel the testimony of a former provincial minister of the Crown. It is not clear whether it would have been different if the witness was still a provincial minister of the Crown. This case is discussed in the text that follows. The degree to which provincial law may bind the federal Crown, and the degree to which federal law may bind the provincial Crown, is discussed later in this chapter, sec. 10.9(c), ''Constitutional limitations'', below.

41 [1982] 2 S.C.R. 686.

42 For most purposes the rules are the same as those applying to private individuals: *Verreault* v. *A.-G. Que.* [1977] 1 S.C.R. 41; *Bank of Montreal* v. *A.-G. Que.* [1979] 1 S.C.R. 565; but there are some special Crown rules: Hogg, note 1, above, ch. 8, and Lordon, note 1, above, ch. 8, are accounts of the law.

43 *Clarke* v. *A.-G. Ont.* [1966] 1 O.R. 539 (C.A.); Hogg, note 1, above, 174-177, discusses the legal position of Crown servants.

forces, but it was later applied to civil servants as well. The Supreme Court of Canada has held that this rule will be displaced by an express provision to the contrary in a contract of employment or collective agreement, or in a statute.[44]

10.7 Liability in tort

In tort, the law developed differently. Although the petition of right included some causes of action which we would now classify as tortious, in the nineteenth century the courts refused to develop the petition of right into a general remedy in tort. The reasoning in those crucial nineteenth century cases — that ''the King can do no wrong'' — we can now see to be misconceived, but the cases became firmly established as the law. Since no remedy other than the petition of right was available to sue the Crown in tort, the Crown became immune. That immunity migrated to Canada as part of the public law received in British North America.

The Crown's immunity from tortious liability did not mean that a person injured by a Crown servant was necessarily without redress. The Crown servant who committed the tort was of course personally liable, even if the servant was acting in the course of employment. The plaintiff could therefore bring action against the particular Crown servant who caused the injury. As early as 1908 in England, it was said that ''in a proper case'' the Crown would defend its servant and pay any damages awarded; and this certainly became the invariable practice later on. Indeed, the practice of the Crown ''standing behind'' any servant who committed a tort in the course of his employment seems to have been general in all jurisdictions in which the Crown was immune from liability in tort, and the practice was probably the reason why the scandalous gap in the law was not filled much earlier. But the practice was not an adequate substitute for the comprehensive legal liability of the Crown, and in 1947 the United Kingdom finally enacted the Crown Proceedings Act, which was a major reform of the procedural and substantive law of Crown liability. The procedural reform of the Act has already been described.[45] The Act also imposed liability in tort on the Crown.

The United Kingdom's Crown Proceedings Act became the model for legislation in Canada, and between 1951 and 1974 similar statutes were enacted by nine provinces. In this way, the Crown became liable in tort in all provinces except Quebec. Quebec did not pass a statute on the United Kingdom model, but the Crown was already liable in tort (delict) in Quebec by virtue of a decision of the Supreme Court of Canada in 1935, which had interpreted Quebec's Code of Civil Procedure as imposing tort liability on the Crown.[46] The Parliament of Canada also did not pass a statute on the United Kingdom model, but it had imposed a

44 *Nova Scotia Govt. Employees Assn.* v. *Civil Service Comm. of Nova Scotia* [1981] 1 S.C.R. 211.

45 Section 10.3, ''Proceedings against the Crown'', above.

46 *The King* v. *Cliche* [1935] S.C.R. 561.

measure of liability on the Crown in a series of statutes commencing in 1887, and it did enact a more comprehensive statute in 1951 which imposed tort liability on the Crown.[47] The result is that the Crown is liable in tort in all Canadian provinces, as well as the federal jurisdiction. Unfortunately, many of the Canadian statutes are defective in that they leave some residues of Crown immunity. As well, there is an extensive body of case-law adapting the private-law rules of tort law to the different situation of the Crown and other public bodies.[48]

10.8 Statutes

(a) Common law immunity

The Crown is, of course, subject to its Parliament[49] or Legislature.[50] So long as a legislative body acts within the limits of its powers, it is free to make its laws applicable to the Crown (or government), just as it is free to make its laws applicable to other legal persons within its jurisdiction.[51] Any other conclusion would be inconsistent with the supremacy of the legislative branch of government. Indeed, it was settled in England as early as 1561 that the Crown was bound by any statute which applied to it,[52] and this is one of the fundamental principles of the British constitution that was received in British North America.

It follows that the Crown is not immune from statutes by virtue of any rule of the constitution. However, the Crown does enjoy a measure of immunity by virtue of a common law rule of statutory construction (or interpretation). The rule is that the Crown is not bound by statute except by express words or necessary implication.[53] What this means is that general language in a statute, such as

47 See now Crown Liability and Proceedings Act, R.S.C. 1985, c. C-50 (as amended by S.C. 1990, c. 8).

48 Accounts of the law may be found in Hogg, note 1, above, chs. 5-7 and Lordon, note 1, above, ch. 9.

49 The Parliament of Canada has power to impose a liability on the Crown in right of Canada, either because that would be an indirect appropriation of federal funds (s. 102), or because that would come within the peace, order, and good government of Canada: Mundell, "Remedies against the Crown" in Law Society of Upper Canada, *Remedies*, Special Lectures 1967, 149, 154-156.

50 The Legislature of a province has power to impose a liability on the Crown in right of the province, because that would be an indirect appropriation of provincial funds (s. 126): Mundell, previous note; *Re Troops in Cape Breton* [1930] S.C.R. 554 (Parliament cannot impose a financial obligation on a province). An alternative basis is the power to amend the constitution of the province (s. 45 of the Constitution Act, 1982).

51 The extent to which Parliament or a Legislature can make laws binding on the Crown in right of a government other than that of the legislating jurisdiction is considered later in this section of the chapter.

52 *Willion* v. *Berkley* (1561), 1 Plowden 223; 75 E.R. 339.

53 The leading case is *Province of Bombay* v. *Municipal Corp. of Bombay* [1947] A.C. 58 (Crown land immune from Act authorizing the laying of water-mains in the city of Bombay). For discussion, see Hogg, note 1, above, ch. 10.

''person'' or ''owner'' or ''landlord'', will be interpreted as not including the Crown, unless that statute expressly states that it applies to the Crown (express words), or unless the context of the statute makes it clear beyond doubt that the Crown must be bound (necessary implication). The rule is often expressed as a ''presumption'' that the Crown is not bound by statute — a presumption that is rebuttable by express words or necessary implication. The rule is sometimes described as a ''prerogative'' of the Crown, which is also accurate, so long as it is understood that the rule is an immunity rather than a power.[54] The rule is not a power to override a statute that applies to the Crown; the rule is a rule of construction, designed to ascertain whether or not the statute does apply to the Crown. Once it is ascertained that the statute does apply to the Crown, then the Crown is bound: the Crown has no prerogative power to escape from the obligations imposed by the statute.

The immunity of the Crown from statutes, like other Crown privileges, extends to public corporations that are ''agents of the Crown''. Thus, the CBC has been held to be immune from the Lord's Day Act and therefore to be free to broadcast on Sundays.[55] Two Crown corporations engaged in the production of uranium have been held to be immune from the Combines Investigation Act and therefore to be free to enter into a price-fixing cartel.[56] A Crown corporation operating a telephone system has been held to be immune from the statute regulating telecommunications.[57] However, if a Crown corporation acts outside its statutory purposes, as the CBC did in broadcasting an obscene film, then the corporation loses its Crown immunity and is bound by the same laws as are applicable to other corporations.[58] The topic of Crown agency was discussed earlier in this chapter.[59]

(b) Effect of Interpretation Acts

The Interpretation Act of Canada[60] and of each Canadian province[61] includes a provision that states when the Crown is bound by statute. All but two of the provisions confirm the common law rule of immunity. The provisions contemplate that the Crown may be bound by express words, but they say nothing about necessary implication. It seems unlikely, however, that the provisions are intended to enlarge Crown immunity by denying that the Crown could be bound by nec-

54 Dicey's definition of prerogative (see sec. 1.9, ''Prerogative'', above) would confine the term to the powers of the Crown, but the better usage includes privileges and immunities of the Crown.

55 *CBC* v. *A.-G. Ont.* [1959] S.C.R. 188.

56 *R.* v. *Eldorado Nuclear* [1983] 2 S.C.R. 551.

57 *Alta. Govt. Telephones* v. *Can.* [1989] 2 S.C.R. 225.

58 *CBC* v. *The Queen* [1983] 1 S.C.R. 339.

59 Section 10.2, ''Crown agency'', above

60 Interpretation Act, R.S.C. 1985, c. I-21, s. 17.

61 E.g., Interpretation Act, R.S.O. 1980, c. 219, s. 11.

essary implication. The requirement of express words should probably be regarded as including any clear indication of an intention to bind the Crown.[62] Indeed, if the Interpretation Act provisions were read as insisting upon only express words, they would constitute an attempted restraint on the future exercise of legislative power, which might be unconstitutional.[63] The question of constitutionality need not be faced if the Interpretation Act provisions are read as rules of interpretation only, giving way not only to express words, but to any clear indication of an intention to bind the Crown.[64] That is the better reading of the provisions.[65]

British Columbia has abolished the common law rule of immunity. The Interpretation Act of British Columbia,[66] which has now been copied by Prince Edward Island,[67] provides that the Crown is bound by statute unless the statute "otherwise specifically provides". This reverses the position at common law and under the standard statutory provisions. Under the unreformed law, and apart from the necessary implication rule, the legislative drafter must deliberately bind the Crown when that is the desired result. Under British Columbia's reformed law, the legislative drafter must deliberately exempt the Crown when that is the desired result. In one sense, the change is merely a question of appropriate drafting techniques. However, there is no reason to suppose that the omission in a statute of a section expressly binding the Crown is always the product of a conscious decision by the government and legislative body that the Crown should be exempt. More likely, it is the product of a failure by anyone to consider the question of whether the Crown should be bound. But the omission carries the serious consequence that the statute will not bind the Crown unless a necessary implication to the contrary can be found. The result is that many statutes do not bind the Crown.

The British Columbia rule is the more appropriate one. In the last century there has been a great increase in both the scope of governmental activity, and in the scope of legislative regulation. In general, where the Crown engages in an activity which is controlled by statute, it should surely be subject to the statutory controls; and where legislation is passed to benefit a class of the community, the benefits should not be denied to some members of that class merely because of

---

62 *Alta. Govt. Telephones* v. *Can.* [1989] 2 S.C.R. 225, 281, holding that s. 17 of the federal Interpretation Act includes necessary implication. Note, however, that s. 17 uses the phrase "mentioned or referred to", which is arguably broader than the phrases "expressly states" or "expressly stated", which are found in the provincial Interpretation Acts.

63 See ch. 12, Parliamentary Sovereignty, under heading 12.3, "Self-imposed restraints on legislative powers", below.

64 Reading down a statute to avoid a constitutional issue is of course a common technique of interpretation: ch. 15, Judicial Review on Federal Grounds, under heading 15.4(j), "Reading down", below.

65 For full discussion of the various Interpretation Act provisions, see Hogg, note 1, above, 205-209.

66 Interpretation Act, R.S.B.C. 1979, c. 206, s. 14.

67 Interpretation Act, R.S.P.E.I. 1988, c. I-8, s. 14.

their relationship with the Crown. There is no good reason, for example, why the Crown should be exempt from planning laws designed to order our environment, or building codes designed to promote health and safety, or speed limits designed to reduce accidents. Of course, the Crown does require many special powers and some immunities in order to govern effectively. But when special powers or immunities are needed, the Parliament or Legislature can and does provide them. In a system of responsible government, the executive branch of government is rarely denied the legislation it wants. When powers and immunities are specifically granted by statute, a powerful tradition insists that their scope be carefully defined. The immunity which is granted by the traditional presumption against the Crown being bound by statute is far broader than is needed by an executive which controls the legislative branch, and because it is not needed it conflicts with the basic constitutional assumption that the Crown should be under the law. It follows that the British Columbia reform is, in my view, an important improvement of the law.

(c) Exceptions to immunity

The desirability of abolishing the Crown's presumption of immunity from statute has not been lost on the courts. Dickson C.J. has commented that the immunity "seems to conflict with basic notions of equality before the law".[68] However, the courts are powerless to change the law. Not only is the rule of immunity well established at common law, in Canada it has been given statutory form in the Interpretation Act provisions that have just been described. Nevertheless, the courts have struggled to find ways of escaping from the rule of immunity. The result has been the creation of many exceptions to the rule. These have been fully examined elsewhere,[69] and will simply be briefly noted here.

There are six classes of statutes that are exempt from immunity. First, of course, are statutes that contain express words binding the Crown. Second are statutes that can be interpreted as giving rise to a necessary implication that the Crown is to be bound.[70] Third are statutes that are beneficial to the Crown (including particular provisions that are burdensome).[71] Fourth are statutes that are incorporated by reference (even if only by implication) into a contract entered

---

68 *R.* v. *Eldorado Nuclear* [1983] 2 S.C.R. 551, 558 (Crown agents immune from prosecution for allegedly entering into an illegal cartel, while private cartel members were liable).

69 Hogg, note 1, above, ch. 10.

70 E.g., *R.* v. *Ouellette* [1980] 1 S.C.R. 568 (Crown bound by costs provision in Criminal Code despite lack of express words); *A.G. Que.* v. *Expropriation Tribunal* [1986] 1 S.C.R. 732 (Crown bound by Expropriation Act despite lack of express words); contrast *Alta. Govt. Telephones* v. *Can.* [1989] 2 S.C.R. 225 (Crown agent not bound by Railway Act because of lack of express words and necessary implication).

71 E.g., *Sparling* v. *Que.* [1988] 2 S.C.R. 1015 (Crown agent bound by corporation law's insider-trading provisions because corporation law beneficial to Crown agent).

into by the Crown.[72] Fifth are statutes incorporated by reference (even if only by implication) into a statute binding on the Crown.[73] Sixth are all statutes relevant to a civil proceeding to which the Crown is a party.[74] Together, these exceptions do not quite eat up the rule, but they do make substantial inroads into the rule, and they yield a body of law that is both complex and uncertain. The law would be simplified and improved if other jurisdictions would follow the lead of British Columbia and Prince Edward Island by amending their Interpretation Acts to abolish the rule of Crown immunity.[75]

10.9 Federal complications

(a) Scope of presumption

The term ''the Crown'' is of course appropriate to describe any of the governments which represent the Crown throughout the Commonwealth. Within Canada alone the Crown is represented by a federal government and ten provincial governments. In this federal context, what is the scope of the presumption that the Crown is not bound by statutes except by express words or necessary implication? Plainly, this rule operates to exempt the Crown in right of the legislating government. Does it also operate to exempt the Crown in right of other governments as well? If an Ontario statute imposed rent controls in general terms upon landlords, the Crown in right of Ontario would of course be exempt from the controls if the statute did not bind the Crown by express words or necessary implication. But what of the Crown in right of Canada?

A wide view of the immunity rule would exempt the Crown in all its capacities from any legislation that did not bind the Crown by express words or necessary implication. A narrow view of the immunity rule would exempt only the Crown in right of the legislating government. If the issue were free from authority, I would argue that the narrow view was the preferable one. The narrow view involves a realistic recognition that each government is a separate legal person from the others.[76] The narrow view also has the advantage of limiting the scope of an immunity that has no justification. There is some authority in favour

72 E.g. *Bank of Montreal* v. *A.G. Que.* [1979] 1 S.C.R. 565 (Crown as customer of bank bound by Bills of Exchange Act).

73 E.g., *Re Mar-Lise Industries* [1969] 2 O.R. 404 (C.A.) (Crown agent authorized to lend money bound by statute regarding chattel mortgages).

74 *Can. Ind. Gas & Oil* v. *Govt. of Sask.* [1979] 1 S.C.R. 37 (Crown bound by statute requiring judgment debtor to pay interest on unsatisfied judgment).

75 So recommended in Ontario Law Reform Commission, *Report on the Liability of the Crown* (1990), 113. I disclose that I was the research director of the project that culminated in the Commission's report.

76 Notes 3 5 and accompanying text, above.

of the narrow view.[77] However, the weight of modern authority is firmly on the side of the wide view.[78] According to this view, the presumption, both in its statutory form and its common law form, benefits an indivisible Crown, making no distinction between the Crown in right of the legislating government and the Crown in right of other governments.

(b) Meaning of the Crown

A related problem concerns the meaning of the term "the Crown" (or "Her Majesty" or any other equivalent) when it is used in a statute. Does this mean the Crown in right of the legislating government only, or does it include the Crown in right of other governments as well? Sometimes the context will suggest an answer. Where it does not, Canadian courts have tended to favour the wide view, sometimes buttressing the view with the rhetoric of an indivisible Crown.[79]

(c) Constitutional limitations

Finally, and most difficult of all, is the question of the extent to which the Parliament or a Legislature has the constitutional power to make laws binding upon other governments in the Canadian federation. If, for example, an Ontario statute did, as a matter of interpretation, purport to bind the Crown in right of Canada, a constitutional question would arise: is it within the power of the Ontario Legislature to pass a statute binding the Dominion? Nor can the constitutional question be kept wholly separate from the questions of interpretation. If it were decided that the Legislature of Ontario has no constitutional power to pass a statute binding the Crown in right of Canada, then this decision might react on the interpretation of the statute because of the doctrine that the prima facie interpretation of a statute should be "read down" so far as is necessary to preserve the statute from invalidity.[80]

---

77 *Dominion Building Corp.* v. *The King* [1933] A.C. 533 (Ontario statute binds Crown in right of Canada).

78 *Gauthier* v. *The King* (1918) 56 S.C.R. 176 (Ontario statute does not bind Crown in right of Canada); *The Queen (Alta.)* v. *Can. Transport Commn.* [1978] 1 S.C.R. 61 (federal statute does not bind Crown in right of Alberta); *Alta. Govt. Telephones* v. *Can.* [1989] 2 S.C.R. 225 (federal statute does not bind Crown in right of Alberta.

79 *A.-G. B.C.* v. *C.P.R.* [1906] A.C. 204; *A.-G. Que.* v. *Nipissing Central Ry. Co.* [1926] A.C. 715; *Nickel Rim Mines Ltd.* v. *A.-G. Ont.* [1967] S.C.R. 672; *The Queen (Alta.)* v. *Can. Transport Commn.* [1978] 1 S.C.R. 61, 71-76; *Alta. Govt. Telephones* v. *Can.* [1989] 2 S.C.R. 225, 274.

80 *The Queen (Alta.)* v. *Can. Transport Comm.* [1978] 1 S.C.R. 61, 71-76; and see note 64, above. In the case cited, Laskin C.J. reasoned in the other direction, holding in effect that the common law rule of immunity should protect the provinces from federal laws because they had no constitutional protection from federal laws: *Id.*, 76.

(d) Provincial laws binding federal Crown

There is no doubt that the federal Parliament may adopt by reference the laws of a province and make them applicable to the federal Crown.[81] What is in doubt is the extent to which the laws of a province may be made binding upon the federal Crown by their own force, that is to say, without any adoption by the federal Parliament. In *Gauthier* v. *The King* (1918),[82] the question was whether the federal Crown was bound by Ontario's Arbitration Act. The Act expressly applied to ''His Majesty'', and therefore undoubtedly bound the Ontario government. But what of the federal government? The Supreme Court of Canada held that the federal Crown was not bound by the Ontario statute. There are three elements to the result in this case. First, as to the proper interpretation of the reference to ''His Majesty'' in the Ontario statute, their lordships held that it should be interpreted as applying only to the Crown in right of Ontario. Secondly, as to the scope of the presumption that the Crown is exempt from statutes, their lordships, while evidently not appreciating that this was an issue, necessarily held that the presumption of Crown immunity extends to the Crown in all its capacities.[83] Thirdly, while one of the three opinions interpreted the Ontario statute without recourse to constitutional questions, the other two opinions placed some reliance upon an alleged constitutional principle that a province was in any event incompetent to make its legislation binding on the federal Crown.[84]

A few years later, however, the Privy Council reached a different result. In *Dominion Building Corp.* v. *The King* (1933),[85] one of the questions to be decided was whether an Ontario statute applied to the federal Crown. The statute was not expressed to be binding on the Crown or Her Majesty, so that the first issue in *Gauthier* did not have to be determined. But the Privy Council determined that the general language of the Ontario statute was applicable to the federal Crown, notwithstanding the absence of express words or a necessary implication to that effect. And by implication the Privy Council also determined that there was no constitutional impediment to a provincial law binding the federal Crown.

These two inconsistent decisions have left in doubt the question whether provincial Legislatures have the constitutional power to enact statutes binding on the federal Crown. Later decisions have not clarified the position,[86] although the

---

81 Gibson ''Interjurisdictional Immunity in Canadian Federalism'' (1969) 47 Can. Bar Rev. 40, 46.

82 (1918) 56 S.C.R. 176.

83 If the presumption applied only to the Crown in right of Ontario (the legislating jurisdiction), then the federal Crown would have been bound by the statute even if the express binding clause did not apply to the federal Crown.

84 *Id.*, 182 per Fitzpatrick C.J., 194 per Anglin J.

85 [1933] A.C. 533.

86 *CNR* v. *Nor-Min Supplies* [1977] 1 S.C.R. 322 decides that provincial mechanics lien legislation applies to land owned by CNR, an agent of the federal Crown. The question whether federal Crown land is immune from provincial law does not seem to have been argued, and was not discussed by the Court.

weight of dicta supports a constitutional immunity from provincial statutes for the federal Crown.[87] In my opinion, however, there should be no such immunity. In general, where the federal Crown is engaging in activity which is regulated by provincial law, it should be bound by the law. This is not a serious impairment of federal power for two reasons: first, only provincial laws in relation to provincial subject matters will be valid, and it may be safely assumed that a provincial law which purported to single out the federal Crown for especially severe treatment would be found to be ultra vires.[88] Secondly, if the federal Parliament wishes to provide immunity from provincial laws for the federal government, the Parliament has the power to do so: an appropriately drafted federal statute which protected a federal activity from provincial law would effectively override any inconsistent provincial law through the doctrine of paramountcy.

(e) Provincial laws binding other provinces

Does a provincial Legislature have the constitutional power to enact a law binding on the Crown in right of another province? This question seems never to have been explicitly decided.[89] It cannot arise very frequently, because the provincial Legislature's powers are confined to the territory of the province, and any attempt to reach into another province would be defeated by the rule of extraterritoriality.[90] However, the Crown in right of a province (or a Crown agent) has the capacity to engage in activities in another province, such as making a contract, holding property or bringing court proceedings.[91] When that happens, there is no rule of constitutional law that would exempt the Crown's activities from the law of the province in which they are carried on.[92] Even if the federal Crown is immune from the law of a province (a dubious proposition, for the reasons given in the previous section), the federal Crown must in the nature of things have a presence in each province, which (it could be argued) justifies some degree of

---

87 *The Queen (Alta.)* v. *Can. Transport Comm.* [1978] 1 S.C.R. 61, 72; *A.-G. Que. and Keable* v. *A.-G. Can.* [1979] 1 S.C.R. 218, 244; see also Laskin, note 1, above, 124-125; Goldenberg, note 6, above, 341, 400-401; McNairn, *Governmental and Intergovernmental Immunity* (1977), 35; cf. ch. 15, Judicial Review on Federal Grounds, under heading 15.4(k) ''Interjurisdictional immunity'', below.

88 See ch. 15, Judicial Review on Federal Grounds, under heading 15.4(b), ''Singling out'', below.

89 In *Re Caisse de Dépt et Placement du Qué.* (1983) 42 O.R. (2d) 561 (Div. Ct.), the Court relied on the indivisible Crown to hold that the Quebec Crown was immune from the Ontario Securities Act by virtue of the presumption of Crown immunity. There was no need to go on to the constitutional question. In 1984, the Act was amended to include a provision binding the Crown. In *Re Asbestos Corp.* (1991) 1 O.R. (3d) 723 (Div. Ct.), the Court held that the Quebec Crown was bound by the Act, but the Court overlooked the constitutional question altogether.

90 See ch. 13, Extraterritorial Competence, under heading 13.3, ''Provincial Legislatures'', below.

91 See ch. 13, Extraterritorial Competence, under heading 13.4, ''The Crown'', below.

92 The rule of statutory interpretation may have that effect, of course: note 89, above. The text contemplates a provincial statute that is apt, as a matter of interpretation, to apply to the Crown in right of another province.

protection from provincial laws. But "it is not imperative for provincial Crowns to engage in activities outside their boundaries, so it is fair to treat them like everyone else in the area when they choose to do so."[93]

(f) Federal laws binding provincial Crown

In contrast to the reluctance to hold that provincial laws bind the federal Crown, the courts have shown no hesitation in holding that federal laws apply to the provincial Crown.[94] Thus, federal customs legislation has been held applicable to the Crown in right of British Columbia as an importer of Scotch whisky,[95] federal railway legislation authorizing expropriation of "lands of the Crown" has been held applicable to provincial Crown lands,[96] federal provision as to the litigation costs of "Her Majesty" has been held applicable to the costs of the provincial Crown,[97] federal railways regulation has been held applicable to the Crown in right of Ontario as operator of the "Go-Train" commuter service on C.N.R. tracks[98], and federal taxing legislation has been held to impose an administrative duty on the provinces to collect and remit the tax.[99] These holdings appear to me to be sound,[100] but they do not sit easily with the suggestions of federal immunity from provincial laws.[101] If anything, the provinces have the stronger claim to judge-made immunity from federal law, because the provinces cannot protect themselves through the doctrine of paramountcy.

---

93 Gibson, note 81, above, 61. Accord, *Re Asbestos Corp.*, note 89, above; McNairn, note 87, above, 33. Contra, Laskin, note 1, above, 124.

94 See generally Lederman in Lang (ed.), *Contemporary Problems of Public Law in Canada* (1968), 116-118; Laskin, note 1, above, 123, but compare 121; Goldenberg, note 6, above, 341, 400-401; Gibson, note 81, above, 59-61.

95 *A.-G. B.C.* v. *A.-G. Can.* (Johnny Walker) [1924] A.C. 222.

96 *A.-G. B.C.* v. *C.P.R.* [1906] A.C. 204; *A.-G. Que.* v. *Nipissing Central Ry. Co.* [1926] A.C. 715; see also *Re Exported Natural Gas Tax* [1982] 1 S.C.R. 1004, 1050-1053.

97 *Nickel Rim Mines Ltd.* v. *A.-G. Ont.* [1967] S.C.R. 672.

98 *The Queen (Ont.)* v. *Bd. of Transport Commrs.* (Go-Train) [1968] S.C.R. 118. See also *Alta. Govt. Telephones* v. *Can.* [1989] 2 S.C.R. 225, 275, 301 (obiter dicta that federal Parliament has power to bind provincial Crown agent).

99 *Re GST* [1992] 2 S.C.R. 445.

100 The more general question of the extent to which the laws of one level of government may apply to matters within the legislative competence of the other level is discussed in sec. 15.4(k), "Interjurisdictional immunity", below.

101 In *The Queen (Alta.)* v. *Can. Transport Comm.* [1978] 1 S.C.R. 61, 72, Laskin C.J. referred to the two different rules with evident approval. See also Laskin, note 1, above, 124, where the author tentatively explains the difference by saying that "the theory . . . may be that the federal Crown is external both to the provincial catalogue of powers as well as to the territorial ambit of provincial legislation". But the first point simply begs the question, and the second point seems wrong since no extraterritorial power is required to make the federal Crown bound by provincial law within the province. That the author was not really satisfied by these explanations is suggested by his closing point: "Nor is logic a constitutional imperative calling for reciprocal authority". (*Ibid.*).

It has been argued that it is implicit in the federal form of government that there be an immunity from federal laws for at least the essential functions of provincial governments.[102] This has been recognized in Australia,[103] although not in the United States.[104] There are two Canadian cases that could be read as supporting the existence of such an immunity,[105] but the weight of authority is against it.[106]

---

102 Laskin, note 1, above, 121, but compare 123; Swinton, ''Federalism and Provincial Government Immunity'' (1979) 29 U. Toronto L.J. 1.

103 *Melbourne* v. *Commonwealth* (State Banking) (1974) 74 C.L.R. 31 (Commonwealth may not prohibit banks from lending money to states); *Queensland Electricity Commission* v. *Commonwealth* (1985) 159 C.L.R. 193 (Commonwealth may not single out state for special labour relations procedure).

104 *Garcia* v. *San Antonio Metropolitan Transit Authority* (1985) 469 U.S. 528 (federal minimum wage law applies to state and local governments).

105 *Re Troops in Cape Breton* [1930] S.C.R. 554 includes an obiter dictum (at p. 562) that the federal Parliament cannot impose a financial obligation on a province. The reason given was that ''the right of appropriation of [provincial revenues] belongs to the legislature of the province exclusively''. *Regional Municipality of Peel* v. *MacKenzie* [1982] 2 S.C.R. 9 decides that the federal Parliament cannot require a municipality to contribute to the support of juvenile delinquents. Martland J. for the Court relied (at p. 20) on *Re Troops in Cape Breton*, and the inability to impose a financial obligation on a province or municipality. It seems unlikely, however, that Martland J. was articulating a general doctrine of immunity, because he also emphasized (at p. 22) that the impugned financial provisions of the Act were ''not truly necessary for the effective exercise of Parliament's legislative authority in these fields [of criminal law or criminal procedure]''. The obvious inference was that, if the provisions had been ''truly necessary'', they would have been valid.

106 *Re Anti-Inflation Act* [1976] 2 S.C.R. 373, 430 (obiter dictum asserting federal power to impose wage and price controls on provincial and local governments); *Alta. Govt. Telephones* v. *Can.* [1989] 2 S.C.R. 225, 275 (obiter dictum expressly rejecting Swinton's argument, note 101 above, for provincial immunity from federal laws). See generally ch. 15, Judicial Review on Federal Grounds, under heading 15.8, ''Interjurisdictional immunity'', below.

11

Treaties

11.1 Definition of treaty

A treaty is an agreement entered into between states which is binding in international law.[1] A treaty may be between only two states (bilateral), or more than two states (multilateral). It may be called a ''treaty'', or it may be called any one of a variety of other names: a ''convention'', a ''charter'', a ''protocol'', and many others, including simply an ''agreement''. For those versed in international diplomacy, each of these names does carry certain connotations as to the nature of the treaty, but the various names are of no legal significance: all agreements between states which are intended to be binding in international law, by whatever name they are called, are treaties.

---

1 For a valuable collection of materials, notes and bibliography on the law of treaties in Canada, see Kindred (ed.), *International Law* (5th ed., 1993), ch. 3.

11.2 Power to make treaties

Because a treaty is an agreement which is binding in international law, a treaty can only be made by an entity having international legal personality. In 1867 the various colonies of the British Empire, although many of them (including those of British North America) were self-governing in domestic affairs, lacked the capacity to enter into treaties. The Empire spoke with one voice, and the voice was that of the imperial government in Great Britain. The common law accorded to the Crown (the executive branch of government in Great Britain) full power to conduct foreign affairs, including the making of treaties, for the entire Empire. In 1867, therefore, it was the British government which entered into treaties binding the Empire, or any part of the Empire. As the Empire became the Commonwealth, and as its members acquired international personality in their own right, the treaty-making powers of the British government were gradually distributed to the independent members of the Commonwealth.[2]

In Canada's case the formal grant of treaty-making power is not to be found in the Constitution Act, 1867 (which did not contemplate that Canada would become an independent nation), but in the instrument by which the King or Queen in Great Britain delegated the prerogative powers over foreign affairs to the Governor General of Canada, who would exercise the powers upon the advice of the Canadian government. The current instrument of delegation is a comprehensive document which was adopted in 1947 and which is entitled Letters Patent constituting the office of Governor General of Canada.[3] In this document, no prerogative power over Canada is withheld: by clause 2 the Governor General is authorized "to exercise all powers and authorities lawfully belonging to Us [the King] in respect of Canada". This language undoubtedly delegates to the federal government of Canada the power to enter into treaties binding Canada.

Even without an express delegation of treaty-making power, Canada's achievement of full independence would necessarily carry with it the power to enter into treaties, and in the absence of any contrary constitutional provision the power would be located with the executive branch of the government which represents the country as a whole, namely, the federal government.[4] In recent years, there has been a claim that the Canadian provinces possess treaty-making competence under the Constitution and in international law. This claim will be examined at the end of this chapter,[5] because it can be understood only in the

2 See Kennedy, *The Constitution of Canada 1534-1937* (2nd ed., 1938), chs. 20, 25 and pp. 510-518; Hopkins, *Confederation at the Crossroads* (1968), ch. 11; Stanley, *A Short History of the Canadian Constitution* (1969), ch. 7; Jacomy-Millette, *Treaty Law in Canada* (1975), Part I; Beaudoin, *Le Constitution du Canada* (1990), ch. 17.

3 It is reproduced in R.S.C. 1985, Appendix II, No. 31.

4 For explanations of the source of federal treaty-making power, see Gotlieb, *Canadian Treaty-Making* (1968), 28-30; Morris, "The Treaty-Making Power" (1967) 45 Can. Bar Rev. 478, 482-484.

5 Section 11.3, "Provincial treaty-making", below.

light of the constitutional law respecting the implementation of treaties. For the moment, it suffices to say that the provincial claim has never been accepted by the federal government, and the federal government does in fact exercise exclusive treaty-making powers.

11.3 Procedure for making treaties

(a) Signing

International law does not prescribe any formal procedures for the making of treaties, and there are a variety of procedures in use. The most formal treaty is in "head of state" form, which means that for Canada the Queen would be named as a party. Until 1947, treaties in head of state form required a formal act by the King in London, but since 1947 it has become possible to conclude all formalities in Canada.[6] However, the treaty in head of state form has become so unusual in international practice that Canada has never since 1947 had occasion to use its new formal powers.[7] The treaty in head of state form has been supplanted by its less formal cousin, the treaty in intergovernmental form, which is a treaty in which the governments (not the formal heads of state) of the agreeing states are named as the parties. Treaties in intergovernmental form are signed by an official (called a plenipotentiary) who acts under the authority of an "instrument of full power", which is a document signed by the foreign minister (for Canada the Secretary of State for External Affairs) granting to the plenipotentiary "full power" to sign the treaty.[8] A third kind of treaty, which is less formal than the treaty in intergovernmental form, and which is now more common, is the treaty in exchange-of-notes form. This is concluded by an exchange of notes (or letters) between the two agreeing states; the notes may be signed by the states' foreign ministers or by ambassadors or high commissioners or even by a minister in charge of a department other than external affairs.[9] A treaty in exchange-of-notes form does not consist of a single formal document, but of two documents: the first is the note in which one state proposes to another the terms of the agreement, and the second is the note in reply in which the other state accepts the proposed terms. Multilateral treaties are rarely concluded in exchange-of-notes form.

---

6 Before 1939 any document which required authentication under the Great Seal of the Realm had to be sealed in London, because Canada had no Great Seal of its own. The Seals Act, S.C. 1939, c. 22, created the Great Seal of Canada, and obviated the necessity to send documents to London for sealing. But treaties in head of state form still had to go to London for the King's approval prior to sealing in Canada, because the Governor General lacked the authority to give this approval. This disability was removed in 1947 with the adoption of new Letters Patent constituting the office of Governor General: note 3 and accompanying text, above.

7 Gotlieb, note 4, above, 40.

8 Gotlieb, note 4, above, 87, gives an example of an instrument of full power.

9 *Id.*, 33.

(b) Ratification

Treaties in exchange-of-notes form and some treaties in intergovernmental form come into force on the signing of the agreement, or the delivery of the second note (the reply to the first note), or on a date specified in the agreement.[10] A treaty of a more formal character will often provide that it does not come into force until it has been ''ratified'' by the states that have signed it. In keeping with the general tendency towards less formality in international relations, only a minority of treaties now require ratification before they come into force. For a Canadian treaty in intergovernmental form which does require ratification, the Secretary of State for External Affairs will sign an ''instrument of ratification'' which certifies that the government of Canada ratifies the treaty. In the case of bilateral treaties, the two states will then exchange the instruments of ratification in a brief formal ceremony. In the case of multilateral treaties, the treaty will provide that instruments of ratification be deposited with a specified government or international organization, and the ''depositary'' will be under a duty to inform all parties of ratifications that have been deposited.[11]

(c) Role of Parliament

The Canadian Parliament plays no necessary role in the making of treaties. The negotiation and conclusion of a treaty is part and parcel of the conduct of international relations, and the conduct of international relations has always been one of the prerogatives of the Crown; in other words, the executive branch of government has the power to make treaties without the necessity of parliamentary authority. There is no legal requirement that the Parliament give its approval to either the signing or the ratification of a treaty.[12] The position in the United States is different. The United States' Constitution, by article 2, s. 2(2), empowers the President to make treaties only with the approval of a two-thirds majority in the Senate. The executive of the United States is therefore obliged by its constitutional law to obtain the approval of one house of the Congress as part of the process of making a treaty.[13]

Despite the absence of any constitutional obligation to obtain parliamentary approval, it has been the practice of Canadian governments to obtain parliamentary approval of the most important treaties in the interval between signing and ratification. The government will lay the treaty before Parliament and move a

---

10 *Id.*, 33-34.

11 *Id.*, 37-49.

12 *Id.*, 14. As we shall notice later in the next section of this chapter, however, the implementation of a treaty, if it involves a change in the internal law of Canada, will require a statute enacted by the Parliament of Canada, or the provincial Legislatures, or both.

13 This requirement may be avoided by the President entering into an ''executive agreement''; see note 18, below.

resolution in each House approving the treaty. The resolution is not in statutory form, and does not receive royal assent. Of all the treaties which Canada ratified between 1946 and 1966 approximately one quarter were submitted to Parliament for approval. However, there is no practice of securing Parliament's approval of treaties which do not require ratification, and these are now the more common kind of treaty.[14]

11.4 Implementing treaties

(a) The need for legislation

The narrative so far has been concerned with the making of treaties, that is to say, the formation of treaty obligations. But the making of a treaty must be distinguished from the implementing of the treaty, that is to say, the performance of the treaty obligations. As soon as a treaty is made and in force, the states that are parties to the treaty come under an obligation in international law to implement the treaty.

Canada's constitutional law, derived in this respect from the United Kingdom, does not recognize a treaty as part of the internal (or ''municipal'') law of Canada. Accordingly, a treaty which requires a change in the internal law of Canada can only be implemented by the enactment of a statute which makes the required change in the law. Many treaties do not require a change in the internal law of the states which are parties. This is true of treaties which do not impinge on individual rights, nor contravene existing laws, nor require action outside the executive powers of the government which made the treaty. For example, treaties between Canada and other states relating to defence, foreign aid, the high seas, the air, research, weather stations, diplomatic relations and many other matters, may be able to be implemented simply by the executive action of the Canadian government which made the treaty.[15] But many treaties cannot be implemented without an alteration in the internal law of Canada. For example, treaties between Canada and other states relating to patents, copyrights, taxation of foreigners, extradition, and many other matters, can often be implemented only by the enactment of legislation to alter the internal law of Canada.[16]

The rule that a statute is needed to implement a treaty which involves a change in Canada's internal law contrasts with the rule in the United States. The United States' Constitution, by article 6, simply makes ''all treaties'' part of ''the supreme law of the land''. The reason for this difference between Canada and the United States lies in the different procedures for making treaties. We have already

14 Gotlieb, note 4, above, 18.

15 However, any expenditure of money requires parliamentary appropriation.

16 See Macdonald, ''International Treaty Law and the Domestic Law of Canada'' (1975) 2 Dal. L.J. 307.

noticed that in the United States the Constitution requires the President to obtain the approval of the Senate before he concludes a treaty.[17] It is therefore easy to understand why the Constitution incorporates the treaty into the internal law of the United States.[18] But in Canada, where there is no constitutional requirement of parliamentary approval prior to the making of a treaty, it would offend against the basic principle of parliamentary supremacy if the executive could alter the law of the land merely by making a treaty.

It follows that the courts of Canada (and of other countries with British-derived constitutions) will not give effect to a treaty unless it has been enacted into law by the appropriate legislative body; or, to put the same proposition in another way, the courts will apply the law laid down by statute or common law, even if it is inconsistent with a treaty which is binding upon Canada.[19] In a case where Canada's internal law is not in conformity with a treaty binding upon Canada, then Canada is in breach of its international obligations and may be liable in international law to pay damages or suffer other sanctions,[20] but the breach of a treaty is irrelevant to the rights of parties to litigation in a Canadian court. The only concession which the Canadian courts have been prepared to make in recognition of Canada's international obligations is to interpret statutes so as to conform as far as possible with international law.[21] But where the language of a

17 Text accompanying note 13, above.

18 Senate approval is not required for an ''executive agreement'', which is an agreement between the President and a foreign country. An executive agreement has been held not to be a ''treaty'' within article 2, s. 2(2), of the U.S. Constitution; and is therefore not subject to the requirement of Senate approval. However, in international law such an agreement is an informal treaty which is just as binding as a formal treaty. Moreover, the courts of the United States have accepted that an executive agreement, while not a treaty under article 2, s. 2(2), is a valid treaty for other purposes and is part of ''the supreme law of the land'' under article 6: *U.S.* v. *Belmont* (1937) 301 U.S. 324; *U.S.* v. *Pink* (1942) 315 U.S. 203.

19 *Francis* v. *The Queen* [1956] S.C.R. 618 (refusal to enforce treaty granting customs exemption to Indians); *Capital Cities Communications* v. *CRTC* [1978] 2 S.C.R. 141, 173 (refusal to enforce radio communications convention).

20 A state cannot . . . plead its municipal law as an excuse for failing to fulfil its international obligations'': Greig, *International Law* (2nd ed., 1976), 53.

21 *Re Tax on Foreign Legations* [1943] S.C.R. 208; Comment, (1943) 21 Can. Bar Rev. 506; Jacomy-Millette, note 2, above, 280-290. The proposition in the text is the orthodox one, and it seems to me to be the law of Canada, but it should be noted that it is not without controversy. La Forest, ''May the Provinces Legislate in Violation of International Law?'' (1961) 39 Can. Bar Rev. 78, argues that the provincial Legislatures (but not the federal Parliament) are incompetent to legislate in violation of customary international law (but not treaties). Vanek, ''Is International Law Part of the Law of Canada?'' (1960) 8 U. Toronto L.J. 251, goes even further, arguing that the federal Parliament and the provincial Legislatures are incompetent to legislate in violation of either customary international law or treaties. These views are inconsistent with conventional notions as to the relationship of international law to internal law and the plenary and ample legislative powers of the Canadian legislative bodies. The power of a province to legislate in violation of international law is discussed inconclusively in *Re Alta. Union of Provincial Employees* (1980) 120 D.L.R. (3d) 590, 607-622 (Alta. Q.B.); affd. (1981) 130 D.L.R. (3d) 191 (Alta. C.A.) (holding that denial of right to strike did not violate international law).

statute is clearly and unmistakably inconsistent with a treaty or other rule of international law, then there is no room for interpreting it into conformity with the international rule and the statute must be applied as it stands.[22]

(b) The federal problem

In a unitary state, there is rarely any difficulty in performing a treaty obligation which necessitates a change in the internal law of the state. In the United Kingdom or New Zealand, for example, once the government has entered into a treaty, it can easily secure the passage of any legislation which is necessary to perform the treaty obligations. There is only one Parliament for the whole country and that Parliament has power to make laws upon all subject matters. Moreover, in a system of responsible government, the government is usually able to control the Parliament. The result is that the government which has the power to form treaty obligations also has the power to see that the obligations are performed through legislative action. The position of a federal state is not so simple. Because legislative power is distributed among a central and several regional legislative bodies, there is the possibility that treaties made by the central government can be performed only by the regional legislative bodies which are not controlled by the central government and which can rarely be persuaded to act in unison.

(c) The United States

In the United States, as we have already noticed, article 6 of the Constitution makes a treaty part of "the supreme law of the land". A treaty made by the central government will therefore become law even if it deals with a subject matter which would otherwise be within the legislative competence of the states; and, if the treaty conflicts with existing or subsequent state laws, the treaty will take precedence.[23]

---

22 The text deals with only a small part of the relationship between international law (which includes both customary and conventional (treaty) law) and domestic law (both statutory and common law). For fuller studies, see Claydon, "The Application of Human Rights Law by Canadian Courts" (1981) 30 Buffalo L. Rev. 727; Claydon, "International Human Rights Law and the Interpretation of the Charter" (1982) 4 Supreme Court L.R. 287; Mendes, "Interpreting the Charter" (1982) 20 Alta. L. Rev. 383; Cohen and Bayefsky, "The Canadian Charter of Rights and Freedoms and Public International Law" (1983) 61 Can. Bar Rev. 265; Schabas, *International Human Rights Law and the Canadian Charter* (2nd ed., 1996). As these works show, the growing body of international human rights law may be an important influence on Canadian domestic law.

23 Where there is conflict between a treaty and a federal statute (an Act of Congress), the rule is that whichever of the two is later in date is deemed to repeal the earlier to the extent of the inconsistency: *Edye* v. *Robertson* (1884) 112 U.S. 580. Of course, if a federal statute does alter or repeal a treaty rule, the United States will be in breach of its treaty obligation in international law.

Article 6 of the Constitution of the United States applies only to those treaties which are "self-executing", that is to say, those treaties which express their obligations in terms which are sufficiently definite and precise to be enforceable like a statute in the courts. Many treaties are not self-executing, either because their terms are vague, or because their terms are more in the nature of promises of future action than immediately binding rules. A treaty which is not self-executing does require the passage of more detailed legislation for its implementation. If the subject matter of the treaty would in any event be within the competence of the federal Congress, then it is obvious that the Congress will be the body with authority to enact the implementing legislation. But what if the subject matter of the treaty would normally be within the competence of the state Legislatures? Does the existence of the treaty alter the distribution of legislative competence? On principle, one would expect the answer to be yes. Since a self-executing treaty will prevail in an area of state legislative competence and even in the face of inconsistent state laws, one would expect the federal Congress to have the power to implement a non-self-executing treaty even when its subject matter would otherwise be within state legislative competence. The authorities are neither numerous nor definitive in their answer, but they indicate that this is probably the position.[24]

(d) Australia

In Australia, there is no provision in the Constitution which gives to treaties the force of internal law, but s. 51(29) of the Constitution allocates to the federal Parliament the power to make laws "with respect to ... external affairs". In a series of cases, the High Court of Australia has decided that the external affairs power includes the power to enact legislation performing treaty obligations, even if in the absence of the treaty the subject matter of the legislation would be within the exclusive competence of the state Legislatures. In *R.* v. *Burgess*; *ex parte Henry* (1936),[25] the Court upheld a federal statute that was designed to implement a treaty concerning air navigation, although the treaty contemplated the regulation of intrastate aviation, a matter that in Australia would otherwise be outside federal legislative power.[26] In *Koowarta* v. *Bjelke-Petersen* (1982),[27] the Court upheld a federal statute that prohibited racial discrimination in (among other things) the disposition of property, another matter that in Australia would otherwise be outside federal legislative power; the statute was upheld on the basis that it

---

24 *Missouri* v. *Holland* (1920) 252 U.S. 416 is the leading case; see generally, Nowak, Rotunda, Young, *Constitutional Law* (3rd ed., 1986), 201-212.

25 (1936) 55 C.L.R. 608.

26 The statute in issue authorized the government to make regulations for the purpose of implementing the treaty. The High Court held that the statute was valid, but that the regulations which had been made under it were ultra vires because they departed from the terms of the treaty.

27 (1982) 153 C.L.R. 168.

implemented a treaty prohibiting racial discrimination. In *Commonwealth* v. *Tasmania* (Franklin Dam) (1983),[28] the Court upheld a federal statute that prohibited the construction of a hydro-electric dam in Tasmania, on the ground that the dam would flood a wilderness area listed for preservation by the ''World Heritage Committee'', an international body acting under a treaty for the protection of the cultural and natural heritage of the world; the construction of the dam would otherwise have been within the jurisdiction of the Tasmanian Legislature (which had in fact purported to authorize construction).

These decisions of the High Court of Australia, and especially the *Franklin Dam* case, indicate that the federal Parliament's external affairs power includes an extensive power to implement the terms of treaties.[29] The dominant school of thought holds that the mere fact that Australia has entered into a treaty in good faith[30] brings the subject matter of that treaty within the external affairs power. A minority school of thought, concerned about an unreviewable expansion of federal power, holds that the subject matter of a treaty must possess some objective (but hard to define) ''international'' element in order to come within the external affairs power. The former school gained the ascendancy in the *Franklin Dam* case, but the Court split four to three,[31] with the three dissenting judges calling for an additional international element which in their view was lacking from the preservation of wilderness in Tasmania.[32]

11.5 Implementing treaties in Canada

(a) Section 132

Canada has a provision in its Constitution which is addressed to the power to perform treaties. Section 132 of the Constitution Act, 1867 provides that:

---

28 (1983) 158 C.L.R. 1; folld. in *Richardson* v. *Forestry Commn.* (1988) 164 C.L.R. 261 (upholding interim protection order under treaty power).

29 For a discussion and commentary on the Australian jurisprudence, see Strom and Finkle, ''Treaty Implementation: The Canadian Game Needs Australian Rules'' (1993), 25 Ottawa L. Rev. 39; Struthers, '''Treaty Implementation . . . Australian Rules': A Rejoinder'' (1994), 26 Ottawa L. Rev. 305.

30 A ''colourable'' treaty, entered into simply to augment legislative power, would not of course satisfy this school, but it is not easy to imagine how colourability would be established, and in practice the problems have arisen with multilateral treaties, where the large number of party states makes a colourability argument completely implausible.

31 The majority consisted of Murphy, Mason, Brennan and Deane JJ.; the dissenters were Gibbs C.J., Wilson and Dawson JJ.

32 In *Burgess*, Evatt and McTiernan JJ. and, perhaps, Latham C.J. took the absolute view; Dixon and Starke JJ., who concurred in the result, insisted upon an additional international element, which they found to be present. In *Koowarta*, Mason, Murphy and Brennan JJ. took the absolute view; Stephen J., who concurred in the result, and Gibbs C.J., Aickin and Wilson JJ., who dissented, insisted upon an additional international element, which Stephen J. found to be present, and the dissenters found to be absent.

> The Parliament and government of Canada shall have all powers necessary or proper for performing the obligations of Canada or of any province thereof, as part of the British Empire, towards foreign countries, arising under treaties between the Empire and such foreign countries.

This provision rather clearly grants to the federal Parliament the power to enact legislation which is necessary to implement treaties but it refers only to treaties between the ''British Empire'' and foreign countries. The reason why s. 132 is framed in these terms is that in 1867 the conduct of international affairs for the entire Empire was still firmly vested in the British (imperial) government, and it was the British government which negotiated, signed and ratified all treaties which applied to the Empire or to any part of the Empire. The treaties were then submitted to the colonial governors for implementation in their colonies. The framers of the Constitution Act, 1867 assumed correctly that the international obligations of the new Dominion of Canada would also be created by the imperial government in Britain. Accordingly, the Constitution Act, 1867 was silent as to the power to make treaties, and contemplated the performance only of ''Empire'' treaties.

What the framers of the Constitution Act, 1867 apparently did not foresee was the evolution of Canada from colonial status to a fully independent member of the international community. This evolution[33] culminated in the Balfour Declaration, made at the imperial conference of 1926, which affirmed that Great Britain and the dominions were ''autonomous communities within the British Empire, equal in status, in no way subordinate one to another in any aspect of their domestic or external affairs''.[34] The imperial conference also specifically addressed the question of treaty-making, resolving that each dominion government had the power to negotiate, sign and ratify treaties on its own behalf.[35] After 1926, although some formal steps necessary for completion of a treaty in head of state form still had to be taken in London, they were taken solely on the advice of the Canadian government. These vestiges of the colonial past were finally removed in 1947,[36] but by then they had been without significance for more than twenty years. Less formal treaties — those in intergovernmental form or exchange-of-notes form — were after 1926 completed by Canadian officials without even formal British intervention.

(b) Labour Conventions case

Once Canada had obtained the power to conclude treaties on its own behalf, the question arose whether s. 132, with its reference to ''Empire'' treaties, could

33 See note 2, above.

34 Ollivier, *Colonial and Imperial Conferences* (1954), vol. 3, 146.

35 Ollivier, 150-155. On the imperial conferences of 1926 and 1930, see ch. 3, Independence, above.

36 Note 6, above.

be interpreted as conferring power to implement Canadian treaties. The answer came in the *Labour Conventions* case (1937).[37] In 1919, 1921 and 1928 the International Labour Organization, of which Canada was a member, adopted three conventions under which the members agreed to enact laws limiting the working hours of employees, and requiring a weekly rest and a minimum wage. These treaties were not to be binding upon a member state until the state had ratified them. The government of Canada ratified the three treaties in 1935. The government then introduced into the federal Parliament the legislation which was necessary to perform the treaty obligations, and the Limitation of Hours of Work Act, the Weekly Rest in Industrial Undertakings Act and the Minimum Wages Act were duly enacted.[38] The Supreme Court of Canada, sitting as a bench of six judges, divided evenly as to the validity of the statutes; but the Privy Council held them to be invalid. Lord Atkin, who wrote the Privy Council's opinion, rejected the argument that s. 132 supplied the power to enact the statutes. Section 132 authorized the performance of treaty obligations that bound Canada "as part of the British Empire", but not those that bound Canada "by virtue of her new status as an international person"; s. 132 authorized the performance of the treaty obligations which arose "under treaties between the Empire and ... foreign countries", but not those which arose under treaties between Canada and foreign countries.[39] On this reasoning, it followed that s. 132 was inapplicable.

If s. 132 did not supply the legislative power to implement Canadian, as opposed to Empire, treaties, where was the power to be found? In effect, Lord Atkin answered that this was the wrong question. For the purpose of the federal distribution of legislative powers, he said, "there is no such thing as treaty legislation as such. The distribution is based on classes of subjects; and as a treaty deals with a particular class of subjects so will the legislative power of performing it be ascertained".[40] In other words, in classifying a statute which was required to implement a Canadian treaty, one was supposed to disregard the fact that the purpose of the statute was to implement a treaty and look to the substantive subject matter of the statute. If the statute which was required for implementation of the treaty related to a matter allocated by s. 91 to the federal Parliament, then the federal Parliament would have the power to implement the treaty. If, on the other hand, the statute which was required for the implementation of the treaty related to a matter allocated by s. 92 to the provincial Legislatures, then the provincial Legislatures would have the power to implement the treaty. In this particular case, disregarding the existence of the treaties (the labour conventions), the statutes related to conditions of employment in industry, a matter within the class of subjects "property and civil rights in the province" which was allocated by s.

37 *A.-G. Can.* v. *A.-G. Ont.* (Labour Conventions) [1937] A.C. 326.
38 These three statutes were part of the "Canadian new deal".
39 [1937] A.C. 326, 349.
40 *Id.*, 351.

92(13) to the provincial Legislatures.[41] The result was, therefore, that it was the provincial Legislatures, and not the federal Parliament, which had the power to enact legislation of the kind necessary to implement the labour conventions. The federal legislation was accordingly unconstitutional.

(c) Evaluation of Labour Conventions case

It was in the *Labour Conventions* case that Lord Atkin used his famous ''watertight compartments'' metaphor: ''while the ship of state now sails on larger ventures and into foreign waters she still retains the watertight compartments which are an essential part of her original structure''.[42] For many critics, this dictum has typified the narrow and inflexible approach of the Privy Council to the interpretation of the Canadian Constitution. The reasoning in the *Labour Conventions* case is certainly open to criticism. It is true that the framers of the Constitution Act, 1867 did not contemplate that Canada would acquire treaty-making power in its own right, but does it follow that s. 132 cannot be ''strained'' or ''tortured'' to cover the uncontemplated event?[43] Section 132 makes abundantly clear that the federal Parliament was to have the power to implement treaties. Surely, it is an unduly narrow and literal interpretation of the section to refuse to allow it to continue to cover what is essentially the same subject matter. The result of the *Labour Conventions* case is that the federal Parliament has the power to implement ''Empire treaties''[44] under s. 132, but no power to implement Canadian treaties under s. 132. As F.R. Scott has said: ''So long as Canada clung to the Imperial apron strings, her Parliament was all powerful in legislating on Empire treaties, and no doctrine of 'watertight compartments' existed; once she became a nation in her own right, impotence descended''.[45] This may overstate the case, but the result is unquestionably anomalous.

Even if one agrees with the proposition that s. 132 cannot be extended to cover Canadian treaties, Lord Atkin's conclusion in the *Labour Conventions* case does not necessarily follow. The key to Lord Atkin's reasoning lies in his assertion, quoted above,[46] that for the purpose of the federal distribution of powers ''there is no such thing as treaty legislation as such''. This means that legislation implementing a treaty may not be classified as ''in relation to'' the treaty, but must be

41 See sec. 20.8, ''Labour relations'', below.

42 [1937] A.C. 326, 354.

43 [1937] A.C. 326, 350.

44 It was not technically accurate even in 1867 to speak of ''treaties between the British Empire and foreign countries''. Treaties were not made in the name of the British Empire. They were made by the King on the advice of his British ministers, and unless they contained provisions to the contrary they automatically bound all of his possessions. The non-technical language reinforces the argument made in the text that the language should not be read excessively literally: see Kennedy, *The Constitution of Canada 1534-1937* (2nd ed., 1938), 552.

45 Scott, ''Labour Conventions Case'' (1956) 34 Can. Bar Rev. 114, 115.

46 Note 40, above.

classified as in relation to the subject matter with which the treaty deals. This sweeping proposition is difficult to defend. Section 132, even if no longer literally applicable to modern treaties, shows by its very existence that treaty legislation is a distinct constitutional ''matter'' or ''value'' under the power-distributing provisions of the Constitution, and that it is no part of provincial legislative power. Once it is accepted that a law may be classified as ''in relation to'' a treaty, as s. 132 seems to insist, then, if s. 132 itself does not apply, the law must fall within the opening words of s. 91, which allocate to the federal Parliament the residuary power ''to make laws for the peace, order, and good government of Canada.''

The argument that legislation to implement a Canadian treaty is within the federal power over the peace, order, and good government of Canada was in fact accepted by the Privy Council in the *Radio Reference* (1932),[47] which was decided shortly before the *Labour Conventions* case. We now know too that this view attracted the support of at least one member of the Privy Council in the *Labour Conventions* case itself, because, although the Privy Council practice of that time did not permit the writing of dissenting opinions,[48] Lord Wright subsequently disclosed in an article in the Canadian Bar Review that he had dissented.[49] Since the abolition of Privy Council appeals there have been several dicta in the Supreme Court of Canada indicating a willingness to reconsider the reasoning in the *Labour Conventions* case,[50] and it may well be that the peace, order, and good government argument will ultimately prevail.

While it is necessary to conclude that the *Labour Conventions* case is a poorly reasoned decision, it is much more difficult to be confident that the result is undesirable as a matter of policy within a federation such as Canada.[51] On the side of criticism, it must be said that not only does the result appear to be in conflict with the spirit if not the literal words of s. 132, but it produces the highly inconvenient result that the government of Canada, which creates treaty obligations, is powerless to ensure the performance of many of those obligations. Of

---

47 [1932] A.C. 304, 312. While this was not the only reason given for the decision, it did seem to be part of the *ratio decidendi*.

48 See ch. 8, Supreme Court of Canada, under heading 8.2, ''Abolition of Privy Council appeals'', above.

49 Wright (1955) 33 Can. Bar Rev. 1123, 1125-1128. It has been suggested that, of the five judges who sat on the *Labour Conventions* case, Lord Wright's dissenting view was shared by Lord MacMillan; that Lord Atkin's view was shared by Lord Thankerton; and that the deciding vote was cast by Sir Sydney Rowlatt, a ''taxation judge'', who ''sat throughout the 1937 hearings in his overcoat making neither note nor comment'': MacKinnon (1956) 34 Can. Bar Rev. 115, 117.

50 *Johannesson* v. *West St. Paul* [1952] 1 S.C.R. 292, 303; *Francis* v. *The Queen* [1956] S.C.R. 618, 621; *Re Offshore Mineral Rights of B.C.* [1967] S.C.R. 792, 815-817; *MacDonald* v. *Vapor Can.* [1977] 2 S.C.R. 134, 167-172; *Schneider* v. *The Queen* [1982] 2 S.C.R. 112, 134-135; see also Rand (1960) 38 Can. Bar Rev. 135, 142-143.

51 For comparative studies, see Wheare, *Federal Government* (4th ed., 1963), ch. 9; Brossard, Patry and Weiser, *Les pouvoirs extérieurs du Québec* (1967); Van De Craen, ''The Federated State and its Treaty-Making Power'' (1983) 1 Revue Belge de Droit International 377.

course, it can still perform without impediment treaties which impose obligations which can be performed solely by the executive action of the federal government, and it can ensure the performance of treaties which require legislation within the legislative competence of the federal Parliament; but the federal government cannot ensure the performance of treaties which require legislation within the legislative competence of the provinces.

This does not mean that Canada is always precluded from signing, ratifying or performing treaties upon subjects within the legislative competence of the provinces. The federal government can consult with the provinces before assuming treaty obligations which would require provincial implementation, and if all provinces (or all affected provinces) agree to implement a particular treaty, then Canada can adhere to the treaty without reservation.[52] Even where prior provincial consent has not been obtained, Canada may feel free to adhere to a treaty because it includes a ''federal state clause''; under such a clause a federal state undertakes to perform only those obligations which are within central executive or legislative competence, and undertakes merely to bring to the notice of the provinces (or states or cantons), ''with a favourable recommendation'' for action, those obligations which are within regional competence.[53] Another device which enables a federal state to adhere to a treaty upon a subject matter outside central legislative competence is a ''reservation''; upon the ratification of the treaty, if it contains no federal state clause, and if provincial agreement has not been obtained, the federal state may add a reservation in respect of obligations within provincial competence, which will make clear that the federal state is not binding itself to those obligations. But when all is said and done it is clear that the *Labour Conventions* decision has impaired Canada's capacity to play a full role in international affairs, and Canada has been unable to accept or in some cases to fulfil treaties in respect of labour, education, the status of refugees, women's rights and human rights generally.[54]

In defence of the constitutional rule laid down by the *Labour Conventions* case, it may be said that Canada's difficulty in making and fulfilling treaty obligations is one of the prices of federalism. Provincial autonomy would be seriously threatened if every treaty made by the federal government led to an automatic increase in the legislative authority of the federal Parliament. One does not need to suppose that the federal government would act in bad faith, or would enter into colourable treaties simply to increase federal legislative power, to be

---

52 For examples, see Gotlieb, *Canadian Treaty-Making* (1968), 77-78.

53 Canada is not alone in seeking the inclusion of such clauses. Although, as explained earlier in this chapter, in the United States and Australia federal power to implement treaties is more extensive than in Canada, the American and Australian governments have exercised caution in the making and implementing of treaties upon subjects which would, apart from a treaty, be outside federal legislative competence. Partly this is because the courts in both countries have hinted at limits on federal power, but primarily the caution stems from a general federal policy of not wishing to intrude too vigorously into matters normally controlled by the states.

54 Bernier, *International Legal Aspects of Federalism* (1973), 152-158.

disturbed at this prospect. The proliferation of multinational treaties concerning health, education, welfare, labour relations, human rights and other matters within provincial jurisdiction which have been sponsored by international organizations of which Canada is a member is a sufficient reason for caution. It is arguable that, while s. 132 may have been the appropriate rule when treaties were confined to such matters as defence, diplomatic relations, boundaries and international trade, it may no longer be the appropriate rule for an era when treaties cover a wide range of domestic affairs as well.

W. R. Lederman[55] has suggested a middle ground between full acceptance of the *Labour Conventions* rule and its complete rejection. He takes the view that the federal Parliament ought to possess the power to implement treaties, but he suggests that the Court should have to make a finding of "national concern" before upholding a federal statute that implements a treaty on a subject matter that would otherwise be within provincial jurisdiction. Normally, he says, the entering into of the treaty would suffice to establish that its subject matter had become of national concern, but where the subject matter of the treaty was "something quite fundamental for provincial automomy" the national concern test would not be satisfied, and the power to implement the treaty would remain provincial.[56] A disadvantage of this thesis is the vagueness of the controlling concepts, which would make it very difficult to identify in advance the appropriate implementing authority for each treaty.

A different approach would be to confine the *Labour Conventions* rule to those treaties that are concerned only with the harmonization of the domestic law of states or the promotion of shared values in domestic law. The conventions in issue in the *Labour Conventions* case were of this kind, seeking to elevate the standards of working conditions in the member states. Such treaties should be contrasted with those under which the party states undertake reciprocal obligations to each other. Treaties on taxation, extradition or trade, for example, will bind each party state to treat the nationals of the other state in particular ways. Each state undertakes its obligations in return for promises that its nationals will receive comparable treatment in the other state. With treaties of this kind, the international character of the obligations cannot be doubted, and the inability of the federal government to ensure the fulfilment of Canada's part of the bargain would be a very serious disability.

Even if the *Labour Conventions* rule continues to govern the implementation of treaties, so that there is no treaty power as such, the federal catalogue of legislative powers is extensive enough to enable many treaties to be implemented by the federal Parliament. Moreover, the existence of a treaty will often be relevant to the characterization of implementing legislation, and will tend to support the federal Parliament's power to enact the legislation. In *R.* v. *Crown Zellerbach*

---

55 Lederman, *Continuing Canadian Constitutional Dilemmas* (1981), ch. 19.

56 *Id.*, 358.

(1988),[57] for example, the Supreme Court of Canada upheld federal legislation that regulated marine pollution. Canada was a party to a treaty on marine pollution, but the legislation did not recite that its purpose was to implement the treaty,[58] and the legislation was broader than the treaty, applying to internal waters, which were not covered by the treaty, as well as to the territorial sea and high sea, which were covered by the treaty. For these reasons, no attempt was made by the Attorney General of Canada to argue that the legislation was supported by a treaty power, and therefore no attack was made on the *Labour Conventions* case. However, the Court described the treaty, and, in holding that the legislation related to a matter of national concern within the peace, order, and good government power, the Court invoked (among other things) the "international character and implications" of the legislation.[59]

The existence of a treaty is not only relevant to the national concern branch of the peace, order, and good government power; it could be relevant to the trade and commerce power. A comprehensive trade agreement, like the Canada-U.S. Free Trade Agreement, must address not only tariffs (customs duties), which are clearly within federal legislative authority, but also practices that discriminate against the goods or services of the other country, and that constitute indirect (non-tariff) barriers to trade between the agreeing countries. Practices that constitute non-tariff barriers to trade may include matters within the legislative power of the provinces, and even the practices of the provinces themselves, such as the pricing policies of a provincial government's liquor stores. Assuming that there is no treaty power, the question whether the federal Parliament can prohibit practices that are proscribed by a comprehensive trade agreement depends upon whether the implementing legislation can be characterized as in relation to a matter coming within international trade. The fact that the prohibited practice was the subject of reciprocal obligations in an international treaty designed to reduce barriers to trade would be powerful (although not conclusive) evidence that the federal law was indeed in relation to international trade.[60]

11.6 Provincial treaty-making

The role which the *Labour Conventions* case gives to the Canadian provinces in the implementing of treaties naturally invites the question whether the provinces have any power to make treaties. There is no doubt that the provinces have the power to enter into arrangements with foreign countries or American states that are not intended to be binding in international law. One example, which has been

57 [1988] 1 S.C.R. 401.

58 Such a recitation is necessary, according to *MacDonald* v. *Vapor Can.* [1977] 2 S.C.R. 134, 171-172.

59 [1988] 1 S.C.R. 401, 419, 438.

60 Cf. Sullivan, "Jurisdiction to Negotiate and Implement Free Trade Agreements in Canada" (1987) 24 U. West. Ont. L. Rev. 63.

judicially considered and approved, is an arrangement that the provinces have made with foreign countries for the reciprocal enforcement of maintenance orders where the dependent spouse is in one jurisdiction and the spouse who is obliged to pay maintenance is in another.[61] Many other reciprocal arrangements have been made, for example, with respect to succession duties, motor vehicle registration, drivers' licences, fire-fighting and tourist information.[62] The provinces have also entered into contracts with governments in foreign jurisdictions, for example, to lease property or to acquire telephone services or electricity.[63] These various arrangements or contracts are not intended to be binding in international law, and therefore they do not involve an assertion of treaty-making power.

In recent years there have been claims that the provinces do have treaty-making power under the Constitution, and at international law. So far as international law is concerned, it seems that the provinces would be accepted by foreign countries as having treaty-making capacity if the Constitution of Canada clearly accorded that capacity.[64] And so the question comes back to the Constitution. The Constitution is completely silent as to the power to make treaties. As explained earlier, this is because the framers did not envisage that Canada would acquire the power of an independent nation to make treaties. Section 132 confers the power to implement British Empire treaties on ''the Parliament and government of Canada'' — a provision which is hardly encouraging to the proponents of provincial treaty-making power. However, in the 1960s Quebec asserted that the provinces did have treaty-making power. The primary argument for this position is that the exclusive right conceded to the provinces by the *Labour Conventions* case to implement treaties upon subjects within provincial legislative competence must carry with it the power to make treaties upon subjects within provincial legislative competence. As the treaty-making power devolved from the imperial government to Canada, the federal government acquired treaty-making power with respect to s. 91 subjects, and the provinces acquired treaty-making power with respect to s. 92 subjects. This conclusion was not affected by the broad delegation to the federal government in the Letters Patent constituting the office of Governor General,[65] because of the doctrine that within Canada executive powers are distributed on substantially the same basis as legislative powers, which normally means that the provincial governments have executive powers which match the provincial legislative powers.[66] So the argument runs.[67]

---

61 *A.-G. Ont.* v. *Scott* [1956] S.C.R. 137.

62 See Gotlieb, *Canadian Treaty-Making* (1968), 25; Jacomy-Millette, *Treaty Law in Canada* (1975), 69-78.

63 Gotlieb, previous note, 30.

64 See Bernier, *International Legal Aspects of Federalism* (1973), ch. 2.

65 Note 3, above.

66 See ch. 9, Responsible Government, under heading 9.2, ''Law and convention'', above.

67 See Morin, Comment (1967) 45 Can. Bar Rev. 160; Jacomy-Millette, note 61, above, 85-94; the argument is criticized by Morris, note 4, above, and Gotlieb, note 61, above, 27-32. The issue is canvassed from a number of points of view in papers contributed to Ontario Advisory

The argument for provincial treaty-making power is far from conclusive, and it has never commanded wide acceptance in Canada. Certainly, it has never been accepted by the federal government.[68] Quebec's initiatives in international affairs in the 1960s were always pre-empted by the federal government. Thus, cultural and educational agreements between Quebec and countries such as France and Belgium were given federal authority by Canada first entering into a treaty with the foreign country authorizing the provinces to make agreements with that country. Provincial claims to attend international conferences on topics such as education have always been rejected by the federal government, although a Canadian delegation may have substantial provincial representation and may even be headed by a provincial official. By such techniques, the federal government has managed to satisfy legitimate provincial interests while remaining firm in its insistence that international affairs are an exclusive federal preserve.

Committee on Confederation, *The Confederation Challenge*, vol. 1 (1967), 101 (Laskin), 115 (Delisle), 149 Confederation (McWhinney); vol. 2 (1970), 115 (McWhinney), 153 (Atkey), and in Levy (1976) 3 Dal. L.J. 70.

68 The federal position is set out in two white papers: Martin, *Federalism and International Relations* (1968); Sharp, *Federalism and International Conferences on Education* (1968).

12

Parliamentary Sovereignty

12.1 Sovereignty in the United Kingdom

The "sovereignty" of the United Kingdom Parliament is said by Dicey to be established by the rule that the Parliament has the power "to make or unmake any law whatever".[1] In the United Kingdom, there are no limits to legislative power: there is no fundamental law which cannot be altered by ordinary parliamentary action;[2] there is no constituent instrument which allocates some subject matters of legislation to the Parliament and denies others to it; and there is no bill of rights which denies to the Parliament the power to destroy or curtail civil liberties. Any law, upon any subject matter, is within the Parliament's competence.

1 Dicey, *The Law of the Constitution* (10th ed., 1965), 39.

2 See generally de Smith and Brazier, *Constitutional and Administrative Law* (6th ed., 1989), ch. 4, where the statement in the text is qualified to some degree. In the first place, the United Kingdom's accession to the European Economic Community has probably subjected even the Parliament to Community law. Secondly, the Parliament is probably bound by "manner and form" rules of the legislative process: cf. sec. 12.3(b), "Manner and form of future laws", below. On these two grounds, judicial review of legislation may be available in the United Kingdom.

The practical consequence of the sovereignty of the United Kingdom Parliament is that there is no judicial review of legislation: the courts have no power to deny the force of law to any statute enacted by the Parliament.[3] A power of judicial review in England was actually asserted by Coke C.J. in 1610, in his famous statement that "when an Act of Parliament is against the common right and reason, or repugnant, or impossible to be performed, the common law [that is, the courts] will control it, and adjudge such Act to be void".[4] But it seems likely that Coke C.J.'s view was never more than an "empty phrase".[5] Certainly, the asserted power to hold an Act of Parliament void was never actually exercised by an English court. According to de Smith, at least by the time of the Revolution of 1688, "the judges had tacitly accepted a rule of obligation to give effect to every Act of Parliament, no matter how preposterous its content".[6] The safeguards against preposterous legislation were "political and conventional, not strictly legal".[7]

In seventeenth century England, Parliament became accepted as superior to the other two branches of government, namely, the King and the courts. All conflicts between Parliament and the other branches were settled in Parliament's favour. This development was an inevitable outcome of the growth of ideas of democracy. Even the judges could see that Parliament's view of "common right and reason" should be preferred to that of the courts. As the franchise was extended and corrupt election practices were eliminated, it seemed even more obvious that the solemnly legislated decisions of an elected Parliament should prevail over the policy preferences of non-elected judges. The unfettered power of the Parliament of the United Kingdom continues to this day, despite periodic calls for a federal system of government, a bill of rights, and an entrenched written constitution. All such calls have been resisted, thus preserving in its purest form the principle of parliamentary sovereignty.

12.2 Sovereignty in Canada

(a) Federalism

At confederation in 1867, the framers of the British North America Act not only contemplated a continuing colonial relationship between the new Dominion of Canada and the United Kingdom, they sought to model the new Dominion's institutions upon those of the United Kingdom. However, the federal character of Canada forced some fundamental departures from British concepts. Legislative

3 *Pickin* v. *British Railways Bd.* [1974] A.C. 765 (H.L.) (courts lacked jurisdiction to consider whether statute had been procured by fraud).
4 *Dr. Bonham's Case* (1610) 8 Co. Rep. 113, 118; 77 E.R. 646, 652 (K.B.).
5 de Smith and Brazier, note 2, above, 72.
6 *Ibid.*
7 *Id.*, 73.

power had to be distributed between the federal Parliament and the provincial Legislatures. This meant that each legislative body was given the power to make laws in relation to certain classes of subjects, and denied the power to make laws in relation to other classes of subjects. Moreover, as we have seen, the courts assumed the power to determine whether or not the Parliament or a Legislature had acted within its powers in enacting a statute, and to declare the statute invalid if it were outside the powers of the enacting body.[8] It followed that there was no legislative body in Canada which was sovereign in the sense of being able to make or unmake any law whatsoever.

While federalism was inconsistent with one omnicompetent Legislature like the United Kingdom Parliament, the idea of parliamentary sovereignty remained an important influence in Canadian constitutional theory.[9] The Constitution Act, 1867 for the most part limited legislative power only to the extent necessary to give effect to the federal principle.[10] Any power withheld from the federal Parliament was possessed by the provincial Legislatures, and vice versa. If there was room for doubt on this point, the Privy Council scotched it by repeatedly enunciating the principle of exhaustive distribution of legislative powers: ''whatever belongs to self-government in Canada belongs either to the Dominion or to the provinces, within the limits of the British North America Act''.[11] The federal Parliament and provincial Legislatures, provided they stayed within the limits

---

8 The history of judicial review in Canada is related in ch. 5, Federalism, under heading 5.5, ''Role of the Courts'', above. As well, until the passage of the Statute of Westminster, 1931, laws enacted by the Canadian Parliament or a provincial Legislature were void to the extent of any repugnancy with any imperial statute extending to Canada: see ch. 3, Independence, under heading 3.2, ''Colonial Laws Validity Act, 1865'', above.

9 Bayefsky, ''Parliamentary Sovereignty and Human Rights in Canada'' (1983) 31 Political Studies 239.

10 The courts have added some corollaries of their own which they have regarded as entailed by the federal principle, for example, the incapacity to preclude judicial review of the unconstitutionality of a statute (discussed in ch. 7, Courts, under heading 7.3(f), ''Privative clauses'', above), the incapacity to delegate powers from one level of government to the other (discussed in ch. 14, Delegation, under heading 14.3(a), ''Legislative inter-delegation'', below), and the incapacity to enact laws that are excessively broad and vague (discussed in ch. 15, Judicial Review on Federal Grounds, under heading 15.5(a), ''Matter'', below).

11 *A.-G. Ont. v. A.-G. Can.* (Reference Appeal) [1912] A.C. 571, 581, 583. Accord, *Bank of Toronto v. Lambe* (1887) 12 App. Cas. 575, 587; *Union Colliery Co. v. Bryden* [1899] A.C. 580, 584-585; *A.-G. Can. v. A.-G. Ont.* (Labour Conventions) [1937] A.C. 326, 353-354; *Murphy v. CPR* [1958] S.C.R. 626, 643; *Jones v. A.-G. N.B.* [1975] 2 S.C.R. 182, 195; Browne, *The Judicial Committee and the British North America Act* (1967), 33-35. Note however the dictum by Laskin C.J. in *Central Can. Potash v. Govt. of Sask.* [1979] 1 S.C.R. 42, 75 that ''it does not follow [from the principle of exhaustive distribution] that legislation of a province held to be invalid may ipso facto be validly enacted by Parliament in its very terms''. In the context of that case, this implies that neither level of government could enact a scheme for the prorationing of potash produced in Saskatchewan — a constitutional hiatus. This must surely be wrong.

imposed by the scheme of federalism, received powers as "plenary and ample" as those of the United Kingdom Parliament.[12]

(b) Charter of Rights

After the newly-independent thirteen American colonies formed their union in 1787, they added ten amendments to the new Constitution in 1789, and these first ten amendments became a Bill of Rights which could not be altered except by further constitutional amendment.[13] When the loyal British North American colonies united in 1867, they did not copy this radical departure from British tradition. Apart from certain educational[14] and language rights,[15] no Bill of Rights was incorporated into the British North America Act.[16] This meant that the Parliament or a Legislature was not limited in its powers to curtail civil liberties.[17]

The adoption in 1982 of the Canadian Charter of Rights and Freedoms has now imposed upon the federal Parliament and the provincial Legislatures a set of limitations on their powers to curtail civil liberties. The civil liberties protected by the Charter include freedom of religion, expression, assembly and association (s. 2), voting rights (s. 3), mobility rights (s. 6), various procedural and other legal rights (ss. 7-14), the right to equal protection of the laws (ss. 15, 28) and new language rights (ss. 16-23). These protected civil liberties cannot be abridged by either the federal Parliament or a provincial Legislature. Since 1982, therefore, the Parliament and the Legislatures have been subject to two principal sets of constitutional limitations on their powers: (1) the federal limitations, mainly dating from 1867, which are designed to protect federal values; and (2) the Charter limitations, dating from 1982, which are designed to protect civil libertarian values.[18]

Canada's Charter of Rights is similar in principle and in much of its content to the American Bill of Rights. But the idea of parliamentary sovereignty influenced the final form of the Charter, and led to a crucial difference between the two instruments. Section 33 of the Charter, which has no counterpart in the American Bill of Rights, enables the Parliament or a Legislature to "override" most of the provisions of the Charter. This is accomplished by including in a

---

12 *Hodge v. The Queen* (1883) 9 App. Cas. 117, 132.

13 The original Bill of Rights was later supplemented by the thirteenth, fourteenth and fifteenth amendments, adopted after the civil war, and by the nineteenth, twenty-fourth and twenty-sixth amendments, adopted this century.

14 Constitution Act, 1867, s. 93; discussed in ch. 54, Education, below.

15 Constitution Act, 1867, s. 133; discussed in ch. 53, Language, below.

16 Other restrictions on legislative power of a non-federal character were (and still are) ss. 96-98 (appointment of judiciary), 99 (independence of judiciary), 121 (free movement of goods) and 125 (intergovernmental taxation).

17 Judicial attempts to find an "implied bill of rights" in the Constitution Act, 1867 are discussed in ch. 31, Civil Liberties, under heading 31.4(c), "Implied bill of rights", below.

18 Not all limitations on legislative powers fit into these two categories: see notes 14 to 16, above; but these are the main categories.

statute an express declaration that the statute is to operate notwithstanding a provision included in s. 2 or ss. 7 to 15 of the Charter.[19] Once this declaration is included, the statute will operate free of the invalidating effect of the Charter provisions specified in the declaration. In this way, the Parliament or a Legislature, provided it is willing to include the express declaration required by the override provision, is able to enact a law that abridges rights guaranteed by s. 2 or ss. 7 to 15 of the Charter. The override provision thus preserves parliamentary supremacy over much of the Charter.

(c) Constitutional amendment

One power that was always withheld from the federal Parliament and the provincial Legislatures was the power to amend the Constitution itself. That power resided with the United Kingdom Parliament until 1982, and since 1982 has been possessed by the various combinations of legislative bodies stipulated in Part V of the Constitution Act, 1982.[20]

If one thinks of the Part V amending procedures as a third legislative process, then it is now literally true that legislative power in Canada is exhaustively distributed among Canadian institutions. Every law is amenable to repeal or amendment by one of three processes: (1) the federal Parliament has authority over all laws within federal legislative power; (2) the provincial Legislatures have authority over all laws within provincial legislative power; and (3) one of the various amending procedures is available to repeal or amend any law that is outside the competence of both the federal Parliament and the provincial Legislatures. Judicial review of legislation occurs when the courts are called upon to determine whether the correct process was employed to enact a particular law.

(d) Extraterritorial competence

The extent of the power of the federal Parliament and provincial Legislatures to legislate with extraterritorial effect will be discussed in chapter 13, Extraterritorial Competence, below.

(e) Delegation

The extent of the power of the federal Parliament and provincial Legislatures to delegate their powers will be discussed in chapter 14, Delegation, below.

---

19 The override clause is analyzed in detail in ch. 36, Override of Rights, below. It does not apply to ss. 3-5 (democratic rights), 6 (mobility), 16-23 (language), 28 (sexual equality).

20 See ch. 4, Amendment, above. As is there explained, some provisions of what is now called the Constitution of Canada were before 1982 and still are amendable by the unilateral action of the federal Parliament or a Legislature.

(f) Retroactive legislation

The extent of the power of the federal Parliament and provincial Legislatures to enact retroactive legislation will be discussed in chapter 48, Rights on Being Charged, below.[21]

(g) Wisdom or policy of legislation

The idea underlying parliamentary sovereignty is that in a democratic society important public policy choices should be made in the elected legislative assemblies, and not by non-elected judges. It is often said, for example, that the courts have no concern with "the wisdom or expediency or policy" of a statute.[22] This follows from the fact that nearly all potential laws, however foolish or ineffective, are competent to one or the other legislative body. But the courts do have to make policy choices in determining the validity of statutes. Even in a distribution-of-powers case, if the text of the Constitution is not clear and there is no clearly governing prior precedent, the court ends up making a choice between the two levels of government which involves an important element of discretion. In Charter cases, the assessment of whether a law has abridged a guaranteed right, and if so whether the law is a "reasonable" limit on the right, and whether the law can be "demonstrably justified in a free and democratic society", plainly calls upon the courts to make discretionary choices.

As related in the earlier discussion of judicial review,[23] it is likely that the personal predilections of the judges have influenced the course of judicial review in the United States, Australia and Canada. It is hardly surprising to discover that judges are human and are not successful in shedding the baggage of prejudices accumulated before their appointment to the bench. However, there is little doubt that most judges make a conscientious attempt to exclude their personal policy preferences from the process of constitutional adjudication. The facts, the precedents, the inferences that can reasonably be drawn from the facts and the precedents, and the implications of the alternative outcomes, are to be assessed in as neutral a fashion as possible. If this counsel of perfection cannot be fully achieved in practice, it is nonetheless the ideal to which a judge must strive. The ideal of professional neutrality is the assumption upon which litigation is conducted; otherwise, why bother with evidence and argument? And the attempt to achieve professional neutrality is what, in a democratic society, justifies the conferral of powers of judicial review on non-elected judges.

---

21 Chapter 48, Rights on Being Charged, under heading 48.8, "Retroactive offences (s. 11(g))", below.

22 *A.-G. Ont. v. A.-G. Can.* (Reference Appeal) [1912] A.C. 571, 583; the point has been repeated many times, e.g., by Laskin C.J. in the *Anti-Inflation Reference* [1976] 2 S.C.R. 373, 424-425.

23 Note 8, above.

12.3 Self-imposed restraints on legislative power

(a) Substance of future laws

Not only may the Parliament or a Legislature, acting within its allotted sphere of competence, make any law it chooses, it may repeal any of its earlier laws.[24] Even if the Parliament or Legislature purported to provide that a particular law was not to be repealed or altered, this provision would not be effective to prevent a future Parliament or Legislature from repealing or amending the "protected" law. The later law, though in conflict with the protecting provision, would unhesitatingly be upheld by the courts.[25] Where two laws of the same legislative body are inconsistent, the general rule is that the later is deemed to impliedly repeal the earlier.[26] In political terms, the rationale of this rule is clear. If a legislative body could bind itself not to do something in the future, then a government could use its parliamentary majority to protect its policies from alteration or repeal. This would lay a dead hand on a government subsequently elected to power in a new election with new issues. In other words, a government while in office could frustrate in advance the policies urged by the opposition.

In *Re Canada Assistance Plan* (1991),[27] a constitutional challenge was made to a federal bill to implement a federal budget proposal that would place a five per cent annual cap on the growth of Canada Assistance Plan transfer payments from the federal government to the three provinces of Alberta, British Columbia and Ontario. (These three provinces were singled out because they were the three wealthiest provinces, as measured by their failure to qualify for equalization payments.) The Canada Assistance Plan (CAP) was a federal statute that authorized cost-sharing agreements to be entered into by the federal government with the provinces, under which the federal government would undertake to pay 50 per cent of the costs incurred by the provinces in the provision of certain stipulated social assistance and welfare programmes. Under this authority, the federal government entered into CAP agreements with all ten provinces. By the terms of both the CAP legislation and each agreement, each agreement could be amended only with the consent of both the federal government and the province. It was argued that the budget proposal, by restricting the federal contributions to less

24 Exceptions are the Constitutions of Manitoba, Alberta and Saskatchewan. These consist of statutes which were enacted by the federal Parliament under s. 2 of the Constitution Act, 1871, but which cannot be repealed or amended by the federal Parliament, because s. 45 of the Constitution Act, 1982 confers on each provincial Legislature the power to amend "the constitution of the province".

25 See *Vauxhall Estates v. Liverpool Corp.* [1932] 1 K.B. 733, 746 (Div. Ct.); *Ellen Street Estates v. Min. of Health* [1934] 1 K.B. 590, 597 (C.A.).

26 See ch. 16, Paramountcy, under heading 16.1, "Problem of inconsistency", below.

27 [1991] 2 S.C.R. 525. The unanimous judgment of the Court was written by Sopinka J. I disclose that I was one of the counsel for the Attorney General of Canada.

than the agreed-upon 50 per cent share,[28] was in effect a unilateral amendment of the three agreements which had not been made with the consent of the three affected provinces.

While there was no doubt that the federal government was obliged to fulfil its side of the CAP agreements so long as the CAP legislation remained unchanged, the effect of the proposed bill, once it was enacted, would be to amend the CAP legislation and thereby place a statutory limit on the federal government's CAP payments. Following the orthodox theory of parliamentary sovereignty, the Supreme Court of Canada held that Parliament remained free to amend the CAP legislation in this way (or any other way) notwithstanding the cost-sharing agreements with the provinces. The Court also considered an ingenious argument that a doctrine of ''legitimate expectations'' applied, not to Parliament itself, but to the federal government. The effect of the doctrine, it was argued, was to constrain the Minister of Finance (or any other member of the government) from introducing a bill into Parliament, if the effect of the bill would be to defeat the legitimate expectations of the provinces that had been created by the terms of the CAP agreements. In rejecting this argument, the Court held, in effect, that the doctrine of parliamentary sovereignty flowed upstream from the legislative chamber to protect from judicial review the process of legislative policy-making by cabinet and the preparation and introduction of bills for consideration by Parliament. The Court pointed out that: ''A restraint on the Executive in the introduction of legislation is a fetter on the sovereignty of Parliament itself.''[29]

(b) Manner and form of future laws

While a legislative body is not bound by self-imposed restraints as to the content, substance or policy of its enactments,[30] it is reasonably clear that a legislative body may be bound by self-imposed procedural (or manner and form) restraints on its enactments.

There is of course no doubt as to the binding character of the rules in the Constitution that define the composition of the legislative bodies and the steps

---

28 Only if the growth in provincial costs exceeded five per cent in a particular year would the federal contribution fall short of the full 50 per cent contribution.

29 [1991] 2 S.C.R. 525, 560. Strictly speaking, a restraint on the Executive would not preclude the introduction into Parliament of a private member's bill, but the reality of the Canadian legislative process is that only government bills stand any real chance of securing parliamentary time, let alone passage. In fact, the bill in issue had been certified by the Speaker as a money bill, which by virtue of s. 54 of the Constitution Act, 1867, can only be a government bill. Sopinka J. (at p. 560) referred to this fact, but only as a reinforcement of the general proposition that the entire legislative process was immune from review.

30 A related issue is whether a legislative body can abdicate its functions or some of them. Even Dicey accepted the legal efficacy of a total abdication: *The Law of the Constitution* (10th ed., 1965), 68-69; but the efficacy of a partial abdication has been more controversial: see ch. 3, Independence, under heading 3.5(d), ''Termination of imperial authority'', above.

required in the legislative process.[31] A bill passed by a provincial legislative assembly which is not presented to the Lieutenant Governor for the royal assent is invalid, because the Lieutenant Governor's assent is part of the legislative process required by the Constitution.[32] A bill passed by Manitoba's Legislature in English only is invalid, because s. 23 of the Manitoba Act, 1870 (which is part of the Constitution of Canada) requires Manitoba's statutes to be enacted in French as well as English.[33]

The foregoing examples involved provisions of the Constitution. Would the Parliament or a Legislature be bound by *self-imposed* rules as to the "manner and form"[34] in which statutes were to be enacted? The answer, in my view, is yes. The Parliament or a Legislature could "re-define itself" by changing the nature of the legislative process. To be sure, the Parliament could not unilaterally abolish the Senate or the requirement of the royal assent, and the provincial Legislatures could not affect the office of Lieutenant Governor; but this is because "the office of the Queen, the Governor General and the Lieutenant Governor of a province" and "the powers of the Senate" are expressly included, by Part V of the Constitution Act, 1982 (ss. 41(a), 42(1)(b)), among the topics that can only be altered by a special amending procedure.[35] But five provinces have abolished their upper houses by ordinary legislation, and a province without an upper house could establish one.[36] The Parliament or a Legislature could add other elements to the legislative process, either for all statutes or just for particular kinds of statutes. For example, the federal Parliament could provide that a law to abolish the office

31 Conklin, "Pickin and its Applicability to Canada" (1975) 25 U. Toronto L.J. 193, 201-204.

32 *Gallant v. The King* [1949] 2 D.L.R. 425 (P.E.I. S.C.) (absence of royal assent prevented bill from becoming law, and could not be corrected by subsequent purported royal assent).

33 *Re Manitoba Language Rights* [1985] 1 S.C.R. 721.

34 The phrase "manner and form" (instead of procedural) has become customary in this branch of the law, because it was used in s. 5 of the Colonial Laws Validity Act, 1865 (U.K.), which authorized colonial legislatures to amend their constitutions, provided that any such amendments were "passed in such manner and form as may from time to time be required by any Act of Parliament . . . in force in the said colony."

35 As well as these explicit restrictions on legislative alterations to the legislative process, there are some implied limits associated with the Constitution Act, 1867's establishment or recognition of the Governor General, the Lieutenant Governors and representative assemblies: see the discussion of the initiative and referendum cases in ch. 14, Delegation, under heading 14.2(d), "Office of Lieutenant Governor or Governor General", below.

36 Quebec, Nova Scotia, New Brunswick, Prince Edward Island and Manitoba each abolished their upper houses, as an amendment to "the constitution of the province" under s. 92(1) of the Constitution Act, 1867: for details, see Forsey, *Freedom and Order* (1974), 227. Section 92(1) was repealed in 1982 and replaced by s. 45 of the Constitution Act, 1982, the similar language of which would confer a similar power. In fact, there is now no province with an upper house. Section 45 could however be used to establish one. In *Re Upper House* [1980] 1 S.C.R. 54, the Court held that the federal Parliament lacked the power to abolish or substantially alter the Senate. This decision was based on s. 91(1) of the Constitution Act, 1867, which was repealed in 1982 and replaced by s. 44 of the Constitution Act, 1982. Section 44, through its express subjection to s. 42(1)(b), clearly withholds the power to amend "the powers of the Senate and the method of selecting Senators".

of Auditor General must first be approved by a referendum of voters, or a provincial Legislature could provide that a law altering the constituencies for elections must be passed by a two-thirds majority in the legislative assembly. These ''manner and form'' laws, which purport to re-define the legislative body, either generally or for particular purposes, are binding for the future. A law which purported to disregard these hypothetical examples of manner and form laws, for example, by purporting to abolish the office of Auditor General without a prior referendum, or to alter the provincial electoral law by a simple majority,[37] would be held to be invalid by the courts.[38] Thus, while the federal Parliament or a provincial Legislature cannot bind itself as to the substance of future legislation, it can bind itself as to the manner and form of future legislation.

The binding nature of self-imposed manner and form requirements is not entirely free from doubt. There is still a school of thought that holds that even a manner and form restriction cannot bind a ''sovereign'' legislature.[39] The effect of this school of thought is to deny to a legislative body the power to change its traditional forms and structures: this would invalidate such things as special-majority rules, the abolition or creation of upper houses, and the addition of referenda to the legislative process.[40] It seems implausible that a legislative body should be disabled from making changes to its present structure and procedures. Moreover, the case-law, while not conclusive, tends to support the validity of self-imposed manner and form requirements.[41]

---

37 The manner and form law could itself be directly repealed in the ordinary way, but it could not be disregarded. Direct repeal can be guarded against by entrenching the entrenching provision, i.e., by stipulating that the new manner and form procedure is also applicable to the repeal or amendment of the entrenching provision itself.

38 For other examples, see Lysyk, Comment (1965) 4 Alta. L. Rev. 154, 156-157; Forsey, *Freedom and Order* (1974) 227; Conklin, note 28, above, 204-206; Swinton, ''Challenging the Validity of an Act of Parliament'' (1976) 14 Osgoode Hall L.J. 345, 379.

39 The classical exposition is Dicey, *The Law of the Constitution* (10th ed., 1965), ch. 1, and the introduction by E.C.S. Wade, the editor of the 10th ed.; also H.W.R. Wade, ''The Basis of Legal Sovereignty'' [1955] Camb. L.J. 172. A Canadian contribution to this side of the issue is Elliot, ''Rethinking Manner and Form'' (1991) 29 Osgoode Hall L.J. 215. The dominant theory now is that manner and form restrictions are effective: Jennings, *The Law and the Constitution* (5th ed., 1959), ch. 4; Marshall, *Parliamentary Sovereignty and the Commonwealth* (1957), passim; Tarnopolsky, *The Canadian Bill of Rights* (2nd ed., 1975), ch. 3; de Smith and Brazier, *Constitutional and Administrative Law* (6th ed., 1989), ch. 4.

40 Elliot, previous note, would invalidate manner and form restrictions ''in all but the most unusual circumstances''; they could be valid if consistent with ''the values of the legal and political culture of the society in question''; but any change in the simple-majority rule would not be valid. Why the simple-majority rule enjoys such extraordinary value, when it is modified for special purposes by most organizations, is not explained.

41 Outside Canada, the leading cases are *A.-G. N.S.W. v. Trethowan* [1932] A.C. 526 (P.C., Australia); *Harris v. Min. of Interior* [1952] 2 S.A.L.R. (A.D.) 428 (S. Africa A.D.); *Bribery Commr. v. Ranasinghe* [1965] A.C. 172 (P.C., Ceylon). None of these cases unequivocally supports the proposition in the text. *Trethowan* is the only case of a self-imposed manner and form restriction, and it could be explained as resting on s. 5 of the Colonial Laws Validity Act.

In Canada, the leading case is *R.* v. *Mercure* (1988),[42] in which the Supreme Court of Canada held that the Saskatchewan Legislature was bound by a statutory requirement that its statutes be enacted in both English and French. The statutory requirement had been enacted in 1876, before the creation of the province of Saskatchewan, by the Parliament of Canada, exercising its authority over the federal territory that in 1905 became Saskatchewan. Although the bilingual requirement had not been enacted by the Legislature itself, it had been enacted by the Legislature's predecessor, and it could be freely repealed or amended by the Legislature. La Forest J., for the majority of the Court, treated the case as no different from a self-imposed manner and form requirement,[43] and held the requirement to be valid and binding. While the Legislature was free to repeal the bilingual requirement, it could not ignore it, and until the requirement was expressly repealed by the correct manner and form[44] the requirement had to be observed. A statute enacted by the Legislature in English only, in disregard of the bilingual requirement, was accordingly struck down.

In Canadian statutes, it is not uncommon to find "primacy clauses" that purport to declare that the statute containing the clause is supreme over other statutes, future as well as past.[45] Such clauses are intended to defeat the doctrine of implied repeal,[46] under which a later statute would impliedly repeal an inconsistent earlier statute to the extent of the inconsistency. The best-known example is the Canadian Bill of Rights, which is a federal statute, which provides in effect that the Canadian Bill of Rights is supreme over any other federal statute unless in the other statute "it is expressly declared . . . that it shall operate notwithstanding the Canadian Bill of Rights". The Supreme Court of Canada has held that this primacy clause has the effect of rendering inoperative inconsistent statutes

---

Harris and *Ranasinghe* involved restrictions in the Constitution itself, although the Constitution was as freely amendable as an ordinary statute.

42 [1988] 1 S.C.R. 234.

43 *Id.*, 278, approving the view of Jennings, note 39, above, and me (in the 2nd edition of this book). On the other hand, La Forest J. did say (at pp. 277, 279) that the manner and form restriction was in the Legislature's "constituent instrument". The issue would be unequivocally raised by Ontario's French Language Services Act, R.S.O. 1990, c. F-32, s. 3(2), which provides that: "The Public Bills of the Legislative Assembly introduced after the 1st day of January, 1991 shall be introduced and enacted in both English and French."

44 After the decision, Saskatchewan enacted a statute in both English and French which validated past English-only statutes, and repealed the requirement for the future: The Language Act, S.S. 1988, c. L-6.1. Alberta, which was in the same situation (*R.* v. *Paquette* [1990] 2 S.C.R. 1103), enacted in both languages a similar statute: Languages Act, S.A. 1988, c. L-7.5.

45 As well as the examples given in the text, see the statutes implementing income tax treaties, e.g., Canada-United States Tax Convention Act, S.C. 1984, c. 20, s. 3(2). In *A.-G. Can.* v. *Public Service Staff Relations Bd.* [1977] 2 F.C. 663 (C.A.), the Court held that s. 28 of the Federal Court Act, authorizing judicial review of federal agencies "notwithstanding . . . the provisions of any other Act", superseded a privative clause in the Public Service Staff Relations Act. The privative clause predated s. 28, but Le Dain J. suggested (at p. 671) that s. 28 might well be effective even against future privative clauses.

46 Note 26, above.

that do not contain the notwithstanding clause.[47] The Quebec Charter of Human Rights and Freedoms, which is a Quebec statute, contains a similar clause making the Charter supreme over other statutes "unless such Act expressly states that it applies despite the Charter". The Supreme Court of Canada has held that this is effective also, rendering inoperative a later Quebec statute that purported to derogate from one of the guaranteed rights.[48] Human Rights Codes (anti-discrimination statutes) in several provinces also contain primacy clauses,[49] and these have been held to be effective by the Supreme Court of Canada.[50] Indeed, the Supreme Court of Canada has gone so far as to hold that human rights legislation takes precedence over inconsistent later statutes even without a primacy clause. The Court said that, because "human rights legislation is of a special nature and declares public policy regarding matters of general concern", it may not be repealed or amended "save by clear legislative pronouncement".[51]

The theory under which primacy clauses are effective has never been articulated by the Court, but it must rest on the principle that a legislative body may bind itself as to manner and form. The primacy clause binds the legislative body not to repeal or amend the protected legislation, except in the manner and form indicated by the primacy clause. That involves using the formula contemplated by the primacy clause, such as the notwithstanding declaration contemplated by the Canadian Bill of Rights. If no particular formula is provided by the primacy clause, then it must be taken as requiring express words, as opposed to mere implication, for the repeal or amendment of the protected statute.

A statutory provision cannot be a manner and form requirement unless it is unmistakably addressed to the future action of the enacting legislative body. In *Re Canada Assistance Plan* (1991),[52] a case that was examined earlier in this chapter,[53] the Supreme Court of Canada had to consider the effect of a statutory provision that required the consent of the provinces for any amendment to certain cost-sharing agreements between Canada and the provinces. It was argued that this provision implicitly precluded any amendment of federal legislation that would have the effect of limiting the federal government's obligations under the agreements, unless the consent of the provinces had first been obtained. The Court

---

47 See ch. 32, Canadian Bill of Rights, under heading 32.3, "Effect on later statutes", below.

48 *Ford* v. *Quebec* [1988] 2 S.C.R. 712; *Devine* v. *Que.* [1988] 2 S.C.R. 790.

49 Bayefsky, note 9, above, 250-252.

50 *Scowby* v. *Glendinning* [1986] 2 S.C.R. 226, 236 (obiter dictum, not referring to the primacy clause in s. 44 of the Saskatchewan Human Rights Code).

51 *Winnipeg School Division No. 1* v. *Craton* [1985] 2 S.C.R. 150, 156. This reasoning is dubious. Much other legislation "declares public policy regarding matters of general concern". Surely, in the absence of a primacy clause, the Court is in no position to create priorities between public policies. Accord, Monahan and Petter, "Developments" (1987) 9 Supreme Court L.R. 69, 143-150. Cf. *MacBain* v. *Lederman* [1985] 1 F.C. 856 (C.A.), holding that the Canadian Bill of Rights rendered inoperative a provision of the federal Human Rights Code; the courts thus seem to be recognizing a hierarchy of statutes.

52 [1991] 2 S.C.R. 525.

53 Note 27, above.

held that the consent requirement was not a manner and form requirement for the simple reason that it expressly applied to amendments to the agreements, not to amendments to the legislation. Since the legislation was silent on the question of the Parliament's power to enact new laws, that power was unimpaired, and could be used to alter the federal government's obligations under the agreements. The Court said that it would require a very clear indication in a statute, especially a non-constitutional statute, before the court would find ''an intention of the legislative body to bind itself in the future.''[54]

A statutory provision that is unmistakably addressed to the future action of the enacting legislative body may be a manner and form provision. But it is not necessarily so. A statutory provision that looks like a manner and form restriction may be one of four other kinds of laws. First, the statutory provision could be regarded as an attempt to restrict the substance of future legislation, which is of course ineffective.[55] Secondly, the statutory provision could be regarded as a ''directory'' procedural requirement; the breach of a directory, as opposed to a mandatory, requirement does not lead to invalidity.[56] Thirdly, the statutory provision could be regarded as a rule of interpretation, which would be displaced by any clear statutory indication to the contrary.[57] Fourthly, the statutory provision could be regarded as an ''internal'' rule of parliamentary procedure; the breach of such a rule does not invalidate the resulting statute.[58] None of these four kinds of provisions forms the basis for judicial review of legislation. A manner and form provision, on the other hand, does form the basis for judicial review, because if a statute is enacted in disregard of an applicable manner and form provision, the purported statute is a nullity and will be so declared by a court.

---

54 [1991] 2 S.C.R. 525, 563.

55 E.g., an ostensibly procedural requirement which is virtually impossible of fulfilment, such as approval by eighty per cent of the voters in a referendum: see Friedmann, ''Trethowan's Case'' (1950) 24 Aust. L.J. 103, 105-105; Marshall, note 36, above, 41-42; de Smith, note 36, above, 92. In *Re Can. Assistance Plan* [1991] 2 S.C.R. 525, 564, the Court held that the consent of the provinces could not be a valid manner and form requirement for the federal Parliament, because this would be a restraint of substance rather than procedure. Cf. the rule that Parliament may not delegate its legislative powers to the provinces: ch. 14, Delegation, under heading 14.3, ''Federal inter-delegation'', above.

56 E.g., *Simpson v. A.-G.* [1955] N.Z.L.R. 271 (N.Z. C.A.); *Clayton v. Heffron* (1960) 105 C.L.R. 215 (H.C. Aust.). In *Re Man. Language Rights* [1985] 1 S.C.R. 721, 740-743, the Court held that s. 23 of the Manitoba Act, 1870, requiring statutes to be enacted in both English and French, was not ''directory'', but was ''mandatory''. See Evans, ''Mandatory and Directory Rules'' (1981) 1 Legal Studies 227.

57 See for example the discussion of the effect of statutory provisions purporting to require the use of express words to bind the Crown: ch. 10, The Crown, under heading 10.8(b), ''Effect of Interpretation Acts'', above; see also discussion of the effect of s. 2 of the Canadian Bill of Rights: ch. 32, Canadian Bill of Rights, under heading 32.2(a), ''Meaning of s. 2'', below.

58 Conklin, note 31, above; Swinton, note 38, above.

13

Extraterritorial Competence

13.1 The issue

Do the Canadian federal Parliament and the provincial Legislatures have power to make laws with extraterritorial effect? It is obvious that they do not have the power to change the law of a foreign country. But the question is whether they have the power to make legal consequences within Canada depend upon facts outside the territory. There is no doubt that the Parliament of the United Kingdom has this power, and it is often regarded as one of the marks of a "sovereign" parliament. Thus, to use a well-known example, the Parliament of the United Kingdom could validly enact that smoking in the streets of Paris is an offence. If it did so, this would not change the law of France: the Paris police would not arrest smokers and the French courts would not punish them. But such a statute would change the law of the United Kingdom. If anyone who had smoked in the streets of Paris came to the United Kingdom, the offender would be liable to be arrested by the police and punished by a United Kingdom court.[1]

---

1 Jennings, *The Law and the Constitution* (5th ed., 1959), 170-171; see also *B.C. Elec. Ry.* v. *The King* [1946] A.C. 527, 541-542.

Legislation of this kind is not normally enacted for reasons of international comity.[2] But every country for reasons of public policy does sometimes wish to attach within its borders legal consequences to acts committed outside its territory by its own subjects or even in some circumstances by aliens. For example, Canada's Criminal Code,[3] while normally confined to acts committed within Canada,[4] includes a number of offences that can be committed outside Canada, for example, hijacking an aircraft, forging a Canadian passport, piracy, bigamy and espionage.[5] Nor is the Criminal Code the only federal statute that purports to reach out beyond the boundaries of Canada: immigration, deportation, extradition, shipping, fishing, arctic pollution, customs and taxation are other areas where Canadian law attaches consequences within Canada to facts occurring outside Canada.

13.2 Federal Parliament

The question whether the Canadian federal Parliament has the power to enact statutes with extraterritorial effect arose in *Croft* v. *Dunphy* (1933).[6] The federal Parliament had enacted as part of the Customs Act an anti-smuggling provision which authorized the seizure of vessels that were found with dutiable goods aboard ''hovering'' off the coast of Canada within a distance of twelve miles, which was in excess of the ordinary territorial limit accepted at that time of three miles. After a vessel with a cargo of rum had been seized on the high seas eleven miles from the coast of Nova Scotia, the validity of the hovering law was challenged in the courts. It was of course undoubted that the United Kingdom Parliament had the power to enact a like statute and had in fact done so. It was also undoubted that the federal Parliament had power under the Constitution Act, 1867 to enact customs laws for Canada.[7] What was in question was whether the federal Parliament could give its laws extraterritorial effect. The Privy Council held that it could: ''Once it is found that a particular topic of legislation is among those upon which the Dominion Parliament may competently legislate . . . their Lordships see no reason to restrict the permitted scope of such legislation by any other consideration than is applicable to the legislation of a fully Sovereign State''.[8] Their lordships declared that the federal Parliament had plenary legislative power within the limits imposed by the Constitution; the Constitution ''imposed no

2 ''Comity'', in this sense, is defined in the Oxford English Dictionary as ''courtesy and friendly agreement and interaction between states''. Laws with extraterritorial effect are generally seen as disrespectful of another nation's sovereignty.
3 R.S.C. 1985, c. C-46.
4 *Id.*, s. 6(2).
5 *Id.*, ss. 7, 46, 57, 58, 74, 75, 290; Official Secrets Act, R.S.C. 1985, c. O-5, s. 13.
6 [1933] A.C. 156.
7 The precise heads of power were not identified, but they are ss. 91(2) and 91(3).
8 [1933] A.C. 156, 163.

[territorial] restriction in terms and their Lordships see no justification for inferring it''.[9]

The recognition of the extraterritorial power of the federal Parliament in *Croft* v. *Dunphy* would probably by itself have put to rest doubts on the question.[10] But, while *Croft* v. *Dunphy* was wending its way up the Canadian courts, the Statute of Westminster, 1931 was enacted by the imperial Parliament.[11] Section 3 of the Statute of Westminster provides:

> It is hereby declared and enacted that the Parliament of a Dominion has full power to make laws having extraterritorial operation.

The Statute of Westminster was in force by the time *Croft* v. *Dunphy* reached the Privy Council, and it was argued that s. 3 had retrospective effect. The Privy Council, having concluded that the federal Parliament had the power which it asserted under the Constitution Act, 1867 alone, did not need to decide the question. Their lordships contented themselves by saying that ''the question of the validity of extra-territorial legislation by the Dominion cannot at least arise in the future''.[12] The combined effects of *Croft* v. *Dunphy* and s. 3 of the Statute of Westminster do indeed affirm beyond question the extraterritorial powers of the federal Parliament.[13]

---

9 *Id.*, 167.

10 Doubts had been raised by the decisions in *Macleod* v. *A.-G. N.S.W.* [1891] A.C. 455 (Aust.) and *Nadan* v. *The King* [1926] A.C. 482, 492. But *Macleod* is explicable as depending upon the rule of statutory interpretation that presumes a statutory intention to legislate intraterritorially (where enforcement is effective), and which requires clear language to infer an intention to legislate extraterritorially. *Nadan*, which was decided primarily on the ground of repugnancy to imperial statutes, appears to be wrong in characterizing the operation of a statute abolishing Privy Council appeals as extraterritorial; such a statute is really an amendment of Canada's own judicial structure: see *British Coal Corp.* v. *The King* [1935] A.C. 500, 522; *Ibralebbe* v. *The Queen* [1964] A.C. 900, 921-922 (Ceylon).

11 See ch. 3, Independence, under heading 3.3, ''Statute of Westminster, 1931'', above.

12 [1933] A.C. 156, 167. Shortly after the decision in *Croft* v. *Dunphy* and the enactment of the Statute of Westminster the federal Parliament enacted the Extraterritorial Act, S.C. 1932-33, c. 39 (now s. 8(3) of the Interpretation Act, R.S.C. 1985, c. I-21), providing that every statute enacted before December 11, 1931 (the date upon which the Statute of Westminster came into force), ''that expressly or by necessary or reasonable implication was intended . . . to have extraterritorial operation shall be construed as if, at the date of its enactment, the Parliament of Canada had full power to make laws having extraterritorial operation''. The purpose of this statute was no doubt to avoid the risk that the courts would through statutory interpretation in effect stultify the doctrine of extraterritorial competence by ''reading down'' pre-1931 statutes so as to confine them to intraterritorial operation. Cf. *Macleod* v. *A.-G. N.S.W.*, note 10, above.

13 *British Coal Corp.* v. *The King* [1930] A.C. 500, 520; *Co-op. Committee on Japanese Canadians* v. *A.-G. Can.* [1947] A.C. 87, 104; *A.-G. Ont.* v. *A.-G. Can.* (Privy Council Appeals) [1947] A.C. 127, 147; *B.C. Elec. Ry.* v. *The King* [1946] A.C. 527, 540-543; *Re Offshore Mineral Rights of B.C.* [1967] S.C.R. 792; *Re Continental Shelf Offshore Nfld.* [1984] 1 S.C.R. 86. It has been suggested that a valid law would still have to have some connection with Canada; otherwise it would not be ''for the peace, order, and good government of Canada''. It may well be, however, that s. 3 of the Statute of Westminster has eliminated even that limitation. The

13.3 Provincial Legislatures

(a) Territorial limitation

What about the provincial Legislatures? Section 3 of the Statute of Westminster did not apply to them.[14] *Croft* v. *Dunphy* was of course concerned with federal power, although its language did not suggest any lesser provincial power. Nevertheless, in a federal system it is obvious that a province, whose government is elected by and responsible to only those people within its territory, should not have extensive powers outside its territory where other provincial governments have a better claim to govern.[15] It is not surprising to find, therefore, that the Constitution Act, 1867 couches provincial legislative power in terms which rather plainly impose a territorial limitation on the scope of the power. The sections allocating power to the provincial Legislatures, namely, ss. 92, 92A, 93 and 95, open with the words ''In each province''; and each class of subjects listed in s. 92 as within provincial legislative power contains the phrase ''in the province'' or some other indication of a territorial limitation. A body of case law has established that these phrases in the Constitution Act, 1867 do impose a territorial limitation on provincial legislative power.[16]

(b) Territory of province

A threshold question concerns the territorial limits of the province. Obviously, these are defined by the boundaries of the province.[17]

---

point is discussed in the Australian case of *Trustees Executors and Agency Co.* v. *Federal Commr. of Taxation* (1933) 49 C.L.R. 220.

14 Section 2 of the Statute of Westminster, conferring the power to legislate repugnantly to imperial statutes, was made applicable to the provincial Legislatures by s. 7(2), but s. 3 applied only to the federal Parliament.

15 This is the position of the state legislatures in the United States, although the territorial restriction has been located in the ''due process'' clause of the fourteenth amendment of the Constitution of the United States: see cases cited, notes 77-79, 98, below. The state legislatures of Australia are also confined by a territorial restriction, although it has been interpreted more liberally than the Canadian restriction: *Cox* v. *Tomat* (1972) 126 C.L.R. 105; *Union Steamship Co.* v. *King* (1988) 166 C.L.R. 1; Australia Act 1986 (U.K.), s. 2(1), conferring extra-territorial power on states, is probably declaratory of the general law: Hanks, *Constitutional Law in Australia* (1991), 175-180.

16 See Lefroy, *Canada's Federal System* (1913), 501-515; Tremblay, *Les compétences législatives au Canada* (1967), 279-295; Laskin, *Canadian Constitutional Law* (5th ed., 1986 by Finkelstein), 548-572; La Forest, ''May the Provinces Legislate in Violation of International Law?'' (1961) 39 Can. Bar Rev. 78; Edinger, ''Territorial Limitations on Provincial Powers'' (1982) 14 Ottawa L. Rev. 57; Sullivan, ''Interpreting the Territorial Limitations on the Provinces'' (1985) 7 Supreme Court L.R. 511. The territorial limitation on the provincial taxing power (s. 92(2)) has developed distinctively and is discussed in ch. 27, Taxation, under the heading 27.4, ''Territorial Limitation'', below.

17 The boundaries of a province will be ascertained by reference to the instruments by which the

With respect to coastal provinces, a question arises as to their jurisdiction over offshore waters. If the definition of a province's boundaries explicitly includes some portion of the offshore, then of course that area is within the province.[18] If the definition of a province's boundaries is not explicit on the point, the general rule is that the territory of the province ends at the low-water mark.[19] The only exceptions are "inland waters", such as harbours, bays, estuaries and other waters lying "between the jaws of the land"; these waters are within the province. The territorial sea and the high sea beyond (over the continental shelf) are outside the territory of the province.[20] The coastal provinces therefore lack either ownership of the seabed (with its minerals) or legislative authority over the territorial sea and continental shelf.[21]

The question whether the airspace above a province is within the province has arisen in a taxation context. In *The Queen (Manitoba)* v. *Air Canada* (1980),[22] the issue was whether Manitoba could levy a consumption tax on the sale of liquor to passengers on aircraft flying across the province. The Supreme Court of Canada held that the sales of liquor did not occur within the province, and the tax was therefore unconstitutional. The Court decided that the passage of aircraft through the airspace above the province was not a sufficiently "substantial" presence in the province to support a tax on the passengers.[23] Even if the aircraft landed in the course of its journey across the province, this "momentary transitory presence" would still be insufficient.[24] The Court expressly refused "to explore

---

province was initially created or defined, to the terms of union with Canada (where applicable), to any modifications of the boundaries after confederation under s. 3 of the Constitution Act, 1871, and to any judicial decisions on boundaries, e.g., *Re Labrador Boundary* [1927] 2 D.L.R. 401 (P.C.); *Re Offshore Mineral Rights of B.C.* [1967] S.C.R. 792; *Re Strait of Georgia* [1984] 1 S.C.R. 388.

18 In *Re Strait of Georgia* [1984] 1 S.C.R. 388, it was held that the United Kingdom statute establishing the colony of British Columbia included within the boundaries of the colony the water between mainland British Columbia and Vancouver Island.

19 This rule was established for England in *R.* v. *Keyn* (1876) 2 Ex. D. 63, and applied to Canada in *Re Offshore Mineral Rights of B.C.* [1967] S.C.R. 792.

20 For detailed analysis of the legal position of the various bodies of water adjacent to a coastal province, see La Forest, *Natural Resources and Public Property under the Canadian Constitution* (1969), ch. 6; Harrison (1979) 17 Osgoode Hall L.J. 469, 501-504.

21 *Re Offshore Mineral Rights of B.C.* [1967] S.C.R. 792 (continental shelf and territorial sea off B.C.); *Re Continental Shelf Offshore Nfld.* [1984] 1 S.C.R. 86 (continental shelf off Nfld.). With respect to the territorial sea off Newfoundland, see ch. 29, Natural Resources, under heading 29.3(c), "Newfoundland Offshore Reference", below.

22 [1980] 2 S.C.R. 303.

23 *Id.*, 316.

24 *Id.*, 319. In *Re CP Airlines and the Queen (B.C.)* (1983) 149 D.L.R. (3d) 519 (B.C. C.A.), it was held that, even on flights that originated or terminated within a province, that province could not tax sales of liquor within the airspace over the province. However, the origination or termination of a flight in the province did provide a sufficiently substantial presence in the province to support a tax on the aircraft. In *Re Lynden Transport* (1981) 119 D.L.R. (3d) 765 (B.C. C.A.), it was held that trucks carrying freight in bond through a province are not subject to provincial sales tax.

the extent to which a province has legislative jurisdiction in the airspace *per se*'',[25] thus leaving open the possibility that an assertion of jurisdiction over the airspace in relation to a matter having a more substantial connection with the province might have been upheld.

(c) Impairment of extraprovincial rights

A line of cases denies provincial power to impair extraprovincial contractual rights.[26]

In *Royal Bank of Canada* v. *The King* (1913),[27] Alberta had enacted a statute expropriating the proceeds of a bond issue which had been made by a railway company in London; the statute provided that the province, which had guaranteed the bonds, should continue to be liable to the bondholders. The reason for the expropriation, recited in the preamble to the statute, was that the company was in default in constructing the railway line for which the money had been borrowed, and in paying interest to the bondholders. The Privy Council held that the statute was invalid. Their lordships assumed that the purpose for which the bondholders had advanced their money had ''ceased to exist'', although there was no evidence that the plan to construct the railway line had been abandoned (and after the decision the railway line was in fact constructed by the province).[28] Proceeding from this assumption, their lordships held that the failure of the purpose would give to the bondholders a common law right to recover back the money they had lent. Their lordships then held that this right of recovery existed in Quebec, because that was the location of the head office of the Royal Bank, in which the proceeds of the bond issue were deposited. In fact, the proceeds were deposited in the Alberta branch of the bank, and a bank account is ordinarily deemed to be located in the branch of the bank that holds the account.[29] The conclusion of this remarkable reasoning process was to characterize the Alberta statute as purporting to destroy a right to recover money in Quebec — ''a civil right outside the province''.[30] On that basis, the statute was held to be unconstitutional.

Even granting the various steps in the reasoning of the *Royal Bank* case, the holding that the statute was invalid represented a very strict application of the extraterritorial limitation. The destruction of the bondholders' contractual or quasi-contractual claim against the head office of the bank was, on any view, a side effect of the statute. Their lordships said that the statute was invalid because

25 [1980] 2 S.C.R. 303, 316.

26 The cases involve a determination of the situs of a right, to determine whether it is located within the province or not: see the discussion of the situs of intangible property in ch. 30, Taxation, under heading 30.11(c), ''Property'', below. For criticism of the use of the situs rules, see Sullivan, note 16, above.

27 [1913] A.C. 283.

28 See *Credit Foncier Franco-Canadien* v. *Ross* [1937] 3 D.L.R. 365, 371 (Alta. C.A.).

29 *The King* v. *Lovitt* [1912] A.C. 212.

30 [1913] A.C. 283, 298.

it "was neither *confined* to property and civil rights within the province nor directed *solely* to matters of a merely local or private nature within it".[31]

Other cases have taken the same strict approach, invalidating provincial statutes with any significant impact outside the province. In *Credit Foncier Franco-Canadien* v. *Ross* (1937),[32] the Alberta Appellate Division held invalid an Alberta statute which purported to reduce or eliminate the interest payable upon certain classes of debt. Among several reasons for striking down the statute, was the territorial limitation on provincial power. This statute exceeded the limitation because it applied to debts payable outside Alberta to creditors resident outside Alberta. The facts that the legislation was designed for the relief of debtors in the depression, that it applied only to debtors in Alberta, and that a debt ordinarily is deemed to be situate where the debtor resides,[33] were not referred to as relevant considerations. In *Beauharnois Light, Heat and Power Co.* v. *Hydro-Electric Power Commission* (1937),[34] the Ontario Court of Appeal struck down an Ontario statute which purported to cancel a contract between Ontario's Hydro-Electric Power Commission and a Quebec power company. The contract had been made in Ontario. It required the company to deliver electric power to the Commission at the boundary between Ontario and Quebec, and required the Commission to pay the company in Toronto. But, despite these strong intraprovincial elements, Middleton J.A. for the Ontario Court of Appeal said that the statute "affected" rights outside Ontario, and was for this reason invalid.[35]

These cases suggest that provincial modification of debt or other contractual rights is effective only if both parties to the contract are resident within the province. Jurisdiction over only one party, such as the debtor, is not sufficient.[36] This "watertight" view of provincial boundaries fails to distinguish the pith and substance of a statute — its "matter" — from its incidental effects. The general rule of constitutional law is that a law is classified by its pith and substance, and incidental effects on subjects outside jurisdiction are not relevant to constitutionality.[37] No one would quarrel with the proposition that a provincial statute whose pith and substance is the destruction or modification of rights outside the province must be unconstitutional. But where the cases go wrong, as it seems to me, is in

---

31 *Ibid.* Emphasis supplied.

32 [1937] 3 D.L.R. 365 (Alta. A.D.).

33 *The King* v. *Lovitt* [1912] A.C. 212; and see La Forest, *The Allocation of Taxing Power under the Canadian Constitution* (2nd ed., 1981), 122.

34 [1937] O.R. 796 (C.A.); see also *Ottawa Valley Power Co.* v. *Hydro-Elec. Power Comm.* [1937] O.R. 265 (C.A.).

35 *Id.*, 821.

36 *A.-G. Ont.* v. *Scott* [1956] S.C.R. 137, 141; Lefroy, *Canada's Federal System* (1913), 506.

37 See ch. 15, Judicial Review on Federal Grounds, under heading 15.5, "Characterization of laws", below. Contra, Sullivan, note 16, above, who argues that the pith and substance rule ought not to govern the extraterritorial issue, which should depend on the effects of the impugned legislation, and should involve an assessment of the severity of the effects outside the enacting province.

refusing to recognize that a statute whose pith and substance is a matter inside the province may incidentally destroy or modify rights outside the province.

The correct approach is exemplified by *Ladore* v. *Bennett* (1939).[38] In that case, the Privy Council upheld an Ontario statute which amalgamated four adjoining municipalities that were in financial difficulties, and incorporated them into a new City of Windsor. The statute compulsorily retired all the old municipalities' debentures and issued the creditors with debentures of the new city bearing a reduced rate of interest. It was objected that the reduction in interest altered the rights of creditors residing outside the province. The Privy Council characterized the Ontario statute as in relation to ''municipal institutions in the province'' (s. 92(8)). This power authorized the dissolution and creation of municipal institutions, which inevitably involved the destruction of old debt and its replacement by new; and, Lord Atkin said, ''if for strictly provincial purposes debts may be destroyed and new debts created, it is inevitable that [creditors] should be affected whether the original creditors reside within or without the province''.[39]

In *Re Upper Churchill Water Rights* (1984),[40] the Supreme Court of Canada accepted the thesis advanced in the previous two paragraphs that the *Royal Bank* line of cases was inconsistent with *Ladore* v. *Bennett*, and that the latter case was the correct one.[41] It is clear, therefore, that the impairment of extraprovincial rights (or other extraprovincial consequences) may be validly accomplished by a provincial Legislature as an incidental effect of a statute that is in relation to a matter territorially within the province and within a head of provincial legislative power.

What was in issue in the *Churchill Falls* case was a Newfoundland statute which expropriated all the assets and water rights of a company generating hydroelectricity at Churchill Falls in Newfoundland (Labrador). The expropriation, for which the company received no compensation,[42] destroyed the ability of the company to perform (or pay damages for the breach of) a 1969 contract (the power contract), under which the company had (with the approval of the Newfoundland government) undertaken to supply nearly all of its production of electricity at a low price to Hydro-Quebec, a Quebec Crown corporation, for a term of 65 years. The power contract had created rights outside Newfoundland, because it called for the delivery of electricity in Quebec, and because it was (by an express provision) enforceable in the courts of Quebec. The expropriating statute made no mention of the power contract, and the province argued that the destruction of

38 [1939] A.C. 468.

39 *Id.*, 481; the word ''creditors'' has been substituted for ''debtors'', which was obviously a verbal slip by Lord Atkin.

40 [1984] 1 S.C.R. 297.

41 *Id.*, 332. The two paragraphs appeared in the first edition (1977) at pp. 209-210.

42 The statute did provide for compensation to be paid to the shareholders for the loss in value of their shares. The shareholders were Hydro-Quebec (34.2 per cent) and Newfoundland and Labrador Hydro (a Newfoundland Crown corporation) (65.8 per cent).

the extraprovincial contractual right was valid under *Ladore* v. *Bennett*, because it was an incidental effect of a statute primarily directed to the expropriation of assets within the province. McIntyre J. for a unanimous Court rejected this argument. He found that the statute was "a colourable attempt to interfere with the power contract and thus to derogate from the rights of Hydro-Quebec to receive an agreed amount of power at an agreed price".[43] This finding promoted the destruction of the extraprovincial right from a merely incidental effect to the pith and substance (or matter) of the statute. On this basis, even following *Ladore* v. *Bennett* (as McIntyre J. insisted he was doing), the statute had to be held unconstitutional as an invalid attempt to impair a civil right outside the province.[44]

(d) Regulation of extraprovincial activity

As a general proposition, it is plain that a province may not regulate extraprovincial activity. What is often difficult is distinguishing extraprovincial activity from intraprovincial activity, and distinguishing the incidental effects of a statute from its pith and substance.[45]

In *Burns Foods* v. *A.-G. Man.* (1973),[46] the Supreme Court of Canada held that Manitoba had no power to authorize a regulation prohibiting meat packers from processing in Manitoba hogs that they had purchased in Saskatchewan. The purpose of the regulation was to prevent the packers from bypassing the Manitoba hog producers' marketing plan. In the Manitoba courts, the regulation was upheld as a valid incident of a local marketing scheme. But in the Supreme Court of Canada, only Ritchie J., who dissented, took this approach. Pigeon J., for the majority, cited the *Royal Bank* case for the proposition that a contract of sale in Saskatchewan "is clearly not within the legislative authority of the Province of

---

43 [1984] 1 S.C.R. 297, 333. For criticism, see Sullivan, note 16, above; Edinger, Comment (1985) 63 Can. Bar Rev. 203.

44 The statute had been enacted and the proceedings commenced before 1982, which is presumably the reason that the Court made no reference to s. 92A(2) of the Constitution Act, 1867, which was added in 1982, and which authorizes a provincial Legislature to make "laws in relation to the export from the province to another part of Canada of . . . the production from facilities in the province for the generation of electrical energy". If the statute were to be re-enacted, would s. 92A(2) save it? Under s. 92A(2), a formerly exclusive federal power, and still a concurrent federal power, it is less clear that the destruction of an extraprovincial contractual right would be a fatal objection.

45 Where a provincial law is in relation to persons or property or transactions within the province, the law may take account of facts occurring outside the province. In *Bank of Toronto* v. *Lambe* (1887) 12 App. Cas. 575, discussed in ch. 30, Taxation, under heading 30.11(b), "Persons", below, it was held that a tax on a person within the province could be computed by reference to facts outside the province; and in *Re Legault* (1975) 8 O.R. (2d) 585 (C.A.) and *Re Underwood McLellan* (1979) 103 D.L.R. (3d) 268 (Sask. C.A.) it was held that the regulation of a profession within the province extended to the disciplining of licensed professionals (a lawyer and an engineer) for unprofessional conduct that took place outside the province.

46 [1975] 1 S.C.R. 494.

Manitoba''.[47] However, it is not clear that this proposition was the ratio decidendi of the decision, because Pigeon J. also held that the impugned regulation was an invalid interference with interprovincial trade and commerce.[48]

In *Interprovincial Cooperatives* v. *The Queen* (1975),[49] the Supreme Court of Canada, by a majority of four to three, held that Manitoba could not create a statutory right of action against out-of-province firms[50] who introduced pollutants into rivers flowing into Manitoba and thereby destroyed Manitoba fisheries. Laskin C.J. (with Judson and Spence JJ.) dissented, holding that the purpose of the legislation was to redress injury suffered in Manitoba, and that the extraterritorial effect was incidental to the main purpose.[51] Again, the ratio decidendi of the majority is not easy to encapsulate. For Ritchie J., the crucial point was that the discharge of pollutants was licensed by statute in the provinces in which it occurred, and those statutory licences were civil rights outside Manitoba which Manitoba was powerless to impair. For Pigeon J. (and Martland and Beetz JJ.), the statutory licences were not relevant, but the mere fact that the discharge of the pollutants occurred outside Manitoba took the discharge outside the legislative authority of Manitoba.

The reasoning of the two majority opinions in *Ipco* is not, in my view, convincing. Ritchie J.'s emphasis on the fact that the discharge of the pollutants was licensed in Ontario and Saskatchewan, where it occurred, is tantamount to giving extraterritorial effect to the licensing statutes: in my view, those statutes should immunize the polluters from liability for damage caused in Ontario and Saskatchewan, but not elsewhere. Pigeon J.'s emphasis on the fact that the discharge of the pollutants occurred outside Manitoba, in my view, ignores the fact that the defendants must have known that the inevitable result of polluting the rivers in Ontario and Saskatchewan was to pollute the water in downstream Manitoba.

Ipco may be contrasted with *The Queen* v. *Thomas Equipment* (1979),[52] in which the Supreme Court of Canada held that a New Brunswick supplier of farm machinery, which supplied machinery to an Alberta retailer for sale in Alberta, was bound by an Alberta statute; the statute required the supplier to purchase back from the retailer any stock that had not been sold by the retailer when the

---

47 *Id.*, 502.

48 *Id.*, 504.

49 [1976] 1 S.C.R. 477; for comment, see Hertz (1976) 26 U. Toronto L.J. 24.

50 Although the pollution took place from plants in Ontario and Saskatchewan, the two corporate defendants also carried on business in Manitoba and had a sufficient presence in Manitoba that the jurisdiction over them of the Manitoba courts was not disputed. The only issue was whether Manitoba law could be applied to the facts. Compare *Moran* v. *Pyle National (Can.)* [1975] 1 S.C.R. 393, discussed at note 69, below, where the jurisdiction of the Court over the defendant was the sole issue.

51 Cf. *Workmen's Comp. Bd.* v. *C.P.R.* [1920] A.C. 184, where the Privy Council held that a British Columbia statute could make workers' compensation payable to workers resident in the province in respect of accidents occurring outside the province.

52 [1979] 2 S.C.R. 529.

supply agreement was terminated. Martland J. for the majority of the Court (Martland, Pigeon, Dickson, Beetz, Estey and Pratte JJ.), in holding that the New Brunswick supplier was bound by the Alberta statute, distinguished *Ipco* on the basis of the New Brunswick supplier's deliberate decision to enter the Alberta marketplace. This decision subjected the supplier to "the rules of the game" in Alberta. But is this a material difference from the facts of *Ipco*? One could as easily characterize the introduction of pollutants into rivers flowing into Manitoba as a deliberate decision to "enter" Manitoba. The minority (Laskin C.J., Ritchie and Spence JJ.) were more faithful to *Ipco* in deciding that the Alberta statute could not constitutionally reach the New Brunswick supplier merely because the supplied goods were sold at retail in Alberta. Yet, surely, notwithstanding *Ipco*, there is force in the majority's view that a person who deliberately avails himself of the Alberta marketplace should be subject to the Alberta law which regulates that marketplace.

In my view, *Thomas Equipment* is more consonant with the flexible approach to extraterritoriality which is exemplified by *Ladore* v. *Bennett*, and which is essential to effective provincial regulation of an interdependent economy and environment. In my view, in *Burns Foods*, Manitoba should have been held competent to regulate the purchase of hogs in Saskatchewan, since the regulation applied only to hogs that were to be processed in Manitoba. In *Ipco*, Manitoba should have been held competent to impose an obligation of compensation on persons introducing pollutants into rivers in Ontario and Saskatchewan, since those rivers flowed into Manitoba. In both those cases, as in *Thomas Equipment*, the provincial law pursued a valid local purpose, and the defendants had made a deliberate choice to avail themselves of the facilities of the legislating province.[53]

(e) Conferral of extraprovincial capacity

The provincial power of incorporation in s. 92(11) of the Constitution Act, 1867 refers to "the incorporation of companies with provincial objects". The full meaning of the phrase "with provincial objects" is discussed in chapter 22, Companies, but there is no doubt that it involves a territorial limitation on the power. It was decided in *Dobie* v. *Temporalities Board* (1881)[54] that Quebec had no power to alter the constitution of a particular company with a pre-confederation charter, because its corporate existence extended to Ontario as well as Quebec. But this holding raised the question whether a provincially-incorporated company

53 Cf. *Moran* v. *Pyle National (Can.)* [1975] 1 S.C.R. 393, discussed at note 70, below. The rule there suggested for provincial court jurisdiction over out-of-province defendants seems equally appropriate for the application of provincial law to out-of-province defendants. Other analogies are *A.-G. Que.* v. *Kellogg's Co. of Can.* [1978] 2 S.C.R. 211 (provincial regulation of imported advertising upheld); *N.S. Bd. of Censors* v. *McNeil* [1978] 2 S.C.R. 662 (provincial regulation of imported films upheld).

54 (1881) 7 App. Cas. 136.

could "walk outside" its province of incorporation and operate elsewhere in Canada.

In *Bonanza Creek Gold Mining Co.* v. *The King* (1916),[55] the Privy Council held that a mining company incorporated in Ontario could operate in the Yukon. While Ontario could not confer "actual powers and rights" which were exercised outside Ontario, it could create corporations with the capacity to acquire powers and rights outside the province. Whether or not such powers and rights were in fact available to the company in another province would depend upon whether that other province chose to recognize the company and permit it to operate. Thus, by authorizing the conferral of extraprovincial capacity the Privy Council served commercial convenience while not detracting from the authority of other provinces to regulate business activity within their borders.

A variant of the *Bonanza* problem arose in *P.E.I. Potato Marketing Board* v. *Willis* (1952).[56] This case established the validity of "administrative inter-delegation", under which the federal Parliament delegates federal power to a provincial agency. The case involved a potato marketing board, which was created by Prince Edward Island and was designed to exercise a totality of regulatory power over potato marketing by receiving a delegation of provincial power from the provincial Legislature and a delegation of federal power from the federal Parliament. The validity of the provincial side of the delegation was unquestionable because of the *Hodge* doctrine, to be discussed in the next chapter, Delegation. But the validity of the federal side of the delegation to the provincial agency was questionable. This administrative inter-delegation raised a number of fundamental federal issues, and these are also discussed in the next chapter. The issue that is relevant to the present topic is whether the Legislature of Prince Edward Island (or any other province) could create a provincial marketing board (or other agency) with capacity to receive a delegation of power from the federal Parliament. The Supreme Court of Canada held that it could, praying in aid the *Bonanza Creek* decision.

13.4 The Crown

The doctrine of extraterritoriality is a restriction on the *legislative* powers of the provinces. It has no application to executive power that does not depend for its validity on a statute. The Crown in right of a province (or the Dominion) has the power of a natural person to enter into contracts and hold property,[57] and is not subject to territorial restraints in exercising such common law powers. Therefore, a province may engage in commercial activity in another province or another

55 [1916] 1 A.C. 566.

56 [1952] 2 S.C.R. 392.

57 *Verreault* v. *A.G. Que.* [1977] 1 S.C.R. 41, 47; *A.G. Que.* v. *Labrecque* [1980] 2 S.C.R. 1057, 1082.

country. Moreover, although the spending of money by the Crown requires an appropriation by the Legislature (or the Parliament), it is clear that the spending power is not subject to the restrictions that apply to other legislative powers, including the extraterritorial restriction.[58] Therefore, a province may spend, or lend, or guarantee, or otherwise dispose of public funds, outside the boundaries of the province.

13.5 Courts

(a) Conflict of laws and the Constitution

Courts often have to decide issues with extraterritorial elements. Three such issues may be identified: (1) the jurisdiction of a provincial court to decide a case in which the facts or the parties are outside the province; (2) the recognition by a provincial court of a judgment obtained outside the province; and (3) the choice of law to be applied by a provincial court to a case with extraprovincial elements once jurisdiction over the case has been assumed. These three topics are governed by a body of law known as "conflicts law" or the "conflict of laws" or "private international law". Each province has its own body of conflicts law, which is partly common law and partly statutory, and a provincial court[59] will determine any conflicts issue which arises before it by applying its own province's conflicts law. In the parlance of the conflict of laws, conflicts questions are settled by the law of the forum. The conflicts law of each Canadian province has developed with little regard for the idea that there are constitutional limits on provincial extraterritorial competence, or the idea that, within a federal state, conflicts law rules might require modification upon constitutional grounds. A small literature has started to develop these ideas,[60] and the Supreme Court of Canada has shown itself receptive to them.[61] These ideas are the topic of this section of this chapter.

---

58 Chapter 6, Financial Arrangements, under heading 6.8, "Spending power", above.

59 The Supreme Court of Canada, when sitting on appeal from a provincial court, is sitting as a court of that province, and is governed by the same rules as the provincial court (although it may differ from the provincial court as to what those rules are or what they mean). In *A.-G. Can.* v. *Canard* [1976] 1 S.C.R. 170, for example, the Supreme Court of Canada, sitting on appeal from Manitoba, denied relief on the ground that the Manitoba courts could not have given the relief, even though on appeal from the Federal Court of Appeal the Supreme Court of Canada could have granted the relief. One difference, however, is that, whereas before a provincial court the law of another province has to be proved in the same manner as the law of a foreign country, once the case has been appealed into the Supreme Court of Canada, the Supreme Court of Canada will take judicial notice of the laws prevailing in any province or territory (provided they have been pleaded), even if they were not proved at trial: *Logan* v. *Lee* (1907) 39 S.C.R. 311, 313; *Pettkus* v. *Becker* [1980] 2 S.C.R. 834, 853-854; *Hunt* v. *T & N* [1993] 4 S.C.R. 289, 317.

60 Castel, *Canadian Conflict of Laws*, (3rd ed., 1994), 6-14; Sharpe, *Interprovincial Product Liability Litigation* (1982), 62-75, 108-114; Hertz, "The Constitution and the Conflict of Laws"

(b) Jurisdiction

The jurisdiction of courts has always been assumed to be territorially limited, even in a unitary state such as the United Kingdom. This assumption was reflected in the rule of the common law that a court could take jurisdiction of a civil suit only if the defendant was personally served with the writ (or other originating process) within the jurisdiction.[62] The common law rule has been expanded in all common law jurisdictions by ''long-arm'' statutes or rules which authorize service ex juris, that is, the service of process on a defendant outside the territory of the issuing court. These rules vary from province to province, but in some provinces the rules authorize service ex juris of civil process in litigation that has minimal connection with the issuing (forum) province.[63] The courts have dealt with this problem, either by asserting a discretion not to permit service ex juris in a case where it would be unfair to the defendant to subject him to the jurisdiction of the forum court, or by declining jurisdiction in a case where the defendant has been served, on the ground of forum non conveniens, that is, that the court is not a convenient (appropriate) forum for the case.[64]

The service *ex juris* rules purport to expand the jurisdiction of the courts to which they apply. Are they subject to constitutional restraints? The answer must be no for rules enacted or authorized by the Parliament of Canada, because (as explained earlier in this chapter) the Parliament's legislative power is not subject to a territorial limit.[65] But rules enacted or authorized by a provincial Legislature must come within the provincial legislative power over ''the administration of justice in the province'' in s. 92(14) of the Constitution Act, 1867.[66] As the words ''in the province'' emphasize, the service ex juris rules must not exceed the territorial limit on provincial legislative power. It is not clear what that limit is. At one extreme, it could be argued that all service ex juris rules must be uncon-

---

(1977) 27 U. Toronto L.J. 1; Edinger, ''Territorial Limitations on Provincial Powers'' (1982) 14 Ottawa L. Rev. 57; Swan, ''The Canadian Constitution, Federalism and the Conflict of Laws'' (1985) 63 Can. Bar Rev. 271; Sullivan, ''Interpreting the Territorial Limitations on the Provinces'' (1985) 7 Supreme Court L.R. 511; Edinger, ''The MacShannon Test for Discretion'' (1986) 64 Can. Bar Rev. 283.

61 *De Savoye* v. *Morguard Investments* [1990] 3 S.C.R. 1077: discussed at notes 73 and 83, below.

62 Castel, note 60, above, 191. This was the rule for actions *in personam*. A similar rule applied to actions *in rem* (admiralty actions against a ship or its cargo), where the thing (*res*) had to be within the jurisdiction.

63 *Id.*, 10-11.

64 *Id.*, 204, 219-226.

65 Federal legislation can also confer extraterritorial jurisdiction on provincial courts, as has been done by the Coastal Fisheries Protection Act: *Re Gordon and The Queen* (1980) 117 D.L.R. (3d) 307 (B.C. C.A.) (American convicted in provincial court of illegally fishing outside Canada's 12-mile territorial sea, but inside Canada's 200-mile fishing zone).

66 As well as powers granted by the provincial Legislature under s. 92(14), the courts of each province that were established before the province's entry to Canada retain all powers possessed at the time of entry, by virtue of s. 129 of the Constitution Act, 1867, unless those powers have, after entry, been abrogated by the provincial Legislature.

stitutional, because each authorizes an act (service of process on the defendant) to be done outside the province. But this view has been implicitly rejected by the many judgments that have been rendered on the basis of service ex juris, although admittedly the constitutional issue has usually been ignored.

At the other extreme, it could be argued that all service ex juris rules must be constitutional, because they have no coercive force outside the province: they cannot and do not purport to compel the out-of-province defendant to defend the action, and if a judgment is pronounced against the out-of-province defendant, the judgment is directly enforceable only inside the forum province. But the judgment can of course be enforced against any assets of the out-of-province defendant that are located inside the forum province. It is not easy to see why those assets should be at risk if the plaintiff's cause of action has no connection with the forum province. Moreover, if there is a risk that the judgment will be recognized (and then enforced) in other provinces, as may well be the case,[67] it is obvious that ''there must be some limits to the exercise of jurisdiction against persons outside the province''.[68] While the test has not been definitively articulated by the Supreme Court of Canada, it now seems clear that the constitutional rule of extraterritoriality requires that the only causes of action in respect of which service ex juris is available are those in which there is a substantial connection between the defendant and the forum province.[69]

The requirement of a substantial connection with the forum province seems to be implicit in the decision of the Supreme Court of Canada in *Moran* v. *Pyle National (Canada)* (1975).[70] In that case, the plaintiff (the dependant of a deceased electrician) sued in Saskatchewan in respect of an accident which occurred in Saskatchewan: the deceased had been electrocuted and killed when he touched an allegedly defective light bulb. The defendant, Pyle, was the manufacturer of the light bulb; the defendant was resident in Ontario, and did not conduct any business operations in Saskatchewan, or even employ sales personnel or agents in Saskatchewan. The Saskatchewan rules regarding service ex juris authorized service of a writ of summons on a defendant outside the jurisdiction whenever ''the action ... is founded on a tort committed within the jurisdiction''. The defendant, who had been served under this rule, objected to the jurisdiction of the Court. The issue before the Supreme Court of Canada was whether the tort alleged was committed within the province of Saskatchewan. Dickson J. for the Court held that the answer was yes. He refused to employ rules which relied upon the place of acting or the place of harm, and instead placed his finding on a very broad policy-based ground:[71]

---

67 See the next section of this chapter, 13.5(c), ''Recognition of judgments'', below.
68 *De Savoye* v. *Morguard Investments* [1990] 3 S.C.R. 1077, 1104.
69 The issue is discussed in the sources listed in note 60, above.
70 [1975] 1 S.C.R. 393.
71 *Id.*, 409.

> Where a foreign defendant carelessly manufactures a product in a foreign jurisdiction which enters into the normal channels of trade and he knows or ought to know both that as a result of his carelessness a consumer may well be injured and it is reasonably foreseeable that the product would be used or consumed where the plaintiff used or consumed it, then the forum in which the plaintiff suffered damage is entitled to exercise judicial jurisdiction over that foreign defendant.

And his lordship justified this rule in these terms:[72]

> By tendering his products in the market place directly or through normal distributive channels, a manufacturer ought to assume the burden of defending those products wherever they cause harm as long as the forum into which the manufacturer is taken is one that he reasonably ought to have had in his contemplation when he so tendered his goods.

In effect, Dickson J. was saying that the occurrence of damage in a province is not by itself sufficient to subject an out-of-province defendant to the jurisdiction of the province's courts, but where it is accompanied by some business activity on the part of the defendant within the province, including the indirect activity which can be foreseen as the result of marketing ''through normal distributive channels'', then the defendant may be subjected to the jurisdiction of the courts where the damage occurred.

In *Moran* v. *Pyle*, Dickson J. emphasized that the ''sole issue'' was whether Saskatchewan's rules regarding jurisdiction based on service ex juris had been complied with. He did not consider whether there were constitutional limits on the jurisdiction which could be conferred by the Saskatchewan Legislature on the Saskatchewan courts.[73] But the rule which he announced could serve satisfactorily as a statement of the constitutional limits of provincial-court jurisdiction over defendants outside the province, requiring as it does a substantial connection between the defendant and the forum province of a kind that makes it reasonable for the courts of the forum province to exercise jurisdiction over litigation against the defendant.

In *De Savoye* v. *Morguard Investments* (1990),[74] the Supreme Court of Canada upheld the validity of an Alberta judgment against a British Columbia defendant who had been served outside the jurisdiction, and who had not consented to the jurisdiction. La Forest J. for the Court held that there was a substantial connection between the defendant and the forum province of Alberta. The action was to enforce repayment of a loan which had been entered into by the defendant in Alberta where he lived at the time, and the loan was secured by a mortgage

---

72 *Ibid.*

73 Nor did Dickson J. consider the choice-of-law issue that would arise once the Saskatchewan court had taken jurisdiction. The case thus presents a different issue from the *Ipco* case, note 49, above, and the *Thomas Equipment* case, note 52, above, where there was no contest as to jurisdiction, and the sole issue was whether the law of the forum was the appropriate law to apply to the facts.

74 [1990] 3 S.C.R. 1077. See Black and Swan, Comment (1991) 12 Advocates' Quarterly 489; Blom, Comment (1991) 70 Can. Bar Rev. 733.

over the defendant's land in Alberta. La Forest J. quoted the previous paragraph of this text,[75] which derived a constitutional requirement of substantial connection from *Moran* v. *Pyle*, and without committing himself to the precise terms of the constitutional requirement, said that he found this approach ''attractive''.[76] It seems fair to conclude that the rule of substantial connection is now established.[77]

The rule of substantial connection bears a striking resemblance to the constitutional law which has developed in the United States with respect to the limits of the ''long-arm'' jurisdiction (based on service ex juris) of the state courts. Those limits are imposed by the due process clause of the fourteenth amendment, which provides that ''nor shall any State deprive any person of life, liberty, or property, without due process of law''. Due process requires, not merely that the non-resident defendant be served with the writ or other initiating process, but that the defendant ''have certain minimum contacts with [the forum state] such that the maintenance of the suit does not offend 'traditional notions of fair play and substantial justice'.''[78] The kind of ''minimum contact'' that will suffice is ''some act by which the defendant purposefully avails itself of the privilege of conducting activities in the forum state, thus invoking the benefits and protections of its laws''.[79] Although the defendant's activities in the forum state must be purposeful, and not merely casual or accidental, they need not be direct. For example, due process is not violated if a state court asserts jurisdiction over a (duly served) non-resident ''corporation that delivers its products into the stream of commerce with the expectation that they will be purchased in the forum State''.[80] While Canada does not have an equivalent to the due process clause of the fourteenth amendment for cases where only economic issues are at stake,[81] in my view, the

75 It appeared in the 2nd edition (1985) at p. 278.

76 [1990] 3 S.C.R. 1077, 1109.

77 If service out of the jurisdiction is unconstitutional with respect to those parties who lack a substantial connection with the forum province, this may prohibit the joinder of some parties as co-defendants or third parties in complex litigation, which would require additional proceedings against those parties in other jurisdictions (where the substantial connection rule would be satisfied). This is a serious drawback of the substantial connection rule, which should be avoided where possible by an expansive definition of substantial connection for the purpose of joining additional parties: see the pre-*Morguard* case of *Jannock Corp.* v. *Tamblyn and Partners* (1975) 8 O.R. (2d) 622, 630 (C.A.), where the difficulties of multiple proceedings are elaborated.

78 *International Shoe Co.* v. *Washington* (1945) 326 U.S. 310, 316 (sales efforts within state subjected non-resident defendant to jurisdiction of state courts).

79 *Hanson* v. *Denckla* (1958) 357 U.S. 235, 253 (absence of activity within state immunized defendant trustee from jurisdiction of state courts).

80 *World-Wide Volkswagen Corp.* v. *Woodson* (1980) 444 U.S. 86, 298 (automobile accident in state insufficient to subject non-resident automobile dealer to jurisdiction of state courts). See also Sharpe, note 60, above, 62-65; Swan note 60, above.

81 Section 7 of the Charter applies only to ''life, liberty and security of the person'', not to property. Note, however, the two cautious suggestions that s. 7 might have a role to play in this context: *De Savoye* v. *Morguard Investments* [1990] 3 S.C.R. 1077, 1110.

due process test, as elaborated in these cases, could as easily serve as a test of extraterritoriality under the Constitution of Canada.

(c) Recognition of judgments

Within a federal state, it seems obvious that, if a provincial court takes jurisdiction over a defendant who is resident in another province, and if the court observes constitutional standards of the kind suggested in the previous section of this chapter, the resulting judgment should be recognized[82] by the courts of the defendant's province.[83] This is the position in the United States, where article IV, s. 1 of the Constitution provides that "full faith and credit shall be given in each state to the public acts, records, and judicial proceedings of every other state". This "full faith and credit" clause means that a state court is constitutionally obliged to recognize a judgment rendered by the court of a sister state, provided that the rendering court acted within its jurisdiction, which means, among other things, that the rendering court must have satisfied the constitutional requirements of due process which were explained in the previous section of this chapter.[84]

The Constitution of Canada contains no explicit "full faith and credit" clause, and, until the decision in *De Savoye* v. *Morguard Investments* (1990),[85] it was widely assumed that each province had the power to protect its residents (and their assets) from the judgments of the courts of other provinces by restrictive rules regarding the recognition of judgments. In fact, the common law rule of recognition of "foreign" judgments was unthinkingly carried over to the Cana-

---

82 Recognition means that the judgment will be accepted as a conclusive resolution of the dispute between the parties, so that the dispute need not be re-litigated in the recognizing jurisdiction. Recognition is all that is necessary for some kinds of judgment, e.g., a judgment in favour of a defendant, or a declaration of rights, or a decision regarding status (such as adoption or divorce). Enforcement is necessary for other kinds of judgments, e.g., a judgment awarding damages to the plaintiff. Recognition is a pre-condition to enforcement, but enforcement requires a further procedure. At common law, enforcement required an action to enforce the judgment (in which the only issue was whether the judgment should be recognized). All provinces now have reciprocal enforcement legislation which, as between reciprocating jurisdictions, for some kinds of judgments, simplifies the procedure by substituting a registration procedure for the common law action. See Castel, note 60, above, 285-300; Swan, "Recognition and Enforcement of Foreign and Extra-provincial Judgments" in Law Society of Upper Canada, *Rights and Remedies in the Law of Creditor and Debtor* (Special Lectures, 1988).

83 The judgments of the Federal Court of Canada are enforceable across Canada: Federal Court Act, R.S.C. 1985, c. F-7, s. 55(1). The problems of recognition of provincial court judgments do not apply. Query about the recognition of judgments of the Supreme Court of Canada, when sitting on appeal from a provincial court: Supreme Court Act, R.S.C. 1985, c. S-26, s. 94(1); and see note 59, above.

84 *D'Arcy* v. *Ketchum* (1850) 52 U.S. (11 How.) 165 (judgment in New York not recognized in Louisiana against Louisiana defendant who had never been served with process). See also the cases cited, notes 78-80, above. Australia has an explicit full faith and credit clause in s. 118 of the Constitution.

85 [1990] 3 S.C.R. 1077.

dian federation. Under the common law rule, a court will recognize the judgment of a foreign court only where, either (1) the defendant was personally served within the territory of the foreign court, or (2) the defendant voluntarily submitted to the jurisdiction of the foreign court (either by agreeing in advance to do so, or by defending the suit on the merits).[86] Under the common law rule, a court will not recognize the judgment of a foreign court against a defendant who has not voluntarily submitted to the jurisdiction, if the foreign court's jurisdiction was based on service ex juris, and that is so even if the foreign court's assertion of jurisdiction was based on a rule which has its counterpart in the rules of the receiving court. Where the common law rule was not satisfied, in order to obtain a judgment that would be recognized in the defendant's province, the plaintiff had to bring a new suit on the original cause of action in the courts of the defendant's province and re-litigate the merits of the cause of action all over again. Such a result could be justified where the first judgment had been obtained in the court of a genuinely foreign jurisdiction, where there might be room for concern that the Canadian defendant had not received a fair trial, but, as between two Canadian provinces, the non-recognition of a judgment obtained on the basis of service ex juris (within constitutional limits) was a ridiculous waste of the litigants' time and money.

In *De Savoye* v. *Morguard Investments* (1990),[87] the question arose whether an Alberta judgment should be recognized in British Columbia. The plaintiffs were mortgagees of land in Alberta. The defendant mortgagor, who owned the land in Alberta, had lived in Alberta when he borrowed the mortgage money, but had subsequently moved to British Columbia. When the defendant defaulted on his mortgage payments, the plaintiffs brought an action against him in Alberta. The plaintiffs served the defendant in British Columbia with the writ in accordance with the rules for service ex juris of the Alberta court. The defendant took no steps to appear or defend the action. The plaintiffs obtained by default an order for the judicial sale of the mortgaged land (which, it will be recalled, was located in Alberta) and a judgment against the defendant for the difference between the value of the land and the amount owing under the mortgage. In order to enforce this judgment, the plaintiffs brought a second action in British Columbia. The question was whether the British Columbia court was obliged to recognize the judgment that the Alberta court had rendered against the non-resident defendant. The Supreme Court of Canada, in a unanimous judgment written by La Forest J., answered yes.

La Forest J. acknowledged that the facts of *De Savoye* would not satisfy the common law rule of recognition, because the defendant was outside the jurisdiction of the Alberta court at the time of the action and had never submitted to the jurisdiction. But La Forest J. said that Canadian courts had in the past "made a serious error in transposing the rules developed for the enforcement of foreign

86 Sharpe, note 60, above, 43-54.
87 [1990] 3 S.C.R. 1077.

judgments to the enforcement of judgments from sister-provinces''.[88] For the purpose of recognizing each other's judgments, the provinces should not be regarded as ''foreign'' jurisdictions; they were part of one nation. Moreover, the courts of each province observed the same standards of procedural fairness, and were subject to review by the same Supreme Court of Canada.[89] It was inherent in the federation that the courts of one province should give full faith and credit to the judgments of a court in another province.

The full faith and credit rule could be oppressive to defendants if it were not accompanied by some limits on the exercise of jurisdiction by provincial courts against persons outside the province. In order to deal with this concern, La Forest J. in *De Savoye* held that the judgment sought to be recognized must be against a defendant[90] with a sufficiently ''substantial connection'' to the forum that it was reasonable for the court to assume the jurisdiction.[91] In this case, the mortgage had been entered into in Alberta by a borrower who was then resident in Alberta, and the mortgaged property was located in Alberta. These facts easily established a substantial connection between the defendant and the forum of Alberta. Therefore, the courts of British Columbia were obliged to recognize the Alberta judgment.

The effect of the *De Savoye* case is that there is now an implicit full faith and credit rule in the Constitution of Canada.[92] The courts of all provinces must recognize a judgment rendered by the court of another province, provided the

---

88 *Id.*, 1098.

89 *Id.*, 1100. La Forest J. added the point that, under s. 96 of the Constitution Act, 1867, the judges of the superior, district and county courts in each province are appointed by the federal government. On the unitary aspects of the administration of justice in Canada, see ch. 7, Courts, above.

90 The test probably does turn on the connection between ''the defendant'' and the forum province, as La Forest J. said (at 1109); but La Forest J. also made reference to the connections with the forum province of ''the subject-matter of the action'' (at 1103, 1104); of the ''damages suffered'' (at 1107); of ''the transaction'' (at 1103); and of ''the transaction or the parties'' (at 1108). The test is not entirely clear: for discussion see Black and Swan, note 74, above; Blom, note 74, above.

91 *Id.*, 1108. La Forest J. (at p. 1104) rejected reciprocity (which would exist if the B.C. Court would have exercised jurisdiction on the same basis as the Alberta Court) as the test for validity. He gave no reason, but two could be given. First, reciprocity focuses on the rules of the two jurisdictions, not on the position of the defendant: even if both jurisdictions had the same service *ex juris* rule, the rule could still be unfair to the defendant. Secondly, reciprocity ignores the territorial restriction on provincial court jurisdiction: an excessive assertion of jurisdiction by a province should not be validated simply because another province has made a similar assertion. See Black and Swan, note 74, above, 499.

92 The reasons for judgment did not make perfectly clear whether the *De Savoye* rule of recognition was a constitutional requirement or simply a new common law rule. In *Hunt* v. *T & N* [1993] 4 S.C.R. 289, which is discussed next in the text, La Forest J. for the Court (at p. 324) explained the *De Savoye* decision as establishing a constitutional requirement that was ''beyond the power of provincial legislatures to override''. Accordingly, a Quebec statute that purported to enact a more restrictive rule was held to be unconstitutional in its application to court orders emanating from other Canadian provinces.

judgment was rendered in compliance with the forum province's jurisdictional rules, and provided that those rules do not offend any constitutional principle. The constitutional principle of extraterritoriality is not offended where the court of one province renders a judgment against a resident of another province, provided the out-of-province defendant was served in compliance with the court's rules for service ex juris, and the defendant has a substantial connection with the forum province.

In *Hunt* v. *T & N* (1993),[93] the Supreme Court of Canada extended the *De Savoye* rule of recognition from final judgments to other types of court orders. At issue was the efficacy of a Quebec statute that prohibited the removal from the province of documents of a business concern in Quebec that were required by a court outside the province. The purpose of the statute, which had a counterpart in Ontario, was to frustrate the enforcement against companies in Quebec of United States anti-trust laws. However, the statute purported to block all out-of-province court orders seeking documents from Quebec companies, whether the orders emanated from the courts of the United States or from the courts of other Canadian provinces. In the *Hunt* case, proceedings had been brought in British Columbia[94] by a plaintiff who alleged that he had suffered injury in British Columbia that had been caused by his exposure to asbestos fibres in products distributed in British Columbia by the defendants, which were Quebec companies engaged in the manufacture and distribution of asbestos products. The plaintiff obtained an order from the trial court in British Columbia for discovery by the defendants of documents in Quebec. When the defendants refused to comply, relying on the Quebec statute, the plaintiff applied to the British Columbia court for an order compelling the defendants to produce all relevant documents. The British Columbia courts held that they could not make this order in the face of the prohibitory terms of the Quebec statute. However, the Supreme Court of Canada, in a unanimous judgment written by La Forest J., held that the Quebec statute was constitutionally ineffective to block the British Columbia court's order for discovery of documents; the Supreme Court of Canada therefore ordered the defendants to comply with the court order to produce the documents.

In *Hunt*, La Forest J. acknowledged that the case did not raise exactly the same issue as *De Savoye*, which concerned the recognition by a court of one province of the final judgment of the court of another province. But La Forest J. held that the constitutional obligation to give full faith and credit to a judgment rendered in another province ''cannot be avoided by a preemptive strike''.[95] The

---

93 [1993] 4 S.C.R. 289.

94 The jurisdiction of the B.C. court had been unsuccessfully challenged in earlier proceedings. La Forest J. (at p. 315) described the affirmation of jurisdiction as ''scarcely surprising'', and noted the close similarity of the facts to *Moran* v. *Pyle National (Can.)*, described at note 70, above. In both cases, La Forest J. said (at p. 316), ''the manufacturer must be taken to have known that the goods would be used outside the province of manufacture in the manner they were''.

95 [1993] 4 S.C.R. 289, 327.

purpose of Quebec's blocking statute was to make it difficult to obtain judgment against Quebec defendants in jurisdictions outside Quebec. That kind of restriction was inconsistent with Canada's federal system, which created a common market and allowed people and products to move freely throughout all provinces (and territories). No province had the power to deny to the citizens of other provinces their normal rights of access to their own courts to resolve the disputes that would inevitably arise out of interprovincial activity. No province had the power to insist, in effect, that its residents be sued only in the courts of their own province. These propositions followed from the *De Savoye* idea that the provinces (and territories) are not foreign jurisdictions to each other, but are parts of a single nation with an ''essentially unitary'' court system.[96] *De Savoye's* full faith and credit rule applied not only to final judgments, but also required each province to respect the normal judicial processes (such as discovery) of the other provinces. If followed that the Quebec statute was ''constitutionally inapplicable to other provinces'',[97] and could not bar the discovery process of the courts of British Columbia.

(d) Choice of law

Once a court has taken jurisdiction of a case which has foreign as well as local elements, the question arises whether the court should apply the law of the forum (the law of the court's own jurisdiction) or the foreign law. This choice-of-law issue is resolved by application of the forum's conflicts law, which may be common law or statutory. If the applicable choice-of-law rule directs the court to the foreign substantive law, then the court will apply the foreign law; if the choice-of-law rule directs the court to the substantive law of the forum, then the court will apply the law of the forum.

Problems of choice of law are not usually seen as raising constitutional questions. If the court of province A determines a case on the basis of the ''foreign'' law of province B, this is not seen as an extraterritorial application of the law of province B. The court of province A is applying its own choice-of-law rule, which has the effect of incorporating the (foreign) substantive law of province B into the (domestic) law of province A.[98] But, in the converse situation, where province A's (the forum's) choice-of-law rule directs the court to apply province A's (the forum's) own substantive law to a case having elements in province B, the question whether province A has given an unconstitutional extra-

96 *Id.*, 322.

97 *Id.*, 331. The Court did need to decide, and did not decide, whether the statute was applicable to other countries. That would have required a decision as to the extent of the province's authority under s. 92(13) to diminish extraprovincial rights in order to protect property (documents) in the province. The issue was inconclusively discussed by La Forest J. at pp. 320-321.

98 This must be the correct analysis, because the choice-of-law rule will often direct the court to apply the law of a foreign country, e.g., Italy, which could not make its laws applicable of their own force in the forum, e.g., Ontario. Accord, Sharpe, note 60, above, 113-114.

territorial application to its law cannot be avoided by the assertion that the result was demanded by province A's (the forum's) choice-of-law rule.[99]

The constitutional limitations on the legislative competence of province A must be observed whenever the substantive law of province A is applied by the courts of province A to a case having elements in province B.[100] That is why the constitutional question had to be faced in the *Ipco* case.[101] In that case, the action had been brought in Manitoba for damages against defendants that had introduced pollutants into rivers outside Manitoba. The Manitoba court[102] could not choose to apply Manitoba law to the defendants, either directly or via a choice-of-law rule, without deciding that such an application would be within the territorial competence of the Manitoba Legislature.[103] A court in Ontario (or Saskatchewan, where the pollution took place) would have a somewhat different issue to consider. The Ontario court would not apply the law of Manitoba (or any other foreign law)[104] as being applicable in Ontario of its own force. The Ontario court would apply Manitoba law only if directed to do so by Ontario's choice-of-law rules. The Ontario court would, therefore, never have to decide the question whether Manitoba's statute went beyond the territorial competence of the Manitoba Legislature.

The choice-of-law rule in tort cases in Canada used to be the rule in *Phillips* v. *Eyre*,[105] which directed that the law of the forum be applied to torts committed elsewhere so long as the act was also "unjustifiable" (which did not necessarily

---

99 If the court concludes that the law of the forum should be interpreted as applying to the facts directly of its own force, then the court will apply the law of the forum, provided that the law of the forum remains within the constitutional rule regarding extraterritoriality. If the court concludes that the law of the forum should not be interpreted as applying to the facts directly of its own force, then the court will invoke the applicable choice-of-law rule of the forum. The choice-of-law rule may direct application of foreign law, or it may direct application of the law of the forum. The latter possibility is a second chance for the law of the forum to apply. For discussion, see Edinger (1982), 14 Ottawa Law Rev. 57, 70; Castel, note 60 above, 7-8; Hertz (1977), 27 U. Toronto L.J. 1, 61.

100 Once again, the position in the United States is instructive. A state's choice-of-law rule will be unconstitutional as a denial of due process (which, as noted earlier, in this context is similar to Canada's doctrine of extraterritoriality) if it directs the choice of the substantive law of the forum to facts and parties that have little contact with the forum state: see *Allstate Insurance Co.* v. *Hague* (1981) 449 U.S. 302 (holding, by majority, that a Minnesota court did not violate due process by applying a Minnesota choice-of-law rule which directed application of Minnesota law to the interpretation of an insurance policy written in Wisconsin).

101 Note 49 and accompanying text, above.

102 The Supreme Court of Canada was a Manitoba Court for this purpose: see note 59, above.

103 For this reason, a constitutional issue was inescapably involved in *The Queen* v. *Thomas Equipment*, note 52 and accompanying text, above, where the Supreme Court of Canada on appeal from Alberta (and therefore sitting as an Alberta Court) decided to apply Alberta law to a case with New Brunswick elements.

104 Pre-confederation laws applicable in Ontario and federal laws applicable in Ontario are not, of course, foreign laws for this purpose.

105 (1870) L.R. 6 Q.B.1. The rule was adopted for Canada in *McLean* v. *Pettigrew* [1945] S.C.R. 62, which was overruled in *Tolofson* v. *Jensen*, next note.

mean that it was actionable) in the place where the act was committed. This rule led to forum-shopping, because a plaintiff who had suffered an injury in one province could often choose to sue in a different province in which the law was more favourable to the plaintiff's claim.

In *Tolofson* v. *Jensen* (1994),[106] two actions were consolidated in which personal injury plaintiffs had brought their actions in a jurisdiction other than that in which the accident occurred. In one case, a resident of British Columbia, who had suffered a car accident in Saskatchewan caused by a resident of Saskatchewan sued for damages in British Columbia. That action was barred by a limitation period in Saskatchewan, but not in British Columbia. As well, Saskatchewan imposed a requirement of proving ''wilful or wanton misconduct'' where the plaintiff had been a passenger in a car driven by the defendant; no similar rule applied in British Columbia. In the other case, a resident of Ontario, who had suffered a car accident in Quebec caused by a resident of Quebec, sued for damages in Ontario. That action was barred in Quebec by Quebec's no-fault automobile liability regime, which restricted a victim to a statutory benefit that was less than common-law damages. When these cases reached the Supreme Court of Canada, the Court took the opportunity to review the rule in *Phillips* v. *Eyre*, and held that it should be overruled for Canada. La Forest J., who wrote for a Court that was unanimous on the main issues, held that the choice-of-law rule for tort cases in Canada should henceforth be that the applicable law is the law of the place where the tort was committed (lex loci delicti). This meant that the plaintiffs in the two cases were governed by the law of the place of the tort and could not take advantage of the more favourable law of the place where they had chosen to sue.[107]

Central to the reasoning of La Forest J. in *Tolofson* v. *Jensen* was the Constitution of Canada. He did not say directly that the new choice-of-law rule (the place of the tort) was required by the Constitution, but he said that the old rule in *Phillips* v. *Eyre* should be rejected because it ''may possibly raise intractable constitutional problems''.[108] What were those constitutional problems? La Forest J. did not give a clear answer to this question, but he did suggest two kinds of constitutional considerations that militated in favour of his new place-of-tort rule. One consideration was extraterritoriality. La Forest J. said that the powers of the courts were limited in the same way as the provincial Legislatures and that ''an attempt by one province to impose liability for negligence in respect of activities that have taken place wholly in another province . . . would give rise to

---

106 [1994] 3 S.C.R. 1022. The opinion of the majority was written by La Forest J., with the agreement of Gonthier, Cory, McLachlin and Iacobucci JJ. A brief concurring opinion was written by Major J., with the agreement of Sopinka J.; Major J. agreed with La Forest J. subject to one reservation not material to the outcome.

107 The Court also decided that limitation periods were to be characterized as substantive (rather than procedural) law, which meant that the limitation period of the province where the tort occurred, not the limitation period of the forum, was the applicable period.

108 [1994] 3 S.C.R. 1022, 1066.

serious constitutional concerns''.[109] The concern identified here is that the forum province should not be permitted, even by a choice-of-law rule, to extend its law to facts occurring outside the province, because that would be in violation of the extraterritoriality prohibition.

Another constitutional consideration was full faith and credit, the doctrine developed by the Court to require the recognition of the judgments of sister provinces. La Forest J. said that in ''a single country with different provinces exercising territorial legislative jurisdiction'', there should be a rule ''that ensures that an act committed in one part of this country will be given the same legal effect throughout the country''.[110] The concern identified here is that the forum province ought to give full faith and credit to the laws of the other province in which the tort was committed, rather than substituting its own laws. If this were the dominant consideration, it would allow a different rule to be applied to torts committed in another country (as opposed to another province), since there would be no constitutional reason to give full faith and credit to the laws of foreign countries. If, on the other hand, extraterritoriality were the dominant consideration, the same rule should be applied to all torts committed anywhere outside the forum province, whether elsewhere in Canada or in a foreign country. This issue did not have to be resolved in the *Tolofson* case, but La Forest J. indicated, obiter, that, while the place-of-tort rule should be invariable for torts committed within Canada, in exceptional cases he was ''not averse to retaining a discretion in the court to apply our own law'' to a tort committed outside Canada.[111] This willingness to distinguish interprovincial litigation from international litigation perhaps suggests that, for La Forest J., it was the full faith and credit rule, rather than the extraterritoriality rule, that was the dominant constitutional principle.

109 *Ibid.*

110 *Id.*, 1064.

111 *Id.*, 1054. This was the point upon which Major J. (with Sopinka J.) entered a reservation. In his view, the Court ought not to foreclose the possibility of an exception to the place-of-tort rule in interprovincial as well as international litigation.

14

Delegation

14.1 Power of delegation

(a) Introduction

It is impossible for the federal Parliament or any provincial Legislature to enact all of the laws that are needed in its jurisdiction for the purpose of government in any given year. When a legislative scheme is established, the Parliament or the Legislature will usually enact the scheme in outline only, and will delegate to a subordinate body the power to make laws on matters of detail. The subordinate body (or delegate) to which this law-making power is delegated is most commonly the Governor in Council or the Lieutenant Governor in Council; each of these bodies is in practice the cabinet of the government concerned.[1] Sometimes a power of law-making is delegated to a single minister, or a public corporation, or a municipality, or a school board, or an administrative agency, or a court. The body of law enacted by these subordinate bodies vastly exceeds in bulk the body of law enacted by the primary legislative bodies.[2]

The legislation of subordinate bodies is called ''subordinate legislation'' or ''delegated legislation''; these terms encompass all laws made by bodies other than the Parliament or a Legislature. Some other terms are used to describe particular kinds of subordinate (or delegated) legislation: a ''regulation'' usually means a law enacted by the Governor in Council or Lieutenant Governor in Council or a minister or agency of the federal or provincial government; a ''by-law'' usually means a law enacted by a municipality; a ''rule'' usually means a law enacted by a court or administrative agency to regulate its procedure; and an ''order'' usually means a direction for a particular case. Terminology is not, however, consistent.

(b) United Kingdom Parliament

It was settled in England in the seventeenth century that the King had no power to make new laws.[3] Only the elected Parliament had the power to make new laws. But the Parliament, as a sovereign body, could enact any law that it chose, and therefore it could enact a law delegating law-making power to the King or to his ministers or to any other official or body.

(c) Provincial Legislatures

Was this power of delegation inherited by the Parliament and Legislatures of Canada? An argument that the power had not been inherited in Canada was based on the premise that the powers of the Canadian legislative bodies had been delegated to them by the imperial Parliament; since the Canadian legislative bodies were themselves mere delegates, they could not further delegate (or sub-delegate) their powers: delegatus non potest delegare.[4] In *Hodge* v. *The Queen* (1883),[5] the Privy Council rejected this argument. In that case, the Ontario Legislature had delegated to a Board of License Commissioners the power to make regulations for licensed taverns. The Privy Council held that the delegation was

---

1 See ch. 9, Responsible Government, above.

2 For useful accounts of delegation in Canada, see Third Report of the Special Committee on Statutory Instruments (House of Commons, Canada, 1969); Cheffins and Tucker, *The Constitutional Process in Canada* (2nd ed., 1976), ch. 3.

3 *Case of Proclamations* (1611) 12 Co. Rep. 74, 77 E.R. 1352.

4 A delegate has no power to delegate. For analysis of this doctrine, see Willis, ''Delegatus non potest delegare'' (1943) 21 Can. Bar Rev. 257.

5 (1883) 9 App. Cas. 117.

valid. It was erroneous, they held, to regard the powers conferred by the Constitution Act, 1867 on the provincial Legislatures as delegated powers. On the contrary, provincial legislative power was "as plenary and as ample within the limits prescribed by section 92 as the Imperial Parliament in the plenitude of its power possessed and could bestow."[6]

The Privy Council's references to the plenitude and amplitude of colonial legislative power, and of its equivalence to that of the Parliament of the United Kingdom, suggested that there were no limits to the power of delegation. But the power actually delegated in *Hodge* — to license and regulate taverns — hardly called for a decision as to the outer limits of legislative power; and the Privy Council described the power at one point as "an authority ancillary to legislation" and as a "limited discretionary authority".[7] Thus the facts and some of the dicta invited an argument that even plenitude and amplitude may have their limits, and that a sweeping delegation might run into some, as yet unidentified, constitutional obstacle.

It seems clear, however, that sweeping delegations by provincial Legislatures are valid. For example, the conventional kind of natural products marketing statute simply confers on the Lieutenant Governor in Council the power to establish marketing schemes and boards to administer them, and leaves to the discretion of the Lieutenant Governor in Council the question of which products should be regulated, by what board and upon what terms. In *Shannon* v. *Lower Mainland Dairy Products Board* (1938),[8] the Privy Council was faced with the argument that such a skeletal statute was an invalid delegation of "legislative powers". This argument was rejected by their lordships as "subversive" of provincial legislative power and as inconsistent with the "supremacy" of the provincial Legislatures.[9]

(d) Federal Parliament

The Privy Council in *Hodge* did not have to determine the extent of the federal Parliament's power of delegation, but their lordships indicated in a dictum that the federal power was just as "plenary and ample" as that of the provincial Legislatures.[10]

In *Re Gray* (1918),[11] the Supreme Court of Canada had to determine the validity of the delegation of legislative power contained in the War Measures

---

6 *Id.*, 132.

7 *Ibid.*

8 [1938] A.C. 708.

9 *Id.*, 722, effectively though not explicitly overruling *Credit Foncier Franco-Canadien* v. *Ross* [1937] 3 D.L.R. 365 (Alta. A.D.), but for further references see note 16, below.

10 (1883) 9 App. Cas. 117, 132. See also *A.-G. Can.* v. *Cain* [1906] A.C. 542, 547. For application of the *Hodge* doctrine outside Canada, see *R.* v. *Burah* (1878), 3 App. Cas. 889 (India); *Powell* v. *Apollo Candle Co.* (1885) 10 App. Cas. 282 (Australia); *Cobb & Co.* v. *Kropp* [1967] 1 A.C. 141 (Australia).

11 (1918) 57 S.C.R. 150.

Act, 1914. That Act, passed at the beginning of the first world war, empowered the Governor in Council to proclaim a state of "real or apprehended war, invasion or insurrection", and then "to make from time to time such orders and regulations, as he may by reason of the existence of real or apprehended war, invasion or insurrection, deem necessary or advisable for the security, defence, peace, order and welfare of Canada".[12] In effect, the War Measures Act transferred to the federal cabinet virtually the whole legislative authority of the Parliament for the duration of the war. The Court held that even a delegation as sweeping as this one was valid. However, the four opinions each contained indications that the power of delegation was not absolute, and that an "abdication", "abandonment" or "surrender" of the Parliament's powers would be invalid.[13] But, since none of the majority judges regarded the War Measures Act as an unconstitutional abdication, abandonment or surrender, it is not easy to imagine the kind of delegation that would be unconstitutional. Nor did the judges indicate how their suggested limitation was to be reconciled with the *Hodge* doctrine of plenary and ample power; or, to put the same question in another way, what principle of constitutional law dictated the suggested limitation.[14]

Another sweeping delegation by the federal Parliament, although one that never seems to have been challenged in the courts, is the grant of extensive powers of self-government to the two federal territories. The Northwest Territories Act and the Yukon Act establish a Council for each territory, and empower the Council to make "ordinances" for the government of its territory in relation to a long list of subjects roughly corresponding to the list of subjects allocated to the provincial Legislatures by s. 92 of the Constitution Act, 1867.[15]

14.2 Limitations imposed by Constitution

(a) Delegation of legislative power

It goes without saying that the Constitution could impose limitations on the power of the Canadian legislative bodies to delegate their powers. What *Hodge*, *Shannon* and *Gray* establish is that the courts will not readily imply any such limitations. In particular, these cases establish that in Canada there is no require-

---

12 The War Measures Act has been upheld as an exercise of the federal Parliament's "peace, order, and good government" power: see ch. 17, Peace, Order and Good Government, under heading 17.4(b), "War" 113 to 116, below.

13 (1918) 57 S.C.R. 150, 157, 165, 171, 176.

14 See Willis, "Administrative Law and the B.N.A. Act" (1939) 53 Harv. L. Rev. 251; Laskin, *Canadian Constitutional Law* (5th ed., 1986 by Finkelstein), 42.

15 See Northwest Territories Act, R.S.C. 1985, c. N-27, ss. 9, 16; Yukon Act, R.S.C. 1985, c. Y-2, ss. 9, 17; for dicta affirming the validity of the delegation, see *Re Gray* (1918) 57 S.C.R. 150, 170. The federal Parliament's power to legislate for the territories comes from the Constitution Act, 1871, s. 4.

ment that ''legislative'' and ''executive'' powers be exercised by separate and independent bodies. A delegation cannot be attacked on the ground that it confers ''legislative'' power on the executive branch of government.[16]

In the United States, the position is otherwise. There, the separation of powers doctrine which is embedded in the federal and state constitutions has been held to prohibit the delegation by the federal Congress or a state Legislature of any of its ''legislative'' powers. In practice, however, this has not proved to be a serious restraint on the conferral of law-making powers upon administrative agencies or officials, because the courts have given a very attenuated meaning to legislative powers. So long as the Congress or Legislature limits the scope of its delegate's law-making authority by reference to some ''standard'', then the grant of power is deemed not to be a forbidden delegation of legislative power. Moreover, the courts have accepted vague phrases such as ''just and reasonable rates'' or ''unfair methods of competition'' as adequate standards. But there is always the danger that an exceptionally broad and vague delegation might be classified as a delegation of legislative power; and in fact there are two decisions of the Supreme Court of the United States in which delegations have been held to be unconstitutional on this ground.[17]

The difference between the Canadian and American systems resides not only in the different language of the two constitutional instruments, but in Canada's retention of the British system of responsible government. The close link between the executive and legislative branches which is entailed by the British system is utterly inconsistent with any separation of the executive and legislative functions.[18] In Australia, where responsible government was also retained, but where the federal constitution (although not the state constitutions) follows the American pattern of making a separate distribution of the legislative, executive and judicial powers, the courts have been forced to conclude that the federal Parliament may delegate legislative power to the executive without offending the constitutional limitation.[19]

---

16 There is one case to the contrary, *Credit Foncier Franco-Canadien* v. *Ross* [1937] 3 D.L.R. 365 (Alta. A.D.) holding that legislative power may not be delegated, but the case has been effectively overruled by the Privy Council (note 8, above) and the Supreme Court of Canada in *Re Criminal Law Amendment Act 1968-69* (Breathalyzer) [1970] S.C.R. 777 (note 99, below), and has never been followed: for discussion, see Willis, note 14, above, 258; Rutherford, ''Delegation of Legislative Power'' (1948) 26 Can. Bar Rev. 533.

17 *Panama Refining Co.* v. *Ryan* (1935) 293 U.S. 388; *Schechter Poultry Corp.* v. *U.S.A.* (1935) 295 U.S. 494.

18 See ch. 9, Responsible Government, under heading 9.4(e), ''The Cabinet'', above. Responsible government is not inconsistent with a separation of the *judicial* function from the two political branches. In Canada the judicature provisions of the Constitution have been construed as imposing limits upon the kinds of bodies which can be invested with some judicial functions: see the next section of this chapter.

19 *Roche* v. *Kronheimer* (1921) 29 C.L.R. 329; *Victorian Stevedoring and Gen. Contracting Co.* v. *Dignan* (1931) 46 C.L.R. 73. With respect to judicial power, however, the separation has been insisted upon: *A.-G. Cwlth.* v. *The Queen* (Boilermakers) (1957) 95 C.L.R. 529.

It is possible that there is one legislative power in Canada that cannot be delegated, and that is the federal Parliament's power to levy taxes. Section 53 of the Constitution Act, 1867 provides that a bill levying a tax must originate in the House of Commons, and s. 54 provides that the House of Commons shall not pass any such bill unless the bill was recommended by message of the Governor General.[20] It is arguable that a delegation of the taxing power is implicitly forbidden by these sections, because a tax levied under a delegated power would not originate in the House of Commons or be recommended by a message of the Governor General.[21]

The argument that the federal taxing power cannot be delegated was made in *Re Agricultural Products Marketing Act* (1978),[22] as part of a constitutional attack on a federal statute that authorized marketing boards to impose levies on farmers. The Supreme Court of Canada held that the levies were not taxes, but administrative charges, and so the Court did not need to determine the issue. However, Pigeon J. for a majority of the Court rejected the argument anyway, on the basis that ss. 53 and 54 could be amended by the federal Parliament,[23] and any inconsistent legislation should be treated as an implicit amendment.[24] This seems an unsatisfactory holding. Surely, the fact that the provisions can be amended by the federal Parliament should not justify their disregard (as opposed to explicit amendment or repeal) by the Parliament. Another possible answer to the argument that ss. 53 and 54 prohibit delegation is that ss. 53 and 54 are merely directory provisions addressed to the ''internal'' procedures of the House of Commons, and (like other such procedures) are not enforceable by the courts. This answer is more plausible, but the presence of ss. 53 and 54 in the Constitution Act, 1867 suggests that they enjoy a higher status than internal parliamentary procedure.

(b) Delegation of judicial power

The absence of any general separation of powers doctrine in Canada means that there is no general prohibition on the delegation of judicial power to bodies other than courts. However, s. 96 of the Constitution Act, 1867 has been interpreted as implicitly prohibiting the delegation of judicial functions analogous to

---

20 Sections 53 and 54 apply to the provinces as well, by virtue of s. 90. Accordingly, exactly the same argument can be made about the existence of provincial capacity to delegate the power to levy taxes.

21 See Cheffins and Tucker, *The Constitutional Process in Canada* (2nd ed., 1976), 58; La Forest, *The Allocation of Taxing Power under the Canadian Constitution* (2nd ed., 1981), 40-41.

22 [1978] 2 S.C.R. 1198.

23 At that time (before 1982) the amendment of ss. 53 and 54 would have been possible under s. 91(1) of the Constitution Act, 1867. That provision has now been repealed and replaced by s. 44 of the Constitution Act, 1982, which would also authorize an amendment of ss. 53 and 54.

24 [1978] 2 S.C.R. 1198, 1291. Laskin C.J. in a separate concurring opinion discussed the argument (at pp. 1227-1229), but did not reach any conclusions on its force.

those performed by a superior, district or county court to a body that is not a superior, district or county court. This prohibition applies to the provincial Legislatures, but not to the federal Parliament, except when the federal Parliament invests a provincial body with judicial functions. The prohibition has been discussed in chapter 7, Courts.[25]

(c) Classification of laws

The Constitution of Canada, as a federal constitution, distributes legislative powers among the federal Parliament and the provincial Legislatures. Every law enacted by the Parliament or a Legislature must fall within one of the classes of subjects allocated by the Constitution to the enacting legislative body. Otherwise it is invalid. This is as true of a law effecting a delegation as it is of any other law. The invalidity of a statute which is ultra vires the enacting legislative body will of course destroy any powers which the statute purported to delegate to the government or to an administrative agency.

This is obvious enough, but a more subtle effect of the federal distribution of powers on the power to delegate is possible. It has been suggested in Australia that a particularly broad or vague delegation by the federal Parliament of law-making power could be held invalid on the ground that "the enactment attempting it is not a law with respect to any particular head or heads of legislative power".[26] In Canada, the same idea surfaced in a famous dictum of Rand J. in *Saumur* v. *Quebec* (1953)[27] as a reason for striking down a municipal by-law that forbade the distribution of literature on the streets of Quebec City without the permission of the chief of police. Because the by-law supplied no standards for the guidance of the chief of police, it was impossible to be sure from its terms whether the by-law was addressed to street regulation of soliciting and littering (in which case it would be valid) or to censorship of the religious and political content of material proposed for distribution (in which case it would be invalid). For Rand J. (none of the other judges took this point), the absence of precision in the drafting of the by-law was by itself a fatal flaw. The relevant passage of his opinion is not easy to summarize, and so I set it out in full:

> Conceding, as in the Alberta Reference, that aspects of the activities of religion and free speech may be affected by provincial legislation, such legislation, as in all other fields, must be sufficiently definite and precise to indicate its subject matter. In our political organization, as in federal structures generally, that is the condition of legislation by any authority within it: the courts must be able from its language and its relevant circumstances, to attribute an enactment to a matter *in relation to which* the legislature acting has been empowered to make laws. That principle inheres in the nature of federalism; otherwise, authority, in broad and general terms, could be

25 Chapter 7, Courts, under heading 7.3, "Implications of Constitution's judicature sections", above.

26 *Victorian Stevedoring and Gen. Contracting Co.* v. *Dignan* (1931) 46 C.L.R. 73, 101.

27 [1953] 2 S.C.R. 299, 333.

> conferred which would end the division of powers. Where the language is sufficiently specific and can fairly be interpreted as applying only to matter within the enacting jurisdiction, that attribution will be made; and where the requisite elements are present, there is the rule of severability. But to authorize action which may be related indifferently to a variety of incompatible matters by means of the device of a discretionary licence cannot be brought within either of these mechanisms; and the Court is powerless, under general language that overlaps exclusive jurisdictions, to delineate and preserve valid power in a segregated form. If the purpose is street regulation, taxation, registration or other local object, the language must, with sufficient precision, define the matter and mode of administration; and by no expedient which ignores that requirement can constitutional limitations be circumvented.

This seems to be the only suggestion in the Canadian cases that a sweeping delegation might run foul of the federal distribution of powers.[28] In most cases, of course, a law can be attributed to a matter coming within a class of subject, such as banking, even if the law includes a delegation to a subordinate body. And more sweeping delegations, covering laws of various classifications, are not necessarily invalid. Thus, the federal delegations to the territorial councils of the Yukon and Northwest Territories are undoubtedly valid as laws in relation to federal territories.[29] It is possible that other sweeping delegations could be upheld, if federal, as in relation to "the peace, order, and good government of Canada"[30] or "the executive government of Canada";[31] and, if provincial, as in relation to the amendment of "the constitution of the province".[32]

(d) Office of Lieutenant Governor or Governor General

Before 1982, each provincial Legislature had, under s. 92(1) of the Constitution Act, 1867, the power to amend "the constitution of the province, except as regards the office of Lieutenant Governor". The office of Lieutenant Governor was thus explicitly withdrawn from the provincial power of amendment. Section 92(1) was repealed in 1982 and replaced by s. 45 of the Constitution Act, 1982, which also confers the power to amend "the constitution of the province". While s. 45 itself does not make an exception for the office of Lieutenant Governor, s. 45 is expressly made subject to s. 41 (the unanimity procedure), and s. 41(a)

---

28 *N.S. Bd. of Censors* v. *McNeil* [1978] 2 S.C.R. 662 presented a similar situation of an absence of standards in a delegation to a censorship board, but the Court "read down" the broad power so that the power excluded censorship of political or religious ideas. The Court sustained the thus-limited power. This approach would have been possible in *Saumur* too. In that case, it could have been said that those exercises of the chief of police's discretion directed to the censorship of political or religious ideas were invalid, while preserving the by-law as a vehicle of street regulation. Since the adoption of the Charter of Rights, there is now, by s. 1, a constitutional requirement of standards in a law that abridges a Charter right: ch. 35, Limitation of Rights, under heading 39.7, "Prescribed by law", below.

29 Note 15, above.

30 Constitution Act, 1867, s. 91 (opening words).

31 Constitution Act, 1982, s. 44.

32 *Id.*, s. 45.

stipulates that an amendment to the Constitution of Canada in relation to "the office of . . . the Lieutenant Governor of a province" may be made only by the unanimity procedure of s. 41.[33] It is probably safe to conclude that the provincial power of amendment under s. 45 is essentially the same as it was under s. 92(1).[34]

The exception of the office of Lieutenant Governor from the provincial power of amendment has been held to limit the provincial power to delegate. The cases defining this limitation arose out of Western Canadian experiments with theories of "direct democracy", in which, through the mechanism of "initiative" and "referendum", the electorate participates directly in the legislative process.

In 1916, Manitoba enacted the Initiative and Referendum Act. This Act allowed the electors to "initiate" a proposed law through a petition signed by eight per cent of the electors and presented to the Legislative Assembly. If the Legislative Assembly did not enact the proposed law, then the law had to be submitted to the electorate in a "referendum". If the proposed law was approved by a majority of the votes cast in the referendum, then it became law without any action on the part of the Manitoba Legislature. The Act also provided a similar procedure for the repeal of existing laws.

The Initiative and Referendum Act left the Manitoba Legislature intact, and in possession of all its powers. It followed that the normal representative process through the Legislature could still be used to enact statutes and indeed it could be used to repeal or alter the initiative and referendum process. But the grant of power to the electors was quite unlimited and appeared to be as plenary as that of the Legislature, so that, for example, the initiative and referendum process could be employed to repeal or alter the normal representative process through the Legislature. This is, as S.A. Scott has commented, "a highly interesting situation: for, two equally competent legislative processes, each independent of the other, may act disharmoniously, each undoing the work of the other (the last to speak laying down, in principle, the governing law) or even engage in a race to the statute book to alter the constitution of the other, restrict its power, or even abolish it outright."[35]

In *Re Initiative and Referendum Act* (1919),[36] the Privy Council held that the statute had to be regarded as an amendment of the constitution of Manitoba, and that it went beyond the power of amendment conferred by the Constitution Act, 1867. Their lordships held that the exception to s. 92(1) of "the office of Lieutenant Governor" was applicable, because the statute purported to alter the

---

33 Sections 41 (unanimity procedure) and 45 (provincial Legislature alone), as well as the other amending procedures, are discussed in ch. 4, Amendment, above.

34 It should be noted however that s. 41 is confined to amendments to the "Constitution of Canada", while s. 45 is not so confined. It could be argued that a change in the office of the Lieutenant Governor that did not involve any change in the instruments that form part of the Constitution of Canada would not be caught by s. 41 and would accordingly be open to the province, either under s. 45 or under one of the other heads of provincial legislative power.

35 Scott, "Constituent Authority and the Canadian Provinces" (1967) 12 McGill L.J. 528, 536.

36 [1919] A.C. 935.

position of the Lieutenant Governor by creating a legislative process in which he played no part.[37] Thus their lordships fastened upon what must be the least important feature of the Initiative and Referendum Act to find it invalid. It must be remembered that, under the conventions of responsible government, the Lieutenant Governor's function of giving royal assent to a bill which has passed the representative house of the Legislature is an automatic formality: the Lieutenant Governor of a province (like the Governor General of Canada) has no power of veto akin to that possessed by the President of the United States or the Governor of a state.[38]

Another attempt to bypass the requirement of royal assent led to invalidity in *Re Manitoba Language Rights* (1985).[39] At issue was a Manitoba statute that purported to provide a two-stage procedure for the enactment of laws in both English and French (which is required in Manitoba by s. 23 of the Manitoba Act, 1870). The statute contemplated that a law could be enacted initially in English only, and the French version would be deemed to be enacted by the later deposit with the Clerk of the House of Assembly of a certified translation of the law. The Supreme Court of Canada pointed out that the certified translation, although given the full force of law, would not have received the royal assent. The Court cited the *Initiative and Referendum Reference*, and held that Manitoba's attempt to do away with the royal assent was ''an unconstitutional attempt to interfere with the powers of the Lieutenant Governor''.[40]

The protected status of the Lieutenant Governor was given a startling application in *Credit Foncier Franco-Canadien* v. *Ross* (1937),[41] where the Appellate Division of the Supreme Court of Alberta held that a delegation of law-making power to the Lieutenant Governor in Council was invalid as ''an interference with the office of the Lieutenant Governor.''[42] Harvey C.J. for the Court purported to follow the *Initiative and Referendum Reference*, saying: ''This case is different only in that it adds to rather than subtracts from the Lieutenant Governor's functions. That difference in my opinion is of no importance.''[43] If this decision were correct, it would destroy most of the delegations on the provincial statute books. In each province, the body to which law-making powers are most frequently delegated by statute is the cabinet, and of course the normal drafting technique for that purpose is to delegate the power to ''the Lieutenant Governor in Council''. It is possible that the Court intended to confine its decision to cases

---

37 *Cf. R.* v. *Nat Bell Liquors* [1922] 2 A.C. 128; discussed, text accompanying note 51, below.

38 The power to refuse the royal assent to a bill exists at law, but has been nullified by convention: see ch. 9, Responsible Government, under heading 9.4(d), ''The Governor General'', above.

39 [1985] 1 S.C.R. 721.

40 *Id.*, 777. The two-stage procedure was held to be unconstitutional on another ground as well, namely, that s. 23 of the Manitoba Act, 1870 implicitly required that the English and French versions of the statute be enacted at the same time: *Id.*, 776.

41 [1937] 3 D.L.R. 365 (Alta. A.D.).

42 *Id.*, 368.

43 *Ibid.*

where the Lieutenant Governor in Council had the power to provide exemptions from the Act itself (a power he was given in *Credit Foncier*), but the Court did not say so. Even so limited, the decision is a most implausible reading of s. 92(1), which did not prohibit all laws with respect to the Lieutenant Governor, but simply prohibited any amendment to the constitution of the province which would affect the office of Lieutenant Governor. Anyway, *Credit Foncier* has been criticized and perhaps overruled; it has never been followed; and many delegations to the Lieutenant Governor in Council have been held or assumed to be valid.[44]

The protection of the office of Lieutenant Governor was before 1982 (under s. 92(1) of the Constitution Act, 1867) and still is (under s. 45 of the Constitution Act, 1982) a limitation on the power of each Legislature to amend ''the constitution of the province''. The comparable power of the federal Parliament before 1982 was s. 91(1) of the Constitution Act, 1867, which did not include any comparable protection for the office of Governor General. Section 91(1) was repealed in 1982 and replaced by s. 44 of the Constitution Act, 1982, which confers the power to amend the Constitution of Canada in relation to ''the executive government of Canada or the Senate and House of Commons''. Section 44 (like s. 45) is expressly made subject to s. 41 (the unanimity procedure), and s. 41(a) stipulates that an amendment to the Constitution of Canada in relation to ''the office of . . . the Governor General'' may be made only by the unanimity procedure of s. 41.[45] The office of Governor General is thus withdrawn from the federal Parliament's amending power, and the ground of decision in the *Initiative and Referendum Reference* would apply to a federal statute establishing a new legislative process that by-passed the Governor General.

(e) Requirement of a Legislature or Parliament

We have seen that the *Initiative and Referendum Reference* was decided on the basis that there was a constitutional prohibition of a legislative process that bypassed the province's Lieutenant Governor. But a more substantial objection could be made to legislation by initiative and referendum, and that is, that the process bypasses the province's legislative assembly. In the *Initiative and Referendum Reference*, the lower court, the Manitoba Court of Appeal, decided that the regime of direct democracy was bad, not merely because it bypassed the Lieutenant Governor, but also because it invested primary powers of legislation in a body (the electorate) which was not a ''Legislature''.[46] In other words, the Constitution contemplated that primary law-making authority could be exercised only by a Legislature, and the term Legislature involved the participation of some

---

44 See note 16, above.

45 Sections 41 (unanimity procedure) and 44 (federal Parliament alone), as well as the other amending procedures, are discussed in ch. 4, Amendment, above.

46 (1916) 27 Man. R. 1 (Man. C.A.); and see Scott, note 35, above, 552-553 for the relevant passages.

form of representative assembly. The Privy Council deliberately refrained from passing upon this ground of decision, but in an obiter dictum they suggested that they agreed with it.[47]

If the initiative and referendum procedure were construed as *delegated* rather than primary law-making power, then it would be immaterial that it were vested in a body other than a ''Legislature''; that, after all, is exactly what *Hodge*[48] decided was permissible.[49] The Privy Council in the *Initiative and Referendum Reference* asserted that, while *Hodge* permitted a provincial Legislature to ''seek the assistance of subordinate agencies'', it did not follow ''that [the Legislature] can create and endow with its own capacity a new legislative power not created by the [Constitution] Act to which it owes its own existence''.[50] One is prompted to ask, why not? And then to ask, why does the Initiative and Referendum Act fall into the forbidden rather than the permitted category? It could hardly be the unrestricted scope of the power conferred on the electorate, because a delegator always retains the power to restrict or withdraw a grant of unrestricted power to a delegate. It could perhaps be the power of the electorate to alter or abolish the powers of the delegator (the Legislature). Certainly, this is a fundamental power, but it is arguable that it is not a sufficient reason to condemn the entire Initiative and Referendum Act; it would be sufficient to ''read down'' the Act by deciding that, while an attempt to turn against the Legislature itself would be invalid, other exercises of the power would be valid.

The Privy Council had another opportunity to pass on these fundamental questions in *R.* v. *Nat Bell Liquors* (1922),[51] when it had to decide whether Alberta's Liquor Act of 1916 was valid. The Alberta Legislature in 1913 had enacted the Direct Legislation Act, which established an initiative and referendum procedure. Under the Alberta procedure, where a proposed statute had been initiated by a proportion of electors, and then approved in a referendum of electors, ''the said proposed statute shall be enacted by the Legislature at its next session without amendment . . . and . . . shall come into force upon receiving royal assent . . .''. The Alberta procedure differed from the Manitoba procedure in its require-

---

47 [1919] A.C. 935, 945. Accord, *OPSEU* v. *Ont.* [1987] 2 S.C.R. 2, 47 (obiter dictum denying provincial power to introduce ''political institutions foreign to and incompatible with the Canadian system''). The argument that law-making power must be exercised by a Legislature is analogous to one that has been accepted in the United States, where the federal and state constitutions attempt to separate the legislative, executive and judicial powers. There the principle of separation of powers has been invoked for the proposition that ''legislative'' power may not be delegated to the executive: note 17, above.

48 Note 5, above.

49 Scott, note 35, above, 548 says that delegation is also an answer to the by-passing of the Lieutenant Governor. But the federal distribution of powers requires us to classify the Initiative and Referendum Act and find a provincial head of power which supports it. Even if the Act is merely a ''delegation'', it probably has to be classified as an amendment of the constitution of the province, and the office of Lieutenant Governor is expressly exempted from the power.

50 [1919] A.C. 935, 945.

51 [1922] 2 A.C. 128.

ment that the statute be enacted by the Legislature. It will be recalled that the Manitoba procedure bypassed the Legislature altogether. However, the Alberta Act clearly contemplated that, after a referendum had approved a proposed statute, the Legislature was under a duty to enact the statute without amendment; in other words, the Legislature's role was to be formal only.

Alberta's initiative and referendum procedure was employed to enact the Liquor Act of 1916, and Nat Bell Liquors was convicted of an offence under the Liquor Act. On appeal from an application to quash this conviction, the Privy Council held that it was no objection to the validity of the Liquor Act that it had been enacted by the initiative and referendum procedure. They relied upon the fact that the procedure had culminated in passage through the Alberta Legislature, including the giving of royal assent. They concluded: "It is impossible to say that [the Liquor Act] was not an Act of the Legislature and it is none the less a statute because it was the statutory duty of the Legislature to pass it."[52] Their lordships' ready acceptance of the idea that the Direct Legislation Act had imposed a "statutory duty" on the Legislature to enact measures approved by referendum is surely inconsistent with their earlier decision in the Manitoba *Initiative and Referendum Reference*[53] (to which they did not refer, although it was referred to in argument). Once it is accepted that the Legislature's role is formal only, simply to place a rubber stamp on the result of the referendum, then the reasoning which appealed to the Privy Council and Manitoba Court of Appeal in the *Initiative and Referendum Reference* seems applicable again, that is to say, the office of Lieutenant Governor is again impaired, and primary legislative power is again granted away from the Legislature. *R.* v. *Nat Bell Liquors* can be reconciled with the earlier case only if the referendum were held to be advisory rather than mandatory, that is, if the apparent attempt by the Direct Legislation Act to impose a statutory duty were held to be ineffective. Then, and only then, would the Liquor Act have been a genuine enactment of the Alberta Legislature.[54]

Another difficulty with the decision in *R.* v. *Nat Bell Liquors* is that it violates a basic rule of parliamentary sovereignty, namely, that a legislative body cannot bind itself as to the substance (as opposed to the manner and form) of its future enactments.[55] Alberta's Direct Legislation Act of 1913, as interpreted by the Privy Council, purported to tie the hands of future Legislatures by imposing upon them a duty to enact whatever policies were determined upon by the initiative and referendum process. Such a self-imposed restraint on the discretion of future Legislatures should not have been upheld.

The argument accepted by the Manitoba Court of Appeal in the *Initiative and Referendum Reference*, namely, that the Constitution Act contemplates that

---

52 *Id.*, 134.
53 Note 36, above.
54 For another (and more charitable) analysis of the *Nat Bell* case, see Scott, note 35, above, 557-561.
55 See ch. 12, Parliamentary Sovereignty, at heading 12.3, "Substance of future laws", above.

primary law-making authority be exercised only by the organs that it establishes or recognizes, would seem to apply with the same force to the federal Parliament as to the provincial Legislatures.[56] Indeed, it was applied, as one of the reasons of the Supreme Court of Canada, in the *Upper House Reference* (1979).[57] In deciding that the federal Parliament had no power to abolish the Senate, the Court characterized such a measure as ''a transfer by Parliament of all its legislative powers to a new legislative body of which the Senate would not be a member'', and the Court cited with approval the reasoning of the Manitoba Court of Appeal in the *Initiative and Referendum Reference*.[58] With respect, this is a rather strained application of the argument. There is little analogy between a regime of direct democracy, which would bypass deliberative assemblies altogether, and the abolition of an upper house, which would leave the elected lower house (and the head of state) in possession of full legislative power. Moreover, such an argument has never been used to prevent a province from abolishing its upper house; and five provinces have in fact abolished their upper houses by ordinary statute, including Quebec, whose upper house was established in the Constitution Act, 1867 itself.[59]

14.3 Federal inter-delegation

(a) Legislative inter-delegation

Federal ''inter-delegation'' is the delegation of federal power to the provinces, or of provincial power to the Dominion.[60] In the 1930s and 1940s, federal

---

56 There is an obiter dictum in *Re Initiative and Referendum* [1919] A.C. 935, 943, suggesting that the federal Parliament's possession of the ''residuary power of legislation'' might give it increased power ''to set up new legislative bodies''.

57 *Re Upper House* [1980] 1 S.C.R. 54. The constitutional background to the case is explained, and the reasoning of the decision criticized, in Hogg, Comment (1980) 58 Can. Bar Rev. 631. The doubt as to the extent of the federal Parliament's power was caused by the breadth and vagueness of s. 91(1) of the Constitution Act, 1867, which was then (before 1982) the federal Parliament's power of unilateral constitutional amendment. Section 91(1) was repealed in 1982 and replaced by s. 44 of the Constitution Act, 1982. Because s. 44 is expressly made subject to s. 42, and because s. 42(1)(b) requires the general amending procedure to be used to alter ''the powers of the Senate and the method of selecting Senators'', it is now clear without judicial interpretation that the federal Parliament alone cannot abolish the Senate.

58 [1980] 1 S.C.R. 54, 72.

59 Constitution Act, 1867, s. 71, established the Legislative Council of Quebec. None of the five provincial abolitions of upper houses (detailed in Forsey, *Freedom and Order* (1974), 227) was challenged in the courts, but in *Re Upper House* [1980] 1 S.C.R. 54, 74, the Supreme Court of Canada referred to them and assumed them to be valid, distinguishing them on grounds that do not touch the present argument.

60 For discussion of federal inter-delegation, see Lederman, ''Some Forms and Limitations of Cooperative Federalism'' (1967) 45 Can. Bar Rev. 409; Weiler, ''The Supreme Court and the Law of Canadian Federalism'' (1973) 23 U. Toronto L.J. 307, 311-318; La Forest, ''Delegation of Legislative Power in Canada'' (1975) 21 McGill L.J. 131; Driedger, ''The Interaction Of Federal and Provincial Laws'' (1976) 54 Can. Bar Rev. 695.

inter-delegation came to be seen as a device by which the Dominion and the provinces could in effect agree for specific purposes to lend each other needed legislative powers. The result of the Privy Council's interpretation of the Canadian Constitution was that in some fields, most notably that of marketing, neither Parliament nor a Legislature was competent to enact effective measures. The Privy Council conceded that this was so, and exhorted the unfortunate Canadian legislative bodies to "cooperate" to produce effective measures.[61]

Cooperation through inter-delegation was first attempted as a solution to the problem of old age pensions. The federal government wanted to establish a scheme of old age pensions which would be financed by contributions from employees as well as from the federal government and the provinces. This proposal ran into two constitutional difficulties. The first was the Privy Council's decision in the *Unemployment Insurance Reference* (1937),[62] which suggested that any contributory pension scheme would be outside the power of the Dominion, although inside the power of the provinces. The second difficulty was that several of the provinces wanted to finance their contribution to the scheme by levying an indirect sales tax, which would be outside the power of the provinces, although inside the power of the Dominion.[63] A suggested solution lay in complementary delegations. The provincial Legislatures would each enact a statute delegating to the federal Parliament the provincial power "to make laws in relation to any matter relating to employment"; and the federal Parliament would enact a statute delegating to the provincial Legislatures the power to levy "a retail sales tax of the nature of indirect taxation". The federal Parliament could then enact the pension scheme, exercising authority delegated to it by the provincial Legislatures; and the provincial Legislatures could then levy the sales taxes, exercising authority delegated to them by the federal Parliament.

Was the proposed inter-delegation constitutional? There is no express power of inter-delegation in the Canadian Constitution,[64] as there is in the Australian Constitution.[65] But since the *Hodge* doctrine allowed the federal Parliament and

---

61 Note 76, below.

62 *A.-G. Can.* v. *A.-G. Ont.* (Unemployment Insurance) [1937] A.C. 355, which was overcome so far as unemployment insurance was concerned by an amendment to the Constitution Act, 1867 in 1940 adding "unemployment insurance" as s. 91(2A) to the list of federal powers.

63 Constitution Act, 1867, ss. 91(3), 92(2); and see ch. 23, Taxation, below.

64 The Fulton-Favreau amendment proposal (1964) would have inserted a power of inter-delegation in the Constitution. The closest provision actually in the Constitution Act, 1867 is s. 94, which appears to contemplate an irrevocable transfer of legislative power from the Legislatures to the Parliament; as Lederman comments, note 60, above, 421, "perhaps this is one reason why it has never been used".

65 Constitution of Australia, s. 51(37), authorizing the states to "refer" powers to the federal Parliament, but not vice versa. Of course, in Australia most federal legislative powers are concurrent with the states anyway, so that there is little need for a corresponding federal power of delegation. Section 51(37) has been used only occasionally. For discussion, see Lumb and Ryan, *The Constitution of the Commonwealth of Australia Annotated* (4th ed., 1986), 193-196; Hanks, *Constitutional Law in Australia* (1991), 364-365.

provincial Legislatures to delegate their powers to subordinate bodies, could they not also delegate their powers to each other? The answer came in the *Nova Scotia Inter-delegation* case (1950).[66] A bill was introduced in the Nova Scotia Legislature to carry out the provincial side of the inter-delegation scheme. The bill was referred to the Supreme Court of Nova Scotia for a decision as to its constitutionality. The Nova Scotia court held that the bill was invalid. On appeal to the Supreme Court of Canada, this decision was affirmed. The reasoning of the two Courts was, essentially, that inter-delegation would disturb the scheme of distribution of powers in the Constitution. The various legislative bodies should not be permitted to agree to alter that scheme in the absence of clear authority in the Constitution itself. There was no express authority, and none should be implied.

This result does seem to follow inexorably from the premise that inter-delegation would involve a change in the distribution of powers effected by the Constitution. But the premise is incorrect. A delegation of power does not divest the delegator of its power; nor does it confer a permanent power on the delegate. The delegator has the continuing power to legislate on the same topic concurrently if it chooses, and it can withdraw the delegation at any time. This being so, why not apply the *Hodge* doctrine and concede that legislative power in Canada is sufficiently ''plenary and ample'' to sustain inter-delegation? The majority judges do not provide a satisfying answer to this line of reasoning. Nor do they explain why, as a matter of policy, Canadian federalism should be denied the flexibility of cooperation through inter-delegation.

Only Rand J. made a brief attempt to grapple with the merits by asserting that the ''continued exercise of delegated power'' would give rise to ''prescriptive claims'' to the permanent possession of the power, and ''the power of revocation might in fact become no more feasible, practically, than amendment of the Act of 1867 of its own volition by the British Parliament''.[67] W.R. Lederman, in an important article in the Canadian Bar Review, agrees, and adds that delegation between the federal Parliament and provincial Legislatures ''could seriously confuse the basic political responsibility and accountability of members of the federal Parliament and the federal Cabinet, and too much of this could destroy these federal institutions''.[68] There is force in these arguments, but they come very close to an enquiry into the wisdom of legislative policy, and it is doubtful whether they are sufficient to warrant carving an exception out of such basic constitutional principles as the *Hodge* doctrine of plenary and ample power[69] and its associated doctrine that the totality of legislative power is distributed to Canadian legislative bodies.[70]

---

66 *A.-G. N.S.* v. *A.-G. Can.* (Nova Scotia Inter-delegation) [1951] S.C.R. 31.
67 [1951] S.C.R 31, 50.
68 Lederman, ''Some Forms and Limitations of Cooperative Federalism'' (1967) 45 Can. Bar Rev. 409, 426.
69 Note 6, above.
70 See ch. 12, Parliamentary Sovereignty, above.

The immediate benefit sought to be achieved by the Nova Scotia inter-delegation, namely, a contributory old age pension scheme, was a long time in coming. After the *Nova Scotia Inter-delegation* decision, the federal government decided to attempt to achieve the desired result through constitutional amendment. It proposed two constitutional amendments, one to confer on the federal Parliament the power to enact a pension scheme, and the other to confer on the provincial Legislatures the power to levy an indirect sales tax. After a lengthy correspondence with the provincial governments, and several changes in the detail of the proposal, the federal government secured the unanimous consent of the ten provincial governments to the pension amendment. However, the sales tax amendment secured the consent of only eight provincial governments, and the two dissenters were Ontario and Quebec. The federal government went ahead with the pension amendment, but refused to continue its support for the sales tax amendment. In the end, therefore, only one address was submitted to the federal Parliament, and only one amendment was enacted by the Parliament at Westminster, in 1951.[71] This amendment became s. 94A of the Constitution Act, 1867, giving authority to the federal Parliament to make "laws in relation to old age pensions".[72] This amendment was followed by the federal enactment of the Old Age Security Act, 1951, which provided for payment of an old age pension financed wholly by federal taxation. The Canada Pension Plan, which is a contributory scheme, was not introduced for another fourteen years in 1965 and after another constitutional amendment in 1964 had replaced the 1951 version of s. 94A with a different version.[73] The delays and difficulties in providing for old age pensions do not by themselves establish the desirability of inter-delegation, because they sprang from a variety of causes. But one of those causes was the difficulty of constitutional adaptation by formal amendment of the Constitution. Governments wanted to be able to adapt the Constitution more easily and less permanently. Consequently governments continued to consider the device of inter-delegation, despite the *Nova Scotia Inter-delegation* case.

(b) Administrative inter-delegation

Two years after *Nova Scotia Inter-delegation*, a slightly different form of inter-delegation came before the courts in *P.E.I. Potato Marketing Board* v. *Willis* (1952).[74] By the Agricultural Products Marketing Act 1949, the federal Parliament gave power to the Governor General in Council (that is, the federal cabinet) to delegate to *provincial* marketing boards the power to regulate the marketing of agricultural products "outside the province in interprovincial and export trade".

---

71 The pre-1982 amending procedure is described in ch. 4, Amendment, above.

72 Added by British North America Act, 1951 (U.K.), R.S.C. 1985, Appendix II, No. 35; for history, see Livingston, *Federalism and Constitutional Change* (1956), 66-68.

73 Added by Constitution Act, 1964 (U.K.), R.S.C. 1985, Appendix II, No. 38; for history, see Lederman, note 68, above, 412.

74 [1952] 2 S.C.R. 392.

Prince Edward Island had earlier enacted a marketing statute which empowered the Lieutenant Governor in Council (that is, the provincial cabinet) to establish schemes to regulate the marketing of agricultural products within the province, and to establish marketing boards to administer such schemes. In 1950, this statute was amended to bring it into line with the federal Act, and in particular to authorize provincial marketing boards, once established by the provincial government, to exercise any powers delegated to them by the federal government. Also in 1950, the government of Prince Edward Island, acting under the authority of the provincial statute, established a scheme for the marketing of potatoes in the province, and established a board of five members, the P.E.I. Potato Marketing Board, to administer the scheme. The federal government, acting under the authority of the federal statute, then delegated to the P.E.I. Potato Marketing Board the authority to regulate the marketing of P.E.I. potatoes outside the province in interprovincial and export trade.

The object of the inter-delegation from the federal Parliament to the provincial marketing board was to ensure that the provincial board was possessed of the totality of regulatory power over P.E.I. potatoes. The Privy Council, in striking down earlier marketing schemes,[75] had explained that effective regulation required "cooperation" between Parliament and the Legislatures.[76] Their lordships did not concern themselves with the great difficulties of securing cooperation, nor did they indicate what forms of cooperation would be constitutionally permissible. We have seen that in the *Nova Scotia Inter-delegation* case in 1950 one form of cooperation, namely, *legislative* inter-delegation, was held to be unconstitutional. Here was a second form of cooperation, namely, *administrative* inter-delegation: the delegate (or recipient of the power) was not the provincial Legislature itself, but an administrative agency created by the provincial Legislature.

On the face of it, the argument for validity did not look promising. If the federal Parliament could not delegate federal power to the provincial Legislature, surely by parity of reasoning the federal Parliament could not delegate federal power to a creature of the provincial Legislature. If the provincial Legislature could not itself accept a delegation of federal power, surely it could not create an administrative agency with capacity to accept a delegation of federal power. Nevertheless, in *P.E.I. Potato Marketing Board* v. *Willis* (1952),[77] the Supreme Court of Canada held that administrative inter-delegation was valid. The federal Parliament could, if it chose, "adopt as its own" a provincial agency and authorize it to exercise federal powers side by side with its provincial powers. And the provincial Legislature could confer on a provincial agency the capacity to accept a delegation of federal powers. Rand J. pointed out that "the Dominion by appropriate words could create a similar Board, composed of the same persons, bearing the same name, and with a similar formal organization, to execute the

75 Marketing is discussed in ch. 20, Property and Civil Rights, below.
76 E.g., *A.-G. B.C.* v. *A.-G. Can.* (Natural Products Marketing) [1937] A.C. 377, 389.
77 [1952] 2 S.C.R. 392.

same Dominion functions''.[78] None of the judges explained why the same reasoning had not prevailed in the *Nova Scotia Inter-delegation* case. Why could not the Dominion select the name, the members and the procedures of a provincial Legislature as the recipient of its delegation?[79]

Lederman takes the view that there is a constitutionally significant difference between legislative inter-delegation and administrative inter-delegation. As noted earlier, he supports the *Nova Scotia Inter-delegation* case on the basis that delegation from one legislative body to another could seriously confuse the ''basic political responsibility and accountability'' for legislative discretion. Delegation to an administrative agency, he argues, does not involve that risk: ''Even when regulation-making power is involved for the subordinate delegate body, if that regulation-making power is properly limited, still there is no threat to responsibility for primary legislative discretions under our federal system''.[80] A preliminary difficulty with this argument is that a delegation by Parliament to a Legislature (or vice versa) can also be ''properly limited'', and it is certain that the courts would declare invalid an attempt by the delegate Legislature to enact federal laws outside the scope of the ''properly limited'' authority. The more fundamental difficulty springs from Lederman's assumption that an administrative inter-delegation must be ''properly limited''. The cases decided after Lederman's article have shown that the federal Parliament need not enact even the skeleton of a regulatory scheme, but can remit the entire matter to the discretion of the provincial Legislature.[81] This is accomplished through a combination of administrative inter-delegation[82] and referential legislation. It is the latter device which must now be considered.

---

78 *Id.*, 414-415.

79 See Ballem, Comment (1952) 30 Can. Bar Rev. 1050, 1057.

80 Lederman, note 68, above, 427.

81 *Coughlin* v. *Ont. Highway Transport Bd.* [1968] S.C.R. 569; *Re Agricultural Products Marketing Act* [1978] 2 S.C.R. 1198, 1222-1226; and see discussion later in this chapter, accompanying note 86, below. The constitutional rule is not a prohibition of the inter-delegation of ''legislative'' power, as the Ontario Court of Appeal wrongly assumed in *Re Peralta* (1985) 49 O.R. (2d) 705 (C.A.); affirmed under name *Peralta* v. *Ont.* [1988] 2 S.C.R. 1045. What is prohibited is the inter-delegation of any kind of power, including administrative power, to a primary law-making body — the Parliament or a Legislature. What is permitted is the inter-delegation of any kind of power, including ''legislative'' power, to a body or official other than a primary law-making body: *R.* v. *Furtney* [1991] 3 S.C.R. 89, 104 (upholding federal delegation to Lieutenant Governor in Council, regardless of whether delegated power is ''administrative'' or ''legislative'').

82 Administrative inter-delegations were upheld in *R.* v. *Wilson* (1980) 119 D.L.R. (3d) 558 (B.C. C.A.) (federal power over young offenders delegated to the provincial Lieutenant Governor in Council); *Peralta* v. *Ont.* [1988] 2 S.C.R. 1045 (federal power over fishing delegated to provincial minister); *R.* v. *S.(S)* [1990] 2 S.C.R. 254 (federal power over diversion programmes for young offenders delegated to provincial Attorney General); *R.* v. *Furtney* [1991] 3 S.C.R. 89 (federal power over gaming delegated to provincial Lieutenant Governor in Council).

14.4 Referential legislation

(a) Incorporation by reference

Incorporation by reference is a technique which is occasionally used by legislative bodies, especially where it is desired to enact the same law as another jurisdiction.[83] Instead of repeating in full the desired rules, the drafter may simply incorporate by reference, or adopt, the rules of another jurisdiction. The leading case on the validity of this technique is *A.-G. Ont.* v. *Scott* (1956),[84] where the Supreme Court of Canada upheld an Ontario statute which provided for the enforcement in Ontario of orders to pay maintenance obtained in England (and some other foreign jurisdictions) by wives who were resident in England against husbands who were resident in Ontario. Section 5(2) of the Ontario statute provided that in proceedings to enforce a foreign maintenance order the husband was entitled "to raise any defence that he might have raised in the original proceedings [in England] had he been a party thereto". In other words, the Ontario Legislature, instead of itself specifying the defences which were available in Ontario to the husband, was accepting whatever defences were specified by the Parliament of the United Kingdom. The Supreme Court of Canada held that this provision was valid. Their lordships denied that there was a delegation involved; all that was involved was the incorporation or adoption of certain English laws into Ontario law.

(b) Anticipatory incorporation by reference

In *Scott*, the Court recognized, but did not attach particular importance to, the fact that the Ontario statute adopted not only the English rules in existence at the time of the enactment of the Ontario statute, but the English rules in existence from time to time in the future. Yet the "anticipatory" character of the incorporation makes the Ontario statute difficult to distinguish from a delegation. The effect of the Ontario statute is that, whenever the Parliament of the United Kingdom alters the laws of England governing defences to maintenance applications, it also alters the law of Ontario. It is important to notice, however, that even if *Scott* were treated as a case of delegation, the result would not necessarily be wrong. As Laskin pointed out in his casebook, the *Nova Scotia Inter-delegation* case did not say anything about the validity of a delegation to a non-Canadian legislative body. Since such a delegation would not disturb the federal distribution of powers, one might well assume that the *Hodge* doctrine would operate to

83 Where the incorporating legislative body is under an obligation to enact statutes in both official languages, the general rule is that the incorporated instrument must also be in both languages: see ch. 53, Language, under heading 53.4(d), "Incorporation by reference", below.

84 [1956] S.C.R. 137.

validate the delegation.[85] The distinction between anticipatory incorporation and delegation would only become significant if it were the enactments of another Canadian legislative body which had been incorporated.

It was not long before the Supreme Court of Canada was confronted with this latter case. Once again, some background may be helpful to appreciate the problem which the various governments were attempting to solve. In *A.-G. Ont.* v. *Winner* (1954),[86] the Privy Council decided that the provinces had no power to regulate motor carrier services which extended beyond the limits of the province. This was an inconvenient decision, because the regulation of motor carriers in Canada, both intraprovincial and interprovincial, was in fact wholly provincial; and the federal government did not have the administrative or physical facilities to assume the task of regulating the interprovincial and international carriers.

The federal government, after conferring with the provinces, decided to avoid the *Winner* decision altogether. In order to do so, it secured the enactment by the federal Parliament of the Motor Vehicle Transport Act. This Act, which was a model of brevity as well as constitutional ingenuity, simply provided that extra-provincial carriers operating in a province had to obtain a licence from the provincial transport board. The provincial transport board, in licensing extra-provincial carriers, was to do so ''upon the like terms and conditions and in the like manner as if the extra-provincial undertaking operated in the province were a local undertaking''. In this way, the federal Parliament not only delegated the unwanted regulatory power back to the provincial transport boards, but directed them to apply the provincial laws in existence from time to time. This was an administrative inter-delegation coupled with an anticipatory incorporation by reference. Was it valid?

In *Coughlin* v. *Ontario Highway Transport Board* (1968),[87] a majority of the Supreme Court of Canada, in an opinion written by Cartwright J., held that the federal Motor Vehicle Transport Act was valid. The delegation to the provincial transport boards was valid on the authority of *P.E.I. Potato Marketing Board* v. *Willis*.[88] The anticipatory incorporation by reference was valid on the authority of *A.-G. Ont.* v. *Scott*.[89] The latter point involved taking *Scott* at its face value, namely, as authority for the proposition that anticipatory incorporation by reference is not delegation. Only Ritchie J., who (with Martland J.) dissented, attempted to penetrate through the form of the statute to its substance. He pointed out that there would ''be no objection to Parliament enacting a statute in which *existing* provincial legislation is incorporated by reference so as to obviate the necessity of re-enacting it verbatim''; but in this case Parliament had ''adopted

---

85 Laskin, *Canadian Constitutional Law* (5th ed., 1986 by Finkelstein), 43. *Cf. Coughlin* v. *Ont. Highway Transport Bd.* [1968] S.C.R. 569, 584.

86 [1954] A.C. 541.

87 [1968] S.C.R. 569.

88 Note 74, above.

89 Note 84, above.

the provisions of the provincial statutes in question as they may be amended from time to time''.[90] In Ritchie J.'s view, the result of this so-called adoption was a delegation of the kind condemned in the *Nova Scotia Inter-delegation* case: the federal Parliament had ''left the power to exercise control of the licensing of extra-provincial undertakings to be regulated in such manner as the Province might from time to time determine''.[91]

The majority of the Court in *Coughlin* did not attempt to meet Ritchie J.'s argument. They said that the difference between this case and *Nova Scotia Inter-delegation* was ''too obvious to require emphasis'',[92] but they did not explain what the difference was. Certainly, *Coughlin* enables *Nova Scotia Inter-delegation* to be readily evaded. Instead of the federal Parliament delegating directly to the provincial Legislature (or vice versa), the federal Parliament simply delegates to an agency of the provincial Legislature and directs that agency to apply provincial law.[93] The trading of powers which was condemned in *Nova Scotia Inter-delegation* can easily be accomplished by the *Coughlin* technique. What *Nova Scotia Inter-delegation* said could not be done directly, *Coughlin* now allows to be done indirectly.[94]

(c) Independent validity of incorporated law

There is nevertheless an important (if not ''obvious'') difference between *Coughlin* and *Nova Scotia Inter-delegation*. The provincial legislation which was incorporated by reference in *Coughlin* was (or would be in the future) enacted by the provincial Legislature within its competence and for its own purposes, namely, to regulate intraprovincial carriers; the provincial legislation was not created just for the federal purpose of regulating extra provincial carriers. Thus Laskin, in summarizing the result of the decisions, says: ''There is no unconstitutional delegation involved where there is no enlargement of the legislative authority of the referred legislature, but rather a borrowing of provisions which are within its competence and which were enacted for its own purposes, and which the referring

---

90 [1968] S.C.R. 569, 582-583.

91 *Id.*, 584.

92 *Id.*, 575.

93 This technique reached its nadir in *Re Agricultural Products Marketing Act* [1978] 2 S.C.R. 1198, where ten provincial marketing boards (and a federal board) drew powers from both levels of government. Laskin C.J. in a concurring opinion (at pp. 1222-1226) held that the provincial boards could be directed to apply provincial law, or could be given federal authority to make regulations which differed from province to province; there was no ''constitutional requirement in the delegation of authority that standards be fixed by Parliament'' (p. 1226). Pigeon J.'s short opinion for the majority (he said at p. 1289 that he was ''pressed for time'') agreed (at p. 1290) with Laskin C.J.'s conclusion on the delegation point, and clearly agreed with the substance of the reasoning. As one of the counsel in the case, I can testify to the impossibility of tracing the lines of responsibility for many of the decisions of the marketing boards back to one level of government or the other.

94 See Lysyk, Comment (1969) 47 Can. Bar Rev. 271.

legislature could have validly spelled out for its own purposes''.[95] In effect, what is being insisted upon is that the legislation which is incorporated by reference should have a validity and significance independent of the scheme of delegation.[96] This element was present in *Coughlin*, because the provincial transportation laws were enacted within provincial competence to regulate intraprovincial carriers. This being so, they could also be ''borrowed'' by the federal Parliament to regulate interprovincial carriers. In *Nova Scotia Inter-delegation*, by contrast, it was contemplated that the legislative bodies to which powers were delegated would each enact laws which would apart from the delegation be outside their competence, and which were solely for the purpose of carrying out the pension plan scheme.

The ratio decidendi of *Nova Scotia Inter-delegation* may also be understood by looking at the case from the standpoint of the primary legislative body that is the *recipient* of the power. What *Nova Scotia Inter-delegation* decides is that the powers of a primary legislative body cannot be enlarged by delegation from another legislative body. The scheme of legislative inter-delegation that was struck down in *Nova Scotia Inter-delegation* contemplated that the federal Parliament and provincial Legislatures would each acquire by delegation the power to do something that was not authorized by ss. 91 and 92 of the Constitution Act, 1867. The schemes that were upheld in *Willis* and *Coughlin* did not contemplate that the Legislature of Prince Edward Island (in *Willis*) or the Legislature of Ontario (in *Coughlin*) would enact a law that went beyond the powers granted by s. 92.[97] The legal test is captured by this question: does the scheme of inter-delegation purport to enlarge the powers of one of the primary legislative bodies? If the answer is yes, the scheme is an invalid legislative inter-delegation (as in *Nova Scotia Inter-delegation*). If the answer is no, the scheme is a valid administrative inter-delegation (as in *Willis* and *Coughlin*) or a valid incorporation by reference (as in *Scott* and *Coughlin*).[98]

---

95 Laskin, note 85, above, 43; accord, Driedger, note 60, above, 709.

96 Cf. the doctrine of ''facts of independent significance'' which has been recognized by American writers on the law of wills; such facts do not need to satisfy the rules for a valid incorporation by reference: see Atkinson, *Law of Wills* (2nd ed., 1973), 394.

97 Note, however, that in practice if not in theory the federal adoption of provincial law in the federal Motor Vehicle Transport Act (the Act upheld in *Coughlin*) does enlarge the powers of the provincial Legislatures. In *R.* v. *Smith* [1972] S.C.R. 359, the Court upheld the Alberta transport board's policy of discriminating between local truckers and extraprovincial truckers. In *National Freight Consultants* v. *Motor Transport Bd.* [1980] 2 S.C.R. 621, the Court upheld the Alberta transport board's restriction on a trucking activity in British Columbia. The federal adoption enabled Alberta law to discriminate against interprovincial transportation in *Smith*, and to have extraterritorial effect in *National Freight Consultants*. Query whether these cases are rightly decided.

98 The anticipatory incorporation by reference in s. 88 of the Indian Act, which is discussed in detail in ch. 27, Aboriginal Peoples, under heading 27.3, ''Section 88 of the Indian Act'', below, was upheld in *Dick* v. *The Queen* [1985] 2 S.C.R. 309. See also *R.* v. *Francis* [1988] 1 S.C.R. 1025 (upholding Indian Reserve Traffic Regulation that incorporated provincial traffic laws); *R.* v. *Furtney* [1991] 3 S.C.R. 89, 105 (upholding Criminal Code provision that incor-

14.5 Conditional legislation

(a) Conditions as delegations

There is no doubt that the Parliament or a Legislature may make the application of its legislation conditional on the doing of some act or the happening of some event. It is very common, for example, for a statute to provide that it shall come into force on a date to be fixed by proclamation of the Governor in Council or the Lieutenant Governor in Council. Such a provision is undoubtedly valid as a condition to the operation of the legislation.[99]

Where the fulfilment of the condition requires the action of some person or body, such as the Governor in Council or Lieutenant Governor in Council, it is obvious that the conditional law also delegates a power to the actor — the power to bring the legislation into force. Sometimes the power delegated in the form of a condition is akin to a power to legislate. In the *Breathalyzer Reference* (1970),[100] a federal statute provided that "this Act or any of the provisions of this Act shall come into force on a day or days to be fixed by proclamation". The Supreme Court of Canada held that this condition enabled the Governor in Council to proclaim in force the part of the Act which provided for the compulsory taking of breath samples from drivers, and to except from the proclamation the part of the Act which stipulated that the suspected driver be provided with a sample. In a case of this kind, the civil libertarian issue must turn on the meaning of the condition in the statute. If the language of the statute authorizes the Governor in Council to proclaim in force the main obligation without the safeguard, then there is the end of the case. The *Hodge* doctrine[101] makes clear that, as a matter of constitutional law, such a delegation of power is within the competence of the Canadian legislative bodies.

(b) Conditions as administrative inter-delegations

Conditional legislation may raise a constitutional issue where the laws of one level of government are conditional upon the actions of another level of

---

porated provincial gaming laws). For further examples, see Dreidger, note 60, above, 708-713 and National Energy Board Act, R.S.C. 1985, c. N-7, s. 114, enacted to overcome *Campbell-Bennett* v. *Comstock Midwestern* [1954] S.C.R. 207. With respect to the requirement of bilingual enactment in s. 133 of the Constitution Act, 1867, see ch. 53, Language, under heading 53.4(d), "Incorporation by reference", above.

99 The most dramatic example of a law which is conditional upon proclamation was the War Measures Act and is now the Emergencies Act, S.C. 1988, c. 29. The Canada Temperance Act, which is conditional upon local adoption by electors, was upheld in *Russell* v. *The Queen* (1882) 7 App. Cas. 829, 835, where it was described as "conditional legislation", and upheld again in *A.-G. Ont.* v. *Can. Temperance Federation* [1946] A.C. 193.

100 *Re Criminal Law Amendment Act, 1968-69* [1970] S.C.R. 777.

101 Note 5, above.

government. Here there is the potential of an argument that the condition is in truth an invalid federal inter-delegation. But the scope which has been allowed to federal inter-delegation by the cases discussed in the preceding sections of this chapter makes clear that even ''interjurisdictional conditions'' are usually valid. For example, there is no reason to doubt the validity of a federal law which comes into force in each province[102] upon a proclamation by the Lieutenant Governor of the province.[103] This is a delegation of power from the federal Parliament to the executive branch of the provincial government,[104] but the federal inter-delegation cases which have been discussed make clear that the only delegation which is inadmissible is to the legislative branch of the provincial government — the one struck down in the *Nova Scotia Inter-delegation* case.[105]

(c) Conditions as legislative inter-delegations

Closer to the forbidden territory marked out by *Nova Scotia Inter-delegation* are the cases where a federal law is conditional upon the existence of a provincial law. In *Gold Seal* v. *Dominion Express Co.* (1921),[106] the Supreme Court of Canada upheld a federal law which prohibited the importation of liquor into any province where its sale for beverage purposes was prohibited by provincial law. Under this provision the applicability of the federal law would depend upon whether the provincial Legislature enacted or repealed a liquor prohibition law. But presumably the Court's decision to uphold the federal law could be justified on the same ground as the incorporation by reference in *Coughlin*, that is to say, any such provincial law would have independent validity and significance.[107] The federal law did not purport to enlarge the powers of the provincial Legislatures.

In *Lord's Day Alliance of Canada* v. *A.-G. B.C.* (1959),[108] however, the Supreme Court of Canada did in my opinion sanction conditional federal legislation which had the effect of enlarging the powers of the provincial Legislatures. The federal Lord's Day Act (like the motor carrier legislation enacted after *Winner*) was enacted to overcome an inconvenient decision of the Privy Council.

---

102 A federal law need not be uniformly applicable throughout Canada, but may apply in some provinces and not others: ch. 17, Peace, Order and Good Government, under heading 17.3(b), ''Definition of national concern'', below.

103 *Ex parte Kleinys* (1965) 49 D.L.R. (2d) 225 (B.C. S.C.) upheld such a delegation; see also *Re Anti-Inflation Act* [1976] 2 S.C.R. 373, 431; cf. *R.* v. *Burah* (1878) 3 App. Cas. 889 (India).

104 See note 82, above. *Re Anti-Inflation Act* [1976] 2 S.C.R. 373, 430-436, while holding that the Anti-Inflation Act could not be brought into force in the provincial public sector by an agreement with the provincial government which was unauthorized by provincial legislation, did not doubt that the federal Parliament could by apt language make its laws applicable in a province subject to a condition to be satisfied by the provincial government.

105 Note 66, above.

106 (1921) 62 S.C.R. 424.

107 Note 96 and accompanying text, above.

108 [1959] S.C.R. 497.

The decision was *A.-G. Ont.* v. *Hamilton Street Railway* (1903),[109] in which the Privy Council struck down Ontario's Lord's Day Act, on the basis that the prohibition of work on Sundays was a ''criminal law'' within exclusive federal jurisdiction under s. 91(27) of the Constitution Act, 1867. Before this decision, it had been widely assumed that Sunday observance was within provincial competence as a matter of ''property and civil rights in the province'' (s. 92(13)) or as a matter of a ''merely local or private nature in the province'' (s. 92(16)). Several provinces had Sunday observance statutes, and the Dominion had none. After the decision, the federal Parliament came under pressure to fill the void, and it exercised the jurisdiction thrust upon it with the same ingenuity which characterized the post-*Winner* scheme many years later. The federal Lord's Day Act of 1906 prohibited various activities on Sunday,[110] but the principal sections each allowed individual provinces to ''opt out'' of the prohibition if they chose. Thus s. 6 provided: ''It is not lawful for any person, on the Lord's Day, *except as provided in any provincial Act or law now or hereafter in force*, to engage in any public game . . . at which any fee is charged . . . for admission . . .''.

The opting-out clause, which I have italicized, appeared to be an invitation to the provinces to reassume the jurisdiction which had been denied them in *Hamilton Street Railway*. What was its true effect? Was it an inadmissible delegation to the provincial Legislatures of the federal power to enact criminal law? Or was it something else, which was admissible under the Constitution? In the *Lord's Day Alliance* case, it was necessary to determine the validity of a British Columbia bill which proposed to amend the Vancouver Charter to allow the City of Vancouver by by-law to permit fee-paying spectator sport on Sunday afternoons. The Supreme Court of Canada held unanimously that the proposed provincial statute was valid. In Rand J.'s words, the opting-out clause was ''a condition of fact in relation to which Parliament itself has provided a limitation for its own legislative Act.''[111]

The description of the opting-out clause in the Lord's Day Act as ''a condition''[112] does not eliminate the possibility that it is also an invalid inter-dele-

109 [1903] A.C. 524; on Sunday observance laws, see ch. 18, Criminal Law, below.

110 The basic prohibition was held to be a valid criminal law in *R.* v. *Big M Drug Mart* [1985] 1 S.C.R. 295, but was held to be unconstitutional for breach of the Charter of Rights guarantee of freedom of religion.

111 [1959] S.C.R. 497, 510; to the same effect, 503 per Kerwin C.J., 511 per Locke J.; see also *Lord's Day Alliance* v. *A.-G. Man.* [1925] A.C. 384 (upholding another similar provision of the Lord's Day Act); *R.* v. *Morgentaler* [1988] 1 S.C.R. 30 (upholding in question 5 of reference Criminal Code provision for provincial law to permit abortions); Osborne and Campbell, ''Recent Amendments to Lottery and Gaming Laws'' (1988) 26 Osgoode Hall L.J. 19 (discussing Criminal Code provision for provincial law to permit lotteries).

112 Another way of looking at the opting-out clause is to treat it as a ''waiver of paramountcy'': see Ontario Law Reform Commission, *Report on Sunday Observance Legislation* (1970), 279. The theory is that there are two inconsistent valid laws, the permissive provincial law and the prohibitory federal law. Apart from the opting-out clause, the federal law would override the provincial law by the doctrine of federal paramountcy. The opting-out clause however avoids

gation. The question remains: does the provincial law have independent provincial validity and significance? If it does not — if it is merely derivative from the Lord's Day Act — then consistently with *Nova Scotia Inter-delegation* it cannot be effective. The judges of the Supreme Court of Canada were obviously troubled by this question. However, they decided that the law permitting Sunday sport was within provincial competence, either as a law in relation to property and civil rights in the province (s. 92(13)), or as a law in relation to matters of a merely local or private nature in the province (s. 92(16)).

In my view, the Court's classification of the law in *Lord's Day Alliance* cannot be supported. The *Hamilton Street Railway* case decided that a Sunday observance law was a criminal law, exclusively within federal competence. That unfortunate ruling (which had been reaffirmed by the Supreme Court of Canada in the *Henry Birks* case of 1955)[113] was accepted without reservation by the Court in *Lord's Day Alliance*. If the making of a Sunday observance law is a matter of criminal law outside provincial competence, then the repealing of a Sunday observance law is equally a matter of criminal law outside provincial competence. To be sure, the British Columbia statute did not purport directly to repeal part of the Lord's Day Act, but its sole purpose was to lift from the people of Vancouver the criminal prohibition imposed by the Lord's Day Act. If the criminal prohibition had not existed, no amendment to the Vancouver Charter would have been needed or desired. The amendment had no significance except as a removal of a criminal prohibition. This is outside provincial competence as surely as the imposition of a criminal prohibition.

The conclusion is that *Lord's Day Alliance* is inconsistent with *Nova Scotia Inter-delegation*, because in *Lord's Day Alliance* the federal statute was in effect held to enlarge the powers of the provincial Legislatures.[114]

14.6 Conclusions on federal inter-delegation

The decision in *Nova Scotia Inter-delegation* (1950) denied to the various Canadian legislative bodies the power to delegate their powers to each other. The reasoning to this conclusion was unpersuasive, and the conclusion was unfortunate as a matter of policy, since it denied to the Canadian federation a flexible

---

this result by waiving paramountcy, and allowing the provincial law to override the federal. There seems no reason to doubt that the federal Parliament can if it chooses waive its paramountcy in a field where concurrent federal and provincial laws are possible. Since the federal Parliament need not legislate at all in the field, thus leaving it open to provincial law, it must also, surely, be able to legislate but waive its paramountcy. However, as noted in the text which follows, whether one describes the opting-out clause in the Lord's Day Act as a condition or a waiver of paramountcy, it is still essential that the provincial law have independent provincial validity and significance.

113 *Henry Birks & Sons* v. *Montreal* [1955] S.C.R. 799.

114 Accord, Lysyk, note 94, above, 273; Weiler, note 60, above, 315; Driedger, note 60, above, 707.

means of constitutional adaptation. The cases which have been decided since 1950, especially, *Willis* (1952), *Scott* (1956), *Lord's Day Alliance* (1959) and *Coughlin* (1968), have reinstated federal inter-delegation as an important tool of cooperative federalism. Indeed, these cases invite the comment that the Canadian legislative bodies, through administrative inter-delegation, or referential legislation, or conditional legislation, or some mixture of these devices, may now do indirectly what they cannot do directly.

The only vestige of a prohibition against inter-delegation which now remains is the rule that one legislative body cannot enlarge the powers of another by authorizing the latter to enact laws which would have no significance and validity independent of the delegation. It is arguable that even this rule can no longer stand in the light of *Lord's Day Alliance*, because that case, according to my analysis (but not according to the Court's analysis), did sanction the enlargement by the federal Parliament of a province's legislative powers. However, since the judges in each of the later cases have been careful to acknowledge the continued viability of *Nova Scotia Inter-delegation*, and since no judge has pushed the analysis to the point of questioning the correctness of the decision, it may well be that the Supreme Court would be reluctant to overrule *Nova Scotia Inter-delegation*. Presumably, too, the Court is unlikely to be faced squarely with the issue, since the inter-delegations of the near future are more likely to tread the safe paths formed by the later cases than they are to take the riskier course of direct legislative inter-delegation with its unavoidable challenge to the correctness of *Nova Scotia Inter-delegation*.

II

DISTRIBUTION OF POWERS

15

Judicial Review on Federal Grounds

15.1 Scope of chapter

This chapter is the beginning of Part II of the book, which is devoted to the distribution of powers. Chapter 5, Federalism, has already introduced the principal ideas of a federal constitution. As has been explained, it is the distribution of powers between a central authority (in Canada, the federal Parliament) and regional authorities (in Canada, the provincial Legislatures) that constitutes the essence of a federal constitution. That distribution of powers has to be contained in a written constitution that is binding on the central and regional authorities, and is unalterable by the unilateral action of either of them. Thus the Constitution of Canada (like all other federal constitutions) defines the kinds of laws that may be enacted by the federal Parliament and the kinds of laws that may be enacted by each provincial Legislature. When a question arises whether the federal Parliament or a provincial Legislature has enacted a law that comes within the Constitution's definition of the powers allocated to the enacting body, an authoritative answer to that question can be provided only by the courts. This is the justification for judicial review of legislation, which is the power to determine whether any particular law is valid or invalid. The law is valid (intra vires) if the court finds that the law was enacted within the powers allocated by the Constitution to whichever legislative body enacted the law, and the law is invalid (ultra vires) if the court finds that the law was enacted outside the powers allocated to the enacting body.

The history and rationale of judicial review of legislation in Canada have been examined in chapter 5, Federalism. This chapter will examine the doctrines, the techniques and the language employed by the courts in carrying out their function of judicial review.

The constitutional provisions distributing power between the federal Parliament and the provincial Legislatures are not the only restraints on legislative power in Canada. As has been explained in chapter 12, Parliamentary Sovereignty, there are other kinds of restraints as well, and the most important of these is the Charter of Rights. These other restraints also give rise to judicial review of legislation. However, this chapter, and indeed the whole of Part II of the book, is confined to judicial review on federal grounds (or distribution-of-powers grounds), because a distinctive set of doctrines, techniques and language has accumulated around this branch of judicial review. Judicial review on Charter grounds will be examined separately in chapter 33, Charter of Rights, which is in Part III of the book, Civil Liberties.

15.2 Priority between federal and Charter grounds

When a law is challenged on both federal and Charter grounds, does the Constitution accord priority to one ground over the other?

It must be conceded that this question has little practical significance, since s. 52 of the Constitution Act, 1982 makes clear that a law that is contrary to any provision of the Constitution of Canada is "of no force or effect". Both the federal distribution of powers and the Charter of Rights are part of the "Constitution of Canada''.[1] A successful challenge to a law on the federal ground that the law is outside the authority of the enacting legislative body is attended by the same consequence of invalidity as a successful challenge on the Charter ground that the law contravenes a provision of the Charter of Rights.

Nevertheless, it is, I think, meaningful and accurate to assert that the provisions of the Constitution distributing powers to the federal Parliament and the provincial Legislatures are logically prior to the Charter of Rights. These provisions create the powers that are exercisable by Canadian legislative bodies. It is impossible for a nation to be governed without bodies possessing legislative powers, but it is possible for a nation to be governed without a Charter of Rights. The Charter of Rights assumes the existence of legislative powers, although admittedly it imposes limits on those powers. I conclude that the argument that a law is invalid because it is outside the powers conferred on the enacting body by the federal part of the Constitution is a prior, or more radical, argument than the argument that a law is invalid because it offends a prohibition contained in the Charter of Rights.[2] In other words, in reviewing the validity of a law, the first question is whether the law is within the law-making power of the enacting body, and the second question is whether the law is consistent with the Charter of Rights.

This way of comparing the status of the federal part of the Constitution with the Charter of Rights finds support in the language of s. 32(1) of the Charter of Rights. Section 32(1) is the provision that makes the Charter applicable to the federal Parliament and the provincial Legislatures.[3] It provides as follows:

> 32.(1) This Charter applies
> (a) to the Parliament and government of Canada in respect of all matters within the authority of Parliament including all matters relating to the Yukon Territory and Northwest Territories; and
> (b) to the legislature and government of each province in respect of matters within the authority of the legislature of each province.

At first reading, the language of s. 32 seems unduly prolix. What is the force of the phrase ''in respect of all matters within the authority of'' the Parliament or the Legislature? The answer is that the quoted phrase limits the application of the Charter to laws within the distribution-of-powers authority of the Parliament or the Legislature. Thus, the Charter does not apply to a law that is ultra vires on federal grounds; such a law is invalid, of course, but only for breach of the power-distributing provisions of the Constitution; it cannot also be invalid for breach of

1 The phrase is defined in s. 52(2); the definition is discussed in ch. 1, Sources, under heading 1.4, ''Constitution of Canada'', above.

2 Accord, *Westendorp* v. *The Queen* [1983] 1 S.C.R. 43, 46 per Laskin C.J. Whyte (1984) 6 Supreme Court L.R. 49, 55-56 criticizes this dictum on the ground that Canada's constitutional law has never hitherto ranked arguments in order of precedence. A possible answer to Professor Whyte is that Canada's constitutional law has never hitherto had a Charter of Rights, and judicial review has hitherto rarely been faced with two different kinds of invalidating constitutional provisions applicable to a single law.

3 See ch. 34, Application of Charter, below.

the Charter. In other words, where there is a distribution-of-powers argument and a Charter argument for the invalidity of a law, the arguments cannot both be successful.

If I am right that a federal ground of judicial review takes priority over a Charter ground, all that this means is that an argument based on a Charter ground should be framed as an alternative, not an addition, to an argument based on a federal ground. The priority of the federal ground does not mean that a court deciding a constitutional case must always dispose of the federal issue before proceeding to the Charter issue. On the contrary, the court can and undoubtedly will do what it has always done in every kind of case, and, that is to decide the case on the ground that seems strongest to the court. Where the opposition to the law is primarily based on a civil libertarian value, and the law is invalid for breach of the Charter of Rights, there is no reason for the court to decide a more tenuous and difficult federalism issue. Even though the federalism issue would be the more fundamental defect were it decided against the law, there is no logical problem in the court deciding the case on the basis of the alternative Charter issue.

There is a well-known line of cases in which laws limiting free expression have been challenged on federal grounds. The challenged laws were: a law imposing on newspapers the obligation to publish a government reply to any criticism of a provincial government, a law restricting the distribution of literature on the streets, a law prohibiting the propagation of ''communism or bolshevism'', a law subjecting films to censorship, and a law prohibiting all public assemblies for a short period of time.[4] These cases genuinely raised federal issues, because neither the text of the Constitution nor any underlying federal principle offers a clear or general answer to the question of which level of government has the authority to restrain the fundamental political freedoms. But commentators have been quick to point out that the results of some of the cases seemed to turn more on a judicial concern to protect freedom of speech than on an assessment of the federalism issues at stake. Paul Weiler has argued, for example, that the Supreme Court of Canada in the 1950s used doctrines of federalism as a kind of surreptitious bill of rights, allocating jurisdiction to that level of government that had not exercised it, in order to invalidate a law that the Court really believed should not have been enacted at all.[5] Now that the Charter of Rights is available as a ground of review, a denial of a fundamental political liberty can be frankly acknowledged as a ground of invalidity under s. 2 of the Charter. The difficult federal issue would not then have to be decided. Of course, if the court decided that the law did not violate the Charter, perhaps by virtue of justification under s. 1, then the federal issue would have to be decided: in that event the alternative road could not be by-passed.

---

4 The cases are described in ch. 31, Expression, under heading 31.1, ''Distribution of powers'', below.

5 Weiler, ''The Supreme Court and the Law of Canadian Federalism'' (1973) 23 U. Toronto L.J. 307, 342-352.

Another point in favour of the logical priority of federalism issues over Charter issues is the presence in the Charter of Rights of the power of override. Section 33 of the Charter of Rights enables the Parliament or a Legislature to override most of the provisions of the Charter of Rights by including in a statute a declaration that the statute is to operate notwithstanding the relevant provision of the Charter of Rights.[6] Such a statute is then valid, despite the breach of the Charter of Rights. There is no similar saving provision for a breach of the federal distribution of powers. A law that is invalid for breach of the federal distribution of powers cannot be re-enacted by the enacting Parliament or Legislature (unless the Constitution is first amended). On the other hand, such a law can be enacted by the other level of government: if by virtue of the federal distribution of powers a law is incompetent to the federal Parliament, the law can be enacted by the provincial Legislatures, and vice versa.[7] The limits of the Charter of Rights, by contrast, apply to both the federal Parliament and the provincial Legislatures. Whatever the Charter denies to one level of government is also denied to the other.

15.3 Procedure

The procedural and evidentiary rules respecting judicial review on federal grounds are mostly the same as those respecting judicial review on Charter grounds. They are dealt with in chapters 56, Procedure, and 57, Proof, below. Those chapters discuss remedies, standing, mootness, ripeness, alternative grounds, notice to Attorneys General, intervention, legislative history and evidence.

15.4 Reasoning

In Canada the distribution of legislative power between the federal Parliament and the provincial Legislatures is mainly set out in ss. 91 and 92 of the Constitution Act, 1867.[8] Section 91 lists the kinds of laws which are competent to the federal Parliament; s. 92 lists the kinds of laws which are competent to the provincial Legislatures.[9] Both sections use a distinctive terminology, giving leg-

---

6 See ch. 36, Override of Rights, below.

7 See ch. 12, Parliamentary Sovereignty, above, and sec. 15.6(e), ''Exhaustiveness'', below.

8 Other sections conferring legislative power include ss. 92A (added 1982), 93, 94, 94A (added 1951, revised 1964), 95, 101, 132 of the Constitution Act, 1867; ss. 2, 3, 4 of the Constitution Act, 1871; ss. 2, 3 of the Statute of Westminster, 1931.

9 Canada's two lists of legislative powers may be contrasted with the Constitutions of the United States and Australia, which list only federal legislative powers, most of which are concurrent with a general, unenumerated state power. This means that the two-step process of judicial review described in the following text is not generally applicable to state laws in the United States and Australia: there are no enumerated classes into which state laws have to be fitted. Judicial review in Australia is compared with judicial review in Canada in Gilbert, *Australian and Canadian Federalism 1867-1984* (1986).

islative authority in relation to ''matters'' coming within ''classes of subjects''. This terminology emphasizes and helps to describe the two steps involved in the process of judicial review:[10] the first step is to identify the ''matter'' (or pith and substance) of the challenged law; the second step is to assign the matter to one of the ''classes of subjects'' (or heads of legislative power).[11] Of course, neither of these two steps has any significance by itself. The challenged statute is characterized (or classified) as in relation to a ''matter'' (step 1) only to determine whether it is authorized by some head of power in the Constitution. The ''classes of subjects'' are interpreted (step 2) only to determine which one will accommodate the matter of a particular statute. The process is, in Laskin's words, ''an interlocking one, in which the British North America Act and the challenged legislation react on one another and fix each other's meaning''.[12] Nevertheless, for purposes of analysis it is necessary to recognize that two steps are involved: the characterization[13] of the challenged law (step 1) and the interpretation of the power-distributing provisions of the Constitution (step 2).

15.5 Characterization of laws

(a) ''Matter''

The first step in judicial review is to identify the ''matter'' of the challenged law.[14] What is the ''matter'' of a law? Laskin says it is ''a distillation of the

10 On the process of judicial review on federal grounds, see Mundell (1954) 32 Can. Bar Rev. 813; Laskin (1955) 11 U. Toronto L.J. 114; Mundell (1955) 33 Can. Bar Rev. 915; Lederman in Lederman (ed.), *The Courts and the Canadian Constitution* (1964), 177; Lederman in Crépeau and Macpherson (eds.), *The Future of Canadian Federalism* (1965), 91; Browne, *The Judicial Committee and the British North America Act* (1967), passim; Abel (1968) 7 West. Ont. L. Rev. 1; Abel (1969) 19 U. Toronto L.J. 487; Lederman (1975) 53 Can. Bar Rev. 597.

11 ''What the process of constitutional adjudication involves is a distillation of the 'constitutional value' represented by challenged legislation (the 'matter' in relation to which it is enacted) and its attribution to a head of power (or 'class of subject')'': Laskin, *Canadian Constitutional Law* (5th ed., 1986 by Finkelstein), 242.

12 Laskin (1955) 11 U. Toronto L.J. 114, 127. Accord, Mundell (1955) 33 Can. Bar Rev. 915, 926; contra, Abel (1969) 19 U. Toronto L.J. 487, 490

13 The term characterization or classification is used in two senses in constitutional writing. The sense used in this chapter is the identification of the ''matter'' (or pith and substance) of a challenged law (step 1). Sometimes, the term is used to refer to the entire process of judicial review, i.e., as including allocation of the matter to a class of subject or head of power (step 2). Both usages are sanctioned by good practice.

14 The challenged law is usually a single statute. The challenged law can be a regulation or by-law or other form of delegated legislation, e.g., *A.-G. Man.* v. *Man. Egg & Poultry Assn.* [1971] S.C.R. 689. The challenged law can be a statute and a regulation made under the statute, e.g., *R.* v. *Morgentaler (No. 3)* [1993] 3 S.C.R. 463, 480, holding that a very general statute and a specific regulation ''must be considered together for the purposes of constitutional characterization''. The challenged law can take the form of a ''legislative scheme'' consisting of several related statutes: note 86, below. The challenged law can be part only of a statute: sec. 15.6 ''Severance'', below.

constitutional value represented by the challenged legislation'';[15] Abel says it is ''an abstract of the statute's content'';[16] Lederman says it is ''the true meaning of the challenged law'';[17] Mundell says it is the answer to the question, ''what in fact does the law do, and why?'';[18] Beetz J. says it is ''a name'' for ''the content or subject matter'' of the law;[19] other judges have sometimes said that it is the ''leading feature'' or ''true nature and character'' of the law, but usually they have described it as ''the pith and substance'' of the law.[20] The general idea of these and similar formulations is that it is necessary to identify the dominant or most important characteristic of the challenged law.[21]

As emphasized earlier, the sole purpose of identifying the ''matter'' of a law is to determine whether the law is constitutional or not. In identifying the ''matter'' of the law, the Courts therefore tend to use concepts that will assist in determining to which head of power the ''matter'' should be alloccted.[22] For example, if a law were characterized as in relation to the regulation of insurance, then it would be clear that the law was competent only to the provinces because it is settled by precedent that the regulation of insurance is a matter coming within ''property and civil rights in the province'', which is a provincial class of subject (s. 92(13)). Indeed, sometimes the ''matter'' of a law will be described in the very language of a class of subject. For example, the federal Bank Act would undoubtedly be characterized as a law in relation to banking, making perfectly clear that it relates to a matter coming within ''banking'', which is a federal class of subject (s. 91(15)). The point is that the identification of the ''matter'' of a statute will often effectively settle the question of its validity, leaving the allocation of the matter to a class of subject little more than a formality.[23]

---

15 Note 11, above.

16 (1969) 19 U. Toronto L.J. 487, 490.

17 Lederman in Lederman (ed.), *The Courts and the Canadian Constitution* (1964), 186.

18 (1955) 33 Can. Bar Rev. 915, 928. Gilbert, note 14, above, 27, comments that the last two words of this quotation sum up the difference between Canadian and Australian characterization techniques; Australian judges do not ask ''and why?''.

19 *Re Anti-Inflation Act* [1976] 2 S.C.R. 373, 450.

20 The phrase ''pith and substance'' seems to have been first used in this context in *Union Colliery Co.* v. *Bryden* [1899] A.C. 580, 587 per Lord Watson.

21 Pith and substance is not relevant to judicial review on Charter grounds. For that purpose, one identifies the ''purpose'' and the ''effect'' of an impugned statute. If either the purpose or the effect of the statute is to abridge a Charter right, then the statute will be invalid, unless it is saved by s. 1: *R.* v. *Big M Drug Mart* [1985] 1 S.C.R. 295, 331. See generally ch. 33, Charter of Rights, under heading 33.6, ''Characterization of laws'', below.

22 Note that a ''matter'' must be sufficiently specific to come within a class of subject: *Saumur* v. *Que.* [1953] 2 S.C.R. 299, 333 per Rand J.; or, if it comes within the national concern branch of the peace, order, and good government power, to serve as a limited, justiciable restraint on federal power: *Re Anti-Inflation Act* [1976] 2 S.C.R. 373, 450-459 per Beetz J.; *R.* v. *Crown Zellerbach* [1988] 1 S.C.R. 401, 432 per Le Dain J.

23 Abel (1969) U. Toronto L.J. 487, 490, while not denying that this is what in fact occurs, argues that the courts should discern the ''matter'' of a statute in disregard of the effect of the characterization on constitutionality.

The difficulty in identifying the ''matter'' of a statute is that many statutes have one feature (or aspect) which comes within a provincial head of power and another which comes within a federal head of power. Clearly, the selection of one or the other feature as the ''matter'' of the statute will dispose of the case; equally clearly, the court in making its selection will be conscious of the ultimate result which is thereby dictated. Take the case of a provincial statute which imposes a direct tax on banks. One feature of this law is ''direct taxation'' which comes within a provincial class of subject (s. 92(2)); but another feature of the law is banking which comes within a federal class of subject (s. 91(15)). If the law is in relation to direct taxation it is good, but if it is in relation to banking it is bad. How does the court make the crucial choice? Logic offers no solution: the law has both the relevant qualities and there is no logical basis for preferring one over the other. What the courts do in cases of this kind is to make a judgment as to which is the most important feature of the law and to characterize the law by that feature: that dominant feature is the ''pith and substance'' or ''matter'' of the law; the other feature is merely incidental, irrelevant for constitutional purposes.[24] In *Bank of Toronto* v. *Lambe* (1887),[25] the Privy Council upheld a provincial law which imposed a tax on banks. The dominant feature of the law was to raise revenue, and accordingly the ''matter'' of the law was taxation, not banking. This distinction is commonly expressed by using the phrase ''in relation to'', which appears in ss. 91 and 92. One would say of the impugned law in *Bank of Toronto* v. *Lambe* that it was ''in relation to'' taxation (the matter) and merely ''affected'' banking.

It is important to recognize that this ''pith and substance'' doctrine enables one level of government to enact laws with substantial impact on matters outside its jurisdiction. The levy of the tax in *Bank of Toronto* v. *Lambe* was, after all, a significant exercise of legislative power over the banks; but because the law was characterized as ''in relation to'' taxation (its pith and substance or matter), it could validly ''affect'' banking. There are many examples of laws which have been upheld despite their ''incidental'' impact on matters outside the enacting body's jurisdiction. A provincial law in relation to insurance (provincial matter) may validly restrict or even stop the activities of federally-incorporated companies (federal matter); a provincial law reorganizing municipalities (provincial matter) may validly alter the interest payable on debt owed to out-of-province creditors (federal matter); a federal law in relation to navigation and shipping (federal matter) may validly regulate labour relations in a port (provincial matter); a federal law in relation to the national capital region (federal matter) may validly regulate land use in Ontario and Quebec (provincial matter). These and other well-known cases are footnoted below.[26]

---

24 Lederman in Lederman (ed.), *The Courts and the Canadian Constitution* (1964), 188-189, 195-197.

25 (1887) 12 App. Cas. 575.

26 *Workmen's Comp. Bd.* v. *CPR* [1920] A.C. 184 (workmen's compensation; international ship-

Needless to say, a different result follows if the pith and substance of the challenged law is adjudged to be a matter outside jurisdiction. *Bank of Toronto* v. *Lambe* may be contrasted with the *Alberta Bank Taxation Reference* (1938),[27] in which the Privy Council struck down an Alberta law which imposed a special tax solely on the banks. Their lordships concluded that the pith and substance of this particular law was to discourage the operation of the banks in Alberta. Its ''matter'' therefore came within ''banking'' and the taxing quality of the law was merely incidental. The province's power to tax could not save the law, because its pith and substance was not taxation.[28]

(b) Singling out

The *Alberta Bank Taxation Reference* is occasionally read as prohibiting the provincial Legislatures from ''singling out'' banks or other federal undertakings for special treatment. The same point is occasionally made by the proposition that provincial laws ''of general application'' may validly apply to banks or other federal undertakings. But in the *Alberta Bank Taxation Reference* the singling out of the banks was only one of the factors which led the Privy Council to characterize the law as in relation to banking. The high rate of tax imposed by the law, and the fact that the law was part of a package of social credit policies inimical to bank credit, were at least equally important. There are a number of cases in which provincial laws have been upheld, although the laws singled out a person or class of persons within federal jurisdiction. For example, in *Bank of*

---

ping; extraprovincial rights); *Lymburn* v. *Mayland* [1932] A.C. 318 (securities regulation; federal companies); *Ladore* v. *Bennett* [1939] A.C. 468 (municipal institutions; property outside province); *Johannesson* v. *West St. Paul* [1952] 1 S.C.R. 292 (aeronautics; land use); *Stevedores Reference* [1955] S.C.R. 529 (navigation and shipping; local labour relations); *A.-G. Ont.* v. *Barfried Enterprises* [1963] S.C.R. 570 (unconscionable contracts; interest); *Oil, Chemical and Atomic Wkrs.* v. *Imperial Oil* [1963] S.C.R. 584 (labour relations; federal elections); *Munro* v. *National Capital Comm.* [1966] S.C.R. 663 (national capital region; land use); *Carnation Co.* v. *Que. Agricultural Marketing Bd.* [1968] S.C.R. 238 (local marketing; interprovincial trade); *Walter* v. *A.-G. Alta.* [1969] S.C.R. 383 (land use; religion); *Papp* v. *Papp* [1970] 1 O.R. 331 (divorce; custody); *Can. Indemnity Co.* v. *A.-G. B.C.* [1977] 2 S.C.R. 504 (insurance; trade and commerce; federal companies); *A.-G. Que.* v. *Kellogg's Co.* [1978] 2 S.C.R. 211 (advertising for children; television); *Construction Montcalm* v. *Minimum Wage Comm.* [1979] 1 S.C.R. 754 (minimum wage; airport); *Four B Manufacturing* v. *United Garment Workers* [1980] 1 S.C.R. 1031 (labour relations; Indian reserve). The same idea as that expressed by the contrasting ''in relation to'' and ''affecting'' has been expressed in terms of an ''ancillary'' doctrine, which is examined later in this chapter. A similar ''trenching'' doctrine has fallen into disuse: see *Papp* v. *Papp* [1970] 1 O.R. 331, 335 per Laskin J.A.; Laskin, *Canadian Constitutional Law* (5th ed., 1986 by Finkelstein), 255; Lederman in Lederman (ed.), *The Courts and the Canadian Constitution* (1964), 197. In particular, the theory that laws passed under the peace, order, and good government power had a lesser capacity to ''trench upon'' provincial classes of subject is no longer accepted, and is contradicted by *Johannesson* v. *West St. Paul* [1952] 1 S.C.R. 292 and *Munro* v. *National Capital Comm.* [1966] S.C.R. 663.

27 *A.-G. Alta.* v. *A.-G. Can.* (Bank Taxation) [1939] A.C. 117.

28 For criticism of the decision, see Mallory (1944) 10 Can. J. Ec. & Pol. Sci. 165, 171-172.

Toronto v. *Lambe*, the leading case referred to earlier,[29] the taxing statute, although it applied to other corporations as well as banks, did impose a special rate of tax on banks alone; yet the Privy Council did not hesitate to characterize the law as in relation to taxation, not banking. Similarly, a provincial tax levied on a single company which operated an international railway bridge (within federal jurisdiction under s. 92(10)) has been upheld.[30] A provincial electoral law has been upheld notwithstanding that it discriminated against certain aliens and naturalized subjects (''naturalization and aliens'' being a federal class of subject (s. 91(25)).[31] A provincial moratorium law has been upheld notwithstanding that it applied only to proceedings against a single federally-incorporated company.[32] A provincial law authorizing compulsory inspection of bank records in civil litigation has been upheld as in relation to civil procedure, notwithstanding that it singled out the banks.[33] A provincial law expropriating the assets of only one of five companies engaged in mining asbestos in the province has been upheld notwithstanding that the company singled out was federally-incorporated.[34]

These cases show that a provincial law need not be of general application to apply validly to undertakings within federal jurisdiction. A law is characterized by its pith and substance (its dominant feature). The singling out of undertakings within federal jurisdiction is not conclusive of pith and substance. Exactly the same principles would apply to federal laws that singled out local works or undertakings or other matters within provincial jurisdiction, although there do not seem to be any illustrative cases.

While a provincial law of special application to undertakings within federal jurisdiction is not necessarily invalid, it is also true that a provincial law of general application is not necessarily valid in its application to undertakings within federal jurisdiction. Normally, as we have seen, a provincial law of general application which is in relation to a provincial matter may validly affect federal matters as well. But the courts have carved out an important exception to this general rule. If the effect of the provincial law would be to impair the status or essential powers of a federally-incorporated company, or to affect a vital part of a federally-regulated enterprise, then the provincial law, although valid in the generality of its applications, will not apply to the federally-incorporated company or federally-regulated enterprise.[35]

---

29 Note 25, above.

30 *Van Buren Bridge Co.* v. *Madawaska* (1958) 15 D.L.R. (2d) 763 (N.B. A.D.).

31 *Cunningham* v. *Tomey Homma* [1903] A.C. 151.

32 *Abitibi Power and Paper Co.* v. *Montreal Trust Co.* [1943] A.C. 536.

33 *Sommers* v. *Sturdy* (1957) 10 D.L.R. (2d) 269 (B.C. C.A.); see also *Gregory Co.* v. *Imperial Bank* [1960] C.S. 204 (Que. S.C.); compare *A.-G. Can.* v. *A.-G. Que.* (Bank Deposits) [1947] A.C. 33.

34 *Société Asbestos* v. *Société nationale de l'amiante* (1981) 128 D.L.R. (3d) 405 (Que. C.A.).

35 See sec. 15.8, ''Interjurisdictional immunity'', below.

(c) Double aspect

One might well ask why a law which presents both federal and provincial characteristics should not be treated as competent to both the federal Parliament and the provincial Legislatures. At first glance, such a result seems inconsistent with the stipulation in ss. 91 and 92 that each list of classes of subject is assigned "exclusively" to either the Parliament or the Legislatures.[36] But the Privy Council early announced that "subjects which in one aspect and for one purpose fall within s. 92, may in another aspect and for another purpose fall within s. 91".[37] This doctrine has become known as the "double aspect" doctrine; it would perhaps be clearer if it had become known as the "double matter" doctrine, because it acknowledges that some kinds of laws have both a federal and a provincial "matter" and are therefore competent to both the Dominion and the provinces.[38]

The courts have not explained when it is appropriate to apply the double aspect doctrine, and when it is necessary to make a choice between the federal and provincial features of a challenged law. Lederman's explanation seems to be the only plausible one: the double aspect doctrine is applicable when "the contrast between the relative importance of the two features is not so sharp".[39] In other words, the double aspect doctrine is the course of judicial restraint. When the court finds that the federal and provincial characteristics of a law are roughly equal in importance, then the conclusion is that laws of that kind may be enacted by either the Parliament or a Legislature.

The Supreme Court of Canada has upheld provincial highway traffic offences of driving without due care and attention and failing to remain at the scene of an accident as laws in relation to conduct on the roads, which is a matter coming within provincial power, probably under "property and civil rights in the province" (s. 92(13)); at the same time the Court has upheld very similar federal offences contained in the Criminal Code as laws in relation to the punishment of crime, which is a matter coming within "criminal law", a federal head of power

36 See sec. 15.9, "Exclusiveness", below.

37 *Hodge* v. *The Queen* (1883) 9 App. Cas. 117, 130.

38 A law can also have a double aspect in that it presents characteristics from more than one class of subject in the same list. Since this does not give any legislative authority to the other level of government, it is normally irrelevant. Occasionally it is relevant, as in *Re Exported Natural Gas Tax* [1982] 1 S.C.R. 1004, 1074 (federal tax on provincial property would escape s. 125 if it were also a trade and commerce measure); *A.-G. Can.* v. *CN Transportation* [1983] 2 S.C.R. 206, 279-280 (Dickson J.'s dissenting view, rejected by majority, that federal criminal law could be enforced federally only if it were also a trade and commerce measure).

39 Lederman, *Continuing Canadian Constitutional Dilemmas* (1981), 244; this formulation was approved by Dickson J. for the majority in *Multiple Access* v. *McCutcheon* [1982] 2 S.C.R. 161, 181 in reaching his conclusion (also at p. 181) that "insider trading provisions have both a securities law and a companies law aspect"; and again by Dickson C.J. for the majority in *Rio Hotel* v. *N.B.* [1987] 2 S.C.R. 59, 65 in reaching his conclusion that prohibitions of nude dancing in taverns have both a liquor-licensing and a criminal law aspect.

(s. 91(27)).[40] It is clear from these cases that laws prescribing rules of conduct on the roads have a ''double aspect'', and are therefore competent to both the Parliament and a Legislature.

Securities regulation is another field where some laws have a double aspect. The Supreme Court of Canada has upheld both a provincial and a federal law, each creating an offence of issuing a false prospectus.[41] The Court has also upheld both a provincial and a federal law, each creating a civil remedy for insider trading.[42] The provincial power in both cases came from the characterization of the provincial laws as regulating the trade in securities, which is a matter coming within ''property and civil rights in the province'' (s. 92(13)). The federal power came from the characterization of the federal false prospectus offence as a ''criminal law'' (s. 91(27)) and the federal insider trading remedy as a corporate law coming within the federal power to incorporate companies (s. 91 opening words).

The effective concurrency of power over the highways and over securities regulation, and over other fields of law,[43] gives rise to the possibility of conflict between a valid federal law and a valid provincial law. The resolution of such conflicts in favour of the federal law is the function of the doctrine of ''federal paramountcy'', which is the subject of the next chapter.

(d) Purpose

The characterization of a law for constitutional purposes is, as we have seen, the identification of the ''matter'' of the law; the matter is often described as the ''pith and substance'' of the law, but is perhaps best described as the dominant or most important characteristic of the law.[44] The process of characterization is not a technical, formalistic exercise, confined to the strict legal operation of the impugned law. As we noticed in the earlier discussion of the *Alberta Bank Taxation Reference* (1938),[45] the fact that a provincial law levies a tax (for example) is not decisive of its classification as a taxing measure. The Court will look beyond the direct legal effects to inquire into the social or economic purposes which the statute was enacted to achieve. If the Court concludes that the purpose

---

40 *O'Grady* v. *Sparling* [1960] S.C.R. 804; *Stephens* v. *The Queen* [1960] S.C.R. 823; *Mann* v. *The Queen* [1966] S.C.R. 238.

41 *Smith* v. *The Queen* [1960] S.C.R. 776.

42 *Multiple Access* v. *McCutcheon* [1982] 2 S.C.R. 161. See generally ch. 21, Property and Civil Rights, under heading 20.10, ''Securities regulation'', below.

43 E.g., insolvency: *A.-G. Ont.* v. *A.-G. Can.* (Voluntary Assignments) [1894] A.C. 189; *Robinson* v. *Countrywide Factors* [1978] 1 S.C.R. 753; temperance: *A.-G. Ont.* v. *A.-G. Can.* (Local Prohibition) [1896] A.C. 348; interest rates: *A.-G. Ont.* v. *Barfried Enterprises* [1963] S.C.R. 570; maintenance of spouses and children and custody of children: *Papp* v. *Papp* [1970] 1 O.R. 331 (C.A.); entertainment in taverns: *Rio Hotel* v. *N.B.* [1987] 2 S.C.R. 59; gaming: *R.* v. *Furtney* [1991] 3 S.C.R. 89.

44 Text accompanying note 21, above.

45 Note 27, above.

of the ostensible tax is to regulate or destroy the banks, then the law will be characterized as being in relation to banking and will be held to be invalid.[46]

The cases on Sunday closing present an interesting illustration of the importance of legislative purpose in characterization. In *R.* v. *Big M Drug Mart* (1985),[47] the Supreme Court of Canada, following earlier authority, held that the federal Lord's Day Act, which prohibited various commercial activities on Sundays, was a valid exercise of the federal Parliament's power over criminal law. (The Act was actually struck down for breach of the Charter of Rights.) The criminal character of the Act flowed from its purpose, which was the religious one of ''the preservation of the sanctity of the Christian sabbath''.[48] The religious purpose could be discovered from the name and history of the Act. The Court acknowledged that if the purpose of the statute had not been religious ''but rather the secular goal of enforcing a uniform day of rest from labour'', then the Act would have fallen under provincial rather than federal competence.[49] The latter case arrived at the Court's doorstep just one year later. In *R.* v. *Edwards Books and Art* (1986)[50] the Court held that Ontario's Retail Business Holidays Act, which prohibited retail stores from opening on Sundays, was a valid exercise of the province's power over property and civil rights in the province. (The Act also survived a Charter attack, by virtue of s. 1.) In this case, the Court discovered the secular purpose of the Act — providing a uniform pause day for retail workers — in the legislative history, which consisted of the parliamentary debates and the law reform commission report that preceded the enactment of the Act. The different outcomes in *Big M* and *Edwards Books* turned on the different purposes of the challenged laws: the prohibition of work on Sunday fell within federal or provincial competence depending upon whether the purpose of the prohibition was religious or secular.[51]

What is meant by the ''purpose'' of a statute? An inanimate object such as a statute can have a purpose in the sense of a function, and sometimes a preamble

---

46 In Australia, the ''pith and substance'' or purposive approach to characterization has been generally rejected in favour of a more formal approach which looks to the strict legal operation of the law, eschewing consideration of social or economic purposes or effects. This formalistic approach has had the effect of expanding the federal enumerated powers, because it permits a law to control indirectly matters within state jurisdiction, so long as the direct legal effect of the law is attributable to a matter within federal jurisdiction. The approach does not have a similarly expansive effect on state powers, because the states do not have enumerated powers, and state laws rarely require characterization: see note 9, above. The differing approaches to characterization in Canada and Australia are analyzed in Gilbert, note 14, above; see also Sawer, *Australian Federation in the Courts* (1967), 109-111.

47 [1985] 1 S.C.R. 295.

48 *Id.*, 354.

49 *Id.*, 355.

50 [1986] 2 S.C.R. 713.

51 See generally ch. 18, Criminal Law, under heading 18.7, ''Sunday observance law'', below.

to the statute will make clear what that purpose is.[52] Sometimes, the courts refer to the "intention" of the statute or of the legislative body that enacted it. This language does no harm as long as it is not taken too literally. A statute cannot have an intention, and a deliberative body such as a legislature is likely to have as many intentions (or purposes) as there are members. As Lederman has said, what is really being sought is "the full or total meaning of the rule", judged "in terms of the consequences of the action called for".[53]

In determining the "purpose" of a statute in this special sense, there is no doubt as to the propriety of reference to the state of law before the statute and the defect in the law (the "mischief") which the statute purports to correct. These may be referred to under ordinary rules of statutory interpretation. Until recently, there was doubt about the propriety of reference to parliamentary debates (Hansard) and other sources of the "legislative history" of the statute. The relevance of legislative history is obvious: it helps to place the statute in its context, gives some explanation of its provisions, and articulates the policy of the government that proposed it. Legislative history has usually been held inadmissible in Canada under ordinary rules of statutory interpretation. But the interpretation of a particular provision of a statute is an entirely different process from the characterization of the entire statute for purposes of judicial review.[54] There seems to be no good reason why legislative history should not be resorted to for the latter purpose, and, despite some earlier authority to the contrary, it is now established that reports of royal commissions and law reform commissions, government policy papers and even parliamentary debates are indeed admissible.[55]

(e) Effect

In characterizing a statute — identifying its "matter" or "pith and substance" — a court will always consider the effect of the statute, in the sense that the court will consider how the statute changes the rights and liabilities of those

---

52 In *Abitibi Power and Paper Co.* v. *Montreal Trust Co.* [1943] A.C. 536, 548, the Privy Council stated that it would require "cogent grounds" before imputing to the enacting body an object other than the one appearing in the preamble on the face of the legislation. To the same effect, *A.-G. Can.* v. *Hallet & Carey* [1952] A.C. 427, 444. Contrast *Re Anti-Inflation Act* [1976] 2 S.C.R. 373, where the existence of a preamble that made no reference to an emergency did not prevent Laskin C.J. (at p. 422) and Ritchie J. (at p. 438), for the majority, from characterizing the Anti-Inflation Act as an emergency measure. Beetz J., who dissented, emphasized (at pp. 465-467) the text of the preamble. In *A.-G. Can. and Dupond* v. *Montreal* [1978] 2 S.C.R. 770, Beetz J. for the majority referred (at p. 795) to the recitals in the preamble to the impugned by-law, and Laskin C.J. for the minority did so too (at p. 774), in support of their differing characterizations.

53 Lederman, *Continuing Canadian Constitutional Dilemmas* (1981), 239.

54 Also to be distinguished, is the use of legislative history for the purpose of interpreting the Constitution Acts, 1867 to 1982: see ch. 57, Proof, under heading 57.1, "Legislative history", below.

55 See ch. 57, Proof, under heading 57.1, "Legislative history", below.

who are subject to it. This simply involves understanding the terms of the statute, and that can be accomplished without going beyond the four corners of the statute. But, as we noticed in the previous section of this chapter, the search for pith and substance will not remain within the four corners of the statute if there is reason to believe that the direct legal effects of the statute are directed to the indirect achievement of other purposes. In such a case, said Lord Maugham L.C. in the *Alberta Bank Taxation Reference*, "the Court must take into account any public general knowledge of which the Court would take judicial notice, and may in a proper case require to be informed by evidence as to what the effect of the legislation will be".[56]

In the *Alberta Bank Taxation Reference*,[57] the Privy Council examined the impact on the banks of the tax which Alberta proposed and used the severity of the tax as one of the reasons for concluding that the statute should be characterized as in relation to banking rather than taxation. In *Texada Mines* v. *A.-G. B.C.* (1960),[58] the Supreme Court of Canada examined the effect of a provincial law imposing a tax on iron ore, and concluded that the tax was so heavy as to make it uneconomic to sell the ore outside the province; the Court accordingly characterized the law as in relation to interprovincial trade, a federal head of power (s. 91(2)), rather than as in relation to direct taxation within the province (s. 92(2)). In *Central Canada Potash Co.* v. *Government of Saskatchewan* (1978),[59] the Court examined the effect of a provincial scheme for the prorationing of potash; finding that nearly all of the province's production was exported, and that the province had abundant reserves, the Court characterized the scheme as in relation to interprovincial and international trade rather than the conservation of a natural resource.[60] Of course, in many cases, evidence as to the likely effect of legislation would not add anything useful to the task of characterization, but would merely bear on the wisdom or efficacy of the statute. In those cases the evidence is not relevant.[61]

There have been cases in which the Court has examined the administration of a statute as an aid to classifying it for constitutional purposes. In *Saumur* v. *Quebec* (1953),[62] there was a constitutional challenge to a municipal by-law which

---

56 *A.-G. Alta.* v. *A.-G. Can.* (Bank Taxation) [1939] A.C. 117, 130. See generally ch. 57, Proof, under heading 57.2, "Evidence". below.

57 *A.-G. Alta.* v. *A.-G. Can.* (Bank Taxation) [1939] A.C. 117; see note 27 and accompanying text, above.

58 [1960] S.C.R. 713.

59 [1979] 1 S.C.R. 42.

60 *In A.-G. Man.* v. *Manitoba Egg and Poultry Assn.* [1971] S.C.R. 689, 704-705, Laskin J. complained about the absence of any "factual underpinning" for a reference of the validity of a provincial egg marketing plan; in particular, the volume of out-of-province eggs in the province's market would have assisted in the characterization of the plan.

61 *Re Anti-Inflation Act* [1976] 2 S.C.R. 373, 424-455, rejecting evidence that federal wage and price controls were unlikely to reduce inflation. On the irrelevance of the wisdom or policy of a law, see ch. 12, Parliamentary Sovereignty, above.

62 [1953] 2 S.C.R. 299.

made it an offence to distribute literature in the streets of the city of Quebec without having previously obtained the written permission of the chief of police. Such a law could have been passed for the purposes of protecting pedestrian traffic or controlling litter in the city streets, and indeed four judges of the Supreme Court did uphold the law as being in relation to the streets, a perfectly legitimate topic of provincial regulation. But the other five judges — a majority — took note of the way in which the by-law was actually administered. They found that, on an application for permission to distribute literature, the chief of police would examine the contents of the material to be distributed, and would make his decision on the basis of whether he found the contents to be objectionable or not. In other words, the chief of police used the by-law as a vehicle of censorship, and the by-law constituted an effective bar to the dissemination of literature by an unpopular minority group such as the Jehovah's Witnesses, who had brought the action challenging the by-law. On the basis of these findings, the majority classified the by-law as in relation to speech or religion, and held that it was incompetent to the province.[63] Of course, the reason for the by-law's invalidity was not its administration by the chief of police, but the fact that its language was apt to authorize a regime of political and religious censorship; and it is possible that the majority judges would have reached the same result solely on the basis of the language of the by-law. But it is obvious that the judges were influenced by the actual use of the by-law, and it is even more obvious that they regarded the facts as to the actual use of the by-law as relevant and admissible on the question of classification.[64]

(f) Colourability

The courts are, of course, concerned with the substance of the legislation to be characterized and not merely its form. The "colourability" doctrine is invoked when a statute bears the formal trappings of a matter within jurisdiction, but in reality is addressed to a matter outside jurisdiction. In the *Alberta Bank Taxation Reference*,[65] for example, the Privy Council held that the legislation, although ostensibly designed as a taxation measure, was in reality directed at banking. Similarly, attempts by the federal Parliament to regulate insurance (a provincial matter) by incorporating provisions into the Criminal Code (criminal law being federal), or by enacting special taxing measures, have been struck down as col-

---

63 Of the five majority judges, only four, namely, Rand, Kellock, Estey, and Locke JJ., held the by-law to be unconstitutional. The fifth member of the majority, Kerwin J., held that it was constitutional, but inapplicable to a religious group such as the Jehovah's Witnesses because it conflicted with the Freedom of Worship Act, a pre-confederation statute which in Kerwin J.'s opinion protected their proselytizing practices.

64 In *A.-G. B.C.* v. *McDonald Murphy Lumber* [1930] A.C. 357, 363, the Privy Council reinforced its conclusion that the challenged provincial tax was an invalid export tax with the fact that the portion of the tax purportedly payable on timber used locally was not actually collected.

65 Note 27 and accompanying text, above.

ourable.[66] A provincial attempt to relieve debtors from the payment of interest (a federal matter) by forgiving part of the principal of the loan has also been condemned as colourable,[67] as has been a provincial attempt to prohibit the propagation of communism (speech being a federal matter) by controlling the use of property.[68]

In *Re Upper Churchill Water Rights* (1984),[69] the Supreme Court of Canada struck down a Newfoundland statute that expropriated the assets of a company that generated hydro-electricity at Churchill Falls in Labrador. On the face of it, the statute seemed valid, because it was clear that Newfoundland had the power to expropriate property situated within its borders. But the Court held that the pith and substance of the statute was to deprive the company of the capacity to fulfil a long-term contract to supply power to Hydro-Quebec at below-market rates. The nullification of this contract was outside the power of Newfoundland, because the contract created rights in Quebec. The statute made no mention of the power contract or of any rights outside the province, and was thus ''cloaked in the proper constitutional form''.[70] The statute was nevertheless held to be invalid as ''a colourable attempt to interfere with the power contract''.[71]

In *R.* v. *Morgentaler (No. 3)* (1993),[72] the Supreme Court of Canada struck down a Nova Scotia statute that required ''designated'' medical procedures to be performed in a hospital. The designation had been accomplished by a regulation, which listed nine medical procedures, of which the fourth was abortion. The statute declared that its purpose was ''to prohibit the privatization of the provision of certain medical services in order to maintain a single high-quality health-care delivery system for all Nova Scotians''. On the face of it, the statute seemed to be a health measure, which would be within the constitutional power of the province. The Supreme Court of Canada, in a unanimous opinion by Sopinka J., pointed to uncontradicted testimony that the stimulus for the statute came from a proposal by Dr. Henry Morgentaler to establish an abortion clinic in the province, and the Court quoted extensively from the legislative history of the statute to show the legislators' preoccupation with stopping the establishment of the Morgentaler clinic. None of this was literally inconsistent with the stated purpose of the legislation. Nor did the Court attempt to resolve ''the intractable dispute between the parties as to whether this legislation will in fact restrict access to abortion in Nova Scotia''.[73] Nevertheless, the Court held that the statute and regulation ''were aimed primarily at suppressing the perceived harm or evil of abortion clinics'', and that they were properly characterized as invalid criminal

---

66 *A.G. Ont.* v. *Reciprocal Insurers* [1924] A.C. 328; *Re Insurance Act of Can.* [1932] A.C. 41.
67 *A.-G. Sask.* v. *A.-G. Can.* (Sask. Farm Security) [1949] A.C. 110.
68 *Switzman* v. *Elbling* [1957] S.C.R. 285.
69 [1984] 1 S.C.R. 297.
70 *Id.*, 332.
71 *Id.*, 333.
72 [1993] 3 S.C.R. 463.
73 *Id.*, 515.

laws.[74] The Court struck down the statute and regulation in their entirety, despite the fact that eight of the nine designated hospital procedures had nothing to do with abortion. By this holding, the Court made clear that it regarded the designation of the eight non-abortion procedures as a smokescreen to conceal from a reviewing court the true purpose of the legislation. This is a remarkable application of the colourability doctrine.[75]

In these colourability cases there is a very fine line between adjudication on policy and adjudication on validity. Indeed, the adjective ''colourable'' carries a strong connotation of judicial disapproval, if not of the policy of the statute, at least of the means by which the legislative body sought to carry out the policy. Such disapproval is entirely out of place, serving only to cast doubt on the neutrality of judicial review. The colourability doctrine can and should be stated without impugning the legislative branch: it simply means that ''form is not controlling in the determination of essential character''.[76]

The colourability doctrine applies the maxim that a legislative body cannot do indirectly what it cannot do directly. However, as is suggested by the paucity of citations in this section of the chapter, arguments of colourability are rarely successful. Often, a legislative body will find a way to do indirectly what it cannot do directly. For example, the federal Parliament cannot regulate the delivery of health care in the provinces, but it can transfer cash and tax points to only those provinces whose health care plans comply with federal standards of universality, accessibility and mobility.[77] Neither the federal Parliament nor the provincial Legislatures can delegate powers to each other, but each can delegate powers to agencies created by the other.[78] A provincial Legislature cannot regulate television programmes or advertising, but it can prohibit certain kinds of advertising in all media, and the prohibition will be valid and effective as a bar to television advertising.[79] A provincial Legislature cannot levy a sales tax on the vendor of a good, because such a tax would be indirect, but the Legislature can impose on the vendor an obligation to collect a tax that is formally levied on the consumer of the good.[80]

(g) Criteria of choice

The characterization of a statute is often decisive of its validity, and the Court will obviously be aware of that fact. The choice between competing char-

74 *Id.*, 512.

75 Sopinka J. (at 496) denied that he was applying the colourability doctrine. This is one of those occasions where the text-writer must rely on what the Court has done rather than on what the Court says it has done!

76 Abel (1969) 19 U. Toronto L.J. 487, 494.

77 See ch. 6, Financial Arrangements, under heading 6.8, ''Spending power'', above.

78 See ch. 14, Delegation, under heading 14.3, ''Federal inter-delegation'', above.

79 *Irwin Toy* v. *Quebec* [1989] 1 S.C.R. 927, 953 (expressly rejecting colourability argument).

80 See ch. 30, Taxation, under heading 30.7, ''Sales taxes'', below.

acteristics of the statute, in order to identify the most important one as the ''matter'', may be nothing less than a choice between validity or invalidity. What are the criteria of importance that will control or at least guide this crucial choice? No doubt, full understanding of the legislative scheme, informed by relevant extrinsic material, will often reveal one dominant statutory policy to which other features are subordinate. No doubt, too, judicial decisions on similar kinds of statutes will often provide some guide. But in the hardest cases the choice is not compelled by either the nature of the statute or the prior judicial decisions. The choice is inevitably one of policy.

The policy choice that lies at the base of a characterization decision is bound to be related to the ultimate consequence of the choice which is, I am assuming, the validity or invalidity of the statute. The choice must be guided by a concept of federalism. Is this the kind of law that should be enacted at the federal or the provincial level?[81] The reasoning at this point should not be affected by judicial approval or disapproval of the particular statute in issue; nor by the political situation which provided the controversy, let alone the political allegiances of the contending parties. The only ''political'' values which may be accepted as legitimate to judicial review are those that have a constitutional dimension to them, that is, values that may reasonably be asserted to be enduring considerations in the allocation of power between the two levels of government.[82]

There would be little dispute as to some of the considerations that it is legitimate for a judge to take account of in resolving an issue of characterization. The allocations of power that are explicit in the Constitution are suggestive of the kinds of new laws that should be allocated to each level of government. The case-law that elaborates the constitutional text offers other suggestions and analogies. But there are many other values to be drawn from history, political science, economics and sociology, which are arguably inherent in Canada's federal system, but which are much more controversial. Simeon[83] has suggested the three values of community, efficiency and democracy as criteria that are helpful to an appraisal of the allocation of power in a federal system. But, as he acknowledges, there is room for much argument as to the existence and relative weight of these values. Conceptions of community, namely, whether Canada or a particular province is

81 Lederman, *Continuing Canadian Constitutional Dilemmas* (1981), 241.

82 This seems to me to be the thesis of Wechsler, ''Toward Neutral Principles of Constitutional Law'' (1959) 73 Harv. L. Rev. 1, but his use of the word ''neutral'' was unfortunate, since it implied a value-free process of reasoning which Wechsler did not intend. His article was an attempt to defend the legitimacy of judicial review by emphasizing the rational side of adjudication, in contrast to the legal realists, who viewed adjudication as a policy choice by (unelected, unaccountable and unrepresentative) judges. The debate continues to this day between the ''interpretivist'' and ''noninterpretivist'' constitutional theorists. For a balanced view, acknowledging both the constraining function of legal texts, principles and rules, and the role of values, see Newman, ''Between Legal Realism and Neutral Principles'' (1984) 72 Calif. L. Rev. 200.

83 Simeon, ''Criteria for Choice in Federal Systems'' (1983) 8 Queen's L.J. 131.

the primary community to which the citizen should feel allegiance, are subject to reasonable disagreement, especially between many English-speaking Canadians and many French-speaking Quebecers. Conceptions of efficiency, namely, whether a particular governmental power is exercised most efficiently by the federal government or by a province, are also subject to reasonable disagreement, with varying weight being given, on the one hand, to economies of scale, national economic policies, nationwide mobility of resources, and uniform access to rights, resources and opportunities by all citizens and, on the other hand, to local diversity and experimentation and smaller bureaucracies. Conceptions of democracy, namely, whether the federal government or a provincial government is more responsive and accountable to the people and more protective of minorities, are also subject to reasonable disagreement.[84]

One cannot say that a judge is wrong to take account of these kinds of considerations. How else is the judge to reach a decision as to the appropriate characterization of a statute, where conventional legal sources fail to supply the answer? But, in assessing these kinds of criteria, the judge has little to provide guidance and may tend to assume that his or her personal preferences are widely shared if not impliedly embodied in the Constitution. In that sense, judicial review can never be wholly neutral, wholly divorced from the predilections of the judges. This is one reason why in federalism cases judicial restraint should be a governing precept.[85] In other words, where the choice between competing characterizations is not clear, the choice which will support the legislation is normally to be preferred.

(h) Presumption of constitutionality

Judicial restraint in determining the validity of statutes may be expressed in terms of a ''presumption of constitutionality''.[86] Such a term transfers from the law of evidence the idea that a burden of demonstration lies upon those who would challenge the validity of a statute which has emerged from the democratic process. The presumption of constitutionality carries three legal consequences. One is the point made in the previous section of the chapter: in choosing between competing, plausible characterizations of a law, the court should normally choose that one that would support the validity of the law. Secondly, where the validity of a law requires a finding of fact (for example, the existence of an emergency), that finding of fact need not be proved strictly by the government; it is enough

84 See generally Monahan, ''At Doctrine's Twilight: The Structure of Canadian Federalism'' (1984) 34 U. Toronto L.J. 47; Swinton, *The Supreme Court and Canadian Federalism* (1990), chs. 5-7.

85 Fuller reasons are offered in ch. 5, Federalism, under heading 5.5, ''Role of the courts'', above.

86 *N.S. Bd. of Censors* v. *McNeil* [1978] 2 S.C.R. 662, 687-688; Magnet, ''The Presumption of Constitutionality'' (1980) 18 Osgoode Hall L.J. 87; Strayer, *The Canadian Constitution and the Courts* (3rd ed., 1988), 251-254; Charles, Cromwell and Jobson, *Evidence and the Charter of Rights and Freedoms* (1989), 35-47.

that there be a "rational basis" for the finding.[87] Thirdly, where a law is open to both a narrow and a wide interpretation, and under the wide interpretation the law's application would extend beyond the powers of the enacting legislative body, the court should "read down" the law so as to confine it to those applications that are within the power of the enacting legislative body.[88] These three doctrines have the effect of reducing judicial interference with the affairs of the legislative branch of government. Where a law is challenged on Charter grounds, as opposed to federal grounds, there is no presumption of constitutionality, except for the third doctrine, "reading down", which also applies in Charter cases. Other than the reading down doctrine, determinations of law and fact in Charter cases are subject to their own set of rules, and those rules are not compatible with a presumption of constitutionality.[89]

15.6 Severance

A statute, however complex, is usually the elaboration of a single legislative plan or scheme. The leading feature of that plan or scheme will be the pith and substance (or the matter) of the entire statute. For constitutional purposes the statute is one law, and it will stand or fall as a whole when its validity is questioned.[90] Occasionally, however, it is possible to say that part only of a statute is invalid, and the balance of the statute would be valid if it stood alone. Of course, the balance does not stand alone; and the question arises whether the court should "sever" the bad part, thereby preserving the good part, or whether the court should declare the entire statute to be bad. The rule which the courts have developed is that severance is inappropriate when the remaining good part "is so inextricably bound up with the part declared invalid that what remains cannot independently survive"; in that event, it may be assumed that the legislative body would not have enacted the remaining part by itself.[91] On the other hand, where the two parts can exist independently of each other, so that it is plausible to regard

87 See ch. 57, Proof, under heading 57.2(f), "Standard of proof", below.

88 See sec. 15.7, "Reading down", later in this chapter.

89 See ch. 35, Limitation of rights, under heading 35.5 "Presumption of constitutionality", below.

90 A "legislative scheme" (as it is called in Australia) exists when a single policy is embodied in more than one statute. In that case, the courts will examine the entire scheme in order to characterize any one statute, and a holding of invalidity will affect all parts of the scheme (the opposite result to severance), e.g., *A.-G. Ont.* v. *Reciprocal Insurers* [1924] A.C. 328; *Re Insurance Act of Canada* [1932] A.C. 41; *Re Alberta Statutes* [1938] S.C.R. 100; affirmed with respect to one statute only in *A.-G. Alta.* v. *A.-G. Can.* (Bank Taxation) [1939] A.C. 117; *Texada Mines* v. *A.-G. B.C.* [1960] S.C.R. 713. This mode of reasoning has not been applied to schemes involving complementary legislation by both levels of government: see ch. 14, Delegation, under heading 14.3, "Federal inter-delegation", above. For a comparative study of legislative schemes in Australia and Canada, see Gilbert, *Australian and Canadian Federalism 1867-1984* (1986), chs. 6, 7.

91 *A.-G. Alta.* v. *A.-G. Can.* (Alta. Bill of Rights) [1947] A.C. 503, 518.

them as two laws with two different ''matters'', then severance is appropriate, because it may be assumed that the legislative body would have enacted one even if it had been advised that it could not enact the other.[92]

The Privy Council and the Supreme Court of Canada have both been difficult to persuade that severance is appropriate. They have usually struck down the entire statute once an adverse conclusion has been reached as to the constitutionality of part. When one considers the large number of cases in which statutes have been held to be unconstitutional, the few cases in which severance has been ordered emphasize how rarely the occasion for its use has been held to arise.[93] Statutes have mostly been held to stand or fall in toto, often without any reference to the possibility of severance. Although the courts have not expressed themselves in these terms, there appears to be a presumption that a statute embodies a single statutory scheme of which all the parts are interdependent. In other words, there seems to be a presumption against severance.

A ''severance clause'' is a section of a statute that provides that, if any part of the statute is judicially held to be unconstitutional, the remainder of the Act is to continue to be effective. At the very least, such a clause should reverse the presumption against severance: instead of the presumption that the various parts of the statute are interdependent and inseverable, the presumption should be that the parts are independent and severable. This is the way severance clauses work in the United States and Australia, where they seem to be more common than they are in Canada.[94] To give some effect to a severance clause seems sound, since the clause indicates the legislative intent with respect to severance, and the courts have always claimed that the inquiry into severability is an inquiry into legislative intent.[95] However, in what seems to be the only Canadian case dealing with a statute containing a severance clause, the Privy Council refused to sever the unconstitutional portion of the statute from the rest. Their lordships applied

---

92 Lederman, *Continuing Canadian Constitutional Dilemmas* (1981), 247-248; Strayer, *The Canadian Constitution and the Courts* (3rd ed., 1988), 301-303.

93 Severance was ordered in *Toronto* v. *York* [1938] A.C. 415; *Roy* v. *Plourde* [1943] S.C.R. 262; *Re s. 5(a) of the Dairy Industry Act* (Margarine) [1949] S.C.R. 1 (the appeal to the Privy Council did not include this issue: *Can. Federation of Agriculture* v. *A.-G. Que.* [1951] 1 A.C. 179); *MacDonald* v. *Vapor Can.* [1977] 2 S.C.R. 134; *N.S. Bd. of Censors* v. *McNeil* [1978] 2 S.C.R. 662; *Re Agricultural Products Marketing Act* [1978] 2 S.C.R. 1198; *Regional Municipality of Peel* v. *McKenzie* [1982] 2 S.C.R. 9. Severance was explicitly refused in *Re Initiative and Referendum Act* [1919] A.C. 935, 944; *A.-G. Can.* v. *A.-G. Ont.* (Unemployment Insurance) [1937] A.C. 355, 367; *A.-G. Man.* v. *A.-G. Can.* (Natural Products Marketing) [1937] A.C. 377, 388-389; *A.-G. Alta.* v. *A.-G. Can.* (Alta. Bill of Rights) [1947] A.C. 503, 518.

94 For the United States, see *Carter* v. *Carter Coal Co.* (1936) 298 U.S. 238, 312-313, 321-322. For Australia, see *Bank of N.S.W.* v. *Commonwealth* (State Banking) (1948) 76 C.L.R. 1, 368-372.

95 To attribute an intention to a deliberative body is artificial enough; when the intention is predicated on a hypothetical situation, the usefulness of the attribution may well be questioned. However, the courts have used this mode of reasoning, and it does convey the sense that severance is an issue closely analogous to statutory interpretation.

the usual rule regarding severance, and seemed to assume that the severance clause (to which their lordships referred) made no difference.[96]

Severance is far more common in Charter cases than in federalism cases. Although the same test is applied, it is highly unusual to find that an entire statute is struck down under the Charter of Rights. Charter review is not based on the pith and substance of a law, but on the question whether either the "purpose" or the "effect" of the law abridges a Charter right.[97] Under this test, it is usually only a single section or a few sections of a statute[98] that abridge a Charter right, and it is usually beyond argument that the rest of the statute can independently survive. For example, it could hardly be argued that the invalidity of the search and seizure power of the Competition Act[99] entailed the striking down of the entire Act, or that the invalidity of the felony-murder rule[100] entailed the striking down of the entire Criminal Code.

There seems to be only one Charter case in the Supreme Court of Canada where the entire statute was struck down, and that was *R.* v. *Big M Drug Mart* (1985),[101] which held that the Lord's Day Act was wholly bad. In other cases the offending provision has been severed from the rest of the statute, usually without argument or discussion.[102] It seems reasonable to conclude that the presumption against severance in federalism cases has been replaced in Charter cases by a presumption in favour of severance. Severance is an important tool of judicial restraint, because it circumscribes the impact of a successful Charter attack on a law. The law that falls is normally only a small portion of the legislative structure, and the rest of the structure remains standing.

15.7 Reading down

The "reading down" doctrine requires that, whenever possible, a statute is to be interpreted as being within the power of the enacting legislative body. What this means in practice is that general language in a statute which is literally apt to extend beyond the power of the enacting Parliament or Legislature will be construed more narrowly so as to keep it within the permissible scope of power. Reading down is simply a canon of construction (or interpretation). It is only

---

96 *A.-G. B.C.* v. *A.-G. Can.* (Natural Products Marketing) [1937] A.C. 377.

97 Note 21, above.

98 Severance can be applied to instuments other than statutes, e.g., *Ross* v. *New Brunswick School District No. 15* [1995] 1 S.C.R. 827 (severing and striking down one part of a human rights tribunal's order as an unjustified infringement of a Charter right).

99 *Hunter* v. *Southam* [1984] 2 S.C.R. 145.

100 *R.* v. *Vaillancourt* [1987] 2 S.C.R. 636.

101 [1985] 1 S.C.R. 295.

102 In some cases, although there is no question of invalidating the entire statute, there is a question as to how much of the statute should be struck down: e.g., *R.* v. *Morgentaler* [1988] 1 S.C.R. 30, 80; *Devine* v. *Que.* [1988] 2 S.C.R. 790, 814. In some cases, the courts have awarded remedies other than severance: see ch. 37, Enforcement of Rights, below.

available where the language of the statute will bear the (valid) limited meaning as well as the (invalid) extended meaning; it then stipulates that the limited meaning be selected. Reading down is like severance in that both techniques mitigate the impact of judicial review; but reading down achieves its remedial purpose solely by the interpretation of the challenged statute, whereas severance involves holding part of the statute to be invalid.[103] Reading down is sometimes said to depend upon a presumption of constitutionality: the enacting legislative body is presumed to have meant to enact provisions which do not transgress the limits of its constitutional powers; general language which appears to transgress the limits must therefore be ''read down'' so that it is confined within the limits.[104]

There are many examples of reading down. The Federal Court Act has been read down to exclude from the jurisdiction of the Federal Court cases that are governed by provincial law, because s. 101 of the Constitution Act, 1867, under which the Federal Court Act was enacted, authorizes the establishment of federal courts only for the purpose of deciding cases governed by federal law.[105] The Family Relations Act of British Columbia, which authorizes the division of family assets on divorce, has been read down to exclude property on an Indian reserve, because the right to property on an Indian reserve is exclusively within federal power.[106] A limitation period in the federal Railway Act has been read down to bar only causes of action created by the Act itself, because the barring of a common law cause of action in tort is exclusively within provincial power.[107] And, as the next section of this chapter[108] will show, provincial statutes have often been read down to exclude federally-regulated undertakings from otherwise valid and ostensibly applicable language.[109]

The general idea that a law should not be held to be wholly invalid just because it overreaches the limits of jurisdiction in certain respects is obviously in accord with a properly restrained role for the courts. Reading down allows the

---

103 Severance is treated in the previous section of this chapter.

104 Reading down is also available to bring a statute into conformity with the Charter of Rights or the Canadian Bill of Rights.

105 E.g., *Que. North Shore Paper Co.* v. *CP* [1977] 2 S.C.R. 1054.

106 *Derrickson* v. *Derrickson* [1986] 1 S.C.R. 285.

107 *Clark* v. *CNR* [1988] 2 S.C.R. 680.

108 Section 15.8, ''Interjurisdictional immunity'', below.

109 For other examples of reading down, see *Re Industrial Relations and Disputes Investigation Act* (Stevedores Reference) [1955] S.C.R. 529, esp. 535, 566, 582 (limiting scope of federal labour relations law); *CBC* v. *Cordeau* [1979] 22 S.C.R. 618, 640 (provincial tribunal's powers read down to exclude s. 96 power to punish for contempt); *The Queen (Man.)* v. *Air Can.* [1980] 2 S.C.R. 303 (provincial sales tax read down to exclude aircraft flying over province); *Friends of Oldman River Society* v. *Can.* [1992] 1 S.C.R. 3 (federal environmental statute read down to limit environmental assessment to matters within federal legislative jurisdiction); *R.* v. *Grant* [1993] 3 S.C.R. 223 (police power to search without warrant read down to apply only in exigent circumstances). On the other hand, a law that is excessively vague and broad so that it cannot be characterized as in relation to a matter within a head of power will not be rehabilitated by a massive exercise in reading down: see *Saumur* v. *Que.* [1953] 2 S.C.R. 299, 333 per Rand J.

bulk of the legislative policy to be accomplished, while trimming off those applications that are constitutionally bad. The trouble is that it is not easy to tell when a law which is valid in most of its applications has trespassed outside its proper field. It must be recalled that the ''pith and substance'' doctrine, exemplified by *Bank of Toronto* v. *Lambe*,[110] is that a law which is in relation to a matter within jurisdiction (in that case taxation) is not objectionable just because it affects a matter outside jurisdiction (in that case banking). The limits of the pith and substance doctrine mark out an ill-defined zone of ''interjurisdictional immunity'', which is discussed in the next section of this chapter.

15.8 Interjurisdictional immunity

(a) Definition

The term interjurisdictional immunity does not have a precise meaning.[111] A law that purports to apply to a matter outside the jurisdiction of the enacting legislative body may be attacked in three different ways. The attack may go to (1) the validity of the law, or (2) the applicability of the law, or (3) the operability of the law.

First, it may be argued that the law is *invalid*, because the matter of the law (or its pith and substance) comes within a class of subjects that is outside the jurisdiction of the enacting legislative body. That is why the provincial law imposing a tax on banks was struck down in the *Alberta Bank Taxation Reference* (1938).[112] The provincial law was classified as in relation to banking (a federal matter), rather than direct taxation in the province (a provincial matter), and was accordingly held to be invalid. The question of validity depends upon the characterization of the law, which has been discussed in earlier sections of this chapter, and will not be revisited in this section of the chapter.

A second way of attacking a law that purports to apply to a matter outside the jurisdiction of the enacting body is to acknowledge that the law is valid in most of its applications, but to argue that the law should be interpreted so as not to apply to the matter that is outside the jurisdiction of the enacting body. If this argument succeeds, the law is not held to be invalid, but simply *inapplicable* to the extra-jurisdictional matter. The technique for limiting the application of the law to matters within jurisdiction is the reading down doctrine, which was discussed in the previous section of this chapter. The occasions when it is appropriate to use the technique will be discussed in this section of the chapter. It is this issue that I treat as interjurisdictional immunity.

---

110 Note 25, above.

111 See Gibson, ''Interjurisdictional Immunity in Canadian Federalism'' (1969) 47 Can. Bar Rev. 40; Elliot, Comment (1988) 67 Can. Bar Rev. 523; Edinger, Comment (1989) 68 Can. Bar Rev. 631.

112 Note 22, above.

A third way of attacking a law that applies to a matter outside the jurisdiction of the enacting body is to argue that the law is *inoperative* through the doctrine of paramountcy. The doctrine of paramountcy stipulates that, where there are inconsistent federal and provincial laws, it is the federal law that prevails; paramountcy renders the provincial law inoperative to the extent of the inconsistency. Thus, paramountcy is a form of attack that is available only against a provincial law, and then only when there is a conflicting federal law in existence. The doctrine of paramountcy is the topic of the next chapter.

It is the second issue — the issue of applicability — that I am treating under the present rubric of interjurisdictional immunity.

(b) Federally-incorporated companies

The idea of interjurisdictional immunity finds its genesis in cases concerning federally-incorporated companies. It has been held that an otherwise valid provincial law may not impair the status or essential powers of a federally-incorporated company. Thus, a provincial law prohibiting all extra-provincial companies from operating in the province,[113] and a provincial law imposing a licensing scheme for the raising of corporate capital,[114] have been "read down" to exempt federally-incorporated companies. On the other hand, provincial laws whose impact on corporate status or powers was deemed less serious have been held applicable to federally-incorporated companies.[115]

(c) Federally-regulated undertakings

From the company cases a similar idea of immunity was carried over to cases concerning federally-regulated undertakings.[116] It is now well settled that undertakings engaged in interprovincial or international transportation or communication, which come within federal jurisdiction under the exceptions to s. 92(10) of the Constitution Act, 1867, are immune from otherwise valid provincial laws which would have the effect of "sterilizing" the undertakings. On this basis,

113 *John Deere Plow Co.* v. *Wharton* [1915] A.C. 330; *Great West Saddlery* v. *The King* [1921] 2 A.C. 91.

114 *A.-G. Man.* v. *A.-G. Can.* (Manitoba Securities) [1929] A.C. 260.

115 *Lymburn* v. *Mayland* [1932] A.C. 318; *Can. Indemnity Co.* v. *A.-G. B.C.* [1977] 2 S.C.R. 504; *Re Upper Churchill Water Rights* [1984] 1 S.C.R. 297. This "status and essential powers" immunity is discussed in ch. 22, Companies, below.

116 The issue is not quite the same. The federal incorporation power does not authorize regulation of the activities of federally-incorporated companies, and therefore there can be no immunity from provincial laws regulating the activities of such companies. Undertakings (whether incorporated federally or provincially or outside Canada or even if unincorporated) operating in fields of federal legislative competence are, by definition, subject to federal regulation of their activities, and therefore some immunity from provincial laws purporting to regulate the activities of such undertakings is possible.

an interprovincial telephone company has been held immune from provincial law requiring the consent of a municipality for the erection of telephone poles and wires,[117] an international bus line has been held immune from provincial regulation as to routes, rates, etc.,[118] and an interprovincial pipeline has been held immune from provincial mechanics liens legislation.[119]

Until 1966, the provincial laws that were held inapplicable to federally-regulated undertakings were laws that asserted a power to sterilize (paralyze or impair) the federally-authorized activity. This possibility, however unlikely in practice, was the basis of each decision. In the *Quebec Minimum Wage* case (1966),[120] the Supreme Court of Canada abandoned the language of sterilization, and held that the Bell Telephone Company (an interprovincial undertaking) was immune from a provincial minimum wage law on the lesser ground that such a law "affects a vital part of the management and operation of the undertaking".[121]

The new "vital part" test carved out a much broader field of immunity from provincial law than the old sterilization test, because the vital part test precluded the application of provincial laws that could not possibly paralyze or even impair the operation of the federally-regulated undertaking. The expansion of the immunity was criticized by commentators, who argued that such an extensive immunity was unnecessary, and undesirable in a federation where so many laws for the protection of workers, consumers and the environment (for example) are enacted and enforced at the provincial level.[122] In the *Quebec Minimum Wage* case itself, the decision meant that workers in federal industries were not protected by minimum wage laws, because at that time there was no federal minimum wage. (There is now.) In a case where there is federal law in existence, the doctrine of paramountcy would of course force any directly conflicting provincial law out of the field, so that no immunity is needed for that situation.

In *Bell Canada* v. *Quebec* (1988),[123] the Supreme Court of Canada reaffirmed its commitment to the vital part test. The case, along with two others decided at

---

117 *Toronto* v. *Bell Telephone Co.* [1905] A.C. 52.

118 *A.-G. Ont.* v. *Winner* [1954] A.C. 541; *Registrar of Motor Vehicles* v. *Can. American Transfer* [1972] S.C.R. 811. On the other hand, less radical regulation, e.g., speed limits and other rules of the road, licence plates, weight limits, etc., are undoubtedly competent to the provinces. The application of provincial laws to aeronautics and to radio and television is discussed in ch. 22, Transportation and Communication, below. With respect to harbours, see *Hamilton Harbour Commrs.* v. *City of Hamilton* (1978) 21 O.R. (2d) 459 (Ont. C.A.) (provincial land-use laws apply).

119 *Campbell-Bennett* v. *Comstock Midwestern* [1954] S.C.R. 207.

120 *Commission du Salaire Minimum* v. *Bell Telephone Co.* [1966] S.C.R. 767.

121 *Id.*, 774 per Martland J. For apt criticism, see Gibson (1969) 47 Can. Bar Rev. 40, 53-56; Weiler (1973) 23 U. Toronto L.J. 307, 340-342; and see ch. 20, Property and Civil Rights, under heading 21.8(b), "Federal power", below.

122 See Gibson, note 111, above, 53-56; Weiler, "The Supreme Court and the Law of Canadian Federalism" (1973) 23 U. Toronto L.J. 307, 340-342; the 2nd ed. (1985) of this book, 329-332, 465-466.

123 [1988] 1 S.C.R. 749.

the same time,[124] presented the question whether provincial occupational health and safety laws could apply to undertakings engaged in interprovincial transportation and communication. The precise question was whether Bell Canada, which is an interprovincial telephone company, was bound in Quebec by a Quebec law that required the protective reassignment of pregnant workers who work with video monitors. The Supreme Court of Canada, in an opinion written by Beetz J., held that the provincial law was constitutionally incapable of applying to the federal undertaking, and had to be read down so that it did not apply to the federal undertaking. Beetz J. acknowledged that a law requiring the reassignment of a small number of workers, like the minimum wage law in the *Quebec Minimum Wage* case, could not paralyze or impair the operation of the federal undertaking. But he held that ''it is sufficient that the provincial statute which purports to apply to the federal undertaking affects a vital or essential part of that undertaking, without necessarily going as far as impairing or paralyzing it''.[125] In his lordship's view, occupational health and safety laws, because they regulated labour relations within a firm, affected a vital part of the management and operation of the firm.[126] Therefore, occupational health and safety laws enacted by a province could not constitutionally apply to a federal undertaking.

In the *Bell Canada* case, Beetz J. rejected the view that there could be concurrent provincial jurisdiction over a vital part of a federal undertaking. In principle, ''a basic, minimum and unassailable content'' had to be assigned to each head of federal legislative power, and, since federal legislative power is exclusive, provincial laws could not affect that unassailable core.[127] In practice, ''twofold jurisdiction'' would encourage a ''proliferation'' of regulations, and the application of the paramountcy rule, far from solving the conflicts between ''rival systems of regulation'', would be a ''source of uncertainty and endless disputes''.[128] With this emphatic language, Beetz J. repudiated the overlapping of authority — the de facto concurrency — that had been urged by the critics of the vital part immunity.[129]

---

124 *CNR* v. *Courtois* [1988] 1 S.C.R. 868 (CNR not bound by provincial law authorizing accident investigation); *Alltrans Express* v. *B.C.* [1988] 1 S.C.R. 897 (Alltrans Express not bound by provincial law requiring safety committee and protective footwear).

125 [1988] 1 S.C.R. 749, 859-860.

126 *Id.*, 762.

127 *Id.*, 839.

128 *Id.*, 843.

129 Note 122, above. In the 2nd edition of this book (1985) I attacked the whole notion of interjurisdictional immunity. Beetz J. quoted extensively from my book, and criticized my views in a detailed fashion more like a law review article than a judgment. My views were also criticized by Elliot, Comment (1988) 67 Can. Bar Rev. 523. I have been persuaded by Beetz J. and Professor Elliot that some degree of interjurisdictional immunity is entailed by the Constitution of Canada's dual lists of exclusive powers. Otherwise, what would be incompetent to a legislative body in a narrowly framed law would be permitted if the law were framed more broadly. That cannot be right. However, I still think that the vital part test casts the immunity too widely. The old sterilization or impairment test would be more appropriate in my view.

Shortly after reaffirming the vital part test in the *Bell Canada* case, the Supreme Court of Canada had to decide whether a Quebec law that prohibited advertising directed at children could apply to advertising on television, which is of course a federally-regulated medium. In *Irwin Toy* v. *Quebec* (1989),[130] the Court held that the law was applicable to advertising on television. The Court acknowledged that advertising was ''a vital part of the operation of a television broadcast undertaking''.[131] But now the Court said that the vital part test applied only to provincial laws that purported to apply *directly* to federal undertakings. Where a provincial law had only an ''indirect effect'' on the undertaking, the law would be inapplicable only if the law impaired, paralyzed or sterilized the undertaking. An indirect effect falling short of impairment, even if it affected a vital part of the undertaking, would not render the provincial law constitutionally inapplicable.[132] In this case, the provincial prohibition on advertising applied to advertisers, not to the media: the advertiser was prohibited from placing the prohibited category of advertising, but the media were not directly prohibited from carrying the advertising.[133] Since the effect of the provincial law on a television undertaking was indirect, it did not matter that the law affected a vital part of the undertaking. Only *impairment* would render the law inapplicable, and the loss of children's advertising could not impair the operation of the television undertaking. Therefore, the provincial law was valid and effective to preclude advertisers in Quebec from placing advertisements directed at children on television.

Irwin Toy constitutes an important qualification of the vital part test, and it makes little sense. If it is the case, as *Bell Canada* held, that any vital part of a federal undertaking is within the unassailable, exclusive core of federal power, upon what basis does that unassailable, exclusive core become vulnerable to the indirect effects of a provincial law? If that core is protected from direct invasion, why should it be exposed to indirect invasion? Dale Gibson[134] speculates that the Court in *Irwin Toy* had become concerned that the vital part test was too tight a restriction on provincial power over federal undertakings operating within the province, and ''saw this new refinement as a way of loosening the constraints''.[135] Gibson argues that it would have been much better to do away with all interjur-

---

130 [1989] 1 S.C.R. 927. The five-judge bench, consisting of Dickson C.J., Beetz, McIntyre, Lamer and Wilson JJ., divided three to two on the Charter issue (the majority upholding the law under s. 1), but were unanimous on the interjurisdictional immunity issue.

131 *Id.*, 957.

132 *Id.*, 955.

133 This had been the basis of the earlier decision in *A.G. Que.* v. *Kellogg's Co. of Can.* [1978] 2 S.C.R. 211, holding that restrictions on advertising directed at children could validly apply to television advertising.

134 Gibson, Comment (1990) 69 Can. Bar Rev. 339.

135 *Id.*, 353. The decision in *Irwin Toy* was rendered only eleven months after the decision in *Bell Canada*, and four of the five judges who sat on *Irwin Toy*, including Beetz J., had also sat on *Bell Canada*.

isdictional immunity of federal undertakings from provincial laws that do not threaten the continuing functioning of the undertakings. I agree with Gibson that this is the only situation where the immunity is needed. What we have instead is the vital part test, which is too broad and too vague, and which is now needlessly complicated by the direct-indirect distinction.

Another suggestion that the Supreme Court of Canada is wavering in its commitment to the vital part test came in *Ontario* v. *Canadian Pacific* (1995).[136] In that case, Canadian Pacific, which operates an interprovincial railway and is an undertaking within federal jurisdiction, was held to be bound by Ontario's Environmental Protection Act. The company was under an obligation, provided by the federal Railway Act, to keep its right-of-way free of dead grass, weeds and other unnecessary combustible matter. In order to accomplish this task on the part of the right-of-way that ran through the town of Kenora, the company conducted a controlled burning of the dry grass on the right-of-way. Some smoke escaped into adjoining residential areas, causing a nuisance to the residents and provoking complaints. The company was charged with discharging a contaminant into the natural environment in breach of the Ontario Act. The Ontario Court of Appeal held that the Act validly applied to the company.[137] The Court pointed out that there were other ways of keeping the right-of-way clear of combustible matter, so that ''controlled burning [was] not essential to the [company's] ability to fulfil its statutory mandate''.[138] The Court also held that the Act was not aimed at the management and control of an undertaking.[139] These tests were much more favourable to the application of the provincial law than the vital part test, which the Court never recited or attempted to apply. And yet it could hardly be doubted that the right-of-way was a vital part of the railway, and that a provincial law that regulated the clearance of the right-of-way affected a vital part of the operation of the railway. The company appealed to the Supreme Court of Canada, which dismissed the appeal on this issue orally without written reasons.[140] The Court's brief oral explanation did not indicate how the outcome could be reconciled with the vital part test.[141]

---

136 [1995] 2 S.C.R. 1028.

137 (1993) 13 O.R. (3d) 389 (C.A.).

138 *Id.*, 393.

139 *Id.*, 397-398.

140 The Court did write at length on whether the Environmental Protection Act was unconstitutionally vague or overbroad: [1995] 2 S.C.R. 1028, 1031.

141 The Court, while affirming the decision of the Court of Appeal, did not express any approval of the reasons of the Court of Appeal. What Lamer C.J. said at the conclusion of the oral argument was: ''We are all of the view that the judgment *CPR* v. *Notre Dame de Bonsecours* [1899] A.C. 367 governs the first issue in this appeal and, accordingly, the appeal with respect to that ground fails'': [1995] 2 S.C.R. 1028, 1029. The *Bonsecours* case had not been referred to by the Court of Appeal. In that case, the Privy Council decided that the Canadian Pacific Railway had to comply with a municipal order, made under provincial law, to clear a drainage ditch on its right-of-way; the ditch was blocked and flooding adjacent land. The case is similar to the 1995 appeal, but one might wonder whether it is still good law since the vital part test

(d) Other federal matters

The doctrine of interjurisdictional immunity also applies outside the fields of transportation and communication.[142] Provincial labour laws have been held inapplicable to postal workers[143] and to teachers on a military base.[144] A provincial driving licence requirement has been held inapplicable to members of the armed forces.[145] Provincial laws respecting inquiries and police discipline have been held inapplicable to the Royal Canadian Mounted Police.[146] A variety of provincial laws respecting hunting, adoption and family property have been held inapplicable to Indians or on Indian reserves.[147] A provincial bus licence requirement has been held inapplicable to a bus service provided by a federal agency in a federal park.[148] A municipal by-law prohibiting the display of signs on residential property has been held inapplicable to federal election signs.[149]

(e) Rationale of immunity

These interjurisdictional immunity cases do not concern provincial laws that single out federal undertakings, works, persons or services for special treatment.[150] On the contrary, in every case the provincial law that was held inapplicable was a law of general application that was indisputably valid in most of its applications. Nor were the decisions based on the paramountcy doctrine: in most of the cases, there was no competing federal law in existence.[151] The theory behind

---

was unknown in 1899, having been invented in 1966 by the Supreme Court of Canada with no prior judicial support (as explained in the text accompanying note 121, above).

142 Not covered in the list that follows are the Crown: see. ch. 10, The Crown, under heading 10.9, "Federal complications", above; and taxation: see ch. 30, Taxation, under heading 30.12, "Interjurisdictional taxation", below.

143 *Re Minimum Wage Act (Sask.)* [1948] S.C.R. 248; *Letter Carriers' Union of Can.* v. *Can. Union of Postal Workers* [1975] 1 S.C.R. 178.

144 *A.G. Can.* v. *St.-Hubert Base Teachers' Assn.* [1983] 1 S.C.R. 498.

145 *R.* v. *Anderson* (1930) 54 C.C.C. 321 (Man. C.A.).

146 *A.G. Que. and Keable* v. *A.G. Can.* [1979] 1 S.C.R. 218; *A.G. Alta.* v. *Putnam* [1981] 2 S.C.R. 267.

147 See ch. 27, Aboriginal Peoples, under heading 27.2, "Provincial legislative power", below.

148 *National Battlefields Commn.* v. *CTCUQ* [1990] 2 S.C.R. 838.

149 *McKay* v. *The Queen* [1965] S.C.R. 798.

150 Singling out would not by itself be a ground of invalidity, but would be a factor indicating that the law should be characterized as "in relation to" the federal undertaking: sec. 15.5(b), "Singling out", above.

151 The rationale of the old cases giving immunity to federally-incorporated companies is equivocal, and Ziegel takes the view that they are based on paramountcy: Ziegel in Ziegel (ed.), *Canadian Company Law* (1967), 165-167. This view involves an extremely broad definition of the inconsistency which will suffice to trigger the paramountcy doctrine, and the recent cases on paramountcy have insisted upon an extremely narrow definition: see ch. 16, Paramountcy, below. The recent interjurisdictional immunity decisions are not based on paramountcy: see *Re Minimum Wage Act (Sask.)* [1948] S.C.R. 248, 253, 257, 269; *Campbell-Bennett* v. *Comstock*

the results is that each head of federal power not only grants power to the federal Parliament but, being exclusive, denies power to the provincial Legislatures. There is no doubt, of course, that a provincial law (or municipal by-law) that specifically prohibited the posting of federal election signs would be invalid, because it would be characterized as in relation to a federal matter (federal elections). The doctrine of interjurisdictional immunity insists that the same result cannot be accomplished by the enactment of a broader law that, by reason of its non-federal applications, could be characterized as in relation to a provincial matter (land use).[152]

The difficulty is to distinguish the occasions when the interjurisdictional immunity doctrine applies from the occasions when the pith and substance doctrine applies. The pith and substance doctrine, it will be recalled, stipulates that a law ''in relation to'' a provincial matter may validly ''affect'' a federal matter.[153] Thus, the *McKay* case (1965),[154] which is the case that held that a municipal sign law could not extend to federal election signs, may be contrasted with the *Oil, Chemical Workers* case (1963),[155] which decided that a provincial prohibition on union donations to political parties could validly prohibit donations to federal as well as provincial parties. A similar decision was given in the *OPSEU* case (1987),[156] where the Court held that a provincial law prohibiting provincial public servants from running as candidates in elections could validly prohibit participation in federal as well as provincial elections.

The pith and substance doctrine, which allows a provincial law to ''affect'' a federal matter, is applied much more frequently than the interjurisdictional immunity doctrine, which reads down the provincial law to exclude the federal matter. As well as the *Oil Chemical Workers* and *OPSEU* cases, there are many other well-known examples.[157] The leading case is, of course, *Bank of Toronto* v. *Lambe* (1887),[158] which decided that a provincial tax could validly apply to a bank, although a bank is a federal undertaking. Provincial taxes do of course routinely apply to federal undertakings operating in the province. Provincial workers compensation laws also apply to federal undertakings.[159] Provincial labour laws have been held to apply to a contractor building a runway for an airport (a federal undertaking) on federal Crown land (also within federal jurisdiction),[160]

Midwestern [1954] S.C.R. 207, 222; *Commission du Salaire Minimum* v. *Bell Telephone Co.* [1966] S.C.R. 767, 771, 776-777; *Natural Parents* v. *Superintendent of Child Welfare* [1976] 2 S.C.R. 751, 760-761; *Bell Can.* v. *Que.* [1988] 1 S.C.R. 749, 867.

152 *McKay* v. *The Queen* [1965] S.C.R. 798. The restriction on freedom of expression would now attract a Charter attack as well.

153 Section 15.5(a), ''Matter'', above.

154 Note 152, above.

155 *Oil, Chemical and Atomic Workers* v. *Imperial Oil* [1963] S.C.R. 584.

156 *OPSEU* v. *Ont.* [1987] 2 S.C.R. 2.

157 Note 26, above.

158 Note 25, above.

159 *Workman's Comp. Bd.* v. *CPR* [1920] A.C. 184.

160 *Construction Montcalm* v. *Minimum Wage Commn.* [1979] 1 S.C.R. 754.

and to a business owned by Indians on an Indian reserve (within federal jurisdiction).[161] A provincial limitation statute has been held applicable to an action against a interprovincial railway (a federal undertaking).[162]

In the *Bell Canada* case,[163] Beetz J. made an effort to define the boundary between the pith and substance doctrine, on the one hand, and the interjurisdictional immunity doctrine, on the other. He suggested that the inapplicability to federal undertakings of provincial occupational safety laws was "one facet of a more general rule", which he expressed in these terms:[164]

> Works, such as federal railways, things, such as land reserved for Indians, and persons, such as Indians, who are within the special and exclusive jurisdiction of Parliament, are still subject to provincial statutes that are general in their application, . . . provided however that the application of these provincial laws does not bear upon those subjects in what makes them specifically of federal jurisdiction.

According to this formulation, provincial laws may validly extend to federal subjects unless the laws "bear upon those subjects in what makes them specifically of federal jurisdiction". This formulation seems to involve a judicial judgment as to the severity of the impact of a provincial law on the federal subject to which the law ostensibly extends. If the provincial law would affect the "basic, minimum and unassailable" core of the federal subject, then the interjurisdictional immunity doctrine stipulates that the law must be restricted in its application (read down) to exclude the federal subject. If, on the other hand, the provincial law does not intrude heavily on the federal subject, then the pith and substance doctrine stipulates that the provincial law may validly apply to the federal subject.

(f) Provincial entities

The cases discussed to this point have all concerned the impact of *provincial* laws on federally-incorporated companies, federally-regulated undertakings and other federal persons or subjects. There is no case applying the doctrine of interjurisdictional immunity to *federal* laws in order to protect provincially-incorporated companies or provincially-regulated undertakings. The doctrine ought to be reciprocal, because the provincial heads of legislative power are just as exclusive as the federal heads of legislative power, although it is true that the federal heads are paramount in the event of conflict between federal and provincial laws.[165] There have occasionally been suggestions that the doctrine is reciprocal,[166]

161 *Four B Manufacturing* v. *United Garment Workers* [1980] 1 S.C.R. 1031.

162 *Clark* v. *CNR* [1988] 2 S.C.R. 680.

163 Note 123, above.

164 [1988] 1 S.C.R. 749, 762.

165 The existence of the paramountcy doctrine cuts both ways. On the one hand, it attributes a superior force to federal power. On the other hand, it suggests the need to protect provincial undertakings from federal law. The federal Parliament can protect its creatures from provincial

but the weight of authority is the other way.[167] Probably, therefore, a federal law in relation to a federal matter may validly extend to the status or essential powers of a provincially-incorporated company, or to the vital part of a provincially-regulated undertaking.

15.9 Interpretation of Constitution

(a) Relevance

Once the matter (or pith and substance) of a challenged law has been identified, the second stage in judicial review is to assign the matter to one of the "classes of subjects" (or heads of legislative power) specified in the Constitution. What is involved here, of course, is the interpretation of the power-distributing language of the Constitution. This is the principal topic of many of the succeeding chapters and so nothing need be said in this chapter about the meaning of particular heads of power. However, there are certain general principles which cut across particular heads of power, and which will be treated in this chapter.

(b) Exclusiveness

Each list of classes of subjects in s. 91 or s. 92 of the Constitution Act, 1867 is exclusive to the Parliament or Legislature to which it is assigned.[168] This means that a particular "matter" will come within a class of subjects in only one list. One corollary of exclusiveness is that if either the Parliament or a Legislature fails to legislate to the full limit of its power this does not have the effect of augmenting the powers of the other level of government.[169] However, the exclu-

---

law by enacting protective laws that will be paramount over conflicting provincial laws. The provincial Legislatures cannot do this.

166 *Caron* v. *The King* [1924] A.C. 999, 1006 (by "parity of reason" the immunity should be reciprocal); *City of Medicine Hat* v. *A.G. Can.* (1985) 18 D.L.R. (4th) 428 (Alta. C.A.) (assuming that vital part test applied to municipality, but holding that federal law did not affect vital part of municipality); Elliot, Comment (1988) 67 Can. Bar Rev. 523, 542 (citing cases where federal laws were read down).

167 Chapter 10, The Crown, under heading 10.9(f), "Federal laws binding provincial Crown", above.

168 This is explicit in the opening words of ss. 91 and 92 and the other power-conferring sections, except for ss. 92A(3), 94A and 95, which confer concurrent powers. Concurrency in the Constitution is discussed in sec. 15.9(d), "Concurrency", below.

169 *Union Colliery Co.* v. *Bryden* [1899] A.C. 580, 588. It is obvious that the powers of one level of government cannot expand or contract depending upon the absence or presence of laws enacted by the other level of government. Nonetheless, courts do occasionally make reference to the absence or presence of such laws, and it seems likely that in practice they are sometimes influenced in favour of validity by the failure of the other jurisdiction to act. See *Fulton* v. *Energy Resources Conservation Bd.* [1981] 1 S.C.R. 153, 162, 164 (explicit references to federal legislative inaction with implication that provincial power augmented).

siveness of the two lists does not mean that similar or even identical laws may not be enacted by both levels of government. Some laws are available to both levels, but that is because such laws have a double aspect (or two matters),[170] not because the classes of subjects duplicate or overlap each other; they do not.[171]

On the face of it, the terse descriptions of the classes of subjects (or heads of power) appear to give rise to a good deal of duplication and overlapping. For example, "property and civil rights in the province" (s. 92(13)) appears apt to include "the regulation of trade and commerce" (s. 91(2)). The courts have dealt with this kind of apparent overlapping by interpreting each head of power as excluding the other. Thus, "trade and commerce" has been narrowed down to interprovincial or international trade and commerce, while "property and civil rights" has been interpreted as including the regulation of only local trade and commerce. Similar accommodations have been made between "property and civil rights" and other heads of federal power, such as "interest" (s. 91(19)) and "bankruptcy and insolvency" (s. 91(21)). Another case of apparent overlapping is the federal class of subject "marriage and divorce" (s. 91(26)) and the provincial class "the solemnization of marriage in the province" (s. 92(12)). In all these cases the courts have narrowed the meaning of the broader class in order to exclude the narrower class. This process of "mutual modification"[172] is necessary in order to place each head of power in its context as part of two mutually exclusive lists.[173]

(c) Ancillary power

In the United States and Australia, the enumerated federal powers include an "ancillary" power. For the United States Congress, it is a power "to make all laws which shall be necessary and proper for carrying into execution the foregoing [enumerated] powers".[174] For the Australian Parliament, it is a power to make laws with respect to "matters incidental to the execution of any power vested by this Constitution in the Parliament".[175] In the United States and Australia, there

170 Section 15.5(c), "Double aspect", above. The pith and substance doctrine occasionally has the same effect, in that a provision that would normally be within the jurisdiction of the provinces (e.g., custody of children) may be validly enacted federally as part of a law the pith and substance of which comes within the jurisdiction of the federal Parliament (e.g., divorce): see *Papp* v. *Papp* [1970] 1 O.R. 331 (Ont. C.A.) and discussion of ancillary power in the next section of this chapter.

171 There is one arguable violation of this proposition, namely, the taxation powers of ss. 91(3) and 92(2): see ch. 30, Taxation, under heading 30.1(b), "For provincial purposes", below.

172 Lederman, *Continuing Canadian Constitutional Dilemmas* (1981), 243.

173 In the Constitutions of the United States, and Australia, where only the federal powers are enumerated (note 9, above), there is no similar basis for limiting the scope of the enumerated powers, with the result in both countries of a more expansive interpretation of federal powers than has occurred in Canada.

174 Constitution of the United States, art. 1, s. 8, cl. 18.

175 Constitution of Australia, s. 51(39).

is no list of enumerated state powers: the states simply retain a general residuary power of legislation,[176] and so there is no ancillary clause applicable to the states.

The Constitution of Canada does not include an ancillary power in the enumerated powers of either the federal Parliament or the provincial Legislatures. There have been suggestions from time to time that an ancillary power should be implied.[177] The better view, however, is that no such power is needed. The pith and substance doctrine enables a law that is classified as "in relation to" a matter within the competence of the enacting body to have incidental or ancillary effects on matters outside the competence of the enacting body. With respect to those incidental or ancillary effects, legislative power is, of course, concurrent rather than exclusive, but it does not seem to be necessary or helpful to introduce the concept of an ancillary power to explain results that can just as easily be regarded as flowing from well-established rules of classification.

The existence of an ancillary power was rejected as redundant in *A.-G. Can.* v. *Nykorak* (1962),[178] in which the Supreme Court of Canada upheld legislation which conferred on the federal Crown a civil right of action for loss of the services of an injured serviceman. Judson J. for a majority of the Court said that "legislation of this kind comes squarely under head 7 of s. 91 [the defence power], notwithstanding the fact that it may incidentally affect property and civil rights within the province". And he added that it was "meaningless" to rely on a "necessarily incidental" (or ancillary) doctrine to support the effect on property and civil rights.[179]

The same point was made by Laskin J.A., sitting alone as the Ontario Court of Appeal, in *Papp* v. *Papp* (1970).[180] In upholding the custody provisions of the federal Divorce Act, his lordship said that he did not favour the language of "necessarily incidental" or "ancillary" to explain the valid impact of a federal law in relation to "divorce" on a provincial matter, such as custody of children:[181]

> Where there is admitted competence, as there is here, to legislate to a certain point, the question of limits (where that point is passed) is best answered by asking whether there is a rational, functional connection between what is admittedly good and what is challenged.

Laskin J.A.'s "rational, functional connection" (or rational connection test, as it will hereafter be described) allows each enumerated head of power to embrace laws that have some impact on matters entrusted to the other level of government, and it provides a flexible standard which gives the enacting body considerable

---

176 Constitution of the United States, tenth amendment; Constitution of Australia, s. 107.

177 *Grand Trunk Ry.* v. *A.G. Can.* [1907] A.C. 65, 68; *R.* v. *Thomas Fuller Construction* [1980] 1 S.C.R. 695, 713; *Fowler* v. *The Queen* [1980] 2 S.C.R. 213, 224, 226; *Regional Municipality of Peel* v. *MacKenzie* [1982] 2 S.C.R. 9, 18.

178 [1962] S.C.R. 331.

179 *Id.*, 335. This dictum was cited with approval in *Papp* v. *Papp* (following text) and *A.-G. Can.* v. *CN Transportation* [1983] 2 S.C.R. 206, 228 per Laskin C.J.

180 [1970] 1 O.R. 331 (Ont. C.A.).

181 *Id.*, 335-336 (page 336 starts at "whether").

leeway to choose the legislative techniques it deems appropriate, while providing a judicial check on an unjustified usurpation of powers. In other words, the rational connection test directly confronts the appropriate questions in interpreting a federal constitution. Not being burdened with the complication of an express ancillary power, why should Canadian courts invent one?

The rational connection test has been applied in two recent decisions of the Supreme Court of Canada. In *R.* v. *Zelensky* (1978),[182] in which the Supreme Court of Canada upheld a provision in the federal Criminal Code authorizing the payment of compensation to a victim of crime, Laskin C.J. for the majority of the Court cited *Papp* v. *Papp* and employed the rational connection test to reject the argument that the criminal law power would not authorize the quasi-civil sanction of compensation.[183] In *Multiple Access* v. *McCutcheon* (1982),[184] the Supreme Court of Canada, in a majority opinion written by Dickson J., upheld a provision of federal corporation law granting a civil remedy for insider trading, on the basis that the provision had a ''rational, functional connection'' with company law.[185]

It would be nice if the discussion of the ancillary power (or rather its absence) could stop at this harmonious point. But, alas, there are some discordant notes to be reported. In several cases, the same Supreme Court of Canada that decided *Zelensky* and *Multiple Access* has referred to an ancillary power.[186] This would not matter — it would just be a question of semantics — if the ancillary power were defined by reference to the rational connection test in *Papp* v. *Papp*. But the references have been accompanied by some heretical doctrine. The most puzzling reference occurs in the dissenting opinion of Laskin C.J. in *A.-G. Que.* v. *Kellogg's Company* (1978),[187] a case in which the majority of the Court held that a provincial law regulating advertising directed at children could validly apply to advertising on television (television being within federal jurisdiction). In dissenting from this result, Laskin C.J. said that ''in so far as the British North America Act may be said to recognize an ancillary power or a power to pass legislation necessarily incidental to enumerated powers, such a power resides only in the Parliament of Canada''.[188] The acknowledgement that there may be an ancillary power after all is surprising, coming from Laskin C.J., who had of course expressly rejected the concept in *Papp* v. *Papp*. The further suggestion that the ancillary power (if it exists) applies only to the federal Parliament is even more surprising. The rational connection test of *Papp* v. *Papp* applies with equal force to provincial as to federal powers, and there are many cases in which provincial laws, held to be in relation to a matter coming within a provincial class of subject, have been held to have a valid incidental effect on a matter within

182 [1978] 2 S.C.R. 940.
183 *Id.*, 955.
184 [1982] 2 S.C.R. 161.
185 *Id.*, 183.
186 Note 177, above.
187 [1978] 2 S.C.R. 211.
188 *Id.*, 216.

federal jurisdiction.[189] I think it is plain both on principle[190] and on authority that the provincial enumerated powers have exactly the same capacity as the federal enumerated powers to ''affect'' matters allocated to the other level of government.[191]

In *R.* v. *Thomas Fuller Construction* (1979),[192] the Supreme Court of Canada held that the Federal Court Act could not confer on the Federal Court jurisdiction to determine an issue of provincial law raised by a third party notice issued in proceedings that otherwise raised issues of federal law. Pigeon J. for the majority referred to ''the ancillary power doctrine'' and said that it was ''limited to what is truly *necessary* for the effective exercise of Parliament's legislative authority''.[193] This is obviously a much stricter test than the rational connection test of *Papp* v. *Papp*, and indeed the result of the case was to impose an inconveniently restrictive interpretation on the federal Parliament's power to establish federal courts under s. 101 of the Constitution Act, 1867.[194] It is tempting to dismiss *Fuller Construction* as an aberration to be explained by the Court's hostility to federal jurisdiction, but the dictum on the ancillary power was cited with approval in *Regional Municipality of Peel* v. *MacKenzie* (1982).[195] In that case, the Court held that the federal Parliament's criminal law power would not extend so far as to impose upon a municipality an obligation to contribute to the support of a juvenile delinquent. Martland J. for a unanimous Court, after citing the *Fuller Construction* dictum,[196] held that it had not been ''demonstrated that it is essential to the operation of the legislative scheme provided in the Juvenile Delinquents Act that the cost of supporting juvenile delinquents must be borne by the municipalities''.[197] Clearly, the stipulation that the impugned provision be ''essential'' to the legislative scheme is stricter than the rational connection test of *Papp* v. *Papp*.

---

189 The cases cited in note 26, above, include more provincial laws than federal laws. If there was any room for doubt before the *Kellogg's* case, it has certainly been resolved by the *Kellogg's* case itself and by the later decisions in *Construction Montcalm* and *Four B Manufacturing* (both cited in note 26), in both of which Laskin C.J. also dissented.

190 Laskin C.J.'s statement may have been an importation of doctrine from the United States or Australia, where only the federal Congress or Parliament is empowered by a list of enumerated powers: notes 173-176, above. In Canada, where both the federal Parliament and the provincial Legislatures are empowered by lists of enumerated powers, there is no basis for a distinction.

191 This statement in the 2nd edition (1985) was approved by Dickson C.J. for the Court in *General Motors* v. *City National Leasing* [1989] 1 S.C.R. 641, 670.

192 [1980] 1 S.C.R. 695.

193 *Id.*, 713 (emphasis in original).

194 The decision is criticized in ch. 7, Courts, under heading 7.2(b), ''Federal Court of Canada'', above.

195 [1982] 2 S.C.R. 9.

196 *Id.*, 18. He also referred to *Fowler* v. *The Queen* [1980] 2 S.C.R. 213 (pollution of water frequented by fish outside federal power over fisheries), where the phrase ''necessarily incidental'' is used (at pp. 224, 226).

197 *Id.*, 19.

In *General Motors* v. *City National Leasing* (1989),[198] Dickson C.J. for a unanimous Court attempted to reconcile the various approaches that the Court had taken to defining the extent of the legislative power to affect matters outside the competence of the enacting body. Dickson C.J. said: ''As the seriousness of the encroachment on provincial powers varies, so does the test required to ensure that an appropriate constitutional balance is maintained''.[199] According to this theory, the Court must measure the degree of encroachment of a legislative scheme on the other government's sphere of power, and then the Court must determine how necessary the impugned provision is to the otherwise valid legislative scheme.[200] For minor encroachments, the rational connection test is appropriate. For major encroachments, a stricter test (such as ''truly necessary'' or ''essential'') is appropriate. In the *General Motors* case itself, the impugned law was the civil remedy in the federal competition statute. This law did intrude into provincial power over property and civil rights, but only ''in a limited way''. Therefore, it was sufficient to test the validity of the law by the rational connection test, and applying that test the Court upheld the validity of the civil remedy.[201] The rational connection to the legislative scheme was that the civil remedy, by providing a means and an incentive to private enforcement, would improve the efficacy of the competition law.

The *General Motors* judgment is a valiant attempt to give coherence to the inconsistent approaches of the Court. With respect, however, it is not satisfactory. If a provision is a rational, functional part of a federal legislative scheme, why should it be regarded as ''encroaching'' or ''intruding'' on provincial powers? Indeed, it may be doubted whether the provincial Legislatures would have been competent to enact the civil remedy provision that was under attack, since its purpose was to improve the enforcement of a federal law. The idea of encroachment or intrusion, however appealing in common sense, does not stand up to analysis. If I am wrong on this, there still remain serious difficulties. How is the encroachment or intrusion, once found, to be measured? And, once measured, how is the unique test for validity[202] to be formulated for that particular encroachment or intrusion? In my view, the *General Motors* approach makes the answer to a simple question too complicated, too discretionary, and therefore too unpredictable.

The two different ways of viewing the ancillary aspects of legislative competence are nicely illustrated by the two concurring judgments in *Re GST* (1992).[203] In that case, the Supreme Court of Canada upheld the collection provisions of the federal Goods and Services Tax, which involved payment of tax

198 [1989] 1 S.C.R. 641.

199 *Id.*, 671.

200 *Id.*, 668-669.

201 *Id.*, 683-684.

202 *Id.*, 669. (''A careful case by case assessment of the proper test is the best approach.'')

203 [1992] 3 S.C.R. 445.

on the value added to a good or service at each stage of production and distribution. Faithful to the approach in *General Motors*, Lamer C.J. for the majority said that the provisions (whose only purpose was to collect the federal tax) were an ''intrusion upon provincial jurisdiction'',[204] but he upheld the provisions under what he described as the ''necessarily incidental'' doctrine.[205] La Forest J.'s concurring opinion was, with respect, the more orthodox one. He avoided all language implying an intrusion upon provincial jurisdiction. Once it was determined that the GST was a valid federal tax, it was ''of no moment'' that the collection provisions affected property and civil rights.[206]

The proper course for the Court is to return to the true path marked out by *Nykorak*, *Papp*, *Zelensky* and *Multiple Access*. Each head of legislative power, whether federal or provincial, authorizes all provisions that have a rational connection to the exercise of that head of power. There is no theoretical or practical need for a separate ancillary power. The rational connection test is to be preferred to stricter alternatives, such as the ''truly necessary'' or ''essential'' tests, simply because it is less strict. The more liberal test respects the limits imposed by the Constitution's distribution of powers by requiring a rational connection, but it still allows considerable leeway to the legislative judgment of both the federal Parliament and the provincial Legislatures. It thus accords with the refrain of this text in favour of judicial restraint.

(d) Concurrency

As noted in the earlier section of this chapter on ''Exclusiveness'',[207] in the Canadian Constitution most of the classes of subjects (heads of legislative power) are exclusive to the Parliament or Legislature to which they are assigned. There are, however, three provisions that explicitly confer concurrent powers. First, s. 92A(2) of the Constitution Act, 1867 (added in 1982) confers on the provincial Legislatures the power to make laws in relation to the export of natural resources, and s. 92A(3) is explicit that the power is concurrent with the federal Parliament's trade and commerce power. Secondly, s. 94A (added in 1951 and revised in 1964) confers on the federal Parliament the power to make laws in relation to old age pensions and supplementary benefits, and the section acknowledges the existence of concurrent provincial power. Thirdly, s. 95 confers on both the federal Parliament and the provincial Legislatures concurrent powers over agriculture and immigration. These three provisions[208] obviously cover only a small portion of

---

204 *Id.*, 471.
205 *Id.*, 469.
206 *Id.*, 490.
207 Section 15.6(b), ''Exclusiveness'', above
208 A fourth case of concurrency could be added, although the concurrency is not express: the provincial taxing powers of s. 92(2) and s. 92A(4) are effectively concurrent with the federal taxing power of s. 91(3): see ch. 30, Taxation, at note 2, below.

the field of legislative power. In the Canadian scheme of distribution, exclusivity is the rule and concurrency the exception.

It is otherwise in the United States and Australia, where concurrency is the rule and exclusivity the exception. In each of the American and Australian Constitutions there is a single list of subjects of legislation; that list is allotted to the federal Congress or Parliament, but for the most part the listed subjects are concurrent with the states. The states do not have a list of powers at all: they simply retain the plenary powers which they possessed prior to the union.[209] This is the contrast which is emphasized in the common description of the American or Australian federal government as being one ''of enumerated powers''. It follows that the American or Australian states, as well as possessing exclusive residual power, also possess concurrent power over most of the topics which have been allotted to the federal Congress or Parliament. The states are free to legislate upon these topics unless and until the federal Congress or Parliament decides to exercise its power. Once a federal law has been enacted, of course, the federal law will prevail over any inconsistent state law.[210] If the federal law is deemed to be comprehensive on a particular topic, state legislation on that topic is precluded altogether; in that case, the federal power, although still formally concurrent, becomes practically exclusive.

The contrast between the two exclusive lists of Canada and the single concurrent list of the United States or Australia is not as sharp as might be thought. There is, in practice, a substantial area of concurrency in Canada, even with respect to topics covered by the two exclusive lists. This result flows from two doctrines that have been explained earlier in this chapter. The first is the ''double aspect'' doctrine, which recognizes that a law may have a double aspect, that is, one aspect (or characteristic) coming within the federal list, and another aspect coming within the provincial list. For example, a law prohibiting careless driving has a criminal (federal) aspect and a highway regulation (provincial) aspect. Such a law is competent to both levels of government. Upon this and other legislative subjects with double aspects, there is in practice concurrent legislative power.[211]

The second judge-made doctrine that leads to concurrency is the ''pith and substance'' doctrine. Under that doctrine, if the ''pith and substance'' of a law comes within the list of the legislative body that enacted it, then the law is valid, and it is no objection to the law that it also incidentally regulates a matter falling within the other list. For example, the custody of children may be regulated incidentally under the federal divorce power, although the custody of children is

---

209 The federal enumerated powers are in art. 1, s. 8, of the United States Constitution and in ss. 51, 52 of the Australian Constitution. The states' plenary power is in the tenth amendment to the United States Constitution and in s. 107 of the Australian Constitution.

210 Federal paramountcy has been held to be implicit in the supremacy clause (art. 6, clause 2) of the United States Constitution, and is explicit in s. 109 of the Australian Constitution.

211 Section 15.5(c), ''Double aspect'', above.

otherwise a matter coming within provincial competence. This is one of many subjects upon which legislative power is in practice concurrent.[212]

Whenever legislative power is concurrent, there is the possibility of conflict between federal and provincial laws. In Canada, as in the United States and Australia, conflict between federal and provincial (or state) laws is resolved by a rule of federal paramountcy. Paramountcy is the topic of the next chapter of this book.

(e) Exhaustiveness

As has been explained in chapter 12, Parliamentary Sovereignty, the distribution of powers between the federal Parliament and the provincial Legislatures is exhaustive: the totality of legislative power is distributed between the federal Parliament and the provincial Legislatures. As the earlier chapter explained, there are important exceptions to the doctrine of exhaustive distribution, including the subjects protected by the Charter of Rights. But the exceptions have not eaten up the rule, and the rule is still helpful in understanding the structure of the Constitution.

It goes without saying that the framers of the Constitution could not foresee every kind of law which has subsequently been enacted; nor could they foresee social, economic and technological developments which have required novel forms of regulation. But they did make provision for new or unforeseen kinds of laws. The last of the enumerated provincial classes of subjects in s. 92 is ''generally all matters of a merely local or private nature in the province'' (s. 92(16)). And for matters which do not come within this or any other enumerated class of subjects, the opening words of s. 91 give to the federal Parliament the residuary power ''to make laws for the peace, order, and good government of Canada in relation to all matters not coming within the classes of subjects assigned exclusively to the Legislatures of the Provinces''. Thus, any matter which does not come within any of the specific classes of subjects will be provincial if it is merely local or private (s. 92(16)) and will be federal if it has a national dimension (s. 91, opening words).[213]

The consequence that is usually claimed to flow from the principle of exhaustive distribution is that every conceivable law is competent to one level of government or the other. That is generally true. But a law that is excessively broad or vague will be incompetent to both levels of government. A law must be sufficiently particular that it can be attributed to a ''matter'' coming within one of the classes of subjects in relation to which the enacting body is authorized to legislate. In *Saumur* v. *Quebec* (1953),[214] Rand J. articulated this doctrine as one

212 The pith and substance doctrine is discussed from this point of view in sec. 15.5(a), ''Matter'', above, and sec. 15.9(c), ''Ancillary power'', above.

213 See ch. 17, Peace, Order, and Good Government, below.

214 [1953] 2 S.C.R. 299.

reason for striking down a municipal by-law that forbade the distribution of literature on the streets of Quebec City without the permission of the chief of police. The by-law could have been administered as a mechanism for the regulation of the streets to prevent harassment of pedestrians and reduce littering, but the evidence showed that the by-law was in fact administered as a vehicle of censorship by the chief of police, whose decisions were based on his attitude towards the contents of the material to be distributed. For Rand J., the absence of any standards in the by-law to guide the chief of police's discretion was, by itself, fatal to the validity of the by-law. Without more precision in the drafting of the by-law, it was impossible to classify it as in relation to any particular matter.[215]

It might perhaps have been thought that a law that did not fit into any of the enumerated classes of subjects (including s. 92(16)) would come within the federal Parliament's residuary peace, order, and good government power. Again, that is generally true. But in the *Anti-Inflation Reference* (1976),[216] Beetz J., speaking for the majority of the Court on this issue (he dissented from the result), denied that a topic as broad as "the containment and reduction of inflation" could be authorized by the peace, order, and good government power. Except in times of emergency, even the p.o.g.g. power would embrace a new matter only where it "was not an aggregate but had a degree of unity that made it indivisible, an identity which made it distinct from provincial matters and a sufficient consistence to retain the bounds of form".[217] The point is that the federal Parliament should not be able to extend its authority into fields of provincial competence by enacting laws upon subjects so diffuse and pervasive that they do not fit within any enumerated power. In other words, a federal law that purports to regulate matters within provincial (as well as federal) competence cannot be saved by classifying the law as in relation to a matter as broad and diffuse as inflation.

(f) Progressive interpretation

Since confederation in 1867, Canada has changed a great deal. Its territory and population have expanded many times. Agriculture has ceased to be the dominant activity, supplanted by mining, manufacturing, financial and service industries. The population has become concentrated in large cities. Technological developments, including electricity, the internal combustion engine, the telephone, aviation, radio, television and now the computer, have transformed the modes of communication and transportation, the appearance of the landscape, and the ways in which people live, work and play. Governments have grown immensely, as they have undertaken the building of railways, roads, dams, air-

---

215 *Id.*, 333. The full text of this dictum is set out in ch. 14, Delegation, under heading 14.2(c), "Classification of Laws", above. None of the other judges used this mode of reasoning.

216 [1976] 2 S.C.R. 373.

217 *Id.*, 458. Accord, *R.* v. *Crown Zellerbach* [1988] 1 S.C.R. 401, 432; Lederman, *Continuing Canadian Constitutional Dilemmas* (1981), 310-311.

ports, pipelines and other public projects; and as the increasing acceptance of egalitarian, collectivist and humanitarian values has required the regulation of industry for the protection of workers, consumers and the environment, the regulation of labour relations to permit collective bargaining, and the expansion of public education, public health and social security systems. While all this change was occurring, the nation also had to endure the first world war, the great depression, the second world war and periodic bouts of inflation.

During this time the Constitution changed very little, and only four small changes were made in the distribution of powers.[218] The doctrine of progressive interpretation is one of the means by which the Constitution Act, 1867 has been able to adapt to the changes in Canadian society. What this doctrine stipulates is that the general language used to describe the classes of subjects (or heads of power) is not to be frozen in the sense in which it would have been understood in 1867. For example, the phrase ''undertakings connecting the provinces with any other or others of the provinces'' (s. 92(10)(a)) includes an interprovincial telephone system, although the telephone was unknown in 1867;[219] the phrase ''criminal law'' (s. 91(27)) ''is not confined to what was criminal by the law of England or of any province in 1867'';[220] the phrase ''banking'' (s. 91(15)) is not confined to ''the extent and kind of business actually carried on by banks in Canada in 1867''.[221] On the contrary, the words of the Act are to be given a ''progressive interpretation'', so that they are continuously adapted to new conditions and new ideas.

It is true that the Privy Council did not always follow this precept, and occasionally denied its validity.[222] Indeed, in the *Labour Conventions* case (1937),[223] Lord Atkin gave eloquent expression to a contrary point of view, saying, ''while the ship of state now sails on larger ventures and into foreign waters she still retains the watertight compartments which are an essential part of her original structure''. That Lord Atkin did not conceive of the ''watertight compartments'' expanding or contracting in response to new developments is made clear from the actual holding in the *Labour Conventions* case, which was an emphatic refusal to give a progressive interpretation to the treaty power. But the authority of the *Labour Conventions* case, even on the point which it decided, is now suspect;[224]

218 In 1940, unemployment insurance was added to the federal list (s. 91(2A)). In 1951, power over old age pensions was granted to the federal Parliament (s. 94A). In 1964, the new power over old age pensions was expanded to include supplementary benefits (s. 94A). In 1982, provincial powers over natural resources were added (s. 92A). The most important changes since 1867, not affecting the federal distribution of powers, have been the adoption of the amending procedures and the Charter of Rights in 1982.

219 *Toronto* v. *Bell Telephone Co.* [1905] A.C. 52.

220 *P.A.T.A.* v. *A.-G. Can.* [1931] A.C. 310, 324. Accord, *R.* v. *Zelensky* [1978] 2 S.C.R. 940, 951 (upholding compensation provision in federal Criminal Code).

221 *A.-G. Alta.* v. *A.-G. Can.* (Alberta Bill of Rights) [1947] A.C. 503, 553.

222 Browne, *The Judicial Committee and the British North America Act* (1967), 20-29.

223 *A.-G. Can.* v. *A.-G. Ont.* (Labour Conventions) [1937] A.C. 326, 354.

224 See ch. 11, Treaties, under heading 11.5(b), ''Labour Conventions case'', above.

and the ''watertight compartments'' metaphor is not a reliable guide to judicial attitudes to the Constitution. Lord Sankey's metaphor would now be more generally accepted: ''the B.N.A. Act planted in Canada a living tree capable of growth and expansion within its natural limits''.[225]

The idea underlying the doctrine of progressive interpretation is that the Constitution Act, 1867, although undeniably a statute, is not a statute like any other: it is a ''constituent'' or ''organic'' statute, which has to provide the basis for the entire government of a nation over a long period of time. An inflexible interpretation, rooted in the past, would only serve to withhold necessary powers from the Parliament or Legislatures. It must be remembered too that the Constitution Act, 1867, like other federal constitutions, differs from an ordinary statute in that it cannot easily be amended when it becomes out of date, so that its adaptation to changing conditions must fall to a large extent upon the courts.[226]

(g) Legislative history

To what extent is the legislative history of the Constitution Act, 1867 admissible as an aid to the interpretation of the language of the Act? This issue is considered in chapter 57, Proof, below.[227]

(h) Precedent

The need for judicial adaptation of a constitution, coupled with the difficulty of amendment, invites the question whether the doctrine of precedent (or stare decisis) should not be relaxed in constitutional cases. This question has been considered in chapter 8, Supreme Court of Canada, above.[228]

---

225 *Edwards* v. *A.-G. Can.* [1930] A.C. 114, 136; Lord Sankey did emphasize that the case was not concerned with the distribution of legislative powers, but his idea was reformulated and approved in *British Coal Corp.* v. *The King* [1935] A.C. 500, 518 and *A.-G. Ont.* v. *A.-G. Can.* (Privy Council Appeals) [1947] A.C. 127, 154, the latter of which did involve the distribution of powers. The Supreme Court of Canada has approved the living tree metaphor in *A.-G. Que.* v. *Blaikie* [1979] 2 S.C.R. 1016, 1029 (interpretation of language rights); *A.-G. B.C.* v. *Can. Trust Co.* [1980] 2 S.C.R. 466, 478 (interpretation of taxing power); *Re Residential Tenancies Act* [1981] 1 S.C.R. 714, 723 (interpretation of s. 96); *Law Society of Upper Can.* v. *Skapinker* [1984] 1 S.C.R. 357, 365 (interpretation of s. 6 of Charter).

226 This position is rejected by some scholars, who argue that the courts are forever bound by the ''original understanding'' of the Constitution. Their view, often called ''originalism'' is criticized in ch. 57, Proof, under heading 57.1, ''Originalism'', below.

227 Chapter 57, Proof, under heading 57.6, 'Legislative history'', below.

228 Chapter 8, Supreme Court of Canada, under heading ''Precedent'', above.

16

Paramountcy

16.1 Problem of inconsistency

Every legal system has to have a rule to reconcile conflicts between inconsistent laws. The solution of the common law, which is applicable in unitary states such as the United Kingdom or New Zealand, is the doctrine of implied repeal: where there are two inconsistent (or conflicting) statutes[1] the later is deemed to have impliedly repealed the earlier to the extent of the inconsistency.[2] The doctrine of implied repeal applies in Canada to resolve conflicts between laws enacted by the same legislative body, for example, conflicts between two statutes of the

1 The rule applies only to statute law, because the normal development of the common law eliminates inconsistencies. Where two inconsistent rules of common law are announced by the courts, a later court will choose one of them as "correct", either overruling the other decision as wrong or declaring it to be applicable only to some narrow set of facts or even "its own" facts.

2 Driedger, *Construction of Statutes* (3rd ed., 1994; by Sullivan), 188-192; Burrows, "Implied Repeal" (1976) 3 Otago L. Rev. 601. An exception of uncertain scope is where the earlier statute is "special" and the later statute is "general"; in that case the general yields to the special, on the basis that the general statute should be construed as allowing an exception for the special statute; e.g., *Re B.C. Teachers' Federation* (1985) 23 D.L.R. (4th) 161 (B.C. C.A.).

federal Parliament[3] or two statutes of the Ontario Legislature.[4] But in a federal system there is also the possibility of conflict between the statutes of different legislative bodies within the federation.[5]

In Canada conflict between the statutes of different provincial Legislatures is unlikely to occur because the legislative authority of each province is confined within its own territory.[6] But conflict between a statute of the federal Parliament and a statute of a provincial Legislature is bound to occur from time to time because federal and provincial laws are applicable in the same territory, and by virtue of the double aspect and pith and substance (incidental effect) doctrines may be applicable to the same facts.[7] The doctrine of implied repeal is of no help in resolving a federal-provincial conflict because neither the federal Parliament nor a provincial Legislature has the power to repeal either expressly or impliedly each other's laws. For the same reason the order in which the two laws were enacted is irrelevant: there is no reason to prefer the later over the earlier, or vice versa.

The rule which has been adopted by the courts is the doctrine of "federal paramountcy":[8] where there are inconsistent (or conflicting) federal and provincial laws, it is the federal law[9] which prevails.[10] A similar rule has been adopted

---

3 E.g., *Can.* v. *Schmidt* [1987] 1 S.C.R. 500.

4 E.g., *Winnipeg School Division No. 1* v. *Craton* [1985] 2 S.C.R. 150.

5 The doctrine of implied repeal also resolves conflicts between a federal statute or a provincial statute and a pre-confederation statute, where the pre-confederation statute is upon a subject within the competence of the body that enacted the post-confederation law: *Moore* v. *Johnson* [1982] 1 S.C.R. 115.

6 In *Interprovincial Cooperatives* v. *The Queen* [1976] 1 S.C.R. 477, an apparent conflict between the laws of two provinces was resolved in three different ways, but each opinion assumed that the two laws could not both be applicable to a single set of facts, and that one of the laws had to be held either invalid or inapplicable by reason of the extraterritorial limitation on provincial legislative power. This case is discussed in ch. 13, Extraterritorial Competence, under heading 13.3(d), "Regulation of extraprovincial activity", above.

7 These doctrines are described, along with the three constitutional provisions that explicitly confer concurrent powers (ss. 92A(2), 94A, 95), in ch. 15, Judicial Review on Federal Grounds, under heading 15.9(d), "Concurrency", above.

8 Lederman, "The Concurrent Operation of Federal and Provincial Laws in Canada" (1963) 9 McGill L.J. 185; Laskin, "Occupying the Field: Paramountcy in Penal Legislation" (1963) 41 Can. Bar Rev. 234; Laskin, *Canadian Constitutional Law* (5th ed., 1986 by Finkelstein), 262-291.

9 Paramountcy is a quality inherent in federal legislative power, and should in my view be attributed only to statutes enacted by the federal Parliament (and to regulations or orders made thereunder), There is, however, some authority that the same paramount status is possessed by a pre-confederation law in a field of federal jurisdiction: *Hellens* v. *Densmore* [1957] S.C.R. 768, 784; *Re Broddy* (1982) 142 D.L.R. (3d) 151, 157 (Alta. C.A.); and even by a rule of the common law in a field of federal jurisdiction: *Bisaillon* v. *Keable* [1983] 2 S.C.R. 60, 108.

10 The Constitution Act, 1867 is curiously silent on the point, though there have been occasional suggestions that paramountcy flows from the notwithstanding clause in the opening words of s. 91 or the concluding clause of s. 91: *Re Exported Natural Gas Tax* [1982] 1 S.C.R. 1004,

in the United States and Australia,[11] and apparently by all modern federal constitutions.[12] The doctrine of paramountcy applies where there is a federal law and a provincial law which are (1) each valid, and (2) inconsistent. Most of this chapter will be devoted to the difficulty of determining when two laws are inconsistent for the purpose of paramountcy, but it should not be overlooked that the issue does not arise unless each law has first been held to be valid as an independent enactment. In determining the validity of each law, the existence and terms of the other law are irrelevant. Validity depends upon the principles discussed in the previous chapter: does the ''matter'' (or pith and substance) of the law come within the ''classes of subjects'' (or heads of power) allocated to the enacting Parliament or Legislature? If one law fails this test, then the problem is resolved without recourse to the doctrine of paramountcy. It is only if each law independently passes the test of validity that it is necessary to determine whether the laws are inconsistent. This may appear to be labouring the obvious, but there are a startling number of judicial opinions which confuse the issue of consistency with the antecedent, and entirely different, issue of validity.[13]

16.2 Definition of inconsistency

When are two laws deemed to be inconsistent (or conflicting) so as to attract the doctrine of paramountcy? The question has profound implications for the scope of judicial review and for the balance of power in the federal system. Given the overriding force of federal law, a wide definition of inconsistency will result in the defeat of provincial laws in ''fields'' which are ''covered'' by federal law; a narrow definition, on the other hand, will allow provincial laws to survive so long as they do not ''expressly contradict'' federal law. The wide definition is the course of judicial activism in favour of central power; the narrow definition is the course of judicial restraint, leaving all but the irreconcilable conflicts to be resolved in the political arena. We shall see that Canadian courts have followed the course of restraint.

1031; Laskin, *Canadian Constitutional Law* (5th ed., 1986 by Finkelstein), 263. Two of the three provisions conferring concurrent powers (note 7, above), namely, ss. 92A and 95, expressly stipulate that the federal power is to be paramount. The third provision, s. 94A, conferring federal power over old age pensions and supplementary benefits, appears to contemplate concurrent operation of federal and provincial laws, although it has been argued that it reverses the normal rule and makes provincial laws paramount: see Laskin, above, 263-264 (rejecting the argument).

11 The result has been held to be implicit in the ''supremacy clause'' in the United States' Constitution, art. 6, cl. 2; and is explicit in s. 109 of the Australian Constitution.

12 Wheare, *Federal Government* (4th ed., 1963), 74.

13 Note 74, below.

16.3 Express contradiction

(a) Impossibility of dual compliance

The only clear case of inconsistency, which I call express contradiction,[14] occurs when one law expressly contradicts the other. For laws which directly regulate conduct, an express contradiction occurs when it is impossible for a person to obey both laws; or, as Martland J. put it in *Smith* v. *The Queen* (1960),[15] ''compliance with one law involves breach of the other''.

The decided cases offer only a few examples of impossibility of dual compliance. Where there are insufficient assets to pay a person's debts, it is impossible to comply with a federal law stipulating the order of priority of payment and a provincial law stipulating a different order of priority.[16] Where a federal law stipulates that Japanese citizens in Canada are to be afforded the same employment opportunities as Canadian citizens, and a provincial law stipulates that Japanese are not to be employed in mines, another express contradiction occurs.[17] Where two spouses are separated, and a court order made under federal law grants custody of their child to the wife, while a court order made under provincial law grants custody to the husband, another express contradiction occurs.[18] Where a federal law stipulates that defined standard weights and measures be used and a provincial law requires purchasers of natural gas to pay a tax by reference to a non-standard unit of measurement, another express contradiction occurs.[19]

In *Bank of Montreal* v. *Hall* (1990),[20] the question arose whether there was a conflict between the federal Bank Act, which provided a procedure for the foreclosure of a mortgage, and the provincial Limitation of Civil Rights Act, which stipulated, as a prelude to foreclosure proceedings, that the creditor must serve on the debtor a notice giving the debtor a last opportunity to repay the loan. In this case, the bank had taken foreclosure proceedings in compliance with the federal law, but had not served the notice required by the provincial law. The Supreme Court of Canada held that the bank was not obliged to comply with the provincial law, because the provincial law was inconsistent with the federal law. La Forest J., who wrote the opinion of the Court, held that there was an express

---

14 Laskin, note 10, above, 264, uses the term ''operating incompatibility'', but he evidently has in mind a broader test than express contradiction because he includes in the test the negative implication which arises when a federal penal law is more restrictive than a provincial penal law, I prefer ''express contradiction'' because it clearly excludes negative implication and duplication, and makes it easier to analyze the three situations separately.

15 [1960] S.C.R. 776, 800.

16 *Royal Bank of Can.* v. *LaRue* [1928] A.C. 187; *Re Bozanich* [1942] S.C.R. 130: *A.-G. Ont.* v. *Policy-holders of Wentworth Ins. Co.* [1969] S.C.R. 779.

17 *A.-G. B.C.* v. *A.-G. Can.* (Employment of Japanese) [1924] A.C. 203.

18 *Gillespie* v. *Gillespie* (1973) 36 D.L.R. (3d) 421 (N.B. C.A.); discussed in ch. 26, The Family, under heading 26.8(a), ''General principles'', below.

19 *Re Min. of Finance (B.C.) and Pacific Petroleums* (1979) 99 D.L.R. (3d) 491 (B.C. CA.).

20 [1990] 1 S.C.R. 121.

contradiction — he described it as an "actual conflict in operation"[21] — between the two laws. "There could be", he said, "no clearer instance of a case where compliance with the federal statute necessarily entails defiance of its provincial counterpart".[22] With respect, this is incorrect. The federal statute did not forbid the bank from serving a notice giving the debtor a last chance to pay, and such a notice could have been served without any breach of the federal statute. The sole effect of compliance with the provincial law would be to delay the bank in realizing its security. There was no express contradiction (or actual conflict in operation), because both laws could be complied with by following the more stringent provincial law.[23]

(b) Secondary rules

The test of impossibility of dual compliance is relatively easy to apply to laws that directly impose duties on persons.[24] As well as these "primary" rules, however, there are "secondary" rules that do not directly impose duties on persons, but are rather facilitative or permissive, for example, the rules for the making of a contract.[25] It may be argued that there cannot be an impossibility of dual compliance with laws that do not impose duties, because two merely permissive laws that seem to be inconsistent can always be complied with by not doing whatever it is that is permitted. Eric Colvin rejects this argument, for the reason that secondary rules can be analyzed as imposing duties, not on persons at large to be sure, but on the officials who will have to administer the law, including the judges. If two rules would require inconsistent responses by a judge to the same set of facts, then there is an impossibility of dual compliance and therefore an express contradiction.[26]

---

21 *Id.*, 152.

22 *Id.*, 153.

23 The case is the same as *O'Grady* v. *Sparling*, note 39, below; *Stephens* v. *The Queen*, note 42, below; *Ross* v. *Registrar of Motor Vehicles*, note 47, below; *Bell* v. *A.G. P.E.I.*, note 48, below; *Provincial Secretary P.E.I.* v. *Egan*, note 49, below; *Construction Montcalm* v. *Minimum Wage Commn.*, note 54, below; *Irwin Toy* v. *Que.*, note 58, below. In each of these cases, provincial law imposed more severe standards than federal law, and in each case the Court held that there was no conflict because both laws could be complied with by following the stricter provincial law.

24 An anomalous class of cases is the "regulated industries" cases, in which an apparent contradiction between the federal Combines Investigation Act (anti-trust law) and provincial laws has been resolved by interpreting the federal law as implicitly permitting anti-competitive practices that are authorized by provincial law: see ch. 18, Criminal Law, under heading 18.6, "Competition law", below. McDonald, "Constitutional Aspects of Canadian Anti-Combines Law Enforcement" (1969) 47 Can. Bar Rev. 161, 205 aptly comments that these interpretative holdings come "close to provincial paramountcy".

25 The distinction comes from Hart, *The Concept of Law* (2nd. ed., 1994), 81.

26 Colvin, "Legal Theory and the Paramountcy Rule" (1979) 25 McGill L.J. 82; Comment (1983)17 U.B.C.L. Rev. 347.

Colvin's theory seems to be the most satisfactory way to explain *Tennant* v. *Union Bank of Canada* (1893).[27] The federal Bank Act provided that a warehouse receipt issued by a saw-miller was effective to give title to goods to a bank, and a provincial law provided that such a receipt was ineffective unless the issuer was engaged in the business of warehousing goods (which a saw-miller would not normally be). The Privy Council, in reasons that are not clear, held that the two laws were inconsistent: a receipt which fulfilled the federal requirements was effective, and the provincial law was inoperative to that extent. On a superficial analysis, the dual compliance test is not satisfied: the laws imposed no duties on banks or saw-millers, and both laws could be complied with by saw-millers not issuing, or banks not accepting, warehouse receipts as documents of title. However, the whole point of the federal law was to facilitate bank credit by validating warehouse receipts from saw-millers. One's intuitive reaction — apparently shared by the Privy Council — is that this policy should not be frustrated by the provincial law. This result is achieved if the rules in *Tennant* are "recast as directives to legal officials on how to decide a question of title to goods".[28] So recast, it is clear that a judge faced with a question of title to goods that depends upon the efficacy of a warehouse receipt issued by a saw-miller to a bank cannot comply with both laws. Dual compliance is impossible, and there is an express contradiction.[29]

Crown Grain Co. v. *Day* (1908)[30] is another example of the express contradiction of secondary rules — rules that impose no duties directly on people. In that case, the federal Supreme Court Act provided that an appeal lay to the Supreme Court of Canada "from any final judgment of the highest court of final resort . . . in any province", and a provincial law provided that in mechanics liens cases there was to be no appeal to the Supreme Court of Canada. The Privy Council held that the two laws were inconsistent, and that the provincial law barring appeals was inoperative. Once again, on a superficial analysis, the dual compliance test is not satisfied: the two laws imposed no duties on the parties to litigation, and both laws could be complied with by the losing litigant in a mechanics lien case not taking an appeal to the Supreme Court. But if the laws are recast as directives to a court that has to determine whether or not an appeal to the Supreme Court is available, the contradiction emerges. A court cannot decide that there is a right of appeal (as directed by federal law) and that there is

---

27 [1894] A.C. 31.

28 Colvin, Comment, note 26, above, 355.

29 While the impossibility of dual compliance does not become clear without some recasting of the rules, the recasting relies only on an implication that all laws (including secondary rules) are to be given effect to by judges (or other officials) with jurisdiction to determine disputes in which their terms are relevant. In that sense the contradiction in *Tennant* was "express", and not an example of the "negative implication" discussed in the next section of this chapter: see Colvin, note 26, above, 355.

30 [1908] A.C. 504.

not a right of appeal (as directed by provincial law). For the court, there is an impossibility of dual compliance and therefore an express contradiction.[31]

In the *Saskatchewan Breathalyzer* case (1958),[32] a federal law provided that "no person is required to give a sample of . . . breath" as evidence of driving while intoxicated, and a provincial law suspended the driving licence of any person who refused to comply with a police request for a sample. If the provincial law were construed as "requiring" the giving of a sample, then it expressly contradicted the federal law which said that no person was "required" to give a sample.[33] In the Supreme Court of Canada, Cartwright J. (with the concurrence of Locke J.) and Martland J. held that the provincial law did require the giving of a sample, because it suspended the licence of any driver who refused. But the other six members of the Court the majority decided otherwise. They held that the provincial sanction for refusal to give a sample was not severe enough — merely the denial of "a questionable privilege" — to amount to a requirement of giving a sample. Therefore, the provincial law did not contradict the federal law. This remarkable decision was the first in a series in which the Court has strained to avoid a finding of inconsistency and thereby keep the provincial law in operation.

16.4 Negative implication

(a) Covering the field

Cases where one law expressly contradicts another obviously call for the application of the paramountcy doctrine. The question to be examined in this section is whether they are the only cases that attract the doctrine or whether lesser kinds of incompatibility will also suffice. Where the federal Parliament has

---

31 The express contradiction of secondary rules is also exemplified by cases involving differing federal and provincial rules with respect to juvenile offenders: *A.-G. B.C.* v. *Smith* [1967] S.C.R. 702 (prosecution under provincial statute inoperative); *R.* v. *Wilson* (1980)119 D.L.R. (3d) 558 (B.C. C.A.) (provincial restrictions on admission to "youth containment centres" inoperative); *A.-G. Que.* v. *Lechasseur* [1981] 2 S.C.R. 253 (provincial diversion procedures inoperative). In each case, the federal and provincial laws did not impose contradictory requirements on the juvenile offender: his duty not to engage in criminal conduct was the same under both laws. But the laws did impose contradictory requirements on the officials charged with administering the law. As Fauteux J. said in *A.-G. B.C.* v. *Smith*, above, at 714, the two laws "clash at the level of law enforcement".

32 *Re s. 92(4) of the Vehicles Act 1957 (Sask.)* [1958] S.C.R. 608.

33 It was of course possible to "comply" with both laws by voluntarily giving a sample, but the point of the federal law was to leave the suspected driver free not to give a sample. This is another situation where it is necessary to recast the permissive federal law as a duty imposed on a judge not to visit sanctions on a person who refuses to comply with a police request for a breath sample. Only after that recasting exercise is there an impossibility of dual compliance by the judge.

enacted a law on a particular topic, does this preclude a province from enacting a different law on the same topic? If the provincial law does not contradict the federal law, but adds to it or supplements it, is the provincial law rendered inoperative by the federal law? And what if the provincial law is exactly the same as the federal law? The short answer to these questions is that only express contradiction suffices to invoke the paramountcy doctrine. A provincial law that is supplementary or duplicative of a federal law is not deemed to be inconsistent with the federal law.

Canadian courts, by confining the doctrine of paramountcy to such a narrow compass, have rejected a ''covering the field'' (or negative implication) test of inconsistency, which is employed by the courts of the United States and Australia.[34] Under this test, a federal law may be interpreted as covering the field and precluding any provincial laws in that field, even if they are not contradictory of the federal law.[35] In other words, a federal law may be read as including not only its express provisions, but also a ''negative implication'' that those express provisions should not be supplemented or duplicated by any provincial law on the same subject. Under this test, the question is whether the provincial law is in the same ''field'', or is upon the same subject, as the federal law: if so, the provincial law is deemed to be inconsistent with the federal law.

The negative implication (or covering the field) test of inconsistency seems to have been applied on one occasion by the Privy Council. In the *Local Prohibition* case (1896),[36] the Privy Council held that federal local-option temperance legislation would render inoperative similar provincial legislation if both laws were ever adopted in the same district. Both laws prohibited the retail sale of liquor, the only differences residing in the definition of quantities which made a sale ''wholesale'' and therefore permitted. It was possible to comply with both laws by complying with the stricter of the two, that is, by selling liquor only in quantities which fitted the narrowest definition of wholesale sale. The direct contradiction test was therefore not satisfied,[37] and their lordships' finding of

---

34 For an authoritative statement of the rule of ''preemption'' (as it is usually called) in the United States, see *Pennsylvania* v. *Nelson* (1956) 359 U.S. 497, 501-505; and for the rule of ''inconsistency'' (as it is usually called) in Australia, see *Ex parte McLean* (1930), 43 C.L.R. 472, 483. These broad definitions of inconsistency are, of course, consistent with the more centralized interpretation of the federal distribution of powers in the United States and Australia. For a detailed comparison of the Australian and Canadian law, see Gilbert, *Australian and Canadian Federalism 1867-1984* (1986), chs. 8, 9.

35 This interpretation is not automatic, but turns on a judicial finding that the federal law was to be the sole and exclusive law in the field. This finding, and the definition of the ''field'' that has been covered, confer a degree of judicial discretion that makes the law quite unpredictable.

36 *A.-G. Ont.* v. *A.G. Can.* (Local Prohibition) [1896] A.C. 348.

37 Contra, Lederman (1963) 9 McGill L.J. 185, 190-191; Laskin (1963) 41 Can. Bar Rev. 234, 243.

inconsistency, although not explained in the opinion, must have been premised on a negative implication or coverage of the field.[38]

A statement of the negative implication (or covering the field) test of inconsistency is to be found in the dissenting opinion of Cartwright J. in *O'Grady* v. *Sparling* (1960).[39] In that case, a federal law (the Criminal Code) made it an offence to drive a motor vehicle recklessly; a provincial law (Manitoba's Highway Traffic Act) made it an offence to drive carelessly ("without due care and attention"). The two laws did not expressly contradict each other because it was possible to obey both of them by adhering to the stricter provincial standard. Nonetheless, Cartwright J. (who had dissented in the *Saskatchewan Breathalyzer* case) would have held that the two laws were inconsistent. With the concurrence of Locke J., he said:[40]

> In my opinion when Parliament has expressed in an Act its decision that a certain kind or degree of negligence in the operation of a motor vehicle shall be punishable as a crime against the state it follows that it has decided that no less culpable kind or degree of negligence in such operation shall be so punishable. By necessary implication the Act says not only what kinds or degrees of negligence shall be punishable but also what kinds or degrees shall not.

The premise of this reasoning is the inference that Parliament covered the field of bad driving when it enacted the Criminal Code offence of reckless driving, and thereby preempted any provincial law in the same field. What Cartwright J. was willing to do was to add to the express terms of the federal statute an implication that there should be no provincial regulation of the same subject matter.

In *O'Grady* v. *Sparling*, Cartwright J.'s opinion was a dissenting one. The majority of the Court, in an opinion written by Judson J., rejected the negative implication (or covering the field) test, holding that "both provisions can live together and operate concurrently".[41] The two laws were therefore not inconsistent and paramountcy did not apply. The negative implication test was also rejected in two other cases which the Court decided at the same time. In *Stephens* v. *TheQueen* (1960),[42] the question was whether there was inconsistency between a federal (Criminal Code) offence of failing to remain at the scene of an accident "with intent to escape civil or criminal liability", and a provincial (Highway Traffic Act) offence of failing to remain at the scene of an accident. In this case, as in *O'Grady*, it was possible to obey both laws by complying with the stricter of the two, which was the provincial one because it lacked the ingredient of intention to escape liability. Again the majority of the Court, in an opinion written this time by Kerwin C.J., held that there was no inconsistency; and again Cart-

---

38 This part of the decision was not obiter, because it formed part of their lordships' answer to one of the questions referred for decision; on the other hand, the existence of inconsistency was described as "obvious" and was not carefully considered.

39 [1960] S.C.R. 804.

40 *Id.*, 820-821.

41 *Id.*, 811.

42 [1960] S.C.R. 823.

wright J. (with Locke J.) dissented on the basis of a negative implication. In *Smith* v. *The Queen* (1960),[43] the two laws were virtually identical in their effect: the federal (Criminal Code) offence was making, circulating or publishing a false prospectus; the provincial (Securities Act) offence was furnishing false information in a prospectus. Again the Court held that the two laws were not inconsistent. Kerwin C.J., who wrote one of the two concurring opinions, said that the two laws could ''co-exist'';[44] Martland J., who wrote the other, made his already-quoted statement that there was ''no conflict in the sense that compliance with one law involves breach of the other'';[45] Cartwright J. again dissented, this time attracting the support of Ritchie J. as well as Locke J.

In *O'Grady*, *Stephens* and *Smith*, none of the majority or concurring opinions attempted to deal with Cartwright J.'s argument that inconsistency could arise by negative implication. In fact, with the exception of Martland J.'s ''compliance'' dictum in *Smith*, none of the opinions even offered a rival definition of inconsistency. These failures left in doubt the exact status of negative implication (or covering the field) as a test of inconsistency. Had the majority judges rejected negative implication in principle for all cases, or had they decided merely that no negative implication should be drawn from the particular federal laws in issue in *O'Grady*, *Stephens* and *Smith*? Since those cases were decided, the Supreme Court of Canada has made clear that the former view is correct. A series of cases has decided that the negative implication test no longer has any place in Canadian constitutional law.

The first case is *Mann* v. *TheQueen* (1966).[46] This case concerned a new federal Criminal Code offence of driving a motor vehicle ''in a manner that is dangerous to the public''. This ''dangerous driving'' offence stipulated a stricter standard of care than the ''reckless driving'' offence which was the federal offence in issue in *O'Grady* v. *Sparling*. Did this new offence render inoperative the provincial ''careless driving'' offences? In *Mann*, the Court held unanimously that paramountcy did not apply. This case was a clearer one for Cartwright J.'s negative implication than *O'Grady* v. *Sparling*, because the federal standard was now so close to the provincial one. But Cartwright J. wrote a concurring opinion in *Mann*, following *O'Grady* v. *Sparling* and not mentioning the negative implication test. Obviously, Cartwright J. was bowing to the doctrine of precedent, but it is significant that he did not consider that the clearer facts of Mann justified his persisting with the negative implication test.

In *Ross* v. *Registrar of Motor Vehicles* (1973)[47] and *Bell* v. *A.-G. P.E.I.* (1973),[48] the question arose whether there was inconsistency between a federal

43 [1960] S.C.R. 776.
44 *Id.*, 781.
45 *Id.*, 800, quoted at note 15, above.
46 [1966] S.C.R. 238.
47 [1975] 1 S.C.R. 5.
48 [1975] 1 S.C.R. 25.

law conferring a judicial discretion to prohibit a convicted ''drunk driver'' from driving and a provincial law imposing an automatic suspension of a convicted drunk driver's driving licence. The question had first arisen in *Provincial Secretary of P.E.I.* v. *Egan* (1941),[49] when the Criminal Code included as a penalty for certain impaired driving offences the power to prohibit the convicted defendant from driving anywhere in Canada for up to three years. Egan was convicted of impaired driving, but the magistrate in imposing sentence exercised his discretion to make no order prohibiting Egan from driving. However, Egan's driving licence had been issued by Prince Edward Island, and that province's Highway Traffic Act automatically suspended for 12 months the licence of anyone who like Egan had been convicted of an impaired driving offence. Egan therefore lost his licence for a year and was effectively prohibited from driving his car for that period of time. The Supreme Court of Canada unanimously decided that Egan had indeed lost his licence: the provincial suspension was not inconsistent with the federal discretion. Cartwright J. was not on the Court in 1941, and no judge made the argument that a federal discretion to prohibit driving carried the negative implication that there should be no automatic suspension of the convicted driver's licence to drive. Although the reasoning of the judges confuses validity with inconsistency and does not clarify the ground for decision on the latter question, the reason for the result must have been that both enactments could be obeyed by Egan by not driving for a year!

The new point which had to be decided in *Ross* and *Bell* arose out of an amendment to the Criminal Code in 1972 which enlarged the discretion of the court in sentencing impaired drivers. Whereas before 1972 any court-imposed prohibition on driving had to be for a continuous period of time, the 1972 amendment authorized the sentencing court to prohibit driving on an intermittent basis ''at such times and places as may be specified in the order''. In *Ross*, the sentencing Court had prohibited the defendant ''from driving for a period of six months, except Monday to Friday, 8 a.m. to 5:45 p.m., in the course of employment and going to and from work''. The purpose of the 1972 amendment, as exemplified by the order in *Ross*, was to enable the sentencing court to tailor its prohibition order to the facts of the case; and, in particular, to impose a more lenient restraint on a defendant who was dependent upon driving for his livelihood. It was obviously contemplated by the amendment, and by the Court which sentenced Ross, that the defendant would be free to drive in those periods which were exempt from the federal prohibition.[50] An automatic, blanket suspension of the defendant's licence would nullify the effect of the amendment and make a mockery of the criminal court's carefully tailored order. Surely, if ever a negative

49 [1941] S.C.R. 396.

50 The sentencing Court in Ross actually held that the provincial licence was not to be suspended. Pigeon J. was surely correct in holding that the Court lacked the power to suspend the operation of a provincial law; Judson J. in dissent did not rely on this aspect of the sentencing Court's order; Spence J. in dissent held that the sentencing Court did have the power it asserted.

implication was warranted, it was here. But the Supreme Court of Canada refused to draw the implication. In *Bell*, where no intermittent order had in fact been made, the Court unanimously followed *Egan* and held operative an automatic provincial suspension of the convicted driver's licence. In *Ross*, where the intermittent order had been made, the Court reached the same conclusion by a majority of five to two. Pigeon J. for the majority admitted that "this means that as long as the provincial licence suspension is in effect, the person concerned gets no benefit from the indulgence granted under the federal legislation", but dismissed the point by asking rhetorically, "is the situation any different in law from that which was considered in the *Egan* case . . . ?"[51] The two dissenting judges, Judson and Spence JJ., held that the making of the intermittent order in Ross did create a "direct conflict"[52] to which the provincial suspension had to yield.

The Supreme Court of Canada's rejection of negative implication (or covering the field) has continued in more recent cases. In *Robinson* v. *Countrywide Factors* (1977),[53] the Court held that a provincial law avoiding fraudulent preferences by insolvent debtors could stand in the face of a federal bankruptcy law. In *Construction Montcalm* v. *MinimumWage Commission* (1978),[54] the Court held that a provincial minimum wage law was applicable to a Crown contractor constructing an airport runway, despite the fact that there was an applicable (less onerous) federal minimum wage law. In *Schneider* v. *TheQueen* (1982),[55] the Court held that a provincial Heroin Treatment Act was not inconsistent with the federal Narcotic Control Act. In *Multiple Access* v. *McCutcheon* (1982),[56] the Court applied a provincial "insider trading" law to shares in a federally incorporated company, despite the existence of an applicable federal law prohibiting insider trading. In *Rio Hotel* v. *New Brunswick* (1987),[57] the Court held that a provincial prohibition of "nude entertainment" in taverns was not inconsistent with the federal Criminal Code offences involving public nudity. In *Irwin Toy* v. *Quebec* (1989),[58] the Court held that a provincial prohibition of advertising directed at children applied to television, despite the existence of federal guidelines for television advertising directed at children. In *Clarke* v. *Clarke* (1990),[59] the Court held that provincial matrimonial property legislation required the sharing of a military pension, despite a federal prohibition on the alienation of the pension.

51 [1975] 1 S.C.R. 5, 13. Pigeon J. went on to suggest (at p.15) that his decision was compatible with the negative implication (or covering the field) test, but it is difficult to see how that test could have produced the same result.

52 *Id.*, 20.

53 [1977] 2 S.C.R. 753.

54 [1979] 1 S.C.R. 754.

55 [1982] 2 S.C.R. 112.

56 [1982] 2 S.C.R. 161.

57 [1987] 2 S.C.R. 59.

58 [1989] 1 S.C.R. 927.

59 [1990] 2 S.C.R. 795.

In each of these cases, there was a federal and a provincial law in the same field. In most of the cases, the provincial law pursued an objective that was inconsistent with that of the federal law. But there was no conflict in the operation of the competing laws, in the sense of impossibility of dual compliance: both laws could be complied with by following whichever rule was stricter. The inexorable conclusion is that there is no room for an imputed inconsistency based on covering the field or negative implication.[60] The sole test of inconsistency in Canadian constitutional law is express contradiction. This is the course of judicial restraint, allowing the fullest possible play to provincial legislation.

(b) Express extension of paramountcy

If the federal Parliament occupied a field of legislation by express words, would that be effective? For example, s. 88 of the federal Indian Act[61] provides that provincial laws are inapplicable to Indians "to the extent that such laws make provision for any matter for which provision is made by or under this Act". On the face of it,[62] this provision purports to extend the doctrine of paramountcy by rendering inoperative provincial laws upon the same matters as the Indian Act, even if the provincial laws do not contradict the Indian Act. Is it open to the federal Parliament to extend the doctrine of paramountcy beyond the case of an actual conflict in operation?

In principle, the answer to this question should be yes. Assuming that the express federal paramountcy provision was valid under federalism rules, that is, it was part of a law in relation to a federal head of power, there seems no reason why it should not be valid. If that is so, then a provincial law in the same field would be inconsistent with the federal law, and would therefore be rendered inoperative by the doctrine of paramountcy. For the most part, it has been assumed that this is indeed the law.[63] However, in *Dick* v. *The Queen* (1985),[64] Beetz J.,

60 A possible counter-example is *Bank of Montreal* v. *Hall* [1990] 1 S.C.R. 121, where paramountcy was applied despite the lack of an express contradiction: see criticism at note 20, above. While the Court did purport to apply the express contradiction test, there are dicta at 154-155 that suggest a covering-the-field test.

61 R.S.C. 1985, c. I-5.

62 The various interpretations of s. 88 are discussed in ch. 27, Aboriginal Peoples, under heading 27.3, "Section 88 of the Indian Act", below. In *Dick* v. *The Queen* [1985] 2 S.C.R. 309, it was held that s. 88 applied only to those provincial laws that could not apply to Indians of their own force. For those laws, Parliament, having made them applicable by referential incorporation, can adopt any paramountcy rule it chooses.

63 *A.-G. B.C.* v. *Smith* [1967] S.C.R. 702, 714 (holding that federal law, which defined juvenile delinquency as including breaches of provincial laws, precluded prosecutions under provincial laws); *R.* v. *Francis* [1988] 1 S.C.R. 1025, 1031 (dictum that "sufficient intent" to cover field would be effective); cf. *Ross* v. *Registrar of Motor Vehicles* [1975] 1 S.C.R. 5, 16 (dictum leaving point open). The cases holding that s. 88 makes Indian treaties override provincial laws also support my view, because they proceed on the assumption that Parliament has the power to expand paramountcy in that way. See ch. 27, Aboriginal Peoples, under heading 27.3(d), "Treaty exception", below.

64 [1985] 2 S.C.R. 309, 327-328.

who wrote the opinion of the five-judge bench, said that ''it would not be open to Parliament in my view to make the Indian Act paramount over provincial laws simply because the Indian Act occupied the field. Operational conflict would be required to this end''. This dictum was not strictly necessary to the decision, but it was part of the reasoning process, and it must be taken as a considered view of the issue.[65] For the reasons given above,[66] I think the better view is that an express covering-the-field clause would be effective.[67]

16.5 Overlap and duplication

(a) Constitutional significance

The four paramountcy cases decided in the 1960s, namely, *O'Grady*, *Smith*, *Stephens* and *Mann* all concerned penal enactments which overlapped. In the case of each pair of laws, many fact situations would constitute an offence under both the federal and the provincial law. However, all of the majority and concurring opinions in the four cases (including that of Martland J. in *Smith*, which contained the ''dual compliance'' dictum) placed emphasis on the fact that the competing federal and provincial laws were different in some respect; by ''different'' they usually seemed to mean that there was some imaginable set of facts to which one law would apply and not the other. The implication of this kind of reasoning is that a provincial law which duplicated the provisions of a federal law would be held to be in-operative. Curiously, none of the majority or concurring judges said this, but their opinions are only explicable on this basis.[68]

There is no reason why duplication should be a case of inconsistency once the negative implication or covering the field test is rejected. On the contrary, duplication is ''the ultimate in harmony''.[69] The argument that it is untidy, wasteful and confusing to have two laws when only one is needed[70] reflects a value which in a federal system often has to be subordinated to that of provincial autonomy. Nor does the latter value disappear when provincial law merely duplicates federal law, because the suspension of a provincial law may create a gap

65 The point was made in support of interpreting s. 88 as applying only to provincial laws that could not apply of their own force to Indians: note 62, above. The case is more fully discussed in ch. 27, Aboriginal Peoples, under heading 27.3(b), ''Laws of general application'', below.

66 Accord, Monahan and Petter, ''Developments'' (1987) 9 Supreme Court L.R. 69, 163.

67 It appears that paramountcy may be expressly waived by the federal Parliament, as it has purported to do in the (now repealed) Juvenile Delinquents Act, R.S.C. 1970, c. J-3, s. 39, and possibly also in the Lord's Day Act: *Lord's Day Alliance of Can.* v. *A.-G. B.C.* [1959] S.C.R. 497; and see also ch. 14, Delegation, under heading 14.5(c), ''Conditions as legislative inter-delegation'', above.

68 Only the dissenting judges in *Smith,* namely Locke, Cartwright, and Ritchie JJ., held that the substantial identity between the two laws in that case amounted to an inconsistency.

69 Lederman (1963)9 McGill I.J. 185, 195.

70 *Id.*, 196.

in a provincial scheme of regulation which would have to be filled by federal law — a situation as productive of untidiness, waste and confusion as duplication.

In any event, arguments against duplication of federal and provincial laws can have little weight once overlapping is admitted. After all, overlapping legislation is duplicative to the extent of the overlap, and yet it is clear that provincial law is not inoperative to the extent of its overlap with federal law. It must be remembered too that the differences between the federal and provincial laws in *O'Grady* and *Stephens* were small, and in *Smith* and *Mann* they were virtually non-existent. If paramountcy does not apply when 999 cases out of 1,000 are covered by both laws, why should paramountcy apply when all 1,000 are covered by both laws? It is submitted that duplication is not a test of inconsistency.

The argument contained in the previous two paragraphs, which appeared in the first edition (1977) of this book,[71] was accepted by Dickson J. for a majority of the Supreme Court of Canada in *Multiple Access* v. *McCutcheon* (1982).[72] He held that the provisions of Ontario securities law relating to insider trading were not rendered inoperative by the substantially identical provisions of federal corporate law. This case is a considered and unequivocal ruling that duplication is not a test of paramountcy, and it probably settles the question, although there are two earlier cases to the contrary,[73] neither of which was referred to by Dickson J. Probably, the two earlier cases should be treated as overruled by *Multiple Access*.

Once it is determined that duplication is not a test of paramountcy, there is obviously no point in searching for minor differences between essentially similar laws, which was the approach taken by the Supreme Court of Canada in *O'Grady*, *Smith*, *Stephens* and *Mann*. This approach, which has not been used in cases decided after *Mann*, seems muddled. Occasionally, the search for differences — any differences — has led judges to point out that the competing laws had different "purposes" or "aspects", and that they were consistent for that reason, even though they were substantially the same in operation. This kind of reasoning confuses validity with consistency.[74] The existence of different purposes or as-

---

71 Pages 110-111.

72 [1982]2 S.C.R. 161, 185-191.

73 *Home Insurance Co. v. Lindal and Beattie* [1934] S.C.R. 33, 40; *N.S. Bd. of Censors v. McNeil* [1978] 2 S.C.R. 662, 699. In both cases, it was assumed without question that duplication would give rise to federal paramountcy. There was no deliberate consideration of the issue, as there was in *Multiple Access.*

74 On the distinction between validity and consistency, see text accompanying note 13, above. For dicta indicating confusion of validity with consistency, either by treating the aspect doctrine as relevant to consistency, or by treating the existence or terms of one law as relevant to the validity of the other, or by treating inconsistency as a withdrawal of provincial power to enact the inconsistent legislation, see *Prov. Secretary of P.E.I.* v. *Egan* [1941] S.C.R. 396, 400-403 per Duff C.J.; *Johnson* v. *A.-G. Alta.* [1954] S.C.R. 127, 136-138 *per Rand J.; Smith v. The Queen* [1960] S.C.R. 776, 781 per Kerwin C.J., 786-787 per Locke *J.; O'Grady v. Sparling* [1960] S.C.R. 804, 811 per Judson J., 821 per Cartwright J.; *Stephens* v. *The Queen* [1960] S.C.R. 823, 829 per Cartwright J.; *A.-G. Ont.* v. *Barfried Enterprises* [1963] S.C.R. 570, 583 per Martland J.; *Mann* v. *The Queen* [1966] S.C.R. 238, 251 per Ritchie J.; *N.S. Bd. of Censors*

pects is relevant only to the question whether each law is valid in the first place. The double aspect doctrine[75] ''opens two gates to the same field'', but it does not help to resolve the subsequent question of whether the two laws are inconsistent.[76] Whether the laws are inconsistent or not depends not on their dominant purpose or aspect but upon whether they are compatible in operation.

(b) Double criminal liability

The existence of overlapping or duplicative penal provisions raises the possibility that a person may be liable to conviction under both a federal law and a provincial law for the same conduct. There is nothing in paramountcy doctrine which precludes multiple prosecutions or convictions under federal and provincial laws.[77]

However, there is no reason why s. 11(h) of the Charter of Rights, which precludes double jeopardy,[78] and the various rules of criminal procedure that have a similar purpose,[79] should not be applicable where an accused is charged with an offence under a federal statute and an offence under a provincial statute.[80] For the purpose of double-jeopardy law, the differing jurisdictional sources of the multiple offences should be irrelevant. In other words, double jeopardy issues should be dealt with as if Canada was a unitary state. Indeed, the administration of criminal justice in each province is to a large extent unitary. It is the provincial police and prosecutors who enforce most of the federal criminal law as well as

v. *McNeil* [1978] 2 S.C.R. 662, 695, 698-699 per Ritchie J.; *Husky Oil Operations* v. *M.N.R.* [1995] 3 S.C.R. 453, para. 87 per Gonthier J., criticized para. 213 per Iacobucci J.

75 See ch. 15, Judicial Review on Federal Grounds, under heading 15.5(c), ''Double aspect'', above.

76 Lederman (1963)9 McGill L.J. 185, 197; accord, Laskin (1963) 41 Can. Bar Rev. 234, 242, 247; Weiler (1973) 23 U. Toronto L.J. 307, 359.

77 *R.* v. *Gautreau* (1978) 88 D.L.R. (3d) 718, 723 (N.B. A.D.).

78 See ch. 48, Rights on Being Charged, under heading 48.9, ''Double jeopardy'', below. There is no comparable guarantee in Australia. In the United States, the fifth amendment includes a guarantee against double jeopardy under federal law, and the same guarantee applies to state law through the due process clause of the fourteenth amendment: *Benton* v. *Maryland (1969)* 395 U.S. 784; but it has been held that the guarantee does not apply where one offence is federal and the other is state: *Bartkus* v. *Illinois* (1959)359 U.S. 121; *Abbate* v. *United States* (1959) 359 U.S. 187; cf. *Can.* v. *Schmidt* [1987] 1 S.C.R. 500 (rejecting argument that extradition to U.S. should be refused, because of this limitation to the double-jeopardy rule).

79 The doctrines of autrefois acquit, autrefois convict, issue estoppel, resjudicata (as expanded in *Kienapple* v. *The Queen* [1975] 1 S.C.R. 729) and, perhaps, abuse of process all bear on issues of double jeopardy. See generally Friedland, *Double Jeopardy* (1969).

80 Accord, *R.* v. *Wigglesworth* [1987] 2 S.C.R. 541, 554, 556, 560 (obiter dicta); Friedland (1967)17 U. Toronto L.J. 66. Contra, *R.* v. *Kissick* [1942] 2 W.W.R. 418 (Man. C.A.). The Criminal Code, R.S.C. 1985, c. C-46, s. 12, prohibiting double punishment for the same offence, is expressly confined to federal offences, but much of the ground covered by s. 12 is now also covered by the *Kienapple* rule.

all provincial penal law, and it is the provincial court system in which both federal and provincial offences are tried.[81] This means that nearly all relevant decisions are taken by the same provincial officials or judges, regardless of whether the offences are federal or provincial. The paucity of case law suggests that the issues of double jeopardy across jurisdictional boundaries are in fact usually resolved by prosecutorial or judicial discretion.

(c) Double civil liability

Double civil liability is also a possibility under overlapping or duplicative federal and provincial laws. The Privy Council has upheld double income taxation, saying that federal and provincial taxes ''may co-exist and be enforced without clashing'', because the Dominion ''reaps part of the field'', while the province ''reaps another part''.[82] The Supreme Court of Canada has upheld duplicative civil remedies for insider trading, one in a federal corporations statute, the other in an Ontario securities statute.[83] To the objection that a plaintiff should not be permitted to recover double damages from the insider, Dickson J. for the majority of the Court pointed out that no court would award damages to a plaintiff who had already been fully compensated.[84] Like the possibility of double criminal liability, the issue of double civil liability did not need to be resolved by the doctrine of paramountcy.[85]

16.6 Effect of inconsistency

Once it has been determined that a federal law is inconsistent with a provincial law, the doctrine of federal paramountcy stipulates that the provincial law must yield to the federal law. The most usual and most accurate way of describing the effect on the provincial law is to say that it is rendered inoperative to the extent of the inconsistency. Notice that the paramountcy doctrine applies only to the extent of the inconsistency. The doctrine will not affect the operation of those parts of the provincial law which are not inconsistent with the federal law, unless of course the inconsistent parts are inseparably linked up with the consistent parts.[86] There is also a temporal limitation on the paramountcy doctrine. It will

---

81 Courts of criminal jurisdiction, policing and prosecution are discussed in ch. 19, Criminal Justice, below.

82 *Forbes* v. *A.-G. Man.* [1937] A.C. 260, 274.

83 *Multiple Access* v. *McCutcheon* [1982] 2 S.C.R. 161.

84 *Id.*, 191.

85 See also *Lamb* v. *Lamb* [1985] 1 S.C.R. 851 (provincial order for exclusive possession of matrimonial home not inconsistent with federal order for maintenance).

86 This would depend upon the ordinary rules as to severance: ch. 15, Judicial Review on Federal Grounds, under heading, 15.6, ''Severance'', above.

affect the operation of the provincial law only so long as the inconsistent federal law is in force. If the federal law is repealed, the provincial law will automatically ''revive'' (come back into operation) without any reenactment by the provincial Legislature.[87]

It is not accurate to describe the effect of the paramountcy doctrine as the ''repeal'' of the provincial law. The federal Parliament cannot repeal a provincial law. Moreover, a repealed law does not revive on the repeal of the repealing law. Nor is it accurate to describe the effect of the paramountcy doctrine as rendering the provincial law ultra vires, invalid or unconstitutional. Such a description confuses validity with consistency.[88] The federal Parliament cannot unilaterally take away from a provincial Legislature any power that the Constitution confers upon the Legislature.[89] The provincial power to enact the law is not lost; it continues to exist (so does the provincial law), although it remains in abeyance until such time as the federal Parliament repeals the inconsistent federal law. This is why the only satisfactory description of the effect of the paramountcy doctrine is that it renders inoperative the inconsistent provincial law.

It is even misleading to describe the effect of the paramountcy doctrine as rendering a provincial law ''inapplicable''. This description is not literally wrong, but it invites confusion with the doctrine of interjurisdictional immunity. The doctrine of interjurisdictional immunity is a limitation on the power of the provincial Legislatures to enact laws that extend into core areas of exclusive federal jurisdiction. In the *Quebec Minimum Wage* case (1966),[90] for example, it was held that Quebec's minimum wage law could not constitutionally apply to the Bell Telephone Company. This was not based on the existence of an inconsistent federal law; there was no federal minimum wage law in existence at that time.[91] The decision was based on the rule that a provincial law cannot affect a ''vital part'' of an undertaking within federal jurisdiction (such as a telephone company). In a case of this kind, the law is said to be inapplicable, not inoperative, which makes clear that the provincial law is yielding not merely to an inconsistent

87 It is otherwise of course if the provincial Legislature has formally repealed the law in the meantime.

88 Note 74, above.

89 Cf. *A.-G. N.S.* v. *A.-G. Can.* (Nova Scotia Inter-delegation) [1951] S.C.R. 31, holding that neither Parliament nor Legislature can confer additional powers on each other; a fortiori, neither can take existing powers away.

90 *Commission du Salaire Minimum* v. *Bell Telephone Co.* [1966] S.C.R. 767; discussed in ch. 15, Judicial Review on Federal Grounds, under heading 15.8, ''Interjurisdictional immunity'', above.

91 Even if there had been a federal minimum wage law, the existence of a different federal standard has been held not to qualify as an inconsistency: *Construction Montcalm v. Minimum Wage Commn.* [1979] 1 S.C.R. 754.

federal law, but to an implied prohibition in the Constitution which makes the application of the law ultra vires.[92]

92 It is sometimes unclear whether a provincial law has been held to be *inapplicable* on account of interjurisdictional immunity or *inoperative* on account of inconsistency with federal law. A line of cases that holds that provincial law cannot alter the ranking of debts in bankruptcy could be explained *either* on the (ultra vires) basis that the law affects a vital part of bankruptcy (a federal head of power) *or* on the (paramountcy) basis that the law is inconsistent with the Bankruptcy Act (a federal law). The cases are discussed in *Husky Oil Operations* v. *MNR* [1995] 3 S.C.R. 453, where Gonthier J. for the majority (at para. 87) uses the word ''inapplicable'' for some (but not all) paramountcy conflicts. Iacobucci J. for the dissenting minority (at para. 213) criticizes Gonthier J.'s usage as ''[confusing] the doctrines of vires and paramountcy, as these have been traditionally understood''.

17

Peace, Order, and Good Government

17.1 Residuary nature of power

The opening words of s. 91 of the Constitution Act, 1867 confer on the federal Parliament the power:

> to make laws for the peace, order, and good government of Canada, in relation to all matters not coming within the classes of subjects by this Act assigned exclusively to the Legislatures of the provinces; . . .

This power to make laws for the "peace, order, and good government of Canada" (hereinafter called the p.o.g.g. power)[1] is residuary in its relationship to the provincial heads of power, because it is expressly confined to "matters not coming

---

1 See Laskin, "Peace, Order and Good Government Re-examined" (1947) 25 Can. Bar Rev. 1054; Abel "What Peace, Order and Good Government?" (1968) 7 West. Ont. L. Rev. 1: Abel, "The Neglected Logic of 91 and 92" (1969) 19 U. Toronto L.J. 487; Lederman, "Unity and Diversity in Canadian Federalism" (1975) 53 Can. Bar Rev. 597; Lysyk, "Constitutional Reform and the Introductory Clause of s. 91" (1979) 57 Can. Bar. Rev. 531; Beaudoin, *La Constitution du Canada* (1990), ch. 8; Tremblay, *Droit Constitutionnel-Principles* (1993), Part II, ch. 1.

within the classes of subjects by this Act assigned exclusively to the Legislatures of the provinces''. It is clear from this language that any matter which does not come within a provincial head of power must be within the power of the federal Parliament. By this means the distribution of legislative powers was to be exhaustive. With only a few exceptions, of which the most important is the Charter of Rights, the residuary nature of the federal power ensures that every possible subject of legislation belongs to one or other of the federal Parliament or the provincial Legislatures.[2]

The residuary nature of the federal power in Canada is in contrast to the distribution of legislative powers in the earlier Constitution of the United States (1787) and the later Constitution of Australia (1900). In those two countries, the federal Congress or Parliament has only enumerated powers and the Legislatures of the States have the residue.[3] There are reasons for supposing that this difference between the Constitution Act, 1867 and its only real precedent, the Constitution of the United States, was part of a design to create a stronger central government in Canada than existed in the United States.[4] Of course, there is no logical reason why this result should follow from the mere fact that the federal Parliament has the residue of power: the actual extent and importance of the residue depends by definition on the extent and importance of the provincial powers which are subtracted from the residue.

In Canada the provincial heads of power include one of great extent and importance. This is s. 92(13), ''property and civil rights in the province'', a phrase which is apt to include most of the private law of property, contracts and torts and their many derivatives. Indeed, at the hands of the Privy Council, s. 92(13) became a kind of residuary power itself, and one which was much more important than the federal peace, order, and good government power.[5] A second potentially sweeping head of provincial power is s. 92(16), ''generally all matters of a merely local or private nature in the province''. Albert S. Abel used the existence of s. 92(16) as the basis for an argument that there is no residuary power in the Constitution Act, 1867 at all. He said that p.o.g.g. and s. 92(16) were two complementary grants of power which distributed the residue between the two levels of government.[6] But, as Abel himself conceded, one might just as easily speak of two residuary clauses as none, and of the two s. 92(16) has in practice turned out to be quite unimportant, because its work has been done for it by s. 92(13).[7]

---

2 See ch. 15, Judicial Review on Federal Grounds, under heading 15.9(e), ''Exhaustiveness,'' above.

3 Constitution of the United States, art. 1, s. 8 (enumerated powers), 10th amendment (residue); Constitution of Australia. ss. 51, 52 (enumerated powers), 107 (residue).

4 See ch. 5, Federalism, under heading 5.3, ''Federalism in Canada'', above.

5 See ch. 20, Property and Civil Rights, below.

6 Abel (1968) 7 West. Ont. L. Rev. 1. This theory is articulated by Lord Watson in *A.-G. Ont.* v. *A.-G. Can.* (Local Prohibition) [1896] A.C. 348, 365.

7 In the same article Abel insisted that the phrase ''peace, order and good government of Canada'' should not be treated as ''a jingle'' (p. 4) or a ''package deal'' (p. 5), but should be unpacked

The exact nature of the relationship between the p.o.g.g. language at the beginning of s. 91, and the enumerated heads of federal legislative power which follow it, has been more controversial. The O'Connor Report (1939) claimed, and other commentators have agreed, that it is incorrect to describe the p.o.g.g. power as residuary in its relationship with the enumerated heads of power.[8] The p.o.g.g. power, in O'Connor's view, does not comprise what is left after subtraction of the federal (as well as the provincial) enumerated heads; on the contrary, the p.o.g.g. power is the entire federal power, that is to say, all power not allocated to the provincial Legislatures. The enumerated heads of federal power are merely examples of the peace, order, and good government of Canada; they are not heads of power which exist independently of the opening words. This thesis finds support in the opening language[9] of s. 91, which asserts that the enumerated heads of federal power are listed "for greater certainty, but not so as to restrict the generality of the foregoing terms of this section [i.e., the p.o.g.g. language]". This thesis has led to the common description of the p.o.g.g. power as the "general" power.

Nevertheless, my view is that this "general" theory of the p.o.g.g. power, as including the whole of federal legislative power, is not a particularly helpful way of reading the Constitution Act, 1867. In the first place, despite the apparent import of the reference in s. 91 to "for greater certainty, etc.", it is reasonably clear that many of the enumerated heads of federal power are not merely examples of the opening words. Topics such as "trade and commerce" (s. 91(2)), "bank-

---

so that a court asks of a statute: "does this involve the peace of Canada? the order of Canada? the good government of Canada?" (p. 6). This suggestion not only finds no support in Canadian case law (as he conceded), it seems to me to be historically inaccurate. The phrase, "peace, order, and good government", or some close variant thereof, is to be found in nearly all the British-derived constitutions, including the constitutions of unitary states such as New Zealand, and the phrase has everywhere been interpreted as "a compendious means of delegating full powers of legislation", subject to any limitations which may be derived from other language of the constitution: Jennings, *Constitutional Law of the Commonwealth* (1957), vol. 1, 49; *Ibralebbe* v. *The Queen* [1964] A.C. 900, 923 (Ceylon). It is consistent with this understanding that s. 4 of the Constitution Act, 1871, intending to confer upon the federal Parliament plenary legislative power over the territories, empowered the Parliament to "make provision for the administration, peace, order, and good government of any territory not for the time being included in any Province". There is no doubt that plenary legislative power was in fact conferred in the sense explained by Jennings: *Riel* v. *The Queen* (1885) 10 App. Cas. 675; see also *A.-G. Sask.* v. *CPR* [1953] A.C. 594; *CLRB* v. *Yellowknife* [1977] 2 S.C.R. 729.

8 *Report of the Parliamentary Counsel relating to the British North America Act, 1867* (Senate of Canada, 1939, Annex I), 61-63. This view was shared by Laskin, among others. See Laskin, *Canadian Constitutional Law* (5th ed., 1986 by Finkelstein), 401; Laskin (1947) 25 Can. Bar Rev. 1054, 1057; this important article includes references to the voluminous earlier commentary on the p.o.g.g. power.

9 The deeming clause in the closing language of s. 91 expressly refers only to the s. 91 enumeration and gives it priority over s. 92(16) or, possibly, all of the s. 92 enumeration. The controversy as to its meaning, and the conflicting dicta, are reported in Browne, *The Judicial Committee and the British North America Act* (1967), 37, 45-46, 59, 165-167. See also Lysyk (1979) 57 Can. Bar Rev. 531, 540-541.

ing'' (s. 91(15)), ''bills of exchange and promissory notes''(s. 91(18)), ''interest'' (s. 91(19)), ''bankruptcy and insolvency'' (s. 91(21)), ''patents of invention and discovery'' (s. 91(22)), ''copyrights'' (s. 91(23)), and ''marriage and divorce'' (s. 91(26)) would probably have been held to come within the provincial head of ''property and civil rights in the province''(s. 92(13)) if they had not been specifically enumerated in the federal list.[10] If not specifically enumerated they would therefore have been excluded from the p.o.g.g. language, since it does not include provincial heads of power. It seems to me, therefore, that W.R. Lederman is correct in his conclusion that ''the federal list was not just superfluous grammatical prudence, it was compelled by historical necessity [the broad scope of ''property and civil rights''] and has independent standing''.[11]

A second reason for rejecting the general theory of the p.o.g.g. power is that it does not accord with the practice of the courts in applying the power-distributing provisions of the Constitution. For whatever a judge or commentator may say about the process of constitutional classification, the normal practice is to start by looking for a particular enumerated head of power which will sustain the impugned statute. Nor is there anything perverse about such a practice. When lawyers are called upon to decide which of two provisions in a text — be it a constitution, statute, deed, contract, will, or whatever — is applicable to a situation, they will usually choose the more specific of the two. This is often assumed to be the author's intention, because it means that there is a sphere of operation for both provisions, not merely the more general provision. It is also a more economical practice since the meaning of the more specific provision is usually clearer. ''The more difficult exploration of the big classes of subjects need not be undertaken if the little ones prove fruitful.''[12]

In my view, therefore, the residuary theory of the p.o.g.g. power is more helpful than the competing general theory. The discussion which follows will proceed on the assumption that matters which come within enumerated federal or provincial heads of power should be located in those enumerated heads, and the office of the p.o.g.g. power is to accommodate the matters which do not come within any of the enumerated federal or provincial heads.[13]

---

10 This point is incontrovertible with respect to one federal head of power, namely, ''unemployment insurance'' (s. 91(2A)), because that topic was held to be within property and civil rights in the province in *A.-G. Can.* v. *A.-G. Ont.* (Unemployment Insurance) [1937] A.C. 355, and was added to s. 91 by an amendment in 1940.

11 Lederman (1975) 53 Can. Bar Rev. 597, 603; Lysyk (1979) 57 Can. Bar Rev. 531, 539.

12 Abel (1969) 19 U. Toronto L.J. 487, 516, and see also 510.

13 The theory that p.o.g.g. is essentially a residuary power, which appears to me to be correct, does not imply that the opening words of s. 91 are subordinate to the enumeration in the sense of conferring a weaker kind of legislative power. Under the ''trenching doctrine'' the enumerated heads of s. 91 were said to have the capacity to authorize encroachments on provincial subject matters (trenching), while the opening words had a lesser capacity to do so. The trenching theory is not useful and it has faded into well-deserved obscurity: Laskin, *Canadian Constitutional Law* (5th ed., 1986 by Finkelstein), 255. The true position is that both enumeration and opening words are subject to the same rules, and the exercise of both powers may have an

The p.o.g.g. power has been the trunk from which three branches of legislative power have grown: (1) the "gap" branch; (2) the "national concern" branch; and (3) the "emergency" branch. Each will be discussed in turn in the text that follows.

17.2 The "gap" branch

One of the offices of the p.o.g.g. power is to fill lacunae or gaps in the scheme of distribution of powers. There are very few undoubted gaps in the scheme of distribution which have to be filled in this way. One gap exists in the provision for the incorporation of companies.[14] The Constitution Act, 1867, by s. 92(11), empowers the provincial Legislatures to make laws in relation to "the incorporation of companies with provincial objects", but there is no equivalent enumerated federal power of incorporation. The courts have held that the power to incorporate companies with objects other than provincial must fall within the federal p.o.g.g. power because of its residuary nature.[15]

A similar argument can be made with respect to the treaty power.[16] Section 132 of the Constitution Act, 1867 confers upon the federal Parliament the power to enact laws for performing the obligations of Canada "as part of the British Empire, towards foreign countries, arising under treaties between the Empire and such foreign countries". The framers of the Constitution Act, 1867 evidently did not contemplate that Canada would eventually acquire the power to enter into treaties on its own behalf. Accordingly, s. 132 is silent about performing the obligations of Canada arising under treaties entered into by Canada in its own right as an international person. In the *Radio Reference* (1932),[17] the Privy Council held that the p.o.g.g. power filled this gap. Viscount Dunedin said that the power to perform Canadian (as opposed to imperial) treaties came within p.o.g.g. because it was "not mentioned explicitly in either s. 91 or s. 92".[18] This reasoning appears to be a faithful reading of the Constitution Act, 1867. However, it was later emphatically rejected by a differently-constituted Privy Council, speaking

---

important impact on property and civil rights in the province or other provincial subject matters. This can occur either by virtue of the "double-aspect" doctrine, e.g. *Munro* v. *National Capital Comm.* [1966] S.C.R. 663, where the p.o.g.g. power gave land use planning power to create a national capital region concurrent with provincial power, or by virtue of the incidental effect doctrine, e.g., *Johannesson* v. *West St. Paul* [1952] 1 S.C.R. 292, where the p.o.g.g. power gave authority over aeronautics which pre-empted municipal zoning by-laws. The double-aspect doctrine and the incidental effect doctrine are discussed in ch. 15, Judicial Review on Federal Grounds, above.

14 This topic is discussed in detail in ch. 22, Companies, below.

15 *Citizens' Insurance Co.* v. *Parsons* (1881) 7 App. Cas. 96.

16 This topic is discussed in detail in ch. 11, Treaties, above.

17 *Re Regulation and Control of Radio Communication in Can.* [1932] A.C. 304.

18 *Id.*, 312.

through Lord Atkin, in the *Labour Conventions* case (1937).[19] Recent dicta by the Supreme Court of Canada suggest that the reasoning in the *Radio Reference* could be returning to judicial favour.[20]

A less obvious example of the gap test is *Jones* v. *A.-G. N.B.* (1974),[21] in which the Supreme Court of Canada upheld the validity of the federal Official Languages Act, an Act which, broadly speaking, attempted to guarantee the equal status of French and English in the institutions of the Parliament and government of Canada. Laskin C.J. for the unanimous Court pointed out that since federal institutions and agencies are ''clearly beyond provincial reach'', they must be within federal reach under the opening p.o.g.g. words of s. 91, ''on the basis of the purely residuary character of the legislative power thereby conferred.''[22] As in the federal company cases and the *Radio Reference*, no definition of p.o.g.g. was offered. It was sufficient to note that the matter of the legislation was not included in any of the enumerated heads of power of ss. 91 and 92.[23]

The cases dealing with legislative jurisdiction over offshore mineral resources have employed a similar analysis. Because the seabed off the shore of British Columbia and the seabed off the shore of Newfoundland lay outside the boundaries of each province, the offshore minerals were outside each province's legislative jurisdiction.[24] The offshore minerals therefore had to come within the federal Parliament's p.o.g.g. power ''in its residual capacity''.[25]

It is of course always possible to classify a law by labelling its ''matter'' or ''pith and substance'' with a name which does not appear to come within any of the enumerated heads of power.[26] This could be said, and has been said, of aeronautics, atomic energy and the national capital region.[27] But the decisions concerning these topics are not based on the same reasoning as the cases on federal incorporation, treaties, official languages and offshore resources. These

19 *A.-G. Can.* v. *A.-G. Ont.* (Labour Conventions) [1937] A.C. 326.

20 See ch. 11, Treaties, under heading 11.5(c), ''Evaluation of Labour Conventions case'', above.

21 [1975] 2 S.C.R. 182.

22 *Id.*, 189.

23 *Jones* was followed in *R.* v. *Appleby (No. 2)* (1976) 76 D.L.R. (3d) 110 (N.B. A.D.) (p.o.g.g. authorizes National Library Act provision for the compulsory taking of two copies of all new books published in Canada) and *Friends of Oldman River Society* v. *Can.* [1992] 1 S.C.R. (p.o.g.g. authorizes procedures for assessment of environmental impact of projects affecting federal heads of power).

24 The provincial Legislatures' lack of extraterritorial competence is explained in ch. 13, Extraterritorial Competence, above.

25 In *Re Offshore Mineral Rights of B.C.* [1967] S.C.R. 792, the Court also buttressed this reasoning with the national concern branch of p.o.g.g., asserting (at p. 817) that the offshore minerals were ''of concern to Canada as a whole and go beyond local or provincial concern or interest''. In *Re Nfld. Continental Shelf* [1984] S.C.R. 86, 127, which is where the quotation in the text comes from, this ''residual capacity'' was the only reason given for federal legislative jurisdiction.

26 Le Dain (1974) 12 Osgoode Hall L.J. 261, 293; quoted with approval by Beetz J. in *Re Anti-Inflation Act* [1976] 2 S.C.R. 373, 451.

27 See notes 44-50 below.

latter cases depend upon a lacuna or gap in the text of the Constitution: a reference to companies with provincial objects but no mention of companies with broader objects; a reference to imperial treaties but no mention of Canadian treaties; references to executive and legislative power but no mention of regulating the agencies that exercise that power; and a withdrawal of provincial extraterritorial competence but no grant of federal extraterritorial competence. In these cases, the Constitution recognizes certain topics as being classes of subjects for distribution-of-powers purposes, but fails to deal completely with each topic. The p.o.g.g. language completes the incomplete assignment of power. The gap branch of p.o.g.g. covers these limited and unusual cases, where the application of the p.o.g.g. power is almost logically required. In most cases a "new" or hitherto unrecognized kind of law does not have any necessary or logical claim to come within p.o.g.g. It might come within property and civil rights in the province (s. 92(13)) or matters of a merely local or private nature in the province (s. 92(16)). Which head of power is appropriate depends on the nature of the "new" matter, and the scope which is attributed to the various competing heads of power of which p.o.g.g. is only one.[28]

17.3 The "national concern" branch

(a) History

The "national concern" branch of p.o.g.g. takes its name from a dictum in the *Canada Temperance Federation* case (1946), a case that will shortly be described. But its roots may be traced back to the previous century.

The history starts with *Russell* v. *The Queen* (1882),[29] although no definition of p.o.g.g. was actually articulated in that case. The statute in issue was the Canada Temperance Act, a federal statute which established a local-option temperance scheme. Sir Montague Smith for the Privy Council upheld the statute on the basis that it did not fall within any of the provincial heads of legislative power. Therefore, he held, it must be within federal power, but he did not commit himself as to which head of federal power was applicable.

The decision in *Russell* was later explained by Lord Watson for the Privy Council in the *Local Prohibition* case (1896)[30] as resting on the p.o.g.g. power, and in the course of this explanation Lord Watson enunciated for the first time a "national dimensions" definition of p.o.g.g.:[31]

> Their Lordships do not doubt that some matters, in their origin local and provincial, might attain such dimensions as to affect the body politic of the Dominion, and to

28 The relevance of "newness" is examined later in this chapter, under heading 17.3(d), "Newness", below.

29 (1882) 7 App. Cas. 829.

30 *A.-G. Ont.* v. *A.-G. Can.* (Local Prohibition) [1896] A.C. 348.

31 *Id.*, 361.

> justify the Canadian Parliament in passing laws for their regulation or abolition in the interest of the Dominion. But great caution must be observed in distinguishing between that which is local or provincial and that which has ceased to be merely local or provincial, and has become a matter of national concern, in such sense as to bring it within the jurisdiction of the Parliament of Canada.

The idea that some matters of legislation, in their origin local and provincial, could acquire "national dimensions" or (as it is usually now expressed) "national concern" and thereby come within the federal Parliament's p.o.g.g. power, is the core of the national concern branch of p.o.g.g.

Ironically, although it was the *Local Prohibition* case which explained *Russell* as resting on the p.o.g.g. power, the two decisions are not easy to reconcile. The *Local Prohibition* case concerned a provincial local-option temperance scheme which was very similar to the federal scheme upheld in *Russell*. In the *Local Prohibition* case, their lordships upheld the provincial statute as being in relation to either "property and civil rights in the province" (s. 92(13)) or "matters of a merely local or private nature in the province" (s. 92(16)). This reasoning is directly contradictory of *Russell*, which was based on the holding that a local-option temperance scheme did not come within s. 92(13) or s. 92(16). By this time, of course, it had been established that the "double aspect" doctrine would sometimes permit both levels of government to enact laws in the same general field.[32] But this would explain the co-existence of *Russell* and *Local Prohibition* only if a federal aspect could be attributed to the Canada Temperance Act. The Privy Council in *Russell* appeared to assume that whenever Parliament regarded a problem as being "one of general concern to the Dominion, upon which uniformity of legislation is desirable", then it acquired the power to deal with it.[33] If this were the law, there would be no limit to the reach of federal power. And yet Lord Watson's national dimensions test, while accompanied by the exhortation to "great caution" in its application, did not indicate what were the limits of the p.o.g.g. power.[34]

In 1911, Viscount Haldane joined the ranks of the law lords and thereby became a member of the Judicial Committee of the Privy Council. He wrote many

---

32 *Hodge* v. *The Queen* (1883) 9 App. Cas. 117; and see ch. 15, Judicial Review on Federal Grounds, under heading 15.5(c), "Double aspect", above.

33 (1882) 7 App. Cas. 829, 841; and see notes 55-64, and accompanying text, below.

34 The authority of *Russell* v. *The Queen* was also impaired by the fact that the case was a private prosecution and neither the federal Attorney-General nor any provincial Attorney-General was represented in the proceedings. Moreover, counsel for Russell conceded that Parliament had the power to enact the Canada Temperance Act without the local-option features. This led Duff J. in *Re Board of Commerce Act* (1920) 60 S.C.R. 456, 507 to describe Russell as "in great part an unargued case". See also *Local Prohibition* case [1896] A.C. 348, 362 per Lord Watson; *Natural Products Marketing Act Reference* [1936] S.C.R. 398, 420, per Duff C.J. Not long after *Russell*, legislation was enacted in Quebec and Ontario requiring, whenever the validity of a statute was challenged, that notice be given to the appropriate Attorney-General, and that he or she be entitled to intervene in the proceedings. These requirements exist now in all Canadian jurisdictions: see ch. 56, Procedure, under heading 56.6, "Intervention", below.

of the opinions in Canadian constitutional appeals until his death in 1928. During this period, the Privy Council severely contracted each of the major federal powers. The impact of the decisions of this period on the criminal law power and the trade and commerce power is related in the later two chapters on those topics. With respect to the p.o.g.g. power, Viscount Haldane's Privy Council ignored Lord Watson's national dimensions dictum, and instead insisted that only an emergency would justify the exercise of the p.o.g.g. power. The decisions that expounded this view are discussed later in this chapter.[35]

Viscount Haldane's view that p.o.g.g. was only an emergency power persisted until after the second world war.[36] Its inconsistency with the national dimensions view of p.o.g.g. was not directly confronted until *A.-G. Ont.* v. *Canada Temperance Federation* (1946).[37] In that case, a frontal attack was mounted against *Russell* v. *The Queen* (1882).[38] The Canada Temperance Act, which had been upheld in *Russell*, was challenged a second time. In opposition to the statute, two alternative arguments were presented: either *Russell* was wrongly decided because it was not based on an emergency, or, if *Russell* was based on an emergency (as Viscount Haldane had claimed in *Toronto Electric Commissioners* v. *Snider*),[39] the alleged emergency of drunkenness had now passed away. In light of the Privy Council's insistence on an emergency in every p.o.g.g. case since 1896, these arguments looked unanswerable. But in the *Canada Temperance* case, the Privy Council, now speaking through Viscount Simon, refused to overrule *Russell*. While stopping short of actually approving the decision, their lordships pointed out that it had stood for over sixty years, and for that reason "must be regarded as firmly embedded in the constitutional law of Canada".[40] Moreover, they held that *Russell* had not been decided on the basis of an emergency, and the p.o.g.g. power was not confined to emergencies.

The *Canada Temperance* case thus repudiated the line of cases that asserted that only an emergency could serve as the basis for an exercise of the p.o.g.g. power. In place of that doctrine, Viscount Simon formulated a new test, in the following words:[41]

> In their Lordships' opinion, the true test must be found in the real subject matter of the legislation: if it is such that it goes beyond local or provincial concern or interests and must from its inherent nature be the concern of the Dominion as a whole (as, for example, in the *Aeronautics* case and the *Radio* case), then it will fall within the

35 Section 17.4, "The "emergency" branch", below.

36 After Viscount Haldane's death in 1928, some fragmentation of opinion in the Privy Council emerged, and the national dimensions test was referred to obiter, without disapproval, in the *Aeronautics Reference* [1932] A.C. 54, the *Radio Reference* [1932] A.C. 304 (at least by implication) and in *CPR* v. *A.-G. B.C.* (Empress Hotel) [1950] A.C. 122.

37 [1946] A.C. 193.

38 Note 29, above.

39 Note 105, below.

40 [1946] A.C. 193, 206.

41 *Id.*, 205-206.

> competence of the Dominion Parliament as a matter affecting the peace, order and good government of Canada, although it may in another aspect touch on matters specially reserved to the provincial legislatures. War and pestilence, no doubt, are instances; so, too, may be the drink or drug traffic, or the carrying of arms. In *Russell* v. *The Queen*, Sir Montague Smith gave as an instance of valid Dominion legislation a law which prohibited or restricted the sale or exposure of cattle having a contagious disease. Nor is the validity of the legislation, when due to its inherent nature, affected because there may still be room for enactments by a provincial legislature dealing with an aspect of the same subject in so far as it specially affects that province.

This dictum, which bears a close resemblance to Lord Watson's "national dimensions" dictum in the *Local Prohibition* case, is now established as the definition of the "national concern" branch of p.o.g.g. The test is whether the matter of the legislation "goes beyond local or provincial concern or interests and must from its inherent nature be the concern of the Dominion as a whole". If this test is satisfied, then the matter comes within the p.o.g.g. power in its national concern branch. Of course, as will be elaborated later in this chapter, the emergency cases are still good law in the sense that an emergency will also provide a basis for legislation under the p.o.g.g. power. But the *Canada Temperance* case established that there was a national concern branch of p.o.g.g. as well as an emergency branch.[42]

The national concern branch of p.o.g.g. has been recognized in many cases since 1946,[43] and it has provided the sole basis for the decision in three cases in the Supreme Court of Canada. The first case was *Johannesson* v. *West St. Paul* (1952),[44] in which the Court held that aeronautics satisfied the national concern test. Of the five opinions written, four cited and relied upon the *Canada Temperance* dictum,[45] but only Locke J. attempted to define the characteristics of aeronautics that he thought were relevant. He pointed to the rapid growth of passenger and freight traffic by air, the use of aircraft for the carriage of mails especially to the more remote northern parts of the country, and the necessity for the devel-

---

42 The relationship between the two branches, that is, the question when an emergency is required and when national concern will suffice, is taken up in the last section of this chapter.

43 At first, it seemed to be destined for oblivion. The emergency test was applied (as the sole test) in *Co-op. Committee on Japanese Canadians* v. *A.-G. Can.* [1947] A.C. 87; *Re Wartime Leasehold Regulations* [1950] S.C.R. 124; *Can. Federation of Agriculture* v. *A.-G. Que.* [1951] A.C. 179.

44 [1952] 1 S.C.R. 292.

45 The *Aeronautics Reference* [1932] A.C. 54 had already decided that the federal Parliament had authority over aeronautics, but the decision had been based primarily on the existence of a British Empire treaty binding Canada. In 1947 the British Empire treaty was denounced and replaced by a new treaty to which Canada was a party in its own right. This rendered the treaty power arguably unavailable (note 19, above), and necessitated the finding of a new basis for legislative jurisdiction. In *Johannesson*, Rinfret C.J. still thought that the issue was concluded by the *Aeronautics Reference*: [1952] 1 S.C.R. 292, 303; but the other four opinions each cited and relied upon the *Canada Temperance* test: [1952] 1 S.C.R. 292, 308-309, 311, 318, 328. On aeronautics, see ch. 21, Transportation and Communication, below.

opment of air services to be controlled by a national government responsive to the needs of the nation as a whole.[46]

The second case was *Munro* v. *National Capital Commission* (1966),[47] in which the Court held that the national capital region — an area around Ottawa designated by federal legislation — satisfied the national concern test. Cartwright J. for a unanimous Court referred to the unsuccessful efforts to zone the national capital region through the cooperative action of the two provinces of Ontario and Quebec.[48] Then, later on, he said:[49]

> I find it difficult to suggest a subject-matter of legislation which more clearly goes beyond local or provincial interests and is the concern of Canada as a whole than the development, conservation and improvement of the National Capital Region in accordance with a coherent plan in order that the nature and character of the seat of the Government of Canada may be in accordance with its national significance. Adopting the words of the learned trial judge, it is my view that the Act "deals with a single matter of national concern".

The third case was *R.* v. *Crown Zellerbach* (1988),[50] in which the Court held that marine pollution satisfied the national concern test. The federal Ocean Dumping Control Act, which prohibited dumping "at sea", was upheld in its application to marine waters within the boundaries of British Columbia. Le Dain J. for the majority of the Court[51] held that[52] "marine pollution, because of its predominantly extra-provincial as well as international character and implications, is clearly a matter of concern to Canada as a whole".

A fourth case could be added to the list, although the national concern branch of p.o.g.g. was not the sole ground of decision. In *Ontario Hydro* v. *Ontario* (1993),[53] the Supreme Court of Canada upheld the federal Atomic Energy Control Act. Federal jurisdiction over atomic energy (or nuclear power) was derived from both the declaratory power of s. 92(10)(c)[54] and the national concern branch of p.o.g.g. With respect to the national concern branch of p.o.g.g., La Forest J. for

---

46 [1952] 1 S.C.R. 292, 326-327.

47 [1966] S.C.R. 663.

48 *Id.*, 667.

49 *Id.*, 671.

50 [1988] 1 S.C.R. 401.

51 Le Dain J. was joined by Dickson C.J., McIntyre and Wilson JJ. La Forest J., joined by Beetz and Lamer JJ., dissented on the ground that the requirement of distinctness (see following text) was not satisfied.

52 [1988] 1 S.C.R. 401, 436.

53 [1993] 3 S.C.R. 327. La Forest., with L'Heureux-Dubé and Gonthier J., held that labour relations in a nuclear-powered electrical generating station were within federal jurisdiction. Lamer C.J., in a separate concurring opinion, reached the same result. Iacobucci J., with Sopinka and Cory JJ., dissented. However, all three opinions agreed that the federal Parliament had regulatory jurisdiction over nuclear power by reason of both the declaratory power and the national concern branch of p.o.g.g.

54 See ch. 22, Transportation and Communication, under heading 22.8, "Works for the general advantage of Canada", below.

the majority of the Court said[55] that "the production, use and application of atomic energy constitute a matter of national concern", because "it is predominantly extra-provincial and international in character and implications"; he also pointed to the "strategic and security aspects of nuclear power in relation to national defence" and to its potential for environmental catastrophes.[56]

The cumulative effect of the cases is to establish firmly the national concern branch of p.o.g.g. In the following sections of the chapter, an attempt will be made to analyze the elements of the national concern branch.

(b) Definition of national concern

When does a subject matter of legislation become "the concern of the Dominion as a whole" so as to satisfy the national concern test?

About all that can be gleaned from the dicta in *Johannesson* and *Munro* is a sense that it is the nation-wide importance of a subject of legislation that determines whether or not it has the requisite national concern. But such a subjective criterion as importance could hardly serve as a justiciable test. Moreover, it would be difficult to argue that matters coming within federal legislative competence are generally more important than matters coming within provincial legislative competence. What could be more important than the law of contract or property, or municipal institutions, or education — all matters within provincial legislative competence? The notion of importance can be refined a little if one adds a geographic dimension to it. A matter of national concern must be "of import or significance to all parts of Canada".[57]

If a geographic sense of national concern is accepted, this could be thought to imply that it is the desirability of uniform legislation across Canada on a particular topic which gives that topic a national dimension. But this cannot be correct either. Uniformity is desirable with respect to many topics, and for many reasons, but of course the distribution of legislative powers in a federal system necessarily involves a substantial subordination of the value of uniformity to that of provincial autonomy even where there is no objective necessity for regional variations. In legislative fields which are entrusted to the provinces, it is for the provinces to decide whether or not they desire uniformity: they can achieve it whenever they wish through the enactment of uniform laws. If, as is common, some provinces do not enact the uniform statute, or enact it with variations, no

---

55 [1993] 3 S.C.R. 327, 379.

56 See also *Re Offshore Mineral Rights of B.C.* [1967] S.C.R. 792 (offshore mineral resources satisfied national concern test and gap test). *Re Can. Metal Co.* (1982) 144 D.L.R. (3d) 124 (Man. Q.B.) (air pollution satisfied national concern test). The curious decision in *The Queen* v. *Hauser* [1979] 1 S.C.R. 984 (upholding the Narcotic Control Act under p.o.g.g. without reference to either the emergency test or the national concern test, but solely on the basis of drug abuse as a "genuinely new problem") is discussed later in this chapter in text accompanying note 79, below.

57 Gibson, "Measuring National Dimensions" (1976) 7 Man. L.J. 15, 31.

great harm is done: a substantial degree of uniformity will still have been achieved and will still be valuable. Even in fields entrusted to the federal Parliament, while uniform laws are usual, federal laws occasionally impose different rules on different parts of the country.[58] There is no constitutional requirement of uniformity.[59]

There are, however, cases where uniformity of law throughout the country is not merely desirable, but essential, in the sense that the problem "is beyond the power of the provinces to deal with it".[60] This is the case when the failure of one province to act would injure the residents of the other (cooperating) provinces. This "provincial inability" test goes a long way towards explaining the cases. The often cited case of an epidemic of pestilence is a good example. The failure by one province to take preventative measures would probably lead to the spreading of the disease into those provinces which had taken preventative measures. The national concern cases can be explained in these terms. In the case of aeronautics (*Johannesson*),[61] the failure of one province to accept uniform procedures for the use of air space and ground facilities would endanger the residents of other provinces engaged in inter-provincial and international air travel. In the case of the national capital region (*Munro*),[62] the failure of either Quebec or Ontario to cooperate in the development of the national capital region would have denied to all Canadians the symbolic value of a suitable national capital. Indeed, in the *Munro* case the Supreme Court of Canada took judicial notice of the fact that the "zoning" of the national capital region was only undertaken federally after unsuccessful efforts by the federal government to secure cooperative action by Ontario and Quebec.[63] In the case of marine pollution (*Crown Zellerbach*),[64] the failure of one province to protect its waters would probably lead to the pollution of the waters of other provinces as well as the (federal) territorial sea and high

58 E.g., introduction of English divorce and annulment law in Ontario: Divorce Act, S.C. 1930, c. 14, (since repealed); differential rates of income tax caused by transfer of tax points to Quebec: ch. 6, Financial Arrangements, under heading 6.7, "Conditional federal grants", above; local-option liquor prohibition: *Russell* v. *the Queen* (1882) 7 App. Cas. 829; *A.-G. Ont.* v. *Can. Temperance Federation* [1946] A.C. 193; and cf. *Gold Seal* v. *Dom. Express Co.* (1921) 62 S.C.R. 424; opting-out clauses in the Lord's Day Act: *Lord's Day Alliance of Can.* v. *A.-G. B.C.* [1959] S.C.R. 497; adoption of provincial highway transport regulation: *Coughlin* v. *Ont. Highway Transport Bd.* [1968] S.C.R. 569; provincial variations in criminal procedure or punishment: *A.-G. B.C.* v. *Smith* [1967] S.C.R. 702, 710-711; *R.* v. *Burnshine* [1975] 1 S.C.R. 693; *R.* v. *Cornell* [1988] 1 S.C.R. 461; *R.* v. *Turpin* [1989] 1 S.C.R. 1296; *R.* v. *S.(S)* [1990] 2 S.C.R. 254.

59 Not only is no requirement of uniformity imposed by federalism principles, challenges to non-uniform federal laws based on the equality guarantees of the Canadian Bill of Rights and the Charter of Rights have also failed: see ch. 52, Equality, under heading 52.16, "Place of residence", below.

60 Gibson, note 57, above, 33.

61 Note 44, above.

62 Note 47, above.

63 Note 48, above.

64 Note 50, above.

sea. In the case of nuclear power (*Ontario Hydro*),[65] the failure of one province to enact adequate regulatory measures would expose the people of other provinces to the risk of an environmental catastrophe as well as the risks created by the proliferation of nuclear weapons.

In the *Crown Zellerbach* case,[66] Le Dain J. for the majority of the Court relied on the provincial inability test as a reason for finding that marine pollution was a matter of national concern. ''It is because of the interrelatedness of the intra-provincial and extra-provincial aspects of the matter that it requires a single or uniform legislative treatment.''[67] It seems, therefore, that the most important element of national concern is a need for one national law which cannot realistically be satisfied by cooperative provincial action because the failure of one province to cooperate would carry with it adverse consequences for the residents of other provinces. A subject-matter of legislation which has this characteristic has the necessary national concern to justify invocation of the p.o.g.g. power.[68]

(c) Distinctness

In the *Anti-Inflation Reference* (1976),[69] a case that is discussed later in this chapter,[70] the Supreme Court of Canada upheld federal wage and price controls under the emergency branch of the p.o.g.g. power. Laskin C.J. (with whom Judson, Spence and Dickson JJ. agreed) left open the possibility that the federal wage and price controls could also have been supported under the national concern branch,[71] but Beetz J. (with whom, on this point, Martland, Ritchie, Pigeon and de Grandpré JJ. agreed) denied that the wage and price controls could have been supported under the national concern branch. Beetz J.'s opinion was that inflation was too broad and diffuse a topic to qualify as a ''matter'' coming within the national concern branch of the p.o.g.g. power. In order to qualify as a matter, a topic must be ''distinct'': it must have ''a degree of unity that makes it indivisible, an identity which makes it distinct from provincial matters and a sufficient con-

65 Note 53, above.

66 Note 50, above.

67 *Id.*, 434. He went on (also at p. 434) to caution against the fallacy ''that there must be plenary jurisdiction in one order of government or the other to deal with any legislative problem''. This is a reference to the requirement of distinctness, which Le Dain J. described as ''singleness or indivisibility'', which is discussed next in the text. He regarded (still at p. 434) the provincial inability test as useful in determining whether a matter has the requisite singleness or indivisibility. I find this passage difficult to understand. To me, the provincial inability test identifies the requirement of national concern, but is not relevant to the requirement of distinctness.

68 As well as the *Crown Zellerbach* case, the provincial inability test is referred to with approval in *Labatt Breweries* v. *A.-G. Can.* [1980] 1 S.C.R. 914, 945; *Schneider* v. *The Queen* [1982] 2 S.C.R. 112, 131; *The Queen* v. *Wetmore* [1983] 2 S.C.R. 284, 296.

69 *Re Anti-Inflation Act* [1976] 2 S.C.R. 373.

70 Note 142, below.

71 [1976] 2 S.C.R. 373, 419.

sistence to retain the bounds of form".[72] This opinion was supported by a majority of five of the nine judges.

The requirement of distinctness was the issue that divided the Supreme Court of Canada in *R.* v. *Crown Zellerbach* (1988).[73] In that case, a majority of the Court[74] upheld the federal Ocean Dumping Control Act, which prohibited dumping "at sea", on the basis that marine pollution[75] was a matter of national concern. La Forest J. dissented, because in his view marine pollution lacked the distinctness required of a matter of national concern. Marine waters intermingled with fresh waters, and were affected by coastal activity and by deposits from the air. The power to regulate marine pollution thus intruded too deeply into industrial and municipal activity, resource development, construction, recreation and other matters within provincial jurisdiction. Le Dain J. for the majority, while not asserting federal authority over pollution in general, held that marine pollution, although obviously affected by the air and by fresh water flowing into the sea, did have "ascertainable and reasonable limits, in so far as its impact on provincial jurisdiction is concerned".[76]

The requirement of distinctness was articulated in the *Crown Zellerbach* case,[77] in Le Dain J.'s usual felicitous style, as follows:

> For a matter to qualify as a matter of national concern . . . it must have a singleness, distinctiveness and indivisibility that clearly distinguishes it from matters of provincial concern and a scale of impact on provincial jurisdiction that is reconcilable with the fundamental distribution of legislative power under the Constitution.

As this passage emphasizes, the requirement of distinctness is an essential safeguard, allaying the justifiable concern that the national concern branch of p.o.g.g. would tend to absorb the entire catalogue of provincial powers if subject matters as broad as inflation and pollution were within federal authority.[78]

The requirement of "distinctness" is a necessary but not a sufficient condition for a matter to be admitted to the national concern branch of p.o.g.g. A distinct matter would also have to satisfy the provincial inability test (or other definition of national concern) in order to be admitted to the national concern

---

72 *Id.*, 457-458.

73 [1988] 1 S.C.R. 401.

74 Note 51, above.

75 Federal jurisdiction over the waters outside the boundaries of any province could not be, and was not, doubted: see ch. 13, Extraterritorial Competence, under heading 13.3(b), "Territory of province", above. The problem was that the Act applied to all dumping "at sea", and "sea" included inland waters within the boundaries of the provinces. The offence alleged against Crown Zellerbach had taken place within the boundaries of British Columbia.

76 [1988] 1 S.C.R. 401, 438.

77 *Id.*, 432.

78 See also *Schneider* v. *The Queen* [1982] 2 S.C.R. 112, 142 ("health" is another "amorphous topic" in the same category); *General Motors* v. *City National Leasing* [1989] 1 S.C.R. 641, 682 ("competition is not a single matter any more than inflation or pollution"); *Friends of Oldman River Society* v. *Can.* [1992] 1 S.C.R. 3, 63-64, (the environment is in the same category).

branch of p.o.g.g. A distinct matter would come within provincial power if it came within ''property and civil rights in the province'' (s. 92(13)) or if it were ''of a merely local or private nature in the province''(s. 92(16)).

(d) Newness

In *The Queen* v. *Hauser* (1979),[79] the Supreme Court of Canada, by a majority of four to three, held that the federal Narcotic Control Act was a valid exercise of the p.o.g.g. power. This was a surprising result, because the Act had previously been upheld by the Supreme Court of Canada as a criminal law.[80] The criminal classification seems more plausible, because nearly all of the Act is concerned to prohibit the production, trafficking and possession of illicit drugs, and to provide for the prosecution and punishment of offenders; indeed, the penalties in the Act go as high as life imprisonment (for trafficking), an extraordinary sanction to find in a regulatory statute. To be sure, in favour of the p.o.g.g. classification, there is an affinity between alcohol and drugs, which suggests an analogy with *Russell* v. *The Queen* (1882),[81] in which a temperance law was upheld under the p.o.g.g. power. But *Russell* has always been an anomaly which was difficult to justify under orthodox constitutional doctrine, and it seemed to have been finally discredited in the *Anti-Inflation Reference* (1976),[82] where Beetz J. described *Russell* as a ''special'' case, an ''extraordinary'' case, a case with a ''chequered'' history, and a case that was ''not easy to reconcile with the *Local Prohibition* case''. It accordingly came as something of a surprise in *Hauser* to find Pigeon J., with the concurrence of Martland, Ritchie and Beetz JJ., referring to *Russell* with approval.[83]

The reasons given in Pigeon J.'s majority opinion for his reliance on the p.o.g.g. power are perfunctory and unsatisfactory.[84] No indication is given of why narcotics have attained the requisite degree of national concern. Indeed, the phrase ''national concern'' is never used, and no reference is made to the *Canada Temperance* case, or to *Johannesson*, *Munro* or the *Anti-Inflation Reference*. (The *Crown Zellerbach* case had not then been decided.) The sum and substance of the reasoning is contained in the following paragraph of the opinion:[85]

> In my view, the most important consideration for classifying the Narcotic Control Act as legislation enacted under the general residual federal power, is that this is

79 [1979] 1 S.C.R. 984.

80 *Industrial Acceptance Corp.* v. *The Queen* [1953] 2 S.C.R. 273.

81 Note 29, above.

82 *Re Anti-Inflation Act* [1976] 2 S.C.R. 373, 453-457.

83 [1979] 1 S.C.R. 984, 997. All of these judges had joined with Beetz J. in his dismissal of *Russell* in the *Anti-Inflation Reference*.

84 Dickson J., with the agreement of Pratte J., dissented. With respect, his opinion is an impeccable account of the constitutional basis (as criminal law) of the Narcotic Control Act. Spence J. wrote a separate concurring opinion, and did not discuss this issue.

85 *Id.*, 1000-1001.

> essentially legislation adopted to deal with a genuinely new problem which did not exist at the time of Confederation and clearly cannot be put in the class of "Matters of a merely local or private nature". The subject-matter of this legislation is thus properly to be dealt with on the same footing as such other new developments as aviation (*Re Aeronautics*) and radio communications (*Re Radio Communication*).

In this passage, the emphasis on "distinctness" which is found in the *Anti-Inflation Reference* (and in the later *Crown Zellerbach* case) is replaced by an emphasis on "newness". To be sure, Beetz J. in the *Anti-Inflation Reference* had referred several times to a "new matter" or "new subject-matter", and had described inflation as "a very ancient phenomenon".[86] But, in context, I think he was referring to a *conceptually* new subject-matter, that is to say, one which was not clearly covered by an enumerated head and had not previously been considered by the courts. He was using the word "new" in the sense of "arising for consideration for the first time": a new matter would therefore be one "that the courts have yet to allocate to either a provincial or a federal head of power".[87] It is hard to accept that a matter comes within the national concern branch of p.o.g.g. only if it is *historically* new. Newness in the historical sense seems to have no relevance in this context. Pigeon J.'s examples of aeronautics and radio do not help his argument. While it is true that aeronautics was placed under p.o.g.g. in *Johannesson*, the Court has held that television (and therefore radio) is not covered by p.o.g.g., but by an enumerated federal power (s. 92(10)(a)).[88] Other new inventions, such as, buses, trucks, telephones and movies have all been located outside p.o.g.g. Aeronautics is an anomaly, not the illustration of a general rule.[89] And, on the other side of the coin, if we accept the rapid (and unexplained) rehabilitation of *Russell*, what is "new" about liquor abuse? What about the actual problem at issue in *Hauser*, namely, drug abuse? Pigeon J. said that "drug abuse did not become a problem in this country during the last century".[90] Yet, surely neither Pigeon J. nor anyone else would disagree with Dickson J.'s dissenting opinion that "drug abuse is a very ancient phenomenon", and the most that can be said is that it was "not a pressing problem at the time of Confederation".[91]

I conclude that "newness" is irrelevant and unhelpful in this context. As Lysyk has said, "the newness, or lack of newness, of the matter ought to be an entirely neutral factor in the process of determining the content of the federal residuary power."[92]

---

86 [1976] 2 S.C.R. 373, 458.

87 Elliot, Note (1979) 14 U.B.C.L. Rev. 163, 197.

88 *Capital Cities Communications* v. *CRTC* [1978] 2 S.C.R. 141.

89 Chapter 21, Transportation and Communications, deals with (inter alia) aeronautics, radio, television, trucks, buses, telephones and movies.

90 [1979] 1 S.C.R. 984, 997.

91 *Id.*, 1059.

92 Lysyk, (1979) 57 Can. Bar Rev. 531, 571-572. Accord, *R.* v. *Crown Zellerbach* [1988] 1 S.C.R. 401, 432 per Le Dain J. for majority, but note the cautious reference to newness by La Forest J. dissenting at 458.

The reader will be wondering why Pigeon J. engaged in such tortured reasoning in order to locate the Narcotic Control Act within p.o.g.g., when the criminal classification was available to sustain the law. The answer is that Pigeon J. was straining to avoid facing the question whether the federal Parliament had the power to provide for the prosecution of criminal laws. At that time, the Court was deeply split on this question. As long as the federal power to prosecute criminal law was thought not to exist or was in doubt, the manifest inconvenience of that disability would inevitably create a tendency in the Court to move laws out of the "criminal" category and into another category, such as p.o.g.g., where federal enforcement power was clear. Since *Hauser*, the Court has decided that the federal government has the same power of enforcement over its criminal laws as it has over its other laws.[93] There is no longer any reason for the Court to shun the criminal classification.

I conclude that *Hauser* was wrongly decided, and should be overruled by the Court when a suitable occasion arises.[94] The Narcotic Control Act is properly to be characterized as a criminal law. It cannot be placed within the national concern branch of p.o.g.g.

The foregoing discussion of *Hauser* was compelled by Pigeon J.'s introduction of the concept of "newness" as a pre-condition for a matter to be admitted to the national concern branch of p.o.g.g. My conclusion, of course, is that there is no requirement of "newness".

17.4 The "emergency" branch

(a) The non-emergency cases

It is now necessary to go back in time to the period from 1911 to 1928, when Lord Haldane sat on the Privy Council. This was the period, it will be recalled, when the Privy Council ignored Lord Watson's "national dimensions" dictum in the *Local Prohibition* case,[95] and instead consistently expounded and applied the view that only an emergency would serve to enable the federal Parliament to exercise its p.o.g.g. power.[96]

---

93 The history of this controversy is related in ch. 19, Criminal Justice, under heading 19.6, "Prosecution", below.

94 In *Schneider* v. *The Queen* [1982] 2 S.C.R. 112, 115, Laskin C.J., in a separate sole concurring opinion, said that "the majority judgment in the *Hauser* case ought not to have placed the Narcotic Control Act under the residuary power", and that there was "good ground to reconsider that basis of decision, resting as it did on a bare majority judgment". That is an unusually direct and powerful criticism, especially from a judge who was sympathetic to the expansion of the national concern branch of p.o.g.g.

95 Note 30, above.

96 The only exemption from this requirement was the incorporation of federal companies, where federal power could be justified as filling a gap in the distribution-of-powers provisions of the Constitution: see the discussion of the "gap branch" earlier in this chapter.

Viscount Haldane's first consideration of the p.o.g.g. power came in the *Insurance Reference* (1916).[97] In that case, the Privy Council, through Viscount Haldane, held that the federal Insurance Act of 1910, which purported to license insurance companies, was unconstitutional. The Privy Council rejected arguments based on the trade and commerce power and the p.o.g.g. power. With respect to the latter, all that Viscount Haldane said was that the p.o.g.g. power "does not . . . enable the Dominion Parliament to trench on the subject-matters entrusted to the provincial Legislatures by the enumeration in s. 92."[98] He did not go on to specify any exceptions to this proposition, not even the case of an emergency; and he did not refer to the national dimensions test or consider the question whether the insurance industry satisfied that test.

The emergency test first emerged in the *Board of Commerce* case (1922),[99] although the word emergency was not used in the opinion. In that case, the Privy Council through Viscount Haldane struck down legislation which, as well as containing anti-combines provisions, prohibited the hoarding of "necessaries of life" (defined as food, clothing and fuel) and required stocks of such necessaries to be sold at fair prices. Their lordships rejected the p.o.g.g. power as authority for the statute on the ground that "highly exceptional" or "abnormal" circumstances would be required to justify the invocation of p.o.g.g.; as examples, they suggested "war or famine".[100]

In *Toronto Electric Commissioners* v. *Snider* (1925),[101] the question arose whether federal legislation for the settlement of industrial disputes — the labour legislation of the period — was valid. The Privy Council through Viscount Haldane held that it was not. The relations between employers and employees was a matter of civil rights in the province, and therefore within provincial jurisdiction. The p.o.g.g. power was available only in "cases arising out of some extraordinary peril to the national life of Canada, such as the cases arising out of a war".[102]

In neither of these two important cases did the Privy Council make any reference to the "national dimensions" test. The difficulty of reconciling *Russell*[103] with the new emergency doctrine was hinted at in *Board of Commerce*,[104] and resolved in *Snider* by characterizing intemperance in Canada as an emergency: an evil "so great and so general that at least for the period it was a menace

97 *A.G. Can.* v. *A.-G. Alta.* (Insurance) [1916] 1 A.C. 588.
98 *Id.*, 595.
99 [1922] 1 A.C. 191.
100 *Id.*, 197, 200.
101 [1925] A.C. 396.
102 *Id.*, 412.
103 Note 29, above.
104 [1922] 1 A.C. 191, 200.

to the national life of Canada so serious and so pressing that the National Parliament was called on to intervene to protect the nation from disaster''.[105]

Lord Haldane died in 1928. In 1932 the national dimensions test briefly surfaced again in the *Aeronautics Reference*.[106] But in the ''new deal'' cases[107] the Privy Council reverted to the emergency doctrine. In the depression of the 1930s, Prime Minister R.B. Bennett had proposed and secured the enactment of a Canadian new deal — a series of statutes designed to effect far-reaching social and economic reforms. However, in 1935, before the statutes could be implemented, his Conservative government was defeated, and the Liberal government of Prime Minister Mackenzie King referred the statutes to the courts for an opinion as to their validity. Most of the statutes were held to be invalid. The Privy Council, now speaking through Lord Atkin, held that laws providing for a weekly rest, minimum wages and maximum hours of labour were simply labour laws which, by virtue of *Snider*, were incompetent to the federal Parliament.[108] Unemployment insurance was also a matter within property and civil rights in the province and incompetent to the federal Parliament.[109] And the same was true of regulating the marketing of natural products.[110] Their lordships neither asked nor answered the question whether the various subject matters of the new deal statutes might not have acquired a ''national dimension'' through the existence of an economic depression requiring national action for its alleviation. On the contrary, they held that only an emergency would justify the invocation of the p.o.g.g. power. One might have thought that the depression would qualify as an emergency,[111] but their lordships denied that the depression was an emergency.[112]

Finally, in the *Margarine Reference* (1951),[113] the Privy Council through Lord Morton of Henryton held that a federal prohibition on the manufacture and

105 [1925] A.C. 396, 412. This ''national binge'' explanation of *Russell* was roundly condemned in *The King* v. *Eastern Terminal Elev. Co.* [1925] S.C.R. 434, 438, by Anglin C.J. whose views were often in conflict with the Privy Council of this period.

106 [1932] A.C. 54, 77.

107 The ''new deal cases'' in the Privy Council consisted of: *A.-G. Can.* v. *A.-G. Ont.* (Labour Conventions) [1937] A.C. 326; *A.-G. Can.* v. *A.-G. Ont.* (Unemployment Insurance) [1937] A.C. 355; *A.-G. B.C.* v. *A.-G. Can.* (Price Spreads) [1937] A.C. 368; *A.-G. B.C.* v. *A.-G. Can.* (Natural Products Marketing) [1937] A.C. 377; *A.-G. B.C.* v. *A.-G. Can.* (Farmers' Creditors Arrangement) [1937] A.C. 391; *A.-G. Ont.* v. *A.-G. Can.* (Canada Standard Trade Mark) [1937] A.C. 405. The decisions are the subject of a symposium in (1937) 15 Can. Bar Rev. 393-507; see also McConnell, ''The Judicial Review of Prime Minister Bennett's New Deal'' (1968) 6 Osgoode Hall L.J. 39; McConnell, ''Some Comparisons of the Roosevelt and Bennett New Deals'' (1971) 9 Osgoode Hall L.J. 221.

108 *A.-G. Can.* v. *A.-G. Ont.* (Labour Conventions) [1937] A.C. 326.

109 *A.-G. Can.* v. *A.-G. Ont.* (Unemployment Insurance) [1937] A.C. 355.

110 *A.-G. B.C.* v. *A.-G. Can.* (Natural Products Marketing) [1937] A.C. 377.

111 In *A.-G.* v. *A.-G. Ont.* (Unemployment Insurance) [1937] A.C. 355, counsel for the federal government included in his factum data showing the unemployment, lost production, lowering of living standards, etc., caused by the depression, but their lordships were unmoved.

112 I think it was also a relevant factor that the new deal legislation was permanent, rather than temporary: see sec. 17.4(e), ''Temporary character of law'', below.

113 *Can. Federation of Agriculture* v. *A.G. Que.* [1951] A.C. 179.

sale of margarine was invalid. Among other arguments, that based on p.o.g.g. was rejected on the basis of the emergency test.[114]

The denials of federal power in the "p.o.g.g. cases" of the Haldane period and the new deal period had profound effects on the nature of the Canadian federation. The *Insurance Reference*[115] confirmed that p.o.g.g. (like trade and commerce) could not be used to regulate a particular industry merely because the industry is nation-wide and important to the national economy. This has ensured that much regulation of industry has to be provincial.[116] The *Board of Commerce* case,[117] as well as reinforcing the lack of federal power over much economic regulation, discouraged the federal Parliament from enacting wage or price controls in peacetime until the Anti-Inflation Act of 1975.[118] The same case forced the substitution of narrower and less effective competition laws which could be upheld as criminal law.[119]

Toronto Electric Commissioners v. *Snider*[120] altered the character of the nation's labour law by remitting most of it to the provinces for enactment, although federal laws continue to govern the federal public sector and industries within federal jurisdiction.[121] The *Labour Conventions* case,[122] as well as extending the holding in *Snider* to labour standards, divided up the power to implement treaties in a way which still controls Canadian treaty-making practices.[123]

The *Unemployment Insurance Reference*[124] carried forward the logic of the insurance and labour cases to preclude the development of federal social security programmes of a contributory insurance character. It was reversed so far as unemployment insurance was concerned by an amendment to the Constitution Act in 1940, which added "unemployment insurance" as head 2A to the list of federal enumerated powers; but it cast its shadow over old age and other pensions, leading to an amendment in 1951 which added s. 94A to the Constitution Act and a further amendment in 1964 altering the new s. 94A. Other national social insurance plans covering health care and welfare services have been established under provincial legislation with the federal government setting the standards and sharing the cost.[125]

The *Natural Products Marketing Reference*[126] confirmed that p.o.g.g. did not offer a solution to the problem of enacting effective marketing schemes, a

---

114 *Id.*, 197-198.
115 Note 97, above.
116 See ch. 21, Property and Civil Rights, under heading 21.5, "Insurance", below.
117 Note 99, above.
118 Note 142, below.
119 See ch. 18, Criminal Law, under heading 18.6, "Competition law", below.
120 Note 101, above.
121 See ch. 21, Property and Civil Rights, under heading 21.8, "Labour relations", below
122 Note 108, above.
123 See ch. 11, Treaties, above.
124 Note 109, above.
125 See ch. 6, Financial Arrangements, under heading 6.7, "Conditional federal grants", above.
126 Note 99, above.

problem to which some partial solutions have been devised — but only partial solutions.[127]

The emergency period of the Privy Council thus wrote an exceedingly important chapter of Canadian constitutional law. While, as we shall see, the pendulum has subsequently tended to swing back to a position which allows larger use of the principal federal powers, it is likely that the broad lines of constitutional authority which were established by the Privy Council will continue to be controlling, and the expectations and patterns of legislative activity which they generated will certainly not be quickly revised. Recognizing this, constitutional lawyers have tended to lose interest in the once-heated debate over whether or not the Privy Council ''misread'' the Constitution in so limiting federal power. One can debate a fait accompli for only so long.

(b) War

The p.o.g.g. power did not entirely wither away in the Haldane and post-Haldane period. There were cases in which the emergency test was satisfied.[128]

During the first world war, the federal Parliament enacted the War Measures Act,[129] a statute which came into force on the issue by the federal government of a proclamation ''that war, invasion, or insurrection, real or apprehended, exists''. The Act then empowered the federal government to make regulations on almost any conceivable subject. The War Measures Act was proclaimed into force for both world wars, and during both wars the federal government embarked on extensive economic and other controls in regulations made under the Act. In the *Fort Frances* case,[130] the Privy Council held that the regime of price control which had been established during the first world war, and which was continued temporarily after the war, was constitutional. In ''a sufficiently great emergency such as that arising out of war'', the p.o.g.g. power would authorize laws which in normal times would be competent only to the provinces.[131] Rent control during and after the second world war was upheld on the same basis by the Supreme

127 See ch. 21, Property and Civil Rights, under heading 21.9, ''Marketing'', below.

128 See generally, Marx, ''The Emergency Power and Civil Liberties'' (1970) 16 McGill L.J. 39; Tarnopolsky, ''Emergency Powers and Civil Liberties'' (1972) 15 Can. Pub. Admin. 194; Weinrib, ''Situations of Emergency in Canadian Constitutional Law'' in *Contemporary Law: Canadian Reports to the 1990 International Congress of Comparative Law* (1990), 466.

129 The War Measures Act was enacted in 1914 and remained in force until 1988, when it was repealed by the Emergencies Act, S.C. 1988, c. 29. The Emergencies Act provides for, in ascending order of threat, four kinds of emergencies: (1) public welfare emergencies (e.g., natural disaster, disease, accident, pollution); (2) public order emergencies (e.g., the October crisis of 1970); (3) international emergencies (e.g., oil shortages caused by wars or embargoes elsewhere); and (4) war emergencies. See Tenofsky, ''The War Measures and Emergency Acts'' (1989) 19 Amer. Rev. of Can. Studies 293. At the time of writing (1997), no part of the Emergencies Act has been proclaimed in force.

130 *Fort Frances Pulp and Power Co.* v. *Man. Free Press Co.* [1923] A.C. 695.

131 *Id.*, 705.

Court of Canada in the *Wartime Leasehold Regulations Reference* (1950).[132] The deportation of Japanese Canadians after the second world war was upheld on the same basis by the Privy Council in the *Japanese Canadians Reference* (1947).[133]

Each of these three wartime cases arose after the actual hostilities had ceased, and one issue was whether wartime measures could be continued in time of peace. In the *Fort Frances* case, Viscount Haldane deferred to the federal government on this point, saying that "very clear evidence" would be required to justify the Court "in overruling the decision of the Government that exceptional measures were still requisite".[134] The other cases gave essentially the same answer.[135]

The cases that upheld the War Measures Act under the emergency branch of p.o.g.g. did not consider any possible role for the federal power over "defence" in s. 91(7). In Australia (where there is no p.o.g.g. power), it is the defence power that has authorized national economic and social regulation in time of war.[136] In Canada, the defence power of s. 91(7) should be regarded as the authority for legislation relating to the armed forces and other traditional military matters.[137] The emergency branch of p.o.g.g. should be confined to the temporary and extraordinary role required for national regulation in time of actual war (or other emergency).[138]

(c) Apprehended insurrection

Apart from the two world wars, the War Measures Act was proclaimed in force on only one other occasion, and that was the "October crisis" of October 1970 when the Front de Libération du Québec, a violent Quebec separatist group, had kidnapped a British diplomat and a Quebec cabinet minister (who was later killed by his captors) and had made various demands as the condition of their release.[139] The federal government responded by issuing a proclamation declaring that "apprehended insurrection exists", and thereby bringing the War Measures

---

132 [1950] S.C.R. 124.

133 *Co-op. Committee on Japanese Canadians* v. *A.-G. Can.* [1947] A.C. 87.

134 [1923] A.C. 695, 706.

135 [1947] A.C. 87, 101-102; [1950] S.C.R. 124, 130-131, 135, 141, 151, 157, 166.

136 The Australian and Canadian wartime powers are compared in Gilbert, "There Will be Wars . . ." (1980) 18 Osgoode Hall L.J. 307. The war power has filled the same function in the United States. See generally Laskin, *Canadian Constitutional Law* (5th ed., 1986 by Finkelstein), 345-347.

137 *A.-G. Can.* v. *Nykorak* [1962] S.C.R. 331, 335, 337 (law conferring cause of action for loss of services of members of armed forces); *McKay* v. *The Queen* [1980] 2 S.C.R. 370, 390 (law providing for trial by court martial of military offenders).

138 In *Re Anti-Inflation Act* [1976] 2 S.C.R. 373, 461, Beetz J. emphasized that "in practice, the emergency doctrine operates as a partial and temporary alteration of the distribution of powers between Parliament and the provincial Legislatures".

139 For an account of the October crisis and the legal measures employed to deal with it, see Tarnopolsky, *The Canadian Bill of Rights* (2nd ed., 1975), 331-348, who also refers to the other literature on the topic.

Act into force. The government then used the powers conferred by the Act to make the Public Order Regulations; these regulations outlawed the F.L.Q., and gave the police new powers of arrest, search, seizure and detention.[140] Under these powers, no fewer than 497 people were arrested and detained. Only 62 of those arrested were charged, and less than one-third of those charged were convicted. It was a remarkable suspension of civil liberties; and the facts which emerged later, especially during the trials of the kidnappers, suggested that there was never any possibility of an insurrection from the small and ill-organized F.L.Q. or from any other group. However, the constitutionality of the invocation of the War Measures Act was never reviewed by the courts,[141] and many of those who had been arrested or mistreated by the police were compensated by the Quebec government.

(d) Inflation

The most recent application of the emergency doctrine is to be found in the *Anti-Inflation Reference* (1976),[142] in which the federal Anti-Inflation Act was upheld as an emergency measure. The Anti-Inflation Act, 1975, and regulations made thereunder, controlled increases in wages, fees, prices, profits, and dividends (''wage and price controls'' for short). The control scheme was administered by federal tribunals and officials. The scheme was temporary, the Act automatically expiring at the end of 1978 unless terminated earlier or extended by the government with parliamentary approval. After the Act had been in force for six months (and many collective agreements and prices had been adjusted under its provisions), the federal government referred the Act to the Supreme Court of Canada for a decision as to its constitutionality. The Court, by a majority of seven to two,

---

140 The proclamation of the War Measures Act and the Public Order Regulations were revoked on December 3, 1970 by the Public Order (Temporary Measures) Act, S.C. 1970-71-72, c. 2, which continued in force a more limited version of the laws previously contained in the regulations. This Act, which enjoys the distinction of being the only example of a statute containing a ''notwithstanding clause'' exempting its provisions from the Canadian Bill of Rights (s. 12), was to expire automatically on April 30, 1971 unless extended by resolution of both Houses of Parliament (s. 15). It never was extended. There are other examples of temporary measures which have been enacted by the federal Parliament under its emergency power, but which have never been litigated: The Emergency Powers Act, S.C. 1950-51, c. 5, enacted during the Korean War; The Energy Supplies Emergency Act, S.C. 1973-74, c. 52, enacted after the 1973 Yom Kippur War when there was a threat of an oil shortage; see Marx, ''The Energy Crisis and the Emergency Power'' (1975) 2 Dalhousie L.J. 446. The Emergencies Act, note 128, above, replaced the War Measures Act in 1988. The Emergencies Act is intended to reserve the most draconic powers for the most serious emergencies and to authorize more limited measures for less serious emergencies.

141 There was some litigation in which lower courts refused to review the government's proclamation of apprehended insurrection: see Marx, ''The Apprehended Insurrection of October 1970'' (1972) 7 U.B.C. Law Rev. 55; Lyon, ''Constitutional Validity of Public Order Regulations'' (1972) 18 McGill L.J. 136.

142 *Re Anti-Inflation Act* [1976] 2 S.C.R. 373.

held that the Act was valid as an exercise of the federal Parliament's emergency power. At the time when the control programme was announced, there had been a period of about twenty months of double-digit inflation in Canada, and the inflation had been accompanied by relatively high rates of unemployment. The majority of the Court held that this situation could be characterized by the government and Parliament as an emergency.[143]

The most serious difficulty with this conclusion[144] was that the Act itself, although it contained a preamble which purported to recite the reasons for the legislation, did not assert the existence of an emergency. This omission pointed to the conclusion, which was accepted only by the two dissenting judges,[145] that the government and Parliament had proceeded on the basis that federal power existed under the national concern branch of p.o.g.g. and that no showing of emergency was required.

The factual material that was filed in the *Anti-Inflation Reference*[146] included an economic study, which was agreed to by a substantial section of Canadian professional economic opinion, and which was not seriously challenged, asserting that Canadian inflation was not only on the wane when the controls were introduced in October 1975 but that it had never been particularly serious in its effects on living standards (which had continued to rise), or by comparison with the United States and other trading nations (whose rates of inflation were similar), or by comparison with other periods of recent Canadian history (this was Canada's third period of double-digit inflation since the second world war).[147]

Nevertheless, Laskin C.J., with whom Judson, Spence and Dickson JJ. agreed, held that the Court "would be unjustified in concluding, on the submissions in this case and on all the material put before it, that the Parliament of

---

143 Laskin C.J. used the word "crisis", but did not suggest that it meant anything different from emergency. Ritchie J. used the term "emergency".

144 My criticism of this decision should be taken with a grain of salt, since I was one of the counsel on the losing side!

145 Beetz J., with whom de Grandpré J. agreed, held that Parliament cannot rely on its emergency power "unless it gives an unmistakable signal that it is acting pursuant to its extraordinary power": [1976] 2 S.C.R. 373, 463. Compare *MacDonald* v. *Vapor Can.* [1977] 2 S.C.R 134, where Laskin C.J. insisted (at p. 171) that an exercise of federal power to implement a treaty "must be manifested in the implementing legislation and not left to inference". Yet Laskin C.J. in the *Anti-Inflation Reference* was content for an exercise of the emergency power to be left to inference.

146 The Canadian Labour Congress annexed to its factum a study of inflation in Canada by Richard G. Lipsey, a professor of economics at Queen's University, and it later filed telegrams from thirty-eight other economists associating themselves with Lipsey's conclusions. See ch. 57, Proof, under heading 57.2, "Evidence", below.

147 The recurring nature of double-digit inflation was demonstrated by its occurrence again in Canada (and other western nations) in 1980-82. However, this time the federal Parliament chose not to exercise the vast emergency powers which it had presumably acquired, contenting itself with wage controls in the federal public sector (five per cent of the workforce) and exhortations to voluntary restraint elsewhere. I cannot resist commenting that, if double-digit inflation really were an emergency, one would expect sterner remedies than these.

Canada did not have a rational basis for regarding the Anti-Inflation Act as a measure which, in its judgment, was temporarily necessary to meet a situation of economic crisis imperilling the well-being of Canada as a whole and requiring Parliament's stern intervention in the interests of the country as a whole''.[148] It will be noted that this passage carefully disclaims any judicial duty to make a definitive finding that an emergency exists. All that the Court need do is to find that a ''rational basis'' exists for a finding of emergency. Moreover, it is not necessary for the proponents of the legislation to establish a rational basis, it is for the opponents of the legislation to establish the absence of a rational basis. Ritchie J., who wrote a concurring opinion with which Martland and Pigeon JJ. agreed, did not use the language of rational basis, but he also cast the burden of proof onto the opponents of the legislation. He adopted the test used in the war measures cases,[149] and held that ''a judgment declaring the Act to be ultra vires could only be justified by reliance on very clear evidence that an emergency had not arisen when the statute was enacted''.[150] And, without discussing the evidence to that effect which had been presented, he held that it did not satisfy his test.[151]

In a constitutional case, where the validity of legislation depends upon findings of fact concerning the social or economic condition of the country, it is obviously impossible for the Court to make definitive findings. Moreover, judicial restraint requires that a degree of deference be paid to the governmental judgment upon which the legislative policy was based. However, the formulations in the *Anti-Inflation Reference*, especially when read in the light of the persuasive factual material before the Court which denied the existence of an emergency, make it almost impossible to challenge federal legislation on the ground that there is no emergency.[152] This means that the federal Parliament can use its emergency power almost at will.

(e) Temporary character of law

There is one important limitation on the federal emergency power: it will support only temporary measures.[153] This is usually regarded as a self-evident proposition, based on the fact that an emergency is a temporary phenomenon. One is entitled to question, however, the usefulness of this limitation. It is in any

148 [1976] 2 S.C.R. 373, 425.
149 Note 134, above.
150 [1976] 2 S.C.R. 373, 439.
151 Beetz J., with whom de Grandpré J. agreed, dissented on the ground that the Act gave no indication that it was enacted to meet an emergency: note 145, above. Accordingly, he did not go on to consider the burden or standard of proof which was appropriate.
152 For full discussion, see Hogg, ''Proof of Facts in Constitutional Cases'' (1976) 26 U. Toronto L.J. 386.
153 *Re Anti-Inflation Act* [1976] 2 S.C.R. 373, 427, 437, 461, 467; *R.* v. *Crown Zellerbach* [1988] 1 S.C.R. 401, 432.

case primarily formal, because an ostensibly temporary measure can always be continued in force by the Parliament, while an ostensibly permanent measure can be repealed at any time. More importantly, an emergency, although itself temporary, may be caused by structural defects in the social or economic order which need to be corrected not only to cure the emergency, but also to prevent the occurrence of future emergencies. Yet preventive legislation would surely have to be permanent.[154]

The new deal statutes, which were enacted to deal with the depression, had this dual character: they were designed not only to help alleviate the immediate suffering of the depression, but also to provide permanent economic security which it was hoped would prevent a similar disaster in the future. Perhaps unemployment insurance is the best example of a permanent preventive measure, but minimum wage laws, anti-combine laws and natural products marketing regulation — other Canadian new deal measures — were also perceived by government in the same way. Nevertheless, in the *Unemployment Insurance Reference* (1937)[155] and companion cases,[156] the Privy Council struck down most of the new deal legislation, and while it appears that their lordships' primary reason was that the depression did not qualify as a genuine emergency, it is a fair inference that they were influenced by the permanent nature of the new deal measures. Similarly, in the *Board of Commerce* case (1922),[157] federal legislation to control hoarding and profiteering caused by the economic dislocation which was the aftermath of the first world war was held to be unconstitutional. Once again, the Privy Council, while also doubting that a peacetime economic problem could be characterized as an emergency, was influenced by the ostensibly permanent character of the proposed controls.[158]

The contrast between the new deal cases and the *Board of Commerce* case, on the one hand, and the *Anti-Inflation Reference*,[159] on the other, is too obvious to require elaboration. It cannot be explained solely in conventional legal terms, but it is the fact that in the former cases the impugned legislation was permanent while in the *Anti-Inflation Reference* the legislation was temporary. No permanent measure has ever been upheld under the emergency power.[160]

---

154 In other contexts "prevention" has been held to be on the same basis as "cure": *A.-G. Ont.* v. *Can. Temperance Federation* [1946] A.C. 193, 207.

155 [1937] A.C. 355.

156 Note 107, above.

157 [1922] 1 A.C. 191.

158 *Id.*, 197 where the point is explicit.

159 Note 142, above.

160 A possible exception is *Lovibond* v. *Grand Trunk Ry. Co.* [1939] O.R. 305 (Ont. C.A.), where the federal expropriation of shares in the Grand Trunk Ry. Co. was upheld. Masten J.A. (at p. 344), delivering one of two concurring opinions, offered the emergency branch of p.o.g.g. as one of two bases for the legislation.

17.5 Relationship between national concern and emergency

The "gap" branch of p.o.g.g. stands on its own and requires no reconciliation with the "national concern" and "emergency" branches. But the relationship between the national concern and emergency branches does require examination.

One point has been settled by the course of decision since the abolition of appeals to the Privy Council. It is clear that the Privy Council was wrong in asserting that only an emergency would justify the invocation of the p.o.g.g. power. *Johannesson*,[161] *Munro*,[162] *Crown Zellerbach*[163] and *Ontario Hydro*[164] establish that the emergency test cannot be the exclusive touchstone. Clearly, for some class of cases the national concern doctrine will suffice to justify the invocation of p.o.g.g. But, unless we are to repudiate the Haldane and post-Haldane decisions altogether, we must accept that there is a class of case for which only an emergency will suffice to found federal power. The problem then is to draw the line between these two different classes.

One possible dividing line must be rejected at the outset. It is not possible to argue that laws affecting property and civil rights must satisfy the emergency test, while laws not affecting property and civil rights need only satisfy the national concern test. In *Johannesson*,[165] what was in issue was the validity of a municipal zoning by-law which purported to limit the establishment of aerodromes in a municipality. In *Munro*,[166] what was in issue was the validity of a federal expropriation of a farmer's land to create a green belt in the national capital region. In *Crown Zellerbach*,[167] what was in issue was a federal law prohibiting the dumping of logging waste in provincial waters. Zoning, expropriation and logging are normally within property and civil rights in the province, and so all three cases had a profound impact upon property and civil rights in the province. Yet it was the national concern doctrine, not the emergency doctrine, which was applied in the cases.

W.R. Lederman, in an article which appeared in the Canadian Bar Review in 1975,[168] suggested a more sophisticated reconciliation of the cases. He pointed out that such subject matters as aviation, the national capital region and atomic energy each had "a natural unity that is quite limited and specific in its extent".[169] He contrasted these "limited and specific" subject matters with such sweeping categories as environmental pollution, culture or language. If the sweeping or

161 Note 44, above.
162 Note 47, above.
163 Note 50, above.
164 Note 53, above.
165 Note 44, above.
166 Note 47, above.
167 Note 50, above.
168 "Unity and Diversity in Canadian Federalism" (1975) 53 Can. Bar Rev. 597; see also Le Dain, "Sir Lyman Duff and the Constitution" (1974) 12 Osgoode Hall L.J. 261, 293.
169 *Id.*, 610.

pervasive categories were enfranchised as federal subject matters simply on the basis of national concern, then there would be no limit to the reach of federal legislative powers and the existing distribution of legislative powers would become unstable. Accordingly, in normal times such categories had to be broken down into more specific and meaningful categories for the purpose of allocating legislative jurisdiction; on this basis some parts of the sweeping categories would be within federal jurisdiction and other parts would be within provincial jurisdiction. Only in an emergency could the federal Parliament assume the plenary power over the whole of a sweeping category.

In the *Anti-Inflation Reference*,[170] Lederman appeared as counsel for one of the unions opposed to the legislation, and he and the other counsel urged his distinction upon the Court with a view to establishing that wage and price controls — a sweeping category — had to satisfy the stricter emergency test. The distinction was accepted by Beetz J., whose opinion constitutes the first, and so far the only,[171] attempt by a Canadian judge to reconcile the emergency cases with the national concern cases. Beetz J.'s opinion was a dissent, but it will be recalled that on this point Ritchie J. agreed with him. (The disagreement was over the question whether the legislation was in fact a recognizable response to an emergency.) This meant that Beetz J.'s opinion on this point enjoyed the support of five members — a majority of the Court, because de Grandpré J. agreed with Beetz J.; and Martland and Pigeon JJ. agreed with Ritchie J. Beetz J.'s opinion also seems to have been accepted by the Court in the later *Crown Zellerbach* case.[172]

In his opinion, Beetz J. expressly acknowledged his indebtedness to Lederman's article.[173] In accordance with the thesis of that article, he refused to accept that a subject matter as broad as "inflation" could be accepted as a new head of federal power: it was "totally lacking in specificity"; it was "so pervasive that

---

170 *Re Anti-Inflation Act* [1976] 2 S.C.R. 373.

171 In *Johannesson* v. *West St. Paul* [1952] 1 S.C.R. 292, *Munro* v. *National Capital Comm.* [1966] S.C.R. 663, and *R.* v. *Crown Zellerbach* [1988] 1 S.C.R. 401, the Court applied the national concern doctrine without reference to the Privy Council cases that had held that only an emergency would suffice. However, in *Crown Zellerbach*, Le Dain J. for the majority said (at p. 431) that the national concern doctrine was "separate and distinct" from the emergency doctrine, and he applied the requirement of distinctness that had been insisted upon by Beetz J. This indicated agreement with Beetz J. La Forest, J., who dissented, also seemed to assume the correctness of Beetz J.'s analysis. In *Re Anti-Inflation Act* [1976] 2 S.C.R. 373, Laskin C.J., with whom Judson, Spence and Dickson JJ. agreed, applied the emergency doctrine without reference to *Johannesson* and *Munro*. Laskin C.J. did suggest (at p. 419) that the national concern test could also have sustained the legislation, but he did not pursue this idea, and in particular he did not explain his disagreement with Beetz J.'s carefully reasoned opinion to the contrary, which was joined in on this point by all the other judges, and which is discussed in the following text.

172 Previous note.

173 [1976] 2 S.C.R. 373, 451; he also acknowledged his indebtedness to the article by Le Dain cited in note 168, above.

it knows no bounds''; the recognition of such a ''diffuse'' subject matter ''would render most provincial powers nugatory'' and ''destroy the equilibrium of the Constitution''.[174] Rather, the Anti-Inflation Act should be classified for constitutional purposes not in terms of the Act's ''ultimate purpose'' (to contain inflation) but in terms of its ''operation'' and ''effects'',[175] and in these more specific terms the Act was in relation to wages, prices and profits, which were matters within property and civil rights in the province. In normal times, therefore, wage and price controls were outside the competence of the federal Parliament. In an emergency, however, the power of the federal Parliament ''knows no limit other than those which are dictated by the nature of the crisis. But one of those limits is the temporary nature of the crisis''.[176]

The thesis advanced by Lederman and adopted by Beetz J. is that the p.o.g.g. power performs two separate functions in the Constitution. First, it gives to the federal Parliament *permanent* jurisdiction over ''distinct subject matters which do not fall within any of the enumerated heads of s. 92 and which, by nature, are of national concern'', for example, aeronautics and the national capital region.[177] Secondly, the p.o.g.g. power gives to the federal Parliament *temporary* jurisdiction over all subject matters needed to deal with an emergency. On this dual function theory, it is not helpful to regard an emergency as being simply an example of a matter of national concern. As Beetz J. said, ''in practice the emergency doctrine operates as a partial and temporary alteration of the distribution of power between Parliament and the provincial Legislatures''.[178]

This theory certainly explains most of the cases. The leading ''emergency'' cases did involve legislation which asserted a sweeping new category of federal power over property, prices, wages or persons, for example, combinations, hoarding, prices and profits in *Board of Commerce*,[179] prices in *Fort Frances*,[180] labour relations and standards in *Snider*[181] and *Labour Conventions*,[182] marketing of natural products in *Natural Products Marketing*,[183] rents in *Wartime Leasehold Regulations*,[184] and deportation in *Japanese Canadians*.[185] Accordingly, in these cases the legislation was upheld only if there was an emergency. The leading ''national concern'' cases each involved legislation over a more distinct and specific subject matter, for example, aeronautics in *Johannesson*,[186] the national

174 *Id.*, 458. Accord, *R.* v. *Crown Zellerbach* [1988] 1 S.C.R. 401, 431-432.
175 *Id.*, 452.
176 *Id.*, 461.
177 *Id.*, 457.
178 *Id.*, 461.
179 Note 99, above.
180 Note 130, above.
181 Note 101, above.
182 Note 108, above.
183 Note 110, above.
184 Note 132, above.
185 Note 133, above.
186 Note 44, above.

capital in *Munro*,[187] atomic energy in *Ontario Hydro*,[188] and marine pollution in *Crown Zellerbach*[189] (where the issue of distinctness divided the Court). Accordingly, in these cases no emergency was called for, and the legislation was upheld if the subject matter was judged to be of national concern.[190]

Not all of the cases fit the theory. *Russell*[191] and *Margarine*[192] do not sit easily together. If the federal prohibition of one product — liquor or margarine — requires an emergency, as *Margarine* implies, then *Russell* is wrong. If, however, the subject matter of liquor or margarine is sufficiently specific that it requires only a showing of national concern, as *Russell* implies, then the courts were wrong to call for an emergency in *Margarine*. On the other hand, even if the national concern test is the appropriate one, one can justify the result of *Margarine* on the ground that the prohibition of a particular product lacking any special strategic importance was not sufficiently national in its dimensions; but it is not easy to see the national concern in *Russell*, especially as the legislation was brought into force by local votes. The *Unemployment Insurance Reference*[193] also gives difficulty. One would have thought that unemployment insurance was sufficiently specific to qualify as a new judge-made head of federal power, and that it had the requisite national concern. And, even if an emergency was necessary for this and the other ''new deal'' statutes, one would have thought that the depression of the 1930s qualified. But *Russell* and the *Unemployment Insurance Reference* are difficult to explain on any theory.[194] Probably, both cases were wrongly decided.

187 Note 47, above.

188 Note 53, above.

189 Note 50, above.

190 Monahan, ''The Structure of Canadian Federalism'' (1984) 34 U. Toronto L.J. 47, 73 has pointed out that the absence of criteria to determine whether a particular topic is distinct and indivisible, on the one hand, or sweeping and divisible, on the other, inevitably requires the judge to balance the national dimensions of the problem against the local or provincial dimensions.

191 Note 29, above.

192 Note 113, above.

193 Note 109, above.

194 *Hauser*, note 79, above, is also difficult to explain on any theory: see criticism in text accompanying note 79, above.

18

Criminal Law

18.1 Distribution of powers

The Constitution Act, 1867, by s. 91(27), confers on the federal Parliament the power to make laws in relation to:

> [t]he criminal law, except the constitution of courts of criminal jurisdiction, but including the procedure in criminal matters.

Under this provision, the criminal law is a federal responsibility. This stands in contrast with the United States and Australia, where the criminal law is a state responsibility. In Canada, since 1892, the criminal law has been codified in one federally-enacted Criminal Code.[1] The argument accepted by the United States and Australia that criminal law should reflect local conditions and sentiments was rejected by the fathers of confederation in favour of a national body of law.[2] However, as will be explained, for the most part, the Criminal Code is enforced by the provinces; and the decisions to investigate, charge and prosecute offences are therefore matters of provincial policy which will no doubt be framed in response to local conditions and sentiments. In this way, the criminal law is not as centralized as other fields of federal legislative competence, where federal administration normally follows federal enactment.

The provincial role in criminal justice derives from s. 92(14) of the Constitution Act, 1867, which confers on the provincial Legislatures the power to make laws in relation to:

> The administration of justice in the province, including the constitution, maintenance, and organization of provincial courts, both of civil and of criminal jurisdiction, and including procedure in civil matters in those courts.

This is the provision that authorizes provincial policing[3] and prosecution[4] of offences under the Criminal Code, although there is (unexercised) concurrent federal power as well on the basis that federal legislative power over the criminal law (or any other subject matter) carries with it the matching power of enforcement.

The establishment of courts of criminal jurisdiction[5] is expressly included in provincial power by s. 92(14), and is expressly excluded from federal power by s. 91(27). Criminal trials accordingly take place in provincial courts. But the rules of procedure and evidence[6] in a criminal trial are federal: the ''procedure in criminal matters'' is expressly included in federal power by s. 91(27).

---

1 R.S.C. 1985, c. C-46. There are as well other federal statutes enacted under the criminal law power, e.g., the Food and Drugs Act, the Hazardous Products Act. There are as well federal statutes enacted under other heads of federal power that also create offences for their enforcement, e.g., the Fisheries Act, the Income Tax Act. The enforcement provisions of the Income Tax Act do not depend upon the criminal law power for their validity: *Knox Contracting* v. *Can.* [1990] 2 S.C.R. 338, 358 per Sopinka J. for majority on this issue; Cory J. for minority held that the enforcement provisions of the Act were criminal law, not tax law. The majority view is the better one: the enforcement provisions of a statutory scheme come under the same constitutional power as the scheme itself. In *Kourtessis* v. *M.N.R.* [1993] 2 S.C.R. 53, 72, 102, the Court was unanimous that the offence provisions of the Income Tax Act were supportable under both the taxation power and the criminal law power. Query whether the reference to the criminal law power is necessary or correct.

2 The legislative history of s. 91(27) is related in Friedland, *A Century of Criminal Justice* (1984), ch. 2; Edwards, ''The Advent of English (Not French) Criminal Law and Procedure into Canada'' (1984) 26 Crim. Law Q. 464.

3 Policing is discussed in the next chapter, Criminal Justice, under heading 19.5, ''Policing'', below.

4 Chapter 19, Criminal Justice, under heading 19.6, ''Prosecution'', below.

5 Chapter 19, Criminal Justice, under heading 19.2, ''Courts of criminal jurisdiction'', below.

6 Chapter 19, Criminal Justice, under headings 19.3, ''Procedure'', and 19.4 ''Evidence'', below.

Jurisdiction over correctional institutions[7] is divided between the two levels of government. Under s. 91(28), the federal Parliament has jurisdiction over "penitentiaries", which hold offenders sentenced to imprisonment for two years or more. Under s. 92(6), the provinces have jurisdiction over "prisons" which hold offenders sentenced to imprisonment for less than two years.

Another provincial head of power is relevant in this context, namely, s. 92(15), which authorizes the provincial Legislatures to make laws in relation to:

> The imposition of punishment by fine, penalty, or imprisonment for enforcing any law of the province made in relation to any matter coming within any of the classes of subjects enumerated in this section.

This provision authorizes the provincial Legislatures to enact penal sanctions for the enforcement of provincial laws.[8] However, the closing language of the provision makes clear that it is an ancillary power, authorizing the creation of provincial offences only for the purpose of enforcing laws which are authorized under some other head of provincial power. Nevertheless, we shall see that s. 92(15) has imported a substantial degree of concurrent provincial jurisdiction to enact penal laws which are indistinguishable from federal criminal laws. This in turn has given rise to difficult issues of paramountcy where similar federal and provincial laws co-exist.

I have divided these topics into two chapters. This chapter, Criminal Law, covers the substantive criminal law, including the provincial power to enact penal laws. The next chapter, Criminal Justice, covers the adjectival aspects of criminal justice from policing through to punishment.

18.2 Definition of criminal law

The federal Parliament's power to enact "criminal law" has proved very difficult to define.[9] In the *Board of Commerce* case (1922),[10] Viscount Haldane held that the power was applicable only "where the subject matter is one which by its very nature belongs to the domain of criminal jurisprudence". Like Viscount Haldane's definitions of the peace, order, and good government power[11] and the trade and commerce power,[12] this definition of criminal law appeared to be too

7 Chapter 19, Criminal Justice, under heading 19.8, "Punishment", below.

8 Section 18.9, "Provincial power to enact penal laws", below.

9 See Leigh, "The Criminal Law Power" (1967) 5 Alta. L. Rev. 237; McDonald, "Constitutional Aspects of Canadian Anti-Combines Law Enforcement" (1969) 47 Can. Bar Rev. 161; Chevrette, "La notion de droit criminel" (1969) 3 Revue Juridique Thémis 17; Laskin, *Canadian Constitutional Law* (5th ed., 1986 by Finkelstein), ch. 14; Beaudoin, *La Constitution du Canada* (1990), ch. 16.

10 [1922] 1 A.C. 191, 198-199; folld. in *Toronto Electric Commrs.* v. *Snider* [1925] A.C. 396.

11 See ch. 17, Peace, Order, and Good Government, above.

12 See ch. 20, Trade and Commerce, below.

narrow.[13] Although Viscount Haldane did not spell out what he meant by a "domain of criminal jurisprudence", the phrase could be read as freezing the criminal law into a mould established at some earlier time, presumably 1867.[14]

After Viscount Haldane's death in 1928, Lord Atkin in the *P.A.T.A.* case (1931)[15] repudiated the domain of criminal jurisprudence theory and made clear that the federal power was "not confined to what was criminal by the law of England or of any Province in 1867", and that "the power may extend to legislation to make new crimes". Lord Atkin in the *P.A.T.A.* case offered a rival definition of criminal law:[16]

> The criminal quality of an act cannot be discerned by intuition; nor can it be discovered by reference to any standard but one: Is the act prohibited with penal consequences?

This definition appeared to be too wide in that it would enable the federal Parliament to expand its jurisdiction indefinitely, simply by framing its legislation in the form of a prohibition coupled with a penalty. Nor was this definition sufficiently qualified when Lord Atkin later said that "the only limitation on the plenary power of the Dominion to determine what shall or shall not be criminal is the condition that Parliament shall not in the guise of enacting criminal legislation in truth and in substance encroach on any of the classes of subjects enumerated in s. 92".[17] This says no more than the trite proposition that a law must be properly classifiable as in relation to the criminal law, and it no doubt contemplates the possibility of a statute in which the prohibition and penalty are unimportant appendages to provisions which really seek to accomplish the legislative goal by other means. Even setting aside this kind of "colourable" statute, which no one would seriously seek to defend as criminal, the *P.A.T.A.* definition is still too wide, because it would uphold any federal law which employs a prohibition and penalty as its primary mode of operation. If the only characteristics of the criminal law are the formal ones of a prohibition and a penalty, then there is no principled basis for denying to a law with those characteristics the criminal classification.

It is clear that a proper balance in the distribution of legislative powers requires some third ingredient in the definition of criminal law. This was demonstrated in the *Margarine Reference* (1951),[18] where the law in issue simply prohibited the manufacture, importation or sale of margarine. It was common

---

13 In fairness to Viscount Haldane, it must be said that the regulatory scheme in issue in the *Board of Commerce* case, administered as it was by an administrative tribunal, could not plausibly be characterized as a criminal law; and Viscount Haldane's only real fault lay in his failure to spell out what he meant by "the domain of criminal jurisprudence".

14 This would be inconsistent with the doctrine of progressive interpretation, discussed in ch. 15, Judicial Review on Federal Grounds, above.

15 *Proprietary Articles Trade Assn.* v. *A.-G. Can.* [1931] A.C. 310, 324.

16 *Ibid.*

17 *A.-G. B.C.* v. *A.-G. Can.* (Price Spreads) [1937] A.C. 368, 375.

18 *Can. Federation of Agriculture* v. *A.-G. Que.* [1951] A.C. 179.

ground that the purpose of this law was to protect the dairy industry. The Privy Council held that, although the law perfectly fitted the criminal form of a prohibition coupled with a penalty, the economic object of protecting an industry from its competitors made the law in pith and substance in relation to property and civil rights in the province.

It follows from the *Margarine Reference* that the elusive third ingredient of a criminal law is a typically criminal public purpose. In the Supreme Court of Canada, Rand J., whose reasoning was adopted by the Privy Council, said that a prohibition was not criminal unless it served "a public purpose which can support it as being in relation to the criminal law".[19] And what were the public purposes which would qualify? "Public peace, order, security, health, morality: these are the ordinary though not exclusive ends served by that law . . .".[20] It will be noticed that Rand J. was careful not to give an exhaustive definition of the purposes of the criminal law. It was enough for him to be confident that the protection of the dairy industry was not a qualifying purpose. But while he characterized that purpose as "to benefit one group of persons as against competitors in business",[21] no doubt the proponents of such protective legislation would deny that such a narrow definition was appropriate and would define the purpose in terms of national economic policy of benefit to all Canadians. Rand J.'s tendentious description of the margarine law, and his failure to provide a test for the identification of a typically criminal public purpose, detract from the value of his much-quoted opinion.[22] Indeed, it is fair to say that the requirement of a typically criminal public purpose is really only a slightly more sophisticated formulation of Viscount Haldane's "domain of criminal jurisprudence".[23]

The *Margarine Reference* should not be read as denying that the criminal law can serve economic ends. A large part of the criminal law is devoted to the protection of private property — a purpose, one might add, which confers a larger benefit on those who own property than on those who do not. But, apart from the traditional crimes of theft and its many variants, various forms of economic regulation have been upheld as criminal law. The *P.A.T.A.* case[24] itself upheld anti-combines (competition) laws under the criminal law power, and under this

---

19 [1949] S.C.R. 1, 50.

20 *Ibid.*

21 *Ibid.*

22 Accord, Weiler, "The Supreme Court and the Law of Canadian Federalism" (1973) 23 U. Toronto L.J. 307, 326.

23 A definition was suggested by Dickson C.J. (dissenting, but not on this issue) in *R.* v. *Hauser* [1979] 1 S.C.R. 984, 1026, which was approved by Cory J. for the majority in *Knox Contracting* v. *Can.* [1990] 2 S.C.R. 338, 348, as follows:

> Head 27 of s. 91 of the B.N.A. Act empowers Parliament to make substantive laws prohibiting, with penal consequences, acts or omissions considered to be harmful to the State, or to persons or property within the State. In this formulation, the typically criminal public purpose is said to be the prevention of harm to the State or to persons or property within the State.

24 Note 15, above.

general rubric a variety of federal laws have been upheld, including prohibitions on price discrimination[25] and resale price maintenance[26] and a judicial power to enjoin some of the prohibited practices.[27] The false prospectus provisions of the Criminal Code have been upheld as criminal law, establishing that securities regulation — at least in crude form — is within the criminal law.[28] In short, there is abundant support for Laskin's assertion that ''resort to the criminal law power to proscribe undesirable commercial practices is today as characteristic of its exercise as has been resort thereto to curb violence or immoral conduct.''[29]

In *Boggs v. The Queen* (1981),[30] the Supreme Court of Canada, in a unanimous opinion written by Estey J., struck down the federal Criminal Code offence of driving a motor vehicle while one's provincial driver's licence was suspended. This offence would have been constitutionally unimpeachable if a provincial driver's licence could be suspended only for breach of Criminal Code provisions concerned with fitness to drive. If that were the case, the offence of driving while disqualified could be related to the public purpose of safety on the roads. In fact, Boggs' licence had been suspended for just such a cause: he had been convicted of the Criminal Code offences of impaired driving and refusing to take a breath test; and under Ontario's highway legislation these convictions had resulted in the automatic suspension of his driver's licence. But Estey J. discovered, on reviewing the highway legislation of all the provinces, that drivers' licences could also be suspended for breach of a variety of provincial regulations, and in particular for failure to pay insurance premiums, civil judgments, taxes and licence fees. These latter grounds for licence suspensions bore ''no relationship in practice or in theory to the owner's ability to drive and hence to public safety on the highways of the nation''.[31] A criminal prohibition premised on such grounds was simply an enforcement measure for a variety of provincial regulatory and taxation regimes, and did not pursue the kind of public purpose required by Rand J. in the *Margarine Reference*. The Criminal Code offence of driving while suspended was accordingly unconstitutional. It is clear that a re-framed version, in which the offence was confined to cases where the provincial disqualification resulted from a violation of a Criminal Code offence, would be sustained.[32]

---

25 *A.-G. B.C.* v. *A.-G. Can.* (Price Spreads) [1937] A.C. 368.

26 *R.* v. *Campbell* (1965) 58 D.L.R. (2d) 673 (S.C.C.).

27 *Goodyear Tire and Rubber Co.* v. *The Queen* [1956] S.C.R. 303. See generally sec. 18.4, ''Competition law'', below.

28 *Smith* v. *The Queen* [1960] S.C.R. 776. See generally ch. 21, Property and Civil Rights, under heading 21.10, ''Securities regulation'', below.

29 Laskin, note 9, above, 849; the whole of ch. 14 is a valuable collection of cases and textual notes on the scope of the criminal law power.

30 [1981] 1 S.C.R. 49.

31 *Id.*, 59.

32 Estey J. held (at p. 65) that the Court itself could not correct the drafting through severance or reading down.

18.3 Food and drugs

(a) Food and drug standards

In the *Margarine Reference* (1951),[33] as we have just noticed, a prohibition on the manufacture or sale of margarine was struck down on the basis that the purpose of the legislation was the economic one of protecting the dairy industry. When the margarine legislation was originally enacted by the federal Parliament in 1886, the statute included a preamble asserting that margarine was "injurious to health". If that had been the continuing basis of the legislation, there is no doubt that it would have satisfied the requirement of a typically criminal public purpose. It is well-established that food and drug legislation making illegal the manufacture or sale of dangerous products, adulterated products or misbranded products is within the criminal law power.[34] But in the *Margarine Reference* it was conceded by the federal government that margarine was not injurious to health. This concession, which had to be made in light of the medical facts, destroyed what was originally a secure criminal law foundation for the legislation.

In *Labatt Breweries* v. *A.-G. Can.* (1979),[35] the Supreme Court of Canada held that the part of the federal Food and Drugs Act that authorized regulations prescribing compositional standards for food was unconstitutional. Regulations made under the Act prescribed the ingredients of "beer" and "light beer" (along with hundreds of other foods and beverages), and in particular stipulated that any product described as "light beer" must contain no more than 2.5 per cent alcohol. Labatt Breweries violated the regulations by retailing a product they described as "lite" beer (which the Court held to be equivalent to "light" beer), which had an alcoholic content of 4 per cent, that is, more than the prescribed standard of 2.5 per cent. The brewery argued that the compositional standard was unconstitutional, and Estey J., writing for a majority of the Supreme Court of Canada, so held.[36] Estey J. acknowledged that the criminal law power could be used to enact laws for the protection of health (and much of the Food and Drugs Act is plainly directed to that end),[37] but he found that the alcoholic requirement for light beer was not related to health. He also acknowledged that the criminal law power could be used to enact laws for the prevention of deception (and some of the Food and Drugs Act is also plainly directed to that end),[38] but he found that the specification of the compositional standards for light beer could not be supported on

33 Note 18, above.

34 *R.* v. *Wetmore* [1983] 2 S.C.R. 284 (federal Food and Drugs Act offences of insanitary storage and deceptive labelling of drugs upheld as criminal law).

35 [1980] 1 S.C.R. 914.

36 Estey J. was joined by Martland, Ritchie, Dickson, Beetz and Pratte JJ. Laskin C.J., Pigeon and McIntyre JJ. dissented. The dissenting opinions relied on the trade and commerce power, not the criminal law power, and are accordingly ignored in the account that follows.

37 E.g., *R.* v. *Wetmore*, note 34, above.

38 *Ibid.*

this ground either. It followed that the compositional standards authorized by the Food and Drugs Act could not be supported under the criminal law power. Since they could not be supported under the peace, order, and good government power,[39] or the trade and commerce power,[40] either, it followed that they were invalid. Although Estey J. confined his ruling to federal compositional standards ''in so far as they relate to malt liquors'',[41] the decision must mean that all the federal standards are invalid, except those few that can be related to health.

The *Labatt* decision is unfortunate in precluding a national regime of compositional standards for food. Most sectors of the food industry (beer is a good example) have become highly concentrated, with a few large manufacturers or suppliers advertising their products on national television and then marketing the products nation-wide. It would be costly and inconvenient for such manufacturers to comply with a variety of provincially-established standards. Of course, manufacturers might be content with no standards at all, and this invites the question: what is the public policy justification for a national regime of compositional standards for food?

In my view, Estey J. rejected too quickly the deception rationale for federal compositional standards. He was impressed by the fact that Labatt Breweries specified on the label of their ''lite'' beer that it contained 4 per cent alcohol. Obviously, this meant that the careful and knowledgeable reader of the label would not be deceived as to the product's alcohol content. But surely Parliament could rationally conclude that consumers often do not read or understand labels, and that consumers should be able to count on the fact that certain product names imply particular characteristics of the product: for example, that ''light beer'' was a low-alcohol beer; that ''mayonnaise'' contained egg; that ''jam'' and ''juice'' were made from fruit, ''ice-cream'' from milk (or cream), and ''chocolate'' from cacao beans; that ''ground beef'' consisted only of beef; and so on.[42] Departures from these standards were not prohibited, but they had to be signalled by calling the unqualified product by a different name. With respect, the denial that this kind of regulation is directed to the prevention of consumer deception[43] is essentially

39 This aspect of the decision is discussed in ch. 17, Peace, Order, and Good Government, under heading 17.3(b), ''Definition of national concern'', above.

40 This aspect of the decision is discussed in ch. 20, Trade and Commerce, under heading 20.3, ''General trade and commerce'', below.

41 [1980] 1 S.C.R. 914, 947.

42 These examples are all taken from the actual regulations of which the ''light beer'' rule was one.

43 Having rejected the legislative purpose of preventing deception, Estey J. did not say what he thought the real purpose was. He described the impugned regulation (at p. 934) as ''this detailed regulation of the brewing industry in the production and sale of its product''. But the production and sale of 4 per cent beer (for example) was only affected in that it had to be described by some term other than ''light'' (or ''lite''). Similarly, a manufacturer of candy could use any ingredients it chose, but could not describe the product as ''chocolate'' unless it contained cacao beans. To describe this as ''detailed regulation'' of an industry does not seem plausible, and in any event the description does not tell us what the purpose of the regulation is and it is the purpose which is critical to the characterization of a law as criminal or not.

the substitution of the Court's opinion as to the nature and likelihood of consumer deception for that of the Parliament.[44] In my view, a proper deference to a rationally defensible legislative policy required the regulation in *Labatt* to be upheld as a criminal law.

(b) Illicit drugs

The non-medical use of drugs such as marijuana, cocaine and heroin is proscribed by the federal Narcotic Control Act, which prohibits the production, importation, sale and possession of a variety of illicit drugs. The Act appears to be the paradigm of a ''criminal'' statute, and in 1953 the Supreme Court of Canada so characterized an earlier version of the Act.[45] In *The Queen* v. *Hauser* (1979),[46] a majority of the Supreme Court of Canada, in an opinion written by Pigeon J., held that the Act was not authorized by the criminal law power. This did not mean that the Act was invalid. The Court assigned the Act to the peace, order, and good government power of the federal Parliament, and upheld the Act on that basis. This characterization of the Act has been criticized in an earlier chapter of this book,[47] and the criticism need not be repeated here. It suffices to say that the decision is so widely regarded as wrong that I believe that on an appropriate occasion it will be repudiated by the Court. The better view is that the Narcotic Control Act is a criminal law.[48]

In *Schneider* v. *The Queen* (1982),[49] the Supreme Court of Canada upheld British Columbia's Heroin Treatment Act, which provided for the compulsory apprehension, assessment and treatment of drug addicts; the treatment could include compulsory detention in a treatment centre for up to six months. The argument that this was really a criminal law was based on the deprivations of liberty that were authorized by the Act. Of course, the Act was designed to treat and cure drug addicts, not to deter or punish them; but in some ways this made the legislation more rather than less oppressive, since the coercive features of the legislation were not accompanied by the procedural safeguards which surround a criminal trial.[50] Nevertheless, the Court was unanimous in classifying the legislation as within provincial competence. Dickson J., who wrote for seven of the nine judges, held that the medical treatment of drug addiction came within pro-

---

44 MacPherson, ''Economic Regulation and the British North America Act'' (1980) 5 Can. Bus. L. J. 172, 183, criticizes the *Labatt* decision on a number of grounds, including this one. The aftermath of the decision is described in Monahan, *Politics and the Constitution* (1987), 228-234.

45 *Industrial Acceptance Corp.* v. *The Queen* [1953] 2 S.C.R. 273.

46 [1979] 1 S.C.R. 984.

47 Chapter 17, Peace, Order, and Good Government, under heading 17.3(b), ''Definition of national concern'', above.

48 The decisions regarding the regulation of alcohol have also followed an anomalous path. They are also discussed in ch. 17, Peace, Order, and Good Government, above.

49 [1982] 2 S.C.R. 112.

50 Section 7 of the Charter of Rights was not considered, because the case pre-dated the Charter.

vincial authority over public health as a ''local or private'' matter within s. 92(16) of the Constitution Act, 1867. The coercive elements of the Act were incidental to its public health purpose.[51] Laskin C.J. and Estey J., in separate concurring opinions, reached similar conclusions.[52]

(c) Tobacco

In *RJR-MacDonald* v. *Canada* (1995),[53] the Supreme Court of Canada had to review the validity of the federal Tobacco Products Control Act, which prohibited the advertising of cigarettes and other tobacco products and required the placement of health warnings on packages. Was this a valid criminal law? The Act contained a prohibition and a penalty, but was there a typically criminal public purpose? In the case of the requirement of warnings, the Court was unanimous that the protection of public health supplied the required purpose to support the exercise of the criminal-law power.[54] But what of the ban on advertising? It was clear that the criminal-law power permitted Parliament to prohibit the manufacture, sale or possession of dangerous products.[55] But Parliament had not done that: the manufacture, sale and possession of tobacco remained lawful, and all that was prohibited was the advertising of tobacco products. Advertising itself was not a dangerous act, and the advertising of consumer goods was normally within the legislative jurisdiction of the provinces under their power over property and civil rights.[56] In the Supreme Court of Canada, Major J.'s dissenting view was that the prohibition of the advertising of a legal product lacked a ''typically criminal purpose'' and was outside the federal criminal-law power. But La Forest J., for the majority, disagreed. In his view, the power to prohibit the use of tobacco on account of its harmful effects on health also encompassed the power to take the lesser step of prohibiting the advertising of tobacco products. Although it was impracticable to ban the product itself in view of the large number of Canadians

---

51 Compulsory detention of the mentally incompetent under provincial law was upheld in the pre-Charter case of *Fawcett* v. *A.-G. Ont.* [1964] S.C.R. 625; but there the compulsion can be more easily justified on the basis that mental incompetence destroys the capacity to consent. This may be the point of Dickson J.'s description in *Schneider* (at p. 138) of narcotic addiction as a ''compulsive condition over which the individual loses control''. Cf. *R.* v. *Swain* [1991] 1 S.C.R. 933 (striking down, under ss. 7 and 9 of Charter, the Criminal Code provisions for detention of those acquitted by reason of insanity).

52 Laskin C.J. agreed generally with Dickson J. Estey J. placed the provincial power in s. 92(7) (hospitals) as well as in s. 92(13) (property and civil rights) and s. 92(16) (local or private matters).

53 [1995] 3 S.C.R. 199. On the criminal-law power, La Forest J.'s opinion is the majority one, attracting the support of six other judges. Major J. dissented on this issue, attracting the support of Sopinka J.

54 *Id.*, para. 41 per La Forest J., para. 196 per Major J.

55 Note 34, above, and previous section of this chapter under heading 18.3(b), ''Illicit drugs'', above.

56 *Irwin Toy* v. *Que.* [1989] 1 S.C.R. 927.

who were smokers,[57] it was clear from the legislative history that the ban on advertising still pursued the same underlying public purpose, namely, the protection of the public from a dangerous product. The fact that Parliament chose a ''circuitous path'' to its destination did not alter the pith and substance of the law, which was criminal. The majority of the Court held accordingly that the Act was within the criminal-law power of Parliament. (The Act was struck down by a majority of the Court under the Charter of Rights, because of the impact of the advertising ban on freedom of expression.)[58]

18.4 Health

Health[59] is not a single matter assigned by the Constitution exclusively to one level of government. Like inflation[60] and the environment,[61] health is an ''amorphous topic'' which is distributed to the federal Parliament or the provincial Legislatures depending on the purpose and effect of the particular health measure in issue.[62] As the previous section of this chapter (food and drugs) illustrates, there is a criminal-law aspect of health, authorizing federal legislation under s. 91(27) to punish conduct that is dangerous to health. The federal Parliament's peace, order, and good government power probably also authorizes legislation regarding health, where a problem has attained a national dimension (air or water pollution perhaps)[63] or where an emergency exists (an ''epidemic of pestilence'' has been suggested).[64] As well, in those sectors of the economy where labour relations and standards are under federal jurisdiction,[65] the federal Parliament has power to enact laws regarding occupational health and safety.[66] The federal Parliament has also used its spending power to impose national standards

57 A similar explanation was given for the exemption from the ban of advertising in foreign media imported into Canada (which meant that Canadians continued to be exposed to a great deal of lawful advertising of tobacco products). La Forest J. said (para. 56) that it would not be practical to censor foreign publications.

58 Chapter 40, Expression, under heading 40.7(c), ''Advertising restrictions'', below.

59 See Lajoie and Molinari, ''Partage constitutionnel des compétences en matière de santé au Canada'' (1978) 56 Can. Bar Rev. 579.

60 *Re Anti-Inflation Act* [1976] 2 S.C.R. 373, 458 per Beetz J.

61 *Friends of Oldman River Society* v. *Can.* [1992] 1 S.C.R. 3, 63, 64, 70 per La Forest J.

62 *Schneider* v. *The Queen* [1982] 2 S.C.R. 112, 142 per Estey J.; *RJR-MacDonald* v. *Can.* [1995] 3 S.C.R. 199, para. 32 per La Forest J.

63 *Re Can. Metal Co.* (1982) 144 D.L.R. (3d) 124 (Man. Q.B.) (upholding federal Clean Air Act under peace, order, and good government and criminal law powers). Cf. *R.* v. *Crown Zellerbach* [1988] 1 S.C.R. 401 (upholding federal Ocean Dumping Control Act under peace, order, and good government power).

64 *Toronto Electric Commrs.* v. *Snider* [1925] A.C. 396, 412.

65 See ch. 21, Property and Civil Rights, under heading 21.8, ''Labour relations'', below.

66 *Bell Can.* v. *Que.* [1988] 1 S.C.R. 749 (upholding federal power and denying the existence of concurrent provincial power).

for hospital insurance and medical care programmes as a condition of federal contributions to these provincial programmes.[67]

On the provincial side, *Schneider* holds that the provinces have extensive authority over public health as a local or private matter under s. 92(16). *Margarine*[68] and *Labatt*[69] hold by implication that the manufacture and sale of food and drugs may be regulated provincially as coming within property and civil rights in the province under s. 92(13). The same power over property and civil rights authorizes the regulation of labour relations in most sectors of the economy, including occupational health and safety requirements.[70] The power over property and civil rights also authorizes the regulation of the medical profession (along with other trades and professions).[71] And s. 92(7) specifically grants to the provinces authority over hospitals.[72]

18.5 Abortion

Canada's Criminal Code used to prohibit abortions, with the exception of an abortion approved by the therapeutic abortion committee of a hospital, which had to certify that the continuation of the pregnancy would be likely to endanger the mother's life or health. In *Morgentaler* v. *The Queen* (1975),[73] the validity of the prohibition was challenged on the basis that the safety of modern techniques of abortion made the prohibition inappropriate as a protection for the health of the pregnant woman. Therefore, the prohibition was not authorized by the criminal law power. Laskin C.J. held that it was open to Parliament under the criminal law power to prohibit the termination of pregnancy, even if the termination would not endanger the health of the woman.[74] The principal objective of the prohibition was "to protect the state interest in the foetus", and that was sufficient to make the prohibition a valid exercise of the criminal law power.[75]

The *Morgentaler* case of 1975 also rejected a challenge to the abortion law based on the Canadian Bill of Rights. But another challenge was brought after

67 See ch. 6, Financial Arrangements, under heading 6.7, "Conditional federal grants", above.

68 Note 18, above.

69 Note 35, above.

70 See ch. 21, Property and Civil Rights, under heading 21.8, "Labour relations", below

71 See ch. 21, Property and Civil Rights, under heading 21.7, "Professions and trades", below.

72 *Fawcett* v. *A.-G. Ont.* [1964] S.C.R. 625 (provincial detention of mental incompetents upheld under s. 92(7)); cf. *R.* v. *Morgentaler (No. 3)* [1993] 3 S.C.R. 463, (provincial law requiring that abortions be performed in hospitals held to be in pith and substance a criminal law, not a health measure, and struck down).

73 [1976] 1 S.C.R. 616.

74 *Id.*, 624-628. Laskin C.J. dissented on another issue, but on this issue the Court was unanimous, although the majority did not express any reasons on the point.

75 *R.* v. *Morgentaler* [1988] 1 S.C.R. 30, 129 per Beetz J. following (and elaborating on) the 1975 *Morgentaler* case. In the 1988 case, all judges except Wilson J. held that the prohibition was within the criminal law power, although the other judgments expressed no reasons on the point; Wilson J. did not mention the point.

the enactment of the Charter of Rights, and in the *Morgentaler* case of 1988[76] the Supreme Court of Canada struck down the law as contrary to s. 7 of the Charter. At the time of writing, Parliament has not enacted a replacement law,[77] and the Criminal Code no longer prohibits abortion. A provincial prohibition would be held to be an invalid attempt to enact a criminal law,[78] even if the Charter obstacle could be surmounted.

18.6 Competition law

The encouragement of competition throughout much of the private sector of the Canadian economy has been a longstanding policy of Canada's federal governments. The argument is that a competitive market is the best means of promoting the efficient use of labour, capital and natural resources; and that in those sectors of the economy where the market is competitive, governmental regulation of industry is less necessary. However, because economic activity ignores provincial boundaries, and labour, capital and technology are highly mobile, it is difficult to regulate anti-competitive practices at a provincial level.[79] It is generally agreed that such regulation has to be federal if it is to be effective.[80]

In the second half of the nineteenth century, many industries became highly concentrated through mergers and other forms of combination which had the effect of limiting or eliminating competition. In the United States, the Congress acted against the combines or ''trusts'' which dominated many industries by enacting the Sherman Anti-Trust Act in 1890. In Canada, the federal Parliament passed a similar law a year earlier, in 1889. The Canadian law, which simply prohibited combinations designed to limit competition, was intended to be a criminal law, and in 1892 it was transferred to the Criminal Code. Machinery for investigation and for cease and desist orders was added in 1910. This first anti-combines (or competition) law was never challenged in the courts.[81]

---

76 Previous note. The case is discussed in ch. 44, Fundamental Justice, under heading 44.8, ''Security of the person'', below.

77 Bill C-43, to introduce a less restrictive law, was passed by the House of Commons, but defeated by the Senate on a 43-43 tie vote at third reading on January 31, 1991.

78 *Re Freedom of Informed Choice (Abortions) Act* (1985) 25 D.L.R. (4th) 751 (Sask. C.A.) (provincial law requiring consent of husband or parents held invalid as criminal law); *R.* v. *Morgentaler (No. 3)* [1993] 3 S.C.R. 463 (provincial law requiring abortions to be performed in hospitals held invalid as criminal law).

79 Where an industry is regulated provincially, this usually involves the sanctioning of anti-competitive practices in that industry; the courts have resolved the potential paramountcy problem by holding that the federal Combines Investigation Act is inapplicable to provincially-regulated industries, e.g. *A.-G. Can.* v. *Law Society of B.C.* [1982] 2 S.C.R. 307, 347-361; McDonald, note 9, above, 200-210.

80 See Safarian, *Canadian Federalism and Economic Integration* (1974), esp. Parts 1 and III.

81 McDonald, note 9, above, is a study of the constitutional issues raised by Canadian combines law.

In 1919, a more ambitious regime of regulation was enacted by the Combines and Fair Prices Act and the Board of Commerce Act. These two statutes prohibited combinations which in the opinion of an administrative agency, the Board of Commerce, were detrimental to the public interest. The Board had powers, not merely of investigation, but also to make cease and desist orders in respect of combinations or practices which it determined to be unlawful. In addition to those competition provisions, the statutes included provisions directed at hoarding and unduly profiting from necessaries of life (defined as staple foods, clothing and fuel), and conferred extensive powers on the board to determine when undue profits were being made and to make cease and desist orders which in effect fixed maximum prices. These two statutes were held to be unconstitutional in the famous *Board of Commerce* case (1921).[82] The Privy Council rejected the arguments in support which were based on the ''peace, order, and good government'' power,[83] the ''trade and commerce'' power[84] and the ''criminal law'' power. In reference to the criminal law power, it will be recalled that this was the case where Viscount Haldane uttered his ''domain of criminal jurisprudence'' dictum.[85]

After the *Board of Commerce* case, the federal Parliament enacted the Combines Investigation Act, 1923. This Act repealed the two statutes of 1919, and replaced them with a simpler prohibition of combines in restraint of trade. The new Act granted investigatory powers to a registrar and commissioners, but these officials were not given the power to order the cessation of anti-competitive activities. In the *P.A.T.A.* case (1931),[86] the Privy Council, now speaking through Lord Atkin, upheld the Act as a valid criminal law. It will be recalled that Lord Atkin repudiated the ''domain of criminal jurisprudence'' theory in this case,[87] and he held that ''if Parliament genuinely determines that commercial activities which can be so described [as contrary to the public interest] are to be suppressed in the public interest, their Lordships see no reason why Parliament should not make them crimes''.[88] This decision established that the criminal law power was capable of expansion into the world of commerce.[89]

The federal Parliament in 1935 enacted the Dominion Trade and Industry Commission Act. This Act established a Commission to administer the Combines Investigation Act and conferred upon the Commission some new powers. One of the new powers was that of ''advance clearance'', under which the Commission could approve of certain agreements or practices and relieve them from prose-

82 [1922] 1 A.C. 191.
83 See ch. 17, Peace, Order, and Good Government, under heading 17.4(a) ''The non-emergency cases'', above.
84 See ch. 20, Trade and Commerce, under heading 20.2(a) ''In the Privy Council'', below.
85 Note 10, above.
86 *P.A.T.A.* v. *A.-G. Can.* [1931] A.C. 310.
87 Note 15, above.
88 [1931] A.C. 310, 323-324.
89 Lord Atkin left open the possibility that the trade and commerce power could also have sustained the legislation, but he did not pursue this line of reasoning: [1931] A.C. 310, 326.

cution. This power was held to be unconstitutional by the Supreme Court of Canada,[90] and the appeal to the Privy Council did not include that part of the decision. The Privy Council upheld the validity of the investigatory and prosecutorial powers of the Commission.[91]

Another statute enacted in 1935 was a prohibition of anti-competitive price discrimination which was added to the Criminal Code. This was upheld by the Privy Council as a criminal law.[92] In 1951, the federal Parliament prohibited resale price maintenance. This was upheld by the Supreme Court of Canada as a criminal law.[93] In 1952, the federal Parliament authorized the courts to make orders prohibiting the continuation of illegal practices or dissolving illegal mergers, in addition to their power to impose conventional criminal sanctions. The constitutionality of a prohibition order was challenged in *Goodyear Tire and Rubber Co.* v. *The Queen* (1956)[94] and upheld by the Supreme Court of Canada as within the criminal law power.

Canada's competition law[95] was radically altered by two phases of amendment, the first enacted in 1975 and the second in 1986. In 1975, the Combines Investigation Act was expanded to apply to the service industries.[96] The Restrictive Trade Practice Commission, which had formerly had only powers of inquiry, report and recommendation, was given the power to make orders compelling the cessation of certain anti-competitive practices. A new civil remedy was added to the Act. In 1986, the name of the Act was changed from the Combines Investigation Act to the Competition Act. The Restrictive Trade Practices Commission was replaced by the Competition Tribunal, which has only adjudicative functions. The Tribunal has power to make a variety of orders, including the cessation of certain anti-competitive trade practices, the prohibition of mergers or their approval subject to conditions, the divestiture of assets or shares, the dissolution of amalgamations, and consent orders. These powers cannot be upheld as criminal law, because the Tribunal is not a court of criminal jurisdiction, and the orders can be made without any prior conviction for a criminal offence. Indeed, the

---

90 *Dominion Trade and Industry Comm. Act* [1936] S.C.R. 379.

91 *A.-G. Ont.* v. *A.-G. Can.* (Canada Standard Trade Mark) [1937] A.C. 405, varying judgment in previous note; this case also upheld, under the trade and commerce power, the creation of a national trade mark: see ch. 20, Trade and Commerce, under heading 20.3, ''General trade and commerce'', below.

92 *A.-G. B.C.* v. *A.-G. Can.* (Price Spreads) [1937] A.C. 368.

93 *R.* v. *Campbell* (1965) 58 D.L.R. (2d) 673 (S.C.C.), affg. (1964) 46 D.L.R. (2d) 83 (Ont. C.A.).

94 [1956] S.C.R. 303.

95 The current law is the Competition Act, R.S.C. 1985, c. C-34, as renamed and amended by S.C. 1986, c. 26, Part II. The Competition Tribunal is established by the Competition Act, S.C. 1986, c. 26, Part I. See Grover and Kwinter, ''The New Competition Act'' (1987) 66 Can. Bar Rev. 267.

96 In *A.-G. Can.* v. *Law Society of B.C.* [1982] 2 S.C.R. 307, 358 the Court upheld the extension of s. 32 of the Act to service industries as valid ''criminal legislation'', although the Court went on to hold that s. 32 did not apply to the Law Society of B.C.

provisions of the Act that are enforced by the Tribunal are civil: they do not carry a criminal sanction.

Although many anti-competitive practices are now de-criminalized, criminal sanctions have been retained for some practices. Obviously, however, the criminal aspect of the Act is greatly diminished in importance, and the criminal law power no longer provides a constitutional foundation for much of the Act. In the United States, the Sherman Act has been upheld under the commerce clause.[97] Canada's counterpart is the trade and commerce power, and the Supreme Court of Canada has now held that the trade and commerce power does provide the constitutional basis for the Act.

The Supreme Court of Canada's ruling came in *General Motors* v. *City National Leasing* (1989).[98] The case involved the civil remedy in the Act, which had been added in 1975. The civil remedy allowed any person who had suffered loss as a result of a breach of the Act to sue the person who committed the breach in a court of competent jurisdiction to recover damages for the loss. The civil remedy was not premised on the conviction of the defendant for a criminal offence, and it was not awarded by a court of criminal jurisdiction. The remedy was available to a private plaintiff in a court of civil jurisdiction in an ordinary action, and was governed by the civil rules of evidence and procedure. The criminal law power could not sustain such a proceeding.[99] Nevertheless, the Supreme Court of Canada upheld the constitutionality of the civil remedy. The Court held that the Act was a valid law under the trade and commerce power.[100] There was no reason, therefore, why its enforcement should be limited to criminal sanctions. The civil remedy was a valid part of the law, because it was designed to provide an incentive to private enforcement of the law, as a supplement to public enforcement.

The *City National Leasing* case did not address the validity of the extensive powers of the Competition Tribunal. The case actually arose before 1986, when those powers were added to the Act. However, the Court emphasized that the Act was an integrated regulatory scheme, and it is safe to assume that all parts, including the 1986 amendments, can be supported under the trade and commerce power. The resolution of this issue has not immunized the Act from constitutional attack, however. Charter attacks on the Tribunal, the investigatory powers in the Act and some of the criminal offences have met with success.[101] The constitutional battles to achieve an effective competition law never seem to end.

---

97 Nowak and Rotunda, *Constitutional Law* (4th ed., 1991), ch. 4.

98 [1989] 1 S.C.R. 641.

99 See sec. 18.9, "Criminal law and civil remedy", below.

100 For more discussion, see ch. 20, Trade and Commerce, under heading 20.3, "General trade and commerce", below.

101 E.g., *Hunter* v. *Southam* [1984] 2 S.C.R. 145 (striking down search and seizure provisions of the pre-1986 Act); *Thomson Newspapers* v. *Can.* [1990] 1 S.C.R. 425 (narrowly upholding examination for discovery provisions); *Stelco* v. *Can.* [1990] 1 S.C.R. 617 (ditto); *Alex Couture* v. *A.G. Can.* (1990) 69 D.L.R. (4th) 635 (Que. S.C.) (striking down merger provisions and Tribunal); *Can.* v. *NutraSweet Co.* (1990) 32 C.P.R. (3d) 1 (Comp. Trib.) (upholding Tribunal);

18.7 Sunday observance law

(a) Federal power

The observance of days of religious significance[102] is obviously a matter upon which attitudes will vary from one locality to another. Moreover, limitations on work or play, albeit with religious motivation, could easily be regarded as in relation to civil rights or local matters in the province, and penalties could be justified under s. 92(15).[103] For these reasons, before 1903 it was generally assumed that laws regarding Sunday observance were competent to the provinces. That assumption was shattered by the Privy Council in *A.-G. Ont. v. Hamilton Street Railway* (1903),[104] in which Ontario's Lord's Day Act was struck down as a criminal law. This holding was re-affirmed, and indeed somewhat extended, by the Supreme Court of Canada in the *Henry Birks* case (1955),[105] in which a law requiring the closing of shops on six days recognized as holy days by the Roman Catholic church was held to be in the same category as a Sunday observance law and therefore unconstitutional. It is therefore clearly established that limitations on work or play which are imposed for religious reasons are criminal laws solely within the competence of the federal Parliament.

After the decision in the *Hamilton Street Railway* case, the federal Parliament moved to fill the void created by the invalidation of provincial Sunday observance laws. In 1906, the Parliament enacted the Lord's Day Act, which prohibited work and other commercial activities on Sunday (which the Act described as "the Lord's Day"). The Act included ingenious provisions enabling the provinces to "opt out" of the prohibitions if they chose. These opting out provisions were upheld under constitutional challenge in *Lord's Day Alliance of Canada* v. *A.-G. B.C.* (1959).[106] The basic prohibitions of the Lord's Day Act were not vulnerable to challenge — at least, not until after the enactment of the Charter of Rights, when they were challenged. In *R.* v. *Big M Drug Mart* (1985),[107] the Supreme Court of Canada confirmed that the Lord's Day Act was a valid exercise of the criminal law power, because it pursued the religious purpose of preserving the sanctity of the Christian sabbath.[108] The law came within the typically criminal

---

R. v. *Wholesale Travel Group* [1991] 3 S.C.R. 154 (striking down part of false advertising offence); *R.* v. *N.S. Pharmaceutical Society* [1992] 2 S.C.R. 606 (upholding conspiracy offence).

102 See Lysyk, Comment (1966) 2 U.B.C. L. Rev. 59, 60; Curtis, "Sunday Observance Legislation in Alberta" (1974) 12 Alta. L. Rev. 236.

103 Section 18.11, "Provincial power to enact penal laws", below.

104 [1903] A.C. 524.

105 *Henry Birks & Sons* v. *Montreal* [1955] S.C.R. 799.

106 [1959] S.C.R. 497; see ch. 14, Delegation, under heading 14.5(c), "Conditions as legislative inter-delegations" above.

107 [1985] 1 S.C.R. 295; see ch. 39, Religion, under heading 39.4, "Freedom of religion", below.

108 *Id.*, 354.

purposes stipulated by Rand J. in the *Margarine Reference*,[109] because it was intended to safeguard morality.

The religious purpose that gave the Lord's Day Act its criminal character was of course essential to its validity as an enactment of the federal Parliament. Absent a religious purpose, the requirement of a uniform day of rest would be outside federal competence, for reasons that are elaborated in the next paragraph. But the same religious purpose that breathed life into the Act under the criminal law power was the kiss of death under the Charter of Rights. The Supreme Court of Canada in the *Big M* case held that the Act offended the Charter guarantee of freedom of religion, because its purpose was to compel the observance of the Christian sabbath. Moreover, a law that pursued a purpose so contradictory of Charter values could not be justified under s. 1. The Court accordingly held that the Lord's Day Act was unconstitutional.

(b) Provincial power

The provinces have the authority to regulate the conduct of most business or recreation in the province, along with labour relations, as matters of property and civil rights or local matters in the province. This authority certainly extends to the imposition of limits on hours of work for labour,[110] and in *Lieberman* v. *The Queen* (1963)[111] it was held that provincial authority also extends to the imposition of limits on the business hours of commercial establishments. In *Lieberman*, the Supreme Court of Canada upheld a provincial law which required the closing of pool rooms and bowling alleys between midnight and six a.m. on any weekday, and all day on Sunday. The Court sustained a conviction for operating a bowling alley on a Sunday. The Court distinguished *Hamilton Street Railway*, *Henry Birks* and other Sunday observance cases on the ground that the prohibition in those cases had a religious motivation, whereas the prohibition in *Lieberman*, including the special rule for Sunday, was "primarily concerned . . . with secular matters".[112] Ritchie J., who wrote the opinion of the Court, did not explain what could be the "secular" purpose of a prohibition of business on Sunday which did not apply to any other day of the week. Nor did he explain how the dominant purpose of such a prohibition was to be ascertained.

Provincial power to enact Sunday closing laws was attacked anew after the enactment of the Charter of Rights. In *R.* v. *Edwards Books and Art* (1986),[113] the Supreme Court of Canada followed *Lieberman* to hold that a law providing a "pause day" for secular purposes "is properly characterized as relating to prop-

---

109 Note 20, above.

110 *Reference re Legislative Jurisdiction over Hours of Labour* [1925] S.C.R. 505; *A.-G. Can.* v. *A.-G. Ont.* (Labour Conventions) [1937] A.C. 326.

111 [1963] S.C.R. 643.

112 *Id.*, 649.

113 [1986] 2 S.C.R. 713.

erty and civil rights in the province''.[114] The Court held that an Ontario law that prohibited retail stores from opening on Sundays had the requisite secular purpose: while Sunday had historically become accepted as the common pause day for religious reasons, the purpose of Ontario's law was now the secular one of providing a uniform pause day for retail workers. The Court made reference to statements in the legislative history of the Act to infer its secular purpose. *Edwards Books* thus confirmed that, provided the provinces proposed and enacted Sunday-closing laws in language that was secular, the provinces had recovered the power that they were denied in the *Hamilton Street Railway* case.[115]

In *Edwards Books*, the principal ground of attack on Ontario's Sunday-closing law was based on the Charter guarantee of freedom of religion. The Court held that, although the purpose of the law was secular, the *effect* of the law was to limit freedom of religion. However, the secular purpose of the law was an objective that could form the basis of justification under s. 1; and the Court held that the Act was justified under s. 1. The secular purpose thus distinguished the case from *Big M*, where the Court had refused to uphold the law under s. 1. In *Edwards Books*, the law was upheld.[116]

18.8 Prevention of crime

(a) Prevention in general

A law may be validly enacted ''in relation to'' the criminal law, although the law itself does not have the characteristics of a criminal law. This would be true, for example, of a law which simply repealed a criminal law. Its most important application, however, is in support of laws aimed at the prevention of crime,[117] for example, binding over a person to keep the peace, controlling the possession of guns,[118] or detaining a person who has not been able to stand trial by reason of insanity.[119] There is no doubt that laws of this kind are valid although they depart from the traditional format of criminal law. The same rationale of

---

114 *Id.*, 740-741.

115 Note 104, above.

116 Sunday-closing is discussed in more detail in ch. 39, Religion, under heading 39.5, ''Sunday observance'', below.

117 Laskin, *Canadian Constitutional Law* (5th ed., 1986 by Finkelstein), 850. The provinces may enact laws with a similar purpose so long as they can be classified as in relation to a provincial matter such as property use: *Bedard* v. *Dawson* [1923] S.C.R. 681 (closing ''disorderly'' houses); or administration of justice: *Di Iorio* v. *Montreal Jail Warden* [1978] 1 S.C.R. 152 (inquiry into organized crime); or the regulation of business: *N.S. Bd. of Censors* v. *McNeil* [1978] 2 S.C.R. 662 (movie censorship); or the regulation of the municipal public domain (parks and streets): *A.-G. Can. and Dupond* v. *Montreal* [1978] 2 S.C.R. 770 (temporary prohibition of assemblies and parades).

118 *A.G. Can.* v. *Pattison* (1981) 123 D.L.R. (3d) 111 (Alta. C.A.).

119 *R.* v. *Swain* [1991] 1 S.C.R. 933 (but striking down law for breach of ss. 7 and 9 of Charter).

prevention has been held to justify a provision in the Combines Investigation Act authorizing the courts to make orders prohibiting future conduct which would constitute an offence under the Act.[120]

(b) Young offenders

For similar reasons, the federal Juvenile Delinquents Act was upheld under the criminal law power, despite its express stipulation that juvenile delinquents were not to be treated as ''criminals'', but were to be ''subjected to such wise care, treatment and control as will tend to check their evil tendencies and strengthen their better instincts.''[121] In 1984, the Juvenile Delinquents Act was replaced by the Young Offenders Act, which is ''more closely tailored to our traditional conception of the criminal law'', but still carries forward a similar curative and preventive philosophy.[122] In pursuit of that philosophy, the Young Offenders Act makes provision for diversion programmes, under which young offenders are diverted away from the criminal courts, and which do not rely upon traditional criminal sanctions. These programmes have been upheld as an exercise of the preventive aspect of the criminal law power.[123]

18.9 Criminal law and civil remedy

(a) Federal power generally to create civil remedies

This section of the chapter will examine the extent to which the federal Parliament's criminal law power will authorize the creation of a civil right of action for breach of a criminal statute. But first it is appropriate to comment on the broader question of the federal Parliament's power to create a civil right of action under other heads of federal power.

The federal Parliament has no independent power to create civil remedies akin to its power over criminal law. This means that if the pith and substance of a federal law is the creation of a new civil cause of action, the law will be invalid as coming within the provincial head of power ''property and civil rights in the province'' (s. 92(13)). In *MacDonald* v. *Vapor Canada* (1976),[124] the Supreme

120 *Goodyear Tire and Rubber Co.* v. *The Queen* [1956] S.C.R. 303, 308-309.

121 *A.-G. B.C.* v. *Smith* [1967] S.C.R. 702. But a provision in the Act purporting to authorize a court to order a municipality to contribute to the support of a delinquent child is invalid as going beyond the scope of criminal law: *Regional Municipality of Peel* v. *MacKenzie* [1982] 2 S.C.R. 9.

122 *R.* v. *S.(S)* [1990] 2 S.C.R. 254, 279 (upholding validity of Act, following *Smith*).

123 *Id.*, 282. The validity of provincial legislation making non-criminal and non-curial provision for young offenders was left open in *A.-G. Que* v. *Lechasseur* [1981] 2 S.C.R.. 253, 259 (diversion procedure under Quebec's Youth Protection Act rendered inoperative through paramountcy on laying of charge under federal Criminal Code).

124 [1977] 2 S.C.R. 134.

Court of Canada held that s. 7(e) of the federal Trade Marks Act was invalid on this basis. Section 7(e) prohibited business practices ''contrary to honest industrial or commercial usage in Canada.'' A later section of the Act authorized a court to grant civil relief — injunction, damages or accounting of profits — for breach of s. 7(e). The Act did not provide a criminal sanction for breach of s. 7(e).[125] Laskin C.J. for the majority of the Court described s. 7(e) as essentially an extension of tortious liability, which therefore came within property and civil rights in the province.[126]

Where the pith and substance of a federal law is not the creation of a civil remedy, but is some other matter within federal power, there is no reason to doubt the validity of a civil remedy provided for enforcement of the law. The remedy is valid as incidental to the main purpose of the law. This point emerges clearly from Laskin C.J.'s opinion in *Vapor*. He was at pains to emphasize that s. 7(e) was a ''detached provision'', and was not part of a broader regulatory scheme.[127] He contrasted another provision in the same Act which provided ''for enforcement of its trade mark provisions at the suit of an injured person'',[128] and he clearly assumed that the trade-mark civil remedy was valid.[129] There is also a dictum in the *Vapor* case to the effect that a civil remedy could be associated with patent or copyright laws,[130] and federal patent[131] and copyright[132] laws do of course confer civil rights of action on persons injured by their breach. Although the reasoning behind the *Vapor* dicta is not spelled out, the assumption is that a law validly enacted in relation to trade marks (trade and commerce power),[133] or patents (s. 91(22)) or copyrights (s. 91(23)) may validly include appropriate means of enforcement.

The cases upholding the corollary relief provisions of the federal Divorce Act of 1968 are suggestive. In *Papp* v. *Papp* (1969),[134] the issue was whether the Divorce Act could validly provide for the custody of the children of a dissolved marriage. It was clearly established that custody of children was a matter coming within property and civil rights in the province, and until 1968 custody had been

---

125 The Criminal Code, R.S.C. 1985, c. C-46, s. 126, does impose a penalty for breach of any federal law that does not include its own penalty provision. The argument that s. 126 converted s. 7(e) into a criminal law was peremptorily rejected by the Court: [1977] 2 S.C.R. 134, 145.

126 *Id.*, 149 (''simply a formulation of the tort of conversion, perhaps writ large and in a business context''), 165 (''supplementing existing tort liability''). Laskin C.J.'s opinion was written for six judges. de Grandpré J. wrote a separate concurring opinion for three judges which agreed with Laskin C.J.'s conclusion and did not indicate any disagreement with Laskin C.J.'s reasoning.

127 *Id.*, 165.

128 *Id.*, 142.

129 *Id.*, 172.

130 *Ibid.*

131 Patent Act, R.S.C. 1985, c. P-4, ss. 54-60.

132 Copyright Act, R.S.C. 1985, c. C-42, ss. 34-41.

133 See *A.-G. Ont.* v. *A.-G. Can.* (Canada Standard Trade Mark) [1937] A.C. 405.

134 [1970] 1 O.R. 331 (C.A.).

exclusively regulated by the provinces. Nevertheless, Laskin J.A., sitting alone as the Ontario Court of Appeal, upheld the custody provisions of the federal Divorce Act. They were valid, he held, because there was a "rational, functional connection" between them and the admittedly valid provisions of the Act concerning divorce.[135] In a series of subsequent cases, *Papp* v. *Papp* has been followed and its reasoning also used to uphold the provisions of the Divorce Act providing for the maintenance of children and spouses and for alimony, despite the fact that maintenance and alimony would in other contexts come within property and civil rights in the province.[136]

Since *Papp* v. *Papp*, the Supreme Court of Canada has used the functional connection test to uphold a civil remedy in federal corporation law, against persons who engage in insider trading,[137] and a civil remedy in federal competition law, against persons who engage in anti-competitive practices.[138] There are also other cases in which civil rights of action in federal statutes have been upheld: a right of action for loss of services to the federal Crown against a person who injures a member of the armed forces;[139] the extension of the civil liability of the federal Crown;[140] a right of action in a "common informer" to recover penalties for bribery in a federal election;[141] a right of action for breach of the federal Railway Act;[142] a provision prohibiting railway companies from contracting out of their liability for negligence;[143] a provision imposing a limitation period on actions against railway companies;[144] and a provision limiting the tortious liability of shipowners.[145]

(b) Criminal law power to create civil remedies

Does the criminal law power, like the other heads of federal power, authorize the federal Parliament to confer a civil right of action for breach of a statutory prohibition? This issue is more difficult, because the criminal law power differs

135 *Id.*, 336.
136 The cases are discussed in ch. 24, Family Law, below.
137 *Multiple Access* v. *McCutcheon* [1982] 2 S.C.R. 161.
138 *General Motors* v. *City National Leasing* [1989] 1 S.C.R. 641; and see discussion at note 98, above.
139 *Nykorak* v. *A.-G. Can.* [1962] S.C.R. 331.
140 Chapter 10, The Crown, above.
141 *Doyle* v. *Bell* (1884) 11 O.A.R. 326 (C.A.).
142 *Curran* v. *Grand Trunk Ry. Co.* (1898) 25 O.A.R. 407 (Ont. C.A.).
143 *Grand Trunk Ry. Co.* v. *A.-G. Can.* [1907] A.C. 65.
144 *Greer* v. *C.P.R.* (1915) 51 S.C.R. 338; *Can. Northern Ry. Co.* v. *Pszenicnzy* (1916) 54 S.C.R. 36; *Williams* v. *CNR* (1976) 75 D.L.R. (3d) 87 (N.S. A.D.). However, a federal limitation period on common law actions against railway companies has been held to be ultra vires as an invasion of property and civil rights in the province: *Clark* v. *CNR* [1988] 2 S.C.R. 680, (reading down limitation period to cover only civil causes of action created by the Railway Act; obiter dictum at p. 710 that such causes of action are valid).
145 *Whitbread* v. *Walley* [1990] 3 S.C.R. 1273.

from the other heads of federal power in that the criminal law power, by its very nature, contemplates public rather than private enforcement.

In *R.* v. *Zelensky* (1978),[146] the Supreme Court of Canada, by a majority of six to three, upheld a provision of the Criminal Code that authorized a criminal court, upon convicting an accused of an indictable offence, to order the accused to pay to the victim compensation for any loss or damage caused by the commission of the offence. This power to award compensation had three civil characteristics: (1) the order was to be made, not at the request of the prosecutor or at the initiative of the court, but only on the application of the victim; (2) the amount of compensation was to be related, not to the degree of blameworthiness of the accused, but to the value of the victim's loss; and (3) the order was to be enforced, not by the state as a fine would be, but by the victim as if it were a civil judgment. The civil characteristics of the compensation provision persuaded Pigeon J., writing for three dissenting judges, that the provision could not be upheld as criminal law. But Laskin C.J., writing for the majority, emphasized the "criminal" characteristics of the provision. The order for compensation was to be made as part of the sentencing process in the criminal proceedings, not in a separate civil action. As well, the order was discretionary, unlike an award of damages in a successful civil action. Indeed, Laskin C.J. held that this was a case where the trial judge should not have exercised his discretion to make the order.[147] There was dispute as to the appropriate amount of compensation, and Laskin C.J. held that this dispute could only be satisfactorily resolved in a separate civil action, in which the parties would have the benefit of discovery and production of documents and a proper trial of issues bearing on the quantum of the defendant's liability. The absence of such procedures from a criminal trial did not make the power to award compensation unconstitutional, but it did call for restraint in its exercise.[148]

What *Zelensky* does not decide is whether the federal Parliament could authorize a person, who had suffered loss as the result of the breach of a criminal law, to bring a separate civil action to recover damages (or other relief) outside

146 [1978] 2 S.C.R. 940.

147 This made a ruling on the constitutional question unnecessary. However, the Court decides constitutional issues that go beyond the necessity of the case even more frequently than it articulates the alleged rule that the Court ought not to do so.

148 Although the constitutional ruling in *Zelensky* applied only to s. 653 (now s. 725) of the Criminal Code, Laskin C.J. (at p. 946) assumed the validity of the restitution provision in s. 655 (now s. 727) of the Code, and it is clear that other sections of the Code providing for compensation or restitution are valid as well: MacPherson, "The Constitutionality of the Compensation and Restitution Provisions of the Criminal Code" (1979) 11 Ottawa L. Rev. 713. Forfeiture of property used in the commission of a criminal offence was upheld in *Industrial Acceptance Corp.* v. *The Queen* [1953] 2 S.C.R. 273. An order prohibiting the repetition of criminal conduct was upheld in *Goodyear Tire and Rubber Co.* v. *The Queen* [1956] S.C.R. 303.

the criminal process.[149] The civil remedy[150] could not, of course, be the only sanction for breach of a criminal statute: the presence of traditional criminal sanctions as the primary mode of enforcement would be essential to the classification of the statute as a criminal law.[151] But it does not follow that the criminal law power will never authorize the creation of a civil remedy. Such a simple proposition ignores the fundamental principle that laws are classified in accordance with their pith and substance, and the corollary that a law which is valid under the pith and substance test may incidentally affect matters which ordinarily lie outside the power of the enacting body.[152] Where a federal statute with all the traditional characteristics of a criminal law purports to confer a civil right of action as a supplementary mode of enforcement, the question of the validity of the civil remedy should depend upon the answer to the question that was posed in *Papp* v. *Papp*, namely, whether there is a ''rational, functional connection between what is admittedly good [the prohibition coupled with a penalty] and what is challenged [the civil remedy]''. However, it must be acknowledged that the fact that the Court divided in *Zelensky*, and the emphasis in the majority opinion of the fact that the compensation order was a discretionary part of the sentencing process, suggest that the Court will be unwilling to uphold a separate civil right of action as ancillary to a criminal law.[153]

18.10 Criminal law and regulatory authority

The question to be considered here is whether the criminal law power will sustain the establishment of a regulatory scheme in which an administrative

149 The federal Competition Act contains just such a provision, but in *General Motors* v. *City National Leasing* [1989] 1 S.C.R. 641, where the provision was upheld, the Court avoided this issue by holding that the Act was valid under the trade and commerce power, not the criminal law power.

150 A related issue is whether there is any constitutional bar to the courts inferring a civil right of action for breach of a federal statute that provides only for criminal penalties. There are conflicting dicta on this issue: *Transport Oil Co.* v. *Imperial Oil Co.* [1935] O.R. 215, 219 (C.A.); *Direct Lumber Co.* v. *Western Plywood Co.* [1962] S.C.R. 646, 649. However, since these dicta were uttered, the Supreme Court has held that a judicially-inferred civil right of action for breach of a statute arises from the common law tort of negligence, not from the statute: *The Queen (Can.)* v. *Sask. Wheat Pool* [1983] 1 S.C.R. 205. Although no constitutional conclusions were drawn in this case, the reasoning would free the federal Parliament from responsibility for the new cause of action and would seem to finesse any constitutional problem. If this is so, however, it means in practice that the federal Parliament may do indirectly (create a civil cause of action by silence through judicial interpretation) what it perhaps may not do directly (create a civil cause of action by express words). This is an argument in favour of a liberal view of the Parliament's ancillary criminal law power (discussed in following text).

151 *MacDonald* v. *Vapor Can.*, note 124, above.

152 Chapter 15, Judicial Review on Federal Grounds, above.

153 Cf. *Regional Municipality of Peel* v. *McKenzie* [1982] 2 S.C.R. 9 (Parliament cannot require municipalities to contribute to support of delinquent child, as ancillary to criminal law power).

agency or official exercises discretionary authority. A criminal law ordinarily consists of a prohibition which is to be self-applied by the persons to whom it is addressed. There is not normally any intervention by an administrative agency or official prior to the application of the law. The law is "administered" by law enforcement officials and courts of criminal jurisdiction only in the sense that they can bring to bear the machinery of punishment after the prohibited conduct has occurred. Lord Atkin's definition of a criminal law as a prohibition coupled with a penalty[154] suggested that these formal characteristics were essential to any law which could be classified as criminal.[155]

The competition and insurance cases encourage the view that the criminal law power will not sustain a regulatory scheme which relies upon more sophisticated tools than a simple prohibition and penalty. It will be recalled from the earlier consideration of federal competition law that in the two cases where the law vested prohibitory or regulatory powers in an administrative agency, the courts held that these powers could not be sustained as criminal law.[156] The insurance cases present a similar picture. After the Privy Council had struck down a federal statute purporting to regulate by licensing the insurance industry, the Parliament added a section to the Criminal Code making it an offence to carry on the business of insurance without a licence from the Minister of Finance. The Privy Council held that the pith and substance of the new law was the establishment of licensing authority in the Minister of Finance and accordingly struck down the law as a colourable attempt to do indirectly what the Parliament could not do directly.[157]

In *Nova Scotia Board of Censors* v. *McNeil* (1978),[158] the Supreme Court of Canada, by the narrow majority of five to four, held that the censorship of films was not criminal. The Court upheld Nova Scotia's censorship law as being the regulation of an industry within the province (property and civil rights under s. 92(13)) or a local or private matter under s. 92(16). Laskin C.J. for the minority held that the law was invalid as being a criminal law. Ritchie J. for the majority pointed out that the censorship law did not take the criminal form of a prohibition

154 Note 16, above.

155 The contrast here is with a regulatory law. Some kinds of laws, e.g., those aimed at the prevention of crime, may be valid laws "in relation to" the criminal law without conforming to the traditional format: see sec. 18.8, "Prevention of crime", above.

156 *Re Board of Commerce Act* [1922] 1 A.C. 191; *Reference re Dominion Trade and Industry Comm. Act*, [1936] S.C.R. 379; and see ch. 19, Criminal Justice, under heading 18.6, "Competition Law", above. It should be noted that s. 96 and associated provisions of the Constitution Act, 1867 would not be an impediment, because those provisions do not restrain the federal Parliament in the establishment of federal courts or tribunals; but if the authority vested in the tribunal were characterized as "criminal jurisdiction", the questions would arise whether the federal Parliament had constituted a court of criminal jurisdiction, and if so whether it had the power to do so: see ch. 19, Criminal Justice, under heading 19.1, "Courts of criminal jurisdiction", below.

157 *A.-G. Ont.* v. *Reciprocal Insurers* [1924] A.C. 328.

158 [1978] 2 S.C.R. 662.

coupled with a penalty. On this issue, I believe that Ritchie J. had the better argument. The salient characteristic of censorship is an administrative process that imposes a prior restraint on material deemed by the censorship tribunal to be offensive. There is, of course, always a prohibition, coupled with a penalty, on the sale or exhibition of uncensored material, but this is designed to enforce recourse to the administrative process. It is true that the suppression of ideas that are contrary to current morality[159] is a typically criminal objective, but the prior case-law indicates a requirement of form as well as a typically criminal objective.

The Criminal Code used to contain an abortion provision which took the form of a prohibition coupled with a dispensation. Abortion was prohibited with a dispensation for abortions approved by the therapeutic abortion committee of a hospital. In 1988, that law was held to be unconstitutional on Charter grounds.[160] There had been a pre-Charter challenge on federalism grounds, which was rejected in *Morgentaler* v. *The Queen* (1975).[161] In the latter case, only Laskin C.J. addressed himself to the point now in issue, asserting that ''Parliament may determine what is not criminal as well as what is, and may hence introduce dispensations or exemptions in its criminal legislation''.[162] This view appears to be too sweeping, since an elaborate regulatory scheme may easily be cast in the form of a ''dispensation'' or ''exemption'' from a ''criminal'' law. Indeed, this was the mechanism unsuccessfully employed to regulate the insurance industry.[163] Perhaps the required qualification is simply that of colourability: the more elaborate the regulatory scheme, the more likely it is that the Court will classify the dispensation or exemption as being regulatory rather than criminal.[164]

In *R.* v. *Furtney* (1991),[165] a challenge was mounted against the Criminal Code provisions respecting lotteries. The Code prohibited lotteries, but made an exception for organizations licensed by the Lieutenant Governor in Council of a province. The five accused were licensed to conduct lotteries, but they were alleged to have violated the conditions stipulated in their provincial licences, which limited the profits that could be made by management. The Supreme Court of Canada held that the Criminal Code provision was a valid criminal law, despite

159 Since the adoption of the Charter of Rights in 1982, Ontario's censorship law has been successfully challenged as abridging freedom of expression under s. 2 of the Charter: *Re Ont. Film and Video Appeciation Society and Ont. Bd. of Censors* (1984) 45 O.R. (2d) 80 (C.A.).

160 Note 70, above.

161 [1976] 1 S.C.R. 616.

162 *Id.*, 626-627. Laskin C.J.'s opinion was dissenting, but on the constitutionality of the abortion law the Court was unanimous, although the majority did not express any reasons on the point. Cf. *Lord's Day Alliance* v. *A.-G. B.C.* [1959] S.C.R. 497, discussed in ch. 14, Delegation, under heading 14.5(c), ''Conditions as legislative inter-delegation'', above.

163 Note 157, above.

164 Cf. *R.* v. *Cosman's Furniture* (1976) 73 D.L.R. (3d) 312 (Man. C.A.) (upholding federal Hazardous Products Act as criminal law); *The Queen* v. *Hauser* [1979] 1 S.C.R. 984 (upholding federal Narcotic Control Act, but not as criminal law, but see criticism accompanying note 46, above).

165 [1991] 3 S.C.R. 89.

the fact that it delegated regulatory power to the provincial Lieutenant Governor in Council. Stevenson J. for the Court accepted my suggestion in an earlier edition of this book that colourability was the issue, and held that "the decriminalization of lotteries licensed under prescribed conditions is not colourable".[166] He viewed the licensing provisions as constituting "a definition of the crime, defining the reach of the offence"; and he held that it was "a constitutionally permissive exercise of the criminal law power, reducing the area subject to criminal law prohibition where certain conditions exist".[167]

18.11 Provincial power to enact penal laws

At the beginning of this chapter, it was explained that the provincial Legislatures have the power under s. 92(15) of the Constitution Act, 1867 to impose "punishment by fine, penalty or imprisonment" for the purpose of enforcing otherwise valid provincial laws.[168] This ancillary power would no doubt have been read into the Constitution by the courts if it had not been expressly included, because it is obvious that the provinces require the power to use penalties for enforcement of their legislation. However, the power requires the courts to draw a distinction between a valid provincial law with an ancillary penalty and a provincial law which is invalid as being in pith and substance a criminal law. The elusiveness of that distinction creates uncertainty about the scope of provincial power under s. 92(15) as well as the scope of federal power under s. 91(27).

The dominant tendency of the case law has been to uphold provincial penal legislation. In *Bedard* v. *Dawson* (1923),[169] the Supreme Court of Canada upheld a provincial law authorizing the closing of "disorderly houses", which were primarily defined as houses in respect of which there had been Criminal Code convictions for gambling or prostitution. On the face of it, the provincial law appeared to be simply supplementing undoubted criminal laws by adding new penalties, but the Court upheld the law as in relation to the use of property, and at most as aimed at suppressing the conditions likely to cause crime rather than

166 *Id.*, 106.

167 *Ibid.*

168 Section 92(15) seems to place no limit on the severity of the sanction provided it is limited to "fine, penalty or imprisonment": *R.* v. *Wason* (1890) 17 O.A.R. 221, 250 (C.A.) (obiter dictum that s. 92(15) confers "power to inflict penalty without limit in amount, and imprisonment without limit in duration"); *R.* v. *Chief* (1963) 42 D.L.R. (2d) 712, affd. (1964) 44 D.L.R. (2d) 108 (Man. C.A.) (maximum five years' imprisonment upheld); *Re Skelley and the Queen* (1982) 140 D.L.R. (3d) 186 (B.C. C.A.) (mandatory imprisonment for seven or fourteen days upheld). This phrase is broad enough to include forfeiture of property: *R.* v. *Nat Bell Liquors Ltd.* [1922] 2 A.C.. 128, 138; but its language excludes some kinds of sanctions, for example, capital punishment: Laskin, *Canadian Constitutional Law* (5th ed., 1986 by Finkelstein), 851.

169 [1923] S.C.R. 681.

at the punishment of crime.[170] In *Provincial Secretary of Prince Edward Island* v. *Egan* (1941),[171] the Supreme Court of Canada upheld a provincial law automatically suspending the driver's licence of anyone convicted of the Criminal Code's impaired driving offences. The Court held that the provincial law was in relation to the regulation of highway traffic and therefore within provincial competence.[172] A paramountcy argument was also resolved in favour of the provincial law.

A series of cases in the 1960s were even more generous to provincial power. Provincial offences of careless driving,[173] failing to remain at the scene of an accident[174] and furnishing false information in a prospectus[175] were each upheld. In each case there existed in the Criminal Code a very similar federal offence, and in each case the Criminal Code offence was upheld as a valid criminal law. Moreover, as we have noticed in an earlier chapter, in each case the existence of similar federal and provincial laws was not regarded by the Court as an inconsistency which would render the provincial law inoperative under the doctrine of paramountcy.[176] The result is that over much of the field which may loosely be thought of as criminal law legislative power is concurrent.

The tendency to uphold provincial penal laws has continued. We have already noticed that in *N.S. Board of Censors* v. *McNeil* (1978),[177] provincial film censorship was upheld over a dissent by Laskin C.J., who regarded censorship as a matter coming within criminal law. In *A.-G. Can. and Dupond* v. *Montreal* (1978),[178] a municipal by-law prohibiting all assemblies, parades or gatherings in the public domain (parks and streets) of Montreal was upheld. Beetz J., for a majority of six judges, held that the by-law was a valid regulation of the municipal public domain, and that its purpose was not punitive, but preventive of public disturbances.[179] Laskin C.J., for a minority of three judges, again dissented on the ground that the by-law was a criminal law: in his view, the by-law did not have

---

170 Legislation for the prevention of crime is within the power of the federal Parliament, but there is an extensive area of concurrency flowing from provincial authority over the administration of justice, property, local businesses, roads, and other local institutions: note 117, above.

171 [1941] S.C.R. 396.

172 The opinions are unspecific as to the appropriate provincial head of power; the opinions of Duff C.J., Hudson and Taschereau JJ. assert the existence of provincial power without reference to any head of s. 92, while that of Rinfret C.J. suggests three heads, namely, ss. 92(9), 92(13) and 92(16) (but not, curiously, s. 92(10)).

173 *O'Grady* v. *Sparling* [1960] S.C.R. 804; *Mann* v. *The Queen* [1966] S.C.R. 238.

174 *Stephens* v. *The Queen* [1960] S.C.R. 823.

175 *Smith* v. *The Queen* [1960] S.C.R. 776.

176 Chapter 16, Paramountcy, under heading 16.4(a), "Covering the field", above.

177 [1978] 2 S.C.R. 662; note 158, above.

178 [1978] 2 S.C.R. 770.

179 Now that the Charter of Rights is in force, such a by-law would be vulnerable as an abridgement of freedom of assembly under s. 2.

a regulatory purpose, but was simply addressed to apprehended breaches of the peace and the maintenance of public order — exclusively criminal concerns.[180]

Laskin C.J.'s view of the criminal law power as a substantial limitation on provincial power to enact penal laws finds little support in the numerous cases upholding provincial laws. However, in *Westendorp* v. *The Queen* (1983),[181] he wrote the opinion for a unanimous Court, unexpectedly striking down a municipal by-law that prohibited a person from remaining on the street for the purpose of prostitution, and from approaching another person for the purpose of prostitution. On the basis of the prior case-law, especially *Bedard* v. *Dawson* and the *Dupond* case, it would seem clear that the Alberta Court of Appeal was right in holding that the by-law was valid as a regulation of the streets. The by-law made no attempt to control prostitution anywhere but on the streets. Its purpose was to protect the users of the streets from the activities of prostitutes and their customers. But Laskin C.J. condemned this line of reasoning as "baffling",[182] and held that the purpose of the by-law was "so patently an attempt to control or punish prostitution as to be beyond question".[183]

Westendorp is a reminder that the provincial power to create offences under s. 92(15) is not as broad as the federal power to create offences under s. 91(27). In all the decisions in which provincial laws were upheld, the penalties were imposed in respect of matters over which the provinces ordinarily have legislative jurisdiction, such as property, streets, parks, business activity or corporate securities. This was an essential element of the decisions, because s. 92(15) confers a power that is merely ancillary to other provincial heads of power. Where, as the Court held in *Westendorp*, the provincial offence cannot be safely anchored in property and civil rights or some other head of provincial power, then it will be invalid.[184]

180 Provincial power to enact penal laws was also upheld in *Montreal* v. *Arcade Amusements* [1985] 1 S.C.R. 368 (regulation of location of video games); *Rio Hotel* v. *N.B.* [1987] 2 S.C.R. 59 (prohibition of "nude entertainment" in taverns); *Devine* v. *Que.* [1988] 2 S.C.R. 790 (requirement of French only in public signs); *Irwin Toy* v. *Que.* [1989] 1 S.C.R. 927 (prohibition of advertising directed at children).

181 [1983] 1 S.C.R. 43.

182 *Id.*, 53.

183 *Id.*, 52. Cf. *Re ss. 193 and 195.1 of Criminal Code* [1990] 1 S.C.R. 1123 (upholding federal prohibition of communicating for purpose of prostitution under s. 1 as measure of street control).

184 See also *Johnson* v. *A.-G. Alta.* [1954] S.C.R. 127, in which the Court divided evenly on the question whether a province could provide for confiscation of slot machines; the tie was broken by Rand J., who held the law inoperative under the paramountcy doctrine. Cf. *R.* v. *Furtney* [1991] 2 S.C.R. 89, 103 (upholding provincial power to regulate gambling).

19

Criminal Justice

19.1 Distribution of power

The previous chapter, Criminal Law, was primarily concerned with the definition of substantive criminal law. This chapter, Criminal Justice, addresses the adjectival aspects of criminal justice in Canada. The central theme is the search for a boundary between, on the one hand, the federal power in s. 91(27) over criminal law and criminal procedure, and, on the other hand, the provincial power in s. 92(14) over the administration of justice in the province.

19.2 Courts of criminal jurisdiction

(a) Establishment of criminal court

The constitution of courts of criminal jurisdiction is expressly included in s. 92(14), so that it is within the provincial power over the administration of justice in the province, and the topic is expressly excluded from s. 91(27), so that it is outside the federal Parliament's authority over criminal law and procedure. The assignment of power is thus perfectly clear. But, of course, the issue of characterization remains: is a particular law in relation to the constitution of courts of criminal jurisdiction, or is the law in relation to criminal law or procedure? And a further issue arises: to what extent does s. 96 of the Constitution Act, 1867, which provides for the federal appointment of the judges of provincial superior, district and county courts, impose constraints on the establishment of courts of criminal jurisdiction?

(b) Investment with criminal jurisdiction

The characterization issue[1] arose in *Re Vancini* (1904),[2] which concerned a federal law that invested a provincial court with criminal jurisdiction. Was the investment of an existing provincial court with criminal jurisdiction equivalent to the constitution of a court of criminal jurisdiction? The Supreme Court of Canada answered no, and upheld the federal law. This decision makes clear that the federal Parliament can, if it chooses to do so, stipulate a provincial court as the forum for adjudication of criminal law cases.[3] In fact, all criminal cases are tried in provincial courts, and it is the federal Criminal Code that confers each court's jurisdiction.[4]

In *Re Vancini*, the criminal jurisdiction was conferred on a police magistrate. The jurisdiction included the power to try indictable offences with the consent of the accused. The present Criminal Code[5] continues to grant to a ''magistrate''

1 In *Ritcey* v. *The Queen* [1980] 1 S.C.R. 1077, the Supreme Court of Canada upheld a provincial law authorizing a county court judge to deliver judgment in a criminal case (or a civil case) for eight weeks after resigning his office. This was a law in relation to the constitution of courts of criminal jurisdiction, not a law in relation to criminal procedure.

2 (1904) 34 S.C.R. 621.

3 It has since become well established that the federal Parliament has power to stipulate the forum of adjudication of matters within its legislative competence: see ch. 7, Courts, under heading 7.1(a), ''Provincial courts'', above.

4 It is possible that the federal Parliament could establish courts of criminal jurisdiction under s. 101: see ch. 7, Courts, under heading 7.2(b), ''Federal Court of Canada'', above.

5 R.S.C. 1985, c. C-46. The sections relevant to the following text are 468 (jurisdiction of superior court), 469 (jurisdiction of superior and inferior courts). 471 (judge and jury), 552 (definition of ''judge'' and ''magistrate''), 553 (absolute jurisdiction of magistrate), 554 (consensual jurisdiction of magistrate) and 558 (superior court).

(any provincially-appointed judge with criminal jurisdiction) an extensive jurisdiction to try indictable (as well as summary) offences. Only a very few indictable offences are excluded from the magistrate's jurisdiction.[6] Most of the magistrate's indictable-offence jurisdiction depends upon the consent of the accused, but some of it is "absolute". All of the indictable-offence jurisdiction is concurrent with that of the superior court in each province. Nevertheless, the overwhelming majority of criminal cases, including most of the serious indictable offences, are tried by provincially-appointed magistrates (who are now called Provincial Court judges in most provinces).[7]

(c) Application of s. 96 to indictable offences

In *Re Vancini*, the attack on the magistrate's jurisdiction was not based on s. 96 of the Constitution Act, 1867,[8] and the Supreme Court of Canada said nothing about s. 96. Obviously, the Criminal Code and the actual administration of criminal justice in each province is premised on the assumption that indictable-offence jurisdiction may be exercised by a court with provincially-appointed judges, without violating s. 96. That assumption has to be questioned after the decision of the Supreme Court of Canada in *McEvoy* v. *A.-G. N.B.* (1982).[9] The question in *McEvoy* was whether the federal Parliament could confer on a proposed "unified criminal court" in New Brunswick the power to try all indictable offences.[10] The proposed court would not be a s. 96 court, because its judges were to be appointed by the provincial government. The Supreme Court of Canada held that the investment in such a court of jurisdiction over all indictable offences would be unconstitutional. The Supreme Court held that jurisdiction over indictable offences was part of superior-court jurisdiction in 1867, and that there was not even concurrent jurisdiction in inferior courts in 1867. Therefore, the jurisdiction could not be granted to a non-s. 96 (inferior) court. The Supreme Court

6 The exclusions (in s. 469) are treason, alarming Her Majesty, intimidating Parliament, mutiny, sedition, piracy and murder.

7 In 1985, Provincial Court judges dealt with 96 per cent of Criminal Code offences in Ontario, 97 per cent in Quebec, and 99 per cent in Saskatchewan: Law Reform Commission of Canada, *Towards a Unified Criminal Court* (Working Paper 59, 1989), 7.

8 Section 96, which simply provides for federal appointment of the judges of the superior, district and county courts of each province, has been interpreted to mean that functions which traditionally belong to superior, district or county courts (s. 96 functions) cannot be conferred upon courts with provincially-appointed judges (non-s. 96 courts). This doctrine is discussed in detail in ch. 7, Courts, under heading 7.3, "Implications of Constitution's judicature sections", above.

9 [1983] 1 S.C.R. 704.

10 The question was referred by the government of New Brunswick to the New Brunswick Court of Appeal under New Brunswick's reference legislation; and was then appealed to the Supreme Court of Canada. The question was hypothetical in that the government of New Brunswick, although a proponent of the project, did not refer to the Court any statute, even in draft form; and the federal government had not agreed to carry out its part of the project. Nevertheless, the Court decided to answer the question.

added that it would make no difference whether the jurisdiction of the unified criminal court was exclusive or concurrent with the superior court; even in the latter case, "what is being attempted here is the transformation by conjoint action of an inferior court into a superior court", and s. 96 was "an insuperable obstacle to such an endeavour".[11]

The Supreme Court of Canada in *McEvoy* made no reference to *Re Vancini*, and made only passing reference to the present Criminal Code.[12] And yet, what is the difference between the jurisdiction of the proposed unified criminal court and the jurisdiction of the magistrate under the present Criminal Code? To be sure, the magistrate's jurisdiction under the Criminal Code is all concurrent with the superior court in each province, but in *McEvoy* the Supreme Court held that concurrency made no difference. To be sure, some (not all) of the magistrate's jurisdiction depends on the consent of the accused, but it is obvious that consent cannot cure a breach of the constitution,[13] and the Supreme Court in *McEvoy* did not even inquire whether election by the accused would be the mechanism for allocating cases between the (concurrent) jurisdiction of the proposed unified criminal court and the superior court.[14] The only remaining difference is the fact that a few indictable offences are withheld by the Criminal Code from the magistrate's jurisdiction, whereas all indictable offences would come within the jurisdiction of the unified criminal court. But it hardly seems reasonable, let alone principled, to say that an allocation of 99 per cent of all indictable offences to an inferior court does not violate s. 96,[15] but an allocation of 100 per cent would do so.

11 *Id.*, 721. The treatment of concurrency was not obiter. The order of reference asked for separate rulings on an investment of exclusive jurisdiction and an investment of concurrent jurisdiction, and the Court held that each would be invalid. In passing, it should be noted that the treatment of concurrency makes clear that the *ratio decidendi* of *McEvoy* is not the withdrawal of indictable-offence jurisdiction from the superior court (for that would not occur under the concurrency alternative), but is the conferral of indictable-offence jurisdiction on the inferior (unified criminal) court.

12 *Id.*, 719 (reference to "one or a few transfers of criminal law power, such as has already been accomplished under the Criminal Code"). This casual reference conveys a misleading impression of limited and exceptional indictable-offence jurisdiction in non-s. 96 courts. As explained in the text, the reverse is the true situation.

13 Cf. *A.-G. N.S.* v. *A.-G. Can.* (Nova Scotia Inter-delegation) [1951] S.C.R. 31 (even the consent of Parliament and the Legislatures could not validate the proposed legislative scheme).

14 Another curious omission from the judgment is any reference to s. 11(f) of the Charter, which guarantees "the benefit of trial by jury" where the maximum penalty is imprisonment for five years or more. If the unified criminal court would sit without a jury, exclusive jurisdiction over all indictable offences would violate s. 11(f); and concurrent jurisdiction would also violate s. 11(f) unless it were organized, at least for the cases covered by s. 11(f), around some form of election by the accused. If the unified criminal court would sit with a jury, at least in the cases covered by s. 11(f), the question would have to be faced whether presiding over a jury is a s. 96 function.

15 The cases over which an inferior court has jurisdiction comprise at least 99 per cent of all Criminal Code offences: see the limited exceptions listed in note 6, above. The cases actually

Because *McEvoy* is such a poorly considered decision, it would be a mistake to take the reasoning at its face value, which would lead to the conclusion that indictable-offence jurisdiction may be exercised only by s. 96 courts. Despite the incautious rulings in *McEvoy*, it seems unlikely that the Supreme Court of Canada intended to cause the upheaval in the criminal justice system that would be attended by the removal of all indictable-offence jurisdiction from the Provincial Court judges who now (as explained above) try the vast majority of indictable offences. The Ontario Court of Appeal has politely refused to draw this alarming conclusion, and has held that the Criminal Code's conferral of jurisdiction on Provincial Court judges does not run afoul of the requirements of s. 96.[16]

One of the things that *McEvoy* indubitably decides is that all criminal jurisdiction cannot be vested, on either an exclusive or a concurrent basis, in a single court — unless the court is a superior court. However, a more modest version of the same idea has survived a s. 96 challenge. The federal Young Offenders Act confers on a ''youth court'' jurisdiction to try all offences committed by ''young persons'' (persons over 11 and under 18). In each province, the court that possesses this unified jurisdiction is to be designated by the provincial government, which can designate either a superior or an inferior court as the province's youth court. In the *Young Offenders Act Reference* (1991),[17] he Supreme Court of Canada held that this scheme successfully escaped the terrible toils of s. 96. If the designated court was a superior court, there was no problem, because s. 96 imposes no restrictions on the jurisdiction that can be conferred on a superior court. If the designated court was an inferior court, the unified jurisdiction was still valid, despite *McEvoy*. The Court by a majority[18] held that, since there was no special jurisdiction over young persons at the time of confederation, the jurisdiction of the youth court was a new kind of jurisdiction that could safely be entrusted to an inferior court. The minority disagreed, pointing out that, at the time of confederation, the trial of most criminal offences, regardless of the age of the offender, could take place only in a superior court. However, the minority concurred in upholding the legislation, because the institutional setting of the Young Offenders Act made the youth court jurisdiction sufficiently different from superior-court jurisdiction at confederation.[19]

---

tried by an inferior court comprise less than 99 per cent of all Criminal Code offences, because of the concurrent jurisdiction of s. 96 courts: see the statistics provided in note 7, above.

16 *R.* v. *Trimarchi* (1987) 63 O.R. (2d) 515 (C.A.).

17 *Re Young Offenders Act* [1991] 1 S.C.R. 252.

18 The plurality opinion was written by Lamer C.J., with whom Gonthier and Cory JJ. agreed. The concurring opinion of La Forest J., with whom L'Heureux Dubé J. agreed, agreed with Lamer C.J. on historical inquiry, thus forming a majority of five. The concurring opinion of Wilson J., with whom McLachlin J. agreed, took the minority position described in the text. The Court was unanimous in result, upholding the Act.

19 The difference of opinion is understandable only to those versed in the arcane jurisprudence of s. 96, and in particular the three-part test established in the *Residential Tenancies* case: ch. 7 Courts, under heading 7.3(e), ''Administrative tribunals'', above. In the *Young Offenders Act*

(d) Application of s. 96 to Parliament

In *McEvoy*,[20] the proposed unified criminal court was to be established by the province, but it was to be invested with jurisdiction by the federal Parliament. This had also been the situation in *Re Vancini*,[21] and, although (as noted above) *Re Vancini* did not address the s. 96 argument, two decisions of the Ontario Court of Appeal had treated *Re Vancini* as authority for the proposition that the federal Parliament was not bound by s. 96, and could therefore confer a s. 96 function on a court or tribunal with provincially-appointed members.[22] In *Papp* v. *Papp* (1969),[23] the later of the two cases, Laskin J.A., sitting as the Ontario Court of Appeal, held that a provincially-established and provincially-appointed court official (a master) could make an interim custody order (assumed to be a s. 96 function), because the power to make the order was granted by the federal Parliament, and "section 96 does not inhibit the federal Parliament".[24] On this basis, the constraints of s. 96 could be avoided, at least in fields of federal legislative authority, by the cooperative action of the two levels of government.

In *McEvoy*, however, the Supreme Court of Canada rejected this position, holding that: "Section 96 bars Parliament from altering the constitutional scheme envisaged by the judicature sections of the Constitution Act, 1867, just as it does the provinces from doing so."[25] This is a direct contradiction of the holding in *Papp* v. *Papp*, to which the Court did not refer.[26] Presumably, *Papp* v. *Papp* must now be regarded as overruled on this point.[27] Any doubt is probably resolved by the *Young Offenders Act Reference* (1991),[28]
which was another case in which the court (the youth court in that case) was to be established by the province, and was to be invested with its criminal jurisdiction by the federal Parliament. Although the Supreme Court of Canada unanimously

---

Reference, the majority decided the case on the first part (the historical inquiry), while the minority had to move on to the third part (the institutional setting). In *MacMillan Bloedel* v. *Simpson* [1995] 4 S.C.R. 725, a majority of the Supreme Court of Canada held that the youth court could not be invested with exclusive jurisdiction over contempt of a superior court, because that was part of a superior court's "core" jurisdiction: ch. 7, Courts, under heading 7.3(e), "Administrative tribunals, above.

20 Note 9, above.

21 Note 2, above.

22 The first case is *R.* v. *McDonald* [1958] O.R. 373 (C.A.) (federal Parliament may empower provincially-appointed "magistrate" to grant bail). The second case is *Papp* v. *Papp*, next note.

23 [1970] 1 O.R. 331 (C.A.).

24 *Id.*, 339. In *Re B.C. Family Relations Act* [1982] 1 S.C.R. 62, 76, Laskin C.J. reiterated that "the Parliament of Canada is not inhibited by s. 96", citing *Re Vancini* in support.

25 [1983] 1 S.C.R. 704, 720.

26 Nor did the Court in *McEvoy* refer to the dictum of Laskin C.J. in *Re B.C. Family Relations Act*, note 24, above, which is also directly contradictory of the holding in *McEvoy*.

27 *R.* v. *McDonald*, note 22, above, is presumably also overruled on this point.

28 [1991] 1 S.C.R. 252; note 17, above.

held that s. 96 did not invalidate the scheme, all three opinions proceeded on the assumption that s. 96 did bind Parliament, and Lamer C.J. said so, citing *McEvoy*.[29]

McEvoy and *Young Offenders* decide that the federal Parliament is bound by s. 96. But the cases do not decide that s. 96 applies to federally-established courts and tribunals, and I think it is plain from the language of s. 96 that s. 96 does not do so.[30] In my view, it was crucial to the decisions in *McEvoy* and *Young Offenders* that in each case the proposed court was to be established by the province. As a provincially-established court that did not satisfy s. 96, it could not be granted a s. 96 function either by the province or — the cases now add — by the federal Parliament. A court that was *both* established by and invested with jurisdiction by the federal Parliament would not be subject to s. 96: such a court could exercise powers traditionally possessed by a superior, district or county court, even if its judges were not appointed in compliance with s. 96. In the field of criminal law, it is not clear whether the federal Parliament could establish such a court, in view of the express allocation to the provinces of the power over the constitution of courts of criminal jurisdiction.[31] But in other fields of federal legislative competence federal courts or tribunals could be constituted free of the constraints of s. 96.

19.3 Procedure

Section 91(27) expressly provides that the federal Parliament's power over criminal law includes ''the procedure in criminal matters''.[32] In fact, the federal Criminal Code[33] provides the rules of procedure for prosecutions of criminal offences.

The laying of an information, which usually initiates the criminal process, has been held to be a matter of criminal procedure, and therefore competent to the federal Parliament.[34] It may be safely assumed that the procedural steps that follow the initiation of the process,[35] including bail (now called judicial interim release), the preliminary inquiry, the trial,[36] appeals, and judicial review,[37] are all

---

29 *Id.*, 264.

30 Chapter 7, Courts, under heading 7.2(e), ''Appointments, payment and tenure of federal judges'', above.

31 Chapter 7, Courts, under heading 7.2(b), ''Federal Court of Canada'', above.

32 See Laskin, *Canadian Constitutional Law* (5th ed., 1986 by Finkelstein), 184-192.

33 R.S.C. 1985, c. C-46.

34 *A.-G. Que.* v. *Lechasseur* [1981] 2 S.C.R. 253.

35 Some matters prior to the initiation of the process are also within criminal law or procedure, for example, police powers of arrest, search and seizure: *R.* v. *Hoffmann-La Roche* (1981) 33 O.R. (2d) 694, 724 (C.A.); *Scowby* v. *Glendinning* [1986] 2 S.C.R. 226, 239.

36 While legal aid in criminal as well as civil cases is within the administration of justice in the province, the federal Parliament may validly provide for the assignment of counsel to an unrepresented accused: *R.* v. *Happeney* (1970) 12 D.L.R. (3d) 538 (Man. C.A.).

37 *R.* v. *Miller* (1989) 61 D.L.R. (4th) 764 (P.E.I.A.D.) (civil procedure rules not applicable to Charter challenge in criminal case).

also matters of criminal procedure. Policing and prosecution, however, are probably not matters of criminal procedure: their constitutional characterization is discussed in two later sections of this chapter.

19.4 Evidence

Section 91(27)'s grant of power to the federal Parliament over "the procedure in criminal matters" includes evidence as well as procedure.[38] In fact, the federal Canada Evidence Act[39] provides the rules of evidence for prosecutions of criminal offences.

The provinces cannot enact laws that would have the effect of excluding evidence from a criminal trial. For example, a province cannot exclude from criminal proceedings evidence of an admission made in civil proceedings.[40] Nor can a province provide that an accident report, made under the compulsion of a provincial statute, is inadmissible in criminal proceedings.[41] Rules of evidence that are peculiar to criminal matters cannot be altered by the provinces, even for the purpose of civil proceedings. For example, it is a rule of the common law that a person charged with murder cannot be compelled to testify at the inquest into the death. This rule cannot be altered by a province.[42] It is also a rule of the common law that a police witness has a "privilege" to withhold the identity of a police informer. This rule also cannot be altered by a province, even for civil proceedings.[43]

19.5 Policing

(a) Provincial power

Provincial power over the administration of justice in the province (s. 92(14)) is not confined to civil justice. It includes criminal justice as well, despite the allocation to the federal Parliament of power over criminal law and procedure (s. 91(27)). In *Di Iorio* v. *Warden of Montreal Jail* (1976),[44] the Supreme Court of Canada upheld the validity of a provincially-established inquiry (with coercive power over witnesses) into organized crime in the province of Quebec. Seven of

---

38 See Laskin, note 32, above, 193-194.

39 R.S.C. 1985, c. C-5. Gaps in coverage are filled by s. 40, which incorporates the laws of evidence of the province in which the proceedings are taken.

40 *Klein* v. *Bell* [1955] S.C.R. 309.

41 *Marshall* v. *The Queen* [1961] S.C.R. 123.

42 *Batary* v. *A.-G. Sask.* [1965] S.C.R. 465. A person not yet charged may be made compellable: *Faber* v. *The Queen* [1976] 2 S.C.R. 9; and see *Di Iorio* v. *Warden of Montreal Jail* [1978] 1 S.C.R. 152, discussed in text accompanying note 44, below.

43 *Bisaillon* v. *Keable* [1983] 2 S.C.R. 60.

44 [1977] 2 S.C.R. 152.

the nine judges explicitly made the point that the administration of justice in the province included criminal justice. Laskin C.J. (with de Grandpré J.) dissented. He would have struck down the provincial legislation establishing the inquiry on the ground that the administration of justice in the province did not include criminal justice. In Laskin C.J.'s view, the enforcement of criminal law, including both policing and prosecution, was the exclusive constitutional responsibility of the federal Parliament.[45]

This section of the chapter will be devoted to policing.[46] The next section will be devoted to prosecution. Apart from Laskin C.J.'s surprising dissent in *Di Iorio*, it never seems to have been doubted that provincial authority over the administration of justice in the province includes the provision of police services. It has always been accepted that each province has the power to establish a police force, and this includes the power to "appoint, control and discipline" the members of the force.[47] A provincial police force would have the power to police not only provincial penal laws enacted under s. 92(15), but also federal criminal laws.[48]

(b) Provincial police forces

Ontario and Quebec have established provincial police forces.[49] These forces police the federal Criminal Code, provincial statutes and municipal by-laws in rural parts of the province. In larger municipal areas, policing is provided either

---

45 In subsequent cases, in which a provincial inquiry into crime was upheld, Laskin C.J. did not persist with his view and the Court was unanimous: *A.-G. Que. and Keable* v. *A.-G. Can.* [1979] 1 S.C.R. 218; *Bisaillon* v. *Keable* [1983] 2 S.C.R. 60. Other dicta affirming provincial power over criminal justice include *The Queen* v. *Hauser* [1979] 1 S.C.R. 984, 996, 1004-1005; *Chartier* v. *A.-G. Que.* [1979] 2 S.C.R. 474, 501; *Ritcey* v. *The Queen* [1980] 1 S.C.R. 1077, 1085; *O'Hara* v. *B.C.* [1987] 2 S.C.R. 591, 610; and see Shamenski, "The Meaning of Administration of Justice before Confederation" (1985) 7 Supreme Court L.R. 441. But note Laskin C.J.'s re-affirmation of the essence of his *Di Iorio* opinion in the context of prosecution in *A.-G. Can.* v. *CN Transportation* [1983] 2 S.C.R. 206 and *R.* v. *Wetmore* [1983] 2 S.C.R. 284, where his view suddenly attracted a majority of the Court. These decisions are discussed in the next section of this chapter on prosecutions. They do not, in my view, cast doubt on provincial authority over inquiries or policing.

46 See Kelly and Kelly, *Policing in Canada* (1976); Grant in Macdonald and Humphrey (eds.), *The Practice of Freedom* (1979), ch. 22; Stenning, *Legal Status of the Police* (1982); Hogg in Beck and Bernier (eds.), *Canada and the New Constitution* (1983), vol. 1, 91, 102 (from which some of the following account is drawn); Talbot, Jayewardene, Juliani, *Canada's Constables* (1985).

47 *A.-G. Alta.* v. *Putnam* [1981] 2 S.C.R. 267, 279, (per Dickson J. dissenting, but not on this point); *O'Hara* v. *B.C.* [1987] 2 S.C.R. 591, 606 (per Dickson C.J. for majority). Dickson J. did not include the *empowering* of the police. As noted in note 35, above, it is clear that the empowering of police officers to make arrests, searches and seizures in the enforcement of criminal law is an exclusive federal responsibility under s. 91(27).

48 *R.* v. *Whiskeyjack* (1984) 16 D.L.R. (4th) 231 (Alta. C.A.).

49 Police Services Act, S.O. 1990, c. 10; Police Act, R.S.Q. 1977, c. P-13; Stenning, note 46, above, 78-81.

by the provincial force or by a municipal force (also established under provincial law).[50]

(c) R.C.M.P. policing contracts

The other eight provinces, that is, all except Ontario and Quebec, have not established provincial police forces. Instead, these provinces have entered into agreements with the federal government to ''rent'' the federal police force, the Royal Canadian Mounted Police (R.C.M.P.). Under these agreements, for a fee, the R.C.M.P. provides police services to the province. The services provided are the enforcement of the federal Criminal Code, of provincial statutes and of municipal by-laws.[51] These agreements do not cover municipalities. Some municipalities in the eight renting provinces have their own police forces, which, of course, are established under provincial law.[52] But most municipalities have also rented the R.C.M.P., so that in those municipalities the R.C.M.P. enforces the Criminal Code, provincial statutes and municipal by-laws.

The policing agreements that have been adopted by the eight provinces and about two hundred municipalities are authorized on the federal side by the Royal Canadian Mounted Police Act,[53] and on the provincial side by a provision in the provincial Police Act.[54] This means that, in performing provincial police services and municipal police services under contract, the R.C.M.P. is authorized by the statute law of the province, as well as by federal statute law. The constitutional authority for this aspect of R.C.M.P. policing can be traced back through the provincial Police Act to s. 92(14) of the Constitution Act, 1867 (the provincial power over the administration of justice in the province).

It is clear in principle that the R.C.M.P., when performing provincial police services and municipal police services under contract, is subject to the direction of the provincial Attorney General (or other provincial minister with authority over policing). However, the R.C.M.P. is also regulated by the Royal Canadian Mounted Police Act and regulations made under that Act, and is subject to the authority of the R.C.M.P. Commissioner in Ottawa, who is in turn responsible to

---

50 Stenning, note 46, above, 84-87.

51 Stenning, note 46, above, 69-77.

52 Stenning, note 46, above, 81-83, 87-90.

53 R.S.C. 1985, c. R-10, s. 20.

54 See the following Police Acts (from west to east):

B.C.:	Police Act, R.S.B.C. 1996, c. 367, s. 14.
Alta.:	Police Act, R.S.A. 1980, c. P-12, s. 2.
Sask.:	Police Act, R.S.S. 1978, c. P-15, s. 3.
Man.:	Provincial Police Act, R.S.M. 1987, c. P150, s. 15.
N.B.:	Police Act, S.N.B. 1977, c. P-9.2, s. 2.
N.S.:	Police Act, R.S.N.S. 1989, c. 348, s. 11.
P.E.I.	Police Act, R.S.P.E.I. 1988, c. P-11, s. 15.
Nfld.	Agreement for Policing the Province Act, R.S. Nfld. 1990, c. A-5, s. 2.

the federal Solicitor General. In *A.-G. Que. and Keable* v. *A.-G. Can.* (1978),[55] where the issue was the validity of a provincial commission of inquiry into activities of the R.C.M.P., the Supreme Court of Canada held that a member of the R.C.M.P., who was alleged to have committed a criminal offence, could be investigated, charged and prosecuted by the Attorney General of a province. It followed that Quebec could establish a commission of inquiry to examine specific incidents of alleged criminal activity on the part of members of the force. But the Court held that the commission could not pursue its inquiry into "the administration and management of the force".[56] In *Keable*, the incidents under investigation arose out of the security-service activities of the force (described below), but it seems clear that the province's exclusion from the administration and management of the force was an absolute bar, unrelated to the activities in which the force happened to be engaged.[57]

In *A.-G. Alta.* v. *Putnam* (1981),[58] it was held that the disciplining of the R.C.M.P. was an exclusive federal responsibility. The case arose out of a complaint, made to a provincial police complaints board, about the conduct of two members of the force who were engaged in the policing of the federal Narcotic Control Act. The two policemen were successful in challenging the constitutional authority of the provincial board: the Court held that they were subject only to the disciplinary procedures of the R.C.M.P. laid down by federal law. In *Putnam* (as in *Keable*), the policemen were engaged in activities outside the scope of contracted police services, which (as explained below) do not include the policing of federal statutes other than the Criminal Code. But Laskin C.J. for eight judges (Dickson J. dissented) said that the decision would have been the same if the policemen had been engaged in contracted police services, that is, the policing of the Criminal Code, or a provincial statute or a municipal by-law. It was not practicable to segregate contracted duties from non-contracted duties for purposes of discipline: all R.C.M.P. duties were exclusively subject to federal disciplinary control.[59] This decision is not very easy to reconcile with the earlier *Keable* decision. As Dickson J. pointed out in his dissenting opinion, it seems anomalous that a province may investigate and prosecute a member of the R.C.M.P. for a criminal offence, as *Keable* acknowledges, but may not take any action with respect to allegations of less serious conduct.[60]

The cumulative result of *Keable's* immunity for the administration and management of the force and *Putnam's* immunity for the discipline of the force

55 [1979] 1 S.C.R. 218.
56 *Id.*, 242.
57 Note, however, the suggestion of Estey J. (at pp. 258-259) that "different principles" might apply where the R.C.M.P. was performing provincial police services under contract.
58 [1981] 2 S.C.R. 267.
59 *Id.*, 277.
60 *Id.*, 299. Cf. *Scowby* v. *Glendinning* [1986] 2 S.C.R. 226 (board of inquiry under Sask. Human Rights Code may not investigate complaint of unlawful arrest against R.C.M.P. members engaged in contract policing).

is a substantial limitation of provincial power over the R.C.M.P. It is clear that the eight provinces that choose to rent the services of the R.C.M.P. have thereby forfeited a good deal of the control that a province could exercise over a provincial police force.[61] Needless to say, if this were a matter of sufficiently serious concern to a province, it could establish its own provincial police force, as Ontario and Quebec have done.[62]

(d) R.C.M.P. policing of territories

The R.C.M.P. was originally formed in 1873 (as the North West Mounted Police) to police the federal territories. It is still the sole police force in the remaining territories, that is, the Yukon and Northwest Territories. The constitutional authority for this function is to be found in the federal Parliament's plenary powers of government over the federal territories, which are conferred by s. 4 of the Constitution Act, 1871.[63]

(e) R.C.M.P. policing of national security

Until 1984, the R.C.M.P. also conducted Canada's Security Service, investigating subversive activities or espionage in all provinces, including Ontario and Quebec, as well as activities outside Canada that are directed against Canada. Such activities are usually offences under the Official Secrets Act, although they may often be Criminal Code offences as well. The Security Service was established on the constitutional basis that national security is a federal responsibility, either under the peace, order, and good government power (s. 91) or under the defence power (s. 91(7)).[64] In 1984, this function was taken away from the R.C.M.P. and entrusted to a civilian body, the Canadian Security Intelligence Service.[65]

---

61 *O'Hara* v. *B.C.* [1987] 2 S.C.R. 591, 606-607, made clear that the immunity of the R.C.M.P. from provincial inquiry and discipline has no application to a provincial or municipal police force. The Court upheld a provincial inquiry into injuries inflicted on a prisoner while in the custody of a municipal police force.

62 All provinces have had their own provincial police forces in the past: Grant, note 46, above, 407.

63 R.S.C. 1985, Appendix II, No. 11.

64 In *A.-G. Que. and Keable* v. *A.-G. Can.* [1979] S.C.R. 218, a case concerning a provincial inquiry into some of the security-service activities of the R.C.M.P. in Quebec, Pigeon J., with the concurrence of five other judges, said (at p. 242) that ''Parliament's authority for the establishment of this force and its management as part of the Government of Canada is unquestioned''. This dictum was quoted and reaffirmed in *A.-G. Alta.* v. *Putnam* [1981] 2 S.C.R. 267, 272, a case concerning a provincial inquiry into some of the narcotic-offence activities of the R.C.M.P., but in which the R.C.M.P.'s provincial contract services were expressly recognized and implicitly approved. The dictum is rather perfunctory, considering the range of functions of the R.C.M.P. and the differing constitutional justifications for those functions.

65 Canadian Security Intelligence Service Act, R.S.C. 1985, c. C-23.

(f) R.C.M.P. policing of federal statutes

The R.C.M.P. also polices all federal statutes other than the Criminal Code, and federal prosecutors undertake the prosecutions entailed.[66] This function of the R.C.M.P. is performed in all provinces: it is performed in the eight renting provinces, although not by virtue of the rental agreements; and it is performed in Ontario and Quebec, even though they have their own police forces. Some of the federal statutes that are federally policed and prosecuted are "criminal" laws in that, like the Criminal Code, they have been enacted under the criminal law power of the federal Parliament. These include, for example, the Narcotic Control Act,[67] the Food and Drugs Act, and the Hazardous Products Act. In addition, even in areas policed by provincial or municipal forces, a few Criminal Code offences are policed by the R.C.M.P. One of these is conspiracy to commit an offence under a statute other than the Criminal Code; the offence of conspiracy is a Criminal Code offence even when the conspiracy is to violate another federal statute. Other examples are fraud or theft against a federal government department, counterfeiting, and a variety of "white-collar" offences such as stock frauds and bankruptcy frauds.[68]

The constitutional authority for the federal policing of offences created by the Criminal Code and other statutes enacted under the criminal law power is now established,[69] but its basis has never been clearly articulated. It probably stems from the federal Parliament's power to enforce its own laws, a power that is included in each federal head of power, and that is concurrent with provincial power over the administration of justice in the province.[70]

As well as statutes enacted by the federal Parliament under the criminal law power, there are many statutes enacted under other powers that contain penal provisions for their enforcement. These include, among many others, the Income Tax Act, the Customs Act, the Bank Act and the Fisheries Act, each of which is enacted under a power other than the criminal law power. These statutes are also

---

66 The Young Offenders Act and its predecessor, the Juvenile Delinquents Act, are anomalous, because they are policed by provincial or municipal police (or by the R.C.M.P. under contract), and they are prosecuted by provincial prosecutors.

67 On the criminal classification of the Narcotic Control Act, see ch. 17, Peace, Order, and Good Government, under heading 17.3(c), "Distinctness", above.

68 See Kelly and Kelly, note 46, above, 63-64, 92.

69 *A.-G. Alta.* v. *Putnam* [1981] 2 S.C.R. 267 (note 61, above). See also *P.A.T.A.* v. *A.-G. Can.* [1931] A.C. 310 (upholding federal investigatory and prosecutorial functions in Combines Investigation Act); *A.-G. Can.* v. *CN Transportation* [1983] 2 S.C.R. 206 (upholding federal prosecution of Combines Investigation Act); *R.* v. *Wetmore* [1983] 2 S.C.R. 284 (upholding federal prosecution of Food and Drugs Act).

70 See note 72, below, dealing with federal authority to prosecute. Cf. *A.-G. Alta.* v. *Atlas Lumber Co.* [1941] S.C.R. 87, 100, where Rinfret J. said: "it has long since been decided that, with respect to matters coming within the enumerated heads of s. 91, the Parliament of Canada may give jurisdiction to provincial courts and regulate proceedings in such courts to the fullest extent". For full discussion, see Laskin, note 32, above, 184-188.

policed by the R.C.M.P. The constitutional authority for the federal policing of these ''non-criminal'' federal statutes is provided by whatever head of power authorized the enactment of the offence that is being prosecuted. In other words, each head of federal power includes a power of enforcement.[71]

19.6 Prosecution

(a) Provincial power

Prosecutions of offences under the federal Criminal Code, as well as under provincial penal statutes, are undertaken by prosecutors who in each province are appointed and paid by the provincial government, and who come within the responsibility of the provincial Attorney General. There are no contracts for the provision of federal prosecutorial services like the contracts under which the R.C.M.P. performs police functions in so many provinces and municipalities. Even in those provinces and municipalities with R.C.M.P. contracts, Criminal Code prosecutions are undertaken by provincial Crown attorneys or Crown prosecutors. Obviously, this is also the situation in those provinces and municipalities with their own police forces. The constitutional authority for provincial prosecution of federal criminal law stems from each province's power over the administration of justice in the province.[72]

---

71 *The Queen* v. *Hauser* [1979] 1 S.C.R. 984, upholding federal prosecution of the Narcotic Control Act, and holding that the Act was enacted under the peace, order, and good government power. (The case is probably wrong on the latter point: see ch. 17, Peace, Order and Good Government, under heading 17.3(d), ''Newness'', above.) See also the authorities cited in note 68, above.

72 *Re Bradley and the Queen* (1975) 9 O.R. (2d) 161 (C.A.) (upholding Ontario's Crown Attorneys Act). In *A.-G. Can.* v. *CN Transportation* [1983] 2 S.C.R. 206, Laskin C.J. (with the concurrence of three other judges) suggested (at pp. 223-226) that federal power to prosecute federal offences was exclusive, and that the provinces had no prosecutorial power save what they retained from before confederation through s. 129 or what was granted them by federal statute. This dictum was unnecessary to the decision of the case (which involved the federal prosecution of a combines offence); is contradictory of the *Bradley* case, above, to which he made no reference; is hard to reconcile with the majority's decision in the *Di Iorio* case (see notes 44 and 45 and accompanying text, above); and is hard to reconcile with the existence of concurrent power over civil justice in fields of federal legislative power: see, e.g., *Board* v. *Board* [1919] A.C. 956 (provincial power over adjudication in divorce). A possible defence of Laskin C.J.'s dictum would be to characterize prosecutions as coming within ''the procedure in criminal matters'' in s. 91(27). But Laskin C.J. did not rely on this ground, and it is contradicted by *Re Dominion Trade and Industry Comm. Act* [1936] S.C.R. 379, 383 and the *Bradley* case, above. The better view is that the federal power of prosecution comes within the phrase ''criminal law'' in s. 91(27), on the basis that each head of federal power includes a power of enforcement, because enforcement has a ''rational, functional connection'' (*Papp v. Papp* [1970] 1 O.R. 331, 336) with the substantive content of each head of power. Accord, MacPherson, ''Developments'' (1980) 1 Supreme Court L.R. 77, 101; Stenning, *Appearing for the Crown* (1986), 188-196.

(b) Federal power

Prosecutions of offences under federal statutes other than the Criminal Code, as well as the offence of conspiracy to commit such an offence, are undertaken by federal prosecutors, that is, counsel employed by the federal Department of Justice. Before 1969, the division of functions between provincial prosecutors and federal prosecutors rested on informal agreement between the federal and provincial governments, and the matter was uncontroversial. In 1969, the division of function was reflected for the first time in an amendment of the Criminal Code. Before 1969, s. 2 of the Criminal Code defined the term "Attorney General" as the Attorney General of each province. The 1969 amendment altered the definition so that, in respect of offences under statutes other than the Criminal Code or conspiracies to commit such offences, the term meant "the Attorney General of Canada". This amendment, in effect, formally substituted the federal Attorney General for the provincial Attorney General in respect of the stipulated classes of offences.[73] It was, therefore, an explicit assertion of federal legislative authority over the prosecutorial function. It squarely raised the constitutional issue of whether the federal Parliament had the authority to legislate concerning the prosecution of offences under federal statutes.[74]

The constitutional issue has now been answered in favour of the federal Parliament's authority. The first case to tackle the issue in the Supreme Court of Canada was *The Queen* v. *Hauser* (1979),[75] in which the Court upheld the 1969 amendment (in its application to that case), holding that the prosecution of a charge of violating the federal Narcotic Control Act was properly instituted by a federal prosecutor. However, this decision was reached on a narrow ground. Pigeon J., with the concurrence of Martland, Ritchie and Beetz JJ., the four judges comprising a majority of the seven-judge bench, held that the Narcotic Control Act was not a "criminal law strictly so called"[76] in that it was not authorized by the federal criminal law power in s. 91(27), but by the federal power over the peace, order, and good government of Canada in the opening words of s. 91. From

---

73 The definition substitutes the federal Attorney General for the provincial Attorney General only when proceedings have been "commenced at the instance of the Government of Canada and conducted by or on behalf of that Government". In that event, the federal Attorney General is given exclusive jurisdiction. If the information is not laid by or on behalf of the Government of Canada, or, even if it is, if counsel for the Government of Canada does not appear to conduct the prosecution, then the provincial Attorney General has the right to conduct the prosecution: *R.* v. *Sacobie and Paul* [1983] 1 S.C.R. 241.

74 So long as there was no legislation defining the role of the federal Attorney General, the role could have been rationalized as analogous to a private prosecutor, who would be subject to the ultimate control of the Attorney General of the province. Dickson J. has suggested that this is the position of the federal Attorney General in his dissenting opinions in *The Queen* v. *Hauser* [1979] 1 S.C.R. 984 and *R.* v. *Wetmore* [1983] 2 S.C.R. 284, which would deny to the federal Parliament the power to legislate for the prosecution of federal criminal law.

75 [1979] 1 S.C.R. 984.

76 *Id.*, 992.

this implausible premise,[77] the majority felt able to confine themselves to deciding that there was a federal power to legislate for the prosecution of offences under federal ''non-criminal'' laws. Without explaining why there should be any difference,[78] they expressly left undecided the question whether there was a federal power to legislate for the prosecution of offences under federal ''criminal'' laws.[79]

The point left undecided in *Hauser* could hardly be left undecided for long, when one considers that all offences under federal statutes other than the Criminal Code were being prosecuted by federal prosecutors.[80] The Court finally grasped the nettle in a pair of cases decided on the same day in 1983. *A.-G. Can.* v. *CN Transportation* (1983)[81] was a federal prosecution of an offence under the federal Combines Investigation Act. The seven-judge bench unanimously upheld the federal power of prosecution, but they divided four to three on their reasons. The majority opinion was written by Laskin C.J., with the concurrence of Ritchie, Estey and McIntyre JJ. Laskin C.J. held that the federal power existed even if (which he did not decide) the Combines Investigation Act was a ''criminal'' law. He explicitly rejected the distinction between offences under ''criminal'' laws and offences under ''non-criminal'' laws: the federal power of prosecution existed over all federal offences, no matter what head of power authorized the law creating the offence. The minority concurring opinion was written by Dickson J., with the concurrence of Beetz and Lamer JJ. Dickson J. held that the Combines Investigation Act was authorized by the federal trade and commerce power.[82] For Dickson J., federal prosecutorial authority existed only on the same narrow basis as in *Hauser*, that is, the authority to prosecute offences under non-criminal laws.

---

77 In my view, this part of the decision is wrong: see ch. 17, Peace, Order, and Good Government, under heading 17.3(d), ''Newness'', above.

78 The administration of justice in the province includes civil as well as criminal justice, and the Constitution's underlying rationale of sensitive local enforcement of nation-wide laws (discussed in the following text) is not applicable only to ''criminal'' laws: see MacPherson, ''Developments'' (1980) 1 Supreme Court L.R. 77, 97-103. I conclude that the distinction between criminal and non-criminal laws has no basis in s. 92(14). Once the distinction is rejected, as it now has been (see following text), the question still remains whether the plenary power of enforcement of federal laws is exclusively provincial or whether there is concurrent federal power as well. The cases after *Hauser* (see following text) establish the existence of federal power.

79 Spence J. concurred on the separate ground (later accepted in the *CN Transportation* and *Wetmore* cases, discussed in the following text) that there was federal prosecutorial power over all offences created by federal law (whether criminal or non-criminal). Dickson J., with Pratte J., dissented, holding that the Narcotic Control Act was a criminal law, and that the legislative authority over the enforcement of criminal law was exclusively provincial.

80 In *The Queen* v. *Aziz* [1981] 1 S.C.R. 188, a federally-prosecuted charge of conspiracy to contravene the Narcotic Control Act, the Court again upheld federal prosecution, but, although conspiracy is a Criminal Code offence, the Court still declined to decide the question left open in *Hauser*.

81 [1983] 2 S.C.R. 206.

82 The constitutional basis of the Combines Investigation Act, now the Competition Act, is considered in sec. 18.6, ''Competition law'', above.

The second case of the pair was *R.* v. *Wetmore* (1983),[83] which was a federal prosecution of an offence under the federal Food and Drugs Act. The same seven-judge bench upheld the federal power of prosecution by a majority of six to one. All seven judges agreed that the relevant provisions of the Food and Drugs Act were criminal laws. For Laskin C.J. and the three judges who agreed with him in the *CN Transportation* case, the question was resolved in favour of federal power by Laskin C.J.'s opinion in that case. But now two more judges, Beetz and Lamer JJ., joined in Laskin C.J.'s view on the basis of precedent: they said that they felt bound by Laskin C.J.'s majority opinion in the *CN Transportation* case. This left Dickson J., who was alone in his dissenting opinion that there was no federal authority to prosecute offences under statutes enacted under the criminal law power.

The *CN Transportation* and *Wetmore* cases establish the existence of federal power to provide for the prosecution of federal offences, whether created under the criminal law power or some other head of federal power. Despite an obiter dictum of Laskin C.J.'s to the effect that this federal power is exclusive,[84] the better view in my opinion is that the federal power is concurrent with provincial prosecutorial authority derived from the administration of justice in the province. Concurrency flows more naturally from the earlier decision in *Di Iorio* where, it will be recalled, the Supreme Court of Canada, over Laskin C.J.'s dissent, upheld provincial power to hold an inquiry into organized crime in the province of Quebec.[85] And concurrency accords more happily with the long history of provincial prosecution of Criminal Code offences. Indeed, as Dickson J. emphasized in his dissenting opinions in *Hauser* and *Wetmore*, it seems plausible to read the history of provincial enforcement as an accurate reflection of the constitutional division of powers over criminal justice. On the one hand, s. 91(27) (federal power over criminal law and procedure) authorizes a single national system of criminal law and procedure, in contrast to the state systems of the United States and Australia. On the other hand, s. 92(14) (provincial power over the administration of justice) authorizes provincial enforcement of the criminal law, so that policing and prosecutorial decisions are made at the local level, ensuring that the national criminal law is sensitively administered in response to local needs, values and sentiments.

The only aspect of Dickson J.'s two dissenting opinions that is definitely inconsistent with the majority opinions in *CN Transportation* and *Wetmore* is Dickson J.'s view that provincial authority over criminal justice is exclusive. The majority opinions make clear that the federal Parliament may also provide for the enforcement of criminal law, on the basis of the general rule that the power to make a law (in this case, criminal law) includes the power to enforce that law. The existence of this federal power means that federal laws cannot be rendered

---

83 [1983] 2 S.C.R. 284.

84 For citation and criticism, see note 72, above.

85 See notes 44 and 45 and accompanying text, above.

ineffectual by inadequate or unwilling provincial enforcement. This would surely be a real risk if (as Dickson J. would have held) the federal government lacked the constitutional authority to enforce its own criminal laws. The disadvantage of concurrent federal power is that the federal Parliament could enact legislation assuming total federal control over the enforcement of criminal law: aptly framed legislation, reinforced by the doctrine of federal paramountcy,[86] could exclude the provinces altogether from their traditional enforcement role.[87] This would be a mischievous development, because centralized criminal law enforcement would probably be insensitive to local values. However, there seems to be no informed sentiment in favour of a federal takeover of criminal law enforcement, and it would be strenuously resisted by the provinces.[88] I think it is safe to conclude that a federal takeover of criminal law enforcement is adequately deterred by political forces.

19.7 Public inquiries

Because provincial authority over the administration of justice extends to criminal justice,[89] the province may establish a commission of inquiry into matters forming part of criminal justice, and may give to the commission powers of investigation that include the compelling of oral testimony and production of documents. What the province may not do is to authorize an inquiry into the commission of a specific crime. That is a matter coming within the exclusive federal jurisdiction over criminal procedure. The main objection to a provincial inquiry into the commission of a crime is that the inquiry would probably have the effect of denying to the suspected person the right to remain silent and other safeguards of federal criminal procedure.

The broad power of the provinces to investigate the operation of the criminal justice system is illustrated by decisions upholding a provincial coroner's inquest into a death by homicide,[90] a provincial inquiry into organized crime in the

86 Cf. *A.-G. Que.* v. *Lechasseur* [1981] 2 S.C.R. 253 (private prosecution under Criminal Code of person under 18 rendered inoperative the procedures of Quebec's Youth Protection Act); for criticism, see Whyte, "Developments" (1983) 5 Supreme Court L.R. 77, 83.

87 For a contrary view, see Friedland, *A Century of Criminal Justice* (1984), 59.

88 As related in the previous section of this chapter, policing is already substantially centralized in eight provinces, not by virtue of unilateral federal action, but by virtue of the voluntary renting of the R.C.M.P. by eight provincial governments. Whether this curious abnegation of provincial power is explained by the special history and high status in Canada of the R.C.M.P., or by the fact that renting the R.C.M.P. is cheaper than operating a separate provincial force, it does cast doubt on the strength of the oft-repeated provincial sentiment in favour of provincial enforcement of criminal law.

89 Note 45, above.

90 *Faber* v. *The Queen* [1976] 2 S.C.R. 9.

province,[91] a provincial inquiry into illegal acts by the police,[92] a provincial inquiry into baby deaths at a hospital,[93] a provincial inquiry into injuries suffered by a prisoner in police custody,[94] and a provincial inquiry into the investigation, charge, prosecution and conviction of a man wrongly convicted of murder.[95] In each of these cases, it was likely that the inquiry would reveal the commission of a crime; that the person suspected of committing the crime would be compelled to testify; and that the person suspected of committing the crime would, after the inquiry, be charged with the crime. But in each case the inquiry was upheld. The Court held that establishing the responsibility for a specific crime was not the main purpose of the inquiry, which was addressed to broader issues associated with the proper functioning of the criminal justice system.

The tendency to uphold provincial public inquiries into criminal justice was checked in *Starr* v. *Houlden* (1990).[96] In that case, the Supreme Court of Canada, by a majority, struck down a provincial inquiry into dealings between public officials and an individual and a corporation, who were both alleged to have made improper payments to public officials. The terms of reference of the inquiry expressly forbade the commissioner from expressing any conclusion as to the criminal responsibility of any individual or organization. Nevertheless, the Court held that the commission of inquiry was, in pith and substance, ''a substitute police investigation and preliminary inquiry into a specific offence''.[97] The Court relied upon three things to support this conclusion: (1) the terms of reference of the inquiry named the individual and the corporation whose activities were to be investigated; (2) the terms of reference described the activities to be investigated in language that was similar to the language of a Criminal Code offence; and (3) a police investigation of the activities was going on at the same time. In these circumstances, the Court held that the inquiry was really an inquiry into the criminal responsibility of the named individual and the named corporation. Therefore, the inquiry was a matter coming within the exclusive federal power over criminal procedure, and was outside the competence of the province.

---

91 *Di Iorio* v. *Warden of Montreal Jail* [1977] 2 S.C.R. 152.

92 *A.G. Que. and Keable* v. *A.G. Can.* [1979] 1 S.C.R. 218; *Bisaillon* v. *Keable* [1983] 2 S.C.R. 60; but note that inquiry could not extend into the administration and management of the federal police force.

93 *Re Nelles and Grange* (1984) 46 O.R. (2d) 210 (C.A.); but note that commissioner could not ''name names''.

94 *O'Hara* v. *B.C.* [1987] 2 S.C.R. 591.

95 *MacKeigan* v. *Hickman* [1989] 2 S.C.R. 796.

96 [1990] 1 S.C.R. 1366. The opinion of the six-judge majority was written by Lamer J. L'Heureux Dubé J. dissented.

97 *Id.*, 1402.

19.8 Punishment

(a) Distribution of powers

Jurisdiction over the punishment of offenders, or ''corrections'' (the more popular current term), is divided between the two levels of government.[98] At the federal level, the power over the criminal law, conferred by s. 91(27), includes the power to prescribe the punishment for breaches of that law. In addition, s. 91(28) gives to the federal Parliament jurisdiction over ''the establishment, maintenance, and management of penitentiaries''. At the provincial level, we have already noticed the power under s. 92(15) to prescribe the punishment for breaches of provincial statutes.[99] We have also noticed the provincial power under s. 92(14) over the administration of justice, which includes the constitution, maintenance and organization of the criminal courts.[100] In addition, under s. 92(6), the provincial Legislatures have power over the ''establishment, maintenance, and management of public and reformatory prisons in and for the province''.

In accordance with the rule that prerogative powers follow the corresponding legislative powers,[101] the prerogative power of pardon is divided between the two levels of government: it belongs to the federal government in respect of offences created by federal law, and to each provincial government in respect of offences created by that province's law.[102]

(b) Imprisonment

Both the federal Parliament, acting under s. 91(27) or under other heads of power, and the provincial Legislatures, acting under s. 92(15), have the power to authorize a court to order imprisonment as a sanction for breach of a law.

Once imprisonment has been ordered, jurisdiction over the offender no longer follows the jurisdiction of enactment of the statute creating the offence. As related above, the federal Parliament has jurisdiction over ''penitentiaries'' under s. 91(28), while the provincial Legislatures have jurisdiction over ''prisons'' under s. 92(6).[103] The Constitution Act, 1867 does not supply definitions

98 See Jaffary, ''Correctional Federalism'' (1965) 7 Can. Jo. of Corrections 362, to which this account is indebted, and Hogg in Beck and Bernier (eds.) *Canada and the New Constitution* (1983), vol. 1, 91, 109, from which this account is partly drawn. This section of this chapter does not deal with the impact of the Charter of Rights.

99 See ch. 18, Criminal Law, under heading 18.11, ''Provincial power to enact penal laws'', above.

100 See the previous sections of this chapter, 19.2, ''Courts of criminal jurisdiction'', 19.3, ''Procedure'', 19.4, ''Evidence'', 19.5, ''Policing'', and 19.6, ''Prosecution'', above.

101 See ch. 10, The Crown, under heading 10.1, ''Definition'', above.

102 *A.-G. Can.* v. *A.-G. Ont.* (Executive Power) (1894) 23 S.C.R. 458; for discussion, see Friedland, *A Century of Criminal Justice* (1984), 63-65.

103 *O'Hara* v. *B.C.* [1987] 2 S.C.R. 591, 611 (s. 92(6) provides authority for provincial inquiry into injuries suffered by a prisoner in a provincial prison).

of penitentiaries or prisons. The distinction that is made by the Criminal Code,[104] and that is maintained in practice, is that offenders who are sentenced to imprisonment for two years or more are confined in a federal institution, that is, a penitentiary; those sentenced to less than two years are confined in a provincial institution, that is, a prison. This "two-year rule" is supported by pre-confederation legislative history: in the united province of Canada, a "penitentiary" meant a place of confinement for those sentenced to two or more years of imprisonment; lesser offenders were confined in local jails.[105]

Needless to say, the great majority of inmates in both provincial prisons and federal penitentiaries are persons who have been convicted of offences under the Criminal Code or other federal law. Under s. 92(15), provincial laws can and many do provide for imprisonment as a punishment for committing an offence against provincial law. But provincial offences tend to be less serious than the major Criminal Code offences, so that a fine is the sanction most commonly imposed for breach of a provincial law. It is possible for a conviction under provincial law to lead to a sentence in a federal penitentiary,[106] but it is unusual for a provincial statute to authorize a sentence as long as two years and very unusual for such a sentence actually to be imposed.[107]

An interesting question is the extent to which the federal power over criminal law will extend into the provincial prison system. Could a federal criminal law make stipulations about the treatment of offenders in provincial prisons? For example, the federal Parliament has enacted the Young Offenders Act,[108] and that Act provides, among other things, for the separate custody of juvenile offenders in provincial institutions. While a law of this kind could be held invalid as a law in relation to provincial prisons, it is arguable that the power to punish by imprisonment carries with it the power to define the nature of the imprisonment, even though that involves the federal imposition of national standards on the provincial prison systems.

In *R.* v. *Casserley* (1982),[109] the question arose whether a province could impose a fee for room and board upon offenders who were serving intermittent, weekend-only sentences in provincial prisons. Casserley, who had been convicted of a Criminal Code offence and sentenced to an intermittent sentence in a prov-

---

104 R.S.C. 1985, c. C-46, s. 731.

105 Friedland, *A Century of Criminal Justice* (1984), 61-62, relates the legislative history of ss. 91(28) and 92(6). The long history of proposals to change the two-year rule, in response to differing correctional philosophies, is related by Needham, "Historical Perspectives on the Federal-Provincial Split in Jurisdiction in Corrections" (1980) 22 Can. J. of Criminology 298.

106 *Dempsey* v. *Can.* [1986] 3 F.C. 129 (C.A.) (prisoner serving 12-year sentence for federal offences in penitentiary entitled to serve 85-day sentence for provincial offences in federal penitentiary).

107 A sentence of less than two years for a provincial offence could be served in a federal penitentiary if it is consecutive to an uncompleted penitentiary term: see previous note.

108 R.S.C. 1985, c. Y-1, s. 24.

109 (1982) 38 O.R. (2d) 313 (C.A.).

incial prison, refused to pay this fee, and was denied by the provincial prison authorities the remission of his sentence that he would otherwise have earned for good behaviour. The Ontario Court of Appeal decided that the denial of remission was invalid. Remission of federal sentences, including those served in provincial prisons, was validly provided for in the federal Prisons and Reformatories Act, which did not contemplate loss of remission for non-payment of fees. The Court left open the question whether the province could impose fees on prisoners if the fees were enforced otherwise than by loss of remission. Would such fees be characterized as additional penalties (and bad), or would they be characterized as part of the administration of the prison (and good)?[110]

(c) Parole

Parole involves the release of a prisoner before the expiry of his sentence so as to enable him to serve the balance of the sentence at large, but subject to conditions and under supervision.[111] Parole is an institution that did not exist in 1867, so that the Constitution Act, 1867 is silent on the division of responsibility for it. There seem to have been only two cases on this point (neither at the level of the Supreme Court of Canada), and they decided that legislative power over parole belonged to the jurisdiction that prescribed the punishment.[112] If that is correct, the federal Parliament has jurisdiction over the parole of all prisoners sentenced for an offence against federal law, regardless of whether the prisoner is confined in a federal penitentiary (because of a sentence of two or more years) or a provincial prison (because of a sentence of less than two years). The provincial Legislatures have jurisdiction over the parole of all prisoners sentenced for an offence against provincial law, regardless of the length of the sentence or the place of confinement.

In corrections' theory, parole is not regarded as a remission of the sentence of the paroled prisoner, but as a continuation of the sentence. A well-known aphorism has it that the prisoner is at large, but is not free. All that has changed are the conditions of the prisoner's custody, and those changes have been made in order to accomplish correctional objectives, that is, to aid the prisoner's rehabilitation and facilitate his or her re-entry to society. Once parole is accepted as a step in the correctional process, it would seem more appropriate for responsi-

110 The Court did say (at p. 320) that a fee that took the form of a deduction from a prisoner's earnings from employment while in custody would be valid, but the Court expressly declined (also at p. 320) to rule on the validity of other kinds of fees.

111 In the text I use the term parole as a general term for supervised release from imprisonment, although various forms of supervised release are in fact called by various other names, such as, ''conditional release'', ''mandatory supervision''.

112 *R.* v. *Casserley*, note 109, above; *R.* v. *P.D.P.* (1979) 94 D.L.R. (3d) 564 (B.C. C.A.) (province lacks authority over parole of young offender in provincial institution serving sentence imposed by federal law).

bility to be divided along the same lines as it is for penitentiaries and prisons.[113] Some steps have been taken in this direction. Under the federal Corrections and Conditional Release Act,[114] the National Parole Board is given authority over all prisoners convicted under federal laws, including prisoners serving time in provincial prisons. However, in those provinces that have established provincial parole boards, the Act delegates authority over prisoners in provincial prisons to the parole board of the province. At the time of writing (1995), three provinces (Ontario, Quebec and British Columbia) have established parole boards, and by virtue of the delegation their parole boards have authority over provincial prisoners who were convicted under federal law, as well as authority over provincial prisoners who were convicted under provincial law. In those provinces that have not established parole boards, the National Parole Board exercises jurisdiction over all offenders sentenced under federal law, including those in provincial prisons. The federal Act also purports to confer on the National Parole Board jurisdiction over prisoners sentenced under provincial law who are (because their sentences are two years or more) serving time in a federal penitentiary.

(d) Probation

Probation is similar to parole in that a convicted offender is at large subject to conditions and under supervision. It differs from parole in two important respects. First, probation is ordered by the sentencing court, not by a parole board. Secondly, probation is ordered in lieu of imprisonment or other punishment; it does not follow a period of imprisonment. Since probation is a form of punishment, the court's power to impose it stems from the jurisdiction that enacted the law that was violated. Only the federal Parliament could empower a court to impose probation for breach of a federal law, and only a provincial Legislature could empower a court to impose probation for breach of a provincial law.

Once probation has been ordered, however, which level of government is responsible for its administration? The Constitution Act, 1867 does not tell us, presumably because probation, like parole, was unknown in 1867. Nor do there appear to be any judicial decisions on the point. The current practice seems to stem from the language of the Criminal Code, which stipulates that an offender placed on probation must "report to and be under the supervision of a probations officer or other person designated by the court".[116] Thus the appointment of the supervisory official is the responsibility of the court, and the over-all supervision of probation is also entrusted to the court by the Criminal Code.[117] In this way

---

113 This position is argued by Jaffary, note 98, above, at 366-369 and by the Canadian Criminology and Corrections Associations, "The Parole System in Canada" (1973) 15 Can. J. of Criminology and Corrections 144.

114 S.C. 1992, c. 20.

116 Criminal Code, R.S.C. 1985, c. C-46, s. 737(2)(a).

117 See especially s. 738.

probation has come to be viewed as part of the provincial court system: all probation services, like other provincial court services, are in fact supplied by the provinces.[118]

The provincial responsibility for probation contrasts awkwardly with the federal responsibility for parole of Criminal Code offenders, since parole and probation are so similar. On the other hand, as long as the provinces continue to be responsible for the custody of offenders sentenced to less than two years' imprisonment, it is arguable that they should be responsible for the control of offenders sentenced to the lesser punishment of probation. On this reasoning, it is parole that is the anomaly. If the parole function followed the custodial function, so that the provinces were responsible for paroling offenders sentenced to less than two years' imprisonment, then the division of responsibilities, although arbitrary in that it would still turn on the arbitrary two-year rule, would be consistent.

118 Jaffary, note 98, above, 369.

20

Trade and Commerce

20.1 Relationship to property and civil rights

Section 91(2) of the Constitution Act, 1867 confers upon the federal Parliament the power to make laws in relation to "the regulation of trade and commerce".[1]

The generality of the language of s. 91(2) contrasts with the restrictive language of the commerce power of the Congress of the United States: "to regulate commerce with foreign nations, and among the several States, and with the Indian tribes".[2] Despite its broader language, the Canadian trade and commerce clause has turned out to be a much more limited power than its American cousin.[3] The divergence in result is the product of judicial interpretation, which

1 See Laskin, *Canadian Constitutional Law* (5th ed., 1986 by Finkelstein), ch. 8.

2 Constitution of the United States, art. 1, s. 8(3).

3 For example, the United States Congress has more extensive powers than the Canadian Parliament over anti-trust, insurance, labour, marketing, securities regulation and transportation and communication. These comparisons are made in the appropriate places in this text. At a technical level, the key to the difference lies in the absence from the Constitution of the United States of any state power equivalent to Canada's s. 92(13). The states possess no enumerated powers, simply an undefined plenary power recognized by the tenth amendment. There is, therefore, no principled way to limit the reach of the commerce clause or of the Congress's other enumerated powers. At a deeper level, the difference undoubtedly reflects the prevalence of a more centralized conception of federalism in the United States.

in Canada has narrowed the scope of the clause, and in the United States has expanded it.[4]

The interpretative problem for Canada lay in the accommodation of the federal power over "the regulation of trade and commerce" (s. 91(2)) with the provincial power over "property and civil rights in the province" (s. 92(13)). On the face of it, these powers appear to overlap. Trade and commerce is carried on by means of contracts which give rise to "civil rights" over "property". However, the courts, by a process of "mutual modification",[5] have narrowed the two classes of subjects so as to eliminate the overlapping and make each power exclusive. The leading case is *Citizens' Insurance Co.* v. *Parsons* (1881),[6] in which the issue was the validity of a provincial statute which stipulated that certain conditions were to be included in all fire insurance policies entered into in the province. The Privy Council, speaking through Sir Montague Smith, held that the statute was a valid law in relation to property and civil rights in the province. It did not come within the federal trade and commerce power, because that power should be read as not including "the power to regulate by legislation the contracts of a particular business or trade, such as the business of fire insurance in a single province".[7] What the phrase "the regulation of trade and commerce" did include was "political arrangements in regard to trade requiring the sanction of Parliament, regulation of trade in matters of inter-provincial concern, and it may be that they would include general regulation of trade affecting the whole dominion".[8]

Since the *Parsons* case, it has been accepted that, in general, intraprovincial trade and commerce is a matter within provincial power, under "property and civil rights in the province" (s. 92(13)),[9] and the federal trade and commerce power is confined to (1) interprovincial or international trade and commerce, and (2) "general" trade and commerce. Each of these categories will be considered in turn.

---

4 For comparisons, see Smith, *The Commerce Power in Canada and the United States* (1963); Mackinnon, *Comparative Federalism* (1964). In Australia, the commerce clause (Constitution s. 51(1)) is very similar to the American clause, but it has not received a similarly expansive interpretation, partly because of s. 92, guaranteeing freedom of interstate trade. For comparison, see Gilbert, *Australian and Canadian Federalism 1867-1984* (1986), chs. 4, 5.

5 Mutual modification is discussed in ch. 15, Judicial Review on Federal Grounds, under heading 15.9(b), "Exclusiveness", above.

6 (1881) 7 App. Cas. 96.

7 *Id.*, 113.

8 *Ibid.*

9 It has been suggested that the appropriate head of power is "matters of a merely local or private nature in the province" (s. 92(16)), because "legislation on 'trade' is not on civil rights as such, and especially so where in the Act the two subjects are expressly differentiated": Rand, Foreword to Smith, *The Commerce Power in Canada and the United States* (1968), xii; *Re Farm Products Marketing Act* [1957] S.C.R. 198, 211-212. The more usual attribution has been to s. 92(13).

20.2 Interprovincial or international trade and commerce

(a) In the Privy Council

The history of the trade and commerce power closely parallels the history of the peace, order, and good government power.[10] In many of the most important constitutional cases, both the peace, order, and good government power and the trade and commerce power were relied upon, and many of the cases examined in the earlier chapter on peace, order, and good government will accordingly be encountered again in this chapter. Like the peace, order, and good government power, the trade and commerce power was severely contracted by the Privy Council, but has been permitted to expand somewhat by the Supreme Court of Canada since the abolition of appeals to the Privy Council.

The *Parsons* case did not define when trade and commerce became sufficiently interprovincial so as to come within the federal power. This definition was left to the Haldane period. The *Insurance Reference* (1916)[11] set the pattern. The federal Insurance Act of 1910 purported to establish a licensing regime for insurance companies, other than provincial companies carrying on business wholly within the province of incorporation. The exemption emphasized that the aim of the Act was to impose federal regulation on an industry which spread across the country without regard for provincial boundaries. But the Privy Council held that the scope of the industry or of particular companies was irrelevant. Viscount Haldane said:[12]

> It must now be taken that the authority to legislate for the regulation of trade and commerce does not extend to the regulation by a licensing system of a particular trade in which Canadians would otherwise be free to engage in the provinces.

The trade and commerce power was also rejected as a support for the legislation in the *Board of Commerce* case (1922).[13] The legislation there included anti-combines provisions, and also provisions regulating hoarding and excessive prices of certain ''necessaries of life'' (food, clothing and fuel). In argument, Viscount Haldane suggested that the trade and commerce power had no independent content and could be invoked only as ancillary to other federal powers.[14] In his actual opinion, Viscount Haldane dismissed the trade and commerce power in one uninformative sentence: s. 91(2) ''did not, by itself, enable interference with particular trades in which Canadians would, apart from any right of interference

10 Chapter 17, Peace, Order, and Good Government, above.

11 *A.-G. Can.* v. *A.-G. Alta.* (Insurance) [1916] 1 A.C. 588.

12 *Id.*, 596. Other attempts by the federal Parliament to regulate the insurance industry were also struck down as colourable versions of what had previously been held invalid: see ch. 21, Property and Civil Rights, under heading 21.5, ''Insurance'', below.

13 *Re Board of Commerce Act* [1922] 1 A.C. 191.

14 Laskin, note 1, above, 425.

conferred by these words above [p.o.g.g.], be free to engage in the Provinces''.[15] The ancillary theory of the trade and commerce power was repeated in *Toronto Electric Commissioners* v. *Snider* (1925),[16] where the power was again rejected, this time as a support for federal labour laws.[17] In these two cases, the interprovincial character of the laws resided in the fact that they attempted to control, not particular trades, but more general aspects of the economy — combinations, prices, labour — which were governed by economic forces that ignored provincial boundaries. But the pervasiveness and interdependence of the legislations' subject matters was not sufficient to carry them out of property and civil rights and into the federal fold.

In the *P.A.T.A.* case (1931),[18] the Privy Council through Lord Atkin upheld as a ''criminal law'' (s. 91(27)) a narrower form of anti-combines law (which had been redrafted following the *Board of Commerce* case). In an obiter dictum, Lord Atkin repudiated Viscount Haldane's ancillary theory of the trade and commerce power, saying that the words of s. 91(2) ''must receive their proper construction where they stand as giving an independent authority to Parliament over the particular subject-matter''.[19] However, he did not cast doubt on the results in *Board of Commerce* and *Snider*, and he expressly forbore from giving any rival definition to s. 91(2).[20]

Federal attempts to use the trade and commerce power to regulate marketing[21] were also struck down by the Privy Council, and by the Supreme Court of Canada while still subject to appeals to the Privy Council. In *The King* v. *Eastern Terminal Elevator Co.* (1925),[22] the Supreme Court of Canada by a majority struck down a statute which regulated the grain trade. As is common knowledge (and was recognized by the judges in the case), very little of Canada's grain is consumed in the province of production, and the great bulk of it is exported. Nevertheless, the federal statute had to fasten onto some local operations, and in particular to license and regulate grain elevators, in order to make the scheme effective. The Court held that the regulation of local works, such as elevators, made the entire scheme invalid.[23] Similarly, in the *Natural Products Marketing*

15 [1922] 1 A.C. 191, 198. See now *General Motors* v. *City National Leasing*, note 81, below; ch. 18, Criminal Law, under heading 18.6, ''Competition law'', above.

16 [1925] A.C. 396, 410.

17 See ch. 21, Property and Civil Rights, under heading 21.8, ''Labour relations'', below.

18 *P.A.T.A.* v. *A.-G. Can.* [1931] A.C. 310.

19 *Id.*, 326.

20 Lord Atkin did leave open the intriguing possibility that the *P.A.T.A.* legislation could have been upheld under s. 91(2), but he did not pursue the point: *Id.*, 326.

21 See ch. 21, Property and Civil Rights, under heading 21.9, ''Marketing'', below.

22 [1925] S.C.R. 434.

23 This decision was overcome by the use of the declaratory power (s. 92(10)(c)). The federal Parliament enacted a statute declaring all grain elevators and warehouses to be for the general advantage of Canada: Canada Grain Act, S.C. 1926, c. 33, s. 234. The current sweeping form of this declaration has been upheld in *Jorgenson* v. *A.-G. Can.* [1971] S.C.R. 725 and *Chamney* v. *The Queen* [1975] 2 S.C.R. 151. See ch. 22, Transportation and Communication, under heading 22.3, ''Works for the general advantage of Canada'', below.

Reference (1937),[24] one of the "new deal" cases,[25] a statute was held invalid which provided for the establishment of marketing schemes for those natural products whose principal market was outside the province of production, or some part of which was for export. The Privy Council through Lord Atkin held that the entire statute was invalid because it included within its purview some transactions which could be completed within the province. That was a matter within property and civil rights in the province.

The Privy Council's last consideration of the trade and commerce power came in the *Margarine Reference* (1951),[26] in which their lordships held that a federal prohibition of the manufacture, sale or possession of margarine (for the purpose of protecting the dairy industry) was wholly invalid, because it proscribed not only interprovincial transactions but also transactions that could be completed within a province. A provision in the statute which prohibited the *importation* of margarine had been upheld by the Supreme Court of Canada as a valid exercise of the trade and commerce power.[27] The appeal to the Privy Council did not include the question of importation, and the Privy Council did not express any opinion on it; but there is no doubt that the federal trade and commerce power will authorize the regulation or prohibition[28] of the importation of goods into Canada.[29]

(b) In the Supreme Court of Canada

Since the abolition of appeals to the Privy Council there has been a resurgence of the trade and commerce power. A new attitude was discernible in the *Ontario Farm Products Marketing Reference* (1957),[30] a case concerning a provincial marketing statute, in which four judges indicated by implication that federal power

---

24 *A.-G. B.C.* v. *A.-G. Can.* (Natural Products Marketing) [1937] A.C. 377.

25 See ch. 17, Peace, Order, and Good Government, under heading 17.4(a), "The non-emergency cases", above.

26 *Can. Federation of Agriculture* v. *A.-G. Que.* [1951] A.C. 179.

27 [1949] S.C.R. 1.

28 There are dicta in early cases to the effect that the "regulation" of trade and commerce does not include its prohibition. Whatever validity this proposition may have in interpreting the powers of a municipality or administrative agency, it cannot be correct for s. 91(2), because it would leave a gap in legislative power: neither the Parliament nor the Legislatures could prohibit interprovincial or international trade in a product. See Laskin, note 1, above, 236.

29 *Gold Seal Ltd.* v. *Dominion Express Co.* (1921) 62 S.C.R. 424; *Caloil* v. *A.-G. Can.* [1971] S.C.R. 543. Custom duties may be justified under s. 91(2) or (3): *A.-G. B.C.* v. *A.-G. Can.* (Johnny Walker) [1924] A.C. 222. In *A.-G. Ont. v. A.-G. Can.* (Local Prohibition) [1896] A.C. 348, the Privy Council held that a provincial Legislature has no power to prohibit the importation of intoxicating liquor into the province. However, it has been held that a provincial law prohibiting (with certain exceptions) the possession of liquor not purchased from the provincial government's liquor store is valid, notwithstanding that it has the effect of prohibiting the importation of liquor into the province: *R.* v. *Gautreau* (1978) 88 D.L.R. (3d) 718 (N.B. A.D.).

30 [1957] S.C.R. 198.

would extend to some transactions which were completed within a province.[31] In *Murphy* v. *C.P.R.* (1958),[32] the Supreme Court of Canada upheld the validity of the federal Canadian Wheat Board Act, which provided for the compulsory purchase by the Canadian Wheat Board of all grain destined for markets outside the province of production, and for the marketing, pooling of proceeds and equalizing of the return to producers. The transaction which gave rise to the *Murphy* litigation was an interprovincial one — a shipment of grain from one province to another in violation of the Act. But in *R.* v. *Klassen* (1959),[33] the Manitoba Court of Appeal had to decide whether the Act could validly apply to a purely local work — a feed mill which processed locally-produced wheat and sold it as feed to local farmers. The Act imposed on producers, and enforced through elevators and mills, a quota system which was designed to ensure equal access to the interprovincial and export market; it also applied to local processing and sale so that a producer could not obtain an unfair advantage by selling grain in excess of his quota to a local mill for locally-sold flour, seed or feed. The Manitoba Court of Appeal held that the application of the Act to such intraprovincial transactions was valid. It was incidental to the principal purpose of the Act, which was to regulate the interprovincial and export trade in grain.

The *Klassen* decision was a striking departure from the course of Privy Council decisions, which had consistently decided that federal regulation under the trade and commerce power could not embrace wholly intraprovincial transactions, even when the main object was to regulate the interprovincial or export trade. Yet the Supreme Court of Canada refused leave to appeal the decision. The new development suggested by *Klassen* was confirmed in *Caloil* v. *A.-G. Can.* (1971),[34] when the Supreme Court of Canada unanimously upheld a federal prohibition on the transportation or sale of imported oil west of the Ottawa Valley. The purpose was to protect the domestic industry in the West from the then cheaper imported product. This prohibition clearly caught many transactions which would otherwise have been completed within a province. Nevertheless, the law was upheld as "an incident in the administration of an extra-provincial marketing scheme" and as "an integral part of the control of imports in the furtherance of an extraprovincial trade policy".[35]

It is not easy to be confident about the implications of these cases. The commodities concerned — grain and oil — flow across provincial lines from the

---

31 *Id.*, 204, 209, 231; the passages are set out in full in *Carnation Co.* v. *Que. Agricultural Marketing Bd.* [1968] S.C.R. 238, 245-246.

32 [1958] S.C.R. 626.

33 (1959) 20 D.L.R. (2d) 406 (Man. C.A.); see Laskin, Comment (1959) 37 Can. Bar Rev. 630.

34 [1971] S.C.R. 543.

35 *Id.*, 551 per Pigeon J. with whom Fauteux C.J., Abbott, Ritchie, Hall and Spence JJ. agreed; Laskin C.J., with whom Martland and Judson JJ. agreed, wrote a very brief separate concurring opinion emphasizing that the impugned law governed the importation of goods.

province of production or importation to the province of consumption or export.[36] The existence of this interprovincial flow enabled the courts to uphold the regulation of intraprovincial transactions on the ground that such regulation was incidental to the main object of regulating the interprovincial flow.[37] It is not yet clear to what extent interprovincial elements of a less obvious kind would provide support for federal regulation. Whenever a market for a product is national (or international) in size, as opposed to local, there is a strong argument that effective regulation of the market can only be national; and this is the position which has been effectively established in the United States.[38] The Canadian decisions do not yet go that far.

In *Re Agricultural Products Marketing Act* (1978),[39] a federal marketing statute was upheld. The statute was the federal element of interlocking federal and provincial statutes (and regulations and orders) that together (1) established and empowered a national egg marketing agency and provincial egg marketing agencies; (2) controlled the supply of eggs by the imposition of quotas on each province and, within each provincial quota, on each producer; (3) provided for the disposal of the surplus product; and (4) imposed levies on producers to finance the cost of the scheme and especially the cost of surplus disposal. The federal agency was elected by all egg producers regardless of whether their business was interprovincial or local; federal quotas were based on volumes of production, not volumes entering interprovincial trade; the purchase and disposal of the surplus product by the federal agency was not confined to interprovincial trade; and federal levies were imposed on all producers, regardless of whether their production was destined for a local or out-of-province market. This intervention in local markets was especially heavy in that evidence showed that 90 per cent of all eggs produced in Canada were consumed within the province of production: it was cheaper to ship the feed for the birds than the fragile, perishable eggs.

On the face of it, the Supreme Court of Canada's decision to uphold the federal Act in *Re Agricultural Products Marketing Act* is a major expansion of federal power into local markets. However, the case is an unusual one, and may

---

36 So does natural gas, and the federal Parliament has power under s. 91(2) to regulate the price when the gas is sold outside the province of production: *Sask. Power Corp.* v. *TransCan. Pipelines* (1988) 56 D.L.R. (4th) 416 (Sask. C.A.).

37 Under the double aspect doctrine, an expanded federal power need not entail a diminished provincial power. Yet the Supreme Court of Canada has severely curtailed the powers of the provinces to regulate the marketing of goods imported from outside the province: *A.-G. Man.* v. *Man. Egg and Poultry Assn.* [1971] S.C.R. 689; *Burns Foods* v. *A.-G. Man.* [1975] 1 S.C.R. 494; or to regulate the production or pricing of goods produced in the province but destined for out-of-province markets: *Can. Industrial Gas and Oil* v. *Govt. of Sask.* [1978] 2 S.C.R. 545; *Central Can. Potash* v. *Govt. of Sask.* [1979] 1 S.C.R. 42. Provincial power over marketing is discussed in ch. 21, Property and Civil Rights, under heading 21.9, ''Marketing'', below.

38 Riker, *Federalism, Origin, Operation, Significance* (1964), 71-75.

39 [1978] 2 S.C.R. 1198. I disclose that I was one of the counsel representing those who were interested in the invalidity of the marketing plan.

not be an important precedent. The Court[40] was impressed by the fact that the federal Act was the centrepiece of a cooperative scheme designed to rationalize the national market in eggs. The scheme had been agreed to by all eleven governments, and had been executed by complementary legislation in all eleven jurisdictions. Indeed, one of the provincial statutes — that of Ontario — was also in issue, and was also upheld. As Pigeon J. remarked with disarming frankness, it was ''a sincere cooperative effort'', and ''it would really be unfortunate if this was all brought to nought''.[41] A related factor was the extreme difficulty of disentangling the federal and provincial elements of the actual marketing plan for eggs that had been established, under the aegis of the statutes, by a complex undergrowth of regulations and orders emanating from the two levels of government. In these circumstances, it was understandable that the Court would place reliance on the frequent references in the federal Act to interprovincial and export trade, even though it was clear that these references did not in practice exclude farmers producing for local markets from the crucial federal rules regarding production quotas,[42] surplus disposal[43] and levies.[44] The result is that the two concurring opinions are very general and abstract and hard to relate to the actual operation of the marketing plan under consideration.[45]

40 Two essentially concurring opinions were written. Laskin C.J. wrote a very long opinion which attracted the agreement of Judson, Spence and Dickson JJ. Pigeon J. wrote a short opinion — he explained at p. 1289 that he was ''pressed for time'' — which essentially reacted to Laskin C.J.'s opinion with which he was in substantial agreement. Pigeon J's opinion, despite its perfunctory nature, attracted the agreement of Martland, Ritchie, Beetz and de Grandpré JJ. and accordingly qualifies as the majority opinion.

41 [1978] 2 S.C.R. 1198, 1296.

42 With respect to production quotas, both federal and provincial rules were upheld. Pigeon J. for the majority said (at p. 1293) that ''the control of production, whether agricultural or industrial, is prima facie a local matter, a matter of provincial jurisdiction''. Nevertheless, Laskin C.J. (with whom Pigeon J. agreed on this issue) said (at p. 1265) that: ''I do not think Parliament is precluded from allocating quotas on an industry-wide basis if it relates them to its regulatory control in relation to interprovincial and export trade''. He did not explain what the qualification meant.

43 With respect to surplus disposal, Pigeon J. for the majority held (at p. 1292) that the federal agency could not be empowered to buy and sell surplus eggs in local trade. In this he disagreed with Laskin C.J. for the minority (at p. 1266). However, Pigeon J. did not explain the implications of his view for the rest of the marketing plan, of which surplus disposal was an important part.

44 With respect to levies, Laskin C.J. (with whom Pigeon J. agreed on this issue) introduced (at p. 1263) the qualification that they be limited to interprovincial and export trade, and suggested that they could be levied at grading stations established to handle eggs in interprovincial and export trade. Laskin C.J. did not explain whether this meant that the actual levies in the case, which were based on production, were bad.

45 The previous three notes illustrate the doubts left by the opinions, which led to further litigation, e.g., *Boulanger* v. *Fédération des producteurs d'oeufs* (1982) 141 D.L.R. (3d) 72 (Que. C.A.). For comment on *Re Agricultural Products Marketing Act*, see Smith in Law Society of Upper Canada, *The Constitution and the Future of Canada*, Special Lectures, 1978, 135.

In *Dominion Stores* v. *The Queen* (1979),[46] the Supreme Court of Canada, by a narrow five to four majority, struck down Part I of the federal Canada Agricultural Products Standards Act. The Act provided for the establishment of grades with appropriate grade names for agricultural products. Part II of the Act made it compulsory to use the grade names for products moving in interprovincial or international trade. Part I of the Act did not make it compulsory to use the grade names for products marketed within the province of production,[47] but it provided that, if the grade names were used in local trade, then the appropriate federal standards had to be complied with. Dominion Stores was charged under Part I with selling apples (which were assumed to be locally produced) under the federally-established grade name ''Canada Extra Fancy'', which did not comply with the standards stipulated for that grade of apples. The company was acquitted on the ground that Part I of the Act was an unconstitutional attempt to regulate local trade.

In my opinion, *Dominion Stores* was wrongly decided. It is incontrovertible that Part II of the Canada Agricultural Products Standards Act, which requires the use of the federal grade names and standards for products moving in interprovincial or international trade, is a valid exercise of power over trade and commerce. But if the same grade names could be used for locally-produced products, without compliance with the federal standards, then the grade names would lose their credibility. It seems to me, therefore, that Part I of the Act was necessary to protect the interprovincial and international scheme: if the grade names were used for locally-produced products, then the federal standards had to be complied with. Surely, such a modest intrusion into local trade has a ''rational, functional connection'' with the regulation of interprovincial and international trade. In rejecting this intrusion into local trade, the Court seems to have inexplicably reverted to the bad old days of the Privy Council's ''watertight compartments''. Indeed, Estey J.'s majority opinion discussed the trade and commerce power by reference only to the old Privy Council decisions that had so narrowed the power. He did not mention any of the developments since the abolition of appeals. However, at the end of the opinion Estey J. said that ''it may well be''

46 [1980] 1 S.C.R. 844.

47 These facts were blurred by the existence in Ontario of provincial legislation which made the use of the same grade names compulsory in local trade. This led Estey J. for the majority to emphasize, correctly, that the use of the federal grade names was in practice mandatory in Ontario. But, in assessing the validity of the federal law, the existence of the provincial law should have been treated as irrelevant. The federal law imposed no compulsion. To the extent that Estey J. relied on the provincial law in assessing the validity of the federal law, he was permitting the scope of the federal trade and commerce power to be contracted by the enactment of provincial legislation. Moreover, this approach assumes that the federal law would be valid in those provinces that did not have matching legislation. It also stands in sharp contrast with the Court's approach in *Re Agricultural Products Marketing Act* [1978] 2 S.C.R. 1198, where the Court was obviously anxious to overlook elements of overreaching by each level of government in order to sustain a marketing plan that had been established by the cooperative action of both levels of government.

that his account of law "is not now a correct description of the federal power under s. 91(2)".[48] This unusual acknowledgment is a welcome caveat against giving too much precedential weight to the reasoning, but it does not meet my criticism, which is that a more "correct description" of the law would have led to a different outcome.[49]

Labatt Breweries v. *A.-G. Can.* (1979)[50] is another case in which the federal trade and commerce power was rejected as a support for federal legislation. In that case, the Court struck down compositional standards for beer enacted under the federal Food and Drugs Act. In the earlier chapter on Criminal Law, where the case is discussed at some length, I argued that the standards should have been upheld under the criminal law power.[51] But, with respect, the Court was right to reject the power to regulate interprovincial trade as a ground of validity. As Estey J. for the majority pointed out, the standards were imposed without regard for the product's movements across provincial boundaries.[52] He also reaffirmed the rule established in the insurance cases that the trade and commerce power will not authorize the regulation of a single trade or industry, even if the industry is dominated by a few large firms which advertise and market their products on a nation-wide basis.[53]

20.3 General trade and commerce

It will be recalled that in the leading case of *Citizens' Insurance Co.* v. *Parsons* the Privy Council had suggested two categories of trade and commerce. The first, namely, interprovincial or international trade and commerce, we have just considered. The second was "general regulation of trade affecting the whole dominion" — the so-called "general" category of trade and commerce.[54]

Until the decision of the Supreme Court of Canada in *General Motors* v. *City National Leasing* (1989), which is discussed later in this chapter,[55] the general category of trade and commerce had been rather consistently rejected as a support for federal policies of economic regulation. For example, it was rejected as a

48 [1980] 1 S.C.R. 844, 866.

49 In my view, the law could also have been upheld under the "general" category of trade and commerce: see the discussion in the next section of this chapter.

50 [1980] 1 S.C.R. 914.

51 See ch. 18, Criminal Law, under heading 18.3(a), "Food and drug standards", above.

52 *Id.*, 939, 943. The "general" category of trade and commerce was also rejected: see the discussion in the next section of this chapter.

53 *Id.*, 941. The brewing industry is in fact highly concentrated. The market is dominated by only three large firms. Estey J. pointed out, however (at p. 839), that the industry's production facilities tend to be local: Labatts had a brewery in every province except Quebec and Prince Edward Island. It is hard to see the relevance of this. Would the federal standards be valid in their application to an industry with centralized production facilities?

54 Note 8, above.

55 Note 81, below.

support for the regulation of the insurance industry in the *Insurance Reference*, the regulation of combines, prices and profits in the *Board of Commerce* case, the regulation of labour relations in *Toronto Electric Commissioners* v. *Snider*, the regulation of marketing in *The King* v. *Eastern Terminal Elevator Co.* and the *Natural Products Marketing Reference*, and the prohibition of margarine in the *Margarine Reference*.[56]

Until 1989, the only unequivocal example of a valid exercise of the general trade and commerce power[57] was the *Canada Standard Trade Mark* case (1937),[58] in which the Privy Council upheld a federal statute which established a national mark called ''Canada Standard''. The use of the mark was voluntary, but if the mark was used, federal standards as to the quality of the product so marked had to be complied with. The use of the mark was not confined to interprovincial and international trade. The case seemed to decide that the general trade and commerce power would authorize federal standards of production or manufacture for products traded locally, provided that the federal standards were tied to the voluntary use of a distinctive mark.[59]

A shadow was cast on the *Canada Standard* case by the decision of the Supreme Court of Canada in *Dominion Stores* v. *The Queen* (1979).[60] That case presented very similar facts. The Canada Agricultural Products Standards Act established a system of grades for agricultural products, and provided that, if the grades were voluntarily used for products traded locally, then the products had to comply with the associated federal standards. The four dissenting judges regarded the *Canada Standard* case as indistinguishable: the grade name ''Canada Extra

56 All of these cases are discussed in the previous section of this chapter, ''Interprovincial or international trade and commerce'', above.

57 In *John Deere Plow Co.* v. *Wharton* [1915] A.C. 330, 340, the Privy Council suggested that the federal Parliament's power over some aspects of the incorporation of companies was derived from the general trade and commerce power; this suggestion is replete with difficulties: see Smith, *The Commerce Power in Canada and the United States* (1963), 96-99; Ziegel in Ziegel (ed.), *Studies in Canadian Company Law* (1967), 159-160; and it is probably better to regard the whole topic of the incorporation of companies with other than provincial objects as derived from the ''peace, order, and good government'' power: see ch. 23, Companies, under heading 23.1, ''Incorporation of companies'', below. Another possible authority is *Re Alberta Statutes* [1938] S.C.R. 100, 116-121, where Duff C.J. and Davis J. gave as one of their reasons for striking down some of Alberta's social credit legislation that the creation of a new system of credit to be used as a means of exchange was a matter within the federal trade and commerce power; the other three opinions in the case did not rely on the trade and commerce power.

58 *A.-G. Ont.* v. *A.-G. Can.* (Canada Standard Trade Mark) [1937] A.C. 405.

59 The Privy Council stated, obiter (at p. 417), that the power to create and regulate trade marks was within the trade and commerce power. The existence of this power is assumed in *MacDonald* v. *Vapor Can.* [1977] 2 S.C.R. 134, and is upheld in *Asbjorn Horgard* v. *Gibbs/Nortac Industries* [1987] 3 F.C. 544 (C.A.). The Constitution Act, 1867, by s. 91(22) and (23), allocates patents and copyrights to federal legislative power, but is silent about trade marks. As to the extent of federal power over patents, see *Smith, Kline & French Laboratories* v. *A.G. Can.* [1986] 1 F.C. 274 (T.D.).

60 [1980] 1 S.C.R. 844; and see text accompanying note 46, above.

Fancy'' when used by Dominion Stores for apples should attract the associated federal regulation in the same way and for the same reasons as the use of the trade mark ''Canada Standard''. But Estey J. for the majority fastened on what seems to me to be a mere difference of machinery, namely, that in the *Canada Standard* case the mark was formally vested in the Crown, and on this ground he distinguished the *Canada Standard* case. This kind of distinction is close to confining a case to its own facts.[61]

In *Labatt Breweries* v. *A.-G. Can.* (1979),[62] the Supreme Court of Canada struck down compositional standards for light beer which had been enacted under the federal Food and Drugs Act. These standards became applicable only through the voluntary use of the description ''light beer''. Two of the dissenting judges (Pigeon J. with whom McIntyre J. agreed) would have upheld the legislation as on all fours with that upheld in the *Canada Standard* case. However, the third dissenting judge (Laskin C.J.) and the six majority judges did not regard the precedent as controlling. Estey J. for the majority referred to the ''arrogation'' by Parliament of ''common names'',[63] and it is certainly arguable that therein lies an essential difference between *Canada Standard* (and *Dominion Stores*) on the one hand and *Labatt Breweries* on the other. In *Canada Standard* (and *Dominion Stores*) the application of the federal standards depended upon the use of a distinctive description, namely, Canada Standard (or Canada Extra Fancy). In *Labatt Breweries* the application of the federal standard depended upon the use of a common description, namely, ''light beer''. As MacPherson has commented, the use of a distinctive description is genuinely voluntary, because it is easy for manufacturers who do not wish to comply with the federal standards to avoid the use of the distinctive description. But the use of a common description is virtually mandatory since it is often not practicable for a manufacturer to produce a marketable product without calling the product by its common name.[64] ''Light beer'' is perhaps not the clearest example, but there are compositional standards prescribed by regulations made under the Food and Drugs Act for ''beer'', ''whisky'', ''gin'', ''rum'', ''brandy'', ''coffee'', ''tea'', ''chocolate'', ''cocoa'', ''ice cream'', ''margarine'', and for dozens of other foods and drinks described by their ordinary names. Such a regulatory regime bears little resemblance to that in issue in the *Canada Standard* case.

The standards laid down under the federal Food and Drugs Act can be supported under the general trade and commerce power only if that power is held to extend to the mandatory prescription of nation-wide standards for the manu-

---

61 A second point of distinction, namely, that the use of the grade names was effectively mandatory by reason of matching provincial legislation seems wrong for the reasons given in note 47, above.

62 [1980] 1 S.C.R. 914; see also text accompanying note 50, above.

63 *Id.*, 926.

64 MacPherson, ''Economic Regulation and the British North America Act'' (1980) 5 Can. Bus. L.J. 172, 187. This article includes an extensive critique of the *Dominion Stores* and *Labatt Breweries* decisions.

facture of foods and drugs. In *Labatt Breweries*, Laskin C.J. in his separate dissent was prepared to go that far. He said that under the general branch of the trade and commerce power Parliament ''should be able to fix standards that are common to all manufacturers of foods, including beer, drugs, cosmetics and therapeutic devices, at least to equalize competitive advantages in the carrying on of businesses concerned with such products''.[65] No other judge agreed with Laskin C.J., although Estey J. did say that the general branch of the trade and commerce power would authorize legislation that ''affected industry and commerce at large or in a sweeping general sense''.[66] The force of this assertion was severely attenuated by Estey J.'s concurrent holding that the Food and Drugs Act is not sufficiently ''sweeping'' or ''general'' in its scope, apparently because the Regulations (not the Act, be it noted) were drafted on a commodity-by-commodity basis. Considering that the Act and Regulations covered most of the common foods and drugs which are consumed in Canada, it is not easy to imagine a more sweeping or general code of regulation.

In *MacDonald* v. *Vapor Canada* (1976),[67] the issue arose as to the validity of a federal law which prohibited, and provided a civil remedy for, any ''act'' or ''business practice'' which was ''contrary to honest industrial or commercial usage in Canada''. The Federal Court of Appeal had upheld the law on the basis that ''a law laying down a set of general rules as to the conduct of businessmen in their competitive activities in Canada'' was within the general category of trade and commerce.[68] The Supreme Court of Canada unanimously reversed this decision. Laskin C.J., who wrote the principal opinion,[69] pointed out that the creation or extension of civil causes of action of an essentially contractual or tortious character was a matter within property and civil rights in the province. While a new civil remedy could be upheld as an incident to an otherwise valid federal law, in this case the remedy stood alone.[70] The only federal aspect which could really be claimed for the law was the fact that it applied throughout Canada, but generality of application has never been sufficient of itself to shift a law dealing with property and civil rights in the province into a federal head of power.[71]

Although the general trade and commerce power proved unavailing once again in *Vapor*, Laskin C.J. did suggest some circumstances where it would be available. He implied several times that the result might well have been different if the law had been part of a ''regulatory scheme'' administered by a ''federally-

---

65 [1980] 1 S.C.R. 914, 921.

66 *Id.*, 943.

67 [1977] 2 S.C.R. 134; for more extended discussion, see Hogg, Comment (1976) 54 Can. Bar Rev. 361.

68 (1972) 33 D.L.R. (3d) 434, 449.

69 Laskin C.J.'s opinion was agreed to by Spence, Pigeon, Dickson and Beetz JJ.; a separate concurring opinion was written by de Grandpré J. and agreed to by Martland and Judson JJ.

70 This aspect of the *Vapor* case is discussed in ch. 18, Criminal Law, under heading 18.9, ''Criminal law and civil remedy'', above.

71 [1977] 2 S.C.R. 134, 156.

appointed agency''.[72] This law was not part of a ''regulatory scheme'' and its enforcement was ''left to the chance of private redress without public monitoring by the continued oversight of a regulatory agency''.[73] His lordship did not define a ''regulatory scheme''; nor did he explain why the existence of such a scheme, administered by a regulatory agency, would satisfy the general trade and commerce power. The suggestion finds no basis in the previous case law. On the contrary, many of the federal statutes which were held unconstitutional by the Privy Council established some form of regulatory scheme administered by a federally-appointed official or agency.[74]

In the *Anti-Inflation Reference* (1976),[75] the federal regime of wage and price control appeared to present the regulatory scheme and the administrative agency called for in Laskin C.J.'s *Vapor* dicta. However, counsel for the federal government chose not to argue that the Act could be upheld under the trade and commerce power, confining their argument to the peace, order, and good government power. The legislation was upheld under the emergency branch of the peace, order, and good government power.[76] In his opinion in the *Anti-Inflation Reference*, Laskin C.J. included one paragraph which indicated that he might have been favourably disposed to an argument that the general trade and commerce power could have sustained the Act.[77] The other opinions in the case made no reference to the trade and commerce power.[78] In the *Labatt Breweries* case, which has just been discussed, where the ''general'' trade and commerce power was relied upon in argument, Estey J.'s majority opinion and Pigeon J.'s dissenting opinion made only passing reference to the *Vapor* case, and the other opinions did not refer to it at all.[79]

Despite the absence of supporting authority, Laskin C.J.'s dicta in *Vapor* have proved to be very important, having become the basis for upholding the

---

72 *Id.*, 156, 158, 163, 165, 167.

73 *Id.*, 165.

74 E.g., *A.-G. Can.* v. *A.-G. Alta.* (Insurance) [1916] 1 A.C. 588; *Re Board of Commerce Act* [1922] 1 A.C. 191; *Toronto Electric Commrs.* v. *Snider* [1925] A.C. 396; *The King* v. *Eastern Terminal Elevator Co.* [1926] S.C.R. 434; *A.-G. Can.* v. *A.-G. Ont.* (Unemployment Insurance) [1937] A.C. 355; *A.-G. B.C.* v. *A.-G. Can.* (Natural Products Marketing) [1937] A.C. 377. Laskin C.J. in *MacDonald* v. *Vapor Can.* [1977] 2 S.C.R. 134, 163 appeared to place the marketing cases in a special category, asserting that in those cases ''regulation by a public authority'' would not alone be sufficient; the regulation must also apply ''to the flow of interprovincial or foreign trade''. Why these cases should be special is not explained, although, of course, marketing cases are numerous and the doctrine is therefore deeply entrenched.

75 *Re Anti-Inflation Act* [1976] 2 S.C.R. 373.

76 See ch. 17, Peace, Order, and Good Government, under heading 17.4(d), ''Inflation'', above.

77 [1976] S.C.R. 373, 426-427.

78 Laskin C.J.'s opinion was agreed with by Judson, Spence and Dickson JJ.; Ritchie J.'s separate concurring opinion was agreed with by Martland and Pigeon JJ.; Beetz J.'s dissenting opinion was agreed with by de Grandpré J.

79 Finkelstein, Comment (1989) 68 Can. Bar Rev. 802 argues that both the *Anti-Inflation Reference* and *Labatt Breweries* should be reconsidered in the light of the *City National Leasing* case, note 81, below.

federal Competition Act. As noted in the earlier chapter on Criminal Law,[80] Canada's competition law had been upheld as a ''criminal'' law, but this characterization had become impossible to sustain after amendments in 1975 and 1986, which had the effect of de-criminalizing much of the law. The constitutionality of the new legislation had to be resolved in *General Motors* v. *City National Leasing* (1989),[81] which was a challenge to the validity of the civil remedy that had been introduced into the legislation in 1975. The Supreme Court of Canada, in a unanimous judgment written by Dickson C.J., held that the Combines Investigation Act (now the Competition Act) was a valid exercise of the ''general'' trade and commerce power.

Dickson C.J. applied the *Vapor* test, which consisted of three elements: (1) the presence of a ''general regulatory scheme'', (2) the ''oversight of a regulatory agency'', and (3) a concern ''with trade as a whole rather than with a particular industry''.[82] To these three elements, Dickson C.J. added a fourth and fifth: (4) ''the legislation should be of a nature that the provinces jointly or severally would be constitutionally incapable of enacting'', and (5) ''the failure to include one or more provinces or localities in a legislative scheme would jeopardize the successful operation of the scheme in other parts of the country''.[83] In the case of the Competition Act, all five elements were present: (1) There was a regulatory scheme. (2) It operated under the oversight of a regulatory agency. (3) It was concerned with trade in general, not with a particular place or a particular industry. Moreover ((4) and (5)), only national regulation of competition could possibly be effective, because of the ability of factors of production to move freely from one province to another.[84]

It is important to notice that the general branch of the trade and commerce power authorizes the regulation of *intraprovincial* trade. Indeed, there would be no need for a general branch of trade and commerce if it did not extend beyond interprovincial and international trade. In *City National Leasing*, the allegations that gave rise to the litigation concerned price discrimination in the financing of the purchase of vehicles by companies that lease fleets of automobiles and trucks. These purchases, and the associated financing arrangements, were transactions that, individually, took place within a single province. Those facts gave rise to an argument that the federal legislation should be read down to exclude such intraprovincial activity, which could be left to provincial law. Dickson C.J.'s answer

---

80 Chapter 18, Criminal Law, under heading 18.6, ''Competition law'', above.

81 [1989] 1 S.C.R. 641.

82 *Id.*, 661.

83 *Id.*, 662. The additional elements, and indeed the general line of reasoning, had been put forward by Dickson J. in *A.G. Can.* v. *CN Transportation* [1983] 2 S.C.R. 206, in which he decided that the federal competition law could be upheld under the general branch of trade and commerce. In that case, however, only two other judges agreed with him. The four-judge majority did not need to, and did not, decide the appropriate constitutional characterization of the legislation.

84 [1989] 1 S.C.R. 641, 679.

to this argument was a reference back to the provincial inability test, captured in elements (4) and (5) of his definition of general trade and commerce: "Competition cannot be successfully regulated by federal legislation which is restricted to interprovincial trade."[85] The conclusion was that Parliament (as well as the provinces) has the constitutional power to regulate intraprovincial aspects of competition.[86]

20.4 Specific topics

This chapter has discussed the federal trade and commerce power in relatively general terms. When attention is directed to more specific topics, for example, the regulation of businesses, the regulation of professions and trades, labour relations, marketing and securities regulation, it is found that trade and commerce is not the dominant source of power: legislative power is for the most part provincial, under property and civil rights in the province. Accordingly, these and other topics are examined in the next chapter, entitled Property and Civil Rights. However, despite its title, the next chapter is not just an examination of provincial power. Under each specific topic, the elements of federal power are examined as well. The peace, order, and good government power, the criminal law power, and, especially, the trade and commerce power, are therefore important subsidiary themes of the next chapter.

---

85 *Id.*, 681.

86 *Id.*, 682, asserting that "competition is not a single matter, any more than inflation or pollution", and the provinces also had the power "to deal with competition in the exercise of their legislative powers in such fields as consumer protection, labour relations, marketing and the like".

21

Property and Civil Rights

21.1 Importance

Section 92(13) of the Constitution Act, 1867 confers upon the provincial Legislatures the power to make laws in relation to "property and civil rights in the province''.[1] This is by far the most important of the provincial heads of power. Indeed, the previous chapters on the three major federal heads of power, namely, peace, order, and good government, trade and commerce and criminal law, have been as much concerned with property and civil rights in the province as they have been with their ostensible topics. Most of the major constitutional cases have turned on the competition between one or more of the federal heads of power, on the one hand, and property and civil rights, on the other.

21.2 History

In chapter 2, Reception, we noticed that the phrase ''property and civil rights'' has a history in British North America which starts before confederation.[2] It will be recalled that the phrase appeared in s. 8 of the Quebec Act, 1774, which restored the French civil law as the private law of the conquered colony of Quebec. In s. 8, the phrase meant the whole body of law governing relationships between individuals — the body of law that did not need to be supplanted by the conquest of a foreign power. It will also be recalled that the phrase occurred again in the first Act of the Legislature of the province of Upper Canada, which in 1792 adopted English law as the private law of the colony. In this context, the phrase plainly had the same meaning as in the Quebec Act, 1774.

The phrase ''property and civil rights in the province'', as a head of provincial power in s. 91(13) of the Constitution Act, 1867, did not have precisely the same meaning as in the pre-confederation instruments, because the phrase now appeared in the context of a federal system in which extensive powers had been accorded to a new central Parliament.[3] But, subject to the qualifications required by the new federal scheme, it is clear that the framers of the Constitution Act understood the familiar phrase in the same sense it obtained in 1792 and 1774, that is to say, as a compendious description of the entire body of private law which governs the relationships between subject and subject, as opposed to the

1 Tremblay, *Les compétences législatives au Canada et les pouvoirs provinciaux en matière de propriété et de droits civils* (1967) is a study of s. 92(13). This important book has no counterpart in the English-language literature, which has tended to concentrate on the federal powers. See also Beaudoin, *La Constitution du Canada* (1990), ch. 9. Section 92(13) has no counterpart in the Constitutions of the United States or Australia because they enumerate only the federal powers. However, Americans often speak of the ''police power'' of the states, meaning the power to promote the health, safety, morals and general welfare of the people: Tribe, *American Constitutional Law* (2nd ed., 1988), 405-406.

2 See ch. 2, Reception, under heading 2.3(b), ''Ontario and Quebec'', above. See also Tremblay, note 1, above, 19-45; *O'Connor Report* (Senate of Canada 1939), Annex I, 109-145; Stanley, *A Short History of the Canadian Constitution* (1969), chs. 2 and 3.

3 In addition, the words ''in the province'' had been added to the phrase: see ch. 13, Extraterritorial Competence, above.

law which governs the relationships between the subject and the institutions of government.[4]

The Constitution Act, 1867 did make some changes in the historical definition of property and civil rights. If it had not done so, it would have left very little for the new central Parliament to do. The enumerated list of federal heads of legislative power in s. 91 included a number of matters which would otherwise have come within property and civil rights in the province, for example, trade and commerce (s. 91(2)), banking (s. 91(15)), bills of exchange and promissory notes (s. 91(18)), interest (s. 91(19)), bankruptcy and insolvency (s. 91(21)), patents of invention and discovery (s. 91(22)), copyrights (s. 91(23)), and marriage and divorce (s. 91(28)). These federal classes of subjects were withdrawn from property and civil rights by their exclusive vesting in the federal Parliament. In addition, the peace, order, and good government phrase in the opening language of s. 91 presumably contemplated that certain matters which would otherwise have come within property and civil rights could attain such a national dimension as to come within federal competence. The zoning of the national capital region has since been held to be an example of this kind of federal subject matter.[5]

It remains true, however, that even after proper accommodation has been made for the catalogue of exclusive federal powers, property and civil rights in the province still covers most of the legal relationships between persons in Canada. The law relating to property, succession, the family, contracts and torts is mainly within provincial jurisdiction under s. 92(13). Moreover, the original distinction between private and public law has tended to break down for constitutional purposes, as governments have increasingly intervened to regulate the economic life of the nation. Labour relations, once a private matter between employer and employee, is now so extensively regulated that it may be thought of as a branch of public law. Much business activity is no longer governed simply by contract, but by statutory rules and the decisions of government officials. These governmental interventions in the marketplace, if they could not be fitted rather clearly into a particular head of legislative power, have for the most part been allocated by the courts to property and civil rights in the province. In other words, the evolution of our laws has now swept much public law into the rubric which was originally designed to exclude public law. This will be described in later sections of this chapter.

21.3 Civil liberties

It will be clear from the history of the phrase "property and civil rights" that the term "civil rights" in this context does not bear the meaning which it has

---

4 *Citizens Insurance Co.* v. *Parsons* (1881) 7 App. Cas. 96, 110-111; Tremblay, note 1, above, passim; *O'Connor Report,* note 2, above, Annex I, 135; Lederman, "Unity and Diversity in Canadian Federalism" (1975) 53 Can. Bar Rev. 597, 601.

5 *Munro* v. *National Capital Comm.* [1966] S.C.R. 663, and see generally ch. 17, Peace, Order and Good Government, above.

acquired in the United States, that is, as meaning the civil liberties which in that country are guaranteed by the Bill of Rights. Civil rights in the sense required by the Constitution Act, 1867 are juristically distinct from civil liberties. The civil rights referred to in the Constitution Act, 1867 comprise primarily proprietary, contractual or tortious rights; these rights exist when a legal rule stipulates that in certain circumstances one person is entitled to something from another. But civil liberties exist when there is an absence of legal rules: whatever is not forbidden is a civil liberty. While it is common to use the term ''right'' in reference to a freedom or liberty, it is important not to overlook the analytical distinction. To say that one has a ''right'' to criticize the government (for example) implies only that no law prohibits criticism of the government.[6] This is quite different from the right to have a loan repaid (for example), because the law of contract creates this right by stipulating that certain kinds of promises must be performed and by imposing sanctions for non-performance.[7]

The term ''civil rights'' in s. 92(13) is used in the older, stricter sense. It does not include the fundamental civil liberties of belief and expression. Of course, many provincial laws impinge on those civil liberties, but a law whose pith and substance is the restraint of belief or expression does not come within property and civil rights in the province.[8]

21.4 Local or private matters

The provincial ''residuary power''[9] in s. 92(16) over ''all matters of a merely local or private nature in the province'' has turned out to be relatively unimportant, because the wide scope of ''property and civil rights in the province'' has left little in the way of a residue of local or private matters.

Section 92(16) has not been completely ignored, but often it is suggested as a possible alternative to s. 92(13), rather than as an independent source of power.

---

6 Under a bill of rights, such as Canada's Charter of Rights, it may carry the further implication that no law could prohibit criticism of the government, that is, any such law would be unconstitutional.

7 The distinction between rights and liberties, which is of course commonplace in legal writing, has been emphasized by Rand J. in *Saumur* v. *Que.* [1953] 2 S.C.R. 299, 329 and *Switzman* v. *Elbling* [1957] S.C.R. 285, 305. Even civil liberties which are guaranteed by an effective bill of rights are juristically distinct from civil rights arising from the law of property, contract or torts. A bill of rights is addressed to legislative bodies, not individuals, and it will prevent the making of, or render invalid, any law which purports to deny the guaranteed civil liberty. The bill of rights will not necessarily give any redress to an individual whose civil liberties are wrongly violated, although s. 24 of the Charter of Rights may well permit the granting of such redress. Section 24 of the Charter is discussed in ch. 37, ''Enforcement of Rights'', below.

8 See ch. 31, Expression, under heading 31.1, ''Distribution of powers'', below. See also ch. 28, Civil Liberties, under heading 28.4(b), ''Distribution of powers'', below, and ch. 35, Equality, under heading 35.1, ''Distribution of powers'', below.

9 The double-residue theory is explained in ch. 17, Peace, Order, and Good Government, under heading 17.1, ''Residuary nature of power'', above.

Jurisdiction over highway traffic, for example, is undoubtedly provincial, but the Supreme Court of Canada has not committed itself to a specific head of power: s. 92(16) has been suggested, along with s. 92(13).[10] A municipal by-law temporarily banning assemblies in the streets and parks of Montreal has been upheld primarily under s. 92(16), with s. 92(13) also relied upon.[11] Jurisdiction over local trade is also undoubtedly provincial, and the power has usually been attributed to s. 92(13), but it has been suggested that s. 92(16) is the more appropriate attribution.[12] Provincial film censorship has been upheld (before the adoption of the Charter of Rights), with s. 92(13) and s. 92(16) offered as alternative sources of power.[13] Section 92(16) has been held to be the sole source of power to sustain the Heroin Treatment Act, a public health measure enacted by British Columbia.[14]

21.5 Insurance

(a) Reasons for regulation

The insurance industry became the arena in which the two levels of government contended for the power to regulate business, or at least that part of business activity over which legislative power was not specifically allocated by the Constitution Act, 1867. Unlike banking (s. 91(15)), insurance is not specifically mentioned in the Constitution Act, 1867; but, like banking, insurance was one of the first industries to attract fundamental regulation.

Because the terms and conditions of insurance policies are in practice stipulated by the insurer, and are not well understood by the insured, governments sought to protect the insured by requiring the inclusion of certain conditions in every policy. Because the financial strength, probity and permanence of an insurer cannot in practice be judged by the insured, and are essential to the fulfilment of the policy, governments sought to control entry to, and supervise the performance of, the industry by licensing insurers, by requiring a security deposit, by limiting the insurers' powers of investment, and by official inspection of their books. Similar considerations apply to banks and loan and trust companies.

---

10 *Provincial Secretary P.E.I.* v. *Egan* [1941] S.C.R. 396 is the leading case, but the opinions of Duff C.J., Hudson and Taschereau JJ. do not refer to any particular head of s. 92, while Rinfret J. refers inconclusively (at p. 413) to three heads, namely, s. 92(9), (13) and (16).

11 *A.-G. Can. and Dupond* v. *Montreal* [1978] 2 S.C.R. 770, 792 (s. 92(8), (14) and (15) are also invoked).

12 See ch. 20, Trade and Commerce, under heading 20.1, "Relationship to property and civil rights", above. Cf. *Rio Hotel* v. *N.B.* [1987] 2 S.C.R. 59, 63, 67 (provincial authority to regulate the sale and consumption of alcohol comes from 92(16) and/or 92(13)).

13 *N.S. Bd. of Censors* v. *McNeil* [1978] 2 S.C.R. 662, 699.

14 *Schneider* v. *The Queen* [1982] 2 S.C.R. 112. This was the view of all judges except Estey J., who in a separate concurrence suggested (at p. 141) s. 92(7) and (13), as well as (16).

(b) Provincial power

In the latter part of the nineteenth century, both levels of government began to regulate the insurance industry. A provincial statute was the first to come before the courts. In the leading case of *Citizens' Insurance Co.* v. *Parsons* (1881),[15] the Privy Council upheld an Ontario statute which required that certain conditions be included in every policy of fire insurance entered into in Ontario. Their lordships held that regulation of the terms of contracts came within property and civil rights in the province (s. 92(13)), and did not come within trade and commerce (s. 91(2)).

The next statute to come before the courts was a federal one, the Insurance Act, 1910, which prohibited any company from carrying on the business of insurance unless it had a licence issued by the federal Minister of Finance; there was also a requirement of a security deposit and provision for official inspection and report upon solvency. Provincially-incorporated companies carrying on business wholly within the province of incorporation were exempt from the Act. The Privy Council in the *Insurance Reference* (1916)[16] held the statute to be unconstitutional. Rejecting the argument based on trade and commerce,[17] their lordships held that the regulation of a particular industry came within property and civil rights in the province, even when the industry and particular firms extended beyond the boundaries of any one province.[18]

The *Insurance Reference* was followed by a series of cases in which the courts had to pass on a variety of federal attempts to regain the jurisdiction which had been denied to the Dominion. The federal government's persistence in this enterprise, the ingenuity of the expedients employed, and the intransigence of provincial opposition, apparently stemmed from rivalries between permanent officials in Ottawa and Toronto.[19] The first response to the Privy Council's decision was an attempt by the federal Parliament to compel the licensing of insurance companies by a provision in the Criminal Code making it an offence to carry on the business of insurance without a licence from the federal Minister of Finance.

---

15 (1881) 7 App. Cas. 96.

16 *A.-G. Can.* v. *A.-G. Alta.* (Insurance) [1916] 1 A.C. 588.

17 In the United States, after an initial ruling that insurance was not "commerce" (*Paul* v. *Virginia* (1868) 75 U.S. 168), the Supreme Court changed its mind and decided that regulation of the insurance industry was competent to the federal Congress under the commerce clause: *U.S.* v. *South-Eastern Underwriters Assn.* (1944) 322 U.S. 533. The Congress in fact delegated the power back to the states: Smith, *The Commerce Power in Canada and the United States* (1963), 266-273; Benson, *The Supreme Court and the Commerce Clause, 1937-1970* (1970), 147-169.

18 In *Can. Indemnity Co.* v. *A.-G. B.C.* [1977] 2 S.C.R. 504, the insurance industry emphasized the interprovincial and international character of its operations in an attempt to defeat a provincial law establishing a provincial monopoly of automobile insurance; the Supreme Court of Canada upheld the law notwithstanding its incidental impact on interprovincial trade and commerce.

19 The fascinating tale is told in Armstrong, "Federalism and Government Regulation: the Canadian Insurance Industry" (1976) 19 Can. Pub. Admin. 88.

This device was condemned by the Privy Council as a colourable attempt to use the cloak of the criminal law "to interfere with the exercise of civil rights in the Provinces".[20] Then the Privy Council struck down provisions which required non-resident British subjects and aliens to obtain a licence to carry on the business of insurance, and which imposed a special tax on persons taking out insurance with unlicensed British and foreign insurers. Here was a reliance on the powers over immigration (non-residents), aliens and taxation; but the Privy Council held that all three powers were being employed colourably "to intermeddle with the conduct of insurance business".[21] The final case in the series concerned another federal statute directed only at British and foreign insurers and coupled with a special tax on the customers of unregistered insurers. The Supreme Court of Canada adopted the reasoning of the Privy Council's last insurance decision to hold this statute also invalid.[22]

In the middle of this series of decisions the Privy Council also struck down the scheme of unemployment insurance which was part of the Canadian "new deal". The brief reasons delivered in the *Unemployment Insurance Reference* (1937)[23] do not make the ground of decision crystal clear, but it seems to have been decided partly on the basis that the scheme related to employment, and partly on the basis that the scheme related to insurance. Both these matters came within property and civil rights in the province. This decision was overcome by an amendment to the Constitution in 1940.[24]

(c) Federal power

Despite all these setbacks in the courts, the federal government continues to regulate a substantial part of the insurance industry[25] under statutes covering British and foreign companies, federally-incorporated companies and, on a voluntary basis,[26] provincially-incorporated companies.[27] Presumably, the provinces

---

20 *A.-G. Ont.* v. *Reciprocal Insurers* [1924] A.C. 328, 336.

21 *Re Insurance Act of Can.* [1932] A.C. 41, 51.

22 *Re s.16 of Special War Revenue Act* [1942] S.C.R. 429; leave to appeal to the P.C. refused [1943] 4 D.L.R. 657. The issue reappeared when British Columbia took over the automobile insurance industry in the province. Once again provincial authority was reaffirmed, this time to uphold the challenged law: note 18, above.

23 *A.-G. Can.* v. *A.-G. Ont.* (Unemployment Insurance) [1937] A.C. 355.

24 Constitution Act, 1940, adding "unemployment insurance" as head 2A of s. 91. On the meaning of this head of power, see *R.* v. *Scheer* [1974] S.C.R. 1046; *Martin Service Station* v. *M.N.R.* [1977] 2 S.C.R. 996.

25 Marine insurance is a special case; it is within federal jurisdiction under s. 91(10) (navigation and shipping): *Triglav* v. *Terrasses Jewellers* [1983] 1 S.C.R. 283.

26 In *Can. Pioneer Management* v. *Labour Relations Bd. Sask.* [1980] 1 S.C.R. 433, it was held that a provinciallyincorporated life insurance company, which was voluntarily registered under the Canadian and British Insurance Companies Act, was still subject to provincial labour relations law.

27 Canadian and British Insurance Companies Act, R.S.C. 1985, c. I-12; Foreign Insurance Companies Act, R.S.C. 1985, c. I-13; Department of Insurance Act, R.S.C. 1985, c. I-14; Pedoe (1950) 15 Law and Contemp. Probs. 5575.

and the industry are now content with, or at least reconciled to, the continued federal presence, because there has been no constitutional attack on it since 1942. The current federal statutes include preambles which indicate that the powers over trade and commerce, aliens and insolvency are relied upon as supporting their constitutionality. The first two of these heads have, of course, been relied upon in the past. But in all the litigation between 1916 and 1942 the federal power over ''insolvency'' (s. 91(21)) was never considered as a possible basis of federal jurisdiction.

In the *Wentworth Insurance* case (1969),[28] a federal law applicable to insolvent insurance companies was upheld. The federal Winding-Up Act provided a certain order of priority for the distribution by the liquidator to creditors of securities which insurance companies are required by provincial law to keep on deposit. The Ontario Insurance Act provided a different administration and a different order of priority for the distribution of the same fund. On the winding-up of the Wentworth Insurance Company, the question arose whether the company's deposit should be administered in accordance with the federal or the provincial law. The Supreme Court of Canada divided sharply on the question, but decided by a majority of five to four to adopt the reasoning of Laskin J.A. in the Ontario Court of Appeal to the effect that the federal law was a valid law in relation to insolvency, and that the federal law was the applicable provision. Hall J. for the minority said that the federal law was ''a foray into the field of insurance, an area forbidden to Parliament'', and that it was ''colourable legislation and, because of this, ultra vires''.[29] Certainly the majority's decision was a startling departure from the course of decision between 1916 and 1942 when so many and various federal attempts to enter the field of insurance were rebuffed. Now entry had been gained through the ''insolvency'' door. Whether the same point of entry would lead to the regulation of solvent companies, for the purpose of preventing insolvency, is of course much more doubtful.

21.6 Business in general

The insurance cases discussed in the previous section of this chapter established the proposition that the regulation of business was ordinarily a matter within property and civil rights in the province. To this proposition there are a number of exceptions. Some industries fall within federal jurisdiction because they are enumerated in s. 91, such as navigation and shipping(s. 91(10)) and banking (s. 91(15)), or because they are excepted from s. 92(10), namely, interprovincial or international transportation and communications undertakings (s. 92(10)(a) and (b)) and works declared to be for the general advantage of Canada (s. 92(10)(c)). Some industries have been held to fall within federal jurisdiction

28 *A.-G. Ont.* v. *Policy-holders of Wentworth Insurance Co.* [1969] S.C.R. 779.
29 *Id.*, 806.

under the peace, order, and good government power, namely, aeronautics and the production of atomic energy. Other federal powers confer a limited power to regulate business, for example, trade and commerce (s. 91(2)), taxation (s. 91(3)), interest (s. 91(19)), the criminal law (s. 91(27)) and peace, order, and good government (s. 91 opening words).

But the gaps in federal power are very important and extensive. The trade and commerce power will authorize a federal prohibition of the importation of margarine, but not a prohibition of its manufacture or sale.[30] The trade and commerce power will also authorize the regulation of interprovincial marketing, but not local marketing.[31] The trade and commerce power will also authorize the regulation of competition, but not the regulation of wages and prices, product standards or particular industries such as insurance.[32] The taxation power may be used to provide various kinds of incentives or disincentives with a view to the control of business activity,[33] but may not be used as a device to assume regulatory control over the insurance industry.[34] The interest power may be used to control interest rates, but not to control other terms of loans.[35] The criminal law power may be used to prohibit undesirable commercial practices, but if the law departs from the conventional criminal format the criminal law power will not sustain it.[36] The criminal law power may also be used to enforce closing hours on businesses for religious reasons, but not for secular reasons.[37] The peace, order, and good government power will authorize the control of rents, prices and profits in times of emergency, but not in normal times.[38]

The previous paragraph is not intended to be an exhaustive list of the gaps in the federal power to regulate business. It is simply a recitation of the better-known arenas of controversy. The gaps in federal power are covered by the provincial power over property and civil rights. The double-aspect doctrine also ensures substantial areas of concurrency even when federal power exists. The point is that the regulation of an industry, or the more general regulation of prices or profits or combinations, has traditionally been regarded by the courts, not in terms of its ultimate, often nation-wide objectives, but in terms of its immediate impact upon freedom of contract and property rights.[39] In these terms, of course,

---

30 *Can. Federation of Agriculture* v. *A.-G. Que.* (Margarine) [1951] 1 A.C. 179.

31 See sec. 21.9, ''Marketing'', below.

32 See ch. 20, Trade and Commerce, under heading 20.3, ''General trade and commerce'', above.

33 *Reader's Digest Assn.* v. *A.-G. Can.* (1965) 59 D.L.R. (2d) 54 (Que. C.A.).

34 *Re Insurance Act of Can.* [1932] A.C. 41.

35 *A.-G. Ont.* v. *Barfried Enterprises* [1963] S.C.R. 570.

36 See ch. 18, Criminal Law, under heading 18.2, ''Definition of criminal law'', above.

37 See ch. 18, Criminal Law, under heading 18.7, ''Sunday observance law'', above.

38 See ch. 17, Peace, Order and Good Government, under heading 17.4, ''The emergency branch'', above. For provincial power to control prices, see *Home Oil Distributors* v. *A.-G. B.C.* [1940] S.C.R. 444; *Carnation Co.* v. *Que. Agricultural Marketing Bd.* [1968] S.C.R. 238.

39 The same approach has been taken in the labour relations cases: see sec. 21.8, ''Labour relations'', below.

restraints on business fall into the category of property and civil rights in the province.[40]

21.7 Professions and trades

Regulation of professions and trades typically takes the form of restrictions on entry, coupled with rules of conduct, which often include fee-setting, and administration by a governing body. Such regulation is no different for constitutional purposes than that of other industries, and comes within property and civil rights in the province.[41]

21.8 Labour relations

(a) Provincial power

The regulation of labour relations[42] over most of the economy is within provincial competence under property and civil rights in the province. The leading case is *Toronto Electric Commissioners* v. *Snider* (1925),[43] which concerned the validity of a federal attempt to regulate labour relations — the Industrial Disputes Investigation Act of 1907. This Act afforded compulsory conciliation procedures for the settlement of industrial disputes in mining, transportation, communication and public service utilities, and optional procedures for the settlement of disputes not compulsorily covered. The Privy Council held that the Act was unconstitutional. We have noticed in earlier chapters that their lordships rejected arguments that the Act could be sustained under the peace, order, and good government power, or the trade and commerce power, or the criminal law power, and held instead that the Act came within property and civil rights in the province.

The decision of the Privy Council in *Snider* seems to have been both unexpected and unwelcome in Canada at the time. The federal Act had been upheld in the Ontario courts, and in previous litigation in the Quebec courts. Immediately after the decision, the federal Act was amended to confine its operation to industries which were otherwise within federal legislative authority, and in this more

40 *N.S. Bd. of Censors* v. *McNeil* [1978] 2 S.C.R. 662 (film censorship characterized as regulation of film business and upheld under s. 92(13)).

41 *Beaule* v. *Corp. of Master Electricians* (1969) 10 D.L.R. (3d) 93 (Que. C.A.) (electricians); *Re Imrie* [1972] 3 O.R. 275 (H.C.) (realtors); *R.* v. *Buzunis* (1972) 26 D.L.R. (3d) 502 (Man. C.A.) (accountants); *Re Levkoe* (1977) 18 O.R. (2d) 265 (Div. Ct.) (pharmacists); *Re Underwood McLellan* (1979) 103 D.L.R. (3d) 268 (Sask. C.A.) (engineers); *A.-G. Can.* v. *Law Society of B.C.* [1982] 2 S.C.R. 307 (lawyers).

42 For discussion, see Tremblay, note 1, above, 227-253; Laskin, *Canadian Constitutional Law* (5th ed., 1986 by Finkelstein), 523-548; Tremblay, *Droit Constitutionnel-Principles* (1993), Part II, ch. 3.

43 [1925] A.C. 396.

limited form the Act was upheld.[44] The amendment also made the Act applicable to any dispute within provincial jurisdiction "which by the legislation of the province is made subject to the provisions of this Act". This invitation to cooperate was accepted by all provinces except Prince Edward Island, each province enacting legislation adopting the federal law and thereby restoring the fact of uniform federal labour law. However, after the Wagner Act of 1935[45] in the United States had introduced the modern model of North American labour law with its concepts of certification, compulsory collective bargaining and unfair labour practices, new legislation came to be enacted in Canada by the provinces. Apart from the second world war, when a uniform federal law on the Wagner model was proclaimed under the War Measures Act,[46] labour law became provincial again. This is the present situation and it shows no sign of changing.[47]

The legislation in *Snider* was concerned with industrial peace — the prevention of strikes and lockouts through compulsory conciliation. In the *Labour Conventions* case (1937),[48] the decision was extended to labour standards legislation. Federal statutes providing for a weekly rest in employment, limitations on working hours and minimum wages were all held to be unconstitutional. Their lordships rejected arguments based on the peace, order, and good government power and the treaty power, and held that laws imposing labour standards came within property and civil rights in the province. A similar decision was rendered in the *Empress Hotel* case (1950),[49] where the Privy Council held that minimum hours of work in a hotel could only be stipulated by the province.[50]

Even a scheme of unemployment insurance, involving as it did compulsory contributions by employers and employees, was held to be incompetent to the federal Parliament in the *Unemployment Insurance Reference* (1937).[51] This decision was overcome by an amendment to the Constitution adding "unemploy-

---

44 *Stevedores Reference*, note 59, below.

45 The Wagner Act (National Labour Relations Act, 1935), a federal statute, was upheld in *Nat. Labour Relations Bd. v. Jones & Laughlin Steel Corp.* (1937) 301 U.S. 1. The federal Fair Labour Standards Act, 1938 was upheld in *U.S. v. Darby* (1941) 312 U.S. 100. Both decisions were based on the commerce clause. In Australia, the Constitution, by s. 51(35), expressly empowers the federal Parliament to make laws with respect to "conciliation and arbitration for the prevention and settlement of industrial disputes extending beyond the limits of any one state".

46 Order-in-Council P.C. 1003, sometimes called the "Canadian Wagner Act", was replaced after the war with the Industrial Relations and Disputes Investigation Act, S.C. 1948, c. 54, which was confined to "federal" industries.

47 The history is related in Scott, "Federal Jurisdiction over Labour Relations" (1960) 6 McGill L.J. 153.

48 *A.-G. Can.* v. *A.-G. Ont.* (Labour Conventions) [1937] A.C. 326.

49 *CPR* v. *A.-G. B.C.* (Empress Hotel) [1950] A.C. 122. Accord, *Re Hours of Labour* [1925] S.C.R. 505.

50 Cf. *OPSEU* v. *Ont.* [1987] 2 S.C.R. 2 (province may legislate conditions of employment in provincial public sector, including restrictions on political activities).

51 *A.-G. Can.* v. *A.-G. Ont.* (Unemployment Insurance) [1937] A.C. 355.

ment insurance'' as a new head of federal power (s. 91(2A)).[52] However, health care plans that call for compulsory contributions by employers or employees have had to be established by provincial legislation, even though they have been initiated, designed and half-funded by the federal government.[53] In the *Oil, Chemical Workers* case (1963),[54] the Supreme Court of Canada held that a province could validly prohibit the use for political contributions of trade union funds obtained by compulsory deduction from wages. This decision and the *Unemployment Insurance Reference* are companions in their insistence that the modification of the employment relationship is exclusively within property and civil rights, notwithstanding the important federal aspects presented by the relief of nationwide unemployment and by the funding of federal election campaigns.

(b) Federal power

Despite the consistent affirmations of provincial power over labour relations, there is still a substantial federal presence in the field. In 1925, immediately after the decision in *Toronto Electric Commissioners* v. *Snider*,[55] the federal Parliament amended its labour legislation to apply only to ''employment upon or in connection with any work, undertaking or business that is within the legislative authority of the Parliament of Canada''.[56] The Act went on to list a number of industries which were within federal authority, such as navigation and shipping and interprovincial transportation and communication, ''but not so as to restrict the generality of the foregoing''. Aside from the period of the second world war,[57] this has been the pattern of coverage for federal labour law ever since, although the drafting has been slightly changed and the list of federal industries expanded.[58]

The theory that the federal Parliament could regulate labour relations in those industries which were otherwise within federal legislative competence seemed plausible and was not directly challenged until the *Stevedores Reference* (1955).[59] In that case, two unions were claiming to represent a group of stevedores in the port of Toronto; one union was certified under provincial law, the other was certified under federal law. The federal law specifically applied to ''businesses carried on for or in connection with navigation or shipping''. The subject of ''navigation and shipping'' is, of course, a federal head of power under s. 91(10) of the Constitution Act, 1867. The Supreme Court of Canada held that the federal law was valid, and that it was applicable to the stevedores because their work of loading and unloading ships was an essential part of navigation and shipping.

52 Constitution Act, 1940.

53 See ch. 6, Financial Arrangements, under heading 6.8, ''Spending power'', above.

54 *Oil, Chemical and Atomic Wkrs.* v. *Imperial Oil* [1963] S.C.R. 584.

55 Note 43, above.

56 Industrial Disputes Investigation Amendment Act, S.C. 1925, c. 14.

57 Note 46, above.

58 See now Canada Labour Code, R.S.C. 1985, c. L-2.

59 *Re Industrial Relations and Disputes Investigation Act (Can.)* [1955] S.C.R. 529.

Since this decision, it has been clear that the federal Parliament has the power to regulate employment in works, undertakings or businesses within the legislative authority of the federal Parliament.[60]

The legislation upheld in the *Stevedores Reference* covered only what may be termed the federal private sector. Needless to say, there is no doubt that the federal Parliament also has jurisdiction to regulate labour relations in the federal public sector, that is to say, employment in the departments and agencies of the federal government.[61]

The *Stevedores Reference* has been followed in many subsequent cases, litigation being caused by doubt as to whether or not a particular bargaining unit of employees is an integral part of an undertaking that is within federal jurisdiction. The required connection with the federal undertaking is a functional or operational one.[62] The fact that the employer is an interprovincial railway will not sweep a group of employees into federal jurisdiction, if they operate a hotel which is functionally separate from the railway.[63] The fact that employees are engaged in constructing a runway at an airport will not sweep them into federal jurisdiction, if their work is simply construction, unrelated to the tasks of design or operation that would be an integral part of aeronautics.[64] The fact that the employer is a company operated by Indians, and the business is on an Indian reserve, will not sweep employees into federal jurisdiction, if their work is simply the manufacturing of shoes.[65] The fact that employees' wages are subsidized by the federal government, as part of a federal job creation programme, will not sweep construction workers into federal jurisdiction.[66] The Court has approached these cases on the basis that provincial competence over labour relations is the rule, and federal competence is the exception.[67] Federal competence exists only where it is found that the work performed by the employees is an integral part of an undertaking within federal jurisdiction, and that finding depends upon ''legislative authority over the operation, not over the person of the employer''.[68]

Issues of constitutional jurisdiction over labour relations usually arise initially before a labour board, which is asked to certify a union as the bargaining agent of a group of employees. If certification is opposed on constitutional

---

60 E.g., *Ont. Hydro* v. *Ont.* [1993] 3 S.C.R. 327 (employees on works, declared under s. 92(10)(c) to be for the general advantage of Canada, are within federal jurisdiction).

61 *Re Hours of Labour* [1925] S.C.R. 505, 510; *Re Minimum Wage Act (Sask.)* [1948] S.C.R. 248; *Letter Carriers' Union* v. *Can. Union of Postal Wkrs.* [1975] 1 S.C.R. 178; *Can. Labour Relations Bd.* v. *Yellowknife* [1977] 2 S.C.R. 729; *A.-G. Can.* v. *St. Hubert Base Teachers' Assn.* [1983] 1 S.C.R. 498.

62 See also ch. 22, Transportation and Communication, under heading 22.7, ''Related undertakings'', below.

63 *CPR* v. *A.-G. B.C.* (Empress Hotel) [1950] A.C. 122.

64 *Construction Montcalm* v. *Minimum Wage Comm.* [1979] 1 S.C.R. 754.

65 *Four B Manufacturing* v. *United Garment Workers* [1980] 1 S.C.R. 1031.

66 *YMHA Jewish Community Centre* v. *Brown* [1989] 1 S.C.R. 1532.

67 *Four B*, note 65, above, 1045.

68 *Can. Labour Relations Bd.* v. *Yellowknife* [1977] 2 S.C.R. 729, 736.

grounds, the labour board must decide the issue of ''constitutional jurisdictional fact'' that is thereby raised: do these employees form an integral part of a federal undertaking? So long as the labour board asks itself the right question, it is surely prudent for the courts to defer to the judgment of the board, informed as it will be by a closer and more expert examination of the facts.[69] The Supreme Court of Canada does not, however, appear to give much weight to the decision of the labour board, even where the issue is a close one upon which reasonable tribunals could be expected to differ.[70]

In the ''federal sectors'' of the economy, where there is federal jurisdiction over labour relations, is the federal jurisdiction exclusive, or is it concurrent with that of the provincial Legislatures? This question did not receive a definitive answer until *Commission du Salaire Minimum* v. *Bell Telephone Co.* (1966).[71] The issue in that case was whether Quebec's minimum wage law applied to the Bell Telephone Company, which was within federal jurisdiction as an interprovincial communications undertaking.[72] At the time when the case arose, there was no federal minimum wage law (there is now). The Supreme Court of Canada held nevertheless that the provincial law was inapplicable to Bell. The Court held that rates of pay and hours of work were ''vital parts'' of the interprovincial undertaking, and that all such vital parts were subject to the exclusive legislative control of the federal Parliament. Therefore, although the provincial law was valid in its application to most employment in the province, it could not constitutionally apply to employment in a federally-regulated industry.[73]

The *Quebec Minimum Wage* case was criticized in earlier editions of this book, on the basis that there was no good reason to immunize federal undertakings from provincial labour standards where the federal standards were lower or (as in the *Quebec Minimum Wage* case) non-existent.[74] However, in *Bell Canada* v. *Quebec* (1988),[75] the Supreme Court of Canada rejected the criticism and followed its earlier decision. The issue in the *Bell Canada* case was whether a provincial occupational health and safety law was applicable to an interprovincial telephone company. The provincial law gave to workers who used video monitors the right to be assigned to other duties while they were pregnant. The Court held that the

---

69 For the same reason, a ruling by a court as to constitutional jurisdiction over a unit of employees would normally be premature until the labour board had considered the issue: *Re 50478 Ont.* (1986) 56 O.R. (2d) 781 (H.C.).

70 E.g., *Can. Labour Relations Bd.* v. *Paul L'Anglais* [1983] 1 S.C.R. 147; *Northern Telecom Can.* v. *Communications Wkrs. of Can.* [1983] 1 S.C.R. 733. In both these cases, the decision of the board was reversed. In my opinion, the dissenting opinion of Beetz J. in the latter case articulates a more appropriately restrained role for the reviewing Court.

71 [1966] S.C.R. 767.

72 *Toronto* v. *Bell Telephone Co.* [1905] A.C. 52.

73 The case was followed in *Letter Carriers' Union of Can.* v. *Can. Union of Postal Wkrs.* [1975] 1 S.C.R. 178.

74 The criticism is summarized in ch. 15, Judicial Review on Federal Grounds, under heading 15.8(c), ''Federally regulated undertakings'', above.

75 [1988] 1 S.C.R. 749.

provincial law was inapplicable to the telephone company. By interfering in the labour relations of the company, the law would affect a vital part of the management and operation of the federal undertaking. The Court thus reaffirmed its position that labour relations in federally-regulated industries is the exclusive preserve of federal law.

Federal jurisdiction over labour relations will extend outside the federal sectors of the economy in times of national emergency.[76] Both of the world wars counted as emergencies, although the depression of the 1930s did not. However, in the *Anti-Inflation Reference* (1976),[77] the Supreme Court of Canada held that a period of double-digit inflation (Canada's third since the second world war) counted as an emergency, and on this basis upheld temporary federal wage (and price) controls which substantially transformed labour relations outside as well as inside the federal sectors of the economy. This decision was rendered in the face of economic evidence that the inflationary situation was not particularly critical, and in spite of the fact that the preamble to the statute did not allege the existence of a crisis. This attenuation of the concept of an emergency makes federal intervention in labour relations an ever present possibility, since the Canadian economy (like that of all other countries) is nearly always beset by some difficulty, whether it be high unemployment, poor growth or an adverse balance of payments, which could be characterized as an emergency with as much (or as little) plausibility as inflation. Needless to say, throughout these ''emergencies'' provincial power is concurrent, and provincial laws will operate unless and to the extent that inconsistent federal laws have been enacted.

21.9 Marketing

(a) Reasons for regulation

The reasons for regulating markets[78] may be found in the interests of both producers and consumers. Producers wanted to combine together to improve their

---

76 See ch. 17, Peace, Order, and Good Government, under heading 17.4, ''The emergency branch'', above.

77 *Re Anti-Inflation Act* [1976] 2 S.C.R. 373.

78 The regulation of marketing raises several constitutional issues in addition to those discussed in the following text. On the federal declaratory power, see ch. 22, Transportation and Communication, under heading 22.8, ''Works for the general advantage of Canada'', below; on marketing levies as indirect taxation, see ch. 30, Taxation, under heading 30.10(b), ''Regulatory charges'', below; on the guarantee of free admission of goods (s. 121), see ch. 43, Mobility, under heading 43.2, ''Goods'', below; on the limited scope of the concurrent power over agriculture (s. 95), see *A.-G. Sask. v. A.-G. Can.* (Farm Security) [1949] A.C. 110; *Can. Federation of Agriculture v. A.-G. Que.* (Margarine) [1951] A.C. 179, 198-200; Laskin, *Canadian Constitutional Law* (5th ed., 1986 by Finkelstein), 500-501; McConnell, *Commentary on the British North America Act* (1977), 300-303; on federal-provincial inter-delegation, see ch. 14, Delegation, above.

bargaining power. They also wanted uniform standards of quality, enforced by grading, inspection and labelling, so that variations in kind or quality would be fairly reflected in prices. Sometimes, they sought a pooling of proceeds and an equalization of returns so that the short-term rises and falls in the market would be shared by all. In some cases, producers, through a producer-controlled board, would seek to control the market itself by determining the time, quantity and place at which the product should be sold, or even by controlling production and directly fixing prices. The interests of consumers, while by no means identical to those of producers, especially in the matter of prices, also called for regulation of some market practices. Uniform standards of quality, enforced by inspection and labelling, were needed to eliminate dangerous or unhealthy goods and deceptive marketing prices.

(b) Federal power

We have already seen that early attempts by the federal Parliament to enact marketing schemes under the trade and commerce power (s. 91(2)) were struck down by the Privy Council.[79] Their lordships started with a strong presumption that any interference with contracts was a matter within property and civil rights in the province. Even where the market to be regulated was primarily interprovincial or international, the Privy Council struck down statutes in their entirety if they had any application to purely local transactions.[80] This attitude made the federal enactment of an effective marketing scheme impossible.

Since the abolition of appeals to the Privy Council, the Canadian courts have interpreted the trade and commerce power more liberally. Federal regulation of the trade in grain[81] and in oil[82] has been upheld, even though the regulation extended to purely local transactions. The reasoning was that the marketing of products which flow across interprovincial boundaries from the province of production or importation to the province of consumption or export could be regulated by the federal Parliament, and that some local transactions could also be regulated where that was an incident of the regulation of the interprovincial trade. These decisions represent a departure from the Privy Council precedents, and a significant expansion of federal power. Whether the power will be permitted to expand to the point of enabling the federal Parliament to regulate any market which extends beyond any one province remains to be seen, but it would be a rational development of the trade and commerce power.

---

79 See ch. 20, Trade and Commerce, above.

80 The Supreme Court of the United States, in contrast, held that where intrastate and interstate transactions were commingled, the Congress was empowered under the commerce clause to regulate the whole: Smith, *The Commerce Power in Canada and the United States* (1963), 142.

81 *Murphy* v. *CPR* [1958] S.C.R. 626; *R.* v. *Klassen* (1959) 20 D.L.R. (2d) 406 (Man. C.A.).

82 *Caloil* v. *A.-G. Can.* [1971] S.C.R. 543.

(c) Provincial power

Contracts of sale and purchase are prima facie matters within ''property and civil rights in the province'' (s. 92(13)), and therefore amenable to provincial legislation. There is no doubt that under s. 92(13) the provinces have the power to regulate intraprovincial trade, although they lack the power to regulate interprovincial trade.[83] In the context of marketing, this distinction is not easy to apply. A provincial marketing scheme will nearly always have an impact on producers or consumers in other provinces. The question is to what extent should a province be permitted to burden interprovincial trade in the course of regulating intraprovincial trade?[84]

In *Shannon* v. *Lower Mainland Dairy Products Board* (1938),[85] the Privy Council upheld a provincial scheme for the compulsory marketing of milk through provincial boards. This scheme applied to all milk sold in the province, including milk produced in other provinces. The application to milk produced out of the province was upheld as an incident of an essentially intraprovincial scheme. In *Home Oil Distributors* v. *A.-G. B.C.* (1940),[86] the Supreme Court of Canada upheld provincial regulation of the prices of all gasoline and fuel oil sold in the province. Once again the application of the scheme to products produced out of the province was upheld. In *Carnation Co.* v. *Quebec Agricultural Marketing Board* (1968),[87] the Supreme Court of Canada upheld a provincial marketing plan for the sale of raw milk by farmers to the Carnation Company which processed the milk. Under this plan, Carnation had to pay higher prices for its milk than would have been payable in a free market, and indeed higher prices than other processors purchasing from farmers in the same area. In fact, Carnation shipped the bulk of its product out of the province. The Supreme Court of Canada held nevertheless that the marketing law was ''in relation to'' intraprovincial trade, and that it merely ''affected'' interprovincial trade.

These three cases, spanning as they do both the Privy Council period and the post-appeals period, suggest a very extensive power to regulate marketing within the province, notwithstanding the burdens incidentally placed on the residents of other provinces. It is true that in the *Ontario Farm Products Marketing Reference* (1957)[88] there were dicta in the Supreme Court of Canada warning that provincial power over intraprovincial transactions would not extend to transactions which were really part and parcel of interprovincial trade. But these dicta

---

83 See ch. 19, Trade and Commerce, above.

84 The language of ''burdens'' on interstate commerce is conventional in the United States, where the essential problem is exactly the same, but is confronted more openly by the courts than in Canada: see Benson, *The Supreme Court and the Commerce Clause, 1937-1970* (1970), ch. 7.

85 [1938] A.C. 708.

86 [1940] S.C.R. 444.

87 [1968] S.C.R. 238; folld. in *Can. Indemnity Co.* v. *A.-G. B.C.* [1977] 2 S.C.R. 504.

88 *Re Farm Products Marketing Act* [1957] S.C.R. 198.

had been cited in the *Carnation* case[89] the following year, and the Court had not regarded them as applicable, despite the fact that in *Carnation* the bulk of the regulated product was destined for export. However, in the *Manitoba Egg Reference* (1971),[90] the Supreme Curt of Canada unexpectedly struck down a provincial scheme to regulate the marketing of eggs. The scheme applied to all eggs sold in Manitoba, including eggs produced elsewhere. The reason for the application of the scheme to eggs produced out-of-province was, no doubt, that the scheme could otherwise be undermined by imports of an unregulated and presumably cheaper product. Moreover, the application of provincial regulation to a product produced outside the province had been upheld in the *Shannon* and *Home Oil* cases.[91] But, without explaining why these precedents and *Carnation* were not controlling, Martland J. for a majority of the Court held that ''the Plan now in issue not only affects interprovincial trade in eggs, but that it aims at the regulation of such trade''.[92] The plan was accordingly held to be unconstitutional in its entirety.[93]

The *Manitoba Egg Reference* arose out of a much-publicized ''chicken and egg war'' between Ontario (which produced a surplus of eggs) and Quebec (which produced a surplus of chickens). Those provinces had established marketing plans for eggs in Quebec and for chickens in Ontario which, according to the press, gave undue preference to the locally-produced product. Manitoba, which as a producer of agricultural surpluses claimed to be injured by both plans, created an egg marketing plan of its own on the Quebec model and referred it to the courts for a judicial decision which would also effectively determine the validity of the Quebec and Ontario plans.[94] This background of the case may be relevant, because, although it is not mentioned in the opinions, it must have been present in the minds of the judges, and it may well have suggested to them that the various marketing plans could be used as vehicles by which a province could discriminate against the out-of-province product. Discrimination would of course make the

89 [1968] S.C.R. 238, 245-246.

90 *A.-G. Man.* v. *Man. Egg & Poultry Assn.* [1971] S.C.R. 689.

91 Notes 85, 86, above.

92 [1971] S.C.R. 689, 703 per Martland J. with whom Fauteux C.J., Abbott, Judson, Ritchie and Spence JJ. agreed. Separate concurring opinions by Laskin J., with whom Hall J. agreed, and Pigeon J. are to the same effect.

93 In *Burns Foods* v. *A.-G. Man.* [1975] 1 S.C.R. 494, the Supreme Court of Canada, by a majority of six to one, reached a similar decision, but held that only that part of the Manitoba Hog Producers' Marketing Plan which purported to bind the product purchased out-of-province was invalid. Even this more restrained result seems open to criticism, however, on the basis that the application to the imported product was necessary to the integrity of the plan and was merely an incidental effect of a plan whose primary purpose was to control the marketing of hogs in the province. This was the basis of Ritchie J.'s dissent.

94 Weiler, *In the Last Resort* (1974), ch. 6, describes the background to the *Manitoba Egg Reference*, criticizes the use by the Manitoba government of the reference in these circumstances, and criticizes the decision of the Supreme Court.

plan unconstitutional, at least in operation,[95] and would be a clear distinction between this case and *Shannon* and *Home Oil*. Unfortunately, none of the opinions clearly stated that the decision was based on the discriminatory character of the plan, and Laskin J. denied that his opinion was based on discrimination against out-of-province producers.[96] A literal reading of the opinions would seem "to bar subjection of extraprovincial products even to a fairly administered, provincial regulatory scheme".[97] Such a principle is inconsistent with prior authority and with any effective provincial capacity to regulate marketing.

The decision in the *Manitoba Egg Reference* was followed by a federal-provincial agreement involving all 11 governments which settled a national marketing plan for eggs. The plan allocated production quotas to each province, and stipulated a higher price for eggs sold outside the province of production. Within each province, production quotas were to be imposed on producers so as to control supply and support prices; the surplus product (surplus to the table market) was to be sold in the industrial market by a marketing board; and the plan was to be financed by levies on all producers. The plan was to be administered by a national marketing board and ten provincial marketing boards. This ambitious national project was set up under the aegis of a federal marketing statute and ten provincial marketing statutes, and each marketing board was granted powers by inter-delegations from both levels of government. Through the cooperative action of both levels of government, it was hoped to fill the gaps in federal and provincial legislative power.

In *Re Agricultural Products Marketing Act* (1978),[98] the Supreme Court of Canada upheld the principal elements of the plan. Both the federal marketing statute and the Ontario statute were upheld, on the basis that the federal statute regulated the interprovincial elements of the plan, and the provincial statute regulated the intraprovincial elements of the plan. As noted in the discussion of

95 However, if discrimination was not inherent in the plan, and it could be administered fairly, then it would follow that only its unfair administration would be unconstitutional, and there would be no basis for the Court to hold invalid the plan itself.

96 [1971] S.C.R. 689, 716, but note Laskin J.'s next paragraph, which refers to a province's "figurative sealing of its borders to entry of goods from others" (717), and which does appear to assume discrimination. The other opinions could be read as regarding the plan as inherently discriminatory: see especially 701 per Martland J., 723 per Pigeon J. In *Burns Foods* v. *A.-G. Man.* [1975] 1 S.C.R. 494, 506, Pigeon J. (with the agreement of Fauteux C.J., Abbott, Martland, Judson and Spence JJ.) referred to "the features of discrimination present in the *[Manitoba] Egg case*". However, he went on to say that discrimination was absent in the *Burns Foods* case, and yet the hog marketing plan in that case could not be extended to hogs purchased out-of-province.

97 Weiler, *In the Last Resort* (1974), 162. One of the many puzzles of the decision is how the Court was able to reach its conclusion without the aid of any factual information as to the actual impact of the plan on out-of-province eggs. It is possible that the impact would have been trivial in that Manitoba appears to have been a net exporter of eggs (Weiler, 156). Laskin J. deplored the absence of any "factual underpinning", but still went on to hold the scheme invalid.

98 [1978] 2 S.C.R. 1198.

the case in the previous chapter,[99] it was doubtful whether each level of government had succeeded in remaining within its proper sphere, but the Court was willing to give the benefit of the doubt to both the federal and the provincial sides of the cooperative enterprise. With respect to the provincial statute, perhaps the most important aspect of the decision is the holding that the provincial statute could impose production quotas on all producers ''irrespective of the destination of their output''.[100]

The Court has not adhered to this ruling about provincial power to control the production of natural resources. In *Central Canada Potash* v. *Government of Saskatchewan* (1978),[101] the Court struck down Saskatchewan's prorationing scheme for potash produced in the province. The scheme, which was established by regulations made under statutory authority, imposed production quotas on producers of potash in the province.[102] The Saskatchewan Court of Appeal upheld the controls as measures ''to protect and maintain the potash industry as a viable economic industry within the province''.[103] But the Supreme Court of Canada reversed. Laskin C.J. for a unanimous Court acknowledged that *Re Agricultural Products Marketing Act* had held that production controls were ''ordinarily'' matters within provincial authority; but he said that ''the situation may be different, however, where a province establishes a marketing scheme with price fixing as its central feature''.[104] He did not explain why price fixing would make the situation different, and it is very hard to see why, since price fixing was also a central feature of the egg marketing plan in *Re Agricultural Products Marketing Act*. The controls in each case pursued exactly the same economic purpose: by reducing the supply of the product, the price could be maintained at a level above its free-market level.[105] The political object in both cases was to increase returns to producers and make the producing industry more prosperous.

In order to account for the different outcomes in the two cases, it seems necessary to look to the destination of the product. In *Re Agricultural Products Marketing Act*, it was established that 90 per cent of the eggs produced in Canada were consumed within the province of production. In *Central Canada Potash*, it was established that virtually all of the potash produced in Saskatchewan was

---

99 Chapter 20, Trade and Commerce, under heading 20.2(b), ''In the Supreme Court of Canada'', above.

100 [1978] 2 S.C.R. 1198, 1296 per Pigeon J. for majority. Laskin C.J. for concurring minority was a little more cautious, upholding production controls (at p. 1286) on the basis that the ''primary object'' of the Act was ''to regulate marketing in intraprovincial trade''.

101 [1979] 1 S.C.R. 42.

102 The case did not concern potash owned by the province itself. As proprietor, a province is free to control production and (if possible) price even if the product is destined for export. In this case, the resource was privately owned, and the controls involved an exercise of legislative, not proprietary power. The distinction is referred to by Laskin C.J. (at p. 72).

103 [1979] 1 S.C.R. 42, 68, quoting the relevant passage from the opinion of the Court of Appeal.

104 *Id.*, 74.

105 Moreover, where supply can be controlled in the relevant market, the power to fix prices is not very significant, since the control of supply is by itself sufficient to manage the price.

exported. This led Laskin C.J. to characterize the prorationing scheme as "directly aimed at the production of potash destined for export".[106] With respect, this is not a plausible characterization. The prorationing controls were imposed at the mine without regard for the ultimate destination of the potash. The controls would have applied in exactly the same way if the fertilizer industry (the consumer of potash) had been located within the province. The purpose of the controls was not to reduce the export trade (though that was certainly their effect), but to protect the local mining industry. The Court's reasoning produces the unfortunate consequence that those provinces that, like Saskatchewan, are mainly primary producers have less control over their natural resources than those provinces that, like Ontario, have more integrated economies.[107]

Neither in *Re Agricultural Products Marketing Act* nor in *Central Canada Potash*, could it be argued that the production controls had a physical (as opposed to economic) conservation purpose. Eggs are a renewable resource that can be produced in any quantity for the indefinite future. Potash is not a renewable resource, of course, but the trial judge found that Saskatchewan possessed reserves sufficient to supply world demand for 1,500 years; so it was plain, as Laskin C.J. held, that the prorationing scheme "could not be said to be a response to threatened shortages of the mineral or to conservation needs".[108] Where production controls are imposed for a physical conservation purpose, there is no doubt about the existence of provincial power. In *Spooner Oils* v. *Turner Valley Gas Conservation Bd.* (1933),[109] the Supreme Court of Canada upheld legislation enacted by Alberta to limit the production of natural gas in the Turner Valley gas field. The purpose of the controls was to prevent producers from extracting large quantities of gas, then separating naphtha from the gas, and then burning the gas. This wasteful practice had developed because there was a strong market for the naphtha, and no market for most of the gas. The Supreme Court of Canada did not discuss the location of the market for the naphtha, but it is safe to assume that it was outside Alberta. The Court rejected the argument that the province was purporting to regulate trade and commerce, saying that the production controls were imposed "from a point of view which is provincial and for a purpose which is provincial

106 [1979] 1 S.C.R. 42, 74.

107 The Court followed its prior decision in *Can. Industrial Gas and Oil* v. *Govt. of Sask.* [1978] 2 S.C.R. 545, where the Court struck down a Saskatchewan law purporting to fix the price of oil at the wellhead. The price was not an "export price", being imposed without regard for the destination of the oil. However, because the evidence showed that 98 per cent of Saskatchewan's oil was exported to eastern Canada, the Court, by majority, held that the province was attempting to fix the price in the export market, which was an unconstitutional attempt to regulate interprovincial trade and commerce. This reasoning is, in my view, open to the same line of criticism as that offered in the text in respect of the *Central Can. Potash case*. The two cases have attracted an extensive and generally critical commentary, of which perhaps the best article is Moull, "Natural Resources: The Other Crisis in Canadian Federalism" (1980) 18 Osgoode Hall L.J. 1.

108 [1979] 1 S.C.R. 42, 50.

109 [1933] S.C.R. 629.

— the prevention of what the legislature conceives to be a waste of natural gas in the working of [the gas wells].''[110]

The Constitution Act, 1982, by s. 50, added a new s. 92A to the Constitution Act, 1867, enlarging provincial powers over natural resources.[111] Two provisions are arguably relevant to production controls in marketing plans. First, s. 92A(1)(b) confers on the provincial Legislatures the power to make laws in relation to:

> development, conservation and management of nonrenewable natural resources and forestry resources in the province, including laws in relation to the rate of primary production therefrom;

It will be noticed that this power applies only to ''non-renewable natural resources and forestry resources''. It therefore has no application to eggs and other agricultural products. It does apply to potash and other minerals, and it does contemplate ''laws in relation to the rate of primary production''. But the references at the beginning of the paragraph to ''development, conservation and management'', and the absence of any reference to the case where the resources are destined for export (which, it will be recalled, was the fatal element of the potash prorationing scheme), suggest that the paragraph may be no more than declaratory of pre-1982 provincial power as determined in *Central Canada Potash*.

The second new provision that may be relevant to production controls in marketing plans is s. 92A(2), which provides:

> In each province, the legislature may make laws in relation to the export from the province to another part of Canada of the primary production from non-renewable natural resources and forestry resources in the province and the production from facilities in the province for the generation of electrical energy, but such laws may not authorize or provide for discrimination in prices or in supplies exported to another part of Canada.

This provision is certainly an enlargement of pre-1982 provincial power, since laws in relation to the export of resources were previously incompetent to the provinces, as is illustrated by *Central Canada Potash*.[112] However, the new power does not extend to agricultural products; and, even with respect to ''non-renewable natural resources'' (and lumber and electricity), the new power only authorizes laws in relation to the export of the resources ''to another part of Canada''. The export of resources from Canada remains outside provincial legislative power.

110 *Id.*, 649.

111 For analysis of s. 92A, see Moull, ''Section 92A of the Constitution Act, 1867'' (1983) 61 Can. Bar Rev. 715; Cairns, Chandler, Moull, ''The Resource Amendment (Section 92A) and the Political Economy of Canadian Federalism'' (1985) 23 Osgoode Hall L.J. 253; Cairns, Chandler, Moull, ''Constitutional Change and the Private Sector: The Case of the Resource Amendment'' (1987) 24 Osgoode Hall L.J. 299.

112 Section 92A(3) provides that the new power is not exclusive: federal power exists as well, and federal laws are paramount over inconsistent provincial laws.

The facts of *Central Canada Potash*, where the bulk of the potash was destined for markets in the United States, would be outside the new power.[113]

21.10 Securities regulation

(a) Provincial power

In line with the insurance cases and the marketing cases, the provinces have the power to regulate the trade in corporate securities.[114] This is a matter within property and civil rights in the province. In fact, the provinces have regulatory regimes which establish securities commissions, and which provide for the licensing of brokers and the regulation of the market for corporate securities.

There is one important exception to the generality of provincial power over the securities industry. It has been held that the province has no power to confer upon a provincial agency discretionary power over the issue of securities by a federally-incorporated company, because the capacity to raise capital is an essential attribute of corporate status.[115] This does not preclude all provincial regulation of the issue of securities by federally-incorporated companies; for example, such companies can be required to issue their securities only through provincially-licensed brokers,[116] and a remedy can be provided for ''insider trading'' in their securities.[117] The question in each case is whether the degree of provincial control amounts to a denial of an essential attribute of corporate status. The scope of this immunity from provincial law is more fully discussed in the later chapter on Companies.[118]

Except for the limited immunity of federally-incorporated companies, the provincial power has been given a broad scope by the courts. The Ontario Securities Act's offence of furnishing false information in a prospectus has been held to be valid and operative, notwithstanding the existence of a similar offence in the federal Criminal Code.[119] The Quebec Securities Act's provision freezing deposits of funds or securities pending an investigation by the Commission has been held to be valid and applicable to a bank, notwithstanding the singling out

113 The facts of *CIGOL*, note 107, above, would be mainly within the new power, since Saskatchewan's oil was mainly exported to eastern Canada, not to the United States.

114 See generally *Report of the A.-G.'s Committee on Securities Legislation in Ontario* (Kimber Report) (1965), Part IX; Anisman and Hogg in Consumer and Corporate Affairs Canada, *Proposals for a Securities Market Law for Canada* (1979), vol. 3, 135.

115 *A.-G. Man.* v. *A.-G. Can.* (Manitoba Securities) [1929] A.C. 260.

116 *Lymburn* v. *Mayland* [1932] A.C. 318.

117 *Multiple Access* v. *McCutcheon* [1982] 2 S.C.R. 161.

118 Chapter 23, Companies, under heading 23.3, ''The status and essential powers immunity'', below.

119 *Smith* v. *The Queen* [1960] S.C.R. 776; see also *Multiple Access* v. *McCutcheon* [1982] 2 S.C.R. 161 (provincial insider trading remedy upheld despite existence of similar federal remedy).

of banks and other institutions holding deposits.[120] The Quebec Act has also been held applicable to a broker operating in the province whose business was confined to customers outside the province;[121] and the Manitoba Act has been held applicable to a broker operating outside the province but selling stock to customers inside the province.[122] In these cases where the provincial legislation has been applied to operations which, overall, are interprovincial, the court may have been influenced by the absence of federal securities legislation.[123]

(b) Federal power

The federal government has commissioned and published a study of the possibility of federal regulation of the securities industry, including a draft bill,[124] but at the time of writing this has not been adopted as federal government policy. The federal incorporation power authorizes the regulation of the issue of securities by federally-incorporated companies,[125] and authorizes some degree of regulation of trading in those securities.[126] The criminal law power authorizes the punishment of fraudulent or deceptive practices in the securities industry,[127] but it would probably not authorize a sophisticated regulatory regime involving licensing of brokers and discretionary powers in an administrative agency.[128] The trade and commerce power would certainly authorize the regulation of interprovincial dealings in securities, despite the recent holdings of concurrent provincial power.[129] The hard question is whether the trade and commerce power could cover even transactions which, regarded individually, begin and end in the one province, on the basis that the securities industry serves a capital market which is interprovincial and indeed international.[130]

---

120 *Gregory & Co.* v. *Imperial Bank* [1960] C.S. 204 (Que. S.C.).

121 *Gregory & Co.* v. *Que. Securities Comm.* [1961] S.C.R. 584. The Court did not determine the constitutionality of this application of the Act.

122 *R.* v. *W. McKenzie Securities Ltd.* (1966) 56 D.L.R. (2d) 56 (Man. C.A.). In this case the constitutional issue was determined in favour of the legislation.

123 The marketing cases suggest that incidents of an interprovincial operation may only be regulated federally: see sec. 21.9, ''Marketing'' above.

124 Consumer and Corporate Affairs Canada, *Proposals for a Securities Market Law for Canada* (1979). See also Anisman, ''The Proposals for a Securities Market Law for Canada: Purpose and Process'' (1981) 19 Osgoode Hall L.J. 329.

125 *A.-G. Man.* v. *A.-G. Can.* (Manitoba Securities) [1929] A.C. 260.

126 *Esso Standard Inc.* v. *J.W. Enterprises* [1963] S.C.R. 144 (provision authorizing take-over offeror to buy out dissenting minority); *Multiple Access* v. *McCutcheon* [1982] 2 S.C.R. 161 (remedy for insider trading).

127 *Smith* v. *The Queen* [1960] S.C.R. 776 (false prospectus offence in Criminal Code upheld).

128 See ch. 18, Criminal Law, under heading 18.10, ''Criminal law and regulatory authority'', above.

129 Notes 121, 122, above.

130 In the United States, federal securities regulation has been upheld under the commerce clause: Smith, *The Commerce Power in Canada and the United States* (1963), 461-465. The case for federal power is argued by Anisman and Hogg, note 114, above; and in *Multiple Access* v.

21.11 Property

(a) General

The creation of property rights, their transfer and their general characteristics are within property and civil rights in the province. Thus, the law of real and personal property and all its various derivatives, such as landlord and tenant, trusts and wills, succession on intestacy, conveyancing, and land use planning, are within provincial power.

Difficulty has arisen, however, in cases where a province has sought to control the ownership or use of property in order to accomplish a non-proprietary objective which it could not accomplish by more direct means. For example, in *Switzman* v. *Elbling* (1957)[131] a provincial law which prohibited the use of a house ''to propagate communism or bolshevism'' was characterized as either a criminal law or a law in relation to speech, and not as a property law. By contrast, in *Bedard* v. *Dawson* (1923)[132] a provincial law which prohibited the use of a house as a ''disorderly house'' was characterized as a property law, and not as a mere supplement to Criminal Code offences in respect of disorderly houses.[133] And in *Johnson* v. *A.-G. Alta.* (1954)[134] the Court divided evenly on the question whether a provincial law which denied property rights in slot machines and provided for the confiscation of slot machines was a property law or a criminal law.[135]

(b) Foreign ownership

The question whether a province can control foreign ownership of land was litigated in *Morgan* v. *A.-G. P.E.I.* (1975),[136] in which the Supreme Court of Canada upheld a statute of Prince Edward Island which provided that ''no person who is not a resident of the province'' could acquire holdings of real property of more than a specified size except with the permission of the provincial cabinet. The qualification for unrestricted landholding was residence, not citizenship, and

---

McCutcheon [1982] 2 S.C.R. 161, there are sympathetic obiter dicta in both Dickson J.'s majority opinion (at pp. 173-174) and Estey J.'s dissenting opinion (at p. 225).

131 [1957] S.C.R. 285.

132 [1923] S.C.R. 681.

133 In *N.S. Bd. of Censors* v. *McNeil* [1978] 2 S.C.R. 662, Ritchie J. for the majority upheld (at p. 688) a provincial film censorship law on the implausible basis that it was ''concerned with dealings in and the use of property (i.e., films) which take place wholly within the province''. He also upheld the law (at p. 688) as the regulation of the ''film business'' and (at p. 699) as the regulation of a local or private matter.

134 [1954] S.C.R. 127.

135 See also *Walter* v. *A.-G. Alta.* [1969] S.C.R. 383, upholding provincial restrictions on the communal holding of land which were intended to limit the expansion of Hutterite ''colonies''.

136 [1976] 2 S.C.R. 349.

so the prohibition applied to non-resident citizens as well as non-resident aliens.[137] The decision would have been more difficult if the discrimination had been against aliens instead of non-residents, because ''naturalization and aliens'' (s. 91(25)) is a federal head of legislative power. The authorities are divided on the extent of provincial power to discriminate against aliens,[138] but a dictum in the *Morgan* case suggests that a provincial law which imposed property-owning restraints on aliens could still be sustained as a valid property law.[139]

The federal Parliament has also asserted jurisdiction over foreign ownership of property in the Investment Canada Act,[140] which provides screening procedures for certain takeovers of Canadian businesses by ''non-Canadians''. In the insurance cases, the ''aliens'' power was never held to be sufficient to authorize the regulation of foreign insurance companies, but there are dicta in those cases to the effect that the federal Parliament could ''by properly framed legislation'' impose restrictions on aliens seeking to do business in Canada.[141] The same dicta suggested that the trade and commerce power would also be available in support of this kind of legislation, and the undoubted federal authority over the import and export of goods[142] provides an analogy. At the time of writing there has been no constitutional challenge to this Act, or to its predecessor, the Foreign Investment Review Act, enacted in 1973.[143]

21.12 Debt adjustment

The law of contract is mainly within provincial power under property and civil rights in the province.[144] Provincial power extends to the annulment or reformation of harsh or unconscionable contracts.[145] But the provincial power to modify creditors' rights is circumscribed by a number of provisions of the Constitution Act, 1867. One is the extraterritorial limitation imposed by the words ''in the province'' in s. 92(13) itself. Another is the allocation of ''interest'' (s.

---

137 *Morgan* was followed in *Re Min. of Revenue (Ont.) and Hala* (1977) 18 O.R. (2d) 88 (Ont. H.C.), upholding a provincial tax on the acquisition of land, which was levied at the rate of less than one per cent on residents and twenty per cent on non-residents. The object of the tax was to discourage absentee ownership.

138 See ch. 35, Equality, under heading 35.1, ''Distribution of powers'', below.

139 [1976] 2 S.C.R. 349, 364-365. Contra, Spencer, ''The Alien Landowner in Canada'' (1973) 51 Can. Bar Rev. 389.

140 S.C. 1985, c. 20, repealing and replacing the Foreign Investment Review Act, 1973.

141 *A.-G. Can.* v. *A.-G. Alta.* (Insurance) [1916] 1 A.C. 588, 597; *A.-G. Ont.* v. *Reciprocal Insurers* [1924] A.C. 328, 346; *Re Insurance Act of Can.* [1932] A.C. 41, 51.

142 See ch. 20, Trade and Commerce, under heading 20.2(a), ''In the Privy Council'', above.

143 For general discussion, see MacNab, ''Constitutionality of Federal Control of Foreign Investment'' (1965) 23 U. Toronto Fac. L. Rev. 95; Arnett, ''Canadian Regulation of Foreign Investment'' (1972) 50 Can. Bar Rev. 213.

144 Note 4, above.

145 *A.-G. Ont.* v. *Barfried Enterprises*, [1963] S.C.R. 570.

91(19)) and "bankruptcy and insolvency" (s. 91(21)) to the federal Parliament, which withdraws those subjects from provincial power. These various infirmities in provincial power have not deterred the provinces from extensive regulation of the debtor-creditor relationship, often with the purpose of protecting local debtors from the enforcement efforts of out-of-province creditors. The resulting constitutional challenges have created a substantial body of case-law, which is described in chapter 25, Bankruptcy and Insolvency, below.[146]

21.13 Consumer protection

Many of the laws that have been upheld within the various rubrics described in this chapter had the purpose of consumer protection. This illustrates that much consumer protection law is open to the province under the power over property and civil rights in the province. For example, provincial restrictions on advertising directed at children have been described as "in relation to consumer protection" and upheld under s. 92(13).[147] But much *federal* law could just as accurately be described as in relation to consumer protection. The phrase consumer protection is too broad and vague to serve as a "matter" for the purpose of the federal distribution of powers. Like inflation, pollution or health, consumer protection must be broken out into smaller, more distinct, concepts, before a consumer protection law can be placed in its correct constitutional slot.

21.14 Extraterritorial competence

The legislative power conferred by s. 92(13) is over property and civil rights in the province. The words "in the province" make clear that there is a territorial limitation on the power. The nature of that limitation has been discussed in chapter 13, Extraterritorial Competence, above.

146 Chapter 25, Bankruptcy and Insolvency, under heading 25.5, "Adjustment of debts", below.
147 *Irwin Toy* v. *Que.* [1989] 1 S.C.R. 927, 953.

22

Transportation and Communication

22.1 Distribution of power

Legislative power over transportation and communication[1] is divided between the federal Parliament and the provincial Legislatures. There is no mention of either transportation or communication in the Constitution Act, 1867, although several modes of transportation and communication are mentioned. The most important of these references occurs in s. 92(10). Section 92(10) is, of course, part of the list of provincial powers. It confers upon the provincial Legislatures the power to make laws in relation to:

> Local works and undertakings other than such as are of the following classes:
> (a) Lines of steam or other ships, railways, canals, telegraphs, and other works and undertakings connecting the province with any other or others of the provinces, or extending beyond the limits of the province;
> (b) Lines of steam ships between the province and any British or foreign country;
> (c) Such works as, although wholly situate within the province, are before or after their execution declared by the Parliament of Canada to be for the general advantage of Canada or for the advantage of two or more of the provinces.

The three listed exceptions from provincial power are heads of federal legislative power by virtue of s. 91(29), which includes in the federal enumeration those classes of subjects which are expressly excepted from the provincial enumeration. Indeed, the exceptions have turned out to be more important than the primary grant of power over ''local works and undertakings'', because the courts have often preferred to rest provincial power on s. 92(13) (property and civil rights in the province) or s. 92(16) (matters of a merely local or private nature in the province), each of which is apt to cover much the same ground as s. 92(10).[2]

The essential scheme of s. 92(10) is to divide legislative authority over transportation and communication on a territorial basis. The specific references in s. 92(10)(a) to ''lines of steam or other ships, railways, canals, telegraphs'' do not allocate those modes of transportation or communication unqualifiedly to the federal Parliament. The references must be read in the context of the later reference to ''other works and undertakings connecting the province with any other or others of the provinces, or extending beyond the limits of the province'', and the whole of paragraph (a) must be read as an exception to the grant of provincial authority over local works and undertakings. The effect is to allocate to the federal

---

1 McNairn, ''Transportation, Communication and the Constitution'' (1969) 47 Can. Bar Rev. 355; McNairn, ''Aeronautics and the Constitution'' (1971) 49 Can. Bar Rev. 411; Mullan and Beaman, ''The Constitutional Implications of the Regulation of Telecommunications'' (1973) 2 Queen's L.J. 67; Fraser, ''Some Comments on Subsection 92(10) of the Constitution Act, 1867'' (1984) 29 McGill L.J. 557; Monahan, ''Constitutional Jurisdiction over Transportation: Recent Developments and Proposals for Change'' in *Directions: Final Report of the Royal Commission on National Passenger Transportation* (1992), vol. 3, c. 9; Laskin, *Canadian Constitutional Law* (5th ed., 1986 by Finkelstein), ch. 9; Beaudoin, *La Constitution du Canada* (1990), ch. 11; Rémillard, *Le Fédéralisme Canadien* (2nd ed., 1983), vol. 1, ch. 4.

2 McNairn (1969) 47 Can. Bar Rev. 355, 356.

Parliament the authority over *interprovincial* or *international* shipping lines, railways, canals, telegraphs and other modes of transportation or communication; and to allocate to the provincial Legislatures the authority over *intraprovincial* shipping lines, railways, canals, telegraphs and other modes of transportation or communication.[3]

Section 92(10)(c) forms an exception to the territorial distinction which generally differentiates federal and provincial jurisdiction under s. 92(10). Paragraph (c) enables the federal Parliament to assume jurisdiction over a purely local work by the simple (and unilateral) device of declaring the work to be ''for the general advantage of Canada or for the advantage of two or more of the provinces''. This declaratory power is available over any local ''works'', and is not confined to works related to transportation or communication.[4] However, the power will be discussed in this chapter. Paragraphs (a) and (b) of s. 92(10), by contrast, are confined to works and undertakings related to transportation or communication.[5]

There are other heads of legislative power which bear on transportation and communication. The peace, order, and good government power, which formed the subject of chapter 17, has been held to give the federal Parliament jurisdiction over aeronautics.[6] Several of the federal Parliament's enumerated powers also cover aspects of transportation and communication: ''beacons, buoys, lighthouses, and Sable Island'' (s. 91(9)); ''navigation and shipping'' (s. 91(10)),[7] and ''ferries between a province and any British or foreign country or between two provinces'' (s. 91(13)).[8] The federal ''trade and commerce'' power, on the other

---

3 For example, local railways are within provincial jurisdiction: *Montreal* v. *Montreal St. Ry.* [1912] A.C. 333; *B.C. Elec. Ry.* v. *CNR* [1932] S.C.R. 161; *UTU* v. *Central Western Ry.* [1990] 3 S.C.R. 1112. Even local shiplines are within provincial jurisdiction, notwithstanding s. 91(10) (''navigation and shipping''); *Agence Maritime* v. *Can. Labour Relations Bd.* [1969] S.C.R. 851.

4 Note 74, below.

5 Section 22.3, ''Transportation and communication'', below.

6 Section 22.11, ''Transportation by air'', below.

7 Section 22.10, ''Transportation by water'', below.

8 Transportation and communication arrangements were crucial to the confederation of the provinces. Section 145 of the British North America Act (repealed in 1893) provided for the construction by the Government of Canada of the Intercolonial Railway, linking the St. Lawrence valley with the ice-free port of Halifax. Section 11 of the B.C. Terms of Union provided for the construction of the Canadian Pacific Railway, ''to connect the seaboard of British Columbia with the railway system of Canada'': see *B.C.* v. *Can.* [1994] 2 S.C.R. 41. The P.E.I. Terms of Union included an undertaking that the Government of Canada would provide ferry service between the Island and the mainland: see *The Queen Can.* v. *The Queen P.E.I.* [1978] 1 F.C. 533 (C.A.); *P.E.I.* v. *CNR* [1991] 1 F.C. 129 (C.A.). Section 31 of the Newfoundland Terms of Union included the takeover by the Government of Canada of (among other things) the Newfoundland Railway and the telecommunications system, which thereby came within federal legislative jurisdiction: *CNR* v. *Commrs. of Public Utilities* [1976] 2 S.C.R. 112. Section 32 was an undertaking by the Government of Canada to provide a ferry service between the mainland and the Island. See Monahan, ''Constitutional Jurisdiction Over Transportation:

hand, has never been held to confer any federal power over transportation or communication.[9] This is in striking contrast with the commerce clause in the Constitution of the United States, which authorizes federal regulation of interstate transportation and communication.[10]

The scheme of this chapter will be, first, to examine the powers over interprovincial or international undertakings and over works for the general advantage of Canada, and, secondly, to examine the powers over each of the principal modes of transportation and communication.

22.2 Works and undertakings

We have already noticed that s. 92(10)(a), read with s. 91(29), of the Constitution Act, 1867 confers on the federal Parliament the power to make laws in relation to:

> Lines of steam or other ships, railways, canals, telegraphs, and other works and undertakings connecting the province with any other or others of the provinces, or extending beyond the limits of the province.

We have also noticed that this power is confined to interprovincial (or international) works and undertakings, and that intraprovincial works and undertakings are within provincial jurisdiction.[11]

Section 92(10)(a) refers to ''works and undertakings'', while s. 92(10)(c) refers only to ''works''. This suggests a distinction between the two terms which has usually been ignored, but has occasionally been adverted to in the cases.It has been said that a work is a ''physical thing'',[12] while an undertaking is''not a physical thing, but an arrangement under which . . . physical things areused''.[13] The term ''undertaking'' is the one which has been most often invoked in the cases under s. 92(10)(a), and it seems to be equivalent to''organization''[14] or ''enterprise'',[15] although in the case of radio and television broadcasting the word has been held apt to encompass the entire broadcasting activity and not just particular broadcasting firms.[16]

Recent Developments and Proposals for Change'' in *Directions: Final Report of the Royal Commission on National Passenger Transportation* (1992), vol. 3, ch. 9.

9 McNairn (1969), note 1, above.

10 The abundant authorities start in the Supreme Court of the United States with *Gibbons* v. *Ogden* (1824) 9 Wheat. (22 U.S.) 1.

11 Note 3, above.

12 *Montreal* v. *Montreal St. Ry.* [1912] A.C. 333, 342; see also text accompanying note 75, below.

13 *Re Regulation and Control of Radio Communication in Can.* [1932] A.C. 304, 315.

14 *CPR* v. *A.-G. B.C.* (Empress Hotel) [1950] A.C. 122, 142.

15 *A.-G. Ont.* v. *Winner* [1954] A.C. 541, 580; and see McNairn (1969) 47 Can. Bar Rev. 355, 358.

16 Text accompanying note 155, below.

22.3 Transportation and communication

Section 92(10)(a) is confined to works and undertakings involved in transportation or communication. The general phrase "other works or undertakings connecting the province with any other", etc., is to be read ejusdem generis with the specific examples which precede it, and the specific examples are all modes of transportation or communication. The word "connecting" in this context is to be confined to connections by transportation or communication. Section 92(10)(a) has never been held applicable to any work or undertaking which is not of a transportation or communication character. It is well established that the regulation of business enterprises which operate in more than one province, such as insurance companies, is for the most part within provincial authority under property and civil rights in the province.[17] The argument that s. 92(10)(a) would authorize federal regulation of labour relations in a construction firm that was participating in a nation-wide federal job creation programme has been rejected on the ground that s. 92(10)(a) covers only works and undertakings involved in transportation or communication.[18]

22.4 Connection with another province

According to s. 92(10)(a), an undertaking in a province is within federal jurisdiction if it is an undertaking "connecting the province with any other or others of the provinces, or extending beyond the limits of the province". The courts have held that the connection (or extension) that is contemplated by s. 92(10)(a) is an operational connection, and not a merely physical connection. For example, a local railway[19] or pipeline[20] does not come within federal jurisdiction just because it is physically connected to an interprovincial railway or pipeline. The local undertaking will remain within provincial jurisdiction despite the physical connection and despite regular cooperation between the two undertakings to facilitate through traffic. An undertaking will come within s. 92(10)(a) only if (1) the undertaking's own business operations extend beyond the provincial border, or (2) the undertaking has a close operational relationship[21] with an interprovincial undertaking.

---

17 *Can. Indemnity Co.* v. *A.G.B.C.* [1977] 2 S.C.R. 504.

18 *YMHA Jewish Community Centre* v. *Brown* [1989] 1 S.C.R. 1532, 1552. Accord, *CPR* v. *A.G.B.C.* (Empress Hotel) [1950] A.C. 122, 142 (obiter dictum); *Re National Energy Bd. Act* [1988] 2 F.C. 196, 220 (C.A.) (contractual arrangements to purchase gas from another province not within s. 92(10)(a)); *Conklin & Garrett* v. *Ont.* (1989) 70 O.R. (2d) 713 (Div. Ct.) (midway rides that are moved around North America to fairs and exhibitions not within s. 92(10)(a)); McNairn (1969), note 1, above.

19 Note 3, above.

20 *Re National Energy Bd. Act* [1988] 2 F.C. 196 (C.A.).

21 The nature of the relationship is described later in this chapter under heading 22.7, "Related undertakings", below.

In *Alberta Government Telephones* v. *CRTC* (1989),[22] the question arose whether Alberta Government Telephones (AGT) was within the regulatory jurisdiction of the federal or provincial government. AGT was an Alberta Crown corporation that operated a telephone system in Alberta. The AGT system connected at the four borders of the province with the telephone companies of British Columbia, Saskatchewan, the Northwest Territories and Montana. The AGT system was confined to the province of Alberta, and could carry telephone messages only within the province. AGT's subscribers could of course make calls to points outside Alberta and receive calls from outside Alberta, but this service was available only through the cooperation of extraprovincial telephone companies, who carried the messages through their own territories. Despite the intraprovincial scope of the AGT system, the Supreme Court of Canada held that AGT was an interprovincial undertaking. The Court said that "the facts demonstrate much more than mere physical interconnection of AGT's system at provincial borders."[23] The facts referred to were the bilateral agreements that AGT had entered into with the four neighbouring carriers, and AGT's membership of Telecom Canada, which was an unincorporated association of the major Canadian telephone companies to form a national telecommunications network. It seems to have been the scope and complexity of these bilateral and multilateral arrangements, enabling AGT to provide interprovincial and international service to its Alberta subscribers, that led the Court to characterize AGT as an interprovincial undertaking.[24]

The result in *AGT* probably owes a good deal to the unique character of telecommunication, which permits instantaneous two-way communication between people in different provinces and different countries. In other contexts, cooperative arrangements between an independently-managed local undertaking and extraprovincial undertakings would not suffice to transform the local undertaking into an interprovincial undertaking. We have already noticed the railway and pipeline cases, which have held that cooperative arrangements with a connecting interprovincial undertaking were insufficient to transform an independently-managed local undertaking into an interprovincial undertaking.[25] The

22 [1989] 2 S.C.R. 225. The majority opinion was written by Dickson C.J., with whom four others agreed. Wilson J. dissented on an issue of Crown immunity, but she agreed with Dickson C.J. on the constitutional issue. I disclose that I was one of the counsel on the losing side.

23 *Id.*, 262.

24 It is not easy to capture exactly what moved the Court to classify AGT as interprovincial: see Hogg, Comment (1990) 35 McGill L.J. 480. In *UTU* v. *Central Western Ry.* [1990] 3 S.C.R. 1112, 1135, Dickson C.J. for the Court said:

> The linchpin in the *A.G.T.* v. *CRTC* decision was this court's finding that A.G.T., by virtue of its role in Telecom Canada and its bilateral contracts with other telephone companies, was able to provide its clients with an interprovincial and, indeed, international telecommunications service.

25 Notes 19, 20, above.

freight-forwarding cases[26] are similar. A freight forwarder, which took delivery of goods in one province, and made all the arrangements necessary to ship the goods to another province by railway, has been held to be a local undertaking. The only interprovincial undertaking was the railway which carried the goods outside the province. The freight forwarder, whose operations took place in a single province, did not become an interprovincial undertaking by virtue of being a shipper on an interprovincial railway.[27]

22.5 Undivided jurisdiction

What is the appropriate classification of a business or group of associated businesses which is engaged in intraprovincial transportation or communication as well as interprovincial (or international) transportation or communication? Does one sever the intraprovincial part from the interprovincial part, and divide legislative jurisdiction accordingly? Or does one look to the dominant characteristic of the business and allocate legislative jurisdiction over the entire business according to whether the dominant characteristic is intraprovincial or interprovincial? We shall see that neither of these approaches has been adopted by the courts; instead, they have held that a business which is engaged in a significant amount of continuous and regular interprovincial transportation or communication is wholly within federal jurisdiction.

The courts early rejected the idea of dividing legislative jurisdiction over a single undertaking. In *Toronto* v. *Bell Telephone Co.* (1905),[28] it was held that the Bell Telephone Company was an interprovincial undertaking within s. 92(10)(a). The Privy Council rejected the argument that the company's long-distance business and its local business should be separated for the purpose of allocating legislative jurisdiction. Their lordships held that the company carried on "one single undertaking", and that it fell within s. 92(10)(a). Nor did their lordships embark on an inquiry as to which aspect of the company's undertaking was dominant: the local or the long-distance. In fact, at the time of the litigation the company had not actually established any connections outside Ontario, and so the interprovincial connection, far from being the dominant feature of the business, was no more than a "paper connection".[29] But their lordships held that the mere fact that the company's objects "contemplate extension beyond the limits of one province"[30] sufficed to stamp the entire undertaking with an interprovincial character.

---

26 The leading case is *Re Cannet Freight Cartage* [1976] 1 F.C. 174 (C.A.).

27 The pipeline and freight forwarding decisions (which were decided below the level of the Supreme Court of Canada) were approved in *UTU* v. *Central Western Ry.* [1990] 3 S.C.R. 1112, 1145-1147.

28 [1905] A.C. 52.

29 *Id.*, 58.

30 *Id.*, 57.

The same resistance to dual jurisdiction over transportation and communication undertakings is evident in *A.-G. Ont.* v. *Winner* (1954).[31] The question in that case was whether the province of New Brunswick had regulatory authority over a bus line which operated from the United States, through New Brunswick, and into Nova Scotia. The bus line picked up and put down passengers at various points within New Brunswick; and the provincial highway board, purporting to act under statutory authority, sought to regulate (in fact, to prohibit) this part of the bus line's business. The Supreme Court of Canada held that the province could not regulate an interprovincial or international journey, even if it began or ended in New Brunswick, but that the province could regulate the journeys which began and ended in New Brunswick without crossing a provincial border. The Privy Council reversed this holding, denying the province even the regulatory authority over the local journeys. The dual legislative authority contemplated by the Supreme Court would be acceptable only "if there were evidence that Mr. Winner was engaged in two enterprises; one within the Province and the other of a connecting character".[32] As it was, however, the same buses carried both the local and the long-distance passengers: the undertaking was "in fact one and indivisible".[33] Their lordships therefore relied on the *Bell Telephone* case to hold that the entire undertaking was within federal jurisdiction.[34]

The *Bell Telephone* and *Winner* cases established an important rule, which has been consistently reaffirmed in later cases, that a transportation or communication undertaking is subject to the regulation of only one level of government. Once an undertaking is classified as interprovincial, all of its services, intraprovincial as well as interprovincial, are subject to federal jurisdiction.[35] And, by the same token, once an undertaking is classified as local, all of its services, including any casual or irregular interprovincial services,[36] are subject to provincial regulation. In this way, the courts have avoided the complications of divided regulation of a single undertaking. However, the one-undertaking-one-regulator rule loads all the freight on the initial question of classification (or characterization): everything turns on whether the undertaking is interprovincial or local. As Dickson C.J. commented in the *AGT* case, the question of jurisdiction is "an all or nothing affair".[37]

---

31 [1954] A.C. 541.

32 *Id.*, 580.

33 *Id.*, 581.

34 The sequel to the *Winner* case was a scheme of inter-delegation under which the federal Parliament delegated its authority over interprovincial road transport back to the provinces: see ch. 14, Delegation, under heading 14.4(b), "Anticipatory incorporation by reference", above.

35 *The Queen (Ont.)* v. *Bd. of Transport Commrs.* [1968] S.C.R. 118 (commuter service on interprovincial railway line); *Sask. Power Corp.* v. *Trans Can. Pipelines* [1979] 1 S.C.R. 297 (local gas delivery in interprovincial pipeline); *Re Ottawa-Carleton Regional Transit Commn.* (1983) 44 O.R. (2d) 560 (C.A.) (labour relations in municipal transit system).

36 If the interprovincial services were continuous and regular, the undertaking would be classified as interprovincial: see the next section of this chapter.

37 [1989] 2 S.C.R. 225, 257.

22.6 Continuous and regular service

In *Winner*, as in *Bell Telephone*, their lordships did not inquire into the volume in dollars or passenger miles of Winner's local New Brunswick business, or make any attempt to compare it with the interprovincial and international business. In later cases, where this kind of information has been available, the courts have not shrunk from the implication of *Winner*, and especially *Bell Telephone*, that an interprovincial connection need not be the major part of the undertaking's activity in order to bring the undertaking within s. 92(10)(a). So long as the interprovincial services are a "continuous and regular" part of the undertaking's operations, the undertaking will be classified as interprovincial.

A good example of the "continuous and regular" rule is *Re Ottawa-Carleton Regional Transit Commission* (1983).[38] In that case, a municipal transit system serving the Ottawa area in Ontario operated some bus routes between Ottawa and Hull in Quebec. The bus routes to and from Quebec accounted for less than one per cent of the total distance travelled by the system's vehicles, and they carried only about three per cent of the system's passengers. This interprovincial service, although small in relation to the local service, was regularly scheduled, and the Ontario Court of Appeal held that it was "continuous and regular". Therefore, the Court concluded that the transit system was an interprovincial undertaking, which meant that its labour relations (among other things) came within federal jurisdiction.

In the *Ottawa-Carleton* case, the interprovincial service was part of the transit system's regularly scheduled bus service. This supported the finding that the interprovincial service was "continuous and regular". In the trucking business, there is typically no published schedule or other predetermined timetable: hauls are made as and when customers call for them. Even in this situation, Ontario courts have been willing to find that a small proportion of interprovincial business satisfied the "continuous and regular" rule. In *Re Tank Truck Transport* (1960),[39] it was held that a trucking company came within s. 92(10)(a), although 94 per cent of its trips were confined to the province and only six per cent were to points outside the province. McLennan J. of the Ontario High Court, whose decision was affirmed by the Court of Appeal, held that the interprovincial connections were "continuous and regular". In that case, there were interprovincial hauls to be made nearly every day. *Tank Truck* was followed in the *Liquid Cargo* case (1965),[40] where another trucking business was held to be within s. 92(10)(a), although its interprovincial business comprised only 1.6 per cent of its trips and ten per cent of its mileage. Haines J. of the Ontario High Court held that the

38 (1983) 44 O.R. (2d) 560 (C.A.).
39 [1960] O.R. 497 (H.C.); affd. without written reasons [1963] 1 O.R. 272 (C.A.).
40 *R.* v. *Cooksville Magistrate's Court; ex parte Liquid Cargo Lines* [1965] 1 O.R. 84 (H.C.).

''continuous and regular'' test was satisfied, despite the fact that as much as two to three weeks could go by between interprovincial hauls.[41]

If the continuous and regular standard is not met, and the interprovincial service is held to be merely casual, then the undertaking will be classified as local (intraprovincial), which will place its activity within provincial regulatory jurisdiction. For example, in *Agence Maritime* v. *Canada Labour Relations Board* (1969),[42] vessels plying coastal ports within Quebec made three trips outside the province over a period of two years. The shipping company was held to be within provincial labour relations jurisdiction.[43]

There is one qualification which must be made to the rule that ''continuous and regular'' interprovincial service constitutes an interprovincial connection within the meaning of s. 92(10)(a). The rule will not apply to a carrier who artificially organizes its business so as to acquire an interprovincial connection, for example, by unnecessarily detouring across a provincial border or by unnecessarily locating a terminal just across a border. Such a ''subterfuge'' or ''camouflage'' will be disregarded by the courts in determining whether or not the undertaking is really interprovincial. As the Privy Council said in *Winner*: ''The question is whether in truth and in fact there is an internal activity prolonged over the border in order to enable the owner to evade provincial jurisdiction or whether in pith and substance it is interprovincial''.[44] In effect this is the colourability doctrine[45] applied to interprovincial undertakings.

22.7 Related undertakings

(a) Common ownership

The decisions in *Bell Telephone*, *Winner*, *Ottawa-Carleton*, *Tank Truck* and *Liquid Cargo* were each premised on the finding that the company (or individual) was engaged in one indivisible undertaking. But a company may engage in more than one undertaking, in which case that company's operations may become subject to dual legislative authority. The fact that various business operations are carried on by a single proprietor does not foreclose inquiry as to whether or not those operations consist of more than one undertaking for constitutional purposes. It is the degree to which the operations are integrated in a functional or business sense that will determine whether they constitute one undertaking or not.

41 See also *Re Pacific Produce Delivery and Warehouses* (1974) 44 D.L.R. (3d) 130 (C.A.); *Re A.-G. Que. and Baillargeon* (1978) 97 D.L.R. (3d) 447 (C.A.).

42 [1969] S.C.R. 851.

43 Cf. *Construction Montcalm* v. *Minimum Wage Comm.* [1979] 1 S.C.R. 754 (construction company with occasional work on airport; held, within provincial jurisdiction).

44 [1954] A.C. 541, 582.

45 See ch. 15, Judicial Review on Federal Grounds, under heading 15.5(f), ''Colourability'', above.

For example, in the *Empress Hotel* case (1950),[46] the Privy Council held that the Empress Hotel in Victoria, although owned by the Canadian Pacific Railway Company, was a separate undertaking from the company's interprovincial railway. It followed that employment in the hotel was regulated by provincial law, while employment on the railway was regulated by federal law. In reaching this conclusion, their lordships examined the business relationship between the hotel and the railway. If the hotel had catered principally to railway travellers, like a station restaurant, then it would have been classified as part of the railway undertaking. But in fact the Empress Hotel carried on a general hotel business, drawing its customers from all sections of the travelling public in the same way as an independently-owned hotel. Their lordships did not doubt that the hotel and the railway complemented each other in the sense that each helped the business of the other, but they concluded that ''that does not prevent them from being separate businesses or undertakings''.[47]

The inconclusiveness of ownership works in both directions. Just as one proprietor may own and operate two separate undertakings, so two (or more) proprietors may own and operate different parts of a single undertaking. A business which, regarded by itself, is entirely local may be so closely tied into another business which is interprovincial that the two businesses will be classified as forming a single interprovincial undertaking. There are two situations in which a local undertaking will be treated for constitutional purposes as part of a separately-owned interprovincial undertaking. One (common management) is where the two undertakings are managed in common as a single enterprise. The other (dependency) is where the interprovincial undertaking is dependent on the local undertaking for the performance of an essential part of the interprovincial transportation or communication services. These two situations are the topics of the next two sections of the chapter.

(b) Common management

The first situation where a local undertaking will be held to be part of a separately-owned interprovincial undertaking is where the two undertakings are actually operated in common as a single enterprise. That was the case in *Luscar Collieries* v. *McDonald* (1927),[48] where a short railway line located within the province of Alberta was held to be part of the interprovincial undertaking of the Canadian Northern Railway. The short line was owned by a colliery, which had built the line in order to be able to move coal onto the interprovincial railway to which the short line was connected (via another branch). Under a formal management agreement, the short line was operated by CNR. Although the Privy Council's reasons for judgment are ambiguous, the case was later explained by

---

46 *CPR* v. *A.-G. B.C.* (Empress Hotel) [1950] A.C. 122.

47 *Id.*, 144.

48 [1927] A.C. 925.

the Supreme Court of Canada as turning on the common management by CNR of both the local and the interprovincial line.[49] Later cases have made clear that a mere physical connection, even combined with regular cooperatively-organized through traffic, will not make a local railway part of an interprovincial railway.[50]

In the *GO-Train* case (1968),[51] the Government of Ontario established the GO-Train commuter rail service, located entirely within the province, to serve the city of Toronto. No new railway track was built. The GO-Train trains made use of a short stretch of the Canadian National Railway's interprovincial network of rail. The Supreme Court of Canada held that the use of the interprovincial railway line made the commuter service part of the interprovincial undertaking. All of the services provided on the interprovincial line came within the same federal jurisdiction. This decision is not exactly a case of common management, because, unlike the *Luscar Collieries* case, the commuter service was not managed by CNR.[52] However, it is close to common management, because of the constraints imposed on the commuter service by CNR's control of the CNR tracks. The Court cited *Luscar Collieries*, and treated it as on all fours.

(c) Dependency

The second situation where a local undertaking will be held to be part of a separately-owned interprovincial undertaking is where the interprovincial undertaking is dependent on the local undertaking for the performance of an essential part of the interprovincial transportation or communication services.[53] The leading example of this situation is the *Stevedores Reference* (1955).[54] The issue in the case was whether employment in a stevedoring company came within federal or provincial jurisdiction. The company furnished stevedoring services (the loading and unloading of ships) to several shipping companies in Canadian ports. It was common ground that the shipping companies were within federal jurisdiction under s. 92(10)(a), or possibly s. 91(10) (''navigation and shipping''). But the stevedoring company was independent of the shipping companies, and its operations in each port were entirely local. Nevertheless, the Supreme Court of Canada, by a majority of eight to one, held that the stevedores came within federal jurisdiction. The Court held that the stevedoring operations were ''part and par-

49 *B.C. Elec. Ry. Co.* v. *CNR* [1932] S.C.R. 161, 169; *UTU* v. *Central Western Ry.* [1990] 3 S.C.R. 1112. 1133.

50 *Ibid.* Also, *Montreal* v. *Montreal St. Ry.* [1912] A.C. 333. Cf. *Kootenay and Elk Ry.* v. *CPR* [1974] S.C.R. 955, 980, 982 (obiter dicta implying that something less than common management would suffice), but note discussion of *Kootenay and Elk* and affirmation of common management requirement in *UTU* case, previous note, at 1133-1135.

51 *The Queen Ont.* v. *Bd. of Transport Commrs.* [1968] S.C.R. 118.

52 Fraser, note 1, above, 605 regards the case as wrongly decided.

53 *UTU* v. *Central Western Ry.* [1990] 3 S.C.R. 1112, 1137.

54 *Re Industrial Relations and Disputes Investigation Act* [1955] S.C.R. 529.

cel'' of a shipping undertaking,[55] and the shipping undertaking was ''entirely dependent'' on the stevedoring activity.[56]

Another example of the dependency rule is provided by the *Letter Carriers* case (1973).[57] In that case, a private company delivered and collected mail under contract with the Post Office. The postal work comprised most of the company's business. The Supreme Court of Canada held that the company's employees came within federal jurisdiction. Ritchie J. for the Court held that the work of the employees was ''essential to the function of the postal service'', and ''an integral part of the effective operation of the Post Office''.[58]

The relationship of dependency that will bring a local undertaking into federal jurisdiction must be a permanent, or at least ongoing, relationship. A casual, exceptional or temporary relationship will not suffice. Otherwise, ''the Constitution could not be applied with any degree of continuity and regularity''.[59] For example, employees of a construction company that had been engaged by Canadian National Railway to replace bridges on the interprovincial railway line were certainly performing a function that was essential to the operation of the interprovincial railway. But the company's relationship with CNR was temporary in that it was limited to the particular construction projects contracted for. The relationship lacked the ongoing character that would have constitutional significance, and the employees were accordingly within provincial labour relations jurisdiction.[60] A more permanent relationship for the purpose of maintenance or repair would have brought the employees into the federal fold as an essential part of the interprovincial undertaking.[61]

The relationship of dependency that will bring a local undertaking into federal jurisdiction is the dependency of the interprovincial undertaking on the local undertaking, not the other way around.[62] A local railway that serves grain elevators is dependent upon its connection with an interprovincial railway that will carry the grain to port.[63] A local pipeline that supplies a factory with natural gas is dependent upon its connection with an interprovincial pipeline for all of its

---

55 *Id.*, 537.

56 *Id.*, 534.

57 *Letter Carriers' Union of Can.* v. *Can. Union of Postal Workers* [1975] 1 S.C.R. 178.

58 *Id.* 183, 186. See also *Northern Telecom Can.* v. *Communications Workers of Can.* [1983] 1 S.C.R. 733 (telephone installation ''an integral element'' of the telephone undertaking); *Bernshine Mobile Maintenance* v. *CLRB* [1986] 1 F.C. 422 (C.A.) (truck washing essential to interprovincial trucking undertaking).

59 *Northern Telecom Can.* v. *Communications Workers (No. 1)* [1980] 1 S.C.R. 115, 132 (obiter dictum); cf. *Construction Montcalm* v. *Minimum Wage Commn.* [1979] 1 S.C.R. 754 (employees of construction firm building runway at airport not within federal authority over aeronautics).

60 *Re Can. Labour Code* [1987] 2 F.C. 30 (C.A.).

61 E.g., *Bernshine Mobile Maintenance* v. *CLRB* [1986] 1 F.C. 422 (C.A.) (company that washed trucks held to be essential part of interprovincial undertaking).

62 Fraser, note 1, above, 605.

63 *UTU* v. *Central Western Ry.* [1990] 3 S.C.R. 1112.

gas.[64] And a freight forwarder that collects goods in Toronto for shipment to the West is dependent upon its connection with an interprovincial railway to carry the goods to their destinations.[65] In each of these cases, the interprovincial undertaking could function effectively without the local undertaking. It was the local undertaking that depended upon the interprovincial undertaking. That relationship of dependency is constitutionally irrelevant. It does not transform the railway, the pipeline and the freight forwarder into parts of interprovincial undertakings. They remain as local undertakings within provincial jurisdiction, as the footnoted cases have decided.

The same cases establish that a connection between a local undertaking and an interprovincial undertaking, combined with a mutually beneficial commercial relationship, is not enough to make the local undertaking a part of the interprovincial undertaking.[66] The only[67] kinds of commercial relationships that will produce this result are (1) where the local undertaking is managed in common with the interprovincial undertaking (the topic of the previous section of this chapter), or (2) where the local undertaking performs a function that is essential to the delivery by the interprovincial undertaking of the interprovincial services (the topic of this section of the chapter).[68]

22.8 Works for the general advantage of Canada

Section 92(10)(c), read with s. 91(29), gives the federal Parliament the power to make laws in relation to:

> (c) Such works as, although wholly situate within the province, are before or after their execution declared by the Parliament of Canada to be for the general advantage of Canada or for the advantage of two or more of the provinces.

---

64 *Re National Energy Bd. Act* [1988] 2 F.C. 196 (C.A.).

65 *Re Cannet Freight Cartage* [1976] 1 F.C. 174 (C.A.).

66 *UTU* v. *Central Western Ry.* [1990] 3 S.C.R. 1112, 1147.

67 The cable television cases, namely, *Capital Cities*, note 184, below, and *Dionne*, note 188, below, do not quite fit the analysis. The cable systems, although located within a province, were held to be within federal jurisdiction. The cable systems were managed independently of the broadcasters (although with respect to broadcast signals the companies could exercise very little management discretion — they were "no more than a conduit for signals from the telecast"). The broadcasters were not dependent upon the cable systems for distribution of the signals, because the signals could be received off the air (although the cable systems provided a better quality of distribution). Critical to the decisions was the avoidance of the awkward dual regulatory jurisdiction that would result if cable reception was provincial and off-air reception was federal.

68 This issue of the correct constitutional classification of an undertaking arises most frequently in a labour relations context, where it is necessary to determine which labour board, federal or provincial, has jurisdiction: see ch. 21, Property and Civil Rights, under heading 21.8, "Labour relations", above.

This ''declaratory power'' enables the federal Parliament to assume jurisdiction over a local work by declaring the work to be ''for the general advantage of Canada''.[69] For example, an intraprovincial railway would be within provincial jurisdiction as a local work or undertaking (s. 92(10)),[70] but if the federal Parliament declared the railway to be a work for the general advantage of Canada, then the railway would be withdrawn from provincial jurisdiction by virtue of s. 92(10)(c) and brought into federal jurisdiction by virtue of s. 91(29).[71] If the declaration were repealed by the federal Parliament, then the railway would revert to provincial jurisdiction.[72]

The declaratory power has been exercised no less than 472 times, the majority of which have been in respect of local railways. Other instances include tramways, canals, bridges, dams, tunnels, harbours, wharves, telegraphs, telephones, mines, mills, grain elevators, hotels, restaurants, theatres, oil refineries and factories of various kinds.[73] Not all of these declarations relate to works involved in transportation or communication, and it is clear that the power is not so limited.[74]

The power under s. 92(10)(c) is confined to ''works'', which contrasts with s. 92(10)(a)'s reference to ''works and undertakings''. We have already noticed that there are dicta which distinguish between a ''work'' and an ''undertaking'', on the basis that a work is a tangible thing while an undertaking is an intangible ''arrangement'' or ''organization'' or ''enterprise''.[75] However, the drafters of federal declarations have not always observed such niceties and there are many federal statutes which contain declarations in respect of ''works and undertakings'' or even ''undertakings'' alone.[76] No declaration has ever been held to be invalid on the ground that it purported to apply to an ''undertaking'', and one

69 Lajoie, *Le pouvoir déclaratoire du Parlement* (1969) is a monograph on the declaratory power. See also MacDonald, Annotation [1943] 1 D.L.R. 1 (also, somewhat altered, in Dominion Law Annotations, vol. 3, 206); Schwartz, ''Fiat by Declaration'' (1960) 2 Osgoode Hall L.J. 1; Hanssen, ''The Federal Declaratory Power'' (1968) 3 Man. L.J. 87; Laskin, *Canadian Constitutional Law* (5th ed., 1986 by Finkelstein), 627-631; and for further literature see Lajoie, above, 153 (bibliography).

70 Note 3, above.

71 *B.C.* v.*Can.* [1994] 2 S.C.R. 41, 116. The declaration will not affect the ownership of the declared work, just legislative jurisdiction over it; although that jurisdiction might authorize a subsequent expropriation by federal statute: see ch. 28, Public Property, under the heading 28.5, ''Expropriation'', below.

72 *UTU* v. *Central Western Ry.* [1990] 3 S.C.R. 1112.

73 Lajoie, note 69, above, 54 and appendix which lists 470 declarations; Hanssen, note 69, above, has a similar appendix although it is less complete. Since Lajoie compiled her list, two more declarations have been made: note 91, below.

74 *Jorgenson* v. *A.-G. Can.* [1971] S.C.R. 725 (grain elevators); *Chamney* v. *The Queen* [1975] 2 S.C.R. 151 (grain elevators); *Ont. Hydro* v. *Ont.* [1993] 3 S.C.R. 327 (electrical generating stations); Laskin, note 69, above, 627.

75 Note 12, above.

76 Hanssen, note 69, above, (appendix) lists many examples; see also McNairn (1969) 47 Can. Bar Rev. 355, 359.

such declaration has been expressly upheld.[77] Lajoie explains the validity of such declarations by suggesting that a declaration may be applied to undertakings linked with works, but not to undertakings which exist without the aid of works, for example, a society of accountants or lawyers or a social service agency.[78]

The distinction between works and undertakings is further blurred by the fact that the effect of a declaration over a work "must surely be to bring within federal authority not only the physical shell of the activity but also the integrated activity carried on therein; in other words, the declaration operates on the work in its functional character".[79] That this is correct is demonstrated by cases in which the declaration has been followed by an assertion of regulatory jurisdiction over the activity related to the work. Perhaps the clearest examples are the declarations that grain elevators and various kinds of mills and warehouses are works for the general advantage of Canada. The purpose of these declarations was to assume the regulatory jurisdiction over the grain trade which had been denied to the federal Parliament by *The King* v. *Eastern Terminal Elevator Co.* (1925).[80] It has been held that these declarations are effective to authorize federal regulation of the delivery, receipt, storage and processing of the grain, that is to say, the activities created on in or about the "works".[81]

In *Ontario Hydro* v. *Ontario* (1993),[82] the Supreme Court of Canada held that a declaration over a work conferred on the federal Parliament jurisdiction over labour relations in the declared work. Ontario Hydro was a provincially-owned and provincially-regulated corporation that produced and distributed electricity. The corporation produced the electricity at 81 generating stations, of which five were operated by nuclear power. The five nuclear plants had been declared to be works for the general advantage of Canada by a provision in the federal Atomic Energy Act. The Supreme Court of Canada, by a majority, held that the declaration conferred on Parliament power over "the work as a going concern", which involved "control over its operation and management".[83] That included "power to regulate the labour relations between management and labour engaged

---

77 *Que. Ry. Light and Power Co.* v. *Beauport* [1945] S.C.R. 16.

78 Lajoie, note 69, above, 61. She also suggests, though less confidently, that the declaratory power would not be available with respect to undertakings in which the physical works are of secondary importance to the provision of services, for example, universities or hospitals. See also Laskin, note 69, above, 628, who says that the declaratory power is not available with respect to "undertakings existing without works".

79 Laskin, note 69, above, 629; Hanssen, note 69, above, 93-95.

80 [1925] S.C.R. 434; see ch. 20, Trade and Commerce, under heading 20.2(a), "In the Privy Council", above.

81 *Jorgenson v. A.-G. Can.* [1971] S.C.R. 725; *Chamney v. The Queen*, [1975] 2 S.C.R. 151.

82 [1993] 3 S.C.R. 327. La Forest J., with L'Heureux-Dubé and Gonthier JJ., wrote the majority opinion. Lamer C.J. wrote a separate concurring opinion. Iacobucci J., with Sopinka and Cory JJ., wrote a dissenting opinion, taking the view that legislative jurisdiction over the declared work did not extend to labour relations.

83 *Id.*, 367.

in operating the work''.[84] It followed that, although the rest of Hydro's workforce was governed by provincial labour law, the workers in the nuclear plants were governed by federal labour law.

The language of s. 92(10)(c) makes clear that a declaration may be made not only in respect of existing works, but also in respect of works to be constructed in the future. Until recently there was some doubt as to how specific a declaration had to be, especially if it was to apply to works not in existence at the time of the declaration. Obviously, any declaration had to sufficiently identify the works to which it applied, but did identification require that each work be individually specified by name or other description? In *Jorgensen* v. *A.-G. Can.* (1971),[85] the Supreme Court of Canada answered no, holding that a declaration which referred to a class of works was valid. At issue were the declarations in the Canada Grain Act and the Canada Wheat Board Act. The first of these applied to ''all [grain] elevators in Canada heretofore or hereafter constructed''; the second applied to ''all flour mills, feed mills, feed warehouses and seed cleaning mills, whether heretofore constructed or hereafter to be constructed''. Both these sweeping ''class'' declarations were upheld.

While the definition of a work is subject to judicial interpretation, the courts have made no attempt to give content to the words ''for the general advantage of Canada''. The courts have treated this phrase as imposing a requirement of form rather than substance. No work is caught by s. 92(10)(c) by implication. There must be an explicit declaration by Parliament that the work is for the general advantage of Canada.[86] Once an explicit declaration has been made, it is conclusive: the question whether a particular work really is for the general advantage of Canada has been seen as an issue of policy for the Parliament, not subject to judicial review.[87]

In the earlier chapter on Federalism, I commented that the federal Parliament's power under s. 92(10)(c) is in conflict with classical principles of federalism because it enables the federal Parliament, by its own unilateral act, to increase its own powers and diminish those of the provinces.[88] The Constitutions of the United States and Australia confer no comparable power on their federal (or state) legislative bodies. The Canadian power has been the subject of provincial objection,[89] and it has been suggested that it should be amended to require the consent of the province in which the work is situated, or the consent of a majority of the provinces.[90] It appears, however, that the federal government and Parliament

84 *Id.*, 368.

85 [1971] S.C.R. 725; also *Chamney* v. *The Queen* [1972] 2 S.C.R. 151. See also *Ont. Hydro* v. *Ont.* [1993] 3 S.C.R. 327 (upholding a class declaration in the Atomic Energy Control Act).

86 *YMHA Jewish Community Centre* v. *Brown* [1989] 1 S.C.R. 1532, 1552.

87 Lajoie, note 69, above, 69-70; Laskin, note 69, above, 628; Hanssen, note 69, above, 102-105.

88 Chapter 5, Federalism, under heading 5.3(i), ''Declaratory power'', above.

89 Lajoie, note 69, above, 70-72.

90 *Id.*, 118. The unsuccessful Charlottetown Accord of 1992 (see ch. 4, Amendment, under heading 4.1(c), ''The failure to accommodate Quebec'', above) proposed the amendment of s. 92(10)(*c*) to require the consent of the province in which the work was situated.

are sensitive to the anomalous character of the power and are now inclined to use the power only sparingly. It has been used very rarely in recent times.[91]

22.9 Transportation by land

Legislative jurisdiction over transportation by land depends upon the principles explained in the previous sections of this chapter. Jurisdiction over trains,[92] buses,[93] trucks,[94] taxis, limousines,[95] pipelines,[96] and electricity transmission lines[97] depends primarily on whether they are operated as part of an interprovincial (or international) undertaking, in which case jurisdiction is federal under s. 92(10)(a), or whether they are operated as part of an intraprovincial undertaking, in which case jurisdiction is provincial under s. 92(10).[98] Some intraprovincial undertakings, including many local railways, have been brought under federal jurisdiction by exercise of the declaratory power under s. 92(10)(c).

22.10 Transportation by water

Jurisdiction over transportation by water depends upon some of the same principles as those applicable to transportation by land. Section 92(10)(a) ex-

---

91 According to my research, the last two declarations are Cape Breton Development Corporation Act, S.C. 1967-68, c. 6, s. 35 and Teleglobe Canada Reorganization and Divestiture Act, S.C. 1987, c. 12, s. 9. Of course, old declarations are re-enacted when a statute that includes a declaration is replaced by a new statute, e.g., National Transportation Act, 1987, S.C. 1987, c. 34, ss. 158(4), 174(6).

92 *Montreal* v. *Montreal St. Ry.* [1912] A.C. 333; *Luscar Collieries* v. *McDonald* [1972] A.C. 925; *B.C. Elec. Ry.* v. *C.N.R.* [1932] S.C.R. 161; *The Queen (Ont.)* v. *Bd. of Transport Commrs.* [1968] S.C.R. 118; *Re Can. Labour Code* [1987] 2 F.C. 30 (C.A.); *UTU* v. *Central Western Ry.* [1990] 3 S.C.R. 1112. For discussion of the development of railways in Canada, and the variety of consitutional provisions which have been called in aid, see McNairn (1969) 47 Can. Bar Rev. 355, esp. 365-373; and see also note 8, above.

93 *A.-G. Ont.* v. *Winner* [1954] A.C. 541; *Re Ottawa-Carleton Regional Transit Comm.* (1983) 44 O.R. (2d) 560 (C.A.); *Ferguson Bus Lines* v. *ATU* [1990] 2 F.C. 586 (C.A.).

94 *Re Tank Truck Transport* [1960] O.R. 497 (H.C.); affd. [1963] 1 O.R. 272 (C.A.); *R.* v. *Cooksville Magistrate's Court; ex parte Liquid Cargo Lines* [1965] 1 O.R. 84 (H.C.); *R.* v. *Man. Lab Bd.; ex parte Invictus* (1968) 65 D.L.R. (2d) 517 (Man. Q.B.); *Re A.-G. Que. and Baillargeon* (1987) 97 D.L.R. (3d) 447 (Que. C.A.); *Bernshine Mobile Maintenance* v. *CLRB* [1986] 1 F.C. 422 (C.A.).

95 *Re Colonial Coach Lines* [1967] 2 O.R. 25 (H.C.); *Re Windsor Airline Limousine Service* (1980) 30 O.R. (2d) 732 (Div. Ct.).

96 *Campbell-Bennett* v. *Comstock Midwestern* [1954] S.C.R. 207; *Sask. Power Corp.* v. *Trans Can. Pipelines* [1979] 1 S.C.R. 297; *Re National Energy Bd. Act* [1988] 2 F.C. 196 (C.A.); *Re Bypass Pipelines* (1988) 64 O.R. (2d) 293 (C.A.).

97 *Fulton* v. *Energy Resources Conservation Bd.* [1981] 1 S.C.R. 153; *Re Town of Summerside and Maritime Electric Co. (No. 2)* (1983) 3 D.L.R. (4th) 577 (P.E.I. S.C. in banco).

98 An undertaking may still be bound by the valid laws of the level of government which lacks primary jurisdiction over the undertaking under the incidental effect doctrine, or the double aspect doctrine, but subject to the interjurisdictional immunity doctrine: see ch. 15, Judicial Review on Federal Grounds, above.

pressly refers to "lines of steam or other ships" and to "canals". In addition, however, s. 91(10) confers on the federal Parliament jurisdiction over "navigation and shipping". The unqualified language of s. 91(10) does not authorize Parliament to regulate labour relations in undertakings engaged in intraprovincial shipping. In *Agence Maritime* v. *Canada Labour Relations Board* (1969),[99] it was held that labour relations on ships plying the waters of the St. Lawrence River within the province of Quebec were within provincial, not federal, jurisdiction. Of course ships with a continuous and regular trade to the ports of more than one province (or more than one country) would be within federal jurisdiction.[100] Labour relations on the ships supplying and servicing the oil drilling rigs off the coast of Newfoundland have been held to be within federal jurisdiction: although each voyage began and ended in a single province (Newfoundland), the major part of the voyage was in international waters.[101] However, ferries passing briefly through American waters on journeys between ports in British Columbia have been held to be within provincial jurisdiction.[102]

The federal power over navigation and shipping in s. 91(10)[103] confers federal legislative competence over navigable waters,[104] works of navigation,[105] harbours,[106] and a far-reaching body of maritime or admiralty law, which includes laws regarding rules of navigation,[107] liability for maritime accidents,[108] liability for loss or delay of a ship's cargo,[109] marine insurance,[110] the sale, purchase and ownership of ships,[111] the construction, repair and maintenance of ships,[112] and pilotage and towage.[113]

---

99 [1969] S.C.R. 851.

100 Federal jurisdiction would flow from s. 92(10)(a). See also s. 91(13) ("ferries between a province and any British or foreign country or between two provinces"). With respect to ferries, see also note 8, above.

101 *Seafarers' International Union* v. *Crosbie Offshore Services* [1982] 2 F.C. 855 (C.A.). The Court relied on s. 91(10), but s. 92(10)(a) seems to be the applicable head of power.

102 *Singbeil* v. *Hansen* (1985) 19 D.L.R. (4th) 48 (B.C.C.A.).

103 On the scope of the power, see Laskin, *Canadian Constitutional Law* (5th ed., 1986 by Finkelstein), 631-639; McConnell, *Commentary on the British North America Act* (1977), 196-201.

104 *Re Waters and Water Powers* [1929] S.C.R. 200.

105 *Ibid.* See also s. 91(9) ("beacons, buoys, lighthouses and Sable Island").

106 *Hamilton Harbour Commrs.* v. *City of Hamilton* (1978) 21 O.R. (2d) 459 (C.A.).

107 *Whitbread* v. *Walley* [1991] 1 S.C.R. 1273.

108 *Ibid.* Federal power extends to tortious liability for "land based activities that are sufficiently connected with navigation and shipping": *Id.*, 1292, citing *ITO-International Terminal Operators* v. *Miida Electronics* [1986] 1 S.C.R. 752.

109 *Tropwood A.G.* v. *Sivaco Wire and Nail Co.* [1979] S.C.R. 157; *Aris Steamship Co.* v. *Associated Metals* [1980] 2 S.C.R. 322.

110 *Triglav* v. *Terrasses Jewellers* [1983] 1 S.C.R. 283.

111 *Antares Shipping Corp.* v. *The Ship "Capricorn"* [1980] 1 S.C.R. 553.

112 *Wire Rope Industries* v. *B.C. Marine Shipbuilders* [1981] 1 S.C.R. 363.

113 *Ibid.*

Federal power over navigation and shipping is not confined to undertakings engaged in interprovincial or international shipping: it applies to vessels engaged in local shipping, and to pleasure boats as well as commercial vessels.[114] Nor is it confined to the high seas, or even to tidal waters: it extends up navigable rivers as well. All waterways are ''part of the same navigational network'' and must be subject to the ''uniform legal regime'' of Canadian maritime law.[115] All boats share that system of waterways, and they must obey the same federal ''rules of the road'' and be subject to the same federal regime of tortious liability.[116] The legislative authority over navigation and shipping that is conferred on the federal Parliament by s. 91(10) is, therefore, much more extensive than the authority over other forms of transportation and communication, where s. 92(10)(a) is the sole source of authority. For example, the tortious liability of a company operating an interprovincial railway is governed by provincial law, while the tortious liability of those engaged in navigation and shipping is (as explained above) governed by Canadian maritime law.[117]

22.11 Transportation by air

(a) Basis of legislative jurisdiction

The subject of aeronautics[118] is not governed by the same principles as apply to other modes of transportation. It started off on a different constitutional track because the first legislation was enacted by the federal Parliament to perform Canada's obligations under an international treaty. In the *Aeronautics Reference* (1931),[119] the Privy Council held that the legislation was valid by virtue of the treaty power in s. 132 of the Constitution Act, 1867.[120] The possibility that the peace, order, and good government power might also sustain the legislation was suggested as an alternative basis of jurisdiction.[121] This suggestion became im-

114 *Whitbread* v. *Walley* [1991] 1 S.C.R. 1273. (Canadian maritime law applied to accident caused by pleasure boat making short journey on intraprovincial waterways).

115 *Id.*, 1295.

116 *Id.*, 1297. Cf. aeronautics, where the shared use of airspace and ground facilities makes it impractical to divide up legislative jurisdiction according to whether the carrier is local or not. Query to what extent provincial and municipal laws may validly affect navigation and shipping: contrast *St-Denis de Brompton* v. *Filteau* (1986) 59 D.L.R. (4th) 84 (Que. C.A.) (municipal by-law prohibiting motor boats on lake invalid for effect on navigation and shipping) with *Windermere Watersport* v. *Invermere* (1989) 59 D.L.R. (4th) 285 (B.C.C.A.) (similar by-law upheld).

117 *Id.*, 1300.

118 See generally McNairn, ''Aeronautics and the Constitution'' (1971) 49 Can. Bar Rev. 411; Paquette, ''Les compétences constitutionnelles en matière d'aeronautique'' (1979) 57 Can. Bar Rev. 281.

119 *Re Regulation and Control of Aeronautics in Can.* [1932] A.C. 54.

120 Chapter 11, Treaties, above.

121 [1932] A.C. 54, 77.

portant when the original treaty, which was a ''British Empire'' treaty to which s. 132 applied, was replaced by a new treaty, which was a ''Canadian'' treaty to which s. 132 did not apply; and it became necessary to attribute jurisdiction to some head of power other than the treaty power. In *Johannesson* v. *West St. Paul* (1952),[122] the Supreme Court of Canada held that the peace, order, and good government power gave the federal Parliament the claimed jurisdiction. This was on the basis that aeronautics was a distinct ''matter'' which satisfied the *Canada Temperance* test, that is to say, ''it goes beyond local or provincial concern or interests and must from its inherent nature be the concern of the Dominion as a whole''.[123]

Johannesson contains surprisingly little discussion of the reasons for attributing aeronautics to the peace, order and good government power. Kerwin, Kellock and Estey JJ. contented themselves with a recitation of the *Canada Temperance* test,[124] apparently regarding it as self-evident that aeronautics satisfied the test. Only Locke J. attempted to spell out some reasons, referring to the growth of the air industry, its role in the carriage of mail and in opening up the more remote parts of the country.[125] But the same points could be made about other modes of transportation, especially the railways in their hey-day, and yet it has never been suggested that the federal Parliament could assume jurisdiction over the railways under the peace, order, and good government power. On the contrary, federal jurisdiction over railways has always been placed under s. 92(10)(a), with the important result that local railways are outside federal jurisdiction.[126] It is true that railways are expressly mentioned in s. 92(10)(a), but road transportation (bus and truck) is not expressly mentioned and yet has been held to be within the same head of power by virtue of the phrase ''other works and undertakings'' in s. 92(10)(a). Why is aeronautics not caught by the same phrase? No court has ever asked or answered this question, and yet it now appears to be accepted without doubt that jurisdiction resides in the peace, order, and good government power, and that s. 92(10)(a) has no application to aeronautics.

(b) Intraprovincial aeronautics

Because jurisdiction over aeronautics has been held to depend upon its national dimension or national concern, the question whether a particular undertaking is interprovincial or merely local is probably irrelevant. There are obiter

122 [1952] 1 S.C.R. 292.

123 *A.-G. Ont.* v. *Can. Temperance Federation* [1946] A.C. 193, 205, citing the *Aeronautics Reference* as an example. In *Johannesson*, four of the five opinions cited and relied upon the *Canada Temperance* test: [1952] 1 S.C.R. 292, 308-309 per Kerwin J., 311 per Kellock J., 318 per Estey J., 328 per Locke J.; while Rinfret C.J. (at 303) thought the issue was concluded by the *Aeronautics Reference*. Peace, Order, and Good Government is the subject of ch. 17, above.

124 See previous note.

125 [1952] 1 S.C.R. 292, 326-327.

126 Note 3, above.

dicta in both the *Aeronautics Reference*[127] and *Johannesson*[128] to the effect that federal jurisdiction extends to purely intraprovincial airlines, and this has been distinctly decided by the British Columbia Court of Appeal in *Jorgenson* v. *North Vancouver Magistrates*.[129] The most plausible reason for subjecting local airlines to the same regime as the interprovincial and international airlines is the fact that both kinds of carriers share the same airspace and ground facilities, so that their operations are necessarily closely integrated.[130] Divided control over navigation and ground facilities would be impossible. It is true that divided control over economic regulation — fares and perhaps routes — would be possible, but it is most unlikely that the courts would at this late stage be willing to fragment the subject of aeronautics into navigational and economic aspects.[131] The better view is that both aspects of aeronautics come within federal jurisdiction.[132]

(c) Provincial jurisdiction

Given that federal legislative jurisdiction exists over aeronautics, there remains the question of the degree to which provincial laws are precluded. Where there are inconsistent federal laws, then provincial laws are of course rendered inoperative by the paramountcy doctrine, but the tendency of the decisions is to deny the application of provincial laws to airports and related activity even where the federal Parliament has not acted.

---

127 [1932] A.C. 54, 77.

128 [1952] 1 S.C.R. 292, 314.

129 (1959) 28 W.W.R. 265 (B.C.C.A.); see McNairn, note 118, above, 418-419; contra, Paquette, note 118, above, 291.

130 This explanation was approved, obiter, in *Whitbread* v. *Walley* [1991] 1 S.C.R. 1273, 1299; see also note 116, above.

131 McNairn, note 118, above, 427-429. Radio and television are close analogies, the argument for unified control of local and long-distance broadcasting depending on the shared use of the frequency spectrum. It has never been suggested that economic regulation should be treated any differently than technical regulation, although there is some room for argument that content regulation should be treated differently: see sec. 22.12(c), ''Content regulation'', below. Another analogy is *The Queen (Ont.)* v. *Bd. of Transport Commrs.* [1968] S.C.R. 118, in which the shared use of interprovincial trackage brought a local rail service within federal jurisdiction, including jurisdiction over fares.

132 There is, of course, room for argument as to where aeronautics ends and related local undertakings begin; for example, a company which services aircraft has been held to be within the federal power over aeronautics: *Field Aviation Co.* v. *Indust. Relations Bd. (Alta.)* [1974] 6 W.W.R. 596 (Alta. A.D.); while a company engaged in constructing airport runways was held to be a separate local undertaking: *Construction Montcalm* v. *Minimum Wage Commn.* [1979] 1 S.C.R. 754. The provision of porter service in the airport, and limousine service to and from the airport, have also been held to be local undertakings outside federal power: *Re Colonial Coach Lines* [1967] 2 O.R. 25 (H.C.); *Murray Hill Limousine Service* v. *Batson* [1965] B.R. 788 (Que. C.A.); McNairn, note 118, above, 431-438. Cf. *Stevedores Reference*, [1955] S.C.R. 529; discussed in text accompanying note 54, above.

The most extreme example is the *Johannesson* case[133] itself. At issue in the case was a municipal by-law, made under the authority of a provincial statute, which prohibited aerodromes in part of the municipality and required a licence for their establishment elsewhere. Johannesson, who owned a small airline, found a site in the municipality which was suitable for an air strip where he planned to establish a service depot for his planes. He purchased the land and brought proceedings to have the by-law declared invalid. The Supreme Court of Canada held that the by-law was invalid because of its interference with aeronautics. It should be noted that there were federal regulations providing for the licensing of a site for use as an aerodrome, and if Johannesson's site had been licensed an issue of paramountcy would have been raised. But Johannesson's site had not been licensed; Johannesson had selected the site because it appeared to him to satisfy general federal regulations with respect to aerodromes, and because it was suitable for his business. When one considers that the control of land use is ordinarily within property and civil rights in the province, and is always a question of vital local concern, it would surely have been wiser for the Court to treat the by-law as valid under the double-aspect doctrine.[134] On this basis, the by-law would override a private business decision to construct an aerodrome, at least until the appropriate federal regulatory authority had directed its construction.[135]

Johannesson was followed by the Ontario Court of Appeal in *Re Orangeville Airport* (1976),[136] in which it was held that municipal zoning by-laws could not apply to an airport. In this case, however, the airport was federally licensed and in operation, and the by-law would have had the effect of preventing the building of new hangars, the plans of which had been approved by the federal Minister of Transport. In *Re Walker and Minister of Housing* (1983),[137] the same Court invalidated height restrictions imposed by the province on land adjacent to an airport. Once again, the airport was federally licensed and in operation. The purpose of the height restrictions was to facilitate the use of the airport by larger aircraft. Both these cases were very much clearer than *Johannesson*, since it was plain that the provincial law in each case affected a vital part of the design or operation of a functioning airport.

In *Construction Montcalm* v. *Minimum Wage Commission* (1978),[138] the question arose whether a provincial minimum wage law could apply to a construction firm that was engaged in building the runways of an airport. The Supreme Court of Canada held that the provincial law was validly applicable. Beetz J. for

---

133 Note 122, above.

134 Cf. *R.* v. *Pearsall* (1977) 80 D.L.R. (3d) 285 (Sask. C.A.), upholding provincial law prohibiting use of aircraft for hunting game; *Re The Queen and Van Gool* (1987) 36 D.L.R. (4th) 481 (B.C.C.A.), upholding municipal by-law permitting use of land as private airport.

135 Weiler (1973) 23 U. Toronto L.J. 207, 324.

136 (1976) 11 O.R. (2d) 546 (C.A.).

137 (1983) 41 O.R. (2d) 9 (C.A.).

138 [1979] 1 S.C.R. 754.

the majority[139] confined the immunity from provincial law to ''an integral part of aeronautics''.[140] The location of an airport (which was the issue in *Johannesson*), its design (which was the issue in *Orangeville)*, and its operation (which was the issue in *Walker*) would each be an integral part of aeronautics from which provincial power was excluded, but the physical construction (in accordance with federal specifications) of the runways was not. Therefore, provincial law regarding minimum wages could validly apply to the construction firm.[141]

22.12 Communication by radio

(a) Basis of legislative jurisdiction

Radio broadcasting[142] (like television broadcasting)[143] takes place by means of electromagnetic waves of various frequencies which are transmitted in space. Only a limited number of frequencies are available, and regulation is therefore necessary to control the use of a scarce public resource. Because radio waves do not observe national boundaries, international agreement on the allocation of frequencies has been necessary to avoid transnational interference with radio reception. The International Radiotelegraph Convention, 1927, was a treaty which assigned frequencies among the various signatory states, one of which was Canada. In order to comply with this treaty, it was necessary for the assignment of radio frequencies in Canada to be regulated by statute. In the *Radio Reference* (1932),[144] decided just four months after the *Aeronautics Reference*,[145] the Privy Council held that the federal Parliament had the ''jurisdiction to regulate and control radio communication''. This jurisdiction existed by virtue of both the power over the peace, order, and good government of Canada (s. 91 opening words) and the power over interprovincial undertakings (s. 92(10)(a)).

---

139 Beetz J.'s opinion was agreed to by Martland, Ritchie, Pigeon, Dickson, Estey and Pratte JJ. Laskin C.J. with Spence J. dissented, holding that provincial law could not apply on an airport or on federal public property. The general issue of interjurisdictional immunity, upon which Laskin C.J. was usually in dissent, is discussed in ch. 15, Judicial Review on Federal Grounds, above.

140 [1979] 1 S.C.R. 754, 770.

141 Beetz J. (at pp. 775-776) also rejected the argument that the construction firm was itself an ''aeronautics undertaking'': its business was that of a general building contractor and its connection with aeronautics was only ''casual or temporary''. Cf. *Re Forest Industries Flying Tankers* (1980) 108 D.L.R. (3d) 686 (B.C. C.A.) (company operating aircraft solely to prevent and fight forest fires held to be an aeronautics undertaking immune from provincial human rights legislation).

142 See Mullan and Beaman, note 1, above, 69-74.

143 Exactly the same constitutional considerations apply to broadcast television as apply to radio: see sec. 22.13, ''Communication by television'', below.

144 [1932] A.C. 304.

145 Note 116, above.

The peace, order, and good government power was treated in the *Radio Reference* as authorizing laws implementing treaties. The treaty of 1927 had been entered into by Canada in its own right. Therefore, it was not a ''British Empire'' treaty, and s. 132 of the Constitution Act, 1867 did not authorize implementing legislation. Their lordships held that the peace, order, and good government power filled the gap and authorized legislation to implement ''Canadian'' treaties. This mode of reasoning was repudiated by a differently constituted Privy Council in the *Labour Conventions* case (1937).[146] But even if we disregard the existence of the treaty (as dictated by *Labour Conventions*), it is possible that the peace, order, and good government power still gives to the federal Parliament the jurisdiction over radio broadcasting.

Aeronautics[147] provides an analogy. It will be recalled that federal jurisdiction over aeronautics was first attributed to the existence of a treaty; then, after the treaty could no longer be relied upon, federal jurisdiction was attributed to the peace, order, and good government power. The attribution to peace, order, and good government was based on the view that aeronautics satisfied the *Canada Temperance* test, that is to say, it ''goes beyond local or provincial concern or interests and must from its inherent nature be the concern of the Dominion as a whole''.[148] It is clear that radio broadcasting has a similar, and perhaps stronger, claim to a national dimension or concern. The fact that radio frequencies do not respect provincial boundaries means that the limited range of frequencies cannot be assigned on a provincial basis, and the role of radio as an interprovincial and international communications link and as a force for national identity and unity also gives it an important national dimension. In *Re CFRB* (1973),[149] the Ontario Court of Appeal decided that the analogy between radio and aeronautics was compelling, and the Court held that radio broadcasting was a matter within federal jurisdiction under the *Canada Temperance* definition of peace, order, and good government. The Supreme Court of Canada refused leave to appeal.[150]

While the analogy with aeronautics has force, it will be recalled that the attribution of aeronautics to the peace, order, and good government power is something of an anomaly: federal jurisdiction over all other modes of transportation has been derived from s. 92(10)(a), the power over ''undertakings connecting the province with any other or others of the provinces, or extending beyond the limits of the province''.[151] In the case of radio, s. 92(10)(a) was suggested as an additional basis of jurisdiction in both the *Radio Reference*[152] and

146 *A.-G. Can.* v. *A.-G. Ont.* (Labour Conventions) [1937] A.C. 326. There are indications that the Supreme Court of Canada will revert to the *Radio Reference* reasoning. The subject of implementing treaties is dealt with in ch. 11, Treaties, above.

147 Section 22.11, ''Transportation by air'', above.

148 *A.-G. Ont.* v. *Can. Temperance Federation* [1946] A.C. 193, 205.

149 [1973] 3 O.R. 819 (C.A.).

150 November 13, 1973.

151 Text accompanying note 126, above.

152 [1932] A.C. 304, 315.

Re CFRB.[153] In *Capital Cities Communications* v. *CRTC* (1977),[154] the Supreme Court of Canada held that s. 92(10)(a) was the basis of jurisdiction over broadcast television — and broadcast radio would obviously be in the same constitutional situation as broadcast television. The Court made no reference at all to peace, order, and good government, an omission that is so striking that it should probably be interpreted as a disapproval of that basis of jurisdiction.

In view of the *Capital Cities* holding, it is probably safe to conclude that federal jurisdiction over radio comes from the federal power over interprovincial or international "undertakings" in s. 92(10)(a). It will be recalled that it was in the *Radio Reference* that Viscount Dunedin gave his often-quoted definition of an undertaking as "not a physical thing, but an arrangement under which . . . physical things are used".[155] But it is clear that the word "arrangement" in this context is not confined to a particular organization or enterprise, which is how the term "undertaking" in s. 92(10)(a) has usually been interpreted.[156] Viscount Dunedin seems to have been thinking of the entire field of radio broadcasting as one vast undertaking. This extraordinarily broad definition of undertaking was accepted without demur in *Re CFRB*, Kelly J.A. for the Ontario Court of Appeal asserting that the *Radio Reference* decided that "the whole of the undertaking of broadcasting" was within federal jurisdiction.[157] Laskin C.J. for the majority in the *Capital Cities* case was less specific, but he seemed to be using the word undertaking in the same broad sense.[158]

(b) Intraprovincial broadcasting

Does federal jurisdiction extend to purely intraprovincial radio broadcasting? In the *Radio Reference*,[159] the Privy Council considered this question and answered it yes. If federal jurisdiction is placed under the peace, order, and good government power, then the analogy of aeronautics[160] suggests that this must be the correct answer. If federal jurisdiction is placed under s. 92(10)(a), the correctness of the answer is less clear. It must be remembered that authority over most forms of transportation and communication — railways, bus lines, trucking lines, pipelines, and telephone systems — is divided on a territorial basis: the intraprovincial systems are within provincial jurisdiction as "local works and

153 [1973] 3 O.R. 819, 822.
154 [1978] 2 S.C.R. 141.
155 [1932] A.C. 304, 315.
156 Note 16, above.
157 [1973] 3 O.R. 819, 822; see also *Re Public Utilities Comm. and Victoria Cablevision* (1965) 51 D.L.R. (2d) 716 (B.C. C.A.).
158 [1978] 2 S.C.R. 141, 161.
159 [1932] A.C. 304, 313. In one of those distressing lapses for which the Privy Council became notorious in Canada, their lordships referred consistently to "inter-provincial" broadcasting, although in the context it is clear that they meant *intra*provincial broadcasting.
160 See sec. 22.11 (b), "Intraprovincial aeronautics", above.

undertakings'' (s. 92(10)), and only interprovincial or international systems are within federal jurisdiction under s. 92(10)(a). And yet radio is different from all of these other modes of transportation or communication in that all radio broadcasters must use the same kind of radio waves in the same frequency spectrum. The shared use of the frequency spectrum does give plausibility to the broader meaning attributed to the term ''undertaking'' in the *Radio Reference*, *CFRB* and *Capital Cities* cases.[161] The need to allocate space in the frequency spectrum in order to avoid interference suggests that the power to regulate the interprovincial broadcaster must carry with it the power to regulate the intraprovincial broadcaster as well.[162] Certainly, the federal Radio and Broadcasting Acts[163] assert federal regulatory jurisdiction over intraprovincial as well as interprovincial and international broadcasters.

(c) Content regulation

The *Radio Reference* was concerned with the technical aspects of transmitting and receiving radio signals, that is, the problem of allocating frequencies and regulating transmission so as to avoid technical interference. In deciding that regulation of this kind could be accomplished at the national level, the Privy Council was not addressing itself to the question whether the federal Parliament could regulate the content of radio broadcasting. It is arguable therefore that the *Radio Reference* leaves open the possibility that the federal Parliament can regulate the medium but not the message.[164]

In *Re CFRB* (1973),[165] the Ontario Court of Appeal had to determine the validity of a provision in the federal Broadcasting Act which prohibited the broadcasting of partisan political programmes on the day before a federal, provincial or municipal election. The radio station which was prosecuted for breach of the provision argued that the federal Parliament's power over broadcasting did not extend to programme content. The Ontario Court of Appeal rejected the argument. The Court said that ''it would be flying in the face of all practical considerations and logic to charge Parliament with the responsibility for the regulation and control of the carrier system and to deny it the right to exercise legislative control over what is the only reason for the existence of the carrier system, i.e., the transmission and reception of intellectual material''.[166] The Court accordingly held that Parliament's jurisdiction over radio did extend to ''the

161 Notes 155-157, above.

162 There is an analogy in the shared use of airspace and ground facilities by aircraft, although aeronautics has not been treated as an undertaking under s. 92(10)(a), jurisdiction having been placed solely under the peace, order, and good government power.

163 Radio Act, R.S.C. 1985, c. R-2; Broadcasting Act, R.S.C. 1985, c. B-9.

164 Cohen (1974) 12 Can. Pat. Rep. (2d) 173, 188.

165 [1973] 3 O.R. 819 (C.A.).

166 *Id.*, 824.

control and regulation of the intellectual content of radio communication''.[167] It followed that the impugned section of the Broadcasting Act was valid. An application was made to the Supreme Court of Canada for leave to appeal this decision, and leave was refused.[168]

In *Capital Cities Communications* v. *CRTC* (1977),[169] the Supreme Court of Canada had to determine the question whether a federal regulatory agency could authorize cable television companies to delete the commercials from American television programmes captured by the cable companies from the air, and to replace the deleted commercials with Canadian commercials; the American programmes with the Canadian commercials would then be distributed by the cable television companies to their subscribers. The question whether this practice could be authorized by the federal agency raised the constitutional question whether the federal Parliament had authority over the content of cable television. The Court held that the cable system was ''no more than a conduit for signals from the telecast'',[170] and that federal power over broadcast television extended to the cable system. Thus, the decision determined the scope of authority over broadcast television — and therefore broadcast radio — as well as cable television. The Court held that Parliament could regulate the content of the programmes. The regulation of programme content was inseparable from the regulation of the technical and economic aspects of television.

The *CFRB* and *Capital Cities* cases settle the question of federal power to regulate programme content. They are consistent with the judge-made policy, evident in earlier cases,[171] of refusing to divide legislative authority over transportation or communications undertakings.

The existence of exclusive federal authority over the programme content of radio and television does not exclude provincial law altogether. Under the pith and substance doctrine, a law that is in pith and substance in relation to a matter within provincial legislative competence may validly have an incidental effect on the programme content of radio or television. This is illustrated by *A.-G. Que*. v. *Kellogg's Co.* (1978),[172] where the question arose whether a Quebec law that prohibited the use of cartoons in advertising intended for children could validly apply to advertising on television. The Attorney General of Quebec had sought an injunction against the Kellogg's Company to restrain it from advertising its cereals on television by animated cartoons. The Supreme Court of Canada granted the injunction. Martland J. for the majority of the Court held that the pith and substance of the law was the control of commercial activity in the province, which was valid under s. 92(13) or s. 92(16). Such a law could incidentally also restrict

167 *Ibid.*
168 November 13, 1973.
169 [1978] 2 S.C.R. 141.
170 *Id.*, 159.
171 See sec. 22.5, ''Undivided jurisdiction'', above.
172 [1978] 2 S.C.R. 211.

what was shown on television. Martland J. suggested the analogy of defamation: just as provincial restrictions on defamatory statements could not be evaded by the use of a federal medium such as television, nor could the provincial restrictions on advertising be so evaded.[173]

In the *Kellogg's* case, the law applied to all advertising media, not just television, although it seems obvious that cartoon advertising for children would be a much less significant problem in any medium other than television. But the more general scope of the law helped the Court to classify the law as in relation to advertising generally, rather than to advertising on television.[174] The Quebec government, the plaintiff in the case, had also employed a wise procedural tactic in not seeking to enjoin the television station that had been showing the offending advertisements. The injunction had been sought only against the Kellogg's Company, the advertiser. Martland J. stressed that he was not forced to decide whether an injunction would lie against the television station, and that he was not deciding that question.[175]

In chapter 40, Expression, the limits on the powers of both levels of government to control the expression of ideas on television or other media, including the limits imposed by the Charter of Rights, are considered more fully.

22.13 Communication by television

(a) Broadcast television

Television[176] was almost unknown as a means of communication in 1932 when the *Radio Reference*[177] was decided. But it had been invented, and the reference to the Court asked for its opinion as to the constitutional jurisdiction not only over sound radio, but also over the transmission and reception of ''pictures''. A report by the Minister of Justice which was placed before the Court described television and included it in the term ''radio''.[178] Thus, although their

173 See also *Irwin Toy* v. *Que.* [1989] 1 S.C.R. 927, following *Kellogg's* and upholding a provincial ban on advertising directed at children, including advertising on television.

174 This was the case in *Irwin Toy*, previous note, as well. If the law had singled out television for special rules, the Court might well have classified the law as in relation to television programming, which would have required a finding of invalidity. On singling out, see ch. 15, Judicial Review on Federal Grounds, above.

175 *Id.*, 225. Martland J. was probably concerned about the rule that a provincial law may not ''sterilize'' a federal undertaking. The issue of an injunction against the television station might have been precluded by that rule. On the sterilization of federal undertakings, see ch. 15, Judicial Review on Federal Grounds, under heading 15.5(k), ''Interjurisdictional Immunity,'' above.

176 See Mullan and Beaman, note 1, above, 80-88; Miazga, ''Cable Television'' (1978) 43 Sask. L. Rev. 1; Wilkie, ''The Radio Reference and Onward'' (1980) 18 Osgoode Hall L.J. 49.

177 [1932] A.C. 304; note 144 and accompanying text, above.

178 [1931] S.C.R. 541, 542.

lordships of the Privy Council made no specific reference to television in their opinion, their answer to the question referred did literally apply to television as well as radio. And, of course, the reasoning in the case applies with the same force to television as to radio. Broadcast television also utilizes electromagnetic waves in space, and its hardware or carrier system requires national regulation just as much as radio and for the same reasons. Moreover, the argument for national regulation of programme content also has exactly the same force in relation to television as it has in relation to radio.

In *Capital Cities Communications* v. *CRTC* (1977),[179] the Supreme Court of Canada held that the *Radio Reference* supplied the same rule for broadcast television (and for cable television) as it did for radio. It is clear that for constitutional purposes there is no distinction between radio and broadcast television, and the preceding discussion of radio is all relevant to broadcast television as well. Indeed, as will be seen in the next section of this text, cable television is also in the same constitutional position as radio and broadcast television, except, perhaps, for cable systems carrying only the local programming that is possible on cable television.

(b) Cable television

Cable television differs from broadcast television in that viewers receive their signals through a cable rather than through the air. A cable television system consists essentially of two parts. The first part is the "head end", which is an antenna placed to pick up the signals from the television-broadcasting stations in the area or from satellites. The second part is the "distribution system", which is the network of cable that carries the signal from the head end into the homes of subscribers who pay rent to the cable company for the service. The notable feature of a cable television system is that it does not require radio frequency space, because it only uses a receiving antenna. The transmitting occurs on the cable, which places a strict geographical limit on the range of the signals, and which ensures that the cable system's signals cannot interfere with the signals of radio or television broadcasting stations or with the signals of other cable systems. It is also possible for programmes to be originated by the cable operator. Programmes can be made in a local studio, or purchased in tape form, or relayed from some local place such as a sports stadium or meeting hall. These "local programmes" can be supplied on one or more "community channels" of the cable system.

In the *Radio Reference*,[180] it was argued by the provinces that, even if radio transmitters had to be regulated federally because of the limitations of the radio frequency spectrum, the receivers did not require regulation because they did not interfere with other users of the radio frequency spectrum. The Privy Council refused to draw a distinction between transmitters and receivers. Their lordships

179 [1978] 2 S.C.R. 141.
180 [1932] A.C. 304.

held that once it was determined that the transmitter came within federal control, the receiver ''must share its fate''.[181]

> Broadcasting as a system cannot exist without both a transmitter and a receiver. The receiver is indeed useless without a transmitter and can be reduced to a nonentity if the transmitter closes. The system cannot be divided into two parts, each independent of the other.[182]

And their lordships added, finally, that ''a divided control between transmitter and receiver could only lead to confusion and inefficiency''.[183] This holding that transmitter and receiver must be treated as parts of one system for constitutional purposes resolves any question about legislative jurisdiction over the head end or receiving apparatus of a cable television system: the jurisdiction must be federal.

In *Capital Cities Communications* v. *CRTC* (1977),[184] the question arose whether the federal Parliament had constitutional authority to regulate the programme content of cable television. It was conceded that the federal Parliament had constitutional authority over the reception of broadcast signals by the cable operator's head end or receiving apparatus. But it was argued that the distribution system — the network of cable that carries the signals from the head end to the television sets in the homes of the cable subscribers — was a separate local undertaking within provincial jurisdiction. This argument was rejected by Laskin C.J. for the majority of the Supreme Court of Canada.[185] He held that the head end and the distribution system were parts of an indivisible communications undertaking within the legislative competence of the federal Parliament. The cable system could not be separated from the telecast, because it was ''no more than a conduit for signals from the telecast''.[186] It would be ''incongruous'', he held, ''to deny the continuation of regulatory authority because the signals are intercepted and sent on to ultimate viewers through a different technology''.[187]

The *Capital Cities* case sustained federal regulation of cable television. On the same day, the Supreme Court of Canada handed down its decision in *Public Service Board* v. *Dionne* (1977),[188] which scotched any argument that there was concurrent provincial authority over cable television. Laskin C.J. for the majority[189] struck down a Quebec law purporting to authorize a provincial agency to license cable television systems within the province. Laskin C.J. affirmed the exclusivity of federal regulatory power over cable television, and reaffirmed the

---

181 *Id.*, 315.
182 *Ibid.*
183 *Id.*, 317.
184 [1978] 2 S.C.R. 141. The case is briefly discussed in note 67, above.
185 Laskin C.J.'s opinion was agreed with by Martland, Judson, Ritchie, Spence and Dickson JJ. Pigeon J., with the agreement of Beetz and de Grandpré JJ., dissented.
186 [1978] 2 S.C.R. 141, 159.
187 *Id.*, 162.
188 [1978] 2 S.C.R. 191.
189 The Court split in the same way as in the *Capital Cities* case, note 185, above.

Court's refusal to countenance "divided constitutional control of what is functionally an inter-related system".[190]

Both *Capital Cities* and *Dionne* were concerned with the distribution by cable of "off-air" signals, that is, programmes that had originated as broadcast signals that had been captured from the air by the cable operator. In both cases, Laskin C.J. emphasized that the Court was not deciding which level of government had jurisdiction over "local" programmes, that is, the programmes produced in a local studio, or purchased in tape form, or relayed by cable from some local place. That question was left open. The important distinction between local programmes and off-air programmes is that the local programmes have never been received by the head end as broadcast signals. So far as local programmes are concerned, the cable system cannot be characterized as "a conduit for signals from the telecast,"[191] and the reasoning of *Capital Cities* and *Dionne* has no obvious application. If we postulate a cable television system which carries only programmes originated by the cable operator, the local origin of all programmes suggests the analogy of a closed-circuit television system of the kind commonly organized in schools or universities, or even a concert hall, theatre or cinema which uses television to serve a spillover audience in an adjoining hall.[192] Here, there does not seem to be any plausible claim to federal jurisdiction. The system is within provincial jurisdiction as a local work or undertaking under s. 92(10).

What most cable operators actually supply, of course, is at most only a few "community channels" carrying local programmes and a larger number of channels carrying programmes received from broadcast television stations. So long as the cable operator provides off-air programmes as well as local programmes, it is arguable that the local programmes are part of one undertaking whose characteristics are predominantly interprovincial. The courts have not been willing, for example, to sever into two undertakings a telephone company or a bus line or a trucking company which does both local and long-distance business.[193] In each

---

190 [1978] 2 S.C.R. 191, 197. A provincial law in relation to a matter within provincial competence could validly apply incidentally to a cable television system: *A.-G. Que. v. Kellogg's Co.* [1978] 2 S.C.R. 211; discussed in text accompanying note 172, above.

191 Note 186, above.

192 Even if intraprovincial broadcasting is within federal jurisdiction, as argued in sec. 22.12(b), "Intraprovincial broadcasting", above, cable transmission presents distinctive features. A cable television system which carries only local programmes differs from a local airline or broadcasting station in that the cable system is self-contained. An intraprovincial airline must compete with interprovincial airlines for airport facilities and air routes. Similarly an intraprovincial radio or television broadcaster must compete with interprovincial broadcasters for frequency space. Clearly, in both cases the need to share facilities and the possibility of interference makes unified control highly desirable if not essential. But a cable television system carrying only local programmes is entirely self-contained. Its signals originate within the cable system and are confined to the system by the cable. The system need not use any facilities in common with broadcasters or other cable systems, and its signals cannot interfere with any broadcast or cabled signals.

193 Section 22.5, "Undivided jurisdiction", above.

case the courts have held that a significant amount of "continuous and regular" interprovincial business turns the entire enterprise into an interprovincial undertaking. It is likely that the courts would view a cable television undertaking in the same light.[194]

(c) Pay television

The term "pay television" encompasses a variety of different systems, although they all utilize a cable to bring their product to their customers. Constitutional jurisdiction over pay television depends upon the same considerations as apply to cable television generally. In essence, this means that a self-contained, purely local, system will be within provincial jurisdiction, while a system which is added to the standard cable television mixed offering will be within federal jurisdiction.

22.14 Communication by telephone

(a) Bell Canada

Legislative authority over communication by telephone (telecommunication)[195] depends upon s. 92(10) of the Constitution Act, 1867. We have already examined *Toronto* v. *Bell Telephone Co.* (1905)[196] and seen that the federal Parliament has legislative authority over the Bell Telephone Company, because it is an interprovincial undertaking under s. 92(10)(a). At the time of the decision, Bell was operating only in Ontario but it was planning to extend its system into Quebec, and the Privy Council took the wish for the deed. Bell did in fact extend its service into Quebec, and later added service in the eastern Northwest Territories. By virtue of the *Bell Telephone* decision, Bell has always been federally regulated.

(b) Other major carriers

Outside Ontario and Quebec, each province has a separate telephone company whose operations do not extend beyond the boundaries of the province. In

194 This line of reasoning is suggested in an obiter dictum in *Public Service Bd.* v. *Dionne* [1978] 2 S.C.R. 191, where Laskin C.J. said (at p. 197) that the case did not involve cable operators that "*limit* their operations to programmes locally produced by them" (my emphasis), and (at p. 198) that "an argument based on relative percentages of original programming and of programmes received from broadcasting stations" would be of no avail.

195 Mullan and Beaman, note 1, above, 74-80. Buchan and others, *Telecommunications Regulation and the Constitution* (Institute for Research on Public Policy, 1982); Brait, "Constitutional Jurisdiction to Regulate Telephone Services" (1981) 13 Ottawa L. Rev. 53; Schultz, "Federalism and Telecommunications" (1982) 20 Osgoode Hall L.J. 745..

196 [1905] A.C. 52; note 28 and accompanying text, above.

British Columbia, the privately-owned British Columbia Telephone Company was brought under federal jurisdiction in 1916 by a declaration under s. 92(10)(c) that it was a work for the general advantage of Canada.[197] Since that time, like Bell, it has been federally regulated. Each of the three prairie provinces has a telephone system that was established and owned by the province as a Crown corporation, although the Alberta system was privatized in 1990. Each of the four Atlantic provinces has a telephone system that is owned and operated by a private company.

Until the decision of the Supreme Court of Canada in the *AGT* case (1989),[198] it was assumed that the three prairie companies and the four Atlantic companies were local undertakings within provincial jurisdiction under s. 92(10). All of the seven companies were in fact regulated provincially. However, in the *AGT* case, which was examined earlier in this chapter,[199] the Supreme Court of Canada held that Alberta Government Telephones (AGT) was within federal jurisdiction. Although AGT's operations did not extend beyond the province of Alberta, the Court held that the company was properly classified as an interprovincial undertaking under s. 92(10)(a). The Court pointed out that the company had the capacity to provide interprovincial and international service to its subscribers. This capacity stemmed from the company's connections at the Alberta border with the telephone systems of neighbouring jurisdictions and the company's membership of Telecom Canada, which is now called the Stentor Network,[200] which is an unincorporated association of the major Canadian telephone companies to form a national telecommunications network. The effect of this decision was to sweep into federal jurisdiction not only AGT, but the other two prairie companies and the four Atlantic companies as well. Each of these six companies had the same characteristics as AGT, namely, cross-border connections and membership in Telecom Canada (now the Stentor Network).

(c) Local carriers

After the *AGT* case, it was clear that the nine major Canadian telephone companies — and over 90 per cent of Canada's telephones — were within federal jurisdiction. What remained for decision was the constitutional status of a number of local telephone companies. In Ontario and Quebec, there are 46 local telephone

---

197 S.C. 1916, c. 66. A declaration has also been made in respect of the Bell Telephone Co., but in *Toronto* v. *Bell Telephone Co.* [1905] A.C. 52, the declaration was held to be "unmeaning" because the planned "works" would not be "wholly situate within the province" as stipulated by s. 92(10)(c).

198 *Alta. Govt. Telephones* v. *CRTC* [1989] 2 S.C.R. 225.

199 Text accompanying note 22, above.

200 In 1921, the major carriers organized the Telephone Association of Canada (TAC) to create a national telecommunications network. In 1931, TAC evolved into the Trans-Canada Telephone System (TCTS), which was renamed Telecom Canada in 1983, and Stentor Canadian Network Management in 1992.

companies existing alongside Bell, and there are a few in other provinces as well. These companies range in size from very small indeed to the large systems that serve Thunder Bay and Edmonton. They are mostly privately owned, but a few (including those in Thunder Bay and Edmonton) are municipally owned. They lack cross-border connections, and they are not members of the Stentor Network. Each company is able to provide full interprovincial and international service to its customers by cooperative arrangements with the major telephone company (the Stentor member) in the same province. The constitutional status of these local telephone companies depended on the correct interpretation of the *AGT* case. If the *AGT* case turned on AGT's cross-border connections and its membership in the Stentor Network, then local companies lacking these characteristics would remain within provincial jurisdiction. If, on the other hand, the *AGT* case turned on AGT's capacity to provide interprovincial and international service to its customers, then the local companies would be in the same federal boat.

The issue arose for decision in *Téléphone Guèvremont* v. *Quebec* (1994).[201] Téléphone Guèvremont was a local telephone company located in Quebec with 5,400 subscribers. It was not a member of the Stentor Network, and it had no connections at any of Quebec's borders (its territory being "in the heart" of the province). The company was interconnected with Bell, and through Bell's facilities the company could send and receive messages to and from anywhere in Canada and the rest of the world. The company, which was being regulated by a provincial agency (the Régie des télécommunications) brought proceedings to obtain a ruling that the province (and therefore the Régie) lacked any regulatory authority over the company. The company was successful in the Superior Court, the Quebec Court of Appeal and the Supreme Court of Canada. The Quebec Court of Appeal,[202] in an opinion written by Rousseau-Houle J.A., held that the company's lack of Stentor membership and cross-border connections was not decisive. What was decisive was that the company was "the medium by which its local subscribers receive interprovincial and international communications".[203] It was therefore an interprovincial telephone system under s. 92(10)(a). This decision was affirmed by the Supreme Court of Canada. Lamer C.J.'s reasons for the unanimous Court read in full as follows:[204]

> We are all of the view that Téléphone Guèvremont Inc. is an interprovincial work and undertaking within the legislative authority of the Parliament of Canada by virtue of ss. 92(10)(a) and 91(29) of the *Constitution Act, 1867* by reason of the nature of the services provided and the mode of operation of the undertaking, which provides a telecommunication signal carrier service whereby its subscribers send and receive interprovincial and international communications as set out in the reasons of Rousseau-Houle J.A.

---

201 [1994] 1 S.C.R. 878. The opinion of the unanimous Court was written by Lamer C.J.
202 (1992) 99 D.L.R. (4th) 241 (Que. C.A.).
203 *Id.*, 256.
204 [1994] 1 S.C.R. 878, 879.

With those few words, the issue was settled. All telephone companies are within federal jurisdiction.

22.15 Communication by other means

(a) Film

The exhibition of films, like most businesses, comes within the legislative competence of the provinces. The location and design of cinemas, safety and health requirements, the qualifications of projectionists and other personnel, the storage and rental of films, advertisements for film showings, times of showings and ticket prices, would all be matters within "property and civil rights in the province" (s. 92(13)) or "matters of a merely local or private nature in the province" (s. 92(16)).[205] This conclusion is not affected by the interprovincial or international elements of the film industry, such as the fact that the films shown may be imported from other countries,[206] or that a particular cinema may be part of a chain of cinemas stretching across the country.[207] Each province is free to impose its own regime of regulation upon the cinemas within its borders.

In *N.S. Bd. of Censors* v. *McNeil* (1978),[208] the Supreme Court of Canada held that provincial authority over the exhibition of films extended to regulating the content of films by a system of censorship administered by a provincial agency with authority to ban films altogether, to permit their exhibition with cuts, and to permit their exhibition with age-based admission restrictions. Ritchie J. for the majority assumed that the provincial agency would limit its powers to issues of primarily local significance, namely, the depiction of violence or sex.[209] Censorship on political or religious grounds would be outside provincial power. In chapter 40, Expression, below, the limits on the powers of both levels of government to control the expression of ideas in film or other media, including the limits imposed by the Charter of Rights, are considered more fully.

(b) Theatre

Live theatre, by which term I mean all forms of stage production, including plays, vaudeville, and concerts,[210] is within provincial regulatory authority upon the same constitutional grounds as film. The degree to which a province can

205 *N.S. Bd. of Censors* v. *McNeil* [1978] 2 S.C.R. 662, discussed in following text.
206 In the *McNeil* case, previous note, the film in issue was imported.
207 Cf. *Can. Indemnity Co.* v. *A.-G. B.C.* [1977] 2 S.C.R. 504 (provincial authority over insurance industry unaffected by national and multi-national scope and operation of insurance companies).
208 [1978] 2 S.C.R. 662.
209 *Id.*, 700-701. The control of commercial advertising is also within provincial power: *A.-G. Que.* v. *Kellogg's Co.* [1978] 2 S.C.R. 211; *Irwin Toy* v. *Que.* [1989] 1 S.C.R. 927.
210 Sporting events and other local entertainments are in the same constitutional category as theatre.

regulate the content of a live production depends upon the same considerations as apply to film and literature, and is examined in chapter 40, Expression, below.

(c) Literature

By literature I mean all forms of written communication, including books, pamphlets, magazines and newspapers.[211] The publication, distribution and sale of all these forms of literature may be regulated by the province within which the publication, distribution or sale occurs. These are matters within property and civil rights in the province. This conclusion is not affected by the fact that the literature was imported from other provinces or countries,[212] or that the publisher or distributor is a nation-wide organization.[213] However, as in the case of film and theatre, the degree to which a province can regulate the content of literature is a difficult question that is considered more fully in chapter 40, Expression, below.

211 Records, tapes, videodiscs, and videotapes are in the same constitutional category as literature.
212 Note 200, above.
213 Note 201, above.

23

Companies

23.1 Incorporation of companies

(a) Distribution of powers

The Constitution Act, 1867, by s. 92(11), confers on the provincial Legislatures the power to make laws in relation to ''the incorporation of companies with provincial objects''. The list of federal legislative powers does not include an incorporating power corresponding to the provincial power.[1] However, it was established in *Citizens' Insurance Co.* v. *Parsons* (1881)[2] that the federal Parliament had an incorporating power by virtue of the residuary character of the peace, order, and good government power in the opening words of s. 91.[3] Since the peace, order, and good government power extended to all matters not assigned to the provinces, and since the provincial power of incorporation was confined to

1 There is only a power to incorporate banks (s. 91(15)): ch. 24, Financial Institutions, under heading 24.4, ''Incorporation of banks'', below.

2 (1881) 7 App. Cas. 96.

3 There is a suggestion in *John Deere Plow Co.* v. *Wharton* [1915] A.C. 330, 340, that the trade and commerce power also supplies part of the federal incorporation power, but this is probably wrong: see ch. 20, Trade and Commerce, under heading 20.3 ''General trade and commerce'', above.

"companies with provincial objects", it followed that the incorporation of companies "for objects other than provincial" came within the legislative competence of the federal Parliament.[4]

This, then, is the distribution of legislative power in relation to the incorporation of companies. The provincial Legislatures may provide for the incorporation of companies with provincial objects; the federal Parliament may provide for the incorporation of companies with objects other than provincial. The precise demarcation between the federal and provincial powers depends upon the meaning of the phrase "with provincial objects" in s. 92(11). It is clear from the cases that this phrase imposes a territorial limitation on the provincial power of incorporation; the nature of that limitation is the topic of the next section of this chapter. That section will be followed by a discussion of whether the phrase also imposes a functional limitation on the provincial power of incorporation.

(b) Territorial limitation

As noted above, the cases decide that there is a territorial limitation on the provincial power to incorporate companies.[5] The leading case on the nature of the territorial limitation is *Bonanza Creek Gold Mining Co.* v. *The King* (1916).[6] The issue in that case was whether a company incorporated in Ontario for the purpose of mining could carry on its operations in the Yukon territory, and for that purpose acquire property and enter into contracts in the Yukon. The argument was made, and accepted by a majority of the Supreme Court of Canada, that since the province's legislative powers were confined to the territory of the province (as is generally true),[7] the province could not create a corporation with a legal existence outside the province; otherwise, the creature of a provincial Legislature would receive more than its creator possessed. The Privy Council rejected this plausible but highly inconvenient argument. Their lordships ruled that there was indeed a territorial limitation on the provincial incorporation power, but one less severe than had been accepted in the Supreme Court of Canada. The words "with provincial objects" in s. 92(11) did "confine the character of the actual powers and rights which the provincial Government can bestow, either by legislation or through the Executive, to powers and rights exercisable within the province".[8] But, their lordships pointed out, "actual powers and rights are one thing and capacity to accept extra-provincial powers and rights is quite another".[9] The

4 This reasoning is effectively criticized by Ziegel in Ziegel (ed.), *Studies in Canadian Company Law* (1967), vol. 1, 153-154, but, as he concedes, the existence of the federal power of incorporation is firmly established.

5 For the early cases, see note 17, below.

6 [1916] 1 A.C. 566.

7 Chapter 13, Extraterritorial Competence, above.

8 [1916] 1 A.C. 566, 583.

9 *Ibid.*

incorporating province could if it chose confer upon a company the capacity to receive powers and rights outside the province. Whether the company did in fact receive powers and rights in another province, territory or country would depend upon whether the other jurisdiction chose to recognize it and permit it to carry on business there. But if the other jurisdiction did accord recognition, the company's provincial incorporation was sufficient to endow it with legal personality in the recognizing jurisdiction.

Applying this doctrine to the facts of the *Bonanza Creek* case, the Privy Council held that the Ontario Companies Act, under which the company had been incorporated, was apt to confer the capacity to acquire extra-provincial powers and rights, and that the company had that capacity. Had the Yukon territory recognized the company and granted it the right to carry on business in the territory? The territory's Foreign Companies Ordinance required any company incorporated outside the territory, other than federally-incorporated companies, to obtain a licence from the territorial government in order to carry on business in the territory. The company had obtained the required licence, and this licence transformed the capacity to accept rights and powers into actual rights and powers. It followed that the corporation could acquire mining claims, leases and other property, could enter into contracts, and could perform all those acts necessary for the carrying on of its business in the Yukon.

Bonanza Creek made clear that a provincially-incorporated company had no right to be recognized as a legal person outside its province of incorporation, but that, in the absence of any limitation in the statute under which the company was incorporated or in the company's charter, an explicit licence to carry on business in another province or territory or country would cure the defect in the licensing jurisdiction. With such a licence, a provincially-incorporated company could validly enjoy the various attributes of legal personality in a province other than the province of incorporation: it could sue and be sued, enter into contracts, hold property, and so on. Other cases have liberalized this rule even further by holding that the recognition (or permission or licensing) of the non-incorporating jurisdiction need not be express (as it was in *Bonanza Creek*). Recognition may be implied, and will be implied in any province which does not impose any prohibition or restriction on the status or powers of companies incorporated in other provinces.[10] In fact, all provinces now have laws requiring the licensing of companies incorporated outside the province which are carrying on business inside the province, and in most cases these statutes impose disabilities as well as penalties on unlicensed companies.[11]

---

10 *Honsberger* v. *Weyburn Townsite Co.* (1919) 59 S.C.R. 281; *Re Anglo-American Fire Ins. Co.* (1919) 16 O.W.N. 150 (H.C.); *Aetna Factors Corp.* v. *Breau* (1957) 15 D.L.R. (2d) 326 (N.B.A.D.); Ross, "The Extra-Provincial Licensing Statutes" (1980) 4 Can. Bus. L.J. 183; and see discussion of the validity of the extraprovincial licensing statutes, at notes 45-49, below.

11 See Castel, *Canadian Conflict of Laws* (3rd ed., 1994), 535-540.

(c) Functional limitation

The phrase "with provincial objects" in s. 92(11) might be thought to impose a functional (as well as a territorial) limitation on the provincial power of incorporation. A functional limitation would confine the power to the incorporation of companies whose objects were within provincial legislative authority: for example, a school or a shop or an insurance company, but not a ferry between two provinces or an airline.

It is a remarkable fact that after all these years commentators are not in agreement as to whether there is, in addition to the territorial limitation, also a functional limitation on the provincial power of incorporation. Wegenast, writing in 1931, says that the dividing line between federal and provincial power "is not as yet fully defined".[12] Laskin in his casebook accepts that there is a territorial limitation on the provincial power, but poses the question whether there is a functional limitation as well.[13] Ziegel says that it is "a commonplace" that the dividing line "runs along both territorial and functional lines".[14] Lederman says that the dividing line is territorial only.[15]

In my opinion, there is no functional limitation on the provincial power of incorporation. The phrase "with provincial objects" imposes only a territorial restriction on the power. The legislative history suggests that this reading is correct,[16] and so do the early cases.[17] In the *AGT* case (1989),[18] the Supreme Court of Canada held that the province of Alberta could incorporate a company and empower it to engage in activity within federal regulatory jurisdiction. The provincially-incorporated company was held to be validly engaged in operating an interprovincial telephone undertaking — a business activity that could be regulated only by the federal Parliament.[19]

---

12 Wegenast, *The Law of Canadian Companies* (1931), 28.

13 Laskin, *Canadian Constitutional Law* (5th ed., 1986 by Finkelstein), 722.

14 Ziegel, note 4, above, 159-160. McNairn (1969) 47 Can. Bar Rev. 353, 361, agrees.

15 Lederman in Lang (ed.), *Contemporary Problems of Public Law in Canada* (1968), 116, 118.

16 Wegenast, note 12, above, 30.

17 Especially, *Citizens Ins. Co.* v. *Parsons* (1881) 7 App. Cas. 96; *Dobie* v. *Temporalities Board* (1881), 7 App. Cas. 136; *Colonial Bldg. and Invt. Assn.* v. *A.-G. Que.* (1883) 9 App. Cas. 157; in each case legislative jurisdiction was assigned on a territorial basis.

18 *Alta. Govt. Telephones* v. *CRTC* [1989] 2 S.C.R. 225, 297.

19 In *Kootenay and Elk Ry. Co.* v. *C.P.R.* [1974] S.C.R. 955, one issue was whether the province of B.C. could incorporate a company to construct and operate a railway running to the U.S. border and linking there to a U.S. railway. The Supreme Court of Canada, by a majority, held that even if the B.C. railway became part of an extraprovincial undertaking within s. 92(10)(a) of the Constitution Act, 1867 and therefore within federal legislative authority, the provincial incorporation would be valid. Hall and Spence JJ. dissented on this point, and while their reasoning is not entirely clear they probably were relying on a functional rather than a territorial limitation on provincial power; cf. their dissenting opinion in *Breckenridge Speedway* v. *The Queen* [1970] S.C.R. 175; ch. 24, Financial Institutions, under heading 24.5, "Incorporation of other financial institutions", below.

As Lederman has pointed out[20] the clearest indication of the absence of any functional limitation on the provincial incorporating power is to be found in the *Bonanza Creek* case. Crucial to the reasoning in the case was the holding that s. 92(11) permits the province to create a company with the legal attributes of a natural person, that is to say, without limitation as to the kinds of activity which it can pursue. In Britain, and before confederation in British North America, the power to create such a corporation had existed; and their lordships held that such a power was carried forward to the provincial Legislatures by s. 92(11).[21] It followed that a province could incorporate companies with powers to do things that fell within federal as well as provincial legislative authority. Of course, like a natural person, the company, even when operating in its province of incorporation, would have to comply with all applicable laws, federal as well as provincial. And, outside its province of incorporation, the company would need recognition of its legal personality from each jurisdiction where it sought to act. But the mere fact of provincial incorporation did not imply any functional limit on the subject matter of its powers.

Reinforcing the cases that reject any functional limitation on the provincial power of incorporation is the consideration that such a limitation would be so vague and uncertain as to be commercially unworkable. The objects of a company, especially if they are numerous and diverse, often could not be confidently classified as within the regulatory authority of one or the other level of government. The functional theory would therefore pose a serious problem for those wishing to incorporate a company and wondering to which jurisdiction they should resort. Even more serious, the functional theory would raise the spectre of an ultra vires challenge every time a company's activity strayed outside the regulatory authority of the jurisdiction of incorporation.[22] Only the territorial theory provides a practical criterion for identifying the jurisdiction of incorporation, and affords security to the full range of corporate activity.

(d) Federal power

The federal power to incorporate companies must correspond with the provincial power, because the federal power is simply the residue of the entire possible power to incorporate companies after subtracting the provincial power.[23] Therefore, if the phrase "with provincial objects" in s. 92(11) imposes only a territorial limit on the provincial power of incorporation, then there must be only a territorial

20 Lederman, note 15, above, 116.

21 [1916] 1 A.C. 566, 584-585.

22 The problem would arise in respect of provincial companies engaged in the postal service, navigation and shipping, aviation, radio or television broadcasting, and all modes of interprovincial or international transportation and communication.

23 Text accompanying note 2, above.

limit on the federal power as well.[24] The federal power is confined to the incorporation of companies with objects that extend beyond the limits of any one province. It follows, although the point has never been directly decided, that a company whose objects were expressly confined within one province could not be incorporated federally.[25] But so long as the company's charter authorizes it to carry on business in more than one province,[26] then it is clear that the company may be incorporated federally. This is so even if the company never does actually extend its operations to more than one province.[27] The subject matter of the company's objects is as unrestricted as it is in the case of a provincially-incorporated company. It may include "objects within provincial authority in more than one province"[28] as well as objects within federal legislative jurisdiction. In fact, of course, the business activities of most federal companies would fall within property and civil rights in the province, a matter within provincial legislative jurisdiction.

The Canada Business Corporations Act,[29] which came into force in 1975, does not recognize any functional limitation on the federal incorporating power. The Act explicitly states in s. 15(1) that "a corporation has the capacity and, subject to this Act, the rights, powers and privileges of a natural person." The existence of the territorial limitation on the federal Parliament's power is implicitly recognized in s. 4 of the Act, which states that a purpose of the Act is to reform "the law applicable to business corporations incorporated to carry on business throughout Canada". Moreover, s. 15(2) expressly provides that "a corporation may carry on business throughout Canada". The form of application for incorporation prescribed by s. 6 makes no provision for listing the objects that the corporation is to pursue.[30] This omission would be constitutionally objection-

24 It is arguable that even if the provincial power of incorporation had a functional as well as a territorial limitation, the federal Parliament's power is not limited functionally because any corporation authorized to carry on business in more than one province (whatever the subject matter of its objects) is outside provincial power and therefore within federal power.

25 This is however implied by *Colonial Bldg. and Invt. Assn.* v. *A.G. Que.* (1883) 9 App. Cas. 157.

26 The practice used to be to insert in the application for federal incorporation a statement that "the operations of the company may be carried on throughout Canada and elsewhere": Wegenast, note 12, above, 45. Since 1975, when the Canada Business Corporations Act, R.S.C. 1985, c. C-44, came into force, this formula is no longer necessary, because s. 15(2) expressly provides that "a corporation may carry on business throughout Canada".

27 *Colonial Building and Invt. Assn.* v. *A.-G. Que.* (1883) 9 App. Cas. 157.

28 *Can. Pioneer Management* v. *Labour Relations Bd. Sask.* [1980] 1 S.C.R. 433, 454 (Parliament has power to provide for the incorporation of trust companies, although it lacks power to regulate their activities); *Life Underwriters Assn.* v. *Que.* [1992] S.C.R. (Parliament has power to incorporate an association of underwriters, and authorize the use by its members of the CLU designation, although it lacks power to regulate life insurers).

29 R.S.C. 1985, c. C-44.

30 The form of application for incorporation prescribed by s. 6 does require disclosure of "any restrictions on the businesses that the corporation may carry on". If an application for incorporation restricted the corporation's businesses to the territory of one province, then the appli-

able if there were any functional limitation on the federal incorporating power. The federal government has obviously been persuaded by its advisers that there is no such limitation.[31] For the reasons given, I believe that the government is correct.

(e) Conclusion

What all this boils down to is that there is very little difference between the federal and provincial incorporating powers. Both powers extend to the full range of possible corporate objects. The only difference lies in the fact that a federally-incorporated company is entitled as of right to recognition as a legal person throughout Canada, while a provincially-incorporated company is entitled to recognition as a legal person only within the province of incorporation. Outside the province of incorporation, the provincial company is dependent upon the laws of each jurisdiction in which it seeks to operate for recognition of its legal personality. However, this difference is rarely important in practice, since each Canadian province affords a simple licensing procedure to enable extra-provincial companies to act within its own boundaries.[32]

23.2 Regulation of corporate activity

It will by now be clear that Canadian constitutional law draws a distinction between the power to incorporate a company and the power to regulate its activities. The incorporation power is the power to bring a company into existence: it obviously authorizes the conferral of legal personality on an association of persons. It also authorizes the regulation of corporate structure, that is, all laws of a company law character, for example, the laws pertaining to corporate powers,[33]

---

cation should not be accepted because it would be outside the constitutional power of the federal Parliament: see note 25, above.

31 The original version of s. 4 stated that the purpose of the Act was to reform the law applicable to ''business corporations incorporated for objects other than provincial''. This phrase avoided any commitment to either a territorial or functional theory, but it was replaced in committee by the phrase ''business corporations incorporated to carry on business throughout Canada''. The Senate Committee accepted that there was no functional limitation on federal power, and that the reference to ''objects other than provincial'' might mislead people unfamiliar with the language of the Constitution Act, 1867: Senate of Canada, Proceedings of the Standing Senate Committee on Banking, Trade and Commerce, February 25, 1975, pp. 27:5-27:13.

32 Note 11, above.

33 In *Can. Pioneer Management* v. *Labour Relations Bd. Sask.* [1980] 1 S.C.R. 433, 453, the Supreme Court of Canada upheld the validity of the federal Trust Companies Act under the federal incorporation power. The federal Parliament could ''impose limitations on their corporate capacity [i.e., that of federally-incorporated trust companies] as conditions of their incorporation''. The Court rejected the argument that the Act ''goes beyond incorporation and rises to the level of regulation''.

organization, internal management[34] and financing.[35] The precise scope of the incorporation power is not clearly settled, and probably never will be, because of the vagueness of the rubric "company law."[36] But it is clear that the incorporation power does not imply a power to regulate the activity of a company once it has been brought into existence. This follows from the fact that both the federal Parliament and a provincial Legislature may create a company with objects whose subject matter is outside the regulatory power of the incorporating jurisdiction.

The power to regulate corporate activity is distributed in accordance with the classes of subjects listed in the Constitution, especially in ss. 91 and 92. Once a company has been incorporated, its activity will be subject to the legislation of whichever order of government has validly enacted laws in respect of that activity. In ascertaining the appropriate regulatory jurisdiction, as opposed to the appropriate incorporating jurisdiction, the territorial extent of the company's objects is not decisive. The mere fact that a company's activity extends beyond the limits of any one province will not by itself bring the activity within federal regulatory jurisdiction.[37] If the activity wears an aspect within provincial legislative jurisdiction such as "property and civil rights" — and most business activity does — then each province will have the power to regulate that part of the company's activity which occurs within the province's borders. Conversely, if the activity wears an aspect which is within federal jurisdiction, then it will be under federal control even if it is local. Some examples may clarify the point. A federally-incorporated company is liable to pay any provincial taxes which are applicable to income or activity of the kind received or carried on by the company, and a provincially-incorporated company is likewise obliged to pay any applicable federal taxes.[38] An insurance company may be incorporated federally, but will be

34 *Montel* v. *Groupe de Consultants P.G.L.* (1982) 142 D.L.R. (3d) 659 (Que. C.A.) (upholding federal provisions respecting receivers and managers and the oppression remedy); *Multiple Access* v. *McCutcheon* [1982] 2 S.C.R. 161, 177 (upholding federal provisions respecting insider trading).

35 *Esso Standard* v. *J.W. Enterprises* [1963] S.C.R. 144 (upholding federal provisions permitting takeover offeror to buy out minority shareholders); *Multiple Access* v. *McCutcheon* [1982] 2 S.C.R. 161 (upholding federal provisions respecting insider trading). These decisions go beyond regulation of the issue and primary distribution of corporate securities, and authorize some degree of regulation of the secondary market in the securities of federally-incorporated companies. In the latter case, Dickson J. for the majority said (at p. 177) that insider malfeasance "affects also financing because shareholders and potential shareholders must be assured the company's affairs will be scrupulously and fairly conducted; otherwise the raising of capital, clearly an element of company law, will be inhibited".

36 The cases cited in the previous three notes suggest that the category of company law, like other constitutional categories, should be given a "progressive interpretation", so that it can expand with changing social and economic conditions. Of course, a valid corporate law would have to have a genuine corporate purpose, rather than a social or economic purpose with no rational connection with corporate structure.

37 *Can. Indemnity Co.* v. *A.-G. B.C.* [1977] 2 S.C.R. 504 (national and multi-national insurance companies remain within provincial jurisdiction).

38 *Bank of Toronto* v. *Lambe* (1887) 12 App. Cas. 575.

subject to provincial laws as to the terms and conditions of its contracts of insurance,[39] and as to the classes of business in which it may engage.[40] An interprovincial telephone company may be incorporated provincially, but its rates will be subject to federal regulation.[41] A hotel may be owned and operated by a federally-incorporated company, but its labour relations will be subject to provincial regulation.[42] The point is that the jurisdiction of incorporation has the power to confer on a company its legal personality, its organization, and its essential powers; but its business will be regulated by whichever jurisdiction possesses and exercises the power to regulate that kind of business.[43]

The importance of the distinction between a law in relation to the incorporation of a company, and a law in relation to the activity of a company is illustrated by *Dobie* v. *Temporalities Board* (1881).[44] In that case, the province of Quebec enacted a statute to alter the administration of a Presbyterian church fund and the constitution of the board which administered the fund. This statute was held to be invalid, because the board had been incorporated before confederation by the united province of Canada, which of course included both Ontario and Quebec, and the board's rights and powers extended throughout both provinces. Because the board had been given a corporate personality which extended beyond any one province, it was in the same constitutional situation as a federally-incorporated company, and the federal Parliament was the only body with power to alter the terms of the board's incorporation. If the board's original incorporation had been confined to the province of Quebec, then a law altering the terms of the incorporation would have been competent to the Legislature.

Although their lordships did not express themselves in these terms, we would now say that the vice of the law in *Dobie* was that it had a "company law" character. Not only was it directed at one corporation, but it purported to alter the corporate structure. It could not therefore be characterized as a law in relation to property and civil rights in the province, or any other provincial subject matter. It was a law in relation to a federal corporation and invalid as such. Similarly, if the federal Parliament purported to alter the company law of the provinces, for example, by requiring a minimum number of shareholders for provincial companies, or by amending the corporate charter of a particular provincial company, the federal statute would be invalid. Such a law (unless it had an equally important federal aspect) would be characterized as a law in relation to the incorporation of

39 *Citizens Ins. Co.* v. *Parsons* (1881) 7 App. Cas. 96.

40 *Can. Indemnity Co.* v. *A.-G. B.C.* [1977] 2 S.C.R. 504.

41 *Alta. Govt. Telephones* v. *CRTC* [1989] 2 S.C.R. 225. Cf. *The Queen (Ont.)* v. *Bd. of Transport Commrs.* [1968] S.C.R. 118 (provincially-incorporated railway company held subject to federal regulation).

42 *CPR* v. *A.-G. B.C.* (Empress Hotel) [1950] A.C. 122.

43 Banking is an exception because s. 91(15) confers on the federal Parliament both the power to incorporate banks and the power to regulate banking: see ch. 24, Financial Institutions, below.

44 (1881) 7 App. Cas. 136.

companies with provincial objects — a matter withdrawn from federal legislative competence.

The propositions considered so far depend upon the familiar principle of federal classification: each law must be classified as within one of the heads of power of the enacting legislative body. In the company law field, it has the effect of protecting companies from the legislation of jurisdictions other than the incorporating jurisdiction. But the protection is a very limited one. If the legislation of the non-incorporating jurisdiction which purports to apply to the company is not of a company law character, and is classified as a law in relation to a matter which is within the competence of the enacting legislative body, then the doctrine of classification will not protect the company. Generally speaking, as has already been emphasized, a company must comply with all of the laws which apply to it, whether they are enacted by the incorporating jurisdiction or by some other jurisdiction.

23.3 The ''status and essential powers'' immunity

(a) Scope of immunity

There is one important exception to the general principle that a company is obliged to obey any valid law which is apt to apply to it. A province may not impair the ''status and essential powers'' of a federally-incorporated company (hereinafter referred to as a federal company). What this means is that if a province enacts a law which is within its legislative competence, but which would have the effect of impairing the status or essential powers of a federal company, then the law will be held inapplicable to any federal company.

This immunity was established by two famous cases, *John Deere Plow Co.* v. *Wharton* (1915)[45] and *Great West Saddlery Co.* v. *The King* (1921).[46] In these cases, the Privy Council had to determine the validity of several provincial statutes, each of which prohibited ''extra-provincial companies'' (defined as all companies not incorporated under the law of the enacting province) from carrying on business within the province unless and until they had obtained a licence from a provincial official. If these extra-provincial companies statutes had been directed solely at federal companies, then no doubt they could have been classified as laws in relation to federal companies and struck down on that basis. But the laws applied indifferently to all companies incorporated outside the province. These included federal companies, to be sure, but they also included companies incorporated in other provinces and in other countries. The Privy Council held nevertheless that the extra-provincial companies laws were inapplicable to federal companies. Although the laws were generally valid laws in relation to property

45 [1915] A.C. 330.
46 [1921] 2 A.C. 91.

and civil rights in the province, they could not sterilize or destroy the essential powers which the Dominion had validly conferred upon its companies.[47]

In *John Deere* and *Great West Saddlery*, it was not the licensing of federal companies by the province which was constitutionally objectionable; it was the fact that failure to obtain a licence resulted in the loss of corporate status or an essential corporate power. There is no constitutional objection to a province providing for the licensing of all foreign companies, including federal companies; for the payment of licence fees; and for financial penalties for non-payment of fees. So long as the penalties for failure to obtain a licence do not include the deprivation of the power to do business in the province, or of the power to sue in the provincial courts,[48] or of any other essential corporate power, then there is no reason why the licensing regime should not apply to federal companies.[49]

In *Great West Saddlery*, in addition to the extra-provincial companies statutes, the Ontario Mortmain Act was challenged. The Mortmain Act prohibited all companies, wherever incorporated, from acquiring or holding land in the province, except with a provincial licence. Such a law was obviously generally valid as a law in relation to property and civil rights in the province, but was it applicable to federal companies? The Privy Council answered yes: "a Dominion company is in no better position than any other corporation which desires to hold land".[50] The Mortmain Act, while it undoubtedly restricted the powers of a federal company in Ontario, did not go so far as to deprive a federal company of powers essential to corporate existence in the province. The power to hold land was not an essential attribute of corporate status, and was therefore subject to provincial laws in relation to land in the province. The extra-provincial companies statutes, on the other hand, by prohibiting all corporate activity in the province, were in effect denying corporate status to federal companies.

The difficult distinction between the denial of an essential corporate attribute (for example, the extra-provincial companies statutes) and the regulation of business activity (for example, the mortmain statute) was drawn again by the Privy Council in the *Manitoba Securities* case (1929)[51] and *Lymburn* v. *Mayland* (1932),[52] two cases concerned with provincial securities statutes. In the *Manitoba Securities* case, the provincial statute purported to regulate the issue of corporate

---

47 This is the rationale of the *Great West Saddlery* case, and it is probably the correct explanation of the *John Deere* case. However, the reasoning in *John Deere* is less clear, and some of the dicta could be read as placing the result on the principle of classification.

48 *Donald E. Hirtle Transport* v. *IAC* (1978) 92 D.L.R. (3d) 87 (N.S.A.D.) (federal company cannot be deprived of power to sue in provincial court).

49 *Re Royalite Oil Co.* [1931] 1 W.W.R. 484. (Alta. A.D.). For a doubt, see Ross, note 10, above, 199. Query whether the province can prohibit a federally-incorporated company from using its corporate name: *Re Constitution Act, 1867, ss. 91 and 92* (1991) 80 D.L.R. (4th) 431 (Man. C.A.) (majority held no).

50 [1921] 2 A.C. 91, 119.

51 *A.-G. Man.* v. *A.-G. Can.* (Manitoba Securities) [1929] A.C. 260.

52 [1932] A.C. 318.

securities by prohibiting any company from issuing stocks, bonds or other securities without first obtaining a licence from a provincial agency. The agency had to examine the company's incorporating documents, its financial condition, its plan of business and other matters; and it could insist upon changes by the company before granting the licence. This statute could not be condemned by classifying it as a law in relation to federal companies, because it included all companies and there was "no discrimination against Dominion companies as such."[53] The correct classification of the statute was as a law in relation to property and civil rights in the province. Nevertheless, the Privy Council held that the statute could not constitutionally apply to federal companies. The capacity of a company to raise capital was so essential to its existence that the application of the statute to a federal company would "impair the status and essential capacities of the company in a substantial degree".[54]

In *Lymburn* v. *Mayland* (1932),[55] a different result was reached. In that case, the statute in issue, which had been enacted by Alberta after the decision in the *Manitoba Securities* case, did not impose a licensing requirement directly on the companies issuing stocks and bonds, but it did impose a licensing requirement on brokers and salesmen; and it prohibited any company from issuing securities to the public unless the company employed for the purpose a licensed broker or salesman. The Privy Council held that this statute was valid as a law in relation to property and civil rights in the province, and that it was applicable to federal companies. By fastening the licensing requirement on the broker or salesman, the Alberta statute avoided the vice of the Manitoba statute. Their lordships said that there was "no reason to suppose that any honest company would have any difficulty in finding registered persons in the Province through whom it could lawfully issue its capital", and therefore there was no ground for a holding that "the functions and activities of a company were sterilized or its status and essential capacities impaired in a substantial degree".[56]

In *Multiple Access* v. *McCutcheon* (1982),[57] the Supreme Court of Canada held that an Ontario law, which provided a remedy against insider trading, was applicable to a federal company. Restrictions on the trading of shares by those with inside knowledge did not impair the federal company's essential power to raise capital.

The sterilization argument was raised in *Canadian Indemnity Co.* v. *A.-G. B.C.* (1976),[58] in which there was a constitutional challenge to British Columbia's

53 [1929] A.C. 260, 265.
54 *Id.*, 267. Accord, *Lukey* v. *Ruthenian Farmers' Elevator Co.* [1924] S.C.R. 56.
55 [1932] A.C. 318.
56 *Id.*, 324-325. Commentators such as Ziegel note 4, above, 168-171, have noted that current provincial securities legislation includes provisions which appear to be closer to the invalid Manitoba model than to the valid Alberta model, and which may therefore be inapplicable to federal companies. See generally Kay, "Constitutional Aspects of Approval of Share Transactions" (1981) 19 Osgoode Hall L.J. 100.
57 [1982] 2 S.C.R. 161, 183-185.
58 [1977] 2 S.C.R. 504.

"Autoplan", a system of compulsory automobile insurance carried by a Crown corporation. The establishment of a Crown monopoly on the provision of automobile insurance involved the elimination of private insurers from that class of insurance. The federally-incorporated insurers argued that the legislation was an impairment of their status and essential powers. On the basis of the case law which has just been described, the Supreme Court of Canada had little difficulty in rejecting the argument. The Court held unanimously that the legislation was validly applicable to federal companies. The Autoplan was a regulation of "a particular business or activity" to which a federal company was subject "in the same way as a natural person or a provincially-incorporated company".[59]

There is a certain unreality in the decisions which have held provincial statutes inapplicable to federal companies on the ground of an impairment of some essential corporate attribute. In none of the cases did the statute single out federal companies for special treatment, or discriminate against them in any way. And, of course, any provincial statute which did single out or discriminate against federal companies would run the risk of being classified as a law in relation to a federal matter.[60] The statutes in issue in *John Deere* and in *Great West Saddlery* applied to all extra-provincial companies seeking entry to the provincial economy, and the statute in the *Manitoba Securities* case applied to all companies issuing securities in the province. There was no reason to suppose that the licensing authorities in any of these cases would be other than even-handed in their dispensation of licences, and indeed any discrimination against federal companies would almost certainly be ultra vires on the basis that, since the provincial Legislature could not itself discriminate against federal companies, it could not authorize its officials to do so. It is reasonable to assume therefore that the provincial licensing requirements which were in issue in these cases would have to be applied to federal companies on the basis of exactly the same criteria as would be applied to companies incorporated provincially or in other countries. Since no province would want to halt economic activity within its boundaries, it is hard to see what realistic ground the Privy Council could have had for its sweeping rhetoric about impairment of corporate status; it is also hard to see why we need a status-and-essential-powers immunity at all.[61]

Those provincial laws which undoubtedly do apply to a federal company will often have a drastic effect on the company. For example, the provincial mortmain statute which was held applicable to federal companies in *Great West*

---

59 *Id.*, 519. See also *Re Upper Churchill Water Rights* [1984] 1 S.C.R. 297, discussed at note 66, below. Note that for companies (whether federally-incorporated or not) that are engaged in activities within federal jurisdiction (for example, interprovincial transportation or communication) there is a degree of immunity from provincial law for their business activities: see the discussion of interjurisdictional immunity in ch. 15, Judicial Review on Federal Grounds, above.

60 On singling out, see ch. 15, Judicial Review on Federal Grounds, above.

61 For more general discussion, and criticism, see discussion of interjurisdictional immunity, ch. 15, Judicial Review on Federal Grounds, above.

Saddlery could have excluded from the province a company whose sole business consisted of the buying, holding and selling of land. The provincial statute requiring the licensing of stockbrokers which was held applicable to federal companies in *Lymburn* v. *Mayland* could have excluded from the province a company whose sole business consisted of the trading of corporate securities. The establishment of the Crown monopoly of automobile insurance in *Canadian Indemnity* could have excluded from the province a company solely engaged in writing automobile insurance.

Laws of the kind described are valid provincial laws, of course, and moreover they apply to federal companies, even when their effect is to put such companies out of business.[62] These laws are applicable to federal companies because they simply regulate or prohibit a corporate activity. A law prohibiting a particular activity, such as landholding, stockbroking or automobile insuring, is not deemed to be totally stultifying to any company. And it is a fact that a company which finds its operations in a province brought to a close by such a law can employ its assets[63] in another line of business in the province, and, if it is not empowered to carry out another line of business, it can easily secure from the incorporating jurisdiction the necessary amendment of its powers to that end.

The company whose particular line of business has been halted has not had its status or essential powers impaired in the sense which the cases stipulate. In *John Deere* and *Great West Saddlery*, the offending law (as interpreted by the Privy Council) prohibited federal companies from engaging in any activity whatever; such a law is equivalent to a denial of corporate status. In the *Manitoba Securities* case, the offending law (again, as interpreted in the Privy Council's inimitable fashion) prohibited federal companies from raising capital; such a law strikes at the most fundamental corporate power. Laws which simply strike at particular kinds of activity do not have any comparable constitutional infirmity. The provincial Legislature has a perfect right to regulate property and civil rights as it sees fit, and all persons to whom the laws apply, including federal companies, are bound by the laws. There is no reason why a corporate person should be in any better position than a human person. It should be remembered that virtually any business can be incorporated federally rather than provincially if its promoters or proprietors so desire. It would be odd if a federal charter rendered the business partially immune from provincial regulation, and any such doctrine would leave the provinces powerless to undertake any radical regulation of business.[64]

62 *Citizens' Ins. Co.*. v. *Parsons* (1881) 7 App. Cas. 96, 117; *A.-G. (Man.)* v. *Man. Licence Holders Assn.* [1902] A.C. 73, 79; *Lymburn* v. *Mayland* [1932] A.C. 318, 324. If the obscure decision in *La Compagnie Hydraulique de St. Francois* v. *Continental Heat and Light Co.* [1909] A.C. 194 is inconsistent with the proposition in the text, then it is wrongly decided: see Ziegel, note 4, above, 178-180.

63 In *Re Upper Churchill Water Rights*, [1984] 1 S.C.R. 297, discussed at note 66, below, it was held that an uncompensated expropriation of all property did not impair corporate status or essential powers. Although the lack of compensation left the federal company without assets, it had not lost the capacity to raise new capital and thereby acquire new assets.

64 Cf. Lederman, note 15, above, 114.

(b) Taking a federal company's assets

Do the principles discussed to this point preclude a province from expropriating the assets of a federal company? A province has the power to enact a law expropriating property by virtue of its legislative power over property and civil rights in the province.[65] The provincial power of expropriation would extend to assets owned by a federal company, unless of course the expropriating law were characterized as a law in relation to the federal company or the expropriating law were held to impair the status or essential powers of the federal company.

In *Re Upper Churchill Water Rights* (1984),[66] the issue was the constitutionality of a Newfoundland statute that purported to expropriate all the assets of the Churchill Falls (Labrador) Corporation, a federal company that operated a hydroelectric generating station at Churchill Falls in Newfoundland (Labrador). The Supreme Court of Canada held that the statute was unconstitutional, because it purported to destroy contractual rights outside the province. But the Act was also attacked on the ground that it impaired the status and essential powers of a federal company. The expropriating statute applied only to the one federal company. The company's only objects were to generate and distribute hydroelectricity. The statute took away all of the company's operating assets, including its water rights, so that the company's objects could no longer be carried out. The statute provided no compensation whatsoever to the company, although it did provide for compensation to shareholders for the decline in the value of their shares.[67] If ever there was a case where an expropriation of assets could be regarded as sterilizing a federal company, this was the case. But the Supreme Court of Canada rejected this ground of attack. McIntyre J. for a unanimous Court pointed out that, although the company had lost its assets, it was "left with its corporate structure intact and with the capability to raise new capital and issue shares".[68] Therefore, he held, the Act did not deny the company's status or essential powers.[69]

McIntyre J. did not explicitly deal with the argument that the Act, by singling out one federal corporation for expropriation, should be characterized as a law in relation to a federal company.[70] But it is clear that the purpose of the statute was to acquire the electrical generating capacity, whoever its owner might be, rather than to strike at the federal company that happened to be the owner. The statute, although not general in its application, was nevertheless not a law in relation to a

---

65 See ch. 28, Public Property, under heading 28.5, "Expropriation", below.

66 [1984] 1 S.C.R. 297.

67 The shares were held: as to 34.2 per cent, by Hydro-Quebec, the Quebec Crown corporation that was the principal purchaser of the power; and as to the remaining 65.8 per cent, by Newfoundland and Labrador Hydro, a Newfoundland Crown corporation.

68 [1984] 1 S.C.R. 297, 327.

69 McIntyre J. did not explicitly deal with the argument that the company's only objects could no longer be carried out. The answer, no doubt, as suggested in the earlier text, is that federal corporate law would permit an alteration of the objects of the company.

70 On singling out, see ch. 15, Judicial Review on Federal Grounds, above.

federal company. In fact, McIntyre J. held that the purpose of the statute was to enable Newfoundland to nullify an improvident contract entered into by the company in 1969 (with the approval of the Newfoundland government) to supply most of the electricity generated at Churchill Falls to Hydro-Quebec at a price far below the market price for a term of 65 years. On this basis, he characterized the statute as being in relation to civil rights outside the province; and held that it was invalid for that reason.

Since the statute in issue in *Churchill Falls* was held to be invalid, the rejection of the federal company argument was not strictly necessary for the decision. But it is a carefully considered part of the opinion, agreed to by the eight judges that participated in the decision; and, in my view, it is consistent with the cases noticed earlier that decide that a provincial Legislature may prohibit a particular activity in the province, even if the prohibition has the effect of stopping a federal company from pursuing its business in the province.[71] As a matter of policy, too, it would be intolerable if a province could not nationalize an industry in which there was some degree of ownership by federal companies. I conclude that the *Churchill Falls* case may safely be taken as authority for the proposition that a federal company enjoys no immunity from a provincial law expropriating its assets.[72]

(c) Immunity of provincial companies

Do provincial companies enjoy immunities analogous to those of federal companies?

The ordinary principles of federal classification apply to protect provincial companies in the same way as they apply to protect federal companies. If a provincial statute is classified by the courts as a law in relation to a company incorporated in another province, then the provincial statute will be invalid. If a federal statute is classified by the courts as a law in relation to a company incorporated in a province, then the federal statute will be invalid. The doctrine of classification would therefore protect a provincial company from any laws emanating from another province or from Ottawa which singled it out for special treatment in such a way as to persuade a court that the law was in pith and substance in relation to the company. Such laws are of course exceedingly rare.

The more important and difficult question is whether a provincial company enjoys the same immunity as a federal company from laws which would impair the status or essential powers of the provincial company. Here we are concerned

71 Text accompanying note 62, above. Note especially *Can. Indemnity Co.* v. *A.-G. B.C.* [1977] 2 S.C.R. 504.

72 Accord, *Société Asbestos* v. *Société nationale de l'amiante* (1981) 128 D.L.R. (3d) 405 (Que. C.A.). There is one case to the contrary, namely, *B.C. Power Corp.* v. *A.-G. B.C.* (1963) 47 D.L.R. (2d) 633 (B.C.S.C.). That decision was criticized at length in the first edition (1977) of this book (at pp. 360-362). It was expressly overruled by McIntyre J. in the *Churchill Falls* case at p. 327.

with laws which do not single out any provincial company for special treatment, but which are held to have the effect of impairing a company's status or essential powers. The question breaks down into two sub-questions. The first is whether a provincial Legislature could impair the status or essential powers of a company incorporated in another province. The second is whether the federal Parliament could impair the status or essential powers of a company incorporated in one of the provinces. Neither question has been the subject of any judicial decision or dictum so far as I can discover. It is therefore necessary to go back to first principles in order to work out the answers.

The first question, which is whether a provincial Legislature has power to impair the status or essential powers of a company incorporated in another province, must be answered yes. The only situation in which this question would arise would be where a company incorporated in one province (the incorporating province) was seeking to operate in another province (the legislating province). So long as a company confines its activities to its province of incorporation there can be no question of another province enacting a law which would impair the status or essential powers of the company.[73] But when a provincial company seeks to extend its activities outside its province of incorporation, the *Bonanza Creek* case[74] decides that its recognition as a corporate entity depends entirely upon the laws applicable in the jurisdictions in which it seeks to operate. Unlike a federal company, which is entitled to recognition as a corporate entity throughout Canada, a provincial company is not entitled to recognition as a corporate entity outside its province of incorporation. The other provinces are under no obligation to accord recognition. It follows that a province could legislate so as to refuse to permit all companies incorporated in other provinces to do business in the legislating province;[75] a province could legislate so as to refuse to permit all companies incorporated in other provinces to raise capital in the legislating province;[76] and it could deny the status or essential powers of companies incorporated in other provinces in other, so far unprecedented, ways.

The second question is whether the federal Parliament has power to impair the status or essential powers of a company incorporated in a province. Again, the answer must be yes when the company is seeking to operate outside its province of incorporation; the *Bonanza Creek* case makes clear that outside its province of incorporation a provincial company is vulnerable to all applicable

---

73 The status and essential powers of a provincial company operating inside the province of incorporation cannot be impaired by other provinces, for this would require provincial laws with substantial extraterritorial effect, and the provinces have no power to enact such laws: see ch. 13, Extraterritorial Competence, above. Needless to say, a provincial company's status and essential powers, both inside and outside the province of incorporation, may be impaired by the province of incorporation.

74 [1916] A.C. 566; note 6, above.

75 Cf. *John Deere Plow Co.* v. *Wharton* [1915] A.C. 330; note 45, above; *Great West Saddlery Co.* v. *The Queen* [1921] 2 A.C. 91; note 46, above.

76 Cf. *A.-G. Man.* v. *A.-G. Can.* (Manitoba Securities) [1929] A.C. 260; note 51, above.

laws, whether provincial or federal, and even if they impair its status or essential powers. But the hard question is whether a federal law could impair the status or essential powers of a provincial company within its province of incorporation. For example, assuming that the federal Parliament could validly enact a securities law which purported to prohibit the primary issue of corporate securities (a law on the model of the *Manitoba Securities* case),[77] would such a law be applicable to a provincial company which sought to issue new shares in its province of incorporation? It is clearly established, as we have seen, that an otherwise valid provincial law is not applicable to a federal company if the effect of the law is to impair the status and essential powers of the company. What is now in question is whether the same doctrine applies in reverse: to protect a provincial company from federal laws which would impair the company's status and essential powers.

The answer to this question must depend upon the conceptual basis of the existing status-and-essential-powers immunity. On the one hand, it could be said that the immunity derives from a limitation on legislative power which is to be implied in the Constitution; this ultra vires rationale should apply in both directions, limiting federal power no less than provincial. On the other hand, it could be said that the immunity derives from the doctrine of federal paramountcy, on the basis that a provincial law stultifying a federal company is deemed to be in conflict with the federal law under which the company was incorporated; this paramountcy rationale would not work in both directions, because the paramountcy doctrine denies effect to provincial but not federal legislation.[78]

The leading cases which define the position of federal companies vis-à-vis provincial law, namely, *John Deere*, *Great West Saddlery*, *Manitoba Securities* and *Lymburn* v. *Mayland*, are not clear on the conceptual basis of the status-and-essential-powers immunity. The opinions suggest the ultra vires rationale, for they are sprinkled with words suggesting a lack of constitutional power, such as "invalid", "incompetent" and "ultra vires", rather than words suggesting paramountcy, such as "inoperative" or "inconsistent". Not too much should be made of this, of course, because their lordships were not attempting to be precise about the rationale of the doctrine. However, recent cases according an analogous immunity to undertakings within federal regulatory jurisdiction have clearly not been based on the paramountcy doctrine,[79] and the narrow operation which courts have given to the paramountcy doctrine in other contexts[80] suggests that it could not be the source of the status-and-essential-powers immunity.[81] It seems likely,

77 *Ibid.*

78 See ch. 16, Paramountcy, above. A dictum in *John Deere Plow Co.* v. *Wharton* [1915] A.C. 330, 341, has been interpreted as supporting a theory of paramountcy in reverse, but this is almost certainly a misreading of the dictum: see Ziegel, note 4, above, 160.

79 See ch. 15, Judicial Review on Federal Grounds, under heading 15.8(e), "Rationale of immunity", above.

80 See ch. 16, Paramountcy, above.

81 Contra, Ziegel, note 4, above, 165-167, 190.

therefore, that the ultra vires rationale is the better one;[82] and that the immunity should be reciprocal, protecting provincial companies (within their province of incorporation) from stultifying federal laws in the same way that it protects federal companies from stultifying provincial laws.[83]

82 There is, in my opinion, no satisfactory rationale for the immunity, nor any satisfactory policy justification. However, since the immunity exists it is necessary to select the least implausible of the two possible rationales. See also ch. 15, Judicial Review on Federal Grounds, under heading 15.5(k), "Interjurisdictional immunity", "Rationale of immunity".

83 The case for provincial corporate immunity is arguably stronger than for federal corporate immunity: see ch. 15, Judicial Review on Federal Grounds, under heading 15.8(f), "Provincial entities", above.

24

Financial Institutions

24.1 Federal power over banking

The Constitution Act, 1867, by s. 91(15), allocates to the federal Parliament legislative power in relation to "banking, incorporation of banks, and the issue of paper money". This makes banking[1] a special case in that the normal bifurcation of legislative authority between the incorporation of a company and the regulation of its business activity does not apply: the federal Parliament has both the power to incorporate banks and the power to regulate banking.

In addition, the federal Parliament has a range of other powers over money and credit. It has powers over "currency and coinage" (s. 91(14)), "savings banks" (s. 91(16)), "bills of exchange and promissory notes" (s. 91(18)), "interest" (s. 91(19)) and "legal tender" (s. 91(20)).

24.2 Definition of banking

(a) Functional test

What is comprised in the term "banking"? In the leading case of *Tennant* v. *Union Bank of Canada* (1894),[2] the Privy Council had to determine the validity

1 See Binavince and Fairley, "Banking and the Constitution" (1986) 65 Can. Car Rev. 328.
2 [1894] A.C. 31.

of a warehouse receipt held by a bank as security for a loan. According to provincial law, the receipt was invalid as a title to the goods represented thereby, but, according to the federal Bank Act, the receipt was valid. Lord Watson for the Privy Council held that the provision in the Bank Act was constitutional, although it had ''the effect of modifying civil rights in the province''.[3] He pointed out that the provision was designed to facilitate loans by banks on the security of goods, and such a loan ''was a proper banking transaction''.[4] The term ''banking'' was ''wide enough to embrace every transaction coming within the legitimate business of a banker''.[5]

The *Tennant* case made clear that Parliament could use its banking power to define a security interest and permit borrowing on the strength of that interest. In *Bank of Montreal* v. *Hall* (1990),[6] the Supreme Court of Canada went a step further to hold that Parliament could also prescribe the steps to be taken by a bank in order to realize its security in the event of default. The Court held that foreclosure proceedings by a bank must be conducted in accordance with the Bank Act, not the general provincial law respecting foreclosure. This impact on property and civil rights in the province was within the federal power over banking, because, following *Tennant*, the lending of money on the security of property was a transaction coming within ''the legitimate business of a banker'',[7] and the provisions for realization of a security interest were inseparable from the provisions creating the security interest.[8]

The rule of ''progressive interpretation''[9] applies to the scope of the phrase ''the legitimate business of a banker''. In the *Alberta Bill of Rights* case (1947),[10] the Privy Council said that this phrase was not confined to the kinds of transactions carried on by banks in 1867 but expanded along with the subsequent expansions of the business of banking.

These definitions of banking, although vague, obviously indicate an extensive federal power. In fact, however, the federal Parliament has exercised the power sparingly. The federal Bank Act[11] applies only to the banks listed in a schedule to the Act, and provides that the Act is the charter of each bank. The Act provides for the incorporation of new banks (either by Act of Parliament or by letters patent), and the organization and regulation of the banks. The Act prohibits companies which are not chartered under the Act from calling themselves banks, but it does not prohibit them from engaging in the business of banking.

3 *Id.*, 47.
4 *Id.*, 46.
5 *Ibid.*
6 [1990] 1 S.C.R. 121.
7 *Id.*, 132.
8 *Id.*, 147.
9 See sec. 15.6(f), ''Progressive interpretation'', above.
10 *A.-G. Alta.* v. *A.-G. Can.* (Alberta Bill of Rights) [1947] A.C. 503, 516-517.
11 S.C. 1991, c. 46.

(b) Institutional test

There are many institutions other than the chartered banks which fill the role of financial intermediaries by borrowing (or otherwise acquiring) funds from people who save and lending them to people who wish to spend. Some of these institutions, notably, the trust companies, the credit unions and the caisses populaires, not only accept short-term and demand deposits from the public which can be withdrawn over the counter in the same way as bank savings accounts, they also accept demand deposits upon which negotiable orders can be drawn in the same way as bank chequing accounts.[12] The credit unions and caisses populaires are all incorporated provincially, as are the majority of the trust companies, and all the provincially-incorporated institutions are primarily regulated by the provinces. None of these institutions is covered by the Bank Act, and only federally-incorporated trust and loan companies are subjected to pervasive federal regulation.[13]

The federal Parliament has never attempted to regulate the activities of the provincially-incorporated near-banks, and provincial regulation has never been challenged. However, the constitutional status of the activities of the near-banks has arisen for decision in a labour relations context. In *Canadian Pioneer Management* v. *Labour Relations Board of Saskatchewan* (1980),[14] a federally-incorporated trust company carried on a business that was for the most part identical to that of a chartered bank. The trust company accepted deposits from the public, opened chequing accounts and term deposits for depositors, made a wide variety of loans including overdrafts, and offered other services of a banking nature, such as money orders and safety deposit boxes. The only function performed by the company that was not also performed by the chartered banks was estate and trust administration, but this function constituted only one per cent of the company's business. The issue in the case was whether the company was subject to federal

12 The legislation of each jurisdiction requires a trust company to hold deposits as a ''trustee'' for the depositors. I suspect that these fiduciary provisions were inserted in order to distinguish the trust companies' chequing and savings accounts from those of the banks. In my view, the fact that the trust company offers a pre-determined rate of interest to its depositors, and assumes the risk of profit or loss on the reinvestment of the funds deposited, is incompatible with a fiduciary relationship between the trust company and its depositors. My view has however been disapproved by Beetz J. for the majority of the Supreme Court of Canada in Can. *Pioneer Management* v. *Labour Relations Bd. Sask.* [1980] 1 S.C.R. 433, 451 (but compare 464), who accepted the existence of a fiduciary relationship. This point was not necessary to the decision of the case in view of the institutional test applied by Beetz J: see following text. In the context of priority of debts, the Court has refused to recognize a statutory trust where the trust property was not identifiable: *Dauphin Plains Credit Union* v. *Xyloid Industries* [1980] 1 S.C.R. 1182, 1196-1198.

13 See generally Baum, ''Near-banks: Trust Companies of Canada'' (1971) 45 Tulane L. Rev. 546; McDonald, ''The B.N.A. Act and the Near Banks'' (1972) 10 Alta. L. Rev. 155. As to the validity of federal regulation, see note 43, below.

14 [1980] 1 S.C.R. 433.

or provincial labour law. This turned on whether the company was engaged in "banking"'. The Supreme Court of Canada held that the company was not engaged in banking, so that it was subject to provincial labour law.[15]

The Court in *Canadian Pioneer Management* had to provide a definition of the term "banking". Beetz J. for the majority[16] rejected a "functional" definition of the term, on the ground that none of the functions of the chartered banks was exclusive to banks. The economic function of financial intermediation was performed by a variety of other institutions, including life insurance companies, loan companies and trust companies. Nor were there any specific functions that should be regarded as exclusive to the business of banking, not even the provision of chequing facilities to depositors.[17] If the *Tennant* definition of banking were applied without qualification, then the provision of financial services, which is part of the "legitimate business" of many kinds of institutions and individuals as well as bankers, would fall under the exclusive legislative competence of Parliament. This would be an extension of federal power that was never intended.[18] Beetz J. concluded that the *Tennant* definition should be reframed in "institutional" terms. In institutional terms, the business of banking meant the business of the institutions authorized by the federal Bank Act to hold themselves out as banks.[19] In effect, Beetz J. deferred to the parliamentary definition of banks in order to define the scope of banking. He acknowledged that this institutional test granted to the federal Parliament the power to define its own power: the scope of banking would expand or contract according to the extent to which Parliament had chosen to legislate.[20]

In *Canadian Pioneer Management*, the institutional test was particularly appropriate, because the entire business of the trust company had to be classified as either federal or provincial, in order to attribute the business to one or the other regime of labour relations. Beetz J. acknowledged that the institutional test might not be appropriate where the issue was the constitutionality of a particular law with some impact on functions performed by banks. In that context, the word "banking" in s. 91(15) might have a "wider" meaning than just those functions performed by chartered banks.[21] Beetz J. did not indicate how the term "banking" should be defined in such a case, or what kinds of laws he had in mind. However, as we noticed earlier, in *Bank of Montreal* v. *Hall* (1990),[22] where the issue was

---

15 The division of constitutional authority over labour relations is discussed in sec. 21.8, "Labour relations", above.

16 Beetz J.'s opinion was agreed to by Martland, Ritchie, Pigeon, Estey and McIntyre JJ. Laskin C.J., with the agreement of Dickson J., wrote a short concurring opinion which was similar in reasoning to Beetz J.'s opinion.

17 [1980] 1 S.C.R. 433, 461.

18 *Id.*, 468

19 *Id.*, 465-466.

20 *Id.*, 468-469, noting that the definitions of penitentiaries (s. 91(28)) and Indians (s. 91(24)) also depend upon federal legislation.

21 *Id.*, 466.

22 Note 6, above.

the validity of provisions of the Bank Act prescribing the steps to be taken to foreclose on a mortgage, the Court went back to the functional test employed in *Tennant*, and asked whether the Parliament was regulating a transaction coming within ''the legitimate business of a banker''.

24.3 Provincial regulation of financial institutions

(a) Banks

A law in relation to banking is incompetent to the provinces, by virtue of the exclusive federal power over banking (s. 91(5)). However, if there are no functions that are exclusive to banking, as *Canadian Pioneer Management* decideit follows that provincial regulation of the activities of financial institutions other than the chartered banks cannot be characterized as in relation to ''banking''. As noted earlier in this chapter, this includes the ''near-banks'', namely, the trust companies, credit unions and caisses populaires that accept deposits from the public and issue savings and chequing accounts. Provincial regulation would come within property and civil rights in the province, in common with the regulation of most business activity.[23]

The existence of the federal power over banking has occasionally led to the invalidation of provincial laws. In the *Alberta Statutes Reference* (1938),[24] the Supreme Court of Canada struck down the Alberta legislation of the 1930s that attempted to establish ''social credit'' in the province, a regime that involved the creation of a new form of credit.[25] To the extent that this decision depended upon the view that the creation of credit is exclusively a banking function, Beetz J. in *Canadian Pioneer Management* doubted its correctness.[26] However, as Beetz J. pointed out, the Court in the *Alberta Statutes Reference* relied on other grounds as well, especially the federal power over ''currency''. Other decisions striking down provincial laws as being in relation to banking seem consistent with Beetz J.'s institutional test. The *Alberta Bank Taxation Reference* (1939)[27] struck down one of Alberta's social credit laws, which levied an oppressively heavy tax on the banks, and only the banks. The *Quebec Bank Deposits Reference* (1946)[28] struck down a Quebec law, which confiscated all deposits in ''credit institutions''

23 See ch. 21, Property and Civil Rights, above.
24 *Re Alberta Statutes* [1938] S.C.R. 100.
25 See also *A.-G. Alta.* v. *A.-G. Can.* (Alberta Bill of Rights) [1947] A.C. 503. The Social Credit government of Premier Aberhart was elected in Alberta in 1935. All the measures enacted to carry out social credit policies were destroyed either by federal disallowances or by judicial decisions: see ch. 25, Bankruptcy and Insolvency, under heading 25.5, ''Adjustment of debts'', below.
26 [1980] 1 S.C.R. 433, 458.
27 *A.-G. Alta.* v. *A.-G. Can.* (Bank Taxation) [1939] A.C. 117.
28 *A.-G. Can.* v. *A.-G. Que.* (Bank Deposits) [1947] A.C. 33.

that had not been claimed for 30 years; the Privy Council emphasized that credit institutions were ''primarily'' banks. In each case, it was the primary impact of the provincial law on the activities of the chartered banks that led to the banking classification of the law and its consequent invalidity.

On the other hand, where the pith and substance of a law comes within a provincial head of power, the law will be competent to the province even if it has an incidental impact on banking (the activities of the chartered banks).[29] Thus, a province may tax the banks, so long as the purpose is to raise revenue[30] and not (as the Privy Council found in the *Alberta Bank Taxation Reference*)[31] to destroy or sterilize the banks. The same kind of reasoning may be seen in other cases involving banks. Provincial laws will apply to the banks except in three classes of cases: (1) where the provincial law is in pith and substance in relation to banking (as in the social credit cases); (2) where the provincial law, although within a provincial head of power, would affect a vital part of the operation of a bank;[32] and (3) where the provincial law is inconsistent with the Bank Act or some other federal law.[33]

(b) Non-bank financial institutions

Apart from the banks, the other three pillars of the financial community are commonly said to be the trust companies, the insurance companies and the securities dealers. To this list must be added the credit unions, caisses populaires and loan companies, all of which are important financial intermediaries in Canada.[34] All of these financial institutions are subject to provincial regulation, whether they are incorporated federally or provincially or in some foreign jurisdiction. The provincial power comes from the authority over property and civil rights in the province.

Trust companies, as their name implies, initially developed to administer trusts and estates. In that capacity, there could be no doubt as to their subjection to provincial regulatory jurisdiction. Doubt was caused by the expansion of the

---

29 See generally ch. 15, Judicial Review on Federal Grounds, above.

30 *Bank of Toronto* v. *Lambe* (1887) 12 App. Cas. 575.

31 Note 27, above.

32 See ch. 15, Judicial Review on Federal Grounds, under heading 15.8, ''Interjurisdictional Immunity'' above. This immunity was examined and held inapplicable on the facts to banks in *Sommers* v. *Sturdy* (1957) 10 D.L.R. (2d) 269 (B.C.C.A.) and *Gregory Co.* v. *Imperial Bank* [1960] C.S. 204 (Que. S.C.).

33 This is simply the doctrine of paramountcy, exemplified in *Tennant* v. *Union Bank of Can.* [1894] A.C. 31 and *Bank of Montreal* v. *Hall* [1990] 1 S.C.R. 121, where provincial laws were held to be inapplicable to banks on the basis of federal paramountcy. These cases are discussed in ch. 16, Paramountcy, under heading 16.3, ''Express contradiction'', above.

34 See Moull, Waitzer, Ziegel, ''The Changing Regulatory Environment for Financial Institutions'' in Ziegel, Waverman, Conklin (eds.), *Canadian Financial Institutions: Changing the Regulatory Environment* (Ontario Economic Council, 1985), 101-170; Daniels, ''Breaking the Logjam: Proposals for Moving Beyond the Equals Approach'' (1993) 22 Can. Bus. L.J. 13.2.

activities of the trust companies into "near-banking": taking deposits from the public and issuing term deposits, savings and chequing accounts that are practically indistinguishable from the term deposits, savings and chequing accounts that are issued by the chartered banks. However, the *Canadian Pioneer Management* case[35] decides that these "near-banking" functions, when performed by institutions other than the chartered banks, are still subject to provincial regulation. This decision also confirms the existence of provincial jurisdiction over the credit unions and caisses populaires, which also take deposits from their members and provide bank-like services to their members. Nor could there be any doubt about provincial jurisdiction over loan companies that raise funds from the public for the purpose of mortgage lending.

Insurance companies charge premiums which are invested in order to provide the funds to cover the insured event, whether it be death, illness, fire, accident or theft. They also issue a variety of endowment policies, annuity contracts and other instruments that are essentially long-term investments, not unlike term deposits. As related in the earlier chapter on Property and Civil Rights,[36] the insurance industry was the battleground upon which federal and provincial regulators fought for control in a series of cases between 1880 and 1942. These cases were all resolved in favour of the provincial power over property and civil rights. Insurance companies are therefore subject to provincial regulation, although there is also a considerable federal presence which seems to be based as much on acquiescence by the provinces and the industry as on constitutional right.

Securities dealers underwrite new issues of stocks, bonds and other corporate securities, distribute new issues and buy and sell securities that are traded on the stock exchanges or over the counter. As related in the earlier chapter on Property and Civil Rights,[37] the provinces have the power to regulate the securities industry, including the stock exchanges, under the provincial power over property and civil rights in the province. Each province has established a securities commission for that purpose. Despite some gaps in provincial power, there is no comprehensive federal regulation even of interprovincial transactions, and no federal securities commission, although there are some prohibitions on fraud and deception in the Criminal Code and some rules respecting the securities of federally incorporated companies.

24.4 Incorporation of banks

Since the federal Parliament has legislative power over the "incorporation of banks" under s. 91(15) of the Constitution Act, it follows that the incorporation of banks is withdrawn from the provincial power of incorporation under s. 92(11)

35 Note 14, above.

36 Chapter 21, under heading 21.5, "Insurance", above.

37 Chapter 21, under heading 21.10, "Securities regulation", above.

of the Constitution Act.[38] This is so, irrespective of whether the phrase ''with provincial objects'' in s. 92(11) has territorial or functional significance.[39]

24.5 Incorporation of other financial institutions

The provinces acting under s. 92(11) (''the incorporation of companies with provincial objects'') have the power to incorporate trust companies, loan companies, credit unions, caisses populaires, insurance companies, securities dealers and other non-bank financial institutions, including the power to authorize them to perform functions similar to the chartered banks. Any doubt on this score[40] has been resolved by the decision in *Canadian Pioneer Management*.[41] Although the trust company in that case had been federally incorporated, the decision makes clear that financial institutions other than the chartered banks are not ''banks'' and their activities are not ''banking'' within the meaning of s. 91(15).

The decision in *Canadian Pioneer Management* also makes clear that the federal Parliament's power of incorporation[42] (not its power over banking) authorizes the incorporation of trust companies and other non-bank financial institutions, provided, of course, that their powers are not limited to a single province. As the previous chapter, Companies, has emphasized, the power of incorporation does not extend to the regulation of the business activity of the federally-incorporated entity. However, the federal power of incorporation does authorize some degree of regulation of federally-incorporated financial institutions as ''conditions of their incorporation''.[43]

38 This is because the heads of power are mutually exclusive: see ch. 15, Judicial Review on Federal Grounds, under heading 15.9(b), ''Exclusiveness'', above.

39 See ch. 23, Companies, under heading 23.1, ''Incorporation of companies'', above.

40 *Re Bergethaler Waisenamt* [1949] 1 D.L.R. 769 (Man. C.A.) upheld the deposit-taking function of a provinciallyincorporated trust company, but implied that the provision of chequing facilities would be unconstitutional as banking. *Breckenridge Speedway* v. *The Queen* [1970] S.C.R. 175 upheld contracts between the ''treasury branches'' of Alberta and their customers, but the majority did not resolve the question whether the treasury branches carried on the business of banking, and the minority held that the treasury branches did carry on the business of banking and were for that reason unconstitutional.

41 Note 14, above.

42 Note 39, above.

43 *Id.*, 453, upholding the federal Trust Companies Act on the ground that its provisions did not go beyond conditions of incorporation and did not rise to ''the level of regulation''.

25

Bankruptcy and Insolvency

25.1 Section 91(21)

Section 91(21) of the Constitution Act, 1867 grants to the federal Parliament the power to enact laws in relation to ''bankruptcy and insolvency''.[1] In the United States, the federal Congress has a similar power: to pass ''uniform laws on the subject of bankruptcies throughout the United States''.[2] The same is true in Australia, where the federal Parliament has legislative power over ''bankruptcy and insolvency''.[3] These grants of power recognize that debtors may move from

1 See *Bankruptcy and Insolvency* (Report of the Study Committee on Bankruptcy and Insolvency Legislation, Government of Canada, 1970); Bohémier, *La faillite en droit constitutionnel canadien* (1972); McConnell, *Commentary on the British North America Act* (1977), 217-220; Carignan, ''La compétence legislative en matière de faillite et d'insolvabilité (1979) 57 Can. Bar Rev. 47; Laskin, *Canadian Constitutional Law* (5th ed., 1986 by Finkelstein), 758-781.

2 Constitution of the United States, article 1, s. 8(4).

3 Constitution of Australia, s. 51(17).

one province to another, and may have property and creditors in more than one province. A national body of law is required to ensure that all of a debtor's property is available to satisfy his debts, that all creditors are fairly treated, and that all are bound by any arrangements for the settlement of the debtor's debts. Indeed, without these assurances, lenders would be reluctant to extend credit to persons who could evade their obligations simply by removing themselves or their assets across a provincial boundary.

25.2 Bankruptcy legislation

The federal Parliament first enacted a comprehensive Bankruptcy Act in 1919.[4] This Act was applicable to corporations and individuals, and to business failures as well as personal insolvency. It was repealed and replaced by a new Act in 1949.[5] The 1949 Act is still in force, although it was substantially modified (and renamed the Bankruptcy and Insolvency Act) in 1992.[6] Under the Bankruptcy and Insolvency Act, there is now provision for insolvent corporations or individuals to make arrangements with their creditors without actually going bankrupt. The Companies Creditors Arrangement Act,[7] which was enacted in 1933 (before the Bankruptcy Act contained adequate provision for an arrangement between an insolvent debtor and creditors), also makes provision for a corporation (but not an individual) to make an arrangement with its creditors. Also existing side by side with the Bankruptcy and Insolvency Act is the Winding-up and Restructuring Act,[8] which was enacted before the Bankruptcy Act, to enable insolvent corporations to be wound up. The Winding-up and Restructuring Act has not been repealed, although the Bankruptcy and Insolvency Act now also provides for the winding up of insolvent corporations.

25.3 Meaning of bankruptcy

''Bankruptcy'' has been judicially defined in these terms:[9]

> Bankruptcy is a well understood procedure by which an insolvent debtor's property is coercively brought under judicial administration in the interests primarily of the creditors. To this proceeding not only a personal stigma may attach but restrictions on freedom in future business activity may result. The relief to the debtor consists in the cancellation of debts which, otherwise, might effectually prevent him from

4 The history of bankruptcy legislation is related in the Report of the Study Committee, note 1, above, ch. 2.

5 Bankruptcy Act, R.S.C. 1985, c. B-3, renamed the Bankruptcy and Insolvency Act by S.C. 1992, c. 27, s. 2.

6 S.C. 1992, c. 27.

7 R.S.C. 1985, c. C-36.

8 R.S.C. 1985, c. W-11; formerly the Winding-up Act, renamed by S.C. 1996, c. 6, s. 3.

9 *Can. Bankers Assn.* v. *A.G. Sask.* [1956] S.C.R. 31, 46 per Rand J.

rehabilitating himself economically and socially. As this passage makes clear, bankruptcy is a technical term referring to a legal status under which a debtor's assets are vested in a trustee whose duty is to realise the assets and make a rateable distribution among the debtor's creditors. At the conclusion of a bankruptcy, the debtor is discharged from bankruptcy, the unpaid portion of the debts is cancelled and the debtor is permitted to resume life free of debt.

25.4 Meaning of insolvency

"Insolvency" is "a broader term" than bankruptcy, meaning "the inability to meet obligations as they mature".[10] An insolvent debtor is unable to pay his debts as they fall due. An insolvent debtor is liable to become bankrupt, and is subject to less radical legislated measures, both under the federal Bankruptcy Act and under provincial law, to protect the creditors and rehabilitate the debtor.

25.5 Adjustment of debts

(a) Federal power

Provincial power over property and civil rights extends to the law of property and contract.[11] However, the courts early recognized that the federal power over bankruptcy and insolvency could not be effective if it did not authorize substantial modifications of the ordinary rights of property and contract.[12] The first major test of the extent of the power came in *Re Companies' Creditors Arrangement Act* (1934),[13] which was a reference to determine the validity of the federal Companies' Creditors Arrangement Act of 1933. The Act authorized an insolvent company to make a composition with its creditors that would alter the normal obligations of contracts. Moreover, the Act did not utilize the technique of bankruptcy; the purpose was to prevent the insolvent company from having to go bankrupt. Nevertheless, the Supreme Court of Canada upheld the Act. Duff C.J. said that "legislation in respect of compositions and arrangements is a natural and ordinary component of a system of bankruptcy and insolvency law".[14]

This decision was followed in the *Farmers' Creditors Arrangement Reference* (1937),[15] in which the Court upheld the federal Farmers' Creditors Arrangement Act. This Act, which was one of Prime Minister R. B. Bennett's "new deal" initiatives, was enacted during the depression to authorize insolvent farmers to

10 *Ibid.*

11 Chapter 21, Property and Civil Rights, above.

12 *Cushing* v. *Dupuy* (1880) 5 App. Cas. 409, 415-416, upholding federal law denying appeals to Privy Council in insolvency matters.

13 [1934] S.C.R. 659.

14 *Id.*, 660; Cannon J. is to the same effect at 664.

15 *A.G.B.C.* v. *A.G. Can.* (Farmers' Creditors Arrangement) [1937] A.C. 391.

make a composition with their creditors that would enable the farmer to keep the farm and would require the creditor to accept less than the full amount owing. Once again, the Act impaired the normal obligations of contracts, and, once again, the Act did not force the debtor into bankruptcy, but instead sought to avoid bankruptcy. The Privy Council emphasized that the word ''insolvency'' was broader than ''bankruptcy'', and that it was open to Parliament to provide for compositions with creditors by techniques less formal than bankruptcy, provided that the legislative scheme was predicated on the insolvency of the debtor. The Privy Council also emphasized that the federal power over bankruptcy and insolvency should be interpreted as authorizing new techniques of providing for insolvency; the power did not confine Parliament to those regulatory instruments that may have been familiar in 1867.

Re Companies' Creditors Arrangement Act and the *Farmers' Creditors Arrangement Reference* covered compositions outside bankruptcy. Once a creditor has become bankrupt there is no doubt that Parliament can provide for the debtor's discharge from bankruptcy and his release from the unpaid portion of his debts.[16] In short, there is no doubt that the federal Parliament has power to adjust debts in order to regulate bankruptcy or insolvency.

In addition to the power over bankruptcy and insolvency, the federal Parliament has legislative authority over ''interest'', granted by s. 91(19) of the Constitution Act, 1867.[17] This enables Parliament to regulate interest rates, or to modify them after they have been agreed upon by the debtor and the creditor.

(b) Provincial power

The provincial power over ''property and civil rights in the province'', which is granted by s. 92(13), extends to most of the law of contract and property, but some aspects of debtor-creditor relationships are outside that power by reason of the grants to the federal Parliament of the exclusive powers over ''bankruptcy and insolvency'' and ''interest''. The provinces are also subject to an extraterritorial restriction imposed by the words ''in the province'' in s. 92(13) itself.[18] These various gaps in provincial power have brought to grief many provincial attempts to modify creditors' rights.

Much of the case law on the modification of creditors' rights arose out of the depression of the 1930s, which was accompanied by a drought in the prairie provinces. The governments of those provinces, with Alberta's Social Credit government (elected in 1935) leading the way, naturally attempted to relieve the burden of debt (which was mainly owed to eastern creditors) from their residents and especially their farmers. Their attempts to make creditors share some part of the losses caused by the depression, and to keep farmland productive, were nearly

16 Note 9, above.

17 See Laskin, *Canadian Constitutional Law* (5th ed., 1986 by Finkelstein), 743-785.

18 Chapter 13, Extraterritorial Competence, above.

all defeated, either by the decisions of the courts or by the federal government's exercise of the power of disallowance. The story has been well told by J. R. Mallory,[19] and it is difficult to resist his conclusion that the laissez-faire prejudices of that time played a role in the judicial decisions as well as the disallowances.

(c) Interest adjustment

One of the Alberta Social Credit government's first responses to the hardship caused by the depression was to reduce the interest charges on farmers and other debtors in the province and on the provincial government. Alberta's Reduction and Settlement of Debts Act, 1936, enacted a formula for the reduction or cancellation of interest on certain specified classes of debts. This was held to be unconstitutional by the Appellate Division of the Alberta Supreme Court[20] as a law in relation to "interest" and to civil rights outside the province (where most of the creditors resided).[21] Another Alberta statute, cutting in half the interest payable on bonds issued by or guaranteed by the province, was struck down by the Privy Council as a law in relation to "interest".[22]

Saskatchewan attempted to circumvent these decisions by providing that "in case of crop failure" (which was defined) the farmer-debtor was not excused from payments of interest to his creditor, but the principal sum was to be automatically reduced by the amount of the interest. This provision was coupled with a postponement of the payment of the principal sum for the period of crop failure. In the *Saskatchewan Farm Security Reference* (1949),[23] the Privy Council held that the statute was colourable; although it purported to deal only with the principal of the debt, in substance it was the interest that was modified. The effect of the statute, their lordships asserted, was "the same" as if the statute had said "in plain terms" that "for the period of suspension there should be no interest charged".[24] This was not quite accurate, because the legislation expressly stipulated that interest continued to be "chargeable, payable and recoverable". No doubt, it was hoped that a creditor would not insist upon payment of interest and would apply unpaid interest to make up the principal sum, but the creditor was fully entitled to insist upon payment of interest on the due day.[25] Their lordships

---

19 Mallory, *Social Credit and the Federal Power* (1954), esp. ch. 6; see also Tollefson in Lang (ed.), *Contemporary Problems of Public Law in Canada* (1968), 49.

20 *Credit Foncier Franco-Canadien* v. *Ross* [1937] 3 D.L.R. 365 (Alta. A.D.).

21 The extraterritorial point seems dubious in light of *Ladore* v. *Bennett* [1939] A.C. 468; discussed in ch. 13, Extraterritorial Competence, under heading 13.3(c), "Impairment of extraprovincial rights", above.

22 *Lethbridge Northern Irrigation Dist. Trustees* v. *I.O.F.* [1940] A.C. 523.

23 *A.-G. Sask.* v. *A.-G. Can.* (Farm Security) [1949] A.C. 110.

24 *Id.*, 125.

25 A second ground of decision was that a reduction in the principal sum was equivalent to an increase in the rate of interest, and was accordingly a law in relation to interest. This line of reasoning is flatly inconsistent with the first line of reasoning, and it was not expressed to be an alternative. And surely the incidental effects on the interest rate should not make a law which only alters principal a law "in relation to" interest.

also gave no weight to the consideration that the statute operated only in the case of crop failure, which would seem to demonstrate a provincial concern that the free exercise of creditors' rights would drive farmers off the land. But their lordships held that the pith and substance of the law was neither ''property'' (s. 92(13)) nor ''agriculture'' (s. 95).[26]

In striking contrast to the *Saskatchewan Farm Security Reference* is the decision of the Supreme Court of Canada in *A.-G. Ont.* v. *Barfried Enterprises* (1963).[27] Ontario's Unconscionable Transactions Relief Act enabled a court to set aside, or revise the terms of, a loan of money where it found that ''the cost of the loan is excessive and that the transaction is harsh and unconscionable''. The ''cost of the loan'' was defined as meaning ''the whole cost to the debtor of money lent'' and it expressly included ''interest, discount, subscription, premium, dues, bonus, commission, brokerage fees and charges''. In commercial terms, of course, whenever a lender advances less than the sum which will have to be repaid by the borrower on redemption, the true rate of return to the lender must take account of the extra sum (whether described as a discount, bonus, premium or whatever). The discount must be amortized over the life of the loan and added to conventional interest in order to ascertain the annual rate of return to the lender. The discount is different from conventional interest only in the unimportant respect that it is not payable until the maturity of the loan. But in *Barfried*, where the mortgage had been granted at a substantial discount, the Supreme Court of Canada held that the ''essential characteristic'' of interest was its ''day-to-day accrual'', and that a discount payable only on maturity was therefore not interest. It followed that a provincial law regulating ''the whole cost'' of a loan was not a law in relation to interest. The Court therefore upheld the legislation as ''relating to annulment or reformation of contract''.[28]

The narrow definition of interest given in *Barfried*, if carried over to cases in which federal legislation is in issue, would rob the interest power of all efficacy, since no regulation of interest could possibly be effective if it did not control all elements of the lender's rate of return. However, in *Tomell Investments* v. *East Marstock Lands* (1977),[29] the Supreme Court of Canada upheld federal legislation controlling the size of the penalty payable to a lender in the event of default by the borrower. Pigeon J. for the majority acknowledged that the legislation did not deal with ''interest in the strict sense of a charge accruing day by day'', but he held that the legislation was ''a valid exercise of ancillary power''.[30] Laskin C.J. in a brief separate concurring opinion made no reference to the narrow *Barfried* definition of interest; he held that the legislation was ''an assertion of the interest

26 This is one of the cases which justifies Laskin's assertion that the courts' construction of the agriculture power ''has drained it of substance'': *Canadian Constitutional Law* (5th ed., 1986 by Finkelstein), 500.
27 [1963] S.C.R. 570; for comment, see Weiler (1973) 23 U. Toronto L.J. 307, 339-340.
28 *Id.*, 577.
29 [1978] 1 S.C.R. 974.
30 *Id.*, 987.

power simpliciter'', and that it was ''unnecessary to invoke any doctrine of ancillary power.''[13]

(d) Principal and interest adjustment

The limitations imposed on provincial power — at least before the *Barfried* decision — by the existence of the federal ''interest'' power are less relevant when debt adjustment takes the form of an administrative power to modify the entire debtor-creditor relationship, reducing or postponing principal as well as interest obligations.[32] But such laws have in any event been struck down on the basis that they relate to the federal subject matter of ''bankruptcy and insolvency'' (s. 91(21)).[33] This was the fate of Alberta's Debt Adjustment Act, 1937, which among other things authorized an administrative agency to impose a settlement on creditors, although the legislation was not predicated upon an act of bankruptcy or the insolvency of the debtor.[34] A different kind of Act, providing for a judicial consolidation of all of a debtor's debts and regular payments into court by the debtor, was also struck down as in relation to bankruptcy and insolvency.[35] But there is no doubt about the validity of provincial laws that empower the courts to give directions for the periodic payment of a single judgment debt.[36]

(e) Moratorium

A province may enact a law suspending a creditor's right to enforce repayment of a loan while a period of notice is given that would provide a last opportunity for the debtor to repay the loan. Such a law is within the provincial power over property and civil rights in the province.[37] Probably, a province could also enact a general self-applying moratorium statute, postponing the rights of creditors for a fixed period of time, but not otherwise altering those rights.[38] But where the power to postpone creditors' rights is vested in a government official or agency with discretion to tailor its order to the facts of individual cases, then this is unconstitutional as authorizing the kind of composition or settlement which is

---

31 *Id.*, 977. See also ch. 15, Judicial Review on Federal Grounds, under heading 15.9(c), ''Ancillary power'', above.

32 The *Sask. Farm Security Reference* suggests that the interest power could be an impediment to provincial laws requiring a composition or settlement of debts: note 25, above; but it seems extreme to characterize such laws as in relation to interest.

33 The federal power under s. 91(21) to authorize compositions, arrangements or settlements between debtors and creditors is clear: text accompanying notes 13-15, above.

34 *A.-G. Alta.* v. *A.-G. Can.* (Debt Adjustment) [1943] A.C. 356.

35 *Re Orderly Payment of Debts Act* [1960] S.C.R. 571.

36 *Schill* v. *Weimer* (1981) 132 D.L.R. (3d) 25 (Sask. C.A.).

37 *Bank of Montreal* v. *Hall* [1990] 1 S.C.R. 121, 131.

38 See *Can. Bankers' Assn.* v. *A.-G. Sask.* [1956] S.C.R. 31, 42, 47.

within exclusive federal power.[39] On the other hand, where a discretionary power to postpone creditors' rights is vested in the court in which those rights have to be enforced, the power has been treated as a power to stay proceedings, which can then be characterized as a matter of civil procedure coming within the administration of justice in the province (s. 92(14)). The judicially-enforced moratorium has been upheld, notwithstanding that the court, in exercising its discretion, was directed to address itself to the ability of the debtor to pay the debt.[40]

25.6 Priority of debts

(a) Federal power

The federal power over bankruptcy and insolvency enables the federal Parliament to provide for the ranking of debts in bankruptcy. Upon bankruptcy, therefore, the priority of creditors is determined by federal bankruptcy law. Provincial law purporting to alter the federally-stipulated order of priority in bankruptcy is unconstitutional, because it affects an essential part of bankruptcy, and would in any event be inoperative, because it would conflict with the Bankruptcy Act's scheme of distribution.[41] However, this does not mean that provincial law is irrelevant to the distribution of assets on bankruptcy. For example, whether the debtor owns a particular asset will depend upon the provincial law of property. Whether the debtor owes a particular debt will depend upon the provincial law of contract.

The Bankruptcy Act[42] establishes a general rule that all creditors rank equally, and those whose claims are proved in a bankruptcy are to be paid rateably.[43] As an exception to the general rule, ten categories of debts are accorded priority, including, for example, the expenses of the trustee in bankruptcy, wages owed to an employee, and rent owed to a landlord.[44] These preferred creditors must be paid, in the order of priority stipulated by the Act, before the ordinary creditors. However, the entire scheme of distribution is "subject to the rights of

39 *A.-G. Alta.* v. *A.-G. Can.* (Debt Adjustment) [1943] A.C. 356; *Can. Bankers Assn.* v. *A.-G. Sask.* [1956] S.C.R. 31.

40 *Roy* v. *Plourde* [1943] S.C.R. 262; cf. *Abitibi Power and Paper Co.* v. *Montreal Trust Co.* [1943] A.C. 536; see generally, Laskin, *Canadian Constitutional Law* (5th ed., 1986 by Finkelstein), 766-768.

41 *Royal Bank of Can.* v. *Larue* [1928] A.C. 187 (assignment for benefit of creditors under Bankruptcy Act takes priority over hypothec under Civil Code); *A.G. Ont.* v. *Policy-holders of Wentworth Insurance Co.* [1969] S.C.R. 779 (priority of claims against insurance fund governed by federal Winding-up Act, not provincial law).

42 R.S.C. 1985, c. B-3.

43 Section 141.

44 Section 136 as amended by S.C. 1992, c. 27, s. 54.

secured creditors''.[45] This phrase enables secured creditors to realize their security as if there were no bankruptcy. The term ''secured creditor'' is defined in s. 2 of the Act, but in terms so general that the validity and effect of ''a mortgage, pledge, charge, lien or privilege'' is left to be determined under the provincial law relating to secured transactions. For example, if a creditor claims to hold a first mortgage on land in Ontario, the trustee in bankruptcy (or, in case of dispute, the courts) will look to Ontario's law of mortgages to determine whether the creditor is indeed a secured creditor and, if, so the extent to which the creditor can resort to the land in priority to all other creditors. In this way, provincial law has a profound, albeit indirect, effect on the distribution of the bankrupt's assets.

(b) Statutory lien

Debts owed to the Crown for unpaid federal and provincial taxes are expressly mentioned in the Bankruptcy and Insolvency Act, and are given the status of preferred debts. However, they are well down in the order of priorities (tenth, in fact), so that Crown claimants are likely to receive less than their full indebtedness.[46] To overcome this disability, provincial Legislatures in their taxing statutes have often attempted to create a statutory lien (or charge or privilege) in favour of the Crown for unpaid taxes. The purpose is to convert the claim for unpaid taxes into a ''secured debt'' and thereby leap ahead of other creditors in bankruptcy. The constitutional argument for this result is that, since the category of secured creditors depends upon provincial law, any change in the provincial law could validly have the indirect result of promoting (or postponing) a creditor's claim in bankruptcy. This argument has not been accepted by the Supreme Court of Canada. In a series of cases,[47] the Court has held that a provincially-legislated statutory lien for unpaid taxes, although undoubtedly effective in all situations outside bankruptcy, was ineffective in bankruptcy. The legislation did not qualify the Crown as a secured creditor, and the Crown's claim simply ranked as a preferred creditor, in accordance with the provisions of the Bankruptcy Act respecting claims of the Crown.

(c) Statutory trust

The property of a bankrupt that is divisible among his or her creditors does not include property held by the bankrupt in trust for a beneficiary.[48] The bene-

---

45 *Ibid.*

46 The federal Parliament has the power to reduce the prerogative priority of Crown debts, including debts owed to the provinces: *Re Silver Bros.* [1932] A.C. 514; cases cited in notes 47, 50, below; see also Hogg, *Liability of the Crown* (2nd ed., 1989), 192, 197.

47 *Deputy Minr. of Revenue* v. *Rainville* [1980] 1 S.C.R. 35; *Deloitte Haskins & Sells* v. *Workers' Comp. Bd.* [1985] 1 S.C.R. 785; *Fed. Bus. Dvlpt. Bank* v. *Que.* [1988] 1 S.C.R. 1061. For discussion, see Roman and Sweatman, ''The Conflict between Canadian Provincial Personal Property Security Acts and the Federal Bankruptcy Act'' (1992) 71 Can. Bar Rev. 77.

48 Bankruptcy and Insolvency Act, s. 67(1)(a) as amended by S.C. 1992, c. 27, s. 33.

ficiary of a trust is the beneficial owner of the trust property, and is not affected by the trustee's personal bankruptcy. As in the case of a secured debt, it falls to the law of each province to determine whether or not a valid trust exists. As in the case of a secured debt, the Supreme Court of Canada has had to face the question whether a trust constructed by statute will protect property claimed by the Crown from the claims of creditors in bankruptcy.

The statutory trust is typically created in this way. Provincial (and federal)[49] taxing statutes often provide for a private person to withhold tax (an employer, for example) or to collect tax (a retailer, for example), and require that the tax withheld or collected be regularly remitted to the Crown. In order to guard against the possibility that the collecting agent may be more dutiful in withholding or collecting than in remitting, it is standard drafting practice for the statute to require the collecting agent to hold the retained taxes on trust for the Crown. The idea is to create a trust of the retained taxes, so that, in the event of the bankruptcy of the collecting agent, the Crown as beneficiary will be entitled to repayment in priority to other creditors.

There is no reason to doubt the efficacy in bankruptcy of these statutory trusts as long as the taxes are in fact retained by the collecting agent, and are kept separate and apart from the collecting agent's personal assets. In that case, there is identifiable property to which the trust obligation can attach. In *British Columbia* v. *Henfrey Samson Belair* (1989),[50] the collecting agent, which was a bankrupt automobile dealer, had collected sales taxes as required by provincial law, but had not kept the retained money in a separate fund. The provincial taxing statute had anticipated this predictable situation (it did not expressly require that the retained money be kept in a separate fund), and the statute provided that the taxes owed to the Crown were to be deemed to be held on trust, and were also deemed to have been kept separate and apart from the collecting agent's personal assets, even if no separate fund had in fact been maintained. The province argued that this provision created a statutory trust of the company's assets to the extent of the value of the unremitted tax. Assets sufficient to pay the Crown in full were therefore to be excluded from the bankrupt's estate and dedicated to the claim of the Crown as beneficiary. The Supreme Court of Canada, by a majority, rejected the province's argument. The statute was ineffective to create a trust because there was no identifiable property to which the trust could attach. McLachlin J. for the majority said that only a trust complying with "general principles of law"

---

49 A statutory deemed trust created by federal law raises no constitutional issue since the federal Parliament has the constitutional power to alter priorities under the Bankruptcy Act. However, as a matter of statutory interpretation, the decision in *B.C.* v. *Henfrey Samson Belair*, next note, suggests that in the absence of a segregated fund even a federal deemed trust would not qualify as a "trust" within the meaning of s. 67(1)(a) of the Bankruptcy and Insolvency Act.

50 [1989] 2 S.C.R. 24. The majority opinion was written by McLachlin J. and agreed to by Lamer, Wilson, La Forest, L'Heureux-Dubé and Gonthier JJ. Cory J. wrote a dissenting opinion. The case is discussed by Roman and Sweatman, note 47, above.

— a ''true trust'' — would take the trust property out of the bankrupt estate.[51] Cory J. in dissent held that, since the law of trusts was within provincial jurisdiction, it was open to the province to abolish the requirement of identifiable property for trusts of retained taxes. In his view, the statutory trust ought to be respected for bankruptcy purposes.

There is no doubt that a statutory deemed trust would be effective in provincial law, even in the absence of identifiable property.[52] The effect of the *Henfrey Samson Belair* decision is to accentuate unnecessarily the disparity between provincial law, which is applicable so long as the debtor has not gone into bankruptcy, and federal law, which becomes applicable if the debtor goes into bankruptcy. In any case of insolvency where the Crown has claims under statutory deemed trusts, the secured and preferred creditors have a great incentive to force the debtor into bankruptcy, because the onset of bankruptcy will invalidate the Crown's statutory trust and reduce the Crown debt to the tenth (bottom) rank of preferred creditors.[53]

(d) Statutory set-off

The federal Bankruptcy Act places unpaid workers' compensation premiums in a preferred category, but one that is well down in the order of priorities. In order to reduce the risk of non-payment when a contractor has failed to pay workers' compensation premiums, it is common for the provinces to impose a deemed liability for the unpaid premiums on a third party who owes money to the contractor, and give to the third party a right of set-off against the debt owed by the third party to the defaulting contractor. Saskatchewan's provisions came before the Supreme Court of Canada in *Husky Oil Operations* v. *Minister of National Revenue* (1995).[54] In that case, Husky Oil Operations employed a contractor to build a heavy oil upgrader, but the contractor went bankrupt before it completed the work. At that time, Husky owed the contractor $800,000. The contractor had not been paying its workers' compensation premiums, and it owed $200,000 to Saskatchewan's Workers' Compensation Board. Saskatchewan's

51 *Id.*, 34. Note also the reference (at 33) to ''the common law attributes of trusts''. This seems to assume that there is a federal law of trusts, and that it is the unmodified common law (meaning equity). But in fact all provinces have enacted Trustee Acts that modify the common law in different ways, and, as Cory J. pointed out (at 40), the civil law trust differs from the common law trust.

52 *Troup* v. *Royal Bank of Can.* [1962] S.C.R. 487, awarding damages for breach of statutory trust. This was not a bankruptcy case, although Judson J. said, obiter (at 494): ''As to bankruptcy, the creation of the trust by s. 3(1) [of the provincial Mechanics' Lien Act] does affect the amount of the property divisible among the creditors but so does any other trust validly created''.

53 Ziegel, ''The Supreme Court of Canada scuttles the deemed trust in bankruptcy'' (1989) 15 Can. Bus. L.J. 498 criticizes the decision on this basis.

54 [1995] 3 S.C.R. 453. Gonthier J. wrote the majority opinion, which was concurred in by Lamer C.J., La Forest, L'Heureux-Dubé and McLachlin JJ. Iacobucci J. wrote the dissenting opinion, which was concurred in by Sopinka, Cory and Major JJ.

Workers' Compensation Act provided that, when a contractor failed to pay its workers' compensation premiums, the principal (in this case, Husky) became liable to the Board for the unpaid premiums. However, the Act also allowed the principal to set off the liability to pay the premiums against any money owed to the contractor.

Outside bankruptcy, there could be no doubt as to the validity and operability of Saskatchewan's deemed-liability-and-set-off provisions: Husky was liable to pay the deemed liability of $200,000 to the Workers' Compensation Board, but could set the deemed liability off against the $800,000 that Husky owed the contractor. Inside bankruptcy, however, it could be argued that the effect of the provisions was to ensure that the Workers' Compensation Board received payment of its debt out of one the bankrupt's assets (the money owed by Husky) ahead of other creditors. This gave to the Board's debt a higher priority than the debt was entitled to under the federal Bankruptcy Act. Gonthier J., writing for a five-four majority of the Supreme Court of Canada, accepted this argument and held that the deemed-liability-and-set-off provisions were ''inapplicable''[55] in the event of the bankruptcy of the contractor. Iacobucci J., who wrote the dissenting opinion, would have held the provisions to be applicable on the basis that the provincial law of set-off was applicable to claims in bankruptcy, and changes in the provincial law should not be regarded as incompatible with the Bankruptcy Act, even if they had an impact on the distribution of the property of a bankrupt.

25.7 Voluntary assignments

Until the enactment of the Bankruptcy Act in 1919, there was no federal insolvency or bankruptcy legislation relating to individuals. The provinces had little choice but to move into the vacuum in order to provide relief for insolvent debtors and equitable treatment for creditors. Lacking jurisdiction over bankruptcy and insolvency, the provinces enacted laws that enabled an insolvent debtor to make an assignment of his property to a trustee licensed by the province. The trustee would then have power to liquidate the assets and pay the proceeds to the creditors. The provincial laws did not compel an insolvent debtor to make an assignment; the assignment had to be a voluntary act. Once an assignment was made, creditors' rights of enforcement were placed in abeyance, but the provincial laws did not permit a composition with creditors that would enable the insolvent debtor to be released from debts that had not been repaid in full.

55 *Id.*, para. 87. This seems to confuse two different rationales for the decision, namely, ultra vires (provincial law is inapplicable to a vital part of a federal head of power, that is, bankruptcy) and paramountcy (provincial law is inoperative to the extent of inconsistency with a federal law, that is, the Bankruptcy Act). Iacobucci J. (para. 213) aptly criticizes the passage on account of this confusion.

In the *Voluntary Assignments* case (1894),[56] the Privy Council upheld Ontario's voluntary assignment law. The Court emphasized that the legislation involved no compulsion on the debtor, and was not predicated on any formal state of insolvency: "the operation of an assignment for the benefit of creditors was precisely the same, whether the assignor was or was not in fact insolvent".[57] The law was held to be a valid exercise of power over property and civil rights in the province. The Privy Council was explicitly influenced by the absence of any federal legislation, and their lordships made clear that provision for voluntary assignments would also be competent to the federal Parliament as an ancillary element of bankruptcy or insolvency legislation.[58] The federal Bankruptcy Act does now make provision for voluntary assignments by insolvent debtors.

25.8 Fraudulent preferences

The Quebec Civil Code has, since before confederation, contained provisions to enable creditors to defeat fraudulent preferences, and after confederation all common law provinces enacted legislation to the same end. A fraudulent preference is a payment (or assignment of property) by a debtor to one creditor, with the purpose of preferring that creditor, when the debtor's assets are insufficient to pay all creditors. Such a preference has the effect of defeating the claims of the other creditors.

The validity of provincial laws respecting fraudulent preferences had been the subject of a variety of opinions in lower courts, and it was not until *Robinson* v. *Countrywide Factors* (1978)[59] that the Supreme Court of Canada definitely settled the question in favour of the legislation. That case involved a Saskatchewan law that provided for the defeat of a payment or assignment made by a debtor in favour of a creditor "with intent to give that creditor preference over his other creditors", if the payment or assignment was made by the debtor "when he is in insolvent circumstances or is unable to pay his debts in full or knows that he is on the eve of insolvency". There was a similar provision in the federal Bankruptcy Act, but the federal provision applied only if the debtor became bankrupt within three months of giving the preference. There was no similar restriction in the provincial law. In this case, the debtor had paid off a pressing creditor two years

56 *A.G. Ont.* v. *A.G. Can.* (Voluntary Assignments) [1894] A.C. 189.

57 *Id.*, 199.

58 *Id.*, 200-201. For doubt as to the correctness of the decision in light of the law's close connexion with insolvency, see *Re Orderly Payment of Debts Act* [1960] S.C.R. 571, 576-577 per Kerwin C.J. However, the Court in *Robinson* v. *Countrywide Factors* [1978] 1 S.C.R. 753, 762-763, 808, did not endorse the criticism; and the actual decision in that case (next note) clearly supports the correctness of the *Voluntary Assignments* case.

59 [1978] 1 S.C.R. 753. Spence J. wrote the majority opinion; Beetz J. added some additional concurring reasons; Laskin C.J. dissented.

before the debtor went bankrupt, so that the transaction could not be impeached under the Bankruptcy Act. Could it be impeached under the provincial law?

The Supreme Court of Canada in *Robinson* v. *Countrywide Factors* answered yes. The Court upheld the provincial law, and held that the law was not rendered inoperative by the similar provision in the Bankruptcy Act.[60] Laskin C.J. dissented, pointing out that the provincial law was explicitly predicated on the insolvency or imminent insolvency of the debtor. He pointed out that in the *Voluntary Assignments* case the provincial voluntary-assignment law had not been expressly predicated on insolvency, and the Privy Council had relied on that feature of the law in upholding its validity. But the majority of the Supreme Court of Canada held that Saskatchewan's fraudulent-preference law was valid despite its references to insolvency. Spence J., who wrote the majority judgment, did not directly address Laskin C.J.'s objection; Spence J. contented himself with the proposition that fraudulent-preference laws ''were still valid provincial enactments in reference to 'property' and 'civil rights' and were valuable aids to trustees in bankruptcy in attacking the validity of such transactions.''[61] But Beetz J., who agreed with Spence J. but added some concurring reasons, pointed out that provincial laws concerning mortgages and other secured transactions ''are implicitly or explicitly predicated on the risk of insolvency'', because they only ''produce their full effect when the risk has been converted into reality''.[62] In his view, which must also be the *ratio decidendi* of the majority's decision, provincial laws that defeat fraudulent preferences in a situation of impending or actual insolvency ''do not cease to be laws in relation to property and civil rights simply . . . because Parliament could enact similar laws in relation to bankruptcy and insolvency''.[63]

---

60 This is consistent with the ''express contradiction'' rule of paramountcy: see ch. 16, Paramountcy, above. Outside the three month period stipulated by the federal Act, the provincial law could operate without any operating conflict with the Bankruptcy Act: [1978] 1 S.C.R. 753, 794 per Spence J., 808 per Beetz J.

61 *Id.*, 794.

62 *Id.*, 804.

63 *Id.*, 803.

26

The Family

26.1 Distribution of powers

In principle, one would expect the bulk of family law to come within provincial power. Family law has little or no effect on trade or transportation or other aspects of the national economy. It rather concerns the ways in which people choose to live their private lives, and may be expected to reflect values which differ from one part of the country to another.

While most family law is within provincial jurisdiction, the Constitution Act, 1867, by s. 91(26), allocates to the federal Parliament the power to make laws in relation to "marriage and divorce". The national interest in marriage and divorce consists in the desirability of nation-wide recognition of marriages and divorces. If marriage and divorce were provincial responsibilities, and if markedly different rules developed among provinces, there would be no assurance that a marriage or divorce performed or obtained in one province would be recognized by the courts of another province. This has been a problem in the United States where marriage and divorce are state responsibilities. Australia has followed the Canadian pattern of allocating marriage and divorce to the federal Parliament.

The Constitution Act, 1867, by s. 92(12), confers on the provincial Legislatures the power to make laws in relation to "the solemnization of marriage in the province". The boundary between this power and the federal power over "marriage" is discussed later in this chapter. Most provincial power over family law is derived from that expansive phrase in s. 92(13), "property and civil rights in the province", which encompasses property and contract law and other private-law relations, including, for example, matrimonial property, succession, support of spouses and children, adoption, guardianship, custody, legitimacy, affiliation and names.

The various federal and provincial powers are discussed in the following sections of this chapter, including the problem of conflict between differing orders of custody or support made under federal and provincial laws. A final section will briefly examine the constitutional problems of the administration of justice in family law matters.

26.2 Crime and delinquency

Juvenile delinquency and criminal charges arising out of family disputes are within the legislative competence of the federal Parliament under the "criminal law" power (s. 91(27)). The validity of the federal Young Offenders Act (and its

---

1 The actual reasons of the framers seem to have included other factors as well, especially a hostility towards divorce, and a feeling that (outside Quebec) a federal regime would be stricter than a provincial regime: Jordan, "The Federal Divorce Act (1968) and the Constitution" (1968) 14 McGill L.J. 209; Bushnell, "Family Law and the Constitution" (1978) 1 Can. J. Fam. L. 202.

2 A constitutional amendment transferring marriage and divorce to the provinces would create serious problems if it were not accompanied by provision for a national rule of recognition. Canada's Constitution does not now even contain an explicit "full faith and credit" clause: see next note.

3 The "full faith and credit" clause in article IV, s. 1, of the Constitution of the United States requires that "full faith and credit" be given in each state to the "public acts, records and judicial proceedings of every other state". But this clause has not solved the problems indicated in the text: see, e.g., *Estin* v. *Estin* (1948) 334 U.S. 541 (Nevada divorce ineffective to alter alimony rights in New York).

4 Constitution of Australia, s. 51(21) ("marriage"), s. 51(22) ("divorce and matrimonial causes").

5 See ch. 20, Property and Civil Rights, above.

6 On the possible impact of the Charter of Rights on family law, see Bala and Redfearn, "Family Law and the 'Liberty Interest'" (1983) 15 Ottawa L. Rev. 274.

predecessor, the Juvenile Delinquents Act) have been specifically upheld on this basis,[7] and family-related offences under the federal Criminal Code,[8] such as corrupting children (s. 172), failing to provide necessaries of life (s. 215), assault (s. 266) and abduction (s. 281), are clearly valid criminal laws. These elements of family law that are sustained by the criminal law power will not be further discussed in this chapter.[9]

26.3 Marriage

(a) Formation of marriage

The federal authority in relation to ''marriage'' — the first branch of s. 91(26) — has to be read side by side with the provincial authority in relation to ''the solemnization of marriage in the province'' (s. 92(12)). In fact, most of the laws concerning marriage have been enacted by the provinces, and the courts have tended to construe the provincial power liberally. The scope of federal power has been left largely undetermined.[10]

The only federal law ever to come before the courts was one which declared that every marriage performed in accordance with the laws of the place where it was performed was to be recognized as a valid marriage everywhere in Canada. In the *Marriage Reference* (1912)[11] the Privy Council through Viscount Haldane held that the law was invalid. According to their lordships, the difficulty with the law was that it assumed that all rules bearing on the validity of a marriage were within the federal power over ''marriage''. But this would relegate the provincial power over ''the solemnization of marriage'' to the laying down of merely directory rules, that is, rules which if broken would not impair the validity of the resulting marriage. Their lordships rejected this view, holding that the provincial power extended to the enactment of ''conditions as to solemnization which may affect the validity of the contract''.[12] Since the provincial power was subtracted from the federal power, it followed that the federal Parliament could not legislate with respect to all questions of validity, and the impugned law was bad.

Following the *Marriage Reference*, it is clear that a province has power to stipulate pre-ceremonial requirements, such as, the issue of a licence or the publication of banns, and to stipulate the qualifications of the person performing

7 *A.-G. B.C.* v. *Smith* [1967] S.C.R. 702; *R.* v. *S.(S)* [1990] 2 S.C.R. 254; and see ch. 18, Criminal Law, under heading 18.8(b), ''Young offenders'', above.

8 R.S.C. 1985, c. C-46.

9 See ch. 18, Criminal Law, above.

10 Katz, ''The Scope of the Federal Legislative Authority in relation to Marriage'' (1975) 7 Ottawa L. Rev. 384; Laskin, *Canadian Constitutional Law* (5th ed., 1986 by Finkelstein), 670-672.

11 *Re Questions Concerning Marriage* [1912] A.C. 880.

12 *Id.*, 887.

13 *Alspector* v. *Alspector* [1957] O.R. 454, 464 (C.A.).

the ceremony, even if breach of the stipulations renders the marriage a nullity. These are matters closely associated with the performance of the ceremony — the solemnization. Much less clearly associated with the ceremony is a requirement of parental consent to the marriage of a minor, but in two cases the Supreme Court of Canada has held that a province may enact that parental consent is a condition of a valid marriage. These cases were decided on the dubious ground that parental consent was a "formality" of marriage rather than a matter governing the capacity of the parties. Laws governing the capacity of the parties are outside provincial power, for example, a law prescribing the prohibited degrees of consanguinity and affinity, or a law prescribing the capacity of divorced people to remarry.

(b) Consequences of marriage

Does the federal power over "marriage" extend to the consequences of marriage, for example, the obligation to support a dependent spouse or children, custody of children, and the property rights of married people? In fact, until 1968 laws on these topics had only been enacted by the provinces, and the laws had been held to be valid as matters coming within "property and civil rights in the province" (s. 92(13)). In 1968, the federal Parliament provided for alimony, maintenance and custody in the new Divorce Act, but only as corollary relief in divorce proceedings. These provisions of the Divorce Act have been upheld as an exercise of the "divorce" power, and it has not been necessary to consider whether they could have been enacted bythe federal Parliament as measures unrelated to divorce. In Australia, thefederal marriage power empowers regulation of the relationship betweenmarried persons and their children, and it is arguable that the Canadianpower is no less broad.

---

14 *Gilham* v. *Steele* [1953] 2 D.L.R. 89 (B.C. C.A.).

15 *Kerr* v. *Kerr* [1934] S.C.R. 72; *A.-G. Alta.* v. *Underwood* [1934] S.C.R. 635. See also *Ross* v. *MacQueen* [1948] 2 D.L.R. 536 (Alta. S.C.) holding that minimum age is also within provincial power. These three cases are acutely criticized by Katz, note 10, above, 386-390.

16 *Teagle* v. *Teagle* [1952] 3 D.L.R. 843, 847-848 (B.C.S.C.); *Re Schepull* [1954] O.R. 67, 71 (H.C.); see Marriage (Prohibited Degrees) Act, S.C. 1990, c. 46. Of course, a provincial law in relation to a matter within provincial authority, such as adoption, could have the valid, incidental effect of altering capacity to marry: *Re Broddy* (1982) 142 D.L.R. (3d) 151, 153 (Alta. C.A.).

17 *Hellens* v. *Densmore* [1957] S.C.R. 768.

18 *Re Adoption Act* [1938] S.C.R. 398.

19 S.C. 1967-68, c. 24; see now Divorce Act, S.C. 1986, c. 4, ss. 15-20.

20 Note 34 and accompanying text, below.

21 Constitution of Australia, s. 51(21), "Marriage", as interpreted in *A.-G. Vic.* v. *Australia* (Marriage Act) (1962) 107 C.L.R. 529 (H.C. Aust.); *Russell* v. *Russell* (1976) 134 C.L.R. 495 (H.C. Aust.).

22 Katz, note 10, above, 392-396; see also note 51 below.

26.4 Divorce

The federal Parliament's power to make laws in relation to "divorce" — the second branch of s. 91(26) — lay almost dormant until 1968 when for the first time a comprehensive, Canada-wide Divorce Act was enacted. Before that time, the law differed from province to province, depending upon the date when English law had been received in the province, the terms of pre-confederation laws on the topic, and several federal statutes which did not apply in all provinces. In Newfoundland and Quebec, and in Ontario until 1930, there was no judicial procedure to obtain a divorce, and a federal statute was necessary in every case.

The Divorce Act confers jurisdiction on the superior court in each province to grant divorces, establishes a procedure by way of "application" (formerly "petition") for obtaining decrees of divorce, and stipulates the grounds upon which decrees may be granted. The constitutionality of these primary parts of the Act cannot be doubted. The Act also contains provisions for the award of corollary relief to the parties: alimony, maintenance and the custody of children. The provisions for corollary relief cover matters which before 1968 had been the responsibility of the provinces, and they have been constitutionally controversial. In the next two sections of this chapter, we shall see that all constitutional challenges have been unsuccessful.

26.5 Custody and support of children

(a) Custody of children

In the *Adoption Reference* (1938), the Supreme Court of Canada held that it was competent to the province to enact laws providing for the adoption of children and for the maintenance of children and deserted wives. Duff C.J. for the Court explained that the welfare and education of children and the protection of the poor and distressed were matters of provincial responsibility. He did not explain to which head of legislative power this responsibility was to be attributed, but it

23 Jordan, note 1, above.

24 S.C., 1967-68, c. 24; see now Divorce Act, S.C. 1986, c. 4.

25 Reception is the subject of ch. 2, above.

26 For description of the complex pre-1968 law, see Mendes da Costa (ed.), *Studies in Canadian Family Law* (1972), vol. 1, 362-365.

27 The Act does not provide for other matrimonial causes such as judicial separation or nullity. These proceedings are accordingly still governed by English law received in the province, pre-confederation laws and provincial laws. Whether the federal Parliament could enact federal laws on these topics is discussed by Jordan, note 1, above, 262-267.

28 *Re Adoption Act* [1938] S.C.R. 398.

29 See also *R.* v. *Chief* (1963) 42 D.L.R. (2d) 712 (Man. Q.B.); affd. 44 D.L.R. (2d) 108 (Man. C.A.).

has subsequently been generally assumed to be "property and civil rights in the province" (s. 92(13)) rather than "matters of a merely local or private nature in the province" (s. 92(16)).

Since the *Adoption Reference* it has never been doubted that adoption, legitimacy, custody, guardianship, child welfare, affiliation and maintenance of children are within provincial power, and of course every province has enacted statutes on these and related topics. What has not been so clear is the extent of federal power on these topics by virtue of the federal Parliament's power over "marriage and divorce" (s. 91(26)). The possibility of some federal authority was raised but not decided by Duff C.J. in the *Adoption Reference*, and the question was not presented for decision until after the enactment of the federal Divorce Act in 1968.

The question of the validity of the corollary relief provisions of the Divorce Act had to be decided in *Papp* v. *Papp* (1969), a case in which a custody order had been made under the Divorce Act. Laskin J.A., sitting alone as the Ontario Court of Appeal, upheld the custody provisions of the Divorce Act. He pointed out that the provisions applied only to the children of the marriage whose dissolution was sought, and that no corollary relief could be awarded at trial if the petition failed. The provisions were valid, he held, because there was a "rational, functional connection" between them and the admittedly valid provisions of the Act concerning divorce. In his view, the custody of children was "bound up with the direct consequences of marriage and divorce" and was "complementary" to the divorce itself.

Papp v. *Papp* concerned an "interim" order of custody, that is, an order of custody made after the application for divorce to cover the period up to the trial. But the decision has been consistently followed in subsequent cases challenging other forms of corollary relief. Appellate courts in Manitoba and Alberta have upheld the constitutionality of "permanent" custody orders, that is, orders made on the granting of the divorce. More difficult is the question of the validity of the

---

30 The interaction between provincial adoption laws and federal laws raised difficult questions in *Natural Parents* v. *Superintendent of Child Welfare* [1976] 2 S.C.R. 751 (adoption law applicable to Indian but ineffective to change Indian status); *Re Broddy* (1982) 142 D.L.R. (3d) 151 (Alta. C.A.) (adoption law "read down" so as not to bring adopted child within prohibited degrees of consanguinity).

31 In *Re B.C. Family Relations Act* [1982] 1 S.C.R. 62 it was assumed that provincial legislative authority extended to adoption, guardianship, custody, and occupancy of and access to the family residence. The only question was whether these jurisdictions could be conferred upon a non-s. 96 court: see sec. 26.9(c), "Provincial courts", below.

32 The statutes of all provinces are collected in the *Canadian Family Law Guide* (CCH loose-leaf service).

33 [1938] S.C.R. 398, 402.

34 [1970] 1 O.R. 331 (C.A.).

35 *Id.*, 336.

36 *Id.*, 338.

37 *Whyte* v. *Whyte* (1969) 7 D.L.R. (3d) 7 (Man. C.A.); *Heikel* v. *Heikel* (1970) 12 D.L.R. (3d) 311 (Alta. A.D.).

authority given by the Divorce Act to the court subsequently to vary a custody order made at the time of the divorce. On an application for variation, the divorce is over, and the only issue for decision is the best interests of the child. Is there still a "rational, functional connection" with the divorce? In *Skjonsby* v. *Skjonsby* (1975) the Appellate Division of the Alberta Supreme Court answered yes, upholding the power of variation.

(b) Support of children

The Divorce Act's provisions authorizing the court to order payments of support (formerly called maintenance) in respect of the children of the marriage are as valid as those concerning custody, and for the same reason, namely, their close connection with the divorce. The power to vary support orders, long after the divorce, is also valid. Moreover, the original order for support need not be finally made at the time of granting the divorce. In *Zacks* v. *Zacks* (1973), a judge of the Supreme Court of British Columbia, on granting a decree nisi for divorce, ordered that the wife and child of the marriage were entitled to support, but directed a reference to the registrar of the Court to recommend the amount. The decree absolute, finalizing the divorce, was entered before the amount was fixed. The Supreme Court of Canada had no difficulty in deciding that both the language of the Divorce Act and the "divorce" power extended to the fixing of quantum after the grant of the divorce. Of course, in that case the application for support had been made in a timely fashion and the trial judge had declared that the respondent wife was entitled to support. The Supreme Court of Canada therefore did not have to decide, and expressly left open, the question whether a divorce court could entertain an application for support which had been made for the first time after the decree absolute had been granted.

26.6 Support of spouse

The previous section of this chapter dealt with the custody and support of children. This section of the chapter is concerned with payments for the support of a dependent spouse. Such payments used to be called either alimony or maintenance. The general distinction between the two terms is that alimony describes payments made to a separated spouse during the marriage, while maintenance

38 (1975) 53 D.L.R. (3d) 602 (Alta. A.D.).

39 *Jackson* v. *Jackson* [1973] S.C.R. 205.

40 *Ibid.*

41 [1973] S.C.R. 891.

42 *Id.*, 914. *Wark* v. *Wark* (1986) 30 D.L.R. (4th) 90 (Man. C.A.) (support may be ordered after the divorce, provided there is a rational, functional connection with the marriage). See also *Whyte* v. *Whyte* (1969) 7 D.L.R. (3d) 7, 13 (Man. C.A.); *Re Rinaldi and Rinaldi* (1975) 9 O.R. (2d) 109, 113 (Div. Ct.); *Vadeboncoeur* v. *Landry* [1977] 2 S.C.R. 179, 187.

describes payments made after the dissolution of the marriage. This usage was adhered to in the Divorce Act of 1968, but the current Act, which was enacted in 1986, uses the term "support" for both kinds of payments.

It is clear that the provinces have the power to provide for payments of support by one spouse to the other. This was one of the points decided in the *Adoption Reference*. All provinces have in fact enacted statutes giving spouses the right to bring proceedings for support. Most provinces also provide for support to be awarded as ancillary relief in actions for judicial separation, annulment or restitution of conjugal rights.

The federal Divorce Act includes, as part of the corollary relief available in divorce proceedings, provisions for alimony and maintenance for the support of a spouse. There is no doubt as to the validity of these provisions. *Zacks* v. *Zacks* (1973), the decision of the Supreme Court of Canada that has already been discussed in connection with support of children, upheld the validity of an order made under the Divorce Act which was for the support of the wife as well as the child of the marriage. Martland J. for the Court spoke of "alimony, maintenance and the custody of children" as subjects which were all "inseparable from [Parliament's] jurisdiction to pass laws governing the change of status resulting from a dissolution of marriage".

26.7 Division of property

The Divorce Act, by s. 15, authorizes the payment of maintenance for the support of a spouse or children by "lump sum" as well as by periodic sums. The power to order payment by lump sum has been interpreted as not including the power to order the transfer of real estate or other specific assets.

It has been suggested that an order for the transfer of specific property would in any case be outside the constitutional power of the federal Parliament, because it would be within "property and civil rights in the province" (s. 92(13)). It is of course true that laws in relation to property, including matrimonial property, are within the competence of the provinces under their power over property and civil rights. But that is also true of support and custody. The federal Parliament has the power to provide for support and custody as corollary relief in divorce pro-

43 Note 28, above.
44 Mendes da Costa (ed.), note 26, above, 352-356.
45 [1973] S.C.R. 891.
46 Note 41, above.
47 [1973] S.C.R. 891, 900.
48 *Chadderton* v. *Chadderton* [1973] 1 O.R. 560 (C.A.). No constitutional issue was discussed.
49 *Osborne* v. *Osborne* (1973) 14 R.F.L. 61, 66 (Sask. Q.B.); *K.* v. *K.* (1975) 53 D.L.R. (3d) 290, 298 (Man. C.A.).
50 *Lamb* v. *Lamb* [1985] 1 S.C.R. 851 (province may authorize order granting exclusive possession of matrimonial home).

ceedings because of the ''rational, functional connection'' between laws which provide for the dissolution of a marriage and laws which provide for these forms of corollary relief. It could surely be argued that a similar connection exists between the dissolution of a marriage and the disposition of the matrimonial property. Thus, while the federal Parliament probably could not enact a comprehensive regime of family property, the cases so far decided under the Divorce Act (all of which have sustained federal power) suggest that there would be no constitutional impediment to the expansion of the Divorce Act's corollary relief provisions to permit the court, on the making of a decree for divorce, to order transfers of specific property from one spouse to the other.

26.8 Conflict between orders made under federal and provincial law

(a) General principles

There is provincial legislation providing for support and custody, and the validity of this legislation is not in doubt. Since the introduction in 1968 of the corollary relief provisions of the federal Divorce Act, there has been the possibility of conflict between orders made under provincial law and orders made under the Divorce Act. In my opinion, the existence of conflict and its consequences should be determined by the relatively well-settled body of constitutional law which resolves conflicts between federal and provincial laws, that is to say, the doctrine of federal paramountcy. Instead, the courts have often disregarded the doctrine of paramountcy and have produced a remarkably inconsistent patchwork of decisions.

Some of the difficulty seems to have been caused by confusion with the rules of conflict of laws (or private international law). In *McKee* v. *McKee* (1951), the Privy Council decided that the Supreme Court of Ontario had jurisdiction to make

51 See Law Reform Commission of Canada, *Family Property* (Working Paper 8, 1975), 1; *Divorce* (Working Paper 13, 1975), 58-61.

52 The ''marriage'' power (s. 91(26)) could be relied on for this purpose: see sec. 26.3(b), ''Consequences of marriage'', above; but in the absence of suggestive case law it seems prudent to doubt that the courts would extend the power so far into the traditionally provincial field of property law.

53 Cf. *Lansell* v. *Lansell* (1964) 110 C.L.R. 353 (H.C. Aust.), holding that the Australian federal Parliament's power over ''divorce and matrimonial causes'' (Constitution, s. 51(22)) extended to division of property on divorce.

54 Sections 26.5, ''Custody and support of children'', and 26.6, ''Support of spouse'', above.

55 Accord, *Lamb* v. *Lamb* [1985] 1 S.C.R. 851, 859. The doctrine of federal paramountcy is discussed in ch. 16, Paramountcy, above.

56 The decisions are acutely analyzed in Ontario Law Reform Commission, *Report on Family Law: Part IV, Support Obligations* (1975), ch. 3.

57 [1951] A.C. 352.

an order for the custody of a child resident in Ontario, despite the existence of an inconsistent custody order made in another jurisdiction (California). Their lordships pointed out that under Ontario law the welfare of the infant was the paramount consideration in questions of custody, and this consideration should prevail over all others, including the existence of a foreign order.

The rule of *McKee* v. *McKee* resolves conflicts as to custody between a province and a foreign jurisdiction, or between two provinces. But where the conflict is between federal and provincial law an issue of constitutional law is presented which cannot be resolved by the rules of the conflict of laws. An order for custody or other corollary relief which is made under the Divorce Act by the superior court of a province is not an order of a ''foreign'' court in other provinces. On the contrary, s. 20 of the Divorce Act provides (and federal legislative power supports the provision) that the order ''has legal effect throughout Canada'', and s. 20 further provides that the order may be registered in any province as an order of the superior court of that province and may then be enforced ''as an order of that court''. Surely any order for corollary relief under the Divorce Act must render inoperative any inconsistent order under provincial law by virtue of the doctrine of paramountcy.

The question then arises: when is an order for corollary relief under the Divorce Act inconsistent with an order under provincial law? Under the ''express contradiction'' test of inconsistency, which has now been accepted by the Supreme Court of Canada, there can be no doubt about custody orders. An order under the Divorce Act granting the custody of a child to spouse W expressly contradicts an order under provincial law granting the custody of the same child to spouse H. Assuming that W and H are living apart, a child cannot be in the custody of both at the same time. The case of support (whether of spouse or children) is not so clear. An order under the Divorce Act requiring spouse H to pay $500 per month to spouse W does not expressly contradict an order under provincial law requiring spouse H to pay $600 to spouse W. Both orders can be complied with by spouse H paying $1,100 to spouse W! This is absurd because it is obvious that each order was intended to occupy the field, exhaustively defining H's obligation, and by implication excluding any additional obligation. It has been decided that there is an inconsistency between two orders requiring the payment of different amounts of support, and that the provincial order is inoperative. The rest of this chapter will proceed on the realistic assumption that

58 S.C. 1986, c. 4. The previous Divorce Act of 1968, by ss. 14 and 15, made similar provision.

59 See ch. 16, Paramountcy, under heading 16.3, ''Express contradiction'', above.

60 *Gillespie* v. *Gillespie* (1973) 36 D.L.R. (3d) 421 (N.B.A.D.).

61 It is perhaps arguable that both orders can be complied with by spouse H paying the larger sum, in this example, $600, to spouse W. Cf. *Lamb* v. *Lamb* [1985] 1 S.C.R. 851 (support order under Divorce Act not inconsistent with order for exclusive possession of matrimonial home under provincial law).

62 *Hughes* v. *Hughes* (1976) 72 D.L.R. (3d) 577 (B.C.C.A.).

this decision is correct. But it should not be overlooked that a relentless application of the express contradiction test would lead to a finding that two orders requiring the payment of different amounts of support are not inconsistent.

(b) Variation under provincial law of orders under Divorce Act

The first situation to be examined is where a divorce has been granted by the superior court of a province, and the court has also made an order for corollary relief (custody or support) under the Divorce Act. Is it later open to a court (in the same or another province), acting under provincial law, to make an order for custody or maintenance which is inconsistent with the pre-existing Divorce Act order?

In *Emerson* v. *Emerson* (1972), a divorce had been granted by the Supreme Court of New Brunswick, and the Court had awarded the wife maintenance for the support of the child of the marriage. The husband lived in New Brunswick, but the wife and child lived in Ontario. The wife wished to vary the amount of maintenance. The Divorce Act includes a power to vary orders for corollary relief, but at that time the Act provided that the power was exercisable only "by the court that made the order". The wife therefore had to go to New Brunswick to take advantage of this provision. Instead, she applied to the Supreme Court of Ontario for maintenance under the provincial Infants Act. Wright J., invoking an earlier decision of his own, applied the conflict of laws rule of *McKee* v. *McKee* to hold that the welfare of the child was the primary consideration and that he was free to order maintenance under the provincial law even in the face of an inconsistent order under the federal Divorce Act.

Wright J.'s decision in *Emerson* v. *Emerson* to grant relief in Ontario where the wife and child lived is certainly understandable. The Divorce Act of 1968 was deficient in only allowing orders to be varied in the province where the divorce was granted. (The current Act, enacted in 1986, permits variation by a court in a province where either former spouse is ordinarily resident, whether or not that court granted the divorce and originally ordered corollary relief.) But the fact remains that the Divorce Act maintenance order, although made in New Brun-

---

63 Provincial law providing an additional means of enforcement of a Divorce Act order has been held not to be inconsistent with the Divorce Act: *Re Pointmeier and Pointmeier* (1982) 133 D.L.R. (3d) 496 (Alta. C.A.); unless it permits recovery of arrears barred by the Divorce Act: *Re Brewer and Brewer* (1981) 125 D.L.R. (3d) 183 (N.B.A.D.).

64 Colvin, Comment (1983) 17 U.B.C.L. Rev. 347 suggests two alternative solutions: (1) that express contradiction should not be regarded as the only test of inconsistency, or (2) that, if express contradiction is the only test, so that both orders are in force, spouse W should only be permitted to enforce one of them (she could choose which one).

65 [1972] 3 O.R. 5 (H.C.).

66 *Bray* v. *Bray* [1971] 1 O.R. 232 (H.C.), discussed in text accompanying note 86, below.

67 Note 57, above.

68 Divorce Act, S.C. 1986, c. 4, s. 5. There is a confirmation procedure for the case where the respondent to the application for variation lives in another province: s. 18.

swick, had legal force in Ontario, and was enforceable in Ontario, by virtue of a valid federal law. Since the Divorce Act of 1968 gave Wright J. no power directly to vary the order made under the Divorce Act, the result of the decision is to produce two inconsistent orders for maintenance, both enforceable in Ontario. This is precisely the situation which the doctrine of paramountcy is designed to resolve, and it dictates that the order made under the federal Act must prevail. Wright J. should have declined jurisdiction, since his order (made under provincial law) would have to be futile.

The authority of *Emerson* v. *Emerson* has been limited and perhaps destroyed by two decisions of provincial courts of appeal. In *Ramsay* v. *Ramsay* (1976), the Ontario Court of Appeal held that an Ontario court had no authority to vary an order for maintenance of a spouse made under the Divorce Act in Manitoba. Their lordships added, obiter, however, that questions of the custody or welfare of children stood on a different footing: in their view the Divorce Act should not be construed as depriving the provincial courts of their ancient *parens patriae* jurisdiction over children within their territorial jurisdiction. Although their lordships did not refer to *Emerson* v. *Emerson*, this dictum could be read as supporting the outcome of that case since the case did involve the welfare of a child.

In *Re Hall and Hall* (1976) the British Columbia Court of Appeal rejected the obiter dictum in *Ramsay* v. *Ramsay* and the decision in *Emerson* v. *Emerson*. The Court held that a British Columbia court had no jurisdiction to vary an order for the custody of a child made under the Divorce Act in Quebec. The Divorce Act of 1968 gave no such jurisdiction, and an order made under provincial law (whether under statute or the *parens patriae* jurisdiction) would simply be inconsistent with the Divorce Act. It seems to me, with respect, that *Re Hall and Hall* is rightly decided and that the obiter dictum in *Ramsay* v. *Ramsay* and the decision in *Emerson* v. *Emerson* (as well as cases which have followed it) are inconsistent with the doctrine of federal paramountcy.

The decisions and dicta which seem to ignore the doctrine of federal paramountcy reflect a concern that an order for corollary relief under the Divorce Act should not preclude forever the making of an inconsistent order under provincial law. It may be possible to construct a sound constitutional basis to avoid that

---

69 But note the doubt recorded in the text accompanying note 64, above, as to whether the express contradiction test of inconsistency is satisfied here.

70 (1976) 13 O.R. (2d) 85 (C.A.).

71 *Parens patriae*, literally "parent of the country", refers to the royal prerogative, eventually exercised by the courts, to act as guardian to persons with legal disabilities, such as infants, idiots and lunatics. Like other prerogative powers, it may be supplanted by legislation, but is still available to fill gaps in the legislation: see, e.g., *Beson* v. *Director of Child Welfare (Nfld.)* [1982] 2 S.C.R. 716.

72 (1976) 70 D.L.R. (3d) 493 (B.C. C.A.).

73 The Court did not refer to *Emerson* v. *Emerson* but the two decisions are in direct conflict.

74 The Court conceded (at 504) that a possible exception to the general rule may be an emergency involving the safety of the child, where a temporary protective order under provincial law may be necessary: *Re D.J.C. and W.C.* (1975) 8 O.R. (2d) 310 (C.A.).

result. It will be recalled that the validity of the corollary relief provisions of the Divorce Act depends upon their "rational, functional connection" with divorce. It is arguable, therefore, that an order for corollary relief is inherently temporary, expiring naturally as the divorce retreats into the past and its impact on the circumstances of the parties diminishes. On this basis, it would eventually be open to a court to decide that the effects of a divorce had been exhausted, and that an order made under the Divorce Act could be reviewed and replaced by a different order made under provincial law.

(c) Orders under provincial law where no order under Divorce Act

The second situation to be examined is where a divorce has been granted by the superior court of a province, but no order for corollary relief (custody or support) has been made. What is the effect of the divorce decree on an order for custody or support made under provincial law? The order under provincial law might have been made before or after the divorce decree.

Wright J.'s decision in *Emerson* v. *Emerson* would clearly assert the Court's power to act under provincial law. I have already given my reasons for thinking that *Emerson* v. *Emerson* is wrongly decided. However, it seems to me that the Ontario Court of Appeal in *Richards* v. *Richards* (1972) went too far in the other direction when Gale C.J.O. for the Court asserted that the Divorce Act, by occupying the "field" of corollary relief, had rendered ineffective all provincial laws "in that field". This dictum was not necessary for the actual decision in *Richards* v. *Richards*, and it conflicts with recent decisions of the Supreme Court of Canada which have consistently rejected the covering-the-field test of inconsistency between federal and provincial laws, and have insisted upon a more direct conflict ("express contradiction") to trigger the paramountcy doctrine. On the basis of the express contradiction test, as long as no order has in fact been made under the Divorce Act, an order made under provincial law would not be deemed inconsis-

75 Note 35, above.

76 This line of argument is suggested in three articles by Colvin, "Custody Orders under the Constitution" (1978) 56 Can. Bar Rev. 1; "Federal Jurisdiction over Support after Divorce" (1979) 11 Ottawa L. Rev. 540; "Family Maintenance" (1979) 2 Can. J. Fam. L. 221; and by Ryan, "The Overlapping Custody Jurisdiction" (1980) 3 Can. J. Fam. L. 95; and Weiler, "The Exercise of Jurisdiction in Custody Disputes" (1980) 3 Can. J. Fam. L. 281.

77 Cf. *Re Clarke and Hutchings* (1976) 71 D.L.R. (3d) 356 (Nfld. C.A.) (custody order under Divorce Act does not preclude order under provincial law in favour of person not party to divorce); *Black* v. *Black* (1981) 123 D.L.R. (3d) 499 (N.S.S.C.) (maintenance order under Divorce Act cannot continue after death of paying spouse); *Re Williams and Hillier* (1981) 130 D.L.R. (3d) 492 (Alta. C.A.) (access order under Divorce Act is extinguished by adoption order under provincial law); *Wark* v. *Wark* (1986) 30 D.L.R. (4th) 90 (Man. C.A.) (power to make new support order or vary old one dependent upon rational, functional connection with divorce).

78 Note 65, above.

79 [1972] 2 O.R. 596, 597 (C.A.).

80 See ch. 16, Paramountcy, above.

tent with the Divorce Act and would therefore be legally effective. Of course, if and when a valid order is made under the Divorce Act, it will render the competing order inoperative.[81]

(d) Variation under Divorce Act of orders under provincial law

The third and final situation to be examined is where an order has been made for support or custody under provincial law before the commencement of divorce proceedings. In subsequent divorce proceedings in the same or another province, can an order for corollary relief be made which is inconsistent with the pre-existing order?[82][83]

This was the situation in *Gillespie* v. *Gillespie* (1973),[84] in which the New Brunswick Appellate Division held that the Supreme Court of New Brunswick had jurisdiction, on the granting of a divorce, to make an order for the custody of a child of the marriage, although the child was in Ontario and was the subject of a custody order made under Ontario's Infants Act. The Court held, correctly in my opinion, that the conflict between the two orders was to be resolved by the doctrine of paramountcy, the order made under the federal Divorce Act prevailing over the order made under the provincial Infants Act.[85]

In *Gillespie* v. *Gillespie*, the Court refused to follow the decision of the Ontario High Court in *Bray* v. *Bray* (1971).[86] In that case, Wright J. held that on granting a divorce in Ontario he was powerless to make an order for the custody of a child of the marriage who was in Quebec and the subject of an order made under Quebec law. He relied on the conflict of laws decision of *McKee* v. *McKee* for the proposition that primary jurisdiction over the custody of a child moves with the child. The decision in *Bray* v. *Bray*, like his lordship's later decision in *Emerson* v. *Emerson*,[87] appears to ignore the nation-wide application of the Divorce Act and of orders made under it. As a matter of judicial discretion, there may often be good grounds for declining to make a custody order in respect of a child in another province, but the court's power to make such an order is not seriously open to doubt. An order made in Ontario under the Divorce Act would be effective in Quebec; it could be registered as an order of the Quebec superior court and

---

81 *Lamb* v. *Lamb* [1985] 1 S.C.R. 851 (order for exclusive possession of matrimonial home, made under provincial law, valid and operative notwithstanding order for support under Divorce Act).

82 Note the doubt as to whether the power to make an order for corollary relief continues after the granting of the divorce: note 42, above.

83 It is assumed that the pre-existing order does not automatically lapse on the dissolution of the marriage: Mendes da Costa (ed.), *Studies in Canadian Family Law* (1972), vol. 1, 354-356.

84 (1972) 36 D.L.R. (3d) 421 (N.B. A.D.).

85 Accord, *Whyte* v. *Whyte* (1969) 7 D.L.R. (3d) 7 (Man. C.A.); *Re Hall and Hall* (1976) 70 D.L.R. (3d) 493 (B.C. C.A.).

86 [1971] 1 O.R. 232 (H.C.).

87 Note 57, above.

88 Note 65, above.

enforced in Quebec; and it would be paramount over any order made under provincial law.

26.9 Jurisdiction of Family Courts

(a) Fragmentation of jurisdiction

In most provinces, matters of family law are adjudicated upon by several different courts. There is now a strong movement to unite the various jurisdictions in a new unified family court. The existing fragmentation of jurisdiction is mainly an accident or series of accidents of history, but part of the explanation, and an impediment to radical reorganization, is the Constitution. Not only does the Constitution divide legislative jurisdiction over family law in the ways already discussed in this chapter, it also imposes restraints on the kinds of courts which can be invested with jurisdiction to determine family disputes.

(b) Federal courts

Section 101 of the Constitution Act, 1867 confers on the federal Parliament the power to establish federal courts. This power has been exercised by the establishment of the Federal Court of Canada, but the Federal Court has not been given any significant jurisdiction in family matters. Section 101 of the Constitution Act, 1867 limits federally-established courts to the adjudication of issues governed by federal law. Since much substantive family law is outside federal legislative competence, no federal court could in any event be given an extensive family jurisdiction. Any court exercising comprehensive family jurisdiction would have to be a provincial court.

(c) Provincial courts invested by province

Section 92(14) of the Constitution Act, 1867 confers on the provincial Legislatures the power to make laws in relation to ''the administration of justice in the province, including the constitution, maintenance, and organization of provincial courts''. Provincial courts established under this provision are not confined to issues governed by provincial law; they may be given jurisdiction to administer

89 Accord, *Hughes* v. *Hughes* (1976) 72 D.L.R. (3d) 577 (B.C. C.A.).

90 Russell, *The Judiciary in Canada* (1987), ch. 9, explains the diverse arrangements that have evolved. The statutes establishing family courts are collected in the *Canadian Family Law Guide* (CCH loose-leaf service).

91 Katz, note 10, above.

92 See ch. 7, Courts, under heading 7.2, ''Federal courts'', above.

93 A minor jurisdiction is conferred by Divorce Act, S.C. 1986, c. 4, ss. 3, 5.

federal as well as provincial law. However, s. 96 (and the associated judicature sections) of the Constitution Act do impose limits on the power of the provincial Legislatures to invest provincial courts with jurisdiction. It has been decided that s. 96 implicitly stipulates that a province may not vest in an inferior court (that is, a court which is not a superior, district or county court) a jurisdiction analogous to that exercised by a superior, district or county court.

Most of what we now regard as family law has come into existence since confederation, and as the provincial Legislatures have created new bodies of law they have tended to vest adjudicatory power in the inferior courts in the province. In the *Adoption Reference* (1938), the Supreme Court of Canada had to determine the constitutionality of provincial statutes which vested in inferior courts powers to grant adoptions, to award "maintenance" to deserted wives and children, to make affiliation orders and award maintenance for illegitimate children and to make orders for the care of children in need of protection. Duff C.J., for the Court, upheld each of these jurisdictions as "broadly conform[ing] to a type of jurisdiction generally exercisable by courts of summary jurisdiction rather than the jurisdiction exercised by courts within the purview of s. 96". In *Re B.C. Family Relations Act* (1982), the Supreme Court of Canada held that, since a province could confer on an inferior court jurisdiction over adoption, it could also confer jurisdiction over guardianship and custody, which were "lesser rungs" on the ladder of family relationships. These two decisions of the Supreme Court of Canada establish that most family law can be administered by inferior courts. Of course, the powers upheld in the two cases could also be vested in a s. 96 court if a province wished to follow that route. All that the two cases decide is that there is no fetter on the provincial competence to confer those powers.

There are still some matters of family law that, although within provincial legislative competence, must be vested in a s. 96 court. In *Re B.C. Family Relations Act*, the Court, while upholding the jurisdiction over guardianship and custody (as related above), struck down an attempt to confer on the inferior court jurisdiction over occupancy of (and access to) the family residence. That jurisdiction could be conferred only on a s. 96 court, because of its impact on proprietary rights and its similarity to injunctive relief. This decision shows that a unified family court really has to be established at the level of a superior, district or county court (so that it is a s. 96 court).

(d) Provincial courts invested by Dominion

There is no doubt that jurisdiction to grant a divorce decree, and probably relief ancillary to a divorce decree, may be conferred by the provincial Legisla-

---

94 See ch. 7, Courts, under heading 7.1, "Provincial courts", above.
95 *Id.*, under heading 7.3, "Implications of Constitution's judicature sections", above.
96 *Re Adoption Act* [1938] S.C.R. 398.
97 *Id.*, 421.
98 [1982] 1 S.C.R. 62.

tures only on a s. 96 court. But, because the substantive law of divorce is within federal legislative authority, the federal Parliament also has the power to invest courts with divorce jurisdiction. Moreover, s. 96 and the associated sections of the Constitution Act, 1867 do not apply to federal courts and tribunals. Therefore, the federal Parliament could if it chose confer divorce jurisdiction on a federally-established court or tribunal which did not satisfy the rules stipulated by ss. 96 to 100.

The federal Parliament has in fact chosen to confer divorce jurisdiction on the superior court in each province. The action of the federal Parliament has not completely eliminated the s. 96 difficulty, however. It can arise, for example, where rules made under provincial law purport to permit some divorce matters to be referred to a master of the court for decision, instead of being determined by a federally-appointed judge. It has been held that the s. 96 difficulty cannot arise where the adjudicator derives his authority from federal law. In *Papp* v. *Papp* (1969), a constitutional challenge was made to rules of the Supreme Court of Ontario which purported to authorize a master to make interim custody orders in divorce cases. Laskin J.A., sitting as the Ontario Court of Appeal, held that the impugned rules had been made under the authority of the federal Divorce Act, and not under provincial law. Since the master's power derived from federal law, the power was valid even if it was a jurisdiction analogous to that of a superior, district or county court. The federal Parliament was free to do what the provincial Legislatures could not do.

Whether or not *Papp* v. *Papp* is still good law is doubtful in light of the recent decision of the Supreme Court of Canada in *McEvoy* v. *A.-G. N.B.* (1983), which holds that even the federal Parliament cannot confer a s. 96 function (in that case it was the power to try indictable offences) on a provincially-established inferior court. However, the Supreme Court of Canada (which included Laskin C.J.) did not disapprove of *Papp* v. *Papp*, and certainly what was proposed in

---

99 *A.-G. B.C.* v. *McKenzie* [1965] S.C.R. 490; *Re Judicature Amendment Act, 1970 (No. 4)* [1971] 2 O.R. 521 (C.A.).

100 See ch. 7, Courts, under heading 7.1(a), ''Establishment of provincial courts'', above.

101 *Id.*, at note 100, above; also, ch. 19, Criminal Justice, under heading 19.2(d), ''Application of s. 96 to Parliament'', above.

102 The federal Parliament probably could not confer divorce jurisdiction on a *provincially-established* court or tribunal that did not satisfy ss. 96 to 100: *McEvoy* v. *A.-G. N.B.* [1983] 1 S.C.R. 704; and see note 108, below.

103 Divorce Act, S.C. 1986, c. 4, s. 3.

104 In *Zacks* v. *Zacks* [1973] S.C.R. 891, the Supreme Court of Canada held that provincial rules of court authorizing the reference to a master of the quantum of maintenance did not offend the judicature provisions of the Constitution Act because the master's power was to inquire and report and not to adjudicate.

105 [1970] 1 O.R. 331 (C.A.).

106 [1983] 1 S.C.R. 704.

107 *Papp* v. *Papp* is not mentioned in the opinion, although it was cited to the Court by counsel for both sides.

McEvoy was a more radical transformation of court jurisdiction than had occurred in *Papp* v. *Papp*.

108 The effect of the proposal in *McEvoy* was described by the Court as ''a complete obliteration of Superior Court criminal law jurisdiction'' (p. 719). To the argument that jurisdiction concurrent with the superior court was proposed, the Court said: ''we think this overlooks the fact that what is being attempted here is the transformation by conjoint action of an inferior court into a superior court'' (p. 721). *McEvoy* is discussed in ch. 19, Criminal Justice, under heading 19.2(c), ''Application of s. 96 to indictable offences'', above.

27

Aboriginal Peoples

27.1 Federal legislative power

(a) Section 91(24)

Section 91(24) of the Constitution Act, 1867 confers upon the federal Parliament the power to make laws in relation to "Indians, and lands reserved for the Indians".[1]

The main reason for s. 91(24) seems to have been a concern for the protection of the Indians against local settlers, whose interests lay in an absence of restrictions on the expansion of European settlement. The idea was that the more distant level of government — the federal government — would be more likely to respect the Indian reserves that existed in 1867, to respect the treaties with the Indians that had been entered into by 1867, and generally to protect the Indians against the interests of local majorities.[2] A second reason was probably the desire to maintain uniform national policies respecting the Indians. The Royal Proclamation of 1763 had established that treaty-making with the Indians was the sole responsibility of the (imperial) Crown in right of the United Kingdom.[3] After confederation, the federal government was the natural successor to that responsibility.[4]

It will be noticed that s. 91(24) contains two heads of power: a power over "Indians" and a power over "lands reserved for the Indians". The first power may be exercised in respect of Indians (and only Indians) whether or not they reside on, or have any connection with, lands reserved for the Indians. The second power may be exercised in respect of Indians and non-Indians so long as the law is related to lands reserved for the Indians.

---

1 See Lysyk, "The Unique Constitutional Position of the Canadian Indian" (1967) 45 Can. Bar Rev. 513; Lysyk "Constitutional Developments relating to Indians and Indian Lands" in Law Society of Upper Canada, *The Constitution and the Future of Canada* (Special Lectures, 1978), 201; Sanders, "Prior Claims: Aboriginal People in the Constitution of Canada" in Beck and Bernier (eds.), *Canada and the New Constitution* (1983), vol. 1, 225; Woodward, *Native Law* (1989); Beaudoin, *La Constitution du Canada* (1990), ch. 15; Reiter, *The Fundamental Principles of Indian Law* (1990, loose-leaf).

2 Sanders, previous note, 238.

3 Note 17, below.

4 Aboriginal peoples did not participate in the confederation process, so that they had no influence over constitutional developments of profound significance to them.

(b) Indians

The federal power over "Indians" — the first branch of s. 91(24) — invites two questions: (1) Who is an Indian? and (2) What kinds of laws may be made in relation to Indians?

Who is an Indian? The federal Indian Act[5] defines the term "Indian" for the purpose of that Act, and establishes a register to record the names of qualified persons. The statutory definition traces Indian status from particular bands whose charter members were normally determined at the time of the establishment of a reserve or the making of a treaty. The status then devolves from these charter members to their descendants.[6] Persons within the statutory definition of the Indian Act are known as "status Indians". They alone enjoy the right to live on Indian reserves[7] and various other Indian Act privileges.[8] There are about 500,000 status Indians in Canada.

It is probable that all status Indians are "Indians" within the meaning of s. 91(24) of the Constitution Act, 1867.[9] But there are also many persons of Indian blood and culture who are outside the statutory definition.[10] These "non-status

5 R.S.C. 1985, c. I-5.

6 The status provisions of the Act were substantially amended in 1985 by S.C. 1985, c. 27. The historical roots of status are now buried in s. 6(1)(a), which brings the charter group forward to those entitled to be registered in 1985. The amendments eliminate certain provisions that had been attacked as discriminatory, in particular, the provision that caused an Indian woman to lose status if she married a non-Indian man: see *A.G. Can.* v. *Lavell* [1974] S.C.R. 1349 (provision upheld under Canadian Bill of Rights); *Lovelace* v. *Can.* (1983) 1 Can. Human Rights Yearbook 305 (U.N. Human Rights Committee) (provision held contrary to International Covenant on Civil and Political Rights). The amendments permit persons who before 1985 lost status under this and other provisions of the Act, including voluntary enfranchisement (which is no longer possible), and their children, to regain status. The amendments also separate Indian status from band membership; control over the latter, but not the former, has been conferred on the bands. See Scarsgard, "Indian Status and Band Membership" (University of Saskatchewan Native Law Centre, Update 1986).

7 Any liberalization of the definition of a status Indian, such as occurred in 1985 (previous note), has the effect of enlarging the population that is entitled to live on the reserves.

8 E.g., exemption from payment of tax on personal property situated on a reserve (s. 87), which has been held to include income tax: *Nowegijick v. The Queen* [1983] 1 S.C.R. 29. Before 1950, status Indians resident on a reserve had no right to vote, so that the voluntary termination of status became known as "enfranchisement". In 1950, the franchise was extended to those Indians who waived their exemption from tax. Only in 1960 was an unconditional right to vote finally extended to status Indians.

9 The Court would accept a statutory definition that could be supported as a reasonable, bona fide definition: see *A.-G. Can. v. Canard* [1976] 1 S.C.R. 170, 206 per Beetz J., implying the validity of the provision (repealed in 1985) under which a white woman became an "instant Indian" on marrying an Indian man.

10 Even a full-blooded Indian does not necessarily have Indian status under the Indian Act. His or her ancestors may not have belonged to the charter group for whom a reserve was established or with whom a treaty was made. Even a "treaty Indian", whose ancestors signed a treaty, could lack status under the Indian Act, because status could be lost in a variety of ways. See

Indians'' are also undoubtedly ''Indians'' within the meaning of s. 91(24), although they are not governed by the Indian Act. The Métis people, who originated in the west from intermarriage between French Canadian men and Indian women during the fur trade period, received ''half-breed'' land grants in lieu of any right to live on reserves, and were accordingly excluded from the charter group from whom Indian status devolved. However, they are probably ''Indians'' within the meaning of s. 91(24).[11] There may be as many as 500,000 Métis and non-status Indians in Canada. The Inuit or Eskimo people are also outside the reserve system, and are therefore not covered by the Indian Act definition, but they have been held to be ''Indians'' within the meaning of s. 91(24).[12] There are about 35,000 Inuit people in Canada. The Parliament is, of course, under no obligation to legislate to the full limit of its authority, and, with respect to Indians, it has certainly not done so: non-status Indians, Métis and Inuit are not governed by the Indian Act.[13]

What kinds of laws may be made in relation to Indians? The federal Parliament has taken the broad view that it may legislate for Indians on matters which otherwise lie outside its legislative competence, and on which it could not legislate for non-Indians. The most conspicuous examples are the provisions of the Indian Act that govern succession to the property of deceased Indians. There are also provisions for the administration of the property of mentally incompetent Indians and infant Indians, and provisions for the education of Indian children. Whether these provisions are valid or not is of course a question of characterization: are they in pith and substance in relation to Indians, or in relation to succession or property or education? Lysyk rightly points out that this inquiry ''will not be concluded by the fact that the enactment is limited in its application to a class of persons mentioned in the B.N.A. Act'',[14] and he expresses doubt as to the validity of the Indian Act's forays into the law of property.

If s. 91(24) merely authorized Parliament to make laws for Indians which it could make for non-Indians, then the provision would be unnecessary. It seems likely, therefore, that the courts would uphold laws which could be rationally related to intelligible Indian policies, even if the laws would ordinarily be outside federal competence. This is not to deny Lysyk's caveat about the danger of assuming that a law which applies only to Indians is a law ''in relation to''

---

generally Woodward, note 1, above, 5-12. As well, some full-blooded Indians were classified as ''half-breeds''.

11 The issue is fully canvassed by Chartier, ''Indian: Analysis of the Term'' (1978) 43 Sask. L.R. 37; see also Bell, ''Who are the Métis People in section 35(2)?'' (1991) 29 Alta. L. Rev. 351.

12 *Re Eskimos* [1939] S.C.R. 104.

13 The guarantees of native rights in ss. 25 and 35 of the Constitution Act, 1982 (discussed later in this chapter) use the phrase ''aboriginal peoples of Canada'', which is defined in s. 35(2) as including ''the Indian, Inuit and Métis peoples of Canada''. As indicated in the text it is probable that ''Indians'' in s. 91(24) encompasses the same people.

14 Lysyk, note 1, above, 533-534. On singling out, see ch. 15, Judicial Review on Federal Grounds, above.

Indians. For example, a law which stipulated a special speed limit for Indians driving automobiles on public highways would be hard to sustain as an ''Indian'' law, because it does not seem to bear any relationship to any intelligible legislative policy in regard to Indians. But laws in regard to Indian property and Indian education have traditionally been part of federal Indian policy, and could no doubt be justified as aiming at peculiarly Indian concerns.[15] Whether such laws are wise or unwise is of course a much-controverted question, but it is not relevant to their constitutional validity.

(c) Lands reserved for the Indians

Section 91(24), by its second branch, confers on the federal Parliament legislative power over ''lands reserved for the Indians''. This phrase[16] obviously includes the lands set aside as Indian reserves in various ways before and after confederation. However, it also includes the huge area of land recognized by the Royal Proclamation of 1763[17] as ''reserved'' for the Indians, that is, all land within the territory covered by the Proclamation that was in the possession of the Indians and that had not been ceded to the Crown. The phrase may extend to all land that is subject to unextinguished aboriginal title.

A grant of legislative power does not carry with it proprietary rights over the subject matter of the power.[18] In the *St. Catherine's Milling* case (1889),[19] the Privy Council held that lands reserved for the Indians were not among the properties transferred to the Dominion by the property provisions of the Constitution Act, 1867.[20] Accordingly, the underlying title to the land remained in the Crown in right of the province.[21] The title of the provincial Crown is subject to the

---

15 The succession provisions were upheld in *A.-G. Can. v. Canard* [1976] 1 S.C.R. 170, where there was a distribution-of-powers challenge as well as a bill-of-rights challenge. This is an important holding, because the succession provisions are among the few provisions that deal with off-reserve property. It has been argued, however, that the off-reserve public drunkenness provisions (repealed in 1985) were unconstitutional (as well as in conflict with the Canadian Bill of Rights) because the racial classification was not reasonable in that context: McDonald, ''Equality before the Law and the Indian Act'' (1977) 3 Dalhousie L.J. 726. In *Brown* v. *The Queen* (1980) 107 D.L.R. (3d) 705 (B.C.C.A.), the Indian Act exemption from tax for personal property situated on a reserve was upheld in its application to provincial tax, following *Canard*.

16 For discussion, see La Forest, *Natural Resources and Public Property under the Canadian Constitution* (1969), ch. 7; Woodward, note 1, above, ch. 8.

17 R.S.C. 1985, Appendix II, No. 1. The Royal Proclamation of 1763 is briefly described in ch. 2, Reception, under heading 2.3(b), ''Ontario and Quebec'', above. With respect to Indians, the Proclamation recognized their rights to unceded lands in their possession, and established that the rights could be ceded only to the Crown.

18 See ch. 25, Public Property, under heading 25.4, ''Legislative power and proprietary interests'', below.

19 *St. Catherine's Milling and Lumber Co.* v. *The Queen* (1888) 14 App. Cas. 46.

20 The property provisions are discussed in ch. 28, Public Property, under heading 28.1, ''Distribution of public property'', below.

21 La Forest, note 16, above, 113-114.

aboriginal rights of the Indians,[22] and those rights, along with other matters pertaining to the control and administration of the reserves, are subject to the legislative authority of the federal Parliament.[23] But if the Indians surrender their rights over particular lands, which they can only do to the Crown, then full title to the lands is assumed by the province, not the Dominion.[24]

(d) Canadian Bill of Rights

The Canadian Bill of Rights, which is the subject of chapter 32, below, applies only to federal laws.[25] It contains, in s. 1(b), a guarantee of ''equality before the law'', and it specifically forbids ''discrimination by reason of race''.

The federal Indian Act[26] appears on its face to offend the guarantee of equality in the Canadian Bill of Rights. Yet special laws for Indians and Indian reserves are clearly contemplated by s. 91(24) of the Constitution Act, 1867. Indeed, legislation enacted in relation to ''Indians'' — the first branch of s. 91(24) — must normally be confined to Indians, that is to say, it must employ a racial classification,[27] in order to be constitutional. Legislation in relation to ''lands reserved for the Indians'' — the second branch of s. 91(24) — need not necessarily employ a racial classification; it could apply to anyone on a reserve.[28]

In *R.* v. *Drybones* (1969),[29] the Supreme Court of Canada held that the use of the racial classification ''Indian'' in s. 95 of the Indian Act, which made it an

---

22 As to the nature of aboriginal rights, see sec. 27.5, ''Aboriginal rights'', below.

23 Federal and provincial legislative authority is now limited by s. 35 of the Constitution Act, 1982, discussed later in this chapter.

24 *St. Catherine's Milling and Lumber Co. v. The Queen* (1889) 14 App. Cas. 46; *A.-G. Can. v. A.-G. Ont.* (Indian Annuities) [1897] A.C. 199; *Smith v. The Queen* [1983] 1 S.C.R. 554. The rule is otherwise in the prairie provinces, where the Dominion retained title to public lands until the Natural Resources Agreements of 1930; those Agreements, while generally transferring public lands to the provinces, provided for reserve lands to continue as federal lands after 1930, even including reserves established after 1930. In the other provinces, except for Quebec, Prince Edward Island and Newfoundland (although there are no reserves in Newfoundland), the provinces have entered into agreements with the Dominion, granting the Dominion the right to manage, sell and lease surrendered lands on reserves. The agreements and other instruments relative to the ownership and management of reserve lands are listed in Sanders, *Legal Aspects of Economic Development on Indian Reserve Lands* (Dept. of Indian and Northern Affairs, Ottawa, 1976), Appendix A.

25 It may apply to provincial laws that are incorporated by reference by s. 88 of the Indian Act (discussed later in this chapter): *Jack and Charlie* v. *The Queen* [1985] 2 S.C.R. 332, 338 (obiter dictum).

26 R.S.C. 1985, c. I-5.

27 Note, however, the leeway accorded to the federal Parliament in defining the term ''Indian'': note 9 above.

28 It is of course arguable that any law that is applicable only on a reserve, even if literally applicable to anyone, is so predominantly applicable to Indians that, in substance if not in form, the law does employ a racial classification. This argument was accepted in *R. v. Hayden*, note 30, below.

29 [1970] S.C.R. 282.

offence for an Indian to be intoxicated on a reserve, violated the equality guarantee in the Canadian Bill of Rights. The majority of the Court did not even notice the problem that the racial classification ''Indian'' seemed to be requisite to the constitutional validity of s. 95, although Pigeon J. emphasized this point in dissent. This decision cast doubt on all of the provisions of the Indian Act,[30] and on the whole principle of a special regime of law for Indians. Later cases, however, have tended to confine *Drybones* ''to its own facts'',[31] and it now appears that the special regime of law for Indians is not threatened by the decision.[32]

(e) Charter of Rights

The Charter of Rights, by s. 15, also contains an equality guarantee. The Indian Act has not yet been challenged under s. 15. It seems likely, however, that the Constitution's various recognitions of Indian special status, reinforced by the long history of the reserve system, and by the desire of aboriginal peoples to preserve their identity and culture through some form of special legal status, would lead the courts to reject an equality challenge, perhaps by recognizing an exception to s. 15, or under the Charter's affirmative action clause (s. 15(2)), or under the Charter's general limitation clause (s. 1), or under the Charter's saving clause for ''aboriginal, treaty or other rights or freedoms that pertain to the aboriginal peoples of Canada'' (s. 25).[33]

(f) Treaties

Before 1982, when s. 35 of the Constitution Act, 1982 was adopted, it was clear that federal legislative power over Indians and lands reserved for the Indians

30 A distinction could of course be drawn between those provisions that (like s. 95 — the off-reserve drunkenness offence) applied only to Indians, and those provisions that (like s. 97 — the on-reserve drunkenness offence) applied on a reserve to non-Indians as well as Indians. At first, s. 97 was upheld on this basis: *R.* v. *Whiteman (No. 1)* [1971] 2 W.W.R. 316 (Sask. Dist. Ct.). In *R. v. Hayden* (1983) 3 D.L.R. (4th) 361 (Man. C.A.), s. 97 was struck down on the ground that, although s. 97 was not confined to Indians, since Indians were the ''predominant residents of reservations'', s. 97 was just as discriminatory as s. 95, and *Drybones* should be followed. In *R.* v. *Lefthand* (1985) 19 D.L.R. (4th) 720 (Alta. C.A.), s. 97 was upheld, following *Whiteman* and disapproving *Hayden*. Sections 95 and 97 were repealed in 1985.

31 *A.-G. Can. v. Lavell* [1974] S.C.R. 1349 (Indian Act status provision upheld); *A.-G. Can. v. Canard* [1976] 1 S.C.R. 170 (Indian Act succession provision upheld). For more discussion of the relationship between s. 91(24) and equality, see Hogg, Comment (1974) 52 Can. Bar Rev. 263; Sanders, ''The Renewal of Indian Special Status'' in Bayefsky and Eberts (eds.), *Equality Rights and the Canadian Charter of Rights and Freedoms* (1985), ch. 12. See also ch. 52, Equality under heading 52.10, ''Race'', below

32 Special status for the aboriginal peoples has been given constitutional recognition by ss. 25, 35 and 35.1 of the Constitution Act, 1982, discussed later in this chapter, under heading 27.3, ''Aboriginal rights'', below.

33 See ch. 52, Equality, under heading 52.10, ''Race'', below. Section 25 is discussed later in sec. 27.9, ''Section 25'', below.

was not limited by the terms of treaties entered into with other countries or with Indian tribes or bands. So far as treaties with other countries are concerned, the general rule is that they have no effect on the internal law of Canada unless they are implemented by legislation.[34] Thus, although a treaty entered into with the United States exempted the Indians from payment of customs duties at the Canadian border, the Supreme Court of Canada held that customs duties were still payable by the Indians, because the Customs Act did not include the agreed-upon exemption.[35]

So far as treaties with Indian tribes or bands are concerned,[36] before 1982 they too could not stand against inconsistent federal[37] legislation. Thus, although a treaty entered into with certain Indian tribes guaranteed their right to hunt for food at any time of the year, the Supreme Court of Canada held that the Indians were still prohibited by federal law from shooting migratory birds out of season, because the Migratory Birds Convention Act did not include the agreed-upon exemption.[38]

Section 35 of the Constitution Act, 1982 now gives constitutional protection to rights created by treaties entered into with Indian tribes or bands and perhaps to rights created by provisions in international treaties. Section 35 operates as a limitation on the powers of the federal Parliament, as well as the provincial Legislatures. Section 35 is the subject of a later section of this chapter.[39]

27.2 Provincial legislative power

(a) General rule

The general rule is that provincial laws apply to Indians and lands reserved for the Indians.[40] In *R.* v. *Hill* (1907),[41] the Ontario Court of Appeal held that a provincial law confining the practice of medicine to qualified physicians applied

34 See ch. 11, Treaties, above.

35 *Francis v. The Queen* [1956] S.C.R. 618; the decision is criticized by Lysyk, note 1, above, 527-528, on the basis that the Customs Act could have been construed as not violating the treaty.

36 The legal status of these treaties is discussed in sec. 27.6, ''Treaty rights'', below.

37 The treaties are effective against provincial legislation, both by reason of their ''Indianness'': note 54, below; and by virtue of s. 88 of the Indian Act, which makes provincial laws ''subject to the terms of any treaty''. However, s. 88 is inapplicable to federal laws: *R.* v. *George* [1966] S.C.R. 267. Section 88 of the Indian Act is discussed later in this chapter in sec. 27.3, ''Section 88 of the Indian Act'', below.

38 *Sikyea v. The Queen* [1964] S.C.R. 642; *R. v. George* [1966] S.C.R. 267. For other cases affirming the effectiveness of the Migratory Birds Convention Act, see *Daniels v. White* [1968] S.C.R. 517; *R. v. Catagas* (1977) 81 D.L.R. (3d) 396 (Man. C.A.).

39 Section 27.8, ''Section 35'', below.

40 See generally the articles cited in note 1, above; also, Hughes, ''Indians and Lands Reserved for the Indians'' (1983) 21 Osgoode Hall L.J. 82.

41 (1907) 15 O.L.R. 406 (C.A.).

to Indians; an Indian was convicted of the offence of the unauthorized practice of medicine. The offence in *Hill* did not take place on a reserve, but the result would have been the same if it had. In *Four B Manufacturing* v. *United Garment Workers* (1979),[42] the Supreme Court of Canada held that provincial labour law applied to a shoe-manufacturing business, which was located on a reserve, which was owned (through a corporation) by Indians, which employed mainly Indians, and which had been funded by the Department of Indian Affairs. In *R.* v. *Francis* (1988),[43] the Supreme Court of Canada held that provincial traffic laws applied to an Indian driving a vehicle on an Indian reserve.[44]

These decisions establish that the provincial Legislatures have the power to make their laws applicable to Indians and on Indian reserves, so long as the law is in relation to a matter coming within a provincial head of power. The situation of Indians and Indian reserves is thus no different from that of aliens, banks, federally-incorporated companies and interprovincial undertakings. These, too, are subjects of federal legislative power, but they still have to pay provincial taxes, and obey provincial traffic laws, health and safety requirements, social and economic regulations and the myriad of other provincial laws which apply to them in common with other similarly-situated residents of the province.[45]

The *Four B* and *Francis* cases definitely rejected the theory that Indian reserves are federal ''enclaves'' from which provincial laws are excluded. This theory was advanced by Laskin as a professor in his casebook,[46] and in a number of his judicial opinions as Chief Justice — all of them in dissent.[47] The theory was always implausible, because it involved a distinction between the first and second branches of s. 91(24) for which there is no textual warrant, and it placed the second branch (''lands reserved for the Indians'') in a privileged position enjoyed by no other federal subject matter.[48] It is plain that there is no constitutional distinction between ''Indians'' and ''lands reserved for the Indians'', and that provincial laws may apply to both subject matters.

---

42 [1980] 1 S.C.R. 1031.

43 [1988] 1 S.C.R. 1025.

44 None of the three decisions relied on s. 88 of the Indian Act, discussed in the next section of this chapter. Section 88 did not exist when the *Hill* case was decided; s. 88 was referred to but not relied upon in the *Four B* case; s. 88 was expressly held to be inapplicable in the *Francis* case. According to *Dick* v. *The Queen*, note 71, below, s. 88 has no application to provincial laws that can apply to Indians of their own force.

45 See ch. 15, Judicial Review on Federal Grounds, under heading 15.5(k), ''Interjurisdictional immunity'', above.

46 Laskin, *Canadian Constitutional Law* (4th ed. rev., 1975), 523 (''provincial laws are inapplicable on a reservation''). This position has been abandoned in the 5th edition by Finkelstein, the editor.

47 *Cardinal v. A.-G. Alta.* [1974] S.C.R. 695; *Natural Parents v. Superintendent of Child Welfare* [1976] 2 S.C.R. 751 (concurring opinion, but dissenting on this issue); *Four B* case, note 42, above.

48 Laskin, note 45, above, 529, appeared to accord a similar status to the federal power over ''the public debt and property'' (s. 91(1A)). The enclave theory has also been rejected in that context: *Construction Montcalm v. Minimum Wage Comm.* [1979] 1 S.C.R. 754 (Laskin C.J. dissenting).

There are five exceptions to the general rule that provincial laws apply to Indians and lands reserved for the Indians.

(b) First exception: singling out

The first exception is singling out. A provincial law that singled out Indians or Indian reserves for special treatment would run the risk of being classified as a law in relation to Indians or Indian reserves; and, if so classified, the law would be invalid.[49]

(c) Second exception: Indianness

The second exception to the general rule that provincial laws apply to Indians and lands reserved for the Indians is ''Indianness''. A provincial law that affects ''an integral part of primary federal jurisdiction over Indians and lands reserved for the Indians''[50] will be inapplicable to Indians and lands reserved for the Indians, even though the law is one of general application that is otherwise within provincial competence. This vague exception, which has been framed as preclud-ing laws that impair the ''status or capacity'' of Indians,[51] or that affect ''Indi-anness'',[52] has its analogy in the immunity from provincial laws that affect a vital part of undertakings within federal jurisdiction.[53]

The Indianness exception means that provincial laws cannot affect aboriginal or treaty rights.[54] Nor can provincial laws affect Indian status. In *Natural Parents*

---

49 *R.* v. *Sutherland* [1980] 2 S.C.R. 451, 455 (provincial law struck down); *Dick* v. *The Queen* [1985] 2 S.C.R. 309, 322 (obiter dictum); *Leighton* v. *B.C.* (1989) 57 D.L.R. (4th) 657 (B.C.C.A.) (provincial law struck down); see ch. 15, Judicial Review on Federal Grounds, under heading 15.5(b), ''Singling out'', above.

50 *Four B Manufacturing v. UGW.* [1980] 1 S.C.R. 1031, 1047 per Beetz J.

51 This is the phraseology used by Dickson J. in *Kruger and Manuel* v. *The Queen* [1978] 1 S.C.R. 104, 110.

52 This is the phraseology used by Laskin C.J. in *Natural Parents v. Superintendent of Child Welfare* [1967] 2 S.C.R. 751, 760-761, and by Beetz J. in *Dick* v. *The Queen* [1985] 2 S.C.R. 309, 326.

53 See ch. 15, Judicial Review on Federal Grounds, under heading 15.5(k), ''Interjurisdictional immunity'', above.

54 *Simon* v. *The Queen* [1985] 2 S.C.R. 387, 411 per Dickson C.J. for the Court:

> It has been held to be within the exclusive power of Parliament under s. 91(24) of the Constitution Act, 1867 to derogate from rights recognized in a treaty agreement made with the Indians.

If provincial law is incompetent to derogate from treaty rights by reason of the impact on Indianness, the same must be true of aboriginal rights as well. With respect to treaty rights, the provincial disability is reinforced by s. 88 of the Indian Act (sec. 27.3, below) and since 1982 by s. 35 of the Constitution Act, 1982 (sec. 27.8, below). With respect to aboriginal rights, the provincial disability is partially removed by s. 88 of the Indian Act, but was fully restored in 1982 by s. 35 of the Constitution Act, 1982. See Slattery, ''Understanding Aboriginal Rights'' (1987) 66 Can. Bar Rev. 727, 774-782.

v. *Superintendent of Child Welfare* (1975),[55] the Supreme Court of Canada held that, while provincial adoption law would permit white parents to adopt an Indian child, the provincial law had to be read down so as not to deprive the child of his Indian status.[56] Provincial laws cannot affect the right to possession of land on an Indian reserve,[57] and probably cannot affect at least some uses of land on a reserve. Hunting on a reserve is such a significant element of traditional Indian ways that it should probably be free of provincial regulation.[58] However, it is less obvious that the construction of housing and other buildings on a reserve should be free of provincial regulation, although there are decisions of provincial courts of appeal that so decide.[59]

Provincial laws that do affect Indianness cannot apply to Indians of their own force. However, as will be explained later in this chapter, some such laws could become applicable to Indians through s. 88 of the Indian Act, which incorporates by reference provincial laws of general application.

(d) Third exception: paramountcy

The third exception to the general rule that provincial laws apply to Indians and lands reserved for the Indians is the doctrine of federal paramountcy. If a provincial law is inconsistent with a provision of the Indian Act (or any other federal law), the provincial law is rendered inoperative by the doctrine of federal paramountcy.[60]

---

55 [1976] 2 S.C.R. 751.

56 This was the end result, although a variety of opinions reached the result by a variety of routes. The protection for Indian status was affirmed, obiter, by Beetz J. in *Four B Manufacturing* v. *UGW*. [1980] 1 S.C.R. 1031, 1047.

57 *Derrickson* v. *Derrickson* [1986] 1 S.C.R. 285 (division of assets on divorce or separation); *Paul* v. *Paul* [1986] 1 S.C.R. 306 (occupancy of family residence).

58 So held in *R.* v. *Jim* (1915) 26 C.C.C. 236 (B.C.S.C.); *R.* v. *Isaac* (1976) 13 N.S.R. (2d) 460 (N.S.A.D.). Query whether hunting by Indians off a reserve is a characteristic of Indianness that is immune from provincial law. Compare *Kruger and Manuel* v. *The Queen* [1978] 1 S.C.R. 104 (held, no) with *Dick* v. *The Queen* [1985] 2 S.C.R. 309, 320-321 (assuming, without deciding, yes). Of course, hunting would be a characteristic of Indianness if hunting were an aboriginal right or a treaty right (note 54, above) or were protected by the Natural Resources Agreements (note 82, below). Does hunting have a different character when none of these cases apply?

59 *Surrey Corp.* v. *Peace Arch Enterprises* (1970) 74 W.W.R. 380 (B.C.C.A.) (zoning and health laws); *Re Whitebear Band Council* (1982) 135 D.L.R. (3d) 128 (Sask. C.A.) (labour law). Compare *Western Industrial Contractors* v. *Sarcee Developments* (1979) 98 D.L.R. (3d) 424 (Alta. C.A.) (provincial builder's lien applies to leasehold interest on reserve lands); *Re Stony Plain Indian Reserve* (1981) 130 D.L.R. (3d) 636, 652 (Alta. C.A.) (reaffirming *Sarcee*). In *Construction Montcalm* v. *Minimum Wage Comm.* [1979] 1 S.C.R. 754, the Supreme Court of Canada held that provincial minimum wage law applied to a construction firm building a runway at an airport. The reasoning of Beetz J. for the majority is difficult to reconcile with the *Peace Arch* and *Whitebear* decisions, because the construction of buildings on a reserve seems only tenuously related to "Indianness".

60 Chapter 16, Paramountcy, above.

(e) Fourth exception: Natural Resources Agreements

The fourth exception to the general rule that provincial laws apply to Indians and lands reserved for the Indians is a right of Indians to take game and fish for food, which is defined and protected in the three prairie provinces by the "Natural Resources Agreements". Provincial laws cannot deprive Indians of this right. The Natural Resources Agreements, which are part of the Constitution of Canada, are discussed in a later section of this chapter.[61]

(f) Fifth exception: section 35

The fifth exception to the general rule that provincial laws apply to Indians and lands reserved for the Indians is the "aboriginal and treaty rights" that since 1982 have been protected by s. 35 of the Constitution Act, 1982. Even before 1982 aboriginal rights and treaty rights were not vulnerable to provincial law, because of the Indianness exception (the second exception, above). As well, in the case of treaty rights, s. 88 of the Indian Act expressly provided that provincial laws of general application must yield to the terms of any treaty. Section 88 is examined in the next section of this chapter. Since 1982, s. 35 of the Constitution Act, 1982 has given constitutional status to aboriginal and treaty rights, constituting yet another basis upon which they are protected from impairment by provincial law. Section 35, unlike the Indianness exception and s. 88, applies to federal laws as well as provincial laws. Section 35 is examined later in this chapter.[62]

27.3 Section 88 of the Indian Act

(a) Text of s. 88

Section 88 of the Indian Act, which was first enacted in 1951 (it was then s. 87), provides as follows:

> Subject to the terms of any treaty and any other Act of the Parliament of Canada, all laws of general application from time to time in force in any province are applicable to and in respect of Indians in the province, except to the extent that such laws are inconsistent with this Act or any order, rule, regulation or by-law made thereunder, and except to the extent that such laws make provision for any matter for which provision is made by or under this Act.

---

61 Section 27.4, "Natural Resources Agreements", below.

62 Section 27.8, "Section 35", below.

Section 88 makes clear that provincial[63] ''laws of general application'' apply to ''Indians''.[64] The section makes no reference to lands reserved for the Indians, but there is no doubt that the section extends to Indians on a reserve.[65] Section 88 operates as a federal adoption, or incorporation by reference, of provincial laws, making the provincial laws applicable as part of federal law. This technique is valid, despite the fact that it comes close to a delegation of federal legislative power to the provinces.[66]

(b) Laws of general application

What is meant by the phrase ''laws of general application''? The phrase certainly excludes provincial laws that single out Indians for special treatment. As noted earlier, such laws are likely to be classified as being in relation to Indians and therefore as invalid.[67] Section 88 does not invigorate such laws.

Does the phrase ''laws of general application'' also exclude laws that, while not singling out Indians for special treatment, have a specially severe effect on Indians by affecting Indianness? As noted earlier, such laws cannot apply to Indians of their own force.[68] The Supreme Court of Canada in 1978 answered no to this question, holding that s. 88 did not make provincial laws affecting Indianness applicable to Indians.[69] Since other provincial laws of general application would apply to Indians of their own force anyway,[70] this interpretation made s. 88 merely declaratory of the general constitutional position, in that s. 88 did not expand the body of provincial law that applied to Indians.

In *Dick* v. *The Queen* (1985),[71] the Court changed its mind about the scope of s. 88. Beetz J. for the Court held that s. 88 did apply to provincial laws that affected Indianness by impairing the status or capacity of Indians. These were the only laws to which s. 88 needed to apply, because these were the laws that could not apply to Indians of their own force. Indeed, Beetz J. held, these were the only

---

63 Section 88 does not apply to federal laws, with the important consequence (before the adoption of s. 35 of the Constitution Act, 1982) that Indian treaties do not take precedence over federal laws: notes 37, 38, above. As noted later in the text, the opening words of s. 88 accord precedence to Indian treaties over provincial laws.

64 Because s. 88 is part of the Indian Act, the word ''Indians'' excludes non-status Indians, and the Inuit and Métis peoples: see sec. 27.1(b), ''Indians'', above.

65 La Forest, note 15, above, 179. Query, however, whether s. 88 would incorporate a provincial law that applied to lands reserved for the Indians: *Derrickson* v. *Derrickson* [1986] 1 S.C.R. 285, 299 (leaving the question open).

66 See ch. 14, Delegation, under heading 14.3(c), ''Referential legislation'', above.

67 This is the first exception to the general rule that provincial laws apply to Indians: text accompanying note 49, above. A valid provincial law of special application to Indians would not be covered by s. 88, but would be applicable of its own force: Lysyk, note 1, above, 536-539.

68 This is the second exception to the general rule that provincial laws apply to Indians: text accompanying note 50, above.

69 *Kruger and Manuel* v. *The Queen* [1978] 1 S.C.R. 104, 110.

70 This is the general rule: text accompanying note 40, above.

71 [1985] 2 S.C.R. 309.

laws to which s. 88 applied. Those ''provincial laws that can be applied to Indians without touching their Indianness, like traffic legislation'', applied to Indians of their own force. Section 88 was not needed to make those laws applicable to Indians, and s. 88 should be interpreted as not extending to those laws.[72]

The *Dick* interpretation of ''laws of general application'' in s. 88 has been reaffirmed in later cases,[73] and seems to be firmly established. It means that s. 88 is not merely declaratory of the existing constitutional position. On the contrary, s. 88 expands the body of provincial law that is applicable to Indians. Provincial laws affecting Indianness, which do not apply to Indians of their own force, are made applicable by s. 88.[74] Provincial laws not affecting Indianness, which do apply to Indians of their own force, are not caught by s. 88.

(c) Paramountcy exception

Section 88, by its opening words, is expressly subject to ''any other Act of the Parliament of Canada'', so that any conflict between a federal statute and a provincial law of general application has to be resolved in favour of the federal statute. A provincial law of general application is also inapplicable where it is ''inconsistent with this Act or any order, rule, regulation or by-law made thereunder''. These two parts of the section seem to be intended to make clear that the paramountcy doctrine applies to provincial laws of general application, notwithstanding their adoption by a federal statute.

The closing language of s. 88 goes on to provide that provincial laws of general application are applicable ''except to the extent that such laws make provision for any matter for which provision is made by or under this Act''. This language in its context seems to contemplate that a provincial law of general application which makes provision for any matter for which provision is made by (or under) the Indian Act must yield to the provisions of the Indian Act. The doctrine of paramountcy, on the other hand, at least as it has been interpreted recently, applies only where there is an express contradiction between a federal and a provincial law. It does not apply where the federal and provincial laws, while not in direct conflict, are merely occupying the same field, or in other words making provision for the same matters.[75] It seems probable therefore that the closing words of s. 88 go further than the paramountcy doctrine and will render inapplicable to Indians some provincial laws of general application which are not in direct conflict with the Indian Act.

It is important to notice that this expansion of the paramountcy doctrine operates as an exception to s. 88. Since the laws of general application to which

72 *Id.*, 326-327.

73 *Derrickson* v. *Derrickson* [1986] 1 S.C.R. 285, 297; *R.* v. *Francis* [1988] 1 S.C.R. 1025, 1030.

74 This is subject to s. 35 of the Constitution Act, 1982, which guarantees aboriginal or treaty rights from impairment by federal law (including s. 88) as well as provincial law: sec. 27.8, below.

75 Chapter 16, Paramountcy, above.

s. 88 applies are only those provincial laws that affect Indianness, it is only those laws that are subject to the wider paramountcy rule.[76] Provincial laws that do not affect Indianness are not caught by s. 88, and are not affected by the exception to s. 88. Provincial laws that do not affect Indianness apply to Indians of their own force, not through s. 88, and they are subject to the ordinary rule of paramountcy, not the expanded rule of s. 88.

(d) Treaty exception

Section 88, by its opening words, is ''subject to the terms of any treaty''. This means that any conflict between a treaty made with the Indians[77] and a provincial law of general application has to be resolved in favour of the treaty provision. Section 88 has been the ground upon which courts have held that provincial laws cannot impair Indian treaty rights.[78] The cases have assumed that s. 88 has this protective effect against all provincial laws, and they have not considered the implications of the *Dick* holding that s. 88 applies only to provincial laws that affect Indianness. According to *Dick*, s. 88 does not apply to provincial laws that do not affect Indianness, and therefore s. 88 would not confer on Indian treaties paramountcy over provincial laws that do not affect Indianness. However, I think it is clear that all provincial laws that purport to impair Indian treaty rights do, by virtue of that impairment, affect Indianness.[79] On that basis, the courts have been correct to assume that s. 88 shields Indian treaties from all provincial laws. This function of s. 88 has become less important with the adoption in 1982 of s. 35 of the Constitution Act, 1982, which gives explicit constitutional protection to aboriginal and treaty rights. Section 35 is examined later in this chapter.[80]

27.4 Natural Resources Agreements

A further limitation on provincial competence to make laws applicable to Indians is to be found in the ''Natural Resources Agreements'', which were entered into between Canada and the three prairie provinces, and which were

76 In *Dick* v. *The Queen* [1985] 2 S.C.R. 309, 328, Beetz J. drew this conclusion. He even asserted that Parliament could not validly enact a broader paramountcy rule for provincial laws that applied to Indians of their own force. This assertion is questioned in ch. 16, Paramountcy, under heading 16.5(a), ''Constitutional significance'', above.

77 According to one dictum, the reference to a treaty in s. 88 does not include international treaties: *Francis* v. *The Queen* [1956] S.C.R. 618, 631 per Kellock J.; note 35, above.

78 *R.* v. *White and Bob* (1965) 52 D.L.R. (2d) 481n (S.C.C.); *Simon* v. *The Queen* [1985] 2 S.C.R. 387; *Saanichton Marina* v. *Tsawout Indian Band* (1989) 57 D.L.R. (4th) 161 (B.C.C.A.); *R.* v. *Sioui* [1990] 1 S.C.R. 1025.

79 Note 54, above.

80 Section 27.8, ''Section 35'', below.

given constitutional status by an amendment to the Constitution Act in 1930.[81] The following clause is to be found in the Agreement with Alberta (clause 12), Saskatchewan (clause 12) and Manitoba (clause 13):[82]

> In order to secure to the Indians of the Province the continuance of the supply of game and fish for their support and subsistence, Canada agrees that the laws respecting game in force in the Province from time to time shall apply to the Indians within the boundaries thereof, provided, however, that the said Indians shall have the right, which the Province hereby assures to them of hunting, trapping and fishing game for food at all seasons of the year on all unoccupied Crown lands and on any other lands to which the said Indians may have a right of access.

In Alberta, Saskatchewan and Manitoba, therefore, the Indians are guaranteed the right to take game and fish "for food" at all seasons of the year on the lands specified.[83] Provincial laws[84] to the contrary are inapplicable to the Indians.

The words "for food" are an important restriction on the hunting and fishing rights conferred by the Natural Resources Agreements. Those Indians in the prairie provinces who, under the numbered treaties, had a right to hunt and fish for commercial purposes as well as for food had their rights cut down by the Agreements. The Supreme Court of Canada in *R.* v. *Horseman* (1990)[85] held that an Alberta Indian's treaty right to hunt commercially, which had been conferred by Treaty 8 in 1899, had been "merged and consolidated" in clause 12 of the Alberta Agreement, and his rights were now only those specified in the Agreement. This meant that Indian treaty rights had been partially extinguished by a constitutional amendment enacted without the consent of the Indians, who were not even consulted on the terms of the Natural Resources Agreements.

27.5 Aboriginal rights

(a) Definition of aboriginal rights

Section 35 of the Constitution Act, 1982 gives constitutional protection to "the existing aboriginal and treaty rights of the aboriginal peoples of Canada".

---

81 Constitution Act, 1930, R.S.C. 1985, Appendix II, No. 26. The history of these agreements is related in ch. 28, Public Property, under heading 28.1, "Distribution of public property", below.

82 There is also an agreement with British Columbia, but it does not include this clause, although there is a clause respecting Indians in the Terms of Union with British Columbia: see *Jack* v. *The Queen* [1980] 1 S.C.R. 294; Lysyk, note 1, above, 522.

83 The clause has been frequently applied or interpreted by the courts: e.g., *Daniels* v. *White* [1968] S.C.R. 517; *Frank v. The Queen* [1978] 1 S.C.R. 95; *The Queen* v. *Mousseau* [1980] 2 S.C.R. 89; *Elk* v. *The Queen* [1980] 2 S.C.R. 166; *The Queen* v. *Sutherland* [1980] 2 S.C.R. 451; *Moosehunter* v. *The Queen* [1981] 1 S.C.R. 282; *R.* v. *Horse* [1988] 1 S.C.R. 187.

84 The clause gives no protection against federal laws: *Daniels* v. *White* [1968] S.C.R. 517; *Elk* v. *The Queen* [1980] 2 S.C.R. 166.

85 [1990] 1 S.C.R. 901.

The nature of that protection is explained later in this chapter.[86] First, however, there is a brief account of the two categories of protected rights. This section of the chapter examines ''aboriginal rights''; the next section examines ''treaty rights''.

Aboriginal rights[87] are rights held by aboriginal peoples, not by virtue of Crown grant, legislation or treaty, but ''by reason of the fact that aboriginal peoples were once independent, self-governing entities in possession of most of the lands now making up Canada''.[88] It is clear that many rights with respect to land survived the reception of English and French law that occurred as the result of European settlement, and it is probable that rights with respect to self-government, customary law and cultural and religious practices also survived. There is still no generally accepted definition of aboriginal rights, and it is probably futile to search for one, in view of the variety of practices, needs and circumstances that gave rise to the rights. Those rights that have been recognized by the courts have been described as ''unique'' and ''sui generis''.[89] These terms acknowledge that aboriginal rights cannot be fitted into categories drawn from English or French law.

(b) Recognition of aboriginal rights

The survival of aboriginal rights with respect to land was placed beyond doubt by the *Calder* case (1973).[90] In that case, six of the seven judges held that the Nishga people of British Columbia possessed aboriginal rights to their lands that had survived European settlement. The actual outcome of the case was inconclusive, because the six judges split evenly on the question of whether the rights had been validly extinguished or not. However, the recognition of the rights was highly significant, and in fact, as will be noted later, caused the Government of Canada to start the negotiation of modern treaties — usually styled land claims agreements — in the regions of Canada where there were no treaties.

Aboriginal rights that have not been extinguished are recognized by the common law and are enforceable by the courts. The leading case is *Guerin* v. *The Queen* (1984),[91] in which the majority of the Supreme Court of Canada recognized the aboriginal title of the Musqueam Indian Band to land in British Columbia.

---

86 Section 27.8, ''Section 35'', below.

87 There is a vast literature on aboriginal rights, much of it emphasizing constitutional aspects. A few particularly useful sources are Slattery, ''The Constitutional Guarantee of Aboriginal and Treaty Rights'' (1983) 8 Queen's L.J. 232; Sanders, ''The Rights of the Aboriginal Peoples in Canada'' (1983) 61 Can. Bar Rev. 314; Slattery, ''Understanding Aboriginal Rights'' (1987) 66 Can. Bar Rev. 727; Pentney, ''The Rights of the Aboriginal Peoples of Canada'' (1988) 22 U.B.C. L. Rev. 21 (Part I), 207 (Part II); Woodward, note 1, above, ch. 2; Reiter, note 1, above, ch. 1; Binnie, ''The Sparrow Doctrine'' (1990) 15 Queen's L.J. 217.

88 Slattery (1983), previous note, 242.

89 *Guerin* v. *The Queen* [1984] 2 S.C.R. 335, 342; *R.* v. *Sparrow* [1990] 1 S.C.R. 1075, 1112.

90 *Calder* v. *A.G.B.C.* [1973] S.C.R. 313.

91 [1984] 2 S.C.R. 335.

Dickson C.J. described aboriginal title as "a legal right derived from the Indians' historic occupation and possession of their tribal lands".[92] The Band had surrendered the land to the Crown in order to enable the Crown to lease it to a golf club. The Crown did lease it to the golf club, but on terms less favourable than those agreed to by the Band. The Court held that the aboriginal title to the land gave rise to a fiduciary duty on the part of the Crown to deal with the land for the benefit of the surrendering Indians. The Court held that this fiduciary duty had been broken, and awarded damages to the Band. It should be noted that this outcome did not depend upon s. 35 of the Constitution Act, 1982, which was not in force at the time of the surrender and which was not relied upon by the Court.

In *R.* v. *Sparrow* (1990),[93] the Supreme Court of Canada unanimously recognized the aboriginal right of a member of the Musqueam Indian Band to fish for salmon in the Fraser River "where his ancestors had fished from time immemorial". Mr. Sparrow had been charged with a violation of the federal Fisheries Act, and, because the charge related to facts occurring after 1982, he was able to invoke s. 35 of the Constitution Act, 1982. The Court held that s. 35 did provide constitutional protection for the aboriginal right, and the Court laid down the principles that govern s. 35; this aspect of the case is addressed later in this chapter.[94] The Court enlarged upon the fiduciary duty that had been recognized in *Guerin*. The purpose of the discussion was to derive principles for the application of s. 35, but the Court made clear that in all dealings with aboriginal peoples (including legislation since the enactment of s. 35) "the Government has the responsibility to act in a fiduciary capacity".[95]

The effect of *Guerin* and *Sparrow* is to confirm that aboriginal rights do exist at common law, and that they are enforceable at the suit of aboriginal peoples.[96] The cases also recognize a fiduciary, or trust-like, obligation on the part of the Crown of ill-defined scope and ramifications.[97] *Sparrow* decides as well that aboriginal rights, including the fiduciary duty, are now constitutionally guaranteed through s. 35 of the Constitution Act, 1982.

---

92 *Id.*, 376 per Dickson C.J.; see also 349 per Wilson J. Only Estey J., who concurred in the result, decided the case on the basis of the law of agency.

93 [1990] 1 S.C.R. 1075.

94 Text accompanying note 128, below.

95 [1990] 1 S.C.R. 1075, 1108 per Dickson C.J. and La Forest J. for the Court.

96 See also *Roberts* v. *Can.* [1989] 1 S.C.R. 322, 340 (aboriginal title is a matter of federal common law and within the jurisdiction of the Federal Court); *Ont.* v. *Bear Island Foundation* [1991] 2 S.C.R. 570 (aboriginal right was established, but it had been extinguished by treaty).

97 In *Guerin* v. *The Queen* [1984] 2 S.C.R. 335, 387, Dickson C.J. said that "the fiduciary obligation which is owed to the Indians by the Crown is *sui generis*". This raises the possibility that it involves duties that are foreign to the traditional meaning of a fiduciary. In particular, an obligation to consult with aboriginal people before their interests are affected by governmental action would seem to be a likely application of the notion in the Indian context: notes 145, 156, below; although a traditional trustee is rarely under any obligation to consult the beneficiaries in the course of administering the trust.

(c) Extinguishment of aboriginal rights

Aboriginal rights can be extinguished in three ways: (1) by surrender, (2) by legislation, and (3) by constitutional amendment. The surrender of aboriginal rights must be voluntary, and must be to the Crown. Surrenders have occurred in treaties entered into between the Crown and an aboriginal nation.[98] The treaty will confer treaty rights on the aboriginal people in substitution for any surrendered aboriginal rights (and in addition to any unsurrendered aboriginal rights). Before 1982, aboriginal rights could also be extinguished by legislation,[99] although, after confederation, only the federal Parliament was competent to enact an extinguishing law.[100] (This power is now removed by s. 35.) Needless to say, aboriginal rights could also be extinguished by constitutional amendment.[101] Extinguishment, whether by voluntary surrender, by statute, or by constitutional amendment, would not be inferred from unclear language; only a ''clear and plain'' intention to extinguish would be accepted by the courts as having that effect. This was decided in the *Sparrow* case,[102] determining the issue that had caused the even division of the Court in *Calder*.[103]

27.6 Treaty rights

(a) Introduction

Before 1982, Indian treaty rights were explicitly protected from derogation by provincial law, but not federal law, by s. 88 of the Indian Act.[104] Since 1982, Indian treaty rights have been protected by s. 35 of the Constitution Act, 1982 from derogation by either federal or provincial law. Section 35 is discussed later in this chapter.[105]

(b) History

In eastern North America, from the earliest stages of French and English settlement, treaties of peace and friendship were entered into with the Indian

---

98 E.g., *Ont.* v. *Bear Island Foundation*, note 96, above; *R.* v.*Howard* [1994] 2 S.C.R. 299 (fishing right extinguished by treaty).

99 *Sikyea* v. *The Queen* [1964] S.C.R. 642 (treaty right); *R.* v. *George* [1966] S.C.R. 267 (treaty right); *R.* v. *Derriksan* (1976) 71 D.L.R. (3d) 159 (S.C.C.) (aboriginal right); *R.* v. *Sparrow* [1990] 1 S.C.R. 1075, 1111 (aboriginal right — obiter dictum).

100 Note 54, above.

101 *R.* v. *Horseman* [1990] 1 S.C.R. 901 (treaty right); note 85, above.

102 Note 93, above.

103 Note 90, above.

104 Section 27.3(d), ''Treaty exception'', above. Treaty rights were also protected from provincial law by the ''Indianness'' exception: note 54, above.

105 Section 27.8, ''Section 35'', below.

nations. These treaties of the seventeenth and eighteenth centuries conferred (among other things) hunting and fishing rights in return for peace, and typically did not involve the cession by the Indians of their lands.[106] As European settlement moved westward, so did treaty-making. In 1850, the Robinson treaties were signed on the shores of Lakes Huron and Superior;[107] and, between 1871 and 1921, a series of 11 numbered treaties were entered into, covering a large part of Canada in Ontario and the prairie provinces.[108] These treaties do on their face cede Indian lands to the Crown[109] in return for (among other things) hunting and fishing rights, as well as the reservation of portions of the treaty lands for the Indians. By the 1920s, when the last of the numbered treaties had been entered into, there remained vast areas of Canada where no treaty-making had taken place. These included Inuit lands in Labrador, northern Quebec and the Northwest Territories, and Indian lands in northern Quebec, British Columbia, the Yukon and the Northwest Territories.

After the *Calder* case (1973)[110] recognized the validity of aboriginal rights, the Government of Canada reversed its policy of 50 years,[111] and resumed the process of treaty-making. Modern treaties — styled land claims agreements — have been entered into with the Inuit and Cree of the James Bay area of northern Quebec, and with a number of the First Nations in the Yukon and Northwest Territories.[112] These land claims agreements reserve large areas of land (settlement land) to the aboriginal signatories as well as considerable sums of money in return for the surrender of aboriginal rights over non-settlement land. As well, however, the agreements constitute sophisticated codes with respect to such matters as development, land use planning, water management, fish and wildlife harvesting, forestry and mining. These codes assure a continuing role for the aboriginal people in the management of the resources of the entire region covered by the agreement, not just their own settlement land.[113]

---

106 *Simon* v. *The Queen* [1985] 2 S.C.R. 387 recognized a treaty of peace and friendship made in 1752.

107 *Ont.* v. *Bear Island Foundation* [1991] 2 S.C.R. 570 recognized the Robinson-Huron Treaty of 1850.

108 *R.* v. *Swimmer* (1971) 17 D.L.R. (3d) 476 (Sask. C.A.) recognized Treaty No. 6 of 1876.

109 There is room for doubt as to whether the written terms of the numbered treaties accurately express the Indian understanding of their terms, and whether there was fully informed consent to the apparent extinguishment of rights: see, e.g., *Re Paulette* (1973) 42 D.L.R. (3d) 8 (N.W.T. S.C.).

110 Note 90, above.

111 Department of Indian Affairs and Northern Development, ''Statement on Claims of Indian and Inuit People'' (Queen's Printer, Ottawa, 1973).

112 Merrit and Fenge, ''The Nunavut Land Claims Settlement'' (1990) 15 Queen's L.J. 255; Thompson, ''Land Claim Settlements in Northern Canada'' (1991) 55 Sask. L. Rev. 127.

113 Self-government agreements have also been negotiated with some aboriginal nations. These have not formed part of constitutionally-protected land claims agreements, but have been separate agreements, implemented by federal legislation.

Section 35 of the Constitution Act, 1982 explicitly includes rights acquired under modern land claims agreements in its protected treaty rights. Therefore, as land claims agreements are ratified, they acquire constitutional status.

(c) Definition of treaty

An Indian treaty has been described as ''unique'' or ''sui generis''.[114] It is not a treaty at international law, and is not subject to the rules of international law. It is not a contract, and is not subject to the rules of contract law. It is an agreement between the Crown and an aboriginal nation with the following characteristics:

1. Parties: The parties to the treaty must be the Crown, on the one side, and an aboriginal nation, on the other side.[115]
2. Agency: The signatories to the treaty must have the authority to bind their principals, namely, the Crown and the aboriginal nation.[116]
3. Intention to create legal relations: The parties must intend to create legally binding obligations.
4. Consideration: The obligations must be assumed by both sides, so that the agreement is a bargain.
5. Formality: there must be ''a certain measure of solemnity''.

The foregoing characteristics are my extrapolation from the two leading cases on the meaning of a treaty. The cases are *Simon* v. *The Queen* (1985) and *R.* v. *Sioui* (1990). Both cases were applying s. 88 of the Indian Act, not s. 35 of the Constitution Act, 1982, but it is safe to assume that the word ''treaty'' would bear the same meaning in both instruments.

In *Simon* v. *The Queen* (1985),[117] the question arose whether legal recognition should be given to a ''peace and friendship'' treaty signed in 1752 by the governor of Nova Scotia and the Chief of the Micmac Indians. The document purported to guarantee to the Indians ''free liberty of hunting and fishing as usual'' in the treaty area. The Supreme Court of Canada held that this was a valid treaty, which, by virtue of s. 88 of the Indian Act, exempted the Micmac defendant from the game laws of Nova Scotia. Dickson C.J. for the Court indicated his definition of an Indian treaty in two passages. At page 401:

---

114 *Simon* v. *The Queen* [1985] 2 S.C.R. 387, 404; *R.* v. *Sioui* [1990] 1 S.C.R. 1025, 1043. These two cases are fully examined in text accompanying notes 117 and 118, below.

115 The argument that an Indian tribe was not an entity possessing the legal personality or the capacity to enter into treaties was summarily rejected in *Simon* (at 398-401) and not raised again in *Sioui*.

116 This was in issue in both *Simon* and *Sioui*, and it was determined in both cases that the signatories possessed the requisite authority.

117 [1985] 2 S.C.R. 387.

> In my opinion, both the Governor and the Micmac entered into the Treaty with the intention of creating mutually binding obligations which would be solemnly respected.

And at p. 410:

> The treaty was an exchange [of] solemn promises between the Micmacs and the King's representative entered into to achieve and guarantee peace. It is an enforceable obligation between the Indians and the white man and, as such, falls within the meaning of the word "treaty" in s. 88 of the Indian Act.

In *R.* v. *Sioui* (1990),[118] what was in issue was a short document signed only by the Governor of Quebec in 1760, which "certified" that the Chief of the Huron Indians had come "in the name of his nation" to make peace, and henceforth the Huron Indians were under his protection and were to be allowed "the free exercise of their religion, their customs and liberty of trading with the English". The Supreme Court of Canada held that this was a valid treaty, which, by virtue of s. 88 of the Indian Act, exempted the Huron defendants, who were practising customary religious rites in a provincial park, from provincial park regulations. Lamer C.J. for the Court quoted the extracts from the *Simon* case, and said at p. 1044:

> From the extracts it is clear that what characterizes a treaty is the intention to create obligations, the presence of mutually binding obligations and a certain measure of solemnity.

These elements, he held, were all satisfied by the document of 1760.

In both *Simon* and *Sioui*, the treaties did not involve a cession of land by the Indians; and in *Sioui*, the right to religious exercise that was successfully asserted by the Huron Indians was not even over their traditional territory. These cases make clear that the surrender of aboriginal rights is not a requirement of a valid treaty. Nor does a treaty have to be concerned with territory; it could be "an agreement about political or social rights".[119] In each case, however, there was consideration moving from the Indian side, namely, a promise to cease hostilities. The Indians had made a bargain, and the Crown should be held to its side of the bargain.

It is a well established principle of interpretation that "treaties and statutes relating to Indians should be liberally construed and doubtful expressions resolved in favour of the Indians".[120] The idea is to construe treaties "in the sense in which they would naturally be understood by the Indians".[121] In *Sioui*, Lamer C.J. for the Court said that the same approach should be applied to the question whether a particular document constituted a treaty: "we should adopt a broad and generous interpretation of what constitutes a treaty",[122] and also "in examining the preli-

118 [1990] 1 S.C.R. 1025.

119 *Id.*, 1043.

120 *Nowegijick* v. *The Queen* [1983] 1 S.C.R. 29, 36 (statute); *Simon* v. *The Queen* [1985] 2 S.C.R. 387, 402 (treaty); *R.* v. *Sioui* [1990] 1 S.C.R. 1025, 1036 (treaty).

121 *Ibid.* (all three citations).

122 *R.* v. *Sioui* [1990] 1 S.C.R. 1025, 1035.

minary question of the capacity to sign a treaty''.[123] The Court has to attempt to transport itself back to the time of signing the treaty to determine whether the Indians had reasonable grounds for believing that they were dealing with an authorized agent of the Crown, and that the resulting document created binding obligations. In *Sioui*, this approach helped the Court to resolve in favour of the Indians any doubt about the Governor's authority and the status of his rather informal certificate.

(d) Extinguishment of treaty rights

Treaty rights may be extinguished in the same three ways as aboriginal rights, that is: (1) by voluntary surrender to the Crown, (2) by federal (but not provincial) legislation, and (3) by constitutional amendment. Extinguishment by any of these means will not be lightly inferred; a ''clear and plain'' intention to extinguish must be established.[124]

In addition, it is probable that treaty rights would be at least voidable in the event of a fundamental breach by one of the parties.[125] However, evidence of longstanding non-exercise of treaty rights does not cause an extinguishment.[126] Nor could international treaties or treaties with other Indian nations cause an extinguishment. Without competent legislation or a constitutional amendment, ''a treaty cannot be extinguished without the consent of the Indians concerned''.[127]

27.7 The need for constitutional protection

Aboriginal and treaty rights suffered from four serious infirmities. One was the uncertainty as to the precise legal status of the rights. Both the relationship of the aboriginal peoples to the land and the treaties between the Crown and the aboriginal peoples lacked close analogies in the common law. This uncertainty has been partially lifted by recent decisions recognizing aboriginal and treaty rights, but uncertainties persist, especially as to the definition of aboriginal rights. The second infirmity was the doctrine of parliamentary sovereignty, which meant that aboriginal rights were vulnerable to change or abolition by the action of the competent legislative body. The third infirmity was the liberal idea of equality, which gained increasing acceptance in Canada after the second world war. As well as creating a political climate unsympathetic to the recognition of special

---

123 *Id.*, 1036.

124 See sec. 27.5(c), ''Extinguishment of aboriginal rights'', above, where the authorities for treaty rights as well as aboriginal rights are cited.

125 Cf. *Simon* v. *The Queen* [1985] 2 S.C.R. 387, 404 (obiter dictum).

126 *R.* v. *Sioui* [1990] 1 S.C.R. 1025, 1066.

127 *Id.*, 1063. Lamer C.J. does not qualify his assertion by reference to legislative extinguishments before 1982 or constitutional extinguishments, but he is not addressing those modes of extinguishment, and it is clear that they do not require the consent of the Indians.

rights peculiar to a group defined by race, the idea of equality, when guaranteed by the Canadian Bill of Rights and, later, by the Charter of Rights, suggested that special status might actually be unconstitutional. The fourth infirmity was that aboriginal and treaty rights could be modified or extinguished by constitutional amendment, and the aboriginal peoples' representatives were not entitled to participate in the decisive phases of the amending process.

The Constitution Act, 1982, supplemented by an amendment adopted in 1984, has taken steps to eliminate these four infirmities. Section 35 of the Constitution Act, 1982 provides that "the existing aboriginal and treaty rights of the aboriginal peoples of Canada are hereby recognized and affirmed". This gives constitutional recognition (but not definition) to "aboriginal and treaty rights", and protects them from legislative attack. Section 25 of the Constitution Act, 1982, which is part of the Charter of Rights, provides that the Charter of Rights is not to be construed as derogating from "aboriginal, treaty or other rights or freedoms that pertain to the aboriginal peoples of Canada". This makes clear that the equality guarantee in s. 15 of the Charter does not invalidate aboriginal or treaty rights. Finally, s. 35.1 declares that constitutional amendments to the native rights provisions of the Constitution Acts, 1867 and 1982 that directly apply to aboriginal peoples will not be made without a prior constitutional conference involving participation by representatives of the aboriginal peoples of Canada. These three provisions — ss. 35, 25 and 35.1 — reinforce s. 91(24) in their recognition of special status for the aboriginal peoples.[128] They are discussed in more detail in the next three sections of this chapter.

27.8 Section 35

(a) Text of s. 35

Section 35 of the Constitution Act, 1982[129] provides as follows:[130]

> 35. (1) The existing aboriginal and treaty rights of the aboriginal peoples of Canada are hereby recognized and affirmed.
>
> (2) In this Act, "aboriginal peoples of Canada" includes the Indian, Inuit and Métis peoples of Canada.
>
> (3) For greater certainty, in subsection (1) "treaty rights" includes rights that now exist by way of land claims agreements or may be so acquired.

128 Sanders, note 31, above, traces the history of special status in the face of these forces.

129 For commentary, see note 87, above.

130 Section 35 was not in the October 1980 version of the Constitution Act, 1982. It was in the April 1981 version, but without the word "existing" in subsection (1). The entire section was dropped, apparently at the request of the Premiers of the resource-based provinces, in the November 5, 1981 federal-provincial agreement. This development attracted severe criticism and, later in November, the first ministers agreed to restore the section, but with the addition of the word "existing". Subsections (3) and (4) were not in the original version; they were added by the Constitution Amendment Proclamation, 1983.

(4) Notwithstanding any other provision of this Act, the aboriginal and treaty rights referred to in subsection (1) are guaranteed equally to male and female persons.

(b) Outside Charter of Rights

Section 35 is outside the Charter of Rights, which occupies ss. 1 to 34 of the Constitution Act, 1982. The location of s. 35 outside the Charter of Rights provides certain advantages. The rights referred to in s. 35 are not qualified by s. 1 of the Charter, that is, the rights are not subject to "such reasonable limits prescribed by law as can be demonstrably justified in a free and democratic society", although, as we shall see, they are subject to reasonable regulation according to principles similar to those applicable to s. 1. Nor are the rights subject to legislative override under s. 33 of the Charter. Nor are the rights effective only against governmental action, as stipulated by s. 32 of the Charter. On the other hand, the location of s. 35 outside the Charter carries the disadvantage that the rights are not enforceable under s. 24, a provision that permits enforcement only of Charter rights.

(c) "Aboriginal peoples of Canada"

The rights referred to in s. 35 are possessed by the "aboriginal peoples of Canada". That phrase, which is also used in ss. 25, 37 and 37.1, is defined in s. 35(2) as including "the Indian, Inuit and Métis peoples of Canada", but none of these three terms is given further definition. It is obvious that the phrase includes not only status Indians, but also non-status Indians, as well as the Inuit (or Eskimo) and Métis peoples. As noted earlier in this chapter,[131] the federal Parliament has the power under s. 91(24) to supply some degree of definition to the word "Indians" in s. 91(24), although it has never attempted a comprehensive definition. The courts would probably accept federally legislated definitions of the words "Indian", "Inuit" and "Métis" in s. 35(2), provided that the definitions employed reasonable criteria.[132]

(d) "Aboriginal and treaty rights"

The rights referred to in s. 35 are "aboriginal and treaty rights". The nature of these rights has been explained very generally in earlier sections of this chapter.[133]

---

131 Note 7, above.

132 The definition of "Indians" in s. 91(24) is discussed, at notes 7-11, above, and the opinion offered that the term would extend to non-status Indians, Inuit and Métis peoples. In other words, the term "Indians" in s. 91(24) is just as wide as the term "aboriginal peoples of Canada" in s. 35(2). The word "Indian" in s. 35(2) has a narrower meaning than the word "Indians" in s. 91(24), because the Inuit and Métis peoples are separately identified in s. 35(2).

133 Section 27.5(d), "Definition of aboriginal rights"; sec. 27.6(c), "Definition of treaty", above.

(e) "Existing"

Section 35 protects "existing aboriginal and treaty rights". What is the force of the word "existing"? The word obviously has reference to April 17, 1982, which is when the Constitution Act, 1982 was proclaimed into force.

It is clear from the text of s. 35 itself that the word "existing" does not exclude rights that come into existence after 1982. Such rights could only be treaty rights, of course, since aboriginal rights pre-date European settlement. Subsection (3) of s. 35 provides:

> For greater certainty, in subsection (1) "treaty rights" includes rights that now exist by way of land claims agreement or may be so acquired.

The last phrase, "or may be so acquired", makes clear that treaty rights acquired after 1982 are protected by s. 35. The first phrase, "For greater certainty", makes clear that, although "land claims agreements" are the only kind of modern treaties expressly mentioned, future treaty rights derived from treaties that did not settle land claims would also be protected.

What is the status of aboriginal or treaty rights that had been extinguished or regulated before 1982? This was the issue that had to be resolved in *R.* v. *Sparrow* (1990).[134] In that case, a member of the Musqueam Indian Band was charged under the federal Fisheries Act with the offence of fishing with a drift net that was longer than permitted by the Band's Indian food fishing licence, which had been issued under regulations made under the Fisheries Act. The Supreme Court of Canada, as noted earlier,[135] held that the Indian defendant was exercising an aboriginal right to fish that was protected by s. 35. However, the question remained: was it an "existing" right? The right to fish had for many years before 1982 been subject to a system of discretionary licensing under the Fisheries Act that, the Crown argued, was inconsistent with the continued existence in 1982 of any right to fish.

The Supreme Court of Canada in *Sparrow* held that the word "existing" in s. 35 meant "unextinguished".[136] A right that had been validly extinguished before 1982 was not protected by s. 35.[137] In other words, s. 35 did not retroactively annul prior extinguishments of aboriginal rights so as to restore the rights to their original unimpaired condition.

The Court in *Sparrow* refused to imply an extinguishment from the admittedly extensive regulatory control of the Fisheries Act. While an aboriginal right could be extinguished by federal statute before 1982,[138] a federal statute would have that effect only if the intention to extinguish was "clear and plain". The

---

134 [1990] 1 S.C.R. 1075.
135 Note 93, above.
136 [1990] 1 S.C.R. 1075, 1091.
137 See also *R.* v. *Howard* [1994] 2 S.C.R. 299 (s. 35 does not protect fishing right extinguished by treaty in 1923).
138 *Id.*, 1111.

Fisheries Act and its regulations (although they prohibited fishing, except under a statutory licence) did not demonstrate "a clear and plain intention to extinguish the Indian aboriginal right to fish".[139] Therefore, the right was an "existing" right within the meaning of s. 35.

The Court in *Sparrow* also refused to treat regulation as a partial extinguishment of the regulated right. Before *Sparrow*, it was arguable that an existing right was only that part of the right that was not regulated in 1982. On that approach, the scope of an existing right would be defined by the regulatory laws that limited the right in 1982. Those laws would, in effect, be frozen and constitutionalized by s. 35. Only the unregulated residue would be an "existing" right. The Court in *Sparrow* rejected this approach, pointing out that it would give constitutional status to a host of statutes and regulations, which might differ from place to place, and which would draw no distinction between the important and the trivial, the permanent and the temporary, or the reasonable and the unreasonable.[140] Instead, the Court held that an aboriginal right, provided it had not been extinguished before 1982 by clear and plain language, should be treated as existing in its unregulated form.

According to *Sparrow*, the effect of the word "existing" in s. 35 was to exclude from constitutional protection those rights that had been validly extinguished before 1982. This was a much less severe restriction of the scope of s. 35 than the incorporation-of-regulations interpretation that the Court rejected, but it was a restriction nonetheless. However, the Court also attributed an expansive or liberalizing effect to the word "existing". The Court held that the word "existing" meant that the guaranteed rights are "affirmed in a contemporary form rather than in their primeval simplicity and vigour".[141] This would mean that aboriginal rights to hunt and fish (for example) were not simply rights to hunt and fish by bow and arrow, bone hook, and other techniques available before European settlement, but were rights that would evolve to take advantage of the progress of technology. Similarly, a right to trade in the form of barter would in modern times extend to the use of currency, credit and the normal commercial facilities of distribution and exchange.

(f) "Recognized and affirmed"

Section 35 provides that existing aboriginal and treaty rights are "recognized and affirmed". What is the effect of this language?

The Court in *Sparrow* held that the phrase "recognized and affirmed" should be interpreted according to the principle that "treaties and statutes relating to Indians should be liberally construed and doubtful expressions resolved in favour

139 *Id.*, 1099.

140 *Id.*, 1092, following Slattery, (1987) 66 Can. Bar Rev. 727, 781-782.

141 *Id.*, 1093, again following Slattery, (1987) 66 Can. Bar Rev. 727, 782.

of the Indians''.[142] The phrase should also be read as incorporating the fiduciary obligation that government owes to the aboriginal peoples. From these two premises, the Court concluded that s. 35 should be interpreted as a constitutional guarantee of aboriginal and treaty rights. As a constitutional guarantee, s. 35 had the effect of nullifying legislation that purported to abridge the guaranteed rights.

Because s. 35 is not part of the Charter of Rights, it is not subject to s. 1 of the Charter of Rights, which makes clear that the guaranteed rights are not absolute, but are subject to ''such reasonable limits prescribed by law as can be demonstrably justified in a free and democratic society''. However, the Court held that the rights protected by s. 35 were not absolute either. They were subject to regulation by federal laws, provided the laws met a standard of justification not unlike that erected by the Court for s. 1 of the Charter.[143] Any law that had the effect of impairing an existing aboriginal right would be subject to judicial review to determine whether it was a justified impairment. A justified impairment would have to pursue an objective that was ''compelling and substantial''.[144] The conservation and management of a limited resource would be a justified objective, but ''the public interest'' would be too vague to serve as a justification.[145] If a sufficient objective was found, then the law had to employ means that were consistent with ''the special trust relationship'' between government and the aboriginal peoples.[146] In the context of the fishery, this would require that the Indian claims be given priority over the claims of other interest groups who could not assert an aboriginal right.[147] In other contexts, other questions would have to be addressed:[148]

> These include the questions of whether there has been as little infringement as possible in order to effect the desired result; whether, in a situation of expropriation, fair compensation is available; and, whether the aboriginal group in question has been consulted with respect to the conservation measures being implemented.

In the *Sparrow* case itself, the Court did not feel able to decide whether the net-length restriction would satisfy the standard of justification. The Court ordered a new trial to permit findings of fact that would enable the issue of justification to be resolved. If the net-length restriction were found to satisfy the standard of justification, then the restriction would be valid and Mr. Sparrow would be guilty as charged. If the net-length restriction were found not to satisfy the standard of justification, then the net-length restriction would be invalid as a violation of s. 35 and Mr. Sparrow would be entitled to an acquittal.

---

142 Note 120, above.
143 Chapter 35, Limitation of Rights, below.
144 [1990] 1 S.C.R. 1075, 1113.
145 *Ibid.*
146 *Ibid.*
147 *Id.*, 1116.
148 *Id.*, 1119.

(g) Application to treaty rights

Sparrow was concerned with an aboriginal right, not a treaty right. Because s. 35 applies to treaty rights as well as aboriginal rights, the doctrine laid down by *Sparrow* probably applies to treaty rights as well as aboriginal rights. The only doubt relates to the doctrine of justified regulation. It might be thought that treaty rights ought to receive absolute protection by s. 35, on the basis that the Crown's fiduciary duty is to do exactly what it voluntarily promised to do in the treaty. Probably, however, treaty rights would have to yield to any federal law that could satisfy the *Sparrow* standard of justification; but it may be taken for granted that the standard of justification for a law impairing a treaty right would be very high indeed.

(h) Application to extinguishment

Before 1982, aboriginal and treaty rights could be extinguished by federal legislation, provided clear and plain words were used for the purpose.[149] It is implicit in *Sparrow* that s. 35 now protects aboriginal and treaty rights from extinguishment by federal legislation. The justificatory tests propounded in *Sparrow* would, if satisfied, save a federal law that purported to *regulate* an aboriginal or treaty right, but not a federal law that purported to *extinguish* the right.[150]

The effect of s. 35 is that aboriginal and treaty rights can only be extinguished in two ways: (1) by surrender and (2) by constitutional amendment.[151] The first involves the consent of the aboriginal right-holders. The second does not, but it would surely be contrary to the federal government's fiduciary duty to the aboriginal peoples to proceed with a constitutional amendment affecting aboriginal or treaty rights without at least the active participation of the aboriginal peoples.[152]

(i) Application to provincial laws

What effect does s. 35 have on provincial laws? The Court in *Sparrow* did not have to consider that question, because the only law at issue, the Fisheries Act, was a federal law. However, the Court said: "It [that is, s. 35] also affords aboriginal people constitutional protection against provincial legislative

---

149 Note 98, above.

150 Note, however, that Dickson C.J. and La Forest J, in the passage quoted at note 148, above, referred to "a situation of expropriation". I assume that what is contemplated here is the expropriation of a parcel of Indian land which, if fully justified and fully paid for, would not be a violation of s. 35, although the aboriginal rights in that parcel of land would be extinguished. This example does, however, show the difficulty of distinguishing justified regulation (valid) from expropriation (invalid).

151 In the case of treaty rights, a fundamental breach of the treaty may be a third mode of extinguishment: note 124, above.

152 Note 162, below.

power''.[153] This should probably be read as meaning that a provincial law cannot impair aboriginal or treaty rights, even if the law could pass the justificatory tests stipulated by the Court for federal laws.[154]

Quite apart from s. 35, we have already noticed that provincial legislative power does not extend to laws that would impair aboriginal or treaty rights, because such laws affect Indianness.[155] By virtue of s. 88 of the Indian Act, provincial laws of general application that affect Indianness may become applicable to Indians.[156] Treaty rights, however, are expressly immunized by s. 88 from the provincial laws that are incorporated by s. 88. Section 88 does not expressly immunize aboriginal rights from the provincial laws that are incorporated by s. 88, and so, through s. 88, a provincial law could impair aboriginal rights. A provincial law to which s. 88 applies is transformed by adoption or incorporation into a federal law. The effect of s. 35 would be to require any provincial law that is adopted by s. 88 to pass the *Sparrow* tests of justification before the law could impair aboriginal rights.

27.9 Section 25

Section 25 of the Constitution Act, 1982[157] is part of the Charter of Rights. It provides:[158]

> 25. The guarantee in this Charter of certain rights and freedoms shall not be construed so as to abrogate or derogate from any aboriginal, treaty or other rights or freedoms that pertain to the aboriginal peoples of Canada including
> (a) any rights or freedoms that have been recognized by the Royal Proclamation of October 7, 1763; and
>
> (b) any rights or freedoms that now exist by way of land claims agreements or may be so acquired.

---

153 [1990] 1 S.C.R. 1075, 1105.

154 In *Mitchell* v. *Peguis Indian Band* [1990] 2 S.C.R. 85, 108-109, Dickson C.J. in a separate concurring judgment made clear, obiter, that the Crown's fiduciary obligation to the Indians was owed by provincial governments as well as the federal government. The other judges said nothing on this point.

155 This is the second exception to the general rule that provincial laws apply to Indians and lands reserved for the Indians: sec. 27.2 (c), ''Second exception: Indianness'', above.

156 See sec. 27.3, ''Section 88 of the Indian Act'', above.

157 For commentary, see note 87, above; also, Wildsmith, ''Aboriginal Peoples and s. 25 of the Charter'' (U. of Sask. Native Law Centre, 1988).

158 Section 25 was not in the October 1980 version of the Charter, although there was a reference to ''rights or freedoms that pertain to the native peoples of Canada'' in the October 1980 version of s. 26. Section 25 was included for the first time in the April 1981 version, and the reference to native peoples was removed from s. 26. Paragraph (b) was substituted by the Constitution Amendment Proclamation, 1983. The former paragraph provided:

> (b) any rights or freedoms that may be acquired by the aboriginal peoples of Canada by way of land claims settlement.

Section 25 is part of the Charter of Rights, but it does not create any new rights. It is an interpretative provision, included to make clear that the Charter is not to be construed as derogating from "any aboriginal, treaty or other rights or freedoms that pertain to the aboriginal peoples of Canada". In the absence of s. 25, it would perhaps have been arguable that rights attaching to groups defined by race were invalidated by s. 15 (the equality clause) of the Charter.

The previous section of this chapter has described s. 35 of the Constitution Act, 1982, under which "the existing aboriginal and treaty rights of the aboriginal peoples of Canada are hereby recognized and affirmed". Section 35 is not merely a saving provision, but affords constitutional protection from legislative impairment for the rights that it covers. Section 35 probably leaves s. 25 with no work to do. It is possible, however, that the class of rights saved by s. 25 is wider than the class of rights guaranteed by s. 35: the class of rights saved by s. 25 is not qualified by the word "existing", and it may be broader in its inclusion of "other" rights or freedoms and in its express mention of the Royal Proclamation of 1763.

Section 25 is the same as s. 35 in its description of the right-holders as the "aboriginal peoples of Canada". As noted in the discussion of s. 35, that phrase is defined by s. 35(2) as including "the Indian, Inuit and Métis peoples of Canada".

27.10 Section 35.1

Section 91(24) of the Constitution Act, 1867 and ss. 25 and 35 of the Constitution Act, 1982 can, of course, be repealed or amended by the process of constitutional amendment. The appropriate procedure would be the general (seven-fifty) amending procedure of s. 38 of the Constitution Act, 1982.[159] That procedure, it will be recalled, requires the assent of the federal Parliament and the Legislatures of two-thirds of the provinces representing 50 per cent of the population of the provinces. Aboriginal peoples have been concerned that their constitutional protections are still vulnerable, in the sense that they could be impaired by a process in which their organizations play no formal role. In fact, ss. 25 and 35 of the Constitution Act, 1982 have already been amended once,[160] but in ways that were agreed to by representatives of the aboriginal peoples at a constitutional conference of first ministers held in March 1983 to which representatives of the aboriginal peoples were invited.[161]

---

159 If an amendment affected aboriginal rights only within a single province, s. 38 would still be the appropriate procedure. Section 43 applies to the amendment of "any provision that applies to one or more, but not all, provinces". Sections 91(24), 25 and 35 are not so limited.

160 Constitution Amendment Proclamation, 1983, R.S.C. 1985, Appendix II, No. 46, substituting new s. 25(b), adding new s. 35(3) and (4), and adding new ss. 35.1, 37.1, 54.1 and 61 of the Constitution Act, 1982.

161 This conference, including the participation of representatives of the native peoples, had been mandated by s. 37 of the Constitution Act, 1982. Section 37.1, agreed to at that same conference,

The changes agreed to in March 1983 did not include a veto for aboriginal peoples on constitutional amendments affecting their rights, but a new section 35.1 was added, which went some distance in that direction. Section 35.1 declares that the federal and provincial governments "are committed to the principle" that, before any amendment is made to s. 91(24) or to s. 35 or to s. 25,[162] a constitutional conference will be convened to which representatives of the aboriginal peoples of Canada will be invited to participate in discussions of the proposed amendment.[163] Through s. 35.1, the aboriginal peoples have gained entry to the constitutional amendment process. This privilege is accorded to no other group outside government, which emphasizes that the special status of the aboriginal peoples is now firmly accepted in Canada.

27.11 Charlottetown Accord

The Charlottetown Accord of 1992[164] proposed an elaborate set of new constitutional provisions respecting aboriginal peoples. A new section 35.1 would recognize that the aboriginal peoples of Canada "have the inherent right of self-government within Canada". This right would not be enforceable in the courts for a period of five years, during which time (as well as afterwards) the federal and provincial governments would be committed to the negotiation of self-government agreements. The self-government agreements would be enforceable, and they would create treaty rights that were protected by s. 35. The Charter of Rights would apply to the institutions of self-government. These provisions were supplemented by ancillary provisions that attempted to give some definition to abor-

---

mandated two further such conferences. These conferences were held in 1985 and 1987, and they attempted to agree on language that would expressly recognize a right of aboriginal self-government. Unfortunately, agreement could not be reached.

162 Section 35.1 probably does not apply to constitutional amendments that make no direct change to any of the identified constitutional provisions but which do impair aboriginal or treaty rights. However, the fiduciary duty of the Crown recognized in *Sparrow* would, in my view, preclude such action without aboriginal participation.

163 Schwartz, *First Principles, Second Thoughts:* ... (Institute for Research on Public Policy, Montreal, 1986), 127-131, argues that s. 35.1 is invalid. The argument is that s. 35.1 is, in effect, an amendment to Part V of the Constitution Act, 1982 (which contains the amending procedures); such an amendment requires unanimous provincial consent (s. 41(e)); and the Constitution Amendment Proclamation, 1983 (which added s. 35.l) was ratified by only nine provincial legislative assemblies because at that time (1983) Quebec was boycotting the constitutional amending process. The premise of this argument is dubious. Section 35.1 is not literally an amendment to Part V, and s. 35.1 is not addressed to the Governor General, Senate, House of Commons or legislative assemblies which are governed by Part V.

164 Chapter 4, Amendment, under heading 4.1(c), "The failure to accommodate Quebec", above. I disclose that I was one of the legal advisers to the Assembly of First Nations in the discussions leading to the Charlottetown Accord, and I have also been giving legal advice to the Council for Yukon Indians and other aboriginal organizations in their land claim and self-government processes.

iginal self-government and to set up the framework for a "political accord" that would guide the process of self-government negotiations.

The defeat of the Charlottetown Accord in the referendum of 1992 spelled the end of the aboriginal provisions of the Accord. However, the Accord will have some lasting effects on the status of aboriginal peoples. In the first place, the leaders of the four national aboriginal organizations,[165] along with the eleven first ministers and the two territorial leaders, were full parties to all the discussions that led up to the Accord. Aboriginal participation was not confined to the aboriginal provisions of the Accord, but extended to all its far-reaching provisions. In this way, the aboriginal organizations were treated as if they were already a third order of government, as was contemplated by the Accord. In the second place, the agreement by all first ministers and territorial leaders that the aboriginal peoples have an "inherent" right of self-government should probably be regarded as an informal recognition that the right exists now, albeit in inchoate form, despite the failure to ratify the express declaration to that effect in the Accord. This recognition by all governments should facilitate the negotiation of self-government agreements between governments and first nations, which can of course take place under the existing constitutional provisions, and which is already in progress in some parts of the country. Nor is there any reason why the provisions of self-government agreements, which are modern treaties, should not have constitutional status as treaty rights protected under s. 35.[166] The movement to self-government can and will proceed despite the failure of the Charlottetown Accord.

---

165 The four organizations that were represented were the Assembly of First Nations, representing most status Indians (Indians, as defined in the Indian Act), the Native Council of Canada, representing mainly non-status Indians, the Métis National Council, representing Métis, and the Inuit Tapirisat of Canada, representing Inuit.

166 Constitutional status as aboriginal rights is also arguable, based on the inherent (aboriginal) right of self-government.

28

Public Property

28.1 Distribution of public property

At the time of confederation, it was necessary to apportion the assets and liabilities of the confederating provinces between the new Dominion and the provinces. This was accomplished by various sections in Part VIII of the Constitution Act, 1867. Section 108 conveyed from the provinces to the Dominion the property listed in the third schedule to the Act. The schedule includes canals, public harbours, lighthouses and piers, steamboats, dredges and public vessels, rivers and lake improvements, railways, military roads, customs houses, post offices and other public buildings, ordinance and military property and lands set apart for general public purposes. Section 117 provided that the provinces should retain their ''public property not otherwise disposed of by this Act'', and s. 109 reinforced this residuary provision by providing that ''all lands, mines, minerals, and royalties belonging to the several provinces'' should continue to belong to the provinces.[1]

These provisions, along with the rest of the Constitution Act, 1867, applied only to the four original provinces of Ontario, Quebec, New Brunswick and Nova Scotia. As new provinces were admitted, special arrangements with respect to

1 For details, see La Forest, *Natural Resources and Public Property under the Canadian Constitution* (1968), chs. 1-7. There is also a note in Laskin, *Canadian Constitutional Law* (5th ed., 1986 by Finkelstein), 662-667.

public property had to be made in each case, but subject to some modifications the terms of the Constitution Act, 1867 were made applicable to each new province. A striking exception to the general application of the Act was the reservation by the Dominion of Crown lands in the provinces which were carved out of federal territories, that is, the three prairie provinces of Alberta, Saskatchewan and Manitoba. The purpose of the reservation was to facilitate federal policies with respect to immigration, land settlement and railways; but it meant that in the prairie provinces the Dominion owned the natural resources that in the other provinces belonged to the province by virtue of ss. 109 and 117. This continued until 1930, when the Natural Resources Agreements were entered into by the Dominion with the three prairie provinces, transferring to the provinces the type of assets which belonged to the other provinces. These agreements were confirmed, and given overriding effect, by the Constitution Act, 1930.[2]

28.2 Legislative power over public property

The federal Parliament has the exclusive power to make laws in relation to "the public debt and property" (s. 91(1A)). This power enables it to enact laws in respect of federally-owned property.[3]

The provincial Legislatures have similar legislative powers in respect of provincial public property.[4] Section 92(5) of the Constitution Act, 1867 confers the power to make laws in relation to "the management and sale of the public lands belonging to the province and of the timber and wood thereon". The general legislative power over "property and civil rights in the province" (s. 92(13)), among its many functions, gives power over provincially-owned property which is not covered by s. 92(5), for example, personal property. These legislative powers over public property enable the provincial Legislature to act like a private proprietor in disposing of the province's own property. This means that the provincial Legislature may legislate terms as to the use or sale of provincial property which it could not legislate in other contexts, for example, a stipulation

2 R.S.C. 1985, Appendix II, No. 26. The Agreements are scheduled to the Act. For commentary, see La Forest, note 1, above, ch. 3. The Constitution Act, 1930 also confirmed an agreement with B.C., under which Canada conveyed back to B.C. the Railway Belt and Peace River Block. These were lands that had been conveyed to Canada to assist in the financing of the Canadian Pacific Railway, but which had not in fact been used for that purpose.

3 La Forest, note 1, above, ch. 8. Note that the existence of exclusive federal power does not exclude provincial laws from federal public property, if the laws are otherwise competent to the province: *Construction Montcalm* v. *Minimum Wage Comm.* [1979] 1 S.C.R. 754 (provincial minimum wage law applicable to construction firm working at an airport on federal Crown land); see ch. 15, Judicial Review on Federal Grounds, under heading 15.5(k), Interjurisdictional Immunity, above.

4 La Forest, note 1, above, ch. 9.

that timber be processed in Canada,[5] or that no Chinese or Japanese labour be employed in cutting timber.[6] This broad legislative power to dispose of a province's own property is consistent with the broad executive powers enjoyed by the province as proprietor.[7] This is the subject of the next section of this chapter.

28.3 Executive power over public property

The federal and provincial governments have full executive powers over their respective public properties. It is neither necessary nor accurate to invoke the royal prerogative to explain the Crown's power over its property. As a legal person,[8] the Crown in right of Canada or the Crown in right of a province has the power to do anything that other legal persons (individuals or corporations) can do.[9] Thus, unless there are legislative[10] or constitutional[11] restrictions applicable to a piece of public property, it may be sold, mortgaged, leased, licensed or

5 *Smylie* v. *The Queen* (1900) 27 O.A.R. 172 (Ont. C.A.). The argument that this stipulation indirectly prohibited the export of unsawn timber to the U.S.A., a matter of ''trade and commerce'' under s. 91(2), was rejected on the basis that the province had the power under s. 92(5) to dictate the terms upon which it disposed of its property.

6 *Brooks-Bidlake* v. *A.-G. B.C.* [1923] A.C. 450. In other contexts this could be a law in relation to ''naturalization and aliens'' under s. 91(25). (Since the adoption of the Charter of Rights, such a law would be invalid for breach of the equality guarantee.)

7 Bushnell, Comment (1980) 58 Can. Bar Rev. 157, argues that provincial legislative power under s. 92(5) is limited in exactly the same way as other provincial legislative powers; and that provincial executive power as proprietor (see following text) is no wider than provincial legislative power. Indeed, he suggests that a province cannot deal with its property without legislative authority. Thring, ''Alberta, Oil, and the Constitution'' (1979) 17 Alta. L. Rev. 69 holds a similar view to Bushnell's. La Forest, note 1, above, 164-170, on the other hand, holds that provincial legislative power under s. 92(5) and executive power as proprietor are both akin to that of a private proprietor. A middle view, espoused by Moull, ''Natural Resources: Provincial Proprietary Rights'' (1983) 21 Alta. L. Rev. 472, 475-480, is that the province has the legislative power under s. 92(5) to *authorize* the inclusion of extraordinary terms in Crown contracts, but the terms will be effective only if inserted into Crown contracts. Section 92(5) would not empower the province to directly impose such terms by legislation. This seems to be the view which accords best with general principles, with the cases cited in notes 5 and 6, above, and with my view of the spending power, discussed in ch. 6, Financial Arrangements, above, which presents a close analogy to the present problem.

8 See ch. 10, The Crown, under heading 10.1, ''Definition'', above.

9 La Forest, note 1, above, 143, 167. For a contrary view, see note 7, above.

10 An example of a legislative restriction would be provincial land acquired or set aside for a hospital. If the hospital purpose was imposed by statute, then any inconsistent executive dealing with the land would be illegal. The Crown's prerogative or common law powers may be displaced by a statute: *A.-G.* v. *De Keysers Royal Hotel* [1920] A.C. 508 (prerogative power of expropriation displaced by statute). Of course, a legislative restriction can always be removed or modified by statute.

11 An example of a constitutional restriction would be lands reserved for the Indians, which, although owned by the province, are subject to federal legislative power under s. 91(24): see ch. 27, Aboriginal Peoples, above.

managed at the pleasure of the responsible government, and without the necessity of legislation.[12] The Crown's power to do these things is not a prerogative power, because the power is not unique to the Crown, but is possessed in common with other legal persons.[13] Moreover, in the role of proprietor, the Crown can (subject to market conditions) insist upon the inclusion in leases, licences or other instruments of any terms that a private proprietor could insist upon. These include terms that in other contexts would be outside the province's power to impose by legislation.[14]

A province's ownership of natural resources, such as oil and gas, or other minerals,[15] gives it much more power over the resources than it possesses over privately-owned resources. The exploitation of a provincially-owned resource can be controlled by the province, either by the province directly producing and selling the resource, or by the province granting permits, leases or licences that authorize private firms to produce and sell the resource. Obviously, the rate of production, the degree of processing within the province and (subject to market conditions) the price at which it is to be sold can be controlled by the province as proprietor. These matters could not necessarily be controlled in the case of privately-owned resources, because legislation would be necessary, and there are limits to provincial legislative power over natural resources, especially those resources destined for export from the province.[16] Similarly, a province can profit from the exploitation of provincially-owned resources in a variety of ways: by direct sales or by licence fees, rents or royalties. A province can profit from the

12 La Forest, note 1, above, 19-21, argues persuasively that no legislative authority is necessary, although in practice of course each jurisdiction regulates the disposition of Crown lands by statute. For a contrary view, see note 7, above.

13 The term prerogative is sometimes used to include all of the common law powers of the Crown, but in my view it should not include those common law powers that are not unique to the Crown: see ch. 1, Sources, under heading 1.9, ''Prerogative'', above.

14 *A.-G. B.C.* v. *Deeks Sand and Gravel Co.* [1956] S.C.R. 336 (royalty that might have been ultra vires if enacted upheld as a contract). The conditions in *Smylie* (note 5, above) and *Brooks-Bidlake* (note 6, above) could have been imposed without authorizing legislation.

15 Throughout Canada, provincial governments have usually retained title to timber lands, issuing licences to permit their exploitation. As a result, most timber lands are still provincially owned. Most mineral rights in Ontario, Quebec and the Atlantic provinces are privately owned. Offshore resources are in effect owned by the federal government, which has the exclusive right to explore for and exploit them. The provinces also have the power to expropriate privately owned lands or mineral rights, as Saskatchewan did in 1973 in order to gain greater control over its oil and gas: note 17, below.

16 *Central Can. Potash* v. *Govt. of Sask.* [1979] 1 S.C.R. 42, striking down provincial scheme for the prorationing of production and fixing the price of potash. Laskin C.J. for the Court emphasized (at p. 72) that the Government of Saskatchewan was acting ''not under proprietary right but in pursuance of legislative and statutory authority directed to proprietary rights of others''. The case is discussed in ch. 21, Property and Civil Rights, under heading 21.9(c), ''Provincial power'', above.

exploitation of privately-owned resources only through taxes, and there are limits to provincial legislative power to levy taxes on natural resources.[17]

All Canadian governments are extensively involved in commercial activities, either directly or through Crown corporations. Governments sell liquor, electricity, insurance, books, wheat, eggs and other natural products. They own railways, airlines, pipelines, telephone systems and radio and television networks. Nor do a government's commercial activities have to coincide with the legislative power of that level of government. The activities are premised on powers which flow from the ownership and control of property, not on the catalogue of legislative powers which are independent of property ownership.[18]

28.4 Legislative power and proprietary interests

While a government's proprietary interests generally confer matching legislative and executive powers (as has been explained above), the converse proposition is not true. The existence of legislative power in respect of a particular subject-matter does not imply any proprietary rights in the subject-matter. In the *Fisheries Reference* (1898),[19] the Privy Council established this proposition by deciding that the grant of power over "fisheries" in s. 91(12) of the Constitution Act, 1867 conferred only legislative powers on the federal Parliament. Proprietary interests in fisheries were not thereby conferred upon the federal government, and proprietary interests could be held by provincial governments or private individuals.

The broad distinction between legislative power and ownership is obvious and may easily be illustrated. For example, the federal Parliament has legislative power over "banking" (s. 91(15)), "patents of invention and discovery" (s. 91(22)), "copyrights" (s. 91(23)) and "lands reserved for the Indians" (s. 91(24)), but the federal government does not own any banks or many patents or copyrights, and it is the provincial governments which have underlying title to Indian reserves.[20] The same point may be made about the power to declare local

17 *Can. Industrial Gas and Oil* v. *Govt. of Sask.* [1978] 2 S.C.R. 545, striking down a "mineral income tax" on oil produced on private land and a "royalty surcharge" on oil produced on Crown land. (Much of the Crown land had been expropriated from private owners, in order to make it subject to royalties, rather than taxation.) The Court held that the "royalty surcharge" was a tax rather than a royalty, because it was imposed on land already subject to oil leases, and the leases did not authorize the additional royalty. The additional royalty could only be imposed by legislation, which meant taxation. Since this decision, provincial power to tax natural resources has been enlarged by s. 92A(4) of the Constitution Act, 1867 (added in 1982): see ch. 30, Taxation, under heading 30.2(i), "Resource taxes", below.

18 Spending, lending, contracting and disposing of property are all alike in this respect: see ch. 6, Financial Arrangements, under heading 6.8, "Spending power", above.

19 *A.-G. Can.* v. *A.-G. Ont.* (Fisheries) [1898] A.C. 700.

20 See ch. 27, Aboriginal Peoples, under heading 27.1(c), "Lands reserved for the Indians", above.

works to be "for the general advantage of Canada" (s. 92(10)(c)); such a declaration will assign to the Dominion the legislative authority over the local work, but will not by itself alter its ownership.[21]

Some of the implications of the distinction between legislative power and proprietary interests are less obvious. The exercise of legislative power over, say, fisheries, may severely limit the owner's enjoyment of the property, for example, by limiting the times and manner of fishing. Such a law is valid notwithstanding its incidental effects on proprietary rights.[22] But a federal law which is in pith and substance a modification of proprietary rights will be invalid as a law in relation to property and civil rights in the province (s. 92(13)).[23] Accordingly, where an exercise of federal legislative power purports to regulate proprietary rights, the issue will arise whether the purported regulation is a law in relation to fisheries (for example), or is a law in relation to property and civil rights in the province.

In the *Fish Canneries Reference* (1930),[24] for example, the Privy Council held that the federal power over fisheries did not extend to the regulation of fish canning and curing plants. In their lordships' judgment, the processing of the fish was a matter which fell within "property and civil rights in the province" rather than "fisheries".[25] The same reasoning has been used to limit the federal power over "agriculture" (s. 95); this power will not authorize laws governing the marketing of agricultural products, because the marketing of the product is a matter of property and civil rights in the province (or "trade and commerce" if it is interprovincial).[26] This reasoning was used as the basis for an attack on the provisions of federal company law which permit a take-over offeror to acquire compulsorily the shares of a dissenting minority of shareholders. It was argued that this was a "property" law, but in *Esso Standard* v. *J.W. Enterprises* (1963),[27] the Supreme Court of Canada upheld the law as one relating to the capital of a federally-incorporated company.

Just as federal powers are limited by the existence of provincial power over property, so the provincial power over property is limited by the existence of federal powers. In the *Bank Deposits* case (1947),[28] the Privy Council had to determine the validity of a Quebec law which confiscated as bona vacantia

21 The federal Parliament may, however, be able to expropriate the local work after it has been brought within its legislative power: note 33, below.

22 *A.-G. Can.* v. *A.-G. Ont.* (Fisheries) [1898] A.C. 700.

23 The federal law will also be held invalid if it is in pith and substance an exercise of proprietary rights. For example, in *A.-G. Can.* v. *A.-G. Ont.* (Fisheries) [1898] A.C. 700 it was held that the federal Parliament could regulate the times and manner of fishing in provincially owned fisheries, but could not grant leases of the fisheries conferring on the lessee the exclusive right to fish; the latter power was proprietary and was held by the province as owner of the fishery.

24 *A.-G. Can.* v. *A.-G. B.C.* (Fish Canneries) [1930] A.C. 111.

25 Fisheries is one of the topics of ch. 29, Natural Resources, below.

26 See ch. 21, Property and Civil Rights, under heading 21.9, "marketing", above.

27 [1963] S.C.R. 144. To the same effect is *Multiple Access* v. *McCutcheon* [1982] 2 S.C.R. 161 (upholding federal "insider trading" law).

28 *A.-G. Can.* v. *A.-G. Que.* (Bank Deposits) [1947] A.C. 33.

deposits in "credit institutions" which had not been claimed or operated for 30 years. Their lordships held that the law was in pith and substance in relation to the federal subject of "banking" (s. 91(15)), not property, and was accordingly invalid. This case, and those cited in the previous paragraph, are illustrative of a pervasive problem in Canadian constitutional law, namely, the drawing of the dividing line between those federal heads of power which contemplate some degree of interference with contractual and proprietary rights, on the one hand, and the provincial head of power over property and civil rights in the province, on the other.[29]

28.5 Expropriation

(a) Federal power

This distinction between federal laws which relate to a head of federal power and laws which relate to the ownership of property is further blurred by the fact that most federal powers will authorize the expropriation of property. Thus, the federal Parliament, in exercise of its power over "navigation and shipping" (s. 91(10)), could expropriate property in order to permit the erection of works for navigation purposes;[30] the federal Parliament, in exercise of its power over the national capital (which comes from the peace, order, and good government clause) may expropriate property to create a "green belt" in the national capital region;[31] the federal Parliament, in exercise of its power over interprovincial transportation, could authorize the expropriation of land for the building of a railway or pipeline;[32] and the federal Parliament could probably exercise its declaratory power to bring a local work into federal jurisdiction (s. 92(10)(c)) and then expropriate the work.[33] It is obvious that any federal expropriation would have to be justified as a law in relation to some head of federal power, and there does not appear to be any federal power which would authorize expropriation at large or for any public purpose. In

29 Most of the leading constitutional cases have at bottom turned on this issue, e.g., the cases on peace, order, and good government (ch. 17, above), criminal law (ch. 18, above), trade and commerce (ch. 20, above) and property and civil rights (ch. 21, above).

30 *Montreal* v. *Montreal Harbour Commrs.* [1926] A.C. 299, 313, 320.

31 *Munro* v. *National Capital Comm.* [1966] S.C.R. 663; see also *R.* v. *Appleby* (No. 2) (1976) 76 D.L.R. (3d) 110 (N.B. A.D.) (federal Parliament, under peace, order, and good government power, may demand two copies of every book published in Canada for the National Library). The emergency branch of peace, order, and good government was suggested as the constitutional basis for the federal expropriation of the shares of the insolvent Grand Trunk Railway in *Lovibond* v. *Grand Trunk Ry.* [1939] O.R. 305, 324 (C.A.); see also *A.-G. Can.* v. *Hallet and Carey* [1952] A.C. 427 (federal expropriation of oats and barley, to prevent profiteering after war, assumed to be valid).

32 *Re Dyke and Cochin Pipe Lines* (1978) 85 D.L.R. (3rd) 607 (Sask. C.A.).

33 Lajoie, *Le pouvoir déclaratoire du Parlement* (1969), 102-106.

other words, the federal power of expropriation appears to be limited to the taking of property for purposes otherwise falling within its legislative authority.[34]

(b) Provincial power

The provincial Legislatures, by contrast, probably have a general power to expropriate property in the province, simply by virtue of the breadth of their legislative power over ''property and civil rights in the province'' (s. 92(13)).[35] Where the expropriation could also be related to another provincial head of power, the provincial power is even clearer. This does not mean that the provincial power of expropriation is unlimited. If the expropriating law is in pith and substance a law in relation to a matter outside provincial competence, then it will be invalid on ordinary federal principles.[36] In principle, an expropriation that would ''sterilize'' a federally-incorporated company[37] or a federally-regulated undertaking[38]

---

34 Laskin, note 1, above, 669. Canadian constitutional law has never recognized a general power of ''eminent domain'' - a power to take private property for public use. It is conceivable that such a power could be found in the federal power over ''the public debt and property'' (s. 91(1A)), but no case goes so far and neither La Forest, note 1, above, 149, nor Lajoie, *Expropriation et fédéralisme au Canada* (1972), 72-73, nor Laskin, note 1, above, 668-670, regard this interpretation of s. 91(1A) as open. The existence in s. 117 of the federal power ''to assume any lands or public property required for fortifications or for the defence of the country'' also tends to negative the existence of any general power of expropriation.

35 *McAfee* v. *Irving Refining* (1970) 17 D.L.R. (3d) 729 (N.B.A.D.) (expropriation of land to construct intraprovincial pipeline upheld); *Can. Industrial Gas and Oil* v. *Govt. of Sask.* [1978] 2 S.C.R. 545, 569 (expropriation of oil and gas rights upheld); *Société Asbestos* v. *Société nationale de l'amiante* (1981) 128 D.L.R. (3d) 405 (Que. C.A.) (expropriation of assets of asbestos mining company upheld). La Forest, note 1, above, 173 and Laskin, note 1, above, 669, both assert an extensive provincial power of expropriation. Lajoie, note 34, above, ch. 4, argues that expropriation is merely a means to an end, and that the end must be within the legislative competence of the province.

36 *Re Upper Churchill Water Rights* [1984] 1 S.C.R. 297 (expropriation of assets of hydro-electric company struck down as a colourable attempt to destroy contractual rights outside province possessed by purchaser of electricity under long-term contract). However, in both the *CIGOL* and *Asbestos* cases, note 35, above, the fact that the expropriated resource was almost entirely destined for export did not affect the validity of the provincial expropriation. As was pointed out in the *Asbestos* case, at pp. 418-419, an expropriation is not by itself an exercise of regulatory power, and the product under its new ownership would remain subject to federal regulatory power.

37 In the *Churchill Falls* case, previous note, the Supreme Court held that even an uncompensated taking of all of the assets of a federally-incorporated company did not amount to sterilization, because the company retained the capacity to raise new capital and (perhaps after amendment of its charter) start a new business.

38 The expropriation would leave the undertaking subject to federal regulatory jurisdiction, even though under provincial ownership: *The Queen (Ont.)* v. *Bd. of Transport Commrs.* (Go-Train) [1968] S.C.R. 118 (commuter service operated by province of Ontario on interprovincial railway line held subject to federal regulatory jurisdiction); *Alta. Govt. Telephones* v. *Can.* [1989] 2 S.C.R. 255 (telephone company owned by province held subject to federal regulatory jurisdiction); and so it may be safe to assert that a change to provincial ownership could never amount to a sterilization.

would be invalid by virtue of the principles of interjurisdictional immunity, but in practice it seems that an expropriation would never be held to have a sterilizing effect.[39]

(c) Crown property

The questions whether the federal Parliament may expropriate property owned by a province, and whether a provincial Legislature may expropriate property owned by the Dominion, probably depend at bottom on the capacity of the Parliament or the Legislatures to enact laws binding on the Crown in right of another government. This topic was considered in the earlier chapter on the Crown.[40] Generally speaking, federal legislative power will extend to bind the Crown in right of a province, and there have been cases in which the federal Parliament has validly expropriated provincial Crown property.[41] Whether provincial legislative power will extend to the expropriation of federal Crown property is much more dubious, the dominant opinion being that provincial legislative power will not extend so far.[42]

(d) Compensation

There is a rule of statutory interpretation in Anglo-Canadian law that a statute which takes private property is to be read as implicitly requiring that compensation be paid to the private owner. "Unless the words of the statute clearly so demand, a statute is not to be construed so as to take away the property of a subject without compensation".[43] This rule was liberally applied by the Supreme Court of Canada in *Manitoba Fisheries* v. *The Queen* (1978).[44] In that case, a company that operated a fish exporting business was put out of business when a federal statute gave to a Crown corporation the exclusive right to export fish. The statute was silent on

39 See previous two notes. See ch. 15, Judicial Review on Federal Grounds, under hading 15.8, "Interjurisdictional immunity", above.

40 See ch. 10, The Crown, under heading 10.9, "Federal complications", above.

41 *A.-G. B.C.* v. *CPR* [1906] A.C. 204; *A.-G. Que.* v. *Nipissing Central Ry. Co.* [1926] A.C. 715; La Forest, note 1, above, 150-155; Lajoie, note 34, above, 139-148. In *Re Exported Natural Gas Tax* [1982] 1 S.C.R. 1004, 1053 the majority of the Court, obiter, emphasized that the federal power of expropriation extended only to "the property absolutely essential to the Dominion undertaking".

42 See ch. 10, The Crown, under heading 10.9(d), "Provincial laws binding federal Crown", above. *Construction Montcalm* v. *Minimum Wage Comm.*, note 3, above, rejects the theory that federal Crown property is an enclave from which provincial law is excluded. The case involved a minimum wage law, not an expropriation, but it may pave the way for recognition of a provincial power of expropriation of federal Crown property.

43 *A.G.* v. *De Keyser's Royal Hotel* [1920] A.C. 508, 542 (H.L.). Cf. *Burmah Oil Co.* v. *Lord Advocate* [1965] A.C. 75 (H.L.), where it was held that a taking authorized by the royal prerogative was accompanied by an obligation to pay compensation.

44 [1979] 1 S.C.R. 101.

the question of compensation. The company sued for compensation. It lost in the lower courts, on the ground that there had been no taking of any of the company's assets. The suit was successful in the Supreme Court of Canada, where Ritchie J. for the Court pointed out that the creation of the statutory monopoly had had the effect of destroying the company's goodwill[45] and rendering its physical assets useless for their purposes. He held that this amounted to a taking of property, which meant that the company was entitled to be compensated.

The Supreme Court of Canada decided another taking case in *The Queen (B.C.)* v. *Tener* (1985).[46] The provincial statute in issue restricted the plaintiffs' ability to exploit their mineral rights over land in a provincial park. The statute said nothing about compensation. The Supreme Court of Canada followed the *Manitoba Fisheries* case to hold that the devaluation of the mineral rights was a taking of property that had to be compensated.[47] This holding actually goes a step beyond *Manitoba Fisheries*. In that case, a Crown corporation had in effect acquired the business of exporting fish. In *Tener*, the Crown acquired nothing — neither the minerals nor the power to exploit the mineral rights. This suggests to me that the provincial statute should have been classified as a regulation of the provincial park rather than as a taking of mineral rights.

Where a statute is regulatory, not involving a taking of property, the general rule is that no compensation is payable for loss caused by the statute.[48] Most forms of regulation impose costs on those who are regulated, and it would be intolerably costly to compensate them. Moreover, much regulation has a redistributive purpose: it is designed to reduce the rights of one group (manufacturers, employers, for example) and increase the rights of another (consumers, employees, for example). A compensation regime would work at cross-purposes to the purpose of the regulation.[49] Nevertheless, there is an indistinct boundary between regulating and taking. *Manitoba Fisheries* and *Tener* have the effect of expanding the class of takings (for which compensation should be provided) and contracting the class of regulations (for which no compensation should be provided).

The rule requiring compensation for a taking of property is in Canada (as in the United Kingdom) only a rule of statutory interpretation. If a statute expressly provides that no compensation is payable, then there is no room for interpretation and the express words of the statute must be applied.[50] In *R.* v. *Appleby (No. 2)*

45 Not folld. in *Home Orderly Services* v. *Man.* (1987) 43 D.L.R. (4th) 300 (Man. C.A.) (business of providing health care terminated when government took over service; held, no goodwill independent of government, and no compensation payable).

46 [1985] 1 S.C.R. 533.

47 Folld. in *Casamiro Resource Corp.* v. *B.C.* (1991) 80 D.L.R. (4th) 1 (B.C.C.A.) (another case involving the devaluation of mineral rights in a provincial park).

48 Hogg, *Liability of the Crown* (2nd ed., 1989), 105.

49 *Id.*, 116.

50 By the same token, a regulatory statute may expressly provide that compensation is payable to those who have borne the costs of the regulation.

(1976),[51] for example, it was held that no compensation was payable to a publisher who, in compliance with the National Library Act, sent two copies of each new book to the National Library. The Act stipulated that two copies of each newly-published book were to be sent to the Library "at his [the publisher's] own expense". The express denial of reimbursement excluded the rule of compensation.[52]

Neither the federal government nor a provincial government is under any constitutional (as opposed to statutory) obligation to pay fair compensation, or any compensation, for property expropriated.[53] In the United States, the fifth amendment to the Constitution requires the federal Congress to pay "just compensation" for property expropriated, and the due process clause of the fourteenth amendment by implication imposes the same obligation on the state Legislatures.[54] In Australia, while there is no comparable limitation on the state Legislatures, the federal Parliament has the power to expropriate property only "on just terms".[55] In Canada, by contrast, neither the Constitution Act, 1867 nor the Charter of Rights[56] contains any guarantee of compensation and, in the absence of any such guarantee, legislative power is unlimited.[57] The position was accurately, if dramatically, put by the judge who said that "the prohibition 'Thou shalt not steal' has no legal force upon the sovereign body".[58]

The Canadian Bill of Rights,[59] which of course is applicable only to federal laws, by s. 1(a), confers a right to "enjoyment of property", and the right not to be deprived thereof "except by due process of law". This language is sufficiently similar to that of the due process clause in the fourteenth amendment to the Constitution of the United States that it could be interpreted (as the American clause has been)[60] as conferring a right to compensation on the deprivation of property. In *Appleby*, discussed above,[61] this point was argued and rejected. The Court refused to import the American notion of substantive (as opposed to pro-

51 (1976) 76 D.L.R. (3d) 110 (N.B.A.D.).

52 A judicial decision awarding compensation may be retroactively annulled by statute, as occurred in the War Damage Act 1965 (U.K.), which reversed the decision in *Burmah Oil*, note 43, above.

53 Note that international trade treaties may provide for compensation of foreign owners in some circumstances.

54 *Chicago, Burlington and Quincy Rd. Co.* v. *Chicago* (1897) 166 U.S. 226.

55 Constitution of Australia, s. 51(31).

56 Sections 7 and 8 of the Charter of Rights are discussed in the following text.

57 La Forest, note 1, above, 149-155; Laskin, note 1, above, 669; Strayer, "Constitutional Aspects of Nationalization of Industry" (1964) 7 Can. B. J. 226, 227.

58 *Florence Mining Co.* v. *Cobalt Lake Mining Co.* (1909) 18 O.L.R. 275, 279 per Riddell J.; aff'd. 43 O.L.R. 474 (P.C.)).

59 The Canadian Bill of Rights is the subject of ch. 32, below.

60 Note 54, above.

61 Note 51, above.

cedural) due process into the Canadian Bill of Rights.[62] Section 7 of the Charter of Rights, which is the nearest thing to a due process clause in the Charter, protects ''life, liberty and security of the person'', but makes no reference to a deprivation of property.[63] Section 8 of the Charter, which protects against ''unreasonable search or seizure'', is probably confined to seizures of property for evidentiary or investigatory purposes,[64] and, if so, has no application to an expropriation.[65]

In rare cases, a failure to provide for compensation will have an indirect impact on the constitutionality of an expropriating statute. In *Re Upper Churchill Water Rights* (1984),[66] a Newfoundland statute expropriated all the assets of a company that operated a hydro-electric generating station at Churchill Falls in Newfoundland (Labrador). The expropriating statute provided for no compensation to the company, although it did provide for compensation to the company's shareholders for the decline in value of their shares. It was argued that the failure to compensate the company rendered the statute unconstitutional as a sterilization of a federally-incorporated company. The Supreme Court of Canada rejected this argument on the ground that the company retained its capacity to raise new capital. However, the Court held that the statute was unconstitutional as an attempt to destroy contractual rights outside the province. The Court mainly relied upon evidence extrinsic to the statute to hold that the true purpose of the statute was to nullify a long-term contract entered into by the company (with the approval of the Newfoundland government) to supply electricity to Quebec at less than the market price. This characterization of the statute was reinforced by the statute's failure to compensate the company: having lost the assets required to generate electricity, the company could no longer fulfil its side of the power contract; and, receiving no compensation, the company could not even pay damages for breach of the contract. Thus, the failure to pay compensation, by indicating a purpose other than the ostensible (and valid) purpose of converting a resource to provincial ownership,[67] contributed to the finding of invalidity.

---

62 The due process clause of the Canadian Bill of Rights was not mentioned in the *Manitoba Fisheries* case, note 44, above, although it was argued. The *Tener* case, note 46, above, involved a provincial law.

63 Section 7 is examined in ch. 44, Fundamental Justice, below.

64 So held in *Re Becker and the Queen (Alta.)* (1983) 148 D.L.R. (3d) 539 (Alta. C.A.). Section 8 is examined in ch. 45, Unreasonable Search and Seizure, below.

65 The Canada-U.S. Free Trade Agreement, by article 1605, requires Canada to pay ''prompt, adequate and effective compensation at fair market value'' for property expropriated from an American investor. However, only the Government of the United States could invoke the article, and only on behalf of the American investor. (Canadian investments in the United States receive the same protection.)

66 [1984] 1 S.C.R. 297.

67 Cf. *Société Asbestos* v. *Société nationale de l'amiante* (1981) 128 D.L.R. (3d) 405 (Que. C.A.) (provincial expropriation of assets of asbestos mining company upheld).

29

Natural Resources

29.1 Onshore minerals: provincial powers

(a) Provincial public property

With respect to minerals[1] owned by a province, we have noticed in the previous chapter on Public Property that the broad range of powers open to a private proprietor is also open to the province as proprietor. This is an important source of regulatory authority over the oil and gas that is found in Alberta and Saskatchewan, because a major part of the oil and gas reserves in each of those provinces is owned by the province.

Once a province ceases to own a resource, its proprietary right is lost. But the provinces of Alberta and Saskatchewan have devised ingenious ways of perpetuating their control through proprietary right. An oil or gas lease, which gives to a private oil producer the right to produce and sell oil or gas from the leased Crown land, may include a ''compliance with laws'' clause, which obligates the lessee to comply with future provincial laws, and a ''variable royalty'' clause, which obligates the lessee to pay whatever royalty is prescribed by future provincial laws.[2] These clauses incorporate into the lease future changes in provincial regulations or royalties. By virtue of these clauses, the grant of the lease does not preclude continued exercise of provincial control by proprietary right. In the absence of these clauses, the lease would be as binding on the Crown as on the private party. Of course, the province by statute could still derogate from the contractual rights and obligations, or regulate or tax the oil and gas after its recovery from the ground (and conversion to private ownership), but this would require the enactment of legislation that would have to satisfy the more stringent tests of validity that are applicable when the province is acting purely as legislator.

---

1 There is a vast literature on the constitutional law relating to minerals, especially, oil and gas. Especially useful are La Forest, *Natural Resources and Public Property under the Canadian Constitution* (1968); Crommelin, ''Jurisdiction over Onshore Oil and Gas in Canada'' (1975) 10 U.B.C. L. Rev. 86; Moull, ''Natural Resource Ownership: Atlantic Canada Perspective'' (1986) 10 Dal. L.J. 103. For commentary on s. 29A (the resource amendment of 1982), see Moull, ''Section 92A of the Constitution Act, 1867'' (1983) 61 Can. Bar. Rev. 715; Cairns, Chandler and Moull, ''The Resource Amendment (Section 92A) and the Political Economy of Canadian Federalism'' (1985) 23 Osgoode Hall L.J. 253; Cairns, Chandler and Moull, ''Constitutional Change and the Private Sector: The Case of the Resource Amendment'' (1987) 24 Osgoode Hall L.J. 299.

2 The use, effect and validity of these clauses are discussed by Harrison, ''The Legal Character of Petroleum Licences'' (1980) 58 Can. Bar Rev. 483: Moull, ''Natural Resources: Provincial Proprietary Rights'' (1983) 21 Alta. L. Rev. 472. The critical point is that the rights and obligations of the lessee must be regarded as stemming from the lease (or other contract) and not from the legislation authorizing the lease. Even so, it is likely that there are some basic terms that cannot be unilaterally changed under these clauses.

(b) Private property

When a province acts as legislator (as opposed to proprietor), in order to regulate the production and marketing of privately-owned minerals, or to obtain revenue from their production, it has to rely on its legislative authority over property and civil rights in the province (s. 92(13)), local works and undertakings (s. 92(10)), matters of a local or private nature (s. 92(16)), natural resources (s. 92A) and taxation (ss. 92(2), 92A(4)). These powers are extensive with respect to resources that are marketed within the province, that is, resources that are consumed, or at least refined or processed, within the province of production. But the *CIGOL* and *Central Canada Potash* cases[3] establish severe limits on provincial power over resources that are mainly exported from the province of production. These cases, and provincial powers over production, marketing and export generally, are examined in chapter 21, Property and Civil Rights, above.[4] The taxation of resources is examined in the next chapter, Taxation.[5]

(c) Pipelines

The province can also regulate pipelines, mines and other facilities by virtue of its power over local works and undertakings (s. 92(10)).[6] However, this power is confined to works and undertakings that do not extend beyond the limits of the province. A pipeline that extends beyond the limits of the province,[7] or that, although local, is connected to and operated as part of an interprovincial system,[8] falls outside provincial jurisdiction (s. 92(10)(a)). These principles are discussed in chapter 22, Transportation and Communication, above.

29.2 Onshore minerals: federal powers

(a) Federal public property

Federal public property also yields minerals (and other resources); and in respect of these resources the Dominion enjoys the same proprietary powers as

3 *Can. Industrial Gas and Oil* v. *Govt. of Sask.* [1978] 2 S.C.R. 545; *Central Can. Potash* v. *Govt. of Sask.* [1979] 1 S.C.R. 42.

4 Chapter 21, under heading 21.9, ''Marketing'', above.

5 Chapter 30, under heading 30.2(i), ''Resource taxes'', below.

6 *Re National Energy Bd. Act* [1988] 2 F.C. 196 (C.A.)

7 *Campbell-Bennett* v. *Comstock Midwestern* [1954] S.C.R. 207; *Sask. Power Corp.* v. *Trans-Can. Pipelines* [1979] 1 S.C.R. 297.

8 The feeder lines that carry the oil and gas from the production fields to the interprovincial trunk lines have been held to be outside provincial jurisdiction for this reason: *Re Westspur Pipeline Co. Gathering System* (1957) 76 C.R.T.C. 158 (Bd. of Transport Commrs.); but a distribution line that carries gas from the interprovincial trunk line to the consumer has been held to be within provincial jurisdiction: *Re National Energy Bd. Act* [1988] 2 F.C. 196 (C.A.).

do the provinces over their publicly-owned resources. Those powers are explained in the previous chapter, Public Property. As will be explained later in this chapter, the Dominion also possesses rights akin to ownership over the resources of the seabed of the territorial sea and continental shelf off the shore of Canada.[9]

(b) Private property

With respect to privately-owned minerals, federal legislative power is plenary in the two federal territories[10] and in the offshore.[11] In the provinces, however, federal legislative power is, of course, confined to the catalogue of federal powers. The important ones are briefly described in the text that follows.

(c) Peace, order, and good government

Under the emergency branch of the power over the peace, order, and good government of Canada, the federal Parliament could assume extensive regulatory powers in the event of an emergency, such as, an interruption of oil supply. Under the national concern branch, the federal Parliament possesses powers over a mineral of special military significance, namely, uranium. The special position of uranium is examined later in this chapter.[12] The peace, order, and good government power, in both of its branches, is the topic of chapter 17, above.

(d) Trade and commerce

Under the trade and commerce power (s. 91(2)), the federal Parliament may regulate the marketing of resources in interprovincial and international trade, which of course includes the import and export of resources. That power is examined in chapter 20, Trade and Commerce, above.

(e) Works and undertakings

Under the power over works and undertakings extending beyond the limits of one province (s. 92(10)(a)), the federal Parliament may regulate pipelines and other means of transportation that cross provincial boundaries.[13] As well, the declaratory power of s. 92(10)(c) enables the federal Parliament to declare a local work, such as a mine, a pipeline or other man-made facility, to be a work for the general advantage of Canada and thereby to assume regulatory authority over the

---

9 Section 29.2, ''Offshore minerals'', below.
10 Constitution Act, 1871, s. 4.
11 Note 9, above.
12 Text at notes 14-21, below.
13 Notes 7-8 and accompanying text, above.

work. The federal powers under s. 92(10)(a) and s. 92(10)(c) are examined in chapter 22, Transportation and Communication, above.

(f) Taxation

Under the taxation power (s. 91(3)), the federal Parliament may levy any kind of tax on resources. That power is discussed in the next chapter, Taxation.

(g) Uranium

Although the mining and production of minerals generally falls within provincial competence, uranium is in a special position.[14] In 1946, after the atomic bombs had been dropped on Japan, the federal Parliament passed the Atomic Energy Control Act.[15] The Act created a category of ''prescribed substances'', which included uranium, and the Act declared that all works and undertakings ''for the production, refining or treatment of prescribed substances'' were works for the general advantage of Canada.[16] This declaration was, of course, an exercise of the declaratory power under s. 92(10)(c) of the Constitution Act, 1867, and it had the effect of shifting the declared works from provincial to federal jurisdiction.[17] The Act created the Atomic Energy Control Board, and gave to the Board regulatory power over prescribed substances, including uranium. The result is that prospecting for, mining, refining and handling uranium requires a licence from the Board, and is regulated by the Board.

The constitutional validity of the Atomic Energy Control Act has been upheld by the Supreme Court of Canada.[18] The federal Parliament's power to enact the Act was found in two sources, namely, the declaratory power under s. 92(10)(c)[19] and the national concern branch of the peace, order, and good government power.[20] The production, refining and marketing of uranium is therefore a federal responsibility.

14 See Sproule, ''The Uranium Mining Industry in Saskatchewan'' (1978) 43 Sask. L. Rev. 65; O'Donnell, ''An Inquiry into Provincial Jurisdiction over Uranium Development in Saskatchewan'' (1984) 48 Sask. L. Rev. 293. As these articles show, in practice, there is a substantial provincial regulatory role.

15 S.C. 1946, c. 37; now R.S.C. 1985, c. A-6.

16 The declaration is now in s. 18.

17 See ch. 22, Transportation and Communication, under heading 22.8, ''Works for the general advantage of Canada'', above.

18 *Ont. Hydro* v. *Ont.* [1993] 3 S.C.R. 327. The Court was unanimous in reaching the conclusion described in the text; the Court divided on the issue in the case, which was whether federal jurisdiction extended to labour relations in an electrical generating station driven by nuclear power.

19 Note 17, above.

20 See sec. 17.3, ''The national concern branch'', above.

29.3 Offshore minerals

(a) International law and constitutional law

Since the nineteenth century, international law has recognized that the territorial sea is part of the territory of the coastal state. The territorial sea originally consisted of the sea within three miles (a cannon's range) of the coast, but it is now accepted that a coastal state may claim a wider territorial sea, and Canada in common with many other states has now established a 12-mile territorial sea.[21] A more recent development in international law is the recognition that coastal states have the exclusive right to explore and exploit the natural resources of the continental shelf. The continental shelf is the shallow part of the ocean which is contiguous to each continent and which may extend for 200 miles or more before the seabed drops sharply to the deep ocean floor. The continental shelf is unlike the territorial sea in that the continental shelf is not part of the territory of the coastal state, and for most purposes the coastal state is not entitled to exercise sovereignty over it. But the coastal state is entitled to exploit the mineral resources of the shelf.

International law has thus settled the question of which sovereign state has the right to exploit offshore minerals. But international law cannot determine which level of government in a federal state possesses the right. That question has to be settled by the domestic law of each federal state. In Canada, however (as in Australia[22] and the United States[23]), the Constitution is silent on the question, no doubt because the exploitation of offshore minerals (except by drilling from the shore) was not possible at confederation and was not contemplated by the framers. In Canada, therefore (as in Australia and the United States), the question had to be resolved by the courts with very little assistance from conventional sources of constitutional law.[24]

(b) B.C. Offshore Reference

The position of Canada's west coast was determined in the *B.C. Offshore Reference* (1967).[25] This was a reference by the federal government to the Su-

21 Territorial Sea and Fishing Zones Act, R.S.C. 1985, c. T-8, s. 3.

22 In Australia, jurisdiction over the offshore was settled in favour of the federal government in *New South Wales* v. *Commonwealth* (1975) 135 C.L.R. 337.

23 In the United States, jurisdiction over the offshore was settled in favour of the federal government in *United States* v. *California* (1947) 332 U.S. 19; *United States* v. *Louisiana* (1950) 339 U.S. 699; *United States* v. *Texas* (1950) 339 U.S. 707; *United States* v. *Maine* (1975) 420 U.S. 515.

24 See Head, "The Canadian Offshore Minerals Reference" (1968) 18 U. Toronto L.J. 131; La Forest, *Natural Resources and Public Property under the Canadian Constitution* (1969), ch. 6; Harrison, "Jurisdiction over the Canadian Offshore" (1979) 17 Osgoode Hall L.J. 469; McEvoy, "Atlantic Canada: The Constitutional Offshore Regions" (1984) 8 Dal. L.J. 284; Cullen, *Federalism in Action: The Australian and Canadian Offshore Disputes* (1990).

25 *Re Offshore Mineral Rights of B.C.* [1967] S.C.R. 792.

preme Court of Canada for a ruling on the constitutional status of the territorial sea and continental shelf off the shore of British Columbia. The Court held that the boundaries of British Columbia ended at the low-water mark. This was the general rule,[26] and the boundaries of British Columbia had never been extended beyond the low-water mark.[27] It followed that British Columbia did not have any property rights in, or rights to explore and exploit, or legislative jurisdiction[28] over, either the territorial sea[29] or the continental shelf. Moreover, since British Columbia had never been a sovereign state recognized by international law, it could not have acquired rights created by international law. With respect to the territorial sea, the Court concluded that the federal government owned the seabed of the territorial sea, and had plenary legislative jurisdiction over it, either under the public property power (s. 91(1A)) or under the peace, order, and good government power (s. 91, opening words). With respect to the continental shelf, the Court concluded that, while the federal government did not own the natural resources of the continental shelf, it had the right to explore for and exploit those resources, and it had legislative jurisdiction over the resources, under the peace, order, and good government power.[30]

(c) Newfoundland Offshore Reference

Although the *B.C. Offshore Reference* dealt only with the coast of British Columbia, its reasoning seemed applicable to the eastern coastal waters as well, with the possible exception of the Newfoundland offshore. The government of Newfoundland took the position that Newfoundland's more recent admission to Canada distinguished Newfoundland from the other provinces. The argument was that Newfoundland had achieved statehood in international law before its admission to Canada, and with that status had acquired the same rights over its territorial sea and continental shelf as were possessed by other sovereign states. These

26 See ch. 13, Extraterritorial Competence, under heading 13.3(b), "Territory of province", above.

27 It has since been decided that there was one exception to this proposition. The status of the water between mainland British Columbia and Vancouver Island had not been explicitly treated in the *B.C. Offshore Reference.* In subsequent litigation, commenced by a reference by the British Columbia government, the Supreme Court of Canada held that this water, although it was not inland water (note 30, below), had been included within the boundaries of British Columbia by the United Kingdom statute that constituted the colony, and were part of the colony in 1871, when it became a province of Canada. Therefore, jurisdiction over this water was provincial: *Re Strait of Georgia* [1984] 1 S.C.R. 388.

28 On the incapacity of the provincial Legislatures to pass laws with extraterritorial effect, see ch. 13, Extraterritorial Competence, above.

29 The territorial sea does not include inland waters, such as harbours, bays, estuaries and other waters lying "between the jaws of the land". These waters are within the boundaries of the province, and their resources (if not privately owned) belong to the province.

30 In the case of the B.C. offshore, no oil has been discovered, and no revenue-sharing agreement has been concluded between the governments of B.C. and Canada. See Cullen, note 25, above, 135-147.

rights, the argument continued, were retained by Newfoundland when it became a province of Canada in 1949. This argument was never accepted by the federal government. The resolution of the dispute became urgent after oil was discovered in the Hibernia field, which was located on the continental shelf about 170 miles east of St. John's. The federal government directed a reference to the Supreme Court of Canada to resolve the question of jurisdiction over the Hibernia field. The question required a decision as to the constitutional status of the continental shelf, but did not require a decision about the territorial sea.

In the *Newfoundland Offshore Reference* (1984),[31] the Court held that Newfoundland was in no different position than British Columbia. Newfoundland, which was being governed by a British Commission at the time of union in 1949,[32] did not then possess the status of a sovereign state; and, in any event, in 1949 international law had not developed to the point of recognizing a coastal state's rights over the resources of the continental shelf.[33] Before union, therefore, Newfoundland was not able to acquire any rights at international law over its continental shelf. After union, when those rights came to be recognized by international law, they devolved upon Canada, not Newfoundland. Thus, the right to explore and exploit the resources of the continental shelf belonged to the federal government, not to Newfoundland. Legislative jurisdiction over the resources could not be possessed by Newfoundland, because the resources lay outside the territory of the province; legislative jurisdiction was possessed by the federal Parliament "under the peace, order, and good government power in its residual capacity".[34]

The *Newfoundland Offshore Reference* determined the status of the continental shelf off the coast of Newfoundland. The Court was not asked to determine, and did not determine, the status of the territorial sea. But the Supreme Court's reaffirmation of the rule that provincial boundaries end at the low-water mark,[35] and its denial to Newfoundland of international statehood at the time of union, make it unlikely that the Court will reach any different decision with respect to the territorial sea.[36] As well, the Court will probably want to avoid the anomaly

---

31 *Re Nfld. Continental Shelf* [1984] 1 S.C.R. 86. I disclose that I was one of the counsel for the federal government in the case.

32 The pre-confederation government of Newfoundland is described in ch. 2, Reception, under heading 2.5(e), "Newfoundland", above.

33 The current doctrine of customary international law, recognizing an exclusive right of exploration and exploitation in the coastal state without the necessity of a claim or other assertion of jurisdiction, is a very recent development, which, the Court held, had not matured by 1949: [1984] 1 S.C.R. 86, 116-127.

34 *Id.*, 127.

35 This rule was accepted again, by both majority and minority in *Re Strait of Georgia* [1984] 1 S.C.R. 388, although the majority held that the definition of the boundaries of British Columbia created an exception to the rule for the water between mainland British Columbia and Vancouver Island.

36 Accord, *Ace Atlantic Container Express* v. *Nfld.* (1992) 92 D.L.R. (4th) 581 (Nfld. C.A.). (territory of province ends at low-water mark). In *Re Mineral and Other Natural Resources of the Continental Shelf* (1983) 145 D.L.R. (3d) 9 (Nfld. C.A.), the Newfoundland Court of Appeal

that the territorial sea off the coast of one province has a different constitutional status than the territorial sea off the coast of the other provinces.[37]

(d) Basis of federal jurisdiction

The reasoning of the Supreme Court of Canada in the *B.C. Offshore Reference* was criticized for sliding too quickly from the proposition that Canada (meaning the state at international law) possessed rights over the offshore under international law to the proposition that Canada (meaning the federal level of government) possessed rights over the offshore under domestic constitutional law.[38] It is true that the second proposition is not logically entailed by the first, as is demonstrated by Canada's divided power to implement treaties.[39] And yet, the highest courts of Australia and the United States have reached exactly the same result — federal jurisdiction over the offshore — as the Supreme Court of Canada, and they have employed similar reasoning.[40] In all three countries, the courts have accepted the idea that it is the nation, as represented by the federal government, and not its constituent units, that possesses the rights and responsibilities of external sovereignty.

While the Constitution Act, 1867 (like the Constitutions of Australia and the United States) is not explicit on the status of offshore resources, it is noteworthy that all those powers affecting external sovereignty that are mentioned are, without exception, confided to the federal Parliament. These include trade and commerce (s. 91(2)), military and naval service and defence (s. 91(7)), beacons, buoys, lighthouses and Sable Island (s. 91(9)), navigation and shipping (s. 91(10)) and the other major offshore resource, namely, seacoast fisheries (s. 91(12)). In all these matters, the Constitution Act, 1867 recognizes that "once low-water mark is passed, the international domain is reached".[41] For domestic constitutional

---

held that the resources of the territorial sea belonged to Newfoundland, although the resources of the continental shelf did not. This case was a provincial reference, and entirely separate from the federal reference regarding the Hibernia oilfield on the continental shelf (note 32, above). The decision in the Hibernia reference, although not an appeal from the decision of the Newfoundland Court of Appeal, effectively affirms the decision of the Newfoundland Court of Appeal on the continental shelf (although the Supreme Court's reasons were different). With respect to the territorial sea, the decision of the Newfoundland Court of Appeal, which relies on Newfoundland being a sovereign state in 1949, was appealed to the Supreme Court of Canada, but the appeal was not proceeded with.

37 In the case of the Newfoundland offshore, where oil has been discovered in the Hibernia field, in 1985 a revenue-sharing and management agreement (the Atlantic Accord) was concluded between the governments of Newfoundland and Canada. In the case of the Nova Scotia offshore, where only non-commercial quantities of oil have so far been discovered, in 1986 an agreement (the Nova Scotia Accord) similar to Newfoundland's was concluded. See Cullen, note 25, above, 178-190.

38 Head, note 25, above, 155.

39 See ch. 11, Treaties, above.

40 Notes 23 and 24, above.

41 *United States* v. *Texas* (1950) 339 U.S. 707, 719.

purposes, as well as for international law purposes, the actor in that domain is the federal government, not the provinces.[42] With respect, the Supreme Court of Canada was right to apply this idea to offshore resources.

29.4 Forestry

(a) Facts

Forests cover approximately 35 per cent of Canada's land mass. Logging, wood, paper and allied industries account for about 14 per cent of all Canadian manufacturing, and Canada is the world's largest exporter of forest products. Although British Columbia is the most heavily dependent upon its forest resources, the industry is important to the economy of every province, except for Prince Edward Island.[43]

(b) Provincial public property

Most forest lands are owned by the provinces. With respect to these lands, the provinces enjoy the same powers of disposition and management as a private proprietor.[44] In each province, the provincially-owned forests are harvested by private firms to whom the provincial Crown issues licences to cut timber. The process is controlled by the province through conditions attached to the licences. A common condition is the ''manufacturing condition'', which requires that timber cut on Crown lands be processed in Canada. We have already noticed that this condition has been held to be a valid exercise of provincial power over provincial property, although, as a restriction on exports, it would probably be invalid if imposed by provincial legislation on private timber lands.[45] Another common condition restricts the number of trees that the licensee may harvest each year. This is undoubtedly valid as an exercise of proprietary right, and would probably also be valid if imposed by legislation on private timber lands, in view of its conservation purpose.[46]

---

42 Surveillance, defence, resolution of disputes with other nations, entering into of treaties with other nations, are all, inevitably, federal responsibilities. Pollution of ocean waters outside the territory of any province is within federal jurisdiction: *R.* v. *Crown Zellerbach* [1988] 1 S.C.R. 401, 417 (obiter dictum). Even the supplying and servicing of offshore oil installations by ship has been held to be within federal jurisdiction: *Seafarers' International Union* v. *Crosbie Offshore Services* [1982] 2 F.C. 855 (C.A.).

43 These facts are taken from Fashler and Thompson, ''Constitutional Change and the Forest Industry'' in Beck and Bernier (eds.), *Canada and the New Constitution* (1983), vol. 2, 55, 57.

44 Chapter 25, Public Property, above.

45 *Smylie* v. *The Queen* (1900) 27 O.A.R. 172 (C.A.); discussed in ch. 25, Public Property, under heading 28.2, ''Legislative power over public property'', above.

46 See following text.

The province can derive revenue from the production of timber on its own lands through sales of timber, rents, licence fees and stumpage fees (which are like royalties). When imposed as proprietor, these charges are valid, even if they would be invalid if levied by legislation as taxes.[47]

(c) Federal public property

Substantial forest lands are owned by the federal government. These include national parks, military reserves and, of course, all the publicly-owned lands in the Yukon and Northwest Territories. The federal government enjoys the same ample powers over its public property as the provinces do over theirs.[48]

(d) Private property

Some forest lands are privately owned, including extensive areas in southern Ontario, Quebec and the maritime provinces. The control of these resources requires legislation under the provincial powers over property and civil rights in the province (s. 92(13)) and over natural resources (s. 92A). Since forest products are often exported from Canada, provincial controls on production could be vulnerable under the doctrine established in the *Central Canada Potash* case.[49] However, controls that have as their purpose the conservation of the resource, as opposed to the support of the price, would be valid. Provincial power over the production of resources is discussed in chapter 21, Property and Civil Rights, above.[50]

In order to derive revenue from the production of timber on privately-owned lands, the province must exercise its powers to tax (ss. 92(2), 92(9), 92A(4)). These powers to tax resources are discussed in the next chapter on Taxation.[51]

(e) Navigation conflicts

Logging activities can interfere with navigation, if logs are stored in log booms on water and transported by water to the mill. When logs are floated on non-navigable waters, the provinces appear to have an exclusive right to regulate floating.[52] On navigable waters, however, there is a federal power of regulation under the power over ''navigation and shipping'' (s. 91(10)). Moreover, the

---

47 See ch. 25, Public Property, under heading 28.3 ''Executive power over public property'', above.

48 Chapter 25, Public Property, above.

49 *Central Can. Potash* v. *Govt. of Sask.* [1979] 1 S.C.R. 42; discussed in ch. 20, Property and Civil Rights, under heading 21.9(c), ''Provincial power'', above.

50 Section 21.9, ''Marketing'', above. Note too that s. 92A(1)(b) and s. 92A(2) which are both discussed there, apply to ''forestry resources'', as well as to ''non-renewable natural resources''.

51 Section 30.2(i), ''Resource taxes'', below.

52 La Forest, *Water Law in Canada* (1973), 30-32 discusses ''floatability''.

federal power also operates as a limitation of provincial power, in that the provinces may not authorize the obstruction of navigable rivers.[53]

(f) Fisheries conflicts

Logging activities can also interfere with fisheries, if the debris from logging enters waters where fish spawn or live. The federal power over "sea coast and inland fisheries" (s. 91(12)) authorizes federal legislation for the protection of the waters in which fish spawn or live, and this includes the regulation of onshore activities that would pollute fish habitats. One section of the federal Fisheries Act dealt specifically with logging, and prohibited the deposit of logging debris "into any water frequented by fish". In *Fowler* v. *The Queen* (1980),[54] this section was held to be unconstitutional, because it was too broad a prohibition, insufficiently linked to any likely harm to fisheries. If the section had stipulated that the logging debris must be harmful to fish, then the connection between the proscribed activity and the fisheries would have caused the law to be upheld as a law in relation to fisheries.[55]

29.5 Fisheries

(a) Section 91(12)

The Constitution Act, 1867, by s. 91(12), confers on the federal Parliament the power to make laws in relation to "sea coast and inland fisheries".[56] This important resource was thus confided to federal jurisdiction, which extends to all fisheries in Canada, including those situated entirely within one province.

---

53 *Queddy River Driving Boom Co.* v. *Davidson* (1883) 10 S.C.R. 222. Such an obstruction may only be authorized by Parliament. The construction of such an obstruction accordingly requires federal permission under the Navigable Waters Protection Act, R.S.C. 1985, c. N-22.

54 *Fowler* v. *The Queen* [1980] 2 S.C.R. 213.

55 *Northwest Falling Contractors* v. *The Queen* [1980] 2 S.C.R. 292, upholding another section of the Fisheries Act, which prohibited the deposit of a "deleterious substance" (it was oil in this case) into water frequented by fish; the definition of a "deleterious substance" restricted the prohibition to deposits that threatened fish. This case and the *Fowler* case are discussed in the next section of this chapter on Fisheries.

56 See Alhéritière, Compétence fédérale sur les pêcheries (1972) 13 Cahiers de Droit (Laval) 53; La Forest, *Water Law in Canada* (1973), 38-42; Fairley, "Canadian Federalism, Fisheries and the Constitution" (1980) 12 Ottawa L. Rev. 257; Scott, "Regulation and the Location of Jurisdictional Powers: The Fishery" (1982) 20 Osgoode Hall L.J. 780.

(b) The right to fish

At both common law and civil law, the right to fish[57] belongs to the owner of the water bed (or solum). The owner of the bed may grant this right to fish to another, thereby severing the right to fish from the bed; the right to fish is recognized as a property right (it is a profit à prendre), which may be disposed of separately from the bed.

Tidal waters are an exception to the general rule that ownership of the bed carries with it the exclusive right to fish. Tidal waters are waters affected by the tide, for example, the sea and its bays, estuaries and the mouths of rivers. In tidal waters, there is a public right to fish. This public right overrides the proprietary right of the owner of the bed; the owner has no exclusive right to fish, and accordingly cannot grant any exclusive right to fish.

The Crown in right of the province is the owner of the bed of many fishing waters within the boundaries of the province:[58] waters on or adjacent to provincial public lands (which are of course extensive); tidal waters on or adjacent to private lands (the private owner does not obtain title to the bed of tidal waters); and, probably, non-tidal waters that are navigable (to which private owners probably do not obtain title).[59]

The Crown in right of Canada is the owner of the bed of fishing waters on or adjacent to federal public property, for example, federal parks and military reserves. The Crown in right of Canada also owns the bed of waters outside the boundaries of any province, for example, waters on public lands in the Yukon and Northwest territories, and offshore waters.[60]

Private persons own the bed of fishing waters that are non-tidal and non-navigable,[61] and that are on or adjacent to private land. The rule of both the common law and the civil law is that the owner of land owns the bed of any stream on that land. If the stream forms the boundary between lands owned by different persons, each riparian owner owns the bed of the stream to a line running

---

57 This account of the right to fish, which seems necessary in order to understand the constitutional law, is derived primarily from Laskin, ''Jurisdictional Framework for Water Management'' in Ministry of Northern Affairs and National Resources, *Resources for Tomorrow* (1961), 211 and La Forest, *Water Law in Canada* (1973), 195-199, 234-247.

58 The general rule is that the boundaries of the province end at the low-water mark of the sea, although bays, harbours, estuaries and other areas ''within the jaws of the land'' are within the boundaries of the province: see ch. 13, Extraterritorial Competence, under heading 13.3(b), ''Territory of province'', above.

59 This point is controversial: see the differing accounts by Laskin, note 58, above, 212 and La Forest, note 58, above, 235-236.

60 See note 59, above. The concept of ownership is appropriate only with respect to the bed of the (formerly three-mile now twelve-mile) territorial sea, which is within the boundaries of Canada: see *Re Offshore Mineral Rights of B.C.* [1967] S.C.R. 792. Canada, however, also asserts a 200-mile jurisdiction over fisheries under the Territorial Sea and Fishing Zones Act, R.S.C. 1985, c. T-8.

61 As to whether there can be private ownership of the bed of navigable waters, see note 60, above.

down the middle of the bed (ad medium filum aquae — to the centre thread of the stream).

The ownership of fishing rights is significant for constitutional purposes, because, in the *Fisheries Reference* (1898),[62] the Privy Council held that the power over fisheries in s. 91(12) conferred legislative jurisdiction only, and did not confer proprietary rights over fisheries. Nor did the fisheries power enable the federal Parliament to legislate in relation to proprietary rights over fisheries. Their lordships held that, while the federal Parliament could regulate the time and manner of fishing, it could not grant exclusive rights to fish in waters belonging to a province or to private individuals, because that would be a conferral of proprietary rights.

(c) Provincial public property

Where fishing rights are owned by a province, the province may, by legislation enacted under s. 92(5) (management and sale of public lands), or simply by contract, grant fishing rights and stipulate the terms and conditions upon which those rights are to be exercised.[63] For example, the province could establish a closed season for fishing in provincial Crown waters.[64] The management of public lands in s. 92(5) must include measures to conserve the stock of fish and to protect the fish environment. In waters owned by a province, and in which the province possesses the fishing rights, legislative jurisdiction is therefore effectively concurrent. In the case of conflict, the rule of federal paramountcy would, of course, give priority to the federal law.[65]

Where there is a public right to fish, that is, in tidal waters and navigable non-tidal waters, provincial ownership of the bed is irrelevant, since it carries with it no proprietary right in the fisheries. The provincial Legislatures cannot grant exclusive rights to fish in such waters, or otherwise regulate fishing. In waters where there is a public right to fish, the federal Parliament has exclusive jurisdiction, even where a province owns the bed of the waters.[66]

---

62 *A.-G. Can.* v. *A.-G. Ont.* (Fisheries) [1898] A.C. 700.

63 *Id.*, 716.

64 *R.* v. *Wagner* [1932] 2 W.W.R. 162 (Man. C.A.) decides the contrary, but the dissenting opinion is to be preferred: La Forest, *Water Law in Canada* (1973), 42. See also *Peralta* v. *Ont.* [1988] 2 S.C.R. 1045, 1046 (asserting, obiter, that the provinces have the power to regulate commercial fishing "in respect of provincially-owned fisheries as an aspect of their power to administer their public property").

65 *Peralta* v. *Ont.* [1988] 2 S.C.R. 1045, 1046 (obiter dictum). In order to minimize conflict at the level of administration, in Ontario the federal government has appointed as fishery officers (who administer the Act and regulations) the provincial officials who are responsible for the administration of the provincial legislation. The interdelegation was upheld in *Re Shoal Lake Band of Indians No. 39* (1979) 25 O.R. (2d) 334 (H.C.). The nature and degree of interdelegation differs from province to province, and there is a separate set of regulations for each province.

66 *A.-G. B.C.* v. *A.-G. Can.* (B.C. Fisheries) [1914] A.C. 153; *A.-G. Can.* v. *A.-G. Que.* (Quebec Fisheries) [1921] A.C. 413. In both cases, the former at p. 171, the latter at p. 428, their lordships

(d) Federal public property

Where fishing rights are owned by the Dominion, as they are in non-tidal and non-navigable waters on or adjacent to federal public lands, the federal Parliament's power over fisheries (s. 91(12)) is supplemented by its power over federal public property (s. 91(1A)), and it possesses power over both the proprietary and the operational aspects of fishing.[67]

(e) Private property

Where fishing rights are owned privately, as they are in non-tidal and non-navigable waters on or adjacent to private lands, jurisdiction is divided. The province is competent to regulate the grant of fishing rights and other proprietary aspects,[68] and the Dominion is competent to regulate the times and manner and all other aspects of fishing.

(f) Preservation of fish

It is well established that Parliament may legislate for the preservation of fish. This means that Parliament may regulate fishing operations by establishing closed seasons, and prohibiting the use of destructive fishing methods, regardless of who owns the fishing rights.[69] It also means that Parliament may act to protect the environment of fish, to ensure that spawning grounds or fish habitats are not polluted.

The power to protect the environment of fish is not a general power to regulate water pollution. In *Fowler* v. *The Queen* (1980),[70] the Supreme Court of Canada struck down a section of the federal Fisheries Act that prohibited the deposit of logging debris "into any water frequented by fish". Martland J. for the Court held that the vice of the law was that it did not link the proscribed conduct to actual or potential harm to fisheries, and there was no evidence that all logging debris was in fact harmful to fisheries.[71] Such a blanket prohibition of

---

made an exception for methods of fishing that make use of the water bed. The public right to fish does not extend to the use of the bed, and the province as proprietor retains the power to regulate the use of the bed.

67 La Forest, note 58, above, 42.

68 *A.-G. Can.* v. *A.-G. Ont.* (Fisheries) [1898] A.C. 700, 716 ("For example, provisions prescribing the mode in which a private fishery is to be conveyed or otherwise disposed of, and the rights of succession in respect of it . . .").

69 *Id.*, 713. Parliament may also pursue purposes other than conservation, for example, the promotion of sport fishing: *Gulf Trollers Assn.* v. *Can.* [1987] 2 F.C. 93 (C.A.).

70 [1980] 2 S.C.R. 213.

71 MacPherson, "Developments" (1981) 2 Supreme Court L.R. 49, 81-86, criticizes the decision on the basis that the fragile life cycle of the salmon made any debris potentially harmful, even if on the present state of knowledge no harm could be proved.

an activity that would normally be subject to provincial jurisdiction was accordingly unconstitutional.

One month after the decision in *Fowler*, the Court reached a different result in *Northwest Falling Contractors* v. *The Queen* (1980).[72] In that case, the Court upheld a section of the federal Fisheries Act that prohibited the deposit of a ''deleterious substance'' into water frequented by fish. The term ''deleterious substance'' was defined as something ''deleterious to fish or fish habitat or to the use by man of fish''. This definition provided the link between the proscribed conduct and the harm to fisheries which had been lacking in the offence struck down in *Fowler*. This enabled Martland J. for the Court to distinguish the earlier case, and uphold the validity of the offence in this case. Taken together, the two cases emphasize that the fisheries power will authorize the regulation of non-fishing activity only when there is clear connection between the regulated activity and a harmful effect on fisheries.[73]

(g) Marketing of fish

Federal power over fisheries does not extend to the processing and marketing of fish. In the *Fish Canneries Reference* (1930),[74] the Privy Council struck down a federal statute that required the licensing of fish canning and curing plants. Their lordships held that, once the fish were caught, they were a commodity like any other, and their processing and marketing came within the provincial jurisdiction over property and civil rights in the province (s. 92(13)).[75] Of course, interprovincial or international marketing would come within the federal jurisdiction over trade and commence (s. 91(2)).

29.6 Electricity

(a) Hydro-electricity

The provincial Legislatures have power over the generation and distribution of hydro-electricity, because dams,[76] generating stations and distribution systems

72 [1980] 2 S.C.R. 292.

73 See also *R.* v. *Crown Zellerbach* [1988] 1 S.C.R. 399 (federal prohibition of dumping of waste at sea cannot be upheld under s. 91(12), because no clear link with harm to fisheries).

74*A.-G. Can.* v. *A.-G. B.C.* (Fish Canneries) [1930] A.C. 111. This case has also been discussed in the previous chapter, Public Property, under heading 28.4, ''Legislative power and proprietary interests'', above.

75 Even the contracts between the processors of fish and the crews of fishing vessels come within provincial labour relations jurisdiction: *B.C. Packers* v. *CLRB* [1976] 1 F.C. 375 (C.A). However, federal jurisdiction continues while the fish are being transported from the fishing grounds to the shore: *R.* v. *Bodmer* (1981) 120 D.L.R. (3d) 699 (B.C. Co. Ct.) (upholding federal regulation of vessels used as fish packers).

76 A dam is also subject to federal jurisdiction under s. 91(10) (''navigation and shipping'') with

are "local works and undertakings" within s. 92(10) of the Constitution Act, 1867.

In *Fulton* v. *Energy Resources Conservation Board* (1981),[77] the Supreme Court of Canada held that a proposed electricity substation and transmission line in Alberta, which would deliver 99 per cent of its output to customers within the province, was a local work or undertaking within provincial jurisdiction, even though it was to connect with a transmission line in British Columbia to enable power to be shared, especially during emergencies or periods of surplus. If a more substantial operational connection had existed between the two systems, the systems would have been classified as a single interprovincial undertaking and would have come within federal jurisdiction under s. 92(10)(a).[78] Jurisdiction over electrical distribution systems is thus governed by the same principles as jurisdiction over other media of transportation and communication, such as railways, pipelines and telephones.[79]

In *Re Upper Churchill Water Rights* (1984),[80] the Newfoundland Legislature purported to expropriate all the assets of a company that generated hydro-electricity at Churchill Falls in Newfoundland (Labrador) and transmitted the bulk of the production into Quebec. The Supreme Court of Canada struck down the legislation, because its purpose was to destroy a contractual right outside Newfoundland, namely, the right to receive power under a long-term contract between the generating company and Hydro-Quebec. The Court did not consider the question whether the continuous and regular transmission of power from Churchill Falls to Quebec converted the operation into a federal undertaking.

(b) Other kinds of electricity

Electricity generated from oil, gas, coal or other sources of energy than water power would be governed by the same constitutional principles as hydro-elec-

---

respect to its effect on navigability: *Smith* v. *Ont. and Minnesota Power Co.* (1918) 44 O.L.R. 43 (A.D.); *Re Waters and Water Powers* [1929] S.C.R. 200, 226; and probably under s. 91(12) ("inland fisheries") with respect to its effect on the movement of fish. It has been suggested that a dam that spans a river forming a boundary between two provinces is within exclusive federal jurisdiction under s. 92(10)(a): [1929] S.C.R. 200, 225; but this is probably wrong, because a dam is not a work of transportation or communication to which s. 92(10)(a) is restricted: see ch. 22, Transportation and Communication, under heading 22.3 "Transportation and communication", above. An analogy is a mine which crosses a provincial boundary: cf. *R.* v. *Belous* [1977] 6 W.W.R. 19 (Man. C.A.) (interprovincial mine within federal jurisdiction, but because of declaration under s. 92(10)(c)).

77 [1981] 1 S.C.R. 153.

78 *Re Town of Summerside and Maritime Electric Co. (No. 2)* (1983) 3 D.L.R. (4th) 577 (P.E.I.S.C. in banco) (submarine cable linking N.B. and P.E.I. electrical systems created federal undertaking).

79 See ch. 22, Transportation and Communication, especially sec. 22.7, "Related undertakings", above.

80 [1984] 1 S.C.R. 297.

tricity. An exception, however, is electricity generated from nuclear power, which would probably come within federal jurisdiction for reasons explained in the earlier discussion of uranium.[81]

(c) Section 92A

It seems likely that the foregoing principles have not been changed by s. 92A(1)(c) of the Constitution Act, 1867, which was added to the Constitution in 1982.[82] Under s. 92A(1)(c), each provincial Legislature has the power to make laws in relation to:

> (c) development, conservation and management of sites and facilities in the province for the generation and production of electrical energy.

As a general proposition, this provision is declaratory of the pre-1982 law. The provision contains no express exception for the case where electricity is generated from nuclear power. However, in that case, the Supreme Court of Canada has held that it is the federal Parliament that has legislative authority over the operation and management of the nuclear plant.[83] Another exception to the provincial jurisdiction recognized by s. 92A(1)(c) would be the case where electricity is generated within an interprovincial undertaking.

The 1982 amendments also provided for the export of resources, including electricity. Before 1982, the province was incompetent to make laws in relation to the export of resources, that being a matter within the federal trade and commerce power.[84] Under s. 92A(2), each provincial Legislature has the power to make laws in relation to ''the export from the province to another part of Canada'' of (among other resources) electricity. This new power only applies to electricity which is exported ''to another part of Canada''.[85] The provinces remain incompetent to regulate the export of electricity from Canada. The new power is concurrent with the federal Parliament's trade and commerce power, and, in the event of conflict between federal and provincial laws, the federal law prevails.[86]

---

81 *Ont. Hydro* v. *Ont.* [1993] 3 S.C.R. 327; note 21, above. This case upholds federal jurisdiction over the nuclear power plant. Whether federal jurisdiction would extend to the distribution of the electricity is much less clear.

82 For analysis, see references in note 1, above.

83 Note 82, above.

84 *Can. Industrial Gas & Oil* v. *Govt. of Sask.* [1978] 2 S.C.R. 545; *Central Can. Potash Co.* v. *Govt. of Sask.* [1979] 1 S.C.R. 42.

85 In the *Churchill Falls* case, note 81, above, the Court did not consider the applicability of s. 92A(2), presumably because the legislation in issue had been enacted before 1982 (although it had never been proclaimed in force). Even if that legislation could not itself be characterized as being in relation to the export of electricity, it seems likely that Newfoundland's objectives could now be achieved under s. 92A(2), by directly regulating the quantity or price of electricity to be exported to Quebec. See Moull, ''Newfoundland Resources'' (1985) 7 Supreme Court L.R. 419.

86 Section 92A(3) explicitly preserves federal power and explicitly declares federal paramountcy.

29.7 Environmental protection

(a) Introduction

The environment,[87] comprising as it does ''all that is around us'', is too diffuse a topic to be assigned by the Constitution exclusively to one level of government.[88] Like inflation,[89] it is an aggregate of matters, which come within various classes of subjects, some within federal jurisdiction and others within provincial jurisdiction.

(b) Federal power

At the federal level, the most obvious sources of power are the following. The criminal law power (s. 91(27)) provides power to prohibit activities that are dangerous to health, but provides only limited power to establish a sophisticated regulatory structure (as opposed to a simple prohibition and penalty).[90] The power over fisheries (s. 91(12)) provides power to regulate the environment of fish.[91] The power over navigation and shipping (s. 91(10)) provides power to regulate the activities of ships, such as the discharge of oil and other harmful substances.[92] As well, the jurisdiction over coastal waters outside the boundaries of the provinces would include the power to control pollution in Canadian waters (s. 91(1A)).[93] There is also federal jurisdiction over international and interprovincial rivers, where pollution in one province will be carried into other provinces or countries.[94] The federal Parliament can also control activities on federal public

87 See Laskin, ''Jurisdictional Framework for Water Management'' in Ministry of Northern Affairs and National Resources, *Resources for Tomorrow* (1961), 211; Gibson, ''The Constitutional Context of Canadian Water Planning'' (1968) 7 Alta. L. Rev. 81; Landis, ''Legal Controls of Pollution in the Great Lakes Basin'' (1970) 48 Can. Bar Rev. 66; Emond, ''The Case for a Greater Federal Role in the Environmental Protection Field'' (1972) 10 Osgoode Hall L.J. 647; Alhéritière, ''Les problèmes constitutionnels de la lutte contre la pollution de l'espace atmospherique au Canada'' (1972) 50 Can. Bar Rev. 561; Gibson, ''Constitutional Jurisdiction over Environmental Management in Canada'' (1973) 23 U. Toronto L.J. 54; Beaudoin, ''La protection de l'environnement et ses implications en droit constitutionnnel'' (1977) 23 McGill L.J. 207.

88 *Friends of Oldman River Society* v. *Can.* [1992] 1 S.C.R. 3, 63, 64, 70.

89 *Re Anti-Inflation Act* [1976] 2 S.C.R. 373, 458.

90 See ch. 18, Criminal Law, especially sec. 18.10, ''Criminal law and regulatory authority'', above.

91 See the earlier section of this chapter, 29.5, ''Fisheries'', above.

92 In *R.* v. *Crown Zellerbach* (1984) 7 D.L.R. (4th) 449 (B.C.C.A.), it was held that a federal prohibition of dumping waste at sea could not be upheld under s. 91(10) without showing some potential harm to shipping or navigation. The s. 91(10) argument was not pursued in the Supreme Court of Canada, where the law was upheld under p.o.g.g.: [1988] 1 S.C.R. 399, 418.

93 *R.* v. *Crown Zellerbach* [1988] 1 S.C.R. 399, 417 (obiter dictum).

94 *Ibid.*; *Interprovincial Cooperatives* v. *The Queen* [1976] 1 S.C.R. 477.

lands (s. 91(1A))[95] and the activities of industries within federal jurisdiction, which include aviation (s. 91, opening words),[96] interprovincial and international transportation and communication (s. 92(10)(a)),[97] nuclear power (s. 92(10)(c))[98] and banking (s. 91(15)),[99] but which do not include most mining and manufacturing industries. The taxing power (s. 91(3)) can be used to discourage polluting activities through higher taxes, and to encourage the installation of anti-pollution equipment through accelerated capital cost allowance and other deductions.[100] The emergency branch of the peace, order, and good government power (s. 91, opening words) is available to deal with an emergency, such as an escape of radioactive waste.[101] The national concern branch of the peace, order, and good government power will support measures to control pollution of air or water that are beyond the capacity of the provinces to control; on this basis, a federal prohibition of dumping waste at sea has been upheld.[102]

In *Friends of Oldman River Society* v. *Canada* (1992)[103] the question arose whether a Guidelines Order, made under the federal Department of the Environment Act, could impose an environmental assessment on the Government of Alberta's project to build a dam on the Oldman River in Alberta. The Guidelines Order required all departments and agencies of the federal government that had decision-making authority, before coming to a decision on a proposal that could have an adverse environmental impact on an area of federal responsibility, to require a public review of the proposal by an environmental assessment panel. The province had in fact applied to the federal Minister of Transport for approval of the dam under the Navigable Waters Protection Act, a federal statute that provides that no work is to be built on navigable waters without the approval of the Minister. The Minister had given his approval after considering the effect of the dam on navigation. He did not subject the project to an environmental assessment under the Guidelines Order. The issue in the proceedings, brought by an environmental group called the Friends of the Oldman River Society, was whether the Guidelines Order was constitutionally valid and effective to enlarge the duties of the Minister of Transport[104] to encompass an environmental assessment of a project that was mainly within provincial jurisdiction.[105]

---

95 Chapter 28, Public Property, above.

96 Chapter 22, Transportation and Communication, above.

97 *Ibid.*

98 Section 29.2(g), ''Uranium'', above.

99 Chapter 24, Financial Institutions, above.

100 See next chapter, Taxation, below.

101 Chapter 17, Peace, Order, and Good Government, above.

102 *R.* v. *Crown Zellerback* [1988] 1 S.C.R. 399; discussed in ch. 17 under heading 17.3 ''The 'national concern' branch'', above. The national concern branch seems to be the basis for the Canada Water Act, R.S.C. 1985, c. C-11; note especially the preamble.

103 [1992] 1 S.C.R. . La Forest J. wrote the opinion of the majority, which on the constitutional issues was agreed to by the Court; Stevenson J. dissented on another issue.

104 The federal Minister of Fisheries and Oceans was also asked by the Friends of the Oldman River Society to order an environmental assessment of the project on account of the impact on

The Supreme Court of Canada held that the Guidelines Order was valid, and that it did impose on the Minister of Transport the duty to require an environmental assessment of the project. The federal Parliament had the power to provide for an environmental assessment as an incident of any institution or activity that was otherwise within federal jurisdiction. However, "the scope of assessment is not confined to the particular head of power under which the Government of Canada has a decision-making responsibility".[106] That responsibility was "a necessary condition to engage the process", but it was open to Parliament to require a review that extended to "the environmental effect on all areas of federal jurisdiction".[107] In this case, the effect of the Guidelines Order was to require the Minister of Transport, in his capacity as a decision-maker under the Navigable Waters Protection Act, "to consider the environmental impact of the dam on such areas of federal responsibility as navigable waters, fisheries, Indians and Indian lands, to name those most obviously relevant in the circumstances here".[108]

What, then, was the head of federal power under which the Department of the Environment Act, and its creature, the Guidelines Order, were enacted? La Forest J.'s answer to this question was prefaced by the proposition that Parliament has the power to enact legislation "under several heads of power at the same time".[109] The power to provide for environmental impact assessment came from all "the relevant subject matters enumerated in s. 91 of the Constitution Act, 1867".[110] That was the authority for "the substance" of the Guidelines Order. As for the "procedural or organizational element that coordinates the process of assessment", that "may be viewed either as an adjunct of the particular legislative powers involved" or as an exercise of "the residuary power in s. 91".[111] Therefore, the Guidelines Order was within the power of the federal Parliament.

The effect of the *Oldman River* decision is to confer on the federal Parliament the power to provide for environmental impact assessment of any project that has any effect on any matter within federal jurisdiction. The dam on the Oldman River had an effect on navigable waters, fisheries and lands reserved for the Indians (there was an Indian reserve downstream from the dam site). These effects justified a wide-ranging environmental assessment encompassing the impact of

---

the fishery, but he refused. The proceedings were also brought against him, but the Supreme Court of Canada confined its reasons to the obligation of the Minister of Transport.

105 If the project were within federal jurisdiction, for example, an airport, then all aspects of environmental assessment would be within federal jurisdiction, because the province would lack the authority to halt the project.

106 [1992] 1 S.C.R. , p. 50.

107 *Id.*, pp. 50-51.

108 *Id.*, p. 50.

109 *Id.*, p. 51.

110 *Ibid.*

111 *Id.*, p. 52, citing *Jones* v. *A.G.N.B.* [1975] 2 S.C.R. 182, 189, where the Court had upheld the federal Official Languages Act under the residuary branch of the peace, order, and good government power. For discussion, see ch. 17, Peace, Order and Good Government, under heading 17.2, "The gap branch", above.

the dam on those three subject matters as well as any other federal matters that turned out to be implicated. The province would also have authority to provide for environmental impact assessment of the project, both under provincial powers over natural resources and property and civil rights, and also by virtue of its power to spend money. In the case of the Oldman River dam, the province had in fact carried out or commissioned studies of the impact of the project on the river basin (salinization, sedimentation, recreation, fish habitat and other matters), the management of water resources, fisheries, wildlife, historical resources, agriculture, irrigation, recreation, the effect on the Indian reserve and transportation systems.[112] Indeed, the province had gone forward on the basis that all legal hurdles had been surmounted, and by the time the Supreme Court of Canada rendered its decision the dam was substantially built. The ruling of the Court rendered the project illegal (by nullifying the approval of the Minister of Transport).[113] The case for environmental impact assessment by a single, jointly-established, federal-provincial agency, with comprehensive powers delegated by both levels of government could not be clearer.

(c) Provincial power

At the provincial level, the most obvious sources of power are the following. The power over property and civil rights (s. 92(13)) authorizes the regulation of land use and most aspects of mining, manufacturing and other business activity, including the regulation of emissions that could pollute the environment.[114] This power, and the power over municipal institutions (s. 92(8)), also authorizes municipal regulation of local activity that affects the environment, for example, zoning, construction, purification of water, sewage, garbage disposal and noise.[115] The provinces can also control activities on provincial public lands (s. 92(5)), which contain much mining and lumbering.[116] The provinces also possess the power to tax (s. 92(2)), and can use it to tax the consumption of products that cause pollution, such as gasoline, and to exempt products that reduce pollution, such as insulation.[117]

---

112 *Id.*, pp. 13-16, relating the facts.

113 The required federal assessment was in fact subsequently done, and was unfavourable, recommending that the completed dam be "decommissioned" by opening tunnels that would allow a normal flow of the river water. The federal Minister of Transport immediately announced that this recommendation was rejected: Government of Canada news release, May 21, 1992; and the project was approved, despite the assessment.

114 See ch. 20, Property and Civil Rights, above. In *R.* v. *Lake Ontario Cement* [1973] 2 O.R. 247 (H.C.), a provincial law prohibiting the emission of contaminants was upheld.

115 *R.* v. *Young* (1973) 1 O.R. (2d) 564 (C.A.) (anti-noise by-law upheld).

116 Chapter 28, Public Property, above.

117 See next chapter, Taxation, below.

30

Taxation

30.1 Distribution of powers

(a) The primary powers

The distribution of powers over taxation[1] has already been briefly described, and their co-operative exercise has been considered in chapter 6, Financial Arrangements. The federal Parliament, under s. 91(3) of the Constitution Act, 1867, has the power to make laws in relation to "the raising of money by any mode or system of taxation". This power[2] extends to any kind of taxation, whether direct or indirect.[3]

The provincial Legislatures, under s. 92(2) of the Constitution Act, 1867, have the power to make laws in relation to "direct taxation within the province in order to the raising of a revenue for provincial purposes". This power limits the provinces to "direct" taxation, to taxation "within the province" and to taxation "for provincial purposes". These three limitations, which apply only to provincial power, will be examined later in this chapter. The Constitution Act, 1982 conferred another taxing power on the provincial Legislatures: a power to employ "any mode or system of taxation" in respect of natural resources in the province. This new power, which extends to indirect as well as direct taxation of resources, will also be examined later in this chapter.

Needless to say, both the federal and provincial taxing powers are subject to the ordinary principles of classification[4] and colourability[5] that apply to all legislative powers. The pith and substance of a law that imposes a charge or a levy may be held to be some matter other than taxation, for example, insurance,[6] unemployment insurance,[7] banking,[8] export trade,[9] labour standards[10] or market-

---

1 See Kennedy and Wells, *The Law of the Taxing Power in Canada* (1931); Laskin, *Canadian Constitutional Law* (5th ed., 1986 by Finkelstein), ch. 13; Magnet, "The Constitutional Distribution of Taxation Powers in Canada" (1978) 10 Ottawa L. Rev. 473; La Forest, *The Allocation of Taxing Power under the Canadian Constitution* (2nd ed., 1981) 1p. and Mintz, *Dividing the Spoils: the Federal-Provincial Allocation of Taxing Powers* (1992).

2 Note the doubt whether the taxing power may be delegated as freely as other legislative powers: see ch. 14, Delegation, under heading 14.2(a), "Delegation of legislative power", above.

3 La Forest, note 1, above.

4 For example, the collection measures authorized by federal taxing legislation have been upheld as validly incidental to the raising of revenue, despite their effect on property and civil rights: *Re GST* [1992] 2 S.C.R. 445; *TransGas* v. *Mid-Plains Contractors* [1994] 3 S.C.R. 753.

5 In *Re Anti-Inflation Act* [1976] 2 S.C.R. 373, 390, Laskin C.J. said: "The Parliament of Canada is authorized to raise money 'by any mode or system of taxation' and it would be an unusual case where this power, so apparently limitless, could be challenged as colourably used and thus make it appropriate for the Court to consider extrinsic material to show colourability". However, the colourability doctrine has been used to strike down a federal tax, which was classified as a disguised attempt to regulate insurance: see next note.

6 *Re Insurance Act of Can.* [1932] A.C. 41.

7 *A.-G. Can.* v. *A.-G. Ont.* (Unemployment Insurance) [1937] A.C. 355.

8 *A.-G. Alta.* v. *A.-G. Can.* (Bank Taxation) [1939] A.C. 117.

9 *Texada Mines* v. *A.-G. B.C.* [1960] S.C.R. 713.

10 *Commn. du Salaire Minimum* v. *Bell Telephone Co.* [1966] S.C.R. 767.

ing.[11] In such cases, the validity of the law turns on whether the enacting legislative body had legislative authority over the true matter of the law. The enacting body's taxing power is irrelevant.[12]

(b) For provincial purposes

We have noticed that the provincial power of taxation in s. 92(2) is subject to three limitations: (1) the tax must be "direct"; (2) the tax must be "within the province"; and (3) the tax must be "for provincial purposes". The first two limitations are of great importance, and are examined at length later in this chapter. The third — that the tax be "in order to the raising of a revenue for provincial purposes" — has turned out to be unimportant. It will be described now so that it can be put aside.

In *Dow* v. *Black* (1875),[13] the Privy Council held that a province could levy a tax to finance the building of an interprovincial railway, although such an undertaking would be outside the legislative power of the province. It was no doubt this case and others like it that led Duff C.J. to assert that the phrase "for provincial purposes" meant only that "the taxing power is given to them [the provinces] for the exclusive disposition of the Legislature".[14] This dictum, although uttered in dissent, is now the established position. In other words, the phrase "for provincial purposes" imports no limits on the purposes for which a province may raise taxes.[15] This is consistent with the rule that the spending power of the provinces is comparable to that of a natural person, extending to purposes that are outside the legislative authority of the provinces.[16]

Nor does the phrase "for provincial purposes" in s. 92(2) constitute an implied restriction on the federal taxing power of s. 91(3). In *Winterhaven Stables* v. *Canada* (1988),[17] it was argued that the federal Income Tax Act was invalid on the ground that the income tax was used for the raising of a revenue for provincial purposes. In support of the argument, it was pointed out that the revenues raised by the income tax contributed to the grants that were made to the provinces out of the Consolidated Revenue fund to subsidize provincial programmes of post-secondary education, health care and welfare. The Alberta Court of Appeal rejected the argument, holding that it was not an objection to a federal taxing statute that some part of the revenue would ultimately be used for provincial purposes. This decision confirmed that there are no limits on the purposes for

---

11 *Re Agricultural Products Marketing Act* [1978] 2 S.C.R. 1198.

12 See also sec. 30.10, "Taxes and charges", below.

13 (1875) L.R. 6 P.C. 272.

14 *Re Employment and Social Insurance Act* [1936] S.C.R. 427, 434, per Duff C.J. dissenting. On appeal, the Privy Council did not address the point: [1937] A.C. 355.

15 *Air Can.* v. *B.C.* [1989] 1 S.C.R. 1161, 1189; Laskin, note 1, above, 838-839; La Forest, note 1, above, 75-76.

16 Section 6.8, "Spending power", above.

17 (1988) 53 D.L.R. (4th) 413 (Alta. C.A.).

which the federal Parliament may raise taxes.[18] The decision also confirmed the corollary proposition that the spending power of the Dominion (like that of the provinces) is comparable to that of a natural person, extending to purposes that are outside the legislative authority of the federal Parliament.[19]

(c) The provincial licensing power

The provinces also have power, under s. 92(9), to make laws in relation to ''shop, saloon, tavern, auctioneer, and other licences in order to the raising of a revenue for provincial, local, or municipal purposes''. Note that this power is explicitly limited to ''the raising of a revenue''. It is a taxing power, not a regulatory power.[20] The provinces can, of course, regulate occupations or activities by licensing, but only under other powers, such as those in respect of natural resources (s. 92A(1)), municipal institutions in the province (s. 92(8)), local works and undertakings (s. 92(10)), property and civil rights in the province (s. 92(13)) or matters of a merely local or private nature in the province (s. 92(16)).[21]

Section 92(9) is not explicitly limited to the raising of a revenue by direct means, which invites the question: to what extent, if at all, does s. 92(9) enlarge s. 92(2) by authorizing indirect taxation in the form of licence fees? There have been considerable, but inconclusive, judicial dicta on this point. La Forest's careful study of the cases leads him to the conclusion that s. 92(9) authorizes indirect licence fees only if they are directed to defraying the expense of an otherwise valid regulatory scheme.[22] It may be objected that the provinces have this power anyway, as an incident to the regulatory scheme,[23] and so this interpretation leaves s. 92(9) with no independent force of its own. But it does seem to be the better view, because of ''the overriding implication of sections 91 and 92 that the power to levy indirect taxation should be reserved to Parliament''.[24]

---

18 La Forest, note 1, above, 52. Contra, Laskin, note 1, above, 788. The question whether Parliament may impose indirect taxation for provincial purposes was raised and left open in *Caron* v. *The King* [1924] A.C. 999, 1004 and in *Re Agricultural Products Marketing Act* [1978] 2 S.C.R. 1198, 1233. But the *Winterhaven* decision, previous note, although dealing with direct taxation, would also apply to indirect taxation, suggesting an affirmative answer.

19 Section 6.8, ''Spending power'', above.

20 La Forest, note 1, above, 162-165.

21 E.g., *Hodge* v. *The Queen* (1884) 9 App. Cas. 117.

22 La Forest, note 1, above, 155-165. Magnet (1978) 10 Ottawa L. Rev. 473, 522-527 reaches a similar conclusion, except that he considers that indirect licence fees are not necessarily limited to expenses.

23 Section 30.10, ''Taxes and charges'', below.

24 La Forest, note 1, above, 164. Section 92(9) authorizes indirect levies provided they are limited to defraying the expenses of a valid regulatory scheme: *Allard Contractors* v. *Coquitlam* [1993] 4 S.C.R. 371, 404; *Ont. Home Builders' Assn.* v. *York Region Bd. of Ed.* [1996] 2 S.C.R. 929, paras. 53, 114.

(d) Limitations on the powers

There are two provisions of the Constitution Act, 1867 which impose restraints on both federal and provincial taxes. Section 121 provides that:

> All articles of the growth, produce, or manufacture of any one of the provinces shall, from and after the union, be admitted free into each of the other provinces.

The purpose of s. 121, supplemented by a common external tariff and common citizenship, was to make Canada a common market. Section 121 certainly precludes customs duties between the provinces.[25] The question whether it goes further and precludes non-fiscal impediments to interprovincial trade has not been definitely decided.[26]

The other express restraint on the taxing powers is s. 125, which provides that:

> No lands or property belonging to Canada or any province shall be liable to taxation.

The purpose of this provision is to exempt each level of government from land or property taxes levied by other levels of government. This provision is considered later in this chapter.[27]

(e) Paramountcy

Federal and provincial powers overlap in the field of direct taxation, which includes the two most lucrative taxes, namely, income taxes and retail sales taxes. Therefore, both levels of government do in fact exploit the same tax bases. For example, the resident of Canada pays an income tax to both the federal government and his or her provincial government; and the taxes are calculated on the same income or, in the case of Quebec, virtually the same income. There is no constitutional objection to this ''double taxation''; nor does it attract the application of the paramountcy doctrine. As Lord Macmillan put it, in a case upholding a Manitoba income tax: ''Both income taxes may be enforced without clashing. The Dominion reaps part of the field of the Manitoba citizen's income. The Province reaps another part of it''.[28] As explained earlier,[29] the Dominion and the provinces have entered into agreements for the ''sharing'' of common tax fields, and for the definition and collection of the taxes, so that double taxation is in practice not much more oppressive or complex than is any system of modern taxation.

---

25 But see *Atlantic Smoke Shops* v. *Conlon* [1943] A.C. 550; note 44, below.

26 See ch. 43, Mobility, under heading 43.2(b), ''Section 121 of the Constitution Act, 1867,'' below.

27 Section 30.13, ''Section 125'', below.

28 *Forbes* v. *A.-G. Man.* [1937] A.C. 260, 274; see generally ch. 16, Paramountcy, above.

29 Chapter 6, Financial Arrangements, above.

30.2 The meaning of direct taxation

(a) Mill's definition

It will be recalled that s. 92(2) of the Constitution Act, 1867 confines the provinces to "direct" taxes.[30] John Stuart Mill, writing in 1848, defined direct and indirect taxes in these terms:[31]

> A direct tax is one which is demanded from the very person who it is intended or desired should pay it. Indirect taxes are those which are demanded from one person in the expectation and intention that he shall indemnify himself at the expense of another.

The courts have accepted this language as the authoritative explanation of the words "direct taxation" in s. 92(2).[32] Although economists would no longer accept the validity of Mill's distinction, the Constitution requires a distinction of some kind to be drawn, and Mill's definition has served as a reasonably justiciable formula. In fact most kinds of taxation can now be confidently assigned to one class or the other, and the room for controversy is accordingly quite limited.[33]

The distinction between a direct and indirect tax has been held to lie in "the general tendencies of the tax and the common understandings of men as to those tendencies".[34] If the general tendency is for the tax to be paid by the very person taxed, then the tax is direct; if the general tendency is for the tax to be paid by someone else, then the tax is indirect. The courts have said that they are not concerned with whether the tax is in fact recouped by the taxpayer in a particular case.[35] In fact, of course, whenever a tax is levied upon a person in business he

30 In Australia, where the states are not confined to direct taxation, they are precluded from levying "duties of customs and of excise" (Constitution, s. 90) and a broad judicial definition of excise has in fact withdrawn from the states most kinds of indirect taxation. In the United States, there is a limitation on federal taxing power in that "direct" taxes must be apportioned among the states in proportion to population (Constitution, art. 1, s. 2(3); art. 1, s. 9(4); not applicable to income tax: 16th amdmt.); but there is no comparable limitation on state taxing power, although implications from the federal commerce clause (Constitution art. 1, s. 8(3)) and the due process clause (14th amdmt.), together with the prohibition on "imposts or duties on imports or exports" (Constitution, art. 1, s. 10(2)), preclude some forms of indirect taxation.

31 *Principles of Political Economy* (1848), Book V, ch. 3.

32 *Bank of Toronto* v. *Lambe* (1887) 12 App. Cas. 575 is the leading case, but Mill's definition is relied upon in nearly all the cases.

33 In *Ont. Home Builders' Assn.* v. *York Region Bd. of Ed.* [1996] 2 S.C.R. 929, paras. 126-146, La Forest J., concurring in the result, held that where a tax falls within an established "direct" category (in that case, land taxes), then it is no longer correct to apply the Mill passing-on test; any variant of the established category is direct regardless of its tendency to be passed on. Iacobucci J. for the majority rejected this view, holding that a tendency to be passed on made even a tax on land indirect.

34 *Id.*, 582.

35 *Id.*, 581; *Brewers' and Maltsters' Assn. of Ont.* v. *A.-G. Ont.* [1897] A.C. 231; *A.-G. B.C.* v. *Kingcome Navigation Co.* [1934] A.C. 45; *Cairns Construction* v. *Govt. of Sask.* [1960] S.C.R. 619.

will seek to recoup the tax as part of the price of the goods or services which he produces. Indeed, he has to do so if he is to make a profit and stay in business. If this recoupment were given constitutional significance, most taxes would be indirect and the tax bases available to the provinces would be seriously inadequate to supply provincial revenue. What the courts have done is to distinguish between, on the one hand, a tax which is likely to be recouped only because, like other expenses, it is a cost of doing business, and, on the other hand, a tax which is likely to be ''passed on'' as an element of the very good or service or transaction which is taxed.

The most useful description of the passing-on characteristic that will make a tax indirect[36] is a dictum of Rand J.'s, as follows:[37]

> If the tax is related or relatable, directly or indirectly, to a unit of the commodity or its price, imposed when the commodity is in course of being manufactured or marketed, then the tax tends to cling as a burden to the unit or the transaction presented to the market.

Take, for example, a tax on the removal of gravel from a quarry. In a case where such a tax was levied on a volumetric basis (26 cents per cubic metres of gravel was the rate of one such tax), the tax was held to be indirect,[38] because the tax would tend to cling to the gravel as part of the resale price when the gravel was sold by the quarry company. The purchaser of the gravel was likely to end up bearing the burden of the tax, because the purchaser was likely to have to pay 26 cents more per cubic metre for the gravel than the price that would have been acceptable to the quarry company had there been no tax. If, on the other hand, the tax on the removal of the gravel had been levied on a flat basis (unrelated to the volume of gravel removed), the tax would have been direct,[39] because it could not be related to each unit of the gravel. A flat tax would form part of the quarry company's expenses of doing business, and, like all such expenses, would if possible be reflected in the quarry company's prices; but that recovery of the tax would not make the tax indirect.

If a tax is related to a unit of a good, the tax will still be direct if it is impossible for the payer of the tax to pass it on to anyone else. That is why Rand J.'s above-quoted test stipulates that an indirect tax is ''imposed when the com-

---

36 In *Re Que. Sales Tax* [1994] 2 S.C.R. 715, 726, Gonthier J. for the Court suggested that ''transparency'' (''everyone know[ing] how much tax they really pay'') was also a characteristic of a direct tax. This does not find support in Mill's definition. Query whether it is correct. If a value-added tax or other form of retail sales tax were embedded in the retail price instead of being charged separately by the retailer, surely this would not convert a direct tax into an indirect one.

37 *C.P.R.* v. *A.-G. Sask.* [1952] 2 S.C.R. 231, 251-252.

38 *Allard Contractors* v. *Coquitlam* [1993] 4 S.C.R. 371, 398 (the impost, although indirect, was upheld as a regulatory charge); folld. in *Ont. Home Builders' Assn.* v. *York Region Bd. of Ed.* [1996] 2 S.C.R. 929 (education development charge imposed on land under development held to be indirect, but upheld as a regulatory charge).

39 *Id.*, 394.

modity is in course of being manufactured or marketed''; in that case, the manufacturer or wholesaler will normally be able to pass on the tax when the good is resold. But if the tax is imposed on the consumer (the last purchaser) of the good, who is not going to resell the good, then the payer of the tax has no way of shifting the burden to anyone else, and the tax is direct. This is the rationale under which the provinces have been able to levy a retail sales tax; it is discussed later in the chapter.[40] A similar rationale supports the directness of a value-added tax imposed on the purchaser of goods or services. Although a value-added tax is imposed at each stage of production and marketing, the tax is reimbursed to each payer in the chain of distribution except for the final purchaser for consumption. Only the final purchaser is not reimbursed; and of course the final purchaser is the only payer who cannot pass the tax on to anyone else. The value-added tax is therefore direct.[41]

(b) Rationale

Why does s. 92(2) limit the provinces to direct taxation? The answer is that the limitation is a corollary to the general principle, discussed later in this chapter, that provincial taxing powers (like other provincial legislative powers) are confined to the territory of the province. The leading feature of an indirect tax is, as we have noticed, that it is likely to be passed on by the initial taxpayer through the incorporation of the tax into the price of goods or services provided by the initial taxpayer. What this means is that a tax that is initially levied on a taxpayer within the province could ultimately be borne by a consumer outside the province. If that occurred, the province would be taxing a person to whom it provided no governmental benefits and to whom it was not accountable. This result is avoided if the province is restricted to direct taxation, where the initial taxpayer within the province is also the person who ultimately bears the tax.

As noticed earlier, even a direct tax will be circuitously recouped if it forms part of the overhead of a business. But it is obviously neither possible nor desirable to exclude from the provincial taxing power all taxes that are in fact recouped by the initial taxpayer. The test of directness is a justiciable means of excluding from provincial power at least those taxes that are most likely to be passed on, and thereby confining provincial power to those taxes the burden of which is most likely to remain within the province.

30.3 Customs and excise duties

A customs duty is a tax on the import of goods. An excise duty is a tax on the manufacture or distribution of goods. These two taxes have been described

40 Section 30.7, ''Sales taxes'', below.
41 *Ibid.*

as the "classical examples of indirect taxation".[42] A customs or excise duty is payable by the importer or manufacturer or distributor, but he will pass it on as part of the price which he charges for the imported or manufactured or distributed goods.[43] Customs and excise duties are therefore competent only to the federal Parliament.[44]

An export tax is a tax on the export of goods. It is analogous to a customs duty, and is sometimes called a customs duty. An export tax is also an indirect tax.[45]

A sales tax, which is discussed more fully later on,[46] is, if imposed on the seller, analogous to an excise tax, and is sometimes called an excise tax. It is also an indirect tax. Other excise-type taxes that have been held to be indirect taxes are: a tax on insurers computed as a percentage of each premium,[47] a tax on building contractors computed as a percentage of each contract price,[48] a tax on the seller of grain futures computed as a percentage of each contract.[49] A tax on the gross revenue of a coal mine has also been held indirect, on the basis that gross revenue is the sum of all of the taxpayer's sales of coal, and is no different from a tax on each sale.[50]

30.4 Income taxes

An income tax is normally a tax on net income, that is, income after deduction of the expenses incurred in gaining the income. A tax on net income is direct.[51] Indeed, "an income tax is the most typical form of direct taxation".[52] This is so,

42 *Atlantic Smoke Shops* v. *Conlon* [1943] A.C. 550, 568.

43 Customs and excise were expressly transferred from the provinces to the Dominion by s. 122 of the Constitution Act, 1867, but s. 122 is now spent and the present power derives from s. 91(3): La Forest, note 1, above, 94-96; Laskin, note 1, above, 782. It has been suggested that customs duties also come within s. 91(2) (trade and commerce): *A.-G. B.C.* v. *A.-G. Can.* (Johnnie Walker) [1924] A.C. 222; and certainly there is a close connection between regulating and taxing the importation of goods.

44 However, notwithstanding this rule, and s. 121 of the Constitution Act, 1867, provincial retail sales taxes may be levied on goods brought into the province along with goods purchased in the province: *Atlantic Smoke Shops* v. *Conlon* [1943] A.C. 550; *Re Marine Petrobulk* (1985) 18 D.L.R. (4th) 451 (B.C.C.A.); see also Beck, Comment (1964) 42 Can. Bar Rev. 490.

45 *A.-G. B.C.* v. *McDonald Murphy Lumber Co.* [1930] A.C. 357; *Can. Industrial Gas and Oil* v. *Govt. of Sask.* [1978] 2 S.C.R. 545.

46 Section 30.7, "Sales taxes", below.

47 *A.-G. Que.* v. *Queen Ins. Co.* (1878) 3 App. Cas. 1090.

48 *Charlottetown* v. *Foundation Maritime* [1932] S.C.R. 589.

49 *A.-G. Man.* v. *A.-G. Can.* (Grain Futures) [1925] A.C. 561.

50 *The King* v. *Caledonian Collieries* [1928] A.C. 358.

51 *Nickel Rim Mines* v. *A.-G. Ont.* [1966] 1 O.R. 345 (C.A.); affd. [1967] S.C.R. 270; La Forest, note 1, above, 101-103.

52 *Forbes* v. *A.-G. Man.* [1937] A.C. 260, 268; and see *Abbott* v. *St. John* (1908) 40 S.C.R. 597; *Caron* v. *The Queen* [1924] A.C. 999; *Kerr* v. *Supt. of Income Tax* [1942] S.C.R. 435.

even if the tax is only on a particular type of income, for example, income from mining.[53]

A tax on gross income would also be direct if the tax could not be passed on to another. For example, a tax on income from employment would be direct, whether the base was defined as gross or net income. The recipient of employment income has no obvious way of passing on the burden of the tax. However, as noted earlier, a tax on the gross revenue from the sale of goods or services is so similar to a tax on each sale that it will tend to cling to the product; it is therefore classified as indirect.[54]

30.5 Business taxes

Business taxes taking the form of a flat fee,[55] or a fee that varies with amount of capital and number of places of business[56] (or any factor other than volume of transactions)[57] have been held to be direct; these taxes are no doubt recouped from the customers of the business, but they are not different in this respect from other costs of production.[58]

30.6 Property taxes

Taxes on land or other fixed assets[59] are direct. Municipal real property taxes fall into this category. Such taxes are of course levied not only on owner-occupiers but also on landlords, and landlords will seek recoupment from their tenants; but this recoupment does not make the tax indirect, being regarded as an overhead expense like the cost of repairs or heating.[60] Even a tax on the stock-in-trade of a business has been held to be direct.[61]

In *Ontario Home Builders' Association* v. *York Region Board of Education* (1996),[62] the taxes in issue were "education development charges", which were imposed under statutory authority by school boards in Ontario. The charges were

---

53 *Nfld. & Labrador Corp.* v. *A.-G. Nfld.* [1982] 2 S.C.R. 260.

54 Note 50, above.

55 *Brewers' and Maltsters' Assn.* v. *A.-G. Ont.* [1897] A.C. 231.

56 *Bank of Toronto* v. *Lambe* (1887) 12 App. Cas. 575.

57 La Forest, note 1, above, 103-104.

58 Text accompanying note 34, above.

59 *A.-G. B.C.* v. *E. & N. Ry.* [1950] A.C. 87; *CPR* v. *A.-G. Sask.* [1952] 2 S.C.R. 231; La Forest, note 1, above, 104-106.

60 *Candow* v. *City of Corner Brook* (1983) 147 D.L.R. (3d) 165 (Nfld. C.A.).

61 *Fortier* v. *Lambe* (1894) 25 S.C.R. 422; *Colpitts Ranches* v. *A.-G. Alta.* [1954] 3 D.L.R. 121 (Alta. S.C.).

62 [1996] 2 S.C.R. 929. The Court was unanimous. Iacobucci J. wrote the majority opinion, which was agreed with by Lamer C.J., Sopinka, Cory and Major JJ. La Forest J. wrote a concurring opinion, which was agreed with by L'Heureux-Dubé, Gonthier and McLachlin JJ.

levied on land undergoing development for residential housing, and were paid on each residential unit on the issue of a building permit. Iacobucci J., for the majority of the Supreme Court of Canada, acknowledged that the charges were ''land taxes'', a category of tax that in the past had been held to be direct. In this case, however, he held that the charges were indirect, because there would be a tendency for the charges to be passed on by the developer to the ultimate purchasers of the new houses. Therefore, the charges were indirect taxes, and were incompetent to the province under the main taxing power of s. 92(2). However, Iacobucci J. upheld the charges on the basis that they were regulatory charges that had been levied for the purpose of defraying the cost of the new school construction that would be entailed by new housing developments.[63] La Forest J. wrote a concurring opinion in which he upheld the charges under the province's main taxing power of s. 92(2). In his view, the education development charges were land taxes and not regulatory charges. The prior cases established that the category of land taxes was a direct category, regardless of the incidence of any particular variant of the tax. In the case of an established direct category, it was not correct to revisit the issue of directness by reference to Mill's passing-on definition. He agreed that the charges were probably indirect on the basis of the passing-on definition,[64] but that was not a relevant question in the case of an established direct category.

30.7 Sales taxes

A sales tax, if imposed upon the seller, is analogous to an excise tax, and it is obvious that the tax will usually tend to enter into the price charged to the purchaser. Such a tax is indirect.[65] If a sales tax is imposed upon the purchaser, the indirect character of the tax is less obvious, although there is an analogy with a customs duty;. In *A.-G. B.C. v. CPR* (1927),[66] the Privy Council held that a provincial tax on the purchaser of fuel oil (one-half cent on each gallon purchased) was indirect. Fuel oil was a marketable commodity; it could be resold by the initial purchaser, and on resale the tax would enter into the price charged. It was established that the Canadian Pacific Railway, the taxpayer, consumed the oil and did not resell it, but their lordships refused to be distracted by what they described as ''the special circumstances of individual cases''; because it was ''practicable'' to pass the tax along, the tax should be classified as indirect and therefore unconstitutional.

After the *Canadian Pacific* case, British Columbia amended its legislation so that the tax on fuel oil (at the same rate as before) was levied on the consumer

63 The regulatory-charge issue in the case is discussed in section 30.10(b), ''Regulatory charges'', below.

64 Note 62, above, para. 146.

65 Section 30.3, ''Customs and excise duties'', above.

66 [1927] A.C. 934. Followed in *Air Can. v. B.C.* [1989] 1 S.C.R. 1191 (similar statute).

instead of the purchaser. In *A.-G. B.C. v. Kingcombe Navigation Co.* (1933),[67] the Privy Council upheld the tax as direct. The distinction between this tax and the old one was that a consumer, unlike a purchaser, cannot resell, and therefore cannot pass along the tax. Of course, commercial users of fuel oil would no doubt recoup the tax as part of the price of their service or product, but their lordships held that because the tax did not fasten onto any transaction with the oil any such subsequent recoupment did not make the tax direct.[68]

In *Kingscombe*, the tax had been levied in accordance with the amount of oil consumed. This emphasized that the tax was levied on consumption, but it made the tax a difficult one to collect. In *Atlantic Smoke Shops* v. *Conlon* (1943),[69] the Privy Council upheld a provincial tax which was levied at the point of retail sale. New Brunswick's tobacco tax was to be paid at the rate of ten per cent of the retail price by any person who purchased for his own consumption, or for the consumption of others at his expense. The tax was also payable by a person who purchased as agent for another, although the agent would obviously be reimbursed by his principal. The problem of collection was solved by the ingenious device of requiring all sellers of tobacco to collect the tax as agents of the provincial government. Indeed, the constitutional challenge was made by a smoke shop which was prosecuted for failing to fulfil its role as provincial tax-collector. The Privy Council held that the tax was direct. Because it was to be paid by the consumer, there was ''no question of further re-sale'', and the tax could not be ''passed on to any other person by subsequent dealing''.[70]

These decisions opened up to the provinces the field of retail sales taxes.[71] All provinces except Alberta have availed themselves of the opportunity to levy a low-rate (but high-yield) general retail sales tax. While rates and exemptions vary, the taxes cover most kinds of ''tangible personal property'' which are purchased at retail sale in the province. They follow the *Conlon* model in applying to purchases for consumption, in providing for the licensing of all retailers, and in constituting each retailer as agent of the province to collect the tax.[72] There is no doubt that these taxes are constitutional.

The competence of the federal Parliament under s. 91(3) to levy a sales tax — whether direct or indirect — is not in doubt: a sales tax is a ''mode of system

67 [1934] A.C. 45. Followed in *Air Can. v. B.C.* [1989] 1 S.C.R. 1191 (similar statute).
68 See also *Cairns Construction v. Sask.* [1960] S.C.R. 619, upholding a retail sales tax in respect of building materials, which were not to be resold as such, but which were to be incorporated by the purchaser into houses build for sale.
69 [1943] A.C. 550.
70 Id., 563.
71 Cf. *Dickenson's Arcade* v. *Tasmania* (1974) 130 C.L.R. 177 (H.C. Aust.), holding that a consumption tax is not a duty of excise and is therefore competent to the states: see note 30, above.
72 Even a tax collected by the wholesaler from the retailer and remitted to the Crown in advance of the retail sale (when the tax was actually imposed) as been held to be direct: *Chehalis Indian Band* v. *B.C.* (1988) 53 D.L.R. (4th) 761 (B.C.C.A.).

of taxation''. However, in *Re GST* (1992),[73] the government of Alberta brought proceedings to challenge the power of the federal Parliament to levy the Goods and Service Tax, which had been introduced in 1991.[74] The Goods and Service Tax is a value-added tax, which is a type of sales tax, but one that is levied on the value added to a good or service at each stage of production and distribution. Each payer of the tax is reimbursed by the government (through the mechanism of an ''input tax credit'') for the tax paid at each stage of production and distribution except for the final retail sale. This is a characteristic of all value-added taxes, which are constructed to avoid the ''cascading'' of tax (the levying of tax on tax) as a good or service moves through the chain of production and distribution. The burden of tax is borne only once, at the point of final retail sale, where the payer (who is, under the GST, the purchaser for consumption) has no right to be reimbursed. It was argued against the tax that, since no revenue was retained by government from the imposition of the GST at stages prior to the final sale, the collection provisions of the tax were not really revenue-raising measures, and were an invalid interference with property and civil rights. The Supreme Court of Canada rejected this argument, holding that the multi-stage collection provisions that were characteristic of value-added taxes was ''simply part and parcel of the mode or system of taxation adopted by Parliament''.[75]

In *Re GST*, it did not matter whether the GST was a direct or indirect tax, because it had been imposed by the federal Parliament. When the GST was introduced in 1991, it replaced a federal sales tax that was imposed at the wholesale level, and that was undoubtedly indirect. However, the GST is imposed on the final purchaser for consumption, and is therefore a direct tax that could be adopted by the provinces. It is true that the GST is also imposed at every stage of production and distribution prior to the point of final retail sale, but this feature would not make the tax indirect. As explained above, each payer of the tax, except for the final purchaser, is reimbursed for the tax paid. The persons who are entitled to reimbursement are really tax collectors rather than taxpayers. They will not pass on the cost of the tax, because they do not bear the cost of the tax. The final purchaser at retail (the consumer) is the only person who bears the cost of the tax, and that person cannot pass it on. In effect, the value-added form of taxation is a method of collecting a retail sales tax in instalments, instead of in a single lump

---

73 [1992] 2 S.C.R. 445. Lamer C.J. wrote the majority opinion with the agreement of five others, La Forest J. wrote a separate concurring opinion with the agreement of one other.

74 S.C. 1990, c. 45, amending the Excise Tax Act.

75 [1992] 2 S.C.R. 445, 492. The Court also rejected an argument that the federal government was under a constitutional obligation to compensate all suppliers of taxable goods and services for the costs involved in collecting the tax as agents of the federal government. The Court held that s. 103 of the Constitution Act, 1867, which was claimed to be the source of this obligation, was simply an appropriation provision, providing authority to pay the costs of tax collection, but imposing no obligation to do so.

sum at the point of retail sale. The tax remains a retail sales tax, and, being imposed on the consumer, it is a direct tax.[76]

30.8 Death taxes

Death taxes[77] come in essentially two forms. An "estate tax" is levied on all the property of a deceased person, irrespective of its location and irrespective of who will inherit it. An "inheritance tax" (or succession duty) is levied on the inheritance received by each beneficiary. There are Canadian precedents for both kinds of tax. The federal Parliament levied a succession duty in 1941, and replaced it with an estate tax in 1958; the estate tax was abolished at the end of 1971 when a capital gains tax, effective on death, was introduced. Various provinces have levied succession duties intermittently since 1892; at the time of writing, there has been a general withdrawal from the field, and no province now levies a succession duty.

An estate tax is incompetent to the provinces, because it is indirect. It is indirect because it must of necessity be levied on the executor (or administrator) of the estate, and it is of course contemplated that he will reimburse himself from the assets of the estate and thereby pass the tax on to the beneficiaries. A further constitutional difficulty with an estate tax is that it will ordinarily include property outside the province and exceed the limitation in s. 92(2) to taxation "in the province"; this point is taken up later in this chapter.[78]

An inheritance tax, or succession duty, is competent to the provinces, because it can be levied directly on the beneficiary, in which case it is direct.[79] However, even an inheritance tax has to be carefully framed to avoid the trap of indirectness (as well as extraterritoriality). Early provincial legislation imposed a liability on the executor and was struck down as indirect.[80] In the case of an inheritance tax, this vice can be corrected by exempting the executor from personal liability and imposing the liability exclusively on each beneficiary whose inheritance is taxed.[81] The collection problem can be resolved by placing the executor under a

---

76 *Re Que. Sales Tax* [1994] 2 S.C.R. 715, upholding amendments to Quebec's sales tax to transform it into a value-added tax similar to the federal GST. A small-supplier exemption, relieving persons with revenue of less than $30,000 per annum from the obligation to collect and remit the tax and denying them input tax credits, did create a small element of indirectness, but that was "an incidental element of the efficient administration of the proposed consumption tax" (p. 740); the exemption did not make the general tendency of the tax indirect.

77 La Forest, note 1, above 106-109.

78 Section 30.11, "Territorial limitation", below.

79 *A.-G. B.C.* v. *Can. Trust Co.* [1980] 2 S.C.R. 466, 472.

80 *Cotton* v. *The King* [1914] A.C. 176; *Burland* v. *The King* [1922] 1 A.C. 215; *Prov. Treas. Alta.* v. *Kerr* [1933] A.C. 710.

81 *Alleyn* v. *Barthe* [1992] 1 A.C. 215. The liability in this case attached to the "transmission" to the beneficiary, but in light of the executor's exemption it could only be paid by the beneficiary.

duty to deduct and remit the tax before distributing the estate,[82] and the executor may probably even be penalized an amount equal to or in excess of the full amount of the tax if he or she fails in the duty of collection.[83] This became the general pattern of succession duty legislation. The history bears a close affinity to that of the retail sales tax,[84] and it is perhaps unnecessary to comment that the limitation to direct taxation is in most contexts now one of form rather than substance, a mere requirement of careful drafting.

30.9 Resource taxes

A tax on the production of a natural resource,[85] such as oil or gas, is an excise tax, which naturally tends to be incorporated into the price of the resource when it is sold by the producer.[86] Such a tax is indirect, and before 1982 was incompetent to the provinces.[87]

---

82 This has not been decided, but so long as the provision avoided the charge of colourability it would be valid under s. 92(15) of the Constitution Act, 1867.

83 This has not been decided, but so long as the provision avoided the charge of colourability it would be valid under s. 92(15) of the Constitution Act, 1867.

84 Section 30.7, ''Sales taxes'', above.

85 With respect to natural resources, the provincial power to tax is usually necessary only where the resources are privately owned. Where resources are owned by the province, the province as proprietor may impose royalties or other charges on their exploitation; and these charges will be valid as an exercise of proprietary right, even if they would have been invalid if imposed as taxes. In the *CIGOL* case, next note, the province of Saskatchewan imposed a ''royalty surcharge'' on oil produced from Crown land and a ''mineral income tax'' on oil produced from private land. The idea was that the royalty surcharge would not have to meet the test of directness. However, the oil produced from Crown land was being produced under leases which already provided for a royalty and did not authorize the additional ''royalty surcharge''. Therefore, the additional levy could not be imposed by proprietary right. The royalty surcharge had to satisfy the same test of directness as the mineral income tax. Since 1982, the new s. 92A(4) authorizes indirect provincial resource taxes, and the distinction between Crown royalties and taxation has become much less significant.

86 E.g., *Allard Contractors* v. *Coquitlam* [1993] 4 S.C.R. 371 (impost on extraction of gravel held to be indirect; but upheld as regulatory charge; s. 92A(4) not considered).

87 *Can. Industrial Gas and Oil* v. *Govt. of Sask.* [1978] 2 S.C.R. 545. In that case, ingenious drafting provided a powerful argument that the normal indirect classification did not apply. In 1974, the province of Saskatchewan appropriated to itself the sudden rise in the international price of oil by levying a tax on every barrel of oil produced in Saskatchewan. The tax was the difference between the cost of producing a barrel of oil before the price increase (a figure specified in the taxing legislation) and the actual well-head price received by the producer. This tax could not be recouped by the producer from the purchaser because any increase in the well-head price would simply increase the tax payable by the producer. The price determined the tax, rather than the other way around. The Saskatchewan Court of Appeal accordingly held the tax to be direct and valid. The Supreme Court of Canada reversed, holding by a majority that the tax formed part of the price paid by the purchaser, and that the tax was indirect.

The Constitution Act, 1982 added a new s. 92A to the Constitution Act, 1867.[88] The new s. 92A, which augmented provincial power over natural resources, included as subsection (4) the following taxing power:

> (4) In each province, the legislature may make laws in relation to the raising of money by any mode or system of taxation in respect of
>
> (a) inon-renewable natural resources and forestry resources in the province and the primary production therefrom, and
>
> (b) sites and facilities in the province for the generation of electrical energy and the production therefrom
>
> whether or not such production is exported in whole or in part from the province, but such laws may not authorize or provide for taxation that differentiates between production exported to another part of Canada and production not exported from the province.

This new power authorizes the taxation of non-renewable natural resources, forestry resources and electricity facilities. These resources may be taxed in place, or their primary production may be taxed. The phrase, "any mode or system of taxation", which is the same language as appears in the federal taxing power of s. 91(3), is apt to include indirect as well as direct taxation. A tax on a resource in place would be a direct tax, which before 1982 would in any event have been competent to the provinces under s. 92(2).[89] But a tax on the production of a resource would be an indirect tax, which before 1982 would have been incompetent to the provinces under s. 92(2). Such a tax is now competent to the provinces under s. 92A(4).

The closing language of s. 92A(4) makes clear that a tax on the production of a resource is valid even if the production is exported in whole or in part from the province.[90] If the tax is indirect, and if the resource is mainly exported, the burden of the tax will fall on the out-of-province purchasers, to whom the taxing government is not accountable. Nevertheless, such a tax is authorized by s. 92A(4).

The proviso to the closing language of s. 92A(4) prohibits taxation that discriminates between "production exported to another part of Canada" and "production not exported from the province". This anti-discrimination proviso would not affect a tax that applied uniformly to all production, regardless of whether or not the production was exported. Nor would the proviso affect a tax that applied only to production that was exported to another country (as opposed

---

88 For commentary on s. 92A, see Moull, "Section 92A of the Constitution Act, 1867" (1983) 61 Can. Bar. Rev. 715; Cairns, Chandler and Moull, "The Resource Amendment (Section 92A) and the Political Economy of Canadian Federalism" (1985) 23 Osgoode Hall L.J. 253; Cairns, Chandler and Moull, "Constitutional Change and the Private Sector: The Case of the Resource Amendment" (1987) 24 Osgoode Hall L.J. 299.

89 Section 30.6, "Property taxes", above.

90 In the *CIGOL* case, note 87, above, the Court characterized the tax as an export tax, because, although the tax applied uniformly to all oil produced in the province, 98 per cent of the oil was in fact exported. Section 92A(4) seems to be expressed in terms that would validate such a tax.

''to another part of Canada''). However, although such a tax is not caught by the anti-discrimination proviso, its validity would not be perfectly clear. A law imposing a tax on resources exported from Canada could be classified as a regulatory measure — an attempt to regulate the export of resources[91] — in which case the law would be unconstitutional.[92] If, however, the taxing law were classified as a revenue measure, then it would be valid under s. 92A(4).

30.10 Taxes and charges

(a) Proprietary charges

Not every impost levied by a province has to satisfy the requirement of being ''direct''. If the charge is not ''taxation'' within the meaning of s. 92(2), and is constitutionally justified under some other provincial power, then it is no objection that the charge is indirect. The most obvious category of permissible charges are those levied by a province in the exercise of proprietary rights over its public property.[93] Thus, a province may levy charges in the form of licence fees, rents or royalties as the price for the private exploitation of provincially-owned natural resources; and a province may charge for the sale of books, liquor, electricity, rail travel or other goods or services which it supplies in a commercial way.[94] Some of these charges are undoubtedly indirect,[95] but they are valid nonetheless, because they are not taxes.

(b) Regulatory charges

A second category of charges are those of a more governmental or compulsory character, which require legislation for their imposition.[96] These charges are

---

91 This is a risk even with respect to the universal tax, where the taxed resource is in fact nearly all exported: *Central Can. Potash* v. *Govt. of Sask.* [1979] 1 S.C.R. 42 (universal production and pricing controls on potash held to be a regulation of export trade, because province's entire production exported).

92 Before 1982, the provinces were incompetent to regulate the export of resources: *CIGOL* case, note 87, above; *Central Can. Potash* case, note 91, above. Since 1982, s. 92A(2) has authorized provincial laws in relation to the export of resources ''to another part of Canada'', but not to a foreign country. For discussion, see ch. 21, Property and Civil Rights, under heading 21.9, ''Marketing'', above.

93 Note that once private rights have been created in provincial public property, for example, by the grant of a lease without the reservation of a provincial power of amendment, legislation is then necessary to derogate from the private rights. This is illustrated by the holding with respect to the ''royalty surcharge'' in the *CIGOL* case, note 86, above. This problem is avoided if the Crown lease includes a ''variable royalty clause'': see ch. 29, Natural Resources, under heading 29.1(a), ''Provincial public property'', above.

94 See ch. 28, Public Property, under heading 28.2, ''Executive power over public property'', above.

95 For example, royalties based on production of a resource: note 86, above.

96 The concepts of ''governmental'' or ''compulsory'' charges are intended to be opposed to

not necessarily taxes, and, if they are not, they need not be direct, even if imposed by a province. They are not taxes if they can be supported as regulatory charges imposed under one of the province's regulatory powers, such as natural resources (s. 92A(1)), municipal institutions in the province (s. 92(8)), local works and undertakings (s. 92(10)), property and civil rights in the province (s. 92(13)) or matters of a merely local or private nature in the province (s. 92(16)).[97] Examples of such charges might be licence fees, registration fees, bridge tolls or water rates. These can be supported as regulatory charges if they are taken in payment for a specific governmental service, and if they bear a reasonable relation to the cost of providing the service — whether it be the issue of a licence,[98] the registration of a deed,[99] the provision of a bridge, or the supply of water.[100] These charges are not taxes because their purpose is to defray expenses, not to raise revenue. Even if a charge proves to be too high and produces a surplus of revenue which is available for general governmental purposes, the charge will still not be characterized as a tax so long as the court is satisfied that it is not a colourable attempt to levy an indirect tax.[101] In other words, the Legislature is permitted "reasonable leeway" in fixing its charges for services.[102]

"commercial" or "voluntary". These words are all admittedly very slippery. There is no principled distinction between the governmental and commercial functions of government; and the distinction between a compulsory and voluntary charge is nearly always a question of degree: even income or sales taxes are voluntary in the sense that they can be avoided by not earning income or buying goods.

97 It is probably better not to describe regulatory charges as "taxes" on the basis that they lack the revenue-raising purpose that characterizes a tax. However, it can certainly be argued that they have a revenue-raising purpose, albeit one that is dedicated to defraying the costs of regulation. In *Allard,* note 103, below, Iacobucci J. for the unanimous Court consistently described the gravel-extraction fees as "taxes", but upheld them despite their indirect character on the ground that they were ancillary to a regulatory scheme. In *Ontario Home Builders*, note 107, below, Iacobucci J. for the majority never clearly said whether or not the education development charges were taxes; La Forest J., concurring, was careful to distinguish a regulatory charge from a tax. While outcomes do not seem to vary with the terminology, the question whether s. 92(9) is needed to sustain a regulatory charge may turn on whether the regulatory charges are taxes or not: see note 24, above.

98 *Shannon* v. *Lower Mainland Dairy Products Bd.* [1938] A.C. 708; *Re Farm Products Marketing Act Reference* [1957] S.C.R. 198; *Re Falardeau* (1985) 21 D.L.R. (4th) 477 (Alta. C.A.). The licensing power in s. 92(9) appears to have little or no independent content, and is usually referred to in the cases in conjunction with other provincial powers. It does not by itself authorize the levying of indirect taxes through licence fees; and it does not by itself authorize the regulation of business activity through licence fees: see text at note 20, above.

99 *A.-G. Can.* v. *Registrar of Titles* [1934] 4 D.L.R. 764 (B.C. C.A.).

100 *Min. of Justice (Can.)* v. *Levis* [1919] A.C. 505. This case and the one in the previous note arose under s. 125 of the Constitution Act, 1867 (sec. 30.13, below), but the same principles apply: text at note 116, below.

101 *Re Farm Products Marketing Act* [1957] S.C.R. 198, 260; *A.-G. Can.* v. *Registrar of Titles* [1934] 4 D.L.R. 764, 774 (B.C. C.A.).

102 *Allard Contractors* v. *Coquitlam* [1993] 4 S.C.R. 371, 411-412; La Forest, note 1, above, 65.

In *Allard Contractors* v. *Coquitlam* (1993),[103] the Supreme Court of Canada upheld fees imposed by by-law by several municipalities in British Columbia on the extraction of gravel. The fees were calculated in accordance with the volume of gravel extracted, and they would have been invalid for indirectness if they were taxes.[104] The authority to impose the fees was conferred by the province's Municipal Act, which did not link the fees to the regulation of the roads or their repair, and which did not require that the funds raised by the fees be used for road repair (or any other purpose). The municipal by-laws that imposed the fees also made no reference to the purpose of the fees. In short, the fees appeared to be free-standing taxes, lacking the connection to a regulatory scheme that would be required to sustain the fees as regulatory charges. Surprisingly, the Supreme Court of Canada held that the fees were regulatory charges. According to Iacobucci J. for the Court, a connection to road repair could be inferred from various scattered provisions of the Municipal Act, and from testimony by municipal officials that they had tried to fix the level of the fees by reference to the cost of repairing the roads over which the gravel trucks would operate. (Iacobucci J. acknowledged that other evidence suggested that the fees raised ''considerably more'' than was needed for the repair of the roads, but he dismissed that as irrelevant on the basis of the reasonable leeway rule.)[105] From these premises, the Court concluded that the extraction fees were ancillary to a regulatory scheme for the repair of the roads and were, despite their indirectness, valid regulatory charges.[106]

In *Ontario Home Builders' Association* v. *York Region Board of Education* (1996),[107] the Supreme Court of Canada upheld ''education development charges'', which were levied by school boards (under statutory authority) on land undergoing development. The purpose of the charges was to fund the construction of new schools. The fees were imposed on the issue of building permits, and their amount was based on the estimated cost of the new schools that would be needed as the result of the development of the land. Iacobucci J., for the majority of the Court, held that the charges were indirect and could not be supported under the main provincial taxing power of s. 92(2). However, he upheld the charges on the ground that they were ''ancillary to a valid regulatory scheme for the provision of educational facilities as a component of land use planning, pursuant to ss. 92(9), (13) and (16)''.[108] The statutory policy was to make new development bear the

---

103 [1993] 4 S.C.R. 371. The opinion of the Court was written by Iacobucci J.

104 Note 38, above.

105 Note 102, above.

106 In view of the difficulty in upholding the fees as regulatory charges, it is surprising that the Court did not consider s. 92A(4) (taxation of the primary production of non-renewable natural resources) as an alternative constitutional basis for the fees; but Iacobucci J. said (at p. 413) that, since he had found the fees to be valid as regulatory charges, it was not necessary to consider s. 92A(4).

107 [1996] 2 S.C.R. 929. The Court was unanimous. Iacobucci J. wrote the majority opinion, which was concurred in by Lamer C.J., Sopinka, Cory and Major JJ. La Forest J. wrote a concurring opinion, which was agreed with by L'Heureux-Dubé, Gonthier and McLachlin JJ.

108 *Id.*, para. 50.

costs of the infrastructure necessitated by the development. The connection to the regulatory scheme was ''easier'' to find than it had been in *Allard,* because the authorizing statute and regulations expressly required that the amount of the charges be based on the estimated costs of building new schools, and also required that the proceeds of the charges could only be used for that purpose.[109] These requirements also ensured that the charges did not raise revenue in excess of the funds required for the regulatory purpose; there was ''no question of excessive recovery''.[110] La Forest J. concurred in the result, but disagreed with the majority's reasoning. In La Forest J.'s view, the charges were not ancillary to any regulatory scheme. The link between land development and new schools was not as close as the link between gravel extraction and road maintenance in *Allard.* However, the charges could be upheld under s. 92(2) as direct taxes, because they were taxes on land, and taxes on land were direct taxes.[111]

It is common for farm product marketing schemes to include levies on the farmers (producers of the regulated product), who are the beneficiaries of the schemes. Two kinds of levies may be involved. An ''expenses'' levy is designed to defray the expenses of administering the scheme, which in the more sophisticated schemes will include losses incurred by a marketing agency in selling off surpluses of the regulated product.[112] An ''equalization'' or ''adjustment'' levy is designed to effect a pooling of proceeds, so that returns to producers are equalized even if the product was actually sold in various markets at various prices. Marketing levies, being imposed on production, tend to be passed on to the consumers of the product. If they are taxes, they are therefore indirect. At first, the courts did classify marketing levies as taxes, and accordingly struck down provincial levies on the ground of indirectness. But the Supreme Court of Canada, overruling these decisions, has held that marketing levies are not taxes, because their function is regulatory rather than revenue-producing.[113] Therefore, marketing levies will be upheld if they are part of an otherwise valid marketing scheme.[114]

---

109 *Id.*, para. 54.

110 *Ibid.*

111 The appropriate classification of taxes on land is discussed under heading 30.6, ''Property taxes'', above.

112 The product that is surplus to the higher-priced table market (for home consumption) has to be sold in the lower-priced industrial market (for manufactured food products). In order to equalize returns to producers who have sold their products in one or the other or both markets, a scheme can provide for the equalization or adjustment levies that are discussed next. But, if all selling has been done by a central marketing agency, it can pay the same price to all producers and then levy all producers for losses incurred on sales in the industrial market. In this way, an expenses levy (the expenses being trading losses) serves the function of an equalization or adjustment levy.

113 *Re Agricultural Products Marketing Act* [1978] 2 S.C.R. 1198, 1234-1257, 1291.

114 *Wayvel Farms* v. *Alta. Pork Producers' Marketing Bd.* (1987) 46 D.L.R. (4th) 72 (Alta. C.A.); La Forest, note 1, above, 60-70.

It is perhaps unnecessary to add that charges imposed by a province which cannot be upheld as direct taxation under s. 92(2) must come within some other head of provincial power. Charges of a direct character may of course be supportable under s. 92(2) as well as under a regulatory power. But the validity of a regulatory charge is likely to depend upon the validity of the regulatory scheme to which it is incident.[115] If the scheme is invalid, even a direct charge is unlikely to be severed off and upheld as a valid tax.

The federal Parliament, not being confined to direct taxation, can impose both direct and indirect charges under its taxation power (s. 91(3)), but a federal regulatory charge, like a provincial regulatory charge, may well have to stand or fall under some head of regulatory power. Thus, the distinction between taxes and charges may become relevant to the validity of a federal law.

The distinction between taxes and charges is relevant to both levels of government in another context as well. Section 125 of the Constitution Act, 1867 provides that ''no lands or property belonging to Canada or any province shall be liable to taxation''. Section 125 will exempt a government from taxes levied by other governments on its lands or property, but not from regulatory charges such as water rates or deed registration fees.[116]

30.11 Territorial limitation

(a) General

The federal taxing power, like other federal powers, will authorize laws with extraterritorial effect.[117] But the provincial taxing power, like other provincial powers, is limited to the territory of the province.[118] This limitation is explicit in s. 92(2), which refers to direct taxation ''within the province''.[119]

Taxes are, of course, always paid by persons, and a narrow view of the territorial limitation on provincial taxing power would confine the power to taxes levied on persons in the province. But the courts have taken a more expansive view, holding that taxes may be levied not only upon persons, but also upon property or transactions or benefits. In determining the constitutionality of a provincial tax, the first step is to ask whether the tax is imposed upon persons or property or transactions or benefits. Having thereby ascertained the subject of the tax, the second step is to ask whether the subject of the tax is within the province.

115 *Cf. Commn. du Salaire Minimum* v. *Bell Telephone Co.* [1966] S.C.R. 767.

116 *Min. of Justice (Can.)* v. *Levis* [1919] A.C. 505; *A.-G. Can. v. Registrar of Titles* [1934] 4 D.L.R. 764 (B.C. C.A.); La Forest, note 1, above, 187-189.

117 *B.C. Electric Ry. Co.* v. *The King* [1946] A.C. 527 (federal income tax on non-residents upheld). See generally ch. 13, Extraterritorial Competence, above.

118 Kennedy and Wells, note 1, above, ch. 5; Laskin, note 1, above, 822-838; La Forest, note 1, above, ch. 5. See generally ch. 13, Extraterritorial Competence, above.

119 Section 92(9) (licensing) is not so explicit, but the territorial limitation is implicit. Section 92A(4) (resource taxation) is explicitly confined to resources ''in the province''.

(b) Persons

A provincial tax on persons in the province may obviously be levied on persons domiciled or resident there. But it may also be levied on persons with more tenuous connections with the province. In the leading case of *Bank of Toronto* v. *Lambe* (1887),[120] the Privy Council held that Quebec could levy a tax on a bank which had a branch in Quebec, although the bank had its head office and the bulk of its capital in Ontario. Their lordships held that the province could tax "any person found within the province"; the person need not "be domiciled or even resident in Quebec"; and in this case the fact that the bank was "found to be carrying on business" in the province provided a sufficient territorial connection.[121] This holding places beyond doubt provincial taxes on non-resident individuals or corporations who carry on business in the province or are employed in the province.[122]

Bank of Toronto v. *Lambe* also established a more subtle point. The tax in that case was computed partly on the basis of the amount of the bank's paid-up capital. The bank objected that only a small part of its capital was employed in Quebec, or owned by persons resident in Quebec, and yet the province was basing its tax on the entire sum. But the Privy Council held that so long as the tax was levied on a person in Quebec the amount of the tax could be computed by reference to extraprovincial facts. Thus, while a tax levied on property outside the province would be unconstitutional, a tax levied on a person inside the province could be calculated by reference to the amount of his property outside the province. This holding enables the provinces to levy income tax on their residents in respect of income earned outside the province.[123] It also enables the provinces to levy succession duty on their residents in respect of property situated outside the province and inherited from a deceased person domiciled outside the province.[124] In each case, of course, a question of interpretation arises as to whether the province is levying tax on extraprovincial property (which would be bad) or is merely employing the extraprovincial property as a factor in computing a tax levied on a subject in the province.[125]

---

120 (1887) 12 App. Cas. 575.

121 *Id.*, 584.

122 La Forest, note 1, above, 114.

123 *Kerr* v. *Supt. of Income Tax* [1942] S.C.R. 436; *CPR v. Prov. Treas. Man.* [1953] 4 D.L.R. 233 (Man. Q.B.). Cf. *Container Corp.* v. *Franchise Tax Bd.* (1983) 463 U.S. 159 (upholding California's "unitary business tax", computed on basis of corporation's world income).

124 This "accessions basis" succession duty has been upheld in *A.-G. B.C.* v. *Can. Trust Co.* [1980] 2 S.C.R. 466 and *Covert* v. *Min. of Finance (N.S.)* [1980] 2 S.C.R. 774.

125 The question whether a tax is levied on a person or on property is not necessarily decided the same way where it arises in a non-constitutional context: *Nowegijick* v. *The Queen* [1983] 1 S.C.R. 29 (income tax, which is a tax on the person for constitutional territorial purposes, is a tax on property for the purpose of a tax exemption in the Indian Act for property situated on a reserve).

An imaginative attempt to apply the principle in *Bank of Toronto* v. *Lambe* was Manitoba's purported imposition of a tax on airlines in respect of the use of aircraft which flew over the province. In *The Queen (Manitoba)* v. *Air Canada* (1980),[126] the Supreme Court of Canada accepted that the tax was imposed on the person of Air Canada, and that Air Canada had offices and service facilities within Manitoba. The use of aircraft on overflights was argued to be merely the means of measuring this personal tax. This argument was rejected by the Court for two reasons. First, on the construction of the taxing statute, it only imposed a tax if property had been brought into the province, and the transitory presence of aircraft above the province (even if they also landed temporarily in the province) did not amount to a bringing into the province.[127] Secondly, however, Laskin C.J. for the Court said that the principle of *Bank of Toronto* v. *Lambe* could not be ''extended to make interprovincial and international aircraft operations as [sic] measuring standards to determine the amount of a tax imposed upon an air carrier which has a business office in the taxing Province''.[128] Why aircraft operations may not be used as ''measuring standards'', while banking operations (also within federal jurisdiction) may be so used, was not explained.[129]

(c) Property

Where a tax is levied on property, as distinct from persons, it is immaterial whether or not the owner upon whom the burden of the tax will fall is within the province. So far as territorial competence is concerned, the question is simply whether or not the property subject to the tax is within the province. It has never been doubted, for example, that municipal taxes on land are valid even when the land is owned by a non-resident of the province. But difficulties have arisen in allocating taxing jurisdiction over property other than land, and especially intangibles, such as stocks, bonds, insurance policies and interests in trusts or estates. Most of the case law concerns provincial succession duty.

It was at one time thought that provincial succession duty could be levied on the foreign movables of a person dying domiciled in the province, on the basis of the conflict-of-laws maxim mobilia sequuntur personam — movable property follows the person of the owner. The theory was that the situs of a deceased person's movable property could be deemed to be the place of his domicile. This

---

126 [1980] 2 S.C.R. 303.

127 See the discussion of the case in ch. 13, Extraterritorial Competence, under heading 13.3(b), ''Territory of province'', above.

128 [1980] 2 S.C.R. 303, 318.

129 *The Queen (Man.)* v. *Air Can.* was followed in *Re Lynden Transport* (1981) 119 D.L.R. (3d) 765 (B.C. C.A.) (trucks carrying freight in bond through province not subject to provincial tax) and *CP Air* v. *B.C.* [1989] 1 S.C.R. 1133 (sales of drinks to airline passengers were not within province, even on flights that originated or terminated in province) and distinguished in *Air Can.* v. *B.C.* [1989] 1 S.C.R. 1161 (sales of gasoline to air carrier were within province, where the sale took place, even though gasoline was consumed in flight).

theory had the advantage of providing a single, simple rule to resolve questions of situs, and the theory did obtain a temporary foothold in the Canadian courts. However, it was decisively rejected by the Privy Council in *Provincial Treasurer of Alberta* v. *Kerr* (1933),[130] which decided that the province of deceased's domicile could not tax property which was ''locally situate'' outside the province. This meant of course that some other rule or rules had to be found to determine where intangible property was ''locally situate''.

It might have been thought that English law would provide little assistance in the resolution of such a peculiarly federal problem. But the ecclesiastical courts in England had developed rules as to the situs of property for the purpose of determining their probate jurisdiction, which extended only to assets found in the local territory of the court. In *The King* v. *National Trust Co.* (1933),[131] Duff C.J. for the Supreme Court of Canada said that the words ''in the province'' in s. 92(2) of the Constitution Act, 1867 must be taken as importing these ''common law'' rules as to situs. This implausible proposition is now firmly established.[132] The result is that a body of arcane rules has been transplanted from England and then elaborated in Canada for the purpose of determining the situs of property.[133] The constitutional status of the situs rules has been confirmed by the further rule that a province may not alter the rules in order to assume taxing jurisdiction over property.[134] The judge-made rules as to situs are therefore immune from provincial legislative change.[135]

(d) Transactions and benefits

Finally, a province may levy taxes on transactions occurring or benefits arising in the province, even if the property involved is outside the province and the person upon whom the tax burden will fall is outside the province. There is little doubt, for example, that a province may tax income earned in a province,

130 [1933] A.C. 710.

131 [1933] S.C.R. 670, 673.

132 *R.* v. *Williams* [1942] A.C. 541.

133 The law has been admirably described and critically analyzed by La Forest, note 1, above, 115-143. For a convenient summary of the principal rules and authorities, see Laskin, note 1, above, 825-828.

134 *The King* v. *Nat. Trust Co.* [1933] S.C.R. 670, 673; *R. v. Williams* [1942] A.C. 541, 559; cf. *Min. of Finance (B.C.)* v. *First Nat. Bank of Nevada* [1975] 1 S.C.R. 525.

135 The rules for tax purposes may incidentally be altered by provincial laws validly enacted in relation to some other matter than taxation. For example, a provincial company law prescribing that the shares of a provincially-incorporated company may only be transferred at the company's head office in the province will have the effect of fixing the situs of the shares: *Erie Beach Co.* v. *A.-G. Ont.* [1930] A.C. 161; and a provincial insurance law prescribing that the proceeds of insurance policies written by provincially-licensed insurers may only be paid in the province will have the effect of fixing the situs of the policy: *Re Lawton* [1945] 4 D.L.R. 8 (Man. C.A.); *Re Youngman* [1971] 1 W.W.R. 576 (B.C.C.A.). Of course, if a law was characterized as in relation to property or civil rights outside the province, it would be invalid: Editorial Note to *Re Lawton* [1945] 4 D.L.R. 8, 9.

even if the income is actually received outside the province by a person resident outside the province.[136] Here, as elsewhere, the most difficult problems have been raised by succession duty legislation. Quebec's legislation used to include a provision taxing "all transmissions" of foreign movable property of a person dying domiciled in the province. Ontario's legislation used to include a provision taxing the "succession" to foreign movable property of a person dying domiciled in the province. These provisions applied to property situated outside the province, and they did not stipulate that the recipient or beneficiary of the property should be domiciled or resident in the province. These provisions could be justified on the basis that the tax was levied on the transmission or succession, not on the property or its recipient. The transmission or succession could be regarded as a transaction occurring or benefit arising in the province in which the deceased was domiciled, since it is the law of that province which stipulates the rules under which the transmission of or succession to movable property is permitted. Both provisions were in fact upheld by the courts, but in cases in which the beneficiary of the deceased's property was domiciled in the same province as the deceased.[137] It was therefore unnecessary to face the hard question whether the tax could have been validly levied on a transmission or succession where the beneficiary as well as the property was outside the province.[138]

30.12 Interjurisdictional taxation

(a) The Crown

The question whether statutes apply to the Crown, including the question whether one level of government in the federation is bound by a statute enacted by another level of government, has been considered in the earlier chapter on the Crown.[139] One of the cases which is usually cited for the proposition that federal

136 *Firestone Tire and Rubber Co.* v. *Commr. of Income Tax* [1942] S.C.R. 476; *Int. Harvester Co.* v. *Prov. Tax Comm.* [1949] A.C. 36; *Alworth* v. *Min. of Finance (B.C.)* [1978] 1 S.C.R. 447.

137 *Alleyn* v. *Barthe* [1922] 1 A.C. 215; *A.-G. Ont.* v. *Baby* (1926) 60 O.L.R. 1 (C.A.). The imposition of succession duties on dispositions made in the province by the deceased in his lifetime has raised a similar issue. In *Re Flavelle* [1943] O.R. 167 Rose C.J. of the Ontario High Court upheld this feature of Ontario's legislation, but he did so on the assumption that a disposition was made in the province if the disponer and disponee were in the province at the time of the disposition; he did not consider whether the tax could be validly levied on a disposition by a disponer in the province to a disponee outside the province.

138 Dicta on the point are divided: in favour of validity, *Cotton* v. *The King* (1911) 45 S.C.R. 469, 505-506; opposed, *Alleyn* v. *Barthe* [1922] 1 A.C. 215, 228; *A.-G. B.C.* v. *Can. Trust Co.* [1980] 2 S.C.R. 466, 481-483; see generally La Forest, note 1, above, 143-147.

139 Chapter 10, under heading 10.8, "Statutes", above. On the Crown as taxpayer, see McNairn, *Governmental and Intergovernmental Immunity in Australia and Canada* (1977), ch. 6; La Forest, note 1, above, 53-54, 175-177.

laws may bind the Crown in right of a province is the *Johnnie Walker* case (1924),[140] in which the government of British Columbia was held to be liable to pay a federal tax (customs duty) in respect of its importation of whisky for sale in provincial liquor outlets. The federal government, on the other hand, according to La Forest, is not liable to pay provincial taxes.[141] La Forest's assertion is based upon the widely-held view that the Dominion is immune from provincial laws. This difference in the treatment of federal and provincial Crowns has been discussed, and its correctness doubted, in the earlier chapter on the Crown.[142]

Section 125 of the Constitution Act, 1867, which provides an explicit intergovernmental immunity from taxation of lands or property belonging to the Crown, is the topic of a later section of this chapter.

(b) Ministers, officials, judges

Federal income taxes may validly be levied on a minister of a provincial government and on a member of the provincial legislative assembly.[143] A fortiori, a provincial Crown servant would be liable. The federal Parliament may also tax the income of judges, whether federally or provincially appointed.[144]

Provincial income taxes may be validly levied on federal officials,[145] and presumably on ministers and members of Parliament as well.[146] With respect to federally-appointed judges, an argument for immunity from provincial tax was built around the guarantee of tenure in s. 99 of the Constitution Act, 1867 and the fact that by s. 100 their salaries must be ''fixed and provided'' by the Parliament of Canada. But the courts have held that neither of these provisions is violated by a provincial income tax, and that both federally and provincially-appointed judges may be taxed by the province.[147]

These propositions have all been established in cases in which it was sought to apply taxing laws of general application to the persons asserting immunity. The cases have been careful to reserve the question whether either level of government could enact a discriminatory tax, or use its taxing power to destroy ''powers'' or ''capacity'' conferred by the other level of government.[148]

---

140 *A.-G. B.C.* v. *A.-G. Can.* (Johnnie Walker) [1924] A.C. 222.

141 La Forest, note 1, above, 176.

142 Chapter 10, under heading 10.9(d), ''Provincial laws binding federal Crown'', above.

143 *Caron* v. *The King* [1924] A.C. 999.

144 This follows inevitably from the cases upholding provincial taxation of judicial incomes: note 147, below.

145 *Abbott* v. *St. John* (1908) 40 S.C.R. 597; *Forbes v. A.-G. Man.* [1937] A.C. 260.

146 Cf. *Caron* v. *The King* [1924] A.C. 999.

147 *Toronto* v. *Morson* (1917) 40 O.L.R. 227 (C.A.); *Judges* v. *A.-G. Sask.* [1937] 2 D.L.R. 209 (P.C.).

148 *Abbott* v. *St. John* (1908) 40 S.C.R. 597, 607; *Caron* v. *The King* [1924] A.C. 999, 1006; *Forbes* v. *A.-G. Man.* [1937] A.C. 260, 271; *Judges* v. *A.-G. Sask.* [1937] 2 D.L.R. 209, 213 (P.C.). See also ch. 15, Judicial Review on Federal Grounds, under headings 15.5(b), ''Singling out'', and 15.8, ''Interjurisdictional immunity'', above.

(c) Business activity outside regulatory control

It will be recalled that in *Bank of Toronto* v. *Lambe* (1887)[149] the Privy Council held that a province could levy a tax on the banks, notwithstanding that "banking" was a federal head of legislative power under s. 91(15) of the Constitution Act, 1867. This case[150] established that for constitutional purposes taxing is not the same as regulating, and each level of government is entitled to look to institutions outside its own regulatory authority for the purpose of levying taxes.[151] On the other hand, a provincial tax which is a disguised attempt to regulate the banking industry (or other federally-regulated undertaking) will be invalid.[152] By the same token, while the federal Parliament may tax the insurance companies, it may not use a tax as a device for regulating the industry.[153] In these cases, invalidity stems not merely from the "singling out" of an enterprise or activity regulated by the other level of government — that alone is not fatal[154] — but from the Court's judgment that the pith and substance of the statute was not taxation, but regulation.

30.13 Section 125

(a) General

Section 125 of the Constitution Act, 1867 provides that:

No lands or property belonging to Canada or any province shall be liable to taxation.

Section 125[155] provides an intergovernmental immunity from taxation,[156] but only from taxation upon "lands or property belonging to Canada or any province". Section 125 provides the same immunity for the lands or property of a province

149 (1887) 12 App. Cas. 575.

150 See also *CPR* v. *Notre Dame de Bonsecours* [1899] A.C. 367.

151 A regulatory charge, as distinct from a tax, will be invalid if the scheme of regulation to which it is incidental is invalid: *Commn. du Salaire Minimum* v. *Bell Telephone Co.* [1966] S.C.R. 767; and see sec. 30.10(b), "Regulatory charges", above.

152 *A.-G. Alta.* v. *A-.G. Can.* (Bank Taxation) [1939] A.C. 117; see also *Texada Mines* v. *A.-G. B.C.* [1960] S.C.R. 713.

153 *Re Insurance Act of Can.* [1932] A.C. 41.

154 *Van Buren Bridge Co.* v. *Madawaska* (1957) 15 D.L.R. (2d) 763 (N.B. A.D.).

155 Section 125 is examined in Laskin, note 1, above, 840-844; McNairn, note 139, above, 137-143; La Forest, note 1, above, 182-194; Bale, "Reciprocal Tax Immunity in a Federation" (1983) 61 Can. Bar Rev. 652; Moull, "Intergovernmental Immunity from Taxation" (1984) 32 Can. Tax J. 54.

156 The Constitution of Australia, s. 114, is similar to s. 125. The Constitution of the United States contains no comparable provision, but there is a judge-made doctrine of intergovernmental immunity, which originated in *McCulloch* v. *Maryland* (1819) 17 U.S. (4 Wheat.) 316. See generally Sackville, "The Doctrine of Immunity of Instrumentalities in the United States and Australia" (1969) 7 Melb. U.L. Rev. 15.

as it does for the lands or property of Canada.[157] Thus, federal taxes cannot apply to the lands or property of a provincial Crown, and provincial taxes cannot apply to the lands or property of the federal Crown or of another provincial Crown.[158] The lands or property of a Crown corporation, provided the corporation is an agent of the Crown,[159] enjoy the same immunity as if the lands or property were owned directly by the Crown.[160]

(b) Taxation

Section 125 provides immunity only from "taxation". The courts have held that taxation means levies imposed under the authority of either the federal or provincial taxing powers. In other words, s. 125 restricts the taxing powers, but does not restrict other legislative powers. Thus, s. 125 has not prevented the federal Parliament from expropriating provincial Crown lands under its power over interprovincial railways.[161] Nor does s. 125 apply to regulatory charges, such as a charge for the supply of water[162] or a fee for registration of title to land.[163] Not being taxes,[164] regulatory charges may be imposed by a province upon the lands or property of the federal Crown or by the federal Parliament on the lands or property of a provincial Crown.

---

157 *Re Exported Natural Gas Tax* [1982] 1 S.C.R. 1004, 1067, rejecting the argument that s. 91(3) overrides s. 125 by reason of the notwithstanding clause in s. 91.

158 It is the legal incidence of the tax, and not its ultimate economic incidence, that is relevant. Thus, s. 125 will not cover a tax imposed on a private person, even if the private person is likely to pass the tax on to a government: *City of Halifax* v. *Fairbanks* [1928] A.C. 117 (private landlord liable to pay property tax although Crown was the tenant); *City of Vancouver* v. *A.-G. Can.* [1944] S.C.R. 23 (same situation); *The King* v. *Bell Telephone Co.* (1935) 59 Que. K.B. 205 (C.A.) (Crown liable to reimburse telephone company for tax levied on company on long-distance calls); *Re GST* [1992] 2 S.C.R. 445 (purchasers from Crown liable to pay GST even if tax forced Crown to lower price or reduce volume of sales). By the same token, s. 125 will cover a tax imposed on the Crown, even if the Crown is likely to pass it on to a private person: *Re Exported Natural Gas Tax* [1982] 1 S.C.R. 1004 (Crown exempt from indirect tax on exported natural gas).

159 See ch. 10, The Crown, under heading 10.2, "Crown agency", above.

160 *City of Halifax* v. *Halifax Harbour Commrs.* [1935] S.C.R. 215 (municipal business tax not applicable to Halifax Harbour Commissioners controlled by federal Crown; s. 125 not referred to); *Re City of Toronto and CBC* [1938] O.W.N. 507 (C.A.) (municipal property tax not applicable to CBC controlled by federal Crown). Even a private corporation which is acting not as an independent contractor but as a controlled servant of the Crown is entitled to the immunity: *Montreal* v. *Montreal Locomotive Works* [1947] 1 D.L.R. 161 (P.C.) (municipal business tax inapplicable to private corporation constructing munitions plant on Crown land, subject to control of Crown); *Regina Industries* v. *City of Regina* [1947] S.C.R. 345 (similar facts and decision); La Forest, note 1, above, 186-187.

161 *A.-G. B.C.* v. *CPR* [1906] A.C. 204; *A.-G. Que. v. Nipissing Central Ry. Co.* [1926] A.C. 715.

162 *Min. of Justice (Can.)* v. *Levis* [1919] A.C. 505. Query correctness of *The Queen* v. *Breton* [1967] S.C.R. 503 (municipal by-law imposing duty to maintain sidewalk held inapplicable to federal Crown on ground that such a duty amounts to a tax and is barred by s. 125).

163 *A.-G. Can.* v. *Registrar of Titles* [1934] 4 D.L.R. 764 (B.C. C.A.).

164 See sec. 30.10, "Taxes and charges", above.

In the *Johnnie Walker* case (1924),[165] the Privy Council held that s. 125 did not apply to exempt the province of British Columbia from liability to pay federal customs duty on the importation by the province of a case of scotch whisky intended for sale in the province's Crown-owned liquor stores. The Privy Council's reasons for denying the application of s. 125 are obscure, but the Supreme Court of Canada has since explained the case as turning on the classification of the customs duty as primarily regulatory of trade and commerce, rather than revenue-raising. Since the law was "primarily" authorized by the trade and commerce power (s. 91(2)), and not the taxing power (s. 91(3)), s. 125 did not apply.[166] This case illustrates that the application of s. 125 to a law imposing a levy will turn on the law's classification. If the primary purpose of the levy is the raising of revenue for general public purposes, then the levy is taxation, and s. 125 applies. If, however, as in *Johnnie Walker*, the primary purpose of the law is regulatory, then the levy is not taxation, and s. 125 does not apply.[167] (A broader immunity, based on principles of federalism, may still be applicable.)[168]

In *Re GST* (1992),[169] the Supreme Court of Canada had to decide whether the federal legislation levying the Goods and Services Tax had any application to the provinces. The GST was imposed on the purchaser of taxable goods and services; the supplier (or vendor) was under a duty to collect the tax as agent for the government and remit it to the government. Under the federal taxing legislation, the provinces were not required to pay the GST when they purchased taxable goods and services, but (like all other suppliers) the provinces were required to collect and remit the GST when they supplied (or sold) taxable goods and services. It was argued that, since the obligation to collect and remit the federal tax would inevitably impose costs on the provinces, this was tantamount to the imposition of a tax. The Court rejected the argument, holding that no tax was imposed on the property of the province,[170] and that it was competent to the federal Parliament to impose "administrative burdens" upon the provinces as an incident of a federal scheme of taxation.[171]

---

165 *A.-G. B.C.* v. *A.-G. Can.* (Johnnie Walker) [1924] A.C. 222.

166 *Re Exported Natural Gas Tax* [1982] 1 S.C.R. 1004, 1068-1070. This explanation is not entirely implausible, given the function of the tariff in influencing foreign trade and protecting Canadian industry.

167 *Re Exported Natural Gas Tax* [1982] 1 S.C.R. 1004, 1070. In this case, the Supreme Court of Canada held that the primary purpose of a federal levy on exported natural gas was to raise revenue for general federal purposes; the levy was therefore a tax, and s. 125 applied to exempt provincial Crown property from the levy.

168 See ch. 15, Judicial Review on Federal Grounds, under heading 15.8, "Interjurisdictional immunity", above.

169 [1992] 2 S.C.R. 445.

170 The fact that in some market situations the burden of the tax might be wholly or partially passed back to the supplier was irrelevant: *Id.*, 480-481; and see note 158, above.

171 Nor was there any provincial immunity from federal law based on s. 126 of the Constitution Act, 1867 (establishing provincial consolidated revenue funds) or on general principles of interjurisdictional immunity: *Id.*, 481-485; and see ch. 10, The Crown, under heading 10.9(f), "Federal laws binding provincial Crown", above.

(c) Lands or property

Section 125's exemption is for "lands or property" belonging to Canada or any province. It might be thought that the jurisprudence on the territorial limit of the provincial taxing power, which distinguishes between taxes on property, taxes on persons and taxes on transactions and benefits,[172] would also be relevant in this context, and that s. 125 would provide exemption only from taxes on property. But this is not so.

In *Re Exported Natural Gas Tax* (1982),[173] the Supreme Court of Canada held that the province of Alberta was liable to pay a federal tax on the export of natural gas which the province itself had produced from its own provincial Crown lands and then exported from Canada. It was argued on behalf of the federal government that the tax was not levied on the gas itself, but rather on the person of the exporter or perhaps (by reason of the way in which the tax was drafted) on the transaction of the exporter's receiving the gas. Since the tax was not levied on property, the argument continued, s. 125 did not apply to exempt the province of Alberta. The Supreme Court of Canada rejected this argument, holding that s. 125 applied, regardless of whether the tax was on property or persons or transactions. The majority of the Court pointed out that the s. 125 immunity would be "illusory" if it applied only to taxes on property. As the jurisprudence on the territorial limit of the provincial taxing power shows, small drafting changes can change the classification of a statute. Any proposed tax on property could easily be framed as a tax on a person or a transaction. These subtle nuances of form should not dictate the scope of the protection afforded by s. 125. The Court held accordingly that s. 125 provided exemption not only from taxes levied on Crown property, but also from taxes levied on persons or transactions in respect of Crown property.[174]

(d) Commercial activity

In *Re Exported Natural Gas Tax* (1982),[175] the federal government made a second argument in its unsuccessful attempt to apply the federal tax on exported natural gas to the province of Alberta. The argument was that the s. 125 immunity, although applicable to the natural gas in the ground, was lost when the province applied industry to the resource by extracting it, processing it and transporting it for sale. The province, the argument went, was liable to pay tax "as a result of having embarked on a commercial activity as an ordinary trader".[176] The majority of the Court rejected this argument, but did so in cautious terms. The Court

---

172 Section 30.11, 'Territorial limitation'', above.
173 [1982] 1 S.C.R. 1004.
174 *Id.*, 1078.
175 [1982] 1 S.C.R. 1004.
176 *Id.*, 1079.

pointed out that the facts disclosed no commercial activity beyond what was necessary to realize by sale the province's own natural resource. Natural resources were intended to be an important source of provincial revenue, and the s. 125 immunity should extend to the industry that was employed to convert resources into marketable condition.[177]

Re Exported Natural Gas Tax leaves open the question whether s. 125 would protect a government from taxes levied by another government in respect of property acquired for or employed in a commercial enterprise, such as the operation of liquor stores, gasoline stations or railways. As a matter of policy, there is merit in the idea, which is accepted in the United States,[178] that, when a government embarks on a commercial enterprise, it should be treated as having accepted the same world of regulation and taxation as a privately-owned enterprise. As well, if intergovernmental tax exemption were extended to property employed in all activities by governments, the expropriation of private industry would be artificially encouraged, and federal and provincial tax bases eroded.[179] On the other hand, there is no satisfactory principle by which a particular governmental activity can be characterized as either ''commercial'' or ''governmental''.[180] As McConnell has noted, government rarely engages in a commercial venture purely in an effort to compete for private profit.[181] The government is usually drawn in by regulatory or public policy objectives. Indeed, the fact that a government has decided to embark on a particular activity indicates a deliberate judgment that the activity should become governmental.[182] Upon what basis could a court decide otherwise?

The text of s. 125 contains no hint of a distinction between commercial and governmental functions. Nor have the Canadian cases developed any such dis-

---

177 *Id.*, 1081. For comment on this aspect of the case, see Moull, ''Alberta Natural Gas Reference'' (1983) 7 Can. Bus. L.J. 485.

178 In the United States, where there is no equivalent of s. 125 in the Constitution, the courts have held that the judge-made intergovernmental tax immunity (note 156, above) does not extend to functions which, although performed by a state, are commercial rather than governmental. The distinction was established in *South Carolina* v. *United States* (1905) 199 U.S. 261, which decided that a state was obliged to pay a federal tax on the sale of liquor in state liquor stores; the state's exemption from federal tax was limited to functions ''of a strictly governmental character'' and did not extend to ''the carrying on of an ordinary private business'' (p. 269). This distinction was applied in many subsequent cases; its utility was doubted in *New York* v. *United States* (1946) 326 U.S. 572; but it was revived and applied in *National League of Cities* v. *Usery* (1976) 426 U.S. 833 (federal labour standards inapplicable to states in ''areas of traditional governmental functions'').

179 *South Carolina* v. *United States* (1905) 199 U.S. 261, 267.

180 This has been a serious problem in the United States, most forcefully articulated in *New York* v. *United States* (1946) 326 U.S. 572.

181 *Commentary on the British North America Act* (1977), 369.

182 Cf. the discussion of the ''functions'' test of Crown agency, which is open to the same objection: ch. 10, The Crown, under heading 10.2(b), ''At common law'', above.

tinction.[183] The *Johnnie Walker* case[184] would have been the perfect opportunity to do so, because the province of British Columbia was there acting as a merchant, buying liquor at wholesale and selling it at retail. In the Supreme Court of Canada,[185] Idington J. placed some reliance on the fact that the province's enterprise would not have been contemplated at the time of confederation.[186] But Brodeur J. considered and rejected the governmental-commercial distinction. He related the history of provincial attempts to control the consumption of liquor, and pointed out that the direct sale of liquor was just the final evolution of that public policy. In assuming the function of direct sale, Brodeur J. said, "nobody can deny that they exercised functions which are of a governmental character".[187] None of the other judges in the Supreme Court of Canada made any reference to the governmental-commercial distinction. Nor did the Privy Council.

I conclude that s. 125 probably covers taxation of all property belonging to Canada or a province, regardless of whether the property is acquired for or employed in a commercial activity or a governmental activity. The section is not limited to non-commercial property.

30.14 Unconstitutional taxes

After a tax has been held to be unconstitutional, what is the legal position of the persons who, believing the tax to be valid, have paid it? Can they recover the payments? Or can the government keep its ill-gotten gains? These questions are examined in the more general context of the effect of an unconstitutional law in chapter 55, Effect of Unconstitutional Law, below.[188]

183 In *Re City of Toronto and CBC* [1938] O.W.N. 507 (C.A.), s. 125 was extended to the Canadian Broadcasting Corporation without discussion of the element of commerce in the CBC's activities.

184 *A.-G. B.C.* v. *A.-G. Can.* (Johnnie Walker) [1924] A.C. 222; discussed in text at note 165, above.

185 (1922) 64 S.C.R. 377.

186 *Id.*, 380.

187 *Id.*, 391.

188 Section 55.6, "Unconstitutional taxes", below.

III

CIVIL LIBERTIES

31

Civil Liberties

31.1 Definition

Civil liberties[1] encompass a broad range of values that support the freedom and dignity of the individual, and that are given recognition in various ways by Canadian law. The political civil liberties include the freedoms of speech, religion, assembly and association; the right to vote and be a candidate for elected office; and the freedom to enter and leave Canada and to move from one province to another. Legal civil liberties include the freedom from search, seizure, arrest, imprisonment, cruel and unusual punishment and unfair trial procedures. Egalitarian civil liberties include equality of access to accommodation, employment, education and other benefits, implying, at least, an absence of racial, sexual or other illegitimate criteria of discrimination. Particular to Canada are language rights, covering the right to use the English or the French language; and educational rights, covering the rights of denominational (or separate) schools.

All of these civil liberties are discussed in the chapters that follow. The basic point to be made here, however, is that all of these civil liberties come into competition with other values recognized by the legal system, and indeed they

1 See Scott, *Civil Liberties and Canadian Federalism* (1959); Schmeiser, *Civil Liberties in Canada* (1964); Tarnopolsky, *The Canadian Bill of Rights* (2nd ed., 1975); Beaudoin and Mendes (eds.), *The Canadian Charter of Rights and Freedoms* (3rd ed., 1996); Tremblay, *Droit Constitutionel-Principes* (1993), Part II, ch. 4.

come into competition with each other. When we speak of the protection of civil liberties in a society, we are really speaking about the nature of the compromises which that society has made between civil libertarian values of the kind described and the competing values recognized by social and economic regulation, which limits individual freedom in pursuit of collective goals, such as public order and morality, health and safety, fair dealing, environmental protection and a more equitable distribution of wealth.

31.2 Common law

The English common law, which was inherited by the colonies of British North America,[2] includes many rules that are protective of civil liberties, but it does not provide any positive guarantees of their continued recognition. The common law's position is that a person is free to do anything that is not positively prohibited, and various doctrines help to narrow the scope of what is positively prohibited. For the common law, civil liberties do not derive from positive law or governmental action, but from an absence of positive law or governmental action. Take freedom of speech as an example. At common law, one is free to speak one's mind so long as there is no positive law prohibiting such action. The laws of defamation, contempt of court, sedition, hate propaganda, obscenity, fraud, false advertising, television and radio licensing are among the laws which prohibit (or regulate) various forms of speech; what is left unprohibited is the civil liberty of speech. The doctrine of parliamentary sovereignty meant that in the United Kingdom those unregulated residues of individual liberty had no constitutional protection. Parliament could make any law whatever, even if it curtailed a cherished civil liberty.[3] Only a bill of rights that was immune from ordinary legislative change could guarantee civil liberties from legislative encroachment, and the United Kingdom has never had a bill of rights of that kind.[4]

After the newly-independent American colonies federated in 1787, they added various guarantees of civil liberties to their new Constitution;[5] these "amendments" became a Bill of Rights which could not be altered except by further constitutional amendment. This was a radical departure from British tradition. When the loyal British North American colonies federated in 1867, they

2 The French civil law was inherited in Quebec, but the criminal law and public law generally were supplanted by the English law: see ch. 2, Reception, under heading 2.3(b), "Ontario and Quebec", above.

3 See ch. 12, Parliamentary Sovereignty, under heading 12.1 "Sovereignty in the United Kingdom", above.

4 The Magna Carta of 1297 and the Bill of Rights of 1689 are simply statutes amenable to ordinary legislative change.

5 The first ten amendments, the original "bill of rights", were passed by Congress in 1789 (the first year of the Union) and ratified by three-fourths of the states in 1791. Other bill of rights amendments, of which the fourteenth (1868) is the most important, were adopted later.

did not include a bill of rights in their Constitution. On the contrary, as recited in the preamble to the Constitution Act, 1867, the Canadian federation was to have "a Constitution similar in principle to that of the United Kingdom". Thus the Canadian Parliament and Legislatures, provided they stayed within the limits of the federal distribution of powers and a few other restraints,[6] received powers as "plenary and ample" as those of the United Kingdom Parliament.[7]

Civil liberties in Canada have now received some direct constitutional protection. In 1960, the Canadian Bill of Rights was adopted, but it was only a statute, not a constitutional amendment, and it was applicable only to the federal level of government, not to the provinces. For these and other reasons, the Canadian Bill of Rights made little change in Canada's law.[8] In 1982, the Charter of Rights was adopted. The Charter is a constitutional instrument; it is applicable to both levels of government, and its brief history makes clear that it fulfils an important role in protecting the civil liberties that it guarantees.[9] But the fact remains that, for most of its history, Canada, like the United Kingdom, Australia and New Zealand, has had few direct constitutional protections of civil liberties.

Despite the lack of a bill of rights, Canada, like the United Kingdom, Australia and New Zealand, has a good record of respect for civil liberties. Tolerance of political and religious dissent, and of racial and linguistic minorities, freedom of movement, control of police powers and fair and open trials are among the criteria by which a nation's record is judged. Canada's record, while far from perfect, seems to be much better than that of most of the countries of the world, although nearly all countries have bills of rights in their constitutions. The basic reason for this has very little to do with the contents of Canada's (or any other country's) constitutional law. It is to be found in the democratic character of Canada's political institutions, supported by long traditions[10] of free elections, opposition parties and a free press. Democracy is without doubt the most important safeguard of civil liberties.[11]

A second safeguard of civil liberties is the independence of the judiciary, which in Canada is partly secured by constitutional provisions, but is most effectively secured by a long political tradition stretching back to the beginning of the eighteenth century in Britain.[12]

A third safeguard of civil liberties is the common law, which, for the most part, tends to favour individual rights and freedoms (as traditionally understood) when they come into conflict with state interests. This is perhaps seen most clearly

---

6 The impact on civil liberties of the Constitution Act, 1867 is discussed in a later section of this chapter.

7 See ch. 12, Parliamentary Sovereignty, under heading 12.2, "Sovereignty in Canada", above.

8 See ch. 32, Canadian Bill of Rights, below.

9 See ch. 33, Charter of Rights, below.

10 There are a few relevant provisions in the Constitution Act, 1867: see note 40, below; and, since 1982, in the Charter of Rights, ss. 3-5: see ch. 42, Voting, below.

11 Russell, "A Democratic Approach to Civil Liberties" (1969) 19 U. Toronto L.J. 109.

12 See ch. 7, Courts, under heading 7.1(c), Tenure of provincial judges", above.

in the criminal law. For example, mens rea (or a guilty mind) was an ingredient of common law offences and is presumed by the courts to be an ingredient of statutory offences; in other respects, the definitions of crime are construed strictly (in favour of the defendant), the defendant is presumed to be innocent and the Crown is required to prove guilt beyond a reasonable doubt, confessions are inadmissible unless they have been freely obtained, the defendant cannot be compelled to testify and no-one can be compelled to incriminate himself.[13]

Outside the realm of criminal law, the state and the individual usually come into conflict as the result of the exercise by officials of governmental powers over persons or private property. In Britain, common law doctrine early developed that the King and his officials had no powers other than those granted by the law. It is true that ''the law'' included certain royal prerogatives as well as statute law, but the courts successfully asserted the power to determine the existence and extent of the prerogatives.[14] With few exceptions, actions which infringe the liberty of the subject require the authority of a statute.[15] This was settled in the great case of *Entick* v. *Carrington* (1765),[16] in which it was held that neither a search warrant signed by a minister of the Crown, nor a claim of ''state necessity'', could justify Crown servants in entering the premises of the plaintiff and seizing his papers. The plaintiff's action in trespass against the Crown servants was successful, because they could not show that their actions were authorized by law.

The principle of validity — that every official act must be justified by law — has to be reaffirmed periodically. One of the best-known modern cases is *Roncarelli* v. *Duplessis* (1959),[17] in which Premier Duplessis of Quebec ordered the cancellation of restaurateur Roncarelli's liquor licence because Roncarelli was a Jehovah's Witness who had made a practice of acting as bondsman for the numerous Jehovah's Witnesses who were arrested for distributing their literature in breach of municipal by-laws. The Supreme Court of Canada awarded damages to Roncarelli. Duplessis could not rely on his high office, nor his judgment as to the demands of the public interest, as justification for his act. Only a statute would suffice to authorize the cancellation of the licence, and the statute which did authorize licence cancellations gave the power to another official, not the Premier.[18] The Duplessis regime in Quebec offered the courts many other opportunities to protect civil liberties. In the present context, we may notice *Chaput* v. *Romain* (1955),[19] in which police broke up an assembly of Jehovah's Witnesses

13 The rule against self-incrimination has been modified by statute in Canada, and as modified, included in the Charter of Rights, s. 13: see ch. 50, Right Against Self-Incrimination, below.

14 *Case of Proclamations* (1610) 12 Co. Rep. 74, 77 E.R. 1352.

15 See ch. 1, Sources, under heading 1.9, ''Prerogative'', above.

16 (1765) 19 St. Tr. 1030, 95 E.R. 807 (K.B.).

17 [1959] S.C.R. 121.

18 In any event, the Court made clear that the exercise of the power by the correct official, but for a purpose extraneous to the service and consumption of liquor, would have been unauthorized.

19 [1955] S.C.R. 834.

who were meeting peacefully in a private house, and *Lamb* v. *Benoit* (1959),[20] in which police arrested a Jehovah's Witness who was distributing pamphlets on a street corner. In both those cases, the Supreme Court of Canada awarded damages against the responsible policemen on the ground that they had acted without legal authority.[21]

A corollary of cases such as *Entick* v. *Carrington* and *Roncarelli* v. *Duplessis* is that the Prime Minister (or Premier) or a Minister of the Crown or any other representative of the government has no power to suspend the operation of a law for a time, or to dispense with a law in favour of a particular person or group. These ''suspending'' and ''dispensing'' powers were asserted by the Stuart Kings, but were abolished by the Bill of Rights of 1688. From time to time, modern governments assert such powers, and the assertions are repudiated by the courts, who always add a stern admonition that the Crown is not above the law.[22]

A second feature of the common law protection of civil liberties is the availability of remedies to citizens injured by illegal official action. If an official acts outside his or her statutory authority, the official enjoys no more powers than a private individual; if the act is tortious, then the official may be sued in an ordinary action in tort by the injured citizen. This is true even if the tort were committed in the course of employment, although in that case the Crown itself will ordinarily be liable as well.[23] In addition to the ordinary action in tort, the courts developed the ''prerogative writs'' for the express purpose of allowing speedy challenge to contested official action or inaction. The most famous of these writs is habeas corpus, to determine the legality of imprisonment; but the writs of mandamus, certiorari, prohibition and quo warranto also provide mechanisms which are available to secure judicial review of administrative action. Of more recent vintage is the action for a declaration (declaratory judgment), which is also often available to review administrative action. In some jurisdictions, a single statutory remedy, often styled an application for judicial review, has been introduced to do the work of several common law remedies.

Because of the doctrine of parliamentary sovereignty, if a statute plainly takes away a civil liberty or plainly authorizes an official to take away a civil liberty, then the courts can provide no protection. The principle of validity is satisfied; no legal wrong has occurred; and no remedy is available. However, it is still the function of the courts to interpret any statute which is relied upon as

20 [1959] S.C.R. 321.

21 Another important decision was *Boucher* v. *The King* [1951] S.C.R. 265 (Jehovah's Witness not guilty of sedition).

22 *Fitzgerald* v. *Muldoon* [1976] 2 N.Z.L.R. 615 (N.Z. S.C.) (N.Z. Prime Minister may not suspend statutory obligation to contribute to state pension plan); *Re Anti-Inflation Act* [1976] 2 S.C.R. 373 (Lieutenant Governor in Council may not change law by agreement with Governor in Council); *Man. Govt. Employees Assn.* v. *Govt. of Man.* [1978] 1 S.C.R. 1123 (same decision); *R.* v. *Catagas* (1977) 81 D.L.R. (3d) 396 (Man. C.A.) (Minister may not dispense with Migratory Birds Convention Act in favour of native people.)

23 See ch. 10, The Crown, under heading 10.7, ''Liability in tort'', above.

the justification for a denial of a civil liberty and many civil libertarian values have been introduced into the law as canons of interpretation.

The governing canon of interpretation is that "statutes which encroach on the rights of the subject, whether as regards person or property, are subject to a 'strict' construction".[24] This is a principle which is no longer universally applauded because of cases where courts have given rein to laissez-faire prejudices and interpreted social legislation so strictly as to stultify its objects.[25] But now that state intervention in the social and economic life of the nation is generally accepted, even by judges, these hostile interpretations have ceased to be a problem. In my opinion, the principle of strict construction is sound: it is reasonable for the courts to insist that invasions of personal or proprietary rights be clearly authorized by the statutory language. For example, there is a presumption against interference with vested rights and a presumption against the retroactive operation of a statute. As well, the courts have confined the scope of official discretion by holding that power conferred in broad terms may not be "abused" by exercise in bad faith or for an improper purpose or upon irrelevant considerations. The courts have also structured the mode of exercise of some statutory powers by insisting upon official compliance with the procedural guarantees of "natural justice". More dubious is the judicial construction of "privative clauses" (which purport to oust judicial review), which has been so strict as to make the clauses largely ineffective. All of these results have been achieved without any denial of parliamentary sovereignty, and without the aid of a bill of rights, simply by "interpreting" statutory language, wherever possible, into conformity with civil libertarian values.[26]

31.3 Statute

(a) Human rights codes

Since the latter part of the second world war, Canadian provincial Legislatures have been active in promoting egalitarian civil liberties by statute. The purpose of the statutes is to prohibit discrimination by landlords and employers on grounds such as race, national origin, colour, religion, sex or age. Early statutes simply prohibited various forms of discrimination and imposed a penalty for breach. But, following the model of a New York statute of 1945, the provinces passed statutes which employed labour relations techniques of investigation, conciliation and arbitration to combat discrimination in accommodation and employment. In 1962, Ontario took the step of consolidating its law into a Human

24 *A.G. Can.* v. *Hallet & Carey* [1952] A.C. 427, 450.

25 See Jennings, *The Law and the Constitution* (5th ed., 1959), 253.

26 See Driedger, *Construction of Statutes* (3rd ed., 1994, by Sullivan), chs. 13, 14.

Rights Code, to be administered by a Human Rights Commission. All of the other provinces followed suit, and, finally, in 1977, the federal Parliament enacted its own Code with a Commission to administer it. These codes prohibit discriminatory practices in hiring and employment, and in the renting of accommodation; they provide for investigation and conciliation of complaints by a commission, and for adjudication by a board of inquiry if conciliation fails. As well as their administrative functions, the commissions have educational and promotional functions.[27]

The importance of the various human rights codes has not been diminished by the adoption in 1982 of the Charter of Rights. The human rights codes apply to discrimination by private individuals or firms, especially in the hiring and paying of employees, and in the renting of commercial and residential accommodation.[28] This fills a gap in the Charter of Rights, which applies only to governmental activity, not private activity.[29] Moreover, the codes' informal and inexpensive procedures, which are initiated by a complaint to the human rights commission, have no counterpart under the Charter, which contemplates judicial enforcement of its provisions.[30]

(b) Statutory bills of rights

Statutory bills of rights are another source of civil liberties. Saskatchewan led the way in 1947 with the Saskatchewan Bill of Rights Act,[31] which went beyond fair employment and accommodation to guarantee the fundamental freedoms of speech, press, assembly, religion and association. In 1960, the federal Parliament enacted the Canadian Bill of Rights,[32] which guaranteed a wide range of civil liberties and had the effect of overriding inconsistent federal (but not provincial) statutes. In 1972, Alberta enacted the Alberta Bill of Rights;[33] and, in

---

27 See Tarnopolsky, *Discrimination and the Law in Canada* (1982), of which ch. 2 relates the history of the legislation. See also Macdonald and Humphrey (eds.), *The Practice of Freedom* (1979), chs. 3 (Cheffins and Tucker), 4 (Leavy), 5 (Hunter), 15 (Tarnopolsky), 16 (Fairweather).

28 The Codes also apply to activity by governments and to that extent overlap with s. 15 of the Charter of Rights. Presumably, the courts would insist that Code remedies be exhausted before exercising their discretion to give a remedy under s. 24 of the Charter.

29 See ch. 34, Application of Charter, below.

30 Days, "Civil Rights in Canada: An American Perspective" (1984) 32 Am. Jo. Comp. Law, 307, 316, is struck by the leadership role played by the Canadian provinces (rather than the federal government, as in the United States) and by the dominance of legislative and administrative bodies (rather than the courts, as in the United States).

31 S.S. 1947, c. 35, but note that the Act did not purport to have overriding effect on inconsistent legislation. It was repealed and replaced by the Saskatchewan Human Rights Code, S.S. 1979, c. S-24.1, s. 44 of which provides that an inconsistent law is inoperative unless the law contains a notwithstanding clause.

32 S.C. 1960, c. 44. See next chapter on Canadian Bill of Rights.

33 S.A. 1972, c. 1.

1975, Quebec enacted the Quebec Charter of Human Rights and Freedoms.[34] Each of these statutes was similar to the Canadian Bill of Rights in guaranteeing a range of civil liberties and overriding inconsistent statutes. These four statutory bills of rights have lost much of their importance since the adoption in 1982 of the Charter of Rights, which is a constitutional instrument applicable to both the federal and provincial levels of government. But the statutory bills of rights remain in force, and remain effective to the extent that they are broader in scope than the Charter, as they are in a few respects.[35]

The Canadian Bill of Rights is the topic of the next chapter.

31.4 Constitution Act, 1867

(a) Express guarantees

We have already noticed that the framers of the Constitution Act, 1867 rejected the American precedent of the Bill of Rights, and sought instead to make an exhaustive distribution of legislative powers.[36] We have also noticed some exceptions to the principle of exhaustion. In the context of civil liberties, the important exceptions are s. 93, guaranteeing rights and privileges of denominational schools;[37] s. 99, guaranteeing the tenure of superior court judges;[38] and s. 133, guaranteeing the English and French languages in legislative and judicial proceedings in Quebec and the federal jurisdiction.[39] These provisions[40] do constitute a small bill of rights.[41]

---

34 S.Q. 1975, c. 6. For commentary, see Macdonald and Humphrey (eds.), *The Practice of Freedom* (1979), ch. 21 (by Brun).

35 E.g.. *Singh* v. *Minr. of Emplt. and Imm.* [1985] 1 S.C.R. 177 (s. 2(e) of Canadian Bill of Rights extends beyond s. 7); *MacBain* v. *Lederman* [1985] 1 F.C. 856 (C.A.) (same point); *Ford* v. *Que.* [1988] 2 S.C.R. 712 (Charter had been overridden under s. 33, but Quebec Charter had not been). The relationship between the statutory bills of rights and the Charter is examined by me in Beaudoin and Rathushny (eds.), *The Canadian Charter of Rights and Freedoms* (2nd ed., 1989), ch. 1; see also ch. 32, Canadian Bill of Rights, under heading 32.1, ''History'', below.

36 See ch. 12, Parliamentary Sovereignty, under heading 12.2, ''Sovereignty in Canada'', above.

37 See ch. 54, Education, below.

38 See ch. 7, Courts, under heading 7.1(b), ''Tenure of provincial judges'', above.

39 See ch. 53, Language, below.

40 See also s. 20 (annual session of Parliament), ss. 50, 91(1) (five year limit to Parliament), ss. 51, 51A, 52 (representation by population), s. 86 (annual sessions of Legislatures of Ontario and Quebec), s. 121 (free admission of goods to provinces), s. 125 (no taxation of land or property belonging to Canada or province).

41 My use in an earlier edition of the phrase ''a small bill of rights'' in reference to denominational school rights was disapproved in *Greater Montreal Protestant School Bd.* v. *Que.* [1989] 1 S.C.R. 377, 401 per Beetz J. for majority; the point was that the school rights should not be given the liberal interpretation that is appropriate to rights guaranteed by the Charter of Rights; otherwise, I think the description is accurate. The suggestion of an ''implied bill of rights'' is discussed later in this chapter, in sec. 31.4(c), ''Implied bill of rights'', below. The suggestion that the federal power of disallowance is available to invalidate provincial violations of civil liberties is referred to in ch. 5, Federalism, under heading 5.3(e), ''Disallowance'', above.

(b) Distribution of powers

The distribution of powers in Canada (or any other federal state) denies plenary power to any one legislative body. This raises impediments to legislative action in many fields, and thus often has the indirect effect of safeguarding civil liberties. For example, the provincial Legislatures have no power to enact criminal law; if a province attempts to suppress gambling[42] or communism[43] or prostitution,[44] and the law is classified as a criminal law, the law will be invalid, and gamblers, communists and prostitutes will remain free to continue their activities. As another example, the federal Parliament has no power to regulate property and civil rights in the province; if the federal Parliament attempts to prohibit the sale of margarine[45] or regulate the labelling of beer,[46] and the law is classified as a law in relation to property and civil rights in the province, the law will be invalid, and sellers of margarine and beer will be free from the purported federal constraints.

The foregoing examples illustrate the obvious proposition that a law affecting civil liberties, like any other law, is valid only if it is authorized by a grant of power in the Constitution Act, 1867. But a more subtle question then calls for an answer: to what extent is the law's impact on civil liberties a relevant factor in determining the appropriate classification of the law? The same question may be reframed by asking, to what extent are civil liberties "matters" (or constitutional values) which must be recognized as coming within the classes of subjects (or heads of power) in ss. 91 and 92 of the Constitution Act, 1867?[47]

The broad range of claims which can be encompassed by the term "civil liberties" renders any single or simple answer impossible.[48] Accordingly, this question is taken up with respect to particular civil liberties in the chapters that follow. However, to anticipate the more detailed discussion, as a broad generalization, it may be said that a law's impact on civil liberties has not been treated by the courts as the leading characteristic in determining the law's classification. The courts have instead relegated the impact of a law on civil liberties to an

---

42 *Johnson* v. *A.-G. Alta.* [1954] S.C.R. 127 (provincial law confiscating slot-machines struck down).

43 *Switzman* v. *Elbling* [1957] S.C.R. 285 (provincial law authorizing padlocking of any house used to propagate communism struck down).

44 *Westendorp* v. *The Queen* [1983] 1 S.C.R. 43 (municipal by-law prohibiting street prostitution struck down).

45 *Can. Federation of Agriculture* v. *A.-G. Que.* [1951] A.C. 179 (federal law prohibiting manufacture or sale of margarine struck down).

46 *Labatt Breweries* v. *A.-G. Can.* [1980] 1 S.C.R. 914 (federal law prescribing compositional standards for product labelled "light beer" struck down).

47 See ch. 15, Judicial Review on Federal Grounds, above. Note also that civil liberties are not equivalent to civil rights in the phrase "property and civil rights in the province" (s. 92(13)): see ch. 21, Property and Civil Rights, under heading 21.3, "Civil liberties", above.

48 On the distribution of powers over civil liberties, see Tarnopolsky, *The Canadian Bill of Rights* (2nd ed., 1975), ch. 2; Swinton, *The Supreme Court and Canadian Federalism* (1990), ch. 6.

incidental or subordinate position. The effect of this approach to classification is that the power to affect civil liberties is distributed between the two levels of government, depending upon which level of government has jurisdiction over the activities regulated by the law. For example, the provincial Legislatures may prohibit racial discrimination in occupations subject to provincial jurisdiction, and the federal Parliament may prohibit discrimination in occupations subject to federal jurisdiction. In other words, it is the nature of the regulated occupation that determines the law's classification, not the law's impact on racial discrimination. It should be added that the federal Parliament could probably enact a universal prohibition of racial discrimination (though not a more sophisticated scheme) under the criminal law power, but this would depend upon the law's classification as a criminal law, and in making that classification, the courts will look for the ingredients of a criminal law — a prohibition, a penalty and a typically criminal public purpose — and not primarily to the law's impact on racial discrimination.[49]

(c) Implied bill of rights

Restraints on legislative power that are derived only from the federal distribution of powers are incomplete, in that a law which is denied to one level of government will be open to the other level of government. For example, when Ontario's Lord's Day Act was held to be unconstitutional, on the ground that the observance of days of religious significance was a matter of criminal law,[50] the federal Parliament enacted a Lord's Day Act that was held to be constitutional for precisely the reason that had defeated it as a provincial measure.[51] Only under a bill of rights can the courts consider the question whether any legislative body should be able to impose Christian days of religious observance upon a pluralistic society.[52]

In the absence of a bill of rights, when a law abridging a civil liberty is challenged, the issue is ''which jurisdiction should have power to work the injustice, not whether the injustice should be prohibited completely''.[53] The theory that there are some ''injustices'' that should be ''prohibited completely'' is, of

---

49 This is offered as an example only. The egalitarian civil liberties are discussed more fully in ch. 35, Equality, under the heading ''Distribution of powers'', below.

50 *A.G. Ont.* v. *Hamilton Street Ry.* [1903] A.C. 524.

51 *Lord's Day Alliance of Can.* v. *A.-G. B.C.* [1959] S.C.R. 497.

52 After the adoption of the Canadian Bill of Rights in 1960, the Lord's Day Act was unsuccessfully challenged under the Bill: *Robertson and Rosetanni* v. *The Queen* [1963] S.C.R. 651; and, after the adoption of the Charter of Rights in 1982, the Act was successfully challenged under the Charter: *R.* v. *Big M Drug Mart* [1985] 1 S.C.R. 295. See ch. 39, Religion, below.

53 Weiler, ''The Supreme Court and the Law of Canadian Federalism'' (1973) 23 U. Toronto L.J. 307, 344, although Weiler points out that the Supreme Court of Canada has occasionally used federalism as a surreptitious bill of rights, allocating jurisdiction to that level of government which has not exercised it in order to invalidate a law which it really believes should not be enacted at all.

course, the impulse to adoption of a bill of rights. Indeed, some judges have professed to find in the Constitution Act, 1867 an "implied bill of rights". In the *Alberta Press* case (1938),[54] where the Supreme Court of Canada held that a province could not require newspapers to give the government a right of reply to criticism of provincial policies, Duff C.J.'s opinion could be read as suggesting that the Constitution Act, 1867 impliedly forbade both the Legislatures and the Parliament from curtailing political speech.[55] In *Switzman* v. *Elbling* (1957),[56] where the Court held that a province could not prohibit the use of a house to propagate communism, Rand J. left open the possibility that Parliament as well as the Legislatures might be incompetent to curtail political speech;[57] but Abbott J. went further, saying explicitly that "Parliament itself could not abrogate this right of discussion and debate".[58] Abbott J.'s obiter dictum was an unequivocal expression of the implied bill of rights theory.

The implied bill of rights theory was forgotten, or at least was never mentioned, by the Supreme Court of Canada from 1963 until 1978, when the Court decided the *Dupond* case (1978).[59] In that case, Beetz J., for the majority, said that none of the fundamental freedoms that were inherited from the United Kingdom "is so enshrined in the Constitution as to be beyond the reach of competent legislation". This seemed to have given the theory its quietus. However, like freeway proposals and snakes, the theory does not die easily. Since the adoption of the Charter of Rights in 1982, it has been revived in a number of obiter dicta, the clearest of which was uttered by Beetz J., who had been so dismissive of the theory in *Dupond*. In the *OPSEU* case (1987),[60] his lordship for the majority quoted with evident approval the dicta in the *Alberta Press* case and *Switzman* v. *Elbling*, and said that "quite apart from Charter considerations, the legislative bodies in this country must conform to these basic structural imperatives and can in no way override them". In context, it is clear that by "basic structural imper-

---

54 *Re Alta. Statutes* [1938] S.C.R. 100; this case is discussed in ch. 40, Expression, under heading 40.1, "Distribution of powers", below.

55 *Id.*, 133-134. This passage was quoted with approval in *Saumur* v. *City of Quebec* [1953] 2 S.C.R. 299 by Rand J. at 331, Kellock J. at 353-354 and Locke J. at 373-374; and Kellock J. at 354 and Locke J. at 363 each suggested the possibility of an implied bill of rights.

56 [1957] S.C.R. 285; this case is discussed in ch. 40, Expression, under heading 40.1, "Distribution of powers", below.

57 *Id.*, 307.

58 *Id.*, 328. He cautiously repeated the proposition in *Oil, Chemical and Atomic Wkrs.* v. *Imperial Oil* [1963] S.C.R. 584, 600.

59 *A.G. Can. and Dupond* v. *Montreal* [1978] 2 S.C.R. 770, 796; this case is discussed in ch. 40, Expression, under heading 40.1, "Distribution of powers", below. The quoted dictum was quoted with approval by Estey J. for the Court in *A.G. Can.* v. *Law Society of B.C.* [1982] 2 S.C.R. 307, 364.

60 *OPSEU* v. *Ont.* [1987] 1 S.C.R. 2, 57 per Beetz J.; 25 per Dickson C.J. is to the same effect. Other implied bill of rights dicta are to be found in *Fraser* v. *Public Service Staff Relations Bd.* [1985] 2 S.C.R. 455, 462-463 per Dickson C.J.; *RWDSU* v. *Dolphin Delivery* [1986] 2 S.C.R. 573, 584 per McIntyre J.

atives'' he meant the political freedoms, including freedom of expression, that were necessary to preserve ''the essential structure of free parliamentary institutions''.

Two reasons have been suggested in the dicta as supporting the existence of an implied bill of rights. The first is the language of the preamble to the Constitution Act, 1867, which refers to ''a Constitution similar in principle to that of the United Kingdom''.[61] The reasoning here is that civil liberties that were enjoyed in the United Kingdom in 1867 were intended to be enjoyed in Canada as well. The difficulty with this reasoning is that the central feature of the Constitution of the United Kingdom, and of its Parliament, was in 1867, and still is, parliamentary sovereignty: any of the civil liberties, including freedom of political speech, can be abolished by the Parliament at Westminster at any time. In the United Kingdom, the tradition of respect for civil liberties is not reflected in the law of the Constitution. It therefore seems likely that ''a Constitution similar in principle to that of the United Kingdom'' would not contain implied guarantees of civil liberties.

A second reason which has been offered in favour of an implied bill of rights is the Constitution Act, 1867's establishment of representative parliamentary institutions. The reasoning here is that free political speech is ''the breath of life of parliamentary institutions'', and therefore the establishment of such institutions must be implicitly accompanied by a guarantee of the conditions that are necessary to the effective functioning of the institutions. This is a stronger argument,[62] but it is subject to a similar difficulty to the argument based on the preamble. When the Canadian Constitution established parliamentary institutions on the Westminster model, the plausible assumption would be that they were intended to exercise powers of the same order as those of the Parliament at Westminster, and, of course, those powers included the power to curtail civil liberties, including freedom of political speech. Any limitations on legislative power, such as those entailed by the federal system, could be expected to be expressed, or at least very clearly implied. This seems especially clear with respect to a bill of rights. The framers of the Constitution had the United States Constitution before them; it was their only useful precedent. They followed its federal character, but they deliberately did not copy its bill of rights.[63]

---

61 Cf. *New Brunswick Broadcasting Co.* v. *N.S.* [1993] 1 S.C.R. 319, 375 per McLachlin J. for majority, holding that preamble incorporates into Constitution of Canada the rules of parliamentary privilege.

62 It can be buttressed by the suggestion in *Re Initiative and Referendum Act* [1919] A.C. 935, 945, that the establishment in the Constitution Act of representative parliamentary institutions guarantees the existence of those institutions. It is conceivable that this argument could be pushed so far as to guarantee freedom of political discussion: see Russell, ''The Political Role of the Supreme Court of Canada in its First Century'' (1975) 53 Can. Bar Rev. 576, 592; although the ironic result would be that the establishment of institutions in a written constitution radically distinguishes the institutions from those upon which they were modelled!

63 The implied bill of rights is supported by Scott, note 1, above, 18-21; Schmeiser, note 1, above, 203 (but compare 15) and Gibson, ''Constitutional Amendment and the Implied Bill of Rights''

The conventional wisdom is that legislative powers are exhaustively distributed in Canada. As has been explained in chapter 12, Parliamentary Sovereignty, while there are undoubted exceptions to exhaustive distribution, the principle is certainly inconsistent with the theory of an implied bill of rights. It seems to me that it is the principle of exhaustive distribution that is more faithful to the history and text of the Constitution Act, 1867. We have noticed that the adoption of the Charter of Rights in 1982 seems to have provoked the Supreme Court of Canada into a renewal of its lagging faith in the implied bill of rights.[64] This is surely a perverse reaction. Since s. 2 of the Charter explicitly guarantees freedom of expression, it is now even harder to argue that an implicit guarantee is to be derived from the Constitution Act, 1867.[65]

31.5 Constitution Act, 1982

The Charter of Rights, which is Part I of the Constitution Act, 1982, is a bill of rights that is part of the Constitution of Canada. It is the topic of chapters 33-54, below.

(1967) 12 McGill L.J. 497; and is opposed by Laskin, ''An Inquiry into the Diefenbaker Bill of Rights'' (1959) 37 Can. Bar Rev. 77, 103 and Weiler, note 52, above, 344.

64 Note 60, above.

65 Such an argument would normally be pointless since the explicit guarantee could be relied upon. Note, however, that s. 2 of the Charter is subject to the power of override in s. 33, while the implied bill of rights (if it exists) would not be subject to override.

32

Canadian Bill of Rights

32.1 History

We have already noticed that the Constitution Act, 1867 did not include a bill of rights.[1] This was an omission which never seems to have been regretted until after the second world war, when concern for civil liberties surfaced publicly and led to suggestions that a bill of rights should be adopted. Similar suggestions were being taken seriously elsewhere in the world. In 1948, the Universal Declaration of Human Rights was adopted by the United Nations; and a bill of rights has become an indispensable part of the constitution of each of the many developing countries which have attained independence since then.

In 1960, the Progressive Conservative government of Prime Minister Diefenbaker secured the enactment of the Canadian Bill of Rights.[2] It was enacted as an ordinary statute of the federal Parliament, and it was made applicable only to federal laws.[3] Apparently the government was reluctant to resort to the anachronistic procedure for amending the Constitution, and was convinced that the

1 See previous chapter, Civil Liberties, under heading 31.4, ''Constitution Act, 1867'', above.
2 The Canadian Bill of Rights, S.C. 1960, c. 44; R.S.C. 1985, Appendix III, is set out in an appendix to this book. For discussion, see Tarnopolsky, *The Canadian Bill of Rights* (2nd ed., 1975); Beaudoin, *La Constitution du Canada* (1990), ch. 22; Tremblay, *Droit Constitutionel-Principes* (1993), 321-325.
3 Section 32.2, ''Application to federal laws'', below.

provinces would not agree to the adoption of a bill of rights which was applicable to them.[4] However, the failure to entrench the Bill of Rights by constitutional amendment meant that it could be amended[5] or repealed at any time by the federal Parliament, and raised the question whether it could be effective at all. The failure to extend the Bill of Rights to the provinces (which would have required an amendment) meant that provincial violations of civil liberties were not covered at all.[6]

The Canadian Bill of Rights lost most of its importance in 1982, with the adoption of the Charter of Rights.[7] Most of the rights and freedoms guaranteed by the Bill are now guaranteed by the Charter. The Charter is part of the Constitution of Canada, and can be amended only by the constitutional amending procedures. The Charter is applicable to the provincial as well as to the federal level of government. In these circumstances, it would not have been surprising if the Charter had repealed the Bill. But it did not do so, and it is plain that the Bill remains in force, despite the fact that most of its provisions are duplicated by the Charter.[8] Those provisions of the Bill that are not duplicated by the Charter are two in number: (1) the Bill's "due process" clause (s. 1(a)), which extends to the protection of property, and (2) the Bill's guarantee (s. 2(e)) of a fair hearing for the determination of rights and obligations.[9] Both these provisions go beyond the guarantees in the Charter, and will therefore continue to be operative restraints on federal (but not provincial) activity.

---

4 Tarnopolsky, note 2, above, 88-92.

5 The Canadian Bill of Rights has been amended once by the ordinary action of the federal Parliament: Statute Law (Canadian Charter of Rights and Freedoms) Amendment Act, S.C. 1985, c. 26, s. 105 (amending s. 3 regarding pre-enactment scrutiny of bills and regulations).

6 It is of course open to the provinces to enact their own bills of rights, and Saskatchewan, Alberta and Quebec have done so: see previous chapter, Civil Liberties, under heading 31.3(b), "Statutory bills of rights", above.

7 See Hogg, "A Comparison of the Charter of Rights with the Canadian Bill of Rights" in Beaudoin and Ratushny (eds.), *The Canadian Charter of Rights and Freedoms* (2nd ed., 1989), ch. 1.

8 In the chapter in the previous note, at p. 4, I argue that duplicative provisions of the Canadian Bill of Rights are of no force and effect. However, this view is not consistent with dicta in *Singh* v. *Minr. of Emplmt. and Immigration* [1985] 1 S.C.R. 177, 224; note 27, below. Nor is my argument consistent with *Ford* v. *Que.* [1988] 2 S.C.R. 712, in which the Court held that s. 58 of Quebec's language law was invalid for conflict with the Quebec Charter of Rights and Freedoms, not the Charter of Rights, which had been overridden under s. 33; and that s. 69 of the language law was invalid for conflict with both the Quebec Charter of Rights and Freedoms and the Charter of Rights. Obviously, the Court treated the Quebec Charter of Rights and Freedoms as operating concurrently with the Charter of Rights. The situation of the Canadian Bill of Rights would be the same.

9 Both these provisions are discussed in ch. 44, Fundamental Justice, under heading 44.9, "Property", below.

32.2 Application to federal laws

The Canadian Bill of Rights applies to every "law of Canada". This phrase is defined in s. 5(2) as follows:

> The expression "law of Canada" in Part I means an Act of the Parliament of Canada enacted before or after the coming into force of this Act, any order, rule or regulation thereunder, and any law in force in Canada or in any part of Canada at the commencement of this Act that is subject to be repealed, abolished or altered by the Parliament of Canada.

This definition covers existing and future federal legislation, including "any order, rule or regulation thereunder", which would include subordinate legislation[10] and all administrative action taken under the authority of primary or subordinate federal legislation.[11] The definition also covers existing (but not future) laws that are "subject to be repealed, abolished or altered by the Parliament of Canada". This phrase is copied from s. 129 of the Constitution Act, 1867, and is intended to catch pre-confederation laws within the legislative authority of the federal Parliament which were continued in force in 1867 by s. 129. Very few of these would still be in force.

The definition does not cover provincial laws, not even provincial laws in fields of concurrent jurisdiction.[12] However, provincial laws that are incorporated by reference into a federal statute would be transformed by the incorporation (or adoption) into federal laws, and would become subject to the Canadian Bill of Rights.[13]

32.3 Effect on inconsistent statutes

(a) Meaning of s. 2

The Canadian Bill of Rights does not expressly state what is to be its effect on a federal statute that violates its precepts. Is the Bill merely a canon of

---

10 In legal theory, this is the status of the laws of the Yukon and Northwest Territories. However, in *Re Branigan* (1986) 26 D.L.R. (4th) 268 (Y.T.S.C.), it was held that the constitutional development of Yukon made it inappropriate to apply the Bill to territorial laws.

11 Query whether the common law in fields of federal legislative jurisdiction is covered. Taman, "The Adversary Process on Trial" (1975) 13 Osgoode Hall L.J. 251, 276 and Lyon, "A Progress Report on the Canadian Bill of Rights" (1976) 3 Dalhousie L.J. 39, 41 say yes.

12 Provincial laws are not covered by the closing language of the definition, because, although provincial laws in fields of concurrent jurisdiction may be rendered inoperative through paramountcy by inconsistent federal laws, it is not accurate to describe a provincial law that has been rendered inoperative by paramountcy as "repealed, abolished or altered": see ch. 16, Paramountcy, under heading 16.6, "Effect of inconsistency", above.

13 *Jack and Charlie* v. *The Queen* [1985] 2 S.C.R. 332, 338 (obiter dictum suggesting that Canadian Bill of Rights might apply to provincial laws adopted by s. 88 of the Indian Act).

interpretation for doubtful or equivocal language in federal statutes? Or is it a ''constitutional'' instrument which will override inconsistent federal statutes? The latter alternative would, of course, raise the constitutional question whether the Parliament could bind itself in this way by enactment of a simple statute.

The effect of the Bill on inconsistent statutes turns on the meaning of the opening words of s. 2, which state:

> Every law of Canada shall, unless it is expressly declared by an Act of the Parliament of Canada that it shall operate notwithstanding the Canadian Bill of Rights, be so construed and applied as not to abrogate, abridge or infringe or to authorize the abrogation, abridgment or infringement of any of the rights or freedoms herein recognized and declared, and in particular, no law of Canada shall be construed or applied so as to. . . .

These opening words are followed by a detailed list of legal civil liberties. A due process clause and the main political and egalitarian civil liberties are ''recognized and declared'' separately in s. 1 of the Act; but it is clear that the s. 1 liberties are included in the phrase in s. 2 ''any of the rights or freedoms herein recognized and declared'' and that they, as well as the s. 2 liberties, accordingly obtain their force from the opening words of s. 2.[14] It is also clear from s. 2 that the federal Parliament may exempt a statute from compliance with the Canadian Bill of Rights by enacting an express declaration that the statute ''shall operate notwithstanding the Canadian Bill of Rights''.[15]

What is not so clear in s. 2 is the meaning of the phrase ''construed and applied''. Does this require the courts simply to ''construe'' each statute so as to avoid as far as possible any conflict with the Bill of Rights, and then ''apply'' the statute as so construed? On this view, s. 2 is merely a rule of construction or interpretation. If a statute plainly infringed the Bill of Rights, so that the conflict could not be avoided by interpretation, then the effect of s. 2 would be exhausted and the statute would have to be applied despite its conflict with the Bill of Rights. This would follow even if the conflicting statute did not include the express declaration that it was to operate notwithstanding the Canadian Bill of Rights. A rule of construction cannot avail against a clear statutory intention to the contrary.

The alternative reading of s. 2 (which has now been judicially accepted) is to give the word ''apply'' in s. 2 some independent force, which can be done by

---

14 *Curr* v. *The Queen* [1972] S.C.R. 889, 896 per Laskin J.; *Miller and Cockriell* v. *The Queen* [1977] 2 S.C.R. 680, 686 per Laskin C.J.

15 The exemption clause has been used only once: Public Order (Temporary Measures) Act, S.C. 1970-71-72, c. 2, s. 12. This is the statute which superseded the Public Order Regulations which were made under the War Measures Act of 1914 to deal with the F.L.Q. ''October crisis'' in Quebec in 1970. The War Measures Act itself was exempted from the Bill of Rights not by a notwithstanding clause (curiously) but by a different form of words in s. 6(5), which was added to the Act by the same statute which enacted the Bill of Rights: S.C. 1960, c. 44, s. 6. The War Measures Act is discussed in ch. 17, Peace, Order, and Good Government, under the headings ''War'' and ''Apprehended insurrection'', above. As noted there, the Act was repealed and replaced by the Emergencies Act, S.C. 1988, c. 29, which contains no notwithstanding clause or other exemption from the Canadian Bill of Rights.

reading it as a direction not to apply a statute which is inconsistent with the Bill of Rights. On this view, the courts should first "construe" a statute to avoid as far as possible any conflict with the Bill of Rights, but if the conflict cannot be avoided by interpretation, then the courts should hold the statute to be inoperative. This reading is strongly supported by the language of the exemption clause in s. 2. A statute is exempt from the Bill of Rights if it is expressly declared that it "shall operate notwithstanding the Canadian Bill of Rights". The use of the word "operate" implies that in the absence of such a declaration the statute would be inoperative. Even more persuasive is the point that the Bill of Rights would hardly have introduced the exemption clause as a formula merely to escape from a rule of construction. A rule of construction will yield to any clear language; no special formula is needed for the purpose.

Anyway, after nearly ten years of doubt reinforced by conflicting judicial opinions, the Supreme Court of Canada by a majority of six to three rejected the view that s. 2 was merely a rule of interpretation and held that s. 2 had the effect of overriding inconsistent federal statutes by rendering them inoperative. This was decided in *R.* v. *Drybones* (1969).[16] In that case, s. 94(b) of the Indian Act, which made it an offence for "an Indian" to be intoxicated anywhere off a reserve, was held to be inconsistent with s. 1(b) of the Bill of Rights, which guarantees to the individual "equality before the law".[17] Ritchie J. for the majority of the Court[18] held that s. 94(b) was rendered inoperative by the Bill of Rights.[19] He held that the term "inoperative" was the appropriate one to describe the effect of the Bill of Rights on an inconsistent statute, and that the effect on the inconsistent statute was "somewhat analogous to a case where valid provincial legislation in an otherwise unoccupied field ceases to be operative by reason of conflicting federal legislation".[20]

The decision in *Drybones* made clear that the Canadian Bill of Rights was not a statute like any other. In *Hogan* v. *The Queen* (1975),[21] Laskin J. described its status in these terms: "The Canadian Bill of Rights is a half-way house between a purely common law regime and a constitutional one; it may aptly be described as a quasi-constitutional instrument". Despite this and other affirmations of the

---

16 [1970] S.C.R. 282.

17 The meaning of "equality before the law" is addressed in ch. 52, Equality, under heading 52.2, "Canadian Bill of Rights", below.

18 Fauteux, Martland, Judson, and Spence JJ. agreed with Ritchie J.; Hall J. wrote a brief concurring opinion, but also expressed his agreement with Ritchie J.; Cartwright C.J., Abbott and Pigeon JJ. each wrote dissenting opinions.

19 *R.* v. *Drybones* was followed in *R.* v. *Hayden* (1983) 3 D.L.R. (4th) 361 (Man. C.A.), in which the Indian Act offence of being drunk on a reserve was held to be inoperative (*Drybones* had concerned the off-reserve offence). However, *Hayden* was not followed in *R.* v. *Lefthand* (1985) 19 D.L.R. (4th) 720 (Alta. C.A.) (upholding the on-reserve offence). Both of these Indian Act drunkenness offences were repealed in 1985.

20 [1970] S.C.R. 282, 294-295; and see note 32, below.

21 [1975] 2 S.C.R. 574, 579.

overriding effect of the Canadian Bill of Rights,[22] Canadian courts continued to be very reluctant to apply the Bill. There have, however, been a few cases where it has been applied.[23]

In *Singh* v. *Minister of Employment and Immigration* (1985),[24] a challenge was brought by persons who claimed to be refugees to the refugee-determination process of the federal Immigration Act. That process could, and did in this case, result in a denial of refugee status without an oral hearing before an official with power to make the determination. The Supreme Court of Canada unanimously granted a remedy to the applicants, holding that they were entitled to an oral hearing notwithstanding the contrary provisions of the Immigration Act. However, the Court divided evenly on the legal basis for its decision. Wilson J., with the concurrence of Dickson C.J. and Lamer J., decided on the basis of s. 7 of the Charter of Rights, and said nothing about the Canadian Bill of Rights. Beetz J., with the concurrence of Estey and McIntyre JJ., decided on the basis of s. 2(e) of the Canadian Bill of Rights. Beetz J. did not rely on s. 7 of the Charter, because of doubt as to whether "life, liberty and security of the person" were affected by the refugee-determination process. (Wilson J. had decided that security of the person was affected.) Beetz J. preferred to rely on s. 2(e) of the Canadian Bill of Rights, because s. 2(e) afforded a right to a fair hearing whenever there was federal power to determine a person's "rights and obligations".

In *Singh*, while Wilson J. held that the offending provisions of the Immigration Act were "of no force or effect" by virtue of their conflict with the Charter of Rights,[25] Beetz J. held that the provisions were "inoperative" by virtue of their conflict with the Canadian Bill of Rights.[26] Beetz J. pointed out that s. 26 of the Charter of Rights expressly preserved "any other rights or freedoms that exist in Canada", which made clear that the Canadian Bill of Rights and the various provincial bills of rights remained in force. "Because these constitutional or quasi-constitutional instruments are drafted differently", he noted, "they are susceptible of producing cumulative effects for the better protection of rights and freedoms".[27] For this reason, these instruments should not be allowed to "fall into neglect".[28]

---

22 For obiter dicta reaffirming the overriding effect of the Bill of Rights, see *Lavell* v. *A.-G. Can.* [1974] S.C.R. 1349, 1364-1365 per Ritchie J., 1374 per Abbott J., 1382 per Laskin J.; *R.* v. *Burnshine* [1975] 1 S.C.R. 693, 714 per Laskin J.; *Hogan* v. *The Queen* [1975] 2 S.C.R. 574, 584 per Ritchie J., 589-590 per Laskin C.J.; *A.-G. Can.* v. *Canard* [1976] 1 S.C.R. 170, 205 per Beetz J.; *R.* v. *Miller and Cockriell* [1977] 2 S.C.R. 680, 686 per Laskin C.J.

23 As well as the *Hayden* case, note 19, above, the *Singh* case, note 24, below, and *MacBain* v. *Lederman*, note 29, below, there are the cases listed in note 49, below.

24 [1985] 1 S.C.R. 177.

25 *Id.*, 221.

26 *Id.*, 239, following *Drybones*. The word inoperative was also used in *MacBain* v. *Lederman* [1985] 1 F.C. 856, 883 (C.A.); note 29, below; following *Drybones* and *Singh*.

27 *Id.*, 224.

28 *Id.*, 224. Beetz J. for a unanimous Court in *Ford* v. *Que.* [1988] 2 S.C.R. 712; note 8, above,

In *MacBain* v. *Lederman* (1985),[29] a challenge was brought to the provisions of the federal Human Rights Code that provided for the appointment of a tribunal to determine complaints under the Code. The objection to the provisions was that they allowed the Commission, which was in effect the prosecutor, to select the members of the tribunal; this gave rise, so it was argued, to a reasonable apprehension of bias. This objection could not be raised under s. 7 of the Charter of Rights, because the tribunal had no power that could affect "life, liberty and security of the person". However, the tribunal did have the power to determine "rights and obligations". The Federal Court of Appeal, taking its cue from Beetz J. in *Singh*, held that s. 2(e) of the Canadian Bill of Rights applied, and that it rendered inoperative the appointment provisions of the Human Rights Code.

(b) Effect on earlier statutes

The Canadian Bill of Rights is a statute of the federal Parliament. What is the constitutional basis for preferring it over another statute of the federal Parliament? The general rule of the common law for resolving conflicts between two laws of the same legislative body is the doctrine of implied repeal: the later is deemed to have impliedly repealed the earlier to the extent of the inconsistency.[30] In *Drybones*, it was the Indian Act which was the earlier of the two statutes. This fact seems to eliminate any constitutional difficulty. To be sure, Ritchie J. denied that the inconsistent provision of the Indian Act was repealed, saying that it was merely "inoperative",[31] but in respect of constitutional power the difference is immaterial: if a later statute can repeal an earlier one, it can surely do something less drastic, such as suspend it or render it inoperative.[32]

(c) Effect on later statutes

What is the effect of the Canadian Bill of Rights on statutes enacted after the Bill of Rights? The Bill of Rights certainly purports to apply to later statutes. Section 5(2) defines "law of Canada" as including a federal statute "enacted before or after the coming into force of this Act", and the exemption clause in s. 2 contemplates that the Bill of Rights will be applicable to later statutes (since earlier statutes obviously could not include the express declaration). The courts have assumed without discussion that the Bill of Rights applies to post-1960

applied the Quebec Charter of Rights and Freedoms to strike down a Quebec law that was protected from Charter attack by a notwithstanding clause under s. 33 of the Charter.

29 [1985] 1 F.C. 856 (C.A.).

30 See ch. 16, Paramountcy, under the heading 16.1, "Problem of inconsistency", above.

31 [1970] S.C.R. 282, 294.

32 He did not explain the difference between repealing and rendering inoperative, but presumably the latter is suspensory only: the inconsistent statute (the Indian Act) would revive if the Canadian Bill of Rights were repealed. That is the effect of the paramountcy doctrine, which also renders statutes "inoperative" and which Ritchie J. suggested was analogous.

statutes. Both *Singh*[33] and *MacBain*[34] applied the Bill of Rights to post-1960 statutes, and no court has suggested that there is any distinction to be drawn between statutes enacted before the Bill of Rights and those enacted after.[35]

What is the constitutional basis for the application of the Bill of Rights to later statutes? The difficulty is that according to the orthodox doctrine of parliamentary sovereignty, the later (and more specific) statute should be regarded as impliedly repealing the earlier statute (the Bill of Rights) to the extent of the inconsistency.[36] On this basis, the Bill of Rights, although effective in rendering inoperative earlier inconsistent statutes, could not be anything more than a canon of construction with respect to later inconsistent statutes. For this reason, early commentators on the Canadian Bill of Rights emphatically denied that the Bill could override future legislation.[37] There is one possible escape from the remorseless logic of parliamentary sovereignty. If it is accepted, as I think it must be, that the federal Parliament can bind itself as to the ''manner and form'' of its future legislation,[38] then it is arguable that the notwithstanding clause in s. 2 of the Bill of Rights is a manner-and-form limitation.[39] The argument would be that Parliament has bound itself to enact laws inconsistent with the Bill of Rights only in a specified manner and form: that manner and form is the inclusion of an express declaration that the statute ''shall operate notwithstanding the Canadian Bill of Rights''. The conclusion of this argument would be that the Bill of Rights is entrenched, and that a later statute inconsistent with it is invalid unless it contains the express declaration described in s. 2 (the exemption clause).

In my view, the manner-and-form analysis has considerable force, although it is not helped at all by the insistence of Ritchie J. in *Drybones*[40] that the Bill of Rights renders inconsistent statutes ''inoperative''. The manner-and-form analysis would force us to say that later statutes inconsistent with the Bill of Rights were not merely inoperative, but invalid; the absence of the exemption clause would have the same effect as the absence of assent by the Governor General (for

33 Note 24, above.
34 Note 29, above.
35 The only exception is *R.* v. *Drybones* [1970] S.C.R. 282, 301, where Pigeon J. (who dissented) said, obiter, that ''different considerations may conceivably apply in the case of subsequent statutes''.
36 Note 30, above.
37 Gordon, ''The Canadian Bill of Rights'' (1961) 4 Can. Bar J. 431, 440 (''the attempt must be futile''); Laskin, ''An Inquiry into the Diefenbaker Bill of Rights'' (1959) 37 Can. Bar Rev. 77, 132 (''an unentrenched non-constitutional enactment [cannot] be given force to limit Parliamentary action''); Schmeiser, *Civil Liberties in Canada* (1964), 42 (the Bill ''cannot possibly apply to future legislation'').
38 See ch. 12, Parliamentary Sovereignty, under heading 12.3, ''Self-imposed restraints on legislative power'', above.
39 Tarnopolsky, note 1, above, 143.
40 Note 31, above. The word ''inoperative'' was also used in the two cases where the Bill of Rights has actually been applied to a post-1960 statute, namely, *Singh* and *MacBain*; the citations are in note 26, above.

example), namely, complete invalidity. Of course, the word ''inoperative' could still be accepted with respect to earlier statutes, for which the manner-and-form argument is irrelevant, since the special manner and form was not part of the law when they were enacted.

If the foregoing analysis is correct, the ironic result is that the exemption clause in the Canadian Bill of Rights, far from detracting from the efficacy of the Bill, is essential to its efficacy, at least in its application to later statutes. If it were not for the exemption clause, the Bill would be unable to prevail over later statutes.[412]

(d) Conclusions

The effect of the Canadian Bill of Rights on prior inconsistent federal statutes is to render them inoperative. The constitutional basis for this effect is the doctrine of implied repeal: since Parliament can repeal an earlier statute, it can do something less than repeal, that is, render a statute inoperative.

The effect of the Bill of Rights on subsequent inconsistent federal statutes which do not include an express declaration of exemption is also said to be to render them inoperative. Probably, however, the Bill of Rights renders such statutes invalid, not inoperative. The constitutional basis for this effect is the manner-and-form doctrine. Parliament has bound itself to enact laws inconsistent with the Bill of Rights only in the manner and form prescribed by the Bill of Rights.

32.4 Contents

The Canadian Bill of Rights guarantees the fundamental freedoms of religion, speech, assembly and association (s. 1(c), (d), (e), (f)). It guarantees a number of legal rights, including protection against arbitrary detention or imprisonment, protection against cruel and unusual treatment or punishment, the right to counsel, protection against self-incrimination, the presumption of innocence, the right to a fair and public trial and the right to an interpreter (s. 2). It guarantees equality before the law (s. 1(b)). As noted at the beginning of this chapter, these guarantees all have their counterparts in the Charter of Rights, which was adopted in 1982, and the replicated provisions of the Bill have lost their importance.[42]

There are two guarantees in the Canadian Bill of Rights that are not substantially replicated in the Charter of Rights. These are s. 1(a), which protects property rights through a ''due process'' clause, and s. 2(e), which guarantees a

41 Note, however, that the Supreme Court of Canada has upheld ''primacy clauses'' in human rights codes which were not accompanief by notwithstanding procedures: ch. 12, Parliamentary Sovereignty, under heading 12.3(b), ''Manner and form of future laws'', above.

42 Note 8, above, and accompanying text.

fair hearing whenever a person's rights and obligations are to be determined. Section 7 of the Charter covers some of the same ground as ss. 1(a) and 2(e) of the Bill, but s. 7 does not protect property rights and does not guarantee a fair hearing where only economic interests are at stake.[43] These provisions are discussed in chapter 44, Fundamental Justice, below.[44] For present purposes, the point is that ss. 1(a) and 2(e) of the Canadian Bill of Rights are the only provisions[45] that still have work to do following the adoption of the Charter of Rights in 1982.

32.5 Judicial interpretation

The Canadian Bill of Rights has, of course, left a legacy of case-law interpreting its provisions.[46] With respect to those provisions of the Bill of Rights that are not replicated by the Charter of Rights (ss. 1(a) and 2(e) are the only ones), the case-law is obviously of continuing relevance. With respect to those provisions of the Bill of Rights that are replicated by the Charter of Rights, the case-law is of little continuing relevance, even where the Bill right is expressed in the same language as the Charter right.

The Supreme Court of Canada was much criticized for its "timid" approach to the Bill of Rights. In the 22 years that elapsed between the Bill's enactment in 1960 and the Charter's adoption in 1982, the *Drybones* case[47] was the only one[48] in which the Supreme Court of Canada held a statute to be inoperative for breach of the Bill.[49] This cautious attitude stemmed in large part from the fact that the Bill was simply a statute,[50] which "did not reflect a clear constitutional mandate

---

43 It was the broader scope of s. 2(e) that caused it, rather than s. 7 of the Charter, to be relied upon in the *Singh* case, note 24, above, and *MacBain* v. *Lederman*, note 29, above. There are no post-Charter cases relying on s.1(a).

44 Section 44.9, "Property", below.

45 The Bill's prohibition (s. 2(a)) of "arbitrary . . . exile" is not reproduced in the Charter, but would be covered by the Charter's mobility clause (s. 6). The Bill's guarantee of "equality before the law" (s. 1(b)) stood on its own for the first three years of the Charter's life (see s. 32(2) of Charter), but on April 17, 1985 s. 1(b) was replicated by the coming into force of the Charter's equality clause (s. 15).

46 See Tarnopolsky, *The Canadian Bill of Rights* (2nd ed., 1975), chs. 5-8.

47 Note 16, above.

48 The *Drybones* case was followed in *R.* v. *Hayden*, note 19, above. Since 1982, there have been two more applications of the Canadian Bill of Rights, namely, the *Singh* case, note 24, above, and *MacBain* v. *Lederman*, note 29, above.

49 In some cases, however, a remedy was afforded which did not involve holding a statute to be inoperative: *Brownridge* v. *The Queen* [1972] S.C.R. 926 (right to counsel before taking breath test); *Lowry and Lepper* v. *The Queen* [1974] S.C.R. 195 (right to hearing before sentencing); *A.-G. Ont.* v. *Reale* [1975] 2 S.C.R. 624 (right to interpreter during judge's charge to jury); *R.* v. *Shelley* [1981] 2 S.C.R. 196 (Crown required to prove additional element of offence notwithstanding "reverse onus" clause).

50 The restrained attitude is well expressed by Laskin J. in *Curr* v. *The Queen* [1972] S.C.R. 889, 899, emphasizing the statutory root of the Bill; quoted with approval by Martland J. in *R.* v. *Burnshine* [1975] 1 S.C.R. 693, 707.

to make judicial decisions having the effect of limiting or qualifying the traditional sovereignty of Parliament''.[51] A reinforcing factor was that the Bill contained no limiting provision comparable to s. 1 of the Charter, so that the courts were inclined to avoid broad interpretations of the rights for fear that reasonable statutory limits on the rights would have to be struck down.[52]

The restraint that led the courts to defer to the legislative choices that were presented for judicial review under the Bill of Rights has not continued under the Charter. The courts have assumed that the constitutional status of the Charter resolves their former uncertainty as to the legitimacy of judicial review. Moreover, broad interpretations of the Charter rights are automatically subject to the qualification that reasonable legislation in derogation of a right may be justified under s. 1. These seem to be the principal reasons[53] why the Supreme Court of Canada has consistently refused to follow its Bill of Rights decisions when the same point has arisen for decision under the Charter.

The Supreme Court of Canada had decided that mandatory Sunday closing did not offend the guarantee of ''freedom of religion'' in the Bill of Rights;[54] but in *R.* v. *Big M Drug Mart* (1985)[55] the Court held that mandatory Sunday closing did offend the guarantee of ''freedom of conscience and religion'' in the Charter of Rights. The Court had decided that a police demand for a breath sample was not a detention, so that there was no right to counsel under the Bill of Rights;[56] but in *R.* v. *Therens* (1985)[57] the Court reached the opposite conclusion under the similar language of the Charter of Rights. The Court had decided that a rational ''reverse onus'' clause did not offend the presumption of innocence in the Bill of Rights;[58] but in *R.* v. *Oakes* (1986)[59] the Court held that all reverse onus clauses offended the presumption of innocence in the Charter of Rights. These cases[60] have made it abundantly clear that there is no presumption that language carried over from the Bill of Rights to the Charter bears the same meaning in its new context. On the contrary, the cautious, restrictive interpretations of the Bill of Rights are more likely to be repudiated in favour of a generous interpretation of Charter rights. In other words, decisions rendered under the Bill of Rights are of little precedential value in determining the meaning of the Charter.

---

51 *R.* v. *Therens* [1985] 1 S.C.R. 613, 639 per Le Dain J.
52 *Ibid.*
53 For extended discussion, see Hogg, note 7, above.
54 *Robertson and Rosetanni* v. *The Queen* [1963] S.C.R. 651 (upholding federal Lord's Day Act).
55 [1985] 1 S.C.R. 295 (striking down federal Lord's Day Act).
56 *Chromiak* v. *The Queen* [1980] 1 S.C.R. 471.
57 [1985] 1 S.C.R. 613.
58 *R.* v. *Appleby* [1972] S.C.R. 303; *R.* v. *Shelley* [1981] 2 S.C.R. 196. These cases established that a reverse onus clause was valid if there was a ''rational connection'' between the proved fact and the presumed fact.
59 [1986] 1 S.C.R. 103 (rational connection relevant only under s. 1). Accord, *R.* v. *Whyte* [1988] 2 S.C.R. 3.
60 See also *Singh* v. *Minr. of Emplmt. and Imm.* [1985] 1 S.C.R. 177, 209 per Wilson J.; *Re B.C. Motor Vehicle Act* [1985] 2 S.C.R. 486, 509-512 per Lamer J.

32.6 Scrutiny by Minister of Justice

The Canadian Bill of Rights contains an interesting noncurial enforcement clause. Section 3 of the Canadian Bill of Rights requires the federal Minister of Justice to scrutinize all proposed federal statutes and regulations "in order to ascertain whether any of the provisions thereof are inconsistent with [the Canadian Bill of Rights]", and it goes on to require that "he shall report any such inconsistency to the House of Commons at the first convenient opportunity".[61] As Peter Russell has noted, it is a weakness of this provision that it "entrusts the government itself with the responsibility of testing its own proposals against the Bill of Rights"; and he points out that "to put real teeth into such a provision, a standing committee of the House of Commons would have to be established".[62] Nevertheless, although only one report of inconsistency has ever been made,[63] the contemplated scrutiny does take place within the Department of Justice, and legislative proposals are sometimes modified before they achieve their final form.[64]

The Charter of Rights contains no obligations of pre-enactment scrutiny and report like those imposed by s. 3 of the Bill of Rights. However, in 1985 the federal Parliament amended the Department of Justice Act to require a similar scrutiny and report for compliance with the Charter.[65] As a result of this amendment (which confirmed a pre-existing practice), the scrutiny by the Minister of Justice of proposed statutes and regulations must encompass compliance with the Charter as well as the Bill.

---

61 Section 3 was repealed and replaced by S.C. 1985, c. 26, s. 105, but the changes were not significant. The quoted language is in both versions.

62 Russell, "A Democratic Approach to Civil Liberties" (1969) 19 U. Toronto L.J. 109, 125-126.

63 Report to the House of Commons by the Minister of Justice pursuant to s. 3 of the Canadian Bill of Rights", March 27, 1975 (a report concerning an amendment to the Feeds Act).

64 Tarnopolsky, note 2, above, 125-128, gives examples.

65 S.C. 1985, c. 26, which by s. 105 repealed and replaced s. 3 of the Canadian Bill of Rights (note 61, above), and by s. 106 added a new s. 4.1 to the Department of Justice Act, R.S.C. 1985, c. J-2. With respect to regulations, the obligation of scrutiny under the foregoing provisions (which cover regulations as well as bills) is duplicated by s. 3 of the Statutory Instruments Act, R.S.C. 1985, c. S-22. The existence of s. 3 is expressly recognized in the 1985 version of s. 3 of the Canadian Bill of Rights - that was the reason for its amendment in 1985 - and in s. 4.1 of the Department of Justice Act.

33

Charter of Rights

33.1 History of Charter

We have already noticed the absence of a bill of rights in the Constitution Act, 1867, the increased interest in bills of rights following the second world war, and the enactment in 1960 of the Canadian Bill of Rights.[1] The enactment of the Canadian Bill of Rights did not satisfy those who advocated a bill of rights for Canada. It was a merely statutory instrument. It did not apply to the provinces. And it had been given little effect even in its application to the federal government. Indeed, the inadequacies of the Canadian Bill of Rights were often offered as reasons for the adoption of a more effective bill.

The most prominent of the advocates of a bill of rights was Pierre Elliott Trudeau, who was elected to Parliament in 1965, became Minister of Justice in the Liberal government of Prime Minister Pearson in 1967, and became Prime Minister in 1968. His government, which remained in office with only one brief interruption from 1968 until his retirement in 1984, steadily sought to achieve provincial consent to an amendment of the Constitution which would include a new amending formula and a new bill of rights. That long quest culminated in November 1981 with an agreement which included nine of the ten provinces (Quebec dissenting), and which was followed by the enactment of the Constitution Act, 1982[2] of which Part I is the Canadian Charter of Rights and Freedoms.[3]

The Charter of Rights[4] has quickly proved itself to be a more effective instrument than the old Canadian Bill of Rights (which has, however, not been repealed).[5] Whereas the Bill is merely a statute, the Charter is part of the Constitution of Canada and can be altered only by constitutional amendment.[6] Whereas

---

1 See previous chapter, Canadian Bill of Rights, under heading 32.1, ''History'', above.

2 The Constitution Act, 1982 is Schedule B of the Canada Act 1982, c. 11 (U.K.).

3 The history of the Constitution Act, 1982 is more fully related in ch. 4, Amendment, under heading 4.1(b), ''The search for a domestic amending procedure'', above. For further discussion, see Bayefsky, *Canada's Constitution Act 1982 and Amendments: A Documentary History* (1989); Weinrib, ''Of Diligence and Dice: Reconstituting Canada's Constitution'' (1992) 42 U.T.L.J. 207.

4 For commentary on the Charter of Rights, see Gibson, *Law of the Charter: General Principles* (1986); Weiler and Elliot (eds.), *Litigating the Values of a Nation: The Canadian Charter of Rights and Freedoms* (1986); Sharpe (ed.), *Charter Litigation* (1987); Finkelstein and Rogers (eds.), *Charter Issues in Civil Cases* (1988); Beaudoin and Mendes (eds.), *The Canadian Charter of Rights and Freedoms* (3rd ed., 1996) Tremblay, *Droit Constitutionnel-Principes* (1993), 325-352. Mandel M., *The Charter of Rights and the Legalization of Politics in Canada* (2nd ed., 1994); Greene, *The Charter of Rights* (1989); Beatty, *Talking Heads and the Supremes* (1990); McLeod, Takach, Morton, Segal, *The Canadian Charter of Rights* (Carswell, loose-leaf service); *Canadian Charter of Rights Annotated* (Canada Law Book, loose-leaf service). The last work contains an excellent bibliography of the periodical literature, which is kept up to date, and I make no attempt to list it here, except for the outstanding article by Peck, ''An Analytical Framework for the Application of the Charter'' (1987) 25 Osgoode Hall L.J. 1.

5 Most of the guarantees of the Canadian Bill of Rights duplicate guarantees now contained in the Charter. However, several provisions do go beyond the Charter, and these provisions will continue to be effective as against the federal government. The relationship between the Bill and the Charter is examined by me in Beaudoin and Ratushny, *The Canadian Charter of Rights and Freedoms* (2nd ed., 1989), ch. 1.

6 The ''Constitution of Canada'' is defined in s. 52(2) of the Constitution Act, 1982, and the definition includes ''this Act'' of which the Charter is Part I. By virtue of s. 52(3), the constitutional amending procedure must be employed to alter the Charter. By virtue of s. 38,

the Bill's effect on inconsistent statutes is (or was) not clear, the Charter expressly overrides inconsistent statutes.[7] And whereas the Bill applies only to the federal level of government, the Charter applies to both levels.[8]

33.2 Protection of civil liberties

The Charter of Rights, like any other bill of rights,[9] guarantees a set of civil liberties that are regarded as so important that they should receive immunity, or at least special protection, from state action. This purpose is partially accomplished through the legislative and executive branches of government, which will normally do their best to avoid actions that would violate Charter rights.[10] Indeed, after the adoption of the Charter, all Canadian jurisdictions except for Quebec (which was protesting the adoption of the Charter) engaged in a review of the statute book and enacted amendments to a large number of statutes to correct perceived violations of Charter rights.[11] In the federal jurisdiction, there is a continuing statutory obligation on the Minister of Justice to review all proposed statutes and regulations for compliance with the Charter, and to report instances of non-compliance to the House of Commons.[12] In each province, some degree of scrutiny (admittedly not followed by any public report) would be undertaken by the Attorney General or Minister of Justice as part of his or her duty to keep governmental action within constitutional limits. It would be a mistake to underestimate the extent of executive and legislative compliance with the Charter, although for the most part it goes unnoticed and unrecorded.

---

the general (seven-fifty) procedure is the appropriate one. This procedure involves the concurrence of the federal Parliament and the Legislatures of two-thirds of the provinces having at least fifty per cent of the population of all the provinces.

7 Constitution Act, 1982, s. 52(1) (supremacy clause). The effect of the Bill on inconsistent statutes is discussed in the previous chapter on the Canadian Bill of Rights, under heading 32.3, "Effect on inconsistent statutes", above.

8 Constitution Act, 1982, s. 32(1), discussed in ch. 34, Application of Charter, below.

9 The purposes and effects of a bill of rights are the subject of a vast literature. Outstanding Canadian contributions are Russell, "A Democratic Approach to Civil Liberties" (1969) 19 U. Toronto L.J. 109; Smiley, "The Case against the Canadian Charter of Human Rights" (1969) 2 Can. J. Pol. Sci. 277; Macdonald, "Postscript and Prelude - the Jurisprudence of the Charter" (1982) 4 Supreme Court L.R. 321; Russell, "The Political Purposes of the Canadian Charter of Rights and Freedoms" (1983) 61 Can. Bar Rev. 30. See also note 4, above.

10 The second edition of this book (1985) was criticized for placing insufficient emphasis on Charter compliance by the legislative and executive branches of government: Slattery, "A Theory of the Charter" (1987) 25 Osgoode Hall L.J. 701.

11 E.g., Statute Law (Canadian Charter of Rights and Freedoms) Amendment Act, S.C. 1985, c. 26. Each province except for Quebec and each territory enacted a comparable statute between 1985 and 1987.

12 Department of Justice Act, R.S.C. 1985, c. J-2, s. 4.1 (added in 1985). This provision is modelled on s. 3 of the Canadian Bill of Rights, discussed in the previous chapter, Canadian Bill of Rights, under heading 32.6, "Scrutiny by Minister of Justice", above.

If the Charter's effect depended exclusively on the voluntary acts of government, there would obviously be no guarantee of compliance. Ultimately, the Charter is enforced by the sanction of nullification administered by the courts. If a law (or a governmental act) is challenged, and if it is found by a court to violate one of the civil liberties guaranteed by the Charter, the court will declare the law (or act) to be nugatory. In that way, the guaranteed civil liberties are protected from the actions of Parliament, Legislatures, government agencies and officials.

The Charter will never become the main safeguard of civil liberties in Canada. The main safeguards will continue to be the democratic character of Canadian political institutions, the independence of the judiciary and a legal tradition of respect for civil liberties. The Charter is no substitute for any of these things, and would be ineffective if any of these things disappeared. This is demonstrated by the fact that in many countries with bills of rights in their constitutions the civil liberties which are purportedly guaranteed do not exist in practice.

33.3 Enhancement of national unity

It is sometimes said that a bill of rights is a centralizing force in a federal state.[13] This is not true in any obvious sense. The Charter of Rights did not confer any additional powers on the federal Parliament. On the contrary, it limited the powers of the federal Parliament as well as the provincial Legislatures. But the Charter is a centralizing force in a subtle sense. It supplies a set of uniform national standards for the protection of civil liberties. These apply throughout the country, and in fields of formerly exclusive provincial jurisdiction. Some of these standards, namely, the mobility rights of s. 6 and the language rights of ss. 16 to 23, are avowedly directed to national unity, facilitating personal mobility and attempting to make the whole of Canada a homeland for French-speaking as well as English-speaking Canadians. But all of the provisions of the Charter give to persons whose civil liberties have been abridged by provincial (or federal) action the right to appeal to national norms which will be enforced by the court system, and ultimately by a national court, the Supreme Court of Canada.

It is true that the decisions of the Supreme Court of Canada on Charter issues will not be unifying in the sense of attracting national concurrence. Judicial decisions on matters such as pornography, school prayers, the funding of denominational schools, Sunday closing, minority language education, the right to strike, police powers and abortion are highly controversial and divisive. But the debates engendered by such decisions are national debates, on issues that transcend the federal-provincial or regional differences that occupy so much of Canada's public

13 Russell (1983), note 9, above, 31-43, to which the following text is indebted. See also Cairns, "Recent Federalist Constitutional Proposals" (1979) 5 Can. Public Policy 348; Hogg, "Federalism Fights the Charter of Rights" in Shugarman and Whitaker (eds.), *Federalism and Political Community* (1989), 249; Weinrib, "Canada's Charter: Rights Protection in the Cultural Mosaic" (1996) 4 Cardozo J of Int'l and Comp. L. 395.

debates. Charter issues do not call in question the legitimacy of Canada as a national political community. They assume that legitimacy, and they strengthen it by the further assumption that on issues of human liberty it is appropriate to have a single Canadian policy.[14]

I conclude that the Charter's conferral of a right to invoke national standards and a national court for the protection of civil liberties adds a dimension of allegiance to Canada as a whole that did not exist before 1982. The Charter is to that extent a unifying instrument.

33.4 Expansion of judicial review

(a) New grounds of review

The major effect of the Charter has been an expansion of judicial review. Judicial review is not new in Canada. Since confederation, Canadian courts have assumed and exercised the power to hold laws and acts to be invalid for inconsistency with the Constitution.[15] Until the adoption of the Charter in 1982, however, the provisions of the Constitution that yielded most of the invalidating inconsistencies were the provisions that distribute legislative powers between the federal Parliament and the provincial Legislatures. The Charter adds a new set of constitutional provisions that will invalidate inconsistent laws. Thus, whereas before 1982 judicial review in Canada was for the most part confined to federalism grounds, since 1982 judicial review can also be based on Charter grounds.

The addition of the Charter's grounds of judicial review has proved to be a substantial expansion of judicial review. Not only are Charter cases much more numerous than federalism cases, they are also more policy-laden. This is because many of the Charter rights are expressed in exceedingly vague terms, and all of the rights come into conflict with other values respected in Canadian society. The result is that judicial review under the Charter involves a much higher component of policy than any other line of judicial work.

(b) Vagueness of concepts

Take the issue of vagueness first. While some of the Charter rights are fairly specific, most are not. They depend upon vague words or phrases, including, ''thought, belief, opinion and expression'', ''assembly'', ''association'', ''life, liberty and security of the person'', ''fundamental justice'', ''fair and public

14 Section 1 of the Charter makes room for some diversity on civil liberties issues, but it also exerts a homogenizing influence on provincial policy-making, because the requirement of ''least drastic means'' discourages variations in provincial laws that derogate from Charter rights: see ch. 35, Limitation of Rights, under heading 35.11, ''Least drastic means'', below.

15 See ch. 5, Federalism, under heading 5.5, ''Role of the Courts'', above.

hearing'', ''cruel and unusual treatment or punishment'' and ''equal protection and equal benefit of the law''. The meaning of these phrases has to be determined by the courts. In performing that task, the judges will inevitably be influenced by their own social, economic and political values. They will also be influenced by their attitudes towards the appropriate relationship between the courts and the other branches of government. An attitude of judicial restraint would be deferential to the decisions of the political branches, resulting in judicial invalidation of political decisions only in clear cases of Charter violations. An attitude of judicial activism would be sympathetic to the expansion of the guaranteed civil liberties, resulting in frequent invalidation of the decisions of the political branches.

The history of the interpretation of the American Bill of Rights[16] teaches us how malleable is the vague language of a bill of rights, and how dramatically its interpretation varies with changes in the attitudes of the judges who have to apply it. Until the school desegregation case of 1954,[17] which brought the ''equal protection'' clause of the fourteenth amendment into prominence, the main area of controversy was the ''due process'' clauses of the fifth and fourteenth amendments. (The fifth amendment applies to the federal Congress; the fourteenth amendment applies to the states.) Those clauses provide that no person is to be deprived of ''life, liberty, or property'' without ''due process of law''. The due process clause of the fifth amendment was one of the grounds of decision in the *Dred Scott* case (1857).[18] In that case, the Supreme Court of the United States held that a federal law purporting to ban slavery from certain parts of the United States could not have the effect of freeing slaves brought into those states, because that would be a deprivation of the owner's property rights in his slaves. The American Bill of Rights thus became an obstacle to the emancipation of the slaves, an obstacle that was removed after the civil war by constitutional amendments.[19]

Another notorious case is *Lochner* v. *New York* (1905),[20] in which the Supreme Court of the United States struck down a New York law that limited hours

16 The American Bill of Rights is made up of the first ten amendments to the Constitution of the United States. These amendments were passed by the Congress in 1789 (the first year of the union) and were ratified by three-fourths of the states in 1791. Other civil rights amendments, of which the fourteenth (1868) is the most important, were added later. The term ''American Bill of Rights'' is often used to include all the civil rights amendments, and that is the usage in this book. There are also some civil rights provisions in the original Constitution, namely, prohibitions on ex post facto laws or bills of attainder (art. I, s. 9, cl. 3; art. I, s. 10, cl. 1), a provision prohibiting the states from impairing the obligation of contracts (art. I, s. 10, cl. 1), and a guarantee of jury trials in federal criminal prosecutions (art. III, s. 2, cl. 3).

17 *Brown* v. *Bd. of Education* (1954) 347 U.S. 483.

18 *Dred Scott* v. *Sandford* (1857) 60 U.S. (19 How.) 393.

19 The thirteenth amendment (1865) proscribed slavery. The fourteenth amendment (1868) conferred citizenship and equality rights on blacks and whites alike. The fifteenth amendment (1870) provided that the right to vote was not to be denied or abridged on account of race, colour, or previous condition of servitude.

20 (1905) 198 U.S. 45.

of work in a bakery to 60 per week and 10 per day. This law violated the due process clause of the fourteenth amendment, because it was a denial of "liberty" — the employer's liberty to contract with his workers — without due process of law. Holmes J.'s dissent has become famous: he pointed out that this legal argument masked a laissez-faire economic theory which had been deliberately rejected by the New York legislature.[21] The *Lochner* case was not an isolated one. In more than a hundred later cases, the Supreme Court of the United States applied broad conceptions of "property", "liberty" and "due process" to strike down state laws attempting to prescribe maximum hours of work, minimum wages, maximum prices and to restrain anti-union activity by employers. Only after President F.D. Roosevelt, in an attempt to save his "New Deal" legislation, had proposed his "court-packing" plan, did the Court change its mind and reverse these decisions.[22]

The American Court's rejection of *Lochner* and the other "substantive due process" cases is sometimes described as the "constitutional revolution" of 1937. That revolution brought to an end a remarkable period of judicial activism. However, in 1953, when Chief Justice Warren was appointed, the Court entered upon another controversial activist phase, which lasted until several years after the Chief Justice's retirement in 1969. The Warren Court gave broad readings to several of the clauses of the American Bill of Rights. The equal protection clause of the fourteenth amendment was held to require the desegregation of segregated schools[23] and the reapportionment of malapportioned state Legislatures.[24] The first amendment prohibition of an establishment of religion was held to require a ban on voluntary school prayers.[25] The fifth and sixth amendments were held to confer a number of rights on criminal defendants, and upon breach to require the exclusion of reliable evidence or the setting aside of convictions.[26] The eighth amendment's ban on cruel and unusual punishments was held to cover capital punishment.[27] Even substantive due process was revived, not to invalidate social

---

21 Holmes' own political views, unlike those of his fiends Brandeis and Frankfurter, were conservative: he had no particular sympathy for the laws that he would have upheld: Novick, *Honourable Justice: The Life of Oliver Wendell Holmes* (1989). His decisions were based on his interpretation of the Constitution, and his belief in the appropriate limits of judicial authority.

22 *West Coast Hotel* v. *Parrish* (1937) 300 U.S. 379. See also Tribe, *American Constitutional Law* (2nd ed., 1988), ch. 8; Nowak and Rotunda, *Constitutional Law* (4th ed., 1991), ch. 11.

23 *Brown* v. *Bd. of Education* (1954) 347 U.S. 483.

24 *Baker* v. *Carr* (1962) 369 U.S. 186; *Reynolds* v. *Sims* (1964) 377 U.S. 533.

25 *Engel* v. *Vitale* (1962) 370 U.S. 421; *Abington School District* v. *Schempp* (1963) 347 U.S. 203.

26 *Mapp* v. *Ohio* (1961) 367 U.S. 643 (excluding illegally obtained evidence); *Gideon* v. *Wainwright* (1963) 372 U.S. 335 (right to counsel); *Escobedo* v. *Illinois* (1964) 378 U.S. 478 (right to be informed of right to remain silent); *Miranda* v. *Arizona* (1966) 384 U.S. 436 (right to be informed of right to counsel).

27 *Furman* v. *Georgia* (19972) 408 U.S. 238. For the revival of capital punishment in the U.S.A., see ch. 49, Cruel and Unusual Punishment, below.

legislation, but to protect from state law a woman's "liberty" to have an abortion.[28]

The constitutional decisions of the Warren Court were, and still are, highly controversial.[29] They differed from the decisions of the *Lochner* era in that the Warren Court decisions vindicated values then current among American liberals, whereas those of the *Lochner* era vindicated values then current among American conservatives. Judicial activism can take any political direction depending in large measure on the political predilections of the judges.

The Canadian Charter of Rights, contains no protection of "property" and no reference to "due process of law" — omissions that are explained by concern about the substantive due process decisions of the *Lochner* era. However, s. 7 does confer protection on "liberty", and s. 7 substitutes for the phrase "due process" the equally vague phrase "fundamental justice". The Charter's other guarantees include language that is similar to, or even wider than, the American Bill, for example, the freedom of religion and freedom of speech clauses of s. 2, the rights of criminal defendants in s. 11, the cruel and unusual punishment clause of s. 12, and the equality clause of s. 15. As the later chapters of this book will show, the Supreme Court of Canada has willingly embraced the new powers conferred on it by this vague language. Ignoring the warning signs posted by the American jurisprudence, the Court has interpreted "fundamental justice" as a substantive concept, and used it to strike down a range of criminal laws,[30] as well as restrictions on abortion.[31] The rights of criminal defendants and the concept of cruel and unusual punishment have been carried well beyond the decisions of the Warren Court (or the Burger and Rehnquist Courts) in the United States.[32] Freedom of religion and expression have also been interpreted more broadly than in the United States.[33] In short, the Charter has ushered in a period of extraordinarily active judicial review. Curiously, this period of judicial activism has not been

---

28 *Roe* v. *Wade* (1973) 410 U.S. 113.

29 After Chief Justice Warren's retirement in 1969, the Court's active phase continued for a few years (see notes 27 and 28, above), but then the Court became more restrained. There were no more civil libertarian initiatives comparable to those cited in the previous notes, and a tendency emerged to qualify some of the criminal defendant rulings. But none of the major decisions has been reversed. Nor have the frequent attempts to overturn the decisions by constitutional amendment been successful.

30 *Re B.C. Motor Vehicle Act* [1985] 2 S.C.R. 486; *R.* v. *Vaillancourt* [1987] 2 S.C.R. 636; *R.* v. *Martineau* [1990] 2 S.C.R. 633; *R.* v. *Logan* [1990] 2 S.C.R. 731; *R.* v. *Hess* [1990] 2 S.C.R. 906.

31 *R.* v. *Morgentaler* [1988] 1 S.C.R. 30.

32 The comparison is carefully documented in Harvie and Foster, "Ties that Bind? The Supreme Court of Canada, American Jurisprudence . . ." (1990) 28 Osgoode Hall L.J. 729.

33 E.g. *R.* v. *Big M Drug Mart* [1985] 1 S.C.R. 295 (holding Sunday closing to be in violation of freedom of religion, notwithstanding American decisions to the contrary). A balanced appraisal of this area would need to factor in s. 1, which has had the effect of qualifying the Court's extremely broad definitions of religion and expression: see chs. 39, Religion, and 40, Expression, below.

accompanied by the public controversy about the role of the Court that has now become the standard fare of politics in the United States. It is not clear whether this is because Canadians are more respectful of their Court or because they are less disturbed by the liberal outcomes. It is probably a bit of both.[34]

(c) Role of s. 1

The previous section has addressed the problem of vagueness in the language of the Charter, and the discretion which vagueness inevitably confers on the courts whose duty it is to apply the Charter. But even if there were perfect agreement on the precise scope of every guaranteed right, the application of the Charter would still be a difficult, policy-laden undertaking. This is because the civil liberties guaranteed by the Charter occasionally come into conflict with each other and frequently come into conflict with other values that are respected in Canadian society. A moment's reflection is enough to show that the Charter's values should not always take precedence over non-Charter values. Take freedom of expression, for example. This freedom is undeniably limited by many laws that restrict what a person is free to say or write, for example, laws respecting fraud, defamation, misleading advertising or labelling, sedition, official secrecy, blasphemy, obscenity and contempt of court. No one would seriously suggest that s. 2 of the Charter should be applied to eliminate all laws limiting expression, because the purposes of some at least of these laws are just as valuable in their place as is freedom of expression. What is called for, obviously, is a compromise between the conflicting values.

Section 1 of the Charter, which is the subject of a later chapter,[35] implicitly authorizes the courts to balance the guaranteed rights against competing societal values. Section 1 provides:

> 1. The Canadian Charter of Rights and Freedoms guarantees the rights and freedoms set out in it subject only to such reasonable limits prescribed by law as can be demonstrably justified in a free and democratic society.

Section 1 makes clear that a law limiting a Charter right is valid if the law is a ''reasonable'' one that ''can be demonstrably justified in a free and democratic society''. Who is to decide whether a law satisfies the requirements of s. 1? Initially, decisions will be made by the government that introduces a bill in derogation of a Charter right, and by the legislative body that enacts the bill into law. But these decisions are not conclusive. When a law is challenged in the courts, the reviewing court will reach its own determination on the question whether s. 1 is satisfied. When appeals have been exhausted, it is the final decision

---

34 The former ground accords with the conventional wisdom, which holds that Canadians are more respectful of authority than Americans; the latter ground is inconsistent with the conventional wisdom, which holds that Americans are more devoted to individual liberty.

35 Chapter 35, Limitation of Rights, below.

of the courts that prevails over the judgment of the government and legislature that enacted the law.

Because of s. 1, judicial review of legislation under the Charter of Rights is a two-stage process. The first stage of judicial review is to determine whether the challenged law derogates from a Charter right. If it does not, then the review is at an end: the law must be upheld. But if the law is held to derogate from a Charter right, then the review moves to the second stage. The second stage is to determine whether the law is justified under s. 1 as a reasonable limit prescribed by law that can be demonstrably justified in a free and democratic society. In the second stage of judicial review, the reviewing court must decide whether the law should be upheld despite the fact that it limits a Charter right. In other words, the Court must decide whether the enacting legislative body has made an appropriate compromise between the civil libertarian value guaranteed by the Charter and the competing social or economic objectives pursued by the law. Before the adoption of the Charter in 1982, that compromise was worked out in the political arena. That will still occur, of course, but, under the Charter, the political judgment will be subject to judicial review. The courts will have to decide whether the Parliament or Legislature, in enacting an abridgement of a civil liberty, has drawn the line in the "right" place. In making that judgment, the courts will receive little guidance from the vague references in s. 1 to reasonable limits and demonstrable justification.[36]

(d) Role of s. 33

Judicial power under a bill of rights is naturally greatest when the court has a conclusive veto over legislation. This is the situation in the United States, of course, where the decisions of the Supreme Court of the United States can be overcome only by the difficult and time-consuming process of constitutional amendment. In Canada, however, the Charter includes, as s. 33, an override power, which enables the Parliament or a Legislature to enact a law that will override the guarantees in s. 2 and ss. 7 to 15 of the Charter.[37] Allthat is necessary is the enactment of a law containing an express declaration that the law is to operate notwithstanding the relevant provision of the Charter. Once this declaration has been enacted, the law that it protects will not be touched by the overridden provision of the Charter. This override power extends to s. 2 (expression), ss. 7 to 14 (legal rights) and s. 15 (equality). It does not extend to ss. 3-5 (democratic rights), s. 6 (mobility), ss. 16 to 23 (language rights) or s. 28 (sexual equality).

---

36 The attempt to develop standards that would limit judicial discretion and render decisions more predictable is described in ch. 35, Limitation of Rights, below.

37 The override power is discussed in ch. 36, Override of Rights, below. The Canadian Bill of Rights, s. 2, includes a similar power, discussed in ch. 32, Canadian Bill of Rights, under heading 32.3, "Effect of inconsistent statutes", above. So does the Alberta Bill of Rights, R.S.A. 1980, c. A-16, s. 2, the Quebec Charter of Human Rights and Freedoms, R.S.Q. 1977, c. C-12, s. 52, and the Saskatchewan Human Rights Code, S.S. 1979, s. S-24.1, s. 44.

With respect to these provisions, no override is possible. With respect to the provisions that can be overridden, any judicial decision could be overcome by the re-enactment of the invalid statute coupled with a declaration of override; in other words, the judicial veto is suspensory only. The fact that the elected legislative bodies have been left with the last word answers a good deal of the concern about the legitimacy of judicial review by unelected judges.[38]

33.5 Political questions

''All constitutional interpretations have political consequences''.[39] By denying government the power to do something it wants to do, or even by affirming the existence of the power, the courts are inescapably important parties to political controversies. Indeed, in Canada many political controversies find their way into courts. It is usually possible to construct an argument that any controversial government policy offends some part of the Constitution; and many organizations and individuals, and even some provincial governments, hold the puzzling view that losing an expensive constitutional case is a good way to advance their political objectives.

A constitutional challenge to a government policy will only succeed if the challenger can persuade a court that the policy is contrary to the Constitution. Inside the courtroom, the issue is determined on the basis of the language of the Constitution. Of course, the language of the Constitution may not speak clearly to the point, and the Court will have to exercise choice in determining what is the best interpretation of vague or ambiguous language. Issues of standing, mootness, ripeness or remedy may also have to be resolved, again involving the exercise of choice. But judges are not free to decide cases in accordance with their personal preferences or their ideological predilections or their sense of political astuteness, although no doubt these factors may unconsciously influence judicial choices. Judges decide cases by the application of standards of legality that are derived from the Constitution, the statutes and the decided cases.[40] Decisions of single judges are or course subject to appeal, as are many decisions of appellate courts until the Supreme Court of Canada is reached, and even the Supreme Court of Canada is subject to professional and academic commentary. Departures from standards of legality are thus open to correction and criticism.

38 If there was an override power in the American Bill of Rights, it would have offered a solution to the substantive due process decisions of the *Lochner* era. President Roosevelt's court-packing plan would not have been necessary. It must be conceded as well that some of the Warren Court decisions would probably have been overridden in some states.

39 This statement by Jackson J. of the Supreme Court of the United States is in his book: Jackson, *The Supreme Court in the American System* (1955), 56.

40 See Slattery, ''Are Constitutional Cases Political?'' (1989) 11 Supreme Court L.R. 507. For reference to the vast literature on the legitimacy of judicial review, see ch. 5, Federalism, under heading 5.5(b), ''Limitations of judicial review'', above.

In the United States, there have been occasional refusals to decide cases on the basis of a "political questions" doctrine.[41] The general idea is that there are some questions that are inherently nonjusticiable because they are too "political" for judicial resolution. American commentators are divided on the question whether there is indeed a political questions doctrine. One school of thought holds that each of the decisions can be explained without recourse to any such doctrine. For example, even where a court has invoked the doctrine, the refusal to grant a remedy may well turn on (1) the court's obligation to respect those decisions of the executive or legislative branches that are made within their constitutional authority, or (2) the court's refusal to impose limitations or prohibitions on government activity where the Constitution does not prescribe any.

Whatever the position in the United States, it is clear that there is no political questions doctrine in Canada. In *Operation Dismantle* v. *The Queen* (1985),[42] an action was brought by a peace organization for a declaration that the Canadian government's decision to permit the United States to test its air-launched "cruise missile" in Canada was a violation of the Charter of Rights. The Supreme Court of Canada struck out the statement of claim as disclosing no cause of action. The Court held that the federal government was acting within its constitutional powers in permitting the tests, and that no prohibition in the Charter (or elsewhere in the Constitution) applied to the tests.[43] However, the Court declined to place its decision on a political questions doctrine. Wilson J., speaking for a unanimous Court on this issue, said that there was no doctrine of political questions in Canadian constitutional law. If a case raised the question whether executive or legislative action violated the Constitution, then the question had to be answered by the Court, regardless of the political character of the controversy.[44]

The question whether the Parliament of Canada could place a five per cent cap on the growth of its payments to the provinces under open-ended cost-sharing agreements was (at least to provincial politicians) a controversial political question in 1990, when the policy was announced in the federal budget. When the policy was challenged in court by four provinces, the federal government argued that the issue was a purely political one that was not suitable for judicial determination. But the reference to the courts had transformed the issue into a legal one: did the Constitution contain any prohibition on the unilateral introduction and enactment of legislation to curb spending by the federal government under shared-cost agreements with the provinces? The Supreme Court of Canada in *Re Canada Assistance Plan* (1991)[45] held that this was a legal question that could be answered by the Court; and the Court went on to hold that there were no prohi-

---

41 See Nowak and Rotunda, *Constitutional Law* (4th ed., 1991), 104-114; Tribe, *American Constitutional Law* (2nd ed., 1988), 96-107.

42 [1985] 1 S.C.R. 441.

43 Section 7 was the basis argued for by the plaintiff.

44 [1985] 1 S.C.R. 441, 472. Wilson J.'s opinion was a separate concurrence, but on this issue Dickson J., who wrote for the rest of the Court, agreed with her: *Id.*, 459.

45 [1991] 2 S.C.R. 525.

bitions in Canada's constitutional law that would preclude the proposed legislation. Of course, if the Court had been asked whether the federal Parliament should as a matter of policy reduce its contributions to provincial social programmes, the Court would have refused to answer. The refusal might have been expressed in terms of the question being "political",[46] but the real point would be that the question was not one of law.

33.6 Characterization of laws

(a) Comparison with federalism review

Under the two-stage process of judicial review of legislation under the Charter of Rights, the first stage is to determine whether the challenged law abridges a Charter right. (If it does, then the second stage is to determine whether the law can be justified under s. 1.) In the first stage of judicial review under the Charter, there are two related issues that have to be resolved in every case: one is the characterization of the challenged law, and the other is the meaning of the asserted right. The first issue requires an examination of the purpose or effect of the challenged law in order to determine whether it limits a Charter right. The second issue requires an interpretation of the language of the Charter of Rights in order to determine whether it has been abridged by the challenged law. Obviously, these two issues are inextricably linked in practice. However, for the purpose of analysis, this section will consider the techniques by which a law is characterized for the purpose of Charter review. Succeeding sections will consider the techniques by which the Charter of Rights is interpreted. (The question of justification under s. 1 is left to a later chapter.)[47]

The characterization of laws for the purpose of *federalism* review has earlier been explained.[48] The courts attempt to ascertain the "matter" (or "pith and substance") of a challenged law; then they decide whether that matter comes within one of the classes of subjects (heads of power) that are conferred upon the enacting legislative body. In determining the pith and substance of a law, the most important consideration is the *purpose* of the law. Once the pith and substance of the law has been held to be within the powers of the enacting legislative body, it is no objection that the law may have some *effect* on matters outside the powers of the enacting legislative body. For example, a provincial law enacted for the purpose of levying a direct tax has been held to be valid and applicable to a bank, notwithstanding that the taxation of a bank has a significant effect on banking, which is a matter that is outside provincial jurisdiction.[49]

---

46 *Id.*, 545, asserting power not to answer a "purely political" question.

47 Chapter 35, Limitation of Rights, below.

48 Chapter 15, Judicial Review on Federal Grounds, under heading 15.5, "Characterization of laws", above.

49 This is the famous case of *Bank of Toronto* v. *Lambe* (1887) 12 App. Cas. 575; discussed in ch. 15, Judicial Review on Federal Grounds, under heading 15.5(a), "Matter", above.

The characterization of laws for the purpose of *Charter* review reflects a similarity and a difference between Charter review and federalism review. If the *purpose* of a law is to abridge a Charter right, then the law will be unconstitutional. That rule is similar to the federalism rule that condemns a law with the purpose of regulating matters outside the jurisdiction of the enacting body. It is in the legal result to be attributed to the *effect* of a law that a crucial distinction emerges between Charter review and federalism review. If the effect of a law is to abridge a Charter right, then the law will be unconstitutional (unless saved by s. 1), even if the purpose of the law was entirely benign and constitutional. This rule is the reverse of the federalism rule that tolerates effects on matters outside the jurisdiction of the enacting legislative body so long as the purpose (more precisely, the matter or pith and substance) of the law is within the jurisdiction of the enacting body.

(b) Purpose or effect

A law will offend the Charter of Rights if either its purpose or its effect is to abridge a Charter right.[50] This point was established by the Sunday-closing cases. In *R.* v. *Big M Drug Mart* (1985),[51] the Supreme Court of Canada held that the federal Lord's Day Act, which prohibited commercial activity on a Sunday, abridged the guarantee of freedom of religion in s. 2(a) of the Charter of Rights. The Court held that the history of the Lord's Day Act established that its purpose was the religious one of compelling the observance of the Christian Sabbath. That purpose was an abridgement of freedom of religion, which invalidated the legislation. It was not necessary to consider whether the effect of the legislation was to abridge freedom of religion, because "effects can never be relied upon to save legislation with an invalid purpose".[52] Moreover, legislation with an invalid purpose could not be justified under s. 1.[53]

In *R.* v. *Edwards Books and Art* (1986),[54] the Court was presented with another Sunday-closing law, this one enacted by a province in a statute that prescribed holidays for retail businesses. The Court held that the history of this law established that its purpose was the secular one of prescribing a uniform pause day for retail workers. Therefore, the law passed the purpose test. However,

50 *R.* v. *Big M Drug Mart* [1985] 1 S.C.R. 295, 331.

51 *Ibid.* Dickson J. wrote the majority judgment. Wilson J. wrote a separate concurrence, arguing that only effect (not purpose) was relevant to the characterization of laws for the purpose of Charter review.

52 *Id.*, 334.

53 *Id.*, 353.

54 [1986] 2 S.C.R. 713. The plurality opinion was written by Dickson C.J. with the concurrence of Chouinard and Le Dain JJ.; they held that the Act abridged freedom of religion, but was saved by s. 1. La Forest J. wrote a separate concurrence, reaching the same conclusions. Beetz J. with the concurrence of McIntyre J. wrote a separate concurrence, but on the ground that the Act did not abridge freedom of religion. Wilson J. dissented in part, because in her view the sabbatarian exemption in the Act was too narrow to be saved by s. 1.

the Court went on to consider the effect of the law, and the majority held that the effect of the law was to impose a burden on those retailers whose religious beliefs required them to abstain from work on a day other than Sunday. That effect was an abridgement of freedom of religion. Therefore, like the Lord's Day Act, this Sunday-closing law also abridged the Charter right. However, a majority of the Court relied on the benign purpose of the law to uphold it under s. 1.[55]

While either purpose or effect can invalidate legislation, Canadian legislative bodies rarely enact laws that have the purpose of abridging a Charter right. The Lord's Day Act has the special distinction of being the only law to fail the purpose test in the Supreme Court of Canada. The purpose of a law is normally benign (as it was in *Edwards Books*), and the breach of the Charter is an incidental effect of the pursuit of the purpose. Where this is the case, the law may satisfy the justificatory standard of s. 1, in which case the law will be upheld as a reasonable limit that is demonstrably justified in a free and democratic society. (This was the outcome in *Edwards Books*.) If the law does not satisfy the justificatory standard of s. 1, then it will be invalid by virtue of its limiting effect on the Charter right.

(c) Trivial effects

In *R.* v. *Jones* (1986),[56] another claim to freedom of religion came before the Court. The accused was charged with a breach of Alberta's School Act, because instead of sending his children to school he was educating them himself in the basement of the fundamentalist church of which he was pastor. Alberta's School Act actually made liberal provision for alternative schooling, but it did require that the accused obtain from the province's Department of Education either approval of his basement operation as a private school or approval in the form of a certificate of efficient instruction for parental education. The accused refused to apply for either of these approvals, because he claimed that it was contrary to his religion to request the State for permission to do what was God's will. La Forest J. for a minority of three held that the School Act did violate freedom of religion in requiring the accused to apply to the State for permission to educate his children. However, he upheld the Act under s. 1. Wilson J. for the majority held that the Act did not violate freedom of religion. In her view, where the effect of a law on a Charter right was ''trivial or insubstantial'',[57] there was no breach of the Charter, and that was the case here.

Jones was decided before *Edwards Books*.[58] In the latter case, the question arose whether the Sunday-closing law had any effect, or any substantial effect, on freedom of religion. The difficulty in the case was that any retailer who

---

55 The two cases also present an interesting contrast of characterization for federalism purposes: see ch. 18, Criminal Law, under heading 18.7, ''Sunday observance law'', above.

56 [1986] 2 S.C.R. 284.

57 *Id.*, 314.

58 [1986] 2 S.C.R. 713; note 52, above.

observed a sabbath placed himself or herself at a competitive disadvantage which would exist even if there was no Sunday-closing law. The Sunday-closing law removed that disadvantage from those retailers who observed Sunday as their sabbath, but that preference for Sunday-observers did not affect the practices of non-Sunday observers. This was the position taken by Beetz and McIntyre JJ. in *Edwards Books*: they held that the Sunday-closing law did not abridge freedom of religion. Dickson C.J.'s answer to this, for the majority, was that the Act, by relieving the Sunday observers of any financial penalty, exacerbated the competitive disadvantage of non-Sunday observers.[59] He went on to hold, after referring to *Jones*, that this increase in competitive advantage caused by the Act was not "insubstantial or trivial".[60]

(d) Severance

In *R.* v. *Big M Drug Mart* (1985),[61] the entire Lord's Day Act was held to be unconstitutional because of its inadmissible religious purpose. In no other Charter case has the entire statute been struck down. In other cases where there has been a holding of unconstitutionality, the vice infected only one or a few provisions of the challenged statute; those provisions were "severed" from the rest of the statute, enabling the rest of the statute to survive. The principles upon which severance is applied in both federalism and Charter cases have been examined in chapter 15, Judicial Review on Federal Grounds.[62]

(e) Reading down

Where the language of a statute will bear two interpretations, one of which would abridge a Charter right, and one of which would not, the Charter can be applied simply by selecting the interpretation that does not abridge the Charter right. This technique is known as "reading down". Its application in both federalism and Charter cases has been examined in chapter 15, Judicial Review on Federal Grounds.[63]

33.7 Interpretation of Charter

(a) Progressive interpretation

A constitution differs from an ordinary statute in that a constitution is expressed in language sufficiently broad to accommodate a wide and unpredictable

---

59 *Id.*, 765.
60 *Id.*, 766.
61 [1985] 1 S.C.R. 295; note 49, above.
62 Section 15.6, "Severance", above.
63 Section 15.7, "Reading down", above.

range of facts; a constitution is difficult to amend; and a constitution is likely to remain in force for a long time. These considerations call for a flexible interpretation, so that the constitution can be adapted over time to changing conditions. That is the source of the doctrine of progressive interpretation, which was elegantly captured in *Edwards* v. *A.-G. Can.* (1930)[64] by Lord Sankey's metaphor of "a living tree capable of growth and expansion within its natural limits". The requirement of flexibility or progressive interpretation obviously applies to the Charter of Rights no less than other constitutional provisions,[65] although the Charter is still so recent that the requirement is not yet apparent.

It is never seriously doubted that progressive interpretation is necessary and desirable in order to adapt the Constitution to facts that did not exist and could not have been foreseen at the time when it was written. For example, in 1967, the Supreme Court of the United States applied the right against unreasonable search and seizure in the fourth amendment to electronic eavesdropping — a practice that could not have been anticipated in the eighteenth century, when the fourth amendment was adopted.[66] However, when progressive interpretation leads to more radical changes in the meaning of rights, it is more controversial. In the United States, a school of thought, sometimes called "originalism" or "interpretivism", holds that the courts ought to adhere faithfully to the "original understanding" of the meaning of the Constitution.[67] Only in this way, it is argued, can the judges' own policy preferences be excluded from constitutional adjudication. Progressive interpretation is illegitimate, it is said, because it grants to unelected judges the power to amend the Constitution without recourse to the amending procedures provided by the Constitution. The amending procedures were included for the very purpose of keeping the Constitution up-to-date, and they constitute the only democratic way of accomplishing that purpose.

There are many theoretical difficulties with originalism, which are discussed elsewhere in this book.[68] From a practical standpoint, however, it is simply

---

64 [1930] A.C. 124, 136. The doctrine of progressive interpretation is discussed in ch. 15, Judicial Review on Federal Grounds, under heading 15.9(f), "Progressive interpretation", above.

65 *A.-G. Que.* v. *Blaikie* [1979] 2 S.C.R. 1016, 1029-1030 (interpreting s. 133 of the Constitution Act, 1867 one of the few bill-of-rights provisions); *Law Society of Upper Can.* v. *Skapinker* [1984] 1 S.C.R. 375, 365-366 (interpreting s. 6 of the Charter); *Hunter* v. *Southam* [1984] 2 S.C.R. 145, 155-157 (interpreting s. 8); *Re B.C. Motor Vehicle Act* [1985] 2 S.C.R. 486, 509 (interpreting s. 7); *Re Prov. Electoral Boundaries (Sask.)* [1991] 2 S.C.R. 158, 180 (interpreting s. 3).

66 *Katz* v. *United States* (1967) 389 U.S. 347. The Supreme Court of Canada, in *R.* v. *Duarte* [1990] 1 S.C.R. 30, has given a similar interpretation to s. 8 of the Charter, but of course s. 8 dates from 1982, when electronic surveillance could reasonably have been assumed to be within the contemplation of the framers.

67 See ch. 55, Constitutional Litigation, under heading 55.7, "Legislative history", above, where originalism is described and criticized. For fuller discussions, see Hogg, "Legislative History in Constitutional Cases" in Sharpe (ed.), *Charter Litigation* (1987), ch. 6; Hogg, "The Charter of Rights and American Theories of Interpretation" (1987) 25 Osgoode Hall L.J. 87.

68 Previous note.

inevitable that judicial interpretations will change with changing societal values. Judges are not historians, and, even if they were, they would be rightly reluctant to decide modern controversies by reference to research as to the attitudes of people long dead and gone. When the deficiencies of a purely formal theory of equality had been demonstrated to the Supreme Court of the United States, should it nevertheless have adhered to the separate-but-equal doctrine and perpetuated the segregation of the races in public schools?[69] When exaggerated notions of an employer's "property" and "liberty" proved to be incompatible with new kinds of regulation of labour standards, even including minimum wage and maximum hours, and much other social and economic regulation, should the Supreme Court of the United States have stood its ground and destroyed Roosevelt's New Deal?[70] As the latter example shows, changes in interpretation need not always take the form of an expansion of the guaranteed rights; in some instances, old interpretations will come to be seen as too broad, and hence too restrictive of legislative policy. In my view, a continuing review by the courts of their former interpretations of the Constitution is essential if a bill of rights is not to become a force of reactionary conservatism.[71] Moreover, in the case of Canada's Charter of Rights, I think it is clear as a matter of fact that the original understanding of many of the framers of 1982 was not that the Charter rights should be frozen in the shape that seemed good in 1982, but rather that the rights should be subject to changing judicial interpretations over time.[72]

(b) Generous interpretation

For Lord Sankey in *Edwards* v. *A.-G. Can.* (1930),[73] the primary implication of his living tree metaphor was that a constitution should receive a generous interpretation. He went on to say that the provisions of the Constitution Act, 1867 should not be "cut down" by "a narrow and technical construction", but should be given "a large and liberal interpretation".[74] This case decided that women were "persons" and accordingly eligible to be appointed to the Senate. It did not concern the federal distribution of powers. However, the dictum was taken up in

69 *Brown* v. *Board of Education* (1954) 347 U.S. 483 overruled *Plessy* v. *Ferguson* (1896) 163 U.S. 537.

70 *West Coast Hotel Co.* v. *Parrish* (1937) 300 U.S. 379 overruled *Lochner* v. *New York* (1905) 198 U.S. 45.

71 Originalism can be reinforced by its close cousin, the theory of "natural rights", which are rights that are rooted in nature and therefore not subject to change. The famous debate between Blackstone, the conservative, and Bentham, the reformer, as to whether natural rights exist was revived by two lesser mortals in reference to Canada's Charter of Rights: Vaughan, "On being a Positivist: Does it really matter?" (1991) 29 Osgoode Hall L.J. 399; Hogg, "On being a Positivist: A Reply" (1991) 29 Osgoode Hall L.J. 411.

72 Chapter 57, Proof, under heading 57.1(f), "Progressive interpretation", below.

73 Note 64, above.

74 *Ibid.*

later cases that did concern the federal distribution of powers.[75] The later cases emphasized that a large and liberal interpretation of the provisions of the Constitution that allocate powers to the federal Parliament and provincial Legislatures has the effect of conferring the ''widest amplitude'' of power on those bodies. In the context of federalism, the large and liberal interpretation is the course of judicial restraint; it tends to uphold challenged legislation, reinforcing a presumption of constitutionality.

The Charter of Rights does not confer power on the Parliament or Legislatures. On the contrary, it denies power to the Parliament and Legislatures. A generous interpretation of the Charter cannot be justified as increasing the powers of the legislative bodies; it will have the effect of reducing their powers. It is the course of judicial activism, since it will lead to more invalidations of laws than a narrow interpretation of the Charter. The justification for a generous interpretation of the Charter is that it will give full effect to the civil liberties that are guaranteed by the Charter. That was the approach of the Supreme Court of Canada in *A.-G. Que.* v. *Blaikie* (1979),[76] in giving a broad interpretation to s. 133 of the Constitution Act, 1867, the language guarantee that is one of the few bill of rights provisions in the 1867 instrument. With respect to the Charter, the Court has agreed that it calls for ''a generous interpretation, avoiding what has been called 'the austerity of tabulated legalism', suitable to give to individuals the full measure of the fundamental rights and freedoms referred to''.[77]

When the judges speak of a generous or broad interpretation of the Charter, they are referring to the scope of the guaranteed rights. It should not be overlooked, however, that there is a second stage to judicial review under the Charter, and that is the application of the standard of justification under s. 1. There is a relationship between the scope of the rights guaranteed by the Charter and the standard of justification under s. 1. In *R.* v. *Oakes* (1986),[78] which is examined at length in chapter 35, Limitation of Rights,[79] the Court decided to prescribe a single standard of justification for all rights, to make that standard a high one, and to cast the

---

75 *British Coal Corp.* v. *The King* [1935] A.C. 500, 518; *A.-G. Ont.* v. *A.-G. Can.* (Privy Council Appeals) [1947] A.C. 127, 154. Both cases gave a liberal interpretation to s. 101, which empowers Parliament to establish a general court of appeal for Canada.

76 [1979] 2 S.C.R. 1016, 1029-1030, justifying the decision that the reference to courts in s. 133 included administrative tribunals.

77 *Min. of Home Affairs* v. *Fisher* [1980] A.C. 319, 328 (P.C., Bermuda) per Lord Wilberforce in reference to Bermuda's bill of rights; quoted in *Hunter* v. *Southam* [1984] 2 S.C.R. 145, 156. To the same effect is *R.* v. *Big M Drug Mart* [1985] 1 S.C.R. 295, 344; *Re B.C. Motor Vehicle Act* [1985] 2 S.C.R. 486, 509; *United States* v. *Cotroni* [1989] 1 S.C.R. 1469, 1480; *Re Prov. Electoral Boundaries (Sask.)* [1991] 2 S.C.R. 158, 179. In the case of language rights, however, which are ''peculiar to Canada'', are ''based on a political compromise'', and are ''expressed in more precise and flexible language'', a more restrained interpretation is said to be called for: *MacDonald* v. *City of Montreal* [1986] 1 S.C.R. 460, 500; *Société des Acadiens* v. *Assn. of Parents* [1986] 1 S.C.R. 549, 578.

78 [1986] 1 S.C.R. 103.

79 Chapter 35, under heading 35.8(b), ''Oakes test'', below.

burden of satisfying it on the government. This insistence that the test of justification be a stringent one is, in practice, inconsistent with the insistence that the guaranteed rights be given a generous (broad) scope. If the scope of the guaranteed rights is wide, they are bound to reach conduct that is not really worthy of constitutional protection. If Parliament or a Legislature attempts to regulate conduct that is guaranteed only by virtue of an artificially wide definition of the Charter rights, the courts are going to strive to uphold the legislation. Since the courts can uphold the legislation only under s. 1, they will strive to find that s. 1 is satisfied, and the inevitable result will be the erosion of the *Oakes* standard of justification.[80]

Freedom of expression may be the most obvious example of the connection between the scope of a right and the stringency of s. 1 justification. It is obvious that any attempt to regulate political debate should have to face a stringent standard of justification under s. 1. But if the Court decides, as it seems to have done, that every communicative act, no matter how trivial, false or harmful, enjoys constitutional protection, then it is inevitable that the Court will relax the standard of s. 1 justification in order to accommodate laws that are generally approved. For example, the Court has held that advertising is constitutionally protected, but has sustained provincial regulation of advertising directed at children — despite a weak case of justification under s. 1.[81] Soliciting for the purpose of prostitution is also protected by the Constitution, which would no doubt surprise many Canadians, but few would be surprised to find that the Criminal Code offence has been upheld under s. 1 — although the case for justification was weak.[82] Similar comments could be made about hate propaganda,[83] obscenity,[84] defamation[85] and nude dancing,[86] which are some of the other activities caught by the broad scope of s. 2(b) of the Charter of Rights.[87]

Does it make much difference whether the Court gives a wide interpretation to rights and relaxes the standard of justification under s. 1, or gives a narrow interpretation[88] to rights and maintains the stringent standard of justification called for by *Oakes*? If we assume that the outcomes of cases will be much the same under either approach, the second approach is surely preferable, because it will

---

80 This thesis is advanced in more detail in Hogg, ''Interpreting the Charter of Rights: Generosity and Justification'' (1990) 28 Osgoode Hall L.J. 817.

81 *Irwin Toy* v. *Que.* [1989] 1 S.C.R. 927; but note the failure of s. 1 justification in *Ford* v. *Que.* [1988] 2 S.C.R. 712, *Rocket* v. *Royal College of Dental Surgeons* [1990] 2 S.C.R. 232 and *RJR-MacDonald* v. *Can.* [1995] 3 S.C.R. 199.

82 *Re ss. 193 and 195.1 of Crim. Code* [1990] 1 S.C.R. 1123.

83 *R.* v. *Keegstra* [1990] 3 S.C.R. 697 (prohibition on hate propaganda upheld under s. 1).

84 *R.* v. *Butler* [1992] 1 S.C.R. 452 (prohibition on obscenity upheld under s. 1).

85 *Hill v. Church of Scientology* [1995] 2 S.C.R. 1130 (tort of defamation upheld under s. 1).

86 E.g., *Re Koumoudouros* (1984) 45 O.R. (2d) 426 (Div. Ct.) (prohibition on nude dancing upheld under s. 1).

87 See ch. 40, Expression, below.

88 I use narrow in contradistinction to wide, but, as I argue in the next section, the correct approach is a purposive one, which will usually (but not always) have the effect of narrowing the right.

reduce the volume of litigation and limit the policy-making role of the courts. If the scope of the guaranteed rights is wide, and the standard of justification is relaxed, then a large number of Charter challenges will come before the courts, and will fall to be determined under s. 1. Since s. 1 requires that the policy of the legislation be balanced against the policy of the Charter, and since it is difficult to maintain meaningful standards to constrain the balancing process, judicial review will become even more unpredictable than it is now. While there are signs that some judges welcome such extensive powers, most judges will be concerned to stem the wasteful floods of litigation, to limit the occasions when they have to review the policy choices of legislative bodies, and to introduce meaningful rules to the process of Charter review. These purposes can be accomplished only by restricting the scope of the Charter rights.[89]

(c) Purposive interpretation

How can the scope of the Charter rights be restricted without abandoning or undermining the civil libertarian values that the Charter protects? The Supreme Court of Canada has answered this question in its insistence on a ''purposive'' interpretation of the Charter rights.[90] What this involves is an attempt to ascertain the purpose of each Charter right, and then to interpret the right so as to include activity that comes within the purpose and exclude activity that does not. Of course, this cannot be anything more than a general approach to interpretation. The actual purpose of a right is usually unknown, and so a court has a good deal of discretion in deciding what the purpose is, and at what level of generality it should be expressed. But some guidance can be obtained from the language in which the right is expressed, from the implications to be drawn from the context in which the right is to be found, including other parts of the Charter, from the pre-Charter history of the right and from the legislative history of the Charter. Moreover, as a body of case-law develops on the meaning of a particular right, the core of the definition tends to become settled.[91]

The Court has generally assumed that a ''purposive'' approach and a ''generous'' approach are one and the same thing — or at least are not inconsistent. Indeed, statements of the purposive approach have nearly always been accompanied — often in the same sentence — by statements of the generous approach.[92]

---

89 In American parlance, I am advocating more ''definitional balancing'' (by applying the purposive approach to yield a definition of the right: see next section) and less ''ad hoc balancing'' (under s. 1): see Peck, note 4, above, 21-31. I here part company with Beatty, note 4, above, who holds the view that the presence of s. 1 in the Charter precludes definitional balancing; on his view, all balancing should take place under s. 1.

90 E.g., *Hunter* v. *Southam* [1984] 2 S.C.R. 145, 156; *R.* v. *Big M Drug Mart* [1985] 1 S.C.R. 295, 344; *Re B.C. Motor Vehicle Act* [1985] 2 S.C.R. 486, 499.

91 For analysis of purposive interpretation, see Peck, note 4, above, 6-31.

92 This is true of each of the citations in the previous note. Note, however, that in *Big M*, which contains the fullest explanation of the purposive approach, Dickson J. warned (at 344) that judges should not ''overshoot'' the purpose of the right.

In the case of some rights, that is correct: a purposive interpretation will yield a broad scope for the right.[93] In the case of most rights, however, the widest possible reading of the right, which is the most generous interpretation, will ''overshoot'' the purpose of the right, by including behaviour that is outside the purpose and unworthy of constitutional protection. The effect of a purposive approach is normally going to be to narrow the scope of the right.[94] Generosity is a helpful idea as long as it is subordinate to purpose. Obviously, the courts in interpreting the Charter should avoid narrow, legalistic interpretations that might be appropriate to a detailed statute.[95] But if the goal of generosity is set free from the limiting framework of purpose, the results of a generous interpretation will normally be inconsistent with the purposive approach.

The purposive approach, it seems to me, works in perfect harmony with the stringent standard of justification under s. 1. Once a right has been confined to its purpose, it seems obvious that a government ought to have to satisfy a stringent standard of justification to uphold legislation limiting the right.

(d) Process as purpose

The undoubted usefulness of a purposive interpretation invites the question whether the Charter has a single over-arching purpose which would illuminate each provision. In the United States, Ely has argued that the purpose of the Bill of Rights is to protect the *process* of decision-making.[96] In the case of some rights, it is process writ small, namely, procedural fairness in the resolution of individual disputes. In the case of other rights, it is process writ large, namely, reinforcing the democratic political process. All rights are ultimately directed to one of these two kinds of process. In principle, Ely's argument could easily be adapted to fit Canada's Charter, and Fairley and Monahan have both taken that step.[97] In Monahan's words, the Charter does not require the courts ''to test the substantive outcomes of the political process against some theory of the right or the good'';

---

93 This is the case for s. 8: *Hunter* v. *Southam* [1984] 2 S.C.R. 145 (stipulating standards of reasonableness); *R.* v. *Duarte* [1990] 1 S.C.R. 30 (extending s. 8 to electronic surveillance).

94 E.g., *Law Society of Upper Can.* v. *Skapinker* [1984] 1 S.C.R. 357 (s. 6 does not guarantee a general right to work); *Andrews* v. *Law Society of B.C.* [1989] 1 S.C.R. 143 (s. 25 prohibits discrimination only on the stated grounds or analogous grounds).

95 Neither the federal nor the provincial Interpretations Acts apply to the Charter: *Law Society of Upper Can.* v. *Spakinker* [1984] 1 S.C.R. 357, 370. Technically, of course, the Charter is Part I of the Constitution Act, 1982, which is a schedule to a U.K. statute, the Canada Act 1982 (U.K.), 1982, c. 11; but the two Acts were entirely drafted in Canada and passed in the form of a resolution by the federal Parliament; it would be absurd to apply the U.K. Interpretation Act to them.

96 Ely, *Democracy and Distrust* (1982).

97 Fairley, ''Enforcing the Charter: Some Thoughts on an Appropriate and Just Standard for Judicial Review'' (1982) 4 Supreme Court L.R. 217; Monahan, ''Judicial Review and Democracy: A Theory of Judicial Review'' (1986) 21 U.B.C. L. Rev. 87.

rather, the Charter guarantees the integrity of the political process itself by enhancing "the opportunities for public debate and collective deliberation".[98]

This process-based theory of judicial review offers two important advantages. The first advantage is that it supplies a helpful context for interpreting particular guarantees. The guarantees of free speech or expression, for example, should be seen not as constitutive of personal autonomy (a substantive value), but as an instrument of democratic government (a process-based value). The guarantees of due process or fundamental justice should be seen not as requiring substantively just (or good) outcomes, but as requiring a fair procedure.

The second advantage of the process-based theory of judicial review is that it offers a solution to the problem of the legitimacy of judicial review. Under this theory, the judges need never take positions on controversial substantive issues, because the constitution does not address such issues. All that the judges are concerned with is the fairness of the process by which legislative bodies or other agencies or officials reach their decisions. It is not the wisdom, justice or rightness of the outcomes of the political process, but the integrity of the process itself, that is the proper subject of judicial review. When a bench of non-elected judges strikes down a statute enacted by an elected legislative body, it is doing so either because the process of enacting the statute was flawed or because the statute itself places impediments in the way of a fair political process. Such decisions may be controversial, but they involve judgments only on matters of process or procedure; they do not trespass on the exclusive power of elected officials to determine the substantive values by which society is to be governed. Viewed in this light, the power of judicial review is not incompatible with democracy; indeed, process-based judicial review casts the judges in the role of "servants of democracy even as they strike down the actions of supposedly democratic governments".[99]

At first glance, the process-based theory is attractive. Even if the crucial distinction between process and substance is hard to draw, the theory provides a means of limiting the scope of some of the broader Charter guarantees and thereby reduces the political element of judicial decision-making. I have no doubt that judicial review is best addressed to process rather than substance, but I do not think that process provides a satisfactory general or comprehensive theory of judicial review, either under the American Bill of Rights or under the Charter of Rights. With respect to the American Bill of rights, Tribe[100] and Dworkin[101] have effectively criticized Ely's thesis. With respect to the Charter of Rights, I have attempted to do the same thing,[102] and I will just summarize the points here. First, many of the broader Charter guarantees are inescapably substantive, or have been

---

98 Monahan, note 96, above, 89. Cf. Fairley, note 96, above, 234.

99 Tribe, "The Puzzling Persistence of Process-Based Constitutional Theories" (1980) 89 Yale L.J. 1063, 1063.

100 *Ibid.*

101 Dworkin, "The Forum of Principle" (1981) 56 N.Y.U.L. Rev. 469.

102 Hogg, "The Charter of Rights and American Theories of Interpretation" (1987) 25 Osgoode Hall L.J. 87.

interpreted to be so; and only a few are truly supportive of the democratic political process.[103] Secondly, the legal rights guarantees, although procedural in form, are ultimately directed to the substantive goal of respect for individual liberty, dignity and privacy. Indeed, all the Charter guarantees respect some aspect of individual liberty, dignity or privacy. They cannot be subsumed under a single process rubric. There is no escaping the fact that judicial review enables the judges to strike down those products of the democratic political process that fail to respect those aspects of individual autonomy that are guaranteed by the Charter.

(e) Hierarchy of rights

The Charter of Rights, by s. 33, provides for the override of some rights by the inclusion of a notwithstanding clause in the overriding statute.[104] The rights that can be overridden in this way are those guaranteed by s. 2 (freedom of religion, expression, assembly and association), ss. 7-14 (legal rights) and s. 15 (equality). The rights that cannot be overridden in this way are those guaranteed by ss. 3-5 (democratic rights), s. 6 (mobility), ss. 16-23 (language) and s. 28 (sexual equality). Section 33 thus creates two tiers of rights: the ''common rights'' that are subject to override, and the ''privileged rights'' that are not. One right, namely, the right to sexual equality (s. 28), may even be exempt from the limitation power of s. 1 as well as the override power of s. 33.[105] That places s. 28 at the top of the hierarchy. Aboriginal and treaty rights, which are guaranteed by s. 35, are similarly privileged in that they are subject to neither s. 1 nor s. 33; this is because s. 35 is outside the Charter of Rights.[106] However, being outside the Charter of Rights, is not entirely beneficial, because it means that s. 24, which provides a remedy for breach of Charter rights, does not provide a remedy for breach of aboriginal and treaty rights.

There seems to be no rational basis for the Charter's distinctions between rights. It could, I think, be argued that the right to vote is more valuable than other rights, but why are mobility rights and language rights also exempt from s. 33? Why is Parliament free to restrict political debate by overriding s. 2, or impose a cruel and unusual punishment by overriding s. 12, but is not free to invoke s. 33 to restrict personal mobility or the guaranteed uses of the English or French language? With respect to equality, the distinctions are even harder to defend. Why is racial discrimination possible by the invocation of s. 33, while sexual discrimination is absolutely precluded? Those who regard the Charter as reflecting

103 Language rights certainly do not fit the model, as both Monahan and Fairley acknowledge. But freedom of conscience and religion, freedom of expression and mobility, while certainly contributing to an open political process, extend well beyond that purpose. Equality, as limited in *Andrews* v. *Law Society of B.C.* [1989] 1 S.C.R. 143, fits the process model better than I acknowledged in my article, which was written before *Andrews*.

104 Chapter 36, Override of Rights, below.

105 Chapter 52, Equality, under heading 52.12, ''Sex'', below.

106 Chapter 27, Aboriginal Peoples, under heading 27.8, ''Section 35'', above.

a transcendent set of norms rooted in nature or stipulated by God ought to have difficulty with these distinctions. Those who regard the Charter as the handiwork of politicians, responding in their usual way to the pressures of interest groups and other practical exigencies, will be less surprised by its irrational structure.

(f) Conflict between rights

The hierarchy of rights that I have described reflects differences in the vulnerability of the right to legislative abridgement. It does not imply that the "privileged rights" must take priority over the "common rights" when they come into conflict. There are two provisions of the Charter that contemplate conflict between rights. One is s. 25, which recognizes that aboriginal and treaty rights, which are available to people who are defined by their race, may be regarded as in conflict with the equality guarantee, which prohibits discrimination on the ground of race. Section 25 recognizes this possibility of conflict, and provides that the aboriginal and treaty rights are to prevail.[107] Another recognized potential for conflict is between the denominational school rights of s. 93, which are available to people who are defined by their religion, and the equality rights of s. 15, which prohibits discrimination on the ground of religion; s. 29 recognizes this possibility of conflict, and provides that the denominational school rights are to prevail.[108]

The Charter makes no provision for other kinds of conflicts between rights.[109] In *B.C. Government Employees' Union* v. *British Columbia* (1988),[110] the Chief Justice of British Columbia had issued an injunction against a union to prohibit its members from picketing the courthouses. The union applied to have the injunction set aside, invoking their members' right to freedom of expression. The government supported the injunction, invoking a right of access to the courts, which is not mentioned in the Charter, but which (it was argued) is implied by the fact that the Charter is enforced through access to the courts. The Supreme Court of Canada unanimously upheld the injunction. Dickson C.J. for the majority seemed to agree that the Charter did guarantee a right of access to the courts, but he did not explicitly recognize that he was faced with a conflict between two rights; he held that the injunction was a limit on freedom of expression, but that it was justified under s. 1 as a reasonable and demonstrably justified limit. McIntyre J., in a separate concurrence, held that a right of access to the court was "Charter-protected", and, therefore, he reasoned, the injunction could not be a breach of freedom of expression. McIntyre J. thus assumed, without saying so,

107 *Id.*, under heading 27.9, "Section 25", above.

108 So held in *Re Bill 30* (Ont. Separate School Funding) [1987] 1 S.C.R. 1148; and see ch. 54, Education, below.

109 See Petter and Hutchinson, "Rights in Conflict" (1989) 23 U.B.C.L. Rev. 531.

110 [1988] 2 S.C.R. 214. Dickson C.J. wrote the majority opinion, which was agreed to by Lamer, Wilson, La Forest and L'Heureux-Dubé JJ. McIntyre J. wrote a concurring opinion.

that freedom of expression should give way to the more specific (but less explicit) right of access to the courts.

In *R.* v. *Keegstra* (1990),[111] a person accused of wilfully promoting hatred against a racial group (Jews in this case), which is the hate propaganda offence of the Criminal Code, attacked the offence as an abridgement of freedom of expression. The prosecution defended the Criminal Code provision on the ground that, by protecting racial groups from hateful messages, it furthered the values of racial equality (in s. 15) and multiculturalism (in s. 27) that were also recognized by the Charter. The Supreme Court of Canada, by a majority, upheld the Criminal Code provision. Dickson C.J. for the majority followed the same approach as in the *BCGEU* case, holding that the provision did abridge freedom of expression, and the rights invoked in support of the legislation were relevant only through s. 1; he held that the law was justified under s. 1. McLachlin J., for the dissenting minority, agreed that the values of equality and multiculturalism were of relevance only through s. 1; she held that the law was not justified under s. 1, not because equality and multiculturalism should be subordinated to freedom of expression, but because in her view the hate propaganda law was neither a rational nor a least drastic means of suppressing racism.

In both the *BCGEU* and *Keegstra* cases, the conflict between rights was resolved through s. 1. Only McIntyre J., concurring separately in *BCGEU*, took the position that the scope of a right (in that case, freedom of expression) should be narrowed to accommodate the exercise of another right (in that case, access to the courts). That technique of ''mutual modification'' is the way in which the conflicting heads of legislative power have been accommodated in federalism cases. For example, the federal Parliament's exclusive power to legislate in relation to ''trade and commerce'' (s. 91(2)) has been held to exclude intraprovincial trade so as not to conflict with the provincial Legislatures' exclusive power to legislate in relation to ''property and civil rights in the province'' (s. 92(13)).[112] But the Court has generally avoided engaging in mutual modification in its Charter jurisprudence. In *Keegstra,* both the majority and minority explicitly rejected this approach to the interpretation of Charter rights.[113] According to that case, the scope of each right should be defined without regard for the existence of other rights. When other rights are invoked in support of a challenged law, the conflict is to be resolved by application of the justificatory principles of s. 1.[114] In that way, the Court does not assign priorities to rights, except in the context of a

111 [1990] 3 S.C.R. 697. Dickson C.J. wrote the majority opinion, which was agreed to by Wilson, L'Heureux-Dubé and Gonthier JJ. McLachlin J. wrote a dissenting opinion, which was agreed to by La Forest and Sopinka JJ.

112 See ch. 15, Judicial Review on Federalism Grounds, under heading 15.6(b), ''Exclusiveness'', above.

113 [1990] 3 S.C.R. 697, 734, 755-758 per Dickson C.J., 833-837 per McLachlin J.

114 Accord *Dagenais* v. *CBC* [1994] 3 S.C.R. 835 (court-ordered publication ban made to protect fair trials of accuseds struck down; Charter right to fair trial taken into account under s.1).

specific law in a particular case. In other words, the Court prefers ''ad hoc balancing'' to ''definitional balancing'' when resolving conflicts between rights.

However the Supreme Court of Canada has not always avoided the definitional balancing of Charter rights. In *R.* v. *O'Connor* (1995),[115] the Court was called upon to decide whether and how an accused in a sexual assault case should be able to gain access to the counselling and medical records of the complainants (or other witnesses). The records sought were not held by the Crown and were not part of the Crown's case; the records were in the possession of the persons and institutions that had provided the therapeutic counselling. Unlike most other Charter cases, here there was no law to be challenged or supported. The Court itself had to establish for the first time the common law principles which would strike the proper balance between the accused's right (under s.7) to full answer and defence, and the witness's right (under s. 7 or s. 8) to a reasonable expectation of privacy. In this context, it would have been nonsensical for the Court to consider full answer and defence without regard for privacy, or privacy without regard to full answer and defence. Instead, the majority of the Court considered how privacy rights could be accommodated to ''reasonably limit'' full answer and defence;[116] the dissenting minority considered how the right to a fair trial could ''demonstrably justify'' limits on privacy.[117] Both the majority and the minority set up procedures for an application to the trial judge for disclosure of third-party records, and stipulated the factors to be weighed by the judge in determining whether to make an order for disclosure. Although the Supreme Court of Canada employs the language of s. 1, the effect of the decision is to narrow the scope of one Charter right to accommodate the exercise of another. *O'Connor* therefore establishes that definitional balancing (or mutual modification) does indeed have a place in Charter jurisprudence, albeit one that only arises in special circumstances.

(g) English-French discrepancies

The rules to deal with discrepancies between the English and French versions of the Charter of Rights are discussed in chapter 53, Language, below.

33.8 Sources of interpretation

(a) Pre-Charter cases

In interpreting the Charter, the doctrine of precedent will apply in the same way as it applies to the interpretation of other constitutional provisions.[118] How-

---

115 [1995] 4 S.C.R. 411. On this issue, the majority judgment was that of Lamer C.J. and Sopinka J. Major J. and Cory J. wrote separate concurring judgements. Iacobucci J. concurred with Cory J. The main dissenting opinion was that of L'Heureux-Dubé J., with the concurrence of La Forest and Gonthier JJ. McLachlin J. concurred with L'Heureux-Dubé J. but wrote a separate opinion.

116 [1995] 4 S.C.R. 411, para. 30 per Lamer C.J. and Sopinka J.

117 *Id.*, para 131 per L'Heureux-Dubé J.

118 See ch. 8, Supreme Court of Canada, under heading 8.7, ''Precedent'', above.

ever, there will be few Canadian cases decided before the adoption of the Charter in 1982 that will be relevant.

The closest cases would appear to be those interpreting the Canadian Bill of Rights. But, as noted in the previous chapter on the Canadian Bill of Rights, the Supreme Court of Canada exercised extraordinary restraint in interpreting the Bill, relying in part on its statutory, as opposed to constitutional, status. The Charter does have constitutional status, and it also contains internal indications that it affords stronger protections for the guaranteed rights than did the Bill.[119] In this new context, the Court has consistently departed from previous decisions interpreting language in the Bill which is similar to language in the Charter.[120]

The cases interpreting the distribution-of-powers provisions of the Constitution Act, 1867 will usually be irrelevant to the interpretation of the Charter.[121] The issue in each of those cases is whether a law is in relation to a matter coming within a class of subject allocated to the enacting legislative body. The answer to that question will rarely have any bearing on the question whether that law (or a similar law) abridges a Charter right. It is true that both questions involve the characterization (or classification) of the impugned statute, but the classes into which laws must be sorted are totally different for the distribution-of-powers decision from what they are for the Charter decision; none of the phrases that distribute power between the federal Parliament and provincial Legislatures are to be found in the Charter.[122] More than that, classification of laws for distribution-of-powers purposes turns on the ''matter'' or ''pith and substance'' of the law; and incidental effects on matters outside jurisdiction are valid.[123] Classification for Charter purposes does not disregard the incidental effects of a law. If the law has the effect of abridging a Charter right, then the Charter is implicated and, if s. 1 does not supply justification, the law will be to that extent invalid.[124]

---

119 See Hogg in Beaudoin and Ratushny, note 4, above, 1, specifically identifying the limitation clause (s. 1), the supremacy clause (s. 52(1)), the remedy clause (s. 24), the absence of ''frozen concepts'' language, and the stronger equality clause (s. 15).

120 See ch. 32, Canadian Bill of Rights, under heading 32.5, ''Judicial interpretation'', above.

121 The contrary position is argued by Finkelstein, ''The Relevance of Pre-Charter Case Law for Post-Charter Adjudication'' (1982) 4 Supreme Court L.R. 267.

122 E.g., *Re Ont. Film and Video Appreciation Soc.* (1984) 45 O.R. (2d) 80 (C.A.), holding that a censorship law violated s. 2 of the Charter. The Court made no reference to *N.S. Bd. of Censors* v. *McNeil* [1978] 2 S.C.R. 662, holding that a similar censorship law was valid as a regulation of business or local matter. Plainly, although *McNeil* was determinative of the distribution-of-powers issue (at least in any court below the Supreme Court of Canada), it was irrelevant to the Charter issue.

123 See sec. 33.6, ''Classification of laws'', above.

124 *Ibid.* As is there explained, classification for Charter purposes does look to the ''purpose'' of a law as well as to its ''effect''. Classification by purpose can yield similar results to classification by pith and substance: e.g., *R.* v. *Big M Drug Mart* [1985] 1 S.C.R. 295; note 50, above.

(b) American cases

The American Bill of Rights[125] was an important source of inspiration for the Charter (as it was for most other countries' bills of rights), and much of the language of the Charter can be traced back to phrases in the American Bill of Rights. Obviously, the decisions of the Supreme Court of the United States interpreting language that is similar to the language of the Charter are useful precedents for Canadian courts. Even where the language is dissimilar, the American cases are a useful source of ideas and parallels. Nor must secondary materials be overlooked. The long American experience with the Bill of Rights has generated a highly sophisticated commentary on civil libertarian values, such as speech or equal protection, and on the role of judicial review in a democratic society, which it would be folly to ignore. The American sources, which are of course set against a familiar common law background, and a social and economic milieu that is also familiar to Canadians, are in fact frequently, but not systematically, referred to in Charter cases.[126]

Despite the obvious usefulness of American cases, their results have not always been followed in Canada. The Supreme Court of Canada has exhorted itself to "be wary of drawing too ready a parallel between constitutions born to different countries in different ages and in different circumstances".[127] Where the Canadian Court has departed from American precedents, it has usually been to give a broader interpretation to the rights in the Charter. Thus, freedom of religion, freedom of expression, fundamental justice (due process) and the rights of persons accused of crime have all been extended beyond the American precedents.[128]

One reason for the broader interpretation of the rights in Canada is the presence of s. 1 in the Canadian Charter of Rights. The Canadian Court regards s. 1 as an important difference between the two constitutions, and one that suggests a broader scope for the guaranteed rights in Canada.[129] The Canadian Court has felt free to give Charter rights a broad interpretation, knowing that s. 1 will allow laws imposing reasonable limits on the rights to be upheld. Without any limitation

125 For definition, see note 16, above.

126 See Bender, "The Canadian Charter and the U.S. Bill of Rights" (1983) 28 McGill L.J. 811; McKercher (ed.), *The U.S. Bill of Rights and the Canadian Charter of Rights and Freedoms* (1983); Bushnell, "The Use of American Cases" (1986) 35 U.N.B.L.J. 157; Cameron, "The Motor Vehicle Reference and the Relevance of American Doctrine" in Sharpe (ed.), *Charter Litigation* (1987), ch. 4; Charles, Cromwell and Jobson, *Evidence and the Charter of Rights and Freedoms* (1989), 27-35; Harvie and Foster, "Ties that Bind? The Supreme Court of Canada, American Jurisprudence . . ." (1990) 28 Osgoode Hall L.J. 729.

127 *R.* v. *Rahey* [1987] 1 S.C.R. 598, 639 per La Forest J.; *R.* v. *Keegstra* [1990] 3 S.C.R. 697, 740 per Dickson C.J.

128 Notes 22-33 and accompanying text, above.

129 *Re B.C. Motor Vehicle Act* [1985] 2 S.C.R. 486, 498 per Lamer J.; *R.* v. *Keegstra* [1990] 3 S.C.R. 697, 743 per Dickson C.J. For my criticism of this approach, see text accompanying notes 87-88, above.

clause like s. 1 of the Charter, the American Court is driven to do more ''definitional balancing'' in which the scope of the rights themselves are narrowed so as to accommodate laws that the Court regards as reasonable limits that ought not to be struck down. The presence in the Canadian Charter of s. 33 — the power of override — probably also tends in the same direction.[130] An overly broad application of the Charter can, after all, be overcome by an ordinary statute containing a notwithstanding clause. An overly broad application of the American Bill of Rights can be overcome only by a constitutional amendment. Once again, the Canadian Court has less reason than the American Court to be cautious in drawing the boundaries of the guaranteed rights.

(c) International sources

Canada is bound by a number of treaties dealing with human rights,[131] of which the most important for present purposes is the International Covenant on Civil and Political Rights,[132] to which Canada became a party in 1976. As treaties, these instruments are only binding at international law. They are not incorporated into Canada's domestic law, and are not enforceable in Canadian courts.[133] However, the International Covenant on Civil and Political Rights covers much of the same ground and, although its provisions are more detailed, uses similar language to the Charter of Rights.[134] The terms of the Covenant are relevant to the interpretation of the Charter, by virtue of the rule that a statute (and presumably a constitution) should be interpreted as far as possible into conformity with international law.[135] Where (as is common) the Covenant makes detailed provision for

---

130 Section 33 is expressly linked with s. 1 in the defence of a more generous interpretation of rights in *Re B.C. Motor Vehicle Act*, previous note.

131 Cohen and Bayefsky, ''The Canadian Charter of Rights and Freedoms and Public International Law'' (1983) 61 Can. Bar Rev. 265, 285 list 23 treaties on human rights that have been ratified by Canada. On the relevance of international human rights law to Canada, see the same article; also, Bayefsky, ''The Impact of the European Convention on Human Rights in the United Kingdom'' (1981) 13 Ottawa L. Rev. 507; Claydon, ''The Application of International Human Rights Law by Canadian Courts'' (1981) 30 Buffalo L. Rev. 727; Claydon, ''International Human Rights Law and the Interpretation of the Charter'' (1982) 4 Supreme Court L.R. 287; Mendes, ''Interpreting the Charter: Applying International and European Jurisprudence'' (1982) 20 Alta. L. Rev. 383; Hayward, ''International Law and the Interpretation of the Charter'' (1985) 23 U. Western Ont. L. Rev. 9; Schabas, *International Human Rights Law and the Canadian Charter* (2nd ed., 1996); Bayefsky, *International Human Rights Law* (1992).

132 The text of the Covenant is set out in Appendix VI to this book.

133 See ch. 11, Treaties, under heading 11.2, ''Implementing treaties'', above.

134 Tarnopolsky, ''A Comparison between the Charter and the International Covenant'' (1983) 8 Queen's L.J. 211. Note that, while Canada's ratification of the International Covenant was one of the reasons urged in Canada for the adoption in 1982 of the Charter, the Charter does not purport to implement the Covenant, although many Charter provisions no doubt do implement particular provisions of the Covenant.

135 *Re Powers to Levy Rates on Foreign Legations* [1943] S.C.R. 208; Jacomy-Millette, *Treaty Law in Canada* (1975), 280-290; Driedger, *Construction of Statutes* (3rd ed., 1994, by Sullivan), 330-333.

a right that is also guaranteed by the Charter, but in language that is less clear or complete, the terms of the Covenant may well indicate the appropriate interpretation of the Charter language.

For example, s. 10(b) of the Charter, which confers upon an arrested person the right "to retain and instruct counsel without delay", does not make clear whether counsel is to be paid for by the accused or by the government. The Covenant, however, by article 14(3)(d), confers upon an accused person the right to "legal assistance", and goes on to stipulate that the legal assistance is to be provided "without payment by him . . . if he does not have sufficient means to pay for it". The terms of the Covenant thus impose upon Canada an obligation under international law to supply legal aid to an indigent accused. Canadian courts could interpret the equivocal language of s. 10(b) of the Charter as having constitutionalized that international obligation.[136] Note, however, that this interpretation of s. 10(b) is not compelled by the terms of the Covenant, because Canada could fulfil the terms of the Covenant by providing legal aid on a statutory, as opposed to a constitutional, basis. The Covenant does not require that all of its stipulations be embodied in the constitutions of the states that are parties to the Covenant. Compliance can take the form of statutory or administrative measures.[137]

The International Covenant on Civil and Political Rights includes an optional protocol,[138] to which Canada is a party, which provides that individuals in the states that are parties to the protocol, who claim that any of their rights under the Covenant have been violated, and who have exhausted all available domestic remedies, may petition the Human Rights Committee of the United Nations. The Committee receives submissions from the petitioner and from the state against which the violation is alleged, and decides whether or not the state has violated the Covenant. The decision cannot be directly enforced, of course, but it is reported to the petitioner, the state and the General Assembly of the United Nations.[139] This procedure yields decisions which constitute a body of jurisprudence interpreting the Covenant.[140] Since this jurisprudence elaborates the terms of obligations at international law which have been accepted by Canada, it is as relevant to the interpretation of the Charter as the terms of the Covenant itself.

---

136 *R.* v. *Brydges* [1990] 1 S.C.R. 190, 214 (obiter dictum). Other references to the International Covenant by Canadian courts are listed in Schabas, note 131, above, Appendix III.

137 Tarnopolsky note 134, above, 212.

138 The text of the optional protocol, to which Canada became a party in 1976, is set out in Appendix VII to this book.

139 The procedure is described by Zuijdwijk, "The Right to Petition the United Nations because of Alleged Violations of Human Rights" (1981) 59 Can. Bar Rev. 103.

140 The Convention and the optional protocol only became effective in 1976, not only for Canada but for other party states as well. So far there is no official series of reports of the decisions of the Human Rights Committee. They are reported, however, in the Human Rights Law Journal; and the decisions on petitions against Canada are reported in the Canadian Human Rights Yearbook.

The decisions of the Human Rights Committee of the United Nations are relevant to the interpretation of the Charter, not only because Canada is a party to the Covenant which they interpret, but also because they are considered interpretations by distinguished jurists of language and ideas that are similar to the language and ideas of the Charter. Even if Canada were not a party to the Covenant, the Committee's decisions would enjoy the same kind of persuasive value for Canadian courts as the decisions of the courts of a foreign country: the search for wisdom is not to be circumscribed by national boundaries.[141]

The European Convention on Human Rights[142] is another source of international jurisprudence that has persuasive value for Canadian courts interpreting the Charter.[143] The European Convention came into force in 1953 and has been adhered to by the United Kingdom and 20 other European countries. Canada is not a party and cannot become one, because the treaty is a regional one. The Convention guarantees many of the same civil liberties as the Charter, although, like the International Covenant, the Convention tends to be more detailed in its provisions. Under the Convention, individuals in party states may petition the European Commission of Human Rights claiming a violation of the Convention, and the Commission has the power to make a decision in the form of a report. The Commission refers some petitions to the European Court of Human Rights for decision, and the Court makes a decision on any petition that is referred. The decisions of the Commission and the Court constitute a body of jurisprudence on the interpretation of the Convention.[144]

(d) Legislative history

The legislative history of the Charter is admissible as an aid to its interpretation. Thus, earlier versions of the Charter, testimony given before the parliamentary committee which examined an earlier version, and debates in the Senate and House of Commons are all relevant and admissible. This topic will be addressed in chapter 57, Proof, below.[145]

33.9 Priority between federal and Charter grounds

When a law is challenged on both federal and Charter grounds, it is the federal ground that is the more fundamental of the two, and that ought to take

141 Claydon, (1982) 4 Supreme Court L.R. 287, 295.

142 The text of the Convention is set out in Schabas, note 131, above, 255.

143 References to the Convention by Canadian courts are listed in Schabas, note 131, above, Appendix III. See also Zellick, ''The European Convention on Human Rights: its Significance for Charter Litigation'' in Sharpe (ed.), *Charter Litigation* (1987), ch. 5.

144 All decisions of the Court and some decisions of the Commission are reported in the European Human Rights Reports. A selection is also reported in the Human Rights Law Journal.

145 Section 56.7, ''Legislative history'', below.

priority over the Charter ground. This point has been argued, and its implications explained, in chapter 15, Judicial Review on Federal Grounds, above.[146]

33.10 Commencement of Charter

Section 58 of the Constitution Act, 1982 provides that the Act is to come into force on a day to be fixed by proclamation. That proclamation was issued by the Queen, who came to Canada for the purpose, at a ceremony in Ottawa on April 17, 1982; and the proclamation fixed April 17, 1982 as the day upon which the Constitution Act, 1982 was to come into force.[147] The Charter of Rights accordingly came into force on that day, and operates only prospectively from that day.

A statute (or regulation or by-law or other legislative instrument) which was enacted before April 17, 1982, and which is inconsistent with the Charter, will be rendered ''of no force or effect'' by the supremacy clause of the Constitution,[148] but only as from April 17, 1982.[149] Action of an executive or administrative kind, such as search, seizure, arrest or detention, which was taken before April 17, 1982, cannot be a violation of the Charter, because the Charter was not in force at the time of the action.[150] No remedy under s. 24(1) would be available in respect of action taken before April 17, 1982, because the remedy is available only to anyone whose rights or freedoms, ''as guaranteed by this Charter'', have been infringed or denied.[151] Even s. 24(2) (exclusion of evidence) would not apply to evidence which, although tendered after April 17, 1982, was obtained before April 17, 1982; s. 24(2) applies only to evidence ''obtained in a manner that infringed or denied any rights or freedoms guaranteed by this Charter'', and no rights or freedoms were guaranteed by the Charter until April 17, 1982.[152]

Some of the provisions of the Charter have been interpreted in such a way that events occurring before April 17, 1982 are relevant to their application, despite the exclusively prospective operation of the Charter. One example is provided by s. 13, which stipulates that a witness who testifies in any proceedings has the right not to have any incriminating evidence that the witness may have given in earlier proceedings used against him or her in the later proceedings. It has been held that this right takes effect at the time of the later proceedings, when the Crown seeks to use the incriminating testimony from the earlier proceedings.

---

146 Section 15.2, ''Priority between federal and Charter grounds'', above.

147 The proclamation is published in a special issue of The Canada Gazette, Part III, September 21, 1982, p. 33.

148 Constitution Act, 1982, s. 52(1) (supremacy clause).

149 *R.* v. *Stevens* [1988] 1 S.C.R. 1153 (accused, charged with an offence that took place before 1982, cannot challenge law on Charter grounds).

150 *R.* v. *James* [1988] 1 S.C.R. 669 (seizure took place before 1982).

151 *Ibid.*

152 *Ibid.*

Therefore, the right can be invoked even if the earlier proceedings took place before April 17, 1982, provided that the later proceedings took place after April 17, 1982.[153] Another example is provided by s. 11(b), which guarantees the right "to be tried within a reasonable time". It has been held that a period of delay occurring before April 17, 1982 should be taken into account in determining whether a person, whose trial had still not occurred by a date after April 17, 1982, had been denied the right to be tried within a reasonable time.[154] Another example is provided by s. 12, which guarantees the right "not to be subjected to any cruel and unusual treatment or punishment". Where a person was sentenced to a cruel and unusual punishment before April 17, 1982, but the sentence continued after April 17, 1982, the continuation of the sentence would constitute a breach of s. 12.[155] But even in these two examples, where events occurring prior to April 17, 1982 are relevant, the application of the Charter is prospective only.

33.11 Undeclared rights

Section 26 of the Charter[156] provides as follows:

> 26. The guarantee in this Charter of certain rights and freedoms shall not be construed as denying the existence of any other rights or freedoms that exist in Canada.

Section 26 is a cautionary provision, included to make clear that the Charter is not to be construed as taking away any existing undeclared rights or freedoms.[157] Rights or freedoms protected by the common law or by statute[158] will continue to

153 *Dubois* v. *The Queen* [1985] 2 S.C.R. 350. The rule is the same for s. 11(h) (double jeopardy): the right becomes effective at the time of the later proceedings, and it is irrelevant that the earlier proceedings took place before April 17, 1982: *Corp. Professionnelle des Médecins* v. *Thibault* [1988] 1 S.C.R. 1033.

154 *R.* v. *Antoine* (1983) 41 O.R. (2d) 607, 613 (C.A.).

155 *Re Mitchell and the Queen* (1983) 42 O.R. (2d) 481 (H.C.); *R.* v. *Konechny* (1983) 6 D.L.R. (4th) 350 (B.C. C.A.). See also *R.* v. *Gamble* [1988] 2 S.C.R. 595 (continuing deprivation of liberty remediable, despite fact that breach of fundamental justice occurred before 1982).

156 In the October 1980 version of the Charter, s. 26 (then numbered s. 24) was included in its present form, but with the addition (at the end, after the word "Canada", which was followed by a comma) of the words "including any rights or freedoms that pertain to the native peoples of Canada". These words were dropped in the April 1981 version of s. 26 (then numbered s. 26), because of the inclusion of s. 25, which appeared for the first time in the April 1981 version.

157 Section 26 has its equivalent in the ninth amendment of the Constitution of the United States, a provision that has rarely been invoked: Goodman, *The Ninth Amendment* (Exposition Press, Smithtown, New York, 1981).

158 Among the statutory rights preserved by s. 26 are those contained in the Canadian Bill of Rights and the statutory bills of rights of Saskatchewan, Alberta and Quebec. *Singh* v. *Minr. of Emplmt. and Immigration* [1985] 1 S.C.R. 177, 224.

exist notwithstanding the Charter.[159] Section 26 does not incorporate these undeclared rights and freedoms into the Charter, or ''constitutionalize'' them in any other way. They continue to exist independently of the Charter, and receive no extra protection from the Charter. They differ from the rights or freedoms guaranteed in the Charter in that, as creatures of common law or statute, the undeclared rights can be altered or abolished by the action of the competent legislative body. As well, the remedy under s. 24 is not available for their enforcement.

159 The Constitution Act, 1867, by s. 133, contains a guarantee of language rights, and, by s. 93, a guarantee of denominational schools. There are also some equivalent provisions in the Manitoba Act, the Alberta Act, the Saskatchewan Act and the Terms of Union of Newfoundland. These rights would also be preserved by s. 26. However, they are the subject of more specific preservation by s. 21 (language) and s. 29 (denominational schools) of the Charter. Aboriginal rights are specifically preserved by ss. 25 and 35.

34

Application of Charter

34.1 Benefit of rights

(a) The issue

Who is entitled to the benefit of the rights guaranteed by the Charter of Rights? In particular, is a corporation entitled to the benefit of all rights? This question turns on the language by which the rights are defined; this language is surprisingly various and surprisingly silent on its applicability to corporations.

(b) Everyone, anyone, any person

Sections 2, 7, 8, 9, 10, 12 and 17 of the Charter open with the phrase, ''Everyone has the right''. In ss. 11 and 19 ''any person'' replaces ''everyone''; s. 20 uses ''any member of the public''; and s. 24 uses ''anyone''. It seems likely that these various terms are synonymous[1] and that each is apt to include a cor-

1 In the French version of the Charter, the word ''chacun'' is used in place of ''everyone'' in ss. 2, 8, 9, 10, 12 and 17; and the same word ''chacun'' is used in place of ''person'' in s. 19. This reinforces the commonsense conclusion that nothing turns on at least the variation between ''everyone'' and ''any person''.

poration as well as an individual.[2] Indeed, some of the rights would be seriously attenuated if they did not apply to corporations. For example, newspapers, television stations and other media of communication require significant capital for their operation and are usually operated by corporations; ''freedom of the press and other media of communication'' (s. 2(b)) would be a hollow right if it could not be invoked by a corporation. Nor is there any reason to assume that the Charter denies to a corporation charged with an offence the basic safeguards of a fair trial (s. 11).

Some of the rights, although guaranteed to ''everyone'' or ''any person'', are by their very nature not available to a corporation. For example, the right to ''freedom of conscience and religion'' in s. 2(a) does not apply to a corporation, because a corporation cannot hold a religious belief or any other belief.[3] The right to fundamental justice under s. 7 does not apply to a corporation, because it is limited to deprivations of ''life, liberty and security of the person'', which are attributes of individuals, not corporations.[4] The right not to be ''arbitrarily detained or imprisoned'' in s. 9, and other rights that arise only on ''arrest or detention'' in s. 10, as well as the right to reasonable bail in s. 11(e), cannot be enjoyed by a corporation, because a corporation cannot be detained, imprisoned or arrested.[5] A corporation cannot testify, so that the right of an accused person not to be compelled to be a witness against himself in s. 11(c),[6] the right against self-incrimination in s. 13,[7] and the right of a witness to an interpreter in s. 14, are not available to a corporation.

Those rights that do not apply to corporations cannot be invoked by a corporation to obtain a remedy under s. 24.[8] Section 24 itself is available to ''anyone'', which includes a corporation,[9] and can therefore be used by a corporation to enforce a right that does apply to a corporation. However, it is wrong to assume that a corporation can never invoke a right that does not apply to a corporation. In *R.* v. *Big M Drug Mart* (1985),[10] the Supreme Court of Canada

---

2 *Hunter* v. *Southam* [1984] 2 S.C.R. 145 (applying s. 8 at suit of corporation); *Edmonton Journal* v. *Alta.* [1989] 2 S.C.R. 1326 (applying s. 2 at suit of corporation). *R.* v. *CIP* [1992] 1 S.C.R. 843 (holding that s. 11(b) applies to corporation). The word ''person'' in the American Bill of Rights (where it appears in the fifth and fourteenth amendments) has been held to include a corporation: *Covington and Lexington Turnpike Road Co.* v. *Sandford* (1896) 164 U.S. 578; *Smyth* v. *Ames* (1897) 169 U.S. 466; *First Nat. Bank of Boston* v. *Bellotti* (1978) 435 U.S. 765.

3 *R.* v. *Big M Drug Mart* [1985] 1 S.C.R. 295, 314.

4 *Irwin Toy* v. *Que.* [1989] 1 S.C.R. 927, 1004; *Dywidag Systems* v. *Zutphen Bros.* [1990] 1 S.C.R. 705, 709.

5 Query correctness of *Re PPG Industries Can.* (1983) 146 D.L.R. (3d) 261 (B.C.C.A.) (corporation not entitled to trial by jury because of reference to imprisonment in s. 11(f)).

6 *R.* v. *Amway Corp.* [1989] 1 S.C.R. 21, 37-40.

7 Cf. *United States* v. *White* (1944) 322 U.S. 694, 698 (privilege against self-incrimination essentially personal, applying only to natural individuals).

8 See ch. 37, Enforcement of Rights, under heading 37.2, ''Standing'', above.

9 *R.* v. *Big M Drug Mart* [1985] 1 S.C.R. 295, 313.

10 [1985] 1 S.C.R. 295.

held that a corporation could invoke the right to freedom of religion in s. 2(a) as a defence to a criminal charge of selling goods on a Sunday. The charge was laid under the federal Lord's Day Act, which the corporation successfully argued was unconstitutional on the ground that the Act abridged the freedom of religion of individuals. The corporation had standing to make this argument, despite the fact that s. 2(a) did not apply to a corporation, because ''no-one can be convicted of an offence under an unconstitutional law''.[11] The corporation was not seeking a remedy under s. 24. As a defendant to a criminal charge, the corporation was entitled to rely on any constitutional defect in the law. This ruling means that rights that do not apply to corporations by their own terms may nevertheless operate to the benefit of corporations. The rationale and limits of this ruling are discussed later in the book.[12]

A foetus is not a legal person, either at common law or civil law, until the child is born by being separated alive from the mother. A foetus is not entitled to a right to life under s. 7, or any other right under the Charter.[13]

(c) Individual

Section 15 confers its equality rights on ''every individual''. This is a more specific term than ''everyone'', ''any person'' or ''anyone'', and it probably excludes a corporation, at least in the context of an instrument which also contains the more general terms. The word ''individual'' was substituted for ''everyone'' during the parliamentary committee's deliberations on the Charter, and the explanation given to the committee was that the change was intended ''to make it clear that this right would apply to natural persons only''.[14] Within s. 15, the reference to ''discrimination based on race, national or ethnic origin, colour, religion, sex, age or mental or physical disability'' also reinforces the exclusion of corporations: the listed attributes are all personal characteristics of human beings, and only ''national origin'' could apply to corporations as well. But in that company, national origin should probably be read down to exclude foreign

---

11 *Id.*, 313.

12 Chapter 56, Constitutional Litigation, under heading 56.2, ''Standing'', below.

13 *Tremblay* v. *Daigle* [1989] 2 S.C.R. 530 (foetus not a ''human being'' for purpose of right to life in Quebec Charter of Rights and Freedoms or for purpose of civil rights under Quebec Civil Code); *R.* v. *Sullivan* [1991] 1 S.C.R. 489 (foetus not a ''person'' within Criminal Code offence of death by criminal negligence); *Borowski* v. *A.G. Can.* (1987) 39 D.L.R. (4th) 731 (Sask. C.A.) (foetus not included in s. 7's ''everyone'' or s. 15's ''individual''). The *Borowski* case went up to the Supreme Court of Canada, but in that Court these rulings were not addressed, because the issue, which was the validity of the abortion provisions of the Criminal Code, had become moot: *Borowski* v. *Can.* [1989] 1 S.C.R. 342. The abortion provisions of the Criminal Code were held to be unconstitutional in *R.* v. *Morgentaler (No. 2)* [1988] 1 S.C.R. 30 on the ground that they infringed the mother's right under s. 7; there was no ruling on whether the foetus had any rights.

14 For reference to the legislative history, see Gibson, *The Law of the Charter: Equality Rights* (1990), 53-55.

corporations.[15] While I think that this is the better view, the position is not clear. It can be argued that the French version of s. 15, which uses the word "personne" in subsection (1) in place of individual (although it uses "individus" in subsection (2)), suggests that artificial persons are covered. It can also be argued that it is anomalous to make the act of incorporation deny to a business proprietor a right that he or she enjoyed before incorporation.[16]

At the time of writing, the Supreme Court of Canada has decided two cases where corporations have invoked s. 15; finding against the equality claim on other grounds, the Court studiously refused to decide this issue,[17] which may indicate that the Court has some doubt as to the answer.[18] Lower courts have held that s. 15 does not extend to corporations.[19]

Even if s. 15 does not extend to corporations, corporations will still be able to rely on s. 15 as a defence to a criminal charge laid under a law that is invalid by virtue of unconstitutional discrimination against individuals. This is the principle established by *Big M Drug Mart*, discussed above.[20]

The word "individual" does not include a foetus.[21]

(d) Citizen

Generally speaking, a person need not be a Canadian citizen in order to invoke Charter rights. "Everyone" in s. 7 has been held to include "every human being who is physically present in Canada and by virtue of such presence amenable to Canadian law".[22] The same would apply to "anyone", "any person" and "individual". Even persons who have entered Canada illegally are entitled to most of the Charter rights simply by virtue of their presence on Canadian soil.[23]

---

15 The stipulated grounds are not exclusive, but only "analogous grounds" can be added, and the common feature of the stipulated grounds may well be the personal characteristic of a human being: see ch. 52, Equality, under heading 52.7, "Discrimination", below.

16 See Gibson, note 14, above; Chipeur, Section 15 of the Charter protects People and Corporations - Equally" (1986) 11 Can. Bus. L.J. 304; Gertner, "Are Corporations entitled to Equality?" (1986) 19 Can. Rts. Reporter 288.

17 *Rudolf Wolff & Co.* v. *Can.* [1990] 1 S.C.R. 695, 703; *Dywidag Systems* v. *Zutphen Bros.* [1990] 1 S.C.R. 705, 709. The decisions hold that the Crown is not an individual.

18 Cf. *R.* v. *Big M Drug Mart* [1985] 1 S.C.R. 293, 313 where Dickson J. uses the word "individuals" to include "real persons or artificial ones"; but he is not referring to s. 15.

19 The cases are referred to in the sources in note 16, above.

20 Note 10, above.

21 Note 13, above.

22 *Singh* v. *Minr. of Emplt. and Immig.* [1985] 1 S.C.R. 177, 202 per Wilson J. for half of the six-judge bench. Beetz J. for the other half decided the case on the basis of the Canadian Bill of Rights rather than the Charter. While Beetz J. said nothing on this point, he probably agreed with it, because he assumed that illegal immigrants were entitled to the rights under the Canadian Bill of Rights.

23 *Ibid.* In *R.* v. *A.* [1990] 1 S.C.R. 995, a majority of the Court seems to have held that even persons outside Canada are entitled to Charter rights. This entitlement must surely be restricted to citizens.

Citizenship is a required qualification for some rights. Voting rights (s. 3), mobility rights (s. 6) and minority language educational rights (s. 23) are conferred upon a ''citizen''.

Canadian citizenship is a relatively recent concept, established for the first time by federal statute in 1947.[24] It is clear that citizenship is a matter coming within the legislative authority of the federal Parliament.[25] Now that the concept has constitutional implications, how will the courts define it? It seems unlikely that the courts would develop their own definition of ''citizen'', since the concept has no meaning apart from statute.[26] Yet it would be unfortunate if the courts were to hold that the statutory rules defining citizenship in 1982 (when the Charter came into force) constituted the rigid, unchangeable definition for constitutional purposes. The best course is for the courts to accept that citizenship is a creature of federal statute law and that it can be changed from time to time by the federal Parliament, even though the consequence of any such change is also to change the scope of ss. 3, 6 and 23 of the Charter.[27] Of course, the courts should review any amendment to the citizenship law to satisfy themselves that it is reasonably related to a legitimate national objective, and is not simply a device to limit Charter rights.

If I am right that the term ''citizen'' essentially means citizenship as legislated from time to time by the federal Parliament, it follows that the term excludes corporations, at least until such time as the Parliament establishes a concept of citizenship for corporations.[28] The contexts in which the term ''citizen'' appears in the Charter reinforce the view that corporate citizenship is not contemplated. The term appears only in ss. 3, 6 and 23. It is obvious that a corporation could not possess the right to vote under s. 3, or the right to educate its ''children'' in the minority language under s. 23. That leaves only the mobility rights of s. 6. Certainly, it is not impossible for mobility rights to be extended to corporations, but this would represent a radical change in Canada's constitutional law, which has hitherto always denied full legal status to a corporation outside its jurisdiction

---

24 Canadian Citizenship Act, S.C. 1946, c. 15; see now Citizenship Act, R.S.C. 1985, c. C-29.

25 It is not clear whether the power is derived from s. 91(25) (naturalization and aliens) or from the opening words of s. 91 (peace, order, and good government): McConnell, *Commentary on the British North America Act* (1977) 227-232.

26 Contrast the word ''Indian'' in s. 91(24), which is obviously not a purely statutory concept, and which has been held to include persons outside the definition in the federal Indian Act: *Re Eskimos* [1939] S.C.R. 104.

27 Cf. *Cunningham* v. *Tomey Homma* [1903] A.C. 151, 156 (Parliament has power to define ''aliens'' in s. 91(25)); *A.-G. Can.* v. *Canard* [1976] 1 S.C.R. 170, 206 (Parliament has power to define ''Indians'' in s. 91(24) although Parliament has not attempted to do so exhaustively: see previous note).

28 If, on the other hand, the courts were prepared to give the term ''citizen'' some significance independent of federal statute law, it is possible that a corporation could be held to be a Canadian citizen, based on either incorporation within Canada or control by Canadian citizens.

of incorporation.[29] A change in this fundamental rule would call for a clearer provision than one applying to "every citizen".

(e) Permanent resident

The mobility rights of s. 6(2) (but not s. 6(1)) apply, not only to "every citizen", but also to "every person who has the status of a permanent resident of Canada".

The term "permanent resident" is to be found in the federal Immigration Act,[30] where it is defined as follows:

> "permanent resident" means a person who
> (a) has been granted landing,
> (b) has not become a Canadian citizen, and
> (c) has not ceased to be a permanent resident pursuant to s. 24(1) [which contemplates a permanent departure].

The term is thus a technical term in immigration law, meaning a person who has been officially admitted to Canada as a permanent resident, but who has not taken out Canadian citizenship. Section 6(2) of the Charter probably uses the term in this technical sense, because it refers to a person who has "the status" of a permanent resident, which seems to imply some official recognition of the status, and not just the fact of permanent residence. If this is correct, then the courts should interpret "permanent resident" as meaning its statutory definition from time to time in the Immigration Act.[31] On that basis, of course, a corporation would not be included.

If, contrary to the opinion just advanced, the courts did not confine the term "permanent resident" to its technical immigration-law meaning, then it could easily encompass a corporation. A corporation can be a "person",[32] and it is well established in income-tax law that a corporation can be a "resident" of Canada,[33] and there seems to be no reason why a corporation could not be a "permanent" resident of Canada. Of course, as noted in the previous discussion of citizenship, the extension of mobility rights to corporations would constitute a radical change in the constitutional law respecting corporate recognition outside the province of

29 See ch. 23, Companies, under heading 23.1(b), "Territorial limitation", above.

30 S.C. 1976-77, c. 52, s. 2(1); now R.S.C. 1985, c. I-2, s. 2(1). The term was not used or defined in the Immigration Act before 1977: see R.S.C. 1970, c. I-2; although there was (and still is) a reference to "permanent residence" in the definition of "landing" in s. 2. The term "permanent resident" was used in the Immigration Appeal Board Act, R.S.C. 1970, c. I-3 (since repealed by S.C. 1976-77, c. 52), where it was defined in s. 2 as "a person who has been granted lawful admission to Canada for permanent residence under the Immigration Act".

31 The problem of a statutory definition controlling the scope of a constitutional right is discussed in the previous section of this chapter with reference to citizenship, note 27, above.

32 Note 2 and accompanying text, above.

33 The leading case, which makes corporate residence depend upon the location of "central management and control", is *De Boers Consolidated Mines* v. *Howe* [1906] A.C. 455 (H.L.).

incorporation, and the courts may be reluctant to take this step in the absence of clearer language in the Charter.[34]

34.2 Burden of rights

(a) Both levels of government

The previous section of this chapter examined who was entitled to the benefit of Charter rights. This section examines who is subject to the burden of Charter rights, or, in other words, who is bound by the Charter. This latter question is governed by s. 32(1) of the Charter,[35] which provides as follows:

> 32.(1) This Charter applies
> (a) to the Parliament and government of Canada in respect of all matters within the authority of Parliament including all matters relating to the Yukon Territory and Northwest Territories; and
> (b) to the legislature and government of each province in respect of all matters within the authority of the legislature of each province.

Section 32(1) expressly provides that the Charter applies to "the Parliament and government of Canada" and to "the legislature and government of each province". This makes clear that both levels of government are bound by the Charter.

It will be recalled that the Canadian Bill of Rights applied only to the federal level of government.[36]

The original American Bill of Rights, namely, the first ten amendments to the Constitution of the United States, was proposed by the first Congress in response to concerns about civil liberties that had been expressed during the debates on the ratification of the Constitution. These concerns seem to have been directed only to the new federal government, and the first ten amendments, which were ratified by the states in 1791,[37] applied only to the federal government. After the civil war, however, the fourteenth amendment was adopted (it was ratified in 1868), and it did apply to the states (and only to the states). The due process clause of the fourteenth amendment has been interpreted as "incorporating" most (but not all) of the guarantees of the first ten amendments. Through this doctrine of "selective incorporation", the incorporated guarantees have become applica-

---

34 Note 29 and accompanying text, above.

35 For commentary on s. 32, see Gibson, *The Law of the Charter: General Principles* (1986), 88-120; Beaudoin and Ratushny (eds.), *The Canadian Charter of Rights and Freedoms* (2nd ed., 1989), ch. 3 (by Tassé); McLeod, Takach, Morton, Segan, *The Canadian Charter of Rights* (Carswell, loose-leaf), ch. 3; *Canadian Charter of Rights Annotated*, (Canada Law Book, loose-leaf), annotation to s. 32. The last work provides a bibliography of the relevant literature.

36 See previous chapter, Canadian Bill of Rights.

37 The Constitution of the United States, by article V, provides that an amendment must be proposed by the federal Congress by a two-thirds majority of both Houses, and must be ratified by the Legislatures (or constitutional conventions) of three-fourths of the states.

ble to the states.[38] In the opposite direction, the equal protection clause of the fourteenth amendment, which has no counterpart in the first ten amendments, has been incorporated into the due process clause of the fifth amendment, and has thereby become applicable to the federal level of government.[39] By these circuitous routes, most of the guarantees of the American Bill of Rights have become applicable to both levels of government.

(b) Parliament or Legislature

The references in s. 32 to the ''Parliament'' and a ''legislature'' make clear that the Charter operates as a limitation on the powers of those legislative bodies.[40] Any statute enacted by either Parliament or a Legislature which is inconsistent with the Charter will be outside the power of (ultra vires) the enacting body and will be invalid.[41]

The word ''Parliament'' means the federal legislative body, which consists (in the language of s. 17 of the Constitution Act, 1867) ''of the Queen, an upper house styled the Senate, and the House of Commons''. Of these three elements, the first, namely the Queen, is represented in Canada by the Governor General, who gives the royal assent. The second element, the Senate, is the upper house, which is an appointed legislative chamber. The third element, the House of Commons, is the lower house, which is an elected legislative chamber.[42]

The word ''legislature'' means the provincial legislative body, which consists, in the case of Ontario (in the language of s. 69 of the Constitution Act, 1867), ''of the Lieutenant Governor and of one house, styled the Legislative Assembly of Ontario''. Ontario's two elements of a Lieutenant Governor, who gives the royal assent, and a Legislative Assembly, which is an elected chamber, have their counterparts in the other nine provinces as well. Five provinces used to have an upper house, styled a Legislative Council, but all five abolished it.[43]

In *New Brunswick Broadcasting Co.* v. *Nova Scotia* (1993),[44], the question arose whether the Nova Scotia legislative assembly, which had prohibited the

38 The Supreme Court of the United States never accepted ''total incorporation'' of the first ten amendments. Selective incorporation covered only the more fundamental guarantees; however, this has steadily been extended to all but a few of the guarantees, thus coming close to total incorporation. The position is well explained in Nowak and Rotunda, *Constitutional Law* (4th ed., 1991), 382-388. A shorter account is in Tribe, *American Constitutional Law* (2nd ed., 1988), 772-774.

39 Nowak, previous note, 569; Tribe, previous note, 1437.

40 On the effect of the phrases ''in respect of all matters'', etc. in both paragraphs, see ch. 15, Judicial Review on Federal Grounds, under heading 15.2, ''Priority between federal and Charter grounds'', above.

41 This result would follow even without the supremacy clause of s. 52(1), but that clause reinforces the ultra vires conclusion.

42 The Parliament is more fully described in chapter 9, Responsible Government, under heading 9.4, ''The legislative branch'', above.

43 Forsey, *Freedom and Order* (1974), 222.

44 [1993] 1 S.C.R. 319.

televising of its proceedings, was bound by the Charter of Rights. The Supreme Court of Canada, by a majority,[45] held that the word ''legislature'' in s. 32 should be interpreted as making the Charter applicable to a legislative assembly, even when the assembly.acted independently of the Lieutenant Governor and was for that reason less than the full Legislature. Presumably, the same conclusion would apply to the word ''Parliament'' in s. 32, making the Charter applicable to actions of the Senate or the House of Commons as well as to those of Parliament as a whole.

What the Supreme Court of Canada in *New Brunswick Broadcasting* gave with the one hand it took away with the other. Having held that the Charter applied to the legislative assembly of Nova Scotia, the Court went on to hold by a majority[46] that the power of the assembly ''to exclude strangers'' (including the television media) from its deliberations was immune from Charter review. This odd result was premised on the theory that the parliamentary privileges that are needed to secure the orderly functioning of a legislative assembly, and which include the power to exclude strangers, are part of the ''Constitution of Canada''. If that was so, then it followed (according to the majority) that the Charter did not apply, because ''one part of the Constitution cannot be abrogated or diminished by another''.[47]

The reasoning in *New Brunswick Broadcasting* is open to criticism. The point has earlier been made that there was insufficient basis to add parliamentary privilege to the definition of the Constitution of Canada, considering that that definition is expressed solely in terms of written instruments and appears (despite the use of the word ''includes'') to be exhaustive.[48] But the next step in the Court's reasoning is even harder to justify. The fact that a power is conferred by the Constitution of Canada does not immunize the power from the Charter of Rights.[49]

---

45 On this issue, only Lamer C.J., who concurred in the result, dissented, holding that ''legislature'' included only the body capable of enacting laws, and not its component parts.

46 McLachlin J. wrote the majority opinion, with the concurrence of La Forest, L'Heureux-Dubé, Gonthier and Iacobucci JJ. Lamer C.J. based his concurring opinion on the interpretation of s. 32: previous note. Sopinka J., concurring, and Cory J., dissenting, both disagreed with McLachlin J. on this issue, holding that the Charter applied to the actions of the legislative assembly in the exercise of parliamentary privilege.

47 [1993] 1 S.C.R. 319, 373.

48 Ch. 1, Sources under heading 1.4, ''Constitution of Canada'', above.

49 McLachlin J. said, [1993] 1 S.C.R. 320, 373, that ''one part of the Constitution cannot be abrogated or diminished by another part of the Constitution''. The words ''or diminished'' are what is wrong in this statement. They reflect a misunderstanding of *Re Bill 30* (Ontario Separate School Funding) [1987] 1 S.C.R. 1148, the case she cites as authority. That case decided that a power to distinguish between school supporters on the basis of religion was implicit in s. 93 of the Constitution Act, 1867, which expressly authorized the establishment of denominational schools, and was not an infringement of s. 15 of the Charter of Rights. The case did not decide that the provincial power over education was in any other respect undiminished by the Charter of Rights. On the contrary, discrimination on any basis other than religion (such as race or sex) would be unconstitutional, and infringements of Charter rights other than those in s. 15 would also be unconstitutional.

On the contrary, the purpose of the Charter of Rights is to diminish the powers of the legislative and executive branches of government, including those powers that are conferred by the Constitution. This is illustrated by the application of the Charter of Rights to the legislative powers of the federal Parliament and the provincial Legislatures. All of the legislative powers of the federal Parliament and the provincial Legislatures are conferred by the Constitution of Canada, chiefly by ss. 91 and 92 of the Constitution Act, 1867. The Charter of Rights applies to these powers. Indeed, there would be no point in applying the Charter to the Parliament and the Legislatures if powers conferred by other parts of the Constitution were exempt from its constraints.

In my opinion, the decision that the legislative assembly of Nova Scotia came within the word ''legislature'' in s. 32 of the Charter of Rights entailed the legal conclusion that all of the assembly's powers, including those conferred by the Constitution, were subject to the Charter of Rights. As a matter of policy too, it is surely unacceptable that every exercise of parliamentary-privilege powers by a legislative assembly should be exempt from Charter review. Could a legislative assembly choose to exclude all members of the public from its deliberations? Could it refuse to allow members of the opposition to speak, or allow them to speak but refuse to record their speeches? These questions answer themselves. This is not to say that a legislative assembly may never act in derogation of a guaranteed right; it is only to say that a rule adopted by a legislative assembly in derogation of a Charter right would have to be justified as a reasonable limit under s. 1. As Sopinka and Cory JJ. pointed out in their opinions in the *New Brunswick Broadcasting* case,[50] restrictions on the use of television cameras in order to maintain order and decorum in the legislative assembly would be readily upheld by the courts under s. 1.

(c) Statutory authority

Because s. 32 makes the Charter of Rights applicable to the federal Parliament and the provincial Legislatures, the Parliament and Legislatures have lost the power to enact laws that are inconsistent with the Charter of Rights. It follows that any body exercising statutory authority, for example, the Governor in Council or Lieutenant Governor in Council, ministers, officials, municipalities, administrative tribunals and police officers, is also bound by the Charter.

Action taken under statutory authority is valid only if it is within the scope of that authority. Since neither Parliament nor a Legislature can itself pass a law in breach of the Charter, neither body can authorize action which would be in breach of the Charter. Thus, the limitations on statutory authority which are imposed by the Charter will flow down the chain of statutory authority and apply to regulations, by-laws, orders, decisions and all other action (whether legislative, administrative or judicial) which depends for its validity on statutory authority.

50 [1993] 1 S.C.R. 320, 397 per Sopinka J. concurring separately, 413-414 per Cory J. dissenting.

That is the way in which limitations on statutory authority imposed by ss. 91 and 92 of the Constitution Act, 1867 (and other distribution-of-powers rules) work. There is no reason to treat limitations on statutory authority imposed by the Charter any differently.

The distinctive characteristic of action taken under statutory authority is that it involves a power of compulsion that is not possessed by a private individual or organization. It is that power of compulsion that must conform to the Charter. A private corporation is a creature of statute in the sense that its existence and powers depend upon the statute that authorized its incorporation. But a private corporation is empowered to exercise only the same proprietary and contractual powers that are available to a natural person. It does not possess the coercive power of governance to which the Charter applies. This is the reason why the Supreme Court of Canada has held that the mandatory retirement policies of a university and a hospital are not reviewable under the Charter. Although the university and the hospital were both established and empowered by statute, the bodies were not possessed of powers any larger than those of a natural person.[51]

Where the Parliament or a Legislature has delegated a power of compulsion to a body or person, then the Charter will apply to the delegate. For example, the Charter has been held to apply to a municipal by-law, made under statutory authority, that purported to prohibit postering on municipal public property.[52] The Charter has been held to apply to an arbitrator awarding a remedy for an unjust dismissal; the adjudicator ordered the employer to provide the dismissed employee with a letter of reference — a requirement that was possible because the adjudicator was exercising powers conferred by statute.[53] Had the adjudicator's authority simply come from the consent of the parties, no exercise of statutory power would have been involved, and the Charter would not have applied. The Charter has been held applicable to the rules of the Law Society of Alberta, which purported to restrict the entry of out-of-province law firms to the legal profession in Alberta — something that required the exercise of statutory authority.[54] The rules of an organization that are binding on the members simply by virtue of their consent are not subject to the Charter.[55] The Charter has also been held applicable to an automobile insurance policy that excluded common-law spouses from spousal accident benefits; although both the insurer and the insured were private

51 *McKinney* v. *U. of Guelph* [1990] 3 S.C.R. 229; *Stoffman* v. *Vancouver General Hospital* [1990] 3 S.C.R. 483. If the bodies had been controlled by government, they would have been covered by the Charter by virtue of s. 32's reference to ''government''. That was the case in *Douglas/Kwantlen Faculty Assn.* v. *Douglas College* [1990] 3 S.C.R. 570 and *Lavigne* v. *OPSEU* [1991] 2 S.C.R. 211, where community colleges were held to be subject to the Charter.

52 *Ramsden* v. *Peterborough* [1993] 2 S.C.R. 1084.

53 *Slaight Communics.* v. *Davidson* [1989] 1 S.C.R. 1038.

54 *Black* v. *Law Society of Alta.* [1989] 1 S.C.R. 591.

55 *Tomen* v. *FWTAO* (1989) 70 O.R. (2d) 48 (C.A.).

parties, the terms of the policy were stipulated by statute.[56] A private person making a citizen's arrest under statutory authority is subject to the Charter.[57]

The foregoing examples illustrate that bodies or persons possessing statutory authority are often independent of the federal government or the provincial government. The Charter applies to the exercise of statutory authority regardless of whether the actor is part of the government or is controlled by the government. It is the exertion of a power of compulsion granted by statute that causes the Charter to apply. As we shall see in the next section of this chapter, the Charter also applies to the action of the federal and provincial governments, including all bodies or persons controlled by a government, even if the governmental action was not based on statutory authority. But, outside the sphere of government, the Charter will apply only to persons or bodies exercising statutory authority.

In *Re Bhindi* (1986),[58] the British Columbia Court of Appeal had to consider whether a ''closed-shop'' provision in a collective agreement violated the guarantee of freedom of association in the Charter of Rights. A closed shop is a workplace in which the employer has agreed to hire only members of the union. The majority of the Court, pointing out that the collective agreement was between a private employer and the union of its employees, held that the collective agreement was a private contract to which the Charter did not apply. The fallacy in this ruling, as the two dissenting judges pointed out, is that the closed-shop provision was not only expressly authorized by the applicable labour legislation, it would have been ineffective without the statutory authority. At common law, a contract is binding by virtue of the consent of the parties. A collective agreement that forces unwilling employees to join the union could not be effective through the common law of contract. In all jurisdictions, collective agreements are authorized by statute so that their terms and conditions will be binding on all employees in the bargaining unit, including those who do not agree with the terms and conditions. The terms and conditions of a collective agreement thus have a coercive force that goes beyond what could be achieved in a common law (or civil law) contract. Therefore, the terms and conditions of a collective agreement should be subject to the Charter.

In *Lavigne* v. *OPSEU* (1991),[59] the Supreme Court of Canada had to consider whether an ''agency-shop'' provision in a collective agreement violated the guarantees of freedom of expression and association in the Charter of Rights. An agency shop is a workplace in which all employees are not required to join the union (as is the case in a closed shop or a union shop), but all employees are

---

56 *Miron* v. *Trudel* [1995] 2 S.C.R. 418.

57 *R.* v. *Lerke* (1986) 25 D.L.R. (4th) 403 (Alta. C.A.).

58 (1986) 29 D.L.R. (4th) 47 (B.C.C.A.). The majority opinion was written by Nemetz C.J. with the agreement of Hinkson and Craig JJ.A. Dissenting opinions were written by Anderson and Hutcheon JJ.A.

59 [1991] 2 S.C.R. 211. On the status of the collective agreement, the majority opinion of La Forest J. attracted the agreement of Sopinka, Gonthier, Cory and McLachlin JJ. Wilson J.'s concurring opinion was agreed with by L'Heureux-Dubé J.

required to pay dues to the union. The Supreme Court of Canada held that the Charter applied, because the employer was an agent of the provincial government, which made the collective agreement a governmental act.[60] But the Court seemed to be unanimous that, if the employer had not been a part of government, then the collective agreement would be a private contract to which the Charter would not have applied. La Forest J. for the majority, after referring to *Bhindi* with approval, said that the fact that the provision for the compulsory payment of dues was authorized (but not required) by statute did not make the Charter applicable. He said that the "parties to collective agreement negotiations would be free to agree to [the agency shop provision] independently of any legislative 'permission' ".[61] With respect, La Forest J. is correct that the Charter should not become applicable by virtue of permissive statutory authority which grants power no greater than would be possessed by a natural person anyway. But that is not this case. Without statutory authority, an obligation to pay union dues could be created only by the agreement of the employee. In my opinion, it is clear that the dissident employee was being subjected to a statutory power of compulsion as surely as if the statute had directly ordered him to pay the dues.

It was not necessary for the Court in *Lavigne* to rule on the status of collective agreements in the private sector. Because the government was a party to the collective agreement, the Charter applied.[62] The discussion of statutory authority was therefore obiter. I hope that when the issue has to be decided, the Court will reconsider its approval of *Bhindi* and its comments on statutory authority. As the cases stand at present, a Legislature that is itself powerless to abridge freedom of association (or any other Charter right) has the mysterious capacity to grant to employers and unions (or anyone else outside of government) the power to abridge the right. That cannot be good law.

(d) Amending procedures

The extent to which s. 32 of the Charter makes the Charter binding on the process of constitutional amendment has been discussed in the earlier chapter on Amendment.[63] Briefly, the position is that those amending procedures that require the concurrence of several legislative houses (under ss. 38, 41, 43) are not con-

60 See text accompanying note 66, below.

61 [1991] 2 S.C.R. 211, 310. Wilson J. was less categorical, saying (at p. 247) that "in a great many instances, 'permissive legislation' does not connote governmental approval of what is permitted but connotes at most governmental acquiescence in it". With respect, the issue is not whether governmental approval or governmental acquiescence (whatever the difference may be) has been given, but whether a statutory power of compulsion has been delegated by the Legislature and exercised by the Legislature's delegates, and the answer to that question is surely yes.

62 This was also the case in *Douglas/Kwantlen Faculty Assn.* v. *Douglas College* [1990] 3 S.C.R. 570, where the Charter was held applicable to a collective agreement.

63 Chapter 4, Amendment, under heading 4.2(d), "Charter of Rights", above.

strained by the Charter. However, the limited powers of amendment that are possessed by the federal Parliament alone (under s. 44) and by each provincial Legislature alone (under s. 45) are constrained by the Charter.

(e) Government

The application of the Charter to all action taken under statutory authority follows simply from the references in s. 32 to ''Parliament'' and ''legislature''. What is added by the references to the ''government'' of Canada and of each province?[64] To the extent that government acts under statutory authority, the reference to government adds nothing. But government sometimes acts under prerogative powers, which are common law powers possessed only by government, for example, when government awards honours, issues passports or conducts foreign affairs. Government also acts under common law powers that are possessed by everyone, for example, when government enters into contracts, or buys or sells property. The references in s. 32 to ''government'' will make the Charter applicable to governmental action taken under both kinds of common law powers. The Supreme Court of Canada has held that the Charter applies to a cabinet decision taken under the prerogative to allow the United States to test its cruise missile in Canada.[65] The Court has also applied the Charter to the making by a Crown agent of a contract of employment with its employees.[66] In the latter case, La Forest J. said: ''To permit government to pursue policies violating Charter

64 The references to government in s. 32 are expressly confined to the governments of Canada and the provinces. Therefore, actions by foreign governments cannot be breaches of the Charter: *R.* v. *Harrer* [1995] 3 S.C.R. 562 (United States' police officers not obliged to comply with Charter). Generally speaking, it is also not a breach of the Charter where Canadian law exposes a person to foreign sanctions, for example, by compelling testimony that violates a foreign secrecy law: *Spencer* v. *The Queen* [1985] 2 S.C.R. 278. However, extradition is a deprivation of liberty, and s. 7 is breached if a fugitive is extradited by Canada to a foreign country where the fugitive may be treated in a fashion that ''shocks the conscience''; *Can.* v. *Schmidt* [1987] 1 S.C.R. 500, 522. But the Court has been reluctant to interfere with extradition orders, and has allowed extraditions to the United States notwithstanding that the penalties faced by the fugitives in question were more severe than penalties for similar crimes in Canada, or were even contrary to our Charter: *Kindler* v. *Can.* [1991] 2 S.C.R. 779 (death penalty); *United States* v. *Jamieson* [1996] 1 S.C.R. 465 (mandatory 20 year sentence); *United States* v. *Whitley* [1996] 1 S.C.R. 467 (mandatory 20 year sentence); *United States* v. *Ross* [1996] 1 S.C.R. 469 (mandatory 15 year sentence). There is an inconclusive discussion of foreign governmental action in *Singh* v. *Minr. of Emplt. and Immig.* [1985] 1 S.C.R. 177.

65 *Operation Dismantle* v. *The Queen* [1985] 1 S.C.R. 441. The claim that ''life, liberty and security of the person'' had been placed at risk was rejected.

66 *Douglas/Kwantlen Faculty Assn.* v. *Douglas College* [1990] 3 S.C.R. 570, 585 (collective agreement contained provision for mandatory requirement); *Lavigne* v. *OPSEU* [1991] 2 S.C.R. 211, 313 (collective agreement required employees to pay union dues, even if they were not union members).

rights by means of contracts or agreements with other persons or bodies cannot be tolerated''.[67]

What is included in the term ''government''? Obviously, it includes action taken by the Governor General in Council or the Lieutenant Governor in Council, by the cabinet, by individual ministers and by public servants within the departments of government. Also included are those Crown corporations and public agencies that are outside the formal departmental structure, but which, by virtue of a substantial degree of ministerial control, are deemed to be ''agents'' of the Crown.[68] Thus, the Supreme Court of Canada has held[69] that a community college in British Columbia was subject to the Charter, because it was subject to a substantial degree of government control.[70] All the members of the governing board were appointed by the Lieutenant Governor in Council, and held office at pleasure. As well, the Minister of Education had power to issue directives to the college. In other cases involving a university and a hospital, the Court has held that both institutions were sufficiently independent of government that they were not subject to the Charter.[71]

The control test looks to an *institutional* or *structural* link with government to determine whether a public body is covered by the Charter. This is a principled approach to the issue, and one that makes use of the jurisprudence defining the Crown and Crown agents. The majority of the Court has wisely rejected a *functional* link with government as the test for the coverage of the Charter.[72] Thus, it was irrelevant that the university and the hospital were each performing a ''public service'', as long as they were performing it independently of government.[73] And it would be irrelevant that a public body was performing a ''private'' function if

---

67 *Ibid.* The same passage is in both cases. There was in fact statutory authority for the collective agreement in both cases, but the Court placed its decision on the presence of a government party to the agreement, and clearly intended to lay down a rule governing common law contracts.

68 See ch. 10, The Crown, under heading 10.2, ''Crown agency'', above.

69 *Douglas/Kwantlen Faculty Assn.* v. *Douglas College* [1990] 3 S.C.R. 570; folld. in *Lavigne* v. *OPSEU* [1991] 2 S.C.R. 211 (Council of Regents, governing Ontario's community colleges, controlled by Minister of Education).

70 The college was also expressly stipulated by statute to be an agent of the Crown, but the Court did not rely on this fact. The rule for Crown-agent status is that an express stipulation will create the status even if the body so stipulated is not controlled by government: ch. 10, The Crown, under heading 10.2(c), ''By statute'', above. It is submitted that the same rule should apply to the application of the Charter as well.

71 *McKinney* v. *U. of Guelph* [1990] 3 S.C.R. 229; *Stoffman* v. *Vancouver General Hospital* [1990] 3 S.C.R. 483.

72 In *McKinney*, previous note, and *Stoffman*, previous note, Wilson J. dissented on the issue of the application of the Charter. In her view, the Court ought to apply three tests (1) a ''control'' test, (2) a ''governmental functions'' test, and (3) a ''government entity'' test; and none of the three tests were to be determinative. Fortunately, the majority rejected this approach, which would have been a recipe for unbridled judicial discretion.

73 *McKinney*, previous note, 269; *Stoffman*, previous note, 511.

it was performing it under the control of government[74] There is no principled way to classify the functions of public bodies into "governmental" (or "public") and "commercial" (or "private") categories. The only useful question is whether government has assumed control of the function. The existence of control is the only sure guide to whether the function is one of government to which the Charter should apply.

It must be emphasized that the scope of the term "government" is important only if the body alleged to have breached the Charter was not relying on a statutory power. If the body alleged to have breached the Charter was relying on a statutory power, the Charter will apply by virtue of that fact,[75] and regardless of whether or not the body is within the term "government".

(f) Courts

Does the Charter apply to the courts? The Supreme Court of Canada has answered this question yes and no.

The no answer came in *Retail, Wholesale and Department Store Union* v. *Dolphin Delivery* (1986).[76] The question in that case was whether Dolphin Delivery, a courier company, could obtain an injunction to restrain a union from picketing Dolphin Delivery's premises. The union represented the employees of another courier company against whom it was on strike. Since Dolphin Delivery was not part of that dispute, the picketing of Dolphin Delivery's premises would be "secondary picketing". The courts in British Columbia held that the picketing would constitute the common law tort of inducing a breach of contract, and they granted an injunction to prevent the picketing. In the Supreme Court of Canada, the union argued that the injunction should be set aside, because it abridged the Charter guarantee of freedom of expression. The Court rejected the argument on the ground that the Charter had no application to the order of a court. McIntyre J., speaking for a unanimous Court on this issue, held that the word "government" in s. 32 meant only the executive branch of government, and did not include the judicial branch.[77] A court order was not governmental action, and therefore the injunction issued by the Supreme Court of British Columbia was not subject to the Charter.

The yes answer came in *R.* v. *Rahey* (1987).[78] In that case, the Supreme Court of Canada had to determine whether a criminal court had denied to a

74 *Lavigne* v. *OPSEU* [1991] 2 S.C.R. 211, 314 ("... government activities which are in form 'commercial' or 'private' transactions are in reality expressions of government policy ...").

75 Section 34.2(b), "Parliament or Legislature", above.

76 [1986] 2 S.C.R. 573. The majority opinion was written by McIntyre J., with the agreement of Dickson C.J., Estey, Chouinard and Le Dain JJ. Concurring opinions were written by Beetz and Wilson JJ., but they both agreed with McIntyre J. on the applicability of the Charter.

77 *Id.*, 598-600.

78 [1987] 1 S.C.R. 588. Four concurring opinions were written: by Lamer J. (with Dickson C.J.), Wilson J. (with Estey J.), Le Dain J. (with Beetz J.) and La Forest J. (with McIntyre J.).

defendant the s. 11(b) right to be tried within a reasonable time. The trial judge had delayed unreasonably in reaching a decision on the application by the defendant, made at the close of the Crown's case, for a directed verdict of acquittal. The trial judge had adjourned the application 19 times and taken 11 months to reach his decision; his decision was to deny the application. The Supreme Court of Canada held that the delay was a breach of s. 11(b) of the Charter and the Court ordered a stay of the proceedings. In this case, the action that was held to be a breach of the Charter was the action of a court, and the remedy was directed to a court. In the Supreme Court of Canada, of the four judges who wrote opinions, only La Forest J. adverted to this point, saying: "it seems obvious to me that the courts, as custodians of the principles enshrined in the Charter, must themselves be subject to Charter scrutiny in the administration of their duties".[79] This statement is, of course, contradictory of the ruling in *Dolphin Delivery*, given only five months earlier, that the Charter does not apply to the courts. Yet *Dolphin Delivery* was not referred to by La Forest J. or by any of the other judges who wrote opinions.

The yes answer was confirmed in *British Columbia Government Employees' Union* v. *British Columbia* (1988).[80] In that case, a union, on lawful strike, had formed picket lines outside the courts in British Columbia, where some of the union members worked. The Chief Justice of British Columbia, discovering the picketers outside the courthouse on his way to work, immediately, on his own motion and without notice to the union, issued an injunction prohibiting the picketing of the courts. The union, on learning of the injunction, applied to have it set aside on the ground that it abridged the s. 2(b) right to freedom of expression. The Supreme Court of Canada refused to set aside the injunction. The majority of the Court held that, although the injunction did limit freedom of expression, it was justified under s. 1. Although the Charter issue was thus resolved in favour of the injunction, Dickson C.J. for a unanimous Court (on this issue), did hold that a court order was subject to Charter review. He referred to *Dolphin Delivery*, distinguishing it on the basis that the injunction in that case was issued to resolve "a purely private dispute".[81] In this case, "the court is acting on its own motion and not at the instance of any private party", and the court's motivation "is entirely 'public' in nature, rather than 'private' ".[82]

The *Rahey* and *BCGEU* decisions have, in effect, repudiated McIntyre J.'s ruling in *Dolphin Delivery* that the word "government" in s. 32 excludes the courts. Obviously, in the circumstances of those two cases, "government" did include the courts. Also, many of the Charter rights contemplate that the courts

79 *Id.*, 633.

80 [1988] 2 S.C.R. 214. Dickson C.J. wrote the majority opinion, with the agreement of Lamer, Wilson, La Forest and L'Heureux-Dubé JJ. McIntyre J. wrote a concurring opinion agreeing with Dickson C.J. that the Charter applied, but disagreeing with Dickson C.J.'s opinion that there had been a violation of freedom of expression.

81 *Id.*, 243.

82 *Id.*, 244. Accord, *UNA* v. *Alta.* (1992) 89 D.L.R. (4th) 609, 635 (S.C.C.).

are bound by the Charter. Nearly all of the rights guaranteed to criminal defendants by s. 11 entail action by courts: holding a trial within a reasonable time (s. 11(b)), not compelling the defendant to testify (s. 11(c)), respecting the presumption of innocence and providing a fair and public trial (s. 11(d)), granting reasonable bail (s. 11(e)) and so on. The same is true of the s. 12 right not to be subjected to cruel and unusual treatment or punishment, the s. 13 right against self-incrimination, and the s. 14 right to an interpreter. These provisions supply a context in which it is reasonable to interpret the word ''government'' in s. 32 as including the judicial branch. The references in s. 32 to ''Parliament'' and ''Legislature'' could also be regarded as catching court action, because courts are established (or continued) by statute, and their powers to grant injunctions and make other orders are granted (or continued) by statute. Since other statutory tribunals have to comply with the Charter, the courts should have to do so too.

If it is impossible to reconcile the definition of ''government'' in *Dolphin Delivery* with the decisions in *Rahey* and *BCGEU*, is it still possible to accommodate the actual decision in *Dolphin Delivery* with the two later cases? There are two elements of the court order in *Dolphin Delivery* that make it distinctive: (1) the court order resolved a dispute between two private parties, and (2) the court order was based upon the common law. No government was involved in the dispute, and no statute applied to the dispute. Therefore, there was no governmental action that could make the Charter applicable, at least up to the point of the making of the court order (the issue of the injunction). The question then becomes: does the making of the court order, supported as it is by ''the full panoply of state power'', supply the requisite element of governmental action?[83] The ratio decidendi of *Dolphin Delivery* must be that a court order, when issued as a resolution of a dispute between private parties, and when based on the common law, is not governmental action to which the Charter applies.[84] And the reason for the decision is that a contrary decision would have the effect of applying the Charter to the relationships of private parties that s. 32 intends to exclude

83 *Shelley* v. *Kraemer* (1948) 334 U.S. 1, 19 (where the quotation comes from) answers the question yes, holding that an injunction to enforce a racially-discriminatory restrictive covenant was ''state action'' to which the Bill of Rights applied. The decision has been much criticized: e.g., in the famous article by Wechsler,''Toward Neutral Principles of Constitutional Law'' (1959) 73 Harv. L. Rev. 1, 29-31. Tribe, *American Constitutional Law* (2nd ed., 1988), 1697, joins the criticism, commenting that ''such reasoning, consistently applied, would require individuals to conform their private agreements to constitutional standards whenever, as almost always, the individuals might later seek the security of potential judicial enforcement''.

84 In *Young* v. *Young* [1993] 4 S.C.R. 3, L'Heureux-Dubé J. (with La Forest and Gonthier JJ.) held that the Charter did not apply to a court order, resolving a dispute between two private parties, granting custody of children to their mother and access to their father (there were restrictions on access relating to religion that were argued to be in breach of s. 2(a)). However, the majority of the Court left open the question whether the Charter applied or not. They did not say why they did not agree with L'Heureux-Dubé J., but it may have been because the court order could be traced to a power in the Divorce Act.

from Charter coverage,[85] and that ought in principle to be excluded from Charter coverage.[86] Where, however, a court order is issued on the court's own motion for a public purpose (as in *BCGEU*), or in a proceeding to which government is a party (as in any criminal case, such as *Rahey*), or in a purely private proceeding that is governed by statute law, then the Charter will apply to the court order.

(g) Common law

Does the Charter apply to the common law? This question is closely related to the question whether the Charter applies to the courts, since the courts "make" the common law. It is not surprising, therefore, that in the *Dolphin Delivery* case (1986)[87] the Supreme Court of Canada answered the question no: the Charter does not apply to the common law, or at least those rules of the common law that regulate relationships between private parties.

In *Dolphin Delivery*, an injunction against picketing had been issued against a union. The basis for the injunction was a rule of the common law that secondary picketing (in the circumstances there presented) would amount to the tort of inducing a breach of contract. The union, seeking to set aside the injunction, argued that this rule of the common law was an unconstitutional abridgement of freedom of expression. McIntyre J., for a Court that was unanimous on this issue, said that the Charter had no application to such a rule: "where . . . private party 'A' sues private party 'B' relying on the common law, and where no act of government is relied upon to support the action, the Charter will not apply".[88] With this language, the Court excluded from Charter review the rules of the common law that regulate relationships between private parties.

The Supreme Court of the United States has decided this issue the other way. The leading case is *New York Times* v. *Sullivan* (1963).[89] In that case, it was held that the Bill of Rights' guarantees of freedom of speech and of the press applied to the common law of defamation, shielding a newspaper from tortious liability for defamatory criticism of a public official, unless the criticism was actuated by malice. In this way, the Bill of Rights modified the common law of Alabama by adding a new ingredient to the tort of defamation, namely, malice, where the defamatory statement took the form of political speech. There is an earlier American case that is on all fours with *Dolphin Delivery*. In *American Federation of*

---

85 This is explicit in McIntyre J.'s opinion: *RWDSU* v. *Dolphin Delivery* [1986] 2 S.C.R. 573, 600 ("To regard a court order as an element of governmental intervention necessary to invoke the Charter would, it seems to me, widen the scope of Charter application to virtually all private litigation"). This is Tribe's point as well, previous note.

86 The rationale for the exclusion of private action is examined in sec. 34.2(h), "Private action", below.

87 *RWDSU* v. *Dolphin Delivery* [1986] 2 S.C.R. 573; discussed at note 76, above.

88 *Id.*, 603.

89 (1963) 376 U.S. 254.

Labour v. *Swing* (1941),[90] the Supreme Court of the United States held that an injunction issued by a state court to restrain a union from secondary picketing was an unconstitutional violation of the guarantee of freedom of speech. The injunction was based on the common law, and the effect of the decision was to modify the common law of the state of Illinois. As the result of these decisions, in the United States, it is well settled ''that common law is state action — that is, that the state 'acts' when its courts create and enforce common law rules''.[91]

In Canada, the exclusion of the common law from Charter review makes it necessary to determine the source of any law that is claimed to abridge a Charter right. If the applicable law is a rule of the common law, the Charter does not apply. If, however, the law is a rule of statute law, the Charter does apply: the statute supplies the needed element of governmental action.[92] This anomaly is starkly presented by the facts of *Dolphin Delivery* itself. Because the prohibition on secondary picketing had not been enacted in the Canada Labour Code,[93] it remained a matter of common law, and the Charter did not apply. But in most jurisdictions, including British Columbia, the prohibition on secondary picketing has been enacted in the Labour Code; in those jurisdictions, the Charter will apply.[94] It seems odd that the applicability of the Charter should turn on the question whether the applicable law is a rule of the common law or a rule of statute law.[95]

In support of the Court's decision in *Dolphin Delivery*, it could be said that the exclusion of private action from the operation of the Charter does entail the exclusion of at least some of the common law. In an expansive sense, the common law could be said to authorize any private action that is not prohibited by a positive rule of law. On this view, if I were to refuse to permit Anglicans to enter my house, my refusal would be an act authorized by the common law, and therefore subject to Charter review. This line of reasoning would make the Charter appl-

90 (1941) 312 U.S. 321.

91 Tribe, *American Constitutional Law* (2nd ed., 1988), 1711.

92 Section 34.2(b), ''Parliament or Legislature'', above.

93 The applicable law was federal, because the union represented employees of an undertaking engaged in interprovincial transportation.

94 Just as a common law rule becomes subject to the Charter if the rule is transformed into statute law, a convention (defined sec. 1.9, ''Conventions'', above) that is enacted into statutory form also becomes subject to the Charter: *Osborne* v. *Can.* [1991] 2 S.C.R. 69 (restrictions on political activity by public servants held unconstitutional).

95 Slattery, ''The Charter's Relevance to Private Litigation: Does Dolphin Deliver?'' (1987) 32 McGill L.J. 905 criticizes the exclusion of the common law from the Charter on the basis that in most Canadian jurisdictions the original reception of the common law from England, and its continuing force, depends upon a statute. He points out as well that the Civil Code of Quebec, which substitutes for the common law in that civilian jurisdiction, is a statute. With respect to the latter point, the Court has now held that the rules of the civil law governing relations between private parties are also exempt from the Charter: *Tremblay* v. *Daigle* [1989] 2 S.C.R. 530, 571. This removes the intolerable anomaly of the Charter having a far more extensive application in Quebec than it has in the nine common law provinces.

icable to all private action. The American courts have not allowed themselves to be beguiled down that slippery slope, but the Supreme Court of Canada is right to be concerned that the application of the Charter to any rule of the common law would later require difficult distinctions to be drawn if a zone of private action is to be shielded from Charter review.[96]

The Charter applies when a Crown prosecutor exercises a common law power to adduce evidence of the accused's insanity, causing the accused to be acquitted but held in custody.[97] The Charter applies when the Crown acts under a prerogative power, for example, by authorizing the testing of American cruise missiles on Canadian soil.[98] The Charter also applies when the Crown acts under a general common law power, for example, by entering into a contract with its employees requiring mandatory retirement[99] or mandatory payment of union dues.[100] It is questionable whether one ought to describe the Charter as applicable to the common law[101] in these situations,[102] because it is the presence of the governmental actor, not the source of the actor's power, that makes the Charter applicable.

While the Charter does not apply directly to the common law (where no governmental actor is involved), the Charter does have an indirect effect on the common law. This was suggested by McIntyre J. in *Dolphin Delivery*, when he asserted that "the judiciary ought to apply and develop the principles of the common law in a manner consistent with the fundamental values enshrined in the Constitution"; and he went on to say that "in this sense, then, the Charter is far from irrelevant to private litigants whose disputes fall to be decided at common law".[103] In that case, McIntyre J. did examine the Charter argument, holding that secondary picketing "would have involved the exercise of the right of freedom of expression",[104] but that the common law's prohibition of the practice would

---

96 The rationale for the exclusion of private action is examined in sec. 34.2(h), "Private action", below.

97 *R.* v. *Swain* [1991] 1 S.C.R. 933 (the breach of the Charter was cured by the Court directly modifying the common law rule).

98 *Operation Dismantle* v. *The Queen* [1985] 1 S.C.R. 441.

99 *Douglas/Kwantlen Faculty Assn.* v. *Douglas College* [1990] 3 S.C.R. 570.

100 *Lavigne* v. *OPSEU* [1991] 1 S.C.R. 211; see notes 64-67 and accompanying text, above.

101 The common law offence of contempt of court is subject to the Charter: *R.* v. *Kopyto* (1987) 62 O.R. (2d) 449 (C.A.); *BCGEU* v. *B.C.* [1988] 2 S.C.R. 214. These were cases of criminal contempt, where the court is, in effect, a party, and the dispute is not a private one. The position is less clear with respect to civil contempt for breach of a court order, where the dispute retains a private character (although the defendant is liable to imprisonment): see *Vidéotron* v. *Industries Microlec* [1992] 2 S.C.R. 1065, 1071, 1079, 1100, where the majority opinions seem to assume that the Charter would apply.

102 McIntyre J.'s opinion in *RWDSU* v. *Dolphin Delivery* [1986] 2 S.C.R. 573 was confusing, because early in the opinion (at 592) he insisted that the Charter did apply to the common law, but he later (at 599) made it clear that he meant only when "the common law is the basis of some governmental act".

103 [1986] 2 S.C.R. 573, 603.

104 *Id.*, 588.

have been justified under s. 1.[105] Although this part of the opinion appeared to be obiter, and was never connected to the dictum about developing the common law, it was clear that the majority of the Court[106] did not believe that the common law respecting secondary picketing was inconsistent with the values of the Constitution. Therefore, that case did not present the occasion for developing the common law so as to make it consistent with the values of the Constitution.

In *Dagenais* v. *CBC* (1994),[107] a Charter challenge was brought to an injunction (publication ban) that had been issued by a trial judge to prohibit the CBC from broadcasting a television programme that could have had the effect of influencing the juries in a series of criminal trials of Christian brothers who were charged with abusing young boys in their care. The applicants for the injunction were the Christian brothers who had been charged with abuse, and the respondent was the CBC, which, although publicly owned, is not an agent of the Crown to which the Charter would apply. Since the legal basis for the injunction was the common law, the case was on all fours with *Dolphin Delivery* in that it was a dispute between private parties governed by the common law.[108] Lamer C.J. for the majority of the Supreme Court of Canada relied upon McIntyre J.'s dictum in *Dolphin Delivery* to hold that the common law should be developed in a manner consistent with the values of the Constitution. After reviewing the common law respecting publication bans, the Chief Justice decided that the law gave insufficient weight to the Charter value of freedom of expression. He held that it was "necessary to reformulate the common law rule . . . in a manner that reflects the

105 Beetz J. wrote a separate concurring opinion, holding that picketing was not a form of expression that was protected under s. 2(b). Wilson J. also wrote a separate concurring opinion disagreeing with McIntyre J.'s opinion on the application of the Charter.

106 Only Wilson J. seemed to decide (the brief opinion is not perfectly clear on the point) that the prohibition on secondary picketing would have violated the Charter had the Charter been applicable.

107 [1994] 3 S.C.R. 835. The majority opinion was written by Lamer C.J., with whom Sopinka, Cory, Iacobucci and Major JJ. agreed; McLachlin J. wrote a separate concurring opinion; La Forest, L'Heureux-Dubé and Gonthier JJ. each wrote concurring opinions. All nine judges agreed that the Charter applied to the publication ban, but there was some diversity in the reasons. Lamer C.J.'s majority opinion is described in the accompanying text. McLachlin J., with whom (on this issue) La Forest J. agreed, held (at p. 944) that the Charter applied to "Court orders in the criminal sphere". Gonthier J. held (at p. 918) that the Charter applied to the common law in "criminal matters". L'Heureux-Dubé J. held (at p. 912) that the Charter applied to the common law without limitation.

108 But see *Hill* v. *Church of Scientology* [1995] 2 S.C.R. 1130, para. 94 (discussed in following text), in which Cory J. said that *Dagenais* should not be regarded as a case of "purely private civil litigation", because "the court was called upon to consider the operations of the court and to determine the extent of its own jurisdiction to consider matters which were essentially public in nature". However, in *Dagenais* itself, this was not the rationale for the application of the Charter in the majority judgment of Lamer C.J. to which Cory J. agreed, or in the opinion of L'Heureux-Dubé J., although it seems closer to the opinion of McLachlin J. with which (on this issue) La Forest J. agreed and perhaps to the opinion of Gonthier J. On the division of opinion, see previous note.

principles of the Charter''.[109] He proceeded to do this by formulating a more restrictive common law rule for the issue of publication bans, and by striking down the ban that was under appeal.[110]

In *Hill* v. *Church of Scientology* (1995),[111] a Crown attorney employed by the government of Ontario brought an action for defamation against the Church of Scientology and its lawyer, who had falsely accused the plaintiff of violating a court order. The defendants argued that their statements were protected by the Charter of Rights. They pointed to the facts that the plaintiff was employed as an agent of the Crown, that the defamatory statements related to his official duties, and that his defamation action was being funded by the Crown. The Supreme Court of Canada held that these facts did not supply the element of governmental action that was required by s. 32 of the Charter. In the context of a defamation action, the plaintiff was a private party, because the action was brought, not as part of his governmental duties, but to vindicate his personal reputation. Since it was the common law that governed the cause of action, it followed that the Charter did not apply. However, although the Charter did not apply directly to the common law of defamation, it was still necessary to consider whether the common law was consistent with ''Charter values'',[112] and to modify the common law if necessary. Cory J., who wrote for the Court on this issue, said that this exercise was not exactly the same as applying the Charter directly to the common law. The balancing of the competing values ''must be more flexible than the traditional s. 1 analysis undertaken in cases involving governmental action'', and the Charter claimant ''should bear the onus of proving both that the common law fails to comply with Charter values and that, when these values are balanced, the common law should be modified''.[113] The concern here was that a private party relying on the common law should not be put in the position of carrying the burden of defending the law against a Charter attack. (Of course, a private party relying on a statute is placed in precisely this position.) Having established these preliminaries, Cory J. went on to balance the competing interests that are accommodated by the common law of defamation, namely, the personal reputation of plaintiffs and the freedom of expression of defendants.[114] The Court concluded that ''in its application to the parties in this action, the common law of defamation complies

109 [1994] 3 S.C.R. 835, 878.

110 For discussion of this aspect of the decision, see ch. 40, Expression, under heading 40.14(b), ''Restrictions on reporting'', below.

111 [1995] 2 S.C.R. 1130 Cory J. wrote the opinion of the majority. L'Heureux-Dubé J., who wrote a short concurring opinion, agreed with Cory J. on all but one issue having nothing to do with the application of the Charter. The Court was therefore unanimous on the application of the Charter.

112 *Id.*, para. 95.

113 *Id.*, paras. 97, 98; there is of course no onus of proof on issues of law (as opposed to fact) in Charter cases (or any other kinds of cases), and the statement about onus of proof is presumably intended to relate only to issues of fact.

114 This part of the opinion is discussed in ch. 40, Expression, under heading 40.10, ''Defamation'', below.

with the underlying values of the Charter and there is no need to amend or alter it''.[115]

The result of these cases is that the exclusion of the common law from Charter review is not particularly significant. When the Charter does not apply directly, it will apply indirectly, and, despite some differences in the way s. 1 justification is assessed, the indirect application is much the same in its effect as the direct application.

(h) Private action

Section 32 provides, as we have seen, that the Charter applies to ''the Parliament and government of Canada'' and to ''the legislature and government of each province''. This is an exhaustive statement of the binding application of the Charter. It follows that the Charter applies only where there has been governmental action of some kind, that is, action by the Parliament or government of Canada or by the Legislature or government of a province. The rights guaranteed by the Charter take effect only as restrictions on the power of government over the persons entitled to the rights. The Charter regulates the relations between government and private persons, but it does not regulate the relations between private persons and private persons.[116] Private action is therefore excluded from the application of the Charter. Such actions as an employer restricting an employee's freedom of speech or assembly, a parent restricting the mobility of a child or a landlord discriminating on the basis of race in his selection of tenants cannot be breaches of the Charter, because in no case is there any action by the Parliament or government of Canada or by the Legislature or government of a province. In cases where private action results in a restriction of a civil liberty, there may be a remedy for the aggrieved person under a human rights code, under labour law, family law, tort law, contract law or property law, or under some other branch of the law governing relations between private persons; but there will be no breach of the Charter.

After the Charter was adopted in 1982 there was some speculation as to whether it was restricted to governmental action. Some commentators took the view that it was not so restricted. Section 32, it was suggested, was a cautionary provision, inserted to make clear that governmental action was covered, but not intended to confine the guaranteed rights to governmental action. This view was never particularly plausible, running into contradictory indications within the text

---

115 [1995] 2 S.C.R. 1130, para. 141.

116 *RWDSU* v. *Dolphin Delivery* [1986] 2 S.C.R. 573 (Charter inapplicable to union picketing of private company); *Tremblay* v. *Daigle* [1989] 2 S.C.R. 530 (Charter inapplicable to father's attempt to stop an abortion); *McKinney* v. *U. of Guelph* [1990] 3 S.C.R. 229 (Charter inapplicable to mandatory retirement rules within university); *Stoffman* v. *Vancouver General Hospital* [1990] 3 S.C.R. 483 (same result within hospital).

of the Charter,[117] in the legislative history of the Charter[118] and in the American jurisprudence, which confines the Bill of Rights to governmental action ("state action").[119] In deciding that the Charter does not extend to private action, the Supreme Court of Canada has affirmed the normal role of a constitution. A constitution establishes and regulates the institutions of government, and it leaves to those institutions the task of ordering the private affairs of the people.

The restriction of the Charter to "governmental action" (which may take the form of a legislative or executive or in some situations a judicial act) is sometimes regarded as creating a public-private distinction in our law. The terms "public" and "private" are no doubt convenient labels, but they reflect a rather complex body of law, and they can be seriously misleading. Much "public" activity is not covered by the Charter, because there is no statutory or governmental presence that would make the Charter applicable.[120] Much "private" activity has been regulated by statute, or been joined by government, and if so the statutory or governmental presence will make the Charter applicable as well. If the Parliament chooses to give a power of arrest to private citizens, a citizen's arrest will be subject to the Charter.[121] If the Parliament chooses to criminalize abortion, its statute will be subject to the Charter, and the Court will investigate the constitutionality of regulating a woman's decision to have an abortion.[122] If the Legislature chooses to prohibit discrimination by sex, its statute will be subject to the Charter, and the Court will investigate the constitutionality of a statutory exemption for boys-only sports teams.[123] If the Government chooses to contract with its employees for mandatory retirement, the contractual provision to which government is a party will be subject to the Charter, and the Court will investigate the constitutionality of mandatory retirement.[124] If the police enlist the aid of a private individual, for example, to obtain information from a prisoner or to obtain medical records, the private informers are regarded as agents of the police, and the Court will investigate the constitutionality of their actions.[125] Therefore, when

---

117 Section 1, for example, affords justification only to Charter limits that are "prescribed by law", which would never be true of private action in derogation of a Charter right.

118 Testimony of F.J.E. Jordan, Senior Counsel, Public Law, federal Department of Justice, in *Minutes of Proceedings and Evidence of the Special Joint Committee of the Senate and of the House of Commons on the Constitution of Canada*, First Session of Thirty-second Parliament, 1980-81, pp. 48:27 (January 29, 1981), 49:47 (January 30, 1981).

119 Tribe, *American Constitutional Law* (2nd ed., 1988), ch. 18; Nowak and Rotunda, *Constitutional Law* (4th ed., 1991), ch. 14.

120 E.g., *McKinney* v. *U. of Guelph* [1990] 3 S.C.R. 229 (public university not covered by Charter); *Stoffman* v. *Vancouver General Hospital* [1990] 3 S.C.R. 483 (public hospital not covered by Charter).

121 *R.* v. *Lerke* (1986) 25 D.L.R. (4th) 403 (Alta. C.A.).

122 *R.* v. *Morgentaler (No. 2)* [1988] 1 S.C.R. 30.

123 *Re Blainey* (1986) 54 O.R. (2d) 513 (C.A.).

124 *Douglas/Kwantlen Faculty Assn.* v. *Douglas College* [1990] 3 S.C.R. 570.

125 *R. v. Broyles* [1991] 3 S.C.R. 595 (statement obtained from prisoner in breach of s. 7); *R. v. Dersch* [1993] 3 S.C.R. 768 (medical records given in breach of s. 8).

it is said that the Charter does not apply to "private" action, the word "private" is really a term of art, denoting a residual category from which it is necessary to subtract those cases where the existence of a statute or the presence of government does make the Charter applicable. Without this understanding, the claim that the Charter does not apply to private action would be grossly misleading.

Even noting that the potential scope of "public" action is not fixed, there remain critics who take issue with the legitimacy of the public/private distinction as it has been applied to the Charter. They assert that government is really everywhere, even if only by facilitation or abstention. Moreover, some of these critics see a nasty bias in the public/private distinction. It is the sphere of the "private", from which the Charter is excluded, that includes the relationships of hierarchy and dominance that serve to oppress workers (in the socialist critique) or women (in the feminist critique).[126] The Charter and Charter jurisprudence are attacked on the grounds that nothing in the Charter addresses the really bad stuff that is left unregulated. But the real risks of unmitigated oppression in the private sphere are rather overstated. Legislatures have never accepted that they are limited in their actions by some mythical divide between public matters and private ones, and have actually extensively regulated the employment relationship (to provide for collective bargaining, employment standards, health and safety standards, pay equity, etc.), family relationships (to regulate marriage, divorce, support, family property, child welfare, physical abuse, etc.) and much else that is "private". If the laws are inadequate, it has little to do with the public/private distinction, and much to do with the power of competing political forces. Indeed the constitutional power (and the evident political willingness) of Canadian governmental institutions to regulate the private spheres out of life makes it unnecessary (and undesirable) to extend the Charter's reach to matters outside the fluid boundaries set by governmental action. If private abuse exists, the democratic political process can drive the legislative bodies to produce the laws that are needed to provide the remedy. A legislative body can design a remedial instrument that is appropriate to the problem — in contrast to the limited range of relatively crude remedies that could be fashioned as Charter remedies by the courts.[127]

It is arguable that if a private abuse exists, there ought to be a Charter remedy, in case no remedy is provided by the competent governmental institutions, or in case the legislated remedy is inadequate. If the Charter were extended to private activity, s. 24 would authorize a court-imposed remedy. This would create an extensive new body of "constitutional tort law", co-existing uneasily with the labour codes, family law, human rights codes and other bodies of law, not for-

126 E.g., Lessard, "The Idea of the Private: A Discussion of State Action Doctrine and Separate Sphere Ideology" (1986) 10 Dal. L.J. 107; Hutchinson and Petter, "Private Rights/Public Wrongs: The Liberal Lie of the Charter" (1988) 38 U. Toronto L.J. 278; Fudge, "The Public/Private Distinction: The . . . Use of Charter Litigation to Further Feminist Struggles" (1987) 25 Osgoode Hall L.J. 485.

127 See Weiler, "The Charter at Work" (1990) 40 U. Toronto L.J. 117, 148-155.

getting the criminal law and the law of torts. The existence of these new remedies would vastly expand the role of the courts. The Charter of Rights, and the judicial review that inescapably accompanies its prescriptions, would be intolerably pervasive, applying to even the most intimate relationship.[128] The effect of the governmental action restriction is that there is a private realm in which people are not obliged to subscribe to ''state'' values, and into which constitutional norms do not intrude.[129] The boundaries of that realm are marked, not by an a priori definition of what is ''private'', but by the absence of statutory or other governmental intervention. The boundaries will expand or contract as the scope of governmental intervention, driven by democratic political forces, contracts or expands. But, at any given time, the boundaries can be ascertained by the courts, and the scope of the Charter can therefore be determined.

128 See *McKinney* v. *U. of Guelph* [1990] 3 S.C.R. 229, 262-263 per La Forest J.

129 See Whyte, ''Is the Private Sector affected by the Charter?'' in Smith (ed.), *Righting the Balance: Canada's New Equality Rights* (1986), 145, 149.

35

Limitation of Rights

35.1 Introduction to s. 1

Section 1 of the Charter of Rights[1] provides as follows:

> The Canadian Charter of Rights and Freedoms guarantees the rights and freedoms set out in it subject only to such reasonable limits prescribed by law as can be demonstrably justified in a free and democratic society.

Section 1 guarantees the rights and freedoms set out in the Charter, but makes clear that they are not absolutes; they are subject ''to such reasonable limits prescribed by law as can be demonstrably justified in a free and democratic society''.[2]

Section 1 of the Charter contemplates that judicial review of legislation under the Charter should proceed in two stages. In the first stage, the court must decide whether the challenged law has the effect of limiting one of the guaranteed rights. If the challenged law does have this effect, the second stage is reached: the court must then decide whether the limit is a reasonable one that can be demonstrably justified in a free and democratic society. The first stage involves the interpretation and application of the provisions of the Charter that define the guaranteed rights. The second stage involves the interpretation and application of s. 1 of the Charter.

The existence of the general limitation clause of s. 1, and the two-stage review process which s. 1 mandates, reflect the influence of international human rights instruments, and especially the European Convention on Human Rights and the International Covenant on Civil and Political Rights. In these instruments, the guaranteed rights are qualified by limitation clauses expressed in terms quite

---

1 There is a huge literature on s. 1: see the up-to-date bibliography in *Canadian Charter of Rights Annotated*, Canada Law Book, looseleaf service, vol. 4. Especially valuable is Gibson, *The Law of the Charter: General Principles* (1986), ch. 4; Peck, ''An Analytical Framework for the Application of the Canadian Charter of Rights and Freedoms'' (1987) 25 Osgoode Hall L.J. 1; Elliot, ''The Supreme Court of Canada and Section 1'' (1987) 12 Queen's L.J. 277; Weinrib, ''The Supreme Court of Canada and Section 1 of the Charter'' (1988) 10 Supreme Court L.R. 469; Mendes, ''In Search of a Theory of Social Justice: The Supreme Court Reconceives the Oakes Test'' (1990) 24 Thémis 1. Some parts of this chapter draw on my article, ''Section 1 Revisited'' (1991) 1 Nat. Jo. Con. Law 1.

2 In the October 1980 version of the Charter, s. 1 was as follows:

> The Canadian Charter of Rights and Freedoms guarantees the rights and freedoms set out in it subject only to such reasonable limits as are generally accepted in a free and democratic society with a parliamentary system of government.

This version of s. 1 attracted a great deal of criticism, and it was amended to its present form in the April 1981 version of the Charter. Three potentially significant changes were made: (1) the phrase ''prescribed by law'' was added; (2) the phrase ''as can be demonstrably justified'' replaced the phrase ''as are generally accepted''; and (3) the phrase ''with a parliamentary system of government'' (which might have implied the irrelevance of American experience) was dropped from the final version. Each of these changes tended to raise the standard of justification under s. 1. See generally Hiebert, ''The Evolution of the Limitation Clause'' (1990) 28 Osgoode Hall L.J. 103.

similar to Canada's s. 1. The cases before the European Court of Human Rights (under the European Convention) and the Human Rights Committee of the United Nations (under the International Covenant) constitute a body of jurisprudence[3] as to the meaning of the limitation clauses[4] which has been relied upon by academic commentators on s. 1 of the Charter and which is starting to be used by Canadian courts.

In contrast to the international instruments which have just been described, the American Bill of Rights contains no limitation clause, and many of the guaranteed rights are expressed in unqualified terms. Since rights to "freedom of speech" and "equal protection" (to name the two most obvious examples) cannot be absolute, the American courts have had to imply qualifications on the rights in order to accommodate legitimate restraints on free speech and legitimate distinctions between different groups. This has been accomplished as a matter of "judicial legislation" and without any express direction in the Bill of Rights. In Canada, the courts can point to s. 1 as authorizing the development of limits on the guaranteed rights. This formal difference between the American Bill and the Canadian Charter does not make the American jurisprudence irrelevant, of course, but it does require the Canadian courts to develop their own patterns of reasoning, which must take into account not only the guaranteed rights but also the limitation clause of s. 1.

During the public debate that preceded the adoption of the Charter, there was controversy about the desirability of a limitation clause, the conventional view being that the clause "weakened" the Charter. But s. 1 has probably had the effect of strengthening the guaranteed rights. As will be explained, s. 1 has been interpreted as imposing stringent requirements of justification. Those requirements may be more difficult for the government to discharge than the requirements that would have been imposed by the courts in the absence of a limitation clause. In any event, there is merit in the frank avowal that the guaranteed rights are not absolutes, and in the establishment of procedural and substantive rules defining the requirements of justification. These rules, which the Court has derived from s. 1, are the topic of this chapter.

It should be remembered that s. 1 is not the only route to the enactment of laws in derogation of Charter rights. Under s. 33 (the override clause), it is possible to enact a law that overrides a Charter right by including in the law a notwithstanding clause. Thus, a law that cannot satisfy the standard of justification required by s. 1 may still be competent to the Parliament or Legislature under s.

---

3 For discussion of this jurisprudence, and its relevance to the Charter, see ch. 33, Charter of Rights, under heading 33.8(c), 30.3(e), "International sources", above.

4 See Hovius, "The Limitation Clauses of the European Convention on Human Rights" (1985) 17 Ottawa L. Rev. 213; Hovius, "The Limitation Clauses of the European Convention on Human Rights and Freedoms" (1986) 6 Yearbook of European Law 1; de Mestral (ed.), *The Limitation of Human Rights in Comparative Constitutional Law* (1986) Yourow; *The Margin of Appreciation Doctrine in the Dynamics of European Human Rights Jurisprudence* (1993).

33. Section 33 is the topic of chapter 36, Override of Rights, which follows this chapter.

35.2 Rationale of s. 1

The idea that rights can be limited in pursuit of other legislative objectives is a difficult one. If a right can be limited, what is its value? Indeed, this question should really be reformulated as, what is a right? In the absence of rights, it is normally a sufficient moral or political justification for a law (or any political decision) that the law is calculated to increase the general welfare. The law may make some people worse off, but so long as these costs are outweighed by the benefits to others, there is a net increase in the general welfare.[5]

In a famous essay, "Taking Rights Seriously" (1970),[6] Dworkin pointed out that rights are not "taken seriously" if they can be overridden simply by an appeal to the general welfare. It should not be possible to take away a right just because, on balance, the benefits to others will outweigh the cost to the right-holder. If a right could be taken away for only the reasons that would be sufficient if no right existed, then the claim to a right is pointless. Dworkin's argument was directed to "moral rights", but his argument has more obvious force to constitutionally protected rights, and its practical significance in that context is clear. Section 1 of the Charter would undermine everything that follows it if it were interpreted as permitting the Court to uphold a limit on a guaranteed right whenever the benefits of the law imposing the limit outweighed the costs. Moreover, there is no reason in a democracy why a non-elected Court should be given the task of re-doing the political calculus of costs and benefits that has already been performed by an elected legislative body. Not only does the Court lack the democratic mandate that is provided by electoral accountability, the Court also lacks the expertise and resources to review the legislative judgment that a particular law will increase the general welfare.[7]

---

5 Utilitarianism holds that the principle of "utility" is the only sure guide to public policy. Jeremy Bentham held that the principle of utility was satisfied if a policy would advance "the greatest happiness of the greatest number". This required that, if a law inflicted some pains, those pains were outweighed by the pleasures that the law produced. Bentham went so far as to catalogue the various pleasures and pains and to provide standards for measuring them, so that the pleasures could be added and the pains subtracted in order to determine whether the principle of utility was satisfied: Bentham, *An Introduction to the Principles of Morals and Legislation* (Burns and Hart eds., 1970), chs. 1-5. Of course, no one now believes that pleasures and pains can be identified and measured in the scientific way suggested by Bentham. But it is probably the case that legislators do attempt some kind of utilitarian calculus, weighing advantages against disadvantages, or benefits against costs, in formulating policy.

6 This essay was originally published in the New York Review of Books. It now forms ch. 7 of Dworkin, *Taking Rights Seriously* (rev. ed., 1978).

7 See Weinrib, note 1, above, esp. 486-492.

In *R.* v. *Oakes* (1986),[8] the Supreme Court of Canada attempted to grapple with these profound questions. Dickson C.J. wrote a brilliant opinion for a Court that was unanimous on this issue. He pointed out[9] that the words "free and democratic society" in s. 1 set the standard of justification under s. 1. Only the values of a free and democratic society would suffice to limit the guaranteed rights. Since the guaranteed rights were themselves derived from the values of a free and democratic society, there was an "identity of values" underlying both the rights and their limits.[10] "The underlying values of a free and democratic society both guarantee the rights in the Charter and, in appropriate circumstances, justify limitations upon those rights".[11] What are these values? Dickson C.J. suggested,[12] as examples:

> respect for the inherent dignity of the human person, commitment to social justice and equality, accommodation of a wide variety of beliefs, respect for cultural and group identity, and faith in social and political institutions which enhance the participation of individuals and groups in society.

It is implicit in the Court's emphasis on the values of a free and democratic society that some kinds of considerations[13] can never justify limits on rights.[14] However, the reference to a free and democratic society is too vague to provide much assistance in assessing the manifold worthy objectives that legislative bodies attempt to pursue in derogation of rights. As we shall see later in the chapter,[15] the Court has accepted a wide variety of legislative objectives as justifications under s. 1.

As well as its reference to a free and democratic society, s. 1 provides other indications as to the relationship between the guaranteed rights and legislated limits on those rights. In *Oakes*, Dickson C.J. pointed out[16] that s. 1 performed two functions. It not only provided for limits on the guaranteed rights; it also, by its opening words, expressly guaranteed the rights and freedoms set out in the Charter. The primacy of the rights and freedoms was also implied by the requirement that limits be "demonstrably" justified. These indications led Dickson C.J. to stipulate strict rules as to the burden and standard of proof of justification, and as to the substantive criteria that would qualify a law as a "reasonable limit" that "can be demonstrably justified in a free and democratic society". Thus, the

8 [1986] 1 S.C.R. 103.
9 *Id.*, 136.
10 Weinrib, note 1, above, 494.
11 *Slaight Communications* v. *Davidson* [1989] 1 S.C.R. 1038, 1056; *R.* v. *Keegstra* [1990] 3 S.C.R. 697, 736.
12 [1986] 1 S.C.R. 103, 136.
13 Cf. Rawls, *A Theory of Justice* (1972), 61, 250, arguing that (except for the maintenance of public order — a vague exception) a right can be defeated only by another right.
14 Weinrib, note 1, above, 494-495.
15 Section 35.9, "Sufficiently important objective", below.
16 [1986] 1 S.C.R. 103, 135.

Court insisted upon a "stringent standard of justification"[17] before it would accept a limit under s. 1. In this way, the Court has attempted to lay down rules that will preserve the guaranteed rights against much legislative encroachment,[18] but will permit the enactment of limits where there is a strong demonstration that the exercise of the rights "would be inimical to the realization of collective goals of fundamental importance".[19] The various elements of this approach are discussed in the balance of this chapter.

35.3 Relationship between s. 1 and rights

There is a close relationship between the standard of justification required under s. 1 and the scope of the guaranteed rights.[20] If the courts give to the guaranteed rights a broad interpretation that extends beyond their purpose, it is inevitable that the court will relax the standard of justification under s. 1 in order to uphold legislation limiting the extended right. For example, if the guarantee of freedom of expression in s. 2(b) were held to protect perjury, fraud, deception and conspiracy — all forms of expression in an extended sense — it would be foolish to require a legislative body to satisfy a high standard of justification in order to regulate or prohibit such obviously harmful behaviour.

In fact, as has been briefly mentioned, and will be more fully described later in this chapter, in *R.* v. *Oakes* (1986),[21] the Supreme Court of Canada decided to prescribe a single standard of justification for all rights, and to make that standard a high one, and to cast the burden of satisfying it on the government. In my opinion, this decision entails a corresponding caution in defining the guaranteed rights. Each right should be so interpreted as not to reach behaviour that is outside the purpose of the right — behaviour that is not worthy of constitutional protection. If this is ignored, the inevitable result will be the erosion of the *Oakes* standard of justification, because it can be taken for granted that the courts will find a way of upholding legislation in the face of Charter claims that are regarded by the judges as weak.

It may well be that it makes little difference in result whether the courts opt for a stringent standard of justification coupled with a purposive interpretation of

---

17 *Id.*, 136.

18 Dworkin has popularized the metaphor that rights are "trumps", because they will defeat a general utilitarian justification for a law: see, e.g., Dworkin, note 6, above, 365. But in Dworkin's theory of rights, the metaphor is not entirely apt, because in bridge the trump card always takes the trick: a trump can be defeated only by another (higher) trump, whereas Dworkin makes clear at 191 that a right can be defeated not only by another (conflicting) right but by a powerful utilitarian justification. Rawls' theory of rights, on the other hand, takes the stronger position that a right can be defeated only by another right: note 13, above.

19 [1986] 1 S.C.R. 103, 136.

20 The argument in this section of the chapter is made more fully in Hogg, "Interpreting the Charter of Rights: Generosity and Justification" (1990) 28 Osgoode Hall L.J. 817.

21 [1986] 1 S.C.R. 103.

rights, or for a relaxed standard of justification coupled with a broad interpretation of rights. However, it certainly makes a great deal of difference to the scope of judicial review. If the rights are broad, and the standard of justification is low, then many more Charter challenges will come before the courts, and will fall to be determined under s. 1. Since the standard of justification under s. 1 would be low, it would be difficult to devise meaningful constraints on the process of judicial review. The result would be that judicial review would become even more pervasive, even more policy-laden, and even more unpredictable than it is now. In my view, therefore, the courts should adhere to the strict standard of justification prescribed by *Oakes*, and should give a purposive (rather than a generous) interpretation to the guaranteed rights.[22] That approach will help to stem the wasteful floods of litigation,[23] to limit the occasions when courts have to review the policy choices of legislative bodies and to introduce meaningful rules to the process of Charter review.

35.4 Burden of proof

Who bears the burden of proof of factual issues in Charter litigation? At the first stage of Charter review, the court must decide whether a Charter right has been infringed. This issue is subject to the normal rules as to burden of proof, which means that the burden of proving all elements of the breach of a Charter right rests on the person asserting the breach. In the case of those rights that are qualified by their own terms, for example, by requirements of unreasonableness or arbitrariness, the burden of proving unreasonableness or arbitrariness, or whatever else is part of the definition of the right, rests on the person asserting the breach.

The second stage of Charter review, which is reached only if a Charter right has been infringed, is the inquiry into justification under s. 1. At this stage, the burden of persuasion shifts to the government (or other party) seeking to support the challenged law. It is for the government to persuade the court that the challenged law is a "reasonable limit", and that it "can be demonstrably justified in a free and democratic society".[24] This was established by the judgment of Dickson C.J. for the unanimous Court in *R.* v. *Oakes* (1986).[25] The standard of proof, the

22 On the difference between a "purposive" interpretation and a "generous" interpretation, see ch. 33, Charter of Rights, under heading 33.7, "Interpretation of Charter", above.

23 An indication of the danger is provided by the flood of equality challenges that entered the judicial system before *Andrews* v. *Law Society of B.C.* [1989] 1 S.C.R. 143 severely narrowed the scope of s. 15. In the first three years that s. 15 was in force, there were 599 cases in which a law was challenged, usually unsuccessfully, under s. 15: Brodsky and Day, *Canadian Charter Equality Rights for Women* (Canadian Advisory Council on the Status of Women, 1989), 277. The great majority of these cases could not even be brought after the ruling in *Andrews*.

24 The question whether a Charter limit is "prescribed by law" is a pure question of law to which no burden of proof could attach.

25 [1986] 1 S.C.R. 103, 136-137.

Court held, was "the civil standard, namely, proof by a preponderance of probability".[26] The criminal standard of proof beyond a reasonable doubt would be too onerous, given the vagueness of the controlling concepts of reasonableness, justifiability and free and democratic society, but "the preponderance of probability test must be applied rigorously".[27]

In order to satisfy the burden of proving justification under s. 1, Dickson C.J. said that evidence would "generally" be required, although he added that "there may be cases where certain elements of the s. 1 analysis are obvious or self-evident".[28] It is risky for a government not to adduce evidence of justification[29] in defence of a Charter challenge, but in several cases the Supreme Court has been prepared to make justificatory findings of a factual nature without evidence,[30] or with very little evidence,[31] relying on the "obvious" or "self-evident" character of the findings. These cases have been criticized,[32] but the Supreme Court of Canada has to make do with the factual record developed at trial, and it would be unfortunate if a law was struck down because of a deficiency in the evidence which could be supplied by a common sense finding.

Evidence in Charter cases gives rise to many problems. One is the point already made, that the validity or invalidity of a law will often turn on the state of the evidentiary record at trial.[33] Another problem is cost. A parade of expert witnesses is extremely costly,[34] and this cost is borne not just by the defending government, but also by the challenger, who, although not bearing the burden of proof, must in all prudence adduce evidence to rebut the government's evidence of justification.[35] For these reasons, in my opinion, it would be desirable for

---

26 *Id.*, 137.

27 *Ibid.*

28 *Id.*, 138.

29 Note that evidence has often been adduced informally in constitutional cases, in the form of social-science briefs, and extracts from studies and reports of various kinds. The admissibility of this material is examined in ch. 57, Proof, under heading 57.2, "Evidence", below.

30 *R.* v. *Jones* [1986] 2 S.C.R. 284, 299-300, 315; *R.W.D.S.U.* v. *Dolphin Delivery* [1986] 2 S.C.R. 573, 590.

31 *R.* v. *Edwards Books and Art* [1986] 2 S.C.R. 713, 769-770.

32 Petter and Monahan, "Developments" (1988) 10 Supreme Court L.R. 61, 71-96.

33 E.g., *Corp. Professionnelle des Médecins* v. *Thibault* [1988] 1 S.C.R. 1033 (Quebec statute allowing prosecutor to appeal from acquittal by way of trial de novo struck down for breach of s. 11(h); s. 1 justification not considered for lack of evidence).

34 As to cheaper modes of proof, see note 29, above.

35 In the normal course, each party to litigation tenders all of that party's evidence at the same time. Therefore, a plaintiff challenging a law on Charter grounds will tender all of the plaintiff's evidence before the defendant government tenders any evidence. The plaintiff's evidence will include not only the stage 1 evidence of the Charter breach, but also the stage 2 evidence in rebuttal of the anticipated evidence of justification. Since the latter evidence is given before the government has tendered any evidence of justification, some of the advantage of the government's burden of proof is lost. It would be better to split the trial, and allow the plaintiff's reply evidence to follow the defendant's evidence. A trial court undoubtedly has the power to organize a Charter trial in that fashion, but no such practice seems to have developed.

Charter review to become less dependent on evidence, even if the courts have to strain somewhat to make ''obvious'' or ''self-evident'' findings.

35.5 Presumption of constitutionality

When a statute is attacked on federal grounds, there is, or ought to be, a presumption of constitutionality.[36] This presumption carries three legal consequences. First, the court should exercise restraint in judicial review, striking down the law only if it clearly offends constitutional restrictions on the power of the enacting Parliament or Legislature. Secondly, where the validity of a law turns on a finding of fact (for example, the existence of an emergency), that finding of fact need not be proved strictly by the government; it is sufficient that there be a ''rational basis'' for the finding.[37] Thirdly, where a law is open to two interpretations, under one of which it would be unconstitutional, and under the other of which it would be constitutional, the latter interpretation is the one that should be selected; this mode of interpretation is known as ''reading down''.[38] These are three doctrines of judicial restraint, designed to minimize intrusion by the judicial branch in the affairs of the legislative branch.

In federalism cases, whatever the form of the litigation, the constitutional contest is essentially between two levels of government: what is denied to one level of government belongs to the other. In that context, a presumption of constitutionality tilts the scale in favour of upholding the law that has been enacted by one of the levels of government. In Charter cases, the constitutional contest is between a government and an individual, who asserts that a right has been violated. In that context, it is not appropriate to tilt the scale in favour of the government. There should be no special obstacles placed in the way of an individual who seeks to vindicate a Charter right. In Charter cases, therefore, there is no presumption of constitutionality,[39] except in the third sense indicated above, namely, reading down.[40] There is no derogation of individual rights if the individual wins through a reading down of the statute as opposed to a holding of invalidity. The general rule that a statute should be interpreted as far as possible to conform to the Constitution would apply to the Charter as well as to the federalism part of the Constitution.

With respect to evidence in Charter cases, in the stage-one inquiry into whether the law infringes a Charter right, the burden of proof does rest on the

36 See ch. 15, Judicial Review on Federal Grounds, under heading 15.5(h), ''Presumption of constitutionality'', above.

37 See ch. 57, Proof, under heading 57.2, ''Standard of proof'', below.

38 See ch. 15, Judicial Review on Federal Grounds, under heading 15.7, ''Reading down'', above.

39 *Man.* v. *Metropolitan Stores* [1987] 1 S.C.R. 110, 121-125 per Beetz J., giving as his reason (at 122) ''the innovative and evolutive character of the Charter''. Contra, Pinard, ''La présumption de constitutionnalité'' (1990) 35 McGill L.J. 305.

40 *Id.*, 125, where Beetz J. leaves the point open.

individual asserting the infringement. That, however, is simply a consequence of the rule of civil procedure that "the one who asserts must prove".[41] The burden of proof is the normal civil one, uncomplicated by any doctrine that the government need have only a "rational basis" for its legislation. Once the stage-one inquiry has been answered yes, there is no presumption that the law is a reasonable limit that can be demonstrably justified in a free and democratic society. On the contrary, the burden is on the government to prove that the elements of s. 1 justification are present.[42]

35.6 Limits

Section 1 provides that the Charter rights are subject "to such reasonable limits prescribed by law as can be demonstrably justified in a free and democratic society". There is one decision of the Supreme Court of Canada that holds that not every Charter infringement is a "limit", and any infringement that is more severe than a limit cannot be justified under s. 1.

This distinction was announced in the *Quebec School Board* case (1984).[43] In that case, the Court had to determine the validity of the "Quebec clause" of Quebec's Charter of the French Language (Bill 101), which limited admission to English-language schools in Quebec to the children of persons who had been educated in English in Quebec. The Quebec clause was inconsistent with s. 23(1)(b) (the "Canada clause") of the Charter of Rights, which guaranteed admission to minority-language schools to the children of persons who had been educated in the minority language anywhere in Canada.[44] The Supreme Court of Canada held that the Quebec clause infringed s. 23(1)(b), but the Court refused to be drawn into any inquiry into justification under s. 1. The opinion of "the Court", pointed out that the detailed definition of the classes of parents entitled to protection was the heart of s. 23 of the Charter. A redefinition of those classes was not a "limit" contemplated by s. 1 of the Charter as open to legislative enactment. The Court concluded that "the provisions of [the Quebec clause] collide directly with those of s. 23 of the Charter, and are not limits which can be legitimized by s. 1 of the Charter".[45]

The distinction invoked by the Court in the *Quebec School Board* case is a distinction between "limits", which can be justified under s. 1, and "denials", which cannot be. The obvious criticism of the distinction is that there is no legal standard by which the various Charter infringements can be sorted into the two

---

41 *Id.*, 124-125.
42 See ch. 57, Proof, under heading 57.2, "Evidence", above.
43 *A.G. Que.* v. *Que. Protestant School Bds.* [1984] 2 S.C.R. 66.
44 See ch. 53, Language, under heading 53.8, "Language of education", below.
45 [1984] 2 S.C.R. 66, 88.

categories.[46] The Court seems to have taken this criticism to heart, and, without actually overruling the *Quebec School Board* case, has signalled that it will no longer use the distinction to obviate the requirement of s. 1 justification, ''apart from the rare case of a truly complete denial'' of a guaranteed right.[47] The result seems to be that even severe restrictions on Charter rights will count as limits, and will therefore be susceptible to s. 1 justification. The severity of the contravention would not be irrelevant, of course, because it would be harder to establish that a severe contravention was reasonable and demonstrably justified.

35.7 Prescribed by law

(a) Definition

Section 1 provides that the Charter rights are subject to ''such reasonable limits *prescribed by law* as can be demonstrably justified in a free and democratic society''. The words ''prescribed by law'' make clear that an act that is not legally authorized can never be justified under s. 1, no matter how reasonable or demonstrably justified it may appear to be.[48] Charter violations that take place on the initiative of a police officer (or other official), acting without clear legal authority,[49] are outside the protection of s. 1.

The requirement that any limit on rights be prescribed by law reflects two values that are basic to constitutionalism or the rule of law. First, in order to preclude arbitrary and discriminatory action by government officials, all official action in derogation of rights must be authorized by law. Secondly, citizens must have a reasonable opportunity to know what is prohibited so that they can act accordingly. Both these values are satisfied by a law that fulfils two requirements: (1) the law must be adequately accessible to the public, and (2) the law must be

46 This criticism was elaborated at undue length in the second edition of this book (1985), 682-684. For approval of the distinction, see Weinrib, note 1, above, 479-483.

47 *Ford* v. *Que.* [1988] 2 S.C.R. 712, 771-774, where the distinction is cogently criticized, the only implausible element being the description (at 773) of the *Quebec School Board* case as exemplifying a ''complete denial'' of the right. Cf. *R.* v. *Big M Drug Mart* [1985] 1 S.C.R. 295, holding that Sunday-closing legislation could not be justified under s. 1, because its purpose was to compel religious observance, which was itself a violation of freedom of religion. This line of reasoning is a possible explanation of the *Quebec School Board* case. See sec. 35.9(d), ''Inadmissible objective'', below.

48 E.g., *R.* v. *Therens* [1985] 1 S.C.R. 613 (no law authorized denial by police of right to counsel); *R.* v. *Mannion* [1986] 2 S.C.R. 272 (no law authorized use by Crown prosecutor of accused's previous incriminating testimony); *R.* v. *Simmons* [1988] 2 S.C.R. 495 (no law authorized denial by customs officials of right to counsel); *R.* v. *Hebert* [1990] 2 S.C.R. 151 (no law authorized denial by police of right to silence); *R.* v. *Broyles* [1991] 3 S.C.R. 595 (no law authorized denial by police of right to silence); *R. v. Dersch* [1993] 3 S.C.R. 768 (no law authorized access by police to medical records).

49 *R.* v. *Hebert* [1990] 2 S.C.R. 151 205 per Sopinka J. (''The word 'prescribe' connotes a mandate for specific action, not merely permission for that which is not prohibited.'')

formulated with sufficient precision to enable people to regulate their conduct by it, and to provide guidance to those who apply the law.

These two requirements have been held to be inherent in the phrase "prescribed by law" by the European Court of Human Rights, interpreting that same phrase in the European Convention on Human Rights.[50] In the *Sunday Times* case (1979),[51] the Court had to decide whether the contempt power of the British courts, which had been exercised to restrain the Sunday Times from publishing an article on pending litigation by thalidomide victims against a drug company, was a breach of the right to freedom of expression, which was guaranteed by the Convention. The Convention provided that the right to freedom of expression was "subject to such . . . restrictions . . . as are prescribed by law and are necessary in a democratic society". It was argued that the law of contempt could not satisfy this limitation clause, because it was a creature of common law and not of legislation. The Court rejected this argument, holding (1) that a common law rule was adequately accessible to the public, and (2) that the common law of contempt was formulated with sufficient precision to enable a newspaper to regulate its reporting of pending judicial proceedings.[52]

The Supreme Court of Canada has not yet essayed a comprehensive analysis of "prescribed by law", but the decisions are consistent with the two requirements of accessibility and precision. As to accessibility, the Court has held that a statute, a regulation or a rule of the common law will qualify.[53] On the other hand, directives or guidelines which, although issued by government departments or agencies, fall outside the class of officially published delegated legislation, will probably not qualify.[54]

As to precision, the Supreme Court of Canada has held that a limit on a right need not be express, but can result "by necessity from the terms of a statute or regulation or from its operating requirements".[55] For example, a statutory requirement that a roadside breath test be administered "forthwith", which in practice precluded contact by the suspected motorist with counsel, was held to be a limit

---

50 See ch. 33, Charter of Rights, under heading 33.8(c), "International sources", above.

51 *Sunday Times* v. *United Kingdom* (1979) 2 European Human Rights Reports 245 (Eur. Ct. of Hum. Rts.). The discussion of "prescribed by law" is at pp. 270-273.

52 The Court held nevertheless that the contempt law was not justified under the limitation clause, because it was not "necessary in a democratic society".

53 *R.* v. *Therens* [1985] 1 S.C.R. 613, 645 (dictum accepting statute, regulation and common law); *R.W.D.S.U.* v. *Dolphin Delivery* [1986] 2 S.C.R. 573 (common law limit accepted); *B.C.E.G.U.* v. *B.C.* [1988] 2 S.C.R. 214 (common law limit accepted); *Irwin Toy* v. *Que.* [1989] 1 S.C.R. 927, 981 (regulation accepted); *R.* v. *Swain* [1991] 1 S.C.R. 933, 968 (common law accepted).

54 *Re Ont. Film and Video Appreciation Society* (1984) 45 O.R. (2d) 80 (C.A.) (standards published by Ont. Board of Censors not a law, because not binding on Board); *Committee for Cth. of Can.* v. *Can.* [1991] 1 S.C.R. 139 (Court divided on issue whether airport's internal directives were law). Cf. *Martineau* v. *Matsqui Institution Inmate Disciplinary Bd.* [1978] 1 S.C.R. 118 (Court divided on issue whether departmental directives were "law" within s. 28 of the Federal Court Act).

55 *R.* v. *Therens* [1985] 1 S.C.R. 613, 645.

"prescribed by law" on the right to counsel, although the statute was silent on the right to counsel.[56]

(b) Discretion

A law that confers a discretion on a board or official to act in derogation of a Charter right will satisfy the prescribed-by-law requirement if the discretion is constrained by legal standards. In *Re Ontario Film and Video Appreciation Society* (1984),[57] a statute authorizing film censorship failed the requirement, because the censor board was given an unfettered discretion to ban or cut films proposed for public exhibition; the statute did not stipulate the criteria to be applied by the board. The board had in fact developed its own criteria, which were publicly available, but those criteria, the Court held, were insufficient, because they were not binding on the board. Had they been contained in the statute itself, or in a regulation, the limit on freedom of expression would have been prescribed by law.

The *Ontario Film and Video* case was a decision of the Ontario Court of Appeal. The Supreme Court of Canada has also held that a statutory discretion in derogation of a Charter right must be subject to an "intelligible standard".[58] However, the Court has upheld discretions that were not constrained by meaningful legal standards. In *R.* v. *Hufsky* (1988),[59] the Court upheld a provincial statute authorizing the police at their unfettered discretion to stop vehicles. The police used the power to stop vehicles at random, in a programme of spot checks for drunkenness and other traffic violations. The Court held that the general discretion conferred by the statute should be interpreted to extend to random stops; and that the statute, so interpreted, was, by implication, a limit prescribed by law on the right not to be arbitrarily detained.

The random stop that led to the arrest in *Hufsky* was part of an organized programme, which took place at a pre-determined location at which several police officers were present. In *R.* v. *Ladouceur* (1990),[60] the Court was presented with a roving random stop, taken at the initiative of an individual police officer, and not part of any organized programme. The Court, by a narrow majority of five to four, followed *Hufsky* and held that the same statute authorized the stop, and that it was a limit prescribed by law on the right not to be arbitrarily detained. The dissenting minority held that the decision in *Hufsky* should be confined to stops at organized check-points, and that s. 1 could not extend to a statute that authorized a police officer to stop any vehicle at any time, at any place and for any reason.

---

56 *R.* v. *Thomsen* [1988] 1 S.C.R. 640. Also, *R.* v. *Hufsky* [1988] 1 S.C.R. 621; note 59, below; *R.* v. *Ladouceur* [1990] 1 S.C.R. 1257; note 60, below; *Slaight Communications* v. *Davidson* [1989] 1 S.C.R. 1038; note 61, below.

57 (1984) 45 O.R. (2d) 80 (C.A.).

58 *Irwin Toy* v. *Que.* [1989] 1 S.C.R. 927, 983.

59 [1988] 1 S.C.R. 621.

60 [1990] 1 S.C.R. 1257.

A similar decision was reached in *Slaight Communications* v. *Davidson* (1989).[61] In that case, an adjudicator found that an employer had unjustly dismissed an employee. The adjudicator ordered the employer to provide a letter of reference to the employee, reciting certain stipulated facts about the employee's achievements, and also ordered the employer not to make any comments other than the stipulated facts in response to any enquiry about the employee's performance. The purpose of the negative order was to prevent the employer from undermining the effect of the positive order. The majority of the Supreme Court of Canada held that both the positive and negative orders, although limits on the employer's freedom of expression, were justified under s. 1. The Court held that the prescribed-by-law requirement was satisfied, because the adjudicator's order was made under the authority of a statute. But the statute simply gave to the adjudicator a general power to order compensation, reinstatement or other equitable remedy. There was no explicit authority to require a letter of reference or otherwise limit freedom of expression. Nevertheless, the statutory discretion was held to be, by implication, a limit prescribed by law on freedom of expression.[62]

(c) Vagueness

It is a principle of fundamental justice in Canada, and of due process in the United States, that a statute is ''void for vagueness'' if its prohibitions are not clearly defined.[63] A vague law offends the values of constitutionalism. It does not provide sufficiently clear standards to avoid arbitrary and discriminatory applications by those charged with enforcement. It does not provide reasonable notice of what is prohibited so that citizens can govern themselves safely. Indeed, as American judges have noted, a vague law may lead citizens to steer far wider of the unlawful zone than they would if the boundaries were clearly marked.[64]

In Canada, the idea that a law may be void for vagueness is also implicit in the requirement that a limit on a Charter right be prescribed by law. That follows from the rule described above[65] that precision is one of the ingredients of the prescribed-by-law requirement.[66]

Irwin Toy v. *Quebec* (1989)[67] was a challenge to a provincial statute that prohibited ''commercial advertising directed at persons under thirteen years of age''. The statute stipulated three factors that were to be taken into account in

61 [1989] 1 S.C.R. 1038.

62 See also *United States* v. *Cotroni* [1989] 1 S.C.R. 1469, 1497-1498 (upholding prosecutorial discretion in the context of extradition); *Irwin Toy* v. *Que.* [1989] 1 S.C.R. 927; note 67, below.

63 Chapter 44, Fundamental Justice, under heading 44.16, ''Vague laws'', below.

64 See *Grayned* v. *City of Rockford* (1972) 408 U.S. 104, 108-109 (holding that an anti-noise by-law was not unconstitutionally vague).

65 Section 35.7(a), ''Definition'', above.

66 A law that was excessively vague would also not be a ''reasonable'' limit within s. 1: *Osborne* v. *Can.* [1991] 2 S.C.R. 69, 94.

67 [1989] 1 S.C.R. 927.

determining whether an advertisement was directed at persons under 13 years of age, but even with these factors, the scope of the prohibited class of advertisements was highly uncertain. It was argued that such a vague prohibition could not be a limit on freedom of expression that was prescribed by law. The majority of the Court held that it was not practicable to seek "absolute precision" in a statute. A law would fail the prescribed-by-law test only "where there is no intelligible standard and where the legislature has given a plenary discretion to do whatever seems best in a wide set of circumstances".[68] That was not the case here, the Court held, because the three statutory factors provided an "intelligible standard" for the application of the prohibition.[69]

It is not possible to provide a general definition of an "intelligible standard". Another formulation that has been suggested is whether the impugned law "is so obscure as to be incapable of interpretation using the ordinary tools".[70] Obviously, the test is not intended to be a demanding one. The Court has upheld a prohibition on communicating for the purpose of prostitution,[71] a prohibition on communicating hatred or contempt towards minorities,[72] a prohibition on political campaigning by civil servants[73] and a prohibition on the sale of obscene materials.[74] In each case, there was a limit on freedom of expression that was couched in relatively vague terms; and, in each case, the Court held that the law supplied a sufficiently intelligible standard to meet the prescribed-by-law requirement of s. 1.

35.8 Reasonable and demonstrably justified

(a) Introduction

Section 1 provides that the Charter rights are subject to "such *reasonable* limits prescribed by law as can be *demonstrably justified* in a free and democratic society". The requirements of reasonableness and demonstrable justification are cumulative, not alternative. Although both must be satisfied, there does not seem to be much point in treating each separately. Indeed, the requirement of reasonableness may be redundant, because a limit that is demonstrably justified must

68 *Id.*, 983.

69 See also *Luscher* v. *Deputy Minr., Revenue Can.* [1985] 1 F.C. 85 (C.A.) (striking down a prohibition of the importation of "immoral or indecent" books; such a vague law could not be a "reasonable limit"); *Re Blainey and Ont. Hockey Assn.* (1986) 54 O.R. (2d) 513 (C.A.) (striking down exemption from Human Rights Code for sex-segregated sport: "It prescribes no limits and provides no guidelines.").

70 *Osborne* v. *Can.* [1991] 2 S.C.R. 69, 94.

71 *Re ss. 193 and 195.1 of Crim. Code* [1990] 1 S.C.R. 1123.

72 *Can.* v. *Taylor* [1990] 3 S.C.R. 892.

73 *Osborne* v. *Can.* [1991] 2 S.C.R. 69.

74 *R.* v. *Butler* [1992] 1 S.C.R. 452.

surely be reasonable. The courts have not attempted to distinguish between the two requirements, but have assumed that the language of reasonableness and demonstrable justification articulates a single standard to be applied to all laws limiting Charter rights.

(b) Oakes test

In *R.* v. *Oakes* (1986),[75] Dickson C.J., for a Court that was unanimous on this issue, laid down the criteria that must be satisfied to establish that a limit is reasonable and demonstrably justified in a free and democratic society. Because this judgment has taken on some of the character of holy writ, I set out below the main passages:[76]

> To establish that a limit is reasonable and demonstrably justified in a free and democratic society, two central criteria must be satisfied. First, the objective, which the measures responsible for a limit on a Charter right or freedom are designed to serve, must be ''of sufficient importance to warrant overriding a constitutionally protected right or freedom'' . . . The standard must be high in order to ensure that objectives which are trivial or discordant with the principles integral to a free and democratic society do not gain s. 1 protection. It is necessary, at a minimum, that an objective relate to concerns which are pressing and substantial in a free and democratic society before it can be characterized as sufficiently important.
>
> Second, once a sufficiently significant objective is recognized, then the party invoking s. 1 must show that the means chosen are reasonable and demonstrably justified. This involves ''a form of proportionality test'' . . . Although the nature of the proportionality test will vary depending on the circumstances, in each case courts will be required to balance the interests of society with those of individuals and groups. There are, in my view, three important components of a proportionality test. First, the measures adopted must be carefully designed to achieve the objective in question. They must not be arbitrary, unfair or based on irrational considerations. In short, they must be rationally connected to the objective. Second, the means, even if rationally connected to the objective in this first sense, should impair ''as little as possible'' the right or freedom in question . . . Third, there must be a proportionality between the *effects* of the measures which are responsible for limiting the Charter right or freedom, and the objective which has been identified as of ''sufficient importance''.

In summary, there are four criteria to be satisfied by a law that qualifies as a reasonable limit that can be demonstrably justified in a free and democratic society:

1. Sufficiently important objective: The law must pursue an objective that is sufficiently important to justify limiting a Charter right.
2. Rational connection: The law must be rationally connected to the objective.
3. Least drastic means: The law must impair the right no more than is necessary to accomplish the objective.

---

75 [1986] 1 S.C.R. 103.

76 *Id.*, 138-139 (emphasis in original).

4. Proportionate effect: The law must not have a disproportionately severe effect on the persons to whom it applies.

Each of these criteria will be examined in turn in the text that follows.

To anticipate the later discussion, it is step 3 — least drastic means — that is the centre of the inquiry into s. 1 justification. Only in a rare case will a court reject the legislative judgment that the objective of the law is sufficiently important to justify limiting a Charter right (step 1). It is an even rarer case where the law is not rationally connected to the objective (step 2). And the inquiry into disproportionate effect (step 4) is normally, if not always, precluded by the judgment that the law's objective is sufficiently important to justify the impact on civil liberties (step 1). What is left for serious inquiry is the question whether the law has impaired the Charter right no more than is necessary to accomplish the objective (step 3). As we shall see, nearly all the s. 1 cases have turned on the answer to this inquiry.

35.9 Sufficiently important objective

(a) Identification of objective

The identification of the objective of a challenged law is a task of considerable practical and theoretical difficulty. At the practical level, the objective of the legislators in enacting the challenged law may be unknown. To be sure, the courts will now willingly receive the legislative history of the law,[77] but this is often silent or unclear with respect to the provision under attack. Courts have not been troubled by this difficulty as much as one might expect. They usually assume that the statute itself reveals its objective, and they may pronounce confidently on the point even if there is no supporting evidence.

Even if one could be absolutely certain of what the legislators were hoping to achieve when they enacted the challenged law, the statement of the objective can be expressed at various levels of generality. Take *Andrews* v. *Law Society of British Columbia* (1989)[78] as an example. The challenged law imposed a requirement of Canadian citizenship for admission to the legal profession of British Columbia. The Supreme Court of Canada was unanimous that the law infringed the guarantee of equality, but the Court divided on the question whether the law could be justified under s. 1. The objective of the law could be expressed at a high level of generality: to restrict entry to the legal profession to persons who are qualified to practise law. Stated in this way, who could doubt that the objective was sufficiently important for the purpose of s. 1? Or the objective of the law could be stated at a low level of generality: to restrict entry to the legal profession

77 See ch. 57, Proof, under heading 57.1, "Legislative history", below.

78 [1989] 1 S.C.R. 143.

to persons who are Canadian citizens. Stated in this way, the value of the objective is by no means obvious. There is no logical or factual basis for preferring one version of the law's objective to the other; they are simply expressed at different levels of generality.

The higher the level of generality at which a legislative objective is expressed, the more obviously desirable the objective will appear to be. This will move the s. 1 inquiry into the proportionality of the means that the law employs to accomplish the objective, that is, steps 2, 3 and 4 of the *Oakes* analysis. However, when step 3 is reached — least drastic means — the high level of generality will become a serious problem for the justification of the law. If the objective has been stated at a high level of generality, it will be easy to think of other ways in which the wide objective could be accomplished with less interference with the Charter right. If the objective has been stated at a low level of generality, perhaps simply restating the terms of the challenged law, then it will be hard to think of other ways in which the narrow objective could be accomplished with less interference with the Charter right. In the *Andrews* case, the difference of opinion between the majority, who held that the citizenship requirement could not be justified under s. 1, and the minority, who held that it could be, can be traced in large part to the different levels of generality employed by the judges in characterizing the purpose of the law.[79]

In arriving at the appropriate level of generality at which to cast a legislative objective, it must be remembered that the only reason for embarking on the search for the legislative objective is to determine whether there is a sufficient justification for an infringement of the Charter. The statement of the objective should therefore be related to the infringement of the Charter, rather than to other goals. In other words, the statement of the objective should supply a reason for infringing the Charter right.[80] In *RJR-MacDonald* v. *Canada* (1995),[81] the challenged law was one that banned the advertising of tobacco products. The infringement of the Charter was the breach of freedom of expression. If Parliament had chosen to ban the harmful product itself, there would have been no basis for a Charter challenge. Instead, Parliament chose the lesser path of banning the advertising of the product, and exposed its law to a Charter challenge. It was not therefore relevant to s. 1

79 Wilson J., with whom Dickson C.J. and L'Heureux-Dubé J. agreed, articulated the purpose at a high level of generality, but held that the proportionality tests were failed (p. 156). McIntyre J., with whom Lamer J. agreed, articulated the purpose at a low level of generality; he acknowledged that it could not meet the ''pressing and substantial'' standard, but he held that that standard was inappropriately high, and that the law was justified under an appropriately lower standard (pp. 184-186). La Forest J. agreed with McIntyre J.'s account of s. 1, but still agreed with Wilson J. that the law could not be justified.

80 C. Sherrin, ''Objectionable Objectives?: An Analysis of the First Branch of the Oakes Test'' (D.Jur. thesis, Osgoode Hall Law School, York University, 1994), 137 (''[The court's] primary focus must remain upon the characterization which most directly relates to the reason for violating the constitutional right.'')

81 [1995] 3 S.C.R. 199.

justification to characterize the objective as the protection of public health from the use of tobacco, and to establish the importance of the objective by reviewing the evidence that showed the harmful effects of tobacco on health. This way of looking at the objective was too broad because it did not focus on the reason for infringing the Charter. McLachlin J., writing for the majority of the Supreme Court of Canada, said that "the objective that is relevant to the s. 1 analysis is *the objective of the infringing measure*"; on that basis, the objective of the advertising ban "must be to prevent people in Canada from being persuaded by advertising and promotion to use tobacco products".[82] This was a narrower and "less significant" objective than the broad objective of protecting the health of Canadians from use of tobacco, but she held that it was still an objective of sufficient importance to justify overriding the right of free expression.[83] She went on to hold, however, that the law failed the least drastic means branch of the s. 1 inquiry, because the total ban encompassed purely informational and brand-recognition advertising that played no role in persuading people to use tobacco products. The law was therefore struck down.

In *Irwin Toy* v. *Quebec* (1989),[84] the majority of the Supreme Court of Canada upheld a Quebec law that prohibited advertising directed at children under 13. The law infringed freedom of expression, but was held to be justified under s. 1. The majority of the Court defined the objective of the law at a very low level of generality, as the protection of children (a vulnerable group) from advertising.[85] No attempt was made to define the objective in terms of the injury to the children that the law was presumably designed to prevent.[86] Nonetheless, the majority held that the objective was "pressing and substantial". Having defined the objective in narrow terms, it was then easy to find that the proportionality tests were satisfied. Indeed, the proportionality reasoning became no more than a pair of tautologies. If the objective of the law was to protect children from advertising, then a ban on advertising directed at children must be rationally connected to the objective,[87] and nothing less than a ban on advertising could possibly satisfy the objective.[88]

The trouble with the reasoning of the majority in *Irwin Toy* is that the narrow statement of the objective of the law, essentially repeating the text of the law, left the proportionality tests with no work to do. The *Oakes* test necessarily implies that it is possible to make independent assessments of the objective of a challenged law and of the means employed by the law to accomplish its objective. This

---

82 *Id.*, para. 144 (emphasis in original).

83 *Id.*, para. 146.

84 [1989] 1 S.C.R. 927.

85 *Id.*, 987.

86 McIntyre J., who, with the agreement of Beetz J., dissented, held that the law could not be justified under s. 1, because there was no evidence that children were harmed by advertising directed at them.

87 *Id.*, 991.

88 *Id.*, 999

requires that the objective of the law be formulated at a higher level of generality than a mere paraphrase of the law. Of course, the question remains: how high a level of generality is appropriate? The answer cannot be captured in any verbal formula. It is inevitably a discretionary choice by the reviewing court. Yet that choice will often dictate the answers to the four *Oakes* questions. Obviously, the attitude of the reviewing court to its function of review — activism or restraint — will play a crucial but inarticulate role in the choice.[89]

(b) Importance of objective

According to *R.* v. *Oakes* (1986),[90] the only kind of law that can serve as a justified limit on a Charter right is one that pursues an objective that is sufficiently important to justify overriding a Charter right. When does an objective achieve this degree of importance? Dickson C.J. in his *Oakes* judgment attempted to provide some guidance on this question. First of all, as emphasized earlier in this chapter,[91] the legislative objective must meet the standard implied in the words "free and democratic society" in s. 1. Only objectives that are consistent with the values of a free and democratic society will qualify. Secondly, he suggested that the objective must "relate to concerns which are "pressing and substantial", rather than merely trivial.[92] Thirdly, the objective must be directed to "the realization of collective goals of fundamental importance".[93]

These phrases all indicate that a reviewing court should engage in a rigorous scrutiny of the legislative objective. In practice, however, the requirement of a sufficiently important objective has been satisfied in all but one or two of the Charter cases that have reached the Supreme Court of Canada. It has been easy to persuade the Court that, when the Parliament or Legislature acts in derogation of individual rights, it is doing so to further values that are acceptable in a free and democratic society, to satisfy concerns that are pressing and substantial and to realize collective goals of fundamental importance. Some of the cases are examined in the sections of this text that follow.

(c) Quebec's distinct society

Quebec's "distinct society" provides the motivation for laws respecting language, education and culture that have no counterparts in the other provinces. When Dickson C.J. in *Oakes* gave examples of the values of a free and democratic society, he included "respect for cultural and group identity".[94] This suggested

---

89 The thesis of Peck's article, note 1, above, is that the *Oakes* test, although clearly intended to mandate active review, is sufficiently malleable to protect restraint as well.

90 [1986] 1 S.C.R. 103, 138.

91 Text accompanying notes 8-14, above.

92 [1986] 1 S.C.R. 103, 138-139.

93 *Id.*, 136.

94 *Ibid.*

that the Court would be willing to use s. 1 to enable the national norms of the Charter to accommodate at least some of the diversity that it is the role of the federal system to permit.[95]

It was perhaps unfortunate that the very first Charter case to reach the Supreme Court of Canada raised a conflict between a Charter right and cultural identity. In the *Quebec School Board* case (1984),[96] the question was whether Quebec could restrict admission to its English-language public schools to the children of persons who had been educated in English in Quebec. This was an infringement of the minority language educational right in s. 23(1)(b) of the Charter.[97] The question was whether it could be justified under s. 1. A lengthy trial was held at which the Attorney General of Quebec adduced evidence of the need to protect the French language and culture and reduce the assimilation of Quebec children into the nationally-dominant English-speaking culture. The trial judge reviewed this evidence, and held that the infringement of s. 23(1)(b) would make such a trivial contribution to Quebec's cultural and linguistic objectives that it could not be regarded as a reasonable limit under s. 1.[98] However, the Supreme Court of Canada finessed the question of justification altogether. As explained earlier in this chapter,[99] the Court held that the Quebec law was such a severe infringement of the Charter right that it should be characterized as a ''denial'' rather than a ''limit'' of the right, and a denial of the right could not be justified under s. 1. The Court therefore discarded the evidence of justification, and refused to even entertain a line of argument based on Quebec's distinct society.

In *Attorney General of Quebec* v. *Ford* (1988),[100] the Court was faced with another of Quebec's unique laws, this one requiring that public signs be solely in the French language. The Court held that the law infringed freedom of expression, and that it could not be justified under s. 1. However, now the Court recognized the vulnerable position of the French language in Quebec, and recognized that the protection and enhancement of the language was a sufficiently important objective to justify a limit on freedom of expression. The law was struck down, not because of any doubt as to the legitimacy of the purpose, but because the banning of English was a disproportionate impairment of the rights of English-speakers. However, the mandatory use of French was valid,[101] and, the Court held,

95 The accommodation of federal values by the Charter of rights is the topic of my essay, ''Federalism Fights the Charter of Rights'' in Shugarman and Whitaker (eds.), *Federalism and Political Community* (1989), 249-266.

96 *A.G. Que.* v. *Que. Protestant School Bds.* [1984] 2 S.C.R. 66.

97 Section 23(1)(b) is discussed in ch. 53, Language, under heading 53.8, ''Language of education'', below.

98 (1982) 140 D.L.R. (3d) 33, 71-90 (Que.S.C.). The trial judge also held, in the alternative, that the Quebec law was the ''denial'' of a right that could not be justified under s. 1. The Quebec Court of Appeal affirmed on the latter ground: (1983) 1 D.L.R. (4th) 573 (Que.C.A.).

99 Section 35.6, ''Limits'', above.

100 [1988] 2 S.C.R. 712.

101 So held in the companion case of *Devine* v. *Que.* [1988] 2 S.C.R. 790.

it would have been valid to require that French be predominant over English. It was the banning of English that went too far. (The sequel to the decision was that Quebec re-enacted a ban on English-language signs, protecting the new law by including in the law the notwithstanding clause that is permitted by s. 33 of the Charter.)[102]

The Meech Lake Accord of 1987[103] would have amended the Constitution by adding a clause recognizing "that Quebec constitutes within Canada a distinct society". This clause turned out to be the most controversial element of the Accord, attracting opposition on account of its vagueness, its possible effect on Charter rights and its suggestion of special status for the province of Quebec. These concerns seemed to me to be exaggerated in light of the Court's willingness in *Ford* to take into account Quebec's distinctness despite the absence of a distinct society clause in the Constitution. Yet it was the distinct society clause, above all, that precluded the Accord from winning the support of all the provincial Legislatures.

(d) Inadmissible objectives

Dickson C.J. in *R.* v. *Oakes* (1986)[104] made it clear that a legislative objective would not count as justification if it was not sufficiently important to override a Charter right. Subsumed in the vague notion of importance were the requirements that the objective would have to be consistent with the values of a "free and democratic society", and relate to concerns that were "pressing and substantial".

Despite the vigour of these strictures, there has so far been only one case in which the Supreme Court of Canada has unequivocally rejected the legislative objective. In *R.* v. *Big M Drug Mart* (1985),[105] the Court held that the Lord's Day Act, which was a federal Sunday-closing law, infringed the guarantee of freedom of religion. Its purpose, the majority of the Court held, was "to compel the observance of the Christian sabbath".[106] That was a purpose that was directly contradictory of the Charter right, and could not be a purpose that justified limiting the right.

The Court in *Big M* acknowledged that the secular objective of providing a common day of rest would be sufficiently important to justify overriding a Charter right, but the Court refused to attribute that purpose to the Lord's Day Act for two reasons. First, the legislative history of the Act indicated that the purpose was religious, not secular. Secondly, under federalism principles, the Act was

---

102 S.Q. 1988, c. 54, An Act to Amend the Charter of the French Language.

103 See ch. 4, Amendment, under heading 4.1, "The failure to accommodate Quebec", above. A distinct society clause was also proposed in the Charlottetown Accord of 1992, which was defeated in a popular referendum.

104 [1986] 1 S.C.R. 103, 138-139.

105 [1985] 1 S.C.R. 295. Query whether the *Quebec School Board* case is another example: see note 45, above.

106 *Id.*, 351.

constitutionally valid as a criminal law only if the purpose was religious.[107] It followed that the legislative objective could not justify the limiting of freedom of religion, and the Act was unconstitutional.[108] Not long after *Big M*, the Court was invited to review a *provincial* Sunday-closing law in the case of *R.* v. *Edwards Books and Art* (1986).[109] The Court held that the provincial law pursued the secular objective of providing a common day of rest for workers in the province. This distinguished the case from *Big M*, and, since the other elements of s. 1 justification were also satisfied, the provincial law was upheld under s. 1.

Three rules emerge from the decision in *Big M*. The first is that an objective cannot provide the basis for s. 1 justification if the objective is incompatible with the values entrenched by the Charter of Rights. The religious objective of compelling the observance of a Christian sabbath was incompatible with the guarantee of freedom of religion. However, as *Edwards Books* held, the objective of providing a common day of rest, although entailing some limitation of freedom of religion, could be accommodated by a society that respected freedom of religion.

The second rule is that an objective cannot provide the basis for s. 1 justification if the objective is ultra vires the enacting legislative body on federal distribution of powers grounds.[110] Therefore, the provision of a common day of rest could not be accepted as the objective of the federal law in *Big M*, although it could be accepted as the objective of the provincial law in *Edwards Books.*

The third rule to be derived from *Big M* is the rule against shifting objectives, which is the topic of the next section.

(e) Shifting objectives

In *R.* v. *Big M Drug Mart* (1985),[111] the Supreme Court of Canada held that an objective cannot provide the basis for s. 1 justification if that objective did not in fact cause the enactment of the law. Dickson C.J. rejected the notion that the purpose of a law might change over time with changing social conditions. This would create uncertainty and invite the relitigation of Charter issues previously settled. Therefore, he held: "Purpose is a function of the intent of those who drafted and enacted the legislation at the time, and not of any shifting variable".[112]

---

107 *Id.*, 352-353.

108 Followed in *Zylberberg* v. *Sudbury Bd. of Ed.* (1988) 65 O.R. (2d) 641 (C.A.) (s. 1 cannot save provincial law requiring religious exercises in the schools); *Can. Civil Libs. Assn.* v. *Ont.* (1990) 71 O.R. (2d) 341 (C.A.) (s. 1 cannot save provincial law requiring religious instruction in the schools if the instruction amounts to Christian indoctrination).

109 [1986] 2 S.C.R. 713.

110 [1985] 1 S.C.R. 295, 353.

111 [1985] 1 S.C.R. 295; note 105, above.

112 *Id.*, 335. This part of the *Big M* opinion is to be found in the first stage of the Charter analysis, when the Court considered whether the law infringed a Charter right. By implication, but not expressly, the Court applied the same rule to the identification of the objective of the law in the section 1 analysis. Query whether the same rule applies to the assessment of purpose for the

This rule was fatal to the legislation in *Big M*, because the religious motivation of the legislators in 1906, when the law was enacted, was clear, although it was certainly arguable that the law had been maintained on the books in recent times only because it fulfilled the secular function of requiring a common day of rest.

The rule against shifting objectives was again considered by the Supreme Court of Canada in *R.* v. *Butler* (1992),[113] in which the Court upheld under s. 1 the anti-obscenity provision of the Criminal Code. Sopinka J., writing for a unanimous Court, acknowledged that the original objective of the provision was the promotion of morality, and he held that this objective was insufficiently important to justify a limit on freedom of expression. However, he went on to uphold the provision on the basis that, as interpreted in recent cases, the provision promoted sexual equality. Was this an impermissible shift in the objective of the law? No, answered Sopinka J. The objective had always been the protection of society from the harms caused by obscene materials. The change in the way in which the courts defined those harms was merely "a permissible shift in emphasis".[114] The modern "emphasis" made the law's objective sufficiently important to serve as a justification under s. 1.

What Sopinka J. did in *Butler* was to formulate the objective of the law at a level of generality that could be regarded as remaining constant over time, even though the "emphasis" (which is really just a more particular formulation of the objective) had changed with changing community values. This technique offers a path around the rule against shifting objectives. In *R.* v. *Zundel* (1992),[115] the majority of the Supreme Court of Canada refused to take that path. At issue was the Criminal Code offence of spreading false news, which was held to be a limit on freedom of expression. The original objective of the law was to protect "the great men of the realm" from malicious lies. In *Zundel*, however, the law had been used to prosecute the purveyor of Holocaust-denial literature that was deeply offensive to Jews. For Cory and Iacobucci JJ., who wrote the dissenting opinion, the false-news law had always had as its purpose the prevention of harm from deliberate falsehoods. Citing *Butler*, they characterized the modern objective of racial harmony as a "permissible shift in emphasis" in response to current values.[116] They would have upheld the law under s. 1. McLachlin J., who wrote for the majority, held that the prevention of harm from deliberate falsehoods was too

---

federal distribution of powers. In the *Margarine Reference, Can. Federation of Agriculture* v. *A.G. Que.* [1951] A.C. 179, the Privy Council struck down a federal prohibition on the manufacture and sale of margarine, although the law had originally been enacted in 1886 on the secure criminal-law basis that margarine was injurious to health. In subsequent reenactments of the statute, a preamble reciting the health rationale was dropped, and the federal Attorney General acknowledged that the original health rationale was false. The Act was judged on the basis that its purpose was the protection of the dairy industry.

113 [1992] 1 S.C.R. 452.

114 *Id.*, 496.

115 [1992] 2 S.C.R. 731.

116 *Id.*, 823.

general a statement of the law's objective. In her view, "to convert [the false-news law] into a provision directed at encouraging racial harmony is to go beyond any permissible shift in emphasis".[117] She applied the rule against shifting objectives to hold that the modern objective could not be attributed to the law. Since the law had not been enacted for an objective that was sufficiently important today to justify a limit on freedom of expression, the law was struck down.

(f) Cost

Is it a possible justification of a limit on a Charter right that the limit will save money?

This was one of the issues in *Singh* v. *Minister of Employment and Immigration* (1984),[118] where the question was whether an oral hearing by a body with decision-making power had to be afforded to every person who arrived at Canada's borders and claimed to be a refugee. It was argued by the Attorney General of Canada that such a procedure, if applied to the many thousands of refugee-claimants who arrive each year, would impose an "unreasonable burden" on the resources of government. Wilson J., who wrote for three of six judges of the Supreme Court of Canada, said:[119]

> I have considerable doubt that the type of utilitarian consideration brought forward by Mr. Bowie [counsel for the Attorney General of Canada] can constitute a justification for a limitation on the rights set out in the *Charter*. Certainly the guarantees of the *Charter* would be illusory if they could be ignored because it was administratively convenient to do so. No doubt considerable time and money can be saved by adopting administrative procedures which ignore the principles of fundamental justice but such an argument, in my view, misses the point of the exercise under s. 1. The principles of natural justice and procedural fairness which have long been espoused by our courts, and the constitutional entrenchment of the principles of fundamental justice in s. 7, implicitly recognize that a balance of administrative convenience does not override the need to adhere to these principles. Whatever standard of review eventually emerges under s. 1, it seems to me that the basis of the justification for the limitation of rights under s. 7 must be more compelling than any advanced in these appeals.

The other three judges in *Singh* did not address this issue — indeed, they did not decide the case on the basis of the Charter — but the Court was unanimous that the full hearing right had to be provided. (Compliance with the Court's ruling in fact proved to be very difficult, leading to a huge backlog of refugee claimants, who endured delays of two years or more awaiting adjudication.)[120]

---

117 *Id.*, 761.

118 [1985] 1 S.C.R. 177.

119 *Id.*, 218-219. See also *Re B.C. Motor Vehicle Act* [1985] 2 S.C.R. 486, 518 per Lamer J. ("administrative expediency" would be relevant under s. 1 "only in cases arising out of exceptional conditions, such as natural disasters, the outbreak of war, epidemics and the like"); *R.* v. *Schwartz* [1988] 2 S.C.R. 443, 472 per Dickson C.J. ("administrative convenience . . . is rarely if ever an objective of sufficient importance").

120 See ch. 44, Fundamental Justice, under heading 44.4(b), "Immigrants", below.

In *R.* v. *Lee* (1989),[121] a challenge was brought against the section of the Criminal Code that provided that an accused who had elected trial by jury, but who had failed to appear for trial without a legitimate excuse, was to be tried by judge alone. Was this the denial of the Charter right to "the benefit of trial by jury" (s. 11(f))? The majority of the Supreme Court of Canada held that the right had been denied, but that the section was saved by s. 1. Lamer J. for the majority held that it was appropriate to deny the right to those who had burdened the system with the cost of futilely empanelling a jury.[122] Wilson J. dissented, holding that "reducing administrative inconvenience and reducing expense are not, in my view, sufficient objectives to override such a vital constitutional right".[123]

In *R.* v. *Chaulk* (1990),[124] the question was whether the Criminal Code's presumption of sanity offended the Charter of Rights. The majority of the Supreme Court of Canada held that the presumption of sanity offended the presumption of innocence guaranteed by s. 11(d), because it relieved the Crown of the burden of proving that an accused person was sane. However, Lamer C.J. (with four others) was willing to uphold the rule under s. 1; in his view, to relieve the Crown of the great difficulty of proving sanity was a sufficient objective.[125] Wilson J. disagreed, holding that a "purely procedural" objective could not be sufficiently important to satisfy s. 1.[126] She acknowledged that the prospect of guilty persons escaping conviction through false pleas of insanity could be a "pressing social problem" that would afford justification under s. 1, but she held that there was no evidence to establish such a concern.[127]

Professor Weinrib must be correct when she says that:[128] "It is inherent in the nature of constitutional rights that they must receive a higher priority in the distribution of available government funds than policies or programmes that do not enjoy that status". She concludes that: "A different preference for allocation of resources cannot justify encroachment on a right". The difficulty is to determine the point at which considerations of cost become so weighty that they would justify the limiting of a Charter right. Even Wilson J. seems to accept that "prohibitive" cost could have this effect.[129]

It should also be noted that cost may have an impact on the content of some of the Charter rights, and thus be relevant to the first stage of Charter review. What is entailed by the principles of fundamental justice may well vary from situation to situation, depending at least in part on the resources involved in

121 [1989] 2 S.C.R. 1384.

122 Id., 1390-1391.

123 *Id.*, 1420.

124 [1990] 3 S.C.R. 1303.

125 *Id.*, 1337.

126 *Id.*, 1373.

127 Three judges held that the presumption of innocence did not offend s. 11(d); they did not need to consider s. 1.

128 Weinrib, note 1, above, 486. See also sec. 35.2, "Rationale of s. 1", above.

129 See *Singh*, note 118, above, 220, where this is strongly implied.

providing hearing and appeal rights of differing extent. Similarly, the right to equal benefit of the law can hardly be defined without regard for the claims on resources of policies and programmes that compete with a challenged programme: all roads cannot be paved at once. The right to a trial within a reasonable time and the right not to be subjected to cruel and unusual punishment do not require that the facilities of criminal justice and corrections should be allocated the resources now allocated to health care or education.

35.10 Rational connection

(a) Definition

The second step in the *Oakes* tests of justification (the first element of proportionality)[130] of a law that limits a Charter right is to determine whether the law is "rationally connected" to the objective of the law. This second step is reached of course only after the first step has been taken and the objective of the law has been found to be sufficiently important to justify in principle the limiting of the Charter right. "The requirement of rational connection calls for an assessment of how well the legislative garment has been tailored to suit its purpose".[131] The law must be "carefully designed to achieve the objective in question"; it should not be "arbitrary, unfair, or based on irrational considerations".[132]

The *Oakes* case itself[133] was determined by the Supreme Court of Canada's finding that the law failed the rational connection requirement. At issue was the validity of a provision of the federal Narcotic Control Act, which provided that proof that the accused was in possession of an illegal drug raised a presumption that the accused was in possession for the purpose of trafficking. The effect of the provision was to cast on the accused the burden of proving that he was not in possession for the purpose of trafficking. The Supreme Court of Canada held that this "reverse onus" clause was an infringement of s. 11(d) of the Charter, which guarantees the presumption of innocence. This moved the Charter inquiry into its second stage: could the reverse onus clause be justified under s. 1?

The Court in *Oakes* readily agreed that the objective of the reverse onus clause — to protect society from drug trafficking — was sufficiently important to justify limiting a Charter right. But the Court held that the law failed the rational connection test. "There must be", Dickson C.J. said, "a rational connection between the basic fact of possession and the presumed fact of possession for the purpose of trafficking".[134] This reverse onus clause could not satisfy this requi-

130 Text accompanying note 75, above.
131 *R.* v. *Edwards Books and Art* [1986] 2 S.C.R. 713, 770.
132 *R.* v. *Oakes* [1986] 1 S.C.R. 103, 139.
133 Previous note.
134 *Id.*, 141.

rement because it did not make any stipulation as to the quantity of narcotics in the possession of the accused: ''possession of a small or negligible quantity of narcotics does not support the inference of trafficking''.[135] The Court stopped the s. 1 inquiry at this point, holding that the reverse onus clause could not be justified under s. 1 and was therefore unconstitutional.

Had the Court moved its inquiry on to step 3 — least drastic means — there is no doubt that the law would have failed that requirement. By raising the presumption of trafficking on the basis of possession of any quantity of narcotics, however small, the law did not impair the presumption of innocence as little as possible. Indeed, the requirement of least drastic means seems to me to provide a much stronger ground for the decision than does the requirement of rational connection.[136] Surely, the defect in the reverse onus clause was that it was too harsh, not that it was irrational. It seems to me that the reverse onus clause would tend to discourage both the possession of drugs (because the possessor would be in jeopardy of the serious charge of trafficking) and the trafficking in drugs (because the Crown's ability to prove a trafficking purpose would be facilitated).[137] Both these tendencies have a rational connection to the objective of protecting society from drug trafficking.

According to my count, at the time of writing (1997), *Oakes* is the only case in the Supreme Court of Canada where a law has been struck down for failure to satisfy the requirement of rational connection.[138] All of the other s. 1 cases where the objective has been approved have turned on the requirement of least drastic means. If I am right that *Oakes* could have been decided more easily on the basis of least drastic means, one is forced to conclude that the requirement of rational connection has very little work to do. Indeed, for a time I held the theory that the requirement of rational connection was redundant, because the few laws that would fail it would also fail the requirement of least drastic means. But I am now persuaded[139] that it is possible to imagine a case where the rational connection test has an independent role to play. A law could be so poorly designed to meet its (important) objective that the law would fail the s. 1 justification, even though it had only a minimal effect on a guaranteed right, and even though a better designed law would have a more severe impact on the guaranteed right. In such

---

135 *Id.*, 142.

136 Accord, Peck, note 1, above, 70; Mendes, note 1, above, 8-10; Beatty, *Talking Heads and the Supremes* (1990), 31.

137 It is difficult to catch a trafficker in the act of selling drugs. That is the reason for the offence of possession for the purpose of trafficking. But it is also difficult to prove the purpose. That is the reason for the reverse onus.

138 In *RJR-MacDonald* v. *Can.* [1995] 3 S.C.R. 199, discussed in text accompanying note 140, below, while the challenged legislation generally satisfied the rational connection test, one provision failed the test: note 142, below.

139 A benefit of teaching, which is much underrated by professors, is that students often challenge cherished professorial ''insights''. I am indebted to first-year student Stephen L. Szikora, class of '92, for the destruction in the classroom of the redundancy theory.

a case, the law would fail the requirement of rational connection even though it would pass the requirement of least drastic means.

A silly variant of *Oakes* might serve as an example. Suppose that the Narcotic Control Act cast on persons accused of drug trafficking the burden of proving their names. This burden would be very easy to discharge (and could be discharged without the accused himself actually testifying), and therefore would be only a minimal infringement of the presumption of innocence. But it would not contribute in any significant way to the goal of impeding the trade in drugs. This law would fail the requirement of rational connection, although it is a less drastic measure than a reverse onus clause affecting an important element of the offence.

(b) Causation

The essence of rational connection is a causal relationship between the objective of the law and the measures enacted by the law. This is often a difficult matter to establish by evidence, and the Supreme Court of Canada has not always insisted on direct proof of the causal relationship.

A striking example of the Court substituting it own intuition for admissible evidence is *RJR-MacDonald* v. *Canada* (1995).[140] In that case, the objective of the law, which banned the advertising of tobacco products, was to reduce the consumption of tobacco. The law was certainly a limit on freedom of expression. Could it be justified under s. 1? At the trial (which took 71 sitting days), a parade of expert witnesses called by both sides from all over the world debated the issue of whether the ban on advertising would indeed reduce consumption. The trial judge found that the steady decline in tobacco use in all developed countries (some of which had enacted advertising bans and some of which had not) was unaffected by the presence or absence of advertising, and he specifically rejected the evidence to the contrary as being unreliable and without probative value. He concluded that there was no rational connection between the advertising ban and the objective of reduced consumption, and that the law (which also failed the minimum impairment test) was unjustified under s. 1. In the Supreme Court of Canada, however, there was unanimity on the position that the rational connection test was satisfied. La Forest J., for the four dissenting judges (who would have upheld the law under s. 1), held that ''the common-sense connection between advertising and consumption'' was ''sufficient to satisfy the rational connection requirement''.[141] McLachlin J., for the five-judge majority (who struck the law down on the basis that it failed the minimum impairment test), agreed with La Forest J. that the rational connection test was satisfied. She said that a causal connection based on ''reason'' or ''logic'' would suffice, even though the evid-

140 [1995] 3 S.C.R. 199.

141 *Id.*, para. 86; he also reviewed the evidence and, in direct contradiction to the careful judgment of the trial judge, held (para. 87) that ''there was, in any event, sufficient evidence adduced at trial to bear out the rational connection between advertising and consumption''.

ence was "admittedly inconclusive".[142] For all the judges, therefore, the finding at trial based on the evidence had to give way to the appellate judges' "common sense", "reason" or "logic".[143]

35.11 Least drastic means

(a) Definition

The requirement of least drastic means is the third step in the *Oakes* tests of justification[144] of a law that limits a Charter right. In *R.* v. *Oakes*,[145] it was described as the second element of proportionality, and it was said to require that the law "should impair 'as little as possible' the right or freedom in question". The idea is that the law should impair the right no more than is necessary to accomplish the desired objective, or, in other words, that the law should pursue the objective by the least drastic means. This branch of the *Oakes* test can also be described as the minimum impairment test, because it insists that the limit on the Charter right be the minimum that is necessary to accomplish the desired objective. It is not, however, accurate (although it has become popular) to describe the test as the *minimal* impairment test, because the word "minimal" carries the connotation of trivial or slight, and a justified limit on a Charter right might be quite a severe limit on the right. The law of defamation, for example, is hardly a "minimal" restraint on freedom of expression, affecting as it does all expression that is critical of others, but it has been held to be the minimum impairment required to safeguard the value of personal reputation.[146]

The requirement of least drastic means has turned out to be the heart and soul of s. 1 justification. We have noticed that courts have usually readily accepted that a legislative purpose is sufficiently important to justify overriding a Charter right (first step).[147] We have also noticed that courts have usually readily accepted that a law is rationally connected to its objective (second step).[148] We shall shortly notice that courts have usually readily accepted that a law does not have a

142 *Id.*, paras. 156-158. She did, however, hold (para. 159) that one provision of the Act, s. 8, which prohibited the use of the tobacco trademark on articles other than tobacco products (such as a tobacco brand logo on a cigarette lighter), did not satisfy even a "causal connection based on logic or reason", and failed the rational connection test.

143 See also *R.* v. *Butler* [1992] 1 S.C.R. 452, 503 ("reasonable to presume" that there is a causal relationship between obscenity and harm to society); *Ross* v. *New Brunswick School District No. 15* [1996] 1 S.C.R. 825, para. 101 ("reasonable to anticipate" that there is a causal relationship between anti-semitic activity by schoolteacher outside school and discriminatory attitudes within school).

144 Text accompanying note 75, above.

145 [1986] 1 S.C.R. 103, 139.

146 *Hill* v. *Church of Scientology* [1995] 2 S.C.R. 1130.

147 See sec. 35.9, "Sufficiently important objective", above.

148 See sec. 35.10, "Rational connection", above.

disproportionately severe impact on the persons to whom it applies (fourth step).[149] In short, for the great majority of cases, the arena of debate is the third step, the requirement of least drastic means.

A number of laws have failed the requirement of least drastic means. The Criminal Code's felony-murder rule has been held to be too drastic a means of discouraging the use of weapons by criminals.[150] Quebec's prohibition of the use of English in commercial signs has been held to be too drastic a means of protecting the French language,[151] although requiring the use of French is acceptable.[152] Alberta's rule prohibiting Alberta lawyers from entering into partnership with lawyers not resident in Alberta has been held to be too drastic a means of regulating the standards of the legal profession.[153] Alberta's prohibition of the publication of accounts of matrimonial litigation has been held to be too drastic a means of safeguarding the privacy of individuals.[154] Ontario's prohibition on advertising by dentists has been held to be too drastic a means of maintaining high professional standards.[155] A federal ban on all advertising of tobacco products was held to be too drastic a means of curtailing the consumption of tobacco.[156] A board of inquiry order that a person employed in a non-teaching position by a school board must be fired if he continued his dissemination of anti-semitic ideas was held to be too drastic a means of rectifying a discriminatory climate in the school.[157] In each of these cases, the Supreme Court of Canada held that other laws were available to the enacting legislative body which would still accomplish the desired objective but which would impair the Charter right less than the law that was enacted.

(b) Margin of appreciation

It is rarely self-evident that a law limiting a Charter right does so by the least drastic means.[158] Indeed, "a judge would be unimaginative indeed if he could not come up with something a little less 'drastic' or a little less 'restrictive' in almost

149 See sec. 35.12, "Proportionate effect", below.

150 *R.* v. *Vaillancourt* [1987] 2 S.C.R. 636. See also *R.* v. *Martineau* [1990] 2 S.C.R. 633; *R.* v. *Logan* [1990] 2 S.C.R. 731; *R.* v. *Hess* [1990] 2 S.C.R. 906, all cases in which Criminal Code provisions failed the least-drastic-means test.

151 *Ford* v. *Que.* [1988] 2 S.C.R. 712.

152 *Devine* v. *Que.* [1988] 2 S.C.R. 790.

153 *Black* v. *Law Society of Alta.* [1989] 1 S.C.R. 591.

154 *Edmonton Journal* v. *Alta.* [1989] 2 S.C.R. 1326.

155 *Rocket* v. *Royal College of Dental Surgeons* [1990] 2 S.C.R. 232.

156 *RJR-MacDonald* v. *Can.* [1995] 3 S.C.R. 199.

157 *Ross* v. *New Brunswick School District No. 15* [1996] 1 S.C.R. 825 (the order removing the person from a teaching position to a non-teaching position did satisfy the least drastic means test).

158 We have noticed that it can be made to appear self-evident by articulating the objective of the law in terms so close to the actual text of the law that no other law could possibly fulfil the objective: notes 78-89 and accompanying text, above.

any situation, and thereby enable himself to vote to strike legislation down''.[159] This is especially so if judges are unaware of the practicalities of designing and administering a regulatory regime, and are indifferent to considerations of cost. If s. 1 is to offer any real prospect of justification, the judges have to pay some degree of deference to legislative choices.

A related point concerns the accommodation by the Charter of federal values. A strict application of the least-drastic-means requirement would allow only one legislative response to an objective that involved the limiting of a Charter right. The law that least impaired the Charter right would be acceptable; all alternatives would fail. In a federal country like Canada, there ought to be some room for distinctive provincial responses to similar social objectives. The uniformity of provincial laws that would be entailed by a stringent requirement of least drastic means is in conflict with the federal values of distinctiveness, diversity and experimentation. If s. 1 is to permit some accommodation of these federal values, the judges have to allow to provincial Legislatures a ''margin of appreciation'',[160] a zone of discretion within which different legislative choices in derogation of a Charter right could be tolerated.[161]

The categorical language that Dickson C.J. employed in *Oakes* to delineate the function of the Supreme Court of Canada under s. 1 appeared to leave little room for even a narrow margin of appreciation. The only law that was qualified to enter into the kingdom of validity was the law that impaired the Charter right ''as little as possible''.[162] In view of the ease with which a less drastic alternative to virtually any law could be imagined, the process of s. 1 justification looked like the camel passing through the eye of the needle.

Not surprisingly, the Supreme Court of Canada quickly recognized that some margin of appreciation had to mitigate the least-drastic-means requirement. The problem became evident in *R.* v. *Edwards Books and Art* (1986).[163] In that case, the Court upheld the Ontario Sunday-closing law that applied to retail businesses in the province. The Court held that the law infringed freedom of religion, but that it was justified under s. 1. The Court held that the objective of the law, which was to provide a common day of rest, was sufficiently important to justify over-

---

159 *Illinois Elections Bd.* v. *Socialist Workers Party* (1979) 440 U.S. 173, 188-189 per Blackmun J.

160 The European Court of Human Rights, interpreting the limitation clauses in the European Convention on Human Rights, has allowed member states ''une marge d'appréciation'', which is usually mechanically rendered into English as ''margin of appreciation'', although measure of discretion would be much better. This concept allows the Court to tolerate different levels of derogation of Convention rights out of respect for the different conditions and values of the European states that adhere to the Convention. See references in note 4, above.

161 This argument is advanced at more length in ''Federalism Fights the Charter of Rights'', which is my contribution to Shugarman and Whitaker (eds.), *Federalism and Political Community* (1989), 249. As noted in the paper, s. 1 is not the only vehicle by which the Charter of Rights can accommodate federal values. Section 33 (the power of override) is also available.

162 Note 145, above.

163 [1986] 2 S.C.R. 713.

riding a Charter right. The question was whether the law satisfied the requirement of least drastic means. The law contained a "sabbatarian exemption" for retailers who observed Saturday as the sabbath. However, only small retailers — those employing no more than seven people and using no more than 5,000 square feet of retail space — were entitled to the exemption. The issue in the case resolved itself into whether the law had made an adequate accommodation of those who observed Saturday as their sabbath. On this point the Court fractured into three camps.

Dickson C.J., who had written the *Oakes* opinion, now softened his language considerably. With the concurrence of Chouinard and Le Dain JJ., he said that the test was whether the law abridged the freedom of religion of Saturday observers "as little as is reasonably possible".[164] The word "reasonably" had not appeared in that phrase in the *Oakes* case. As to the precise form of the legislative limit, it was "one that was reasonable for the legislature to impose".[165] The courts were "not called upon to substitute judicial opinions for legislative ones as to the place at which to draw a precise line".[166] The exemption in the Act "represents a satisfactory effort on the part of the Legislature of Ontario to that end [the accommodation of Saturday observers] and is, accordingly, permissible".[167] La Forest J. was even more deferential in his attitude to the province's policy choice. He would have upheld the law, even if it had contained no sabbatarian exemption. He said that "a legislature must be given reasonable room to manoeuvre".[168] In particular, it seemed to him that "the choice of having or not having an exemption for those who observe a day other than Sunday must remain, in essence, a legislative choice".[169] Only Wilson J. applied the remorseless logic of "least drastic means" to insist that the law must contain a sabbatarian exception, and that the exception must extend to all Saturday-observing retailers, not just those with no more than seven employees and 5,000 square feet of space.[170]

The majority opinions in *Edwards Books* in effect recognized a margin of appreciation, which would tolerate a variety of different Sunday-closing laws. Indeed, the Court has since used the phrase "margin of appreciation" to describe its approach to the requirement of least drastic means.[171] Certainly, the cases after *Edwards Books* have applied the requirement in a flexible fashion, looking for a reasonable legislative effort to minimize the infringement of the Charter right, rather than insisting that only the least possible infringement could survive.

---

164 *Id.* 772.
165 *Id.*, 781-782.
166 *Id.* 782.
167 *Ibid.*
168 *Id.*, 795.
169 *Id.*, 796.
170 *Id.*, 810. Beetz J. (with McIntyre J.) did not discuss s. 1 at all, because in his view the Sunday closing law did not breach freedom of religion.
171 *Irwin Toy* v. *Que.* [1989] 1 S.C.R. 927, 999.

In *R.* v. *Whyte* (1988),[172] the Court upheld the Criminal Code provision that presumes that a person occupying the driver's seat of a vehicle has the care and control of the vehicle for the purpose of the drunk driving offence. This reverse onus clause infringed the presumption of innocence in order to make it easier to secure convictions. Dickson C.J. for the Court described[173] the clause as a "restrained parliamentary response to a pressing social problem" and "a minimal interference with the presumption of innocence".

In *Canadian Newspapers Co.* v. *Attorney General of Canada* (1988),[174] the Court upheld a Criminal Code provision authorizing a court order banning the disclosure of the identity of the complainant in a case of sexual assault. The making of the order by the Court was mandatory if it was requested by the complainant or the prosecutor. It was argued that a discretionary ban would be a less severe limit on freedom of the press. Lamer J. for the Court held[175] that only a mandatory ban would provide assurance to a complainant that her identity would not be disclosed, and therefore only a mandatory ban would serve the purpose of fostering complaints by victims of sexual assault.

In *British Columbia Government Employees' Union* v. *Attorney General of British Columbia* (1988),[176] the Court upheld an injunction prohibiting the union, which was on strike, from picketing the courts of British Columbia, where some of its members worked. Holding that "a picket line *ipso facto* impedes public access to justice",[177] Dickson C.J. for the Court held that the injunction limited freedom of expression by the least drastic means because the union was free to picket workplaces other than the courts.

In *United States* v. *Cotroni* (1989),[178] the Court upheld the extradition to the United States of a Canadian citizen. Extradition infringed the citizen's mobility right under s. 6 of the Charter, but the objective of suppressing crime was sufficiently important to support a limit on the right. Wilson and Sopinka JJ., who dissented, held that in this case extradition did not limit the right as little as possible, because the accused was charged with a crime that had allegedly been committed in Canada; he could therefore have been prosecuted in Canada as an alternative to his extradition. La Forest J. for the majority answered this by insisting that the requirement of least drastic means must be applied "flexibly".[179]

---

172 [1988] 2 S.C.R. 3.

173 *Id.*, 26-27.

174 [1988] 2 S.C.R. 122.

175 *Id.*, 130-133.

176 [1988] 2 S.C.R. 214.

177 *Id.*, 231. The *ipso facto* is important, because the evidence established that, in addition to everyone's normal ability to cross the picket line, those with business in the courts could obtain a pass from the picketers. In my view, these facts showed that the injunction was an unnecessarily severe response to the picketing, and s. 1 should have been held to be unavailable to save the injunction.

178 [1989] 1 S.C.R. 1469.

179 *Id.*, 1489.

Because there could be procedural or evidentiary reasons why the other country was a preferable forum, he held that the right "is infringed as little as possible, or at the very least as little as reasonably possible".[180]

In the *Prostitution Reference* (1990),[181] the Court upheld the offence of communicating for the purpose of prostitution. This was a limit on freedom of expression that was justified by the objective of eliminating the nuisance of street solicitation. Wilson J. in dissent pointed out[182] that the law prohibited communications between prostitutes and customers regardless of whether or not traffic congestion, noise, or any other form of nuisance was caused by the activity; she thought that the law failed the least-drastic-means test. Dickson C.J. and Lamer J. for the majority emphasized the difficulty of devising legislative solutions, and the Court's inability "to second-guess the wisdom of policy choices made by our legislators".[183] They held that the law passed the least-drastic-means test.

In each of the foregoing cases,[184] it does not take a vivid imagination to devise a law that would be less intrusive of the applicable Charter right than the law that was enacted. But the Court was willing to defer to the legislative choice on the basis that the choice was within a margin of appreciation, a zone of discretion in which reasonable legislators could disagree while still respecting the Charter right. The result makes for an unpredictable jurisprudence, but there is no practical way to avoid uncertainty in the application of the requirement of least drastic means.

35.12 Proportionate effect

The requirement of proportionate effect is the fourth and last step in the *Oakes* tests of justification.[185] In *R.* v. *Oakes*,[186] it was described by Dickson C.J. as the third element of proportionality, and it was said to require "a proportionality between the *effects* of the measures which are responsible for limiting the Charter right or freedom, and the objective which has been identified as of 'sufficient importance'". In *R.* v. *Edwards Books and Art* (1986),[187] Dickson C.J. rephrased the requirement by saying that "their effects [that is, the effects of the limiting

180 *Id.*, 1490. This approach was unanimously affirmed by the Court in two subsequent cases involving the extradition of Canadian citizens to be tried for crimes in the United States: *United States* v. *Whitley* [1996] 1 S.C.R. 467; *United States* v. *Ross* [1996] 1 S.C.R. 469.

181 *Re ss. 193 and 195.1 of Criminal Code* [1990] 2 S.C.R. 1123.

182 *Id.*, 1214-1215.

183 *Id.*, 1199 per Lamer J; 1138 per Dickson C. J. is to the same effect.

184 Many other cases could be added to this account, e.g., cases respecting hate propaganda laws (sec. 40.9, below), pornography laws (sec. 40.11, below) and mandatory retirement laws (sec. 52.13, below), all of which have survived the least-drastic-means test and been upheld under s. 1.

185 Text accompanying note 75, above.

186 [1986] 1 S.C.R. 103, 139 (emphasis in original).

187 [1986] 2 S.C.R. 713, 768.

measures] must not so severely trench on individual or group rights that the legislative objective, albeit important, is nevertheless outweighed by the abridgement of rights''. In *Dagenais* v. *CBC* (1994),[188] Lamer C.J. added to the requirement by saying that the third element of proportionality should also take into account the ''proportionality between the deleterious and the salutory effects of the measures''.

Although this fourth step is offered as a test of the means rather than the objective of the law, it has nothing to do with means. The fourth step is reached, it must be remembered, only after the means have already been judged to be rationally connected to the objective (second step), and to be the least drastic of all the means of accomplishing the objective (third step). What the requirement of proportionate effect requires is a balancing of the objective sought by the law against the infringement of the civil liberty. It asks whether the Charter infringement is too high a price to pay for the benefit of the law.

Obedient to *Oakes*, when the Court engages in s. 1 analysis, it always goes through the motion of this fourth step. So far as I can tell, however, this step has never had any influence on the outcome of any case. And I think that the reason for this is that it is redundant. It is really a restatement of the first step, the requirement that a limiting law pursue an objective that is sufficiently important to justify overriding a Charter right. If a law is sufficiently important to justify overriding a Charter right (first step), and if the law is rationally connected to the objective (second step), and if the law impairs the Charter right no more than is necessary to accomplish the objective (third step), how could its effects then be judged to be too severe? A judgment that the effects of the law were too severe would surely mean that the objective was *not* sufficiently important to justify limiting a Charter right. If the objective is sufficiently important, and the objective is pursued by the least drastic means, then it must follow that the effects of the law are an acceptable price to pay for the benefit of the law.[189] I conclude, therefore, that an affirmative answer to the first step — sufficiently important objective — will always yield an affirmative answer to the fourth step — proportionate effect.[190] If this is so, then the fourth step has no work to do, and can safely be ignored.

---

188 [1994] 3 S.C.R. 835, 889.

189 Contra, *Rocket* v. *Royal College of Dental Surgeons* [1990] 2 S.C.R. 232, where McLachlin J. for Court held that the impugned law (restricting advertising by dentists) pursued a sufficiently important objective (first step) but failed the fourth step. Even here, however, the fourth step seemed redundant, because the supporting reasons basically repeated the reasons given under least-drastic-means (third step).

190 This conclusion follows only insofar as the full proportionality analysis has indeed been completed by step (3). If the assessment of the objective of the legislation (step (1)) has been done in a rather general way, not focusing on the precise nature of the Charter breach or on the effects of the legislation, there may be some work for step (4) to do. Moreover, it is arguable that it is more likely that Dickson C.J. in *Oakes* intended step (1) to be no more than a general threshold test, since it is only if his step (1) is read in that way does his step (4) make sense,

35.13 Application to equality rights

The *Oakes* test is offered by Dickson C.J. as a universal rule, applicable to all Charter infringements. Whether this is indeed the position has been left in some doubt by *Andrews* v. *Law Society of British Columbia* (1989).[191] In that case, McIntyre J. took the view that the *Oakes* test was ''too stringent for application in all cases''.[192] That was an equality case, in which the question was whether British Columbia's requirement of Canadian citizenship as a qualification for admission to the legal profession infringed s. 15 of the Charter. The Court held unanimously that it did, but the Court then divided on the question whether the law was saved by s. 1. McIntyre J., who dissented, in effect rejected the *Oakes* test, at least for equality cases. He said:[193]

> There is no single test under s. 1; rather, the Court must carefully engage in the balancing of many factors in determining whether an infringement is reasonable and demonstrably justified.

What McIntyre J. was concerned about was the fact that legislative bodies had to make ''innumerable distinctions'' between groups and individuals in the pursuit of ''desirable social goals'', and in making these distinctions it was not reasonable to demand ''the standard of perfection'' that was contemplated by *Oakes*.[194] Applying a more flexible standard, McIntyre J. held that the citizenship requirement was justified under s. 1. Lamer J., the other dissenter, agreed with McIntyre J. La Forest J. said that he was ''in general agreement'' with McIntyre J.'s views on s. 1, although he held that, even on the basis of a lower standard than *Oakes*, the citizenship requirement could not be justified under s. 1.[195] La Forest J. therefore voted with the majority to strike down the citizenship requirement.

There would be a great deal of force to McIntyre J.'s argument if it were the case that s. 15 condemned innumerable legislative distinctions, and required that each be justified under s. 1. But, as will be explained in chapter 52, Equality,[196] the decision in *Andrews* severely limited the scope of s. 15, confining it to the listed categories of ''race, national or ethnic origin, colour, religion, sex, age or mental or physical disability'', and to ''analogous grounds''. This restriction led Wilson J. to hold that the *Oakes* test ''remains an appropriate standard'' for s. 15 cases: ''Given that s. 15 is designed to protect those groups that suffer social,

---

and we should not lightly conclude that a clear thinker like Dickson C.J. said something that did not make sense. I am indebted to first-year student, Jacob Bakan, class of 1998, for these points.

191 [1989] 1 S.C.R. 143.

192 *Id.*, 184.

193 *Id.*, 185.

194 *Ibid.*

195 *Id.*, 197.

196 Chapter 52, Equality, below.

political and legal disadvantage in our society, the burden resting on government is appropriately an onerous one''.[197] She therefore applied the *Oakes* test, and held that the citizenship requirement could not pass it. Her opinion was concurred with by Dickson C.J. and L'Heureux-Dubé J.

In the result, the six judges in *Andrews* voted by a majority of four to two to strike down the British Columbia law. But, because La Forest J., although voting with the majority, expressed himself as in general agreement with McIntyre J.'s statement of s. 1 principles (although not his application of those principles), the Court actually divided evenly on whether the *Oakes* test should apply in equality cases. This issue must obviously be regarded as unresolved, but in my view the argument of Wilson J. is the more persuasive one. Given the restrictions on the scope of s. 15, an infringement of s. 15 calls for the same stringent standard of justification as does the infringement of any other Charter right. The *Oakes* test ought to apply to s. 15 cases.[198]

35.14 Application to qualified rights

(a) Scope of s. 1

Does s. 1 have a role to play in justifying infringements of Charter rights that are by their own terms qualified by notions of reasonableness or regularity? The general answer is yes.[199] The principal qualified rights are examined in the text that follows.

(b) Section 7

Section 7 of the Charter guarantees the right not to be deprived of life, liberty and security of the person ''except in accordance with the principles of fundamental justice''. It is clear from the text of s. 7 that the right to life, liberty and security of the person can be limited by a law that conforms to the principles of fundamental justice. Does s. 1 permit other limits? Could a law that violated the principles of fundamental justice still be upheld under s. 1 as a reasonable limit prescribed by law that could be demonstrably justified in a free and democratic society?

In the *B. C. Motor Vehicle Reference* (1985),[200] Lamer J. said, obiter, that the answer was yes, ''but only in cases arising out of exceptional conditions, such

197 [1989] 1 S.C.R. 143, 154.

198 Another question about the application of the *Oakes* test is whether it applies to those Charter rights, such as ss. 7, 8, 9 and 12, which are by their own terms limited by notions of reasonableness or regularity. This is really a broader question about the application of s. 1, and is accordingly treated separately later in the chapter: sec. 35.14, ''Application to qualified rights'', below.

199 Gibson, note 1, above, 135-142.

200 *Re B.C. Motor Vehicle Act* [1985] 2 S.C.R. 486.

as natural disasters, the outbreak of war, epidemics, and the like''.[201] Wilson J. took the contrary view, also obiter, that a law that violated the principles of fundamental justice could never be either ''reasonable'' or ''demonstrably justified in a free and democratic society''.[202]

In *R.* v. *Morgentaler (No. 2)* (1988),[203] the Supreme Court of Canada, by a majority, held that the abortion offence in the Criminal Code infringed s. 7 of the Charter. Each of the three majority opinions, including that of Wilson J., went on to consider whether the law could nonetheless be justified under s. 1 (and held that it could not be). I think it is fair to say, however, that the discussions of s. 1 justification essentially rehearsed points already discussed under fundamental justice.[204] The finding that the abortion law offended fundamental justice virtually entailed a finding that the law was not a ''reasonable limit'' and was not ''demonstrably justified in a free and democratic society''.

In other cases, the Supreme Court of Canada has routinely applied s. 1 before holding that a breach of s. 7 invalidated a law.[205] The s. 1 justification has been upheld in minority opinions,[206] but never by a majority of the Court.

(c) Section 8

Section 8 of the Charter guarantees the right to be secure against ''unreasonable'' search and seizure. One may well question whether a search that is ''unreasonable'' within the meaning of s. 8 could be justified as ''reasonable'' within the meaning of s. 1. On the other hand, the Supreme Court of Canada in *Hunter* v. *Southam* (1984)[207] has elaborated a set of requirements for legislation that authorizes a search or seizure, and by this ruling has given a particular meaning to the word ''unreasonable'' in s. 8. The word ''reasonable'' in the entirely different context of s. 1 is not restricted in the same fashion. Although the words are the same, the tests they require are different. In principle, therefore,

201 *Id.*, 518. In context, it is possible that Lamer J. was dealing only with infringements of s. 7 for ''administrative expediency'', in which case he was not restricting the use of s. 1 in justification of laws pursuing more lofty objectives.

202 *Id.*, 523. Wilson J. repeated this view in *R.* v. *Jones* [1986] 2 S.C.R. 284, 322; *Re ss. 193 and 195.1 of Criminal Code* (Prostitution Reference) [1990] 1 S.C.R. 1123, 1223; *R.* v. *Swain* [1991] 1 S.C.R. 933, 1034.

203 [1988] 1 S.C.R. 30.

204 This is clear in the case of the opinions of Dickson, C.J. (with whom Lamer J. agreed) and Beetz J. (with whom Estey J. agreed). Wilson J.'s opinion arguably applies a somewhat different analysis to the s. 1 reasoning (at 180-184) than to the fundamental justice reasoning (at 174-180).

205 *R.* v. *Vaillancourt* [1987] 2 S.C.R. 636; *R.* v. *Logan* [1990] 2 S.C.R. 731; *R.* v. *Hess* [1990] 2 S.C.R. 906.

206 *R.* v. *Penno* [1990] 2 S.C.R. 865 per Lamer J. concurring; *R.* v. *Hess*, previous note, per McLachlin J. dissenting.

207 [1984] 2 S.C.R. 145; see ch. 45, Unreasonable Search or Seizure, under heading 45.7, ''Reasonableness'', below.

it is possible to imagine a law that fails the narrow test of reasonableness in s. 8, but passes the broader test of reasonableness in s. 1.[208] Finkelstein is correct, it seems to me, when he argues that, after a law has been found in violation of s. 8, ''s. 1 must then become operative to allow the Crown to lead evidence of reasonableness and demonstrable justification to support the search or seizure''.[209]

(d) Section 9

Section 9 of the Charter guarantees the right not to be ''arbitrarily'' detained or imprisoned. Can an arbitrary detention be reasonable and demonstrably justified under s. 1?

That question arose in *R.* v. *Hufsky* (1988).[210] The case involved a Charter challenge to a spot-check programme by police, under which motor vehicles were stopped at random at a check-point to check for drunkenness and other traffic violations. The Supreme Court of Canada held that a driver stopped by police under the spot-check programme had been arbitrarily detained in breach of s. 9, but the Court held that the procedure was justified under s. 1. The objective of preventing highway accidents was sufficiently important to justify arbitrary detentions, and nothing less than a random stopping procedure would be as effective in detecting and deterring the commission of traffic offences. The Court assumed without discussion that s. 1 was applicable to salvage an infringement of s. 9.[211]

(e) Section 11

Several of the rights of accused persons in s. 11 are qualified by requirements of reasonableness. A person charged with an offence has the right: to be informed without ''unreasonable'' delay of the specific offence (s. 11(a)); to be tried within a ''reasonable'' time (s. 11(b)); and not to be denied ''reasonable'' bail without just cause (s. 11(e)). It seems probable that infringements of these rights could, perhaps only in the rarest of cases, be ''reasonable'' limits under s. 1. As was argued with respect to s. 8,[212] the requirement of reasonableness takes on a unique meaning in the context of the definition of a particular Charter right. Therefore, it is in principle possible for a law to fail a requirement of reasonableness in s. 11 and still pass the more generous requirement of reasonableness in the different context of s. 1.

---

208 Contra, *R.* v. *Noble* (1984) 48 O.R. (2d) 643, 667-668 (C.A.). Cf. *Hunter* v. *Southam* [1984] 2 S.C.R. 145, 169 (''I leave to another day the difficult question of the relationship between these two sections [ss. 1 and 8] . . .'').

209 Finkelstein, Comment on Hunter v. Southam (1985) 63 Can. Bar Rev. 178, 197.

210 [1988] 1 S.C.R. 621.

211 Followed in *R.* v. *Ladouceur* [1990] 1 S.C.R. 1257 (roving random stop upheld under s. 1).

212 Section 35.14(c), ''Section 8'', above.

(f) Section 12

It may simply be the failure of my imagination, but I find it difficult to accept that the right not to be subjected to any "cruel and unusual treatment or punishment" could ever be justifiably limited.[213] This may be an absolute right. Perhaps it is the only one.

35.15 Application to common law

The *Oakes* test applies to common law limits on rights. It is well established that a rule of the common law may be a limit "prescribed by law" under s. 1,[214] and in two cases common law rules in derogation of Charter rights have been held to be justified under s. 1.[215] In both cases, it was assumed that the *Oakes* tests applied, but the tests were not applied with much care. It is hard to apply the various tests to a rule of the common law, where there is no specific enactment that can be examined in terms of objective, rational connection, least drastic means and proportionate effect.

In *R.* v. *Swain* (1991),[216] however, the Supreme Court of Canada applied the *Oakes* tests to the common law rule that a Crown prosecutor may adduce evidence of the insanity of the accused against the wish of the accused. This rule was a violation of s. 7 of the Charter, because the evidence of insanity, if led by the Crown, limited the accused's right to control his or her own defence. The majority of the Court held that the rule failed the least-drastic-means branch of the *Oakes* tests, and could not, therefore, be upheld under s. 1. At this point, an interesting difference emerged between a rule of statute law and a rule of the common law. While a rule of statute law that violated the Charter would have to be struck down, a rule of the common law could be amended by the Court itself. A less drastic rule, which would satisfy s. 1, would allow the Crown to adduce evidence of insanity only after the accused had been found otherwise guilty of the offence charged. The issue of insanity would then be tried (in front of the same trier of fact) before any final verdict was entered. Lamer C.J., speaking for the majority of the Court, said that he could see "no conceptual problem with the Court simply enunciating such a rule to take the place of the old rule".[217] With those words,

213 Contra, *R.* v. *Smith* [1987] 1 S.C.R. 1045, where majority of Court, having decided that a minimum prison sentence for importing narcotics was cruel and unusual, proceeded to consider (and reject) s. 1 justification. Only Le Dain J., concurring (at 1111) and McIntyre J., dissenting (at 1085), regarded s. 1 as unavailable to justify a limit on s. 12.

214 Note 53, above.

215 *RWDSU* v. *Dolphin Delivery* [1986] 2 S.C.R. 573 (common law tort of inducing breach of contract by secondary picketing upheld); *BCEGU* v. *B.C.* [1988] 2 S.C.R. 214 (common law prohibition of picketing of courthouses based on contempt of court upheld).

216 [1991] 1 S.C.R. 933.

217 *Id.*, 978; Wilson J. agreed at 1036.

the offending rule of the common law was immediately transformed into a new rule that was compatible with the Charter of Rights![218]

In *R.* v. *Daviault* (1994),[219] the Supreme Court of Canada held, by a majority, that the common law rule that self-induced intoxication was no defence to a criminal charge offended ss. 7 and 11(d) of the Charter. The Court immediately constructed a new rule, that extreme intoxication was a defence, and that the defence had to be established by the accused on the balance of probabilities. The imposition of the onus of proof on the accused was a breach of the presumption of innocence of s. 11(d), but the Court held that it was justified under s. 1. The s.1 analysis was very brief, and did not follow the *Oakes* tests at all.[220]

Swain and *Daviault* were criminal cases in which the Charter of Rights applied by virtue of the presence of the Crown as a party to the proceedings. The Charter of Rights does not apply to the common law in its application to private parties, that is, where no governmental actor is involved.[221]. However, the Supreme Court of Canada has held that the Charter of Rights applies indirectly to the common law, because the Court will examine whether the common law is consistent with "Charter values", and, if it is not, the Court will modify the common law to make it consistent with Charter values. In *Hill* v. *Church of Scientology* (1995),[222] which was a defamation action between private parties, the Supreme Court of Canada considered whether the common law of defamation was consistent with Charter values. Cory J., who wrote for the Court on this issue, said that it was not appropriate to apply "the traditional s.1 analysis" in cases where the Charter was not directly applicable. Instead, he said, there should be a "more flexible" balancing of the competing values, and the onus rested with the Charter claimant to persuade the Court that the common law should be modified.[223] He concluded that the law of defamation struck an appropriate balance between the Charter value of freedom of expression and the non-Charter (but important) value of personal reputation; therefore, there was no need to modify the common law.[224]

---

218 After this decision, Parliament enacted legislation which details the conditions under which a court may order the accused to undergo a mental assessment. According to this legislation, a court may make such an order either of its own motion, on application of the accused, or on application of the Crown prosecutor. Unless the accused has put his or her mental capacity in issue, the court may only make an order for assessment on application of the prosecutor if the prosecutor satisfies the court that there are "reasonable grounds to doubt that the accused is criminally responsible for the alleged offence, on account of mental disorder": S.C. 1991, c. 43, s. 672.12(3)(b). This provision does not limit the prosecutor to applying for an assessment only after the trier of fact has found the accused to be otherwise guilty.

219 [1994] 3 S.C.R. 63.

220 *Id.*, 101-102.

221 Chapter 34, Application of Charter, under heading 34.2(f), "Common law", above.

222 [1995] 2 S.C.R. 1130.

223 *Id.*, paras. 97, 98.

224 See also *Dagenais* v. *CBC* [1994] 3 S.C.R. 835 (modifying common law power to issue publication ban injunction).

35.16 Emergency measures

The Charter of Rights makes no explicit provision for the enactment of emergency measures.[225] On the three occasions when the War Measures Act has been proclaimed in force — during the first world war, the second world war and the "October crisis" of 1970 — civil liberties were severely restricted by regulations made under the Act.[226] The War Measures Act was repealed in 1988, and replaced by the Emergencies Act,[227] which also authorizes restrictions on civil liberties. It will be for the courts to decide, in a situation of emergency, whether such restrictions are reasonable and demonstrably justified in a free and democratic society.[228]

---

225 The Canadian Bill of Rights, by s. 6, amended the War Measures Act to exempt it from the provisions of the Canadian Bill of Rights. The War Measures Act has since been repealed by the Emergencies Act, S.C. 1988, c. 29, which does not, however, contain a similar exemption.

226 See ch. 17, Peace, Order and Good Government, under heading 17.4, "The 'emergency' branch", above.

227 S.C. 1988, c. 29.

228 In *Re B.C. Motor Vehicle Act* [1985] 2 S.C.R. 486, 518, Lamer J. suggests an expanded role for s. 1 in a situation of emergency; for commentary, see Weinrib, note 1, above, 489-491.

36

Override of Rights

36.1 Section 33

Section 33 of the Charter of Rights[1] provides as follows:

> 33.(1) Parliament or the legislature of a province may expressly declare in an Act of Parliament or of the legislature, as the case may be, that the Act or a provision thereof shall operate notwithstanding a provision included in section 2 or sections 7 to 15 of this Charter.

1 See Scott, ''Entrenchment by Executive Action'' (1982) 4 Supreme Court L.R. 303 (arguing that the Lieutenant Governor should be instructed to refuse royal assent to any bill containing a s. 33 declaration); Slattery, ''Override Clauses under Section 33'' (1983) 61 Can. Bar Rev. 391 (arguing that s. 33 is subordinate to s. 1); Arbess, ''Limitations on Legislative Override'' (1983) 21 Osgoode Hall L.J. 113 (also arguing that s. 33 is subordinate to s. 1); LaSelva, ''Only in Canada: Reflections on the Charter's Notwithstanding Clause'' (1983) 63 Dalhousie Review 383 (arguing that s. 33 leaves a law exposed to review under pre-Charter federalism principles); Weiler, ''Rights and Judges in a Democracy: A New Canadian Version'' (1984) 18 Jo. of Law Reform, 51 (general discussion); Greschner and Norman, ''The Courts and Section 33'' (1987) 12 Queen's L.J. 155 (arguing that s. 33 can only be used to protect a law after a judicial decision invalidating the law); Weinrib, ''Learning to Live with the Override'' (1990) 35 McGill L.J. 541 (comment on *Ford* case); Gibson, *The Law of the Charter: General Principles* (1986), 124-131 (general discussion); Beaudoin and Ratushny (eds.), *The Canadian Charter of Rights and Freedoms* (1989), 102-108 (by Tassé) (general discussion); Whyte, ''On Not Standing for Notwithstanding'' (1990) 28 Alta. L. Rev. 347 (criticism of s. 33); Russell, ''Standing Up for Notwithstanding'' (1991) 29 Alta. L. Rev. 293 (defence of s. 33); T. Macklem, ''Engaging the Override'' (1991) 1 Nat. J. Con. Law 274 (criticism of s. 33).

(2) An Act or a provision of an Act in respect of which a declaration made under this section is in effect shall have such operation as it would have but for the provision of this Charter referred to in the declaration.
(3) A declaration made under subsection (1) shall cease to have effect five years after it comes into force or on such earlier date as may be specified in the declaration.
(4) Parliament or a legislature of a province may re-enact a declaration made under subsection (1).
(5) Subsection (3) applies in respect of a re-enactment made under subsection (4).

Section 33 enables the Parliament or a Legislature to ''override'' s. 2 or ss. 7 to 15 of the Charter. If a statute contains an express declaration that it is to operate notwithstanding a provision included in s. 2 or ss. 7 to 15 of the Charter, then by virtue of s. 33(2) the statute will operate free from the invalidating effect of the Charter provision referred to in the declaration. Through the use of this override power, the Parliament or a Legislature is enabled to enact a statute limiting (or abolishing) one or more of the rights or freedoms guaranteed by s. 2 or ss. 7 to 15. If the override power did not exist (or if it were not exercised), such a statute would be valid only if it came within s. 1 of the Charter: a court would have to be persuaded, in accordance with the rules described in the previous chapter, that the statute came within ''such reasonable limits prescribed by law as can be demonstrably justified in a free and democratic society''. The override power, if exercised, would remove the statute containing the express declaration from the reach of the Charter provisions referred to in the declaration without the necessity of any showing of reasonableness or demonstrable justification.[2]

36.2 History of s. 33

Section 33 was not in any of the earlier versions of the Charter. It was the crucial element of the federal-provincial agreement of November 5, 1981 that secured the consent of those provinces (other than Quebec) that had until then been opposed to the Charter on the ground that it limited the sovereignty of their Legislatures.[3] Section 33 preserved that sovereignty, provided the Legislature satisfied the requirements of the section.

Quebec was the one province that did not join the agreement of November 5, 1981, and the province has never given its assent to the Constitution Act, 1982, including the Charter of Rights. After the Charter came into force on April 17, 1982, Quebec's Parti Québécois Government secured the passage by the Legis-

2 This point has been the subject of some controversy: see sec. 36.7, ''Judicial review'', below.

3 The other major concession achieved by the seven provinces was the substitution of their preferred amending formula for the one preferred by the federal government and its two provincial allies (Ontario and New Brunswick). The history of the Constitution Act, 1982 is related in ch. 4, Amendment, under heading 4.1(b), ''The search for a domestic amending procedure'', above.

lature of Bill 62, entitled An Act respecting the Constitution Act, 1982.[4] This Act, which was intended to be a protest against the Charter,[5] added a standard-form notwithstanding clause to each of the statutes in force in Quebec on April 16, 1982.[6] In addition, each new Act enacted by the Quebec Legislature routinely included a standard-form notwithstanding clause. The latter practice was discontinued after December 2, 1985, when a provincial election installed a Liberal Government in Quebec City with a policy of reaching a constitutional accommodation with the rest of Canada.[7] The Liberal Government also allowed the blanket override to lapse in 1987, when it came to the end of its five-year life; no attempt was made to re-enact it for another five-year term.

The Liberal Government of Quebec that was elected on December 2, 1985, while not continuing the previous government's routine uses of s. 33, did nevertheless insert a notwithstanding clause in five statutes in order to preclude Charter attacks on the statutes.[8] These uses of the clause seem to have attracted no controversy, with one notable exception. The controversial use of s. 33 was in Bill C-178, entitled An Act to Amend the Charter of the French language,[9] in which the Legislature of Quebec prohibited the use of English in outside commercial signs. This was a response to the decision of the Supreme Court of Canada in *Ford* v. *Quebec* (1988),[10] which had held that a law banning the use of languages other than French in commercial signs was an infringement of the Charter right to freedom of expression. After this decision, the Legislature re-enacted the prohibition with respect to exterior signs (while allowing bilingual interior signs), and protected the new prohibition with a notwithstanding clause. Section 33 was thus used to support a language policy that enjoyed widespread support among French-speakers within Quebec, although the law (and the use of s. 33) was very unpopular outside Quebec and contributed to opposition to the then-unratified Meech Lake Accord.[11] In 1993 when the notwithstanding clause reached the end of its five-year life, the Quebec Legislature lifted the ban on English language signs and replaced it with legislation that required only that French be predominant. This new legislation was not protected by a notwithstanding clause.[12]

4 S.Q. 1982, c. 21.

5 The Act did not override the Quebec Charter of Human Rights and Freedoms, thus making clear that the purpose was not to abridge civil liberties, but only to protest the imposed national Charter.

6 The validity of this use of the override was upheld in *Ford* v. *Que.* [1988] 2 S.C.R. 712; the case is discussed in the text that follows.

7 That policy caused the Government to agree to the Meech Lake Accord, which, however, failed to achieve two of the required eleven legislative ratifications in the three-year period allowed for ratifications, and therefore lapsed. See ch. 4, Amendment, under heading 4.1(c), "The failure to accommodate Quebec", above.

8 The four non-controversial exercises of s. 33 are described in Bayefsky, "The Judicial Function under the Canadian Charter of Rights and Freedoms" (1987) 32 McGill L.J. 791, 823-825.

9 S.Q. 1988, c. 54.

10 [1988] 2 S.C.R. 712.

11 Note 7, above.

12 S.Q. 1993, c. 40.

Outside Quebec, the power of override has been used just once. That was by Saskatchewan to protect a back-to-work law[13] of a kind that the Saskatchewan Court of Appeal in an earlier case[14] had held was contrary to the guarantee of freedom of association (s. 2(d)). When Saskatchewan enacted the override clause, the Government was in the process of appealing the earlier case to the Supreme Court of Canada. The Supreme Court of Canada later allowed the appeal, vindicating the Saskatchewan Government's view that the back-to-work law did not offend the Charter.[15] Thus, the use of the power of override was shown to be unnecessary. No other province except Quebec has ever used the power; nor has the federal Parliament.

36.3 Rights that may be overridden

Not all Charter rights may be overridden by the use of s. 33. The section applies only to the rights in s. 2 and ss. 7 to 15 of the Charter. This includes the fundamental freedoms (s. 2), the legal rights (ss. 7 to 14) and the equality rights (s. 15). It does not include the democratic rights (ss. 3 to 5), the mobility rights (s. 6), the language rights (ss. 16 to 23), the enforcement provision (s. 24) or the sexual equality clause (s. 28). As well, in order to be effective under s. 33(2), the declaration must refer specifically to the Charter provision that is to be overridden. It is clear that more than one provision can be referred to, or even all of the provisions contained in s. 2 and ss. 7 to 15,[16] but a declaration that did not specify any particular Charter provision would not be effective.

36.4 Five-year limit

The override power is subject to a temporal restriction. Section 33(3) is a sunset clause, under which an express declaration will automatically expire at the end of five years. Section 33(4) permits the express declaration to be re-enacted, but the re-enacted declaration will also expire at the end of five years (s. 33(5)). It is not perfectly clear whether a re-enacted declaration can be re-enacted a second time (to add a third period of five years), because s. 33(4) authorizes the re-enactment of only ''a declaration *made* under subsection (1)''. However, a declaration re-enacted under subsection (3) should probably be regarded as a declaration made under subsection (1), in which case the declaration is perpetually renewable. The purpose of the sunset clause is to force reconsideration by the

13 The SGEU Dispute Settlement Act, S.S. 1984-85-86, c. 111, s. 9.

14 *RWDSU* v. *Govt. of Sask.* [1985] 5 W.W.R. 97 (Sask. C.A.).

15 *RWDSU* v. *Sask.* [1987] 1 S.C.R. 460.

16 *Ford* v. *Que.* [1988] 2 S.C.R. 712, 737-742; discussed in sec. 36.5, ''Specificity of declaration'', below.

Parliament or Legislature of each exercise of the power at five-year intervals (intervals in which elections must be held).

36.5 Specificity of declaration

Section 33 stipulates that the Parliament or Legislature must "expressly" declare that a statute is to operate notwithstanding a Charter right. The exercise of the override power must therefore be express. It is not to be inferred by implication from the fact that a particular statute has been enacted in violation of the Charter. The express declaration contemplated by s. 33(1) thus becomes a "manner and form" requirement[17] that is essential to the validity of any statute enacted in violation of a provision contained in s. 2 or ss. 7 to 15 of the Charter.

Secondly, the express declaration contemplated by s. 33(1) must be specific as to the statute[18] that is thereby exempted from the provisions of the Charter. Indeed, the express declaration must be in the statute itself, although it can be added to a pre-existing statute by amendment (on the basis that an amending statute is construed as part of the statute that it amends). Whether s. 33(1) would authorize a blanket declaration which purported to apply to all statutes, or to a class of statutes described in general terms, is a question that was raised by Quebec's Bill 62, entitled An Act respecting the Constitution Act, 1982. This was the Act, mentioned earlier,[19] that was passed by Quebec as a kind of protest against the Charter of Rights (to which Quebec had not agreed). The Act added a standard-form notwithstanding clause to "each of the Acts adopted [by the National Assembly of Quebec] before 17 April 1982". The Acts referred to were not listed; they were identified only by the quoted phrase. In *Ford* v. *Quebec* (1988),[20] the Supreme Court of Canada held that this exercise of the override power was legally sufficient; the express declaration had been effectively inserted in each of the Acts coming within the omnibus description.

Thirdly, the express declaration contemplated by s. 33(1) must be specific as to the Charter right which is to be overridden. In the *Ford* case,[21] it was argued that the declaration should refer to the very right that was infringed by the particular Act in which the declaration appeared. That argument would have been fatal to the standard form of declaration that was in issue in that case. That

---

17 Manner and form requirements are discussed in ch. 12, Parliamentary Sovereignty, under heading 12.3(b), "Manner and form of future laws", above.

18 The express declaration must be contained in a statute. In the context of s. 33, "an Act of Parliament or of the legislature" would not extend to regulations, by-laws or other forms of delegated legislation, because that would enable the Charter to be overridden without full parliamentary debate: Gibson, note 1, above, 127-128; Beaudoin and Ratushny, note 1, above, 103-104 (by Tassé).

19 Note 4, above.

20 [1988] 2 S.C.R. 712, 742-743.

21 *Id.*, 740-742.

declaration referred to ''the provisions of sections 2 and 7 to 15 of the Constitution Act, 1982'',[22] which is, of course, a reference to all of the Charter rights that s. 33 makes vulnerable to the override. The Supreme Court of Canada held[23] that this omnibus reference to the rights was sufficient. It was not reasonable to require a reference that was particular to the statute containing the declaration, because a legislative body ''might not be in a position to judge with any degree of certainty what provisions of the [Charter] might be successfully invoked against various aspects of the Act in question''. For this reason, a legislative body ''must be permitted in a particular case to override more than one provision of the Charter and indeed all of the provisions which it is permitted to override by the terms of s. 33''.[24] Nor did the word ''expressly'' in s. 33 require that the Charter rights be identified in words (such as ''freedom of expression''). A reference to the numbers of the sections of the Charter was ''sufficiently express''.

36.6 Retroactive effect

In the *Ford* case,[25] the Supreme Court of Canada had to rule on the validity of Bill 62, entitled An Act respecting the Constitution Act, 1982, which was the Quebec statute that purported to insert a standard override clause in every one of Quebec's statutes. In the previous section of this chapter, we noticed that the Court upheld this exercise of the override power, despite the omnibus character of its specification of the statutes that it would protect and the rights that it would override. In one respect, however, Bill 62 was held to be unconstitutional, and that was its attempt to make the declaration retroactive. Bill 62 was enacted on June 23, 1982, but was expressed to take effect from April 17, 1982, which was the date when the Charter of Rights came into force. The Court held that the normal presumption against retroactivity should be applied to the language of s. 33, and the section should be construed as permitting ''prospective derogation only''.[26] The derogation of rights therefore came into force on June 23, 1982, the date of enactment, not on April 17, 1982, the date stipulated in Bill 62.

There is considerable appeal to the idea that rights should not be able to be taken away retroactively. As Weinrib has commented, the rule of law requires that a person be aware of his or her constitutional rights at the time of taking action, and not be vulnerable to retroactive change.[27] However, the ruling against retroactivity will probably encourage the use of s. 33. Before the *Ford* case was decided, it had always been assumed that a decision striking down a statute for

22 There were actually two declarations in issue in the case; both were in the language quoted in the text.
23 [1988] 2 S.C.R. 712, 741.
24 For criticism, see Weinrib, note 1, above.
25 [1988] 2 S.C.R. 712.
26 *Id.*, 744.
27 Weinrib, note 1, above, 559.

breach of the Charter could be retroactively reversed by the competent legislative body by the exercise of its override power. Indeed, one learned article had argued that this was the *only* permissible use of s. 33.[28] Now that this option is no longer open, it is to be expected that legislative bodies, when limiting rights, will sometimes include cautionary override clauses to insure against the risk of an adverse judicial decision on s. 1 justification.[29]

36.7 Judicial review

To what extent is the exercise of the override power subject to judicial review?

A declaration under s. 33 will be held to be invalid by the courts if it fails to satisfy the various requirements of s. 33 that have been described earlier in this chapter. The declaration must be confined to the rights specified in s. 33; it must be specific as to the statute that is exempted from the Charter, and as to the rights that are overridden; and it may not be given retroactive effect. These requirements are mainly formal, and, as we have noticed, are not very demanding.

Are there any other grounds upon which a declaration under s. 33 could be successfully attacked? It has been suggested that any declaration under s. 33 would have to satisfy the s. 1 standards of reasonableness and demonstrable justification.[30] Of course, those standards would have to be lower than they are for statutes unprotected by s. 33, because otherwise there would be no point in a legislative body exercising the power of override. But the application of s. 1 would introduce a degree of judicial review to the exercise of the override power, enabling courts to strike down those statutes that were in fundamental conflict with the values of a free and democratic society.

The thesis that s. 33 is subject to s. 1 is a difficult one to sustain. It is true that s. 33 does not expressly state that s. 1 of the Charter can be overridden. However, it is implicit in s. 33 that, once a Charter provision has been overridden by an express declaration in a statute, the Charter provision has no application whatsoever to the statute, and therefore there is no need for any showing of reasonableness or justification under s. 1. This view seems to have been accepted in the *Ford* case. Although the Court made no explicit reference to the s. 1 argument, the Court upheld the validity of the s. 33 override without considering its reasonableness or demonstrable justification. And the Court said[31] that s. 33

---

28 Greschner and Norman, note 1, above.

29 Where the statute deals with a temporary problem, such as an emergency, or a labour dispute, the damage may be irremediable by the time a court has ruled on the Charter issue. In other cases, it may be reasonable to await the Charter decision, even though it can only be overturned prospectively.

30 Slattery, note 1, above; Arbess, note 1, above.

31 [1988] 2 S.C.R. 712, 740.

''lays down requirements of form only'', and that there was ''no warrant for importing into it grounds for substantive review''.[32]

36.8 Evaluation of s. 33

Section 33 is viewed by many as an anomaly that is simply incompatible with constitutionally guaranteed rights. Certainly, s. 33 invites the question whether it is meaningful to speak about rights when the principal provisions of the Charter can be overcome by the enactment of an ordinary statute containing a notwithstanding declaration. A similar question was earlier addressed under s. 1,[33] but under s. 1 the decision whether a law can survive conflict with a guaranteed right is made by a court upon a showing that the law is a reasonable limit that can be demonstrably justified in a free and democratic society. Under s. 33, the Parliament or Legislature makes the decision for whatever reasons seem good to it.

The fact is, however, that if we put to one side the special case of Quebec, which has never given its approval to the Charter of Rights, we are left with only one use of the power of override. That use, by Saskatchewan, was cautionary only and was later established to be unnecessary when it became clear that the protected statute did not in fact abridge any Charter right.[34] It is clear that governments are exceedingly reluctant to use s. 33. The reluctance stems partly from a principled commitment to the Charter (not at present shared by Quebec) and partly from the political resistance that could be expected from opposition parties, the press, the organized bar and civil liberties groups. In practice, therefore, it seems clear that s. 33 will be used infrequently and only when the legislating government is persuaded that there are powerful reasons of public policy to justify its use. Despite s. 33, the fact that a right is in the Charter constitutes a significant obstacle to its abridgement, and places it in a much stronger position than a right that is not in the Charter.

We have earlier noticed the longstanding debate about the legitimacy of judicial review.[35] Of course, there is widespread agreement that certain rights ought to take priority over the wish of the majority, and that result can only be accomplished by giving to courts the power to strike down the majority's legislation when it unjustifiably abridges those rights. The difficulty is that in a civilized society like Canada the courts are rarely confronted with unequivocal

32 The thesis of Greschner and Norman, note 1, above, which would restrict the use of s. 33 to situations where there had been a prior judicial invalidation of a statute, is also contradicted by *Ford*, where there had been no such prior decision.

33 Chapter 35, Limitation of Rights, under heading 35.3, ''Relationship between s. 1 and rights'', above.

34 Section 36.2, ''History of s. 33'', above.

35 See ch. 33, Charter of Rights, under heading 33.4, ''Expansion of judicial review'', above.

examples of majority oppression. What tends to come before the courts are delicate questions of public policy in which community objectives are in opposition to individual rights. Aid to Catholic schools, Sunday closing, hate propaganda, obscenity, prostitution, mandatory retirement and the protection of the French language are examples, taken almost at random from recent cases. There is no general agreement as to the appropriate legislative response to such issues, because there is no general agreement on the weight to be accorded the various competing values. When legislation is enacted, it inevitably finds its way into the courts as a Charter case. There is no clear answer to such a case, either in morality or in law. The question of legitimacy is this: why should the views of non-elected judges prevail over the views of the elected legislators?

Once it is acknowledged that the definition of rights is often unclear, and that even clearly acknowledged rights must occasionally yield to other values, it is obvious that there is room for argument over the question of which institutions should have the power to determine questions of rights. The British solution is the doctrine of parliamentary sovereignty, under which there is no judicial review of statutes, and judgments of the Parliament are final. The American solution is judicial review, under which the courts have the power to review the legislative choices, and the judgments of the courts are final. The power of override places Canada in an intermediate position. Judicial review of statutes is, of course, a longstanding part of the Canadian Constitution, because it has been needed since 1867 to impose the rules of federalism on the two levels of government. But judicial review on Charter grounds dates only from 1982, and, by virtue of s. 33, a judicial decision to strike down a law for breach of s. 2 or ss. 7 to 15 of the Charter is not final. The judicial decision is subject to legislative review. If the competent legislative body still wants the law, it can re-enact it by including the notwithstanding clause contemplated by s. 33.

It is wrong to assume that a judicial decision on a rights issue closes the debate on that issue. On the contrary, citizens and their elected representatives will inevitably want to continue the debate, and in some cases there will be a strong sentiment in favour of reversing the decision of the Court. This can, of course, be accomplished by constitutional amendment, but this is such a difficult process that it can rarely be invoked with any prospect of success. In the United States, where the Bill of Rights is unqualified by an override power, the political response to a decision considered unjust or harmful is to attack the Court, and to attempt to change its composition. We have noticed that the threat of packing the Supreme Court of the United States was used by President Roosevelt to influence the Court in favour of his new deal legislation. And in recent times a series of appointments by Republican Presidents has been made with the avowed purpose of reversing some of the controversial civil libertarian decisions of the Warren Court. These kinds of reactions, which draw the Court itself deeply into the realm of partisan politics, are much less likely in Canada, where the power of legislative override is always on standby. The override power is exercised after a reasoned debate in a public forum addressed to a particular issue of justice and public policy, and this is preferable (I think) to the court-bashing and the court-packing that is a staple of federal politics in the United States.

It is also wrong to assume that a judicial decision at the highest level is always "right". There are no right and wrong decisions on the issues that reach the Supreme Court of Canada. More than this, however, judges have their biases and blind spots, like the rest of humanity. And they are often poorly informed about the costs and other consequences of their decisions. If the judges have the last word on the issues of social and political justice that arise in the form of Charter litigation, there is no guarantee that the issues will always be decided more wisely than if the last word rests with the peoples' elected representatives. The power of override allows for the rare case where the elected representatives are convinced that a judicial decision is an inappropriate answer to the rights issue. By that device, citizens are able to participate in the policy choices for their political community.[36]

While s. 33 looks odd to non-Canadian observers, it has precedents in the Canadian Bill of Rights[37] and in the statutory bills of rights enacted by Saskatchewan,[38] Alberta[39] and Quebec.[40] Each of those instruments confers a power of override on the Parliament or Legislature. The power of override seems to be a uniquely Canadian invention, which makes judicial review suspensory only. So long as the last word remains with the competent legislative body, there can be no acute or longstanding conflict between the judicial and legislative branches, and much of the American debate over the legitimacy of judicial review is

36 For a defence of s. 33 to which the foregoing account is indebted, see Russell, note 1, above.

37 Canadian Bill of Rights, R.S.C. 1985, Appendix III. By s. 2, the Bill applies "unless it is expressly declared by an Act of the Parliament of Canada that it shall operate notwithstanding the Canadian Bill of Rights". This provision undoubtedly provided the model for s. 33 of the Charter. But the override power in the Bill is a less refined instrument in that it applies to all of the provisions of the Bill (instead of just some of them), it does not require that particular provisions be referred to in the declaration, and it does not impose any time-limit on the duration of the declaration. The override power in the Bill has been used just once: Public Order (Temporary Measures) Act, S.C. 1970-71-72, c. 2, s. 12.

38 The Saskatchewan Human Rights Code, S.S. 1979, c. S-24.1, includes an override power (s. 44) which is similar to the one in the Canadian Bill of Rights. It has been used once, in the same Act that overrode the Charter of Rights, namely, the SGEU Dispute Settlement Act, S.S. 1984-85-86, c. 111, s. 9; note 13, above, and accompanying text.

39 The Alberta Bill of rights, R.S.A. 1980, c. A-16, includes an override power (s. 2) which is similar to the one in the Canadian Bill of Rights. It has never been used.

40 Quebec's Charter of Human Rights and Freedoms, R.S.Q. 1977, c. C-12, includes an override power. Section 52 provides:

> Sections 9 to 38 prevail over any provision of any subsequent act which may be inconsistent therewith unless such act expressly states that it applies despite the Charter.

This override power had been used nine times by 1981. The nine statutes are listed in Herbert Marx, Débats de l'Assemblée nationale, Quebec, October 6, 1981, p. B1286.

rendered irrelevant. That is why Professor Weiler has described s. 33 as ''an intrinsically sound solution to the dilemma of rights and courts''.[41]

---

41 Weiler, ''Rights and Judges in a Democracy: A New Canadian Version'' (1984) 18 Jo. of Law Reform 51, 80.

37

Enforcement of Rights

37.1 Supremacy clause

(a) Section 52(1)

Section 52(1) of the Constitution Act, 1982[1] provides as follows:

1 For commentary on ss. 24(1) and 52(1), see Gibson, *The Law of the Charter: General Principles* (1986), chs. 6, 8; Beaudoin and Mendes (eds.), *The Canadian Charter of Rights and Freedoms* (3rd ed., 1996), 2-49–2-70 (by Tassé and Tassé), ch. 19 (by Gibson and Gee); McLeod, Takach, Morton, Segal, *The Canadian Charter of Rights* (Carswell, loose-leaf), chs. 28, 30; Fitzgerald, *Understanding Charter Remedies* (Carswell, loose-leaf); Roach, *Constitutional Remedies in Canada* (Canada Law Book, loose-leaf); *Canadian Charter of Rights Annotated* (Canada Law Book, loose-leaf), annotations to ss. 24 and 52. The last work provides a bibliography of the relevant literature.

> The Constitution of Canada is the supreme law of Canada, and any law that is inconsistent with the provisions of the Constitution is, to the extent of the inconsistency, of no force or effect.

This supremacy clause gives to the Charter overriding effect. Since the Charter is part of the "Constitution of Canada",[2] any law that is inconsistent with the Charter is "of no force or effect". Since it inevitably falls to the courts to determine whether or not a law is inconsistent with the Charter, s. 52(1) provides an explicit basis for judicial review of legislation in Canada. Of course, as related in chapter 5 on Federalism,[3] Canadian courts long ago assumed and exercised the power of judicial review to enforce the distribution-of-powers rules of federalism and other restrictions contained in the British North America Act, and they would have enforced the Charter in the same way. Section 52(1) merely articulates the previous practice.

Before the adoption of the Charter of Rights in 1982, judicial review of legislation could take place in a wide variety of legal proceedings; for example, review could occur on a reference for an advisory opinion, an action for a declaratory judgment or an injunction, an application to review the decision of an administrative agency or official, or as a collateral issue in a criminal or civil proceeding. Whenever the constitutionality of a statute was properly placed in issue, and was relevant to the outcome of the case, the presiding court was obliged to determine the constitutional question.[4] This continues to be true under the Charter: all the remedies that have been available in the past continue to be available.

(b) Section 24(1) compared

As noted in the previous section, the effect of the supremacy clause (s. 52(1)) is to preserve all pre-existing remedies for unconstitutional action and to extend those remedies to the Charter of Rights. In addition, however, the Charter contains its own remedy clause, namely, s. 24. Section 24(1) authorizes a court of competent jurisdiction to award a remedy for breach of the Charter. Section 24(2) authorizes a court of competent jurisdiction to exclude evidence obtained in breach of the Charter; the power to exclude evidence is the topic of the next chapter.[5]

The remedy clause of s. 24(1) is examined in the latter part of this chapter.[6] However, it is worth setting it out here, and briefly noting the differences between s. 24(1) and s. 52(1). Section 24(1) provides:

---

2 The term "Constitution of Canada" is defined in s. 52(2)(a) as including the Constitution Act, 1982, of which the Charter is Part I.

3 Chapter 5, Federalism, under heading 5.5, "Role of the Courts", above.

4 See ch. 56, Procedure, below.

5 Chapter 38, Exclusion of Evidence, below.

6 Section 37.2, "Remedy clause", below.

> Anyone whose rights or freedoms, as guaranteed by this Charter, have been infringed or denied may apply to a court of competent jurisdiction to obtain such remedy as the court considers appropriate and just in the circumstances.

The differences between s. 24(1) and s. 52(1), which will be elaborated as the chapter progresses, may be briefly noted at this point. First, s. 24(1) is applicable only to breaches of the Charter of Rights; s. 52(1) is applicable to the entire Constitution of Canada, including the Charter of Rights. Secondly, s. 24(1) is available only to a person whose rights have been infringed; s. 52(1) is available in some circumstances to persons whose rights have not been infringed.[7] Thirdly, s. 24(1) may be applied only by a "court of competent jurisdiction"; s. 52(1) may be applied by any court or tribunal with power to decide questions of law.[8] Fourthly, s. 24(1) authorizes the award of a wide range of remedies; s. 52(1) appears to authorize only a holding of invalidity, leaving it to the general law to authorize the particular remedy. Fifthly, s. 24(1) confers a discretion on the court as to whether any remedy should be awarded; s. 52(1) appears to confer no discretion on the court, requiring the court to make a holding of invalidity if it concludes that a law or act is inconsistent with the Constitution.

In the fourth and fifth propositions of the previous paragraph, I have pointed out that s. 52(1) expressly contemplates only a holding of invalidity as a remedy for inconsistency between a statute and the Constitution of Canada and that s. 52(1) does not in terms confer any discretion on the courts. However, in Charter cases, the courts have in fact developed a number of variations on a simple declaration of invalidity, and have assumed the power to choose from a range of possible remedies.[9] There are in fact six choices available to a court under s. 52(1):

1. Nullification, that is, striking down (declaring invalid) the statute that is inconsistent with the Constitition;
2. Temporary validity, that is, striking down the statute that is inconsistent with the Constitution, but temporarily suspending the coming into force of the declaration of invalidity;
3. Severance, that is, holding that only part of the statute is inconsistent with the Constitution, striking down only that part and severing it from the valid remainder;
4. Reading in, that is, adding words to a statute that is inconsistent with the Constitution so as to make the statute consistent with the Constitution and valid;
5. Reading down, that is, interpreting a statute that could be interpreted as inconsistent with the Constitution so that it is consistent with the Constitution; and
6. Constitutional exemption, that is, creating an exemption from a statute that is partly inconsistent with the Constitution so as to exclude from the statute the application that would be inconsistent with the Constitution.

Each of these six remedies is discussed in the text that follows. It must be emphasized that each of the six remedies is authorized by the supremacy clause of s. 52(1), and does not require the authority of the remedy clause of s. 24(1). The distinctive role of s. 24(1) is the topic of the latter part of this chapter.[10]

---

7 Section 37.2(d), "Standing", below.

8 Section 37.3, "Administrative tribunals", below.

9 The remedies available, and the criteria of choice, are fully discussed by Lamer C.J. in *Schachter v. Can.* [1992] 2 S.C.R. 679, 695-719.

10 Section 37.2, "Remedy clauses", below.

(c) Nullification

Section 52(1) (the supremacy clause) stipulates that "any law that is inconsistent with the provisions of the Constitution is, to the extent of the inconsistency, of no force or effect". This language requires a court to hold that an unconstitutional law is invalid. If a law is found by a court to be inconsistent with the Charter of Rights, the court is obliged to strike the law down. The effect of such a holding is that the litigation will be determined as if the unconstitutional law did not exist.[11] If the litigation is a criminal prosecution, the person charged under the invalid law will be entitled to be acquitted. If the litigation is a civil action, the party relying on the invalid law will lose the legal basis for his or her case.

(d) Temporary validity

While s. 52(1) requires a court to hold that an unconstitutional statute is invalid, the courts have assumed the power to postpone the operation of the declaration of invalidity. When a court exercises this power, the effect is to grant a period of temporary validity to an unconstitutional statute, because the statute will remain in force until the expiry of the period of postponement.

In *Re Manitoba Language Rights* (1985),[12] a case that is discussed more fully later in this book,[13] the Supreme Court of Canada assumed the power to hold that unconstitutional laws were to be given "temporary force and effect" to allow the Legislature time to enact the required corrective legislation. That was a highly unusual case in that the Manitoba Legislature's failure to enact laws in French as well as English had invalidated the entire Manitoba statute book. The Court invoked the "rule of law" ("necessity" would have been the more conventional rubric) to keep the unconstitutional laws temporarily in force in order to avoid a vacuum of law in the province. This was a radical exercise of judicial power, because a body of unconstitutional law was maintained in force solely by virtue of the Court's order.

The *Manitoba Language* case appeared to be unique at the time. However, it turned out that the laws of Saskatchewan and Alberta were in a similar plight, because a pre-confederation statute required that they be enacted in French as well as English, and the laws had in fact been enacted in English only. The Supreme Court of Canada followed its earlier decision and filled the vacuum of law by declaring a period of temporary validity to allow the two Legislatures the

---

11 The effect of an unconstitutional law is examined in more detail in chapter 55, Effect of Unconstitutional Law, below.

12 [1985] 1 S.C.R. 721.

13 Chapter 55, Effect of Unconstitutional Law, under heading 55.8(a), "The Manitoba Language Rights Reference", below. That same chapter, under heading 55.1, "Invalidity of unconstitutional law", discusses the technique of prospective overruling, which bears a close affinity to the remedy ordered in the *Manitoba Language* case.

time to take curative action.[14] In yet another case,[15] the Court employed the same technique to maintain in force the by-laws and other acts of a Quebec municipality that had been invalidly incorporated, but which had in fact been functioning for a period of six years. These cases are discussed more fully later in this book.[16]

The *Manitoba Language* case and its companions were not Charter cases. In each case, the invalidity flowed from a failure to comply with a non-Charter rule of the Constitution. But the Supreme Court of Canada has several times given delayed effect to a Charter ruling in order to allow governmental authorities time to accommodate to the ruling. In *R.* v. *Brydges* (1990),[17] Lamer J. for the majority of the Supreme Court of Canada, after deciding that the police were under a constitutional duty to advise all persons under arrest of the availability of legal aid, allowed a ''transition period'' of 30 days to enable the police forces to prepare new cautions.[18] In *R.* v. *Askov* (1990),[19] Cory J. for the majority of the Supreme Court of Canada, after deciding that the District of Peel in Ontario had unreasonable systemic delay in its criminal court process, raised the possibility of ''a transitional period of lenient treatment of systemic delay''.[20] Unfortunately, he decided not to allow any such period of leniency, which caused thousands of criminal charges to be stayed over the next few months, because the District's huge backlog of cases could not be cleared overnight.

Brydges and *Askov* did not involve unconstitutional legislation; but there is now a series of cases in which courts have maintained legislation in force after holding it to be invalid for breach of the Charter of Rights. In *Dixon* v. *British Columbia* (1989),[21] McLachlin C.J., who was then the Chief Justice of the Supreme Court of British Columbia (she was later elevated to the Supreme Court of Canada), held that the provincial legislation prescribing electoral districts for the province was unconstitutional; the disparity between the voting populations of different districts was so great as to violate s. 3 of the Charter (which guarantees the right to vote). Having reached this decision, she pointed out that the nullification of the legislation would leave the province without the means of holding an election, and in a system of responsible government it was possible for an election to be called at any time. This qualified as ''an emergency'' comparable to that recognized in *Re Manitoba Language Rights*, and a similar order was

---

14 *R.* v. *Mercure* [1988] 1 S.C.R. 234 (Sask.); *R.* v. *Paquette* [1990] 2 S.C.R. 1103 (Alta.).

15 *Sinclair* v. *Que.* [1992] 1 S.C.R. 579.

16 Chapter 55, Effect of Unconstitutional Law, under headings 55.8(c), ''The Mercure case,'' and 55.8(d), ''The Paquette case'', below.

17 [1990] 1 S.C.R. 190. Lamer J. wrote for the majority of four. La Forest J. wrote a concurring judgment for a minority of three; he found it unnecessary to deal with the question of whether the police needed to prepare new cautions.

18 *Id.*, 217.

19 [1990] 2 S.C.R. 1199. Cory J. wrote for five judges. There were four short concurring opinions which made no reference to the possibility of a transitional period.

20 *Id.*, 1231.

21 (1989) 59 D.L.R. (4th) 247 (B.C.S.C.).

required.[22] She therefore held that the unconstitutional legislation "will stay provisionally in place to avoid the constitutional crisis which would occur should a precipitate election be required".[23] The legislation would remain in place for the time that "may reasonably be required to remedy the legislation", and she left that period to be fixed by a later order of the court.[24] An order was subsequently sought before another judge, who declined to impose any deadline on the Legislature, holding that the Legislature should be left "to do what is right in its own time".[25] New legislation was in fact enacted in time for the next provincial election,[26] which took place more than two years later — in October, 1991.

In *R.* v. *Swain* (1991),[27] the majority of the Supreme Court of Canada struck down the provisions of the Criminal Code that required the detention in a psychiatric facility of a person acquitted on the ground of insanity. The Criminal Code provisions were held to be contrary to ss. 7 and 9 of the Charter. The invalidity of the provisions meant that a person acquitted on the ground of insanity would simply be released like any other accused who had been found not guilty at his or her trial. Since a person acquitted on the ground of insanity has usually committed a serious offence, and may well be a continued danger to the public, his or her release into the community would often involve serious risks. (This, of course, was the reason for the provisions requiring the detention of a person acquitted on the ground of insanity.) The Court held that there was to be a six-month "period of temporary validity" so that judges would not be compelled to release into the community all insanity acquittees.[28] The Court evidently assumed that the six-month period would enable the federal government to prepare, and Parliament to enact, replacement provisions which, perhaps by providing additional standards and a separate hearing on the necessity for detention, could overcome the constitutional disabilities of its predecessor.[29]

In *R.* v. *Bain* (1992),[30] the majority of the Supreme Court of Canada struck down the provisions of the Criminal Code that allowed the Crown prosecutor, but not the accused, to "stand by" prospective jurors. The provisions were held to be contrary to the guarantee of a fair trial in s. 11(d) of the Charter, because they gave the Crown more influence than the accused in the selection of the jury. In this case too, the declaration of invalidity was suspended for six months in

---

22 *Id.*, 283.
23 *Id.*, 284.
24 *Ibid.*
25 (1989) 60 D.L.R. (4th) 445, 448 (B.C.S.C.).
26 S.B.C. 1990, c. 39.
27 [1991] 1 S.C.R. 933.
28 *Id.*, 1021, 1037.
29 Seven months after the Court handed down its decision, Parliament repealed the offending provisions and replaced them with provisions that established more comprehensive standards and mandatory hearings on the necessity for detention: S.C. 1991, c. 43, adding new Part XX.1 (Mental Disorder) to the Criminal Code.
30 [1992] 1 S.C.R. 91.

order to "provide an opportunity for Parliament to remedy the situation if it considers it appropriate to do so".[31] There was no explanation of how the six-month period was arrived at, or, indeed, why the declaration of invalidity should be suspended. The invalidity of the stand-by provisions certainly did not pose a danger to the public or a threat to the rule of law.

In *Schachter* v. *Canada* (1992),[32] the Supreme Court of Canada held that a provision of the federal Unemployment Insurance Act offended the guarantee of equality s. 15 of the Charter of Rights, because the provision allowed more generous child care benefits to adoptive parents than to natural parents.[33] This meant that the statute was "under-inclusive",[34] meaning that it failed to include a class of people (natural parents, in this case) that had an equality-based constitutional right to be included. Lamer C.J. for the majority of the Court pointed out that striking down an under-inclusive statute would have the perverse result of denying the statutory benefits to the deserving class that was covered by the statute (adoptive parents in this case), while granting no benefit to the class that was unconstitutionally excluded (natural parents in this case). He concluded that: "The logical remedy is to strike down but suspend the declaration of invalidity to allow the government to determine whether to cancel or extend the benefits".[35] In fact, by the time the Court rendered its decision in *Schachter*, Parliament had amended the Act so as to equalize the position of adoptive and natural parents. The Court held, therefore, that there was "no need for a declaration of invalidity or a suspension thereof".[36]

In *Schachter*, although the Court was willing to grant a temporary period of validity in that case, Lamer C.J. recognized the radical character of the remedy. In the first place, it maintains in force a statute that has been found to be unconstitutional. In the second place, it is a "serious interference" with the legislative process, because the delayed nullification "forces the matter back onto the legislative agenda at a time not of the choosing of the legislature, and within time limits under which the legislature would not normally be forced to act".[37] For these reasons, Lamer C.J. held that it was preferable for the Court to rectify the

---

31 *Id.*, 104, 165. Parliament did remedy the situation by repealing the Crown's power of stand-by and giving the Crown the same powers as the accused with respect to jury selection: S.C. 1992, c. 41, s. 2, amending s. 634 of the Criminal Code.

32 [1992] 2 S.C.R. 679. The opinion of Lamer C.J. was concurred in by Sopinka, Gonthier and McLachlin JJ. La Forest J. wrote a short concurring opinion that was concurred in by L'Heureux-Dubé J.

33 This point was actually conceded by the Government of Canada, and the Court proceeded on the basis of the concession, despite doubt as to whether the concession was correct: *Id.*, 695, 727.

34 *Id.*, 715.

35 *Id.*, 716.

36 *Id.*, 725. The result was that the Court granted no remedy at all to the unfortunate plaintiff, despite his success on the substantive issue of equality rights. However, the Court did order the Crown to pay his costs.

37 *Id.*, 716-717.

statute by severance (discussed next) or reading in (discussed after severance) where those remedies were appropriate. Where those remedies were not appropriate (as in this case), and a declaration of invalidity had to be made, then the Court could provide for a temporary suspension of the declaration of invalidity in certain cases. Those cases were those in which the immediate striking down of the legislation (1) ''would pose a danger to the public'' (as in *Swain*), (2) ''would threaten the rule of law'' (as in the *Manitoba Language* case), or (3) ''would result in the deprivation of benefits from deserving persons'' (as in *Schachter* itself).[38]

(e) Severance

The topic of severance, in Charter cases as well as other constitutional cases, has been examined earlier.[39] Severance is the appropriate remedy when only part of the statute is held to be invalid, and the rest can independently survive. In that case, a court will hold that the bad part of the statute should be struck down and severed from the good part, thereby preserving the part that complies with the Constitution. Severance occurs in most Charter cases because it is unusual for a Charter breach to taint a statute in its entirety. For example, the invalidity of the search and seizure power of the Competition Act does not entail the striking down of the entire Act,[40] and the invalidity of the felony-murder rule of the Criminal Code does not entail the striking down of the entire Criminal Code.[41] Severance is a doctrine of judicial restraint, because its effect is to minimize the impact of a successful Charter attack on a law: the court's intrusion into the legislative process goes no further than is necessary to vindicate the Charter right.

Severance, as traditionally employed, is not designed to alter the meaning or effect of the remainder of the statute that survives. The remainder of the statute survives on its own merits, because in the form that it was enacted it was from the beginning consistent with the Constitution (and severable from the unconstitutional part). In a few Charter cases, however, the Supreme Court of Canada has started to use the doctrine of severance in order to repair a statutory provision that was invalid in the language in which it was enacted. In these cases, severance is used to amend the defective statutory provision by deleting the words that caused the constitutional problem.

In *R.* v. *Hess* (1990),[42] the Supreme Court of Canada reviewed the statutory rape provision of the Criminal Code. The provision made it an offence for a male person to have intercourse with a female person under 14 years of age, ''whether

38 *Id.*, 719. These ''guidelines'' will accommodate the *Manitoba Language* case, note 12, above, *Dixon* v. *B.C.*, note 21, above, and *R.* v. *Swain* note 27, above, but not *R.* v. *Bain*, note 30, above, although that case was decided only six months before *Schachter*.

39 Chapter 15, Judicial Review on Federal Grounds, under heading 15.6, ''Severance'', above.

40 *Hunter* v. *Southam* [1984] 2 S.C.R. 145.

41 *R.* v. *Vaillancourt* [1987] 2 S.C.R. 636.

42 [1990] 2 S.C.R. 906.

or not he believes that she is fourteen years of age or more''. The quoted language caused the offence to violate s. 7, because it eliminated the requirement of mens rea for an essential element of the offence, namely, the age of the girl. The constitutional problem could be corrected by excising the quoted words. The rest of the section would make sense without the words, and the normal requirement of mens rea would apply if there was no longer any language eliminating the requirement. The Court accordingly invoked the power of severance to strike out the unconstitutional words. No new words had to be inserted in order to import the requirement of mens rea. The result, of course, was a significant change in the statutory provision. The alternative would have been to strike down the entire offence, which would mean that intercourse with a girl under fourteen would no longer be an offence, even for a man who was aware of the girl's age — least until Parliament amended the Criminal Code to reintroduce the offence.

In *Tétreault-Gadoury* v. *Canada* (1991),[43] the Supreme Court of Canada held that it was a breach of s. 15 of the Charter to restrict unemployment insurance benefits to persons under the age of 65. There was an age-65 bar in the Unemployment Insurance Act, which took the form of an exception to the general rules of entitlement. If the age-65 bar were excised from the Act, the normal rules of entitlement would operate without any limitation as to age. The Court therefore simply invoked the power of severance to remove the age-65 bar from the Act. The effect of this was to require payment of unemployment insurance benefits to persons over 65. This meant that the plaintiff became entitled to benefits, because she was a person over 65 who was otherwise qualified. As in *Hess*, the Court's decision caused a significant change in the statutory provision.

What is new about the use of severance in *Hess* and *Tétreault-Gadoury* is that in both those cases words were deleted from a statutory provision that were integral to the operation of the provision. The rest of the provision could survive only because it had been altered by the Court's deletion of the severed words. The provision was invalid in the language in which it was enacted by Parliament, and could be upheld only after the Court had amended it. In *Hess*, Parliament had created the offence of statutory rape as one of absolute liability, in which the accused's ignorance of the girl's true age was no defence. The Court used the technique of severance to amend the offence from one of absolute liability to one of mens rea. In that new form, which was never enacted by Parliament, the offence could be upheld. The same analysis holds in *Tétreault-Gadoury*: the deletion of the age-65 bar to unemployment insurance benefits was a deliberate amendment by the Court of the unemployment insurance scheme that had been enacted by Parliament. Only after the judicial amendment had been made could the scheme be upheld.[44]

---

43 [1991] 2 S.C.R. 22.

44 For further discussion, see Hogg, ''Judicial Amendment of Statutes to Conform to the Charter of Rights'' in Baudouin and others (eds.) *Mélanges Jean Beetz* (Les Éditions Thémis, 1995), 497.

In *Tétreault-Gadoury*, the statutory scheme of unemployment insurance was "under-inclusive", meaning that the scheme failed to include a class of people (those over 65) who had a constitutional right to be included. In such a case, the obvious remedy is to hold the statute unconstitutional, but this produces the harsh result of denying unemployment insurance benefits to persons under 65. The alternative[45] is to "extend"[46] the statutory benefits to persons over 65 by striking out the words that make the statutory scheme under-inclusive. However, the remedy of extension directly alters the statutory scheme and requires new expenditures by the federal government that have never been authorized by Parliament. Thus, a court faced with an under-inclusive statute has an unpalatable choice between the draconic remedy of nullification and the radical remedy of extension. In choosing the remedy of extension, the Court in *Tétreault-Gadoury* was influenced by the fact that by the time the case was decided Parliament had repealed the age-bar (although not with retroactive effect so as to entitle the applicant).[47] La Forest J. for the Court also said (rather cryptically) that "there was no evidence put forth that the government could not afford to extend benefits to those over sixty-five".[48]

(f) Reading in

Although the remedy in *Tétreault-Gadoury*[49] was a radical one, it did not involve adding new words to the Unemployment Insurance Act. The age-65 bar was simply deleted by the exercise of the Court's power of severance, leaving the plaintiff in a position to rely upon the general rules of entitlement. A much more difficult problem was presented to the Supreme Court of Canada in *Schachter* v. *Canada* (1992).[50] In that case, a claim was made by natural parents to child care benefits that were conferred only on adoptive parents by the federal Unemployment Insurance Act. The Act treated adoptive parents more generously than natural parents, which was agreed on appeal to be a denial of equal benefit of the law in violation of s. 15 of the Charter of Rights. But what was the remedy? There was no severable provision excluding natural parents from the child care benefits.

45 Another option is the suspended declaration of invalidity, which was held to be the appropriate remedy for an under-inclusive statute in the *Schachter* case, discussed at note 32, above, and note 50, below.

46 For American writing on the remedy of extension, see Beers, "Extension versus Invalidiation of Underinclusive Statutes" (1975) 12 Columbia J. Law and Soc. Problems 115; Caminker, "A Norm-Based Remedial Model for Underinclusive Statutes" (1986) 95 Yale L.J. 1185. The remedy of extension in Canada is discussed further in the next section, "Reading in", text accompanying note 67, below.

47 [1991] 2 S.C.R. 22, 46.

48 *Ibid.* His lordship did not indicate what kind of evidence he would find persuasive. It is not clear whether he was unwilling to take judicial notice of the notorious federal deficit, or whether he did not regard the deficit as making new expenditures unaffordable.

49 Note 43, above.

50 [1992] 2 S.C.R. 679; the case is also discussed at note 32, above.

The Act simply limited the benefits to adoptive parents. If that provision were excised, the perverse result would be to deny child care benefits to all adoptive parents.

In *Schachter*, the Supreme Court of Canada held that it possessed the power not only to sever language from a statute, but also to "read in" new language if that were necessary to remedy a constitutional defect. In principle, therefore, the defect in *Schachter* could be cured by "reading in" the class of natural parents to the statutory provision benefiting adoptive parents. Lamer C.J., speaking for a unanimous Court on this issue, explained that reading in would be a "legitimate remedy akin to severance",[51] despite the fact that it involved adding to a statute words that had never been enacted by Parliament. In other words, a judicial remedy was available to cure the under-inclusive statutory scheme even if new language had to be added to the statute in order to accommodate the unconstitutionally excluded class.

The Court in *Schachter* acknowledged that caution was called for in exercising the newly-assumed power of reading in. Reading in would be appropriate only in "the clearest of cases",[52] which seemed to mean cases where (1) the addition of the excluded class was consistent with the legislative objective, (2) there seemed to be little choice as to how to cure the constitutional defect, (3) the reading in would not involve a substantial change in the cost or nature of the legislative scheme, and (4) the alternative of striking down the under-inclusive provision would be an inferior remedy.[53] The Court concluded that the *Schachter* case was not an appropriate one for correction by reading in. The objective of the Act in making special provision for adoptive parents was not clear, and therefore it could not be assumed that the addition of natural parents to the provision would be consistent with the legislative objective. Furthermore, the reading in of natural parents (who are of course more numerous than adoptive parents) would cause a major increase in the scope and cost of the child care benefits legislated by Parliament. The Court concluded that "to read in natural parents would in these circumstances constitute a substantial intrusion into the legislative domain".[54] Instead, as related earlier in this chapter,[55] the Court held that the appropriate remedy was a declaration of invalidity suspended for a sufficient time to enable Parliament to amend the Act into conformity with the Constitution.

In *Haig* v. *Canada* (1992),[56] the Ontario Court of Appeal held that the Canadian Human Rights Act's prohibition of discrimination in employment was

51 *Id.*, 702. Reading *in*, which involves adding new words to a statute to remove a constitutional defect, should not be confused with reading *down*, which involves giving a narrow interpretation to a statute in order to avoid a constitutional defect. Reading down is the topic of the next section of this chapter.

52 *Id.*, 718 per Lamer C.J., 727 per La Forest J.

53 *Id.*, 718.

54 *Id.*, 723 per Lamer C.J.; La Forest J. agreed.

55 Text accompanying note 32, above.

56 (1992) 9 O.R. (3d) 495 (C.A.). The opinion of the Court was written by Krever J.A.

unconstitutional because it did not include sexual orientation as a ground of discrimination. The case had been brought by a plaintiff who had been discharged from the armed forces by reason of his homosexuality. He complained that, while the Canadian Human Rights Act afforded protection against discrimination based on "race, national or ethnic origin, colour, religion, age, sex, marital status, family status, disability and conviction for which a pardon has been granted", it did not cover discrimination based on sexual orientation. The Court agreed that the failure to include sexual orientation was a denial of the plaintiff's equality rights under s. 15 of the Charter. The plaintiff therefore succeeded in his claim that the Canadian Human Rights Act was constitutionally under-inclusive in excluding homosexuals from its protection. But what was the appropriate remedy? The Court, in an opinion written by Krever J.A., held that this was a case for reading in. The Court ordered that the Act was to be "interpreted, applied and administered as though it contained 'sexual orientation' as a prohibited ground of discrimination".[57]

In *Haig*, Krever J.A. gave a number of reasons for reading sexual orientation into the Canadian Human Rights Act. He said that this addition to the Act would be consistent with the objective of the Act and "would be less intrusive than the total destruction of the objective that would result from striking the provision down".[58] The Court did not have evidence of the estimated cost to government of extending the protection of the Canadian Human Rights Act to persons who complain of discrimination because of their sexual orientation, but Krever J.A. thought that it was "safe to assume that it cannot be so great as substantially to change the nature of the legislative scheme created by the Act."[59] In this case, unlike *Schachter*, the class to be added was much smaller than the class originally benefited. Krever J.A. concluded that it was "inconceivable" that "Parliament would have preferred no human rights Act over one that included sexual orientation as a prohibited ground of discrimination".[60] All these reasons suggested that reading in was the appropriate remedy.

The decision in *Haig* was not appealed by the Crown to the Supreme Court of Canada. Once reading in is admitted as a legitimate tool of judicial review, as *Schachter* has ruled, *Haig* does seem to be an appropriate case for the remedy. It should be noticed, however, that the remedy is a good deal more radical than Krever J.A. acknowledged. The Court's reasoning would apply with equal force to *all* grounds of discrimination that are analogous to those listed in s. 15 of the Charter of Rights. We know, for example, that "citizenship" is an analogous ground,[61] and other grounds will in due course be recognized by courts. Thus, the

57 *Id.*, 508.
58 *Id.*, 506.
59 *Id.*, 507.
60 *Id.*, 508.
61 See ch. 52, Equality, under heading 52.7, "Discrimination", below.

Court's decision to read into the Act the added ground of sexual orientation has the potential to extend the scope of the Act in ways that are difficult to predict.

In *Miron* v. *Trudel* (1995),[62] the Supreme Court of Canada applied the remedy of reading in.[63] The Court in that case held that Ontario's Insurance Act, which stipulated the terms of the compulsory automobile insurance policies in the province, contained an unconstitutional provision for an accident benefit that was payable to the "spouse" of an insured person. Because the definition of spouse in the Act was restricted to a person who was legally married to the insured person, the Court held by a majority that this provision discriminated against the claimant, who was the common-law spouse of an insured person. The exclusion of common-law spouses was discrimination on the basis of marital status, which was a denial of the claimant's s. 15 equality rights.[64] The Court held that the appropriate remedy for the constitutional defect was to read into the definition of spouse new language that would include the unconstitutionally-excluded class of common-law spouses.[65] The problem of formulating the appropriate language to read into the Act was solved by the fact that the Legislature had already amended the definition by adding common-law spouses, although it had done so after the claimant's cause of action arose by an amendment that was only prospective in its effect. This amendment also indicated how the Legislature would have remedied the constitutional defect had it been required to do so in time to qualify the claimant. The Court accordingly ordered that the language of the subsequent amendment be made retroactive to cover the claimant's claim of spousal status.[66]

Haig and *Miron* are both examples of the remedy of "extension". As in *Tétreault-Gadoury*,[67] in each of *Haig* and *Miron* the Court had to review an "under-inclusive" statute, that is, a statute that conferred a benefit on a class that failed to include all persons who had an equality-based right to be included. Unlike *Tétreault-Gadoury*, however, in *Haig* and *Miron* the extensions could not be accomplished by severing words from the statute; the extensions in *Haig* and

62 [1995] 2 S.C.R. 418. The majority opinion was written by McLachlin J., with the agreement of Sopinka, Cory and Iacobucci JJ. L'Heureux-Dubé J. wrote a separate concurring opinion, agreeing with McLachlin J. as to remedy. Gonthier J. dissented, with the agreement of Lamer C.J., La Forest and Major JJ.

63 See also *R.* v. *Laba* [1994] 3 S.C.R. 965 (unconstitutional reverse onus clause saved by striking out language imposing burden of persuasion on accused and reading in new language to substitute an evidentiary burden).

64 The case is discussed in ch. 52, Equality, under heading 52.7(b), "Must be on listed or analogous grounds", below.

65 This would also have been the remedy of the dissenting minority in *Egan* v. *Can.* [1995] 2 S.C.R. 513, 620, para. 220, per Iacobucci J., who would have held that the exclusion of same-sex couples from the spouse's allowance under the federal Old Age Security programme was a breach of s. 15.

66 [1995] 2 S.C.R. 418, 510, para. 180 per McLachlin J. The Court did not provide the time limit of retroactivity, but presumably the read-in language would take effect from April 17, 1985, when s. 15 of the Charter came into force (three years after the rest of the Charter).

67 Note 43, above.

Miron required the Court to read new words into the statute in order to extend its benefits to those who had been unconstitutionally excluded.

Once it is accepted that severance is available to extend the reach of a statute to make it conform to the Charter of Rights, it is only a short step to reading in. If severance allows the Court to delete something improperly included in a statute, it seems only appropriate to allow a Court to add something improperly excluded from a statute. As Lamer C.J. commented in *Schachter*,[68] it seems wrong that the "style of drafting" of a statute should be "the single critical factor in the determination of a remedy".[69] This line of reasoning leads inexorably to *Haig*, where the constitutional deficiency lay not in what the statute included, but in what the statute excluded. The Court corrected the deficiency by reading in the new ground of sexual orientation. The same kind of constitutional deficiency was present in *Miron* and was corrected in the same way, namely, by reading in the class of unconstitutionally-excluded common-law spouses.

There is no doubt that reading in is a serious intrusion by the courts on the functions of the legislative branch of government. So is severance, when it is employed (as in *Tétreault-Gadoury*) to extend the reach of an under-inclusive statute. However, the alternative of striking down the unconstitutional legislative scheme is also very intrusive. This is illustrated by *Nova Scotia* v. *Phillips* (1986).[70] In that case, the Nova Scotia Court of Appeal held that a welfare benefit that was available only to single mothers was in breach of s. 15, because the benefit was not available to single fathers as well. Being unwilling to extend the statutory provision by reading in the excluded group of single fathers, the Court was driven to nullify the provision, which denied the benefit to single mothers. This restored equality, but it was obviously an ironic and harsh result. Moreover, while the decision does not directly amend the unconstitutional statute, it does force the Legislature to act promptly to restore the nullified benefits, as well as to correct the constitutional defect.

A variation on the remedy of striking down an unconstitutional statute is to declare the statute unconstitutional, but suspend the declaration of invalidity for a stipulated period of time. As explained earlier,[71] this was held to be the appropriate remedy in the *Schachter* case. The attraction of the suspended declaration of invalidity is that it avoids the disruptive effects of the immediate retroactive nullification of a statutory programme, which is the normal consequence of a declaration of invalidity. However, the making of a suspended declaration of invalidity is close to a legislative function. To be sure, the court does not directly amend the unconstitutional statute, as the court does when it exercises its powers of severance and reading in. But the court takes upon itself the power to maintain in force for a temporary period a statute that is unconstitutional. And the time

68 Note 32, above.

69 [1992] 2 S.C.R. 689, 698.

70 (1986) 34 D.L.R. (4th) 633 (N.S.C.A.).

71 Text accompanying notes 32 and 55, above.

limit on the suspension has the effect of imposing on the competent legislative body a deadline to which it must conform on pain of the declaration of invalidity taking effect. Obviously, this is a major interference by the judicial branch of government with the agenda, priorities and procedures of the legislative branch.

One way or another, a group that has been unconstitutionally excluded from a legislated programme has to be added. None of the solutions is free from difficulty. In cases like *Tétreault-Gadoury, Haig* and *Miron*, where severance or reading in effects the necessary repair in a straight-forward fashion that seems consistent with the legislative objective, and that does not significantly alter the legislative scheme, there is much to be said for the direct judicial amendment of the statute by severance or reading in. Although severance takes away words that the legislative body enacted, and reading in adds words that the legislative body did not enact, these radical results need not be other than temporary. It is always open to the competent legislative body to enact a new legislative scheme — in compliance with constitutional requirements, needless to say — if the legislators are not content with the scheme as amended by the court. In this sense, the democratic legislative process retains the last word.

(g) Reading down

The topic of reading down, in Charter cases as well as other constitutional cases, has been examined earlier.[72] Reading down is the appropriate remedy when a statute will bear two interpretations, one of which would offend the Charter of Rights and the other of which would not. In that case, a court will hold that the latter interpretation, which is normally the narrower one (hence reading *down*), is the correct one. When a statute is read down to avoid a breach of the Charter, there is no holding of invalidity. The vindication of the Charter right is accomplished solely by interpretation. Reading down is another doctrine of judicial restraint, because it minimizes the impact of a successful Charter attack on a law.

Reading down should not be confused with reading *in*, which was the topic of the previous section of this chapter. Reading in involves the insertion into a statute of words that Parliament never enacted. It is not a technique of interpretation, but rather a technique of judicial amendment, altering the statute to make it conform to the Constitution. Reading in usually has the effect of extending the scope of the statute. Reading down, on the other hand, involves giving a statute a narrow interpretation in order to avoid a constitutional problem that would arise if the statute were given a broad interpretation.

---

72 Chapter 15, Judicial Review on Federal Grounds, under heading 15.7, ''Reading down'', above. While reading down is commonly used in federalism cases, its use in Charter cases has been less common; where it has been seen as tantamount to a reconstruction of the statute, the Court has been wary of the technique: Sharpe (ed.), *Constitutional Litigation* (1987), 248 (by Rogerson); *Osborne* v. *Can.* [1991] 2 S.C.R. 69, 76-77 per Wilson J., 101 per Sopinka J. The ''constitutional exemption'' is similar to reading down, and the Court has also been wary of this technique: sec. 37.1(h), ''Constitutional exemption'', below.

(h) Constitutional exemption

The Supreme Court of Canada has occasionally indicated, obiter, that it might be willing to grant a "constitutional exemption" from "otherwise valid legislation" that would be unconstitutional in its application to particular individuals or groups.[73] In the context of Sunday closing, the dicta seemed to indicate that a prohibition of retailing on a Sunday could be salvaged by reading into the legislation an exemption for those who observed some day other than Sunday as the sabbath. With this exemption, the Sunday-closing law would no longer offend the guarantee against freedom of religion. The advantage of the constitutional exemption is that it enables the Court to uphold a law that is valid in most of its applications by creating an exemption for those applications that would offend the Charter. The disadvantage of the constitutional exemption is that its scope must be defined by the Court, and the task of definition is likely to involve choice among a range of equally constitutional solutions; that is the kind of choice that should be made by the legislative body itself.

In *R.* v. *Seaboyer* (1991),[74] the Supreme Court of Canada considered the constitutional validity of the Criminal Code provision restricting the evidence that may be adduced by the accused in sexual assault cases of the past sexual activity of the complainant. This provision, which has been enacted in most jurisdictions of the United States, is known as a rape-shield law, because its main purpose is to shield the complainant in a sexual assault (or rape) case from cross-examination at trial. The Ontario Court of Appeal[75] had taken the view that in some situations the rape-shield section would violate s. 7 (or s. 11(d)) of the Charter, because it would deprive the accused of the right to make full answer and defence. Nonetheless, the Court of Appeal, following American authority, had upheld the section on the basis that there would only be rare cases where the section would exclude relevant evidence, and those cases could be accommodated by the doctrine of the constitutional exemption. In that way, the section could remain in force for the generality of cases, while leaving it open to an accused to establish that in the circumstances of a particular case the section should not be applied.

The Supreme Court of Canada reversed the Ontario Court of Appeal. The Court, by a majority, agreed that in some situations the rape-shield section would deprive an accused of the right to make full answer and defence.[76] However, the

---

73 *R.* v. *Big M Drug Mart* [1985] 1 S.C.R. 295, 315; *R.* v. *Edwards Books and Art* [1986] 2 S.C.R. 713, 783. A constitutional exemption from a Sunday closing law was granted in *R.* v. *Westfair Foods* (1989) 65 D.L.R. (4th) 56 (Sask. C.A.). See also *Osborne* v. *Can.* [1991] 2 S.C.R. 69, 77 per Wilson J. obiter (constitutional exemption not available), 105 per Sopinka J. obiter (constitutional exemption available).

74 [1991] 2 S.C.R. 577.

75 (1987) 61 O.R. (2d) 290 (C.A.).

76 L'Heureux-Dubé J. who, with Gonthier J., dissented, would have upheld the rape-shield section on the ground that it excluded only evidence that was either irrelevant or, if relevant, unduly prejudicial to the fairness of the trial.

Supreme Court of Canada held that this made the section unconstitutional. McLachlin J., who wrote for the majority, refused to salvage the section through the doctrine of constitutional exemption. The constitutional exemption would operate by importing into the section a discretionary power of dispensation by the trial judge. In her view, since Parliament deliberately chose to exclude any discretion on the part of the trial judge, the importation into the section of judicial discretion, "while perhaps saving the law in one sense, dramatically alters it in another".[77] In her view, the constitutional exemption would have much the same effect as striking down the section, because the admissibility of evidence under the constitutional exemption would be governed by common law notions of relevance. Finally (and perhaps inconsistently with the previous point), she noted that it would be difficult to define the scope of the constitutional exemption so as to provide guidance to trial judges.[78]

Seaboyer thus rejects the constitutional exemption as the salvation of what the Court regarded as the overbroad rape-shield law, but McLachlin J. made clear that she was not rejecting the solution in principle, and she said that "it may be appropriate in some other case".[79]

(i) Reconstruction

So far this chapter has been devoted to reporting the various techniques that are available to a court that finds a statute to be unconstitutional. Some of these techniques are highly intrusive of the legislative function, and two of them, namely, severance and reading in, have occasionally been used by courts to directly amend a statute in order to bring the statute into conformity with the Charter of Rights. After all this, it may seem disingenuous to claim that the general rule is that the courts may not reconstruct an unconstitutional statute in order to render it constitutional. That, however, is the general rule; and the creative use of the techniques of temporary validity, severance, reading in, reading down and the constitutional exemption should be seen as exceptions to the general rule.

There is a point at which a court will recognize that an unconstitutional statute cannot be salvaged except by changes that are too profound, too policy-laden and too controversial to be carried out by a court. It is all a matter of degree, which is difficult to articulate and to predict. As Lamer C.J. commented in *Schachter* v. *Canada* (1991):[80]

---

77 [1991] 2 S.C.R. 577, 628.

78 *Id.* 629.

79 *Id.*, 630. McLachlin J. found that "other case" in *Rodriguez* v. *B.C.* [1993] 3 S.C.R. 519, where she and three others, Lamer C.J., L'Heureux-Dubé and Cory JJ., all dissenting, would have allowed a constitutional exemption from the prohibition of assisting suicide for persons physically unable to commit suicide unassisted. However, Lamer C.J. (by himself) asserted (at 577) that a constitutional exempton could only be granted in concert with a suspended declaration of invalidity. Sopinka J. for the majority upheld the prohibition without any constitutional exemption.

80 [1992] 2 S.C.R. 679, 705.

> In some cases, the question of how the statute ought to be extended in order to comply with the Constitution cannot be answered with a sufficient degree of precision on the basis of constitutional analysis. In such a case, it is the legislature's role to fill in the gaps, not the court's.

This dictum serves as a reminder of the caution that should be exercised by non-elected courts in fashioning new laws. In a democracy, the primary responsibility for the enactment of new laws must always be that of the elected legislative bodies.

The general rule prohibiting a court from reconstructing an unconstitutional statute is illustrated by *Hunter* v. *Southam* (1984).[81] In that case, the Supreme Court of Canada held that the search and seizure power in the Competition Act was unconstitutional under s. 8 of the Charter, because the Act did not stipulate a standard of reasonable and probable cause for the issue of a search warrant, and did not invest an impartial judicial body with the power to issue the warrant. It was argued that the Court should "read in" the required standards, and uphold the power as judicially modified. Dickson J. for the Court refused to salvage the provision in this way; he asserted that "it is the legislature's responsibility to enact legislation that embodies appropriate safeguards to comply with the Constitution's requirements".[82] The Court therefore struck down the statutory provision, leaving Parliament to enact an amendment that would satisfy the constitutional requirements. Parliament did in fact amend the Act to that end.[83]

A similar argument in favour of the reconstruction of unconstitutional legislation was made and rejected in *Singh* v. *Minister of Employment and Immigration* (1985).[84] The Supreme Court of Canada held that the refugee-determination provisions of the Immigration Act were unconstitutional, because they did not provide for a hearing by an official with power to decide.[85] It was suggested that this result could be achieved by a cleverly designed order of the Court. But Beetz J. pointed out that there was "probably more than one way to remedy the constitutional shortcomings of the Immigration Act", and it was "not the function of this Court to re-write the Act".[86] There were occasions when "crude surgery" could be performed by the Court, "but not plastic or re-constructive surgery".[87] The Court accordingly struck down the refugee-determination procedure, leaving

81 [1984] 2 S.C.R. 145.

82 *Id.*, 169.

83 S.C. 1986, c. 26.

84 [1985] 1 S.C.R. 177.

85 Beetz J. with two others reached his conclusion — technically, that the Act was inoperative rather than unconstitutional — on the basis of s. 2(e) of the Canadian Bill of Rights. Only Beetz J. commented on the Court's refusal to reconstruct the offending provision. Wilson J. with two others reached her conclusion on the basis of s. 7 of the Charter, and her principal reason was the Minister's failure to disclose reasons for rejection to the refugee claimant.

86 [1985] 1 S.C.R. 177, 235.

87 *Id.*, 236.

it to Parliament to fill the lacuna with a new, and constitutional, provision. Parliament did in fact enact the required amendment.[88]

The Supreme Court of Canada again refused to reconstruct defective legislation in *Rocket* v. *Royal College of Dental Surgeons* (1990).[89] The offending legislation was a prohibition on advertising by dentists, with some limited exceptions. The Court held that the prohibition was a breach of freedom of expression and was not saved by s. 1. The Court made clear that some restrictions on professional advertising would be saved by s. 1, but it still struck the prohibition down in its entirety. McLachlin J. for the Court said that it was ''for the legislators'' to determine what kinds of advertising should be prohibited.[90]

There is one exception to the general rule that a court will not redraft a law in order to bring the law into compliance with the Charter. This is the rare case where the offending law is a rule of the common law. In *R.* v. *Swain* (1991),[91] the Supreme Court of Canada reviewed the common law rule that allows the Crown prosecutor in a criminal trial to adduce evidence of the accused's insanity against the wish of the accused. The Court held that this rule violated s. 7 of the Charter, because the evidence of insanity, if believed, would limit the right of the accused to conduct his or her own defence. The Court held that the rule would be saved by s. 1 if the issue of insanity were raised by the Crown in a separate hearing, in front of the same trier of fact, which would take place after the conclusion of the criminal trial, and which would only take place if the accused had been found otherwise guilty of the offence charged. The Court held that it was not necessary to strike down the existing law. Because the existing law was a rule of the judge-made common law, not statute, the Court had the power to replace the existing rule with a new rule that complied with the Charter. The Court therefore simply declared that a new rule, fashioned by it to comply with the Charter, was now the law![92]

37.2 Remedy clause

(a) Section 24(1)

Section 24(1) of the Charter[93] provides as follows:

> Anyone whose rights or freedoms, as guaranteed by this Charter, have been infringed or denied may apply to a court of competent jurisdiction to obtain such remedy as the court considers appropriate and just in the circumstances.

---

88 S.C. 1986, c. 13.
89 [1990] 2 S.C.R. 232.
90 *Id.*, 252.
91 [1991] 1 S.C.R. 933.
92 *Id.*, 978, 1036.
93 For commentary on s. 24(1), see note 1, above.

Section 24(1) provides for the granting of a remedy to enforce the rights or freedoms guaranteed by the Charter.[94]

(b) Applicable to Charter only

Section 24(1) is available only for a breach of the Charter. It is not a remedy for unconstitutional action in general. Breaches of other parts of the Constitution of Canada may only be challenged by the traditional methods referred to in the earlier discussion of the supremacy clause. In respect of enforcement, the Charter is thus in a preferred position. While many of the rights or freedoms guaranteed by the Charter existed before the Charter, in the sense that before April 17, 1982 Canadian law afforded some protection to them, the inclusion of a pre-existing right or freedom in the Charter has the effect of significantly strengthening the right: it becomes part of "the supreme law of Canada" to which inconsistent laws must yield (s. 52(1)), it becomes entrenched (alterable only by the process of constitutional amendment) (s. 52(3)), and it becomes enforceable under s. 24.

(c) Non-exclusive remedy

Section 24(1) is not the exclusive remedy for a breach of the Charter of Rights.[95] It will be recalled that the supremacy clause of s. 52(1), which is the topic of the earlier part of this chapter, renders "of no force or effect" any law that is inconsistent with the Constitution of Canada. As has been explained, s. 52(1) authorizes a court to hold that a law that abridges a Charter right is invalid. Whenever the validity of a statute (or other official act) is relevant to the outcome of a dispute, the court that is seized of the dispute has the power and the duty to determine whether or not the statute (or other act) is valid. For example, a court trying a criminal case is obliged to rule on the validity of the statute creating the offence if the defendant argues that the statute violates the Charter of Rights; if the court accepts the defendant's argument, then the court will acquit the defendant on the ground that the offence charged is not known to the law.[96] In this example, the ruling of invalidity is authorized by s. 52(1) and the remedy of acquittal is authorized by the Criminal Code. Section 24(1) is not needed in such a case, and it is not applicable.

As will be explained later in this chapter, an administrative tribunal may or may not be a "court of competent jurisdiction", depending upon the scope of its statutory powers. If an administrative tribunal is not a court of competent jurisdiction, then it lacks the remedial powers granted by s. 24(1). But, provided the tribunal has power to decide questions of law, the tribunal may still rule on the validity of a statute that is potentially applicable and that is argued to be in

94 The legislative history of s. 24(1) is related by Gibson, note 1, above, 192-195.
95 *R. v. Big M Drug Mart* [1985] 1 S.C.R. 295, 313.
96 *Ibid.*

violation of the Charter.[97] For example, if a union applies to a labour board for certification as the collective bargaining agent of agricultural workers, and a statute excludes agricultural workers from collective bargaining, the labour board would have the power to rule on the question whether the statutory exclusion of agricultural workers violated the Charter.[98] If the board held that the statutory exclusion was a violation of the Charter, then the board would also have the power to certify the union. In this example, the ruling of invalidity is authorized by s. 52(1), and the remedy of certification is authorized by the board's empowering statute. Section 24(1) is not applicable and it does not matter whether or not the board is a court of competent jurisdiction.

As these examples show, s. 24(1) is not needed to provide a remedy for a Charter infringement where a holding of invalidity is all that the applicant needs in order to obtain an appropriate remedy that is available under the general law. Section 24(1) is needed only where a remedy provided by the general law is not available for some reason, or will not provide satisfactory redress.

(d) Standing

Standing to apply for a remedy under s. 24(1) is granted to ''anyone''[99] whose Charter rights ''have been infringed or denied''. This imposes stricter requirements of standing than are applicable to many remedies under the general law.[100]

Section 24(1) contemplates that it is the applicant's own rights that have been infringed or denied. For example, it has been held that an accused could not complain about an unreasonable search of his girlfriend's apartment, even though the search yielded evidence (a cache of drugs) that was relied upon by the Crown as part of its case against the accused. Since the accused had no reasonable expectation of privacy in someone else's apartment, the search was not a breach of the accused's s. 8 right to be secure against unreasonable search or seizure. Only the tenant of the apartment could pursue a remedy under s. 24.[101]

A corporation cannot obtain a remedy under s. 24(1) for a denial of freedom of religion, because a corporation cannot hold a religious belief. But, in *R.* v. *Big M Drug Mart* (1985),[102] the Supreme Court of Canada held that a corporation could defend a criminal charge under a Sunday closing law on the ground that the law was a denial of the freedom of religion of individuals. The Court held that a defendant to a criminal charge was at liberty to raise any constitutional

97 Section 37.3, ''Administrative tribunals'', below.

98 *Cuddy Chicks* v. *Ont.* [1991] 2 S.C.R. 5.

99 The meaning of ''anyone'' is examined in ch. 34, Application of Charter, under heading 34.1, ''Benefit of rights'', above.

100 Standing under the general law is examined in ch. 56, Constitutional Litigation, under heading 56.2, ''Standing'', above.

101 *R.* v. *Edwards* [1996] 1 S.C.R. 128.

102 [1985] 1 S.C.R. 295.

defect in the law under which the charge is laid, because "no one can be convicted of an offence under an unconstitutional law".[103] The fact that the corporation had no standing under s. 24(1) to challenge the law was irrelevant. The challenge was based on the supremacy clause of s. 52(1): "Where, as here, the challenge is based on the unconstitutionality of legislation, recourse to s. 24 is unnecessary and the particular effect on the challenged party is irrelevant".[104]

In *R.* v. *Big M Drug Mart*, the corporation was allowed to invoke a right that did not extend to corporations in order to escape criminal liability under a statute that purported to apply to it. Sometimes a person, motivated by public interest, wishes to make a Charter challenge to a statute that does not even apply to the challenger. This cannot be done under s. 24(1). However, in *Minister of Justice* v. *Borowski* (1981),[105] the Supreme Court of Canada granted standing to an anti-abortion activist to bring an action for a declaration that the Criminal Code's abortion provisions were unconstitutional. Those provisions could never actually be applied to the applicant, who was neither a doctor nor a woman, but he was granted standing nevertheless. This illustrates that the availability of a declaration of invalidity under the general law is governed by more generous standing requirements than are the remedies authorized by s. 24(1).

(e) Apprehended infringements

Section 24(1) stipulates that the applicant's rights "have been" infringed or denied, which contemplates that the infringement has occurred at the time of the application. It does not authorize an application in respect of a merely apprehended future infringement. For example, no one could bring a s. 24(1) application after nothing more than an announcement of a new police interrogation procedure, even if the announced procedure was going to infringe the Charter. However, it seems to be generally accepted that the imminent threat of a Charter violation will satisfy s. 24(1).[106] For example, s. 24(1) will authorize a remedy for English-speaking parents who are denied by statute their Charter right under s. 23 to send their children to an English-speaking school, even if the application is made before the school year has started, and therefore before any parent's child has actually been refused admission.[107] It is not clear whether s. 24(1) will extend as

103 *Id.*, 313.

104 *Ibid.* Accord, *R.* v. *Morgentaler* [1988] 1 S.C.R. 30 (male doctor acquitted of performing an illegal abortion on ground that women's Charter right to liberty or security of the person infringed by law); *R.* v. *Wholesale Travel Group* [1991] 3 S.C.R. 154 (corporation successfully attacked part of law under which it was charged on ground that it infringed liberty of individual).

105 [1981] 2 S.C.R. 575.

106 E.g. Gibson, note 1, above, 195-198; Cromwell, *Locus Standi* (1986), 99-100.

107 *Que. Assn. of Protestant School Bds.* v. *A.-G. Que.* (1982) 140 D.L.R. (3d) 33 (Que. S.C.). This decision was affirmed by the Quebec Court of Appeal ((1983) 1 D.L.R. (4th) 573) and by the Supreme Court of Canada ([1984] 2 S.C.R. 66), although neither appellate court commented on the remedial issue.

far as the general remedies of declaration and injunction, which are both available in respect of threatened violations of rights.[108]

(f) Court of competent jurisdiction

Section 24(1)'s remedies may be granted only by a ''court of competent jurisdiction''. We have already noticed the important point that the power to make a finding of invalidity on Charter grounds under the supremacy clause of s. 52(1) is not restricted to a court of competent jurisdiction, but is possessed by any court or tribunal (with power to decide questions of law) before which the validity of the law is brought into contention.[109] The meaning of the phrase ''court of competent jurisdiction'' is thus relevant only to the availability of a remedy under s. 24(1).

A superior court, which is a court of general jurisdiction, is always a court of competent jurisdiction.[110] Therefore, an application for a remedy under s. 24(1) can always be made to a superior court. This does not mean that the application will always be successful if a Charter violation is established, because the award of a remedy under s. 24(1) is discretionary. If, for example, the applicant interrupted a trial in an inferior court in order to bring a s. 24(1) application before a superior court, the superior court should normally refuse the application on the ground that the trial court is the most convenient forum to hear the s. 24(1) application.[111]

A trial court, even if it is not a superior court, is a court of competent jurisdiction to hear an application for a remedy that relates to the conduct of the trial, for example, the exclusion of evidence that has been obtained in violation of the Charter or a stay of proceedings that have gone on for an unreasonable time. It is not necessary to make a separate application to a superior court, although a superior court would also be a court of competent jurisdiction. If a separate application were made to a superior court, the superior court should generally decline to grant any remedy, because it is the trial judge who is in the best position to assess what is the remedy that is just and appropriate.[112] However, a defendant to a criminal charge who has not been given a trial date, and is not likely to get one for a long time, has no trial court within reach, and therefore may apply to a superior court to stay the proceedings on the ground of unreasonable delay.[113] Even after the trial has commenced, an application to a superior court may be appropriate if it is the action of the trial judge that is the subject of the complaint;

108 de Smith, *Judicial Review of Administrative Action* (4th ed., 1980), 435, 480.
109 Section 37.1, ''Supremacy clause'', above.
110 *R.* v. *Rahey* [1987] 1 S.C.R. 588; *R.* v. *Smith* [1989] 2 S.C.R. 1120.
111 *R.* v. *Smith* [1989] 2 S.C.R. 1120, 1129.
112 *Ibid.*
113 *Ibid.*

for example, when the trial judge has failed to render a decision on a motion for a directed verdict.[114]

The Supreme Court of Canada has held that a judge conducting a preliminary inquiry into a criminal charge is not a court of competent jurisdiction.[115] This means that a preliminary inquiry judge has no power to stay proceedings on the ground of unreasonable delay under s. 11(b), and no power to exclude evidence on the ground that the evidence was obtained in breach of the Charter.[116] This is a rather surprising result when one considers that the preliminary inquiry judge would have to rule on non-Charter grounds on the validity of the charge and the admissibility of the evidence adduced.[117] In the case where the defendant claims that the trial of a criminal charge has been unreasonably delayed because too much time has elapsed even before the preliminary inquiry has been held, the defendant can make a separate application to a superior court to stay the proceedings.[118] But, in the normal course of events, Charter applications have to await the trial.

An administrative tribunal is a court of competent jurisdiction if its constituent statute gives it power over (1) the parties to the dispute, (2) the subject matter of the dispute, and (3) the Charter remedy that is sought. This was the ruling in *Weber* v. *Ontario Hydro* (1995),[119] in which a majority of the Supreme Court of Canada held that a labour arbitrator was a court of competent jurisdiction which could grant a declaration and damages under s. 24(1) for a breach of the Charter. In that case, Ontario Hydro was alleged to have engaged in unlawful surveillance of one of its employees who was drawing sickness benefits from the employer and who was suspected by the employer of malingering. On the assumption that the facts were as alleged and that the Charter applied, the surveillance by the employer would have been a breach of the plaintiff employee's right to be secure from unreasonable search and seizure. Did the labour arbitrator have the power to grant remedies under s. 24(1), or was the superior court the correct forum? Ontario's labour relations statute conferred on the arbitrator exclusive power to adjudicate "all differences" between an employer and an employee

---

114 *R.* v. *Rahey* [1987] 1 S.C.R. 588.

115 *Mills* v. *The Queen* [1986] 1 S.C.R. 863.

116 In *Mills*, previous note, Lamer J. alone took the view (obiter) (at p. 889) that the preliminary inquiry judge would be a court of competent jurisdiction "for the purpose of excluding evidence under s. 24(2)". The majority disagreed. Lamer C.J. repeated this opinion in *Mooring* v. *Can.* [1996] 1 S.C.R. 75, para. 6, relying on the later holdings (notes 87, 88, below) that administrative tribunals could be courts of competent jurisdiction.

117 Even more surprising is the holding in *R.* v. *Seaboyer* [1991] 2 S.C.R. 577 that the preliminary inquiry judge has no power to determine Charter issues under s. 52(1): see text accompanying note 167, below.

118 *R.* v. *Smith* [1989] 2 S.C.R. 1120.

119 [1995] 2 S.C.R. 929. McLachlin J. wrote the majority opinion which was agreed with by L'Heureux-Dubé, Gonthier and Major JJ. Iacobucci J. wrote the dissenting opinion which was agreed with by La Forest and Sopinka JJ. The dissenting view was that only a court could be a court of competent jurisdiction.

arising out of a collective agreement. This provided power over the parties and the subject matter. And the Act conferred on the arbitrator power to award a declaration and damages, which supplied the necessary power over the remedies sought by the plaintiff. Therefore, the labour arbitrator was a court of competent jurisdiction, and was the correct forum for the plaintiff's Charter claim.

In *Mooring* v. *Canada* (1996),[120] the National Parole Board revoked the parole of the applicant, who was a former prisoner on parole. The Board's decision was based in part on evidence (housebreaking equipment and a gun) discovered in an illegal search of the applicant's van. The applicant applied to the courts to quash the Board's decision on the ground that the Board ought to have excluded the evidence that had been obtained in breach of the Charter. This raised the question whether the National Parole Board was a court of competent jurisdiction, because only a court of competent jurisdiction would have the power to exclude evidence on Charter grounds. The Board had power over the parties and the subject matter of the dispute, but, according to a majority of the Supreme Court of Canada, the Board did not have power to grant the remedy sought. The Board's constituent statute required the Board to take into account "all available information that is relevant to a case". The majority's view was that this language disabled the Board from excluding any relevant information.[121] Therefore, the Board had no power to award the remedy sought, and was not a court of competent jurisdiction.

Weber and *Mooring* both emphasize that an *administrative tribunal* is not a court of competent jurisdiction unless it has jurisdiction, not only over (1) the parties and (2) the subject matter, but also over (3) the remedy sought. It was the third requirement that led to the different outcomes of the two cases. In the case of an administrative tribunal, it seems wise to confine the tribunal to its normal range of remedies, so that a Charter claim does not move it beyond its statutory mandate, which alone is the sphere of its undoubted competence. When it is a *court* that is claimed to be a court of competent jurisdiction, does the third requirement still apply? Putting the same question in another way, is a court to which a s. 24(1) application has been made, confined to remedies within its usual jurisdiction? The weight of authority favours an affirmative answer to this question: a court cannot grant a remedy under s. 24(1) unless it possesses jurisdiction, independently of the Charter, to grant that remedy.[122] The example which is commonly given to illustrate the value of this rule is the case of a criminal court asked to award damages against a police officer at the conclusion of a criminal

---

120 [1996] 1 S.C.R. 75. Sopinka J. wrote the majority opinion in which, on this issue, Lamer C.J., La Forest, L'Heureux-Dubé, Gonthier, Cory and Iacobucci JJ. concurred. Major J., with McLachlin J.'s agreement, dissented on the ground explained in the next note.

121 Major J., who dissented, pointed out that on the majority view the parolee was deprived of any remedy for the breach of his Charter rights. Major J.'s view was that the statutory language should be read as including a power to exclude evidence.

122 *Mills* v. *The Queen* [1986] 1 S.C.R. 863, 884-887 per Lamer J., obiter, dissenting, but not on this issue, citing many lower-court decisions.

trial in which it was established that the police officer's actions infringed the accused's Charter rights. It would be unfair for the criminal court to award damages against a person who has not been represented by counsel, who has not had the normal civil-action benefits of pleadings, discovery and production of documents or even a proper trial of the issue of his liability to damages. Plainly, a separate action in a civil court is the appropriate forum to dispose of the issue of the police officer's liability to damages.

Despite these powerful arguments, on balance, I incline to the view that the phrase "court of competent jurisdiction" does not limit the remedies which may be granted by a court on a s. 24(1) application. My view is based on three reasons. The first turns on the wording of s. 24(1). As Gibson has pointed out,[123] s. 24(1) deals separately with the questions of court of competent jurisdiction and remedy. After directing applicants to a court of competent jurisdiction, the section then empowers the court to grant "such remedy as the court considers appropriate and just in the circumstances". This structure invites the interpretation that s. 24(1) is itself the source of the court's remedial power, and a court which is competent as to subject matter and parties has a power, conferred by s. 24(1), to grant any remedy that the court considers appropriate and just in the circumstances. Secondly, s. 24(1) provides a constitutional right to a remedy. Legislative limitations on the remedial power of particular courts should not limit the power of those courts to grant a constitutional remedy. This has been recognized by courts that have held that the Crown cannot invoke its normal immunity from mandamus or injunction in order to shield an unconstitutional act.[124] Finally, it seems to me that s. 24(1) should be interpreted as enabling the courts to fashion completely new remedies for Charter violations, something that would not be possible if a court required a pre-existing remedial competence. In the hypothetical police officer case, for example, it might be appropriate and just for the criminal court to reprimand the police officer or to refer his actions to a police discipline board; a criminal court would not possess even those powers if it was confined to its normal remedial jurisdiction. For these reasons, I prefer to read s. 24(1) as a sufficient source of a court's remedial power.

---

123 Gibson, note 1, above, 283.

124 *Société Asbestos* v. *Société Nationale de l'amiante* [1979] C.A. 342 (Que. C.A.) (injunction granted against Crown to prevent implementation of unconstitutional law); *Van Mulligen* v. *Sask. Housing Corp.* (1982) 23 Sask. R. 66 (Q.B.) (injunction granted against Crown to prevent unconstitutional transfer of civil servant); *Levesque* v. *A.G. Can.* [1986] 2 F.C. 287 (mandamus issued against Crown to compel right to vote by prison inmates); *Air Can.* v. *B.C.* [1986] 2 S.C.R. 539 (mandamus issued against Crown to compel issue of fiat for proceedings to recover unconstitutional tax); see generally, Hogg, *Liability of the Crown* (2nd ed., 1989), 26, 34-35. *Mulligen* and *Levesque* were s. 24 cases; the others were invoking the general law of remedies, not s. 24.

(g) Range of remedies

The argument made in the previous section was that the phrase "court of competent jurisdiction" did not limit the range of remedies available under s. 24(1). Section 24(1) does limit the range of remedies by the phrase "such remedy as the court considers appropriate and just in the circumstances". While this phrase confers a discretion on the court, the cases are slowly developing principles that will structure and limit the discretion. For example, the courts have usually insisted that existing procedures be employed for s. 24(1) applications, so that well-understood procedural values are not ignored simply because a constitutional point is in issue.[125] This is why applications respecting the conduct of a trial should normally be made to the trial judge, who is in the best position to determine whether a trial should be delayed or interrupted.[126] For the same reason, the courts have generally refused to countenance the creation of new procedural mechanisms, such as the pre-trial motion to suppress evidence, despite its common use in the United States.[127] This kind of procedural caution would obviously bar the award of damages or other civil remedies in a criminal trial, where the person against whom the remedy is sought was not represented by counsel and has not received the normal civil safeguards of pleadings, discovery and the like, which ensure a proper trial of the issue of civil liability.[128]

Subject to the important qualification that a remedy must be appropriate and just in all the circumstances of the case, there is no limit to the remedies that may be ordered under s. 24(1).[129] They include "defensive" remedies,[130] where the court nullifies or stops some law or act, for example, by dismissing a charge, staying a proceeding, quashing a search warrant or a committal or a conviction, enjoining an act, or declaring a law to be invalid.[131] The exclusion of evidence obtained in breach of the Charter also falls into the defensive category, but the exclusion of evidence is subject to a special set of rules under s. 24(2), and it is discussed in the next chapter.[132] The remedies available under s. 24(1) also include

---

125 See Gibson, note 1, above, 284-286.

126 Note 111, above.

127 *Re Blackwoods Beverages* (1984) 15 D.L.R. (4th) 231 (Man. C.A.).

128 *Mills* v. *The Queen* [1986] 1 S.C.R. 863, 971 per La Forest J., obiter. Cf. *R.* v. *Zelinsky* [1978] 2 S.C.R. 940 (upholding validity of Criminal Code provision providing for compensation to victim, but suggesting circumstances in which compensation award should not be made).

129 The numerous cases in which remedies have been awarded by courts are collected in the two loose-leaf services cited in note 1, above.

130 The distinction between defensive and affirmative constitutional remedies is made by Hill, "Constitutional Remedies" (1969) 69 Columb. L. Rev. 1109 and Dellinger, "Of Rights and Remedies: the Constitution as a Sword" (1972) 85 Harv. L. Rev. 1532.

131 Note that defensive remedies will often be available under s. 52(1) (the supremacy clause), and no recourse to s. 24(1) will be necessary: sec. 37.1, "Supremacy clause", above.

132 Chapter 38, Exclusion of Evidence, below.

''affirmative'' remedies, such as ordering the return of goods improperly seized,[133] a mandatory injunction requiring positive action[134] or the award of damages.[135] In one case,[136] the court contemplated ordering a provincial Legislature to enact legislation to make provision for absentee voting, but the court contented itself with issuing a declaration that the absence of any provision for absentee voting was a breach of s. 3 of the Charter. The declaration can be a useful remedy which does not actually order the taking of positive action by a government, but which would almost invariably be obeyed by a government that was declared to be in default of its Charter duties.[137]

Selecting from the broad range of remedies which are possible under s. 24(1) of the Charter presents the courts with a difficult and value-laden task. As L'Heureux-Dubé J. has eloquently stated:[138]

> It is important to recognize that the *Charter* has now put into judges' hands a scalpel instead of an axe: a tool that may fashion, more carefully than ever, solutions taking into account the sometimes complementary and sometimes opposing concerns of fairness to the individual, societal interests, and the integrity of the judicial system.

It has been suggested that the court's discretion should be governed by three factors: (1) the redress of the wrong suffered by the applicant; (2) the encouragement of future compliance with the Constitution; and (3) the avoidance of unnecessary interference with the exercise of governmental power.[139] To these might be added: (4) the ability of the court to administer the remedy awarded. But, as L'Heureux-Dubé J. has emphasized, each case will also present its own unique set of considerations.

(h) Appeals

Section 24(1) does not authorize an appeal from the decision of a court of competent jurisdiction.[140] The existence of a right of appeal will depend upon the

133 E.g., *Re Chapman* (1984) 46 O.R. (2d) 65 (C.A.); *Lagiorgia* v. *Can.* [1987] 3 F.C. 28 (C.A.).

134 See Sharpe, ''Injunctions and the Charter'' (1984) 22 Osgoode Hall L.J. 473. As the author explains, in the United States, despite the absence of any equivalent of s. 24, it has been held that the ''civil rights injunction'' is available to enforce the Bill of Rights.

135 See Pilkington, ''Damages as a Remedy for Infringement of the Canadian Charter of Rights and Freedoms'' (1984) 62 Can. Bar Rev. 517; Cooper-Stephenson, ''Tort Theory for the Charter Damages Remedy (1988) 52 Sask. L. Rev. 1; Cooper-Stephenson, *Charter Damages Claims* (1990). As these sources explain, in the United States, despite the absence of any equivalent of s. 24, it has been held that damages are available for a breach of the Bill of Rights, which has created a class of ''constitutional torts'' by government officials. See also Hogg, *Liability of the Crown* (2nd ed., 1989), 112, 113.

136 *Re Hoogbruin* (1985) 24 D.L.R. (4th) 718 (B.C.C.A.).

104 E.g., *Re Gamble* [1988] 2 S.C.R. 595 (declaration that prisoner held in violation of s. 7 was eligible for parole).

138 *R.* v. *O'Connor* [1995] 4 S.C.R. 411, para. 69.

139 Pilkington, note 135, above.

140 *Mills* v. *The Queen* [1986] 1 S.C.R. 863; *James Doyle* v. *Anderson* (1990) 71 D.L.R. (4th) 731 (Nfld. C.A.).

rules of the court to which the s. 24(1) application was made. Where there is no existing right of appeal, as will often be the case in applications in criminal proceedings before the trial is over, there will be no appeal from the Charter ruling by the court of competent jurisdiction.[141]

In *Knox Contracting* v. *Canada* (1990),[142] the Supreme Court of Canada, by a majority, held that there was no appeal from a refusal by a judge to quash a search warrant issued under the Income Tax Act. The Court held that, because neither the Income Tax Act nor the Criminal Code provided for any right of appeal, there was no right of appeal, despite the fact that the applicant claimed that the warrant had been issued in breach of the Charter of Rights.[143] In *Kourtessis* v. *Minister of National Revenue* (1993),[144] another attempt was made to quash a search warrant issued under the Income Tax Act. This time the applicant applied for a declaration that the statutory provision authorizing the warrant and the warrant itself were unconstitutional for breach of the Charter. The Supreme Court of Canada was unanimous that an appeal was available in these proceedings. An application (or action) for a declaration of invalidity was a civil proceeding. The declaration "is not transformed from a civil remedy to a criminal remedy merely because the declaration relates to a criminal statutory provision".[145] It followed that the application for a declaration in this case was governed by the provincial rules of civil procedure, which made provision for an appeal. In this way, the rules of criminal procedure were bypassed, although the Court emphasized that there would be a discretion to refuse to issue the declaration if another procedure were available to resolve the constitutional issue.[146]

37.3 Administrative tribunals

(a) With power to decide questions of law

Can administrative tribunals decide Charter issues? The Supreme Court of Canada has answered yes to this question. In *Douglas/Kwantlen Faculty Asso-*

141 A wrong decision on a Charter issue by a court of competent jurisdiction, unless "manifestly and palpably wrong", will not be a jurisdictional error giving rise to judicial review by prerogative writ or other extraordinary remedy: *Re Corbeil* (1986) 27 C.C.C. (3d) 245 (Ont. C.A.). Of course, if the court of competent jurisdiction is a superior court, the prerogative writs and other extraordinary remedies would not normally be available to review the decision, although it is possible that the invocation of the Charter would remove the superior court's immunity: *Kourtessis v. M.N.R.* [1993] 2 S.C.R. 53, 90 per La Forest J., obiter; cf. cases cited in note 124, above.

142 [1990] 2 S.C.R. 338.

143 Sopinka J., dissenting, would have avoided this unfortunate result by classifying the Income Tax Act as a taxation law rather than a criminal law, and by allowing the appellant to invoke the appeal procedures allowed by provincial law.

144 [1993] 2 S.C.R. 53.

145 *Id.*, 114 per Sopinka J.

146 *Id.*, 86, 115.

ciation v. *Douglas College* (1990),[147] the Court held that an arbitration board, which had been appointed by the parties under a collective agreement, but which was empowered by statute to decide questions of law, had the power to determine the constitutionality of a mandatory retirement provision in the collective agreement. In *Cuddy Chicks* v. *Ontario* (1991),[148] the Court held that a labour relations board, which had been created and empowered by statute to decide questions of law, had the power to determine the constitutionality of a provision in the empowering statute that denied collective bargaining rights to agricultural workers. In both cases, it was necessary for the tribunal to resolve the constitutional issue in order to exercise its statutory jurisdiction. In the *Douglas College* case, La Forest J., for the Court, said: ''A tribunal must respect the Constitution so that if it finds invalid a law that it is called upon to apply, it is bound to treat it as having no force or effect''.[149] This conclusion was entailed by the supremacy clause in s. 52(1) of the Constitution Act, 1982. In effect, the tribunal was obliged to apply all of the relevant law, which included the Constitution as well as the relevant portions of contracts and statutes.

The power to decide the Charter issues in *Douglas College* and *Cuddy Chicks* did not come from the remedial provision in s. 24 of the Charter. Section 24's remedies are available only to a court of competent jurisdiction. In both cases, the Supreme Court of Canada expressly refused to decide whether an administrative tribunal could be a court of competent jurisdiction. Section 24 was irrelevant, because the applicants were not seeking any remedy for breach of the Charter, not even a declaration of invalidity.[150] The applicant was seeking a remedy that the tribunal was empowered to grant in the normal course of its jurisdiction: the reinstatement of wrongfully dismissed employees in *Douglas College* and the certification of a union in *Cuddy Chicks*. The Charter issue arose in the course of determining whether the remedy should be granted, because the Charter if applicable directed the tribunal to disregard a law that would otherwise bar the tribunal from granting the remedy sought. Thus, in *Douglas College*, the professors who had been mandatorily retired were entitled to be reinstated only if the mandatory retirement provision was invalid; and, in *Cuddy Chicks*, the union that had organ-

147 [1990] 3 S.C.R. 570. On the ability of the arbitrator to decide Charter issues, all judges agreed with La Forest J.'s opinion, except that Wilson J. (with L'Heureux-Dubé J.) preferred ''to leave open the question whether a tribunal may have such jurisdiction even in the absence of specific provisions in the governing legislation'' (606-607). (This reservation related to the fact that the arbitrator had express power to decide questions of law.)

148 [1991] 2 S.C.R. 5. The principal opinion was written by La Forest J., with whom all judges agreed, although Wilson J. (with L'Heureux-Dubé J.) added brief concurring reasons, making the same reservation as she had made in *Douglas College*, previous note.

149 [1990] 3 S.C.R. 570, 594.

150 The power to make a general declaration of invalidity is part of the jurisdiction of a superior court, but unless specifically granted by statute is not possessed by an inferior court or an administrative tribunal: [1990] 3 S.C.R. 570, 592. The determination by a tribunal that a law, which it is called upon to apply, is unconstitutional is not equivalent to a formal declaration of invalidity: *Id.*, 599.

ized the agricultural workers was entitled to certification only if the agricultural workers exclusion was invalid. But the applicants did not look to s. 24 for any remedy. Once s. 52(1) had invalidated the apparently applicable law, the exercise of the tribunal's ordinary statutory jurisdiction over the parties, the subject matter and the remedy would give to the applicants all that they asked for.

Where an administrative tribunal decides a constitutional question, its decision will be subject to judicial review by a superior court.[151] Indeed, an attempt by Parliament or a Legislature to enact a privative clause to bar judicial review would be unconstitutional.[152] Nevertheless, the tribunal's initial determination of the constitutional question is likely to make a useful contribution to the ultimate resolution of the issue. The tribunal's expert knowledge of the regulated field is likely to produce a well informed assessment of the strength of the constitutional arguments.[153] This fact was acknowledged by La Forest J. in both *Douglas College*[154] and *Cuddy Chicks*[155] but he also added in both cases that constitutional determinations by administrative decisions should receive "no curial deference".[156] In other words, a superior court, when reviewing the decision of an administrative tribunal on a Charter issue, should not defer to the decision of the tribunal, even if the tribunal has made a reasonable interpretation of the Charter. The superior court should decide the constitutional question in the way that the superior court believes to be correct.

(b) Without power to decide questions of law

In both *Douglas College* and *Cuddy Chicks,* the tribunals' empowering statutes expressly granted to the tribunal the power to decide questions of law.[157]

---

151 There is no right to appeal from a decision of an administrative tribunal unless the right has been conferred by statute. However, all administrative tribunals are subject to judicial review by superior courts, not to reconsider the merits, but to determine whether jurisdiction has been exceeded, and, depending on the review remedy sought, to correct some other kinds of errors, often including errors of law.

152 Chapter 7, Courts, under heading 7.3(f), "Privative clauses", above.

153 See generally Evans, "Administrative Tribunals and Charter Challenges" (1988) 2 Can. J. of Admin. Law and Practice 13; McAllister, "The Role of Administrative Tribunals in Charter Adjudication" (1991) Nat. J. Con. Law 25; Anisman, "Jurisdiction of Administrative Tribunals to Apply the Canadian Charter of Rights and Freedoms" (LSUC Special Lectures, 1992); Priest, "Charter Procedure in Administrative Cases: The Tribunal's Perspective" (1994) 7 Can. J. Admin. Practice 151.

154 *Id.*, 605.

155 [1991] 2 S.C.R. 5, 18.

156 *Id.*, 17; [1990] 3 S.C.R. 570, 605.

157 The express power to decide questions of law was mentioned but not particularly emphasized by La Forest J. in the *Douglas College* case [1990] 3 S.C.R. 570, 596, although Wilson J. reserved judgment on the significance of the express power: note 148, above. In *Cuddy Chicks* [1991] 2 S.C.R. 5, 14, La Forest J. said that the jurisdiction to rule on Charter questions "must have expressly or impliedly been conferred on the tribunal by its enabling statute or otherwise". Despite this softer formulation, Wilson J. (at 20) again repeated her reservation.

That express power is not granted to all tribunals, and in particular is not granted to the Board of Referees under the Unemployment Insurance Act. In *Tétreault-Gadoury* v. *Canada* (1991),[158] the question arose whether a Board of Referees could decide a Charter issue, which had been raised by a person who had been denied benefits on account of her having reached the age of 65. The applicant was not seeking any special remedy that would involve relying on s. 24 of the Charter. She simply wanted the Board of Referees to award her the unemployment insurance benefits to which she would be entitled if the statutory provision barring payments to persons over 65 was disregarded. The Supreme Court of Canada held that the Board of Referees could not consider the Charter issue. Because the Unemployment Insurance Act did not grant to the Board of Referees the express power to decide questions of law, the Board was precluded from deciding a Charter issue. Moreover, the Federal Court, from which the applicant sought judicial review of the Board's decision, was equally disabled from considering the Charter issue, because its powers were ''limited to overseeing and controlling the legality of decisions of administrative bodies and to referring back to those bodies for redetermination, with directions if appropriate''.[159]

In *Tétreault-Gadoury*, La Forest J., who wrote for the majority, was influenced by the fact that some administrative tribunals were poorly equipped to decide Charter issues, for example, those that were staffed by non-lawyers, or had to deal with a large caseload.[160] But these prudential considerations seem to me inadequate to overcome the theoretical objections to the Court's ruling. The Court's ruling means that the federal Parliament (and the same would be true of a provincial Legislature), which is itself powerless to enact a law in violation of the Charter, has the power to create an administrative tribunal that can — indeed, must — apply a law that is in violation of the Charter. In *Tétreault-Gadoury* itself, for example, the Court went on to hold that the statutory provision excluding persons over 65 from unemployment insurance benefits was unconstitutional. Yet, the Court insisted that the Board of Referees had been under a duty to apply the unconstitutional law, and its decision could not be upset on judicial review.

---

158 [1991] 2 S.C.R. 22. The principal opinion was written by La Forest J., with whom all judges agreed, although L'Heureux-Dubé J. added brief concurring reasons, repeating (at 48) Wilson J.'s reservation in *Douglas College* and *Cuddy Chicks*, notes 148, 149, above. (Wilson J. had retired from the court by the time this case was argued.)

159 *Id.*, 37. The applicant was not left without a remedy, because there was an appeal (which she had not taken) from the Board of Referees to the Umpire, who did have express power to decide questions of law. Of course, a right of appeal of this kind would not be available from the decisions of all administrative tribunals. Where it was not available, presumably the aggrieved person could apply to a court of competent jurisdiction under s. 24 of the Charter. This remedy, it should be noted, is available only for Charter breaches. If the tribunal were in breach of the federalism part of the Constitution, or s. 96 of the Constitution Act, 1867, or s. 35 of the Constitution Act, 1982, s. 24 would not be available. If the constitutional infirmity was in the enabling statute (as it was in *Tétreault-Gadoury*), proceedings could be brought to obtain a declaration that the statutory provision was unconstitutional.

160 [1991] 2 S.C.R. 22, 36.

The remedy for the Charter breach could be obtained only by an appeal to a body that had express power to decide questions of law, which would only be possible if such an appeal was provided for by statute, or, if there was no such right of appeal, by an application to a court of competent jurisdiction under s. 24.[161] With respect, this seems an unnecessarily circuitous alternative to simply allowing the administrative tribunal to decide the Charter issue in the first place.

In *Tétreault-Gadoury*, La Forest J.'s reason for not allowing the administrative tribunal to decide the Charter issue was that the enabling statute of the administrative tribunal (the Board of Referees) did not contain an express power to decide questions of law. But it must be remembered that any statutory tribunal, whether or not it has an express power to decide questions of law, must decide all questions of law or fact that are necessary to determine a dispute that is properly before it.[162] A tribunal cannot fold its hands and refuse to determine a dispute just because the dispute raises a question of law. This is so, whether or not the tribunal has an express power to decide questions of law. In effect, all tribunals with power to decide anything have an *implied* power to decide all related questions of law. Their decisions on questions of law may be subject to appeal, or to judicial review, or both, but the power (and duty)[163] of the tribunal to render them cannot be doubted.

Once it is accepted that all administrative tribunals have an implied power (and duty) to decide questions of law, it is hard to justify placing limits on the body of law that the tribunal may consider. It is clear that the tribunal must respect not only its own empowering statute, but also other applicable legislation.[164] If that is so, then surely the tribunal should not be able to ignore the Constitution which, according to s. 52, is ''the supreme law of Canada''. La Forest J. conceded in *Douglas College* that it would be anomalous if there were one law for administrative tribunals and another for courts.[165] But that is the inevitable result of the decision in *Tétreault-Gadoury*. If there is no express power to decide questions of law, a tribunal with power to determine disputes over eligibility to unemployment insurance benefits (for example) must still apply all applicable laws, *except for the Charter*, even if the effect of the Charter is to invalidate some of the apparently applicable law. A court, or a tribunal with express power to decide questions of law, would have to apply all applicable laws, including the Charter. This is an anomaly that, in my view, cannot be justified by policy doubts about

161 Note 160, above.

162 Evans, note 154, above, 19-20. I leave out of account the possible, but highly unusual, case of a tribunal expressly debarred from deciding questions of law, and required to adjourn and refer the legal question to another tribunal or court.

163 A tribunal would have control of its own proceedings and could adjourn to enable a ruling to be obtained from a superior court.

164 *McLeod* v. *Egan* [1975] 1 S.C.R. 517 (arbitrator under collective agreement bound to interpret any statute potentially applicable to the dispute).

165 [1990] 3 S.C.R. 570, 597.

the talents, expertise, experience and time of the members of administrative tribunals.

(c) Preliminary inquiry judge

In *R.* v. *Seaboyer* (1991),[166] the *Tétreault-Gadoury* decision was taken a long step further, all the way to a court of criminal jurisdiction. The Supreme Court of Canada held that the judge presiding at the preliminary inquiry of an indictable offence had no jurisdiction under s. 52(1) of the Constitution Act, 1982 to determine the constitutionality of a rape-shield law which purported to limit the accused's right to cross-examine the victim of a sexual assault. The Court acknowledged that the preliminary inquiry judge would in the course of conducting the inquiry have the power (and the duty) to rule on the admissibility of the evidence presented at the inquiry. But this power did not extend to determining the constitutionality of a statute that purported to prohibit the admission of evidence. In order to determine whether there was sufficient evidence to make the accused stand trial, the preliminary inquiry judge was obliged "to accept the rules of evidence as they stand".[167] Any Charter challenge to the rules of evidence had to await the trial, where the trial judge would be permitted to look at the Constitution of Canada as part of the body of law to be applied.[168]

As in *Tétreault-Gadoury*, the decision in *Seaboyer* seemed to be the product of a policy concern by the Supreme Court of Canada, in this case, that constitutional rulings at preliminary inquiries would lead to interlocutory appeals and the delay of trials. But, one way or another, important constitutional issues have to be resolved, and it is hard to see why the preliminary inquiry should not start the process of decision. Indeed, it is hard to see how the preliminary inquiry judge can properly determine whether the accused should stand trial if the judge must blindly follow unconstitutional legislation. That, however, is the present state of the law.

37.4 Scrutiny by Minister of Justice

The Charter of Rights makes no provision for the pre-enactment scrutiny of proposed statutes and regulations to ensure that they comply with the Charter. The Canadian Bill of Rights, it will be recalled, imposes an obligation of scrutiny on the Minister of Justice, including an obligation to report to the House of Commons any inconsistency between the Bill and a proposed statute or regula-

166 [1991] 2 S.C.R. 577. The decision is also examined in the discussion of constitutional exemption, at note 32, above.

167 *Id.*, 638.

168 It has been held that a preliminary inquiry judge is not a court of competent jurisdiction within s. 24(1): note 115, above; but this was irrelevant in *Seaboyer*, where it was s. 52(1), not s. 24(1), that was being relied upon by the accused.

tion.[169] In 1985, the Department of Justice Act[170] was amended to require that the Minister of Justice's scrutiny and report encompass compliance with the Charter as well as with the Bill.[171]

37.5 Legislative enforcement

The federal Parliament and the provincial Legislatures, acting within their own legislative jurisdictions, are of course free to make whatever provision they choose for the better enforcement of Charter rights. But the Charter of Rights does not confer any new legislative power. Section 31 declares that "nothing in this Charter extends the legislative powers of any body or authority".

Section 93(4) of the Constitution Act, 1867 expressly authorizes the federal Parliament to enact "remedial laws" to redress a breach by a province of the denominational school rights guaranteed by s. 93.[172] The American Bill of Rights expressly authorizes the federal Congress to enact laws to "enforce" against the states the guarantee against slavery,[173] the rights to due process and equal protection[174] and the right to vote without discriminatory restrictions.[175] It is clear from s. 31 of the Charter that no similar remedial or enforcement power in the federal Parliament is to be inferred from the provisions of the Charter. Enforcement of the Charter is the function of the courts, by virtue of s. 52(1) or s. 24.

---

169 This provision is discussed in ch. 32, Canadian Bill of Rights, under heading 32.6 "Scrutiny by Minister of Justice", above.

170 R.S.C. 1985, c. J-2.

171 Section 4.1 was added by Statute Law (Canadian Charter of Rights and Freedoms) Amendment Act, S.C. 1985, c. 26, s. 105. With respect to regulations, the scrutiny obligation is duplicated by the Statutory Instruments Act, R.S.C. 1985, c. S-22, s. 3(2)(c).

172 See ch. 54, Education, under heading 54.2, "Federal power to enact remedial laws", below.

173 Thirteenth amendment, s. 2.

174 Fourteenth amendment, s. 5.

175 Fifteenth amendment, s. 2.

38

Exclusion of Evidence

38.1 Scope of chapter

The previous chapter, Enforcement of Rights, has considered the remedies that are available for breach of the Charter of Rights. That chapter omitted one remedy, namely, the exclusion of evidence that has been obtained in breach of the Charter. The reason for the omission is that the exclusion of evidence is separately provided for in s. 24(2) of the Charter, and has accumulated its own distinctive body of case-law. This chapter is devoted to s. 24(2) and its exegesis.

38.2 Origin of s. 24(2)

Before the adoption of the Charter of Rights in 1982, Canadian courts followed the rule of the English common law that evidence obtained by illegal means was admissible if relevant.[1] The Canadian Bill of Rights of 1960 was silent on the question of the admissibility of evidence, and the Supreme Court of Canada held that even a breach of the Canadian Bill of Rights did not render inadmissible any evidence obtained by the breach.[2]

The Canadian rule of admissibility stood in contrast with the American exclusionary rule. The American courts held that evidence obtained in violation of the Bill of Rights was inadmissible.[3] When Canada's Charter of Rights was being drafted, a debate ensued as to whether the American exclusionary rule should be adopted. In favour of the American rule, it could be argued that lawless behaviour by law enforcement officers should not be rewarded by allowing them to use the fruits of such behaviour. On the other side of the argument was the point that when reliable evidence is excluded, a guilty person usually goes free; it is arguable that it would be more sensible to discipline the police officer directly than to confer such a windfall on the undeserving accused.[4] However, despite widespread popular and academic hostility to the exclusionary rule, American courts have persisted with it on the theory, which is controversial, that it is required in order to deter police misconduct. In the United States, deterrence is the rationale of the exclusionary rule.[5]

In Canada, the outcome of the debate between admission and exclusion was a compromise between the two alternatives.[6] The compromise is embodied in s. 24(2) of the Charter of Rights.

38.3 Text of s. 24(2)

Section 24(2) of the Charter of Rights[7] provides as follows:

> Where, in proceedings under subsection (1), a court concludes that evidence was obtained in a manner that infringed or denied any rights or freedoms guaranteed by

---

1 *The Queen* v. *Wray* [1971] S.C.R. 272, following *Kuruma* v. *The Queen* [1955] A.C. 197 (P.C.). In *Wray*, the majority denied the existence of a discretion to exclude evidence where its admission would bring the administration of justice into disrepute.

2 *Hogan* v. *The Queen* [1975] 2 S.C.R. 574.

3 *Mapp* v. *Ohio* (1961) 367 U.S. 643.

4 "Our way of upholding the Constitution is not to strike at the man who breaks it, but to let off somebody else who broke something else": *Wigmore on Evidence* (1961), vol. 8, 31.

5 *Segura* v. *United States* (1984) 468 U.S. 796; *Illinois* v. *Krull* (1987) 480 U.S. 340.

6 In the October 1980 version of the Charter, there was no provision for the exclusion of evidence obtained in breach of the Charter. Indeed, there was a section affirming the pre-existing law:

> 26. No provision of this Charter, other than section 13 [privilege against self-incrimination], affects the laws respecting the admissibility of evidence in any proceedings or the authority of the Parliament or a legislature to make laws in relation thereto.

This section was deleted and the present s. 24(2) was inserted in the April 1981 version.

7 For commentary on s. 24(2), see Gibson, *The Law of the Charter: General Principles* (1986), ch. 7; Charles, Cromwell and Jobson, *Evidence and the Charter of Rights and Freedoms (1989), ch. 3; Beaudoin and Mendes (eds.), The Canadian Charter of Rights and Freedoms* (3rd ed.,

the Charter, the evidence shall be excluded if it is established that, having regard to all the circumstances, the admission of it in the proceedings would bring the administration of justice into disrepute.

Section 24(2) bases its exclusionary rule on the good reputation of the administration of justice, rather than the deterrence of official misconduct.[8] If the admission of evidence obtained in breach of the Charter "would bring the administration of justice into disrepute", then the evidence must ("shall") be excluded. If the admission of the evidence would not bring the administration of justice into disrepute, then the general rule of admissibility will apply.[9] Of course, if the evidence was obtained without any breach of the Charter of Rights, even if the police action involved a trick[10] or an illegality, then the general rule of admissibility will apply.

In *R.* v. *Calder* (1996),[11] a statement had been obtained from the accused in breach of his right to counsel, and had been excluded by the trial judge under s. 24(2). This meant, of course, that the Crown could not use the statement as part of its case in chief. However, when the accused testified in his own defence, he told a story that differed from the earlier excluded statement. The Crown applied to have the statement admitted for the sole purpose of cross-examining the accused as to his credibility. This raised the question whether evidence that had been excluded for one purpose (establishing the guilt of the accused) could be admitted for another purpose (impeaching the accused's credibility). Section 24(2) calls for the court to have regard to "all the circumstances" in determining whether

1996), 19-30–19-61 (by Gibson and Gee); Stuart, *Charter Justice in Canadian Criminal Law* (2nd ed., 1996); Sopinka, Lederman, Bryant, *The Law of Evidence in Canada* (1992), ch. 9; Schiff, *Evidence in the Litigation Process* (1993); Roach, *Constitutional Remedies in Canada* (Canada Law Book, loose-leaf) McLeod, Takach, Morton, Segal, *The Canadian Charter of Rights* (Carswell, loose-leaf), ch. 29; *Canadian Charter of Rights Annotated* (Canada Law Book, loose-leaf), annotation to s. 24(2). The last work provides a bibliography of the relevant literature.

8 *R.* v. *Collins* [1987] 1 S.C.R. 265, 281 ("s. 24(2) is not a remedy for police misconduct").

9 In *R.* v. *Therens* [1985] 1 S.C.R. 613, 648, Le Dain J., with the agreement of five of the seven other judges on this issue, held that, after a finding that the admission of the evidence would not bring the administration of justice into disrepute, the court had no discretion to exclude the evidence, even if the court concluded that the exclusion of the evidence would be an "appropriate and just" remedy under s. 24(1). This point did not have to be decided in *Therens*, and Dickson C.J. (at p. 619) and Lamer J. (at p. 626) left the point open.

10 A police tactic that was in use before the Charter of Rights was the placing of a police officer disguised as a prisoner in the same cell as the accused. In apparently casual conversation, the police officer would attempt to elicit an incriminating statement from an unsuspecting accused. Before the Charter of Rights, such a statement was admissible: *Rothman* v. *The Queen* [1981] 1 S.C.R. 640 (statement admitted). The position now is that this tactic is a breach of s. 7 of the Charter of Rights, and the statement is therefore vulnerable to exclusion under s. 24(2): *R.* v. *Hebert* [1990] 2 S.C.R. 151 (statement excluded).

11 [1996] 1 S.C.R. 660. The majority opinion was that of Sopinka J., with the concurrence of Gonthier, Cory, Iacobucci and Major JJ. La Forest J. wrote a brief concurring opinion. McLachlin J. dissented.

the admission of evidence would bring the administration of justice into disrepute. Was the accused's inconsistent testimony one of the relevant circumstances? And could evidence have different effects on the administration of justice depending on the purposes for which it was used? Sopinka J., writing for the majority of the Supreme Court of Canada, gave a cautious yes answer to both questions. He left open the possibility that evidence that, if admitted without restriction, would tend to bring the administration of justice into disrepute might be admissible if its use in the proceedings were restricted. However, he said that the admission of evidence for the restricted purpose of impeaching credibility would be appropriate only in ''very limited circumstances'', and he did not say what those circumstances would be.[12] In this case, he held that the Crown's application to use the evidence for the purpose of impeaching credibility had been correctly denied by the trial judge, although the trial (on sexual misconduct charges) essentially turned on whether the accused (a police officer) or the complainant (a prostitute) was telling the truth. The jury had acquitted the accused, and this verdict was upheld by the majority of the Supreme Court of Canada. The dissenting opinion of McLachlin J. was that the inability of the Crown to cross-examine the accused on his earlier statement would tend to bring the administration of justice into disrepute.

Section 24(2) provides for the exclusion of evidence, not the inclusion of evidence. For example, the Criminal Code prohibits the use of wire-tap evidence not obtained in conformity with the Code; such evidence is inadmissible by virtue of its express statutory exclusion, whether or not its admission would bring the administration of justice into disrepute.[13] Section 24(2) has no application to evidence that is excluded by a common law or statutory exclusionary rule. A statutory exclusionary rule may be vulnerable to Charter attack, but not under s. 24(2). For example, in *R.* v. *Seaboyer* (1991),[14] the Supreme Court of Canada held that the ''rape-shield'' law, which excluded from a criminal trial for sexual assault evidence of the complainant's past sexual activity, was unconstitutional. Because the law excluded evidence that might be necessary to make full answer and defence, the law violated ss. 7 and 11 (d) of the Charter.[15]

38.4 Causation

Section 24(2) applies when evidence has been ''obtained in a manner'' that infringed or denied a Charter right. This requirement would be satisfied if the evidence was obtained as a result of the Charter infringement. For example, a

---

12 *Id.*, para. 35. La Forest J., concurring, said (para. 1) that he could not envisage any circumstances where the distinction would be appropriate.

13 *R.* v. *Thompson* [1990] 2 S.C.R. 1111.

14 [1991] 2 S.C.R. 577.

15 See also Paciocco, ''The Constitutional Right to Present Defence Evidence in Criminal Cases'' (1985) 63 Can. Bar Rev. 519.

weapon may be found during an unreasonable search. In that case, there would be a causal connection between the Charter violation and the discovery of the evidence.[16] But the Supreme Court of Canada in *R.* v. *Strachan* (1988)[17] has held that a causal connection is not necessary. It is not necessary to show that the evidence was discovered by reason of the Charter violation. And it is certainly not necessary to show that the evidence would not have been discovered but for the Charter violation. It is sufficient that there be a temporal connection between the Charter violation and the discovery of the evidence.

The facts of the *Strachan* case were these. The police held a valid search warrant to search the accused's apartment for illegal drugs. When they arrived at the apartment they arrested the accused for possession of marijuana, and they searched the apartment, where they found drugs. The Supreme Court of Canada held that the police had denied the accused's right to counsel, because, although they had advised the accused of his right to retain and instruct counsel, they had not allowed him to contact a lawyer until after the search was over and they had taken him back to the police station. The question then arose whether the evidence found in the search should be excluded. It was clear that there was no causal relationship between the breach of the Charter and the discovery of the evidence. The police held a valid search warrant, and they would have searched the apartment and found the evidence even if the accused's counsel had been present. Nevertheless, the Court held that s. 24(2) applied. The Charter violation and the discovery of the evidence were part of a single "chain of events";[18] the Charter violation occurred "in the course of" obtaining the evidence.[19] This temporal connection between the Charter violation and the discovery of the evidence was enough to establish that the evidence was "obtained in a manner" that infringed or denied a Charter right. (The Court went on to admit the evidence on the ground that there were extenuating circumstances that mitigated the police conduct, so that the admission of the evidence would not bring the administration of justice into disrepute.)

In *Strachan*, the Court was intentionally vague about the precise nature of the connection between the Charter violation and the discovery of the evidence. The temporal connection that existed in that case sufficed, but such a connection was not "determinative":[20] "there can be no hard and fast rule for determining when evidence obtained following the infringement of a Charter right becomes too remote".[21] For example, there might be a causal connection, but not a temporal

16 E.g., *R.* v. *I. (L.R.)* [1993] 4 S.C.R. 504 (first confession obtained in breach of Charter; second confession excluded on basis of causal connection to first confession).

17 [1988] 2 S.C.R. 980; followed in *R.* v. *Debot* [1989] 2 S.C.R. 1140 (reasonable "frisk" search not preceded by advice of right to counsel).

18 *Id.*, 1005.

19 *Ibid.* Cf. *R.* v. *Graham* (1991) 1 O.R. (3d) 499 (C.A.) (lapse of seven days between Charter violation and inculpatory statement negated any temporal connection).

20 *Ibid.*

21 *Id.*, 1006.

connection. This would be so with respect to ''secondary'' (or ''derivative'') evidence, which is evidence obtained as an indirect result of a Charter violation. An example of secondary evidence would be a weapon found elsewhere as the result of lawful police work based on information discovered during an unreasonable search. The secondary evidence may be found some time after the Charter violation, but it would be causally connected to the Charter violation.[22] In the United States, the exclusionary rule applies to secondary evidence (''the fruit of the poisoned tree'') as well as to the primary product of a constitutional violation.[23] This seems to be a reasonable interpretation of s. 24(2) as well.[24] Of course, as the causal connection between the Charter violation and the discovery of the evidence becomes more tenuous, the likelihood increases that a court would hold that the evidence was not obtained in a manner that infringed a Charter right.

The facts of *R.* v. *Grant* (1993)[25] presented another situation where there was no causal connection between the breach of the Charter and the obtaining of the evidence. In that case, the police had conducted two warrantless searches of the perimeter of the accused's house, which the police suspected was being used to cultivate marijuana. Having observed indications that the basement of the house was being used to cultivate something, the police applied for and obtained a warrant to search the house itself. They searched the house and found and seized marijuana plants, marijuana and drug paraphernalia. The Supreme Court of Canada, in an opinion written by Sopinka J., held that the warrantless perimeter searches had been made in breach of s. 8 of the Charter, but he also held that the search warrant for the house itself was valid, because the police had presented to the issuing judge sufficient evidence of reasonable and probable cause for a search of the house quite apart from the perimeter-search observations, which should not have been relied upon. Sopinka J. held, nonetheless, that the valid warrant did not wash away the sins of the past. There was ''a sufficient temporal connection between the warrantless perimeter searches and the evidence ultimately offered at trial to require a determination as to whether the evidence should be excluded''.[26] (He went on to admit the evidence on the grounds that it was real evidence and it had been obtained in good faith, so that the admission of the evidence would not bring the administration of justice into disrepute.)

In *R.* v. *Burlingham* (1995),[27] police persuaded a murder suspect to provide a statement and to lead them to the murder weapon in violation of his right to

---

22 *Id.*, 1004, using derivative evidence as an example of a causal connection.

23 *Silverthorne Lumber Co.* v. *United States* (1920) 251 U.S. 385; *Wong Sun* v. *United States* (1963) 371 U.S. 471.

24 Note 22, above (obiter dictum recognizing application of s. 24(2) to derivative evidence).

25 [1993] 3 S.C.R. 223. The opinion of the Court was written by Sopinka J. Two other cases raising the same issues were decided at the same time, namely, *R.* v. *Wiley* [1993] 3 S.C.R. 263 and *R.* v. *Plant* [1993] 3 S.C.R. 281.

26 [1993] 3 S.C.R. 223, 255.

27 [1995] 2 S.C.R. 206; see also ch. 47, Rights on Arrest or Detention, under heading 47.4, ''Right to counsel'', below.

counsel under s. 10(b) of the Charter. Obviously, the direct fruits of the unconstitutional police actions (the accused's statement and the weapon) required a determination as to their admissibility under s. 24(2) (all of this evidence was ultimately excluded). However, the accused had also recounted to his girlfriend how he had led police to the weapon, and, at his trial, she testified about that conversation. The accused's statement to his girlfriend was voluntary, and, since the girlfriend was not a police agent, the statement to her had not been elicited by the police and was not in violation of the right to counsel. Nevertheless, the Supreme Court of Canada held that the statement to the girlfriend was caught by s. 24(2). The Court reasoned from *Strachan* that there was a sufficient temporal connection with the breach of the accused's Charter rights to taint the statement to the girlfriend.[28] The Court went on to hold that the admission of the girlfriend's testimony would bring the administration of justice into disrepute, and a new trial was ordered from which her testimony was to be excluded.

38.5 Burden of proof

The exclusionary rule of s. 24(2) applies ''if it is established'' that the admission of the evidence would bring the administration of justice into disrepute. The phrase ''if it is established'' casts the burden of proving that the admission of the evidence would bring the administration of justice into disrepute onto the person seeking to exclude the evidence.[29] The standard of proof is the civil standard of the balance of probability.[30] Thus, the person seeking to exclude the evidence must persuade the trial court that it is more probable than not that the admission of the evidence would bring the administration of justice into disrepute. Of course, without a clear definition of the matter to be proved, namely, disrepute, the location of the burden of proof and the standard of proof are not of much significance. Certainly, the cases in the Supreme Court of Canada, to be described shortly, do not suggest that the Court uses the burden of proof to resolve uncertainty. Rather, they suggest a leaning in favour of exclusion, even when one would expect at least a division of opinion among reasonable people as to whether disrepute had been established.[31] In fact, the Court has frankly acknowledged that, while ''theoretically'' the burden is placed on the accused to establish that the administration of justice would be brought into disrepute, ''in practice'' the

---

28 The Court was unanimous that a sufficient proximate connection to the Charter breach existed, but L'Heureux-Dubé J., the lone dissenter, felt that the testimony should still have been admitted. A majority of six judges concurred with Iacobucci J.'s opinion that the evidence was both tainted by the Charter breach and should have been excluded.

29 *R.* v. *Collins* [1987] 1 S.C.R. 265, 280.

30 *Ibid.*

31 E.g., the cases where the police acted in good faith, in ignorance that they were in violation of the Charter, and obtained reliable evidence. The Court had often excluded the evidence in these circumstances: see cases cited in notes 80-86, below.

burden will fall on the Crown when the Crown ''possesses superior knowledge''. For instance, under the ''discoverability'' rule, which is discussed later,[32] it will be for the Crown to demonstrate that the police could have obtained a particular piece of evidence independently of the Charter breach, not for an accused to prove that police could not have obtained the evidence ''but for'' their unconstitutional methods.[33]

38.6 Reasonable person test

When s. 24(2) speaks of bringing the administration of justice ''into disrepute'', it does not say in whose eyes the disrepute must appear. Disrepute to a police officer (for example) might be quite different from disrepute to a law professor. In *R.* v. *Collins* (1987),[34] where Lamer J. for the majority of the Supreme Court of Canada laid down the basic guidelines for s. 24(2), his lordship said that it is disrepute in the ''community at large'' that is the touchstone. But he hastened to add that no attempt should be made to ascertain the actual state of opinion in the community at large, whether by opinion polls or other direct evidence. Instead, he stipulated a ''reasonable person'' test: the trial court would have to decide whether the admission of the evidence would bring the administration of justice into disrepute in the eyes of a reasonable person.[35] ''The reasonable person is usually the average person in the community, but only when the community's current mood is reasonable''.[36]

It is difficult to know how a judge is to ascertain the views of the ''average person''. Indeed, the whole exercise is so hypothetical that it is doubtful whether it is even meaningful to ask what the average person would think about the admission of evidence in a particular case. It seems inevitable that judges will regard themselves as barometers of public opinion for the purpose of s. 24(2), so that disrepute is likely to reflect ''the views of the judiciary more closely then that of the citizenry at large''.[37] And yet, this is one topic upon which the attitudes of the judiciary, nurtured in a professional climate of concern for scrupulous adherence to constitutional norms, are unlikely to be shared by the citizenry at large, who would probably give much greater weight to securing the conviction of criminals.[38]

32 Section 38.8(d), ''The discoverability rule'', below.

33 *R.* v. *Burlingham* [1995] 2 S.C.R. 206, para. 32 per Iacobucci J. Four others concurred in Iacobucci J.'s majority opinion. For further discussion of this point, see sec. 38.8, ''Nature of evidence'', below.

34 [1987] 1 S.C.R. 265.

35 *Id.*, 282.

36 *Ibid.*

37 Gibson, ''Shocking the Public'' (1983) 1 Man. L.J. 495, 498.

38 Bryant and others, ''Public Attitudes towards the Exclusion of Evidence'' (1990) 69 Can. Bar Rev. 1; Gold and others, ''Public Support for the Exclusion of Unconstitutionally Obtained

38.7 Definition of disrepute

There were suggestions in the pre-Charter case-law that evidence obtained by a dirty trick (such as by a police officer impersonating a priest) should be excluded on the ground that its admission would "shock" the community.[39] In *R.* v. *Collins* (1987),[40] Lamer J. said that community shock was not the standard of disrepute under s. 24(2). A lower standard was sufficient, for two reasons. One reason is that s. 24(2) contemplates that a breach of the Charter has taken place, which is much more serious than a trick,[41] and does not call for such a powerful additional ground of exclusion. The other reason is to be found in the softer language of the French version of s. 24(2). The English version uses the phrase "would bring the administration of justice into disrepute". In the French version, the word "would" is replaced by "est susceptible de". The French version is closer to "could" than "would", which implies a less onerous standard than that of community shock.

While *Collins* establishes the negative proposition that community shock is not the test of disrepute, the case does not provide a positive definition of disrepute. However, Lamer J. did set out three factors to be weighed in determining disrepute. The factors were as follows: (1) the nature of the evidence; (2) the nature of the conduct by which the evidence was obtained; and (3) the effect on the system of justice of excluding the evidence.[42] Each of these factors will be considered next.

38.8 Nature of evidence

(a) Unreliable evidence

The first branch of the *Collins* test calls for an examination of the nature of the evidence that has been obtained in breach of the Charter. The Supreme Court of Canada has viewed this branch of the test as driven by a concern with the fairness of the trial. If the evidence is of a kind that its admission would make the trial unfair, then it follows that its admission would tend to bring the administration of justice into disrepute.

The core of unfairness encompasses evidence that is unreliable. Unreliable evidence carries with it the risk that a trial may not arrive at the truth, and that an innocent person might be convicted. To admit unreliable evidence that has been

Evidence" (1990) 1 Supreme Court L.R. (2d) 555. In *R.* v. *Burlingham* [1995] 2 S.C.R. 206, para. 74, L'Heureux-Dubé J., dissenting, suggested that public opinion surveys did constitute a periodic "reality check" that was both "healthy and necessary" for the judges. No other judge agreed with her opinion!

39 *Rothman* v. *The Queen* [1981] 1 S.C.R. 640, 697 per Lamer J.

40 [1987] 1 S.C.R. 265, 286-288.

41 Note, however, that some "tricks" are breaches of the Charter: note 10, above.

42 [1987] 1 S.C.R. 265, 284-286.

obtained in breach of the Charter would always bring the administration of justice into disrepute.[43] It is arguable that unreliable evidence is the only kind of evidence that, by its nature, should be *automatically* excluded.[44] However, the Court has extended the first branch of the *Collins* test far beyond unreliable evidence. Indeed, most of the cases in which evidence has been excluded under this branch of the test have concerned evidence that seemed exceedingly reliable, and in some cases constituted conclusive proof that the accused had committed the offence charged. In *Collins,* Lamer J. did not insist that all evidence coming within the first branch of his test should be automatically excluded; he left open the possibility that other factors might lead to the admission of the evidence.[45] However, the Court has nearly always excluded evidence that comes within the first branch of the test. Having found that the evidence would, by its nature, affect the fairness of the trial, the Court has naturally felt constrained to exclude it. ''Once impugned evidence has been found to come within the trial fairness rationale, exclusion is virtually certain to follow.''[46]

(b) Independent of Charter violation

Within the category of reliable evidence, the Court initially distinguished two subcategories.[47] One is evidence that, although discovered in the course of a Charter violation, existed independently of the Charter violation. The cases in the Supreme Court of Canada that illustrated this kind of evidence concerned drugs[48] or weapons[49] found in the course of an unreasonable search, stolen property[50] obtained after an arbitrary arrest,[51] and a blood sample obtained by a hospital for

---

43 *R.* v. *Evans* [1991] 1 S.C.R. 869 (unreliable statement by mentally deficient accused excluded).

44 *R.* v. *Burlingham* [1995] 2 S.C.R. 206, paras. 75-89 per L'Heureux-Dubé J. dissenting; Paciocco, ''The Judicial Repeal of s. 24(2) and the Development of the Canadian Exclusionary Rule'' (1990) 32 Crim. L.Q. 326.

45 *R.* v. *Collins* [1987] 1 S.C.R. 265, 284 per Lamer J. for majority (''If the admission of the evidence in some way affects the fairness of the trial, then the admission of the evidence would *tend* to bring the administration of justice into disrepute and, subject to a consideration of other factors, the evidence generally should be excluded.'')

46 *R.* v. *Burlingham* [1995] 2 S.C.R. 206, para. 29 per Iacobucci J. for majority.

47 *Id.*, 284-285; R. v. *Simmons* [1988] 2 S.C.R. 495, 534.

48 *R.* v. *Collins* [1987] 1 S.C.R. 265 (new trial ordered to determine whether drugs should be admitted); *R.* v. *Sieben* [1987] 1 S.C.R. 295 (drugs admitted); *R.* v. *Hamill* [1987] 1 S.C.R. 301 (new trial ordered to determine whether drugs should be admitted); *R.* v. *Simmons* [1988] 2 S.C.R. 495 (drugs admitted); *R.* v. *Strachan* [1988] 2 S.C.R. 980 (drugs admitted); *R.* v. *Debot* [1989] 2 S.C.R. 1140 (drugs admitted); *R.* v. *Greffe* [1990] 1 S.C.R. 755 (drugs excluded); *R.* v. *Kokesch* [1990] 3 S.C.R. 3 (drugs excluded); *R.* v. *Généreux* [1992] 1 S.C.R. 259 (drugs admitted); *R.* v. *Grant* [1993] 3 S.C.R. 223 (drugs admitted); *R.* v. *Wiley* [1993] 3 S.C.R. 263 (drugs admitted); *R.* v. *Plant* [1993] 3 S.C.R. 281 (drugs admitted).

49 *R.* v. *Genest* [1989] 1 S.C.R. 59 (weapons excluded); *R.* v. *Black* [1989] 2 S.C.R. 138 (weapon admitted).

50 *R.* v. *Duguay* [1989] 1 S.C.R. 93 (stolen property excluded).

51 See also *R.* v. *Wise* [1992] 1 S.C.R. 527 (evidence of location of vehicle admitted).

medical purposes.[52] The Court initially took the view that the use of this evidence would not make the trial unfair; therefore, its use would not tend to bring the administration of justice into disrepute; and, therefore, it should be admitted unless there are other circumstances (for example, the conduct of the police) that would tend to bring the administration of justice into disrepute.

(c) Created by Charter violation

The other kind of reliable evidence is that which would not exist apart from the Charter violation, for example, a confession given while drunk,[53] a confession given before the accused had been warned of his right to counsel,[54] and a confession given in response to police questioning that continued after the accused had asked to see a lawyer.[55] In these cases, the Court is fond of saying that the accused has been "conscripted against himself",[56] but in fact the cases involve voluntary confessions to which the term conscripted is inaccurate. What can be said about the evidence without exaggeration is that it is self-incriminatory,[57] and that it would not exist had there been no Charter violation. This evidence is usually, but not always, excluded on the ground that its admission would make the trial "unfair".[58]

The Supreme Court of Canada has placed in the same noxious category real evidence that has been obtained from the accused by a breach of the Charter, for example, a breath sample obtained before the accused had been warned of or been given a reasonable opportunity to exercise his right to counsel,[59] a blood sample taken from an unconscious accused,[60] fingerprints obtained after an arbi-

---

52 *R.* v. *Colarusso* [1994] 1 S.C.R. 20 (blood sample admitted); cf. *R.* v. *Borden* [1994] 3 S.C.R. 145 (blood sample taken by police with consent of accused, but for another investigation, excluded).

53 *Clarkson* v. *The Queen* [1986] 1 S.C.R. 383 (confession excluded).

54 *R.* v. *Evans* [1991] 1 S.C.R. 869 (confession excluded); *R.* v. *Elshaw* [1991] 3 S.C.R. 24 (confession excluded).

55 *R.* v. *Manninen* [1987] 1 S.C.R. 1233 (confession excluded); *R.* v. *Black* [1989] 2 S.C.R. 138 (confession excluded); cf. *R.* v. *Brydges* [1990] 1 S.C.R. 190 (confession excluded); *R.* v. *Hebert* [1990] 2 S.C.R. 151 (confession excluded); *R.* v. *Broyles* [1991] 3 S.C.R. 595 (confession excluded).

56 E.g., *R.* v. *Collins* [1987] 1 S.C.R. 265, 284; *R.* v. *Broyles* [1991] 3 S.C.R. 595, 618, 620.

57 Cf. *R.* v. *Smith* [1991] 1 S.C.R. 714 (non-incriminatory statement admitted).

58 *Ibid.*

59 *R.* v. *Therens* [1985] 1 S.C.R. 613 (breath sample excluded); *R.* v. *Tremblay* [1987] 2 S.C.R. 435 (breath sample admitted); *R.* v. *Bartle* [1994] 3 S.C.R. 173 (breath sample excluded); *R.* v. *Prosper* [1994] 3 S.C.R. 236 (breath sample excluded). In all these cases, breath samples were taken under the authority of the Criminal Code, which requires a demand for a sample to be complied with. The advice of counsel could only confirm the obligation. Therefore, absent other factors, the case for excluding a breath sample obtained in breach of the right to counsel seems to me to be very weak.

60 *R.* v. *Pohoretsky* [1987] 1 S.C.R. 945 (blood sample excluded); *R.* v. *Dyment* [1988] 2 S.C.R. 417 (blood sample excluded).

trary arrest,[61] and (implausibly) identification evidence obtained from a line-up held before the accused could retain counsel.[62] Although this evidence is real, it is like a confession in that it is evidence that the accused created, as opposed to pre-existing evidence that the accused merely located or identified.[63] The evidence is therefore self-incriminatory, and would not exist had it not been for the Charter violation. This evidence is usually, but not always, excluded on the ground that its admission would make the trial unfair.

(d) The discoverability rule

In *R.* v. *Mellenthin* (1992),[64] the Supreme Court of Canada blurred or erased the distinction between real evidence created by the accused and real evidence merely located or identified by the accused. In that case, drugs found in a bag on the front seat of the accused's car (as a result of an unreasonable search) were excluded under s. 24(2) of the Charter. Although the accused had merely located or identified the evidence when asked by a police officer what was in the bag, the Court still excluded the evidence. Writing for the unanimous Court, Cory J. held that, because the evidence would not have been discovered without the aid of the accused, it was in the same category as evidence that the accused had created as the result of a Charter violation. Cory J. concluded that the use of the evidence would make the trial unfair, and that it should be excluded.

In *R.* v. *Burlingham* (1995),[65] a majority of the Supreme Court of Canada confirmed that *Mellenthin* had indeed changed the law. The evidence that would make a trial unfair now included all evidence that would not have been discovered ''but for'' the Charter violation. Even if the evidence was real evidence that existed independently of the Charter violation, it was now objectionable by its nature if it was not ''discoverable'' apart from the Charter violation. In *Burlingham*, a murder case, the police had obtained self-incriminatory statements from the accused in breach of his right to counsel. They had also persuaded the accused, again in breach of his right to counsel, to take them to the scene of the crime, where the police were able to find a well-concealed murder weapon (a gun that had been thrown into a river). The trial judge excluded the statements (evidence created by the accused), but admitted the gun (real evidence existing independently of the Charter breach). The accused was convicted of murder. On

61 *R.* v. *Duguay* [1989] 1 S.C.R. 93 (confessions and fingerprints excluded).

62 *R.* v. *Ross* [1989] 1 S.C.R. 3 (line-up identification excluded).

63 See the discussion in *Thomson Newspapers* v. *Can.*, [1990] 1 S.C.R. 425, 552 per La Forest J.; *R.* v. *Meddoui* (1990) 61 C.C.C. (3d) 345, 363 per Kerans J.A.

64 [1992] 3 S.C.R. 615.

65 [1995] 2 S.C.R. 206. Iacobucci J. wrote the majority opinion, which was concurred in by La Forest, Sopinka, Cory and Major JJ. Sopinka J. added some supplementary reasons. Gonthier J. wrote a separate concurring opinion. L'Heureux-Dubé J. dissented, arguing strongly against the adoption of the discoverability rule. I am indebted to her reasons in the criticism of the rule that follows.

appeal to the Supreme Court of Canada, Iacobucci J., for the majority of the Court, held that the key to the admissibility of the gun was the new discoverability rule. Iacobucci J. took the view that the gun would not have been found if the accused had not taken the police to the scene of the crime. Since the visit to the scene of the crime was a breach of the accused's right to counsel, it followed that the gun would not have been discovered but for the breach of the Charter. Therefore, the admission of the gun in evidence made the accused's trial unfair. Therefore, its admission in evidence would bring the administration of justice into disrepute. The conclusion was that the accused's conviction had to be set aside and a new trial ordered.

The discoverability rule purports to be an elaboration of the first branch of the *Collins* test, which calls for an inquiry into the nature of the evidence that was obtained in breach of the Charter. However, as L'Heureux-Dubé J. pointed out in her dissent in *Burlingham*, the discoverability rule cannot be reconciled with the reasoning in the *Collins* case itself.[66] In that case, a police officer seized the accused in a hotel bar, using a "throat hold" to prevent her from swallowing drugs. She did in fact have some heroin in her hand, and she was prevented from swallowing the drug by the officer's action. The Supreme Court of Canada held that the officer's action was a breach of the Charter, because he had no warrant for the arrest of the accused and no evidence had been adduced at trial as to whether he had reasonable grounds to believe that the accused was holding a drug. (The Court was not prepared to regard the successful interception of the drug as itself establishing reasonable grounds.) The Court went on to hold that the heroin should be excluded from evidence, because its admission would bring the administration of justice into disrepute. However, this finding was based on the *conduct of the police officer*, which Lamer J. for the majority described as "a flagrant and serious violation of the rights of an individual".[67] Lamer J. did not regard the *nature of the evidence* as calling for its exclusion. Indeed, he expressly held that the evidence would not make the trial unfair, pointing out that it was real evidence that "existed irrespective of the violation of the Charter".[68] Yet this was a clear case in which the evidence would not have been discovered but for the police officer's breach of the Charter.

The discoverability rule is a huge expansion of the concept of unfairness that governs the first branch of the *Collins* test. Because evidence that would affect the fairness of the trial usually has to be excluded, the discoverability rule will expand the categories of evidence that are excluded. Only where the Crown is able to establish on the balance of probabilities that the evidence would have been discovered if no Charter breach had occurred,[69] will the evidence be treated

---

66 *R.* v. *Collins* [1987] 1 S.C.R. 265.

67 *Id.*, 288.

68 *Id.*, 284.

69 The placing of the burden of proof in the Crown is another departure from *Collins*, which ruled ([1987] 1 S.C.R. 265, 280) that the burden of proving that the admission of the evidence would

as not affecting the fairness of the trial, so that the second and third branches of the *Collins* inquiry can be given dispositive weight.

Because of the discoverability rule, in every case where evidence has been obtained in breach of the Charter, it will now be necessary for the Crown to lead evidence to support an argument that the evidence would have been discovered anyway.[70] This wholly hypothetical inquiry will require evidence of police methods of investigation and successful discoveries of evidence in like cases. As the Crown discovered in *Burlingham*, failure to adduce enough evidence to persuade the trial judge of discoverability will normally result in the exclusion of any Charter-tainted evidence. (Of course, the Crown did not attempt to adduce any such evidence in *Burlingham,* because the Supreme Court of Canada had not yet discovered the discoverability rule.) My view is that the inquiry into discoverability will prove to be a time-consuming distraction from the various considerations that the Court laid down in *Collins*, which surely are far more relevant to the issue of disrepute than theoretical evidence about the likely success of police investigations on the basis of a hypothetical postulate that no Charter breach had taken place.

The inappropriateness of premising the admission of evidence on discoverability was dramatically illustrated by a case decided at the same time as *Burlingham*. In *R.* v. *Silveira* (1995),[71] police officers had arrested the accused on drug-related charges, and had then gone to his house without a search warrant to ''secure'' it until a search warrant could be obtained. The police entered the house and restricted the movements of the occupants until a search warrant had been obtained and brought to the house. They did this to prevent anyone in the house from removing or destroying evidence of drugs that the police believed (correctly, as it turned out) to be inside the house. The Supreme Court of Canada held that the securing of the house was a breach of s. 8 of the Charter, and that the discovery and seizure under the search warrant of drugs that were inside the house were tainted by the same breach. The question that faced the Court was whether the evidence of the drugs should be excluded. Cory J., writing for the majority of the Supreme Court of Canada, held that the evidence should be admitted. He accepted the Crown's position that the immediate securing of the house was based on a well-founded fear that it was necessary to save the evidence, and he held that the admission of the evidence would not bring the administration of justice into disrepute. But what of the discoverability rule? The Crown had not established on the balance of probabilities that the evidence would have been discovered

---

bring the administration of justice into disrepute rested on the person seeking to exclude the evidence: sec. 38.5, ''Burden of proof'', above.

70 This evidence could not be led in front of the jury, because, if it were, the jury would become aware of the potentially inadmissible evidence. It would require a voir dire, a separate trial before the judge alone, to determine the discoverability issue.

71 [1995] 2 S.C.R. 297. Cory J. wrote the majority opinion, in which Sopinka, Gonthier, Iacobucci and Major JJ. concurred. L'Heureux-Dubé J. wrote a concurring opinion. La Forest J. wrote a dissenting opinion.

without the Charter breach. The Crown's position was the exact opposite, namely, that the evidence would probably have disappeared but for the Charter breach. The Court must have recognized that it would be outrageous if the accused were to escape punishment solely because the police had made it impossible for him to arrange for the disposal of his drug stash. But in order to avoid this unsavoury conclusion, Cory J. was forced to make the dubious claim that the evidence would have been discovered without the Charter breach.[72] This was not consistent with the Court's finding that the risk to the evidence provided the exigent circumstances that excused the police breach of the Charter. Had it not been for the majority opinion in *Burlingham* (Cory J. had been part of that majority), there would have been no need to bother with the question of discoverability, which on the facts of this case can be seen as an irrelevant distraction.[73]

38.9 Nature of official conduct

(a) Deliberate violations

The second factor that was identified by Lamer J. in *R.* v. *Collins* as relevant to determining disrepute is the conduct by which the evidence was obtained. Where the police have deliberately violated the Charter in order to obtain incriminating evidence, then the use of the evidence would tend to bring the administration of justice into disrepute. Where the police arrested several accuseds without reasonable and probable cause, in circumstances where the police must have been aware of the absence of a legal basis for the arrests, the Court excluded the confessions, fingerprints and stolen property that the police obtained after the arrest.[74] Where the police made a search under an invalid warrant, and also used excessive force in executing the search, the Court excluded the evidence of the illegal weapons that were found in the search.[75] Where the police entered private property without a warrant and made a "perimeter search" of a house, the Court excluded the evidence of the marijuana plants that were later found in the house.[76] In each of these cases, the police knew or ought to have known that they were acting in breach of the Charter.

---

72 *Id.*, para. 146 (describing the discoverability point as "hardly a submission which is likely to succeed").

73 *R.* v. *Evans* [1996] 1 S.C.R. 8, discussed in chapter 45, Unreasonable Search or Seizure, under heading 45.4(d), "Plain view", below, is another case where the Court made a highly implausible finding of discoverability in order to rescue evidence, which plainly should have been admitted, from the exclusionary consequence of the discoverability rule. In that case, the police officers had testified that they had exhausted all normal investigative techniques without success until the visit to the accused's house when the Charter breach took place.

74 *R.* v. *Duguay* [1989] 1 S.C.R. 93.

75 *R.* v. *Genest* [1989] 1 S.C.R. 59.

76 R. v. *Kokesch* [1990] 3 S.C.R. 3.

(b) Extenuating circumstances

On the other hand, where the action in breach of the Charter was taken in circumstances that were particularly difficult or complicated, the Court has been willing to excuse the breach to the extent of admitting the evidence. In *R.* v. *Tremblay* (1987),[77] the accused was being obstructive, and the police thought that he was using the opportunity to contact a lawyer as a delaying tactic; the Court admitted the evidence of a breath test, despite the fact that it had been administered before there had been enough time for the lawyer to be contacted by the accused's wife. In *R.* v. *Strachan* (1988),[78] the police, after arresting the accused in his apartment, exercised a tight control over him and two other people in the apartment, because the police feared that attempts would be made to use weapons or destroy drugs that they thought (correctly as it turned out) were concealed in the apartment; the Court admitted the evidence of the drugs found by the police, despite the fact that the police delayed too long in allowing the accused to call his lawyer. In *R.* v. *Silveira* (1995),[79] police officers entered the accused's home without a search warrant and exercised control over its occupants (who did not include the accused) while a search warrant was being obtained. The officers had already arrested the accused in a public place, and they feared that, unless they secured the house immediately, someone connected to the accused might destroy or remove evidence of drugs before they could get a warrant to search the house. Although the Crown did not contest that the securing of the house was a breach of the accused's Charter right to be secure from unreasonable search or seizure, a majority of the Supreme Court of Canada admitted the evidence on the basis that the police action was a reaction to a real risk that evidence might be destroyed.

(c) Good faith

In the absence of the extenuating circumstances that are illustrated by *Tremblay* and *Strachan*, the Supreme Court of Canada initially showed itself to be surprisingly impervious to a plea of good faith on the part of police officers who gathered evidence in inadvertent breach of the Charter. This situation arose in several of the early cases, where the precise requirements of the Charter were unsettled at the time when the police acted, and were only settled when the accused's appeal reached the Supreme Court of Canada several years later.

In *R.* v. *Therens* (1985),[80] the police took a breath sample from the accused, who was suspected of impaired driving, without first informing him of his right to retain and instruct counsel. Most lower courts had held that the accused was not ''detained'' in this situation, so that s. 10(b) of the Charter did not apply and

77 [1987] 2 S.C.R. 435.
78 [1988] 2 S.C.R. 980.
79 [1995] 2 S.C.R. 297.
80 [1985] 1 S.C.R. 613.

there was no right to retain and instruct counsel. Indeed, the Supreme Court of Canada itself, in *Chromiak* v. *The Queen* (1980),[81] had recently held that in this situation there was no right to counsel under the similar language of the Canadian Bill of Rights. In these circumstances, the police could surely be forgiven for assuming that they need not offer the accused the opportunity to retain and instruct counsel, which would of course delay the taking of the breath test. The Supreme Court of Canada disagreed. The Court overruled its earlier decision in *Chromiak*, and held that, when a breath test was demanded at the police station, there was a detention and a right to counsel. Then, in an astonishing passage, the majority of the Court said that the police had ''flagrantly violated a Charter right'', and that such an ''overt violation'' would bring the administration of justice into disrepute.[82] The breath sample was therefore excluded. This condemnation of the police action seems to have been based solely on the police's inability to predict that the Supreme Court of Canada would overrule its earlier decision in *Chromiak*.

The Supreme Court of Canada excluded evidence in a number of other early Charter cases that were similar to *Therens*. The Court excluded two other breath samples that had been taken without prior warning of the right to counsel.[83] The Court excluded a vial of blood taken by a doctor from an unconscious accused.[84] The Court excluded a statement made by an accused who was intoxicated,[85] and a statement made by an accused who had said that he wished to exercise his right to counsel but who had made no attempt to do so.[86] In each of these cases, the police action, although held to be a breach of the Charter, had never been so characterized at the time when the police acted. In each case, the action fell into a grey area where reasonable lawyers and judges could and did disagree. In each case, the police did not know, and could not have known, that they were violating the rights of the accused. In these circumstances, the conclusion that the use of the evidence would bring the administration of justice into disrepute was quite implausible.

The *Therens* line of cases appears to hold that the question whether the police acted in good faith or not is irrelevant to bringing the administration of justice into disrepute. This is certainly a rather startling conclusion, especially as the American courts have carved a good-faith exception out of their exclusionary rule.[87] Fortunately, it is too early to say that good faith is irrelevant in Canadian law.

---

81 [1980] 1 S.C.R. 471.

82 [1985] 1 S.C.R. 613, 621 per Estey J. Le Dain J., with the agreement of McIntyre J., dissented on the basis of the police's good-faith reliance on *Chromiak*.

83 *Trask* v. *The Queen* [1985] 1 S.C.R. 655; *Rahn* v. *The Queen* [1985] 1 S.C.R. 659.

84 *R.* v. *Dyment* [1988] 1 S.C.R. 417.

85 *Clarkson* v. *The Queen* [1986] 1 S.C.R. 383.

86 *R.* v. *Manninen* [1987] 1 S.C.R. 1233.

87 *United States* v. *Leon* (1984) 468 U.S. 897 (police relied in good faith on apparently valid warrant); *Massachusetts* v. *Sheppard* (1984) 468 U.S. 981 (same result); *Illinois* v. *Krull* (1987) 480 U.S. 340 (police relied in good faith on a statute subsequently held to be unconstitutional).

In *R.* v. *Simmons* (1988),[88] the accused, who was charged with importing illegal drugs into Canada, had been searched at the airport without having first been informed of her right to retain and instruct counsel. The drugs were found taped to her body. The majority of the Supreme Court of Canada held that the search violated the accused's right to counsel, and was therefore in breach of the Charter. Should the evidence be excluded? In a 180-degree turn from the *Therens* line of cases, the Court said no. Dickson C.J. pointed out that at the time when the search was conducted, the customs officers had no way of knowing that they were in breach of the Charter. He said:[89]

> The breaches occurred not long after the Charter came into force and several years before the decision of this Court in *Therens* on the meaning of detention in s. 10(b). At the time of this search the decision of this Court in *Chromiak*, *supra*, stood for the proposition that investigative detentions of this sort were not detentions of the type requiring persons to be advised of their right to counsel.

With respect, this seems eminently sensible. But, of course, every word of the quotation would apply with even greater force to *Therens* itself, where the police failure to advise of the right to counsel was described as a ''flagrant'' breach of the Charter.

In *Simmons*, the Chief Justice did not attempt to explain the Court's characterization of the police action in *Therens*, but he did offer an explanation for the different outcome in *Therens*. *Therens*, he said, was a case where the accused was ''conscripted against [himself]'', and the use of the breath sample would ''tend to affect adversely the fairness of the trial process''.[90] By this he meant that Therens had been forced to create incriminating evidence in the form of the breath sample. In *Simmons*, he pointed out, ''the evidence obtained as a result of the search was real evidence that existed irrespective of the Charter violations''.[91] In other words, it was not the police conduct that caused the exclusion of the evidence in the *Therens* line of cases, but rather the nature of the evidence — self-incriminatory evidence that would not have existed apart from the Charter violation.[92] This explanation of the cases paves the way to the development of a good-faith doctrine under s. 24(2).

As well as *Simmons*, there are other cases in which the Supreme Court of Canada has held that good-faith action by the police justified the admission of the evidence. Two cases[93] involved evidence discovered in searches conducted under writs of assistance (writs that authorized warrantless searches) that had

88 [1988] 2 S.C.R. 495.

89 *Id.*, 535.

90 *Id.*, 534.

91 *Ibid.*

92 See also *R.* v. *Hebert* [1990] 2 S.C.R. 151 (good faith action by police, but Charter violation caused self-incrimination); *R.* v. *Broyles* [1991] 3 S.C.R. 595 (same result).

93 *R.* v. *Sieben* [1987] 1 S.C.R. 295; *R.* v. *Hamill* [1987] 1 S.C.R. 301.

been issued under the federal Narcotic Control Act. The Supreme Court of Canada held that the writs of assistance had been rendered unconstitutional by the adoption of s. 8 of the Charter of Rights in 1982, so that the evidence had been obtained in breach of the Charter. However, the Court held that the admission of the evidence would not bring the administration of justice into disrepute, because the police ''believed in good faith'' that the writs of assistance, which at the time of the searches had not been challenged under the Charter, were valid.[94] Three cases[95] involved warrantless searches made under the authority of another provision of the Narcotic Control Act. The Supreme Court of Canada held that the statutory provision violated s. 8 of the Charter, but held that the police could not be expected to predict the outcome of a Charter challenge to their statutory power of search. The police had acted in good faith in relying on the statute, and the evidence resulting from the search should not be excluded.

Four other cases involved evidence obtained by various types of surreptitious electronic surveillance.[96] The Supreme Court of Canada held that surreptitious electronic surveillance was a breach of s. 8 of the Charter, but noted that this was not clear at the time when the police obtained their evidence. The Court held that the admission of the evidence would not bring the administration of justice into disrepute. The police officers who conducted the surveillance were acting ''in good faith . . . in accordance with what they had good reason to believe was the law''.[97] In another case,[98] police had a warrant to seize drugs, but, because the warrant was grounded on information which had been discovered through a previous and unreasonable ''olfactory search'', s. 8 of the Charter had been breached. A majority of the Court found that the police had acted in good faith on an honest but mistaken understanding of the scope of their investigatory powers. The majority concluded that the administration of justice would not be brought into disrepute by admitting the evidence.

In the end, therefore, one can say with some confidence that good-faith action by the police, in reliance on the ostensible state of the law at the time of obtaining the evidence, is a factor that weighs in the scale on the side of admitting the evidence.

---

94 [1987] 1 S.C.R. 295, 299.

95 *R.* v. *Grant* [1993] 3 S.C.R. 223; *R.* v. *Wiley* [1993] 3 S.C.R. 263; *R.* v. *Plant* [1993] 3 S.C.R. 281.

96 *R.* v. *Duarte* [1990] 1 S.C.R. 30; *R.* v. *Wiggins* [1990] 1 S.C.R. 62; *R.* v. *Thompson* [1990] 2 S.C.R. 1111; *R.* v. *Wong* [1990] 3 S.C.R. 36.

97 [1990] 1 S.C.R. 30, 59. Similar findings were made in the three other electronic surveillance cases. Similar findings were also made in *R.* v. *Généreux* [1992] 1 S.C.R. 259 (drugs admitted); *R,* v. *Wise* [1992] 1 S.C.R. 527 (evidence of location of car admitted); *R.* v. *Colarusso* [1994] 1 S.C.R. 20 (blood sample admitted).

98 *R.* v. *Evans* [1996] 1 S.C.R. 8. This case is discussed in more detail in ch. 45, Unreasonable Search or Seizure, in sec. 45.4(d) ''Plain view'', below.

38.10 Effect of excluding evidence

It will be recalled that in *R.* v. *Collins*[99] Lamer J. identified three factors as relevant to the question whether the admission of evidence would bring the administration of justice into disrepute. The first two factors were the nature of the evidence and the nature of the official conduct, and these have just been discussed. The third factor was "the effect of excluding the evidence".[100] What his lordship seemed to have in mind under this head was the significance of the evidence to the prosecution's case and the seriousness of the offence charged. The more significant the evidence and the more serious the offence the greater is the social cost of excluding the evidence, and this generally weighs in the scale in favour of admission.[101] This factor has rarely been explicitly considered by the Court, and it is obviously regarded by the Court as less significant than the first two factors.[102] In most of the cases where evidence has been excluded, the evidence appeared to be reliable, it appeared to be crucial to the prosecution's case, and the offence charged was a serious one. And yet the Court typically did not discuss the cost of excluding the evidence, and plainly placed little weight on this factor.

38.11 Conclusion

Given the vague language of s. 24(2), it is not surprising that the Supreme Court of Canada has had difficulty in developing a consistent body of jurisprudence. The early decisions, especially *Therens*, treated s. 24(2) as if it were an absolute exclusionary rule. This was ironic, because s. 24(2) was intended to be a compromise between the American exclusionary rule and the Canadian inclusionary rule. And yet, the American Court, true to its rationale of deterrence, had created a good-faith exception to the American rule, and would almost certainly have admitted the breath sample in *Therens*. After *Therens*, Canada had a stricter exclusionary rule than the United States.

In *Collins*, Lamer J. suggested a set of guidelines for the application of s. 24(2), under which the nature of the evidence, the nature of the police conduct

---

99 [1987] 1 S.C.R. 265.

100 *Id.*, 285.

101 Lamer J. (*Id.*, 286) pointed out, however that where the admission of the evidence would make the trial unfair, then the importance of the evidence and the seriousness of the offence would weigh in the opposite scale, namely, in favour of exclusion. This may be another explanation of the *Therens* line of cases, notes 80–86, above.

102 In *R.* v. *Colarusso* [1994] 1 S.C.R. 20, 78, La Forest J. for the majority, in deciding to admit a blood sample taken in breach of the Charter, placed some weight on what he described as the "appalling" and "shocking" nature of the accused's offence. In *R.* v. *Evans* [1996] 1 S.C.R. 8, Sopinka J., for the majority, in deciding to admit evidence obtained in an unreasonable search placed some weight on the consideration that the crime was a serious drug offence for which the accused stood to be acquitted if the evidence was excluded.

and the cost of excluding the evidence would all be taken in to consideration. While the strict *Therens* approach lingered on in a few cases, *Collins* provided a framework for a recognition that some kinds of evidence were more unfair to the accused than others, that police conduct in breach of the Charter varied in its culpability, and that the social costs of allowing persons accused of serious crimes to go unprosecuted could also be taken into account. The early decisions had recognized none of these propositions. The *Collins* guidelines provided a more nuanced approach to the exclusion of evidence, which was truer to the idea of a compromise between the extremes of invariable inclusion and invariable exclusion.

Regrettably, as the "discoverability rule" has become incorporated into the first branch of the *Collins* test, that nuanced approach is being lost. In place of an inquiry into the nature and circumstances of each Charter breach, a body of jurisprudence is beginning to reject entire classes of evidence on the ground that they would not have been discovered "but for" a breach of the Charter. This is leading us back to a more rigid exclusionary rule. The discoverability rule will also have the effect of side-tracking criminal trials into hypothetical inquiries into what would have happened if the Charter breach had not occurred. These are unfortunate developments. Section 24(2) calls for evidence to be excluded only where "having regard to all of the circumstances, the admission of it in the proceedings would bring the administration of justice into disrepute". Both the language and the spirit of s. 24(2) suggest that the exclusion of evidence should be based on a more exacting and a more relevant standard than a mere finding that the evidence would not have been discovered but for the Charter breach.

39

Religion

39.1 Distribution of powers

Which legislative body — the federal Parliament or the provincial Legislatures — has the power to enact laws in relation to religion?

This question first arose in the litigation over the validity of Sunday observance laws. As has been explained in chapter 18, Criminal Law, a long line of cases has held that laws compelling the observance of Sundays or holy days are within the exclusive competence of the federal Parliament under its power over criminal law.[1] Of course, these laws took the classical criminal law form of a prohibition coupled with a penalty, and there was a long history of the criminalization of profaning the Sabbath. These cases need not be interpreted as holding that all laws with a religious purpose are within federal jurisdiction. There are, however, other cases where it has been held or assumed that any law restricting freedom of religion is within exclusive federal competence.[2] On the other hand, s. 92(12) expressly allocates to the provincial Legislatures the power over the

---

1 Chapter 18, Criminal Law, under heading 18.7, ''Sunday observance law'', above.

2 In *Saumur* v. *City of Quebec* [1953] 2 S.C.R. 299, Rand, Kellock, Locke, Estey, Cartwright and Fauteux JJ. all took this position, although Rinfret, C.J., Taschereau and Kerwin JJ. rejected it. Federal jurisdiction over religion is also assumed in *Walter* v. *A.G. Alta.* [1969] S.C.R. 383 (communal property law not in relation to religion, despite its special impact on Hutterite colonies).

solemnization of marriages, a subject with important religious dimensions; and s. 93(3) makes clear that the provincial Legislature's power over education extends to the establishment of denominational schools.

In *R. v. Edwards Books and Art* (1986),[3] the Supreme Court of Canada upheld provincial legislation that prohibited retail stores from opening on Sundays. The law came within provincial power over property and civil rights, the Court said, because it pursued the secular purpose of providing a pause day for retail workers, rather than the religious purpose of compelling observance of the Christian sabbath. However, the law contained an exemption for stores of less than a specified size that observed Saturday as a holiday. This ''sabbatarian'' exemption admittedly had the religious purpose of accommodating those who observed Saturday as their sabbath. Did the religious purpose render the exemption unconstitutional? Dickson J., speaking for the whole Court on this issue, held that it did not. It was open to a provincial Legislature ''to attempt to neutralize or minimize the adverse effects of otherwise valid provincial legislation on human rights such as freedom of religion''.[4]

Dickson J. in *Edwards Books* concluded that ''the Constitution does not contemplate religion as a discrete constitutional 'matter' falling exclusively within either a federal or provincial class of subjects''.[5] Legislation concerning religion could therefore be competent to either the federal Parliament or the provincial Legislatures, depending upon the other characteristics of the law. In other words, in classifying a law for the purpose of the federal distribution of powers, the law's impact on religion would not necessarily be the critical factor. In *Edwards Books*, the requirement of a common pause day for retail workers could be relieved for some groups for religious reasons without destroying the law's classification as coming within property and civil rights in the province. The power to make laws respecting religion is thus like the power to make laws respecting other civil liberties, which is also for the most part divided between the two levels of government, and is not the exclusive preserve of either one.[6]

Since the adoption of the Charter of Rights in 1982, any law that affects freedom of religion will be vulnerable to challenge under s. 2(a) of the Charter. The rest of this chapter is addressed to s. 2(a) of the Charter.

39.2 Section 2(a) of the Charter

Section 2(a) of the Charter of Rights[7] guarantees to ''everyone''[8] the ''fundamental freedom'' of ''freedom of conscience and religion''.[9]

---

3 [1986] 2 S.C.R. 713.

4 *Id.*, 751.

5 *Id.*, 750.

6 Chapter 31, Civil Liberties, under heading 31.4(b), ''Distribution of powers'', above.

7 For commentary on s. 2(a), see Beaudoin and Mendes (eds.), *The Canadian Charter of Rights and Freedoms* (3rd ed., 1996), ch. 4 (by Swinton); McLeod, Takach, Morton, Segal, *The*

Section 2(a), like other Charter rights, is subject to s. 1 (the limitation clause) of the Charter. A law that limits freedom of conscience and religion will be valid under s. 1 if it comes within the phrase ''such reasonable limits prescribed by law as can be demonstrably justified in a free and democratic society''. Section 1 was examined in chapter 35, Limitation of Rights, above.

The comparable provision of the American Bill of Rights is the first amendment, which on the topic of religion provides that ''Congress shall make no law respecting an establishment of religion, or prohibiting the free exercise thereof''. This provision contains no reference to freedom of conscience. With respect to religion, the provision contains two clauses, an ''establishment'' clause and a ''free exercise'' clause.[10] The first amendment by its terms binds the federal Congress only, but it is also applicable to the states through the fourteenth amendment.[11] The establishment clause, which was intended to prohibit the establishment of an official church or religion in the United States, has no counterpart in s. 2(a). The free exercise clause is closer to s. 2(a).

39.3 Freedom of conscience

Section 2(a)'s reference to ''conscience'', which is not found in the first amendment, would protect systems of belief which are not theocentric (centred on a deity), and which might not be characterized as religions for that reason (or for some other reason).[12]

Canadian Charter of Rights (Carswell, loose-leaf service), ch. 23; *Canadian Charter of Rights Annotated* (Canada Law Book, loose-leaf service), annotation to s. 2(a). The last work contains a bibliography of the relevant literature.

8 On the meaning of ''everyone'', see ch. 34, Application of Charter, under heading 34.1, ''Benefit of rights'', above.

9 The comparable provision of the Canadian Bill of Rights is s. 1(c), which guarantees ''freedom of religion''.

10 For commentary on the religion clauses of the first amendment, see Tribe, *American Constitutional Law* (2nd ed., 1986), ch. 14; Nowak and Rotunda, *Constitutional Law* (4th ed., 1991), ch. 17.

11 The doctrine of ''selective incorporation'', which accomplishes this result, is explained in ch. 34, Application of Charter, under heading 34.2(a), ''Both levels of government'', above.

12 In *R.* v. *Morgentaler* [1988] 1 S.C.R. 30, where the Court struck down the abortion provisions of the Criminal Code, Wilson J. in a separate concurring judgment held that the regulation of abortion was a denial of freedom of conscience, which she defined (at p. 178) as ''personal morality which is not founded in religion'' and as ''conscientious beliefs which are not religiously motivated''. The decision to terminate a pregnancy was (at pp. 175-176) a ''matter of conscience'', which was accordingly protected. None of the other judges made any reference to freedom of conscience.

39.4 Freedom of religion

The leading case on freedom of religion is *R.* v. *Big M Drug Mart* (1985),[13] in which the Supreme Court of Canada struck down the Lord's Day Act, a federal statute that prohibited (with exceptions) commercial activity on Sunday. Dickson J. for the majority of the Court held that the purpose of the Act, which he derived from the history and terms of the Act, was "to compel the observance of the Christian Sabbath".[14] That purpose was an infringement of the freedom of religion of non-Christians, because, by virtue of the guarantee of freedom of religion, "government may not coerce individuals to affirm a specific religious practice for a sectarian purpose".[15]

In *Big M*, Dickson J. offered the following definition of freedom of religion:[16]

> The essence of the concept of freedom of religion is the right to entertain such religious beliefs as a person chooses, the right to declare religious beliefs openly and without fear of hindrance or reprisal, and the right to manifest religious belief by worship and practice or by teaching and dissemination.

The last part of this quotation makes clear that s. 2(a) protects religious practices as well as religious beliefs. Dickson J.'s language borrows from the International Covenant on Civil and Political Rights, which, by article 18, provides that freedom of religion includes the right "to manifest [one's] religion or belief in worship, observance, practice or teaching".

39.5 Sunday observance

We have already noticed the decision in *R.* v. *Big M Drug Mart* (1985),[17] in which the Supreme Court of Canada struck down the federal Lord's Day Act, which prohibited (with exceptions) commercial activity on Sunday. The decision was made easier than it would otherwise have been by the Court's finding from the legislative history and text of the Act that the *purpose* of the Act was "to compel the observance of the Christian Sabbath".[18] Such a purpose was not compatible with s. 2(a). The Court did not have to wait long for the hard case, which was *R.* v. *Edwards Books and Art* (1986),[19] in which Ontario's Retail Business Holidays Act was under challenge. The Act prohibited retail stores from opening on Sunday. The legislative history of this Act showed that its purpose

---

13 [1985] 1 S.C.R. 295. Dickson J. wrote the opinion for the majority. Wilson J. wrote a separate concurrence, disagreeing only with Dickson J.'s reliance on the purpose of the Act, as opposed to its effect, to show the breach of the Charter.

14 *Id.*, 351.

15 *Id.*, 347; see also 350 for a different formulation of the same idea.

16 *Id.*, 336.

17 [1985] 1 S.C.R. 295; discussed at note 12, above.

18 *Id.*, 351.

19 [1986] 2 S.C.R. 713; discussed with reference to the distribution of powers at note 3, above.

was the secular one of providing a common pause day for retail workers. The Court held nonetheless that the law infringed s. 2(a), because its *effect* was to impose an economic burden on those retailers who observed a sabbath on a day other than Sunday. That effect created a "competitive pressure"[20] to abandon a non-Sunday sabbath, which was an abridgement of freedom of religion.[21]

In *Edwards Books*, the law was not actually struck down, because the Court upheld the law under s. 1 of the Charter. The secular purpose of providing a common pause day was sufficiently important to justify a limit on freedom of religion. However, some division of the Court occurred on the question whether the Legislature had used the least drastic means of accomplishing the objective. The answer to that question turned on the extent to which the law should have made accommodation for non-Sunday observers. As has already been explained,[22] the Act did in fact contain a "sabbatarian exemption" for retailers who closed their stores on Saturdays, but the exemption was hedged with a size restriction that made it applicable only to small stores.[23] Having regard to the restriction on the availability of the exemption, could it be said that the law pursued its objective by the least drastic means, that is, with the minimum intrusion on freedom of religion? The majority of the Court answered yes to that question, allowing the Legislature some leeway in designing the exemption.[24] Wilson J., however, dissenting on this point, would have required the exemption to be extended to all Saturday-observing retailers, large as well as small, and she would have struck down the size limits in the exemption.

Although the Ontario Act with its restricted sabbatarian exemption was upheld by the majority in *Edwards Books*, the Ontario Legislature later amended the Act in the fashion called for in Wilson J.'s dissent by removing the size limits on the exemption. Now the Act exempted any retail store that closed on a day other than Sunday by reason of the religion of the owner of the store; such a store was free to open on Sunday. The amended Act was challenged and upheld by the Ontario Court of Appeal in *Peel* v. *Great Atlantic and Pacific Co.* (1991).[25] The Court held that the opening up of the exemption eliminated the "competitive pressure" on non-Christians that the Supreme Court in *Edwards Books* had held to be an infringement of freedom of religion. Therefore, the amended Act did not fall foul of s. 2(a) of the Charter, and was valid without recourse to s. 1.[26]

---

20 *Id.*, 766.

21 See the discussion of these cases in ch. 33, Charter of Rights, under the headings 33.6(b), "Purpose or effect", and 33.6(c), "Trivial effects", above.

22 Text accompanying note 3, above.

23 The exemption also did not cover those who observed a weekday as the sabbath, but apparently no evidence was adduced and no attack mounted on this ground, which was not discussed by the Court.

24 The s. 1 reasoning is discussed more fully in ch. 35, Limitation of Rights, under heading 35.11, "Least drastic means", above.

25 (1991) 2 O.R. (3d) 65 (C.A.).

26 Accord, *London Drugs* v. *Red Deer* (1988) 52 D.L.R. (4th) 203 (Alta C.A.) (Sunday closing

39.6 Other religious practices

The previous section of this chapter discussed the Sunday-closing cases, which establish that there is a constitutional obligation under s. 2(a) to accommodate those persons whose religion calls for observance of a sabbath on a day other than Sunday. This section of the chapter considers the extent to which freedom of religion entails the tolerance of other minority religious practices. In *R.* v. *Big M. Drug Mart* (1985),[27] Dickson J. said that freedom of religion included the right "to manifest religious belief by worship and practice". However, he added the proviso that "such manifestations do not injure his or her neighbours or their parallel rights to hold and manifest beliefs and opinions of their own".[28] The proviso implies that freedom of religion would not protect minority religious groups in such practices as human sacrifice, or refusals of schooling or medical treatment of children. However, there are many other practices that have a religious compulsion for a minority religion, such as (to take examples from pre-Charter cases), refusing to salute the flag or sing the national anthem,[29] distributing proselytizing tracts,[30] chanting a mantra,[31] or holding land communally.[32] Such practices could, and therefore should, be tolerated by the majority. Where there is no compelling governmental interest to the contrary, s. 2(a) of the Charter would require the law to accommodate minority religions by according exemptions for their practices.[33]

In *Young* v. *Young* (1993),[34] a judge had granted custody to the mother of three young children, and had granted access to the father, but with the restriction that the father not discuss the Jehovah's Witness religion with the children, or take them to religious services. The reason for the restriction was that the father's strong religious views were not shared by the mother, and were a source of conflict between them. The father attacked the restriction on the ground, among others, that it denied his right to freedom of religion. The British Columbia Court of

law with wide exemption not in breach of s. 2(a)); cf. *R.* v. *Westfair Foods* (1989) 65 D.L.R. (4th) 56 (Sask. C.A.) (Sunday closing law without sabbatarian exemption upheld by creating a "constitutional exemption" for non-Sunday observers).

27 [1985] 1 S.C.R. 295, 336.

28 *Id.*, 346.

29 *Donald* v. *Hamilton Bd. of Education* [1945] O.R. 518 (C.A.) (Jehovah's Witnesses held exempt from flag salute and national anthem).

30 *Saumur* v. *City of Quebec* [1953] 2 S.C.R. 299 (Jehovah's Witnesses held exempt from municipal street by-law).

31 *R.* v. *Harrold* (1971) 19 D.L.R. (3d) 471 (B.C. C.A.) (Hare Krishnas held bound by municipal anti-noise by-law).

32 *Walter* v. *A.-G. Alta.* [1969] S.C.R. 383 (Hutterites held bound by landholding statute).

33 This is essentially the position that has developed in the United States as the result of the free exercise clause of the first amendment: Tribe, note 10, above, 1242-1275; Nowak, note 10, above, 1206-1242.

34 [1993] 4 S.C.R. 3. Concurring opinions were written by McLachlin J., Cory and Iacobucci JJ. and Sopinka J.; dissenting opinions were written by La Forest and L'Heureux-Dubé JJ.

Appeal struck down the restriction, holding that it was a breach of freedom of religion to preclude a parent from sharing his religious beliefs with his children. On appeal to the Supreme Court of Canada, the British Columbia Court of Appeal's decision was upheld by a narrow majority of four to three, but only Sopinka J. followed the same line of reasoning as the British Columbia Court of Appeal. According to Sopinka J., the restriction on religious communication, although imposed in the best interests of the children, would offend freedom of religion, unless it could be shown that the restriction was needed to avoid a "risk of substantial harm" to the children; since, in his view, the evidence established no such risk, the restriction should be struck down. The other six members of the Court held that no order respecting custody or access that was made in the best interests of the children could violate freedom of religion.[35] The right to freedom of religion did not guarantee any religious activity that would not be in the best interests of the children. Because s. 2(a) was inherently limited in this way, no consideration of s. 1 was needed, and the propriety of the judge's order was to be determined without reference to the Charter. McLachlin J. (with Cory and Iacobucci JJ.) still agreed with the British Columbia Court of Appeal that the restriction should be struck down, because in her view the restriction was not in the best interests of the children. L'Heureux-Dubé J. (with La Forest and Gonthier JJ.) dissented on the ground that the trial judge's finding that the restriction was in the best interests of the children should be upheld.[36]

The idea that freedom of religion authorizes religious practices only so far as they do not injure others has been abandoned by the Supreme Court of Canada in favour of an unqualified right to do anything that is dictated by a religious belief. In *B.(R.)* v. *Children's Aid Society* (1995),[37] a majority of the Supreme Court of Canada held that the decision of parents to prohibit doctors from giving a blood transfusion to their baby daughter was protected by freedom of religion, because it was dictated by their beliefs as Jehovah's Witnesses. The doctors attending the child, who was in hospital, considered that her life would be in danger if she did not receive a blood transfusion. In the face of this advice, an application was made under Ontario's child welfare statute to make the child a temporary ward of the Children's Aid Society. The application was granted by a provincial court judge, and the Children's Aid Society consented to the blood transfusion, which was duly given to the child. The order was then terminated

35 There was a question whether the Charter applied to a court order resolving a dispute between two private parties. L'Heureux-Dubé J., dissenting, held that the Charter did not apply; but the majority assumed without deciding that the Charter did apply.

36 In the companion case of *P.(D.)* v. *S.(C.)* [1993] 4 S.C.R. 141, the Court, by a majority, upheld a prohibition on the access parent "continually" indoctrinating the child with the Jehovah's Witness religion; in this case, a majority (Sopinka and McLachlin JJ. dissenting) accepted the trial judge's view that the prohibition on indoctrination was in the best interests of the child.

37 [1995] 1 S.C.R. 315. On the freedom of religion issue, the opinion of La Forest J. attracted the support of L'Heureux-Dubé, Sopinka, Gonthier and McLachlin JJ. The contrary opinion of Iacobucci and Major JJ. attracted the support of Lamer C.J. and Cory J.

and the child was returned to her parents. The parents challenged this procedure as a violation of their freedom of religion, and five judges (a majority) of the Supreme Court of Canada agreed. Speaking for the majority, La Forest J. said that the right of a parent to choose the medical treatment of the child in accordance with the parent's religious beliefs was a "fundamental aspect of freedom of religion",[38] and that the statutory procedure that had been employed in this case was a "serious" infringement of the parents' rights.[39] However, he held that the statutory procedure was justified under s. 1. Iacobucci and Major JJ., with the agreement of two others, took the view that there were intrinsic limits on freedom of religion, and "a parent's freedom of religion does not include the imposition on the child of religious practices which threaten the safety, health or life of the child".[40]

In *Ross* v. *New Brunswick School District No. 15* (1996),[41] the Supreme Court of Canada again held that a damaging practice was protected by freedom of religion. Ross was a schoolteacher who publicly disseminated (not in his teaching, but in the form of books, letters to the newspaper and television appearances) the opinion that Christian civilization was being destroyed by an international Jewish conspiracy. The Supreme Court of Canada held unanimously that this activity was protected by freedom of religion. La Forest J., who wrote the opinion of the Court, did not articulate which of the tenets of Christianity called for this anti-semitic activity. He recited no evidence on the issue, other than that of Ross himself, who had described his writings as "honest religious statements". And La Forest J. relied on his opinion in *B.(R.)* v. *Children's Aid Society* for the proposition that freedom of religion was to be given a broad interpretation, unlimited by consideration of the impact of an allegedly religious practice on the rights of other people.[42] In this case, Ross had been removed from his teaching position by the order of a board of inquiry constituted under New Brunswick's human rights statute. The board of inquiry, after hearing the evidence of Jewish students and their parents, had found that the school board's failure to dismiss or discipline Ross amounted to discrimination in the provision of educational services. The Court held that the board of inquiry's order infringed Ross's freedom of religion (as well as his freedom of expression). However, the Court held that most of the board's order could be justified under s. 1 as a measure to remedy an anti-semitic environment in the school. This justified the removal of Ross from his teaching position to a non-teaching position with the school board, but it did not justify a part of the order that required that Ross be dismissed from a non-teaching position if he resumed his anti-semitic activity. That part of the

38 *Id.*, para. 105.
39 *Id.*, para. 111.
40 *Id.*, para. 225.
41 [1996] 1 S.C.R. 825. La Forest J. wrote the opinion of the nine-judge Court.
42 *Id.*, para. 73. Note that the judges who rejected this proposition in the *B.(R.)* v. *Children's Aid Society*, note 37, above, agreed with La Forest J.'s opinion in this case.

order was therefore held to be unconstitutional and was severed from the rest of the order.

39.7 Religion in public schools

In *Zylberberg* v. *Sudbury Board of Education* (1988),[43] a challenge was brought to an Ontario regulation, made under statutory authority, that required a public school to open or close each school day with "religious exercises consisting of the reading of the Scriptures or other suitable readings and the repeating of the Lord's Prayer or other suitable prayers". The regulation conferred a right on each pupil not to participate in the religious exercises. The Ontario Court of Appeal, by a majority, held that the regulation was unconstitutional, because it "imposed Christian observances upon non-Christian pupils and religious observances on non-believers".[44] The regulation was not saved by the fact that it was wide enough to authorize non-Christian prayers and readings. In Sudbury, where the case originated, the school board had in fact prescribed only Christian exercises (which was what had caused the litigation); but the Court held that, even if the school board had in fact prescribed non-Christian exercises as well as Christian exercises, the regulation would still be bad because it authorized a school board to prescribe only Christian exercises. Nor was the regulation saved by a pupil's right to be exempted from the religious exercises. The regulation still exerted an indirect coercion[45] on pupils to participate, because of the pressure to conform to the majority's norms, which would make it difficult in practice for a minority pupil to claim the exemption.

Ontario did not appeal the decision in *Zylberberg* and the province removed the requirement of "religious exercises" from its public school regulations. However, the province kept in place a regulation dating from 1944 that required a public school to devote two periods per week to "religious education". A parent had the right to apply to the principal of the school to exempt a pupil from the religious education. In *Canadian Civil Liberties Association* v. *Ontario* (1990),[46] the Ontario Court of Appeal struck down this regulation too. The Court concluded from the legislative history of the regulation and the curricula that were placed before it that the purpose of the regulation was the indoctrination of Christian belief, as opposed to education about many religions. The Court followed *Zylberberg* to hold that the regulation was an unconstitutional attempt to impose the majority's Christian beliefs on all school children, and that it was not saved by the provision for exemption, which parents would be reluctant to utilize for fear of embarrassing their children.

---

43 (1988) 65 O.R. (2d) 641 (C.A.).

44 *Id.*, 654.

45 Cf. the indirect coercion imposed by the "competitive pressure" in *Edwards Books*: note 19, above.

46 (1990) 71 O.R. (2d) 341 (C.A.).

In the United States, the Supreme Court has struck down many attempts to introduce religious exercises or instruction in the public schools, including a government-written ''nondenominational'' prayer,[47] voluntary Christian prayer and bible reading,[48] the posting of the ten commandments on classroom walls,[49] a period of silence for ''meditation or voluntary prayer'',[50] and equal time for the teaching of ''creation science'' and evolution.[51] All of these cases were decided under the establishment clause of the first amendment, not the free exercise clause.[52] What was unconstitutional was the active support of government for religious views or practices, which tended to ''an establishment of religion''. This line of reasoning cannot be directly transferred to s. 2(a) of the Charter, which lacks an establishment clause.

In the United States, judges and commentators have speculated as to whether the decisions barring religious exercises or instruction in the public schools could have been reached under the free exercise clause, which is much closer to s. 2(a). This turns on the question whether a mandatory programme with a power of exemption (or a voluntary programme) is sufficiently coercive in practice to constrain a minority child's freedom not to participate. As we have noticed, the Ontario Court of Appeal in the *Zylberberg* and *Canadian Civil Liberties* cases, after hearing evidence on the point, took the view that the embarrassment of non-conformity did operate as a significant practical barrier to the exercise by minority children (or their parents) of a power of exemption from religious exercises or instruction. That finding, which seems sound, means that programmes of religious exercises or instruction in public schools will normally violate the guarantee of freedom of religion. What would not violate the guarantee is a course on religion that examined various religions in a neutral way, not promoting any one religion or assuming the superiority of any one religion.

39.8 Denominational schools

It goes without saying that private schools may offer religious exercises and instruction, and of course that is a major appeal of private schools to many parents. The Supreme Court of Canada has implied that s. 2(a) requires a province to permit children to be educated outside the secular public system,[53] although the

47 *Engel* v. *Vitale* (1962) 370 U.S. 421.

48 *Abingdon School District* v. *Schempp* (1963) 374 U.S. 203.

49 *Stone* v. *Graham* (1980) 449 U.S. 39.

50 *Wallace* v. *Jaffree* (1985) 472 U.S. 38.

51 *Edwards* v. *Aguillard* (1987) 482 U.S. 578.

52 The text of the two clauses is set out in sec. 39.2, ''Section 2(a) of the Charter'', above.

53 *R.* v. *Jones* [1986] 2 S.C.R. 284 held by a majority of four to three that it was not a violation of s. 2(a) to require that an application be made to the provincial Department of Education for approval of a private school or a certificate of efficient instruction for teaching at home. The minority held that this requirement was contrary to s. 2(a) (although it was saved by s. 1) for a

province must have the right to regulate alternative schools, including denominational schools, in order to ensure that a core curriculum and adequate facilities and standards of teaching are offered.

In the United States, the establishment clause prohibits most state aid to denominational schools.[54] In Canada, systems of state aid to minority Protestant and Catholic schools have existed since confederation and are actually guaranteed by s. 93 of the Constitution Act, 1867.[55] Moreover, the Protestant and Catholic schools that are recognized by s. 93 may receive public funding that is denied to the schools of religious denominations not recognized by s. 93.[56] In *R.* v. *Big M Drug Mart* (1985),[57] Dickson J. left open the question whether s. 2(a), despite its lack of an establishment clause, prohibits state aid to denominational schools other than those entitled under s. 93. It is hard to see why s. 2(a) should be regarded as infringed by a programme of state aid, provided all religions are treated equally.[58]

---

person who believed on religious grounds that he ought to be able to teach his children without reference to the state. It is a reasonable inference that for both majority and minority a prohibition on alternative, religious schooling would violate s. 2(a).

54 Tribe, note 10, above, 1215; Nowak, note 10, above, 1168.

55 Section 93 and its counterparts are discussed in ch. 53, Education, below.

56 *Re Bill 30* (Ontario Separate School Funding) [1987] 1 S.C.R. 1148.

57 [1985] 1 S.C.R. 295, 340-341.

58 The requirement of equal treatment would probably flow from s. 2(a), having regard to *R.* v. *Big M Drug Mart*, previous note (preference for Christian sabbath violated s. 2(a)). As well, ''religion'' is expressly named as a prohibited ground of discrimination in s. 15.

40

Expression

40.1 Distribution of powers

(a) Introduction

Laws abridging civil liberties, like all other laws, are subject to the federal distribution of powers. A law is valid only if it is classified as in relation to a matter coming within a class of subjects allocated by the Constitution to the enacting Parliament or Legislature. As noted in chapter 31, Civil Liberties, generally speaking, a law's impact on civil liberties has not been treated by the courts as the leading characteristic in determining the law's classification; the impact on civil liberties has been treated as an incidental or subordinate feature of the law.[1] Freedom of expression does not fit the general rule perfectly. As we shall see, *political* speech may well be a distinct matter that is assigned exclusively to the federal Parliament. Other kinds of speech are distributed between the two levels of government by reference to the facility or activity wherein the speech is regulated. This makes the position quite complicated. For example, commercial advertising is generally within provincial jurisdiction as an incident of the sale of goods or services in the province; but advertising in a federally-regulated medium, such as radio or television, is within federal jurisdiction. As a further complication, a general prohibition of false or misleading advertising could be enacted by the federal Parliament as a criminal law.

(b) Political speech

With respect to political speech,[2] the story begins with the *Alberta Press* case (1938),[3] in which the Supreme Court of Canada struck down an Alberta statute that compelled newspapers in Alberta to publish a government reply to any criticism of provincial government policies.[4] In that case, Duff C.J. and

1 Chapter 31, Civil Liberties, under heading 31.4(b), ''Distribution of powers'', above.

2 For discussion of the cases, see Schmeiser, *Civil Liberties* in Canada (1964), chs. 4, 5; Tarnopolsky, *The Canadian Bill of Rights* (2nd ed., 1975), 37-46.

3 *Re Alta. Statutes* [1938] S.C.R. 100.

4 Five of the six judges gave as their primary reason that the law was ancillary to and dependent upon other social credit legislation which was invalid. Duff C.J. (with Davis J.) added, obiter, the remarks that are described in the text. Cannon J., who alone did not rely on the ancillary point, found the law invalid on the grounds described in the text. An appeal was taken to the Privy Council, but their lordships decided that the validity of the Press bill (and another bill) was moot, and the appeal proceeded only on a third bill, the Bank Taxation bill: *A.-G. Alta.* v. *A.-G. Can.* (Bank Taxation) [1939] A.C. 117.

Cannon J. asserted that free political discussion ("the breath of life of parliamentary institutions")[5] was so important to the nation as a whole that it could not be regarded as a value that was subordinate to other legislative objectives; nor could it be regarded as a local or private matter (s. 92(16)) or as a civil right "in the province" (s. 92(13)). It followed that it was outside the power of the provinces, and within the exclusive power of the federal Parliament. In Cannon J.'s view, the federal power stemmed from the criminal law power; Duff C.J. did not commit himself as to which head of federal legislative power would be applicable, but he appeared to assume that it would be the peace, order, and good government power.

In *Saumur* v. *City of Quebec* (1953),[6] in which the Court struck down a by-law that required the permission of the Chief of Police for the distribution of pamphlets in the city streets, three of the five majority judges, namely, Rand, Kellock and Locke JJ., used the dicta of Duff C.J. and Cannon J. in the *Alberta Press* case as the basis for their decision.[7]

In *Switzman* v. *Elbling* (1957),[8] the Supreme Court of Canada had to determine the validity of Quebec's "Padlock Act", which made it illegal to use a house "to propagate communism or bolshevism by any means whatever". The Act had been upheld in the Quebec courts, but the Supreme Court of Canada, by a majority of eight to one, held it to be invalid. The dissenting judge, Taschereau J., classified the statute as a law in relation to the use of property, and upheld it on that basis. But the other eight judges held that the control of the use of property was colourable, and that the pith and substance of the law was the prohibition of certain political ideas. However, only three of the eight majority judges, namely, Rand, Kellock and Abbott JJ., classified the law as in relation to speech and assigned it to the federal jurisdiction on that basis. The other five judges, namely, Kerwin C.J., Locke, Cartwright, Fauteux and Nolan JJ., did not express an opinion as to legislative jurisdiction over speech, because they held that the prohibition of the propagation of communism with sanctions for breach was tantamount to the creation of a new crime and was within federal jurisdiction as a criminal law.

It seems plausible to conclude from this line of cases, which ended in the 1950s, that at least some forms of regulation of political speech should be characterized as the denial of a fundamental freedom of national dimensions, which is competent only to the federal Parliament, either under its criminal law power or under its peace, order, and good government power. Weiler has criticized the decisions, arguing that the Court was using doctrines of federalism as a kind of surreptitious bill of rights, allocating jurisdiction to that level of government that had not exercised it, in order to invalidate a law that the Court really believed

---

5 [1938] S.C.R. 100, 133 per Duff C.J.

6 [1953] 2 S.C.R. 299.

7 Estey J. held that the by-law was in relation to religion and invalid on that ground. Kerwin J. held that the by-law was inconsistent with a pre-confederation statute and was invalid on that ground. The four minority judges held that the by-law was in relation to the use of the streets and was valid on that ground.

8 [1957] S.C.R. 285.

should not be enacted at all.[9] However, the cases did not suggest that the entire topic of speech was competent only to the federal Parliament.[10] Since the 1950s, the tendency of the cases has been to expand provincial power over speech, even in cases where the power was exercised in derogation of civil libertarian values.

(c) Provincial power

The provincial power over speech, while it will not extend to the regulation or prohibition of political ideas, does authorize the regulation of speech on commercial or local grounds. The tort of defamation, for example, is provincial, despite its impact on speech, because the redress of injury to reputation supplies a dominant tortious aspect to the law, and the law of torts is within provincial power (s. 92(13)). As another example, advertising is within provincial jurisdiction, because it is part of the regulation of business and of consumer protection that is within provincial power (s. 92(13)).[11]

The first case taking an expansive view of provincial power over speech was *Nova Scotia Board of Censors* v. *McNeil* (1978).[12] In that case, the Supreme Court of Canada upheld provincial censorship of films, on the basis that the exhibition of films was a business within provincial jurisdiction and censorship was part of the regulation of the business (s. 92(13)), or, alternatively, was a regulation of a local matter (s. 92(16)). A difficulty with these characterizations of the censorship law was that the law did not supply any criteria for the censor board, which could therefore have exercised its power to suppress political or religious ideas. But Ritchie J. for the majority of the Court finessed this difficulty by holding that the powers of the censor board should be "read down" to exclude the censorship of political or religious ideas.[13] The censor board's power was thus limited to applying moral standards to the depiction of sex and violence, issues of primarily local significance.[14]

9 Weiler, "The Supreme Court and the Law of Canadian Federalism" (1973) 23 U. Toronto L.J. 307, 342-352. Compare the discussion of the "implied bill of rights" in ch. 31, Civil Liberties, under heading 31.4(c), "Implied bill of rights", above.

10 For example, in the *Alberta Press* case, Duff C.J. was not sure whether the impugned law passed beyond the legitimate provincial realm of regulating newspapers and into the forbidden free speech category: [1938] S.C.R. 100, 135.

11 E.g., *A.-G. Que.* v. *Kellogg's Co.* [1978] 2 S.C.R. 211 (upholding provincial regulation of advertising directed to children); *A.G. Can.* v. *Law Society of B.C.* [1982] 2 S.C.R. 307 (upholding provincial regulation of advertising by lawyers); *Irwin Toy* v. *Que.* [1989] 1 S.C.R. 927 (upholding provincial regulation of advertising directed to children). Cf. *Devine* v. *Que.* [1988] 2 S.C.R. 790 (upholding provincial regulation of the language of commercial signs).

12 [1978] 2 S.C.R. 662.

13 Contrast Rand J.'s comments on the breadth of discretion of the chief of police in *Saumur* v. *City of Que.* [1953] 2 S.C.R. 299, 333.

14 Cf. *Rio Hotel* v. *N.B.* [1987] 2 S.C.R. 59 (upholding provincial prohibition of "nude entertainment" in taverns).

In *A.-G. Can. and Dupond* v. *Montreal* (1978),[15] the Supreme Court of Canada upheld a Montreal by-law that imposed a temporary prohibition on assemblies, parades and gatherings on municipal parks and streets. Beetz J. for the majority of the Court held that this was a regulation of the municipal public domain that was within the provincial power over local matters (s. 92(16)). He also said that ''none of [the freedoms of speech, of assembly and association, of the press and of religion] is a single matter coming within exclusive federal or provincial competence''.[16] However, this was probably not intended as a rejection of the 1950s cases, because he went on to hold that the by-law's prohibition did not involve a denial of free speech, saying that ''demonstrations are not a form of speech but of collective action''.[17] Of course, the by-law did not just ban ''demonstrations'', but would have had the effect of prohibiting an assembly that had gathered quietly to listen to speakers.

Civil libertarian concerns about the extensive powers ceded to the provinces by the *McNeil* and *Dupond* decisions are now of primarily historical interest. Such laws would now have to survive Charter review based on freedom of expression and assembly. What the cases establish, however, is an extensive provincial power to regulate speech or assembly in local parks and streets, and to regulate speech in the media that come within provincial jurisdiction, including films, live theatre, books, magazines, newspapers, tapes and records. That power does not extend to the denial of political speech, but this is a narrow category after *McNeil* and *Dupond.*

(d) Federal power

The federal Parliament has the power to regulate political speech for the reasons given earlier.[18] The federal Parliament also has the power, by a prohibition coupled with a sanction, to make particular kinds of speech criminal, as it has done, for example, in the crimes of sedition, obscenity and fraud. And the federal Parliament has the power to regulate speech in the media that come within federal jurisdiction, namely, radio and television.[19]

15 [1978] 2 S.C.R. 770.

16 *Id.*, 796-797.

17 *Id.*, 797.

18 The dicta in the *Alberta Press* case were referred to with approval by Martland J. for a majority of the Court in *Gay Alliance Toward Equality* v. *Vancouver Sun* [1979] 2 S.C.R. 435, 455 (upholding a newspaper's power to refuse to publish an advertisement for a magazine directed to homosexuals).

19 *Capital Cities Communications* v. *CRTC* [1978] 2 S.C.R. 141 (upholding federal content regulation of television).

40.2 Section 2(b) of the Charter

Section 2(b) of the Charter of Rights[20] guarantees to "everyone"[21] the "fundamental freedom" of:

> freedom of thought, belief, opinion and expression, including freedom of the press and other media of communication;

Section 2(b),[22] like other Charter rights, is subject to s. 1 (the limitation clause) of the Charter. A law that limits freedom of expression will be valid under s. 1 if it comes within the phrase "such reasonable limits prescribed by law as can be demonstrably justified in a free and democratic society". Because of s. 1, judicial review under the Charter is a two-stage process: first is the question whether the law (or action) has the purpose or effect of limiting a guaranteed right; and, secondly, if the law does have that purpose or effect, the question is whether the law satisfies the standards of justification under s. 1. A law will be held to be unconstitutional only if both questions are answered adversely to the law. While this two-stage process is appropriate for judicial review under all the Charter rights, we shall see that the unqualified language of s. 2(b), reinforced by the broad interpretation that has been given to that language, means that, in most of the freedom of expression cases, it is easy to decide that, yes, the impugned law does limit s. 2(b). In that case, the constitutionality of the law will turn on the outcome of the second stage of review, that is, the s. 1 inquiry. However, this chapter is not concerned directly with the s. 1 inquiry. Section 1 was examined in ch. 35, Limitation of Rights, above. This chapter is about the scope of s. 2(b).

40.3 Comparison with first amendment

The comparable provision of the American Bill of Rights is the first amendment, which on the topic of expression provides that "Congress shall make no law . . . abridging the freedom of speech, or of the press".[23] This provision by its

---

20 For commentary on s. 2(b), see Anisman and Linden (eds.), *The Media, the Courts and the Charter* (1986); Beaudoin and Mendes (eds.), *The Canadian Charter of Rights and Freedoms* (3rd ed., 1996), ch. 5 (by Beckton); Schneiderman (ed.), *Freedom of Expression and the Charter* (1991); McLeod, Takach, Morton, Segal, *The Canadian Charter of Rights* (Carswell, loose-leaf service), ch. 23; *Canadian Charter of Rights Annotated* (Canada Law Book, loose-leaf service), annotation to s. 2(b). The last work contains a bibliography of the relevant literature.

21 On the meaning of "everyone", see ch. 34, Application of Charter, under heading 34.1, "Benefit of rights", above.

22 The comparable provisions of the Canadian Bill of Rights are s. 1(d), which guarantees "freedom of speech", and s. 1(f), which guarantees "freedom of the press".

23 For commentary on the guarantee of free speech in the first amendment, see Tribe *American Constitutional Law* (2nd ed., 1986), ch. 12; Nowak and Rotunda, *Constitutional Law* (4th ed., 1991), ch. 16.

terms binds only the federal Congress, but it is applicable to the states as well through the fourteenth amendment.[24]

The first amendment uses the word "speech". Section 2(b) uses the phrase "thought, belief, opinion and expression". The references to "thought, belief, opinion" will have little impact, since even a totalitarian state cannot suppress unexpressed ideas. It is the reference to "expression" in s. 2(b) that is the critical one, and the word expression is very broad — broader than "speech".

Because the first amendment is framed in absolute language, and the American Bill of Rights contains no limitation clause like s. 1, American courts have had difficulty in supplying a principled justification for upholding laws that restrict speech.[25] No attempt will be made here to describe the complex American jurisprudence, except to note that laws restraining speech have often been upheld.

40.4 Reasons for protecting expression

What is the rationale for a guarantee of freedom of expression?

Perhaps the most powerful rationale for the constitutional protection of freedom of expression is its role as an instrument of democratic government. This rationale was well expressed by Rand J. in *Switzman* v. *Elbling* (1957),[26] when he said that parliamentary government was "ultimately government by the free public opinion of an open society", and that it demanded "the condition of a virtually unobstructed access to and diffusion of ideas".[27] In the same case, Abbott J. said that "the right of free expression of opinion and of criticism" were "essential to the working of a parliamentary democracy such as ours".[28] Canadian judges have always placed a high value on freedom of expression as an element of parliamentary democracy and have sought to protect it with the limited tools that were at their disposal before the adoption of the Charter of Rights.[29] It is obvious that political speech is at the core of s. 2(b) of the Charter, and could be curtailed under s. 1 only in service of the most compelling governmental interest.

---

24 The doctrine of "selective incorporation", which accomplishes this result, is explained in ch. 34, Application of Charter, under heading 34.2(a), "Both levels of government", above.

25 For example, the Supreme Court of the United States upheld restrictions on falsehoods, on insulting, profane or fighting words, on advertising and on obscenity by the bizarre expedient of denying that these things were speech at all! The Court has recently backed away from that position, and now accords a degree of first amendment protection to all these things, except for obscenity: *New York Times* v. *Sullivan* (1964) 376 U.S. 254 (false and defamatory statement in newspaper protected); *Cohen* v. *California* (1971) 403 U.S. 15 (profane slogan on jacket protected); *Virginia State Bd. of Pharmacy* v. *Virginia Citizens Consumer Council* (1976) 425 U.S. 748 (advertising protected).

26 [1957] S.C.R. 285.

27 *Id.*, 358.

28 *Id.*, 369.

29 See the discussion of the *Alberta Press* case, the *Saumur* case and *Switzman* v. *Elbling* in text accompanying notes 6 to 10, above.

A second, broader rationale for the constitutional protection of freedom of expression is its role as an instrument of truth. It was John Stuart Mill in his essay *On Liberty* (1859) who argued that suppression of opinion was wrong, because it is only by "the collision of adverse opinions" that truth is discovered or confirmed. This idea became Oliver Wendell Holmes's rationale for the guarantee of freedom of speech in the first amendment: the truth was to be found in a "free trade in ideas", in "the power of thought to get itself accepted in the competition of the market".[30] This "marketplace of ideas" rationale for freedom of expression would include political speech, of course, but would also extend to the ideas of philosophy, history, the social sciences, the natural sciences, medicine and all the other branches of human knowledge. It is obvious that the expression of all these ideas is also protected by s. 2(b) of the Charter.

A third, even broader, rationale for the constitutional protection of freedom of expression is its role as an instrument of personal fulfilment. On this theory, which is to be found in some American judicial decisions, expression is protected not just to create a more perfect polity, and not just to discover the truth, but to "enlarge the prospects for individual self-fulfilment",[31] or to allow "personal growth and self-realization".[32] If expression is conceived in these broad terms, it covers much that is not speech at all: art, music and dance, for example.

The idea of expression as an instrument of personal fulfilment goes too far if it does not include a communicative purpose. After all, any act could be characterized as an instrument of personal fulfilment. Both "speech" and "expression" should be limited to attempts to communicate ideas. The courts of both the United States and Canada have insisted upon a communicative purpose to qualify an act as protected speech or expression. It might be thought that the word "speech", which is narrower than "expression", would exclude even some acts that were done with a communicative purpose. But the Supreme Court of the United States has readily accepted a variety of forms of "expressive conduct" as being "symbolic speech", which is entitled to first amendment protection, for example, a refusal to salute the flag,[33] the burning of a flag,[34] the burning of a draft card,[35] the covering of a motto on a car licence plate,[36] and the wearing of a black armband.[37] If "speech" will go this far, it is clear that "expression" in s. 2(b) of the Charter will do so as well.

---

30 *Abrams* v. *United States* (1919) 250 U.S. 616, 630 (dissenting).
31 Nowak, note 23, above, 940.
32 Tribe, note 23, above, 787.
33 *West Virginia State Bd. of Education* v. *Barnette* (1943) 319 U.S. 624.
34 *Texas* v. *Johnson* (1989) 491 U.S. 397.
35 *United States* v. *O'Brien* (1968) 391 U.S. 367.
36 *Wooley* v. *Maynard* (1977) 430 U.S. 705 (the New Hampshire plate's motto was "Live free or die"!).
37 *Tinker* v. *Des Moines School District* (1969) 393 U.S. 503.

In *Irwin Toy* v. *Quebec* (1989),[38] Dickson C.J., Lamer and Wilson JJ., in their joint majority judgment, embraced all of the three reasons for protecting freedom of expression, which they summarized in the following terms:[39]

> (1) seeking and attaining the truth is an inherently good activity; (2) participation in social and political decision-making is to be fostered and encouraged; and (3) the diversity in forms of individual self-fulfilment and human flourishing ought to be cultivated . . . .

The acceptance of all three reasons as the basis for the right to freedom of expression entails a very broad definition of the right. That is the topic of the next section of this chapter.

40.5 Meaning of expression

(a) Definition

The Supreme Court of Canada has defined "expression" in these terms: "Activity is expressive if it attempts to convey meaning".[40] This broad definition has been supported by a willing acceptance of the broadest rationale for the protection of expression — the realization of individual self-fulfilment[41] — as well as the Court's view that the Charter should be given a generous interpretation.[42]

Is there any activity that is *not* expression under the Court's definition? The answer is not much, because "most human activity combines expressive and physical elements"; what is excluded is that which is "purely physical and does not convey or attempt to convey meaning".[43] Obviously, all forms of art are sufficiently communicative to be protected: novels, plays, films, paintings, dances and music.[44] A speaker's choice of language is protected, so that a requirement that commercial signs be in French only is a violation of s. 2(b).[45] Indeed, the Court has acknowledged that parking a car would be an expressive activity, and therefore protected under s. 2(b), if it were done with an expressive purpose —

38 [1989] 1 S.C.R. 927, 968-971; see also *RWDSU* v. *Dolphin Delivery* [1986] 2 S.C.R. 573, 583-586; *R.* v. *Keegstra* [1990] 3 S.C.R. 697, 727-728, 827-828.

39 *Id.*, 976.

40 *Id.*, 968. Accord, *Re ss. 193 and 195.1 of Criminal Code* (Prostitution Reference) [1990] 1 S.C.R. 1123, 1180; *Rocket* v. *Royal College of Dental Surgeons* [1990] 2 S.C.R. 232, 244; *R.* v. *Keegstra* [1990] 3 S.C.R. 697, 729, 826.

41 Note 38, above.

42 Chapter 33, Charter of Rights, under heading 33.7(b), "Generous interpretation", above.

43 *Irwin Toy* v. *Que.* [1989] 1 S.C.R. 927, 969.

44 *Re ss. 193 and 195.1 of Criminal Code* (Prostitution Reference) [1990] 1 S.C.R. 1123, 1182.

45 *Ford* v. *Que.* [1988] 2 S.C.R. 712.

and a protest against the parking regulations would be a sufficiently expressive purpose![46]

(b) Criminal expression

In the *Prostitution Reference* (1990),[47] the Court held that communicating for the purpose of prostitution, which was an offence under the Criminal Code, was protected expression under s. 2(b). (A majority of the Court upheld the law under s. 1.) Lamer J. in a concurring judgment pointed out that activities should not be denied s. 2(b) protection "solely because they have been made the subject of criminal offences",[48] and he listed 25 Criminal Code offences that prohibited some form of expression. In other words, s. 2(b) protects falsehoods (perjury or fraud, for example) and other harmful (but communicative) activity (counselling a suicide, for example). Lamer J.'s dictum was confirmed in the later cases of *R.* v. *Keegstra* (1990)[49] and *R.* v. *Zundel* (1992),[50] in which the Criminal Code offences of publishing hate propaganda and publishing false news were held to be in violation of s. 2(b). (The hate-propaganda offence, but not the false news offence, was upheld under s. 1 by a narrow majority of the Court.) So long as the activity is communicative, and falls short of the direct infliction of violence, it is protected by s. 2(b).

(c) Violence

Expressive activity that takes the *form* of violence is not protected by s. 2(b): "a murderer or a rapist cannot invoke freedom of expression in justification of the form of expression he has chosen".[51] Initially, the Court said that "threats of violence" were also unprotected,[52] but the Court has since repented of this temporary failure of nerve to hold that threats of violence are protected by s. 2(b).[53] A communication could be classified as a threat of violence only by reference to its *content*, and there are no content-related restrictions on the s. 2(b) right.[54]

---

46 *Irwin Toy* v. *Que.* [1989] 1 S.C.R. 927, 969. Fortunately, most drivers are unaware of their constitutional right to disregard parking restrictions of which they disapprove.

47 *Re ss. 193 and 195.1 of Criminal Code* (Prostitution Reference) [1990] 1 S.C.R. 1123. Dickson C.J., with whom La Forest and Sopinka JJ. agreed, wrote the plurality opinion. Lamer J. wrote a concurring opinion. Wilson J., with the agreement of L'Heureux-Dubé J., dissented.

48 *Id.*, 1183.

49 [1990] 3 S.C.R. 697.

50 [1992] 2 S.C.R. 731.

51 *Id.*, 1185; *Irwin Toy* v. *Que.* [1989] 1 S.C.R. 927, 970; *R.* v. *Keegstra* [1990] 3 S.C.R. 697, 731.

52 *RWDSU* v. *Dolphin Delivery* [1986] 2 S.C.R. 573, 588.

53 *R.* v. *Keegstra* [1990] 3 S.C.R. 697, 733 per Dickson C.J. for majority; McLachlin J. at 829 disagreed.

54 *Id.*, 732.

(d) Content neutrality

It will be evident from the preceding text that content neutrality is the governing principle of the Supreme Court of Canada's definition of expression. "The content of a statement cannot deprive it of the protection accorded by s. 2(b), no matter how offensive it may be".[55] Therefore, in *R.* v. *Keegstra* (1990),[56] the Supreme Court of Canada held unanimously that the promotion of hatred against the Jews or another racial group, which is a Criminal Code offence, is protected by s. 2(b). The offence was upheld under s. 1, but by the bare majority of four to three. In *Keegstra*, the Court even rejected the argument that s. 2(b) should be narrowed by reference to other provisions of the Charter, such as the guarantee of equality in s. 15 and the recognition of multiculturalism in s. 27. The fact that the Criminal Code provision was attempting to vindicate the values reflected in ss. 15 and 27 was relevant only to the s. 1 inquiry.[57]

In *R.* v. *Zundel* (1992),[58] the Supreme Court of Canada struck down the false-news provision of the Criminal Code, which made it an offence for a person to "wilfully publish a statement, tale or news that he knows is false and causes or is likely to cause injury or mischief to a public interest". This prohibition covered only statements that were false, and that were known by the accused to be false. Zundel, who had published a pamphlet denying that the Holocaust occurred, was convicted under the false-news law. The Supreme Court of Canada reversed the conviction on the ground that the law was unconstitutional. The Court was unanimous that s. 2(b)'s protection extended to deliberate falsehoods, because the truth or falsity of a statement can be determined only by reference to its content. The principle of content-neutrality therefore dictated the answer. The Court, by a bare majority of four to three, also held that the law could not be justified under s. 1. The law was therefore struck down, and Zundel was acquitted and left free to continue his dissemination of deliberate falsehoods under the protection of the Constitution.[59]

The principle of content neutrality means that s. 2(b) extends to much activity that is not worthy of constitutional protection. Indeed, the Court has acknowledged that "not all expression is equally worthy of protection".[60] The evaluation of the worthiness of the expression is however relevant only to the s. 1 inquiry. If the

---

55 *Id.*, 828.

56 *Ibid.*

57 *Id.*, 734, 755-758, 833.

58 [1992] 2 S.C.R. 731.

59 Zundel had not been charged under the hate-propaganda offence that was upheld in *Keegstra*, because a prosecution for that offence requires the consent of the Attorney General, and the Attorney General of Ontario, perhaps fearing that Holocaust denial was not caught by the hate-propaganda offence, refused to give his consent. That refusal was followed by the laying of a charge by a private citizen under the false-news provision, which does not require that the consent of the Attorney General be obtained.

60 *Id.*, 760.

Court regards a particular kind of expression as of little value, then this makes the objective of a limiting law easier to justify, and invites more relaxed standards of proportionality. Because communicating for the purpose of prostitution, or promoting racial hatred, are of ''limited importance'',[61] it is relatively easy to justify laws that prohibit those activities.[62] This illustrates my earlier point that the expansion of the guaranteed right, in this case, s. 2(b), inevitably leads to an erosion of the severe standards of justification that the Court originally erected for s. 1. That in turn leads to decisions that depend heavily on the judges' balancing of costs and benefits, a process that is unprincipled and unpredictable.[63]

40.6 Ways of limiting expression

(a) Prior restraint

Expression may be restricted in a variety of different ways. The restriction that is usually regarded as the most severe is a ''prior restraint'' on publication. Expression that is never published cannot contribute in any way to the democratic process, to the marketplace of ideas or to personal fulfilment. The courts have taken under review a variety of prior restraints, including the censorship of films,[64] restrictions on the importation of books and magazines,[65] restrictions on access to the courts[66] and the reporting of judicial proceedings,[67] a publication ban on a fictional television programme,[68] restrictions on access to public property[69] and injunctions against picketing.[70] Needless to say, in all these cases, it was held that the prior restraint was a limit on freedom of expression. The courts have also held that a restriction on election campaign expenditures, which would be used to purchase time or space in the media for campaign messages, is a form of prior restraint that is prohibited by s. 2(b).[71] In contrast to the United States, where prior restraints are nearly (but not quite) always struck down,[72] in Canada the general

---

61 *Id.*, 762.

62 Note, however, that the Court divided on the issue of s. 1 justification in both the prostitution and the hate propaganda cases.

63 Chapter 35, Limitation of Rights, under heading 35.3, ''Relationship between s. 1 and rights'', above.

64 *Re Ont. Film and Video Appreciation Society* (1984) 41 O.R. (2d) 583 (C.A.) (struck down).

65 *Luscher* v. *Revenue Can.* [1985] 1 F.C. 85 (C.A.) (struck down).

66 *Re Southam and The Queen (No. 1)* (1983) 41 O.R. (2d) 113 (C.A.) (struck down); *Re Southam and The Queen (No. 2)* (1986) 53 O.R. (2d) 663 (C.A.) (saved under s. 1).

67 *Canadian Newspapers Co.* v. *Can.* [1988] 1 S.C.R. 122 (saved under s. 1); *Edmonton Journal* v. *Alta.* [1989] 2 S.C.R. 1326 (struck down).

68 *Dagenais* v. *CBC* [1994] 3 S.C.R. 835 (struck down).

69 *Committee for Cth. of Can.* v. *Can.* [1991] 1 S.C.R. 139 (struck down).

70 *BCGEU* v. *B.C.* (Vancouver Courthouse) [1988] 2 S.C.R. 214.

71 *Nat. Citizens Coalition* v. *A.G. Can.* (1984) 11 D.L.R. (4th) 481 (Alta. Q.B.) (struck down).

72 Tribe, note 23, above, 1039-1061; Nowak, note 23, above, 969-990.

standards of s. 1 justification are applicable to prior restraints as well as to other limits on expression, and a number of prior restraints have been upheld under s. 1.[73]

(b) Penal prohibition

The most common restriction on speech is a prohibition coupled with a penal sanction, for example, the Criminal Code offences of perjury or counselling suicide. To the extent that the prospect of punishment deters the uttering of the prohibited expression, a legal prohibition operates in the same way as a prior restraint. However, some speakers may not be deterred, and their ideas will enter the public domain. The courts have struck down a prohibition on advertising by dentists,[74] and a prohibition on the advertising of tobacco products.[75] The courts have upheld under s. 1 a prohibition on advertising directed at children,[76] a prohibition on communicating for the purpose of prostitution[77] and a prohibition on hate propaganda.[78]

Falling just short of a criminal prohibition is the prohibition of "discriminatory practices" in the Canadian Human Rights Act. One of those practices is the use of the telephone to spread messages of hatred against minority groups. A discriminatory practice does not give rise to an immediate penalty, but a Human Rights Tribunal has the power to order that the practice cease. Once the order has been made, it can be entered as an order of the Federal Court, and disobedience is then punishable as a contempt of court. In *Canada* v. *Taylor* (1990),[79] this entire process was followed, and, when Mr. Taylor continued his telephonic messages of anti-semitism in defiance of the court order, he was committed to prison for contempt. He appealed the committal on constitutional grounds up to the Supreme Court of Canada, which held that the ban on telephone messages violated s. 2(b). However, the Court held that the ban was justified under s. 1, and so Mr. Taylor stayed in prison.[80]

In *Ross* v. *New Brunswick School District No. 15* (1996),[81] the public dissemination (outside the classroom) by a schoolteacher of anti-semitic messages was found to be a prohibited discriminatory practice by a board of inquiry constituted under New Brunswick's human rights statute. The board of inquiry ordered the school board that employed the teacher to remove him from his teaching

73 The outcomes of the prior restraint cases are indicated in notes 61-67, above.
74 *Rocket* v. *Royal College of Dental Surgeons* [1990] 2 S.C.R. 232.
75 *R.J.R.-MacDonald* v. *Can.* [1995] 3 S.C.R. 199.
76 *Irwin Toy* v. *Que.* [1989] 1 S.C.R. 927.
77 *Re ss. 193 and 195.1 of Criminal Code* (Prostitution Reference) [1990] 1 S.C.R. 1123.
78 *R.* v. *Keegstra* [1990] 3 S.C.R. 697.
79 [1990] 3 S.C.R. 892.
80 Cf. *BCGEU* v. *B.C.* (Vancouver Courthouse) [1988] 2 S.C.R. 214 (injunction issued against courthouse picketing on basis that picketing was a contempt of court).
81 [1996] 1 S.C.R. 825.

position to a non-teaching position. The Supreme Court of Canada held that the order of the board of inquiry was a breach of s. 2(b), but that it was justified under s.1 as a measure to reduce the climate of anti-semitism that had developed at the school. However, the Court held that the board of inquiry had overstepped the reasonable limit of s. 1 in also ordering the school board to dismiss the teacher from his non-teaching post if at any time in the future he were to resume his anti-semitic activities. That part of the order was struck down as an unjustified breach of s. 2(b).

(c) Civil prohibition

A prohibition on expression that is sanctioned by only a civil remedy is exemplified by the tort of defamation or a contract to keep some matter confidential. Breach of a civil obligation does not attract a penal sanction, such as a fine or imprisonment; the breach entitles the aggrieved party to recover damages or to obtain some other civil remedy such as an injunction. Where a civil obligation is created by the common law (which includes the law of contract), there will normally be no Charter remedy, because the Charter does not apply to the rules of the common law that govern relations between private parties.[82] Where the civil prohibition is created by statute, the Charter will apply, and the prohibition will offend s. 2(b).[83]

(d) Forced expression

Occasionally a person is forced by law to make a statement. For example, in *R.J.R.-MacDonald* v. *Canada* (1995),[84] a federal statute, the Tobacco Products Control Act, required cigarettes and other tobacco products to be sold in packages that displayed prescribed warnings of the health dangers of smoking. The warnings were unattributed, so that they could be interpreted as coming from the manufacturers (instead of the true author, the federal government), and the manufacturers were prohibited from displaying any information of their own on the packages (except for the name of the product). The Supreme Court of Canada, by a majority, held that the requirement of unattributed warnings was a breach of s.2(b), on the basis that ''freedom of expression necessarily entails the right to say nothing or the right not to say certain things''.[85] The majority of the Court held that a simple requirement of health warnings on cigarette packages could be

82 *RWDSU* v. *Dolphin Delivery* [1986] 2 S.C.R. 573 (Charter inapplicable to tort of inducing breach of contract).

83 See ch. 34, Application of Charter, above.

84 [1995] 3 S.C.R. 199.

85 *Id.*, para. 124 per McLachlin J. for the majority. La Forest J. for the dissenting minority would have held that warnings of danger on packaging that were not expressly attributed to the manufacturers did not infringe their freedom of expression, and required no justification under s.1: *Id.* para. 115.

justified under s.1, but that the government had failed to establish the justification for the non-attribution of the warnings or for the prohibition of additional information on the packages. The requirement of unattributed warnings was therefore struck down.

In *Slaight Communications* v. *Davidson* (1989),[86] an adjudicator, exercising statutory powers conferred by the Canada Labour Code, ordered an employer to provide a letter of reference to an unjustly dismissed employee, and also stipulated the facts that were to be recited in the mandatory letter of reference. The Supreme Court of Canada, by a majority, held that it was a breach of s. 2(b) to order a person to make a statement, but, because the statement included ''only objective facts that are not in dispute'', the order was justified under s. 1.

In *Lavigne* v. *OPSEU* (1991),[87] the question arose whether an ''agency shop'' clause in a collective agreement, which required non-members of the union to pay union dues, was a breach of s. 2(b). The evidence established that the union used some of its funds, which included the forced dues, to promote left-wing causes of which the complaining non-member (Lavigne) disapproved. La Forest J. for the majority of the Supreme Court of Canada held that the payments to the union were not expressive activity, and therefore did not come within s. 2(b). Wilson J. for the concurring minority held that a voluntary payment of dues could be expressive activity, but that the forced payment of dues under an agency shop requirement did not imply support for the union's views or preclude the payer from holding and expressing contrary views; she therefore agreed that there was no breach of s. 2(b).[88]

(e) Language requirement

A Quebec law requiring that public signs and advertisements be in French only has been struck down as a violation of s. 2(b). The law did not restrict the content of signs or advertisements; they could contain any message at all, provided the message was in the French language. In *Ford* v. *Quebec* (1988),[89] the Supreme Court of Canada rejected the argument that language was ''merely a means or medium of expression''; rather, the Court held, ''it colours the content and meaning of expression''.[90] The Court concluded that freedom of expression included ''the freedom to express oneself in the language of one's choice''.[91] On that basis, the requirement of the exclusive use of French, involving as it did a prohibition of the use of any language other than French, was unconstitutional. In *Devine* v.

86 [1989] 1 S.C.R. 1038.
87 [1991] 2 S.C.R. 211.
88 Accord, *McKay* v. *Man.* [1989] 2 S.C.R. 357 (public funding of candidates for election does not abridge the freedom of expression of taxpayers).
89 [1988] 2 S.C.R. 712.
90 *Id.*, 748.
91 *Ibid.* The same argument is advanced in Green, ''Freedom of Expression and Choice of Language'' (1991) 13 Law and Policy 215.

Quebec (1988),[92] the Court considered a Quebec law requiring the non-exclusive use of French for brochures, orders, invoices and other business documents; the documents had to be in French, but English (or any other language) could be used as well. The Court held that this law was also a breach of s. 2(b): ''freedom consists in the absence of compulsion as well as an absence of restraint''.[93] However, the Court did uphold the non-exclusive requirement under s. 1.

(f) Search of press premises

In two cases,[94] the Supreme Court of Canada has reviewed the issue of a search warrant to the police to obtain film taken by television crews of a crime in progress. It was argued, and accepted by McLachlin J. in dissent, that the search warrant was invalid as a breach of freedom of the press, because of the chilling effect on newsgathering that would be caused if the information gathered was available to the police. However, the majority of the Court, while suggesting caution in the issue of search warrants for press premises, upheld the warrants, placing emphasis on the fact that the film had already been shown. For the majority, there was no breach of s. 2(b).

(g) Time, manner and place

The least severe form of restriction on expression is the regulation of the time, manner or place of expression. For example, a law might prohibit the use of cartoons in advertising directed at children, or a law might authorize a public official to stipulate the time and route of a parade. These laws restrict expression, and are therefore in violation of s. 2(b); but, because they do not regulate the content of expression, a court would be likely to uphold the laws under s. 1.

The regulation of time, manner and place can be so broad as to amount to a significant restriction on expression. This was the case in *Ramsden* v. *Peterborough* (1993),[95] where a municipal by-law prohibited the placing of posters anywhere on municipal public property. The by-law was content-neutral, and it prohibited only one kind of expression (postering) on only one kind of property (municipal public property). Nonetheless, the by-law did close off the most obvious public places to affix posters, such as utility poles. Moreover, because public postering is inexpensive, it has traditionally been used by poorly-funded groups to publicize new ideas or causes. These considerations persuaded the Supreme Court of Canada that the ban on postering was too broad to be upheld under s. 1, although the Court implied that a narrower by-law, more carefully targeted at such legitimate concerns as littering, aesthetic blight, traffic hazards and impediments to persons repairing utility poles, would be upheld.

---

92 [1988] 2 S.C.R. 790.

93 *Id.*, 813.

94 *CBC* v. *Lessard* [1991] 3 S.C.R. 421; *CBC* v. *N.B.* [1991] 3 S.C.R. 459.

95 [1993] 2 S.C.R. 1084. The opinion of the Court was written by Iacobucci J.

40.7 Commercial expression

(a) Introduction

''Commercial expression'',[96] of which the most important example is advertising, is expression that is designed to promote the sale of goods and services. Because of the obvious public need to forbid false or misleading claims, to require warnings of danger and disclosure of other matters (such as food ingredients), commercial expression is in all jurisdictions subject to a good deal of regulation. Indeed, the Supreme Court of the United States, not wanting to inhibit regulation, initially held that commercial expression was not speech at all, so that it was unprotected by the guarantee of ''freedom of speech'' in the first amendment.[97] In 1976, the Court reversed this implausible position, and held that commercial speech was protected by the first amendment.[98] The Court made clear that it would still uphold laws against false or deceptive claims, and reasonable restrictions as to the time, place and manner of speech.[99] But restrictions on the content of commercial speech have since 1976 generally been struck down.[100]

There are two reasons why commercial expression ought to be protected under a guarantee of freedom of expression (in Canada) or speech (in the United States). First, it does literally fall within the meaning of the word ''expression'' (or ''speech''), and it does make a contribution to the ''marketplace of ideas'' that is fostered by the constitutional guarantee. Secondly, it is very difficult to distinguish commercial speech from other kinds of speech, in that a variety of political, economic and social ideas are inevitably inherent in commercial speech. However, to the extent that commercial expression deals with ascertainable facts regarding price, quality, effectiveness and safety, regulation designed to ensure that consumers have sufficient, accurate information to make informed choices must be upheld. In Canada, the balancing of the value of free expression against the value of consumer protection has to take place within s. 1 of the Charter.

(b) Language requirements

The Supreme Court of Canada has held from the beginning that commercial expression is protected by the guarantee of freedom of expression in s. 2(b). The first case to reach the Court was *Ford* v. *Quebec* (1988),[101] in which the Court

96 See Sharpe, ''Commercial Expression and the Charter'' (1987) 37 U. Toronto L.J. 229; Weinrib, ''Does Money Talk?: Commercial Expression in the Canadian Constitutional Context'' in Schneiderman (ed.) *Freedom of Expression and the Charter* (1991).

97 *Valentine* v. *Chrestenson* (1942) 316 U.S. 52.

98 *Virginia State Bd. of Pharmacy* v. *Virginia Citizens Consumer Council* (1976) 425 U.S. 748.

99 *Id.*, 771, 777-778.

100 Tribe, note 23, above, 890-904; Nowak, note 23, above, 1011-1035.

101 [1988] 2 S.C.R. 712. A single opinion of ''the Court'' was rendered.

held that a Quebec law requiring commercial signs to be in French only was unconstitutional. The Court discussed the American commercial speech cases, and reviewed some of the American literature. While not expressly approving the detail of the American jurisprudence, the Court concluded that:[102]

> Over and above its intrinsic value as expression, commercial expression which, as has been pointed out, protects listeners as well as speakers plays a significant role in enabling individuals to make informed economic choices, an important aspect of individual self-fulfilment and personal autonomy.

The Court held that the language-of-signs law violated s. 2(b) by prohibiting signs in the English language. The Court held that the law could not be justified under s. 1, because, although it pursued an important purpose, namely, the protection of the French language, it impaired the rights of English-speakers more than was necessary to accomplish the purpose. A requirement of French, even a requirement that French be predominant, would have been a ''reasonable limit'' under s. 1, but a complete prohibition of English went too far.[103]

(c) Advertising restrictions

In *Irwin Toy* v. *Quebec* (1989),[104] the Court upheld a Quebec law that prohibited all commercial advertising directed at children under 13 years of age. The Court followed its earlier decision in *Ford* to decide that advertising was constitutionally protected by s. 2(b) of the Charter. In this, the Court was unanimous. However, the Court divided on the issue whether this law could be justified as a ''reasonable limit'' under s. 1. By a majority of three to two, the Court held that the protection of a particularly vulnerable group, namely, young children, was a sufficiently important purpose, and the Quebec Legislature should be allowed some leeway in deciding to accomplish that purpose by a ban on advertising directed at children. The ban was not an absolute one, in the sense that products such as toys and breakfast cereals could still be advertised, provided the advertising did not use cartoons and other techniques directed at children. The majority of the Court accordingly upheld the law.

Professionals such as lawyers, doctors and dentists are typically subject to restrictions on advertising of varying degrees of stringency. The object of the restrictions is to maintain the dignity of a learned profession, although the implausible claim that advertising of professional services is inevitably misleading is sometimes made as well. In *Rocket* v. *Royal College of Dental Surgeons* (1990),[105] a particularly severe regulation came under judicial review. Under

---

102 *Id.*, 767.

103 In the companion case of *Devine* v. *Que.* [1988] 2 S.C.R. 790, the Court held that a requirement of French for various business forms was also a breach of s. 2(b), but, because other languages were not prohibited, the requirement was upheld under s. 1.

104 [1989] 1 S.C.R. 927. A joint opinion of Dickson C.J., Lamer and Wilson JJ. was the majority opinion. McIntyre J., with Beetz J., dissented.

105 [1990] 1 S.C.R. 232. McLachlin J. wrote the opinion of the Court.

Ontario's Health Disciplines Act, dentists were prohibited from advertising their services, with only trivial exceptions for an exterior sign, business cards and the like. The Supreme Court of Canada held unanimously that the dental regulation was a violation of s. 2(b). With respect to s. 1, the Court held that the objective of maintaining high standards of professional conduct would justify the regulation of advertising by professionals, but this particular regulation was far broader than was necessary to accomplish that purpose. For example, the regulation prohibited a dentist from advertising office hours or languages spoken — "information which would be useful to the public and present no serious danger of misleading the public or undercutting professionalism".[106] The Court struck down the regulation.

In *RJR-MacDonald* v. *Canada* (1995),[107] the federal Tobacco Products Control Act was held to be unconstitutional. The Act prohibited the advertising of cigarettes and other tobacco products.[108] Obviously, the Act infringed s. 2(b). With respect to s. 1, the main difficulty for the federal government was that the product itself was lawful. The government argued that a ban on the product was impracticable, because so many Canadians were smokers. Instead, Parliament chose the weaker alternative of banning advertising, intending thereby to reduce consumption, which would reduce the harmful effects of smoking.[109] The Quebec Superior Court, at the conclusion of a long trial, held that the evidence failed to establish a causal connection between a ban on advertising and a reduction in smoking. In the face of this finding, the Supreme Court of Canada was still unanimously prepared to find that there was enough evidence to establish a rational connection between the advertising ban and the objective of reducing consumption. However, a majority of the Court could not accept that a total ban on all forms of advertising, including purely informational advertising, was the least drastic means of accomplishing the objective. The majority concluded that the Act could not be justified under s. 1, and held that it was unconstitutional. The Court would have upheld a ban more carefully targeted at the recruitment of new smokers, for example, advertising directed to young people or advertising associating smoking with an attractive lifestyle.[110]

106 *Id.*, 250.

107 [1995] 3 S.C.R. 199. The principal majority opinion was written by McLachlin J.; Lamer C.J., Sopinka, Iacobucci and Major JJ. each wrote concurring opinions. The principal dissenting opinion was written by La Forest J., with the agreement of L'Heureux-Dubé and Gonthier JJ.; Cory J. wrote a brief dissenting opinion, agreeing with La Forest J. except on one point.

108 The Act also required that unattributed health warnings be displayed on the packaging: see text accompanying note 84, above.

109 This invited the question of whether Parliament could use the criminal-law power to ban advertising of a harmful but legal product. The Court, by a majority of seven to two, held that the criminal-law power did authorize a law of this kind: see ch. 18, Criminal Law, under heading 18.3(c), "Tobacco," above.

110 [1995] 3 S.C.R. 199, paras. 164, 191.

(d) Prostitution

Prostitution, like tobacco, is lawful in Canada. However, the Criminal Code makes it an offence to communicate in a public place for the purpose of engaging in prostitution. The Supreme Court of Canada, in the *Prostitution Reference* (1990),[111] held that this type of ''commercial speech'' is protected by s. 2(b). However, a majority of the Court upheld the Criminal Code provision under s. 1. For the majority, the purpose of eradicating the nuisance of street-solicitation justified the limit on expression. For the dissenting minority, the law was overbroad, because it prohibited communications between prostitutes and customers regardless of whether they were causing any harm to others.

40.8 Picketing

Picketing is the activity of members of a trade union on strike, who will assemble outside a workplace, often carrying signs.[112] The purposes of picketing are to advise the public that the picketers are on strike, to dissuade strikebreakers from entering the workplace, and to encourage consumers to boycott the goods or services produced by the struck firm. Picketing is a form of industrial action that is intended to bring economic pressure to bear on the struck employer in order to encourage the employer to settle its differences with its workers.[113] There is also a communicative element to a picket line, and therefore it constitutes ''expression'' within s. 2(b) of the Charter. Picketing is probably best regarded as a kind of commercial expression, since its main purpose is to encourage employees not to work and consumers not to buy. However, like other kinds of commercial expression, the picket line may also convey an implicit, or even explicit, political message. Of course, under the broad definition of ''expression'' established by the Supreme Court of Canada,[114] it does not matter whether the expression is categorized as commercial or political: both kinds are protected.

In the *Dolphin Delivery* case (1986),[115] a union challenged the constitutionality of an injunction that had been issued by the courts of British Columbia to

111 *Re ss. 193 and 195.1 of Criminal Code* (Prostitution Reference) [1990] 1 S.C.R. 1123. Dickson C.J., with La Forest and Sopinka JJ., wrote the plurality opinion; Lamer J. concurred separately; Wilson J., with L'Heureux-Dubé J., dissented.

112 The term is sometimes extended to demonstrations outside the labour relations setting, where persons carrying signs assemble at a particular location to protest against the policies of a government or a corporation that has offices at that location.

113 The Supreme Court of the United States has described picketing as ''speech plus'', and has accorded it a lower level of constitutional protection on the basis that the ''plus'' could be regulated: Tribe, note 23, above, 826. In Canada, the interplay of s. 2(b) and s. 1 is likely to produce similar outcomes.

114 Section 40.5, ''Meaning of expression'', above.

115 *RWDSU* v. *Dolphin Delivery* [1986] 2 S.C.R. 573. McIntyre J., with Dickson C.J., Estey, Chouinard and Le Dain JJ., wrote the majority judgment. Beetz and Wilson JJ. wrote short concurring opinions.

prohibit the members of the union, which was on strike, from picketing the workplace of a firm that was not their employer. This "secondary picketing" was not provided for by the applicable federal labour law legislation, but the British Columbia courts had held that secondary picketing in the circumstances of this case was prohibited by the common law; it constituted the tort of inducing a breach of contract. The courts had issued the injunction in order to stop the commission of the tort. The Supreme Court of Canada held that the Charter of Rights had no application to a dispute between two private parties that was governed by the common law. Therefore, the Court refused to discharge the injunction. However, McIntyre J. for the majority of the Court, in an extended obiter dictum, recognized the "element of expression in picketing",[116] and held that it was protected expression under the Charter. He also went on to indicate that a prohibition on secondary picketing would be justified under s. 1 as a measure to prevent industrial conflict from spreading beyond the parties in dispute.

In the *Vancouver Courthouse* case (1988),[117] the Chief Justice of British Columbia, who had encountered a picket line at the courthouse on his way to work, as soon as he reached his chambers, on his own motion, and without notice to the union, issued an injunction to prohibit the picketing of the courts. The union was on lawful strike, and was picketing the courts because that was where some of their members worked. The union made application to have the injunction set aside on constitutional grounds, and this application was denied by the Supreme Court of Canada. The Court held that there was a legal basis for the injunction in that the picketing was a criminal contempt of court. The Court also held that the Charter applied to an injunction to prevent a criminal contempt of court; and that this injunction, by prohibiting picketing, was a limit on freedom of expression. However, the Court held that the injunction was justified under s. 1. "Assuring unimpeded access to the courts" was a sufficiently important objective, and the injunction was not overly broad because it "left the union and its members free to express themselves in other places and other ways so long as they did not interfere with the right of access to the courts".[118] These two cases make clear that picketing is protected by s. 2(b) of the Charter. But the readiness with which the courts were prepared to accept the rather slender s. 1 justification in the two cases[119] indicates that laws or court orders limiting picketing in order to avoid the spread of an industrial dispute, or to facilitate access to a public facility, or to

116 *Id.*, 588.

117 *BCGEU* v. *B.C.* [1988] 2 S.C.R. 214. Dickson C.J., with Lamer, Wilson, La Forest and L'Heureux-Dubé JJ., wrote the majority opinion. McIntyre J. wrote a concurring opinion.

118 *Id.*, 248. McIntyre J. in a concurring opinion held the right of access to the courts was protected by the Charter, and therefore an injunction to secure access could not be a breach of s. 2(b).

119 In *Dolphin Delivery*, McIntyre J. said (at 590) that this was a case "where certain elements of the s. 1 analysis are obvious or self-evident", meaning that they did not require evidence. In *Vancouver Courthouse*, Dickson C.J. recited uncontradicted evidence (at 221) that indicated that the picketers were not impeding access to the courts.

reduce the risk of violent confrontations, or for some other purpose, are likely to be upheld under s. 1.

40.9 Hate propaganda

Hate propaganda is material that promotes hatred against minority groups. Racial and religious minorities seem to be the most common targets. Hate propaganda is usually called ''group libel'' in the United States, where it probably may not be banned without offence to the first amendment.[120]

Hate propaganda is prohibited by the Criminal Code, which makes it an offence to wilfully promote hatred against ''any section of the public distinguished by colour, race, religion or ethnic origin.'' This is of course a limit on expression, albeit expression of a worthless and harmful kind. The purpose of the ban is to promote the value of equality, because the effect of hate propaganda is to reinforce the malign attitudes towards minorities that are important barriers to the achievement of equality. It is arguable that the scope of s. 2(b) should be narrowed to make way for a ban on expression that has as its purpose the advancement of equality, which is of course guaranteed by s. 15. That approach would support a ban on hate propaganda without recourse to s. 1.[121]

In *R.* v. *Keegstra* (1990),[122] the Supreme Court of Canada was faced with a challenge to the hate propaganda section of the Criminal Code. The Court rejected the notion that there were any content-based restrictions on the s. 2(b) right. Section 2(b) covered all messages, ''however unpopular, distasteful or contrary to the mainstream''.[123] The Court also rejected the notion that s. 2(b) could be narrowed by reference to the equality rights of s. 15 (or any other rights).[124] It followed that Mr. Keegstra, a schoolteacher who had been found guilty of making anti-semitic statements to his students, had been engaged in constitutionally protected activity. For the purpose of the s. 1 inquiry, however, it was relevant to take account of the competing equality values, which tended to strengthen the

120 Compare *Beauharnais* v. *Illinois* (1952) 343 U.S. 250 (group libel law upheld) with *R.A.V.* v. *St. Paul* (1992) U.S. Lexis 3863 (group libel law struck down but four of nine judges would have upheld a narrower law).

121 This was the mode of reasoning employed by McIntyre J. in the Vancouver Courthouse case, but it was not adopted by the majority: note 116, above.

122 [1990] 3 S.C.R. 697. Dickson C.J., with Wilson, L'Heureux-Dubé and Gonthier JJ., wrote the majority opinion; McLachlin J., with La Forest and Sopinka JJ. dissented. The companion case of *Can.* v. *Taylor* [1990] 3 S.C.R. 892 upheld a ban imposed by the Canadian Human Rights Act on hate propaganda over the telephone. The same judges split the same way on the s. 1 issue. For commentary on the *Keegstra* case, see Weinrib, ''Hate Promotion in a Free and Democratic Society: *R.* v. *Keegstra*'' (1991) 36 McGill L.J. 1416.

123 *Id.*, 729.

124 *Id.*, 734, 755-758.

importance of the law's objective, and thus make it easier to uphold under s. 1.[125] The Court did go on to uphold the law under s. 1, but only by the slim margin of four to three.[126]

The Criminal Code used to contain the offence of spreading false news, which was committed by anyone who published a statement that he knew was false and that caused or was likely to cause injury to a public interest. In *R.* v. *Zundel* (1992),[127] the accused was charged with this offence.[128] He had published a pamphlet that claimed that the Holocaust was a fraud invented by an international conspiracy of Jews. The accused was convicted at trial, but the Supreme Court of Canada, by a majority, held that he was entitled to be acquitted on the ground that the false-news prohibition was unconstitutional. The Court was unanimous in deciding that the accused's activity of publishing deliberate falsehoods was protected by s. 2(b). The doctrine of content-neutrality protected falsehoods as well as truths, because the question whether a statement is true or false can be determined only by reference to the content of the statement. The Court divided four to three on the s. 1 issue, the majority holding that the false-news offence could not be justified under s. 1. The offence was therefore struck down.

The different results in *Keegstra* and *Zundel* depended on the different outcomes of the s. 1 reasoning. The hate-propaganda law that was upheld in *Keegstra* was specifically directed at the wilful promotion of hatred against identifiable groups and it was easy to accept that the prevention of harm caused by that activity was an important objective. The false-news law that was struck down in *Zundel* did not specify any particular type of statement and did not specify what type of injury to the public interest was contemplated. The false-news law was so broad that it was difficult to identify an objective that was

---

125 Accord, *Ross* v. *New Brunswick School District No. 15* [1996] 1 S.C.R. 825, in which the Supreme Court of Canada upheld under s. 1 the order of a human rights tribunal that required the removal from his teaching post of a schoolteacher who disseminated anti-semitic statements outside the classroom. The unanimous Court included the judges who had dissented in *Keegstra* and *Taylor,* note 122, above.

126 After being convicted, Keegstra appealed the conviction and the case went on to the Supreme Court of Canada. Keegstra unsuccessfully applied for leave to re-argue s. 2(b) (and ss. 7 and 15): *R.* v. *Keegstra (No. 2)* [1995] 2 S.C.R. 381. He was able to re-argue s. 11(d) in *R.* v. *Keegstra (No. 3)* [1996] 1 S.C.R. 458, albeit without success in the outcome: ch. 48, Rights On Being Charged, under heading 48.5(b), ''Reverse onus clauses'', below.

127 [1992] 2 S.C.R. 731. McLachlin J., with La Forest, L'Heureux-Dubé and Sopinka JJ., wrote the majority opinion; Cory and Iacobucci JJ., with Gonthier J., wrote the dissenting opinion.

128 The accused was not prosecuted under the hate-propaganda provision of the Criminal Code, because that provision requires the consent of the Attorney General to the laying of a charge. The Attorney General of Ontario had refused his consent, presumably because he was unsure whether denying the Holocaust constituted an offence under that provision. A private citizen then laid a charge under the false-news provision, which had no requirement of consent by the Attorney General. The Attorney General, who in Ontario always intervenes in private prosecutions of indictable offences, decided not to stay the proceedings and instead continued the prosecution, despite his earlier decision not to consent to the laying of a charge under the hate-propaganda provision.

sufficiently important to justify the limit on freedom of expression. Indeed, the objective of the false-news law in its original 13th-century form in England was to prevent the spreading of falsehoods concerning the ''great men of the realm''. The majority of the Court held that this could not serve as an adequate purpose today, and they refused to reinterpret the purpose as the pursuit of racial harmony (as the minority would have done) on the ground that this would be a departure from the actual historical purpose.

40.10 Defamation

The tort of defamation provides a civil remedy for a person whose reputation has been damaged by false statements made by the defendant. Under the content-neutral definition of expression, the defendant's freedom of expression is abridged by this prohibition against statements that are both false and harmful. In the United States, while there does not seem to have been a challenge to the law of defamation in general, the case where the defamed person is a public official has been held to attract the protection of the first amendment right to freedom of speech.

In *New York Times* v. *Sullivan* (1964),[129] the plaintiff, a public official of the city of Montgomery, Alabama, sued the New York Times newspaper for publishing an advertisement which criticized his handling of civil rights demonstrations in Montgomery. The criticism included falsehoods which were defamatory of the plaintiff. Under the common law, which constituted the law of defamation in Alabama, proof of a false and defamatory statement, without more, entitled the plaintiff to damages; and the Alabama courts accordingly awarded damages. The Supreme Court of the United States reversed. Because the defamatory speech was critical of a public official, it was entitled to a degree of first amendment protection. That protection took the form of a requirement of ''malice'': a public official could successfully sue for defamation only if he established that the defendant made the defamatory statement with malice, that is, with the knowledge that the statement was false or at least with a reckless disregard of whether or not the statement was false. The presence of malice was required to strip the speech of its constitutional protection. In this case, the plaintiff was able to show that, if the defendant newspaper had taken the trouble to check the facts stated in the advertisement against its own news stories, it would have become aware that the facts stated in the advertisement were false. But the Court held that this carelessness on the part of the newspaper did not rise to the level of recklessness. Therefore, no malice was present; the statement was protected by the first amendment; and the plaintiff recovered nothing.

---

129 (1964) 376 U.S. 254. The opinion of the majority was written by Brennan J. Black, Douglas and Goldberg JJ. concurred in the dismissal of the plaintiff's action, but they favoured an absolute bar on defamation actions by public officials.

The demonstrated falsity of the speech in *New York Times* v. *Sullivan* did not disqualify the speech from constitutional protection. However, the point of the decision was not to protect false statements. The tort of defamation is anomalous in that it is a tort of absolute liability. Outside privileged occasions, there is no requirement of either intention or negligence. Truth (or "justification") is the only defence for factual statements, and truth must be proved by the defendant by admissible evidence. The Court in *New York Times* v. *Sullivan* recognized that, under the common law of defamation, "would-be critics of official conduct may be deterred from voicing their criticism, even though it is believed to be true and even though it is in fact true, because of doubt whether it can be proved in court or fear of the expense of having to do so."[130] The tendency of the law of defamation to deter the publishing of statements critical of public officials is the "libel chill" that has caused a constitutional restriction to be engrafted onto the common law where the plaintiff is a public official. Later cases have extended the constitutional requirement of proof of malice to public figures other than public officials, for example, a prominent university football coach[131] and a retired army general.[132]

The High Court of Australia has adopted a variant of *New York Times* v. *Sullivan*. *Theophanous* v. *Herald & Weekly Times* (1994)[133] was an action for defamation brought by an Australian member of parliament against a newspaper that had published a letter critical of the plaintiff's views on Australia's immigration policies. The majority of the High Court[134] relied on *New York Times* v. *Sullivan* to hold that the common law of defamation had a "chilling effect" on political speech.[135] However, the Court held that "the protection of free communication does not necessitate such a subordination of the protection of individual reputation as appears to have occurred in the United States".[136] The Court accordingly adopted for Australia the rule in *New York Times* v. *Sullivan*, with two important changes, both favourable to the plaintiff. The first change concerned the burden of proof. The Court rejected the United States rule that placed on

130 *Id.*, 279 per Brennan J.

131 *Curtis Publishing Co.* v. *Butts* (1967) 388 U.S. 130.

132 *Associated Press* v. *Walker* (1967) 388 U.S. 130 (same report as *Curtis Publishing Co.* v. *Butts*). For an account of the United States' law, see Tribe, note 23, above, 861-886; Nowak, note 23, above, 1037-1052; Brown, *The Law of Defamation in Canada* (2nd ed., 1994), vol. 2, ch. 27.

133 (1994) 124 A.L.R. 1 (H.C. of Aust.).

134 The plurality opinion of Mason C.J., Toohey and Gaudron JJ. prevailed. The four-three majority was created by Deane J., who (like Black, Douglas and Goldberg JJ. in *New York Times* v. *Sullivan*) favoured an absolute bar on defamation actions by public officials, but who concurred in the order proposed by the plurality. Dissenting opinions were written by Brennan, Dawson and McHugh JJ., who would not have modified the common law.

135 There is no express bill of rights in the Constitution of Australia, but this case affirmed earlier decisions of the High Court of Australia holding that there was an implied guarantee of freedom of expression.

136 (1994) 124 A.L.R. 1, 23.

the public-official-plaintiff the burden of proving that the defendant either knew that its story was false or was reckless as to whether it was false. Instead, the judges held, the defendant should bear the burden of proving that it did not know that the defamatory statement was false and was not reckless as to whether it was false. The second change in the rule of *New York Times* v. *Sullivan* concerned the substance of the constitutional defence. In the opinion of the Australian judges in *Theophanous*, the defendant should have to prove not only that it did not know that the statement was false and was not reckless as to its falsity, but also that "the publication was reasonable in the circumstances".[137] What was involved in the defence of reasonableness was a showing that the defendant had taken reasonable steps to verify the truth of the published statement. In effect, the Court in *Theophanous* allowed a defence of due diligence to the publisher of a statement critical of a public official.

When the issue arose in Canada, the Supreme Court of Canada had the advantage of the American and Australian cases, which suggested three possible approaches to the modification of the common law of defamation in order to provide some constitutional protection for the criticism of public officials. The most radical approach is an absolute bar on defamation actions by public officials (the minority view in both *New York Times* and *Theophanous*).[138] A middle ground is the requirement that the public-official-plaintiff prove that the defendant knew the criticism was false or was reckless as to whether it was false (*New York Times*). A less severe modification is a defence of due diligence (or reasonableness) on the part of a defendant to a defamation action by a public official (*Theophanous*). Surprisingly, the Canadian Court took none of these routes, electing instead to adhere to the pristine common law.

The case in which the Supreme Court of Canada refused to alter the common law of defamation to protect criticism of public officials was *Hill* v. *Church of Scientology* (1995).[139] The plaintiff, Hill, was a crown attorney employed by the Ministry of the Attorney General in Ontario, who was accused by the Church of Scientology of having violated court orders sealing certain documents belonging to the Church that had been seized under a search warrant. The Church of Scientology held a press conference at which its lawyer described the allegations and announced that contempt proceedings were being brought against Hill. After the

137 *Id.*, 26.

138 Notes 129, 134, above. See also *Derbyshire County Council* v. *Times Newspapers* [1993] A.C. 534 (H.L.) (barring defamation action by local body, relying on reasoning in *New York Times*, despite absence of bill of rights in United Kingdom).

139 [1995] 2 S.C.R. 1130. The seven-judge bench was unanimous. Cory J. wrote the majority opinion, with the agreement of La Forest, Gonthier, McLachlin, Iacobucci and Major JJ. L'Heureux-Dubé J. wrote a short concurring opinion, agreeing with Cory J. except on one point which did not affect the outcome. I disclose that I appeared as counsel for a coalition of media organizations that intervened in the appeal at the level of the Supreme Court of Canada to argue that the common law should be modified to place more weight on freedom of political expression.

contempt proceedings exonerated Hill, he sued the Church of Scientology and its lawyer for defamation, and a jury awarded him $1.6 million in damages. This huge sum was made up of $300,000 of general damages, $500,000 of aggravated damages and $800,000 of punitive damages. The award was upheld by the Supreme Court of Canada. The Court held that the Charter of Rights did not directly apply to the proceedings (despite Hill's public position), but that the common law should be reviewed, and modified if necessary, to make it consistent with "Charter values".[140] The Court held that the common law of defamation was consistent with Charter values, and did not need to be modified.

Cory J., who wrote the majority opinion in *Hill* v. *Church of Scientology*, acknowledged that the common law of defamation represented an accommodation between the competing values of personal reputation and freedom of expression: whatever is "added to the field of libel is taken from the field of free debate".[141] Of the two values, only freedom of expression was protected by the Charter, but it did not follow that freedom of expression should predominate. Ignoring the libel chill argument that had been accepted in *New York Times* and *Theophanous*, the Court held that false and injurious statements were not deserving of much protection. Reputation, on the other hand, although not explicitly protected by the Charter, reflected "the innate dignity of the individual" and was "related to the right to privacy which has been accorded constitutional protection".[142] Having weighed the competing values in this fashion, Cory J. concluded that the law of defamation was not "unduly restrictive or inhibiting."[143] As well, the Court upheld the $1.6 million damages award, and refused to place a cap on damages in defamation suits. This maintained an anomaly, because there is a cap on non-pecuniary damages in personal injury suits, although in personal injury suits no Charter value is affected and in the extreme cases to which the cap would apply the suffering of the victim is much greater.[144] The Court's upholding of the high award will escalate the level of damages that public officials can expect to recover in future defamation suits, and increase the incentive for caution in criticizing or reporting the activities of public officials.

---

140 This aspect of the decision is discussed in ch. 34, Application of the Charter, under heading 34.2(f), "Common law", above.

141 [1995] 2 S.C.R. 1130, para. 100.

142 *Id.*, paras. 120-121.

143 *Id.*, para. 137. On one point, the Court, by a majority, did find the common law to be unduly restrictive or inhibiting. The Court extended the qualified privilege that attaches to reports of judicial proceedings held in open court to pleadings and other documents publicly filed: *Id.*, paras. 143-156. This was the issue upon which L'Heureux-Dubé disagreed with the majority. It did not affect the outcome, because the majority held that the press conference at which the contempt proceedings were announced exceeded the bounds of the privilege.

144 Setting aside the aggravated and punitive damages (although aggravated damages are supposed to be compensatory), the general damages of $300,000 exceeded the cap on non-pecuniary personal injury damages, which was set at $100,000 in 1978, and with inflation was described by Cory J. (para. 173) as having a value of about $250,000 in 1991. The maximum figure would, of course, be reserved for the most serious personal injury cases.

40.11 Pornography

Attempts to ban the description or depiction of sexual activity have traditionally been justified as protecting public morality by preventing the dissemination of material that is morally objectionable. They have been a serious threat to freedom of expression, resulting in many jurisdictions in the banning of the works of some of the greatest novelists, including D. H. Lawrence, James Joyce and Vladimir Nabokov. Another way of looking at pornography that has been suggested by feminist writers and is now widely accepted is as a first cousin to hate propaganda. On this basis, what is offensive about pornography is not the explicit portrayal of sex, nor the flouting of conventional morality, but rather the reinforcement of discrimination against women.[145] On this basis, the emphasis of pornography law would shift to focus on the depiction of violence, cruelty, degradation and humiliation which is apparently a feature of much pornography, and which promotes the attitudes that help to bar the achievement of equality by women. Even on this basis, laws banning pornography raise major problems of definition and create risks of the suppression of serious ideas. However, the advancement of the value of equality does constitute a far more important objective than the protection of conventional morality, and greatly strengthens the argument that can be made for s. 1 justification.

The Supreme Court of the United States has distinguished between pornography and obscenity, and has held that the latter is not speech at all. Obscenity is therefore unprotected by the first amendment, provided that it is "utterly without redeeming social importance".[146] This test has been refined in later cases, but it is extraordinarily difficult to apply. The Court has often been reduced to reading the book or watching the film to determine whether an unconstitutional ban had taken place. Stewart J. was disarmingly frank when he acknowledged that he could not succeed in defining obscenity, but "I know it when I see it".[147]

The expression cases in the Supreme Court of Canada make clear that pornography, including obscenity, is protected expression in Canada. Pornography, however defined, can only be identified by reference to the content of the challenged material. Since there are no content-based restrictions on s. 2(b),[148] it follows that pornography is covered by the guarantee.

In *R.* v. *Butler* (1992),[149] the accused, who operated a sex shop, was found guilty of various charges of selling obscene material and possessing obscene

145 See, E.G., Lahey, "The Charter and Pornography" in Weiler and Elliot (eds.) *Litigating the Values of a Nation* (1986), 265; other points of view are developed in the essays by Arbour (at 294) and Elliot (at 308).

146 *Roth* v. *United States* (1957) 354 U.S. 476, 484.

147 *Jacobellis* v. *Ohio* (1964) 378 U.S. 184, 197. See generally Tribe, note 23, above, 904-928; Nowak, note 23, above, 1136-1156.

148 Section 40.4, "Meaning of expression", above.

149 [1992] 1 S.C.R. 452. The majority opinion was written by Sopinka J. with the concurrence of six others. A concurring opinion was written by Gonthier J. with the concurrence of L'Heureux-

material for sale. He challenged the constitutionality of these prohibitions of obscenity, which were enacted by the Criminal Code. The Code's definition of obscenity was as follows:

> For the purposes of this Act, any publication a dominant characteristic of which is the undue exploitation of sex, or of sex and any one or more of the following subjects, namely, crime, horror, cruelty and violence, shall be deemed to be obscene.

The Supreme Court of Canada held unanimously that the prohibition of obscenity offended s. 2(b) of the Charter. The purpose and the effect of the prohibition was "to restrict the communication of certain types of materials based on their content".[150] Since there are no content-based restrictions on s. 2(b), it followed that obscene material was covered by the guarantee. The Court held, however, that the prohibition could be upheld under s. 1.

Sopinka J. for the majority of the Supreme Court of Canada held that the "undue" exploitation of sex contemplated material that (1) portrayed explicit sex with violence, or (2) portrayed explicit sex without violence, but in a degrading or dehumanizing manner by "[placing] women (and sometimes men) in positions of subordination, servile submission or humiliation".[151] These forms of pornography, when not required by the internal necessities of a serious work of art, were intolerable to the Canadian community, "not because [they offended] against morals but because [they were] perceived by public opinion to be harmful to society, particularly to women".[152] Sopinka J. acknowledged that the perception of harm was "not susceptible of exact proof", but he referred to "a substantial body of opinion that holds that the portrayal of persons being subjected to degrading or dehumanizing sexual treatment results in harm, particularly to women and therefore to society as a whole", and he said that "it would be reasonable to conclude that there is an appreciable risk of harm to society in the portrayal of such material".[153]

These findings could not of course overcome the rule that all expressive activity, no matter how repulsive its content, was protected by s. 2(b). However, they did provide the basis to allow the Court to uphold the obscenity law under s. 1. Section 1 requires that a limit on a right be "prescribed by law", which means that a law must not be excessively vague; and this has been a fatal flaw in some attempts to control pornography.[154] Sopinka J. pointed out that the test of vagueness had to be applied to the language of a statute as it had been interpreted,

---

Dubé J. Gonthier J. generally agreed with Sopinka J., but would have interpreted the definition of obscenity and the prospect of harm to society somewhat more broadly than Sopinka J.

150 *Id.*, 489.

151 *Id.*, 479.

152 *Ibid.*

153 *Id.*, 479-480.

154 *Re Ont. Film and Video Appreciation Society* (1984) 41 O.R. (2d) 583 (C.A.) (film censorship law invalid for failure to supply standards of censorship); *Luscher* v. *Revenue Can.* [1985] 1 F.C. 85 (C.A.) (prohibition of importation of "immoral" or "indecent" books too vague to satisfy s. 1).

and the gloss of harmfulness placed by judicial decisions on the language of the Code gave it enough precisio to count as an "intelligible standard".[155]

The same judicial gloss enabled Sopinka J. to hold that the objective of the Code was not merely moral disapprobation but "the avoidance of harm to society".[156] This was a sufficiently important objective to justify a limit on freedom of expression. It was similar to the prevention of the influence of hate propaganda, which had been accepted as a legitimate reason for the limitation of freedom of expression in the *Keegstra* case.[157] The prohibition also satisfied the proportionality tests stipulated by *Oakes* in that it did not extend beyond material that created a risk of harm to society, and in particular did not prohibit sexually explicit material that was neither accompanied by violence nor degrading or dehumanizing. Nor did it prohibit material that was required by the internal necessities of serious artistic work. Nor did the Code's prohibition touch the private possession or viewing of the obscene materials. Therefore, the prohibition was no wider than was necessary to accomplish the legislative purpose of preventing harm to society. For these reasons, Sopinka J. concluded that the prohibition of obscenity was justified under s. 1.

40.12 Access to public property

Does s. 2(b) confer a right to use public property as a forum of expression?

With respect to *private* property, the general rule (of both the common law and the civil law) is that the owner has the power to determine who uses the property and for what purpose. This means that the owner has the power to determine the extent if at all that the property can be used as the location of signs, placards, pickets, speeches or other forms of expression. This rule of proprietary power obviously affects the kind and amount of expression in our society. But the rule is not affected by s. 2(b) of the Charter, because the Charter does not apply to private action. It is therefore clear that s. 2(b) confers no right to use private property as a forum of expression.[158]

With respect to *public* property, since the Charter applies to governmental action, s. 2(b) is potentially applicable.[159] In *Committee for the Commonwealth of Canada* v. *Canada* (1991),[160] the question arose whether the manager of Crown-

155 [1992] 1 S.C.R. 452, (p. 491).

156 *Id.*, (p. 493).

157 Note 122, above.

158 *Committee for Cth. of Can.* v. *Can.* [1991] 1 S.C.R. 139, 228 per McLachlin J.

159 Note, however, that not all "public" institutions are covered by the Charter. Universities and hospitals, for example, are sufficiently independent of government to be outside the application of the Charter: see ch. 34, Application of Charter, above. Their property therefore counts as private property for this purpose.

160 [1991] 1 S.C.R. 139. While the seven-judge bench was unanimous, there were three concurring opinions: Lamer C.J.'s opinion was agreed to by Sopinka and Cory JJ.; McLachlin J.'s opinion was concurred in by La Forest and Gonthier JJ.; L'Heureux-Dubé J. wrote a third opinion.

owned Dorval Airport in Montreal could prohibit the distribution of political leaflets in the Airport. The Supreme Court of Canada held unanimously that the prohibition was unconstitutional. The Court was unanimous that s. 2(b) conferred a right to use public property for expression purposes; the government did not possess the absolute power of a private owner to control access to and use of public property. However, the Court splintered into three camps in its attempt to define the scope of the right of expression.

The most expansive view of the right of expression on public property was taken by L'Heureux-Dubé J., who held that s. 2(b) conferred a right to use all governmental property for purposes of expression. In her view, any limitation of access or use, even in respect of places not generally accessible by the public, would have to be justified under s. 1. McLachlin J. disagreed with her colleague, but proposed an alternative that in my view is virtually indistinguishable. She said that a prohibition on expression on governmental property would violate s. 2(b) only if the person seeking access was pursuing one of the three purposes of the guarantee of freedom of expression. Those purposes, it will be recalled, are (1) seeking truth, (2) participation in decision-making, and (3) individual self-fulfilment.[161] McLachlin J. assumed that a person or group demanding an audience in "the Prime Minister's office, an airport control tower, a prison cell or a judge's private chambers" would be unable to fit within one of the three purposes. But why not? The purposes are easily wide enough to embrace any statement or demonstration in any imaginable forum. In the end, therefore, McLachlin J. is in the same camp as L'Heureux-Dubé: any restriction on access for the purpose of expression anywhere on government property would need to be justified under s. 1. Nor should it be assumed that justification under s. 1 would necessarily be easy to establish. Where access to a particular building or office is not governed by carefully formulated rules, but is controlled on an ad hoc basis, the exclusion of religious proselytizers or political protesters (for example) would probably not satisfy s. 1's requirement of "prescribed by law".[162]

It seems obvious to me that proprietary control over government property ought not to disappear entirely even in the face of an assertion of expression rights. That was the view of Lamer C.J. in the *Commonwealth of Canada* case. Lamer C.J. would allow proprietary controls over access or use to the extent necessary to carry out the principal function of the governmental place. Thus a rule of silence in the parliamentary library would not violate s. 2(b), and would not need to be justified under s. 1, because silence is essential to the function of the library. Only if expression would be compatible with the function of the place,

---

161 *Id.*, 238-239, following the *Irwin Toy* dictum, quoted at note 39, above.

162 Even a carefully framed rule, if it took the form only of an "internal directive or policy", would not satisfy "prescribed by law", according to Lamer J. (with two others) in this case. McLachlin J. (also with two others) on the other hand, held that internal directives as to the management of Crown property would qualify as "prescribed by law". The seventh judge, L'Heureux-Dubé, did not express an opinion on this issue.

would a limitation on expression offend s. 2(b) and require justification under s. 1. Lamer C.J.'s functional test is not free of difficulty. As McLachlin J. pointed out, it does involve identifying and defining the function of any governmental place in which expression rights have been asserted; it involves determining what degree of expressive activity would be compatible with the function; and, because these inquiries take place within s. 2(b) rather than s. 1, the onus of proof rests on the person asserting freedom of expression. However, the functional test provides more certainty than the s. 1 inquiry that would be required by the opinions of L'Heureux-Dubé and McLachlin JJ. Nor is the functional test unduly restrictive of the guarantee of freedom of expression. It is far wider than the American doctrine of "public forum", under which restrictions on speech on public property require substantial justification (strict scrutiny) only if they apply to places that have traditionally been used for free speech, such as streets, sidewalks and parks.[163] Lamer C.J.'s functional test would extend the constitutional guarantee to expression on any governmental property so long as the expression was compatible with the principal function of the property. In the *Commonwealth* case itself, because the distribution of political leaflets was compatible with the airport's function of serving the travelling public, Lamer C.J. concluded that the plaintiffs had a constitutional right to carry out the practice. L'Heureux-Dubé and McLachlin JJ., relying on their wider views of the constitutional right of access, reached the same conclusion, so that the Court was unanimous in its result.

In *Ramsden* v. *Peterborough* (1993),[164] the Supreme Court of Canada struck down a municipal by-law that prohibited the placing of posters "on any public property" within the municipality. The defendant was a musician who advertised performances of his band by placing posters on hydro poles (utility poles carrying electrical transmission lines) on public property in the municipality. He was charged with a breach of the by-law. He defended the charge on the basis that the by-law was unconstitutional. The opinion of the Supreme Court of Canada was written by Iacobucci J., who had not been a member of the Court at the time of the *Commonwealth* case. There was no doubt, of course, that "postering" was a form of expression. Was postering on public property protected by s. 2(b)? In answering this question, Iacobucci J. noted the three different approaches that were taken in the *Commonwealth* case, but made no attempt to resolve the conflict. Instead, he held that, under each of the three approaches, postering on at least some kinds of public property, including utility poles, would be protected by s. 2(b). That moved the issue to s. 1. His lordship recognized that the municipality's objectives in enacting the by-law, which were to reduce littering, aesthetic blight, traffic hazards and hazards to persons engaged in the repair of utility poles, were sufficiently important to justify some limitation of freedom of expression. He held, however, that a complete ban on postering on all public property was broader

163 Tribe, *American Constitutional Law* (2nd ed., 1988), 986.

164 [1993] 2 S.C.R. 1084. The opinion of the Court was written by Iacobucci J.

than necessary to accomplish the objectives. The by-law therefore failed the least-drastic-means requirement of s. 1 justification, and was unconstitutional.[165]

40.13 Access to courts

(a) Competing values

Section 2(b) expressly provides that freedom of expression includes "freedom of the press and other media of communication". The freedom of the press occasionally comes into conflict with the right of persons accused of crime to receive a fair trial.[166] For example, pre-trial publicity may bias potential jurors or judges, and may damage the reputation of someone subsequently exonerated of the charge. As well, extensive publicity of pending cases, and intemperate criticism of decisions, may tend to draw the courts into political controversy and impair their capacity, or public perception of their capacity, for neutral adjudication.

(b) Restrictions on reporting

Freedom of the press includes the freedom to publish reports of proceedings in court. For example, in *Edmonton Journal* v. *Alberta* (1989),[167] the Supreme Court of Canada struck down an Alberta statute that prohibited, with some limited exceptions, press reports of matrimonial litigation. The Court was unanimous that the statute violated s. 2(b): "the courts must be open to public scrutiny and to public criticism of their operation by the public".[168] With respect to s. 1, the Court agreed that the protection of the privacy of individuals engaged in matrimonial litigation would justify some limits on the right to report judicial proceedings. However, a majority of the Court held that the Alberta ban was wider than was necessary to safeguard privacy, and could not be upheld under s. 1.[169]

In *Canadian Newspapers Co.* v. *Canada* (1988),[170] the Criminal Code made provision for a court order prohibiting the media from disclosing the identity of the complainant in a case of sexual assault. The making of the order was mandatory

165 A by-law prohibiting postering on utility poles and buildings and a by-law prohibiting postering on roads were both struck down as too broad in *Toronto* v. *Quickfall* (1994) 16 O.R. (3d) 665 (C.A.)

166 See generally Lepofsky, *Open Justice* (1985).

167 [1989] 2 S.C.R. 1326. The principal judgment was written by Cory J., with whom Dickson C.J. and Lamer J. agreed; Wilson J. wrote a separate concurring opinion; La Forest J., with L'Heureux-Dubé and Sopinka JJ., dissented on the s. 1 issue.

168 *Id.*, 1337.

169 Parliament subsequently repealed s. 166 of the Criminal Code, which was similar to the Alberta legislation: S.C. 1994, c. 44, s. 9. Although the Court seemed to indicate that a more carefully drafted provision was what was needed, there has been no replacement legislation.

170 [1988] 1 S.C.R. 122. Lamer J. wrote the opinion of the Court.

if it was requested by the complainant or the prosecutor; in other cases, the making of the order was discretionary. The Supreme Court of Canada held that the Criminal Code section was valid. Although it limited the freedom of the press as guaranteed by s. 2(b), the limit was justified under s. 1. The purpose of fostering complaints by victims of sexual assault justified some limit on s. 2(b). The mandatory nature of the ban did not limit the right excessively, because only a mandatory ban would provide assurance to the complainant that her identity would not be disclosed. A merely discretionary ban would not eliminate the fear of publication that it was the purpose of the section to eliminate.

In *Dagenais* v. *CBC* (1994),[171] a superior court had issued an injunction prohibiting the CBC from broadcasting a television programme called "The Boys of St. Vincent". This publication ban did not apply to reports of judicial proceedings, because the programme was a fictional one. The programme portrayed the abuse of children in a Catholic institution and the subsequent trials of the priests who were responsible for the abuse. The injunction was sought by four Catholic priests who had been charged with the abuse of children under their care in circumstances resembling those depicted in the programme. The injunction had been granted under a common-law power to prevent "a real and substantial risk of interference with the fairness of the trial," and was limited to the period of the four trials. At the conclusion of the fourth trial, the injunction would be at an end, and the CBC would be free to air the programme.

The Supreme Court of Canada, by a majority, struck down the injunction. Lamer C.J., who wrote the opinion of the majority, held that the common law rule gave too much weight to the right to a fair trial and not enough weight to freedom of expression. Since the injunction was a limit on freedom of expression, the injunction had to be justified under s. 1 of the Charter by reference to *Oakes*-derived standards of justification. This required, among other things, a judicial finding that "reasonably available alternative measures" would not prevent the risk to the fairness of the trial.[172] In this case, he held, alternative measures were available, namely, "adjourning trials, changing venues, sequestering jurors, allowing challenges for cause and voir dires during jury selection, and providing strong judicial direction to the jury".[173] Therefore, the injunction could not be justified under s. 1.

Gonthier J. wrote the dissenting opinion. He accepted the trial judge's finding, based on the evidence, that there was a risk of influencing potential jurors, and he was reluctant to require a prolonged, American-style jury-selection process

171 [1994] 3 S.C.R. 835. The majority opinion was written by Lamer C.J., with whom Sopinka, Cory, Iacobucci and Major JJ. agreed. A concurring opinion was written by McLachlin J., and dissenting opinions by La Forest J., L'Heureux-Dubé J., and Gonthier J. On the issue of the validity of the publication ban, both McLachlin J. and La Forest J. were essentially in agreement with Lamer C.J. to strike down the ban, while L'Heureux-Dubé J. and Gonthier J. would have upheld the ban.

172 *Id.*, 878.

173 *Id.*, 881.

as an alternative remedy. He pointed out that the only effect of the ban was to delay the presentation of the programme for the duration of the trials, which was expected to be about eight months, when it would be just as timely and interesting to its audience. Not being a news programme, its value was not premised on immediate publication. Nor did the ban affect access to the courts or the publication of their proceedings. Therefore, in his dissenting view, the impact of the ban on freedom of the press was minor, and was justified by the objective of securing a fair trial for the four accused.

(c) Restrictions on access

Freedom of the press also includes the right of the press and the public to be present in court.[174] That right was not affected in the *Edmonton Journal* and *Canadian Newspaper* cases, where the press were not denied access to the courtroom; they were simply prohibited from reporting part of the proceedings.

In *Re Southam and the Queen (No. 1)* (1983),[175] the Ontario Court of Appeal had to consider the validity of s. 12(1) of the Juvenile Delinquents Act, which provided that ''the trials of children shall take place without publicity''. (The phrase ''without publicity'' had been held to require a trial closed to the press and the general public.) A newspaper challenged the validity of this provision, claiming that freedom of expression entailed a right of access to the courts.[176] The Court upheld the newspaper's claim, and struck down the closed-court provision. The Court acknowledged that in some cases the interests of the child would justify restrictions on press access to the trial, but the Court held that an absolute ban could not be justified under s. 1, because it did not pursue the ''least restrictive means'' of attaining its objective. The Court refused to reconstruct the Act by reading a judicial discretion into it. The Juvenile Delinquents Act has since been replaced by the Young Offenders Act, which replaces the absolute requirement of a closed hearing for trials of young offenders with a requirement that hearings be open to the press and public subject to a discretion in the judge to order that a hearing be closed. In *Re Southam and the Queen (No. 2.)* (1986),[177] the new provision was upheld under s. 1.

The Criminal Code provides for a ''pre-inquiry'' by a justice of the peace into whether to commence criminal proceedings against a person against whom an information has been laid. The person accused is not entitled to be present at a pre-inquiry, and any hearing is also closed to the public. In *Southam* v. *Coulter*

---

174 *Edmonton Journal* v. *Alta.* [1989] 2 S.C.R. 1326, 1337 (obiter dictum). Cf. *BCGEU* v. *B.C.* (Vancouver Courthouse) [1988] 2 S.C.R. 214 (injunction to stop picketing outside courthouses upheld in order to provide access to courts).

175 (1983) 41 O.R. (2d) 113 (C.A.).

176 The newspaper could not invoke s. 11(d) of the Charter, which requires a ''public'' criminal trial, because s. 11(d) is available only to the ''person charged with an offence''.

177 (1986) 53 O.R. (2d) 663 (C.A.).

(1990),[178] a private citizen had sworn an information against several cabinet ministers and senior police officers alleging bribery and corruption. Because of the prominence of the accused persons, the press were anxious to attend the pre-inquiry into the charges. The Ontario Court of Appeal held that the constitutional right of public access to the court included pre-trial proceedings as well as trials. However, the Court held that the protection of a falsely accused person and risk to a properly accused person that the subsequent trial would be prejudiced by pre-trial publicity were values that justified the closure of the pre-inquiry. The Court upheld the closure under s. 1.

40.14 Access to legislative assembly

In *New Brunswick Broadcasting Co.* v. *Nova Scotia* (1993),[179] the Supreme Court of Canada, by a majority, upheld a ban on television cameras in the legislative chamber that had been imposed by the Nova Scotia House of Assembly. The reasoning was that parliamentary privilege included the power of a legislative assembly to exclude ''strangers'' from the legislative chamber, and that power was not subject to the Charter of Rights. Sopinka J., who wrote a separate concurring opinion, and Cory J., who dissented, would have held that the Charter applied, and that s. 2(b) conferred a right of access to a legislative assembly on the press and other media. But the majority, by denying that the Charter was applicable at all, effectively rejected any such right.[180]

40.15 Contempt of court

A contempt of court is an act that offends against the administration of justice. A failure to obey a court order is the most common form of contempt. A failure to obey a court order may have no significance beyond the parties to the order, in which case the contempt is a ''civil contempt''. If the court order resolved a dispute between two private parties, and if it was based on the common law, the Charter of Rights will have no application to the court order,[181] or to any proceedings between the private parties to enforce the order by civil contempt proceedings. Therefore, even if the effect of the contempt proceedings were to enforce a restraint on freedom of expression (such as an injunction against picketing), the Charter cannot be called in aid to resist the contempt proceedings.

---

178 (1990) 75 O.R. (2d) 1 (C.A.).

179 [1993] 1 S.C.R. 319. The majority opinion was written by McLachlin J. with the agreement of La Forest, L'Heureux-Dubé, Gonthier and Iacobucci JJ.; Lamer C.J. and Sopinka J. wrote separate concurring opinions; Cory J. dissented.

180 The majority's reasoning is more fully explained, and criticized, in ch. 34, Application of Charter, under heading 34.2(b), ''Parliament or Legislature'', above.

181 *RWDSU* v. *Dolphin Delivery* [1986] 2 S.C.R. 573.

A ''criminal contempt'' is one where the offence to the administration of justice has a public significance that goes beyond the immediate parties. Criminal contempt is a criminal offence at common law that has been preserved in Canada by s. 8 of the Criminal Code.[182] There are two kinds of criminal contempt. A ''direct contempt'' is a contempt i the face of the court. This is committed by words or acts inside the courtroom that are intended to disrupt the proceedings, for example, where a person insults the judge, interrupts the proceedings, refuses to be swor as a witness or refuses to testify. An ''indirect contempt'' is a contempt not in the face of the court. This is committed by words or acts outside the courtroom that are intended to obstruct the administration of justice, for example, an article in a newspaper that would prejudice the fairness of an ongoing or pending trial. Although criminal contempt is a matter of common law, and the Charter does not generally apply to the common law, the public character of criminal contempt makes the Charter applicable.

In the *Vancouver Courthouse* case (1988),[183] the Chief Justice of British Columbia issued an injunction prohibiting a union from picketing the courthouses where some of the striking employees worked. The basis for the injunction was the offence of criminal contempt, which was allegedly being committed by the picketers by restricting access to the courts. The Supreme Court of Canada held that the Charter applied to a injunction for criminal contempt, and that the injunction was a limit on freedom of expression. However, the Court went on to decide that the assurance of unimpeded access to the courts was a sufficiently important objective to justify a limit on freedom of expression, and the injunction in this case was justified as a reasonable limit under s. 1.

In *R.* v. *Kopyto* (1987),[184] a lawyer, after his client had lost a civil suit against police officers, made a statement to the press in which he claimed that: ''The courts and the RCMP are sticking so close together you'd think they were put together with Krazy Glue''. Mr. Kopyto was charged with, and convicted of, ''scandalizing the court'', which was a branch of criminal contempt that had been recognized by the common law since 1900, although it had been rarely invoked. The Ontario Court of Appeal allowed Kopyto's appeal, holding by a majority that the offence of scandalizing the court had not survived Canada's adoption of the Charter of Rights. The critical feature of Kopyto's statement was that it was made *after* the end of a judicial proceeding, so that it could not prejudice an ongoing or pending trial. The only effect of the statement was therefore its general tendency to lower the reputation and the authority of the court. The Ontario Court of Appeal held that criticism of the courts, however unrestrained, made after a decision had

---

182 The lack of a statutory definition of the criminal offence is not a breach of fundamental justice under s. 7: *UNA* v. *Alta.* (1992) 89 D.L.R. (4th) 609 (S.C.C.).

183 *BCGEU* v. *B.C.* (Vancouver Courthouse) [1988] 2 S.C.R. 214.

184 (1987) 62 O.R. (2d) 449 (C.A.). The majority judgments were written by Cory, Goodman and Houlden JJ.A.; Dubin and Brooke JJ.A. dissented on the constitutional issue, although they gave a narrow definition of the (constitutional) offence, and held that Kopyto had not committed it.

been rendered, was constitutionally protected expression, and a law attempting to restrict such criticism could not be justified under s. 1.

40.16 Public service

Public servants in all jurisdictions in Canada are subject to restrictions on their partisan political activities. This is because the entire public service is a professional career service that is supposed to serve governments of all political stripes with equal diligence, and to be impervious to partisan political considerations in the administration of government programmes. The maintenance of the political neutrality of the service is necessary for its effective functioning, both in its relationships with its political masters and in its relationships with the public. While the general rule of neutrality is widely if not universally accepted, it does not provide a sure answer to the question of how much political activity by an individual public servant could be tolerated without serious risk to the integrity of the service.

In *OPSEU* v. *Ontario* (1986),[185] public servants in Ontario challenged provisions in Ontario's Public Service Act that prohibited public servants from engaging in a variety of political activities, including running for the federal Parliament without taking a leave of absence, fund-raising on behalf of federal political parties, and expressing opinions in pubic on federal political issues. This was a pre-Charter case, and so the plaintiffs took aim at the restrictions on political activity only insofar as they precluded *federal* political activity. The plaintiffs argued that such restrictions were outside the powers of a provincial Legislature. The argument was unsuccessful. The Supreme Court of Canada held unanimously that the province had the power to regulate its own public service,[186] and in pursuit of political neutrality the regulation could extend to restrictions on federal as well as provincial political activity.

The inevitable Charter challenge[187] came in *Osborne* v. *Canada* (1991),[188] in which federal public servants attacked provisions in the federal Public Service Employment Act that prohibited them from ''engaging in work'' for or against a candidate for election to Parliament or for or against a federal political party. The Supreme Court of Canada held that the Act did limit freedom of expression under s. 2(b), and that it was not justified under s. 1. The objective of maintaining a

185 [1987] 2 S.C.R. 2.

186 There was some disagreement as to the source of the power. Beetz J., writing with the agreement of McIntyre, Le Dain and La Forest JJ., held that the political restrictions were not simply labour relations laws but were part of the constitution of the province under s. 92(1) (now s. 45 of the Constitution Act, 1982) or the tenure of provincial offices under s. 92(4). Dickson C.J., concurring, relied on s. 92(4) and s. 92(13). Lamer J., concurring, relied only on s. 92(4).

187 The Ontario legislation was challenged unsuccessfully under the Charter in *OPSEU* v. *Ont.* (1988) 65 O.R. (2d) 689 (H.C.).

188 [1991] 2 S.C.R 69.

neutral public service would justify limits on expression, but these limits did not pursue that objective by the least drastic means; the Act was over-inclusive as to both the range of activity that was prohibited, and the range of public servants who were covered. A narrower prohibition would have been sufficient to protect the value of neutrality with less impact on freedom of expression.

40.17 Mandatory letters of reference

Occasionally, labour boards or adjudicators order an employer to give a letter of reference to an employee who has been unjustly dismissed. Such an order is a breach of the employer's Charter right to freedom of expression. Where the order requires the employer to provide an opinion about the employee that the employer does not truly hold, then the breach of the Charter right cannot be justified under s. 1.[189] However, where the stipulated letter of reference contains ''only objective facts that are not in dispute'', then the order can be justified under s. 1.[190]

40.18 Election expenditures

Restrictions on election expenditures are indirect restrictions on political speech, because expenditures are required to purchase time or space in the media for campaign messages. Restrictions on expenditures are therefore bound to diminish the capacity of candidates to communicate their ideas, and thereby diminish the quantity of political speech. This has caused the Supreme Court of the United States to strike down a variety of restrictions on campaign expenditures on the basis that they offend the first amendment guarantee of freedom of speech.[191] There is, however, a powerful reason for such restrictions, and that is to reduce the risk that wealthy or well-financed candidates will have an unfair advantage by reason of their greater access to the media. The well-financed point of view may drown out opposing views.

The federal Canada Elections Act imposes spending limits on parties and candidates during an election. As well, by an amendment enacted in 1983, the Act absolutely prohibited anyone who was not a candidate for election, and who was not acting on behalf of a registered party or a candidate for election, from incurring ''election expenses'' during the period from the date of the issue of the writ for the election to polling day. Election expenses were defined as money paid ''for the purpose of promoting or opposing . . . a particular registered party

189 *National Bank of Can.* v. *RCIU* [1984] 1 S.C.R. 269 (Canada Labour Code should not be interpreted as conferring power to order employer to state opinion not held; Charter not relied upon directly).

190 *Slaight Communications* v. *Davidson* [1989] 1 S.C.R. 1038.

191 The cases are described by Tribe, note 23, above, 1132-1153; Nowak, note 23, above, 1117-1126.

or the election of a particular candidate''. In *National Citizens' Coalition* v. *A.-G. Can.* (1984),[192] a court challenge was mounted against the prohibition on third-party election expenditures that had been enacted by the 1983 amendment. Medhurst J. of the Alberta Court of Queen's Bench had little difficulty in deciding that the prohibition was a breach of the guarantee of freedom of expression in s. 2(b) of the Charter. The more difficult issue was whether the prohibition could be justified under s. 1 of the Charter. The purpose of the prohibition was to sustain the integrity of the spending limits on parties and candidates. (Those spending limits were not challenged.) The spending limits would be undermined if the ''friends'' of a candidate (or party) could spend as much as they pleased in support of his or her campaign. Indeed, without wealthy friends, a candidate opposed by a special interest group would be placed at an unfair disadvantage, since the candidate would be subject to restrictions which did not apply to his or her opponent. Medhurst J. held that the government had not sufficiently established the actual or likely occurrence of the evils that the limit on expression was designed to defeat. He therefore held that the limit had not been shown to be reasonable or demonstrably justified in a free and democratic society. Accordingly, the prohibition on third-party election expenditures was held to be invalid for violation of s. 2(b) of the Charter.[193]

The *National Citizens* decision was rendered not long before the federal election that was held on September 4, 1984. Because of the imminence of the election, the federal government decided not to appeal the decision, and so the issue did not advance to a higher court. The 1984 election was held without any prohibition on third-party expenditures, and so was the 1988 federal election, in which the main issue was free trade with the United States, an issue that provoked heavy spending by lobby groups.

40.19 Voting

The right to vote is guaranteed by s. 3 of the Charter, but the right is limited to elections of the members of the federal House of Commons and of the provincial legislative assemblies.[194] In *Haig* v. *Canada* (1993),[195] the plaintiff, a Canadian

192 (1984) 11 D.L.R. (4th) 481 (Alta. Q.B.).

193 Cf. *Lavigne* v. *OPSEU* [1991] 2 S.C.R. 211 (compelled payment of union dues not a denial of payer's freedom of expression, although dues were used for advocacy purposes); *MacKay* v. *Man.* [1989] 2 S.C.R. 357 (statutory funding of candidates for election not a denial of taxpayer's freedom of expression).

194 Chapter 42, Voting, under heading 42.1(b), ''Section 3 of Charter'', below.

195 [1993] 2 S.C.R. 995. On the point in the text, seven members of the Court agreed with the majority opinion of L'Heureux-Dubé J.; Iacobucci J. wrote a dissenting opinion that was concurred in by Lamer C.J.

citizen who had slipped through the cracks of the residency requirements,[196] found himself unable to vote in the federal referendum that was held to approve the set of constitutional amendments known as the Charlottetown Accord. Being unable to rely on s. 3 of the Charter, he argued that the failure of the federal Parliament to make provision for him to vote was a breach of freedom of expression, guaranteed by s. 2(b) of the Charter. The Supreme Court of Canada agreed that the casting of a ballot in a referendum was a means of expression. However, the majority of the Court held that s. 2(b) did not impose on the federal (or a provincial) government any positive duty to consult its citizens by referendum, and, if a government did choose to hold a referendum, there was no duty to consult everyone.[197] The plaintiff could complain of his exclusion only if it amounted to a breach of his s. 15 equality right, but the majority of the Court held that the exclusion of citizens who did not satisfy the residency requirement was not discrimination that was prohibited by s. 15.[198] The conclusion was that the plaintiff had no constitutional right to vote in the referendum.

40.20 Access to government

In *Native Women's Assn. of Canada* v. *Canada* (1994),[199] the Native Women's Association of Canada (NWAC) argued that the Government of Canada had denied its right to freedom of expression[200] by providing funding to other aboriginal organizations but not to NWAC, and by inviting other aboriginal organizations, but not NWAC, to participate in the constitutional discussions that eventually led to the constitutional proposals known as the Charlottetown Accord. NWAC, which promoted the rights of aboriginal women, argued that the other aboriginal organizations were dominated by men, and the exclusion of NWAC would deny a voice to aboriginal women. As in the earlier *Haig* case,[201] this raised the question whether s. 2(b) imposed positive duties on governments, in this case,

---

196 The problem was created by the fact that two referenda were held, a federal one in nine provinces and a provincial one in Quebec. The plaintiff had moved from Ontario to Quebec in August of 1992. When the referendum was held in October, he was not qualified to vote in the federal referendum, because in October he was not resident in Ontario or any of the other eight provinces where the federal referendum was held (the federal law's requirement). He was not qualified to vote in the Quebec referendum, because he had not been resident in Quebec for six months (the Quebec law's requirement).

197 This was the point upon which Iacobucci J., with Lamer C.J., dissented. In his view (at 1066-1067), s. 2(b) conferred a right to participate in the referendum.

198 See ch. 52, Equality, under heading 52.16, ''Place of residence'', below.

199 [1994] 3 S.C.R. 627. The Court was unanimous. The opinion of the majority was written by Sopinka J., with the agreement of Lamer C.J., La Forest, Gonthier, Cory, Iacobucci and Major JJ. Brief concurring opinions were written by L'Heureux-Dubé and McLachlin JJ.

200 Sections 15 and 28 were invoked as well as s. 2(b). The Court gave some indication of the respective roles of ss. 2(b) and 15 (see note 203, below), but said nothing of substance about s. 28.

201 Note 195, above.

a duty to fund and consult with particular groups. Sopinka J. for the majority of the Supreme Court of Canada held that *Haig* ''establishes the principle that generally the government is under no obligation to fund or provide a specific platform of expression to an individual or a group''.[202] The government could not provide access or funding in a fashion that amounted to discrimination under s. 15,[203] but s. 15 should not be interpreted as constraining the government in its choice of advisers, or requiring the government to listen to every point of view. In any event, in this case, the Court held, the evidence did not support NWAC's contentions that the funded groups were not representative of aboriginal women and were adopting positions inimical to the interests of aboriginal women.

---

202 [1994] 3 S.C.R. 627, 655. L'Heureux-Dubé J.'s separate concurring opinion (at p. 666) disagreed with this reading of *Haig*, but the difference of opinion was very slight, since Sopinka J. acknowledged (at p. 655) that the government must not act ''in a discriminatory fashion'', which was L'Heureux-Dubé J.'s concern. McLachlin J.'s separate concurring opinion was that governments were not constrained by the Charter (including, presumably, s. 15) in choosing and funding their advisers on matters of policy.

203 *Id.*, 664 (discriminatory treatment should be examined under s. 15, not s. 2(b)).

41

Assembly and Association

41.1 Distribution of powers

Legislative authority over *assembly* is divided between the two levels of government, depending upon the type of assembly. For example, the provincial Legislatures have the power to regulate meetings, parades and gatherings on parks and streets by virtue of the provincial legislative authority over ''matters of a merely local or private nature in the province'' (s. 92(16)).[1] The federal Parliament has the power to prohibit riots and other breaches of the peace by virtue of the federal legislative authority over criminal law (s. 91(27)). The regulation of picketing is a matter of labour law, which comes within the power of whichever level of government has authority over the industry in which the picketers are employed.[2]

Legislative authority over *association* is also divided between the two levels of government, depending upon the type of association. For example, the provincial Legislatures have the power to regulate clubs, societies, partnerships and other unincorporated associations, by virtue of the provincial legislative authority over property and civil rights in the province (s. 91(13)).[3] The federal Parliament

---

1 A.G. Can and Dupond v. *Montreal* [1978] 2 S.C.R. 770 (municipal by-law restricting public meetings and parades upheld).

2 See ch. 21, Property and Civil Rights, under heading 21.8, ''Labour relations'', above.

3 Legislative power over the incorporation of companies depends upon s. 92(11) (provincial) and the opening words of s. 91 (federal): see ch. 23, Companies, above.

has the power to prohibit conspiracies to commit offences by virtue of the federal legislative authority over criminal law (s. 91(27)), and the power to regulate mergers and monopolies in restraint of trade by virtue of federal legislative authority over criminal law (s. 91(27)) and trade and commerce (s. 91(2)).[4] In the labour field, the power to regulate trade unions is possessed by the level of government that has authority over the particular industry in which the trade union members are employed. This means that most trade union regulation is provincial; but in the federal public service and in federally-regulated industries, such as banking and interprovincial transportation and communication, where federal labour law applies, the regulation of trade unions is federal.[5]

41.2 Freedom of assembly

Section 2(c) of the Charter of Rights[6] guarantees to "everyone"[7] the "fundamental freedom" of "freedom of peaceful assembly". The word "peaceful", which is not used in the Canadian Bill of Rights,[8] is closer to the first amendment of the United States Constitution ("the right of the people peaceably to assemble"), and is presumably included to make clear that no doubt is cast on laws regarding breaches of the peace or riots. However, municipal by-laws restricting public meetings or parades will be limitations on s. 2(c) that will have to be justified under s. 1.[9] Section 1 was examined in chapter 35, Limitation of Rights, above.

Picketing by striking workers has been held to be an exercise of freedom of expression.[10] For that reason, it is a constitutionally protected activity, and any restrictions have to be justified under s. 1. The Supreme Court of Canada has not treated picketing as an exercise of the right of assembly, although that would also be a plausible analysis.

---

4 See ch. 18, Criminal Law, under heading 18.6, Competition law, above.

5 Note 2, above.

6 For commentary on s. 2(c) and (d), see Beaudoin and Mendes (eds.), *The Canadian Charter of Rights and Freedoms* (3rd ed., 1996), ch. 6 (by Norman); McLeod, Takach, Morton, Segal, *The Canadian Charter of Rights* (Carswell, loose-leaf service), ch. 23; *Canadian Charter of Rights Annotated* (Canada Law Book, loose-leaf service), annotations to s. 2(c) and (d). The last work contains a bibliography of the relevant literature.

7 On the meaning of "everyone", see ch. 34, Application of Charter, under heading 34.1, "Benefit of rights", above.

8 The comparable provision of the Canadian Bill of Rights is s. 1(e), which guarantees "freedom of assembly".

9 *A.G. Can. and Dupond* v. *Montreal*, note 1, above, was a pre-Charter case.

10 See ch. 40, Expression, under heading 40.8, Picketing, above.

41.3 Freedom of association

(a) Section 2(d) of Charter

Section 2(d) of the Charter of Rights[11] guarantees to "everyone"[12] the "fundamental freedom" of "freedom of association".[13]

Section 2(d), like other Charter rights, is subject to s. 1 (the limitation clause) of the Charter, which means that limits on freedom of association will be valid if they come within the phrase "such reasonable limits prescribed by law as can be demonstrably justified in a free and democratic society". Section 1 was examined in chapter 35, Limitation of Rights, above.

Freedom of association is not explicitly guaranteed by the first amendment of the United States Constitution, but it has been held to be guaranteed by implication as a derivative of the guarantees of free speech and assembly.[14]

(b) Formation of association

Freedom of association in s. 2(d) includes "the freedom to establish, belong to and maintain an association".[15] In the labour context, for example, s. 2(d) accords to employees the right to form a trade union.

(c) Purpose of association

Freedom of association is an individual right, not a collective right. It is possessed by individuals and not associations. This means that an association, once formed, is not guaranteed the right to engage in a particular activity "solely

---

11 For commentary on s. 2(d), see note 6, above. For references to freedom of association in contexts not discussed in the text that follows, see *Catholic Children's Aid Society* v. *S.(T)* (1989) 69 O.R. (2d) 189 (C.A.) (s. 2(d) is not applicable to family relationships, and does not protect adopted child's access to natural parents); *Black* v. *Law Society of Alta.* [1989] 1 S.C.R. 591, 636 (minority per McIntyre J. held that restrictions on legal partnerships with out-of-province lawyers violated s. 2(d); majority rested decision only on mobility right of s. 6); *R.* v. *Skinner* [1990] 1 S.C.R. 1235, 1250-1251 (minority per Wilson J. held that prohibition on communication for the purpose of prostitution violated s. 2(d) as well as s. 2(b); majority at 1234 rejected s. 2(d)); *Alex Couture* v. *Can.* (1991) 83 D.L.R. (4th) 477 (Que. C.A.) (s. 2(d) not violated by merger restrictions in Competition Act).

12 Note 7, above.

13 The comparable provision of the Canadian Bill of Rights is s. 1(e), which also guarantees "freedom of association".

14 *NAACP* v. *Alabama* (1958) 357 U.S. 449; see generally Tribe, *American Constitutional Law* (2nd ed., 1988), 1010-1022; Nowak and Rotunda, *Constitutional Law* (4th ed., 1991), 1062-1069.

15 *Professional Institute* v. *N.W.T.* [1990] 2 S.C.R. 367, 402 per Sopinka J., whose opinion (at 401-403) contains an excellent review of the law.

on the ground that the activity is a foundational or essential purpose of the association''.[16]

In the labour context, the Supreme Court of Canada has held in *Professional Institute* v. *Northwest Territories* (1990)[17] that freedom of association is not infringed by legislation establishing a public service union and denying to any other union the power to bargain collectively with the employer. The employees had not lost their right to form a second union, although the legislation would preclude the second union from engaging in collective bargaining. The Court has also held, in the *Labour Trilogy* (1987),[18] that freedom of association is not infringed by legislation denying the right to strike to public sector employees,[19] nor by legislation imposing caps on future wage increases of public sector employees,[20] nor by legislation ordering striking dairyworkers to go back to work.[21] In each of these cases, an association's power to undertake effective action in pursuit of its objectives had been seriously impaired. But the Court held that there was no breach of freedom of association. The individuals' right to form an association did not guarantee to the association the power to carry out the essential objectives of the association. The reason why this step could not be taken was because it would confer on an association rights more extensive than those possessed by individuals.

(d) Exercise of constitutional rights

The logic of freedom of association as merely an individual right does protect one class of associational activity. The right protects the exercise in association of the *constitutional* rights of individuals. Individual rights such as freedom of expression, or freedom of religion, do not lose their constitutional protection when they are exercised in common with others. No decision yet illustrates this point, but it has been widely recognized in dicta.[22]

---

16 *Ibid.*

17 *Ibid.* Sopinka J. wrote the plurality opinion, which was generally agreed with by L'Heureux-Dubé and La Forest JJ. Dickson C.J. wrote a separate concurring opinion. Cory J., with Wilson and Gonthier JJ., dissented.

18 The three decisions cited in the next three notes were handed down on the same day, and are often referred to as the ''Labour Trilogy''.

19 *Re Public Service Employees Relations Act* [1987] 1 S.C.R. 313.

20 *PSAC* v. *Can.* [1987] 1 S.C.R. 424. I disclose that I was one of the counsel for the union in this case.

21 *RWDSU* v. *Sask.* [1987] 1 S.C.R. 460. See also *ILWU* v. *Can.* [1994] 1 S.C.R. 150 (holding that back-to-work legislation does not violate the liberty of the employees under s. 7).

22 *Professional Institute* v. *N.W.T.* [1990] 2 S.C.R. 367, 402-403 per Sopinka J. referring to supporting dicta.

(e) Exercise of non-constitutional rights

Does freedom of association also protect the exercise in association of the *lawful but non-constitutional* rights of individuals? In the *Labour Trilogy*,[23] three of the six judges asserted that freedom of association protected any activity by an association that was permitted for an individual. However, the other three judges pointedly made no reference to this element of the right. In *Professional Institute* v. *Northwest Territories*,[24] two of the six judges made the same claim for freedom of association but over the silence of the other four. In none of the cases did the point have to be decided, because the judges all took the view that the point was not raised by the *Labour Trilogy* or the *Professional Institute* case. But this view is disputable. It is at least arguable that the right to strike is simply the associational analogue of an individual's right to withdraw his or her services at the termination of an individual contract of employment (a common phenomenon in the world of professional sport, for example), and the right to bargain collectively is simply the associational analogue of the right to bargain individually.[25]

The fact is that the costs (and benefits) of collective action are so different from those of individual action that different regimes of regulation are often appropriate. The fixing of prices is a good example: what is lawful for an individual seller is properly prohibited by our competition law when performed in concert with other sellers. It is surely an undue extension of freedom of association to expand its protection to every activity by an association that is permitted to an individual.[26] If the right is so extended, we must expect to find judges denying analogies between collective activity and apparently similar individual activity in order to avoid conferring constitutional protection on collective activity that legislators have reasonably decided to regulate.[27]

---

23 *Re Public Service Employees Relations Act* [1987] 1 S.C.R. 313, 366-367 per Dickson J. (with Wilson J.), 408-409 per McIntyre J. These opinions were repeated in the *PSAC* and *Dairyworkers* cases, notes 20 and 21, above.

24 [1990] 2 S.C.R. 367, 403 per Sopinka J. (with L'Heureux-Dubé J.). La Forest J., who otherwise agreed with Sopinka J., at 390-391 reserved his opinion on this point.

25 This issue can be argued either way, depending upon how many characteristics of the statutory rights to strike and bargain collectively are taken into account. In support of the analogy (and of the extended right) is Beatty and Kennett, ''Striking Back'' (1988) 67 Can. Bar Rev. 573, 589-593. Also in support of the analogy (but not of the extended right) is Weiler, ''The Charter at Work'' (1990) 40 U. Toronto L.J. 117, 146-147.

26 Accord, Weiler, previous note, 146-147.

27 Alternatively, a relaxation of the standards of justification under s. 1 could be used to uphold regulation of collective activity. The better approach, in my opinion, is to confine the right to those activities worthy of protection (because within the purpose of the right), and maintain strict standards of justification under s. 1 This approach is argued for in ch. 35, Limitation of Rights, under heading 35.3, ''Relationship between s. 1 and rights'', above.

(f) Freedom not to associate

Does freedom of association include the freedom not to associate — freedom *from* association? This issue is raised by the union security arrangements that Canadian labour laws typically permit and sometimes require. The strictest arrangement is the "closed shop", under which a person must be a member of the union before he or she can be hired by the employer. The "union shop" does not require an employee to be a member of the union before being hired, but does require that all employees join the union after being hired. The "agency shop", which is the most common arrangement, does not require that all employees be members of the union, but does require that all employees, including non-members, pay dues to the union. In all three cases, an employee who would prefer not to belong to (or pay dues to) a union is compelled to do so on pain of losing his or her job.

The Supreme Court of Canada has so far had to consider only the third type of union security arrangement, that is, the agency shop. In *Lavigne* v. *OPSEU* (1991),[28] the plaintiff, Lavigne, was a teacher at a community college. The collective agreement between the college and the teachers' union included an agency shop provision, under which all employees had to pay dues to the union. Lavigne, who was not a member of the union, did not directly challenge the agency shop provision. He brought an action for a declaration that his obligation to pay dues was a breach of his Charter right to freedom of association to the extent that the dues were used by the union to fund political parties or causes unrelated to the representation of employees. This was not a frontal attack on the agency shop provision: the plaintiff made no objection to his obligation to pay for the union's services as his bargaining agent. What he objected to was the use of the compelled funds to contribute to the New Democratic Party and to various left-wing causes of which Lavigne disapproved. This kind of objection has been sustained under the first amendment in the United States.[29] The Supreme Court of Canada was unanimous in upholding the agency shop provision without any conditions as to the uses to which the compelled dues could be put. However, the Court divided on the reasons for this result.

In *Lavigne*, a narrow majority of the Supreme Court of Canada held that the right to freedom of association included the right not to associate. This was the view of four judges. La Forest J. (with Sopinka and Gonthier JJ.) followed the American approach in holding that the forced payment of dues was not a forced association to the extent that it only required the employee to pay for the union's

---

28 [1991] 2 S.C.R. 211.

29 In the United States, it has been held that the first amendment is infringed by agency shop collective agreements to the extent that the compelled dues are available to the union for political purposes unrelated to the union's duty of representation of the employees: *Abood* v. *Detroit Bd. of Education* (1977) 431 U.S. 209; *Chicago Teachers' Union* v. *Hudson* (1986) 475 U.S. 292; *Lehnert* v. *Ferris Faculty Assn.* (1991) 111 S. Ct. 1950.

services as the employees' bargaining representative, but was a forced association to the extent that the dues were used to support purposes other than employee representation. Therefore, the agency shop provision did limit Lavigne's freedom of association. However, La Forest J. held that the provision was justified under s. 1 as a measure to encourage healthy democratic debate. McLachlin J. was the fourth judge who agreed that the right to freedom of association included the right not to associate. However, in her view, the forced payment of dues was not a forced association, because the payments to the union did not indicate support by the payor for the causes financed by the union. Therefore, in McLachlin J.'s view, the agency shop provision did not limit Lavigne's freedom of association. Wilson J., with L'Heureux-Dubé J. and, on this issue, Cory J., formed a minority of three to hold that freedom of association did not include a right not to associate.

In *Lavigne*, the three-way split of the Supreme Court of Canada came together in the result, producing a unanimous decision that the agency shop provision was valid.[30] However, there is a narrow majority for the view that the right to freedom of association includes the right not to associate. That view would entail the finding that closed shop and union shop arrangements are limits on s. 2(d) of the Charter. However, this does not mean that the arrangements are unconstitutional. In the first place, it must be remembered that many of these arrangements will not be caught by the Charter of Rights at all: an arrangement that is contained in a collective agreement with a private employer is deemed to be ''private action'' to which the Charter has no application.[31] Secondly, where the Charter does apply (because the arrangement is stipulated by statute, or because the employer is an agency of government), there will be a powerful s. 1 defence to the closed shop or union shop. Such arrangements are designed to strengthen the bargaining power of employees and to avoid free-riding by non-union employees who would otherwise share all the benefits of collectively improved terms of employment without sharing any of the burdens of union membership.

30 The Court was also unanimous that there was no breach of freedom of expression: see ch. 40, Expression, under heading 40.18, ''Election expenditures'', above.

31 In *Lavigne*, the Charter of Rights applied to the collective agreement, because the governing body of the college was an agent of the Crown. A contract or collective agreement between private parties is not covered by the Charter, and closed shop provisions have been upheld on that basis: ch. 34, Application of Charter, under heading 34.2(c), ''Statutory authority'', above.

42

Voting

42.1 Voting

(a) Pre-Charter law

Despite the fundamental importance of the right to vote, and the central position of democratic institutions in the Canadian system of government, there was no constitutional right[1] to vote before the adoption of the Charter. Each legislative body was free to enact its own voting qualifications,[2] and these could exclude certain classes of citizens, such as citizens of Japanese or Chinese origin (who once could not vote in British Columbia),[3] or women (who could not vote in federal elections until 1918),[4] or Indians (who could not vote in federal elections

1 The right to vote was protected by the courts to the extent possible through statutory interpretation: clear statutory language was required to take away the right: Boyer, *Political Rights* (1981), 124. The right was (and still is) also protected by the Quebec Charter of Rights and Freedoms, s. 22, and by the Saskatchewan Human Rights Code, s. 8. The right was not (and still is not) protected by the Canadian Bill of Rights or by the Alberta Bill of Rights.

2 The federal Parliament's power was derived from the peace, order, and good government power until 1949, when s. 91(1) was adopted, and after 1949 from s. 91(1), which has now been replaced by s. 44 of the Constitution Act, 1982. The provincial Legislatures' powers were derived from s. 92(1), which has now been replaced by s. 45 of the Constitution Act, 1982. See ch. 4, Amendment, above, for discussion of ss. 44 and 45.

3 *Cunningham* v. *Tomey Homma* [1903] A.C. 151 (disqualification of Japanese and Chinese upheld).

4 Women were granted the right to vote in federal elections in 1918 by S.C. 1918, c. 20.

until 1960),[5] or persons under the age of 18 (who still cannot vote in federal elections).[6]

(b) Section 3 of Charter

Section 3 of the Charter of Rights[7] provides as follows:

> 3. Every citizen of Canada has the right to vote in an election of members of the House of Commons or of a legislative assembly and to be qualified for membership therein.

Section 3 confers on ''every citizen''[8] the right to vote in federal and provincial elections. The right does not extend to municipal elections or referenda or plebiscites.[9]

Section 3 of the Charter is among those provisions that are not subject to override under s. 33.[10]

However, s. 3 is subject to s. 1.[11] The right to vote can be limited by any law that comes within the phrase ''such reasonable limits prescribed by law as can be demonstrably justified in a free and democratic society''.[12] In every jurisdiction, the qualifications for voting are prescribed by statute, and various people are disqualified. The federal statute[13] used to exclude from the franchise not only persons who are not Canadian citizens and persons who are under the age of 18, but also (1) persons who are mentally incompetent, (2) federally-appointed judges, (3) inmates of penal institutions, and (4) most citizens who are absent from Canada. Each of these four categories of exclusion has been held to be unconsti-

---

5 Indians were granted the right to vote in federal elections in 1960 by S.C. 1960, c. 39.

6 Canada Elections Act, R.S.C. 1985, c. E-2, s. 50. The qualifying age was reduced from twenty-one to eighteen by S.C. 1969-70, c. 49.

7 For commentary on ss. 3 to 5 of the Charter, see Beaudoin and Ratushny (eds.), *The Canadian Charter of Rights and Freedoms* (2nd ed., 1989), ch. 8 (by Beaudoin); McLeod, Takach, Morton, Segal, *The Canadian Charter of Rights* (Carswell, loose-leaf), ch. 27; *Canadian Charter of Rights Annotated* (Canada Law Book, loose-leaf service), annotations to ss. 3-5; The last work contains a bibliography of the relevant literature.

8 On the meaning of ''citizen'' see ch. 34, Application of Charter, under heading 34.1, ''Benefit of rights'', above.

9 *Haig* v. *Can.* [1993] 2 S.C.R. 995 (s. 3 confers no right to vote in federal referendum; arguments based on ss. 2(b) and 15 also rejected).

10 See ch. 36, Override of Rights, above.

11 See ch. 35, Limitation of Rights, above.

12 Section 3 of the Charter was in the October 1980 version in the following terms:

> 3. Every citizen of Canada has, without unreasonable distinction or limitation, the right to vote in an election of members of the House of Commons or of a legislative assembly and to be qualified for membership therein.

The April 1981 version contained the final version of s. 3. In the final version the words ''without unreasonable distinction or limitation'' are deleted. The reason for the deletion was, no doubt, that the words were redundant having regard to s. 1.

13 Canada Elections Act, R.S.C. 1985, c. E-2, ss. 50-51.

tutional.[14] In 1993, the federal statute was amended[15] to remove the disqualifications of mentally incompetent persons and judges. The disqualification of prisoners was retained but restricted to inmates "serving a sentence of two years or more".[16] The disqualification of absent citizens was removed for those citizens who had been absent from Canada for less than five years and who intended to return to Canada as residents. Provincial and territorial requirements of six months' or 12 months' residency as a qualification for voting in provincial or territorial elections have been upheld under s. 1 by the courts.[17] The disqualification of non-citizens is of course in conformity with s. 3 of the Charter.

The American Bill of Rights contains no right to vote couched in such sweeping terms as s. 3 of the Charter. However, it is provided in the American Bill of Rights that the right to vote may not be denied "on account of race, colour, or previous condition of servitude" (fifteenth amendment), or "on account of sex" (nineteenth amendment), or "by reason of failure to pay any poll tax or other tax" (twenty-fourth amendment), or "on account of age" greater than 18 years (twenty-sixth amendment). In addition, the Supreme Court of the United States has held that the fourteenth amendment's guarantee of "equal protection of the laws" is violated when malapportioned electoral districts make some votes weightier than others.[18] These decisions, constitutionalizing the principle that each vote should be of equal weight, have led to judicial orders reapportioning state legislatures so that each electoral district contains an approximately equal number of voters.[19]

(c) One person, one vote

To what extent does the Charter require that each vote be of equal weight? As noted in the previous paragraph, the American courts have derived a principle of equality of voting power from the equal protection clause of the fourteenth

---

14 *Can. Disability Rights Council* v. *The Queen* [1988] 3 F.C. 622 (T.D.) (mentally incompetent persons); *Muldoon* v. *Can.* [1988] 3 F.C. 628 (T.D.) (judges); *Sauvé* v. *Can.* [1993] 2 S.C.R. 438 (prison inmates); *Re Hoogbruin* (1985) 24 D.L.R. (4th) 718 (B.C.C.A.) (temporary absentees); the last case involved a provincial statute, but it suggested that the federal disqualification of absent citizens would be hard to justify under s. 1.

15 S.C. 1993, c. 19, amending s. 51 and adding a new s. 51.1.

16 In *Sauvé* v. *Can.*, note 14, above, this provision had been enacted by the time of the argument in the Supreme Court of Canada, but it was inapplicable to the case under appeal and the Court did not comment on it. Query whether the new provision can be justified under s. 1.

17 *Re Yukon Election Residency Requirement* (1986) 27 D.L.R. (4th) 146 (Y.T.C.A.) (12 months upheld); *Arnold* v. *Ont.* (1987) 61 O.R. (2d) 481 (H.C.) (six months upheld); *Haig* v. *Can.* [1993] 2 S.C.R. 995, 1029 (obiter dictum approving six months). Cf. *Re Weremchuk* (1986) 35 D.L.R. (4th) 278 (B.C.C.A.) (requirement of cross on ballot upheld). Note that, as in the last case, some degree of administrative regulation is required to make the right to vote effective, and would not require justification under s. 1.

18 *Baker* v. *Carr* (1962) 369 U.S. 186; *Reynolds* v. *Sims* (1964) 377 U.S. 533.

19 See generally Tribe, *American Constitutional Law* (1978), ch. 13; Nowak and Rotunda, *Constitutional Law* (4th ed., 1991), 816-868.

amendment. The Supreme Court of Canada has held that a similar principle is to be derived, not from s. 15 (the equality guarantee),[20] but from s. 3 (the voting guarantee).

In the *Saskatchewan Electoral Boundaries Reference* (1991),[21] the Supreme Court of Canada was presented with a challenge to the electoral boundaries for Saskatchewan's legislative assembly. The province's Electoral Boundaries Commission Act called for 66 electoral districts (ridings, constituencies), of which two had to be ''northern'', 35 ''rural'' and 29 ''urban''. The two northern districts were allowed to vary from the electoral quotient (the number of voters divided by the number of districts) by 50 per cent. The other districts were allowed to vary by 25 per cent. An electoral commission, working under this mandate, drew the electoral boundaries, which were translated into law by a second Act. The resulting districts ranged from a northern district with a voting population of 6,309 — 38 per cent below the quotient of 10,147 — to an urban district with a voting population of 12,567 — 24 per cent above the quotient. Although these were the extremes, the permissible variation of 25 per cent above or below the quotient produced considerable voter population disparities between districts. Also, the statutory requirement that 35 of the 66 districts be rural, while it did not cause any breach of the 25-per-cent-variance rule, did result in rural voters being somewhat over-represented: the rural districts on average were under the quotient, while the urban districts on average were over the quotient. This last point, which was the primary basis of the dissenting opinion, was particularly emphasized in support of the Charter challenge, because the Progressive Conservative government of Saskatchewan, which had caused the enactment of the 35-rural-districts requirement, drew more electoral support from rural voters than did the New Democratic opposition.

The Court held that the purpose of the right to vote in s. 3 was to confer on each citizen ''effective representation'' in the Legislature.[22] Effective representation in the Legislature did not require absolute parity of voting power, although parity of voting power was ''of prime importance''.[23] Deviations from parity that could be justified on the grounds of effective representation were not breaches of s. 3.[24] Sparsely populated regions could have districts with lower voting populations than densely populated regions, because of the greater difficulty of repre-

---

20 Despite the success of the equal protection argument in the U.S.A., s. 15 might not extend to disparities in voting power because of the need to show discrimination on the basis of the listed or analogous grounds: see ch. 52 Equality, under heading 51.7, ''Discrimination'', below.

21 *Re Prov. Electoral Boundaries (Sask.)* [1991] 2 S.C.R. 158. The majority judgment was written by McLachlin J. and concurred in by La Forest, Gonthier, Stevenson, Iacobucci JJ and ''substantially'' by Sopinka J., who wrote brief concurring reasons. Cory J. dissented with the agreement of Lamer C.J. and L'Heureux-Dubé J.

22 *Id.*, 183. Cory J.'s dissent did not seem to quarrel with this basic proposition, although he placed greater weight than the majority on the ideal of parity.

23 *Id.*, 184.

24 *Id.*, 185.

senting the larger area. For this reason, the special treatment of the northern districts was constitutionally acceptable, as was the rural-urban disparity. Special geographic features, such as rivers and hills, and even municipal boundaries that formed natural community boundaries, did not have to be disregarded in order to achieve better voter parity. Population growth projections could also justify deviations that were projected to diminish through the life of a set of electoral boundaries.

For these reasons, the majority of the Court held that s. 3 was not violated by the liberal allowances for voter population disparities in the Saskatchewan legislation, nor by the actual boundaries drawn by the electoral commission. There was no need to rely on s. 1 to uphold either the legislation or the boundaries. This was so, despite the fact that (as we have noticed) the most populous Saskatchewan district was nearly double the size of the least populous district.[25] Obviously, the principle of effective representation is highly deferential to any electoral apportionment stipulated by a legislative body.[26]

42.2 Candidacy

Section 3 of the Charter covers candidacy as well as voting. It confers upon every citizen the right to be ''qualified for membership'' in the federal House of Commons or a provincial legislative assembly. The qualifications of a member of the House of Commons or a legislative assembly are prescribed by statute in each jurisdiction,[27] and various citizens are disqualified. A disqualification of provincial civil servants was unsuccessfully challenged before the Charter was adopted in a case that went to the Supreme Court of Canada.[28] All disqualifications of citizens are, of course, now contrary to the Charter, unless they can be justified under s. 1.[29]

Section 3 does not refer to the Senate. (None of the provinces has an upper house.) The qualifications of a Senator are prescribed by ss. 23 and 24 of the Constitution Act, 1867, as interpreted by *Edwards* v. *A.-G. Can.* (1930),[30] which held that ''persons'' who were qualified for appointment include women.

---

25 See also*Re Electoral Boundaries Commission Act (Alta.)* (1991) 86 D.L.R. (4th) 447 (Alta. C.A.) (upholding electoral apportionment involving similar deviations to Saskatchewan, but an even more pronounced preference for rural voters).

26 The principle of effective representation is criticized as too deferential by Charney, ''Sask. Election Boundary Reference: One Person — Half a Vote'' (1991) 1 Nat. J. Con. Law 225. An examination of conflicting electoral values in Canada is undertaken by Smith, MacKinnon and Courtney (eds.) in *Drawing Boundaries: Legislatures, Courts* and *Electoral Values* (1992).

27 The source of power is the same as that to prescribe voting qualifications: note 2, above.

28 *OPSEU* v.*Ont.* [1987]) 2 S.C.R. 2 (disqualification upheld as incident of restrictions on political activity by public servants).

29 *MacLean* v.*A.G.N.S.* (1987) 35 D.L.R. (4th) 306 (N.S.S.C., T.D.) (disqualification of convicted criminals struck down).

30 [1930] A.C. 124.

42.3 Duration of legislative bodies

Section 4 of the Charter of Rights[31] provides as follows:

> 4.(1) No House of Commons and no legislative assembly shall continue for longer than five years from the date fixed for the return of the writs at a general election of its members.
>
> (2) In time of real or apprehended war, invasion or insurrection, a House of Commons may be continued by Parliament and a legislative assembly may be continued by the legislature beyond five years if such continuation is not opposed by the votes of more than one-third of the members of the House of Commons or the legislative assembly, as the case may be.

Section 4(1) prescribes a maximum duration of five years for the House of Commons[32] and each provincial legislative assembly.[33] The purpose, of course, is to ensure that there are elections to those bodies at least every five years. The five-year period is a maximum term, not a fixed term. Under the conventions of responsible government, the Prime Minister or Premier has the power to advise an earlier dissolution, either because his or her government has lost the confidence of the house, or (usually) because he or she thinks the time is ripe for an election.[34] This important power of the Prime Minister or Premier is not disturbed by s. 4, except that the power must be exercised within five years of the previous election.

Section 4(2) enables the five-year period to be extended by the Parliament or a Legislature, but only "in time of real or apprehended war, invasion or insurrection", and only if the extension "is not opposed by the votes of more than one-third of the members of the House of Commons or the legislative assembly".

42.4 Annual sittings of legislative bodies

Section 5 of the Charter of Rights[35] provides as follows:

> 5. There shall be a sitting of Parliament and of each Legislature at least once every twelve months.

31 For commentary on s. 4, see note 7, above.

32 Section 4 does not change the law applicable in the federal jurisdiction. Sections 50 and 91(1) of the Constitution Act, 1867 (s. 91(1) was added by amendment in 1949) contained similar provisions to s. 4 of the Charter. Section 91(1) (but not s. 50) is one of the few provisions which were expressly repealed by s. 53 of the Constitution Act, 1982 (see Schedule, Item 1).

33 Section 85 of the Constitution Act, 1867 prescribed a four-year maximum term for the legislative assemblies of Ontario and Quebec, but in both provinces that term was extended to five years by statutes enacted under the provincial amending power of s. 92(1). Section 19 of the Manitoba Act, 1870 prescribes a four-year maximum term for the legislative assembly of Manitoba. None of these provisions was expressly repealed or amended by s. 53 of the Constitution Act, 1982.

34 See ch. 9, Responsible Government, under heading 9.3(c), "The Prime Minister", above.

35 For commentary on s. 5, see note 7, above.

Section 5 stipulates that there shall be a sitting of Parliament and of each Legislature "at least once every twelve months".[36] Section 5 does not say how long the sitting must continue; a very short sitting (one day, for example) would satisfy the requirement.

36 Section 5 has its counterparts in ss. 20 (Parliament) and 86 (Ontario and Quebec) of the Constitution Act, 1867 and in s. 20 of the Manitoba Act. Section 20 (but not s. 86) of the Constitution Act, 1867 and s. 20 of the Manitoba Act are repealed by s. 53 of the Constitution Act, 1982 (see Schedule, Items 1, 2).

43

Mobility

43.1 Persons

(a) Section 6(1) of Charter

Section 6(1) of the Charter of Rights[1] provides as follows:

> Every citizen of Canada has the right to enter, remain in and leave Canada.

Section 6(1) grants to every ''citizen of Canada''[2] the right ''to enter, remain in and leave Canada''. The right does not extend to non-citizens, who can be refused

---

1 For commentary on s. 6, see Beaudoin and Mendes (eds.), *The Canadian Charter of Rights and Freedoms* (3rd ed., 1996), ch. 8 (by Blache); McLeod, Takach, Morton, Segal, *The Canadian Charter of Rights* (Carswell, loose-leaf), ch. 24; *Canadian Charter of Rights Annotated* (Canada Law Book, loose-leaf), annotation to s. 6. The last work includes a bibliography of the relevant literature.

2 On the meaning of ''citizen'', see ch. 34, Application of Charter, under heading 34.1, ''Benefit of rights'', above.

entry to Canada, and who can be admitted subject to conditions that do not apply to citizens. In *Chiarelli* v. *Canada* (1992)[3] the Supreme Court of Canada upheld the deportation of a non-citizen permanent resident, who had been convicted of a serious criminal offence. The Court held that the Immigration Act, which conferred the power of deportation, did not offend s. 6 (or ss. 7 and 15) in prescribing the conditions under which non-citizens were permitted to remain in Canada.

Section 6, like other Charter rights, is subject to s. 1 (the limitation clause) of the Charter. A law that limits the right will be valid under s. 1 if it comes within the phrase "such reasonable limits prescribed by law as can be demonstrably justified in a free and democratic society". Section 1 was examined in chapter 35, Limitation of Rights, above.

Section 6 is one of the privileged rights that is not subject to s. 33 (the override clause) of the Charter. Section 6 cannot be overcome by enactment of a notwithstanding clause. Section 33 was examined in chapter 36, Override of Rights, above.

(b) International movement

The right to enter Canada was recognized before the Charter by the federal Immigration Act,[4] which afforded to Canadian citizens an unrestricted right to enter Canada.[5] The right to remain in Canada was also recognized by implication, since the Act's powers of deportation did not extend to citizens.[6] These rights are now constitutionalized by s. 6(1) of the Charter, so that future legislation providing for the exile, banishment or deportation of citizens is precluded. The right to leave Canada was not entirely clear before the Charter. No law inhibited foreign travel, but in practice a passport is required for entry to most foreign countries, and there was no right to a passport. The issue of a passport was a function of the Secretary of State for External Affairs, which was not regulated by statute, but was one of the few remaining powers still flowing from the royal prerogative. This is still the case. It is arguable that s. 6(1) confers a constitutional right to a passport.[7]

3 *Can.* v. *Chiarelli* [1992] 0 S.C.R. 000.

4 The federal Parliament and provincial Legislatures have concurrent legislative powers in relation to immigration, under s. 95 of the Constitution Act, 1867.

5 See now Immigration Act, R.S.C. 1985, c. I-2, s. 4(1). As well, the Canadian Bill of Rights, although containing no guarantee like s. 6 of the Charter, includes a prohibition on "arbitrary . . . exile" (s. 2(a)).

6 Sections 5, 32, 33. However, in 1945, before Canadian citizenship existed (it was created in 1946), deportation orders against "naturalized British subjects of the Japanese race" were made under the War Measures Act and were upheld in *Co-op. Committee on Japanese Canadians* v. *A.-G. Can.* [1947] A.C. 87.

7 Laskin, "Mobility Rights under the Charter" (1982) 4 Supreme Court L.R. 89, 91. In the United States, the right to travel abroad has been held to be a "liberty" protected by the due process clause of the fifth amendment, giving rise to a right to a passport. However, the right is not as fundamental as the right of interstate travel and can be limited, for example, by a

In *Re Federal Republic of Germany and Rauca* (1983),[8] the Ontario Court of Appeal upheld the extradition of a Canadian citizen to West Germany to face trial there for crimes allegedly committed during the second world war. It was obvious that the federal Extradition Act limited the right to remain in Canada, as guaranteed by s. 6(1). But the Court held that the Act was justified under s. 1, on the grounds that: (1) crimes committed abroad should not go unpunished, (2) Canada's international obligations under its extradition treaty with West Germany should be fulfilled, and (3) extradition was accepted by other free and democratic societies.

In *Rauca*, the alleged crime had been committed outside Canada. In *United States* v. *Cotroni* (1989),[9] the Supreme Court of Canada was faced with the question whether a Canadian citizen could be extradited to the United States to stand trial for a crime (conspiracy to import drugs into the United States) that had been committed in Canada. The Court agreed with the *Rauca* decision that extradition was a limit on s. 6(1), but the Court divided on the issue of s. 1 justification. For Wilson and Sopinka JJ., extradition could not be justified under s. 1 where, as here, it was possible to try the offender in Canada; a prosecution in Canada would make a breach of s. 6(1) unnecessary. But this was the dissenting view. La Forest J. for the majority held that it was not appropriate to insist upon prosecution in Canada, because there could be a variety of evidentiary or procedural reasons why the other country was the preferable forum of trial. In the majority view, the Extradition Act was justified under s. 1 even in its application to Canadian citizens who had committed the alleged crime in Canada.[10]

The right to enter and remain in Canada is, as noted above, expressly confined to citizens. A non-citizen does not possess any right under s. 6(1). However, once a non-citizen arrives on Canadian soil, even if the entry is illegal, the non-citizen is entitled to those Charter rights that are not confined to citizens — and most of the rights are not so confined. In *Singh* v. *Minister of Employment and Immigration* (1985),[11] the Supreme Court of Canada held that illegal immigrants claiming refugee status were entitled to the procedural requirements of fundamental justice

---

prohibition of travel to Cuba (*Zemel* v. *Rusk* (1965) 381 U.S. 1), or by a power to revoke the passport of an American whose activities threatened national security (*Haig* v. *Agee* (1981) 453 U.S. 280). See generally Nowak and Rotunda, *Constitutional Law* (4th ed., 1991), 868-873.

8 (1983) 41 O.R. (2d) 225 (C.A.).

9 [1989] 1 S.C.R. 1469. La Forest J. wrote the majority opinion, which was agreed to by four others. Wilson and Sopinka JJ. each wrote a dissenting opinion.

10 Extradition was unsuccessfully resisted on other constitutional grounds in *Can.* v. *Schmidt* [1987] 1 S.C.R. 500 (double jeopardy argument rejected); *Argentina* v. *Mellino* [1987] 1 S.C.R. 536 (unreasonable delay argument rejected); *United States* v. *Allard* [1987] 1 S.C.R. 564 (unreasonable delay argument rejected); *Kindler* v. *Can.* [1991] S.C.R. (cruel and unusual punishment argument rejected).

11 [1985] 1 S.C.R. 177. The bench of six judges was unanimous in according fundamental justice to the immigrants, but Beetz, J., with two others, placed his decision on s. 2(e) of the Canadian Bill of Rights, while Wilson J., with two others, placed her decision on s. 7 of the Charter.

under either s. 7 of the Charter of Rights or s. 2(e) of the Canadian Bill of Rights. The difficulty of implementing this decision for all of the large numbers of refugee-claimants has led to giant backlogs of illegal immigrants whose deportation is constitutionally barred until they have been afforded the full hearing that *Singh* requires. During the long wait for their hearings (which can run into years), refugee claimants do in practice enjoy a constitutional right to remain in Canada.

(c) Interprovincial movement

Subsections (2), (3) and (4) of s. 6 of the Charter of Rights[12] provide as follows:

> (2) Every citizen of Canada and every person who has the status of a permanent resident of Canada has the right
> (a) to move to and take up residence in any province; and
> (b) to pursue the gaining of a livelihood in any province.
>
> (3) The rights specified in subsection (2) are subject to
> (a) any laws or practices of general application in force in a province other than those that discriminate among persons primarily on the basis of province of present or previous residence; and
> (b) any laws providing for reasonable residency requirements as a qualification for the receipt of publicly provided social services.
>
> (4) Subsections (2) and (3) do not preclude any law, program or activity that has as its object the amelioration in a province of conditions of individuals in that province who are socially or economically disadvantaged if the rate of employment in that province is below the rate of employment in Canada.

Section 6(2), like s. 6(1), applies to ''every citizen of Canada'', but s. 6(2), unlike s. 6(1), also applies to ''every person who has the status of a permanent resident of Canada''. The meaning of these phrases has been considered in an earlier chapter, and the conclusion reached that neither phrase includes a corporation.[13]

Paragraph (a) of s. 6(2) confers the right ''to move to and take up residence in any province''.[14] This freedom existed in practice before the Charter, in that people have always been free to travel from one province to another without the necessity for documentation or border checks. However, it had never been squarely held that there was a constitutional right to move freely between provinces.[15] There were dicta asserting that such a right existed as an attribute of Canadian citizenship;[16] but the right asserted was effective only against provincial legisla-

12 For commentary on s. 6, see note 1, above.

13 Chapter 34, Application of Charter, under heading 34.1, ''Benefit of rights'', above.

14 By s. 30 of the Charter, the word ''province'' includes a federal territory.

15 Section 121 of the Constitution Act, 1867, discussed later in this chapter, does not create such a right, because it applies only to goods.

16 *Winner* v. *S.M.T. (Eastern)* [1951] S.C.R. 889, 920 per Rand J., 935 per Estey J. On the appeal to the Privy Council, this issue was not mentioned: *A.-G. Ont.* v. *Winner* [1954] A.C. 541.

tion, and could be denied by the federal Parliament.[17] Section 6(2)(a) of the Charter creates a right that is effective against federal as well as provincial legislation, and that attaches not only to citizenship but to permanent residence.[18]

In the Constitution of the United States, there is no explicit guarantee of a right to travel, but a right of interstate travel has been recognized as a fundamental right existing by implication from several provisions of the Constitution.[19] The leading case is *Shapiro* v. *Thompson* (1969),[20] in which the Supreme Court of the United States struck down a state statute which required a period of one year's residence in the state as a condition of entitlement to state welfare benefits. The Court held that such a requirement burdened interstate travel, because it would deter indigent persons from moving to the state.[21] *Shapiro* has been followed in a number of other cases, in which a state has purported to require a period of residence as a qualification for voting in county or state elections,[22] for public medical care[23] or for a share in state oil revenues.[24]

Section 6(2)(a) of the Charter is likely to generate similar doctrine to that which has developed in the United States. A provincial law that discriminates against ''new'' residents of the province will probably be classified as a breach of the right to move to and take up residence in the province.[25] Such a law would not be saved by s. 6(3)(a), which protects laws of general application, because it makes an exception for laws that discriminate ''primarily on the basis of province

---

17 The power to deny the right would come from the federal power over citizenship. Citizenship is a matter within federal authority, probably under s. 91(25) (naturalization and aliens), but possibly under the peace, order, and good government power: *Winner* v. *S.M.T. (Eastern)* [1951] S.C.R. 889, 919 per Rand J.; McConnell, *Commentary on the British North America Act* (1977), 227-232.

18 Query whether s. 6(2)(a) creates a right of mobility *within* a province. The English text suggests no: so held in *McDermott* v. *Nackawis* (1988) 53 D.L.R. (4th) 150 (N.B.C.A.); although the French text suggests yes: Beaudoin and Ratushny, note 1, above, 312-313. In *Re Mia* (1985) 17 D.L.R. (4th) 385 (B.C.S.C.) and *Wilson* v. *B.C. Medical Services Commn.* (1988) 53 D.L.R. (4th) 171 (B.C.C.A.), it was held that s. 7, but not s. 6, conferred a right of free mobility within a province to practise as a doctor.

19 Tribe, *American Constitutional Law* (2nd ed., 1986), 1455-1457; Nowak and Rotunda, *Constitutional Law* (4th ed., 1991), 873-886. A right of international travel has also been recognized, although it is regarded as less fundamental and more easily limited: see note 6, above.

20 (1969) 394 U.S. 618.

21 Because the right of interstate travel was a fundamental one, the law's distinction based on duration of residency would violate the equal protection clause of the fourteenth amendment, unless it could be justified by a ''compelling governmental interest'': *Id.*, 634. The state was unable to establish any such interest: the exclusion of poor persons certainly did not qualify.

22 *Dunn* v. *Blumstein* (1972) 405 U.S. 330.

23 *Memorial Hospital* v. *Maricopa County* (1974) 415 U.S. 250.

24 *Zobel* v. *Williams* (1982) 457 U.S. 55.

25 Contra, *Re Allman and Commr. of N.W.T.* (1983) 8 D.L.R. (4th) 230, 237 (N.W.T. C.A.) (three-year residency requirement for voting in a plebiscite on the division of the Northwest Territories does not violate s. 6(2)(a)). Residence requirements for voting in provincial and territorial elections have also been upheld: ch. 42, Voting, under heading 42.1(b), ''Section 3 of the Charter'', above.

of present or previous residence''. However, s. 6(3)(b) protects ''any laws providing for reasonable residency requirements as a qualification for the receipt of publicly provided social services''. This would apply to a case like *Shapiro* v. *Thompson*, where the state law imposed a one-year residency requirement for the receipt of welfare. For a Canadian court, the issue would be whether the qualification period of one year is a ''reasonable'' residency requirement.[26] What is reasonable depends a good deal on the weight to be attributed to the right of interprovincial travel. As noted, the American courts have placed considerable weight on the right of interstate travel, which they always describe as ''fundamental''. Such an approach, if followed in Canada, would indicate that only a rather short period could be regarded as a reasonable residency requirement for the receipt of publicly provided social services.[27]

(d) Gaining a livelihood

Paragraph (b) of s. 6(2) confers the right ''to pursue the gaining of a livelihood in any province''.[28] While Canadians are unrestricted by law (as opposed to personal or financial considerations) in their freedom to move to and take up residence in any province (a right now guaranteed by paragraph (a)), the power ''to pursue the gaining of a livelihood'' is a different story. Each province has a distinctive regime of law for each industry, trade, profession or occupation; and variations in the certification and licensing requirements constitute barriers to personal mobility.[29] In Quebec, there is the further barrier of language requirements. As well, health and pension benefits are often not portable between provinces.

Barriers to personal mobility that are caused simply by variations in provincial laws will not be removed by s. 6(2)(a) because s. 6(3)(a) exempts ''laws or practices of general application in force in a province other than those that discriminate among persons primarily on the basis of province of present or previous

26 In the absence of s. 6(3)(b), or for laws to which s. 6(3)(b) does not apply, the issue would be whether the law could be justified under s. 1 as coming within the phrase ''such reasonable limits prescribed by law as can be demonstrably justified in a free and democratic society''. The effect of s. 6(3)(b) is to retain the requirement of reasonableness, but to omit the requirement that the law be able to be demonstrably justified in a free and democratic society.

27 Many provincial social services are provided under shared-cost agreements with the federal government, e.g., those made under the Canada Health Act and the Canada Assistance Plan, and these agreements contain mobility-related stipulations, including prohibitions on qualifying periods of provincial residence.

28 By s. 30 of the Charter, the word ''province'' includes a federal territory.

29 Safarian, *Canadian Federalism and Economic Integration* (1974); Chrétien, *Securing the Canadian Economic Union in the Constitution* (1980); Bernier, ''Législation et pratiques relatives a la libre circulation des marchandises, personnes, services et capitaux au Canada'' (1980) 3 Journal of European Integration 267; Trebilcock and others, *Federalism and the Canadian Economic Union* (1983); Lee and Trebilcock, ''Economic Mobility and Constitutional Reform'' (1987) 37 U. Toronto L.J. 268.

residence''.[30] This makes clear that provincial laws which restrict entry to certain occupations to residents of the province are now vulnerable under s. 6(2).[31] But most certification, licensing, language, health-benefit or pension laws would easily fit into s. 6(3)(a). For example, a chartered accountant who was entitled to practise in Ontario could not invoke s. 6(2)(b) to provide an entitlement to practise in Saskatchewan; Saskatchewan's more stringent laws were protected by s. 6(3)(a) because they applied to residents and non-residents alike.[32] Indeed, s. 6(3)(a) even contemplates provincial laws which explicitly discriminate against non-residents, provided that residency is not the primary factor of discrimination. And s. 6(4) also contemplates provincial laws which explicitly discriminate against non-residents, provided the law is for the amelioration of conditions of socially or economically disadvantaged individuals in a province whose unemployment is higher than the Canadian average.[33] The latter provision was apparently inserted to accommodate Newfoundland's requirement that its residents be given preference in employment in the offshore oil industry.[34]

Section 6(2)(b)'s right ''to pursue the gaining of a livelihood in any province'', if read literally and apart from its context, could be interpreted as conferring a ''right to work'' on every citizen and permanent resident of Canada. It would be odd to find such a right in a Charter that generally eschews the protection of economic rights, and especially odd to find such a right buried in a section headed ''Mobility Rights''. The question whether s. 6(2)(b) could bear this meaning was raised in *Law Society of Upper Canada* v. *Skapinker* (1984).[35] At issue was a requirement of Ontario's Law Society Act that members of the bar of Ontario must be Canadian citizens. Skapinker, who was qualified for admission to the Ontario bar in all other respects, was not a citizen, although he was a permanent resident of Canada. On being refused admission to the bar, he sued for a declaration that the citizenship requirement was invalid, on the ground that it violated the Charter. Skapinker could not rely on the equality right of s. 15, because his

30 Laskin, note 6, above, 100, argues cogently that ''laws or practices of general application'' in this context means ''laws or practices that do not focus on non-residents as a group''.

31 *Island Equine Clinic* v. *P.E.I.* (1991) 81 D.L.R. (4th) 350 (P.E.I.S.C., A.D.) (denial of veterinary subsidy to new arrival to province is a breach of s. 6(2)(b)).

32 *Taylor* v. *Institute of Chartered Accountants* (1989) 59 D.L.R. (4th) 656 (Sask. C.A.).

33 Laskin, note 6, above, 103 points out that affirmative action programs under s. 6(4) will have to be ''tailored to benefit those individuals in the province who are in fact socially or economically disadvantaged. A general preference for all provincial residents would seem over-inclusive, in that it would benefit the highly skilled and the well off as well as the disadvantaged''. Cf. *Hicklin* v. *Orbeck* (1978) 437 U.S. 518 (state statute requiring that preference be given to Alaska residents in employment in the Alaska oil industry held invalid).

34 Subsections (1), (2) and (3) of s. 6 were in the October 1980 and April 1981 versions of the Charter. Subsection (4) was not in those versions, but was part of the November 5, 1981 agreement between the federal government and nine provinces.

35 [1984] 1 S.C.R. 357.

case arose before s. 15 had come into force.[36] He relied on s. 6(2)(b), arguing that he was a permanent resident of Canada who had been denied the right "to pursue the gaining of a livelihood" in Ontario. The Supreme Court of Canada, in a unanimous opinion written by Estey J., rejected the argument. The Court held that s. 6(2)(b) did not confer an unqualified right to pursue the gaining of a livelihood in the province. The Court held that s. 6(2)(b) was qualified by a mobility element. Since there was no mobility element to the facts presented by Skapinker, he was unsuccessful in asserting the breach of s. 6(2)(b).

What was the mobility element to be implied into s. 6(2)(b)? Estey J. seemed to contemplate two classes of citizens and permanent residents who would possess the requisite mobility element. The first class would comprise any persons denied a livelihood because they had previously resided in another province; this class would cover the persons who had exercised their right under s. 6(2)(a) to move to and take up residence in the province of work.[37] The second class would comprise any persons denied a livelihood because they were not residents of the province; this class would cover the persons who had not exercised their right under s. 6(2)(a) and had instead continued to reside outside the province of work, but who wished to work in the province without becoming a resident of the province, for example, by commuting across the border. Skapinker fitted into neither of these two classes: he had not moved to Ontario from another province and he was not a resident of another province. Therefore, he possessed no right to a livelihood under s. 6(2)(b).

If Skapinker had moved to Ontario from another province or if he resided outside the province, he would have been protected by s. 6(2)(b). But his proceedings would still have been unsuccessful. The Law Society Act did not discriminate against the persons protected by s. 6(2)(b): it discriminated against non-citizens, regardless of their province of present or previous residence. It would be absurd if s. 6(2)(b) gave to recent arrivals or non-residents greater rights to work in a province than those possessed by residents of the province. This result is precluded by s. 6(3), which makes clear that s. 6(2) does not disturb "laws or practices of general application in force in a province other than those that discriminate among persons primarily on the basis of province of present or previous residence". The Law Society Act's requirement of citizenship would be preserved by s. 6(3). (This requirement is, however, now contrary to s. 15, the equality right, of the Charter.)[38]

36 By virtue of s. 32(2) of the Charter, s. 15 came into force three years after the rest of the Charter. After s. 15 came into force, the requirement of citizenship in B.C.'s legal profession legislation was successfully challenged as a breach of s. 15: *Andrews* v. *Law Society of B.C.* [1989] 1 S.C.R. 143.

37 *Re Mia* (1985) 17 D.L.R. (4th) 385 (B.C.S.C.) (discrimination against new residents of province in allocation of licences to practise medicine held contrary to s. 6(2)(b)).

38 Note 35, above.

The right of an out-of-province resident to gain a livelihood in the province was vindicated in *Black* v. *Law Society of Alberta* (1989).[39] The Law Society of Alberta had enacted two regulations, the purpose of which was to discourage law firms from Ontario (or anywhere else outside Alberta) from establishing branch offices in Alberta. The first regulation prohibited members of the Alberta bar who were resident in Alberta from entering into partnership with members who were not resident in Alberta. The second regulation prohibited members of the Alberta bar from being partners in more than one firm. These regulations were challenged by a group of lawyers, all members of the Alberta bar, some of whom were resident in Alberta while others were resident in Ontario. They wished to form an Alberta law firm. As well, all members of the Alberta law firm would also be members of an Ontario law firm. In that way, the Ontario firm, McCarthy & McCarthy (now McCarthy, Tétrault), would have established a branch office in Alberta. The Supreme Court of Canada, by a majority,[40] held that the two Law Society regulations were invalid as violations of s. 6(2)(b)). The effect of the regulations was to impair the ability to gain a livelihood in Alberta of those members of the Alberta bar who did not reside in Alberta. The regulations were not saved by s. 6(3)(a), because they discriminated among lawyers primarily on the basis of the lawyer's province of residence.

(e) Property ownership

Neither paragraph (a) nor paragraph (b) of s. 6(2) confers the right to acquire or hold property in a province. In *Morgan* v. *A.-G. P.E.I.* (1976),[41] the Supreme Court of Canada upheld a provincial law which discriminated against non-residents in limiting their allowable holdings of real estate. That decision is not disturbed by the Charter.

(f) Corporations

Before the Charter, corporations were even more vulnerable than individuals to provincial restrictions on their activities. Since s. 6 of the Charter does not extend to corporations, this situation is unchanged. Within each province, only a corporation incorporated under the law of the province or under federal law is

---

39 [1989] 1 S.C.R. 591. The majority opinion was written by La Forest J. and concurred in by Dickson C.J. and Wilson J. The minority opinion was written by McIntyre J. and concurred in by L'Heureux-Dubé J.

40 McIntyre J. for the minority held that there was no breach of s. 6(2)(b), because no-one was prohibited from entering Alberta or from practising law in Alberta. However, he held that the two regulations did abridge freedom of association (s. 2(d)), although one of the two regulations, the one prohibiting an Alberta lawyer from belonging to more than one firm, was justified under s. 1.

41 [1976] 2 S.C.R. 349; discussed in ch. 21, Property and Civil Rights, under heading 21.11(b), ''Foreign ownership'', above.

entitled to be recognized as a legal entity. For a corporation incorporated in another province or another country, recognition is within the discretion of any province in which it seeks to carry on its business. A province could, if it chose, prevent a corporation incorporated elsewhere from carrying on business in the province. This would disable not only the corporation, but also its officers and servants acting in the course of their employment. No province has done this, no doubt because it would be contrary to economic self-interest, but all provinces do impose licensing requirements on extra-provincial corporations which carry on business in the province.[42]

43.2 Goods

(a) Section 6(2) of Charter

Neither paragraph (a) nor paragraph (b) of s. 6(2) of the Charter confers the right of free movement of goods, as opposed to persons. However, the right to move to and take up residence in another province (s. 6(2)(a)) would probably include the right to bring those personal effects that were needed for the establishment of a new residence. And the right to pursue the gaining of a livelihood in another province (s. 6(2)(b)) would probably include the right to bring business assets, such as equipment or inventory, that were needed for the gaining of a livelihood. It is probable that there is a right to move business assets to another province even if the owner does not actually go there, because, as *Black* v. *Law Society of Alberta*[43] decides, s. 6(2)(b) "does not require the physical presence of the person . . . as the exclusive method of gaining a livelihood".[44]

(b) Section 121 of Constitution Act, 1867

Section 121 of the Constitution Act, 1867 requires that "all articles of the growth, produce or manufacture of any one of the provinces shall . . . be admitted free into each of the other provinces". Section 121 precludes customs duties between the provinces. However, s. 121 has never been used to strike down non-fiscal impediments to interprovincial trade,[45] although its use for that purpose in

---

42 See ch. 23, Companies, under heading 23.1(b), "Territorial limitation", above.

43 Note 38, above.

44 Binavince, "The Impact of the Mobility Rights" (1982) 14 Ottawa L. Rev. 340, 356.

45 In both *Gold Seal* v. *A.-G. Alta.* (1921) 62 S.C.R. 424 and *Atlantic Smoke Shops* v. *Conlon* [1943] A.C. 550, arguments based on s. 121 were rejected on the ground that s. 121 prohibited only customs duties between provinces and no other kinds of impediments to interprovincial mobility of goods.

a gross case of provincial protectionism has been raised as a possibility in cases concerning marketing schemes.[46]

(c) Interprovincial transportation, trade and commerce

The existence of exclusive federal power over interprovincial transportation and interprovincial trade and commerce is the main reason why a province cannot close its borders to the admission of goods. It has been held that a province cannot impose substantial regulation on interprovincial or international carriers, even when they engage in local transportation as well.[47] And there are important restrictions on the power of a province to regulate the marketing of goods whose market extends beyond the boundaries of the province.[48] Since barriers to the interprovincial mobility of goods (or other resources) are most likely to be erected by the provinces, these restrictions on provincial power favour the interprovincial mobility of goods. However, since the restrictions on provincial power flow from the federal distribution of powers, what is withheld from the provinces is possessed by the federal Parliament. When the federal Parliament has enacted barriers to the mobility of goods, either alone[49] or in concert with the provinces,[50] the laws have been upheld. The only limitation on federal power would be s. 121, which applies to federal as well as provincial laws,[51] but, as noted above, that section has proved to be an ineffective guarantee of the interprovincial mobility of goods.

(d) Product standards

A province's authority over property and civil rights in the province enables it to stipulate standards of quality of goods sold in the province for the protection

---

46 *Murphy* v. *CPR* [1958] S.C.R. 626, 642 per Rand J. ("What is forbidden is a trade regulation that in its essence and purpose is related to a provincial boundary."); *Re Agricultural Products Marketing Act* [1978] 2 S.C.R. 1198, 1268 per Laskin C.J. for whole Court on this issue (accepting Rand J.'s dictum). See generally La Forest, *The Allocation of Taxing Power under the Canadian Constitution* (2nd ed., 1981), 178-182.

47 *A.-G. Ont.* v. *Winner* [1954] A.C. 541; discussed in ch. 22, Transportation and Communication, under heading 22.5, "Undivided jurisdiction", above.

48 *A.-G. Man.* v. *Man. Egg and Poultry Assn.* [1971] S.C.R. 689; *Can. Industrial Gas and Oil* v. *Govt. of Sask.* [1978] 2 S.C.R. 545; *Central Can. Potash Co.* v. *Govt. of Sask.* [1979] 1 S.C.R. 42; discussed in ch. 21, Property and Civil Rights, under heading 21.9, "Marketing", above.

49 *Caloil* v. *A.-G. Can.* [1971] S.C.R. 543 (upholding federal prohibition on shipment of imported oil west of the Ottawa Valley, to protect the then dearer domestic product).

50 The power to regulate international and interprovincial transportation has been delegated to provincial agencies by federal legislation: *Coughlin* v. *Ont. Highway Transport Bd.* [1968] S.C.R. 569; so that a carrier has to satisfy a variety of standards in order to move from one province to another: see, e.g., *R.* v. *Smith* [1972] S.C.R. 359. Provincial boundaries have been used as barriers to movement of the factors of production of eggs by complementary federal and provincial legislation: *Re Agricultural Products Marketing Act* [1978] 2 S.C.R. 1198.

51 *Atlantic Smoke Shops* v. *Conlon* [1943] A.C. 550, 569; *Re Agricultural Products Marketing Act* [1978] 2 S.C.R. 1198, 1267.

of the health and safety of consumers, as well as standards for advertising, labelling and selling, to ensure fair dealing in consumer transactions. Obviously, the existence of divergent standards from province to province is a barrier to mobility of goods. For example, in *Attorney General of Quebec* v. *Kellogg's Co.* (1978)[52] the Supreme Court of Canada held that a Quebec law prohibiting the use of cartoons in advertising directed to children was a valid law, and that it was effective to preclude the use within Quebec of television commercials produced and used in Ontario. In *Nova Scotia Board of Censors* v. *McNeil* (1978),[53] the Court held that a Nova Scotia law establishing a regime of motion-picture censorship was a valid law and that it was effective to preclude the screening within Nova Scotia of a motion picture produced in the United States and screened elsewhere in Canada.

The federal Parliament has only limited authority over product standards under the criminal law power,[54] and even less authority under the trade and commerce power.[55] But where a single national standard has been validly enacted by the federal Parliament, this will not preclude the provinces from establishing a variety of stricter standards; the fact that a federal law has "occupied the field" does not render inoperative or preempt otherwise valid provincial laws in the same field.[56]

43.3 Services

Services are supplied by individuals and corporations. A citizen or permanent resident for whom the supply of services is his or her means of livelihood is covered by s. 6(2). Section 6(2) guarantees to a citizen or permanent resident the right to pursue the gaining of a livelihood in any province.[57] The mobility of services supplied by a citizen or permanent resident is thus guaranteed. This is illustrated by *Black* v. *Law Society of Alberta* (1989),[58] where the Supreme Court

52 [1978] 2 S.C.R. 211; folld. in *Irwin Toy* v. *Que.* [1989] 1 S.C.R. 927 (provincial prohibition on advertising directed at children upheld as within provincial power; a Charter attack was also unsuccessful by virtue of s. 1).

53 [1978] 2 S.C.R. 662. Note that this was a pre-Charter case.

54 *Labatt Breweries* v. *A.-G. Can.* [1980] 1 S.C.R. 914 (compositional standards for light beer, not required for health or safety, struck down); see ch. 18, Criminal Law, under heading 18.3, "Food and drugs", above.

55 *Dominion Stores* v. *The Queen* [1980] 1 S.C.R. 844 (federal grades for agricultural products struck down, except where product moved in interprovincial or international trade); *Labatt Breweries* v. *A.-G. Can.* [1980] 1 S.C.R. 914 (federal compositional standards unrelated to the product's movement across provincial boundaries struck down); see ch. 20, Trade and Commerce, above.

56 *Construction Montcalm* v. *Minimum Wage Comm.* [1979] 1 S.C.R. 754 (federal minimum wage did not displace higher provincial minimum wage); see ch. 16, Paramountcy, above.

57 Section 6(2)'s application to the gaining of a livelihood is discussed in sec. 43.1(c), "Gaining a livelihood", above

58 Note 38, above.

of Canada struck down regulations enacted by the Law Society of Alberta that were intended to make it more difficult for a non-resident member of the Alberta Bar to practise law — that is, supply legal services — in Alberta.

Section 6(2)'s guarantee of mobility of services is a weak one, however, because, by s. 6(3), it is subject to "any laws or practices of general application in force in a province other than those that discriminate primarily on the basis of province of present or previous residence". The regulations in *Black* did discriminate on the basis of residence in Alberta, and so were not saved by s. 6(3). But laws of general application that do not discriminate on the basis of provincial residence will not be affected by s. 6(2). Therefore, most provincial restrictions on entry to professions, trades and businesses will not be caught by s. 6(2), despite the fact that they often constitute important barriers to mobility.[59]

Individuals who are not citizens or permanent residents of Canada are not covered by s. 6(2). Nor are corporations. Their mobility is not protected by any constitutional guarantee, and, if they supply services, restrictions on their mobility are also restrictions on the supply of services.

43.4 Capital

(a) Section 6(2) of Charter

The mobility of capital, like the mobility of services, is afforded the protection of s. 6(2) of the Charter, where the capital is integral to the gaining of a livelihood by a citizen or permanent resident. But, by virtue of s. 6(3), s. 6(2) is subject to "any laws or practices of general application in force in a province other than those that discriminate primarily on the basis of province of present or previous residence". Where s. 6(2) does not apply, no constitutional guarantee protects the mobility of capital.

(b) Federal powers over capital

In fact, there are no direct restrictions on the movement of capital from one province to another. Indeed, there are no direct restrictions on the movement of capital to foreign jurisdictions, although the federal Investment Canada Act[60] regulates some of the traffic in the other direction. Direct restrictions on the movement of capital across provincial or international borders would come within the exclusive power of the federal Parliament, and would be incompetent to the provinces.[61]

---

59 Note 28, above.

60 R.S.C. 1985, c.28 (1st supp.).

61 As well as the federal trade and commerce power (s. 91(2)), there is a cluster of federal powers over money, banking and credit. The invalidation of Alberta's social credit policies in the 1930s, e.g., *Re Alta. Statutes* [1938] S.C.R. 100, illustrates the exclusiveness of federal power.

Laws encouraging the nation-wide mobility of capital obviously can only be enacted by the federal Parliament. Yet it has only recently been established that the federal Parliament has the power to enact an effective competition (anti-trust) policy that goes beyond mere criminal prohibitions.[62] It is still not clearly established that the federal Parliament has the power to regulate the securities market, and the securities market is in fact regulated by the provinces.[63] The banks come within federal jurisdiction, but most other financial intermediaries, such as, insurance companies, trust companies and mutual funds, are primarily within provincial jurisdiction.[64] Thus, the Constitution itself contributes to the maintenance of barriers to the mobility of capital.

(c) Restrictions on mobility

The economist's ideal of perfect mobility of capital, leading to the most efficient utilization of resources, is never likely to be espoused as policy by those provinces that would stand to lose by it. Nor is it likely to be espoused by the federal government, which has always accepted the obligation to encourage development in the less favoured regions of the country. A host of federal and provincial programmes are in place to provide incentives to the location of the means of production in regions that would be abandoned in a free market. This phenomenon is not reflected in the case law, but is amply supported by the constitutional powers of both levels of government to levy taxes (and give relief from taxes), to spend money (and subsidize particular businesses) and to purchase goods and services (preferably from local suppliers).[654]

In addition, provincial powers to regulate local markets, most industries, most labour relations and standards, and the trades and professions, often have the effect of favouring the local business (or at least the national or multi-national business which is already in place) by directly or indirectly discouraging the entry to the province of new producers or suppliers. Often too, when provincial policies to protect local industries have fallen afoul of the Constitution, the federal Parliament has been willing to lend its aid. After New Brunswick's attempt to protect its bus industry from foreign competition was held invalid in the *Winner* case,[66] the federal Parliament immediately delegated to the provinces the powers that the Privy Council had just denied New Brunswick. This delegation was upheld by the Supreme Court of Canada.[67]

Perhaps the most dramatic case of federal-provincial cooperation to preclude the mobility of capital is egg marketing. After the ''chicken and egg war'' between

62 See ch. 18, Criminal Law, under heading 18.6, ''Competition law'', above.

63 See ch. 21, Property and Civil Rights, under heading 21.10, ''Securities regulation'', above.

64 See ch. 21, Property and Civil Rights, under heading 21.5, ''Insurance'', above; ch. 24, Financial Institutions, above.

65 Note 28, above.

66 *A.-G. Ont.* v. *Winner* [1954] A.C. 541.

67 *Coughlin* v. *Ont. Highway Transport Bd.* [1968] S.C.R. 569.

Ontario and Quebec in the 1960s, which culminated in a judicial decision denying to the provinces the power to protect their local industries,[68] the 11 Ministers of Agriculture met and allocated egg production quotas to each province. Those quotas were then imposed by complementary federal and provincial laws. The effect was to protect egg producers in each province by prohibiting the shifts in the location of egg production which a free market would produce. This scheme was upheld by the Supreme Court of Canada.[69]

(d) Conclusions

With regard to capital, one must conclude: (1) that only the crudest and most direct provincial restrictions on the mobility of capital are prohibited by the Canadian Constitution; (2) that federal powers to improve mobility through competition law, securities regulation and the regulation of financial institutions are incomplete or at least in doubt; and (3) that, where the federal government is willing to cooperate with the provinces, substantial direct restrictions on mobility are constitutional.

---

68 *A.-G. Man.* v. *Man. Egg and Poultry Assn.* [1971] S.C.R. 689.

69 *Re Agricultural Products Marketing Act* [1978] 2 S.C.R. 1198.

44

Fundamental Justice

44.1 Distribution of powers over legal rights

This chapter deals with s. 7 of the Charter of Rights, which is the first of eight sections (ss. 7 to 14) of the Charter that are grouped under the heading

"Legal Rights". The term legal rights does not have a precise legal or popular meaning. It certainly includes the rights of persons within the system of criminal justice, limiting the powers of the state with respect to search, seizure, arrest, detention, trial and punishment. However, as we shall see, s. 7 in particular spills over into civil justice as well.

The distribution of powers between the federal Parliament and the provincial Legislatures over the matters loosely encompassed by the vague term "legal rights" depends upon the characterization of each law. In characterizing a law, the law's impact on civil liberties is generally irrelevant, or at least of only subordinate importance. If the law is in relation to criminal law or criminal procedure, it will be within federal power under s. 91(27) of the Constitution Act, 1867. The various stages of a criminal trial from arrest and charge through to acquittal or conviction and sentence are accordingly within federal legislative authority. On the other hand, provincial authority over the administration of justice in the province (s. 92(14)) includes the constitution of criminal and civil courts and civil procedure, and extends to some aspects of the investigation and prosecution of crime.[1] If a law establishes a legislative scheme, for example, for the raising of taxes, securities regulation or traffic regulation, the law may provide for investigation and enforcement of the scheme. The validity of these adjectival provisions depends upon the validity of the scheme to which they are incidental. There is no suggestion in the cases that the severity of the law's impact on civil liberties is of importance in assigning legislative jurisdiction.[2]

44.2 Section 7 of Charter

Section 7 of the Charter of Rights[3] provides as follows:

> 7. Everyone has the right to life, liberty and security of the person and the right not to be deprived thereof except in accordance with the principles of fundamental justice.

Section 7 protects the right of "everyone" to "life, liberty and security of the person", and imposes the requirement that any deprivation be "in accordance with the principles of fundamental justice".

It is arguable that s. 7 confers two rights: (1) a right to "life, liberty and security of the person" that is unqualified, except by s. 1 (the limitation clause)

---

1 See chs. 7, Courts, and 19, Criminal Justice, above.

2 On the distribution of legislative power over legal civil liberties, see Tarnopolsky, *The Canadian Bill of Rights* (2nd ed., 1975), 55-56.

3 For commentary on s. 7, see Paciocco, *Charter Principles and Proof in Criminal Cases* (1987); Beaudoin and Ratushny (eds.), *The Canadian Charter of Rights and Freedoms* (2nd ed., 1989), ch. 10 (by Garant); Finkelstein and Finkelstein, *Constitutional Rights in the Investigative Process* (1991), chs. 2, 3; Stuart, *Charter Justice in Canadian Criminal Law* (2nd ed., 1996), ch. 2; McLeod, Takach, Morton, Segal, *The Canadian Charter of Rights* (Carswell, loose-leaf) ch. 5; *Canadian Charter of Rights Annotated* (Canada Law Book, loose-leaf), annotation to s. 7; the last work provides a bibliography of the relevant literature.

of the Charter; and (2) a right not to be deprived of life, liberty and security of the person except in accordance with the principles of fundamental justice. If this were correct, then every deprivation of life, liberty or security of the person would be a breach of s. 7, even if the principles of fundamental justice had been complied with. This two-rights interpretation of s. 7, although supported by the grammatical structure of the English (but not the French) version of the section,[4] is otherwise an unnatural reading of the section, and one that would give s. 7 an extraordinarily broad sweep. The better view is that s. 7 confers only one right, namely, the right not to be deprived of life, liberty or security of the person except in accordance with the principles of fundamental justice. The cases generally assume that the single-right interpretation is the correct one, so that there is no breach of s. 7 unless there has been a failure to comply with the principles of fundamental justice.[5]

The Canadian Bill of Rights, by s. 1(a) guarantees:

> the right of the individual to life, liberty and security of the person and enjoyment of property, and the right not to be deprived thereof except by due process of law. . . .

In addition, s. 2(e) provides that no law of Canada is to be construed or applied so as to:

> deprive a person of the right to a fair hearing in accordance with the principles of fundamental justice for the determination of his rights and obligations. . . .

Section 7 of the Charter can be seen as an amalgam of these two provisions, but s. 7 is significantly narrower in scope than either s. 1(a), which extends to ''enjoyment of property'', or s. 2(e), which extends to any determination of ''rights and obligations''. Section 7's protection is limited to ''life, liberty and security of the person'', a phrase which does not include property and which does not include a determination of rights and obligations respecting economic interests. As has earlier been explained, the Canadian Bill of Rights (which applies only to federal laws) remains in force, and ss. 1(a) and 2(e) are of continuing importance because their coverage is broader than s. 7.[6]

The Constitution of the United States, by the fifth amendment, which applies to the federal government, provides that no person ''shall be deprived of life,

---

4 Contrast the grammatical structure of the fifth and fourteenth amendments of the Constitution of the United States, which clearly confer only one right, namely, the right not to be deprived of life, liberty or property without due process of law.

5 E.g., *Can.* v. *Chiarelli* [1992] 0 S.C.R. 000 (denial of liberty in compliance with fundamental justice is not a breach of s. 7). However, in *Re B.C. Motor Vehicle Act* [1985] 2 S.C.R. 486, Lamer C.J. (at 500) expressly left the issue open, and Wilson J. (at 523) seemed to accept the two-right interpretation, because she said that even if fundamental justice were satisfied s. 1 would *also* have to be satisfied. Both positions are puzzling: Lamer J.'s elaborate discussion of fundamental justice would have little point if *any* denial of life, liberty or security of the person was a breach of s. 7; and Wilson J. had previously doubted the two-right interpretation in *Operation Dismantle* v. *The Queen* [1985] 1 S.C.R. 441, 487.

6 Chapter 32, Canadian Bill of Rights, under heading, 32.4, ''Contents'', above.

liberty, or property, without due process of law''. The fourteenth amendment, which applies to the states, also guarantees against the deprivation of ''life, liberty, or property, without due process of law.'' These guarantees are also broader than s. 7, because they extend to ''property'', although they make no reference to ''security of the person''. Another difference is that the American guarantees refer to ''due process of law'' whereas s. 7 refers to ''the principles of fundamental justice''. The significance of this change is examined in the later discussion of fundamental justice.[7]

44.3 Application of s. 1

Section 7 makes clear that a law can deprive a person of life, liberty or security of the person if the law conforms to the principles of fundamental justice.[8] Could a law that did not conform to the principles of fundamental justice be upheld under s. 1? Could a violation of fundamental justice ever be a reasonable limit that can be demonstrably justified in a free and democratic society? Wilson J. has several times expressed the view that the answer to this question is no: a violation of fundamental justice could never be justified under s. 1. However, for the most part, the Court has routinely moved on to the issue of s. 1 justification before finding a breach of s. 7, and some judges (although never a majority) have held that a particular breach of s. 7 was justified under s. 1. The issue is examined in chapter 35, Limitation of Rights, above.[9]

44.4 Benefit of s. 7

(a) Corporations

Section 7 is applicable to ''everyone'', a word that is normally apt to include a corporation as well as an individual.[10] However, the Supreme Court of Canada has held that in the context of s. 7 ''everyone'' does not include a corporation. An artificial person such as a corporation is incapable of possessing ''life, liberty or security of the person'', because these are attributes of natural persons.[11] Therefore, s. 7 does not apply to a corporation.

---

7 Section 44.9, ''Fundamental justice'', below.

8 Note, however, that the two-right interpretation of s. 7 calls for s. 1 justification even if the principles of fundamental justice are satisfied: text accompanying note 4, above.

9 Chapter 35, Limitation of Rights, under heading 35.13, ''Application to qualified rights'', above.

10 Chapter 34, Application of Charter, under heading 34.1, ''Benefit of rights'', above.

11 *Irwin Toy* v. *Que.* [1989] 1 S.C.R. 927, 1004; *Dywidag Systems* v. *Zutphen Bros.* [1990] 1 S.C.R. 705, 709.

This does not mean that a corporation can never invoke s. 7.[12] When a corporation is a defendant to a prosecution, the corporation is entitled to defend the charge on the basis that the law is a nullity. In *R.* v. *Wholesale Travel Group* (1991),[13] the Supreme Court of Canada held that this principle allows a corporation to defend a criminal charge on the ground that the law under which the charge was laid would be a violation of s. 7 in its application to an individual. The Court rejected the argument that a law could be unconstitutional for individuals, but constitutional for corporations. The Court also rejected the argument that a corporation could be convicted under an unconstitutional law, even though the defect in the law (a denial of ''liberty'' in breach of fundamental justice) was not one that was relevant to a corporation (because a corporation has no right to ''liberty'').[14]

(b) Immigrants

''Everyone'' in s. 7 includes illegal immigrants to Canada. In *Singh* v. *Minister of Employment and Immigration* (1985),[15] Wilson J. said that s. 7 rights could be asserted by ''every human being who is physically present in Canada and by virtue of such presence amenable to Canadian law''.[16] What that meant, she held, was that any illegal immigrant who claimed to be a refugee was entitled to a hearing before an official or tribunal with authority to determine the issue. The argument that such a procedure would make it impossible to deal expeditiously with the many thousands of refugee claimants who arrive in Canada each year was rejected as an inadmissible ''utilitarian'' or ''administrative'' concern, which could not be permitted to vitiate individual rights.[17] In fact, after *Singh*, refugee claimants arrived in Canada at the rate of about 36,000 a year, and the federal government was not able to comply with the *Singh* rule in a timely fashion. As a result, a huge backlog of refugee claimants developed, and they endured delays of two or more years awaiting adjudication.[18]

---

12 An individual may invoke s. 7, even when appearing as a witness as a representative of a corporation: *Thomson Newspapers* v. *Can.* [1990] 1 S.C.R. 425.

13 [1991] 3 S.C.R. 154.

14 See also ch. 56, Constitutional Litigation, under heading 56.2, ''Standing'', below.

15 [1985] 1 S.C.R. 177.

16 *Id.*, 202 per Wilson J. for half of the six-judge bench. Beetz J. for the other half decided the case on the basis of the Canadian Bill of Rights rather than the Charter, but he assumed that illegal immigrants were entitled to the rights under the Canadian Bill of Rights.

17 *Id.*, 218-219.

18 See, for example, the reports of refugee backlogs in The Globe and Mail newspaper, February 23, 26 and 27, 1991. At that time, the refugee-determination procedures occupied a 276-member Immigration and Refugee Board and 773 civil servants.

(c) Foetus

"Everyone" in s. 7 does not include a foetus, and so a foetus is not entitled to a right to life.[19] The Supreme Court of Canada has in fact used s. 7 to strike down *restrictions* on abortion, the reasoning being that the restrictions deprived the mother of her right to liberty or security of the person.[20]

44.5 Burden of s. 7

Section 7, like all the other Charter rights, applies only to "governmental action", as defined in s. 32 of the Charter. This is the subject of chapter 34, Application of Charter, above.[21]

44.6 Life

Section 7 protects "life, liberty and security of the person". So far as "life" is concerned, the section has little work to do.[22] Even the issue of abortion, which is sometimes characterized as implicating a "right to life", meaning a right possessed by a foetus, does not have to be decided in these terms, because the s. 7 right is possessed by "everyone", and everyone does not include a foetus.[23] However, the Supreme Court of Canada has struck down restrictions on abortion, reasoning that they infringed the liberty and security of the person of the mother, and did not comply with the principles of fundamental justice.[24]

44.7 Liberty

(a) Physical liberty

Section 7 protects "life, liberty and security of the person". What is included in "liberty"?

---

19 Chapter 34, Application of Charter, under heading 34.1(b), "Everyone, anyone, any person", above.

20 *R.* v. *Morgentaler (No. 2)* [1988] 1 S.C.R. 30.

21 On the extent to which s. 7 could be infringed by the action of a foreign government, an issue that arises in extradition cases, among others, see ch. 34, Application of Charter, under heading 34.2(d), "Government", above.

22 With respect to capital punishment, which has been eliminated from the Criminal Code, see ch. 50, Cruel and Unusual Punishment, under heading 50.15, "Death penalty", below.

23 Note 19, above.

24 Note 20, above.

''Liberty'' certainly includes freedom from physical restraint. Any law that imposes the penalty of imprisonment, whether the sentence is mandatory[25] or discretionary,[26] is by virtue of that penalty a deprivation of liberty, and must conform to the principles of fundamental justice. A law that imposes only the penalty of a fine is not a deprivation of liberty, and need not conform to the principles of fundamental justice.[27] As well as imprisonment, statutory duties to submit to fingerprinting,[28] to produce documents,[29] to give oral testimony[30] and not to loiter in or near schoolgrounds, playgrounds, public parks and bathing areas,[31] are also deprivations of liberty attracting the rules of fundamental justice.

Once a criminal defendant has been convicted and sentenced to a term of imprisonment, will a change in the terms of the sentence amount to a deprivation of liberty? In *Cunningham* v. *Canada* (1993),[32] the defendant had been sentenced in 1981 to 12 years' imprisonment for manslaughter. Under the Parole Act in force at the time of his sentencing, he was entitled to be released on mandatory supervision after serving two-thirds of the sentence, provided he had been of good behaviour. Before he reached the two-thirds point of his sentence (which was 1989), the Parole Act was amended (in 1986) to empower the National Parole Board to cancel the conditional release and require the continued detention of the prisoner for the rest of his sentence. This power was exercisable where there was reason to believe that the inmate, if released, was likely to commit an offence causing death or serious harm during the unexpired portion of his sentence. The Board exercised its new power in this case, and the defendant was accordingly not released on mandatory supervision in 1989. He applied for habeas corpus. The Supreme Court of Canada held that, although the amendment of the Parole Act had not had the effect of lengthening the defendant's 12-year sentence, it had altered the manner in which the sentence was to be served. Serving time on mandatory supervision was a lesser deprivation of liberty than serving time in prison. This change in the law should be treated as the deprivation of a liberty interest, making s. 7 of the Charter potentially applicable. The Court went on to

---

25 *Re B.C. Motor Vehicle Act* [1985] 2 S.C.R. 486, 515, 529 (mandatory term of imprisonment a denial of liberty); *R. v. Swain* [1991] 1 S.C.R. 933 (automatic detention of person acquitted on ground of insanity a denial of liberty.)

26 *Re ss. 193 and 195.1 of Criminal Code* (Prostitution Reference) [1990] 1 S.C.R. 1123, 1140, 1215 (''possibility of imprisonment'' a denial of liberty).

27 *Re B.C. Motor Vehicle Act* [1985] 2 S.C.R. 486, 529, but note that Lamer J. (at 515) left open the question of ''imprisonment as an alternative to the non-payment of a fine'', and (at 516) left open the question whether there could be a breach of s. 7 even if imprisonment was not available as a sentence. These reservations by Lamer J. raise the possibility of a huge scope for ''liberty'' in s. 7, since even civil orders are ultimately enforceable by imprisonment (for contempt).

28 *R.* v.*Beare* [1988] 2 S.C.R. 387.

29 *Thomson Newspapers* v.*Can.* [1990] 1 S.C.R. 425.

30 *Ibid.*; *Stelco* v.*Can.* [1990] 1 S.C.R. 617.

31 *R.* v. *Heywood* [1994] 3 S.C.R. 761.

32 [1993] 2 S.C.R. 143. The opinion of the Court was written by McLachlin J.

hold that the change in the law was not a breach of the principles of fundamental justice,[33] so that the defendant remained in prison.

(b) Economic liberty

The Supreme Court of Canada has refused to extend liberty beyond freedom from physical restraint.[34] There are good reasons for this caution.

One reason is the unhappy experience of the United States during the *Lochner* era. Between 1905, when *Lochner* v. *New York*[35] was decided, and 1937, when the case was overruled, the Supreme Court of the United States protected the liberties of the owners of factories and mines against the efforts of Congress and the state Legislatures to limit hours of work, to require the payment of minimum wages, to impose health and safety standards and to protect union activity. As Oliver Wendell Holmes pointed out in his brilliant dissenting opinions, the Court used the Constitution to enforce a laissez-faire economic theory that had been rejected by the elected legislators. The Court had taken sides in a political conflict that was suitable for resolution only by elected legislators. In 1937, after an exasperated President Roosevelt had proposed his court-packing plan, the Court changed its mind and reversed these decisions. Since then, the Court has been extremely reluctant to review social and economic regulation, despite its inevitable interferences with the property and contract rights that the Constitution of the United States expressly guarantees.[36]

All this happened in the United States, but the *Lochner* era cast its shadow over Canada as well. The framers of Canada's Charter of Rights deliberately omitted any reference to property in s. 7, and they also omitted any guarantee of the obligation of contracts. These departures from the American model, as well as the replacement of ''due process'' with ''fundamental justice'' (of which more will be said later), were intended to banish *Lochner* from Canada.[37] The product

---

33 This part of the decision is discussed at note 90, below.

34 A notable exception was Wilson J., who consistently advocated a broad definition of liberty: *Singh* v. *Minr. of Emplt. and Imm.* [1985] 1 S.C.R. 177, 205; *Operation Dismantle* v. *The Queen* [1985] 1 S.C.R. 441, 488; *R.* v. *Jones* [1986] 2 S.C.R. 284, 318-319; *R.* v. *Morgentaler (No. 2)* [1988] 1 S.C.R. 30, 164-166. Wilson J.'s definition has been receiving increasing support, but has not yet attracted a majority of the Supreme Court of Canada: *B.(R.)* v. *Children's Aid Society* [1995] 1 S.C.R. 315, para. 80 per La Forest J. with the concurrence of L'Heureux-Dubé, Gonthier and McLachlin JJ. (liberty includes right to choose medical treatment of one's children); *R.* v. *O'Connor* [1995] 4 S.C.R. 411, para. 111 per L'Heureux-Dubé J. with the concurrence of La Forest, Gonthier and McLachlin JJ. (liberty includes privacy; the other five judges acknowledged that privacy was a constitutional right but were silent as to its source).

35 (1905) 198 U.S. 45 (maximum hours of work law struck down over eloquent dissent of Holmes J.).

36 The story is told in Tribe, *American Constitutional Law* (2nd ed., 1986), ch. 8; Nowak and Rotunda, *Constitutional Law* (4th ed., 1991), ch. 11.

37 The legislative history is reviewed by Lamer J. in *Re B.C. Motor Vehicle Act* [1985] 2 S.C.R. 486, 504-505.

is a s. 7 in which liberty must be interpreted as not including property, as not including freedom of contract, and, in short, as not including *economic* liberty.[38]

Another reason for caution in the definition of liberty is the placement of s. 7 within the Charter of Rights. Section 7 leads off a group of sections (ss. 7 to 14) entitled ''Legal Rights''. These provisions are mainly addressed to the rights of individuals in the criminal justice system: search, seizure, detention, arrest, trial, testimony and imprisonment are the concerns of ss. 8 to 14. It seems reasonable to conclude, as Lamer J. has done, that ''the restrictions on liberty and security of the person that s. 7 is concerned with are those that occur as a result of an individual's interaction with the justice system, and its administration''.[39] This line of reasoning also excludes economic liberty from s. 7.

The Supreme Court of Canada has held that s. 7 does not apply to corporations, because ''liberty'' does not include corporate activity.[40] Nor does ''liberty'' include the right to do business, for example, by selling goods on a Sunday.[41] Does ''liberty'' include the right of an individual to work? Despite some lower court decisions[42] to the contrary, which emphasize the role of work as an instrument of self-fulfilment, the regulation of trades and professions should be regarded as restrictions on economic liberty that are outside the scope of s. 7.[43]

(c) Political liberty

''Liberty'' does not include freedom of conscience and religion, freedom of expression, freedom of assembly, freedom of association, the right to vote and be

38 *Re ss. 193 and 195.1 of Criminal Code* (Prostitution Reference) [1990] 1 S.C.R. 1123, 1163-1166 per Lamer J.

39 *Id.*, 1173.

40 Note 11, above.

41 *R.* v. *Edwards Books and Art* [1986] 2 S.C.R. 713, 786 (s. 7 does not confer ''an unconstrained right to transact business whenever one wishes'').

42 E.g. *Wilson* v.*Medical Services Commn.* (1988) 53 D.L.R. (4th) 171 (B.C.C.A.) (s. 7 violated by restrictions on the practice of medicine); criticized by Lepofsky, Comment (1989) 68 Can. Bar Rev. 591.

43 *Re ss. 193 and 195.1 of Criminal Code* (Prostitution Reference) [1990] 1 S.C.R. 1123, 1170-1171 per Lamer J. (disapproving *Wilson*, previous note); *ILWU* v.*Can.* [1994] 1 S.C.R. 150 (holding that back-to-work legislation does not violate the liberty of the employees). But see *Ruffo* v. *Conseil de la Magistrature* [1995] 4 S.C.R. 267, para. 38, where Gonthier J., for the majority of the Court, asserted without discussion that s. 7 demanded that a provincial court judge's conduct be examined by ''an independent and impartial tribunal''. The disciplinary committee charged with investigating the matter had the power to recommend the judge's dismissal. The case could have been decided under s. 23 of Quebec's Charter of Human Rights and Freedoms, which guaranteed an independent and impartial tribunal for a ''determination of... rights and obligations'' and without reference to life, liberty or security of the person. In any case, no remedy was granted, because the Court rejected the allegation that the committee was biased.

a candidate for election, or the right to travel. These rights are all guaranteed elsewhere in the Charter of Rights, and should be excluded from s. 7.[44]

44.8 Security of the person

Section 7 protects ''life, liberty and security of the person''. What is included in ''security of the person''?

In *R.* v. *Morgentaler (No. 2)* (1988),[45] the Supreme Court of Canada, by a majority of five to two, held that the Criminal Code's restrictions on abortion, which required that the abortion be approved by the therapeutic abortion committee of an approved hospital, were unconstitutional. The evidence showed that the requirement of approval by a therapeutic abortion committee restricted access to the procedure of an abortion (because some hospitals would not set up the required committees) and caused delays in treatment, which increased the risk to the health of the woman. All five majority judges agreed that the risk to health that was caused by the law was a deprivation of security of the person.[46] The breach of fundamental justice consisted (for four of the majority judges) in the unnecessarily restrictive procedural requirements for a therapeutic abortion and (for Wilson J.) in the deprivation of the woman's freedom of conscience. As the result of this decision, Canada no longer has any restrictions on abortion.[47]

Does security of the person go beyond health and safety? In *Morgentaler*, three of the five majority judges were willing to find a deprivation of security of the person, not only in the risk to the woman's health created by the law-related delays, but also in the loss of her control over the termination of the pregnancy.[48] On this basis, security of the person would include some requirement of personal autonomy, at least with respect to medical treatment.

---

44 *Ibid.* But see *B.(R.)* v. *Children's Aid Society* [1995] 1 S.C.R. 315, para. 83 per La Forest J. (with the concurrence of three others) (liberty includes the right of parents who were Jehovah's Witnesses to refuse a blood transfusion for their child, although this right was also included in freedom of religion); the overlap between ss. 7 and 2 was rejected by Lamer C.J. at para. 30.

45 [1988] 1 S.C.R. 30. Four opinions were written: by Wilson J.; Dickson C.J. (with Lamer J.); by Beetz J. (with Estey J.); and, dissenting, by McIntyre J. (with La Forest J.). For a case commentary see Weinrib, ''The *Morgantaler* Judgment: Constitutional Rights, Legislative Intention and Institutional Design'' (1992) 42 U.T.L.J. 207.

46 This was the lowest common denominator of the majority reasoning, espoused by Beetz J. and concurred in by Wilson J. and Dickson C.J. For Wilson J., the loss of control over the termination of pregnancy was a deprivation of liberty; and both she and Dickson C.J. regarded the loss of control as another aspect of the deprivation of security of the person. It has been suggested that a risk to ''psychological integrity'' or mental health can also be a deprivation of security of the person: *Mills* v. *The Queen* [1986] 1 S.C.R. 863, 920 per Lamer J, *R.* v. *O'Connor* [1995] 4 S.C.R. 411, para. 111 per L'Heureux-Dubé J.

47 The Government of Canada introduced a less restrictive bill to re-criminalize abortion, which as Bill C-43 passed the House of Commons but was defeated by the Senate on a 43-43 tie vote on January 31, 1991.

48 Note 46, above.

The extension of security of the person to include control over one's body was confirmed in *Rodriguez* v. *British Columbia* (1993).[49] In that case, a plaintiff who was terminally ill (with Lou Gehrig's disease) challenged the constitutionality of the Criminal Code offence of assisting a person to commit suicide. She pointed out that the law deprived a disabled person of the ability to commit suicide (which was not an offence); she wanted to commit suicide, but could not do so without medical assistance, because she was (or soon would be) too disabled by her illness. Eight of the nine judges of the Supreme Court of Canada held that the removal from the plaintiff of an aspect of the control over her body was a deprivation of security of the person under s. 7. However, the plaintiff was not successful in her challenge to the law, because five of the nine judges held that the law did not offend the principles of fundamental justice. That part of the decision is discussed later in this chapter.[50]

It has been suggested that "security of the person" includes the economic capacity to satisfy basic human needs.[51] Whyte says that "state action which deprives a person of all (or a substantial portion) of his or her capacity to produce an income could be seen as invading security of the person". He gives the examples of "the removal of a person from the welfare scheme, the confiscation of property (tools, equipment, etc.) essential to a person's work, or the cancellation of a licence which is essential to the pursuit of one's occupation (taxi driver, lawyer or engineer)".[52] The trouble with this argument is that it accords to s. 7 an economic role that is incompatible with its setting in the legal rights portion of the Charter — a setting that the Supreme Court of Canada has relied upon as controlling the scope of s. 7.[53] The suggested role also involves a massive expansion of judicial review, since it would bring under judicial scrutiny all of the elements of the modern welfare state, including the regulation of trades and professions, the adequacy of labour standards and bankruptcy laws and, of course, the level of public expenditures on social programmes. As Oliver Wendell Holmes would have pointed out, these are the issues upon which elections are won and lost; the judges need a clear mandate to enter that arena, and s. 7 does not provide that clear mandate.

---

49 [1993] 3 S.C.R. 519. The majority opinion was written by Sopinka J. (with La Forest, Gonthier, Iacobucci, and Major JJ.). Dissenting opinions were written by McLachlin J. (with L'Heureux-Dubé J.), Lamer C.J. and Cory J. For the majority, Sopinka J. rejected arguments based on ss. 7, 12 and 15 of the Charter. Of the dissenting opinions, McLachlin J. relied on s. 7, Lamer C.J. on s. 15, and Cory J. on both ss. 7 and 15. Lamer C.J. expressed no view on security of the person or fundamental justice.

50 Note 94, below.

51 *Singh* v. *Minr. of Emplmt. and Imm.* [1985] 1 S.C.R. 177, 207 per Wilson J. (obiter dictum, with supporting citations); *Irwin Toy* v. *Que.* [1989] 1 S.C.R. 927, 1003 per Dickson C.J. (obiter dictum, leaving issue open).

52 Whyte, "Fundamental Justice" (1983) 13 Man. L.J. 455, 474.

53 Note 39, above.

44.9 Property

Section 7 protects "life, liberty and security of the person". The omission of property[54] from s. 7 was a striking and deliberate departure from the constitutional texts that provided the models for s. 7.[55] The due process clauses in the fifth and fourteenth amendments of the Constitution of the United States protect "life, liberty or property". And the due process clause in s. 1(a) of the Canadian Bill of Rights protects "life, liberty, security of the person and enjoyment of property".

The omission of property rights from s. 7 greatly reduces its scope. It means that s. 7 affords no guarantee of compensation or even of a fair procedure for the taking of property by government.[56] It means that s. 7 affords no guarantee of fair treatment by courts,[57] tribunals or officials with power over the purely economic interests of individuals or corporations.[58] It also requires, as we have noticed in the earlier discussions of "liberty" and "security of the person", that those terms be interpreted as excluding economic liberty and economic security; otherwise, property, having been shut out of the front door, would enter by the back.[59]

The omission of property rights from s. 7 also ensures a continuing role for the Canadian Bill of Rights, which continues to apply to federal (but not provincial) laws.[60] In the Canadian Bill of Rights, "enjoyment of property" is guaranteed by the due process clause of s. 1(a); there is also, in s. 2(e), a guarantee of "a fair hearing in accordance with the principles of fundamental justice for the determination of his rights and obligations". Although s. 2(e) has been held to be only

54 The gap is not filled by s. 8's prohibition of unreasonable "seizure". Section 8 applies only to a seizure of property for investigatory or evidentiary purposes: *Re Becker* (1983) 148 D.L.R. (3d) 539 (Alta. C.A.) (s. 8 does not apply to an expropriation of property).

55 However, the International Covenant on Civil and Political Rights, which in articles 6-11 includes elaborate provisions regarding life, liberty and security of the person, also omits any guarantee of property rights.

56 The courts will imply these rights in the absence of an express legislative provision to the contrary: see ch. 28, Public Property, under heading 28.5, "Expropriation", above; but there is no constitutional impediment to an express legislative provision to the contrary, except for s. 1(a) of the Canadian Bill of Rights, which is applicable only to the federal Parliament.

57 Section 7 does not protect the right of action for damages: *Wittman* v. *Emmott* (1991) 77 D.L.R. (4th) 77 (B.C.C.A.); *Budge* v. *Alta.* (1991) 77 D.L.R. (4th) 361 (Alta. C.A.).

58 The courts will imply a duty to observe the rules of "natural justice" in the absence of an express legislative provision to the contrary, but there is no constitutional impediment to an express legislative provision to the contrary. Once again, an exception must be made for the federal jurisdiction, because s. 2(e) of the Canadian Bill of Rights requires compliance with "the principles of fundamental justice" for the determination of "rights and obligations". Note also *Morguard Investments v. De Savoye* [1990] 3 S.C.R. 1077, 1110 (obiter suggestions by La Forest J. that s. 7, "though not made expressly applicable to property", might play a role in conflict of laws cases in the courts).

59 See *Irwin Toy* v. *Que.* [1989] 1 S.C.R. 927, 1003.

60 Chapter 32, Canadian Bill of Rights, above.

a guarantee of a fair procedure,[61] the reference to the determination of ''rights and obligations'' extends beyond s. 7's ''life, liberty and security of the person''. For example, in *Singh* v. *Minister of Employment and Immigration* (1985),[62] where the question was whether refugee claimants had been accorded a sufficient hearing under federal law, Beetz J., for half of the six-judge bench, being undecided whether life, liberty or security of the person was implicated, decided the case under s. 2(e) of the Canadian Bill of Rights. Wilson J., for the other half of the bench, held that s. 7 did apply, and she decided the case on that basis. Both judges were agreed in the result, which was that the Immigration Act's procedures did not measure up to the standard of fundamental justice, and were therefore inoperative or invalid.

MacBain v. *Lederman* (1985)[63] is another example of the broad reach of s. 2(e). The issue in that case was whether the federal Human Rights Code violated fundamental justice in the provisions establishing an adjudicatory tribunal. The Code provided that the members of the tribunal were to be appointed by the Human Rights Commission. It was argued that this mode of appointment gave rise to a reasonable apprehension of bias because the Commission was also in effect the prosecutor of the complaint. The Federal Court of Appeal upheld the claim of bias, and struck down the appointment provisions of the Code. The Court relied upon s. 2(e), which was clearly applicable, because the tribunal had the power to make a determination of the respondent's rights and obligations. The Court did not rely upon s. 7, presumably because the tribunal had no power over life, liberty or security of the person.[64] Most litigation, whether before the courts or tribunals, is about money or property or other purely economic interests. Section 7 does not apply to this kind of litigation, but s. 2(e) does apply, so long as the dispute is governed by federal law.

44.10 Fundamental justice

(a) Procedure and substance

A deprivation of life, liberty or security of the person is a breach of s. 7 of the Charter only if the deprivation is not in accordance with ''the principles of fundamental justice''.[65]

When the Charter was adopted in 1982, the phrase ''the principles of fundamental justice'' did not have a firmly established meaning in Anglo-Canadian

61 This is clear from the context; and see note 66 and accompanying text, below.

62 [1985] 1 S.C.R. 177.

63 [1985] 1 F.C. 856 (C.A.).

64 Query the correctness of *Sask. Human Rts. Commn.* v. *Kodellas* (1989) 60 D.L.R. (4th) 143 (Sask. C.A.) (security of the person is denied by the anxiety of awaiting a long-delayed human rights adjudication).

65 This assumes that s. 7 confers only a single right: see note 5 and accompanying text, above.

law. The phrase did appear in s. 2(e) of the Canadian Bill of Rights, which guarantees to a person "the right to a fair hearing in accordance with the principles of fundamental justice for the determination of his rights and obligations". In that context, which included a reference to "a fair hearing", the term fundamental justice was equivalent to natural justice,[66] a term that does have an established meaning in Anglo-Canadian law. The rules of natural justice are rules of procedure only: they require a hearing, unbiased adjudication and (a recent development) a fair procedure.[67] Therefore, if fundamental justice in s. 7 meant natural justice, the courts would be entitled to review the appropriateness and fairness of the *procedures* enacted for a deprivation of life, liberty or security of the person — but that would be all. The courts would not be entitled to review the *substantive* justice of the deprivation.

The legislative history of s. 7 makes clear that the framers thought that "fundamental justice" meant natural justice, and were anxious to avoid judicial review that went beyond issues of procedure. The concern, expressed at the hearings of the Special Joint Committee that examined the text of the Charter,[68] was to avoid any risk of the importation to Canada of the substantive due process doctrine of the *Lochner* era in the United States.[69] At that time (1905 to 1937), the Supreme Court of the United States applied a notion of substantive due process to strike down state and federal laws providing for maximum hours of work, minimum wages, health and safety standards, and the protection of union activity. These decisions were overruled in 1937,[70] but they demonstrated the hazard of granting to the judges the power to review legislation on a ground as inherently indeterminate as substantive due process. It is plain from the testimony before the Special Joint Committee that the phrase "due process" was omitted from s. 7 in order to make sure that s. 7 did not give rise to a Canadian doctrine of substantive due process.

The trouble was that the phrase that was selected to replace due process was not "natural justice", which would certainly have been restricted to procedure, but "fundamental justice", a term that lacked any substantial body of defining case-law. It was arguable that the term fundamental justice in s. 7, when liberated from the procedural context of s. 2(e) of the Canadian Bill of Rights, was apt to

66 *Duke* v. *The Queen* [1972] S.C.R. 917, 923.

67 See de Smith, Woolf and Jowell *Judicial Review of Administrative Action* (5th ed., 1995), chs. 4, 5.

68 The principal passages in the proceedings of the Special Joint Committee are referred to in *Re B.C. Motor Vehicle Act* [1985] 2 S.C.R. 486, 504-505.

69 Text accompanying notes 35-36, above.

70 Substantive due process is no longer used to review social and economic legislation, but it is still alive and well in other contexts, for example, the incorporation into the fourteenth amendment of most of the guarantees of the first ten amendments, the incorporation into the fifth amendment of the equal protection clause of the fourteenth amendment, and the recognition of a right of privacy. See Tribe, note 36, above, chs. 11, 15; Nowak and Rotunda, note 36, above, ch. 11.

reach substantive as well as procedural justice. In the *B.C. Motor Vehicle Reference* (1985),[71] the Supreme Court of Canada held that fundamental justice did indeed cover substantive as well as procedural justice. The case was a reference by the government of British Columbia to determine the validity of a provision in the province's Motor Vehicle Act which made it an offence to drive a car while prohibited from driving or while one's driving licence was suspended. The Act imposed a mandatory term of imprisonment on anyone found guilty of the offence. The controversial provision was a subsection that declared that the offence was one of "absolute liability" in which "guilt is established by proof of driving, whether or not the defendant knew of the prohibition or suspension". The Court held that it was a breach of fundamental justice to impose a term of imprisonment for an offence that lacked the element of mens rea (a guilty mind). The Court made no attempt to characterize this as a procedural defect in the law; the absence of mens rea created a substantive injustice. Section 7 prohibited substantive as well as procedural injustice.

Lamer J., who wrote the principal opinion in the *B.C. Motor Vehicle Reference*, referred to the testimony in the Special Joint Committee in which fundamental justice was equated with natural justice, and in which the concern of the framers to avoid substantive due process was explained.[72] But he brushed this aside as being of "minimal weight"[73] in comparison to the reasons for giving fundamental justice a more extended meaning.

Lamer J.'s opinion gives three reasons for extending fundamental justice beyond procedure. The first reason is that the words "fundamental justice" are literally broader in scope than other formulations that could have been used, such as, "natural justice". The second reason is that the expansion of the concept of fundamental justice has the effect of expanding the protection of life, liberty and security of the person. These two reasons are without doubt strong considerations cutting in the opposite direction to the legislative history. However, the third reason given by Lamer J. for extending fundamental justice beyond procedure into substance is much more dubious, and Wilson J. in her concurring opinion specifically disagreed with it. Lamer J. held that s. 7 is a kind of general residuary clause for all of the "legal rights" of the Charter. Sections 8 to 14 are merely "illustrative" of deprivations of fundamental justice that could just as easily be caught by s. 7. Since ss. 8 to 14 go beyond merely procedural guarantees (as in "unreasonable" search or seizure in s. 8, "arbitrary" detention or imprisonment in s. 9 and "cruel and unusual" treatment or punishment in s. 12), it follows that s. 7 also must go beyond a merely procedural guarantee.[74]

---

71 *Re B.C. Motor Vehicle Act* [1985] 2 S.C.R. 486. The seven-judge bench was unanimous on this issue, and on the result, but three opinions were written: by Lamer J. with the agreement of four others; by McIntyre J.; and by Wilson J.

72 *Id.*, 504-505.

73 *Id.*, 509. The admissibility and weight of legislative history is examined in ch. 55, Constitutional Litigation, under heading 55.7, "Legislative history", below.

74 *Id.*, 502-503,

There are two difficulties with the residuary theory of s. 7, under which ss. 8 to 14 of the Charter are merely examples or illustrations of s. 7. One difficulty, which was pointed out by Wilson J., is that ss. 8 to 14 of the Charter are not in fact drafted in that way, but as ''self-standing provisions''.[75] A second difficulty is the fact that ss. 8 to 14 are not confined to life, liberty and security of the person, as s. 7 is. Thus, s. 8, which protects property from unreasonable search or seizure, is not premised on a denial of life, liberty or security of the person; this is why s. 8 applies to corporations, while s. 7 does not.[76] Section 11, with its long list of protections for ''any person charged with an offence'', is not confined to offences for which imprisonment is a penalty, but would also apply to offences punishable by a fine; such offences do not implicate life, liberty or security of the person.[77] The guarantees of s. 13 (self-incrimination) and s. 14 (interpreter) are also not confined to proceedings where life, liberty or security of the person is at stake.[78]

The theory that ss. 8 to 14 of the Charter are simply illustrations of s. 7 may help to provide some limits to the new substantive fundamental justice; the values protected by the term ''fundamental justice'' could be derived by analogy from the values explicitly protected by ss. 8 to 14. In the *B.C. Motor Vehicle Reference* itself, for example, the proposition that ''a law that has the potential to convict a person who has not really done anything wrong offends the principles of fundamental justice'' (which was Lamer J.'s opening comment)[79] is a proposition which has affinities to s. 11(d) (presumption of innocence) and s. 12 (cruel and unusual treatment or punishment). But a case such as *Lochner* v. *New York* (1905),[80] where the Supreme Court of the United States applied substantive due process to strike down a law that limited the hours of work in bakeries, could not show affinities to anything in ss. 8 to 14. Thus, the Court's link between s. 7 and ss. 8 to 14, however implausible for other interpretative purposes, may help to shield social and economic legislation from judicial review under s. 7.[81] We have already noticed the usefulness of the link in interpreting ''liberty'' and ''security of the person'' in s. 7.[82]

The question whether the Court was right to extend fundamental justice into the substance of laws is not an easy one. If the Court had followed the legislative

75 *Id.*, 530.

76 Compare *Hunter* v. *Southam* [1984] 2 S.C.R. 145 (s. 8 applies to corporations) with *Irwin Toy* v. *Que.* [1989] 1 S.C.R. 927 (s. 7 does not).

77 It cannot seriously be contended that, just because a minor traffic offence leads to a very slight consequence, perhaps only a small fine, that offence does not fall within s. 11'': *R.* v. *Wigglesworth* [1987] 2 S.C.R. 541, 559 per Wilson J.

78 The force of this criticism seems to be recognized in *R.* v. *CIP* [1992] S.C.R., 843, 854, (p. 6) where Stevenson J. for a unanimous Court that included Lamer C.J. ''explained'' the residuary theory as relating only to the scope of the principles of fundamental justice, not the scope of life, liberty or security of the person.

79 [1985] 2 S.C.R. 486, 492.

80 (1905) 198 U.S. 45.

81 Accord, Colvin, ''Section 7 of the Charter of Rights'' (1989) 68 Can. Bar Rev. 560.

82 Notes 39, 53 and accompanying texts, above.

history and confined fundamental justice to procedural requirements, the distinction between procedure and substance would undoubtedly have proved to be unstable and indeterminate. The distinction has never been clear, and the courts would be constantly urged to characterize this or that unjust result as procedural so as to make it remediable under s. 7.[83] The Court's decision in the *B.C. Motor Vehicle Reference* does spare us that order of argument.

(b) Definition of fundamental justice

In the *B.C. Motor Vehicle Reference*,[84] the only definition of fundamental justice that was provided by the Court was Lamer J.'s assertion that "the principles of fundamental justice are to be found in the basic tenets of the legal system".[85] The inadequacy of this formulation to provide any real guidance for the future was acknowledged by Lamer J. when he said that "those words [fundamental justice] cannot be given any exhaustive content or simple enumerative definition, but will take on concrete meaning as the courts address alleged violations of s. 7".[86] Indeed, the Court never explained why absolute liability, which has long been a familiar (if unloved) part of Canada's system of criminal justice,[87] was now contrary to the basic tenets of the legal system. All that can be discerned from the opinions is the view that absolute liability is morally repugnant.

As will be seen in succeeding sections of this chapter, subsequent decisions have not succeeded in giving better definition to the basic tenets of the legal system. On the contrary, later decisions have demonstrated that there is little agreement as to what are the basic tenets of the legal system or even as to the sources from which the basic tenets might be derived. In *Thomson Newspapers* v. *Canada* (1990),[88] for example, a case that is discussed later,[89] five judges gave five different opinions as to the applicable basic tenet of the legal system!

The Supreme Court of Canada has not even been consistent in describing the principles of fundamental justice as the basic tenets of the legal system. In *Cunningham* v. *Canada* (1993),[90] the Supreme Court of Canada had to decide whether an amendment to the federal Parole Act was a breach of the principles

---

83 *R.* v. *Morgentaler (No. 2)* [1988] 1 S.C.R. 30 illustrates the difficulty: were the invalid restrictions on obtaining an abortion procedural requirements (as Dickson C.J. and Beetz J. claimed) or substantive requirements (as Wilson J. claimed)?

84 Note 71, above.

85 [1985] 2 S.C.R. 486, 503; Lamer J. (at 512) gives another, similar formulation; Wilson J. seems to accept this definition, referring (at 530) to "a fundamental tenet of our justice system"; McIntyre J. said (at 521-522) only that fundamental justice "includes as well a substantive element".

86 *Id.*, 513.

87 Note the inclusion of absolute liability in Dickson C.J.'s taxonomy of criminal offences in *R.* v. *Sault Ste. Marie*, note 110, below.

88 [1990] 1 S.C.R. 425.

89 Text accompanying note 105, below.

90 [1993] 2 S.C.R. 143. The opinion of the Court was written by McLachlin J.

of fundamental justice. The amendment empowered the National Parole Board to deny to a prisoner his release on mandatory supervision for the last one-third of his sentence. The new power was exercisable when there was reason to believe that the prisoner was likely to commit an offence causing death or serious harm if he was released for the unexpired portion of the sentence. Having determined that this change in the law was the deprivation of a liberty interest,[91] the Court had to decide whether it was a breach of the principles of fundamental justice. The Court, in an opinion written by McLachlin J., made no reference to the basic tenets of the legal system. Here is how McLachlin J. posed the question of fundamental justice.[92]

> The . . . question is whether, from a substantive point of view, the change in the law strikes the right balance between the accused's interests and the interests of society.

In other words, whenever a law deprives an individual of life, liberty or security of the person, the courts must determine whether the Parliament or Legislature struck ''the right balance'' between the competing values that the legislators had sought to reconcile. In this case, the Court agreed that ''the balance is fairly struck'',[93] and upheld the impugned law. Of course, if the legislators had got the balance wrong, then the law would have been struck down. For example, a total abolition of release on mandatory supervision would presumably strike the wrong balance, and would be unconstitutional. It is difficult to resist the conclusion that the Court was here interpreting substantive fundamental justice as justifying the Court in striking down a law whenever the Court disagreed with the policy implemented by the law. What else could ''the right balance'' or even ''a fair balance'' mean? At least the basic tenets of the legal system suggested, however vaguely, that there should be some basis in legal history or legal doctrine for the principles of fundamental justice.

The Supreme Court of Canada's broad approach to fundamental justice was evident again in *Rodriguez* v. *British Columbia* (1993).[94] In that case, the Court, on an application by a person who was terminally ill, had to decide whether the Criminal Code's prohibition of assisting a person to commit suicide offended the principles of fundamental justice. One might have thought that this issue would be rather easily resolved by pointing to the common law, which had always prohibited assisting suicide, as well as counselling suicide, attempting suicide and even committing suicide. (The successful suicide could not be directly punished,

---

91 This part of the decision is discussed at note 32, above.

92 [1993] 2 S.C.R. 143, 152. A little earlier on the same page she had required ''a fair balance''.

93 *Id.*, 153. The Court also held that the procedure established for making the determinations of the National Parole Board satisfied procedural fundamental justice.

94 [1993] 3 S.C.R. 519; note 49, above. On s. 7, Sopinka J. (with four others) wrote the majority opinion; McLachlin J. (with one other) and Cory J. wrote dissenting opinions. Lamer C.J. did not discuss s. 7; he also dissented, but he relied on s. 15. For commentary on the *Rodriguez* case, see Weinrib, ''The Body and the Body Politic: Assisted Suicide Under the *Canadian Charter of Rights and Freedoms*'' (1994) 39 McGill LJ 618.

of course, but the deceased's property was forfeited and indignities were visited on the body.) The modern Criminal Code, which no longer made attempted suicide or suicide an offence, was already a substantial liberalization of the common law. The effort to further liberalize the law should surely be characterized as directed to *changing* the basic tenets of the legal system rather than vindicating them. At bottom, this may well be the reason why Sopinka J., who wrote for the majority, held that the law did not offend the principles of fundamental justice. Certainly, he emphasized that the law was simply declaratory of the common law position. But he also asserted that the principles of fundamental justice must be "'fundamental' in the sense that they would have general acceptance among reasonable people",[95] and he found no such consensus on the issue of euthanasia. Surely, a more orthodox view would be that the search for a consensus among reasonable people is a task that is more appropriate to Parliament than the courts; and, in any case, it is hard to see how it would illuminate any basic tenets of the legal system. The principal dissenting opinion in *Rodriguez* was written by McLachlin J. with the agreement of L'Heureux-Dubé J. and the "substantial" agreement of Cory J. In their view, a law would violate fundamental justice if the law was "arbitrary"[96] or "unfair".[97] They held that the Criminal Code provision was arbitrary or unfair, because it precluded a disabled person (who would need assistance) from committing suicide while permitting an able-bodied person to do so. They would have struck down the prohibition on assisting suicide, thereby legalizing euthanasia despite the absence of any legislation to regulate the practice.[98]

The Supreme Court of Canada has allowed s. 7 to drift even further away from the "basic tenets of the legal system" in its Charter review of extradition cases. Sections 11 and 12 of the Charter are not applicable to charges or punishments under foreign law,[99] and have no direct bearing on extradition cases. The Court has maintained, however, that courts do have the right to overturn extradition decisions (which are an executive function of the federal Minister of Justice) if extradition would violate a fugitive's right to fundamental justice. In *Canada* v. *Schmidt* (1987),[100] the Court held that s. 7 would be breached by an extradition

---

95 *Id.*, 607. There is also a passage (at 590) in which he acknowledges that "the principles of fundamental justice leave a great deal of scope for personal judgment".

96 *Id.*, 619. She added (at 619-620) that a limit will be arbitrary "if it bears no relation to, or is inconsistent with, the objective that lies behind the legislation".

97 *Id.*, 621: "The principles of fundamental justice require that each person, considered individually, be treated fairly by the law".

98 The dissenters were not indifferent to the risks of abuse. They would have delayed the coming into force of the declaration of invalidity for one year. They proposed an elaborate code of safeguards to permit the plaintiff in the case to receive assistance in committing suicide. However, after one year, the prohibition would have fallen completely and, unless Parliament had in the meantime acted to permit and control euthanasia, there would have been no prohibition of euthanasia and no safeguards to regulate the practice!

99 *Can.* v. *Schmidt* [1987] 1 S.C.R. 500 (s. 11 does not apply); *Kindler* v. *Can.* [1991] 2 S.C.R. 779 (s. 12 does not apply).

100 [1987] 1 S.C.R. 500, 522.

order where a fugitive faced a punishment under foreign law which would "shock the conscience" of, or be "simply unacceptable" to, reasonable Canadians. How do judges determine whether or not foreign laws are "shocking" or "unacceptable"? One might think that such determinations would be governed by the Supreme Court of Canada's jurisprudence under s. 12 of the Charter, which prohibits "cruel and unusual" punishments. But the Court has upheld extradition orders where fugitives faced drug charges in the United States carrying mandatory penalties of 15 to 20 years imprisonment,[101] despite the fact that the Court has held that a seven-year minimum sentence for similar offences in Canada's Criminal Code is cruel and unusual.[102] This means that long mandatory minimum sentences for drug offences are cruel and unusual, but are not shocking or unacceptable![103] This counterintuitive proposition simply underlines the enormous discretion that the Supreme Court of Canada has assumed for itself under the rubric of fundamental justice.[104]

The point has already been made that the scope of fundamental justice could be restricted by the placement of s. 7 in the legal rights portion of the Charter. The Court's residuary theory of s. 7, under which ss. 8 to 14 are simply illustrations of s. 7, emphasizes that s. 7 is directed to the protection of only those values that are reflected in the legal rights.[105] That offers some assurance that social and economic regulation, even if disliked by a majority of the Court, is not vulnerable to attack under s. 7. It must be remembered as well that a breach of fundamental justice is of no constitutional import if it does not cause a deprivation of life, liberty or security of the person. Outside the general sphere of criminal justice, only a few laws touch life, liberty or security of the person.

The Supreme Court of Canada's residuary theory of s. 7, under which ss. 8 to 14 are merely illustrations of s. 7, has a limiting effect on the scope of fundamental justice, as explained in the previous paragraph. But, on balance, the

101 *United States v. Jamieson* [1996] 1 S.C.R. 465; *United States* v. *Whitley* [1996] 1 S.C.R. 467; *United States* v. *Ross* [1996] 1 S.C.R. 469. In each of the three cases, the Court delivered no opinion other than to uphold the extradition order "substantially for the reasons" of the court of appeal. With respect, this seems a perfunctory disposition of such important issues. If the Supreme Court of Canada does not fully agree with the reasons of the court below it should provide its own reasons.

102 *R.* v. *Smith* [1987] 1 S.C.R. 1045.

103 In *Kindler* v. *Can.* [1991] 2 S.C.R. 779, and *Re Ng Extradition* [1991] 2 S.C.R. 858, the Court had previously held that it did not shock the Canadian conscience to extradite a fugitive to face charges which were punishable by the death penalty. The death penalty is probably cruel and unusual under s. 12: ch. 50, Cruel and Unusual Punishment, under heading 50.7, "Death penalty", below.

104 In *United States* v. *Ross* (1994) 119 D.L.R. (4th) 333, 370-371 (B.C.C.A.), Finch J.A. politely indicated that he found it difficult to apply the *Schmidt* test, and he sensibly suggested that the notion of the "reasonable man", however useful in determining standards of care, was not useful in assessing sentencing guidelines. In affirming the decision of the Court of Appeal, the Supreme Court of Canada did not address this opinion, rather they disposed of the case "substantially for the reasons" of Taylor J.A., with whom Finch J.A. had concurred.

105 Text accompanying notes 79-82, above.

residuary theory introduces additional uncertainty to the interpretation of s. 7 and especially of ss. 8 to 14. The effect of the residuary theory is that the precise language of ss. 8 to 14 becomes relatively unimportant. If it is found that none of those provisions apply to a set of facts, that is not the end of the inquiry; on the contrary, the inquiry moves to s. 7, where it must be determined whether the facts of the case, although outside ss. 8 to 14, are within "the principles of fundamental justice".

In *Thomson Newspapers* v. *Canada* (1990),[106] for example, a corporation and its officers objected to a demand made under the Combines Investigation Act for oral examination of the officers. Although the purpose of the demand was to inquire into the possible commission of an offence by the corporation, neither of the two Charter guarantees against self-incrimination was applicable. Section 11(c), which provides that a person charged with an offence is not a compellable witness against himself, was not applicable, because no one had been charged with an offence. Section 13, which provides that self-incriminatory evidence given in one proceeding cannot be used against the witness in another proceeding, was not applicable, because this inquiry was the first proceeding. If ss. 11(c) and 13 expressed the full measure of the Charter's right against self-incrimination, then there would be no grounds upon which the demand for testimony could be resisted. But the five-judge bench of the Supreme Court of Canada, obedient to the logic of the *B.C. Motor Vehicle Reference*, was unanimous that the "principles of fundamental justice" in s. 7 could still contain some "residual" elements of the right against self-incrimination. In other words, the scope of the right was to be discerned not from the relatively precise language of ss. 11(c) and 13, which explicitly deal with the right, but from the vague language of s. 7, which refers only to the principles of fundamental justice.[107]

It is obvious that the residuary theory of s. 7 introduces great uncertainty into all the legal rights, especially those that are couched in very specific language. With respect to each right, there is a possibility of a residue in s. 7, defined by the phrase "the principles of fundamental justice", which has been defined no more precisely than "the basic tenets of the legal system".[108] In effect, the residuary theory of s. 7 authorizes the judges to redraft the provisions of ss. 8 to 14 of the

---

106 [1990] 1 S.C.R. 425.

107 Accord, *R.* v. *Lyons* [1987] 2 S.C.R. 309, 354 (no right to trial by jury under s. 11(f), but necessary to consider whether s. 7 conferred the right "for s. 11 does not limit s. 7 but simply serves to illustrate and, perhaps, amplify its potential applications"); *Dehghani* v. *Can.* [1993] 1 S.C.R. 1053, 1076 ("there may be residual protection of the right to counsel under s. 7 in situations which do not fall within the parameters of "arrest or detention" in s. 10(b)"); *B.C. Securities Commn.* v. *Branch* [1995] 2 S.C.R. 3 (s. 7 guarantees right to silence that goes beyond ss.11(c) and 13). Contra, *R.* v. *Généreux* [1992] 1 S.C.R. 259, 310 (rejecting s. 7 argument on basis that "s. 7 does not offer greater protection than the highly specific guarantee under s. 11(d)", but noting that in some unspecified circumstances "s. 7 provides a more compendious protection than these sections [ss. 8 to 14] combined").

108 Note 85, above.

Charter. In *Thomson Newspapers*, the five judges came up with no less than five different theories as to what additional content s. 7 added to ss. 11(c) and 13: a right to remain silent (Sopinka J.), a right not to give an incriminating answer (Lamer J.), a right to have all evidence derived from the compelled testimony excluded from subsequent proceedings (Wilson J.), a right to have only that derivative evidence that could not have been discovered apart from the compelled testimony excluded from subsequent proceedings (La Forest J.), no right additional to ss. 11(c) and 13 (L'Heureux-Dubé J.). The range of opinion is remarkable. Yet, each of the judges was confident that he or she was articulating a principle or tenet of the justice system that was so basic that, through s. 7, it should prevail over the inconsistent enactment of the Parliament of Canada.[109]

44.11 Absolute and strict liability

In the pre-Charter case of *R.* v. *City of Sault Ste. Marie* (1978),[110] Dickson J. for the Supreme Court of Canada divided offences into three categories:

1. Offences of ''absolute liability'', in which the offence consists simply of doing the prohibited act. There is no requirement of fault, either mens rea or negligence. The defendant could be convicted even if he or she had no intention of breaking the law and also exercised reasonable care to avoid doing so.
2. Offences of ''strict liability'', in which the offence again consists simply of doing the prohibited act; however, it is a defence if the defendant proves to the civil standard of the balance of probabilities that he or she exercised reasonable care to avoid committing the offence. In effect, there is a fault requirement of negligence, because only the accused who cannot prove the exercise of reasonable care is liable.
3. Offences of ''mens rea'', in which the offence consists not only of doing the prohibited act, but of doing so with the guilty intent (mens rea) of intending to break the law (or being reckless as to whether or not the law would be broken).

The first category, *absolute liability*, came under judicial review in the *B.C. Motor Vehicle Reference* (1985).[111] That case concerned a section of the B.C. Motor Vehicle Act that made it an offence to operate a motor vehicle while one was prohibited or suspended from driving. A subsection explicitly stated that the offence was to be interpreted as ''an absolute liability offence, for which guilt is established by proof of driving, whether or not the defendant knew of the prohi-

109 The Court, in subsequent cases, has continued the lively debate as to the existence of a residual right to silence in s. 7: sec. 44.15, ''Right to silence'', below.

110 [1978] S.C.R. 1299, 1325-1326.

111 [1985] 2 S.C.R. 486; and see text accompanying note 71, above.

bition or suspension''.[112] The Supreme Court of Canada held that absolute liability was a denial of ''the principles of fundamental justice''. Since the offence carried a short term of imprisonment, a conviction would mean a deprivation of ''liberty''. The offence was therefore declared to be in violation of s. 7 and of no force or effect.[113]

Another absolute liability case was *R.* v. *Hess* (1990),[114] which was a challenge to the statutory rape provision of the Criminal Code. This provision made it an offence for a male person to have intercourse with a female person under the age of 14, ''whether or not he [the accused] believes that she is fourteen years of age or more''. This offence was one of absolute liability, since it was no defence for the accused to show that he reasonably believed his act to be innocent: the accused's conduct could be lacking in mens rea and non-negligent. The offence carried a penalty of imprisonment. The Supreme Court of Canada followed the *B.C. Motor Vehicle Reference* to hold unanimously that an absolute liability offence that carried the penalty of imprisonment was a breach of fundamental justice in violation of s. 7. The result was not to strike down the offence entirely, since the deletion of the words ''whether or not he believes that she is fourteen years of age or more'' was sufficient to remove the element of absolute liability.[115]

The second category in Dickson C.J.'s *Sault Ste. Marie* taxonomy is *strict liability*. This came under judicial review in *R.* v. *Wholesale Travel Group* (1991).[116] In that case, the accused corporation[117] was charged with the offence of false or misleading advertising under the Competition Act. The Crown alleged

---

112 Motor Vehicle Act, R.S.B.C. 1979, c. 288 s. 94(2). After the decision, this subsection was repealed: S.B.C. 1986, c. 19. However the Court later held that the amended offence was still an absolute liability offence: *R.* v. *Pontes* [1995] 3 S.C.R. 44; discussed in text accompanying notes 123 and 124, below.

113 One way in which the B.C. Legislature responded to the decision in *B.C. Motor Vehicle Reference* was to enact a new section 4.1 of the Offence Act (R.S.B.C. 1979, c. 305 as am. by S.B.C. 1990, c. 34, s. 10), which states:

> 4.1 Notwithstanding section 4 or the provisions of any other Act, no person is liable to imprisonment with respect to an absolute liability offence.

This enactment proved important to the outcome in *R.* v. *Pontes* : note 112, above. Although the Court ruled in that case that a driving offence was one of absolute liability, the Court simply ''read out'' the penalty of imprisonment which attached to the offence in accordance with s. 4.1 of the Offence Act. This prevented the offence from being declared unconstitutional.

114 [1990] 2 S.C.R. 906. The Court was unanimous that s. 7 was violated, and held by a majority that s. 1 did not save the provision.

115 In *R.* v. *Penno* [1990] 2 S.C.R. 865, it was held that the offence of driving while impaired did not offend fundamental justice, although the offence excluded the defence of intoxication. The mental element of voluntarily becoming intoxicated was a sufficiently guilty mind to satisfy the *B.C. Motor Vehicle Reference*.

116 [1991] 3 S.C.R. 154.

117 The corporation was able to invoke s. 7, despite the fact that s. 7 does not apply to corporations, because the corporation was a defendant to a criminal prosecution, and the law was applicable to individuals as well as to corporations: sec. 44.4(b), ''Corporations'', above.

that the company had advertised travel packages at ''wholesale'' prices, while in fact charging ''retail'' prices. The Act made clear that there was no requirement of mens rea: the only defence was one of reasonable care, and the burden of proving reasonable care rested with the accused. The offence therefore followed the conventional pattern of strict liability. The penalty for the offence was a fine or imprisonment for up to five years or both. The accused relied on the *B.C. Motor Vehicle Reference* to argue that it was a violation of fundamental justice to place an individual in jeopardy of imprisonment for any lesser fault than mens rea. The Crown agreed that the *B.C. Motor Vehicle Reference* required an element of fault for an offence carrying the penalty of imprisonment, but the Crown argued that an absence of reasonable care (negligence) satisfied the requirement.

The Supreme Court of Canada in *Wholesale Travel* was unanimous in its view that the offence of false or misleading advertising in the Competition Act was not a ''true crime'', but was merely a ''regulatory offence'' or ''public welfare offence''. Cory J. explained that the characteristic of a ''true crime'' was that ''inherently wrongful conduct'' was punished.[118] A regulatory offence, on the other hand, was designed to establish standards of conduct for activity that could be harmful to others; it did not imply moral blameworthiness; and it attracted less social stigma. Therefore, the Court reasoned, it was not a constitutional objection to the offence that it was premised on negligence rather than mens rea. The Court treated it as obvious that the offence of misleading advertising fell into the ''regulatory'' category, despite the fact that it carried a maximum penalty of five years' imprisonment — quite a stretch for doing something that did not imply moral blameworthiness and attracted little social stigma![119]

The Competition Act contained a ''reverse onus'' clause which required the defendant to a charge of false or misleading advertising to prove (to the civil standard of the balance of probabilities) that he or she had exercised reasonable care to avoid making the false or misleading claims. Even if the Act had been silent as to the defence and the burden of proof, the effect of the *Sault Ste. Marie* decision[120] was that a regulatory offence was to be regarded as one of strict liability, and two characteristics of strict liability were (1) that there was a defence of reasonable care, and (2) that the burden of proving reasonable care rested on

118 [1991] 3 S.C.R. 154, 219.

119 As the discussion of the cases in the next section of this chapter (sec. 44.12, ''Murder'', below) will show, the Supreme Court of Canada likes to premise radical constitutional results on findings of stigma. There is never any evidence on the point. In my view, the stigma attaching to a particular offence is unknown and perhaps unknowable, since it would depend upon such a host of circumstances related to both the offence and the offender, and would vary according to the eye of the beholder. The concept is too uncertain to attract any constitutional consequence of any kind. In my view, the Court ought to abandon this idea completely and rely on more objective considerations. In this context, it would be preferable to use the presence of the penalty of imprisonment as the dividing line between those offences that require mens rea and those that require only negligence.

120 Note 110, above.

the defendant. Therefore, in order to uphold the offence in *Wholesale Travel* (or any other strict liability offence involving imprisonment), the Court also had to decide whether the reversal of the burden of proof was defeated by the Charter of Rights. This issue was governed, not by s. 7 but by s. 11(d), the presumption of innocence clause, and the Court's decision will be described in this book's later discussion of the presumption of innocence.[121] However, for present purposes, we may note that the Court by a five to four majority upheld the reversal of the burden of proof.

The effect of the *Wholesale Travel* case is to settle the validity of strict liability.[122] In the case of a ''regulatory offence'' or a ''public welfare offence'', including those that carry the penalty of imprisonment, fundamental justice does not require that mens rea be an element of the offence. Fundamental justice is satisfied if there is a defence of reasonable care, and the burden of proving reasonable care (to the civil standard) may be cast on the defendant. In the case of ''true crimes'', however, fundamental justice requires that mens rea be an element of the offence, and the burden of proving mens rea (to the criminal standard) would have to be on the Crown.

The difference between an offence of strict liability and an offence of absolute liability is that an offence of strict liability allows for a defence of reasonable care (or due diligence) while an offence of absolute liability does not. In *R.* v. *Pontes* (1995)[123], the Supreme Court of Canada had to classify an offence in British Columbia's Motor Vehicle Act. The offence was driving while prohibited from driving. The Act provided that any driver who was convicted of a driving-related Criminal Code offence was ''automatically and without notice'' prohibited from operating a motor vehicle for 12 months. Cory J., for the majority of the Court, held that ''automatically and without notice'' meant that a duly diligent driver could be unaware of the prohibition, and could innocently commit the offence of driving while prohibited. The principle that ignorance of the law is not an excuse would preclude the accused from raising his or her ignorance of the statutory suspension as a defence. Cory J. concluded that the statute effectively barred a defence of due diligence and that the offence was therefore one of absolute liability.[124] Gonthier J., for the dissenting minority, acknowledged that an accused driver could not be heard to say that he or she was ignorant of the law. But Gonthier J. pointed out that the driver might be unaware of the fact that he had

121 Chapter 48, Rights on Being Charged, under heading 48.5(b), ''Reverse onus clauses'', above.

122 *R.* v. *Martin* [1992] S.C.R. 838 (strict liability upheld, following *Wholesale Travel*); *R. v. Ellis-Don* [1992] 1 S.C.R. 840 (same decision).

123 [1995] 3 S.C.R. 44. The majority opinion was written by Cory J. with the concurrence of Lamer C.J. and Sopinka, Iacobucci, and Major JJ. The minority opinion was written by Gonthier J., with the concurrence of La Forest, L'Heureux-Dubé, and McLachlin JJ.

124 The Motor Vehicle Act purported to impose a term of imprisonment for the offence, which would be an unconstitutional deprivation of liberty under s. 7 of the Charter. However, the offence was saved by ''reading out'' the penalty in accordance with s. 4.1 of British Columbia's Offence Act: note 113, above.

been convicted of one of the underlying offences to which the statutory prohibition attached. That would be a mistake of fact, not of law, and, if it were a reasonable mistake, it could provide a due diligence defence. The dissenters would have held that the Motor Vehicle Act offence was one of strict liability.

Wholesale Travel insisted on a distinction between "true crimes" (which include mens rea) and regulatory offences (for which a defence of reasonable care suffices). This distinction depends upon vague notions of moral blameworthiness and social stigma, not upon objective considerations such as the severity of the penalty. The offence in the *Wholesale Travel* case carried a penalty of up to five years imprisonment, but it was still classified as a regulatory offence.

The offence of dangerous driving causing death is in the Criminal Code, and it carries a maximum penalty of 14 years imprisonment. Surely, this must be a "true crime" for which mens rea would be constitutionally required. The Supreme Court of Canada held otherwise in *R.* v. *Hundal* (1993).[125] In that case, the accused had driven his truck through a red light and collided with another car in the intersection, killing the driver. The accused testified that he believed that he did not have time to stop safely when the light turned amber, so that he believed that his driving through the intersection was the prudent course of action. This evidence raised the question whether the accused had to be subjectively aware that his driving was dangerous in order to be convicted of dangerous driving. The Court cited *Wholesale Travel* for the proposition that "in the appropriate context, negligence can be an acceptable basis of liability which meets the fault requirement of s. 7 of the Charter".[126] That proposition governed this case: all that the Crown needed to establish was an objective departure by the accused from the appropriate standard of care. The fact that the accused believed that he was driving safely was irrelevant.

The opinion of the majority in *Hundal* was written by Cory J., who relied on *Wholesale Travel* for the holding that objective negligence was a sufficient fault requirement for dangerous driving causing death. In a puzzling attack of reticence, Cory J. did not actually describe the offence of dangerous driving causing death as a "regulatory offence", although that classification had formed the ratio decidendi of his opinion in *Wholesale Travel*. However, he did claim that "driving can only be undertaken by those who have a licence", and he described driving as a "regulated activity".[127] On the face of it, these statements seem irrelevant since unlicensed drivers can be (and often are) found guilty of dangerous driving. Presumably, Cory J. was using the licensing requirement to force driving offences into the "regulatory" category. McLachlin and La Forest JJ. each agreed with Cory J. but added brief concurring reasons. McLachlin J. added nothing on the appropriate classification of the offence. La Forest J. des-

125 [1993] 1 S.C.R. 867. Cory J. wrote the majority opinion; McLachlin J. (with Lamer C.J.) and La Forest J. agreed with Cory J. but added short concurring opinions.

126 *Id.*, 882.

127 *Id.*, 884.

cribed dangerous driving causing death as a ''quasi-regulatory offence'',[128] but he did not expand on the characteristics of this new class of offence.

In *R.* v. *Nova Scotia Pharmaceutical Society* (1992),[129] the Supreme Court of Canada rejected a challenge to the Competition Act offence of conspiring to lessen competition unduly. The Act expressly eliminated the element of mens rea by providing that it was not necessary for the prosecution to prove that the accused intended that his actions would have the effect of lessening competition unduly. Did this provision violate the principles of fundamental justice guaranteed by s. 7 of the Charter?[130] Gonthier J., writing for a unanimous Court, answered no. He held that the challenged provision contained both a subjective mental element, namely, the requirement that the accused intended to enter into an agreement, and an objective mental element, namely, the requirement that the accused *ought to have known* that the agreement would lessen competition. This was enough, he held, to satisfy the ''minimum fault requirement'' of s. 7.[131]

Gonthier J.'s word ''minimum'' was certainly the word to describe the fault requirement that he held was constitutionally sufficient. He pointed out[132] that proof by the Crown that the accused had entered into an agreement that had the effect of lessening competition unduly would ''in most cases'' be all that was needed, because the ''logical inference'' from proof that the accused had entered into such an agreement would be that the accused ought to have known that the agreement would have the effect of lessening competition unduly. The ''objective'' mental element — consisting of what the accused ought to have known — is close to no mental element at all. A businessperson who entered into an agreement that he or she believed would *enhance* competition would have committed the offence if a criminal court concluded that the actual effect of the agreement was to lessen competition unduly.

The opinion in *Nova Scotia Pharmaceutical*, like the opinions in *Hundal*, did not describe the offence under challenge as a ''regulatory offence''. On the contrary, Gonthier J. said that the offence of conspiring to lessen competition unduly was ''at the core of the *criminal* part of the [Competition] Act''.[133] If by that he meant that the offence was a ''true crime'', then the decision in *Nova Scotia Pharmaceutical* cannot stand with *Wholesale Travel*, which was as clear as it could be that true crimes required subjective mens rea. Gonthier J. purported to rely on *Wholesale Travel*, which he described as establishing a minimum fault requirement for ''every criminal or regulatory offence''.[134] If by that he meant that the minimum fault requirement was the same for a ''criminal'' offence as it

128 *Id.*, 876.
129 [1992] 2 S.C.R. 606. Gonthier J. wrote the opinion of the Court.
130 The offence was also unsuccessfully challenged on the basis of the vagueness inherent in the word ''unduly''. This part of the decision is discussed at note 207, below.
131 [1992] 2 S.C.R. 606, 659.
132 *Id.*, 660.
133 *Id.*, 649 (emphasis added).
134 *Id.*, 659.

was for a "regulatory" offence, then it is not an accurate description of the holding in *Wholesale Travel*, which carefully distinguished the fault requirement for the two different categories of offences. Gonthier J. did not mention the stigma or the maximum penalty (it was five years imprisonment) that was attached to the Competition Act offence, and did not offer any other reasons why he regarded a departure from an objective standard as a sufficient fault requirement to satisfy s. 7.

In *R.* v. *Finlay* (1993),[135] the Supreme Court of Canada reviewed the validity of the Criminal Code offence of storing a firearm "in a careless manner". The maximum penalty was two years' imprisonment for a first offence and five years' imprisonment for a second or subsequent offence. Once again, it was necessary to decide whether negligence was a sufficient fault requirement for a Criminal Code offence. Lamer C.J. for the Court repeated the dictum in *Hundal*[136] that "in the appropriate context, negligence can be an acceptable basis of liability which meets the fault requirement of s. 7 of the Charter".[137] In a section of the opinion headed "Stigma Analysis" (an oxymoron in my view), Lamer C.J. held that the offence "does not give rise to sufficient stigma to require a subjective mens rea under s. 7 of the Charter".[138] His lordship did not describe the offence as a regulatory offence, although he did make reference to *Wholesale Travel* as supporting the result. The fault requirement of negligence was upheld.

In *R.* v. *Naglik* (1993),[139] the provision under challenge was the Criminal Code offence of failing to provide necessaries of life to a child under the age of 16 years. The accused's baby had in fact been brutally beaten either by the accused or her common law spouse over a period of several weeks, and they had given the baby no medical treatment. The Supreme Court of Canada, in an opinion written by Lamer C.J., held that the offence did not require subjective mens rea: whether a parent had failed to provide necessaries of life to a child was to be measured by an "objective, societal standard", and not by the subjective belief of the accused. In other words, a negligent failure to provide necessaries of life was as culpable as an intentional failure to do so. Did this objective standard satisfy s. 7 of the Charter? The Court held that it did, relying again on the *Hundal* proposition[140] that "in the appropriate context" negligence will satisfy s. 7.[141] Why was this the appropriate context? Lamer C.J. did not claim that the offence was a "regulatory" one; and it seems obvious that it was a "true crime" — and

135 [1993] 3 S.C.R. 103. The opinion of Lamer C.J. was concurred in by all members of the Court, except for one point of disagreement not germane to the present account.
136 Note 126, above.
137 [1993] 3 S.C.R. 103, 116-117.
138 *Id.*, 119.
139 [1993] 3 S.C.R. 122. The opinion of Lamer C.J. on the constitutional issue was agreed with by all members of the Court, except for one point of disagreement not germane to the present account.
140 Note 126, above.
141 [1993] 3 S.C.R. 122, 144.

a very serious one at that.[142] As for stigma, one would have guessed (it can only be a guess, of course) that the stigma associated with failing to obtain medical treatment for a battered baby was far greater than theft and comparable to attempted murder and murder, which indeed on these facts it closely resembled. But this was not Lamer C.J.'s approach. He acknowledged that the conviction would "stigmatize" the accused, but he held that "this stigmatization is neither unfairly disproportionate nor unrelated to the culpable conduct of which the accused was found guilty".[143] He also pointed out that "the sentencing judge can tailor the sentence to the circumstances of the particular offence and offender, eliminating the danger of the accused being punished to a degree out of proportion to the level of fault actually found to exist."[144] These comments apply with equal force to nearly every offence in the Criminal Code.[145]

It is not easy to summarize the present state of the law. *B.C. Motor Vehicle Reference* still stands for the proposition that s. 7 of the Charter requires that offences that carry the penalty of imprisonment must include an element of fault. According to *Wholesale Travel*, that element of fault must be subjective mens rea if the offence is a true crime, but need only be negligence (departure from an objective standard) if the offence is a regulatory offence. The acceptance of negligence as a sufficient element of fault is an abandonment of the broader principle of *B.C. Motor Vehicle* that the morally innocent should not be punished, because the merely negligent offender may sincerely believe that his or her conduct is lawful. Yet in *Hundal*, the Court held that negligence was the only constitutional requirement for an offence that carried a punishment of 14 years imprisonment, and the Court did not clearly state that the offence was a regulatory one. In *Nova Scotia Pharmaceutical* and *Naglik*, the Court also accepted that a departure from an objective standard was the only constitutional requirement for an offence that the Court implied was a true crime. The Court thus seems to be abandoning its silly distinction between true crimes and regulatory offences. However, the Court leaves us with no guidance as to when subjective mens rea is constitutionally required and when a merely objective standard of fault will suffice.

The narrowest statement of the *B.C. Motor Vehicle* holding is that the absence of any element of fault in an offence that carries the penalty of imprisonment is a breach of fundamental justice. This causes offences of absolute liability to violate s. 7. The later cases have cast no doubt on this holding. Of course, s. 7 has no application to an offence that carries only the penalty of a fine, even a very large fine, because in that case "liberty" is not affected. Therefore, so long as no

---

142 Oddly, the maximum penalty was only two years' imprisonment; however, Lamer C.J. did not suggest that the offence was not very serious.

143 [1993] 3 S.C.R. 122, 144.

144 *Id.*, 145.

145 As noted in the text accompanying note 156, below, murder may be the only serious offence for which the penalty is non-discretionary (and constitutionally valid).

sentence of imprisonment is provided for, it is still possible for the Parliament or Legislature to create offences of absolute liability.

As the preceding text has explained, an absolute liability offence that carries the penalty of imprisonment is an infringement of s. 7 of the Charter. However, it does not follow that the offence must necessarily be struck down. There are other remedial options open to the court.[146] One option is to use the power of severance (or reading in) to convert the offence into one of mens rea (if it is a "true crime") or strict liability (if it is a regulatory offence). This is what happened in *R.* v. *Hess* (1990),[147] where the Supreme Court of Canada severed from the Criminal Code offence of statutory rape the words that denied to an accused the defence that he was unaware of the age of the victim. That change converted the offence from one of absolute liability into one of mens rea, which made it constitutional. Another remedial option is to use the power of severance to eliminate the penalty of imprisonment. This is what happened in *R.* v. *Pontes* (1995),[148] where the Supreme Court of Canada severed the penalty of imprisonment from a Motor Vehicle Act offence (driving while prohibited) that the majority of the Court had decided was an absolute liability offence. That did not change the nature of the offence, but it meant that a convicted driver was only liable to a fine; since there was no longer any risk of a deprivation of liberty, there was no infringement of s. 7.[149]

44.12 Murder

The Criminal Code's definition of murder[150] used to include the so-called felony-murder rule (sometimes called the constructive murder rule). If an accused caused a death in the course of committing certain serious offences, including robbery, while armed with a weapon, then the accused was guilty of murder. There was no requirement that the accused intended to cause the death, or that he knew that his actions were likely to cause the death (subjective foreseeability), or even that he ought to have know that his actions were likely to cause the death (objective foreseeability). In place of these culpable states of mind, the felony-

146 The topic of remedies for unconstitutional statutes is addressed more fully in ch. 37, Enforcement of Rights, above.

147 [1990] 2 S.C.R. 906; discussed in text accompanying note 114, above.

148 [1995] 3 S.C.R. 44; discussed in text accompanying note 112, above.

149 This remedial choice was actually mandated by the Legislature of British Columbia, which had (after the decision in the *B.C. Motor Vehicle Reference*) enacted the following new provision in its Offence Act: "Notwithstanding . . . the provisions of any other Act, no person is liable to imprisonment with respect to an absolute liability offence". The notwithstanding clause made this provision prevail over the imprisonment requirement in the Motor Vehicle Act. This modification to the Motor Vehicle Act offence saved it from unconstitutionality.

150 In *R.* v. *Arkell* [1990] 2 S.C.R. 695, the Supreme Court of Canada rejected a s. 7 challenge to the distinction between "first degree murder" and "second degree murder".

murder rule required only proof of the felony, the use or carrying of the weapon and the ensuing death.

In *R.* v. *Vaillancourt* (1987),[151] the accused was charged with murder as the result of a poolroom robbery in which the accused's accomplice shot and killed a customer of the poolroom. The accused knew that his accomplice was carrying a gun, and of course he intended to rob the poolroom. He was charged under the felony-murder branch of murder,[152] and the appeal proceeded on the assumption that he did not foresee that a death was likely to ensue from the robbery (subjective foresight), and that there was at least a reasonable doubt as to whether he *ought* to have foreseen that a death was likely to ensue (objective foresight). The Supreme Court of Canada held that the felony-murder rule was a violation of fundamental justice under s. 7 of the Charter. The fact that an accused must have mens rea (a guilty mind) with respect to the underlying offence, in this case, the robbery, was not sufficient to satisfy s. 7. Before an accused could be found guilty of murder, s. 7 required that there be mens rea with respect to the death. Therefore, the felony-murder rule was unconstitutional.

The majority opinion in *Vaillancourt* was written by Lamer J. The ratio decidendi of the opinion is contained in the following passage:[153]

> there are, though very few in number, certain crimes where, because of the stigma attached to the conviction therefor or the available penalties, the principles of fundamental justice require a mens rea reflecting the particular nature of that crime. Such is theft, where, in my view, a conviction requires proof of some dishonesty. Murder is another such offence. The punishment for murder is the most severe in our society and the stigma that attaches to a conviction for murder is similarly extreme.

Thus, it was the extreme stigma and severe punishment associated with murder that entailed the requirement that the accused have some level of mens rea with respect to the death.

McIntyre J., who dissented, pointed out[154] that it must surely be open to Parliament to decide that a robbery that causes a death is a more serious offence than a robbery that does not cause a death. If this is so, then the objection to the felony-murder rule is simply an objection to the use of the name "murder". That objection could be corrected by changing the name of the offence to (for example)

---

151 [1987] 2 S.C.R. 636. The principal opinion was written by Lamer J. with the concurrence of Dickson C.J., Estey and Wilson JJ., and, in separate opinions giving cautious agreement, Beetz, Le Dain and La Forest JJ. McIntyre J. dissented.

152 Under s. 21(2) of the Criminal Code, Vaillancourt was a party to the accomplice's crime, because they were functioning in concert, and the commission of the robbery (not the death) was foreseeable. In effect, there were two constructive elements to the charge of murder against Vaillancourt, namely, the felony-murder rule and the party rule. The constitutionality of the latter rule was not reviewed in *Vaillancourt*, but it was in *R.* v. *Logan* [1990] 2 S.C.R. 731; discussed in text accompanying note 162, below.

153 [1987] 2 S.C.R. 636, 653-654.

154 *Id.*, 663.

''manslaughter'' or ''killing during the commission of an offence''. McIntyre J. took the view that the use of the word ''murder'' to classify an unintentional killing ought not to be regarded as a breach of fundamental justice. McIntyre J.'s point is illustrated by Lamer J.'s example of theft, which by reason of its stigma, was said to require proof of some dishonesty.[155] Obviously, an offence of a different name, such as conversion of a motor vehicle, would not require proof of dishonesty. On this view, fundamental justice controls the names by which offences can be called, prohibiting those names that suggest a higher degree of culpability than is warranted.

Lamer J.'s theft example indicates that stigma is more important than penalty in attracting the *Vaillancourt* doctrine. The great majority of offences, including theft, carry discretionary penalties; and a sentencing court would tailor the penalty to fit the actual culpability of the accused.[156] Murder is exceptional in carrying a mandatory penalty of life imprisonment. It is a possible objection to the felony-murder rule that the same penalty must be applied to offenders whose culpability varies widely. Lamer J. did not seem to rely on this argument, although he did make reference to the severity of the punishment for murder. The trouble with this argument is that there is another guarantee of the Charter that is specifically addressed to unduly harsh penalties, and that is s. 12, the prohibition on cruel and unusual punishment. The Supreme Court of Canada[157] has held that a mandatory sentence of imprisonment that is disproportionately severe is unconstitutional for breach of s. 12. This means that s. 12 is the correct rubric under which to bring a complaint that a mandatory sentence is disproportionately severe. Section 7 is not needed to control penalties. That leaves only the control of the names of offences (based on stigma) as a rule for s. 7 in this context. But the control of names is a relatively trivial function that could well be left to the judgment of Parliament and excluded from judicial review, as McIntyre J. argued.

In *Vaillancourt*, the Supreme Court of Canada decided that ''some level of mens rea''[158] with respect to the victim's death was required for the crime of murder. The Court did not have to decide, and did not decide, whether the required level of mens rea was *subjective* foreseeability, meaning that the accused did in fact foresee the likelihood of causing death, or was the lower level of *objective* foreseeability, meaning that the accused did not in fact foresee but ought to have foreseen the likelihood of causing death. In *R.* v. *Martineau* (1990),[159] the Supreme

155 Quotation accompanying note 153, above.

156 This was acknowledged by Lamer C.J. in *R.* v. *Logan* [1990] 2 S.C.R. 731, 743 (''. . . the social stigma associated with a conviction is the most important consideration, not the sentence'').

157 R. v. *Smith* [1987] 1 S.C.R. 1045; discussed in ch. 49, Cruel and Unusual Punishment, under heading 50.4, ''Minimum sentence'', below.

158 [1987] 2 S.C.R. 636, 653-654.

159 [1990] 2 S.C.R. 633. Lamer C.J. wrote for himself and four others; Sopinka J. concurred, but on the basis that it was not necessary to resolve the subjective-objective question; L'Heureux-Dubé J. dissented. The decision was followed in *R.* v. *Sit* [1991] 3 S.C.R. 124, where the Court was unanimous.

Court of Canada, by a majority, held that it was the higher level of mens rea — subjective foreseeability — that was required by s. 7. However, L'Heureux-Dubé J., who dissented, pointed out that it ought to be open to Parliament to enact that "flagrant, callous, ruthless or selfish acts, perpetrated by one whose purpose is already criminal, will be treated more harshly than a mere accidental killing".[160] That is a proposition that surely cannot be denied, and it reinforces the point made earlier that it is only Parliament's use of the name "murder" that offends s. 7.

In *Martineau*, L'Heureux-Dubé J. also pointed out that subjective foresight of death has never before been the exclusive standard for murder in Canada or in the other countries that inherited English principles of criminal law.[161] How then did it suddenly become a basic tent of the legal system? The question points up the indeterminacy of the new doctrine of substantive fundamental justice, and its dependence on the moral attitudes of the judges.

The ruling in *Martineau*, that the mens rea requirement for murder was subjective foresight of the likely death, quickly led to a s. 7 challenge to s. 21(2) of the Criminal Code, which defines who is a "party" to an offence. This provision makes persons party to an offence if they are carrying out an unlawful purpose together, and, although only one of them actually commits the offence, the others "knew *or ought to have known* that the commission of the offence would be a probable consequence of carrying out the common purpose". In *R. v. Logan* (1990),[162] the two accuseds were participants in the armed robbery of a store, in the course of which a third participant shot and severely injured the sales clerk of the store. The two accuseds were convicted as parties under s. 21(2) to the crime of attempted murder, on the basis that they ought to have known that the shooting was a probable consequence of their common purpose. The Supreme Court of Canada set aside their convictions.

In *Logan*, the Supreme Court of Canada held that the crime of attempted murder was one of those "very few offences" for which s. 7 stipulated a requirement of subjective mens rea. There was no mandatory penalty for attempted murder, but that did not matter because it was not the penalty, but "the social stigma associated with a conviction" for attempted murder that was "the most important consideration".[163] Since subjective mens rea was required by s. 7 for a conviction for attempted murder, the same level of mens rea was required for the conviction of a party to the offence. Therefore, the phrase "or ought to have known" in s. 21(2), which purported to make objective mens rea sufficient for the conviction of a party, was inapplicable whenever the principal offence was attempted murder or any other offence for which subjective mens rea was constitutionally required.

---

160 [1990] 2 S.C.R. 633, 657 and see also 662.
161 Id., 674.
162 [1990] 2 S.C.R. 731. Lamer C.J. wrote the majority judgment. L'Heureux-Dubé J. dissented. The decision was followed in *R.* v. *Sit* [1991] 3 S.C.R. 124, where the Court was unanimous.
163 [1990] 2 S.C.R. 731, 743.

What then are the offences for which subjective mens rea is constitutionally required? We know that they include murder, because *Martineau* so decides, and attempted murder, because *Logan* so decides. They also include war crimes and crimes against humanity committed outside Canada.[164] We are told that they are "very few" in number, and are identified primarily by the "social stigma" that is associated with them.[165] We are told that the sentence for the offence is not the decisive consideration, and this is made clear by Lamer C.J.'s example of theft, which he gave in *Vaillancourt* and repeated in *Logan*.[166] Theft is one of the least severely punished offences in the Criminal Code: in some circumstances, theft attracts a *maximum* penalty of six months' imprisonment.[167] In these circumstances, it is difficult to identify which other offences fall into this small category. What is the status of treason, sabotage, mutiny, sedition, forgery, piracy, hijacking, perjury, fabricating evidence, bribery, fraud, cheating, procuring for prostitution, abandoning a child, infanticide, aggravated assault, sexual assault, kidnapping, abduction, torture, bigamy, extortion, breach of trust, breaking and entering and false pretences? How is a prosecutor to decide whether persons can be charged under the objective language of s. 21(2) as parties to these offences? If a charge is laid, how is a judge to decide whether it was properly laid? If it all depends upon the social stigma, how is that to be measured and compared, bearing in mind that only a "very few" offences qualify?[168]

In my opinion, it is most unsatisfactory to make radical constitutional consequences flow from such a vague, unproved and unprovable notion as social stigma. In any case, the notion cannot plausibly be derived from the basic tenets of the legal system, which have always countenanced the conviction for crimes such as murder and attempted murder of those who engage in flagrant, callous, ruthless or selfish acts in pursuit of criminal purposes. Whether it is morally wrong to continue to do so seems to me to be an issue that could safely be left to the Parliament to decide. If, however, it must be accepted that fundamental justice requires that certain offences carry a constitutional requirement of subjective mens rea, then those offences should be identified, not by reference to their names,

164 *R.* v. *Finta* [1994] 1 S.C.R. 701 (holding by majority that the stigma required subjective knowledge of the facts that made the offence a war crime or crime against humanity).

165 *Ibid.*

166 *Id.*, 744.

167 *Ibid.*

168 The answer, of course, is that nothing short of a ruling by a majority of the Supreme Court of Canada can measure the stigma attached to each offence and then determine whether there is a constitutional requirement of subjective mens rea. So far, this has been the issue in the following cases, each of which has determined (after extensive discussion) that subjective mens rea is not required: *R.* v. *Wholesale Travel Group* [1991] 3 S.C.R. 154 (false advertising); *R.* v. *Nova Scotia Pharmaceutical Society* [1992] 2 S.C.R. 606 (conspiring to lessen competition); *R.* v. *DeSousa* [1992] 2 S.C.R. 944 (unlawfully causing bodily harm); *R.* v. *Hundal* [1993] 1 S.C.R. 867 (dangerous driving causing death); *R.* v. *Creighton* [1993] 3 S.C.R. 3 (manslaughter by unlawful act); *R.* v. *Finlay* [1993] 3 S.C.R. 103 (storing a firearm in a careless manner); *R.* v. *Naglik* [1993] 3 S.C.R. 122 (failing to provide necessaries of life to a child).

nor by reference to their social stigma, but by reference to an objective standard, which would have to be framed on the basis of the severity of the sentence.[169]

44.13 Unforeseen Consequences

There are Criminal Code offences in which the consequences of an unlawful act dictate the severity of the punishment for which the accused is liable. For example, the maximum term of imprisonment for dangerous driving is five years; but for dangerous driving causing bodily harm the maximum term is ten years; and for dangerous driving causing death the maximum term is 14 years. Assuming that the accused's mental state is the same for all three offences, is it a breach of fundamental justice to make an unintended and unforeseen consequence (bodily harm or death) the basis of a more serious charge?

In the previous section of this chapter, entitled "Murder", we noticed that the Supreme Court of Canada has held that, where an accused is charged with the offences of murder or attempted murder, then it is a requirement of fundamental justice that the accused must have actually intended or foreseen the death of the victim. However, the Court indicated that this requirement of subjective foresight of the consequences of an unlawful act applied only to "very few" offences, which were to be identified by reference to the "social stigma" and the penalty attaching to the offence.[170] I have already commented on the difficulty of identifying this narrow class of offences. Outside this narrow class, what mens rea elements are required by s. 7 for an offence that makes a person liable for the consequences of an unlawful act?

In *R.* v. *DeSousa* (1992),[171] the accused, while in a fight, threw a glass bottle that shattered against a wall, causing fragments of glass to injure an innocent bystander. The accused neither intended nor foresaw this injury. However, the injury was used as the basis of a Criminal Code charge of unlawfully causing bodily harm. This offence carried a penalty of imprisonment (ten years in fact), so that s. 7 of the Charter was applicable. The Supreme Court of Canada, in an opinion written by Sopinka J., held that the only mental element that was constitutionally required for the offence of unlawfully causing bodily harm was embedded in the word "unlawfully". That required an unlawful act, which Sopinka J. held must be a statutory offence with a constitutionally sufficient mental element. This ingredient of the offence was not in dispute. What was in dispute was the mental element required for causing bodily harm. Sopinka J. held that there was "no constitutional requirement that intention, either on an objective or sub-

169 Cf. note 119, above, where a similar argument is made with respect to the distinction between "regulatory offences" and "true crimes".

170 Text accompanying note 163, above.

171 [1992] 2 S.C.R. 944. Sopinka J. wrote the opinion for the Court.

jective basis, extend to the consequences of unlawful acts in general''.[172] Therefore, the accused was properly convicted of unlawfully causing bodily harm despite his lack of intention or foresight with respect to the bodily harm.

Sopinka J. in *DeSousa* distinguished the line of cases involving murder and attempted murder,[173] on the basis that murder and attempted murder were among ''those few offences which due to [their] stigma and penalty require fault based on a subjective standard''.[174] The offence of unlawfully causing bodily harm did not carry sufficient stigma or penalty to be one of ''those few offences''. For all of the less serious offences, the element of mens rea that was required by the principles of fundamental justice did not include any foresight (subjective or objective) of the consequences of an unlawful act. In other words, under s. 7 of the Charter, ''it is acceptable to distinguish between criminal responsibility for equally reprehensible acts on the basis of the harm that is actually caused''.[175]

The ruling in *DeSousa* was reinforced in *R.* v. *Hundal* (1993),[176] where the Supreme Court of Canada reviewed the Criminal Code offence of dangerous driving causing death. In that case, the three concurring opinions were devoted exclusively to the mental element involved in dangerous driving.[177] Having decided that the mental element was an objective one, so that the accused's subjective belief that he was driving safely was no defence, the Court affirmed his conviction. Without even referring to *DeSousa*, the Court took for granted that the accused could be convicted of dangerous driving *causing death*, even though it was plain that the accused had no intention or foresight with respect to the death that he had caused. (He had gone through a red light and killed another motorist in the intersection.) Yet, the death elevated the maximum penalty from five years (for simple dangerous driving) to 14 years (for dangerous driving causing death). Evidently, neither the stigma of having killed an innocent person by dangerous driving nor the penalty of 14 years were sufficient to impose any constitutional requirement of a mental element with respect to the fatal consequence of the accused's dangerous driving.

In *R.* v. *Creighton* (1993),[178] the Supreme Court of Canada had to determine what was the mental element of the offence of manslaughter by unlawful act, which consisted of causing the death of a human being by an unlawful act. The

---

172 Sopinka J. held (at p. 961) that, as a matter of statutory intepretation, the Criminal Code offence required *objective* foresight of bodily harm, meaning that the accused *ought* to have foreseen the risk of the injury that ensued. But His Lordship emphasized in the language quoted in the text (at p. 965) that not even objective foresight was required by s. 7.

173 The cases are discussed in the previous section of this chapter, under heading 44.12, ''Murder'', above.

174 [1992] 2 S.C.R. 944, 962.

175 *Id.*, 967.

176 [1993] 1 S.C.R. 867.

177 This aspect of the case is discussed at note 125, above.

178 [1993] 3 S.C.R. 3. Concurring opinions were written by Lamer C.J. with three others, McLachlin J. with three others, and La Forest J.

logical possibilities were: (1) the accused actually foresaw the risk of death (subjective foresight of death), (2) the accused ought (as a reasonable person) to have foreseen the risk of death (objective foresight of death), (3) the accused actually foresaw the risk of bodily harm (subjective foresight of bodily harm), and (4) the accused ought (as a reasonable person) to have foreseen the risk of bodily harm (objective foresight of bodily harm). The Criminal Code, as interpreted by the courts, imposed only requirement (4). In the world of substantive fundamental justice, the Court was free to substitute (1), (2) or (3), invoking s. 7 to justify the overruling of Parliament's choice. The Court approached the task by engaging in a long and subtle debate, uninformed by any evidence or social-science information, as to the degree of social stigma[179] that attached to a conviction for manslaughter. According to Lamer C.J. (with three others), the stigma was not enough for (1), but was too much for (3) and (4); it was just right for (2), and so the offence was unconstitutional in requiring only (4). According to McLachlin J. (with three others), the stigma was just right for (4), and so the offence was constitutional. La Forest J. (who alone did not measure the stigma) broke the tie by also coming out in favour of (4). In the end, therefore, the Court, by a five-four majority, upheld the constitutionality of the Criminal Code's requirement of objective foresight of bodily harm as the mental element of unlawful act manslaughter.[180] Foresight of the death was not required, despite the fact that the maximum penalty for manslaughter was imprisonment for life.

44.14 Intoxication

In *R.* v. *Daviault* (1994),[181] the Supreme Court of Canada held that s. 7 requires that extreme intoxication be a defence to a criminal charge. Before this decision, a person could not escape responsibility for offences of general intent by pleading drunkenness. An offence of general intent is one for which the mental element of the offence (mens rea) is simply an intention to do the prohibited act (actus reus). An offence of specific intent is one for which there is a required mental element in addition to the intention to do the act. For example, assault to resist arrest is an offence of specific intent (because the intention to resist arrest is an added mental element), while simple assault is an offence of general intent (because the only mental element is the intention to commit the act of assault). In the case of an offence of specific intent, extreme intoxication may negative the additional intent and lead to the acquittal of the accused, but the accused would

---

179 For those who can stand the tedious repetition of my criticisms of this concept as a constitutional ''standard'', see note 119, above, and text accompanying note 169, above.

180 Accord, *R.* v. *Jackson* [1993] 4 S.C.R. 573, 587.

181 [1994] 3 S.C.R. 63. The opinion of the majority was written by Cory J., with whom L'Heureux-Dubé, McLachlin and Iacobucci JJ. agreed. Short concurring opinions were written by Lamer C.J. and La Forest J., essentially agreeing with Cory J. The opinion of the dissenting minority was written by Sopinka J., with whom Gonthier and Major JJ. agreed.

not normally escape criminal responsibility, because the accused could still be convicted of a lesser offence (such as simple assault) for which no specific intent was required.

The theory by which the courts refused to permit intoxication as a defence to offences of general intent was that the mental element required for an offence of general intent was so minimal that even a drunken person was capable of forming the intent. The fact that drunkenness might have caused the accused to give way more readily to a violent impulse was not enough to negative the mental element of an offence of general intent. What about those cases where it is claimed that the accused's intoxication was so extreme that he or she acted as an automaton without any awareness of doing the forbidden act? The courts rejected even that defence on the pragmatic ground that self-induced drunkenness was sufficiently blameworthy to substitute for the intention to perform the forbidden act. The intention or recklessness involved in voluntarily drinking so much alcohol that the drinker loses control over his or her actions was regarded as a sufficiently guilty mind to support a conviction for an offence of general intent. This rule undoubtedly reflected a policy of protecting the public from drunken offenders, who could not escape responsibility for violent acts by becoming extremely drunk. It probably also reflected some scepticism as to the factual basis of the claim that drunkenness could rob a person so completely of any willed responsibility for his criminal act, especially where that act was a relatively complicated one, such as a rape.

In *R.* v. *Daviault*, the accused was charged with a sexual assault. The complainant, who was confined to a wheelchair, testified that the accused (who had been drinking in her apartment) had wheeled her into her bedroom, had thrown her onto the bed and sexually assaulted her. The accused testified that he had been drinking heavily during the day and evening, and that he awoke without any clothes on in the complainant's bed, but had no recollection of what had happened before that. An expert called by the accused testified that the accused had drunk so much alcohol that he could have been in a state akin to automatism when he committed the assault (if he committed the assault). The trial judge found that the accused had committed the act of sexual assault, but he acquitted the accused on the basis of a reasonable doubt as to whether the accused had the intent necessary to commit the offence. The Quebec Court of Appeal substituted a verdict of guilty on the ground that self-induced intoxication was no defence to a crime of general intent, and sexual assault was a crime of general intent.

The Supreme Court of Canada, by a majority of six to three, held that ss. 7 and 11(d) of the Charter were offended by the rule that self-induced intoxication was no defence to a criminal charge. Cory J., who wrote for the majority, held that, under s. 7, the requirement of mens rea for a crime of general intent could only be the intention to commit the prohibited act. The intention to become drunk could not be substituted for the intention to commit the forbidden act. Having derived this premise from the Charter, he reasoned that to eliminate the only permissible mental element from the crime was a breach of fundamental justice resulting in a breach of s. 7. Section 11(d) was also infringed, because the denial of the defence of drunkenness would enable an accused to be convicted notwithstanding a reasonable doubt as to whether the accused possessed the only permissible mental element of the crime. In short, the Charter required that self-induced intoxication, if it was so extreme as to be akin to automatism, must free the accused from criminal liability. Sopinka J., who wrote the dissenting opinion, took the view that self-induced intoxication was sufficiently blameworthy to count as the mental element for a crime of general intent, and that there were sound policy reasons for not permitting drunken offenders to escape criminal liability for acts of violence.

There are two passages near the end of Cory J.'s majority judgment that evidently seek to allay concerns about the public dangers of a constitutional requirement that has the effect of freeing extremely drunken offenders from criminal liability. The first passage requires the accused to establish the defence of extreme intoxication on the balance of probabilities.[182] By reversing the usual onus of proof in a criminal case, Cory J. created a new rule that offends the presumption of innocence in s. 11(d), and that preserves what he had earlier offered as one of the constitutional vices of the old law, namely, that a person could be convicted of a criminal offence notwithstanding a reasonable doubt as to whether he had the mens rea to commit the offence. But Cory J. explained that the reversal of the onus of proof (but apparently not the old common law) could be justified under s. 1 of the Charter.[183]

The second passage is one where Cory J. asserts "that it is always open to Parliament to fashion a remedy which would make it a crime to commit a prohibited act while drunk".[184] This passage is a puzzle, because every word of the opinion to this point has argued that it is not open to Parliament to make it a crime to commit a prohibited act while drunk. That, surely, is the state of the law that the Court is now striking down. What would the mens rea of this new crime be? It could hardly be the intention or recklessness of getting drunk, since that has been ruled constitutionally insufficient as a replacement for the intention of committing the prohibited act. This problem could hardly be overcome by describing drunkenness as the crime, rather than the prohibited act, since that is a transparent evasion of the constitutional rule laid down in this case. If the only problem with the prosecution of Daviault is that he could not be charged with drunkenness rather than the sexual assault, which is the actual reason for wanting to punish him, then all the words in the majority judgment add up to nothing of substance. Why not simply uphold the present state of the law, instead of insisting on Parliament switching the names of the offences?

---

182 *Id.*, 101.

183 *Ibid.*, citing *R.* v. *Chaulk* [1990] 3 S.C.R. 1303, which upheld under s. 1 the statutory reversal of the onus of proving the defence of insanity.

184 *Id.*, 100.

The decision in *Daviault* attracted very unfavourable public comment. Public concern that drunken offenders would escape liability for violent acts was intensified when the newspapers reported three successful uses of the drunkenness defence within days of the Court's decision. The federal government was forced to take the issue up as a matter of urgency. The government did not follow Cory J.'s suggestion that Parliament could make drunkenness an offence. Instead, Parliament enacted an amendment to the Criminal Code that described extreme self-induced intoxication as a marked departure from "the standard of reasonable care generally recognized in Canadian society", and provided that this departure constituted the fault required for conviction of offences of violence.[185] This essentially enacts the common law rule that the majority in *Daviault* had struck down as offending the Charter of Rights. On the face of it, the amendment is subject to the same constitutional objections as the common law rule. Yet the amendment does not invoke the override power of s. 33: there is no notwithstanding clause to override ss. 7 and 11(d) of the Charter. It will be interesting to see whether the Court will uphold the amendment, which it could only do under s. 1.[186]

44.15 Overbroad laws

In *R.* v. *Heywood* (1994),[187] the Supreme Court of Canada established a new doctrine of "overbreadth",[188] which is a breach of the principles of fundamental justice, and therefore a basis for a finding of unconstitutionality in a law that affects life, liberty or security of the person.

The law under challenge in *Heywood* was a provision of the Criminal Code that made it an offence (of "vagrancy") for a person who had been previously found guilty of the offence (among others) of sexual assault to be "found loitering in or near a schoolground, playground, public park or bathing area". The law obviously restricted the liberty of those convicted sex offenders to whom the prohibition applied. Was it also a breach of the principles of fundamental justice? The majority of the Supreme Court of Canada, in an opinion written by Cory J., held that the purpose of the law was to protect the safety of children. Cory J.

---

185 S.C. 1995, c. 32, adding new s. 33.1 to the Criminal Code.

186 The amending Act contains a two-page preamble which recites what is close to a factual and legal rebuttal of the Court's reasoning, and which emphasizes the close association of intoxication and violence, especially violence against women and children. Recall, however, the Court's reluctance to employ s. 1 to overcome a breach of s. 7: ch. 35, Limitation of Rights, under heading 35.14(b), "Section 7", above.

187 [1994] 3 S.C.R. 761. The opinion of the majority was written by Cory J., with the agreement of Lamer C.J., Sopinka, Iacobucci and Major JJ. The opinion of the dissenting minority was written by Gonthier J., with the agreement of La Forest, L'Heureux-Dubé and McLachlin JJ.

188 In *R.* v. *Nova Scotia Pharmaceutical Society* [1992] 2 S.C.R. 606, 632 ("overbreadth has no independent existence"), Gonthier J. for the Court had denied that there was such a doctrine in Canada.

acknowledged that a restriction on liberty for the purpose of protecting the safety of children would not be a breach of fundamental justice. But, he held, a law that restricted liberty more than was necessary to accomplish its purpose would be a breach of fundamental justice by reason of "overbreadth". In this case, the law was overbroad for three reasons: (1) its geographic scope was too wide, because parks and bathing areas included places where children were not likely to be found; (2) its duration was too long, because it applied for life without any possibility of review; and (3) the class of persons to whom it applied was too wide, because some of the offenders to whom it applied would not be a continuing danger to children.[189] Because the law was overbroad, it offended the principles of fundamental justice. It could not be upheld under s.1, because its overbreadth would cause it to fail the minimum impairment (least drastic means) branch of the s.1 analysis. The law was therefore struck down in its entirety.

Overbreadth is not the same as vagueness (a topic that is treated in the next section of this chapter). A law could be perfectly clear (in which case it would not be vague) and still use means that went further than necessary to accomplish the law's purpose (in which case it would be overbroad). Of course, a law that was excessively vague might also be excessively broad, and thus fail both requirements. Overbreadth and vagueness have this in common: either deficiency results in the invalidity of the entire law, including the part that is consistent with the purpose of the law and clear in its application.

It is hard to disagree with the basic premise of Cory J.'s opinion in *Heywood*, which is that a law that restricts liberty "for no reason" (to use Cory J.'s phrase)[190] offends the principles of fundamental justice. But the doctrine of overbreadth, as applied by the Court, raises serious practical and theoretical difficulties, and confers an exceedingly discretionary power of review on the Court. The doctrine requires that the terms of a law be no broader than is necessary to accomplish the purpose of the law. But the purpose of a law is a judicial construct, which can be defined widely or narrowly as the reviewing court sees fit. In this case, for example, Cory J., who wrote for the majority, defined the purpose of the law as being for the protection of children, while Gonthier J., who wrote for the dissenting minority, defined the purpose of the law as being for the protection of adults as well as children. Much of the difference of opinion between majority and minority depended on these competing purposes, because the law was apt to cover persons and situations that presented a danger to adults as well as children. Even if

189 A fourth reason for holding that the law offended the principles of fundamental justice was that it made no provision for notice of the loitering prohibition to be given to those convicted offenders who came under the terms of the prohibition. This has nothing to do with overbreadth. The theory that a requirement of notice is a principle of fundamental justice, namely, a basic tenet of the legal system, is not only novel, but contradicts what is undeniably a basic tenet of the legal system that ignorance of the law is no excuse. This was the dissenting view of Gonthier J. (In fact, the accused in this case had been given notice of the law when he was warned by police and not charged on an earlier occasion of loitering near a playground.)

190 [1994] 3 S.C.R. 761, 793.

agreement could be reached on the purpose of a law, the question whether the terms of the law are no broader than is needed to carry out the purpose raises a host of interpretative, policy and empirical questions. In this case, for example, Cory J. interpreted loitering as not involving anything more than mere presence in the prohibited areas, while Gonthier J. interpreted the term as requiring some malevolent intent. The two judges also disagreed on such issues as whether sex offenders can be reliably diagnosed as cured, and whether there is a pattern of crossover from one kind of past offence (for example, against adults) to a different kind (for example, against children). These kinds of disagreements among judges are not unusual and are not surprising. It must be recognized, however, that a judge who disapproves of a law will always be able to find that it is overbroad.

A feature of Cory J.'s opinion is his use of hypothetical cases to demonstrate the overbreadth of the law. He was concerned about the application of the law to ''remote wilderness parks'',[191] and to ''a man convicted at age 18 of sexual assault of an adult woman who was known to him in a situation aggravated by alcohol''.[192] The case before the Court, however, was a man, who had been previously convicted of sexual assault, who was found standing at the edge of a children's playground in a public park in Victoria, taking photographs of the children with a camera with a telephoto lens; the film in the camera, and photographs found in his home, showed that he was taking pictures of young girls with their clothing disarranged from play so that their crotches, although covered by underclothes, were visible. The trial judge regarded the behaviour as sufficiently sinister to impose a three-month prison sentence followed by three years of probation. The Supreme Court of Canada could hardly have been indifferent to these facts, but the majority's analysis is based entirely on hypothetical cases involving the most innocent possible offenders.[193] This mode of reasoning is a very powerful tool of judicial review, since there must be few laws indeed in which it would not be possible to design a hypothetical case (disregarding the realities of police and prosecutorial discretion)[194] that is caught by the law although it falls outside the apparent purpose of the law. What law can withstand an attack of this kind?[195]

Why should the Supreme Court of Canada be in such a hurry to strike down a law for overshooting its purpose in a case where the law is clearly accomplishing

191 *Id.*, 795.

192 *Id.*, 799.

193 The most innocent possible offender principle has also been used to strike down minimum sentence requirements under s. 12 of the Charter's prohibition on cruel and unusual treatment or punishment. The law is described (and similar criticism is offered) in ch. 50, Cruel and Unusual Punishment, under heading 50.4, ''Minimum sentence'', below.

194 The majority opinion is completely silent on the issue of police and prosecutorial discretion, although that discretion is likely to keep the wilderness bird watcher out of court, just as it protects the speeding motorist who is rushing a sick child to the hospital.

195 Early in the opinion (at p. 793), Cory J. says that in analyzing a statutory provision to determine whether it is overbroad, a ''measure of deference'' should be paid to the means selected by the legislature. While a measure of deference is not (apparently) very much deference, this dictum should shield those laws whose overbreadth depends upon particularly fanciful hypotheticals.

its purpose?[196] After all, if the hypothetical cases are realistic, there will be future opportunities to review the law when it is applied too broadly. The reliance on hypothetical cases turns the courts into ''roving commissions assigned to pass judgment on the validity of the Nation's laws''.[197] The American courts have not allowed this to happen. In the United States, it is well established that ''a person to whom a statute may constitutionally be applied will not be heard to challenge that statute on the ground that it may conceivably be applied unconstitutionally to others, in other situations not before the Court''.[198] Surely, this reflects a more appropriately restrained role for the courts.

In *Heywood*, the law that was struck down was a direct restraint on the liberty of those to whom it applied, because their access to schoolyards, playgrounds, public parks and bathing areas was restricted. Such laws are unusual. But it must be remembered that any law that carries the possible sanction of imprisonment is deemed by the Supreme Court of Canada to be a deprivation of liberty requiring compliance with s. 7.[199] And it must also be remembered that a corporation, although not itself liable to the sanction of imprisonment, is permitted to rely on s. 7 as a defence to a criminal charge if the defence would be available to an individual.[200] The effect of these rules is to expose not only the criminal law, but virtually all regulatory law to s. 7 review, including review for overbreadth. Any law that includes the sanction of imprisonment is unconstitutional if a court determines, relying on hypothetical cases, that the scope of the law is broader than is required to carry out its purpose.

In *Ontario* v. *Canadian Pacific* (1995),[201] Canadian Pacific was charged with an offence under Ontario's Environmental Protection Act of discharging a contaminant, namely, smoke, into the natural environment. The company had been clearing the part of its railway right-of-way that ran through the town of Kenora, by burning the grass and weeds growing on the right-of-way. The resulting smoke caused some nuisance and discomfort to residents of the town whose complaints led to the laying of the charge. When the case reached the Supreme Court of

---

196 It is possible that the majority was emboldened by the fact that Parliament (responding to the decision of the British Columbia Court of Appeal in this case, which also struck down the law) had already replaced the law with a narrower version that amended the various characteristics of the law that the majority regarded as overbroad: S.C. 1993, c. 45, s. 1 (referred to by Cory J. at p.801). Therefore, although Heywood was acquitted, a valid law was in place for the future.

197 *Broadrick* v. *Oklahoma* (1973) 413 U.S. 601, 611 per White J.

198 *Id.*, 610-611; the United States' law is described, and rejected, by Lamer C.J. and Gonthier J. in *Ont.* v. *Canadian Pacific* [1995] 2 S.C.R. 1031, paras. 6-7, 73-78, although they do agree not to accept hypothetical cases in order to hold a statute unconstitutionally vague (as opposed to overbroad).

199 Section 44.7(a), ''Physical liberty'', above.

200 Chapter 56, Procedure, under heading 56.2(e), ''Enforcing other people's rights'', below.

201 [1995] 2 S.C.R. 1031. The Court was unanimous as to the outcome, upholding the law and its applicability to Canadian Pacific. The majority opinion was written by Gonthier J., with the agreement of La Forest, L'Heureux-Dubé, McLachlin, Iacobucci and Major JJ. A concurring opinion was written by Lamer C.J., with the agreement of Sopinka and Cory JJ.

Canada, the new doctrine of overbreadth had to be considered, which involved assessing the impact of the law on the most innocent possible offender. The discharge of smoke in a wilderness area (instead of in Kenora), or the placing of sand on icy sidewalks by homeowners (since the hypothetical case need have nothing to do with the actual facts) gave Lamer C.J. enormous difficulty, since they appeared to be discharges of contaminants that were caught by the literal words of the Act. And he explicitly recognized that the fact that police and prosecutors would not lay charges based on the wilderness smoke or the sandy sidewalks was irrelevant under the most innocent possible offender principle. Of course, recognition of the overbreadth argument in this case would be a serious blow to effective environmental regulation, which must rely on broad general language to capture the multitude of polluting activities that ought to be prohibited. Lamer C.J. solved the problem by invoking the presumption of constitutionality and adopting an artificially narrow interpretation of the Act that, he said, exempted the wilderness smoke and the sandy sidewalks. Gonthier J., who wrote the other opinion on the unanimous Court, also managed to find an interpretation of the Act (a different one) that, he said, excluded speculative or imaginary uses of the environment. For both judges, then, the Act was not overbroad, and Ontario was permitted to continue to try to regulate its environment.

44.16 Vague laws

(a) Void for vagueness

A vague law[202] violates the principles of fundamental justice, which causes a breach of s. 7 if the law is a deprivation of life, liberty or security of the person. A vague law offends two values that are fundamental to the legal system. First, the law does not provide fair notice to persons of what is prohibited, which makes it difficult for them to comply with the law. Secondly, the law does not provide clear standards for those entrusted with enforcement, which may lead to arbitrary enforcement.

In the *Prostitution Reference* (1990),[203] it was argued (among other things) that the offence of communicating for the purpose of engaging in prostitution was

202 Vagueness can also have an invalidating effect under the federal distribution of powers, because it can cause difficulty in classifying the law as in relation to a matter coming within one of the heads of power of the enacting legislative body: *Saumur* v. *Que.* [1953] 2 S.C.R. 299, 333; discussed in ch. 15, Judicial Review on Federal Grounds, under heading 15.9(e), ''Exhaustiveness'', above. Vagueness also does not satisfy the requirement ''prescribed by law'' in s. 1 of the Charter, which means that a vague law in derogation of a Charter right cannot be saved by s. 1: ch. 35, Limitation of Rights, under heading 35.7(c), ''Vagueness'', above.

203 *Re ss. 193 and 195.1 of Criminal Code* (Prostitution Reference) [1990] 1 S.C.R. 1123. The discussion of vagueness is in the concurring judgment of Lamer J., with whom Dickson C.J. for the majority agreed on this issue. Wilson J., dissenting in the result, also rejected the argument based on vagueness, but did not express agreement (or disagreement) with Lamer J.

in breach of s. 7, because the offence was unconstitutionally vague. The Supreme Court of Canada, while acknowledging that the prohibition was "broad and far reaching", denied that it was so vague that a court could not give "sensible meaning" to its terms.[204] This attack on the provision was therefore rejected, as were the attacks based on freedom of expression and freedom of association.

In *United Nurses of Alberta* v. *Alberta* (1992),[205] it was argued that the criminal offence of contempt of court was unconstitutionally vague under s. 7. The offence of contempt of court is unique in Canada in that it has not been reduced to statutory form. Section 9 of the Criminal Code, while abolishing common law offences, makes an exception for contempt of court, which accordingly survives as a common law offence. The Supreme Court of Canada held that it was not a requirement of fundamental justice that a criminal offence be codified in statutory form. Although the elements of the common law offence were not as clear as could be achieved in a statutory definition, the offence was "neither vague nor arbitrary".[206]

In *R.* v. *Nova Scotia Pharmaceutical Society* (1992),[207] the Competition Act offence of conspiring to lessen competition "unduly" was attacked under s. 7 on the ground that the crucial word "unduly" was unconstitutionally vague. Once again, the argument was rejected by the Supreme Court of Canada. Gonthier J., for a unanimous Court, reviewed the cases that had interpreted the word "unduly", and concluded that "Parliament has sufficiently delineated the area of risk and the terms of debate to meet the constitutional standard".[208]

In *Ontario* v. *Canadian Pacific* (1995),[209] a challenge was brought to a provision in Ontario's Environmental Protection Act, which made it an offence to discharge a "contaminant" into the "natural environment" that could impair the quality of the environment "for any use that can be made of it". It was argued that the controlling concepts of "contaminant", "natural environment" and "use" were so vague that the offence was void for vagueness under s. 7. Gonthier J., for a Court that was unanimous on this issue, held that, although the legislation was very broad and general, its scope was "reasonably delineated" so that "legal debate can occur as to the application of the provision in a specific fact situation".[210] That was all that s. 7 required, and the challenge therefore failed.

As was related in the previous section of this chapter, in the *Canadian Pacific* case, the law was also challenged for overbreadth. An overbreadth challenge

---

204 *Id.*, 1160.

205 [1992] 1 S.C.R. 901. The majority opinion was written by McLachlin J. Dissenting opinions were written by Cory and Sopinka JJ., but they did not discuss the vagueness issue.

206 *Id.*, 933.

207 [1992] 2 S.C.R. 606. Gonthier J. delivered the opinion of the Court.

208 *Id.*, 657.

209 [1995] 2 S.C.R. 1031. The majority opinion was written by Gonthier J., with whom La Forest, L'Heureux-Dubé, McLachlin, Iacobucci and Major JJ. agreed. A concurring opinion was written by Lamer C.J., with whom Sopinka and Cory JJ. agreed.

210 *Id.*, para. 70.

relies, not on the vagueness of the law, but on the argument that the terms of the law are broader than is necessary to accomplish the purpose of the law. It will be recalled that the analysis employed by the Court to determine the overbreadth argument, is to examine hypothetical cases. If a hypothetical case can be imagined that is outside the purpose of the law, but is nevertheless caught by the terms of the law, then the law is overbroad and is unconstitutional in its entirety. I have already made the comment that the use of imaginary hypothetical cases makes it difficult to defend a law against a claim of overbreadth (although the claim was, with difficulty, successfully defended in the *Canadian Pacific* case). The Court in *Canadian Pacific* made an important distinction between overbreadth and vagueness. In the case of vagueness, the use of hypothetical cases is not permitted. Once the law has been determined to apply to the defendant on the facts of the case before the court, the defendant is not permitted to point to the vagueness of the law in its application to other (hypothetical) cases not before the court. As explained in the previous section of this chapter, I believe the same rule of restraint should have been applied to the overbreadth argument, but at least the issue is settled correctly for the vagueness argument: the use of hypothetical cases is not permitted.

(b) Standard of precision

What is the "constitutional standard" of precision that a law must meet in order to avoid the vice of vagueness? In the *Nova Scotia Pharmaceutical* case, Gonthier J. said:[211]

> A vague provision does not provide an adequate basis for legal debate, that is for reaching a conclusion as to its meaning by reasoned analysis applying legal criteria. It does not sufficiently delineate any area of risk, and thus can provide neither fair notice to the citizen nor a limitation of enforcement discretion. Such a provision is not intelligible, to use the terminology of previous decisions of this Court, and, therefore it fails to give sufficient indications that could fuel a legal debate.

A number of tests are suggested in this passage: whether the law is "intelligible", whether the law sufficiently delineates "an area of risk", and whether the law provides "an adequate basis for legal debate". Of these, the last — the legal debate test — seems to me to be the least useful, because almost any provision, no matter how vague, could provide a basis for legal debate. However, it was the legal debate test that Gonthier J. evidently preferred, that he applied in his conclusion, and that the Supreme Court of Canada has employed in subsequent cases.[212]

---

211 *Id.*, 639-640.

212 *R.* v. *Morales*, note 216, below; *Ont.* v. *Can. Pacific*, note 209, above; *R.* v. *Finta* [1994] 1 S.C.R. 701 (rejecting vagueness attack on Criminal Code's war-crimes provisions); *Ruffo* v. *Conseil de la Magistrature* [1995] 4 S.C.R. 267 (rejecting vagueness attack on Quebec Courts of Justice Act requirement that judges act in a "reserved manner").

What is perhaps most useful in giving some content to the rule against vagueness is to refer back to the two values that the rule protects, namely, fair notice to citizens and limitation of enforcement discretion. A law is unconstitutionally vague if it fails to give fair notice of what conduct is prohibited by the law, and if it fails to impose real limitations on the discretion of those charged with enforcement of the law. These are the standards that are intended to be captured by the various shorthand tests, including the legal debate test.

However formulated, the constitutional standard of precision cannot be very exacting. Gonthier J. in the *Nova Scotia Pharmaceutical* case said that it was important not to require a law "to achieve a standard of precision to which the subject matter does not lend itself."[213] Certainly, there is no requirement that a law be "absolutely certain", because "no law can meet that standard."[214] Nor is the vagueness doctrine offended if a law is open to more than one interpretation. A law is unconstitutionally vague only if it cannot, even with judicial interpretation, provide meaningful standards of conduct.[215]

(c) Application to other Charter rights

Vagueness, in a law that deprives a person of life, liberty or security of the person, is a breach of s. 7, because it is a principle of fundamental justice that a law should not be too vague. In *R.* v. *Morales* (1992),[216] the Supreme Court of Canada held that the doctrine of vagueness also applies to s. 11(e) of the Charter. Section 11(e) guarantees the right "not to be denied reasonable bail without just cause." Lamer C.J. for the majority of the Court said that "there cannot be just cause for a denial of bail within the meaning of s. 11(e) if the statutory criteria for denying bail are vague and imprecise".[217] At issue in the *Morales* case was a Criminal Code provision that authorized a judge to deny bail to an accused person on the ground "that his detention is necessary in the public interest." Lamer C.J. acknowledged that the value of "fair notice to the citizen" was "not relevant to a provision . . . which does not prohibit conduct".[218] However, the value of limiting the discretion of those charged with enforcement was relevant. The "public interest" criterion would authorize a "standardless sweep", because under that criterion "a court can order imprisonment whenever it sees fit".[219]

---

213 [1992] 2 S.C.R. 606, 642; accord *Ruffo* v. *Conseil de la Magistrature* [1995] 4 S.C.R. 267, para. 111-112 (judicial duty to act in a "reserved manner" is an ethical principle which defies a more precise definition).

214 *Re ss. 193 and 195.1 of Criminal Code* (Prostitution Reference) [1990] 1 S.C.R. 1122, 1156.

215 *Id.*, 1157-1161; to the same effect is *R.* v. *Nova Scotia Pharmaceutical Society* [1992] 2 S.C.R. 606, 626-627.

216 [1992] 3 S.C.R. 711. Lamer C.J. wrote the majority opinion. Gonthier J. wrote the dissenting opinion, disagreeing on the issue of vagueness.

217 *Id.*, 728.

218 *Ibid.*

219 *Id.*, 732.

Lamer C.J. concluded that the bail provision provided ''no guidance for legal debate'', and was therefore void for vagueness.[220]

Morales makes clear that the doctrine of vagueness is not confined to s. 7, but applies to any Charter right that carries an implicit requirement that laws not be vague. In *Morales*, it was the ''just cause'' standard in s. 11(e) that called for legislative precision. Similar holdings can be expected under Charter provisions that call for laws that are not unreasonable (s. 8) and laws that are not arbitrary (s. 9); vague laws could not satisfy those standards. Moreover, a law that limits *any* of the guaranteed rights can be upheld under s. 1 only if the limit is ''prescribed by law.'' As had been explained earlier in the book, the requirement that a limit be prescribed by law also calls for fair notice to the citizen and limitations on enforcement discretion. Section 1 cannot be satisfied by a vague law.[221]

44.17 Wrong laws

In *R.* v. *Gamble* (1988),[222] the accused was tried and convicted for murder, and sentenced to life imprisonment. She was tried, convicted and sentenced under the Criminal Code provisions in force at the time of the trial, which was a mistake, because those provisions had just come into force, and were not in force at the time of the commission of the offence. Not only had the elements of the offence been changed, so had the rules regarding eligibility for parole. Had she been convicted under the old (correct) law, she would have been eligible for parole after ten years. Under the new (incorrect) law, she was ineligible for parole for 25 years. The trial and conviction took place in 1976, long before the Charter of Rights was in force. In 1986, when the Charter of Rights was in force, and she had served ten years of her sentence, she applied for habeas corpus to remove from her sentence the condition that she be ineligible for parole for 25 years. The Supreme Court of Canada granted the application.

In *Gamble*, Wilson J. for the majority of the Supreme Court of Canada held that the continued detention of the prisoner without eligibility for parole was a breach of s. 7.[223] The principles of fundamental justice were to be found in ''the basic tenets of our legal system''.[224] It was a basic tenet of any legal system ''that an accused must be tried and punished under the law in force at the time the offence is committed''.[225] Since that did not happen in this case, there was a

220 *Ibid.*

221 Note 202 above. The standard of precision seems to be the same under s. 1 as it is under ss. 7 and 11(e): *R.* v. *Nova Scotia Pharmaceutical Society* [1992] 2 S.C.R. 606, 631.

222 [1988] 2 S.C.R. 595.

223 Dickson C.J. dissented, on the basis (at 610) that the majority's decision would be ''a retrospective application of the Charter''.

224 *Id.*, 647, citing the *B.C. Motor Vehicle Reference.*

225 *Ibid.*

breach of s. 7, and the accused was entitled to be declared eligible for parole forthwith.

44.18 Right to silence

In *R.* v. *Hebert* (1990),[226] the accused had been arrested and advised of his right to counsel. He did retain counsel, and he advised the police that he did not wish to make a statement. However, he was then placed in custody with an undercover police officer, disguised as another prisoner, who engaged the accused in conversation, and to whom the accused made an incriminating statement. The Supreme Court of Canada held that the statement had been obtained in breach of the Charter. The obvious route to that result was the right to counsel in s. 10(b), because it is clear that the right to counsel is violated if the police continue questioning an accused who has exercised his right to counsel.[227] But the route the Court in fact took was a ''right to silence'', which was a principle of fundamental justice in s. 7.

In *Hebert*, the right to silence was said to be a ''basic tenet of the legal system'', although it was no part of the legal system as recently as 1981, when the Court had, in a pre-Charter case,[228] admitted a statement made by an accused to an undercover police officer posing as a prisoner. This new right to silence arose, according to the majority, only upon detention,[229] and it precluded only statements elicited by police questioning. A voluntary statement to another prisoner,[230] or even to an undercover police officer,[231] would not offend the right if the police officer were merely a passive listener. In this case, however, the accused's statement had been elicited by the questioning of the undercover police officer. In effect, the police had used a trick to subvert the accused's election not

226 [1990] 2 S.C.R. 151. The Court was unanimous; McLachlin J. wrote for seven judges; Sopinka and Wilson JJ. wrote separate concurring opinions.

227 See ch. 47, Rights on Arrest or Detention, under heading 47.4(g), ''Duty to refrain from questioning'', below.

228 *Rothman* v. *The Queen* [1981] 1 S.C.R. 640.

229 [1990] 2 S.C.R. 151, 184 per McLachlin J. for majority. Sopinka J.'s concurring opinion held (at 201) that the right arose ''whenever the coercive power of the state is brought to bear against the individual — either formally (by arrest or charge) or informally (by detention or accusation); according to this view (with which Wilson J. also agreed), the right could arise prior to detention. In *R.* v. *Broyles* [1991] 3 S.C.R. 595, 606, discussed in the next paragraph of the text, Iacobucci J. for the Court said that ''the right is triggered when the accused is subjected to the coercive powers of the state *through his or her detention*'' (my emphasis).

230 *R.* v. *Gray* (1991) 4 O.R. (3d) 33 (C.A.) (statement made to fellow prisoner, who afterwards volunteered it to police, admitted).

231 *R.* v. *Logan* [1990] 2 S.C.R. 731 (statements made to undercover police officers posing as prisoners admitted; Lamer C.J. said (at 737) that the police officers ''did not encourage the [accuseds] to talk, but merely provided the opportunity for the making of the statements''); *R.* v. *Johnston* (1991) 2 O.R. (3d) 771 (C.A.) (statement made to police informer in prison admitted; police informer did not ''elicit'' statement).

to make a statement to the police. This was a breach of s. 7. The statement was excluded.[232]

R. v. *Broyles* (1991)[233] was another jailhouse confession case. In that case, the accused made a statement while in custody to a friend who visited him in the jail. Unknown to the accused, the friend had been recruited as a police informer, and was wearing a body pack upon which the accused's statement was recorded. These facts differed from *Hebert* in that the informer in *Broyles* was not a police officer. However, the Supreme Court of Canada held that the informer was acting as an agent of the state, and should be covered by the same constitutional restraints as a police officer. Since the recording showed that the informer had actively elicited the statement by his questions to the accused, the statement was obtained in breach of the right to silence. The statement was excluded.

Hebert and *Broyles* concerned the right to silence before trial. At the trial stage of criminal proceedings, the Charter of Rights contains two specific guarantees that are aspects of a right to silence. One is s. 11(c), which provides that an accused person is not a compellable witness at his or her own trial. The other is s. 13, which provides that a witness who gives self-incriminatory evidence has the right not to have that evidence used against him or her in other proceedings. In the face of these two specific guarantees, does s. 7 afford any additional right to silence at the trial stage? The answer is yes, according to the Supreme Court of Canada: s. 7 contains a residue of the right to silence, and it supplements ss.11(c) and 13.

Section 11(c),[234] which applies only to the accused in a criminal trial (making the accused non-compellable as a witness), is supplemented by a s. 7 right, which applies to any witness in any proceeding, and which makes the witness non-compellable if the true purpose of calling the witness was to obtain incriminating evidence against the witness.[235] For example, if a commission of inquiry was established with the purpose of inquiring into some public issue, and if the commission summoned a witness for the purpose, not of advancing the inquiry, but of obtaining incriminating testimony from the witness, s. 11(c) would not make the witness non-compellable, but s. 7 would. The basis of the witness's residual s. 7 right not to have to testify is that it would be a breach of fundamental justice for the coercive power of the state to be used for the purpose of obtaining self-incriminating testimony from a witness.[236]

---

232 *Hebert* was distinguished in *R.* v. *Jones* [1994] 2 S.C.R. 229 (statements made at pre-trial psychiatric assessment admissible in dangerous offender hearing, because it was a sentencing hearing). See also *R.* v. *Crawford* [1995] 1 S.C.R. 858 (accused's pre-trial silence could be used by a co-accused to impeach his testimony at trial, but not as evidence of guilt).

233 [1991] 3 S.C.R. 595.

234 Chapter 48, Rights on Being Charged, under heading 48.4, ''Non-compellability (s.11(c))'', below.

235 *B.C. Securities Commn.* v. *Branch* [1995] 2 S.C.R. 3, 15.

236 Note, however, that if the evidence were admitted, s. 13 would apply, and the evidence would be inadmissible in later criminal proceedings against the witness.

R. v. *Fitzpatrick* (1995),[237] concerned the requirement of the federal Fisheries Act that records be kept by fishers and supplied to government on a daily basis detailing their daily catch of fish. The question was whether these records, which were required by government to regulate the fishery, could be used as evidence at the trial of a fisher for the offence of overfishing (catching fish in excess of statutory quotas), which carried the penalty of imprisonment. There was no breach of s. 11(c), because the accused was not being compelled to be a witness at his own trial. However, the accused argued that it would be a breach of s. 7 for the Crown to make use of the accused's own compelled statements about his fishing activities as evidence against him. The Supreme Court of Canada rejected the argument, holding that the records could be used at the accused's trial. In the context of a regulatory scheme to which the accused had voluntarily submitted by engaging in the business of fishing, fundamental justice did not provide an immunity against the use of statutorily compelled information.

Section 13,[238] which applies only to self-incriminatory evidence given by a witness (making it inadmissible to incriminate the witness in other proceedings), is supplemented by a s. 7 right, which applies to "derivative" or "secondary" evidence. Derivative evidence is evidence that is discovered as the result of the witness's testimony. Derivative evidence is not *self*-incriminatory because it was not created by the witness but existed independently of the witness's testimony. The s. 7 right excludes derivative evidence that would probably not have been discovered but for the witness's testimony.[239f] For example, on a trial for murder, the gun that is tendered by the Crown as the murder weapon may have been found in a hiding place that was discovered only because it was disclosed in the accused's compelled testimony when he was a witness in earlier proceedings against a person charged with the same crime. In this example, the murder weapon would not be excluded by s. 13, but it will be excluded by s. 7. The basis for the accused's residual s. 7 right to exclude the evidence is that it would be a breach of fundamental justice for the Crown to make use of evidence with such a direct connection to the compelled self-incriminatory testimony.

44.19 Fair trial

The principles of fundamental justice obviously require that a person accused of a crime receive a fair trial. In this respect, s. 7 overlaps with s. 11(d), which also guarantees to a person charged with an offence "a fair and public hearing by an independent and impartial tribunal".[240]

---

237 [1995] 4 S.C.R. 154. La Forest J. wrote the opinion of the Court.

238 Chapter 51, Self-Incrimination, below.

239 *B.C. Securities Commn.* v. *Branch*, note 235, above, 13-14, interpreting *R.* v. *S.(R. J.)* [1995] 1 S.C.R. 451.

240 Section 7 will be applicable only if the offence is punishable by imprisonment, which is a deprivation of "liberty." Section 11(d) will be applicable even if the offence is only punishable

The right to a fair trial does not mean that all existing rules of procedure and evidence that are directed to a fair trial are constitutionalized and consequently immutable. The Supreme Court of Canada has upheld a provision of the Criminal Code that allows for the videotaping of the evidence of a witness who is under the age of 18, so that at the trial the witness need only adopt the contents of the tape instead of going over the whole story again.[241] The Court has also upheld another provision that allows a witness under the age of 18 to testify from behind a one-way screen, so that the witness cannot see the accused (although the accused can see the witness).[242] The Court upheld these departures from the traditional trial format on the ground that they would reduce the stress on young witnesses and enhance the reliability of their evidence. In both cases, the accused's right to cross-examine the witness was preserved. Neither innovation prejudiced the fairness of the trial in any other respect. However, if an unforeseen case should arise in which the use of the videotape or the screen would prejudice the fairness of the trial, the Court took comfort from the fact that the trial judge had been given a discretion to deny the use of the videotape or screen in that case.

In *R.* v. *Seaboyer* (1991),[243] the Supreme Court of Canada held that both ss. 7 and 11(d) guaranteed to an accused "the right to present full answer and defence". The Court by a majority held that this right was abridged by a "rape-shield" provision in the Criminal Code, which restricted the right of a person charged with sexual assault to cross-examine the complainant about her past sexual activity. According to McLachlin J. for the majority, this provision would occasionally have the effect of excluding relevant evidence that was required to enable the accused to make full answer and defence.[244] According to L'Heureux-Dubé J. for the dissenting minority, the rape-shield provision would exclude only evidence that was either irrelevant or so prejudicial to the fairness of the trial that it could properly be excluded. The majority view prevailed, of course, and the rape-shield provision was struck from the Criminal Code.[245]

---

by a fine. A civil action for damages is not caught by either s. 7 or s. 11(d): *Wittman* v. *Emmott* (1991) 77 D.L.R. (4th) 77 (B.C.C.A.); *Budge* v. *Alta.* (1991) 77 D.L.R. (4th) 361 (Alta. C.A.).

241 *R.* v. *L.(D.O.)* [1993] 4 S.C.R. 419.

242 *R.* v. *Levogiannis* [1993] 4 S.C.R. 475.

243 [1991] 2 S.C.R. 577.

244 Cf. *R.* v. *Corbett* [1988] 1 S.C.R. 670 (no breach of fundamental justice to allow Crown to question accused about previous convictions for the purpose of assessing credibility); *R.* v. *Potvin* [1989] 1 S.C.R. 525 (no breach of fundamental justice to admit at trial Crown evidence given at preliminary inquiry, provided accused had an opportunity to cross-examine at preliminary inquiry).

245 Parliament subsequently replaced the rape-shield provisions with a set of provisions that closely followed the principles laid down in the majority judgment in *Seaboyer*: S.C. 1992, c. 38, s. 2, amending s. 276 of the Criminal Code. The new provisions render inadmissible any of the complainant's past sexual history either with a third party or with the accused. The latter exclusion is a significant step beyond the legislation that was struck down in *Seaboyer*, which rendered inadmissible all of the past sexual history of the complainant *except* that between the complainant and the accused. In order to comply with the Charter, however, the new provisions

Criminal proceedings are unlike civil proceedings in that there is no statutory provision for pre-trial discovery in criminal proceedings. In most jurisdictions, however, a practice of voluntary disclosure by the Crown developed. In *R.* v. *Stinchcombe* (1991)[246] the Supreme Court of Canada held that pre-trial disclosure by the Crown[247] of all information relevant to the conduct of the defence[248] is a constitutional obligation, entailed by the accused's right to make full answer and defence.[249] The obligation applies not only to statements obtained from witnesses that the Crown intends to call at trial, but also to statements obtained from persons that the Crown does not intend to call as witnesses.[250] The breadth of the duty is demonstrated by this case, where the Crown had failed to disclose statements obtained from a person whom the Crown did not call as a witness. The person had in fact testified at the preliminary inquiry so that her existence, identity and the general nature of her knowledge were all known to the defence, who could obviously have called her as a witness. Nevertheless, the Court held that the defence's right to make full answer and defence might have been impaired by the failure of the Crown to produce to the defence statements derived from Crown interviews of the person.[251] The Court ordered a new trial.[252]

---

essentially give the trial judge the discretion to determine whether evidence of the complainant's past sexual history should be admitted, in exception to the general rule, in circumstances where it is ''relevant to an issue at trial'' and ''has significant probative value that is not substantially outweighed by the danger of prejudice to the proper administration of justice''. This exception requires judges to rule on the admissibility of the evidence at the beginning of the trial, which not only requires some speculation as to the probable course of the defence, but also potentially biases the trier of fact against the complainant on the basis of evidence that is later found to be irrelevant.

246 [1991] 3 S.C.R. 326. The opinion of the Court was written by Sopinka J.

247 ''In contrast, the defence has no obligation to assist the prosecution and is entitled to assume a purely adversarial role towards the prosecution.'': *Id.*, 333, but note passage earlier on same page reserving question whether ''the duty should be reciprocal''.

248 There is no duty to disclose irrelevant information, or privileged information; and the Crown retains a discretion as to the timing of disclosure, since premature disclosure could impede an ongoing investigation: *Id.*, 339.

249 *Id.*, 336, referring to s. 7, but not s. 11(d); and see also 342, referring again only to s. 7, and indicating some doubt as to the application of the duty to summary conviction offences (as opposed to the indictable offences in issue in the case).

250 Note however that the Crown does not have an obligation to ''produce'' its witnesses for oral discovery by the accused; the Crown cannot control people as it can physical evidence: *R.* v. *Khela* [1995] 4 S.C.R. 201, para. 18 per Sopinka and Iacobucci JJ. for a Court that was unanimous on this point.

251 Accord, *R.* v. *Egger* [1993] 2 S.C.R. 451 (Crown must disclose to accused its possession of a second blood sample and its availability to the accused, even though the Criminal Code prescribed that Crown must take second sample to permit analysis by accused); *R.* v. *Durette* [1994] 1 S.C.R. 469 (excessive editing of wiretap affidavits before disclosure to accused held to be a denial of right to make full answer and defence.); *R.* v. *Chaplin* [1995] 1 S.C.R. 727 (Crown need not disclose whether accused had been target of wiretap when accused had failed to establish that the fact was potentially relevant to the defence).

252 Cf. *R.* v. *Swain* [1991] 1 S.C.R. 933, 972 (Crown's presentation of evidence of accused's

In *R.* v. *O'Connor* (1995),[253] the Supreme Court of Canada had to consider whether an accused's constitutional right to make full answer and defence included a right to obtain documents which were not in the Crown's possession, but were held by third parties. The case arose out of charges of rape and indecent assault brought against a Catholic Bishop who had been the principal of a native residential school at the time of the alleged offences. The complainants were four women, all former students who were employees of the school at the time. The accused sought an order requiring disclosure of the complainants' counsellors' records, medical records and school records, all of which were in the possession of third parties. Because these records were not in the possession of the Crown, *Stinchcombe* imposed no obligation on the Crown to disclose them, which the Crown would in any case be unable to do. As well, the fact that the records were not in the possession of the Crown meant that they were not being relied upon by the Crown, so that they did not form part of the accused's ''case to meet'', and therefore might not be necessary for full answer and defence. Furthermore, the disclosure of the records would implicate constitutional rights besides those of the accused. The complainants, in common with other witnesses, had a right to a reasonable expectation of privacy in the confidential records of persons and institutions who had provided counselling and medical advice.[254] The Court also appreciated that there was a risk of a breach of equality rights: disclosure in sexual assault cases would bear disproportionately on women and could be premised on discriminatory stereotypes about how past sexual activity or psychological counselling might affect issues of consent and credibility.[255]

The Court held unanimously that access to private records in the possession of third parties *could* be necessary to an accused's right to make full answer and defence. However, this did not give an accused person an automatic right of access to the records. Rather, the Court ruled that production must be governed by a procedure which would strike the proper balance between full answer and defence on the one hand, and the witness's privacy and equality rights on the other. The Court in *O'Connor* divided five to four over how to achieve this balance.[256] The majority view was as follows. The defence must apply to the trial

---

insanity against wish of accused violates s. 7, because it is a basic tenet of the legal system that ''an accused person have the right to control his or her own defence''.)

253 [1995] 4 S.C.R. 411. *A.(L.L.)* v. *B.(A.)* [1995] 4 S.C.R. 536 was a companion case, also involving sexual assault charges, which was decided at the same time with the same outcome.

254 The source of this right was not entirely clear. L'Heureux-Dubé J. ([1995] 4 S.C.R. 411, paras. 110-119) placed it in s. 7; the others were not specific as to its source.

255 L'Heureux-Dubé J., referring to the ''rape shield'' provision of the Criminal Code, which restricts the evidence which may be adduced in court about a complainant's sexual activities, stated that ''we must not allow the defence to do indirectly what it cannot do directly'': [1995] 4 S.C.R. 411, para. 122.

256 The majority opinion on this issue was that of Lamer C.J. and Sopinka J., which attracted the support of Cory, Iacobucci, and Major JJ. The main dissenting opinion was that of L'Heureux-Dubé J., which was concurred in by La Forest and Gonthier JJ. McLachlin J. wrote a separate dissent in which she agreed wholly with L'Heureux-Dubé J.

judge for a disclosure order, and must establish on a balance of probabilities that the records are "likely relevant" to making full answer and defence. If likely relevance is established, the records must be produced into court, but at this stage only for the private inspection of the judge. The judge must inspect the records and determine whether a disclosure order should be made. That determination should be made only after considering the following five factors: (1) the records' importance for full answer and defence; (2) their "probative value"; (3) the nature and extent of privacy vested in them; (4) whether production would be premised on a discriminatory belief or bias; and (5) the effect that production would have on a witness's dignity, privacy and security of the person.[257] In this way, the majority of the Court[258] sought to accommodate the competing values. *O'Connor* makes clear that the right to make full answer and defence is not an absolute right, but one that must at times yield to other constitutional values.

44.20 Fair administrative procedures

Earlier in this chapter we noticed the debate on the question whether "fundamental justice" in s. 7 was synonymous with "natural justice" at common law. That debate was settled by the *B.C. Motor Vehicle Reference*,[259] which held that s. 7 extended to substantive as well as procedural justice. As the bulk of this chapter illustrates, s. 7 goes far beyond natural justice, which is a requirement that administrative tribunals observe rules of *procedural* fairness.[260] However, s. 7 also includes a requirement of procedural fairness.[261] This requirement attaches only where a decision-maker has a power of decision over life, liberty or security of the person.[262] Where this is so, s. 7 will impose rules of procedural

257 Security of the person would be threatened if disclosure would cause psychological harm to the witness: see sec. 44.8, "Security of the person", at note 46, above.

258 L'Heureux-Dubé J., dissenting on this issue, took the view that the records should not be produced in court for inspection on the sole basis of likely relevance. She would have had the trial judge balance the salutary and deleterious effects of production into court *before* deciding to examine the records. With respect to the balancing process, she would have added two additional factors to the five stipulated by the majority, namely, (1) society's interest in encouraging the reporting of sexual offences, and (2) the integrity of the trial process. If a trial judge decided that the documents should be produced into court for inspection, L'Heureux-Dubé J. would have had the judge then reconsider all seven factors before deciding whether to make the order for disclosure which would release the records to defence counsel.

259 Note 71, above.

260 Note 67, above.

261 *Singh* v. *Minr. of Emplt. and Imm.* [1985] 1 S.C.R. 177, 212 per Wilson J.; *Pearlman* v. *Man. Law Society* [1991] 2 S.C.R. 869, 882 per Iacobucci J.; *Idziak* v. *Can.* [1992] 3 S.C.R. 631, 656 per Cory J.

262 This explains the continuing significance of s. 2(e) of the Canadian Bill of Rights, which imposes on federal decision-makers with power to determine "rights and obligations" a duty to observe the procedural side of fundamental justice: *Singh* v. *Minr. of Emplt. and Imm.* [1985] 1 S.C.R. 177; *MacBain* v. *Lederman* [1985] 1 F.C. 856 (C.A.).

fairness on the decision-maker. Those rules are probably the same as those that would be required by the common law. The common law rules are in fact basic tenets of the legal system, and they have evolved in response to the same values and objectives as s. 7.[263] Of course, common law rules of procedural fairness must yield to any inconsistent statutory provision. Where s. 7 applies, the rules of procedural fairness have constitutional status and will prevail over inconsistent statutory provisions.[264]

---

263 Note 261, above, the latter citation in that note relying on Evans, ''The Principles of Fundamental Justice'' (1991) 29 Osgoode Hall L.J. 51.

264 *Singh* v. *Minr. of Emplmt. and Imm.* [1985] 1 S.C.R. 177 (striking down refugee-determination provisions of Immigration Act; Wilson J. for half the Court used s. 7; Beetz J. for the other half used s. 2(e)); *R.* v. *Swain* [1991] 1 S.C.R. 933 (striking down insanity procedures of Criminal Code). As to whether s. 1 could save a law that denied a principle of fundamental justice, see sec. 44.3, ''Application of s. 1'', above.

45

Unreasonable Search or Seizure

45.1 Section 8 of Charter

Section 8 of the Charter of Rights[1] provides as follows:

> 8. Everyone has the right to be secure against unreasonable search or seizure.

---

1 For commentary on s. 8, see Beaudoin and Mendes (eds.), *The Canadian Charter of Rights and Freedoms* (3rd ed., 1996), 10-1–10-61 (by Chevrette and Cyr); Hutchison and Morton, *Search and Seizure Law in Canada* (Carswell, loose-leaf); Finkelstein and Finkelstein, *Constitutional Rights in the Investigative Process* (1991), ch. 4; Stuart, *Charter Justice in Canadian Criminal Law* (2nd ed., 1996), ch. 3; Fontana, *The Law of Search and Seizure in Canada* (4th ed., 1997); McLeod, Takach, Morton, Segal, *The Canadian Charter of Rights* (Carswell, loose-leaf), ch. 6; *Canadian Charter of Rights Annotated* (Canada Law Book, loose-leaf), annotation to s. 8; the last work provides a bibliography of the relevant literature.

Section 8 guarantees the right to be secure against unreasonable search or seizure.

Section 8 imposes a requirement of reasonableness on the techniques available to the police (or other agents of the state) to look for and obtain evidence of crime (or other legal wrong). When a breach of s. 8 occurs, any evidence discovered by the unreasonable search or seizure has obviously been obtained in breach of the Charter of Rights. This does not necessarily render the evidence inadmissible. Section 24(2) of the Charter provides that evidence obtained in breach of the Charter of Rights shall be excluded only if its admission would bring the administration of justice into disrepute. Section 24(2) is the topic of chapter 38, Exclusion of Evidence, above. As that chapter shows, if the police acted in good faith and were unaware that they were acting in violation of the Charter, courts will sometimes admit evidence obtained in breach of s. 8. However, a deliberate violation of the Charter, and any violation of settled law (which the police are assumed to be aware of), will nearly always lead to exclusion. Thus, s. 24(2) does not operate to license searches or seizures that are unreasonable according to settled law. For practical purposes, it is reasonably safe to assume that once the Court has characterized a particular investigatory technique as an unreasonable search or seizure that technique is then foreclosed to the police.

Legislation can sometimes overcome a judicial ruling that a particular investigatory technique violates s. 8. Of course, no law can override s. 8, but a law can introduce safeguards, perhaps in the form of a requirement of a warrant to be issued by a court on the basis of reasonable and probable grounds. As later sections of this chapter will show, safeguards of this kind would normally convert an unreasonable search or seizure into a reasonable one.

It is theoretically possible that a law that provides for an "unreasonable" search or seizure could still be upheld as a "reasonable" limit under s. 1 of the Charter. There is no illustrative case, but it is possible to imagine a law that fails the special requirement of reasonableness in s. 8, and yet passes the general requirement of reasonableness in s. 1.[2]

45.2 Common Law

The common law rule is that a police officer or government official has no authority to enter private property for the purpose of searching for evidence, and no authority to seize private property for use as evidence, unless authorized by law. The common law itself authorized search for, and seizure of, evidence without warrant as an incident of a lawful arrest,[3] and it authorized search for, and seizure of, stolen goods upon a warrant issued by a justice upon sworn evidence that there was strong cause to believe that the goods were concealed in

2 See ch. 35, Limitation of Rights, under heading 35.14, "Application to qualified rights", above.

3 A search incident to a lawful arrest is still governed by the common law in Canada; the law is reviewed in *Cloutier* v. *Langlois* [1990] 1 S.C.R. 158.

the place to be searched. But, aside from these two situations, the famous case of *Entick* v. *Carrington* (1765)[4] established that even the officers of the King, authorized by a minister of the King, could not enter upon private property to search for evidence of crime.

The common law continues to apply in the common law provinces of Canada[5] unless it has been overridden by statute. In a system of parliamentary sovereignty, common law safeguards can be overridden by statute. In every jurisdiction in Canada, many powers of search and seizure have been created by statute, and some do omit safeguards such as the requirement of a warrant.[6] Section 8 now limits the power of Canadian legislative bodies, by prohibiting ''unreasonable'' searches and seizures.

45.3 Fourth Amendment of U.S. Constitution

The American Bill of Rights, by the fourth amendment (applicable to the states by the fourteenth amendment), provides:

> The right of the people to be secure in their persons, houses, paper, and effects, against unreasonable searches and seizures, shall not be violated, and no warrants shall issue, but upon probable cause, supported by oath or affirmation, and particularly describing the place to be searched, and the persons or things to be seized.

The fourth amendment is like s. 8 of the Charter in its prohibition of unreasonable searches and seizures.[7] But s. 8 has no equivalent of the fourth amendment's explicit requirements of judicial authorization for each search and seizure, a standard of ''probable cause'', and particularity in the description of the place to be searched and the things to be seized. These requirements would obviously defeat ''writs of assistance'', which are described later in this chapter,[8] and indeed the use of writs of assistance was one of the grievances of the American colonists leading to the revolution. However, the Supreme Court of the United States has carved out a variety of exceptions to the warrant requirement, including a search incident to a lawful arrest,[9] a search conducted in the course of a ''hot pursuit'',[10] a ''stop and frisk'' search for concealed weapons,[11] a search of a vehicle which could be quickly removed from police surveillance,[12] a search at the international

4 (1765) 19 St. Tr. 1030; 95 E.R. 807 (K.B.).

5 *R.* v. *Kokesch* [1990] 3 S.C.R. 3 (entry by police on private property without statutory authority prohibited by common law).

6 A list of federal powers to search without a warrant is appended to *R.* v. *Rao* (1984) 46 O.R. (2d) 80 111 (C.A.).

7 For commentary on the fourth amendment, see LaFave, *Search and Seizure* (3rd ed., 1996); LaFave and Israel, *Criminal Procedure* (2nd ed., 1992), chs. 3-4.

8 Section 45.7(e), ''Writs of assistance'', below.

9 *Chimel* v. *California* (1969) 395 U.S. 752.

10 *Warden* v. *Hayden* (1967) 387 U.S. 294.

11 *Terry* v. *Ohio* (1968) 392 U.S. 1.

12 *Carroll* v. *United States* (1925) 267 U.S. 132.

border[13] and a seizure of evidence "in plain view".[14] The lesson from the American experience is that criteria of reasonableness are bound to be somewhat flexible, since they must take account of not only an individual's right to privacy and peaceful enjoyment of property but also the practicalities of law enforcement.

45.4 Search or seizure

(a) Definitions

A search is an examination, by the agents of the state, of a person's person or property in order to look for evidence. A seizure is the actual taking away, by the agents of the state, of things[15] that could be used as evidence.[16]

The word "seizure" in s. 8 takes its colour from its association with the word "search". A seizure within the meaning of s. 8 is a seizure of property for investigatory or evidentiary purposes. Section 8 is not a general guarantee of property rights, filling the gap created by the omission of property rights from s. 7. For example, s. 8 does not extend to the taking of property by expropriation.[17]

The word "seizure" is also affected by its context within the Charter of Rights. While it is clear that the word "search" will extend to searches of persons[18] as well as of property, the word "seizure" only extends to seizures of property. The seizure of a person would be a detention or imprisonment, and s. 9 of the Charter guarantees "the right not to be arbitrarily detained or imprisoned".[19]

(b) From property to privacy

The reason why the common law imposed such strict restrictions on searches and seizures[20] was because they involved an invasion of property rights: an entry

13 *Almeida-Sanchez* v. *United States* (1973) 413 U.S. 266.

14 *Texas* v. *Brown* (1983) 103 S.Ct. 1535.

15 A seizure involves the taking of a thing, which includes a document; but an order to testify is not a seizure: *Thomson Newspapers* v. *Can* [1990] 1 S.C.R. 425, 569-570 per L'Heureux-Dubé J. (there is general agreement on this point).

16 *R.* v. *Dyment* [1988] 2 S.C.R. 417, 431 per La Forest J. ("As I see it, the essence of a seizure under s. 8 is the taking of a thing from a person by a public authority without that person's consent".).

17 *Re Becker* (1983) 148 D.L.R. (3d) 539 (Alta. C.A.).

18 Cf. *R.* v. *Alderton* (1985) 49 O.R. (2d) 257 (C.A.) (search incidental to a lawful arrest can include taking samples of accused's hair).

19 In the United States, the fourth amendment's prohibition of "unreasonable searches and seizures" applies to seizures of the person, that is, detentions and arrests, as well as to seizures of property: La Fave and Israel, *Criminal Procedure* (2nd ed, 1992), ch. 3. But the Constitution of the United States, unlike the Charter, contains no separate provisions regarding detentions and arrests. Cf. *R.* v. *Silveira* [1995] 2 S.C.R. 297, para. 44 per La Forest J. dissenting (obiter suggestion that "securing" a house, including restraints on the movement of persons in the house, constitutes a seizure of the entire household).

20 Section 45.2, "Common law", above.

onto private premises was a trespass, and the taking away of goods or papers was a conversion. However, neither the eye nor the ear could by themselves commit a trespass or a conversion, so that there was no prohibition on anything seen or heard by the agents of the state that did not result from an invasion of property rights. The protection of property rights was the rationale for, and the organizing principle of, the common law prohibition of search or seizure.

Property has now been replaced by privacy as the value protected by the law of search and seizure. This important change took place in the United States in a case called *Katz* v. *United States* (1967).[21] In that case, police had placed an electronic bug (listening device) on the outside of a public telephone booth, and had listened in to and recorded the accused's end of a telephone conversation that he made from the telephone booth. The question was whether the recording of the accused's conversation had been obtained in breach of the fourth amendment, which (as noted earlier) prohibits "unreasonable searches and seizures". If the fourth amendment covered only an invasion of property rights, then it was inapplicable here, because the telephone booth was public property, and the police did not even enter the booth to plant the bug. The Supreme Court of the United States held that the fourth amendment was not confined to the protection of property. On the contrary, the Court held that "the fourth amendment protects people, not places".[22] In this case, although there had been no trespass, there had been an invasion of a reasonable expectation of privacy upon which the accused had relied in using the telephone booth. This invasion of privacy was a "search and seizure" forbidden by the fourth amendment.

The Supreme Court of Canada has enthusiastically embraced the privacy rationale for the guarantee against unreasonable search or seizure. The first case under s. 8 to reach the Canadian Court was *Hunter* v. *Southam* (1984),[23] which was a challenge to a search and seizure authorized by the federal Combines Investigation Act. The Court followed *Katz* v. *United States* to hold that the guarantee against unreasonable search or seizure in s. 8, like its American counterpart, protected a "reasonable expectation of privacy".[24] In *Hunter* v. *Southam*, there was an actual entry on the business premises of a corporation, and so the issue of the outer limits of s. 8 did not have to be decided. However, the Court assumed without discussion that a corporation possessed the same constitutionally protected expectation of privacy as an individual. For reasons that will be explained later in this chapter, the Court held that s. 8 had been infringed.

In *R.* v. *Plant* (1993),[25] the Calgary police, who suspected the accused of cultivating marijuana in the basement of his home, looked up the records of the

---

21 (1967) 389 U.S. 347.

22 *Id.*, 351.

23 [1984] 2 S.C.R. 145.

24 *Id.*, 159.

25 [1993] 3 S.C.R. 281. The Court was unanimous on the outcome, but the issue discussed in the text divided the seven-judge bench, with Sopinka J.'s opinion attracting the support of five others, and McLachlin J. writing a separate opinion.

City of Calgary's electricity utility, and found that the accused's consumption of electricity was four times higher than that of comparable homeowners. The electricity records were stored in the City's computer to which the police had access through a terminal located at the police station. The City had agreed to give the police access to its computerized records. The accused had not been asked, and, at his trial for the unlawful cultivation of marijuana, he argued that the police inspection of the City's computerized records was an unreasonable search under s. 8. There had, of course, been no entry onto private property, and no inspection of the accused's own private records. The Supreme Court of Canada held unanimously that an individual would have a reasonable expectation of privacy with respect to computerized information that was "personal and confidential". But the Court divided on the correct characterization of information about electricity consumption. Sopinka J., for the majority, held that the information was not personal and confidential, because electricity consumption reveals so little about "the personal lifestyle or private decisions of the occupant of the residence".[26] McLachlin J. disagreed; she took the view that the records disclosed enough information about the lifestyle of the occupant that the occupant had a reasonable expectation that the records would be used solely for the purpose of supplying and billing for electricity.[27] In the result, the majority view prevailed: there was no reasonable expectation of privacy with respect to the records, and therefore the police had not made an unreasonable search within the meaning of s. 8.

In *R.* v. *Dersch* (1993),[28] the police requested from a hospital the results of a blood alcohol test that had been done, for medical reasons, on the victim of a highway accident. A doctor at the hospital prepared a report on the level of alcohol in the victim's blood, including the diagnosis that the victim had been intoxicated at the time of his admission to the hospital. This report was given to the police, who charged the accident victim with impaired driving. The accused, who had not agreed to the release of the information, claimed that the police had made an unreasonable search under s. 8. The case was very similar to *Plant*, in that the police had been provided with the evidence by the voluntary act of a third party, and had made no entry onto the accused's property and no inspection of the accused's own records. In this case, however, the Supreme Court of Canada held that the accused had a reasonable expectation of privacy with respect to his hospital records, including the blood alcohol test results, which he was justified in assuming would be kept confidential by the hospital. Therefore, the obtaining of the information by the police was an unreasonable search within the meaning of s. 8.[29] Other cases have confirmed the rule that a search or seizure need not

---

26 *Id.*, 293.

27 *Id.*, 302.

28 [1993] 3 S.C.R. 768. The majority opinion was written by Major J. L'Heureux Dubé and Gonthier JJ. wrote concurring opinions. On the issue discussed in the text, the Court was unanimous.

29 The Court excluded the evidence under s. 24(2) on the basis that its admission would bring the administration of justice into disrepute.

involve an entry onto property or a forced taking of property: it is the invasion of a reasonable expectation of privacy that constitutes the search or seizure.[30]

(c) Gathering evidence

In *R.* v. *Dyment* (1988),[31] a doctor collected a vial of blood from the freely flowing wound of an unconscious traffic accident victim. The sample was taken for medical purposes. However, the doctor gave the vial to a police officer, who had it analyzed; and, as a result of the analysis, the victim was charged with impaired driving. The question was whether there had been an infringement of s. 8. It was clear that there had been no ''search'' within s. 8, because the initial collection of the blood had been done by the doctor, acting on medical grounds; and the Charter had no application to such a private act.[32] However, the Supreme Court of Canada held that s. 8 contemplated that there could be a ''seizure'' without a search. The Court held that a seizure did take place when the police officer obtained the vial from the doctor. Although the vial was voluntarily handed over by the doctor, this was done without the knowledge or consent of the accused. The accused had ''a reasonable expectation of privacy'' with respect to the vial; and the police infringement of that expectation of privacy was a seizure within s. 8. The Court went on to hold that the seizure was unreasonable, because it had been made without a warrant.[33] Therefore, there was a breach of s. 8.

In *Dyment*, the Court distinguished the case where the police obtained a sample of blood from the front seat of the vehicle that the accident victim was driving. In that case, the accused had ''abandoned his blood''; he had ''ceased to have a reasonable expectation of privacy with respect to it''. Therefore, the evidence was ''gathered'' from the vehicle, not seized.[34] The presence of a reasonable expectation of privacy thus became the dividing line between a *seizure* of evidence, to which s. 8 was potentially applicable, and a *gathering* of evidence, to which s. 8 had no application.

Evidence that is voluntarily given up by an accused person is obviously not seized. However, the courts will treat a giving up of evidence as voluntary only

---

30 *R.* v. *Colarusso* [1994] 1 S.C.R. 20 (blood and urine samples taken by hospital with consent for medical purposes; samples validly seized by coroner for investigation of a death; samples given by coroner to police; held, unreasonable seizure by police); *R.* v. *Borden* [1994] 3 S.C.R. 145 (blood sample taken by police with consent for investigation of offence A, and used by police for investigation of offence B; held, latter use an unreasonable seizure by police; query correctness).

31 [1988] 2 S.C.R. 417. Lamer J., with the concurrence of Beetz and Wilson JJ., and La Forest J., with the consent of Dickson C.J., wrote the majority opinions. McIntyre J. dissented.

32 The taking by the police of a blood sample from a person, without the consent of the person, for use in evidence, would be a search or seizure within s. 8: *R.* v.*Dyment* [1988] 2 S.C.R. 417, 431.

33 Cf. *R.* v.*Katsigiorgis* (1987) 62 O.R. (2d) 441 (C.A.) (blood sample taken by hospital for medical purposes can be seized from hospital pursuant to a search warrant).

34 [1985] 2 S.C.R. 417, 435.

if the accused was aware of the purpose for which the evidence was to be used. Thus, a consent to the taking of a blood or urine sample by a hospital for medical purposes is not a consent to the use of the sample by the police for the purpose of investigating or proving the commission of a crime. Even when the police obtained the sample by the voluntary act of the hospital (or anyone other than the accused), their obtaining of the property is still deemed to be a seizure .... because it invades a reasonable expectation of privacy on the part of the accused. The seizure will be reasonable within s. 8 if it was authorized by a search warrant,[35] but it will be unreasonable if it was not authorized by a search warrant.[36]

(d) Plain view

A person has no reasonable expectation of privacy in respect of things that are in plain view. If a police officer on a public road observes a field of marijuana simply by looking over a fence, the police officer is not engaged in a search. Nor should it make any difference which of the senses has been used to detect something. A police officer does not engage in a search simply by hearing a gunshot or a cry for help. Nor is there a search if a police officer smells gunpowder or blood. So long as the police officer is lawfully present at the vantage point, the use of any of the senses of sight, hearing or smell is not a search; no warrant or other justification is required for the use of any of the senses. (In order to *seize* an object in plain view, a warrant is normally required, and the sensory observations of the police officer will provide the evidence to obtain the warrant.)[37]

The foregoing propositions are well settled in American jurisprudence,[38] and seem so obvious that they must be the law of Canada as well. However, it is necessary to report the strange decision in *R.* v. *Evans* (1996).[39] In that case, the police had received a tip from an unidentified informer that the accused couple were growing marijuana in the basement of their home. The police attempted to verify the tip by checking electricity consumption, and by observing the house from the street, but these steps disclosed nothing. As a last resort, the police decided to knock on the door of the house and (if anyone answered) to question

---

35 Note 33, above.

36 *R.* v. *Dersch*, note 28, above; *R.* v. *Colarusso*, note 30, above; *R.* v. *Borden*, note 30, above.

37 In certain circumstances, American courts have permitted the warrantless seizure of an object in "plain view": W.R. LaFave, *Search and Seizure* (3rd ed., 1996), vol. 1, 396-7; see also note 14. In this situation, the taking of the item is a seizure, albeit one that needs no warrant. As LaFave points out, this is an entirely different doctrine than the rule, also well established in American law, and also described as the "plain view" doctrine, that the observation by the unaided senses of an object in plain view requires no warrant, because it is not a search at all: LaFave, above, 396.

38 LaFave, previous note, vol. 1, 396.

39 [1996] 1 S.C.R. 8. The principal majority opinion was written by Sopinka J. with the agreement of Cory and Iacobucci; La Forest J. wrote a short concurring opinion. The dissenting opinion was written by Major J. with the agreement of Gonthier and L'Heureux-Dubé JJ.

the occupants. Two police officers did knock on the door of the house; it was opened by one of the accused; and when the door was opened the police officers smelled marijuana. They immediately arrested the accused. They applied for a search warrant, and after the warrant was obtained they searched the house, finding marijuana plants and drug paraphernalia. The Supreme Court of Canada unanimously agreed that the police officers had the right to knock on the door of the house and ask questions of the occupants. However, the majority of the Court held that the smelling of the marijuana was a search, and since the initial smell was not authorized by a search warrant, it was an unreasonable search in breach of s. 8 of the Charter. The subsequent search warrant did not cure the violation, because without the olfactory observation the only basis for suspicion was the anonymous tip which by itself would not have been a sufficient basis for the issue of the warrant.

Catch-22 is the only message that the unfortunate police officers can take from this decision. Before going to the front door they had insufficient evidence to obtain a warrant, and after going to the front door, when they had sufficient evidence, they were not allowed to use their observations to obtain a warrant! Moreover, only those engaged in illegal activities can benefit from the decision. No civil libertarian value was at stake, since the police were not asserting any right to enter the house without a warrant or to require answers to their questions from the occupants. No law-abiding person would object to a visit from the police under these conditions.[40] Surely, the correct answer was the one given in dissent by Major J. Since the police were lawfully at the front door of the house, it was not a search to make use of their sense of smell from that vantage point. Nor would it have been a search if the police had observed a dead body that had been lying in plain view of the doorway. When the police knock on the door of a suspect's house to ask questions, it is ridiculous to require them to close their eyes and block their noses. But if they fail to do that, according to the majority, they run the risk that they will detect something of evidentiary value, which would be an unreasonable search in breach of s. 8 of the Charter.

45.5 Electronic surveillance

(a) Third party surveillance

The Supreme Court of Canada has followed the American decision in *Katz* v. *United States*[41] to hold that electronic surveillance is a search or seizure within

40 The majority held that the evidence should be admitted, because the police acted in good faith and its admission would not bring the administration of justice into disrepute. This avoided an acquittal in the case, but now that the law is settled the police will have to follow the settled law, and evidence of police sight or smell would be excluded in future cases.

41 Note 21, above.

s. 8, just as it is within the fourth amendment.[42] The basis for this conclusion is that the purpose of the prohibition on unreasonable search or seizure is to protect a reasonable expectation of privacy. A reasonable expectation of privacy is violated when a third party intercepts a telephone conversation without the knowledge or consent of the participants.[43] The Criminal Code does, however, make provision for the electronic interception of private telephone conversations (wiretaps) under a warrant issued by a superior court judge based on reasonable and probable grounds. When the Criminal Code's regime of judicial authorization is complied with, the wiretap, although obviously still a search and seizure, is not only lawful but is not unreasonable under s. 8.[44]

The previous paragraph deals with "third party" electronic surveillance, where none of the participants to a conversation or transaction has knowledge of, or has given consent to, the surreptitious eavesdropping or recording. It was a third party surveillance that prompted the decision of the Supreme Court of the United States in *Katz* v. *United States*;[45] the police interception of the accused's telephone call in that case was unknown to both the accused and the person on the other end of the line. That was an invasion of the accused's reasonable expectation of privacy, and was therefore a search or seizure.

(b) Participant surveillance

"Participant" electronic surveillance is the case where one of the participants consents to the surreptitious electronic recording of a conversation or transaction. In *R.* v. *Duarte* (1990),[46] a police informer allowed the police to instal secret audio-visual equipment in his apartment, and he consented to the recording of a drug transaction that took place with the accused in the apartment. In a companion case, *R.* v. *Wiggins* (1990),[47] a police informer wore a concealed body pack which transmitted to the police the informer's conversations with the accused about drug dealings. In both these cases, a majority of the Supreme Court of Canada held that the surreptitious electronic surveillance was an unreasonable search or seizure under s. 8. The majority refused to draw any distinction between participant electronic surveillance (these cases) and third party electronic surveillance (*Katz*). In both situations, the surreptitious recording invaded a reasonable expectation of privacy.

---

42 *R.* v. *Duarte* [1990] 1 S.C.R. 30.

43 *R.* v. *Thompson* [1990] 2 S.C.R. 1111.

44 *Ibid.*; *R.* v. *Garofoli* [1990] 2 S.C.R. 1421; *R.* v. *Lachance* [1990] 2 S.C.R. 1490; *Dersch* v. *Can.* [1990] 2 S.C.R. 1505; *R.* v. *Zito* [1990] 2 S.C.R. 1520.

45 Note 21, above.

46 [1990] 1 S.C.R. 30. La Forest J. wrote the majority opinion for himself and five others. Lamer J. held that there was no breach of s. 8.

47 [1990] 1 S.C.R. 62. The composition and voting of the bench was the same as in *Duarte*, previous note.

In any conversation, no matter how confidential its subject matter, each participant runs the risk that his interlocutor will betray the confidence by repeating the conversation to someone else. If a participant is charged with a crime, and the conversation is relevant to the charge, then his interlocutor is free to talk to the police, and to testify in court about the conversation; indeed, the interlocutor can be compelled to testify about the conversation in court. Since the disclosure of a private conversation is admissible in a court of law, then surely the recording of a conversation by a participant ought to be admissible too. The recording simply improves the participant's power of recollection, making the evidence more reliable. For this reason, the Supreme Court of the United States has held that participant surveillance is not a search and seizure within the fourth amendment.[48] When the accused discloses a confidence to someone else, he assumes the risk that his interlocutor will reveal the confidence to the police, and therefore there is no breach of a reasonable expectation of privacy when the interlocutor does reveal the confidence to the police, even when electronic aid is employed. By rejecting this distinction, the Supreme Court of Canada has produced an ironic result. The police informers in *Duarte* and *Wiggins* are free to testify in court about their conversations with the accuseds, where their memory and credibility will no doubt be challenged by the accused; but the electronic records of the conversations, which would set all doubts at rest, are inadmissible![49]

In the participant surveillance cases, it is not the listening to the accused's statement that constitutes the invasion of privacy, because the police agent hears only what the accused voluntarily chooses to tell him. Nor is it the disclosure of the accused's statement to the police or a court, because the Court in *Duarte* made clear that the police agent was free to disclose what he heard or experienced. Therefore, the invasion of privacy must consist in the electronic recording or transmitting of the statement that the accused made to the police agent. If this is so, then there would be an invasion of privacy even if the electronic record was not in fact tendered in evidence. It follows that the police would be in breach of the Charter of Rights if they used a body pack or other electronic surveillance techniques for the *protection* of undercover officers or police informers. In the past, it has apparently been standard police practice to equip undercover officers or informers with radio transmitters so that dangerous situations can be monitored by a back-up squad, who are ready to rush to the rescue if needed.[50] This prudent

48 *Lopez* v. *United States* (1963) 373 U.S. 427; *United States* v. *White* (1971) 401 U.S. 745.

49 In *Duarte* and *Wiggins*, the recordings were in fact admitted, because the police had acted in good faith, and under s. 24(2) the administration of justice would not be brought into disrepute by their admission. The force of my criticism is underlined by La Forest J.'s reason for admitting the recordings: he pointed out in *Duarte* (at 59) that the police "could have proceeded without resorting to electronic surveillance and relied solely on the evidence of the undercover officer as the informer". (In future cases, now that the law is settled, the police will not be able to rely on good faith, and the evidence will be inadmissible under s. 24(2).)

50 Globe and Mail newspaper, July 26, 1991, p. A1.

practice has been outlawed by *Duarte* and *Wiggins*, because the use of the radio transmitter would be an invasion of the privacy of the police suspect.[51]

The Supreme Court of Canada was presented with an opportunity to repent of its decisions in *Duarte* and *Wiggins*, or at least to place some limits on its extravagant notion of privacy, in *R.* v. *Wong* (1990).[52] In that case, the police had installed a concealed video camera in a hotel room that was used for illegal gaming. The hotel consented to the installation of the camera. Was the tape of an illegal gambling session obtained in breach of s. 8 of the Charter? The Court answered yes, reaffirming its decisions in *Duarte* and *Wiggins*, and repeating its rejection of the theory that a participant accepts the risk of disclosure by another participant. In fact, the case is an extension of *Duarte* and *Wiggins*, where the conversations were between people who knew each other, and the conversations took place in private. Here, the camera recorded a hotel room, to which general invitations had been widely distributed, and in which a crowd of people, many of whom were strangers to each other, had gathered. The Supreme Court of Canada held by a majority[53] that the participants in the illegal gambling had a reasonable expectation of privacy in the hotel room[54] that was infringed by the concealed camera. Therefore, the tape was obtained in breach of s. 8 of the Charter.[55]

---

51 The Criminal Code has been amended to provide specifically for state-initiated participant surveillance. Participant surveillance is now lawful as long as peace officers obtain prior judicial authorization based on reasonable grounds: S.C. 1993, c. 40, s. 4, adding ss. 184.1-184.6 to the Criminal Code. In exceptional circumstances, where the peace officer believes on reasonable grounds that the urgency of the situation is such that an authorization could not be obtained ''with reasonable diligence'', the peace officer may resort to participant surveillance without prior judicial authorization. Participant surveillance without prior judicial authorization is also allowed where the agent of the state ''believes on reasonable grounds that there is a risk of bodily harm to the person who consented to the interception'' and ''the purpose of the interception is to prevent bodily harm''. This provision is clearly aimed at protecting undercover police officers and informers. In an effort to balance agent safety with privacy, the new legislation provides that evidence obtained in such a manner is only admissible ''for the purposes of proceedings in which actual, attempted or threatened bodily harm is alleged'', and evidence that does not suggest actual, attempted or threatened bodily harm must be destroyed.

52 [1990] 3 S.C.R. 36.

53 Lamer C.J. and McLachlin J. dissented on this issue.

54 Followed in *R.* v. *Mercer* (1992) 7 O.R. (3d) 9 (C.A.) (search of hotel room without warrant but with consent of hotel manager violated s. 8).

55 La Forest J., writing for himself and three others, held that the tape should nonetheless be admitted under s. 24(2), because its admission would not bring the administration of justice into disrepute. This was because the police had acted in good faith. Lamer C.J. and McLachlin J. also agreed with the outcome, because in their view there had been no breach of s. 8. Wilson J. would have excluded the evidence. Note that La Forest J.'s admission of the evidence was based on the case being one of first impression. With the law now settled, the police would be expected to discontinue the use of surreptitious videotaping; they could not rely on good faith again. However, since the decision in *Wong*, the Criminal Code has been amended to authorize the issue of a warrant, not only for participant surveillance (note 51, above), but also for video surveillance or the use of any other ''device or investigative technique or procedure'': S.C. 1993, c. 40, s. 15, adding ss. 487.01-487.03 to the Criminal Code.

The use of participant electronic surveillance is not totally ruled out by the decisions of the Supreme Court of Canada. The police could use the technique in a situation where there was no reasonable expectation of privacy, although *Wong* makes it difficult to be confident of where that might be. A conversation or transaction taking place on the street, in a shopping mall or in a restaurant might still be deemed to attract the Court's reasonable expectation of privacy. A *private* individual or corporation could surreptitiously record a conversation or transaction, and there would be no breach of s. 8, because the Charter of Rights applies only to governments. The robbery of a bank, a store or a home could be captured on tape by a concealed camera, and the tape (though invading the privacy of the robber) would be admissible in evidence. This would be particularly important if no one was on the premises at the time of the crime, or if the only person on the premises was killed; the tape might then be the only evidence of the crime. Note, however, that if the camera had been installed at the suggestion of the police (made perhaps after an earlier robbery), then this would probably transform the proprietor of the premises into a police agent for this purpose.[56] That would probably mean that the tape had been obtained in breach of s. 8 of the Charter,[57] rendering the evidence inadmissible.[58]

45.6 Production of documents

(a) Licences and permits

An order to produce documents is a search or seizure within s. 8, provided that there is a reasonable expectation of privacy with respect to the documents.

All provinces have legislation requiring the driver of a motor vehicle, upon demand by a police officer, to produce for inspection the driver's licence of the driver and the certificate of insurance of the vehicle. In *R.* v. *Hufsky* (1988),[59] the Ontario law was challenged by a driver, who argued that the requirement to produce his licence and certificate constituted a search,[60] and that the absence of any rules restricting the police power to demand the documents made the search

56 Cf. *R.* v. *Broyles* [1991] 3 S.C.R. 595 (friend of suspect, visiting suspect in prison at suggestion of police, and recording conversation, is a police agent).

57 There would be room for argument as to whether there was a reasonable expectation of privacy in that particular location.

58 There would be room for argument as to whether the evidence should be admitted under s. 24(2), on the ground that the police were unaware that their suggestion violated the Charter and were acting in good faith. This argument can be used in the first case to reach the Supreme Court of Canada. Once the law has been settled, the police are expected to comply.

59 [1988] 1 S.C.R. 621. Le Dain J. delivered the judgment of the Court. The decision was followed in *R.* v. *Ladouceur* [1990] 1 S.C.R. 1257 (same issue).

60 The argument that it was a search rather than a seizure presumably reflected the temporary purpose of the production, which was to enable the police officer to inspect the documents.

unreasonable. The Supreme Court of Canada held that the requirement to produce the documents was not a search within the meaning of s. 8, ''because it did not constitute an intrusion on a reasonable expectation of privacy''.[61] There was no such intrusion ''where a person is required to produce a licence or permit or other documentary evidence of a status or compliance with some legal requirement that is a lawful condition of the exercise of a right or privilege''.[62]

(b) Business records

In *Thomson Newspapers* v. *Canada* (1990),[63] a company and several of its officers were ordered by an official, exercising powers conferred by the federal Combines Investigation Act, to produce business documents in order to make them available for an inquiry into whether there had been a breach of the Act. The Supreme Court of Canada, by a majority, held that the order to produce documents was a seizure within s. 8. To be sure, there was no search, and no entry on premises, but the order was a seizure nonetheless. La Forest J. commented that there was ''little difference between taking a thing and forcing a person to give it up''.[64]

The difference between the driver's licence in *Hufsky* and the business records in *Thomson Newspapers* is that there is no reasonable expectation of privacy in a driver's licence, but there is in a business proprietor's records. However, the Court in *Thomson Newspapers* acknowledged that an order to produce documents was far less intrusive of privacy than a search of premises. Therefore, it was appropriate to insist upon a lower standard of reasonableness[65] for an order to produce documents than would be appropriate for a search or seizure involving an entry onto premises. For this reason,[66] the Court held that the order was a reasonable seizure within the meaning of s. 8, despite the fact that it had been issued by the investigating agency itself (rather than a court), and there had been no judicial finding that there were reasonable and probable grounds that an offence had been committed.

Thomson Newspapers was followed in *R.* v. *McKinlay Transport* (1990).[67] In that case, the Minister of National Revenue, exercising powers conferred by

61 [1988] 1 S.C.R. 621, 638.

62 *Ibid.*

63 [1990] 1 S.C.R. 425. Five separate opinions were written by the five judges who sat on the case. On the question whether an order to produce documents was a seizure, there was a majority of four, with only Sopinka J. dissenting.

64 [1990] 1 S.C.R. 425, 505; also, 442, 493, 592 to the same effect; Sopinka J.'s dissenting view is at 610-615.

65 The requirement of reasonableness is examined in sec. 45.7, ''Reasonableness'', below.

66 On the question whether the statute was ''regulatory'' rather than ''criminal'' (which would also lower the standard of reasonableness), the Court split two/two, Sopinka J. not having to decide the issue.

67 [1990] 1 S.C.R. 627. The composition and voting of the Court was the same as in *Thomson Newspapers*, note 62, above.

the federal Income Tax Act, ordered two companies to produce documents as part of an income tax audit. The Supreme Court of Canada held that the Minister's order was a seizure. As in the earlier case, however, the Court upheld the Minister's power as reasonable within s. 8, on the basis that there was a lower standard of reasonableness for a demand for documents[68] than for a search or seizure that involved an entry onto the taxpayer's premises.[69]

45.7 Reasonableness

(a) Requirement of warrant

When is a search or seizure "unreasonable" within the meaning of s. 8 of the Charter?

In *Hunter* v. *Southam* (1984),[70] the Supreme Court of Canada held that a power of search and seizure in the Combines Investigation Act was contrary to s. 8, because it authorized unreasonable searches and seizures. The Act authorized the Director of the Combines Investigation Branch, or his representative, "to enter any premises on which the Director believes there may be evidence relevant to [an inquiry under the Act]", to search for evidence on the premises and to seize evidence found there. The Act qualified this power by requiring the Director, before exercising the power, to obtain an authorization from a member of the Restrictive Trade Practices Commission. In this case, the statutory power had been employed to search the premises of the Edmonton Journal, one of the Southam newspapers, as part of a combines inquiry into the newspaper industry in Edmonton. The search of the newspaper's files was interrupted by Southam's application for an injunction. That application raised the constitutional question that found its way up to the Supreme Court of Canada.

The Supreme Court of Canada, in a unanimous opinion written by Dickson J., held that a search of the kind in issue was reasonable only if it were authorized by statute, and three conditions were stipulated by the authorizing statute: (1) a requirement of a search warrant or other authorization, to be obtained in advance of the search; (2) a requirement that the warrant be issued by a person who must be "capable of acting judicially", that is, who must not be involved in the investigation; and (3) a requirement that the warrant be issued only after it has been established upon oath that "reasonable and probable grounds" exist to believe that an offence has been committed and that evidence is to be found in

---

68 As well, four of the five judges (Sopinka J. not having to decide the point) agreed that the Income Tax Act was a "regulatory" statute to which lower standards of reasonableness were applicable: see sec. 45.7(d), "Regulatory inspections", below.

69 Accord, *Comité paritaire* v. *Potash* [1994] 2 S.C.R. 406 (power of labour standards inspectors to examine documents and take copies upheld); *B.C. Securities Commn.* v. *Branch* [1995] 2 S.C.R. 3 (power of securities commission to demand documents upheld). Compare *Baron* v. *Can.* [1993] 1 S.C.R. 416; discussed in text accompanying note 76, below.

70 [1984] 2 S.C.R. 145.

the place to be searched. In this case, only the first of the three conditions — the requirement of a warrant — was satisfied by the Act. The second condition — the requirement of an impartial issuer — was not satisfied: the person entitled to issue the warrant was a member of the Restrictive Trade Practices Commission, and, because that body was entrusted with investigatory functions by the Act, its members could not be sufficiently impartial in passing on the Director's application for a warrant. The third condition — the requirement of reasonable and probable cause established on oath — was also not satisfied: the Act did not stipulate upon what standard or by what means of proof the member of the Commission should decide whether there was sufficient reason to issue a warrant.

Hunter v. *Southam* establishes that a search and seizure is reasonable[71] if undertaken in compliance with a statutory power that requires (1) a prior warrant, (2) issued by an impartial arbiter, (3) on a sworn showing of reasonable and probable cause.[72] Before this decision, many lower courts had held that s. 8 required only that the courts should judge the reasonableness of any challenged search or seizure after the fact, on a case-by-case basis. Dickson C.J. said that "such a *post facto* analysis" would not adequately fulfil the purpose of s. 8, which is "to protect individuals from unjustified state intrusions upon their privacy".[73] That purpose, he held, "requires a means of preventing unjustified searches before they happen, not simply of determining, after the fact, whether they ought to have occurred in the first place".[74] Only a system of prior authorization would adequately fulfil the purpose of s. 8.

Shortly after the decision in *Hunter* v. *Southam*, the search and seizure provisions of the Income Tax Act were found to possess manifold constitutional defects. The search warrant was to be issued by a minister (not a judge); and, although a judge had to "approve" the warrant, it was the opinion of the minister (not the judge) as to the existence of reasonable and probable grounds that authorized the warrant. In addition, although the minister had to have grounds for believing that an offence had been committed, there was no requirement that the minister had grounds to believe that evidence would be found in the place to be searched. Nor was the minister required to specify the things to be searched for. Finally, although the warrant could be issued when the minister had grounds to believe that one offence had been committed, the Act gave the warrant-holder the power to search for violations of "any" of the provisions of the Act. For all these

71 In the case of a search of press premises for information gathered by reporters or film crews, the risk to freedom of expression involves additional requirements of reasonableness: *CBC* v. *Lessard* [1991] 3 S.C.R. 421; *CBC* v. *N.B.* [1991] 3 S.C.R. 459.

72 See also *R.* v. *Généreux* [1992] 1 S.C.R. 259 (striking down search warrant issued without sworn showing of reasonable and probable cause); *Baron* v. *Can.* [1993] 1 S.C.R. 416, 446-447 (holding that "reasonable grounds" were equivalent to "reasonable and probable grounds"; the former phrase implicitly imported a requirement of probability).

73 [1984] 2 S.C.R. 145, 160.

74 *Ibid.*

reasons, the search and seizure provisions of the Income Tax Act were struck down.[75]

The Income Tax Act was amended and all of these defects were corrected. The Act now required a judge (not a minister) to be satisfied that an offence had been committed; the judge also had to be satisfied that evidence was likely to be found in the place searched; the judge also had to specify what documents or things were to be searched for; and the search had to be confined to evidence of the particular offence. The careful drafting of the new section was not, however, sufficient to "Charterproof" it. In *Baron* v. *Canada* (1993),[76] the Supreme Court of Canada struck down part of the new section. The problem was that the provision was framed in imperative language that left the issuing judge with no choice but to issue a warrant once he or she was satisfied that the statutory criteria of reasonable and probable grounds were satisfied. The Court held that the constitutional requirement of an impartial arbiter was not satisfied if the issuing judge was obliged "to act as a rubber stamp".[77] The absence of judicial discretion in the issuing of the warrant was a breach of s. 8 of the Charter.

In *R.* v. *Grant* (1993),[78] the Supreme Court of Canada reviewed the validity of a provision of the federal Narcotic Control Act that authorized a warrantless search of "any place other than a dwellinghouse" in which a peace officer believed on reasonable grounds that illegal drugs were present. The Court followed *Hunter* v. *Southam* to hold that the absence of any requirement of a warrant issued by a judge made the statutory authorization unconstitutional in its unqualified form. The Court did not strike down the statutory provision, however. The Court used the remedy of "reading down" to limit the provision "to situations in which exigent circumstances render obtaining a warrant impracticable".[79] Exigent circumstances would be present "where there exists an imminent danger of the loss, removal, destruction or disappearance of the evidence sought in a narcotics investigation if the search or seizure is delayed in order to obtain a warrant".[80] In this case, where the police had conducted two "perimeter searches" of a house that they reasonably (and rightly) suspected was being used to cultivate marijuana, there were no exigent circumstances. Therefore, the searches were unauthorized by the statute (now that it had been read down), and were unreasonable within s. 8.

In the *Grant* case, the observations that the police made during their unconstitutional perimeter searches were used as evidence of reasonable grounds to obtain a search warrant for the house itself. The warrant was issued by a judge,

---

75 *M.N.R.* v. *Kruger* [1984] 2 F.C. 535 (C.A.); *Re Print Three* (1985) 51 O.R. (2d) 321 (C.A.).

76 [1993] 1 S.C.R. 416. The judgment of the Court was written by Sopinka J.

77 *Id.*, 439.

78 [1993] 3 S.C.R. 223. The opinion of the Court was written by Sopinka J. Two other cases raising the same issues were decided at the same time, namely, *R.* v. *Wiley* [1993] 3 S.C.R. 263 and *R.* v. *Plant* [1993] 3 S.C.R. 281.

79 [1993] 3 S.C.R. 233, 241.

80 *Id.*, 241-242.

the house was searched and marijuana plants were found in the house and seized. Was this search and seizure, although authorized by a warrant, also unreasonable, considering that the information placed before the issuing judge had been obtained in breach of s. 8? Sopinka J., who wrote the opinion of the Supreme Court of Canada, held that the test for the validity of a warrant obtained with unconstitutional evidence was whether the judge would have been justified in issuing the warrant ''had the improperly obtained facts been excised from the information sworn to obtain the warrant''.[81] In this case, the police had not relied solely on the perimeter-search observations as their basis for the warrant. The police had also provided the judge with other grounds for suspecting the existence and location of the accused's marijuana operation: a tip by a reliable informer, a sighting of cultivation equipment in the accused's truck, other observations of the accused's movements and high electricity consumption. Sopinka J. held that this other information was sufficient to justify a judge in finding reasonable grounds for the issue of a search warrant. Therefore, the warrant was valid, and the ensuing search and seizure were reasonable.[82]

The opposite result was reached in *R.* v. *Evans* (1996),[83] which was another case in which a house had been searched and marijuana plants discovered in the basement. A warrant had been obtained based on an anonymous tip and the olfactory observation of a police officer, who had smelled the plants while questioning the accused at their front door. The Supreme Court of Canada held that the observation of the police officer was an unreasonable search. If that evidence had been excised from the information sworn to obtain the warrant, all that would have remained was the anonymous tip, which would have been insufficient to justify the issue of a search warrant. Therefore, the warrant was invalid, and the search and seizure was unreasonable.

(b) Warrantless searches

In *Hunter* v. *Southam*, Dickson C.J. recognized the obvious fact that prior authorization is not feasible in every situation. By implication, he acknowledged that a warrantless search could be upheld as reasonable in some situations. But, he held, the party seeking to justify a warrantless search would have to rebut a ''presumption of unreasonableness''.[84] He did not pursue this point, because in

81 *Id.*, 251.

82 The Court still considered that there was a sufficient connection between the unconstitutional perimeter searches and the obtaining of the evidence to make s. 24(2) of the Charter applicable to the evidence; however, the Court held that the admission of the evidence would not bring the administration of justice into disrepute, and that it should not be excluded. This aspect of the decision is described in Ch. 38, Exclusion of Evidence, under heading 38.4, ''Causation'', above.

83 [1996] 1 S.C.R. 8. The case is more fully discussed under heading 45.4(d), ''Plain view'', above.

84 *Id.*, 161.

the instant case it was obvious that prior authorization was feasible. Indeed, it was required by the Act; it was the nature of the prior authorization, not its absence, that had run afoul of s. 8. However, the courts have held that prior authorization is not feasible in the case of a search incident to lawful arrest,[85] a search of a vehicle that could be quickly moved away,[86] or a seizure of property "in plain view" of police officers lawfully on premises.[87] In these cases, a warrantless search or seizure has been held to be reasonable.

While a search of a motor vehicle that could be quickly moved away does not require a warrant, it does require a basis of reasonable and probable grounds. In *R.* v. *Mellenthin* (1992),[88] a police officer, having lawfully stopped a car for a roadside check, asked the driver what was in an open gym bag on the front seat. When the driver produced some empty glass vials of a kind commonly used to store cannabis resin, the police officer searched the bag and found that it contained illegal drugs. The Supreme Court of Canada held that this was an unreasonable search in breach of s. 8. It was true that the police officer had reasonable and probable grounds for the search once he had been shown the glass vials, but the initial inquiry as to what was in the gym bag was "improper", and this contaminated the entire search. On a random roadside check, the only questions that the police officer was allowed to ask were questions relating to driving offences. The stop was justified only by concerns for highway safety,[89] and the police officer could not use the occasion of the stop to pursue an unrelated inquiry for which there was no reasonable basis of suspicion. The search that followed the inquiry about the contents of the gym bag was therefore unreasonable.

A warrantless search or seizure during a random traffic stop would be reasonable if it were based on reasonable and probable grounds. For example, a police officer could seize incriminating evidence that was inside the car "in plain view" of the officer.[90] In *Mellenthin*, however, although the gym bag on the front seat was open, the contents were not visible from outside the car. For another example, the driver of the stopped car might voluntarily say or do something that created a reasonable suspicion in the mind of the police officer. This would make a subsequent search and seizure reasonable for the purpose of s. 8. In *Mellenthin*, the Crown argued that the accused's disclosure of the glass vials was voluntary,

---

85 *R.* v. *Longtin* (1983) 41 O.R. (2d) 545 (C.A.); *Cloutier* v. *Langlois* [1990] 1 S.C.R. 158. Cf. *R.* v. *Beare* [1988] 2 S.C.R. 387 (fingerprinting of person charged with an offence not a breach of s. 8).

86 *R.* v. *Rao* (1984) 46 O.R. (2d) 80, 109 (C.A.).

87 *R.* v. *Longtin* (1983) 41 O.R. (2d) 545, 549 (C.A.); *Solvent Petroleum Extraction* v. *M.N.R.* [1990] 1 F.C. 20 (C.A.). Cf. *R.* v. *Boersma* [1994] 2 S.C.R. 488 (viewing by police of marihuana plantation in plain sight from road not a search).

88 [1992] 3 S.C.R. 615. The opinion of the Court was written by Cory. J.

89 This ruling was based on *R.* v. *Ladouceur* [1990] 1 S.C.R. 1257, where it was held that the random stopping of a vehicle was an arbitrary detention under s. 9 of the Charter, but was justified under s. 1 as a contribution to highway safety: see ch. 46, Arbitrary Detention and Imprisonment, under heading, 46.3(a), "Requirement of standards", below.

90 [1992] 3 S.C.R. 615, 629.

since the accused was under no legal duty to respond to the police officer's question. But the Court held that a driver would probably feel compelled to answer police questions, despite his legal right to remain silent, and that it was not appropriate to treat the accused's disclosure of the glass vials as voluntary.

Another circumstance that will lower the standard of reasonableness imposed by s. 8, and will often excuse the absence of a warrant, is a diminished expectation of privacy. Of course, if there is *no* reasonable expectation of privacy, then there is no search or seizure within s. 8 and no requirement of reasonableness.[91] There are, however, situations where there is a reasonable expectation of privacy, but the expectation is not sufficiently high to require fulfilment of the warrant requirements of *Hunter* v. *Southam*.[92] This is the case in a prison, for example, where inmates, although retaining some expectation of privacy, must expect routine or random frisk searches of their person, and routine or random surveillance and inspection of their cells.[93] There is also a diminished expectation of privacy in a school, where a warrantless search by the principal of a student's person for drugs has been held to be reasonable.[94]

(c) Border searches

The international border is another situation where it has been held that travellers have a diminished expectation of privacy. In *R.* v. *Simmons* (1988),[95] the Supreme Court of Canada upheld a strip search of a female traveller arriving from Jamaica at Toronto's international airport; the search, which had been prompted by indications that the traveller was nervous and the bulky nature of her clothing, revealed packages of illegal drugs strapped to her abdomen. The federal Customs Act authorized such a search where the customs officer had reasonable grounds (as she did in this case) to believe that the traveller was concealing contraband. The Act did not require the customs officer to obtain a warrant or other prior authorization of the search. The Court held that the absence of a warrant requirement was reasonable,[96] because of the diminished expectation of privacy of travellers crossing international borders. A person entering Canada must expect to be subjected to screening procedures, including in cases of suspicion a strip search, provided that the search was conducted (as this one had been) in private by a customs officer of the same sex.

---

91 E.g., *R.* v. *Hufsky*, note 59, above (production of driver's licence).

92 Cf. *Thomson Newspapers* v. *Can.*, note 63, above, and *R.* v. *McKinley Transport*, note 67, above, where there was a reasonable expectation of privacy in documents, but the intrusion was not sufficiently severe to require a warrant.

93 *Weatherall* v. *Can.* [1993] 2 S.C.R. 872.

94 *R.* v. *J.M.G.* (1986) 56 O.R. (2d) 705 (C.A.).

95 [1988] 2 S.C.R. 495.

96 The Court held nevertheless that the search was unreasonable, because it involved a detention, which attracted the right to counsel of s. 10(b), and that right had been denied.

(d) Regulatory inspections

A person who engages in a regulated activity has a diminished expectation of privacy with respect to that activity. It could hardly be argued, for example, that annual filing requirements for incorporated companies breach any reasonable expectation of privacy. Where an activity requires a licence (or permit), as is the case for driving a motor vehicle, the production on official demand of the licence is so obviously necessary to monitor compliance that it involves no breach of a reasonable expectation of privacy; therefore, there is no search or seizure when the licence or permit is demanded by the proper official.[97] In the case of a regulated business, the proprietor's expectation of privacy with respect to the commercial premises, equipment and records is attenuated by the obligation to comply with the regulations and to tolerate the administrative inspections that are an inseparable part of an effective regime of regulation. In effect, the proprietor's expectations of privacy must adjust to accommodate the regulatory regime. The inevitable impairment of privacy is not wholly burdensome: it wears a beneficial aspect insofar as it offers some assurance of compliance by the proprietor's competitors, so that all participants in the industry bear the cost of complying with the regulatory requirements.

The administration of most regimes of regulation involves the use of inspectors who regularly visit the locations of the regulated activity in order to check for compliance with the law. These routine or random inspections are in the nature of spot checks. They are not premised on the suspicion that an offence is being committed; and therefore there would be no point in requiring inspectors to obtain a warrant or other prior authorization for each visit to a building site, restaurant, factory, office, recreation area or other place subject to regulation. This is the position that the courts have generally taken. Administrative inspections, during normal business hours, of commercial premises, or even private homes, in order to check for compliance with building standards, zoning rules, public health and safety requirements and the like, are not unreasonable searches;[98] and, when an illegal or dangerous or diseased thing is discovered by an inspector, the warrantless confiscation of the thing is not an unreasonable seizure.[99]

In *R.* v. *McKinley Transport* (1990),[100] the Supreme Court of Canada held that the federal Income Tax Act was a "regulatory" statute,[101] and the Minister

---

97 *R.* v.*Hufsky*, note 59, above.

98 E.g., *Re Belgoma Transportation* (1985) 51 O.R. (2d) 509 (C.A.) (employment standards inspection); *R.* v.*Quesnel* (1985), 53 O.R. (2d) 338 (C.A.) (marketing board inspection); *R.* v.*Bichel* (1986) 33 D.L.R. (4th) 254 (B.C.C.A.) (building inspection of private home); *Ont. Chrysler* v.*Ont.* (1990) 72 O.R. (2d) 106 (C.A.) (business practices inspection); *Comité paritaire* v. *Potash* [1994] 1 S.C.R. 406 (labour standards inspection).

99 E.g., *R.* v.*Bertram S. Miller* [1986] 3 F.C. 291 (C.A.) (confiscation and destruction of diseased plants); *Re Ozubko* (1986) 33 D.L.R. (4th) 714 (Man. C.A.) (confiscation at racetrack of illegal syringe); *Re Milton* (1986) 37 D.L.R. (4th) 694 (B.C.C.A.) (confiscation of illegal fishing nets).

100

of National Revenue needed powers of spot-checking in order to supervise self-reporting by taxpayers of their income. The Court upheld the warrantless demand by the Minister for a taxpayer's private documents and information. In effect, this case holds that taxpayers have a diminished expectation of privacy with respect to all records relating to the earning of income (or other taxable transactions).[102] However, the "regulatory" nature of the Income Tax Act was not sufficient to relax the requirement of a warrant to authorize an entry upon private premises in order to search for evidence that an offence had been committed. That was the decision of the Supreme Court of Canada in *Baron* v. *Canada* (1993).[103] The search in that case was not a routine monitoring of compliance with the Act, but was based on suspicion that an offence had been committed and was intended to yield evidence for the prosecution of the offence.

(e) Writs of assistance

A "writ of assistance" is in effect a blanket search warrant. It authorizes the holder to search for evidence of a particular kind of crime at any time and place for as long as the holder of the writ occupies the office of police officer (or other official to whom the writ was issued). The federal Narcotics Control Act and three other drug-related statutes formerly authorized the issue of writs of assistance, and writs were in fact issued to members of the Royal Canadian Mounted Police. Once a writ of assistance had been issued to a police officer, the officer did not need to obtain a search warrant or any other form of authority to carry out a particular search or seizure of the kind authorized by the writ.

Challenges to writs of assistance based upon s. 8 of the Charter initially met with mixed success. But, after the Supreme Court of Canada decided *Hunter* v. *Southam* (1984),[104] it became clear that the three requirements of reasonableness that were stipulated in that case would not be satisfied by the statutes that authorize writs of assistance. Parliament accordingly acted to repeal the statutory provisions that authorized the writs.[105] The issue of constitutionality later reached the Supreme Court of Canada in two cases[106] where searches had been conducted under writs of assistance before the statutory provisions had been repealed. The Crown acknowledged that the statutory provisions were unconstitutional, and the Court "assumed" that to be the case. Writs of assistance have therefore disappeared from the Canadian legal system, and their future re-emergence is barred by s. 8.

---

101 Cf. *Thomson Newspapers* v. *Can.* [1990] 1 S.C.R. 425 (Court divided evenly on question whether Combines Investigation Act was a regulatory statute).

102 Followed in *B.C. Securities Commn.* v. *Branch* [1995] 2 S.C.R. 3 (warrantless demand for documents by securities commission upheld as regulatory inspection).

103 [1993] 1 S.C.R. 416.

104 Note 70, above.

105 S.C. 1985, c. 19, s. 200.

106 *R.* v. *Sieben* [1987] 1 S.C.R. 295; *R.* v. *Hamill* [1987] 1 S.C.R. 301.

(f) Illegal searches

Section 8, while prohibiting unreasonable search or seizure, does not make clear whether a violation of the law always makes a search or seizure unreasonable.[107] However, the Supreme Court of Canada has held that conformity with the law is an essential ingredient of reasonableness, so that an illegal search or seizure is per se unreasonable.[108] The point is important, because evidence obtained by an illegal act that is not a contravention of the Charter is admissible and cannot be excluded. Section 24(2) of the Charter (discussed next) only authorizes the exclusion of evidence obtained in contravention of the Charter.

45.8 Remedy for breach

(a) Exclusion of evidence

The normal remedy for an unreasonable search or seizure under s. 8[109] is the exclusion of the evidence discovered or seized. This is not an automatic remedy, because s. 24(2) of the Charter of Rights stipulates that evidence obtained in breach of the Charter is to be excluded only if its admission would bring the administration of justice into disrepute. However, the jurisprudence under s. 24(2) suggests that any breach of s. 8 by the police, where the police knew or ought to have known that they were acting in violation of the Charter, would normally lead to the exclusion of the evidence. Section 24(2) is examined in chapter 38, Exclusion of Evidence, above.

(b) Return of property

Section 24(1) of the Charter of Rights authorizes a court of competent jurisdiction to award remedies other than the exclusion of evidence for breach of

---

107 Section 8 was in the October 1980 version of the Charter in the following terms:

> 8. Everyone has the right not to be subjected to search or seizure except on grounds, and in accordance with procedures, established by law.

In this version, constitutionality was determined simply by compliance with the law, no matter how oppressive a particular law might be. The final version, which appeared in the April 1981 version of the Charter, substituted the test of reasonableness, and did not repeat the requirement of conformity to law.

108 *R.* v. *Kokesch*]1990 3 S.C.R. 3 (unlawful entry by police on private property rendered an otherwise reasonable search unreasonable). Cf. the inconsistent decisions in *R.* v. *Simmons* [1988] 2 S.C.R. 495 (denial of right to counsel on detention rendered an otherwise reasonable search unreasonable) and *R.* v. *Debot* [1989] 2 S.C.R. 1140 (denial of right to counsel on detention did not render search unreasonable).

109 It goes without saying that, if a law authorizes a search or seizure without the safeguards that would make the search or seizure reasonable, the law itself is unconstitutional: *Hunter* v. *Southam* [1984] 2 S.C.R. 145.

the Charter. Under this power, courts have ordered the return of documents seized in violation of s. 8.[110] A truly egregious violation of s. 8 could also lead to an award of damages under s. 24(1). Section 24(1) is examined in chapter 37, Enforcement of Rights, above.

110 *Lagiorgia* v. *Can.* [1987] 3 F.C. 28 (C.A.) (ordering return of documents seized as well as any copies made by Crown); *Commodore Business Machines* v. *Can.* (1988) 63 O.R. (2d) 737 (C.A.) (ordering return of documents seized, but allowing Crown to retain copies).

46

Arbitrary Detention or Imprisonment

46.1 Section 9 of Charter

Section 9 of the Charter of Rights[1] provides as follows:

> 9. Everyone has the right not to be arbitrarily detained or imprisoned.

Section 9 confers "the right not to be arbitrarily detained or imprisoned".

The Canadian Bill of Rights, by s. 2(a), provides that no law shall be construed or applied so as to "authorize or effect the arbitrary detention, imprisonment or exile of any person". Apart from the reference to "exile", which is not carried forward into s. 9 of the Charter (although exile would be prohibited by s. 6(1)), the language of s. 2(a) is very similar to s. 9 of the Charter.

The American Bill of Rights contains no prohibition of arbitrary detentions or imprisonments, but the fourth amendment's prohibition of "unreasonable . . . seizures" applies to seizures of the person, that is, arrests and detentions, as well as to seizures of property. This has given rise to a body of constitutional law regarding arrests and detentions.[2]

---

1 For commentary on s. 9, see Beaudoin and Mendes (eds), *The Canadian Charter of Rights and Freedoms* (3rd ed., 1996), 10-61–10-71 (by Chevrette and Cyr); Young, "All Along the Watchtower: Arbitrary Detention and the Police Function" (1991) 29 Osgoode Hall L.J. 329; Stuart, *Charter Justice in Canadian Criminal Law* (2nd ed., 1996) ch. 4; McLeod, Takach, Morton, Segal, *The Canadian Charter of Rights* (Carswell, loose-leaf), ch. 5; *Canadian Charter of Rights Annotated* (Canada Law Book, loose-leaf), annotation to s. 9; the last work provides a bibliography of the relevant literature.

2 LaFave and Israel, *Criminal Procedure* (2nd ed., 1992), ch. 3.

46.2 Detention or imprisonment

Section 9 applies only if a person has been ''detained or imprisoned''. An action by a police officer or other official that is not a detention or imprisonment cannot be a breach of s. 9, even if the action is arbitrary. The critical word here is ''detained'', because it is broader than ''imprisoned''. The word ''detained'' in s. 9 has the same meaning as the word ''detention'' in s. 10.[3] Section 10 is the provision that confers the right to counsel (as well as to reasons and habeas corpus) ''on arrest or detention''. What kind of restraint will qualify as a detention so as to attract the right against arbitrariness in s. 9, and the right to counsel in s. 10? Because most of the cases have arisen under s. 10, the meaning of detention is examined in the next chapter, chapter 47, Rights on Arrest or Detention, below.

46.3 Arbitrariness

(a) Requirement of standards

When is a person ''arbitrarily'' detained or imprisoned? In *R.* v. *Hufsky* (1988),[4] Le Dain J. for the Supreme Court of Canada said: ''A discretion is arbitrary if there are no criteria, express or implied, which govern its exercise''.

That case concerned the constitutionality of a police programme of random stopping of motorists in order to check the driver's licence, the certificate of insurance, the mechanical fitness of the vehicle and the sobriety of the driver. The stops were not based on suspicion that an offence was being committed; they were made at random as a spot check for compliance with highway traffic laws. The police had statutory authority to stop vehicles,[5] and there was a penalty if a motorist failed to comply. The Court held that the stopping of a motorist by the police was a detention,[6] and that stopping at random was arbitrary within s. 9. The stopping at random for the purpose of the spot check procedure was arbitrary ''because there were no criteria for the selection of the drivers to be stopped''; selection ''was in the absolute discretion of the police officer''.[7] Therefore, the

3 *R.* v. *Hufsky* [1988] 1 S.C.R. 621, 632.

4 [1988] 1 S.C.R. 621, 633.

5 In *Dedman* v. *The Queen* [1985] 2 S.C.R. 2, it was held that even without statutory authority the police had a power to stop vehicles at random which was derived as a matter of common law from their general duties to prevent crime and protect life and property.

6 The definition of detention is elaborated in the next chapter, ch. 47, Rights on Arrest or Detention, under sec. 47.2, ''Arrest or detention'', below.

7 [1988] 1 S.C.R. 621, 633.

ot check programme was in breach ofs. 9. However, the Court upheld the programme under s. 1, on the basis of its contribution to highway safety.[8]

In *R.* v. *Swain* (1991),[9] an accused was found not guilty by reason of insanity of charges of assault and aggravated assault. He challenged the provision of the Criminal Code that required the detention in a psychiatric facility of a person who was acquitted of a criminal charge on the ground of insanity. The Ontario Court of Appeal had twice upheld this provision on the basis that a finding of not guilty by reason of insanity raised a reasonable concern that the accused may remain a danger to the public and be in need of treatment.[10] The Supreme Court of Canada struck down the provision as an arbitrary detention in breach of s. 9. According to Lamer C.J. for the majority of the Court: "The duty of the trial judge is unqualified by any standards whatsoever".[11] And, in a remarkable comment on the contrary opinions of the Court of Appeal and of L'Heureux-Dubé J. who dissented, Lamer C.J. added: "I cannot imagine a detention being ordered on a more arbitrary basis"![12]

In *R.* v. *Lyons* (1987),[13] the "dangerous offender" provisions of the Criminal Code were upheld. Under those provisions, where an offender has been found guilty of a "serious personal injury offence", and the sentencing court has found that "the offender constitutes a threat to the life, safety or physical or mental well-being of other persons", the sentencing court may designate the offender a "dangerous offender", in which case he would be sentenced to a penitentiary for an indeterminate period. The Supreme Court of Canada held that these provisions

---

8 *Hufsky* was followed in *R.* v. *Ladouceur* [1990] 1 S.C.R. 1257, where a roving random stop was also held to be arbitrary, but justified under s. 1. In *R.* v. *Mellenthin* [1992] 3 S.C.R. 615, it was held that the only questions that a police officer could ask a stopped driver were questions about traffic offences; a question about the contents of a bag in the car (which turned out to contain drugs) was therefore an unreasonable search.

9 [1991] 1 S.C.R. 933. On the s. 9 issue, Lamer C.J.'s opinion attracted the support of all judges, except for L'Heureux-Dubé J., who dissented from the s. 9 reasoning and from the result.

10 *R.* v. *Saxell* (1980) 33 O.R. (2d) 78 (C.A.) (under the Canadian Bill of Rights); *R.* v. *Swain* (1986) O.R. (2d) 609 (C.A.) (this case). The Court had also emphasized the requirement on detention of a psychiatric assessment of the accused's dangerousness and his therapeutic needs, and regular reviews of his detention thereafter.

11 [1991] 1 S.C.R. 933, 1012.

12 *Ibid.* In apparent inconsistency with this picture of the standardless assignment of people to psychiatric facilities, Lamer C.J. postponed the holding of invalidity for six months so that judges would not be compelled to release into the community all persons who had been acquitted of offences by reason of insanity. Seven months after the decision was handed down, Parliament repealed the offending provision and replaced it with a more comprehensive scheme of mental assessments and disposition hearings. A presumption against detention was enacted with respect to the period of mental assessment, along with provisions to ensure that only those found to pose a significant threat to the safety of the public would be detained following the conclusion of the criminal trial: S.C. 1991, c. 43, adding new Part XX.1 (Mental Disorder) to the Criminal Code.

13 [1987] S.C.R. 309. The majority opinion was written by La Forest J. Lamer and Wilson JJ. each wrote dissenting opinions, but not on the s. 9 issue, upon which they agreed with the majority.

did not give rise to an arbitrary detention, because the Criminal Code supplied criteria for the classification of an offender as dangerous, and those criteria were carefully tailored to the legislative purpose. The difference between this case and *Swain* is the requirement of a finding of continued danger to the public at the time of sentencing,[14] which was not a requirement of the insanity provision in *Swain*. An amendment to the Criminal Code, enacted after the decision in *Swain* now requires an assessment of persons acquitted on the ground of insanity, to ensure that only those who pose a threat to the public are detained.[15]

The Criminal Code authorizes a peace officer to arrest without warrant "a person who has committed an indictable offence or who, on reasonable and probable grounds, he believes has committed or is about to commit an indictable offence". This provision has been challenged under s. 9, but, the reader will be relieved to learn, the Supreme Court of Canada has held that the standard of "reasonable and probable grounds" saves the power from the charge of arbitrariness.[16] The standard of reasonable and probable grounds is an objective requirement, so that an arrest by a peace officer, who honestly but mistakenly believes that there are reasonable and probable grounds to believe that an offence has been or is about to be committed, is subject to judicial review. If the reviewing court holds that the peace officer's subjective belief did not rise to the objective level of reasonable and probable grounds, then the arrest is unlawful.[17]

It is probably not widely understood in the public at large that in Canada the police possess no general power to detain a person, even for a short time, for the purpose of answering questions. Of course, the police often do stop a person for questioning or ask the person to come to the police station for questioning. But if police suspicion does not rise to the level of the reasonable and probable grounds that are required for an arrest, the police are forced to rely on voluntary compliance.[18]

It is implicit in the cases insisting on standards (or criteria) to govern a power of detention that not just any standard, however irrational, would pass constitutional muster. Would a police power to stop cars escape the charge of arbitrariness if it were restricted to stopping every third blue car? Such a rule would surely be

---

14 Cf. *Webb* v. *B.C.* (1988) 51 D.L.R. (4th) 726 (B.C.C.A.) (upholding detention under warrant of illegal immigrant who poses a danger to the public or who would not otherwise appear for an immigration inquiry).

15 S.C. 1991, c. 43, s. 4, adding a new s. 672.54 to the Criminal Code.

16 *R.* v. *Storrey* [1990] 1 S.C.R. 241. Cory J. wrote the opinion of the Court. In circumstances where an arrest is justified, if the police are in "hot pursuit" of the suspect, and the suspect takes refuge in a private home, the police may make forcible entry into the home if that is necessary in order to make the arrest: *R.* v. *Macooh* [1993] 2 S.C.R. 802 (such an arrest is not a breach of ss. 7 or 9).

17 *Id.*, 251, not making clear whether the objective requirement stems from only the language of the Criminal Code, or whether it is constitutionally required by s. 9.

18 Young, note l, above, 365-374 argues for legislative recognition and regulation of investigative detention.

as arbitrary as an unrestricted discretion. What is required are standards that are rationally related to the purpose of the power of detention.[19]

(b) Illegality

It is not clear whether an *unlawful* detention or imprisonment is for that reason alone arbitrary within s. 9. In the power of arrest without warrant example (previous section), where the peace officer has acted in good faith on grounds that fall just short of reasonable and probable cause, an argument could be made that the arrest, although unlawful, is not arbitrary within s. 9.[20] Probably, however, strict compliance with the law is a necessary (although not a sufficient) condition for compliance with s. 9.[21] In other words, any arrest that is not authorized by law is arbitrary, because the absence of legal authority means that the arrest is not made in accordance with the legal standards that save an exercise of discretion from arbitrariness.[22] The point is important, because a breach of the Charter gives rise to remedies under s. 24, including the exclusion of evidence obtained as the result of the Charter breach,[23] that are not available if the arrest is merely unlawful.

(c) Procedural unfairness

A detention or imprisonment that is not preceded by a proper hearing or other procedural safeguards should probably be regarded as a breach of s. 7, rather than s. 9. The concept of fundamental justice in s. 7 looks to the absence of adequate *procedural* standards for the exercise of a power or duty of detention. To be sure, the concept of fundamental justice in s. 7 is not limited to procedural standards,[24] but, in order to minimize duplication in cases to which s. 9 is also applicable, the substantive/procedural dichotomy is a sensible division of labour.

---

19 Young, note 1, above, 374-387, discusses the issue of standards.

20 *R.* v. *Duguay* (1985) 50 O.R. (2d) 375, 382 (C.A.) (obiter dictum).

21 Section 9 was in the October 1980 version of the Charter in the following terms:

> 9. Everyone has the right not to be detained or imprisoned except on grounds, and in accordance with procedures, established by law.

In the April 1981 version the section achieved its final form: the word ''arbitrarily'' was introduced in place of the phrase ''except on grounds, and in accordance with procedures, established by law''. Under the old language, compliance with the law was a necessary and sufficient condition of the constitutionality of a detention or imprisonment. Under the new language, compliance with the law is not sufficient, because a detention or imprisonment which was authorized by law could still be arbitrary. What is not explicit in the new language is whether compliance with the law is still a necessary condition.

22 This the position under s. 8: an illegal search is for that reason unreasonable: ch. 45, Unreasonable Search or Seizure, under heading 45.7(f), ''Illegal searches'', above.

23 For example, evidence may have been discovered in a warrantless search made incident to the arrest.

24 See ch. 44, Fundamental Justice, above.

That was the approach of the Supreme Court of Canada in *R.* v. *Swain* (1991),[25] where there was a challenge to the provision of the Criminal Code that required the detention of persons acquitted of a criminal charge on the ground of insanity. The majority of the Court held that the absence of a hearing or other procedural safeguards was a breach of s. 7, while the absence of substantive standards was a breach of s. 9.

(d) Duration of imprisonment

Arbitrariness under s. 9 is concerned with the adequacy of the standards prescribed by law for a detention or imprisonment. Section 9 is not concerned with the nature or duration of the detention or imprisonment. The question whether a detention or imprisonment is disproportionately severe for the offence for which it was imposed is not an issue under s. 9. Under the Charter, the severity of a treatment or punishment is to be reviewed under s. 12, which prohibits ''cruel and unusual treatment or punishment''.[26]

25 Note 9, above.

26 See ch. 50, Cruel and Unusual Punishment, below.

47

Rights on Arrest or Detention

47.1 Section 10 of Charter

Section 10 of the Charter of Rights[1] provides as follows:

> 10. Everyone has the right on arrest or detention
> (a) to be informed promptly of the reasons therefor;
> (b) to retain and instruct counsel without delay and to be informed of that right; and to have the validity of the detention determined by way of habeas corpus and to be released if the detention is not lawful.

1 For commentary on s. 10, see Paciocco, *Charter Principles and Proof in Criminal Cases* (1987), ch. 9; M. Finkelstein, *The Right to Counsel* (1988); Beaudoin and Mendes (eds.), *The Canadian Charter of Rights and Freedoms* (3rd ed., 1996), 10-71–10-94 (by Chevrette and Cyr), 11-2–11-40 (by Boisvert), 451-477 (by Ratushny); Stuart, *Charter Justice in Canadian Criminal Law* (2nd ed., 1996), ch. 5; McLeod, Takach, Morton, Segal, *The Canadian Charter of Rights* (Carswell, loose-leaf), chs. 8-10; *Canadian Charter of Rights Annotated* (Canada Law Book, loose-leaf), annotation to s. 10; the last work provides a bibliography of the relevant literature.

This chapter first examines the meaning of "arrest or detention", which is the event upon which the rights are conditioned. Then each of the three rights is considered in turn: the right to reasons, the right to counsel and the right to habeas corpus.[2]

47.2 Arrest or detention

(a) Requirement of compulsion

Section 10 applies only "on arrest or detention". An arrest or detention involves "some form of compulsion or coercion".[3] The rights conferred by s. 10 will therefore not be possessed by a person who has voluntarily co-operated with the police, for example, by inviting the police into his or her home and answering questions,[4] or by voluntarily accompanying the police to the police station to answer questions.[5] The general rule of Canadian law is that a police officer has no general power to detain a person for questioning, and no power to compel a person to answer questions. If a police officer does question a person, and the person declines to answer, the police officer must allow the person to proceed on his or her way, unless the police officer has reasonable and probable grounds to arrest the person, in which case the police officer could make an arrest.[6] If the police officer does make an arrest, the arrested person may be held in custody for up to 24 hours before being brought before a court, but the person will still have the right to remain silent,[7] as well as the rights conferred by s. 10.

(b) Requirement of restraint

When a person acts in response to a demand from a police officer, it is often difficult to distinguish what is compulsory from what is voluntary.[8] In *R.* v. *Therens* (1985),[9] a police officer demanded that the accused driver accompany him to the police station, and provide a breath sample in order to test the accused's sobriety. The accused co-operated with the police, supplied the sample, and was

2 The Canadian Bill of Rights, by s. 2(c), contains three similar guarantees.
3 *R.* v. *Therens* [1985] 1 S.C.R. 613, 642.
4 *R.* v. *Esposito* (1985) 53 O.R. (2d) 356 (C.A.).
5 *R.* v. *Smith* (1986) 26 D.L.R. (4th) 666 (Man. C.A.).
6 *R.* v. *Esposito*, note 4, above, 362.
7 This is a common law right, which has also been recognized as a principle of fundamental justice under s. 7: see ch. 44, Fundamental Justice, under heading 44.15, "Right to silence", above.
8 Cf. *Dedman* v. *The Queen* [1985] 2 S.C.R. 2 (police have common law power to stop vehicles at random; presumably, a refusal to stop would be the offence of obstruction).
9 [1985] 1 S.C.R. 613. The principal opinion was written by Le Dain J., although he dissented in the result (he would have admitted the evidence), and all judges agreed with Le Dain J. on the question whether there was a "detention".

charged with driving a vehicle with more than the maximum level of alcohol in his blood. He was never informed of any right to retain and instruct counsel. This was a breach of s. 10 only if the demand for the breath sample gave rise to a "detention". The Supreme Court of Canada held unanimously that there was a detention, and excluded the breath sample from the evidence.[10]

The demand for a breath sample in *Therens* differed from most police requests for evidence (in the absence of an arrest or a search warrant) in that it was specifically authorized by the Criminal Code, which imposed a penalty on anyone who refused to comply with a police demand for a breath sample. For Le Dain J., who wrote the unanimous opinion of the Court on this issue, the criminal liability for refusal to comply supplied the element of compulsion that was required for a detention.[11] A detention included not only a "restraint on liberty" in the obvious form of a "physical constraint". There was also a detention "when a police officer or other agent of the state assumes control over the movement of a person by a demand or direction which may have significant legal consequences and which prevents or impedes access to counsel".[12] By this test, the accused in *Therens* had been detained within s. 10 of the Charter, and therefore the breath sample had been obtained in breach of the right to counsel.

The Criminal Code actually contains two provisions authorizing police demands for breath samples. One contemplates a test that is administered at the police station, and which yields admissible evidence. The other contemplates a test that is administered at the roadside, and which (because it is less accurate) does not yield admissible evidence, although it may provide the basis for a demand for a police-station test. *Therens* concerned the police-station test, but Le Dain J. said, obiter, that a demand for the roadside test would also give rise to a detention, because there was the same compulsion, sanctioned by a penalty, for failure to submit to the roadside test. The roadside test involved a briefer restraint, and carried less serious consequences (since the resulting sample was not admissible), but the difference between the roadside test and the police-station test was "a mere difference of degree".[13]

The case of the roadside test reached the Supreme Court of Canada in *R.* v. *Thomsen* (1988),[14] where Le Dain J. for the Court confirmed that this was indeed

---

10 Although unanimous that the breath sample had been obtained in breach of the Charter, the Court divided on whether it should be excluded under s. 24(2); the majority excluded it.

11 [1985] 1 S.C.R. 613, 643; Le Dain J. added, obiter (at 644), that there would be a detention even in the absence of any legal obligation to comply with the police demand if a person reasonably believed that he or she had no choice but to comply with the police demand. This suggestion was applied in *R.* v. *Keats* (1987) 48 D.L.R. (4th) 87 (Nfld. C.A.) (holding that "psychological compulsion" is sufficient).

12 [1985] 1 S.C.R. 613, 642. Cf. *R.* v. *Schmautz* [1990] 1 S.C.R. 398 (demand for breath test gave rise to detention even though demand was disobeyed, so that accused was never under restraint and was not restricted in his access to counsel).

13 [1985] 1 S.C.R. 613, 637.

14 [1988] 1 S.C.R. 640.

a detention. There was, however, this difference between the two statutory provisions: the demand for the roadside test, but not the police-station test, had to be complied with ''forthwith''. The Court held that the word ''forthwith'', in the context of a roadside demand, excluded any right to contact with counsel before submitting to the test. This was a reasonable limit on the s. 10 right, which the Court upheld under s. 1.

In *R.* v. *Hufsky* (1988),[15] the question arose whether a driver had been detained when he was stopped by police as part of a programme of random stopping of vehicles to carry out spot checks of drivers for driver's licences, insurance certificates, vehicle condition and, especially, the sobriety of drivers. The police had statutory authority under the provincial Highway Traffic Act to stop vehicles, and there was a penalty for refusal to comply with a police demand to stop. The penal liability placed *Hufsky* on all fours with *Therens*. Once again, there was an assumption of control over the movement of the accused by a police demand that was sanctioned by a penalty. Therefore, the random stop was a detention.

The issue in *Hufsky* was whether a random stop was an arbitrary detention in breach of s. 9 of the Charter. (The Court held that it was an arbitrary detention, but that the arbitrariness was saved by s. 1.)[16] The Court in *Hufsky* made clear, however, that the concept of detention has the same meaning in s. 10,[17] so that the ruling makes s. 10 applicable to the stopping of a motor vehicle by police. It follows that even a police request to see a driver's licence is supposed to be accompanied by a warning of the right to counsel. The Charter is thus introduced into the brief restraints that form part of the normal day to day contacts between the police and members of the public.[18]

Another situation where a brief restraint may occur is at an international airport or other border crossing location. The federal Customs Act provides that, where a customs officer has reasonable cause to suspect that a traveller entering Canada has contraband secreted about his or her person, the traveller may be subjected to a search of his or her person. In *R.* v. *Simmons* (1988),[19] the Supreme Court of Canada, by a majority, held that as soon as a decision was made by a customs officer to order the strip search of a suspected traveller there was a detention. In that case, there was a legally sanctioned assumption of control over

---

15 [1988] 1 S.C.R. 621. The opinion of the Court was given by Le Dain J. The decision in *Hufsky* was followed in *R.* v. *Ladouceur* [1990] 1 S.C.R. 1257 (roving random stop upheld).

16 See ch. 46, Arbitrary Detention or Imprisonment, under heading 46.3(a), ''Requirement of standards'', above.

17 [1988] 1 S.C.R. 621, 632.

18 For this reason, provincial courts of appeal had before *Hufsky* tended to hold that there was no detention where the police restraint was of a brief and routine nature.

19 [1988] 2 S.C.R. 495. The opinion of the majority was written by Dickson C.J.; Wilson J., who concurred in the result, did not agree that there was a detention in this case. *R.* v. *Jacoy* [1988] 2 S.C.R. 548 was a companion case, raising the same issue at a highway checkpoint on the international border; it was decided the same way by the same bench.

the traveller by a customs officer.[20] That was a detention on the authority of *Therens*. It followed that s. 10 of the Charter applied, and s. 10 required that the suspected traveller be warned of her right to counsel before the search was administered. In this case, no such warning had been given to the suspected traveller, who was found to have plastic bags of illegal drugs concealed under her dress. The majority of the Court held that the failure to give the warning converted the search into an unreasonable one, which caused a breach of s. 8 of the Charter and rendered the evidence that had been discovered liable to be excluded.[21]

It is difficult to identify any civil libertarian values that are served by the definition of detention that is applied in *Therens*,[22] *Thomsen*,[23] *Hufsky*[24] and *Simmons*.[25] These cases introduce a right to counsel into every situation, however brief or routine, in which there is a duty to comply with a demand by a police officer (or other official). In every case, the detained person has no choice but to obey the demand, and legal advice could only confirm that duty to obey.[26] There is nothing that counsel could do to protect the innocent, who will in any case be exculpated by the breath test or other inspection or search that he or she is required by law to undergo. The sole effect of the right to counsel seems to be to create opportunities for delay by those who have reason to fear the outcome of the demanded test. Either that delay must be filled by custodial requirements that absorb police resources or the police must take the risk that incriminating evidence will disappear. Would it not be better to restrict the term ''detention'' to those official restraints that are neither routine nor transitory and in which the detained person faces choices that could be assisted by legal advice?

The insecure foundation of the reasoning in *Therens*, *Thomsen*, *Hufsky* and *Simmons* became apparent in *R.* v. *Debot* (1989).[27] In that case, the police, acting on reasonable grounds under a power conferred by the federal Food and Drug Act, made a ''frisk'' (pat-down) search of the accused, which yielded illegal drugs on the accused's person. At the time of the search, the accused had not been arrested, and no warning of the right to counsel accompanied the search. The majority of the Supreme Court of Canada was driven by *Simmons* to decide that the lawful search involved a detention. Therefore, there was a right to counsel

---

20 Routine questioning by customs or immigration officers at a point of entry to Canada does not involve a detention, even if the arriving passenger is diverted from the primary examination line to an interview room for a second examination: *Dehghani* v. *Can.* [1993] 1 S.C.R. 1053.

21 The Court admitted the evidence, because of the unclear state of the law at the time when the customs officer acted. Its admission would not bring the administration of justice into disrepute, as stipulated in s. 24(2).

22 Note 9, above.

23 Note 14, above.

24 Note 15, above.

25 Note 19, above.

26 This is true by definition, because it is the duty to obey that converts the conduct of the person under demand into a detention.

27 [1989] 2 S.C.R. 1140. The majority opinion was written by Lamer J.; concurring opinions were written by Wilson and Sopinka JJ.

under s. 10 at the time of the search. Now, however, the majority held that the search could proceed without waiting for the detained person to exercise his right to counsel. Sopinka J., who concurred in the result, could not accept this notion of a useless right. He agreed that it was pointless to consult counsel if the search was entitled to go on anyway; but, in his view, it was better to hold that there was no right to counsel. Sopinka J. had not been in any of the earlier cases, and it may now be too late for his reasoning to prevail. But there is much to be said for the proposition that there is no detention in a submission to a lawful police demand where the obligation is of brief duration and it would be pointless to consult counsel.

47.3 Right to reasons

Section 10(a) of the Charter confers the right on arrest or detention "to be informed promptly of the reasons therefor".

A breach of the right to reasons guaranteed by s. 10(a) occurred in *R.* v. *Smith* (1991).[28] The accused knew that he had shot a man, but did not know that the victim had died. The police arrested the accused, telling him only that he was under arrest for "a shooting incident". Only after he had made a statement to them did the police tell him that the victim had died. They then charged him with murder. In the Supreme Court of Canada, the Crown conceded that the failure to tell the accused that his victim had died was a breach of s. 10(a), because it meant that he was not informed promptly of the reasons for his arrest.[29]

47.4 Right to counsel

(a) Section 10(b) of Charter

Section 10(b) of the Charter confers the right on arrest or detention "to retain and instruct counsel without delay and to be informed of that right".[30]

(b) Fifth amendment of U.S. Constitution

Section 10(b) enacts for Canada the rule laid down in the United States by *Miranda* v. *Arizona* (1966),[31] in which the Supreme Court of the United States

28 [1991] 1 S.C.R. 714. McLachlin J. wrote the opinion of the Court.

29 Cf. *R.* v. *Evans* [1991] 1 S.C.R. 869 (Sopinka J. alone thought that accused was not informed when, during interrogation, the police became suspicious that the accused, arrested only on a drug charge, was implicated in a murder); *R.* v. *Borden* [1994] 3 S.C.R. 145 (s. 10(a) breached when accused, arrested for one offence, was not told that he was also under suspicion for a second offence).

30 Note that, under the residuary theory of s. 7, s. 7 may require a right to counsel in some situations that are outside the meaning of arrest or detention in s. 10(b): *Dehghani* v. *Can.* [1993] 1 S.C.R. 1053, 1076.

31 (1966) 384 U.S. 436.

interpreted the fifth amendment privilege against self-incrimination as requiring that a suspect be informed of his right to counsel prior to police questioning. After this decision, police forces in the United States required their officers to carry a "Miranda card" from which the officer, before questioning a suspect, had to read to him his constitutional rights, including the right to counsel.[32] Police in Canada now follow a similar practice.

(c) Timeliness of warning

In s. 10(b), it is explicit that there is a right "to retain and instruct counsel without delay". The paragraph goes on to say "and to be informed of that right", so that the words "without delay" do not literally qualify the duty to warn the accused of the right to counsel. It is clear however that the words without delay do apply to the duty to warn, because that interpretation is the only one that would make the right to be informed effective. The warning must be given without delay.[33]

The opening words of s. 10 confer the right to counsel (as well as the right to reasons and habeas corpus) "on arrest or detention". They do not contemplate a warning being given *before* an arrest or detention takes place. Nevertheless, a warning given before an arrest or detention is a valid one, provided that there is "a close factual connection relating the warning to the detention and the reasons therefor".[34] On this basis, a warning that was given about ten minutes before a demand for a breath test (the detention) has been upheld as "part of a single incident at which the [accused] was fully made aware of his rights".[35]

(d) Content of warning

Section 10(b) requires that a detained person be advised of the right "to retain and instruct counsel without delay". The Supreme Court of Canada has

32 The ruling in *Miranda*, previous note, was (at p. 444) that:

> Prior to any questioning, the person must be warned that he has a right to remain silent, that any statement he does make may be used in evidence against him, and that he has the right to the presence of an attorney, either retained or appointed.

It will be noted that, under this ruling, the accused has to be informed not only of his right to counsel, but also of his right to remain silent, a right which also has constitutional status in the United States: *Escobedo* v. *Illinois* (1964) 378 U.S. 478; *Miranda* v. *Arizona*, previous note. In Canada, there is a common law right to remain silent, and it has also been held to be a principle of fundamental justice under s. 7: *R.* v. *Hebert* [1990] 2 S.C.R. 151; but there is no constitutional obligation to inform the accused of his right of silence. In practice, however, Canadian police do warn suspects of their right to silence at the same time as they warn suspects of their right to counsel.

33 *R.* v. *Schmautz* [1990] 1 S.C.R. 398, 416.

34 *Ibid.*

35 *Id.*, 416-417.

added an elaborate gloss to this requirement, so that a police officer who actually warned a detained person in the language of s. 10(b) would commit a breach of s. 10(b). In *R.* v. *Brydges* (1990),[36] Lamer C.J. for the majority of the Court, said that the police warning should also include references to the availability of free duty counsel and legal aid. The fact that this was only an obiter dictum did not deter the Court from instructing the police to get their warning cards into compliance, a task for which the Court allowed a period of 30 days.

Evidently, the police obeyed their instructions, and in *R.* v. *Bartle* (1994),[37] a police officer, before administering a breathalyser test warned the suspect in these terms:

> You have the right to retain and instruct counsel without delay. You have the right to telephone any lawyer that you wish. You also have the right to free legal advice from a Legal Aid lawyer. If you are charged with an offence, you may apply to the Ontario Legal Aid Plan for legal assistance.

The suspect to whom this warning was twice given, once at the roadside and once at the police station, said no, that he did not want to call a lawyer. He was given the breathalyser test, which he failed. The Supreme Court of Canada held that the suspect's s. 10(b) right had been infringed, and that the breathalyser test was inadmissible. Why? Because the police officer had not included in the warning a telephone number by which free duty counsel could be contacted at night. It was immaterial that the suspect had shown no interest in contacting counsel, or that the advice of counsel could do nothing but confirm the statutory duty to provide a breathalyser sample. The telephone number had to be provided, not merely to assist a suspect who indicated an interest in contacting counsel (which is all that had been decided in earlier cases), but as part of the warning to every detained person. After all, the Court pointed out, it was possible that the availability of the telephone number might encourage the suspect to decide to contact counsel, and that would be a good thing.[38]

In *Bartle*, the suspect was arrested at 1.00 a.m. on a Saturday morning. In Ontario, where this occurred, there was a toll-free legal aid number, from which

---

36 [1990] 1 S.C.R. 190, 215.

37 [1994] 3 S.C.R. 173. The majority opinion was written by Lamer C.J., with whom Sopinka, Cory, Iacobucci and Major JJ. agreed. La Forest and McLachlin JJ. wrote concurring opinions. Gonthier J. wrote a brief dissenting opinion, but his disagreement went only to the exclusion of the evidence. L'Heureux-Dubé J. wrote a dissenting opinion, disagreeing both with the scope of the s. 10(b) duty and the exclusion of the evidence. Three other cases were decided at the same time as *Bartle*, raising exactly the same issue: *R.* v. *Pozniak* [1994] 3 S.C.R. 310; *R.* v. *Harper* [1994] 3 S.C.R. 343; *R.* v. *Cobham* [1994] 3 S.C.R. 360. All were decided the same way.

38 The reality is that, in the breathalyser cases, the right to counsel is a needless burden on the police, who are required by law to administer the breathalyser regardless of what counsel would say to the suspect. The right is of no use to the suspect, except to confirm that he or she is under a legal duty to comply with the police request. The only beneficiary is the legal profession for whom the right provides additional employment.

immediate, free legal advice could be obtained from duty counsel who were on 24-hour stand-by. Lamer C.J. said that, while there was no constitutional obligation on a province to establish such a service, if the service did exist, then its availability and the telephone number had to be included in the police warning of the right to counsel. L'Heureux-Dubé J., who dissented, pointed out that s. 10(b) required only that the suspect be informed of ''that right'', which obviously referred back to the constitutional right. She would have decided that there was no duty to advise suspects of services that the province was under no constitutional obligation to provide. For L'Heureux-Dubé J., it was enough to provide the information about legal services, including telephone numbers, after the suspect had indicated an interest in contacting counsel, when the police should cooperate in helping the suspect to exercise the right of which he had been informed.

In *Bartle*, the majority agreed that, in a jurisdiction where no single 24-hour telephone number was available to contact duty counsel, the suspect did not have to be warned of the existence of a non-existent service. However, the majority said that in that case the suspect would have to be provided with information on whatever did exist in the jurisdiction, for example ''a list of telephone numbers for lawyers acting as duty counsel''.[39] That situation came up in *R.* v. *Prosper* (1994),[40] which was decided by the Supreme Court of Canada at the same time as *Bartle*. That was another breathalyser case, the accused having been arrested on a Saturday afternoon in Nova Scotia. In Nova Scotia, there was no 24-hour toll-free telephone number for the provision of free legal advice. It was held that the police satisfied the information component of the s.10(b) right by including in their warning the information that they would provide the accused with a list of legal aid lawyers' home telephone numbers, which they did in fact supply.[41] In *R.* v. *Matheson* (1994),[42] yet another breathalyser case decided by the Court at the same time as *Bartle* and *Prosper*, the arrest took place at 1.00 a.m. on a Saturday morning in Prince Edward Island, where there was no system of any kind in place for the provision of free legal advice after hours. It was held that a police warning that made no mention of the availability of duty counsel was in compliance with s. 10(b).[43]

---

39 [1994] 3 S.C.R. 173, 201. Note that this is still part of the information component of s.10(b), not the exercise of the right to counsel.

40 [1994] 3 S.C.R. 236. The plurality opinion was written by Lamer C.J., with whom Sopinka, Cory and Iacobucci JJ. agreed. McLachlin J. wrote a concurring opinion. The principal dissenting opinion was written by L'Heureux-Dubé J. Dissenting opinions were also written by La Forest, Gonthier and Major JJ.

41 The police were still held to be in breach of the s. 10(b) right by administering the test after the accused was unsuccessful in contacting any of the lawyers on the police list. (They were ''on strike'' and not taking after-hours calls.) The majority of the Court took the view that the police should have waited until a lawyer was available, even if that involved the loss of the breathalyser evidence. The accused's breathalyser test result was excluded.

42 [1994] 3 S.C.R. 328.

43 In that case, the majority of the Court held that there was no breach of s. 10(b), and the accused's breathalyser test result was accordingly admissible.

(e) Comprehension of warning

A warning of the right to counsel must be understood by the detained person. A person who was mentally unfit to stand trial would not be able to exercise the s. 10(b) right, because such a person would not have enough cognitive capacity to understand the warning or to retain and instruct counsel.[44] Section 10(b) was breached in a case[45] where the detained person, who was of low intelligence, said that he did not understand the warning of his right to counsel. The Supreme Court of Canada held that the police should have explained the right to him until they were confident that he understood it. By proceeding to question him without further explanation the police violated his right to counsel.[46]

(f) Comprehension of extent of jeopardy

We have already noticed that s. 10(a) confers a right on arrest or detention ''to be informed promptly of the reasons therefor''. A breach of the right to reasons in s. 10(a) may also cause a breach of the right to counsel in s. 10(b). The detained person must understand in a general way ''the extent of his jeopardy'' in order to be validly warned of the right to counsel. A failure to convey the extent of the jeopardy tainted the warning in *R.* v. *Greffe* (1990),[47] where the police arrested a person, and advised him that he was being arrested on outstanding traffic warrants; in fact, he was suspected of (and was later charged with) importing heroin. The point is, of course, that an accused person cannot make an informed judgment about the need for the assistance of counsel if the accused does not appreciate the seriousness of the charge upon which the arrest was based.

It often happens that a person is arrested on one charge, and subsequent events or more information lead the police to add or substitute a more serious charge. For example, a charge of attempted murder will be increased to murder if the victim subsequently dies. In that case, the accused must be informed of the death, and re-warned of the right to counsel.[48] Another example is the case where

---

44 *R.* v.*Whittle* [1994] 2 S.C.R. 914 (holding that accused did have enough cognitive capacity).

45 *R.* v. *Evans* [1991] 1 S.C.R. 869; folld. in *R.* v. *Borden* [1994] 3 S.C.R. 145 (police investigating detained accused's involvement in two offences advised him of only one investigation). Compare *R.* v.*Jones* [1994] 2 S.C.R. 229 (general warning given at pre-trial psychiatric assessment hearing sufficed to make accused's statement admissible in dangerous offender proceedings, the latter not being a new charge).

46 As a corollary of the requirement that detained persons must understand their right to counsel, the right to counsel is infringed if police attempt to discourage a detainee from exercising the right, or attempt to persuade a detainee not to take counsel's advice to remain silent: *R.* v. *Burlingham* [1995] 2 S.C.R. 206 (police persuaded a murder suspect to accept a plea bargain while his lawyer was out of town).

47 [1990] 1 S.C.R. 755.

48 *R.* v. *Black* [1989] 2 S.C.R. 138. Contrast *R.* v. *Smith* [1991] 1 S.C.R. 714 (accused had shot a man, but did not know, and was not told by the police, that the victim had died; held, he had a sufficient knowledge of the extent of his jeopardy to waive his right to counsel).

the accused was arrested for a drug offence, and warned of his right to counsel. During questioning the accused revealed a possible involvement in a murder, and he was later charged with the murder. It was held that as soon as the police switched the focus of their investigation to the murder, they were under a duty to advise the accused of the change in the extent of his jeopardy, and repeat the initial warning of the right to counsel.[49]

(g) Opportunity to exercise right

The s. 10(b) duty to warn a detained person of the right to counsel does not include a duty to offer the person the use of a telephone or to offer other help in contacting counsel.[50] If, however, the accused indicates that he or she wishes to exercise the right to counsel, then he or she must be provided with a ''reasonable opportunity to retain and instruct counsel without delay''.[51] A reasonable opportunity is denied if the accused is not offered the use of a telephone or other facility to make contact with counsel.[52] A reasonable opportunity is also denied if the police proceed to question the accused[53] or demand a breath sample[54] or place him in a line-up[55] before there has been enough time for the accused to make contact with counsel. However, where the accused does not make a ''reasonably diligent'' effort to contact counsel, for example, by refusing to make a telephone call to a lawyer outside office hours, the police are free to proceed to question him.[56] Otherwise, the accused could needlessly delay the investigation of the crime.[57]

---

49 *R.* v. *Evans* [1991] 1 S.C.R. 869; folld. in *R. v. Borden* [1994] 3 S.C.R. 145 (police investigating detained accused's involvement in two offences advised him of only one investigation). Compare *R. v. Jones* [1994] 2 S.C.R. 229 (general warning given at pre-trial psychiatric assessment hearing sufficed to make accused's statement admissible in dangerous offender proceedings, the latter not being a new charge).

50 *R.* v. *Baig* [1987] 2 S.C.R. 537. But note *R.* v. *Bartle*, note 37, above, on the obligation to provide information about the existence and availability of any system of free legal advice, including telephone numbers.

51 *R.* v. *Manninen* [1987] 1 S.C.R. 1233, 1241.

52 *Ibid.* Cf. *R.* v. *Strachan* [1988] 2 S.C.R. 980 (police justified in refusing use of telephone while they secured a potentially dangerous situation).

53 *R.* v. *Manninen* [1987] 1 S.C.R. 1233.

54 *R.* v. *Tremblay* [1987] 2 S.C.R. 435.

55 *R.* v. *Ross* [1989] 1 S.C.R. 3.

56 *R.* v. *Smith* [1989] 2 S.C.R. 368.

57 What happens if the accused does make reasonably diligent efforts to contact a lawyer and is unsuccessful? In *R.* v. *Prosper* [1994] 3 S.C.R. 236, 269-278, Lamer C.J., speaking for himself and three others (not a majority of the nine-judge bench), said that the police had to continue to ''hold off'' questioning or eliciting other evidence until free legal advice was available. This is a most unfortunate ruling, especially in drunk driving cases (which is what *Prosper* was), which usually occur outside business hours, and where breathalyser tests must be administered before the accused has sobered up. Lamer C.J. said (at p. 275) that this was one of ''the prices which has to be paid by governments'' that fail to ensure that free legal advice is available on

(h) Duty to refrain from questioning

Section 10(b) ''imposes on the police the duty to cease questioning or otherwise attempting to elicit evidence from the detainee until he has had a reasonable opportunity to retain and instruct counsel''. This rule was established in *R.* v. *Manninen* (1987),[58] where the questioning of the accused by the police continued after the accused had indicated that he wished to retain counsel, and the accused made an incriminating statement in response to a police question. There was no doubt that the accused's statement was perfectly voluntary and that it ''clearly established'' his guilt. Nevertheless, the Supreme Court of Canada held that the statement had been obtained in breach of s. 10(b) of the Charter, and that it should be excluded from evidence for that reason.[59] The same reasoning has been used to exclude evidence identifying two accused as the persons who committed the crime, because the line-up in which the accused were identified was held shortly after their arrest in the small hours of the morning, and before they had been successful in contacting counsel.[60]

A voluntary statement by an accused person before he has had a reasonable opportunity to retain counsel, or in contravention of the advice of counsel, is not always the result of a breach of s. 10(b). What s. 10(b) prohibits is the continuation of questioning by the police (or other state agents). Therefore, if the accused makes a voluntary statement to another prisoner, or to a visitor, or even directly to the police, provided the statement was not elicited by police questioning, there is no breach of s. 10(b)[61] (or s. 7).[62] Section 10(b) prohibits the police from actively pursuing information from the accused, but it does not prohibit the role of a passive listener, and the listener may testify as to what he or she heard the accused say.

The warning of the right to counsel is a most unsatisfactory way of regulating police custodial interrogation. It places the police in a false position. Their goal is to obtain a statement from each suspect, because that is the best, and most economical, proof of guilt. Yet they are expected to administer a warning that, if heeded, will cause the suspect not to make a statement. Since a lawyer will nearly always advise an accused person not to talk to the police, it would be more logical

---

a 24-hour basis. One might question whether it is correct to describe ''governments'' (as opposed to victims) as paying the price for ineffective enforcement of drunk driving and other criminal laws.

58 [1987] 1 S.C.R. 1233, 1242 per Lamer J. for the Court.

59 Accord, *R.* v. *Black* [1989] 2 S.C.R. 138 (police re-warned accused of her right to counsel after charge raised from attempted murder to murder, but they questioned her, eliciting a statement, before she was successful in re-contacting counsel; statement excluded); *R.* v. *Burlingham* [1995] 2 S.C.R. 206 (police continued to attempt to obtain a statement and a plea bargain after accused asserted his right to counsel).

60 *R.* v. *Ross* [1989] 1 S.C.R. 3.

61 *R.* v. *Logan* [1990] 2 S.C.R. 731; *R.* v. *Graham* (1991) 1 O.R. (3d) 499 (C.A.).

62 See ch. 44, Fundamental Justice, under heading 44.15, ''Right to silence'', above.

to simply prohibit all statements to the police. Such a rule would be honest and straightforward, and would ensure that all suspects, whether or not represented by counsel, were treated equally. It would also gravely hinder police investigations, leave many crimes unsolved, and reduce guilty pleas and guilty verdicts. These important social costs explain no doubt why we perpetuate "a system which relies on confessions as an important element of proof yet purports to offer everyone complete freedom not to engage in pre-trial questioning by police".[63]

(i) Waiver of right

Section 10(b) confers the right to retain and instruct counsel, but it does not *compel* an accused to retain and instruct counsel. An accused person who does not wish to be represented by counsel may waive the right. When the right has been waived, the police are free to question the accused without offending s. 10(b). The accused has the right to remain silent,[64] but if the accused does answer the questions of the police the answers can be used in evidence against the accused.[65]

A waiver of the right to counsel must be "clear and unequivocal".[66] It has been held that the voluntary answering of police questions after an unsuccessful attempt to contact counsel did not amount to a waiver; the questions should not have been asked in the first place.[67] Another invalid waiver occurred in a case where the accused said that he did not wish to retain counsel, but indicated that this was because he could not afford to pay for a lawyer. Since the police did not explain to him the availability of legal aid or duty counsel, the waiver was not clear and unequivocal.[68]

A waiver of the right to counsel must also be based on a "full knowledge" of "the extent of [the accused's] jeopardy".[69] A waiver made by an accused who was too drunk to appreciate the consequences of waiving the right to counsel has been held to be invalid; police questioning of the accused after the purported waiver was held to be a breach of s. 10(b).[70] For the same reason, a waiver by a person who was mentally unfit to stand trial would also be invalid.[71] On the other hand, a waiver by an accused who had shot a man, but who did not know that the

---

63 Beaudoin and Ratushny (eds), *The Canadian Charter of Rights and Freedoms* (2nd ed., 1989), 477 (by Ratushny).

64 This is a common law right that has also been recognized as a principle of fundamental justice under s. 7: note 62, above.

65 *R.* v. *Upston* [1988] 1 S.C.R. 1083.

66 *Clarkson* v. *The Queen* [1986] 1 S.C.R. 383, 394 per Wilson J. for majority.

67 *R.* v. *Black* [1989] 2 S.C.R. 138, following *R.* v. *Manninen*, note 58, above.

68 *R.* v. *Brydges* [1990] 1 S.C.R. 190; folld. in *R.* v. *Bartle* [1994] 3 S.C.R. 173; *R.* v. *Prosper* [1994] 3 S.C.R. 236.

69 *R.* v. *Smith* [1991] 1 S.C.R. 714, 727 per McLachlin J. for the Court.

70 *Clarkson* v. *The Queen* [1986] 1 S.C.R. 383.

71 *R.* v. *Whittle* [1994] 2 S.C.R. 914 (holding that accused was fit to stand trial and waiver was valid).

victim had died, was held to be valid; he did not know the precise extent of his jeopardy, but he did know that he was in jeopardy for a very serious offence, and that was enough.[72]

(j) Choice of counsel

The right to counsel conferred by s. 10(b) is not a right to conscript the services of any lawyer whom the accused may choose. The accused cannot use s. 10(b) to insist upon the services of a lawyer who is either unable or unwilling to represent him. For example, a lawyer with a conflict of interest would be barred by the bar's rules of professional ethics.[73] Of course, where the accused himself cannot find a lawyer who is able and willing to represent him, the police or the court, depending upon the stage of the proceedings, would be under a constitutional obligation to assist him to find a lawyer.

Where the accused *has retained* a lawyer, the accused must be given a reasonable opportunity to contact that lawyer for advice on new developments relating to the case. In *R.* v. *Burlingham* (1995),[74] the Supreme Court of Canada held that, where a plea bargain is offered, s. 10(b) requires that the offer be made to or in the presence of the lawyer who has been retained and who is familiar with the case. It is not sufficient, where the accused's lawyer is temporarily unavailable, to offer the accused the services of a ''random'' lawyer.[75]

(k) Legal aid

Does s. 10(b) require that counsel be paid for out of public funds? In *Re Ewing* (1974),[76] the British Columbia Court of Appeal held that s. 2(c) of the Canadian Bill of Rights, which refers to ''the right to retain and instruct counsel without delay'', does not require that counsel be provided at public expense; a breach of s. 2(c) would occur only if some impediment (such as the refusal of an adjournment) were placed in the way of the arrested person privately retaining counsel. However, such a narrow definition of the right is unlikely to be followed under the Charter of Rights.[77] The International Covenant on Civil and Political Rights (to which Canada is a party),[78] by article 11(d), provides a right to legal assistance ''without payment'' by the person charged ''if he does not have sufficient means to pay for it''. In the United States, the famous case of *Gideon* v.

72 *R.* v. *Smith* [1991] 1 S.C.R. 714.
73 *Re R. and Speid* (1983) 43 O.R. (2d) 596 (C.A.)
74 [1995] 2 S.C.R. 206.
75 *Id.*, para 31 per Iacobucci J. (for the majority), para 62 per L'Heureux-Dubé J. (concurring on this point).
76 (1974) 49 D.L.R. (3d) 619 (B.C. C.A.)
77 See ch. 32, Canadian Bill of Rights, under heading 32.5, ''Judicial interpretation'', above.
78 The relevance of the International Covenant to the interpretation of the Charter is discussed in ch. 33, Charter of Rights, under heading 33.8(c), ''International sources'', above.

Wainwright (1963)[79] decided that an accused's sixth amendment right "to have the assistance of counsel for his defence" includes the right to have counsel provided at public expense, at least where the defendant is unable to afford counsel and the offence charged carries the penalty of imprisonment.[80]

All provinces do in fact have statutory legal aid plans, which are funded under cost-sharing agreements by both levels of government, and which provide free legal services to persons who are charged with indictable offences and who meet stipulated financial conditions. All provinces also operate a system of duty counsel, who are available to provide legal advice on a temporary basis to those who cannot afford or do not know a lawyer; duty counsel would be able to explain the legal aid plan to an indigent accused. In most provinces too, duty counsel are available through a toll-free telephone number to provide free advice on a 24-hour basis to those who are arrested outside normal business hours. We have already noticed the decisions of the Supreme Court of Canada in *Brydges*[81] and *Bartle*,[82] which require the police warning of the right to counsel to include reference to the availability of duty counsel and legal aid.

In *R.* v. *Prosper* (1994),[83] the accused was arrested on suspicion of drunk driving on a Saturday afternoon in Nova Scotia. Nova Scotia did not have in place a single toll-free telephone number that would provide after-hours access to duty counsel, but the police provided to the accused a list of the home telephone numbers of legal aid lawyers who were prepared to provide legal advice outside business hours. Unfortunately, at that time, the legal aid lawyers were "on strike" and the accused's efforts to contact one of them were unsuccessful. In another case decided at the same time, *R.* v. *Matheson* (1994),[84] the accused was arrested on suspicion of drunk driving in the early hours of Saturday morning in Prince Edward Island. Prince Edward Island had no system, not even a list of home telephone numbers, to provide immediate free after-hours legal advice. These two cases prompted the Supreme Court of Canada in *Prosper* to consider whether the province was under a constitutional obligation to make available the free services of duty counsel to those detained outside normal business hours. Although the nine-judge bench was divided on other issues, Lamer C.J.'s opinion on this point was unanimous. He held that there was no such obligation, relying on the legislative history of s. 10(b), which indicated that s. 10(b) was not intended to extend to an obligation to provide legal aid. He also pointed to the difficulty of enforcing an obligation to provide 24-hour duty counsel services against a government that was found to be in default.

In *Prosper*, Lamer C.J. went on to say, although with the support of only three other judges, that any government that did not provide 24-hour duty counsel

79 (1963) 372 U.S. 335.
80 The last point was decided in *Argersinger* v. *Hamlin* (1972) 407 U.S. 25.
81 Note 36, above.
82 Note 37, above.
83 [1994] 3 S.C.R. 236.
84 [1994] 3 S.C.R. 328.

services should have to "endure" a "trade-off", or "pay" a "price"; that trade-off or price was a requirement that the police hold off the taking of a breathalyser test (or eliciting any other evidence) until duty counsel was available.[85] Since this would render breathalyser testing ineffective, and severely impair the effectiveness of programmes against drunk driving, Lamer C.J. thought that this trade-off or price would be sufficiently distasteful to encourage provinces to establish 24-hour duty counsel services. With respect, it seems an extraordinary use of judicial power to frustrate law enforcement efforts against drunk driving in order to persuade a province to put its resources into a duty counsel programme that the province is under no constitutional obligation to provide.

Prosper decides that there is no constitutional right to 24-hour free duty counsel services. Lamer C.J. pointed out that "the issue of whether the Charter guarantees a right to state-funded counsel *at trial* and *on appeal* does not arise here".[86] That issue would be presented by a case where the accused did not qualify for legal aid, and claimed that the denial of legal aid deprived him of the right to retain and instruct counsel under s. 10(b), and probably the right to make full answer and defence under s. 7, and probably the right to a fair hearing under s.11(d).[87] All three bases for the claim to free legal services are obviously strong. However, the reasons given by Lamer C.J. for rejecting the constitutional right to free duty counsel services were couched in language that would apply with equal force to free legal services at trial and on appeal. The problem of enforcement against a government in default is especially difficult. The judicial grant of legal aid to a person who was disqualified by the province's legal aid plan would amount to redesigning the legal aid plan, which would require additional resources from the province and probably other administrative arrangements. A court would, I think, require a clear case of injustice before overriding the rules of a province's legal aid plan.[88]

(l) Exclusion of evidence

The cases in which the right to counsel under s. 10(b) is litigated are usually concerned with the admissibility of evidence. Often, the issue is whether an inculpatory statement by an accused, made in police custody without the advice of counsel, is admissible at the trial of the accused. Occasionally, a breath sample,

85 [1994] 3 S.C.R. 236, 268, 275.

86 *Id.*, 266 (emphasis in original).

87 *R.* v. *Rowbotham* (1988) 63 C.R. (3d) 113 (Ont. C.A.) is that case; the accused was denied legal aid on the ground that her annual income of $24,000 disqualified her, although the trial took 12 months; held, she lacked the means to employ counsel, which was a breach of s. 7 and 11(d) (s. 10(b) was not relied upon), and on a new trial (which was ordered on other grounds) legal aid must be provided.

88 *R.* v. *Rowbotham*, previous note, presents that case of injustice; there is extensive discussion of the issues at pp. 165-177; also in *R.* v. *Robinson* (1989) 63 D.L.R. (4th) 289 (Alta. C.A.) (denying funding for counsel to appeal a criminal conviction).

or the product of a search, is in issue. If evidence has been obtained in violation of the right to counsel, it is not necessarily inadmissible. Section 24(2) of the Charter provides that evidence obtained in breach of the Charter shall be excluded only if its admission would bring the administration of justice into disrepute. However, the Supreme Court of Canada has made s. 24(2) into a broader exclusionary rule than its language might indicate, and evidence obtained in breach of the right to counsel, especially if it is self-incriminatory (as it often is), is usually excluded. Section 24(2) is the topic of chapter 38, Exclusion of Evidence, above.

47.5 Right to habeas corpus

Section 10(c) confers the right on arrest or detention ''to have the validity of the detention determined by way of habeas corpus and to be released if the detention is not lawful''. This right exists now, of course, but its inclusion in the Charter would mean that it could not be denied or suspended by legislation[89] unless s. 1 (the limitation clause) were held applicable, or unless s. 33 (the override clause) were invoked. The right to habeas corpus is less important in the light of s. 24(1), the remedial section of the Charter, which is also available to secure the release of a person unlawfully detained,[90] and which obviously could not be denied or suspended by legislation. However, as has been explained in chapter 37, Enforcement of Rights, above, which deals with s. 24(1), s. 24(1) has strict standing requirements: a person other than the person detained probably could not apply under s. 24(1), whereas third party applications for habeas corpus are allowed.[91]

---

89 This is so even if the legislation provides for better remedies than habeas corpus: *Re Procedures and the Mental Health Act* (1984) 5 D.L.R. (4th) 577 (P.E.I. S.C. in banco).

90 Cf. *R.* v. *Gamble* [1988] 2 S.C.R. 595 (declaration made under s. 24(1) of eligibility to parole). Note that s. 24(1) is available only if a breach of the Charter has occurred, but any unlawful detention would be an arbitrary detention and therefore a breach of s. 9 of the Charter.

91 Sharpe, *The Law of Habeas Corpus* (2nd ed., 1989), 222.

48

Rights on Being Charged

48.1 Person charged with an offence

(a) Opening words of s. 11

Section 11 of the Charter lists nine paragraphs ((a) to (i)) of rights. These rights apply to ''any person charged with an offence''.

The word ''person'' has been discussed in an earlier chapter, and the conclusion reached that it includes a corporation.[1]

(b) Charged

The word ''charged'' is satisfied ''when a formal written complaint has been made against the accused and a prosecution initiated''.[2] That formal written complaint is the laying of an information or the preferring of an indictment.[3] A person who is merely suspected of an offence is not charged.

In *R.* v. *Kalanj* (1989),[4] the two accused persons were arrested and told that charges would be laid against them. They were released without being charged. Eight months later, an information was sworn laying charges of theft against them. Two years later, the case came on for trial, and the accused moved to quash the indictment for breach of their s. 11(b) right to be tried within a reasonable time. The trial judge did quash the indictment, holding that the delay was unreasonable when the eight-month pre-information delay was added to the two-year post-information delay. When the case reached the Supreme Court of Canada, the majority held that the accused were not charged with an offence until the swearing of the information that formally laid the charges against them. It followed that the delay from charge to trial was to be measured from the date of the information, not the date of the arrest.[5] The Court therefore excluded the eight-month period between arrest and information, and held that their trial had taken place within a ''reasonable time'' as required by s. 11(b).

There is no new ''charge'' against an accused when the Crown applies to have the accused designated a ''dangerous offender''. That application, if successful, subjects the offender to an increased penalty, namely, imprisonment for an indeterminate period. The Supreme Court of Canada,[6] by a majority, has

---

1 Chapter 34, Application of Charter, under heading 34.1, ''Benefit of rights'', above.

2 *R.* v. *Chabot* [1980] 2 S.C.R. 985, 1005, interpreting the word ''charge'' in the Criminal Code.

3 *R.* v. *Kalanj* [1989] 1 S.C.R. 1594, 1607 per McIntyre J. (''I would therefore hold that a person is ''charged with an offence'' within the meaning of s. 11 of the Charter when an information is sworn alleging an offence against him, or where a direct indictment is laid against him when no information is sworn.'')

4 [1989] 1 S.C.R. 1594. The majority opinion was written by McIntyre J. Lamer and Wilson JJ. each wrote dissenting opinions.

5 Lamer and Wilson JJ., who dissented, held that a person was charged ''when the impact of the criminal process is felt by the accused'' (p. 1621), which occurred at the time of the arrest.

6 *R.* v. *Lyons* [1987] 2 S.C.R. 309. The majority opinion was written by La Forest J. Lamer and Wilson JJ. each wrote dissenting opinions; but Lamer J. was the only dissenter on this issue.

characterized a dangerous-offender application as part of the sentencing process, so that it does not attract the guarantees of s. 11.[7] Therefore, the accused is not entitled to insist that the application be tried by a jury under s. 11(f). The Court[8] has also held that the issue of an injunction to prevent the picketing of courthouses, although based on the commission by the picketers of the offence of criminal contempt of court, does not constitute a charge against any individual picketer. ''Had the injunction been disobeyed and had proceedings been taken against the individual for such disobedience, then obviously at that stage [the guarantees of s. 11] would apply''.[9]

Extradition proceedings, which are brought in Canada to surrender a fugitive to a foreign country to stand trial there, do not attract the guarantees of s. 11.[10] The reference in s. 11 to a ''person charged with an offence'' means a person charged with an offence in Canada. A person subject to extradition proceedings has of course been charged with an offence in the foreign country, but he or she has not been charged with an offence in Canada. An extradition hearing is not a trial to determine whether the fugitive is guilty of the offence; it is a proceeding to determine whether there is sufficient evidence to warrant the surrender of the fugitive to stand trial. If there is sufficient evidence, then the fugitive will be tried in the foreign country and will be subject to the rules of that country's criminal justice system.[11]

(c) Offence

The word ''offence'' includes any breach of law, whether federal or provincial, to which a penal sanction is attached.[12] As a matter of constitutional law, an offence could be created by the federal Parliament, either under its criminal law power in s. 91(27), or as an ancillary enforcement measure under any of the

---

7 *Lyons*, previous note, was followed in *R.* v. *Jones* [1994] 2 S.C.R. 229 (evidence of pre-trial psychiatric assessment admissible in dangerous offender hearing, because it was a sentencing hearing).

8 *BCGEU* v. *B.C.* [1988] 2 S.C.R. 214.

9 *Id.*, 246 per Dickson C.J. for Court. Cf. *R.* v. *Cohn* (1984) 48 O.R. (2d) 65 (C.A.) (person cited for contempt of court is charged with an offence); *Man.* v. *Groupe Quebecor* (1987) 45 D.L.R. (4th) 80 (opposite decision; *Cohn* not foll'd.); *Vidéotron* v. *Industries Microlec* [1992] 2 S.C.R. 1065, 1071, 1079, 1100 (obiter dicta as to whether person cited for civil contempt of court is charged with an offence).

10 *Can.* v. *Schmidt* [1987] 1 S.C.R. 500. The majority opinion was written by La Forest J. Lamer and Wilson JJ. each wrote separate concurring opinions. On this issue, however, Lamer J. disagreed that s. 11 did not apply, and Wilson J. was not sure.

11 The actual decision to surrender a fugitive to a foreign country is made by the Minister of Justice, and takes into account a number of factors including Canada's treaty obligations, the impact of the decision on the administration of justice, and human rights considerations. The Minister's determination is subject to judicial review, but under s. 7, not s. 11, of the Charter: see ch. 34, Application of Charter, under heading 34.2(d), ''Government'', above.

12 *R.* v. *Wigglesworth* [1987] 2 S.C.R. 541, 554, 556, 560; *Corp. Professionnelle des Médecins* v. *Thibault* [1988] 1 S.C.R. 1033, 1040.

other heads of federal power.[13] An offence could also be created by provincial law as an ancillary enforcement measure under s. 92(15).[14]

What is the status of proceedings before disciplinary or regulatory bodies? In *R.* v. *Wigglesworth* (1987),[15] an R.C.M.P. constable, who had assaulted a prisoner in the course of an interrogation, was charged with a ''major service offence'' under the Royal Canadian Mounted Police Act. He was tried by a police tribunal, found guilty and fined $300. Were these proceedings subject to s. 11? The Supreme Court of Canada answered yes, but only because the punishment that the tribunal was authorized to impose included a sentence of up to one year's imprisonment. Wilson J., for a Court that was unanimous on this issue, said that a person is charged with an offence under s. 11 if the proceeding against the person is (1) ''by its very nature'' a ''criminal proceeding'', or (2) ''may lead to a true penal consequence''.[16] By reason of the risk of a sentence of imprisonment, the latter test was satisfied by the proceedings before the police tribunal. Therefore, Constable Wigglesworth was a ''person charged with an offence'' who was entitled to the protections of s. 11, including the protection against double jeopardy in s. 11(h) (which was the issue in the litigation).[17]

The first test stipulated by Wilson J. for an offence under s. 11 is the ''by nature'' test. A law sanctioned by a penalty will by its very nature be an offence if the law is ''intended to promote public order and welfare within a public sphere of activity''.[18] This would include an offence that carried only a small fine, for example, a parking infraction. However, the ''by nature'' test would not be satisfied by ''private, domestic or disciplinary matters which are regulatory, protective or corrective and which are primarily intended to maintain discipline, professional integrity and professional standards or to regulate conduct within a limited private sphere of activity''.[19] A service offence under the R.C.M.P. Act fell into this ''private sphere'' and was not ''by nature'' an offence within s. 11.

The second test stipulated by Wilson J. for an offence under s. 11 is the ''true penal consequence'' test. A law that fell into the private sphere would still be an offence under s. 11 if its breach attracted a true penal consequence. A fine would be a true penal consequence if, ''by its magnitude'', it ''would appear to be imposed for the purpose of redressing the wrong done to society at large rather than to the maintenance of internal discipline within the limited sphere of activ-

13 *The Queen* v. *Hauser* [1979] 1 S.C.R. 984.

14 See generally ch. 18, Criminal Law, above.

15 [1987] 2 S.C.R. 541. Wilson J. wrote the majority opinion, which on this issue was unanimous; Estey J. dissented on the double jeopardy issue.

16 *Id.* 559.

17 The issue was whether a charge for common assault under the Criminal Code should be quashed for breach of s. 11(h), the guarantee against double jeopardy. This turned in part on whether the earlier disciplinary proceeding was an ''offence'' within s. 11.

18 [1987] 2 S.C.R. 541, 570.

19 *Ibid.*

ity''.[20] But a fine was not necessarily a true penal consequence,[21] because a fine might only be directed to a disciplinary purpose in a private sphere. In the case of the R.C.M.P. Act, any fines were payable to the Force, not to the Consolidated Revenue Fund, which indicated a disciplinary purpose. Imprisonment, on the other hand, was ''a true penal consequence''. Disciplinary proceedings for a major service offence under the R.C.M.P. Act could lead to a sentence of imprisonment of up to one year. Therefore, although the proceedings before the police tribunal in this case failed the ''by nature'' test, they passed the ''true penal consequence'' test.

Wigglesworth makes clear that most disciplinary proceedings are outside the protection of s. 11. It will be only a rare regulatory or disciplinary statute that will attract the ''true penal consequence'' of a fine of public magnitude or a sentence of imprisonment. In three other cases[22] decided at the same time as *Wigglesworth*, the Court held that s. 11 had no application to proceedings for a disciplinary offence before a police tribunal established under the Ontario Police Act which had the power to reprimand, forfeit pay or leave, reduce in rank or dismiss. Unlike the R.C.M.P. tribunal in *Wigglesworth*, the Ontario tribunal had no power of imprisonment. It followed that in each of the three Ontario cases the accused police constable had not been charged with an offence under s. 11, and the guarantee of an independent and impartial tribunal in s. 11(d) (which was the claimed right) did not apply to him. Similar reasoning has been used to deny the application of s. 11 to proceedings before professional disciplinary tribunals with powers of disqualification, suspension and fine,[23] to a disciplinary hearing before a prison superintendent with power to order solitary confinement,[24] and to proceedings before securities commissions with power to issue cease-trading orders.[25]

In *R.* v. *Généreux* (1992),[26] the Supreme Court of Canada had to decide whether a member of the armed forces, who was charged before a court martial with a breach of the military Code of Service Discipline enacted by the National Defence Act, was a person charged with an offence in s. 11. The Court held unanimously that s. 11 was applicable. The first test of *Wigglesworth* was satisfied, because the court martial proceedings were ''by nature'' criminal. The Code of

20 *Id.*, 561.

21 Accord, *Re Kay Cee Kay Restaurants* (1986) 55 O.R. (2d) 189 (Div. Ct.) (assessment Minister of penalty for false statements in tax return not covered by s. 11); *Lavers* v. *B.C.* (1989) 64 D.L.R. (4th) 193 (B.C.C.A.) (same decision). Cf. *R.* v. *Amway Corp.* [1989] 1 S.C.R. 21, 37 (assuming without deciding that a defendant to a civil action for a statutory forfeiture was a person charged with an offence within s. 11).

22 *Burnham* v. *Metro Toronto Police* [1987] 2 S.C.R. 572; *Trumbley and Pugh* v. *Metro. Toronto Police* [1987] 2 S.C.R. 577; *Trimm* v. *Durham Regional Police* [1987] 2 S.C.R. 582.

23 E.g. *Pearlman* v. *Man. Law Society* [1991] 2 S.C.R. 869.

24 *R.* v. *Shubley* [1990] 1 S.C.R. 3 (Cory J. dissented because he thought that, even in a prison setting, solitary confinement should be regarded as a true penal consequence).

25 E.g., *Holoboff* v. *Alta.* (1991) 80 D.L.R. (4th) 603 (Alta. C.A.).

26 [1992] S.C.R. . The majority opinion of Lamer C.J. seems to have been agreed with by all judges on this issue.

Service Discipline was concerned not only with the maintenance of discipline in the armed forces, but also with public order and welfare in the public sphere. The Code made it a service offence to do anything that was punishable under the Criminal Code or any other Act of Parliament, and a person tried by a court martial or other service tribunal could not be charged in the ordinary courts. Three of the charges in this case were for breaches of the Narcotic Control Act. "Service tribunals thus serve the purpose of the ordinary criminal courts, that is, punishing wrongful conduct, in circumstances where the offence is committed by a member of the [armed forces]".[27] The Court added that the second test of *Wigglesworth* was also satisfied, because the accused soldier faced a "true penal consequence" in that the court martial possessed the power to impose a sentence of imprisonment. It followed that the accused soldier was entitled to invoke the protections of s. 11, specifically, the guarantee of an independent and impartial tribunal in s. 11(d).

48.2 Specific Information (s. 11(a))

Section 11(a) of the Charter of Rights[28] provides:

> 11. Any person charged with an offence has the right
> (a) to be informed without unreasonable delay of the specific offence;

Under s. 11(a), a person charged with an offence must be informed without unreasonable delay[29] of the specific offence. This right also exists under the Criminal Code, under provincial laws and at common law.[30] Before the Charter, of course, this right could be changed by statute. Now it cannot be.[31] For example, a vague description of an offence, without reference to the statute or regulation creating the offence, is a breach of s. 11(a), even if this form of description is authorized by a province's Summary Proceedings Act.[32] However, the provision of the Criminal Code that authorizes a preliminary inquiry judge to order an

---

27 *Id.*, (p. 18).

28 For commentary on s. 11(a), see Beaudoin and Mendes (eds.), *The Canadian Charter of Rights and Freedoms* (3rd ed., 1996), 11-43 (by Boisvert); Stuart, *Charter Justice in Canadian Criminal Law* (2nd ed.,1996), 298-300; McLeod, Takach, Morton, Segal, *The Canadian Charter of Rights* (Carswell, loose-leaf), ch. 11; *Canadian Charter of Rights Annotated* (Canada Law Book, loose-leaf), annotation to s. 11(a). The last work provides a bibliography of the relevant literature.

29 Section 11(a) was in the October 1980 version of the Charter, except that the word "promptly" was in place of "without unreasonable delay". The present version appeared in the April 1981 version of the Charter.

30 *Cotroni* v. *Que. Police Comm.* [1981] 1 S.C.R. 1048. However, s. 11(a) has no counterpart in the Canadian Bill of Rights. The American Bill of Rights, by the sixth amendment, gives to an accused the right "to be informed of the nature and cause of the accusation".

31 Even after the Charter, a statute would be valid if it could be justified under s. 1 (the limitation clause), or if s. 33 (the override clause) were invoked.

32 *R.* v. *Lucas* (1983) 150 D.L.R. (3d) 118 (N.S. A.D.).

accused person to stand trial not only for the offence charged in the original indictment, but also for any other indictable offence in respect of the same transaction, has been held not to be a violation of s. 11(a).[33]

The right conferred by s. 11(a), in common with all the other rights conferred by s. 11, is possessed only by "a person charged with an offence". Therefore, s. 11(a) does not provide a remedy for delay in the bringing of the charge. Nor is there a remedy under s. 11(b), which confers the right "to be tried within a reasonable time", because the reasonable time is measured from the time that the accused is charged.[34] Only if excessive pre-charge delay had the effect of impairing the accused's right to make full answer and defence would the delay be a breach of the Charter; the right to make full answer and defence is guaranteed by ss. 7 and 11(d).[35]

48.3 Trial within reasonable time (s. 11(b))

Section 11(b) of the Charter of Rights provides as follows:

> 11. Any person charged with an offence has the right
>
> . . .
>
> (b) to be tried within a reasonable time;

The right to be tried within a reasonable time has become the most frequently invoked of all the Charter rights. This is because the courts automatically grant a stay of proceedings (rather than an early trial) to an accused person whose trial has been delayed beyond a reasonable time. The volume of cases has caused me to cover the topic in a separate chapter: chapter 49, Trial within Reasonable Time, below.

48.4 Non-compellability (s. 11(c))

(a) Section 11(c)

Section 11(c) of the Charter of Rights[36] provides as follows:

> 11. Any person charged with an offence has the right

33 *R.* v. *Cancor Software Corp.* (1990) 74 O.R. (2d) 65 (C.A.).

34 Chapter 49, Trial Within Reasonable Time, under heading 49.6(a), "Pre-charge delay", below.

35 Chapter 44, Fundamental Justice, under heading 44.19, "Fair trial", above.

36 For commentary on s. 11(c), see Paciocco, *Charter Principles and Proof in Criminal Cases* (1987), ch. 8; Beaudoin and Mendes, note 28, above, 11-44–11-59 (by Boisvert); Stuart, note 28, above, 320-325; Sopinka, Lederman, Bryant, *The Law of Evidence in Canada* (1992), 600-610; 760-765; McLeod, note 28, above, ch. 13; *Canadian Charter of Rights Annotated*, note 28, above, annotation to s. 11(c); the last work provides a bibliography of the relevant literature.

. . .

(c) not to be compelled to be a witness in proceedings against that person in respect of the offence;

Section 11(c) provides that a person charged with an offence has the right not to be compelled to be a witness against himself.[37] At common law, the accused was not only not a compellable witness for the Crown, but was not even a competent witness for the defence. The latter rule was changed in Canada in 1893 by what is now s. 4(1) of the Canada Evidence Act,[38] which provides that an accused "is a competent witness for the defence". (A similar rule has been enacted in every province for the trial of provincial penal offences.) The Canada Evidence Act did not go so far as to make the accused a compellable witness for the Crown, and the accused remained non-compellable as a matter of common law. Section 11(c) is thus declaratory of the common law. One consequence of the inclusion in the Charter of the non-compellability rule is that a statute purporting to make the accused a compellable witness would be invalid.[39]

(b) Rule against self-incrimination

If an accused does decide to testify at his own trial, he cannot refuse to answer any question on the ground that the answer might incriminate him. The common law right to refuse to answer has been abolished in Canada, and replaced by the rule that the incriminating answer cannot be used against the witness in other proceedings. This rule is now in the Charter, s. 13, and is discussed in chapter 51, Self-Incrimination, below.

(c) Adverse inference from accused's silence

The Canada Evidence Act, by s. 4(6), prohibits any comment to the jury (the prohibition applies only to jury trials), by counsel for the Crown or the trial judge, on an accused's failure to testify. "The section is intended to prevent comments to the effect that an innocent person could have been expected to take the stand in his or her own defence."[40] However, the section prohibits *any* comment, so that the trial judge cannot warn the jury not to draw any adverse inference from

---

37 The Canadian Bill of Rights did not include a guarantee of non-compellability, unless it could be inferred from the reference in s. 2(d) to "protection against self crimination or other constitutional safeguards", as was suggested by Laskin J. in *Curr* v. *The Queen* [1972] S.C.R. 889, 912. The American Bill of Rights, by the fifth amendment (applicable to the states through the fourteenth amendment), provides that no person "shall be compelled in any criminal case to be a witness against himself".

38 R.S.C. 1985, c. C-5.

39 The statute would be valid if it could be justified under s. 1 (the limitation clause), or if s. 33 (the override clause) were invoked.

40 Sopinka, note 36, above, 760

the accused's failure to testify; and it is clear that the jury is fully entitled, of its own accord, to draw an adverse inference.[41]

The possibility that an adverse inference may be drawn from a failure to testify imposes some tactical pressure on the accused to testify in his own defence. It has been argued that s. 11(c) requires that these common law rules be modified: in order to remove any penalty from the exercise by the accused of his constitutional right not to testify, the trial judge ought to have to instruct the jury not to draw any adverse inference from the accused's failure to testify. The Ontario Court of Appeal[42] has rejected this argument, holding that s. 11(c) prohibits only rules that create a legal obligation to testify. The constitutional prohibition does not apply to rules that create merely a tactical obligation to testify. The Court held that there had been no breach of s. 11(c) when counsel for a co-accused (who had testified), attempting to shift the blame to the accused, commented on the failure of the accused to testify; and the trial judge did not direct the jury not to draw an adverse inference from the failure of the accused to testify.

In *R.* v. *Crawford* (1995),[43] there was a joint trial of two co-accused, each of whom sought to cast the blame on the other. Accused #1 had made a statement to the police before the trial, but he did not testify at the trial. Accused #2 had made no statement to the police before the trial, but he did testify at the trial. The question in the case was whether counsel for Accused #1 could cross-examine and comment on Accused #2's failure to tell his story to the police before the trial. Was this inconsistent with Accused #2's right to silence? The right to silence in issue here was a right to *pre-trial* silence, which is not protected by s. 11(d), because s. 11(d) protects only the right to silence at the trial. However, it has been held that s. 7 guarantees a right of pre-trial silence.[44] In *Crawford*, the Supreme Court of Canada held by a majority that Accused #2's right to silence did not protect him from cross-examination and adverse comment on his failure to tell his story to the police. However, the Court held that the accused's silence could only be used to impeach his credibility and not as evidence of guilt. Sopinka J. for the majority acknowledged that this subtle distinction ''may not be easily understood by a jury'',[45] but he held that it struck an appropriate balance between Accused #1's right to make full answer and defence and Accused #2's right to pre-trial silence.

---

41 *Id.*, 761.

42 *R.* v. *Boss* (1988) 46 C.C.C. (3d) 523 (Ont. C.A.); *R.* v. *Naglik* (1991) 3 O.R. (3d) 385 (C.A.). The latter case was reversed on another point, and the majority of the Supreme Court of Canada expressly declined to decide the right-to-silence issue: *R.* v. *Naglik* [1993] 3 S.C.R. 122, 137; L'Heureux-Dubé J. agreed with the Court of Appeal.

43 [1995] 1 S.C.R. 858. Sopinka J. wrote the opinion of the eight-judge majority. McLachlin J. dissented.

44 Chapter 44, Fundamental Justice, under heading 44.18, ''Right to silence'', above.

45 [1995] 1 S.C.R. 858, 883. McLachlin J., who dissented, would have excluded any adverse inference from the accused's silence ''either as to guilt or credibility''.

(d) Compulsion of other evidence

Section 11(c) confers the right not to be compelled "to be a witness" against oneself. This is a privilege against testimonial compulsion, not against compulsion generally. Thus the use, in evidence for the prosecution, of a breath test, taken from the accused under the compulsion of the Criminal Code, does not offend s. 11(c).[46] It is a privilege against testimonial compulsion, not against the compulsion of testimony generally. Thus, a "reverse onus" clause, which casts the burden of proving certain exculpatory facts upon the accused, does not offend s. 11(c), because the accused could discharge his burden by calling witnesses other than himself.[47]

(e) Compulsion in other proceedings

Section 11(c) confers the right not to be compelled to be a witness "in proceedings against that person in respect of the offence". The quoted language makes clear that s. 11(c) does not preclude the accused from being made compellable in proceedings that are not against him, or are not in respect of the offence.[48] For example, two persons charged with the same crime, but tried separately, can each be compelled to testify against the other at the other's trial (and preliminary inquiry).[49] As another example, a person charged with an offence can be compelled to be a witness in a civil action brought against him as the result of the same facts that led to the criminal charge.[50]

A person charged with murder could be made a compellable witness at an inquest into the death of the person with whose murder he is charged. At common

46 *R.* v. *Altseimer* (1982) 38 O.R. (2d) 783 (C.A.).

47 *R.* v. *Stanger* (1983) 2 D.L.R. (4th) 121, 125-127 (Alta. C.A.) per McClung J.A. dissenting, but not on this issue, which majority did not address. The reverse onus clause in that case, and in many other cases, has been successfully attacked under s. 11(d) of the Charter (presumption of innocence), which is the topic of the next section of this chapter.

48 However, if "the predominant purpose for seeking the evidence is to obtain incriminating evidence against the person compelled to testify," then a residual right to silence in s. 7 of the Charter will render the person non-compellable: *B.C. Securities Commn.* v. *Branch* [1995] 2 S.C.R. 3, 15; ch. 44, Fundamental Justice, under heading 44.18, "Right to silence", above.

49 *R.* v. *S.(R.J.)* [1995] 1 S.C.R. 451 (trial); *R.* v. *Primeau* [1995] 2 S.C.R. 60 (preliminary inquiry); *R.* v. *Jobin* [1995] 2 S.C.R. 78 (preliminary inquiry). At the trial of the second accused, the prosecution would have to prove the commission of the offence all over again, and s. 13 of the Charter would render inadmissible incriminating evidence given by the second accused when he was a witness at the trial of the first accused.

50 *Caisse Populaire Laurier* v. *Guertin* (1983) 43 O.R. (2d) 91, 96 (H.C.); varied without reference to this issue (1984) 46 O.R. (2d) 422 (C.A.); *Saccomano* v. *Swanson* (1987) 34 D.L.R. (4th) 462 (Alta. Q.B.) (accused a compellable witness in civil action against him). To the same effect is *Re Clarkson Co. and Bookman* (1984) 49 C.B.R. (N.S.) 267 (Ont. H.C.) (accused is compellable in an examination under the Bankruptcy Act); Cf. *Vidéotron* v. *Industries Microlec* [1992] 2 S.C.R. 1065 (person charged with civil contempt for breach of court order not a compellable witness).

law, the person charged with murder is not a compellable witness at the inquest, but this common law rule could be changed by aptly framed federal legislation.[51] Section 11(c) would not preclude such federal legislation, because the inquest is not "proceedings against that person in respect of the offence". If the person called upon to testify at the inquest has not been charged with an offence in respect of the death, then the common law rule does not apply and the person can be made compellable by provincial legislation.[52] Section 11(c) would not preclude such provincial legislation, for two reasons: (1) the inquest is not "proceedings against that person in respect of the offence", and (2) the witness is not a "person charged with an offence", which is the overriding requirement for all of s. 11's guarantees.

(f) Application to corporations

The point has already been made that s. 11's reference to "any person" includes a corporation.[53] However, the non-compellability rule would not apply to an employee of a corporation charged with an offence, just as it does not apply to an employee of a natural person charged with an offence. The employee is compellable, because the employee is not the person charged with the offence.[54] Since a corporation cannot itself testify, it follows that s. 11(c) will have little application to corporations. In *R.* v. *N. M. Paterson & Sons* (1980),[55] the Supreme Court of Canada held that a senior employee of a corporation charged with an offence could not invoke the common law rule that an accused person is not a compellable witness for the prosecution. The employee was therefore held to be a compellable witness for the prosecution. However, the offence in *Paterson* was not one involving mens rea, and the Court expressly refrained from deciding the question whether an officer or employee who was the "directing mind"[56] of the corporation would be a compellable witness in a prosecution of the corporation for an offence involving mens rea. That is the single case where the common law rule against compellability might apply to a witness in the prosecution of a corporation, and s. 11(c) might apply in that case too.[57]

---

51 *Batary* v. *A.-G. Sask.* [1965] S.C.R. 465.

52 *Faber* v. *The Queen* [1976] 2 S.C.R. 9.

53 Note 1, above.

54 *R.* v. *Amway Corp.* [1989] 1 S.C.R. 21 (employee of accused corporation compellable on discovery, even though on discovery employee may testify as to information obtained from the corporation that is outside the witness's personal knowledge); *B.C. Securities Commn.* v. *Branch* [1995] 2 S.C.R. 3 (employees of company compellable at securities commission hearing into conduct of company).

55 [1980] 2 S.C.R. 679.

56 *Canadian Dredge & Dock Co.* v. *The Queen* [1985] 1 S.C.R. 662 (upholding theory of identification to attribute to corporation the guilty mind of senior officer or employee).

57 However, in *R.* v. *Amway Corp.* [1989] 1 S.C.R. 21, 37, Sopinka J. for the Court implied that the directing mind would be as compellable as any other officer or employee.

(g) Application of s. 7 to compelled testimony

The application of s. 11(c) to the directing mind of an accused corporation is an area of doubt as to the meaning of s. 11(c). As the foregoing text has shown, the meaning of s. 11(c) is reasonably clear in most situations. However, in *Thomson Newspapers* v. *Canada* (1990),[58] the Supreme Court of Canada held that the guarantee of fundamental justice in s. 7 of the Charter included ''residual'' elements of a rule against compellability that was broader than s. 11(c). Just what that broader rule might be is unclear, because the principles of fundamental justice have been defined no more specifically than ''the basic tenets of our justice system'', and there is no agreement on what those basic tenets are.[59] In *Thomson Newspapers* itself, each of the five opinions had a different view as to what if any additional content was added to s. 11(c) (and s. 13) by s. 7. In the result, a bare majority upheld the validity of a provision in the Combines Investigation Act that obligated the officers of a corporation to undergo oral examination in an inquiry into the possible commission of an offence by the corporation.

In *Thomson Newspapers*, it was obvious that s. 11(c) did not apply: no one had been charged with an offence, and if anyone were to be charged with an offence it would be the corporation, not the individual officers. However, all judges agreed that the fact that s. 11(c) did not apply was not the end of the inquiry; the inquiry simply moved to s. 7; and two of the five judges (for entirely different reasons) held that the obligation to undergo an oral examination infringed a basic tenet of the legal system under s. 7.[60] It is an unfortunate consequence of this ''residual'' interpretation of s. 7 that it renders relatively unimportant the precise language with which s. 11 has been carefully drafted. If a particular guarantee does not apply, s. 7 will still apply if life, liberty or security of the person is affected and a court can be persuaded that a hitherto unrecognized basic tenet of the legal system has been infringed.

48.5 Presumption of innocence (s. 11(d))

(a) Section 11(d)

Section 11(d) of the Charter of Rights[61] provides as follows:

> 11. Any person charged with an offence has the right

58 [1990] 1 S.C.R. 425.

59 See ch. 44, Fundamental Justice, under heading 44.10 ''Fundamental justice'', above.

60 *Ibid.*, where the five different points of view are described.

61 For commentary on s. 11(d), see Morton and Hutchison, *Presumption of Innocence* (1987); Charles, Cromwell and Jobson, *Evidence and the Charter of Rights and Freedoms* (1989), ch. 2; Beaudoin and Mendes, note 28, above, 11-59–11-69 (by Boisvert); Stuart, note 28, above, 325-354; McLeod, note 28, above, ch. 15; *Canadian Charter of Rights Annotated*, note 28, above, annotation to s. 11(d); the last work provides a bibliography of the relevant literature.

. . .

(d) to be presumed innocent until proven guilty according to law in a fair and public hearing by an independent and impartial tribunal;

Section 11(d) is very similar to s. 2(f) of the Canadian Bill of Rights. There is no provision quite like s. 11(d) in the American Bill of Rights, although the due process clauses of the fifth and fourteenth amendments have been held to include a presumption of innocence[62] and the sixth amendment gives to an accused the right to a ''public'' trial by an ''impartial'' jury.

(b) Reverse onus clauses

The presumption of innocence, which is conferred by s. 11(d) upon any person charged with an offence, exists at common law, and finds expression in the rule that the Crown bears the burden of proving the guilt of the accused (instead of the accused having to prove his innocence), reinforced by the further rule that the standard of proof that must be satisfied by the Crown is proof beyond a reasonable doubt (instead of proof on the balance of probabilities).

Common law rules can of course be changed by apt legislation, and ''reverse onus'' clauses, which cast the burden of proof of some matters on the accused, are to be found in some statutes. In *R.* v. *Oakes* (1986),[63] the Supreme Court of Canada struck down a reverse onus clause in the federal Narcotic Control Act. The clause provided that proof that the accused was in possession of an illegal drug raised a presumption that the accused was in possession for the purpose of trafficking. The Supreme Court of Canada held that s. 11(d) required that the Crown must bear the burden of proving the guilt of a person charged with an offence, and the standard of the Crown's proof must be the criminal standard of proof beyond a reasonable doubt. Any provision that imposed on the accused ''the burden of disproving on a balance of probabilities an essential element of an offence'' would be a breach of s. 11(d), because it would make it ''possible for a conviction to occur despite the existence of a reasonable doubt''.[64]

The effect of the presumption in the Narcotic Control Act was that once the Crown proved beyond a reasonable doubt that the accused was in possession of an illegal drug (the proved fact), then the trier of fact was required[65] to make the

---

62 *Re Winship* (1970) 397 U.S. 358 (due process requires proof of guilt beyond a reasonable doubt).

63 [1986] 1 S.C.R. 103. The majority opinion was written by Dickson C.J. with the concurrence of four others. Estey J., with whom McIntyre J. agreed, wrote a concurring opinion.

64 Id., 132. Cf. *R.* v. *Bray* (1983) 40 O.R. (2d) 766 (C.A.) (reverse onus with respect to grounds for bail, not an essential element of the offence, upheld); *R.* v. *Potvin* [1989] 1 S.C.R. 525 (reverse onus with respect to admission of evidence, not an essential element of the offence, upheld).

65 This was a ''mandatory'' presumption, because the trier of fact was required to infer the presumed fact (purpose of trafficking) from the proved fact (possession). A ''permissive'' presumption merely permits the trier of fact to make the inference of the presumed fact. A permissive presumption does not infringe s. 11(d): *R.* v. *Downey* [1992] 2 S.C.R. 10, 29 per Cory J. obiter for majority.

inference that the accused was in possession for the purpose of trafficking (the presumed fact). This inference made the accused guilty of the offence of possession for the purpose of trafficking, which was a more serious offence than simple possession. The accused could rebut the presumption by proving that the presumed fact (purpose of trafficking) was not true. It is a general rule of the criminal law that, when an element of a criminal offence has to be disproved by the accused, the standard of proof is not the criminal one of proof beyond a reasonable doubt but the civil one of proof on the balance of probabilities. But the Court held that the lowering of the standard of proof did not make a reverse onus clause constitutional, because the clause still relieved the Crown of its constitutional duty to prove all elements of the offence to the criminal standard of proof beyond a reasonable doubt. In the case of the Narcotic Control Act's reverse onus clause, the accused might adduce sufficient evidence to raise a reasonable doubt as to whether the presumed fact (purpose of trafficking) was untrue, but not enough evidence to persuade the trier of fact on a balance of probabilities that the presumed fact was untrue. In that event, the reverse onus clause would require the accused to be convicted of possession for the purpose of trafficking, despite the fact that there was a reasonable doubt as to the existence of an essential element of the offence. It followed that the reverse onus clause violated s. 11(d), and the Court went on to hold that it was not saved by s. 1; the clause was therefore unconstitutional.

The reversal of the onus in *Oakes* related to ''an essential element of the offence''. In *R.* v. *Whyte* (1988),[66] the Supreme Court of Canada had to consider a reverse onus clause that did not relate to an essential element of the offence. The Criminal Code made it an offence to have the ''care or control'' of a motor vehicle while intoxicated. The Code provided that, where an accused occupied the driver's seat of a motor vehicle, he was deemed to have the care or control of the vehicle unless he established (proved on the balance of probabilities) ''that he did not enter or mount the vehicle for the purpose of setting it in motion''. The Crown argued that this clause did not infringe the presumption of innocence, because the intention of setting the vehicle in motion was not an element of the offence. The Court rejected the argument, holding that the presumption of innocence was infringed not only by a requirement to disprove an essential element of the offence but also by this requirement to disprove ''a fact collateral to the substantive offence''.[67] It made no difference whether the fact to be proved was characterized as ''an essential element, a collateral factor, an excuse, or a defence''.[68] If the accused was required to prove some fact on the balance of probabilities in order to avoid conviction, then there was an infringement of the presumption of innocence, because the requirement ''permits a conviction in spite

66 [1988] 2 S.C.R. 3. Dickson C.J. wrote the unanimous opinion of the Court.
67 *Id.*, 18
68 *Ibid.*

of a reasonable doubt in the mind of the trier of fact as to the guilt of the accused''.[69] This reverse onus clause therefore infringed s. 11(d), although the Court went on to uphold the clause under s. 1 as a measure to prevent drunken driving.

The prohibition against reverse onus clauses applies even to excuses or defences.[70] It is an infringement of the presumption of innocence to impose on an accused person the burden of establishing (proving on the balance of probabilities) an excuse or a defence. The hate propaganda offence of the Criminal Code makes truth a defence, but casts upon the accused the burden of proving that the impugned statements are true. That is a breach of s. 11(d).[71] Many regulatory offences (public welfare offences) are offences of strict liability,[72] to which due diligence is a defence, but the burden of proving due diligence is imposed on the accused. That is also a breach of s. 11(d).[73] Even the defence of insanity infringes s. 11(d), because the Criminal Code enacts a presumption of sanity[74] and requires insanity to be proved by the accused.[75] In all these cases, the burden of proving the defence could not be placed on the accused, because that would ''permit a conviction in spite of a reasonable doubt in the mind of the trier of fact as to the guilt of the accused''.[76] However, in all these cases, the Court's bark was worse than its bite, because in each footnoted case the reversal of the onus of proving the defence was upheld under s. 1.

In all the reverse onus cases discussed so far, the challenged provision imposed on the accused a burden of persuasion — a burden of proving (or disproving) some fact on the balance of probabilities. In *R.* v. *Downey* (1992),[77]

69 *Ibid.*

70 But note *R.* v. *Holmes* [1988] 1 S.C.R. 914 and *R.* v. *Schwartz* [1988] 2 S.C.R. 443, where a majority of the Court held that an excusing provision was not a reverse onus clause.

71 *R.* v. *Keegstra* [1990] 3 S.C.R. 697 (upholding the clause by a majority on the basis of s. 1); *R.* v. *Keegstra (No. 3)* [1996] 1 S.C.R. 458 (clause again upheld under s. 1 by a unanimous Court).

72 For an explanation of strict liability, see ch. 44, Fundamental Justice, under heading 44.11, ''Absolute and strict liability'', above.

73 *R.* v. *Wholesale Travel Group* [1991] 3 S.C.R. 154 (a majority of seven to two held that the reverse onus clause infringed s. 11(d), but the clause was upheld by the two votes that held that there was no breach of s. 11(d) plus the three votes that held that the clause should be upheld under s. 1).

74 The relevant section of the Criminal Code has since been amended, the primary difference between the new sections and the old being that the term ''insanity'' has been replaced by the term ''mental disorder''.

75 *R.* v. *Chaulk* [1990] 3 S.C.R. 1303 (a majority of seven to two held that the reverse onus clause infringed s. 11(d), but all seven held that the clause should be upheld under s. 1); foll'd. in *R.* v. *Ratti* [1991] 1 S.C.R. 68; *R.* v. *Romeo* [1991] 1 S.C.R. 86. In *R.* v. *Daviault* [1994] 3 S.C.R. 63, the Court created a reverse onus clause, holding (without any statutory provision) that the defence of extreme intoxication had to be established by the accused on the balance of probabilities; the defence was said to be akin to insanity, so that the reversal of the onus was justified under s. 1.

76 *Id.*, 1330-1331.

77 [1992] 2 S.C.R. 10. The majority opinion was written by Cory J. with the concurrence of L'Heureux-Dubé, Sopinka and Gonthier JJ. McLachlin J., with the concurrence of Iacobucci J. and La Forest J., wrote dissenting opinions.

the Supreme Court of Canada had to review a provision that did not impose on the accused a burden of persuasion, but did impose a burden of adducing (or pointing to) evidence. The Criminal Code made it an offence to live off the avails of prostitution. The Code went on to provide that evidence that the accused "lives with or is habitually in the company of prostitutes" constituted, in the absence of evidence to the contrary, "proof that the [accused] lives on the avails of prostitution". This provision, upon proof that the accused lived with a prostitute (the proved fact), cast upon the accused the burden of *raising a reasonable doubt* that the accused lived on the avails of prostitution (the presumed fact). At the most, the provision would require the accused to adduce evidence to raise a reasonable doubt as to whether he was living on the avails of prostitution. The provision would not require the accused himself to testify, since the testimony of other defence witnesses might suffice. The provision would not even require the accused to call defence evidence if a reasonable doubt emerged from the defence's cross-examination of the Crown witnesses who testified as to the accused's living with a prostitute (the fact that the Crown had to prove). Nevertheless, the Court held unanimously that this evidentiary presumption infringed the presumption of innocence in s. 11(d). According to Cory J. for the majority, "the fact that someone lives with a prostitute" (the proved fact) "does not lead inexorably to the conclusion that the person is living on avails" (the presumed fact).[78] The absence of an "inexorable" connection between the proved fact and the presumed fact "can result in the conviction of an accused despite the existence of a reasonable doubt".[79] This possibility (however unlikely) caused the evidentiary presumption to infringe s. 11(d). However, Cory J. upheld the provision under s. 1, relying on the Crown's difficulty in getting prostitutes to testify against their pimp, and the ease with which an innocent accused could rebut the merely evidentiary presumption.[80]

In *R.* v. *Osolin* (1993),[81] there was a challenge to a provision of the Criminal Code that provided that, where an accused claimed that he had an honest belief that the complainant consented to his actions (it was a sexual assault in that case), the judge should put the defence to the jury "if satisfied that there is sufficient evidence and that, if believed by the jury, the evidence would constitute a defence". It was objected that, by its requirement of "sufficient evidence", this provision imposed a burden on the accused that was inconsistent with the presumption of innocence. The Supreme Court of Canada unanimously upheld the provision. Unlike the provision in *Downey*, this provision did not create any

78 *Id.*, 30.

79 *Ibid.* La Forest and McLachlin JJ., who dissented on the issue of s. 1 justification, expressly agreed with Cory J. on this issue.

80 Cf. *R.* v. *Laba* [1994] 3 S.C.R. 965 (reverse onus clause casting burden of persuasion on accused could be justified under s. 1 if it only cast evidentiary burden on accused; held, clause should be modified accordingly).

81 [1993] 4 S.C.R. 595. The Court was unanimous on the point discussed in the text, although five opinions were written and the Court was divided on the outcome of the appeal.

presumption. It simply required the accused to adduce or point to some evidence on the basis of which a jury could find that there was a reasonable doubt as to the existence of an honest belief. Indeed, although the Criminal Code provision addressed only the defence of mistaken belief, the same threshold had to be crossed in the case of all criminal defences before the trial judge could properly leave them to the jury. The *Osolin* case decides that the presumption of innocence is not infringed by a provision that does no more than impose on the accused the burden of adducing sufficient evidence to raise a reasonable doubt as to the presence or absence of some fact that is a defence (or an element of the offence, a collateral factor or an excuse). An evidentiary burden of this kind does not infringe s.11(d), because the burden of proving all elements of the offence beyond a reasonable doubt remains on the Crown.

While s. 11(d) prohibits the reversal of the burden of proof of a fact that is an element of the offence, s. 11(d) has nothing to say about the *elimination* of an element of the offence. If Parliament were to take the more radical step of eliminating an element of an offence, the accused would be worse off than if the burden of disproving that element had been reversed. Yet the accused would be unable to invoke s. 11(d), because there would have been no interference with the presumption of innocence. Under s. 7, however, there are restrictions on the power of Parliament to eliminate elements of offences for which imprisonment is a punishment (imprisonment being a deprivation of ''liberty'').[82] For example, it is a violation of s. 7 to eliminate all requirement of fault (mens rea or negligence) from the elements of an offence;[83] in the case of ''true crimes'' (as opposed to ''regulatory offences''), it is a violation of s. 7 to eliminate the requirement of mens rea;[84] in the case of murder and some other offences carrying special stigma, the Court has insisted on special levels of mens rea.[85] Thus, the elements of a serious criminal offence (one involving imprisonment) may include not only those enacted by the Parliament or Legislature, but also additional elements called for by s. 7's requirement of fundamental justice. Section 11(d) then reinforces s. 7 by requiring that all the elements of the offence, including those added under s. 7, must be proved by the Crown to the criminal standard of proof beyond a reasonable doubt.[86]

(c) Fair and public hearing

Section 11(d) provides that a person charged with an offence is entitled to a ''fair and public hearing''.

The requirement that a hearing be ''fair'' is explicit in s. 11(d), but that has not deterred the Supreme Court of Canada from holding that the same requirement

---

82 See ch. 44, Fundamental Justice, above.
83 E.g., *Re B.C. Motor Vehicle Act* [1985] 2 S.C.R. 486.
84 *R.* v. *Wholesale Travel Group* [1991] 3 S.C.R. 154.
85 E.g., *R.* v. *Vaillancourt* [1987] 2 S.C.R. 636.
86 *R.* v. *Penno* [1990] 2 S.C.R. 865, 897 (explaining relationship between ss. 7 and 11(d)).

is implicit in the guarantee of fundamental justice of s. 7. In order to avoid repetition, I have discussed the cases in chapter 44, Fundamental Justice, above.[87]

The requirement of s. 11(d) that a hearing be ''public'' would entail a trial in open court, without restrictions on reporting by the media.[88] However, it is likely that s. 1 of the Charter would sustain limited statutory provisions for closed trials, or for suppression of names or details where important privacy interests are at stake.

(d) Independent and impartial tribunal

Section 11(d) confers upon a person charged with an offence a right to a fair and public hearing by ''an independent and impartial tribunal''. The question of the degree of independence that must be possessed by the judges of courts of criminal jurisdiction, in order to satisfy the requirement of ''an independent and impartial tribunal'', has been considered in connection with the independence of the judiciary in chapter 7, Courts, above.[89]

The word ''tribunal'' by itself obviously does not call for a jury, but s. 11(f) does call for a jury ''where the maximum punishment for the offence is imprisonment for five years or a more severe punishment''.[90]

48.6 Reasonable bail (s. 11(e))

Section 11(e) of the Charter of Rights[91] provides as follows:

> 11. Any person charged with an offence has the right
>
> . . .
>
> (e) not to be denied reasonable bail without just cause;

---

87 See ch. 44, Fundamental Justice, under heading 44.19, ''Fair trial'', above.

88 *R.* v. *Sophonow (No. 2)* (1983) 150 D.L.R. (3d) 590 (Man. C.A.) (accused not entitled to pretrial suppression of publicity regarding his case); *R.* v. *D.(G.)* (1991) 2 O.R. (3d) 498 (C.A.) (accused not entitled to suppression of his identity at trial). The issue of press access to trials has been raised by the press, not under s. 11(d) (since the press is not a ''person charged with an offence''), but under s. 2(b) (freedom of expression). This is discussed in ch. 40, Expression, under heading 40.13, ''Access to courts'', above.

89 Section 7.1(c), ''Tenure of provincial judges'', above. See also *R.* v. *Cohn* (1984) 48 O.R. (2d) 65 (C.A.) (trial of contempt charge by judge before whom contempt took place not a breach of s. 11(d)).

90 Section 11(f) is discussed later in this chapter: sec. 48.7, ''Trial by jury (s. 11(f))'', below.

91 For commentary on s. 11(e), see Beaudoin and Mendes, note 28, above, 10-86–10-94 (by Chevrette and Cyr); Stuart, note 28, above, 272-278; McLeod, note 28, above, ch. 16; *Canadian Charter of Rights Annotated*, note 28, above, annotation to s. 11(e); the last work includes a bibliography of the relevant literature.

Section 11(e) confers on any person charged with an offence the right ''not to be denied reasonable bail without just cause''.[92] This is very similar to s. 2(f) of the Canadian Bill of Rights, which provides that a person charged with a criminal offence is not to be deprived of ''the right to reasonable bail without just cause''.[93] The American Bill of Rights, by the eighth amendment, provides that ''excessive bail shall not be required''.[94]

The term ''bail'' has not actually been used in the Criminal Code since the enactment of the Bail Reform Act[95] in 1971, which replaced the term bail with the term ''judicial interim release'', and which replaced the provisions for bail in the Criminal Code with new provisions for judicial interim release. However, the Supreme Court of Canada has held that the word ''bail'' in s. 11(e) refers to all forms of judicial interim release.[96] What s. 11(e) requires is that pre-trial release from custody, by whatever name called, must be ''reasonable'' and must not be denied ''without just cause''. The right conferred by s. 11(e) is ''a basic entitlement to be granted reasonable bail unless there is just cause to do otherwise''.[97]

What is ''reasonable'' bail? The term ''reasonable'' refers to the terms of bail. The amount must be reasonable, and so must be the restrictions on the liberty of the accused while out on bail.[98]

What is ''just cause'' for a denial of bail? The term ''just cause'' imposes a constitutional standard on the reasons for denying bail. The Supreme Court of Canada has said that a law authorizing the denial of bail will meet the constitutional standard of just cause if (1) the law denies bail ''only in a narrow set of circumstances'', and (2) ''the denial of bail is necessary to promote the proper functioning of the bail system and is not undertaken for any purpose extraneous to the bail system''.[99]

The Criminal Code (since its amendment in 1971) establishes a regime under which an accused must normally be granted bail (judicial interim release). The

---

92 Section 11(e) was in the October 1980 version of the Charter (as s. 11(d)) in a watered-down form:

> (d) not to be denied reasonable bail except on grounds, and in accordance with procedures, established by law;

In this version there is no requirement that bail be denied only for just cause; a denial in accordance with the law (even if not for just cause) would be unreviewable. The present language of s. 11(e) was included in the April 1981 version of the Charter.

93 For discussion of s. 2(f), see Tarnopolsky, *The Canadian Bill of Rights* (2nd ed., 1975), 276-277. In *R.* v. *Bray* (1983) 40 O.R. (2d) 766, 770 (C.A.), the Court said that ''the language of s. 11(e) of the Charter is virtually identical to that of s. 2(f) and has the same meaning''.

94 For discussion of this right, see La Fave and Israel, *Criminal Procedure* (2nd ed., 1992), 600-606.

95 S.C. 1970-71-72, c. 37; see now Criminal Code, R.S.C. 1985, c. C-46, ss. 515-526.

96 *R.* v. *Pearson* [1992] 3 S.C.R. 665, 690.

97 *Id.*, 691.

98 *Id.*, 689.

99 *Id.*, 693; *R.* v. *Morales* [1992] 3 S.C.R. 711, 726.

Code provides for a denial of bail where either (1) the accused's detention is necessary to ensure his attendance in court, or (2) his detention is necessary for the protection or safety of the public, having regard to the likelihood that he would commit further crimes pending his trial. It has been held that these two grounds constitute ''just cause'' for a denial of bail within the meaning of s. 11(e).[100] The Criminal Code used to include a third ground, namely, where the detention of the accused is ''necessary in the public interest''. In *R.* v. *Morales* (1992),[101] the Supreme Court of Canada, by a majority, held that this third ground was void for vagueness. The statutory criterion of ''the public interest'' was too ''vague and imprecise'' to satisfy the constitutional standard of just cause.[102]

The Criminal Code generally places the onus on the prosecution to establish that the pre-trial detention of the accused is justified on one of the two grounds for the denial of bail stipulated by the Code. However, there are certain exceptional provisions that shift the onus to the accused, who must establish that his detention is not justified under either of the two grounds. The Supreme Court of Canada has held that these reverse-onus provisions, by denying the ''basic entitlement to bail'', are to be regarded as denials of bail; they are therefore invalid unless they meet the constitutional standard of ''just cause'' under s. 11(e). In *R. v. Morales* (1992),[103] the Supreme Court of Canada, which was unanimous on this issue, upheld a reversal of the onus of proof in the case where an accused was charged with committing an indictable offence while at large and awaiting trial on an earlier indictable offence. In this situation, where there are reasonable grounds to believe that the accused has already committed an offence while out on bail, the Court held that there is just cause for requiring the accused to bear the onus of persuading the Court that he is not likely to do so again.

R. v. *Pearson* (1992)[104] was another reverse-onus case, and a more difficult one. At issue was a provision of the Criminal Code that imposed on persons charged with drug trafficking (and certain other narcotics offences) the onus of establishing that they should be released until their trial. The Supreme Court of Canada, by a majority, upheld this provision. According to Lamer C.J. for the majority, those engaged in drug trafficking often have access to funding and sophisticated organizations that could assist in a flight from justice. The greater risk of an accused drug trafficker absconding before trial amounted to just cause for requiring the accused to bear the onus of persuading the Court that he should be released. McLachlin J., for the dissenting minority, would have struck down

100 *R.* v. *Bray* (1983) 40 O.R. (2d) 766, 769 (C.A.).

101 [1992] 3 S.C.R. 711. Lamer C.J. wrote the majority opinion with the concurrence of La Forest, Sopinka, McLachlin and Iacobucci JJ.; Gonthier J., with the concurrence of L'Heureux-Dubé J., wrote a dissenting opinion.

102 *Id.*, 728.

103 Note 101, above.

104 [1992] 3 S.C.R. 665. Lamer C.J. wrote the majority opinion with the concurrence of L'Heureux-Dubé, Sopinka, Gonthier and Iacobucci JJ.; McLachlin J., with the concurrence of La Forest J., wrote a dissenting opinion.

the reverse-onus provision on the ground that it was broader than necessary. In her view, the rationale for reversing the onus did not extent to the small scale drug trafficker, and yet the reverse-onus provision made no distinction between small and large operators.

48.7 Trial by jury (s. 11(f))

(a) Section 11(f)

Section 11(f) of the Charter of Rights[105] provides as follows:

> 11. Any person charged with an offence has the right
>
> . . .
>
> (f) except in the case of an offence under military law tried before a military tribunal, to the benefit of trial by jury where the maximum punishment for the offence is imprisonment for five years or a more severe punishment;

Section 11(f) confers upon any person charged with an offence[106] the right to the benefit of trial by jury ''where the maximum punishment for the offence is imprisonment for five years or a more severe punishment''. This is a new right, which before the Charter had never been recognized in Canada. The Canadian Bill of Rights contains no right to the benefit of trial by jury. The American Bill of Rights, by the sixth amendment (applicable to the states through the fourteenth amendment), confers upon an accused the right to trial ''by an impartial jury of the state and district wherein the crime shall have been committed''. This right has been judicially restricted to ''serious'' offences, meaning those that carry a penalty of more than six months' imprisonment.[107]

(b) Punishment

The word ''punishment'' in s. 11(f)[108] was interpreted by the British Columbia Court of Appeal in *R.* v. *S.B.* (1983).[109] In that case, the Court held that a

105 For commentary on s. 11(f), see Beaudoin and Mendes, note 28, above, 12-13 (by Morel); Stuart, note 28, above, 362-370; McLeod, note 28, above, ch. 17; *Canadian Charter of Rights Annotated*, note 28, above, annotation to s. 11(f); the last work contains a bibliography of the relevant literature.

106 Cf. *R.* v. *Lyons* [1987] 2 S.C.R. 309 (application by Crown to designate accused a dangerous offender is not equivalent to charging him with an offence; application need not be tried by a jury); *Man.* v. *Groupe Quebecor* (1987) 45 D.L.R. (4th) 80 (Man. C.A.) (contempt of court not an offence within s. 11, and not attracting right to trial by jury); *R.* v. *Cohn*, note 108, below.

107 *Blanton* v. *City of North Las Vegas* (1989) 489 U.S. 538. For general discussion of the right to trial by jury, see La Fave and Israel, *Criminal Procedure* (2nd ed., 1992), ch. 22.

108 It is the ''maximum'' punishment that triggers the right. *R.* v. *Cohn* (1984) 48 O.R. (2d) 65 (C.A.), holding that there is no right to trial by jury on a charge of contempt of court, was based on actual sentencing practices, which seems to be incorrect. Cf. *Man.* v. *Groupe Quebecor*, note 106, above.

109 (1983) 146 D.L.R. (3d) 69 (B.C. C.A.).

young accused, charged with an offence under the Juvenile Delinquents Act, was not entitled to the benefit of trial by jury. The accused was liable to be sentenced to confinement in an ''industrial school'' for more than five years. The Court held that the purpose of the confinement was to treat the offender, not to punish him; therefore, the sentence would not constitute ''punishment'' within the meaning of s. 11(f); therefore, the accused was not entitled to the benefit of trial by jury under s. 11(f). This result is open to the criticism that the Court was unduly influenced by the euphemisms in which Parliament had couched the provisions of the Juvenile Delinquents Act. The compulsory incarceration of a person who has committed a crime, even in a place which is described as an industrial school rather than a penitentiary or a prison, should surely be characterized as a ''punishment''.[110] If there are sound policy reasons for not permitting young offenders to be tried by a jury, then the limitation of the s. 11(f) right should be justified under s. 1 (the limitation clause) of the Charter.

(c) Application to corporations

Any ''person'' charged with an offence would generally include a corporation.[111] But in *Re PPG Industries* (1983),[112] the British Columbia Court of Appeal held that a corporation was not entitled to the benefit of trial by jury under s. 11(f). The accused corporation had been charged with bid-rigging, an offence under the Combines Investigation Act, which carried a penalty of imprisonment for five years or a fine. The Act expressly provided that ''a corporation charged with an offence under this Act shall be tried without the intervention of a jury''. The court held that this provision was not a denial of the right conferred by s. 11(f). Since a corporation could not be imprisoned, the ''maximum punishment'' for a corporation could only be the alternative of a fine. Therefore, the right to the benefit of trial by jury could not be possessed by a corporation. A dissenting opinion pointed out that the right to trial by jury was one that a corporation could enjoy (unlike, for example, the right under s. 11(e) not to be denied reasonable bail); and the purpose of s. 11(f), to provide the benefit of a jury trial for the most serious offences, was as relevant to a corporation as an individual.

(d) Waiver of right

Section 11(f) confers the right to ''the benefit'' of trial by jury. This makes clear that the right to trial by jury can be waived.[113] If the law makes provision

---

110 Cf. *Re Gault* (1967) 387 U.S. 1, 27 (juvenile offender liable to committal to ''industrial school'' entitled to full due process rights, including right to counsel).

111 Chapter 34, Application of Charter, under heading 34.1, ''Benefit of rights'', above.

112 (1983) 146 D.L.R. (3d) 261 (B.C. C.A.).

113 *R.* v. *Turpin* [1989] 1 S.C.R. 1296, 1314-1316. On the waiver of rights under the Criminal Code, see *Korponay* v. *A.-G. Can.* [1982] 1 S.C.R. 41. In the United States, it has been held that the sixth amendment right to trial by jury may be waived by the accused: *Patton* v. *United States* (1930) 281 U.S. 276.

for an accused to elect against trial by jury, as the Criminal Code does, there is no breach of s. 11(f). So long as a trial by judge alone (or any other mode of trial) depends upon the choice of the accused (and not the Crown or the court), the accused may be said to have the benefit of trial by jury.

Section 11(f) confers only a right to trial by jury. It does not confer a right to a choice of the mode of trial. The Criminal Code used to make a trial by jury mandatory for the most serious offences, including murder. In *R.* v. *Turpin* (1989),[114] the two accused, who were charged with murder, applied to be tried by judge alone, invoking s. 11(f). The Supreme Court of Canada agreed that they had waived their constitutional right to trial by jury. But the effect of the waiver was not to confer a right to trial by judge alone. The effect of the waiver was simply to make s. 11(d) inapplicable. The Criminal Code continued to govern the proceedings, and the Criminal Code stipulated that the trial must be by jury. Section 11(f) did not create a constitutional right to elect a mode of trial other than by jury, or a constitutional right to be tried by a judge alone.

A waiver of the right to trial by jury, like the waiver of any other constitutional right, must be "clear and unequivocal" and must be made with full awareness of the consequences of the waiver.[115] The failure of an accused to appear for his trial does not constitute a waiver of the right to trial by jury. On this basis, the Supreme Court of Canada[116] has held that s. 11(f) was violated by a provision of the Criminal Code that provided for the trial by judge alone of an accused who had elected trial by jury but who had failed to appear for his trial without a legitimate excuse. The effect of the provision was to impose on the accused a mode of trial that he had not chosen — or had not chosen in a "clear and unequivocal" way. However, a majority of the Court upheld the provision under s. 1: it was appropriate, they decided, to deny the right to trial by jury to an accused who had burdened the system with the cost of futilely empanelling a jury.

(e) Jury

The word "jury" is not defined. Laws changing the composition or function of the jury, for example, reducing the number of jurors, or changing the rule of unanimity, could be vulnerable on the ground that the resulting panel would not be a "jury" within the meaning of s. 11(f).[117] It is likely however that a court would concede to the Parliament a considerable leeway in regulating the composition of a jury. In the United States, a body of case law has accumulated on

---

114 [1989] 1 S.C.R. 1296. Wilson J. wrote for the Court.

115 *R.* v. *Lee* [1989] 2 S.C.R. 1384, 1411.

116 *Ibid.* Wilson J. for six of the seven judges held that s. 11(f) had been infringed;. Gonthier J. dissented on this issue. Lamer J. for four of the six judges held that the provision was saved by s. 1. Wilson J., with Sopinka J., dissented on this issue; Gonthier J. did not reach this issue, having held that there was no denial of the right.

117 Cf. *R.* v. *Bain* [1992] 1 S.C.R. 91 (jury selection process allowing Crown but not defence to "stand by" jurors violates right to independent and impartial tribunal under s. 11(d)).

the interpretation of the word ''jury'' in the sixth amendment. It has been held that the states (to which the sixth amendment applies only through the fourteenth amendment) have more leeway than the Congress in departing from the standard model of the unanimous decision by a twelve-member jury. A state can reduce the number of jurors from 12 to six,[118] but cannot go as low as five.[119] A state can abolish the rule of unanimity for a 12-member jury,[120] but not for a six-member jury.[121]

(f) Offence under military law

Section 11(f) is explicit that the right to trial by jury does not apply ''in the case of an offence under military law tried before a military tribunal''.

What is an ''offence under military law''? The National Defence Act[122] contains a very broad definition of the ''service offences'' that under that Act are triable by a military tribunal. The definition includes not only a breach of military law, but any breach by a member of the armed forces of the Criminal Code, the Narcotic Control Act and other statutes applicable to the public at large. For the purpose of s. 11(f), this definition should be read down to include only offences which are committed in circumstances connected to military service.[123]

(g) Role of judge

In *R.* v. *Osolin* (1993),[124] a challenge was brought to a requirement of the Criminal Code that there be ''sufficient evidence'' before a defence of honest belief in consent to a sexual assault be put to the jury. The accused, who was tried and convicted of a sexual assault by a jury, complained that his right to a trial by jury under s. 11(f) had been violated, because the trial judge did not put to the jury the accused's (highly implausible) defence that he mistakenly believed that

118 *Williams* v. *Florida* (1970) 399 U.S. 78.

119 *Ballew* v. *Georgia* (1978) U.S. 223.

120 *Apodaca* v. *Oregon* (1972) 406 U.S. 404.

121 *Burch* v. *Louisiana* (1979) 441 U.S. 130. See generally LaFave and Israel, *Criminal Procedure* (2nd ed., 1992) ch. 22.

122 R.S.C. 1985, c. N-5.

123 This was suggested by McIntyre J. in his concurring opinion in *MacKay* v. *The Queen* [1980] 2 S.C.R. 370, 380, a pre-Charter case, in which the Court held that the trial of a soldier by a military tribunal did not offend the Canadian Bill of Rights guarantees of equality before the law (s. 1(b)) or a fair hearing (s. 2(f)). In *R.* v. *McDonald* (1983) 150 D.L.R. (3d) 620 (Court Martial Appeal Court), it was held that, to come within the phrase ''offence under military law'' in s. 11(f), an offence must be within the definition in the National Defence Act and have ''a military nexus''. See generally Lunau, ''Military Tribunals under the Charter'' (1992) 2 Nat. J. Con. Law 197.

124 The Court was unanimous on the point discussed in the text, although five opinions were written and the Court was divided on the outcome of the appeal.

the complainant had consented to his act. The Supreme Court of Canada unanimously rejected the argument. In a jury trial, among the supervisory duties of the trial judge was the duty to determine whether there was sufficient evidence to put a defence to the jury. That was an issue of law that lay within the domain of the judge. Its determination by the judge was not a violation of the accused's right to trial by jury.

48.8 Retroactive offences (s. 11(g))

Section 11(g) of the Charter of Rights[125] provides as follows:

> 11. Any person charged with an offence has the right
>
> (g) not to be found guilty on account of any act or omission unless, at the time of the act or omission, it constituted an offence under Canadian or international law or was criminal according to the general principles of law recognized by the community of nations;

Section 11(g) limits the power of the federal Parliament or provincial Legislatures[126] to create retroactive (or ex post facto) offences.[127] If the Parliament or a Legislature does purport to pass a law which creates such an offence, the law will be effective retroactively only if the newly-illegal act or omission constituted at the time of its occurrence an offence under international law or was criminal according to the general principles of law recognized by the community of nations. Needless to say, s. 11(g) does not change the fundamental principle that a person cannot be found guilty of an offence in Canada merely because his act or omission was a breach of a principle of international law or a principle of law recognized by the community of nations. Only if such a principle were translated into Canadian statute law would a person be exposed to penalty (or any other legal consequence) within Canada. However, s. 11(g) does permit such a principle to

---

125 For commentary on s. 11(g), see Beaudoin and Ratushny, note 28, above, 434-444 (by Chevrette); Stuart, note 28, above, 370-371; McLeod, note 28, above, ch. 18; *Canadian Charter of Rights Annotated*, note 28, above, annotation to s. 11(g); the last work contains a bibliography of the relevant literature.

126 Where a person commits a breach of a law that has previously been declared by a court to be unconstitutional, and after the commission of the breach the earlier decision is reversed or overruled by a court that upholds the validity of the law, s. 11(g) would probably preclude a conviction for the breach: see ch. 55, Effect of Unconstitutional Law, under heading 55.1, "Invalidity of unconstitutional law", below.

127 Section 11(g) would also apply to amendments to existing offences, including defences, at least if the substantive law is made more onerous to the accused. Section 11(g) would not, however, apply to changes in the law respecting evidence or procedure. See Beaudoin and Mendes, note 28, above, 10-94–10-108 (by Chevrette and Cyr).

be translated into Canadian law retroactively, if the competent legislative body does so by apt language.[128]

Canada's Criminal Code contains provisions that were enacted in 1987,[129] following the recommendation of a Commission of Inquiry,[130] to punish crimes against humanity and war crimes, even though the crimes were committed outside Canada and before 1987. The Code provisions apply to any act or omission committed outside Canada that constitutes a "crime against humanity" or a "war crime" that would also have been a crime under Canadian domestic law had it been committed in Canada. In *R.* v. *Finta* (1994),[131] the Code provisions were invoked against an accused who had emigrated to Canada after the Second World War and become a Canadian citizen. The accused was alleged to have participated in the unlawful confinement, robbery, kidnapping and manslaughter of 8,617 Jews in Hungary in 1944 when the accused (then a Hungarian citizen) was a captain in a Hungarian police force carrying out the Nazi policy of eliminating the Jews. He was charged with unlawful confinement, robbery, kidnapping and manslaughter, all of which were Criminal Code offences in Canada in 1944, and the indictment added that the accused's actions constituted crimes against humanity and war crimes within the meaning of the 1987 Criminal Code provisions. The accused was tried by a jury in Ontario and acquitted. On appeal by the Crown, the acquittal was affirmed by a majority of the Supreme Court of Canada.

In *Finta*, although the Court divided four to three on several issues of interpretation of the war-crimes provisions, six of the seven judges[132] upheld the constitutionality of the provisions against a variety of attacks.[133] In particular, the attack based on retroactivity was rejected. Cory J. (with Gonthier and Major JJ.) held that the provisions were retroactive in their effect, but for reasons that were

---

128 Section 11(g) was in the October 1980 version of the Charter (as s. 11(e)) in the following terms:

> (e) not to be found guilty on account of any act or omission that at the time of the act or omission did not constitute an offence;

This was an absolute prohibition of ex post facto penal laws. The final version, which appeared in the April 1981 version of the Charter, contains the two exceptions which have been discussed.

129 S.C. 1987, c. 37. The War Crimes Act, S.C. 1946, c. 73, which also punishes war crimes, was not repealed. Finta was not charged under the latter statute.

130 Commission of Inquiry on War Criminals, *Report* (Deschênes Report) (Ottawa, 1986).

131 [1994] 1 S.C.R. 70. The majority opinion was written by Cory J., with whom Gonthier and Major JJ. agreed. Lamer C.J. agreed with Cory J. to dismiss the appeal, but would have dismissed the cross-appeal by the accused "as being moot" (at p. 723). The dissenting opinion was written by La Forest J., with whom L'Heureux-Dubé and McLachlin JJ. agreed. The dissenters would have ordered a new trial.

132 Lamer C.J. should be regarded as withholding any opinion on the constitutional issues, since he would have dismissed the cross-appeal (which raised the constitutional issues) as being moot: see previous note. However, he did not indicate any disagreement with Cory J. on these issues.

133 As well as retroactivity, the provisions were attacked for removing a defence of obedience to de facto law (s. 7), for vagueness (s. 7), for delay in laying the charges (s. 7), and for discrimination against non-residents of Canada (s. 15).

not very clear he held that the retroactivity did not offend s. 11(g) or s. 7 of the Charter. La Forest J. (with L'Heureux-Dubé and McLachlin JJ.) held that the provisions were not retroactive at all, because the accused was charged with offences that were in the Criminal Code in 1944. Of course, the Canadian Criminal Code did not apply in Hungary in 1944, but the concepts of "war crimes" and "crimes against humanity", which were used by the 1987 Code provisions to make Canadian law extraterritorial, were well established in international law in 1944. Enforcing international law was not retroactive, as was confirmed by the specific reference in s. 11(g) to "the general principles of law recognized by the community of nations".

Where the penalty for an offence has been changed between the time when the offence was committed and the time when the offender is sentenced, s. 11(i) applies, entitling the offender to the benefit of the lesser punishment.[134]

Apart from s. 11(g), Canadian constitutional law contains no prohibition of retroactive (or ex post facto) laws. There is a presumption of statutory interpretation that a statute should not be given retroactive effect,[135] but, if the retroactive effect is clearly expressed, then there is no room for interpretation and the statute is effective according to its terms. Retroactive statutes are in fact common. For example, a taxation law is often made retroactive to budget night, when the law was publicly proposed; otherwise, there would often be room for avoidance action by taxpayers during the hiatus between the budget and the enactment of the law. Another common example is a retroactive statute to change the law as it was declared to be in a judicial decision: a law that has been interpreted in an unexpected way, or has been held to be invalid on remediable grounds, may be amended or validated retroactively to restore the legal position to what it had been believed to be prior to the judicial decision. The power to enact retroactive laws, if exercised with appropriate restraint, is a proper tool of modern government. Section 11(g) diminishes this power only by excluding the creation of retroactive criminal offences. Other kinds of laws may still be made retroactive.

The Constitution of the United States[136] explicitly bans any "ex post facto law", but the ban has been construed as applying only to penal laws.[137] Given that limited interpretation, Canadian law under s. 11(g) will now be similar to the American law, except for the exceptions recognized in s. 11(g) for acts or omissions recognized as criminal by international law or by general principles of law recognized by the community of nations.

---

134 Section 11(i) is discussed later in this chapter, under heading 48.9, "Variation of penalty (s. 11(i))", below.

135 Driedger, *The Construction of Statutes* (3rd ed., 1994, by Sullivan), 508-525; Coté, *The Interpretation of Legislation in Canada* (2nd ed., 1991), 115-137.

136 Article 1, ss. 9(3), 10(1).

137 Tribe, *American Constitutional Law* (2nd ed., 1986), 632-641; Nowak and Rotunda, *Constitutional Law* (4th ed., 1991), 417-419.

48.9 Double jeopardy (s. 11(h))

(a) Section 11(h)

Section 11(h) of the Charter of Rights[138] provides as follows:

> 11. Any person charged with an offence has the right
>
> . . .
>
> (h) if finally acquitted of the offence, not to be tried for it again and, if finally found guilty and punished for the offence, not to be tried or punished for it again;

Section 11(h)[139] enshrines a rule against double jeopardy in the Constitution.[140] Once an accused has been tried for an offence and finally acquitted or convicted, he may not be placed in jeopardy a second time by being tried again for the same offence. The Canadian Bill of Rights contains no protection against double jeopardy. The American Bill of Rights by the fifth amendment (applicable to the states through the fourteenth amendment) provides that ''nor shall any person be subject for the same offence to be twice put in jeopardy of life or limb''.[141]

(b) Two offences

Section 11(h), like the other guarantees of s. 11, applies to a person charged with an ''offence''. In the structure of s. 11(h), that is a reference to the *first* proceedings. If the first proceedings were not proceedings for an offence, then s.

---

138 For commentary on s. 11(h), see Beaudoin and Mendes, note 28, above, 12-41–12-49 (by Morel); Stuart, note 28, above, 372-381; McLeod, note 28, above, ch. 19; *Canadian Charter of Rights Annotated*, note 28, above, annotation to s. 11(h); the last work contains a bibliography of the relevant literature.

139 Section 11(h) was in the October 1980 version of the Charter (as s. 11(f)) in the following terms:

> (f) Not to be tried or punished more than once for an offence of which he or she has been finally convicted or acquitted.

The provision achieved its final form in the April 1981 version. The October 1980 version would have protected from second prosecution a person who had been finally convicted or acquitted of an offence before the coming into force of the Charter and perhaps even outside Canada, so that it might operate to protect a war criminal who has been tried in absentia in some other jurisdiction. The final version of s. 11(h) is addressed to the first trial, and would therefore provide protection against a second prosecution only to a person acquitted or convicted after the coming into force of the Charter.

140 Double jeopardy is also proscribed by a cluster of rules outside the Charter of Rights: the special pleas of autrefois acquit or autrefois convict, res judicata as expanded in *Kienapple* v. *The Queen* [1975] 1 S.C.R. 729, issue estoppel, and, possibly, abuse of process: see *R.* v. *Van Rassel* [1990] 1 S.C.R. 225, 233-239.

141 For discussion of double jeopardy in the United States see LaFave and Israel, *Criminal Procedure* (2nd ed., 1992), ch. 25.

11(h) will have no application. For example, a prison inmate, who attacked another prisoner and who was found guilty after a hearing before the prison superintendent of a breach of prison discipline and punished, could not invoke s. 11(h) to resist later being tried for the Criminal Code offence of assault.[142] In this case, the first proceedings, being purely disciplinary in nature, were not a trial for an offence.[143] Section 11(h) also requires that the *second* proceedings be a trial for an offence (the same offence). For example, a person convicted of an offence in the United States could not invoke s. 11(h) to bar extradition proceedings in Canada to return him to the United States for trial for what he claimed was essentially the same offence.[144] In this case, the second proceedings were not a trial for an offence, because an extradition hearing is not a trial to determine guilt or innocence but is merely to determine whether there is sufficient evidence to warrant the extradition of the fugitive. The accused's objection to being tried again would have to await his appearance before the foreign court, where the objection would be determined by the foreign law.

(c) Previous acquittal or conviction

The word "finally" in s. 11(h) makes clear that a second trial is barred only if there was a final disposition of the charge against the accused in the earlier proceedings.[145] If the earlier proceedings ended in a stay of proceedings, the accused can be charged again and tried for the same offence.[146] If a trial ended in a mistrial, or if a new trial was ordered on appeal as the result of an error at trial, a second trial for the same offence would not be barred.

An accused is not "finally" acquitted or found guilty until after all appellate procedures have been completed. In other words, an appeal from a trial verdict is not itself a second trial for the same offence, even if the verdict was one of acquittal.[147] However, the Supreme Court of Canada[148] has struck down a provi-

---

142 *R.* v. *Shubley* [1990] 1 S.C.R. 3.

143 See also *R.* v. *Yes Holdings* (1987) 48 D.L.R. (4th) 642 (Alta. C.A.) (civil penalty imposed by Minister for breach of Income Tax Act does not bar later prosecution for offence under Act); *Lavers* v. *B.C.* (1989) 64 D.L.R. (4th) 193 (B.C.C.A.) (same decision).

144 *Can.* v. *Schmidt* [1987] 1 S.C.R. 500 (accused had been convicted of a federal offence, and was later charged with a state offence; in the United States the fifth amendment protection against double jeopardy does not apply where one offence is federal and the other state: *Bartkus* v. *Illinois* (1959) 359 U.S. 121).

145 In *R.* v. *T.R. (No. 2)* (1984) 7 D.L.R. (4th) 263 (Alta. Q.B.), it was held that a young offender, who had been finally "found guilty" at an earlier trial, had not been finally "punished", because he had been placed on probation in circumstances which did not amount to punishment. Therefore the accused was not protected from a second trial by s. 11(h).

146 *Re Burrows* (1983) 150 D.L.R. (3d) 317 (Man. C.A.).

147 *R.* v. *Century 21* (1987) 58 O.R. (2d) 737, 766-769 (C.A.); *R.* v. *Morgentaler (No. 2)* [1988] 1 S.C.R. 30, 45, 129, 156.

148 *Corp. Professionnelle des Médecins* v. *Thibault* [1988] 1 S.C.R. 1033. Lamer J. delivered the judgment of the Court.

sion of Quebec's Summary Convictions Act that allowed a prosecutor to appeal by way of trial de novo from an acquittal of an accused charged with a provincial offence. The trial de novo was not confined to the record of the trial: the evidence had to be adduced all over again, and could even be supplemented if either party wished to make up a deficiency. The Court held that this was "not a true appeal, but actually a new trial disguised as an appeal".[149] The appeal provision violated s. 11(h).

(d) Identity of offences

It has been held that the language of s. 11(h), with its pairing of "the offence" and "it", requires that the later charge be for an offence substantially identical to (or included in) the offence of which the accused was previously acquitted or convicted.[150] For this reason, in *R.* v. *Wigglesworth* (1987),[151] the majority of the Supreme Court of Canada held that the conviction of a police officer for a "service offence" under the Royal Canadian Mounted Police Act did not bar a subsequent trial for common assault under the Criminal Code. Because the elements of the two offences were different, s. 11(h) did not apply. Estey J. dissented on the ground that both charges arose out of the same factual assault, and the punishment at the first trial ought to preclude any further punishment for the same act.[152]

48.10 Variation of penalty (s. 11(i))

Section 11(i) of the Charter of Rights[153] provides as follows:

> 11. Any person charged with an offence has the right
>
> . . .
>
> (i) if found guilty of the offence and if the punishment for the offence has been varied between the time of commission and the time of sentencing, to the benefit of the lesser punishment.

---

149 *Id.*, 1044.

150 It would not matter that one offence was created by federal law and the other by provincial law: see ch. 16, Paramountcy, under heading 16.5(b), "Double criminal liability", above. See also *R.* v. *Van Rassel* [1990] 1 S.C.R. 225, 232-233 (inconclusive discussion about whether s. 11(h) applies when one offence was created by foreign law).

151 [1987] 2 S.C.R. 541. The majority opinion was written by Wilson J.; Estey J. alone wrote a dissenting opinion.

152 The same-offence requirement was applied in *R.* v. *Van Rassel* [1990] 1 S.C.R. 225 (acquittal on bribery charges did not bar trial for breach of trust as a police officer).

153 For commentary on s. 11(i), see Beaudoin and Mendes, note 28, above, 10-108–10-113 (by Chevrette and Cry); Stuart, note 28, above, 381-383; McLeod, note 28, above, ch. 20; *Canadian Charter of Rights Annotated*, note 28, above, annotation to s. 11(i); the last work includes a bibliography of the relevant literature.

The case for which s. 11(i)[154] is designed is where the penalty for an offence has been changed after an accused person committed the offence, but before he is sentenced.[155] Section 11(i) provides that the accused is entitled to "the benefit of the lesser punishment". If the penalty was increased, the old penalty applies; if the penalty was reduced, the new penalty applies.[156]

In the United States, the same result has been achieved through judicial interpretation of the constitutional prohibition of ex post facto laws.[157] An increase in penalty cannot be applied to offences already committed without offending the prohibition on ex post facto laws,[158] but a reduction in penalty falls outside the prohibition.[159]

---

154 Section 11(i) appeared in the October 1980 version of the Charter (as s. 11(g)) in the following terms:

> (g) to the benefit of the lesser punishment where the punishment for an offence of which he or she has been convicted has been varied between the time of commission and the time of sentencing.

The Canadian Bill of Rights contains no counterpart of s. 11(i). The final version of the provision appeared in the April 1981 version. The changes in language do not appear to make any change of substance.

155 Cf. *R.* v. *Gamble* [1988] 2 S.C.R. 595 (accused mistakenly tried and sentenced under law that came into force after the commission of the offence; held, breach of s. 7).

156 Cf. *Re Bulmer* (1987) 36 D.L.R. (4th) 688 (Alta. Q.B.) (suspension of driver's licence is a civil consequence, not a "punishment"; therefore, when the period of suspension is increased before sentencing, the accused is not entitled to the shorter period).

157 Note 135, above.

158 *Lindsey* v. *Washington* (1937) 301 U.S. 397.

159 *Malloy* v. *South Carolina* (1915) 237 U.S. 180.

49

Trial Within Reasonable Time

49.1 Section 11(b) of Charter

Section 11(b) of the Charter of Rights[1] provides as follows:

> 11. Any person charged with an offence has the right
>
> . . .
>
> (b) to be tried within a reasonable time;

Section 11(b) confers the right "to be tried within a reasonable time". This is a new right created by the Charter. Before the Charter there was no similar right,

1 For commentary on s. 11(b), see Beaudoin and Mendes (eds.), *The Canadian Charter of Rights and Freedoms* (3rd ed., 1996), 12-2–12-13 (by Morel); Stuart, *Charter Justice in Canadian Criminal Law* (2nd ed., 1996), 300-320; Code, *Trial within a Reasonable Time* (1992); McLeod, Takach, Morton, Segal, *The Canadian Charter of Rights* (Carswell, loose-leaf), ch. 12; *Canadian Charter of Rights Annotated* (Canada Law Book, loose-leaf), annotation to s. 11(b). The last work provides a bibliography of the relevant literature.

either at common law or under statute;[2] and there was no such right in the Canadian Bill of Rights.

Like all the rights conferred by s. 11, the right to be tried within a reasonable time is possessed only by a person ''charged with an offence''.[3] This means that the right has no application in civil proceedings, or before administrative tribunals.[4] Unless a person has been charged with an offence, there is no constitutional requirement that a trial or hearing take place within a reasonable time.[5]

49.2 Purpose of right

The right to be tried within a reasonable time serves three purposes: (1) to minimize the time spent by an accused person in pre-trial custody (or under restrictive bail conditions); (2) to minimize the anxiety experienced by a person awaiting trial; and (3) to minimize the deterioration of evidence necessary to enable the accused to make full answer and defence.[6] The Supreme Court of Canada now seems to be agreed on these purposes, although for a long time Lamer C.J. argued for the position that the impact of delay on the fairness of the trial (purpose (3)) was irrelevant to s. 11(b); in his view, any impairment of an accused's right to make full answer and defence would be cognizable under s. 7 ors. 11(d), but not s. 11(b).[7] However, he has now accepted the majority view that one of the purposes of s. 11(b) is to prevent the deterioration of evidence through the death or disappearance of witnesses and the inevitable decline in memory that occurs over time.[8]

The Supreme Court of Canada has occasionally exhibited a tendency to draw a rather romantic picture of the eagerness of accused persons to be tried; Cory J., for example, has emphasized the ''exquisite agony'' of an accused awaiting trial.[9] It must be unpleasant to wait for a criminal trial, but for an accused who is not in

2 However, habeas corpus was available to counter lengthy delays while awaiting trial: Beaudoin and Mendes, note 1, above, 12-2 (by Morel).

3 The meaning of this phrase, including its application to disciplinary proceedings, is discussed in the previous chapter: under heading 48.1, ''Person charged with an offence'', above.

4 *Akthar* v. *Can.* [1991] 3 F.C. 32 (C.A.) (no right to refugee-determination hearing within reasonable time).

5 Where life, liberty or security of the person is at stake, s. 7 would prohibit unreasonable delays that had the effect of making the trial unfair: ch. 44, Fundamental Justice, under heading 44.19, ''Fair trial'', above. Most civil and administrative proceedings concern money or other economic interests and do not implicate life, liberty or security of the person. There are no constitutional requirements of procedure for such proceedings.

6 *R.* v. *CIP* [1992] 1 S.C.R. 843, 855-859.

7 *R.* v. *Rahey* [1987] 1 S.C.R. 588, 610.

8 *R.* v. *CIP* [1992] 1 S.C.R. 843. The issue had to be determined in this case, because it was the possible impairment of fair-trial values by delay that led the Court to hold that s. 11(b) applied to corporations: see the next section of this chapter.

9 *R.* v. *Askov* [1990] 2 S.C.R. 1199, 1219; but note the scepticism in *R.* v. *Morin* [1992] S.C.R. , , per Sopinka J. (p. 31) per McLachlin J. (p. 4).

custody the wait may be preferable to the trial, with its risk of conviction and sentence. Since the burden of proof is on the prosecution, and the standard of proof is high, even the risk that witnesses may disappear or forget is one that can sometimes be endured with fortitude. It is only realistic to accept that a speedy trial is not desired by many accused persons, and a court-ordered stay of proceedings by reason of delay is a highly attractive windfall.

49.3 Application to corporations

The s. 11(b) right to be tried within a reasonable time is one that can be invoked by a corporation. That was decided by the Supreme Court of Canada in *R.* v. *CIP* (1992).[10] All the s. 11 rights are available to "any person charged with an offence", and the word "person" is in most contexts apt to include a corporation. A corporation would nevertheless be excluded from the benefit of any guarantee if corporate interests lay outside the purpose of the guarantee. In the case of s. 11(b), two of the purposes[11] — the minimization of pre-trial detention, and the minimization of pre-trial anxiety — were inapplicable to corporations. But the third purpose was the preservation of an accused's ability to make full answer and defence, and that purpose extended to all accused, whether corporate or individual. Therefore, there was no reason to exclude a corporation from the benefit of s. 11(b).

What the Court in the *CIP* case gave to the accused corporation with one hand it almost took away with the other. In that case, the corporation had been awaiting trial for 19 months, a delay mainly caused by court congestion. But the Court held that the "presumption of prejudice" that could be relied upon by an individual who suffered delay did not apply to a corporation. In the case of an individual, it was to be presumed that prejudice had been suffered. This was obvious if the accused was in prison, but it also applied to an accused who was at large, because of his or her presumed anxiety about the forthcoming trial.[12] In the case of a corporation, which could suffer neither imprisonment nor anxiety, no presumption of prejudice should be applied. A corporate accused had to affirmatively establish prejudice, and the only kind that would count would be an impairment of its ability to make full answer and defence. Since the corporate accused in the *CIP* case had not established that the delay would impair its ability to make full answer and defence, no breach of s. 11(b) was made out.

The *CIP* case establishes a severe limitation on the availability of s. 11(b) to corporations. For an accused corporation, a delay is unreasonable only if the delay would impair the corporation's ability to make full answer and defence. But it is well established that an impairment of an accused's ability to make full answer

---

10 [1992] S.C.R. . Stevenson J. delivered the judgment of the Court.

11 Text accompanying note 6, above.

12 Text accompanying note 56, below.

and defence is a breach of ss. 7 and 11(d).[13] Delay that impaired an accused corporation's ability to make full answer and defence would be a breach of the guarantee of a fair hearing in ss. 7 and 11(d). Therefore, for an accused corporation, the guarantee of a trial within a reasonable time in s. 11(b), as restricted in the *CIP* case, adds nothing to the guarantee of a fair hearing in ss. 7 and 11(d).[14]

49.4 Application to regulatory offences

A ''regulatory offence'' (or public welfare offence) is one that punishes conduct, not because it is ''inherently wrongful'', but because it has to be regulated in the public interest. The Supreme Court of Canada has distinguished between regulatory offences and ''true crimes'' in the context ofs. 7, holding that negligence is a sufficient requirement of fault for regulatory offences, while mens rea is constitutionally required for true crimes.[15] In *R.* v. *CIP* (1992),[16] the accused corporation was charged with a failure to observe safety precautions required by provincial legislation regulating occupational health and safety. This was a regulatory offence; and it was argued by the Crown that a longer period of delay would be reasonable for regulatory offences than would be reasonable for true crimes. The Supreme Court of Canada rejected the argument, holding that an accused's interest in a speedy trial was no less where the charge was for a regulatory offence.

The *CIP* case involved a corporate accused. As the previous section of this chapter has explained, a corporation can invoke s. 11(b) only if the delay has created a risk of an unfair trial. It is obvious that the risk of an unfair trial calls for a constitutional remedy regardless of the offence charged. However, an *individual* accused can invoke s. 11(b) if the delay has done nothing more than cause him or her a longer period of anxiety; moreover, that anxiety is presumed, and need not be proved.[17] Where the accused's presumed anxiety is the only basis for a constitutional remedy, it seems to me that the distinction between regulatory offences and true crimes might well be relevant, suggesting a longer period of reasonable delay in the case of regulatory offences. Needless to say, if an individual accused was in custody or subject to severe bail restrictions (which would rarely be the case if the accused was only charged with a regulatory offence), or

13 Chapter 44, Fundamental Justice, under heading 44.19, ''Fair trial'', above. Section 7, while generally inapplicable to corporations, is applicable to a corporation charged with an offence: *R.* v. *Wholesale Travel Group* [1991] 3 S.C.R. 154.

14 This overlap of paras. (b) and (d) would be avoided if it were held, as Lamer C.J. argued for a time (note 7, above), that s. 11(b) does not protect fair-trial values. On this approach, s. 11(b) would presumably be inapplicable to corporations.

15 *R.* v. *Wholesale Travel Group* [1991] 2 S.C.R. 154; discussed ch. 44, Fundamental Justice, under heading 44.11, ''Absolute and strict liability'', above.

16 [1992] S.C.R. ; discussed at note 7, above.

17 Section 49.9, ''Prejudice to accused'', below.

if the delay had impaired the individual accused's ability to make full answer and defence, s. 11(b) should be rigorously applied regardless of the offence charged.

49.5 Reasonableness of delay

How long a delay is "reasonable"? The Supreme Court of Canada has refused to stipulate a fixed period of time within which all trials must be held. Instead, the Court has identified various factors which have to be weighed and balanced in order to determine whether or not a period of delay is reasonable. Unfortunately, in the early cases, the Court could not agree on the relevant factors; this produced concurring and dissenting opinions arguing for rival lists of factors.[18] However, in 1989, the judges agreed on the following four factors: (1) the length of the delay; (2) any waivers of time periods; (3) the reasons for the delay; and (4) prejudice to the accused.[19] Each of these factors is described in the text that follows.

It is hardly necessary to comment that this four-factor approach is exceedingly vague. Naturally, it produces highly variable results. This has led commentators[20] to urge the enactment by Parliament[21] of fixed time-limits for trials. Time-limits could be set in accordance with the status quo for a transitional period, and then gradually reduced until satisfactory standards were achieved. Any time-limits would allow for extensions in defined circumstances. Parliament has not heeded these recommendations, which has left the criminal justice system at the mercy of unpredictable and poorly-informed judicial rulings.[22]

49.6 Length of delay

(a) Pre-charge delay

The right to be tried within a reasonable time, like the other rights conferred by s. 11, is possessed by "a person charged with an offence". The Supreme Court

---

18 E.g., *R.* v.*Rahey* [1987] 1 S.C.R. 588.

19 *R.* v.*Smith* [1989] 2 S.C.R. 1120, 1131; this list has been followed in all subsequent cases.

20 Baar, "Time Limit Legislation in Criminal Cases; A Follow-up Assessment" (Department of Justice, Ottawa, 1984); Shetreet, "Time Standards for Justice" (1979) 5 Dal. L.J. 729; Code, *Trial Within a Reasonable Time* (1992), 115-118.

21 Code, previous note, 117, asserts that "primary responsibility for enacting speedy trial standards must lie with the federal government under its s. 91(27) 'criminal procedure' power"; and he adds that if Parliament leaves the field unoccupied, "it is an interesting question as to whether the province could legislate such standards under its s. 92(14) power over the 'administration of justice'."

22 The *Ascov* decision, note 36, below, refused to acknowledge any transitional phase for overburdened courts, and established standards that required the dismissal of 47,000 charges in Ontario and the immediate expenditure by the provincial government of $39 million in additional judges, court staff, Crown attorneys and other resources: Code, note 20, above, 114. At the next opportunity, the *Morin* decision, note 47, below, the Court, in effect, resiled from this ill-considered ruling!

of Canada has inferred from this language that the reasonable time under s. 11(b) is to be measured from the time when a person is charged, that is, when the information is laid or the indictment preferred.[23] Section 11(b) does not provide a remedy for delay in laying the charge,[24] and pre-charge delay is not counted in computing the period of delay to the time of the trial.[25] However, in assessing the reasonableness of post-charge delay, pre-charge delay would in some circumstances be relevant.[26] For example, if the laying of the charge had been preceded by a long investigation, this would weaken the argument that a long post-charge delay was justified by the complexity of the case. Needless to say, if delay in the laying of the charge impaired the accused's ability to defend the charge, the pre-charge delay would be a breach of the fair-trial guarantee of ss. 7 and 11(d).[27]

(b) Appellate delay

Does the right to be tried within a reasonable time apply only to the trial, or does it extend to the final disposition of the case? On the latter view, appeals would have to be disposed of within a reasonable time. In *R.* v. *Potvin* (1993),[28] the Supreme Court of Canada divided on this question, but the majority of the Court, in an opinion written by Sopinka J., held that s. 11(b) did not apply to appellate delay. According to the majority, once a criminal trial has been held, the accused ceases to be a ''person charged with an offence'', and the s. 11(b) clock stops running. This is so whether the trial has resulted in a conviction or an acquittal. The Court in *Potvin* held that the same rule applied to a stay of proceedings, on the ground that a stay was tantamount to an acquittal. This led the Court to decide that an appeal by the Crown from a stay of proceedings did not have to be disposed of within a reasonable time, even though the accused had never had a trial. If the result of an appeal from a conviction or an acquittal was an order for a new trial, or some other order was made directing the continuation

---

23 Chapter 48, Rights on Being Charged, under heading 48.1(b), ''Charged'', above.

24 *R.* v.*L. (W.K.)* [1991] 1 S.C.R. 1091 (no remedy for delay of 30 years from alleged offence to charge); *R.* v. *Finta* [1994] 1 S.C.R. 701 (no remedy for delay of 45 years from alleged offence to charge); *R.* v. *Burke* [1996] 1 S.C.R. 474 (affirming lower court decision of no remedy for delay of 14 years from initial investigation to laying of charges).

25 *Carter* v.*The Queen* [1986] 1 S.C.R. 981; *R.* v.*Kalanj* [1989] 1 S.C.R. 1594; *R.* v.*Morin* [1992] 1 S.C.R. 771.

26 *R.* v.*Morin* [1992] 1 S.C.R. 771, 789.

27 *R.* v.*L. (W.K.)* [1991] 1 S.C.R. 1091, 1100 (pointing out that pre-charge delay will not necessarily have this effect, and may work to the advantage of the accused); *R.* v. *Finta* [1994] 1 S.C.R. 701, 875 (pointing out that pre-charge delay was more likely to have prejudiced the Crown's case than that of the defence); *R.* v. *Burke* [1996] 1 S.C.R. 474 (affirming lower court decision that applicant bore onus of showing prejudicial effect of pre-charge delay before stay of proceedings should be granted).

28 [1993] 2 S.C.R. 880. The majority opinion was written by Sopinka J., with the concurrence of four others. La Forest J. wrote a separate concurring opinion. McLachlin J., with the concurrence of two others, wrote an opinion that concurred in the result but dissented on the application of s. 11(b) to appellate delay.

of the trial proceedings, then "the constitutional clock would be rewound at the time of the order by the appellate court".[29]

The *Potvin* ruling means that s. 11(b) does not apply to the deliberation time of the Supreme Court of Canada, which is occasionally prolonged for periods that are hard to understand. There have been three cases in which the Court has taken more than a year after oral argument to dispose of appeals by accused persons who were still awaiting trial.[30]

Where appellate delay affects the fairness of a subsequent trial, the accused, although lacking a remedy under s. 11(b), would have a remedy under s. 7, since the principles of fundamental justice require that an accused person receive a fair trial.[31]

49.7 Waiver of delay

Periods of delay that are waived by the accused are not counted in computing the reasonable time within s. 11(b). For example, an accused may explicitly waive the s. 11(b) right in order to secure an adjournment or a later trial date. Indeed, any request by the defence for an adjournment or for a particular trial date would normally be treated as an implicit waiver of any delay entailed by the requested postponement.

A waiver of delay "must be clear and unequivocal, with full knowledge of the rights the procedure was enacted to protect and of the effect that waiver will have on those rights".[32] Defence consent to an adjournment or to a late trial date will be waiver if it is clear that the defence counsel must have been conscious of the issue of waiver, but will not be waiver "if consent to a date amounts to mere acquiescence in the inevitable".[33] However, as the next section of this chapter will explain, conduct of the accused that falls short of waiver, but that does make a contribution to delaying the proceedings, will be taken into account in evaluating the reasonableness of the delay: defence consents to adjournments or trial dates may well have the effect of lengthening the period of reasonableness. Delays caused by adjournments or late trial dates that are granted over the strenuous

---

29 *Id.*, 913.

30 *Mills* v. *The Queen* [1986] 1 S.C.R. 863 (24 months, including a rehearing); *Carter* v. *The Queen* [1986] 1 S.C.R. 981 (14 months); *R.* v. *Kalanj* [1989] 1 S.C.R. 1594 (15 months). In *R.* v. *Rahey* [1987] 1 S.C.R. 588, the Court was justifiably critical of a trial judge who took 11 months to render a decision on a Crown motion for a directed verdict, but it took the Court 11 months after oral argument to reach its own decision that the trial judge's delay was unreasonable.

31 *R.* v. *Potvin* [1993] 2 S.C.R. 880, 899, 915. The Court did not mention the guarantee of a fair trial in s. 11(d), but that guarantee would presumably also be applicable.

32 *R.* v. *Morin* [1992] 1 S.C.R. 771, 790.

33 *Ibid.*; *R.* v. *CIP* [1992] 1 S.C.R. 843 (defence consent to a two-week adjournment amounted to implicit waiver; defence consent to a late trial date did not).

objection of defence counsel will of course have to meet an unrelaxed standard of reasonableness.

49.8 Reasons for delay

(a) Types of delay

In fixing the period of delay that is reasonable, the Supreme Court of Canada has distinguished four types of delay: (1) delay that is inherent to the proceedings; (2) delay that is attributable to the Crown; (3) delay that is attributable to the accused; and (4) delay that is institutional or systemic to the court system. The Court will take any period of delay, break it down into these four categories, and try and assess what is reasonable under each head.[34]

(b) Inherent delay

Under the heading of delay that is inherent to the proceedings, the Court takes account of the time required for the preparation of the prosecution case, the preparation of the defence case, and the processing of the case by the court, including applications for bail and other pre-trial procedures. Under this head, a complex case will have longer inherent requirements than a simple case; and a case involving a preliminary inquiry will have longer inherent requirements than a case that proceeds directly to trial. Delay that is judged to be inherent is reasonable.

(c) Crown delay

Under the heading of delay that is attributable to the Crown, the Court takes into account all actions by the Crown that contribute to delay, for example, adjournments requested by the Crown, change of venue motions, or failure or delay in disclosure of the Crown case. For the most part, delays attributable to the Crown will not serve to lengthen the period of reasonableness.

(d) Defence delay

Under the heading of delay that is attributable to the accused, the Court takes into account all actions by the accused that contribute to delay, for example, adjournments requested by the defence (not amounting to waiver), change of venue motions, attacks on search warrants or attacks on wiretap packages. These actions by the defence have the effect of lengthening the period of reasonableness. As noted in the previous section of this chapter, any action by the defence that

34 R. v. *Morin* [1992] 1 S.C.R. 771, 791-800, contains a full explanation of the reasons for delay.

amounts to a waiver of delay means that any consequential delay is wholly within the period of reasonableness. What we are concerned with here are actions of the defence that do not amount to waiver of delay, but which are voluntary contributions to delay.

(e) Systemic delay

Under the heading of institutional or systemic delay, is delay caused by court congestion: this occurs where there are not enough judges or courtrooms or there are inadequate case management procedures to handle the volume of criminal charges with reasonable expedition. The Supreme Court of Canada has made clear that it will not tolerate excessive delay based on the plea of inadequate resources. "The government has a constitutional obligation to commit sufficient resources to prevent unreasonable delay, which distinguishes this obligation from many others that compete for funds with the administration of justice".[35]

In *R.* v. *Askov* (1990),[36] the Supreme Court of Canada stayed proceedings against four accused for unreasonable delay in bringing them to trial. The delay was systemic to the judicial district of Peel, a region near Toronto in which there had been a rapid population growth and in which Toronto's international airport was located. Cory J., for a Court that was unanimous on this issue, said that "a period of [systemic] delay in a range of some six to eight months between committal and trial might be deemed to be the outside limit of what is reasonable".[37] This limit of six to eight months from committal (not charge) to trial went well beyond the necessity of the case, where the time elapsed from charge to trial was two years and ten months. Moreover, it was clear from statistics filed with the Court that in Ontario many thousands of other accused persons would also be entitled to stays, because they had already experienced systemic delay of more than six to eight months. And yet the Court explicitly rejected the establishment of "a transitional period to allow for a temporary period of lenient treatment of systemic delay".[38] The reason was that the judicial district's problems went back at least to 1981, and should have been remedied long ago. With respect, this ignored the fact that the Supreme Court of Canada had been unsuccessful to that time in agreeing on a consistent approach to the definition of reasonable delay, and nothing like the six to eight months' limit had ever been suggested before.

The refusal of a transitional period of leniency naturally required that stays of proceedings be granted to many thousands of other persons awaiting trial in the judicial district of Peel and other congested districts. Although the Attorney General of Ontario acted promptly to appoint more judges (they became known

---

35 *Id.*, 795.

36 [1990] 2 S.C.R. 1199. Cory J. wrote the majority opinion for himself and four others; Lamer C.J., Wilson, Sopinka and McLachlin JJ. each wrote short concurring opinions.

37 *Id.*, 1240.

38 *Id.*, 1231.

as "Askov judges") and otherwise increase the resources available to the court system, in the 12 months that followed the *Askov* decision, over 47,000 charges were stayed or withdrawn in Ontario.[39] In other situations, the Court has been willing to grant a transitional period to enable governments to come into compliance with constitutional norms,[40] and it seems obvious to me that this would have been a wiser solution to the *Askov* problem than the virtual amnesty for accused persons that the Court in effect required.

The *Askov* ruling that six to eight months was the outside limit of systemic delay referred to the period from "committal" to trial. This was a puzzling way of expressing the limit, because the previous cases had been clear that the time was to be measured from the date of the *charge*.[41] The ruling therefore failed to address the total period from charge to trial, and it was not clear whether it was also intended as an outside limit for summary proceedings, where there is no preliminary inquiry and no committal. In *R.* v. *Morin* (1992),[42] the Supreme Court of Canada, now speaking through Sopinka J., did not disavow the *Askov* ruling, but the Court emphasized that what Cory J. had referred to as "the outside limit" was "a guideline" rather than a "fixed limitation period".[43] And, although the Court reaffirmed the *Askov* ruling that no transitional period of tolerance should be accorded, the Court held that the fact that a judicial district was experiencing "unusual strain on its resources" was a "factor" in assessing reasonableness.[44] And, although the Court did not disturb the *Askov* guidelines of six to eight months between committal and trial, the Court suggested "a period of institutional delay of between eight to ten months as a guide to Provincial Courts".[45] The longer period for Provincial Courts reflected the fact that the vast majority of cases are disposed of in summary proceedings, placing greater demands on the Provincial Courts.

49.9 Prejudice to accused

Prejudice to the accused is the last of the four factors[46] that are taken into account in assessing the reasonableness of the period between charge and trial. If the accused is awaiting trial in custody, or under restrictive bail conditions, there is an ongoing deprivation of liberty which ought to be reflected in a period of

39 *R.* v. *Morin* [1992] 1 S.C.R. 771, 779.

40 Chapter 37, Enforcement of Rights, under heading 37.1(i), "Temporary validity", above.

41 Note 25, above.

42 [1992] 1 S.C.R. 771. Sopinka J. wrote the majority opinion for himself and three others; Gonthier and McLachlin JJ. wrote short concurring opinions; Lamer C.J. wrote a dissenting opinion. Cory J. was not on the seven-judge panel.

43 *Id.*, 797.

44 *Id.*, 798.

45 *Id.*, 799.

46 Text accompanying note 19, above.

reasonableness that is at the short end of the spectrum. If delay might lead to the impairment of defence evidence, for example, the death or incapacity of a very old or sick defence witness, the period of reasonableness should be short to preclude the prejudice to the fairness of the trial. Where these sources of actual prejudice are absent, there is still the anxiety presumed to be experienced by a person awaiting trial. In *R.* v. *Askov* (1990),[47] Cory J. spoke of the ''exquisite agony'' of a person awaiting trial,[48] and said there was a ''presumption of prejudice to the accused resulting from the passage of time''; in the case of long delays, the presumption would be ''virtually irrebuttable''.[49] This passage made clear that it was unnecessary for the accused to show actual prejudice in order to obtain a stay of the proceedings under s. 11(b). This ruling was another element in the decision that made inevitable the wholesale staying of proceedings that in fact followed the decision in *Askov*.[50]

The *Askov* presumption of prejudice may be undergoing reconsideration by the Court. In the later case of *R.* v. *Morin* (1992),[51] Sopinka J. for the majority made the points that ''in many cases an accused person is not interested in a speedy trial and delay works to the advantage of the accused''.[52] He implied that delay by itself might not support the inference of sufficient prejudice to justify a stay of proceedings. And McLachlin J., in a concurring opinion, said that ''the accused may have to call evidence if he or she is to displace the strong public interest in bringing those charged with an offence to trial''.[53] Lamer C.J. interpreted the opinions of Sopinka and McLachlin JJ. as casting a burden of proving prejudice on the accused, which was a ''fundamental change'' from the position taken in *Askov*.[54] He dissented on the basis that the Court should not depart from its recent ruling in *Askov*. Only future decisions will tell whether the Court has in fact abandoned the ''presumption of prejudice'' that was established in *Askov*.[55]

49.10 Remedy for delay

What is the remedy for a failure to bring the accused to trial within a reasonable time? The Supreme Court of Canada (following the Supreme Court

47 [1990] 2 S.C.R. 1199.
48 *Id.*, 1219.
49 *Id.*, 1232.
50 Text accompanying note 39, above.
51 [1992] 1 S.C.R. 771.
52 *Id.*, 801.
53 *Id.*, 812.
54 *Id.*, 778.
55 In *R.* v. *CIP* [1992] 1 S.C.R. 843, Stevenson J. for a unanimous Court (which included McLachlin J. but not Sopinka J.) repeated the presumption of prejudice language from *Askov*, but held that the presumption did not apply to a corporation, which had to establish actual prejudice: see text accompanying note 7, above.

of the United States)[56] seems to have committed itself to the position that a stay of proceedings[57] is the only possible remedy.[58] This has been supported by an implausible argument that after a reasonable time has elapsed no court has jurisdiction to try the accused.[59] The remedy of a stay could also be supported by an argument that any lesser remedy would provide insufficient incentive for governments to strip the delays from their court systems. But the stay of proceedings gives no weight at all to the public interest in bringing an accused person to trial. The 47,000 Ontario stays (or withdrawals of charges) that followed the *Askov* ruling dramatically illustrated the downside of the Court's rigid approach to remedies.

In my view, Amsterdam is right when he argues that ''the primary form of judicial relief against denial of a speedy trial should be to expedite the trial, nor to abort it''.[60] Of course, where unreasonable delay has impaired the accused's ability to mount a defence, then a stay of proceedings is indeed the only remedy. But the deprivation of liberty while awaiting a trial in custody, or the anxiety caused by delay, are as well remedied by a speedy trial as by a stay of proceedings. It should be remembered as well that prejudice to the accused is only one of the four factors to be taken into account in assessing the reasonableness of delay, and is in any case often presumed rather than proved. A finding of prejudice is not a necessary condition of a ruling of unreasonable delay.[61] Where there is no prejudice, it seems obvious to me that the Court ought to order a speedy trial rather than a stay of proceedings.

---

56 *Strunk* v. *United States* (1973) 412 U.S. 434, 440.

57 A stay of proceedings is like an acquittal in that it is a final determination of the criminal proceedings, precluding further proceedings on the same charge and sustaining a plea of autrefois acquit. It is unlike an acquittal in that a stay is not a determination of the merits of the charge against the accused. See *R.* v. *Potvin* [1993] 2 S.C.R. 880, 891, 914.

58 *R.* v. *Rahey* [1987] 1 S.C.R. 588; *R.* v. *Askov* [1990] 2 S.C.R. 1199. In the latter case, the Court even rejected the notion of a transitional period to permit a congested court system to correct systemic delay: text accompanying note 34, above.

59 *R.* v. *Rahey* [1987] 1 S.C.R. 588, 614 per Lamer J., 620 per Wilson J; but note the more flexible approach of Le Dain J. at 618 and La Forest J. at 648. If s. 11(b) really did deprive a trial court of jurisdiction, *Askov* should have been followed by the release (if necessary on habeas corpus) of thousands of convicted prisoners whose trials had taken place beyond the *Askov* time-limit. Surely, this is too radical a remedy for s. 11(b).

60 Amsterdam, ''Speedy Criminal Trial: Rights and Remedies'' (1975) 27 Stanford L. Rev. 525, 535. The author also argues (at p. 539) that the dismissal remedy, because it is so repugnant to judges, encourages judges to hold that ''shockingly long delays do not 'violate' the sixth amendment''. In Canada, the Court does not appear to find the dismissal remedy repugnant, and has not tolerated shockingly long delays.

61 This seems to be the current state of the law, although it is not entirely settled: see sec. 49.9, ''Prejudice to accused'', above.

50

Cruel and Unusual Punishment

50.1 Section 12 of Charter

Section 12 of the Charter of Rights[1] provides as follows:

> 12. Everyone has the right not to be subjected to any cruel and unusual treatment or punishment.

Section 12 prohibits any "cruel and unusual treatment or punishment". Section 2(b) of the Canadian Bill of Rights also prohibits any "cruel and unusual treatment or punishment".[2] The eighth amendment of the Constitution of the United States prohibits "cruel and unusual punishments". (The eighth amendment omits reference to "treatment".)

50.2 Treatment or punishment

What s. 12 prohibits is cruel and unusual "treatment or punishment". Unless a particular sanction amounts to "treatment or punishment", s. 12 has no appli-

---

1 For commentary on s. 12, see Beaudoin and Mendes (eds.), *The Canadian Charter of Rights and Freedoms* (3rd ed., 1996), 12-49–12-64 (by Morel); Stuart, *Charter Justice in Canadian Criminal Law* (2nd ed., 1996), ch. 7; McLeod, Takach, Morton, Segal, *The Canadian Charter of Rights* (Carswell, loose-leaf), ch. 21; *Canadian Charter of Rights Annotated* (Canada Law Book, loose-leaf), annotation to s. 12; the last work provides a bibliography of the relevant literature.

2 For commentary on s. 2(b) of the Canadian Bill of Rights, see Tarnopolsky, *The Canadian Bill of Rights* (2nd ed., 1975), 238-239; Tarnopolsky, "Just Deserts or Cruel and Unusual Treatment or Punishment?" (1978) 10 Ottawa L. Rev. 1; Berger, "The Application of the Cruel and Unusual Punishment clause under the Canadian Bill of Rights" (1978) 24 McGill L.J. 161.

cation. The automatic suspension of a driver's licence is a civil sanction that is neither "treatment" nor "punishment".[3] The deportation of a non-citizen who has committed a serious crime has been held not to be "punishment", although the Court acknowledged that it might be "treatment" — the issue did not have to be decided, because deportation was held not to be cruel and unusual in any event.[4]

In *Rodriguez* v. *British Columbia* (1993),[5] it was argued that the Criminal Code prohibition on assisted suicide was cruel and unusual treatment or punishment for a terminally ill plaintiff who wished to commit suicide, but who anticipated that she would soon be too disabled to do it without assistance. The majority of the Supreme Court of Canada regarded it as obvious that the plaintiff's predicament could not be regarded as a "punishment". Nor could a "mere prohibition" be regarded as "treatment"; some "more active state process", involving "an exercise of state control over the individual", was required to constitute treatment within the meaning of s. 12.[6] The plaintiff's attack on the Criminal Code provision therefore failed.

50.3 Cruel and unusual

The phrase "cruel and unusual" has never been satisfactorily defined. There has been inconclusive debate about whether the phrase is disjunctive (so that a punishment that was either cruel or unusual, but not necessarily both, would violate s. 12) or conjunctive (so that a punishment would have to be both cruel and unusual to violate s. 12). The Supreme Court of Canada has now approved the proposition that the words "cruel and unusual" are "interacting expressions colouring each other, so to speak, and hence to be considered together as a compendious description of a norm".[7] This is not particularly helpful, but it seems to accept the conjunctive alternative, requiring that a punishment have elements of both cruelty and unusualness. The Court has also approved, as the test of cruel and unusual punishment, "whether the punishment prescribed is so excessive as to outrage standards of decency".[8] This is not helpful either, since there seems to be no way of defining "standards of decency". However, it is clear that the phrase

3 *R.* v. *Miller* (1988) 65 O.R. (2d) 746 (C.A.); cf. *Re Bulmer* (1987) 36 D.L.R. (4th) 688 (Alta. Q.B.) (similar decision, but under s. 11(i)).

4 *Can.* v. *Chiarelli* [1992] 1 S.C.R. 711, 736.

5 [1993] 3 S.C.R. 519. The majority opinion was written by Sopinka J. and concurred in by four others. The majority rejected arguments based on ss. 7 and 15, as well as s. 12.

6 *Id.*, 611-612.

7 *R.* v. *Miller and Cockriell* [1977] 2 S.C.R. 680, 690 per Laskin C.J., referring to s. 2(b) of the Canadian Bill of Rights. This dictum was accepted by all of the judges in *R.* v. *Smith* [1987] 1 S.C.R. 1045, 1072, 1088, 1109.

8 This also comes from Laskin C.J. in *R.* v. *Miller and Cockriell* [1977] 2 S.C.R. 680, 688, and was also accepted by all the judges in *R.* v. *Smith* [1987] 1 S.C.R. 1045, 1072, 1089, 1109.

includes two classes of treatment or punishment: (1) those that are barbaric in themselves, and (2) those that are grossly disproportionate to the offence.[9]

The first category of prohibited punishments (or treatments) comprises those that are barbaric in themselves. As examples of such punishments, Lamer J. has suggested corporal punishment such as the lash, the lobotomization of dangerous offenders and the castration of sexual offenders.[10] These are punishments (or treatments) that would be cruel and unusual as the penalty for any offence, no matter how heinous, or for any offender, no matter how dangerous.

The second category of prohibited punishments (or treatments) comprises those that are grossly disproportionate to the offence. In *R.* v. *Smith* (1987),[11] it was held that a minimum sentence of seven years' imprisonment for importing narcotics fell into this category. The defendant in that case had been found guilty of importing a substantial quantity of cocaine, and had been sentenced to eight years' imprisonment — more than the statutory minimum.[12] Nevertheless, the majority of the Supreme Court of Canada seized the opportunity to rule on the validity of the minimum sentence. By postulating the most innocent possible offender — a young person returning to Canada from a vacation with what Lamer J. described as "his or her first 'joint of grass' "[13] — the Court held that the minimum sentence was grossly disproportionate to the offence. The minimum sentence was not saved by s. 1 despite the importance of deterring the importation of illegal drugs: "We do not need to sentence small offenders to seven years in prison in order to deter the serious offender".[14]

---

9 The adequacy of procedural or substantive standards for the imposition of imprisonment is best regarded as reviewable under s. 9, which prohibits arbitrary detention or imprisonment. This was the view of Lamer J. in *R.* v. *Smith* [1987] 1 S.C.R. 1045, 1075. Of the six-judge bench, Dickson C.J. agreed with Lamer J; La Forest J. (at 1113) preferred to say nothing about arbitrariness; McIntyre J. (at 1104), Wilson J. (at 1109) and Le Dain J. (at 1111) each thought that arbitrariness was relevant under s. 12. In *R.* v. *Goltz* [1991] 3 S.C.R. 485, 500, Gonthier J. for the majority sided with Lamer J.

10 *R.* v. *Smith* [1987] 1 S.C.R. 1045, 1074.

11 [1987] 1 S.C.R. 1045. The principal opinion was written by Lamer J., with whom only Dickson C.J. agreed entirely. Wilson and La Forest JJ. wrote concurring opinions agreeing with Lamer J. except on the relevance of arbitrariness to s. 12 (see note 7, above). Le Dain J. also wrote a concurring opinion, but he agreed generally with McIntyre J.'s discussion of the law, although rejecting McIntyre J.'s conclusion. McIntyre J. dissented, holding that the minimum sentence was not cruel and unusual punishment.

12 The sentence was not influenced by the seven-year minimum, because the trial judge anticipated the Supreme Court of Canada's ruling that the minimum sentence was unconstitutional.

13 *Id.*, 1053. Lamer J. acknowledged (at 1054) that "no such case has occurred to my knowledge". No doubt, this is because of police or prosecutorial discretion.

14 *Id.*, 1080. Note, however that the Court has not found that extraditing fugitives to face the possibility of much longer minimum sentences for drug offences in the United States "shocks the Canadian conscience" enough to constitute grounds (under s. 7) for overturning extradition orders: *United States* v. *Jamieson* [1996] 1 S.C.R. 465 (20 year minimum sentence); *United States* v. *Whitley* [1996] 1 S.C.R. 467 (20 year minimum sentence); *United States* v. *Ross* [1996] 1 S.C.R. 469 (15 year minimum sentence).

50.4 Minimum sentence

In the previous section of this chapter, we noticed the decision of the Supreme Court of Canada in *R.* v. *Smith* (1987),[15] holding that the minimum sentence of seven years' imprisonment was cruel and unusual as the punishment for importing narcotics, because the punishment was grossly disproportionate to that offence. The test employed in *Smith* was the test of the most innocent possible offender: is it possible to imagine a hypothetical case for which the minimum sentence would be grossly disproportionate? It does not matter that the hypothetical case has never arisen, and is never likely to arise having regard to police and prosecutorial discretion.[16] Nor does it matter that the minimum sentence is appropriate (or too low) for the offender actually before the Court.[17] As McIntyre J. pointed out in dissent, the decision in effect entrenches the discretion of the sentencing judge to take account of all the circumstances of the offender and of the offence. Parliament is not permitted to establish a sentencing rule that significantly restricts that discretion, even when Parliament decides that the gravity of an offence and the protection of the public requires a minimum sentence. It is quite possible, as the Court implies in its discussion of s. 1, that a minimum sentence is not an effective deterrent anyway. But Parliament evidently thought that it was, and the Court does not suggest any alternative way of reducing the importation of drugs.

In *Smith*, Lamer J. made clear that he did not regard all minimum sentences as cruel and unusual.[18] However, the effect of the most innocent possible offender principle was to place in jeopardy any restrictions on the system of individualized sentencing by judges. Individualized sentencing has always been the standard Canadian way. Minimum sentences are rare; maximums tend to be high; and sentencing judges are left with a wide range of discretion to tailor each sentence to the particular offence, the individual offender, and their views about retribution, deterrence, rehabilitation, the protection of society and other social objectives.

The trouble with individualized sentencing is that there is no agreement among judges on the relevance and weight to be accorded the many factors that go into sentencing. Studies of sentencing practices uniformly show outrageous disparities in the sentences that judges impose in similar cases.[19] The position is further complicated by parole and other early release programmes, which are not necessarily well understood by judges when they fix sentences. The situation has been the same in the United States, where it has led to the establishment in the federal jurisdiction and in several states of a sentencing commission, which

15 Note 9, above.

16 Note 13, above.

17 Note 12, above.

18 [1987] 1 S.C.R. 1045, 1077 (''A minimum mandatory term of imprisonment is obviously not in and of itself cruel and unusual''.)

19 The classic study is still Hogarth, *Sentencing as a Human Process* (1971); for references to more recent studies, see Palys and Divorski, ''Explaining Sentence Disparity'' (1986) 28 Can. J. Crim. 347.

establishes guidelines for sentencing that severely reduce (but do not entirely eliminate) judicial discretion. This shift away from individualized sentencing has survived constitutional challenge.[20] For present purposes, the point to be made is that the idealized view of individualized sentencing, which is the foundation of the decision in *Smith*,[21] is one that is not widely shared outside the small community of judges and advocates who operate the present system. It would be a pity if reform of sentencing practices in Canada were to be precluded by constitutional norms that have been erected on such an insecure foundation.[22]

In *R.* v. *Goltz* (1991),[23] the issue was the validity of a minimum sentence of seven *days'* imprisonment. The sentence was required by provincial law for driving a motor vehicle while prohibited from driving. As in *Smith*, there was little doubt that the actual accused was appropriately punished: he had earned his prohibition from driving by a series of traffic violations that under provincial law had accumulated enough "points" to warrant a prohibition, and he had deliberately flouted the prohibition. Moreover, the sentencing judge had directed that the sentence be served on weekends. But the trial court, obedient to the reasoning process in *Smith*, postulated, as the most innocent possible offender, a person who, although prohibited from driving, had driven a vehicle whose driver had become disabled in an accident a few feet off the highway in order "to permit other cars backed up for miles to get by".[24] And yes, for that accused, a seven-day sentence would be grossly disproportionate! (*Smith*, of course, required the courts to disregard the fact that the hypothetical offender would never be charged with the offence.) Therefore, the seven-day minimum sentence was cruel and unusual. The British Columbia Court of Appeal affirmed this decision.

There could be no doubt that the reasoning of the lower courts in *Goltz* was perfectly faithful to *Smith*. However, *Goltz* demonstrated that no minimum sentence, however short, could possibly survive the relentless application of the most innocent possible offender principle. Nevertheless, when the decision came up to the Supreme Court of Canada, McLachlin J., invoking the trial court's Good Samaritan example, would have affirmed the decision that the sentence was cruel and unusual. She was disarmingly frank in her commitment to individualized sentencing, pointing out that the minimum sentence "deprives the judge of the

---

20 *Mistretta* v. *United States* (1989) 488 U.S. 361, rejecting challenge based on separation of powers principles. No argument was made on the basis of cruel and unusual punishment, which in the United States would have had no hope of success: *Harmelin* v. *Michigan* (1991) 501 U.S. 957 (mandatory sentence of life imprisonment without parole for possession of cocaine held not to be cruel and unusual).

21 Note 11, above.

22 It is possible that mandatory sentencing guidelines could survive the most innocent possible offender principle if there was provision for deviation from the guidelines for exceptional cases, perhaps with a requirement of written justification for the deviation by the sentencing judge.

23 [1991] 3 S.C.R. 485. Gonthier J. wrote the majority opinion, with the agreement of five others; McLachlin J. dissented, with the agreement of two others.

24 *Id.*, 530 per McLachlin J., relying on the same example.

range of discretion which is appropriate having regard to the gravity of the offence and the potential circumstances which may arise''.[25] However, McLachlin J.'s opinion was a dissenting opinion that was agreed with by only two others — Lamer C.J. and Stevenson J. Gonthier J. wrote for the majority, and he held that the sentence was not cruel and unusual. He agreed that *Smith* made it necessary to test the proportionality of the sentence by reference to a ''hypothetical example'', but he held that the example had to be ''reasonable'', and not ''far-fetched''.[26] He made no reference to the Good Samaritan moving the car off the accident site, which he presumably regarded as far-fetched.[27] ''The applicable standard'', he said, ''must focus on imaginable circumstances which could commonly arise in day-to-day life''.[28] By that standard, the ''high threshold of gross disproportionality'' had not been crossed.[29]

Murder is an offence that carries a mandatory sentence of life imprisonment. Obviously, a mandatory sentence is a minimum sentence. The culpability of murderers must vary as much as, and perhaps more than, the culpability of those guilty of any other crime. At one end of the spectrum is the evil, cold-blooded, premeditated act of cruelty that is the staple of the murder mystery novel. At the other end of the spectrum is an act of panic, impulse or passion, perhaps involving elements of provocation, self-defence, mental illness, intoxication or bad luck (that are not sufficient to afford a defence). It is also possible for the person who was not the actual killer to be convicted as a party to murder. Therefore, even if the most innocent possible offender principle is confined to ''imaginable circumstances which could commonly arise in day-to-day life'',[30] there is a strong case that life imprisonment as the mandatory penalty for murder is cruel and unusual. Curiously, however, the criminal defence bar, normally so inventive (and effective) in making full use of the Charter, has not yet challenged the mandatory sentence of life imprisonment.

What has been challenged is the distinction drawn by the Criminal Code between ''first degree murder'' and ''second degree murder''. First degree murder includes three types of murder: (1) murder that is ''planned and deliberate''; (2) murder of a police officer or prison officer, whether or not the crime is planned and deliberate; and (3) murder committed in the course of hijacking an aircraft,

---

25 *Id.*, 531.

26 *Id.*, 506, 515.

27 He did however refer (at 518) to the example of the single mother under suspension rushing her sick child to the hospital, and (at 519) to the example of the grandfather under prohibition driving his sick grandchild from a lake to a nearby town. He implied that these examples might not be ''reasonable'', but he answered the first case by saying that it was a suspension rather than a prohibition, and the second by saying that the defence of necessity would be available. The first answer seems rather weak, as McLachlin J. (at 523-528) pointed out.

28 [1991] 3 S.C.R. 485, 515-516.

29 *Id.*, 520. See also *R.* v. *Brown* [1994] 3 S.C.R. 749 (upholding minimum sentence for use of a firearm in the course of committing indictable offence, but decision limited to case where underlying offence is robbery).

30 Note 24, above.

sexual assault, kidnapping and forcible confinement, whether or not the crime is planned and deliberate. First degree murder carries a penalty of life imprisonment, but with the condition that the prisoner is ineligible for parole for 25 years. Second degree murder also carries the penalty of life imprisonment, but without the condition as to eligibility for parole. In *R.* v. *Luxton* (1990),[31] the Supreme Court of Canada held that the parole condition that was attached to a sentence for first degree murder did not constitute cruel and unusual punishment. Lamer C.J. for the Court declared: "The punishment is not excessive and clearly does not outrage our standards of decency."[32]

Luxton was decided before the Court in *Goltz* confined the most innocent possible offender principle to "imaginable circumstances which could commonly arise in day-to-day life". But, even using this stricter standard, in my opinion, the mandatory sentence of 25 years without parole is so severe that it cannot meet the standard. Two of the three categories of first degree murder do not include any element of premeditation, and therefore would encompass a wide range of moral turpitude. For example, it is not "far-fetched" to postulate a hypothetical offender — one who killed in panic, perhaps, or one who was merely an accomplice of the killer, perhaps — for whom the 25 years without parole would be grossly disproportionate. And yet the Court in *Luxton* did not test the sentence by reference to any hypothetical cases, or otherwise explain why the punishment was not grossly disproportionate.

Although it is no longer possible to state the law respecting minimum sentences with any confidence, the Court has obviously abandoned the most innocent possible offender principle. In assessing the proportionality of a minimum sentence, the Court has not returned to the safe ground of considering only the case before it. The Court will still consider hypothetical cases, but it will exclude those that are unreasonable or far-fetched. The Court has not said what cases are unreasonable or far-fetched. Presumably, they are those cases that no reasonable police officer is likely to charge and no reasonable prosecutor is likely to prosecute. The effect of this standard is to permit Parliament and the Legislatures to impose some restrictions on judicial discretion in sentencing.

50.5 Indeterminate sentence

It has been held that a sentence of imprisonment of indeterminate duration is cruel and unusual punishment, when imposed under the Criminal Code's "habitual criminal" provisions. These provisions, which were repealed in 1977, applied to an offender who had been convicted of an indictable offence at least three times and was "leading persistently a criminal life". In the case, at least, of an offender who was not dangerous, but was merely a "social nuisance", an

31 [1990] 2 S.C.R. 711.
32 *Id.*, 724.

indeterminate sentence was "cruel and unusual" within the meaning of s. 12 of the Charter.[33]

The Criminal Code's "habitual criminal" provisions were in 1977 replaced by "dangerous offender" provisions. The new provisions also authorize an indeterminate sentence of imprisonment, but only where the offender has committed a serious personal injury offence and it is established that the offender is a danger to society. Each person who is classified as a dangerous offender must be reviewed by the National Parole Board three years after his classification, and every two years thereafter, and the Parole Board has power to release the offender when it is satisfied that he is no longer an undue risk to society.

In *R.* v. *Lyons* (1987),[34] the Supreme Court of Canada held that the dangerous offender provisions were not cruel and unusual within s. 12 of the Charter. La Forest J. for the Court held that the preventive purpose of the detention was not disproportionate, because those classified as dangerous offenders possessed "the very characteristics that render [preventive] detention necessary".[35] The indeterminate duration of the detention, while severe, was not disproportionate because of the preventive purpose and the requirement of regular review by the Parole Board. And, in language very different in tone from that of Lamer J. in the earlier *Smith* case, La Forest J. added that "gross" disproportionality was not an "exacting" standard, and did not "require punishments to be perfectly suited to accommodate the moral nuances of every crime and every offender".[36]

50.6 Prison conditions

The prohibition against cruel and unusual treatment or punishment applies not only to the penalties prescribed by the Criminal Code or other statutes creating offences. It applies to the actual conditions under which offenders are confined. No doubt, the Charter, like the American Bill of Rights, "does not mandate comfortable prisons",[37] but oppressive conditions or severe disciplinary measures

33 *Re Mitchell and the Queen* (1983) 42 O.R. (2d) 481 (H.C.). The applicant had been classified as an habitual criminal in 1970, before the provisions were repealed. The repeal did not affect those persons already under sentence. The federal government later released 71 of the 87 persons still being held as habitual criminals: Globe and Mail, May 24, 1984.

34 [1987] 2 S.C.R. 309. The majority opinion was written by La Forest J. with the agreement of four others; Lamer and Wilson JJ. each wrote dissenting opinions, but they agreed with La Forest J. on the s. 12 issue.

35 *Id.*, 339.

36 *Id.*, 344-345. *Lyons* was followed in *R.* v. *Milne* [1987] 2 S.C.R. 512. In *Steele* v. *Mountain Institution* [1990] 2 S.C.R. 309, the Court reviewed the decision of the Parole Board not to release a dangerous offender; finding the decision to be wrong, the Court held that his continued detention was cruel and unusual; habeas corpus was issued to release the prisoner. Cf. *R.* v. *Swain* [1991] 1 S.C.R. 933 (striking down Criminal Code provisions for the detention of an accused found not guilty by reason of insanity; ss. 7 and 9 were relied upon, but s. 12 was not considered).

37 *Rhodes* v. *Chapman* (1981) 452 U.S. 337, 349.

in penitentiaries or prisons could amount to cruel and unusual punishment.[38] Where oppressive conditions are caused by overcrowding, a judicial order that the conditions were cruel and unusual might require releasing some prisoners or building new facilities. These are serious consequences, and they tend to interpose the courts into the fixing of governmental spending priorities and the running of a correctional system.

50.7 Death penalty

The death penalty is the most controversial of penalties currently in force. The Canadian Parliament in 1976 abolished the death penalty for all the Criminal Code offences to which it had been attached, namely, murder, treason and piracy.[39] However, the Parliament left the death penalty in place for two offences under the National Defence Act,[40] namely, espionage and mutiny with violence, and for war crimes committed during World War Two.[41]

Before its abolition in 1976, the death penalty for murder was attacked as being cruel and unusual in violation of s. 2(b) of the Canadian Bill of Rights, but in *R.* v. *Miller and Cockriell* (1977),[42] the Supreme Court of Canada unanimously upheld the penalty. This decision, like other decisions under the Canadian Bill of Rights,[43] is not a reliable guide to the likely outcome of a Charter challenge. The better view and the likely outcome is that the death penalty is cruel and unusual, not because it is disproportionate to the offences of espionage, mutiny or war crimes, but because it is barbaric in itself[44] and therefore unavailable even for the most heinous offences.[45]

---

38 *McCann* v. *The Queen* [1976] 1 F.C. 570 (Fed. T.D.) (conditions in solitary confinement held to be cruel and unusual under s. 2(b) of the Canadian Bill of Rights); *Collin* v. *Kaplan* [1983] 1 F.C. 496 (Fed. T.D.) (double-celling held not to be cruel and unusual under s. 12 of Charter; *R.* v. *Olson* (1987) 62 O.R. (2d) 321 (C.A.) (administrative segregation of prisoner at risk from other inmates held not to be cruel and unusual); *R.* v. *McC.(T)* (1991) 4 O.R. (3d) 203 (Ont. Ct. Prov. Div.) (dirty, overcrowded holding cells for young offenders held to be cruel and unusual).

39 S.C. 1974-75-76, c. 105.

40 R.S.C. 1985, c. N-4, s. 78 (espionage), s. 79 (mutiny with violence).

41 War Crimes Act, S.C. 1946, c. 73, s. 11.

42 [1977] 2 S.C.R. 680. The penalty had been abolished by the time the Court decided the case.

43 See ch. 32, Canadian Bill of Rights, under heading 32.5, "Judicial interpretation", above.

44 The two categories of cruel and unusual are explained in text accompanying note 9, above.

45 In *Kindler* v. *Can.* [1991] 2 S.C.R. 779, the Court, by a majority of four to three, held that s. 12 was not applicable to a decision by the Canadian government to surrender a fugitive to a jurisdiction where he might suffer the death penalty; and s. 12 did not require the Canadian government to seek an assurance that the death penalty would not be imposed. The majority's reasoning was that the death penalty, if imposed, would flow from foreign law, not Canadian law. Cory J. dissented, holding that the extradition of a fugitive to face cruel and unusual punishment was itself cruel and unusual punishment in breach of s. 12. Sopinka J. also dissented, holding that the extradition was a breach of s. 7. Lamer C.J. agreed with both dissenting opinions. Both Cory and Sopinka JJ. (and therefore Lamer C.J.) held that capital punishment

In the United States, a series of decisions has held that the death penalty is cruel and unusual if the sentencing court has an unfettered discretion as to its imposition,[46] or if the sentencing court has no discretion as to its imposition,[47] or if it is the punishment for rape (as opposed to murder),[48] or if it is imposed upon an accomplice to a murder (as opposed to the actual killer)[49] or if it is imposed on a person under the age of 16.[50] But the death penalty is not cruel and unusual as the penalty for murder, where the sentencing court has a discretion as to its imposition, provided that statutory guidelines are supplied to control the exercise of that discretion,[51] so long as those guidelines do not unduly circumscribe the range of mitigating circumstances to be taken into account[52] and so long as the sentence is subject to appellate review.[53] A majority of American states continue to impose the death penalty under statutes tailored to fit the difficult reasoning in these cases.

---

was cruel and unusual. The majority opinions of La Forest and McLachlin JJ., both concurred in by L'Heureux-Dubé and Gonthier JJ., did not consider whether capital punishment was cruel and unusual.

46 *Furman* v. *Georgia* (1972) 408 U.S. 238.

47 *Woodson* v. *North Carolina* (1976) 428 U.S. 280.

48 *Coker* v. *Georgia* (1977) 433 U.S. 584.

49 *Enmund* v. *Florida* (1982) 458 U.S. 782.

50 *Thompson* v. *Oklahoma* (1988) 487 U.S. 815.

51 *Gregg* v. *Georgia* (1976) 428 U.S. 153.

52 *Lockett* v. *Ohio* (1978) 438 U.S. 586.

53 *Pulley* v. *Harris* (1984) 465 U.S. 37. The statistical fact that the death penalty is imposed on a disproportionate number of African-American offenders is not a violation of either the cruel and unusual punishment clause or the equal protection clause: *McCleskey* v. *Kemp* (1987) 481 U.S. 279.

51

Self-Incrimination

51.1 Section 13

Section 13 of the Charter of Rights[1] provides as follows:

> 13. A witness who testifies in any proceedings has the right not to have any incriminating evidence so given used to incriminate that witness in any other proceedings, except in a prosecution for perjury or for the giving of contradictory evidence.

Section 13[2] does not give to a witness the right to refuse to answer a question on the ground that the answer might incriminate him. That right, which existed

---

1 For commentary on s. 13, see Paciocco, *Charter Principles* and Proof in Criminal Cases (1987), ch. 7; Stuart, *Charter Justice in Canadian Criminal Law* (2nd ed., 1996), ch. 8; Sopinka, Lederman, Bryant, *The Law of Evidence in Canada* (1992), 734-768; McLeod, Takach, Morton, Segal, *The Canadian Charter of Rights* (Carswell, loose-leaf), ch. 5; *Canadian Charter of Rights Annotated* (Canada Law Book, loose-leaf), annotation to s. 13. The latter work provides a bibliography of the relevant literature.

2 Section 13 of the Charter was in the October 1980 version of the Charter in the following terms:

> 13. A witness has the right when compelled to testify not to have any incriminating evidence so given used to incriminate him or her in any other proceedings, except a prosecution for perjury or for the giving of contradictory evidence.

Under this version of s. 13 the privilege would have been available only if the witness were ''compelled to testify'' in the earlier proceedings. This limitation on s. 13 was eliminated in the April 1981 version. This (final) version is applicable to ''a witness who testifies'', regardless of whether the witness testifies under compulsion or not: notes 10, 11 below.

at common law, was abolished in Canada in 1893 by what is now s. 5(1) of the Canada Evidence Act.[3] (The right has also been abolished by each provincial Evidence Act.) The right has not been restored by the Charter of Rights[4] or by the Canadian Bill of Rights.[5] The right not to answer on the ground of self-incrimination still exists in the common law of the United Kingdom, and in the constitutional law of the United States under the fifth amendment (applicable to the Congress) and the fourteenth amendment (applicable to the states). In Canada, however, a witness may not refuse to answer a question on the ground that the answer might incriminate him. What s. 13 of the Charter does is to give to the witness "the right not to have any incriminating evidence so given used to incriminate that witness in any other proceedings, except in a prosecution for perjury or for the giving of contradictory evidence".

51.2 Invoking the right

Section 13 essentially declares the law as it now exists in s. 5(2) of the Canada Evidence Act (and its provincial counterparts), but with one important change. Under s. 5(2), the incriminating evidence could be excluded from the subsequent proceedings only if the witness had claimed the privilege against self-incrimination at the time of giving the testimony in the earlier proceedings.[6] Under s. 13 of the Charter, the privilege is available to exclude the incriminating testimony from the later proceedings, even if no objection were taken at the time of giving the testimony in the earlier proceedings.[7]

---

3 R.S.C. 1985, c. C-5.

4 It has been held that the common law right to remain silent before the trial is guaranteed by s. 7, despite the failure to include such a right in s. 11(c) or s. 13: *R.* v. *Hebert* [1990] 2 S.C.R. 151. However, by reason of the specific language of s. 13, s. 7 should not be interpreted as granting a right against self-incrimination to a witness in legal proceedings: *Thomson Newspapers* v. *Can.* [1990] 1 S.C.R. 425, 442 (Lamer J. says there is such a right in s. 7), 482 (Wilson J. says no), 538 (La Forest J. says no), 585-585 (L'Heureux-Dubé J. implies no), 601 (Sopinka J. says no); *R.* v. *S.(R.J.)* [1995] 1 S.C.R. 451 (Court now seems unanimous on this point). However, s. 7 will render a witness non-compellable if "the predominant purpose for seeking the evidence is to obtain incriminating evidence against the person compelled to testify": *B.C. Securities Commn.* v. *Branch* [1995] 2 S.C.R. 3, 15.

5 The Canadian Bill of Rights, by s. 2(d), refers to "protection against self-incrimination". This has not been interpreted as restoring the pre-1893 common law right, but has been interpreted as declaratory of the pre-existing federal law (that is, the law as modified by the Canada Evidence Act): Tarnopolsky, *The Canadian Bill of Rights* (2nd ed., 1975), 255-259; *R.* v. *Forrester* (1982) 144 D.L.R. (3d) 558 (Ont. C.A.); *Ziegler* v. *Hunter* [1984] 2 F.C. 608 (C.A.).

6 *Tass* v. *The King* [1947] S.C.R. 103.

7 *Dubois* v. *The Queen* [1985] 2 S.C.R. 350, 360. In other respects, the scope of protection afforded by s. 5(2) is identical to s. 13: *R.* v. *Kuldip* [1990] 3 S.C.R. 618, 642.

51.3 Application to accused

It will be recalled that s. 11(c) of the Charter, which is declaratory of pre-existing common law, confers on a ''person charged with an offence'' the right ''not to be compelled to be a witness'' at his own trial.[8] By the exercise of this right (and the right to remain silent before the trial),[9] an accused can avoid incriminating himself. But if the accused does decide to testify at his own trial, he cannot refuse to answer any question on the ground that the answer might incriminate him. By deciding to testify, the accused assumes the risk that his testimony may be used to incriminate him on the trial of that charge. The only protection that he obtains from s. 13 is that his testimony cannot be used to incriminate him ''in any other proceedings''.

51.4 Compelled and voluntary evidence

An earlier version of s. 13 applied only if the witness was ''compelled to testify'' in the earlier proceedings.[10] That form of the privilege would not have been available to an accused who had testified at his own trial, or to any other witness who had testified voluntarily in a civil or criminal trial. Only evidence given under the compulsion of a subpoena (summons to witness) would have been protected by s. 13. The version of s. 13 that was enacted applies to ''a witness who testifies in any proceedings''. This phrase makes no distinction between voluntary and compelled evidence, and it is clear that the former is covered as well as the latter.[11]

51.5 Incriminating evidence

Section 13 applies to ''incriminating'' evidence. The position in s. 13 of the word ''incriminating'' seems to indicate that the evidence must be incriminating in the first proceedings — the proceedings in which the evidence was originally given — as well as in the second proceedings for which s. 13 now provides the privilege.[12] Both the common law privilege and s. 5(2) of the Canada Evidence Act required the quality of self-incrimination at the time the witness originally spoke. However the Supreme Court of Canada has held that the evidence need not be incriminating in the first proceedings in which it was originally given. All that is necessary is that the evidence be incriminating in the second proceedings

8 See ch. 48, Rights on Being Charged, under heading 48.4, ''Non-compellability'', above.
9 Note 4, above.
10 Note 2, above.
11 *Dubois* v. *The Queen* [1985] 2 S.C.R. 350, 360.
12 This is the position taken by Schiff in *Evidence in the Litigation Process* (4th ed., 1993), ch. 15, sec. 1.

when the Crown seeks to use it.[13] In those second proceedings, all of the evidence for the prosecution is deemed to be incriminating: ''The Crown tenders evidence to support its case and obtain a conviction; it knows best what is incriminating''.[14]

51.6 Other proceedings

(a) Non-criminal proceedings

The privilege conferred by s. 13 applies ''in any other proceedings''. Unlike s. 11, s. 13 is not explicitly confined to a ''person charged with an offence''. However, for s. 13 to apply, there must be a possibility of incrimination in the later, ''other proceedings''. Does this mean that the witness must be a ''person charged with an offence'' in the later proceedings? The answer to this is probably yes, so that s. 13 could only be invoked if the later proceedings against the witness were (1) ''by nature'' criminal or (2) could lead to a ''true penal consequence''.[15] This means that evidence that had been given by a witness in an earlier civil or criminal trial could be used in subsequent *disciplinary* proceedings against the witness. For example, it has been held that a nurse could be barred from practice by a disciplinary tribunal on the basis of a transcript of evidence given by the nurse at her earlier criminal trial on a charge of theft. The evidence satisfied the disciplinary tribunal that the nurse was unfit to practise the nursing profession, but the evidence was not ''incriminating'' in the discipline proceedings, because the discipline proceedings were not ''by nature'' criminal and could not lead to a ''true penal consequence''. Therefore, the nurse could not invoke s. 13 to exclude her earlier testimony from the disciplinary proceedings.[16]

(b) Re-trial

It has been held that the later proceedings — the ''other proceedings'' — may be a second trial on the same charge following a mistrial or successful appeal. In *Dubois* v. *The Queen* (1985),[17] the accused was tried on a charge of murder. He testified in his own defence, admitting that he was the killer of the victim but alleging circumstances of justification. He was convicted, but on appeal a new trial was ordered on the ground that the trial judge had misdirected the jury. At

13 [1985] 2 S.C.R. 350, 364.

14 *Ibid.*

15 This is the definition of an ''offence'' within s. 11, as established by *R.* v. *Wigglesworth* [1987] 2 S.C.R. 541; for discussion, see ch. 48, Rights On Being Charged, under heading 48.1(c), ''Offence'', above.

16 *Knutson* v. *Sask. Reg. Nurses Assn.* (1990) 75 D.L.R. (4th) 723 (Sask. C.A.). Contra, *Re Donald* (1983) 2 D.L.R. (4th) 385 (B.C.C.A.) (applying s. 13 to subsequent disciplinary proceedings).

17 [1985] 2 S.C.R. 350.

the new trial, the accused did not testify. However, the Crown tendered the accused's testimony from the first trial as evidence for the prosecution. The trial judge admitted the evidence, and the accused was again convicted. The Supreme Court of Canada allowed the accused's appeal. Lamer J. for the majority of the Court held that the second trial, although its purpose was simply to resolve the original charge against the accused, counted as "other proceedings" in s. 13. Therefore, the use by the Crown at the second trial of the testimony given by the accused at the first trial was precluded by s. 13.[18]

51.7 Cross-examination

In *R.* v. *Mannion* (1986),[19] the accused was tried on a charge of rape. He testified in his own defence. He was convicted, but on appeal a new trial was ordered. At the new trial, the Crown did not tender the accused's testimony from the first trial as part of the Crown's case in chief. However, the accused testified again at the new trial, and, when he did so, the Crown cross-examined him on statements he had made in his testimony at the first trial. Did this use of the earlier testimony violate s. 13? The Supreme Court of Canada answered yes. McIntyre J. for a unanimous Court held that the testimony from the first trial, although only brought into the second trial on cross-examination, was "used to incriminate" the accused in the second trial. Therefore, there had been a breach of s. 13.

R. v. *Kuldip* (1990)[20] appeared at first glance to be on all fours with *R.* v. *Mannion*. Once again, the question was whether the Crown could cross-examine the accused at a re-trial on testimony given by the accused at the first trial. However, in *Kuldip* the Supreme Court of Canada held that s. 13 did not preclude the cross-examination. The Court held that the case differed from *Mannion* in that the purpose of the cross-examination in *Kuldip* was not to incriminate the accused, but merely to impeach his credibility as a witness. This use of inconsistent statements from the accused's earlier testimony was not precluded by s. 13.

It seems obvious that most questions posed to the accused in cross-examination cannot be confidently classified as being either for the purpose of attacking the witness's credibility or for the purpose of incriminating the accused. Both purposes are likely to be present. It seems artificial, if not impossible, to have to make the choice.[21] What the *Kuldip* rule requires is that the trier of fact must pay

---

18 This ruling was followed in *R.* v. *Mannion* [1986] 2 S.C.R. 272; discussed in text accompanying next note. Curiously, neither in *Dubois* nor *Mannion* did the Court make reference to *R.* v. *Sophonow* [1984] 2 S.C.R. 524, affg. (1984) 11 D.L.R. (4th) 24 (Man. C.A.), in which the Court affirmed a decision (saying that it was in "substantial agreement" with the majority judgment) that a second trial for the same offence was not "other proceedings" within s. 13.

19 [1986] 2 S.C.R. 272

20 [1990] 3 S.C.R. 618

21 This is especially so in light of the Court's broad definition of "incriminating evidence" in s. 13: note 14, above.

no attention to the answers on cross-examination for the purpose of determining whether the accused is guilty. Lamer C.J. said in *Kuldip:*[22] ''A trial judge will have to be very clear in his or her instructions to the jury when setting out the uses to which previous testimony can be put and the uses to which such testimony must not be put''. In other words, the trial judge must instruct the jury not to use the accused's answers on cross-examination on previous testimony to incriminate the accused. Lamer C.J. acknowledged that his contemplated instruction would be ''somewhat troublesome'' to the jury.[23]

It might be thought that the *Kuldip* rule is a needless refinement on the simple and defensible rule that the Court appeared to have adopted in *Mannion*. It is obviously arguable that a prohibition of *all* cross-examination on an accused's inconsistent statements in prior testimony is the only safe way to protect the accused from the prejudice that s. 13 seeks to prevent. To allow cross-examination solely for the purpose of impeaching credibility, as *Kuldip* now does, requires credibility and incrimination to be kept separate in the minds of counsel and triers of fact, which is obviously impossible to police. Nevertheless, there is much to be said for the distinction insisted upon by *Kuldip*, especially in the case of a second trial on the same charge. If there were a total prohibition on cross-examination on prior testimony, the accused would be able to tell a different story at the second trial from the one he told at the first trial, and the accused would be able to rely on s. 13 to insulate the first story from exposure at the second trial. To allow an accused to employ tactics of his kind, without any risk of being confronted on cross-examination with the earlier testimony, would (as Lamer C.J. has commented)[24] '' 'stack the deck' too highly in favour of the accused''.

51.8 Derivative evidence

Section 13 applies to self-incriminatory evidence, and stipulates that such evidence may not be used to incriminate the witness in other proceedings. Section 13 does not apply to evidence that existed independently of the witness's testimony, even if it was discovered as the result of clues obtained from the testimony. This ''derivative'' or ''secondary'' evidence is not literally self-incriminatory, because it was not created by the witness. However, the Supreme Court of Canada has decided that s. 13 does not define exhaustively the scope of the constitutional protection against self-incrimination. There is a residue of protection in s. 7, which supplements s. 13 by conferring on the trial judge a discretion to exclude derivative evidence that would not have been discovered but for the witness's testimony. This ''derivative-use immunity'' does not cover all derivative evidence, because it does not exclude evidence that is in fact discovered as the result

---

22 [1990] 3 S.C.R. 618, 635.

23 *Ibid.*

24 *Id.*, 636.

of the witness's testimony if the evidence would probably be discovered in any event without the witness's testimony. In the case of evidence that would probably not have been discovered "but for" the witness's testimony, the Court's reasoning is that it would be a breach of the principles of fundamental justice guaranteed by s. 7 to allow the Crown to bolster its case with evidence that was so directly connected to the self-incriminatory testimony.[25]

51.9 Perjury

The privilege conferred by s. 13 does not apply where the later proceeding is "a prosecution for perjury or for the giving of contradictory evidence". The reason for this exception is that the offence of perjury or the giving of contradictory evidence could not be proved if the Crown was unable to adduce as evidence the prior testimony that the Crown alleges was perjured or contradictory.

Section 5(2) of the Canada Evidence Act made an exception only for perjury. The Ontario Court of Appeal held in *R.* v. *Chaperon* (1979),[26] that perjury did not include the giving of contradictory evidence (which is a separate offence under the Criminal Code); the accused was therefore entitled to the protection of the privilege in a subsequent prosecution for the giving of contradictory evidence. It seems obvious that perjury and the giving of contradictory evidence[27] should both be excepted from the protection and s. 13 accomplishes that result.

---

25 *R.* v. *S.(R.J.)* [1995] 1 S.C.R. 451, as reinterpreted in *B.C. Securities Commn.* v. *Branch* [1995] 2 S.C.R. 3.

26 (1979) 52 C.C.C. (2d) 85 (Ont. C.A.).

27 This includes not just the Criminal Code offence of the giving of contradictory evidence, but any offence the essence of which is the giving of false or contradictory testimony under oath; the earler testimony is available to the prosecution in the later proceedings: *R.* v. *Staranchuk* [1985] 1 S.C.R. 439, affg. (1983) 3 D.L.R. (4th) 574 (Sask. C.A.) (charge under Bankruptcy Act of making false statements in bankruptcy proceedings).

52

Equality

52.1 Distribution of powers

The distribution of powers over egalitarian values[1] presents two issues. The first issue is the extent to which each level of government may deny or limit egalitarian values, for example, by the enactment of laws that discriminate on the basis of characteristics such as race, national origin or sex. The second issue is the extent to which each level of government may promote egalitarian values, for example, by the enactment of laws that forbid discrimination in employment, accommodation and facilities open to the public.

On the first issue — the power to enact discriminatory laws — the position before April 17, 1985, when s. 15 of the Charter of Rights came into force, was dictated by the doctrine of parliamentary sovereignty: generally speaking, the Parliament or a Legislature could discriminate as it pleased in enacting otherwise competent legislation. Discrimination on the basis of sex, for example, has been upheld.[2] There are, however, some heads of legislative power which have enabled the courts to introduce egalitarian values into decisions reviewing the validity of statutes on federal grounds. The existence of federal power over ''naturalization and aliens'' (s. 91(25)) led the Privy Council in *Union Colliery* v. *Bryden* (1899)[3] to strike down a British Columbia law which prohibited the employment of Chinese persons in mines; their lordships reasoned that the pith and substance of the law was the imposition of a disability on aliens and naturalized subjects.[4] The existence of federal legislative power over ''Indians, and lands reserved for the Indians'' (s. 91(24)) would tend to preclude provincial laws which singled out

1 See Schmeiser, *Civil Liberties in Canada* (1964), ch. 6; Tarnopolsky, *The Canadian Bill of Rights* (2nd ed., 1975), 46-55.

2 *A.-G. Can.* v. *Lavell* [1974] S.C.R. 1349. Even a challenge based on the Canadian Bill of Rights failed: see text accompanying note 15, below.

3 [1899] A.C. 580.

4 But compare *Cunningham* v. *Tomey Homma* [1903] A.C. 151; *Quong-Wing* v. *The King* (1914) 49 S.C.R. 440; *Brooks-Bidlake and Whittall* v. *A.-G. B.C.* [1923] A.C. 450, where similarly discriminatory laws were upheld on the basis that the discrimination was merely incidental. Cf. *A.-G. B.C.* v. *A.-G. Can.* (Japanese Employment) [1924] A.C. 203; *Co-op. Committee on Japanese Canadians* v. *A.-G. Can.* [1947] A.C. 87; *Morgan* v. *A.-G. P.E.I.* [1976] 2 S.C.R. 349. For discussion, see Schmeiser, note 1, above, 257-262.

Indians for special treatment. In all these cases, one must remember that what is denied to one level of government is allowed to the other. Before the coming into force of s. 15, discrimination against aliens and naturalized subjects, and against Indians, was undoubtedly competent to the federal Parliament.

The real threat to egalitarian civil liberties in Canada comes not from legislative and official action, but from discrimination by private persons, such as employers, trade unions, landlords, realtors, restaurateurs and other suppliers of goods or services. The economic liberties of freedom of property and contract, which imply a power to deal with whomever one pleases, come into direct conflict with egalitarian values, and in all Canadian jurisdictions the former have now been subordinated to the latter by the enactment of human rights legislation, which forbids various discriminatory practices on pain of a penalty, and establishes a commission to administer the legislation. The authority to enact legislation of this kind is distributed between the federal Parliament and the provincial Legislatures according to which has jurisdiction over the employment, accommodation, restaurants and other businesses or activities in which discrimination is forbidden. Most of the field is accordingly provincial under property and civil rights in the province (s. 92(13)). However, there is little doubt that the federal Parliament could if it chose exercise its criminal law power (s. 91(27)) to outlaw discriminatory practices generally.

52.2 Canadian Bill of Rights

The Canadian Bill of Rights, by s. 1(b), guarantees ''equality before the law''. This provision, which applies only to the federal Parliament, was on April 17, 1985 superseded by s. 15 of the Charter of Rights, which applies to the federal Parliament and to the provincial Legislatures.

The Supreme Court of Canada held only once that the equality clause in s. 1(b) of the Canadian Bill of Rights had the effect of nullifying a statutory provi-

5 The singling out would not be decisive of the law's classification: see ch. 15, Judicial Review on Federal Grounds under heading 15.5(b), ''Singling out'', above.

6 Some kinds of discrimination by the federal Parliament (not the provincial Legislatures) were (after 1960) rendered inoperative by the equality clause in the Canadian Bill of Rights, which is the subject of the next section of this chapter. Saskatchewan, Alberta and Quebec also have bills of rights: see ch. 31, Civil Liberties, under heading 31.3(b), ''Statutory bills of rights'', above.

7 For a comprehensive survey of the law, see Tarnopolsky and Pentney, *Discrimination and the Law in Canada* (rev. ed., 1985).

8 *Id.*, ch. 3.

9 The analogy here is the prohibition of undesirable commercial practices, as in competition law: see ch. 18, Criminal Law, under heading 18.6, ''Competition law'', above.

10 The Canadian Bill of Rights is the topic of ch. 32, above.

11 For discussion of s. 1(b), see Tarnopolsky, note 1, above, ch. 8; Gold, ''Equality before the Law in the Supreme Court of Canada'' (1980) 18 Osgoode Hall L.J. 336; Gibson, *The Law of the Charter: Equality Rights* (1990), 23-36.

sion. That was in the case of *R.* v. *Drybones* (1969), in which the Court struck down a provision of the Indian Act that made it an offence for ''an Indian'' to be intoxicated off a reserve. (A companion provision made it an offence to be intoxicated on a reserve.) Ritchie J. for the majority of the Court held that the racial classification ''Indian'', which was employed by the challenged provision, was a breach of s. 1(b). This ruling cast doubt on all of the provisions of the Indian Act, which is for the most part applicable only to Indians. Indeed, on principles of federalism, that racial classification is prerequisite to the validity of the Act, which has been enacted under the federal power (s. 91(24)) over ''Indians, and lands reserved for the Indians''.

Drybones predictably led to challenges to other parts of the Indian Act. These were unsuccessful. In *A. G. Can.* v. *Lavell* (1973), the majority of the Court upheld the provisions of the Act that defined the term ''Indian'', although the Act employed a patrilineal concept that discriminated against women. In *A.G. Can.* v. *Canard* (1975), the Court upheld the provisions of the Act that established a special regime of succession to the property of deceased Indians, although the Act required estates to be administered by an official of the Department of Indian Affairs rather than a relative of the deceased. In both these cases, *Drybones*, although not overruled, was distinguished on implausible grounds, and equality in s. 1(b) was defined in a variety of inconsistent ways. The end result was that the validity of the Indian Act (apart from the drunkenness provision) was settled, but the definition of equality in s. 1(b) was in serious disarray.

After the Indian Act cases, the Supreme Court of Canada began to develop a consistent definition of equality under s. 1(b). The definition relied on the cryptic notion of a ''valid federal objective''. If a law pursued a valid federal objective, then it was not in breach of s. 1(b). In *R.* v. *Burnshine* (1974), this doctrine enabled the Court to uphold sentencing provisions that exposed young offenders to longer

---

12 [1970] S.C.R. 282

13 Ritchie J.'s opinion was agreed to by five other judges; Hall J., who was one of the five, also added a separate concurring opinion. Cartwright C.J., Abbott and Pigeon JJ. dissented.

14 See ch. 27, Aboriginal Peoples, above; see also sec. 52.9, ''Discrimination permitted by Constitution'', below.

15 [1974] S.C.R. 1349. Ritchie J.'s opinion was agreed to by three other judges. The fifth member of the majority, Pigeon J., expressed no opinion on whether the impugned provision was in conflict with the equality guarantee; he agreed in the result, because he persisted in the view he had expressed in dissent in *Drybones* that the Canadian Bill of Rights could not in any event override inconsistent legislation. Laskin C.J. dissented, on the basis that *Drybones* was controlling; and his opinion was agreed to by three other judges.

16 [1976] 1 S.C.R. 170. Four concurring opinions were written: by Ritchie J., Martland J. with whom Judson J. agreed, Pigeon J. and Beetz J. Laskin C.J., with whom Spence J. agreed, dissented. The bench comprised only seven judges.

17 For more expansive criticism of these cases, see the 2nd edition of this book (1985), 787-789.

18 [1975] 1 S.C.R. 693. Martland J.'s majority opinion was agreed with by five other judges, two of whom, Ritchie and Pigeon JJ., added brief additional reasons. Laskin J., with Spence and Dickson JJ., dissented.

sentences than adult offenders; the young offenders were to serve "indeterminate" sentences in special correctional facilities which would be dedicated to the rehabilitation of the unfortunate inmates. The Court held that the rehabilitation of young offenders was a valid federal objective that justified the age-based distinction in the statute. In *Bliss* v. *A.G. Can.* (1975), the Court upheld a provision of the Unemployment Insurance Act that denied benefits to a woman whose employment had been interrupted by pregnancy. An unspecified valid federal objective was invoked to justify the denial of benefits in that situation. In *MacKay* v. *The Queen* (1980), the Court upheld a provision of the National Defence Act that exposed members of the armed forces to trial by military tribunal for offences for which a civilian would be tried in the ordinary courts. Because the National Defence Act had been enacted for a valid federal objective, it followed that any differentiation between members of the armed forces and other citizens could not be attacked.

The valid federal objective doctrine was unsatisfactory in two ways. First, the Court never clarified what the term meant, although the Court always accepted that a statute containing a challenged provision did pursue a valid federal objective. Secondly, the Court (at least in *Bliss* and *MacKay*) did not relate the valid federal objective to the particular provision that was under challenge; if the Act as a whole pursued a valid federal objective, then every detailed provision was invulnerable to attack on equality grounds. In effect, the Court automatically deferred to the Parliament's judgment as to the distinctions that were required in order to establish a legislative scheme of sentencing, unemployment insurance, military justice or anything else.

With the coming into force of s. 15 of the Charter of Rights, s. 1(b) of the Canadian Bill of Rights, although still in force, has been rendered irrelevant. Moreover, in applying s. 15, the Supreme Court of Canada has turned over a new leaf. The language of valid federal objective has been banished, and replaced by

---

19 [1979] 1 S.C.R. 183. Ritchie J. wrote the judgment of the Court.

20 [1980] 2 S.C.R. 370. Ritchie J.'s opinion was agreed with by four other judges. McIntyre J., with Dickson J., wrote a separate concurring opinion. Laskin C.J., with Estey J., dissented.

21 This brief account inevitably omits some complexities, including the valiant efforts of Beetz J. (in *Canard*), McIntyre J. (in *MacKay*) and Laskin J. (in *Lavell*, *Canard* and *Burnshine*) to introduce more sophistication into the reasoning. An expanded account of the cases is provided in the 2nd edition of this book (1985), 787-794.

22 In *Beauregard* v. *Can.* [1986] 2 S.C.R. 56, a case which had arisen before s. 15 came into force, the Court by majority rejected a challenge under s. 1(b) to an amendment to the Judges Act that required newly appointed judges to contribute to the cost of their pensions while exempting existing judges from the obligation. Dickson C.J. for the majority said (at 90) that "the day has passed when it might have been appropriate . . . to reassess the direction this Court has taken in interpreting that document [the Canadian Bill of Rights]". Beetz J., with McIntyre J., dissented.

23 On the relationship between the Canadian Bill of Rights and the Charter of Rights, see ch. 32, Canadian Bill of Rights, under heading 32.1, "History".

new doctrine that is less deferential to the legislative will. That new doctrine is the subject of later sections of this chapter. First, however, is a brief description of the American equal protection jurisprudence.

52.3 American Bill of Rights

The fourteenth amendment to the Constitution of the United States provides that no state shall deny to any person within its jurisdiction "the equal protection of the laws". Although the fourteenth amendment applies only to the states, the guarantee of equal protection has been held to be incorporated in the due process clause of the fifth amendment, which applies to the federal Congress. In the result, both levels of government are bound by a guarantee of "equal protection of the laws".

This guarantee of equal protection is unqualified in its terms; and the Constitution of the United States contains no equivalent of s. 1 of the Canadian Charter of Rights, under which reasonable limits on rights are authorized, provided that they "can be demonstrably justified in a free and democratic society". And yet, recognizing that nearly all laws impose burdens or confer benefits on special groups, and deny the benefits or burdens to other groups, the Supreme Court of the United States has developed the doctrine of "reasonable classification", which saves those legislative classifications that are a reasonable means of achieving a legitimate legislative purpose.

In applying the doctrine of reasonable classification, the Court has developed a "two-tier" standard of review. The upper tier includes laws that classify by race or national origin, which the Court describes as "suspect" classifications. Also included in the upper tier are laws which, although employing other kinds of classifications, abridge a "fundamental" right, such as the right to vote or the right of interstate travel. For laws coming within the upper tier, the standard of review is usually described as "strict scrutiny". It is presumed that such laws are not a reasonable means of securing a legitimate legislative purpose. Such laws are held to be unconstitutional unless the government establishes that the classification was justified by a "compelling state interest", and that there was no alternative means of vindicating that state interest. Because it is hard for the government to discharge this burden, the practical effect of including a law in the upper tier is that it is very likely to be held to be unconstitutional. In particular,

---

24 The leading case is *Andrews* v. *Law Society of B.C.* [1989] 1 S.C.R. 143; see esp. 170, rejecting Canadian Bill of Rights doctrine.

25 The applicability of the American Bill of Rights to both levels of government is explained in ch. 34, Application of Charter, under heading 34.2(a), "Both levels of government", above.

26 For accounts of the equal protection jurisprudence, see Tussman and tenBroek, "The Equal Protection of the Laws" (1949) 37 Calif. L. Rev. 341; Tribe, *American Constitutional Law* (2nd ed., 1986), ch. 16; Nowak and Rotunda, *Constitutional Law* (4th ed., 1991), ch. 14.

with the exception of the wartime case of the detention of Japanese Americans, the modern Supreme Court of the United States has invariably struck down laws which classified by race. *Brown* v. *Board of Education* (1954), the school desegregation case, is the most famous example.

The lower tier of judicial review under the equal protection clause includes all legislative classifications that are not "suspect" and that do not affect fundamental rights. For these laws, a more relaxed standard of judicial review, usually described as "minimal scrutiny", is employed. It is sufficient if there is a "rational basis" for the classification. A good example is *Massachusetts Board of Retirement* v. *Murgia* (1976), in which the Court upheld a state law requiring police officers to retire at age 50. The plaintiff police officer, who had been compulsorily retired at age 50, established that he was still in excellent physical and mental health and fully capable of continuing to serve in the police force. Nonetheless, the Court held that the mandatory retirement law satisfied the rational basis test. To remove from police service those officers whose competence had presumptively diminished with age was a reasonable means of achieving a legitimate legislative purpose, namely, securing the physical preparedness of the state's police officers. The Court explicitly rejected the argument that age ("a stage that each of us will reach if we live out our normal span") was a suspect category, inviting strict scrutiny. As this case illustrates, it is not difficult for a government to find a rational basis for a law, so that the minimal scrutiny entailed by including a classification in the lower tier only occasionally results in a holding of unconstitutionality.

Not all equal protection cases fit the neat two-tier analysis. In particular, classifications by sex, which used to be placed on the lower tier, have recently been subjected to a stricter standard of review than the rational basis test. The leading case is *Craig* v. *Boren* (1976), where the Court struck down a state law that prohibited the sale of beer to males under 21 and females under 18. This discrimination against males aged 18 to 21 was supported by evidence showing a much higher incidence of drunkenness arrests and alcohol-related car accidents for young males than for young females. Despite this evidence, the Court held that the law was unconstitutional. Brennan J. for the majority of the Court said that "the showing offered by the [government] does not satisfy us that sex represents a legitimate, accurate proxy for the regulation of drinking and driving". In getting to this result, Brennan J. articulated a standard of judicial review that fell somewhere in between strict scrutiny and minimal scrutiny. He said that "classifications by gender must serve important governmental objectives and

---

27 *Korematsu* v. *United States* (1944) 323 U.S. 214.
28 (1954) 347 U.S. 483.
29 (1976) 427 U.S. 307.
30 *Id.*, 313-314.
31 (1976) 429 U.S. 190.
32 *Id.*, 204.

must be substantially related to achievement of those objectives''. This test, which has come to be described as ''intermediate scrutiny'', has been applied in other cases. However, it may turn out to be just a way station on the journey from the lower tier to the upper tier. It is quite possible that sex will soon be treated as no different from race and national origin, in which case few sexual classifications would survive judicial review under the equal protection clause.

The American cases are not directly relevant to the Canadian Charter of Rights, because the interaction of ss. 15, 28 and 1 of the Charter call for a development of indigenous Canadian doctrine. But the philosophic problem of determining which legislative classifications are bad and which are good is essentially the same. The rich American jurisprudence and commentary, to which the foregoing brief account does not begin to do justice, will obviously be helpful in developing Canadian doctrine.

52.4 Section 15 of Charter

Section 15 of the Charter of Rights provides as follows:

> 15.(1) Every individual is equal before and under the law and has the right to the equal protection and equal benefit of the law without discrimination and, in particular, without discrimination based on race, national or ethnic origin, colour, religion, sex, age or mental or physical disability.
>
> (2) Subsection (1) does not preclude any law, program or activity that has as its object the amelioration of conditions of disadvantaged individuals or groups including those that are disadvantaged because of race, national or ethnic origin, colour, religion, sex, age or mental or physical disability.

Section 15 confers its right on an ''individual''. Equality is expressed in four different ways: equality before the law, equality under the law, equal protection

33 *Id.*, 197.

34 For an account of the cases, see Tribe, note 27, above, 1558-1588; Nowak, note 27, above, 733-753.

35 The most comprehensive study of s. 15, to which I am much indebted, is Gibson, *The Law of the Charter: Equality Rights* (1990). For other commentary on s. 15, see Bayefsky and Eberts (eds.), *Equality Rights and the Charter of Rights* (1985); Smith (ed.), *Righting the Balance: Canada's New Equality Rights* (1986); Weiler and Elliot (eds.), *Litigating the Values of a Nation* (1986), Part II; Boyle and others (eds.), *Charterwatch: Reflections on Equality* (1986); Mahoney and Martin, *Equality and Judicial Neutrality* (1987); Brodsky and Day, *Canadian Charter Equality Rights for Women* (1989); Beaudoin and Mendes (eds.), *The Canadian Charter of Rights and Freedoms* (3rd ed., 1996), ch. 14 (by Black and Smith); Stuart, *Charter Justice in Canadian Criminal Law* (2nd ed., 1996), ch. 10; McLeod, Takach, Morton, Segal, *The Canadian Charter of Rights* (Carswell, loose-leaf), ch. 25; *Canadian Charter of Rights Annotated* (Canada Law Book, loose-leaf), annotation to s. 15. The last work provides a bibliography of the periodical literature.

36 Section 15 was in the October 1980 version of the Charter, but in the following terms:

> (1) Everyone has the right to equality before the law and to the equal protection of the

of the law and equal benefit of the law. The section also guarantees against "discrimination based on race, national or ethnic origin, colour, religion, sex, age or mental or physical disability". These are the named or listed grounds of discrimination. (The common practice of referring to them as "enumerated" grounds is not quite accurate, because the grounds are not numbered.) The section makes clear, by the phrase "in particular", that the named grounds are not exhaustive. Subsection (2) of s. 15 authorizes the creation of affirmative action programmes that have the purpose of ameliorating the conditions of disadvantaged groups. The function of each of the elements of s. 15, and the ways in which the various elements relate to each other and to s. 1 of the Charter, occupy the rest of this chapter.

Section 32(2) of the Charter delayed the coming into force of s. 15 for three years after the coming into force of the rest of the Charter. That brought s. 15 into force on April 17, 1985. The purpose of the delay was to provide time for the federal government and each province to review its body of laws and make those amendments that were necessary to bring the laws into conformity with s. 15. This review did take place in all Canadian jurisdictions except for Quebec, and each jurisdiction enacted amendments to a large number of statutes to correct perceived violations of s. 15 and other Charter rights.

52.5 Application of s. 15

(a) Individual

The *benefit* of the equality rights in s. 15 is conferred upon "an individual". The word individual has been analyzed earlier in this book, and the conclusion reached that it probably excludes a corporation.

(b) "Law" in s. 15

The *burden* of the equality rights, like all other Charter rights, is imposed by s. 32 on the Parliament and government of Canada and the Legislature and

---

law without discrimination because of race, national or ethnic origin, colour, religion, age or sex.

(2) This section does not preclude any law, program or activity that has as its object the amelioration of conditions of disadvantaged persons or groups.

The final version appeared in the April 1981 version. In the final version "every individual" replaced "everyone"; new and more various formulations of the idea of equality were substituted; the words "in particular" made clear that the specified grounds of discrimination were not exhaustive; "mental or physical disability" were added to the specified grounds of discrimination; and the "including" clause was added to s. 15(2).

37 Chapter 33, Charter of Rights, under heading 33.2, "Protection of civil liberties", above.

38 Chapter 34, Application of Charter, under heading 34.1, "Benefit of rights", above. This does not mean that a corporation can never invoke s. 15: see c. 55, Constitutional Litigation, under heading 55.2, "Standing", below.

government of each province. Section 32 has been analyzed earlier in this book, and the conclusion reached that it includes, among other things, all action taken under statutory authority. Does the reference to ''law'' in the various formulations of the equality rights in s. 15 have the effect of narrowing the application of s. 15 so as to exclude governmental action that is not law?

This question arose in *R.* v. *S.(S.)* (1990). The federal Young Offenders Act authorized the Attorney General of each province to establish a programme of ''alternative measures'' to divert young offenders away from proceedings in the courts. The contemplated diversion programmes were established in nine provinces, but not in Ontario. A young person accused of a crime in Ontario argued that the failure of the Attorney General to establish a programme in Ontario was a violation of the accused's equality rights under s. 15. The Supreme Court of Canada rejected this argument on the ground that s. 15 applied only to ''the law''. Section 15 did not apply to an exercise of discretion conferred by law, but only to the enabling law itself. Therefore, the Attorney General of Ontario's decision not to establish a diversion programme could not be impeached under s. 15. In a companion case, *R.* v. *S.(G.)* (1990), the Court also rejected an equality attack on a diversion programme that had been established, on the ground that the programme was an exercise of discretion under the Act.

These holdings that s. 15 has no application to an exercise of discretion conferred by a statute must surely be wrong. It makes no sense to say that Parliament itself lacks the power to abridge equality rights, but Parliament can confer on a delegate the power to abridge equality rights. The better view is that Parliament is unable to delegate a power that Parliament does not possess. Restrictions on the power of Parliament (or a Legislature) must apply to all bodies that draw their powers from the Parliament (or the Legislature). This does seem to be the latest view of the Supreme Court of Canada, because six months after the *S.* cases a majority of the Court asserted that the requirement of ''law'' in s. 15 is satisfied by conduct taken under the authority of law, and a majority of the

---

39 Chapter 34, Application of Charter, under heading 34.2(b), ''Parliament or Legislature'', above.

40 The issue is briefly and inconclusively raised in *Andrews* v. *Law Society of B.C.* [1989] 1 S.C.R. 143, 164, 193.

41 [1990] 2 S.C.R. 254. Dickson C.J. wrote the unanimous opinion of the Court.

42 The Court held as well, following *R.* v. *Turpin* [1989] 1 S.C.R. 1296, that province of residence was not a ground of discrimination under s. 15: sec. 52.16, ''Place of residence'', below. On this basis, the reasoning about ''law'' in s. 15 was not strictly necessary to the decision.

43 [1990] 2 S.C.R. 294. Dickson C.J. wrote the unanimous opinion of the Court.

44 *McKinney* v. *U. of Guelph* [1990] 2 S.C.R. 229, 276-278 per La Forest J. (with whom Dickson C.J. and Gonthier J. agreed), 380-386 per Wilson J. (with whom on this issue Cory J. agreed); Sopinka J. left the issue open at 444. Both La Forest and Wilson JJ. in the passages referred to assumed that even governmental action taken under common law authority, e.g., by contract, would be covered by ''law'' in s. 15 and caught by s. 15. They referred in support to the reference to ''program or activity'' in s. 15(2).

Court held that a collective agreement is ''law'' within s. 15. In these two cases, no reference was made to the contrary rulings in the two *S.* cases. However, the later expression of opinion is the better one.

While the position is not entirely clear, it seems likely that the reference to law in s. 15 does not have the effect of excluding anything from the application of s. 15. In other words, s. 15 applies to the same range of governmental action as other Charter rights. The range of governmental action is that defined in s. 32.

(c) Private action

There is no doubt that s. 32 of the Charter excludes private action from the application of the Charter. This means that s. 15 does not apply to private acts of discrimination, as where an employer hires only male employees, or a landlord rents only to white people, or a shopkeeper refuses to serve children. However, in all Canadian jurisdictions, Human Rights Codes have been enacted that prohibit private acts of discrimination in employment, accommodation and the provision of services. The Codes are typically enforced by human rights commissions through investigation, mediation and, if necessary, adjudication. The Human Rights Codes are simply statutes. They do not enjoy constitutional status. However, some of the Codes contain primacy clauses making them superior to other statutes, and even without a primacy clause the Supreme Court of Canada has held that a Human Rights Code takes precedence over other statutes.

The Human Rights Codes, as statutes, are themselves subject to the Charter of Rights. In *Blainey* v. *Ontario Hockey Association* (1986), a girl, who had been excluded by the Ontario Hockey Association from a boy's hockey team, challenged a provision of the Ontario Human Rights Code that permitted single-sex sports teams. The Code generally prohibited discrimination by sex, but made an exception for single-sex sports teams. The Ontario Court of Appeal by a majority held that the exception was a breach of s. 15, because it denied to the plaintiff the benefit of the Human Rights Code by reason of her sex. The effect of nullifying the exception was to make the general prohibition of discrimination applicable to sports teams, which gave the plaintiff a remedy under the Human Rights Code.

45 *Douglas/Kwantlen Faculty Assn.* v. *Douglas College* [1990] 3 S.C.R. 570, 585 per La Forest J. (with whom Dickson C.J. and Gonthier J. and on this issue Cory J. agreed), 614 per Wilson J. (with whom L'Heureux-Dubé J. agreed); Sopinka J. took the view at 616 that a consensual act could not be law within s. 15.

46 This would include not only governmental action taken under statutory authority, but also governmental action taken under common law authority: previous two notes.

47 See ch. 32, Application of Charter, above.

48 See Tarnopolsky and Pentney, *Discrimination and the Law* (rev. ed., 1985).

49 *Winnipeg School Division No. 1* v. *Craton* [1985] 2 S.C.R. 150; see ch. 12, Parliamentary Sovereignty, under heading 12.3(b), ''Manner and form of future laws'', above.

50 See Juriansz, ''Section 15 and the Human Rights Codes'' in Beaudoin (ed.), *Your Clients and the Charter* (1988), ch. 12.

51 (1986) 54 O.R. (2d) 513 (C.A.).

The Charter of Rights did not apply directly to the action of the Ontario Hockey Association because the Association was a private organization. But by extending the scope of the Human Rights Code to action that the Code left unregulated, the Charter did have an indirect impact on private action.

The argument that succeeded in *Blainey* was tried again in *McKinney* v. *University of Guelph* (1990), in which a university professor who had reached the age of 65 challenged the mandatory retirement retirement of his university. The Charter did not apply to the university, because by virtue of its independence from government the university was held to be a private body. However, the Charter did apply to the Ontario Human Rights Code, which indirectly permitted mandatory retirement: the Code's prohibition of discrimination by age in employment applied only up to age 65. The Supreme Court of Canada held that the age-65 limit was a breach of s. 15. However, the Court went on to hold that the limit was justified by s. 1. Therefore, the limit was upheld, and the Charter did not have the effect of extending the Code to cover mandatory retirement at age 65.

52.6 Equality

(a) Four equalities of s. 15

Section 15 provides that every individual is ''equal before and under the law and has the right to the equal protection and equal benefit of the law''. The reason for having four formulations of the idea of equality was to reverse the restrictive interpretations placed by the Supreme Court of Canada on the phrase ''equality before the law'', which, as we have already noticed, is the phrase used in s. 1(b) of the Canadian Bill of Rights. Section 15 of the Charter speaks of being equal ''before and under the law''. The words ''and under'' were intended to abrogate a suggestion by Ritchie J. in the *Lavell* case, that judicial review on equality grounds did not extend to the substance of the law but only to the way in which it was administered. Section 15 also speaks of ''equal benefit of the law''; this phrase was intended to abrogate a suggestion by Ritchie J. in the *Bliss* case that the legislative provision of ''benefits'' was not subject to equality standards. Finally, s. 15 uses the phrase ''equal protection . . . of the law''. This is very

52 The Charter also had an indirect impact on the common law, which, by virtue of the exception to the Human Rights Code, governed the selection of members to sports teams. The effect of the Charter was to replace the common law rule permitting discrimination with the statutory rule prohibiting discrimination.

53 [1990] 3 S.C.R. 229.

54 The ''four equalities'' are analyzed by Bayefsky in Bayefsky and Eberts, note 36, above, 3-25.

55 Section 52.2, ''Canadian Bill of Rights'', above.

56 Note 15, above, 1366.

57 Note 19, above, 191.

similar to the phrase "equal protection of the laws", which, as we have already noticed, is the phrase used in the fourteenth amendment of the Constitution of the United States.[58]

(b) Absolute equality

What is meant by a guarantee of equality? It cannot mean that the law must treat everyone equally. The Criminal Code imposes punishments on persons convicted of criminal offences; no similar burdens are imposed on the innocent. Education Acts require children to attend school; no similar obligation is imposed on adults. Manufacturers of food and drugs are subject to more stringent regulations than the manufacturers of automobile parts. The legal profession is regulated differently from the accounting profession. The Wills Act prescribes a different distribution of the property of a person who dies leaving a will from that of a person who dies leaving no will. The Income Tax Act imposes a higher rate of tax on those with high incomes than on those with low incomes. Indeed, every statute or regulation employs classifications of one kind or another for the imposition of burdens or the grant of benefits. Laws never provide the same treatment for everyone.

(c) Aristotle's definition

Aristotle said that "justice considers that persons who are equal should have assigned to them equal things",[59] and "there is no inequality when unequals are treated in proportion to the inequality existing between them".[60] According to Aristotle's conception of equality, persons who are alike (similarly situated) should be treated alike, and persons who are not alike should be treated differently in proportion to the difference. Laws that single out groups for special treatment do not offend the principle of equality if they employ classifications that appropriately distinguish between people who are not alike, and if they provide for appropriately different treatment for those who are not alike. For example, a person who has committed a crime deserves to be punished, whereas a person who is innocent does not; and a person who has committed a serious crime deserves to be punished more severely than a person who has committed a minor offence. These people are not alike in respect of their liability to punishment, and the law need not — indeed, must not — treat them equally.

The trouble with Aristotle's idea of equality is that the idea is stated at too high a level of generality to be useful. It provides no criteria to determine whether one person is "like" another, or even as to who should be compared to whom; and it provides no criteria to assess the appropriateness of different legislative

58 Section 52.3, "American Bill of Rights", above.

59 *The Politics of Aristotle* (trans. E. Barker, Oxford U.P., 1946), Book III, xii, 1282b.

60 *Id.*, Book V, i, 1301a.

treatment of those who are not alike. Even the simple example of the treatment of persons who have committed a criminal offence illustrates these problems. What kind of conduct should be treated as criminal? How does one compare the seriousness of different kinds of criminal conduct? What variations in punishment are appropriate to different degrees of seriousness? We normally think of these questions as questions of criminal justice, not equality. The concept of equality is not really useful in answering the questions. This has led commentators to describe equality as an "empty idea". The idea is empty in the sense that it cannot be applied without first working out the criteria of likeness and like treatment, and the idea of equality cannot by itself supply those criteria.

(d) Similarly situated

Before the Supreme Court of Canada decided the *Andrews* case, Canadian courts were applying a version of the Aristotelian principle of equality known as the "similarly situated" test. According to that test, a denial of equality was made out if it could be shown that the law accorded the complainant worse treatment than others who were similarly situated. In *Andrews*, McIntyre J. said that this test was "seriously deficient", and that it could be used to justify laws that discriminated against Jews or blacks. He concluded that the similarly situated test should no longer be used, at least "as a fixed rule or formula for the resolution of equality questions". With respect, this criticism is somewhat exaggerated. Equality is an inescapably "comparative concept" (as McIntyre J. acknowledged). A person is treated unequally only if that person is treated worse than others, and those others (the comparison group) must surely be those who are similarly situated to the complainant. As Gibson has noticed, "no court facing an equality issue can avoid somehow determining whether the person or group relying on section 15 is sufficiently similar to other persons or groups in relevant respects to merit equal treatment". The similarly situated test is not wrong in principle. Its vice is the one identified in the previous paragraph: the test does not supply the crucial criteria that are required to determine who is similarly situated to whom, and what kinds of differences in treatment are appropriate to those who are not similarly situated. The test is deficient in the sense that it provides too little guidance to a reviewing court.

---

61 Westen, "The Empty Idea of Equality" (1982) 95 Harv. L. Rev. 537; Bayefsky, note 35, above, 2-3; contra, Gibson, note 35, above, 59-62.

62 *Andrews* v. *Law Society of B.C.* [1989] 1 S.C.R. 143; an account of the case is given at note 78, below.

63 E.g., *R.* v. *Ertel* (1987) 20 O.A.C. 257 (C.A.).

64 [1989] 1 S.C.R. 143, 166.

65 *Id.*, 168.

66 *Id.*, 164.

67 Gibson, note 35, above, 74. See also *Catholic Children's Aid Society* v. *S.(T.)* (1989) 69 O.R. (2d) 189, 205-206 per Tarnopolsky J.A., vigorously defending the similarly situated test *after* its repudiation in *Andrews*!

(e) Reasonable classification

American courts, as we have seen, have found the criteria of equality in a doctrine of reasonable classification. If a law pursues a legitimate state purpose, and it employs classifications that are reasonably related to the accomplishment of that purpose, there is no violation of equal protection. This approach concentrates on the purpose of the law, and tests likeness by reference to that purpose. If the purpose of a law is to safeguard health, then it is appropriate to impose more stringent regulation on the manufacturers of food and drugs than on the manufacturers of products that are not eaten. However, that purpose could not justify a distinction between individual and corporate manufacturers, because risks to health turn on the nature of the product, not on the organizational form of the manufacturer.

The American doctrine of reasonable classification is like the similarly situated test in that it operates at a very high level of generality. Views will differ as to how the purpose of a law is to be ascertained and stated, and as to how perfectly the law's classifications must fit the purpose. The impact of judicial review will therefore depend upon whether the courts are prepared to accept the legislators' judgments on these inherently disputable issues, or whether the courts are prepared to substitute their own views for those of the legislators. As we have noticed, the American courts have developed ''levels of scrutiny'' that impose strict standards of review (strict scrutiny) on laws that use ''suspect'' classifications, such as race, or which burden the exercise of fundamental rights, and lax standards of review (minimal scrutiny) on laws that employ classifications that are not suspect and that regulate activities that are less fundamental. In that way, some measure of certainty has been introduced into judicial review on equal protection grounds in the United States.

(f) Valid federal objective

Before the adoption of the Charter of Rights, Canadian courts applied the guarantee of equality in the Canadian Bill of Rights. As we have seen, the approach that became dominant in the Supreme Court of Canada was to uphold any distinction in a statute if the statute pursued a ''valid federal objective''. This test brought a high degree of judicial deference to the Court's review of the choices made by Parliament. It was even more deferential than the American standard of minimal scrutiny. The Court was severely criticized for its ''timidity'' in applying the Canadian Bill of Rights, and the legislative history of s. 15 of the Charter of Rights made abundantly clear that it was not to be given the same minimal effect as the Canadian Bill of Rights.

---

68 Section 52.3, ''American Bill of Rights'', above.
69 Section 52.2, ''Canadian Bill of Rights'', above.
70 Bayefsky, note 54, above.

(g) Early applications of s. 15

With the adoption of the Charter of Rights, Canadian courts faced a dilemma. On the one hand, they could not apply s. 15 so deferentially as to rob it of any serious force; that was the criticism of their decisions under the Canadian Bill of Rights. On the other hand, they could hardly review every distinction in the statute book; that would not be a wise use of judicial resources, and would constantly involve the courts in issues of legislative policy. Until the *Andrews* case was decided by the Supreme Court of Canada, most courts followed both approaches, that is, they assumed that every legislative distinction was a proper subject for equality review, but they upheld every distinction. The volume of cases was truly disturbing. A study prepared in 1988, only three years after the coming into force of s. 15 (which occurred on April 17, 1985), found 591 cases (two-thirds of which were reported in full) in which a law had been challenged on the basis of s. 15. Most of the challenges seemed unmeritorious, and most were unsuccessful; but the absence of any clear standards for the application of s. 15 encouraged lawyers to keep trying to use s. 15 whenever a statutory distinction worked to the disadvantage of a client.

In the *Andrews* case, which will be described more fully in the next section of this chapter, the Supreme Court of Canada started to develop rules to control the floodgates opened by s. 15. In fact, the text of s. 15 offered some clues to its scope that were missing from its counterparts in the Canadian Bill of Rights and the fourteenth amendment. The listed grounds of ''race, national or ethnic origin, colour, religion, sex, age or mental or physical disability'' pointed to personal characteristics of individuals which could not be changed (or could not easily be changed), and which have often been the targets of prejudice and stereotyping. The reference in subsection (2) (the affirmative action clause) to ''disadvantaged individuals or groups'' suggested that the role of s. 15 was to correct discrimination against disadvantaged individuals or groups. These references suggested that the purpose of s. 15 was not to eliminate all unfairness from our laws, let alone all classifications that could not be rationally defended, but rather to eliminate discrimination based on immutable personal characteristics. These considerations led the Court in *Andrews* to interpret s. 15 as a prohibition of discrimination, and to define discrimination as disadvantage caused by the classifications listed in s. 15 and analogous classifications. This has the merit of avoiding any inquiry into the abstract concept of equality, and the further merit of excluding from equality review those statutes that do not employ the listed classifications, or analogous classifications.

---

71 Brodsky and Day, note 35, above, 277.
72 Charter of Rights, s. 32(2).
73 Note 78, below.

52.7 Discrimination

(a) Discrimination is the operative concept

Section 15 of the Charter of Rights guarantees equality, but goes on to stipulate "without discrimination and, in particular, without discrimination based on race, national or ethnic origin, colour, religion, sex, age or mental or physical disability". It is now clear that s. 15 should be read as prohibiting only those violations of equality that amount to "discrimination". Discrimination is therefore the operative concept. What does it mean?

In my view, the following ten rules can be derived from the cases:

Discrimination must be on listed or analogous grounds.
Discrimination may be justified only under s. 1.
Discrimination need not be invidious.
Analogous grounds involve immutable personal characteristics.
Particular disadvantage is required.
General disadvantage is not required.
Discrimination may be unintended.
It may be systemic.
It may require reasonable accommodation.
It need not appear on the face of the law.

Each of these rules is discussed in the text that follows.

(b) Must be on listed or analogous grounds

What kinds of legislative distinctions count as discrimination, and are therefore prohibited by s. 15? Before the *Andrews* case, a variety of views had been articulated by courts and commentators. At one extreme was the position taken by me in the second edition of this book.[74] According to this view, any legislative distinction should be treated as discrimination in violation of s. 15; the question whether the distinction was justified or not would be determined under s. 1. At the other extreme was the position taken by McLachlin J. in the British Columbia Court of Appeal in *Andrews*.[75] According to this view, the only legislative distinctions that would amount to discrimination were those that were "unreasonable or unfair". Under this approach, s. 15 contained its own implicit requirement of justification, and the question whether a legislative distinction was justified or not would be determined within s. 15 itself. When *Andrews* reached the Supreme Court of Canada, McIntyre J. criticized both these positions.[76] The Hogg position, he pointed out, virtually denied any function to s. 15, because all issues of

74 (2nd ed., 1985), 799-801.
75 (1986) 27 D.L.R. (4th) 600, 610 (B.C.C.A.).
76 [1989] 1 S.C.R. 143, 181-182.

justification would be remitted to s. 1. The McLachlin position, on the other hand, virtually denied any function to s. 1, because issues of justification would be resolved within s. 15.

McIntyre J. adopted a ''middle ground'' between the two competing positions. The middle ground was to interpret discrimination in s. 15 as including only the distinctions listed in s. 15 and ''analogous'' distinctions. ''This enumerated and analogous grounds approach'', he said, ''most closely accords with the purposes of s. 15'', and ''leaves questions of justification to s. 1''.[77] This approach differed from my position in that it narrowed the range of distinctions that would qualify as discrimination. However, once s. 15 had been narrowed in that fashion, issues of reasonableness or fairness would be excluded from s. 15 and remitted entirely to s. 1, as I had urged.

The *Andrews* case[78] concerned the validity of one of the requirements of the British Columbia statute regulating entry to the legal profession in that province. The statute restricted membership of the profession to Canadian citizens. Andrews, who was not a Canadian citizen but who was otherwise qualified for admission, sued for a declaration that the requirement of Canadian citizenship violated s. 15 of the Charter. The Supreme Court of Canada held unanimously that the citizenship requirement did violate s. 15, and held by a majority that the requirement was not saved by s. 1. The principal judgment was written by McIntyre J., with whom all the other judges agreed as to the interpretation of s. 15 and its relationship with s. 1. The judgment is in fact the dissenting judgment, because McIntyre lost the support of the majority for his opinion that the requi-

---

77 *Id.*, 182. In my view, this passage should be read as an adoption of the ''enumerated and analogous grounds'' approach. Gibson, note 35, above, 147-149, takes the view that the case leaves open the possibility that non-analogous grounds of distinction are also covered. There are some passages in the opinions of McIntyre and Wilson JJ. that could be read as casting doubt on the restriction to analogous grounds, but I think the better reading of both judgments is as stated in the text. La Forest J. did, however, (at p. 194) leave open the question whether s. 15 extended beyond analogous grounds. This debate, and perhaps even La Forest J.'s reservation, seems to be resolved by the *Workers' Compensation Reference*, note 114, below, in which La Forest J. for a unanimous Court rejected a s. 15 claim on the basis that the impugned statute did not discriminate on the basis of a named or analogous ground. See also *R.* v. *Turpin* [1989] 1 S.C.R. 1296, 1332, where Wilson J. for a unanimous Court approved the ''enumerated and analogous grounds'' approach; *R.* v. *Swain* [1990] 1 S.C.R. 933, 992, where Lamer C.J., with the agreement of Sopinka and Cory JJ., also approved the ''enumerated and analogous grounds'' approach; *R.* v. *Généreux* [1992] 1 S.C.R. 259, 311, where Lamer C.J. approved the restriction to analogous grounds. In *Miron* v. *Trudel* [1995] 2 S.C.R. 418, and *Egan* v. *Can.* [1995] 2 S.C.R. 513, both of which are discussed later in this section at notes 79 and 85, below, eight of the nine judges accepted the restriction to analogous grounds; only L'Heureux-Dubé J. rejected that interpretation of s. 15.

78 *Andrews* v. *Law Society of B.C.* [1989] 1 S.C.R. 143. The Court comprised six judges. Wilson J.'s majority opinion was agreed with by Dickson C.J. and L'Heureux-Dubé J. La Forest J. wrote a separate concurring opinion. McIntyre J.'s dissenting opinion was agreed with by Lamer J.

rement of citizenship could be justified under s. 1. Wilson and La Forest JJ. also wrote judgments, essentially agreeing with McIntyre J. except on the issue of s. 1.

Andrews was able to establish discrimination under s. 15, because he had suffered a disadvantage by reason of his non-Canadian citizenship. To be sure, citizenship was not one of the grounds of discrimination expressly listed in s. 15, but it was analogous to those grounds. The scope of analogous grounds (a topic that is taken up later in this chapter) received surprisingly little discussion in the opinions, although all judges were clear that citizenship qualified as an analogous ground. Having established discrimination, Andrews had established a breach of s. 15. Nothing more was required. The question whether citizenship was a reasonable requirement for admission to the bar of British Columbia was not a relevant inquiry within s. 15, although it was a relevant inquiry under s. 1.

Discrimination, according to *Andrews*, consists in the imposition of some disadvantage on an individual by reason of the individual's possession of a listed or analogous s. 15 characteristic. The question whether the discrimination is justified is examined under s. 1. This straightforward approach, which had seemed to be well settled, was followed by only four of the nine members of the Supreme Court of Canada in two cases decided in 1995. In those cases, the Court divided into three camps, each with a different approach to s. 15.

The first case was *Miron* v. *Trudel*,[79] in which the plaintiff, who had suffered an automobile accident, claimed an accident benefit under his common-law wife's automobile insurance policy, the terms of which were prescribed by Ontario's Insurance Act. The benefit was available to a spouse of the insured, but the definition of spouse in the policy (as prescribed by the Act) was limited to legally-married persons and therefore excluded the plaintiff, who was living in a common-law relationship with the insured. He sued the insurance company for the benefit, arguing that the restriction on the availability of the benefit discriminated against him in violation of s. 15.[80] The Supreme Court of Canada, by a five to four majority, accepted the plaintiff's argument that the restriction on the availability of the spousal accident benefit discriminated against the plaintiff in violation of s. 15, and could not be justified under s. 1. The Court repaired the constitutional defect by simply adding common-law spouses to the definition actually enacted by the Legislature.[81]

The principal majority opinion was written by McLachlin J. with whom Sopinka, Cory and Iacobucci JJ. agreed. McLachlin J. reached her conclusion by the orthodox *Andrews* route. She held that the plaintiff had suffered a disadvantage (the denial of the accident benefit) by reason of his marital status, and that marital

---

79 [1995] 2 S.C.R. 418.

80 The Charter applied to this action between private parties, because the terms of the insurance policy were precribed by statute: ch. 34, Application of Charter, under heading 34.2(b), ''Parliament or Legislature'', above.

81 The power of a court to salvage an unconstitutional statute by ''reading in'' corrective language is explained in ch. 37, Enforcement of Rights, under heading 37.1(f), ''Reading in'', above.

status was a ground of discrimination that was analogous to those listed in s. 15.[82] Therefore, there was a breach of s. 15, and, she held, that breach could not be justified under s. 1.

The fifth majority judge was L'Heureux-Dubé J., whose concurring opinion followed a different route to the same result. She (alone of the nine judges) rejected the restriction of s. 15 to listed and analogous grounds. Instead, she held, the question whether discrimination existed should be determined on a case-by-case basis by analyzing (1) the nature of the group affected by the distinction and (2) the nature of the interest affected by the distinction. In this case, she held, the group affected was ''persons in non-traditional relationships'', and those persons ''have suffered, and continue to suffer, some degree of disadvantage and marginalization from the mainstream''.[83] The interest affected was the protection of the family from the economic consequences of an automobile injury. She concluded that the effect of the law was discriminatory within s. 15 of the Charter. She also held that the law could not be justified under s. 1.

The third approach in *Miron* v. *Trudel* was that followed by the four dissenting judges. Gonthier J. wrote the dissenting opinion, which was agreed with by Lamer C.J., La Forest and Major JJ. Gonthier J. took the view that a legislative distinction would qualify as discrimination under s. 15 only if it was based on a listed or analogous ground *and* the distinction was ''irrelevant'' to ''the functional values of the legislation''.[84] Gonthier J. held that marital status could be an analogous ground, and would be irrelevant to some kinds of laws, for example, laws respecting qualifications for employment. But the law conferring accident benefits on a spouse was related to the reciprocal support obligations of marriage. In defining support obligations or other attributes of marriage, marital status was not an irrelevant ground of distinction. Therefore, for Gonthier J. and the other dissenting judges, there was no discrimination and no breach of s. 15. It was unnecessary to advance to the s. 1 inquiry.

A second case was decided on the same day as *Miron* v. *Trudel* and by the same full bench of nine judges of the Supreme Court of Canada. *Egan* v. *Canada* (1995)[85] also related to a statutory definition of spouse, this time in the federal Old Age Security Act, which provides pensions for persons who have reached the age of 65. The Act provides a spouse's allowance to the spouse of a pensioner if the spouse has reached the age of 60 and if the combined income of the two spouses is below a threshold stipulated by the Act. Unlike the Insurance Act in *Miron* v. *Trudel*, the Old Age Security Act defined spouse to include common-law spouses (based on one year of living together). However, the definition did stipulate that the spouses be ''of the opposite sex'', and that restriction was the basis of the constitutional challenge in the case. The plaintiffs were two men who

82 This part of the decision is discussed in the text accompanying note 123, below.
83 [1995] 2 S.C.R. 418, 474-475, para. 103.
84 *Id.*, 447, para. 37.
85 [1995] 2 S.C.R. 513.

lived together in a homosexual relationship. One was a pensioner and the other had reached the age of 60; the latter would have qualified for the spouse's allowance were it not for the requirement that the partners be of the opposite sex. The plaintiffs sued for a declaration that the Old Age Security Act violated s. 15. The Supreme Court of Canada, by a majority of five to four, rejected the challenge and upheld the restriction on the availability of the spouse's allowance. Although the result of the case differed from *Miron* (where the constitutional challenge had been successful), the judges lined up in the same way on the s. 15 issue. The different result in *Egan* was caused by the presence of a narrow majority in favour of upholding the law under s. 1.

The four judges who in *Miron* had followed the orthodox *Andrews* approach did the same in *Egan*. This time it was Cory J. who wrote the opinion on s. 15, with the concurrence of Sopinka, McLachlin and Iacobucci JJ. Cory J. held that the plaintiffs had suffered a disadvantage (the denial of the spouse's allowance) by reason of their sexual orientation, and that sexual orientation was a ground of discrimination analogous to those listed in s. 15.[86] Therefore, there was a breach of s. 15. Three of the four judges went on to hold that the law could not be justified under s. 1,[87] but Sopinka J. held that the law could be justified under s. 1.

L'Heureux-Dubé J. followed the same approach as she had taken in *Miron*, rejecting the restriction of s. 15 to listed and analogous grounds. Instead, she assessed the nature of the group affected (homosexuals are a "socially vulnerable group", and the plaintiffs were "elderly and poor" to boot),[88] and the nature of the interest affected (the provision of a basic shared standard of living), which led her to the conclusion that the law was discriminatory in violation of s. 15. She also concluded that the law could not be justified under s. 1.

The four judges who had insisted on "irrelevance" in *Miron* repeated the requirement in *Egan*, and again found that it was not satisfied. La Forest J., writing with the concurrence of Lamer C.J., Gonthier and Major JJ., agreed that sexual orientation was an analogous ground, but held that it was relevant to "the functional values underlying the law". The law, he held, was designed to support heterosexual relationships, because heterosexual couples have the unique ability to procreate, and the requirement of an ability to procreate was relevant to the purpose of the law. The exclusion of homosexual couples, along with other couples who live together but not in a sexual relationship (friends, siblings, parent and child, for example), was not based on an irrelevant ground and therefore was not discriminatory under s. 15. La Forest J. went on to say, without giving any reasons, that if he had decided otherwise under s. 15, he would have upheld the law under s. 1. Since Sopinka J. had also upheld the law under s. 1, there was a five-judge majority for this position, and the law was upheld.

---

86 This part of the decision is discussed in the text accompanying note 127, below.

87 Iacobucci J. wrote the opinion on s. 1, with the agreement of Cory and McLachlin JJ.

88 [1995] 2 S.C.R. 513, 566-567, para. 89.

Perhaps it is unrealistic to expect a clear body of doctrine to emerge quickly from the Supreme Court of Canada on a concept so difficult as equality. Perhaps, as well, the differences between the judges are not, in practice, as significant as they appear. The extreme departures from *Andrews* are L'Heureux-Dubé J.'s opinions in *Miron* and *Egan*,[89] which entirely reject analogous grounds as a controlling concept, and remit the issue of discrimination to a weighing of the effects on the group affected and the interest affected. L'Heureux-Dubé J. is alone in this view of s. 15, which relies heavily on judicial discretion. If it were generally adopted, L'Heureux-Dubé J.'s approach would produce quite variable results from judges who would place different weights on the values in play. On the other hand, it must be acknowledged that the inability of other eight judges to find common ground on a useful definition of analogous grounds (a point that is discussed later in the chapter) also supplies very little certainty.

The importation of the requirement of irrelevance into s. 15 by Gonthier J. in *Miron* and La Forest J. in *Egan* (in both cases with the support of the other and of Lamer C.J. and Major J.) also seems to me to be a departure from *Andrews*. To ask whether a legislative distinction is ''irrelevant'' is very close to asking whether a legislative distinction is unreasonable or unfair, which is a question that the Court in *Andrews* banished from s. 15. The question of irrelevance is also very close to the s. 1 inquiry, where the objective of the legislation and the proportionality of the legislative means are examined.[90] In principle, once a legislative distinction has been found to be based on listed or analogous grounds, it is surely better to leave all issues of justification to s. 1, where the *Oakes* standards of review have to be satisfied, and where the burden of proof rests with the government (or other proponent of the law).

The technical differences in the judges' reasoning in *Miron* and *Egan* undoubtedly reflect more fundamental divisions within the Supreme Court of Canada as to the appropriateness of judicial intervention in policy issues of great social significance. The effect of *Miron* is that all of the attributes of a legal

89 Her dissenting opinion in *Thibaudeau* v.*Can.* [1995] 2 S.C.R. 627, which was released on the same day as *Miron* and *Egan*, is to the same effect.

90 In *Miron* v. *Trudel* [1995] 2 S.C.R. 418, 444-447, paras. 31-38, Gonthier J. is at pains to point out that the requirement of irrelevance in s. 15 still leaves s. 1 with some work to do. Part of his argument (para. 37) is that the ''functional values'' of the impugned law (which is what s. 15 irrelevance is addressed to) are not necessarily the same as the objective of the law (which is what s. 1 proportionality is addressed to). This is a very refined distinction. In *Thibaudeau* v. *Can.* [1995] 2 S.C.R. 627, 682, para. 106, Gonthier J. acknowledged that ''relevance is to be determined in light of the underlying objectives of the legislation''. In *Egan* v.*Can.* [1995] 2 S.C.R. 513, 546-548, paras. 42-45, L'Heureux-Dubé J. acutely criticizes the irrelevance requirement, pointing out (among other things) that the objective of the law (or its ''functional values'' or ''underlying objectives'') may itself be discriminatory, that the burden of proof of irrelevance would fall on the rights claimant, and that the requirement of irrelevance imposes an ''internal limitation'' on s. 15. For similar criticisms, see *Miron* v. *Trudel*, above, 491, para. 137 per McLachlin J.; *Thibaudeau* v.*Can.*, above, 700-701, paras. 154-156 per Cory and Iacobucci JJ.

marriage must now be extended to unmarried couples. Any failure to do so would discriminate on the basis of marital status, and would be unconstitutional, except in the unlikely event that the law could be justified under s. 1.[91] While individuals will no doubt continue to get married for social, religious or personal reasons, their choice cannot be invested with any legal consequences, for example, with respect to spousal support obligations, spousal property rights, or tax or benefit programmes. This could be regarded as no more than the logical culmination of many piecemeal legislated recognitions of common-law relationships. However, it is a radical result, which would certainly be controversial if made in a legislative body. For example, it is a result that may not be desired by those couples who made a choice to live together without becoming formally married, whether because of reservations as to the permanence of their relationship, or because of a joint desire to remain outside the legal regime of marriage (with respect to property rights, for example).

Egan takes *Miron* a step further. While the exclusion of same-sex couples from spousal pension benefits was upheld in *Egan*, the five-four majority rested on Sopinka J.'s s. 1 ruling. That ruling was based on a concern that Parliament should be permitted to proceed incrementally in recognizing same-sex relationships (''still generally regarded as a novel concept''),[92] and a concern about the cost implications of the expansion of spending programmes. The ruling was expressed in tentative language, which suggested that, in due course, benefit programmes would have to equate same-sex couples with opposite-sex couples. The five-four majority holding of s. 1 justification is, therefore, much less important for the future than the five-four majority holding that the exclusion of same-sex couples from the spousal pension benefits amounts to discrimination on the basis of sexual orientation, which is prohibited by s. 15. It follows that the denial of any attribute of marriage to a same-sex couple will certainly offend s. 15, and will probably not be saved by s. 1, especially if no government spending is involved.

With respect to tax and benefit programmes (at least), it is unlikely that the constitutionally-required extension of spousal recognition to common-law couples (*Miron*) and same-sex couples (*Egan*) will end the constitutional challenges based on underinclusiveness. What is the justification for excluding those people who live in relationships of mutual support and dependence, but without a sexual aspect? Households comprising two friends, or two siblings or a parent and child (for example) will probably have to be added to those programmes that now make use of concepts such as spouse or family. Their exclusion is based on something

91 Where it is beneficial to be married, the challenge will come from a person who is unmarried, as in *Miron*. Where it is detrimental to be married (which will be a common situation), the challenge will come from a person who is married, as in *Schachtschnieder* v.*The Queen* [1994] 1 F.C. 40 (F.C.A.) (a pre-*Miron* case upholding an income tax credit that was available only to an unmarried taxpayer). In either case, there is discrimination on the basis of marital status, which would have to be justified under s. 1.

92 [1995] 2 S.C.R. 513, 576, para. 111.

like marital status and sexual orientation, involving as it does stereotypical assumptions as to what counts as a marriage or a family, and an irrational preference for sexual relationships over others that may be just as deserving of support. There are difficulties of definition and of cost, but these pragmatic problems are less likely to deter judicial designers of legislation than elected politicians.

(c) May be justified only under s. 1

The respective roles of s. 15 and s. 1 were settled by the *Andrews* decision. Before the decision, many courts (including, as noted above, the British Columbia Court of Appeal in *Andrews* itself)[93] had held that s. 15 prohibited only unreasonable distinctions. In other words, s. 15 called for some assessment of the purpose and justification of a distinction. This was an understandable position as long as s. 15 applied to virtually any legislative distinction. It would be inappropriate to require justification under s. 1, with its burden of proof on the government and its strict standard of review (as stipulated in *Oakes*), for every law that drew any kind of distinction.[94] But once s. 15 was confined to the named grounds and analogous grounds, then it became much more plausible to insist upon justification under s. 1 for every law that distinguished on the basis of one of those grounds. In *Andrews*, the Court accepted that position. The Court unanimously held that any assessment of the reasonableness of an impugned distinction should take place, not in applying s. 15, but in applying s. 1. Under s. 15, the only inquiry was whether there was discrimination on the basis of the named or analogous grounds. It was the role of s. 1 to admit the issue of whether the discrimination could be justified as a reasonable limit that could be demonstrably justified in a free and democratic society.

As explained in the previous section of this chapter, in the *Miron*[95] and *Egan*[96] cases, which were decided in 1995, four of the nine judges would have imported some elements of justification back into s. 15 by requiring that the rights claimant establish that a legislative distinction not only be based on listed or analogous grounds but that the legislative distinction also be ''irrelevant''. In my opinion, this requirement represents an unfortunate blurring of the respective roles of ss. 15 and 1. The better view, which is adhered to by the other five judges, who have criticized and rejected the requirement of irrelevance, is that all issues of justification should be addressed under s. 1.

---

93 Note 75, above.

94 I had urged this position in the 2nd edition of this work: see note 74, above; but this was written before *Oakes*. The single, strict standard of justification prescribed by *Oakes* entails some narrowing of the guaranteed rights: see ch. 35, Limitation of Rights, under heading 35.3, ''Relationship between s. 1 and rights'', above.

95 Note 79, above.

96 Note 85, above.

The Court in *Andrews* split evenly on the question whether it was appropriate to apply the strict *Oakes* standard of justification[97] to laws that violated s. 15. This disagreement is rather surprising to me, since it seems obvious that Wilson J. was right in her view that, once s. 15 is limited to discrimination on the listed and analogous grounds, "the burden resting on government to justify the type of discrimination against such groups is appropriately an onerous one".[98] Applying the onerous *Oakes* standard, Wilson J. (with whom two other judges agreed) held that the citizenship requirement could not be justified under s. 1. But McIntyre J. (with whom one other judge agreed) took the view that the *Oakes* test was too stringent for s. 15 violations,[99] and on the basis of a lower standard of review he held that the citizenship requirement could be justified under s. 1. La Forest J. agreed with McIntyre J. that a lower standard of review under s. 1 was appropriate,[100] but he held that even on the lower standard of review the citizenship requirement could not be justified under s. 1. In the result, there was a four to two majority on the six-judge bench for the position that the citizenship requirement, which all agreed was a breach of s. 15, was not justified under s. 1 and was therefore invalid.[101]

(d) Need not be invidious

It follows from what has been said about the relationship between s. 15 and s. 1 that discrimination in s. 15 need not be invidious. Of course, a person cannot complain of discrimination under s. 15 unless that person has suffered some disadvantage by virtue of the challenged law. But the complainant does not have to establish that the law draws an unreasonable, irrational, unfair, unjustified or invidious distinction. It is enough to show that the disadvantageous treatment is caused by a law that employs one of the distinctions listed in s. 15 or an analogous distinction.[102]

For example, in *Andrews*, all of the judges agreed that the law excluding non-citizens from membership of the bar was a violation of s. 15, although two of the judges held that the exclusion of non-citizens was reasonable and justified under s. 1. All judges agreed that the weighing of justificatory factors must take place only as part of the s. 1 inquiry. Section 15 was exhausted once the complainant had established that he had been denied a benefit available to others (membership of the bar) by reference to a distinction (citizenship) which was either stated in s. 15 or was (as in the case of citizenship) analogous to the distinctions stated in s. 15.

---

97 Chapter 35, Limitation of Rights, above.

98 [1989] 1 S.C.R. 143, 154.

99 *Id.*, 184.

100 *Id.*, 197-198.

101 As to the break-down of voting, see note 78, above.

102 Note 77, above.

As explained earlier in this chapter, in the *Miron*[103] and *Egan*[104] cases, which were decided in 1995, four of the nine judges would have imported some elements of justification back into s. 15, but this remains a minority position on the Court. The majority still insists that all issues of justification be addressed under s. 1.

(e) Analogous grounds involve immutable personal characteristics

Discrimination in s. 15 may be based either on the grounds listed in s. 15 or on grounds analogous to those listed. This much is established by the cases in the Supreme Court of Canada.[105] What are analogous grounds? The answer must be: grounds that are similar to the listed grounds. The listed grounds are "race, national or ethnic origin, colour, religion, sex, age or mental or physical disability". These are all *personal characteristics* of individuals. Moreover, all but one are personal characteristics that are *immutable*, at least in the sense that they cannot be changed by the choice of the individual.

Of the grounds listed in s. 15, only "religion" arguably fails the immutable test. Religion is unlike all the other listed characteristics in that there is no natural or legal impediment to a change of religion, and some people do in fact switch from one religion to another. In the case of most individuals, however, a religious affiliation was acquired early and became deeply embedded in the individual's consciousness, so that "the changes of inner conviction that often accompany such conversions may . . . be considered "beyond the individual's conscious control".[106] Gibson suggests that immutability should be considered a test for characteristics analogous to those specified in s. 15 only if the term is interpreted to mean something like: "not immediately changeable except with great difficulty or cost".[107]

Another way of looking at immutability as the common element of the listed personal characteristics is to notice that the characteristics are inherent, rather than acquired. They do not reflect a voluntary choice by anyone, but rather an involuntary inheritance. They describe what a person is, rather than what a person does. Section 15 prohibits laws that distinguish between people on the basis of their inherent attributes as opposed to their behaviour. Section 15 therefore does not prohibit laws that make special provision for those who have committed a crime, become insolvent, manufactured food or drugs, joined the legal profession, made a will, purchased a taxable good or service, etc. It is true that individuals may claim to be treated unfairly by the law for conditions that are their own responsibility, but this kind of claim even if fully justified does not warrant a constitutional remedy. This kind of claim is the daily fare of politics, and is best

103 Note 79, above.
104 Note 85, above.
105 *Ibid.*
106 Gibson, note 35, above, 158.
107 *Ibid.*

remedied not by judges but by those who are politically accountable. What does warrant a constitutional remedy is the claim that a person has been unfairly treated by reason of a condition over which the person has no control. In that case, forces of prejudice may well have distorted the political process, and it is appropriate for judges to review the challenged distinction.

In *Andrews* v. *Law Society of British Columbia* (1989),[108] the Supreme Court of Canada held that citizenship was an analogous ground. McIntyre J. never offered a definition of analogous grounds, although he made clear that discrimination must be based on a ''personal characteristic'' of an individual or group,[109] and he obviously assumed that citizenship was such a personal characteristic. Wilson J. also offered no definition, but she said that she agreed with McIntyre J. that the law ''discriminates against them [that is, non-citizens] on the ground of their personal characteristics, i.e., their non-citizen status''.[110]

In *Andrews*, La Forest J. (who alone had questioned the restriction of s. 15 to analogous grounds)[111] was the only judge who carried the analysis beyond a reference to personal characteristics. He said[112] that citizenship was ''a personal characteristic which shares many similarities with those enumerated in s. 15''. He evidently regarded immutability as one of those similarities, because he went on to explain:[113]

> The characteristic of citizenship is one typically not within the control of the individual and, in this sense, is immutable. Citizenship is, at least temporarily, a characteristic of personhood not alterable by conscious action and in some cases not alterable except on the basis of unacceptable costs.

Thus, for La Forest J., it was not enough that citizenship was a ''personal characteristic''; it was important that the characteristic be ''immutable'', meaning that it could not be changed. Of course, citizenship can be changed, but La Forest J. meant that the change is not wholly within the control of the individual, who must wait for the statutorily-prescribed effluxion of time, and perhaps the satisfaction of other statutory conditions, on top of the individual's admittedly voluntary choice of Canadian residence.

In the *Workers' Compensation Reference* (1989),[114] a s. 15 challenge was mounted against the provision in the Workers' Compensation Act of Newfoundland that denies to an injured worker the right to sue his or her employer in tort. It was argued that the denial of the tort action was a violation of s. 15, because other accident victims, for example, those injured on the roads, could bring a tort action for damages against the person whose fault caused the accident. The

---

108 [1989] 1 S.C.R. 143; discussed at note 78, above.

109 *Id.*, 174

110 *Id.*, 151.

111 *Id.*, 194; see note 77, above.

112 *Id.*, 195.

113 *Ibid.*

114 *Re Workers' Compensation Act, 1983 (Nfld.)* [1989] 1 S.C.R. 922.

Supreme Court of Canada disposed of the case in a single paragraph. Since the singling out of work-related accident victims did not depend upon any of the grounds of discrimination named in s. 15, and was not analogous to those named grounds, there could be no breach of s. 15. This defeated the challenge, and avoided the need for the Court to proceed to s. 1, which would have entailed an evaluation of the policy reasons for the standard Canadian workers' compensation system.

The brevity of the reasons in the *Workers' Compensation Reference* is unfortunate, because the Court did not explain why the distinction in the workers' compensation legislation was not analogous to those listed in s. 15. The denial of the right of action turned on the employment status of the injured person. That is surely a "personal characteristic". What must be lacking is the element of immutability. Employment is not an immutable status, depending as it does on the choice and effort of the employed individual. On the other hand, the only way in which an individual in Newfoundland (or any of the other provinces) could avoid the restrictions imposed by the workers' compensation scheme was by choosing not to be employed at all. Since that is not a practical choice for those who lack independent wealth, one could well argue that the status of being employed is (to use La Forest J.'s phrase from *Andrews*) "not alterable except on the basis of unacceptable costs". However, the ratio decidendi of the case must be that employment status is not an analogous ground.[115]

In *Rudolf Wolff & Co.* v. *Canada* (1990),[116] the question arose whether the Federal Court Act infringed s. 15 by conferring on the Federal Court of Canada exclusive jurisdiction over actions against the Crown in right of Canada. The inability to bring such actions in the superior courts of the provinces (which has since been permitted) did involve some serious disadvantages for persons with claims against the federal Crown. However, the Supreme Court of Canada held that s. 15 did not supply any remedy. The individuals who were disadvantaged by the Federal Court Act were "a disparate group with the sole common interest of seeking to bring a claim against the Crown before a court".[117] The interest in bringing a claim against the Crown was not an immutable personal characteristic analogous to those listed in s. 15.[118]

---

115 Accord, *Municipal Contracting* v. *IUOE* (1989) 60 O.R. (4th) 323 (N.S.A.D.) (employment in construction industry not an analogous ground); *OPSEU* v. *National Citizens' Coalition* (1990) 74 O.R. (2d) 260 (C.A.) (earning of employment income not an analogous ground); *Can.* v. *Taylor* (1991) 81 D.L.R. (4th) 679 (F.C.A.) (employment as a teacher not an analogous ground); *R.* v. *Généreux* [1992] 1 S.C.R. 259, 311 (membership in the armed forces not an analogous ground, but obiter dictum that special circumstances could change this conclusion). Contra, Gibson, note 35, above, 257.

116 [1990] 1 S.C.R. 695.

117 *Id.*, 702 per Cory J. for Court.

118 Accord, *Mirhadizadeh* v. *Ont.* (1989) 69 O.R. (2d) 422 (C.A.) (upholding limitation period on actions against public authorities).

What about place of residence? That was the ground of discrimination relied upon in *R.* v. *Turpin* (1989).[119] In that case, a provision of the Criminal Code that made a difference in the treatment of accused persons, depending upon whether they were charged in Alberta or elsewhere in Canada, was challenged under s. 15. The Supreme Court of Canada rejected the challenge for reasons that are examined later in this chapter.[120] The unanimous opinion of the Court was written by Wilson J., who left open the question whether place of residence was an analogous ground. She said:[121]

> I would not wish to suggest that a person's province of residence or place of trial could not in some circumstances be a personal characteristic of the individual or group capable of constituting a ground of discrimination. I simply say that it is not so here.

This is a rather opaque statement, from which it is probably unwise to draw any strong inferences. However, she does imply that province of residence could "in some circumstances" be an analogous ground. Clearly, as she notes, it is a personal characteristic, and the question is whether it is sufficiently immutable to qualify as similar to the listed grounds. I would have thought that place of residence is a matter of personal choice, and is not immutable for that reason.[122]

Is marital status an analogous ground? In *Miron* v. *Trudel* (1995),[123] the Supreme Court of Canada said maybe. The Court held by a five-four majority that it was a breach of s. 15 for a statutory automobile insurance policy that provided accident benefits to the "spouse" of the insured to restrict the definition of spouse to persons who were legally married. The claimant, who was the common-law spouse of an insured, was successful in securing the accident benefit. Only four judges decided that marital status was an analogous ground. This was the position of McLachlin J., with the concurrence of Sopinka, Cory and Iacobucci JJ. She held that immutability was not an absolute requirement but only an "indicator" of an analogous ground (along with historical disadvantage and membership of a discrete and insular minority).[124] She held that immutability was a characteristic of marital status "albeit in attenuated form", because there are "often" impediments to marriage that are outside the control of the individual.[125] For example, one partner in a common-law union might want to marry while the other did not, or they might not be free to marry because of an undissolved previous marriage. The fifth member of the majority, L'Heureux-Dubé J., rejected

119 [1989] 1 S.C.R. 1296.
120 Note 156, below.
121 [1989] 1 S.C.R. 1296, 1333.
122 Contra Gibson, note 35, above, 159, emphasizing "the powerful deterrents to migration that so frequently exist in the real world". See also sec. 52.16, "Place of residence", below.
123 [1995] 2 S.C.R. 418. The case is more fully discussed in the text accompanying note 79, above.
124 This use of various "indicators" to identify analogous grounds was also employed by McLachlin J. dissenting in *Thibaudeau* v. *Can.* [1995]. 2 S.C.R. 627, 722-723, paras. 206-212; none of the other judges addressed the issue.
125 [1995] 2 S.C.R. 418, 498, para. 153.

the concept of analogous grounds as a requirement for s. 15, and therefore did not address the issue. The dissenting opinion was written by Gonthier J., with the agreement of Lamer C.J., La Forest and Major JJ. Gonthier J. held that marital status was not an analogous ground. While he did not expressly invoke immutability, he emphasized that the decision to marry was a joint choice, which carried burdens as well as benefits; indeed, the burdens of marriage might well outweigh the benefits. It was not discriminatory to deny to a common-law couple attributes of marriage that were available to them by entering into the contract of marriage.[126]

Is sexual orientation an analogous ground? In *Egan* v. *Canada* (1995),[127] the Supreme Court of Canada said yes. The claimants, a homosexual couple, who claimed the spouse's allowance under the federal Old Age Security program, did not actually succeed, for reasons that were fully explained earlier in the chapter. But eight of the nine judges[128] agreed that sexual orientation was an analogous ground that could in principle be the basis of a s. 15 equality claim.[129] This ruling was not very fully reasoned, no doubt because the Attorney General of Canada conceded the point. La Forest J., with whom Lamer C.J., Gonthier and Major JJ. agreed, said that sexual orientation "is a deeply personal characteristic that is either unchangeable or changeable only at unacceptable personal costs".[130] Cory J., with whom Sopinka, Iacobucci and McLachlin JJ. agreed (on this issue), made no reference to immutability or any other definition of analogous grounds and simply referred to the historical disadvantage suffered by homosexuals (which he said was not decisive) and the growing recognition by courts and legislators that sexual orientation should be treated as an analogous ground.[131]

Of all the distinctions to be found in the statute books, there must be very few that are based on the named grounds of discrimination, and only a few more that are based on immutable personal characteristics that would be regarded as analogous to the named grounds. The interpretation of discrimination that restricts s. 15 to distinctions based on the named or analogous grounds has caused a dramatic reduction in the reach of s. 15. However, there is much to be said for the view, articulated so well in *Andrews*, that the narrower version of s. 15 is much better targeted to its purpose, which is to correct disadvantages imposed through prejudices that may have distorted the political process. Complaints of

---

126 *Id.*, 451-452, paras. 47-49. However, Gonthier J. left open the possibility that marital status might be an analogous ground in a law that had nothing to do with the attributes of marriage: *Id.*, 429, para. 2.

127 [1995] 2 S.C.R. 513. The case is more fully discussed in the text accompanying note 85, above.

128 For L'Heureux-Dubé J., the issue did not arise, and she did not need to decide it. She used other criteria to determine that the exclusion of same sex-couples from the spouse's allowance was a breach of s. 15: see text accompanying note 85, above.

129 Accord, *Haig* v. *Can.* (1992) 9 O.R. (3d) 495 (C.A.) (Canadian Human Rights Act offended s. 15 by failing to include sexual orientation as a prohibited ground of discrimination).

130 [1995] 2 S.C.R. 513, 528, para. 5.

131 *Id.*, 599-603, paras. 171-178.

unequal treatment that cannot be related to a named or analogous ground must be addressed to elected officials, not to the courts.

(f) Particular disadvantage is required

In order to establish discrimination under s. 15, it is obvious that an individual must show that he or she has suffered a disadvantage by reason of his or her possession of one of the characteristics named in s. 15 or an analogous characteristic. In *Andrews*,[132] McIntyre J. said that, in order for a legislative distinction to amount to discrimination against an individual or group, the distinction must be one ''which has the effect of imposing burdens, obligations or disadvantages on such individual or group not imposed on others, or which withholds or limits access to opportunities, benefits and advantages available to other members of society''. It is the requirement of disadvantage that involves a comparison with others — others who are similarly situated to the complainant except for the presence of an immutable personal characteristic. In *Andrews* itself, this requirement was easily satisfied. The plaintiff's non-Canadian citizenship denied him access to the legal profession, while permitting access to others whose qualifications to practise law were no different from his, except for their possession of Canadian citizenship.

In *Thibaudeau* v. *Canada* (1995),[133] the claimant was unable to establish that she had suffered a disadvantage by reason of her marital status. The claimant was a divorced woman who had custody of the children of the marriage and who received child-support payments from her former husband. She objected to a provision of the Income Tax Act that required her to pay income tax on the support payments that she received from her ex-spouse. She argued that the tax provision discriminated against separated custodial parents, because in an intact family the income tax on money spent on child support would be paid by the spouse who earned the income. The Supreme Court of Canada, by a majority, rejected the argument. The Court pointed out that the inclusion requirement on the recipient spouse was matched by a deduction for the payor spouse. Since the payor spouse was usually in a higher tax bracket than the recipient spouse, the tax saved by the deduction would normally exceed the tax incurred by the inclusion. This resulted in a reduction of tax for the majority of separated couples — a reduction that cost the treasury over $300 million per year.

While it was the payor who received the benefit of the deduction, and the recipient who bore the burden of the tax, the family law system required that the tax consequences be taken into account in fixing the amount of child support.

---

132 [1989] 1 S.C.R. 143, 174.

133 [1995] 2 S.C.R. 627. The principal majority opinion of the seven-judge bench was written by Gonthier J. Short concurring opinions were written by Sopinka J., with whom La Forest J. agreed, and by Cory and Iacobucci JJ. McLachlin J. and L'Heureux-Dubé J. each wrote dissenting opinions.

Therefore, in fixing the amount of child support, the payor's enhanced ability to pay should be recognized, and the amount of child support should be grossed-up to fully compensate the recipient for her additional tax liability. In Thibaudeau's case, the family court that made the support order had taken her additional tax liability into account, but it appeared that the liability had been underestimated, and the gross-up for tax was insufficient.[134] But the majority of the Supreme Court of Canada held that this deficiency should be remedied by a review of the support order by the family court. Although some separated custodial parents did not benefit from the deduction-inclusion system, as a group separated custodial parents did benefit.[135] Therefore, the Income Tax Act did not discriminate against them, and there was no breach of s. 15 of the Charter of Rights.

How does one measure disadvantage? Is it a purely economic calculus, or are non-economic disadvantages also relevant? This question was presented by *Egan* v. *Canada* (1995),[136] in which, it will be recalled, a homosexual couple challenged the spouse's allowance that was payable under the federal Old Age Security Act to the "spouse" of a pensioner. The term spouse included persons in common-law relationships, but only if they were "of the opposite sex". The awkward element of the facts, however, was that in British Columbia, where the claimants lived, the combined effect of the provincial social assistance entitlements and the Old Age Security pension left the claimants better off than they would be if they were recognized as spouses under the Old Age Security Act. The Supreme Court of Canada denied the claim to spousal status by a majority of five to four for reasons that have earlier been explained.[137] But all nine judges accepted the proposition that the denial of the federal spousal allowance was a disadvantage that could in principle be the basis of a s. 15 equality right.

In *Egan*, none of the judges considered that the economic advantage of the claimants' non-recognition as spouses should defeat their s. 15 claim. La Forest J., who wrote for four of the five judges who upheld the legislation, dismissed the point by saying that, while there might be an advantage "in this specific instance" (which was the only one before the Court), "there was nothing to show that this is generally the case with homosexual couples" (meaning, presumably, couples in other provinces who were not before the Court).[138] Cory J., who

134 The Court did not consider the question, upon which no evidence seemed to have been led, as to how much lower the support order would have been if the payor's deduction did not exist. Without some estimate of this, it is not apparent merely from the inadequacy of the tax gross-up that Thibaudeau was worse off than she would have been in a world without the deduction-inclusion system.

135 McLachlin and L'Heureux-Dubé JJ. dissented primarily on the ground that the family-law system could not be relied upon to shift the tax benefit forward to the custodial spouse. By conferring the benefit of the deduction on the non-custodial spouse, and imposing the burden of the tax on the custodial spouse, the Act was discriminatory.

136 [1995] 2 S.C.R. 513; discussed at note 85, above.

137 Text accompanying note 85, above.

138 [1995] 2 S.C.R. 513, 531, para.12.

dissented, but who on this point attracted the agreement of Sopinka J., as well as Iacobucci and McLachlin JJ., said that "the concept of equal benefit of the law should not be restricted to a simple calculation of economic profit or loss".[139] And L'Heureux-Dubé J. agreed that "it would take too narrow a view of the phrase "benefit of the law" [in s. 15] to define it strictly in terms of economic interests".[140] These sentiments are admirable, but it must not be overlooked that many people, especially those who are poor, place a higher value on additional income than on less tangible considerations. In *Egan*, if the s. 15 argument had prevailed, as the four dissenters would have held, the law would have been invalidated not only for Egan and his partner, but for all other same-sex couples in like circumstances. Those who preferred the extra money that came from their non-spousal status would have to accept the lower benefits that their newly acquired spousal status had brought. Nor is this a unique or unusual situation as La Forest J. implied. It is common for social legislation to combine spousal incomes for the purpose of determining eligibility for income-tested social programs, and common-law spouses are included for the very reason that two single individuals would draw higher benefits than a married couple.

Another way of framing the issue in *Egan* is to ask whether the presence of disadvantage is to be judged from the *subjective* standard of the individual who makes the claim of discrimination, or from an *objective* standard determined by the reviewing court. The Supreme Court of Canada was implicitly applying a subjective standard in *Egan*: the claimants were disadvantaged because, according to their subjective calculus of costs and benefits, the disadvantage of not being officially recognized as spouses outweighed the advantage of higher single-status social assistance. The same subjective standard seems to have been the (unarticulated) premise of the finding of disadvantage in *McKinney* v. *University of Guelph* (1990),[141] in which the Supreme Court of Canada held that mandatory retirement at age 65 constituted discrimination on the basis of age. The Court assumed without discussion that mandatory retirement was a disadvantage to employees aged 65. From an *objective* standpoint, this is probably wrong. The evidence in *McKinney* suggested that in a regime of mandatory retirement, wages rise faster with seniority than they would if there were no definite end to an individual's employment, continuous performance assessment is not usually im-

---

139 *Id.*, 593, para.158. Cory J. also asserted that the economic advantage was "highly speculative and may well be incorrect" (593, para.157), although the factual issue was not regarded as speculative by La Forest J. or L'Heureux-Dubé J. He also held that the provincial law should be ignored in assessing the validity of the federal law (592, paras.155-156), a point that seems inconsistent with *Thibaudeau*, note 133, above, where the provincial family law rescued the Income Tax Act from discrimination. In *Thibaudeau*, Cory and Iacobucci JJ. explained the difference on the basis that the Income Tax Act "explicitly" incorporated family law, whereas in *Egan* the spousal allowance was allotted "independently of any reference to provincial social insurance legislation" (note 133, above, 703, para.161).

140 [1995] 2 S.C.R. 513, 565, para.86.

141 [1990] 3 S.C.R. 229, see also sec. 52.13, "Age", below.

posed upon older workers and pension rights are usually agreed to and contributed to by the employer. Assuming this to be so, one might well conclude that a person of 65, who admittedly now confronts the downside of the regime, has nonetheless received overall a net benefit from mandatory retirement. But none of the judges doubted that the individual plaintiffs, who had reached 65 and wished to continue their work, were disadvantaged by the obligation to retire. From their own subjective standpoint, the plaintiff professors were disadvantaged.

If the subjective standard of disadvantage is the correct approach, then disadvantage will be present in all but the most unusual cases, since plaintiffs do not bring Charter cases (or any other legal proceedings) unless they believe that they have suffered a disadvantage. The case for the subjective standard would be conclusive if Charter decisions affected only the parties to those decisions. Who, one might ask, is in the position to do the calculus of costs and benefits for someone else? But Charter decisions do not affect only the parties who believe they are disadvantaged. If mandatory retirement had been struck down in *McKinney*, then its benefits would have been denied to all employees,[142] including those whose unions had voluntarily sought and negotiated mandatory retirement in their collective agreements. This radical result was in fact avoided in *McKinney*, because the Court held, by a majority, that mandatory retirement was justified under s. 1. As part of the s. 1 inquiry, the Court did attempt an objective weighing of the costs and benefits of mandatory retirement. The Court concluded that mandatory retirement offered significant benefits to individual university professors, as well as to the universities as centres of teaching and research. In the end, therefore, the Court's (objective) calculus of costs and benefits, rather than the (subjective) calculus of the plaintiffs, is the one that prevailed. Mandatory retirement was upheld.

The subjective standard of disadvantage in s. 15 (as opposed to s. 1) was not applied in *Thibaudeau*,[143] the case (discussed earlier) that upheld the Income Tax Act's deduction-inclusion system for taxing child support. In that case, it will be recalled, the claimant Thibaudeau regarded herself as disadvantaged by the Income Tax Act provisions, and she probably was disadvantaged by them since the amount of her support had not been grossed-up sufficiently to enable her to pay the additional income tax to which the support payments rendered her liable. But the Supreme Court of Canada held that the deduction-inclusion system was, on the whole, beneficial to separated custodial parents. Therefore, the Court did not want to strike the system down. But this reasoning all took place within s. 15. In contrast to *McKinney*, the Court did not need to advance to the s. 1 inquiry. In effect, without saying so, the Court in *Thibaudeau* applied an objective measure of disadvantage to the s. 15 equality claim. The claim failed for lack of objective disadvantage, despite the claimant's subjective sense of disadvantage.

---

142 The ruling applied to all workplaces, not just those of government, because the challenge was to the Human Rights Code, which applied to private as well as public workplaces.

143 Note 133, above.

The objective approach to disadvantage was also applied in *R.* v. *Swain* (1991),[144] where one of the issues was whether a person accused of a criminal offence, who had chosen not to raise the defence of insanity, would be discriminated against by a rule that permitted the Crown against the wish of the accused to raise the issue of insanity. If the accused were convicted of the criminal offence, he would be subject to a finite sentence imposed under the Criminal Code. If the accused were acquitted on the ground of insanity, he would be detained indefinitely at the pleasure of the Lieutenant Governor. One can easily understand why an accused would regard the indefinite detention as a worse alternative than the finite sentence. And this alternative, obviously, is triggered by the mental disability of the accused, which is one of the grounds of discrimination named in s. 15. Nevertheless, Lamer C.J. for a majority of the Supreme Court of Canada held that there was no discrimination because the accused who was acquitted on the ground of insanity did not really suffer a disadvantage; rather, he was spared the disadvantage of being convicted of an offence for which by reason of insanity he did not have the requisite guilty mind.[145] This conclusion obviously involved a rejection of the subjective measurement of disadvantage: the accused, who with the advice of counsel deliberately refused to use the defence of insanity, obviously feared the indeterminate detention more than the stigma of conviction. I agree that the point of view of the accused ought not to be decisive, but the Court's view that the stigma of a criminal conviction (coupled with a finite sentence) would be a greater detriment to the accused than an indefinite detention seems to me to be wrong on any basis.[146]

In assessing disadvantage, the question is whether an individual has suffered a disadvantage by reason of his or her possession of one of the named or analogous s. 15 characteristics. Thus, in *Thibaudeau*,[147] while a separated custodial parent did bear the burden of having to pay tax on support payments, the separated custodial parent could expect the family law system to fully offset this burden by delivering to her higher support payments, more faithfully paid. Therefore, there was no net disadvantage, so the Supreme Court of Canada decided.

Following *Thibaudeau*, to what extent is it appropriate to net out the advantages and disadvantages that flow from an individual's possession of one of the listed or analogous s. 15 characteristics? In *Miron* v. *Trudel* (1995),[148] it will be recalled that the Supreme Court of Canada held that Ontario's Insurance Act

---

144 [1991] 1 S.C.R. 933.

145 *Id.*, 995-996. Lamer C.J. wrote for himself, Sopinka and Cory JJ., and his opinion on this issue was agreed with by Gonthier and La Forest JJ. Wilson and L'Heureux-Dubé JJ. did not need to, and did not, consider this issue.

146 This is another example of the Supreme Court of Canada's confidence that it is able to identify and measure the stigma of a criminal conviction, and the Court's view that radical constitutional results should flow from a finding of stigma: see ch.44, Fundamental Justice, ss. 44.1-44.13, above.

147 Note 133, above.

148 [1995] 2 S.C.R. 418; discussed at note 79, above.

discriminated on the basis of marital status by limiting accident benefits to the legally-married spouse of the insured, thereby excluding the plaintiff, who was living in a common-law relationship with the insured. MacLachlin J. for the majority of the Court held that the plaintiff's case presented a clear disadvantage: as a common-law spouse of the insured, he was denied the accident benefit to which a legally-married spouse of the insured would have been entitled.[149] But Gonthier J., in his dissenting judgment, pointed out that the position was not quite so simple. While ''unmarried persons who live together do not possess some of the important rights that married persons have'' (including the right to spousal automobile accident benefits), ''they are not subject to many of the legal burdens and obligations of married persons''; therefore, it could not be said that ''their overall position nets out as one of disadvantage''.[150] Of course, the majority view, regarding the burden of the denial of accident benefits in isolation from other legal attributes of common-law relationships, was the view that prevailed.

(g) General disadvantage is not required

In *Andrews*,[151] it will be recalled, the Supreme Court of Canada struck down a British Columbia law that excluded non-citizens from admission to the bar. Three opinions were written, and all three suggested that disadvantage or powerlessness was characteristic of the groups protected by s. 15. Both Wilson and McIntyre JJ. referred to non-citizens as an example of a ''discrete and insular minority'', [152] an obscure phrase which in the United States has become a code word to describe groups that typically experience discrimination.[153] Wilson J. elaborated by explaining that non-citizens were ''a group lacking in political power and as such vulnerable to having their interests overlooked and their rights to equal concern and respect violated''.[154] La Forest J. described non-citizens as ''an example without parallel'' of a group ''who are relatively powerless politically, and whose interests are likely to be compromised by legislative decisions''.[155]

In *R.* v. *Turpin* (1989),[156] a s. 15 challenge was mounted to a provision of the Criminal Code that stipulated that certain of the most serious offences, including murder, were to be tried by a judge and jury, and that gave no right to elect a trial by judge alone. The s. 15 argument was based on another provision

---

149 *Id.*, 493, para.143.

150 *Id.*, 453, para.53, quoting from *Leroux* v. *Co-Operators General Insurance Co.* (1991) 4 O.R. (3d) 609, 620-621 (C.A.). While Gonthier J. approved the statement, he said ''I do not propose to dispose of the case at bar on this basis''.

151 Note 78, above.

152 [1989] 1 S.C.R. 143, 152, 157, 183.

153 Text accompanying note 162, below.

154 [1989] 1 S.C.R. 143, 152.

155 *Id.*, 195.

156 [1989] 1 S.C.R. 1296.

of the Criminal Code, which was applicable only in Alberta, and which gave to an accused person the right to elect a trial by judge alone for all indictable offences, including murder.[157] In *Turpin*, there were three accused who were charged with murder in Ontario. They wished to be tried by judge alone, and they argued that the failure of the Criminal Code to accord that right to an accused person in Ontario was discriminatory, because the right was available to an accused person in Alberta.

In *Turpin*, the Supreme Court of Canada rejected the s. 15 argument on the basis of the second element of discrimination suggested by *Andrews*, namely, the presence of disadvantage. Wilson J. for a unanimous Court said that it was not sufficient for the equality claimant to show that he or she was disadvantaged by the impugned law. That, obviously, was necessary, but it was not sufficient. The claimant had to go further and show that the distinction employed by the statute was one that defined a group that was disadvantaged in other respects. Wilson J. put it this way:[158]

> A finding that there is discrimination will, I think, in most but perhaps not all cases necessarily entail a search for disadvantage that exists apart from and independent of the particular legal distinction being challenged.

Province of residence (or trial) did not, at least in the context of this case, identify a disadvantaged group. It was impossible to identify ''indicia of discrimination such as stereotyping, historical disadvantage or vulnerability to political and social prejudice''.[159] The claim would not, Wilson J. said, ''advance the purposes of s. 15 in remedying or preventing discrimination against groups suffering social, political and legal disadvantage in our society''.[160] Since the claim was outside the purpose of s. 15, it was also outside the scope of s. 15, and the claim accordingly was rejected.[161]

The view that systemic disadvantage and political powerlessness are essential characteristics of the groups protected by s. 15 reflects a theory of equality that finds its origin in the famous footnote 4 of *United States* v. *Caroline Products Co.* (1938).[162] In that footnote, Stone J. of the Supreme Court of the United States pointed out that ''prejudice against discrete and insular minorities'' could have the effect of distorting ''those political processes ordinarily to be relied upon to

---

157 This curious provision has since been amended to extend throughout Canada the right to elect for trial by judge alone.

158 [1989] 1 S.C.R. 1296, 1332.

159 *Id.*, 1333.

160 *Ibid.* This line of reasoning was followed by L'Heureux-Dubé J. for the majority in *Haig* v. *Can.* [1993] 2 S.C.R. 995, 1043-1044, to hold again that place of residence was not an analogous ground.

161 Cf. *McKinney* v. *U. of Guelph* [1990] 3 S.C.R. 229, 293, where Wilson J. said that even a disadvantage imposed by reference to a named ground of discrimination (age in that case) would be discrimination only if there was also a finding of ''prejudice''. La Forest J. seems to reject the point in an inconclusive reference at 279.

162 (1938) 304 U.S. 144

protect minorities''.[163] The point is that discrimination against blacks (or other minorities) may reflect a flawed political process from which blacks are effectively excluded. From this perspective, judicial review of discriminatory laws can be viewed as the correction of a failure of the political process — the failure to represent adequately a ''discrete and insular minority''. This line of reasoning has been offered in the United States by John Hart Ely as a defence of the legitimacy of judicial review on equal protection grounds.[164] According to Ely, when the judges strike down a discriminatory law, what they are really doing is removing impediments to access to the democratic political process. This view of equality casts the judges ''in the role of servants of democracy even as they strike down the actions of supposedly democratic governments''.[165]

The view of equality review as a correction of political powerlessness undoubtedly contains a valuable insight as to why discrimination by legislative bodies may properly be corrected by courts. But it is doubtful whether it is appropriate to regard the political powerlessness of a group as an essential ingredient of discrimination under s. 15. For one thing, a court is not normally in a position to measure the relative power of groups within society. Wilson J.'s insistence in *Turpin* on a ''search for disadvantage that exists apart from and independent of the particular legal distinction being challenged'' would carry courts far beyond the facts and the law relevant to a particular case and into some of the most hotly contested areas of political science.[166]

Wilson J. herself acknowledged in *Andrews* that ''the range of discrete and insular minorities has changed and will continue to change with changing political and social circumstances''.[167] But how could a court possibly measure such changes? Would the economic success of some recently-arrived visible minorities from Asia, who have already achieved incomes higher than the national average,[168] disentitle an immigrant from Asia to a s. 15 remedy? Would the growing proportion of old people in the Canadian population be judged sufficient to disentitle an

163 *Id.*, 153, footnote 4.

164 Ely, *Democracy and Distrust* (1982), ch. 6. This same theory is espoused in Canada by Fairley, ''Enforcing the Charter'' (1982) 4 Supreme Court L.R. 217, 243, 249-250 and Monahan, ''Judicial Review and Democracy'' (1986) 21 U.B.C.L. Rev. 87, 89-97.

165 Tribe, ''The Puzzling Persistence of Process-based Constitutional Theories'' (1980) 89 Yale L.J. 1063, 1063. Tribe goes on to criticize the process-based theories. For criticism from a Canadian standpoint, see Hogg, ''The Charter of Rights and American Theories of Interpretation'' (1987) 25 Osgoode Hall L.J. 87.

166 For example, it is widely held that discrete and insular minorities are relatively effective in the American political process, in comparison with anonymous and diffuse minorities (or majorities): Ackerman, ''Beyond Caroline Products'' (1985) 98 Harv. L. Rev. 713 (criticizing the phrase ''discrete and insular minorities'' in U.S. equal protection law).

167 [1989] 1 S.C.R. 143, 152.

168 On the basis of average incomes, one would be forced to conclude that many visible minority groups are not disadvantaged, and some invisible (white) groups are: see the review of some of the data in Juriansz, ''Employment Equity and Pay Equity'' in Tarnopolsky, *Discrimination in the Law and the Administration of Justice* (1993).

old person to a s. 15 remedy? Would the growing influence of women's groups on legislative agendas be judged sufficient to disentitle a woman to a s. 15 remedy? Of course, the answers to these questions should be no if an immigrant, an old person or a woman could show that a particular statute imposed a burden or denied a benefit solely by reason of the race, national origin, age or sex of the complainant. In my view, nothing more should have to be established.

Assuming that general disadvantage could be identified with particular groups, the awkward question arises as to how to deal with an individual who has been discriminated against on a named or analogous ground, although the individual belongs to a group that is in other respects not subject to disadvantage. The implication of *Turpin* is that an individual member of the advantaged part of a named or analogous group would not invoke s. 15, even if the individual could establish unjust treatment based on a named or analogous ground. Whatever the theoretical justification for such a stern doctrine, it is hard to square with the unqualified language of s. 15,[169] and it has in fact been rejected by the Supreme Court of Canada.

In *R.* v. *Hess* (1990),[170] a s. 15 attack was mounted against the statutory rape offence in the Criminal Code. This provision, since repealed, made it an offence for a male person to have intercourse with a female person under the age of fourteen. The s. 15 attack was based on discrimination by sex: the provision applied only to male offenders and protected only female victims. McLachlin J., with the agreement of three others, frankly noted that Wilson J.'s dictum in *Turpin* suggested that "a distinction against men as compared with women" could not be discrimination under s. 15, because men could "rarely show discrimination apart from the provision they are challenging". She rejected this view, saying that "these arguments take the language in *Turpin* further than is justified".[171] She held that the statutory rape provision did offend s. 15, because of its discrimination against men, although she went on to uphold the provision under s. 1. Wilson J., with the agreement of four other judges, held that the provision did not offend s. 15, because the definition of intercourse used the concept of penetration, which could as a matter of biological fact be committed only by a man; therefore, she held, it was not discriminatory to apply the offence only to men. This dubious reasoning is discussed later in the chapter.[172] For present purposes, the point to notice is that Wilson J., although finding no discrimination, did not repeat her general disadvantage argument from *Turpin*, and clearly assumed that discrimination against men was contrary to s. 15.

---

169 Accord, Gibson, note 35, above, 152-157.

170 [1990] 2 S.C.R. 906. Wilson J.'s opinion was agreed to by Lamer C.J., La Forest and L'Heureux-Dubé JJ.; McLachlin J.'s opinion was agreed to by Gonthier J.; Sopinka J. wrote a concurring opinion siding with McLachlin J. on the s. 1 issue. There was also a s. 7 issue, upon which the Court divided: Wilson J. struck down the law; McLachlin J. dissented, upholding the law under s. 1; Sopinka J. agreed with Wilson J. on the s. 7 issue.

171 *Id.*, 943.

172 Text accompanying note 229, below.

In *Weatherall* v. *Canada* (1993),[173] an inmate in a federal penitentiary brought a constitutional challenge under s. 15 to the penitentiary's practice of allowing female guards to perform frisk searches and observe the cells (and toilets) of male prisoners. These ''cross-gender'' indignities were not visited on female prisoners, who were always searched and observed by female guards. The Court held that there ''may be'' no discrimination against the male prisoners in this situation. The Court did not reach a definite conclusion, falling back on s. 1 to justify the challenged practice.[174] However, in the course of his brief (and probably obiter) comments about the probable lack of discrimination, La Forest J. for the Court did use the language of general disadvantage. He said that ''women generally occupy a disadvantaged position in society in relation to men''.[175] In my opinion, this proposition, however true of society in general, should play no role in the denial of redress to a male prisoner who complains of his treatment at the hands of female guards. In the prison setting, the man is the disadvantaged party. It is cold comfort to him that other men (not in prison) have nothing to complain about.

The question whether a showing of general (or group) disadvantage is a prerequisite to a s. 15 equality claim has probably been settled by *Miron* v. *Trudel* (1995)[176] and *Egan* v. *Canada* (1985),[177] two cases that were described earlier in this chapter. The claim of discrimination in each case was made by a member of a group that, the Court held, was generally disadvantaged. (It was common-law couples in *Miron* and same-sex couples in *Egan*.) In neither case, therefore, was it necessary to pronounce on the issue whether general disadvantage was a prerequisite to a s. 15 claim. Nonetheless, in *Miron*, eight judges said that membership in a disadvantaged group was not a prerequisite, but merely an ''indicator''[178] or ''indicium''[179] of an analogous ground. The ninth judge, L'Heureux-Dubé J., who rejected analogous grounds as a necessary basis for a s. 15 claim, said that the nature of the group affected should be considered but that it was a ''factor'' that was not by itself determinative.[180] In *Egan*, three judges agreed with Cory J., who said that: ''while historical disadvantage or a group's position as a discrete and insular minority may serve as indicators of an analogous ground, they are not

---

173 [1993] 2 S.C.R. 872.

174 The justification (unsupported by any reference to evidence) was that the presence of female guards would ''humanize'' the institutions, and would aid in the achievement of ''employment equity'' in the correctional system.

175 [1993] 2 S.C.R. 872, 877.

176 [1995] 2 S.C.R. 418; the case is discussed at note 79, above.

177 [1995] 2 S.C.R. 513; the case is discussed at note 85, above.

178 [1995] 2 S.C.R. 418, 496, para. 149 per McLachlin J., with the agreement of Sopinka, Cory and Iacobucci JJ.

179 *Id.*, 436, 455, paras. 15, 57 per Gonthier J. dissenting, with the agreement of Lamer C.J., La Forest and Major JJ.

180 *Id.*, 468, para 90 per L'Heureux-Dubé J. concurring.

prerequisites for finding an analogous ground.''[181] That dictum sums up the current position of the Court.

The law respecting general disadvantage may be stated as follows: An individual who invokes s. 15 need show only that a law imposes some disadvantage on him or her, and does so by reason of a named or analogous (immutable) personal characteristic. That is discrimination within s. 15. It is not necessary for the individual to show that he or she is a member of a group that is disadvantaged in other respects. Of course, there may be a sound reason for a discriminatory law, especially if the burdened group is one that is generally advantaged in other respects, but that is relevant under s. 1. In *Hess*, for example, McLachlin J. would have upheld the statutory rape provision under s. 1. In the case of affirmative action, if the conditions stipulated by subsection (2) of s. 15 are satisfied, there is no breach of s. 15. Affirmative action under s. 15(2) is discussed later in this chapter.[182]

(h) May be unintended

Discrimination is not necessarily intentional. In the *Andrews* case,[183] McIntyre J., in the course of defining discrimination, used the phrase ''whether intentional or not''.[184] He also made clear that the Court's decisions interpreting the Human Rights Codes were transferable to s. 15,[185] and (as he expressly acknowledged)[186] those decisions establish that discrimination under the Human Rights Codes need not be intentional.[187] It follows that it is not necessary to show that the *purpose* of the challenged law was to impose a disadvantage on a person by reason of his or her race, national or ethnic origin, etc. It is enough to show that the *effect* of the law is to impose a disadvantage on a person by reference to one of the listed or analogous characteristics.

In *Andrews*,[188] for example, it was never seriously suggested that the object of the British Columbia Legislature was to disadvantage non-citizens; on the contrary, all judges assumed that the legislators thought that citizenship was a bona fide occupational requirement for the practice of law, and the disadvantage to non-citizens was simply an inevitable by-product of the requirement. Never-

181 [1995] 2 S.C.R. 513, 599, para 171, per Cory J. dissenting (but not on this issue), with the agreement of Sopinka, McLachlin and Iacobucci JJ. L'Heureux-Dubé J. took the same view as in *Miron*, namely, that the nature of the group affected was an important factor in finding discrimination. La Forest J., who wrote the majority opinion, with the agreement of Lamer C.J., Gonthier and Major JJ., did not discuss general disadvantage.

182 Section 52.8, Affirmative action, below.

183 Note 78, above.

184 [1989] 1 S.C.R. 143, 174.

185 *Id.*, 175, 176.

186 *Id.*, 173.

187 *Ont. Human Rights Commn.* v. *Simpsons-Sears* [1985] 2 S.C.R. 536; *CNR* v. *Can.* [1987] 1 S.C.R. 1114; *Brooks* v. *Can. Safeway* [1989] 1 S.C.R. 1219.

188 Note 78, above.

theless, the fact that the effect of the law was to disadvantage a person on the basis of citizenship (an analogous ground) was enough to establish a breach of s. 15. The benign purpose of the law was irrelevant under s. 15. The benign purpose was however relevant to the s. 1 inquiry, and was considered by all judges in that context — and, of course, two of six judges held that the law was justified under s. 1.

The rule that discrimination under s. 15 need not be intentional is consistent with the rule that has developed under other Charter rights. It is well established that a law is in breach of a Charter right if *either* the purpose of the law *or* the effect of the law is to abridge the right.[189] Applied to s. 15, this rule yields the conclusion that a discriminatory effect constitutes a breach of s. 15, even if the effect is an incidental by-product of a benign intention. Purpose is, however, always a relevant factor under s. 1, because a law cannot be justified under s. 1 unless it serves an important purpose that is compatible with the values of a free and democratic society.[190] Obviously, an intention to disadvantage one of the protected categories would not qualify as a permissible objective under s. 1. Only unintended discrimination could ever be justified under s. 1.

(i) May be systemic

In *Andrews*,[191] McIntyre J. made clear that the Supreme Court of Canada's decisions under the Human Rights Codes were transferable to s. 15.[192] He also made prominent reference to cases where the Court had held that systemic discrimination was prohibited by the Human Rights Codes.[193] It is clear, therefore, that s. 15 prohibits not only direct discrimination but also systemic discrimination.

Systemic discrimination is caused by a law that does not expressly employ any of the categories prohibited by s. 15, if the law nevertheless has a disproportionately adverse effect on persons defined by any of the prohibited categories. In other words, a law that is neutral (non-discriminatory) on its face may operate in a discriminatory fashion; if it does, the discrimination is systemic. An example is a law imposing height or weight requirements on persons entering the police force. If such a law had the effect of excluding women from entry to the force, it would count as discrimination on the basis of sex, even though the law made reference only to height or weight, and said nothing about sex.

Systemic discrimination may be unintended, as would be the case in my police example if the framers of the height or weight requirements believed the requirements to be bona fide occupational qualifications for a police officer. Systemic discrimination may also be intended, as would be the case if the height

189 Chapter 33, Charter of Rights, under heading 33.6(b), ''Purpose or effect'', above.

190 Chapter 35, Limitation of Rights, under heading 35.9, ''Sufficiently important objective'', above.

191 Note 78, above.

192 Note 185, above.

193 Note 187, above.

or weight requirements were a covert device to exclude women from the police force. Because intention is not an ingredient of discrimination under s. 15,[194] it is not necessary to make any judgment about whether a case of systemic discrimination is intended or not. The mere fact that the law has the effect of discriminating against persons defined by a prohibited category is enough to establish the breach of s. 15. (As noted earlier, however, for the purpose of s. 1, intention will be relevant.)

(j) May require reasonable accommodation

Another concept that has become established in decisions under the Human Rights Codes, and which will apply under s. 15 as well, is "reasonable accommodation". As Gibson points out,[195] it is a necessary corollary of the rule that discrimination may be indirect and unintended that a law may have to make reasonable accommodation for those who, by reason of religious affiliation or disability (for example), are discriminated against by otherwise neutral laws.

For example, the Supreme Court of Canada has held[196] that an employer (a retailer) was under a duty to make reasonable adjustments to employee work schedules so that an employee who was a Seventh Day Adventist would not have to work on Friday evenings and Saturdays. The rule requiring employees to be available for work at those times was a reasonable requirement for a retailer, because those times were particularly busy in the retail trade. However, the rule had a disproportionately adverse effect on those observing a Saturday sabbath, and therefore constituted discrimination on the basis of religion. The discrimination could be cured by making reasonable accommodation for the person whose religious beliefs called for some deviation from the general rule. Or, to turn the proposition around, the discrimination consisted in the failure to make reasonable accommodation for a person whose religious practices were specially burdened by an otherwise neutral rule. This was a Human Rights Code case, but the same principle would apply under s. 15 as well.

(k) Need not appear on face of law

A law may be discriminatory in three different ways. First, a law may be discriminatory *on its face*. A law that expressly excluded women from admission to the police force would be discriminatory on its face. Secondly, a law may be discriminatory *in its effect*. A law that imposed height or weight requirements for admission to the police force would be discriminatory in its effect if the effect of the law (whether intended or not) was to exclude a disproportionate number of female applicants.[197] Thirdly, a law may be discriminatory *in its application*. A

194 See previous section 52.7(h), "May be unintended", above.
195 Gibson, note 35, above, 133.
196 *Ont. Human Rights Commn.* v. *Simpsons-Sears* [1985] 2 S.C.R. 536.
197 See sec. 52.7(f), "May be systemic", above.

law that was neutral on its face and, if administered fairly, would also be neutral in its effect, would be discriminatory in its application if it were administered unfairly, for example, if the police recruitment procedures led to the rejection of a disproportionate number of female applicants.

In the last case, where it is the application of the law that is discriminatory, s. 15 will not affect the validity of the law itself; s. 15 will affect the validity of particular past applications of the law, and it will require that gender-neutral procedures be established for its future administration.[198] In the first two cases, where a law is discriminatory on its face or in its effect, the law itself will be invalid for breach of s. 15.

52.8 Affirmative action

Subsection (2) of s. 15[199] provides as follows:

> 15.(2) Subsection (1) does not preclude any law, program or activity that has as its object the amelioration of conditions of disadvantaged individuals or groups including those that are disadvantaged because of race, national or ethnic origin, colour, religion, sex, age or mental or physical disability.

Subsection (2) of s. 15 is an exception to the general prohibition of discrimination in subsection (1) of s. 15. It makes clear that s. 15 does not preclude ''affirmative action'' programmes in favour of ''disadvantaged individuals or groups''. Such programmes inevitably involve some element of reverse discrimination in the sense that a member of a disadvantaged group will be preferred to a person who is equally or better qualified but who is not a member of the disadvantaged group. If it were not for subsection (2), such programmes would be vulnerable to attack on equality grounds by an individual who was passed over in favour of a member of a disadvantaged group defined by race or sex (for example).[200] Section 1 is of course available to sustain a law that uses a racial or sexual classification for a benign purpose, but subsection (2) of s. 15 makes it unnecessary to go to s. 1. Provided that a law, programme or activity meets the conditions stipulated by subsection (2) of s. 15,[201] it cannot be attacked under s. 15.

---

198 As to the application of s. 15 to action taken under statutory discretion, see text accompanying notes 41-47, above.

199 For commentary on s. 15(2), see Gibson, note 35, above, ch. 7; Blache, ''Affirmative Action'' in Weiler and Elliot, note 35, above, 165-186; Juriansz, ''Equality Rights, Affirmative Action'' in Finkelstein and Rogers (eds.), *Charter Issues in Civil Cases* (1988), 109-150.

200 In the United States, where there is no equivalent to s. 15(2), there is continuous litigation over the constitutionality (under the equal protection clause of the fourteenth amendment) and the legality (under the Civil Rights Act, 1964) of affirmative action programmes: see Tribe, *American Constitutional Law* (2nd ed., 1986), 1521-1544; Nowak and Rotunda, *Constitutional Law* (4th ed., (1991), 655-698.

201 Note the requirement that the beneficiaries be ''disadvantaged'', and the difficulty of giving content to that term: notes 166, 168, above.

The Human Rights Codes of most Canadian jurisdictions expressly authorize affirmative action programmes, thus relieving such programmes from the Code's general prohibitions on discrimination in employment. These statutory authorizations are important, because the Charter of Rights, including s. 15, does not apply to private acts of discrimination; the validity of voluntarily undertaken private affirmative action would have to be determined by reference to the applicable Human Rights Code, not the Charter of rights. To the extent that a Human Rights Code qualified its general prohibition on discrimination in employment (for example) with a provision creating a broader exception for affirmative action than that provided in s. 15(2) of the Charter, the provision of the Human Rights Code would be open to attack under s. 15. For example, affirmative action programmes might be authorized without the requirement that the beneficiaries be "disadvantaged". If such an attack were successful under s. 15, and if s. 1 did not save the provision, then the law authorizing the programme would fall, the Code's general prohibition on discrimination in employment would apply, and the programme would become illegal. In that indirect way, the Charter would reach voluntary private action.[202]

52.9 Discrimination permitted by Constitution

(a) Age in ss. 23, 29, 99

What is the position if the Constitution itself requires or permits discrimination? For example, the Constitution Act, 1867, provides that a person under the age of 30 cannot be appointed to the Senate (s. 23), and that a senator must retire at the age of 75 (s. 29); it also provides that a judge must retire at the age of 75 (s. 99). These provisions impose a burden by reference to a ground of discrimination that is listed in s. 15, namely, age. The provisions would therefore be contrary to s. 15, and hence invalid (unless saved by s. 1), if they were contained in an official instrument other than the Constitution itself. Are the provisions sheltered from Charter attack by reason of their constitutional status? The answer to this question is yes.

(b) Race in s. 91(24)

This issue arose under the equality clause of the Canadian Bill of Rights. In *R.* v. *Drybones* (1969),[203] the Supreme Court of Canada struck down a provision

202 See the earlier discussion of the impact of s. 15 on private action through the invalidating of exceptions in the Human Rights Codes: text accompanying note 50, above.

203 [1970] S.C.R. 282. Ritchie J., with the agreement of five others, wrote the majority opinion; Hall J., who was one of the five, added a separate concurring opinion. Cartwright C.J., Abbott and Pigeon JJ. each wrote a dissenting opinion.

of the Indian Act that made it an offence for "an Indian" to be drunk off a reserve. (The offence was matched by another offence for being drunk on a reserve; both provisions have since been repealed.) The majority of the Court held that the use of the racial classification "Indian" as an ingredient of an offence was contrary to the equality clause of the Canadian Bill of Rights. What was not addressed by Ritchie J.'s opinion for the majority, although it was the basis of Pigeon J.'s dissent, was that the use of the racial classification "Indian" was prerequisite to the validity of all of the provisions of the Indian Act. The Constitution Act, 1867, by s. 91(24), confers on the federal Parliament the power to make laws in relation to "Indians, and lands reserved for the Indians". Obviously, any law enacted under this power will be explicitly restricted to "Indians" or will have a disproportionate impact on Indians who live on "lands reserved for the Indians". Did *Drybones* mean that the entire Indian Act was inoperative, and that s. 91(24) could no longer be used by the federal Parliament?

Drybones was predictably followed by attacks on other provisions of the Indian Act, and two of the cases went on to the Supreme Court of Canada. The Court quickly repented of its boldness in *Drybones*, and upheld, first, the status provisions of the Indian Act (which defined the term "Indian"),[204] and, secondly, the succession provisions of the Act (which governed succession to the property of deceased Indians residing on reserves).[205] In the second case, Ritchie J. for the majority held that differences between Indians and non-Indians were contemplated by s. 91(24) of the Constitution, and such differences should not be eradicated under the equality guarantee of the Canadian Bill of Rights.[206] This was flatly contradictory of his opinion in *Drybones*,[207] where he had held that a difference between Indians and non-Indians did have to be eradicated under the equality guarantee of the Canadian Bill of Rights. However, obviously, the later view had won over most of the Court.[208]

(c) Religion in s. 93

After the coming into force of s. 15 of the Charter of Rights, no new challenges were brought to the Indian Act. However, a similar issue arose in the *Ontario Separate School Funding* case (1987).[209] That case reviewed the validity of an Ontario statute that extended full public funding to Roman Catholic separate

---

204 *A.G. Can.* v. *Lavell* [1974] S.C.R. 1349.

205 *A.G. Can.* v. *Canard* [1976] 1 S.C.R. 170.

206 *Id.*, 191-192.

207 *Id.*, 192, attempting to distinguish *Drybones*, on the basis that it arose in the Northwest Territories, where both Indians and non-Indians were covered by federal law.

208 Ritchie J.'s opinion on this issue was agreed to by Martland, Judson and Pigeon JJ. Beetz J. wrote a separate concurring opinion. Laskin C.J., with whom Spence J. agreed, dissented.

209 *Re Bill 30* (Ontario Separate School Funding) [1987] 1 S.C.R. 1148. The principal opinion was written by Wilson J. with three others; Estey J. with one other wrote a concurring opinion; Lamer J. also wrote a concurring opinion.

secondary schools, which at the time were being funded to grade 10 only. This was attacked on the ground that it was a violation of s. 15 to confer a benefit on Roman Catholic separate school supporters, a class defined by their religion. In Ontario, at that time, the non-denominational public school system also received full public funding, but denominational schools other than the Roman Catholic schools did not. The Supreme Court of Canada unanimously upheld the statute on the basis that the distinctive treatment of Roman Catholic school supporters was expressly permitted by the Constitution.

The province's power to enact laws in relation to education came from s. 93 of the Constitution Act, 1867. However, s. 93 went on to guarantee the rights of Roman Catholic and Protestant school supporters that existed at the time of confederation,[210] and subsection (3) of s. 93 made reference to any system of separate schools "thereafter established", meaning established after confederation. The Supreme Court of Canada held, in the words of Estey J., that this language "contemplates that after confederation the Legislature may establish a new system of separate schools or may enlarge an existing system of separate schools".[211] This power, if it was to be exercised, required the Legislature to distinguish between school supporters on the basis of religion. Estey J. drew an analogy with s. 91(24) (Indians, and lands reserved for the Indians), pointing out (without referring to *Drybones*) that s. 91(24) "authorizes the Parliament of Canada to legislate for the benefit of the Indian population in a preferential, discriminatory, or distinctive fashion vis à vis others".[212] The Charter of Rights, he held, "cannot be interpreted as rendering unconstitutional distinctions that are expressly permitted by the Constitution Act, 1867".[213]

It seems clear, therefore, that the Charter of Rights, although adopted later in time than the Constitution Act, 1867, is not to be read as impliedly repealing or amending those provisions of the earlier instrument that are inconsistent with the unqualified language of s. 15 (or any other guarantee). Rather, s. 15 is to be read as qualified by the language of the earlier instrument.

(d) Province of residence in ss. 91, 92

A closely related issue, which is discussed more fully in a later section of this chapter,[214] is whether distinctions based on a person's province of residence could amount to discrimination under s. 15. To the extent that a claim of discri-

---

210 Wilson J., but not Estey or Lamer JJ., gave as a second reason for decision that full funding was a right guaranteed by s. 93(1), and protected from Charter attack by s. 29 of the Charter of Rights. This ground of decision is discussed in ch. 54, Education, under heading 54.4(c), "Regulation", below.

211 [1987] 1 S.C.R. 1148, 1202; Wilson J. at 1176 is to the same effect; and Lamer J. at 1209 agrees with Wilson J. on this issue.

212 *Id.*, 1206.

213 *Id.*, 1207.

214 Section 52.16, "Place of residence", below.

mination involves comparing the treatment accorded by the law of the claimant's province with the (more beneficial) treatment accorded by the law of another province, such a claim is a contradiction of the federal principle, under which the laws of each province are permitted to differ from each other. Differences between provincial laws cannot amount to discrimination under s. 15, because that would require a uniformity of provincial laws which would be inconsistent with the distribution of legislative powers in ss. 91 and 92 (and some other sections) of the Constitution Act, 1867. The federal system thus operates as a general qualification of s. 15's guarantee of equality.

(e) Citizenship in s. 6

The Charter of Rights itself contains some implicit qualifications of s. 15's guarantee of equality. Because s. 6(1)'s guarantee of the right to remain in Canada applies only to a "citizen", it has been held that the Immigration Act may validly provide for the deportation of non-citizens who have committed criminal offences.[215] The imposition of a burden on non-citizens that does not also apply to citizens would normally be a breach of s. 15,[216] but in the case of the right to remain in Canada a difference in treatment was specifically contemplated by s. 6(1).

(f) Language in ss. 16-23

Another qualification of s. 15 is created by the language rights of ss. 16 to 23 of the Charter. These implement a notion of equality of the French and English languages. However, by implication, they accord a "special status" to French and English "in comparison to all other linguistic groups in Canada".[217] For example, the right to minority language education in s. 23, which is explicitly limited to French and English, does not extend to other minority language speakers by the operation of s. 15.[218] The conferral of a benefit on French-speaking citizens that was denied to German-speaking citizens (for example) would normally be a breach of s. 15,[219] but in the case of the right to minority language education a difference in treatment is specifically contemplated by s. 23.

---

215 *Can.* v. *Chiarelli* [1992] S.C.R. .

216 Citizenship was held to be an analogous ground of discrimination in *Andrews* v. *Law Society of B.C.* [1989] 1 S.C.R. 143

217 *Mahe* v. *Alta.* [1990] 1 S.C.R. 342, 369 per Dickson C.J.

218 *Ibid.*

219 I am assuming that language would be an analogous ground of discrimination; in some circumstances, there might be room for argument about whether a person's language is an immutable personal characteristic.

52.10 Race

"Race", as well as "national or ethnic origin" and "colour", is one of the grounds of discrimination that is expressly prohibited by s. 15. A racial distinction in a statute would be upheld if the statute established an affirmative action programme within the terms of s. 15(2), and might be upheld under s. 1 if the statute fell outside the strict terms of s. 15(2) but pursued a benign purpose of an affirmative action kind. Otherwise, it is difficult to imagine a situation in which racial discrimination could possibly be upheld.

The situation of the aboriginal peoples[220] is a special one. The Constitution Act, 1867, by s. 91(24), empowers the federal Parliament to make laws in relation to "Indians, and lands reserved for the Indians". We have already noticed the point that any law enacted under that head will either explicitly employ the racial classification "Indian" or will have disparate impact on Indians who live on "lands reserved for the Indians".[221] The special status of aboriginal peoples has been reinforced by the adoption of s. 35 of the Constitution Act, 1982, which guarantees "aboriginal and treaty rights". Such rights are restricted to aboriginal peoples, who are of course defined by their race. This is recognized by s. 25 of the Charter of Rights, which provides that the Charter should not be construed so as to abrogate or derogate from "any aboriginal, treaty or other rights or freedoms that pertain to the aboriginal peoples of Canada". By reason of these provisions, s. 15 has only a limited role to play with respect to aboriginal peoples. A law enacted by the federal Parliament under s. 91(24) for the benefit of Indian people, and laws enacted to give effect to aboriginal or treaty rights, are not affected by s. 15 of the Charter.

52.11 Religion

"Religion" is another of the grounds of discrimination that is expressly prohibited by s. 15. The public funding of the schools of a religious denomination without comparable provision for the supporters of the schools of other religious denominations would be forbidden by s. 15.[222] However, we have already noticed[223] the special provisions of s. 93 of the Constitution Act, 1867, which guarantee the rights of the supporters of denominational schools that existed at the time of confederation, and which authorize the enlargement of those rights. To the extent that a denominational school system is protected, or even contemplated, by s. 93, no s. 15 challenge is open.

The Charter of Rights, by s. 2(a), guarantees "freedom of conscience and religion". In chapter 39, Religion, we noticed that s. 2(a) has been held to be

220 See generally ch. 27, Aboriginal Peoples, above.
221 Section 52.9(b), "Race in s. 91(24)", above.
222 See also ch. 39, Religion, under heading 39.8, "Denominational schools", above.
223 Section 52.9(c), "Religion in s. 93", above.

abridged by Sunday observance laws and by religious exercises in public schools. In very general terms, the reasoning was that the endorsement of Christian beliefs indirectly burdened those who did not accept those beliefs. These cases could easily be viewed as equality cases in which benefits are conferred on Christians that are denied to the adherents of other religions.

52.12 Sex

(a) Direct discrimination

"Sex" is another of the grounds of discrimination that is expressly prohibited by s. 15.

The equality guarantee of the Canadian Bill of Rights gave rise to two cases of sexual discrimination. The first case was *A.G. Can.* v. *Lavell* (1973),[224] in which a challenge was brought against the provisions of the Indian Act that provide for the transmission of Indian status. The Act provided that an Indian woman who married a non-Indian man lost her Indian status, whereas an Indian man who married a non-Indian woman did not. This challenge was rejected by the Court on the basis of a theory of equality[225] that need not detain us since it is obviously indefensible and was later abandoned by the Court. The discriminatory provisions of the Indian Act were subsequently held by an international tribunal to be in violation of the International Covenant on Civil and Political Rights; and they were repealed in 1985.[226]

The second case was *Bliss* v. *A.G. Can.* (1979),[227] in which a challenge was brought to a provision of the Unemployment Insurance Act, which denied ordinary unemployment benefits to women whose employment was interrupted by pregnancy. (The Act did provide maternity benefits, but there was a longer period of qualification for them, a period designed to limit the benefits to women who were already employed when they became pregnant.) This challenge was rejected by the Court on the basis that the disadvantaged class was defined by pregnancy rather than by sex. This reasoning has been generally criticized. Since pregnancy is a condition to which only women are vulnerable, any disadvantage premised on pregnancy should be characterized as discrimination by sex. This criticism has been accepted by the Supreme Court of Canada, which in a Human Rights Code decision has overruled *Bliss*.[228]

---

224 [1974] S.C.R. 1349.

225 The theory was that "equality *before* the law", the phrase used in s. 1(b) of the Canadian Bill of Rights, only prohibited discrimination in the administration of a law, and did not permit the law itself to be struck down. Of course, in the earlier case of *R.* v. *Drybones* [1970] S.C.R. 282, the law itself had been struck down.

226 See ch. 27, Aboriginal Peoples, under heading 27.1(b), "Indians", above.

227 [1979] 1 S.C.R. 183.

228 *Brooks* v. *Can. Safeway* [1987] 1 S.C.R. 1219 (exclusion of pregnant women from employee group health insurance plan held to be discrimination on the basis of sex).

Although *Bliss* itself has been overruled, its line of reasoning has been employed under s. 15 of the Charter of Rights. In *R.* v. *Hess* (1990),[229] a majority of the Supreme Court of Canada held that the offence of statutory rape (intercourse with a female person under the age of 14) did not offend s. 15, although the offence could only be committed by ''a male person''. Wilson J. for the majority held that, since the prohibited act (''intercourse'') was defined by reference to penetration, it could as a matter of biological fact be committed only by males. Therefore, she concluded, it was not discriminatory to subject only male persons to the offence. Is this not the *Bliss* argument all over again? The imposition of a disability by reference to a biological characteristic of only one sex (such as pregnancy or penetration) is held not to be discrimination by sex. The offence could easily have been recast to include acts of intercourse by older women with young boys. McLachlin J. for a concurring minority did not accept Wilson J.'s reasoning. In McLachlin J.'s view, the offence did constitute discrimination by sex, although it could be justified under s. 1 as a measure for the protection of young females who, unlike young males, would run the risk of pregnancy through intercourse. With respect, McLachlin J.'s reasoning seems sound.

In *Weatherall* v. *Canada*,[230] a prisoner in a federal penitentiary for men challenged the constitutionality of frisk searches and cell surveillance of male prisoners by female guards.[231] This was said to be an affront to the dignity of the prisoners, and to be discriminatory, because female prisoners were searched and observed only by guards of the same sex. La Forest J. for the Supreme Court of Canada pointed out (without referring to s. 28) that equality did not demand that men and women always be treated in the same way, and the effect of cross-gender searching was ''different and more threatening for women than for men''.[232] He did not seem to be entirely convinced by this reasoning, because he concluded only that there ''may not be'' discrimination, and that it was ''doubtful'' that s. 15 had been violated.[233] But he held that, even if there was a breach of s. 15, it was saved by s. 1. The ''humanizing effect'' of having women in male prisons and the enhancement of ''employment equity'' constituted sufficient justification[234] for the practices.[235]

---

229 [1990] 2 S.C.R. 906; see also the fuller discussion at note 170, above.

230 [1993] 2 S.C.R. 872.

231 A challenge under s. 8 was rejected on the ground that a prisoner had no reasonable expectation of privacy with respect to the searches and surveillance.

232 [1993] 2 S.C.R. 872, 877.

233 *Id.*, 877-878.

234 *Id.*, 878. No evidence was referred to in support of these findings; nor was it explained why these findings outweighed the assumed breach of equality rights; nor was it explained how the ''prescribed by law'' requirement of s. 1 was satisfied.

235 See also *Native Women's Assn. of Can.* v. *Can.* [1994] 3 S.C.R. 627 (claim of sex discrimination in funding rejected); the case is discussed in ch. 40, Expression, under heading 40.20, ''Access to government'', above.

(b) Systemic discrimination

The raising of consciousness about the position of women in society has led to the removal from the Canadian statute books of most provisions that create formal inequalities between the sexes. Those few that remain will undoubtedly be reviewed by the courts under s. 15. Where a statutory provision that is gender-neutral on its face gives rise to a disproportionately adverse impact on women, s. 15 review will also be available by reason of the rules, discussed earlier,[236] that discrimination may be unintended, that discrimination may be systematic and that discrimination may require reasonable accommodation to be made to accommodate a special condition (such as pregnancy). To the extent that discrimination against women takes place in the private sphere from which the Charter is excluded, any remedy would have to lie under the Human Rights Codes. In fact, as we have already noticed,[237] it has been in proceedings initiated by women under the Human Rights Codes that the Supreme Court of Canada has established the expansive rules respecting discrimination which now apply to s. 15 as well as to the Codes.[238]

In *Symes* v. *Canada* (1993),[239] it was argued that the Income Tax Act offended s. 15 of the Charter by not allowing businesspersons to deduct the full cost of child care. The Act allowed a deduction for child care, but it was limited to $2,000 per child in 1985 (the taxation year in issue). The taxpayer, a self-employed female lawyer with two children, had in fact paid $13,000 to a nanny to care for her children. In the Supreme Court of Canada, L'Heureux-Dubé and McLachlin JJ. (the only two female judges) held that, because women were more likely than men to bear child care responsibilities, the Act's denial of full deductibility for child care expenses had an adverse impact on women. The two judges concluded that the statutory provision, although neutral on its face, was in its effect discriminatory on the basis of sex. However, this was a dissenting view. The majority of the Court, in an opinion written by Iacobucci J., acknowledged that women disproportionately bore the *social* costs of child care, but held that the taxpayer had not established that women disproportionately bore the *financial* costs of child care. Since the deduction would be available with respect only to the financial costs of child care, it would benefit men as much as women, and its restriction did not amount to discrimination on the basis of sex.

---

236 These rules have been discussed in sec. 52.7, ''Discrimination'', above.

237 *Ibid.*

238 Note as well that s. 15 can sometimes reach private action indirectly by extending the reach of a Human Rights Code. This happened in *Blainey* v. *Ont. Hockey Assn.* (1986) 54 O.R. (2d) 513 (C.A.) (striking down provision of Human Rights Code permitting sex-segregated hockey teams). See generally text accompanying note 50, above.

239 [1993] 4 S.C.R. 695. Iacobucci J. wrote the opinion of the majority. L'Heureux-Dubé and McLachlin JJ. wrote dissenting opinions.

(c) Section 28

Section 28 of the Charter of Rights[240] provides as follows:

28. Notwithstanding anything in this Charter, the rights and freedoms referred to in it are guaranteed equally to male and female persons. Section 28 provides that the rights and freedoms referred to in the Charter ''are guaranteed equally to male and female persons''.[241] This falls short of a requirement of the equal treatment of ''male and female persons'', presumably because that objective is attained by the general equality clause of s. 15. All that s. 28 seems to require is that the other provisions of the Charter[242] be implemented without discrimination between the sexes. To the extent that the other provisions of the Charter would apply equally to male and female persons anyway, s. 28 has very little work to do.

Within its narrow sphere of application, s. 28 is a stronger guarantee than s. 15 in at least two, and perhaps three, respects: (1) the three-year delay in the coming into force of s. 15 (by virtue of s. 32(2)) did not apply to s. 28; (2) the power of legislative override (under s. 33) applies to s. 15, but not to s. 28;[243] and (3) it is possible that even the limitation clause (s. 1) does not qualify s. 28, having regard to s. 28's opening words, ''Notwithstanding anything in this Charter''.

240 For commentary on s. 28, see Gibson, note 35, above, 206-212; Bayefsky and Eberts, note 35, above, ch. 11 (by de Jong); Beaudoin and Mendes, note 35, above, 14-69–14-71 (by Black and Smith); McLeod, note 35, above, ch. 27; *Canadian Charter of Rights Annotated*, note 35, above, annotation to s. 28.

241 Section 28 has no equivalent in the Canadian Bill of Rights or in the American Bill of Rights. However, it was inspired by the Equal Rights Amendment, which was proposed by the Congress of the United States on March 22, 1972, and which was still being considered for ratification by the states when the Charter was drafted. The proposal subsequently lapsed, because it failed to secure ratification by three-fourths of the state legislatures by the deadline of June 30, 1982. The terms of the proposed amendment were as follows:

> Article —
>
> Section 1. Equality of rights under the law shall not be denied or abridged by the United States or by any State on account of sex.
>
> Section 2. The Congress shall have the power to enforce, by appropriate legislation, the provisions of this article.
>
> Section 3. This amendment shall take effect two years after the date of ratification.

242 The Charter does not include s. 35 of the Constitution Act, 1982, which guarantees native rights. However, by an amendment in 1984, s. 35(4) was added, which provides that:

> Notwithstanding any other provision of this Act, the aboriginal and treaty rights referred to in subsection (1) are guaranteed equally to male and female persons.

243 Section 28 was not in the October 1980 version of the Charter, but was in the April 1981 version. At the federal-provincial agreement of November 5, 1981, when the override clause of s. 33 was first agreed to, the first draft of the override clause authorized the override not only of ss. 2 and 7 to 15, but also of ''section 28 of this Charter in its application to discrimination based on sex referred to in section 15''. This provoked a vigorous round of lobbying by women's groups, and the reference to s. 28 was removed from s. 33.

52.13 Age

"Age" is another of the grounds of discrimination that is expressly prohibited by s. 15.

Like the other grounds of discrimination, age is a personal characteristic that is immutable in the sense that it cannot be changed by the choice of the individual. There are, however, two differences between age and the other named grounds of discrimination.[244] First, age is a characteristic shared by everyone. In the course of a normal life span, each individual passes through the various stages of childhood, youth, adulthood, middle age and old age. Each individual of any age has personally experienced all earlier ages and expects to experience the later ages. A minority defined by age is much less likely to suffer from the hostility, intolerance and prejudice of the majority than is a minority defined by race or religion or any other characteristic that the majority has never possessed and will never possess.

A second difference between age and most of the other named characteristics is that there is some correlation between age and ability. That is not true of race, national or ethnic origin, colour, religion or sex, although it is true of mental or physical disability. In fact, our laws are replete with provisions in which age is employed as the qualification for pursuits that require skill or judgment. Consider the laws regulating voting, driving, drinking, marrying, contracting, will-making, leaving school, being employed, etc. In regulating these matters, all jurisdictions impose disabilities on young people, employing age as a proxy for ability. Such stereotyping is inevitably inaccurate, because individuals mature at different rates. In principle, the use of age could be eliminated, because each individual could be tested for performance of each function. Age is used as a qualification for no other reason than to avoid or reduce the administrative burden of individualized testing.

Disabilities imposed on young people by reference to the attainment of a qualifying age do have to be regarded as discrimination under s. 15, since a disadvantage is imposed by reference to a named ground of discrimination, but it is to be hoped that the Supreme Court of Canada would readily uphold them under s. 1, despite the Court's ill-considered claim that administrative expediency does not count towards s. 1 justification.[245]

Advancing age also leads to a decline in ability, culminating in death. This is reflected in the widespread adoption in workplaces of mandatory retirement rules, typically requiring an employee to retire at the age of 65. These rules are reinforced by pay scales that increase with seniority, by relatively lax assessment procedures for workers drawing near to retirement, by private and public pension

---

244 See the discussion by La Forest J. in *McKinney* v. *U. of Guelph* [1990] 3 S.C.R. 229, 296-297.

245 See the discussion of "cost" in ch. 35, Limitation of Rights, under heading 35.9, "Sufficiently important objective", above.

schemes that commence payment at the retirement age and by Human Rights Codes that withdraw their prohibitions on age discrimination at the age of 65.

The Supreme Court of Canada decided a group of four mandatory requirement cases in 1990. The principal decision was *McKinney* v. *University of Guelph* (1990),[246] in which a number of university professors in Ontario challenged the mandatory retirement policies of their universities. The second case[247] involved the same issue in universities in British Columbia. The third case[248] involved the admitting privileges of doctors at a hospital in British Columbia. The fourth case[249] involved professors at a community college in British Columbia. The first three cases were all held to be outside the scope of the Charter, because the universities and the hospital operated outside the control of government. Only the fourth case was within the scope of the Charter, because the community college was more tightly controlled by government than the other institutions. (These are leading cases on the application of the Charter, and are discussed from that standpoint in chapter 34, Application of Charter, above.) Despite the fact that the Charter did not apply to the universities and the hospital, the Court went on to examine the constitutionality of mandatory retirement in those institutions[250] as if s. 15 did apply. The Court held unanimously that mandatory retirement was discrimination by age and was therefore in violation of s. 15, but the Court by a majority[251] went on to decide that mandatory retirement was saved by s. 1. The result, therefore, was that mandatory retirement was upheld.

The Supreme Court of Canada in *McKinney* and the other mandatory retirement cases had no difficulty in finding discrimination within s. 15 of the Charter. The mandatory retirement rules imposed a disadvantage (retirement)[252] on a defined group by its age (65), and age was one of the grounds of discrimination named in s. 15. Therefore, there was a breach of s. 15. The issue then moved to s. 1. Could the mandatory retirement rules be justified as a reasonable limit that was demonstrably justified in a free and democratic society? The majority of the Court answered yes. Within the universities, the rules permitted faculty renewal

---

246 [1990] 3 S.C.R. 229.

247 *Harrison* v. *U.B.C.* [1990] 3 S.C.R. 451.

248 *Stoffman* v. *Vancouver General Hospital* [1990] 3 S.C.R. 483.

249 *Douglas/Kwantlen Faculty Assn.* v. *Douglas College* [1990] 3 S.C.R. 570.

250 In *Douglas*, previous note, the issue was not reached, because the only question before the Court was whether an arbitration board had jurisdiction to determine the Charter issue; the Court held that the board did have jurisdiction.

251 In *McKinney*, note 246, above, on the s. 1 issue, La Forest J., with the agreement of Dickson C.J. and Gonthier J., wrote the plurality judgment; Sopinka and Cory JJ. wrote separate concurring judgments; Wilson and L'Heureux-Dubé JJ. wrote dissenting opinions. (The Court divided differently on the s. 32 issue.) The same division occurred in Harrison, note 247, above, where the issues were exactly the same. The same division occurred in *Stoffman*, note 248, above, except that Cory J. moved into the dissenting camp, because of the absence of tenure for doctors in hospitals.

252 As to whether mandatory retirement is a disadvantage, see note 134 and accompanying test, above.

by opening up positions for younger faculty, and they supported tenure (or employment security) by minimizing the need for continuous performance assessments of older faculty.[253] Within the hospital, the arguments were essentially the same: the termination of admitting privileges for doctors who had reached 65 created openings for younger doctors, and (despite the absence of a formal system of tenure) reduced the need for regular assessments of the competence of older doctors.

In *Tétreault-Gadoury* v. *Canada* (1991),[254] the question arose whether a provision of the Unemployment Insurance Act, which denied benefits to persons over 65, was in breach of s. 15. The Supreme Court of Canada followed *McKinney* to hold that the provision violated s. 15. However, the Court departed from *McKinney* to hold that the age-65 bar could not be justified under s. 1. The result was to strike from the Act the provision imposing the age-65 bar.

The rejection of s. 1 justification in *Tétreault-Gadoury* suggests that age distinctions are vulnerable to Charter attack, and even that mandatory retirement in workplaces other than universities (and hospitals) may be unjustified under s. 1. The Court distinguished *McKinney* on three grounds: (1) that a university was ''a closed system with limited resources''; (2) that ''faculty renewal'' was ''crucial to extending the frontiers of knowledge''; and (3) that ''academic freedom'' required a minimum of performance review up to retirement age.[255] These points, especially the second and third, would be inapplicable in non-university workplaces, both public and private. Of course, other justifications might be persuasive in other contexts. In *Tétreault-Gadoury*, however, the Court rejected what seemed to me to be a powerful justification for the age-bar, which was to prevent the doubling up of pension income and unemployment insurance benefits. The applicant in that case was in fact receiving pension income, presumably as a consequence of having attained age 65.

In *Tétreault-Gadoury*, the Court seemed to forget the salutary point that judicial intervention in the complex field of employee retirement is bound to be clumsy, and is likely to produce counterproductive results. If mandatory retirement is unconstitutional in some workplaces, and if benefit programmes cannot be stopped (or started?) at age 65, various consequences are likely to follow. If an employee cannot be counted upon to leave at age 65 (or other arbitrary age),

253 A provision of Ontario's Human Rights Code, which excluded persons aged over 65 from the protection against age discrimination in employment, was also upheld on the basis that it was designed to permit (not require) mandatory retirement. In *Dickason* v. *U. of Alta.* [1992] 2 S.C.R. 1003, the Supreme Court of Canada upheld mandatory retirement at the University of Alberta in the face of Alberta's Human Rights Code, which prohibited age discrimination in employment (without any upper limit to the age), but which authorized ''reasonable and justifiable'' arrangements; the majority of the Court followed *McKinney* to hold that mandatory retirement was reasonable and justifiable.

254 [1991] 2 S.C.R. 22. The opinion of La Forest J. was agreed to by all members of the Court. L'Heureux-Dubé J. added brief concurring reasons not germane to the s. 15 issue.

255 *Id.*, 44.

then employee incomes would have to rise more slowly with seniority than they now do, employee performance would have to be monitored more closely than it is now, and the incentive for employers and governments to provide adequate pensions for retired workers would be diminished. No court can adequately measure these effects and weigh them against age-based mandatory retirement.

52.14 Mental or physical disability

Mental or physical disability is another of the grounds of discrimination that is expressly prohibited by s. 15. Like the other grounds of discrimination, mental or physical disability is immutable in the sense that it cannot be changed by the choice of the individual. It is not necessarily immutable in an absolute sense, since the condition may be curable. Unlike the other grounds of discrimination, mental or physical disability is, by definition, an impairment in ability; and some legal restrictions may properly be predicated on mental or physical disability. For example, a blind person is properly disqualified from holding a driver's licence; and a mentally incompetent person is properly disqualified from making a will. On the other hand, many disabilities can be accommodated by changes to workplaces and public facilities that permit those who are blind, deaf or in wheelchairs (for example) to function effectively. Thus, the rules that discrimination may be unintended, may be systemic, and may require reasonable accommodation,[256] are of special importance for this ground of discrimination.

In *Rodriguez* v. *British Columbia* (1993),[257] a plaintiff, who suffered from a debilitating, fatal disease (Lou Gehrig's disease), challenged the constitutionality of the Criminal Code offence of assisting a person to commit suicide. She pointed out that this provision had the effect of prohibiting the commission of suicide by a person who was so physically disabled that she was unable to kill herself without assistance. Able-bodied persons, by contrast, were free to commit suicide (neither suicide nor attempted suicide is a Criminal Code offence), because they could do so without assistance. She argued that the prohibition on assisting suicide discriminated on the ground of physical disability, and was unconstitutional by virtue of s. 15.[258] In the Supreme Court of Canada, this argument was accepted by Lamer C.J. and Cory J., who dissented.[259] Sopinka J., who wrote for the majority, did not deal with the argument, contenting himself with the holding that the prohibition would in any case be justified under s. 1. The prohibition was therefore upheld.

---

256 See sec. 52.7, "Discrimination", above.

257 [1993] 3 S.C.R. 519.

258 The law was also unsuccessfully challenged under s. 7 (see secs. 44.8, 44.10(b), above) and s. 12 (see sec. 50.2, above).

259 McLachlin J., with L'Heureux-Dubé J., also dissented, but she relied exclusively on s. 7, asserting (rather cryptically) (at 616) that "this is not at base a case about discrimination under s. 15". However, her reasoning under s. 7 was strikingly similar to Lamer C.J.'s under s. 15.

52.15 Citizenship

Citizenship is not a ground of discrimination that is expressly mentioned in s. 15, but we know that it is analogous to those that are expressly mentioned, because the Supreme Court of Canada so held in *Andrews* v. *Law Society of British Columbia* (1989).[260] In that case, the Court decided that the requirement of British Columbia law that a person be a Canadian citizen as a qualification for admission to the bar of the province was a breach of s. 15 (and was not justified by s. 1). The case establishes the rule that s. 15 prohibits discrimination on the basis not only of the named grounds but also of grounds analogous to the named grounds. The case is the leading case on the interpretation of s. 15, and it has been fully examined earlier in this chapter, mostly in the discussion of the concept of ''discrimination''.[261]

52.16 Place of residence

Does s. 15 prohibit distinctions between individuals based on their place of residence? Place of residence is not one of the grounds of discrimination listed in s. 15. We have already noticed the case of *R.* v. *Turpin* (1989),[262] in which there is an inconclusive reference to the possibility that place of residence could ''in some circumstances'' be a ground of discrimination analogous to those listed in s. 15, in which case it would be prohibited by s. 15. However, in my discussion of that case, I suggested that the better view is that place of residence lacks the element of immutability that is common to the listed grounds, and is required for the analogous grounds. If that view is correct, then distinctions based on an individual's place of residence could never offend s. 15. In case that view is incorrect, it is worth pointing out that place of residence raises some distinctive considerations in a federal state.

Differences in the treatment of individuals that are caused by federalism must be able to be accommodated by the Charter of Rights.[263] It cannot be a breach of s. 15 that the minimum wage is higher in Manitoba than it is in Prince Edward Island, or that nurses have the right to strike in Ontario but not in Alberta. These differences flow from the fact that labour law is a matter coming within property and civil rights in the province, which is one of the topics allocated to the jurisdiction of provincial Legislatures by s. 92 of the Constitution Act, 1867. The federal distribution of powers is a fundamental characteristic of the Constitution of Canada. Differences between provincial laws are the inevitable outcome of ten provincial Legislatures, each exercising extensive legislative authority,

260 [1989] 1 S.C.R. 143.

261 See sec. 52.7, ''Discrimination'', above.

262 [1989] 1 S.C.R. 1296; discussed at note 119, above.

263 See sec. 52.9, ''Discrimination permitted by Constitution'', above.

each acting independently, and each accountable to a different local population. "There can be no question, then, that unequal treatment which stems solely from the exercise, by provincial legislators, of their legitimate jurisdictional powers cannot be the subject of a s. 15(1) challenge on the basis only that it creates distinctions based on province of residence".[264]

If federalism must be an exception to the guarantee of equality, how far does the exception extend? As a minimum, federalism must preclude an argument that involves comparing the law of one province with the law of another province. As argued in the previous paragraph, that line of argument is inadmissible under s. 15. The same conclusion would seem to follow when the Charter claim involves a comparison between a federal law and a provincial law. Once again, two independent legislative bodies, exercising the jurisdictions conferred on them by the Constitution Act, 1867, responding to different electorates, will inevitably produce different outcomes, and s. 15 ought not to be interpreted as denying such a basic federal fact.[265]

Does s. 15 require that federal laws be uniform across the country? In areas of federal jurisdiction, the federal Parliament has the authority to enact uniform national laws. However, apart from the effect of the equality guarantee, there is no constitutional requirement that federal laws must apply uniformly across the country, and in fact many federal laws do not do so.[266] In *R.* v. *S.(S.)* (1990),[267] the Supreme Court of Canada considered the question of whether the Parliament of Canada could make distinctions between different provinces without offending the equality guarantee.[268] At issue was a provision of the federal Young Offenders Act, which authorized the Attorney General of each province to establish a programme of "alternative measures" to divert young offenders away from the courts. Not only did this provision contemplate that different provinces would establish different programmes, it also permitted a province to establish no programme at all. A young offender in Ontario, where there was no programme, argued that the failure of Ontario to establish a programme, when nine other

---

264 *R.* v. *S.(S.)* [1990] 2 S.C.R. 254, 288 per Dickson C.J. (obiter dictum).

265 This issue arose in two cases under the Canadian Bill of Rights, in which the federal Indian Act was compared with the law applicable to non-Indians, which was territorial law in *R.* v. *Drybones* [1970] S.C.R. 282 (Indian Act drunkenness offence struck down), and provincial law in *A.G. Can.* v. *Canard* [1976] 1 S.C.R. 170 (Indian Act succession rules upheld). The issue was ignored by the majority in *Drybones*, although adverted to by Pigeon J. in dissent; and the issue attracted a variety of opinions in *Canard*.

266 See ch. 17, Peace, Order, and Good Government, under heading 17.3(b), "Definition of national concern", above.

267 [1990] 2 S.C.R. 254.

268 Province-based distinctions in federal laws had been upheld under the equality guarantee of the Canadian Bill of Rights: *R.* v. *Burnshine* [1975] 1 S.C.R. 693; *R.* v. *Cornell* [1988] 1 S.C.R. 461. However, the pre-*Andrews* cases in provincial courts of appeal had sometimes struck down such distinctions under s. 15: e.g., *R.* v. *Hamilton* (1986) 57 O.R. (2d) 412 (C.A.); *R.* v. *Frohman* (1987) 60 O.R. (2d) 125 (C.A.); *Re French in Criminal Proceedings* (1987) 44 D.L.R. (4th) 16 (Sask. C.A.).

provinces had done so, was a violation of his equality right under s. 15. This argument was rejected by the Court for reasons not germane to the present topic.[269]

In *S.*, no challenge was actually made to the provisions of the Young Offenders Act that authorized the establishment (or non-establishment) of differing provincial diversion programmes. However, Dickson C.J., for a unanimous Court, went on to discuss the question. After noting that differences between *provincial* laws could never amount to discrimination because of the federal principle,[270] he pointed out that province-based distinctions in *federal* laws could also be "a legitimate means of forwarding the values of a federal system".[271] This was especially so in the field of criminal justice, where "the balancing of national interests and local concerns has been accomplished by a constitutional structure that both permits and encourages federal-provincial co-operation".[272] He concluded that the diversion-programmes authority in the Young Offenders Act was an appropriate reflection of federal values, allowing as it did the adoption of diversion programmes that were suitable to the particular needs of local communities. Therefore, the distinctions in the Young Offenders Act based on province of residence did not constitute discrimination within s. 15.

In *Haig* v. *Canada* (1993),[273] an equality challenge was made to the federal referendum that was held to approve the set of constitutional amendments known as the Charlottetown Accord. The referendum was held under the authority of a federal statute, which authorized the federal government (the Governor in Council) to hold a referendum in "one or more provinces". The government held the federal referendum in all provinces (and territories) except for Quebec. The reason for the exclusion of Quebec was that Quebec had enacted its own referendum statute, and the province held a provincial referendum on the same question on the same date. Unfortunately, the dual referendums left a gap in coverage. The qualification for voting in the federal election was residence on voting day in one of the nine provinces and two territories that were covered by the federal referendum. The qualification for voting in the Quebec election was residence in Quebec for six months prior to voting day. The plaintiff in *Haig* moved to Quebec from Ontario two months before voting day. The move disqualified him from the federal franchise and did not qualify him for the Quebec franchise. He challenged the constitutionality of the federal referendum's exclusion of Quebec. L'Heureux-Dubé J., who wrote for the majority of the Supreme Court of Canada, quoted and followed Dickson C.J.'s opinion in *S.* Without examining the reasons that led to the exclusion of Quebec from the federal referendum, she assumed that the decision not to apply the federal referendum law in all of the provinces was a

269 Note 41, above, and accompanying text.

270 Note 264, above.

271 [1990] 2 S.C.R. 254, 289.

272 *Id.*, 290.

273 [1993] 2 S.C.R. 995. The opinion of the majority was written by L'Heureux-Dubé J. The two concurring opinions of Cory and McLachlin JJ. and the two dissenting opinions of Lamer C.J. and Iacobucci J. did not need to address the equality argument.

legitimate reflection of "the values of a federal system";[274] she concluded that the decision could not be attacked under s. 15.

The opinions in *S.* and *Haig* do not say that every province-based distinction in a federal law is invulnerable to s. 15 attack. However, the opinions make clear that differences between the provinces do not disappear in fields of federal jurisdiction. Even if province of residence is a personal characteristic that could be the basis of discrimination under s. 15, it seems obvious that distinctions in federal laws based on province of residence would usually be accepted as a proper reflection of federal values. Distinctions based on province of residence that are caused by different laws in different provinces will always be accepted as an inevitable outcome of a federal system.

274 *Id.*, 1047.

53

Language

53.1 Introduction

Language[1] has been a controversial issue throughout the history of British North America, and the controversy continues to this day. It could hardly be

1 See Hogg, ''Constitutional Power over Language'' in Law Society of Upper Canada, *The Constitution and the Future of Canada* (Special Lectures, 1978), 229. Parts of the following text are based on this article.

otherwise in a country settled by two different language groups. Because English-speakers constitute a majority in the country as a whole, and French-speakers constitute a majority in the province of Quebec, it is important to determine the distribution-of-powers question of which level of government has the constitutional authority to legislate in respect of language. Because French-speakers constitute a minority in the country as a whole and in every province except Quebec, and English-speakers constitute a minority in the province of Quebec, it is important to determine whether there is constitutional protection for the language of the minority. While English and French, as the languages of the European founders, have been given special constitutional recognition, it must not be overlooked that these questions are also important for the aboriginal peoples, who were here long before the European ''founders'',[2] and for those immigrant groups that have arrived since confederation and have continued to use their language of origin.

The scheme of this chapter will be, first, to examine the distribution of powers over language, and, secondly, to examine the constitutional protections for minority languages.

53.2 Distribution of powers

It is a remarkable fact that language is not one of the classes of subjects (or heads of legislative power) which the Constitution Act, 1867 enumerates and distributes to the two levels of government. Of course, language could still be held to be a ''matter'' coming within one of the classes of subjects which are enumerated. The most likely candidate is ''property and civil rights in the province'' (s. 92(13)), which would mean that the provincial Legislatures had the legislative power. Or language could be held to be a matter which is outside any of the enumerated classes of subjects and which therefore comes within the peace, order, and good government power (s. 91's opening words); this would mean that the federal Parliament had the legislative power.

It is now clear from the decided cases that neither of these solutions is correct. The cases decide that language is not an independent matter of legislation (or constitutional value). Therefore, there is no single plenary power to enact laws in relation to language. Instead, the power to enact a law affecting language is divided between the two levels of government by reference to criteria other than the impact of the law upon language. On this basis, a law prescribing that a particular language or languages must or may be used in certain situations will be classified

2 The right to speak aboriginal languages is probably protected by s. 35 of the Constitution Act, 1982, which guarantees aboriginal and treaty rights. See generally ch. 27, Aboriginal Peoples, above.

for constitutional purposes not as a law in relation to language, but as a law in relation to the institutions or activities that the provision covers.[3]

In *Jones* v. *Attorney General of New Brunswick* (1974),[4] the Supreme Court of Canada upheld the federal Official Languages Act. The Act purported to make the English and French languages the official languages of Canada "in the institutions of the Parliament and Government of Canada". In a unanimous opinion written by Laskin C.J., the Court held that the law was authorized by federal power over federal governmental and parliamentary institutions (which stemmed from the peace, order, and good government power). Provisions recognizing both languages in federal courts could also be authorized by federal power over federal courts (s. 101), and provisions concerning languages in criminal proceedings in provincial courts could also be authorized by the federal power over criminal procedure (s. 91(27)). In the same case, the Court upheld a section of New Brunswick's Official Languages Act, which provided for the use of both official languages in the courts of New Brunswick; this section was authorized by the provincial power over the administration of justice in the province (s. 92(14)).[5]

It is true that in *Jones* the Court did not have to decide, and expressly left open, the question whether the federal Parliament would have the power "to give official status and equality to English and French throughout Canada and in respect of any operations or activities which are otherwise within provincial competence".[6] This dictum does leave open the possibility that a broader language law might be sustainable on the footing that the subject of language had attained a national concern which brought it within the peace, order, and good government power of the federal Parliament. However, since *Jones* was decided, the Court has held that the peace, order, and good government power should be confined to subjects of legislation that are relatively narrow and specific;[7] and it seems likely that the subject of language would be too broad to qualify.[8]

In *Devine* v. *Quebec* (1988),[9] the Supreme Court of Canada upheld various provisions of Quebec's Charter of the French Language that regulated the language of commerce; they required the use of the French language in public signs, commercial advertising, catalogues, brochures, orders, invoices, receipts and other commercial forms. The Court accepted the view, expressed in an earlier edition of this book, that "for constitutional purposes language is ancillary to the purpose for which it is used, and the language law is for constitutional purposes

3 This passage in the 2nd edition (1985) of this book was approved by the Supreme Court of Canada in *Devine* v. *Que.* [1988] 2 S.C.R. 790, 807-808.

4 [1975] 2 S.C.R. 182.

5 Some of the provisions of the two Official Languages Acts have now been constitutionalized in ss. 16-20 of the Charter of Rights, which are discussed later in this chapter.

6 [1975] 2 S.C.R. 182, 187.

7 Chapter 17, Peace, Order and Good Government, under heading 17.3, "The national concern branch", above.

8 Lederman, *Continuing Canadian Constitutional Dilemmas* (1981), 298.

9 [1988] 2 S.C.R. 790.

a law in relation to the institutions or activities to which the law applies''.[10] In this case, the challenged provisions were in relation to commerce within the province, which was a matter within the provincial jurisdiction over property and civil rights in the province(s. 92(13)).[11]

If it seems odd that such an important topic as language is not one of the classes of subjects enumerated by the Constitution Act, 1867, and is not even an independent ''matter'' or constitutional value, it should be noticed that the division of legislative power over language, by denying to either level of government full power over language, constitutes an indirect protection of minority language rights.[12] Of course the protection is quite insufficient, but it is not insignificant. For example, the province of Quebec, in legislating to make French the official language of the province,[13] may be incompetent to apply its law to undertakings within the legislative jurisdiction of the federal Parliament, such as federal governmental agencies, federal Crown corporations, banks, shipping lines, airlines, railways, radio and television stations and other undertakings engaged in interprovincial or international transportation or communication, or otherwise within federal regulatory authority.[14]

I shall now turn to the more direct constitutional protections of minority language rights.

---

10 *Id.*, 808.

11 For distribution of powers purposes, there was no difference between those provisions that required the exclusive use of French (prohibiting English), and those that required the non-exclusive use of French (permitting English as well). However, although all the provisions were held to infringe s. 2(b) of the Charter of Rights (freedom of expression), the exclusive requirements were not saved by s. 1, while the non-exclusive requirements were saved by s. 1. The Charter aspect of the case is discussed in sec. 53.7, ''Language of commerce'', below.

12 This is also true of laws respecting other civil liberties; the impact on civil liberties is normally relegated to an incidental or subordinate position for purposes of constitutional classification: see ch. 31, Civil Liberties, under heading 31.4(b), ''Distribution of powers'', above.

13 Quebec's Charter of the French Language, S.Q. 1977, c. 5, which was enacted in 1977 to give effect to the language policy of the Parti Québécois government, is by far the most sweeping legislation on language which has ever been attempted by a province. It makes French ''the official language of Quebec''; it provides that in most situations everyone has ''a right'' to use, or be communicated with, in French; it makes French ''the language of the legislature and the courts in Quebec'', of the ''civil administration'', of the professions, of work, of commerce and business and of instruction in the schools. All this is laid out in a wealth of detail (there are 232 sections in the Act), including exceptions, transitional provisions and elaborate mechanisms of enforcement by various administrative agencies. The provisions of the Act respecting the Legislature and courts were held to be unconstitutional in *A.-G. Que.* v. *Blaikie* [1979] 2 S.C.R. 1016, note 32, below. The provisions respecting access to English-language schools were held to be unconstitutional in *A.-G. Que.* v. *Que. Protestant School Bds.* [1984] 2 S.C.R. 66, note 142, below. The provisions respecting the language of commercial signs and advertisements were held to be unconstitutional in *Ford* v. *Que.* [1988] 2 S.C.R. 712; note 116, above. For the recent history of language rights in Quebec, see Tetley, ''Language and Education Rights in Quebec and Canada'' (1982) 45 Law and Contemp. Problems 177.

14 See ch. 15, Judicial Review on Federal Grounds, under heading 15.6, ''Interjurisdictional immunity'', above.

53.3 Language of Constitution

The Constitution Act, 1867, like all other constitutional instruments emanating from the United Kingdom before 1982, was enacted in English only.[15] The French version that is to be found in the Appendix to the Revised Statutes of Canada[16] is unofficial.

Section 55 of the Constitution Act, 1982 directs the Minister of Justice to prepare a French version of the English-only parts of the Constitution of Canada, and to put it forward for adoption as an official text by the appropriate amending procedures. Although a French text has been drafted and tabled in Parliament by the Minister of Justice,[17] it has not yet been introduced into the amendment process. So long as the French version of the Constitution Act, 1867 remains unofficial, any discrepancy between the English and French version would have to be resolved by recourse to the English version, because that is the only authoritative one.

The Canada Act 1982 and the Constitution Act, 1982 were enacted by the United Kingdom Parliament in both languages.[18] The Charter of Rights, being Part I of the Constitution Act, 1982, is therefore in both languages. Section 57 of the Constitution Act, 1982 provides that the English and French versions of that Act are ''equally authoritative'', and s. 56 provides that the English and French versions of other parts of the Constitution of Canada that have been enacted in English and French are also ''equally authoritative''. The rule of equal authority is, of course, the only appropriate one for a bilingual country, but it does not tell us how to resolve discrepancies between the English and French versions.

Since confederation, federal statutes have been enacted in both languages, because that was required by s. 133 of the Constitution Act, 1867.[19] The Courts

---

15 The instruments listed in the schedule to the Constitution Act, 1982, which comprise the ''Constitution of Canada'' (see s. 52(2)), include seven Canadian statutes. These were enacted in both English and French, as required by s. 133 of the Constitution Act, 1867. All the other instruments were enacted or made in English only.

16 R.S.C. 1985, Appendix II, No. 5; see also Department of Justice, *A Consolidation of the Constitution Acts, 1867 to 1982* (1996).

17 The Final Report of the French Constitutional Drafting Committee (Department of Justice, Ottawa, 1990) contains a French version of all the parts of the Constitution of Canada that were enacted in English only. The Minister of Justice tabled the report in the House of Commons on December 19, 1990.

18 To be precise, the Canada Act 1982 was enacted in English only, but a French version was appended as Schedule A, and the French version was declared in s. 3 to have ''the same authority *in Canada* as the English version''. The Constitution Act, 1982 was appended as Schedule B; it consisted of an English and a French version, and both versions were declared by s. 57 to be ''equally authoritative''. See generally McEvoy, ''The Charter as a Bilingual Instrument'' (1986) 64 Can. Bar Rev. 155, arguing that the task of interpretation should always start with a consideration of both language versions of the provision to be interpreted.

19 The federal requirement is now repeated by s. 18(1) of the Constitution Act, 1982. Section 133 imposes a similar obligation of bilingual enactment on Quebec, but there is a statutory requi-

have held that the English and French versions are equally authoritative,[20] and have developed rules for resolving discrepancies.[21] These are the rules that should be applied to the bilingual texts of the Constitution of Canada.[22] The rule that is most helpful is addressed to the case where one language version is doubtful or ambiguous and the other is clear; in that case, the doubt or ambiguity is resolved by reference to the clear version.[23] This rule is really a species of the more general rule that, where there is divergence between the two language versions, that meaning should be selected that is compatible with both versions.[24] However, the meaning selected must be reasonable in the context of the statute. If one language version gives better effect to the purpose of the statute, then that version should be selected, even if a narrower meaning would be common to both versions.[25] This last rule would also provide the approach to resolving the rare case of irreconcilable conflict between the two language versions.

53.4 Language of statutes

(a) Constitutional requirements

The only explicit guarantee of language rights in the Constitution Act, 1867 is contained in s. 133,[26] which provides as follows:

> 133. Either the English or the French language may be used by any person in the debates of the Houses of the Parliament of Canada and of the Houses of the Legis-

---

rement of doubtful validity giving preference to the French version: Cté, *The Interpretation of Legislation in Canada* (2nd ed., 1991), 274. Section 23 of the Manitoba Act, 1870 imposes a similar obligation on Manitoba. Section 18(2) of the Constitution Act, 1982 imposes a similar obligation on New Brunswick. The remaining seven provinces are under no constitutional obligation of bilingual enactment. Cf. *R.* v. *Mercure* [1988] 1 S.C.R. 234; *R.* v. *Paquette* [1990] 2 S.C.R. 1103; both cases are discussed in note 31, below.

20 *The King* v. *Dubois* [1935] S.C.R. 378.

21 See Beaupré, *Interpreting Bilingual Legislation* (2nd ed., 1986); Dreidger, *Construction of Statutes* (3rd ed., 1994 by Sullivan), ch. 10; Coté, note 19, above, 272-279.

22 See Gautron, ''French/English Discrepancies in the Charter'' (1982) 12 Man L.J. 220; Beaupré, ''Vers l'interpretation d'une constitution bilingue'' (1984) 25 Les Cahiers Droit 939; Charles, Cromwell, Jobson, *Evidence and the Charter of Rights and Freedoms* (1989), 62-66; Beaudoin and Ratushny (eds.), *The Canadian Charter of Rights and Freedoms* (2nd ed., 1989), 37-39 (by Pentney).

23 *The King* v. *Dubois* [1935] S.C.R. 378. This rule has been applied to the Constitution Act, 1982 in *R.* v. *Conway* [1989] 1 S.C.R. 1659, 1706-1707; *Mahe* v. *Alta.* [1990] 1 S.C.R. 342, 370; *R.* v. *Schmautz* [1990] 1 S.C.R. 398, 415-416.

24 *Jones and Maheux* v. *Gamache* [1969] S.C.R. 119.

25 *The Queen* v. *Compagnie ImmobilièreBCN* [1979] 1 S.C.R. 865. This rule has been applied to the Constitution Act, 1982 in *R.* v. *Collins* [1987] 1 S.C.R. 265, 287; *R.* v. *Turpin* [1989] 1 S.C.R. 1296, 1314.

26 For discussion of s. 133, see Royal Commission on Bilingualism and Biculturalism, *Report*, Book 1 (1967), 52-55; Bastarache (ed.), *Language Rights in Canada* (1987), ch. 2. Magnet, *Official Languages of Canada* (1995).

> lature of Quebec; and both those languages shall be used in the respective records and journals of those Houses; and either of those languages may be used by any person or in any pleading or process in or issuing from any Court of Canada established under this Act, and in or from all or any of the Courts of Quebec. The Acts of the Parliament of Canada and of the Legislature of Quebec shall be printed and published in both those languages.

Section 133 permits either English or French to be used in debates in the Houses of the federal Parliament and Quebec Legislature; it requires both English and French to be used in the records and journals of those Houses; and it requires the statutes of the federal Parliament and Quebec Legislature to be printed and published in both languages. (Section 133 also provides that either English or French may be used in any pleading or process in the federal courts and the Quebec courts: this part of s. 133 is discussed in a later section of this chapter.)[27]

Section 133 applies only to the legislative bodies (and courts) of the federal government and of Quebec. It does not apply to the Legislature (and courts) of any province other than Quebec. However, the Manitoba Act, 1870 includes, as s. 23, a provision that provides for the use of English and French in the Legislature (and courts) of Manitoba in terms very similar to s. 133. None of the other provinces that were created or admitted after 1867 had language guarantees written into their constituent instruments or terms of union.[28]

The Charter of Rights, which is Part I of the Constitution Act, 1982, includes, as ss. 16 to 23, a variety of language provisions.[29] Sections 17 to 19 virtually duplicate the provisions of s. 133 in their application to the legislative bodies (and courts) of the federal government, although not of Quebec. Curiously, however, the Constitution Act, 1982 does not expressly repeal any part of s. 133. Sections 17 to 19 of the Charter of Rights also apply to New Brunswick, so that New Brunswick is now in a similar position to Quebec and Manitoba (as well as being bound by additional language provisions in the Charter).[30]

---

27 Section 53.5, ''Language of courts'', below.

28 Cf. *R.* v. *Mercure* [1988] 1 S.C.R. 234; *R.* v. *Paquette* [1990] 2 S.C.R. 1103; both cases are discussed in note 31, below. The Canadian Bill of Rights and statutory provincial bills of rights also contain no protection for language rights, except that the Canadian Bill of Rights, by s. 2(g), and the Quebec Charter of Human Rights and Freedoms, by s. 36, require an interpreter in court proceedings. An interpreter is also required by the Charter of Rights, s. 14.

29 For discussion of ss. 16-23 see Beaudoin and Mendes (eds.), *The Canadian Charter of Rights and Freedoms* (3rd ed., 1996), chs. 15 (by Tremblay), 16 (by Foucher); Bastarache, note 26, above, chs. 3-5; *Charter of Rights Annotated* (Carswell, loose-leaf), annotation to ss. 16-23; the latter work includes a bibliography of the relevant literature.

30 The provisions of s. 133, s. 23 and ss. 17-19 are all entrenched in the sense that they cannot be *diminished* by the unilateral action of any of the legislative bodies to which they apply: Constitution Act, 1982, ss. 41(c), 43(b). This was true even before the enactment of the amending procedures in 1982: *A.G. Que.* v. *Blaikie* [1979] 2 S.C.R. 1016. However, the provisions do not prohibit the *expansion* of the guaranteed rights: *Jones* v. *A.G. N.B.* [1975] 2 S.C.R. 182; *MacDonald* v. *City of Montreal* [1986] 1 S.C.R. 460, 496; see also Constitution Act, 1982, s. 16(3).

Confining ourselves for the moment to the enactment of statutes, the effect of the constitutional provisions that have been described is that the federal Parliament, the Quebec Legislature, the Manitoba Legislature and the New Brunswick Legislature are each subject to a constitutional requirement that their statutes must be ''printed and published'' in both English and French.[31] The meaning of this requirement has been considered in cases arising out of the attempts by Quebec and Manitoba to enact their statutes in one language only. Those cases are considered next.

(b) Quebec's Charter of the French Language

In *Attorney General of Quebec* v. *Blaikie* (1979),[32] the Supreme Court of Canada struck down those provisions of Quebec's Charter of the French Language[33] that purported to make French the language of the Legislature. The Act provided that bills were to be drafted and enacted in French only, and that only the French version was to be official, although an English translation was to be printed and published. The Court held that these provisions contravened s. 133. It was not sufficient to produce an unofficial English translation of the statutes. Section 133's requirement that the statutes be ''printed and published'' in both languages should be interpreted as a requirement of ''enactment in both languages'',[34] especially in light of the requirement that the ''records and journals'' of the Legislature should be in both languages. Exactly what would be involved in ''enactment'' was not spelled out by the Court, but it would certainly involve bilingual texts of all bills and all amendments at all stages of the legislative process.[35]

The decision in *Blaikie* meant, among other things, that all of Quebec's statutes enacted after the passage of Quebec's Charter of the French Language in

---

31 In *R.* v. *Mercure* [1988] 1 S.C.R. 234, it was held that a pre-confederation statute imposed a requirement of bilingual enactment on the Saskatchewan Legislature, and in *R.* v. *Paquette* [1990] 2 S.C.R. 1103, it was held that the same requirement applied to the Alberta Legislature. However, the Court made clear that the requirement could be repealed by the Legislature itself, acting in the correct bilingual manner and form; and each Legislature did in fact repeal the requirement: The Language Act, S.S. 1988, c. L-6.1; Languages Act, S.A. 1988, c. L-7.5. Ontario has moved in the opposite direction, imposing on itself a requirement starting in 1991 of bilingual enactment: French Language Services Act, R.S.O. 1990, c. F.32, s. 3(2); of course, this requirement could also be repealed by the Legislature, provided it acted in the correct bilingual manner and form.

32 [1979] 2 S.C.R. 1016. The opinion was rendered by ''the Court''.

33 Note 13, above.

34 [1979] 2 S.C.R. 1016, 1022.

35 Bills and amendments would also be within the phrase ''records and journals'', which s. 133 requires to be kept in both languages. The phrase ''records and journals'', which also appears in s. 23 of the Manitoba Act, 1870 and s. 18 of the Constitution Act, 1982, has never been authoritatively defined, although it was examined by Deschênes C.J. in *Blaikie* at first instance, (1978) 85 D.L.R. (3d) 252, 257-260.

1977 were in violation of s. 133.[36] These statutes had been enacted in French only, and were therefore invalid. Fortunately, however, Quebec's Charter had insisted upon the publication of an unofficial English translation, so that the task of translating the statutes into English had been accomplished. The decision in *Blaikie* came down on December 13, 1979. The Quebec Legislature sat overnight to re-enact the statutes in both their French text and their English translation. The enactment of the curative statute was completed the next day.[37] Quebec's prompt and effective remedial action stands in contrast to Manitoba's reaction to a similar problem. The situation in Manitoba is the topic of the next section of this chapter.

(c) Manitoba's Official Language Act

We have already noticed that s. 23 of the Manitoba Act, 1870[38] provides for the use of English and French in the Legislature (and courts) of Manitoba in terms similar to s. 133 of the Constitution Act, 1867.[39] The reason for s. 23, of course, was to guarantee the rights of the French-speaking minority in Manitoba.[40] Its text is so similar to that of s. 133 of the Constitution Act, 1867 that it can be safely assumed that all the points of interpretation of s. 133 that have been discussed in the previous section of this chapter are equally relevant to s. 23.

In 1890, the Manitoba Legislature enacted the Official Language Act.[41] The Act provided that ''the English language only'' shall be used in the records and journals of the Legislature, and in pleadings and process in the Manitoba courts; the Act also provided that Manitoba statutes ''need only be printed and published in the English language''. In effect, the Act was an attempt to repeal most of s. 23 of the Manitoba Act. The Act was held to be invalid by county courts in 1892[42]

36 The Charter of the French Language itself was in a similar plight, having been enacted in French only.

37 S.Q. 1979, c. 61.

38 R.S.C. 1985, Appendix II, No. 8. The Manitoba Act, 1870 is a federal statute which created the province of Manitoba in 1870. It was ratified by the Constitution Act, 1871, R.S.C. 1985, Appendix II, No. 11. It is part of the ''Constitution of Canada'': Constitution Act, 1982, s. 52(2).

39 The text of s. 23 is as follows:

> 23. Either the English or the French languages may be used by any person in the debates of the Houses of the Legislature, and both those languages shall be used in the respective records and journals of those Houses; and either of those languages may be used by any person, or in any pleading or process, in or issuing from any Court of Canada established under the British North America Act, 1867, or in or from all or any of the Courts of the Province. The Acts of the Legislature shall be printed and published in both those languages.

40 In 1870, French-speakers were actually in a slight majority in the Red River settlement. The Riel provisional government, rightly fearing an influx of English-speakers, insisted upon s. 23 as one of the terms of provincehood. See Tetley, (1982) 45 Law and Contemp. Problems 177, 180.

41 S.M. 1890, c. 14.

42 *Pellant* v. *Hebert* (1892), reported in 1981 in 12 R.G.D. 242 (Man. Co. Ct.).

and 1909,[43] but these decisions were not appealed, were not reported, and were completely disregarded by the authorities in Manitoba. In 1976, a third attack was mounted against the Official Language Act, and the Act was again held to be invalid by a county court.[44] The Attorney General of Manitoba announced that: "The Crown does not accept the ruling of the Court with respect to the constitutionality of the Official Language Act"; but he declined to appeal the decision to a higher court.[45] The Legislature and Courts of Manitoba continued the unilingual procedures purportedly authorized by the Official Language Act of 1890, as if that Act were valid.

In 1978, the Official Language Act was challenged for the fourth time. This time, the French-speaking plaintiff brought an action in the Manitoba Court of Queen's Bench seeking a declaration that the Act was invalid, and he was fortunate enough to lose at first instance (for lack of standing), thus giving him the carriage of an appeal to the Manitoba Court of Appeal. He succeeded in the Manitoba Court of Appeal, and this time the Attorney General of Manitoba elected to appeal to the Supreme Court of Canada. The Supreme Court of Canada rendered its judgment in *Attorney General of Manitoba Man.* v. *Forest* (1979)[46] on the same day as it rendered its judgment in *Blaikie*.[47] The Court wrote a brief opinion, essentially adopting its reasoning in *Blaikie* to hold that s. 23 of the Manitoba Act could not be amended by the unilateral action of the Manitoba Legislature; Manitoba's Official Language Act was therefore unconstitutional.

The *Forest* decision had not expressly ruled on the constitutional status of the Manitoba statutes that had been enacted in English only. That ruling came in *Re Manitoba Language Rights* (1985)[48] when the Supreme Court of Canada confirmed that the failure to comply with s. 23's requirement of bilingual enactment resulted in the invalidity of the purported statute. This meant that nearly all of the laws of the province were unconstitutional, because statutes had been enacted in English only from 1890 (when the Official Language Act was enacted) until 1979 (when the *Forest* case was decided), and even since 1979 many statutes had been enacted in English only. In order to save the province from the vacuum of law that would be caused by the Court's finding of wholesale invalidity, the Court declared that the province's statutes were to be "deemed to have temporary force and effect for the minimum period necessary for their translation, re-enactment, printing and publication".[49] This provided a transitional period, the duration

43 *Bertrand* v. *Dussault* (1909), reported in 1977 in 77 D.L.R. (3d) 458 (Man. Co. Ct.).
44 *R.* v. *Forest* (1976) 74 D.L.R. (3d) 704 (Man. Co. Ct.).
45 In a later case, Monnin J.A. described this as an "arrogant abuse of authority": *Re Forest* (1977) 77 D.L.R. (3d) 445, 458 (Man. C.A.).
46 [1979] 2 S.C.R. 1032.
47 Note 32, above.
48 [1985] 1 S.C.R. 721. The opinion was rendered by "the Court". I disclose that I was one of the counsel for the Attorney General of Canada.
49 *Id.*, 782.

of which was later settled with precise dates directed by the Court,[50] during which the existing body of Manitoba laws would remain in force. Future laws, that is, those enacted after the date of the Court's opinion (June 13, 1985), had to comply with s. 23's requirement of bilingual enactment; they did not benefit from the period of temporary validity.[51]

In *Re Manitoba Language Rights*, the Court also considered a two-stage procedure for bilingual enactment that had been established by the Manitoba Legislature after the *Forest* decision in order to facilitate compliance with s. 23 of the Manitoba Act. The first stage of the procedure was the enactment of a bill in English only; the second stage was the preparation of a French translation of the bill, which on deposit in the Legislature would have full legal effect. This procedure did not satisfy s. 23, the Court held, because it denied to French-speakers participation in the legislative process. ''Simultaneity in the use of both English and French is therefore required throughout the process of enacting bills into law''.[52] This conclusion was reinforced by s. 23's requirement that both languages were to be used in the ''records and journals'' of the Legislature. Therefore, the statute prescribing the two-stage procedure was unconstitutional.

The Manitoba statute prescribing the two-stage procedure provided that in case of conflict the original (English) enactment prevailed over the subsequently deposited (French) translation. This provision was also invalid, because s. 23 implicitly required that both language versions be ''equally authoritative''.[53] The preference for one language version ''renders the non-preferred text legally irrelevant, since it cannot safely be relied upon''.[54] Any mechanism that attributed ''superior status'' to one language version of a statute would violate s. 23.[55]

Section 23 is so similar to s. 133 of the Constitution Act, 1867 and to ss. 17 to 19 of the Charter of Rights that these interpretations of s. 23 would undoubtedly apply to the other provisions.

(d) Incorporation by reference

Where a statute makes reference to another document, so as to incorporate (or adopt) the document as part of the statute,[56] then the general rule is that, if

---

50 *Re Man. Language Rights Order No. 1* [1985] 2 S.C.R. 347 (for most statutes, the deadline was December 31, 1988); *Re Man. Language Rights Order No. 2* [1990] 3 S.C.R. 1417 (extending the period of validity for some instruments); *Re Man. Language Rights Order No. 3* [1992] 1 S.C.R. 212 (clarifying original order and further extending the period of validity).

51 The aftermath of *Re Manitoba Language Rights* is more fully discussed in ch. 55, Effect of Unconstitutional Law, under heading 55.8, ''Wholesale invalidity of laws'', below.

52 [1985] 1 S.C.R. 721, 775. Another constitutional flaw was the absence of any requirement of royal assent for the translation: *Id.*, 777.

53 *Id.*, 774.

54 *Id.*, 778.

55 *Ibid.*

56 Incorporation by reference is discussed in ch. 14, Delegation, under heading 14.3(c), ''Referential legislation'', below.

there is a constitutional requirement that the incorporating statute be in both languages, then the requirement will apply to the incorporated document as well. In *Attorney General of Quebec* v. *Collier* (1985),[57] two Quebec statutes fixed public sector wages and other terms of employment. They did so by reference to session papers that had been tabled in the Legislature; the details of the wages and other terms of employment were to be found not in the statutes, but in the session papers to which the statutes referred. The statutes had been enacted in both French and English, but the session papers were in French only. The Quebec Court of Appeal, in a decision that was affirmed by the Supreme Court of Canada, held that the two statutes were unconstitutional. The session papers were an integral part of the statutes. Since the session papers had been tabled in one language only, the statutes could not be said to have been enacted in both languages as required by s. 133 of the Constitution Act, 1867.[58]

In *Collier*, it was important that the incorporated session papers contained the substance of the legislative scheme. It would have been a clear denial of access by English-speakers to the Legislature and its laws if the substance of a legislative scheme had been allowed to be embodied in a document that was in French only. However, where a statute refers to an extrinsic document that is not essential to the operation of the statute, so that the document is not an ''integral part'' of the statute, then there is no ''true incorporation'', and the document would not be subject to the requirement of bilingual texts.[59]

When a statute refers to a document that is essential to the operation of the statute, the general rule is, as noted above, that the document comes under the same language requirements as the statute itself. The Supreme Court of Canada has indicated, however, that this is not an absolute rule. There could be bona fide reasons for exempting the incorporated document from the requirement of bilingual texts. This would be the case where (unlike *Collier*) the incorporated document emanated from a source that was under no obligation of translation, and where (unlike *Collier*) it was not practicable for the legislative body to produce translations.[60]

In *R.* v. *Massia* (1991),[61] a challenge was brought to the federal Government Property Traffic Regulations, which applied on federal Crown property (such as military bases), and which provided that drivers must observe the law of the province in which the Crown property was situated. The Regulations (and the enabling Act) had been enacted in both languages. The accused, who was con-

---

57 (1985) 23 D.L.R. (4th) 339 (Que. C.A.); affirmed under name *Que.* v. *Brunet* [1990] 1 S.C.R. 260.

58 Followed in *Sinclair* v. *Que.* [1992] 1 S.C.R. 212 (statute operated by reference to a unilingual document to be issued in future; held breach of s. 133).

59 *Re Man. Language Rights Order No. 3* [1992] 1 S.C.R. 212, (p. 19).

60 *Id.*, (pp. 19-23) (suggesting as examples the incorporation of the legislation of another jurisdiction and the incorporation of safety standards set by a non-governmental body).

61 (1991) 4 O.R. (3d) 705 (C.A.). The majority opinion was written by Galligan J.A., with the agreement of Brooke J.A.; Doherty J.A. dissented.

victed under the Regulations of driving a vehicle while his licence was suspended on a miliary base in Ontario, challenged the relevant regulation on the basis that it incorporated by reference a law of Ontario (prohibiting driving while under suspension) that had been enacted in English only. The majority of the Ontario Court of Appeal rejected the challenge. They pointed out that Ontario's prohibition of driving while under suspension had been enacted by a body that was at the time of enactment[62] under no obligation to produce bilingual texts, and, although the charge was laid under the federal Regulations, the Ontario prohibition was capable of operating of its own force on federal Crown property. They might have added that the sensible scheme of subjecting military personnel to local traffic laws could not be effective if it were necessary to continuously produce translations of the changing bodies of provincial traffic laws.[63]

(e) Delegated legislation

In *Attorney General of Quebec* v. *Blaikie* (1979),[64] the Supreme Court of Canada decided that s. 133's requirement that "Acts" be printed and published in both languages applied to delegated legislation as well as to statutes.[65] On this point, the Court simply said that "it would truncate the requirement of s. 133 if account were not taken of the growth of delegated legislation".[66] This brief observation appeared to impose the requirement of bilingual enactment on all kinds of delegated legislation. Quebec immediately applied to the Court for a rehearing to determine whether some kinds of delegated legislation were exempt from s. 133.

In *Attorney General of Quebec* v. *Blaikie (No. 2)* (1981),[67] the Court qualified the earlier ruling by holding that only regulations made by "the Government" were subject to s. 133. By "the Government" the Court meant the Lieutenant Governor, the Executive Council and Ministers; the Court took notice of the conventions of responsible government as creating "a considerable degree of integration between the Legislature and the Government", so that the enactments of the Government "must be viewed as an extension of the legislative power of the Legislature" and accordingly as being within s. 133.[68] In the same category,

---

62 The facts arose before the coming into force of s. 3(2) of the French Language Services Act, R.S.O. 1990, c. F.32.

63 This case was decided before *Re Man. Language Rights Order No. 3*, notes 59, 60, above, indicated a rather flexible approach to the question of translation of incorporated documents. In light of the later decision, the dissenting opinion of Doherty J., who would have held that the incorporation was unconstitutional for breach of the language requirements, is wrong.

64 [1979] 2 S.C.R. 1016; discussed at note 32, above.

65 The same word, "Acts", is used in s. 23 of the Manitoba Act, 1870. The word "statutes" is used in s. 18 of the Charter of Rights; this change in nomenclature would not, in my view, change the interpretation.

66 [1979] 2 S.C.R. 1016, 1027.

67 [1981] 1 S.C.R. 312.

68 *Id.*, 319-321.

the Court held, were regulations which, although made by officials or bodies outside the Government, were subject to the approval of the Government; they too were subject to s. 133.[69] Regulations which were neither made by the Government nor subject to approval by the Government were not subject to s. 133. Also not subject to s. 133 were the by-laws of local municipalities and school boards, even if they were subject to the approval of the Government.[70] Another special category was court rules of practice: these rules, although made by the judges not the Government, were subject to s. 133; and so were the rules of those administrative tribunals whose functions were ''quasi-judicial''.[71]

In *Re Manitoba Language Rights* (1985),[72] the Supreme Court of Canada made clear that the scope of s. 23 of the Manitoba Act was the same as the scope of s. 133 of the Constitution Act, 1867. This meant that Manitoba was under an obligation to translate and re-enact not only the statutes that had been enacted in English only, but also the categories of delegated legislation that were defined in *Blaikie No. 2*.[73] In due course, the Government of Manitoba returned to the Court for a further clarification of this ruling. Did it include orders in council? An order in council clearly emanated from ''the Government'', as stipulated in *Blaikie No. 2*, because an order in council is a formal instrument made by the Lieutenant Governor in Council, acting on the ''advice'' (that is, direction) of the Executive Council (that is, the cabinet). Many regulations are required by their enabling statute to be made by the Lieutenant Governor in Council. Obviously, any order in council that enacted a regulation would be covered by *Blaikie No. 2*. But what of those orders in council that were of an executive rather than a legislative nature, for example, an order appointing a person to an office, or an order authorizing the granting of a contract or permit?

In *Re Manitoba Language Rights Order No. 3* (1992),[74] the Supreme Court of Canada held that s. 23 applied only to ''instruments of a legislative nature''.[75] An instrument would have the following three characteristics: (1) it would establish a ''rule of conduct''; (2) it would have the ''force of law''; and (3) it would be ''of general application rather than directed at specific individuals or situations''.[76] The obligation of bilingual enactment applied only to instruments possessing those three characteristics. Of course, ''Legislatures will often find it

69 *Id.*, 329. However, the Court explained that regulations which were subject to disallowance by the Government, being effective unless and until disallowed, were not subject to s. 133.

70 *Id.*, 321-326.

71 *Id.*, 330-333.

72 [1985] 1 S.C.R. 721; discussed at note 48, above.

73 *Id.*, 744. (''All types of subordinate legislation that in Quebec would be subject to s. 133 of the Constitution Act, 1867, are, in Manitoba, subject to s. 23 of the Manitoba Act, 1870.'')

74 [1992] 1 S.C.R. 212. For Orders Nos. 1 and 2, see note 50, above.

75 *Id.*, (p. 12).

76 *Id.*, (p. 14) (adapting a parliamentary committee's definition of regulation as ''a rule of conduct, enacted by a regulation-making authority pursuant to an Act of Parliament, which has the force of law for an undetermined number of persons'').

appropriate or desirable to translate instruments that go beyond those criteria'',[77] but they would be under no constitutional obligation to do so.

The Court had an opportunity to apply its definition of instruments of a legislative nature in *Sinclair* v. *Quebec* (1992),[78] where the issue was whether the Government of Quebec, acting under statutory authority, could create a new municipality by the issue of letters patent in the French language only.[79] The Court held that the creation of local government institutions, which would have among other things legal powers over the residents of the municipality, was not like the incorporation of a private company, which would simply have the powers of an individual. In this case, the purpose of s. 133 of making laws accessible in both languages would be violated if the structure and powers of local government institutions could be ascertained only from a document that was not in the English language. The Court held, therefore, that the new municipality had not been validly established.[80]

53.5 Language of courts

(a) Constitutional requirements

With respect to the courts, s. 133 of the Constitution Act, 1867 requires that either French or English ''may be used by any person or in any pleading or process in or issuing from any Court of Canada established under this Act, and in or from all or any of the Courts of Quebec''. This gives a choice of either French or English to litigants in the federal courts and the courts of Quebec.[81] Section 23 of the Manitoba Act, 1870 imposes a similar requirement on the courts of Manitoba.[82] Section 19(2) of the Charter of Rights imposes a similar requirement on the courts of New Brunswick. The courts of the other seven provinces are under no similar constitutional obligation.[83]

Quebec's Charter of the French Language provided that, in the courts of Quebec, French was to be the language of pleading and process, except in certain

---

77 *Ibid.*

78 [1992] 1 S.C.R. 579. The judgment was rendered by ''the Court''.

79 The Court described the statute that authorized the letters patent as merely ''a shell''; the detail of the new municipality was all contained in the letters patent and two other related documents, all three of which were in French only. The Court held that all three documents had to be in both languages.

80 In deference to the fact that the municipality had actually been functioning for five years, the Court held that the invalid instruments were to have legal effect for one year in order to permit the Legislature of Quebec to take curative action.

81 The structure of the federal courts and the provincial courts is explained in ch. 7, Courts, above.

82 The text of s. 23 is set out in note 39, above.

83 There are, however, a variety of statutory obligations imposed by the Criminal Code, R.S.C. 1985, c. C-46, ss. 530-534 (language of criminal trials), and by provincial law, e.g., Courts of Justice Act, R.S.O. 1990, c. C.43, ss. 125, 126.

defined circumstances. Like the other assaults on s. 133 that were mounted by the Quebec language law,[84] this one was repulsed by the Supreme Court of Canada in *Attorney General of Quebec* v. *Blaikie* (1979).[85] The Court held that it was not sufficient to give litigants the option of using English in defined circumstances only. Section 133 gave to litigants in the courts of Quebec the option of using English in *any* pleading or process.

(b) Definition of courts

Which courts are covered by s. 133? In *Blaikie*, the Supreme Court of Canada held that the reference to "the Courts of Quebec" included not onlys. 96 courts (with federally-appointed judges), and courts with provincially appointed judges, but also administrative tribunals established by statute that exercised "adjudicative" functions. The Court said that "it would be overly technical to ignore the modern development of noncurial adjudicative agencies which play so important a role in our society, and to refuse to extend to proceedings before them the guarantee of the right to use either French or English by those subject to their jurisdiction".[86]

(c) Language of process

In *MacDonald* v. *City of Montreal* (1986),[87] an English-speaking Quebecer defended a charge of speeding on the ground that the summons, which included the charge, had been issued by the Quebec court in the French language only. The majority of the Supreme Court of Canada, speaking through Beetz J., held that the unilingual summons did not infringe s. 133.[88] Section 133, by providing that "either" of the two languages may be used in any process issuing from a Quebec court, gave to the issuing court the choice of either the English or the French language. The express provision for choice of language made clear that court process need not be bilingual. Nor was the choice of language by the court to be governed by the wishes of the recipient of court process, which would in any case not necessarily be known to the issuing court. Beetz J. said that s. 133, where it conferred a choice of language, "does not guarantee that the speaker, writer or issuer of proceedings or processes will be understood in the language of his choice by those he is addressing".[89]

---

84 Note 13, above.

85 [1979] 2 S.C.R. 1016; discussed at note 32, above.

86 *Id.*, 1029.

87 [1986] 1 S.C.R. 460. Beetz J. wrote the majority opinion with the agreement of four others; Dickson C.J. wrote a short concurring opinion; Wilson J. dissented.

88 The decision was followed with respect to s. 23 of the Manitoba Act in *Bilodeau* v. *A.G. Man.* [1986] 1 S.C.R. 449 (summons issued by Manitoba court in English only; held valid).

89 [1986] 1 S.C.R. 460, 496

In the *MacDonald* case, Wilson J., who dissented, was willing to find by implication in s. 133 a duty in the court to accommodate both English and French speakers. That duty could be discharged by a bilingual summons, or even a French document with some explanation in English; but it was breached by a summons that was wholly in French. Beetz J. for the majority rejected this view, adhering to the more literal interpretation of s. 133 as permitting the court to issue its process in one language only. Beetz J. defended the narrower approach to s. 133 by drawing a distinction between language rights and other human rights. While both types of rights were constitutionally protected, most human rights had a quality of universality, in that they were recognized by all democratic societies; language rights, on the other hand, were ''peculiar to Canada'':[90]

> They are based on a political compromise rather than on principle and lack the universality, generality and fluidity of basic rights resulting from the rules of natural justice. They are expressed in more precise and less flexible language.

This suggestion that language rights should receive a more restrained interpretation than other Charter rights[91] was reiterated and applied in the *Acadiens* case, which is discussed next.

(d) Language of proceedings

In *Société des Acadiens* v. *Association of Parents* (1986),[92] Beetz J., again speaking for the majority of the Supreme Court of Canada, repeated that language rights were ''based on political compromise''; this distinguished them from legal rights, which ''tend to be seminal in nature because they are rooted in principle''.[93] That case arose in New Brunswick, where s. 19(2) of the Charter of Rights imposed on the courts language requirements in terms very similar to those of s. 133. The Société des Acadiens claimed that s. 19(2) was breached when an application made by the Society in French to the New Brunswick Court of Appeal was heard by a panel of three judges one of whom, the Society alleged, was not capable of understanding the French language. The Supreme Court of Canada held unanimously that the Society had not established their allegation that the judge was incompetent in French. However, Beetz J. for the majority held that s. 19(2) did not in any case confer on a French-speaking litigant the right to be heard

---

90 *Id.*, 500, rejecting the view that the requirements of natural justice should be imported into s. 133; see also 496, where the distinction is also stressed.

91 The distinction between language rights and other rights has found little favour among commentators: see Green, ''Are Language Rights Fundamental?'' (1987) 25 Osgoode Hall L.J. 639; Green and Réaume, ''Second Class Rights? Principle and Compromise in the Charter'' (1990) 13 Dal. L.J. 564.

92 [1986] 1 S.C.R. 549. Beetz J. wrote the majority opinion with the agreement of four others. Dickson C.J. and Wilson J. each wrote concurring opinions, disagreeing with Beetz J. that s. 19(2) conferred no right to a judge who understood French, but agreeing with the result on the basis that it had not been established that one of the judges did not understand French.

93 *Id.*, 578.

by a judge who understood French. Following *MacDonald*, he said that, while the litigant had the constitutional right to use either English or French, neither s. 19(2) nor s. 133 conferred any guarantee that the litigant ''will be heard or understood, or that he has the right to be heard or understood in the language of his choice''.[94] Dickson C. J. and Wilson J. each disagreed with Beetz J. They held that the litigant's right to use either English or French impliedly included the right to be understood in the litigant's language of choice by the judge hearing the case.[95]

The reader by now will have conjured up the image of a unilingual judge presiding impassively over a trial in which the witnesses and their counsel are all speaking in a language that the judge cannot understand! Only Franz Kafka could appreciate such a disturbing possibility. Needless to say, Beetz J. in the *Acadiens* case did not intend such a result. He pointed out that the right to a fair hearing, which was recognized by the common low rules of natural justice, and which was protected in part by ss. 7 to 14 of the Charter, would be offended by a presiding judge's failure to comprehend the evidence or argument. But the fair-hearing right to be heard and understood by a court was not a language right, and it extended to those who spoke or understood neither official language.[96] It had not been breached in this case, because the judge's alleged incompetence in French had not been established as a matter of fact.

(e) Right to interpreter

The right of a party or witness to an interpreter is expressly dealt with bys. 14 of the Charter of Rights.[97] Section 14 provides:

> A party or witness in any proceedings who does not understand or speak the language in which the proceedings are conducted or who is deaf has the right to the assistance of an interpreter.

Section 14 confers upon a witness who does not understand or speak the language of the proceeding, or who is deaf,[98] the right to an interpreter. There is a similar right in s. 2(g) of the Canadian Bill of Rights, although deafness is not a qualification under s. 2(g).[99] There is a common law right to an interpreter, which is

94 *Id.*, 574-575. The decision was followed with respect to a pre-confederation statutory language right in *R.* v. *Mercure* [1988] 1 S.C.R. 234.

95 This is clearly Dickson C.J.'s view, although he left open the question whether the right could be satisfied by the use of an interpreter or simultaneous translation. Wilson J.'s opinion is less clear, but seems to be the same.

96 *Id.*, 577

97 For commentary on s. 14, see Beaudoin and Mendes, note 29, above, 12-27–12-41 (by Morel); *Canadian Charter of Rights Annotated*, note 6, above, annotation to s. 14; the last work includes a bibliography of the relevant literature.

98 Section 14 was in the October 1980 version of the Charter, but without the words ''or who is deaf''. These words were added in the April 1981 version.

99 For discussion of s. 2(g), see Tarnopolsky, *The Canadian Bill of Rights* (2nd ed., 1975), 277; *R.* v. *Sadjade* [1983] 2 S.C.R. 361.

possessed by any person who cannot speak or understand the language of proceedings where that person's rights may be affected, because the failure to provide interpretation would be a breach of the rules of natural justice.[100] There is also a statutory right to an interpreter, which is possessed by an accused person in a criminal trial, because the Criminal Code requires that an accused person "be present in court during the whole of his trial", and an accused person is not "present" if he or she cannot understand what is going on.[101]

Under s.14 of the Charter, a party or witness is entitled to an interpreter if the person "does not understand or speak the language in which the proceedings are conducted or who is deaf". It is for the trial judge to determine whether the need for an interpreter has been established, and in case of dispute the person asserting the right would have to establish the need on the balance of probabilities. But it is the duty of the trial judge to take the initiative in supplying an interpreter to a party or witness who needs the help but who through ignorance or timidity does not assert the right.[102]

In *R.* v. *Tran* (1994),[103] the accused, a native of Vietnam who could not speak or understand English, was provided with a Vietnamese interpreter for a trial that took place in English. For most of the trial, the interpretation followed the normal pattern of "consecutive" interpretation, in which words spoken in English by counsel, witnesses or the judge were immediately followed by a translation of those words. This pattern was broken in the case of a witness called by the defence (who happened to be the interpreter himself). This witness testified in English and then gave a brief summary of his testimony in Vietnamese at the end of his direct examination and then again at the end of his cross-examination. The accused was convicted of the offences charged, and he appealed the convictions on the ground that there had been a breach of his s. 14 right to an interpreter. The Supreme Court of Canada held that there had been a breach of s. 14. The Court held that the quality of the interpretation had to meet the standard of "continuity, precision, impartiality, competence and contemporaneousness".[104] In this case, continuity was not observed, because of the break in interpretation during the defence evidence. Precision was not observed, because the little summaries at the end did not convey everything that was said. Contemporaneousness was also not observed, because the interpretation was not contemporaneous with the asking of questions and the giving of answers. (The impartiality and competence of the interpreter were not put in issue). The constitutional standard of interpretation had to be maintained throughout the trial, except at points where the vital interests of the accused were not involved, for example, a discussion of scheduling. Therefore, although the lapse affected only one witness (and that one called by the

---

100 *R.* v.*Tran* [1994] 2 S.C.R. 951, 967.
101 *Id.*, 971.
102 *Id.*, 979.
103 [1994] 2 S.C.R. 951. The opinion of the Court was written by Lamer C.J.
104 *Id.*, 979.

defence), that was enough to offend s. 14. Nor was it necessary for the accused to show that he had suffered any prejudice in his ability to make full answer and defence; the mere fact that he was unable to follow some of the proceedings in which his vital interests were involved was itself prejudicial. It followed that the accused's s. 14 right had been infringed, and the Court ordered a new trial.

Under s. 14, the right to an interpreter applies ''in any proceedings'', which would include civil as well as criminal proceedings and probably proceedings before administrative tribunals as well as courts. Whether the right exists only at the hearing or also applies to an investigatory or even merely preparatory phase of the proceedings will eventually require judicial decision. The interpreter should probably be paid for out of public funds, at least for a party or witness who cannot afford to pay the cost himself.[105]

53.6 Language of government

(a) Section 16 of Charter

The previous sections of this chapter have addressed the constitutional requirements, in the federal jurisdiction, Quebec, Manitoba and New Brunswick, with respect to the use of the English and French languages in legislative bodies and courts. We have noticed the limited form of bilingualism that is required by s. 133 of the Constitution Act, 1867, s. 23 of the Manitoba Act, 1870 and ss. 16 to 22 of the Charter of Rights. The first two sources, namely s. 133 and s. 23, do not go beyond legislative bodies and courts; they say nothing about government services. But two of the provisions of the Charter of Rights, namely, ss. 16 and 20, do go beyond legislative bodies and courts.

Section 16 of the Charter provides as follows:

> 16.(1) English and French are the official languages of Canada and have equality of status and equal rights and privileges as to their use in all institutions of the Parliament and government of Canada.
>
> (2) English and French are the official languages of New Brunswick and have equality of status and equal rights and privileges as to their use in all institutions of the legislature and government of New Brunswick.
>
> (3) Nothing in this Charter limits the authority of Parliament or a legislature to advance the equality of status or use of English and French.

This section makes English and French the ''official languages'' of Canada and New Brunswick. It is not clear what, if any, practical consequences flow from official status.[106] The section also confers on English or French ''equality of status and equal rights and privileges as to their use in all institutions of the Parliament

105 Compare the right to counsel in s. 10(b): ch. 47, Rights on Arrest or Detention, under heading 47.4(j), ''Legal aid'', above.

106 The issue is inconclusively discussed, obiter, in *Société des Acadiens* v. *Assn. of Parents* [1986] 1 S.C.R. 549, 565, 579, 613-621.

and government of Canada'' (subs. (1)), and ''in all institutions of the legislature and government of New Brunswick'' (subs. (2)).[107] These subss. (1) and (2) ofs. 16 are probably not addressed to communications between government and the public, because that topic is addressed by s. 20 (to be considered in the next paragraph). Subsections (1) and (2) of s. 16 may well have the effect, however, of conferring on public servants, in the institutions of the federal Parliament and government and the New Brunswick Legislature and government, the right to use either the English or the French language as the language of work.[108]

Subsection (3) of s. 16 provides that nothing in the Charter ''limits the authority of Parliament or a legislature to advance the equality of status or use of English and French''. This provision has been described as a ''codification''[109] of the existing constitutional rule that authorizes the Parliament and Legislatures to create language rights above and beyond those conferred by the Constitution.[110] In other words, the constitutional language rights are a ''minimum not a maximum'', and they ''can be complemented by federal and provincial legislation''.[111]

(b) Section 20 of Charter

Section 20 of the Charter of Rights provides as follows:

> 20.(1) Any member of the public in Canada has the right to communicate with, and to receive available services from, any head or central office of an institution of the Parliament or government of Canada in English or French, and has the same right with respect to any other office of any such institution where
> (a) there is a significant demand for communications with and services from that office in such language; or
> (b) due to the nature of the office, it is reasonable that communications with and services from that office be available in both English and French.
>
> (2) Any member of the public in New Brunswick has the right to communicate with, and to receive available services from, any office of an institution of the legislature or government of New Brunswick in English or French.

This section imposes an obligation on government to provide bilingual services to the public.[112]

---

107 The phrase ''the Parliament and government of Canada'' also appears in s. 32 of the Charter of Rights, which is discussed in ch. 34, Application of Charter, under heading 34.2, ''Burden of rights'', above. However, in s. 16 and in s. 20 (discussed next in text) the phrase is preceded by ''institutions of'', which would give a much narrower scope to ''Parliament'', although it may not alter the scope of ''government''.

108 The issue is discussed in the context of s. 2 of the Official Languages Act in *Assn. des Gens de l'Air du Qué.* v. *Lang* [1978] 2 F.C. 371 (Fed. C.A.); *Joyal* v. *Air Can.* [1982] C.A. 39 (Que. C.A.).

109 *Société des Acadiens* v. *Assn. of Parents* [1986] 1 S.C.R. 549, 579.

110 Note 30, above.

111 *MacDonald* v. *City of Montreal* [1986] 1 S.C.R. 460, 496.

112 The phrase used is ''any member of the public'', which would probably include a corporation: see ch. 34, Application of Charter, under heading 34.1, ''Benefit of rights'', above.

In the federal jurisdiction, the obligation attaches to any ''head or central office'' of an institution of the Parliament or government of Canada without qualification. It attaches to other federal government offices (those that are not head or central offices) only where either (a) there is a ''significant demand'' for bilingual services from that office, or (b) due to the ''nature of the office'', it is ''reasonable'' that bilingual services be provided by that office. The alternative tests of significant demand and reasonableness are not elaborated by s. 20. Ultimately, it will be for the courts to give meaning to the tests.

In New Brunswick, the obligation to provide bilingual services attaches to ''any office of an institution of the legislature or government of New Brunswick''. The obligation is unqualified by standards of significant demand or reasonableness.

In the other nine provinces, there is no constitutional obligation to provide government services in both official languages, although some provinces by statute or administrative practice do in fact provide some services in both languages.[113]

53.7 Language of commerce

None of the *language* rights in the Constitution of Canada protects the use of the English or French language in commercial (or private) settings.[114] However, statutory language requirements may offend the guarantee of freedom of expression in s. 2(b) of the Charter of Rights.[115] In *Ford* v. *Quebec* (1988),[116] the Supreme Court of Canada struck down the provisions of Quebec's Charter of the French Language[117] that required commercial signs and advertisements to be in French only. The Court held that freedom of expression included ''the freedom to express oneself in the language of one's choice''.[118] It followed that the prohibition of the use of any language other than French was a breach of freedom of expression.

113 Quebec may provide the most extensive services in fact to its (English-speaking) linguistic minority. However, by s. 1 of the Charter of the French Language (note 13, above), French is declared to be the ''official language of Quebec''. While some parts of this legislation have been held to be unconstitutional, no doubt has been cast on the validity of s. 1. Apart from New Brunswick, where s. 16(2) of the Charter of Rights (discussed above) and s. 2 of the Official Languages of New Brunswick Act, R.S. N.B. 1973, c. O-1, both make English and French the official languages of the province, none of the other provinces has made statutory provision for an ''official'' language or languages. Manitoba's (unconstitutional) Official Language Act, 1890 (note 41 and accompanying text, above), despite its title, did not provide that English was the official language of Manitoba.

114 The power to regulate the use of language is discussed in sec. 53.2, ''Distribution of powers'', above.

115 See ch. 40, Freedom of Expression, above.

116 [1988] 2 S.C.R. 712. The opinion was rendered by ''the Court''.

117 Note 13, above.

118 [1988] 2 S.C.R. 712, 748.

The Court also held that, while s. 1 would save some laws designed to protect the French language, the total prohibition of other languages on commercial signs and advertisements was a disproportionately severe measure that could not be saved under s. 1. The law was therefore held to be invalid.

In a companion case, *Devine* v. *Quebec* (1988),[119] the Court held that other provisions of Quebec's Charter of the French Language, which required the non-exclusive use of French in brochures, orders, invoices and other business documents also offended freedom of expression, even though for those documents there was no prohibition of English (or any other language). The Court explained that "freedom consists in the absence of compulsion as well as an absence of restraint".[120] However, the Court held that s. 1 saved the non-exclusive requirements. The provisions were therefore upheld.

The Government of Quebec could not accept the nullification of its sign-language law in the *Ford* decision. The Government caused the Legislature of Quebec to re-enact the prohibition of English on outside commercial signs and advertisements (while allowing bilingual interior signs).[121] The new law was protected from judicial review by a notwithstanding clause, as authorized by s. 33 (the override power) of the Charter of Rights. This use of s. 33 illustrated an important difference between the guarantees of language rights, none of which is subject to override, and the guarantee of freedom of expression, which is subject to override.[122]

53.8 Language of education

(a) Section 93 of Constitution Act, 1867

Section 93 of the Constitution Act, 1867 confers upon the provincial Legislatures the power to make laws in relation to education,[123] but the section prohibits the Legislatures from prejudicially affecting rights or privileges with respect to denominational (or separate) schools existing by law at the time of confederation. The section applies to each of the original confederating provinces, namely, Ontario, Quebec, New Brunswick and Nova Scotia; and to British Columbia (admitted in 1871) and Prince Edward Island (1873) as well.[124] Slightly

---

119 [1988] 2 S.C.R. 790. The opinion was rendered by "the Court".

120 *Id.*, 813.

121 Bill C-178, An Act to amend the Charter of the French Language, enacted as S.Q. 1988, c. 54.

122 Section 33 permits the override of only ss. 2 and 7-15 of the Charter. This excludes all the language rights of ss. 16-23, as well as s. 133 of the Constitution Act, 1867 and s. 23 of the Manitoba Act, 1870. See ch. 36, Override of Rights, above.

123 Education is the topic of the next chapter of this book.

124 British Columbia and Prince Edward Island were each admitted by order in council under s. 146 of the Constitution Act, 1867. Each order in council provided that the terms of the Constitution Act, 1867 (including s. 93) were to apply to the newly admitted province: British Columbia Terms of Union, R.S.C. 1985, Appendix II, No. 10, s. 10; Prince Edward Island Terms of Union, R.S.C. 1985, Appendix II, No. 12, second-last unnumbered para.

different versions of s. 93 were negotiated upon the creation or admission of the remaining provinces, and these are to be found in the statutes which constituted Manitoba (1870),[125] Alberta (1905)[126] and Saskatchewan (1905)[127] and in the Terms of Union of Newfoundland (1949).[128]

Because s. 93 (and its counterparts) confers upon the provincial Legislatures the power to make laws in relation to education, it follows from the ancillary nature of the power over language that the provincial Legislatures have the power to prescribe the language of instruction in the schools. However, s. 93 prohibits the provincial Legislatures from prejudicially affecting ''any right or privilege with respect to denominational schools which any class of persons have by law in the province at the union.'' If, therefore, a particular language of instruction was a right or privilege of denominational schools in a particular province at the time of confederation (or admission), then the province would be disabled from compelling the denominational schools to instruct in a different language.

(b) Mackell case

The question whether language rights are guaranteed to the denominational schools of a particular province cannot be answered in the abstract. It will depend upon an analysis of the legal position of the denominational schools in the province at the time of confederation. However, the question has been determined for Ontario, and the determination has implications for the other provinces. In *Ottawa Roman Catholic Separate School Trustees* v. *Mackell* (1916),[129] the Privy Council held that Ontario had the power to require that English be the language of instruction in hitherto French-speaking Roman Catholic separate schools in the province. Their lordships examined the statute law governing the separate schools in Ontario at the time of confederation, and concluded that the law did not confer upon the separate schools the legal right to use French as the language of instruction. Since no such right existed at confederation, it followed that no such right was preserved by s. 93.

Their lordships in *Mackell* pointed out that s. 93 reserves the rights with respect to denominational schools of a ''class of persons'', and they held that the ''class of persons'' in s. 93 meant a ''class of persons determined according to religious belief, and not according to race or language''.[130] Since the Roman Catholics in Ontario comprised both French-speaking and English-speaking people, the French-speakers could not claim to be a class of persons entitled to rights under s. 93. This part of their lordships' reasoning is obviously unfavourable to

125 Manitoba Act, 1870, R.S.C. 1985, Appendix II, No. 8, s. 22.
126 Alberta Act, R.S.C. 1985, Appendix II, No. 20, s. 17.
127 Saskatchewan Act, R.S.C. 1985, Appendix II, No. 21, s. 17.
128 Terms of Union of Newfoundland, s. 17; schedule to Newfoundland Act, R.S.C. 1985, Appendix II, No. 32.
129 [1917] A.C. 62.
130 *Id.*, 69.

the recognition of language rights under s. 93 in any province. But it is wrong to assume that *Mackell* completely precludes the recognition of language rights under s. 93. After defining the "class of persons" referred to in s. 93, their lordships in *Mackell* went on to examine an argument that the French language was guaranteed to the entire class of Roman Catholics by statutory provisions conferring upon the trustees of separate schools the right to *choose* the language of instruction. This argument was rejected on the ground that the statute law of Ontario at the time of confederation did not confer that right on the trustees of the Roman Catholic separate schools. The implication from the discussion of this point is that, if the law at confederation had conferred that right, then s. 93 would have preserved (and entrenched) it, and the province would have been unable to stipulate to the trustees of separate schools the language of instruction in any of their schools.

It seems a fair conclusion from *Mackell* that s. 93 would preserve from legislative change the language of instruction in denominational schools if it could be established that the trustees of those schools had at the time of confederation (or admission) a legal right to choose the language of instruction in their schools. *Mackell* decides that no such right exists in Ontario, and it is reasonably clear that no such right would be held to exist in New Brunswick, Nova Scotia, Prince Edward Island and British Columbia,[131] but the point is still open in the other provinces.[132]

(c) Section 23 of the Charter

Minority language educational rights have now been provided for in s. 23 of the Charter.[133] Section 23 provides:

> 23.(1) Citizens of Canada
> (a) whose first language learned and still understood is that of the English or French linguistic minority population of the province in which they reside, or
> (b) who have received their primary school instruction in Canada in English or French and reside in a province where the language in which they received that instruction is the language of the English or French linguistic minority population of the province,
>
> have the right to have their children receive primary and secondary school instruction in that language in that province.
>
> (2) Citizens of Canada of whom any child has received or is receiving primary or secondary school instruction in English or French in Canada, have the right to

131 Schmeiser, *Civil Liberties in Canada* (1964), 155-156.

132 *Id.*, ch. 4. A decision of Quebec's Superior Court denies the existence of the right in Quebec: *Protestant School Bd. of Montreal* v. *Min. of Education of Que.* (1976) 83 D.L.R. (3d) 645 (Que. S.C.); appeal dismissed on ground that statute in issue had been repealed: (1978) 83 D.L.R. (3d) 679n (Que. C.A.).

133 For commentary on s. 23, see note 29, above.

have all their children receive primary and secondary school instruction in the same language.

(3) The right of citizens of Canada under subsections (1) and (2) to have their children receive primary and secondary school instruction in the language of the English or French linguistic minority population of a province

(a) applies wherever in the province the number of children of citizens who have such a right is sufficient to warrant the provision to them out of public funds of minority language instruction; and

(b) includes, where the number of those children so warrants, the right to have them receive that instruction in minority language educational facilities provided out of public funds.

Section 23 confers upon "citizens of Canada" who are members of the English-speaking minority in Quebec or the French-speaking minority in the other provinces "the right to have their children receive primary and secondary school instruction in [the minority] language in that province." This right,[134] which applies to denominational and non-denominational schools,[135] is possessed by parents[136] who fit into one of the three categories established by s. 23. Those categories are defined by (1) the mother tongue of the parent (s. 23(1)(a)); (2) the language of primary school instruction in Canada of the parent (s. 23(1)(b)); and (3) the language of instruction in Canada of one child of the parent (s. 23(2)). Each of these categories is examined in the text that follows.

(d) Mother tongue of parent

The first category of parent entitled to minority language educational rights is defined by the mother tongue of the parent. Paragraph (a) of s. 23(1) applies to citizens "whose first language learned and still understood is that of the English or French linguistic minority population of the province[137] in which they reside". For example, in Ontario (or any of the other provinces with English-speaking majorities), a Canadian citizen whose mother tongue ("first language learned and still understood") is French has the right under para. (a) to have his or her children receive primary and secondary school instruction in French. Paragraph (a) will include French-speakers from other parts of Canada and from outside Canada (provided that they have become citizens). It will not include persons whose mother tongue is English or persons whose mother tongue is neither English nor French. The mother tongue criterion would be satisfied by an Ontario parent who

---

134 This right cannot be made subject to the discretion of school boards: *Re Education Act (Ont.)* (1984) 47 O.R. (2d) 1, 30 (C.A.).

135 *Id.*, 50-51; and see sec. 53.8(h), "Denominational schools", below.

136 The right is conferred upon parents. The section does not require that the children be French-speaking: *Id.*, 29.

137 Note that the right depends upon membership of the linguistic minority population *of the province*. It does not apply to a person who is a member of the linguistic majority population of the province, even if he resides in a region of the province where his language is in the minority, for example, an English-speaker in northern New Brunswick or northern Ontario.

could establish (1) that his or her "first language learned" was French and (2) that this language is "still understood". Neither of these stipulations will be easy to apply, and the second (if disputed) seems to require the use of language tests: how else would one establish that a language is "still understood"?

Paragraph (a) is drafted to apply to English-speakers in Quebec as well as to French-speakers elsewhere in Canada. But, by virtue of s. 59 of the Constitution Act, 1982, the paragraph does not apply in Quebec until the legislative assembly or government of Quebec decides to adopt it.[138] This exemption was added in recognition of the fact that Quebec alone of the provinces did not join in the constitutional agreement of November 5, 1981, which accepted (among other things) the terms of the Charter, including s. 23. Since the mother tongue clause would be the most controversial of the minority language educational rights, the decision was made to exempt Quebec from it, until Quebec itself decided that it was willing to be bound by the clause.[139] The effect of the exemption is that English-speaking parents in Quebec have no right to send their children to English-speaking schools, unless they fit into the second or third category of parent recognized by s. 23. For example, a person of English mother tongue, who received her own schooling outside Canada, and who did not already have a child in an English-language school in Canada, would have no right to send her children to an English-language school in Quebec. If and when Quebec opts into the mother tongue clause, that person would become entitled to send her children to an English-language school in Quebec.

(e) Language of instruction of parent in Canada

The second category of parent entitled to minority language educational rights is defined by the language of primary school instruction in Canada of the parent. Paragraph (b) of s. 23(1) applies to citizens who have received their primary school instruction in Canada in the minority language of the province[140] where they now reside. Paragraph (b) has become known as the "Canada clause" because, under paragraph (b), Canadian citizens, who move from one province to another, retain the right to have their children educated in the same language as that in which the parent was educated anywhere in Canada. Quebec is not exempted from paragraph (b). Thus, a Canadian citizen who had been educated in English in Nova Scotia, and who moved to Quebec, would have the right under paragraph (b) to send his children to English-language schools in Quebec. Paragraph (b) would not apply to that person in Quebec if he had been educated in

138 By An Act respecting the Constitution Act, 1982, S.Q. 1982, c. 21, s. 4, the Quebec Legislature has purported to require that the adoption requires the consent of the Legislature, and not just of the "government", as s. 59 contemplates as an alternative.

139 Section 59 was not part of the constitutional agreement of November 5, 1981, but was one of the additional points agreed to shortly afterwards by the Prime Minister and the nine agreeing Premiers.

140 Note 132, above.

Nova Scotia in French (instead of English), or if he had been educated outside Canada.

Quebec's Charter of the French Language, a statute enacted in 1977 to give effect to provincial language policies,[141] limited admission to English-language schools in Quebec to the children of persons who had been educated in English in Quebec. In *Attorney General of Quebec* v. *Quebec Protestant School Boards* (1984),[142] the Supreme Court of Canada held that this ''Quebec clause'', which excluded the children of persons who had been educated in English in provinces other than Quebec, was in conflict with the ''Canada clause'' (s. 23(1)(b)) of the Charter of Rights. Therefore, the Quebec clause had to yield to the Canada clause, and school boards in Quebec were obliged to admit to English-language schools the children of parents who had been educated in English anywhere in Canada.[143]

(f) Language of instruction of child in Canada

The third category of parent entitled to minority language educational rights is defined by the language of instruction in Canada of one child in the family. Subsection (2) of s. 23 applies to citizens who have a child who has received or is receiving primary or secondary school instruction in English or French in Canada. Such persons have the right to have all their children receive their schooling in the same language. Quebec is not exempted from this clause either. Subsection (2) would include a Quebecer who already had a child in an English-language school in Quebec. It would also include an Albertan who moved to Quebec and who before the move had a child in an English-language school in Alberta. In the English-speaking provinces, subsection (2) will confer a right to French-language education on any citizen who has, or has had, a child in a French-language school anywhere in Canada.

(g) Where numbers warrant

The right to minority language education that is conferred on the three categories of parents that have just been described is not an absolute right. By virtue of paragraph (3)(a) of s. 23, the right to ''instruction'' is limited to ''wherever in the province the number of children of citizens who have such a right is sufficient to warrant the provision to them out of public funds of minority language instruction''. By virtue of paragraph (3)(b) of s. 23, the right ''includes, where the number of those children so warrants, the right to have them receive that

141 Note 13, above.

142 [1984] 2 S.C.R. 66. The opinion was rendered by ''the Court''

143 The province's attempt to justify the Quebec clause under s. 1 of the Charter failed, on the ground that the Quebec clause was such a direct denial of the right guaranteed by s. 23(1)(b) that s. 1 had no application: for discussion, see ch. 35, Limitation of Rights, under heading 35.6, ''Limits'', above.

instruction in minority language educational facilities provided out of public funds''.

In *Mahe* v. *Alberta* (1990),[144] the Supreme Court of Canada, speaking through Dickson C.J., held that the effect of paragraphs (a) and (b) of subsection (3) of s. 23 was to establish a ''sliding scale'' of entitlement,[145] based on the number of children whose parents qualify under s. 23.[146] At one end of the scale, the number of children might be so small that the where-numbers-warrant threshold of paragraph (a) would not be crossed, and no programme of minority language instruction would be required. It is arguable, however, that a very small number of minority language students would warrant the provision of bus transportation to a minority language school, if there is one within reasonable driving distance. A somewhat larger number of students would warrant the provision of classroom space and some intensive minority language instruction within a majority language school. A larger number would cross the where-numbers-warrant threshold of paragraph (b), which requires the provision out of public funds of ''minority language educational facilities''. Those facilities might include part of a school or an entire school. At the high end of the scale, the number of children might be so large that paragraph (b)'s requirement of ''minority language educational facilities'' would require the establishment of a minority language school board. ''The idea of a sliding scale is simply that s. 23 guarantees whatever type and level of rights and services is appropriate in order to provide minority language instruction for the particular number of students involved.''[147]

The issue in *Mahe* was the extent of the s. 23 right near the high end of the sliding scale. In Edmonton, there were about 4,000 children whose parents had s. 23 rights, and there was a French-language school in operation with 242 students and space for another 480 students. The sole question was the entitlement of the s. 23 parents to powers of management and control over their children's French-language education. The Court rejected the argument that the phrase ''minority language educational facilities'' in paragraph (b) of subsection (3) referred only to physical facilities. The phrase did of course include physical facilities, which in this case was satisfied by the provision of Edmonton's French-language school. The phrase also included public funding on a basis at least equivalent to that of the majority's schools, which in this case also seems to have been satisfied.[148] But the phrase extended beyond physical facilities to a degree of management and control that was proportionate to the number of qualifying children.

---

144 [1990] 1 S.C.R. 342. The opinion of the Court was given by Dickson C.J.

145 *Id.*, 366.

146 The application of the where-numbers-warrant test cannot be based solely on the numbers of qualified children in a single school district; s. 23(3)(a) uses the phrase ''wherever in the province'', which transcends the territorial limits of school boards: *Id.*, 386; *Re Education Act (Ont.)* (1984) 47 O.R. (2d) 1, 33 (C.A.).

147 [1990] 1 S.C.R. 342, 366.

148 *Id.*, 378. There was no complaint in the proceedings about the level of funding.

The degree of management and control that was required by s. 23 could include a minority language school board, but in *Mahe* Dickson C.J. was ''not satisfied on the basis of present evidence that the number of students likely to attend Francophone schools in Edmonton is sufficient to mandate the establishment of an independent Francophone school board''.[149] However, he concluded that the numbers did warrant a guaranteed number of Francophone representatives on the school board that operated the existing French-language school (and other programmes of French-language instruction). Those representatives should (subject to provincial regulation) be given exclusive control over the French-language instruction, including the expenditure of funds for that purpose, the appointment of administrators and teachers, and the design of programmes of instruction.

Mahe was followed in *Re Public Schools Act (Man.)* (1993),[150] in which the Supreme Court of Canada struck down Manitoba's legislation respecting French-language schools, because it made no provision for the parents of French-language students to have management and control over French-language education. The Court, speaking through Lamer C.J., estimated that the number of potential French-language students in Manitoba was 5,617 at the minimum, with a possibility that the number was much higher. The Court held that, even on the basis of the low figure, the number warranted the establishment of an independent French-language school board in Manitoba under the exclusive management and control of the French-language minority.

(h) Denominational schools

In *Mahe*, most of the s. 23 parents were Roman Catholic separate school supporters, and the French-language school was operated by the separate school board. Under s. 19 of the Charter, nothing in the Charter was to abrogate or derogate from the denominational school rights conferred on separate school supporters by the Constitution of Canada, which in the case of Alberta meant s. 17 of the Alberta Act.[151] This raised the question whether the exclusive powers of management and control that the Court required to be vested in the representatives of the s. 23 parents would derogate from denominational school rights. The Court pointed out that the representatives of the s. 23 parents on the separate school board would also be denominational trustees, so that there was no requirement that the separate school board cede any powers to non-denominational trustees, and there was no interference with the denominational character of the board. The Court took the view that the vesting of exclusive powers of management and control in the s. 23 representatives ''amounts to the *regulation* of a non-denominational aspect of education, namely, the language of instruction, a form

149 *Id.*, 388-389.

150 [1993] 1 S.C.R. 839. The opinion of the Court was given by Lamer C.J.

151 Note 126, above.

of regulation which the courts have long held to be valid''.[152] Therefore, the Court held that denominational school rights were not prejudiced — they were merely ''regulated''[153] — by the vesting of some exclusive powers of management and control in trustees who represented French-speaking parents.

152 [1990] 1 S.C.R. 342, 382 (emphasis in original).

153 On the ''regulation'' of denominational schools, see ch. 54, Education, under heading 54.4(c), ''Regulation'', below.

54

Education

54.1 Provincial power

Section 93 of the Constitution Act, 1867 confers on the provincial Legislatures the exclusive power to make "laws in relation to education". By virtue of this power, the establishment and administration of schools and universities is a provincial responsibility.[1]

Apart from the remedial power of s. 93(4), which is discussed in the next section of this chapter, federal power over education is limited to what is incidental to particular heads of federal power. For example, schools are operated on military bases under the authority of the federal National Defence Act, and this is probably authorized by s. 91(7) ("militia, military and naval service, and defence").[2] Schools are also operated on Indian reserves under the authority of the federal Indian Act, and this is probably authorized by s. 91(24) ("Indians, and lands reserved for the Indians").[3] But such federal interventions are narrow and minor exceptions to the general rule of provincial power over education.

---

1 See Beaudoin, *La Constitution du Canada* (1990), 437-451.

2 *A.-G. Can.* v. *St. Hubert Base Teachers' Assn.* [1983] 1 S.C.R. 498, 510 (raising but not deciding issue).

3 On the extent of federal power under s. 91(24), see ch. 27, Aboriginal Peoples, under heading 27.1, "Federal legislative power", above.

Section 93 restricts the provincial power to make laws in relation to education by the addition of four qualifying subsections. Subsection (1) provides that "nothing in any such law shall prejudicially affect any right or privilege with respect to denominational schools which any class of persons have by law in the province at the union". Subsection (2) provides that the dissentient schools for Protestants and Roman Catholics in Quebec are to be on the same footing as the separate schools for Roman Catholics in Ontario.[4] Subsection (3) gives to the "Protestant or Roman Catholic minority" in any province an appeal to the Governor General in Council from any act or decision of any provincial authority affecting any right or privilege of the minority group in relation to education. Subsection (4) gives the federal Parliament the power to enact "remedial laws" to give effect to any decision of the Governor General in Council under this section.

At the time of confederation, it was a matter of concern that the new Province of Ontario (formerly Canada West) would be controlled by a Protestant majority that might exercise its power over education to take away the rights of its Roman Catholic minority. There was a similar concern that the new Province of Quebec (formerly Canada East), which would be controlled by a Roman Catholic majority, might not respect the rights of its Protestant minority. The same concerns existed with respect to *linguistic* minorities, who in 1867 were more or less the same as religious minorities — French-speakers being mainly Catholic and English-speakers being mainly Protestant. The constitutional protections for linguistic minorities that were adopted at confederation have been discussed in the previous chapter, 53, Language. With respect to religious minorities, the solution was to guarantee their rights to denominational education, and to define those rights by reference to the state of law at the time of confederation. In that way, the existing denominational school rights of the Catholic minority in Ontario could not be impaired by the Legislature; and the Protestant minority in Quebec would be similarly protected. This is the reason for the guarantees of denominational school rights in s. 93.[5]

Section 93 applies not only to Ontario and Quebec, but also to the other original provinces, namely, New Brunswick and Nova Scotia. It also became applicable to British Columbia (admitted in 1871) and to Prince Edward Island (admitted in 1873). Slightly different versions of s. 93 were negotiated upon the creation or admission of the remaining provinces, and these are to be found in the statutes which constituted Manitoba (1870), Alberta (1905) and Saskatchewan (1905) and in the Terms of Union of Newfoundland (1949).[6]

Section 93 is unusual in two respects. First, by qualifying provincial power to legislate in relation to education, s. 93 amounts to a small bill of rights for the

4 See *Greater Montreal Protestant School Bd.* v. *Que.* [1989] S.C.R. 377, 418 (explaining relationship between s. 93(1) and s. 92(2)).

5 See *Re Bill 30 (Ont. Separate School Funding)* [1987] 1 S.C.R. 1148, 1173-1174 per Wilson J.

6 See the previous chapter, 53, Language, under heading 53.8(a), "Section 93 of Constitution Act, 1867", for the relevant references on the applicability of s. 93 and its variants.

protection of minority religious groups;[7] the meaning of these educational guarantees will be the chief topic of the text which follows. Secondly, by allowing a minority group to appeal to the Governor in Council (the federal cabinet), and by authorizing the federal Parliament to enact remedial laws to give effect to a decision on appeal, s. 93 subordinates the provinces to the federal government and Parliament. We have already noticed that this element of provincial subordination is anomalous in a federal system.[8]

54.2 Federal power to enact remedial laws

The federal power to enact remedial laws, which is conferred by subsection (4) of s. 93, has never actually been used. The one time when a remedial law nearly was enacted was in 1896 to resolve the Manitoba school question, which arose out of Manitoba's abolition of its denominational school system in 1890. A remedial bill was introduced into Parliament by the Conservative government; but an election intervened to change the federal government, and the new Liberal government under Prime Minister Laurier persuaded the Manitoba government to change the objectionable law itself.[9] The courts also became involved in the Manitoba school question, and they decided that the aggrieved minority could pursue both a remedy in the courts under s. 93(1) to secure a ruling that a law is invalid, as well as the appeal to the Governor General in Council under s. 93(3) to secure a remedial law under s. 93(4). Neither remedy had the effect of ousting its companion. However, it was held that the aggrieved minority had no remedy under s. 93(1), because no protected right or privilege had been impaired;[10] but that an appeal still lay to the Governor General in Council under s. 93(3), because s. 93(3) protected a broader range of rights and privileges than s. 93(1).[11]

54.3 Protected rights and privileges

Section 93(1) provides:

> Nothing in any such law [i.e., any law in relation to education] shall prejudicially affect any right or privilege with respect to denominational schools which any class of persons have by law in the province at the union.

---

7 My description in an earlier edition of s. 93 as containing ''a small bill of rights'' was disapproved in *Greater Montreal Protestant School Bd.* v. *Que.* [1989] 1 S.C.R. 377, 401 per Beetz J. for majority. Beetz J.'s point was not really that the description was wrong, but rather that s. 93(1) protects only rights and privileges guaranteed by law in 1867 — a fixed statutory benchmark — and does not attract the liberal interpretation that is appropriate for the rights guaranteed by the Charter of Rights.

8 See ch. 5, Federalism, under heading 5.3, ''Federalism in Canada'', above.

9 Schmeiser, *Civil Liberties in Canada* (1964), 164-167; Bale, ''Law, Politics and the Manitoba School Question'' (1985) 63 Can. Bar Rev. 461.

10 *City of Winnipeg* v. *Barrett* [1892] A.C. 445.

11 *Brophy* v. *A.-G. Man.* [1895] A.C. 202; see also *Tiny Roman Catholic Separate School Trustees* v. *The King* [1928] A.C. 363, 369-373 for analysis of the differences between s. 93(1) and s. 93(3).

The protected rights and privileges are defined by a number of phrases in the section. The phrase ''with respect to denominational schools'' confines the protection to denominational schools; provincial power over non-denominational schools is quite unlimited.[12] Even with respect to denominational schools, the protection does not extend to aspects of the curriculum that have no denominational significance.[13] The phrase ''any class of persons'' means a class of persons ''determined according to religious belief, and not according to race or language'';[14] in other words, the only protected rights are those possessed by the entire class of Roman Catholics or Protestants. The phrase ''by law'' means that only rights and privileges established by statute are entitled to protection; longstanding practices or customs do not qualify for protection.[15] The phrase ''at the union'' means that only rights and privileges in existence at confederation (or admission to Canada)[16] are entitled to protection; rights and privileges created subsequently do not qualify.

The exact scope of the protected rights and privileges in each province can only be ascertained by examining the law regarding denominational or separate schools which was in force in that province when it joined Canada. The protected rights and privileges will therefore vary from province to province depending upon the state of its pre-confederation law.[17]

For example, in *Ottawa Separate School Trustees* v. *Mackell* (1917),[18] the question arose whether the province of Ontario had the power to enact the notorious regulation 17, which required hitherto French-speaking separate schools to

---

12 *Hirsch* v. *Montreal Protestant School Commrs.* [1928] A.C. 200.

13 *Greater Montreal Protestant School Bd.* v. *Que.* [1989] 1 S.C.R. 377 (upholding uniform curriculum for non-denominational subjects; uniform curriculum did not apply to denominational subjects; and there was some power to adapt the uniform curriculum to local needs).

14 *Ottawa Separate School Trustees* v. *Mackell* [1917] A.C. 62, 69, holding that the section would not protect rights and privileges possessed only by the French-speaking Roman Catholics.

15 *Maher* v. *Town of Portland* (1874) reported only in *Wheeler's Confederation Law of Canada* (1896), 338. Section 22 of the Manitoba Act, 1870, which is Manitoba's equivalent of s. 93, defines the protected rights as those existing ''by law or practice''. But the added words ''or practice'' were virtually ignored in *City of Winnipeg* v. *Barrett* [1892] A.C. 445, where the Privy Council refused to accord protection to rights and privileges with respect to denominational schools which had been enjoyed in practice (though not in law) since before Manitoba's admission to confederation. A sequel case, *Brophy* v. *A.-G. Man.* [1895] A.C. 202, although concerned with the different question of the scope of the appeal to the Governor General in Council, indicated some relaxation of the narrow view taken in *Barrett*. These cases, and the Manitoba school question generally, are discussed in Schmeiser, note 9, above, 160-166.

16 The date of admission is the point of reference for those provinces admitted after 1867.

17 An account of the situation in each province is contained in Schmeiser, note 9, above, ch. 4. See also the full discussion by Deschênes C.J. in *Protestant School Bd. of Greater Montreal* v. *Min. of Education of Que.* (1976) 83 D.L.R. (3d) 645 (Que. S.C.).

18 [1917] A.C. 62. This case and the issue of language of instruction in general, is more fully discussed in the previous chapter 53, Language, under heading 53.8, ''Language of education'', above.

shift to English-speaking instruction.[19] The Privy Council held that the regulation was valid. Their lordships examined the law in force in Ontario at confederation and concluded that it did not confer upon the separate school trustees any legal power to choose the language of instruction in the schools. (The fact that the trustees had enjoyed that power in practice was irrelevant.) It followed that the choice of the language of instruction was not protected by s. 93(1), and it could therefore be taken away by the province.[20]

The exclusion from s. 93(1) of denominational school rights that were not in existence at confederation does not mean, of course, that new rights and privileges cannot be conferred. The plenary power over education in the opening words of s. 93 provides each provincial Legislature with the continuing power to confer new denominational school rights. Such rights, created by post-confederation legislation, are not guaranteed by s. 93(1), and therefore can be amended or repealed by the same Legislature that enacted them. However, post-confederation rights do enjoy a measure of political protection in that, if they are amended or repealed, an appeal lies to the Governor in Council under s. 93(3), and a remedial law could be enacted by the federal Parliament under s. 93(4).

In the *Ontario Separate School Funding Reference* (1987),[21] the question arose whether the Charter of Rights had limited the power of a provincial Legislature to confer new denominational school rights. At issue was an Ontario statute which purported to provide full public funding for Roman Catholic secondary schools (which had previously not been funded beyond grade 10). Before the adoption of the Charter, no constitutional objection could have been made to such a statute. But now the argument was advanced that the funding statute, by conferring benefits only on Roman Catholic school supporters, discriminated on the basis of religion and offended the equality rights in s. 15 of the Charter. The Supreme Court of Canada rejected this argument. The Court reasoned that the language of subsection (3) of s. 93 (providing for the appeal to the Governor in Council) explicitly contemplated the establishment by a province of new denominational school systems, and implicitly contemplated future additions to existing denominational school systems. The power to establish or add to a denominational school system inevitably involved the use of religion as a basis of distinction. The Charter was not to be interpreted as rendering unconstitutional a distinction

19 A full discussion of this turbulent episode is contained in Schmeiser, note 9, above, 143-146. Regulation 17 was repealed in 1926, and French-language schools re-emerged.

20 See also *Protestant School Bd. of Greater Montreal* v. *Min. of Education of Que.* (1976) 83 D.L.R. (3d) 645 (Que. S.C.) (holding that the same situation obtained in Quebec).

21 *Re Bill 30 (Ont. Separate School Funding)* [1987] 1 S.C.R. 1148. The majority opinion was written by Wilson J., with the agreement of Dickson C.J., McIntyre and LaForest JJ. Estey J. wrote a concurring opinion with the agreement of Beetz J. Lamer J. wrote a concurring opinion. I disclose that I was one of the counsel for the Attorney General of Ontario. For comment on the decision, see Bale (1986) 18 Ottawa L. Rev. 533; Bale (1989) 11 Supreme Court L.R. 399.

that was expressly permitted by another part of the Constitution.[22] This line of reasoning was accepted by all seven sitting judges. (As will be explained later in this chapter, four of the seven judges were also prepared to support the funding law as being the return of rights possessed by Roman Catholic school supporters at confederation.[23] On this basis, the funding statute did not confer new rights, but vindicated old ones, and was shielded from Charter review by s. 93(1).)[24]

It does not follow from the *Ontario Separate School Funding Reference* that the Charter of Rights has no application to a law establishing or extending a denominational school system of a kind contemplated by s. 93(3). On the contrary, all of the Charter guarantees, including the equality guarantee, apply to such a law, with just one exception. The exception is that the law may discriminate on the basis of religion to the extent necessary to give the school system its denominational character. The exception is what is decided by the *Ontario Separate School Funding Reference*. But a denominational school law could not authorize discrimination on the basis of race, or any other ground that was not necessary to the denominational character of the schools. Nor could the law provide for unreasonable search or seizure, or cruel and unusual punishment, or anything else prohibited by the Charter, unless the provision was necessary to the denominational character of the schools.

54.4 Prejudicial effect

(a) Benign laws

The laws condemned by s. 93 are those that "prejudicially affect" the protected rights and privileges. It follows, and the courts have held, that laws having a beneficial effect on the rights and privileges of denominational schools are unimpeachable. Thus, an Ontario statute which changed the method of election of separate school trustees was held to be valid because the court found that the statute was an improvement over the pre-confederation law.[25] An Alberta statute

22 The reasoning was not based on s. 29 of the Charter, which shields from judicial review only denominational school rights that are "guaranteed" by or under the Constitution of Canada. Assuming that the funding statute conferred new denominational school rights, the rights were not "guaranteed" in the sense contemplated by s. 29; [1987] 1 S.C.R. 1148, 1197 per Wilson J., 1209 per Estey J. The reasoning was based on a reading of the Constitution as a whole, with the specific authority over denominational schools in s. 93 prevailing over the more general prohibition of religious discrimination in s. 15 of the Charter.

23 On this basis, the provision for funding was not only valid, but could not be repealed by a future Legislature: [1987] 1 S.C.R. 1148, 1198 per Wilson J.

24 On this basis, the rights were "guaranteed" within the meaning of s. 29 of the Charter, and s. 29 accordingly applied: [1987] 1 S.C.R. 1148, 1196 per Wilson J. However, s. 29 was not necessary to protect the funding statute from Charter review: even without s. 29, rights protected by s. 93(1) could not be affected by the Charter of Rights: *Id.*, 1197 per Wilson J.

25 *Belleville Separate School Trustees* v. *Grainger* (1878) 25 Gr. 570 (Ont. Ch.).

which altered the allocation of school taxes paid by corporations was held to be valid because it increased the separate schools' share of the taxes.[26]

(b) Neutral laws

The courts have been reluctant to find a prejudicial effect even in the case of legislation which is not benign. They have recognized a class of "neutral" legislation which, although it affects protected rights and privileges, is still valid because it lacks the element of prejudicial effect. The extent to which the courts have leaned against a finding of prejudicial effect is shown by *Ottawa Separate Schools Trustees* v. *Quebec Bank* (1920),[27] where the separate schools were forced by statute to assume liabilities incurred by a provincially-appointed commission which had operated the separate schools for a short period of time.[28] It seems obvious that the imposition of a new financial burden could not be regarded as beneficial, but the Privy Council held that it was not prejudicial either. Their lordships pointed out that the liabilities had been incurred by the commission for school purposes, and would have been incurred by the trustees if they had been operating the schools. The force of this reasoning is not apparent, but the general idea seems to be that a reasonable detriment should not be accounted prejudicial.

(c) Regulation

Other kinds of separate school regulation have been countenanced by the courts. In *Tiny Roman Catholic Separate School Trustees* v. *The King* (1928),[29] the Privy Council said that Ontario had the power to "regulate" instruction in the separate schools. In other words, the protected rights and privileges were subject to a degree of provincial regulation. On this basis, their lordships upheld a provincial law which prohibited the separate schools in Ontario from offering secondary (or high school) education beyond grade 10, although there was no such restriction on the separate schools at the time of confederation.

The reasoning in *Tiny* was based on the fact that, at confederation, separate schools were subject to regulation by a provincial body called the Council of Public Instruction. The Privy Council assumed that this power of regulation was sufficiently broad that it could have been exercised to prohibit secondary instruction. Although this power had never been exercised prior to confederation, its existence was sufficient to deny s. 93(1) protection to secondary-level instruction. The result of this reasoning was to empower the province to severely curtail rights that Roman Catholic school supporters undoubtedly possessed at confederation. Moreover, the reasoning had the potential to render the s. 93(1) guarantee almost

26 *Re Calgary Bd. of Education and A.-G. Alta.* (1981) 122 D.L.R. (3d) 249 (Alta. C.A.).
27 [1920] A.C. 230.
28 See note 37 and accompanying text, below.
29 [1928] A.C. 363.

illusory, because the Privy Council said that the only limit on the power of regulation was that it did not extend to the abolition of the separate schools: ''the power to regulate does not imply a power to abolish''.[30]

In the *Ontario Separate School Funding Reference* (1987),[31] the Supreme Court of Canada reconsidered the *Tiny* case. As noted earlier, the statute in issue provided full public funding of secondary education in Roman Catholic separate schools. This represented a reversal by the Ontario Legislature of the policy that had been upheld in *Tiny*. The Ontario funding statute was attacked as being discrimination on the basis of religion in violation of s. 15 of the Charter. The statute was defended as a vindication of rights that were constitutionally protected by s. 93(1) of the Constitution Act, 1867. But the difficulty with this defence was that the *Tiny* case had decided that the provision of secondary education was not a right that was protected by s. 93(1). In the *Ontario Separate School Funding Reference*, a majority of the Supreme Court of Canada overruled the *Tiny* case. The majority held that the Privy Council had been wrong to decide that the power of regulation possessed by the Council of Public Instruction could have been exercised to radically curtail the level of instruction in the separate school system: the prohibition of secondary education should have been held to be a breach of a s. 93(1) right. It followed from this rejection of *Tiny* that Ontario's funding statute simply restored to Roman Catholic school supporters a constitutional right that had been unconstitutionally withheld from them by the pre-*Tiny* legislation. Since the modern funding statute came within s. 93(1), it was shielded from Charter review. (A minority of the Court, while upholding the funding statute on other grounds,[32] refused to reopen the *Tiny* case.)

The *Ontario Separate School Funding Reference* does not disturb the general rule that denominational school rights are subject to regulation.[33] What the case decides is that regulation does not extend to a denial of any of the fundamental characteristics of denominational education as established by pre-confederation law. In Ontario, one of the fundamental characteristics is the level of instruction.

(d) Withdrawal of management

Another fundamental pre-confederation characteristic of denominational education is the power of denominational trustees to manage the denominational

30 [1928] A.C. 363, 389.

31 [1987] 1 S.C.R. 1148; see note 21, above.

32 See text accompanying note 21, above.

33 See also *Toronto Corp.* v. *Roman Catholic Schools Trustees* [1926] A.C. 81 (zoning by-law and building code applicable); *Moose Jaw Bd. of Education* v. *A.-G. Sask.* (1975) 57 D.L.R. (3d) 315 (Sask. C.A.) (collective bargaining for teachers upheld); *Greater Montreal Protestant School Bd.* v. *Que.* [1989] 1 S.C.R. 377, 388 (Wilson J.'s concurring opinion was that the curriculum could be regulated, provided it did not ''undermine the denominational character of the separate schools''); *Mahe* v. *Alta.* [1990] 1 S.C.R. 342, 382 (language rights conferred by s. 23 of Charter could be applied to denominational schools as a ''regulation of a non-denominational aspect of education'').

schools. *Ottawa Roman Catholic Separate Schools* v. *Ottawa Corporation* (1916),[34] was a case that arose out of the province of Ontario's attempts to enforce obedience to regulation 17, the English-language requirement which (we have earlier noticed) was upheld by the Privy Council in *Mackell*.[35] In Ottawa, the trustees of French-speaking separate schools refused to open the schools rather than comply with regulation 17. The province thereupon enacted a statute which authorized the province to withdraw from the school trustees all powers over the schools and vest the powers in a commission appointed by the provincial government. The Privy Council held that the statute authorizing the commission prejudicially affected the right of management, which was part of Ontario's law at the time of confederation. The statute therefore violated s. 93(1) and was invalid.[36]

The Ontario Legislature then enacted a second statute to force the trustees to obey regulation 17. The second statute was very similar to its invalid predecessor, employing the same device of a provincially-appointed commission to take over the schools. But the second statute was more precise as to when the powers could be assumed and when they had to be relinquished (the first statute had left these decisions to the discretion of the Minister of Education). In *Re Ottawa Separate Schools* (1917),[37] the Appellate Division of the Supreme Court of Ontario held that the second statute was valid. In the Court's view, it was the indefinite and discretionary nature of the suspending power in the first statute which made it bad. The more limited suspending power in the second statute was good. A provision calculated only to secure the observance of the law by separate school trustees was not inconsistent with the trustees' power of management, because that power should not be treated as enabling the trustees to conduct their schools in defiance of the law.

While the Ontario Court upholding the second statute did not expressly rely on a provincial power of regulation, the decision is consistent with the later cases that hold that even a protected right or privilege (in this case the power of management) is subject to provincial regulation. However, the Privy Council decision striking down the first statute establishes that a total suspension of the trustees' powers of management for an indefinite time goes beyond regulation and is (at least in Ontario) a violation of s. 93(1). It is easy to see why this is so: if it were possible for a province to appoint managers in lieu of the elected trustees of the denominational schools, then the schools' character could be destroyed.

---

34 [1917] A.C. 76.

35 Note 18 and accompanying text, above.

36 A commission had been appointed, and had taken over the management of the schools. The result of the decision was that the commission had to relinquish its powers to the separate school trustees. This led to litigation as to which body was liable for debts incurred by the commission: the litigation is described in the text accompanying note 27, above.

37 (1917) 41 O.L.R. 259 (A.D.).

(e) Withdrawal of exclusivity

Another fundamental pre-confederation characteristic of denominational education is the dedication of the denominational schools to members of the denomination. *Hirsch* v. *Montreal Protestant School Commissioners* (1928)[38] involved a Quebec statute of 1903 which deemed Jews to be Protestants. The effect of the law on the Protestant denominational schools in Quebec would have been to enable Jews to join with Protestants in the establishment of a denominational school and the election of its trustees, to enable Jews to be appointed as school trustees, and to compel the schools to accept Jewish children. These applications of the 1903 statute were held to have a prejudicial effect on the pre-confederation right of the Protestant minority to establish its own schools under the exclusive management of Protestant trustees for the exclusive use of Protestant children. These applications of the 1903 statute were accordingly unconstitutional for inconsistency with s. 93(1).[39]

The *Hirsch* case emphasizes that the right of a Roman Catholic or Protestant minority to establish and support denominational schools which will be managed by their own elected trustees is a fundamental characteristic of a separate school system. If the schools could be compelled to serve other sections of the population, then they would retain their denominational character only by the grace of the Legislature. Section 93(1) precludes any breach of this principle of exclusivity.[40] Needless to say, the voluntary acceptance by a denominational school board of persons outside the denomination is an entirely different matter, raising no constitutional question.

(f) Reduction in funding

One of the elements of the scheme of ''regulation'' of separate schools that was upheld by the Privy Council in *Tiny*[41] was a reduction in the separate schools' share of the province's funding for education. In *Attorney General of Quebec* v. *Greater Hull School Board* (1984),[42] the Supreme Court of Canada had to consider a Quebec law that repealed a pre-confederation law which stipulated that denominational schools must share in provincial grants for education on a basis proportionate to the number of children attending denominational schools compared to the number of children attending non-denominational schools. The Court held

38 [1928] A.C. 200.

39 The 1903 statute was valid to the extent that it did not impinge on the rights and privileges of the denominational schools; in particular, it was valid in its application to nondenominational schools.

40 Cf. *A.-G. Que.* v. *Greater Hull School Bd.* [1984] 2 S.C.R. 575, (striking down law providing for referendum on denominational school taxes, on ground that non-denominational school supporters were eligible to vote); this case is discussed in text accompanying note 41, below.

41 Note 29, above.

42 [1984] 2 S.C.R. 575.

unanimously that the freeing of the granting power from this restriction was a violation of s. 93(1), and the new law was accordingly struck down.

The decision in the *Greater Hull School Board* case seemed to be inconsistent with the *Tiny* case, which had granted extensive provincial discretion to depart from pre-confederation rules in fixing the funding of separate schools. However, the Court in *Greater Hull* did not question the *Tiny* case, and the majority even cited it with apparent approval at one point.[43] In the *Ontario Separate School Funding Reference* (1987),[44] the majority of the Court drew the logical inference and overruled the reasoning of the *Tiny* case with respect to funding (as well as the level of instruction). The Court held that at confederation in Ontario, as in Quebec, separate school supporters had the right to a proportionate share of public funding for education. The Privy Council in *Tiny* had been wrong to uphold a reduction in that share. The Ontario Legislature in now granting full funding to the separate schools was restoring to Roman Catholic school supporters a right that was constitutionally guaranteed by s. 93(1).

Another provision of the law in issue in the *Greater Hull School Board* case required denominational school boards to obtain approval by referendum for taxation beyond a stipulated amount. This was a change from the school boards' pre-confederation powers of taxation, which were not so limited. The Court also struck down this provision, but the judges divided in their reasons. For Chouinard J., writing for himself and Dickson C.J., Beetz, Estey, McIntyre and Wilson JJ., the requirement of a referendum was invalid, because those eligible to vote in the referendum included non-denominational school supporters; had the referendum been limited to denominational school supporters, Chouinard J. would have upheld it as a valid regulation of denominational schools. For Le Dain J., writing for himself and Lamer J., the new requirement of a referendum was a sufficient fetter on the taxing power of denominational school boards that it was prejudicial to the effective management of the denominational schools; the requirement was therefore invalid, and would not have been saved if those eligible to vote were restricted to denominational school supporters.

In *Ontario Home Builders' Association* v. *York Region Board of Education* (1996),[45] a challenge was brought to Ontario's system of education development charges, which were charges that could be levied by public and separate school boards on land undergoing residential development. The purpose of the charges was to fund the construction of the new schools that would be needed when the land was developed. The system was challenged under s. 93(1) on two alternative bases. If the charges were regarded as assessments for the support of the school systems, there was no attempt to distinguish between separate school supporters and public school supporters. Education development charges levied on developers by a public school board, for example, would be passed on to the purchasers

43 *Id.*, 594.

44 [1987] 1 S.C.R. 1148, 1196.

45 [1996] 2 S.C.R. 929. The opinion of the Court on this issue was written by Iacobucci J.

of the new houses, some of whom would be separate school supporters. This was contrary to the right of denominational school supporters to be exempt from assessments for the support of the public school system. If, on the other hand, the charges were regarded as part of the provincial government's grant to the public and separate school systems, there was no statutory guarantee that the separate school board's entitlement to the proceeds of the charges would be proportionate on a per pupil basis with that of the public school board. This was contrary to the right of denominational school supporters to a proportionate share of the provincial grant for education. The Supreme Court of Canada unanimously rejected both arguments. The Court held that the education development charges were neither an assessment nor a grant, but a "new source of funds" that was not contemplated at the time of Confederation, and which was outside the scope of the denominational school rights protected by s. 93(1).[46] The Court also held that, if the charges were regarded as part of the provincial grant for education, the requirement of proportionality no longer called for a strict per pupil comparison (as it certainly did at Confederation), but simply a "fair and non-discriminatory" distribution.[47] The statutory system of education development charges was, the Court held, fair and non-discriminatory as between the separate and the public school systems.

(g) Expropriation of resources

In *Re Education Act (Quebec)* (1993),[48] the Supreme Court of Canada upheld what may be the most radical of all the many statutes that, over the years, have affected denominational schools. At issue was a Quebec statute that transformed the educational structure of the province from one organized according to religion to one organized according to language. The statute divided the province into two sets of territories, one set for French-language school boards and the other set for English-language school boards; a school board was established for each linguistic territory. All of the schools, equipment and other assets of the Protestant and Catholic school boards (except those serving Montreal and Quebec City), along with their teachers and administrators, were taken without compensation and transferred to the new linguistic school boards. The Court held that s. 93(1) did not confer on denominational school supporters any constitutional right to the assets that their school boards had built up with their taxes over the years. The right conferred by s. 93(1) was the right to dissent, and that was preserved, at least in theory, by the new statute. Within each linguistic territory, a Protestant or Roman Catholic minority could establish its own denominational school board, and the denominational board and the linguistic board were then obliged to agree upon a sharing of the linguistic school board's assets with the denominational

46 *Id.*, para. 75.
47 *Id.*, para. 74.
48 [1993] 2 S.C.R. 511. The opinion of the Court was written by Gonthier J.

board. The Minister of Education was to serve as an arbiter of the fairness of the division of the assets in the event that the two boards could not agree, and the Minister was obliged to ensure that the denominational board had the assets it required.

The new right of dissent differed radically from that existing in 1867, because the new right depended upon the dissenters being a minority within one of the statutorily-created linguistic territories; for example, English-speaking Protestants would be unlikely ever to be a minority within an English-language school territory. Moreover, the right of dissent, when it was available, forced the minority denomination to start from scratch, with no guarantee of the assets accumulated in the past by their supporters, with no guarantee of the same teachers and schoolhouses, and in practice ultimately dependent upon the decisions of the Minister of Education as to the resources that they received. The Court acknowledged these differences, but held that the new right of dissent was sufficient to satisfy s. 93(1).[49]

---

49 The Court also upheld a host of other changes, many of which seemed calculated to make the right of dissent at least less attractive than it had been, including a prohibition on the denominational schools accepting students who were not of that denomination, a governmental power to alter the territories of denominational school boards, and an assignment to a central agency of the powers to borrow for school boards and allocate taxes among school boards.

IV

PRACTICE

55

Effect of Unconstitutional Law

55.1 Invalidity of unconstitutional law

What is the effect of a judicial decision that a law is unconstitutional? Section 52(1) of the Constitution Act, 1982 (the supremacy clause) provides that the Constitution of Canada is "the supreme law of Canada", and that "any law that is inconsistent with the provisions of the Constitution" is "of no force or effect". This supremacy clause dates only from 1982, but it states a principle that has always been part of Canadian constitutional law. A law enacted outside the authority granted by the Constitution is ultra vires, invalid, void, a nullity. As Field J. said in the Supreme Court of the United States in 1886: "An unconstitutional act is not a law; it confers no rights; it imposes no duties; it affords no protection; it creates no office; it is, in legal contemplation, as inoperative as though it had never been passed".[1]

A judicial decision that a law is unconstitutional is retroactive in the sense that it involves the nullification of the law from the outset. Indeed, any judicial decision must be retroactive in order to apply to the facts before the court, since those facts must have already occurred. That a court makes new law when it

1 *Norton* v. *Shelby County* (1886) 118 U.S. 425, 442.

overrules prior doctrine or even when it decides an unprecedented case is not open to doubt; but a court does not make new law in the same way as a legislative body, that is, for the future only.

The Supreme Court of the United States, a more pragmatic body than its Canadian counterpart, has not felt constrained by this traditional difference between a court and a legislative body. In cases involving criminal defendants who have been convicted under statutes or practices which the Court has found for the first time to be unconstitutional, the Court has abandoned Field J.'s relentless logic and held that it has a discretion to make a constitutional ruling prospective only,[2] with the result that facts occurring before the decision are not to be governed by the "new" ruling.[3] This practice of "prospective overruling" is difficult to justify in theory,[4] however attractive it may appear in practice, and it has never been accepted by Canadian courts. For a Canadian court, a constitutional restriction operates of its own force, even if judicial recognition of the fact has been delayed.[5]

Once the Supreme Court of Canada has held that a law is unconstitutional, there can be no doubt about the status of the law: it is invalid, and need not be obeyed. The same result follows from a holding of invalidity by a lower court. Moreover, it is unlikely that the government would succeed in obtaining a stay of judgment, or an injunction compelling obedience to the law, pending an appeal.[6] Of course, the holding of unconstitutionality might be reversed on appeal,[7] in

---

2 The leading cases are *Linkletter* v. *Walker* (1965) 381 U.S. 618; *Stovall* v. *Denno* (1967) 388 U.S. 293; see Traynor, "Transatlantic Reflections on Leeways and Limits of Appellate Courts" [1980] Utah L. Rev. 225; Tribe, *American Constitutional Law* (2nd ed., 1988), 26-32.

3 If the ruling is exclusively prospective, then the party successfully asserting the new constitutional right has to be denied relief. If the party is granted relief, the question arises whether any other past events are caught by the new ruling. American courts have differed on these issues, which raise grave questions of equity between similarly-situated litigants.

4 Both the legislative character of the judicial lawmaking (discussed in text) and the determination of the cut-off time (previous note) are serious theoretical problems: see Weiler, "Legal Values and Judicial Decision-Making" (1970) 48 Can. Bar Rev. 1, 29-33.

5 Friedland, "Prospective and Retrospective Lawmaking" (1974) 24 U. Toronto L.J. 170, suggests that there might be some room for prospective overruling in Canadian constitutional cases, but he acknowledges (at p. 179) that the short time for appeal and the limited opportunity for collateral attack on criminal convictions in Canada render the American concern about re-opening convictions of little practical significance. Prospective overruling was considered and rejected in *Re Edward and Edward* (1987) 39 D.L.R. (4th) 654 (Sask. C.A.) (a matrimonial property case).

6 See the next section of this chapter, under heading 55.2, "Stay of proceedings", below.

7 In the case of federal laws that are enforced in the provincial courts, there is also the possibility that a holding of invalidity in one province might not be followed in another province. The general rule is that the courts of one province are not bound by decisions of the courts of another province. This rule applies to the interpretation of federal laws: *Wolf* v. *The Queen* [1975] 2 S.C.R. 107; so that the same law can have different meanings in different provinces - until the Supreme Court of Canada rules on the issue. Query whether this carries over to rulings as to constitutionality. Can a federal law be valid in one province and invalid in another? Whatever the theoretical difficulty, this situation does occasionally arise.

which case the theory would be that the law had always been constitutional. Anyone disobeying a law, in reliance on the judgment of a lower court that the law is unconstitutional, does take the risk that the law will ultimately be held to be constitutional. However, it is unlikely that such a person would be exposed to criminal liability by the retroactive effect of the appellate court's reversal of the holding of unconstitutionality.[8]

55.2 Stay of proceedings

When proceedings are brought to obtain a ruling that a law is unconstitutional, or when an appeal is brought from a ruling that a law is constitutional, will a court stay or enjoin the continued enforcement of the law pending a decision as to its validity? The short answer to this question is usually no. The applicable principles were laid down in *Manitoba* v. *Metropolitan Stores* (1987).[9] In that case, an employer, who was resisting the imposition by the Manitoba Labour Relations Board of a first collective agreement, brought proceedings in the Manitoba Court of Queen's Bench to have the relevant provisions of Manitoba's Labour Relations Act declared unconstitutional. The employer then applied to the Court to stay the proceedings of the Manitoba Labour Relations Board until the issue of the validity of the legislation had been determined by the Court. The application went on up to the Supreme Court of Canada, which denied the stay. Beetz J. for the Court said that a stay of proceedings pending a trial (or appeal) was essentially the same as an interlocutory injunction and should be governed by the same rules. Those rules would require the applicant to establish: (1) that there is a serious issue to be determined at the trial (or appeal); (2) that the applicant would suffer irreparable harm if the stay was not granted; and (3) that the balance of convenience favours granting the stay. On the last issue, Beetz J. pointed out that in constitutional cases the balance of convenience must take into account not only the private interests of the litigants, but also the public interest. The public interest, he held, is usually better served by the continued enforcement of the laws than by their (admittedly temporary) suspension. It followed that "in a case where the authority of a law enforcement agency is constitutionally challenged, no interlocutory injunction or stay should issue to restrain that authority from performing its duties to the public unless, in the balance of convenience, the public interest is taken into consideration and given the weight it should carry".[10] In that case, he held that the public interest in the continued operation of the labour laws was not outweighed by any countervailing public interest or by the private interest of the employer, and no stay of proceedings should be granted.

---

8 Charter of Rights, s. 11(g); discussed sec. 48.8, "Retroactive offences (s. 11(g))", above.
9 [1987] 1 S.C.R. 110. The opinion of the Court was written by Beetz J.
10 *Id.*, 149.

In *RJR-MacDonald* v. *Canada* (1994),[11] the Supreme Court of Canada refused to stay a judgment of the Quebec Court of Appeal upholding the constitutionality of the federal Tobacco Products Control Act. The Act had been held to be unconstitutional by the Quebec Superior Court, but that decision had been reversed by the Court of Appeal. The tobacco companies that had brought the proceedings to challenge the constitutionality of the Act appealed to the Supreme Court of Canada. While that appeal was pending, the federal government promulgated new regulations respecting the packaging of cigarettes, which required the companies to incur substantial unrecoverable expenses in redesigning and producing new packages. The new regulations were made under an enabling section of the challenged Tobacco Products Control Act. The companies pointed out that if the Supreme Court of Canada were to restore the judgment of the Superior Court, the new regulations would fall with the Act, and the cost of producing new packages would be wasted; indeed, further costs would be incurred in restoring the packages to their former design. Even on these facts, the Supreme Court of Canada refused a stay. Following the three-part inquiry required by *Metropolitan Stores*, the Court held (1) that the constitutionality of the Act was a serious issue to be determined on appeal; (2) that the companies would suffer irreparable harm if they were forced to comply with the new regulations; but (3) that the public interest in the continued enforcement of measures designed to promote public health outweighed the economic interests of the companies. The stay of proceedings was therefore denied.[12]

In *143471 Canada Inc.* v. *Quebec* (1994),[13] the Supreme Court of Canada upheld an order of the Quebec Superior Court impounding documents that had been seized by officials investigating evasion of Quebec's meals and hotels tax. The taxpayers had brought proceedings to challenge the constitutionality of the statutory provisions under which the seizures had purportedly been authorized. The impounding order required that the seized documents be sealed and kept in custody pending a final judgment on the constitutionality of the seizures. The impounding order was not literally a stay of proceedings, but it was an interlocutory order the effect of which was to suspend the operation of the taxing legislation against the taxpayers until the constitutionality of the legislation had been determined. The Supreme Court of Canada was unanimous that the three-part inquiry required by *Metropolitan Stores* was the analytical framework under which the impounding order should be reviewed. The Court agreed as well on the answer to the first question, holding that the main proceedings raised a serious constitutional issue for decision. The Court divided on the second question, which

---

11 [1994] 1 S.C.R. 311. The opinion of the Court was written by Sopinka and Cory JJ.

12 When the appeal on the merits reached the Supreme Court of Canada, the Court struck the Act down: *RJR-MacDonald v. Can.* [1995] 3 S.C.R. 199.

13 [1994] 2 S.C.R. 339. The opinion of the majority was written by Cory J., with whom Sopinka and Iacobucci JJ. agreed. Lamer C.J. wrote a concurring opinion in which he was "generally in agreement" with Cory J. The dissenting opinion was written by La Forest J., with whom L'Heureux-Dubé and McLachlan JJ. agreed.

was whether the taxpayers would suffer irreparable harm if the documents were not temporarily impounded. Cory J. for the majority took the view that the mere invasion of privacy involved in the searches that yielded the documents and in the access to the documents amounted to irreparable harm. La Forest J. for the minority took the view that the invasion of privacy was minor in view of the business character of the documents seized (which consisted of invoices, cheque stubs and other financial records) and that the taxpayers would not suffer any significant harm if the documents were inspected by the tax authorities. The Court also divided on the third question, which was where the balance of convenience lay. Cory J. for the majority held that the public interest in the enforcement of the province's taxing legislation would not be much affected, because the impounding orders applied only to those taxpayers who were challenging the constitutionality of the statute and did not involve a general suspension of the statute. La Forest J. for the minority took the view that the public interest in the continued enforcement of the statute ought to predominate. Cory J.'s majority view prevailed, of course, and the impounding order was affirmed.

Once a law has actually been held to be unconstitutional, even if the holding is under appeal, the public interest in the continued enforcement of the law is enormously diminished. The government is therefore usually unsuccessful in obtaining a stay of judgment to keep the law in force pending the decision on appeal.[14] An unusual case is *Thibaudeau* v. *The Queen* (1994),[15] in which the Supreme Court of Canada stayed a judgment of the Federal Court of Appeal that declared unconstitutional a provision of the Income Tax Act imposing income tax on child support payments. Although no reasons were given, the striking down of the law would have affected the tax liability of all payors and recipients of child support and would have required the variation of most support orders and agreements. Faced with so much disruption, the public interest favoured placing the decision on hold until the appeal could be decided by the Supreme Court of Canada. When the Supreme Court of Canada did decide the appeal, it reversed the Federal Court of Appeal and upheld the law.[16]

55.3 Notice requirements in litigation

If the Constitution operates of its own force, and not by virtue of its application by the courts, how are we to explain the efficacy of the notice requirements enacted by all Canadian jurisdictions? As will be explained in the next chapter, Procedure,[17] all jurisdictions have laws which purport to preclude a court from

---

14 E.g., *Regional Municipality of Peel* v. *Great Atlantic and Pacific Co.* (1990) 74 O.R.(2d) 161 (C.A.) (refusing stay of court order declaring Sunday closing law unconstitutional).

15 The decision on the stay is only reported in the *Supreme Court of Canada Bulletin*, 1994, p. 1036.

16 *Thibaudeau* v. *Can.* [1995] 2 S.C.R. 627.

17 Section 56.6, "Intervention", below.

considering the constitutional validity of a statute unless prior notice has been given to the Attorney General. These requirements are respected by the courts, so that it is not unusual for a court to refuse to consider the constitutionality of a statute on the ground that the requisite notice has not been given.[18] The effect of such a refusal will often be to apply a statute that at least one of the litigants wishes to argue is unconstitutional.

It could be argued that a notice requirement that has the effect of precluding judicial review of the constitutionality of a statute is invalid. If a notice requirement were treated as equivalent to a privative clause, that would indeed be the result.[19] But, unlike a privative clause, a notice requirement does not preclude judicial review; it only interposes a simple procedural step as a precondition to judicial review. The purpose of that procedural step is not to impede judicial review, but to facilitate it by ensuring that the constitutional issue is fully argued, not only by the private litigants, but by the appropriate Attorney General, who has the resources and the interest to mount an argument in support of the legislation. It must be remembered that judicial review is always hedged by procedural rules: a proper proceeding must be brought within the proper time by a proper party before a proper court. The raising of a constitutional issue, however plausible, will not cure a procedural infirmity, even though the infirmity will (unless corrected) preclude judicial review. It seems reasonable to characterize the notice requirements as procedural (or perhaps jurisdictional) rules validly enacted for the administration of justice in the courts to which the rules apply.[20]

55.4 Acts done under unconstitutional law

One consequence of the retroactive nullification of a statute that is held to be unconstitutional is that a public official who performs an act under the authority of the statute loses the protection of the statute. If the act would have been tortious[21] if unauthorized by a statute, then the act must now be treated as tortious, and the official will be liable in damages as if the act had been committed privately.[22] The subjection of public officials to the private law of torts was, for Dicey, an

---

18 Strayer, *The Canadian Constitution and the Courts* (3rd ed., 1988), 78-79, supplies citations. A preferable course would often be to adjourn until notice has been given, awarding costs against the party who failed to give timely notice.

19 See ch. 7, Courts, under heading 7.3(f), ''Privative clauses'', above.

20 Provincial power would come from s. 92(14) (the administration of justice in the province). Federal power would come from s. 101 (federal courts). See Strayer, note 18, above, 83-86; Cavarzan, Comment (1984) 62 Can. Bar Rev. 75.

21 Criminal liability is unlikely, by reason of the absence of mens rea and the retroactive nature of the liability: note 8, above.

22 There are some statutory provisions that protect police officers and public officials from personal liability for acts performed in reliance on a statute that is subsequently held to be unconstitutional: Strayer, note 18, above, 106-107; Hogg, *Liability of the Crown* (2nd ed., 1989), 91.

important element of the "rule of law", leading him to claim with pride that "every official, from the Prime Minister down to a constable or a collector of taxes, is under the same responsibility for every act done without legal justification as any other citizen".[23]

While there are many examples of public officials being held personally liable for acting in excess of their legal powers,[24] there seem to be no reported Canadian cases in which an official was held personally liable for acting under an unconstitutional statute.[25] I therefore fall back on a leading Australian case to illustrate the proposition. In *James* v. *Commonwealth* (1939),[26] officials of the federal government of Australia, relying in good faith on powers contained in a federal marketing statute, seized quantities of dried fruit from a producer who was thought to be in breach of the statute. After the marketing statute had been held to be unconstitutional, the producer sued the Crown in right of Australia for damages in tort for the conversion of his property. He succeeded. The retroactive nullification of the statute deprived the enforcing officials of the protection of the statute, and rendered them personally liable for acts that would, apart from the statute, have been tortious. The Crown was vicariously liable for the torts of its servants.

James v. *Commonwealth* illustrates another implication of the subjection of public officials to the private law of torts: the public official is liable only if he or she has committed an act that would in the absence of statutory authority be a tort. There was no doubt, of course, that the seizure of the dried fruit fulfilled this requirement: the seizure constituted the tort of conversion. But, in the same action, the plaintiff producer also claimed damages for "the general loss to his trade or business caused by the continual effect of the administration of the [unconstitutional] Dried Fruits Act and the regulations". He failed in this claim, because the general hindrance to his business, although unauthorized, did not fall within a recognized head of tortious liability.

Where a plaintiff can bring his action within a recognized head of tortious liability, if he voluntarily submitted to the act complained of, he may find that the defendant official (or the Crown) has a good defence. This point is illustrated by another Australian case, *McClintock* v. *Commonwealth* (1947).[27] In that case, the plaintiff, a pineapple grower, had submitted to the directions of federal officials that he deliver up a portion of his crop for Australian troops abroad. He later decided to challenge the validity of the directions, and he sued the Crown in right of Australia for conversion of the pineapples. His action failed on the ground that,

---

23 Dicey, *The Law of the Constitution* (10th ed., 1959), 193.

24 The best-known Canadian example is *Roncarelli* v. *Duplessis* [1959] S.C.R. 121, discussed with other cases in ch. 31, Civil Liberties, under heading 31.2, "Common law", above.

25 There are plenty of American and Australian cases: see Pannam, "Tortious Liability for Acts performed under an Unconstitutional Statute" (1966) 5 Melb. U.L. Rev. 113.

26 (1939) 62 C.L.R. 339.

27 (1947) 75 C.L.R. 1.

even if the official directions were invalid, the tort of conversion had not been committed, because the plaintiff had voluntarily delivered up his pineapples.

It may be thought a harsh rule that exposes public officials to personal liability for acts done under an unconstitutional statute. After all, public officials are expected to carry out faithfully the duties imposed upon them by statute, and should not be placed at risk of personal liability when a statute is subsequently held to be unconstitutional. This line of reasoning would suggest that there should be a defence to a tort action for an official who acted in good faith upon the presumed validity of a statute that had not been declared unconstitutional. On the other hand, such a defence would deny redress to the injured party. The rule of liability shifts the loss to the public official. No doubt, the Crown or other public body would usually be the actual defendant, rendered liable through its vicarious liability for its employees.[28] And, where the individual official is sued and found liable, presumably the Crown or other public body would in practice "stand behind" the official and indemnify him or her.[29] Finally, for those officials who do run some risk of actually having to pay damages, there is insurance. I conclude that, as between the innocent public official and the innocent injured citizen, it is better that the public official bear the cost of unconstitutional activity. The exposure to tortious liability of officials who act under an unconstitutional statute seems, on balance, preferable to a special good-faith-reliance defence for such officials.[30]

Central Canada Potash Co. v. *Government of Saskatchewan* (1978)[31] is an unusual case in that the existence of an unconstitutional statute had the effect of immunizing an enforcing official from tortious liability. The statute in question[32] established a prorationing scheme for potash, which imposed production quotas on potash producers in Saskatchewan. In seeking to enforce the statute against a producing company that was exceeding its quota, the deputy minister in charge of the scheme threatened the company with the cancellation of its mineral lease from the Crown. The lease was, by its terms, subject to cancellation for breach of valid production quotas, and the company reduced its production as the consequence of this threat. The company challenged the constitutionality of the prorationing scheme, and it sued the provincial Crown for damages for the tort of intimidation allegedly committed by the deputy minister. The Supreme Court of

28 The Crown was the defendant in the *James* and *McClintock* cases, discussed in the preceding text, and in the *Central Can. Potash* case, discussed in the following text. On the liability of the Crown in tort, see ch. 10, The Crown, above.

29 Before the Crown was made liable in tort, a party injured by governmental activity always had to sue the individual employee who caused the damage. I believe that it was standard practice in all jurisdictions for the Crown to indemnify any employee held liable.

30 See Hogg, *Liability of the Crown* (2nd ed., 1989), 144-146.

31 [1979] 1 S.C.R. 42.

32 The detail of the prorationing scheme was actually contained in regulations, but nothing turns on that, and for simplicity the text will continue to describe the scheme as statutory.

Canada held that the prorationing scheme was unconstitutional.[33] However, the Court, in a unanimous opinion written by Martland J., dismissed the action for damages. The tort of intimidation required a threat of unlawful action. The deputy minister's threat was to exercise powers that he reasonably believed he possessed for the enforcement of legislation that had not then been held to be unconstitutional and that it was his duty to enforce. The deputy minister's conduct was to be assessed in the light of the circumstances existing at the time. The subsequent holding that the legislation was unconstitutional did not convert the deputy minister's enforcement efforts into the tort of intimidation.

The decision in *Central Canada Potash* gives some legal effect to legislation that was later held to be unconstitutional, and Martland J. cited with approval dicta in the House of Lords to the effect that a regulation had the force of law ''unless and until it has been found to be ultra vires''.[34] Martland J.'s opinion could perhaps be read as the precursor of a special good-faith-reliance defence for public officials acting in reliance on unconstitutional statutes. But I think the opinion is best understood as turning on the ingredients of the tort of intimidation. All that the case decides is that the threat that will form the basis of the tort of intimidation cannot merely be a threat to enforce legislation that appeared to be valid at the time of enforcement. If, instead of a mere threat, a seizure of goods or a trespass to land or an imprisonment had occurred in reliance on the legislation, the subsequent holding of unconstitutionality would have exposed the enforcing official to tortious liability for damages.

55.5 Res judicata

The doctrine of res judicata stipulates that a judicial decision is binding on the parties to the litigation, so that the same issue may not be re-litigated by the losing party. Once decided by a court of competent jurisdiction, an issue is said to be res judicata. The doctrine of res judicata is needed in order to bring disputes to an end. The doctrine precludes the re-opening of a decided case, even if it later becomes clear that the case was wrongly decided. The doctrine can have the effect of preserving the consequences of an unconstitutional law. After a law has been held to be unconstitutional, prior judicial decisions in which the law was applied remain binding and unreviewable (unless there is still time to appeal).[35]

In *R.* v. *Vaillancourt* (1987),[36] the Supreme Court of Canada held that the Criminal Code offence of felony-murder was unconstitutional, because it violated

---

33 This aspect of the decision is discussed in ch. 20, Property and Civil Rights, under heading 20.9, ''Marketing'', above.

34 [1979] 1 S.C.R. 42, 89.

35 *Re Man. Language Rights* [1985] 1 S.C.R. 721, 757 (''*res judicata* would preclude the re-opening of cases decided by the courts on the basis of invalid laws''); Gibson, *The Law of the Charter: General Principles* (1986), 179.

36 [1987] 2 S.C.R. 636.

the accused's right to fundamental justice under s. 7 of the Charter of Rights. The accused in that case, who had been convicted of the offence at trial, was therefore entitled to be acquitted. But what was to become of all the other persons already serving prison sentences for the non-existent offence of felony-murder?

In *R.* v. *Thomas* (1990),[37] this question was raised by an accused who had been convicted of felony-murder in 1984 — three years before the Court's ruling in *Vaillancourt* — and who had unsuccessfully appealed to the British Columbia Court of Appeal (where he had not raised any constitutional issue). After the Supreme Court of Canada's ruling in *Vaillancourt*, Mr. Thomas applied to the Supreme Court of Canada for leave to appeal from the affirmation of his conviction by the British Columbia Court of Appeal. The time limit for such an application was 21 days, and Mr. Thomas was three years out of time. However, the Supreme Court of Canada had power to extend the time where there were "special reasons" to do so. A three-judge bench of the Supreme Court of Canada refused to extend the time and grant leave to appeal. Sopinka J. held that relief was precluded, because the accused was no longer "in the judicial system". An accused would be in the judicial system if there was still time to appeal, but an application for an extension of time should be granted only on "the criteria that normally apply in such cases". These criteria required that an intention to appeal be formed within the stipulated time, and that there be an adequate explanation for the delay. The fact that the accused had been convicted under a law subsequently held to be unconstitutional was not a sufficient reason to bring him "artificially" into the system.

In *R.* v. *Thomas*, the accused, although unsuccessful, had chosen the most promising route to review his conviction, that is, a *direct* attack in the form of an appeal. An appeal is not precluded by the doctrine of *res judicata*. The doctrine of *res judicata* would be a conclusive answer to a *collateral* attack on the accused's conviction, for example, an application for habeas corpus, an action for a declaration that the accused was illegally in custody, an action for damages for false imprisonment or a defence to a charge of escaping from lawful custody. All such collateral attacks would fail on the ground that the accused was in custody pursuant to the judgment of a court of competent jurisdiction.[38] The fact that the convicting court had made an error of law in applying an unconstitutional statute would not deprive the court of jurisdiction.[39] Only an absence of jurisdiction, rendering a decision a nullity, would expose a judicial decision to collateral attack.[40]

37 [1990] 1 S.C.R. 713.

38 *Turigan* v. *Alta.* (1988) 53 D.L.R. (4th) 321 (Alta. C.A.) (person convicted under unconstitutional law cannot recover fine, because fine is *res judicata*).

39 *Ibid.*

40 See generally Rubinstein, *Jurisdiction and Illegality* (1965), esp. ch. 1.

55.6 De facto officers

The de facto officer doctrine protects from collateral attack the act of an officer who has apparent (de facto) authority to act, but who lacks the legal (de jure) authority.[41] The doctrine does not prevent a direct attack on the legality of the officer's title to the position: a direct attack would be a proceeding to remove the officer. Nor does the doctrine protect the officer himself from liability: we have already noticed that the personal liability of an officer who acts without legal authority is a basic tenet of the rule of law.[42] What the doctrine does is to protect third parties, who are not normally in a position to verify the lawfulness of an officer's appointment, and who are therefore entitled to rely on the ostensibly official acts of a person acting as an officer, even though he holds an invalid or non-existent appointment. For example, a seizure of property under a search warrant issued to a person who had not been properly appointed a police constable has been upheld on the ground that the holder of the warrant had performed the functions of a police constable for several years, and held the office de facto.[43] The Court said[44] that "the acts of a person assuming to exercise the functions of an office to which he has no legal title are, as regards third persons . . . legal and binding".

The de facto officer doctrine has traditionally been limited to preventing attacks on the regularity of an officer's appointment to his office. The doctrine could not be used to validate the office itself, or the powers vested in the office. This traditional limitation would make the doctrine of little utility in preserving the consequences of an unconstitutional statute, because the doctrine would only apply in the unusual case where an officer's appointment, but not his office or powers, came from an unconstitutional statute. And yet, the public ought to be able to rely upon the efficacy of things done under a statute that is subsequently held to be unconstitutional without having to make fine distinctions between offices, powers and appointments.

The Supreme Court of Canada has recently articulated the de facto officer doctrine in these broad terms: "There is only one true condition precedent to the application of the doctrine: the de facto officer must occupy his or her office under colour of authority".[45] The doctrine gives effect to "the justified expectations of those who have relied upon the acts of those administering the invalid laws and to the existence and efficacy of public and private bodies corporate,

---

41 Constantineau, *A Treatise on the De Facto Doctrine* (1910); Rubinstein, note 40, above, 205-208; Pannam, "Unconstitutional Statutes and De Facto Officers" (1966) 2 Fed. L. Rev. 37; Gibson, note 35, above, 176-178.

42 Note 23, above. *Crown Trust Co.* v. *The Queen* (1986) 54 O.R. (2d) 79 (Div. Ct.) applies the de facto doctrine to immunize the officer from personal liability. That is wrong.

43 *O'Neil* v. *A.G. Can.* (1896) 26 S.C.R. 122.

44 *Id.*, 130.

45 *Re Man. Language Rights* [1985] 1 S.C.R. 721, 756.

though irregularly or illegally organized''.[46] These statements go well beyond the curing of defects in an officer's appointment.[47] The Court has applied these statements to uphold a summons issued by a court in the purported exercise of a power granted by an unconstitutional statute.[48] The summons was valid, because it had been issued by a court acting under colour of the authority of the unconstitutional statute.

The Supreme Court of Canada's expansion of the de facto officer doctrine will have the effect of saving much that has been done under an unconstitutional statute. The doctrine will preclude subsequent attacks on the validity of the acts of those administering the unconstitutional statute. The doctrine will not (as explained above) protect the administering officers from personal liability. Nor will the doctrine validate the unconstitutional statute itself, or (probably) transactions under the statute that were completed without the intervening act of an ''officer''.[49]

55.7 Unconstitutional taxes

Where a tax has been paid to government under a statute subsequently held to be unconstitutional, can the tax be recovered by the taxpayer?[50] In principle, the answer should be yes. The government's right to the tax was destroyed by the holding of unconstitutionality, and the tax should be refunded to the taxpayer. Neither governments nor courts have so far embraced this simple solution. Governments have usually tried to retain taxes paid under an unconstitutional statute, and taxpayers have often been unsuccessful in enforcing recovery in the courts.

Where taxes have been levied under a regulation or by-law that was invalid, not on constitutional grounds, but in the administrative-law sense that it was unauthorized by an enabling statute, the courts have applied private-law rules of quasi-contract or restitution to resolve the taxpayer's claim to recover the taxes.[51] The principal private-law rule is that payments made under a mistake of law are irrecoverable, while payments made under a mistake of fact are recoverable. Translated into a taxing context, it can be said that a person who pays a tax that was levied without statutory authority has made a mistake of law, that is, a mistake as to the validity of the tax. Consequently, the payment is irrecoverable. This

46 *Id.*, 757.

47 See the discussion by Harradence J.A., concurring separately, in *Turigan* v. *Alta.* (1988) 53 D.L.R. (4th) 321, 340-348 (Alta. C.A.).

48 *Bilodeau* v. *A.G. Man.* [1986] 1 S.C.R. 449. The issuing court was probably also invalidly created, although the Supreme Court of Canada made no finding on that issue.

49 Contra, Gibson, note 35, above, 177-178.

50 This section of the chapter borrows heavily from Hogg, *Liability of the Crown* (2nd ed., 1989), 181-186, where more extensive footnote references may be found.

51 Cf. *Peel* v. *Can.* [1992] 3 S.C.R. 762 (municipality unsuccessful in restitutionary claim to recover payments for the support of young offenders required to be made by unconstitutional federal statute, because no ''benefit'' had been conferred on the defendant government).

result has little intuitive appeal, and courts have struggled to find ways of finding for the taxpayer. In one case, the Supreme Court of Canada held that a payment had been made under a mistake as to the existence of a by-law, which the Court characterized as a mistake of fact.[52] In another case, the Court held that the taxes had been paid under duress, which is an exception to the mistake-of-law rule.[53] But for the most part payments of invalid taxes have been held to be irrecoverable.[54]

Where a tax is invalid because the taxing statute has been held to be unconstitutional, the courts initially started to recognize that the holding of unconstitutionality ought to entitle the taxpayer to recover any payments made under the statute. In *Amax Potash* v. *Government of Saskatchewan* (1976),[55] the Supreme Court of Canada held that the Saskatchewan Legislature could not enact a statute purporting to bar the recovery of taxes that had been paid to the Saskatchewan government under an unconstitutional statute. This decision was said to be demanded by a principle of federalism: a restriction on the province's legislative power to tax could not be evaded by the indirect means of barring recovery of taxes levied in violation of the restriction.[56] The Court did not have to decide, and did not decide, whether the taxes paid were recoverable at common law (having regard to the mistake-of-law doctrine).

In *Air Canada* v. *British Columbia* (1989),[57] Air Canada (and other airlines) sued the Crown in right of British Columbia to recover gasoline taxes paid by the airline between 1974 and 1976. The taxes were unconstitutional, because they were ''indirect'', and the provincial power of taxation is confined to ''direct'' taxes. The unconstitutional levy stopped in 1976, when the province enacted a new statute that imposed a similar tax, but one that was a valid direct tax. By an amendment in 1981, the new valid tax was made retroactive, so that it covered the 1974 to 1976 period; the 1981 amendment also provided that the taxes collected between 1974 and 1976 were ''confiscated''. Was this 1981 amendment

---

52 *George (Porky) Jacobs Enterprises* v. *City of Regina* [1964] S.C.R. 326.

53 *Eadie* v. *Township of Brantford* [1967] S.C.R. 573. An alternative ground of decision was another obscure exception to the mistake-of-law rule,namely, that the parties were not *in pari delicto*; this ground seems to have been disapproved in the *Nepean* case, next note.

54 E.g. *Hydro Electric Commn. of Nepean* v. *Ont. Hydro* [1982] 1 S.C.R. 347. Note, however, the dissenting reasoning rejecting the mistake-of-law defence. In *Air Can.* v. *B.C.* [1989] 1 S.C.R. 1161, La Forest J. and two other judges preferred this part of the dissenting reasoning: see text accompanying note 58, below. In *Can. Pacific Airlines* v. *B.C.* [1989] 1 S.C.R. 1133, it seems that all six judges must have denied the mistake-of-law defence, although the concurrences of Beetz and McIntyre JJ. expressly reserved the point: see note 62, below.

55 [1977] 2 S.C.R. 576. For discussion, see Strayer, *The Canadian Constitution and the Courts* (3rd ed., 1988), 103-107; Gibson, *The Law of the Charter: General Principles* (1986), 170-172.

56 *Amax Potash* was followed in *Air Can.* v. *B.C. (A.G.)* [1986] 2 S.C.R. 539 (petition of right to recover unconstitutional taxes, levied at a time when the petition of right was the only means of suing the Crown, cannot be blocked by refusal of fiat).

57 [1989] 1 S.C.R. 1161.

effective to bar the recovery by the taxpayer of the unconstitutional taxes? The Supreme Court of Canada by a majority[58] said yes. The majority held that this was a different case from *Amax Potash*. In *Amax Potash*, the Saskatchewan Legislature had simply tried to immunize itself from suit to avoid repaying an unconstitutional tax. In this case, the British Columbia Legislature had imposed a new valid tax, had made the new tax retroactive, and had collected the new tax by retaining (confiscating) the moneys collected under the old invalid tax.

The *Air Canada* case shows that the imposition of a new, valid, retroactive tax is a way around the restriction of *Amax Potash*. That was a sufficient reason for the majority to deny recovery of the unconstitutional tax. But La Forest J. went on to give an additional reason to deny recovery. He said that recovery would in any case be barred by the common law of restitution. That bar would not be the result of the mistake-of-law doctrine, which in his lordship's view ought to be stricken from the law of restitution. Instead, there should be a special rule of restitution applicable to unconstitutional taxes: the rule should be that such taxes are irrecoverable by the taxpayers, because of the potential disruption of governmental finances that recovery would cause. La Forest J.'s opinion on this point was agreed to by two of the other judges, namely, Lamer and L'Heureux-Dubé JJ. It was not agreed to by the other two judges in the majority, namely, Beetz and McIntyre JJ., who based their decision exclusively on the retroactive tax. Nor was it agreed to by the dissenting judge, Wilson J., who took the opposing view that unconstitutional taxes should generally be recoverable by the taxpayer.

The new rule of irrecoverability suggested by La Forest J. would apply, he said, to ''ultra vires taxes, at least in the case of unconstitutional statutes''.[59] The qualification leaves in doubt the question whether the new rule would extend to taxes that are ultra vires in only the administrative-law sense. However, La Forest J. did make clear that ''this rule should not apply where a tax is extracted from a taxpayer through a misapplication of the law''.[60] In the latter case, the tax would be recoverable, provided the mistake-of-law doctrine is abrogated, as La Forest J. also suggested. Indeed, in *Canadian Pacific Airlines* v. *British Columbia* (1989),[61] a companion case that was decided at the same time as *Air Canada*, the Court permitted an airline to recover retail sales taxes paid to British Columbia on aircraft entering the province in the course of interprovincial and international

58 The majority judgment of the six-judge bench was written by La Forest J., which on this point was agreed to by four other judges. Wilson J. dissented on the ground that the confiscation provision contaminated the arrangements, showing that the true purpose was to give effect to an unconstitutional statute - the very thing prohibited in *Amax Potash*.

59 [1989] 1 S.C.R. 1161, 1206.

60 *Id.*, 1207.

61 [1989] 1 S.C.R. 1133.

flights.[62] That was a case of misapplication of the law, because the taxing statute on its true interpretation did not apply to the aircraft. However, the Court invoked constitutional considerations in giving a narrow interpretation to the taxing statute, which was literally capable of applying to the aircraft. The Court could have held that the statute did purport to apply to the aircraft, but could not do so because of a lack of constitutional power to tax aircraft in interprovincial and international transit. On that reasoning, the new rule of irrecoverability would have been engaged. Surely, the taxpayer's ability to recover illegal taxes ought not to turn on such an illusory distinction.

There is no authority to support a rule that unconstitutional taxes are irrecoverable, and, in my view, the rule is inconsistent with *Amax Potash*. To be sure, *Amax Potash* did not literally decide that the taxes paid in that case were recoverable, but what is the point of denying validity to the province's attempt to make the taxes irrecoverable if the taxes were already irrecoverable anyway? Moreover, the reason for the decision in *Amax Potash* is that constitutional restrictions on the province's taxing power should not be able to be evaded by retaining unconstitutional taxes. If that reasoning applies to a statutory bar, as *Amax Potash* decides, then it applies with equal force to a common law bar of the kind propounded by La Forest J.[63]

The policy reason advanced by La Forest J. seems to me to be quite inadequate to support his rule of irrecoverability. As Wilson J. pointed out in dissent,[64] the idea of fiscal disruption hardly seems sufficient to cast the burden of governmental error on the innocent taxpayer. Moreover, as Wilson J. also pointed out,[65] it seems wrong to require the taxpayer to refuse to pay or to pay under protest in order to avoid losing his or her money. Citizens are expected to be law-abiding, but, under La Forest J.'s rule, the compliant citizen is punished by the loss of his or her taxes.

To my mind, the constitutional principle that ought to dominate all others in this context is the principle that the Crown may not levy a tax except by the authority of the Parliament or Legislature. This principle, enshrined in the Bill of Rights of 1688,[66] ensures not merely that the executive branch is subject to the rule of law, but also that the executive branch must call the legislative branch into

62 In order to reach this result, upon which the six-judge court was unanimous, it was necessary to reject the province's mistake-of-law defence. La Forest J., with the agreement of Lamer, L'Heureux Dubé and Wilson JJ did so explicitly. However, Beetz and McIntyre, JJ. must have done so too, although their concurrences purported to reserve the issue.

63 Exactly the same points may be made about *Air Can.* v. *B.C. (A.G.)*, note 56, above. What is the point of deciding that the Attorney General of B.C. must advise the grant of the royal fiat to allow the initiation of proceedings to recover unconstitutional taxes if the proceedings are doomed to failure?

64 [1989] 1 S.C.R. 1161, 1215.

65 *Id.*, 1214.

66 Article 4; and see *Bowles* v. *Bank of England* [1913] 1 Ch. 57 (resolution of legislative committee, approved by House of Commons, but not by House of Lords and King, cannot authorize levy of tax).

session to raise taxes (and vote supply). To permit the Crown to retain a tax that has been levied without legislative authority is to condone a breach of one of the most fundamental constitutional principles. That principle applies not only to the tax that is invalid on constitutional grounds, but also to the tax that is invalid on non-constitutional grounds. In both situations, the tax should be recoverable. Neither La Forest J.'s new rule nor the mistake-of-law doctrine ought to preclude recovery.

The argument made in the previous paragraph derives support from a well-settled rule that the Crown may recover moneys paid out of the consolidated revenue fund without legislative authority.[67] The unauthorized expenditure is recoverable, even if it was made under a mistake of law, and even if the recipient could have raised the defences of estoppel or change of position to an action by a private plaintiff. In this situation, the governing rule is the fundamental constitutional principle that prohibits the Crown from spending public funds except under the authority of the Parliament or Legislature.[68] To apply the ordinary rules of restitution so as to render an unauthorized expenditure irrecoverable would in effect permit an important constitutional safeguard to be evaded. In my view, this line of reasoning ought also to apply when it is the subject suing the Crown to recover a payment made to the Crown, and when the constitutional principle in issue is the prohibition on the levying of taxes without legislative authority.

55.8 Wholesale invalidation of laws

(a) The Manitoba Language Rights Reference

A peculiarly difficult problem arises when a large number of laws are held to be unconstitutional.[69] In *Re Manitoba Language Rights* (1985),[70] the Supreme Court of Canada held that nearly all of the laws of the province of Manitoba were unconstitutional. There was no plausible way of escaping from this alarming conclusion. Section 23 of the Manitoba Act, 1870, which is the constitution of the province of Manitoba, provided that Manitoba statutes were to be enacted in both the English and the French languages. In 1890, Manitoba enacted the Official Language Act, which provided that Manitoba statutes need only be enacted in the English language. In effect, this Act was an attempt to repeal a constitutional requirement. Yet it was not until 1979 that the Supreme Court of Canada, in the

67 *Auckland Harbour Bd.* v. *The King* [1924] A.C. 318 (N.Z.); *The King* v. *Toronto Terminals Ry. Co.* [1948] Ex. C.R. 563; *Breckenridge Speedway* v. *The Queen* [1970] S.C.R. 175; Hogg, note 50, above, 185.

68 *Auckland Harbour Bd.* v. *The King* [1924] A.C. 318, 326-327.

69 This section of the chapter draws on my articles "Necessity in Manitoba" in Shetreet (ed.), *Role of Courts in Society* (1988), 7-24, and "Necessity in a Constitutional Crisis" (1989) 15 Monash U. L. Rev. 253.

70 [1985] 1 S.C.R. 721.

Forest case (1979),[71] held that the Official Language Act was invalid by reason of its conflict with s. 23 of the Manitoba Act.

The *Forest* decision meant that the Manitoba Legislature had to enact its statutes in both the English and the French languages. This requirement applied not only to statutes enacted after the *Forest* decision, but to statutes enacted before the decision as well. Manitoba's statutes had been enacted in English only ever since 1890, when the Official Language Act was passed. Moreover, Manitoba had not been preparing unofficial French translations of its statutes. Manitoba was therefore faced with a massive task of translation and re-enactment. It embarked on this task rather slowly. In 1984, five years after the *Forest* decision, the Legislature was still enacting some current statutes in English only, and none of the body of statutes enacted before 1979 had been re-enacted in the required bilingual form.

The *Forest* case had not had to rule on the legal status of the large body of statutes that had been enacted in English only. This issue arose when a motorist named Bilodeau, who was charged with the offence of speeding, defended the charge on the ground that Manitoba's highway speed limits had been imposed by a statute that was invalid, because the statute had been enacted in English only.[72] When the *Bilodeau* appeal reached the Supreme Court of Canada, the federal government became concerned that the appeal might not yield a comprehensive ruling on the validity of Manitoba's statutes. The federal government accordingly directed a reference to the Supreme Court of Canada for an opinion as to the validity of all of Manitoba's statutes that had been enacted in English only. In *Re Manitoba Language Rights* (1985),[73] the Supreme Court of Canada, rejecting the argument advanced by the government of Manitoba that the constitutional requirement of bilingual enactment was ''directory'' only, held that the consequence of failure to comply with the constitutional requirement was invalidity. It followed that all of Manitoba's past and present statute law, except for those statutes enacted in both languages (all pre-1890 statutes and some post-1979 statutes), was invalid.

If the Supreme Court of Canada in the *Manitoba Language Rights Reference* had stopped at the point of its holding of general invalidity, the consequences would have been a vacuum of law in Manitoba. Under the federal distribution of powers, the provinces have responsibility for most of the private law, including contracts, torts, property, commercial law, succession, labour relations, industrial regulation and consumer protection. In Manitoba, the laws on all these topics, and many others, if enacted since 1890 in English only, would be invalid. The provinces also have responsibility for the courts, municipal institutions, school boards and many other regulatory or public bodies. In Manitoba, all these bodies, to the extent that they derived their existence or powers from laws enacted in English only, would be acting without legal authority.

---

71 *A.-G. Man.* v. *Forest* [1979] 2 S.C.R. 1032.

72 *Bilodeau* v. *A.-G. Man.* [1986] 1 S.C.R. 449.

73 [1985] 1 S.C.R. 721. I disclose that I was one of the counsel for the Attorney General of Canada.

The Legislature of Manitoba would also be an invalid body. Although the Legislature was established by the Manitoba Act, 1870 (the constitution), the structure of the legislative assembly had been radically changed by laws passed since 1890 in English only: the size of the assembly had been increased from 24 to 57 members, women had been granted the right to vote and sit in the assembly, and persons aged 18 to 20 had also been granted the right to vote. If the laws pertaining to the franchise and the Legislature were invalid, then Manitoba would lack a Legislature. If this were so, the vacuum of law could never be filled. Past laws could not be re-enacted in both languages. Future laws could not be enacted, even in both languages. Even a remedial constitutional amendment seemed to be unavailable, because s. 43 of the Constitution Act, 1982 stipulated that an amendment affecting only one province must be agreed to by "resolutions of the Senate and House of Commons and of the legislative assembly of each province to which the amendment applies". If Manitoba lacked a lawful legislative assembly, it could not pass the requisite resolution.

There were some common law doctrines that could provide some relief from the consequences of the invalidity of Manitoba's laws. The res judicata doctrine would preclude the re-opening of cases decided by the courts on the basis of invalid laws.[74] The de facto doctrine would sometimes give validity to the acts of a public official with ostensible (but not legal) authority to perform his duties.[75] The mistake of law doctrine might preclude the recovery by taxpayers of taxes paid under an invalid law.[76] The trouble with these three doctrines is that each is quite limited in its scope, and, as the Court acknowledged,[77] the doctrines would not cover all of the situations that could be questioned.

The Supreme Court of Canada in the *Manitoba Language Rights Reference* faced an awkward dilemma. On the one hand, the integrity of Canada's Constitution, with its protections for the French-speaking minority, required the Court to hold that Manitoba statutes enacted only in English were invalid. On the other hand, the Court could not thrust upon the people of Manitoba the chaos and disorder that seemed inevitable if the Court were to deny the efficacy of the legal system that was in fact in place. The solution devised by the Court was to hold that the Acts of the Legislature that were enacted only in English were invalid, but to hold as well that the Acts were to be "deemed to have temporary force and effect for the minimum period necessary for their translation, re-enactment, printing and publication".[78] The latter holding protected the existing body of Manitoba laws, and all things done on the basis of past laws. Future laws, that is, the laws enacted after the date of the Court's opinion (June 13, 1985), had to comply with

74 See sec. 55.5, "Res judicata", above.

75 See sec. 55.6, "De facto officers", above.

76 See sec. 55.7, "Unconstitutional taxes", above.

77 [1985] 1 S.C.R. 721, 757.

78 *Id.*, 782.

the constitutional requirements and did not benefit from the period of temporary validity.[79]

The Court's holding of temporary validity entailed a ruling as to the duration of the minimum period necessary for the translation and re-enactment of Manitoba's unilingual laws. This ruling was provided at a later hearing, at which the Court fixed December 31, 1988 as the date by which Manitoba's consolidated statutes and regulations and rules of court were to be translated and re-enacted, and December 31, 1990 as the date by which all other laws were to be translated and re-enacted.[80] Generally speaking, the effect of this order was to allow (1) a period of just over three years for the translation and re-enactment of all of the important current laws, and (2) a period of just over five years for the translation and re-enactment of less important current laws (private laws and unconsolidated public laws) and repealed or spent laws (some at least of which were to be translated and re-enacted to preclude the re-opening of transactions dependent upon their validity).[81] In the result, therefore, for several years the people of Manitoba were bound by laws that were never constitutionally enacted. The laws derived their force exclusively from the order of the Supreme Court of Canada.

What is the justification for this radical exercise of power by the Supreme Court of Canada? The reason offered by the Court for the temporary validation of Manitoba's unilingual statutes was that a legal vacuum in the province would "undermine the principle of the Rule of Law".[82] According to the Court, there were two aspects to the rule of law. First, the rule of law required that the law be supreme over officials of the government as well as private individuals. This aspect of the rule of law is of course basic to constitutionalism, justifying courts in restraining arbitrary power by insisting upon fidelity to the constitution and other laws. The second aspect of the rule of law, which was even more basic than the first, required simply that a community be governed by law. In this sense, the rule of law recognized that "law and order are indispensable elements of civilized life".[83]

In the Manitoba situation, the two requirements of the rule of law contradicted each other. The first requirement — the supremacy of the law over the organs of government — entailed that Manitoba's unilingual laws, since they had not been enacted in compliance with the law of the constitution, be held invalid. But the effect of such a holding was to deny to Manitoba an operating legal system

---

79 *Id.*, 768.

80 *Re Man. Language Rights Order No. 1* [1985] 2 S.C.R. 347; see also *Re Man. Language Rights Order No. 2* [1990] 3 S.C.R. 1417 (extending the period of validity for some instruments); *Re Man. Language Rights Order No. 3* [1992] S.C.R. (clarifying original order and further extending the period of validity).

81 Manitoba proposed to translate all repealed and spent laws back to and including the 1970 revision of the Manitoba Statutes. Perfect safety required the province to go all the way back to 1890, but such a task was impossible.

82 [1985] 1 S.C.R. 721, 748.

83 *Id.*, 749.

in violation of the second requirement of the rule of law. The Court's resolution of this conflict was to accord temporary force to the existing body of Manitoba laws until such time as the Manitoba Legislature could comply with the law of the constitution.

The Court's decision thus made the concept of the "rule of law", which is usually a mere rhetorical flourish, the central justification for its preservation of Manitoba's de facto legal system. The Court claimed that the rule of law had "constitutional status", because it was referred to in the preamble to the Constitution Act, 1982, and because it was "implicit in the very nature of a Constitution".[84] The Court did not directly rely upon a doctrine of "necessity", although courts in various parts of the common-law world had invoked such a doctrine to justify departures from constitutional legality.[85] The Court referred to these cases, but treated them as supplying only "analogous support" for its order.[86] However, the decision could as easily have been framed in terms of necessity as of the rule of law.[87]

(b) The Bilodeau case

An ironic consequence of the Supreme Court of Canada's ruling in the *Manitoba Language Rights Reference* was that it entailed the conviction of Mr. Bilodeau, the man who had originally brought the issue to the Court. He had been vindicated in his contention that the English-language statute under which he had been convicted was invalid. But, by virtue of the *Manitoba Language Rights Reference*, the statute was deemed to have been in force when Bilodeau committed his offence; therefore, he was properly convicted under the Act. The Supreme Court of Canada was accordingly obliged to affirm his conviction, and, after a long delay which was perhaps intended to signal the Court's discomfort, the Court did affirm his conviction.[88]

(c) The Mercure case

One could be forgiven for assuming that the situation in Manitoba was unique. But it turned out that a similar vacuum of law existed in Saskatchewan as well. The province of Saskatchewan had been created by federal statute in 1905,[89] when it had been carved out of the Northwest Territories. In 1877, when

84 [1985] 1 S.C.R. 721, 750.

85 There are cases arising out of the American civil war, Pakistan, Cyprus and Southern Rhodesia. The cases are discussed in the articles referred to in note 69, above.

86 [1985] 1 S.C.R. 721, 758.

87 That is the thesis argued in the articles referred to in note 69, above.

88 *Bilodeau* v. *A.-G. Man.* [1966] 1 S.C.R. 449. The appeal had been argued at the same time as the reference (June 1984), but the decision on the appeal was handed down eleven months after the decision on the reference.

89 Saskatchewan Act, 1905.

the small population of the Territories was half French-speaking, the federal Parliament enacted a law, similar to s. 23 of the Manitoba Act, 1870, that required the ordinances of the Legislative Assembly of the Territories to be enacted in both the English and the French languages. By the time Saskatchewan was created in 1905, the wave of immigration to the prairies had greatly increased the population, and reduced the proportion of French-speakers to less than five per cent of the population. (It is about two per cent today.) The 1877 language law was apparently assumed to be inapplicable to the new province, and from the beginning the Legislature enacted statutes in English only.

It was not until the 1980s that anyone brought a legal challenge to the Saskatchewan Legislature's practice of English-only enactment. In *R.* v. *Mercure* (1988),[90] a French-speaking resident of Saskatchewan defended a charge of speeding on the ground that Saskatchewan's highway legislation had been invalidly enacted. The case rose to the Supreme Court of Canada, where a majority held that the 1877 language law was still part of the law of Saskatchewan, and that it prescribed the manner and form of enactment of statutes by the Legislature. Since all Saskatchewan statutes had been enacted in English only, which was the wrong manner and form, they were all invalid. However, the principle of the *Manitoba Language Rights Reference* applied here, too, "to keep the existing laws temporarily in effect for the minimum period of time necessary for the statutes to be translated, re-enacted, printed and published in French".[91]

Mercure thus decided that in Saskatchewan, as in Manitoba, the statute books were full of invalid statutes. However, the Court noted an important difference between the two provinces. In the case of Manitoba, the language requirement was an entrenched part of the constitution of the province, requiring a constitutional amendment for its repeal or alteration. In the case of Saskatchewan, however, the language requirement was not part of the constitution. As a pre-confederation law, received at the creation of the province, it could be repealed or amended by the Saskatchewan Legislature — acting in the correct manner and form, needless to say. The Court actually suggested this solution in its reasons for judgment: "the Legislature may resort to the obvious, if ironic, expedient of enacting a bilingual statute removing the restrictions imposed on it by [the 1877 language law] and then declaring all existing provincial statutes valid notwithstanding that they were enacted, printed and published in English only".[92] To the distress of its French-speaking minority, the government of Saskatchewan took up this suggestion, and secured the enactment by the Legislature, in both English and French, of a statute that repealed the two-language requirement for the future and validated all the statutes invalidly enacted in the past.[93]

---

90 [1988] 1 S.C.R. 234.

91 *Id.*, 280.

92 [1988] 1 S.C.R. 234, 280-281.

93 The Language Act, S.S. 1988, c. L-6.1.

(d) The Paquette case

The province of Alberta was established at the same time as the province of Saskatchewan,[94] and was carved out of the same federal territories. Alberta, like Saskatchewan, had always enacted statutes in English only and had never repealed or amended the 1877 language law. It was clear that the *Mercure* ruling must apply to Alberta as well, and, in *R.* v. *Paquette* (1990),[95] the Supreme Court of Canada so held. Therefore, Alberta was also faced with a wholly invalid body of statutes, although no doubt the statutes were temporarily in effect for the time needed to translate and re-enact them. Alberta, like Saskatchewan, took the easy route of enacting, in both languages, a curative statute.[96]

(e) The Sinclair case

In *Sinclair* v. *Quebec* (1992),[97] the Supreme Court of Canada held that a Quebec statute that authorized the amalgamation of two municipalities into a new municipality was unconstitutional. The problem was the familiar one of the failure to use both languages in the constituting instruments. The statute itself had been enacted in both languages, but its operation depended upon letters patent and other instruments that were in French only. The Court held that this was a breach of the requirement of bilingual enactment that was imposed on the Quebec Legislature by s. 133 of the Constitution Act, 1867.[98] It followed that the new municipality had been invalidly constituted, and everything done by the municipality was a nullity.

The decision of the Supreme Court of Canada in *Sinclair* was given in 1992. The new municipality had in fact been operating on the faith of its purported constituting instruments since 1986. Here was yet another case for a period of temporary validity! The Court said:[99]

> It would be wrong to throw the affairs of the citizens of Rouyn and Noranda into a state of chaos on account of the procedure chosen by the National Assembly of Quebec to effect their purported amalgamation into the new city of Rouyn-Noranda. This is an appropriate case for this Court to exercise its suspensive power by declaring that the instruments in this appeal, while invalid for non-compliance with s. 133 of the Constitution Act, 1867, shall continue in force for a period of time in order to permit the National Assembly to take what steps it sees fit to remedy the constitutional defects. This period of time shall be one year from the date of this judgment.

---

94 Alberta Act, 1905.

95 [1990] 2 S.C.R. 1103.

96 Languages Act, S.A. 1988, c. L-7.5.

97 [1992] S.C.R. . The opinion is the opinion of "the Court".

98 The case is described in ch. 53, Language, under heading 53.4(e), "Delegated legislation", above.

99 [1992] S.C.R. , (p. 19).

What was contemplated, of course, was that the Legislature would re-incorporate the municipality by a properly bilingual statute, which it would make retroactive to 1986. In order to permit this to happen, for a period of one year, all of the purported by-laws and other invalid municipal acts made or done since 1986 were maintained in force by virtue of the Court's order.

56

Procedure

56.1 Procedure

Judicial review of legislation can occur whenever a statute is potentially applicable to facts in proceedings before a court. If the party resisting the application of the statute argues that the statute is invalid, a constitutional issue is presented that must be resolved by the court. Judicial review of legislation can thus occur in any proceedings, before courts of all levels, and even before administrative tribunals. That this is so is made plain by s. 52(1) of the Constitution Act, 1982 (the supremacy clause), which provides that ''any law that is inconsistent with the provisions of the Constitution is, to the extent of the inconsistency, of no force or effect''. This supremacy clause must be obeyed, not only by the Supreme Court of Canada, but also by lower courts and administrative tribunals: all bodies with power to decide questions of law possess the power — indeed, the duty — to review the validity of legislation when the issue arises in proceedings before them.[1]

1 See generally chs. 15, Judicial Review on Federal Grounds, and 37, Enforcement of rights, above.

Judicial review of legislation will occur in a criminal prosecution if the defendant argues that the statute under which the charge was laid is invalid. Judicial review will occur in a civil action if a relevant statute is challenged as invalid by a party whose interest it is to avoid the effect of the statute; for example, the plaintiff in a civil action may allege that a statute of limitation, which apparently bars the action, is unconstitutional. Judicial review will occur before an administrative tribunal if a party claims that the tribunal is acting under, or proposing to apply, an invalid statute. Judicial review of legislation will occur in proceedings to review the decision of an administrative tribunal if the party seeking to overturn the tribunal's decision argues that the tribunal's power stemmed from an unconstitutional statute. It is even possible to bring proceedings in which the only relief sought is a declaration that a statute is invalid. Liberal rules of standing have made declaratory proceedings available to individuals or groups who oppose a particular statute, but who cannot show that the statute has any special impact upon them. The rules of standing are discussed in the next section of this chapter. There is also the uniquely Canadian procedure of the "reference", by which a government (but not a private individual) may refer questions of law to a court for an advisory opinion; although the reference procedure is not confined to constitutional questions, it has been widely used for that purpose.[2]

Apart from the declaratory action and the reference procedure, which account for only a small proportion of the constitutional cases decided by the Supreme Court of Canada, judicial review usually occurs on the initiative of a private individual (or corporation) who is attempting to resist the application of a statute which appears to apply to him or her. The private party who makes a constitutional challenge to a statute is attempting to avoid, by whatever legal means are at hand, the duty ostensibly imposed upon him or her by the statute. Mallory is accurate for most of the cases when he says that "the force that starts our interpretive machinery in motion is the reaction of a free economy against regulation".[3] The risk of constitutional issues being resolved by the courts without argument from the interested government has been reduced by rules requiring the party raising a constitutional issue to give notice to the Attorney General, and allowing the Attorney General to intervene in the proceedings. The notice and intervention provisions are discussed later in this chapter.[4]

Much of the practice and procedure of judicial review is simply the practice and procedure of whatever kind of litigation happens to yield the constitutional issue. The balance of this chapter is concerned with those issues that are distinctive to constitutional cases: standing, mootness, ripeness, alternative grounds and intervention.[5] The next chapter, Proof, deals with legislative history and evidence.

---

2 See ch. 8, Supreme Court of Canada, under heading 8.6, Reference jurisdiction, above.

3 Mallory, "The Courts and the Sovereignty of the Canadian Parliament" (1944) 10 Can. J. Ec. Pol. Sci. 165.

4 Section 56.6, Intervention, below.

5 As to costs, see Fox, "Costs in Public-Interest Litigation" (1989) 10 Advocates' Quarterly 385.

56.2 Standing

(a) Definition

The question whether a person has "standing" (or locus standi)[6] to bring legal proceedings is a question about whether the person has a sufficient stake in the outcome to invoke the judicial process. The question of standing focuses on the position of the party seeking to sue, not on the issues that the lawsuit is intended to resolve.

Restrictions on standing are intended (1) to avoid opening the floodgates to unnecessary litigation; (2) to ration scarce judicial resources by applying them to real rather than hypothetical disputes; (3) to place limits on the exercise of judicial power by precluding rulings that are not needed to resolve disputes; (4) to avoid the risk of prejudice to persons who would be affected by a decision but are not before the court; (5) to avoid the risk that cases will be inadequately presented by parties who have no real interest in the outcome; and (6) to avoid the risk that a court will reach an unwise decision of a question that comes before it in a hypothetical or abstract form, lacking the factual context of a real dispute. In constitutional cases, however, there is the countervailing idea of constitutionalism (or rule of law), which dictates that remedies ought to be available when governments fail to abide by the law of the constitution. This idea often suggests that a private litigant who, for public rather than private reasons, wishes to raise a constitutional question ought to be allowed to do so. This is probably the reason for the remarkable relaxation in the Canadian law of public interest standing that will be described in the text that follows.

Where a constitutional issue arises in the course of ordinary civil or criminal litigation, a question of standing is rarely controversial.[7] The validity of a statute (or some other official instrument or act) must be determined in order to resolve the issue between the parties. It goes without saying that only the party who would be affected by the application of the statute has any right to raise the issue of its constitutionality. That person has standing to attack the validity of the statute.

The issue of standing may become controversial where a private individual or firm initiates legal proceedings for the sole purpose of challenging the consti-

---

6 See Thio, *Locus Standi and Judicial Review* (1971); Law Reform Commission of British Columbia, *Report on Civil Litigation in the Public Interest* (1980); Blake, "Standing to Litigate Constitutional Rights and Freedoms in Canada and the United States" (1984) 16 Ottawa L. Rev. 66; Sharpe (ed), *Charter Litigation* (1987), ch. 1 (by Bogart); Cromwell, *Locus Standi* (1986); Strayer, *The Canadian Constitution and the Courts* (3rd ed., 1988), ch. 6; Ontario Law Reform Commission, *Report on the Law of Standing* (1989); Sharpe, *The Law of Habeas Corpus* (2nd ed., 1989), 222-224. For the (more restrictive) law of the United States, see Tribe, *American Constitutional Law* (2nd ed., 1988), 107-156.

7 But note sec. 56.2(e), "Enforcing other people's rights", below.

tutionality of a statute (or other official instrument).[8] For the private party,[9] the proceeding of choice for this purpose[10] is an action for a declaration.[11] In all Canadian jurisdictions, a superior court may make ''binding declarations of right, whether or not any consequential relief is or could be claimed''.[12] This means that a court can make a declaration as to the rights of the parties even in cases where the plaintiff has no cause of action in the sense of an entitlement to coercive relief in the form of damages, an injunction, specific performance or the like. The declaration has become a popular remedy to challenge official action of various kinds, because the aggrieved party often lacks a cause of action in the traditional sense, and yet the absence of coercive relief is rarely a problem when the defendant is the government or a public body that can normally be relied upon to obey the declaratory judgment.

(b) Exceptional prejudice

Although it is clear in principle that a declaration can be issued at the suit of a party who has no right to damages or other coercive relief, the courts have imposed a requirement of standing on the availability of the declaration. The general rule is that the Attorney General is the guardian of the public interest, and only the Attorney General has standing to bring proceedings to vindicate the public interest.[13]

In the context of a challenge to the validity of a statute, this rule denies standing to an individual who is affected by the statute no differently from any other member of the public. If, however, an individual is ''exceptionally prejud-

8 The rules of standing differ depending upon the remedy sought, and the area of law involved: see the works by Thio, Cromwell, Strayer, note 6, above. This account is confined to the remedy of declaration in constitutional cases. Note, however, that in *Finlay* v. *Can.* [1986] 2 S.C.R. 607, discussed in text accompanying note 29, below, the Court held (at pp. 634-635) that the same rule of standing extended to an ancillary injunction.

9 For a Canadian government, the proceeding of choice is a reference, a proceeding which is not available to a private litigant: see ch. 8, Supreme Court of Canada, under heading 8.6, Reference jurisdiction, above.

10 Standing to seek a remedy under s. 24 of the Charter of rights is discussed in ch. 37, Enforcement of Rights, below. As that chapter explains, s. 24(1) does not preclude the traditional declaration of invalidity in Charter cases; the latter remedy depends upon s. 52 of the Constitution Act, 1982.

11 See Zamir, *The Declaratory Judgment* (1962).

12 The history of this provision is related in Zamir, previous note, ch. 2. The current Canadian references are collected in Cromwell, note 6, above, 121.

13 The Attorney General can either bring proceedings of his or her own motion (ex officio), or can consent to a private litigant bringing a ''relator action'' in the name of the Attorney General. A relator action is expressed as having been brought by the Attorney General ''at the relation of'' the private litigant (the relator). The relator has the carriage of the proceedings, and is responsible for costs. However, the Attorney General retains some rights to control the litigation. See Zamir, note 11, above, 262-267; Edwards, *The Attorney General, Politics and the Public Interest* (1984), 130-145, 286-295.

iced'' by the statute, that is, the statute applies to him or her differently from the public generally, then the individual has standing to bring a declaratory action to challenge the validity of the statute.[14]

(c) Role of the Attorney General

Underlying the exceptional prejudice rule is the assumption that the Attorney General can be counted on to act as guardian of the public interest. If there is no individual who is exceptionally prejudiced, a public wrong will not necessarily go unredressed, because the Attorney General has the power to bring remedial proceedings.

The Attorney General's role as plaintiff in public interest litigation developed in England in cases involving such matters as obstructions of public highways or waterways, public nuisances or misapplications of the funds of charitable trusts.[15] In such cases, no policy of the Attorney General's own government is in issue, and the Attorney General may reasonably be expected to exercise a wise discretion as to whether or not to institute legal proceedings. But this is not so where the gravamen of the complaint is the unconstitutionality of a statute, or the illegality of some policy or act of the government. The problem is that the Attorney General is a member of the government. Like other ministers, he or she is committed to the policies of the government, and will normally be obliged to defend the legality of those policies.[16]

The Supreme Court of Canada has recognized the conventional constraints that preclude the Attorney General from bringing proceedings to challenge the policies of his or her own government.[17] This recognition has been an important factor influencing the court to create a discretionary category of public interest standing which may be conferred on an individual who wishes to challenge the constitutionality of a statute despite the fact that he or she has not been exceptionally prejudiced by the statute.

---

14 *Smith* v. *A.G. Ont.* [1924] S.C.R. 331, 337.

15 Zamir, note 11, above, 257.

16 In Sharpe (ed.), note 6, above, 52-53, Professor J.Ll.J. Edwards seems to argue for a more independent role for the Attorney General, asserting that: ''The Attorney General is entitled to oppose the policy of his ministerial colleagues at every stage of its formulation and implementation, including discussions within the appropriate cabinet committee or in the cabinet itself.'' Obviously, the Attorney General or any other minister is free to express his or her independent views when policy is being formulated within cabinet or cabinet committees. But, in my view, once the policy has been formulated the Attorney General like any other cabinet minister is bound by the convention of collective responsibility and would have to resign the office if he or she wished to continue to oppose the policy.

17 *Thorson* v. *A.-G. Can.* [1975] 1 S.C.R. 138, 146. This case is discussed in the text accompanying note 19, below.

(d) Discretionary public interest standing

The exceptional prejudice rule, which was established in 1924,[18] is still the law of Canada in that only exceptional prejudice *entitles* a plaintiff to the standing needed to bring a declaratory action to challenge the validity of a statute. But in a series of cases the Supreme Court of Canada has held that there is a discretion to grant standing to a private plaintiff who seeks to vindicate a public interest and who is not exceptionally prejudiced.

The first case is *Thorson* v. *Attorney General of Canada* (1974).[19] In that case, the plaintiff sued for a declaration that the federal Official Languages Act was invalid. The plaintiff was not exceptionally prejudiced by the Act, which applied to him no differently than to other Canadians. Nonetheless, the Supreme Court of Canada by a majority granted standing to the plaintiff. The Court held that it had a discretion to grant standing to a plaintiff who was not exceptionally prejudiced, and that the discretion should be exercised in this plaintiff's favour.

Laskin, J., writing for the majority of the Court in *Thorson*, pointed out that, because the Official Languages Act was declaratory and directory, not even imposing penalties for its breach, no-one would be able to establish exceptional prejudice. Moreover, it was not realistic to suppose that the federal Attorney General would exercise his undoubted right to bring proceedings, since he was a member of the government that had secured the passage of the Act, and indeed he was the minister responsible for its implementation. Therefore, the effect of the traditional standing rules would be to immunize the Act from constitutional challenge. Laskin J. asserted[20] that it would be a cause for alarm if the legal system provided no route by which a question concerning the constitutionality of a statute could be determined by the courts.[21]

The second case in the series of public interest standing cases is *Nova Scotia Board of Censors* v. *McNeil* (1975),[22] in which the plaintiff brought an action for a declaration that Nova Scotia's film censorship statute was invalid. This statute differed from the Official Languages Act in that the censorship statute was not merely declaratory. The statute was regulatory, and film exhibitors were subject to the regulatory regime and liable to penalties for non-compliance. An exhibitor would be entitled to standing under the exceptional prejudice rule. The plaintiff, however, was not an exhibitor; he was a member of the public who objected to the banning in Nova Scotia of "Last Tango in Paris".

---

18 Note 14, above.

19 [1975] 1 S.C.R. 138. The Court divided six to three, with Laskin J. writing for the majority, and Judson J. writing for the minority.

20 *Id.*, 145.

21 The issue reached the Supreme Court of Canada on the merits in a reference in which Mr. Thorson appeared as counsel for one of the intervenors: *Jones* v. *A.G.N.B.* [1975] 2 S.C.R. 182, where the legislation was upheld.

22 [1976] 2 S.C.R. 265.

Did the new discretion to grant standing extend to a plaintiff who had not suffered exceptional prejudice, when the object of the challenge was a regulatory statute and those regulated by the statute had chosen not to sue? The Supreme Court of Canada, now speaking unanimously through Laskin C.J., answered yes. The Court took the view that the plaintiff was asserting an interest different from that of the exhibitors, in that the statute controlled what the public could see at the movies. Since the statute had not been challenged by the exhibitors (or by the Attorney General), there was no practical way in which the public's interest in what it could see at the movies could be translated into a constitutional challenge. Therefore, the Court held, it should exercise its discretion in favour of granting standing to the plaintiff.[23]

The third case in the series of public interest standing cases is *Minister of Justice of Canada* v. *Borowski* (1981),[24] in which the plaintiff sued for a declaration that the therapeutic abortion provisions of the Criminal Code were inoperative through conflict with the Canadian Bill of Rights (the Charter of Rights not being in the Constitution at this time). This case differed from the previous two cases in that the impugned legislation was neither declaratory (as in *Thorson*) nor regulatory (as in *McNeil*), but rather exculpatory: abortion was a criminal offence, but the constitutional challenge was brought against provisions that exempted therapeutic abortions from the offence. The other new element of the case was that the impugned provisions could have no direct impact on the plaintiff,[25] because he was male, and was not a doctor. Nevertheless, the Supreme Court of Canada, by a seven to two majority, exercised its discretion to grant standing to the plaintiff. Martland J., who wrote for the majority of the Court, pointed out that neither doctors performing abortions nor women seeking abortions would want to challenge provisions that were exculpatory. He summarized *Thorson* and *McNeil* in these terms:[26]

> I interpret these cases as deciding that to establish status as a plaintiff in a suit seeking a declaration that legislation is invalid, if there is a serious issue as to its invalidity, a person need only to show that he is affected by it directly or that he has a genuine interest as a citizen in the validity of the legislation and that there is no other reasonable and effective manner in which the issue may be brought before the Court.

---

23 The action reached the Supreme Court of Canada on the merits in *N.S. Bd. of Censors* v. *McNeil* [1978] 2 S.C.R. 662, where the legislation was upheld.

24 [1981] 2 S.C.R. 575. The Court divided seven to two, with Martland J. writing for the majority, and Laskin C.J. writing for the minority.

25 Public interest standing was granted to a corporation in *Energy Probe* v. *Can.* (1989) 68 O.R. (2d) 449 (C.A.) and *Can. Council of Churches* v. *Can.* [1990] 2 F.C. 534 (C.A.); reversed on other grounds [1992] 1 S.C.R. 236; although the challenged legislation could not in either case affect the corporation. These cases establish that the public interest plaintiff may sue through a corporate vehicle.

26 [1981] 2 S.C.R. 575, 598.

Laskin C.J., who had written the judgments in *Thorson* and *McNeil*, now dissented, holding[27] that the plaintiff had no ''judicially cognizable interest in the matter he raises''.[28]

The fourth case in the series of public interest standing cases is *Finlay* v. *Minister of Finance of Canada* (1986).[29] In that case, the plaintiff sought a declaration that payments by the federal government to the province of Manitoba were illegal, on the ground that Manitoba was not fulfilling the conditions of the cost-sharing agreement between the two governments under which the payments were made. The plaintiff was a recipient of income support under provincial legislation that he contended did not fulfil the agreed-upon conditions. However, success in his action would have no direct effect on his own (or anyone else's) entitlement to support, because that entitlement arose under the provincial legislation, and the validity of the provincial legislation would not be affected by the illegality of the federal funding. (The plaintiff's hope, of course, was that success in the action would persuade the province to amend the provincial legislation.)

Finlay raised the question whether the public interest standing discretion could be extended to a non-constitutional challenge to the legality of a federal public expenditure. The Supreme Court of Canada, in a unanimous judgment written by Le Dain J., answered yes. Although the plaintiff's claim raised no constitutional issue, it did raise a question of law that was justiciable. Then, taking Martland J.'s summary of the cases in *Borowski* (quoted earlier)[30] as his text, Le Dain J. held[31] that the plaintiff was ''a person with a genuine interest in these issues and not a mere busybody''; and there was ''no other reasonable and effective manner in which the issue may be brought before a court''.[32]

The result of these four cases is to establish a very liberal rule for public interest standing. While it is still the case that a private plaintiff has no right to bring a declaratory action when he or she has no special personal interest in an issue of constitutional or public law, the courts will grant standing as a matter of

---

27 *Id.*, 587.

28 The plaintiff's case was never decided by the Supreme Court of Canada on the merits. It did reach the Court, but by that time the entire Criminal Code section respecting abortion, the offence part (which Borowski wanted to preserve) as well as the exculpatory part (which Borowski attacked) had been struck down in *R.* v. *Morgentaler (No. 2)* [1988] 1 S.C.R. 30 (a criminal prosecution of doctors for performing abortions without complying with the exculpatory provisions). The Court dismissed Borowski's appeal on the grounds that (1) the issue he raised was moot, and (2) he had lost standing. On the latter ground, the Court held that the standing cases (*Thorson, McNeil, Borowski*) required an individual to challenge a specific law or a specific government act, which Borowski could no longer do: *Borowski* v. *Can.* [1989] 1 S.C.R. 342.

29 [1986] 2 S.C.R. 607.

30 Quotation in text accompanying note 26, above.

31 [1986] 2 S.C.R. 607, 633.

32 The issue reached the Supreme Court of Canada on the merits in *Finlay* v. *Can.* [1993] 1 S.C.R. 1080, where a majority held that Manitoba was not in breach of the federal conditions; the declaration was therefore denied.

discretion to the plaintiff who establishes (1) that the action raises a serious legal question, (2) that the plaintiff has a genuine interest in the resolution of the question, and (3) that there is no other reasonable and effective manner in which the question may be brought to court.

The third requirement — that there is no other reasonable and effective manner in which the question may be brought to court — is a corollary of the purpose of granting public interest standing, which is to make sure that governments and legislative bodies adhere to the Constitution and other applicable laws. If there is no obstacle to judicial review at the suit of someone who is directly affected by a particular government measure, then it is not a wise use of scarce judicial resources to permit proceedings by persons or bodies that have no special interest in the measure. In *Canadian Council of Churches* v. *Canada* (1992),[33] the Canadian Council of Churches brought an action for a declaration of invalidity in respect of newly-enacted provisions of the Immigration Act that stipulated the procedure for determining claims by immigrants of refugee status. The Supreme Court of Canada struck out the statement of claim on the ground that the Council lacked standing to pursue it. The first two requirements for public interest standing were satisfied, because (1) the action raised a serious issue as to the validity of the new refugee determination procedures, and (2) the Council had a genuine interest in the issue, because it provided services to refugees and other recent immigrants. But the third requirement was not satisfied, because individual refugee claimants, who had been arriving at the rate of about 3,000 per month, each had standing to challenge the legislation, and some of them had in fact done so. It was clear therefore that persons with a direct interest in the issue could bring it to court, and there was no possibility that the legislation would be immunized from judicial review by a denial of standing to the Canadian Council of Churches. The Council was therefore denied standing.[34]

(e) Enforcing other people's rights

As has been explained, a constitutional issue will arise in the course of ordinary civil or criminal litigation if a party alleges that an ostensibly applicable statute is unconstitutional. When the validity of a statute is attacked by a private person on federalism (distribution of powers) grounds, the private challenger is asserting that the statute is outside the power of the enacting legislative body. If the challenged statute is a provincial one, a successful challenge would mean only that the power to enact the statute was possessed by the federal Parliament rather than by the provincial Legislature. It is arguable that only the federal government

33 [1992] 1 S.C.R. 236. Cory J. wrote the opinion for the unanimous Court.

34 See also *CARAL* v. *N.S.* (1990) 69 D.L.R. (4th) 241 (N.S.A.D.) (public interest standing to challenge abortion law denied, because criminal charge under law had been laid against doctor who was also challenging law); *Hy and Zel's* v. *Ont.* [1993] 3 S.C.R. 675 (public interest standing to challenge Sunday-closing law denied, because of other (unspecified) ways of bringing the issue to court).

has the requisite interest in defending the federal domain from encroachment by provincial Legislatures. If this argument were accepted, it would follow that a private individual, motivated only by a desire to avoid compliance with the law, ought to be denied standing to challenge the statute.

Although it has been argued that private persons ought not to be permitted to challenge a statute on federalism grounds,[35] the argument has never been considered by the courts. On the contrary, it has always been assumed that a private person does have standing to challenge on federalism grounds a law that purportedly applies to him. This assumption, although never articulated and defended, accords with a basic notion of constitutionalism that insists that governments must stay within the limits of their legal powers. When a private person challenges a law on federalism grounds, no matter how selfish the motive of the challenger, the private person is enforcing a regime of constitutionalism that requires governments to obey the Constitution.

When the validity of a statute is attacked by a private person on Charter grounds, the challenger is usually enforcing a constitutional right that applies to the challenger. For example, people who were stopped from distributing leaflets at an airport challenged the law prohibiting the activity on the basis that the law deprived the distributors of their right to freedom of expression.[36] In that case, the distributors were vindicating their own right to freedom of expression, a right that is conferred on "everyone" by s. 2(b) of the Charter of Rights. No issue of standing arose, because it was obvious that the distributors had standing to challenge the law. But not all cases are so obvious. Can a private person challenge a law on the ground that it violates *someone else's* Charter rights?

Freedom of conscience and religion is a right which, although guaranteed to "everyone" by s. 2(a) of the Charter, cannot apply to a corporation, because a corporation has no conscience and no religion. Nevertheless, in *R.* v. *Big M Drug Mart* (1985),[37] a corporation, Big M Drug Mart Ltd., successfully invoked the right to freedom of religion as a defence to a criminal charge. The charge was one of selling goods on a Sunday in violation of the federal Lord's Day Act. The Supreme Court of Canada held that the Lord's Day Act violated s. 2(a) of the Charter, because the purpose of the Act was to compel the observance of the Christian sabbath. It was irrelevant whether a corporation could enjoy or exercise freedom of religion. The law was unconstitutional because it abridged the right of *individuals* to freedom of religion. Therefore, the law was of no force or effect by virtue of the supremacy clause of s. 52. The "undoubted corollary" of the principle that the Constitution is supreme is that "no one can be convicted of an

---

35 Weiler, *In the Last Resort* (1974), ch. 6. The argument is criticized in Swinton, *The Supreme Court and Canadian Federalism* (1990), ch. 2.

36 *Committee for Cth. of Can.* v. *Can.* [1991] 1 S.C.R. 139.

37 [1985] 1 S.C.R. 295. The opinion of Dickson J. was agreed to by all members of the Court, except Wilson J., who wrote a separate concurring opinion, disagreeing with one part of Dickson J.'s opinion. On the issue discussed here, the Court was unanimous.

offence under an unconstitutional law''.[38] It followed that ''any accused, whether corporate or individual, may defend a criminal charge by arguing that the law under which the charge is brought is constitutionally invalid''.[39] The Court held that the Lord's Day Act was unconstitutional, and acquitted the accused corporation.

Big M Drug Mart establishes the rule that a defendant to a criminal charge may raise any constitutional defect in the law under which the charge was laid. This redounded to the benefit of a corporation in that case, but the rule applies to individuals as well. In *Big M Drug Mart* itself, Dickson J. gave the example of an ''accused atheist'', who ''would be equally entitled to resist a charge under the Act''.[40] In *R.* v. *Morgentaler (No. 2)* (1988),[41] a male doctor, who was charged under the abortion provisions of the Criminal Code, successfully defended the charge on the ground that the abortion provisions violated the Charter rights of pregnant women. Similarly, an individual would be entitled to defend a charge laid under a discriminatory law that was invalid under s. 15, even though the defendant was not one of the persons discriminated against.[42] As McLachlin J. has said:[43]

> Any constitutional defect may be raised in the defence of a criminal charge. This is only just. A person should not be convicted under an invalid law.

The Court in *Big M Drug Mart* pointed out that the defendant corporation was not seeking a special Charter remedy under s. 24. Under s. 24, it would be necessary for the corporation to show that its rights had been infringed or denied.[44] Therefore, no remedy under s. 24 would be available to a corporation for the infringement or denial of rights, such as freedom of religion, that do not extend to a corporation. The same rule would apply to individuals who are not within the class of persons protected by a right, such as the atheist in Dickson J.'s example; they too could not invoke s. 24. But, as Dickson J. pointed out: ''Where, as here [that is, in *Big M Drug Mart*], the challenge is based on the unconstitutionality of legislation, recourse to s. 24 is unnecessary and the particular effect on the challenging party is irrelevant''.[45] The Court thus excluded the s. 24 remedy

38 *Id.*, 313.
39 *Id.*, 313-314.
40 *Id.*, 314.
41 [1988] 1 S.C.R. 30.
42 *R.* v. *Hess* [1990] 2 S.C.R. 906, 945 per McLachlin J. dissenting but not on this point.
43 *Ibid.* Cf. *Boggs* v. *The Queen* [1981] 1 S.C.R. 49 (accused successfully claimed that offence of driving while suspended was not a valid criminal law on the ground that suspension could occur for such reasons as non-payment of licence fees, although accused's suspension was for impaired driving); *R.* v. *Smith* [1987] 1 S.C.R. 1045 (convicted drug importer successfully attacked minimum sentence on ground that it would be cruel and unusual in some hypothetical case, although the accused's own situation merited a severe sentence).
44 See ch. 37, Enforcement of Rights, under heading 37.2(d), ''Standing'', above.
45 [1985] 1 S.C.R. 295, 313.

from the rule of *Big M Drug Mart*, but did not otherwise indicate when corporations could invoke Charter rights that do not apply to corporations.

In *Irwin Toy* v. *Quebec* (1989),[46] a corporation, Irwin Toy Ltd., applied for a declaration that a Quebec law, which prohibited advertising that was directed at children, was unconstitutional. The declaration was sought on a number of constitutional grounds, all of which were unsuccessful. For present purposes, the point of interest was the Court's response to the corporation's argument that the law infringed s. 7 of the Charter. Section 7 provides that "everyone" has the right to "life, liberty and the security of the person", and the right not to be deprived thereof except in accordance with the principles of fundamental justice. The Court refused to address this argument on the merits, because a corporation by its nature could not enjoy "life, liberty or security of the person", and therefore could not invoke s. 7 in support of its declaration of invalidity.[47] The Court distinguished its earlier decision in *Big M Drug Mart*: "There are no penal proceedings pending in the case at hand, so the principle articulated in *Big M Drug Mart* is not involved".[48]

What are the limits of "the principle articulated in *Big M. Drug Mart*"? It is clear that the principle catches the case where a corporation is charged with a criminal offence. In *R.* v. *Wholesale Travel Group* (1991),[49] a corporation was allowed to invoke s. 7 as a defence to a charge of false advertising laid under the federal Competition Act. The Supreme Court of Canada did in fact strike down one element of the offence — a requirement that the defendant make a timely retraction of the false claim — on the ground that it created the potential for absolute (no-fault) liability in breach of s. 7. Although s. 7 did not apply to corporations, the corporation was entitled to attack the law unders. 7, because the law applied to individuals as well as corporations, and was capable of depriving an individual of his or her liberty (imprisonment being a possible penalty for an individual under the law).[50] Lamer C.J., who spoke for the entire Court on this issue,[51] rejected the argument that a law could be unconstitutional for individuals

46 [1989] 1 S.C.R. 927. The joint opinion of Dickson C.J., Lamer and Wilson JJ. is the majority opinion. McIntyre J., with whom Beetz J. agreed, wrote a dissenting opinion.

47 *Id.*, 1004 per joint opinion of majority; McIntyre J. for the minority (at 1009) agreed that s. 7 could not be invoked by the plaintiff corporation.

48 *Ibid.Irwin Toy* was followed in *Dywidag Systems* v. *Zutphen Bros.* [1990] 1 S.C.R. 705, 709 (refusing to allow a corporation to invoke s. 7 in non-penal proceedings). But note the obscure dictum of Stevenson J. for the Court in *R.* v. *CIP* [1992] 0 S.C.R. 000, 000 (p. 5): "In *Irwin Toy* it was not the absence of penal proceedings per se that precluded the respondent corporation from invoking s. 7".

49 [1991] 3 S.C.R. 154.

50 Accord, *Ont.* v. *CP* [1995] 2 S.C.R. 1031 (allowing a corporation to argue that environmental law with sanction of imprisonment was void for overbreadth and vagueness under s. 7; both arguments were rejected on the merits).

51 All judges, except for Cory, J. (with whom L'Heureux-Dubé J. agreed) said that they agreed with Lamer C.J. on the issue of standing, and the Court was unanimous in striking down the timely retraction provision for breach of s. 7 at the instance of the corporation.

but constitutional for corporations.[52] He added, in an obiter dictum,[53] that, if a statutory provision were drafted so as to apply only to corporations, a corporation would not be able to challenge the law under s. 7.[54] This would follow, because there would no longer be any threat of imprisonment, and therefore no deprivation of "liberty". (The same result would follow if a provision were left applicable to individuals as well as corporations, but was made punishable only by fine.)[55]

The difference between *Irwin Toy*, where the Court held that a corporation could not invoke s. 7, and *Wholesale Travel*, where the Court held that a corporation could invoke s. 7, is that Irwin Toy Ltd. was a civil plaintiff seeking a declaration while Wholesale Travel Group Inc. was a defendant in a criminal proceeding. But why should this difference be important? The plaintiff corporation in *Irwin Toy* was not relying on s. 24 of the Charter for its remedy. The corporation was simply seeking a declaration that the law was unconstitutional. It has always been regarded as axiomatic in Canadian constitutional law that an individual or corporation may seek a declaration of invalidity on *federal* grounds, despite the fact that no individual or corporation is directly implicated in the question whether a law should properly be enacted by one level of government rather than the other.[56] Indeed, in *Irwin Toy* itself, the plaintiff corporation, in addition to Charter grounds, attacked the law on a federal ground (that the provincial law could not apply to advertising in the federal medium of television), and the Court without any preliminary discussion addressed that ground on the merits (rejecting it in the result).

It is difficult to see what principle allows a plaintiff to bring an action for a declaration of invalidity on federal grounds, but not on Charter grounds. Assuming that the plaintiff has a sufficient interest in the validity of the law, which evidently was the case in *Irwin Toy* where the plaintiff's business of manufacturing and selling toys would be especially affected by the law, the plaintiff ought to be able to obtain a declaration that the law is unconstitutional on the basis of any part of the Constitution. To be sure, the plaintiff corporation in *Irwin Toy* could deliberately flout the law so as to bring on a prosecution. Then *Big M Drug Mart* would apply, and the corporation would be entitled to defend the charge on the basis of

---

52 [1991] 3 S.C.R. 154, 180-181.

53 *Id.*, 182.

54 McLachlin J., while generally agreeing with Lamer C.J. on the issue of standing, added (at 260) that she found it unnecessary to consider "the application of the Charter to a provision dealing with corporations only".

55 This method of salvaging a statute that violates s. 7 could be employed by the Court itself. Instead of striking down the substantive offence, the Court could simply strike down the penalty of imprisonment. Or the Court could hold that imprisonment is available only if the prosecution establishes a fault-requirement that would satisfy s. 7 (even though the statute does not require it); otherwise, imprisonment is not available. Both these approaches would be more restrained, preserving more of the statute, than the striking down of the offence.

56 The leading case is *A.G. Can.* v. *Law Society of B.C.* [1982] 2 S.C.R. 307, holding that the superior courts cannot be deprived of their powers to grant declarations of invalidity at the suit of private individuals. See also the earlier discussion accompanying note 35, above.

s. 7 or any other Charter right, whether or not it applied to a corporation. But why should the corporation have to subject itself to criminal proceedings in order to eradicate an invalid law? The principle of constitutionalism is surely offended by the erection of artificial barriers to constitutional challenges to legislation. At the very least, there should be no difference between federal and Charter grounds. Both grounds have the effect of withholding power from legislative bodies, and both grounds lead to invalidity under the supremacy clause.

The correct principle, it seems to me, is that a challenge to the constitutionality of a law (assuming that it involves no remedy other than a finding of invalidity) should be governed by the same rules of standing and procedure, regardless of whether the challenge is based on federal or Charter grounds.[57] This would mean not only that the challenge could be made as a defence to a criminal charge (as in *Big M Drug Mart*), but in any other proceedings, civil or criminal, where the law is potentially relevant, including proceedings for a declaration of invalidity.[58] However, unless and until the Supreme Court of Canada repents of its ruling in *Irwin Toy*, the position seems to be as follows. The general rule of *Irwin Toy* is that a Charter right that invalidates a law may be invoked by a person affected by the law only if the person affected by the law is also a person entitled to the benefit of the Charter right. If the person affected by the law is not a person entitled to the benefit of the Charter right, then the general rule will preclude the person from challenging the law, except in the case where the person is the defendant in a criminal prosecution for breach of the law. In that case, the *Big M Drug Mart* exception to the general rule will apply to prevent the person from being convicted under the unconstitutional law.[59]

---

57 In *R.* v. *Big M Drug Mart* [1985] 1 S.C.R. 295, 313, Dickson J. said:

> Standing and jurisdiction to challenge the validity of a law pursuant to which one is being prosecuted is the same regardless of whether that challenge is with respect to ss. 91 and 92 of the Constitution Act, 1867 or with respect to the limits imposed on the legislatures by the Constitution Act, 1982.

With respect, this seems to me to be correct, except for the phrase ''pursuant to which one is being prosecuted''. Why should the rule be limited to that situation?

58 This passage from the 3rd edition (1992) was approved by L'Heureux-Dubé J., dissenting with McLachlin J., in *Hy and Zel's* v. *Ont.* [1993] 3 S.C.R. 675, 715; the majority did not address this point.

59 Query whether other forms of compulsion, e.g., an order to produce documents, an injunction, an order to pay damages, would also entitle the person under compulsion to defend on the basis that no-one should be forced to obey an unconstitutional law.

56.3 Mootness

(a) Definition

A case is "moot" when there is no longer any dispute between the parties.[60] Mootness is like an absence of standing in that the court is being invited to rule on an issue that has no direct impact on the parties to the proceedings. The difference is that standing is judged at the commencement of the proceedings, whereas mootness is judged after the commencement of the proceedings. The parties to a moot case had a real dispute when the proceedings commenced, but the passage of time caused the dispute to disappear. A case becomes moot when the repeal of a statute,[61] the expiry of a lease,[62] the death of a party,[63] or some other new circumstance,[64] resolves the dispute or makes it irrelevant.

(b) General rule

Normally, of course, the parties to litigation will not wish to proceed after their case has become moot. If they do, it will usually be because they perceive that some principle is at stake, although the mundane question of who is to be responsible for costs is for some parties a sufficient incentive. If the parties do wish to proceed with the litigation, should they be permitted to do so? The general rule is no: a court should not decide a case that has become moot.

The general rule is illustrated by *Borowski* v. *Attorney General for Canada* (1989).[65] In that case, the plaintiff had brought proceedings for a declaration that the provisions of the Criminal Code that permitted therapeutic abortions were unconstitutional. His standing to bring the proceedings was challenged, but was upheld by the Supreme Court of Canada in what is now a leading case on standing, discussed earlier in this chapter.[66] The case proceeded to the merits, but after it had been decided by the Saskatchewan Court of Appeal and leave had been granted to appeal to the Supreme Court of Canada, the Supreme Court of Canada in the *Morgentaler* case[67] struck down all the abortion provisions of the Criminal

---

60 See Macklem and Gertner, "Re Skapinker and the Mootness Doctrine" (1984) 6 Supreme Court L. Rev. 369; Sharpe, note 6, above, ch. 12 (by Sharpe); Strayer, note 6, above, 211-215. For the (more restrictive) law of the United States, see Tribe, note 6, above, 82-93.

61 E.g., *A.-G. Alta* v. *A.-G. Can.* (Bank Taxation) [1939] A.C. 117.

62 E.g., *Switzman* v. *Elbling* [1957] S.C.R. 285.

63 E.g., *R.* v. *Mercure* [1988] 1 S.C.R. 234.

64 E.g., *Phillips* v. *N.S.* [1995] 2 S.C.R. 97 (application for stay of inquiry, on ground that pre-trial publicity would prejudice jury in criminal proceedings, rendered moot when applicants elected trial by judge alone).

65 [1989] 1 S.C.R. 342.

66 *Minr. of Justice (Can.)* v. *Borowski* [1981] 2 S.C.R. 575; discussed in text accompanying note 24, above.

67 *R.* v. *Morgentaler (No. 2)* [1988] 1 S.C.R. 30.

Code, those that created the offence of abortion, as well as those that permitted therapeutic abortions. This made Mr. Borowski even more unhappy, because it meant that non-therapeutic abortions as well as therapeutic abortions were permitted. He wished to continue his proceedings in order to secure a ruling that the foetus was entitled to constitutional protection. It was clear that any ruling by the Supreme Court of Canada would in fact influence the shape of any new abortion law that would be enacted by Parliament to replace the old law. Nevertheless, the Court refused to decide the case, holding that it had become moot. Sopinka J. for the unanimous Court said[68] that there was no longer a ''live controversy'' to resolve, because ''the substratum of Mr. Borowski's appeal had disappeared''.[69]

The rule against deciding moot cases flows from the same policy considerations as those that support restrictions on standing. The major purpose is to ration scarce judicial resources by applying them to real issues. A subsidiary purpose is to limit the power of the courts to make pronouncements of constitutional law that are not required to resolve a dispute. There is also the risk that a moot case would not be properly presented and argued by parties who lack an interest in the outcome. Another risk is that the court might come to an unwise decision of a question that comes in a hypothetical or abstract form, lacking the concreteness of a genuine controversy.[70]

(c) Discretion to decide

These counsels of restraint have not proved to be particularly compelling in the context of standing. In that context, we have seen that the Court has often chosen to grant standing to a party with no special interest in the proceedings, in order to enable a constitutional issue to be litigated.[71] The same is true of mootness. The Court has a discretion to decide a moot case, and, at least in constitutional cases, usually exercises the discretion in favour of deciding the case. Indeed, *Borowski*, despite its clear affirmation of the rule against deciding moot cases, is one of only a small group of cases in which the Court has actually applied the rule.[72]

Borowski may be contrasted with another abortion case decided in the same year. In *Tremblay* v. *Daigle* (1989),[73] the issue of the constitutional right of the

68 [1989] 1 S.C.R. 342, 357.

69 The court also held that the plaintiff had lost his standing. Query whether this is indeed a separate issue. Mootness, it has been said, is ''the doctrine of standing set in a time frame'': Tribe, note 6, above, 83.

70 [1989] 1 S.C.R. 342, 358-363.

71 See ch. 38, under heading 38.2, ''Standing'', above.

72 The scanty precedents are referred to by Sopinka J. in [1989] 1 S.C.R. 342, 354-356; another example is *Phillips* v. *N.S.*, note 64, above.

73 [1989] 2 S.C.R. 530.

foetus[74] was raised in proceedings by a man to obtain an injunction against his girlfriend to restrain her from having an abortion. During the oral argument in the Supreme Court of Canada, the Court discovered that the defendant had already had the abortion, thereby rendering the case moot. The Court exercised its discretion to decide the case, and denied the injunction. The Court's reason was to remove from other pregnant women the threat of injunctive proceedings by their husbands and boyfriends.[75]

I have footnoted below a number of constitutional cases which were moot by the time they reached the Supreme Court of Canada, but which were decided nevertheless.[76] In these cases, the Court was obviously persuaded that (1) there was a serious legal question to be decided,[77] and (2) the question, despite its mootness, would be properly argued on both sides. Where both these factors are present, the Court will usually exercise its discretion to decide a moot case.

56.4 Ripeness

A case is not ''ripe'' for decision if it depends upon future events that may or may not occur.[78] In that situation, the case would involve a premature determination of what is still only a hypothetical question. For example, a challenge

---

74 The Court did not rule on the Charter of Rights issue, because the Charter was inapplicable to ''a civil action between two private parties'' (p. 571). The Court did rule on the effect of the Quebec Charter of Human Rights and Freedoms and the Civil Code.

75 This case was highly unusual in that it reached the Supreme Court of Canada well within the period of gestation. In the normal course of events, that is too short a time to reach an appellate court. American courts, which take mootness much more seriously than do Canadian courts, do not apply the mootness bar to cases that are inherently ''evasive of review'': see *Roe* v. *Wade* (1973) 410 U.S. 113, 125 (''Pregnancy provides a classic justification for a conclusion of non-mootness. It truly could be 'capable of repetition, yet evading review'.'') In *Borowski*, note 65, above, Sopinka J. (at p. 361) recognized that this category of case ought to be decided.

76 *Switzman* v. *Elbling* [1957] S.C.R. 285 (tenant's challenge to Quebec's Padlock law became moot when tenant's lease expired); *Re Objection by Que. to Resolution to Amend the Constitution* [1982] 2 S.C.R. 793 (Quebec's claim that a convention had been broken became moot when the Canada Act 1982 was enacted); *Law Society of Upper Can.* v. *Skapinker* [1984] 1 S.C.R. 357 (law graduate's challenge to citizenship requirement for admission to bar became moot when he became a citizen and was admitted); *R.* v. *Mercure* [1988] 1 S.C.R. 234 (defendant's challenge to a speeding ticket became moot when the defendant died).

77 In *Borowski*, note 65, above, the disappearance of the Criminal Code provisions respecting abortion not only made the proceedings moot, but converted a concrete constitutional issue into an abstract one. All that the Court could have provided was a general opinion on the interpretation of the Charter without reference to any statute or any facts. This was the unusual feature of *Borowski*. Most moot cases retain the concrete issue that formerly divided the parties.

78 See Sharpe (ed.), note 6, above, 340-342 (by Sharpe); Strayer, note 6, above, 211-215. For the law of the United States, see Tribe, note 6, above, 77-82.

to the constitutionality of a bill that has not been enacted would not be ripe: the bill may never be enacted or may be significantly amended before enactment.[79]

There do not seem to be any Canadian cases that are unequivocal precedents for a doctrine of ripeness, although there is a well developed American jurisprudence. The Canadian rule undoubtedly is the same as the rule for mootness.[80] A court should not decide a case that is unripe for adjudication, but the court would have a discretion to do so.

56.5 Alternative grounds

A case that is properly before a court may be capable of decision on a non-constitutional ground or a constitutional ground or both. The course of judicial restraint is to decide the case on the non-constitutional ground.[81] That way, the dispute between the litigants is resolved, but the impact of a constitutional decision on the powers of the legislative or executive branches of government is avoided. For the same reason, if a case can be decided on a narrow constitutional ground or a wide ground, the narrow ground is to be preferred. If a case can be decided either on a rule of federalism or under the Charter, the federalism ground is the narrower one,[82] because it leaves the other level of government free to act, whereas a Charter decision striking down a law does not.[83] The general idea is that a proper deference to the other branches of government makes it wise for the courts, as far as possible, to frame their decisions in ways that do not intrude gratuitously on the powers of the other branches.

The courts have often articulated counsels of restraint of this kind,[84] but they have also frequently disregarded them. If a constitutional issue has in fact been fully argued on the basis of an adequate factual record, and if the issue is likely to recur, there is much to be said for deciding the issue then and there, even if the case could be disposed of on a non-constitutional or narrower constitutional basis. A decision takes advantage of argument and evidence that would otherwise be wasted, in the sense that fresh argument and fresh evidence would be needed in a later case where the issue recurred. And a decision settles the issue, providing certainty and rendering relitigation unnecessary. Therefore, in the appropriate

79 Governments occasionally direct references to determine in advance the constitutionality of an unenacted bill. Since the answers to reference questions are advisory only, on a reference, no doctrine of ripeness restrains the courts from answering hypothetical questions.

80 See sec. 56.3, Mootness, above.

81 See Sharpe, note 6, above, 342-345 (by Sharpe); Strayer, note 6, above, 199-211.

82 See also ch. 15, Judicial Review on Federal Grounds, under heading 15.2, "Priority between federal and Charter grounds", above.

83 Sharpe, note 6, above, 343-344 (by Sharpe). This point could be disputed on the basis that a Charter decision can be overridden by the use of a notwithstanding clause under s. 33, whereas a federalism decision can be overridden only by a constitutional amendment.

84 Davis, *Canadian Constitutional Law Handbook* (1985), 578-583, collects many quotations; see also note 82, above.

case, a court is not to be faulted for basing its decision on reasons that are more expansive than are strictly required to give judgment.

56.6 Intervention

(a) By Attorney General

When a constitutional issue arises, it is usually in litigation in which the Crown (or the Attorney General) is a party. In that case, the Attorney General will be represented in court to participate in the constitutional argument. A constitutional issue can, however, arise in litigation to which the Crown is not a party. Of course, the parties to the litigation will normally be interested in arguing both sides of the constitutional issue, and they may make the arguments very well. However, obviously there are no guarantees that a constitutional issue will be properly argued in private litigation.[85] The Attorneys General have the incentive, the expertise and the resources to present an argument that would usually be superior to the argument that could be presented by a private party. Moreover, it seems wrong that a finding of invalidity could be made by a court without hearing from counsel representing the government of the enacting jurisdiction.[86]

Neither at common law nor in equity was the Attorney General permitted to intervene in litigation to which the Crown was not a party. Any general right of intervention would rightly be seen as subversive of the independence of the judiciary. But litigation in which the constitutionality of a statute is in issue is a universally recognized exception to the policy against governmental intervention.[87]

In Canada, all provinces[88] have now enacted statutes that require notice to be given to the Attorney General of the province of any proceedings in which the

---

85 The example usually given is *Russell* v. *The Queen* (1882) 7 App. Cas. 829, in which the federal Canada Temperance Act was upheld under the peace, order, and good government power. This controversial ruling was made in litigation between a private prosecutor and an accused person. No Attorney General was present. This decision stimulated the enactment of the notice provisions that are described in the text following: Strayer, note 6, above, 73-74.

86 For detailed discussion on the role of the Attorney General, see Huscroft, "The Attorney General and *Charter* Challenges to Legislation: Advocate or Adjudicator" (1995) 5 N.J.C.L. 125.

87 See Strayer, note 6, above, 73-86.

88 The references are as follows: B.C.: Constitutional Question Act, R.S.B.C. 1979, c. 63, s. 8, as amended by S.B.C. 1982, c. 5; Alta.: Judicature Act, R.S.A. 1980, c. J-1, s. 25, as amended by S.A. 1981, c. 51, s. 2; Sask.: Constitutional Questions Act, R.S.S. 1978, c. C-29, s. 8, as amended by S.S. 1983-84, c. 31; Man.: Constitutional Questions Act, C.C.S.M., c. C-180, s. 7; Ont.: Courts of Justice Act, R.S.O. 1990, c. C.43, s. 109; Que.: Code of Civil Procedure, R.S.Q. 1977, c. C-25, s. 95, as amended by S.Q. 1985, c. 29; N.B.: Judicature Act, R.S.N.B. 1973, c. J-2, s. 22, as amended by S.N.B. 1980, c. 28, S.N.B. 1982, c. 3; N.S.: Constitutional Questions Act, R.S.N.S. 1989, c. 89, s. 10; P.E.I.: Supreme Court Act, R.S.P.E.I. 1988, c. S-10, s. 41; Nfld.: Judicature Act, R.S.N. 1990, c. J-4, s. 57.

constitutionality of a statute is in issue.[89] Most provinces require that notice be given to the Attorney General of Canada as well. The statutes prohibit the court from determining the constitutional question until the requisite notices have been served.[90] The statutes give to the Attorneys General the right to intervene in the proceedings. In the Supreme Court of Canada,[91] the Federal Court of Canada[92] and federal tribunals,[93] there is similar provision for notices to be given, although in those courts and tribunals all 11 Attorneys General must be served, and all have the right of intervention.

The extent of the rights of an intervening Attorney General depends upon the terms of the statute permitting the intervention. An intervenor is not a party to the proceedings, unless the statute so provides. If an intervenor is not made a party to the proceedings, then of course he or she lacks the rights (and liabilities) that the rules of court accord to (or impose on) parties, the most important of these (in lower courts) normally being the right of appeal.[94] All the notice statutes give to the intervenor Attorneys General the right to be heard and some specifically mention the right to adduce evidence. Two provinces[95] make the intervenor Attorneys General parties for all purposes; five provinces[96] and the Federal Court Act confer a right of appeal; two six provinces[97] withhold all attributes other than the right to be heard.[98]

(b) By private party

The notice requirements that have just been described apply only to Attorneys General, and give only Attorneys General a right of intervention.

89 There is some variation in the definition of the issues that give rise to the obligation to give notice: (1) Constitutional validity (all jurisdictions); (2) Constitutional applicability (all but N.B. and Nfld.); (3) Operability under paramountcy doctrine (only Man., Que., N.B., S.C.C., F.C.C.); and (4) Constitutional remedy (only B.C., Sask., Man., N.S., S.C.C.). For discussion, see Strayer, note 6, above, 80-81.

90 Strayer, note 6, above, 78-79. The constitutional validity of this prohibition is discussed in ch. 55, Effect of Unconstitutional Law, under heading 55.3, "Notice requirements in litigation", above.

91 Supreme Court Act, R.S.C. 1985, c. S-26, s. 53 (applicable only to references); Rules of the Supreme Court of Canada, 1983, Rule 18 (appeals and references), Rule 32 (appeals). For commentary on the Act and Rules, see Crane and Brown, *Supreme Court of Canada Practice 1991-92* (Carswell, 1991).

92 Federal Court Act, R.S.C. 1985, c. F-7, s. 57, as amended by S.C. 1990, c. 8.

93 *Ibid.*

94 On the liability side, a non-party would not be liable to costs (unless that had been made a condition of the intervention), and no relief could be awarded against him or her.

95 B.C. and Man.

96 Alta. Ont., Que., N.S., P.E.I. and Nfld.

97 Sask. and N.B.

98 An intervenor is different from an amicus curiae in that the intervenor has some kind of interest in the outcome of the proceedings, whereas an amicus curiae does not. An amicus curiae (friend of the court) is a person who appears in proceedings with the permission of the court to make an oral or written submission that may assist the court. Rules of court often recognize amicus curiae, but they do not give the amicus the status of a party or any right of appeal.

In references,[99] where there are no parties in the ordinary sense, the notice requirements will enable the Attorneys General to participate.[100] The various reference statutes also contemplate other "interested" persons being granted leave to intervene in a reference,[101] and unions, aboriginal organizations, civil liberties associations, and a variety of other organizations, special interest groups and individuals are in practice often granted leave.[102]

In proceedings other than references, courts have authority, usually explicit in their rules of procedure, sometimes not, to admit "interested" non-parties[103] as intervenors.[104] Even in a criminal trial it is not uncommon for private parties (such as victims or the media) or special interest groups to seek and obtain status as intervenors, often to seek or oppose a publication ban on all or part of the proceedings.[105] In the Supreme Court of Canada, the rules expressly provide for intervention by "any person interested" in an appeal.[106] Leave to intervene must be granted by a judge of the Court. It has been a source of complaint that written reasons have not been given for granting or denying an application for leave to intervene, so that no body of jurisprudence has developed to constrain the discretion of the Court and to guide would-be intervenors.[107] Since these criticisms were published a written judgment has been issued,[108] and presumably others will be issued from time to time.

---

99 References are discussed in ch. 8, Supreme Court of Canada, under heading 8.6, "Reference jurisdiction", above.

100 Notes 89-99, above.

101 In the Supreme Court of Canada, Rule 18 of the Rules of the Supreme Court of Canada provides for the admission of intervenors in both references and appeals. There is also provision for the admission of intervenors in references in the Supreme Court Act, R.S.C. 1985, c. S-26, s. 53(6).

102 See Strayer, note 6, above, 170-174.

103 The requirement of interest distinguishes an intervenor from an amicus curiae: note 94, above.

104 See Welch, "No Room at the Top: Interest Group Intervenors and Charter Litigation in the Supreme Court of Canada" (1985) 43 U. Toronto Faculty L. Rev. 204; Sharpe, note 6, above, ch. 2 (by Swan); Bryden, "Public Interest Intervention in the Courts" (1987) 66 Can. Bar Rev. 490; Strayer, note 6, above, 195-197; Muldoon, *Law of Intervention* (1989); Ontario Law Reform Commission, *Report on the Law of Standing* (1989), ch. 5; Lavine, "Advocating Values: Public Interest Intervention in Charter Litigation" (1992) 2 NJCL 27.

105 The Supreme Court of Canada has shown an extraordinary solicitude to private intervenors in criminal trials, even allowing them to appeal interlocutory rulings directly to the Supreme Court of Canada: *Dagenais* v. *CBC* [1994] 3 S.C.R. 835, 872 per Lamer C.J. (setting up a code of procedure for publication bans). Such an appeal is not available to the parties, and would postpone or disrupt the trial of the accused. The intervention itself, even if no appeals are brought, is a distraction from the issue of the accused's guilt or innocence, raising concerns on the part of Crown and defence that trials can be prolonged (even "hijacked") by third-party Charter claimants.

106 Note 102, above.

107 Welch, note 76, above; Sharpe, note 76, above.

108 *Re Workers' Compensation Act, 1983 (Nfld.) (Application to Intervene)* [1989] 2 S.C.R. 335.

57

Proof

57.1 Legislative history

(a) Definition

The term "legislative history"[1] does not have a precise meaning. In the account that follows, I use the term to mean the documentary evidence of the events that occurred during the drafting and enactment of a statute. It may include the following elements:

1 See Kyer, "Has History a Role to Play in Constitutional Adjudication: Some Preliminary Considerations" (1981) 15 Law Society of Upper Canada Gazette 135; Sharpe (ed.), *Charter Litigation* (1987), ch. 6 (by Hogg); Monahan, *Politics and the Constitution* (1987), ch. 5; Strayer, *The Canadian Constitution and the Courts* (3rd ed., 1988), 275-283; Charles, Cromwell and Johnson, *Evidence and the Charter of Rights and Freedoms* (1989), 75-124; Swinton, *The Supreme Court and Canadian Federalism* (1990), ch. 4.

1. the report of a royal commission or law reform commission or parliamentary committee recommending that a statute be enacted;
2. a government policy paper (whether called a white paper, green paper, budget paper or whatever) recommending that a statute be enacted;
3. a report or study produced outside government which existed at the time of the enactment of the statute and was relied upon by the government that introduced the legislation;
4. earlier versions of the statute, either before or after its introduction into Parliament or the Legislature;
5. statements by ministers or members of Parliament and testimony of expert witnesses before a parliamentary committee charged with studying the bill; and
6. speeches in the Parliament or Legislature when the bill is being debated.

The foregoing list does not include the state of the law, whether common law or statutory, before the enactment of the statute. This is an important part of the context within which the language of a statute must be read. However, the prior state of the law is not an event occurring during the drafting and enactment of a statute, and it is not normally described as part of the legislative history. The admissibility of the prior state of the law as an aid to statutory interpretation or constitutional adjudication is perfectly clear and uncontroversial.

Also excluded from my definition are social-science data and other factual material which has played no role in the legislative process, even though such material may bear on the purpose or likely efficacy of a statute, and may be tendered to a court in aid of statutory interpretation or constitutional adjudication. The relevance and admissibility of factual material extrinsic to the legislative process are taken up in the next section of this chapter.[2]

There are two different categories of legislative history which may be relevant in constitutional adjudication. The first is the legislative history of a challenged statute, which may shed light on the purpose of the statute and other matters relevant to its constitutional validity. The second is the legislative history of the Constitution of Canada itself, which may shed light on the meaning of the relevant constitutional text. These two categories of legislative history will be dealt with separately in the account that follows.

(b) Classification of statutes

There are three purposes for which the legislative history of a challenged statute is admissible. First, in constitutional cases raising federalism issues, legislative history may be used to help identify the ''matter'' of the challenged statute to determine whether the statute comes within the legislative authority of the

2 Section 57.2, Evidence, below.

enacting body.[3] Secondly, in Charter cases, legislative history may be used to help determine whether the purpose of the challenged statute was to infringe a Charter right.[4] Thirdly, again in Charter cases, where a statute has been found to infringe a Charter right, legislative history may be used to determine whether the statute is justified as a reasonable limit under s. 1.[5]

Legislative history has usually been held inadmissible in Canada under ordinary rules of statutory interpretation.[6] But the interpretation of a particular provision of a statute is an entirely different process from the classification of the statute for purposes of judicial review. There seems to be no good reason why legislative history should not be resorted to for the latter purpose. In the 1960s, there were two decisions of the Supreme Court of Canada that did prohibit resort to the legislative history of a statute for purposes of constitutional classification.[7] However, there were earlier decisions that permitted resort to legislative history,[8] and since 1976 the permissive rule has become firmly established.[9] Legislative history is now routinely admitted for the three purposes described in the previous paragraph. All categories of legislative history are admissible, including parliamentary debates (Hansard).[10]

The radical change in the attitude of the Supreme Court of Canada to legislative history is illustrated by *RJR-MacDonald* v. *Canada* (1995).[11] In that case,

---

3 Re Anti-Inflation Act [1976] 2 S.C.R. 373, 438-439 (white paper), 471-472 (parliamentary debates); *Re Residential Tenancies Act* [1981] 1 S.C.R. 714, 721-723 (law reform commission report, green paper); *Re Exported Natural Gas Tax* [1982] 1 S.C.R. 1004, 1048 (government policy paper, budget documents); *Schneider v. The Queen* [1982] 2 S.C.R. 112, 131 (government report); *Re Upper Churchill Water Rights* [1984] 1 S.C.R. 297, 315-319 (government information pamphlet admitted, but public speeches excluded as unreliable); *General Motors* v. *City National Leasing* [1989] 1 S.C.R. 641, 679-681, 686-688 (report of Economic Council of Canada, study commissioned by government); *R.* v. *Morgentaler (No. 3)* [1993] 3 S.C.R. 463, 485 (parliamentary debates); *RJR-MacDonald* v. *Can.* [1995] 3 S.C.R. 199, paras. 30, 35-37 (parliamentary debates; legislative committee report; government policy papers).

4 *R.* v. *Edwards Books and Art* [1986] 2 S.C.R. 713, 745-749 (parliamentary debates, law reform commission report).

5 *Id.*, 769-772, 796-800 (law reform commission report); *R.* v. *Whyte* [1988] 2 S.C.R. 3, 24-25 (parliamentary debates); *Irwin Toy* v. *Que.* [1989] 1 S.C.R. 927, 983-984 (parliamentary debates); *R.* v. *Keegstra* [1990] 3 S.C.R. 697, 745 (report of special committee on hate propaganda).

6 Kilgour, ''The Rule against the Use of Legislative History'' (1952) 30 Can. Bar Rev. 769; Corry, ''The Use of Legislative History in the Interpretation of Statutes'' (1954) 32 Can. Bar Rev. 624; Charles, ''Extrinsic Evidence and Statutory Interpretation'' (1983) 7 Dal. L.J. 7.

7 *Texada Mines* v. *A.-G. B.C.* [1960] S.C.R. 713, 720; *A.-G. Can.* v. *Reader's Digest* [1961] S.C.R. 775, 782, 791.

8 *P.A.T.A.* v. *A.-G. Can.* [1931] A.C. 310, 317; *A.-G. B.C.* v. *A.-G. Can.* [1937] A.C. 368, 376; *Ladore* v. *Bennett* [1939] A.C. 468, 477; *Home Oil Distributors* v. *A.-G. B.C.* [1940] S.C.R. 444, 447-448.

9 Notes 3-5, above. The current practice was started by *Re Anti-Inflation Act*, note 3, above.

10 Despite a dictum to the contrary in *Re Residential Tenancies Act*, note 3, above, at 721, parliamentary debates at the time of enactment of a challenged statute have often been examined in constitutional cases by the Supreme Court of Canada: see notes 3-5, above.

11 [1995] 3 S.C.R. 199.

McLachlin J., writing for the majority of the Supreme Court of Canada, rebuked the Attorney General of Canada for *not* producing a piece of legislative history (it was a government policy paper for which Crown privilege had been asserted) that might have cast light on whether the government had considered ways of discouraging tobacco consumption that were less invasive of freedom of expression than the total ban on tobacco advertising that was in issue in the case.[12] Her ladyship said that she was ''hard pressed not to infer'' that the government's motive in withholding the document was because it would have shown that a less intrusive measure was available! She then used this inference as one of the important reasons for finding that the government had not satisfied the minimum-impairment branch of the *Oakes* test, which meant that the law could not be justified under s. 1.

Legislative history is not admitted to prove the truth of the facts that may be asserted in the material, but merely to show what considerations moved the enacting legislative body to enact the challenged statute. The courts have accordingly not required legislative history to be proved like other facts in litigation; they have received it without formal proof.

(c) Interpretation of Constitution Act, 1867

To what extent is the legislative history of the Constitution Act, 1867 (formerly the British North America Act, 1867) admissible as an aid to the interpretation of the language of the Act?

This issue has not arisen very frequently, probably because of the sparse records which exist of the legislative history. There are no verbatim records of the discussions that preceded confederation at the conferences at Charlottetown (1864), Quebec (1864) and London, England (1866). The records of the Charlottetown conference are very scanty indeed. The 72 resolutions passed at the Quebec conference survive, and these formed the basis of the scheme of confederation, but there is little record of discussion. The 69 resolutions of the London conference also survive, but again there is little record of discussion. The Confederation Debates in the legislative assembly of the united province of Canada (1865) are preserved in full, but of course these are not the debates of the drafters, but of the members of the legislative assembly of one of the three uniting provinces. There were no debates in the legislative assemblies of the other two uniting provinces, namely, Nova Scotia and New Brunswick. The debate in the Parliament of the United Kingdom is of course available in the United Kingdom Hansard for 1867.[13]

Until recently, the weight of authority was against the admissibility of the legislative history of the Constitution Act, 1867 as an aid to its interpretation.[14]

---

12 *Id.*, para. 166. The concurring opinion of Iacobucci J. is to the same effect (para. 186).

13 The most comprehensive collection of confederation documents is Browne, *Documents on the Confederation of British North America* (1969). See also references in note 1, above.

14 Laskin, *Canadian Constitutional Law* (5th ed., 1986 by Finkelstein), 296.

This was not surprising in light of the rule that legislative history was not admissible as an aid to the interpretation of statutes.[15] However, in a series of recent cases, the Supreme Court of Canada has referred to the legislative history of the Constitution Act, 1867,[16] and these cases now settle the question in favour of the admissibility of the material.[17] The cases draw no distinction between parliamentary debates (Hansard) and other kinds of legislative history: it is clear that all kinds are admissible. Nor do the cases limit the purposes for which the material may be used; it may be used even for the meaning of particular words and phrases.

(d) Interpretation of Constitution Act, 1982

To what extent is the legislative history of the Constitution Act, 1982 admissible as an aid to the interpretation of its provisions, which include the Canadian Charter of Rights and Freedoms?

Unlike the scanty records of the legislative history of the Constitution Act, 1867, there are abundant records of the legislative history of the Constitution Act, 1982. We have the text of no less than seven versions of the Constitution Act, 1982, starting with a discussion draft of August 22, 1980 and culminating in the version that was enacted on March 29, 1982.[18] There are extensive passages in the debates of the Canadian House of Commons and Senate from the introduction into the House of Commons of the ''Proposed Resolution for a Joint Address to Her Majesty the Queen respecting the Constitution of Canada'' on October 6, 1980 until the passage of the much-amended resolution on December 2, 1981

15 Note 6, above.

16 *Jones* v. *A.-G. N.B.* [1975] 2 S.C.R. 182, 194 (Quebec Resolutions); *Di Iorio* v. *Warden of Montreal Jail* [1978] 1 S.C.R. 152, 200 (speech in U.K. Parliament); *A.-G. Que.* v. *Blaikie* [1979] 2 S.C.R. 1016, 1017 (approving lower court in ''matters of detail and history'', which included consideration of Confederation Debates); *Re Upper House* [1980] 1 S.C.R. 54, 66-67 (Confederation Debates); *A.G. Can.* v. *CN Transportation* [1983] 2 S.C.R. 206, 226 (Confederation Debates); *MacDonald* v. *City of Montreal* [1986] 1 S.C.R. 460, 494 (Quebec Resolutions).

17 One further case is worthy of note, although it is so unusual that it may not constitute a useful precedent. In *Reference re Resolution to Amend the Constitution* [1981] 1 S.C.R. 753 the Supreme Court of Canada made a number of references to legislative history. On the issue whether there was a legal requirement of provincial consent to constitutional amendments, the seven-judge majority on that issue referred (at pp. 789-797) to the proceedings of the Imperial Conferences of 1926 and 1930 which preceded the enactment of the Statute of Westminster, 1931; and the two-judge minority referred (at p. 846) to a speech in the House of Commons in 1949. On the issue whether there was a conventional requirement of provincial consent to constitutional amendments, the six-judge majority on that issue referred (at pp. 892, 901-904) to speeches in the House of Commons in 1938, 1940, 1943 and 1960, (at p. 896) to a speech in the U.K. House of Commons in 1907, (at pp. 898-900) to a federal government white paper, and (at pp. 906-908) to speeches at a federal-provincial conference in 1931; and the three-judge minority referred (at p. 866) to parliamentary debate in the House of Commons in 1940.

18 The text of all versions is set out in Elliot, ''Interpreting the Charter - Use of the Earlier Versions as an Aid'' (1982) U.B.C. L. Rev. (Charter ed.) 11, together with argument in favour of their admissibility.

(Commons) and December 8, 1981 (Senate).[19] There is the testimony given by witnesses to the Special Joint Committee of the Senate and House of Commons on the Constitution of Canada, which sat from November 6, 1980 to February 13, 1981; the minutes of the proceedings and evidence of the Committee, which occupies several volumes, includes explanations of the text by the Justice Department lawyers who drafted it.[20] There is the federal-provincial agreement of November 5, 1981, in which an accommodation was reached between the federal government (and Ontario and New Brunswick) and seven of the eight provinces that had been opposed to the proposals.[21] And finally there are the debates in the United Kingdom House of Commons from the introduction of the Canada Bill on December 14, 1981 to its passage on March 8, 1982, and in the House of Lords from its introduction on March 8, 1982 to its passage on March 25, 1982.[22] The Canada Act 1982 became law on March 29, 1982, when the Queen gave her assent.

Since legislative history is freely admissible for the purpose of interpreting the Constitution Act, 1867, it must also be admissible for the purpose of interpreting the Constitution Act, 1982. There is no legal difference between the status of the two Acts. This position has been affirmed by the Supreme Court of Canada.[23]

(e) Originalism

Assuming that the legislative history of the Constitution Act, 1982 is admissible as an aid to the interpretation of the constitutional text, what *weight* ought to be given to the legislative history?

The strongest possible position would be that the legislative history is conclusive. In other words, once the Court is clear about the meaning indicated by the legislative history, the Court is bound to give the text that meaning. This position — that a court is bound by the ''original understanding'' of a constitutional text — is held by some constitutional scholars in the United States, where

19 This material is too voluminous to list in a footnote. The index to the *Commons Debates*, 1980-83 has 19 pages of entries under ''Constitution''. The Senate references are also extensive.

20 *Minutes of Proceedings and Evidence of the Special Joint Committee of the Senate and of the House of Commons on the Constitution of Canada*, First Session of the Thirty-second Parliament, 1980-81, November 6, 1980 to February 13, 1981.

21 See McWhinney, *Canada and the Constitution 1979-1982* (1982); Romanow, Whyte, Leeson, *Canada . . . Notwithstanding* (1984).

22 Once again there are extensive references, but the dates given in the text make them relatively easy to find in the *Debates* of the House of Commons and the House of Lords.

23 *Dubois* v. *The Queen* [1985] 2 S.C.R. 350, 360 (earlier version of Charter); *Re B.C. Motor Vehicle Act* [1985] 2 S.C.R. 486, 504-507 (testimony at special joint committee); *United States* v. *Cotroni* [1989] 1 S.C.R. 1469, 1479-1480 (testimony at special joint committee); *Mahe* v. *Alta.* [1990] 1 S.C.R. 342, 369 (Hansard); *R.* v. *Prosper* [1994] 3 S.C.R. 236, 266-267 (minutes of special joint committee).

it is sometimes described as "originalism".[24] The argument is that a constitutional text should be read in the sense intended by its framers, because it is only the values of the framers that have achieved supremacy over other values through the process of constitution-making. Originalism, it is argued, would produce consistency and predictability in judicial review, because the interpretation of the Constitution would remain constant over time, not changing with changes in the composition of the Supreme Court.

Originalism also offers an answer to the problem of the legitimacy of judicial review. If judicial review is merely giving effect to the original understanding of the framers, then non-elected judges do not trespass on democratic values when they strike down a statute enacted by an elected legislative body. As to the admitted necessity of adapting the Constitution to new conditions and new values, the originalist argues that this should be accomplished by the democratic amending process, not by the "interpretations" of judges.

Originalism has never enjoyed any significant support in Canada.[25] Indeed, as has been narrated, while Americans have debated whether the "original understanding" should be binding, Canadians have debated whether evidence of the "original understanding" should even be disclosed to the Court![26] Originalism is also rejected by a majority of American scholars,[27] and by the practice of American courts, which (as the originalists acknowledge — and deplore) do not regard themselves as bound by the original understanding. Nevertheless, originalism presents a plausible case for giving great weight to legislative history.

There are powerful arguments against originalism, so powerful in my view that they lead to the conclusion that legislative history ought to be accorded little weight in constitutional interpretation.[28] The main problem is that it is not possible to be confident of the "intention of the framers" or the "original understanding". This is caused by the fact that the process of constitutional amendment engaged a large number of people. Of these people, who are to count as framers? Whose original understanding or intention is important? Even if the framers could be

---

24 Berger, *Government by Judiciary* (1977), esp. ch. 20, is the best-known and most uncompromising exposition of originalism; Bork, "Neutral Principles and Some First Amendment Problems" (1971) 47 Ind. L.J. 2 is often cited as well, but in fact Bork does not make his attitude towards legislative history perfectly clear, although he implies (at 4, 13) that the original understanding is binding; Kay, "Adherence to the Original Intentions in Constitutional Adjudication" (1988) 82 Northwestern U.L. Rev. 226 is an elegant defence of originalism.

25 For a soft Canadian Variant of originalism, see Morton and Knopff, "Permanence and Change in a Written Constitution: The "Living Tree" Doctrine and the Charter of Rights" (1990) 1 Supreme Court L.R. (2nd ed.) 533.

26 Note 12, above, and accompanying text.

27 See Brest, "The Misconceived Quest for the Original Understanding" (1980) 60 Boston U.L. Rev. 204; Dworkin, "The Forum of Principle" (1981) 56 N.Y.U.L Rev. 469; Powell, "The Original Understanding of Original Intent" (1985) 98 Harv. L. Rev. 885; Wroth, "The Constitution and the Common Law" (1988) 22 Suffolk U. Law Rev. 553.

28 These views are expressed at more length in my contribution to Sharpe, note 1, above, 150-157.

identified, their collective intention as to points not written down in the constitutional text could not be ascertained with certainty for two reasons. One is the difficulty of attributing any particular opinion to a large group of people who did not actually vote on the point at issue. Another is the difficulty of historical research and analysis, which makes unreliable any findings about beliefs and attitudes in 1867 (although this is not yet a problem for 1982).[29] Yet another is the inherently dynamic process of judicial review, which makes some degree of ''progressive interpretation'' inevitable; that is the topic of the next section of this chapter.

(f) Progressive interpretation

In Canada, it is well established that the language of the Constitution Act, 1867 is not to be frozen in the sense in which it would have been understood in 1867. Rather, the language is to be given a ''progressive interpretation'' so that it is continuously adapted to new conditions and new ideas.[30] The principle of progressive interpretation is flatly inconsistent with originalism, the whole point of which is to deny that the courts have the power to adapt the Constitution to new conditions and new ideas. It would be wrong to conclude that the principle of progressive interpretation is necessarily inconsistent with the intentions of the framers. What originalism ignores is the possibility that the framers were content to leave the detailed application of the Constitution to the courts of the future, and were content that the process of adjudication would apply the text in ways unanticipated at the time of drafting.[31]

With respect to the Constitution Act, 1867, it is quite likely that the ''interpretative intention''[32] of the framers was something like the doctrine of progressive interpretation. They knew that their handiwork would have to adapt to changes in society, and yet they did not seem to contemplate amendment as a frequent method of adaptation, because they made no provision for amendment of the constitutional text, and amendment was in fact only possible by the agency of the imperial Parliament of Great Britain. With respect to the Constitution Act, 1982, the proceedings of the Special Joint Committee of the Senate and House of Commons on the Constitution of Canada indicate rather clearly that the civil servants who drafted the text and the ministers and members of Parliament who

---

29 Kyer, note 1, above.

30 See ch. 15, Judicial Review on Federal Grounds, under heading 15.9(f), Progressive interpretation, above.

31 The thesis of Wroth, note 26, above, is (at 567) ''that all involved in the constitutional decision-making process, whether as framers, ratifiers, opponents, or ordinary citizens, fully understood the open-ended and creative powers of the courts in developing and applying rules of law based on analysis of basic principles found in precedent''.

32 Brest, note 26, above, 215-216 distinguishes between ''substantive intent'', by which he means intent as to the meaning of a particular provision of the constitutional text, and ''interpretive intent'', by which he means intent as to the role of the courts in interpreting the text over time.

adopted it assumed that the courts would not be bound by the views of the framers, and would interpret the text in ways that could not be predicted with certainty.[33]

The principle of progressive interpretation means that the views of the framers about the meaning of particular provisions of the constitutional text become less and less relevant with the passage of time. As Beetz J. has pointed out, legislative history is a "starting point", but it cannot be conclusive in interpreting "essential dynamic" provisions.[34]

(g) Weight of legislative history

In the *B.C. Motor Vehicle Reference* (1985),[35] the Supreme Court of Canada had to decide whether the phrase "fundamental justice" in s. 7 of the Charter of Rights meant procedural justice only, or whether it included substantive justice as well. The question had been the subject of considerable testimony before the Special Joint Committee, and the witnesses, who included those responsible for drafting s. 7, all agreed that fundamental justice was procedural only. Lamer J. for the majority of the Court quoted these statements. But he went on to reject the position taken by the witnesses. He concluded from the language and context of s. 7 that the better interpretation of the phrase extended to substantive justice as well. In reaching this conclusion, he emphasized that the legislative history, although admissible, was entitled to little weight. He pointed to the difficulty in assuming that the views of witnesses to a parliamentary committee were shared by the "multiplicity of actors" who had negotiated, drafted and adopted the Charter.[36] And, in direct contradiction of the originalist argument, he cautioned against the risk that adherence to legislative history would cause the meaning of the Charter to "become frozen in time to the moment of adoption with little or no possibility of growth, development and adjustment to changing societal needs".[37] Such a result would "stunt the growth" of the "newly planted 'living tree' that is the Charter".[38]

Lamer J.'s conclusion that legislative history should be used with great caution and given little weight is, in my opinion, generally the correct approach. In that particular case, however, I think that the legislative history ought to have been respected. Not only was the legislative history unanimous, but it went to the fundamental question of why s. 7 had been included in the Charter in the first place.[39] The lesson to be drawn from *B.C. Motor Vehicle* is that, if legislative

33 Monahan, note 1, above, 78-82, draws this conclusion from his analysis of the proceedings of the special joint committee.

34 *Martin Service Station* v. *MNR* [1977] 2 S.C.R. 996, 1006.

35 *Re B.C. Motor Vehicle Act* [1985] 2 S.C.R. 486.

36 *Id.*, 507-509.

37 *Id.*, 509.

38 *Ibid.*

39 Monahan, note 1, above, 84-85.

history was entitled to little weight in that case, it will rarely be influential.[40] The reality is that only the Court can supply an authoritative interpretation of the constitutional text, relying on the language that was actually enacted.

57.2 Evidence

(a) Modes of proof

How are facts to be proved in constitutional cases?[41]

The general rule is that a court may make findings of fact on the basis of either sworn evidence or judicial notice. Judicial notice may be taken only of ''facts which are (a) so notorious as not to be the subject of dispute among reasonable persons, or (b) capable of immediate and accurate demonstration by resorting to readily accessible sources of indisputable accuracy''.[42] Because the requirements of judicial notice are so restrictive, any dispute about facts must be resolved by a court on the basis of sworn evidence, using the rules regarding the burden and standard of proof to deal with gaps or conflicts in the evidence.[43]

In principle, the general rules regarding the proof of facts in litigation ought to apply to constitutional cases no less than to non-constitutional cases, and they ought to apply to both ''adjudicative facts'' and ''legislative facts''.[44] Adjudicative facts are facts about the immediate parties to the litigation: ''who did what, where, when, how, and with what motive or intent?'' Legislative facts are the facts of the social sciences, concerned with the causes and effects of social and economic phenomena. Legislative facts are rarely in issue in most kinds of litigation, but they are often in issue in constitutional litigation, where the constitutionality of a law may depend upon such diverse facts as the existence of an emergency,[45] the effect of segregated schooling on minority children,[46] the rela-

40 *Mahe* v. *Alta.* [1990] 1 S.C.R. 342, 369 (placing ''no weight'' on Hansard). But contrast *R.* v. *Prosper* [1994] 3 S.C.R. 236, 266-267 (relying on minutes of special joint committee.).

41 See Hogg, ''Proof of Facts in Constitutional Cases'' (1976) 26 U. Toronto L.J. 386; Sharpe, note 1, above, chs. 7 (by Morgan), 8 (by Swinton), 9 (by Hagan); Strayer, note 1, above, 263-297; Charles, note 1, above, 106-124.

42 Sopinka, Lederman and Bryant, *The Law of Evidence in Canada* (1992), 976.

43 Legislative history, which was the topic of the previous section of this chapter (sec. 57.1), is an exception to the general rules of proof. It is admitted, not to prove the truth of the facts contained therein, but to prove what considerations were taken into account in the process of enactment of a statute. The courts will receive legislative history without formal proof.

44 The terminology was coined by Professor Kenneth Culp Davis: see Davis, *Administrative Law Treatise* (1958), vol. 2, s. 15.03; Davis, ''Facts in Lawmaking'' (1980) 80 Columbia L. Rev. 931. The terminology was recognized by Sopinka J. for the Court in *Danson* v. *Ont.* [1990] 2 S.C.R. 1086, 1099.

45 *Re Anti-Inflation Act* [1976] 2 S.C.R. 373.

46 *Brown* v. *Board of Education* (1954) 347 U.S. 483.

tionship between alcohol consumption and road accidents,[47] the susceptibility to advertising of young children,[48] the affect of pornography on behaviour,[49] or the affect of advertising on tobacco consumption.[50]

Legislative facts obviously cannot be proved by the testimony of eye witnesses, but they can be proved by the opinion testimony of persons expert in the relevant field of knowledge. Like other witnesses, experts are subject to cross-examination, and their testimony may be contradicted by the testimony of other experts. These safeguards provide some assurance of reliability for factual findings of controverted legislative facts. However, it has been suggested that an appellate court may interfere with a finding of legislative fact by a trial judge more readily than is permissible with respect to a finding of adjudicative fact. With respect to a finding of adjudicative fact, the trial judge is in a privileged position, because he or she has seen the witnesses and is best able to assess their credibility. The trial judge's finding will therefore be upset on appeal only if the appellate court concludes that the finding is clearly wrong. A finding of legislative fact is not normally as dependent on assessments of the credibility of witnesses, and, at least in some cases, the appellate court may be in as good a position as the trial judge to weigh competing social-science evidence.[51]

(b) Brandeis briefs in the United States

According to the traditional requirements of judicial notice, legislative facts cannot be the subject of judicial notice unless they are indisputable. Most of the time, that is not the case. However, in the United States, there has been some relaxation of the requirements of judicial notice for findings of legislative fact in constitutional cases. In *Muller* v. *Oregon* (1908),[52] Louis D. Brandeis, counsel for the state of Oregon, filed a brief (we would call it a factum in Canada) in the Supreme Court of the United States which included social-science data drawn from books, articles and reports in support of the constitutionality of a state law limiting the hours of female labour. The data contained in the brief had not been proved in the conventional way. Yet the Court received the brief, summarized its

---

47 *Craig* v. *Boren* (1976) 429 U.S. 190; *R.* v. *Seo* (1986) 54 O.R. (2d) 293 (C.A.); *R.* v. *Hufsky* [1988] 1 S.C.R. 621; *R.* v. *Thomsen* [1988] 1 S.C.R. 640.

48 *Irwin Toy* v. *Que.* [1989] 1 S.C.R. 927.

49 *R.* v. *Butler* [1992] 1 S.C.R. 452.

50 *RJR-MacDonald* v. *Can.* [1995] 3 S.C.R. 199.

51 *RJR-MacDonald* v. *Can.* [1995] 3 S.C.R. 199, paras. 79-81 per La Forest J. with the concurrence on this issue of Lamer C.J., L'Heureux-Dubé, Gonthier, Cory and Iacobucci JJ. (rejecting the finding of the trial judge that there was no connection between advertising and consumption of tobacco products). McLachlin J., with the concurrence on this issue of Sopinka and probably Major JJ., is more cautious, but she acknowledges (para. 141) that "a lesser degree of deference may be required where the trial judge has considered social science and other policy oriented evidence".

52 (1908) 208 U.S. 412.

contents in a footnote,[53] and acknowledged that it had considered the brief as a matter of ''judicial cognizance'' in reaching its decision.[54]

Since *Muller* v. *Oregon*, this type of brief has been in common use, and is often called a ''Brandeis brief''. Its best-known use was in the famous school desegregation case, *Brown* v. *Board of Education* (1954),[55] where a Social Science Statement, signed by 32 social scientists, was appended to the brief of counsel for the appellants. The Statement summarized the general fund of psychological and sociological knowledge of the effects of the segregation of the black and white races. The Court, which held that segregation of the schools was unconstitutional, made reference[56] to some of the sources referred to in the brief (and to one source that was not referred to in the brief).[57]

The reception by American courts of Brandeis briefs seems to rest on an expanded notion of judicial notice. The courts take notice of the state of expert knowledge in a field of social science, even though the facts do not have the indisputable character that is the traditional prerequisite for judicial notice. As a practical matter, the Brandeis brief can expose the court to a broad canvass of the state of social-science knowledge without the parties incurring the costs associated with a trial involving a lengthy parade of expert witnesses.[58] However, despite the wide acceptance of the Brandeis brief in the United States, no clear rules have emerged as to when it is an appropriate vehicle of proof, as to the appropriate procedures to allow for rebuttal by the other side, or as to the weight to be given to ''facts'' in a Brandeis brief, which are inevitably less reliable than those adduced by sworn testimony.[59]

(c) Social-science briefs in references

In Canada, in references,[60] it is not uncommon for the ''case'', or the factums (briefs of legal argument) of counsel, to include social-science data, occasionally

---

53 *Id.*, 419, note 1.

54 *Id.*, 420-421.

55 (1954) 347 U.S. 483.

56 *Id.*, 494, footnote 11.

57 Another well-known American case is *Craig* v. *Boren* (1976) 429 U.S. 190, in which a Brandeis brief was filed in support of an Oklahoma law which established a higher drinking age for males (21) than for females (18). The brief used statistics to show the correlations between the use of alcohol by young males and traffic accidents. Brennan J. for the majority of the Court made reference to the brief (at pp. 200-204), but still held that the law was unconstitutional.

58 Another justification of the Brandeis brief is that on some constitutional issues it is not necessary to prove legislative facts as strictly as adjudicative facts. In order to support legislation, a court may require no more than a showing that there was a rational basis for any underlying premise of legislative fact. See Schiff, *Evidence in the Litigation Process* (1988), vol. 2, 711-712. See also next section, 57.2(f), ''Standard of proof'', below.

59 Davis, ''Facts in Lawmaking'' (1980) 80 Columbia L. Rev. 931; Woolhandler, ''Rethinking the Judicial Reception of Legislative Facts'' (1988) 41 Vanderbilt L. Rev. 111.

60 References are examined in sec. 8.6, Reference jurisdiction, above. A reference by the federal

in affidavit form, but more often in the form of unsworn statements by experts or unsworn extracts from books, articles and reports.

In the *Anti-Inflation Reference* (1976),[61] where one of the issues was whether a high rate of inflation qualified as an emergency, the Supreme Court of Canada received and considered an unsworn statement by an economist that was appended to the factum of the Canadian Labour Congress, which was one of the intervenors in the reference opposed to the validity of the legislation. In that case, before the hearing, the Chief Justice had given directions for the filing of factual material so that each side would have an opportunity to file rebuttal material. The supporters of the legislation did file rebuttal material. The admissibility of such material is usually taken to be established by the *Anti-Inflation Reference*. In the *Residential Tenancies Act Reference* (1981),[62] Dickson J. for the Court confirmed that ''in constitutional references'', there was no inflexible rule governing the admissibility of extrinsic materials.[63] ''Material relevant to the issues before the court, and not inherently unreliable or offending against public policy should be admissible, . . .''[64] However, he approved ''the practice followed in the *Anti-Inflation Reference*'' of giving ''timely directions'' with respect to the filing of the material.[65]

A practical justification for the reception of unsworn factual material in a reference is that the procedure of a reference does not include a trial or any other procedure for the taking of evidence. It is true that a court that is seized of a reference could direct the trial of a factual issue, or could direct the filing of affidavits and the cross-examination of deponents. But such directions are very unusual indeed. I have been able to discover only three cases in which evidence was given on a reference. In *Re Eskimos* (1939),[66] where the issue was whether the Inuit people came within the word ''Indians'' in the Constitution, the Supreme Court of Canada directed the registrar of the Court to conduct a hearing of the issue. The hearing was held, and the transcript was transmitted to the Court. In *Re Truscott* (1967),[67] where the issue was whether a criminal conviction should be set aside, the Supreme Court of Canada, sitting as a full bench of nine judges, heard oral evidence itself. *Re Milgaard* (1992)[68] was another reference to the Supreme Court of Canada to review a criminal conviction outside the appeal period, and the Court, this time sitting as a bench of five judges, again heard oral

---

government is directed to the Supreme Court of Canada. A reference by a provincial government is directed to the Court of Appeal of the province, from which it may be appealed as of right to the Supreme Court of Canada.

61 [1976] 2 S.C.R. 373.

62 [1981] 1 S.C.R. 714.

63 *Id.*, 722.

64 *Id.*, 733.

65 *Id.*, 722-723

66 [1939] S.C.R. 104.

67 [1967] S.C.R. 309.

68 (1992) 71 C.C.C. (3d) 260 (S.C.C.).

evidence. These three cases are quite outside the normal practice on references, which makes no provision for the formal proof of facts. In these circumstances, the reception of Brandeis briefs, or other informal vehicles of proof, is a practical necessity.

(d) Social-science briefs in appeals

Occasionally, a constitutional issue in a case is recognized for the first time on appeal. In such a case, the appeal resembles a reference, in that there is no practical way to receive factual material other than through the case on appeal or the factums of counsel. In these cases, the Supreme Court of Canada has accepted factual material that was filed, without formal proof, in the Court of Appeal or the Supreme Court of Canada.[69]

(e) Social-science briefs in trials

At trial (or other first-instance proceeding), where there is an opportunity to adduce the ''best evidence'', that is, sworn testimony, it seems obvious that it is the best evidence that should be adduced. All facts, whether ''legislative'' or ''adjudicative'', should be proved in the conventional manner. To the extent that the insights of social science are relevant, they should be proved by the expert testimony of social scientists, subject to the normal safeguards of the oath, cross-examination and rebuttal.[70]

However, the relaxation of the rules for legislative facts in constitutional cases has certainly spilled over from references and appeals to trials.[71] For example, in *R.* v. *Morgentaler (No. 2)* (1988),[72] in which the Criminal Code provisions respecting abortion were held to be unconstitutional on Charter grounds, the judges in the majority referred to a variety of evidence respecting abortion without questioning its admissibility or drawing any distinction between material adduced through sworn testimony and unsworn material. It seems that both categories were received by the trial court. McIntyre J., who dissented, made this comment:[73]

> While I recognize that in constitutional cases a greater latitude has been allowed concerning the reception of such material, I would prefer to place principal reliance upon the evidence given under oath in court in my consideration of the factual matters.

---

69 E.g., *R.* v. *Seo* (1986) 54 O.R. (2d) 293, 302-303 (C.A.); *R.* v. *Hufsky* [1988] 1 S.C.R. 621, 634-635; *R.* v. *Thomsen* [1988] 1 S.C.R. 640, 654-655; *Ford* v. *Que.* [1988] 2 S.C.R. 712, 774-777; *Irwin Toy* v. *Que.* [1989] 1 S.C.R. 927, 983-984.

70 Accord, Laskin, *Canadian Constitutional Law* (5th ed., 1986 by Finkelstein), vol. 2, 1008.

71 Sharpe, note 1, above, 178 (by Morgan).

72 [1988] 1 S.C.R. 30.

73 *Id.*, 149.

It seems clear that a trial court, when asked to make findings of legislative fact, has a discretion to admit unsworn evidence that is "not inherently unreliable".[74] The court could take into account such matters as whether the legislative facts are essential to the case; whether they are disputed; and whether it would be impossible, or very costly, to prove them by conventional means.[75] The court should also provide appropriate procedural directions so that there is the opportunity for each side to file reply material.

(f) Standard of proof

The *Anti-Inflation Reference* (1976)[76] decides that, in distribution-of-powers (or federalism) constitutional cases, the proponent of legislation need show no more than a rational basis for legislative facts that are prerequisite to the validity of the legislation. The issue in the case was whether a high rate of inflation qualified as an emergency so as to enable the federal Parliament to invoke the emergency branch of the peace, order, and good government power. As related earlier,[77] the Court accepted unsworn social-science briefs on this issue. Laskin C.J., with whom Judson, Spence and Dickson JJ. agreed, said[78] that "the extrinsic material need only go so far as to persuade the Court that there is *a rational basis for the legislation* which it is attributing to the head of power invoked in this case in support of its validity". Ritchie J., with whom Martland and Pigeon JJ. agreed, said [79]that the facts that would support the legislation should be rejected by the Court only on the basis of "very clear evidence that an emergency had not arisen when the statute was enacted".

The rational basis test (and the very-clear-evidence-to-the-contrary test amounts to much the same thing) erects a presumption of constitutionality that is exceedingly difficult for the challenger of legislation to overcome. The rational basis test enables a court to uphold the validity of legislation without the necessity for strict proof of the underlying facts. It enables a court to resolve conflicting evidence without the need to make a definitive ruling on the conflict. Therefore, the rational basis test could be regarded as a justification for the reception of unsworn factual material.

---

74 The quoted words come from *Re Residential Tenancies Act*, note 64, above. In *R.* v. *Squires (No. 1)* (1985) 25 C.C.C. (3d) 32 (Ont. Prov. Ct., Crim. Div.), the Court rejected unsworn evidence on the basis that it was not "inherently reliable".

75 Another factor is whether the legislative facts have to be proved only to a rational-basis standard: see next section, 38.8(d), Standard of proof, below.

76 *Re Anti-Inflation Act* [1976] 2 S.C.R. 337.

77 Note 61, above, and accompanying text.

78 [1976] 2 S.C.R. 337, 423 (my emphasis). Two pages later, at 425, Laskin J. repeats the rational basis test, but with the significant twist that he places the burden on the opponent of the legislation to show that there was no rational basis for the legislation. With respect, this latter formulation seems too deferential, because it places too high a burden on the party seeking judicial review.

79 *Id.*, 439.

The rational basis test is not appropriate in Charter cases. For those attacking the validity of a law on Charter grounds, a breach of the Charter would obviously have to be affirmatively established. For those upholding the validity of a law under s. 1 of the Charter, the *Oakes* tests of justification would have to be satisfied. In *R.* v. *Oakes* (1986),[80] Dickson C.J., for a Court that was unanimous on this issue, said[81] that ''the onus of proving'' justification was on the party seeking to uphold the challenged law. The standard of proof, he held,[82] was ''the civil standard, namely, proof on a preponderance of probability''. And he added[83] that ''a very high degree of probability'', though not the criminal standard, was required. This makes clear that the rational basis test does not define the standard of proof of legislative facts in Charter cases.[84]

---

80 [1986] 1 S.C.R. 103.
81 *Id.*, 136-137.
82 *Id.*, 137.
83 *Id.*, 138.
84 See also ch. 35, Limitation of Rights, under heading 35.4, ''Burden of proof'', above. Accord, Sharpe, note 1, above, 206 (by Swinton); Strayer, note 1, above, 293.

APPENDIX I

Constitution Act, 1867

U.K., 30 & 31 Victoria, c. 3.

(Consolidated with amendments)

An Act for the Union of Canada, Nova Scotia, and New Brunswick, and the Government thereof; and for Purposes connected therewith.

(29th March, 1867.)

WHEREAS the Provinces of Canada, Nova Scotia and New Brunswick have expressed their Desire to be federally united into One Dominion under the Crown of the United Kingdom of Great Britain and Ireland, with a Constitution similar in Principle to that of the United Kingdom:

And whereas such a Union would conduce to the Welfare of the Provinces and promote the Interests of the British Empire:

And whereas on the Establishment of the Union by Authority of Parliament it is expedient, not only that the Constitution of the Legislative Authority in the Dominion be provided for, but also that the Nature of the Executive Government therein be declared:

And whereas it is expedient that Provision be made for the eventual Admission into the Union of other Parts of British North America:(1)

(1) The enacting clause was repealed by the *Statute Law Revision Act, 1893,* 56-57 Vict., c. 14 (U.K.). It read as follows:

> Be it therefore enacted and declared by the Queen's Most Excellent Majesty, by and with the Advice and Consent of the Lords Spiritual and Temporal, and Commons, in this present Parliament assembled, and by the Authority of the same, as follows:

I. — Preliminary.

1. This Act may be cited as the *Constitution Act, 1867.*(2)

2. Repealed.(3)

II. — Union.

3. It shall be lawful for the Queen, by and with the Advice of Her Majesty's Most Honourable Privy Council, to declare by Proclamation that, on and after a Day therein appointed, not being more than Six Months after the passing of this Act, the Provinces of Canada, Nova Scotia, and New Brunswick shall form and be One Dominion under the Name of Canada; and on and after that Day those Three Provinces shall form and be One Dominion under that Name accordingly.(4)

4. Unless it is otherwise expressed or implied, the Name Canada shall be taken to mean Canada as constituted under this Act.(5)

5. Canada shall be divided into Four Provinces, named Ontario, Quebec, Nova Scotia, and New Brunswick.(6)

---

(2) As enacted by the *Constitution Act, 1982*, which came into force on April 17, 1982. The section, as originally enacted, read as follows:

> **1.** This Act may be cited as The British North America Act, 1867.

(3) Section 2, repealed by the *Statute Law Revision Act, 1893*, 56-57 Vict., c. 14 (U.K.), read as follows:

> **2.** The Provisions of this Act referring to Her Majesty the Queen extend also to the Heirs and Successors of Her Majesty, Kings and Queens of the United Kingdom of Great Britain and Ireland.

(4) The first day of July, 1867, was fixed by proclamation dated May 22, 1867.

(5) Partially repealed by the *Statute Law Revision Act, 1893*, 56-57 Vict., c. 14 (U.K.). As originally enacted the section read as follows:

> **4.** The subsequent Provisions of this Act, shall, unless it is otherwise expressed or implied, commence and have effect on and after the Union, that is to say, on and after the Day appointed for the Union taking effect in the Queen's Proclamation; and in the same Provisions, unless it is otherwise expressed or implied, the Name Canada shall be taken to mean Canada as constituted under this Act.

(6) Canada now consists of ten provinces (Ontario, Quebec, Nova Scotia, New Brunswick, Manitoba, British Columbia, Prince Edward Island, Alberta, Saskatchewan and Newfoundland) and two territories (the Yukon Territory and the Northwest Territories).

The first territories added to the Union were Rupert's Land and the North-Western Territory,

6. The Parts of the Province of Canada (as it exists at the passing of this Act) which formerly constituted respectively the Provinces of Upper Canada and Lower Canada shall be deemed to be severed, and shall form Two separate Provinces. The Part which formerly constituted the Province of Upper Canada shall constitute the Province of Ontario; and the Part which formerly constituted the Province of Lower Canada shall constitute the Province of Quebec.

7. The Provinces of Nova Scotia and New Brunswick shall have the same Limits as at the passing of this Act.

8. In the general Census of the Population of Canada which is hereby required to be taken in the Year One thousand eight

---

(subsequently designated the Northwest Territories), which were admitted pursuant to section 146 of the *Constitution Act, 1867* and the *Rupert 's Land Act, 1868*, 31-32 Vict., c. 105 (U.K.), by the *Rupert's Land and North-Western Territory Order* of June 23, 1870, effective July 15, 1870. Prior to the admission of those territories the Parliament of Canada enacted *An Act for the temporary Government of Rupert's Land and the North-Western Territory when united with Canada* (32-33 Vict., c. 3), and the *Manitoba Act, 1870*, (33 Vict., c. 3), which provided for the formation of the Province of Manitoba.

British Columbia was admitted into the Union pursuant to section 146 of the *Constitution Act, 1867*, by the *British Columbia Terms of Union*, being Order in Council of May 16, 1871, effective July 20, 1871.

Prince Edward Island was admitted pursuant to section 146 of the *Constitution Act, 1867*, by the *Prince Edward Island Terms of Union*, being Order in Council of June 26, 1873, effective July 1, 1873.

On June 29, 1871, the United Kingdom Parliament enacted the *Constitution Act, 1871* (34-35 Vict., c. 28) authorizing the creation of additional provinces out of territories not included in any province. Pursuant to this statute, the Parliament of Canada enacted the *Alberta Act* (July 20, 1905, 4-5 Edw. VII, c. 3) and the *Saskatchewan Act*, (July 20, 1905, 4-5 Edw. VII, c. 42), providing for the creation of the provinces of Alberta and Saskatchewan, respectively. Both these Acts came into force on Sept. 1, 1905.

Meanwhile, all remaining British possessions and territories in North America and the islands adjacent thereto, except the colony of Newfoundland and its dependencies, were admitted into the Canadian Confederation by the *Adjacent Territories Order* dated July 31, 1880.

The Parliament of Canada added portions of the Northwest Territories to the adjoining provinces in 1912 by *The Ontario Boundaries Extension Act*, 1912, 2 Geo. V, c. 40, *The Quebec Boundaries Extension Act,* 1912, 2 Geo. V, c. 45 and *The Manitoba Boundaries Extension Act*, 1912, 2 Geo. V, c. 32, and further additions were made to Manitoba by *The Manitoba Boundaries Extension Act*, 1930, 20-21 Geo. V., c. 28.

The Yukon Territory was created out of the Northwest Territories in 1898 by The *Yukon Territory Act*, 61 Vict., c. 6, (Canada).

Newfoundland was added on March 31, 1949, by the *Newfoundland Act* (U.K.), 12-13 Geo. VI, c. 22, which ratified the Terms of Union between Canada and Newfoundland.

hundred and seventy-one, and in every Tenth Year thereafter, the respective Populations of the Four Provinces shall be distinguished.

III. — EXECUTIVE POWER.

9. The Executive Government and Authority of and over Canada is hereby declared to continue and be vested in the Queen.

10. The Provisions of this Act referring to the Governor General extend and apply to the Governor General for the Time being of Canada, or other the Chief Executive Officer or Administrator for the Time being carrying on the Government of Canada on behalf and in the Name of the Queen, by whatever Title he is designated.

11. There shall be a Council to aid and advise in the Government of Canada, to be styled the Queen's Privy Council for Canada; and the Persons who are to be Members of that Council shall be from Time to Time chosen and summoned by the Governor General and sworn in as Privy Councillors, and Members thereof may be from Time to Time removed by the Governor General.

12. All Powers, Authorities, and Functions which under any Act of the Parliament of Great Britain, or of the Parliament of the United Kingdom of Great Britain and Ireland, or of the Legislature of Upper Canada, Lower Canada, Canada, Nova Scotia, or New Brunswick, are at the Union vested in or exerciseable by the respective Governors or Lieutenant Governors of those Provinces, with the Advice, or with the Advice and Consent, of the respective Executive Councils thereof, or in conjunction with those Councils, or with any Number of Members thereof, or by those Governors or Lieutenant Governors individually, shall, as far as the same continue in existence and capable of being exercised after the Union in relation to the Government of Canada, be vested in and exerciseable by the Governor General, with the Advice or with the Advice and Consent of or in conjunction with the Queen's Privy Council for Canada, or any Member thereof, or by the Governor General individually, as the Case requires, subject nevertheless (except with respect to such as exist under Acts of the Parliament of Great Britain or of the Parliament of the United Kingdom of

Great Britain and Ireland) to be abolished or altered by the Parliament of Canada.(7)

13. The Provisions of this Act referring to the Governor General in Council shall be construed as referring to the Governor General acting by and with the Advice of the Queen's Privy Council for Canada.

14. It shall be lawful for the Queen, if Her Majesty thinks fit, to authorize the Governor General from Time to Time to appoint any Person or any Persons jointly or severally to be his Deputy or Deputies within any Part or Parts of Canada, and in that Capacity to exercise during the Pleasure of the Governor General such of the Powers, Authorities, and Functions of the Governor General as the Governor General deems it necessary or expedient to assign to him or them, subject to any Limitations or Directions expressed or given by the Queen; but the Appointment of such a Deputy or Deputies shall not affect the Exercise by the Governor General himself of any Power, Authority or Function.

15. The Command-in-Chief of the Land and Naval Militia, and of all Naval and Military Forces, of and in Canada, is hereby declared to continue and be vested in the Queen.

16. Until the Queen otherwise directs, the Seat of Government of Canada shall be Ottawa.

IV. — Legislative Power

17. There shall be One Parliament for Canada, consisting of the Queen, an Upper House styled the Senate, and the House of Commons.

18. The privileges, immunities, and powers to be held, enjoyed, and exercised by the Senate and by the House of Commons, and by the Members thereof respectively, shall be such as are from time to time defined by Act of the Parliament of Canada, but so that any Act of the Parliament of Canada defining such privileges, immunities, and powers shall not confer any privileges, immunities, or powers exceeding those at the passing of such Act held, enjoyed, and exercised by the Commons House

(7) See the notes to section 129, *infra*.

of Parliament of the United Kingdom of Great Britain and Ireland, and by the Members thereof.(8)

19. The Parliament of Canada shall be called together not later than Six Months after the Union.(9)

20. Repealed.(10)

The Senate.

21. The Senate shall, subject to the Provisions of this Act, consist of One Hundred and four Members, who shall be styled Senators.(11)

22. In relation to the Constitution of the Senate Canada shall be deemed to consist of Four Divisions:—

---

(8) Repealed and re-enacted by the *Parliament of Canada Act, 1875*, 38-39 Vict., c. 38 (U.K.). The original section read as follows:

> **18.** The Privileges, Immunities, and Powers to be held, enjoyed, and exercised by the Senate and by the House of Commons and by the Members thereof respectively shall be such as are from Time to Time defined by Act of the Parliament of Canada, but so that the same shall never exceed those at the passing of this Act held, enjoyed, and exercised by the Commons House of Parliament of the United Kingdom of Great Britain and Ireland and by the Members thereof.

(9) Spent. The first session of the first Parliament began on November 6, 1867.

(10) Section 20, repealed by the Schedule to the *Constitution Act, 1982*, read as follows:

> 20. There shall be a Session of the Parliament of Canada once at least in every Year, so that Twelve Months shall not intervene between the last Sitting of the Parliament in one Session and its first Sitting in the next Session.
>
> Section 20 has been replaced by section 5 of the *Constitution Act, 1982*, which provides that there shall be a sitting of Parliament at least once every twelve months.

(11) As amended by the *Constitution Act, 1915*, 5-6 Geo. V, c. 45 (U.K.) and modified by the *Newfoundland Act*, 12-13 Geo. VI, c. 22 (U.K.), and the *Constitution Act (No. 2), 1975*, S.C. 1974-75-76, c. 53.

The original section read as follows:

> **21.** The Senate shall, subject to the Provisions of this Act, consist of Seventy-two Members, who shall be styled Senators.

The *Manitoba Act, 1870*, added two for Manitoba; the *British Columbia Terms of Union* added three; upon admission of Prince Edward Island four more were provided by section 147 of the *Constitution Act, 1867*; the *Alberta Act* and the *Saskatchewan Act* each added four. The Senate was reconstituted at 96 by the *Constitution Act, 1915*. Six more Senators were added upon union with Newfoundland, and one Senator each was added for the Yukon Territory and the Northwest Territories by the *Constitution Act (No. 2), 1975*.

1. Ontario;
2. Quebec;
3. The Maritime Provinces, Nova Scotia and New Brunswick, and Prince Edward Island;
4. The Western Provinces of Manitoba, British Columbia. Saskatchewan, and Alberta;

which Four Divisions shall (subject to the Provisions of this Act) be equally represented in the Senate as follows: Ontario by twenty-four senators; Quebec by twenty-four senators; the Maritime Provinces and Prince Edward Island by twenty-four senators, ten thereof representing Nova Scotia, ten thereof representing New Brunswick, and four thereof representing Prince Edward Island; the Western Provinces by twenty-four senators, six thereof representing Manitoba, six thereof representing British Columbia, six thereof representing Saskatchewan, and six thereof representing Alberta; Newfoundland shall be entitled to be represented in the Senate by six members; the Yukon Territory and the Northwest Territories shall be entitled to be represented in the Senate by one member each.

In the Case of Quebec each of the Twenty-four Senators representing that Province shall be appointed for One of the Twenty-four Electoral Divisions of Lower Canada specified in Schedule A. to Chapter One of the Consolidated statutes of Canada.(12)

23. The Qualification of a Senator shall be as follows:

---

(12) As amended by the *Constitution Act, 1915*, the *Newfoundland Act*, 12-13 Geo. VI, c. 22 (U.K.), and the *Constitution Act (No. 2), 1975*, S.C. 1974-75-76, c. 53. The original section read as follows:

> 22. In relation to the Constitution of the Senate, Canada shall be deemed to consist of Three Divisions:
>
> 1. Ontario;
>
> 2. Quebec;
>
> 3. The Maritime Provinces, Nova Scotia and New Brunswick;
>
> which Three Divisions shall (subject to the Provisions of this Act) be equally represented in the Senate as follows: Ontario by Twenty-four Senators; Quebec by Twenty-four Senators; and the Maritime Provinces by Twenty-four Senators, Twelve thereof representing Nova Scotia, and Twelve thereof representing New Brunswick.
>
> In the case of Quebec each of the Twenty-four Senators representing that province shall be appointed for One of the Twenty-four Electoral Divisions of Lower Canada specified in Schedule A. to Chapter One of the Consolidated Statutes of Canada.

(1) He shall be of the full age of Thirty Years:

(2) He shall be either a natural-born Subject of the Queen, or a Subject of the Queen naturalized by an Act of the Parliament of Great Britain, or of the Parliament of the United Kingdom of Great Britain and Ireland, or of the Legislature of One of the Provinces of Upper Canada, Lower Canada, Canada, Nova Scotia, or New Brunswick, before the Union, or of the Parliament of Canada, after the Union:

(3) He shall be legally or equitably seised as of Freehold for his own Use and Benefit of Lands or Tenements held in Free and Common Socage, or seised or possessed for his own Use and Benefit of Lands or Tenements held in Franc-alleu or in Roture, within the Province for which he is appointed, of the Value of Four thousand Dollars, over and above all Rents, Dues, Debts, Charges, Mortgages, and Incumbrances due or payable out of or charged on or affecting the same:

(4) His Real and Personal Property shall be together worth Four thousand Dollars over and above his Debts and Liabilities:

(5) He shall be resident in the Province for which he is appointed:

(6) In the case of Quebec he shall have his Real Property Qualification in the Electoral Division for which he is appointed, or shall be resident in that Division.(13)

24. The Governor General shall from Time to Time, in the Queen's Name, by Instrument under the Great Seal of Canada, summon qualified Persons to the Senate; and, subject to the Provisions of this Act, every Person so summoned shall become and be a Member of the Senate and a Senator.

25. Repealed.(14)

---

(13) Section 2 of the *Constitution Act (No. 2), 1975*, S.C. 1974-75-76, c. 53 provided that for the purposes of that Act (which added one Senator each for the Yukon Territory and the Northwest Territories) the term ''Province'' in section 23 of the *Constitution Act, 1867*, has the same meaning as is assigned to the term ''province'' by section 28 of the *Interpretation Act*, R.S.C. 1985, c. I-21, which provides that the term ''province'' means ''a province of Canada, and includes the Yukon Territory and the Northwest Territories.''

(14) Repealed by the *Statute Law Revision Act, 1893*, 56-57 Vict., 14 (U.K.). The section read as follows:

> **25.** Such Persons shall be first summoned to the Senate as the Queen by Warrant under Her Majesty's Royal Sign Manual thinks fit to approve, and their Names shall be inserted in the Queen's Proclamation of Union.

26. If at any Time on the Recommendation of the Governor General the Queen thinks fit to direct that Four or Eight Members be added to the Senate, the Governor General may by Summons to Four or Eight qualified Persons (as the Case may be), representing equally the Four Divisions of Canada, add to the Senate accordingly.(15)

27. In case of such Addition being at any Time made, the Governor General shall not summon any Person to the Senate, except upon a further like Direction by the Queen on the like Recommendation, to represent one of the Four Divisions until such Division is represented by Twenty-four Senators and no more.(16)

28. The Number of Senators shall not at any Time exceed One Hundred and twelve.(17)

29. (1) Subject to subsection (2), a Senator shall, subject to the provisions of this Act, hold his place in the Senate for life.

(2) A Senator who is summoned to the Senate after the coming into force of this subsection shall, subject to this Act, hold his place in the Senate until he attains the age of seventy-five years.(18)

---

(15) As amended by the *Constitution Act, 1915*, 5-6 Geo. V, c. 45 (U.K.). The original section read as follows:

> **26.** If at any Time on the Recommendation of the Governor General the Queen thinks fit to direct that Three or Six Members be added to the Senate, the Governor General may by Summons to Three or Six qualified Persons (as the Case may be), representing equally the Three Divisions of Canada, add to the Senate accordingly.

(16) As amended by the *Constitution Act, 1915*, 5-6 Geo. V, c. 45 (U.K.). The original section read as follows:

> **27.** In case of such Addition being at any Time made the Governor General shall not summon any Person to the Senate except on a further like Direction by the Queen on the like Recommendation, until each of the Three Divisions of Canada is represented by Twenty-four Senators and no more.

(17) As amended by the *Constitution Act, 1915*, 5-6 Geo. V, c. 45 (U.K.), and the *Constitution Act (No. 2), 1975*, S.C. 1974-75-76, c. 53. The original section read as follows:

> **28.** The Number of Senators shall not at any Time exceed Seventy-eight.

(18) As enacted by the *Constitution Act, 1965*, Statutes of Canada, 1965, c. 4 which came into force on the 1st of June 1965. The original section read as follows:

> **29.** A Senator shall, subject to the Provisions of this Act, hold his Place in the Senate for Life.

[Sections 30 to 36 are omitted.]

The House of Commons.

37. The House of Commons shall, subject to the Provisions of this Act, consist of two hundred and eighty-two members of whom ninety-five shall be elected for Ontario, seventy-five for Quebec, eleven for Nova Scotia, ten for New Brunswick, fourteen for Manitoba, twenty-eight for British Columbia, four for Prince Edward Island, twenty-one for Alberta, fourteen for Saskatchewan, seven for Newfoundland, one for the Yukon Territory and two for the Northwest Territories.(20)

38. The Governor General shall from Time to Time, in the Queen's Name, by Instrument under the Great Seal of Canada, summon and call together the House of Commons.

[Sections 39 to 49 are omitted.]

50. Every House of Commons shall continue for Five Years from the Day of the Return of the Writs for choosing the House (subject to be sooner dissolved by the Governor General), and no longer.(26)

[Section 51 is omitted.]

51A. Notwithstanding anything in this Act a province shall always be entitled to a number of members in the House of Commons not less than the number of senators representing such province.(29)

---

(20) The figures given here result from the application of section 51, as enacted by the *Constitution Act, 1985 (Representation)*, S.C., 1986, c. 8, Part I, and readjusted pursuant to the *Electoral Boundaries Readjustment Act*, R.S.C. 1985, c. E-3. The original section (which was altered from time to time as the result of the addition of new provinces and changes in population) read as follows:

> **37.** The House of Commons shall, subject to the Provisions of this Act, consist of one hundred and eighty-one members, of whom Eighty-two shall be elected for Ontario, Sixty-five for Quebec, Nineteen for Nova Scotia, and Fifteen for New Brunswick.

(26) The term of the twelfth Parliament was extended by the *British North America Act, 1916*, 6-7 Geo. V, c. 19 (U.K.), which Act was repealed by the *Statute Law Revision Act, 1927*, 17-18 Geo. V, c. 42 (U.K.). See also subsection 4(1) of the *Constitution Act, 1982*, which provides that no House of Commons shall continue for longer than five years from the date fixed for the return of the writs at a general election of its members, and subsection 4(2) thereof, which provides for continuation of the House of Commons in special circumstances.

(29) As enacted by the *Constitution Act, 1915*, 5-6 Geo. V, c. 45 (U.K.).

52. The Number of Members of the House of Commons may be from Time to Time increased by the Parliament of Canada, provided the proportionate Representation of the Provinces prescribed by this Act is not thereby disturbed.

Money Votes; Royal Assent.

53. Bills for appropriating any Part of the Public Revenue, or for imposing any Tax or Impost, shall originate in the House of Commons.

54. It shall not be lawful for the House of Commons to adopt or pass any Vote, Resolution, Address, or Bill for the Appropriation of any Part of the Public Revenue, or of any Tax or Impost, to any Purpose that has not been first recommended to that House by Message of the Governor General in the Session in which such Vote, Resolution, Address, or Bill is proposed.

55. Where a Bill passed by the Houses of the Parliament is presented to the Governor General for the Queen's Assent, he shall declare, according to his Discretion, but subject to the Provisions of this Act and to Her Majesty's Instructions, either that he assents thereto in the Queen's Name, or that he withholds the Queen's Assent, or that he reserves the Bill for the Signification of the Queen's Pleasure.

56. Where the Governor General assents to a Bill in the Queen's Name, he shall by the first convenient Opportunity send an authentic Copy of the Act to one of Her Majesty's Principal Secretaries of State, and if the Queen in Council within Two Years after Receipt thereof by the Secretary of State thinks fit to disallow the Act, such Disallowance (with a Certificate of the Secretary of State of the Day on which the Act was received by him) being signified by the Governor General, by Speech or Message to each of the Houses of the Parliament or by Proclamation, shall annul the Act from and after the Day of such Signification.

57. A Bill reserved for the Signification of the Queen's Pleasure shall not have any Force unless and until, within Two Years from the Day on which it was presented to the Governor General for the Queen's Assent, the Governor General signifies, by Speech or Message to each of the Houses of the Parliament or by Proclamation, that it has received the Assent of the Queen in Council.

An Entry of every such Speech, Message, or Proclamation shall be made in the Journal of each House, and a Duplicate thereof duly attested shall be delivered to the proper Officer to be kept among the Records of Canada.

V. — PROVINCIAL CONSTITUTIONS.

Executive Power.

58. For each Province there shall be an Officer, styled the Lieutenant Governor, appointed by the Governor General in Council by Instrument under the Great Seal of Canada.

59. A Lieutenant Governor shall hold Office during the Pleasure of the Governor General; but any Lieutenant Governor appointed after the Commencement of the First Session of the Parliament of Canada shall not be removeable within Five Years from his Appointment, except for Cause assigned, which shall be communicated to him in Writing within One Month after the Order for his Removal is made, and shall be communicated by Message to the Senate and to the House of Commons within One Week thereafter if the Parliament is then sitting, and if not then within One Week after the Commencement of the next Session of the Parliament.

60. The Salaries of the Lieutenant Governors shall be fixed and provided by the Parliament of Canada.(30)

61. Every Lieutenant Governor shall, before assuming the Duties of his Office, make and subscribe before the Governor General or some Person authorized by him Oaths of Allegiance and Office similar to those taken by the Governor General.

62. The Provisions of this Act referring to the Lieutenant Governor extend and apply to the Lieutenant Governor for the Time being of each Province, or other the Chief Executive Officer or Administrator for the Time being carrying on the Government of the Province, by whatever Title he is designated.

63. The Executive Council of Ontario and of Quebec shall be composed of such Persons as the Lieutenant Governor from Time to Time thinks fit, and in the first instance of the following Officers, namely, — the Attorney General, the Secretary and Registrar of the Province, the Treasurer of the Province, the

---

(30) Provided for by the *Salaries Act*, R.S.C. 1985, c. S-3.

Commissioner of Crown Lands, and the Commissioner of Agriculture and Public Works, with in Quebec, the Speaker of the Legislative Council and the Solicitor General.(31)

64. The Constitution of the Executive Authority in each of the Provinces of Nova Scotia and New Brunswick shall, subject to the Provisions of this Act, continue as it exists at the Union until altered under the Authority of this Act.(32)

65. All Powers, Authorities, and Functions which under any Act of the Parliament of Great Britain, or of the Parliament of the United Kingdom of Great Britain and Ireland, or of the Legislature of Upper Canada, Lower Canada, or Canada, were or are before or at the Union vested in or exerciseable by the respective Governors or Lieutenant Governors of those Provinces, with the Advice or with the Advice and Consent of the respective Executive Councils thereof, or in conjunction with those Councils, or with any Number of Members thereof, or by those Governors or Lieutenant Governors individually, shall, as far as the same are capable of being exercised after the Union in relation to the Government of Ontario and Quebec respectively, be vested in and shall or may be exercised by the Lieutenant Governor of Ontario and Quebec respectively, with the Advice or with the Advice and consent of or in conjunction with the respective Executive Councils, or any Members thereof, or by the Lieutenant Governor individually, as the Case requires, subject nevertheless (except with respect to such as exist under Acts of the Parliament of Great Britain, or of the Parliament of the United Kingdom of Great Britain and Ireland,) to be abolished or altered by the respective Legislatures of Ontario and Quebec.(33)

66. The Provisions of this Act referring to the Lieutenant Governor in Council shall be construed as referring to the Lieutenant Governor of the Province acting by and with the Advice of the Executive Council thereof.

---

(31) Now provided for in Ontario by the *Executive Council Act*, R.S.O. 1990, c. E.25, and in Quebec by the *Executive Power Act*, R.S.Q. 1977, c. E-18.

(32) A similar provision was included in each of the instruments admitting British Columbia, Prince Edward Island, and Newfoundland. The Executive Authorities for Manitoba, Alberta and Saskatchewan were established by the statutes creating those provinces. See the notes to section 5, *supra*.

(33) See the notes to section 129, *infra*.

67. The Governor General in Council may from Time to Time appoint an Administrator to execute the office and Functions of Lieutenant Governor during his Absence, Illness, or other Inability.

68. Unless and until the Executive Government of any Province otherwise directs with respect to that Province, the Seats of Government of the Provinces shall be as follows, namely, — of Ontario, the City of Toronto; of Quebec, the City of Quebec; of Nova Scotia, the City of Halifax; and of New Brunswick, the City of Fredericton.

Legislative Power.

1.—ONTARIO.

69. There shall be a Legislature for Ontario consisting of the Lieutenant Governor and of One House, styled the Legislative Assembly of Ontario.

[Section 70 is omitted.]

2.—QUEBEC.

71. There shall be a Legislature for Quebec consisting of the Lieutenant Governor and of Two Houses, styled the Legislative Council of Quebec and the Legislative Assembly of Quebec.(35)

[Sections 72 to 85 are omitted.]

86. There shall be a Session of the Legislature of Ontario and of that of Quebec once at least in every Year, so that Twelve Months shall not intervene between the last Sitting of the Legislature in each Province in one Session and its first Sitting in the next Session.(41)

[Section 87 is omitted.]

---

(35) The Act respecting the Legislative Council of Quebec, S.Q. 1968, c. 9, provided that the Legislature for Quebec shall consist of the Lieutenant Governor and the National Assembly of Quebec, and repealed the provisions of the *Legislature Act*, R.S.Q. 1964, c. 6, relating to the Legislative Council of Quebec. Sections 72 to 79 following are therefore completely spent.

(41) See also section 5 of the *Constitution Act, 1982*, which provides that there shall be a sitting of each legislature at least once every twelve months.

4.—NOVA SCOTIA AND NEW BRUNSWICK.

88. The Constitution of the Legislature of each of the Provinces of Nova Scotia and New Brunswick shall, subject to the Provisions of this Act, continue as it exists at the Union until altered under the Authority of this Act.(42)

89. Repealed.(43)

6.—THE FOUR PRONVICES.

90. The following Provisions of this Act respecting the Parliament of Canada, namely, — the Provisions relating to Appropriation and Tax Bills, the Recommendation of Money Votes, the Assent to Bills, the Disallowance of Acts, and the Signification of Pleasure on Bills reserved, — shall extend and apply to the Legislatures of the several Provinces as if those

---

(42) Partially repealed by the *Statute Law Revision Act, 1893*, 56-57 Vict., c. 14 (U.K.), which deleted the following concluding words of the original enactment:

> and the House of Assembly of New Brunswick existing at the passing of this Act shall, unless sooner dissolved, continue for the Period for which it was elected.

A similar provision was included in each of the instruments admitting British Columbia, Prince Edward Island and Newfoundland. The Legislatures of Manitoba, Alberta and Saskatchewan were established by the statutes creating those provinces. See the footnotes to section 5, *supra*.

See also sections 3 to 5 of the *Constitution Act, 1982*, which prescribe democratic rights applicable to all provinces, and subitem 2(2) of the Schedule to that Act, which sets out the repeal of section 20 of the *Manitoba Act, 1870*. Section 20 of the *Manitoba Act, 1870*, has been replaced by section 5 of the *Constitution Act, 1982*.

Section 20 reads as follows:

> **20.** There shall be a Session of the Legislature once at least in every year, so that twelve months shall not intervene between the last sitting of the Legislature in one Session and its first sitting in the next Session.

(43) Repealed by the *Statute Law Revision Act, 1893*, 56-57 Vict., c. 14 (U.K.). The section read as follows:

> 5. — Ontario, Quebec, and Nova Scotia.
>
> **89.** Each of the Lieutenant Governors of Ontario, Quebec and Nova Scotia shall cause Writs to be issued for the First Election of Members of the Legislative Assembly thereof in such Form and by such Person as he thinks fit, and at such Time and addressed to such Returning Officer as the Governor General directs, and so that the First Election of Member of Assembly for any Electoral District or any Subdivision thereof shall be held at the same Time and at the same Places as the Election for a Member to serve in the House of Commons of Canada for the Electoral District.

Provisions were here re-enacted and made applicable in Terms to the respective Provinces and the Legislatures thereof, with the Substitution of the Lieutenant Governor of the Province for the Governor General, of the Governor General for the Queen and for a Secretary of State, of One Year for Two Years, and of the Province for Canada.

VI. — DISTRIBUTION OF LEGISLATIVE POWERS.

Powers of the Parliament.

91. It shall be lawful for the Queen, by and with the Advice and Consent of the Senate and House of Commons, to make Laws for the Peace, Order, and good Government of Canada, in relation to all Matters not coming within the Classes of Subjects by this Act assigned exclusively to the Legislatures of the Provinces; and for greater Certainty, but not so as to restrict the Generality of the foregoing Terms of this Section, it is hereby declared that (notwithstanding anything in this Act) the exclusive Legislative Authority of the Parliament of Canada extends to all Matters coming within the Classes of Subjects next hereinafter enumerated; that is to say, —

1. Repealed.(44)

1A. The Public Debt and Property.(45)

2. The Regulation of Trade and Commerce.

---

(44) Class 1 was added by the *British North America (No. 2) Act, 1949,* 13 Geo. VI, c. 8 (U.K.). That Act and class 1 were repealed by the *Constitution Act, 1982*. The matters referred to in class 1 are provided for in subsection 4(2) and Part V of the *Constitution Act, 1982*. As enacted, class 1 read as follows:

> 1. The amendment from time to time of the Constitution of Canada, except as regards matters coming within the classes of subjects by this Act assigned exclusively to the Legislatures of the provinces, or as regards rights or privileges by this or any other Constitutional Act granted or secured to the Legislature or the Government of a province, or to any class of persons with respect to schools or as regards the use of the English or the French language or as regards the requirements that there shall be a session of the Parliament of Canada at least once each year, and that no House of Commons shall continue for more than five years from the day of the return of the Writs for choosing the House: provided, however, that a House of Commons may in time of real or apprehended war, invasion or insurrection be continued by the Parliament of Canada if such continuation is not opposed by the votes of more than one-third of the members of such House.

(45) Re-numbered by the *British North America (No. 2) Act, 1949.*

2A. Unemployment insurance.(46)
3. The raising of Money by any Mode or System of Taxation.
4. The borrowing of Money on the Public Credit.
5. Postal Service.
6. The Census and Statistics.
7. Militia, Military and Naval Service, and Defence.
8. The fixing of and providing for the Salaries and Allowances of Civil and other Officers of the Government of Canada.
9. Beacons, Buoys, Lighthouses, and Sable Island.
10. Navigation and Shipping.
11. Quarantine and the Establishment and Maintenance of Marine Hospitals.
12. Sea Coast and Inland Fisheries.
13. Ferries between a Province and any British or Foreign Country or between Two Provinces.
14. Currency and Coinage.
15. Banking, Incorporation of Banks, and the Issue of Paper Money.
16. Savings Banks.
17. Weights and Measures.
18. Bills of Exchange and Promissory Notes.
19. Interest.
20. Legal Tender.
21. Bankruptcy and Insolvency.
22. Patents of Invention and Discovery.
23. Copyrights.
24. Indians, and Lands reserved for the Indians.
25. Naturalization and Aliens.
26. Marriage and Divorce.
27. The Criminal Law, except the Constitution of Courts of Criminal Jurisdiction, but including the Procedure in Criminal Matters.
28. The Establishment, Maintenance, and Management of Penitentiaries.
29. Such Classes of Subjects as are expressly excepted in the Enumeration of the Classes of Subjects by this Act assigned exclusively to the Legislatures of the Provinces.

---

(46) Added by the *Constitution Act, 1940*, 3-4 Geo. VI, c. 36 (U.K.).

And any Matter coming within any of the Classes of Subjects enumerated in this Section shall not be deemed to come within the Class of Matters of a local or private Nature comprised in the Enumeration of the Classes of Subjects by this Act assigned exclusively to the Legislatures of the Provinces.(47)

---

(47) Legislative authority has been conferred on Parliament by other Acts as follows:

1. The *Constitution Act, 1871*, 34-35 Vict., c. 28 (U.K.).

2. The Parliament of Canada, may from time to time establish new Provinces in any territories forming for the time being part of the Dominion of Canada, but not included in any Province thereof, and may, at the time of such establishment, make provision for the constitution and administration of any such Province, and for the passing of laws for the peace, order, and good government of such Province, and for its representation in the said Parliament.

3. The Parliament of Canada may from time to time, with the consent of the Legislature of any province of the said Dominion, increase, diminish, or otherwise alter the limits of such Province, upon such terms and conditions as may be agreed to by the said Legislature, and may, with the like consent, make provision respecting the effect and operation of any such increase or diminution or alteration of territory in relation to any Province affected thereby.

4. The Parliament of Canada may from time to time make provision for the administration, peace, order, and good government of any territory not for the time being included in any Province.

5. The following Acts passed by the said Parliament of Canada, and intituled respectively, — ''An Act for the temporary government of Rupert's Land and the North Western Territory when united with Canada''; and ''An Act to amend and continue the Act thirty-two and thirty-three Victoria, chapter three, and to establish and provide for the government of ''the Province of Manitoba'', shall be and be deemed to have been valid and effectual for all purposes whatsoever from the date at which they respectively received the assent, in the Queen's name, of the Governor General of the said Dominion of Canada.

6. Except as provided by the third section of this Act, it shall not be competent for the Parliament of Canada to alter the provisions of the last-mentioned Act of the said Parliament in so far as it relates to the Province of Manitoba, or of any other Act hereafter establishing new Provinces in the said Dominion, subject always to the right of the Legislature of the Province of Manitoba to alter from time to time the provisions of any law respecting the qualification of electors and members of the Legislative Assembly, and to make laws respecting elections in the said Province.

The *Rupert's Land Act, 1868*, 31-32 Vict., c. 105 (U.K.) (repealed by the *Statute Law Revision Act, 1893*, 56-57 Vict., c. 14 (U.K.)) had previously conferred similar authority in relation to Rupert's

Exclusive Powers of Provincial Legislatures.

92. In each Province the Legislature may exclusively make Laws in relation to Matters coming within the Classes of Subject next hereinafter enumerated; that is to say, —

1. Repealed.(48)
2. Direct Taxation within the Province in order to the raising of a Revenue for Provincial Purposes.
3. The borrowing of Money on the sole Credit of the Province.
4. The Establishment and Tenure of Provincial Offices and the Appointment and Payment of Provincial Officers.
5. The Management and Sale of the Public Lands belonging to the Province and of the Timber and Wood thereon.
6. The Establishment, Maintenance, and Management of Public and Reformatory Prisons in and for the Province.
7. The Establishment, Maintenance, and Management of Hospitals, Asylums, Charities, and Eleemosynary Institutions in and for the Province, other than Marine Hospitals.

Land and the North Western Territory upon admission of those areas.

2. The *Constitution Act, 1886*, 49-50 Vict., c. 35 (U.K.).

> **1.** The Parliament of Canada may from time to time make provision for the representation in the Senate and House of Commons of Canada, or in either of them, of any territories which for the time being form part of the Dominion of Canada, but are not included in any province thereof.

3. The *Statute of Westminster, 1931*, 22 Geo. V, c. 4 (U.K.).

> **3.** It is hereby declared and enacted that the Parliament of a Dominion has full power to make laws having extra-territorial operation.

4. Section 44 of the *Constitution Act, 1982*, authorizes Parliament to amend the Constitution of Canada in relation to the executive government of Canada or the Senate and House of Commons. Sections 38, 41, 42, and 43 of that Act authorize the Senate and House of Commons to give their approval to certain other constitutional amendments by resolution.

(48) Class 1 was repealed by the *Constitution Act, 1982*. As enacted, it read as follows:

> 1. The Amendment from Time to Time, notwithstanding anything in this Act, of the Constitution of the province, except as regards the Office of Lieutenant Governor.

Section 45 of the *Constitution Act, 1982*, now authorizes legislatures to make laws amending the constitution of the province. Sections 38, 41, 42, and 43 of that Act authorize legislative assemblies to give their approval by resolution to certain other amendments to the Constitution of Canada.

8. Municipal Institutions in the Province.
9. Shop, Saloon, Tavern, Auctioneer, and other Licences in order to the raising of a Revenue for Provincial, Local, or Municipal Purposes.
10. Local Works and Undertakings other than such as are of the following Classes: —
(*a*) Lines of Steam or other Ships, Railways, Canals, Telegraphs, and other Works and Undertakings connecting the Province with any other or others of the Provinces, or extending beyond the Limits of the Province;
(*b*) Lines of Steam Ships between the Province and any British or Foreign Country;
(*c*) Such Works as, although wholly situate within the Province, are before or after their Execution declared by the Parliament of Canada to be for the general Advantage of Canada or for the Advantage of Two or more of the Provinces.
11. The Incorporation of Companies with Provincial Objects.
12. The Solemnization of Marriage in the Province.
13. Property and Civil Rights in the Province.
14. The Administration of Justice in the Province, including the Constitution, Maintenance, and Organization of Provincial Courts, both of Civil and of Criminal Jurisdiction, and including Procedure in Civil Matters in those Courts.
15. The Imposition of Punishment by Fine, Penalty, or Imprisonment for enforcing any Law of the Province made in relation to any matter coming within any of the Classes of Subjects enumerated in this Section.
16. Generally all Matters of a merely local or private Nature in the Province.

Non-Renewable Natural Resources, Forestry Resources and Electrical Energy.

92A. (1) In each province, the legislature may exclusively make laws in relation to

(*a*) exploration for non-renewable natural resources in the province;

(*b*) development, conservation and management of non-renewable natural resources and forestry resources in the province, including laws in relation to the rate of primary production therefrom; and

(*c*) development, conservation and management of sites and facilities in the province for the generation and production of electrical energy.

(2) In each province, the legislature may make laws in relation to the export from the province to another part of Canada of the primary production from non-renewable natural resources and forestry resources in the province and the production from facilities in the province for the generation of electrical energy, but such laws may not authorize or provide for discrimination in prices or in supplies exported to another part of Canada.

(3) Nothing in subsection (2) derogates from the authority of Parliament to enact laws in relation to the matters referred to in that subsection and, where such a law of Parliament and a law of a province conflict, the law of Parliament prevails to the extent of the conflict.

(4) In each province, the legislature may make laws in relation to the raising of money by any mode or system of taxation in respect of

(*a*) non-renewable natural resources and forestry resources in the province and the primary production therefrom, and

(*b*) sites and facilities in the province for the generation of electrical energy and the production therefrom,

whether or not such production is exported in whole or in part from the province, but such laws may not authorize or provide for taxation that differentiates between production exported to another part of Canada and production not exported from the province.

(5) The expression ''primary production'' has the meaning assigned by the Sixth Schedule.

(6) Nothing in subsections (1) to (5) derogates from any powers or rights that a legislature or government of a province had immediately before the coming into force of this section.(49)

Education.

93. In and for each Province the Legislature may exclusively make Laws in relation to Education, subject and according to the following Provisions: —

(49) Added by the *Constitution Act, 1982*.

(1) Nothing in any such Law shall prejudicially affect any Right or Privilege with respect to Denominational Schools which any Class of Persons have by Law in the Province at the Union:

(2) All the Powers, Privileges, and Duties at the Union by Law conferred and imposed in Upper Canada on the Separate Schools and School Trustees of the Queen's Roman Catholic Subjects shall be and the same are hereby extended to the Dissentient Schools of the Queen's Protestant and Roman Catholic Subjects in Quebec:

(3) Where in any Province a System of Separate or Dissentient Schools exists by Law at the Union or is thereafter established by the Legislature of the Province, an Appeal shall lie to the Governor General in Council from any Act or Decision of any Provincial Authority affecting any Right or Privilege of the Protestant or Roman Catholic Minority of the Queen's Subjects in relation to Education:

(4) In case any such Provincial Law as from Time to Time seems to the Governor General in Council requisite for the due Execution of the Provisions of this Section is not made, or in case any Decision of the Governor General in Council on any Appeal under this Section is not duly executed by the proper Provincial Authority in that Behalf, then and in every such Case, and as far only as the Circumstances of each Case require, the Parliament of Canada may make remedial Laws for the due Execution of the Provisions of this Section and of any Decision of the Governor General in Council under this Section.(50)

---

(50) Altered for Manitoba by section 22 of the *Manitoba Act, 1870*, 33 Vict., c. 3 (Canada), (confirmed by the *Constitution Act, 1871*), which reads as follows:

> **22.** In and for the Province, the said Legislature may exclusively make Laws in relation to Education, subject and according to the following provisions: —
>
> (1) Nothing in any such Law shall prejudicially affect any right or privilege with respect to Denominational Schools which any class of persons have by Law or practice in the Province at the Union:
>
> (2) An appeal shall lie to the Governor General in Council from any Act or decision of the Legislature of the Province, or of any Provincial Authority, affecting any right or privilege, of the Protestant or Roman Catholic minority

Uniformity of Laws in Ontario, Nova Scotia and New Brunswick.

94. Notwithstanding anything in this Act, the Parliament of Canada may make Provision for the Uniformity of all or any

---

of the Queen's subjects in relation to Education:

(3) In case any such Provincial Law, as from time to time seems to the Governor General in Council requisite for the due execution of the provisions of this section, is not made, or in case any decision of the Governor General in Council on any appeal under this section is not duly executed by the proper Provincial Authority in that behalf, then, and in every such case, and as far only as the circumstances of each case require, the Parliament of Canada may make remedial Laws for the due execution of the provisions of this section, and of any decision of the Governor General in Council under this section.

Altered for Alberta by section 17 of the *Alberta Act*, 4-5 Edw. VII, c. 3, 1905 (Canada), which reads as follows:

17. Section 93 of the *Constitution Act, 1867*, shall apply to the said province, with the substitution for paragraph (1) of the said section 93 of the following paragraph: —

(1) Nothing in any such law shall prejudicially affect any right or privilege with respect to separate schools which any class of persons have at the date of the passing of this Act, under the terms of chapters 29 and 30 of the Ordinances of the Northwest Territories, passed in the year 1901, or with respect to religious instruction in any public or separate school as provided for in the said ordinances.

2. In the appropriation by the Legislature or distribution by the Government of the province of any moneys for the support of schools organized and carried on in accordance with the said chapter 29 or any Act passed in amendment thereof, or in substitution therefor, there shall be no discrimination against schools of any class described in the said chapter 29.

3. Where the expression "by law" is employed in paragraph 3 of the said section 93, it shall be held to mean the law as set out in the said chapters 29 and 30, and where the expression "at the Union" is employed, in the said paragraph 3, it shall be held to mean the date at which this Act comes into force.

Altered for Saskatchewan by section 17 of the *Saskatchewan Act*, 4-5 Edw. VII, c. 42, 1905 (Canada), which reads as follows:

17. Section 93 of the *Constitution Act, 1867*, shall apply to the said province, with the substitution for paragraph (1) of the said section 93, of the following paragraph: —

(1) Nothing in any such law shall prejudicially affect any right or privilege with respect to separate schools which any class of persons have at the date of the passing of this Act, under the terms of chapters 29 and 30 of the Ordinances of the Northwest Territories, passed in the year 1901, or with respect to religious instruction in any public or separate school as provided

of the Laws relative to Property and Civil Rights in Ontario, Nova Scotia, and New Brunswick, and of the Procedure of all or any of the Courts in Those Three Provinces, and from and after the passing of any Act in that Behalf the Power of the Parliament of Canada to make Laws in relation to any Matter comprised in any such Act shall, notwithstanding anything in this Act, be unrestricted; but any Act of the Parliament of Canada making Provision for such Uniformity shall not have effect in

---

for in the said ordinances.

2. In the appropriation by the Legislature or distribution by the Government of the province of any moneys for the support of schools organized and carried on in accordance with the said chapter 29, or any Act passed in amendment thereof or in substitution therefor, there shall be no discrimination against schools of any class described in the said chapter 29.

3. Where the expression "by law" is employed in paragraph (3) of the said section 93, it shall be held to mean the law as set out in the said chapters 29 and 30; and where the expression "at the Union" is employed in the said paragraph (3), it shall be held to mean the date at which this Act comes into force.

Altered by Term 17 of the Terms of Union of Newfoundland with Canada (confirmed by the *Newfoundland Act*, 12-13 Geo. VI, c. 22 (U.K.)), which reads as follows:

17. In lieu of section ninety-three of the *Constitution Act, 1867*, the following term shall apply in respect of the Province of Newfoundland:

In and for the Province of Newfoundland the Legislature shall have exclusive authority to make laws in relation to education, but the Legislature will not have authority to make laws prejudicially affecting any right or privilege with respect to denominational schools, common (amalgamated) schools, or denominational colleges, that any class or classes of persons have by law in Newfoundland at the date of Union, and out of public funds of the Province of Newfoundland, provided for education,

(*a*) all such schools shall receive their share of such funds in accordance with scales determined on a non-discriminatory basis from time to time by the Legislature for all schools then being conducted under authority of the Legislature; and

(*b*) all such colleges shall receive their share of any grant from time to time voted for all colleges then being conducted under authority of the Legislature, such grant being distributed on a non-discriminatory basis.

See also sections 23, 29, and 59 of the *Constitution Act, 1982*. Section 23 provides for new minority language educational rights and section 59 permits a delay in respect of the coming into force in Quebec of one aspect of those rights. Section 29 provides that nothing in the *Canadian Charter of Rights and Freedoms* abrogates or derogates from any rights or privileges guaranteed by or under the Constitution of Canada in respect of denominational, separate or dissentient schools.

any Province unless and until it is adopted and enacted as Law by the Legislature thereof.

Old Age Pensions.

94A. The Parliament of Canada may make laws in relation to old age pensions and supplementary benefits, including survivors, and disability benefits irrespective of age, but no such law shall affect the operation of any law present or future of a provincial legislature in relation to any such matter.(51)

Agriculture and Immigration.

95. In each Province the Legislature may make Laws in relation to Agriculture in the Province, and to Immigration into the Province; and it is hereby declared that the Parliament of Canada may from Time to Time make Laws in relation to Agriculture in all or any of the Provinces, and to Immigration into all or any of the Provinces; and any Law of the Legislature of a Province relative to Agriculture or to Immigration shall have effect in and for the Province as long and as far only as it is not repugnant to any Act of the Parliament of Canada.

VII. — JUDICATURE.

96. The Governor General shall appoint the Judges of the Superior, District, and County Courts in each Province, except those of the Courts of Probate in Nova Scotia and New Brunswick.

97. Until the laws relative to Property and Civil Rights in Ontario, Nova Scotia, and New Brunswick, and the Procedure of the Courts in those Provinces, are made uniform, the Judges of the Courts of those Provinces appointed by the Governor General shall be selected from the respective Bars of those Provinces.

---

(51) Added by the *Constitution Act, 1964*, 12-13 Eliz. II, c. 73 (U.K.). As originally enacted by the *British North America Act, 1951*, 14-15 Geo. VI, c. 32 (U.K.), which was repealed by the *Constitution Act, 1982*, section 94A read as follows:

> **94A.** It is hereby declared that the Parliament of Canada may from time to time make laws in relation to old age pensions in Canada, but no law made by the Parliament of Canada in relation to old age pensions shall affect the operation of any law present or future of a Provincial Legislature in relation to old age pensions.

98. The Judges of the Courts of Quebec shall be selected from the Bar of that Province.

99. (1) Subject to subsection two of this section, the Judges of the Superior Courts shall hold office during good behaviour, but shall be removable by the Governor General on Address of the Senate and House of Commons.

(2) A Judge of a Superior Court, whether appointed before or after the coming into force of this section, shall cease to hold office upon attaining the age of seventy-five years, or upon the coming into force of this section if at that time he has already attained that age.(52)

100. The Salaries, Allowances, and Pensions of the Judges of the Superior, District, and County Courts (except the Courts of Probate in Nova Scotia and New Brunswick), and of the Admiralty Courts in Cases where the Judges thereof are for the Time being paid by Salary, shall be fixed and provided by the Parliament of Canada.(53)

101. The Parliament of Canada may, notwithstanding anything in this Act, from Time to Time provide for the Constitution, Maintenance, and Organization of a General Court of Appeal for Canada, and for the Establishment of any additional Courts for the better Administration of the Laws of Canada.(54)

VIII. — Revenues; Debts; Assets; Taxation.

[Sections 102 to 104 are omitted.]

105. Unless altered by the Parliament of Canada, the Salary of the Governor General shall be Ten thousand Pounds Sterling Money of the United Kingdom of Great Britain and Ireland, payable out of the Consolidated Revenue Fund of Canada, and the same shall form the Third Charge thereon.(55)

---

(52) Repealed and re-enacted by the *Constitution Act, 1960*, 9 Eliz. II, c. 2 (U.K.), which came into force on the 1st day of March, 1961. The original section read as follows:

> **99.** The Judges of the Superior Courts shall hold Office during good Behaviour, but shall be removable by the Governor General on Address of the Senate and House of Commons.

(53) Now provided for in the *Judges Act*, R.S.C. 1985, c. J-l.

(54) See the *Supreme Court Act*, R.S.C. 1985, c. S-26, and the *Federal Court Act*, R.S.C. 1985, c. F-7 and the *Tax Court of Canada Act*, R.S.C. 1985, c. T-2.

(55) Now covered by the *Governor General's Act*, R.S.C. 1985, c. G-9.

[Sections 106 and 107 are omitted.]

108. The Public Works and Property of each Province, enumerated in the Third Schedule to this Act, shall be the Property of Canada.

109. All Lands, Mines, Minerals, and Royalties belonging to the several Provinces of Canada, Nova Scotia, and New Brunswick at the Union, and all Sums then due or payable for such Lands, Mines, Minerals, or Royalties, shall belong to the several Provinces of Ontario, Quebec, Nova Scotia, and New Brunswick in which the same are situate or arise, subject to any Trusts existing in respect thereof, and to any Interest other than that of the Province in the same.(56)

[Sections 110 to 116 are omitted.]

117. The several Provinces shall retain all their respective Public Property not otherwise disposed of in this Act, subject to the Right of Canada to assume any Lands or Public Property required for Fortifications or for the Defence of the Country.

[Sections 118 to 120 are omitted.]

121. All Articles of the Growth, Produce, or Manufacture of any one of the Provinces shall, from and after the Union, be admitted free into each of the other Provinces.

122. The Customs and Excise Laws of each Province shall, subject to the Provisions of this Act, continue in force until altered by the Parliament of Canada.(60)

[Sections 123 and 124 are omitted.]

125. No Lands or Property belonging to Canada or any Province shall be liable to Taxation.

[Section 126 is omitted.]

---

(56) The three prairie provinces were placed in the same position as the original provinces by the *Constitution Act, 1930*, 21 Geo. V, c. 26 (U.K.).

(60) Spent. Now covered by the *Customs Act*, R.S.C. 1985, c. 1 (2nd Supp.), the *Customs Tariff*, R.S.C. 1985, c. 41 (3rd Supp.), the *Excise Act*, R.S.C. 1985, c. E-14 and the *Excise Tax Act*, R.S.C. 1985, c. E-15.

IX. — MISCELLANEOUS PROVISIONS.

General.

[Sections 127 and 128 are omitted.]

129. Except as otherwise provided by this Act, all Laws in force in Canada, Nova Scotia, or New Brunswick at the Union, and all Courts of Civil and Criminal Jurisdiction, and all legal Commissions, Powers, and Authorities, and all Officers, Judicial, Administrative, and Ministerial, existing therein at the Union, shall continue in Ontario, Quebec, Nova Scotia, and New Brunswick respectively, as if the Union had not been made; subject nevertheless (except with respect to such as are enacted by or exist under Acts of the Parliament of Great Britain or of the Parliament of the United Kingdom of Great Britain and Ireland), to be repealed, abolished, or altered by the Parliament of Canada, or by the Legislature of the respective Province, according to the Authority of the Parliament or of that Legislature under this Act.(64)

[Sections 130 and 131 are omitted.]

132. The Parliament and Government of Canada shall have all Powers necessary or proper for performing the Obligations of Canada or of any Province thereof, as Part of the British Empire, towards Foreign Countries, arising under Treaties between the Empire and such Foreign Countries.

133. Either the English or the French Language may be used by any Person in the Debates of the Houses of the Parliament of Canada and of the Houses of the Legislature of Quebec; and both those Languages shall be used in the respective Records and Journals of those Houses; and either of those Languages may be used by any Person or in any Pleading or Process in or issuing from any Court of Canada established under this Act, and in or from all or any of the Courts of Quebec.

---

(64) The restriction against altering or repealing laws enacted by or existing under statutes of the United Kingdom was removed by the *Statute of Westminster, 1931*, 22 Geo. V, c. 4 (U.K.) except in respect of certain constitutional documents. Comprehensive procedures for amending enactments forming part of the Constitution of Canada were provided by Part V of the *Constitution Act, 1982*, (U.K.) 1982, c. 11.

The Acts of the Parliament of Canada and of the Legislature of Quebec shall be printed and published in both those Languages.(66)

[Sections 134 to 145 are omitted.]

XI. — ADMISSION OF OTHER COLONIES.

146. It shall be lawful for the Queen, by and with the Advice of Her Majesty's Most Honourable Privy Council, on Addresses from the Houses of the Parliament of Canada, and from the Houses of the respective Legislatures of the Colonies or Provinces of Newfoundland, Prince Edward Island, and British Columbia, to admit those Colonies or Provinces, or any of them, into the Union, and on Address from the Houses of the Parliament of Canada to admit Rupert's Land and the North-western Territory, or either of them, into the Union, on such Terms and Conditions in each Case as are in the Addresses expressed and as the Queen thinks fit to approve, subject to the Provisions of this Act; and the Provisions of any Order in Council in that Behalf shall have effect as if they had been enacted by the Parliament of the United Kingdom of Great Britain and Ireland.(75)

[Section 147 is omitted.]

---

(66) A similar provision was enacted for Manitoba by Section 23 of the *Manitoba Act, 1870*, 33 Vict., c. 3 (Canada), (confirmed by the *Constitution Act, 1871*). Section 23 read as follows:

> **23.** Either the English or the French language may be used by any person in the debates of the Houses of the Legislature, and both those languages shall be used in the respective Records and Journals of those Houses; and either of those languages may be used by any person, or in any Pleading or Process, in or issuing from any Court of Canada established under the British North America Act, 1867, or in or from all or any of the Courts of the Province. The Acts of the Legislature shall be printed and published in both those languages.

Sections 17 to 19 of the *Constitution Act, 1982*, restate the language rights set out in section 133 in respect of Parliament and the courts established under the *Constitution Act, 1867*, and also guarantees those rights in respect of the legislature of New Brunswick and the courts of that province.

Section 16 and sections 20, 21 and 23 of the *Constitution Act, 1981*, recognize additional language rights in respect of the English and French languages. Section 22 preserves language rights and privileges of languages other than English and French.

(75) All territories mentioned in this section are now part of Canada. See the notes to section 5, *supra*.

SCHEDULES

[The first and second schedules are omitted.]

THE THIRD SCHEDULE.

Provincial Public Works and Property to be the Property of Canada.

1. Canals, with Lands and Water Power connected therewith.
2. Public Harbours.
3. Lighthouses and Piers, and Sable Island.
4. Steamboats, Dredges, and public Vessels.
5. Rivers and Lake Improvements.
6. Railways and Railway Stocks, Mortgages, and other Debts due by Railway Companies.
7. Military Roads.
8. Custom Houses, Post Offices, and all other Public Buildings, except such as the Government of Canada appropriate for the Use of the Provincial Legislature and Governments.
9. Property transferred by the imperial Government, and known as Ordinance Property.
10. Armouries, Drill Sheds, Military Clothing, and Munitions of War, and Lands set apart for general Public Purposes.

[The fourth and fifth schedules are omitted.]

THE SIXTH SCHEDULE. (78)

Primary Production from Non-Renewable Natural Resources and Forestry Resources.

1. For the purposes of section 92A of this Act,

(*a*) production from a non-renewable natural resource is primary production therefrom if

(i) it is in the form in which it exists upon its recovery or severance from its natural state, or

(ii) it is a product resulting from processing or refining the resource, and is not a manufactured product or a product resulting from refining

---

(78) As enacted by the *Constitution Act, 1982*.

crude oil, refining upgraded heavy crude oil, refining gases or liquids derived from coal or refining a synthetic equivalent or crude oil; and

(*b*) production from a forestry resource is primary production therefrom if it consists of sawlogs, poles, lumber, wood chips, sawdust or any other primary wood product, or wood pulp, and is not a product manufactured from wood.

APPENDIX II

Canada Act 1982

U.K., 1982, c. 11

An Act to give effect to a request by the Senate and House of Commons of Canada

Loi donnant suite à une demande du Sénat et de la Chambre des communes du Canada

Whereas Canada has requested and consented to the enactment of an Act of the Parliament of the United Kingdom to give effect to the provisions hereinafter set forth and the Senate and the House of Commons of Canada in Parliament assembled have submitted an address to Her Majesty requesting that Her Majesty may graciously be pleased to cause a Bill to be laid before the Parliament of the United Kingdom for that purpose.

Be it therefore enacted by the Queen's Most Excellent Majesty, by and with the advice and consent of the Lords Spiritual and Temporal, and Commons, in this present Parliament assembled, and by the authority of the same as follows:

Sa Très Excellente Majesté la Reine, considérant:

qu'à la demande et avec le consentement du Canada, le Parlement du Royaume-Uni est invité à adopter une loi visant à donner effet aux dispositions énoncées ci-après et que le Sénat et la Chambre des communes du Canada réunis en Parlement ont présenté une adresse demandant à Sa Très Gracieuse Majesté de bien vouloir faire déposer devant le Parlement du Royaume-Uni un projet de loi à cette fin,

sur l'avis et du consentement des Lords spirituels et temporels *et des Communes réunis en Parlement, et par l'autorité de celui-ci, édicte :*

Constitution Act, 1982 enacted

1. *The Constitution Act, 1982* set out in Schedule B to this Act is hereby enacted for and shall have the force of law in Canada and shall come into force as provided in that Act.

Adoption de la *Loi constitutionnelle de 1982*

1. La *Loi constitutionnelle de 1982*, énoncée à l'annexe B, est édictée pour le Canada et y a force de loi. Elle entre en vigueur conformément à ses dispositions.

Termination of power to legislate for Canada

2. No Act of the Parliament of the United Kingdom passed after the *Constitution Act, 1982* comes into force shall extend to Canada as part of its law.

2. Les lois adoptées par le Parlement du Royaume-Uni aprés l'entrée en vigueur de la *Loi constitutionnelle de 1982* ne font pas partie du droit du Canada.

Cessation du pouvoir de légiférer pour le Canada

French version

3. So far as it is not contained in Schedule B, the French version of this Act is set out in Schedule A to this Act and has the same authority in Canada as the English version thereof.

3. La partie de la version française de la présente loi qui figure à l'annexe A a force de loi au Canada au même titre que la version anglaise correspondante.

Version française

Short title

4. This Act may be cited as the *Canada Act 1982*.

4. Titre abrégé de la présente loi: *Loi de 1982 sur le Canada.*

Titre abrégé

APPENDIX III

Constitution Act, 1982

Schedule B to Canada Act 1982 (U.K.)

PART I

CANADIAN CHARTER OF RIGHTS AND FREEDOMS

Whereas Canada is founded upon principles that recognize the supremacy of God and the rule of law:

Guarantee of Rights and Freedoms

Rights and freedoms in Canada

1. The *Canadian Charter of Rights and Freedoms* guarantees the rights and freedoms set out in it subject only to such reasonable limits prescribed by law as can be demonstrably justified in a free and democratic society.

Fundamental Freedoms

Fundamental freedoms

2. Everyone has the following fundamental freedoms:

(*a*) freedom of conscience and religion;

(*b*) freedom of thought, belief, opinion and expression, including freedom of the press and other media of communication;

(*c*) freedom of peaceful assembly; and

(*d*) freedom of association.

PARTIE I

CHARTE CANADIENNE DES DROITS ET LIBERTÉS

Attendu que le Canada est fondé sur des principes qui reconnaissent la suprématie de Dieu et la primauté du droit:

Garantie des droits et libertés

Droits et libertés au Canada

1. La Charte canadienne des droits et libertés garantit les droits et libertés qui y sont énoncés. Ils ne peuvent être restreints que par une règle de droit, dans des limites qui soient raisonnables et dont la justification puisse se démontrer dans le cadre d'une société libre et démocratique.

Libertés fondamentales

Libertés fondamentales

2. Chacun a les libertés fondamentales suivantes:

a) liberté de conscience et de religion;

b) liberté de pensée, de croyance, d'opinion et d'expression, y compris la liberté de la presse et des autres moyens de communication;

c) liberté de réunion pacifique;

d) liberté d'association.

Democratic Rights	*Droits démocratiques*
Democratic rights of citizens — **3.** Every citizen of Canada has the right to vote in an election of members of the House of Commons or of a legislative assembly and to be qualified for membership therein.	Droits démocratiques des citoyens — **3.** Tout citoyen canadien a le droit de vote et est éligible aux élections législatives fédérales ou provinciales.
Maximum duration of legislative bodies — **4.** (1) No House of Commons and no legislative assembly shall continue for longer than five years from the date fixed for the return of the writs at a general election of its members.(80)	Mandat maximal des assemblées — **4.** (1) Le mandat maximal de la Chambre des communes et des assemblées législatives est de cinq ans à compter de la date fixée pour le retour des brefs relatifs aux élections générales correspondantes.
Continuation in special circumstances — (2) In time of real or apprehended war, invasion or insurrection, a House of Commons may be continued by Parliament and a legislative assembly may be continued by the legislature beyond five years if such continuation is not opposed by the votes of more than one-third of the members of the House of Commons or the legislative assembly, as the case may be.(81)	Prolongations spéciales — (2) Le mandat de la Chambre des communes ou celui d'une assemblée législative peut être prolongé respectivement par le Parlement ou par la législature en question au-delà de cinq ans en cas de guerre, d'invasion ou d'insurrection, réelles ou appréhendées, pourvu que cette prolongation ne fasse pas l'objet d'une opposition exprimée par les voix de plus du tiers des députés de la Chambre des communes ou de l'assemblée législative.
Annual sitting of legislative bodies — **5.** There shall be a sitting of Parliament and of each legislature at least once every twelve months.(82)	Séance annuelle — **5.** Le Parlement et les législatures tiennent une séance au moins une fois tous les douze mois.

(80) See section 50 and the footnotes to sections 85 and 88 of the *Constitution Act, 1867*.

(81) Replaces part of Class I of section 91 of the *Constitution Act, 1867*, which was repealed as set out in subitem 1(3) of the Schedule to this Act.

(82) See the footnotes to sections 20, 86 and 88 of the *Constitution Act, 1867*.

Mobility Rights

Mobility of citizens

6. (1) Every citizen of Canada has the right to enter, remain in and leave Canada.

Rights to move and gain livelihood

(2) Every citizen of Canada and every person who has the status of a permanent resident of Canada has the right

(*a*) to move to and take up residence in any province; and

(*b*) to pursue the gaining of a livelihood in any province.

Limitation

(3) The rights specified in subsection (2) are subject to

(*a*) any laws or practices of general application in force in a province other than those that discriminate among persons primarily on the basis of province of present or previous residence; and

(*b*) any laws providing for reasonable residency requirements as a qualification for the receipt of publicly provided social services.

Affirmative action programs

(4) Subsections (2) and (3) do not preclude any law, program or activity that has as its object the amelioration in a province of conditions of individuals in that province who are socially or economically disadvantaged if the rate of employment in that province is below the rate of employment in Canada.

Liberté de circulation et d'établissement

Liberté de circulation

6. (1) Tout citoyen canadien a le droit de demeurer au Canada, d'y entrer ou d'en sortir.

Liberti d'établissement

(2) Tout citoyen canadien et toute personne ayant le statut de résident permanent au Canada ont le droit:

a) de se déplacer dans tout le pays et d'établir leur résidence dans toute province;

b) de gagner leur vie dans toute province.

Restriction

(3) Les droits mentionnés au paragraphe (2) sont subordonnés:

a) aux lois et usages d'application générale en vigueur dans une province donnée, s'ils n'établissent entre les personnes aucune distinction fondée principalement sur la province de résidence antérieure ou actuelle;

b) aux lois prévoyant de justes conditions de résidence en vue de l'obtention des services sociaux publics.

Programmes de promotion sociale

(4) Les paragraphes (2) et (3) n'ont pas pour objet d'interdire les lois, programmes ou activités destinés à améliorer, dans une province, la situation d'individus défavorisés socialement ou économiquement, si le taux d'emploi dans la province est inférieur à la moyenne nationale.

Legal Rights

Life, liberty and security of person

7. Everyone has the right to life, liberty and security of the person and the right not to be deprived thereof except in accordance with the principles of fundamental justice.

Search or seizure

8. Everyone has the right to be secure against unreasonable search or seizure.

Detention or imprisonment

9. Everyone has the right not to be arbitrarily detained or imprisoned.

Arrest or detention

10. Everyone has the right on arrest or detention

(*a*) to be informed promptly of the reasons therefor;

(*b*) to retain and instruct counsel without delay and to be informed of that right; and

(*c*) to have the validity of the detention determined by way of *habeas corpus* and to be released if the detention is not lawful.

Proceedings in criminal and penal matters

11. Any person charged with an offence has the right

(*a*) to be informed without unreasonable delay of the specific offence;

(*b*) to be tried within a reasonable time;

Garanties juridiques

Vie. liberté et sécurité

7. Chacun a droit à la vie, à la liberté et à la sécurité de sa personne; il ne peut être porté atteinte à ce droit qu'en conformité avec les principes de justice fondamentale.

Fouilles, perquisitions ou saisies

8. Chacun a droit à la protection contre les fouilles, les perquisitions ou les saisies abusives.

Détention ou emprisonnement

9. Chacun a droit à la protection contre la détention ou l'emprisonnement arbitraires.

Arrestation ou détention

10. Chacun a le droit, en cas d'arrestation ou de détention:

a) d'être informé dans les plus brefs délais des motifs de son arrestation ou de sa détention;

b) d'avoir recours sans délai à l'assistance d'un avocat et d'être informé de ce droit;

c) de faire contrôler, par *habeas corpus*, la légalité de sa détention et d'obtenir, le cas échéant, sa libération.

Affaires criminelles et pénales

11. Tout inculpé a le droit:

a) d'être informé sans délai anormal de l'infraction précise qu'on lui reproche;

b) d'être jugé dans un délai raisonnable;

(*c*) not to be compelled to be a witness in proceedings against that person in respect of the offence;

(*d*) to be presumed innocent until proven guilty according to law in a fair and public hearing by an independent and impartial tribunal;

(*e*) not to be denied reasonable bail without just cause;

(*f*) except in the case of an offence under military law tried before a military tribunal, to the benefit of trial by jury where the maximum punishment for the offence is imprisonment for five years or a more severe punishment;

(*g*) not to be found guilty on account of any act or omission unless, at the time of the act or omission, it constituted an offence under Canadian or international law or was criminal according to the general principles of law recognized by the community of nations;

c) de ne pas être contraint de témoigner contre lui-même dans toute poursuite intentée contre lui pour l'infraction qu'on lui reproche;

d) d'être présumé innocent tant qu'il n'est pas déclaré coupable, conformément à la loi, par un tribunal indépendant et impartial à l'issue d'un procès public et équitable;

e) de ne pas être privé sans juste cause d'une mise en liberté assortie d'un cautionnement raisonnable;

f) sauf s'il s'agit d'une infraction relevant de la justice militaire, de bénéficier d'un procès avec jury lorsque la peine maximale prévue pour l'infraction dont il est accusé est un emprisonnement de cinq ans ou une peine plus grave;

g) de ne pas être déclaré coupable en raison d'une action ou d'une omission qui, au moment où elle est survenue, ne constituait pas une infraction d'après le droit interne du Canada ou le droit international et n'avait pas de caractère criminel d'après les principes généraux de droit reconnus par l'ensemble des nations;

(*h*) if finally acquitted of the offence, not to be tried for it again and, if finally found guilty and punished for the offence, not to be tried or punished for it again; and

(*i*) if found guilty of the offence and if the punishment for the offence has been varied between the time of commission and the time of sentencing, to the benefit of the lesser punishment.

h) d'une part de ne pas être jugé de nouveau pour une infraction dont il a été définitivement acquitté, d'autre part de ne pas être jugé ni puni de nouveau pour une infraction dont il a été définitivement déclaré coupable et puni;

i) de bénéficier de la peine la moins sévère, lorsque la peine qui sanctionne l'infraction dont il est déclaré coupable est modifiée entre le moment de la perpétration de l'infraction et celui de la sentence.

Treatment or punishment

12. Everyone has the right not to be subjected to any cruel and unusual treatment or punishment.

Cruauté

12. Chacun a droit à la protection contre tous traitements ou peines cruels et inusités.

Self-crimination

13. A witness who testifies in any proceedings has the right not to have any incriminating evidence so given used to incriminate that witness in any other proceedings, except in a prosecution for perjury or for the giving of contradictory evidence.

Témoignage incriminant

13. Chacun a droit à ce qu'aucun témoignage incriminant qu'il donne ne soit utilisé pour l'incriminer dans d'autres procédures, sauf lors de poursuites pour parjure ou pour témoignages contradictoires.

Interpreter

14. A party or witness in any proceedings who does not understand or speak the language in which the proceedings are conducted or who is deaf has the right to the assistance of an interpreter.

Interprète

14. La partie ou le témoin qui ne peuvent suivre les procédures, soit parce qu'ils ne comprennent pas ou ne parlent pas la langue employée, soit parce qu'ils sont atteints de surdité, ont droit à l'assistance d'un interprète.

Equality Rights

Equality before and under law and equal protection and benefit of law

15. (1) Every individual is equal before and under the law and has the right to the equal protection and equal benefit of the law without discrimination and, in particular, without discrimination based on race, national or ethnic origin, colour, religion, sex, age or mental or physical disability.

Affirmative action programs

(2) Subsection (1) does not preclude any law, program or activity that has as its object the amelioration of conditions of disadvantaged individuals or groups including those that are disadvantaged because of race, national or ethnic origin, colour, religion, sex, age or mental or physical disability.(83)

Droits à légalité

Égalité devant la loi, égalité de bénéfice et protection égale de la loi

15. (1) La loi ne fait acception de personne et s'applique Également à tous, et tous ont droit à la même protection et au même bénéfice de la loi, indépendamment de toute discrimination, notamment des discriminations fondées sur la race, l'origine nationale ou ethnique, la couleur, la religion, le sexe, l'âge ou les déficiences mentales ou physiques.

Programmes de promotion sociale.

(2) Le paragraphe (1) n'a pas pour effet d'interdire les lois, programmes ou activités destinés à améliorer la situation d'individus ou de groupes défavorisés, notamment du fait de leur race, de leur origine nationale ou ethnique, de leur couleur, de leur religion, de leur sexe, de leur âge ou de leurs déficiences mentales ou physiques.

Official Languages of Canada

Official languages of Canada

16. (1) English and French are the official languages of Canada and have equality of status and equal rights and privileges as to their use in all institutions of the Parliament and government of Canada.

Langues officielles du Canada

Langues ofiicielles du Canada

16. (1) Le français et l'anglais sont les langues officielles du Canada; ils ont un statut et des droits et privilèges égaux quant à leur usage dans les institutions du Parlement et du gouvernement du Canada.

---

(83) Subsection 32(2) provides that section 15 shall not have effect until three years after section 32 comes into force. Section 32 came into force on April 17, 1982; therefore, section 15 had effect on April 17, 1985.

Official languages of New Brunswick

(2) English and French are the official languages of New Brunswick and have equality of status and equal rights and privileges as to their use in all institutions of the legislature and government of New Brunswick.

(2) Le français et l'anglais sont les langues officielles du Nouveau-Brunswick; ils ont un statut et des droits et privilèges égaux quant à leur usage dans les institutions de la Législature et du gouvernement du Nouveau-Brunswick.

Languer officielles du Nouveau-Brunswick.

Advancement of status and use

(3) Nothing in this Charter limits the authority of Parliament or a legislature to advance the equality of status or use of English and French.

(3) La présente charte ne limite pas le pouvoir du Parlement et des législatures de favoriser la progression vers l'égalité de statut ou d'usage du français et de l'anglais.

Progression vers l'égalité

English and French linguistic communities in New Brunswick

16.1 (1) The English linguistic community and the French linguistic community in New Brunswick have equality of status and equal rights and privileges, including the right to distinct educational institutions and such distinct cultural institutions as are necessary for the preservation and promotion of those communities.

16.1 (1) La communauté linguistique française et la communauté linguistique anglaise du Nouveau-Brunswick ont un statut et des droits et privilèges égaux, notamment le droit à des institutions d'enseignement distinctes et aux institutions culturelles distinctes nécessaires à leur protection et à leur promotion.

Communautés linguistiques française et anglaise du Nouveau-Brunswick

Role of the legislature and government of New Brunswick

(2) The role of the legislature and government of New Brunswick to preserve and promote the status, rights and privileges referred to in subsection (1) is affirmed.(83.1)

(2) Le rôle de la législature et du gouvernement du Nouveau-Brunswick de protéger et de promouvoir le statut, les droits et les privilèges visés au paragraphe (1) est confirmé.

Rôle de la législature et du gouvernement du Nouveau-Brunswick

Proceedings of Parliament

17. (1) Everyone has the right to use English or French in any debates and other proceedings of Parliament.(84)

17. (1) Chacun a le droit d'employer le français ou l'anglais dans les débats et travaux du Parlement.

Travaux du Parlement

(83.1) Section 16.1 was added by *Constitution Amendment, 1993 (New Brunswick)*. See SI/93-54.

(84) See section 133 of the *Constitution Act, 1967*, and the footnote thereto.

Proceedings of New Brunswick legislature

(2) Everyone has the right to use English or French in any debates and other proceedings of the legislature of New Brunswick.(85)

Travaux de la Législature du Nouveau-Brunswick

(2) Chacun a le droit d'employer le français ou l'anglais dans les débats et travaux de la Législature du Nouveau-Brunswick.

Parliamentary statute and records

18. (1) The statutes, records and journals of Parliament shall be printed and published in English and French and both language versions are equally authoritative.(86)

Documents parlementaires

18. (1) Les lois, les archives, les comptes rendus et les procès-verbaux du Parlement sont imprimés et publiés en français et en anglais, les deux versions des lois ayant également force de loi et celles des autres documents ayant même valeur.

New Brunswick statutes and records

(2) The statutes, records and journals of the legislature of New Brunswick shall be printed and published in English and French and both language versions are equally authoritative.(87)

Documents de la Législature du Nouveau-Brunswick

(2) Les lois, les archives, les comptes rendus et les procès-verbaux de la Législature du Nouveau-Brunswick sont imprimés et publiés en français et en anglais, les deux versions des lois ayant également force de loi et celles des autres documents ayant même valeur.

Proceedings in courts established by Parliament

19. (1) Either English or French may be used by any person in, or in any pleading in or process issuing from, any court established by Parliament.(88)

Procédures devant les tribunaux établis par le Parlement

19. (1) Chacun a le droit d'employer le français ou l'anglais dans toutes les affaires dont sont saisis les tribunaux établis par le Parlement et dans tous les actes de procédure qui en découlent.

---

(85) *Id.*
(86) *Id.*
(87) *Id.*
(88) *Id.*

Proceedings in New Brunswick courts

(2) Either English or French may be used by any person in, or in any pleading in or process issuing from, any court of New Brunswick.(89)

Procédures devant les tribunaux du Nouveau-Brunswick

(2) Chacun a le droit d'employer le français ou l'anglais dans toutes les affaires dont sont saisis les tribunaux du Nouveau-Brunswick et dans tous les actes de procédure qui en découlent.

Communications by public with federal institutions

20. (1) Any member of the public in Canada has the right to communicate with, and to receive available services from, any head or central office of an institution of the Parliament or government of Canada in English or French, and has the same right with respect to any other office of any such institution where

(*a*) there is a significant demand for communications with and services from that office in such language; or

(*b*) due to the nature of the office, it is reasonable that communications with and services from that office be available in both English and French.

Communications entre les administrés et les institutions fédérales

20. (1) Le public a, au Canada, droit à l'emploi du français ou de l'anglais pour communiquer avec le siège ou l'administration centrale des institutions du Parlement ou du gouvernement du Canada ou pour en recevoir les services; il a le même droit à l'égard de tout autre bureau de ces institutions là où, selon le cas:

a) l'emploi du français ou de l'anglais fait l'objet d'une demande importante;

b) l'emploi du français et de l'anglais se justifie par la vocation du bureau.

Communications by public with New Brunswick institutions

(2) Any member of the public in New Brunswick has the right to communicate with, and to receive available services from, any office of an institution of the legislature or government of New Brunswick in English or French.

Communications entre les administrés et les institutions du Nouveau-Brunswick

(2) Le public a, au Nouveau-Brunswick, droit à l'emploi du français ou de l'anglais pour communiquer avec tout bureau des institutions de la législature ou du gouvernement ou pour en recevoir les services.

(89) *Id.*

Continuation of existing constitutional provisions

21. Nothing in sections 16 to 20 abrogates or derogates from any right, privilege or obligation with respect to the English and French languages, or either of them, that exists or is continued by virtue of any other provision of the Constitution of Canada.(90)

Rights and privileges preserved

22. Nothing in sections 16 to 20 abrogates or derogates from any legal or customary right or privilege acquired or enjoyed either before or after the coming into force of this Charter with respect to any language that is not English or French.

Minority Language Educational Rights

Language of instruction

23. (1) Citizens of Canada

(*a*) whose first language learned and still understood is that of the English or French linguistic minority population of the province in which they reside, or

(*b*) who have received their primary school instruction in Canada in English or French and reside in a province where the language in which they received that instruction is the language of the English or French linguistic minority population of the province,

Maintien en vigueur de certaines dispositions

21. Les articles 16 à 20 n'ont pas pour effet, en ce qui a trait à la langue française ou anglaise ou à ces deux langues, de porter atteinte aux droits, privilèges ou obligations qui existent ou sont maintenus aux termes d'une autre disposition de la Constitution du Canada.

Droits préservés

22. Les articles 16 à 20 n'ont pas pour effet de porter atteinte aux droits et privilèges, antérieurs ou postérieurs à l'entrée en vigueur de la présente charte et découlant de la loi ou de la coutume, des langues autres que le français ou l'anglais.

Droits à l'instruction dans la langue de la minorité

Langue d'instruction

23. (1) Les citoyens canadiens:

a) dont la premiére langue apprise et encore comprise est celle de la minorité francophone ou anglophone de la province où ils résident,

b) qui ont reçu leur instruction, au niveau primaire, en français ou en anglais au Canada et qui résident dans une province ou la langue dans laquelle ils ont reçu cette instruction est celle de la minorité francophone ou anglophone de la province,

(90) See, for example, section 133 of the *Constitution Act, 1867*, and the *Manitoba Act, 1870*, in the footnote thereto.

have the right to have their children receive primary and secondary school instruction in that language in that province.(91)

ont, dans l'un ou l'autre cas, le droit d'y faire instruire leurs enfants, aux niveaux primaire et secondaire, dans cette langue.

Continuity of language instruction

(2) Citizens of Canada of whom any child has received or is receiving primary or secondary school instruction in English or French in Canada, have the right to have all their children receive primary and secondary school instruction in the same language.

(2) Les citoyens canadiens dont un enfant a reçu ou reçoit son instruction, au niveau primaire ou secondaire, en français ou en anglais au Canada ont le droit de faire instruire tous leurs enfants, aux niveaux primaire et secondaire, dans la langue de cette instruction.

Continuité d'emploi de la langue d'instruction

Application where numbers warrant

(3) The right of citizens of Canada under subsections (1) and (2) to have their children receive primary and secondary school instruction in the language of the English or French linguistic minority population of a province

(*a*) applies wherever in the province the number of children of citizens who have such a right is sufficient to warrant the provision to them out of public funds of minority language instruction; and

(*b*) includes, where the number of those children so warrants, the right to have them receive that instruction in minority language educational facilities provided out of public funds.

(3) Le droit reconnu aux citoyens canadiens par les paragraphes (1) et (2) de faire instruire leurs enfants, aux niveaux primaire et secondaire, dans la langue de la minorité francophone ou anglophone d'une province:

a) s'exerce partout dans la province où le nombre des enfants des citoyens qui ont ce droit est suffisant pour justifier à leur endroit la prestation, sur les fonds publics, de l'instruction dans la langue de la minorité;

b) comprend, lorsque le nombre de ces enfants le justifie, le droit de les faire instruire dans des établissements d'enseignement de la minorité linguistique financés sur les fonds publics.

Justification par le nombre

(91) Paragraph 23(1)(*a*) is not in force in respect of Quebec. See section 59 *infra*.

Enforcement

Enforcement of guaranteed rights and freedoms

24. (1) Anyone whose rights or freedoms, as guaranteed by this Charter, have been infringed or denied may apply to a court of competent jurisdiction to obtain such remedy as the court considers appropriate and just in the circumstances.

Exclusion of evidence bringing administration of justice into disrepute

(2) Where, in proceedings under subsection (1), a court concludes that evidence was obtained in a manner that infringed or denied any rights or freedoms guaranteed by this Charter, the evidence shall be excluded if it is established that, having regard to all the circumstances, the admission of it in the proceedings would bring the administration of justice into disrepute.

General

Aboriginal rights and freedoms not affected by Charter

25. The guarantee in this Charter of certain rights and freedoms shall not be construed so as to abrogate or derogate from any aboriginal, treaty or other rights or freedoms that pertain to the aboriginal peoples of Canada including

Recours

Recours en cas d'atteinte aux droits et libertés

24. (1) Toute personne, victime de violation ou de négation des droits ou libertés qui lui sont garantis par la présente charte, peut s'adresser à un tribunal compétent pour obtenir la réparation que le tribunal estime convenable et juste eu égard aux circonstances.

Irrecevabilité d'éléments de preuve qui risqueraient de déconsidérer l'administration de la justice

(2) Lorsque, dans une instance visée au paragraphe (1), le tribunal a conclu que des éléments de preuve ont été obtenus dans des conditions qui portent atteinte aux droits ou libertés garantis par la présente charte, ces éléments de preuve sont écartés s'il est établi, eu égard aux circonstances, que leur utilisation est susceptible de déconsidérer l'administration de la justice.

Dispositions générales

Maintien des droits et libertés des autochtones

25. Le fait que la présente charte garantit certains droits et libertés ne porte pas atteinte aux droits ou libertés — ancestraux, issus de traités ou autres — des peuples autochtones du Canada, notamment:

(*a*) any rights or freedoms that have been recognized by the Royal Proclamation of October 7, 1763; and

(*b*) any rights or freedoms that now exist by way of land claims agreements or may be so acquired.(92)

a) aux droits ou libertés reconnus par la Proclamation royale du 7 octobre 1763;

b) aux droits ou libertés existants issus d'accords sur des revendications territoriales ou ceux susceptibles d'être ainsi acquis.(1)

Other rights and freedoms not affected by Charter

26. The guarantee in this Charter of certain rights and freedoms shall not be construed as denying the existence of any other rights or freedoms that exist in Canada.

Maintien des autres droits et libertés

26. Le fait que la présente charte garantit certains droits et libertés ne constitue pas une négation des autres droits ou libertés qui existent au Canada.

Multicultural heritage

27. This Charter shall be interpreted in a manner consistent with the preservation and enhancement of the multicultural heritage of Canadians.

Maintien du patrimoine culturel

27. Toute interprétation de la présente charte doit concorder avec l'objectif de promouvoir le maintien et la valorisation du patrimoine multiculturel des Canadiens.

Rights guaranteed equally to both sexes

28. Notwithstanding anything in this Charter, the rights and freedoms referred to in it are guaranteed equally to male and female persons.

Égalité de garantie des droits pour les deux sexes

28. Indépendamment des autres dispositions de la présente charte, les droits et libertés qui y sont mentionnés sont garantis également aux personnes des deux sexes.

Rights respecting certain schools preserved

29. Nothing in this Charter abrogates or derogates from any rights or privileges guaranteed by or under the Constitution of Canada in respect of denominational, separate or dissentient schools.(93)

Maintien des droits relatifs à certaines écoles

29. Les dispositions de la présente charte ne portent pas atteinte aux droits ou privilèges garantis en vertu de la Constitution du Canada concernant les écoles séparées et autres écoles confessionnelles.

---

(92) Paragraph 25(*b*) was repealed and re-enacted by the *Constitution Amendment Proclamation, 1983. See* SI/84-102

Paragraph 25(*b*) as originally enacted read as follows:

"(*b*) any rights or freedoms that may be acquired by Canada by way of land claim settlement."

(93) See section 93 of the *Constitution Act, 1867*, and the footnote thereto.

Application to territories and territorial authorities

30. A reference in this Charter to a province or to the legislative assembly or legislature of a province shall be deemed to include a reference to the Yukon Territory and the Northwest Territories, or to the appropriate legislative authority thereof, as the case may be.

Application aux territoires

30. Dans la présente charte, les dispositions qui visent les provinces, leur législature ou leur assemblée législative visent également le territoire du Yukon, les territoires du Nord-Ouest ou leurs autorités législatives compétentes.

Legislative powers not extended

31. Nothing in this Charter extends the legislative powers of any body or authority.

Non-élargissement des compétences législatives

31. La présente charte n'élargit pas les compétences législatives de quelque organisme ou autorité que ce soit.

Application of Charter

Application de la charte

Application of Charter

32. (1) This Charter applies

(*a*) to the Parliament and government of Canada in respect of all matters within the authority of Parliament including all matters relating to the Yukon Territory and Northwest Territories; and

(*b*) to the legislature and government of each prov∞ce in respect of all matters within the authority of the legislature of each province.

Application de la charte

32. (1) La présente charte s'applique:

a) au Parlement et au gouvernement du Canada, pour tous les domaines relevant du Parlement, y compris ceux qui concernent le territoire du Yukon et les territoires du Nord-Ouest;

b) à la législature et au gouvernement de chaque province, pour tous les domaines relevant de cette législature.

Exception

(2) Notwithstanding subsection (1), section 15 shall not have effect until three years after this section comes into force.

Restriction

(2) Par dérogation au paragraphe (1), l'article 15 n'a d'effet que trois ans aprés l'entrée en vigueur du présent article.

Exception where express declaration

33. (1) Parliament or the legislature of a province may expressly declare in an Act of Parliament or of the legislature, as the case may be, that the Act or a provision thereof shall operate notwithstanding a provision included in section 2 or sections 7 to 15 of this Charter.

Dérogation par déclaration expresse

33. (1) Le Parlement ou la législature d'une province peut adopter une loi où il est expressément déclaré que celle-ci ou une de ses dispositions a effet indépendamment d'une disposition donnée de l'article 2 ou des articles 7 à 15 de la présente charte.

Operation of exception

(2) An Act or a provision of an Act in respect of which a declaration made under this section is in effect shall have such operation as it would have but for the provision of this Charter referred to in the declaration.

Effet de la dérogation

(2) La loi ou la disposition qui fait l'objet d'une déclaration conforme au présent article et en vigueur a l'effet qu'elle aurait sauf la disposition en cause de la charte.

Five year limitation

(3) A declaration made under subsection (1) shall cease to have effect five years after it comes into force or on such earlier date as may be specified in the declaration.

Durée de validité

(3) La déclaration visée au paragraphe (1) cesse d'avoir effet à la date qui y est précisée ou, au plus tard, cinq ans aprés son entrée en vigueur.

Re-enactment

(4) Parliament or the legislature of a province may re-enact a declaration made under subsection (1).

Nouvelle adoption

(4) Le Parlement ou une législature peut adopter de nouveau une déclaration visée au paragraphe (1).

Five year limitation

(5) Subsection (3) applies in respect of a re-enactment made under subsection (4).

Durée de valdité

(5) Le paragraphe (3) s'applique à toute déclaration adoptée sous le régime du paragraphe (4).

Citation

Citation

34. This Part may be cited as the *Canadian Charter of Rights and Freedoms*.

Titre

Titre

34. Titre de la présente partie: *Charte canadienne des droits et libertés*.

PART II

RIGHTS OF THE ABORIGINAL PEOPLES OF CANADA

Recognition of existing aboriginal and treaty rights

35. (1) The existing aboriginal and treaty rights of the aboriginal peoples of Canada are hereby recognized and affirmed.

Definition of "aboriginal peoples of Canada"

(2) In this Act, "aboriginal peoples of Canada" includes the Indian, Inuit and Métis peoples of Canada.

Land claims agreements

(3) For greater certainty, in subsection (1) "treaty rights" includes rights that now exist by way of land claims agreements or may be so acquired.

Aboriginal and treaty rights are guaranteed equally to both sexes

(4) Notwithstanding any other provision of this Act, the aboriginal and treaty rights referred to in subsection (1) are guaranteed equally to male and female persons.(94)

Commitment to participation in constitutional conference

35.1 The government of Canada and the provincial governments are committed to the principle that, before any amendment is made to Class 24 of section 91 of the "*Constitution Act, 1867*", to section 25 of this Act or to this Part,

PARTIE II

DROITS DES PEUPLES AUTOCHTONES DU CANADA

Confirmation des droits existants des peuples autochtones

35. (1) Les droits existants — ancestraux ou issus de traités — des peuples autochtones du Canada sont reconnus et confirmés.

Définition de «peuples autochtones du Canada»

(2) Dans la présente loi, «peuples autochtones du Canada» s'entend notamment des Indiens, des Inuit et des Métis du Canada.

Accords sur des revendications territoriales

(3) Il est entendu que sont compris parmi les droits issus de traités, dont il est fait mention au paragraphe (1), les droits existants issus d'accords sur des revendications territoriales ou ceux susceptibles d'être ainsi acquis.

Égalité de garantie des droits pour les deux sexes

(4) Indépendamment de toute autre disposition de la présente loi, les droits — ancestraux ou issus de traités — visés au paragraphe (1) sont garantis également aux personnes des deux sexes.(2)

Engagement relatif à la participation à une conférence constitutionnelle

35.1 Les gouvernements fédéral et provinciaux sont liés par l'engagement de principe selon lequel le premier ministre du Canada, avant toute modification de la catégorie 24 de l'article 92 de la «*Loi constitutionnelle de 1867*», de l'article 25 de la présente loi ou de la présente partie:

(94) Subsections 35(3) and (4) were added by the *Constitution Amendment Proclamation, 1983*. *See* SI/84-102.

(*a*) a constitutional conference that includes in its agenda an item relating to the proposed amendment, composed of the Prime Minister of Canada and the first ministers of the provinces, will be convened by the Prime Minister of Canada; and

(*b*) the Prime Minister of Canada will invite representatives of the aboriginal peoples of Canada to participate in the discussions on that item.(95)

a) convoquera une conférence constitutionnelle réunissant les premiers ministres provinciaux et lui-même et comportant à son ordre du jour la question du projet de modification;

b) invitera les représentants des peuples autochtones du Canada à participer aux travaux relatifs à cette question.(3)

PART III

EQUALIZATION AND REGIONAL DISPARITIES

Commitment to promote equal opportunities

36. (1) Without altering the legislative authority of Parliament or of the provincial legislatures, or the rights of any of them with respect to the exercise of their legislative authority, Parliament and the legislatures, together with the government of Canada and the provincial governments, are committed to

(*a*) promoting equal opportunities for the well-being of Canadians;

(*b*) furthering economic development to reduce disparity in opportunities; and

PARTIE III

PÉRÉQUATION ET INÉGALITÉS RÉGIONALES

Éngagements relatifs a l'égalité des chances

36. (1) Sous réserve des compétences législatives du Parlement et des législatures et de leur droit de les exercer, le Parlement et les législatures, ainsi que les gouvernements fédéral et provinciaux, s'engagent à:

a promouvoir l'égalité des chances de tous les Canadiens dans la recherche de leur bien-être;

b) favoriser le développement économique pour réduire l'inégalité des chances;

(95) Section 35.1 was added by the *Constitution Amendment Proclamation, 1983*. *See* SI/84-102.

(*c*) providing essential public services of reasonable quality to all Canadians.

c) fournir à tous les Canadiens, à un niveau de qualité acceptable, les services publics essentiels.

Commitment respecting public services

(2) Parliament and the government of Canada are committed to the principle of making equalization payments to ensure that provincial governments have sufficient revenues to provide reasonably comparable levels of public services at reasonably comparable levels of taxation.(96)

Engagement relatif aux services publics

(2) Le Parlement et le gouvernement du Canada prennent l'engagement de principe de faire des paiements de péréquation propres à donner aux gouvernements provinciaux des revenus suffisants pour les mettre en mesure d'assurer les services publics à un niveau de qualité et de fiscalité sensiblement comparables.

PART IV

CONSTITUTIONAL CONFERENCE

37. (97)

PARTIE IV

CONFÉRENCE CONSTITUTIONNELLE

37. Abrogé.

---

(96) See footnotes to sections 114 and 118 of the *Constitution Act, 1867*.

(97) Section 54 provided for the repeal of Part IV one year after Part VIII came into force. Part VII came into force on April 17, 1982 thereby repealing Part IV on April 17, 1983.

Part IV, as originally enacted, read as follows:

> (1) A constitutional conference composed of the Prime Minister of Canada and the first ministers of the provinces shall be convened by the Prime Minister of Canada within one year after this Part comes into force.
>
> (2) The conference convened under subsection (1) shall have included in its agenda an item respecting constitutional matters that directly affect the aboriginal peoples of Canada, including the identification and definition of the rights of those peoples to be included in the Constitution of Canada, and the Prime Minister of Canada shall invite representatives of those peoples to participate in the discussions on that item.
>
> (3) The Prime Minister of Canada shall invite elected representatives of the governments of the Yukon Territory and the Northwest Territories to participate in the discussions on any item on the agenda of the conference convened under subsection (1) that, in the opinion of the Prime Minister, directly affects the Yukon Territory and the Northwest Territories.

PART IV.1

CONSTITUTIONAL CONFERENCES

37.1 (98)

PARTIE IV.1

CONFÉRENCES CONSTITUTIONNELLES

37.1 Abrogé.

PART V

PROCEDURE FOR AMENDING CONSTITUTION OF CANADA(99)

PARTIE V

PROCÉDURE DE MODIFICATION DE LA CONSTITUTION DU CANADA

General procedure for amending Constitution of Canada

38. (1) An amendment to the Constitution of Canada may be made by proclamation issued by the Governor General under the Great Seal of Canada where so authorized by

(*a*) resolutions of the Senate and House of Commons; and

Procédure normale de modification

38. (1) La Constitution du Canada peut être modifiée par proclamation du gouverneur général sous le grand sceau du Canada, autorisée à la fois:

a) par des résolutions du Sénat et de la Chambre des communes;

(98) Part IV.1, which was added by the *Constitution Amendment Proclamation, 1983* (see SI/84-102), was repealed on April 18, 1987 by section 54.1.

Part IV.1, as originally enacted read as follows:

> **37.1** (1) In addition to the conference convened in March 1983, at least two constitutional conferences composed of the Prime Minister of Canada and the first ministers of the provinces shall be convened by the Prime Minister of Canada, the first within three years after April 17, 1982 and the second within five years after that date.
>
> (2) Each conference convened under subsection (1) shall have included in its agenda constitutional matters that directly affect the aboriginal peoples of Canada, and the Prime Minister of Canada shall invite representatives of those peoples to participate in the discussions on those matters.
>
> (3) The Prime Minister of Canada shall invite elected representatives of the governments of the Yukon Territory and the Northwest Territories to participate in the discussions on any item on the agenda of a conference convened under subsection (1) that, in the opinion of the Prime Minister, directly affects the Yukon Territory and the Northwest Territories.
>
> (4) Nothing in this section shall be construed so as to derogate from subsection 35(1).

(99) Prior to the enactment of Part V certain provisions of the Constitution of Canada and the provincial consultations could be amended pursuant to the *Constitution Act, 1867*. See the footnotes in section 91, Class 1 and section 92, Class 1 thereof, *supra*. Other amendments to the Constitution could only be made by enactment of the Parliament of the United Kingdom.

(*b*) resolutions of the legislative assemblies of at least two-thirds of the provinces that have, in the aggregate, according to the then latest general census, at least fifty per cent of the population of all the provinces.

b) par des résolutions des assemblées législatives d'au moins deux tiers des provinces dont la population confondue représente, selon le recensement général le plus récent à l'époque, au moins cinquante pour cent de la population de toutes les provinces.

Majority of members

(2) An amendment made under subsection (1) that derogates from the legislative powers, the proprietary rights or any other rights or privileges of the legislature or government of a province shall require a resolution supported by a majority of the members of each of the Senate, the House of Commons and the legislative assemblies required under subsection (1).

Majorité simple

(2) Une modification faite conformément au paragraphe (1) mais dérogatoire à la compétence législative, aux droits de propriété ou à tous autres droits ou privilèges d'une législature ou d'un gouvernement provincial exige une résolution adoptée à la majorité des sénateurs, des députés fédéraux et des députés de chacune des assemblées législatives du nombre requis de provinces.

Expression of dissent

(3) An amendment referred to in subsection (2) shall not have effect in a province the legislative assembly of which has expressed its dissent thereto by resolution supported by a majority of its members prior to the issue of the proclamation to which the amendment relates unless that legislative assembly, subsequently, by resolution supported by a majority of its members, revokes its dissent and authorizes the amendment.

Désaccord

(3) La modification visée au paragraphe (2) est sans effet dans une province dont l'assemblée législative a, avant la prise de la proclamation, exprimé son désaccord par une résolution adoptée à la majorité des députés, sauf si cette assemblée, par résolution également adoptée à la majorité, revient sur son désaccord et autorise la modification.

Revocation of dissent

(4) A resolution of dissent made for the purposes of subsection (3) may be revoked at any time before or after the issue of the proclamation to which it relates.

Levée du désaccord

(4) La résolution de désaccord visée au paragraphe (3) peut être révoquée à tout moment, indépendamment de la date de la proclamation il laquelle elle se rapporte.

Restriction on proclamation.

39. (1) A proclamation shall not be issued under subsection 38(1) before the expiration of one year from the adoption of the resolution initiating the amendment procedure thereunder, unless the legislative assembly of each province has previously adopted a resolution of assent or dissent.

Restriction

39. (1) La proclamation visée au paragraphe 38(1) ne peut être prise dans l'année suivant l'adoption de la résolution à l'origine de la procédure de modification que si l'assemblée législative de chaque province a préalablement adopté une résolution d'agrément ou de désaccord.

Idem

(2) A proclamation shall not be issued under subsection 38(1) after the expiration of three years from the adoption of the resolution initiating the amendment procedure thereunder.

Idem

(2) La proclamation visée au paragraphe 38(1) ne peut être prise que dans les trois ans suivant l'adoption de la résolution à l'origine de la procédure de modification.

Compensation

40. Where an amendment is made under subsection 38(1) that transfers provincial legislative powers relating to education or other cultural matters from provincial legislatures to Parliament, Canada shall provide reasonable compensation to any province to which the amendment does not apply.

Compensation

40. Le Canada fournit une juste compensation aux provinces auxquelles ne s'applique pas une modification faite conformément au paragraphe 38(1) et relative, en matière d'éducation ou dans d'autres domaines culturels, à un transfert de compétences législatives provinciales au Parlement.

Amendment by unanimous consent

41. An amendment to the Constitution of Canada in relation to the following matters may be made by proclamation issued by the Governor General under the Great Seal of Canada only where authorized by resolutions of the Senate and House of Commons and of the legislative assembly of each province:

(*a*) the office of the Queen, the Governor General and the Lieutenant Governor of a province;

(*b*) the right of a province to a number of members in the House of Commons not less than the number of Senators by which the province is entitled to be represented at the time this Part comes into force;

(*c*) subject to section 43, the use of the English or the French language;

(*d*) the composition of the Supreme Court of Canada; and

(*e*) an amendment to this Part.

Consentement unanime

41. Toute modification de la Constitution du Canada portant sur les questions suivantes se fait par proclamation du gouverneur général sous le grand sceau du Canada, autorisée par des résolutions du Sénat, de la Chambre des communes et de l'assemblée législative de chaque province:

a) la charge de Reine, celle de gouverneur général et celle de lieutenant-gouverneur;

b) le droit d'une province d'avoir à la Chambre des communes un nombre de députés au moins égal à celui des sénateurs par lesquels elle est habilitée à être représentée lors de l'entrée en vigueur de la présente partie;

c) sous réserve de l'anicle 43, l'usage du français ou de l'anglais;

d) la composition de la Cour suprême du Canada;

e) la modification de la présente partie.

Amendment by general procedure

42. (1) An amendment to the Constitution of Canada in relation to the following matters may be made only in accordance with subsection 38(1):

(*a*) the principle of proportionate representation of the provinces in the House of Commons prescribed by the Constitution of Canada;

Procédure normale de modification

42. (1) Toute modification de la Constitution du Canada portant sur les questions suivantes se fait conformément au paragraphe 38(1):

a) le principe de la représentation proportionnelle des provinces à la Chambre des communes prévu par la Constitution du Canada;

(*b*) the powers of the Senate and the method of selecting Senators;
(*c*) the number of members by which a province is entitled to be represented in the Senate and the residence qualifications of Senators;
(*d*) subject to paragraph 41(*d*), the Supreme Court of Canada;
(*e*) the extension of existing provinces into the territories; and
(*f*) notwithstanding any other law or practice, the establishment of new provinces.

b) les pouvoirs du Sénat et le mode de sélection des sénateurs;
c) le nombre des sénateurs par lesquels une province est habilitée à être représentée et les conditions de résidence qu'ils doivent remplir;
d) sous réserve de l'alinéa 41*d*), la Cour suprême du Canada;
e) le rattachement aux provinces existantes de tout ou partie des territoires;
f) par dérogation à toute autre loi ou usage, la création de provinces.

Exception

(2) Subsections 38(2) to (4) do not apply in respect of amendments in relation to matters referred to in subsection (1).

(2) Les paragraphes 38(2) à (4) ne s'appliquent pas aux questions mentionnées au paragraphe (1).

Exception

Amendment of provisions relating to some but not all provinces

43. An amendment to the Constitution of Canada in relation to any provision that applies to one or more, but not all, provinces, including

(*a*) any alteration to boundaries between provinces, and

(*b*) any amendment to any provision that relates to the use of the English or the French language within a province, may be made by proclamation issued by the Governor General under the Great Seal of Canada only where so authorized by resolutions of the Senate and House of Commons and of the legislative assembly of each province to which the amendment applies.

Modification à l'égard de certaines provinces

43. Les dispositions de la Constitution du Canada applicables à certaines provinces seulement ne peuvent être modifiées que par proclamation du gouverneur général sous le grand sceau du Canada, autorisée par des résolutions de Sénat, de la Chambre des communes et de l'assemblée législative de chaque province concernée. Le présent article s'applique notamment:

a) aux changements du tracé des frontières interprovinciales;

b) aux modifications des dispositions relatives à l'usage du français ou de l'anglais dans une province.

Amendments by Parliament

44. Subject to sections 41 and 42, Parliament may exclusively make laws amending the Constitution of Canada in relation to the executive government of Canada or the Senate and House of Commons.

Modification par le Parlement

44. Sous réserve des articles 41 et 42, le Parlement a compétence exclusive pour modifier les dispositions de la Constitution du Canada relatives au pouvoir exécutif fédéral, au Sénat ou à la Chambre des communes.

Amendments by provincial legislatures

45. Subject to section 41, the legislature of each province may exclusively make laws amending the constitution of the province.

Modification par les législatures

45. Sous réserve de l'article 41, une législature a compétence exclusive pour modifier la constitution de sa province.

Initiation of amendment procedures

46. (1) The procedures for amendment under sections 38, 41, 42 and 43 may be initiated either by the Senate or the House of Commons or by the legislative assembly of a province

Initiative des procédures

46. (1) L'initiative des procédures de modification visées aux articles 38, 41, 42 et 43 appartient au Sénat, à la Chambre des communes ou à une assemblée législative.

Revocation of authorization

(2) A resolution of assent made for the purposes of this Part may be revoked at any time before the issue of a proclamation authorized by it.

Possibilité de révocation

(2) Une résolution d'agrément adoptée dans le cadre de la présente partie peut être révoquée à tout moment avant la date de la proclamation qu'elle autorise.

Amendments without Senate resolution

47. (1) An amendment to the Constitution of Canada made by proclamation under section 38, 41, 42 or 43 may be made without a resolution of the Senate authorizing the issue of the proclamation if, within one hundred and eighty days after the adoption by the House of Commons of a resolution authorizing its issue, the Senate has not adopted such a resolution and if, at any time after the expiration of that period, the House of Commons again adopts the resolution.

Modification sans résolution du Sénat

47. (1) Dans les cas visés à l'article 38, 41, 42 ou 43, il peut être passé outre au défaut d'autorisation du Sénat si celui-ci n'a pas adopté de résolution dans un délai de cent quatre-vingts jours suivant l'adoption de celle de la Chambre des communes et si cette dernière, après l'expiration du délai, adopte une nouvelle résolution dans le même sens.

Computation of period

(2) Any period when Parliament is prorogued or dissolved shall not be counted in computing the one hundred and eighty day period referred to in subsection (1).

Computation du délai

(2) Dans la computation du délai visé au paragraphe (1), ne sont pas comptées les périodes pendant lesquelles le Parlement est prorogé ou dissous.

Advice to issue proclamation

48. The Queen's Privy Council for Canada shall advise the Governor General to issue a proclamation under this Part forthwith on the adoption of the resolutions required for an amendment made by proclamation under this Part.

Demande de proclamation

48. Le Conseil privé de la Reine pour le Canada demande au gouverneur général de prendre, conformément à la présente partie, une proclamation dés l'adoption des résolutions prévues par cette partie pour une modification par proclamation.

Constitutional conference

49. A constitutional conference composed of the Prime Minister of Canada and the first ministers of the provinces shall be convened by the Prime Minister of Canada within fifteen years after this Part comes into force to review the provisions of this Part.

Conference constitutionnelle

49. Dans le quinze ans suivant l'entrée en vigueur de la présente partie, le premier ministre du Canada convoque une conférence constitutionnelle réunissant les premiers ministres provinciaux et lui-même, en vue du réexamen des dispositions de cette partie.

PART VI

AMENDMENT TO THE CONSTITUTION ACT, 1867

PARTIE VI

MODIFICATION DE LA LOI CONSTITUTIONNELLE DE 1867

[Sections 50 and 51 are omitted. They added a new s. 92A and a new Sixth Schedule to the Constitution Act, 1867. The new provisions have been reproduced as part of the Constitution Act, 1867.]

PART VII

GENERAL

PARTIE VII

DISPOSITIONS GÉNÉRALES

Primacy of Constitution of Canada

52. (1) The Constitution of Canada is the supreme law of Canada, and any law that is inconsistent with the provisions of the Constitution is, to the extent of the inconsistency, of no force or effect.

Primauté de la Constitution du Canada

52. (1) La Constitution du Canada est la loi suprême du Canada; elle rend inopérantes les dispositions incompatibles de toute autre règle de droit.

Constitution of Canada

(2) The Constitution of Canada includes

(*a*) the Canada Act 1982, including this Act;

(*b*) the Acts and orders referred to in the schedule; and

(*c*) any amendment to any Act or order referred to in paragraph (*a*) or (*b*).

Constitution du Canada

(2) La Constitution du Canada comprend :

a) la *Loi de 1982 sur le Canada*, y compris la présente loi;

b) les textes législatifs et les décrets figurant à l'annexe;

c) les modifications des textes législatifs et des décrets mentionnés aux alinéas *a*) ou *b*).

Amendments to Constitution of Canada

(3) Amendments to the Constitution of Canada shall be made only in accordance with the authority contained in the Constitution of Canada.

Modification

(3) La Constitution du Canada ne peut être modifée que conformément aux pouvoirs conférés par elle.

Repeals and new names

53. (1) The enactments referred to in Column I of the schedule are hereby repealed or amended to the extent indicated in Column II thereof and, unless repealed, shall continue as law in Canada under the names set out in Column III thereof.

Abrogation et nouveaux titres

53. (1) Les textes législatifs et les décrets énumérés à la colonne I de l'annexe sont abrogés ou modifiés dans la mesure indiquée à la colonne II. Sauf abrogation, ils restent en vigueur en tant que lois du Canada sous les titres mentionnés à la colonne III.

Consequential amendments

(2) Every enactment, except the *Canada Act 1982*, that refers to an enactment referred to in the schedule by the name in Column I thereof is hereby amended by substituting for that name the corresponding name in Column III thereof, and any British North America Act not referred to in the schedule may be cited as the *Constitution Act* followed by the year and number, if any, of its enactment.

Modifications corrélatives

(2) Tout texte législatif ou réglementaire, sauf la *Loi de 1982 sur le Canada*, qui fait mention d'un texte législatif ou décret figurant à l'annexe par le titre indiqué à la colonne I est modifié par substitution à ce titre du titre correspondant mentionné à la colonne III; tout Acte de l'Amérique du Nord britannique non mentionné à l'annexe peut être cité sous le titre de *Loi constitutionnelle* suivi de l'indication de l'année de son adoption et éventuellement de son numéro.

Repeal and consequential amendments

54. Part IV is repealed on the day that is one year after this Part comes into force and this section may be repealed and this Act renumbered, consequentially upon the repeal of Part IV and this section, by proclamation issued by the Governor General under the Great Seal of Canada.(102)

Abrogation et modifications qui en découlent

54. La partie IV est abrogée un an aprés l'entrée en vigueur de la présente partie et le gouverneur général peut, par proclamation sous le grand sceau du Canada, abroger le présent article et apporter en conséquence de cette double abrogation les aménagements qui s'imposent à la présente loi.

(102) Part VII came into force on April 17, 1982. *See* SI/82-97.

Repeal of Part IV.1 and this section

54.1(103)

54.1 Abrogé.

French version of Constitution of Canada

55. A French version of the portions of the Constitution of Canada referred to in the schedule shall be prepared by the Minister of Justice of Canada as expeditiously as possible and, when any portion thereof sufficient to warrant action being taken has been so prepared, it shall be put forward for enactment by proclamation issued by the Governor General under the Great Seal of Canada pursuant to the procedure then applicable to an amendment of the same provisions of the Constitution of Canada.

Version française de certains textes constitutionnels

55. Le ministre de la Justice du Canada est chargé de rédiger, dans les meilleurs délais, la version française des parties de la Constitution du Canada qui figurent à l'annexe; toute partie suffisamment importante est, dès qu'elle est prête, déposée pour adoption par proclamation du gouverneur général sous le grand sceau du Canada, conformément à la procédure applicable à l'époque à la modification des dispositions constitutionnelles qu'elle contient.

English and French versions of certain constitutional texts

56. Where any portion of the Constitution of Canada has been or is enacted in English and French or where a French version of any portion of the Constitution is enacted pursuant to section 55, the English and French versions of that portion of the Constitution are equally authoritative.

Versions française et anglaise de certains textes constitutionnels

56. Les versions française et anglaise des parties de la Constitution du Canada adoptées dans ces deux langues ont également force de loi. En outre, ont également force de loi, dès l'adoption, dans le cadre de l'article 55, d'une partie de la version française de la Constitution, cette partie et la version anglaise correspondante.

English and French versions of this Act

57. The English and French versions of this Act are equally authoritative.

Versions française et anglaise de la présente loi

57. Les versions française et anglaise de la présente loi ont également force de loi.

---

(103) Section 54.1, which was added by the *Constitution Amendment Proclamation, 1983* (see SI/84-102), provided for the repeal of Part IV.1 and section 54.1 on April 18, 1987.

Section 54.1, as originally enacted, read as follows:

54.1 Part IV.1 and this section are repealed on April 18, 1987.

Commencement

58. Subject to section 59, this Act shall come into force on a day to be fixed by proclamation issued by the Queen or the Governor General under the Great Seal of Canada.(104)

Entrée en vigueur

58. Sous réserve de l'article 59, la présente loi entre en vigueur à la date fixée par proclamation de la Reine ou du gouverneur général sous le grand sceau du Canada.

Commencement of paragraph 23(1)(*a*) in respect of Quebec

59. (1) Paragraph 23(1)(*a*) shall come into force in respect of Quebec on a day to be fixed by proclamation issued by the Queen or the Governor General under the Great Seal of Canada.

Entrée en vigueur de l'alinéa 23(1)*a*) pour le Québec

59. (1) L'alinéa 23(1)*a*) entre en vigueur pour le Québec à la date fixée par proclamation de la Reine ou du gouverneur général sous le grand sceau du Canada.

Authorization of Quebec

(2) A proclamation under subsection (1) shall be issued only where authorized by the legislative assembly or government of Quebec.(105)

Autorisation du Québec

(2) La proclamation visée au paragraphe (1) ne peut être prise qu'après autorisation de l'assemblée législative ou du gouvernement du Québec.

Repeal of this section

(3) This section may be repealed on the day paragraph 23(1)(*a*) comes into force in respect of Quebec and this Act amended and renumbered, consequentially upon the repeal of this section, by proclamation issued by the Queen or the Governor General under the Great Seal of Canada.

Abrogation du présent article

(3) Le présent article peut être abrogé à la date d'entrée en vigueur de l'alinéa 23(1)*a*) pour le Québec, et la présente loi faire l'object, dés cette abrogation, des modifications et changements de numérotation qui en découlent, par proclamation de la Reine ou du gouverneur général sous le grand sceau du Canada.

Short title and citations

60. This Act may be cited as the Constitution Act, 1982, and the Constitution Acts 1867 to 1975 (No. 2) and this Act may be cited together as the Constitution Acts, 1867 to 1982.

Titres

60. Titre abrégé de la présente loi : *Loi constitutionnelle de 1982*; titre commun des lois constitutionnelles de 1867 à 1975 (no 2) et de la présente loi : *Lois constitutionnelles de 1867 à 1982*.

(104) The Act, with the exception of paragraph 23(1)(*a*) in respect of Quebec, came into force on April 17, 1982 by proclamation issued by the Queen. *See* SI/82-97.

(105) No proclamation has been issued under section 59.

References

61. A reference to the "*Constitution Acts, 1867 to 1982*" shall be deemed to include a reference to the "*Constitution Amendment Proclamation, 1983*".(106)

Mentions

61. Toute mention des «*Lois constitutionnelles de 1867 à 1982*» est réputée constituer également une mention de la «*Proclamation de 1983 modifiant la Constitution*».

(106) Section 61 was added by the *Constitution Amendment Proclamation, 1983. See* SI/84-102. See also section 3 of the *Constitution Act, 1985 (Representation)*, S.C. 1986, c. 8, Part I and the *Constitution Amendment, 1987 (Newfoundland Act)* SI/88-11.

APPENDIX III

SCHEDULE

to the

Constitution Act, 1982

Modernization of the Constitution

Item	Column I Act Affected	Column II Amendment	Column III New Name
1.	British North America Act, 1867, 30-31 Vict., c. 3 (U.K.)	(1) Section 1 is repealed and the following substituted therefor: "1. This Act may be cited as the *Constitution Act. 1867*." (2) Section 20 is repealed. (3) Class 1 of section 91 is repealed. (4) Class 1 of section 92 is repealed.	Constitution Act, 1867
2.	An Act to amend and continue the Act 32-33 Victoria chapter 3; and to establish and provide for the Government of the Province of Manitoba, 1870, 33 Vict., c. 3 (Can.)	(1) The long title is repealed and the following substituted therefor: "*Manitoba Act, 1870*." (2) Section 20 is repealed.	Manitoba Act, 1870
3.	Order of Her Majesty in Council admitting Rupert's Land and the North-Western Territory into the union, dated the 23rd day of June, 1870		Rupert's Land and North-Western Territory Order
4.	Order of Her Majesty in Council admitting British Columbia into the Union, dated the 16th day of May, 1871		British Columbia Terms of Union

SCHEDULE

to the

Constitution Act, 1982 – *Continued*

Item	Column I Act Affected	Column II Amendment	Column III New Name
5.	British North America Act, 1871, 34-35 Vict., c. 28 (U.K.)	Section 1 is repealed and the following substituted therefor: "1. This Act may be cited as the *Constitution Act, 1871.*"	Constitution Act, 1871
6.	Order of Her Majesty in Council admitting Prince Edward Island into the Union, dated the 26th day of June, 1873		Prince Edward Island Terms of Union
7.	Parliament of Canada Act, 1875, 38-39 Vict., c. 38 (U.K.)		Parliament of Canada Act, 1875
8.	Order of Her Majesty in Council admitting all British possessions and Territories in North America and islands adjacent thereto into the Union, dated the 31st day of July, 1880		Adjacent Territories Order
9.	British North America Act, 1886, 49-50 Vict., c. 35 (U.K.)	Section 3 is repealed and the following substituted therefor: "3. This Act may be cited as the *Constitution Act, 1886.*"	Constitution Act, 1886
10.	Canada (Ontario Boundary) Act, 1889, 52-53 Vict., c. 28 (U.K.)		Canada (Ontario Boundary) Act, 1889

SCHEDULE

to the

Constitution Act, 1982 – *Continued*

Item	Column I Act Affected	Column II Amendment	Column III New Name
11.	Canadian Speaker (Appointment of Deputy) Act, 1895, 2nd Sess., 59 Vict., c. 3 (U.K.)	The Act is repealed.	
12.	The Alberta Act, 1905, 4-5 Edw. VII, c. 3 (Can.)		Alberta Act
13.	The Saskatchewan Act, 1905, 4-5 Edw. VII, c. 42 (Can.)		Saskatchewan Act
14.	British North America Act, 1907, 7 Edw. VII, c. 11 (U.K.)	Section 2 is repealed and the following substituted therefor: "2. This Act may be cited as the *Constitution Act, 1907*."	Constitution Act, 1907
15.	British North America Act, 1915, 5-6 Geo. V, c. 45 (U.K.)	Section 3 is repealed and the following substituted therefor: "3. This Act may be cited as the *Constitution Act, 1915*.	Constitution Act, 1915
16.	British North America Act, 1930, 20-21 Geo. V, c. 26 (U.K.)	Section 3 is repealed and the following substituted therefor: "3. This Act may be cited as the *Constitution Act, 1930*."	Constitution Act, 1930

SCHEDULE

to the

Constitution Act, 1982 – *Continued*

Item	Column I Act Affected	Column II Amendment	Column III New Name
17.	Statute of Westminster, 1931, 22 Geo. V, c. 4 (U.K.)	In so far as they apply to Canada, (*a*) section 4 is repealed; and (*b*) subsection 7(1) is repealed.	Statute of Westminster, 1931
18.	British North America Act, 1940, 3-4 Geo. VI, c. 36 (U.K.)	Section 2 is repealed and the following substituted therefor: "2. This Act may be cited as the *Constitution Act, 1940*."	Constitution Act, 1940
19.	British North America Act, 1943, 6-7 Geo. VI, c. 30 (U.K.)	The Act is repealed.	
20.	British North America Act, 1946, 9-10 Geo. VI, c. 63 (U.K.)	The Act is repealed.	
21.	British North America Act, 1949, 12-13 Geo. VI, c. 22 (U.K.)	Section 3 is repealed and the following substituted therefor: "3. This Act may be cited as the *Newfoundland Act*."	Newfoundland Act
22.	British North America (No. 2) Act, 1949, 13 Geo. VI, c. 81 (U.K.)	The Act is repealed.	
23.	British North America Act, 1951, 14-15 Geo. VI, c. 32 (U.K.)	The Act is repealed.	

SCHEDULE

to the

Constitution Act, 1982 – *Continued*

Item	Column I Act Affected	Column II Amendment	Column III New Name
24.	British North America Act, 1952, 1 Eliz. II, c. 15 (Can.)	The Act is repealed.	
25.	British North America Act, 1960, 9 Eliz. II, c. 2 (U.K.)	Section 2 is repealed and the following substituted therefor: "2. This Act may be cited as the *Constitution Act, 1960*."	Constitution Act, 1960
26.	British North America Act, 1964, 12-13 Eliz. II, c. 73 (U.K.)	Section 2 is repealed and the following substituted therefor: "2. This Act may be cited as the *Constitution Act*, 1964."	Constitution Act, 1964
27.	British North America Act, 1965, 14 Eliz. II, c. 4, Part I (Can.)	Section 2 is repealed and the following substituted therefor: "2. This Part may be cited as the *Constitution Act, 1965*."	Constitution Act, 1965
28.	British North America Act, 1974, 23 Eliz. II, c. 13, Part I (Can.)	Section 3, as amended by 25-26 Eliz. II, c. 28, s. 38(1) (Can.), is repealed and the following substituted therefor: "3. This Part may be cited as the *Constitution Act, 1974*."	Constitution Act, 1974

SCHEDULE

to the

Constitution Act, 1982 – *Concluded*

Item	Column I Act Affected	Column II Amendment	Column III New Name
29.	British North America Act, 1975, 23-24 Eliz. II, c. 28, Part I (Can.)	Section 3, as amended by 25-26 Eliz. II, c. 28, s. 31 (Can.), is repealed and the following substituted therefor: "3. This Part may be cited as the *Constitution Act (No. 1), 1975.*"	Constitution Act (No. 1), 1975
30.	British North America Act (No. 2), 1975, 23-24 Eliz. II, c. 53 (Can.)	Section 3 is repealed and the following substituted therefor: "3. This Act may be cited as the *Constitution Act (No. 2), 1975.*"	Constitution Act (No. 2), 1975

APPENDIX IV

Canadian Bill of Rights

S.C. 1960, c. 44

The Parliament of Canada, affirming that the Canadian Nation is founded upon principles that acknowledge the supremacy of God, the dignity and worth of the human person and the position of the family in a society of free men and free institutions;

Affirming also that men and institutions remain free only when freedom is founded upon respect for moral and spiritual values and the rule of law;

And being desirous of enshrining these principles and the human rights and fundamental freedoms derived from them, in a Bill of Rights which shall reflect the respect of Parliament for its constitutional authority and which shall ensure the protection of these rights and freedoms in Canada:

THEREFORE Her Majesty, by and with the advice and consent of the Senate and House of Commons of Canada, enacts as follows:

PART I

BILL OF RIGHTS

1. It is hereby recognized and declared that in Canada there have existed and shall continue to exist without discrimination by reason of race, national origin, colour, religion or sex, the following human rights and fundamental freedoms, namely,

(a) the right of the individual to life, liberty, security of the person and enjoyment of property, and the right not to be deprived thereof except by due process of law;
(b) the right of the individual to equality before the law and the protection of the law;
(c) freedom of religion;
(d) freedom of speech;
(e) freedom of assembly and association; and
(f) freedom of the press.

2. Every law of Canada shall, unless it is expressly declared by an Act of the Parliament of Canada that it shall operate notwithstanding the Canadian Bill of Rights, be so construed and applied as not to abrogate, abridge or infringe or to authorize the abrogation, abridgment or infringement of any of the rights or freedoms herein recognized and declared, and in particular, no law of Canada shall be construed or applied so as to

(a) authorize or effect the arbitrary detention, imprisonment or exile of any person;

(b) impose or authorize the imposition of cruel and unusual treatment or punishment;

(c) deprive a person who has been arrested or detained

(i) of the right to be informed promptly of the reason for his arrest or detention,

(ii) of the right to retain and instruct counsel without delay, or

(iii) of the remedy by way of *habeas corpus* for the determination of the validity of his detention and for his release if the detention is not lawful;

(d) authorize a court, tribunal, commission, board or other authority to compel a person to give evidence if he is denied counsel, protection against self crimination or other constitutional safeguards;

(e) deprive a person of the right to a fair hearing in accordance with the principles of fundamental justice for the determination of his rights and obligations;

(f) deprive a person charged with a criminal offence of the right to be presumed innocent until proved guilty according to law in a fair and public hearing by an independent and impartial tribunal, or of the right to reasonable bail without just cause; or

(g) deprive a person of the right to the assistance of an interpreter in any proceedings in which he is involved or in which he is a party or a witness, before a court, commission, board or other tribunal, if he does not understand or speak the language in which such proceedings are conducted.

3. (1) Subject to subsection (2), the Minister of Justice shall, in accordance with such regulations as may be prescribed by the Governor in Council, examine every regulation transmitted to the Clerk of the Privy Council for registration pursuant to the *Statutory Instruments Act* and every Bill introduced in or presented to the House of Commons by a Minister of the Crown, in order to ascertain whether any of the provisions thereof are inconsistent with the purposes and provisions of this Part and he shall report any such inconsistency to the House of Commons at the first convenient opportunity.

(2) A regulation need not be examined in accordance with subsection (1) if prior to being made it was examined as a proposed regulation in accordance with section 3 of the *Statutory Instruments Act* to ensure that it was not inconsistent with the purposes and provisions of this Part.(1)

4. The provisions of this Part shall be known as the *Canadian Bill of Rights.*

---

(1) Section 3 was repealed and replaced by S.C. 1985, c. 26, s. 105.

PART II

5. (1) Nothing in Part I shall be construed to abrogate or abridge any human right or fundamental freedom not enumerated therein that may have existed in Canada at the commencement of this Act.

(2) The expression "law of Canada" in Part I means an Act of the Parliament of Canada enacted before or after the coming into force of this Act, any order, rule or regulation thereunder, and any law in force in Canada or in any part of Canada at the commencement of this Act that is subject to be repealed, abolished or altered by the Parliament of Canada.

(3) The provisions of Part I shall be construed as extending only to matters coming within the legislative authority of the Parliament of Canada.

APPENDIX V

American Bill of Rights

AMENDMENTS TO THE CONSTITUTION OF THE UNITED STATES

First Ten Amendments passed by Congress September 25, 1789.
Ratified by three-fourths of the States December 15, 1791.

ARTICLE I

Congress shall make no law respecting an establishment of religion, or prohibiting the free exercise thereof; or abridging the freedom of speech, or of the press; or the right of the people peaceably to assemble, and to petition the government for a redress of grievances.

ARTICLE II

A well regulated militia, being necessary to the security of a free State, the right of the people to keep and bear arms, shall not be infringed.

ARTICLE III

No soldier shall, in time of peace be quartered in any house, without the consent of the owner, nor in time of war, but in a manner to be prescribed by law.

ARTICLE IV

The right of the people to be secure in their persons, houses, papers, and effects, against unreasonable searches and seizures, shall not be violated, and no warrants shall issue, but upon probable cause, supported by oath or affirmation, and particularly describing the place to be searched, and the persons or things to be seized.

ARTICLE V

No person shall be held to answer for a capital, or otherwise infamous crime, unless on a presentment or indictment of a grand jury, except in cases arising in the land or naval forces, or in the militia, when in actual service in time of war or public danger; nor shall any person be subject for the same offense to be twice put in jeopardy of life or limb; nor shall be compelled in any criminal case to be a witness against himself, nor be deprived of life, liberty, or property, without due process of law; nor shall private property be taken for public use without just compensation.

ARTICLE VI

In all criminal prosecutions, the accused shall enjoy the right to a speedy and public trial, by an impartial jury of the State and district wherein the crime shall have been committed, which district shall have been previously ascertained by law, and to be informed of the nature and cause of the accusation; to be confronted with the witnesses against him; to have compulsory process for obtaining witnesses in his favor, and to have the assistance of counsel for his defense.

ARTICLE VII

In suits at common law, where the value in controversy shall exceed twenty dollars, the right of trial by jury shall be preserved, and no fact tried by a jury shall be otherwise reexamined in any court of the United States, than according to the rules of the common law.

ARTICLE VIII

Excessive bail shall not be required, nor excessive fines imposed, nor cruel and unusual punishments inflicted.

ARTICLE IX

The enumeration in the Constitution of certain rights shall not be construed to deny or disparage others retained by the people.

ARTICLE X

The powers not delegated to the United States by the Constitution, nor prohibited by it to the States, are reserved to the States respectively, or to the people.

ARTICLE XIII

Passed by Congress January 31, 1865. Ratified December 6, 1865.

SECTION 1. Neither slavery nor involuntary servitude, except as punishment for crime whereof the party shall have been duly convicted, shall exist within the United States, or any place subject to their jurisdiction.

SECTION 2. Congress shall have power to enforce this article by appropriate legislation.

ARTICLE XIV

Passed by Congress June 13, 1866. Ratified July 9, 1868.

SECTION 1. All persons born or naturalized in the United States, and subject to the jurisdiction thereof, are citizens of the United States and of the State wherein they reside. No State shall make or enforce any law which shall abridge the privileges or immunities of citizens of the United States; nor shall any State deprive any person of life, liberty, or property, without due process of law; nor deny to any person within its jurisdiction the equal protection of the laws. . . .

SECTION 5. The Congress shall have power to enforce, by appropriate legislation, the provisions of this article.

ARTICLE XV

Passed by Congress February 26, 1869. Ratified February 3, 1870.

SECTION 1. The right of citizens of the United States to vote shall not be denied or abridged by the United States or by any State on account of race, color, or previous condition of servitude.

SECTION 2. The Congress shall have power to enforce this article by appropriate legislation.

ARTICLE XIX

Passed by Congress June 4, 1919. Ratified August 18, 1920.

The right of citizens of the United States to vote shall not be denied or abridged by the United States or by any State on account of sex.

The Congress shall have power by appropriate legislation to enforce the provisions of this article.

ARTICLE XXIV

Passed by Congress August 27, 1962. Ratified January 23, 1964.

SECTION 1. The right of citizens of the United States to vote in any primary or other election for President or Vice President, for electors for President or Vice President, or for Senator or Representative in Congress, shall not be denied or abridged by the United States or any State by reason of failure to pay any poll tax or other tax.

SECTION 2. The Congress shall have the power to enforce this article by appropriate legislation.

ARTICLE XXVI

Passed by Congress March 23, 1971. Ratified June 30, 1971.

SECTION 1. The right of citizens of the United States, who are eighteen years of age or older, to vote shall not be denied or abridged by the United States or any State on account of age.

SECTION 2. The Congress shall have the power to enforce this article by appropriate legislation.

they reside. No State shall make or enforce any law which shall abridge the privileges or immunities of citizens of the United States; nor shall any State deprive any person of life, liberty, or property, without due process of law; nor deny to any person within its jurisdiction the equal protection of the laws.

SECTION 5. The Congress shall have power to enforce, by appropriate legislation, the provisions of this article.

ARTICLE XV

Passed by Congress February 26, 1869. Ratified February 3, 1870.

SECTION 1. The right of citizens of the United States to vote shall not be denied or abridged by the United States or by any State on account of race, color, or previous condition of servitude.

SECTION 2. The Congress shall have power to enforce this article by appropriate legislation.

ARTICLE XIX

Passed by Congress June 4, 1919. Ratified August 18, 1920.

The right of citizens of the United States to vote shall not be denied or abridged by the United States or by any State on account of sex.

The Congress shall have power by appropriate legislation to enforce the provisions of this article.

ARTICLE XXIV

Passed by Congress August 27, 1962. Ratified January 23, 1964.

SECTION 1. The right of citizens of the United States to vote in any primary or other election for President or Vice President, for electors for President or Vice President, or for Senator or Representative in Congress, shall not be denied or abridged by the United States or any State by reason of failure to pay any poll tax or other tax.

SECTION 2. The Congress shall have the power to enforce this article by appropriate legislation.

ARTICLE XXVI

Passed by Congress March 23, 1971. Ratified June 30, 1971.

SECTION 1. The right of citizens of the United States, who are eighteen years of age or older, to vote shall not be denied or abridged by the United States or any State on account of age.

SECTION 2. The Congress shall have the power to enforce this article by appropriate legislation.

APPENDIX VI

International Covenant on Civil and Political Rights

THE STATES PARTIES TO THE PRESENT COVENANT,

Considering that, in accordance with the principles proclaimed in the Charter of the United Nations, recognition of the inherent dignity and of the equal and inalienable rights of all members of the human family is the foundation of freedom, justice and peace in the world,

Recognizing that these rights derive from the inherent dignity of the human person,

Recognizing that, in accordance with the Universal Declaration of Human Rights, the ideal of free human beings enjoying civil and political freedom and freedom from fear and want can only be achieved if conditions are created whereby everyone may enjoy his civil and political rights, as well as his economic, social and cultural rights,

Considering the obligations of States under the Charter of the United Nations to promote universal respect for, and observance of, human rights and freedoms,

Realizing that the individual, having duties to other individuals and to the community to which he belongs, is under a responsibility to strive for the promotion and observance of the rights recognized in the present Covenant,

Agree upon the following articles:

PART I

Article 1

1. All peoples have the right of self-determination. By virtue of that right they freely determine their political status and freely pursue their economic, social and cultural development.
2. All peoples may, for their own ends, freely dispose of their natural wealth and resources without prejudice to any obligations arising out of international economic co-operation, based upon the principle of mutual benefit, and international law. In no case may a people be deprived of its own means of subsistence.
3. The States Parties to the present Covenant, including those having responsibility for the administration of Non-Self-Governing and Trust Territories, shall promote the realization of the right of self-determination, and shall respect that right, in conformity with the provisions of the Charter of the United Nations.

PART II

Article 2

1. Each State Party to the present Covenant undertakes to respect and to ensure to all individuals within its territory and subject to its jurisdiction the rights

recognized in the present Covenant, without distinction of any kind, such as race, colour, sex, language, religion, political or other opinion, national or social origin, property, birth or other status.

2. Where not already provided for by existing legislative or other measures, each State Party to the present Covenant undertakes to take the necessary steps, in accordance with its constitutional processes and with the provisions of the present Covenant, to adopt such legislative or other measures as may be necessary to give effect to the rights recognized in the present Covenant.

3. Each State Party to the present Covenant undertakes:

(*a*) To ensure that any person whose rights or freedoms as herein recognized are violated shall have an effective remedy, notwithstanding that the violation has been committed by persons acting in an official capacity;

(*b*) To ensure that any person claiming such a remedy shall have his right thereto determined by competent judicial, administrative or legislative authorities, or by any other competent authority provided for by the legal system of the State, and to develop the possibilities of judicial remedy;

(*c*) To ensure that the competent authorities shall enforce such remedies when granted.

Article 3

The States Parties to the present Covenant undertake to ensure the equal right of men and women to the enjoyment of all civil and political rights set forth in the present Covenant.

Article 4

1. In time of public emergency which threatens the life of the nation and the existence of which is officially proclaimed, the States Parties to the present Covenant may take measures derogating from their obligations under the present Covenant to the extent strictly required by the exigencies of the situation, provided that such measures are not inconsistent with their other obligations under international law and do not involve discrimination solely on the ground of race, colour, sex, language, religion or social origin.

2. No derogation from articles 6, 7, 8 (paragraphs 1 and 2), 11, 15, 16 and 18 may be made under this provision.

3. Any State Party to the present Covenant availing itself of the right of derogation shall immediately inform the other States Parties to the present Covenant, through the intermediary of the Secretary-General of the United Nations, of the provisions from which it has derogated and of the reasons by which it was actuated. A further communication shall be made, through the same intermediary, on the date on which it terminates such derogation.

Article 5

1. Nothing in the present Covenant may be interpreted as implying for any State, group or person any right to engage in any activity or perform any act aimed at

the destruction of any of the rights and freedoms recognized herein or at their limitation to a greater extent than is provided for in the present Covenant.
2. There shall be no restriction upon or derogation from any of the fundamental human rights recognized or existing in any State Party to the present Covenant pursuant to law, conventions, regulations or custom on the pretext that the present Covenant does not recognize such rights or that it recognizes them to a lesser extent.

PART III

Article 6

1. Every human being has the inherent right to life. This right shall be protected by law. No one shall be arbitrarily deprived of his life.
2. In countries which have not abolished the death penalty, sentence of death may be imposed only for the most serious crimes in accordance with the law in force at the time of the commission of the crime and not contrary to the provisions of the present Covenant and to the Convention on the Prevention and Punishment of the Crime of Genocide. This penalty can only be carried out pursuant to a final judgement rendered by a competent court.
3. When deprivation of life constitutes the crime of genocide, it is understood that nothing in this article shall authorize any State Party to the present Covenant to derogate in any way from any obligation assumed under the provisions of the Convention on the Prevention and Punishment of the Crime of Genocide.
4. Anyone sentenced to death shall have the right to seek pardon or commutation of the sentence. Amnesty, pardon or commutation of the sentence of death may be granted in all cases.
5. Sentence of death shall not be imposed for crimes committed by persons below eighteen years of age and shall not be carried out on pregnant women.
6. Nothing in this article shall be invoked to delay or to prevent the abolition of capital punishment by any State Party to the present Covenant.

Article 7

No one shall be subjected to torture or to cruel, inhuman or degrading treatment or punishment. In particular, no one shall be subjected without his free consent to medical or scientific experimentation.

Article 8

1. No one shall be held in slavery; slavery and the slave-trade in all their forms shall be prohibited.
2. No one shall be held in servitude.
3. (*a*) No one shall be required to perform forced or compulsory labour;
   (*b*) Paragraph 3(*a*) shall not be held to preclude, in countries where imprisonment with hard labour may be imposed as a punishment for a crime, the perform-

ance of hard labour in pursuance of a sentence to such punishment by a competent court;

(*c*) For the purpose of this paragraph the term "forced or compulsory labour" shall not include:

(i) Any work or service, not referred to in sub-paragraph (*b*), normally required of a person who is under detention in consequence of a lawful order of a court, or of a person during conditional release from such detention;

(ii) Any service of a military character and, in countries where conscientious objection is recognized, any national service required by law of conscientious objectors;

(iii) Any service exacted in cases of emergency or calamity threatening the life or well-being of the community;

(iv) Any work or service which forms part of normal civil obligations.

Article 9

1. Everyone has the right to liberty and security of person. No one shall be subjected to arbitrary arrest or detention. No one shall be deprived of his liberty except on such grounds and in accordance with such procedure as are established by law.

2. Anyone who is arrested shall be informed, at the time of arrest, of the reasons for his arrest and shall be promptly informed of any charges against him.

3. Anyone arrested or detained on a criminal charge shall be brought promptly before a judge or other officer authorized by law to exercise judicial power and shall be entitled to trial within a reasonable time or to release. It shall not be the general rule that persons awaiting trial shall be detained in custody, but release may be subject to guarantees to appear for trial, at any other stage of the judicial proceedings, and, should occasion arise, for execution of the judgement.

4. Anyone who is deprived of his liberty by arrest or detention shall be entitled to take proceedings before a court, in order that that court may decide without delay on the lawfulness of his detention and order his release if the detention is not lawful.

5. Anyone who has been the victim of unlawful arrest or detention shall have an enforceable right to compensation.

Article 10

1. All persons deprived of their liberty shall be treated with humanity and with respect for the inherent dignity of the human person.

2. (*a*) Accused persons shall, save in exceptional circumstances, be segregated from convicted persons and shall be subject to separate treatment appropriate to their status as unconvicted persons;

(*b*) Accused juvenile persons shall be separated from adults and brought as speedily as possible for adjudication.

3. The penitentiary system shall comprise treatment of prisoners the essential aim of which shall be their reformation and social rehabilitation. Juvenile offenders shall be segregated from adults and be accorded treatment appropriate to their age and legal status.

Article 11

No one shall be imprisoned merely on the ground of inability to fulfil a contractual obligation.

Article 12

1. Everyone lawfully within the territory of a State shall, within that territory, have the right to liberty of movement and freedom to choose his residence.
2. Everyone shall be free to leave any country, including his own.
3. The above-mentioned rights shall not be subject to any restrictions except those which are provided by law, are necessary to protect national security, public order (*ordre public*), public health or morals or the rights and freedoms of others, and are consistent with the other rights recognized in the present Covenant.
4. No one shall be arbitrarily deprived of the right to enter his own country.

Article 13

An alien lawfully in the territory of a State Party to the present Covenant may be expelled therefrom only in pursuance of a decision reached in accordance with law and shall, except where compelling reasons of national security otherwise require, be allowed to submit the reasons against his expulsion and to have his case reviewed by, and be represented for the purpose before, the competent authority or a person or persons especially designated by the competent authority.

Article 14

1. All persons shall be equal before the courts and tribunals. In the determination of any criminal charge against him, or of his rights and obligations in a suit at law, everyone shall be entitled to a fair and public hearing by a competent, independent and impartial tribunal established by law. The Press and the public may be excluded from all or part of a trial for reasons of morals, public order (*ordre public*) or national security in a democratic society, or when the interest of the private lives of the parties so requires, or to the extent strictly necessary in the opinion of the court in special circumstances where publicity would prejudice the interests of justice; but any judgement rendered in a criminal case or in a suit at law shall be made public except where the interest of juvenile persons otherwise requires or the proceedings concern matrimonial disputes or the guardianship of children.
2. Everyone charged with a criminal offence shall have the right to be presumed innocent until proved guilty according to law.

3. In the determination of any criminal charge against him, everyone shall be entitled to the following minimum guarantees, in full equality:

(*a*) To be informed promptly and in detail in a language which he understands of the nature and cause of the charge against him;

(*b*) To have adequate time and facilities for the preparation of his defence and to communicate with counsel of his own choosing;

(*c*) To be tried without undue delay;

(*d*) To be tried in his presence, and to defend himself in person or through legal assistance of his own choosing; to be informed, if he does not have legal assistance, of this right; and to have legal assistance assigned to him, in any case where the interests of justice so require, and without payment by him in any such case if he does not have sufficient means to pay for it;

(*e*) To examine, or have examined, the witnesses against him and to obtain the attendance and examination of witnesses on his behalf under the same conditions as witnesses against him;

(*f*) To have the free assistance of an interpreter if he cannot understand or speak the language used in court;

(*g*) Not to be compelled to testify against himself or to confess guilt.

4. In the case of juvenile persons, the procedure shall be such as will take account of their age and the desirability of promoting their rehabilitation.

5. Everyone convicted of a crime shall have the right to his conviction and sentence being reviewed by a higher tribunal according to law.

6. When a person has by a final decision been convicted of a criminal offence and when subsequently his conviction has been reversed or he has been pardoned on the ground that a new or newly discovered fact shows conclusively that there has been a miscarriage of justice, the person who has suffered punishment as a result of such conviction shall be compensated according to law, unless it is proved that the non-disclosure of the unknown fact in time is wholly or partly attributable to him.

7. No one shall be liable to be tried or punished again for an offence for which he has already been finally convicted or acquitted in accordance with the law and penal procedure of each country.

Article 15

1. No one shall be held guilty of any criminal offence on account of any act or omission which did not constitute a criminal offence, under national or international law, at the time when it was committed. Nor shall a heavier penalty be imposed than the one that was applicable at the time when the criminal offence was committed. If, subsequent to the commission of the offence, provision is made by law for the imposition of a lighter penalty, the offender shall benefit thereby.

2. Nothing in this article shall prejudice the trial and punishment of any person for any act or omission which, at the time when it was committed, was criminal according to the general principles of law recognized by the community of nations.

Article 16

Everyone shall have the right to recognition everywhere as a person before the law.

Article 17

1. No one shall be subjected to arbitrary or unlawful interference with his privacy, family, home or correspondence, nor to unlawful attacks on his honour and reputation.
2. Everyone has the right to the protection of the law against such interference or attacks.

Article 18

1. Everyone shall have the right to freedom of thought, conscience and religion. This right shall include freedom to have or to adopt a religion or belief of his choice, and freedom, either individually or in community with others and in public or private, to manifest his religion or belief in worship, observance, practice and teaching.
2. No one shall be subject to coercion which would impair his freedom to have or to adopt a religion or belief of his choice.
3. Freedom to manifest one's religion or beliefs may be subject only to such limitations as are prescribed by law and are necessary to protect public safety, order, health, or morals or the fundamental rights and freedoms of others.
4. The States Parties to the present Covenant undertake to have respect for the liberty of parents and, when applicable, legal guardians to ensure the religious and moral education of their children in conformity with their own convictions.

Article 19

1. Everyone shall have the right to hold opinions without interference.
2. Everyone shall have the right to freedom of expression; this right shall include freedom to seek, receive and impart information and ideas of all kinds, regardless of frontiers, either orally, in writing or in print, in the form of art, or through any other media of his choice.
3. The exercise of the rights provided for in paragraph 2 of this article carries with it special duties and responsibilities. It may therefore be subject to certain restrictions, but these shall only be such as are provided by law and are necessary:

(*a*) For respect of the rights or reputations of others;

(*b*) For the protection of national security or of public order (*ordre public*), or of public health or morals.

Article 20

1. Any propaganda for war shall be prohibited by law.
2. Any advocacy of national, racial or religious hatred that constitutes incitement to discrimination, hostility or violence shall be prohibited by law.

Article 21

The right of peaceful assembly shall be recognized. No restrictions may be placed on the exercise of this right other than those imposed in conformity with the law and which are necessary in a democratic society in the interests of national security or public safety, public order (*ordre public*), the protection of public health or morals or the protection of the rights and freedoms of others.

Article 22

1. Everyone shall have the right to freedom of association with others, including the right to form and join trade unions for the protection of his interests.
2. No restrictions may be placed on the exercise of this right other than those which are prescribed by law and which are necessary in a democratic society in the interests of national security or public safety, public order (*ordre public*), the protection of public health or morals or the protection of the rights and freedoms of others. This article shall not prevent the imposition of lawful restrictions on members of the armed forces and of the police in their exercise of this right.
3. Nothing in this article shall authorize States Parties to the International Labour Organisation Convention of 1948 concerning Freedom of Association and Protection of the Right to Organize to take legislative measures which would prejudice, or to apply the law in such a manner as to prejudice, the guarantees provided for in that Convention.

Article 23

1. The family is the natural and fundamental group unit of society and is entitled to protection by society and the State.
2. The right of men and women of marriageable age to marry and to found a family shall be recognized.
3. No marriage shall be entered into without the free and full consent of the intending spouses.
4. States Parties to the present Covenant shall take appropriate steps to ensure equality of rights and responsibilities of spouses as to marriage, during marriage and at its dissolution. In the case of dissolution, provision shall be made for the necessary protection of any children.

Article 24

1. Every child shall have, without any discrimination as to race, colour, sex, language, religion, national or social origin, property or birth, the right to such measures of protection as are required by his status as a minor, on the part of his family, society and the State.
2. Every child shall be registered immediately after birth and shall have a name.
3. Every child has the right to acquire a nationality.

Article 25

Every citizen shall have the right and the opportunity, without any of the distinctions mentioned in article 2 and without unreasonable restrictions:

(*a*) To take part in the conduct of public affairs, directly or through freely chosen representatives;

(*b*) To vote and to be elected at genuine periodic elections which shall be by universal and equal suffrage and shall be held by secret ballot, guaranteeing the free expression of the will of the electors;

(*c*) To have access, on general terms of equality, to public service in his country.

Article 26

All persons are equal before the law and are entitled without any discrimination to the equal protection of the law. In this respect, the law shall prohibit any discrimination and guarantee to all persons equal and effective protection against discrimination on any ground such as race, colour, sex, language, religion, political or other opinion, national or social origin, property, birth or other status.

Article 27

In those States in which ethnic, religious or linguistic minorities exist, persons belonging to such minorities shall not be denied the right, in community with the other members of their group, to enjoy their own culture, to profess and practise their own religion, or to use their own language.

PART IV

Article 28

1. There shall be established a Human Rights Committee (hereafter referred to in the present Covenant as the Committee). It shall consist of eighteen members and shall carry out the functions hereinafter provided.
2. The Committee shall be composed of nationals of the States Parties to the present Covenant who shall be persons of high moral character and recognized competence in the field of human rights, consideration being given to the usefulness of the participation of some persons having legal experience.
3. The members of the Committee shall be elected and shall serve in their personal capacity. . . .

APPENDIX VII

Optional Protocol to International Covenant on Civil and Political Rights

THE STATES PARTIES TO THE PRESENT PROTOCOL,

Considering that in order further to achieve the purposes of the Covenant on Civil and Political Rights (hereinafter referred to as the Covenant) and the implementation of its provisions it would be appropriate to enable the Human Rights Committee set up in part IV of the Covenant (hereinafter referred to as the Committee) to receive and consider, as provided in the present Protocol, communications from individuals claiming to be victims of violations of any of the rights set forth in the Covenant,

Have agreed as follows:

Article 1

A State Party to the Covenant that becomes a party to the present Protocol recognizes the competence of the Committee to receive and consider communications from individuals subject to its jurisdiction who claim to be victims of a violation by that State Party of any of the rights set forth in the Covenant. No communication shall be received by the Committee if it concerns a State Party to the Covenant which is not a party to the present Protocol.

Article 2

Subject to the provisions of article 1, individuals who claim that any of their rights enumerated in the Covenant have been violated and who have exhausted all available domestic remedies may submit a written communication to the Committee for consideration.

Article 3

The Committee shall consider inadmissible any communication under the present Protocol which is anonymous, or which it considers to be an abuse of the rights of submission of such communications or to be incompatible with the provisions of the Covenant.

Article 4

1. Subject to the provisions of article 3, the Committee shall bring any communications submitted to it under the present Protocol to the attention of the State Party to the present Protocol alleged to be violating any provisions of the Covenant.

2. Within six months, the receiving State shall submit to the Committee written explanations or statements clarifying the matter and the remedy, if any, that may have been taken by that State.

Article 5

1. The Committee shall consider communications received under the present Protocol in the light of all written information made available to it by the individual and by the State Party concerned.
2. The Committee shall not consider any communication from an individual unless it has ascertained that:

(*a*) The same matter is not being examined under another procedure of international investigation or settlement;

(*b*) The individual has exhausted all available domestic remedies. This shall not be the rule where the application of the remedies is unreasonably prolonged.
3. The Committee shall hold closed meetings when examining communications under the present Protocol.
4. The Committee shall forward its views to the State Party concerned and to the individual. . . .

Bibliography

This bibliography lists only books with substantial direct relevance to Canadian constitutional law. It accordingly includes few English, Australian or American books, despite their occasional citation in the text. Even within its narrow scope, the bibliography makes no claim to completeness.

Abel A.S., Towards a Constitutional Charter for Canada (U. Toronto, Toronto, 1982)

Advisory Commission on Intergovernmental Relations, In Search of Balance — Canada's Intergovernmental Experience (U.S. Government Printing Office, 1971)

Anisman P. and Linden A.M. (eds.), The Media, the Courts and the Charter (Carswell, Toronto, 1986)

Ashley C.A. and Smails R.G.H., Canadian Crown Corporations (Macmillan of Canada, Toronto, 1965)

Atrens J., The Charter and Criminal Procedure (Butterworths, Toronto, 1989)

Banting K.G. and Simeon R.E.B. (eds.), And No One Cheered (Methuen, Agincourt, Ont., 1983)

Bastarache M. (ed.), Language Rights in Canada (Yvon Blais, Montreal, Que., 1987)

Bastien R., Federalism and Decentralization: Where Do We Stand (Minister of Supply and Services Canada, Ottawa, 1981)

Bayefsky A.F. (ed.), Canada's Constitution Act, 1982 and Amendments: A Documentary History (McGraw-Hill Ryerson, Toronto, 1989)

Bayefsky A.F., International Human Rights Law (Butterworths, Toronto, 1992)

Bayefsky A.F. and Eberts M. (eds.), Equality Rights and the Canadian Charter of Rights and Freedoms (Carswell, Toronto, 1985)

Beatty D.M., Talking Heads and the Supremes (Carswell, Toronto, 1990)

Beaudoin G.-A. and Mendes E. (eds.), The Canadian Charter of Rights and Freedoms (Carswell, Toronto, 3rd ed., 1996)

Beaudoin G.-A. and Ratushny E. (eds.), The Canadian Charter of Rights and Freedoms (Carswell, Toronto, 2nd ed., 1989)

Beaudoin G.-A., La Constitution du Canada: institutions, partage des pouvoirs, droits et libertés (Wilson & Lafleur, Montréal, 1990)

Beaudoin G.-A., Essais sur la Constitution (U. Ottawa, Ottawa, 1979)

Beaudoin G.-A. (ed.), Your Clients and the Charter — Liberty and Equality (Yvon Blais, Cowansville, Que., 1987)

Beaudoin G.-A. (ed.), The Supreme Court of Canada (Yvon Blais, Cowansville, Que., 1986)

Beck J.M., The Government of Nova Scotia (U. Toronto, Toronto, 1957)

Beck S.M. and Bernier I. (eds.), Canada and the New Constitution (Institute for Research on Public Policy, Montreal, 1983)

Behiels M.D. (ed.), The Meech Lake Primer (U. Ottawa, Ottawa, 1989)

Benson E.J., The Taxing Power and the Constitution of Canada (Government of Canada Working Paper on the Constitution, Queen's Printer, Ottawa, 1969)

Berlin M.L. and Pentney W.F., Human Rights and Freedoms in Canada (Butterworths, Toronto, 1987)

Bernier I., International Legal Aspects of Federalism (Longman, London, 1973)

Birch A.H., Federalism, Finance and Social Legislation (Oxford, London, 1955)

Birks S.M., The Survival of the Crown in the Canadian State (LL.M. thesis, Osgoode Hall Law School, York University, Toronto, 1980)

Black E.R., Divided Loyalties: Canadian Concepts of Federalism (McGill-Queens U.P., Montreal, 1975)

Bohémier A., La faillite en droit constitutionnel canadien (U. Montréal, Montréal, 1972)

Bourinot J.G., A Manual of the Constitutional History of Canada from the earliest period to 1901 (Copp Clark, Toronto, rev. ed., 1901)

Bourinot J.G., Parliamentary Procedure and Practice (Dawson Bros., Montreal, 2nd ed., 1892)

Boyer J.P., Lawmaking by the People: Referendums and Plebiscites in Canada (Butterworths, Toronto, 1982)

Boyer J.P., Money and Message (Butterworths, Toronto, 1983)

Boyer J.P., Political Rights (Butterworths, Toronto, 1981)

Boyle C.L.M. and others (eds.), Charterwatch: Reflections on Equality (Carswell, Toronto, 1986).

Brodsky G. and Day S., Canadian Charter Equality Rights for Women (Can. Advisory Council on the Status of Women, Ottawa, 1989)

BIBLIOGRAPHY

Brossard J., L'accession à la souveraineté et le cas du Québec (U. Montréal, Montréal, 1995)

Brossard J., La cour suprême et la constitution (U. Montréal, Montréal, 1983)

Brossard J., L'Immigration. Les droits et pouvoirs du Canada et du Québec (U. Montréal, Montréal, 1967)

Brossard J., Petry A. and Weiser E., Les pouvoirs extérieurs du Québec (U. Montréal, Montréal, 1967)

Browne G.P., Documents on the Confederation of British North America (McClelland & Stewart, Toronto, 1969)

Browne G.P., The Judicial Committee and the British North America Act (U. Toronto, Toronto, 1967)

Brun H. and Tremblay G., Droit Constitutionnel (Yvon Blais Inc., Cowansville, Quebec, 2nd ed., 1990)

Buchan R.J. and others, Telecommunications Regulation and the Constitution (Institute for Research on Public Policy, Montreal, 1982)

Burns R.M., One Country or Two? (McGill-Queens U., Montreal, 1971)

Bushnell, I., The Captive Court: A Study of the Supreme Court of Canada (McGill-Queens U., Montreal, 1992)

Byers R.B. and Reford R.W. (eds.), Canada Challenged: The Viability of Confederation (Canadian Institute of International Affairs, Toronto, 1979)

Cameron E.R., The Canadian Constitution as interpreted by the Judicial Committee of the Privy Council in its Judgments (vol. 1, Butterworths, Winnipeg, 1915; vol. 2, Carswell, Toronto, 1930)

Canadian Bar Association, Committee on the Constitution, Towards a New Canada (Canadian Bar Foundation, Ottawa, 1978)

Canadian Bar Association, Committee on the Supreme Court of Canada, Report (Canadian Bar Foundation, Ottawa, 1987)

Canadian Charter of Rights Annotated (Canada Law Book, Toronto, 1985, looseleaf)

Charles W.H., Cromwell T.A. and Jobson K., Evidence and the Charter of Rights and Freedoms (Butterworths, Toronto, 1989)

Cheffins R.I. and Johnson P.A., The Revised Canadian Constitution (McGraw-Hill Ryerson, Toronto, 1986)

Chevrette F. and Marx H., Droit Constitutionnel (U. Montréal, Montréal, 1982)

Chrétien J., Securing the Canadian Economic Union in the Constitution (Minister of Supply and Services Canada, Ottawa, 1980)

Clement W.H.P., The Law of the Canadian Constitution (Carswell, Toronto, 3rd ed., 1916)

Code M.A., Trial within a Reasonable Time (Carswell, Toronto, 1992)

Conklin W.E., Images of a Constitution (U. Toronto, Toronto, 1989)

Conklin W.E., In Defence of Fundamental Rights (Sijthoff & Noordhoff, The Netherlands, 1979)

Constantineau A., A Treatise on the De Facto Doctrine (Canada Law Book, Toronto, 1910)

Constitutional Committee of the Quebec Liberal Party, A New Canadian Federation (Quebec Liberal Party, Montreal, 1980)

Cooper-Stephenson K., Charter Damages Claims (Carswell, Toronto, 1990)

Creighton D., The Road to Confederation (Macmillan of Canada, Toronto, 1964)

Crépeau P.-A. and Macpherson C.B. (eds.), The Future of Canadian Federalism (U. Toronto, Toronto, 1965)

Cromwell T.A., Locus Standi (Carswell, Toronto, 1986)

Cullen R., Federalism in Action: the Australian and Canadian Offshore Disputes (Federation, Sydney, 1990)

Davenport P. and Leach R.T. (eds.), Reshaping Confederation (Duke U., Durham, N.C., 1984)

Davis L.B.Z., Canadian Constitutional Law Handbook (Canada Law Book, Aurora, Ont., 1985)

Dawson R.M., Constitutional Issues in Canada 1900-1931 (Oxford, London, 1933)

Dawson R.M., The Development of Dominion Status 1900-1936 (F. Cass, London, 1965)

de Mestral A. and others (eds.), The Limitation of Human Rights in Comparative Constitutional Law (Yvon Blais, Cowansville, Que., 1986)

Department of Justice, A Consolidation of the Constitution Acts 1867-1982 (Minister of Supply and Services Canada, Ottawa, 1996)

Donnelly M.S., The Government of Manitoba (U. Toronto, Toronto, 1963)

Edwards J.Ll.J., The Attorney General, Politics and the Public Interest (Sweet & Maxwell, London, 1984)

Evatt H.V., The King and his Dominion Governors (Cheshire, Australia, 2nd ed., 1967, introduction by Z. Cowen)

Evatt H.V., The Royal Prerogative (Law Book Co., Sydney, Australia, 1987, introduction by L. Zines)

Faribault M. and Fowler R.M., Ten to One: The Confederation Wager (McClelland and Stewart, Toronto, 1965)

Favreau G., The Amendment of the Constitution of Canada (Queen's Printer, Ottawa, 1965)

Finkelstein M., The Right to Counsel (Butterworths, Toronto, 1988)

Finkelstein N. and Finkelstein M., Constitutional Rights in the Investigative Process (Butterworths, Toronto, 1991)

Finkelstein N. and Rogers B.M. (eds.), Charter Issues in Civil Cases (Carswell, Toronto, 1988)

Finkelstein N. and Rogers B.M. (eds.), Administrative Tribunals and the Charter (Carswell, Toronto 1990)

Fitzgerald O., Understanding Charter Remedies (Carswell, Toronto, 1994, looseleaf service)

Fogarty K.H., Equality Rights and their Limitations in the Charter (Carswell, Toronto, 1987)

Forest R.-A. (ed.), L'adhésion du Québec à l'Accord du Lac Meech (Les Editions Thémis, Montréal, Que., 1988)

Forsey, E.A., Freedom and Order (McClelland & Stewart, Toronto, 1974)

Forsey E.A., The Royal Power of Dissolution of Parliament in the British Commonwealth (Oxford, Toronto, 1943; reprinted, 1968)

Foucher P., Constitutional Language Rights of Official-Language Minorities in Canada (Canadian Law Information Council, Ottawa, 1985)

Friedland M.L., A Place Apart: Judicial Independence and Accountability in Canada (Canadian Judicial Council, Ottawa, 1995)

Funston B.W. and Meehan E., Canadian Constitutional Documents Consolidated (Carswell, Toronto, 1994)

Gérin-Lajoie P., Constitutional Amendment in Canada (U. Toronto, Toronto, 1950)

Gibbins R. and others (eds.), Meech Lake and Canada: Perspectives from the West (Academic Printing, Edmonton, 1988)

Gibson D., The Law of the Charter: Equality Rights (Carswell, Toronto, 1990)

BIBLIOGRAPHY

Gibson D., The Law of the Charter: General Principles (Carswell, Toronto, 1986)

Gilbert C.D., Australian and Canadian Federalism 1867-1984 (Melbourne U., Melbourne, 1986)

Gotlieb A.E., Canadian Treaty-Making (Butterworths, Toronto, 1968)

Gotlieb A.E. (ed.), Human Rights, Federalism and Minorities (Canadian Institute of International Affairs, Toronto, 1970)

Grand Council of the Crees, Sovereign Injustice (Grand Council of the Crees, Montreal, 1995)

Greene I., The Charter of Rights (James Lorimer, Toronto, 1989)

Grenier B., La Declaration Canadienne Des Droits, Une loi bien ordinaire? (U. Laval, Quebec, 1979)

Hassard A.R., Canadian Constitutional History and Law (Carswell, Toronto, 1900)

Hawkins G. (ed.), Concepts of Federalism (Canadian Institute of Public Affairs, Toronto, 1965)

Heard A.D., Canadian Constitutional Conventions (Oxford U.P., Toronto, 1991)

Hendry J. McL., Memorandum on the Office of Lieutenant-Governor of a Province: its Constitutional Character and Functions (Department of Justice, Ottawa, 1955)

Hogg P.W., Canada Act 1982 Annotated (Carswell, Toronto, 1982)

Hogg P.W., Liability of the Crown (Carswell, Toronto, 2nd ed., 1989)

Hogg P.W., Meech Lake Constitutional Accord Annotated (Carswell, Toronto, 1988)

Hopkins E.R., Confederation at the Crossroads (McClelland & Stewart, Toronto, 1968)

Ip I. and Mintz J.M., Dividing the Spoils: the Federal-Provincial Allocation of Taxing Powers (C.D. Howe Institute, Toronto, 1992)

Jacomy-Millette A., Treaty Law in Canada (U. Ottawa, Ottawa, 1975)

Kennedy W.P.M., The Constitution of Canada 1534-1937 (Oxford, London, 2nd ed., 1938)

Kennedy W.P.M., Essays in Constitutional Law (Oxford, London, 1934)

Kennedy W.P.M. and Wells D.C., The Law of the Taxing Power in Canada (U. Toronto, Toronto, 1931)

Kwavnick D. (ed.), The Tremblay Report (McClelland & Stewart, Toronto, 1973)

BIBLIOGRAPHY

La Forest G.V., The Allocation of Taxing Power under the Canadian Constitution (Canadian Tax Foundation, Toronto, 2nd ed., 1981)

La Forest G.V., Disallowance and Reservation of Provincial Legislation (Queen's Printer, Ottawa, 1965)

La Forest G.V., Natural Resources and Public Property under the Canadian Constitution (U. Toronto, Toronto, 1969)

Lajoie A., Expropriation et fédéralisme au Canada (U. Montréal, Montréal, 1972)

Lajoie A., Le pouvoir déclaratoire du Parlement (U. Montréal, Montréal, 1969)

Lalonde M. and Basford R., The Canadian Constitution and Constitutional Amendment (Federal-Provincial Relations Office, Ottawa, 1978)

Lamontagne M., Le fédéralisme canadien: évolution et problèmes (U. Laval, Québec, 1954)

Lang O.E. (ed.), Contemporary Problems of Public Law in Canada (U. Toronto, Toronto, 1968)

Laskin B., The British Tradition in Canadian Law (Stevens, London, 1969)

Laskin B., Canadian Constitutional Law (Carswell, Toronto, 3rd ed. rev., 1969 by B. Laskin; 4th ed. rev. 1975 by A.S. Abel; 5th ed., 1986 by N. Finkelstein)

Law Society of Upper Canada, The Constitution and the Future of Canada (Special Lectures, 1978: De Boo, Toronto, 1978)

L'Ecuyer G., La Cour Suprême du Canada et le Partage des Compétences 1949-1978 (Gouvernement du Québec, Ministère des Affaires intergouvernementales, 1978)

Lederman W.R., Continuing Canadian Constitutional Dilemmas (Butterworths, Toronto, 1981)

Lederman W.R. (ed.), The Courts and the Canadian Constitution (McClelland & Stewart, Toronto, 1964)

Lefroy A.H.F., Canadian Constitutional Law (Carswell, Toronto, 1918)

Lefroy A.H.F., Canada's Federal System (Carswell, Toronto, 1913)

Lefroy A.H.F., Leading Cases in Canadian Constitutional Law (Carswell, Toronto, 2nd ed. by R.F. McWilliams, 1920)

Lefroy A.H.F., Legislative Power in Canada (Toronto Law Book Co., Toronto, 1897-8)

Lepofsky M.D., Open Justice (Butterworths, Toronto, 1985)

Livingston W.S., Federalism and Constitutional Change (Clarendon, Oxford, 1956, reprinted Greenwood, Westport, Conn., 1974)

Livingston W.S. (ed.), Federalism in the Commonwealth (Cassel & Co., London, 1963)

Lordon P. (ed.), Crown Law (Butterworths, Toronto, 1991)

Lower A.R.M. and others, Evolving Canadian Federalism (Duke U., Durham, N.C., 1958)

Lyon J.N. and Atkey R.G., Canadian Constitutional Law in a Modern Perspective (U. Toronto, Toronto, 1970)

MacDonald L.G., A Contemporary Analysis of the Prerogative (LL.M. thesis, Osgoode Hall Law School, York University, Toronto, 1988)

Macdonald R. St. J. and Humphrey J.P. (eds.), The Practice of Freedom (Butterworths, Toronto, 1979)

MacKinnon F., The Crown in Canada (Glenbow-Alberta Institute, McClelland & Stewart West, Calgary, 1976)

MacKinnon F., The Government of Prince Edward Island (U. Toronto, Toronto, 1951)

MacKinnon V.S., Comparative Federalism (Martinus Nijhoff, The Hague, 1964)

Magnet J.E., Constitutional Law of Canada (Yvon Blais, Montreal, 5th ed., 1993)

Mahoney K.E. and Martin S.L., Equality and Judicial Neutrality (Carswell, Toronto, 1987)

Mallory J.R., Social Credit and the Federal Power in Canada (U. Toronto, Toronto 1954; reprinted 1976)

Mallory J.R., The Structure of Canadian Government (Gage, Toronto, rev. ed, 1984)

Mandel M., The Charter of Rights and the Legalization of Politics in Canada (Thompson; rev. ed. 1994)

Manning M., Rights, Freedoms and the Courts (Emond-Montgomery, Toronto, 1983)

Marshall G., Constitutional Conventions (Clarendon, Oxford, 1984)

Marshall G., Constitutional Theory (Clarendon, Oxford, 1980)

Marshall G., Parliamentary Sovereignty and the Commonwealth (Clarendon, Oxford, 1962)

BIBLIOGRAPHY

Marshall G. and Moodie G.C., Some Problems of the Constitution (Hutchison, London, 4th rev. ed., 1967)

Martin P.J.J., Federalism and International Relations (Dept. of External Affairs, Ottawa, 1968)

McConnell W.H., Commentary on the British North America Act (Macmillan of Canada, Toronto, 1977)

McDonald D.C., Legal Rights in the Canadian Charter of Rights and Freedoms (Carswell, Toronto, 2nd ed., 1989)

McKercher W.R., The U.S. Bill of Rights and the Canadian Charter of Rights and Freedoms (Ontario Economic Council, Toronto, 1983)

McLeod R.M. and others, The Canadian Charter of Rights (Carswell, Toronto, 1983, loose-leaf service)

McNairn C.H.H., Governmental and Intergovernmental Immunity in Australia and Canada (U. Toronto, Toronto, 1977)

McRoberts K. and Monahan P.J. (eds.), The Charlottetown Accord, the Referendum and the Future of Canada (U. Toronto, 1993)

McRuer Report: Royal Commission of Inquiry into Civil Rights, Report (Ontario, 1968-71)

McWhinney E., Canada and the Constitution 1979-1982 (U. Toronto, Toronto, 1982)

McWhinney E., Constitution-making: Principles, Process, Practice (U. Toronto, Toronto, 1981)

McWhinney E., Judicial Review (U. Toronto, Toronto, 4th ed., 1969)

McWhinney E., Quebec and the Constitution 1960-1978 (U. Toronto, Toronto, 1979)

McWhinney E., Supreme Courts and Judicial Law-making: Constitutional Tribunals and Constitutional Review (Martinus Nijhoff, Dordrecht, The Netherlands, 1985)

Meehan E. and others (eds), The 1995 Annotated Charter of Rights and Freedoms (Carswell, Toronto, 1995)

Meekison J.P., Canadian Federalism: Myth or Reality (Methuen, Toronto, 3rd ed., 1977)

Milne D.A., The Canadian Constitution (James Lorimer, Toronto, 2nd ed., 1991)

Monahan P., Meech Lake: The Inside Story (U. Toronto, Toronto, 1991)

Monahan P., Politics and the Constitution (Carswell, Toronto, 1987)

Morton J.C. and Hutchison S.C., Presumption of Innocence (Carswell, Toronto, 1987)

Munro J.E.C., The Constitution of Canada (Camb. U., Cambridge, 1889)

Newcombe E.L., The British North America Acts (King's Printer, Ottawa, 1908)

O'Connor Report: Senate of Canada, Parliamentary Counsel, Report Relating to the British North America Act, 1867 (Canada, 1939; reprinted, 1961)

O'Hearn P.J.T., Peace, Order and Good Government (Macmillan of Canada, Toronto, 1964)

Ollivier M. (ed.), British North America Acts and Selected Statutes 1867-1962 (Queen's Printer, Ottawa, 1962)

Ollivier M. (ed.), The Colonial and Imperial Conferences from 1887 to 1937 (Queen's Printer, Ottawa, 1954)

Olmsted R.A. (ed.), Decisions of the Judicial Committee of the Privy Council relating to the British North America Act and the Canadian Constitution 1867-1954 (Queen's Printer, Ottawa, 1954)

Ontario Advisory Committee on Confederation, The Confederation Challenge (Background Papers and Reports) (Ontario, 1967 (vol. 1), 1970 (vol. 2))

Ontario Advisory Committee on Confederation, First Report (April 1978), Second Report (March 1979) (Ontario, 1978, 1979)

O'Sullivan D.A., Government in Canada (Carswell, Toronto, 2nd ed., 1887)

Paciocco D.M., Charter Principles and Proof in Criminal Cases (Carswell, Toronto, 1987)

Patenaude P., La preuve, les techniques modernes et le respect des valeurs fondamentales (Les Editions revue de droit, Sherbrooke, Que., 1990)

Pelletier B., La modification constitutionnelle au Canada (Carswell, 1997)

Pépin G., Les tribunaux administratifs et la constitution (U. Montréal, Montréal, 1969)

Plaxton C.P. (ed.), Canadian Constitutional Decisions of the Privy Council, 1930 to 1939 (Queen's Printer, Ottawa, 1939)

Pope J., Confederation: Being a Series of Hitherto Unpublished Documents Bearing on the British North America Act (Carswell, Toronto, 1895)

Rémillard G., Le Fédéralisme Canadien (Québec/Amérique, Montréal), vol. 1 (1983), vol. 2 (1985)

Richard J.D. and Robertson S.M., The Charter and the Media (Canadian Bar Foundation, Ottawa, 1985)

Riddell W.R., The Canadian Constitution in Form and in Fact (Columbia U., New York, 1923)

Riddell W.R., The Constitution of Canada (Yale U.P., New Haven, Conn., 1917)

Roach K., Constitutional Remedies in Canada (Canada Law Book, Aurora, 1994, loose-leaf service)

Romanow R., White J. and Leeson H., Canada . . . Notwithstanding (Carswell/ Methuen, Toronto, 1984)

Rowell-Sirois Report: Royal Commission on Dominion-Provincial Relations, Report (Canada, 1940)

Royal Commission on Bilingualism and Biculturalism, Report (Canada, 1967-1970)

Royal Commission of Inquiry into Civil Rights, Report (McRuer Report) (Ontario, 1968-1971)

Royal Commission of Inquiry on Constitutional Problems, Report (Tremblay Report) (Quebec, 1956)

Royal Commission on Dominion-Provincial Relations, Report (Rowell-Sirois Report) (Canada, 1940)

Royal Commission on the Economic Union and Development Prospects for Canada, Report (Macdonald Report) (Canada, 1985)

Russell P.H., Constitutional Odyssey (U. Toronto, Toronto, 2nd ed., 1993)

Russell P.H., The Judiciary in Canada: The Third Branch of Government (McGraw-Hill Ryerson, Toronto, 1987)

Russell P.H., Knopff R. and Morton F.L., Leading Constitutional Decisions (Carleton U.P., Ottawa, 5th ed., 1989)

Russell P.H., The Supreme Court of Canada as a Bilingual and Bicultural Institution (Documents of the Royal Commission on Bilingualism and Biculturalism, Queen's Printer, Ottawa, 1969)

Safarian A.E., Canadian Federalism and Economic Integration (Queen's Printer, Ottawa, 1974)

Salhany R.E., The Origin of Rights (Carswell, Toronto, 1986)

Saywell J.T., The Office of Lieutenant-Governor (U. Toronto, Toronto, 1957)

Schabas W.A., International Human Rights Law and the Canadian Charter (Carswell, Toronto, 2nd ed., 1996)

Schindeler F.F., Responsible Government in Ontario (U. Toronto, Toronto, 1969)

Schmeiser D.A., Civil Liberties in Canada (Oxford, London, 1964)

Schneiderman D. (ed.), Freedom of Expression and the Charter (Carswell, Toronto, 1991)

Schwartz B., Fathoming Meech Lake (Legal Research Institute of University of Manitoba, Winnipeg, Man. 1987)

Scott F.R., Civil Liberties and Canadian Federalism (U. Toronto, Toronto, 1959)

Scott F.R., Essays on the Constitution (U. Toronto, Toronto, 1977)

Senate and House of Commons of Canada, Special Joint Committee, Report on the Constitution of Canada (Canada, 1972)

Senate of Canada, Parliamentary Counsel, Report relating to the British North America Act 1867 (O'Connor Report) (Canada, 1939; reprinted, 1961)

Sharp M., Federalism and International Conferences on Education (Dept. of External Affairs, Ottawa, 1968)

Sharpe R.J. (ed.), Charter Litigation (Butterworths, Toronto, 1987)

Sharpe R.J., The Law of Habeas Corpus (Clarendon, Oxford, 2nd ed., 1989)

Sharpe R.J., Interprovincial Product Liability Litigation (Butterworths, Toronto, 1982)

Sherrin C., Objectionable Objectives?: An Analysis of the First Branch of the *Oakes* Test (D. Jur. thesis Osgoode Hall Law School of York University, 1994)

Simeon R.E.B., Federal-Provincial Diplomacy (U. Toronto, Toronto, 1972)

Simeon R.E.B. (ed.), Must Canada Fail? (McGill-Queen's U., Montreal, 1977)

Smiley D.V., Canada in Question (McGraw-Hill Ryerson, Toronto, 3rd ed., 1980)

Smiley D.V., The Canadian Charter of Rights and Freedoms (Ontario Economic Council, Toronto, 1981)

Smiley D.V., The Canadian Political Nationality (Methuen, Toronto, 1967)

Smiley D.V., Conditional Grants and Canadian Federalism (Canadian Tax Foundation, Toronto, 1963)

Smiley D.V., Constitutional Adaptation and Canadian Federalism since 1945 (Document of the Royal Commission on Bilingualism and Biculturalism, Queen's Printer, Ottawa, 1970)

Smiley D.V., The Federal Condition in Canada (McGraw-Hill Ryerson, Toronto, 1987)

Smiley D.V. (ed.), The Rowell-Sirois Report (McClelland and Stewart, Toronto, 1963)

Smith A., The Commerce Power in Canada and the United States (Butterworths, Toronto, 1963)

Smith D.E., MacKinnon P. and Courtney J.C., Drawing Boundaries: Legislatures, Courts and Electoral Values (Fifth House, Saskatoon, 1992)

Smith L. (ed.), Righting the Balance: Canada's New Equality Rights (Canadian Human Rights Reporter, Saskatoon, 1986)

Snell J.G. and Vaughan F., The Supreme Court of Canada: History of the Institution (Osgoode Society, Toronto, 1985)

Stanley G.F.G., A Short History of the Canadian Constitution (Ryerson, Toronto, 1969)

Strayer B.L., The Canadian Constitution and the Courts (Butterworths, Toronto, 3rd ed., 1988)

Strayer B.L., The Patriation and Legitimacy of the Canadian Constitution (Cronkite Memorial Lectures, College of Law, U. Saskatchewan, 1982)

Stuart D., Charter Justice in Canadian Criminal Law (Carswell, Toronto, 2nd ed., 1996)

Swinton K.E. and Rogerson C.J. (eds.), Competing Constitutional Visions: The Meech Lake Accord (Carswell, Toronto, 1988)

Swinton K.E., The Supreme Court and Canadian Federalism (Carswell, Toronto, 1990)

Tarnopolsky W.S., The Canadian Bill of Rights (McClelland & Stewart, Toronto, 2nd ed., 1975)

Task Force on Canadian Unity, A Future Together (Pepin-Robarts Report, Minister of Supply and Services Canada, Ottawa, 1979)

Trakman L.E., Reasoning With the Charter (Butterworths, Toronto, 1993)

Trebilcock M.J., Prichard J.R.S., Courchene T.J. and Whalley J. (eds.), Federalism and the Canadian Economic Union (U. Toronto, Toronto, 1983)

Tremblay A., Les compétences législatives au Canada et les pouvoirs provinciaux en matière de propriété et de droits civils (U. Ottawa, Ottawa, 1967)

Tremblay A., Droit Constitutionnel-Principes (Les Éditions Thémis, Montréal, 1992)

Tremblay A., La Réforme de la Constitution au Canada (Les Éditions Thémis, Montréal, 1995)

BIBLIOGRAPHY

Tremblay Report: Royal Commission of Inquiry on Constitutional Problems, Report (Quebec, 1956)

Trudeau P.E., A Canadian Charter of Human Rights (Government of Canada Working Paper on the Constitution, Queen's Printer, Ottawa, 1968)

Trudeau P.E., The Constitution and the People of Canada (Government of Canada Working Paper on the Constitution, Queen's Printer, Ottawa, 1969)

Trudeau P.E., Federalism and the French Canadians (Macmillan of Canada, Toronto, 1968)

Trudeau P.E., Federal-Provincial Grants and the Spending Power of Parliament (Government of Canada Working Paper on the Constitution, Queen's Printer, Ottawa, 1969)

Trudeau P.E., Income Security and Social Services (Government of Canada Working Paper on the Constitution, Queen's Printer, Ottawa, 1969)

Varcoe F.P., The Constitution of Canada (Carswell, Toronto, 2nd ed., 1965)

Walker M. (ed.), Canadian Confederation at the Crossroads (Fraser Institute, Vancouver, B.C., 1978)

Ward N., Dawson's The Government of Canada (U. Toronto P., Toronto, 6th ed., 1987)

Weiler J.M. and Elliot R.M. (eds.), Litigating the Values of a Nation: The Canadian Charter of Rights and Freedoms (Carswell, Toronto, 1986)

Weiler P.C., In the Last Resort (Carswell Methuen, Toronto, 1974)

Wheare K.C., The Constitutional Structure of the Commonwealth (Clarendon, Oxford, 1960)

Wheare K.C., Federal Government (Oxford, London, 4th ed., 1963)

Wheare K.C., Modern Constitutions (Oxford, London, 2nd ed., 1966)

Wheare K.C., The Statute of Westminster and Dominion Status (Oxford, London, 5th ed., 1953)

Wheeler G.J., Confederation Law of Canada (Eyre and Spottiswoode, London, 1896)

Whitley S.J., Criminal Justice and the Constitution (Carswell, Toronto, 1989)

Whyte J.D. and Lederman, W.R., Canadian Constitutional Law (Butterworths, Toronto, 3rd ed., 1992)

Wintemute R., Sexual Orientation and Human Rights: The United States Constitution, the European Convention, and the Canadian Charter (Clarendon, Oxford, 1995)

Witkor C.L. and Tanguay G., Constitutions of Canada (Oceana Publications, Dobbs Ferry, N.Y., 1978)

Young R.A., The Secession of Quebec and the Future of Canada (McGill-Queens U., Montreal, 1995)

Index

References are to sections, not pages

INDEX

References are to sections, not pages

INDEX

References are to sections, not pages

INDEX

References are to sections, not pages

INDEX

References are to sections, not pages

INDEX

References are to sections, not pages

INDEX

References are to sections, not pages

INDEX

References are to sections, not pages

INDEX

References are to sections, not pages

INDEX

References are to sections, not pages

INDEX

References are to sections, not pages

INDEX

References are to sections, not pages

INDEX

References are to sections, not pages

INDEX

References are to sections, not pages